135TH YEAR

WISDEN

CRICKETERS' ALMANACK

1998

EDITED BY MATTHEW ENGEL

PUBLISHED BY JOHN WISDEN & CO LTD

Cased edition ISBN 0 947766 44 8   £27.50

Soft cover edition ISBN 0 947766 45 6   £27.50

Leather bound edition ISBN 0 947766 43 X   £200
(Limited edition of 150)

JOHN WISDEN & CO LTD
25 Down Road, Merrow, Guildford, Surrey GU1 2PY
Tel: 01483 570358   Fax: 01483 533153

WISDEN CRICKETERS' ALMANACK

Editor: Matthew Engel, The Oaks, Newton St Margarets, Herefordshire HR2 0QN.

Deputy editor: Harriet Monkhouse. Production editor: Christine Forrest.
Assistant editor: Simon Briggs.
Managing director: Christopher Lane. Advertisement manager: Colin Ackehurst.

Computer typeset by Spottiswoode Ballantyne Ltd, Colchester

Printed and bound in Great Britain by Clays Ltd, St Ives plc
Distributed by The Penguin Group
Distributed in Australia by Hardie Grant Books

PREFACE

It is possible to become quite famous writing or, above all, talking about cricket: these days, opinionated commentators can be more recognisable than many of the anonymous helmeted players.

Other people in the cricket media may be every bit as important, but less celebrated. *Wisden's* production editor Christine Forrest has been associated with the past 20 editions of the Almanack; in that time there have been four editors, but Christine has remained staunch.

Everyone connected with *Wisden* is aware that, but for her, its sequence of 135 years of continuous publication would probably have been broken years ago. It would certainly have been a far less accurate and reliable book. Together with the deputy editor, Harriet Monkhouse, she has been devoted to maintaining *Wisden's* internal logic and coherence.

Though she is ridiculously young, and looks younger, Christine has decided it is time for a sort of retirement. She has promised to give any help we need, which is reassuring. But if *Wisden* fails to appear next year, you can guess the reason. We will miss her doggedness, her organisational skills and her kindness in equal measure.

Three of *Wisden's* most senior and valued county correspondents have also retired. In the spring, Brian Bearshaw gave up covering Lancashire for the Almanack after 15 seasons. In the autumn, John Callaghan at Yorkshire retired (after 22 seasons), as did Eric Hill, Somerset correspondent for 32 seasons, since *Wisden* 1967. An article by him, The Story of Somerset, appeared as early as 1959.

All three of these writers have provided authoritative, accurate and often trenchant commentary. Each has deep local roots and knowledge and, in Eric's case, the experience of playing for the county. These have given their reporting added weight and passion. None of them has been able to write the story for *Wisden* that would have given them most pleasure: their county winning the Championship.

We will miss them too. Likewise Roy Smart, who has retired as our computer wizard, John Kitchin, who has put tremendous effort into the obituaries over the past decade, and the management and staff of Spottiswoode Ballantyne, whose era as our typesetters has now ended.

Years like this are inevitable in an inherently stable institution. I welcome their successors and look forward to travelling with them into the new millennium. My thanks go too to Sir Paul Getty, and the board and management committee of John Wisden and Co, Christopher Lane in particular; to my deputy Harriet; to the assistant editor Simon Briggs; to Peter Bather, Mike Smith and Gordon Burling, whose roles have again been crucial; to our teammates at *Wisden Cricket Monthly* and my colleagues on *The Guardian*; and, as ever, to my wife and mainstay Hilary, and my son Laurie, who in his sixth summer discovered, like others before him, that his dad's bowling was very hittable.

MATTHEW ENGEL

Newton St Margarets, Herefordshire,
January 1998

LIST OF CONTRIBUTORS

Luke Alfred
Andy Arlidge
Chris Aspin
Philip Bailey
Jack Bannister
Colin Bateman
Greg Baum
Mike Berry
Lee Besford
Edward Bevan
Peter Bidwell
J. Watson Blair
Trent Bouts
Tim Bradford
Robert Brooke
Philip Brown
Colin Bryden
Winston Bynorth
John Callaghan
Ken Casellas
Graham Chadwick
Hugh Chevallier
Richard Colbey
Mike Coward
Lord Cowdrey
Craig Cozier
Tony Cozier
Robert Craddock
Brian Croudy
John Curtis
Gareth A. Davies
Ian Davies
Geoffrey Dean
Tim de Lisle

Ralph Dellor
Norman de Mesquita
Patrick Eagar
John Etheridge
Colin Evans
David Foot
Bill Frindall
David Frith
Nigel Fuller
Andrew Gidley
Chris Goddard
Gideon Haigh
David Hallett
David Hardy
Peter Hargreaves
Norman Harris
Eric Hill
Philip Hoare
Grenville Holland
David Hopps
Gerald Howat
John Illman
Peter Johnson
Abid Ali Kazi
Frank Keating
David Llewellyn
David Lloyd
A. Lokuhapuarachchi
Andrew Longmore
Nick Lucy
David McKie
John MacKinnon
Christopher Martin-Jenkins
Clive Mason

R. Mohan
Geoffrey Moorhouse
Graham Morris
Gerald Mortimer
David Munden
Mike Neasom
Terry Power
Derek Pringle
Qamar Ahmed
Charles Randall
Mark Ray
Dicky Rutnagur
Carol Salmon
Andrew Samson
Derek Scott
Utpal Shuvro
Jasmer Singh
Bill Smith
Rob Steen
Sa'adi Thawfeeq
Leslie Thomas
Andrew Tong
David Townsend
Jan Traylen
Chris Turvey
Sudhir Vaidya
Gerry Vaidyasekera
John Ward
Paul Weaver
Tim Wellock
Marcus Williams
Bruce Wilson
John Woodcock
Graeme Wright

Round the World: Trevor Bayley, Steve Bunce, Antony Coster, Olivier de Braekeleer, John Duncan, Geoff Edwards, Brian Fell, T. J. Finlayson, Tony Fisher, Simone Gambino, Bob Gibb, Simon Hewitt, Peter Knight, David Parsons, Bryan Pattison, Stanley Perlman, Chris Pianca, Jimmy Powell, Jai Kumar Shah, Mark Stafford, Derek Thursby, Vinod Vetath, Colin Wolfe and Clive Woodbridge.

Thanks are accorded to the following for checking the scorecards of first-class matches: Keith Booth, Len Chandler, Bill Davies, Alex Davis, Byron Denning, Jack Foley, Keith Gerrish, Neil Harris, Brian Hunt, Vic Isaacs, David Kendix, Tony Kingston, Reg May, David Norris, David Oldam, Gordon Stringfellow, Stan Tacey, Mike Walsh, Roy Wilkinson, Ken Workman and Graham York.

The editor also acknowledges with gratitude assistance from the following: the ACS e-mail group, Tanya Aldred, Bill Andersson, David Armstrong, Brian Austin, Jack Bailey, Peter Barnes, Richard Beal, David Bishop, Jeremy Brade, Dick Brittenden, Clem Burgmann, Gerry Byrne, Marion Collin, Bill Cook, Bob Cristofani, Prakash Dahatonde, Robert Eastaway, Pat Fenech, Ric Finlay, Craig Francis, Sujoy Ghosh, Ghulam Mustafa Khan, David C. Gibbs, Ray Goble, Robin Gordon-Walker, Peter Griffiths, Kate Hanson, Bob Harragan, Les Hatton, Col. Malcolm Havergal, Keith Hayhurst, Steve Hill, Mohammad Ali Jafri, Ann Jameson, Kate Jamieson, Pat Keane, John Kitchin, Rajesh Kumar, David Lamming, Tony Lewis, Malcolm Lorimer, Robert Low, Steven Lynch, Ken McEwan, Clive Mansell, Mahendra Mapagunaratne, Mohandas Menon, Allan Miller, Roger Packham, Francis Payne, Ken Piesse, Jack Pollard, S. Pervez Qaiser, Andrew Radd, Rex Roberts, Major R. W. K. Ross-Hurst, Geoffrey Saulez, Ian Smith, Philip Snow, Richard Streeton, Mike Turner, Gordon Vince, J. F. Walker, David Walsh, Charlie Wat, Jason Weare, John White, Geoffrey Wilde, Wendy Wimbush and Peter Wynne-Thomas.

The production of *Wisden* would not be possible without the support and co-operation of many other cricket officials, writers and lovers of the game. To them all, many thanks.

CONTENTS

Part One: Comment

Part Two: The Players

Part Three: Records

Part Four: English Cricket in 1997

Part Five: Overseas Cricket in 1996-97

Part Six: Administration and Laws

Part Seven: Miscellaneous

Addresses of first-class and minor counties can now be found on page 1332.

A more detailed index to Cricket Records appears on pages 175-179. The index to the Laws may be found on pages 1332-1333 and an index of Test matches played in 1996-97 on pages 1450-1451.

Index of Fillers and Inserts

PART ONE: COMMENT

NOTES BY THE EDITOR

On May 2, 1997, Tony Blair, the leader of the Labour Party, became Britain's Prime Minister as a result of the General Election, and moved into Downing Street. John Major moved out and immediately went to watch Surrey play the universities.

At this moment, and for some weeks thereafter, it appears that Britain had, for the first time ever, a prime minister (born 1953) younger than a current county cricketer (John Emburey, born 1952). It also had one who, in contrast to his mad-keen predecessor, regarded cricket as something he had put away when he was a teenager, after a brief fling in which he memorised all the statistics of England's Tests in the mid-1960s.

Unlike fox-hunting, cricket was not in immediate danger of being made illegal under the new Government. But among the many subtexts of the election campaign was the one in which the struggling Tories were depicted as the party of England past, wedded to warm beer and cricket, while Labour was hip and youthful, representing cold lager and the people's game. Blair took care to be seen on football grounds.

It was all pretty bogus. But the perception that cricket was a tired old sport remained strong throughout 1997. This was not true everywhere. Whereas cricket was in crisis in England, West Indies, Zimbabwe, and perhaps New Zealand, it flourished in the countries where people had more cause to cheer their national teams. In Sri Lanka, in particular, the boom kept reverberating: when TV showed an interview with Sanath Jayasuriya, the country's electricity demand broke 1,000 megawatts for the first time. In Australia, the traditional Boxing Day start of the Melbourne Test attracted its largest crowd in 22 years, 73,812, and a CD making fun of Bill Lawry's commentaries sold 100,000 copies in no time. Across the globe and into cyberspace, cricketing Internet sites were consistently among the busiest on the entire web.

And what was striking even in Britain was the extent to which the public's residual passion for the game could be mobilised. After Denis Compton died in April, the demand for tickets at his memorial service exceeded anything Westminster Abbey had experienced since the death of the TV presenter Richard Dimbleby, at the height of his celebrity, in 1965. Then there was Dickie Bird's autobiography. Here was a book that contained no revelations, no sex (famously so) and a collection of very well-aired anecdotes. By mid-January 1998, it had sold 287,432 copies in hardback. This is an extraordinary figure.

There was a yearning: a need for heroes. English cricket was still awaiting a new one. When he comes, Tony Blair will rush to embrace him. In his absence, a hero from half a century ago and a lovable umpire provided substitutes.

Mr Dalmiya goes to Lord's

World cricket, meanwhile, acquired not a new prime minister but its first president. In 1996, the possibility that the Indian businessman Jagmohan Dalmiya might take control of the International Cricket Council had caused such consternation that it was almost split asunder. In 1997 he assumed office as President of ICC for a three-year term without a murmur of dissent. And the first public utterance of a man previously painted as a sort of money-mad barbarian was to congratulate Colin Cowdrey on his elevation to the House of Lords. ("The most radical revolutionary will become a conservative on the day after the revolution" – Hannah Arendt.)

Dalmiya's job had never existed before. His predecessor, Sir Clyde Walcott, had been called chairman. Dalmiya's title sounded grander, but the reality was less imposing. The work done by Sir John Anderson, head of New Zealand Cricket, in reconstructing ICC's decision-making processes had ensured a presidency with influence rather than power. There is now an 18-member executive board, with subsidiary committees covering cricket, finance and development. At long last, there are the glimmerings of a proper decision-making structure.

None the less, the game over which Dalmiya presided was one he had played a major part in creating, as Indian cricket's chief power-broker. There were 110 one-day internationals played in 1997 (plus two washouts). Most blurred into each other. The most significant may well have been the least noticed: those in Nairobi during October between Zimbabwe, Kenya and Bangladesh in front of tiny crowds and no TV cameras. After the ICC Trophy earlier in the year, when Bangladesh beat Kenya in the final, both countries had been promoted to a new, intermediate status, above the other Associate countries but behind the Test-playing nations. This enabled them to play one-day internationals, as a possible preliminary move to full Test status – very soon, officials hoped.

In Nairobi, the two aspirants proved themselves hopelessly inferior to the newest of the nine Test-playing teams. Zimbabwe's professionalism and athleticism totally outclassed their rivals, and it rapidly became clear that neither would be ready for Test status in the near future.

It is important not to be dog-in-the-manger about this. There is huge interest in cricket in Bangladesh (which should be harnessed when all the major countries visit for a quickie tournament in October this year), and great playing potential in Kenya. Both countries need an injection of resources to develop stars capable of playing Tests, and ICC is right to encourage them and others. Toronto and Singapore now stage one-day internationals; ICC is salivating about the potential of playing in Florida. The more countries that play cricket the better.

But sports politicians can get carried away by their own rhetoric. Dalmiya was quoted as saying this January that the game had to spread to all corners of the world to survive. That is nonsense. If cricket were to mutate into something different simply to try and sell itself to the American market, or anywhere else, it wouldn't be cricket and it wouldn't be worth having.

If you're broke, fix it

It might be healthier if cricket officials spent a little less time reaching for the sky and paid more attention to what was going on in the gutter. As 1998 began, the rumours that results in one-day internationals were being twisted to suit the interests of betting syndicates operating illegally, mainly in Mumbai and the Gulf, were moving from a murmur to something nearer a roar. Nobody now doubts that this gambling takes place, for large sums, and that cricketers are involved in the process.

This does not necessarily mean that players have deliberately thrown matches. It is possible that the substantial number who have made allegations – Tim May, Shane Warne, Manoj Prabhakar, Aamir Sohail and so on – are making mischief or a mistake. Possible, but increasingly implausible. ICC needs to set up a credible international investigation designed to discover the truth, not what everyone wants to hear.

Anyone with experience of gambling will feel that the amount of smoke billowing out of this story is a pretty reliable indicator of fire. The international programme, particularly as played by India and Pakistan, is a guaranteed recipe for jiggery-pokery. The one-day tournaments of which these countries are so fond have no real meaning. No one remembers who wins them, so honour can never overcome profit. And the actual rewards for victory are hardly exciting. England's success in the Sharjah Champions Trophy in December won them just £25,000 between a squad of 14. Champion golfers tip their waiters better than that, never mind their caddies.

The present system bears a resemblance to the one that was prevalent in tennis a decade or so ago. The top players would turn up in some hick town for what was billed as a showdown. They would split the profits amiably and put on a show for the locals. It was not that they didn't try, but no one except the poor saps watching cared who won. The difference is that the cricketers are not getting rich – not from cricket. A handful do manage to turn their fame to good commercial advantage, but that is not the same thing. It would be astonishing if some of the others had not been tempted by villainy.

One day, we will get it right

As is now well known, *Wisden* has a solution for the problems of Test cricket. The Wisden World Championship, devised in 1996, has now become widely accepted as the best – or at any rate the least worst – method of ranking the teams (see page 1460). The principle of an official Championship has now been agreed by ICC, and details will supposedly be announced in 1998.

Unfortunately, many officials, including Dalmiya, have become seduced by the idea that such a Championship should operate along the lines of the World Cup, as a separate tournament at a fixed time in the calendar, possibly even in a fixed place. Leaving aside the logistical horrors of such an exercise, it would entirely defeat the main purpose.

The idea is to make all Test matches more meaningful, popular and attractive. A tournament-style Championship would have the reverse effect, making all other Tests second-rate. The Australians, currently the runaway leaders of the Wisden table, would have years of effort negated if they happened to play badly in one arbitrarily designated fixture. A World Cup works for football and one-day cricket. It would be grotesquely inappropriate for Test cricket.

A proper Test Championship would force ICC to introduce supervision of grounds to avoid fiascos like the Sabina Park Test this January, which was abandoned because the pitch was dangerous. I am now also inclined to take the plan further. A World Championship for one-day internationals would do a great deal to avoid the alleged criminality discussed above by giving purpose to games that are now just passing shows. As with the Test Championship, it could be custom-made to allow for varying fixture lists. It would also enhance ICC's global vision by offering a context comprehensible to non-traditional audiences.

The right way forward is for every international cricket match to be part of one of three events: the World Cup, the Test World Championship or the one-day World Championship. Millenarianism is the fanciful belief in a future period of peace and happiness and common sense on earth. Well, it so happens we are approaching the millennium.

The age of near-miracles

The summer of 1997 briefly promised something to rank with peace on earth among possible miracles: England winning the Ashes. It did not work out, which was hardly surprising. The Australian team which toured England under Mark Taylor was one of the great all-round sides, not as thrilling as the 1963 West Indians, but maybe stronger in some respects even than the 1948 Australians. Admittedly, Taylor never had a Bradman, but he had the incomparable Shane Warne, an Aussie battler for the ages in Steve Waugh, and Ian Healy, a wicket-keeper/batsman of ferocious efficiency and competitiveness.

In these circumstances, England's achievement in losing only 3-2 was outstanding. It was their fifth successive defeat in an Ashes series, but every time the result has been a little less humiliating: 4-0, 3-0, 4-1, 3-1, 3-2. That might suggest England are certainties at least to draw in 1998-99. The contest was more one-sided than it might seem, though. England's successes came on the first and last days of the series, when Australia were either disorientated or over-relaxed. In the middle, the Aussies were overwhelming.

Shock! Horror! Praise for England!

These Notes always pose special problems in a winter when England are touring the West Indies. I am writing this less than two months before *Wisden* is published (the fact that this is possible is an astonishing tribute to everyone involved on the production side of a 1472-page volume), just after the débâcle at Sabina Park. But in the next seven weeks England are scheduled to play five Tests. For the editor of a UK-based book, it would be useful to produce two alternative sets of Notes: one to encompass the glory-glory mood that would exist if England won the series, after 25 years of hurt, the Wisden Trophy; another to allow for the more familiar outcome.

Let us, however, deal in known facts and the events of 1997. Sensible English observers of the Ashes accentuated the positive, instead of jeering. This series was determined by Australia's brilliance rather than England's incompetence. Last year, the England set-up was better run than it had been for a generation.

The retirement of Ray Illingworth led to a new panel of selectors, chaired by David Graveney – the first chairman since Harry Altham, in 1954, not to have played Test cricket and, at 44, the youngest since Freddie Brown in 1953. His two fellow-selectors, Graham Gooch and Mike Gatting, were both still playing at the start of the season. Thus there was a sense of the torch being passed to a new generation of administrators.

The torch had passed to the men most closely identified with the two English rebel tours to the old South Africa: the captains (Gooch and Gatting), Graveney (the manager on the second trip) and Emburey (the only player to go twice), who this winter became the assistant coach to David Lloyd. But at least that spared us any cant about rewarding loyalty. What one had was a sense that more often than not they were getting things right.

Of course, the selections were not perfect. Everyone accepted in hindsight that the omission of Andy Caddick at Headingley was a mistake. In my view, the panel consistently underestimated the importance of Nick Knight's catching. But the selectors knew what they wanted, and usually wanted the same thing. This was a dramatic, and very welcome, change.

Even more important was the improvement inside the dressing-room. David Lloyd, the coach, lost his formal role as a selector but his role inside the camp increased. As he gained confidence, the strengths of his personality came through too. He may not have Brearley's qualifications in psychotherapy, but his human warmth was vital. Far too often in the past, players have come into the Test team, wandered about looking lost, been almost ignored, sensed the panic and self-centredness that pervaded the team, failed, then been dropped and forgotten. Cricketers need to be cuddled – metaphorically or otherwise – the same as anyone else. Lloyd seemed to understand this instinctively.

Graveney's tact was another factor. In his Journal of the Season in *The Cricketer*, the Glamorgan batsman Hugh Morris, who was in form early in the season, reported how he had had a call from Graveney apologising for his exclusion from the First Test. The chairman's first words were: ''This isn't the call you've been waiting for.'' Morris was impressed and grateful. Graveney was only an average sort of cricketer himself; Lloyd was less than an all-time great. Perhaps this enables them to empathise more with players' aspirations than some of their loftier predecessors could.

One at a time, please

At Lord's, Mike Atherton became England's longest-serving captain when he led the team for the 42nd time. It was inevitable, given modern scheduling, that Peter May's record would be passed eventually. Atherton has done it without ever commanding the wholehearted support of the public.

There were two main reasons for this: the team's indifferent record, which was not his fault – no one could have been more dedicated to improving that; and his customary scowl, even when there was no reason for it, which his mum should have told him about years ago.

Atherton came close to resigning in August, but the selectors wanted him to stay, and prevailed. They did consider splitting the job, giving the one-day leadership to Adam Hollioake, who proved a popular and successful captain in Sharjah when Atherton took a break, but in the end decided that Atherton should be captain for the whole West Indies tour, both Tests and one-dayers. The Australians blazed a trail by dropping Mark Taylor from their World Series team and making Steve Waugh captain, with patchy success. Fashionable opinion has been all in favour of such schemes. I suspect it's a recipe for confusion and rampant dressing-room politics. Captains have to be allowed to do the job properly, and Atherton had earned the right to carry on.

Then raise the tattered standard high . . .

Even so, England's run of three defeats understandably led to the kind of panic attack to which English cricket has been prone throughout the past decade of extreme ill-health. And in this atmosphere the England and Wales Cricket Board (ECB), which replaced the old TCCB at the start of 1997, first poked its head over the parapet and launched a blueprint for the future of English cricket: "Raising the Standard".

The details of this document are recorded on page 1371. Popular history already seems to have decided that it included the case for a two-divisional County Championship with promotion and relegation, which was rejected by the selfish and parochial counties. Indeed, I read somewhere that Lord MacLaurin, the ECB chairman, was staging a crusade.

Well, it was a funny sort of crusade, because Lord MacLaurin never went into battle, never raised his standard. His actual proposal was for the 18 counties to be divided into three conferences of equal standing, with the champions emerging after a series of play-offs in September.

Fortunately, the various anomalies, complexities and idiocies that would have arisen from this nonsense are now of only academic interest, because the conference plan was thrown out. For a start, the scheme meant that teams in the same division would never have played each other, thus creating the least interesting formula for any sporting competition ever devised.

The ECB's reasoning derived solely from the theory that 14 four-day matches (12 in the main season plus two play-offs for every county to decide placings down the order) was the correct amount for each team, rather than the present 17. This might be so. However, at the same time the Board planned to increase the number of one-day games to an average of 28 (compared to six for the Australian states). This would have wholly negated Lord MacLaurin's stated aim: to improve the England team.

The solution that emerged was certainly more sensible though, in the hysterical atmosphere that followed the Ashes, it was widely rubbished. In 1998, the Championship will be essentially unchanged except that teams who finish in the top eight will compete for a Super Cup in 1999, and the bottom four will play each other, rather than a minor team, before they can progress in the following year's NatWest Trophy. *Wisden* can hardly criticise the idea of a Super Cup, since it was first proposed in these Notes in 1995.

It will replace the Benson and Hedges Cup, with its time-wasting zonal games, and enable the season to be more sensibly skewed so that one-day games can be concentrated later in the summer, when weather and crowds are better. This will leave April and May, when players need to get into nick, much freer for the Championship.

Meanwhile, what was the Sunday League and is becoming the any-day-of-the-week League is not going to have the big increases in fixtures originally envisaged. It will, however, be in two divisions with promotion and relegation. And here's the snag. This means the crucial objective for counties each season will henceforth be to ensure that they stay in the top division of this league. Their recruitment policies will be amended accordingly, making it improbable that any county will dare to concentrate on the first-class game, the way, for instance, Glamorgan and Middlesex did in 1997. Any prospective Shane Warnes can forget their chance of a contract if there is competition from a bowler who hits the deck from a few paces and can knock the ball around a bit at No. 7.

Divide and rule

So the next incarnation of county cricket will be lop-sided: it will force the counties to over-stress the one-day game. Thus one begins to think a two-division Championship is inevitable and will constitute an improvement. Naïve enthusiasts still need to be aware of the drawbacks of such a system (mentioned here in past years) and the unnerving agendas that exist in the minds of some of those who support the same reform. There are men in key positions in English cricket who dream of an elite Championship catering only for big-city clubs and played only on the Test grounds. Nothing would be more guaranteed to kill the appeal of the game once and for all.

Lord MacLaurin apparently did want two divisions but was without the support of all his closest advisers. And, having received negative responses when he hawked the idea round the counties before the season, he did not have the courage to fight for it. The absurd thing is that he could have won. Once the conference plan had been jeered off the table, the counties were asked to vote on two divisions. The motion went down 11–7.

Yet I know of at least three counties who would have changed sides – and thus changed the result – had the following three conditions been met:

1. Sensible, and legally watertight, regulation of the transfer market.
2. Guarantees protecting the future of clubs in the second division. 3. A
convincing cost/benefit analysis of the subject. No such document was sighted.
Like many businessmen, MacLaurin proved politically inept.

For profit . . .

In its first year the ECB did convey, much of the time, an air of efficiency and
progressiveness. It became, however, increasingly obsessed with its efforts to
persuade the Government to remove Test cricket from the list of events that
have to be seen on terrestrial TV, so the rights can be sold to the highest bidder.
Ideally, the Board wants Test cricket to stay on the BBC so it can be seen by
the widest audience. But it understandably and rightly wants more money, and
argues that 180 hours of Test cricket a year cannot be compared to 12 minutes
for the Grand National and Derby. This is a tightrope walk, though. Rugby's
viewing figures have plummeted since it moved to Sky TV. The financial
gains are short-term. The damage is not.

There was no attempt to reform the most pernicious evil within English
cricket. One always feels slightly uneasy at charity fundraisers when well-
heeled people eat and drink to raise money for, say, the starving. But it is
legitimate and effective charity. When they do this to raise money for
sportsmen taking advantage of a tax anomaly, whose employers are simply too
skinflint to pay them properly, one just feels sick.

The benefit system, with its emphasis on time-serving and de-emphasis on
excellence, is profoundly corrosive. While this goes on, argument about the
format of the Championship is like those fierce debates between mediaeval
scholars about how many angels can dance on a pinhead.

The ECB's preferred norm of 14 games would be meaningless in the current
circumstances. Hugh Morris again: "Glamorgan have a week off, something
of a contradiction in terms as Colin Metson has three benefit games and a
dinner organised, and I will be playing for MCC against Ynysygerwn."

. . . and pleasure

There was no argument about the bulk of detail in "Raising the Standard"; the
plans for reforming the amateur game. The advantages of Premier Leagues
should outweigh the small loss of tradition. And the idea of a group of, say, six
elite cricketing universities instead of two is a brilliant one.

Oxford, Cambridge, Durham and (probably) Loughborough would be
obvious choices. If a couple of the newest, not very academic, universities
could also be funded to become elite cricketing centres, there is the potential
for a system that could be an appropriate equivalent of the Australian
Academy, catering for excellent cricketers of varying scholastic ability.

A league of these six universities playing three-day matches on good pitches
from April to June would be a far more sensible use of everyone's time and
money than the farcical non-games between Oxbridge and the counties, which
are an insult to the concept of first-class status.

Underlying all the ideas, however, is a delusion: the notion that part of
English cricket's problem is that it is a closed shop. If only amateurs were

allowed to rise through the system, goes the theory, without necessarily making an early choice of a cricketing career, England teams would improve.

Only English cricket could believe, at the end of the 20th century, that the answer to its troubles is more comic-book dilettantism. The Essex League one week, bash the Aussies the next, hey-ho.

What is really required is the exact reverse: a sound career structure in which the most promising talents are nurtured by the counties, with the help of the elite universities, and are given the prospect of clear and top-notch rewards for success at both domestic and international level, instead of the vague promise of a benefit and the chance of ancillary deals if they get a good agent. We seem to be going backwards.

Eyes wrong

There was too much looking back in more routine matters in 1997. I have never been an enthusiast for the third umpire, but I know when I'm licked. TV replays have added an element of dramatic tension to decision-making, which has been very popular. But this is an insidious addition to cricket, and it keeps occupying new territory.

During the Oval Test against Australia, a four scored by Greg Blewett was converted into a six a day later following close examination of the video evidence, when not merely Blewett but the whole Australian team were already out. The total was changed to 220 after the morning papers reported 218. Where does this stop? Will we start changing results after the match?

During the Warwickshire–Somerset Sunday League game (the first to be floodlit), Trevor Penney's cap dropped off while he was chasing the ball into a dark corner of the field, and helped stop the ball's progress. Ian Botham, acting as *deus ex machina* just as he did in the old days, saw the incident while commentating on TV, replayed it over and over, and alerted the umpires who awarded five penalty runs retrospectively.

The decision seemed wrong anyway, since Law 41.1 says stopping the ball with something other than your person has to be wilful to merit a penalty. However, the problem was not the error, but the retrospection. Luckily, this was not a tight contest. Otherwise, the tactics of both teams could have been seriously affected.

Both these events derived from taking pernickety examination of the evidence too far. These were games of cricket, not murder investigations. If the third umpire cannot instantly advise on such matters, the decision of the man in charge on the field should stand. Right or wrong.

Duck soup

It is of course desirable that a cricket match should produce the fairest possible result. But that cannot be the only consideration. This volume faithfully reports that Glamorgan, batting second in a rain-affected Sunday League match against Warwickshire, scored 81 for three against 147 for seven, and thus won by 17 runs.

As editor of *Wisden*, I would like to be able to explain why this is so. Trouble is, I haven't got the foggiest idea. It is, of course, all tied up with the Duckworth/Lewis system that is used on these occasions and tormented the lives of players, umpires, scorers, journalists and spectators alike in 1997. It is said to be fairer than any other system yet devised.

Unfortunately, virtually everyone except the inventors have to take that on trust, because if we understand the principles which govern the system, we get lost when it comes to its implementation. If the average, reasonably well-informed spectator cannot understand what is happening at an event, then it is not a credible entertainment.

A graceless anniversary

This *Wisden* includes an article to mark the 150th anniversary of the birth of W. G. Grace, which falls on July 18 this year. The author, Geoffrey Moorhouse, has his own view of the great 19th-century champion. My own line would be more charitable.

But even Moorhouse wants to raise a glass to the greatest of sporting Victorians. Cricket, it seems, does not. W.G.'s 50th birthday in 1898 was marked by a special celebration Gents v Players match at Lord's, with the man himself playing. A similar match was arranged for his centenary in 1948 (without his presence). By happy chance, July 18, 1998 is a Saturday with no Test or cup final, when Middlesex are away and, indeed, a special MCC v Rest of the World fixture at Lord's has been scheduled.

Nothing to do with W.G. though. It is a memorial match for Diana, Princess of Wales. Her tragic death last year affected millions of people (though only one county was sufficiently affected to postpone a home fixture the day it happened). But her connection with cricket was somewhat remote, it has to be said, and, of all the many worthy causes which deserve support, her Memorial Fund is perhaps not the one in most urgent need of cricket's patronage. I am sorry that MCC has, uncharacteristically, opted for the obsession of the moment, rather than a rare chance both to honour English cricket's most lustrous star and to choose its own charitable priorities.

The manure business

In 1949 Group Captain A. J. Holmes, the chairman of England's selectors, remarked: "The buttons of the mushrooms of a new era in English cricket are just showing through." He was talking about young players like May, Graveney, Trueman and Bailey who would help make England the top team in the world for most of the 1950s. Maybe we are now at a similar stage in the cycle. It looked that way when 19-year-old Ben Hollioake was smashing the Australian bowling to all corners of Lord's in the one-day international last May, and again when England won the Under-19 World Cup in February. As *Wisden* went to press, England had just lost the first Port-of-Spain Test having looked certain of victory; before they can flourish, mushrooms always have to disappear beneath loads of muck.

GOOCH: CRICKET'S No. 1 RUN MACHINE

By CHRISTOPHER MARTIN-JENKINS

The golfer Joyce Wethered was once playing a crucial shot in a major championship when an express train suddenly thundered past. "Didn't the train put you off?" she was asked later. "What train?" she replied. The ability to forget the clutter of everything else and concentrate this completely is surprisingly rare, even among great performers in sport. But Graham Gooch had it in full measure.

And this skill, more the result of mental steel than any natural gift, was the single most important reason for the fact that, by the time he started his final match for Essex on July 23, 1997, Graham Alan Gooch, born at Whipps Cross in Leytonstone exactly 44 years before, had become the most prolific player in history.

One had sensed that he must be somewhere near, when all his limited-overs runs had been added to his final tally of 44,841 in first-class games at an average of 49.11, but it took the computations of Robert Brooke to confirm for *Wisden* this stupendous fact. No single batsman, not Grace, nor Hobbs, nor Woolley, nor Boycott, nor any of his contemporaries in an age of proliferating fixtures, had made so many runs in top-class cricket as the pink-faced, heavy-limbed yeoman of Essex. He had, in fact, unnoticed, overtaken Jack Hobbs's total of 61,237 runs when he reached 67 in a Benson and Hedges Cup game between Essex and Gloucestershire at Chelmsford on May 9, 1995. He finished with 65,928 at 45.81. It is hard to imagine who might ever overtake him.

Gooch, unfortunately, chose to release the news of his retirement through a Sunday newspaper whose chief business is scandal-mongering, but he was always acutely aware of his own worth and the need to make the most of that. In cricketing terms that made him the dedicated professional *par excellence*: steady, sound, sober, solid. It is still a revelation to know that he was not just the latest, perhaps the last, in a long line of that sort of English professional batsman, but, by numerical proof, the hungriest and most acquisitive of them all. He surpassed men like Sutcliffe, Hutton and Boycott from the north; Grace, Hayward, Hobbs and Mead, from the south.

It seems natural to exclude Woolley, Hendren, Hammond and Graveney of the other leading batsmen, because they were somehow different in their nature and approach: more artists than accountants. Yet Gooch himself – and this makes his achievement all the more remarkable – belongs more truly with the entertainers: he was a magnificent sight in full sail. This was no dabber of singles, no delicate leg-glancer or specialist in the smooth caress of a half-volley through extra cover. On the contrary, he was a bold, imposing player: a mighty driver and fierce square-cutter, who looked at the crease to be taller and bulkier than he actually was, with a bat apparently broader than the law permits.

When I first saw him, for MCC against the Australians in 1975, he was still only 21 but he pull-drove Jeff Thomson into the Lord's Grand Stand

for six, before repeating the treatment on Gary Gilmour. Six years later at
Sabina Park, in the final Test of England's 1980-81 tour of the West Indies,
he temporarily obliterated a ferocious attack of Holding, Marshall, Croft
and Garner. Croft, hitherto bullyingly successful, was savaged for 56 runs
in eight overs on a pitch which was hard and bouncy. Gooch cut him over
third man for one six and hooked Marshall for another. He had made 103
out of 155 for two in the 40th over and 153 out of 249 when he was fifth
out.

His greatest innings was one run higher and also against West Indies, at
Headingley in grey weather on a tricky pitch in June 1991. It took him
seven and a half hours. The forces arrayed against him were no less fierce:
Ambrose, Patterson, Walsh and Marshall. Gooch was captain and more than
just the backbone of his side. Throughout England's second innings, he
virtually was the side. He carried his bat for 154 out of 252 and England
went on to win. So they had, too, of course, when he made his 333 and 123
in a single Test at Lord's against India in 1990. These, however, constituted
easier pickings.

This is all well documented. It is the all-round consistency, the
excellence of his figures against all types of bowler – Terry Alderman's
supremacy over him in 1989 was the result of a technical fault assiduously
worked out and corrected – and, above all, in all types of cricket, which
placed him above the players of his own era. Time and again, he shone on
the major one-day occasion. He won nine NatWest match awards and 22 in
the Benson and Hedges, both records. His 129 not out against West Indies
at Port-of-Spain in 1985-86 was the most exciting, sustained one-day
innings I have ever seen.

Viv Richards played these sort of innings more often. Gordon Greenidge,
who played three more internationals than Gooch's 125, and Desmond
Haynes, who played many more, scored more one-day international runs,
and so have plenty of others, but no other Englishman. Of the top ten
scorers in one-day internationals, all have played county cricket and know
what it is to switch so often between first-class games and one-day matches
of differing lengths. But when the totals of the modern greats are totted up,
Haynes, Richards, Greenidge, Boycott, Amiss, Javed Miandad, Salim
Malik, Border, Jones, Boon and the rest all fall short of Gooch. The nearest
in terms of innings played, Dennis Amiss, scored more than 10,000 fewer
runs overall (55,462) from only 41 fewer innings. In all the categories
except one-day internationals – Amiss played only 18 of them – his average
is significantly lower than Gooch's. The difference is most marked in the
NatWest and Benson and Hedges, in which Gooch averaged 48.98 and
52.28 to Amiss's 39.00 and 34.86.

All this does not, of course, make Graham Gooch the greatest player of
his time but, even if we judge him only by the timeless yardstick of first-
class cricket, ignoring the mind-wearying, sinew-stretching demands of the
limited-overs game, his stature is clear. After the reduction in Championship matches in 1969, he alone scored above 2,000 runs in more than three
seasons. He did so in five: 1984, 1985, 1988, 1990 and 1993; another 56
runs in his last full season, 1996, would have made it six. He made eight

[*Patrick Eagar*   [*Patrick Eagar*

The Gooch Years: The 1975 model (*above*); the 1991 model, during his epic 154 not out at Headingley (*below left*) . . . but some things never changed (*below right*).

[*Patrick Eagar*   [*Tim Bradford* (The Observer)

first-class hundreds that year and, had he not promised his dying father that he would play one more year, it would have been the right note on which to finish.

It was one of the few occasions when he allowed emotion to supersede his cricketing judgment. What made him special was his capacity for hard work and rigid self-discipline. He earned every run.

GOOCH: THE NUMBERS

	R	I	NO	HS	100s	Avge
First-class	44,841	988	75	333	128	49.11
One-day internationals	4,290	122	6	142	8	36.98
Sunday League	8,573	268	23	176	12	34.99
Benson and Hedges	5,176	114	15	198*	15	52.28
Gillette/NatWest	2,547	56	4	144	6	48.98
Refuge Assurance Cup	42	2	0	31	0	21.00
Nissan Shield (South Africa)	297	9	0	60	0	33.00
SA rebel one-day games	162	3	0	114	1	54.00
	65,928	1,562	123	333	170	45.81

THE TOP TWELVE

The following table shows the leading run-scorers in first-class and top-level limited-overs cricket:

Player	R	I	NO	HS	100s	Avge
1 **G. A. Gooch (10)**	**65,928**	**1,562**	**123**	**333**	**170**	**45.81**
2 J. B. Hobbs (1)	61,237	1,315	106	316*	197	50.65
3 F. E. Woolley (2)	58,969	1,532	85	305*	145	40.75
4 G. Boycott (8)	58,030	1,302	203	261*	158	52.80
5 E. H. Hendren (3)	57,611	1,300	166	301*	170	50.80
6 D. L. Amiss (12)	55,462	1,521	159	262*	115	40.72
7 C. P. Mead (4)	55,061	1,340	185	280*	153	47.67
8 W. G. Grace (5)	54,896	1,493	105	344	126	39.55
9 C. G. Greenidge (24)	53,094	1,311	105	273*	123	44.02
10 I. V. A. Richards (32)	52,755	1,248	122	322	139	46.85
11 W. R. Hammond (6)	50,551	1,005	104	336*	167	56.10
12 H. Sutcliffe (7)	50,138	1,088	123	313	149	51.95

Figures in brackets denote position in first-class run-scoring table (see page 190).
The table includes all first-class matches, one-day internationals, Gillette Cup/NatWest Trophy, Benson and Hedges Cup, Sunday League, Refuge Assurance Cup, domestic one-day competitions in South Africa and the West Indies and one-day matches on the 1981-82 rebel tour of South Africa.

Statistics: Robert Brooke

Christopher Martin-Jenkins is cricket correspondent of the Daily Telegraph *and a BBC commentator. Robert Brooke is a freelance statistician.*

DENIS COMPTON: ENTRANCING PLAYER . . .

By LORD COWDREY OF TONBRIDGE

Denis Compton's death in April 1997 touched a chord with many people who never knew him. They instinctively realised that for someone who lived a full and disorganised life, seldom out of the public gaze, he was a wonderfully simple and friendly character. What was surprising was that behind the apparently happy-go-lucky, serene temperament lurked an apprehensive soul, racked with big-occasion nerves as he waited to go in to bat.

I found this a real consolation, for it showed his human touch. Every top sportsman has butterflies in his tummy when faced with important challenges, but I had never expected him to look so agitated. When I first batted with him in Australia, it was this simple, unashamed expression of nerves – the enchanting smile never far away – that immediately warmed me to him.

It was the smile rather than the nerves that came through to the public. Everyone could also see his breathtaking genius for producing the unexpected and his exceptional gifts of touch and timing – at any ball game. He was so quick on his feet and could move yards down the wicket, sometimes before the bowler had let go of the ball, and get away with it. He piloted the ball through gaps in the field with an effortless ease, the bat ringing with a mellow sound. Fielders watched helplessly whilst bowlers tried to curb their temper. But at the same time his technique was sound and his defence correct; he had the straightest bat in the team, and watched the ball closely on to it. Only when a fast bowler dropped the ball short would we see the power in his strong right hand. But it was the timing and fleetness of foot, the lock of hair flopping down over his perspiring brow, that entranced his army of followers.

The modesty of the man also came through. I was a 15-year-old schoolboy when I saw him play for the first time. I shall never forget the innings he played, nor his charm as he gave time afterwards signing my autograph book. Little did I realise we would be playing Tests together less than seven years later, and sharing a memorable partnership at Adelaide in the match when we retained the Ashes.

A few months after that, he was batting against South Africa in 1955 at Old Trafford. With a borrowed old Gunn & Moore belonging to Freddie Titmus, he scored 158 in the first innings, but an even more brilliant 71 in the second. Hugh Tayfield, the most accurate of off-spinners, would never forget it. He maintained that he bowled the perfect over: every ball on the same spot as planned. Denis pushed the first one back down the wicket, and then proceeded to despatch the next five balls for four to five different parts of Old Trafford. The crowd rose to him, leaving Denis to shake hands with the bowler before he hid himself away at long leg.

But Denis also had the gift of making anyone who batted with him feel better. "You will have to teach me that shot, young Colin," he shouted to me in our first big innings together. "How did you learn that one?" It did wonders for my morale and confidence.

John Warr, in his superb address at Westminster Abbey at the Service of Thanksgiving for Denis's life, referred to his famously bad running between the wickets: "Denis called you for a run, and shouted a despairing 'Good luck' as you hurried by." Happily, I never experienced this first-hand. My only problems were off the field: thanks to alphabetical order, we often shared hotel rooms or adjoining pegs in dressing-rooms. Denis would start a match, or indeed a tour, with very little clothing. I would have to fill the gaps. But he borrowed them all in such a delightful way that it was very hard to ask for them back.

He never could find the time to write letters, or keep a diary of engagements. He received an enormous pile of mail every day, and he relied on a few of us to keep it all in good order. In this way, he was something of an eccentric, but everyone seemed to make allowances for him. The same with his idea of practice and preparation for the big match. There was no gain from interfering with his natural pattern. If it was his day, he could set the team on the path to victory.

Denis would have thrived in any era. I am certain he would have coped with the fast short-pitched bowling of the modern age as well as anyone. And he would have been one of the greatest one-day batsmen, such was his relish for a challenge and his skill at innovation. And he would have enjoyed it all so much. This was at the heart of Denis Compton, the cricketer of exceptional charm.

Lord Cowdrey of Tonbridge, formerly Colin Cowdrey, played 114 Tests for England, 11 of them alongside Denis Compton.

. . . DELIGHTFUL MAN

By FRANK KEATING

The timing, impeccable to the last, was poignant. The news came on the morning the cricketers of England were preparing to call "Play!" on the first day of 1997's County Championship. Then, one by one, the pavilion flags were lowered to half-mast and young men in cream flannels, who knew him not, stood to attention for a minute because they knew who he was all right, and what he had contributed everlastingly to the innate goodness as well as the grandeur of their game.

Compton was an all-time great and, as those standards dipped at Canterbury, Chelmsford, Old Trafford, Trent Bridge and Hove – which in his bonny prime he had sunnily beguiled – bells metaphorically tolled the world over at places happy to accept that team-game players can lift spirits by their skill and chivalry.

Because of the drab days he so illuminated, Denis was almost a cultural icon to Britain of the immediate post-war, a valorous talisman of gaiety and of hope. As Chesterton had it: "There is a great man who makes every man feel small. But the really great man is the one that makes every man feel great."

I was always awestruck in the presence of this cigarette-card monarch of my infancy. We last spoke when Alec Bedser won his New Year knighthood. "No doubt about it," said Denis, "Alec was the best medium-pacer I ever saw, and the greatest trier of the lot." And then he added "Lovely chap, too." There were very few men Denis remembered of whom he would not add: "Lovely chap, too."

The Compton style: At The Oval in the 1953 Test against Australia (*above*) and at a gala night held in his honour at the Empress Hall in London in 1949 (*below*).

We spoke as well that day of the death a few months before of Jack Robertson, the opening batsman who had laid down the markers for the entrance of Compton and Edrich and their string of voluptuous partnerships for Middlesex ("Dear Jack . . . lovely chap with it") and Denis at once became croaky and saddened with age. "There are very few of my vintage left any more. The awfulness of age is that every day you wake up and quite expect to hear another lifelong chum has gone . . ."

Fifty years before he died, to the week, at his beloved Lord's, he set forth on his summer of summers. England was still war-cowering and uncertain: scant, skint lives being put back together in monochrome. In glorious Technicolor, Compton's genius – the whistling happy-go-lucky errand-boy, his feet on the handlebars – lightened the load, and Neville Cardus acclaimed: "Never have I been so deeply touched on a cricket ground as in this heavenly summer, when I went to Lord's to see a pale-faced crowd, existing on rations, the rocket-bomb still in the ears of most, and see the strain of anxiety and affliction passed from all hearts and shoulders at the sight of Compton in full sail . . . each stroke a flick of delight, a propulsion of happy, sane, healthy life. There were no rations in an innings by Compton."

John Arlott wrote his first cricket book in that summer of 1947. It ended: "To close the eyes is to see again that easy, happy figure at the wicket, pushing an unruly forelock out of the eye and then, as it falls down again, playing off the wrong foot a stroke which passes deep-point like a bullet . . . never again will the boyish delight in hitting a ball with a piece of wood flower directly into charm and gaiety and all the wealth of achievement."

Compton's own favourite innings that year – "probably the most memorable of all, I think" – was for Middlesex against Kent at Lord's, "a run-chase, 390-odd at over 100 an hour; we just failed, but it was such glorious fun going for them." Typical Compo. His 300 in three hours in Benoni, South Africa, was always passed off with a chuckle and "Ooh, great fun". Of his 17 Test match centuries he would not disagree when you said that context was all, and the best was 145 at Old Trafford in 1948, at the beginning of which a bumper from Ray Lindwall had cut his eyebrow like a boxer's.

Movietone News the next week gave over its whole bulletin to that innings and Leslie Mitchell's evocative dulcets ended the commentary: "Shaky and ill as he must have been, Compton plays like an utter master. Great as Compton is, never has he been greater." Denis would tell how, groggy, he only continued that epic innings after a few slugs of doctor's-orders brandy.

It was apt, too, that he died on St George's Day, because, Chesterton again:

> St George he was for England
> And before he slayed the dragon
> He drank a pint of English ale
> Out of an English flagon.

Lovely chap, too.

Frank Keating is sports columnist on The Guardian, *where this article first appeared. Compton is featured in his new book,* Frank Keating's Sporting Century.

WOODCOCK'S HUNDRED

In the early summer of 1997, *The Times* published a series of articles naming the 100 Greatest Cricketers of all time. It ran over a period of five weeks, listing the players in ascending order, and reached a climax on the Saturday of the Old Trafford Test, when the paper named W. G. Grace rather than Sir Donald Bradman as the greatest of all. Many Australians present expressed surprise and annoyance, and Shane Warne (No. 13) and Steve Waugh (95) promptly destroyed England on the field.

The list was compiled by John Woodcock, the paper's cricket correspondent for 34 years, the former editor of *Wisden* and the man believed to have seen more Test cricket than anyone else in history. None the less, even Woodcock did not see Grace play, still less Alfred Mynn of Kent (died 1861, No. 4 on the list) or Billy Beldham and John Small of Hambledon (Nos. 39 and 61).

No one, least of all Woodcock, pretended the list was definitive: "Inevitably invidious and essentially provocative," he said. It was, however, a very well-informed basis for many splendid arguments.

1. W. G. Grace	35. K. S. Ranjitsinhji	68. C. V. Grimmett
2. D. G. Bradman	36. F. M. M. Worrell	69. M. D. Marshall
3. G. S. Sobers	37. A. R. Border	70. J. C. Laker
4. A. Mynn	38. C. L. Walcott	71. Waqar Younis
5. J. B. Hobbs	39. W. Beldham	72. D. I. Gower
6. S. F. Barnes	40. G. A. Lohmann	73. C. T. B. Turner
7. W. R. Hammond	41. G. H. Hirst	74. A. C. MacLaren
8. I. V. A. Richards	42. H. Sutcliffe	75. G. L. Jessop
9. I. T. Botham	43. M. J. Procter	76. A. Shaw
10. D. C. S. Compton	44. G. S. Chappell	77. J. B. Statham
11. L. Hutton	45. F. S. Trueman	78. V. A. P. van der Bijl
12. F. E. Woolley	46. H. J. Tayfield	79. C. G. Macartney
13. S. K. Warne	47. T. Richardson	80. R. B. Simpson
14. V. T. Trumper	48. M. C. Cowdrey	81. C. E. L. Ambrose
15. B. A. Richards	49. Kapil Dev	82. Fazal Mahmood
16. Imran Khan	50. B. S. Bedi	83. W. H. Ponsford
17. K. R. Miller	51. R. N. Harvey	84. Hanif Mohammad
18. R. Benaud	52. R. B. Kanhai	85. F. S. Jackson
19. D. K. Lillee	53. G. A. Gooch	86. R. G. D. Willis
20. A. V. Bedser	54. C. B. Fry	87. W. W. Armstrong
21. G. A. Headley	55. A. P. E. Knott	88. D. L. Underwood
22. R. R. Lindwall	56. A. K. Davidson	89. S. Ramadhin
23. S. M. Gavaskar	57. K. F. Barrington	90. L. R. Gibbs
24. E. R. Dexter	58. Javed Miandad	91. W. W. Hall
25. S. R. Tendulkar	59. I. M. Chappell	92. V. Mankad
26. W. J. O'Reilly	60. Wasim Akram	93. H. Larwood
27. E. D. Weekes	61. J. Small	94. J. M. Gregory
28. B. C. Lara	62. G. Boycott	95. S. R. Waugh
29. R. J. Hadlee	63. A. G. Steel	96. H. W. Taylor
30. R. G. Pollock	64. T. G. Evans	97. A. A. Donald
31. A. Shrewsbury	65. M. A. Holding	98. S. J. McCabe
32. F. R. Spofforth	66. L. N. Constantine	99. P. A. de Silva
33. P. B. H. May	67. C. H. Lloyd	100. J. R. Reid
34. W. Rhodes		

W.G. GRACE: 150 YEARS ON

By GEOFFREY MOORHOUSE

On July 18, it will be 150 years since W.G. Grace was born, but there are other ways of measuring how distant he is in time. For one thing, no one still alive, not even Jim Swanton, can remember seeing him play (although in *Sort of a Cricket Person*, E.W.S. notes that "I am supposed to have watched [him] from my perambulator on the Forest Hill ground around 1910"). Eight decades have passed since Grace died, yet he dogs us still, demanding our attention at regular intervals.

The statistics of his career are alone enough to explain why – more than 54,000 first-class runs (there are at least two different versions of the precise figure, so let's leave it at that) spread across 44 seasons, including 839 in just eight days of 1876, when he hit a couple of triple-centuries, and only one other batsman managed to top a thousand runs in the entire season; a thousand in May in 1895, when he was nearly 47; and 2,800-odd wickets costing less than 18 runs apiece. I suppose we might wonder why his bowling average wasn't even more impressive, given the ropy pitches on which Dr Grace played. No modern cricketer would deign to turn out on them, which makes his batting all the more wondrous, and comparisons with Bradman or anyone since quite pointless.

But there was not that much to Grace apart from these skills and his devotion to his family. A hand of whist appears to have marked the limit of his capacity for cerebration, and if one wished to be rude to suburbia one might identify Grace as suburban man incarnate, fluctuating mentally as well as physically between the fringes of Bristol and the London Counties, ultimately coming to rest in Eltham. His one inherited asset was that he came from a clan which was dotty about a great game and dutiful (but in some cases no more) about the general practice of medicine, with no doubt in its collective mind which came first at all times and in all places. His brother E.M. Grace, who was a coroner, once had a corpse put on ice until he could attend to it at close of play, and W.G. himself must have had one of the most prolonged medical trainings in history because he so frequently interrupted it in order to exercise his major talent at the crease. He began to study as a bachelor of 19, and was a father of three in his thirties before taking his final qualification at Westminster Hospital. His most conspicuous act as a doctor is thought to have occurred when an unfortunate fieldsman impaled himself on the boundary fence at Old Trafford.

It was simply because the cricketing Grace totally dominated his own era that an exasperated C.L.R. James could not understand why standard history books of the period never mentioned him. This man, for heaven's sake, opened for England at the age of 50 – and at the age of 18 he had scored 224 not out for England against Surrey, in a match which he left halfway through in order to win a quarter-mile hurdles championship at the Crystal Palace! No wonder he was the best-known Englishman apart from Mr Gladstone, so much so that Evelyn Waugh's friend, Monsignor Ronnie

Knox, waggishly suggested that Gladstone and Grace were really one and the same celebrity.

Athletic is not a word that obviously comes to mind when contemplating Grace in his prime, though a slim young man did precede the pot-bellied genius who in middle age was far too heavy for any horse to bear. I have often wondered how stylishly he played his strokes, ever since I saw some film in which he appeared to be brandishing his bat as though he was about to poke the fire with it. Something tells me that he never hit the ball as gracefully as Victor Trumper did in the famous photo of his straight drive; Grace, I suspect, was much more about power than aesthetics.

That, at any rate, would fit what we know of his character in general. Apart from tenderness to his relatives and a generous soft spot for children, he was not, I think, a particularly attractive man, though he could sometimes (and it is usually recorded as remarkable) encourage a young player on his own side with – as the saying went in his day – bluff good humour. After the Australians had experienced him for the first time, a commentator Down Under observed that, "For so big a man, he is surprisingly tenacious on very small points." He was notorious for employing, in order to pursue victory or personal achievement, a variety of wiles and tricks that may be thought of as, well, hardly cricket. He was also, throughout his career, quite breathtakingly grasping when his eye caught the glint of hard cash.

It was the social historian Eric Midwinter who, some years ago, pointed out that on Grace's first tour of Australia in 1873-74 (when he was a medical student simultaneously enjoying his honeymoon) he extracted a fee of £1,500 from the organisers, which would be well over £100,000 at present values. On his second tour in 1891-92, one-fifth of the entire cost of transporting 13 English cricketers across the world, supporting them in Australia and paying them for what they did there, went into Grace's pocket. He regularly collected testimonials – one, worth £1,458, was organised by MCC so that he might buy a medical practice – and overall probably took something like £1 million in today's currency out of the game; and, remember, there was no sponsorship nor endorsements in those days to inflate a star's income. This was in a period when the prosperous middle classes were earning no more than £1,000 a year, a highly skilled artisan £200, and a labourer half as much if he was lucky. A good professional county cricketer in the second half of the 19th century saw his wages rise from £100 to £250. No wonder it cost twice as much to get into some English grounds if Grace was playing than if he was not.

The astonishing thing about the mercenary Grace, of course, is that he was classified and has ever since been glorified as an amateur. Nothing more exposed the humbug that used to smother the entire topic of Gents v Players than an examination of Grace's financial rewards from the game; and nothing more reveals the intellectual dishonesty at the heart of that humbug than something Grace once said when trying to argue the Gloucestershire committee into playing more amateurs than professionals.

[*Popperfoto*   [*Popperfoto*

W.G. Grace, who was born 150 years ago in July, collected more than 54,000 runs and 2,800 wickets in a career that spanned 44 seasons.

He declared his fear for the future of cricket if it became wholly professional. ''Betting and all kindred evils will follow in its wake, and instead of the game being followed up for love, it will simply be a matter of £ s d.'' Prophetic words, perhaps; but it ill became W.G. Grace to mouth them.

It will be gathered from the above that he has never been a hero of mine, not since the day in adolescence when I discovered that he was sometimes a shameless cheat in a game that, I was being asked to believe, was wholly honourable. I shall nevertheless drink to his memory on July 18 because his tremendous gifts, especially his phenomenal batting, were largely responsible for the elevation of cricket from just another 19th-century game, which had become popular partly because it lent itself to gambling.

Grace's towering presence, more than any other single factor, transformed it into the unrivalled spectator sport of summer, first of all in England, subsequently in other lands spread widely across the world. I would even suggest that a true measurement of W.G.'s unique stature is that he is instantly identifiable, even by some who are uninterested in his vocation, by his initials alone. I cannot think of another human being in any sphere, not even W.C. Fields, of whom this is also true.

Geoffrey Moorhouse's books include The Best Loved Game *and* Lord's. *His latest,* Sun Dancing, *is an imaginative reconstruction of life in a remote Irish monastery. He was book reviewer for* Wisden *in 1994.*

AND LORD'S SAID: "LET THERE BE LIGHTS" . . .

By ROB STEEN

"The idea that the poor should have leisure," observed Bertrand Russell, "has always been shocking to the rich." He might well have had cricket in mind. Inevitably, much cricket goes on while most people are working. But in England they have lately left bank holidays blank. The guardians of the greensward have not moved rapidly to take the opportunity of staging the game at sociable hours.

Happily, times are at last changing. In the nethermost crannies of the minutes of the International Cricket Council's meeting in July 1997 lurked an item of inestimable significance to the future of Test cricket. In the event of bad light, ICC said, play could continue under floodlights. And at Perth in November, between Australia and New Zealand, it happened for the first time. At a time when the game's highest form of expression is struggling in several countries to justify its existence as a commercial entity, the advent of Tests with supper intervals cannot be far away.

Of all the advances in the competitive arts since the Second World War, nothing, not even the satellite dish, can match the cultural significance of the pylon. Here is sport freed from the tyrannies of the working day. Here, moreover, is sport in Technicolor and Sensurround. The lights do not merely illuminate; they appear to magnify and intensify. To be among the 15,000 present at Edgbaston on a balmy Wednesday night in July 1997, for English cricket's first floodlit flannelled foolery of any consequence, was to wonder why the counties had dallied for so long. Here was cricket without an exclusion zone, a family affair complete with crèche and bouncy castle.

All this happened a mere 119 years after floodlights were first tried on an English cricket ground. The ground, though, was Bramall Lane, Sheffield, and the sport was football: in October 1878, 12,000 paid to see a game featuring two Sheffield representative teams and the novelty of electricity; another 8,000 sneaked in free, because no one thought to light the entrances.

The nearest cricket came to such an experiment was at The Oval in 1889, when the second day of Yorkshire's Championship match with Surrey was extended until 7 p.m. because the game was almost over and neither captain wanted to come back next day. It was late August and daylight saving had not been invented, so it was already dark. The players had to rely on the gas lamps from the streets of Kennington.

Typically, it was America which really blazed the trail. When he went there in the 1930s to turn professional, Fred Perry found himself lobbing and smashing in exhibition halls and skating rinks. In 1935 the Cincinnati Reds hosted baseball's first major league night game. English sport was slower on the uptake. When the Arsenal manager, Herbert Chapman, tried to push the idea to meet the growing challenge of greyhound racing, he was rebuffed by football officials. The first floodlit Football League match did not come until February 1956.

Cricket, inevitably, endured an even lengthier awakening. In 1932, the Western Suburbs grade players in Sydney practised under lights, but the bowlers complained that the dew made the white ball hard to grip. There was the odd experiment in the 1950s: the enterprising Middlesex spinner Jack Young staged a benefit match at Highbury, and there was one mid-summer night's frolic in Brisbane, but it took Kerry Packer to transform the ugly gosling into a golden goose.

Spurred by the initial public apathy towards World Series Cricket and the promise of a prime-time television audience, toes were dipped at VFL Park on December 14, 1977. Late arrivals from offices and factories swelled the gate to 6,300, the largest to date for Packer's seemingly vainglorious revolution. The sightscreens were turned around and painted black. The lights were switched on at 6.30, after which a white ball was used, yellow and orange having been deemed unsuitable. Tony Greig, the World XI captain, opted to bat first, reasoning that any voluntary confrontation with Dennis Lillee under such unfamiliar conditions, even though bouncers were to be barred, would be an act of hubris; the Australians still prevailed at a canter. For the defence, a skier held with aplomb by Imran Khan served as Exhibit A. Exhibit B was Ian Chappell's decisive 69, compiled first in bright sunlight, then in the twilight, then lit by high-wattage bulbs.

English reactions ranged from distaste to prescience. John Woodcock observed that Australians, "being always early in their evening meal", were "well-suited by night-time sport". David Frith attributed his nausea to fatigue: "If I'm prejudiced at all perhaps it is in favour of cricket in God's sunshine." Alan Lee's conclusion was unarguable. Packer had "struck gold" and "would arouse the envy of the traditional authorities".

Before long, Dayglo kit was *de rigueur* and WSC was attracting the young and unjaundiced, expanding the audience. State funds provided pylons in Brisbane and Perth. English concessions to all this garish modernity were hesitant and fleeting. There was the Lambert and Butler Cup, held at football grounds in 1981; even though Clive Lloyd, Ian Botham and David Gower were on parade, the semi-finals and final at Stamford Bridge drew a paltry 2,500. By the 1990s, portable pylons were a possibility, so cricket grounds could get temporary lighting. But a Sixes event at The Oval in 1994 was the least propitious attempt yet. It was cancelled halfway through when the principals demanded payment, which the organisers could not provide. The headline in *The Times* alluded to a broader scepticism: "Rotten enterprise worthy of contempt."

The Indian Board of Control used profits from the last World Cup to install floodlights at its principal venues. Dennis Amiss, the Warwickshire chief executive, has estimated the total cost of equipping every first-class county headquarters at £4 million, a far from prohibitive sum. But after unveiling his blueprint for the future of the game Lord MacLaurin, chairman of the ECB, admitted that the possibility had not even been discussed. Given the unalloyed success of Edgbaston, an encouraging attempt in poor weather at Hove and a reasonably well-attended Roses friendly at Old Trafford, it was an astonishing oversight. Here, surely, was the sugar to coat the pill of a two-divisional Championship for the reluctant counties.

[*Patrick Eagar*

Moonrise in Melbourne: The scene at one of cricket's pioneering floodlit games, under Kerry
Packer's aegis at VFL Park in 1978-79.

Technically, the main problem is the ball. Since the white model used in
the one-day game is felt to lack durability, the preferred projectile for the
Sheffield Shield's inaugural day/night fixture, between Western Australia
and Queensland at Perth in November 1994, was a traditional model tanned
in yellow. Some batsmen complained about visibility; but the damp
atmosphere and seaming pitch apparently had rather more to do with their
tribulations. In Britain, dew is also a concern, hence the dispensation
granted to Sussex to drag a rope through the outfield, though Tony Pigott,
the club's chief executive, maintains that, when he inspected the pitch at
10 p.m. the previous evening, it was "as dry as a bone".

Such objections, Pigott argues, are petty, so typical of the game's
aversion to change. It is hard to disagree. Some estimate that batting first in
a day/night international is worth a start of 20 to 30 runs, but in a longer
game of cricket, there is a stronger likelihood of any imbalances evening
out. Besides, the vagaries and uncertainties can only add spice to our
favourite dish. Further self-denial is senseless. Unless, that is, the aim is to
prove Bertrand Russell right.

*Rob Steen is a freelance journalist and the author of five cricket books. The
latest,* Poms and Cobbers, *is a diary of the 1997 Ashes series.*

THE END OF CHIVALRY

By ANDREW LONGMORE

Now that Eton v Harrow is no longer the great social occasion of an English summer, cricket between English public schools rarely gets much space in the national press. The 1997 match between Marlborough and Radley was different.

On a rain-hit day, Marlborough, who were put in to bat, spent 68.3 overs scoring 170, leaving Radley a mere 18 overs in reply. The Marlborough innings was marred by verbal abuse of the batsmen and a number of deliberate no-balls, while on the boundary tempers flared among the spectators. The Warden of Radley admitted that the match "was not played in an attractive atmosphere" and fixtures in major sports between these two historic schools were cancelled for the foreseeable future.

Though the most publicised, this was not the only instance of bad sportsmanship to emerge from schools who once epitomised the Corinthian spirit so absolutely that they would remove their goalkeeper if they conceded a penalty, on the grounds that to defend the consequences of foul play would be improper. In an Under-17 match in Kent, a boy spat at the wicket-keeper after being bowled and had to be forced into the opposition dressing-room at the end of play to apologise.

A match between two crack cricketing schools, Tonbridge of Kent and Grey High School from Port Elizabeth, South Africa, with both sides protecting unbeaten records, quickly degenerated from competitiveness into verbal intimidation, and highlighted a clash of prevailing sporting cultures. Tonbridge won, but only after an unpleasant afternoon. One of the umpires deemed the South Africans 80 per cent responsible.

"Most schools will now play two or three overseas sides a season," Paul Taylor, the Tonbridge cricket master, said. "That has an influence on the boys. Grey were competitive to a degree our players had not seen before and one of our boys was drawn into that."

Here, in microcosm, is English cricket's dilemma. "We have to get a bit of nastiness into our game," the England vice-captain Nasser Hussain said the day after Australia had secured the Ashes for the fifth consecutive series. "In Australia, even in grade cricket, they are abusing you, rucking you and making it very clear they want you back in the pavilion pretty quick." There is a danger that, because Australia have been winning and England losing, the courtesies which the English gave to the cricketing world get blamed for the problems.

Umpires at every level of the English game report that teams are more voluble, more excitable, harder to control than once they were. Very few batsmen walk; bowlers pout and teapot when decisions go against them. Encouragement by the fielding side too often crosses the thin line between morale-boosting and naked intimidation – an average of three times in each county match, according to one first-class umpire – and ordinary league clubs are framing their own disciplinary code to enforce standards which, old timers will tell you, were once instinctive.

In a NatWest Trophy match, two Devon batsmen were treated to premeditated verbal – and personal – abuse by the Leicestershire players. And an incident of persistent intimidation of the umpires, in a Bassetlaw and District League match, resulted in a nine-match ban for one captain, a deduction of points and the ostracism by his club of one of the umpires.

Some people say that the game merely reflects modern society, which is louder and more aggressive. Cricket's reputation for good manners has always been a convenient mask for skulduggery, from W.G. onwards. If, as the anecdote claims, W.G. was bowled and replaced the bails blaming the wind, these days 15 television cameras would have proved him a cheat. Is it too cynical to suggest that a similar thought passed through the head of Ian Healy, the brilliant Australian wicket-keeper, who disclaimed a dubious catch at Lord's and was applauded for his sportsmanship by umpire David Shepherd on the field and by the entire national press the following morning? Healy is not a cheat, but he may be a pragmatist.

The Australians won, however, without any excesses. The series, given the intense scrutiny, was remarkably free of rancour. That is as it should be. Cricket is a contact sport no less than rugby or football, but it is contact of the mind. Its skills are subtler, its rituals more pronounced. The umpires take the field first, the batsmen leave first, generally applauded by the fielding side. In between, the action is more sedate, calculating and thoughtful. There is time for respect and, as Mark Ilott and Robert Croft would doubtless confirm after their puerile shoving match in the NatWest Trophy semi-final, embarrassment. If protocol is breached, if some fielders slip into the pavilion before the opposing batsmen, the game will not collapse in a heap, it will simply be more anarchic and less attractive.

Test cricket ceased to be a metaphor for fair play long before the systematic assault on a batsman's confidence which has become known as sledging became fashionable. The sadness is that the practice has been lauded, mistaken as a prerequisite for excellence. There is an excuse for Test players, earning a hard living from the game, going over the top. There is none for schoolboys.

"We don't want public school cricket to go back ten years, we've got to move to playing the game relevantly," says Paul Taylor of Tonbridge. "But you can make opposing batsmen feel uncomfortable by bowling and fielding tightly, not by abusing them. Players must respect their opponents as cricketers and people."

The responsibility lies with the headmasters and cricket masters, who in the current cut-throat educational climate can fall prey to the same fear of losing as many football managers. The move towards employing recently retired first-class cricketers as coaches has also consciously or subconsciously encouraged a misplaced sense of professionalism. They, like cricketers from Lord's to Little Snoring, need to be reminded: England did not lose to Australia because they were too well-mannered; they lost because they were not good enough.

Andrew Longmore is cricket correspondent and chief sports feature writer of the Independent on Sunday.

COURT ON THE BOUNDARY

By RICHARD COLBEY

John Wisden, the founder of this Almanack, was sued by a Mr Page in 1869 over the copyright presumed to exist in a cricket scorecard. Wisden won the case, but the first words of the judgment convey the tone of a weary judicial sigh: "This," said the judge, "is a very small matter."

Yet, in the years since then, the game in which the umpire's word is supposed to be unarguable law has developed a habit of arguing its most contentious disputes before judges in robes rather than umpires in white coats. Within the past three years cricket has been rocked by two high-profile cases.

First, Devon Malcolm and Phillip DeFreitas sued Wisden's successors, the publishers of *Wisden Cricket Monthly*, over an article questioning their patriotism. The publishers dissociated themselves from the article and paid damages. (See *Wisden* 1996, page 1373). Then Ian Botham and Allan Lamb got themselves embroiled in a marathon libel case against Imran Khan, which they lost. (See *Wisden* 1997, page 1378).

There are many other aspects of the game which have not yet troubled the judiciary, but may do so before long. Cricketers expend a great deal of nervous energy resenting criticism by journalists. It is an occupational hazard; and a player cannot sue for libel simply because a writer says he has played badly and should be dropped.

But if the writer is motivated by malice, the doctrine of fair comment, which normally protects journalists, would not apply. Once there is a challenge to more than mere sporting prowess, as the Malcolm case showed, the courts could probably step in. The distinction between "X looks as if he isn't trying" and "X isn't trying" is one that commentators might bear in mind.

It is also easy to imagine a player going to court against the game's authorities. Allan Lamb and Jack Russell have both appeared to be close to a legal showdown over attempts to censor their autobiographies. The restraint of trade doctrine espoused in *Greig* v *Insole* could come to the aid of a player if the authorities attempted to deprive him of his livelihood because of something written, or said, off the field.

Many people within the game have remained surprised that the Inland Revenue have never challenged the consequences of *Reed* v *Seymour* and have allowed benefits to remain untaxed. And, despite all the "very small matters", there has been surprisingly little litigation over the horrendous injuries that can occur on the cricket field. The precedent set in the rugby-based case of *Smolden* v *Whitfield* in 1996 could easily be applied in a cricketing context. Ben Smolden was crippled when a scrum collapsed. He sued the referee, who was alleged to have lost control of the game. Although the rugby authorities hoped that the courts would find some basis for giving referees immunity in this situation, substantial damages were awarded. An umpire who fails to give a batsman adequate protection against repeated dangerous bowling may find himself the next entrant in cricket's legal hall of fame.

The most significant cricketing decisions are perhaps:

Page v Wisden 1869
After the cricketer and entrepreneur Frederick Lillywhite was bankrupted in 1866, the copyright in the scoresheet he had designed was assigned to a Mr Page. However, John Wisden, who was then in business producing cricket equipment, sold a virtually identical scoresheet. Evidence was given by three "eminent cricketers", Parr, Pickering and Dean, that scoresheets had been in circulation since before 1851. In the light of that, Page's claim was restricted to a copyright in the "runs at the fall of each wicket" section, which was a Lillywhite innovation. But the court rejected even this, and said no copyright existed in a standard scoresheet.

Reed v Seymour 1927
James Seymour was a Kent professional. In the words of the Law Lord, Viscount Cave, he played "fine cricket", and in 1920 was given a benefit match which raised £939. The tax inspector assessed Seymour on that amount. He would be liable if it had been paid to him by way of salary or remuneration but not if it were a personal gift. In a decision that set a precedent for which countless cricketers have been grateful, the House of Lords held Seymour's benefit was an expression of gratitude from the public for the services he had already rendered, and was not intended to spur him on to further successes. Accordingly, it was purely a gift and he did not have to pay tax on it.

Re: Patten 1929
William Patten left £300 in his will to help establish a nursery fund at the Sussex County Club. For reasons that are buried in the obscurities of trusts law, the gift was only effective if this were a charitable purpose. A trust merely for the promotion of sport has never been charitable, although modern lawyers have no problems finding ways around that. It could, however, qualify if it had been set up for the "supportation aid and help of young tradesmen handicraftsmen and persons decayed". Mr Justice Romer decided that young cricketers fell into none of those categories, and that it was thus not charitable, setting a precedent that prevailed until 1980, when the House of Lords decided the FA Youth Trust could be a charity.

Bolton v Stone 1951
On August 9, 1947, the day Denis Compton scored 137 not out in front of 30,000 spectators in a Championship match at The Oval, a batsman at the Cheetham Cricket Club in Kent hit a six out of the ground. Unfortunately, his blow struck Bessie Stone, who had just left her house on the nearby Beckenham Road. She was injured, and sued the club. The House of Lords eventually determined that the club was not liable. About six balls had been hit out of the ground in the previous thirty years, so there clearly was some risk of injury to passers-by. But the Lords decided that the mere fact that an activity involves some risk to non-participants does not make those who carry it on negligent; the benefits of that activity have to be weighed against the risks. This was not a blanket ruling that a club is not liable for

injuries caused in this situation: the length of the boundary, the volume of
people in the area into which balls would be hit and the precautions taken
would be taken into account in any given case.

Miller v Jackson 1977

In another case involving balls being hit out of the ground, a Mr and Mrs
Miller sought an injunction to prevent the Lintz club in Durham playing on
a ground next to their garden. Their house had been built four years
previously; the club had played at the ground for 70 years. Although the
highest possible fence was erected, about eight balls a season would still
land in the Millers' garden; no one had been hurt, but they felt unable to
use the garden when cricket was being played. The Court of Appeal
awarded the Millers £400 damages for the nuisance but said there should
not be an injunction preventing the game being played. A balancing act had
to be struck between preserving the Millers' private rights and allowing a
"commendable" communal activity to continue as it had done for decades.

Greig v Insole 1978

The longest piece of cricketing litigation occupied the High Court for 32
days and arose out of the businessman Kerry Packer's attempts to set up
World Series Cricket, his alternative to Test matches, after he failed to gain
exclusive television rights to Test cricket in Australia. The TCCB,
supported by ICC, announced in 1977 that players remaining contracted
with Packer would be banned from first-class cricket after October. Actions
were brought to quash this ban by the players, in the names of Tony Greig,
John Snow and Mike Procter, and by WSC. Doug Insole was the first
representative defendant on the part of the TCCB.

  Mr Justice Slade granted the orders sought. He held that by announcing
the bans in advance the TCCB had been unlawfully attempting to make the
players breach their contractual obligations to WSC. He also ruled that the
ban would prevent the players from earning their living, and so was
unlawful for being in restraint of trade. Indeed, the TCCB was held to have
breached its own constitution by imposing the ban: it should just have
considered the interests of English cricket, which would be only
peripherally affected by WSC's activities in Australia. It was also obliged
to consider the effect of depriving the cricketing public of seeing the
players involved and the resulting loss of gate money. Had the TCCB done
so, said the judge, it was inconceivable that it would have decided the ban
was appropriate.

Lacey v Parker 1994

Although only a county court decision, Judge Hague's ruling in favour of
the Jordans cricket club in Buckinghamshire was seen by many as proof
that the doctrine of *Miller* v *Jackson* had survived. Neighbours had
demanded that the club put up a 25ft fence, but the judge rejected the
application, despite a decision in 1980, restricting noise made by a
waterskiing club, which had seemed a little ominous for cricket clubs.

Richard Colbey is a barrister and enthusiastic cricket follower.

THE APPLIANCE OF SCIENCE

1. A VIEW FROM THE LAB

By JOHN ILLMAN

When Ray Illingworth was England manager, he was up against teams that had dietitians, exercise specialists, physiotherapists and doctors. Illingworth gave the impression he could do everything himself. England kept losing. With David Lloyd at the helm for England against the South Africans this summer, there will not be such a marked contrast in management style.

But while the new methods are widely accepted in South Africa and Australia, they continue to attract hostile criticism from the other Barmy Army – the diehard English traditionalists. They insist that Len Hutton and Denis Compton and David Gower and Ian Botham made the record books without the benefit of computer analysis, nutritional programmes and the psychological "immersion approach".

Would science have made them any better? Possibly not. According to one theory, great players perform well within their limits and may therefore benefit less from stretching those limits than lesser mortals who have to do their utmost all the time. So perhaps the key question is: can science help the mortals play like gods? The answer lies in two related strands of scientific endeavour. The first is tailored to the individual, and addresses issues like diet, training, coaching, physiotherapy and psychology; the second relates to broader issues of human potential, which science is only just beginning to unravel.

Cricketers' diets are certainly starting to improve. Until recently, English cricketers ranked second only to sumo wrestlers among the world's most overfed sportsmen. They were badly fed too, and some still are. Professor Ron Maughan, chair of the British Olympic Association's Nutrition Steering Group, says: "In an Olympic final, there is only a small difference between a gold medal and obscurity. Sports nutritionists argue that the right food can make all the difference between first and last."

In cricket, he claims, all other things being equal, diet could be the difference between victory and defeat. The evidence is based partly on research into carbohydrates, the main muscle fuel during strenuous exercise. Carbohydrate foods include bread, potatoes, pasta and rice. A Swedish study compared one group of footballers who ate their normal diet between games with another who took carbohydrate supplements. The carbohydrate group ran much faster and further, especially in the second half, and spent more time sprinting and less time walking.

Coaches and players have long talked about the effect of psychology on the game. Remember Mike Brearley? But, while science may be winning the battle for the cricketer's stomach, the battle for his mind highlights the innate conservatism of the English game. Perhaps, at heart, we all see ourselves as amateur psychologists: coaches do not want to concede their territory to other experts. But how many of them can help all those young players who look great in the nets but crumble under pressure? The

[*Chris Turvey, Empics*

The new regime: England train the modern way at their camp in Lanzarote. Darren Gough does a
scuba diving exercise (*above*), and (*below*) Barbro Nybraten stretches the players.

[*Chris Turvey, Empics*

evidence speaks for itself in the number of promising youngsters rejected as "not having what it takes".

We can all quote examples of top players with formidable psychological abilities. Ian Botham apparently taught himself to focus his concentration into the few seconds before bowling and then to switch off and relax between deliveries. It sounds so simple and obvious, but why don't more people do it? Desmond Haynes studied stress management and "positive thinking" – telling himself over and over again that he was the best batsman in the world and that the bowlers were second-rate. Again it sounds simple, but it can take years to develop these skills. Sports psychologists claim young players can be taught them and thus bypass the extended process of learning by experience. This might not be cricket as we have known it, but the most advanced coaches are all ears.

The increasing use of mind games in cricket is based on research which has been shown to have practical value. But so-called "basic research" often begins without anyone knowing where it might lead. It is the glorious pursuit of knowledge for knowledge's sake – the basis of all scientific progress from the development of the wheel to the heart transplant. For instance, work has been done lately into the gift of timing. A player like Geoff Boycott does not delight us the way David Gower or Brian Lara might at their best. As an article in *New Scientist* put it, they seem to "conjure with time", bringing an unhurried genius to the game.

But what is their real secret? Research shows that raw reaction times do not appear to be the answer. When top athletes take standard reaction time tests, such as hitting a switch as soon as it lights up, they are no quicker than average. And yet a cricketer has about five thousandths of a second to hit a fast-moving ball. If he is quicker or slower, he will miss. So the real mystery, as *New Scientist* points out, is not that some people are so skilful, but that anyone ever hits a cricket ball at all.

Research has produced a partial, if bizarre-sounding, answer. Top batsmen, it seems, commit themselves to playing on either the front or back foot at least a tenth of a second before a fast bowler releases the ball. It is hard to believe, but that is true of most scientific discoveries. And it poses another intriguing question: what do the players react to? They themselves cannot explain. "Anticipation studies" seem to suggest that the superior reactions of top players are due more to learning than to any innate factor. But this does not explain what distinguishes a Gower from a run-of-the-mill county performer.

Perhaps we will never know the answer. And maybe the game will be the richer. Mystery and uncertainty, above all else, are what give cricket its appeal. In a recent lecture to the Institute of Political Science in Sydney, Peter Fitzsimons, a former Wallaby rugby player, coined the word "seriousisation". Australian sport, he maintained, had become too systematic, and had lost its romance. He had a point in a country which runs counselling sessions not only for potential national rugby players, but also for their wives and girlfriends. This may be scientific, but it's not cricket.

John Illman is medical correspondent of The Observer, *a keen club cricketer and an accredited coach.*

2. A VIEW FROM THE DRESSING-ROOM

By DEREK PRINGLE

Until recently, cricket's ties with science had gone little beyond a basic understanding of the aerodynamics of swing. And the use of daring technology peaked with the bowling machine and the cat's cradle – a contraption used for practising slip catching but which doubled, far more usefully, as a place for tired bowlers to catch some shut-eye.

What has science now brought to the sport? The answer is probably not much. Surrounding the players with psychologists, nutritionists and fitness gurus may seem a thoroughly professional move but, in a game that is still dominated by skill, their effectiveness is hard to measure. And, as even the most inattentive schoolchild knows, science has to be measured by results. In cricket, with its myriad variables and imponderables, this is impossible, and even the converted must see there can be little point in measuring Shane Warne's fitness levels or body-fat content, unless he intends swapping wrist-spin for steeplechasing.

The progressives – among them England coach David Lloyd, South African coach Bob Woolmer and former England captain Bob Willis – have embraced science with enthusiasm. And the change of attitude in the England dressing-room has been dramatic. Actual change has been a bit slower. Tea and coffee (now considered bad for hand-eye co-ordination and the healing of injuries) and a post-match beer (bad for recovering muscles) are out of favour; even Jack Russell is now only a ten-cup-a-day man. Fruit juice and pizza are the latest to be dispensed with science's blessing.

Yet if the theory behind the rehydration and carbo-loading makes perfect sense to those spending their working lives cooped up with laboratory rats, the comfort zone for those who regard cricket as a sport with a social dimension is visibly shrinking on and off the field. As the economic pariahs of professional sport, cricketers have never found it easy to sacrifice their lifestyle; many regard the difference between fitness and fatness as nothing more than a changed vowel.

Individual players have often gone against the herd mentality of the dressing-room. Geoff Boycott swore by ginseng. Willis first used hypnotherapy in 1977 to help him relax between high-pressure matches. Having been injury-prone for much of his early career, Willis then hardly missed a Test until he retired in 1984. Richard Hadlee, another great fast bowler, became an advocate of "visualisation", a common technique beloved by sports psychologists, and a simple one. It involves re-running a personal best performance through your mind in minuscule detail: how you felt; wind direction; what you had for breakfast etc.

But this is never going to work for everyone. It is in the treatment of injuries that science is most likely to work for the average player. In recent years, the physiotherapist has emerged from being an old football-style sponge man into a dominant figure with an arsenal of machines and a say in everything from a player's training regime to his lifestyle. (In the current England team, Wayne Morton even gives guitar lessons.) Indeed, with players' careers now shorter than they were, the physio has more or less replaced the senior pro as the person unofficially in charge of dispensing wisdom. It is a far cry from the days when "Tonker" Taylor, the Essex captain, dismissed physiotherapists with the statement: "Good players don't need them. Bad players aren't worth it."

Scientific advance has also helped to contribute to the fixture overload that now exists, especially at international level. This would be impossible without the powerful anti-inflammatory drugs and pain-killing injections which allow players to feel they have recovered sooner than nature would have intended. These may cause cricketers terrible problems in later life.

Past players insist that serious injury is largely a modern phenomenon. Trevor Bailey bowled fast-medium for England on five long tours, but missed just one Test match out of 29: with a broken thumb. "The cricket was less intensive and we could get our niggles properly sorted out." Bailey bowled in boots the Mafia would consider ideal for sinking unwanted corpses, and says he relied on nothing more technological than a corset to support his back, and a spot of massage. Keith Fletcher, who began his Essex career as Bailey was ending his, remembers the physio rubbing ash into Bailey's back. "I thought it was some kind of voodoo ritual," recalls Fletcher, a view many have taken over England's recent training and bonding sessions, outings which have included scuba diving and driving Land Rovers blindfold.

Most current players are more enthusiastic. They are particularly keen on video as an analytical tool. Mike Atherton, the England captain, heaped praise on the "Statmaster" which kept a record of every ball bowled in the 1997 Ashes series. He requested and was given a video of every short ball Glenn McGrath had bowled to him. It was ready in a day and, despite the gruesome viewing, Atherton found it helpful.

But where does this no-stone-unturned pact with science leave the game? English cricket has found itself wanting as big money has rolled in from television: an amateurish blot on a sporting landscape paved with gold. Science could be seen as the game's response to its guilty conscience. It will not guarantee better results, but at least it shows that the game is willing to respond to external pressures. However, science can only try to create ever-efficient machines out of players. This is a game whose appeal relies on its unpredictability. They may be able to clone sheep. Eleven Ian Bothams would keep the bar well and truly propped up after play, but they would not make the game any more intoxicating.

Derek Pringle played 30 Tests for England as a super-fit athlete, honed to machine-like perfection. He is now cricket correspondent of The Independent.

FIVE CRICKETERS OF THE YEAR

MATTHEW ELLIOTT

Amid the euphoria at Edgbaston when England won the First Test last June came a salutary reminder of the unedifying face of patriotism. As the Australians trudged off the field, beaten and broody, a pie-eyed partisan relieved Matthew Elliott of his cherished baggy green cap. Giving chase, he hauled the thief to the turf and retrieved it, then found himself assailed by assorted boots and fists.

Those so-called fans did their nation a huge disservice, and not merely in terms of image. They could scarcely have done more, after all, to strengthen Elliott's resolve. Come summer's end, all England had come to fear and admire this intelligent, laconic left-hander. Gaunt, lofty, and prominent of chin (and, for Poms of a certain age, unnervingly reminiscent of another stubborn Victorian opening southpaw, Bill Lawry), Elliott, in a series dominated by the ball, had emerged as the most prolific batsman in either camp. In all, there were 556 Test runs at 55.60, among them the decisive innings of the rubber. It may not be any consolation to his opponents to know that, had he obeyed his instincts, he would have stayed at home.

Two days before reporting to Sydney for the outbound flight, an abortive attempt to jog the few hundred yards to his local corner shop prompted Elliott to believe that his knees, the left especially, were in no shape for the mission. He wanted to inform the selectors there and then. Fears temporarily assuaged by a specialist, he was advised to keep *stumm* and take the risk. So he did. But for him the tour had an inescapable background: he was never quite certain whether his body would answer opportunity's next knock.

MATTHEW THOMAS GRAY ELLIOTT was born on September 28, 1971, in Chelsea, south-east Melbourne, but moved to Kyabram, in Victoria's Golden Valley, at the age of four. He and his two younger brothers cut their teeth on a half-length concrete pitch laid by their father, John, a secondary school teacher and qualified coach. Those spindly arms inhibited the usual cross-batted swipes of the beginner, and ensured that Matthew seldom veered from the V. "We'd bat in order of age, youngest first," he recalls. "They'd run off when it was my turn, and I'd end up chasing after them." How could he not want to open, to get in first?

In 1990, he gave up studying physiotherapy, and was invited to enlist at the Australian Cricket Academy – in the same intake as Shane Warne – only to be persuaded that his cause would be better served by a summer in Eastcote and Leighton Buzzard. When his form dipped the following winter, the Melbourne *Sunday Age* sneeringly cited an "overdose of mediocre club cricket in England". Rejecting the Academy arrested his progress, yet district cricket, where men delight in putting boys in their place, encouraged a wider awareness and greater self-reliance. Foregoing such a head start also did wonders for the motivation.

Equally assured on front foot or back, and far from inelegant, he scored his maiden Sheffield Shield century in 1993-94, extending it to an unbeaten 175, which suggested a yen for substance. Returning from a solid but seldom imposing tour of the shires with Young Australia in 1995, he overcame an injury to his right knee to lead the domestic averages in 1995-96 with 1,233 runs at 68.50, gleaning Player of the Year garlands from peers and umpires alike. But with Mark Taylor and Michael Slater apparently entrenched as the national opening pair, patience seemed to be his paramount need.

In the event, Slater fell from grace after the one-off Test in India in October 1996, and a vacancy arose. Embarking with a duck against West Indies in Brisbane, Elliott atoned in Sydney, only to retire hurt for 78 following a mid-pitch collision with Mark Waugh that bordered on the tragi-comic. He sat out the next eight weeks, left knee incapacitated, embarrassment giving way to depression, if not self-doubt, as Matthew Hayden filled the breach with some success. Yet so vivid an impression had Elliott left that the First Test in Johannesburg saw him return at No. 3, the latest applicant to fill David Boon's shoes.

He seized an initiative his compatriots would not relinquish until the series was won, racing to 85 off 113 balls, and at one juncture hooking Allan Donald for six – off the front foot. Further audacity was apparent in England, notably at Lord's and Leeds, where he scored centuries. On both occasions the fates smiled benignly as chances went a-begging. As ever, an ability to shrug off misadventure served him admirably.

Obliged to press on with so much time lost to rain, he swept to the second fifty of his 112 at Lord's with a flurry of fours, nerves undetectable, selflessness plain. At Headingley, he was on 29, his side a creaky 50 for three, when he survived a gift to slip – and Steve Waugh fell next ball. Darren Gough and Dean Headley were pumped up and bumper-happy, but there was no thought of backing down. On the eve of the match, though frustrated by his erratic hooking to date, he had resolved to pick up the gauntlet, whoever did the flinging. Urged on by the puckish Ricky Ponting, he swatted Headley for a magisterial six and swept on to 199, turning the tide of the series for good.

True, one swirling hook was downed at long leg shortly after he reached three figures, yet the abiding image was one of unshakeable conviction. Here were the fruits of courage, of enterprise, of self-belief. Of the Australian Way. – ROB STEEN.

STUART LAW

At least one selector thought Stuart Law should have been on Australia's Ashes tour of England. Graham Gooch said he was "gobsmacked" to learn that Law had been overlooked, though delighted for Essex's sake, and England's. It was the last time that summer that anyone was to be lost for words to, about or from Law. He opened with a withering attack on the Australian selectors, saying he had already consistently outplayed the Australian batsmen and English bowlers who would feature in the Ashes series, and that if he was being ignored because of his attitude, they could "get stuffed".

He then made good his promise to take out his disaffection on the counties, smashing 1,482 runs in the Championship, and 1,088 more in the one-day competitions, including 80 not out in the NatWest Trophy final at Lord's to win the match for Essex and the match award for himself. It was not just the volume of runs he made, but how he made them, that had such an impact. Without departing too far from the orthodox technique he had crafted from schooldays, he scored at nearly a run a ball in all competitions, reminding himself constantly that cricket had to be above all an entertainment, for himself as well as for the spectators. His full-bladed driving through the off side was intimidating for opposition cover fieldsmen. So, for that matter, was his manner. An unashamed sledger, he was as energetic and rasping with his tongue as he was with his strokes. Late in the season, in a NatWest semi-final at Chelmsford, Glamorgan's Darren Thomas up-ended him with a beamer, whereupon the pair clashed heatedly. Law, of course, had the last word: Essex won.

STUART GRANT LAW was born on October 18, 1968, in suburban Brisbane. His father, Grant, was a redoubtable grade cricketer in Brisbane, and had also captained Queensland's Country XI. At 18 months, young Law got his first cricket bat, and, before he was in double figures, this admonition from his father: "If you're going to play this game, you might as well play it correctly." Thus his father impressed on him at a young age the importance of technique; later study of classicists like Greg Chappell and Martin Crowe reinforced it. Law rose speedily through the conventional ranks, playing first grade in Brisbane at 15, appearing for state under-age and colts teams, and playing in the 1987-88 Youth World Cup in the Australian Riverina. At Berri, he took the liberty of driving the Indian leg-spinner Narendra Hirwani for a couple of long sixes only weeks after Hirwani had taken 16 West Indian wickets on his Test debut. The next season, 1988-89, Law made his debut for Queensland, and scored 179 in his second match. By September 1997, he had made almost 10,000 first-class runs as well as 1,145 in one-day internationals for Australia. He has also taken 64 first-class wickets, at first with medium-pacers and latterly with a crude form of leg-spin that had its highest expression in two overs in a World Cup semi-final at Mohali in 1996.

Law's list of achievements is as diverse as it is distinguished, and sorting out a single highlight is difficult. He captained Young Australia on their tour of England in 1995. He has made a one-day century for Australia and appeared in a World Cup final, the memory tarnished only by the fact that Australia lost to Sri Lanka. Law is, and this is a particular point of pride, the only man to have captained Queensland to the Sheffield Shield – and he has done it twice. He was watching on television as a 16-year-old when Queensland tumbled to another heart-breaking defeat in the final. He remembers thinking that there was still a chance for him to play in the historic first win, though did not imagine for a moment that he would be captain by then, and moreover would have Allan Border, Test cricket's longest serving captain, as his lieutenant. He holds dear the NatWest trophy triumph of last season, if only because it gave him the chance Australia had never afforded him to perform in front of a full house at Lord's. His abiding memory is of Gooch, whom he regards as a kind of mentor, whispering to him just before he walked out to bat that afternoon: "Stewy, just be the best! That's what I used to tell myself. Just be better than anyone else out there."

Most of all, though, Law cherishes his one Test appearance, against Sri Lanka in Perth in December 1995, in which he made an unbeaten and effortless half-century in Australia's only innings (and so, of course, he does not have a Test average). "To actually don the baggy green cap . . . I can take that to the grave with me," he said. By the next Test, Steve Waugh was fit again, Australia were not quite ready to drop David Boon, and Law was jettisoned. Sometimes he dwelt on the injustice, believing that he should have had three Tests to prove or disprove himself. He contests the idea that he is a one-day specialist, yet has to live with it.

In a peculiar sense, he is a victim. In an era of batting plenty in Australia, a man's destiny is determined as much by lucky breaks as anything else, and Law has not had them. It may be that his independent spirit has worked against him. He is from cricket's new age, but not of it. He is what Australians call a knockabout bloke. His values are rugged and timeless: play your shots, speak your mind, back your mates, do anything it takes to win and have a drink with friend and foe alike when it is done. He frowns on the gym culture and treats fitness training as a duty rather than a vocation, while pointing out that he rarely misses a match because of injury and is never less than cricket-fit.

Australia's excess has been Essex's gain. Recommended to the county by Mark Waugh, he has made such appeal on and off the field in the last two seasons that Essex did not hesitate to re-engage him in preference to Waugh at the end of last season; the irony was lost on no one, but nor was the compliment. His batting still has the cavalier flourish of youth but, at nearly 30, he is mellowing and maturing. By the end of his second season at Essex, he had called a truce in his war with the Australian selectors, and for that matter with his inner self.

"Even if I don't play international cricket again, I've had a great career. I can look back and think that, maybe, in another time and place, I would have played more," he said. "But I made it. I've been considered for a number of years now to play for Australia, the best team in the world. That's a feather in anyone's cap." And, as he says, at least he has a cap. – GREG BAUM.

GLENN McGRATH

Friends who were there recall a day last year, deep in the Queensland bush "out the back of Longreach", on a pig-shooting weekend with the man they call "Pigeon" and the cricketing world knows as Glenn McGrath. The tall fast bowler had spotted a large boar, and he disappeared into the bush in hot pursuit. Three shots were heard, and McGrath came loping back into view, reached into the four-wheel drive, said "Out of ammo," and loped off again, all at the same relentless, steady pace. He got the pig. It is a story many who have played against him will recognise uneasily; wild boar or batsman, Glenn McGrath tends to get what he is hunting.

He was demonstrably the best quick bowler on either side in the Ashes series of 1997 and, but for the presence of one Shane Warne, could claim to be the best bowler of all; indeed, it is a claim he might make anyway, if he were a different kind of man. To do so, though, would be ''big-noting'' and, where McGrath comes from, there are few greater sins.

GLENN DONALD McGRATH was born on February 9, 1970, in Dubbo, New South Wales, first of three children of Kevin and Beverley. He carries on the great Australian bush cricketing litany, most famously represented by Sir Donald Bradman, and movingly depicted in Sir Russell Drysdale's painting of two bush kids playing against a stone wall in the sombre ochre of the Australian outback. Dubbo is a wheat and sheep farming centre a couple of hundred miles north-west of Sydney, not quite the real bush, but McGrath's father farmed in a succession of tiny settlements outside Dubbo with names smelling of gum-leaves: Eumungerie, Galgandra, Narromine. It was at the last that the young Glenn went to primary and high school, and where he started to play cricket.

McGrath recalls that there was only one turf wicket available; concrete was more usual. He was on the fringe of the game, and says that he only started to take the sport seriously when he was about 15. His captain in the local club side ''thought I couldn't bowl''. The captain's name is Shane Horsborough and, says McGrath, ''he still reckons I can't bowl''. You get very little chance to become big-headed in the Australian bush. Still, someone thought he could bowl because, at 17, he was picked in the Under-24 Far West selection and then for Western Districts in the annual NSW Country Cup. It was then he was spotted by various good judges, above all Doug Walters. At 19, at Walters's instigation, McGrath moved to Sydney and the Sutherland club. Odd jobs and living in a caravan followed, and four seasons of weekend cricket, until, in January 1993, he was selected for New South Wales against Tasmania. He took five for 79, and was away. By November, he was playing his first Test, against New Zealand at Perth: three wickets for quite a lot.

Since then, he has become Australia's strike bowler, with Warne. At the end of 1997, McGrath had 164 wickets at the remarkable average of 23.43 from 36 Tests. It is a figure very close to the man upon whom McGrath has based his career, Dennis Lillee, whose 355 Test wickets came at 23.92. Of those Australians who have 100 or more Test wickets, the only quicks with better averages than McGrath are Lindwall, Miller and Davidson. In four series completed in 1997, McGrath took 82 wickets: 26 at 17.42 in five home Tests against West Indies; 13 at 22.23 in three against South Africa away; 36 at 19.47 against England in the Ashes series; and seven at 18.28 in one Test against New Zealand before he was injured.

He arrived in May with a huge reputation, especially after his feats against West Indies, when he had considerably better figures than Ambrose, Walsh and Bishop. Yet, after the First Test at Edgbaston and England's famous win, people were asking what all the fuss was about. McGrath's match figures of two for 149 were a fair indication of how he bowled. He

THE WARNE WIGGLE

[*David Munden*

Shane Warne celebrates in his own way in front of the Trent Bridge pavilion after Australia secure the Ashes for the fifth series in a row.

[*Clive Mason/Allsport*]

Phil Tufnell, after five Tests on the sidelines, was finally picked for England at The Oval and took 11 wickets. He won the Man of the Match award and Clive Mason won the Veuve Clicquot Champagne Moment photograph of the season competition.

SUMMER OF SUCCESS . . .

[Patrick Eagar

Mark Taylor holds up the replica Ashes trophy at The Oval.

. . . MOMENT OF GLORY

[Philip Brown

John Crawley on the boundary at Trent Bridge after a briefer but more spectacular triumph: a blinding catch to dismiss Australian opener Matthew Elliott.

THE GOOD BARD . . .

[*Winston Bynorth*

Robert Croft is initiated into the Bardic Circle at the Eisteddfod in Bala, and welcomed by fellow-Bard and former Welsh rugby star Ray Gravell.

. . . AND THE UGLY

[*Graham Morris*

Robert Croft and Mark Ilott square up in the twilight at Chelmsford as the Essex–Glamorgan
NatWest Trophy semi-final reaches a bad-tempered climax.

CITY LIGHTS

Not Sydney . . . not Melbourne . . . but Birmingham. Edgbaston on the warm summer's night of July 23, 1997, a triumphant moment for floodlit cricket in England.

[Lee Besford/Newsteam]

SOMEWHERE . . .

[*Patrick Eagar*

A rainbow, traditional harbinger of fairer weather ahead, appears over Lord's during the Second Test. For English cricket, the good times were to be delayed again.

FIVE CRICKETERS OF THE YEAR

[*Patrick Eagar*

MATTHEW ELLIOTT

FIVE CRICKETERS OF THE YEAR

[*Jan Traylen/Patrick Eagar*

STUART LAW

[*Patrick Eagar*

GLENN McGRATH

FIVE CRICKETERS OF THE YEAR

[*Graham Morris*

MATTHEW MAYNARD

FIVE CRICKETERS OF THE YEAR

[*Graham Morris*

GRAHAM THORPE

failed to understand the nature of that wicket and what needed to be done on it. But he learned, as all the good ones do, very quickly.

On a wicket made for line-and-length fast bowling at Lord's, McGrath had eight for 38 in England's humiliating first innings. The question "Who is this Glenn McGrath anyway?" had been roundly answered. He was integral to Australia's wins in the Third and Fifth Tests, and took seven for 76 in the first innings of a losing cause at The Oval. He was the only Australian quick to play in all six Tests. He had Mike Atherton's number, in particular, dismissing him seven times. Atherton, in fact, was McGrath's 150th Test wicket, at The Oval.

There is a thousand-dollar bet in the Australian dressing-room about whether McGrath will make a first-class fifty – ever. Yet he practises his batting with the same purpose he puts into dismissing batsmen or killing wild boars. So far his best attempt is 24. But if determination is going to count, the wise money would be on McGrath. He is a fine outfielder and, if he has a flaw, it is his apparently unstoppable habit of sledging opponents. It is odd, really, because off the field he is a quiet, modest man. He has the odd extravagance: he recently purchased 30,000 acres of wild bush in western New South Wales where he can go to be alone with his mates. Good news for them; tough on the pigs. – BRUCE WILSON.

MATTHEW MAYNARD

It was September 20, 1997; dusk was approaching fast; and all Wales was starting to get a bit irritated. The Somerset tailenders were delaying Glamorgan's march to the County Championship, and the umpires warned the captain, Matthew Maynard, that they might have to offer the batsmen the light. Then the game would go into the Sunday. It might rain. Kent could yet steal their title. Maynard had to take off his quicks, and bring on his young slow left-armer Dean Cosker. That was not Plan A. But Cosker took the wicket, Somerset were all out, and Glamorgan needed just 11 runs to be champions. Maynard knew they had done it: "It was the biggest moment of my sporting life by far," he said.

And Glamorgan had a third title-winning captain. Unlike the other two, Wilf Wooller and Tony Lewis, this one did not go to Cambridge. He is not even Welsh. He is notoriously nervy. Until 1997, he had a reputation as something of a cricketing wastrel. No one in the modern domestic game – not even Wayne Larkins – has converted so much talent into so few England caps: just four, with a batting average below 11.

Yet Maynard was the man whose firm, positive, unselfish and sometimes surprisingly thoughtful leadership turned Glamorgan, no-hopers for so long, into champions. Steve James was Glamorgan's main run-scorer in 1997. But, when the chips were really down in the last two matches, it was Maynard who played two very different but equally decisive match-winning innings: a steadfast 75 not out against Essex, a breathtaking 142 against Somerset. He is the embodiment of Glamorgan's triumph.

MATTHEW PETER MAYNARD was born on March 21, 1966, in Oldham. (Lloyd George was born in Manchester, so this is no bar to heroism in Wales.) Eight years later, his father took a pub in Anglesey. Dad was a useful cricketer; so was Matthew's elder brother Charles and, at 11, Matthew began to get the odd game in the Menai Bridge village team. At the time, Charles looked the better player. But he became increasingly interested in classical music – he is now a composer. Matthew went in the other direction: he packed away his trumpet, forgot his days as a boy soprano at Bangor Cathedral and concentrated on his cricket. He joined the Bangor club, where the groundsman-pro Bill Clutterbuck became his cricketing mentor.

Maynard began getting games for Kent's Second Eleven. But they were batting him down the order and he made little progress. As he made the long journey home in 1984, the future seemed very bleak. Academically, he had been a washout. He thought his only career option was eventually taking over the pub.

Then Glamorgan rang. In 1985, he was leading scorer in their second team. Late in August, with Glamorgan's season drifting into its customary mediocrity, they thought this 19-year-old was worth a go in the first team, against Yorkshire at Swansea. The game was rain-affected. He did not get a bat until Glamorgan were already on the way to defeat. He scored 102 in 87 minutes, the last 18 of them by hitting successive balls from Phil Carrick back over his head into the terraces. "There can have been few more remarkable maiden centuries in first-class cricket," said *Wisden*. The next June, Maynard scored another quick century at Edgbaston. That cemented his place. He scored 1,002 in the season. In 1987 he upped that to 1,626, and was top of the national list of both catches and six-hits (30 of each). At The Oval in 1988, he was in the Test team, aged just 22. It seemed like a natural progression. Here was a young batting star to take on the world.

And then, of course, it went wrong. Maynard might be a case study for England's failures of the past decade. He came into an already demoralised dressing-room at the fag-end of a disastrous series against West Indies. People told him to play his natural game. So he took on Curtly Ambrose, and was caught behind for three ("a rash stroke" – *Wisden*), failed again second time round, and got dropped. No one said a word.

But two people did the following year. Maynard was in nick, and the England manager Micky Stewart told him: "Just keep going and you'll be in." So he did keep going: a brilliant unbeaten 191 against Gloucestershire at Cardiff followed. Nothing. The next call was from David Graveney, recruiting for the last rebel tour to South Africa. Maynard and his wife Sue had a new baby, and he said yes: "This tour was my pension, that was the way I looked at it." He still thinks he was right. "Look at Rob Bailey. He said no. England never showed him any commitment."

So he was banned from Test cricket and, though his game solidified with the encouragement of Glamorgan's new recruit, Viv Richards, it would be 1993 before England were in touch again. He was recalled at Edgbaston, Mike Atherton's first Test in charge. At 3.40 a.m. on the morning of the match, Sue rang to say she now had a baby daughter. A few hours later he was caught at silly point for a duck. Quite a day. This time he played three successive Tests, including the first next winter at Kingston. But 35 in the first innings there was the nearest he came to success. He was dropped again and, when he realised he was not coming back, spent the rest of the tour in a non-approved manner. "I hit the booze button," he admits.

He had a terrible season in 1994, and it took a period out with injury to convince him he wanted to carry on. In 1996 came the Glamorgan captaincy, and a recall for the one-day internationals. But batting mid-order in these games is no shop window. Last year, David Graveney – in his new, official eminence – did not get in touch. At 32, Maynard takes some comfort in Graham Gooch's career. In the meantime, he has his own national team to worry about: the Welsh team.

At school in Anglesey, Welsh was one of the many subjects at which Matthew Maynard was hopeless. Now he can sing "Land of My Fathers" as loudly and lustily as anyone. And on the night of September 20, 1997, he did. – MATTHEW ENGEL.

GRAHAM THORPE

There are few quieter men in the England dressing-room than Graham Thorpe, and even fewer with more to shout about. The Farnham boy has the face and demeanour of a poker player. The eyes say nothing, the straight-set mouth betrays no emotion. He does not believe in small talk. Yet the runs have piled up in front of him like columns of chips.

Ask any England follower to name the leading batsmen of recent years and they will reel off Mike Atherton and Alec Stewart. Nasser Hussain might get a mention too, and, oh yes, that little left-hander . . . Thorpe. None has contributed more consistently over the past four years than that little left-hander, who has the scoreboard ticking over before you have even noticed he has taken guard. Accumulation is the name of the game. Unspectacular and uncomplicated, Thorpe reached the end of 1997 with a Test average of 42, better than any of his contemporaries in the England side.

He ushered in the New Year of 1997 with something of a reputation as a nearly man. Since scoring a century on Test debut, he had reached 50 on 20 further occasions in 33 more Tests, but only once made it through to three figures again.

Thorpe might have made a New Year's resolution to do something about it. Three centuries came in the next four Tests, two against New Zealand and one against Australia. That brought a rhetorical question from him, at one of his rare press conferences: "I didn't notice too much of a mental barrier today, did you?" Even in an Ashes series that brought more disappointment for England, Thorpe topped the home batting with an average of 50.33, while none of his colleagues could reach the 40s. He scored 453 runs in the six-Test series, which was bettered only by Australian opener Matthew Elliott. To round off his summer, he signed off with a career-best 222 in the vital Championship match against Glamorgan.

More than anything, though, Thorpe had faced the best team in the world and come out with his reputation enhanced. Even then, during a sticky mid-summer patch while the Australians were winning three straight Tests, his place in the middle order had been called into doubt again, while other, more high-profile, players escaped criticism.

Thorpe insists he will not change for the sake of the image-builders being brought in by the ECB's new regime. The only spin doctor he is interested in is one who can help him identify Shane Warne's variations. "If you're naturally enthusiastic and a showman, that's fine, but I'm not, and I think it is important not to try to be something you are not. That way, you only fall into traps," says Thorpe. "Others may attract the publicity, but I don't need that. In sport, you can get envy and jealousy in a dressing-room, but thankfully I've never felt that. You've just got to enjoy it your own way."

GRAHAM PAUL THORPE started in the archetypal English way. Born on August 1, 1969, into a sports-mad family, by the age of 13 he was playing with the men of Wrecclesham, a village team in the heart of Surrey. Two years later, he followed his older brothers, Ian and Alan, into the Farnham first team in the Surrey Championship, and at 16 he was invited up to The Oval.

Cricket, though, was only half of it for Thorpe, as he worked his way towards a PE diploma at Farnham Sixth Form College. By winter, he was a highly promising footballer, good enough to make the England Under-18s as a "nip-your-ankles midfielder", to use his own description. When it came to the time to make a career move, however, Thorpe had not progressed up the soccer ladder. Only Brentford had shown a passing interest, and cricket won the day.

His early development was moulded at Surrey by Micky Stewart and Geoff Arnold, two more characters interested in spit and polish rather than flash and dash. Typically, his role models were not two high-fliers but doughty opener Ray Alikhan and left-arm spinner Keith Medlycott, a man whose own playing career nose-dived but is now back at The Oval as coach. "It was their attitude that I admired most. I liked them as blokes," says Thorpe. "They weren't bothered about who they were playing against or who they were playing under, they were not in awe of anyone – they just got on with their job."

Thorpe, having played for England sides from the age of 15, made the natural progression through to the A team. But there the progress faltered a little. He made four successive England A tours from 1989-90, but did not progress until England were enduring another demolition job by the Australian bowlers in the summer of 1993.

Beaten in the first two Tests, England called up Mark Ilott, Mark Lathwell, Martin McCague and Thorpe for their debuts in the Third at Trent Bridge. The other three made only a passing impact on the international scene, but Thorpe announced himself with a second-innings 114 not out. He was the first England player in 20 years – since Frank Hayes against West Indies – to score a century on debut.

Apart from a broken thumb, which kept him out of the last Test of that 1993 Ashes series, and a brief spell in 1994 when he was dropped, Thorpe has been one of the few constants in the England side of the past four years. Despite problems off the field in 1997 which troubled him deeply – the death of Surrey colleague Graham Kersey in a car accident and Sunday newspaper allegations about his private life – Thorpe remained the most single-mindedly successful of English batsmen. – COLIN BATEMAN.

PART TWO: THE PLAYERS

TEST CRICKETERS

FULL LIST FROM 1877 TO AUGUST 23, 1997

These lists have been compiled on a home and abroad basis, appearances abroad
being printed in *italics*.

Abbreviations. E: England. A: Australia. SA: South Africa. WI: West
Indies. NZ: New Zealand. In: India. P: Pakistan. SL: Sri Lanka. Z: Zimbabwe.

All appearances are placed in this order of seniority. Hence, any England
cricketer playing against Australia in England has that achievement recorded first
and the remainder of his appearances at home (if any) set down before passing to
matches abroad. The figures immediately following each name represent the total
number of appearances in *all* Tests.

The two Tests played between Sri Lanka and India in 1997-98 have been
included.

Where the season embraces two different years, the first year is given; i.e.
1876 indicates 1876-77.

ENGLAND

Number of Test cricketers: 588

Abel, R. 13: v A 1888 (3) 1896 (3) 1902 (2); *v A 1891 (3); v SA 1888 (2)*
Absolom, C. A. 1: *v A 1878*
Agnew, J. P. 3: v A 1985 (1); v WI 1984 (1); v SL 1984 (1)
Allen, D. A. 39: v A 1961 (4) 1964 (1); v SA 1960 (2); v WI 1963 (2) 1966 (1); v P 1962 (4);
    *v A 1962 (1) 1965 (4); v SA 1964 (4); v WI 1959 (5); v NZ 1965 (3); v In 1961 (5); v P
    1961 (3)*
Allen, G. O. B. 25: v A 1930 (1) 1934 (2); v WI 1933 (1); v NZ 1931 (3); v In 1936 (3); *v A
    1932 (5) 1936 (5); v WI 1947 (3); v NZ 1932 (2)*
Allom, M. J. C. 5: *v SA 1930 (1); v NZ 1929 (4)*
Allott, P. J. W. 13: v A 1981 (1) 1985 (4); v WI 1984 (3); v In 1982 (2); v SL 1984 (1); *v In
    1981 (1); v SL 1981 (1)*
Ames, L. E. G. 47: v A 1934 (5) 1938 (2); v SA 1929 (1) 1935 (4); v WI 1933 (3); v NZ 1931
    (3) 1937 (3); v In 1932 (1); *v A 1932 (5) 1936 (5); v SA 1938 (5); v WI 1929 (4) 1934 (4);
    v NZ 1932 (2)*
Amiss, D. L. 50: v A 1968 (1) 1975 (2) 1977 (2); v WI 1966 (1) 1973 (3) 1976 (1); v NZ 1973
    (3); v In 1967 (2) 1971 (1) 1974 (3); v P 1967 (1) 1971 (3) 1974 (3); *v A 1974 (5) 1976 (1);
    v WI 1973 (5); v NZ 1974 (2); v In 1972 (3) 1976 (5); v P 1972 (3)*
Andrew, K. V. 2: v WI 1963 (1); *v A 1954 (1)*
Appleyard, R. 9: v A 1956 (1); v SA 1955 (1); v P 1954 (1); *v A 1954 (4); v NZ 1954 (2)*
Archer, A. G. 1: *v SA 1898*
Armitage, T. 2: *v A 1876 (2)*
Arnold, E. G. 10: v A 1905 (4); v SA 1907 (2); *v A 1903 (4)*
Arnold, G. G. 34: v A 1972 (3) 1975 (1); v WI 1973 (3); v NZ 1969 (1) 1973 (3); v In 1974 (2);
    v P 1967 (2) 1974 (3); *v A 1974 (4); v WI 1973 (3); v NZ 1974 (2); v In 1972 (4); v P
    1972 (3)*
Arnold, J. 1: v NZ 1931
Astill, W. E. 9: *v SA 1927 (5); v WI 1929 (4)*
Atherton, M. A. 73: v A 1989 (2) 1993 (6) 1997 (6); v SA 1994 (3); v WI 1991 (5) 1995 (6);
    v NZ 1990 (3) 1994 (3); v In 1990 (3) 1996 (3); v P 1992 (3) 1996 (3); *v A 1990 (5) 1994 (5);
    v SA 1995 (5); v WI 1993 (5); v NZ 1996 (3); v In 1992 (1); v SL 1992 (1); v Z 1996 (2)*

Athey, C. W. J. 23: v A 1980 (1); v WI 1988 (1); v NZ 1986 (2); v P 1987 (4); *v A 1986 (5) 1987 (1); v WI 1980 (2); v NZ 1987 (1); v P 1987 (3)*

Attewell, W. 10: v A 1890 (1); *v A 1884 (5) 1887 (1) 1891 (3)*

Bailey, R. J. 4: v WI 1988 (1); *v WI 1989 (3)*

Bailey, T. E. 61: v A 1953 (5) 1956 (4); v SA 1951 (2) 1955 (5); v WI 1950 (2) 1957 (4); v NZ 1949 (4) 1958 (4); v P 1954 (3); *v A 1950 (4) 1954 (5) 1958 (5); v SA 1956 (5); v WI 1953 (5); v NZ 1950 (2) 1954 (2)*

Bairstow, D. L. 4: v A 1980 (1); v WI 1980 (1); v In 1979 (1); *v WI 1980 (1)*

Bakewell, A. H. 6: v SA 1935 (2); v WI 1933 (1); v NZ 1931 (2); *v In 1933 (1)*

Balderstone, J. C. 2: v WI 1976 (2)

Barber, R. W. 28: v A 1964 (1) 1968 (1); v SA 1960 (1) 1965 (3); v WI 1966 (2); v NZ 1965 (3); *v A 1965 (5); v SA 1964 (4); v In 1961 (5); v P 1961 (3)*

Barber, W. 2: v SA 1935 (2)

Barlow, G. D. 3: v A 1977 (1); *v In 1976 (2)*

Barlow, R. G. 17: v A 1882 (1) 1884 (3) 1886 (3); *v A 1881 (4) 1882 (4) 1886 (2)*

Barnes, S. F. 27: v A 1902 (1) 1909 (3) 1912 (3); v SA 1912 (3); *v A 1901 (3) 1907 (5) 1911 (5); v SA 1913 (4)*

Barnes, W. 21: v A 1880 (1) 1882 (1) 1884 (2) 1886 (2) 1888 (3) 1890 (2); *v A 1882 (4) 1884 (5) 1886 (1)*

Barnett, C. J. 20: v A 1938 (3) 1948 (1); v SA 1947 (3); v WI 1933 (1); v NZ 1937 (3); v In 1936 (1); *v A 1936 (5); v In 1933 (3)*

Barnett, K. J. 4: v A 1989 (3); v SL 1988 (1)

Barratt, F. 5: v SA 1929 (1); *v NZ 1929 (4)*

Barrington, K. F. 82: v A 1961 (5) 1964 (5) 1968 (5); v SA 1955 (2) 1960 (4) 1965 (3); v WI 1963 (5) 1966 (2); v NZ 1965 (2); v In 1959 (5) 1967 (3); v P 1962 (4) 1967 (3); *v A 1962 (5) 1965 (5); v SA 1964 (5); v WI 1959 (5) 1967 (5); v NZ 1962 (3); v In 1961 (5) 1963 (1); v P 1961 (2)*

Barton, V. A. 1: *v SA 1891*

Bates, W. 15: *v A 1881 (4) 1882 (4) 1884 (5) 1886 (2)*

Bean, G. 3: *v A 1891 (3)*

Bedser, A. V. 51: v A 1948 (5) 1953 (5); v SA 1947 (2) 1951 (5) 1955 (1); v WI 1950 (3); v NZ 1949 (2); v In 1946 (3) 1952 (4); v P 1954 (2); *v A 1946 (5) 1950 (5) 1954 (1); v SA 1948 (5); v NZ 1946 (1) 1950 (2)*

Benjamin, J. E. 1: v SA 1994

Benson, M. R. 1: v In 1986

Berry, R. 2: v WI 1950 (2)

Bicknell, M. P. 2: v A 1993 (2)

Binks, J. G. 2: *v In 1963 (2)*

Bird, M. C. 10: *v SA 1909 (5) 1913 (5)*

Birkenshaw, J. 5: v WI 1973 (2); v In 1972 (2); v P 1972 (1)

Blakey, R. J. 2: *v In 1992 (2)*

Bligh, Hon. I. F. W. 4: *v A 1882 (4)*

Blythe, C. 19: v A 1905 (1) 1909 (2); v SA 1907 (3); *v A 1901 (5) 1907 (1); v SA 1905 (5) 1909 (2)*

Board, J. H. 6: *v SA 1898 (2) 1905 (4)*

Bolus, J. B. 7: v WI 1963 (2); *v In 1963 (5)*

Booth, M. W. 2: *v SA 1913 (2)*

Bosanquet, B. J. T. 7: v A 1905 (3); *v A 1903 (4)*

Botham, I. T. 102: v A 1977 (2) 1980 (1) 1981 (6) 1985 (6) 1989 (3); v WI 1980 (5) 1984 (5) 1991 (1); v NZ 1978 (3) 1983 (4) 1986 (1); v In 1979 (4) 1982 (3); v P 1978 (3) 1982 (3) 1987 (5) 1992 (2); v SL 1984 (1) 1991 (1); *v A 1978 (6) 1979 (3) 1982 (5) 1986 (4); v WI 1980 (4) 1985 (5); v NZ 1977 (3) 1983 (3) 1991 (1); v In 1979 (1) 1981 (6); v P 1983 (1); v SL 1981 (1)*

Bowden, M. P. 2: *v SA 1888 (2)*

Bowes, W. E. 15: v A 1934 (3) 1938 (2); v SA 1935 (4); v WI 1939 (2); v In 1932 (1) 1946 (1); *v A 1932 (1); v NZ 1932 (1)*

Bowley, E. H. 5: v SA 1929 (2); *v NZ 1929 (3)*

Boycott, G. 108: v A 1964 (4) 1968 (3) 1972 (2) 1977 (3) 1980 (1) 1981 (6); v SA 1965 (2); v WI 1966 (4) 1969 (3) 1973 (3) 1980 (5); v NZ 1965 (2) 1969 (3) 1973 (3) 1978 (2); v In 1967 (2) 1971 (1) 1974 (1) 1979 (4); v P 1967 (1) 1971 (2); *v A 1965 (5) 1970 (5) 1978 (6) 1979 (3); v SA 1964 (5); v WI 1967 (5) 1973 (5) 1980 (4); v NZ 1965 (2) 1977 (3); v In 1979 (1) 1981 (4); v P 1977 (3)*

Bradley, W. M. 2: *v A 1899 (2)*

Braund, L. C. 23: v A 1902 (5); v SA 1907 (3); *v A 1901 (5) 1903 (5) 1907 (5)*

Brearley, J. M. 39: v A 1977 (5) 1981 (4); v WI 1976 (2); v NZ 1978 (3); v In 1979 (4); v P 1978 (3); *v A 1976 (1) 1978 (6) 1979 (3); v In 1976 (5) 1979 (1); v P 1977 (2)*
Brearley, W. 4: v A 1905 (2) 1909 (1); v SA 1912 (1)
Brennan, D. V. 2: v SA 1951 (2)
Briggs, John 33: v A 1886 (3) 1888 (3) 1893 (2) 1896 (1) 1899 (1); *v A 1884 (5) 1886 (2) 1887 (1) 1891 (3) 1894 (5) 1897 (5); v SA 1888 (2)*
Broad, B. C. 25: v A 1989 (2); v WI 1984 (4) 1988 (2); v P 1987 (4); v SL 1984 (1); *v A 1986 (5) 1987 (1); v NZ 1987 (3); v P 1987 (3)*
Brockwell, W. 7: v A 1893 (1) 1899 (1); *v A 1894 (5)*
Bromley-Davenport, H. R. 4: *v SA 1895 (3) 1898 (1)*
Brookes, D. 1: *v WI 1947*
Brown, A. 2: *v In 1961 (1); v P 1961 (1)*
Brown, D. J. 26: v A 1968 (4); v SA 1965 (2); v WI 1966 (1) 1969 (3); v NZ 1969 (1); v In 1967 (2): *v A 1965 (4); v WI 1967 (4); v NZ 1965 (2); v P 1968 (3)*
Brown, F. R. 22: v A 1953 (1); v SA 1951 (5); v WI 1950 (1); v NZ 1931 (2) 1937 (1) 1949 (2); v In 1932 (1); *v A 1950 (5); v NZ 1932 1950 (2)*
Brown, G. 7: v A 1921 (3); *v SA 1922 (4)*
Brown, J. T. 8: v A 1896 (2) 1899 (1); *v A 1894 (5)*
Brown, S. J. E. 1: v P 1996
Buckenham, C. P. 4: *v SA 1909 (4)*
Butcher, A. R. 1: v In 1979
Butcher, M. A. 5: v A 1997 (5)
Butcher, R. O. 3: *v WI 1980 (3)*
Butler, H. J. 2: v SA 1947 (1); *v WI 1947 (1)*
Butt, H. R. 3: *v SA 1895 (3)*

Caddick, A. R. 16: v A 1993 (4) 1997 (5); v P 1996 (1); *v WI 1993 (4); v NZ 1996 (2)*
Calthorpe, Hon. F. S. G. 4: *v WI 1929 (4)*
Capel, D. J. 15: v A 1989 (1); v WI 1988 (2); v P 1987 (1); *v A 1987 (1); v WI 1989 (4); v NZ 1987 (3); v P 1987 (3)*
Carr, A. W. 11: v A 1926 (4); v SA 1929 (2); *v SA 1922 (5)*
Carr, D. B. 2: *v In 1951 (2)*
Carr, D. W. 1: v A 1909
Cartwright, T. W. 5: v A 1964 (2); v SA 1965 (1); v NZ 1965 (1); *v SA 1964 (1)*
Chapman, A. P. F. 26: v A 1926 (4) 1930 (4); v SA 1924 (2); v WI 1928 (3); *v A 1924 (4) 1928 (4); v SA 1930 (5)*
Charlwood, H. R. J. 2: *v A 1876 (2)*
Chatterton, W. 1: *v SA 1891*
Childs, J. H. 2: v WI 1988 (2)
Christopherson, S. 1: v A 1884
Clark, E. W. 8: v A 1934 (2); v SA 1929 (1); v WI 1933 (2); *v In 1933 (3)*
Clay, J. C. 1: v SA 1935
Close, D. B. 22: v A 1961 (1); v SA 1955 (1); v WI 1957 (2) 1963 (5) 1966 (1) 1976 (3); v NZ 1949 (1); v In 1959 (1) 1967 (3); v P 1967 (3); *v A 1950 (1)*
Coldwell, L. J. 7: v A 1964 (2); v P 1962 (2); *v A 1962 (2); v NZ 1962 (1)*
Compton, D. C. S. 78: v A 1938 (4) 1948 (5) 1953 (5) 1956 (1); v SA 1947 (5) 1951 (4) 1955 (5); v WI 1939 (3) 1950 (1); v NZ 1937 (1) 1949 (4); v In 1946 (3) 1952 (2); v P 1954 (4); *v A 1946 (5) 1950 (4) 1954 (4); v SA 1948 (5) 1956 (5); v WI 1953 (5); v NZ 1946 (1) 1950 (2)*
Cook, C. 1: v SA 1947
Cook, G. 7: v In 1982 (3); *v A 1982 (3); v SL 1981 (1)*
Cook, N. G. B. 15: v A 1989 (3); v WI 1984 (3); v NZ 1983 (2); *v NZ 1983 (1); v P 1983 (3) 1987 (3)*
Cope, G. A. 3: *v P 1977 (3)*
Copson, W. H. 3: v SA 1947 (1); v WI 1939 (2)
Cork, D. G. 19: v WI 1995 (5); v In 1996 (3); v P 1996 (3); *v SA 1995 (5); v NZ 1996 (3)*
Cornford, W. L. 4: *v NZ 1929 (4)*
Cottam, R. M. H. 4: *v In 1972 (2); v P 1968 (2)*
Coventry, Hon. C. J. 2: *v SA 1888 (2)*
Cowans, N. G. 19: v A 1985 (1); v WI 1984 (1); v NZ 1983 (4); *v A 1982 (4); v NZ 1983 (2); v In 1984 (5); v P 1983 (2)*
Cowdrey, C. S. 6: v WI 1988 (1); *v In 1984 (5)*

Cowdrey, M. C. 114: v A 1956 (5) 1961 (4) 1964 (3) 1968 (4); v SA 1955 (1) 1960 (5) 1965 (3); v WI 1957 (5) 1963 (2) 1966 (4); v NZ 1958 (4) 1965 (3); v In 1959 (5); v P 1962 (4) 1967 (2) 1971 (1); *v A 1954 (5) 1958 (5) 1962 (5) 1965 (4) 1970 (3) 1974 (5); v SA 1956 (5); v WI 1959 (5) 1967 (5); v NZ 1954 (2) 1958 (2) 1962 (3) 1965 (3) 1970 (1); v In 1963 (3); v P 1968 (3)*

Coxon, A. 1: v A 1948

Cranston, J. 1: v A 1890

Cranston, K. 8: v A 1948 (1); v SA 1947 (3); *v WI 1947 (4)*

Crapp, J. F. 7: v A 1948 (3); *v SA 1948 (4)*

Crawford, J. N. 12: v SA 1907 (2); *v A 1907 (5); v SA 1905 (5)*

Crawley, J. P. 22: v A 1997 (5); v SA 1994 (3); v WI 1995 (3); v P 1996 (2); *v A 1994 (3); v SA 1995 (1); v NZ 1996 (3); v Z 1996 (2)*

Croft, R. D. B. 10: v A 1997 (5); v P 1996 (1); *v NZ 1996 (2); v Z 1996 (2)*

Curtis, T. S. 5: v A 1989 (3); v WI 1988 (2)

Cuttell, W. R. 2: *v SA 1898 (2)*

Dawson, E. W. 5: *v SA 1927 (1); v NZ 1929 (4)*

Dean, H. 3: v A 1912 (2); v SA 1912 (1)

DeFreitas, P. A. J. 44: v A 1989 (1) 1993 (1); v SA 1994 (3); v WI 1988 (3) 1991 (5) 1995 (1); v NZ 1990 (2) 1994 (3); v P 1987 (1) 1992 (2); v SL 1991 (1); *v A 1986 (4) 1990 (3) 1994 (4); v WI 1989 (2); v NZ 1987 (2) 1991 (3); v In 1992 (1); v P 1987 (2)*

Denness, M. H. 28: v A 1975 (1); v NZ 1969 (1); v In 1974 (3); v P 1974 (3); *v A 1974 (5); v WI 1973 (4); v NZ 1974 (2); v In 1972 (5); v P 1972 (3)*

Denton, D. 11: v A 1905 (1); *v SA 1905 (5) 1909 (5)*

Dewes, J. G. 5: v A 1948 (1); v WI 1950 (2); *v A 1950 (2)*

Dexter, E. R. 62: v A 1961 (5) 1964 (5) 1968 (2); v SA 1960 (5); v WI 1963 (5); v NZ 1958 (1) 1965 (2); v In 1959 (2); v P 1962 (5); *v A 1958 (2) 1962 (5); v SA 1964 (5); v WI 1959 (5); v NZ 1958 (2) 1962 (3); v In 1961 (5); v P 1961 (3)*

Dilley, G. R. 41: v A 1981 (3) 1989 (2); v WI 1980 (3) 1988 (4); v NZ 1983 (1) 1986 (2); v In 1986 (2); v P 1987 (4); *v A 1979 (2) 1986 (4) 1987 (1); v WI 1980 (4); v NZ 1987 (3); v In 1981 (4); v P 1983 (1) 1987 (1)*

Dipper, A. E. 1: v A 1921

Doggart, G. H. G. 2: v WI 1950 (2)

D'Oliveira, B. L. 44: v A 1968 (2) 1972 (5); v WI 1966 (4) 1969 (3); v NZ 1969 (3); v In 1967 (2) 1971 (3); v P 1967 (3) 1971 (3); *v A 1970 (6); v WI 1967 (5); v NZ 1970 (2); v P 1968 (3)*

Dollery, H. E. 4: v A 1948 (2); v SA 1947 (1); v WI 1950 (1)

Dolphin, A. 1: *v A 1920*

Douglas, J. W. H. T. 23: v A 1912 (1) 1921 (5); v SA 1924 (1); *v A 1911 (5) 1920 (5) 1924 (1); v SA 1913 (5)*

Downton, P. R. 30: v A 1981 (1) 1985 (6); v WI 1984 (5) 1988 (3); v In 1986 (1); v SL 1984 (1); *v WI 1980 (3) 1985 (5); v In 1984 (5)*

Druce, N. F. 5: *v A 1897 (5)*

Ducat, A. 1: v A 1921

Duckworth, G. 24: v A 1930 (5); v SA 1924 (1) 1929 (4) 1935 (1); v WI 1928 (1); v In 1936 (3); *v A 1928 (5); v SA 1930 (3); v NZ 1932 (1)*

Duleepsinhji, K. S. 12: v A 1930 (4); v SA 1929 (1); v NZ 1931 (3); *v NZ 1929 (4)*

Durston, F. J. 1: v A 1921

Ealham, M. A. 6: v A 1997 (4); v In 1996 (1); v P 1996 (1)

Edmonds, P. H. 51: v A 1975 (2) 1985 (5); v NZ 1978 (3) 1983 (2) 1986 (3); v In 1979 (4) 1982 (3) 1986 (2); v P 1978 (3) 1987 (5); *v A 1978 (1) 1986 (5); v WI 1985 (3); v NZ 1977 (3); v In 1984 (5); v P 1977 (2)*

Edrich, J. H. 77: v A 1964 (3) 1968 (5) 1972 (5) 1975 (4); v SA 1965 (1); v WI 1963 (3) 1966 (1) 1969 (3) 1976 (2); v NZ 1965 (1) 1969 (3); v In 1967 (2) 1971 (3) 1974 (3); v P 1971 (3) 1974 (3); *v A 1965 (5) 1970 (6) 1974 (4); v WI 1967 (5); v NZ 1965 (3) 1970 (2) 1974 (2); v In 1963 (2); v P 1968 (3)*

Edrich, W. J. 39: v A 1938 (4) 1948 (5) 1953 (3); v SA 1947 (4); v WI 1950 (2); v NZ 1949 (4); v In 1946 (1); v P 1954 (1); *v A 1946 (5) 1954 (4); v SA 1938 (5); v NZ 1946 (1)*

Elliott, H. 4: v WI 1928 (1); *v SA 1927 (1); v In 1933 (2)*

Ellison, R. M. 11: v A 1985 (2); v WI 1984 (1); v In 1986 (1); v SL 1984 (1); *v WI 1985 (3); v In 1984 (3)*

Emburey, J. E. 64: v A 1980 (1) 1981 (4) 1985 (6) 1989 (3) 1993 (1); v WI 1980 (3) 1988 (3) 1995 (1);
v NZ 1978 (1) 1986 (2); v In 1986 (3); v P 1987 (4); v SL 1988 (1); *v A 1978 (4) 1986 (5) 1987 (1);*
v WI 1980 (4) 1985 (4); v NZ 1987 (3); v In 1979 (1) 1981 (3) 1992 (1); v P 1987 (3); v SL 1981 (1)
1992 (1)

Emmett, G. M. 1: v A 1948

Emmett, T. 7: *v A 1876 (2) 1878 (1) 1881 (4)*

Evans, A. J. 1: v A 1921

Evans, T. G. 91: v A 1948 (5) 1953 (5) 1956 (5); v SA 1947 (5) 1951 (3) 1955 (3); v WI 1950 (3) 1957
(5); v NZ 1949 (4) 1958 (5); v In 1946 (1) 1952 (4) 1959 (2); v P 1954 (4); *v A 1946 (4) 1950 (5)*
1954 (4) 1958 (3); v SA 1948 (3) 1956 (5); v WI 1947 (4) 1953 (4); v NZ 1946 (1) 1950 (2) 1954 (2)

Fagg, A. E. 5: v WI 1939 (1); v In 1936 (2); *v A 1936 (2)*

Fairbrother, N. H. 10: v NZ 1990 (3); v P 1987 (1); *v NZ 1987 (2); v In 1992 (2); v P 1987 (1);*
v SL 1992 (1)

Fane, F. L. 14: *v A 1907 (4); v SA 1905 (5) 1909 (5)*

Farnes, K. 15: v A 1934 (2) 1938 (4); *v A 1936 (2); v SA 1938 (5); v WI 1934 (2)*

Farrimond, W. 4: v SA 1935 (1); *v SA 1930 (2); v WI 1934 (1)*

Fender, P. G. H. 13: v A 1921 (2); v SA 1924 (2) 1929 (1); *v A 1920 (3); v SA 1922 (5)*

Ferris, J. J. 1: *v SA 1891*

Fielder, A. 6: *v A 1903 (2) 1907 (4)*

Fishlock, L. B. 4: v In 1936 (2) 1946 (1); *v A 1946 (1)*

Flavell, J. A. 4: v A 1961 (2) 1964 (2)

Fletcher, K. W. R. 59: v A 1968 (1) 1972 (1) 1975 (2); v WI 1973 (3); v NZ 1969 (2) 1973 (3); v In
1971 (2) 1974 (3); v P 1974 (3); *v A 1970 (5) 1974 (5) 1976 (1); v WI 1973 (4); v NZ 1970 (1)*
1974 (2); v In 1972 (5) 1976 (3) 1981 (6); v P 1968 (3) 1972 (3); v SL 1981 (1)

Flowers, W. 8: v A 1893 (1); *v A 1884 (5) 1886 (2)*

Ford, F. G. J. 5: *v A 1894 (5)*

Foster, F. R. 11: v A 1912 (3); v SA 1912 (3); *v A 1911 (5)*

Foster, N. A. 29: v A 1985 (1) 1989 (3) 1993 (1); v WI 1984 (1) 1988 (2); v NZ 1983 (1) 1986 (1);
v In 1986 (1); v P 1987 (5); v SL 1988 (1); *v A 1987 (1); v WI 1985 (3); v NZ 1983 (2); v In 1984 (2);*
v P 1983 (2) 1987 (2)

Foster, R. E. 8: v SA 1907 (3); *v A 1903 (5)*

Fothergill, A. J. 2: *v SA 1888 (2)*

Fowler, G. 21: v WI 1984 (5); v NZ 1983 (2); v P 1982 (1); v SL 1984 (1); *v A 1982 (3); v NZ 1983 (2);*
v In 1984 (5); v P 1983 (2)

Fraser, A. R. C. 32: v A 1989 (3) 1993 (1); v SA 1994 (2); v WI 1995 (5); v NZ 1994 (3); v In 1990 (3);
v A 1990 (3) 1994 (3); v SA 1995 (3); v WI 1989 (2) 1993 (4)

Freeman, A. P. 12: v SA 1929 (3); v WI 1928 (3); *v A 1924 (2); v SA 1927 (4)*

French, B. N. 16: v NZ 1986 (3); v In 1986 (2); v P 1987 (4); *v A 1987 (1); v NZ 1987 (3); v P 1987 (3)*

Fry, C. B. 26: v A 1899 (5) 1902 (3) 1905 (4) 1909 (3) 1912 (3); v SA 1907 (3) 1912 (3); *v SA 1895 (2)*

Gallian, J. E. R. 3: v WI 1995 (2); *v SA 1995 (1)*

Gatting, M. W. 79: v A 1980 (1) 1981 (6) 1985 (6) 1989 (1) 1993 (2); v WI 1980 (4) 1984 (1) 1988 (2);
v NZ 1983 (2) 1986 (3); v In 1986 (3); v P 1982 (3) 1987 (5); *v A 1986 (5) 1987 (1) 1994 (5); v WI*
1980 (1) 1985 (1); v NZ 1977 (1) 1983 (2) 1987 (3); v In 1981 (3) 1984 (5) 1992 (3); v P 1977 (1)
1983 (3) 1987 (3); v SL 1992 (1)

Gay, L. H. 1: *v A 1894*

Geary, G. 14: v A 1926 (2) 1930 (1) 1934 (2); v SA 1924 (1) 1929 (2); *v A 1928 (4); v SA 1927 (2)*

Gibb, P. A. 8: v In 1946 (2); *v A 1946 (1); v SA 1938 (5)*

Gifford, N. 15: v A 1964 (2) 1972 (3); v NZ 1973 (2); v In 1971 (2); v P 1971 (2); *v In 1972 (2); v P*
1972 (2)

Gilligan, A. E. R. 11: v SA 1924 (4); *v A 1924 (5); v SA 1922 (2)*

Gilligan, A. H. H. 4: *v NZ 1929 (4)*

Gimblett, H. 3: v WI 1939 (1); v In 1936 (2)

Gladwin, C. 8: v SA 1947 (2); v NZ 1949 (1); *v SA 1948 (5)*

Goddard, T. W. 8: v A 1930 (1); v WI 1939 (2); v NZ 1937 (2); *v SA 1938 (3)*

Gooch, G. A. 118: v A 1975 (2) 1980 (1) 1981 (5) 1985 (6) 1989 (5) 1993 (6); v SA 1994 (3); v WI
1980 (5) 1988 (5) 1991 (5); v NZ 1978 (3) 1986 (3) 1990 (3) 1994 (3); v In 1979 (4) 1986 (3)
1990 (3); v P 1978 (2) 1992 (5); v SL 1988 (1) 1991 (1); *v A 1978 (6) 1979 (2) 1990 (4) 1994 (5);*
v WI 1980 (4) 1985 (5) 1989 (2); v NZ 1991 (3); v In 1979 (1) 1981 (6) 1992 (2); v P 1987 (3);
v SL 1981 (1)

Gough, D. 21: v A 1997 (4); v SA 1994 (3); v WI 1995 (3); v NZ 1994 (1); *v A 1994 (3); v SA 1995 (2); v NZ 1996 (3); v Z 1996 (2)*

Gover, A. R. 4: v NZ 1937 (2); v In 1936 (1) 1946 (1)

Gower, D. I. 117: v A 1980 (1) 1981 (5) 1985 (6) 1989 (6); v WI 1980 (1) 1984 (5) 1988 (4); v NZ 1978 (3) 1983 (4) 1986 (3); v In 1979 (4) 1982 (3) 1986 (2) 1990 (3); v P 1978 (3) 1982 (3) 1987 (5) 1992 (3); v SL 1984 (1); *v A 1978 (6) 1979 (3) 1982 (5) 1986 (5) 1990 (5); v WI 1980 (4) 1985 (5); v NZ 1983 (3); v In 1979 (1) 1981 (6) 1984 (5); v P 1983 (3); v SL 1981 (1)*

Grace, E. M. 1: v A 1880

Grace, G. F. 1: v A 1880

Grace, W. G. 22: v A 1880 (1) 1882 (1) 1884 (3) 1886 (3) 1888 (3) 1890 (2) 1893 (2) 1896 (3) 1899 (1); *v A 1891 (3)*

Graveney, T. W. 79: v A 1953 (5) 1956 (2) 1968 (5); v SA 1951 (1) 1955 (5); v WI 1957 (4) 1966 (4) 1969 (1); v NZ 1958 (4); v In 1952 (4) 1967 (3); v P 1954 (3) 1962 (4) 1967 (3); *v A 1954 (2) 1958 (5) 1962 (3); v WI 1953 (5) 1967 (5); v NZ 1954 (2) 1958 (2); v In 1951 (4); v P 1968 (3)*

Greenhough, T. 4: v SA 1960 (1); v In 1959 (3)

Greenwood, A. 2: *v A 1876 (2)*

Greig, A. W. 58: v A 1972 (5) 1975 (4) 1977 (5); v WI 1973 (3) 1976 (5); v NZ 1973 (3); v In 1974 (3); v P 1974 (3); *v A 1974 (6) 1976 (1); v WI 1973 (5); v NZ 1974 (2); v In 1972 (5) 1976 (5); v P 1972 (3)*

Greig, I. A. 2: v P 1982 (2)

Grieve, B. A. F. 2: *v SA 1888 (2)*

Griffith, S. C. 3: *v SA 1948 (2); v WI 1947 (1)*

Gunn, G. 15: v A 1909 (1); *v A 1907 (5) 1911 (5); v WI 1929 (4)*

Gunn, J. 6: v A 1905 (1); *v A 1901 (5)*

Gunn, W. 11: v A 1888 (2) 1890 (2) 1893 (3) 1896 (1) 1899 (1); *v A 1886 (2)*

Haig, N. E. 5: v A 1921 (1); *v WI 1929 (4)*

Haigh, S. 11: v A 1905 (2) 1909 (1) 1912 (1); *v SA 1898 (2) 1905 (5)*

Hallows, C. 2: v A 1921 (1); v WI 1928 (1)

Hammond, W. R. 85: v A 1930 (5) 1934 (5) 1938 (4); v SA 1929 (4) 1935 (5); v WI 1928 (3) 1933 (3) 1939 (3); v NZ 1931 (3) 1937 (3); v In 1932 (1) 1936 (2) 1946 (3); *v A 1928 (5) 1932 (5) 1936 (5) 1946 (4); v SA 1927 (5) 1930 (5) 1938 (5); v WI 1934 (4); v NZ 1932 (2) 1946 (1)*

Hampshire, J. H. 8: v A 1972 (1) 1975 (1); v WI 1969 (2); *v A 1970 (2); v NZ 1970 (2)*

Hardinge, H. T. W. 1: v A 1921

Hardstaff, J. 5: *v A 1907 (5)*

Hardstaff, J. jun. 23: v A 1938 (2) 1948 (1); v SA 1935 (1); v WI 1939 (3); v NZ 1937 (3); v In 1936 (1) 1946 (2); *v A 1936 (5) 1946 (1); v WI 1947 (3)*

Harris, Lord 4: v A 1880 (1) 1884 (2); *v A 1878 (1)*

Hartley, J. C. 2: *v SA 1905 (2)*

Hawke, Lord 5: *v SA 1895 (3) 1898 (2)*

Hayes, E. G. 5: v A 1909 (1); v SA 1912 (1); *v SA 1905 (3)*

Hayes, F. C. 9: v WI 1973 (3) 1976 (2); *v WI 1973 (4)*

Hayward, T. W. 35: v A 1896 (2) 1899 (5) 1902 (1) 1905 (5) 1909 (1); v SA 1907 (3); *v A 1897 (5) 1901 (5) 1903 (5); v SA 1895 (3)*

Headley, D. W. 3: v A 1997 (3)

Hearne, A. 1: *v SA 1891*

Hearne, F. 2: *v SA 1888 (2)*

Hearne, G. G. 1: *v SA 1891*

Hearne, J. T. 12: v A 1896 (3) 1899 (3); *v A 1897 (5); v SA 1891 (1)*

Hearne, J. W. 24: v A 1912 (3) 1921 (1) 1926 (1); v SA 1912 (2) 1924 (3); *v A 1911 (5) 1920 (2) 1924 (4); v SA 1913 (3)*

Hemmings, E. E. 16: v A 1989 (1); v NZ 1990 (3); v In 1990 (3); v P 1982 (2); *v A 1982 (3) 1987 (1) 1990 (1); v NZ 1987 (1); v P 1987 (1)*

Hendren, E. H. 51: v A 1921 (2) 1926 (5) 1930 (2) 1934 (4); v SA 1924 (5) 1929 (5); v WI 1928 (1); *v A 1920 (5) 1924 (5) 1928 (5); v SA 1930 (5); v WI 1929 (4) 1934 (4)*

Hendrick, M. 30: v A 1977 (3) 1980 (1) 1981 (2); v WI 1976 (2) 1980 (2); v NZ 1978 (2); v In 1974 (3) 1979 (4); v P 1974 (2); *v A 1974 (2) 1978 (5); v NZ 1974 (1) 1977 (1)*

Heseltine, C. 2: *v SA 1895 (2)*

Hick, G. A. 46: v A 1993 (3); v SA 1994 (3); v WI 1991 (4) 1995 (5); v NZ 1994 (3); v In 1996 (3); v P 1992 (4) 1996 (1); *v A 1994 (3); v SA 1995 (5); v WI 1993 (5); v NZ 1991 (3); v In 1992 (3); v SL 1992 (1)*

Higgs, K. 15: v A 1968 (1); v WI 1966 (5); v SA 1965 (1); v In 1967 (1); v P 1967 (3); *v A 1965 (1); v NZ 1965 (3)*

Hill, A. 2: *v A 1876 (2)*

Hill, A. J. L. 3: *v SA 1895 (3)*

Hilton, M. J. 4: v SA 1951 (1); v WI 1950 (1); *v In 1951 (2)*

Hirst, G. H. 24: v A 1899 (1) 1902 (4) 1905 (3) 1909 (4); v SA 1907 (3); *v A 1897 (4) 1903 (5)*

Hitch, J. W. 7: v A 1912 (1) 1921 (1); v SA 1912 (1); *v A 1911 (3) 1920 (1)*

Hobbs, J. B. 61: v A 1909 (3) 1912 (3) 1921 (1) 1926 (5) 1930 (5); v SA 1912 (3) 1924 (4) 1929 (1); v WI 1928 (2); *v A 1907 (4) 1911 (5) 1920 (5) 1924 (5) 1928 (5); v SA 1909 (5) 1913 (5)*

Hobbs, R. N. S. 7: v In 1967 (3); v P 1967 (1) 1971 (1); *v WI 1967 (1); v P 1968 (1)*

Hollies, W. E. 13: v A 1948 (1); v SA 1947 (3); v WI 1950 (2); v NZ 1949 (4); *v WI 1934 (3)*

Hollioake, A. J. 2: v A 1997 (2)

Hollioake, B. C. 1: v A 1997

Holmes, E. R. T. 5: v SA 1935 (1); *v WI 1934 (4)*

Holmes, P. 7: v A 1921 (1); v In 1932 (1); *v SA 1927 (5)*

Hone, L. 1: *v A 1878*

Hopwood, J. L. 2: v A 1934 (2)

Hornby, A. N. 3: v A 1882 (1) 1884 (1); *v A 1878 (1)*

Horton, M. J. 2: v In 1959 (2)

Howard, N. D. 4: *v In 1951 (4)*

Howell, H. 5: v A 1921 (1); v SA 1924 (1); *v A 1920 (3)*

Howorth, R. 5: v SA 1947 (1); *v WI 1947 (4)*

Humphries, J. 3: *v A 1907 (3)*

Hunter, J. 5: *v A 1884 (5)*

Hussain, N. 23: v A 1993 (4) 1997 (6); v In 1996 (3); v P 1996 (2); *v WI 1989 (3); v NZ 1996 (3); v Z 1996 (2)*

Hutchings, K. L. 7: v A 1909 (2); *v A 1907 (5)*

Hutton, L. 79: v A 1938 (3) 1948 (4) 1953 (5); v SA 1947 (5) 1951 (5); v WI 1939 (3) 1950 (3); v NZ 1937 (3) 1949 (4); v In 1946 (3) 1952 (4); v P 1954 (2); *v A 1946 (5) 1950 (5) 1954 (5); v SA 1938 (4) 1948 (5); v WI 1947 (2) 1953 (5); v NZ 1950 (2) 1954 (2)*

Hutton, R. A. 5: v In 1971 (3); v P 1971 (2)

Iddon, J. 5: v SA 1935 (1); *v WI 1934 (4)*

Igglesden, A. P. 3: v A 1989 (1); *v WI 1993 (2)*

Ikin, J. T. 18: v SA 1951 (3) 1955 (1); v In 1946 (2) 1952 (2); *v A 1946 (5); v NZ 1946 (1); v WI 1947 (4)*

Illingworth, R. 61: v A 1961 (2) 1968 (3) 1972 (5); v SA 1960 (4); v WI 1966 (2) 1969 (3) 1973 (3); v NZ 1958 (1) 1965 (1) 1969 (3) 1973 (3); v In 1959 (2) 1967 (3) 1971 (3); v P 1962 (1) 1967 (1) 1971 (3); *v A 1962 (2) 1970 (6); v WI 1959 (5); v NZ 1962 (3) 1970 (2)*

Illingworth, R. K. 9: v WI 1991 (2) 1995 (4); *v SA 1995 (3)*

Ilott, M. C. 5: v A 1993 (3); *v SA 1995 (2)*

Insole, D. J. 9: v A 1956 (1); v SA 1955 (1); v WI 1950 (1) 1957 (1); *v SA 1956 (5)*

Irani, R. C. 2: v In 1996 (2)

Jackman, R. D. 4: v P 1982 (2); *v WI 1980 (2)*

Jackson, F. S. 20: v A 1893 (2) 1896 (3) 1899 (5) 1902 (5) 1905 (5)

Jackson, H. L. 2: v A 1961 (1); v NZ 1949 (1)

Jameson, J. A. 4: v In 1971 (2); *v WI 1973 (2)*

Jardine, D. R. 22: v WI 1928 (2) 1933 (2); v NZ 1931 (3); v In 1932 (1); *v A 1928 (5) 1932 (5); v NZ 1932 (1); v In 1933 (3)*

Jarvis, P. W. 9: v A 1989 (2); v WI 1988 (2); *v NZ 1987 (2); v In 1992 (2), v SL 1992 (1)*

Jenkins, R. O. 9: v WI 1950 (2); v In 1952 (2); *v SA 1948 (2)*

Jessop, G. L. 18: v A 1899 (1) 1902 (4) 1905 (1) 1909 (2); v SA 1907 (3) 1912 (2); *v A 1901 (5)*

Jones, A. O. 12: v A 1899 (1) 1905 (2) 1909 (2); *v A 1901 (5) 1907 (2)*

Jones, I. J. 15: v WI 1966 (2); *v A 1965 (4); v WI 1967 (5); v NZ 1965 (3); v In 1963 (1)*

Jupp, H. 2: *v A 1876 (2)*

Jupp, V. W. C. 8: v A 1921 (2); v WI 1928 (2); *v SA 1922 (4)*

Keeton, W. W. 2: v A 1934 (1); v WI 1939 (1)

Kennedy, A. S. 5: *v SA 1922 (5)*

Kenyon, D. 8: v A 1953 (2); v SA 1955 (3); *v In 1951 (3)*

Killick, E. T. 2: v SA 1929 (2)
Kilner, R. 9: v A 1926 (4); v SA 1924 (2); *v A 1924 (3)*
King, J. H. 1: v A 1909
Kinneir, S. P. 1: *v A 1911*
Knight, A. E. 3: *v A 1903 (3)*
Knight, B. R. 29: v A 1968 (2); v WI 1966 (1) 1969 (3); v NZ 1969 (2); v P 1962 (2); *v A 1962 (1) 1965 (2); v NZ 1962 (3) 1965 (2); v In 1961 (4) 1963 (5); v P 1961 (2)*
Knight, D. J. 2: v A 1921 (2)
Knight, N. V. 11: v WI 1995 (2); v In 1996 (1); v P 1996 (3); *v NZ 1996 (3); v Z 1996 (2)*
Knott, A. P. E. 95: v A 1968 (5) 1972 (5) 1975 (4) 1977 (5) 1981 (2); v WI 1969 (3) 1973 (3) 1976 (5) 1980 (4); v NZ 1969 (3) 1973 (3); v In 1971 (3) 1974 (3); v P 1967 (2) 1971 (3) 1974 (3); *v A 1970 (6) 1974 (6) 1976 (1); v WI 1967 (2) 1973 (5); v NZ 1970 (1) 1974 (2); v In 1972 (5) 1976 (5); v P 1968 (3) 1972 (3)*
Knox, N. A. 2: v SA 1907 (2)

Laker, J. C. 46: v A 1948 (3) 1953 (3) 1956 (5); v SA 1951 (2) 1955 (1); v WI 1950 (1) 1957 (4); v NZ 1949 (1) 1958 (4); v In 1952 (4); v P 1954 (1); *v A 1958 (4); v SA 1956 (5); v WI 1947 (4) 1953 (4)*
Lamb, A. J. 79: v A 1985 (6) 1989 (1); v WI 1984 (5) 1988 (4) 1991 (4); v NZ 1983 (4) 1986 (1) 1990 (3); v In 1982 (3) 1986 (2) 1990 (3); v P 1982 (3) 1992 (2); v SL 1984 (1) 1988 (1); *v A 1982 (5) 1986 (5) 1990 (3); v WI 1985 (5) 1989 (4); v NZ 1983 (3) 1991 (3); v In 1984 (5); v P 1983 (3)*
Langridge, James 8: v SA 1935 (1); v WI 1933 (2); v In 1936 (1) 1946 (1); *v In 1933 (3)*
Larkins, W. 13: v A 1981 (1); v WI 1980 (1); *v A 1979 (1) 1990 (3); v WI 1989 (4); v In 1979 (1)*
Larter, J. D. F. 10: v SA 1965 (2); v NZ 1965 (1); v P 1962 (1); *v NZ 1962 (3); v In 1963 (3)*
Larwood, H. 21: v A 1926 (2) 1930 (3); v SA 1929 (3); v WI 1928 (2); v NZ 1931 (1); *v A 1928 (5) 1932 (5)*
Lathwell, M. N. 2: v A 1993 (2)
Lawrence, D. V. 5: v WI 1991 (2); v SL 1988 (1) 1991 (1); *v NZ 1991 (1)*
Leadbeater, E. 2: *v In 1951 (2)*
Lee, H. W. 1: *v SA 1930*
Lees, W. S. 5: *v SA 1905 (5)*
Legge, G. B. 5: *v SA 1927 (1); v NZ 1929 (4)*
Leslie, C. F. H. 4: *v A 1882 (4)*
Lever, J. K. 21: v A 1977 (3); v WI 1980 (1); v In 1979 (1) 1986 (1); *v A 1976 (1) 1978 (1) 1979 (1); v NZ 1977 (1); v In 1976 (5) 1979 (1) 1981 (2); v P 1977 (3)*
Lever, P. 17: v A 1972 (1) 1975 (1); v In 1971 (1); v P 1971 (3); *v A 1970 (5) 1974 (2); v NZ 1970 (2) 1974 (2)*
Leveson Gower, H. D. G. 3: *v SA 1909 (3)*
Levett, W. H. V. 1: *v In 1933*
Lewis, A. R. 9: v NZ 1973 (1); *v In 1972 (5); v P 1972 (3)*
Lewis, C. C. 32: v A 1993 (2); v WI 1991 (2); v NZ 1990 (1); v In 1990 (2) 1996 (3); v P 1992 (5) 1996 (2); v SL 1991 (1); *v A 1990 (1) 1994 (2); v WI 1993 (5); v NZ 1991 (2); v In 1992 (3); v SL 1992 (1)*
Leyland, M. 41: v A 1930 (3) 1934 (5) 1938 (1); v SA 1929 (5) 1935 (4); v WI 1928 (1) 1933 (1); v In 1936 (2); *v A 1928 (1) 1932 (5) 1936 (5); v SA 1930 (5); v WI 1934 (3)*
Lilley, A. A. 35: v A 1896 (3) 1899 (4) 1902 (5) 1905 (5) 1909 (5); v SA 1907 (3); *v A 1901 (5) 1903 (5)*
Lillywhite, James jun. 2: *v A 1876 (2)*
Lloyd, D. 9: v In 1974 (2); v P 1974 (3); *v A 1974 (4)*
Lloyd, T. A. 1: v WI 1984
Loader, P. J. 13: v SA 1955 (1); v WI 1957 (2); v NZ 1958 (3); v P 1954 (1); *v A 1958 (2); v SA 1956 (4)*
Lock, G. A. R. 49: v A 1953 (2) 1956 (4) 1961 (3); v SA 1955 (3); v WI 1957 (3) 1963 (3); v NZ 1958 (5); v In 1952 (2); v P 1962 (3); *v A 1958 (4); v SA 1956 (1); v WI 1953 (5) 1967 (2); v NZ 1958 (2); v In 1961 (5); v P 1961 (2)*
Lockwood, W. H. 12: v A 1893 (2) 1899 (1) 1902 (4); *v A 1894 (5)*
Lohmann, G. A. 18: v A 1886 (3) 1888 (3) 1890 (2) 1896 (1); *v A 1886 (2) 1887 (1) 1891 (3); v SA 1895 (3)*
Lowson, F. A. 7: v SA 1951 (2) 1955 (1); *v In 1951 (4)*
Lucas, A. P. 5: v A 1880 (1) 1882 (1) 1884 (2); *v A 1878 (1)*
Luckhurst, B. W. 21: v A 1972 (4); v WI 1973 (2); v In 1971 (3); v P 1971 (3); *v A 1970 (5) 1974 (2); v NZ 1970 (2)*
Lyttelton, Hon. A. 4: v A 1880 (1) 1882 (1) 1884 (2)

Macaulay, G. G. 8: v A 1926 (1); v SA 1924 (1); v WI 1933 (2); *v SA 1922 (4)*
MacBryan, J. C. W. 1: v SA 1924
McCague, M. J. 3: v A 1993 (2); *v A 1994 (1)*
McConnon, J. E. 2: v P 1954 (2)
McGahey, C. P. 2: *v A 1901 (2)*
MacGregor, G. 8: v A 1890 (2) 1893 (3); *v A 1891 (3)*
McIntyre, A. J. W. 3: v SA 1955 (1); v WI 1950 (1); *v A 1950 (1)*
MacKinnon, F. A. 1: *v A 1878*
MacLaren, A. C. 35: v A 1896 (2) 1899 (4) 1902 (5) 1905 (4) 1909 (5); *v A 1894 (5) 1897 (5) 1901 (5)*
McMaster, J. E. P. 1: *v SA 1888*
Makepeace, J. W. H. 4: *v A 1920 (4)*
Malcolm, D. E. 40: v A 1989 (1) 1993 (1) 1997 (4); v SA 1994 (1); v WI 1991 (2) 1995 (2); v NZ 1990 (3) 1994 (1); v In 1990 (3); v P 1992 (3); *v A 1990 (5) 1994 (4); v SA 1995 (2); v WI 1989 (4) 1993 (1); v In 1992 (2); v SL 1992 (1)*
Mallender, N. A. 2: v P 1992 (2)
Mann, F. G. 7: v NZ 1949 (2); *v SA 1948 (5)*
Mann, F. T. 5: *v SA 1922 (5)*
Marks, V. J. 6: v NZ 1983 (1); v P 1982 (1); *v NZ 1983 (1); v P 1983 (3)*
Marriott, C. S. 1: v WI 1933
Martin, F. 2: v A 1890 (1); *v SA 1891 (1)*
Martin, J. W. 1: v SA 1947
Martin, P. J. 8: v A 1997 (1); v WI 1995 (3); v In 1996 (1); *v SA 1995 (3)*
Mason, J. R. 5: *v A 1897 (5)*
Matthews, A. D. G. 1: v NZ 1937
May, P. B. H. 66: v A 1953 (2) 1956 (5) 1961 (4); v SA 1951 (2) 1955 (5); v WI 1957 (5); v NZ 1958 (5); v In 1952 (4) 1959 (3); v P 1954 (4); *v A 1954 (5) 1958 (5); v SA 1956 (5); v WI 1953 (5) 1959 (3); v NZ 1954 (2) 1958 (2)*
Maynard, M. P. 4: v A 1993 (2); v WI 1988 (1); *v WI 1993 (1)*
Mead, C. P. 17: v A 1921 (2); *v A 1911 (4) 1928 (1); v SA 1913 (5) 1922 (5)*
Mead, W. 1: v A 1899
Midwinter, W. E. 4: *v A 1881 (4)*
Milburn, C. 9: v A 1968 (2); v WI 1966 (4); v In 1967 (1); v P 1967 (1); *v P 1968 (1)*
Miller, A. M. 1: *v SA 1895*
Miller, G. 34: v A 1977 (2); v WI 1976 (1) 1984 (2); v NZ 1978 (2); v In 1979 (3) 1982 (1); v P 1978 (3) 1982 (1); *v A 1978 (6) 1979 (1) 1982 (5); v WI 1980 (1); v NZ 1977 (3); v P 1977 (3)*
Milligan, F. W. 2: *v SA 1898 (2)*
Millman, G. 6: v P 1962 (2); *v In 1961 (2); v P 1961 (2)*
Milton, C. A. 6: v NZ 1958 (2); v In 1959 (2); *v A 1958 (2)*
Mitchell, A. 6: v SA 1935 (2); v In 1936 (1); *v In 1933 (3)*
Mitchell, F. 2: *v SA 1898 (2)*
Mitchell, T. B. 5: v A 1934 (2); v SA 1935 (1); *v A 1932 (1); v NZ 1932 (1)*
Mitchell-Innes, N. S. 1: v SA 1935
Mold, A. W. 3: v A 1893 (3)
Moon, L. J. 4: *v SA 1905 (4)*
Morley, F. 4: v A 1880 (1); *v A 1882 (3)*
Morris, H. 3: v WI 1991 (2); v SL 1991 (1)
Morris, J. E. 3: v In 1990 (3)
Mortimore, J. B. 9: v A 1964 (1); v In 1959 (2); *v A 1958 (1); v NZ 1958 (2); v In 1963 (3)*
Moss, A. E. 9: v A 1956 (1); v SA 1960 (2); v In 1959 (3); *v WI 1953 (1) 1959 (2)*
Moxon, M. D. 10: v A 1989 (1); v WI 1988 (2); v NZ 1986 (2); v P 1987 (1); *v A 1987 (1); v NZ 1987 (3)*
Mullally, A. D. 9: v In 1996 (3); v P 1996 (3); *v NZ 1996 (1); v Z 1996 (2)*
Munton, T. A. 2: v P 1992 (2)
Murdoch, W. L. 1: *v SA 1891*
Murray, J. T. 21: v A 1961 (5); v WI 1966 (1); v In 1967 (3); v P 1962 (3) 1967 (1); *v A 1962 (1); v SA 1964 (1); v NZ 1962 (1) 1965 (1); v In 1961 (3); v P 1961 (1)*

Newham, W. 1: *v A 1887*
Newport, P. J. 3: v A 1989 (1); v SL 1988 (1); *v A 1990 (1)*
Nichols, M. S. 14: v A 1930 (1); v SA 1935 (4); v WI 1933 (1) 1939 (1); *v NZ 1929 (4); v In 1933 (3)*

Oakman, A. S. M. 2: v A 1956 (2)
O'Brien, Sir T. C. 5: v A 1884 (1) 1888 (1); *v SA 1895 (3)*
O'Connor, J. 4: v SA 1929 (1); *v WI 1929 (3)*
Old, C. M. 46: v A 1975 (3) 1977 (2) 1980 (1) 1981 (2); v WI 1973 (1) 1976 (2) 1980 (1); v NZ 1973 (2) 1978 (1); v In 1974 (3); v P 1974 (3) 1978 (3); *v A 1974 (2) 1976 (1) 1978 (1); v WI 1973 (4) 1980 (1); v NZ 1974 (1) 1977 (2); v In 1972 (4) 1976 (4); v P 1972 (1) 1977 (1)*
Oldfield, N. 1: v WI 1939

Padgett, D. E. V. 2: v SA 1960 (2)
Paine, G. A. E. 4: *v WI 1934 (4)*
Palairet, L. C. H. 2: v A 1902 (2)
Palmer, C. H. 1: *v WI 1953*
Palmer, K. E. 1: *v SA 1964*
Parfitt, P. H. 37: v A 1964 (4) 1972 (3); v SA 1965 (2); v WI 1969 (1); v NZ 1965 (2); v P 1962 (5); *v A 1962 (2); v SA 1964 (5); v NZ 1962 (3) 1965 (3); v In 1961 (2) 1963 (3); v P 1961 (2)*
Parker, C. W. L. 1: v A 1921
Parker, P. W. G. 1: v A 1981
Parkhouse, W. G. A. 7: v WI 1950 (2); v In 1959 (2); *v A 1950 (2); v NZ 1950 (1)*
Parkin, C. H. 10: v A 1921 (4); v SA 1924 (1); *v A 1920 (5)*
Parks, J. H. 1: v NZ 1937
Parks, J. M. 46: v A 1964 (5); v SA 1960 (5) 1965 (3); v WI 1963 (4) 1966 (4); v NZ 1965 (3); v P 1954 (1); *v A 1965 (5); v SA 1964 (5); v WI 1959 (1) 1967 (3); v NZ 1965 (2); v In 1963 (5)*
Pataudi sen., Nawab of, 3: v A 1934 (1); *v A 1932 (2)*
Patel, M. M. 2: v In 1996 (2)
Paynter, E. 20: v A 1938 (4); v WI 1939 (2); v NZ 1931 (1) 1937 (2); v In 1932 (1); *v A 1932 (3); v SA 1938 (5); v NZ 1932 (2)*
Peate, E. 9: v A 1882 (1) 1884 (3) 1886 (1); *v A 1881 (4)*
Peebles, I. A. R. 13: v A 1930 (2); v NZ 1931 (3); *v SA 1927 (4) 1930 (4)*
Peel, R. 20: v A 1888 (3) 1890 (1) 1893 (1) 1896 (1); *v A 1884 (5) 1887 (1) 1891 (3) 1894 (5)*
Penn, F. 1: v A 1880
Perks, R. T. D. 2: v WI 1939 (1); *v SA 1938 (1)*
Philipson, H. 5: *v A 1891 (1) 1894 (4)*
Pigott, A. C. S. 1: *v NZ 1983*
Pilling, R. 8: v A 1884 (1) 1886 (1) 1888 (1); *v A 1881 (4) 1887 (1)*
Place, W. 3: *v WI 1947 (3)*
Pocock, P. I. 25: v A 1968 (1); v WI 1976 (2) 1984 (2); v SL 1984 (1); *v WI 1967 (2) 1973 (4); v In 1972 (4) 1984 (5); v P 1968 (1) 1972 (3)*
Pollard, R. 4: v A 1948 (2); v In 1946 (1); *v NZ 1946 (1)*
Poole, C. J. 3: *v In 1951 (3)*
Pope, G. H. 1: v SA 1947
Pougher, A. D. 1: *v SA 1891*
Price, J. S. E. 15: v A 1964 (2) 1972 (1); v In 1971 (3); v P 1971 (1); *v SA 1964 (4); v In 1963 (4)*
Price, W. F. F. 1: v A 1938
Prideaux, R. M. 3: v A 1968 (1); *v P 1968 (2)*
Pringle, D. R. 30: v A 1989 (2); v WI 1984 (3) 1988 (4) 1991 (4); v NZ 1986 (1); v In 1982 (3) 1986 (3); v P 1982 (1) 1992 (3); v SL 1988 (1); *v A 1982 (3); v NZ 1991 (2)*
Pullar, G. 28: v A 1961 (5); v SA 1960 (3); v In 1959 (3); v P 1962 (2); *v A 1962 (4); v WI 1959 (5); v In 1961 (3); v P 1961 (3)*

Quaife, W. G. 7: v A 1899 (2); *v A 1901 (5)*

Radford, N. V. 3: v NZ 1986 (1); v In 1986 (1); *v NZ 1987 (1)*
Radley, C. T. 8: v NZ 1978 (3); v P 1978 (3); *v NZ 1977 (2)*
Ramprakash, M. R. 20: v A 1993 (1) 1997 (1); v WI 1991 (5) 1995 (2); v P 1992 (3); v SL 1991 (1); *v A 1994 (1); v WI 1993 (4); v SA 1995 (2)*
Randall, D. W. 47: v A 1977 (5); v WI 1984 (1); v NZ 1983 (3); v In 1979 (3) 1982 (3); v P 1982 (3); *v A 1976 (1) 1978 (6) 1979 (2) 1982 (4); v NZ 1977 (3) 1983 (3); v In 1976 (4); v P 1977 (3) 1983 (3)*
Ranjitsinhji, K. S. 15: v A 1896 (2) 1899 (5) 1902 (3); *v A 1897 (5)*
Read, H. D. 1: v SA 1935
Read, J. M. 17: v A 1882 (1) 1890 (2) 1893 (1); *v A 1884 (5) 1886 (2) 1887 (1) 1891 (3); v SA 1888 (2)*

Read, W. W. 18: v A 1884 (2) 1886 (3) 1888 (3) 1890 (2) 1893 (2); *v A 1882 (4) 1887 (1); v SA 1891 (1)*

Reeve, D. A. 3: *v NZ 1991 (3)*

Relf, A. E. 13: v A 1909 (1); *v A 1903 (2); v SA 1905 (5) 1913 (5)*

Rhodes, H. J. 2: v In 1959 (2)

Rhodes, S. J. 11: v SA 1994 (3); v NZ 1994 (3); *v A 1994 (5)*

Rhodes, W. 58: v A 1899 (3) 1902 (5) 1905 (4) 1909 (4) 1912 (3) 1921 (1) 1926 (1); v SA 1912 (3); *v A 1903 (5) 1907 (5) 1911 (5) 1920 (5); v SA 1909 (5) 1913 (5); v WI 1929 (4)*

Richards, C. J. 8: v WI 1988 (2); v P 1987 (1); *v A 1986 (5)*

Richardson, D. W. 1: v WI 1957

Richardson, P. E. 34: v A 1956 (5); v WI 1957 (5) 1963 (1); v NZ 1958 (4); *v A 1958 (4); v SA 1956 (5); v NZ 1958 (2); v In 1961 (5); v P 1961 (3)*

Richardson, T. 14: v A 1893 (1) 1896 (3); *v A 1894 (5) 1897 (5)*

Richmond, T. L. 1: v A 1921

Ridgway, F. 5: *v In 1951 (5)*

Robertson, J. D. 11: v SA 1947 (1); v NZ 1949 (1); *v WI 1947 (4); v In 1951 (5)*

Robins, R. W. V. 19: v A 1930 (2); v SA 1929 (1) 1935 (3); v WI 1933 (2); v NZ 1931 (1) 1937 (3); v In 1932 (1) 1936 (2); *v A 1936 (4)*

Robinson, R. T. 29: v A 1985 (6) 1989 (1); v In 1986 (1); v P 1987 (5); v SL 1988 (1); *v A 1987 (1); v WI 1985 (4); v NZ 1987 (3); v In 1984 (5); v P 1987 (2)*

Roope, G. R. J. 21: v A 1975 (1) 1977 (2); v WI 1973 (1); v NZ 1973 (3) 1978 (1); v P 1978 (3); *v NZ 1977 (3); v In 1972 (2); v P 1972 (2) 1977 (3)*

Root, C. F. 3: v A 1926 (3)

Rose, B. C. 9: v WI 1980 (3); *v WI 1980 (1); v NZ 1977 (2); v P 1977 (3)*

Royle, V. P. F. A. 1: *v A 1878*

Rumsey, F. E. 5: v A 1964 (1); v SA 1965 (1); v NZ 1965 (3)

Russell, A. C. 10: v A 1921 (2); *v A 1920 (4); v SA 1922 (4)*

Russell, R. C. 49: v A 1989 (6); v WI 1991 (4) 1995 (3); v NZ 1990 (3); v In 1990 (3) 1996 (3); v P 1992 (3) 1996 (2); v SL 1988 (1) 1991 (1); *v A 1990 (3); v SA 1995 (5); v WI 1989 (4) 1993 (5); v NZ 1991 (3)*

Russell, W. E. 10: v SA 1965 (1); v WI 1966 (2); v P 1967 (1); *v A 1965 (1); v NZ 1965 (3); v In 1961 (1); v P 1961 (1)*

Salisbury, I. D. K. 9: v SA 1994 (1); v P 1992 (2) 1996 (2); *v WI 1993 (2); v In 1992 (2)*

Sandham, A. 14: v A 1921 (1); v SA 1924 (2); *v A 1924 (2); v SA 1922 (5); v WI 1929 (4)*

Schultz, S. S. 1: *v A 1878*

Scotton, W. H. 15: v A 1884 (1) 1886 (3); *v A 1881 (4) 1884 (5) 1886 (2)*

Selby, J. 6: *v A 1876 (2) 1881 (4)*

Selvey, M. W. W. 3: v WI 1976 (2); *v In 1976 (1)*

Shackleton, D. 7: v SA 1951 (1); v WI 1950 (1) 1963 (4); *v In 1951 (1)*

Sharp, J. 3: v A 1909 (3)

Sharpe, J. W. 3: v A 1890 (1); *v A 1891 (2)*

Sharpe, P. J. 12: v A 1964 (2); v WI 1963 (3) 1969 (3); v NZ 1969 (3); *v In 1963 (1)*

Shaw, A. 7: v A 1880 (1); *v A 1876 (2) 1881 (4)*

Sheppard, Rev. D. S. 22: v A 1956 (2); v WI 1950 (1) 1957 (2); v In 1952 (2); v P 1954 (2) 1962 (2); *v A 1950 (2) 1962 (5); v NZ 1950 (1) 1963 (3)*

Sherwin, M. 3: v A 1888 (1); *v A 1886 (2)*

Shrewsbury, A. 23: v A 1884 (3) 1886 (3) 1890 (2) 1893 (3); *v A 1881 (4) 1884 (5) 1886 (2) 1887 (1)*

Shuter, J. 1: v A 1888

Shuttleworth, K. 5: v P 1971 (1); *v A 1970 (2); v NZ 1970 (2)*

Sidebottom, A. 1: v A 1985

Silverwood, C. E. W. 1: *v Z 1996*

Simpson, R. T. 27: v A 1953 (3); v SA 1951 (3); v WI 1950 (3); v NZ 1949 (2); v In 1952 (2); v P 1954 (3); *v A 1950 (5) 1954 (1); v SA 1948 (1); v NZ 1950 (2) 1954 (2)*

Simpson-Hayward, G. H. 5: *v SA 1909 (5)*

Sims, J. M. 4: v SA 1935 (1); v In 1936 (1); *v A 1936 (2)*

Sinfield, R. A. 1: v A 1938

Slack, W. N. 3: v In 1986 (1); *v WI 1985 (2)*

Smailes, T. F. 1: v In 1946

Small, G. C. 17: v A 1989 (1); v WI 1988 (1); v NZ 1986 (2) 1990 (3); *v A 1986 (2) 1990 (4); v WI 1989 (4)*

Smith, A. C. 6: *v A 1962 (4); v NZ 1962 (2)*

Smith, A. M. 1: v A 1997

Smith, C. A. 1: *v SA 1888*

Smith, C. I. J. 5: v NZ 1937 (1); *v WI 1934 (4)*

Smith, C. L. 8: v NZ 1983 (2); v In 1986 (1); *v NZ 1983 (2); v P 1983 (3)*

Smith, D. 2: v SA 1935 (2)

Smith, D. M. 2: *v WI 1985 (2)*

Smith, D. R. 5: *v In 1961 (5)*

Smith, D. V. 3: v WI 1957 (3)

Smith, E. J. 11: v A 1912 (3); v SA 1912 (3); *v A 1911 (4); v SA 1913 (1)*

Smith, H. 1: v WI 1928

Smith, M. J. K. 50: v A 1961 (1) 1972 (3); v SA 1960 (4) 1965 (3); v WI 1966 (1); v NZ 1958 (3) 1965 (3); v In 1959 (2); *v A 1965 (5); v SA 1964 (5); v WI 1959 (5); v NZ 1965 (3); v In 1961 (4) 1963 (5); v P 1961 (3)*

Smith, R. A. 62: v A 1989 (5) 1993 (5); v WI 1988 (2) 1991 (4) 1995 (4); v NZ 1990 (3) 1994 (3); v In 1990 (3); v P 1992 (5); v SL 1988 (1) 1991 (1); *v A 1990 (5); v SA 1995 (5); v WI 1989 (4) 1993 (5); v NZ 1991 (3); v In 1992 (3); v SL 1992 (1)*

Smith, T. P. B. 4: v In 1946 (1); *v A 1946 (2); v NZ 1946 (1)*

Smithson, G. A. 2: *v WI 1947 (2)*

Snow, J. A. 49: v A 1968 (5) 1972 (5) 1975 (4); v SA 1965 (1); v WI 1966 (3) 1969 (3) 1973 (1) 1976 (3); v NZ 1965 (1) 1969 (2) 1973 (3); v In 1967 (3) 1971 (2); v P 1967 (1); *v A 1970 (6); v WI 1967 (4); v P 1968 (2)*

Southerton, J. 2: *v A 1876 (2)*

Spooner, R. H. 10: v A 1905 (2) 1909 (2) 1912 (3); v SA 1912 (3)

Spooner, R. T. 7: v SA 1955 (1); *v In 1951 (5); v WI 1953 (1)*

Stanyforth, R. T. 4: *v SA 1927 (4)*

Staples, S. J. 3: *v SA 1927 (3)*

Statham, J. B. 70: v A 1953 (1) 1956 (3) 1961 (4); v SA 1951 (2) 1955 (4) 1960 (5) 1965 (1); v WI 1957 (3) 1963 (2); v NZ 1958 (2); v In 1959 (3); v P 1954 (4) 1962 (3); *v A 1954 (5) 1958 (4) 1962 (5); v SA 1956 (4); v WI 1953 (4) 1959 (3); v NZ 1950 (1) 1954 (2); v In 1951 (5)*

Steel, A. G. 13: v A 1880 (1) 1882 (1) 1884 (3) 1886 (3) 1888 (1); *v A 1882 (4)*

Steele, D. S. 8: v A 1975 (3); v WI 1976 (5)

Stephenson, J. P. 1: v A 1989

Stevens, G. T. S. 10: v A 1926 (2); *v SA 1922 (1) 1927 (5); v WI 1929 (2)*

Stevenson, G. B. 2: *v WI 1980 (1); v In 1979 (1)*

Stewart, A. J. 69: v A 1993 (6) 1997 (6); v SA 1994 (3); v WI 1991 (1) 1995 (3); v NZ 1990 (3) 1994 (3); v In 1996 (2); v P 1992 (5) 1996 (3); v SL 1991 (1); *v A 1990 (5) 1994 (2); v SA 1995 (5); v WI 1989 (4) 1993 (5); v NZ 1991 (3) 1996 (3); v In 1992 (3); v SL 1992 (1); v Z 1996 (2)*

Stewart, M. J. 8: v WI 1963 (4); v P 1962 (2); *v In 1963 (2)*

Stoddart, A. E. 16: v A 1893 (3) 1896 (2); *v A 1887 (1) 1891 (3) 1894 (5) 1897 (2)*

Storer, W. 6: v A 1899 (1); *v A 1897 (5)*

Street, G. B. 1: *v SA 1922*

Strudwick, H. 28: v A 1921 (2) 1926 (5); v SA 1924 (1); *v A 1911 (1) 1920 (4) 1924 (5); v SA 1909 (5) 1913 (5)*

Studd, C. T. 5: v A 1882 (1); *v A 1882 (4)*

Studd, G. B. 4: *v A 1882 (4)*

Subba Row, R. 13: v A 1961 (5); v SA 1960 (4); v NZ 1958 (1); v In 1959 (1); *v WI 1959 (2)*

Such, P. M. 8: v A 1993 (5); v NZ 1994 (3)

Sugg, F. H. 2: v A 1888 (2)

Sutcliffe, H. 54: v A 1926 (5) 1930 (4) 1934 (4); v SA 1924 (5) 1929 (5) 1935 (2); v WI 1928 (3) 1933 (2); v NZ 1931 (2); v In 1932 (1); *v A 1924 (5) 1928 (4) 1932 (5); v SA 1927 (5); v NZ 1932 (2)*

Swetman, R. 11: v In 1959 (3); *v A 1958 (2); v WI 1959 (4); v NZ 1958 (2)*

Tate, F. W. 1: v A 1902

Tate, M. W. 39: v A 1926 (5) 1930 (5); v SA 1924 (5) 1929 (3) 1935 (1); v WI 1928 (3); v NZ 1931 (1); *v A 1924 (5) 1928 (5); v SA 1930 (5); v NZ 1932 (1)*

Tattersall, R. 16: v A 1953 (1); v SA 1951 (5); v P 1954 (1); *v A 1950 (2); v NZ 1950 (2); v In 1951 (5)*

Tavaré, C. J. 31: v A 1981 (2) 1989 (1); v WI 1980 (2) 1984 (1); v NZ 1983 (4); v In 1982 (3); v P 1982 (3); v SL 1984 (1); *v A 1982 (5); v NZ 1983 (2); v In 1981 (6); v SL 1981 (1)*

Taylor, J. P. 2: v NZ 1994 (1); *v In 1992 (1)*

Taylor, K. 3: v A 1964 (1); v In 1959 (2)

Taylor, L. B. 2: v A 1985 (2)

Taylor, R. W. 57: v A 1981 (3); v NZ 1978 (3) 1983 (4); v In 1979 (3) 1982 (3); v P 1978 (3) 1982 (3); *v A 1978 (6) 1979 (3) 1982 (5); v NZ 1970 (1) 1977 (3) 1983 (3); v In 1979 (1) 1981 (6); v P 1977 (3) 1983 (3); v SL 1981 (1)*

Tennyson, Hon. L. H. 9: v A 1921 (4); *v SA 1913 (5)*

Terry, V. P. 2: v WI 1984 (2)

Thomas, J. G. 5: v NZ 1986 (1); *v WI 1985 (4)*

Thompson, G. J. 6: v A 1909 (1); *v SA 1909 (5)*

Thomson, N. I. 5: *v SA 1964 (5)*

Thorpe, G. P. 43: v A 1993 (3) 1997 (6); v SA 1994 (2); v WI 1995 (6); v In 1996 (3); v P 1996 (3); *v A 1994 (5); v SA 1995 (5); v WI 1993 (5); v NZ 1996 (3); v Z 1996 (2)*

Titmus, F. J. 53: v A 1964 (5); v SA 1955 (2) 1965 (3); v WI 1963 (4) 1966 (3); v NZ 1965 (3); v P 1962 (2) 1967 (2); *v A 1962 (5) 1965 (5) 1974 (4); v SA 1964 (5); v WI 1967 (2); v NZ 1962 (3); v In 1963 (5)*

Tolchard, R. W. 4: *v In 1976 (4)*

Townsend, C. L. 2: v A 1899 (2)

Townsend, D. C. H. 3: *v WI 1934 (3)*

Townsend, L. F. 4: *v WI 1929 (1); v In 1933 (3)*

Tremlett, M. F. 3: *v WI 1947 (3)*

Trott, A. E. 2: *v SA 1898 (2)*

Trueman, F. S. 67: v A 1953 (1) 1956 (2) 1961 (4) 1964 (4); v SA 1955 (1) 1960 (5); v WI 1957 (5) 1963 (5); v NZ 1958 (5) 1965 (2); v In 1952 (4) 1959 (5); v P 1962 (4); *v A 1958 (3) 1962 (5); v WI 1953 (3) 1959 (5); v NZ 1958 (2) 1962 (2)*

Tufnell, N. C. 1: *v SA 1909*

Tufnell, P. C. R. 28: v A 1993 (2) 1997 (1); v SA 1994 (1); v WI 1991 (1); v P 1992 (1); v SL 1991 (1); *v A 1990 (4) 1994 (4); v WI 1993 (2); v NZ 1991 (3) 1996 (3); v In 1992 (2); v SL 1992 (1); v Z 1996 (2)*

Turnbull, M. J. 9: v WI 1933 (2); v In 1936 (1); *v SA 1930 (5); v NZ 1929 (1)*

Tyldesley, E. 14: v A 1921 (3) 1926 (1); v SA 1924 (1); v WI 1928 (3); *v A 1928 (1); v SA 1927 (5)*

Tyldesley, J. T. 31: v A 1899 (2) 1902 (5) 1905 (5) 1909 (4); v SA 1907 (3); *v A 1901 (5) 1903 (5); v SA 1898 (2)*

Tyldesley, R. K. 7: v A 1930 (2); v SA 1924 (4); *v A 1924 (1)*

Tylecote, E. F. S. 6: v A 1886 (2); *v A 1882 (4)*

Tyler, E. J. 1: *v SA 1895*

Tyson, F. H. 17: v A 1956 (1); v SA 1955 (2); v P 1954 (1); *v A 1954 (5) 1958 (2); v SA 1956 (2); v NZ 1954 (2) 1958 (2)*

Ulyett, G. 25: v A 1882 (1) 1884 (3) 1886 (3) 1888 (2) 1890 (1); *v A 1876 (2) 1878 (1) 1881 (4) 1884 (5) 1887 (1); v SA 1888 (2)*

Underwood, D. L. 86: v A 1968 (4) 1972 (2) 1975 (4) 1977 (5); v WI 1966 (2) 1969 (2) 1973 (3) 1976 (5) 1980 (1); v NZ 1969 (2) 1973 (1); v In 1971 (1) 1974 (3); v P 1967 (2) 1971 (1) 1974 (3); *v A 1970 (5) 1974 (5) 1976 (1) 1979 (3); v WI 1973 (4); v NZ 1970 (2) 1974 (2); v In 1972 (4) 1976 (5) 1979 (1) 1981 (6); v P 1968 (3) 1972 (2); v SL 1981 (1)*

Valentine, B. H. 7: *v SA 1938 (5); v In 1933 (2)*

Verity, H. 40: v A 1934 (5) 1938 (4); v SA 1935 (4); v WI 1933 (2) 1939 (1); v NZ 1931 (2) 1937 (1); v In 1936 (3); *v A 1932 (4) 1936 (5); v SA 1938 (5); v NZ 1932 (1); v In 1933 (3)*

Vernon, G. F. 1: *v A 1882*

Vine, J. 2: *v A 1911 (2)*

Voce, W. 27: v NZ 1931 (1) 1937 (1); v In 1932 (1) 1936 (1) 1946 (1); *v A 1932 (4) 1936 (5) 1946 (2); v SA 1930 (5); v WI 1929 (4); v NZ 1932 (2)*

Waddington, A. 2: *v A 1920 (2)*

Wainwright, E. 5: v A 1893 (1); *v A 1897 (4)*

Walker, P. M. 3: v SA 1960 (3)

Walters, C. F. 11: v A 1934 (5); v WI 1933 (3); *v In 1933 (3)*

Ward, A. 5: v WI 1976 (1); v NZ 1969 (3); v P 1971 (1)

Ward, A. 7: v A 1893 (2); *v A 1894 (5)*

Wardle, J. H. 28: v A 1953 (3) 1956 (1); v SA 1951 (2) 1955 (3); v WI 1950 (1) 1957 (1); v P 1954 (4); *v A 1954 (4); v SA 1956 (4); v WI 1947 (1) 1953 (2); v NZ 1954 (2)*

Warner, P. F. 15: v A 1909 (1) 1912 (1); v SA 1912 (1); *v A 1903 (5); v SA 1898 (2) 1905 (5)*

Warr, J. J. 2: *v A 1950 (2)*

Warren, A. R. 1: v A 1905

Washbrook, C. 37: v A 1948 (4) 1956 (3); v SA 1947 (5); v WI 1950 (2); v NZ 1937 (1) 1949 (2); v In 1946 (3); *v A 1946 (5) 1950 (5); v SA 1948 (5); v NZ 1946 (1) 1950 (1)*

Watkin, S. L. 3: v A 1993 (1); v WI 1991 (2)

Watkins, A. J. 15: v A 1948 (1); v NZ 1949 (1); v In 1952 (3); *v SA 1948 (5); v In 1951 (5)*

Watkinson, M. 4: v WI 1995 (3); *v SA 1995 (1)*

Watson, W. 23: v A 1953 (3) 1956 (2); v SA 1951 (5) 1955 (1); v NZ 1958 (2); v In 1952 (1); *v A 1958 (2); v WI 1953 (5); v NZ 1958 (2)*

Webbe, A. J. 1: *v A 1878*

Wellard, A. W. 2: v A 1938 (1); v NZ 1937 (1)

Wells, A. P. 1: v WI 1995

Wharton, A. 1: v NZ 1949

Whitaker, J. J. 1: *v A 1986*

White, C. 8: v SA 1994 (1); v WI 1995 (2); v NZ 1994 (3); *v NZ 1996 (1); v Z 1996 (1)*

White, D. W. 2: *v P 1961 (2)*

White, J. C. 15: v A 1921 (1) 1930 (1); v SA 1929 (3); v WI 1928 (1); *v A 1928 (5); v SA 1930 (4)*

Whysall, W. W. 4: v A 1930 (1); *v A 1924 (3)*

Wilkinson, L. L. 3: *v SA 1938 (3)*

Willey, P. 26: v A 1980 (1) 1981 (4) 1985 (1); v WI 1976 (2) 1980 (5); v NZ 1986 (1); v In 1979 (1); *v A 1979 (3); v WI 1980 (4) 1985 (4)*

Williams, N. F. 1: v In 1990

Willis, R. G. D. 90: v A 1977 (5) 1981 (6); v WI 1973 (1) 1976 (2) 1980 (4) 1984 (3); v NZ 1978 (3) 1983 (4); v In 1974 (1) 1979 (3) 1982 (3); v P 1974 (1) 1978 (3) 1982 (2); *v A 1970 (4) 1974 (5) 1976 (1) 1978 (6) 1979 (3) 1982 (5); v WI 1973 (3); v NZ 1970 (1) 1977 (3) 1983 (3); v In 1976 (5) 1981 (5); v P 1977 (3) 1983 (1); v SL 1981 (1)*

Wilson, C. E. M. 2: *v SA 1898 (2)*

Wilson, D. 6: *v NZ 1970 (1); v In 1963 (5)*

Wilson, E. R. 1: *v A 1920*

Wood, A. 4: v A 1938 (1); v WI 1939 (3)

Wood, B. 12: v A 1972 (1) 1975 (3); v WI 1976 (1); v P 1978 (1); *v NZ 1974 (2); v In 1972 (3); v P 1972 (1)*

Wood, G. E. C. 3: v SA 1924 (3)

Wood, H. 4: v A 1888 (1); *v SA 1888 (2) 1891 (1)*

Wood, R. 1: *v A 1886*

Woods S. M. J. 3: *v SA 1895 (3)*

Woolley, F. E. 64: v A 1909 (1) 1912 (3) 1921 (5) 1926 (5) 1930 (2) 1934 (1); v SA 1912 (3) 1924 (5) 1929 (3); v NZ 1931 (1); v In 1932 (1); *v A 1911 (5) 1920 (5) 1924 (5); v SA 1909 (5) 1913 (5) 1922 (5); v NZ 1929 (4)*

Woolmer, R. A. 19: v A 1975 (2) 1977 (5) 1981 (2); v WI 1976 (5) 1980 (2); *v A 1976 (1); v In 1976 (2)*

Worthington, T. S. 9: v In 1936 (2); *v A 1936 (3); v NZ 1929 (4)*

Wright, C. W. 3: *v SA 1895 (3)*

Wright, D. V. P. 34: v A 1938 (3) 1948 (1); v SA 1947 (4); v WI 1939 (3) 1950 (1); v NZ 1949 (1); v In 1946 (2); *v A 1946 (5) 1950 (5); v SA 1938 (3) 1948 (3); v NZ 1946 (1) 1950 (2)*

Wyatt, R. E. S. 40: v A 1930 (1) 1934 (4); v SA 1929 (2) 1935 (5); v WI 1933 (2); v In 1936 (1); *v A 1932 (5) 1936 (2); v SA 1927 (5) 1930 (5); v WI 1929 (2) 1934 (4); v NZ 1932 (2)*

Wynyard, E. G. 3: v A 1896 (1); *v SA 1905 (2)*

Yardley, N. W. D. 20: v A 1948 (5); v SA 1947 (5); v WI 1950 (3); *v A 1946 (5); v SA 1938 (1); v NZ 1946 (1)*

Young, H. I. 2: v A 1899 (2)

Young, J. A. 8: v A 1948 (3); v SA 1947 (1); v NZ 1949 (2); *v SA 1948 (2)*

Young, R. A. 2: *v A 1907 (2)*

AUSTRALIA

Number of Test cricketers: 372

a'Beckett, E. L. 4: v E 1928 (2); v SA 1931 (1); *v E 1930 (1)*
Alderman, T. M. 41: v E 1982 (1) 1990 (4); v WI 1981 (2) 1984 (3) 1988 (2); v NZ 1989 (1); v P 1981 (3) 1989 (2); v SL 1989 (2); *v E 1981 (6) 1989 (6); v WI 1983 (3) 1990 (1); v NZ 1981 (3) 1989 (1); v P 1982 (1)*
Alexander, G. 2: v E 1884 (1); *v E 1880 (1)*
Alexander, H. H. 1: v E 1932
Allan, F. E. 1: v E 1878
Allan, P. J. 1: v E 1965
Allen, R. C. 1: v E 1886
Andrews, T. J. E. 16: v E 1924 (3); *v E 1921 (5) 1926 (5); v SA 1921 (3)*
Angel, J. 4: v E 1994 (1); v WI 1992 (1); *v P 1994 (2)*
Archer, K. A. 5: v E 1950 (3); v WI 1951 (2)
Archer, R. G. 19: v E 1954 (4); v SA 1952 (1); *v E 1953 (3) 1956 (5); v WI 1954 (5); v P 1956 (1)*
Armstrong, W. W. 50: v E 1901 (4) 1903 (5) 1907 (5) 1911 (5) 1920 (5); v SA 1910 (5); *v E 1902 (5) 1905 (5) 1909 (5) 1921 (5); v SA 1902 (3)*

Badcock, C. L. 7: v E 1936 (3); *v E 1938 (4)*
Bannerman, A. C. 28: v E 1878 (1) 1881 (3) 1882 (4) 1884 (4) 1886 (1) 1887 (1) 1891 (3); *v E 1880 (1) 1882 (1) 1884 (3) 1888 (3) 1893 (3)*
Bannerman, C. 3: v E 1876 (2) 1878 (1)
Bardsley, W. 41: v E 1911 (4) 1920 (5) 1924 (3); v SA 1910 (5); *v E 1909 (5) 1912 (3) 1921 (5) 1926 (5); v SA 1912 (3) 1921 (3)*
Barnes, S. G. 13: v E 1946 (4); v In 1947 (3); *v E 1938 (1) 1948 (4); v NZ 1945 (1)*
Barnett, B. A. 4: *v E 1938 (4)*
Barrett, J. E. 2: *v E 1890 (2)*
Beard, G. R. 3: *v P 1979 (3)*
Benaud, J. 3: v P 1972 (2); *v WI 1972 (1)*
Benaud, R. 63: v E 1954 (5) 1958 (5) 1962 (5); v SA 1952 (4) 1963 (4); v WI 1951 (1) 1960 (5); *v E 1953 (3) 1956 (5) 1961 (4); v SA 1957 (5); v WI 1954 (5); v In 1956 (3) 1959 (5); v P 1956 (1) 1959 (3)*
Bennett, M. J. 3: v WI 1984 (2); *v E 1985 (1)*
Bevan, M. G. 17: v E 1994 (1); v WI 1996 (4); *v E 1997 (3); v SA 1996 (3); v In 1996 (1); v P 1994 (3)*
Bichel, A. J. 2: v WI 1996 (2)
Blackham, J. McC. 35: v E 1876 (2) 1878 (1) 1881 (4) 1882 (4) 1884 (2) 1886 (1) 1887 (1) 1891 (3) 1894 (1); *v E 1880 (1) 1882 (1) 1884 (3) 1886 (3) 1888 (3) 1890 (2) 1893 (3)*
Blackie, D. D. 3: v E 1928 (3)
Blewett, G. S. 22: v E 1994 (2); v WI 1996 (4); v P 1995 (3); *v E 1997 (6); v SA 1996 (3); v WI 1994 (4)*
Bonnor, G. J. 17: v E 1882 (4) 1884 (3); *v E 1880 (1) 1882 (1) 1884 (3) 1886 (2) 1888 (3)*
Boon, D. C. 107: v E 1986 (4) 1987 (1) 1990 (5) 1994 (5); v SA 1993 (3); v WI 1984 (3) 1988 (5) 1992 (5); v NZ 1985 (3) 1987 (3) 1989 (1) 1993 (3); v In 1985 (3) 1991 (5); v P 1989 (2) 1995 (3); v SL 1987 (1) 1989 (2) 1995 (3); *v E 1985 (4) 1989 (6) 1993 (6); v SA 1993 (3); v WI 1990 (5) 1994 (4); v NZ 1985 (3) 1989 (1) 1992 (3); v In 1986 (3); v P 1988 (3) 1994 (3); v SL 1992 (3)*
Booth, B. C. 29: v E 1962 (5) 1965 (3); v SA 1963 (4); v P 1964 (1); *v E 1961 (2) 1964 (5); v WI 1964 (5); v In 1964 (3); v P 1964 (1)*
Border, A. R. 156: v E 1978 (3) 1979 (3) 1982 (5) 1986 (5) 1987 (1) 1990 (5); v SA 1993 (3); v WI 1979 (3) 1981 (3) 1984 (3) 1988 (5) 1992 (5); v NZ 1980 (3) 1985 (3) 1987 (3) 1989 (1) 1993 (3); v In 1980 (3) 1985 (3) 1991 (5); v P 1978 (2) 1981 (3) 1983 (5) 1989 (3); v SL 1987 (1) 1989 (2); *v E 1980 (1) 1981 (6) 1985 (6) 1989 (6) 1993 (6); v WI 1983 (5) 1990 (5); v NZ 1981 (3) 1985 (3) 1989 (1) 1992 (3); v In 1979 (6) 1986 (3); v P 1979 (3) 1982 (3) 1988 (3); v SL 1982 (1) 1992 (3)*
Boyle, H. F. 12: v E 1878 (1) 1881 (4) 1882 (1) 1884 (1); *v E 1880 (1) 1882 (1) 1884 (3)*
Bradman, D. G. 52: v E 1928 (4) 1932 (4) 1936 (5) 1946 (5); v SA 1931 (5); v WI 1930 (5); v In 1947 (5); *v E 1930 (5) 1934 (5) 1938 (4) 1948 (5)*
Bright, R. J. 25: v E 1979 (1); v WI 1979 (1); v NZ 1985 (1); v In 1985 (3); *v E 1977 (3) 1980 (1) 1981 (5); v NZ 1985 (2); v In 1986 (3); v P 1979 (3) 1982 (2)*

Bromley, E. H. 2: v E 1932 (1); *v E 1934 (1)*

Brown, W. A. 22: v E 1936 (2); v In 1947 (3); *v E 1934 (5) 1938 (4) 1948 (2); v SA 1935 (5); v NZ 1945 (1)*

Bruce, W. 14: v E 1884 (2) 1891 (3) 1894 (4); *v E 1886 (2) 1893 (3)*

Burge, P. J. 42: v E 1954 (1) 1958 (1) 1962 (3) 1965 (4); v SA 1963 (5); v WI 1960 (2); *v E 1956 (3) 1961 (5) 1964 (5); v SA 1957 (1); v WI 1954 (1); v In 1956 (3) 1959 (2) 1964 (3); v P 1959 (2) 1964 (1)*

Burke, J. W. 24: v E 1950 (2) 1954 (2) 1958 (5); v WI 1951 (1); *v E 1956 (5); v SA 1957 (5); v In 1956 (3); v P 1956 (1)*

Burn, K. E. 2: *v E 1890 (2)*

Burton, F. J. 2: v E 1886 (1) 1887 (1)

Callaway, S. T. 3: v E 1891 (2) 1894 (1)

Callen, I. W. 1: v In 1977

Campbell, G. D. 4: v P 1989 (1); v SL 1989 (1); *v E 1989 (1); v NZ 1989 (1)*

Carkeek, W. 6: *v E 1912 (3); v SA 1912 (3)*

Carlson, P. H. 2: v E 1978 (2)

Carter, H. 28: v E 1907 (5) 1911 (5) 1920 (2); v SA 1910 (5); *v E 1909 (5) 1921 (4); v SA 1921 (2)*

Chappell, G. S. 87: v E 1970 (5) 1974 (6) 1976 (1) 1979 (3) 1982 (5); v WI 1975 (6) 1979 (3) 1981 (3); v NZ 1973 (3) 1980 (3); v In 1980 (3); v P 1972 (3) 1976 (3) 1981 (3) 1983 (5); *v E 1972 (5) 1975 (4) 1977 (5) 1980 (1); v WI 1972 (5); v NZ 1973 (3) 1976 (2) 1981 (3); v P 1979 (3); v SL 1982 (1)*

Chappell, I. M. 75: v E 1965 (2) 1970 (6) 1974 (6) 1979 (2); v WI 1968 (5) 1975 (6) 1979 (1); v NZ 1973 (3); v In 1967 (4); v P 1964 (1) 1972 (3); *v E 1968 (5) 1972 (5) 1975 (4); v SA 1966 (5) 1969 (4); v WI 1972 (5); v NZ 1973 (3); v In 1969 (5)*

Chappell, T. M. 3: *v E 1981 (3)*

Charlton, P. C. 2: *v E 1890 (2)*

Chipperfield, A. G. 14: v E 1936 (3); *v E 1934 (5) 1938 (1); v SA 1935 (5)*

Clark, W. M. 10: v In 1977 (5); v P 1978 (1); *v WI 1977 (4)*

Colley, D. J. 3: *v E 1972 (3)*

Collins, H. L. 19: v E 1920 (5) 1924 (5); *v E 1921 (3) 1926 (3); v SA 1921 (3)*

Coningham, A. 1: v E 1894

Connolly, A. N. 29: v E 1965 (1) 1970 (1); v SA 1963 (3); v WI 1968 (5); v In 1967 (3); *v E 1968 (5); v SA 1969 (4); v In 1964 (2) 1969 (5)*

Cooper, B. B. 1: v E 1876

Cooper, W. H. 2: v E 1881 (1) 1884 (1)

Corling, G. E. 5: *v E 1964 (5)*

Cosier, G. J. 18: v E 1976 (1) 1978 (2); v WI 1975 (3); v In 1977 (4); v P 1976 (3); *v WI 1977 (3); v NZ 1976 (2)*

Cottam, J. T. 1: v E 1886

Cotter, A. 21: v E 1903 (2) 1907 (2) 1911 (4); v SA 1910 (5); *v E 1905 (3) 1909 (5)*

Coulthard, G. 1: v E 1881

Cowper, R. M. 27: v E 1965 (4); v In 1967 (4); v P 1964 (1); *v E 1964 (1) 1968 (4); v SA 1966 (5); v WI 1964 (5); v In 1964 (2); v P 1964 (1)*

Craig, I. D. 11: v SA 1952 (1); *v E 1956 (2); v SA 1957 (5); v In 1956 (2); v P 1956 (1)*

Crawford, P. 4: *v E 1956 (1); v In 1956 (3)*

Darling, J. 34: v E 1894 (5) 1897 (5) 1901 (3); *v E 1896 (3) 1899 (5) 1902 (5) 1905 (5); v SA 1902 (3)*

Darling, L. S. 12: v E 1932 (2) 1936 (1); *v E 1934 (4); v SA 1935 (5)*

Darling, W. M. 14: v E 1978 (4); v In 1977 (1); v P 1978 (1); *v WI 1977 (3); v In 1979 (5)*

Davidson, A. K. 44: v E 1954 (3) 1958 (5) 1962 (5); v WI 1960 (4); *v E 1953 (5) 1956 (2) 1961 (5); v SA 1957 (5); v In 1956 (1) 1959 (5); v P 1956 (1) 1959 (3)*

Davis, C. I. C. 15: v E 1970 (1); v NZ 1973 (3); v P 1976 (3); *v E 1977 (3); v NZ 1973 (3) 1976 (2)*

Davis, S. P. 1: *v NZ 1985*

De Courcy, J. H. 3: *v E 1953 (3)*

Dell, A. R. 2: v E 1970 (1); v NZ 1973 (1)

Dodemaide, A. I. C. 10: v E 1987 (1); v WI 1988 (2); v NZ 1987 (1); v SL 1987 (1); *v P 1988 (3); v SL 1992 (2)*

Donnan, H. 5: v E 1891 (2); *v E 1896 (3)*

Dooland, B. 3: v E 1946 (2); v In 1947 (1)

Duff, R. A. 22: v E 1901 (4) 1903 (5); *v E 1902 (5) 1905 (5); v SA 1902 (3)*

Duncan, J. R. F. 1: v E 1970

Dyer, G. C. 6: v E 1986 (1) 1987 (1); v NZ 1987 (3); v SL 1987 (1)

Dymock, G. 21: v E 1974 (1) 1978 (3) 1979 (3); v WI 1979 (2); v NZ 1973 (1); v P 1978 (1); *v NZ 1973 (2); v In 1979 (5); v P 1979 (3)*

Dyson, J. 30: v E 1982 (5); v WI 1981 (2) 1984 (3); v NZ 1980 (3); v In 1977 (3) 1980 (3); *v E 1981 (5); v NZ 1981 (3); v P 1982 (3)*

Eady, C. J. 2: v E 1901 (1); *v E 1896 (1)*

Eastwood, K. H. 1: v E 1970

Ebeling, H. I. 1: *v E 1934*

Edwards, J. D. 3: *v E 1888 (3)*

Edwards, R. 20: v E 1974 (5); v P 1972 (2); *v E 1972 (4) 1975 (4); v WI 1972 (5)*

Edwards, W. J. 3: v E 1974 (3)

Elliott, M. T. G. 11: v WI 1996 (2); *v E 1997 (6); v SA 1996 (3)*

Emery, P. A. 1: *v P 1994*

Emery, S. H. 4: *v E 1912 (2); v SA 1912 (2)*

Evans, E. 6: v E 1881 (2) 1882 (1) 1884 (1); *v E 1886 (2)*

Fairfax, A. G. 10: v E 1928 (1); v WI 1930 (5); *v E 1930 (4)*

Favell, L. E. 19: v E 1954 (4) 1958 (2); v WI 1960 (4); *v WI 1954 (2); v In 1959 (4); v P 1959 (3)*

Ferris, J. J. 8: v E 1886 (2) 1887 (1); *v E 1888 (3) 1890 (2)*

Fingleton, J. H. 18: v E 1932 (3) 1936 (5); v SA 1931 (1); *v E 1938 (4); v SA 1935 (5)*

Fleetwood-Smith, L. O'B. 10: v E 1936 (3); *v E 1938 (4); v SA 1935 (3)*

Fleming, D. W. 4: v E 1994 (3); *v P 1994 (1)*

Francis, B. C. 3: *v E 1972 (3)*

Freeman, E. W. 11: v WI 1968 (4); v In 1967 (2); *v E 1968 (2); v SA 1969 (2); v In 1969 (1)*

Freer, F. W. 1: v E 1946

Gannon, J. B. 3: v In 1977 (3)

Garrett, T. W. 19: v E 1876 (2) 1878 (1) 1881 (3) 1882 (3) 1884 (3) 1886 (2) 1887 (1); *v E 1882 (1) 1886 (3)*

Gaunt, R. A. 3: v SA 1963 (1); *v E 1961 (1); v SA 1957 (1)*

Gehrs, D. R. A. 6: v E 1903 (1); v SA 1910 (4); *v E 1905 (1)*

Giffen, G. 31: v E 1881 (3) 1882 (4) 1884 (3) 1891 (3) 1894 (5); *v E 1882 (1) 1884 (3) 1886 (3) 1893 (3) 1896 (3)*

Giffen, W. F. 3: v E 1886 (1) 1891 (2)

Gilbert, D. R. 9: v NZ 1985 (3); v In 1985 (2); *v E 1985 (1); v NZ 1985 (1); v In 1986 (2)*

Gillespie, J. N. 9: v WI 1996 (2); *v E 1997 (4); v SA 1996 (3)*

Gilmour, G. J. 15: v E 1976 (1); v WI 1975 (5); v NZ 1973 (2); v P 1976 (3); *v E 1975 (1); v NZ 1973 (1) 1976 (2)*

Gleeson, J. W. 29: v E 1970 (5); v WI 1968 (5); v In 1967 (4); *v E 1968 (5) 1972 (3); v SA 1969 (4); v In 1969 (3)*

Graham, H. 6: v E 1894 (2); *v E 1893 (3) 1896 (1)*

Gregory, D. W. 3: v E 1876 (2) 1878 (1)

Gregory, E. J. 1: v E 1876

Gregory, J. M. 24: v E 1920 (5) 1924 (5) 1928 (1); *v E 1921 (5) 1926 (5); v SA 1921 (3)*

Gregory, R. G. 2: v E 1936 (2)

Gregory, S. E. 58: v E 1891 (1) 1894 (5) 1897 (5) 1901 (5) 1903 (4) 1907 (2) 1911 (1); *v E 1890 (2) 1893 (3) 1896 (3) 1899 (5) 1902 (5) 1905 (3) 1909 (5) 1912 (3); v SA 1902 (3) 1912 (3)*

Grimmett, C. V. 37: v E 1924 (1) 1928 (5) 1932 (3); v SA 1931 (5); v WI 1930 (5); *v E 1926 (3) 1930 (5) 1934 (5); v SA 1935 (5)*

Groube, T. U. 1: *v E 1880*

Grout, A. T. W. 51: v E 1958 (5) 1962 (2) 1965 (5); v SA 1963 (5); v WI 1960 (5); *v E 1961 (5) 1964 (5); v SA 1957 (5); v WI 1964 (5); v In 1959 (4) 1964 (1); v P 1959 (3) 1964 (1)*

Guest, C. E. J. 1: v E 1962

Hamence, R. A. 3: v E 1946 (1); v In 1947 (2)

Hammond, J. R. 5: *v WI 1972 (5)*

Harry, J. 1: v E 1894

Hartigan, R. J. 2: v E 1907 (2)

Hartkopf, A. E. V. 1: v E 1924

Harvey, M. R. 1: v E 1946

Harvey, R. N. 79: v E 1950 (5) 1954 (5) 1958 (5) 1962 (5); v SA 1952 (5); v WI 1951 (5) 1960 (4); v In 1947 (2); *v E 1948 (2) 1953 (5) 1956 (5) 1961 (5); v SA 1949 (5) 1957 (4); v WI 1954 (5); v In 1956 (3) 1959 (5); v P 1956 (1) 1959 (3)*

Hassett, A. L. 43: v E 1946 (5) 1950 (5); v SA 1952 (5); v WI 1951 (4); v In 1947 (4); *v E 1938 (4) 1948 (5) 1953 (5); v SA 1949 (5); v NZ 1945 (1)*

Hawke, N. J. N. 27: v E 1962 (1) 1965 (4); v SA 1963 (4); v In 1967 (1); v P 1964 (1); *v E 1964 (5) 1968 (2); v SA 1966 (2); v WI 1964 (5); v In 1964 (1); v P 1964 (1)*

Hayden, M. L. 7: v WI 1996 (3); *v SA 1993 (1) 1996 (3)*

Hazlitt, G. R. 9: v E 1907 (2) 1911 (1); *v E 1912 (3); v SA 1912 (3)*

Healy, I. A. 94: v E 1990 (5) 1994 (5); v SA 1993 (3); v WI 1988 (5) 1992 (5) 1996 (5); v NZ 1989 (1) 1993 (3); v In 1991 (5); v P 1989 (3) 1995 (3); v SL 1989 (2) 1995 (3); *v E 1989 (6) 1993 (6) 1997 (6); v SA 1993 (3) 1996 (3); v WI 1990 (5) 1994 (4); v NZ 1989 (1) 1992 (3); v In 1996 (1); v P 1988 (3) 1994 (2); v SL 1992 (3)*

Hendry, H. L. 11: v E 1924 (1) 1928 (4); *v E 1921 (4); v SA 1921 (2)*

Hibbert, P. A. 1: v In 1977

Higgs, J. D. 22: v E 1978 (5) 1979 (1); v WI 1979 (1); v NZ 1980 (3); v In 1980 (2); *v WI 1977 (4); v In 1979 (6)*

Hilditch, A. M. J. 18: v E 1978 (1); v WI 1984 (2); v NZ 1985 (1); v P 1978 (2); *v E 1985 (6); v In 1979 (6)*

Hill, C. 49: v E 1897 (5) 1901 (5) 1903 (5) 1907 (5) 1911 (5); v SA 1910 (5); *v E 1896 (3) 1899 (3) 1902 (5) 1905 (5); v SA 1902 (3)*

Hill, J. C. 3: *v E 1953 (2); v WI 1954 (1)*

Hoare, D. E. 1: v WI 1960

Hodges, J. 2: v E 1876 (2)

Hogan, T. G. 7: v P 1983 (1); *v WI 1983 (5); v SL 1982 (1)*

Hogg, G. B. 1: *v In 1996*

Hogg, R. M. 38: v E 1978 (6) 1982 (3); v WI 1979 (2) 1984 (4); v NZ 1980 (2); v In 1980 (2); v P 1978 (2) 1983 (4); *v E 1981 (2); v WI 1983 (4); v In 1979 (6); v SL 1982 (1)*

Hohns, T. V. 7: v WI 1988 (2); *v E 1989 (5)*

Hole, G. B. 18: v E 1950 (1) 1954 (3); v SA 1952 (4); v WI 1951 (5); *v E 1953 (5)*

Holland, R. G. 11: v WI 1984 (3); v NZ 1985 (3); v In 1985 (1); *v E 1985 (4)*

Hookes, D. W. 23: v E 1976 (1) 1982 (5); v WI 1979 (1); v NZ 1985 (2); v In 1985 (2); *v E 1977 (5); v WI 1983 (5); v P 1979 (1); v SL 1982 (1)*

Hopkins, A. J. 20: v E 1901 (2) 1903 (5); *v E 1902 (5) 1905 (3) 1909 (2); v SA 1902 (3)*

Horan, T. P. 15: v E 1876 (1) 1878 (1) 1881 (4) 1882 (4) 1884 (4); *v E 1882 (1)*

Hordern, H. V. 7: v E 1911 (5); v SA 1910 (2)

Hornibrook, P. M. 6: v E 1928 (1); *v E 1930 (5)*

Howell, W. P. 18: v E 1897 (3) 1901 (4) 1903 (3); *v E 1899 (5) 1902 (1); v SA 1902 (2)*

Hughes, K. J. 70: v E 1978 (6) 1979 (3) 1982 (5); v WI 1979 (3) 1981 (3) 1984 (4); v NZ 1980 (3); v In 1977 (2) 1980 (3); v P 1978 (2) 1981 (3) 1983 (5); *v E 1977 (1) 1980 (1) 1981 (6); v WI 1983 (5); v NZ 1981 (3); v In 1979 (6); v P 1979 (3) 1982 (3)*

Hughes, M. G. 53: v E 1986 (4) 1990 (4); v WI 1988 (4) 1992 (5); v NZ 1987 (1) 1989 (1); v In 1985 (1) 1991 (5); v P 1989 (3); v SL 1987 (1) 1989 (2); *v E 1989 (6) 1993 (6); v SA 1993 (2); v WI 1990 (5); v NZ 1992 (3)*

Hunt, W. A. 1: v SA 1931

Hurst, A. G. 12: v E 1978 (6); v NZ 1973 (1); v In 1977 (1); v P 1978 (2); *v In 1979 (2)*

Hurwood, A. 2: v WI 1930 (2)

Inverarity, R. J. 6: v WI 1968 (1); *v E 1968 (2) 1972 (3)*

Iredale, F. A. 14: v E 1894 (5) 1897 (4); *v E 1896 (2) 1899 (3)*

Ironmonger, H. 14: v E 1928 (2) 1932 (4); v SA 1931 (4); v WI 1930 (4)

Iverson, J. B. 5: v E 1950 (5)

Jackson, A. A. 8: v E 1928 (2); v WI 1930 (4); *v E 1930 (2)*

Jarman, B. N. 19: v E 1962 (3); v WI 1968 (4); v In 1967 (4); v P 1964 (1); *v E 1968 (4); v In 1959 (1) 1964 (2)*

Jarvis, A. H. 11: v E 1884 (3) 1894 (4); *v E 1886 (2) 1888 (2)*

Jenner, T. J. 9: v E 1970 (2) 1974 (2); v WI 1975 (1); *v WI 1972 (4)*

Jennings, C. B. 6: *v E 1912 (3); v SA 1912 (3)*

Johnson I. W. 45: v E 1946 (4) 1950 (5) 1954 (4); v SA 1952 (1); v WI 1951 (4); v In 1947 (4); *v E 1948 (4) 1956 (5); v SA 1949 (5); v WI 1954 (5); v NZ 1945 (1); v In 1956 (2); v P 1956 (1)*

Johnson, L. J. 1: v In 1947

Johnston W. A. 40: v E 1950 (5) 1954 (4); v SA 1952 (5); v WI 1951 (5); v In 1947 (4); *v E 1948 (5) 1953 (3); v SA 1949 (5); v WI 1954 (4)*

Jones, D. M. 52: v E 1986 (5) 1987 (1) 1990 (5); v WI 1988 (3); v NZ 1987 (3) 1989 (1); v In 1991 (5); v P 1989 (3); v SL 1987 (1) 1989 (2); *v E 1989 (6); v WI 1983 (2) 1990 (5); v NZ 1989 (1); v In 1986 (3); v P 1988 (3); v SL 1992 (3)*

Jones, E. 19: v E 1894 (1) 1897 (5) 1901 (2); *v E 1896 (3) 1899 (5) 1902 (2); v SA 1902 (1)*

Jones, S. P. 12: v E 1881 (2) 1884 (4) 1886 (1) 1887 (1); *v E 1882 (1) 1886 (3)*

Joslin, L. R. 1: v In 1967

Julian, B. P. 7: v SL 1995 (1); *v E 1993 (2); v WI 1994 (4)*

Kasprowicz, M. S. 5: v WI 1996 (2); *v E 1997 (3)*

Kelleway, C. 26: v E 1911 (4) 1920 (5) 1924 (5) 1928 (1); v SA 1910 (5); *v E 1912 (3); v SA 1912 (3)*

Kelly, J. J. 36: v E 1897 (5) 1901 (5) 1903 (5); *v E 1896 (3) 1899 (5) 1902 (5) 1905 (5); v SA 1902 (3)*

Kelly, T. J. D. 2: v E 1876 (1) 1878 (1)

Kendall, T. 2: v E 1876 (2)

Kent, M. F. 3: *v E 1981 (3)*

Kerr, R. B. 2: v NZ 1985 (2)

Kippax, A. F. 22: v E 1924 (1) 1928 (5) 1932 (1); v SA 1931 (4); v WI 1930 (5); *v E 1930 (5) 1934 (1)*

Kline L. F. 13: v E 1958 (2); v WI 1960 (2); *v SA 1957 (5); v In 1959 (3); v P 1959 (1)*

Laird, B. M. 21: v E 1979 (2); v WI 1979 (3) 1981 (3); v P 1981 (3); *v E 1980 (1); v NZ 1981 (3); v P 1979 (3) 1982 (3)*

Langer, J. L. 8: v WI 1992 (2) 1996 (2); *v NZ 1992 (3); v P 1994 (1)*

Langley, G. R. A. 26: v E 1954 (2); v SA 1952 (5); v WI 1951 (5); *v E 1953 (4) 1956 (3); v WI 1954 (4); v In 1956 (2); v P 1956 (1)*

Laughlin, T. J. 3: v E 1978 (1); *v WI 1977 (2)*

Laver, F. 15: v E 1901 (1) 1903 (1); *v E 1899 (4) 1905 (5) 1909 (4)*

Law, S. G. 1: v SL 1995

Lawry, W. M. 67: v E 1962 (5) 1965 (5) 1970 (5); v SA 1963 (5); v WI 1968 (5); v In 1967 (4); v P 1964 (1); *v E 1961 (5) 1964 (5) 1968 (4); v SA 1966 (5) 1969 (4); v WI 1964 (5); v In 1964 (3) 1969 (5); v P 1964 (1)*

Lawson, G. F. 46: v E 1982 (5) 1986 (1); v WI 1981 (1) 1984 (5) 1988 (1); v NZ 1980 (1) 1985 (2) 1989 (1); *v P 1983 (5); v SL 1989 (1); v E 1981 (3) 1985 (6) 1989 (6); v WI 1983 (5); v P 1982 (3)*

Lee, P. K. 2: v E 1932 (1); v SA 1931 (1)

Lillee, D. K. 70: v E 1970 (2) 1974 (6) 1976 (1) 1979 (1) 1982 (1); v WI 1975 (5) 1979 (5) 1981 (3); v NZ 1980 (3); v In 1980 (3); v P 1972 (3) 1976 (3) 1981 (3) 1983 (5); *v E 1972 (5) 1975 (4) 1980 (1) 1981 (6); v WI 1972 (1); v NZ 1976 (2) 1981 (3); v P 1979 (3); v SL 1982 (1)*

Lindwall, R. R. 61: v E 1946 (4) 1950 (5) 1954 (4) 1958 (2); v SA 1952 (4); v WI 1951 (5); v In 1947 (5); *v E 1948 (5) 1953 (5) 1956 (4); v SA 1949 (4); v WI 1954 (5); v NZ 1945 (1); v In 1956 (3) 1959 (2); v P 1956 (1) 1959 (2)*

Love, H. S. B. 1: v E 1932

Loxton, S. J. E. 12: v E 1950 (3); v In 1947 (1); *v E 1948 (3); v SA 1949 (5)*

Lyons, J. J. 14: v E 1886 (1) 1891 (3) 1894 (3) 1897 (1); *v E 1888 (1) 1890 (2) 1893 (3)*

McAlister, P. A. 8: v E 1903 (2) 1907 (4); *v E 1909 (2)*

Macartney, C. G. 35: v E 1907 (5) 1911 (1) 1920 (2); v SA 1910 (4); *v E 1909 (5) 1912 (3) 1921 (5) 1926 (5); v SA 1912 (3) 1921 (2)*

McCabe, S. J. 39: v E 1932 (5) 1936 (5); v SA 1931 (5); v WI 1930 (5); *v E 1930 (5) 1934 (5) 1938 (4); v SA 1935 (5)*

McCool, C. L. 14: v E 1946 (5); v In 1947 (3); *v SA 1949 (5); v NZ 1945 (1)*

McCormick, E. L. 12: v E 1936 (4); *v E 1938 (3); v SA 1935 (5)*

McCosker, R. B. 25: v E 1974 (3) 1976 (1) 1979 (2); v WI 1975 (4) 1979 (1); v P 1976 (3); *v E 1975 (4) 1977 (5); v NZ 1976 (2)*

McDermott, C. J. 71: v E 1986 (1) 1987 (1) 1990 (2) 1994 (5); v SA 1993 (3); v WI 1984 (2) 1988 (2) 1992 (5); v NZ 1985 (2) 1987 (3) 1993 (3); v In 1985 (2) 1991 (5); v P 1995 (3); v SL 1987 (1) 1995 (3); *v E 1985 (6) 1993 (2); v SA 1993 (3); v WI 1990 (5); v NZ 1985 (2) 1992 (3); v In 1986 (2); v P 1994 (2); v SL 1992 (3)*

McDonald, C. C. 47: v E 1954 (2) 1958 (5); v SA 1952 (5); v WI 1951 (1) 1960 (5); *v E 1956 (5) 1961 (3); v SA 1957 (5); v WI 1954 (5); v In 1956 (2) 1959 (5); v P 1956 (1) 1959 (3)*

McDonald, E. A. 11: v E 1920 (3); *v E 1921 (5); v SA 1921 (3)*

McDonnell, P. S. 19: v E 1881 (4) 1882 (3) 1884 (2) 1886 (2) 1887 (1); *v E 1880 (1) 1884 (3) 1888 (3)*

McGrath, G. D. 34: v E 1994 (2); v SA 1993 (1); v WI 1996 (5); v NZ 1993 (2); v P 1995 (3); v SL 1995 (3); *v E 1997 (6); v SA 1993 (2) 1996 (3); v WI 1994 (4); v In 1996 (1); v P 1994 (2)*

McIlwraith, J. 1: *v E 1886*

McIntyre, P. E. 2: v E 1994 (1); *v In 1996 (1)*

Mackay, K. D. 37: v E 1958 (5) 1962 (3); v WI 1960 (5); *v E 1956 (3) 1961 (5); v SA 1957 (5); v In 1956 (3) 1959 (5); v P 1959 (3)*

McKenzie, G. D. 60: v E 1962 (5) 1965 (4) 1970 (3); v SA 1963 (5); v WI 1968 (5); v In 1967 (2); v P 1964 (1); *v E 1961 (3) 1964 (5) 1968 (5); v SA 1966 (5) 1969 (3); v WI 1964 (5); v In 1964 (3) 1969 (5); v P 1964 (1)*

McKibbin, T. R. 5: v E 1894 (1) 1897 (2); *v E 1896 (2)*

McLaren, J. W. 1: v E 1911

Maclean, J. A. 4: v E 1978 (4)

McLeod, C. E. 17: v E 1894 (1) 1897 (5) 1901 (2) 1903 (3); *v E 1899 (1) 1905 (5)*

McLeod, R. W. 6: v E 1891 (5); *v E 1893 (3)*

McShane, P. G. 3: v E 1884 (1) 1886 (1) 1887 (1)

Maddocks, L. V. 7: v E 1954 (3); *v E 1956 (2); v WI 1954 (1); v In 1956 (1)*

Maguire, J. N. 3: v P 1983 (1); *v WI 1983 (2)*

Mailey, A. A. 21: v E 1920 (5) 1924 (5); *v E 1921 (3) 1926 (5); v SA 1921 (3)*

Mallett, A. A. 38: v E 1970 (2) 1974 (5) 1979 (1); v WI 1968 (1) 1975 (6) 1979 (1); v NZ 1973 (3); v P 1972 (2); *v E 1968 (1) 1972 (2) 1975 (4) 1980 (1); v SA 1969 (1); v NZ 1973 (3); v In 1969 (5)*

Malone, M. F. 1: *v E 1977*

Mann, A. L. 4: v In 1977 (4)

Marr, A. P. 1: v E 1884

Marsh, G. R. 50: v E 1986 (5) 1987 (1) 1990 (5); v WI 1988 (5); v NZ 1987 (3); v In 1985 (3) 1991 (4); v P 1989 (2); v SL 1987 (1); *v E 1989 (6); v WI 1990 (5); v NZ 1985 (3) 1989 (1); v In 1986 (3); v P 1988 (3)*

Marsh, R. W. 96: v E 1970 (6) 1974 (6) 1976 (1) 1979 (3) 1982 (5); v WI 1975 (6) 1979 (3) 1981 (3); v NZ 1973 (3) 1980 (3); v In 1980 (3); v P 1972 (3) 1976 (3) 1981 (3) 1983 (5); *v E 1972 (5) 1975 (4) 1977 (5) 1980 (1) 1981 (6); v WI 1972 (5); v NZ 1973 (3) 1976 (2) 1981 (3); v P 1979 (3) 1982 (3)*

Martin, J. W. 8: v SA 1963 (1); v WI 1960 (3); *v SA 1966 (1); v In 1964 (2); v P 1964 (1)*

Martyn, D. R. 7: v SA 1993 (2); v WI 1992 (4); *v NZ 1992 (1)*

Massie, H. H. 9: v E 1881 (4) 1882 (3) 1884 (1); *v E 1882 (1)*

Massie, R. A. L. 6: v P 1972 (2); *v E 1972 (4)*

Matthews, C. D. 3: v E 1986 (2); v WI 1988 (1)

Matthews, G. R. J. 33: v E 1986 (4) 1990 (5); v WI 1984 (1) 1992 (2); v NZ 1985 (3); v In 1985 (3); v P 1983 (2); *v E 1985 (1); v WI 1983 (1) 1990 (2); v NZ 1985 (3); v In 1986 (3); v SL 1992 (3)*

Matthews, T. J. 8: v E 1911 (2); *v E 1912 (3); v SA 1912 (3)*

May, T. B. A. 24: v E 1994 (3); v SA 1993 (3); v WI 1988 (1) 1992 (1); v NZ 1987 (1) 1993 (2); *v E 1993 (5); v SA 1993 (1); v P 1988 (3) 1994 (2)*

Mayne, E. R. 4: *v E 1912 (1); v SA 1912 (1) 1921 (2)*

Mayne, L. C. 6: *v SA 1969 (2); v WI 1964 (3); v In 1969 (1)*

Meckiff, I. 18: v E 1958 (4); v SA 1963 (1); v WI 1960 (2); *v SA 1957 (4); v In 1959 (5); v P 1959 (2)*

Meuleman, K. D. 1: *v NZ 1945*

Midwinter, W. E. 8: v E 1876 (2) 1882 (1) 1886 (2); *v E 1884 (3)*

Miller, K. R. 55: v E 1946 (5) 1950 (5) 1954 (4); v SA 1952 (4); v WI 1951 (5); v In 1947 (5); *v E 1948 (5) 1953 (5) 1956 (5); v SA 1949 (5); v WI 1954 (5); v NZ 1945 (1); v P 1956 (1)*

Minnett, R. B. 9: v E 1911 (5); *v E 1912 (3); v SA 1912 (3)*

Misson, F. M. 5: v WI 1960 (3); *v E 1961 (2)*

Moody, T. M. 8: v NZ 1989 (1); v In 1991 (1); v P 1989 (1); v SL 1989 (2); *v SL 1992 (3)*

Moroney, J. 7: v E 1950 (1); v WI 1951 (1); *v SA 1949 (5)*

Morris, A. R. 46: v E 1946 (5) 1950 (5) 1954 (4); v SA 1952 (5); v WI 1951 (4); v In 1947 (4); *v E 1948 (5) 1953 (5); v SA 1949 (5); v WI 1954 (4)*

Morris, S. 1: v E 1884

Moses, H. 6: v E 1886 (2) 1887 (1) 1891 (2) 1894 (1)

Moss, J. K. 1: v P 1978

Moule, W. H. 1: *v E 1880*

Murdoch, W. L. 18: v E 1876 (1) 1878 (1) 1881 (4) 1882 (4) 1884 (1); *v E 1880 (1) 1882 (1) 1884 (3) 1890 (2)*

Musgrove, H. 1: v E 1884

Nagel, L. E. 1: v E 1932
Nash, L. J. 2: v E 1936 (1); v SA 1931 (1)
Nitschke, H. C. 2: v SA 1931 (2)
Noble, M. A. 42: v E 1897 (4) 1901 (5) 1903 (5) 1907 (5); *v E 1899 (5) 1902 (5) 1905 (5) 1909 (5); v SA 1902 (3)*
Noblet, G. 3: v SA 1952 (1); v WI 1951 (1); *v SA 1949 (1)*
Nothling, O. E. 1: v E 1928

O'Brien, L. P. J. 5: v E 1932 (2) 1936 (1); *v SA 1935 (2)*
O'Connor, J. D. A. 4: v E 1907 (3); *v E 1909 (1)*
O'Donnell, S. P. 6: v NZ 1985 (1); *v E 1985 (5)*
Ogilvie, A. D. 5: v In 1977 (3); *v WI 1977 (2)*
O'Keeffe, K. J. 24: v E 1970 (2) 1976 (1); v NZ 1973 (3); v P 1972 (2) 1976 (3); *v E 1977 (3); v WI 1972 (5); v NZ 1973 (3) 1976 (2)*
Oldfield, W. A. 54: v E 1920 (3) 1924 (5) 1928 (5) 1932 (4) 1936 (5); v SA 1931 (5); v WI 1930 (5); *v E 1921 (1) 1926 (5) 1930 (5) 1934 (5); v SA 1921 (1) 1935 (5)*
O'Neill, N. C. 42: v E 1958 (5) 1962 (5); v SA 1963 (4); v WI 1960 (5); *v E 1961 (5) 1964 (4); v WI 1964 (4); v In 1959 (5) 1964 (2); v P 1959 (3)*
O'Reilly, W. J. 27: v E 1932 (5) 1936 (5); v SA 1931 (2); *v E 1934 (5) 1938 (4); v SA 1935 (5); v NZ 1945 (1)*
Oxenham, R. K. 7: v E 1928 (3); v SA 1931 (1); v WI 1930 (3)

Palmer, G. E. 17: v E 1881 (4) 1882 (4) 1884 (2); *v E 1880 (1) 1884 (3) 1886 (3)*
Park, R. L. 1: v E 1920
Pascoe, L. S. 14: v E 1979 (2); v WI 1979 (1) 1981 (1); v NZ 1980 (3); v In 1980 (3); *v E 1977 (3) 1980 (1)*
Pellew, C. E. 10: v E 1920 (4); *v E 1921 (5); v SA 1921 (1)*
Phillips, W. B. 27: v WI 1984 (2); v NZ 1985 (3); v In 1985 (3); v P 1983 (5); *v E 1985 (6); v WI 1983 (5); v NZ 1985 (3)*
Phillips, W. N. 1: v In 1991
Philpott, P. I. 8: v E 1965 (3); *v WI 1964 (5)*
Ponsford, W. H. 29: v E 1924 (5) 1928 (2) 1932 (3); v SA 1931 (4); v WI 1930 (5); *v E 1926 (2) 1930 (4) 1934 (4)*
Ponting, R. T. 9: v WI 1996 (2); v SL 1995 (3); *v E 1997 (3); v In 1996 (1)*
Pope, R. J. 1: v E 1884

Rackemann, C. G. 12: v E 1982 (1) 1990 (1); v WI 1984 (1); v NZ 1989 (1); v P 1983 (2) 1989 (3); v SL 1989 (1); *v WI 1983 (1); v NZ 1989 (1)*
Ransford, V. S. 20: v E 1907 (5) 1911 (5); v SA 1910 (5); *v E 1909 (5)*
Redpath, I. R. 66: v E 1965 (1) 1970 (6) 1974 (6); v SA 1963 (1); v WI 1968 (5) 1975 (6); v In 1967 (3); *v P 1972 (3); v E 1964 (5) 1968 (5); v SA 1966 (5) 1969 (4); v WI 1972 (5); v NZ 1973 (3); v In 1964 (2) 1969 (5); v P 1964 (1)*
Reedman, J. C. 1: v E 1894
Reid, B. A. 27: v E 1986 (5) 1990 (4); v WI 1992 (1); v NZ 1987 (2); v In 1985 (3) 1991 (2); *v WI 1990 (2); v NZ 1985 (3); v In 1986 (2); v P 1988 (3)*
Reiffel, P. R. 29: v SA 1993 (2); v WI 1996 (3); v NZ 1993 (2); v In 1991 (1); v P 1995 (3); v SL 1995 (2); *v E 1993 (3) 1997 (4); v SA 1993 (1); v WI 1994 (4); v NZ 1992 (3); v In 1996 (1)*
Renneberg, D. A. 8: v In 1967 (3); *v SA 1966 (5)*
Richardson, A. J. 9: v E 1924 (4); *v E 1926 (5)*
Richardson, V. Y. 19: v E 1924 (3) 1928 (2) 1932 (5); *v E 1930 (4); v SA 1935 (5)*
Rigg, K. E. 8: v E 1936 (3); v SA 1931 (4); v WI 1930 (1)
Ring, D. T. 13: v SA 1952 (5); v WI 1951 (5); v In 1947 (1); *v E 1948 (1) 1953 (1)*
Ritchie, G. M. 30: v E 1986 (4); v WI 1984 (1); v NZ 1985 (3); v In 1985 (2); *v E 1985 (6); v WI 1983 (5); v NZ 1985 (3); v In 1986 (3); v P 1982 (3)*
Rixon, S. J. 13: v WI 1984 (3); v In 1977 (5); *v WI 1977 (5)*
Robertson, W. R. 1: v E 1884
Robinson, R. D. 3: *v E 1977 (3)*
Robinson, R. H. 1. v E 1936
Rorke, G. F. 4: v E 1958 (2); *v In 1959 (2)*
Rutherford, J. W. 1: *v In 1956*
Ryder, J. 20: v E 1920 (5) 1924 (3) 1928 (5); *v E 1926 (4); v SA 1921 (3)*

Saggers, R. A. 6: *v E 1948 (1); v SA 1949 (5)*

Saunders, J. V. 14: *v* E 1901 (1) 1903 (2) 1907 (5); *v E 1902 (4); v SA 1902 (2)*

Scott, H. J. H. 8: *v* E 1884 (2); *v E 1884 (3) 1886 (3)*

Sellers, R. H. D. 1: *v In 1964*

Serjeant, C. S. 12: *v* In 1977 (4); *v E 1977 (3); v WI 1977 (5)*

Sheahan, A. P. 31: *v* E 1970 (2); *v* WI 1968 (5); *v* NZ 1973 (2); *v* In 1967 (4); *v* P 1972 (2); *v E 1968 (5) 1972 (2); v SA 1969 (4); v In 1969 (5)*

Shepherd, B. K. 9: *v* E 1962 (2); *v* SA 1963 (4); *v* P 1964 (1); *v WI 1964 (2)*

Sievers, M. W. 3: *v* E 1936 (3)

Simpson, R. B. 62: *v* E 1958 (1) 1962 (5) 1965 (3); *v* SA 1963 (5); *v* WI 1960 (5); *v* In 1967 (3) 1977 (5); *v E 1961 (5) 1964 (5); v SA 1957 (5) 1966 (5); v WI 1964 (5) 1977 (5); v In 1964 (3); v P 1964 (1)*

Sincock, D. J. 3: *v* E 1965 (1); *v* P 1964 (1); *v WI 1964 (1)*

Slater, K. N. 1: *v* E 1958

Slater, M. J. 34: *v* E 1994 (5); *v* SA 1993 (3); *v* NZ 1993 (3); *v* P 1995 (3); *v* SL 1995 (3); *v E 1993 (6); v SA 1993 (3); v WI 1994 (4); v In 1996 (1); v P 1994 (3)*

Sleep, P. R. 14: *v* E 1986 (3) 1987 (1); *v* NZ 1987 (3); *v* P 1978 (1) 1989 (1); *v* SL 1989 (1); *v In 1979 (2); v P 1982 (1) 1988 (1)*

Slight, J. 1: *v E 1880*

Smith, D. B. M. 2: *v E 1912 (2)*

Smith, S. B. 3: *v WI 1983 (5)*

Spofforth, F. R. 18: *v* E 1876 (1) 1878 (1) 1881 (1) 1882 (4) 1884 (3) 1886 (1); *v E 1882 (1) 1884 (3) 1886 (3)*

Stackpole, K. R. 43: *v* E 1965 (2) 1970 (6); *v* WI 1968 (5); *v* NZ 1973 (3); *v* P 1972 (1); *v E 1972 (5); v SA 1966 (5) 1969 (4); v WI 1972 (4); v NZ 1973 (3); v In 1969 (5)*

Stevens, G. B. 4: *v In 1959 (2); v P 1959 (2)*

Taber, H. B. 16: *v* WI 1968 (1); *v E 1968 (1); v SA 1966 (5) 1969 (4); v In 1969 (5)*

Tallon, D. 21: *v* E 1946 (5) 1950 (5); *v* In 1947 (5); *v E 1948 (4) 1953 (1); v NZ 1945 (1)*

Taylor, J. M. 20: *v* E 1920 (5) 1924 (5); *v E 1921 (5) 1926 (3); v SA 1921 (2)*

Taylor, M. A. 87: *v* E 1990 (5) 1994 (5); *v* SA 1993 (3); *v* WI 1988 (2) 1992 (4) 1996 (5); *v* NZ 1989 (1) 1993 (3); *v* In 1991 (3); *v* P 1989 (3) 1995 (3); *v* SL 1989 (2) 1995 (3); *v E 1989 (6) 1993 (6) 1997 (6); v SA 1993 (2) 1996 (3); v WI 1990 (5) 1994 (4); v NZ 1989 (1) 1992 (3); v In 1996 (1); v P 1994 (3); v SL 1992 (3)*

Taylor, P. L. 13: *v* E 1986 (1) 1987 (1); *v* WI 1988 (2); *v* In 1991 (2); *v* P 1989 (2); *v* SL 1987 (1); *v WI 1990 (1); v NZ 1989 (1); v P 1988 (2)*

Thomas, G. 8: *v* E 1965 (3); *v WI 1964 (5)*

Thoms, G. R. 1: *v* WI 1951

Thomson, A. L. 4: *v* E 1970 (4)

Thomson, J. R. 51: *v* E 1974 (5) 1979 (1) 1982 (4); *v* WI 1975 (6) 1979 (1) 1981 (2); *v* In 1977 (5); *v* P 1972 (1) 1976 (1) 1981 (3); *v E 1975 (4) 1977 (5) 1985 (2); v WI 1977 (5); v NZ 1981 (3); v P 1982 (3)*

Thomson, N. F. D. 2: *v* E 1876 (2)

Thurlow, H. M. 1: *v* SA 1931

Toohey, P. M. 15: *v* E 1978 (5) 1979 (1); *v* WI 1979 (1); *v* In 1977 (5); *v WI 1977 (3)*

Toshack, E. R. H. 12: *v* E 1946 (5); *v* In 1947 (2); *v E 1948 (4); v NZ 1945 (1)*

Travers, J. P. F. 1: *v* E 1901

Tribe, G. E. 3: *v* E 1946 (3)

Trott, A. E. 3: *v* E 1894 (3)

Trott, G. H. S. 24: *v* E 1891 (3) 1894 (5) 1897 (5); *v E 1888 (3) 1890 (2) 1893 (3) 1896 (3)*

Trumble, H. 32: *v* E 1894 (1) 1897 (5) 1901 (5) 1903 (4); *v E 1890 (2) 1893 (3) 1896 (3) 1899 (5) 1902 (3); v SA 1902 (1)*

Trumble, J. W. 7: *v* E 1884 (4); *v E 1886 (3)*

Trumper, V. T. 48: *v* E 1901 (5) 1903 (5) 1907 (5) 1911 (5); *v* SA 1910 (5); *v E 1899 (5) 1902 (5) 1905 (5) 1909 (5); v SA 1902 (3)*

Turner, A. 14: *v* WI 1975 (6); *v* P 1976 (3); *v E 1975 (3); v NZ 1976 (2)*

Turner, C. T. B. 17: *v* E 1886 (2) 1887 (1) 1891 (3) 1894 (3); *v E 1888 (3) 1890 (2) 1893 (3)*

Veivers, T. R. 21: *v* E 1965 (4); *v* SA 1963 (3); *v* P 1964 (1); *v E 1964 (5); v SA 1966 (4); v In 1964 (3); v P 1964 (1)*

Veletta, M. R. J. 8: *v* E 1987 (1); *v* WI 1988 (2); *v* NZ 1987 (3); *v* P 1989 (1); *v* SL 1987 (1)

Waite, M. G. 2: *v E 1938 (2)*

Walker, M. H. N. 34: v E 1974 (6) 1976 (1); v WI 1975 (3); v NZ 1973 (1); v P 1972 (2) 1976 (2); *v E 1975 (4) 1977 (5); v WI 1972 (5); v NZ 1973 (3) 1976 (2)*

Wall, T. W. 18: v E 1928 (1) 1932 (4); v SA 1931 (3); v WI 1930 (1); *v E 1930 (5) 1934 (4)*

Walters, F. H. 1: v E 1884

Walters, K. D. 74: v E 1965 (5) 1970 (6) 1974 (6) 1976 (1); v WI 1968 (4); v NZ 1973 (3) 1980 (3); v In 1967 (2) 1980 (3); v P 1972 (1) 1976 (3); *v E 1968 (5) 1972 (4) 1975 (4) 1977 (5); v SA 1969 (4); v WI 1972 (5); v NZ 1973 (3) 1976 (2); v In 1969 (5)*

Ward, F. A. 4: v E 1936 (3); *v E 1938 (1)*

Warne, S. K. 58: v E 1994 (5); v SA 1993 (3); v WI 1992 (4) 1996 (5); v NZ 1993 (3); v In 1991 (2); v P 1995 (3); v SL 1995 (3); *v E 1993 (6) 1997 (6); v SA 1993 (3) 1996 (3); v WI 1994 (4); v NZ 1992 (3); v P 1994 (3); v SL 1992 (2)*

Watkins, J. R. 1: v P 1972

Watson, G. D. 5: *v E 1972 (2); v SA 1966 (3)*

Watson, W. J. 4: v E 1954 (1); *v WI 1954 (3)*

Waugh, M. E. 69: v E 1990 (2) 1994 (5); v SA 1993 (3); v WI 1992 (5) 1996 (5); v NZ 1993 (3); v In 1991 (4); v P 1995 (3); v SL 1995 (3); *v E 1993 (6) 1997 (6); v SA 1993 (3) 1996 (3); v WI 1990 (5) 1994 (4); v NZ 1992 (2); v In 1996 (1); v P 1994 (3); v SL 1992 (3)*

Waugh, S. R. 95: v E 1986 (5) 1987 (1) 1990 (3) 1994 (5); v SA 1993 (3); v WI 1988 (5) 1992 (5) 1996 (4); v NZ 1987 (3) 1989 (1) 1993 (3); v In 1985 (2); v P 1989 (3) 1995 (3); v SL 1987 (1) 1989 (2) 1995 (2); *v E 1989 (6) 1993 (6) 1997 (6); v SA 1993 (3) 1996 (3); v WI 1990 (2) 1994 (4); v NZ 1985 (3) 1989 (1) 1992 (3); v In 1986 (3) 1996 (1); v P 1988 (3) 1994 (2)*

Wellham, D. M. 6: v E 1986 (1); v WI 1981 (1); v P 1981 (2); *v E 1981 (1) 1985 (1)*

Wessels, K. C. 24: v E 1982 (4); v WI 1984 (5); v NZ 1985 (1); v P 1983 (5); *v E 1985 (6); v WI 1983 (2); v SL 1982 (1)*

Whatmore, D. F. 7: v P 1978 (2); *v In 1979 (5)*

Whitney, M. R. 12: v WI 1988 (1) 1992 (1); v NZ 1987 (1); v In 1991 (3); *v E 1981 (2); v WI 1990 (2); v SL 1992 (2)*

Whitty, W. J. 14: v E 1911 (2); v SA 1910 (5); *v E 1909 (1) 1912 (3); v SA 1912 (3)*

Wiener, J. M. 6: v E 1979 (2); v WI 1979 (2); *v P 1979 (2)*

Wilson, J. W. 1: *v In 1956*

Wood, G. M. 59: v E 1978 (6) 1982 (1); v WI 1981 (3) 1984 (5) 1988 (3); v NZ 1980 (3); v In 1977 (1) 1980 (3); v P 1978 (1) 1981 (3); *v E 1980 (1) 1981 (6) 1985 (5); v WI 1977 (5) 1983 (1); v NZ 1981 (3); v In 1979 (2); v P 1982 (3) 1988 (3); v SL 1982 (1)*

Woodcock, A. J. 1: v NZ 1973

Woodfull, W. M. 35: v E 1928 (5) 1932 (5); v SA 1931 (5); v WI 1930 (5); *v E 1926 (5) 1930 (5) 1934 (5)*

Woods, S. M. J. 3: *v E 1888 (3)*

Woolley, R. D. 2: *v WI 1983 (1); v SL 1982 (1)*

Worrall, J. 11: v E 1884 (1) 1887 (1) 1894 (1) 1897 (1); *v E 1888 (3) 1899 (4)*

Wright, K. J. 10: v E 1978 (2); v P 1978 (2); *v In 1979 (6)*

Yallop, G. N. 39: v E 1978 (6); v WI 1975 (3) 1984 (1); v In 1977 (1); v P 1978 (1) 1981 (1) 1983 (5); *v E 1980 (1) 1981 (6); v WI 1977 (4); v In 1979 (6); v P 1979 (3); v SL 1982 (1)*

Yardley, B. 33: v E 1978 (4) 1982 (5); v WI 1981 (3); v In 1977 (1) 1980 (2); v P 1978 (1) 1981 (3); *v WI 1977 (5); v NZ 1981 (3); v In 1979 (3); v P 1982 (2); v SL 1982 (1)*

Young, S. 1: *v E 1997*

Zoehrer, T. J. 10: v E 1986 (4); *v NZ 1985 (3); v In 1986 (3)*

SOUTH AFRICA

Number of Test cricketers: 266

Adams, P. R. 9: v E 1995 (2); v A 1996 (2); v In 1996 (2); *v In 1996 (3)*

Adcock, N. A. T. 26: v E 1956 (5); v A 1957 (5); v NZ 1953 (5) 1961 (2); *v E 1955 (4) 1960 (5)*

Anderson, J. H. 1: v A 1902

Ashley, W. H. 1: v E 1888

Bacher, A. 12: v A 1966 (5) 1969 (4); *v E 1965 (3)*
Bacher, A. M. 5: v A 1996 (2); v In 1996 (3)
Balaskas, X. C. 9: v E 1930 (2) 1938 (1); v A 1935 (3); *v E 1935 (1); v NZ 1931 (2)*
Barlow, E. J. 30: v E 1964 (5); v A 1966 (5) 1969 (4); v NZ 1961 (5); *v E 1965 (3); v A 1963 (5);*
  v NZ 1963 (3)
Baumgartner, H. V. 1: v E 1913
Beaumont, R. 5: v E 1913 (2); *v E 1912 (1); v A 1912 (2)*
Begbie, D. W. 5: v E 1948 (3); v A 1949 (2)
Bell, A. J. 16: v E 1930 (3); *v E 1929 (3) 1935 (3); v A 1931 (5); v NZ 1931 (2)*
Bisset, M. 3: v E 1898 (2) 1909 (1)
Bissett, G. F. 4: v E 1927 (4)
Blanckenberg, J. M. 18: v E 1913 (5) 1922 (5); v A 1921 (3); *v E 1924 (5)*
Bland, K. C. 21: v E 1964 (5); v A 1966 (1); v NZ 1961 (5); *v E 1965 (3); v A 1963 (4); v NZ 1963 (3)*
Bock, E. G. 1: v A 1935
Bond, G. E. 1: v E 1938
Bosch, T. 1: *v WI 1991*
Botten, J. T. 3: *v E 1965 (3)*
Brann, W. H. 3: v E 1922 (3)
Briscoe, A. W. 2: v E 1938 (1); v A 1935 (1)
Bromfield, H. D. 9: v E 1964 (3); v NZ 1961 (5); *v E 1965 (1)*
Brown, L. S. 2: *v A 1931 (1); v NZ 1931 (1)*
Burger, C. G. de V. 2: v A 1957 (2)
Burke, S. F. 2: v E 1964 (1); v NZ 1961 (1)
Buys, I. D. 1: v E 1922

Cameron, H. B. 26: v E 1927 (5) 1930 (5); *v E 1929 (4) 1935 (5); v A 1931 (5); v NZ 1931 (2)*
Campbell, T. 5: v E 1909 (4); *v E 1912 (1)*
Carlstein, P. R. 8: v A 1957 (1); *v E 1960 (5); v A 1963 (2)*
Carter, C. P. 10: v E 1913 (2); v A 1921 (3); *v E 1912 (2) 1924 (3)*
Catterall, R. H. 24: v E 1922 (5) 1927 (5) 1930 (4); *v E 1924 (5) 1929 (5)*
Chapman, H. W. 2: v E 1913 (1); v A 1921 (1)
Cheetham, J. E. 24: v E 1948 (1); v A 1949 (3); v NZ 1953 (5); *v E 1951 (5) 1955 (3); v A 1952 (5);*
  v NZ 1952 (2)
Chevalier, G. A. 1: v A 1969
Christy, J. A. J. 10: v E 1930 (1); *v E 1929 (2); v A 1931 (5); v NZ 1931 (2)*
Chubb, G. W. A. 5: *v E 1951 (5)*
Cochran, J. A. K. 1: v E 1930
Coen, S. K. 2: v E 1927 (2)
Commaille, J. M. M. 12: v E 1909 (5) 1927 (2); *v E 1924 (5)*
Commins, J. B. 3: v NZ 1994 (2); v P 1994 (1)
Conyngham, D. P. 1: v E 1922
Cook, F. J. 1: v E 1895
Cook, S. J. 3: v In 1992 (2); *v SL 1993 (1)*
Cooper, A. H. C. 1: v E 1913
Cox, J. L. 3: v E 1913 (3)
Cripps, G. 1: v E 1891
Crisp, R. J. 9: v A 1935 (4); *v E 1935 (5)*
Cronje, W. J. 36: v E 1995 (5); v A 1993 (3) 1996 (3); v NZ 1994 (3); v In 1992 (3) 1996 (3);
  v P 1994 (1); *v E 1994 (3); v A 1993 (3); v WI 1991 (1); v NZ 1994 (1); v In 1996 (3); v SL 1993 (3);*
  v Z 1995 (1)
Cullinan, D. J. 28: v E 1995 (5); v NZ 1994 (3); v In 1992 (1) 1996 (3); v P 1994 (1);
  v E 1994 (1); v A 1993 (3); v NZ 1994 (1); v In 1996 (3); v SL 1993 (3); v Z 1995 (1)
Curnow, S. H. 7: v E 1930 (3); *v A 1931 (4)*

Dalton, E. L. 15: v E 1930 (1) 1938 (4); v A 1935 (1); *v E 1929 (1) 1935 (4); v A 1931 (2); v NZ*
  1931 (2)
Davies, E. Q. 5: v E 1938 (3); v A 1935 (2)
Dawson, O. C. 9: v E 1948 (4); *v E 1947 (5)*
Deane, H. G. 17: v E 1927 (5) 1930 (2); *v E 1924 (5) 1929 (5)*
de Villiers, P. S. 16: v A 1993 (3); v NZ 1994 (3); v P 1994 (1); *v E 1994 (3); v A 1993 (3);*
  v NZ 1994 (1); v In 1996 (2)

Dixon, C. D. 1: v E 1913
Donald, A. A. 33: v E 1995 (5); v A 1993 (3) 1996 (3); v In 1992 (4) 1996 (3); v P 1994 (1); *v E 1994 (3); v A 1993 (3); v WI 1991 (1); v NZ 1994 (1); v In 1996 (2); v SL 1993 (3); v Z 1995 (1)*
Dower, R. R. 1: v E 1898
Draper, R. G. 2: v A 1949 (2)
Duckworth, C. A. R. 2: v E 1956 (2)
Dumbrill, R. 5: v A 1966 (2); *v E 1965 (3)*
Duminy, J. P. 3: v E 1927 (2); *v E 1929 (1)*
Dunell, O. R. 2: v E 1888 (2)
Du Preez, J. H. 2: v A 1966 (2)
Du Toit, J. F. 1: v E 1891
Dyer, D. V. 3: *v E 1947 (3)*

Eksteen, C. E. 6: v E 1995 (1); v NZ 1994 (2); v P 1994 (1); *v NZ 1994 (1); v SL 1993 (1)*
Elgie, M. K. 3: v NZ 1961 (3)
Endean, W. R. 28: v E 1956 (5); v A 1957 (5); v NZ 1953 (5); *v E 1951 (1) 1955 (5); v A 1952 (5); v NZ 1952 (2)*

Farrer, W. S. 6: v NZ 1961 (3); *v NZ 1963 (3)*
Faulkner, G. A. 25: v E 1905 (5) 1909 (5); *v E 1907 (3) 1912 (3) 1924 (1); v A 1910 (5) 1912 (3)*
Fellows-Smith, J. P. 4: *v E 1960 (4)*
Fichardt, C. G. 2: v E 1891 (1) 1895 (1)
Finlason, C. E. 1: v E 1888
Floquet, C. E. 1: v E 1909
Francis, H. H. 2: v E 1898 (2)
Francois, C. M. 5: v E 1922 (5)
Frank, C. N. 3: v A 1921 (3)
Frank, W. H. B. 1: v E 1895
Fuller, E. R. H. 7: v A 1957 (1); *v E 1955 (2); v A 1952 (2); v NZ 1952 (2)*
Fullerton, G. M. 7: v A 1949 (2); *v E 1947 (2) 1951 (3)*
Funston, K. J. 18: v E 1956 (3); v A 1957 (3); v NZ 1953 (3); *v A 1952 (5); v NZ 1952 (2)*

Gamsy, D. 2: v A 1969 (2)
Gibbs, H. H. 4: v A 1996 (1); v In 1996 (1); *v In 1996 (2)*
Gleeson, R. A. 1: v E 1895
Glover, G. K. 1: v E 1895
Goddard, T. L. 41: v E 1956 (5) 1964 (5); v A 1957 (5) 1966 (5) 1969 (3); *v E 1955 (5) 1960 (5); v A 1963 (5); v NZ 1963 (3)*
Gordon, N. 5: v E 1938 (5)
Graham, R. 2: v E 1898 (2)
Grieveson, R. E. 2: v E 1938 (2)
Griffin, G. M. 2: *v E 1960 (2)*

Hall, A. E. 7: v E 1922 (4) 1927 (2) 1930 (1)
Hall, G. G. 1: v E 1964
Halliwell, E. A. 8: v E 1891 (1) 1895 (3) 1898 (1); v A 1902 (3)
Halse, C. G. 3: *v A 1963 (3)*
Hands, P. A. M. 7: v E 1913 (5); v A 1921 (1); *v E 1924 (1)*
Hands, R. H. M. 1: v E 1913
Hanley, M. A. 1: v E 1948
Harris, T. A. 3: v E 1948 (1); *v E 1947 (2)*
Hartigan, G. P. D. 5: v E 1913 (3); *v E 1912 (1); v A 1912 (1)*
Harvey, R. L. 2: v A 1935 (2)
Hathorn, C. M. H. 12: v E 1905 (5); v A 1902 (3); *v E 1907 (3); v A 1910 (1)*
Hearne, F. 4: v E 1891 (1) 1895 (3)
Hearne, G. A. L. 3: v E 1922 (2); *v E 1924 (1)*
Heine, P. S. 14: v E 1956 (5); v A 1957 (4); v NZ 1961 (1); *v E 1955 (4)*
Henry, O. 3: v In 1992 (3)
Hime, C. F. W. 1: v E 1895
Hudson, A. C. 32: v E 1995 (5); v A 1993 (3) 1996 (1); v NZ 1994 (2); v In 1992 (4) 1996 (3); *v E 1994 (2); v A 1993 (3); v WI 1991 (1); v NZ 1994 (1); v In 1996 (3); v SL 1993 (3); v Z 1995 (1)*
Hutchinson, P. 2: v E 1888 (2)

Ironside, D. E. J. 3: v NZ 1953 (3)
Irvine, B. L. 4: v A 1969 (4)

Jack, S. D. 2: v NZ 1994 (2)
Johnson, C. L. 1: v E 1895

Kallis, J. H. 5: v E 1995 (2); v A 1996 (3)
Keith, H. J. 8: v E 1956 (3); *v E 1955 (4); v A 1952 (1)*
Kempis, G. A. 1: v E 1888
Kirsten, G. 29: v E 1995 (5); v A 1993 (3) 1996 (3); v NZ 1994 (3); v In 1996 (3); v P 1994 (1); *v E 1994 (3); v A 1993 (3); v NZ 1994 (1); v In 1996 (3); v Z 1995 (1)*
Kirsten, P. N. 12: v A 1993 (3); v In 1992 (4); *v E 1994 (3); v A 1993 (1); v WI 1991 (1)*
Klusener, L. 7: v A 1996 (2); v In 1996 (3); *v In 1996 (2)*
Kotze, J. J. 3: v A 1902 (2); *v E 1907 (1)*
Kuiper, A. P. 1: *v WI 1991*
Kuys, F. 1: v E 1898

Lance, H. R. 13: v A 1966 (5) 1969 (3); v NZ 1961 (2); *v E 1965 (3)*
Langton, A. B. C. 15: v E 1938 (5); v A 1935 (5); *v E 1935 (5)*
Lawrence, G. B. 5: v NZ 1961 (5)
le Roux, F. L. 1: v E 1913
Lewis, P. T. 1: v E 1913
Lindsay, D. T. 19: v E 1964 (3); v A 1966 (5) 1969 (2); *v E 1965 (3); v A 1963 (3); v NZ 1963 (3)*
Lindsay, J. D. 3: *v E 1947 (3)*
Lindsay, N. V. 1: v A 1921
Ling, W. V. S. 6: v E 1922 (3); v A 1921 (3)
Llewellyn, C. B. 15: v E 1895 (1) 1898 (1); v A 1902 (3); *v E 1912 (3); v A 1910 (5) 1912 (2)*
Lundie, E. B. 1: v E 1913

Macaulay, M. J. 1: v E 1964
McCarthy, C. N. 15: v E 1948 (5); v A 1949 (5); *v E 1951 (5)*
McGlew, D. J. 34: v E 1956 (1); v A 1957 (5); v NZ 1953 (5) 1961 (5); *v E 1951 (2) 1955 (5) 1960 (5); v A 1952 (4); v NZ 1952 (2)*
McKinnon, A. H. 8: v E 1964 (2); v A 1966 (2); v NZ 1961 (1); *v E 1960 (1) 1965 (2)*
McLean, R. A. 40: v E 1956 (5) 1964 (2); v A 1957 (4); v NZ 1953 (4) 1961 (5); *v E 1951 (3) 1955 (5) 1960 (5); v A 1952 (5); v NZ 1952 (2)*
McMillan, B. M. 31: v E 1995 (5); v A 1993 (3) 1996 (2); v NZ 1994 (3); v In 1992 (4) 1996 (3); v P 1994 (1); *v E 1994 (3); v A 1993 (1); v In 1996 (3); v SL 1993 (2); v Z 1995 (1)*
McMillan, Q. 13: v E 1930 (5); *v E 1929 (2); v A 1931 (4); v NZ 1931 (2)*
Mann, N. B. F. 19: v E 1948 (5); v A 1949 (5); *v E 1947 (5) 1951 (4)*
Mansell, P. N. F. 13: *v E 1951 (2) 1955 (4); v A 1952 (5); v NZ 1952 (2)*
Markham, L. A. 1: v E 1948
Marx, W. F. E. 3: v A 1921 (3)
Matthews, C. R. 18: v E 1995 (3); v A 1993 (3); v NZ 1994 (2); v In 1992 (3); *v E 1994 (3); v A 1993 (2); v NZ 1994 (1); v Z 1995 (1)*
Meintjes, D. J. 2: v E 1922 (2)
Melle, M. G. 7: v A 1949 (2); *v E 1951 (1); v A 1952 (4)*
Melville, A. 11: v E 1938 (5) 1948 (1); *v E 1947 (5)*
Middleton, J. 6: v E 1895 (2) 1898 (2); v A 1902 (2)
Mills, C. 1: v E 1891
Milton, W. H. 3: v E 1888 (2) 1891 (1)
Mitchell, B. 42: v E 1930 (5) 1938 (5) 1948 (5); v A 1935 (5); *v E 1929 (5) 1935 (5) 1947 (5); v A 1931 (5); v NZ 1931 (2)*
Mitchell, F. 3: *v E 1912 (1); v A 1912 (2)*
Morkel, D. P. B. 16: v E 1927 (5); *v E 1929 (5); v A 1931 (5); v NZ 1931 (1)*
Murray, A. R. A. 10: v NZ 1953 (4); *v A 1952 (4); v NZ 1952 (2)*

Nel, J. D. 6: v A 1949 (5) 1957 (1)
Newberry, C. 4: v E 1913 (4)
Newson, E. S. 3: v E 1930 (1) 1938 (2)
Nicholson, F. 4: v A 1935 (4)

Nicolson, J. F. W. 3: v E 1927 (3)
Norton, N. O. 1: v E 1909
Nourse, A. D. 34: v E 1938 (5) 1948 (5); v A 1935 (5) 1949 (5); *v E 1935 (4) 1947 (5) 1951 (5)*
Nourse, A. W. 45: v E 1905 (5) 1909 (5) 1913 (5) 1922 (5); v A 1902 (3) 1921 (3); *v E 1907 (3) 1912 (3) 1924 (5); v A 1910 (5) 1912 (3)*
Nupen, E. P. 17: v E 1922 (4) 1927 (5) 1930 (3); v A 1921 (2) 1935 (1); *v E 1924 (2)*

Ochse, A. E. 2: v E 1888 (2)
Ochse, A. L. 3: v E 1927 (1); *v E 1929 (2)*
O'Linn, S. 7: v NZ 1961 (2); *v E 1960 (5)*
Owen-Smith, H. G. 5: *v E 1929 (5)*

Palm, A. W. 1: v E 1927
Parker, G. M. 2: *v E 1924 (2)*
Parkin, D. C. 1: v E 1891
Partridge, J. T. 11: v E 1964 (3); *v A 1963 (5); v NZ 1963 (3)*
Pearse, O. C. 3: *v A 1910 (3)*
Pegler, S. J. 16: v E 1909 (1); *v E 1912 (3) 1924 (5); v A 1910 (4) 1912 (3)*
Pithey, A. J. 17: v E 1956 (3) 1964 (5); *v E 1960 (2); v A 1963 (4); v NZ 1963 (3)*
Pithey, D. B. 8: v A 1966 (2); *v A 1963 (3); v NZ 1963 (3)*
Plimsoll, J. B. 1: *v E 1947*
Pollock, P. M. 28: v E 1964 (5); v A 1966 (5) 1969 (4); v NZ 1961 (3); *v E 1965 (3); v A 1963 (5); v NZ 1963 (3)*
Pollock, R. G. 23: v E 1964 (5); v A 1966 (5) 1969 (4); *v E 1965 (3); v A 1963 (5); v NZ 1963 (1)*
Pollock, S. M. 10: v E 1995 (5); v A 1996 (2); v In 1996 (3)
Poore, R. M. 3: v E 1895 (3)
Pothecary, J. E. 3: *v E 1960 (3)*
Powell, A. W. 1: v E 1898
Prince, C. F. H. 1: v E 1898
Pringle, M. W. 4: v E 1995 (1); v In 1992 (2); *v WI 1991 (1)*
Procter, M. J. 7: v A 1966 (3) 1969 (4)
Promnitz, H. L. E. 2: v E 1927 (2)

Quinn, N. A. 12: v E 1930 (1); *v E 1929 (4); v A 1931 (5); v NZ 1931 (2)*

Reid, N. 1: v A 1921
Rhodes, J. N. 29: v E 1995 (5); v A 1993 (3) 1996 (1); v NZ 1994 (3); v In 1992 (4); v P 1994 (1); *v E 1994 (3); v A 1993 (3); v NZ 1994 (1); v In 1996 (1); v SL 1993 (3); v Z 1995 (1)*
Richards, A. R. 1: v E 1895
Richards, B. A. 4: v A 1969 (4)
Richards, W. H. 1: v E 1888
Richardson, D. J. 37: v E 1995 (5); v A 1993 (3) 1996 (3); v NZ 1994 (3); v In 1992 (4) 1996 (3); *v P 1994 (1); v E 1994 (3); v A 1993 (3); v WI 1991 (1); v NZ 1994 (1); v In 1996 (3); v SL 1993 (3); v Z 1995 (1)*
Robertson, J. B. 3: v A 1935 (3)
Rose-Innes, A. 2: v E 1888 (2)
Routledge, T. W. 4: v E 1891 (1) 1895 (3)
Rowan, A. M. B. 15: v E 1948 (5); *v E 1947 (5) 1951 (5)*
Rowan, E. A. B. 26: v E 1938 (4) 1948 (4); v A 1935 (3) 1949 (5); *v E 1935 (5) 1951 (5)*
Rowe, G. A. 5: v E 1895 (2) 1898 (2); v A 1902 (1)
Rushmere, M. W. 1: *v WI 1991*

Samuelson, S. V. 1: v E 1909
Schultz, B. N. 8: v E 1995 (1); v A 1996 (1); v In 1992 (2); *v SL 1993 (3); v Z 1995 (1)*
Schwarz, R. O. 20: v E 1905 (5) 1909 (4); *v E 1907 (3) 1912 (1); v A 1910 (5) 1912 (2)*
Seccull, A. W. 1: v E 1895
Seymour, M. A. 7: v E 1964 (2); v A 1969 (1); *v A 1963 (4)*
Shalders, W. A. 12: v E 1898 (1) 1905 (5); v A 1902 (3); *v E 1907 (3)*
Shepstone, G. H. 2: v E 1895 (1) 1898 (1)
Sherwell, P. W. 13: v E 1905 (5); *v E 1907 (3); v A 1910 (5)*
Siedle, I. J. 18: v E 1927 (1) 1930 (5); v A 1935 (5); *v E 1929 (3) 1935 (4)*

Sinclair, J. H. 25: v E 1895 (3) 1898 (2) 1905 (5) 1909 (4); v A 1902 (3); *v E 1907 (3); v A 1910 (5)*
Smith, C. J. E. 3: v A 1902 (3)
Smith, F. W. 3: v E 1888 (2) 1895 (1)
Smith, V. I. 9: v A 1949 (3) 1957 (1); *v E 1947 (4) 1955 (1)*
Snell, R. P. 5: v NZ 1994 (1); *v A 1993 (1); v WI 1991 (1); v SL 1993 (2)*
Snooke, S. D. 1: *v E 1907*
Snooke, S. J. 26: v E 1905 (5) 1909 (5) 1922 (3); *v E 1907 (3) 1912 (3); v A 1910 (5) 1912 (2)*
Solomon, W. R. 1: v E 1898
Stewart, R. B. 1: v E 1888
Steyn, P. J. R. 3: v NZ 1994 (1); v P 1994 (1); *v NZ 1994 (1)*
Stricker, L. A. 13: v E 1909 (4); *v E 1912 (2); v A 1910 (5) 1912 (2)*
Susskind, M. J. 5: *v E 1924 (5)*
Symcox, P. L. 10: v A 1996 (1); *v A 1993 (2); v In 1996 (3); v SL 1993 (3); v Z 1995 (1)*

Taberer, H. M. 1: v A 1902
Tancred, A. B. 2: v E 1888 (2)
Tancred, L. J. 14: v E 1905 (5) 1913 (1); v A 1902 (3); *v E 1907 (1) 1912 (2); v A 1912 (2)*
Tancred, V. M. 1: v E 1898
Tapscott, G. L. 1: v E 1913
Tapscott, L. E. 2: v E 1922 (2)
Tayfield, H. J. 37: v E 1956 (5); v A 1949 (5) 1957 (5); v NZ 1953 (5); *v E 1955 (5) 1960 (5); v A 1952 (5); v NZ 1952 (2)*
Taylor, A. I. 1: v E 1956
Taylor, D. 2: v E 1913 (2)
Taylor, H. W. 42: v E 1913 (5) 1922 (5) 1927 (5) 1930 (4); v A 1921 (3); *v E 1912 (3) 1924 (5) 1929 (3); v A 1912 (3) 1931 (5); v NZ 1931 (1)*
Theunissen, N. H. 1: v E 1888
Thornton, P. G. 1: v A 1902
Tomlinson, D. S. 1: *v E 1935*
Traicos, A. J. 3: v A 1969 (3)
Trimborn, P. H. J. 4: v A 1966 (3) 1969 (1)
Tuckett, L. 9: v E 1948 (4); *v E 1947 (5)*
Tuckett, L. R. 1: v E 1913
Twentyman-Jones, P. S. 1: v A 1902

van der Bijl, P. G. V. 5: v E 1938 (5)
Van der Merwe, E. A. 2: v A 1935 (1); *v E 1929 (1)*
Van der Merwe, P. L. 15: v E 1964 (2); v A 1966 (5); *v E 1965 (3); v A 1963 (3); v NZ 1963 (2)*
Van Ryneveld, C. B. 19: v E 1956 (5); v A 1957 (4); v NZ 1953 (5); *v E 1951 (5)*
Varnals, G. D. 3: v E 1964 (3)
Viljoen, K. G. 27: v E 1930 (3) 1938 (4) 1948 (2); v A 1935 (4); *v E 1935 (4) 1947 (5); v A 1931 (4); v NZ 1931 (1)*
Vincent, C. L. 25: v E 1927 (5) 1930 (5); *v E 1929 (4) 1935 (4); v A 1931 (5); v NZ 1931 (2)*
Vintcent, C. H. 3: v E 1888 (2) 1891 (1)
Vogler, A. E. E. 15: v E 1905 (5) 1909 (5); *v E 1907 (3); v A 1910 (2)*

Wade, H. F. 10: v A 1935 (5); *v E 1935 (5)*
Wade, W. W. 11: v E 1938 (3) 1948 (5); v A 1949 (3)
Waite, J. H. B. 50: v E 1956 (5) 1964 (2); v A 1957 (5); v NZ 1953 (5) 1961 (5); *v E 1951 (4) 1955 (5) 1960 (5); v A 1952 (5) 1963 (4); v NZ 1952 (2) 1963 (3)*
Walter, K. A. 2: v NZ 1961 (2)
Ward, T. A. 23: v E 1913 (5) 1922 (5); v A 1921 (3); *v E 1912 (2) 1924 (5); v A 1912 (3)*
Watkins, J. C. 15: v E 1956 (2); v A 1949 (3); v NZ 1953 (3); *v A 1952 (5); v NZ 1952 (2)*
Wesley, C. 3: *v E 1960 (3)*
Wessels, K. C. 16: v A 1993 (1); v In 1992 (4); *v E 1994 (3); v A 1993 (2); v WI 1991 (1); SL 1993 (3)*
Westcott, R. J. 5: v A 1957 (2); v NZ 1953 (3)
White, G. C. 17: v E 1905 (5) 1909 (4); *v E 1907 (3) 1912 (2); v A 1912 (3)*
Willoughby, J. T. 2: v E 1895 (2)
Wimble, C. S. 1: v E 1891
Winslow, P. L. 5: v A 1949 (2); *v E 1955 (3)*
Wynne, O. E. 6: v E 1948 (3); v A 1949 (3)

Zulch, J. W. 16: v E 1909 (5) 1913 (3); v A 1921 (3); *v A 1910 (5)*

WEST INDIES

Number of Test cricketers: 217

Achong, E. 6: v E 1929 (1) 1934 (2); *v E 1933 (3)*

Adams, J. C. 29: v E 1993 (5); v A 1994 (4); v SA 1991 (1); v NZ 1995 (2); *v E 1995 (4); v A 1992 (3) 1996 (5); v NZ 1994 (2); v In 1994 (3)*

Alexander, F. C. M. 25: v E 1959 (5); v P 1957 (5); *v E 1957 (2); v A 1960 (5); v In 1958 (5); v P 1958 (3)*

Ali, Imtiaz 1: v In 1975

Ali, Inshan 12: v E 1973 (2); v A 1972 (3); v In 1970 (1); v P 1976 (1); v NZ 1971 (3); *v E 1973 (1); v A 1975 (1)*

Allan, D. W. 5: v A 1964 (1); v In 1961 (2); *v E 1966 (2)*

Allen, I. B. A. 2: *v E 1991 (2)*

Ambrose, C. E. L. 72: v E 1989 (3) 1993 (5); v A 1990 (5) 1994 (4); v SA 1991 (1); v NZ 1995 (2); v In 1988 (4) 1996 (5); v P 1987 (3) 1992 (3); v SL 1996 (2); *v E 1988 (5) 1991 (5) 1995 (5); v A 1988 (5) 1992 (5) 1996 (4); v NZ 1994 (2); v P 1990 (3); v SL 1993 (1)*

Arthurton, K. L. T. 33: v E 1993 (5); v A 1994 (3); v SA 1991 (1); v In 1988 (4); v P 1992 (3); *v E 1988 (1) 1995 (5); v A 1992 (5); v NZ 1994 (2); v In 1994 (3); v SL 1993 (1)*

Asgarali, N. 2: *v E 1957 (2)*

Atkinson, D. St E. 22: v E 1953 (4); v A 1954 (4); v P 1957 (1); *v E 1957 (2); v A 1951 (2); v NZ 1951 (1) 1955 (4); v In 1948 (4)*

Atkinson, E. St E. 8: v P 1957 (3); *v In 1958 (3); v P 1958 (2)*

Austin, R. A. 2: v A 1977 (2)

Bacchus, S. F. A. F. 19: v A 1977 (2); *v E 1980 (5); v A 1981 (2); v In 1978 (6); v P 1980 (4)*

Baichan, L. 3: *v A 1975 (1); v P 1974 (2)*

Baptiste, E. A. E. 10: v E 1989 (1); v A 1983 (3); *v E 1984 (5); v In 1983 (1)*

Barrett, A. G. 6: v E 1973 (2); v In 1974 (2); *v In 1974 (2)*

Barrow, I. 11: v E 1929 (1) 1934 (1); *v E 1933 (3) 1939 (1); v A 1930 (5)*

Bartlett, E. L. 5: *v E 1928 (1); v A 1930 (4)*

Benjamin, K. C. G. 24: v E 1993 (5); v A 1994 (4); v SA 1991 (1); *v E 1995 (5); v A 1992 (1) 1996 (3); v NZ 1994 (2); v In 1994 (3)*

Benjamin, W. K. M. 21: v E 1993 (5); v A 1994 (4); v In 1988 (1); v P 1987 (3) 1992 (2); *v E 1988 (3); v NZ 1994 (1); v In 1987 (1); v SL 1993 (1)*

Best, C. A. 8: v E 1985 (3) 1989 (3); *v P 1990 (2)*

Betancourt, N. 1: v E 1929

Binns, A. P. 5: v A 1954 (1); v In 1952 (1); *v NZ 1955 (3)*

Birkett, L. S. 4: *v A 1930 (4)*

Bishop, I. R. 37: v E 1989 (4); v NZ 1995 (2); v In 1988 (4) 1996 (4); v P 1992 (2); v SL 1996 (2); *v E 1995 (6); v A 1992 (5) 1996 (5); v P 1990 (3)*

Boyce, K. D. 21: v E 1973 (4); v A 1972 (4); v In 1970 (1); *v E 1973 (3); v A 1975 (4); v In 1974 (3); v P 1974 (2)*

Browne, C. O. 13: v A 1994 (1); v NZ 1995 (2); v In 1996 (3); v SL 1996 (2); *v E 1995 (2); v A 1996 (3)*

Browne, C. R. 4: v E 1929 (2); *v E 1928 (2)*

Butcher, B. F. 44: v E 1959 (2) 1967 (5); v A 1964 (5); *v E 1963 (5) 1966 (5) 1969 (3); v A 1968 (5); v NZ 1968 (3); v In 1958 (5) 1966 (3); v P 1958 (3)*

Butler, L. 1: v A 1954

Butts, C. G. 7: v NZ 1984 (1); *v NZ 1986 (1); v In 1987 (3); v P 1986 (2)*

Bynoe, M. R. 4: v In 1966 (3); v P 1958 (1)

Camacho, G. S. 11: v E 1967 (5); v In 1970 (2); *v E 1969 (2); v A 1968 (2)*

Cameron, F. J. 5: *v In 1948 (5)*

Cameron, J. H. 2: *v E 1939 (2)*

Campbell, S. L. 23: v A 1994 (1); v NZ 1995 (2); v In 1996 (5); v SL 1996 (2); *v E 1995 (6); v A 1996 (5); v NZ 1994 (2)*

Carew, G. M. 4: v E 1934 (1) 1947 (2); *v In 1948 (1)*

Carew, M. C. 19: v E 1967 (1); v NZ 1971 (3); v In 1970 (3); *v E 1963 (2) 1966 (1) 1969 (1); v A 1968 (5); v NZ 1968 (3)*

Challenor, G. 3: *v E 1928 (3)*

Chanderpaul, S. 21: v E 1993 (4); v NZ 1995 (2); v In 1996 (5); *v E 1995 (2); v A 1996 (5); v NZ 1994 (2); v In 1994 (1)*

Chang, H. S. 1: *v In 1978*

Christiani, C. M. 4: v E 1934 (4)

Christiani, R. J. 22: v E 1947 (4) 1953 (1); v In 1952 (2); *v E 1950 (4); v A 1951 (5); v NZ 1951 (1); v In 1948 (5)*

Clarke, C. B. 3: *v E 1939 (3)*

Clarke, S. T. 11: v A 1977 (1); *v A 1981 (1); v In 1978 (5); v P 1980 (4)*

Constantine, L. N. 18: v E 1929 (3) 1934 (3); *v E 1928 (3) 1933 (1) 1939 (3); v A 1930 (5)*

Croft, C. E. H. 27: v E 1980 (4); v A 1977 (2); v P 1976 (5); *v E 1980 (3); v A 1979 (3) 1981 (3); v NZ 1979 (3); v P 1980 (4)*

Cuffy, C. E. 3: *v A 1996 (1); v In 1994 (2)*

Cummins, A. C. 5: v P 1992 (2); *v A 1992 (1); v In 1994 (2)*

Da Costa, O. C. 5: v E 1929 (1) 1934 (1); *v E 1933 (3)*

Daniel, W. W. 10: v A 1983 (2); v In 1975 (1); *v E 1976 (4); v In 1983 (3)*

Davis, B. A. 4: v A 1964 (4)

Davis, C. A. 15: v A 1972 (2); v NZ 1971 (5); v In 1970 (4); *v E 1969 (3); v A 1968 (1)*

Davis, W. W. 15: v A 1983 (1); v NZ 1984 (2); v In 1982 (1); *v E 1984 (1); v In 1983 (6) 1987 (4)*

De Caires, F. I. 3: v E 1929 (3)

Depeiza, C. C. 5: v A 1954 (3); *v NZ 1955 (2)*

Dewdney, T. 9: v A 1954 (2); v P 1957 (3); *v E 1957 (1); v NZ 1955 (3)*

Dhanraj, R. 4: v NZ 1995 (1); *v E 1995 (1); v NZ 1994 (1); v In 1994 (1)*

Dillon, M. 2: v In 1996 (2)

Dowe, U. G. 4: v A 1972 (1); v NZ 1971 (1); v In 1970 (2)

Dujon, P. J. L. 81: v E 1985 (4) 1989 (4); v A 1983 (5) 1990 (5); v NZ 1984 (4); v In 1982 (5) 1988 (4); v P 1987 (3); *v E 1984 (5) 1988 (5) 1991 (5); v A 1981 (3) 1984 (5) 1988 (5); v NZ 1986 (3); v In 1983 (6) 1987 (4); v P 1986 (3) 1990 (3)*

Edwards, R. M. 5: *v A 1968 (2); v NZ 1968 (3)*

Ferguson, W. 8: v E 1947 (4) 1953 (1); *v In 1948 (3)*

Fernandes, M. P. 2: v E 1929 (1); *v E 1928 (1)*

Findlay, T. M. 10: v A 1972 (1); v NZ 1971 (5); v In 1970 (2); *v E 1969 (2)*

Foster, M. L. C. 14: v E 1973 (1); v A 1972 (4) 1977 (1); v NZ 1971 (3); v In 1970 (2); v P 1976 (1); *v E 1969 (1) 1973 (1)*

Francis, G. N. 10: v E 1929 (1); *v E 1928 (3) 1933 (1); v A 1930 (5)*

Frederick, M. 1: v E 1953

Fredericks, R. C. 59: v E 1973 (5); v A 1972 (5); v NZ 1971 (5); v In 1970 (4) 1975 (4); v P 1976 (5); *v E 1969 (3) 1973 (3) 1976 (5); v A 1968 (4) 1975 (6); v NZ 1968 (3); v In 1974 (5); v P 1974 (2)*

Fuller, R. L. 1: v E 1934

Furlonge, H. A. 3: v A 1954 (1); *v NZ 1955 (2)*

Ganteaume, A. G. 1: v E 1947

Garner, J. 58: v E 1980 (4) 1985 (5); v A 1977 (2) 1983 (5); v NZ 1984 (4); v In 1982 (4); v P 1976 (5); *v E 1980 (5) 1984 (5); v A 1979 (3) 1981 (3) 1984 (5); v NZ 1979 (3) 1986 (2); v P 1980 (3)*

Gaskin, B. B. M. 2: v E 1947 (2)

Gibbs, G. L. 1: v A 1954

Gibbs, L. R. 79: v E 1967 (5) 1973 (5); v A 1964 (5) 1972 (5); v NZ 1971 (2); v In 1961 (5) 1970 (1); v P 1957 (4); *v E 1963 (5) 1966 (5) 1969 (3) 1973 (3); v A 1960 (3) 1968 (5) 1975 (6); v NZ 1968 (3); v In 1958 (1) 1966 (3) 1974 (5); v P 1958 (3) 1974 (2)*

Gibson, O. D. 1: *v E 1995*

Gilchrist, R. 13: v P 1957 (4); *v In 1958 (4)*

Gladstone, G. 1: v E 1929

Goddard, J. D. C. 27: v E 1947 (4); *v E 1950 (4) 1957 (5); v A 1951 (4); v NZ 1951 (2) 1955 (3); v In 1948 (5)*

Gomes, H. A. 60: v E 1980 (4) 1985 (5); v A 1977 (3) 1983 (2); v NZ 1984 (4); v In 1982 (5); *v E 1976 (2) 1984 (5); v A 1981 (3) 1984 (5); v NZ 1986 (3); v In 1978 (6) 1983 (6); v P 1980 (4) 1986 (3)*

Gomez, G. E. 29: v E 1947 (4) 1953 (4); v In 1952 (4); *v E 1939 (2) 1950 (4); v A 1951 (5); v NZ 1951 (1); v In 1948 (5)*

Grant, G. C. 12: v E 1934 (4); *v E 1933 (3); v A 1930 (5)*

Grant, R. S. 7: v E 1934 (4); *v E 1939 (3)*

Gray, A. H. 5: *v NZ 1986 (2); v P 1986 (3)*

Greenidge, A. E. 6: v A 1977 (2); *v In 1978 (4)*

Greenidge, C. G. 108: v E 1980 (4) 1985 (5) 1989 (4); v A 1977 (2) 1983 (5) 1990 (5); v NZ 1984 (4); v In 1982 (5) 1988 (4); v P 1976 (5) 1987 (3); *v E 1976 (5) 1980 (5) 1984 (5) 1988 (4); v A 1975 (2) 1979 (3) 1981 (2) 1984 (5) 1988 (5); v NZ 1979 (3) 1986 (3); v In 1974 (5) 1983 (6) 1987 (3); v P 1986 (3) 1990 (3)*

Greenidge, G. A. 5: v A 1972 (3); v NZ 1971 (2)

Grell, M. G. 1: v E 1929

Griffith, A. F. G. 1: *v A 1996*

Griffith, C. C. 28: v E 1959 (1) 1967 (4); v A 1964 (5); *v E 1963 (5) 1966 (5); v A 1968 (3); v NZ 1968 (2); v In 1966 (3)*

Griffith, H. C. 13: v E 1929 (3); *v E 1928 (3) 1933 (2); v A 1930 (5)*

Guillen, S. C. 5: *v A 1951 (3); v NZ 1951 (2)*

Hall, W. W. 48: v E 1959 (5) 1967 (4); v A 1964 (5); v In 1961 (5); *v E 1963 (5) 1966 (5); v A 1960 (5) 1968 (2); v NZ 1968 (3); v In 1958 (5) 1966 (3); v P 1958 (3)*

Harper, R. A. 25: v E 1985 (2); v A 1983 (4); v NZ 1984 (1); *v E 1984 (5) 1988 (3); v A 1984 (2) 1988 (1); v In 1983 (2) 1987 (1); v P 1986 (3); v SL 1993 (1)*

Haynes, D. L. 116: v E 1980 (4) 1985 (5) 1989 (4) 1993 (4); v A 1977 (2) 1983 (5) 1990 (5); v SA 1991 (1); v NZ 1984 (4); v In 1982 (5) 1988 (4); v P 1987 (3) 1992 (3); *v E 1980 (5) 1984 (5) 1988 (4) 1991 (5); v A 1979 (3) 1981 (3) 1984 (5) 1988 (5) 1992 (5); v NZ 1979 (3) 1986 (3); v In 1983 (6) 1987 (4); v P 1980 (4) 1986 (3) 1990 (3); v SL 1993 (1)*

Headley, G. A. 22: v E 1929 (4) 1934 (4) 1947 (1) 1953 (1); *v E 1933 (3) 1939 (3); v A 1930 (5); v In 1948 (1)*

Headley, R. G. A. 2: *v E 1973 (2)*

Hendriks, J. L. 20: v A 1964 (4); v In 1961 (1); *v E 1966 (3) 1969 (1); v A 1968 (5); v NZ 1968 (3); v In 1966 (3)*

Hoad, E. L. G. 4: v E 1929 (1); *v E 1928 (1) 1933 (2)*

Holder, R. I. C. 7: v In 1996 (5); v SL 1996 (2)

Holder, V. A. 40: v E 1973 (1); v A 1972 (3) 1977 (3); v NZ 1971 (4); v In 1970 (3) 1975 (1); v P 1976 (1); *v E 1969 (3) 1973 (2) 1976 (4); v A 1975 (3); v In 1974 (4) 1978 (6); v P 1974 (2)*

Holding, M. A. 60: v E 1980 (4) 1985 (4); v A 1983 (3); v NZ 1984 (3); v In 1975 (4) 1982 (5); *v E 1976 (4) 1980 (5) 1984 (4); v A 1975 (5) 1979 (3) 1981 (3) 1984 (3); v NZ 1979 (3) 1986 (1); v In 1983 (6)*

Holford, D. A. J. 24: v E 1967 (4); v NZ 1971 (5); v In 1970 (1) 1975 (2); v P 1976 (1); *v E 1966 (5); v A 1968 (2); v NZ 1968 (3); v In 1966 (1)*

Holt, J. K. 17: v E 1953 (5); v A 1954 (5); *v In 1958 (5); v P 1958 (2)*

Hooper, C. L. 64: v E 1989 (3); v A 1990 (5) 1994 (4); v In 1996 (5); v P 1987 (3) 1992 (3); v SL 1996 (5); *v E 1988 (5) 1991 (5) 1995 (5); v A 1988 (5) 1992 (4) 1996 (5); v In 1987 (3) 1994 (3); v P 1990 (3); v SL 1993 (1)*

Howard, A. B. 1: v NZ 1971

Hunte, C. C. 44: v E 1959 (5); v A 1964 (5); v In 1961 (5); v P 1957 (5); *v E 1963 (5) 1966 (5); v A 1960 (5); v In 1958 (5) 1966 (3); v P 1958 (1)*

Hunte, E. A. C. 3: v E 1929 (3)

Hylton, L. G. 6: v E 1934 (4); *v E 1939 (2)*

Johnson, H. H. H. 3: v E 1947 (1); *v E 1950 (2)*

Johnson, T. F. 1: *v E 1939*

Jones, C. M. 4: v E 1929 (1) 1934 (3)

Jones, P. E. 9: v E 1947 (1); *v E 1950 (2); v A 1951 (1); v In 1948 (5)*

Julien, B. D. 24: v E 1973 (5); v In 1975 (4); v P 1976 (1); *v E 1973 (3) 1976 (2); v A 1975 (3); v In 1974 (4); v P 1974 (2)*

Jumadeen, R. R. 12: v A 1972 (1) 1977 (2); v NZ 1971 (1); v In 1975 (4); v P 1976 (1); *v E 1976 (1); v In 1978 (2)*

Kallicharran, A. I. 66: v E 1973 (5); v A 1972 (5) 1977 (5); v NZ 1971 (2); v In 1975 (4); v P 1976 (5); *v E 1973 (3) 1976 (3) 1980 (5); v A 1975 (6) 1979 (3); v NZ 1979 (3); v In 1974 (5) 1978 (6); v P 1974 (2) 1980 (4)*

Kanhai, R. B. 79: v E 1959 (5) 1967 (5) 1973 (5); v A 1964 (5) 1972 (5); v In 1961 (5) 1970 (5); v P 1957 (5); *v E 1957 (5) 1963 (5) 1966 (5) 1973 (3); v A 1960 (5) 1968 (5); v In 1958 (5) 1966 (3); v P 1958 (3)*

Kentish, E. S. M. 2: v E 1947 (1) 1953 (1)

King, C. L. 9: v P 1976 (1); *v E 1976 (3) 1980 (1); v A 1979 (1); v NZ 1979 (3)*

King, F. M. 14: v E 1953 (3); v A 1954 (4); v In 1952 (5); *v NZ 1955 (2)*

King, L. A. 2: v E 1967 (1); v In 1961 (1)

Lambert, C. B. 1: *v E 1991*

Lara, B. C. 45: v E 1993 (5); v A 1994 (4); v SA 1991 (1); v NZ 1995 (2); v In 1996 (5); v P 1992 (3); v SL 1996 (2); *v E 1995 (6); v A 1992 (5) 1996 (5); v NZ 1994 (2); v In 1994 (3); v P 1990 (1); v SL 1993 (1)*

Lashley, P. D. 4: *v E 1966 (2); v A 1960 (2)*

Legall, R. 4: v In 1952 (4)

Lewis, D. M. 3: v In 1970 (3)

Lloyd, C. H. 110: v E 1967 (5) 1973 (5) 1980 (4); v A 1972 (3) 1977 (2) 1983 (4); v NZ 1971 (2); v In 1970 (5) 1975 (4) 1982 (5); v P 1976 (5); *v E 1969 (3) 1973 (3) 1976 (5) 1980 (4) 1984 (5); v A 1968 (4) 1975 (6) 1979 (2) 1981 (3) 1984 (5); v NZ 1968 (3) 1979 (3); v In 1966 (3) 1974 (5) 1983 (6); v P 1974 (2) 1980 (4)*

Logie, A. L. 52: v E 1989 (3); v A 1983 (1) 1990 (5); v NZ 1984 (4); v In 1982 (5) 1988 (4); v P 1987 (2); *v E 1988 (5) 1991 (4); v A 1988 (5); v NZ 1986 (3); v In 1983 (3) 1987 (4); v P 1990 (3)*

McMorris, E. D. A. St J. 13: v E 1959 (4); v In 1961 (4); v P 1957 (1); *v E 1963 (2) 1966 (2)*

McWatt, C. A. 6: v E 1953 (5); v A 1954 (1)

Madray, I. S. 2: v P 1957 (2)

Marshall, M. D. 81: v E 1980 (1) 1985 (5) 1989 (2); v A 1983 (4) 1990 (5); v NZ 1984 (4); v In 1982 (5) 1988 (3); v P 1987 (2); *v E 1980 (4) 1984 (4) 1988 (5) 1991 (5); v A 1984 (5) 1988 (5); v NZ 1986 (3); v In 1978 (3) 1983 (6); v P 1980 (4) 1986 (3) 1990 (3)*

Marshall, N. E. 1: v A 1954

Marshall, R. E. 4: *v A 1951 (2); v NZ 1951 (2)*

Martin, F. R. 9: v E 1929 (1); *v E 1928 (3); v A 1930 (5)*

Martindale, E. A. 10: v E 1934 (4); *v E 1933 (3) 1939 (3)*

Mattis, E. H. 4: v E 1980 (4)

Mendonca, I. L. 2: v In 1961 (2)

Merry, C. A. 2: *v E 1933 (2)*

Miller, R. 1: v In 1952

Moodie, G. H. 1: v E 1934

Moseley, E. A. 2: v E 1989 (2)

Murray, D. A. 19: v E 1980 (4); v A 1977 (3); *v A 1981 (2); v In 1978 (6); v P 1980 (4)*

Murray, D. L. 62: v E 1967 (5) 1973 (5); v A 1972 (4) 1977 (2); v In 1975 (4); v P 1976 (5); *v E 1963 (5) 1973 (3) 1976 (5) 1980 (5); v A 1975 (6) 1979 (3); v NZ 1979 (3); v In 1974 (5); v P 1974 (2)*

Murray, J. R. 28: v E 1993 (5); v A 1994 (3); v In 1996 (2); v P 1992 (2); *v E 1995 (4); v A 1992 (3) 1996 (2); v NZ 1994 (2); v In 1994 (3); v SL 1993 (1)*

Nanan, R. 1: *v P 1980*

Neblett, J. M. 1: v E 1934

Noreiga, J. M. 4: v In 1970 (4)

Nunes, R. K. 4: v E 1929 (1); *v E 1928 (3)*

Nurse, S. M. 29: v E 1959 (1) 1967 (5); v A 1964 (4); v In 1961 (1); *v E 1966 (5); v A 1960 (3) 1968 (5); v NZ 1968 (3); v In 1966 (2)*

Padmore, A. L. 2: v In 1975 (1); *v E 1976 (1)*

Pairaudeau, B. H. 13: v E 1953 (2); v In 1952 (5); *v E 1957 (2); v NZ 1955 (4)*

Parry, D. R. 12: v A 1977 (5); *v NZ 1979 (1); v In 1978 (6)*

Passailaigue, C. C. 1: v E 1929

Patterson, B. P. 28: v E 1985 (5) 1989 (1); v A 1990 (5); v SA 1991 (1); v P 1987 (1); *v E 1988 (2) 1991 (3); v A 1988 (4) 1992 (1); v In 1987 (4); v P 1986 (1)*

Payne, T. R. O. 1: v E 1985

Phillip, N. 9: v A 1977 (3); *v In 1978 (6)*

Pierre, L. R. 1: v E 1947

Rae, A. F. 15: v In 1952 (2); *v E 1950 (4); v A 1951 (3); v NZ 1951 (1); v In 1948 (5)*

Ramadhin, S. 43: v E 1953 (5) 1959 (4); v A 1954 (4); v In 1952 (4); *v E 1950 (4) 1957 (5); v A 1951 (5) 1960 (2); v NZ 1951 (2) 1955 (4); v In 1958 (2); v P 1958 (2)*

Reifer, F. L. 2: v SL 1996 (2)

Richards, I. V. A. 121: v E 1980 (4) 1985 (5) 1989 (3); v A 1977 (2) 1983 (5) 1990 (5); v NZ 1984 (4); v In 1975 (4) 1982 (5) 1988 (4); v P 1976 (5) 1987 (2); *v E 1976 (4) 1980 (5) 1984 (5) 1988 (5) 1991 (5); v A 1975 (6) 1979 (3) 1981 (3) 1984 (5) 1988 (5); v NZ 1986 (3); v In 1974 (5) 1983 (6) 1987 (4); v P 1974 (2) 1980 (4) 1986 (3)*

Richardson, R. B. 86: v E 1985 (5) 1989 (4) 1993 (4); v A 1983 (5) 1990 (5) 1994 (4); v SA 1991 (1); v NZ 1984 (4); v In 1988 (4); v P 1987 (3) 1992 (3); *v E 1988 (3) 1991 (5) 1995 (6); v A 1984 (5) 1988 (5) 1992 (5); v NZ 1986 (3); v In 1983 (1) 1987 (4); v P 1986 (3) 1990 (3); v SL 1993 (1)*

Rickards, K. R. 2: v E 1947 (1); *v A 1951 (1)*

Roach, C. A. 16: v E 1929 (4) 1934 (1); *v E 1928 (3) 1933 (3); v A 1930 (5)*

Roberts, A. M. E. 47: v E 1973 (1) 1980 (3); v A 1977 (2); v In 1975 (2) 1982 (5); v P 1976 (5); *v E 1976 (5) 1980 (3); v A 1975 (5) 1979 (3) 1981 (2); v NZ 1979 (2); v In 1974 (5) 1983 (2); v P 1974 (2)*

Roberts, A. T. 1: *v NZ 1955*

Rodriguez, W. V. 5: v E 1967 (1); v A 1964 (1); v In 1961 (2); *v E 1963 (1)*

Rose, F. A. 7: v In 1996 (5); v SL 1996 (2)

Rowe, L. G. 30: v E 1973 (5); v A 1972 (3); v NZ 1971 (4); v In 1975 (4); *v E 1976 (2); v A 1975 (6) 1979 (3); v NZ 1979 (3)*

St Hill, E. L. 2: v E 1929 (2)

St Hill, W. H. 3: v E 1929 (1); *v E 1928 (2)*

Samuels, R. G. 6: v NZ 1995 (2); *v A 1996 (4)*

Scarlett, R. O. 3: v E 1959 (3)

Scott, A. P. H. 1: v In 1952

Scott, O. C. 8: v E 1929 (2); *v E 1928 (2); v A 1930 (5)*

Sealey, B. J. 1: *v E 1933*

Sealy, J. E. D. 11: v E 1929 (2) 1934 (4); *v E 1939 (3); v A 1930 (2)*

Shepherd, J. N. 5: v In 1970 (2); *v E 1969 (3)*

Shillingford, G. C. 7: v NZ 1971 (2); v In 1970 (3); *v E 1969 (2)*

Shillingford, I. T. 4: v A 1977 (1); v P 1976 (3)

Shivnarine, S. 8: v A 1977 (3); *v In 1978 (5)*

Simmons, P. V. 25: v E 1993 (2); v SA 1991 (1); v NZ 1995 (2); v P 1987 (1) 1992 (3); *v E 1991 (5); v A 1992 (5) 1996 (1); v In 1987 (1) 1994 (3); v SL 1993 (1)*

Singh, C. K. 2: v E 1959 (2)

Small, J. A. 3: v E 1929 (1); *v E 1928 (2)*

Small, M. A. 2: v A 1983 (1); *v E 1984 (1)*

Smith, C. W. 5: v In 1961 (1); *v A 1960 (4)*

Smith, O. G. 26: v A 1954 (4); v P 1957 (5); *v E 1957 (5); v NZ 1955 (4); v In 1958 (5); v P 1958 (3)*

Sobers, G. S. 93: v E 1953 (5) 1959 (5) 1967 (5) 1973 (4); v A 1954 (4) 1964 (5); v NZ 1971 (5); v In 1961 (5) 1970 (5); v P 1957 (5); *v E 1957 (5) 1963 (5) 1966 (5) 1969 (3) 1973 (3); v A 1960 (5) 1968 (5); v NZ 1955 (4) 1968 (3); v In 1958 (5) 1966 (3); v P 1958 (3)*

Solomon, J. S. 27: v E 1959 (2); v A 1964 (5); v In 1961 (5); *v E 1963 (2); v A 1960 (5); v In 1958 (4); v P 1958 (3)*

Stayers, S. C. 4: v In 1961 (4)

Stollmeyer, J. B. 32: v E 1947 (2) 1953 (5); v A 1954 (2); v In 1952 (5); *v E 1939 (3) 1950 (4); v A 1951 (5); v NZ 1951 (2); v In 1948 (4)*

Stollmeyer, V. H. 1: *v E 1939*

Taylor, J. 3: v P 1957 (1); *v In 1958 (1); v P 1958 (1)*

Thompson, P. I. C. 2: v NZ 1995 (1); *v A 1996 (1)*

Trim, J. 4: v E 1947 (1); *v A 1951 (1); v In 1948 (2)*

Valentine, A. L. 36: v E 1953 (3); v A 1954 (3); v In 1952 (5) 1961 (2); v P 1957 (1); *v E 1950 (4) 1957 (2); v A 1951 (5) 1960 (5); v NZ 1951 (2) 1955 (4)*

Valentine, V. A. 2. *v E 1933 (2)*

Walcott, C. L. 44: v E 1947 (4) 1953 (5) 1959 (2); v A 1954 (5); v In 1952 (5); v P 1957 (4); *v E 1950 (4) 1957 (5); v A 1951 (3); v NZ 1951 (2); v In 1948 (5)*

Walcott, L. A. 1: v E 1929

Walsh, C. A. 93: v E 1985 (1) 1989 (3) 1993 (5); v A 1990 (5) 1994 (4); v SA 1991 (1); v NZ 1984 (1) 1995 (2); v In 1988 (4) 1996 (4); v P 1987 (3) 1992 (3); v SL 1996 (2); *v E 1988 (5) 1991 (5) 1995 (6); v A 1984 (5) 1988 (5) 1992 (5) 1996 (5); v NZ 1986 (3) 1994 (2); v In 1987 (4) 1994 (3); v P 1986 (3) 1990 (3); v SL 1993 (1)*

Watson, C. 7: v E 1959 (5); v In 1961 (1); *v A 1960 (1)*

Weekes, E. D. 48: v E 1947 (4) 1953 (4); v A 1954 (5) v In 1952 (5); v P 1957 (5); *v E 1950 (4) 1957 (5); v A 1951 (5); v NZ 1951 (2) 1955 (4); v In 1948 (5)*

Weekes, K. H. 2: *v E 1939 (2)*

White, W. A. 2: v A 1964 (2)

Wight, C. V. 2: v E 1929 (1); *v E 1928 (1)*

Wight, G. L. 1: v In 1952

Wiles, C. A. 1: *v E 1933*

Willett, E. T. 5: v A 1972 (3); *v In 1974 (2)*

Williams, A. B. 7: v A 1977 (3); *v In 1978 (4)*

Williams, D. 3: v SA 1991 (1); *v A 1992 (2)*

Williams, E. A. V. 4: v E 1947 (3); *v E 1939 (1)*

Williams, S. C. 19: v E 1993 (1); v A 1994 (4); v In 1996 (5); v SL 1996 (2); *v E 1995 (2); v NZ 1994 (2); v In 1994 (3)*

Wishart, K. L. 1: v E 1934

Worrell, F. M. M. 51: v E 1947 (3) 1953 (4) 1959 (4); v A 1954 (4); v In 1952 (5) 1961 (5); *v E 1950 (4) 1957 (5) 1963 (5); v A 1951 (5) 1960 (5); v NZ 1951 (2)*

NEW ZEALAND

Number of Test cricketers: 201

Alabaster, J. C. 21: v E 1962 (2); v WI 1955 (1); v In 1967 (4); *v E 1958 (2); v SA 1961 (5); v WI 1971 (2); v In 1955 (4); v P 1955 (1)*

Allcott, C. F. W. 6: v E 1929 (2); v SA 1931 (1); *v E 1931 (3)*

Allott, G. I. 4: v E 1996 (2); v Z 1995 (2)

Anderson, R. W. 9: v E 1977 (3); *v E 1978 (3); v P 1976 (3)*

Anderson, W. M. 1: v A 1945

Andrews, B. 2: *v A 1973 (2)*

Astle, N. J. 11: v E 1996 (3); v SL 1996 (2); v Z 1995 (2); *v WI 1995 (2); v P 1996 (2)*

Badcock, F. T. 7: v E 1929 (3) 1932 (2); v SA 1931 (2)

Barber, R. T. 1: v WI 1955

Bartlett, G. A. 10: v E 1965 (2); v In 1967 (2); v P 1964 (1); *v SA 1961 (5)*

Barton, P. T. 7: v E 1962 (3); *v SA 1961 (4)*

Beard, D. D. 4: v WI 1951 (2) 1955 (2)

Beck, J. E. F. 8: v WI 1955 (4); *v SA 1953 (4)*

Bell, W. 2: *v SA 1953 (2)*

Bilby, G. P. 2: v E 1965 (2)

Blain, T. E. 11: v A 1992 (2); v P 1993 (3); *v E 1986 (1); v A 1993 (3); v In 1988 (2)*

Blair, R. W. 19: v E 1954 (1) 1958 (2) 1962 (2); v SA 1952 (2) 1963 (3); v WI 1955 (2); *v E 1958 (3); v SA 1953 (4)*

Blunt, R. C. 9: v E 1929 (4); v SA 1931 (2); *v E 1931 (3)*

Bolton, B. A. 2: v E 1958 (2)

Boock, S. L. 30: v E 1977 (3) 1983 (2) 1987 (1); v WI 1979 (3) 1986 (2); v P 1978 (3) 1984 (2) 1988 (1); *v E 1978 (3); v A 1985 (1); v WI 1984 (3); v P 1984 (3); v SL 1983 (3)*

Bracewell, B. P. 6: v P 1978 (1) 1984 (1); *v E 1978 (3); v A 1980 (1)*

Bracewell, J. G. 41: v E 1987 (3); v A 1985 (2) 1989 (1); v WI 1986 (3); v In 1980 (1) 1989 (2); v P 1988 (2); *v E 1983 (4) 1986 (3) 1990 (3); v A 1980 (3) 1985 (2) 1987 (3); v WI 1984 (1); v In 1988 (3); v P 1984 (2); v SL 1983 (2) 1986 (1)*

Bradburn, G. E. 5: v SL 1990 (1); *v P 1990 (3); v SL 1992 (1)*

Bradburn, W. P. 2: v SA 1963 (2)

Brown, V. R. 2: *v A 1985 (2)*

Burgess, M. G. 50: v E 1970 (1) 1977 (3); v A 1973 (1) 1976 (2); v WI 1968 (2); v In 1967 (4) 1975 (3); v P 1972 (3) 1978 (3); *v E 1969 (2) 1973 (3) 1978 (3); v A 1980 (3); v WI 1971 (5); v In 1969 (3) 1976 (3); v P 1969 (3) 1976 (3)*

Burke, C. 1: v A 1945

Burtt, T. B. 10: v E 1946 (1) 1950 (2); v SA 1952 (1); v WI 1951 (2); *v E 1949 (4)*

Butterfield, L. A. 1: v A 1945

Cairns, B. L. 43: v E 1974 (1) 1977 (1) 1983 (3); v A 1976 (1) 1981 (3); v WI 1979 (3); v In 1975 (1) 1980 (3); v P 1978 (3) 1984 (3); v SL 1982 (2); *v E 1978 (2) 1983 (4); v A 1973 (1) 1980 (3) 1985 (1); v WI 1984 (2); v In 1976 (2); v P 1976 (2); v SL 1983 (2)*

Cairns, C. L. 23: v E 1991 (3) 1996 (3); v A 1992 (2); v P 1993 (1) 1995 (1); v SL 1990 (1) 1996 (2); v Z 1995 (2); *v A 1989 (1) 1993 (2); v In 1995 (3); v P 1996 (2)*

Cameron, F. J. 19: v E 1962 (3); v SA 1963 (3); v P 1964 (3); *v E 1965 (2); v SA 1961 (5); v In 1964 (1); v P 1964 (2)*

Cave, H. B. 19: v E 1954 (2); v WI 1955 (3); *v E 1949 (4) 1958 (2); v In 1955 (5); v P 1955 (3)*

Chapple, M. E. 14: v E 1954 (1) 1965 (1); v SA 1952 (1) 1963 (3); v WI 1955 (1); *v SA 1953 (5) 1961 (2)*

Chatfield, E. J. 43: v E 1974 (1) 1977 (1) 1983 (3) 1987 (3); v A 1976 (2) 1981 (1) 1985 (3); v WI 1986 (3); v P 1984 (3) 1988 (2); v SL 1982 (2); *v E 1983 (3) 1986 (1); v A 1985 (2) 1987 (2); v WI 1984 (4); v In 1988 (3); v P 1984 (1); v SL 1983 (2) 1986 (1)*

Cleverley, D. C. 2: v SA 1931 (1); v A 1945 (1)

Collinge, R. O. 35: v E 1970 (2) 1974 (2) 1977 (3); v A 1973 (3); v In 1967 (2) 1975 (3); v P 1964 (3) 1972 (2); *v E 1965 (3) 1969 (1) 1973 (3) 1978 (1); v In 1964 (2) 1976 (1); v P 1964 (2) 1976 (2)*

Colquhoun, I. A. 2: v E 1954 (2)

Coney, J. V. 52: v E 1983 (3) 1987 (2); v A 1973 (2) 1981 (3) 1985 (3); v WI 1979 (3) 1986 (3); v In 1980 (3); v P 1978 (3) 1984 (3); v SL 1982 (2); *v E 1983 (4) 1986 (3); v A 1973 (2) 1980 (2) 1985 (3); v WI 1984 (4); v P 1984 (3); v SL 1983 (3)*

Congdon, B. E. 61: v E 1965 (3) 1970 (2) 1974 (2) 1977 (3); v A 1973 (3) 1976 (2); v WI 1968 (3); v In 1967 (4) 1975 (3); v P 1964 (3) 1972 (3); *v E 1965 (3) 1969 (3) 1973 (3) 1978 (3); v A 1973 (3); v WI 1971 (5); v In 1964 (3) 1969 (3); v P 1964 (1) 1969 (3)*

Cowie, J. 9: v E 1946 (1); v A 1945 (1); *v E 1937 (3) 1949 (4)*

Cresswell G. F. 3: v E 1950 (2); *v E 1949 (1)*

Cromb, I. B. 5: v SA 1931 (2); *v E 1931 (3)*

Crowe, J. J. 39: v E 1983 (3) 1987 (2); v A 1989 (1); v WI 1986 (3); v P 1984 (3) 1988 (2); v SL 1982 (2); *v E 1983 (2) 1986 (3); v A 1985 (3) 1987 (3) 1989 (1); v WI 1984 (4); v P 1984 (3); v SL 1983 (3) 1986 (1)*

Crowe, M. D. 77: v E 1983 (3) 1987 (3) 1991 (3); v A 1981 (3) 1985 (3) 1992 (3); v SA 1994 (1); v WI 1986 (3); v In 1989 (3); v P 1984 (3) 1988 (2); v SL 1990 (2); *v E 1983 (4) 1986 (3) 1990 (3) 1994 (3); v A 1985 (3) 1987 (3) 1989 (1) 1993 (1); v SA 1994 (3); v WI 1984 (4); v In 1995 (3); v P 1984 (3) 1990 (3); v SL 1983 (3) 1986 (1) 1992 (2); v Z 1992 (2)*

Cunis, R. S. 20: v E 1965 (3) 1970 (2); v SA 1963 (1); v WI 1968 (2); *v E 1969 (1); v WI 1971 (5); v In 1969 (3); v P 1969 (3)*

D'Arcy, J. W. 5: *v E 1958 (5)*

Davis, H. T. 4: v E 1996 (1); v SL 1996 (2); *v E 1994 (1)*

de Groen, R. P. 5: v P 1993 (2); *v A 1993 (2); v SA 1994 (1)*

Dempster, C. S. 10: v E 1929 (4) 1932 (2); v SA 1931 (2); *v E 1931 (2)*

Dempster, E. W. 5: v SA 1952 (1); *v SA 1953 (4)*

Dick, A. E. 17: v E 1962 (3); v SA 1963 (2); v P 1964 (2); *v E 1965 (2); v SA 1961 (5); v P 1964 (3)*

Dickinson, G. R. 3: v E 1929 (2); v SA 1931 (1)

Donnelly, M. P. 7: *v E 1937 (3) 1949 (4)*

Doull, S. B. 18: v E 1996 (3); v WI 1994 (3); v P 1993 (3); v SL 1996 (2); *v A 1993 (2); v SA 1994 (3); v P 1996 (2); v Z 1992 (1)*

Dowling, G. T. 39: v E 1962 (3) 1970 (2); v SA 1963 (1); v WI 1968 (3); v In 1967 (4); v P 1964 (2); *v E 1965 (3) 1969 (3); v SA 1961 (4); v WI 1971 (2); v In 1964 (4) 1969 (3); v P 1964 (3) 1969 (3)*

Dunning, J. A. 4: v E 1932 (1); *v E 1937 (3)*

Edgar, B. A. 39: v E 1983 (3); v A 1981 (3) 1985 (3); v WI 1979 (3); v In 1980 (3); v P 1978 (3); v SL 1982 (2); *v E 1978 (3) 1983 (4) 1986 (3); v A 1980 (3) 1985 (3); v P 1984 (3)*

Edwards, G. N. 8: v E 1977 (1); v A 1976 (2); v In 1980 (3); *v E 1978 (2)*

Emery, R. W. G. 2: v WI 1951 (2)

Fisher, F. E. 1: v SA 1952
Fleming, S. P. 27: v E 1996 (3); v SA 1994 (1); v WI 1994 (2); v In 1993 (1); v P 1995 (1); v SL 1994
    (2) 1996 (2); v Z 1995 (2); *v E 1994 (3); SA 1994 (3); v WI 1995 (2); v In 1995 (3); v P 1996 (2)*
Foley, H. 1: v E 1929
Franklin, T. J. 21: v E 1987 (3); v A 1985 (1) 1989 (1); v In 1989 (3); v SL 1990 (3); *v E 1983 (1)*
    1990 (3); v In 1988 (3); v P 1990 (3)
Freeman, D. L. 2: v E 1932 (2)

Gallichan, N. 1: *v E 1937*
Gedye, S. G. 4: v SA 1963 (3); v P 1964 (1)
Germon, L. K. 12: v E 1996 (2); v P 1995 (1); v Z 1995 (2); *v WI 1995 (2); v In 1995 (3); v P 1996 (2)*
Gillespie, S. R. 1: v A 1985
Gray, E. J. 10: *v E 1983 (2) 1986 (3); v A 1987 (1); v In 1988 (1); v P 1984 (2); v SL 1986 (1)*
Greatbatch, M. J. 41: v E 1987 (2) 1991 (1); v A 1989 (1) 1992 (3); v In 1989 (3) 1993 (1); v P 1988 (1)
    1992 (1) 1993 (3); v SL 1990 (2) 1994 (2); *v E 1990 (3) 1994 (1); v A 1989 (1) 1993 (3); v In*
    1988 (3) 1995 (3); v P 1990 (3) 1996 (2); v Z 1992 (2)
Guillen, S. C. 3: v WI 1955 (3)
Guy, J. W. 12: v E 1958 (2); v WI 1955 (2); *v SA 1961 (2); v In 1955 (5); v P 1955 (1)*

Hadlee, D. R. 26: v E 1974 (2) 1977 (1); v A 1973 (3) 1976 (1); v In 1975 (3); v P 1972 (2);
    v E 1969 (2) 1973 (3); v A 1973 (3); v In 1969 (3); v P 1969 (3)
Hadlee, R. J. 86: v E 1977 (3) 1983 (3) 1987 (1); v A 1973 (2) 1976 (2) 1981 (3) 1985 (3) 1989 (1);
    v WI 1979 (3) 1986 (3); v In 1975 (2) 1980 (3) 1989 (3); v P 1972 (1) 1978 (3) 1984 (3) 1988 (2);
    v SL 1982 (2); *v E 1973 (1) 1978 (3) 1983 (4) 1986 (3) 1990 (3); v A 1973 (3) 1980 (3) 1985 (3)*
    1987 (3); v WI 1984 (4); v In 1976 (3) 1988 (3); v P 1976 (3); v SL 1983 (3) 1986 (1)
Hadlee, W. A. 11: v E 1946 (1) 1950 (2); v A 1945 (1); *v E 1937 (3) 1949 (4)*
Harford, N. S. 8: *v E 1958 (4); v In 1955 (2); v P 1955 (2)*
Harford, R. I. 3: v In 1967 (3)
Harris, C. Z. 9: v A 1992 (1); v P 1992 (1); *v A 1993 (1); v WI 1995 (2); v P 1996 (2); v SL 1992 (2)*
Harris, P. G. Z. 9: v P 1964 (1); *v SA 1961 (5); v In 1955 (1); v P 1955 (2)*
Harris, R. M. 2: v E 1958 (2)
Hart, M. N. 14: v SA 1994 (1); v WI 1994 (2); v In 1993 (1); v P 1993 (2); *v E 1994 (3); v SA 1994 (3);*
    v In 1995 (2)
Hartland, B. R. 9: v E 1991 (3); v In 1993 (1); v P 1992 (1) 1993 (1); *v E 1994 (1); v SL 1992 (2)*
Haslam, M. J. 4: *v In 1995 (2); v Z 1992 (2)*
Hastings, B. F. 31: v E 1974 (2); v A 1973 (3); v WI 1968 (3); v In 1975 (1); v P 1972 (3); *v E 1969 (3)*
    1973 (3); v A 1973 (3); v WI 1971 (5); v In 1969 (2); v P 1969 (3)
Hayes, J. A. 15: v E 1950 (2) 1954 (1); v WI 1951 (2); *v E 1958 (4); v In 1955 (5); v P 1955 (1)*
Henderson, M. 1: v E 1929
Horne, M. J. 3: v E 1996 (1); v SL 1996 (2)
Horne, P. A. 4: v WI 1986 (1); *v A 1987 (1); v P 1990 (1); v SL 1986 (1)*
Hough, K. W. 2: v E 1958 (2)
Howarth, G. P. 47: v E 1974 (2) 1977 (3) 1983 (3); v A 1976 (2) 1981 (3); v WI 1979 (3); v In
    1980 (3); v P 1978 (3) 1984 (3); v SL 1982 (2); *v E 1978 (3) 1983 (4); v A 1980 (2); v WI 1984 (4);*
    v In 1976 (2); v P 1976 (2); v SL 1983 (3)
Howarth, H. J. 30: v E 1970 (2) 1974 (2); v A 1973 (3) 1976 (2); v In 1975 (2); v P 1972 (3); *v E*
    1969 (3) 1973 (2); v WI 1971 (5); v In 1969 (3); v P 1969 (3)

James, K. C. 11: v E 1929 (4) 1932 (2); v SA 1931 (2); *v E 1931 (3)*
Jarvis, T. W. 13: v E 1965 (1); v P 1972 (3); *v WI 1971 (4); v In 1964 (2); v P 1964 (3)*
Jones, A. H. 39: v E 1987 (1) 1991 (3); v A 1989 (1) 1992 (3); v WI 1994 (2); v In 1989 (3);
    v P 1988 (2) 1992 (1) 1993 (3); v SL 1990 (3); *v E 1990 (3); v A 1987 (3) 1993 (3); v In 1988 (3);*
    v SL 1986 (1) 1992 (2); v Z 1992 (2)

Kennedy, R. J. 4: v Z 1995 (2); *v WI 1995 (2)*
Kerr, J. L. 7: v E 1932 (2); v SA 1931 (1); *v E 1931 (2) 1937 (2)*
Kuggeleijn, C. M. 2: *v In 1988 (2)*

Larsen, G. R. 8: v SA 1994 (1); v P 1995 (1); v SL 1994 (2); v Z 1995 (1); *v E 1994 (1); v WI 1995 (2)*
Latham, R. T. 4: v E 1991 (1); v P 1992 (1); *v Z 1992 (2)*

Lees, W. K. 21: v E 1977 (2); v A 1976 (1); v WI 1979 (3); v P 1978 (3); v SL 1982 (2); *v E 1983 (2); v A 1980 (2); v In 1976 (3); v P 1976 (3)*

Leggat, I. B. 1: *v SA 1953*

Leggat, J. G. 9: v E 1954 (1); v SA 1952 (1); v WI 1951 (1) 1955 (1); *v In 1955 (3); v P 1955 (2)*

Lissette, A. F. 2: v WI 1955 (2)

Loveridge, G. R. 1: v Z 1995

Lowry, T. C. 7: v E 1929 (4); *v E 1931 (3)*

McEwan, P. E. 4: v WI 1979 (1); *v A 1980 (2); v P 1984 (1)*

MacGibbon, A. R. 26: v E 1950 (2) 1954 (2); v SA 1952 (1); v WI 1955 (3); *v E 1958 (5); v SA 1953 (5); v In 1955 (5); v P 1955 (3)*

McGirr, H. M. 2: v E 1929 (2)

McGregor, S. N. 25: v E 1954 (2) 1958 (2); v SA 1963 (3); v WI 1955 (4); v P 1964 (2); *v SA 1961 (5); v In 1955 (4); v P 1955 (3)*

McLeod E. G. 1: v E 1929

McMahon T. G. 5: v WI 1955 (1); *v In 1955 (3); v P 1955 (1)*

McRae, D. A. N. 1: v A 1945

Matheson, A. M. 2: v E 1929 (1); *v E 1931 (1)*

Meale, T. 2: *v E 1958 (2)*

Merritt, W. E. 6: v E 1929 (4); *v E 1931 (2)*

Meuli, E. M. 1: v SA 1952

Milburn, B. D. 3: v WI 1968 (3)

Miller, L. S. M. 13: v SA 1952 (2); v WI 1955 (3); *v E 1958 (4); v SA 1953 (4)*

Mills, J. E. 7: v E 1929 (3) 1932 (1); *v E 1931 (3)*

Moir, A. M. 17: v E 1950 (2) 1954 (2) 1958 (2); v SA 1952 (1); v WI 1951 (2) 1955 (1); *v E 1958 (2); v In 1955 (2); v P 1955 (3)*

Moloney D. A. R. 3: *v E 1937 (3)*

Mooney, F. L. H. 14: v E 1950 (2); v SA 1952 (2); v WI 1951 (2); *v E 1949 (3); v SA 1953 (5)*

Morgan, R. W. 20: v E 1965 (2) 1970 (2); v WI 1968 (1); v P 1964 (2); *v E 1965 (3); v WI 1971 (3); v In 1964 (4); v P 1964 (3)*

Morrison, B. D. 1: v E 1962

Morrison, D. K. 48: v E 1987 (3) 1991 (3) 1996 (1); v A 1989 (1) 1992 (3); v SA 1994 (1); v WI 1994 (2); v In 1989 (3) 1993 (1); v P 1988 (1) 1992 (1) 1993 (2) 1995 (1); v SL 1990 (3) 1994 (1); *v E 1990 (3); v A 1987 (3) 1989 (1) 1993 (3); v SA 1994 (2); v WI 1995 (2); v In 1988 (1) 1995 (3); v P 1990 (3)*

Morrison, J. F. M. 17: v E 1974 (2); v A 1973 (3) 1981 (3); v In 1975 (3); *v A 1973 (3); v In 1976 (1); v P 1976 (2)*

Motz, R. C. 32: v E 1962 (2) 1965 (3); v SA 1963 (2); v WI 1968 (3); v In 1967 (4); v P 1964 (3); *v E 1965 (3) 1969 (3); v SA 1961 (5); v In 1964 (3); v P 1964 (1)*

Murray, B. A. G. 13: v E 1970 (1); v In 1967 (4); *v E 1969 (2); v In 1969 (3); v P 1969 (3)*

Murray, D. J. 8: v SA 1994 (1); v WI 1994 (2); v SL 1994 (2); *v SA 1994 (3)*

Nash, D. J. 14: v SA 1994 (1); v WI 1994 (1); v In 1993 (1); v P 1995 (1); v SL 1994 (1); *v E 1994 (3); v SA 1994 (1); v In 1995 (3); v SL 1992 (1); v Z 1992 (1)*

Newman J. 3: v E 1932 (2); v SA 1931 (1)

O'Sullivan, D. R. 11: v In 1975 (1); v P 1972 (1); *v A 1973 (3); v In 1976 (3); v P 1976 (3)*

Overton, G. W. F. 3: *v SA 1953 (3)*

Owens, M. B. 8: v A 1992 (2); v P 1992 (1) 1993 (1); *v E 1994 (2); v SL 1992 (2)*

Page, M. L. 14: v E 1929 (4) 1932 (2); v SA 1931 (2); *v E 1931 (3) 1937 (2)*

Parker, J. M. 36: v E 1974 (2) 1977 (3); v A 1973 (3) 1976 (2); v WI 1979 (3); v In 1975 (3); v P 1972 (1) 1978 (2); *v E 1973 (3) 1978 (2); v A 1973 (3) 1980 (3); v In 1976 (3); v P 1976 (3)*

Parker, N. M. 3: *v In 1976 (2); v P 1976 (1)*

Parore, A. C. 34: v E 1991 (1) 1996 (3); v A 1992 (1); v SA 1994 (1); v WI 1994 (2); v In 1993 (1); v P 1992 (1) 1995 (1); v SL 1994 (2) 1996 (2); v Z 1995 (2); *v E 1990 (1) 1994 (3); v SA 1994 (3); v WI 1995 (1); v In 1995 (3); v P 1996 (2); v SL 1992 (2); v Z 1992 (2)*

Patel, D. N. 37: v E 1991 (1) 1996 (2); v A 1992 (3); v SA 1994 (1); v WI 1986 (3); v P 1988 (1) 1992 (1) 1995 (1); v SL 1990 (2) 1994 (1) 1996 (2); v Z 1995 (2); *v A 1987 (3) 1989 (1) 1993 (3); v WI 1995 (1); v P 1990 (3) 1996 (2); v Z 1992 (2)*

Petherick, P. J. 6: v A 1976 (1); *v In 1976 (3); v P 1976 (2)*

Petrie, E. C. 14: v E 1958 (2) 1965 (3); *v E 1958 (5); v In 1955 (2); v P 1955 (2)*

Playle, W. R. 8: v E 1962 (3); *v E 1958 (5)*

Pocock, B. A. 11: v E 1996 (3); v P 1993 (2); v SL 1996 (2); *v E 1994 (1); v A 1993 (3)*

Pollard, V. 32: v E 1965 (3) 1970 (1); v WI 1968 (3); v In 1967 (4); v P 1972 (1); *v E 1965 (3) 1969 (3) 1973 (3); v In 1964 (4) 1969 (1); v P 1964 (3) 1969 (3)*

Poore, M. B. 14: v E 1954 (1); v SA 1952 (1); *v SA 1953 (5); v In 1955 (4); v P 1955 (3)*

Priest, M. W. 1: *v E 1990*

Pringle, C. 14: v E 1991 (1); v In 1993 (1); v P 1993 (1); v SL 1990 (2) 1994 (1); *v E 1994 (2); v SA 1994 (2); v P 1990 (3); v SL 1992 (1)*

Puna, N. 3: v E 1965 (3)

Rabone, G. O. 12: v E 1954 (2); v SA 1952 (1); v WI 1951 (2); *v E 1949 (4); v SA 1953 (3)*

Redmond, R. E. 1: v P 1972

Reid, J. F. 19: v A 1985 (3); v In 1980 (3); v P 1978 (1) 1984 (3); *v A 1985 (3); v P 1984 (3); v SL 1983 (3)*

Reid, J. R. 58: v E 1950 (2) 1954 (2) 1958 (2) 1962 (3); v SA 1952 (3) 1963 (3); v WI 1951 (2) 1955 (4); v P 1964 (3); *v E 1949 (2) 1958 (5) 1965 (3); v SA 1953 (5) 1961 (5); v In 1955 (5) 1964 (4); v P 1955 (3) 1964 (3)*

Roberts, A. D. G. 7: v In 1975 (2); *v In 1976 (3); v P 1976 (2)*

Roberts, A. W. 5: v E 1929 (1); v SA 1931 (2); *v E 1937 (2)*

Robertson, G. K. 1: v A 1985

Rowe, C. G. 1: v A 1945

Rutherford, K. R. 56: v E 1987 (2) 1991 (2); v A 1985 (3) 1989 (1) 1992 (3); v SA 1994 (1); v WI 1986 (2) 1994 (2); v In 1989 (3) 1993 (1); v P 1992 (1) 1993 (3); v SL 1990 (3) 1994 (2); *v E 1986 (1) 1990 (2) 1994 (3); v A 1987 (1) 1993 (3); v SA 1994 (3); v WI 1984 (4); v In 1988 (2); v P 1990 (3); v SL 1986 (1) 1992 (2); v Z 1992 (2)*

Scott, R. H. 1: v E 1946

Scott, V. J. 10: v E 1946 (1) 1950 (2); v A 1945 (1); v WI 1951 (2); *v E 1949 (4)*

Shrimpton, M. J. F. 10: v E 1962 (2) 1965 (3) 1970 (2); v SA 1963 (1); *v A 1973 (2)*

Sinclair, B. W. 21: v E 1962 (3) 1965 (3); v SA 1963 (3); v In 1967 (2); v P 1964 (2); *v E 1965 (3); v In 1964 (2); v P 1964 (3)*

Sinclair, I. M. 2: v WI 1955 (2)

Smith, F. B. 4: v E 1946 (1); v WI 1951 (1); *v E 1949 (2)*

Smith, H. D. 1: v E 1932

Smith, I. D. S. 63: v E 1983 (3) 1987 (3) 1991 (2); v A 1981 (3) 1985 (3) 1989 (1); v WI 1986 (3); v In 1980 (3) 1989 (3); v P 1984 (3) 1988 (2); v SL 1990 (3); *v E 1983 (2) 1986 (2) 1990 (2); v A 1980 (1) 1985 (3) 1987 (3) 1989 (1); v WI 1984 (4); v In 1988 (3); v P 1984 (3) 1990 (3); v SL 1983 (3) 1986 (1)*

Snedden, C. A. 1: v E 1946

Snedden, M. C. 25: v E 1983 (1) 1987 (2); v A 1981 (3) 1989 (1); v WI 1986 (1); v In 1980 (3) 1989 (3); v SL 1982 (2); *v E 1983 (1) 1990 (3); v A 1985 (1) 1987 (1) 1989 (1); v In 1988 (1); v SL 1986 (1)*

Sparling, J. T. 11: v E 1958 (2) 1962 (1); v SA 1963 (2); *v E 1958 (3); v SA 1961 (3)*

Spearman, C. M. 5: v P 1995 (1); v Z 1995 (2); *v WI 1995 (2)*

Stirling, D. A. 6: *v E 1986 (2); v WI 1984 (1); v P 1984 (3)*

Su'a, M. L. 13: v E 1991 (2); v A 1992 (2); v WI 1994 (1); v P 1992 (1); v SL 1994 (1); *v A 1993 (2); v SL 1992 (2); v Z 1992 (2)*

Sutcliffe, B. 42: v E 1946 (1) 1950 (2) 1954 (2) 1958 (2); v SA 1952 (2); v WI 1951 (2) 1955 (2); *v E 1949 (4) 1958 (4) 1965 (1); v SA 1953 (5); v In 1955 (5) 1964 (4); v P 1955 (3) 1964 (3)*

Taylor, B. R. 30: v E 1965 (1); v WI 1968 (3); v In 1967 (3); v P 1972 (3); *v E 1965 (2) 1969 (2) 1973 (3); v WI 1971 (4); v In 1964 (3) 1969 (2); v P 1964 (3) 1969 (1)*

Taylor, D. D. 3: v E 1946 (1); v WI 1955 (2)

Thomson, K. 2: v In 1967 (2)

Thomson, S. A. 19: v E 1991 (1); v WI 1994 (2); v In 1989 (1) 1993 (1); v P 1993 (3); v SL 1990 (2) 1994 (1); *v E 1994 (3); v SA 1994 (3); v In 1995 (2)*

Tindill, E. W. T. 5: v E 1946 (1); v A 1945 (1); *v E 1937 (3)*

Troup, G. B. 15: v A 1981 (2) 1985 (2); v WI 1979 (3); v In 1980 (2); v P 1978 (2); *v A 1980 (2); v WI 1984 (1); v In 1976 (1)*

Truscott, P. B. 1: v P 1964

Turner, G. M. 41: v E 1970 (2) 1974 (2); v A 1973 (3) 1976 (2); v WI 1968 (3); v In 1975 (3); v P 1972 (3); v SL 1982 (2); *v E 1969 (2) 1973 (3); v A 1973 (2); v WI 1971 (5); v In 1969 (3) 1976 (3); v P 1969 (1) 1976 (2)*

Twose, R. G. 7: v P 1995 (1); v Z 1995 (2); *v WI 1995 (2); v In 1995 (2)*

Vance, R. H. 4: v E 1987 (1); v P 1988 (2); *v A 1989 (1)*

Vaughan, J. T. C. 6: v E 1996 (1); *v WI 1995 (2); v P 1996 (2); v SL 1992 (1)*

Vettori, D. L. 4: v E 1996 (2); v SL 1996 (2)

Vivian, G. E. 5: *v WI 1971 (4); v In 1964 (1)*

Vivian, H. G. 7: v E 1932 (1); v SA 1931 (1); *v E 1931 (2) 1937 (3)*

Wadsworth, K. J. 33: v E 1970 (2) 1974 (2); v A 1973 (3); v In 1975 (3); v P 1972 (3); *v E 1969 (3) 1973 (3); v A 1973 (3); v WI 1971 (5); v In 1969 (3); v P 1969 (3)*

Wallace, W. M. 13: v E 1946 (1) 1950 (2); v A 1945 (1); v SA 1952 (2); *v E 1937 (3) 1949 (4)*

Walmsley, K. P. 2: v SL 1994 (2)

Ward, J. T. 8: v SA 1963 (1); v In 1967 (1); v P 1964 (1); *v E 1965 (1); v In 1964 (4)*

Watson, W. 15: v E 1991 (1); v A 1992 (2); v SL 1990 (3); *v E 1986 (2); v A 1989 (1) 1993 (1); v P 1990 (3); v Z 1992 (2)*

Watt, L. 1: v E 1954

Webb, M. G. 3: v E 1970 (1); v A 1973 (1); *v WI 1971 (1)*

Webb, P. N. 2: v WI 1979 (2)

Weir, G. L. 11: v E 1929 (3) 1932 (2); v SA 1931 (2); *v E 1931 (3) 1937 (1)*

White, D. J. 2: *v P 1990 (2)*

Whitelaw, P. E. 2: v E 1932 (2)

Wright, J. G. 82: v E 1977 (3) 1983 (3) 1987 (3) 1991 (3); v A 1981 (3) 1985 (2) 1989 (1) 1992 (3); v WI 1979 (3) 1986 (3); v In 1980 (3) 1989 (3); v P 1978 (3) 1984 (3) 1988 (2); v SL 1982 (2) 1990 (3); *v E 1978 (2) 1983 (3) 1986 (3) 1990 (3); v A 1980 (3) 1985 (3) 1987 (3) 1989 (1); v WI 1984 (4); v In 1988 (3); v P 1984 (3); v SL 1983 (3) 1992 (2)*

Young, B. A. 25: v E 1996 (3); v SA 1994 (1); v WI 1994 (2); v In 1993 (1); v P 1993 (3) 1995 (1); v SL 1994 (2) 1996 (2); *v E 1994 (3); v A 1993 (1); v SA 1994 (3); v In 1995 (1); v P 1996 (2)*

Yuile, B. W. 17: v E 1962 (2); v WI 1968 (3); v In 1967 (1); v P 1964 (3); *v E 1965 (1); v In 1964 (3) 1969 (1); v P 1964 (1) 1969 (2)*

INDIA

Number of Test cricketers: 213

Abid Ali, S. 29: v E 1972 (4); v A 1969 (1); v WI 1974 (2); v NZ 1969 (3); *v E 1971 (3) 1974 (3); v A 1967 (4); v WI 1970 (5); v NZ 1967 (4)*

Adhikari, H. R. 21: v E 1951 (3); v A 1956 (2); v WI 1948 (5) 1958 (1); v P 1952 (2); *v E 1952 (3); v A 1947 (5)*

Amarnath, L. 24: v E 1933 (3) 1951 (3); v WI 1948 (5); v P 1952 (5); *v E 1946 (3); v A 1947 (5)*

Amarnath, M. 69: v E 1976 (2) 1984 (5); v A 1969 (1) 1979 (1) 1986 (3); v WI 1978 (2) 1983 (3) 1987 (3); v NZ 1976 (3); v P 1983 (2) 1986 (5); v SL 1986 (2); *v E 1979 (2) 1986 (2); v A 1977 (5) 1985 (3); v WI 1975 (4) 1982 (5); v NZ 1975 (3); v P 1978 (3) 1982 (6) 1984 (2); v SL 1985 (2)*

Amarnath, S. 10: v WI 1976 (2); *v WI 1975 (2); v NZ 1975 (3); v P 1978 (3)*

Amar Singh 7: v E 1933 (3); *v E 1932 (1) 1936 (3)*

Amir Elahi 1: *v A 1947*

Amre, P. K. 11: v E 1992 (3); v Z 1992 (1); *v SA 1992 (4); v SL 1993 (3)*

Ankola, S. A. 1: *v P 1989*

Apte, A. L. 1: *v E 1959*

Apte, M. L. 7: v P 1952 (2); *v WI 1952 (5)*

Arshad Ayub 13: v WI 1987 (4); v NZ 1988 (3); *v WI 1988 (4); v P 1989 (2)*

Arun, B. 2: v SL 1986 (2)

Arun Lal 16: v WI 1987 (4); v NZ 1988 (3); v P 1986 (1); v SL 1982 (1); *v WI 1988 (4); v P 1982 (3)*

Azad, K. 7: v E 1981 (3); v WI 1983 (2); v P 1983 (1); *v NZ 1980 (1)*

Azharuddin, M. 85: v E 1984 (3) 1992 (3); v A 1986 (3) 1996 (1); v SA 1996 (3); v WI 1987 (3) 1994 (3); v NZ 1988 (3) 1995 (3); v P 1986 (5); v SL 1986 (1) 1990 (1) 1993 (3); v Z 1992 (1); *v E 1986 (3) 1990 (3) 1996 (3); v A 1985 (3) 1991 (5); v SA 1992 (4) 1996 (3); v WI 1988 (3) 1996 (5); v NZ 1989 (3) 1993 (1); v P 1989 (4); v SL 1985 (3) 1993 (3) 1997 (2); v Z 1992 (1)*

Baig, A. A. 10: v A 1959 (3); v WI 1966 (2); v P 1960 (3); *v E 1959 (2)*
Banerjee, S. A. 1: v WI 1948
Banerjee, S. N. 1: v WI 1948
Banerjee, S. T. 1: *v A 1991*
Baqa Jilani, M. 1: *v E 1936*
Bedi, B. S. 67: v E 1972 (5) 1976 (5); v A 1969 (5); v WI 1966 (2) 1974 (4) 1978 (3); v NZ 1969 (3) 1976 (3); *v E 1967 (3) 1971 (3) 1974 (3) 1979 (3); v A 1967 (2) 1977 (5); v WI 1970 (5) 1975 (4); v NZ 1967 (4) 1975 (2); v P 1978 (3)*
Bhandari, P. 3: v A 1956 (1); v NZ 1955 (1); *v P 1954 (1)*
Bhat, A. R. 2: v WI 1983 (1); v P 1983 (1)
Binny, R. M. H. 27: v E 1979 (1); v WI 1983 (6); v P 1979 (6) 1983 (2) 1986 (3); *v E 1986 (3); v A 1980 (1) 1985 (2); v NZ 1980 (1); v P 1984 (1); v SL 1985 (1)*
Borde, C. G. 55: v E 1961 (5) 1963 (5); v A 1959 (5) 1964 (3) 1969 (1); v WI 1958 (4) 1966 (3); v NZ 1964 (4); v P 1960 (5); *v E 1959 (4) 1967 (3); v A 1967 (4); v WI 1961 (5); v NZ 1967 (4)*

Chandrasekhar, B. S. 58: v E 1963 (4) 1972 (5) 1976 (5); v A 1964 (2); v WI 1966 (3) 1974 (4) 1978 (4); v NZ 1964 (2) 1976 (3); *v E 1967 (3) 1971 (3) 1974 (2) 1979 (1); v A 1967 (2) 1977 (5); v WI 1975 (4); v NZ 1975 (3); v P 1978 (3)*
Chauhan, C. P. S. 40: v E 1972 (2); v A 1969 (1) 1979 (6); v WI 1978 (6); v NZ 1969 (2); v P 1979 (6); *v E 1979 (4); v A 1977 (4) 1980 (3); v NZ 1980 (3); v P 1978 (3)*
Chauhan, R. K. 16: v E 1992 (3); v WI 1994 (2); v NZ 1995 (2); v SL 1993 (3); v Z 1992 (1); *v NZ 1993 (1); v SL 1993 (3) 1997 (1)*
Chowdhury, N. R. 2: v E 1951 (1); v WI 1948 (1)
Colah, S. H. M. 2: v E 1933 (1); *v E 1932 (1)*
Contractor, N. J. 31: v E 1961 (5); v A 1956 (1) 1959 (5); v WI 1958 (5); v NZ 1955 (4); v P 1960 (5); *v E 1959 (4); v WI 1961 (2)*

Dani, H. T. 1: v P 1952
Desai, R. B. 28: v E 1961 (4) 1963 (2); v A 1959 (3); v WI 1958 (1); v NZ 1964 (3); v P 1960 (5); *v E 1959 (5); v A 1967 (1); v WI 1961 (3); v NZ 1967 (1)*
Dilawar Hussain 3: v E 1933 (2); *v E 1936 (1)*
Divecha, R. V. 5: v E 1951 (2); v P 1952 (1); *v E 1952 (2)*
Doshi, D. R. 33: v E 1979 (1) 1981 (6); v A 1979 (6); v P 1979 (6) 1983 (1); v SL 1982 (1); *v E 1982 (1); v A 1980 (3); v NZ 1980 (2); v P 1982 (4)*
Dravid, R. 16: v A 1996 (1); v SA 1996 (3); *v E 1996 (2); v SA 1996 (3); v WI 1996 (5); v SL 1997 (2)*
Durani, S. A. 29: v E 1961 (5) 1963 (5) 1972 (3); v A 1959 (1) 1964 (3); v WI 1966 (1); v NZ 1964 (3); *v WI 1961 (5) 1970 (3)*

Engineer, F. M. 46: v E 1961 (4) 1972 (5); v A 1969 (5); v WI 1966 (1) 1974 (5); v NZ 1964 (4) 1969 (2); *v E 1967 (3) 1971 (3) 1974 (3); v A 1967 (4); v WI 1961 (3); v NZ 1967 (4)*

Gadkari, C. V. 6: *v WI 1952 (3); v P 1954 (3)*
Gaekwad, A. D. 40: v E 1976 (4) 1984 (3); v WI 1974 (3) 1978 (5) 1983 (6); v NZ 1976 (3); v P 1983 (3); *v E 1979 (2); v A 1977 (1); v WI 1975 (3) 1982 (5); v P 1984 (2)*
Gaekwad, D. K. 11: v WI 1958 (1); v P 1952 (2) 1960 (2); *v E 1952 (1) 1959 (4); v WI 1952 (2)*
Gaekwad, H. G. 1: v P 1952
Gandotra, A. 2: v A 1969 (1); v NZ 1969 (1)
Ganesh, D. 4: *v SA 1996 (2); v WI 1996 (2)*
Ganguly, S. C. 14: v A 1996 (1); v SA 1996 (2); *v E 1996 (2); v SA 1996 (3); v WI 1996 (4); v SL 1997 (2)*
Gavaskar, S. M. 125: v E 1972 (5) 1976 (5) 1979 (1) 1981 (6) 1984 (5); v A 1979 (6) 1986 (3); v WI 1974 (2) 1978 (6) 1983 (6); v NZ 1976 (3); v P 1979 (6) 1983 (3) 1986 (4); v SL 1982 (1) 1986 (3); *v E 1971 (3) 1974 (3) 1979 (4) 1982 (3) 1986 (3); v A 1977 (5) 1980 (3) 1985 (3); v WI 1970 (4) 1975 (4) 1982 (5); v NZ 1975 (3) 1980 (3); v P 1978 (3) 1982 (6) 1984 (2); v SL 1985 (3)*
Ghavri, K. D. 39: v E 1976 (3) 1979 (1); v A 1979 (6); v WI 1974 (3) 1978 (6); v NZ 1976 (2); v P 1979 (6); *v E 1979 (4); v A 1977 (3) 1980 (3); v NZ 1980 (1); v P 1978 (1)*

Ghorpade, J. M. 8: v A 1956 (1); v WI 1958 (1); v NZ 1955 (1); *v E 1959 (3); v WI 1952 (2)*

Ghulam Ahmed 22: v E 1951 (2); v A 1956 (2); v WI 1948 (3) 1958 (2); v NZ 1955 (1); v P 1952 (4); *v E 1952 (4); v P 1954 (4)*

Gopalan, M. J. 1: v E 1933

Gopinath, C. D. 8: v E 1951 (3); v A 1959 (1); v P 1952 (1); *v E 1952 (1); v P 1954 (2)*

Guard, G. M. 2: v A 1959 (1); v WI 1958 (1)

Guha, S. 4: v A 1969 (3); *v E 1967 (1)*

Gul Mahomed 8: v P 1952 (2); *v E 1946 (1); v A 1947 (5)*

Gupte, B. P. 3: v E 1963 (1); v NZ 1964 (1); v P 1960 (1)

Gupte, S. P. 36: v E 1951 (1) 1961 (2); v A 1956 (3); v WI 1958 (5); v NZ 1955 (5); v P 1952 (2) 1960 (3); *v E 1959 (5); v WI 1952 (5); v P 1954 (5)*

Gursharan Singh 1: *v NZ 1989*

Hafeez, A. 3: *v E 1946 (3)*

Hanumant Singh 14: v E 1963 (2); v A 1964 (3); v WI 1966 (2); v NZ 1964 (4) 1969 (1); *v E 1967 (2)*

Hardikar, M. S. 2: v WI 1958 (2)

Hazare, V. S. 30: v E 1951 (5); v WI 1948 (5); v P 1952 (3); *v E 1946 (3) 1952 (4); v A 1947 (5); v WI 1952 (5)*

Hindlekar, D. D. 4: *v E 1936 (1) 1946 (3)*

Hirwani, N. D. 17: v SA 1996 (2); v WI 1987 (1); v NZ 1988 (3) 1995 (1); v SL 1990 (1); *v E 1990 (3); v WI 1988 (3); v NZ 1989 (3)*

Ibrahim, K. C. 4: v WI 1948 (4)

Indrajitsinhji, K. S. 4: v A 1964 (3); v NZ 1969 (1)

Irani, J. K. 2: *v A 1947 (2)*

Jadeja, A. D. 11: v NZ 1995 (3); *v E 1996 (2); v SA 1992 (3); v WI 1996 (2); v SL 1997 (1)*

Jahangir Khan, M. 4: *v E 1932 (1) 1936 (3)*

Jai, L. P. 1: v E 1933

Jaisimha, M. L. 39: v E 1961 (5) 1963 (5); v A 1959 (1) 1964 (3); v WI 1966 (2); v NZ 1964 (4) 1969 (1); v P 1960 (4); *v E 1959 (1); v A 1967 (2); v WI 1961 (4) 1970 (3); v NZ 1967 (4)*

Jamshedji, R. J. 1: v E 1933

Jayantilal, K. 1: *v WI 1970*

Johnson, D. J. 2: v A 1996 (1); *v SA 1996 (1)*

Joshi, P. G. 12: v E 1951 (2); v A 1959 (1); v WI 1958 (1); v P 1952 (1) 1960 (1); *v E 1959 (3); v WI 1952 (3)*

Joshi, S. B. 9: v A 1996 (1); v SA 1996 (3); *v E 1996 (1); v WI 1996 (4)*

Kambli, V. G. 17: v E 1992 (3); v WI 1994 (3); v NZ 1995 (3); v SL 1993 (3); v Z 1992 (1); *v NZ 1993 (1); v SL 1993 (3)*

Kanitkar, H. S. 2: v WI 1974 (2)

Kapil Dev 131: v E 1979 (1) 1981 (6) 1984 (4) 1992 (3); v A 1979 (6) 1986 (3); v WI 1978 (6) 1983 (6) 1987 (4); v NZ 1988 (3); v P 1979 (6) 1983 (3) 1986 (5); v SL 1982 (1) 1986 (3) 1990 (1) 1993 (3); v Z 1992 (1); *v E 1979 (4) 1982 (3) 1986 (3) 1990 (3); v A 1980 (3) 1985 (3) 1991 (5); v SA 1992 (4); v WI 1982 (5) 1988 (4); v NZ 1980 (3) 1989 (3) 1993 (1); v P 1978 (3) 1982 (6) 1984 (2) 1989 (4); v SL 1985 (3) 1993 (3); v Z 1992 (1)*

Kapoor, A. R. 4: v A 1996 (1); v SA 1996 (1); v WI 1994 (1); v NZ 1995 (1)

Kardar, A. H. (*see* Hafeez)

Kenny, R. B. 5: v A 1959 (4); v WI 1958 (1)

Kirmani, S. M. H. 88: v E 1976 (5) 1979 (1) 1981 (6) 1984 (5); v A 1979 (6); v WI 1978 (6) 1983 (6); v NZ 1976 (3); v P 1979 (6) 1983 (3); v SL 1982 (1); *v E 1982 (3); v A 1977 (5) 1980 (3) 1985 (3); v WI 1975 (4) 1982 (5); v NZ 1975 (3) 1980 (3); v P 1978 (3) 1982 (6) 1984 (2)*

Kischenchand, G. 5: v P 1952 (1); *v A 1947 (4)*

Kripal Singh, A. G. 14: v E 1961 (1) 1963 (2); v A 1956 (2) 1964 (1); v WI 1958 (1); v NZ 1955 (4); *v E 1959 (1)*

Krishnamurthy, P. 5: *v WI 1970 (5)*

Kulkarni, N. M. 1: *v SL 1997*

Kulkarni, R. R. 3: v A 1986 (1); v P 1986 (2)

Kulkarni, U. N. 4: *v A 1967 (3); v NZ 1967 (1)*

Kumar, V. V. 2: v E 1961 (1); v P 1960 (1)

Kumble, A. 40: v E 1992 (3); v A 1996 (1); v SA 1996 (3); v WI 1994 (3); v NZ 1995 (3); v SL 1993 (3); v Z 1992 (1); *v E 1990 (1) 1996 (3); v SA 1992 (4) 1996 (3); v WI 1996 (5); v NZ 1993 (1); v SL 1993 (3) 1997 (2); v Z 1992 (1)*

Kunderan, B. K. 18: v E 1961 (1) 1963 (5); v A 1959 (3); v WI 1966 (2); v NZ 1964 (1); v P 1960 (2); *v E 1967 (2); v WI 1961 (2)*

Kuruvilla, A. 7: *v WI 1996 (5); v SL 1997 (2)*

Lall Singh 1: *v E 1932*

Lamba, R. 4: v WI 1987 (1); v SL 1986 (3)

Laxman, V. V. S. 8: v SA 1996 (2); *v SA 1996 (2); v WI 1996 (4)*

Madan Lal 39: v E 1976 (2) 1981 (6); v WI 1974 (2) 1983 (3); v NZ 1976 (1); v P 1983 (3); v SL 1982 (1); *v E 1974 (2) 1982 (3) 1986 (1); v A 1977 (2); v WI 1975 (4) 1982 (2); v NZ 1975 (3); v P 1982 (3) 1984 (1)*

Maka, E. S. 2: v P 1952 (1); *v WI 1952 (1)*

Malhotra, A. 7: v E 1981 (2) 1984 (1); v WI 1983 (3); *v E 1982 (1)*

Maninder Singh 35: v A 1986 (3); v WI 1983 (4) 1987 (3); v P 1986 (4); v SL 1986 (3); v Z 1992 (1); *v E 1986 (3); v WI 1982 (3); v P 1982 (5) 1984 (1) 1989 (3); v SL 1985 (2)*

Manjrekar, S. V. 37: v SA 1996 (1); v WI 1987 (1) 1994 (3); v NZ 1995 (1); v SL 1990 (1) 1993 (3); *v E 1990 (3) 1996 (2); v A 1991 (5); v SA 1992 (4); v WI 1988 (4); v NZ 1989 (3) 1993 (1); v P 1989 (4); v Z 1992 (1)*

Manjrekar, V. L. 55: v E 1951 (2) 1961 (5) 1963 (4); v A 1956 (3) 1964 (3); v WI 1958 (4); v NZ 1955 (5) 1964 (1); v P 1952 (3) 1960 (5); *v E 1952 (4) 1959 (2); v WI 1952 (4) 1961 (5); v P 1954 (5)*

Mankad, A. V. 22: v E 1976 (1); v A 1969 (5); v WI 1974 (1); v NZ 1969 (2) 1976 (3); *v E 1971 (3) 1974 (1); v A 1977 (3); v WI 1970 (3)*

Mankad, V. 44: v E 1951 (5); v A 1956 (3); v WI 1948 (5) 1958 (2); v NZ 1955 (4); v P 1952 (4); *v E 1946 (3) 1952 (3); v A 1947 (5); v WI 1952 (5); v P 1954 (5)*

Mansur Ali Khan (*see* Pataudi)

Mantri, M. K. 4: v E 1951 (1); *v E 1952 (2); v P 1954 (1)*

Meherhomji, K. R. 1: *v E 1936*

Mehra, V. L. 8: v E 1961 (1) 1963 (2); v NZ 1955 (2); *v WI 1961 (3)*

Merchant, V. M. 10: v E 1933 (3) 1951 (1); *v E 1936 (3) 1946 (3)*

Mhambrey, P. L. 2: *v E 1996 (2)*

Milkha Singh, A. G. 4: v E 1961 (1); v A 1959 (1); v P 1960 (2)

Modi, R. S. 10: v E 1951 (1); v WI 1948 (5); v P 1952 (1); *v E 1946 (3)*

Mohanty, D. S. 1: *v SL 1997*

Mongia, N. R. 27: v A 1996 (1); v SA 1996 (3); v WI 1994 (3); v NZ 1995 (3); v SL 1993 (3); *v E 1996 (3); v SA 1996 (3); v WI 1996 (5); v NZ 1993 (1); v SL 1997 (2)*

More, K. S. 49: v E 1992 (3); v A 1986 (2); v WI 1987 (4); v NZ 1988 (3); v P 1986 (5); v SL 1986 (3) 1990 (1); *v E 1986 (3) 1990 (3); v A 1991 (3); v SA 1992 (4); v WI 1988 (4); v NZ 1989 (3); v P 1989 (4); v SL 1993 (3); v Z 1992 (1)*

Muddiah, V. M. 2: v A 1959 (1); v P 1960 (1)

Mushtaq Ali, S. 11: v E 1933 (2) 1951 (1); v WI 1948 (3); *v E 1936 (3) 1946 (2)*

Nadkarni, R. G. 41: v E 1961 (1) 1963 (5); v A 1959 (5) 1964 (3); v WI 1958 (1) 1966 (1); v NZ 1955 (1) 1964 (4); *v E 1959 (4); v A 1967 (3); v WI 1961 (5); v NZ 1967 (4)*

Naik, S. S. 3: v WI 1974 (2); *v E 1974 (1)*

Naoomal Jeoomal 3: v E 1933 (2); *v E 1932 (1)*

Narasimha Rao, M. V. 4: v A 1979 (2); v WI 1978 (2)

Navle, J. G. 2: v E 1933 (1); *v E 1932 (1)*

Nayak, S. V. 2: *v E 1982 (2)*

Nayudu, C. K. 7: v E 1933 (3); *v E 1932 (1) 1936 (3)*

Nayudu, C. S. 11: v E 1933 (2) 1951 (1); *v E 1936 (2) 1946 (2); v A 1947 (4)*

Nazir Ali, S. 2: v E 1933 (1); *v E 1932 (1)*

Nissar, Mahomed 6: v E 1933 (2); *v E 1932 (1) 1936 (3)*

Nyalchand, S. 1: v P 1952

Pai, A. M. 1: v NZ 1969

Palia, P. E. 2: *v E 1932 (1) 1936 (1)*

Pandit, C. S. 5: v A 1986 (2); *v E 1986 (1); v A 1991 (2)*

Parkar, G. A. 1: *v E 1982*

Parkar, R. D. 2: v E 1972 (2)
Parsana, D. D. 2: v WI 1978 (2)
Patankar, C. T. 1: v NZ 1955
Pataudi sen., Nawab of, 3: *v E 1946 (3)*
Pataudi jun., Nawab of (now Mansur Ali Khan) 46: v E 1961 (3) 1963 (5) 1972 (3); v A 1964 (3) 1969 (5); v WI 1966 (3) 1974 (4); v NZ 1964 (4) 1969 (3); *v E 1967 (3); v A 1967 (3); v WI 1961 (3); v NZ 1967 (4)*
Patel, B. P. 21: v E 1976 (5); v WI 1974 (3); v NZ 1976 (3); *v E 1974 (2); v A 1977 (2); v WI 1975 (3); v NZ 1975 (3)*
Patel, J. M. 7: v A 1956 (2) 1959 (3); v NZ 1955 (1); *v P 1954 (1)*
Patel, R. 1: v NZ 1988
Patiala, Yuvraj of, 1: v E 1933
Patil, S. M. 29: v E 1979 (1) 1981 (4) 1984 (2); v WI 1983 (2); v P 1979 (2) 1983 (3); v SL 1982 (1); *v E 1982 (2); v A 1980 (3); v NZ 1980 (3); v P 1982 (4) 1984 (2)*
Patil, S. R. 1: v NZ 1955
Phadkar, D. G. 31: v E 1951 (4); v A 1956 (1); v WI 1948 (4) 1958 (1); v NZ 1955 (4); v P 1952 (2); *v E 1952 (4); v A 1947 (4); v WI 1952 (4); v P 1954 (3)*
Prabhakar, M. 39: v E 1984 (2) 1992 (3); v WI 1994 (3); v NZ 1995 (3); v SL 1990 (1) 1993 (3); v Z 1992 (1); *v E 1990 (3); v A 1991 (5); v SA 1992 (4); v NZ 1989 (3); v P 1989 (4); v SL 1993 (3); v Z 1992 (1)*
Prasad, B. K. V. 17: v A 1996 (1); v SA 1996 (3); *v E 1996 (3); v SA 1996 (3); v WI 1996 (5); v SL 1997 (2)*
Prasanna, E. A. S. 49: v E 1961 (1) 1972 (3) 1976 (4); v A 1969 (5); v WI 1966 (1) 1974 (5); v NZ 1969 (3); *v E 1967 (3) 1974 (2); v A 1967 (4) 1977 (4); v WI 1961 (1) 1970 (3) 1975 (1); v NZ 1967 (4) 1975 (3); v P 1978 (2)*
Punjabi, P. H. 5: *v P 1954 (5)*

Rai Singh, K. 1: *v A 1947*
Rajinder Pal 1: v E 1963
Rajindernath, V. 1: v P 1952
Rajput, L. S. 2: *v SL 1985 (2)*
Raju, S. L. V. 24: v E 1992 (3); v WI 1994 (3); v NZ 1995 (2); v SL 1990 (1) 1993 (3); *v E 1996 (1); v A 1991 (4); v SA 1992 (2); v NZ 1989 (2) 1993 (1); v SL 1993 (1); v Z 1992 (1)*
Raman, W. V. 11: v SA 1996 (1); v WI 1987 (1); v NZ 1988 (1); *v SA 1992 (1) 1996 (2); v WI 1988 (1); v NZ 1989 (3); v Z 1992 (1)*
Ramaswami, C. 2: *v E 1936 (2)*
Ramchand, G. S. 33: v A 1956 (3) 1959 (5); v WI 1958 (3); v NZ 1955 (5); v P 1952 (3); *v E 1952 (4); v WI 1952 (5); v P 1954 (5)*
Ramji, L. 1: v E 1933
Rangachari, C. R. 4: v WI 1948 (2); *v A 1947 (2)*
Rangnekar, K. M. 3: *v A 1947 (3)*
Ranjane, V. B. 7: v E 1961 (3) 1963 (1); v A 1964 (1); v WI 1958 (1); *v WI 1961 (1)*
Rathore, V. 6: v A 1996 (1); *v E 1996 (3); v SA 1996 (2)*
Razdan, V. 2: *v P 1989 (2)*
Reddy, B. 4: *v E 1979 (4)*
Rege, M. R. 1: v WI 1948
Roy, A. 4: v A 1969 (2); v NZ 1969 (2)
Roy, Pankaj 43: v E 1951 (5); v A 1956 (3) 1959 (5); v WI 1958 (5); v NZ 1955 (3); v P 1952 (3) 1960 (1); *v E 1952 (4) 1959 (5); v WI 1952 (4); v P 1954 (5)*
Roy, Pranab 2: v E 1981 (2)

Sandhu, B. S. 8: v WI 1983 (1); *v WI 1982 (4); v P 1982 (3)*
Sardesai, D. N. 30: v E 1961 (1) 1963 (5) 1972 (1); v A 1964 (3) 1969 (1); v WI 1966 (2); v NZ 1964 (3); *v E 1967 (1) 1971 (3); v A 1967 (2); v WI 1961 (3) 1970 (5)*
Sarwate, C. T. 9: v E 1951 (1); v WI 1948 (2); *v E 1946 (1); v A 1947 (5)*
Saxena, R. C. 1: *v E 1967*
Sekar, T. A. P. 2: *v P 1982 (2)*
Sen, P. 14: v E 1951 (2); v WI 1948 (5); v P 1952 (2); *v E 1952 (2); v A 1947 (3)*
Sen Gupta, A. K. 1: v WI 1958
Sharma, Ajay 1: v WI 1987

Sharma, Chetan 23: v E 1984 (3); v A 1986 (2); v WI 1987 (3); v SL 1986 (2); *v E 1986 (2); v A 1985 (2); v WI 1988 (4); v P 1984 (2); v SL 1985 (3)*

Sharma, Gopal 5: v E 1984 (1); v P 1986 (2); v SL 1990 (1); *v SL 1985 (1)*

Sharma, P. 5: v E 1976 (2); v WI 1974 (2); *v WI 1975 (1)*

Sharma, Sanjeev 2: v NZ 1988 (1); *v E 1990 (1)*

Shastri, R. J. 80: v E 1981 (6) 1984 (5); v A 1986 (3); v WI 1983 (6) 1987 (4); v NZ 1988 (3); v P 1983 (2) 1986 (5); v SL 1986 (3) 1990 (1); *v E 1982 (3) 1986 (3) 1990 (3); v A 1985 (3) 1991 (3); v SA 1992 (3); v WI 1982 (5) 1988 (4); v NZ 1980 (3); v P 1982 (2) 1984 (2) 1989 (4); v SL 1985 (3); v Z 1992 (1)*

Shinde, S. G. 7: v E 1951 (3); v WI 1948 (1); *v E 1946 (1) 1952 (2)*

Shodhan, R. H. 3: v P 1952 (1); *v WI 1952 (2)*

Shukla, R. C. 1: v SL 1982

Sidhu, N. S. 42: v E 1992 (3); v WI 1983 (2) 1994 (3); v NZ 1988 (3) 1995 (2); v SL 1993 (3); v Z 1992 (1); *v E 1990 (3); v A 1991 (3); v WI 1988 (4) 1996 (4); v NZ 1989 (1) 1993 (1); v P 1989 (4); v SL 1993 (3) 1997 (2)*

Sivaramakrishnan, L. 9: v E 1984 (5); *v A 1985 (2); v WI 1982 (1); v SL 1985 (1)*

Sohoni, S. W. 4: v E 1951 (1); *v E 1946 (2); v A 1947 (1)*

Solkar, E. D. 27: v E 1972 (5) 1976 (1); v A 1969 (4); v WI 1974 (4); v NZ 1969 (1); *v E 1971 (3) 1974 (3); v WI 1970 (5) 1975 (1)*

Sood, M. M. 1: v A 1959

Srikkanth, K. 43: v E 1981 (4) 1984 (2); v A 1986 (3); v WI 1987 (4); v NZ 1988 (3); v P 1986 (5); v SL 1986 (3); *v E 1986 (3); v A 1985 (3) 1991 (4); v P 1982 (2) 1989 (4); v SL 1985 (3)*

Srinath, J. 27: v SA 1996 (3); v WI 1994 (3); v NZ 1995 (3); *v E 1996 (3); v A 1991 (5); v SA 1992 (3) 1996 (3); v NZ 1993 (1); v SL 1993 (2); v Z 1992 (1)*

Srinivasan, T. E. 1: *v NZ 1980*

Subramanya, V. 9: v WI 1966 (2); v NZ 1964 (1); *v E 1967 (2); v A 1967 (2); v NZ 1967 (2)*

Sunderram, G. 2: v NZ 1955 (2)

Surendranath, R. 11: v A 1959 (2); v WI 1958 (2); v P 1960 (2); *v E 1959 (5)*

Surti, R. F. 26: v E 1963 (1); v A 1964 (2) 1969 (1); v WI 1966 (2); v NZ 1964 (1) 1969 (2); v P 1960 (2); *v E 1967 (2); v A 1967 (4); v WI 1961 (5); v NZ 1967 (4)*

Swamy, V. N. 1: v NZ 1955

Tamhane, N. S. 21: v A 1956 (3) 1959 (1); v WI 1958 (4); v NZ 1955 (4); v P 1960 (2); *v E 1959 (2); v P 1954 (5)*

Tarapore, K. K. 1: v WI 1948

Tendulkar, S. R. 55: v E 1992 (3); v A 1996 (1); v SA 1996 (3); v WI 1994 (3); v NZ 1995 (3); v SL 1990 (1) 1993 (3); v Z 1992 (1); *v E 1990 (3) 1996 (3); v A 1991 (5); v SA 1992 (4) 1996 (3); v WI 1996 (5); v NZ 1989 (3) 1993 (1); v P 1989 (4); v SL 1993 (3) 1997 (2); v Z 1992 (1)*

Umrigar, P. R. 59: v E 1951 (5) 1961 (4); v A 1956 (3) 1959 (3); v WI 1948 (1) 1958 (5); v NZ 1955 (5); v P 1952 (5) 1960 (5); *v E 1952 (4) 1959 (4); v WI 1952 (5) 1961 (5); v P 1954 (5)*

Vengsarkar, D. B. 116: v E 1976 (1) 1979 (1) 1981 (6) 1984 (5); v A 1979 (6) 1986 (2); v WI 1978 (6) 1983 (5) 1987 (3); v NZ 1988 (3); v P 1979 (5) 1983 (1) 1986 (5); v SL 1982 (1) 1986 (3) 1990 (1); *v E 1979 (4) 1982 (3) 1986 (3) 1990 (3); v A 1977 (5) 1980 (3) 1985 (3) 1991 (5); v WI 1975 (2) 1982 (5) 1988 (4); v NZ 1975 (3) 1980 (3) 1989 (2); v P 1978 (3) 1982 (6) 1984 (2); v SL 1985 (3)*

Venkataraghavan, S. 57: v E 1972 (2) 1976 (1); v A 1969 (5) 1979 (3); v WI 1966 (2) 1974 (2) 1978 (6); v NZ 1964 (4) 1969 (2) 1976 (3); v P 1983 (2); *v E 1967 (1) 1971 (3) 1974 (2) 1979 (4); v A 1977 (1); v WI 1970 (5) 1975 (3) 1982 (5); v NZ 1975 (1)*

Venkataramana, M. 1: *v WI 1988*

Viswanath, G. R. 91: v E 1972 (5) 1976 (5) 1979 (1) 1981 (6); v A 1969 (4) 1979 (6); v WI 1974 (5) 1978 (6); v NZ 1976 (3); v P 1979 (6); v SL 1982 (1); *v E 1971 (3) 1974 (3) 1979 (4) 1982 (3); v A 1977 (5) 1980 (3); v WI 1970 (3) 1975 (4); v NZ 1975 (3) 1980 (3); v P 1978 (3) 1982 (6)*

Viswanath, S. 3: *v SL 1985 (3)*

Vizianagram, Maharaj Kumar of, Sir Vijay A. 3: *v E 1936 (3)*

Wadekar, A. L. 37: v E 1972 (5); v A 1969 (5); v WI 1966 (2); v NZ 1969 (3); *v E 1967 (3) 1971 (3) 1974 (3); v A 1967 (4); v WI 1970 (5); v NZ 1967 (4)*

Wassan, A. S. 4: *v E 1990 (1); v NZ 1989 (3)*

Wazir Ali, S. 7: v E 1933 (3); *v E 1932 (1) 1936 (3)*

Yadav, N. S. 35: v E 1979 (1) 1981 (1) 1984 (4); v A 1979 (5) 1986 (3); v WI 1983 (3); v P 1979 (5) 1986 (4); v SL 1986 (2); *v A 1980 (2) 1985 (3); v NZ 1980 (1); v P 1984 (1)*
Yadav, V. S. 1: v Z 1992
Yajurvindra Singh 4: v E 1976 (2); v A 1979 (1); *v E 1979 (1)*
Yashpal Sharma 37: v E 1979 (1) 1981 (2); v A 1979 (6); v WI 1983 (1); v P 1979 (6) 1983 (3); v SL 1982 (1); *v E 1979 (3) 1982 (3); v A 1980 (3); v WI 1982 (5); v NZ 1980 (1); v P 1982 (2)*
Yograj Singh 1: *v NZ 1980*

Note: Hafeez, on going later to Oxford University, took his correct name, Kardar.

PAKISTAN

Number of Test cricketers: 144

Aamer Malik 14: v E 1987 (2); v A 1988 (1) 1994 (1); v WI 1990 (1); v In 1989 (4); *v A 1989 (2); v WI 1987 (1); v NZ 1988 (2)*
Aamir Nazir 6: v SL 1995 (1); *v SA 1994 (1); v WI 1992 (1); v NZ 1993 (1); v Z 1994 (2)*
Aamir Sohail 34: v A 1994 (3); v SL 1995 (3); v Z 1993 (3) 1996 (2); *v E 1992 (5) 1996 (2); v A 1995 (3); v SA 1994 (1); v WI 1992 (2); v NZ 1992 (1) 1993 (3) 1995 (1); v SL 1994 (2); v Z 1994 (3)*
Abdul Kadir 4: v A 1964 (1); *v A 1964 (1); v NZ 1964 (2)*
Abdul Qadir 67: v E 1977 (3) 1983 (3) 1987 (3); v A 1982 (3) 1988 (3); v WI 1980 (2) 1986 (3) 1990 (2); v NZ 1984 (3) 1990 (2); v In 1982 (5) 1984 (1) 1989 (4); v SL 1985 (3); *v E 1982 (3) 1987 (4); v A 1983 (5); v WI 1987 (3); v NZ 1984 (2) 1988 (2); v In 1979 (3) 1986 (3); v SL 1985 (2)*
Afaq Hussain 2: v E 1961 (1); *v A 1964 (1)*
Aftab Baloch 2: v WI 1974 (1); v NZ 1969 (1)
Aftab Gul 6: v E 1968 (2); v NZ 1969 (1); *v E 1971 (3)*
Agha Saadat Ali 1: v NZ 1955
Agha Zahid 1: v WI 1974
Akram Raza 9: v A 1994 (2); v WI 1990 (1); v In 1989 (1); v SL 1991 (1); *v NZ 1993 (2); v SL 1994 (1); v Z 1994 (1)*
Alim-ud-Din 25: v E 1961 (2); v A 1956 (1) 1959 (1); v WI 1958 (1); v NZ 1955 (1); v In 1954 (5); *v E 1954 (3) 1962 (3); v WI 1957 (5); v In 1960 (1)*
Amir Elahi 5: *v In 1952 (5)*
Anil Dalpat 9: v E 1983 (3); v NZ 1984 (3); *v NZ 1984 (3)*
Anwar Hussain 4: *v In 1952 (4)*
Anwar Khan 1: *v NZ 1978*
Aqib Javed 21: v A 1994 (1); v NZ 1990 (3); v SL 1991 (3) 1995 (3); *v E 1992 (5); v A 1989 (1); v SA 1994 (1); v NZ 1988 (1) 1992 (1); v Z 1994 (2)*
Arif Butt 3: *v A 1964 (1); v NZ 1964 (2)*
Ashfaq Ahmed 1: v Z 1993
Ashraf Ali 8: v E 1987 (3); v In 1984 (2); v SL 1981 (2) 1985 (1)
Asif Iqbal 58: v E 1968 (3) 1972 (3); v A 1964 (1); v WI 1974 (2); v NZ 1964 (3) 1969 (3) 1976 (3); v In 1978 (3); *v E 1967 (3) 1971 (3) 1974 (3); v A 1964 (1) 1972 (3) 1976 (3) 1978 (2); v WI 1976 (5); v NZ 1964 (3) 1972 (3) 1978 (2); v In 1979 (6)*
Asif Masood 16: v E 1968 (2) 1972 (1); v WI 1974 (2); v NZ 1969 (1); *v E 1971 (3) 1974 (3); v A 1972 (3) 1976 (1)*
Asif Mujtaba 25: v E 1987 (1); v WI 1986 (2); v Z 1993 (3); *v E 1992 (5) 1996 (2); v SA 1994 (1); v WI 1992 (3); v NZ 1992 (1) 1993 (2); v SL 1994 (2) 1996 (2); v Z 1994 (1)*
Ata-ur-Rehman 13: v SL 1995 (1); v Z 1993 (3); *v E 1992 (1) 1996 (2); v WI 1992 (3); v NZ 1993 (2) 1995 (1)*
Atif Rauf 1: *v NZ 1993*
Azam Khan 1: v Z 1996
Azeem Hafeez 18: v E 1983 (2); v NZ 1984 (3); v In 1984 (2); *v A 1983 (5); v NZ 1984 (3); v In 1983 (3)*
Azhar Khan 1: v A 1979
Azmat Rana 1: v A 1979

Basit Ali 19: v A 1994 (2); v SL 1995 (1); v Z 1993 (3); *v A 1995 (3); v WI 1992 (3); v NZ 1993 (3) 1995 (1); v SL 1994 (2); v Z 1994 (1)*

Burki, J. 25: v E 1961 (3); v A 1964 (1); v NZ 1964 (3) 1969 (1); *v E 1962 (5) 1967 (3); v A 1964 (1); v NZ 1964 (3); v In 1960 (5)*

D'Souza, A. 6: v E 1961 (2); v WI 1958 (1); *v E 1962 (3)*

Ehtesham-ud-Din 5: v A 1979 (1); *v E 1982 (1); v In 1979 (3)*

Farooq Hamid 1: *v A 1964*
Farrukh Zaman 1: v NZ 1976
Fazal Mahmood 34: v E 1961 (1); v A 1956 (1) 1959 (2); v WI 1958 (3); v NZ 1955 (2); v In 1954 (4); *v E 1954 (4) 1962 (2); v WI 1957 (5); v In 1952 (5) 1960 (5)*

Ghazali, M. E. Z. 2: *v E 1954 (2)*
Ghulam Abbas 1: *v E 1967*
Gul Mahomed 1: v A 1956

Hanif Mohammad 55: v E 1961 (3) 1968 (3); v A 1956 (1) 1959 (1) 1964 (1); v WI 1958 (1); v NZ 1955 (3) 1964 (3) 1969 (1); v In 1954 (5); *v E 1954 (4) 1962 (5) 1967 (3); v A 1964 (1); v WI 1957 (5); v NZ 1964 (3); v In 1952 (5) 1960 (5)*
Haroon Rashid 23: v E 1977 (3); v A 1979 (2) 1982 (3); v In 1982 (1); v SL 1981 (2); *v E 1978 (3) 1982 (1); v A 1976 (1) 1978 (1); v WI 1976 (5); v NZ 1978 (1)*
Hasan Raza 1: v Z 1996
Haseeb Ahsan 12: v E 1961 (2); v A 1959 (1); v WI 1958 (1); *v WI 1957 (3); v In 1960 (5)*

Ibadulla, K. 4: v A 1964 (1); *v E 1967 (2); v NZ 1964 (1)*
Ijaz Ahmed, sen. 36: v E 1987 (3); v A 1988 (3) 1994 (1); v WI 1990 (3); v NZ 1996 (2); v Z 1996 (2); *v E 1987 (4) 1996 (3); v A 1989 (3) 1995 (2); v SA 1994 (1); v WI 1987 (2); v NZ 1995 (1); v In 1986 (1); v SL 1996 (2); v Z 1994 (3)*
Ijaz Ahmed, jun. 2: v SL 1995 (2)
Ijaz Butt 8: v A 1959 (2); v WI 1958 (3); *v E 1962 (3)*
Ijaz Faqih 5: v WI 1980 (1); *v A 1981 (1); v WI 1987 (2); v In 1986 (1)*
Imran Khan 88: v A 1979 (2) 1982 (3); v WI 1980 (4) 1986 (3) 1990 (3); v NZ 1976 (3); v In 1978 (3) 1982 (6) 1989 (4); v SL 1981 (1) 1985 (3) 1991 (3); *v E 1971 (1) 1974 (3) 1982 (3) 1987 (5); v A 1976 (3) 1978 (2) 1981 (3) 1983 (2) 1989 (3); v WI 1976 (5) 1987 (3); v NZ 1978 (2) 1988 (2); v In 1979 (5) 1986 (5); v SL 1985 (3)*
Imtiaz Ahmed 41: v E 1961 (3); v A 1956 (1) 1959 (3); v WI 1958 (3); v NZ 1955 (3); v In 1954 (5); *v E 1954 (4) 1962 (4); v WI 1957 (5); v In 1952 (5) 1960 (5)*
Intikhab Alam 47: v E 1961 (2) 1968 (3) 1972 (3); v A 1959 (1) 1964 (1); v WI 1974 (2); v NZ 1964 (3) 1969 (3) 1976 (3); *v E 1962 (3) 1967 (3) 1971 (3) 1974 (3); v A 1964 (1) 1972 (3); v WI 1976 (1); v NZ 1964 (3) 1972 (3); v In 1960 (3)*
Inzamam-ul-Haq 37: v A 1994 (3); v NZ 1996 (2); v SL 1995 (3); v Z 1993 (3); *v E 1992 (4) 1996 (3); v A 1995 (3); v SA 1994 (1); v WI 1992 (3); v NZ 1992 (1) 1993 (3) 1995 (1); v SL 1994 (2) 1996 (2); v Z 1994 (3)*
Iqbal Qasim 50: v E 1977 (3) 1987 (3); v A 1979 (3) 1982 (2) 1988 (3); v WI 1980 (4); v NZ 1984 (3); v In 1978 (3) 1982 (2); v SL 1981 (3); *v E 1978 (3); v A 1976 (3) 1981 (2); v WI 1976 (2); v NZ 1984 (1); v In 1979 (6) 1983 (1) 1986 (3)*
Israr Ali 4: v A 1959 (2); *v In 1952 (2)*

Jalal-ud-Din 6: v A 1982 (1); v In 1982 (2) 1984 (2); v SL 1985 (1)
Javed Akhtar 1: *v E 1962*
Javed Miandad 124: v E 1977 (3) 1987 (3); v A 1979 (3) 1982 (3) 1988 (3); v WI 1980 (4) 1986 (3) 1990 (2); v NZ 1976 (3) 1984 (3) 1990 (3); v In 1978 (3) 1982 (6) 1984 (2) 1989 (4); v SL 1981 (3) 1985 (3) 1991 (3); v Z 1993 (3); *v E 1978 (3) 1982 (3) 1987 (5) 1992 (5); v A 1976 (3) 1978 (2) 1981 (3) 1983 (5) 1989 (3); v WI 1987 (1) 1992 (3); v NZ 1978 (3) 1984 (3) 1988 (2) 1992 (1); v In 1979 (6) 1983 (3) 1986 (4); v SL 1985 (3)*

Kabir Khan 4: *v SA 1994 (1); v SL 1994 (1); v Z 1994 (2)*
Kardar, A. H. 23: v A 1956 (1); v NZ 1955 (1); v In 1954 (5); *v E 1954 (4); v WI 1957 (5); v In 1952 (5)*
Khalid Hassan 1: *v E 1954*
Khalid Wazir 2: *v E 1954 (2)*

Khan Mohammad 13: v A 1956 (1); v NZ 1955 (3); v In 1954 (4); *v E 1954 (2); v WI 1957 (2); v In 1952 (1)*

Liaqat Ali 5: v E 1977 (2); v WI 1974 (1); *v E 1978 (2)*

Mahmood Hussain 27: v E 1961 (1); v WI 1958 (3); v NZ 1955 (1); v In 1954 (5); *v E 1954 (2) 1962 (3); v WI 1957 (3); v In 1952 (4) 1960 (5)*

Majid Khan 63: v E 1968 (3) 1972 (3); v A 1964 (1) 1979 (3); v WI 1974 (2) 1980 (4); v NZ 1964 (3) 1976 (3); v In 1978 (3) 1982 (1); v SL 1981 (1); *v E 1967 (3) 1971 (2) 1974 (3) 1982 (1); v A 1972 (3) 1976 (3) 1978 (2) 1981 (3); v WI 1976 (5); v NZ 1972 (3) 1978 (2); v In 1979 (6)*

Mansoor Akhtar 19: v A 1982 (3); v WI 1980 (2); v In 1982 (3); v SL 1981 (1); *v E 1982 (3) 1987 (5); v A 1981 (1) 1989 (1)*

Manzoor Elahi 6: v NZ 1984 (1); v In 1984 (1); *v In 1986 (2); v Z 1994 (2)*

Maqsood Ahmed 16: v NZ 1955 (2); v In 1954 (5); *v E 1954 (4); v In 1952 (5)*

Masood Anwar 1: v WI 1990

Mathias, Wallis 21: v E 1961 (1); v A 1956 (1) 1959 (2); v WI 1958 (3); v NZ 1955 (1); *v E 1962 (3); v WI 1957 (5); v In 1960 (5)*

Miran Bux 2: v In 1954 (2)

Mohammad Akram 6: v NZ 1996 (1); v SL 1995 (2); *v E 1996 (1); v A 1995 (2)*

Mohammad Aslam 1: *v E 1954*

Mohammad Farooq 7: v NZ 1964 (3); *v E 1962 (2); v In 1960 (2)*

Mohammad Hussain 1: v Z 1996 (1)

Mohammad Ilyas 10: v E 1968 (2); v NZ 1964 (3); *v E 1967 (1); v A 1964 (1); v NZ 1964 (3)*

Mohammad Munaf 4: v E 1961 (2); v A 1959 (2)

Mohammad Nazir 14: v E 1972 (1); v WI 1980 (4); v NZ 1969 (3); *v A 1983 (3); v In 1983 (3)*

Mohammad Wasim 2: v NZ 1996 (2)

Mohammad Zahid 3: v NZ 1996 (1); *v SL 1996 (2)*

Mohsin Kamal 9: v E 1983 (1); v A 1994 (2); v SL 1985 (1); *v E 1987 (4); v SL 1985 (1)*

Mohsin Khan 48: v E 1977 (1) 1983 (3); v A 1982 (3); v WI 1986 (3); v NZ 1984 (2); v In 1982 (6) 1984 (2); v SL 1981 (2) 1985 (2); *v E 1978 (3) 1982 (3); v A 1978 (1) 1981 (2) 1983 (5); v NZ 1978 (1) 1984 (3); v In 1983 (3); v SL 1985 (3)*

Moin Khan 26: v A 1994 (1); v WI 1990 (2); v NZ 1996 (2); v SL 1991 (3) 1995 (3); v Z 1996 (2); *v E 1992 (4) 1996 (2); v A 1995 (2); v SA 1994 (1); v WI 1992 (2); v SL 1996 (2)*

Mudassar Nazar 76: v E 1977 (3) 1983 (1) 1987 (3); v A 1979 (3) 1982 (3) 1988 (3); v WI 1986 (2); v NZ 1984 (3); v In 1978 (2) 1982 (6) 1984 (2); v SL 1981 (1) 1985 (3) ; *v E 1978 (3) 1982 (3) 1987 (5); v A 1976 (1) 1978 (1) 1981 (3) 1983 (5); v WI 1987 (3); v NZ 1978 (1) 1984 (3) 1988 (2); v In 1979 (5) 1983 (3); v SL 1985 (3)*

Mufasir-ul-Haq 1: *v NZ 1964*

Munir Malik 3: v A 1959 (1); *v E 1962 (2)*

Mushtaq Ahmed 28: v A 1994 (3); v WI 1990 (2); v NZ 1996 (2); v Z 1993 (2); *v E 1992 (5) 1996 (3); v A 1989 (1) 1995 (2); v WI 1992 (1); v NZ 1992 (1) 1993 (1) 1995 (1); v SL 1994 (2) 1996 (2)*

Mushtaq Mohammad 57: v E 1961 (3) 1968 (3) 1972 (3); v WI 1958 (1) 1974 (2); v NZ 1969 (3) 1976 (3); v In 1978 (3); *v E 1962 (5) 1967 (3) 1971 (3) 1974 (3); v A 1972 (3) 1976 (3) 1978 (2); v WI 1976 (5); v NZ 1972 (2) 1978 (3); v In 1960 (5)*

Nadeem Abbasi 3: v In 1989 (3)

Nadeem Ghauri 1: *v A 1989*

Nadeem Khan 1: *v WI 1992*

Nasim-ul-Ghani 29: v E 1961 (2); v A 1959 (2) 1964 (1); v WI 1958 (3); *v E 1962 (5) 1967 (2); v A 1964 (1) 1972 (1); v WI 1957 (5); v NZ 1964 (3); v In 1960 (4)*

Naushad Ali 6: v NZ 1964 (3); *v NZ 1964 (3)*

Naved Anjum 2: v NZ 1990 (1); v In 1989 (1)

Nazar Mohammad 5: *v In 1952 (5)*

Nazir Junior (*see* Mohammad Nazir)

Niaz Ahmed 2: v E 1968 (1); *v E 1967 (1)*

Pervez Sajjad 19: v E 1968 (1) 1972 (2); v A 1964 (1); v NZ 1964 (3) 1969 (3); *v E 1971 (3); v NZ 1964 (3) 1972 (3)*

Qasim Omar 26: v E 1983 (3); v WI 1986 (3); v NZ 1984 (3); v In 1984 (2); v SL 1985 (3); *v A 1983 (5); v NZ 1984 (3); v In 1983 (1); v SL 1985 (3)*

Ramiz Raja 57: v E 1983 (2) 1987 (3); v A 1988 (3); v WI 1986 (3) 1990 (2); v In 1989 (4); v SL 1985 (1) 1991 (3) 1995 (3); *v E 1987 (2) 1992 (5); v A 1989 (2) 1995 (3); v WI 1987 (3) 1992 (3); v NZ 1992 (1) 1995 (1); v In 1986 (5); v SL 1985 (3) 1996 (2)*

Rashid Khan 4: v SL 1981 (2); *v A 1983 (1); v NZ 1984 (1)*

Rashid Latif 19: v A 1994 (2); v Z 1993 (3); *v E 1992 (1) 1996 (1); v A 1995 (1); v WI 1992 (1) 1993 (3) 1995 (1); v SL 1994 (2); v Z 1994 (3)*

Rehman, S. F. 1: *v WI 1957*

Rizwan-uz-Zaman 11: v WI 1986 (1); v SL 1981 (2); *v A 1981 (1); v NZ 1988 (2); v In 1986 (5)*

Sadiq Mohammad 41: v E 1972 (3) 1977 (2); v WI 1974 (1) 1980 (3); v NZ 1969 (3) 1976 (3); v In 1978 (1); *v E 1971 (3) 1974 (3) 1978 (3); v A 1972 (3) 1976 (2); v WI 1976 (5); v NZ 1972 (3); v In 1979 (3)*

Saeed Ahmed 41: v E 1961 (3) 1968 (3); v A 1959 (3) 1964 (1); v WI 1958 (3); v NZ 1964 (3); *v E 1962 (5) 1967 (3) 1971 (1); v A 1964 (1) 1972 (2); v WI 1957 (5); v NZ 1964 (3); v In 1960 (5)*

Saeed Anwar 21: v A 1994 (2); v WI 1990 (1); v NZ 1996 (2); v SL 1995 (2); v Z 1996 (2); *v E 1996 (3); v SA 1994 (1); v NZ 1993 (1); v SL 1994 (2); v Z 1994 (2)*

Salah-ud-Din 5: v E 1968 (1); v NZ 1964 (3) 1969 (1)

Saleem Jaffer 14: v E 1987 (1); v A 1988 (2); v WI 1986 (1); v NZ 1990 (1); v In 1989 (1); v SL 1991 (2); *v WI 1987 (1); v NZ 1988 (2); v In 1986 (2)*

Salim Altaf 21: v E 1972 (3); v NZ 1969 (2); v In 1978 (1); *v E 1967 (2) 1971 (2); v A 1972 (3) 1976 (2); v WI 1976 (3); v NZ 1972 (3)*

Salim Elahi 4: *v A 1995 (2); v SL 1996 (2)*

Salim Malik 96: v E 1983 (3) 1987 (3); v A 1988 (3) 1994 (3); v WI 1986 (1) 1990 (3); v NZ 1984 (3) 1990 (3) 1996 (2); v In 1982 (6) 1984 (2) 1989 (4); v SL 1981 (2) 1985 (3) 1991 (3); v Z 1996 (2); *v E 1987 (5) 1992 (5) 1996 (3); v A 1983 (3) 1989 (1) 1995 (2); v SA 1994 (1); v WI 1987 (3); v NZ 1984 (3) 1988 (2) 1992 (1) 1993 (3) 1995 (1); v In 1983 (3) 1986 (5); v SL 1985 (3) 1994 (2) 1996 (2); v Z 1994 (3)*

Salim Yousuf 32: v A 1988 (3); v WI 1986 (3) 1990 (1); v NZ 1990 (1); v In 1989 (1); v SL 1981 (1) 1985 (2); *v E 1987 (5); v A 1989 (3); v WI 1987 (3); v NZ 1988 (2); v In 1986 (5)*

Saqlain Mushtaq 9: v NZ 1996 (1); v SL 1995 (2); v Z 1996 (2); *v A 1995 (2); v SL 1996 (2)*

Sarfraz Nawaz 55: v E 1968 (1) 1972 (2) 1977 (2) 1983 (3); v A 1979 (3); v WI 1974 (2) 1980 (2); v NZ 1976 (3); v In 1978 (3) 1982 (6); *v E 1974 (3) 1978 (2) 1982 (1); v A 1972 (2) 1976 (2) 1978 (2) 1981 (3) 1983 (3); v WI 1976 (4); v NZ 1972 (3) 1978 (3)*

Shadab Kabir 3: v NZ 1996 (1); *v E 1996 (2)*

Shafiq Ahmed 6: v E 1977 (3); v WI 1980 (2); *v E 1974 (1)*

Shafqat Rana 5: v E 1968 (2); v A 1964 (1); v NZ 1969 (2)

Shahid Israr 1: v NZ 1976

Shahid Mahboob 1: v In 1989

Shahid Mahmood 1: *v E 1962*

Shahid Nazir 6: v NZ 1996 (2); v Z 1996 (2); *v SL 1996 (2)*

Shahid Saeed 1: v In 1989

Shakeel Ahmed 3: *v WI 1992 (1); v Z 1994 (2)*

Sharpe, D. 3: v A 1959 (3)

Shoaib Mohammad 45: v E 1983 (1) 1987 (1); v A 1988 (3); v WI 1990 (3); v NZ 1984 (1) 1990 (3); v In 1989 (4); v SL 1985 (1) 1991 (3) 1995 (3); v Z 1993 (3); *v E 1987 (4) 1992 (1); v A 1989 (3); v WI 1987 (3); v NZ 1984 (1) 1988 (2); v In 1983 (2) 1986 (3)*

Shuja-ud-Din 19: v E 1961 (2); v A 1959 (3); v WI 1958 (3); v NZ 1955 (3); v In 1954 (5); *v E 1954 (3)*

Sikander Bakht 26: v E 1977 (2); v WI 1980 (1); v NZ 1976 (1); v In 1978 (2) 1982 (1); *v E 1978 (3) 1982 (2); v A 1978 (2) 1981 (3); v WI 1976 (1); v NZ 1978 (3); v In 1979 (5)*

Tahir Naqqash 15: v A 1982 (3); v In 1982 (2); v SL 1981 (3); *v E 1982 (2); v A 1983 (1); v NZ 1984 (1); v In 1983 (3)*

Talat Ali 10: v E 1972 (3); *v E 1978 (2); v A 1972 (1); v NZ 1972 (1) 1978 (3)*

Taslim Arif 6: v A 1979 (3); v WI 1980 (2); *v In 1979 (1)*

Tauseef Ahmed 34: v E 1983 (2) 1987 (2); v A 1979 (3) 1988 (3); v WI 1986 (3); v NZ 1984 (1) 1990 (2); v In 1984 (1); v SL 1981 (3) 1985 (1); v Z 1993 (1); *v E 1987 (2); v A 1989 (3); v NZ 1988 (1); v In 1986 (4); v SL 1985 (2)*

Waqar Hassan 21: v A 1956 (1) 1959 (1); v WI 1958 (1); v NZ 1955 (3); v In 1954 (5); *v E 1954 (4); v WI 1957 (1); v In 1952 (5)*

Waqar Younis 44: v A 1994 (2); v WI 1990 (3); v NZ 1990 (3) 1996 (1); v In 1989 (2); v SL 1991 (3) 1995 (1); v Z 1993 (3) 1996 (2); *v E 1992 (5) 1996 (3); v A 1989 (3) 1995 (3); v WI 1992 (3); v NZ 1992 (1) 1993 (3) 1995 (1); v SL 1994 (2)*

Wasim Akram 72: v E 1987 (2); v A 1994 (2); v WI 1986 (2) 1990 (3); v NZ 1990 (2); v In 1989 (4); v SL 1985 (3) 1991 (3) 1995 (2); v Z 1993 (2) 1996 (2); *v E 1987 (5) 1992 (4) 1996 (3); v A 1989 (3) 1995 (3); v SA 1994 (1); v WI 1987 (3) 1992 (3); v NZ 1984 (2) 1992 (1) 1993 (3) 1995 (1); v In 1986 (5); v SL 1985 (3) 1994 (2); v Z 1994 (3)*

Wasim Bari 81: v E 1968 (3) 1972 (3) 1977 (3); v A 1982 (3); v WI 1974 (2) 1980 (2); v NZ 1969 (3) 1976 (2); v In 1978 (3) 1982 (6); *v E 1967 (3) 1971 (3) 1974 (3) 1978 (3) 1982 (3); v A 1972 (3) 1976 (3) 1978 (2) 1981 (3) 1983 (5); v WI 1976 (5); v NZ 1972 (3) 1978 (3); v In 1979 (6) 1983 (3)*

Wasim Raja 57: v E 1972 (1) 1977 (3) 1983 (3); v A 1979 (3); v WI 1974 (2) 1980 (4); v NZ 1976 (1) 1984 (1); v In 1982 (1) 1984 (1); v SL 1981 (3); *v E 1974 (2) 1978 (3) 1982 (1); v A 1978 (1) 1981 (3) 1983 (2); v WI 1976 (5); v NZ 1972 (3) 1978 (3) 1984 (2); v In 1979 (6) 1983 (3)*

Wazir Mohammad 20: v A 1956 (1) 1959 (1); v WI 1958 (3); v NZ 1955 (2); v In 1954 (5); *v E 1954 (2); v WI 1957 (5); v In 1952 (1)*

Younis Ahmed 4: v NZ 1969 (2); *v In 1986 (1)*

Zaheer Abbas 78: v E 1972 (2) 1983 (3); v A 1979 (2) 1982 (3); v WI 1974 (2) 1980 (3); v NZ 1969 (1) 1976 (3) 1984 (3); v In 1978 (3) 1982 (6) 1984 (2); v SL 1981 (1) 1985 (2); *v E 1971 (3) 1974 (3) 1982 (3); v A 1972 (3) 1976 (3) 1978 (2) 1981 (2) 1983 (5); v WI 1976 (3); v NZ 1972 (3) 1978 (2) 1984 (2); v In 1979 (5) 1983 (3)*

Zahid Fazal 9: v A 1994 (2); v WI 1990 (3); v SL 1991 (3) 1995 (1)

Zahoor Elahi 2: v NZ 1996 (2)

Zakir Khan 2: v In 1989 (1); *v SL 1985 (1)*

Zulfiqar Ahmed 9: v A 1956 (1); v NZ 1955 (3); *v E 1954 (2); v In 1952 (3)*

Zulqarnain 3: *v SL 1985 (3)*

SRI LANKA

Number of Test cricketers: 69

Ahangama, F. S. 3: v In 1985 (3)

Amalean, K. N. 2: v P 1985 (1); *v A 1987 (1)*

Amerasinghe, A. M. J. G. 2: v NZ 1983 (2)

Anurasiri, S. D. 17: v A 1992 (3); v WI 1993 (1); v NZ 1986 (1) 1992 (2); v P 1985 (2); *v E 1991 (1); v In 1986 (1) 1993 (3); v P 1991 (3)*

Arnold, R. P. 3: v P 1996 (2); *v WI 1996 (1)*

Atapattu, M. S. 9: v A 1992 (1); v In 1997 (2); v P 1996 (2); *v WI 1996 (1); v NZ 1996 (1); v In 1990 (1) 1993 (1)*

Dassanayake, P. B. 11: v SA 1993 (3); v WI 1993 (1); v P 1994 (2); *v In 1993 (3); v Z 1994 (2)*

de Alwis, R. G. 11: v A 1982 (1); v NZ 1983 (3); v P 1985 (2); *v A 1987 (1); v NZ 1982 (1); v In 1986 (3)*

de Mel, A. L. F. 17: v E 1981 (1); v A 1982 (1); v In 1985 (3); v P 1985 (3); *v E 1984 (1); v In 1982 (1) 1986 (1); v P 1981 (3) 1985 (3)*

de Silva, A. M. 3: v E 1992 (1); v In 1993 (2)

de Silva, D. S. 12: v E 1981 (1); v A 1982 (1); v NZ 1983 (3); *v E 1984 (1); v NZ 1982 (2); v In 1982 (1); v P 1981 (3)*

de Silva, E. A. R. 10: v In 1985 (1); v P 1985 (1); *v A 1989 (2); v NZ 1990 (3); v In 1986 (3)*

de Silva, G. R. A. 4: v E 1981 (1); *v In 1982 (1); v P 1981 (2)*

de Silva, K. S. C. 5: v In 1997 (1); v P 1996 (1); *v WI 1996 (2); v NZ 1996 (1)*

de Silva, P. A. 63: v E 1992 (1); v A 1992 (3); v SA 1993 (3); v WI 1993 (1); v NZ 1992 (2); v In 1985 (3) 1993 (3) 1997 (2); v P 1985 (3) 1994 (2) 1996 (2); v Z 1996 (2); *v E 1984 (1) 1988 (1) 1991 (1); v A 1987 (1) 1989 (2) 1995 (3); v WI 1996 (2); v NZ 1990 (3) 1994 (2) 1996 (2); v In 1986 (3) 1990 (1) 1993 (3); v P 1985 (3) 1991 (3) 1995 (2); v Z 1994 (3)*

Dharmasena, H. D. P. K. 15: v SA 1993 (2); v P 1994 (2) 1996 (1); v Z 1996 (1); *v A 1995 (2); v WI 1996 (2); v NZ 1996 (1); v P 1995 (2); v Z 1994 (2)*

Dias, R. L. 20: v E 1981 (1); v A 1982 (1); v NZ 1983 (2) 1986 (1); v In 1985 (3); v P 1985 (1); *v E 1984 (1); v In 1982 (1) 1986 (3); v P 1981 (3) 1985 (3)*
Dunusinghe, C. I. 5: *v NZ 1994 (2); v P 1995 (3)*

Fernando, E. R. N. S. 5: v A 1982 (1); v NZ 1983 (2); *v NZ 1982 (2)*

Goonatillake, H. M. 5: v E 1981 (1); *v In 1982 (1); v P 1981 (3)*
Gunasekera, Y. 2: *v NZ 1982 (2)*
Guneratne, R. P. W. 1: v A 1982
Gurusinha, A. P. 41: v E 1992 (1); v A 1992 (3); v SA 1993 (1); v NZ 1986 (1) 1992 (2); v In 1993 (3); v P 1985 (2) 1994 (1); v Z 1996 (2); *v E 1991 (1); v A 1989 (2) 1995 (3); v NZ 1990 (3) 1994 (2); v In 1986 (3) 1990 (1); v P 1985 (1) 1991 (3) 1995 (3); v Z 1994 (3)*

Hathurusinghe, U. C. 24: v E 1992 (1); v A 1992 (3); v SA 1993 (3); v NZ 1992 (2); v In 1993 (3); *v E 1991 (1); v A 1995 (3); v NZ 1990 (2); v P 1991 (3) 1995 (3)*

Jayasekera, R. S. A. 1: *v P 1981*
Jayasuriya S. T. 27: v E 1992 (1); v A 1992 (2); v SA 1993 (2); v WI 1993 (1); v In 1993 (1) 1997 (2); v P 1994 (1) 1996 (2); v Z 1996 (2); *v E 1991 (1); v A 1995 (1); v WI 1996 (2); v NZ 1990 (2) 1996 (2); v In 1993 (1); v P 1991 (3); v Z 1994 (1)*
Jayawardene, D. R. M. 2: v In 1997 (2)
Jeganathan, S. 2: *v NZ 1982 (2)*
John, V. B. 6: v NZ 1983 (3); *v E 1984 (1); v NZ 1982 (2)*
Jurangpathy, B. R. 2: v In 1985 (1); *v In 1986 (1)*

Kalpage, R. S. 9: v SA 1993 (1); v WI 1993 (1); v In 1993 (1); v P 1994 (1) 1996 (1); *v In 1993 (3); v Z 1994 (1)*
Kaluperuma, L. W. 2: v E 1981 (1); *v P 1981 (1)*
Kaluperuma, S. M. S. 4: v NZ 1983 (3); *v A 1987 (1)*
Kaluwitharana, R. S. 16: v A 1992 (2); v In 1993 (1) 1997 (2); v P 1996 (2); v Z 1996 (2); *v A 1995 (3) v WI 1996 (2); v NZ 1996 (2)*
Kuruppu, D. S. B. P. 4: v NZ 1986 (1); *v E 1988 (1) 1991 (1); v A 1987 (1)*
Kuruppuarachchi, A. K. 2: v NZ 1986 (1); v P 1985 (1)

Labrooy, G. F. 9: *v E 1988 (1); v A 1987 (1) 1989 (2); v NZ 1990 (3); v In 1986 (1) 1990 (1)*
Liyanage, D. K. 8: v A 1992 (2); v SA 1993 (1); v NZ 1992 (2); v In 1993 (2); *v In 1993 (1)*

Madugalle, R. S. 21: v E 1981 (1); v A 1982 (1); v NZ 1983 (3) 1986 (1); v In 1985 (3); *v E 1984 (1) 1988 (1); v A 1987 (1); v NZ 1982 (2); v In 1982 (1); v P 1981 (3) 1985 (3)*
Madurasinghe, A. W. R. 3: v A 1992 (1); *v E 1988 (1); v In 1990 (1)*
Mahanama, R. S. 45: v E 1992 (1); v A 1992 (3); v SA 1993 (3); v WI 1993 (1); v NZ 1986 (1) 1992 (2); v In 1993 (3) 1997 (2); v P 1985 (2) 1994 (2); v Z 1996 (2); *v E 1991 (1); v A 1987 (1) 1989 (2) 1995 (2); v WI 1996 (2); v NZ 1990 (1) 1996 (2); v In 1990 (1) 1993 (3); v P 1991 (2) 1995 (3); v Z 1994 (2)*
Mendis, L. R. D. 24: v E 1981 (1); v A 1982 (1); v NZ 1983 (3) 1986 (1); v In 1985 (3); v P 1985 (3); *v E 1984 (1) 1988 (1); v In 1982 (1) 1986 (3); v P 1981 (3) 1985 (3)*
Muralitharan, M. 32: v E 1992 (1); v A 1992 (2); v SA 1993 (3); v WI 1993 (1); v NZ 1992 (1); v In 1993 (2) 1997 (2); v P 1994 (1) 1996 (1); v Z 1996 (2); *v A 1995 (2); v WI 1996 (2); v NZ 1994 (2) 1996 (2); v In 1993 (3); v P 1995 (3); v Z 1994 (2)*

Pushpakumara, K. R. 12: v In 1997 (2); v P 1994 (1); v Z 1996 (1); *v A 1995 (1); v WI 1996 (2); v NZ 1994 (2); v P 1995 (1); v Z 1994 (2)*

Ramanayake, C. P. H. 18: v E 1992 (1); v A 1992 (3); v SA 1993 (2); v NZ 1992 (1); v In 1993 (1); *v E 1988 (1) 1991 (1); v A 1987 (1) 1989 (2); v NZ 1990 (3); v P 1991 (2)*
Ranasinghe, A. N. 2: *v In 1982 (1); v P 1981 (1)*
Ranatunga, A. 71: v E 1981 (1) 1992 (1); v A 1982 (1) 1992 (3); v SA 1993 (3); v WI 1993 (1); v NZ 1983 (3) 1986 (1) 1992 (2); v In 1985 (3) 1993 (3) 1997 (2); v P 1985 (3) 1994 (2) 1996 (2); v Z 1996 (2); *v E 1984 (1) 1988 (1); v A 1987 (1) 1989 (2) 1995 (2); v WI 1996 (2); v NZ 1990 (3) 1994 (2) 1996 (2); v In 1982 (1) 1986 (3) 1990 (1) 1993 (3); v P 1981 (2) 1985 (3) 1991 (3) 1995 (3); v Z 1994 (3)*

Ranatunga, D. 2: *v A 1989 (2)*
Ranatunga, S. 9: v P 1994 (1); *v A 1995 (1); v WI 1996 (1); v NZ 1994 (2); v P 1995 (1); v Z 1994 (3)*
Ratnayake, R. J. 23: v A 1982 (1); v NZ 1983 (1) 1986 (1); v In 1985 (3); v P 1985 (1); *v E 1991 (1); v A 1981 (1); v NZ 1982 (2) 1990 (3); v In 1986 (2) 1990 (1); v P 1985 (3) 1991 (3)*
Ratnayeke, J. R. 22: v NZ 1983 (2) 1986 (1); v P 1985 (3); *v E 1984 (1) 1988 (1); v A 1987 (1) 1989 (2); v NZ 1982 (2); v In 1982 (1) 1986 (3); v P 1981 (2) 1985 (3)*

Samarasekera, M. A. R. 4: *v E 1988 (1); v A 1989 (1); v In 1990 (1); v P 1991 (1)*
Samaraweera, D. P. 7: v WI 1993 (1); v P 1994 (1); *v NZ 1994 (2); v In 1993 (3)*
Senanayake, C. P. 3: *v NZ 1990 (3)*
Silva, K. J. 5: v In 1997 (1); v P 1996 (1); v Z 1996 (2); *v A 1995 (1)*
Silva, S. A. R. 9: v In 1985 (3); v P 1985 (1); *v E 1984 (1) 1988 (1); v NZ 1982 (1); v P 1985 (2)*

Tillekeratne, H. P. 43: v E 1992 (1); v A 1992 (1); v SA 1993 (3); v WI 1993 (1); v NZ 1992 (2); v In 1993 (1) v P 1994 (2) 1996 (2); v Z 1996 (2); *v E 1991 (1); v A 1989 (1) 1995 (3); v WI 1996 (1); v NZ 1990 (3) 1994 (2) 1996 (2); v In 1990 (1) 1993 (3); v P 1991 (3) 1995 (3); v Z 1994 (3)*

Vaas, W. P. U. J. C. 20: v In 1997 (2); v P 1994 (1) 1996 (2); v Z 1996 (2); *v A 1995 (3); v NZ 1994 (2) 1996 (2); v P 1995 (3); v Z 1994 (3)*

Warnapura, B. 4: v E 1981 (1); *v In 1982 (1); v P 1981 (2)*
Warnaweera, K. P. J. 10: v E 1992 (1); v NZ 1992 (2); v In 1993 (3); v P 1985 (1) 1994 (1); *v NZ 1990 (1); v In 1990 (1)*
Weerasinghe, C. D. U. S. 1: v In 1985
Wettimuny, M. D. 2: *v NZ 1982 (2)*
Wettimuny, S. 23: v E 1981 (1); v A 1982 (1); v NZ 1983 (3); v In 1985 (3); v P 1985 (3); *v E 1984 (1); v NZ 1982 (2); v In 1986 (3); v P 1981 (3) 1985 (3)*
Wickremasinghe, A. G. D. 3: v NZ 1992 (2); *v A 1989 (1)*
Wickremasinghe, G. P. 24: v A 1992 (1); v SA 1993 (2); v WI 1993 (1); v In 1993 (2); v P 1994 (1); *v A 1995 (3); v NZ 1994 (2) 1996 (1); v In 1993 (3); v P 1991 (3) 1995 (3); v Z 1994 (2)*
Wijegunawardene, K. I. W. 2: *v E 1991 (1); v P 1991 (1)*
Wijesuriya, R. G. C. E. 4: *v P 1981 (1) 1985 (3)*
Wijetunge, P. K. 1: v SA 1993

Zoysa, D. N. T. 3: v P 1996 (1); *v NZ 1996 (2)*

ZIMBABWE

Number of Test cricketers: 34

Arnott, K. J. 4: v NZ 1992 (2); v In 1992 (1); *v In 1992 (1)*
Brain, D. H. 9: v NZ 1992 (1); v P 1994 (3); v SL 1994 (2); *v In 1992 (1); v P 1993 (2)*
Brandes, E. A. 9: v E 1996 (1); v NZ 1992 (1); v In 1992 (1); *v NZ 1995 (2); v In 1992 (1); v P 1993 (3)*
Briant, G. A. 1: *v In 1992*
Bruk-Jackson, G. K. 2: *v P 1993 (2)*
Burmester, M. G. 3: v NZ 1992 (2); v In 1992 (1)
Butchart, I. P. 1: v P 1994
Campbell, A. D. R. 22: v E 1996 (2); v SA 1995 (1); v NZ 1992 (2); v In 1992 (1); v P 1994 (3); v SL 1994 (3); *v NZ 1995 (2); v In 1992 (1); v P 1993 (3) 1996 (2); v SL 1996 (2)*
Carlisle, S. V. 6: v E 1996 (1); v P 1994 (3); *v NZ 1995 (2)*
Crocker, G. J. 3: v NZ 1992 (2); v In 1992 (1)
Dekker, M. H. 14: v E 1996 (1); v SA 1995 (1); v P 1994 (2); v SL 1994 (3); *v P 1993 (3) 1996 (2); v SL 1996 (2)*
Evans, C. N. 1: *v SL 1996*

Flower, A. 22: v E 1996 (2); v SA 1995 (1); v NZ 1992 (2); v In 1992 (1); v P 1994 (3); v SL 1994 (3); *v NZ 1995 (2); v In 1992 (1); v P 1993 (3) 1996 (2); v SL 1996 (2)*

Flower, G. W. 22: v E 1996 (2); v SA 1995 (1); v NZ 1992 (2); v In 1992 (1); v P 1994 (3); v SL 1994 (3); *v NZ 1995 (2); v In 1992 (1); v P 1993 (3) 1996 (2); v SL 1996 (2)*

Houghton, D. L. 20: v E 1996 (2); v SA 1995 (1); v NZ 1992 (2); v In 1992 (1); v P 1994 (3); v SL 1994 (3); *v NZ 1995 (2); v In 1992 (1); v P 1993 (3) 1996 (2)*

James, W. R. 4: v SL 1994 (3); *v P 1993 (1)*

Jarvis, M. P. 5: v NZ 1992 (1); v In 1992 (1); v SL 1994 (3)

Lock, A. C. I. 1: v SA 1995

Matambanadzo, E. 1: *v P 1996*

Mbangwa, M. 1: *v P 1996*

Olonga, H. K. 7: v E 1996 (2); v P 1994 (1); *v NZ 1995 (1); v P 1996 (1); v SL 1996 (2)*

Peall, S. G. 4: v SL 1994 (2); *v P 1993 (2)*

Pycroft, A. J. 3: v NZ 1992 (2); v In 1992 (1)

Ranchod, U. 1: *v In 1992*

Rennie, J. A. 3: v SL 1994 (1); *v P 1993 (2)*

Shah, A. H. 3: v NZ 1992 (1); *v In 1992 (1); v SL 1996 (1)*

Strang, B. C. 9: v E 1996 (1); v SA 1995 (1); v P 1994 (2); *v NZ 1995 (2); v P 1996 (2); v SL 1996 (1)*

Strang, P. A. 13: v E 1996 (2); v SA 1995 (1); v P 1994 (3); v SL 1994 (1); *v NZ 1995 (2); v P 1996 (2); v SL 1996 (2)*

Streak, H. H. 15: v E 1996 (2); v SA 1995 (1); v P 1994 (3); v SL 1994 (3); *v NZ 1995 (2); v P 1993 (3); v SL 1996 (1)*

Traicos, A. J. 4: v NZ 1992 (2); v In 1992 (1); *v In 1992 (1)*

Waller, A. C. 2: v E 1996 (2)

Whittall, A. R. 3: *v P 1996 (1); v SL 1996 (2)*

Whittall, G. J. 18: v E 1996 (2); v SA 1995 (1); v P 1994 (3); v SL 1994 (3); *v NZ 1995 (2); v P 1993 (3) 1996 (2); v SL 1996 (2)*

Wishart, C. B. 6: v SA 1995 (1); *v NZ 1995 (1); v P 1996 (2); v SL 1996 (2)*

TWO COUNTRIES

Fourteen cricketers have appeared for two countries in Test matches, namely:

Amir Elahi, *India and Pakistan.*
J. J. Ferris, *Australia and England.*
S. C. Guillen, *West Indies and NZ.*
Gul Mahomed, *India and Pakistan.*
F. Hearne, *England and South Africa.*
A. H. Kardar, *India and Pakistan.*
W. E. Midwinter, *England and Australia.*

F. Mitchell, *England and South Africa.*
W. L. Murdoch, *Australia and England.*
Nawab of Pataudi, sen., *England and India.*
A. J. Traicos, *South Africa and Zimbabwe.*
A. E. Trott, *Australia and England.*
K. C. Wessels, *Australia and South Africa.*
S. M. J. Woods, *Australia and England.*

ENGLAND v REST OF THE WORLD

In 1970, owing to the cancellation of the South African tour to England, a series of matches was arranged, with the trappings of a full Test series, between England and the Rest of the World. It was played for the Guinness Trophy.

The following were awarded England caps for playing against the Rest of the World in that series, although the five matches played are now generally considered not to have rated as full Tests: D. L. Amiss (1), G. Boycott (2), D. J. Brown (2), M. C. Cowdrey (4), M. H. Denness (1), B. L. D'Oliveira (4), J. H. Edrich (2), K. W. R. Fletcher (4), A. W. Greig (3), R. Illingworth (5), A. Jones (1), A. P. E. Knott (5), P. Lever (1), B. W. Luckhurst (5), C. M. Old (2), P. J. Sharpe (1), K. Shuttleworth (1), J. A. Snow (5), D. L. Underwood (4), A. Ward (1), D. Wilson (2).

The following players represented the Rest of the World: E. J. Barlow (5), F. M. Engineer (2), L. R. Gibbs (5), Intikhab Alam (5), R. B. Kanhai (5), C. H. Lloyd (5), G. D. McKenzie (3), D. L. Murray (3), Mushtaq Mohammad (2), P. M. Pollock (1), R. G. Pollock (5), M. J. Procter (5), B. A. Richards (5), G. S. Sobers (5).

LIMITED-OVERS INTERNATIONAL CRICKETERS

The following players have appeared for Test-playing countries in limited-overs internationals but had not represented their countries in Test matches by September 21, 1997:

England A. D. Brown, A. F. Giles, I. J. Gould, G. W. Humpage, T. E. Jesty, G. D. Lloyd, J. D. Love, M. A. Lynch, M. J. Smith, N. M. K. Smith, S. D. Udal, C. M. Wells.

Australia G. A. Bishop, A. C. Dale, M. J. Di Venuto, A. C. Gilchrist, S. F. Graf, S. Lee, D. S. Lehmann, R. J. McCurdy, K. H. MacLeay, G. D. Porter, G. R. Robertson, J. D. Siddons, A. M. Stuart, G. S. Trimble, A. K. Zesers.

South Africa N. Boje, R. E. Bryson, D. J. Callaghan, D. N. Crookes, L. J. Koen, G. F. J. Liebenberg, S. J. Palframan, C. E. B. Rice, M. J. R. Rindel, D. B. Rundle, T. G. Shaw, E. O. Simons, E. L. R. Stewart, P. J. R. Steyn, C. J. P. G. van Zyl, M. Yachad.

West Indies H. A. G. Anthony, B. St A. Browne, V. C. Drakes, R. S. Gabriel, R. C. Haynes, R. D. Jacobs, N. A. M. McLean, M. R. Pydanna, D. Ramnarine, P. A. Wallace, L. R. Williams.

New Zealand B. R. Blair, P. G. Coman, M. W. Douglas, B. G. Hadlee, R. T. Hart, R. L. Hayes, B. J. McKechnie, C. D. McMillan, E. B. McSweeney, J. P. Millmow, S. B. O'Connor, A. J. Penn, R. G. Petrie, R. B. Reid, S. J. Roberts, L. W. Stott, R. J. Webb, J. W. Wilson.

G. R. Larsen appeared for New Zealand in 55 limited-overs internationals before making his Test debut.

India A. C. Bedade, Bhupinder Singh, sen., G. Bose, V. B. Chandrasekhar, U. Chatterjee, N. David, P. Dharmani, R. S. Ghai, S. S. Karim, S. C. Khanna, S. P. Mukherjee, A. K. Patel, Randhir Singh, R. P. Singh, R. R. Singh, H. S. Sodhi, S. Somasunder, Sudhakar Rao, P. S. Vaidya.

Pakistan Aamer Hameed, Aamer Hanif, Abdur Razzaq, Arshad Khan, Arshad Pervez, Azhar Mahmood, Ghulam Ali, Haafiz Shahid, Hasan Jamil, Iqbal Sikandar, Irfan Bhatti, Javed Qadir, Mahmood Hamid, Mansoor Rana, Maqsood Rana, Masood Iqbal, Moin-ul-Atiq, Mujahid Jamshed, Naeem Ahmed, Naeem Ashraf, Naseer Malik, Parvez Mir, Saadat Ali, Saeed Azad, Sajid Ali, Sajjad Akbar, Salim Pervez, Shahid Afridi, Shahid Anwar, Shakil Khan, Sohail Fazal, Tanvir Mehdi, Wasim Haider, Zafar Iqbal, Zahid Ahmed.

Sri Lanka U. D. U. Chandana, D. L. S. de Silva, G. N. de Silva, S. K. L. de Silva, E. R. Fernando, T. L. Fernando, U. N. K. Fernando, J. C. Gamage, F. R. M. Goonatillake, A. A. W. Gunawardene, P. D. Heyn, S. A. Jayasinghe, S. H. U. Karnain, C. Mendis, A. M. N. Munasinghe, A. R. M. Opatha, S. P. Pasqual, K. G. Perera, H. S. M. Pieris, S. K. Ranasinghe, N. Ranatunga, N. L. K. Ratnayake, A. P. B. Tennekoon, M. H. Tissera, K. E. A. Upashantha, D. M. Vonhagt, A. P. Weerakkody, S. R. de S. Wettimuny, R. P. A. H. Wickremaratne.

Zimbabwe G. B. Brent, R. D. Brown, K. M. Curran, S. G. Davies, K. G. Duers, E. A. Essop-Adam, D. A. G. Fletcher, J. G. Heron, V. R. Hogg, G. C. Martin, M. A. Meman, G. A. Paterson, G. E. Peckover, P. W. E. Rawson, G. J. Rennie, D. P. Viljoen.

BIRTHS AND DEATHS OF CRICKETERS

The qualifications for inclusion are as follows:

1. All players who have appeared in a Test match.

2. All players who have appeared in a one-day international for a Test-match playing country and are no longer playing first-class cricket.

3. County players who appeared in 200 or more first-class matches during their careers, or 100 after the Second World War and are no longer playing first-class cricket.

4. English county captains who captained their county in three seasons or more since 1890 and are no longer playing first-class cricket.

5. All *Wisden* Cricketers of the Year, including the Public Schoolboys chosen for the 1918 and 1919 Almanacks. Cricketers of the Year are identified by the italic notation *CY* and year of appearance. A list of the Cricketers of the Year from 1889 to 1998 appears on pages 172-174.

6. Players or personalities not otherwise qualified who are thought to be of sufficient interest to merit inclusion.

Details of current leading first-class players who are not Test cricketers or *Wisden* Cricketers of the Year are no longer listed in this section but may be found in the Register of Players on pages 153-171.

Key to abbreviations and symbols

CU – Cambridge University, OU – Oxford University.

Australian states: NSW – New South Wales, Qld – Queensland, S. Aust. – South Australia, Tas. – Tasmania, Vic. – Victoria, W. Aust. – Western Australia.

Indian teams: Eur. – Europeans, Guj. – Gujarat, H'bad – Hyderabad, H. Pradesh – Himachal Pradesh, Ind. Rlwys – Indian Railways, Ind. Serv. – Indian Services, J/K – Jammu and Kashmir, Karn. – Karnataka (Mysore to 1972-73), M. Pradesh – Madhya Pradesh (Central India [C. Ind.] to 1939-40, Holkar to 1954-55, Madhya Bharat to 1956-57), M'tra – Maharashtra, Naw. – Nawanagar, Raja. – Rajasthan, S'tra – Saurashtra (West India [W. Ind.] to 1945-46, Kathiawar to 1949-50), S. Punjab – Southern Punjab (Patiala to 1958-59, Punjab since 1968-69), TC – Travancore-Cochin (Kerala since 1956-57), TN – Tamil Nadu (Madras to 1959-60), U. Pradesh – Uttar Pradesh (United Provinces [U. Prov.] to 1948-49), Vidarbha (CP & Berar to 1949-50, Madhya Pradesh to 1956-57).

New Zealand provinces: Auck. – Auckland, Cant. – Canterbury, C. Dist. – Central Districts, N. Dist. – Northern Districts, Wgtn – Wellington.

Pakistani teams: ADBP – Agricultural Development Bank of Pakistan, B'pur – Bahawalpur, Customs – Pakistan Customs, F'bad – Faisalabad, HBFC – House Building Finance Corporation, HBL – Habib Bank Ltd, I'bad – Islamabad, IDBP – Industrial Development Bank of Pakistan, Kar. – Karachi, MCB – Muslim Commercial Bank, NBP – National Bank of Pakistan, NWFP – North-West Frontier Province, PACO – Pakistan Automobile Corporation, Pak. Rlwys – Pakistan Railways, Pak. Us – Pakistan Universities, PIA – Pakistan International Airlines, PNSC – Pakistan National Shipping Corporation, PWD – Public Works Department, R'pindi – Rawalpindi, UBL – United Bank Ltd, WAPDA – Water and Power Development Authority.

South African provinces: E. Prov. – Eastern Province, E. Tvl – Eastern Transvaal (Easterns since 1995-96), Griq. W. – Griqualand West, N. Tvl – Northern Transvaal, NE Tvl – North-Eastern Transvaal, OFS – Orange Free State (Free State [FS] since 1995-96), Rhod. – Rhodesia, Tvl – Transvaal, W. Prov. – Western Province, W. Tvl – Western Transvaal (North West since 1995-96).

Sri Lankan teams: Ant. – Antonians, Bloom. – Bloomfield Cricket and Athletic Club, BRC – Burgher Recreation Club, CCC – Colombo Cricket Club, Mor. – Moratuwa Sports Club, NCC – Nondescripts Cricket Club, Pan. – Panadura Sports Club, Seb. – Sebastianites, SLAF – Air Force, SSC – Sinhalese Sports Club, TU – Tamil Union Cricket and Athletic Club, Under-23 – Board Under-23 XI, WPC – Western Province (City), WPN – Western Province (North), WPS – Western Province (South).

West Indies islands: B'dos – Barbados, BG – British Guiana (Guyana since 1966), Comb. Is. – Combined Islands, Jam. – Jamaica, T/T – Trinidad & Tobago.

Zimbabwean teams: Mash. – Mashonaland, Mat. – Matabeleland, MCD – Mashonaland Country Districts, Under-24 – Mashonaland Under-24, Zimb. – Zimbabwe.

* Denotes Test player. ** Denotes appeared for two countries. There is a list of Test players country by country from page 53.
† Denotes also played for team under its previous name.

Aamer Hameed (Pak. Us, Lahore, Punjab & OU) b Oct. 18, 1954
*Aamer Malik (ADBP, PIA, Multan & Lahore) b Jan. 3, 1963
*Aamir Nazir (I'bad, Lahore & Allied Bank) b Jan. 2, 1971
*Aamir Sohail (HBL, Sargodha, Lahore & Allied Bank) b Sept. 14, 1966
Abberley, R. N. (Warwicks) b April 22, 1944
*a'Beckett, E. L. (Vic.) b Aug. 11, 1907, d June 2, 1989
*Abdul Kadir (Kar. & NBP) b May 10, 1944
*Abdul Qadir (HBL, Lahore & Punjab) b Sept. 15, 1955
*Abel, R. (Surrey; *CY 1890*) b Nov. 30, 1857, d Dec. 10, 1936
*Abid Ali, S. (H'bad) b Sept. 9, 1941
Abrahams, J. (Lancs) b July 21, 1952
*Absolom, C. A. (CU & Kent) b June 7, 1846, d July 30, 1889
Acfield, D. L. (CU & Essex) b July 24, 1947
*Achong, E. (T/T) b Feb. 16, 1904, d Aug. 29, 1986
Ackerman, H. M. (Border, NE Tvl, Northants, Natal & W. Prov.) b April 28, 1947
Adam, Sir Ronald, 2nd Bt (Pres. MCC 1946-47) b Oct. 30, 1885, d Dec. 26, 1982
*Adams, J. C. (Jam. & Notts) b Jan. 9, 1968
*Adams, P. R. (W. Prov.) b Jan. 20, 1977
Adams, P. W. (Cheltenham & Sussex; *CY 1919*) b Sept. 5, 1900, d Sept. 28, 1962
*Adcock, N. A. T. (Tvl & Natal; *CY 1961*) b March 8, 1931
*Adhikari, H. R. (Guj., Baroda & Ind. Serv.) b July 31, 1919
*Afaq Hussain (Kar., Pak Us, PIA & PWD) b Dec. 31, 1939
Afford, J. A. (Notts) b May 12, 1964
*Aftab Baloch (PWD, Kar., Sind, NBP & PIA) b April 1, 1953
*Aftab Gul (Punjab U., Pak. Us & Lahore) b March 31, 1946
*Agha Saadat Ali (Pak. Us, Punjab, B'pur & Lahore) b June 21, 1929, d Oct. 26, 1995
*Agha Zahid (Pak Us, Punjab, Lahore & HBL) b Jan. 7, 1953

*Agnew, J. P. (Leics; *CY 1988*; broadcaster) b April 4, 1960
*Ahangama, F. S. (SSC) b Sept. 14, 1959
Aird, R. (CU & Hants; Sec. MCC 1953-62, Pres. MCC 1968-69) b May 4, 1902, d Aug. 16, 1986
Aislabie, B. (Surrey, Hants, Kent & Sussex; Sec. MCC 1822-42) b Jan. 14, 1774, d June 2, 1842
Aitchison, Rev. J. K. (Scotland) b May 26, 1920, d Feb. 13, 1994
*Akram Raza (Lahore, Sargodha, F'bad, WAPDA & HBL) b Nov. 22, 1964
*Alabaster, J. C. (Otago) b July 11, 1930
Alcock, C. W. (Sec. Surrey CCC 1872-1907; Editor *Cricket* 1882-1907) b Dec. 2, 1842, d Feb. 26, 1907
Alderman, A. E. (Derbys) b Oct. 30, 1907, d June 4, 1990
*Alderman, T. M. (W. Aust., Kent & Glos; *CY 1982*) b June 12, 1956
Alexander of Tunis, 1st Lord (Pres. MCC 1955-56) b Dec. 10, 1891, d June 16, 1969
*Alexander, F. C. M. (CU & Jam.) b Nov. 2, 1928
*Alexander, G. (Vic.) b April 22, 1851, d Nov. 6, 1930
*Alexander, H. H. (Vic.) b June 9, 1905, d April 15, 1993
Alikhan, R. I. (Sussex, PIA, Surrey & PNSC) b Dec. 28, 1962
*Alim-ud-Din (Rajputana, Guj., Sind, B'pur, Kar. & PWD) b Dec. 15, 1930
*Allan, D. W. (B'dos) b Nov. 5, 1937
*Allan, F. E. (Vic.) b Dec. 2, 1849, d Feb. 9, 1917
Allan, J. M. (OU, Kent, Warwicks & Scotland) b April 2, 1932
*Allan, P. J. (Qld) b Dec. 31, 1935
*Allcott, C. F. W. (Auck.) b Oct. 7, 1896, d Nov. 19, 1973
Allen, B. O. (CU & Glos) b Oct. 13, 1911, d May 1, 1981
*Allen, D. A. (Glos) b Oct. 29, 1935

*Allen, Sir George O. B. (CU & Middx; Pres. MCC 1963-64) b July 31, 1902, d Nov. 29, 1989

*Allen, I. B. A. (Windwards) b Oct. 6, 1965

Allen, M. H. J. (Northants & Derbys) b Jan. 7, 1933, d Oct. 6, 1995

*Allen, R. C. (NSW) b July 2, 1858, d May 2, 1952

Alletson, E. B. (Notts) b March 6, 1884, d July 5, 1963

Alley, W. E. (NSW & Som; Test umpire; *CY 1962*) b Feb. 3, 1919

Allom, M. J. C. (CU & Surrey; Pres. MCC 1969-70) b March 23, 1906, d April 8, 1995

*Allott, G. I. (Cant.) b Dec. 24, 1971

*Allott, P. J. W. (Lancs & Wgtn) b Sept. 14, 1956

Altham, H. S. CBE (OU, Surrey & Hants; historian; Pres. MCC 1959-60) b Nov. 30, 1888, d March 11, 1965

*Amalean, K. N. (SL) b April 7, 1965

*Amarnath, Lala (N. B.) (N. Ind., S. Punjab, Guj., Patiala, U. Pradesh & Ind. Rlwys) b Sept. 11, 1911

*Amarnath, M. (Punjab & Delhi; *CY 1984*) b Sept. 24, 1950

*Amarnath, S. (Punjab & Delhi) b Dec. 30, 1948

*Amar Singh, L. (Patiala, W. Ind. & Naw.) b Dec. 4, 1910, d May 20, 1940

*Ambrose, C. E. L. (Leewards & Northants; *CY 1992*) b Sept. 21, 1963

*Amerasinghe, A. M. J. G. (Nomads & Ant.) b Feb. 2, 1954

*Ames, L. E. G. CBE (Kent; *CY 1929*) b Dec. 3, 1905, d Feb. 26, 1990

**Amir Elahi (Baroda, N. Ind., S. Punjab & B'pur) b Sept. 1, 1908, d Dec. 28, 1980

*Amiss, D. L. MBE (Warwicks; *CY 1975*) b April 7, 1943

*Amre, P. K. (Ind. Rlwys, Raja., Bombay & Bengal) b Aug. 14, 1968

Anderson, I. S. (Derbys & Boland) b April 24, 1960

*Anderson, J. H. (W. Prov.) b April 26, 1874, d March 11, 1926

*Anderson, R. W. (Cant., N. Dist., Otago & C. Dist.) b Oct. 2, 1948

*Anderson, W. M. (Cant.) b Oct. 8, 1919, d Dec. 21, 1979

*Andrew, K. V. (Northants) b Dec. 15, 1929

*Andrews, B. (Cant., C. Dist. & Otago) b April 4, 1945

*Andrews, T. J. E. (NSW) b Aug. 26, 1890, d Jan. 28, 1970

Andrews, W. H. R. (Som) b April 14, 1908, d Jan. 9, 1989

*Angel, J. (W. Aust.) b April 22, 1968

Angell, F. L. (Som) b June 29, 1922

*Anil Dalpat (Kar. & PIA) b Sept. 20, 1963

*Ankola, S. A. (M'tra & †Mumbai) b March 1, 1968

*Anurasiri, S. D. (Pan. & WPS) b Feb. 25, 1966

*Anwar Hussain (N. Ind., Bombay, Sind & Kar.) b July 16, 1920

*Anwar Khan (Kar., Sind & NBP) b Dec. 24, 1955

*Appleyard, R. (Yorks; *CY 1952*) b June 27, 1924

*Apte, A. L. (Ind. Us, Bombay & Raja.) b Oct. 24, 1934

*Apte, M. L. (Bombay & Bengal) b Oct. 5, 1932

*Aqib Javed (Lahore, PACO, Hants, I'bad & Allied Bank) b Aug. 5, 1972

*Archer, A. G. (Worcs) b Dec. 6, 1871, d July 15, 1935

*Archer, K. A. (Qld) b Jan. 17, 1928

*Archer, R. G. (Qld) b Oct. 25, 1933

*Arif Butt (Lahore & Pak. Rlwys) b May 17, 1944

Arlott, John OBE (Writer & broadcaster) b Feb. 25, 1914, d Dec. 14, 1991

*Armitage, T. (Yorks) b April 25, 1848, d Sept. 21, 1922

Armstrong, N. F. (Leics) b Dec. 22, 1892, d Jan. 19, 1990

*Armstrong, W. W. (Vic.; *CY 1903*) b May 22, 1879, d July 13, 1947

Arnold, A. P. (Cant. & Northants) b Oct. 16, 1926

*Arnold, E. G. (Worcs) b Nov. 7, 1876, d Oct. 25, 1942

*Arnold, G. G. (Surrey & Sussex; *CY 1972*) b Sept. 3, 1944

*Arnold, J. (Hants) b Nov. 30, 1907, d April 4, 1984

*Arnold, R. P. (NCC) b Oct. 25, 1973

*Arnott, K. J. (MCD) b March 8, 1961

Arnott, T. (Glam) b Feb. 16, 1902, d Feb. 2, 1975

*Arshad Ayub (H'bad) b Aug. 2, 1958

Arshad Pervez (Sargodha, Lahore, Pak. Us, Servis Ind., HBL & Punjab) b Oct. 1, 1952

*Arthurton, K. L. T. MBE (Leewards) b Feb. 21, 1965

*Arun, B. (TN) b Dec. 14, 1962

*Arun Lal (Delhi & Bengal) b Aug. 1 1955

*Asgarali, N. (T/T) b Dec. 28, 1920

Ashdown, W. H. (Kent) b Dec. 27, 1898, d Sept. 15, 1979

*Ashfaq Ahmed (PACO & PIA) b June 6, 1973

*Ashley, W. H. (W. Prov.) b Feb. 10, 1862, d July 14, 1930

*Ashraf Ali (Lahore, Income Tax, Pak. Us, Pak. Rlwys & UBL) b April 22, 1958

Ashton, C. T. (CU & Essex) b Feb. 19, 1901, d Oct. 31, 1942

Ashton, G. (CU & Worcs) b Sept. 27, 1896, d Feb. 6, 1981

Ashton, Sir Hubert (CU & Essex; *CY 1922;* Pres. MCC 1960-61) b Feb. 13, 1898, d June 17, 1979

Asif Din, M. (Warwicks) b Sept. 21, 1960

*Asif Iqbal (H'bad, Kar., Kent, PIA & NBP; *CY 1968*) b June 6, 1943

*Asif Masood (Lahore, Punjab U. & PIA) b Jan. 23, 1946

*Asif Mujtaba (Kar. & PIA) b Nov. 4, 1967

Aslett, D. G. (Kent) b Feb. 12, 1958

*Astill, W. E. (Leics; *CY 1933*) b March 1, 1888, d Feb. 10, 1948

*Astle, N. J. (Cant. & Notts) b Sept. 15, 1971

*Atapattu, M. S. (SSC & WPC) b Nov. 22, 1970

*Ata-ur-Rehman (Lahore, PACO & Allied Bank) b March 28, 1975

*Atherton, M. A. OBE (CU & Lancs; *CY 1991*) b March 23, 1968

*Athey, C. W. J. (Yorks, Glos & Sussex) b Sept. 27, 1957

*Atif Rauf (I'bad & ADBP) b March 3, 1964

Atkinson, C. R. M. CBE (Som) b July 23, 1931, d June 25, 1991

*Atkinson, D. St E. (B'dos & T/T) b Aug. 9, 1926

*Atkinson, E. St E. (B'dos) b Nov. 6, 1927

Atkinson, G. (Som & Lancs) b March 29, 1938

*Attewell, W. (Notts; *CY 1892*) b June 12, 1861, d June 11, 1927

Austin, Sir Harold B. G. (B'dos) b July 15, 1877, d July 27, 1943

*Austin, R. A. (Jam.) b Sept. 5, 1954

Avery, A. V. (Essex) b Dec. 19, 1914, d May 10, 1997

Aylward, James (Hants & All-England) b 1741, *buried* Dec. 27, 1827

*Azad, K. (Delhi) b Jan. 2, 1959

*Azam Khan (Kar., PNSC, Customs) b March 1, 1969

*Azeem Hafeez (Kar., Allied Bank & PIA) b July 29, 1963

*Azhar Khan (Lahore, Punjab, Pak. Us, PIA & HBL) b Sept. 7, 1955

*Azharuddin, M. (H'bad & Derbys; *CY 1991*) b Feb. 8, 1963

*Azmat Rana (B'pur, PIA, Punjab, Lahore & MCB) b Nov. 3, 1951

*Bacchus, S. F. A. F. (Guyana, W. Prov. & Border) b Jan. 31, 1954

*Bacher, Dr A. (Tvl; Managing Director UCBSA) b May 24, 1942

*Bacher, A. M. (Tvl) b Oct. 29, 1973

*Badcock, C. L. (Tas. & S. Aust.) b April 10, 1914, d Dec. 13, 1982

*Badcock, F. T. (Wgtn & Otago) b Aug. 9, 1895, d Sept. 19, 1982

Baggallay, R. R. C. (Derbys) b May 4, 1884, d Dec. 12, 1975

*Baichan, L. (Guyana) b May 12, 1946

*Baig, A. A. (H'bad, OU & Som) b March 19, 1939

Bailey, J. (Hants) b April 6, 1908, d Feb. 9, 1988

Bailey, J. A. (Essex & OU; Sec. MCC 1974-87) b June 22, 1930

*Bailey, R. J. (Northants) b Oct. 28, 1963

*Bailey, T. E. CBE (Essex & CU; *CY 1950*) b Dec. 3, 1923

Baillie, A. W. (Sec. MCC 1858-63) b June 22, 1830, d May 10, 1867

Bainbridge, H. W. (Surrey, CU & Warwicks) b Oct. 29, 1862, d March 3, 1940

Bainbridge, P. (Glos & Durham; *CY 1986*) b April 16, 1958

*Bairstow, D. L. (Yorks & Griq. W.) b Sept. 1, 1951, d Jan. 5, 1998

Baker, C. S. (Warwicks) b Jan. 5, 1883, d Dec. 16, 1976

Baker, G. R. (Yorks & Lancs) b April 18, 1862, d Dec. 6, 1938

*Bakewell, A. H. (Northants; *CY 1934*) b Nov. 2, 1908, d Jan. 23, 1983

*Balaskas, X. C. (Griq. W., Border, W. Prov., Tvl & NE Tvl) b Oct. 15, 1910, d May 12, 1994

*Balderstone, J. C. (Yorks & Leics) b Nov. 16, 1940

Baldry, D. O. (Middx & Hants) b Dec. 26, 1931

*Banerjee, S. A. (Bengal & Bihar) b Nov. 1, 1919, d Sept. 14, 1992

*Banerjee, S. N. (Bengal, Naw., Bihar & M. Pradesh) b Oct. 3, 1911, d Oct. 14, 1980

*Banerjee, S. T. (Bihar & Bengal) b Feb. 13, 1969

*Bannerman, A. C. (NSW) b March 22, 1854, d Sept. 19, 1924

*Bannerman, Charles (NSW) b July 23, 1851, d Aug. 20, 1930

Bannister, J. D. (Warwicks) b Aug. 23, 1930

*Baptiste, E. A. E. (Kent, Leewards, Northants & E. Prov.) b March 12, 1960

*Baqa Jilani, M. (N. Ind.) b July 20, 1911, d July 2, 1941

*Barber, R. T. (Wgton & C. Dist.) b June 3, 1925

*Barber, R. W. (Lancs, CU & Warwicks; *CY 1967*) b Sept. 26, 1935

*Barber, W. (Yorks) b April 18, 1901, d Sept. 10, 1968

Barclay, J. R. T. (Sussex & OFS) b Jan. 22, 1954

*Bardsley, W. (NSW; *CY 1910*) b Dec. 6, 1882, d Jan. 20, 1954

Barker, G. (Essex) b July 6, 1931

Barling, T. H. (Surrey) b Sept. 1, 1906, d Jan. 2, 1993

*Barlow, E. J. (Tvl, E. Prov., W. Prov., Derbys & Boland) b Aug. 12, 1940

*Barlow, G. D. (Middx) b March 26, 1950

*Barlow, R. G. (Lancs) b May 28, 1851, d July 31, 1919

Barnard, H. M. (Hants) b July 18, 1933

Barnes, A. R. OBE (Sec. Aust. Cricket Board 1960-81) b Sept. 12, 1916, d March 14, 1989

*Barnes, S. F. (Warwicks & Lancs; *CY 1910*) b April 19, 1873, d Dec. 26, 1967

*Barnes, S. G. (NSW) b June 5, 1916, d Dec. 16, 1973

*Barnes, W. (Notts; *CY 1890*) b May 27, 1852, d March 24, 1899

*Barnett, B. A. (Vic.) b March 23, 1908, d June 29, 1979

*Barnett, C. J. (Glos; *CY 1937*) b July 3, 1910, d May 28, 1993

*Barnett, K. J. (Derbys & Boland; *CY 1989*) b July 17, 1960

Baroda, Maharaja of (Manager, Ind. in Eng. 1959) b April 2, 1930, d Sept. 1, 1988

*Barratt, F. (Notts) b April 12, 1894, d Jan. 29, 1947

*Barrett, A. G. (Jam.) b April 5, 1942

*Barrett, Dr J. E. (Vic.) b Oct. 15, 1866, d Feb. 6, 1916

Barrick, D. W. (Northants) b April 28, 1926

*Barrington, K. F. (Surrey; *CY 1960*) b Nov. 24, 1930, d March 14, 1981

Barron, W. (Lancs & Northants) b Oct. 26, 1917

*Barrow, I. (Jam.) b Jan. 6, 1911, d April 2, 1979

*Bartlett, E. L. (B'dos) b March 10, 1906, d Dec. 21, 1976

*Bartlett, G. A. (C. Dist. & Cant.) b Feb. 3, 1941

Bartlett, H. T. (CU, Surrey & Sussex; *CY 1939*) b Oct. 7, 1914, d June 26, 1988

Bartley, T. J. (Test umpire) b March 19, 1908, d April 2, 1964

Barton, M. R. (OU & Surrey) b Oct. 14, 1914

*Barton, P. T. (Wgtn) b Oct. 9, 1935

*Barton, V. A. (Kent & Hants) b Oct. 6, 1867, d March 23, 1906

Barwick, S. R. (Glam) b Sept. 6, 1960

Base, S. J. (W. Prov., Glam, Derbys, Boland & Border) b Jan. 2, 1960

*Basit Ali (Kar. & UBL) b Dec. 13, 1970

Bates, D. L. (Sussex) b May 10, 1933

Bates, L. A. (Warwicks) b March 20, 1895, d March 11, 1971

*Bates, W. (Yorks) b Nov. 19, 1855, d Jan. 8, 1900

Bates, W. E. (Yorks & Glam) b March 5, 1884, d Jan. 17, 1957

*Baumgartner, H. V. (OFS & Tvl) b Nov. 17, 1883, d April 8, 1938

*Bean, G. (Notts & Sussex) b March 7, 1864, d March 16, 1923

Bear, M. J. (Essex & Cant.) b Feb. 23, 1934

*Beard, D. D. (C. Dist. & N. Dist.) b Jan. 14, 1920, d July 15, 1982

*Beard, G. R. (NSW) b Aug. 19, 1950

Beauclerk, Lord Frederick (Middx, Surrey & MCC) b May 8, 1773, d April 22, 1850

Beaufort, 10th Duke of (Pres. MCC 1952-53) b April 4, 1900, d Feb. 5, 1984

*Beaumont, R. (Tvl) b Feb. 4, 1884, d May 25, 1958

*Beck, J. E. F. (Wgtn) b Aug. 1, 1934

*Bedi, B. S. (N. Punjab, Delhi & Northants) b Sept. 25, 1946

*Bedser, Sir Alec V. (Surrey; *CY 1947*) b July 4, 1918

Bedser, E. A. (Surrey) b July 4, 1918

Beet, G. (Derbys; Test umpire) b April 24, 1886, d Dec. 13, 1946

*Begbie, D. W. (Tvl) b Dec. 12, 1914

Beldham, W. (Hambledon & Surrey) b Feb. 5, 1766, d Feb. 20, 1862

*Bell, A. J. (W. Prov. & Rhod.) b April 15, 1906, d Aug. 1, 1985

Bell, R. V. (Middx & Sussex) b Jan. 7, 1931, d Oct. 26, 1989

*Bell, W. (Cant.) b Sept. 5, 1931

Bellamy, B. W. (Northants) b April 22, 1891, d Dec. 22, 1985

*Benaud, J. (NSW) b May 11, 1944

*Benaud, R. OBE (NSW; *CY 1962*) b Oct. 6, 1930

*Benjamin, J. E. (Warwicks & Surrey) b Feb. 2, 1961

*Benjamin, K. C. G. (Leewards & Worcs) b April 8, 1967

*Benjamin, W. K. M. (Leewards, Leics & Hants) b Dec. 31, 1964

Bencraft, Sir H. W. Russell (Hants) b March 4, 1858, d Dec. 25, 1943

Bennett, D. (Middx) b Dec. 18, 1933

*Bennett, M. J. (NSW) b Oct. 6, 1956

*Benson, M. R. (Kent) b July 6, 1958

Berry, L. G. (Leics) b April 28, 1906, d Feb. 5, 1985

*Berry, R. (Lancs, Worcs & Derbys) b Jan. 29, 1926

*Best, C. A. (B'dos & W. Prov.) b May 14, 1959

Bestwick, W. (Derbys) b Feb. 24, 1875, d May 2, 1938

*Betancourt, N. (T/T) b June 4, 1887, d Oct. 12, 1947

*Bevan, M. G. (NSW & Yorks) b May 8, 1970

Bhalekar, R. B. (M'tra) b Feb. 17, 1952

*Bhandari, P. (Delhi & Bengal) b Nov. 27, 1935

*Bhat, A. R. (Karn.) b April 16, 1958

*Bichel, A. J. (Qld) b Aug. 27, 1970

Bick, D. A. (Middx) b Feb. 22, 1936, d Jan. 13, 1992

*Bicknell, M. P. (Surrey) b Jan. 14, 1969

*Bilby, G. P. (Wgtn) b May 7, 1941

*Binks, J. G. (Yorks; *CY 1969*) b Oct. 5, 1935

*Binns, A. P. (Jam.) b July 24, 1929

*Binny, R. M. H. (Karn.) b July 19, 1955

Birch, J. D. (Notts) b June 18, 1955

Bird, H. D. MBE (Yorks & Leics; Test umpire) b April 19, 1933

*Bird, M. C. (Lancs & Surrey) b March 25, 1888, d Dec. 9, 1933

Bird, R. E. (Worcs) b April 4, 1915, d Feb. 20, 1985

*Birkenshaw, J. (Yorks, Leics & Worcs) b Nov. 13, 1940

*Birkett, L. S. (B'dos, BG & T/T; *oldest living Test cricketer at end 1997*) b April 14, 1904

Bishop, G. A. (S. Aust.) b Feb. 25, 1960

*Bishop, I. R. (T/T & Derbys) b Oct. 24, 1967

*Bisset, Sir Murray (M.) (W. Prov.) b April 14, 1876, d Oct. 24, 1931

*Bissett, G. F. (Griq. W., W. Prov. & Tvl) b Nov. 5, 1905, d Nov. 14, 1965

Bissex, M. (Glos) b Sept. 28, 1944

*Blackham, J. McC. (Vic; *CY 1891*) b May 11, 1854, d Dec. 28, 1932

*Blackie, D. D. (Vic.) b April 5, 1882, d April 18, 1955

*Blain, T. E. (C. Dist.) b Feb. 17, 1962

Blair, B. R. (Otago) b Dec. 27, 1957

*Blair, R. W. (Wgtn & C. Dist.) b June 23, 1932

*Blakey, R. J. (Yorks) b Jan. 15, 1967

*Blanckenberg, J. M. (W. Prov. & Natal) b Dec. 31, 1892, dead

*Bland, K. C. (Rhod., E. Prov. & OFS; *CY 1966*) b April 5, 1938

Blenkiron, W. (Warwicks) b July 21, 1942

*Blewett, G. S. (S. Aust.) b Oct. 29, 1971

*Bligh, Hon. Ivo (I. F. W.) (8th Earl of Darnley) (CU & Kent; Pres. MCC 1900) b March 13, 1859, d April 10, 1927

Blofeld, H. C. (CU; writer & broadcaster) b Sept 23, 1939

*Blunt, R. C. MBE (Cant. & Otago; *CY 1928*) b Nov. 3, 1900, d June 22, 1966

*Blythe, C. (Kent; *CY 1904*) b May 30, 1879, d Nov. 8, 1917

*Board, J. H. (Glos) b Feb. 23, 1867, d April 15, 1924

*Bock, E. G. (Griq. W., Tvl & W. Prov.) b Sept. 17, 1908, d Sept. 5, 1961

*Bolton, B. A. (Cant. & Wgtn) b May 31, 1935

*Bolus, J. B. (Yorks, Notts & Derbys) b Jan. 31, 1934

*Bond, G. E. (W. Prov.) b April 5, 1909, d Aug. 27, 1965

Bond, J. D. (Lancs & Notts; *CY 1971*) b May 6, 1932

*Bonnor, G. J. (Vic. & NSW) b Feb. 25, 1855, d June 27, 1912

*Boock, S. L. (Otago & Cant.) b Sept. 20, 1951

*Boon, D. C. MBE (Tas. & Durham; *CY 1994*) b Dec. 29, 1960

Boon, T. J. (Leics) b Nov. 1, 1961

*Booth, B. C. MBE (NSW) b Oct. 19, 1933

Booth, B. J. (Lancs & Leics) b Dec. 3, 1935

Booth, C. (CU & Hants) b May 11, 1842, d July 14, 1926

*Booth, M. W. (Yorks; *CY 1914*) b Dec. 10, 1886, d July 1, 1916

Booth, R. (Yorks & Worcs) b Oct. 1, 1926

*Borde, C. G. (Baroda & M'tra) b July 21, 1933

*Border, A. R. (NSW, Glos, Qld & Essex; *CY 1982*) b July 27, 1955

Bore, M. K. (Yorks & Notts) b June 2, 1947

Borrington, A. J. (Derbys) b Dec. 8, 1948

*Bosanquet, B. J. T. (OU & Middx; *CY 1905*) b Oct. 13, 1877, d Oct. 12, 1936

*Bosch, T. (N. Tvl & Natal) b March 14, 1966

Bose, G. (Bengal) b May 20, 1947

Boshier, B. S. (Leics) b March 6, 1932

*Botham, I. T. OBE (Som, Worcs, Durham & Qld; *CY 1978*) b Nov. 24, 1955

*Botten, J. T. (NE Tvl & N. Tvl) b June 21, 1938

Boucher, J. C. (Ireland) b Dec. 22, 1910, d Dec. 25, 1995

Bowden, J. (Derbys) b Oct. 8, 1884, d March 1, 1958

*Bowden, M. P. (Surrey & Tvl) b Nov. 1, 1865, d Feb. 19, 1892

Bowell, A. (Hants) b April 27, 1880, d Aug. 28, 1957

*Bowes, W. E. (Yorks; *CY 1932*) b July 25, 1908, d Sept. 5, 1987

*Bowley, E. H. (Sussex & Auck.; *CY 1930*) b June 6, 1890, d July 9, 1974

Bowley, F. L. (Worcs) b Nov. 9 1873, d May 31, 1943

Box, T. (Sussex) b Feb. 7, 1808, d July 12, 1876

*Boyce, K. D. (B'dos & Essex; *CY 1974*) b Oct. 11, 1943, d Oct. 11, 1996

*Boycott, G. OBE (Yorks & N. Tvl; *CY 1965*) b Oct. 21, 1940

Boyd-Moss, R. J. (CU & Northants) b Dec. 16, 1959

Boyes, G. S. (Hants) b March 31, 1899, d Feb. 11, 1973

*Boyle, H. F. (Vic.) b Dec. 10, 1847, d Nov. 21, 1907

*Bracewell, B. P. (C. Dist., Otago & N. Dist.) b Sept. 14, 1959

*Bracewell, J. G. (Otago & Auck.) b April 15, 1958

*Bradburn, G. E. (N. Dist.) b May 26, 1966

*Bradburn, W. P. (N. Dist.) b Nov. 24, 1938

*Bradley, W. M. (Kent) b Jan. 2, 1875, d Nov. 19, 1944

*Bradman, Sir Donald G. (NSW & S. Aust.; CY 1931) b Aug. 27, 1908

Brain, B. M. (Worcs & Glos) b Sept. 13, 1940

*Brain, D. H. (Mash.) b Oct. 4, 1964

Bramall, Field-Marshal The Lord (Pres. MCC 1988-89) b Dec. 18, 1923

*Brandes, E. A. (Mash.) b March 5, 1963

Brann, G. (Sussex) b April 23, 1865, d June 14, 1954

*Brann, W. H. (E. Prov.) b April 4, 1899, d Sept. 22, 1953

Brassington, A. J. (Glos) b Aug. 9, 1954

*Braund, L. C. (Surrey & Som; CY 1902) b Oct. 18, 1875, d Dec. 23, 1955

Bray, C. (Essex) b April 6, 1898, d Sept. 12, 1993

Brayshaw, I. J. (W. Aust.) b Jan. 14, 1942

Breakwell, D. (Northants & Som) b July 2, 1948

*Brearley, J. M. OBE (CU & Middx; CY 1977) b April 28, 1942

*Brearley, W. (Lancs; CY 1909) b March 11, 1876, d Jan. 13, 1937

*Brennan, D. V. (Yorks) b Feb. 10, 1920, d Jan. 9, 1985

*Briant, G. A. (Mash.) b April 11, 1969

Bridges, J. J. (Som) b June 28, 1887, d Sept. 26, 1966

Brierley, T. L. (Glam, Lancs & Canada) b June 15, 1910, d Jan. 7, 1989

Briers, N. E. (Leics; CY 1993) b Jan. 15, 1955

*Briggs, John (Lancs; CY 1889) b Oct. 3, 1862, d Jan. 11, 1902

*Bright, R. J. (Vic.) b July 13, 1954

*Briscoe, A. W. (Tvl) b Feb. 6, 1911, d April 22, 1941

*Broad, B. C. (Glos & Notts) b Sept. 29, 1957

Broadbent, R. G. (Worcs) b June 21, 1924, d April 26, 1993

*Brockwell, W. (Surrey & Kimberley; CY 1895) b Jan. 21, 1865, d June 30, 1935

Broderick, V. (Northants) b Aug. 17, 1920

*Bromfield, H. D. (W. Prov.) b June 26, 1932

*Bromley, E. H. (W. Aust. & Vic.) b Sept. 2, 1912, d Feb. 1, 1967

*Bromley-Davenport, H. R. (CU, Eur., & Middx) b Aug. 18, 1870, d May 23, 1954

*Brookes, D. (Northants; CY 1957) b Oct. 29, 1915

Brookes, Wilfrid H. (Editor of Wisden 1936-39) b Dec. 5, 1894, d May 28, 1955

*Brown, A. (Kent) b Oct. 17, 1935

Brown, A. D. (Surrey) b Feb. 11, 1970

Brown, A. S. (Glos) b June 24, 1936

*Brown, D. J. (Warwicks) b Jan. 30, 1942

*Brown, F. R. MBE (CU, Surrey & Northants; CY 1933; Pres. MCC 1971-72) b Dec. 16, 1910, d July 24, 1991

*Brown, G. (Hants) b Oct. 6, 1887, d Dec. 3, 1964

Brown, J. MBE (Scotland) b Sept. 24, 1931

*Brown, J. T. (Yorks; CY 1895) b Aug. 20, 1869, d Nov. 4, 1904

*Brown, L. S. (Tvl, NE Tvl & Rhod.) b Nov. 24, 1910, d Sept. 1, 1983

Brown, R. D. (Mash.) b March 11, 1951

*Brown, S. J. E. (Northants & Durham) b June 29, 1969

Brown, S. M. (Middx) b Dec. 8, 1917, d Dec. 28, 1987

*Brown, V. R. (Cant. & Auck.) b Nov. 3, 1959

*Brown, W. A. (NSW & Qld; CY 1939) b July 31, 1912

Brown, W. C. (Northants) b Nov. 13, 1900, d Jan. 20, 1986

*Browne, C. O. (B'dos) b Dec. 7, 1970

*Browne, C. R. (B'dos & BG) b Oct. 8, 1890, d Jan. 12, 1964

*Bruce, W. (Vic.) b May 22, 1864, d Aug. 3, 1925

*Bruk-Jackson, G. K. (MCD) b April 25, 1969

Bryan, G. J. CBE (Kent) b Dec. 29, 1902, d April 4, 1991

Bryan, J. L. (CU & Kent; CY 1922) b May 26, 1896, d April 23, 1985

Bryan, R. T. (Kent) b July 30, 1898, d July 27, 1970

*Buckenham, C. P. (Essex) b Jan. 16, 1876, d Feb. 23, 1937

Bucknor, S. A. (Test umpire) b May 31, 1946

Buckston, R. H. R. (Derbys) b Oct. 10, 1908, d May 16, 1967

Budd, E. H. (Middx & All-England) b Feb. 23, 1785, d March 29, 1875

Budd, W. L. (Hants; Test umpire) b Oct. 25, 1913, d Aug. 23, 1986

Bull, F. G. (Essex; CY 1898) b April 2, 1875, d Sept. 16, 1910

Buller, J. S. MBE (Yorks & Worcs; Test umpire) b Aug. 23, 1909, d Aug. 7, 1970

Burden, M. D. (Hants) b Oct. 4, 1930, d Nov. 9, 1987

*Burge, P. J. (Qld; CY 1965) b May 17, 1932

*Burger, C. G. de V. (Natal) b July 12, 1935

Burgess, G. I. (Som) b May 5, 1943

*Burgess, M. G. (Auck.) b July 17, 1944

*Burke, C. (Auck.) b March 22, 1914, d Aug. 4, 1997

*Burke, J. W. (NSW; CY 1957) b June 12, 1930, d Feb. 2, 1979

*Burke, S. F. (NE Tvl & OFS) b March 11, 1934

*Burki, Javed (Pak. Us, OU, Punjab, Lahore, Kar., R'pindi & NWFP) b May 8, 1938

*Burmester, M. G. (Mash.) b Jan. 24, 1968

*Burn, K. E. (Tas.) b Sept. 17, 1862, d July 20, 1956

Burns, N. D. (Essex, W. Prov., Som) b Sept. 19, 1965

Burns, W. B. (Worcs) b Aug. 29, 1883, d July 7, 1916

Burnup, C. J. (CU & Kent; *CY 1903*) b Nov. 21, 1875, d April 5, 1960

Burrough, H. D. (Som) b Feb. 6, 1909, d April 9, 1994

Burrows, R. D. (Worcs) b June 6, 1871, d Feb. 12, 1943

Burton, D. C. F. (Yorks) b Sept. 13, 1887, d Sept. 24, 1971

*Burton, F. J. (Vic. & NSW) b Nov. 2, 1865, d Aug. 25, 1929

*Burtt, T. B. (Cant.) b Jan. 22, 1915, d May 24, 1988

Buse, H. T. F. (Som) b Aug. 5, 1910, d Feb. 23, 1992

Buss, A. (Sussex) b Sept. 1, 1939

Buss, M. A. (Sussex & OFS) b Jan. 24, 1944

*Butchart, I. P. (MCD) b May 9, 1960

*Butcher, A. R. (Surrey & Glam; *CY 1991*) b Jan. 7, 1954

*Butcher, B. F. (Guyana; *CY 1970*) b Sept. 3, 1933

Butcher, I. P. (Leics & Glos) b July 1, 1962

*Butcher, M. A. (Surrey) b Aug. 23, 1972

*Butcher, R. O. (Middx, B'dos & Tas.) b Oct. 14, 1953

*Butler, H. J. (Notts) b March 12, 1913, d July 17, 1991

*Butler, L. (T/T) b Feb. 9, 1929

*Butt, H. R. (Sussex) b Dec. 27, 1865, d Dec. 21, 1928

*Butterfield, L. A. (Cant.) b Aug. 29, 1913

*Butts, C. G. (Guyana) b July 8, 1957

Buxton, I. R. (Derbys) b April 17, 1938

*Buys, I. D. (W. Prov.) b Feb. 3, 1895, dead

*Bynoe, M. R. (B'dos) b Feb. 23, 1941

Byrne, J. F. (Warwicks) b June 19, 1871, d May 10, 1954

Caccia, Lord (Pres. MCC 1973-74) b Dec. 21, 1905, d Oct. 31, 1990

*Caddick, A. R. (Som) b Nov. 21, 1968

Cadman, S. (Derbys) b Jan. 29, 1877, d May 6, 1952

Caesar, Julius (Surrey & All-England) b March 25, 1830, d March 6, 1878

Caffyn, W. (Surrey & NSW) b Feb. 2, 1828, d Aug. 28, 1919

Caine, C. Stewart (Editor of *Wisden* 1926-33) b Oct. 28, 1861, d April 15, 1933

*Cairns, B. L. (C. Dist., Otago & N. Dist.) b Oct. 10, 1949

*Cairns, C. L. (N. Dist., Notts & Cant.) b June 13, 1970

Calder, H. L. (Cranleigh; *CY 1918*) b Jan. 24, 1901, d Sept. 15, 1995

*Callaway, S. T. (NSW & Cant.) b Feb. 6, 1868, d Nov. 25, 1923

*Callen, I. W. (Vic. & Boland) b May 2, 1955

*Calthorpe, Hon. F. S. Gough- (CU, Sussex & Warwicks) b May 27, 1892, d Nov. 19, 1935

*Camacho, G. S. (Guyana; Chief Exec. WICB) b Oct. 15, 1945

*Cameron, F. J. (Jam.) b June 22, 1923, d Feb. 1995

*Cameron, F. J. MBE (Otago) b June 1, 1932

*Cameron, H. B. (Tvl, E. Prov. & W. Prov.; *CY 1936*) b July 5, 1905, d Nov. 2, 1935

*Cameron, J. H. (CU, Jam. & Som) b April 8, 1914

*Campbell, A. D. R. (Mash.) b Sept. 23, 1972

*Campbell, G. D. (Tas.) b March 10, 1964

*Campbell, S. L. (B'dos & Durham) b Nov. 1, 1970

*Campbell, T. (Tvl) b Feb. 9, 1882, d Oct. 5, 1924

Cannings, V. H. D. (Warwicks & Hants) b April 3, 1919

*Capel, D. J. (Northants & E. Prov.) b Feb. 6, 1963

Cardus, Sir Neville (Writer) b April 3, 1888, d Feb. 27, 1975

*Carew, G. M. (B'dos) b June 4, 1910, d Dec. 9, 1974

*Carew, M. C. (T/T) b Sept. 15, 1937

*Carkeek, W. (Vic.) b Oct. 17, 1878, d Feb. 20, 1937

*Carlisle, S. V. (Zimb. U-24) b May 10, 1972

*Carlson, P. H. (Qld) b Aug. 8, 1951

*Carlstein, P. R. (OFS, Tvl, Natal & Rhod.) b Oct. 28, 1938

Carpenter, D. (Glos) b Sept. 12, 1935

Carpenter, H. A. (Essex) b July 12, 1869, d Dec. 12, 1933

Carpenter, R. (Cambs & Utd England XI) b Nov. 18, 1830, d July 13, 1901

*Carr, A. W. (Notts; *CY 1923*) b May 21, 1893, d Feb. 7, 1963

*Carr, D. B. OBE (OU & Derbys; *CY 1960*; Sec. TCCB 1974-86) b Dec. 28, 1926

*Carr, D. W. (Kent; *CY 1910*) b March 17, 1872, d March 23, 1950

Carr, J. D. (OU & Middx) b June 15, 1963

Carrick, P. (Yorks & E. Prov.) b July 16, 1952

*Carter, C. P. (Natal & Tvl) b April 23, 1881, d Nov. 8, 1952

*Carter, H. (NSW) b March 15, 1878, d June 8, 1948

Carter, R. G. M. (Worcs) b July 11, 1937

Cartwright, T. W. (Warwicks, Som & Glam) b July 22, 1935

Case, C. C. C. (Som) b Sept. 7, 1895, d Nov. 11, 1969

Cass, G. R. (Essex, Worcs & Tas.) b April 23, 1940

Catt, A. W. (Kent & W. Prov.) b Oct. 2, 1933

*Catterall, R. H. (Tvl, Rhod., Natal & OFS; *CY 1925*) b July 10, 1900, d Jan. 3, 1961

*Cave, H. B. (Wgtn & C. Dist.) b Oct. 10, 1922, d Sept. 15, 1989

Chalk, F. G. H. (OU & Kent) b Sept. 7, 1910, d Feb. 17, 1943

*Challenor, G. (B'dos) b June 28, 1888, d July 30, 1947

Chamberlain, W. R. F. (Northants; Chairman TCCB 1990-94) b April 13, 1925

*Chanderpaul, S. (Guyana) b Aug. 18, 1974

*Chandrasekhar, B. S. (†Karn.; *CY 1972*) b May 17, 1945

*Chang, H. S. (Jam.) b July 22, 1952

Chaplin, H. P. (Sussex & Eur.) b March 1, 1883, d March 6, 1970

*Chapman, A. P. F. (Uppingham, OU & Kent; *CY 1919*) b Sept. 3, 1900, d Sept. 16, 1961

*Chapman, H. W. (Natal) b June 30, 1890, d Dec. 1, 1941

Chapman, J. (Derbys) b March 11, 1877, d Aug. 12, 1956

*Chappell, G. S. MBE (S. Aust., Som & Qld; *CY 1973*) b Aug. 7, 1948

*Chappell, I. M. (S. Aust. & Lancs; *CY 1976*) b Sept. 26, 1943

*Chappell, T. M. (S. Aust., W. Aust. & NSW) b Oct. 21, 1952

*Chapple, M. E. (Cant. & C. Dist.) b July 25, 1930, d July 31, 1985

Charlesworth, C. (Warwicks) b Feb. 12, 1875, d June 15, 1953

*Charlton, P. C. (NSW) b April 9, 1867, d Sept. 30, 1954

*Charlwood, H. R. J. (Sussex) b Dec. 19, 1846, d June 6, 1888

*Chatfield, E. J. MBE (Wgtn) b July 3, 1950

*Chatterton, W. (Derbys) b Dec. 27, 1861, d March 19, 1913

*Chauhan, C. P. S. (M'tra & Delhi) b July 21, 1947

*Chauhan, R. K. (M. Pradesh) b Dec. 19, 1966

*Cheetham, J. E. (W. Prov.) b May 26, 1920, d Aug. 21, 1980

Chester, F. (Worcs; Test umpire) b Jan. 20, 1895, d April 8, 1957

*Chevalier, G. A. (W. Prov.) b March 9, 1937

*Childs, J. H. (Glos & Essex; *CY 1987*) b Aug. 15, 1951

*Chipperfield, A. G. (NSW) b Nov. 17, 1905, d July 29, 1987

Chisholm, R. H. E. (Scotland) b May 22, 1927

*Chowdhury, N. R. (Bihar & Bengal) b May 23, 1923, d Dec. 14, 1979

*Christiani, C. M. (BG) b Oct. 28, 1913, d April 4, 1938

*Christiani, R. J. (BG) b July 19, 1920

*Christopherson, S. (Kent; Pres. MCC 1939-45) b Nov. 11, 1861, d April 6, 1949

*Christy, J. A. J. (Tvl & Qld) b Dec. 12, 1904, d Feb. 1, 1971

*Chubb, G. W. A. (Border & Tvl) b April 12, 1911, d Aug. 28, 1982

Clark, D. G. (Kent; Pres. MCC 1977-78) b Jan. 27, 1919

Clark, E. A. (Middx) b April 15, 1937

*Clark, E. W. (Northants) b Aug. 9, 1902, d April 28, 1982

Clark, T. H. (Surrey) b Oct. 5, 1924, d June 14, 1981

*Clark, W. M. (W. Aust.) b Sept. 19, 1953

*Clarke, Dr C. B. OBE (B'dos, Northants & Essex) b April 7, 1918, d Oct. 14, 1993

Clarke, R. W. (Northants) b April 22, 1924, d Aug. 3, 1981

*Clarke, S. T. (B'dos, Surrey, Tvl, OFS & N. Tvl) b Dec. 11, 1954

Clarke, William (Notts; founded All-England XI & Trent Bridge ground) b Dec. 24, 1798, d Aug. 25, 1856

Clarkson, A. (Yorks & Som) b Sept. 5, 1939

*Clay, J. C. (Glam) b March 18, 1898, d Aug. 12, 1973

Clay, J. D. (Notts) b Oct. 15, 1924

Clayton, G. (Lancs & Som) b Feb. 3, 1938

*Cleverley, D. C. (Auck.) b Dec. 23, 1909

Clift, Patrick B. (Rhod., Leics & Natal) b July 14, 1953, d Sept. 2, 1996

Clift, Phil B. (Glam) b Sept. 3, 1918

Clinton, G. S. (Kent, Surrey & Zimb.-Rhod.) b May 5, 1953

*Close, D. B. CBE (Yorks & Som; *CY 1964*) b Feb. 24, 1931

Cobb, R. A. (Leics & N. Tvl) b May 18, 1961

Cobham, 10th Visct (Hon. C. J. Lyttelton) (Worcs; Pres. MCC 1954) b Aug. 8, 1909, d March 20, 1977

*Cochrane, J. A. K. (Tvl & Griq. W.) b July 15, 1909, d June 15, 1987

Coe, S. (Leics) b June 3, 1873, d Nov. 4, 1955

*Coen, S. K. (OFS, W. Prov., Tvl & Border) b Oct. 14, 1902, d Jan. 28, 1967

*Colah, S. M. H. (Bombay, W. Ind. & Naw.) b Sept. 22, 1902, d Sept. 11, 1950

Colchin, Robert (''Long Robin'') (Kent & All-England) b Nov. 1713, d April 1750

*Coldwell, L. J. (Worcs) b Jan. 10, 1933, d Aug. 6, 1996

*Colley, D. J. (NSW) b March 15, 1947

*Collinge, R. O. (C. Dist., Wgtn & N. Dist.) b April 2, 1946

Collins, A. E. J. (Clifton Coll. & Royal Engineers) b Aug. 18, 1885, d Nov. 11, 1914

Collins, G. C. (Kent) b Sept. 21, 1889, d Jan. 23, 1949

*Collins, H. L. (NSW) b Jan. 21, 1888, d May 28, 1959

Collins, R. (Lancs) b March 10, 1934

*Colquhoun, I. A. (C. Dist.) b June 8, 1924

Coman, P. G. (Cant.) b April 13, 1943

*Commaille, J. M. M. (W. Prov., Natal, OFS & Griq. W.) b Feb. 21, 1883, d July 28, 1956

*Commins, J. B. (Boland & W. Prov.) b Feb. 19, 1965

*Compton, D. C. S. CBE (Middx & Holkar; *CY 1939*) b May 23, 1918, d April 23, 1997

Compton, L. H. (Middx) b Sept. 12, 1912, d Dec. 27, 1984

*Coney, J. V. MBE (Wgtn; *CY 1984*) b June 21, 1952

*Congdon, B. E. OBE (C. Dist., Wgtn, Otago & Cant.; *CY 1974*) b Feb. 11, 1938

*Coningham, A. (NSW & Qld) b July 14, 1863, d June 13, 1939

*Connolly, A. N. (Vic. & Middx) b June 29, 1939

Constable, B. (Surrey) b Feb. 19, 1921, d May 15, 1997

Constant, D. J. (Kent & Leics; Test umpire) b Nov. 9, 1941

*Constantine, L. N. (later Baron Constantine of Maraval and Nelson) (T/T & B'dos; *CY 1940*) b Sept. 21, 1902, d July 1, 1971

Constantine, L. S. (T/T) b May 25, 1874, d Jan. 5, 1942

*Contractor, N. J. (Guj. & Ind. Rlwys) b March 7, 1934

*Conyngham, D. P. (Natal, Tvl & W. Prov.) b May 10, 1897, d July 7, 1979

*Cook, C. (Glos) b Aug. 23, 1921, d Sept. 4, 1996

*Cook, F. J. (E. Prov.) b 1870, d Nov. 30, 1914

*Cook, G. (Northants & E. Prov.) b Oct. 9, 1951

Cook, L. W. (Lancs) b March 28, 1885, d Dec. 2, 1933

*Cook, N. G. B. (Leics & Northants) b June 17, 1956

*Cook, S. J. (Tvl & Som; *CY 1990*) b July 31, 1953

Cook, T. E. R. (Sussex) b Jan. 5, 1901, d Jan. 15, 1950

*Cooper, A. H. C. (Tvl) b Sept. 2, 1893, d July 18, 1963

*Cooper, B. B. (Middx, Kent & Vic.) b March 15, 1844, d Aug. 7, 1914

Cooper, E. (Worcs) b Nov. 30, 1915, d Oct. 29, 1968

Cooper, F. S. Ashley- (Historian) b March 17, 1877, d Jan. 31, 1932

Cooper, G. C. (Sussex) b Sept. 2, 1936

Cooper, K. E. (Notts & Glos) b Dec. 27, 1957

*Cooper, W. H. (Vic.) b Sept. 11, 1849, d April 5, 1939

*Cope, G. A. (Yorks) b Feb. 23, 1947

*Copson, W. H. (Derbys; *CY 1937*) b April 27, 1908, d Sept. 14, 1971

Cordle, A. E. (Glam) b Sept. 21, 1940

*Cork, D. G. (Derbys; *CY 1996*) b Aug. 7, 1971

*Corling, G. E. (NSW) b July 13, 1941

Cornford, J. H. (Sussex) b Dec. 9, 1911, d June 17, 1985

*Cornford, W. L. (Sussex) b Dec. 25, 1900, d Feb. 6, 1964

Cornwallis, W. S. (later 2nd Baron) (Kent) b March 14, 1892, d Jan. 4, 1982

Corrall, P. (Leics) b July 16, 1906, d Feb. 1994

*Corran, A. J. (OU & Notts) b Nov. 25, 1936

*Cosier, G. J. (Vic., S. Aust. & Qld) b April 25, 1953

*Cottam, J. T. (NSW) b Sept. 5, 1867, d Jan. 30, 1897

*Cottam, R. M. H. (Hants & Northants) b Oct. 16, 1944

*Cotter, A. (NSW) b Dec. 3, 1884, d Oct. 31, 1917

Cotton, J. (Notts & Leics) b Nov. 7, 1940

*Coulthard, G. (Vic.; Test umpire) b Aug. 1, 1856, d Oct. 22, 1883

*Coventry, Hon. C. J. (Worcs) b Feb. 26, 1867, d June 2, 1929

*Cowans, N. G. (Middx & Hants) b April 17, 1961

*Cowdrey, C. S. (Kent & Glam) b Oct. 20, 1957

*Cowdrey, M. C. (later Baron Cowdrey of Tonbridge) (OU & Kent; *CY 1956;* Pres. MCC 1986-87) b Dec. 24, 1932

*Cowie, J. OBE (Auck.) b March 30, 1912, d June 3, 1994

Cowley, N. G. (Hants & Glam) b March 1, 1953

*Cowper, R. M. (Vic. & W. Aust.) b Oct. 5, 1940

Cox, A. L. (Northants) b July 22, 1907, d Nov. 13, 1986

Cox, G., jun. (Sussex) b Aug. 23, 1911, d March 30, 1985

Cox, G., sen. (Sussex) b Nov. 29, 1873, d March 24, 1949

*Cox, J. L. (Natal) b June 28, 1886, d July 4, 1971

*Coxon, A. (Yorks) b Jan. 18, 1916

*Craig, I. D. (NSW) b June 12, 1935

Cranfield, L. M. (Glos) b Aug. 29, 1909, d Nov. 18, 1993

Cranmer, P. (Warwicks & Eur.) b Sept. 10, 1914, d May 29, 1994

*Cranston, J. (Glos) b Jan. 9, 1859, d Dec. 10, 1904

*Cranston, K. (Lancs) b Oct. 20, 1917

*Crapp, J. F. (Glos; Test umpire) b Oct. 14, 1912, d Feb. 15, 1981

*Crawford, J. N. (Surrey, S. Aust., Wgtn & Otago; *CY 1907*) b Dec. 1, 1886, d May 2, 1963

*Crawford, P. (NSW) b Aug. 3, 1933

Crawford, V. F. S. (Surrey & Leics) b April 11, 1879, d Aug. 21, 1922

Crawley, A. M. MBE (OU & Kent; Pres. MCC 1972-73) b April 10, 1908, d Nov. 3, 1993

*Crawley, J. P. (Lancs & CU) b Sept. 21, 1971
Cray, S. J. (Essex) b May 29, 1921
Creese, W. L. (Hants) b Dec. 27, 1907, d March 9, 1974
*Cresswell, G. F. (Wgtn & C. Dist.) b March 22, 1915, d Jan. 10, 1966
*Cripps, G. (W. Prov.) b Oct. 19, 1865, d July 27, 1943
*Crisp, R. J. (Rhod., W. Prov. & Worcs) b May 28, 1911, d March 3, 1994
*Crocker, G. J. (MCD) b May 16, 1962
*Croft, C. E. H. (Guyana & Lancs) b March 15, 1953
*Croft, R. D. B. (Glam) b May 25, 1970
*Cromb, I. B. (Cant.) b June 25, 1905, d March 6, 1984
*Cronje, W. J. (†FS & Leics) b Sept. 25, 1969
Croom, A. J. (Warwicks) b May 23, 1896, d Aug. 16, 1947
*Crowe, J. J. (S. Aust. & Auck.) b Sept. 14, 1958
*Crowe, M. D. MBE (Auck., C. Dist., Som & Wgtn; *CY 1985*) b Sept. 22, 1962
Crump, B. S. (Northants) b April 25, 1938
Cuffe, J. A. (NSW & Worcs) b June 26, 1880, d May 16, 1931
*Cuffy, C. E. (Windwards & Surrey) b Feb. 8, 1970
*Cullinan, D. J. (Border, W. Prov., Tvl & Derbys) b March 4, 1967
Cumbes, J. (Lancs, Surrey, Worcs & Warwicks) b May 4, 1944
*Cummins, A. C. (B'dos & Durham) b May 7, 1966
*Cunis, R. S. (Auck. & N. Dist.) b Jan. 5, 1941
*Curnow, S. H. (Tvl) b Dec. 16, 1907, d July 28, 1986
*Curtis, T. S. (Worcs & CU) b Jan. 15, 1960
Cutmore, J. A. (Essex) b Dec. 28, 1898, d Nov. 30, 1985
*Cuttell, W. R. (Lancs; *CY 1898*) b Sept. 13, 1864, d Dec. 9, 1929

*Da Costa, O. C. (Jam.) b Sept. 11, 1907, d Oct. 1, 1936
Dacre, C. C. (Auck. & Glos) b May 15, 1899, d Nov. 2, 1975
Daft, H. B. (Notts) b April 5, 1866, d Jan. 12, 1945
Daft, Richard (Notts & All-England) b Nov. 2, 1835, d July 18, 1900
Dalmeny, Lord (later 6th Earl of Rosebery) (Middx, Surrey & Scotland) b Jan. 8, 1882, d May 30, 1974
Dalmiya, J. (President ICC 1997-   ) b May 30, 1940
*Dalton, E. L. (Natal) b Dec. 2, 1906, d June 3, 1981
*Dani, H. T. (M'tra & Ind. Serv.) b May 24, 1933
*Daniel, W. W. (B'dos, Middx & W. Aust.) b Jan. 16, 1956

*D'Arcy, J. W. (Cant., Wgtn & Otago) b April 23, 1936
Dare, R. (Hants) b Nov. 26, 1921
*Darling, J. (S. Aust.; *CY 1900*) b Nov. 21, 1870, d Jan. 2, 1946
*Darling, L. S. (Vic.) b Aug. 14, 1909, d June 24, 1992
*Darling, W. M. (S. Aust.) b May 1, 1957
*Dassanayake, P. B. (Bloom. & C. Prov.) b July 11, 1970
Davey, J. (Glos) b Sept. 4, 1944
*Davidson, A. K. OBE (NSW; *CY 1962*) b June 14, 1929
Davidson, G. (Derbys) b June 29, 1866, d Feb. 8, 1899
Davies, Dai (Glam; Test umpire) b Aug. 26, 1896, d July 16, 1976
Davies, Emrys (Glam; Test umpire) b June 27, 1904, d Nov. 10, 1975
*Davies, E. Q. (E. Prov., Tvl & NE Tvl) b Aug. 26, 1909, d Nov. 11, 1976
Davies, H. G. (Glam) b April 23, 1912, d Sept. 4, 1993
Davies, J. G. W. OBE (CU & Kent; Pres. MCC 1985-86) b Sept. 10, 1911, d Nov. 5, 1992
Davies, S. G. (Mat.) b May 12, 1977
Davies, T. (Glam) b Oct. 25, 1960
*Davis, B. A. (T/T & Glam) b May 2, 1940
*Davis, C. A. (T/T) b Jan. 1, 1944
Davis, E. (Northants) b March 8, 1922
*Davis, H. T. (Wgtn) b Nov. 30, 1971
*Davis, I. C. (NSW & Qld) b June 25, 1953
Davis, P. (Northants) b May 24, 1915
Davis, R. C. (Glam) b Jan. 1, 1946
*Davis, S. P. (Vic.) b Nov. 8, 1959
*Davis, W. W. (Windwards, Glam, Tas., Northants & Wgtn) b Sept. 18, 1958
Davison, B. F. (Rhod., Leics, Tas. & Glos) b Dec. 21, 1946
Davison, I. J. (Notts) b Oct. 4, 1937
Dawkes, G. O. (Leics & Derbys) b July 19, 1920
*Dawson, E. W. (CU & Leics) b Feb. 13, 1904, d June 4, 1979
*Dawson, O. C. (Natal & Border) b Sept. 1, 1919
Day, A. P. (Kent; *CY 1910*) b April 10, 1885, d Jan. 22, 1969
*de Alwis, R. G. (SSC) b Feb. 15, 1959
*Dean, H. (Lancs) b Aug. 13, 1884, d March 12, 1957
Dean, J., sen. (Sussex) b Jan. 4, 1816, d Dec. 25, 1881
*Deane, H. G. (Natal & Tvl) b July 21, 1895, d Oct. 21, 1939
*De Caires, F. I. (BG) b May 12, 1909, d Feb. 2, 1959
*De Courcy, J. H. (NSW) b April 18, 1927
*DeFreitas, P. A. J. (Leics, Lancs, Boland & Derbys; *CY 1992*) b Feb. 18, 1966

*de Groen, R. P. (Auck. & N. Dist.) b Aug. 5, 1962

*Dekker, M. H. (Mat.) b Dec. 5, 1969

*Dell, A. R. (Qld) b Aug. 6, 1947

*de Mel, A. L. F. (SL) b May 9, 1959

*Dempster, C. S. (Wgtn, Leics, Scotland & Warwicks; *CY 1932*) b Nov. 15, 1903, d Feb. 14, 1974

*Dempster, E. W. (Wgtn) b Jan. 25, 1925

*Denness, M. H. (Scotland, Kent & Essex; *CY 1975*) b Dec. 1, 1940

Dennett, G. (Glos) b April 27, 1880, d Sept. 14, 1937

Denning, P. W. (Som) b Dec. 16, 1949

Dennis, F. (Yorks) b June 11, 1907

Dennis, S. J. (Yorks, OFS & Glam) b Oct. 18, 1960

*Denton, D. (Yorks; *CY 1906*) b July 4, 1874, d Feb. 16, 1950

Deodhar, D. B. (M'tra) b Jan. 14, 1892, d Aug. 24, 1993

*Depeiza, C. C. (B'dos) b Oct. 10, 1928, d Nov. 10, 1995

*Desai, R. B. (Bombay) b June 20, 1939

*de Silva, A. M. (CCC) b Dec. 3, 1963

de Silva, D. L. S. (SL) b Nov. 17, 1956, d April 12, 1980

*de Silva, D. S. (Bloom.) b June 11, 1942

*de Silva, E. A. R. (NCC & Galle) b March 28, 1956

de Silva, G. N. (SL) b March 12, 1955

*de Silva, G. R. A. (SL) b Dec. 12, 1952

*de Silva, K. S. C. (Seb. & NCC) b Jan. 11, 1971

*de Silva, P. A. (NCC & Kent; *CY 1996*) b Oct. 17, 1965

de Smidt, R. W. (W. Prov.; *believed to be longest-lived first-class cricketer*) b Nov. 24, 1883, d Aug. 3, 1986

De Trafford, C. E. (Lancs & Leics) b May 21, 1864, d Nov. 11, 1951

Devereux, L. N. (Middx, Worcs & Glam) b Oct. 20, 1931

*de Villiers, P. S. (N. Tvl & Kent) b Oct. 13, 1964

Dewdney, C. T. (Jam.) b Oct. 23, 1933

*Dewes, J. G. (CU & Middx) b Oct. 11, 1926

Dews, G. (Worcs) b June 5, 1921

*Dexter, E. R. (CU & Sussex; *CY 1961*) b May 15, 1935

*Dhanraj, R. (T/T) b Feb. 6, 1969

*Dharmasena, H. D. P. K. (TU, Ant. & Bloom.) b April 24, 1971

*Dias, R. L. (CCC) b Oct. 18, 1952

Dibbs, A. H. A. (Pres. MCC 1983-84) b Dec. 9, 1918, d Nov. 28, 1985

*Dick, A. E. (Otago & Wgtn) b Oct. 10, 1936

*Dickinson, G. R. (Otago) b March 11, 1903, d March 17, 1978

*Dilawar Hussain (C. Ind. and U. Prov.) b March 19, 1907, d Aug. 26, 1967

*Dilley, G. R. (Kent, Natal & Worcs) b May 18, 1959

Dillon, E. W. (Kent & OU) b Feb. 15, 1881, d April 20, 1941

*Dillon, M. (T/T) b June 5, 1974

*Dipper, A. E. (Glos) b Nov. 9, 1885, d Nov. 7, 1945

*Divecha, R. V. (Bombay, OU, Northants, Vidarbha & S'tra) b Oct. 18, 1927

Diver, A. J. D. (Cambs., Middx, Notts & All-England) b June 6, 1824, d March 25, 1876

Diver, E. J. (Surrey & Warwicks) b March 20, 1861, d Dec. 27, 1924

Dixon, A. L. (Kent) b Nov. 27, 1933

*Dixon, C. D. (Tvl) b Feb. 12, 1891, d Sept. 9, 1969

Dixon, J. A. (Notts) b May 27, 1861, d June 8, 1931

Dodds, T. C. (Essex) b May 29, 1919

*Dodemaide, A. I. C. (Vic. & Sussex) b Oct. 5, 1963

*Doggart, G. H. G. OBE (CU & Sussex; Pres. MCC 1981-82) b July 18, 1925

*D'Oliveira, B. L. OBE (Worcs; *CY 1967*) b Oct. 4, 1931

D'Oliveira, D. B. (Worcs) b Oct. 19, 1960

*Dollery, H. E. (Warwicks & Wgtn; *CY 1952*) b Oct. 14, 1914, d Jan. 20, 1987

*Dolphin, A. (Yorks) b Dec. 24, 1885, d Oct. 23, 1942

*Donald, A. A. (†FS & Warwicks; *CY 1992*) b Oct. 20, 1966

*Donnan, H. (NSW) b Nov. 12, 1864, d Aug. 13, 1956

*Donnelly, M. P. (Wgtn, Cant., OU, Middx & Warwicks; *CY 1948*) b Oct. 17, 1917

*Dooland, B. (S. Aust. & Notts; *CY 1955*) b Nov. 1, 1923, d Sept. 8, 1980

Dorrinton, W. (Kent & All-England) b April 29, 1809, d Nov. 8, 1848

Dorset, 3rd Duke of (Kent) b March 24, 1745, d July 19, 1799

*Doshi, D. R. (Bengal, Notts, Warwicks & S'tra) b Dec. 22, 1947

*Douglas, J. W. H. T. (Essex; *CY 1915*) b Sept. 3, 1882, d Dec. 19, 1930

Douglas, M. W. (C. Dist. & Wgtn) b Oct. 20, 1968

*Doull, S. B. (N. Dist.) b Aug. 6, 1969

Dovey, R. R. (Kent) b July 18, 1920, d Dec. 27, 1974

*Dowe, U. G. (Jam.) b March 29, 1949

*Dower, R. R. (E. Prov.) b June 4, 1876, d Sept. 15, 1964

*Dowling, G. T. OBE (Cant.) b March 4, 1937

*Downton, P. R. (Kent & Middx) b April 4, 1957

*Draper, R. G. (E. Prov & Griq. W.) b Dec. 24, 1926

*Dravid, R. S. (Karn.) b Jan. 11, 1973

Dredge, C. H. (Som) b Aug. 4, 1954

*Druce, N. F. (CU & Surrey; *CY 1898*) b Jan. 1, 1875, d Oct. 27, 1954

Drybrough, C. D. (OU & Middx) b Aug. 31, 1938

*D'Souza, A. (Kar., Peshawar & PIA) b Jan. 17, 1939

*Ducat, A. (Surrey; *CY 1920*) b Feb. 16, 1886, d July 23, 1942

*Duckworth, C. A. R. (Natal & Rhod.) b March 22, 1933

*Duckworth, G. (Lancs; *CY 1929*) b May 9, 1901, d Jan. 5, 1966

Dudleston, B. (Leics, Glos & Rhod.; Test umpire) b July 16, 1945

Duers, K. G. (Mash.) b June 30, 1960

*Duff, R. A. (NSW) b Aug. 17, 1878, d Dec. 13, 1911

*Dujon, P. J. L. (Jam.; *CY 1989*) b May 28, 1956

*Duleepsinhji, K. S. (CU & Sussex; *CY 1930*) b June 13, 1905, d Dec. 5, 1959

*Dumbrill, R. (Natal & Tvl) b Nov. 19, 1938

*Duminy, J. P. (OU, W. Prov. & Tvl) b Dec. 16, 1897, d Jan. 31, 1980

*Duncan, J. R. F. (Qld & Vic.) b March 25, 1944

*Dunell, O. R. (E. Prov.) b July 15, 1856, d Oct. 21, 1929

*Dunning, J. A. (Otago & OU) b Feb. 6, 1903, d June 24, 1971

*Dunusinghe, C. I. (Ant. & NCC) b Oct. 19, 1970

*Du Preez, J. H. (Rhod. & Zimb.) b Nov. 14, 1942

*Durani, S. A. (S'tra, Guj. & Raja.) b Dec. 11, 1934

*Durston, F. J. (Middx) b July 11, 1893, d April 8, 1965

*Du Toit, J. F. (SA) b April 5, 1868, d July 10, 1909

Dye, J. C. J. (Kent, Northants & E. Prov.) b July 24, 1942

*Dyer, D. V. (Natal) b May 2, 1914, d June 18, 1990

*Dyer, G. C. (NSW) b March 16, 1959

*Dymock, G. (Qld) b July 21, 1945

Dyson, A. H. (Glam) b July 10, 1905, d June 7, 1978

Dyson, Jack (Lancs) b July 8, 1934

*Dyson, John (NSW) b June 11, 1954

*Eady, C. J. (Tas.) b Oct. 29, 1870, d Dec. 20, 1945

Eagar, E. D. R. (OU, Glos & Hants) b Dec. 8, 1917, d Sept. 13, 1977

Ealham, A. G. E. (Kent) b Aug. 30, 1944

*Ealham, M. A. (Kent) b Aug. 27, 1969

East, D. E. (Essex) b July 27, 1959

East, R. E. (Essex) b June 20, 1947

Eastman, L. C. (Essex & Otago) b June 3, 1897, d April 17, 1941

*Eastwood, K. H. (Vic.) b Nov. 23, 1935

*Ebeling, H. I. MBE (Vic.) b Jan. 1, 1905, d Jan. 12, 1980

Eckersley, P. T. (Lancs) b July 2, 1904, d Aug. 13, 1940

*Edgar, B. A. (Wgtn) b Nov. 23, 1956

Edinburgh, HRH Duke of (Pres. MCC 1948-49, 1974-75) b June 10, 1921

Edmeades, B. E. A. (Essex) b Sept. 17, 1941

*Edmonds, P. H. (CU, Middx & E. Prov.) b March 8, 1951

Edrich, B. R. (Kent & Glam) b Aug. 18, 1922

Edrich, E. H. (Lancs) b March 27, 1914, d July 9, 1993

Edrich, G. A. (Lancs) b July 13, 1918

*Edrich, J. H. MBE (Surrey; *CY 1966*) b June 21, 1937

*Edrich, W. J. (Middx; *CY 1940*) b March 26, 1916, d April 24, 1986

*Edwards, G. N. (C. Dist.) b May 27, 1955

*Edwards, J. D. (Vic.) b June 12, 1862, d July 31, 1911

Edwards, M. J. (CU & Surrey) b March 1, 1940

*Edwards, R. (W. Aust. & NSW) b Dec. 1, 1942

*Edwards, R. M. (B'dos) b June 3, 1940

*Edwards, W. J. (W. Aust.) b Dec. 23, 1949

*Ehtesham-ud-Din (Lahore, Punjab, PIA, NBP & UBL) b Sept. 4, 1950

*Eksteen, C. E. (Tvl) b Dec. 2, 1966

*Elgie, M. K. (Natal) b March 6, 1933

Elliott, C. S. MBE (Derbys; Test umpire) b April 24, 1912

Elliott, Harold (Lancs; Test umpire) b June 15, 1904, d April 15, 1969

Elliott, Harry (Derbys) b Nov. 2, 1891, d Feb. 2, 1976

*Elliott, M. T. G. (Vic; *CY 1998*) b Sept. 28, 1971

*Ellison, R. M. (Kent & Tas.; *CY 1986*) b Sept. 21, 1959

*Emburey, J. E. (Middx, W. Prov. & Northants; *CY 1984*) b Aug. 20, 1952

*Emery, P. A. (NSW) b June 25, 1964

*Emery, R. W. G. (Auck. & Cant.) b March 28, 1915, d Dec. 18, 1982

*Emery, S. H. (NSW) b Oct. 16, 1885, d Jan. 7, 1967

*Emmett, G. M. (Glos) b Dec. 2, 1912, d Dec. 18, 1976

*Emmett, T. (Yorks) b Sept. 3, 1841, d June 30, 1904

*Endean, W. R. (Tvl) b May 31, 1924

*Engineer, F. M. (Bombay & Lancs) b Feb. 25, 1938

Enthoven, H. J. (CU & Middx) b June 4, 1903, d June 29, 1975

Essop-Adam, E. A. (Mash.) b Nov. 16, 1968

*Evans, A. J. (OU, Hants & Kent) b May 1, 1889, d Sept. 18, 1960

*Evans, C. N. (Mash.) b Nov. 29, 1969

Evans, D. G. L. (Glam; Test umpire) b July 27, 1933, d March 25, 1990

*Evans, E. (NSW) b March 26, 1849, d July 2, 1921

*Evans, T. G. CBE (Kent; *CY 1951*) b Aug. 18, 1920

Evershed, Sir Sydney H. (Derbys) b Jan. 13, 1861, d March 7, 1937

Every, T. (Glam) b Dec. 19, 1909, d Jan. 20, 1990

Eyre, T. J. P. (Derbys) b Oct. 17, 1939

*Fagg, A. E. (Kent; Test umpire) b June 18, 1915, d Sept. 13, 1977

*Fairbrother, N. H. (Lancs & Tvl) b Sept. 9, 1963

*Fairfax, A. G. (NSW) b June 16, 1906, d May 17, 1955

Fairservice, W. J. (Kent) b May 16, 1881, d June 26, 1971

*Fane, F. L. (OU & Essex) b April 27, 1875, d Nov. 27, 1960

*Farnes, K. (CU & Essex; *CY 1939*) b July 8, 1911, d Oct. 20, 1941

*Farooq Hamid (Lahore & PIA) b March 3, 1945

*Farrer, W. S. (Border) b Dec. 8, 1936

*Farrimond, W. (Lancs) b May 23, 1903, d Nov. 14, 1979

*Farrukh Zaman (Peshawar, NWFP, Punjab & MCB) b April 2, 1956

*Faulkner, G. A. (Tvl) b Dec. 17, 1881, d Sept. 10, 1930

*Favell, L. E. MBE (S. Aust.) b Oct. 6, 1929, d June 14, 1987

*Fazal Mahmood (N. Ind., Punjab & Lahore; *CY 1955*) b Feb. 18, 1927

Fearnley, C. D. (Worcs; bat-maker) b April 12, 1940

Featherstone, N. G. (Tvl, N. Tvl, Middx & Glam) b Aug. 20, 1949

'Felix', N. (Wanostrocht) (Kent, Surrey & All-England) b Oct. 4, 1804, d Sept. 3, 1876

*Fellows-Smith, J. P. (OU, Tvl & Northants) b Feb. 3, 1932

Feltham, M. A. (Surrey & Middx) b June 26, 1963

Felton, N. A. (Som & Northants) b Oct. 24, 1960

*Fender, P. G. H. (Sussex & Surrey; *CY 1915*) b Aug. 22, 1892, d June 15, 1985

*Ferguson, W. (T/T) b Dec. 14, 1917, d Feb. 23, 1961

*Fernandes, M. P. (BG) b Aug. 12, 1897, d May 8, 1981

Fernando, E. R. (SL) b Feb. 22, 1944

*Fernando, E. R. N. S. (SLAF) b Dec. 19, 1955

Fernando, T. L. (Colts & BRC) b Dec. 27, 1962

Ferreira, A. M. (N. Tvl & Warwicks) b April 13, 1955

**Ferris, J. J. (NSW, Glos & S. Aust.; *CY 1889*) b May 21, 1867, d Nov. 21, 1900

*Fichardt, C. G. (OFS) b March 20, 1870, d May 30, 1923

Fiddling, K. (Yorks & Northants) b Oct. 13, 1917, d June 19, 1992

Field, F. E. (Warwicks) b Sept. 23, 1874, d Aug. 25, 1934

*Fielder, A. (Kent; *CY 1907*) b July 19, 1877, d Aug. 30, 1949

*Findlay, T. M. MBE (Comb. Is. & Windwards) b Oct. 19, 1943

Findlay, W. (OU & Lancs; Sec. Surrey CCC 1907-19; Sec. MCC 1926-36) b June 22, 1880, d June 19, 1953

*Fingleton, J. H. OBE (NSW; writer) b April 28, 1908, d Nov. 22, 1981

*Finlason, C. E. (Tvl & Griq. W.) b Feb. 19, 1860, d July 31, 1917

Finney, R. J. (Derbys) b Aug. 2, 1960

Firth, Canon J. D'E. E. (Winchester, OU & Notts; *CY 1918*) b Jan. 21, 1900, d Sept. 21, 1957

Firth, J. (Yorks & Leics) b June 27, 1917, d Sept. 7, 1981

*Fisher, F. E. (Wgtn & C. Dist.) b July 28, 1924, d June 19, 1996

*Fishlock, L. B. (Surrey; *CY 1947*) b Jan. 2, 1907, d June 26, 1986

Fishwick, T. S. (Warwicks) b July 24, 1876, d Feb. 21, 1950

Fitzgerald, R. A. (CU & Middx; Sec. MCC 1863-76) b Oct. 1, 1834, d Oct. 28, 1881

Fitzroy-Newdegate, Hon. J. M. (Northants) b March 20, 1897, d May 7, 1976

*Flavell, J. A. (Worcs; *CY 1965*) b May 15, 1929

*Fleetwood-Smith, L. O'B. (Vic.) b March 30, 1908, d March 16, 1971

*Fleming, D. W. (Vic.) b April 24, 1970

*Fleming, S. P. (Cant.) b April 1, 1973

Fletcher, D. A. G. (Rhod. & Zimb.) b Sept. 27, 1948

Fletcher, D. G. W. (Surrey) b July 6, 1924

*Fletcher, K. W. R. OBE (Essex; *CY 1974*) b May 20, 1944

Fletcher, S. D. (Yorks & Lancs) b June 8, 1964

*Floquet, C. E. (Tvl) b Nov. 3, 1884, d Nov. 22, 1963

*Flower, A. (Mash.) b April 28, 1968

*Flower, G. W. (Mash.) b Dec. 20, 1970

*Flowers, W. (Notts) b Dec. 7, 1856, d Nov. 1, 1926

*Foley, H. (Wgtn) b Jan. 28, 1906, d Oct. 16, 1948

Folley, I. (Lancs & Derbys) b Jan. 9, 1963, d Aug. 30, 1993

Forbes, C. (Notts) b Aug. 9, 1936

*Ford, F. G. J. (CU & Middx) b Dec. 14, 1866, d Feb. 7, 1940

Foreman, D. J. (W. Prov. & Sussex) b Feb. 1, 1933

*Foster, F. R. (Warwicks; *CY 1912*) b Jan. 31, 1889, d May 3, 1958

Foster, G. N. (OU, Worcs & Kent) b Oct. 16, 1884, d Aug. 11, 1971

*Foster, H. K. (OU & Worcs; *CY 1911*) b Oct. 30, 1873, d June 23, 1950

Foster, M. K. (Worcs) b Jan. 1, 1889, d Dec. 3, 1940

*Foster, M. L. C. (Jam.) b May 9, 1943

*Foster, N. A. (Essex & Tvl; *CY 1988*) b May 6, 1962

*Foster, R. E. (OU & Worcs; *CY 1901*) b April 16, 1878, d May 13, 1914

*Fothergill, A. J. (Som) b Aug. 26, 1854, d Aug. 1, 1932

Fowke, G. H. S. (Leics) b Oct. 14, 1880, d June 24, 1946

*Fowler, G. (Lancs & Durham) b April 20, 1957

*Francis, B. C. (NSW & Essex) b Feb. 18, 1948

Francis, D. A. (Glam) b Nov. 29, 1953

*Francis, G. N. (B'dos) b Dec. 11, 1897, d Jan. 7, 1942

*Francis, H. H. (Glos & W. Prov.) b May 26, 1868, d Jan. 7, 1936

Francke, F. M. (SL & Qld) b March 29, 1941

*Francois, C. M. (Griq. W.) b June 20, 1897, d May 26, 1944

*Frank, C. N. (Tvl) b Jan. 27, 1891, d Dec. 25, 1961

*Frank, W. H. B. (SA) b Nov. 23, 1872, d Feb. 16, 1945

*Franklin, T. J. (Auck.) b March 18, 1962

*Fraser, A. R. C. (Middx; *CY 1996*) b Aug. 8, 1965

*Frederick, M. (B'dos, Derbys & Jam.) b May 6, 1927

*Fredericks, R. C. (†Guyana & Glam; *CY 1974*) b Nov. 11, 1942

*Freeman, A. P. (Kent; *CY 1923*) b May 17, 1888, d Jan. 28, 1965

*Freeman, D. L. (Wgtn) b Sept. 8, 1914, d May 31, 1994

*Freeman, E. W. (S. Aust.) b July 13, 1944

Freeman, J. R. (Essex) b Sept. 3, 1883, d Aug. 8, 1958

*Freer, F. W. (Vic.) b Dec. 4, 1915

*French, B. N. (Notts) b Aug. 13, 1959

Frost, G. (Notts) b Jan. 15, 1947

*Fry, C. B. (OU, Sussex & Hants; *CY 1895*) b April 25, 1872, d Sept. 7, 1956

*Fuller, E. R. H. (W. Prov.) b Aug. 2, 1931

*Fuller, R. L. (Jam.) b Jan. 30, 1913, d May 3, 1987

*Fullerton, G. M. (Tvl) b Dec. 8, 1922

*Funston, K. J. (NE Tvl, OFS & Tvl) b Dec. 3, 1925

*Furlonge, H. A. (T/T) b June 19, 1934

Gabriel, R. S. (T/T) b June 5, 1952

*Gadkari, C. V. (M'tra & Ind. Serv.) b Feb. 3, 1928, d Jan. 12, 1998

*Gaekwad, A. D. (Baroda) b Sept. 23, 1952

*Gaekwad, D. K. (Baroda) b Oct. 27, 1928

*Gaekwad, H. G. (†M. Pradesh) b Aug. 29, 1923

Gale, R. A. (Middx) b Dec. 10, 1933

*Gallian, J. E. R. (Lancs & OU) b June 25, 1971

*Gallichan, N. (Wgtn) b June 3, 1906, d March 25, 1969

*Gamsy, D. (Natal) b Feb. 17, 1940

*Gandotra, A. (Delhi & Bengal) b Nov. 24, 1948

*Ganesh, D. (Karn.) b June 30, 1973

*Ganguly, S. C. (Bengal) b July 8, 1972

*Gannon, J. B. (W. Aust.) b Feb. 8, 1947

*Ganteaume, A. G. (T/T) b Jan. 22, 1921

Gard, T. (Som) b June 2, 1957

Gardner, F. C. (Warwicks) b June 4, 1922, d Jan. 12, 1979

Gardner, L. R. (Leics) b Feb. 23, 1934

Garland-Wells, H. M. (OU & Surrey) b Nov. 14, 1907, d May 28, 1993

Garlick, R. G. (Lancs & Northants) b April 11, 1917, d May 16, 1988

*Garner, J. MBE (B'dos, Som & S. Aust.; *CY 1980*) b Dec. 16, 1952

Garnham, M. A. (Glos, Leics & Essex) b Aug. 20, 1960

*Garrett, T. W. (NSW) b July 26, 1858, d Aug. 6, 1943

*Gaskin, B. B. M. (BG) b March 21, 1908, d May 1, 1979

*Gatting, M. W. OBE (Middx; *CY 1984*) b June 6, 1957

*Gaunt, R. A. (W. Aust. & Vic.) b Feb. 26, 1934

*Gavaskar, S. M. (Bombay & Som; *CY 1980*) b July 10, 1949

*Gay, L. H. (CU, Hants & Som) b March 24, 1871, d Nov. 1, 1949

*Geary, G. (Leics; *CY 1927*) b July 9, 1893, d March 6, 1981

*Gedye, S. G. (Auck.) b May 2, 1929

*Gehrs, D. R. A. (S. Aust.) b Nov. 29, 1880, d June 25, 1953

*Germon, L. K. (Cant.) b Nov. 4, 1968

Ghai, R. S. (Punjab) b June 12, 1960

*Ghavri, K. D. (S'tra & Bombay) b Feb. 28, 1951

*Ghazali, M. E. Z. (M'tra & Pak. Serv.) b June 15, 1924

*Ghorpade, J. M. (Baroda) b Oct. 2, 1930, d March 29, 1978

*Ghulam Abbas (Kar., NBP & PIA) b May 1, 1947

*Ghulam Ahmed (H'bad) b July 4, 1922

*Gibb, P. A. (CU, Scotland, Yorks & Essex) b July 11, 1913, d Dec. 7, 1977

Gibbons, H. H. (Worcs) b Oct. 10, 1904, d Feb. 16, 1973

*Gibbs, G. L. (BG) b Dec. 27, 1925, d Feb. 21, 1979

*Gibbs, H. H. (W. Prov.) b Feb. 23, 1974

*Gibbs, L. R. (†Guyana, S. Aust. & Warwicks; CY 1972) b Sept. 29, 1934

Gibbs, P. J. K. (OU & Derbys) b Aug. 17, 1944

Gibson, C. H. (Eton, CU & Sussex; CY 1918) b Aug. 23, 1900, d Dec. 31, 1976

Gibson, D. (Surrey) b May 1, 1936

*Gibson, O. D. (B'dos, Border & Glam) b March 16, 1969

*Giffen, G. (S. Aust.; CY 1894) b March 27, 1859, d Nov. 29, 1927

*Giffen, W. F. (S. Aust.) b Sept. 20, 1861, d June 29, 1949

*Gifford, N. MBE (Worcs & Warwicks; CY 1975) b March 30, 1940

*Gilbert, D. R. (NSW, Tas. & Glos) b Dec. 29, 1960

*Gilchrist, R. (Jam. & H'bad) b June 28, 1934

Giles, R. J. (Notts) b Oct. 17, 1919

Gilhouley, K. (Yorks & Notts) b Aug. 8, 1934

*Gillespie, J. N. (S. Aust.) b April 19, 1975

*Gillespie, S. R. (Auck.) b March 2, 1957

Gilliat, R. M. C. (OU & Hants) b May 20, 1944

*Gilligan, A. E. R. (CU, Surrey & Sussex; CY 1924; Pres. MCC 1967-68) b Dec. 23, 1894, d Sept. 5, 1976

*Gilligan, A. H. H. (Sussex) b June 29, 1896, d May 5, 1978

Gilligan, F. W. (OU & Essex) b Sept. 20, 1893, d May 4, 1960

Gillingham, Canon F. H. (Essex) b Sept. 6, 1875, d April 1, 1953

*Gilmour, G. J. (NSW) b June 26, 1951

*Gimblett, H. (Som; CY 1953) b Oct. 19, 1914, d March 30, 1978

*Gladstone, G (see Marais, G. G.)

*Gladwin, Cliff (Derbys) b April 3, 1916, d April 10, 1988

*Gleeson, J. W. (NSW & E. Prov.) b March 14, 1938

*Gleeson, R. A. (E. Prov.) b Dec. 6, 1873, d Sept. 27, 1919

Glover, A. C. S. (Warwicks) b April 19, 1872, d May 22, 1949

*Glover, G. K. (Kimberley & Griq. W.) b May 13, 1870, d Nov. 15, 1938

*Goddard, J. D. C. OBE (B'dos) b April 21, 1919, d Aug. 26, 1987

*Goddard, T. L. (Natal & NE Tvl) b Aug. 1, 1931

*Goddard, T. W. (Glos; CY 1938) b Oct. 1, 1900, d May 22, 1966

Goel, R. (Patiala & Haryana) b Sept. 29, 1942

*Gomes, H. A. (T/T & Middx; CY 1985) b July 13, 1953

*Gomez, G. E. (T/T) b Oct. 10, 1919, d Aug. 6, 1996

*Gooch, G. A. OBE (Essex & W. Prov.; CY 1980) b July 23, 1953

Goodwin, K. (Lancs) b June 25, 1938

Goodwin, T. J. (Leics) b Jan. 22, 1929

Goonatillake, F. R. M. de S. (SL) b Aug. 15, 1951

*Goonatillake, H. M. (SL) b Aug. 16, 1952

Goonesena, G. (Ceylon, Notts, CU & NSW) b Feb. 16, 1931

*Gopalan, M. J. (Madras) b June 6, 1909

*Gopinath, C. D. (Madras) b March 1, 1930

*Gordon, N. (Tvl) b Aug. 6, 1911

Gore, A. C. (Eton & Army; CY 1919) b May 14, 1900, d June 7, 1990

Gough, D. (Yorks) b Sept. 18, 1970

Gould, I. J. (Middx, Auck. & Sussex) b Aug. 19, 1957

*Gover, A. R. MBE (Surrey; CY 1937; oldest surviving CY) b Feb. 29, 1908

*Gower, D. I. OBE (Leics & Hants; CY 1979) b April 1, 1957

Gowrie, 1st Lord (Pres. MCC 1948-49) b July 6, 1872, d May 2, 1955

Grace, C. B. (London County; son of W. G.) b March 1882, d June 6, 1938

*Grace, Dr E. M. (Glos; brother of W. G.) b Nov. 28, 1841, d May 20, 1911

*Grace, G. F. (Glos; brother of W. G.) b Dec. 13, 1850, d Sept. 22, 1880

Grace, Dr Henry (Glos; brother of W. G.) b Jan. 31, 1833, d Nov. 15, 1895

Grace, Dr H. M. (father of W. G.) b Feb. 21, 1808, d Dec. 23, 1871

Grace, Mrs H. M. (mother of W. G.) b July 18, 1812, d July 25, 1884

*Grace, Dr W. G. (Glos; CY 1896) b July 18, 1848, d Oct. 23, 1915

Grace, W. G., jun. (CU & Glos; son of W. G.) b July 6, 1874, d March 2, 1905

Graf, S. F. (Vic., W. Aust. & Hants) b May 19, 1957

*Graham, H. (Vic. & Otago) b Nov. 22, 1870, d Feb. 7, 1911

Graham, J. N. (Kent) b May 8, 1943

*Graham, R. (W. Prov.) b Sept. 16, 1877, d April 21, 1946

*Grant, G. C. (CU, T/T & Rhod.) b May 9, 1907, d Oct. 26, 1978

*Grant, R. S. (CU & T/T) b Dec. 15, 1909, d Oct. 18, 1977

Graveney, D. A. (Glos, Som & Durham) b Jan. 2, 1953

Graveney, J. K. (Glos) b Dec. 16, 1924

*Graveney, T. W. OBE (Glos, Worcs & Qld; CY 1953) b June 16, 1927

Graves, P. J. (Sussex & OFS) b May 19, 1946

*Gray, A. H. (T/T, Surrey & W. Tvl) b May 23, 1963

*Gray, E. J. (Wgtn) b Nov. 18, 1954

Gray, J. R. (Hants) b May 19, 1926

Gray, L. H. (Middx) b Dec. 15, 1915, d Jan. 3, 1983

*Greatbatch, M. J. (C. Dist.) b Dec. 11, 1963

Green, A. M. (Sussex & OFS) b May 28, 1960

Green, D. M. (OU, Lancs & Glos; CY 1969) b Nov. 10, 1939

Green, Major L. (Lancs) b Feb. 1, 1890, d March 2, 1963

*Greenhough, T. (Lancs) b Nov. 9, 1931

*Greenidge, A. E. (B'dos) b Aug. 20, 1956

*Greenidge, C. G. MBE (Hants & B'dos; CY 1977) b May 1, 1951

*Greenidge, G. A. (B'dos & Sussex) b May 26, 1948

Greensmith, W. T. (Essex) b Aug. 16, 1930

*Greenwood, A. (Yorks) b Aug. 20, 1847, d Feb. 12, 1889

Greetham, C. (Som) b Aug. 28, 1936

*Gregory, D. W. (NSW; first Australian captain) b April 15, 1845, d Aug. 4, 1919

*Gregory, E. J. (NSW) b May 29, 1839, d April 22, 1899

*Gregory, J. M. (NSW; CY 1922) b Aug. 14, 1895, d Aug. 7, 1973

*Gregory, R. G. (Vic.) b Feb. 28, 1916, d June 10, 1942

Gregory, R. J. (Surrey) b Aug. 26, 1902, d Oct. 6, 1973

*Gregory, S. E. (NSW; CY 1897) b April 14, 1870, d Aug. 1, 1929

*Greig, A. W. (Border, E. Prov. & Sussex; CY 1975) b Oct. 6, 1946

*Greig, I. A. (CU, Border, Sussex & Surrey) b Dec. 8, 1955

*Grell, M. G. (T/T) b Dec. 18, 1899, d Jan. 11, 1976

*Grieve, B. A. F. (Eng.) b May 28, 1864, d Nov. 19, 1917

Grieves, K. J. (NSW & Lancs) b Aug. 27, 1925, d Jan. 3, 1992

*Grieveson, R. E. (Tvl) b Aug. 24, 1909

*Griffin, G. M. (Natal & Rhod.) b June 12, 1939

*Griffith, A. F. G. (B'dos) b Nov. 19, 1971

*Griffith, C. C. (B'dos; CY 1964) b Dec. 14, 1938

Griffith, G. ("Ben") (Surrey & Utd England XI) b Dec. 20, 1833, d May 3, 1879

*Griffith, H. C. (B'dos) b Dec. 1, 1893, d March 18, 1980

Griffith, M. G. (CU & Sussex) b Nov. 25, 1943

*Griffith, S. C. CBE (CU, Surrey & Sussex; Sec. MCC 1962-74; Pres. MCC 1979-80) b June 16, 1914, d April 7, 1993

Griffiths, B. J. (Northants) b June 13, 1949

Griffiths, W. H. (later Rt Hon. The Lord) (CU & Glam; Pres. MCC 1990-91) b Sept. 26, 1923

*Grimmett, C. V. (Wgtn, Vic., & S. Aust.; CY 1931) b Dec. 25, 1891, d May 2, 1980

*Groube, T. U. (Vic.) b Sept. 2, 1857, d Aug. 5, 1927

*Grout, A. T. W. (Qld) b March 30, 1927, d Nov. 9, 1968

Grove, C. W. (Warwicks & Worcs) b Dec. 16, 1912, d Feb. 15, 1982

Grundy, James (Notts & Utd England XI) b March 5, 1824, d Nov. 24, 1873

*Guard, G. M. (Bombay & Guj.) b Dec. 12, 1925, d March 13, 1978

*Guest, C. E. J. (Vic. & W. Aust.) b Oct. 7, 1937

*Guha, S. (Bengal) b Jan. 31, 1946

**Guillen, S. C. (T/T & Cant.) b Sept. 24, 1924

**Gul Mahomed (N. Ind., Baroda, H'bad, Punjab & Lahore) b Oct. 15, 1921, d May 8, 1992

*Gunasekera, Y. (SL) b Nov. 8, 1957

*Guneratne, R. P. W. (Nomads) b Jan. 26, 1962

*Gunn, G. (Notts; CY 1914) b June 13, 1879, d June 29, 1958

Gunn, G. V. (Notts) b June 21, 1905, d Oct. 14, 1957

*Gunn, J. (Notts; CY 1904) b July 19, 1876, d Aug. 21, 1963

*Gunn, W. (Notts; CY 1890) b Dec. 4, 1858, d Jan. 29, 1921

*Gupte, B. P. (Bombay, Bengal & Ind. Rlwys) b Aug. 30, 1934

*Gupte, S. P. (Bombay, Bengal, Raja. & T/T) b Dec. 11, 1929

*Gursharan Singh (Punjab) b March 8, 1963

*Gurusinha, A. P. (SSC & NCC) b Sept. 16, 1966

*Guy, J. W. (C. Dist., Wgtn, Northants, Cant., Otago & N. Dist.) b Aug. 29, 1934

Haafiz Shahid (WAPDA) b May 10, 1963

Hadlee, B. G. (Cant.) b Dec. 14, 1941

*Hadlee, D. R. (Cant.) b Jan. 6, 1948

*Hadlee, Sir Richard J. (Cant., Notts & Tas.; CY 1982) b July 3, 1951

*Hadlee, W. A. CBE (Cant. & Otago) b June 4, 1915

*Hafeez, A. (see Kardar)

*Haig, N. E. (Middx) b Dec. 12, 1887, d Oct. 27, 1966

*Haigh, S. (Yorks; CY 1901) b March 19, 1871, d Feb. 27, 1921

Halfyard, D. J. (Kent & Notts) b April 3, 1931, d Aug. 23, 1996

*Hall, A. E. (Tvl & Lancs) b Jan. 23, 1896, d Jan. 1, 1964

*Hall, G. G. (NE Tvl & E. Prov.) b May 24, 1938, d June 26, 1987

Hall, I. W. (Derbys) b Dec. 27, 1939

Hall, L. (Yorks; *CY 1890*) b Nov. 1, 1852, d Nov. 19, 1915

*Hall, W. W. (B'dos, T/T & Qld) b Sept. 12, 1937

Hallam, A. W. (Lancs & Notts; *CY 1908*) b Nov. 12, 1869, d July 24, 1940

Hallam, M. R. (Leics) b Sept. 10, 1931

Halliday, H. (Yorks) b Feb. 9, 1920, d Aug. 27, 1967

*Halliwell, E. A. (Tvl & Middx; *CY 1905*) b Sept. 7, 1864, d Oct. 2, 1919

*Hallows, C. (Lancs; *CY 1928*) b April 4, 1895, d Nov. 10, 1972

Hallows, J. (Lancs; *CY 1905*) b Nov. 14, 1873, d May 20, 1910

*Halse, C. G. (Natal) b Feb. 28, 1935

*Hamence, R. A. (S. Aust.) b Nov. 25, 1915

Hamer, A. (Yorks & Derbys) b Dec. 8, 1916, d Nov. 3, 1993

Hammond, H. E. (Sussex) b Nov. 7, 1907, d June 16, 1985

*Hammond, J. R. (S. Aust.) b April 19, 1950

*Hammond, W. R. (Glos; *CY 1928*) b June 19, 1903, d July 1, 1965

*Hampshire, J. H. (Yorks, Derbys & Tas.; Test umpire) b Feb. 10, 1941

*Hands, P. A. M. (W. Prov.) b March 18, 1890, d April 27, 1951

*Hands, R. H. M. (W. Prov.) b July 26, 1888, d April 20, 1918

*Hanif Mohammad (B'pur, Kar. & PIA; *CY 1968*) b Dec. 21, 1934

*Hanley, M. A. (Border & W. Prov.) b Nov. 10, 1918

*Hanumant Singh (M. Pradesh & Raja.) b March 29, 1939

Hardie, B. R. (Scotland & Essex) b Jan. 14, 1950

*Hardikar, M. S. (Bombay) b Feb. 8, 1936, d Feb. 4, 1995

*Hardinge, H. T. W. (Kent; *CY 1915*) b Feb. 25, 1886, d May 8, 1965

*Hardstaff, J. (Notts; Test umpire) b Nov. 9, 1882, d April 2, 1947

*Hardstaff, J., jun. (Notts & Auck.; *CY 1938*) b July 3, 1911, d Jan. 1, 1990

Hardy, J. J. E. (Hants, Som, W. Prov. & Glos) b Oct. 2, 1960

*Harford, N. S. (C. Dist. & Auck.) b Aug. 30, 1930, d March 30, 1981

*Harford, R. I. (Auck.) b May 30, 1936

Hargreave, S. (Warwicks) b Sept. 22, 1875, d Jan. 1, 1929

Harman, R. (Surrey) b Dec. 28, 1941

*Haroon Rashid (Kar., Sind, NBP, PIA & UBL) b March 25, 1953

*Harper, R. A. (Guyana & Northants) b March 17, 1963

*Harris, 4th Lord (OU & Kent; Pres. MCC 1895) b Feb. 3, 1851, d March 24, 1932

Harris, C. B. (Notts) b Dec. 6, 1907, d Aug. 8, 1954

*Harris, C. Z. (Cant.) b Nov. 20, 1969

Harris, David (Hants & All-England) b 1755, d May 19, 1803

Harris, M. J. (Middx, Notts, E. Prov. & Wgtn) b May 25, 1944

*Harris, P. G. Z. (Cant.) b July 18, 1927, d Dec. 1, 1991

*Harris, R. M. (Auck.) b July 27, 1933

*Harris, T. A. (Griq. W. & Tvl) b Aug. 27, 1916, d March 7, 1993

Harrison, L. (Hants) b June 8, 1922

*Harry, J. (Vic.) b Aug. 1, 1857, d Oct. 27, 1919

*Hart, M. N. (N. Dist.) b May 16, 1972

Hart, R. T. (C. Dist. & Wgtn) b Nov. 7, 1961

*Hartigan, G. P. D. (Border) b Dec. 30, 1884, d Jan. 7, 1955

*Hartigan, R. J. (NSW & Qld) b Dec. 12, 1879, d June 7, 1958

*Hartkopf, A. E. V. (Vic.) b Dec. 28, 1889, d May 20, 1968

*Hartland, B. R. (Cant.) b Oct. 22, 1966

Hartley, A. (Lancs; *CY 1911*) b April 11, 1879, d Oct. 9, 1918

*Hartley, J. C. (OU & Sussex) b Nov. 15, 1874, d March 8, 1963

Hartley, S. N. (Yorks & OFS) b March 18, 1956

Harvey, J. F. (Derbys) b Sept. 27, 1939

*Harvey, M. R. (Vic.) b April 29, 1918, d March 20, 1995

Harvey, P. F. (Notts) b Jan. 15, 1923

*Harvey, R. L. (Natal) b Sept. 14, 1911

*Harvey, R. N. MBE (Vic. & NSW; *CY 1954*) b Oct. 8, 1928

Hasan Jamil, (Kalat, Kar., Pak. Us & PIA) b July 25, 1952

*Hasan Raza (Kar.) b March 11, 1982

*Haseeb Ahsan (Peshawar, Pak. Us, Kar. & PIA) b July 15, 1939

*Haslam, M. J. (Auck.) b Sept. 26, 1972

Hassan, B. (Notts) b March 24, 1944

*Hassett, A. L. MBE (Vic.; *CY 1949*) b Aug. 28, 1913, d June 16, 1993

*Hastings, B. F. (Wgtn, C. Dist. & Cant.) b March 23, 1940

*Hathorn, C. M. H. (Tvl) b April 7, 1878, d May 17, 1920

*Hathurusinghe, U. C. (TU) b Sept. 13, 1968

*Hawke, 7th Lord (CU & Yorks; *CY 1909*; Pres. MCC 1914-18) b Aug. 16, 1860, d Oct. 10, 1938

*Hawke, N. J. N. (W. Aust., S. Aust. & Tas.) b June 27, 1939

Hawker, Sir Cyril (Essex; Pres. MCC 1970-71) b July 21, 1900, d Feb. 22, 1991

Hawkins, D. G. (Glos) b May 18, 1935

*Hayden, M. L. (Qld & Hants) b Oct. 29, 1971

*Hayes, E. G. (Surrey & Leics; *CY 1907*) b Nov. 6, 1876, d Dec. 2, 1953

*Hayes, F. C. (Lancs) b Dec. 6, 1946

*Hayes, J. A. (Auck. & Cant.) b Jan. 11, 1927

Hayes, R. L. (N. Dist.) b May 9, 1971

Haygarth, A. (Sussex; Historian) b Aug. 4, 1825, d May 1, 1903

*Haynes, D. L. (B'dos, Middx & W. Prov.; *CY 1991*) b Feb. 15, 1956

Haynes, R. C. (Jam.) b Nov. 11, 1964

Hayward, T. (Cambs. & All-England) b March 21, 1835, d July 21, 1876

*Hayward, T. W. (Surrey; *CY 1895*) b March 29, 1871, d July 19, 1939

*Hazare, V. S. (M'tra, C. Ind. & Baroda) b March 11, 1915

Hazell, H. L. (Som) b Sept. 30, 1909, d March 31, 1990

Hazlerigg, Sir A. G. Bt (later 1st Lord) (Leics) b Nov. 17, 1878, d May 25, 1949

Hazlitt, G. R. (Vic. & NSW) b Sept. 4, 1888, d Oct. 30, 1915

*Headley, D. W. (Middx & Kent) b Jan. 27, 1970

*Headley, G. A. MBE (Jam.; *CY 1934*) b May 30, 1909, d Nov. 30, 1983

*Headley, R. G. A. (Worcs & Jam.) b June 29, 1939

*Healy, I. A. (Qld; *CY 1994*) b April 30, 1964

Heane, G. F. H. (Notts) b Jan. 2, 1904, d Oct. 24, 1969

Heap, J. S. (Lancs) b Aug. 12, 1882, d Jan. 30, 1951

Hearn, P. (Kent) b Nov. 18, 1925

*Hearne, A. (Kent; *CY 1894*) b July 22, 1863, d May 16, 1952

**Hearne, F. (Kent & W. Prov.) b Nov. 23, 1858, d July 14, 1949

*Hearne, G. A. L. (W. Prov.) b March 27, 1888, d Nov. 13, 1978

*Hearne, G. G. (Kent) b July 7, 1856, d Feb. 13, 1932

*Hearne, J. T. (Middx; *CY 1892*) b May 3, 1867, d April 17, 1944

*Hearne, J. W. (Middx; *CY 1912*) b Feb. 11, 1891, d Sept. 14, 1965

Hearne, T. (Middx) b Sept. 4, 1826, d May 13, 1900

Heath, G. E. M. (Hants) b Feb. 20, 1913

Heath, M. (Hants) b March 9, 1934

Hedges, B. (Glam) b Nov. 10, 1927

Hedges, L. P (Tonbridge, OU, Kent & Glos; *CY 1919*) b July 13, 1900, d Jan. 12, 1933

*Heine, P. S. (NE Tvl, OFS & Tvl) b June 28, 1928

*Hemmings, E. E. (Warwicks, Notts & Sussex) b Feb. 20, 1949

Hemsley, E. J. O. (Worcs) b Sept. 1, 1943

*Henderson, M. (Wgtn) b Aug. 2, 1895, d June 17, 1970

Henderson, R. (Surrey; *CY 1890*) b March 30, 1865, d Jan. 29, 1931

*Hendren, E. H. (Middx; *CY 1920*) b Feb. 5, 1889, d Oct. 4, 1962

*Hendrick, M. (Derbys & Notts; *CY 1978*) b Oct. 22, 1948

*Hendriks, J. L. (Jam.) b Dec. 21, 1933

*Hendry, H. L. (NSW & Vic.) b May 24, 1895, d Dec. 16, 1988

*Henry, O. (W. Prov., Boland, OFS & Scotland) b Jan. 23, 1952

Herman, O. W. (Hants) b Sept. 18, 1907, d June 24, 1987

Herman, R. S. (Middx, Border, Griq. W. & Hants) b Nov. 30, 1946

Heron, J. G. (Zimb.) b Nov. 8, 1948

*Heseltine, C. (Hants) b Nov. 26, 1869, d June 13, 1944

Hever, N. G. (Middx & Glam) b Dec. 17, 1924, d Sept. 11, 1987

Hewett, H. T. (OU & Som; *CY 1893*) b May 25, 1864, d March 4, 1921.

Heyhoe-Flint, Rachael (England Women) b June 11, 1939

Heyn, P. D. (SL) b June 26, 1945

*Hibbert, P. A. (Vic.) b July 23, 1952

*Hick, G. A. (Worcs, Zimb., N. Dist. & Qld; *CY 1987*) b May 23, 1966

*Higgs, J. D. (Vic.) b July 11, 1950

*Higgs, K. (Lancs & Leics; *CY 1968*) b Jan. 14, 1937

Hignell, A. J. (CU & Glos) b Sept. 4, 1955

*Hilditch, A. M. J. (NSW & S. Aust.) b May 20, 1956

Hill, Alan (Derbys & OFS) b June 29, 1950

Hill, Allen (Yorks) b Nov. 14, 1843, d Aug. 29, 1910

*Hill, A. J. L. (CU & Hants) b July 26, 1871, d Sept. 6, 1950

*Hill, C. (S. Aust.; *CY 1900*) b March 18, 1877, d Sept. 5, 1945

Hill, E. (Som) b July 9, 1923

Hill, G. (Hants) b April 15, 1913

*Hill, J. C. (Vic.) b June 25, 1923, d Aug. 11, 1974

Hill, M. (Notts, Derbys & Som) b Sept. 14, 1935

Hill, N. W. (Notts) b Aug. 22, 1935

Hill, W. A. (Warwicks) b April 27, 1910, d Aug. 11, 1995

Hill-Wood, Sir Samuel H. (Derbys) b March 21, 1872, d Jan. 4, 1949

Hillyer, W. R. (Kent & Surrey) b March 5, 1813, d Jan. 8, 1861

Hilton, C. (Lancs & Essex) b Sept. 26, 1937

*Hilton, M. J. (Lancs; *CY 1957*) b Aug. 2, 1928, d July 8, 1990
*Hime, C. F. W. (Natal) b Oct. 24, 1869, d Dec. 6, 1940
*Hindlekar, D. D. (Bombay) b Jan. 1, 1909, d March 30, 1949
Hinks, S. G. (Kent & Glos) b Oct. 12, 1960
Hipkin, A. B. (Essex) b Aug. 8, 1900, d Feb. 11, 1957
*Hirst, G. H. (Yorks; *CY 1901*) b Sept. 7, 1871, d May 10, 1954
*Hirwani, N. D. (M. Pradesh & Bengal) b Oct. 18, 1968
*Hitch, J. W. (Surrey; *CY 1914*) b May 7, 1886, d July 7, 1965
Hitchcock, R. E. (Cant. & Warwicks) b Nov. 28, 1929
*Hoad, E. L. G. (B'dos) b Jan. 29, 1896, d March 5, 1986
*Hoare, D. E. (W. Aust.) b Oct. 19, 1934
*Hobbs, Sir John B. ''Jack'' (Surrey; *CY 1909, special portrait 1926*) b Dec. 16, 1882, d Dec. 21, 1963
*Hobbs, R. N. S. (Essex & Glam) b May 8, 1942
*Hodges, J. (Vic.) b Aug. 11, 1855, death unknown
Hodgson, A. (Northants) b Oct. 27, 1951
Hodgson, G. D. (Glos) b Oct. 22, 1966
*Hogan, T. G. (W. Aust.) b Sept. 23, 1956
*Hogg, G. B. (W. Aust.) b Feb. 6, 1971
*Hogg, R. M. (S. Aust.) b March 5, 1951
*Hohns, T. V. (Qld) b Jan. 23, 1954
Holder, J. W. (Hants; Test umpire) b March 19, 1945
*Holder, R. I. C. (B'dos) b Dec. 22, 1967
*Holder, V. A. (B'dos, Worcs & OFS) b Oct. 8, 1945
*Holding, M. A. (Jam., Lancs, Derbys, Tas. & Cant.; *CY 1977*) b Feb. 16, 1954
*Hole, G. B. (NSW & S. Aust.) b Jan. 6, 1931, d Feb. 14, 1990
*Holford, D. A. J. (B'dos & T/T) b April 16, 1940
Holland, F. C. (Surrey) b Feb. 10, 1876, d Feb. 5, 1957
*Holland, R. G. (NSW & Wgtn) b Oct. 19, 1946
*Hollies, W. E. (Warwicks; *CY 1955*) b June 5, 1912, d April 16, 1981
*Hollioake, A. J. (Surrey) b Sept. 5, 1971
*Hollioake, B. C. (Surrey) b Nov. 11, 1977
Holmes, Gp Capt. A. J. (Sussex) b June 30, 1899, d May 21, 1950
*Holmes, E. R. T. (OU & Surrey; *CY 1936*) b Aug. 21, 1905, d Aug. 16, 1960
Holmes, G. C. (Glam) b Sept. 16, 1958
*Holmes, P. (Yorks; *CY 1920*) b Nov. 25, 1886, d Sept. 3, 1971
Holt, A. G. (Hants) b April 8, 1911, d July 28, 1994

*Holt, J. K., jun. (Jam.) b Aug. 12, 1923, d July 2, 1997
Home of the Hirsel, Lord (Middx; Pres. MCC 1966-67) b July 2, 1903, d Oct. 9, 1995
*Hone, L. (MCC) b Jan. 30, 1853, d Dec. 31, 1896
Hooker, R. W. (Middx) b Feb. 22, 1935
*Hookes, D. W. (S. Aust.) b May 3, 1955
*Hooper, C. L. (Guyana & Kent) b Dec. 15, 1966
*Hopkins, A. J. (NSW) b May 3, 1874, d April 25, 1931
Hopkins, J. A. (Glam & E. Prov.) b June 16, 1953
Hopkins, V. (Glos) b Jan. 21, 1911, d Aug. 6, 1984
*Hopwood, J. L. (Lancs) b Oct. 30, 1903, d June 15, 1985
*Horan, T. P. (Vic.) b March 8, 1854, d April 16, 1916
*Hordern, Dr H. V. (NSW & Philadelphia) b Feb. 10, 1884, d June 17, 1938
Hornby, A. H. (CU & Lancs) b July 29, 1877, d Sept. 6, 1952
*Hornby, A. N. (Lancs) b Feb. 10, 1847, d Dec. 17, 1925
*Horne, M. J. (Auck. & Otago) b Feb. 5, 1970
*Horne, P. A. (Auck.) b Jan. 21, 1960
Horner, N. F. (Yorks & Warwicks) b May 10, 1926
*Hornibrook, P. M. (Qld) b July 27, 1899, d Aug. 25, 1976
Horsfall, R. (Essex & Glam) b June 26, 1920, d Aug. 25, 1981
Horton, H. (Worcs & Hants) b April 18, 1923
*Horton, M. J. (Worcs & N. Dist.) b April 21, 1934
*Hough, K. W. (Auck.) b Oct. 24, 1928
*Houghton, D. L. (Mash.) b June 23, 1957
*Howard, A. B. (B'dos) b Aug. 27, 1946
*Howard, N. D. (Lancs) b May 18, 1925, d May 31, 1979
Howard, Major R. (Lancs; MCC Team Manager) b April 17, 1890, d Sept. 10, 1967
*Howarth, G. P. OBE (Auck., Surrey & N. Dist.) b March 29, 1951
*Howarth, H. J. (Auck.) b Dec. 25, 1943
*Howell, H. (Warwicks) b Nov. 29, 1890, d July 9, 1932
*Howell, W. P. (NSW) b Dec. 29, 1869, d July 14, 1940
*Howorth, R. (Worcs) b April 26, 1909, d April 2, 1980
Hubble, J. C. (Kent) b Feb. 10, 1881, d Feb. 26, 1965
*Hudson, A. C. (Natal) b March 17, 1965
Huggins, H. J. (Glos) b March 15, 1877, d Nov. 20, 1942
Hughes, D. P. (Lancs & Tas.; *CY 1988*) b May 13, 1947

*Hughes, K. J. (W. Aust. & Natal; *CY 1981*) b Jan. 26, 1954

*Hughes, M. G. (Vic. & Essex; *CY 1994*) b Nov. 23, 1961

Hughes, S. P. (Middx, N. Tvl & Durham) b Dec. 20, 1959

Huish, F. H. (Kent) b Nov. 15, 1869, d March 16, 1957

Hulme, J. H. A. (Middx) b Aug. 26, 1904, d Sept. 26, 1991

Humpage, G. W. (Warwicks & OFS; *CY 1985*) b April 24, 1954

Humphrey, T. (Surrey) b Jan. 16, 1839, d Sept. 3, 1878

Humphreys, E. (Kent & Cant.) b Aug. 24, 1881, d Nov. 6, 1949

Humphreys, W. A. (Sussex & Hants) b Oct. 28, 1849, d March 23, 1924

Humphries, D. J. (Leics & Worcs) b Aug. 6, 1953

*Humphries, J. (Derbys) b May 19, 1876, d May 7, 1946

Hunt, A. V. (Scotland & Bermuda) b Oct. 1, 1910

Hunt, G. E. (Som) b Sept. 30, 1896, d Jan. 22, 1959

*Hunt, W. A. (NSW) b Aug. 26, 1908, d Dec. 30, 1983

*Hunte, C. C. (B'dos; *CY 1964*) b May 9, 1932

*Hunte, E. A. C. (T/T) b Oct. 3, 1905, d June 26, 1967

Hunter, D. (Yorks) b Feb. 23, 1860, d Jan. 11, 1927

*Hunter, J. (Yorks) b Aug. 3, 1855, d Jan. 4, 1891

*Hurst, A. G. (Vic.) b July 15, 1950

Hurst, R. J. (Middx) b Dec. 29, 1933, d Feb. 10, 1996

*Hurwood, A. (Qld) b June 17, 1902, d Sept. 26, 1982

*Hussain, N. (Essex) b March 28, 1968

*Hutchings, K. L. (Kent; *CY 1907*) b Dec. 7, 1882, d Sept. 3, 1916

Hutchinson, J. M. (Derbys; *believed to be oldest living county cricketer at end 1997*) b Nov. 29, 1896

*Hutchinson, P. (SA) b Jan. 26, 1862, d Sept. 30, 1925

*Hutton, Sir Leonard (Yorks; *CY 1938*) b June 23, 1916, d Sept. 6, 1990

*Hutton, R. A. (CU, Yorks & Tvl) b Sept. 6, 1942

*Hylton, L. G. (Jam.) b March 29, 1905, d May 17, 1955

*Ibadulla, K. (Punjab, Warwicks, Tas. & Otago) b Dec. 20, 1935

*Ibrahim, K. C. (Bombay) b Jan. 26, 1919

Iddison, R. (Yorks & Lancs) b Sept. 15, 1834, d March 19, 1890

*Iddon, J. (Lancs) b Jan. 8, 1902, d April 17, 1946

*Igglesden, A. P. (Kent & W. Prov.) b Oct. 8, 1964

*Ijaz Ahmed, sen. (Gujranwala, PACO, HBL, I'bad & Lahore) b Sept. 20, 1968

*Ijaz Ahmed, jun. (F'bad, ADBP & Pak. Rlwys) b Feb. 2, 1969

*Ijaz Butt (Pak. Us, Punjab, Lahore, R'pindi & Multan) b March 10, 1938

*Ijaz Faqih (Kar., Sind, PWD & MCB) b March 24, 1956

*Ikin, J. T. (Lancs) b March 7, 1918, d Sept. 15, 1984

*Illingworth, R. CBE (Yorks & Leics; *CY 1960*) b June 8, 1932

*Illingworth, R. K. (Worcs & Natal) b Aug. 23, 1963

*Ilott, M. C. (Essex) b Aug. 27, 1970

*Imran Khan (Lahore, Dawood, Worcs, OU, PIA, Sussex & NSW; *CY 1983*) b Nov. 25, 1952

*Imtiaz Ahmed (N. Ind., Comb. Us, NWFP, Pak. Servs, Peshawar & PAF) b Jan. 5, 1928

*Imtiaz Ali (T/T) b July 28, 1954

Inchmore, J. D. (Worcs & N. Tvl) b Feb. 22, 1949

*Indrajitsinhji, K. S. (S'tra & Delhi) b June 15, 1937

Ingle, R. A. (Som) b Nov. 5, 1903, d Dec. 19, 1992

Ingleby-Mackenzie, A. C. D. (Hants; Pres. MCC 1996-   ) b Sept. 15, 1933

Inman, C. C. (Ceylon & Leics) b Jan. 29, 1936

*Inshan Ali (T/T) b Sept. 25, 1949, d June 24, 1995

*Insole, D. J. CBE (CU & Essex; *CY 1956*) b April 18, 1926

*Intikhab Alam (Kar., PIA, Surrey, PWD, Sind, Punjab) b Dec. 28, 1941

*Inverarity, R. J. (W. Aust. & S. Aust.) b Jan. 31, 1944

*Inzamam-ul-Haq (Multan, UBL & F'bad) b March 3, 1970

*Iqbal Qasim (Kar., Sind & NBP) b Aug. 6, 1953

*Irani, J. K. (Sind) b Aug. 18, 1923, d Feb. 25, 1982

*Irani, R. C. (Lancs & Essex) b Oct. 26, 1971

*Iredale, F. A. (NSW) b June 19, 1867, d April 15, 1926

Iremonger, J. (Notts; *CY 1903*) b March 5, 1876, d March 25, 1956

*Ironmonger, H. (Qld & Vic.) b April 7, 1882, d June 1, 1971

*Ironside, D. E. J. (Tvl) b May 2, 1925

*Irvine, B. L. (W. Prov., Natal, Essex & Tvl) b March 9, 1944

*Israr Ali (S. Punjab, B'pur & Multan) b May 1, 1927
*Iverson, J. B. (Vic.) b July 27, 1915, d Oct. 24, 1973
*Jack, S. D. (Tvl) b Aug. 4, 1970
*Jackman, R. D. (Surrey, W. Prov. & Rhod.; CY 1981) b Aug. 13, 1945
*Jackson, A. A. (NSW) b Sept. 5, 1909, d Feb. 16, 1933
Jackson, A. B. (Derbys) b Aug. 21, 1933
Jackson, Rt Hon. Sir F. Stanley (CU & Yorks; CY 1894; Pres. MCC 1921) b Nov. 21, 1870, d March 9, 1947
Jackson, G. R. (Derbys) b June 23, 1896, d Feb. 21, 1966
*Jackson, H. L. (Derbys; CY 1959) b April 5, 1921
Jackson, J. (Notts & All-England) b May 21, 1833, d Nov. 4, 1901
Jackson, P. F. (Worcs) b May 11, 1911
Jackson, V. E. (NSW & Leics) b Oct. 25, 1916, d Jan. 30, 1965
*Jadeja, A. (Haryana) b Feb. 1, 1971
*Jahangir Khan (N. Ind. & CU) b Feb. 1, 1910, d July 23, 1988
*Jai, L. P. (Bombay) b April 1, 1902, d Jan. 29, 1968
*Jaisimha, M. L. (H'bad) b March 3, 1939
Jakeman, F. (Yorks & Northants) b Jan. 10, 1920, d May 18, 1986
*Jalal-ud-Din (PWD, Kar., IDBP & Allied Bank) b June 12, 1959
James, A. E. (Sussex) b Aug. 7, 1924
James, C. L. R. (Writer) b Jan. 4, 1901, d May 31, 1989
*James, K. C. (Wgtn & Northants) b March 12, 1904, d Aug. 21, 1976
*James, W. R. (Mat.) b Aug. 27, 1965
*Jameson, J. A. (Warwicks) b June 30, 1941
*Jamshedji, R. J. (Bombay) b Nov. 18, 1892, d April 5, 1976
*Jardine, D. R. (OU & Surrey; CY 1928) b Oct. 23, 1900, d June 18, 1958
*Jarman, B. N. (S. Aust.) b Feb. 17, 1936
*Jarvis, A. H. (S. Aust.) b Oct. 19, 1860, d Nov. 15, 1933
Jarvis, K. B. S. (Kent & Glos) b April 23, 1953
*Jarvis, M. P. (Mash.) b Dec. 6, 1955
*Jarvis, P. W. (Yorks & Sussex) b June 29, 1965
*Jarvis, T. W. (Auck. & Cant.) b July 29, 1944
*Javed Akhtar (R'pindi & Pak. Serv.) b Nov. 21, 1940
*Javed Miandad (Kar., Sind, Sussex, HBL & Glam; CY 1982) b June 12, 1957
*Jayantilal, K. (H'bad) b Jan. 13, 1948
*Jayasekera, R. S. A. (SL) b Dec. 7, 1957
Jayasinghe, S. (Ceylon & Leics) b Jan. 19, 1931

Jayasinghe, S. A. (SL) b July 15, 1955, d April 20, 1995
*Jayasuriya, S. T. (CCC & Bloom.; CY 1997) b June 30, 1969
*Jayawardene, D. P. M. (SSC) b May 27, 1977
Jeeves, P. (Warwicks) b March 5, 1888, d July 22, 1916
Jefferies, S. T. (W. Prov., Derbys, Lancs, Hants & Boland) b Dec. 8, 1959
*Jeganathan, S. (SL) b July 11, 1951, d May 14, 1996
*Jenkins, R. O. (Worcs; CY 1950) b Nov. 24, 1918, d July 21, 1995
*Jenner, T. J. (W. Aust. & S. Aust.) b Sept. 8, 1944
*Jennings, C. B. (S. Aust.) b June 5, 1884, d June 20, 1950
Jennings, R. V. (Tvl & N. Tvl) b Aug. 9, 1954
Jephson, D. L. A. (CU & Surrey) b Feb. 23, 1871, d Jan. 19, 1926
Jepson, A. (Notts; Test umpire) b July 12, 1915, d July 17, 1997
*Jessop, G. L. (CU & Glos; CY 1898) b May 19, 1874, d May 11, 1955
Jesty, T. E. (Hants, Border, Griq. W., Cant., Surrey & Lancs; CY 1983) b June 2, 1948
Jewell, Major M. F. S. (Worcs & Sussex) b Sept. 15, 1885, d May 28, 1978
*John, V. B. (SL) b May 27, 1960
*Johnson, C. L. (Tvl) b 1871, d May 31, 1908
*Johnson, D. J. (Karn.) b Oct. 16, 1971
Johnson, G. W. (Kent & Tvl) b Nov. 8, 1946
*Johnson, H. H. H. (Jam.) b July 17, 1910, d June 24, 1987
Johnson, H. L. (Derbys) b Nov. 8, 1927
*Johnson, I. W. OBE (Vic.) b Dec. 8, 1917
Johnson, L. A. (Northants) b Aug. 12, 1936
*Johnson, L. J. (Qld) b March 18, 1919, d April 20, 1977
Johnson, P. R. (CU & Som) b Aug. 5, 1880, d July 1, 1959
*Johnson, T. F. (T/T) b Jan. 10, 1917, d April 5, 1985
Johnston, Brian A. CBE (Broadcaster) b June 24, 1912, d Jan. 5, 1994
*Johnston, W. A. (Vic.; CY 1949) b Feb. 26, 1922
Jones, A. MBE (Glam, W. Aust., N. Tvl & Natal; CY 1978) b Nov. 4, 1938
Jones, A. A. (Sussex, Som, Middx, Glam, N. Tvl & OFS) b Dec. 9, 1947
*Jones, A. H. (Wgtn & C. Dist.) b May 9, 1959
*Jones, A. L. (Glam) b June 1, 1957
Jones, A. N. (Sussex, Border & Som) b July 22, 1961
*Jones, A. O. (Notts & CU; CY 1900) b Aug. 16, 1872, d Dec. 21, 1914
*Jones, C. M. (BG) b Nov. 3, 1902, d Dec. 10, 1959
*Jones, D. M. (Vic., Durham & Derbys; CY 1990) b March 24, 1961

*Jones, Ernest (S. Aust. & W. Aust.) b Sept. 30, 1869, d Nov. 23, 1943

Jones, E. C. (Glam) b Dec. 14, 1911, d April 14, 1989

Jones, E. W. (Glam) b June 25, 1942

*Jones, I. J. (Glam) b Dec. 10, 1941

Jones, K. V. (Middx) b March 28, 1942

*Jones, P. E. (T/T) b June 6, 1917, d Nov. 21, 1991

Jones, P. H. (Kent) b June 19, 1935

*Jones, S. P. (NSW, Qld & Auck.) b Aug. 1, 1861, d July 14, 1951

Jones, W. E. (Glam) b Oct. 31, 1916, d July 25, 1996

Jordon, R. C. (Vic.) b Feb. 17, 1937

*Joshi, P. G. (M'tra) b Oct. 27, 1926, d Jan. 8, 1987

*Joshi, S. B. (Karn.) b June 6, 1969

Joshi, U. C. (S'tra, Ind. Rlwys, Guj. & Sussex) b Dec. 23, 1944

*Joslin, L. R. (Vic.) b Dec. 13, 1947

*Julian, B. P. (W. Aust. & Surrey) b Aug. 10, 1970

Julian, R. (Leics) b Aug. 23, 1936

*Julien, B. D. (T/T & Kent) b March 13, 1950

*Jumadeen, R. R. (T/T) b April 12, 1948

*Jupp, H. (Surrey) b Nov. 19, 1841, d April 8, 1889

*Jupp, V. W. C. (Sussex & Northants; *CY 1928*) b March 27, 1891, d July 9, 1960

*Jurangpathy, B. R. (CCC) b June 25, 1967

*Kabir Khan (HBFC) b April 12, 1974

*Kallicharran, A. I. (Guyana, Warwicks, Qld, Tvl & OFS; *CY 1983*) b March 21, 1949

*Kallis, J. H. (W. Prov. & Middx) b Oct. 16, 1975

*Kalpage, R. S. (NCC & Bloom.) b Feb. 19, 1970

*Kaluperuma, L. W. (SL) b May 25, 1949

*Kaluperuma, S. M. S. (SL) b Oct. 22, 1961

*Kaluwitharana, R. S. (Seb., Galle & Colts) b Nov. 24, 1969

*Kambli, V. G. (†Mumbai) b Jan. 18, 1972

*Kanhai, R. B. (†Guyana, T/T, W. Aust., Warwicks & Tas.; *CY 1964*) b Dec. 26, 1935

*Kanitkar, H. S. (M'tra) b Dec. 8, 1942

*Kapil Dev (Haryana, Northants & Worcs; *CY 1983*) b Jan. 6, 1959

*Kapoor, A. R. (TN & Punjab) b March 25, 1971

*Kardar, A. H. (formerly Abdul Hafeez) (N. Ind., OU, Warwicks & Pak. Serv.) b Jan. 17, 1925, d April 21, 1996

Karnain, S. H. U. (NCC & Moors) b Aug. 11, 1962

*Kasprowicz, M. S. (Qld & Essex) b Feb. 10, 1972

*Keeton, W. W. (Notts; *CY 1940*) b April 30, 1905, d Oct. 10, 1980

*Keith, H. J. (Natal) b Oct. 25, 1927, d Nov. 17, 1997

*Kelleway, C. (NSW) b April 25, 1886, d Nov. 16, 1944

*Kelly, J. J. (NSW; *CY 1903*) b May 10, 1867, d Aug. 14, 1938

Kelly, J. M. (Lancs & Derbys) b March 19, 1922, d Nov. 13, 1979

*Kelly, T. J. D. (Vic.) b May 3, 1844, d July 20, 1893

*Kempis, G. A. (Natal) b Aug. 4, 1865, d May 19, 1890

*Kendall, T. (Vic. & Tas.) b Aug. 24, 1851, d Aug. 17, 1924

Kennedy, A. (Lancs) b Nov. 4, 1949

*Kennedy, A. S. (Hants; *CY 1933*) b Jan. 24, 1891, d Nov. 15, 1959

*Kennedy, R. J. (Otago) b June 3, 1972

*Kenny, R. B. (Bombay & Bengal) b Sept. 29, 1930, d Nov. 21, 1985

*Kent, M. F. (Qld) b Nov. 23, 1953

*Kentish, E. S. M. (Jam. & OU) b Nov. 21, 1916

*Kenyon, D. MBE (Worcs; *CY 1963*) b May 15, 1924, d Nov. 12, 1996

Kenyon, M. N. (Lancs) b Dec. 25, 1886, d Nov. 21, 1960

*Kerr, J. L. (Cant.) b Dec. 28, 1910

*Kerr, R. B. (Qld) b June 16, 1961

Key, Sir Kingsmill J. (Surrey & OU) b Oct. 11, 1864, d Aug. 9, 1932

*Khalid Hassan (Punjab & Lahore) b July 14, 1937

*Khalid Wazir (Pak.) b April 27, 1936

*Khan Mohammad (N. Ind., Pak. Us, Som, B'pur, Sind, Kar. & Lahore) b Jan. 1, 1928

Khanna, S. C. (Delhi) b June 3, 1956

Killick, E. H. (Sussex) b Jan. 17, 1875, d Sept. 29, 1948

*Killick, Rev. E. T. (CU & Middx) b May 9, 1907, d May 18, 1953

Kilner, N. (Yorks & Warwicks) b July 21, 1895, d April 28, 1979

*Kilner, R. (Yorks; *CY 1924*) b Oct. 17, 1890, d April 5, 1928

King, B. P. (Worcs & Lancs) b April 22, 1915, d March 31, 1970

*King, C. L. (B'dos, Glam, Worcs & Natal) b June 11, 1951

*King, F. M. (B'dos) b Dec. 14, 1926, d Dec. 23, 1990

King, J. B. (Philadelphia) b Oct. 19, 1873, d Oct. 17, 1965

*King, J. H. (Leics) b April 16, 1871, d Nov. 18, 1946

*King, L. A. (Jam. & Bengal) b Feb. 27, 1939

*Kinneir, S. P. (Warwicks; *CY 1912*) b May 13, 1871, d Oct. 16, 1928

*Kippax, A. F. (NSW) b May 25, 1897, d Sept. 4, 1972

Kirby, D. (CU & Leics) b Jan. 18, 1939

*Kirmani, S. M. H. (†Karn.) b Dec. 29, 1949

*Kirsten, G. (W. Prov.) b Nov. 23, 1967
*Kirsten, P. N. (W. Prov., Sussex, Derbys & Border) b May 14, 1955
*Kischenchand, G. (W. Ind., Guj. & Baroda) b April 14, 1925, d April 16, 1997
Kitchen, M. J. (Som; Test umpire) b Aug. 1, 1940
*Kline, L. F. (Vic.) b Sept. 29, 1934
*Klusener, L. (Natal) b Sept. 4, 1971
*Knight, A. E. (Leics; *CY 1904*) b Oct. 8, 1872, d April 25, 1946
*Knight, B. R. (Essex & Leics) b Feb. 18, 1938
*Knight, D. J. (OU & Surrey; *CY 1915*) b May 12, 1894, d Jan. 5, 1960
*Knight, N. V. (Essex & Warwicks) b Nov. 28, 1969
Knight, R. D. V. (CU, Surrey, Glos & Sussex; Sec. MCC 1994-) b Sept. 6, 1946
Knight, W. H. (Editor of *Wisden* 1870-79) b Nov. 29, 1812, d Aug. 16, 1879
*Knott, A. P. E. (Kent & Tas.; *CY 1970*) b April 9, 1946
Knott, C. J. (Hants) b Nov. 26, 1914
Knowles, J. (Notts) b March 25, 1910
*Knox, N. A. (Surrey; *CY 1907*) b Oct. 10, 1884, d March 3, 1935
Kortright, C. J. (Essex) b Jan. 9, 1871, d Dec. 12, 1952
*Kotze, J. J. (Tvl & W. Prov.) b Aug. 7, 1879, d July 7, 1931
*Kripal Singh, A. G. (Madras & H'bad) b Aug. 6, 1933, d July 23, 1987
*Krishnamurthy, P. (H'bad) b July 12, 1947
*Kuggeleijn, C. M. (N. Dist.) b May 10, 1956
*Kuiper, A. P. (W. Prov., Derbys & Boland) b Aug. 24, 1959
*Kulkarni, N. M. (†Mumbai) b April 3, 1973
*Kulkarni, R. R. (Bombay) b Sept. 25, 1962
*Kulkarni, U. N. (Bombay) b March 7, 1942
*Kumar, V. V. (†TN) b June 22, 1935
*Kumble, A. (Karn. & Northants; *CY 1996*) b Oct. 17, 1970
*Kunderan, B. K. (Ind. Rlwys & Mysore) b Oct. 2, 1939
*Kuruppu, D. S. B. P. (BRC) b Jan. 5, 1962
*Kuruppuarachchi, A. K. (NCC) b Nov. 1, 1964
*Kuruvilla, A. (†Mumbai) b Aug. 8, 1968
*Kuys, F. (W. Prov.) b March 21, 1870, d Sept. 12, 1953
Kynaston, R. (Middx; Sec. MCC 1846-58) b Nov. 5, 1805, d June 21, 1874

*Labrooy, G. F. (CCC) b June 7, 1964
Lacey, Sir Francis E. (CU & Hants; Sec. MCC 1898-1926) b Oct. 19, 1859, d May 26, 1946
*Laird, B. M. (W. Aust.) b Nov. 21, 1950
*Laker, J. C. (Surrey, Auck. & Essex; *CY 1952*) b Feb. 9, 1922, d April 23, 1986

*Lall Singh (S. Punjab) b Dec. 16, 1909, d Nov. 19, 1985
*Lamb, A. J. (W. Prov., Northants & OFS; *CY 1981*) b June 20, 1954
Lamb, Hon. T. M. (OU, Middx & Northants; Chief Exec. ECB, 1997-) b March 24, 1953
*Lamba, R. (Delhi) b Jan. 2, 1958
*Lambert, C. B. (Guyana & N. Tvl) b Feb. 10, 1962
Lambert, G. E. (Glos & Som) b May 11, 1918, d Oct. 31, 1991
Lambert, R. H. (Ireland) b July 18, 1874, d March 24, 1956
Lambert, Wm (Surrey) b 1779, d April 19, 1851
*Lance, H. R. (NE Tvl & Tvl) b June 6, 1940
Langdon, T. (Glos) b Jan. 8, 1879, d Nov. 30, 1944
*Langer, J. L. (W. Aust.) b Nov. 21, 1970
Langford, B. A. (Som) b Dec. 17, 1935
*Langley, G. R. A. (S. Aust.; *CY 1957*) b Sept. 14, 1919
*Langridge, James (Sussex; *CY 1932*) b July 10, 1906, d Sept. 10, 1966
Langridge, John MBE (Sussex; Test umpire; *CY 1950*) b Feb. 10, 1910
Langridge, R. J. (Sussex) b April 13, 1939
*Langton, A. B. C. (Tvl) b March 2, 1912, d Nov. 27, 1942
*Lara, B. C. (T/T & Warwicks; *CY 1995*) b May 2, 1969
*Larkins, W. (Northants, E. Prov. & Durham) b Nov. 22, 1953
*Larsen, G. R. (Wgtn) b Sept. 27, 1962
*Larter, J. D. F. (Northants) b April 24, 1940
*Larwood, H. MBE (Notts; *CY 1927*) b Nov. 14, 1904, d July 22, 1995
*Lashley, P. D. (B'dos) b Feb. 11, 1937
Latchman, H. C. (Middx & Notts) b July 26, 1943
*Latham, R. T. (Cant.) b June 12, 1961
*Lathwell, M. N. (Som) b Dec. 26, 1971
*Laughlin, T. J. (Vic.) b Jan. 30, 1951
*Laver, F. (Vic.) b Dec. 7, 1869, d Sept. 24, 1919
Lavis, G. (Glam) b Aug. 17, 1908, d July 29, 1956
*Law, S. G. (Qld & Essex; *CY 1998*) b Oct. 18, 1968
*Lawrence, D. V. (Glos) b Jan. 28, 1964
*Lawrence, G. B. (Rhod. & Natal) b March 31, 1932
Lawrence, J. (Som) b March 29, 1914, d Dec. 10, 1988
*Lawry, W. M. (Vic.; *CY 1962*) b Feb. 11, 1937
*Lawson, G. F. (NSW & Lancs) b Dec. 7, 1957
Lawton, A. E. (Derbys & Lancs) b March 31, 1879, d Dec. 25, 1955

*Laxman, V. V. S. (H'bad) b Nov. 1, 1974
Leach, G. (Sussex) b July 18, 1881, d Jan. 10, 1945
Leadbeater, B. (Yorks) b Aug. 14, 1943
*Leadbeater, E. (Yorks & Warwicks) b Aug. 15, 1927
Leary, S. E. (Kent) b April 30, 1933, d Aug. 21, 1988
Lee, C. (Yorks & Derbys) b March 17, 1924
Lee, F. S. (Middx & Som; Test umpire) b July 24, 1905, d March 30, 1982
Lee, G. M. (Notts & Derbys) b June 7, 1887, d Feb. 29, 1976
*Lee, H. W. (Middx) b Oct. 26, 1890, d April 21, 1981
Lee, J. W. (Middx & Som) b Feb. 1, 1904, d June 20, 1944
Lee, P. G. (Northants & Lancs; *CY 1976*) b Aug. 27, 1945
*Lee, P. K. (S. Aust.) b Sept. 15, 1904, d Aug. 9, 1980
*Lees, W. K. MBE (Otago) b March 19, 1952
*Lees, W. S. (Surrey; *CY 1906*) b Dec. 25, 1875, d Sept. 10, 1924
Leese, Sir Oliver, Bt (Pres. MCC 1965-66) b Oct. 27, 1894, d Jan. 20, 1978
Lefebvre, R. P. (Holland, Som, Cant. & Glam) b Feb. 7, 1963
*Legall, R. (B'dos & T/T) b Dec. 1, 1925
*Leggat, I. B. (C. Dist.) b June 7, 1930
*Leggat, J. G. (Cant.) b May 27, 1926, d March 9, 1973
*Legge, G. B. (OU & Kent) b Jan. 26, 1903, d Nov. 21, 1940
Lenham, L. J. (Sussex) b May 24, 1936
*le Roux, F. L. (Tvl & E. Prov.) b Feb. 5, 1882, d Sept. 22, 1963
le Roux, G. S. (W. Prov. & Sussex) b Sept. 4, 1955
*Leslie, C. F. H. (OU & Middx) b Dec. 8, 1861, d Feb. 12, 1921
Lester, E. (Yorks) b Feb. 18, 1923
Lester, G. (Leics) b Dec. 27, 1915
Lester, Dr J. A. (Philadelphia) b Aug. 1, 1871, d Sept. 3, 1969
*Lever, J. K. MBE (Essex & Natal; *CY 1979*) b Feb. 24, 1949
*Lever, P. (Lancs & Tas.) b Sept. 17, 1940
*Leveson Gower, Sir H. D. G. (OU & Surrey) b May 8, 1873, d Feb. 1, 1954
*Levett, W. H. V. (Kent) b Jan. 25, 1908, d Nov. 30, 1995
*Lewis, A. R. (Glam & CU) b July 6, 1938
Lewis, A. E. (Som) b Jan. 20, 1877, d Feb. 22, 1956
Lewis, C. BEM (Kent) b July 27, 1908, d April 26, 1993
*Lewis, C. C. (Leics, Notts & Surrey) b Feb. 14, 1968
*Lewis, D. M. (Jam.) b Feb. 21, 1946
Lewis, E. J. (Glam & Sussex) b Jan. 31, 1942

*Lewis, P. T. (W. Prov.) b Oct. 2, 1884, d Jan. 30, 1976
*Leyland, M. (Yorks; *CY 1929*) b July 20, 1900, d Jan. 1, 1967
*Liaqat Ali (Kar., Sind, HBL & PIA) b May 21, 1955
Lightfoot, A. (Northants) b Jan. 8, 1936
*Lillee, D. K. MBE (W. Aust., Tas. & Northants; *CY 1973*) b July 18, 1949
*Lilley, A. A. (Warwicks; *CY 1897*) b Nov. 28, 1866, d Nov. 17, 1929
Lilley, A. W. (Essex) b May 8, 1959
Lilley, B. (Notts) b Feb. 11, 1895, d Aug. 4, 1950
Lillywhite, Fred (Sussex; Editor of *Lillywhite's Guide to Cricketers*) b July 23, 1829, d Sept. 15, 1866
Lillywhite, F. W. (''William'') (Sussex) b June 13, 1792, d Aug. 21, 1854
*Lillywhite, James, jun. (Sussex) b Feb. 23, 1842, d Oct. 25, 1929
*Lindsay, D. T. (NE Tvl, N. Tvl & Tvl) b Sept. 4, 1939
*Lindsay, J. D. (Tvl & NE Tvl) b Sept. 8, 1909, d Aug. 31, 1990
*Lindsay, N. V. (Tvl & OFS) b July 30, 1886, d Feb. 2, 1976
*Lindwall, R. R. MBE (NSW & Qld; *CY 1949*) b Oct. 3, 1921, d June 23, 1996
*Ling, W. V. S. (Griq. W. & E. Prov.) b Oct. 3, 1891, d Sept. 26, 1960
*Lissette, A. F. (Auck. & N. Dist.) b Nov. 6, 1919, d Jan. 24, 1973
Lister, W. H. L. (CU & Lancs) b Oct. 7, 1911
Livingston, L. (NSW & Northants) b May 3, 1920, d Jan. 1998
Livingstone, D. A. (Hants) b Sept. 21, 1933, d Sept. 8, 1988
Livsey, W. H. (Hants) b Sept. 23, 1893, d Sept. 12, 1978
*Liyanage, D. K. (Colts & WPS) b June 6, 1972
*Llewellyn, C. B. (Natal & Hants; *CY 1911*) b Sept. 26, 1876, d June 7, 1964
Llewellyn, M. J. (Glam) b Nov. 27, 1953
Lloyd, B. J. (Glam) b Sept. 6, 1953
*Lloyd, C. H. OBE (†Guyana & Lancs; *CY 1971*) b Aug. 31, 1944
Lloyd, D. (Lancs) b March 18, 1947
*Lloyd, T. A. (Warwicks & OFS) b Nov. 5, 1956
Lloyds, J. W. (Som, OFS & Glos) b Nov. 17, 1954
*Loader, P. J. (Surrey & W. Aust.; *CY 1958*) b Oct. 25, 1929
Lobb, B. (Warwicks & Som) b Jan. 11, 1931
*Lock, A. C. I. (Mash.) b Sept. 10, 1962
*Lock, G. A. R. (Surrey, W. Aust. & Leics; *CY 1954*) b July 5, 1929, d March 29, 1995
Lockwood, Ephraim (Yorks) b April 4, 1845, d Dec. 19, 1921

*Lockwood, W. H. (Notts & Surrey; *CY 1899*) b March 25, 1868, d April 26, 1932

Lockyer, T. (Surrey & All-England) b Nov. 1, 1826, d Dec. 22, 1869

Logan, J. D., jun. (SA) b June 24, 1880, d Jan. 3, 1960

*Logie, A. L. (T/T) b Sept. 28, 1960

*Lohmann, G. A. (Surrey, W. Prov. & Tvl; *CY 1889*) b June 2, 1865, d Dec. 1, 1901

Lomax, J. G. (Lancs & Som) b May 5, 1925, d May 21, 1992

Long, A. (Surrey & Sussex) b Dec. 18, 1940

Longrigg, E. F. (Som & CU) b April 16, 1906, d July 23, 1974

Lord, Thomas (Middx; founder of Lord's) b Nov. 23, 1755, d Jan. 13, 1832

*Love, H. S. B. (NSW & Vic.) b Aug. 10, 1895, d July 22, 1969

Love, J. D. (Yorks) b April 22, 1955

*Loveridge, G. R. (C. Dist.) b Jan. 15, 1975

*Lowry, T. C. (Wgtn, CU & Som) b Feb. 17, 1898, d July 20, 1976

*Lowson, F. A. (Yorks) b July 1, 1925, d Sept. 8, 1984

*Loxton, S. J. E. (Vic.) b March 29, 1921

*Lucas, A. P. (CU, Surrey, Middx & Essex) b Feb. 20, 1857, d Oct. 12, 1923

Luckes, W. T. (Som) b Jan. 1, 1901, d Oct. 27, 1982

*Luckhurst, B. W. (Kent; *CY 1971*) b Feb. 5, 1939

Lumb, R. G. (Yorks) b Feb. 27, 1950

*Lundie, E. B. (E. Prov., W. Prov. & Tvl) b March 15, 1888, d Sept. 12, 1917

Lupton, A. W. (Yorks) b Feb. 23, 1879, d April 14, 1944

Lyon, B. H. (OU & Glos; *CY 1931*) b Jan. 19, 1902, d June 22, 1970

Lyon, M. D. (CU & Som) b April 22, 1898, d Feb. 17, 1964

*Lyons, J. J. (S. Aust.) b May 21, 1863, d July 21, 1927

*Lyttelton, Hon. Alfred (CU & Middx; Pres. MCC 1898) b Feb. 7, 1857, d July 5, 1913

Lyttelton, Rev. Hon. C. F. (CU & Worcs) b Jan. 26, 1887, d Oct. 3, 1931

Lyttelton, Hon. C. G. (CU) b Oct. 27, 1842, d June 9, 1922

Lyttelton, Hon. C. J. (*see* 10th Visct Cobham)

*McAlister, P. A. (Vic.) b July 11, 1869, d May 10, 1938

*Macartney, C. G. (NSW & Otago; *CY 1922*) b June 27, 1886, d Sept. 9, 1958

*Macaulay, G. G. (Yorks; *CY 1924*) b Dec. 7, 1897, d Dec. 13, 1940

*Macaulay, M. J. (Tvl, W. Prov., OFS, NE Tvl & E. Prov.) b April 1939

*MacBryan, J. C. W. (CU & Som; *CY 1925*) b July 22, 1892, d July 14, 1983

*McCabe, S. J. (NSW; *CY 1935*) b July 16, 1910, d Aug. 25, 1968

*McCague, M. J. (Kent & W. Aust.) b May 24, 1969

*McCarthy, C. N. (Natal & CU) b March 24, 1929

*McConnon, J. E. (Glam) b June 21, 1922

*McCool, C. L. (NSW, Qld & Som) b Dec. 9, 1916, d April 5, 1986

McCorkell, N. (Hants) b March 23, 1912

*McCormick, E. L. (Vic.) b May 16, 1906, d June 28, 1991

*McCosker, R. B. (NSW; *CY 1976*) b Dec. 11, 1946

McCurdy, R. J. (Vic., Derbys, S. Aust., E. Prov. & Natal) b Dec. 30, 1959

*McDermott, C. J. (Qld; *CY 1986*) b April 14, 1965

*McDonald, C. C. (Vic.) b Nov. 17, 1928

*McDonald, E. A. (Tas., Vic. & Lancs; *CY 1922*) b Jan. 6, 1891, d July 22, 1937

*McDonnell, P. S. (Vic., NSW & Qld) b Nov. 13, 1858, d Sept. 24, 1896

McEwan, K. S. (E. Prov., W. Prov., Essex & W. Aust.; *CY 1978*) b July 16, 1952

*McEwan, P. E. (Cant.) b Dec. 19, 1953

*McGahey, C. P. (Essex; *CY 1902*) b Feb. 12, 1871, d Jan. 10, 1935

*MacGibbon, A. R. (Cant.) b Aug. 28, 1924

McGilvray, A. D. (NSW; broadcaster) b Dec. 6, 1909, d July 16, 1996

*McGirr, H. M. (Wgtn) b Nov. 5, 1891, d April 14, 1964

*McGlew, D. J. (Natal; *CY 1956*) b March 11, 1929

*McGrath, G. D. (NSW; *CY 1998*) b Feb. 9, 1970

*MacGregor, G. (CU & Middx; *CY 1891*) b Aug. 31, 1869, d Aug. 20, 1919

*McGregor, S. N. (Otago) b Dec. 18, 1931

*McIlwraith, J. (Vic.) b Sept. 7, 1857, d July 5, 1938

*McIntyre, A. J. (Surrey; *CY 1958*) b May 14, 1918

*McIntyre, P. E. (S. Aust.) b April 27, 1966

*Mackay, K. D. MBE (Qld) b Oct. 24, 1925, d June 13, 1982

McKechnie, B. J. (Otago) b Nov. 6, 1953

*McKenzie, G. D. (W. Aust. & Leics; *CY 1965*) b June 24, 1941

*McKibbin, T. R. (NSW) b Dec. 10, 1870, d Dec. 15, 1939

*McKinnon, A. H. (E. Prov. & Tvl) b Aug. 20, 1932, d Dec. 1, 1983

*MacKinnon, F. A. (CU & Kent; *believed to be longest-lived Test cricketer*) b April 9, 1848, d Feb. 27, 1947

*MacLaren, A. C. (Lancs; *CY 1895*) b Dec. 1, 1871, d Nov. 17, 1944

*McLaren, J. W. (Qld) b Dec. 24, 1887, d Nov. 17, 1921

MacLaurin of Knebworth, Lord (Chairman ECB 1997-   ) b March 30, 1937
*Maclean, J. A. (Qld) b April 27, 1946
*McLean, R. A. (Natal; *CY 1961*) b July 9, 1930
MacLeay, K. H. (W. Aust. & Som) b April 2, 1959
*McLeod, C. E. (Vic.) b Oct. 24, 1869, d Nov. 26, 1918
*McLeod, E. G. (Auck. & Wgtn) b Oct. 14, 1900, d Sept. 14, 1989
*McLeod, R. W. (Vic.) b Jan. 19, 1868, d June 14, 1907
McMahon, J. W. (Surrey & Som) b Dec. 28, 1919
*McMahon, T. G. (Wgtn) b Nov. 8, 1929
*McMaster, J. E. P. (Eng.) b March 16, 1861, d June 7, 1929
*McMillan, B. M. (Tvl, W. Prov. & Warwicks) b Dec. 22, 1963
*McMillan, Q. (Tvl) b June 23, 1904, d July 3, 1948
*McMorris, E. D. A. (Jam.) b April 4, 1935
*McRae, D. A. N. (Cant.) b Dec. 25, 1912, d Aug. 10, 1986
*McShane, P. G. (Vic.) b 1857, d Dec. 11, 1903
McSweeney, E. B. (C. Dist. & Wgtn) b March 8, 1957
McVicker, N. M. (Warwicks & Leics) b Nov. 4, 1940
*McWatt, C. A. (BG) b Feb. 1, 1922, d July 12, 1997
*Madan Lal (Punjab & Delhi) b March 20, 1951
*Maddocks, L. V. (Vic. & Tas.) b May 24, 1926
*Madray, I. S. (BG) b July 2, 1934
*Madugalle, R. S. (NCC) b April 22, 1959
*Madurasinghe, A. W. R. (Kurunegala & NWP) b Jan. 30, 1961
*Maguire, J. N. (Qld, E. Prov. & Leics) b Sept. 15, 1956
*Mahanama, R. S. (CCC & Bloom.) b May 31, 1966
Maher, B. J. M. (Derbys) b Feb. 11, 1958
*Mahmood Hussain (Pak. Us, Punjab, Kar., E. Pak. & NTB) b April 2, 1932, d Dec. 25, 1991
*Mailey, A. A. (NSW; writer) b Jan. 3, 1886, d Dec. 31, 1967
*Majid Khan (Lahore, Pak. Us, CU, Glam, PIA, Qld, Punjab; *CY 1970*) b Sept. 28, 1946
*Maka, E. S. (Bombay) b March 5, 1922
*Makepeace, H. (Lancs) b Aug. 22, 1881, d Dec. 19, 1952
*Malcolm, D. E. (Derbys; *CY 1995*) b Feb. 22, 1963
*Malhotra, A. (Haryana, Bengal & Delhi) b Jan. 26, 1957

*Mallender, N. A. (Northants, Otago & Som) b Aug. 13, 1961
*Mallett, A. A. (S. Aust.) b July 13, 1945
*Malone, M. F. (W. Aust. & Lancs) b Oct. 9, 1950
*Maninder Singh (Delhi) b June 13, 1965
*Manjrekar, S. V. (†Mumbai) b July 12, 1965
*Manjrekar, V. L. (Bombay, Bengal, Andhra, U. Pradesh, Raja. & M'tra) b Sept. 26, 1931, d Oct. 18, 1983
*Mankad, A. V. (Bombay) b Oct. 12, 1946
*Mankad, V. (M. H.) (W. Ind., Naw., M'tra, Guj., Bengal, Bombay & Raja.; *CY 1947*) b April 12, 1917, d Aug. 21, 1978
*Mann, A. L. (W. Aust.) b Nov. 8, 1945
*Mann, F. G. CBE (CU & Middx; Pres. MCC 1984-85) b Sept. 6, 1917
*Mann, F. T. (CU & Middx) b March 3, 1888, d Oct. 6, 1964
*Mann, N. B. F. (Natal & E. Prov.) b Dec. 28, 1920, d July 31, 1952
Manning, J. S. (S. Aust. & Northants) b June 11, 1924, d May 5, 1988
Manning, T. E. (Northants) b Sept. 2, 1884, d Nov. 22, 1975
*Mansell, P. N. F. MBE (Rhod.) b March 16, 1920, d May 9, 1995
Mansoor Akhtar (Kar., UBL & Sind) b Dec. 25, 1956
Mansur Ali Khan (*see* Pataudi, Mansur Ali, Nawab of)
*Mantri, M. K. (Bombay & M'tra) b Sept. 1, 1921
*Manzoor Elahi (Multan, Pak. Rlwys & IDBP) b April 15, 1963
*Maqsood Ahmed (S. Punjab, R'pindi & Kar.) b March 26, 1925
*Marais, G. G. (G. Gladstone'') (Jam.) b Jan. 14, 1901, d May 19, 1978
Marchant, F. (Kent & CU) b May 22, 1864, d April 13, 1946
*Markham, L. A. (Natal) b Sept. 12, 1924
*Marks, V. J. (OU, Som & W. Aust.; writer) b June 25, 1955
Marlar, R. G. (CU & Sussex; writer) b Jan. 2, 1931
Marlow, F. W. (Sussex) b Oct. 8, 1867, d Aug. 7, 1952
Marner, P. T. (Lancs & Leics) b March 31, 1936
*Marr, A. P. (NSW) b March 28, 1962, d March 15, 1940
*Marriott, C. S. (CU, Lancs & Kent) b Sept. 14, 1895, d Oct. 13, 1966
Marsden, Tom (Eng.) b 1805, d Feb. 27, 1843
*Marsh, G. R. (W. Aust.) b Dec. 31, 1958
*Marsh, R. W. MBE (W. Aust.; *CY 1982*) b Nov. 11, 1947
Marshal, Alan (Qld & Surrey; *CY 1909*) b June 12, 1883, d July 23, 1915
*Marshall, M. D. (B'dos, Hants & Natal; *CY 1983*) b April 18, 1958

*Marshall, N. E. (B'dos & T/T) b Feb. 27, 1924

*Marshall, R. E. (B'dos & Hants; *CY 1959*) b April 25, 1930, d Oct. 27, 1992

Marsham, C. H. B. (OU & Kent) b Feb. 10, 1879, d July 19, 1928

Martin, E. J. (Notts) b Aug. 17, 1925

*Martin, F. (Kent; *CY 1892*) b Oct. 12, 1861, d Dec. 13, 1921

*Martin, F. R. (Jam.) b Oct. 12, 1893, d Nov. 23, 1967

Martin, G. C. (Mash.) b May 30, 1966

*Martin, J. W. (NSW & S. Aust.) b July 28, 1931, d July 16, 1992

*Martin, J. W. (Kent) b Feb. 16, 1917, d Jan. 4, 1987

*Martin, P. J. (Lancs) b Nov. 15, 1968

Martin, S. H. (Worcs, Natal & Rhod.) b Jan. 11, 1909, d Feb. 17, 1988

*Martindale, E. A. (B'dos) b Nov. 25, 1909, d March 17, 1972

Martin-Jenkins, Christopher (Writer & broadcaster) b Jan. 20, 1945

*Martyn, D. R. (W. Aust.) b Oct. 21, 1971

*Marx, W. F. E. (Tvl) b July 4, 1895, d June 2, 1974

*Mason, J. R. (Kent; *CY 1898*) b March 26, 1874, d Oct. 15, 1958

*Masood Anwar (UBL, Multan & F'bad) b Dec. 12, 1967

Masood Iqbal (Lahore, Punjab U., Pak. Us & HBL) b April 17, 1952

*Massie, H. H. (NSW) b April 11, 1854, d Oct. 12, 1938

*Massie, R. A. L. (W. Aust.; *CY 1973*) b April 14, 1947

*Matambanadzo, E. (Mash.) b April 13, 1976

*Matheson, A. M. (Auck.) b Feb. 27, 1906, d Dec. 31, 1985

*Mathias, Wallis (Sind, Kar. & NBP) b Feb. 4, 1935, d Sept. 1, 1994

*Matthews, A. D. G. (Northants & Glam) b May 3, 1904, d July 29, 1977

*Matthews, C. D. (W. Aust. & Lancs) b Sept. 22, 1962

*Matthews, C. R. (W. Prov.) b Feb. 15, 1965

*Matthews, G. R. J. (NSW) b Dec. 15, 1959

*Matthews, T. J. (Vic.) b April 3, 1884, d Oct. 14, 1943

*Mattis, E. H. (Jam.) b April 11, 1957

*May, P. B. H. CBE (CU & Surrey; *CY 1952*; Pres. MCC 1980-81) b Dec. 31, 1929, d Dec. 27, 1994

*May, T. B. A. (S. Aust.) b Jan. 26, 1962

Mayer, J. H. (Warwicks) b March 2, 1902, d Sept. 6, 1981

Maynard, C. (Warwicks & Lancs) b April 8, 1958

*Maynard, M. P. (Glam, N. Dist. & Otago; *CY 1998*) b March 21, 1966

*Mayne, E. R. (S. Aust. & Vict.) b July 2, 1882, d Oct. 26, 1961

*Mayne, L. C. (W. Aust.) b Jan. 23, 1942

*Mbangwa, M. (Mat.) b June 26, 1976

*Mead, C. P. (Hants; *CY 1912*) b March 9, 1887, d March 26, 1958

*Mead, W. (Essex; *CY 1904*) b March 25, 1868, d March 18, 1954

Meads, E. A. (Notts) b Aug. 17, 1916

*Meale, T. (Wgtn) b Nov. 11, 1928

*Meckiff, I. (Vic.) b Jan. 6, 1935

Medlycott, K. T. (Surrey & N. Tvl) b May 12, 1965

*Meherhomji, K. R. (W. Ind. & Bombay) b Aug. 9, 1911, d Feb. 10, 1982

*Mehra, V. L. (E. Punjab, Ind. Rlwys & Delhi) b March 12, 1938

*Meintjes, D. J. (Tvl) b June 9, 1890, d July 17, 1979

*Melle, M. G. (Tvl & W. Prov.) b June 3, 1930

Melluish, M. E. L. (CU & Middx; Pres. MCC 1991-92) b June 13, 1932

*Melville, A. (OU, Sussex, Natal & Tvl; *CY 1948*) b May 19, 1910, d April 18, 1983

Meman, M. A. (Zimb.) b June 26, 1952

Mendis, G. D. (Sussex & Lancs) b April 20, 1955

*Mendis, L. R. D. (SSC) b Aug. 25, 1952

Mendis, M. C. (Colts) b Dec. 28, 1968

*Mendonca, I. L. (BG) b July 13, 1934

Mercer, J. (Sussex, Glam & Northants; *CY 1927*) b April 22, 1895, d Aug. 31, 1987

*Merchant, V. M. (Bombay; *CY 1937*) b Oct. 12, 1911, d Oct. 27, 1987

*Merritt, W. E. (Cant. & Northants) b Aug. 18, 1908, d June 9, 1977

*Merry, C. A. (T/T) b Jan. 20, 1911, d April 19, 1964

*Meuleman, K. D. (Vic. & W. Aust.) b Sept. 5, 1923

*Meuli, E. M. (C. Dist.) b Feb. 20, 1926

Meyer, B. J. (Glos; Test umpire) b Aug. 21, 1932

Meyer, R. J. O. OBE (CU, Som & W. Ind.) b March 15, 1905, d March 9, 1991

*Mhambrey, P. L. (†Mumbai) b June 20, 1972

Mian Mohammed Saeed (N. India, Patiala & S. Punjab) b Aug. 31, 1910, d Aug. 23, 1979

*Middleton, J. (W. Prov.) b Sept. 30, 1865, d Dec. 23, 1913

Middleton, T. C. (Hants) b Feb. 1, 1964

**Midwinter, W. E. (Vic. & Glos) b June 19, 1851, d Dec. 3, 1890

*Milburn, B. D. (Otago) b Nov. 24, 1943

*Milburn, C. (Northants & W. Aust.; *CY 1967*) b Oct. 23, 1941, d Feb. 28, 1990

*Milkha Singh, A. G. (Madras) b Dec. 31, 1941

*Miller, A. M. (Eng.) b Oct. 19, 1869, d June 26, 1959

Miller, F. P. (Surrey) b July 29, 1828, d Nov. 22, 1875

*Miller, G. (Derbys, Natal & Essex) b Sept. 8, 1952

*Miller, K. R. MBE (Vic., NSW & Notts; *CY 1954*) b Nov. 28, 1919

*Miller, L. S. M. (C. Dist. & Wgtn) b March 31, 1923, d Dec. 17, 1996

Miller, R. (Warwicks) b Jan. 6, 1941, d May 7, 1996

*Miller, R. C. (Jam.) b Dec. 24, 1924

*Milligan, F. W. (Yorks) b March 19, 1870, d March 31, 1900

*Millman, G. (Notts) b Oct. 2, 1934

Millmow, J. P. (Wgtn) b Sept. 22, 1967

*Mills, C. H. (Surrey, Kimberley & W. Prov.) b Nov. 26, 1867, d July 26, 1948

*Mills, J. E. (Auck.) b Sept. 3, 1905, d Dec. 11, 1972

Mills, P. T. (Glos) b May 7, 1879, d Dec. 8, 1950

*Milton, C. A. (Glos; *CY 1959*) b March 10, 1928

*Milton, Sir William H. (W. Prov.) b Dec. 3, 1854, d March 6, 1930

*Minnett, R. B. (NSW) b June 13, 1888, d Oct. 21, 1955

Minshull, John (scorer of first recorded century) b *circa* 1741, d Oct. 1793

*Miran Bux (Pak. Serv., Punjab & R'pindi) b April 20, 1907, d Feb. 8, 1991

*Misson, F. M. (NSW) b Nov. 19, 1938

*Mitchell, A. (Yorks) b Sept. 13, 1902, d Dec. 25, 1976

*Mitchell, B. (Tvl; *CY 1936*) b Jan. 8, 1909, d July 2, 1995

**Mitchell, F. (CU, Yorks & Tvl; *CY 1902*) b Aug. 13, 1872, d Oct. 11, 1935

*Mitchell, T. B. (Derbys) b Sept. 4, 1902, d Jan. 27, 1996

*Mitchell-Innes, N. S. (OU & Som) b Sept. 7, 1914

*Modi, R. S. (Bombay) b Nov. 11, 1924, d May 17, 1996

*Mohammad Akram (R'pindi, Allied Bank & Northants) b Sept. 10, 1974

*Mohammad Aslam (N. Ind. & Pak. Rlwys) b Jan. 5, 1920

*Mohammad Farooq (Kar.) b April 8, 1938

*Mohammad Hussain (Lahore & UBL) b Oct. 8, 1976

*Mohammad Ilyas (Lahore & PIA) b March 19, 1946

*Mohammad Munaf (Sind, E. Pak., Kar. & PIA) b Nov. 2, 1935

*Mohammad Nazir (Pak. Rlwys) b March 8, 1946

*Mohammad Wasim (R'pindi) b Aug. 8, 1977

*Mohammad Zahid (PIA) b Aug. 2, 1976

*Mohanty, D. S. (Orissa) b July 20, 1976

*Mohsin Kamal (Lahore, Allied Bank & PNSC) b June 16, 1963

*Mohsin Khan (Pak. Rlwys, Kar., Sind, Pak. Us & HBL) b March 15, 1955

*Moin Khan (Kar. & PIA) b Sept. 23, 1971

Moin-ul-Atiq (UBL, Kar. & HBL) b Aug. 5, 1964

*Moir, A. M. (Otago) b July 17, 1919

*Mold, A. (Lancs; *CY 1892*) b May 27, 1863, d April 29, 1921

*Moloney, D. A. R. (Wgtn, Otago & Cant.) b Aug. 11, 1910, d July 15, 1942

Monckton of Brenchley, 1st Visct (Pres. MCC 1956-57) b Jan. 17, 1891, d Jan. 9, 1965

*Mongia, N. R. (Baroda) b Dec. 19, 1969

*Moodie, G. H. (Jam.) b Nov. 25, 1915

*Moody, T. M. (W. Aust., Warwicks & Worcs) b Oct. 2, 1965

*Moon, L. J. (CU & Middx) b Feb. 9, 1878, d Nov. 23, 1916

*Mooney, F. L. H. (Wgtn) b May 26, 1921

Moore, H. I. (Notts) b Feb. 28, 1941

Moore, R. H. (Hants) b Nov. 14, 1913

Moorhouse, R. (Yorks) b Sept. 7, 1866, d Jan. 7, 1921

*More, K. S. (Baroda) b Sept. 4, 1962

Morgan, D. C. (Derbys) b Feb. 26, 1929

*Morgan, R. W. (Auck.) b Feb. 12, 1941

*Morkel, D. P. B. (W. Prov.) b Jan. 25, 1906, d Oct. 6, 1980

*Morley, F. (Notts) b Dec. 16, 1850, d Sept. 28, 1884

*Moroney, J. (NSW) b July 24, 1917

*Morris, A. R. MBE (NSW; *CY 1949*) b Jan. 19, 1922

*Morris, H. (Glam) b Oct. 5, 1963

Morris, H. M. (Essex & CU) b April 16, 1898, d Nov. 18, 1984

*Morris, J. E. (Derbys, Griq. W. & Durham) b April 1, 1964

*Morris, S. (Vic.) b June 22, 1855, d Sept. 20, 1931

*Morrison, B. D. (Wgtn) b Dec. 17, 1933

*Morrison, D. K. (Auck. & Lancs) b Feb. 3, 1966

*Morrison, J. F. M. (C. Dist. & Wgtn) b Aug. 27, 1947

Mortensen, O. H. (Denmark & Derbys) b Jan. 29, 1958

*Mortimore, J. B. (Glos) b May 14, 1933

Mortlock, W. (Surrey & Utd Eng. XI) b July 18, 1832, d Jan. 23, 1884

Morton, A., jun. (Derbys) b May 7, 1883, d Dec. 19, 1935

*Moseley, E. A. (B'dos, Glam, E. Prov. & N. Tvl) b Jan. 5, 1958

Moseley, H. R. (B'dos & Som) b May 28, 1948

*Moses, H. (NSW) b Feb. 13, 1858, d Dec. 7, 1938

*Moss, A. E. (Middx) b Nov. 14, 1930

*Moss, J. K. (Vic.) b June 29, 1947

*Motz, R. C. (Cant.; *CY 1966*) b Jan. 12, 1940

*Moule, W. H. (Vic.) b Jan. 31, 1858, d Aug. 24, 1939

*Moxon, M. D. (Yorks & Griq. W.; *CY 1993*) b May 4, 1960

*Mudassar Nazar (Lahore, Punjab, Pak. Us, HBL, PIA & UBL) b April 6, 1956

*Muddiah, V. M. (Mysore & Ind. Servs) b June 8, 1929

*Mufasir-ul-Haq (Kar., Dacca, PWD, E. Pak. & NBP) b Aug. 16, 1944, d July 27, 1983

Mukherjee, S. P. (Bengal) b Oct. 5, 1964

*Mullally, A. D. (W. Aust., Vic., Hants & Leics) b July 12, 1969

Munasinghe, A. M. N. (SSC) b Dec. 10, 1971

Muncer, B. L. (Glam & Middx) b Oct. 23, 1913, d Jan. 18, 1982

Munden, V. S. (Leics) b Jan. 2, 1928

*Munir Malik (Punjab, R'pindi, Pak. Serv. & Kar.) b July 10, 1934

*Munton, T. A. (Warwicks; *CY 1995*) b July 30, 1965

*Muralitharan, M. (TU) b April 17, 1972

**Murdoch, W. L. (NSW & Sussex) b Oct. 18, 1854, d Feb. 18, 1911

*Murray, A. R. A. (E. Prov.) b April 30, 1922, d April 17, 1995

*Murray, B. A. G. (Wgtn) b Sept. 18, 1940

*Murray, D. A. (B'dos) b Sept. 29, 1950

*Murray, D. J. (Cant.) b Sept. 4, 1967

*Murray, D. L. (T/T, CU, Notts & Warwicks) b May 20, 1943

*Murray, J. R. (Windwards) b Jan. 20, 1968

*Murray, J. T. MBE (Middx; *CY 1967*) b April 1, 1935

Murray-Wood, W. (OU & Kent) b June 30, 1917, d Dec. 21, 1968

Murrell, H. R. (Kent & Middx) b Nov. 19, 1879, d Aug. 15, 1952

Musgrove, H. (Vic.) b Nov. 27, 1860, d Nov. 2, 1931

*Mushtaq Ahmed (UBL, Multan, Lahore & Som; *CY 1997*) b June 28, 1970

*Mushtaq Ali, S. (C. Ind., Guj., †M. Pradesh & U. Pradesh) b Dec. 17, 1914

*Mushtaq Mohammad (Kar., Northants & PIA; *CY 1963*) b Nov. 22, 1943

Mynn, Alfred (Kent & All-Eng.) b Jan. 19, 1807, d Nov. 1, 1861

*Nadkarni, R. G. (M'tra & Bombay) b April 4, 1932

*Nadeem Abbasi (R'pindi) b April 15, 1964

*Nadeem Ghauri (Lahore, Pak. Rlwys & HBL) b Oct. 12, 1962

*Nadeem Khan (Kar. & NBP) b Dec. 10, 1969

Naeem Ahmed, (Kar., Pak Us, NBP, UBL & PIA) b Sept. 20, 1952

*Nagel, L. E. (Vic.) b March 6, 1905, d Nov. 23, 1971

*Naik, S. S. (Bombay) b Feb. 21, 1945

*Nanan, R. (T/T) b May 29, 1953

*Naoomal Jeoomal, M. (N. Ind. & Sind) b April 17, 1904, d July 18, 1980

*Narasimha Rao, M. V. (H'bad) b Aug. 11, 1954

Naseer Malik (Khairpair & NBP) b Feb. 1, 1950

*Nash, D. J. (N. Dist., Otago & Middx) b Nov. 20, 1971

*Nash, L. J. (Tas. & Vic.) b May 2, 1910, d July 24, 1986

Nash, M. A. (Glam) b May 9, 1945

*Nasim-ul-Ghani (Kar., Pak. Us, Dacca, E. Pak., PWD & NBP) b May 14, 1941

*Naushad Ali (Kar., E. Pak., R'pindi, Peshawar, NWFP, Punjab & Pak. Serv.) b Oct. 1, 1943

*Naved Anjum (Lahore, UBL & HBL) b July 27, 1963

*Navle, J. G. (Rajputna, C. Ind., Holkar & Gwalior) b Dec. 7, 1902, d Sept. 7, 1979

*Nayak, S. V. (Bombay) b Oct. 20, 1954

*Nayudu, Col. C. K. (C. Ind., Andhra, U. Pradesh & Holkar; *CY 1933*) b Oct. 31, 1895, d Nov. 14, 1967

*Nayudu, C. S. (C. Ind., Holkar, Baroda, Bengal, Andhra & U. Pradesh) b April 18, 1914

*Nazar Mohammad (N. Ind. & Punjab) b March 5, 1921, d July 12, 1996

*Nazir Ali, S. (S. Punjab & Sussex) b June 8, 1906, d Feb. 18, 1975

*Neale, P. A. (Worcs; *CY 1989*) b June 5, 1954

Neale, W. L. (Glos) b March 3, 1904, d Oct. 26, 1955

*Neblett, J. M. (B'dos & BG) b Nov. 13, 1901, d March 28, 1959

Needham, A. (Surrey & Middx) b March 23, 1957

*Nel, J. D. (W. Prov.) b July 10, 1928

Nelson, R. P. (Middx, CU & Northants) b Aug. 7, 1912, d Oct. 29, 1940

*Newberry, C. (Tvl) b 1889, d Aug. 1, 1916

Newell, M. (Notts) b Feb. 25, 1965

*Newham, W. (Sussex) b Dec. 12, 1860, d June 26, 1944

Newland, Richard (Sussex) b *circa* 1718, d May 29, 1791

*Newman, Sir Jack (Wgtn & Cant.) b July 3, 1902, d Sept. 23, 1996

Newman, J. A. (Hants & Cant.) b Nov. 12, 1884, d Dec. 21, 1973

Newman, P. G. (Derbys) b Jan. 10, 1959

*Newport, P. J. (Worcs, Boland & N. Tvl) b Oct. 11, 1962

*Newson, E. S. OBE (Tvl & Rhod.) b Dec. 2, 1910, d April 24, 1988

Newstead, J. T. (Yorks; *CY 1909*) b Sept. 8, 1877, d March 25, 1952

Newton, A. E. (OU & Som) b Sept. 12, 1862, d Sept. 15, 1952

*Niaz Ahmed (Dacca, E. Pak., PWD & Pak. Rlwys) b Nov. 11, 1945

Nicholas, M. C. J. (Hants) b Sept. 29, 1957

Nicholls, D. (Kent) b Dec. 8, 1943

Nicholls, R. B. (Glos) b Dec. 4, 1933, d July 21, 1994

*Nichols, M. S. (Essex; *CY 1934*) b Oct. 6, 1900, d Jan. 26, 1961

Nicholson, A. G. (Yorks) b June 25, 1938, d Nov. 4, 1985

*Nicholson, F. (Griq. W.) b Sept. 17, 1909, d July 30, 1982

*Nicolson, J. F. W. (Natal & OU) b July 19, 1899, d Dec. 13, 1935

*Nissar, Mahomed (Patiala, S. Punjab & U. Pradesh) b Aug. 1, 1910, d March 11, 1963

*Nitschke, H. C. (S. Aust.) b April 14, 1905, d Sept. 29, 1982

*Noble, M. A. (NSW; *CY 1900*) b Jan. 28, 1873, d June 22, 1940

*Noblet, G. (S. Aust.) b Sept. 14, 1916

*Noreiga, J. M. (T/T) b April 15, 1936

Norfolk, 16th Duke of (Pres. MCC 1957-58) b May 30, 1908, d Jan. 31, 1975

Norman, M. E. J. C. (Northants & Leics) b Jan. 19, 1933

*Norton, N. O. (W. Prov. & Border) b May 11, 1881, d June 27, 1968

*Nothling, O. E. (NSW & Qld) b Aug. 1, 1900, d Sept. 26, 1965

*Nourse, A. D. (''Dudley'') (Natal; *CY 1948*) b Nov. 12, 1910, d Aug. 14, 1981

*Nourse, A. W. (''Dave'') (Natal, Tvl & W. Prov.) b Jan. 26, 1878, d July 8, 1948

Nugent, 1st Lord (Pres. MCC 1962-63) b Aug. 11, 1895, d April 27, 1973

*Nunes, R. K. (Jam.) b June 7, 1894, d July 22, 1958

*Nupen, E. P. (Tvl) b Jan. 1, 1902, d Jan. 29, 1977

*Nurse, S. M. (B'dos; *CY 1967*) b Nov. 10, 1933

Nutter, A. E. (Lancs & Northants) b June 28, 1913, d June 3, 1996

*Nyalchand, S. (W. Ind., Kathiawar, Guj., & S'tra) b Sept. 14, 1919, d Jan. 3, 1997

Nyren, John (Hants) b Dec. 15, 1764, d June 28, 1837

Nyren, Richard (Hants & Sussex; Proprietor Bat & Ball Inn, Broadhalfpenny Down) b 1734, d April 25, 1797

Oakes, C. (Sussex) b Aug. 10, 1912

Oakes, J. (Sussex) b March 3, 1916, d July 4, 1997

*Oakman, A. S. M. (Sussex) b April 20, 1930

Oates, T. W. (Notts) b Aug. 9, 1875, d June 18, 1949

Oates, W. F. (Yorks & Derbys) b June 11, 1929

*O'Brien, L. P. J. (Vic.) b July 2, 1907, d March 13, 1997

*O'Brien, Sir Timothy C. (OU & Middx) b Nov. 5, 1861, d Dec. 9, 1948

*Ochse, A. E. (Tvl) b March 11, 1870, d April 11, 1918

*Ochse, A. L. (E. Prov.) b Oct. 11, 1899, d May 5, 1949

*O'Connor, J. (Essex) b Nov. 6, 1897, d Feb. 22, 1977

*O'Connor, J. D. A. (NSW & S. Aust.) b Sept. 9, 1875, d Aug. 23, 1941

*O'Donnell, S. P. (Vic.) b Jan. 26, 1963

Ogilvie, A. D. (Qld) b June 3, 1951

O'Gorman, T. J. G. (Derbys) b May 15, 1967

*O'Keeffe, K. J. (NSW & Som) b Nov. 25, 1949

*Old, C. M. (Yorks, Warwicks & N. Tvl; *CY 1979*) b Dec. 22, 1948

*Oldfield, N. (Lancs & Northants; Test umpire) b May 5, 1911, d April 19, 1996

Oldfield, W. A. MBE (NSW; *CY 1927*) b Sept. 9, 1894, d Aug. 10, 1976

Oldham, S. (Yorks & Derbys) b July 26, 1948

Oldroyd, E. (Yorks) b Oct. 1, 1888, d Dec. 27, 1964

*O'Linn, S. (Kent, W. Prov. & Tvl) b May 5, 1927

Oliver, L. (Derbys) b Oct. 18, 1886, d Jan. 22, 1948

*Olonga, H. K. (Mat.) b July 3, 1976

*O'Neill, N. C. (NSW; *CY 1962*) b Feb. 19, 1937

Ontong, R. C. (Border, Tvl, N. Tvl & Glam) b Sept. 9, 1955

Opatha, A. R. M. (SL) b Aug. 5, 1947

Ord, J. S. (Warwicks) b Aug. 12, 1912

*O'Reilly, W. J. OBE (NSW; *CY 1935*) b Dec. 20, 1905, d Oct. 6, 1992

Ormrod, J. A. (Worcs & Lancs) b Dec. 22, 1942

Oscroft, W. (Notts) b Dec. 16, 1843, d Oct. 10, 1905

O'Shaughnessy, S. J. (Lancs & Worcs) b Sept. 9, 1961

Oslear, D. O. (Test umpire) b March 3, 1929

*O'Sullivan, D. R. (C. Dist. & Hants) b Nov. 16, 1944

Outschoorn, L. (Worcs) b Sept. 26, 1918, d Jan. 9, 1994

*Overton, G. W. F. (Otago) b June 8, 1919, d Sept. 7, 1993

Owen, H. G. P. (CU & Essex) b May 19, 1859, d Oct. 20, 1912

*Owens, M. B. (Cant.) b Nov. 11, 1969

*Owen-Smith, H. G. (W. Prov., OU & Middx; *CY 1930*) b Feb. 18, 1909, d Feb. 28, 1990

Owen-Thomas, D. R. (CU & Surrey) b Sept. 20, 1948

*Oxenham, R. K. (Qld) b July 28, 1891, d Aug. 16, 1939

*Padgett, D. E. V. (Yorks) b July 20, 1934

*Padmore, A. L. (B'dos) b Dec. 17, 1946

Page, J. C. T. (Kent) b May 20, 1930, d Dec. 14, 1990

Page, M. H. (Derbys) b June 17, 1941

*Page, M. L. (Cant.) b May 8, 1902, d Feb. 13, 1987

*Pai, A. M. (Bombay) b April 28, 1945

*Paine, G. A. E. (Middx & Warwicks; *CY 1935*) b June 11, 1908, d March 30, 1978

*Pairaudeau, B. H. (BG & N. Dist.) b April 14, 1931

*Palairet, L. C. H. (OU & Som; *CY 1893*) b May 27, 1870, d March 27, 1933

Palairet, R. C. N. (OU & Som) b June 25, 1871, d Feb. 11, 1955

*Palia, P. E. (Parsis, Madras, U. Prov., Bombay, Mysore & Bengal) b Sept. 5, 1910, d Sept. 9, 1981

*Palm, A. W. (W. Prov.) b June 8, 1901, d Aug. 17, 1966

*Palmer, C. H. CBE (Worcs & Leics; Pres. MCC 1978-79) b May 15, 1919

*Palmer, G. E. (Vic. & Tas.) b Feb. 22, 1859, d Aug. 22, 1910

*Palmer, K. E. (Som; Test umpire) b April 22, 1937

Palmer, R. (Som; Test umpire) b July 12, 1942

*Pandit, C. S. (Bombay, M. Pradesh & Assam) b Sept. 30, 1961

Pardon, Charles F. (Editor of *Wisden* 1887-90) b March 28, 1850, d April 18, 1890

Pardon, Sydney H. (Editor of *Wisden* 1891-1925) b Sept. 23, 1855, d Nov. 20, 1925

*Parfitt, P. H. (Middx; *CY 1963*) b Dec. 8, 1936

Paris, C. G. A. (Hants; Pres. MCC 1975-76) b Aug. 30, 1911

Parish, R. J. (Aust. Administrator) b May 7, 1916

*Park, Dr R. L. (Vic.) b July 30, 1892, d Jan. 23, 1947

*Parkar, G. A. (Bombay) b Oct. 24, 1955

*Parkar, R. D. (Bombay) b Oct. 31, 1946

Parkar, Z. (Bombay) b Nov. 22, 1957

*Parker, C. W. L. (Glos; *CY 1923*) b Oct. 14, 1882, d July 11, 1959

*Parker, G. M. (SA) b May 27, 1899, d May 1, 1969

Parker, J. F. (Surrey) b April 23, 1913, d Jan. 27, 1983

*Parker, J. M. (N. Dist. & Worcs) b Feb. 21, 1951

*Parker, N. M. (Otago & Cant.) b Aug. 28, 1948

*Parker, P. W. G. (CU, Sussex, Natal & Durham) b Jan. 15, 1956

*Parkhouse, W. G. A. (Glam) b Oct. 12, 1925

*Parkin, C. H. (Yorks & Lancs; *CY 1924*) b Feb. 18, 1886, d June 15, 1943

*Parkin, D. C. (E. Prov., Tvl & Griq. W.) b Feb. 20, 1873, d March 20, 1936

Parks, H. W. (Sussex) b July 18, 1906, d May 7, 1984

*Parks, J. H. (Sussex & Cant.; *CY 1938*) b May 12, 1903, d Nov. 21, 1980

*Parks, J. M. (Sussex & Som; *CY 1968*) b Oct. 21, 1931

Parks, R. J. (Hants & Kent) b June 15, 1959

*Parore, A. C. (Auck. & N. Dist.) b Jan. 23, 1971

Parr, George (Notts & All-England) b May 22, 1826, d June 23, 1891

*Parry, D. R. (Comb. Is. & Leewards) b Dec. 22, 1954

*Parsana, D. D. (S'tra, Ind. Rlwys & Guj.) b Dec. 2, 1947

Parsons, A. B. D. (CU & Surrey) b Sept. 20, 1933

Parsons, Canon J. H. (Warwicks) b May 30, 1890, d Feb. 2, 1981

*Partridge, J. T. (Rhod.) b Dec. 9, 1932, d June 7, 1988

Partridge, N. E. (Malvern, CU & Warwicks; *CY 1919*) b Aug. 10, 1900, d March 10, 1982

Partridge, R. J. (Northants) b Feb. 11, 1912, d Feb. 1, 1997

Parvez Mir (R'pindi, Lahore, Punjab, Pak. Us, Derbys, HBL & Glam) b Sept. 24, 1953

*Pascoe, L. S. (NSW) b Feb. 13, 1950

Pasqual, S. P. (SL) b Oct. 15, 1961

*Passailaigue, C. C. (Jam.) b Aug. 1902, d Jan. 7, 1972

*Patankar, C. T. (Bombay) b Nov. 24, 1930

**Pataudi, Iftiqar Ali, Nawab of (OU, Worcs, Patiala, N. Ind. & S. Punjab; *CY 1932*) b March 16, 1910, d Jan. 5, 1952

*Pataudi, Mansur Ali, Nawab of (Sussex, OU, Delhi & H'bad; *CY 1968*) b Jan. 5, 1941

Patel, A. K. (S'tra) b March 6, 1957

*Patel, B. P. (Karn.) b Nov. 24, 1952

*Patel, D. N. (Worcs & Auck.) b Oct. 25, 1958

*Patel, J. M. (Guj.) b Nov. 26, 1924, d Dec. 12, 1992

*Patel, M. M. (Kent) b July 7, 1970

*Patel, R. G. M. (Baroda) b June 1, 1964

Paterson, G. A. (Zimb.) b June 9, 1960

*Patiala, Maharaja of (N. Ind., Patiala & S. Punjab) b Jan. 17, 1913, d June 17, 1974

*Patil, S. M. (Bombay & M. Pradesh) b Aug. 18, 1956

*Patil, S. R. (M'tra) b Oct. 10, 1933

*Patterson, B. P. (Jam., Tas. & Lancs) b Sept. 15, 1961

Patterson, W. H. (OU & Kent) b March 11, 1859, d May 3, 1946

*Payne, T. R. O. (B'dos) b Feb. 13, 1957

*Paynter, E. (Lancs; *CY 1938*) b Nov. 5, 1901, d Feb. 5, 1979

Payton, W. R. D. (Notts) b Feb. 13, 1882, d May 2, 1943

Peach, H. A. (Surrey) b Oct. 6, 1890, d Oct. 8, 1961

*Peall, S. G. (MCD) b Sept. 2, 1969

Pearce, T. N. (Essex) b Nov. 3, 1905, d April 10, 1994

*Pearse, O. C. (Natal) b Oct. 10, 1884, d May 7, 1953

Pearson, F. (Worcs & Auck.) b Sept. 23, 1880, d Nov. 10, 1963

*Peate, E. (Yorks) b March 2, 1855, d March 11, 1900

Peckover, G. E. (Zimb.) b June 2, 1955

*Peebles, I. A. R. (OU, Middx & Scotland; writer; *CY 1931*) b Jan. 20, 1908, d Feb. 28, 1980

*Peel, R. (Yorks; *CY 1889*) b Feb. 12, 1857, d Aug. 12, 1941

*Pegler, S. J. (Tvl) b July 28, 1888, d Sept. 10, 1972

*Pellew, C. E. (S. Aust.) b Sept. 21, 1893, d May 9, 1981

Penn, C. (Kent) b June 19, 1963

*Penn, F. (Kent) b March 7, 1851, d Dec. 26, 1916

Pepper, C. G. (NSW & Aust. Serv.; umpire) b Sept. 15, 1916, d March 24, 1993

Perkins, H. (CU & Cambs; Sec. MCC 1876-97) b Dec. 10, 1832, d May 6, 1916

*Perks, R. T. D. (Worcs) b Oct. 4, 1911, d Nov. 22, 1977

Perrin, P. A. (Essex; *CY 1905*) b May 26, 1876, d Nov. 20, 1945

Perryman, S. P. (Warwicks & Worcs) b Oct. 22, 1955

Pervez Sajjad (Lahore, PIA & Kar.) b Aug. 30, 1942

*Petherick, P. J. (Otago & Wgtn) b Sept. 25, 1942

*Petrie, E. C. (Auck. & N. Dist.) b May 22, 1927

Pettiford, J. (NSW & Kent) b Nov. 29, 1919, d Oct. 11, 1964

*Phadkar, D. G. (M'tra, Bombay, Bengal & Ind. Rlwys) b Dec. 10, 1925, d March 17, 1985

Phebey, A. H. (Kent) b Oct. 1, 1924

Phelan, P. J. (Essex) b Feb. 9, 1938

*Philipson, H. (OU & Middx) b June 8, 1866, d Dec. 4, 1935

*Phillip, N. (Comb. Is., Windwards & Essex) b June 12, 1948

Phillips, H. (Sussex) b Oct. 14, 1844, d July 3, 1919

Phillips, R. B. (NSW & Qld) b May 23, 1954

*Phillips, W. B. (S. Aust.) b March 1, 1958

*Phillips, W. N. (Vic.) b Nov. 7, 1962

Phillipson, C. P. (Sussex) b Feb. 10, 1952

Phillipson, W. E. (Lancs; Test umpire) b Dec. 3, 1910, d Aug. 24, 1991

*Philpott, P. I. (NSW) b Nov. 21, 1934

Pieris, H. S. M. (SL) b Feb. 16, 1946

*Pierre, L. R. (T/T) b June 5, 1921, d April 14, 1989

*Pigott, A. C. S. (Sussex, Wgtn & Surrey) b June 4, 1958

Pilch, Fuller (Norfolk & Kent) b March 17, 1804, d May 1, 1870

Pilling, H. (Lancs) b Feb. 23, 1943

*Pilling, R. (Lancs; *CY 1891*) b July 5, 1855, d March 28, 1891

*Pithey, A. J. (Rhod. & W. Prov.) b July 17, 1933

*Pithey, D. B. (Rhod., OU, Northants, W. Prov., Natal & Tvl) b Oct. 4, 1936

*Place, W. (Lancs) b Dec. 7, 1914

Platt, R. K. (Yorks & Northants) b Dec. 21, 1932

*Playle, W. R. (Auck. & W. Aust.) b Dec. 1, 1938

Pleass, J. E. (Glam) b May 21, 1923

Plews, N. T. (Test umpire) b Sept. 5, 1934

*Plimsoll, J. B. (W. Prov. & Natal) b Oct. 27, 1917

*Pocock, B. A. (N. Dist.) b June 18, 1971

Pocock, N. E. J. (Hants) b Dec. 15, 1951

*Pocock, P. I. (Surrey & N. Tvl) b Sept. 24, 1946

*Pollard, R. (Lancs) b June 19, 1912, d Dec. 16, 1985

*Pollard, V. (C. Dist. & Cant.) b Sept. 7, 1945

*Pollock, P. M. (E. Prov.; *CY 1966*) b June 30, 1941

*Pollock, R. G. (E. Prov. & Tvl; *CY 1966*) b Feb. 27, 1944

Pollock, S. M. (Natal & Warwicks) b July 16, 1973

*Ponsford, W. H. MBE (Vic.; *CY 1935*) b Oct. 19, 1900, d April 6, 1991

Pont, K. R. (Essex) b Jan. 16, 1953

*Ponting, R. T. (Tas.) b Dec. 19, 1974

*Poole, C. J. (Notts) b March 13, 1921, d Feb. 11, 1996

Pooley, E. (Surrey & first England tour) b Feb. 13, 1838, d July 18, 1907

*Poore, M. B. (Cant.) b June 1, 1930

*Poore, Brig-Gen. R. M. (Hants & SA; *CY 1900*) b March 20, 1866, d July 14, 1938

Pope, A. V. (Derbys) b Aug. 15, 1909, d May 11, 1996

*Pope, G. H. (Derbys) b Jan. 27, 1911, d Oct. 29, 1993

*Pope, Dr R. J. (NSW) b Feb. 18, 1864, d July 27, 1952

Popplewell, N. F. M. (CU & Som) b Aug. 8, 1957

Portal of Hungerford, 1st Lord (Pres. MCC 1958-59) b May 21, 1893, d April 22, 1971

Porter, G. D. (W. Aust.) b March 18, 1955

Pothecary, A. E. (Hants) b March 1, 1906, d May 21, 1991

*Pothecary, J. E. (W. Prov.) b Dec. 6, 1933

Potter, L. (Kent, Griq. W., Leics & OFS) b Nov. 7, 1962

*Pougher, A. D. (Leics) b April 19, 1865, d May 20, 1926

*Powell, A. W. (Griq. W.) b July 18, 1873, d Sept. 11, 1948

*Prabhakar, M. (Delhi & Durham) b April 15, 1963

Prasad, B. K. V. (TN & Karn.) b Aug. 5, 1969

*Prasanna, E. A. S. (†Karn.) b May 22, 1940

Prentice, F. T. (Leics) b April 22, 1912, d July 10, 1978

Pressdee, J. S. (Glam & NE Tvl) b June 19, 1933

Preston, Hubert (Editor of *Wisden* 1944-51) b Dec. 16, 1868, d Aug. 6, 1960

Preston, K. C. (Essex) b Aug. 22, 1925

Preston, Norman (Editor of *Wisden* 1952-80) b March 18, 1903, d March 6, 1980

Pretlove, J. F. (CU & Kent) b Nov. 23, 1932

*Price, J. S. E. (Middx) b July 22, 1937

*Price, W. F. (Middx; Test umpire) b April 25, 1902, d Jan. 13, 1969

*Prideaux, R. M. (CU, Kent, Northants, Sussex & OFS) b July 31, 1939

Pridgeon, A. P. (Worcs) b Feb. 22, 1954

*Priest, M. W. (Cant.) b Aug. 12, 1961

*Prince, C. F. H. (W. Prov., Border & E. Prov.) b Sept. 11, 1874, d Feb. 2, 1949

*Pringle, C. (Auck.) b Jan. 26, 1968

*Pringle, D. R. (CU & Essex) b Sept. 18, 1958

*Pringle, M. W. (OFS & W. Prov.) b June 22, 1966

Pritchard, T. L. (Wgtn, Warwicks & Kent) b March 10, 1917

*Procter, M. J. (Glos, Natal, W. Prov., Rhod. & OFS; *CY 1970*) b Sept. 15, 1946

Prodger, J. M. (Kent) b Sept. 1, 1935

*Promnitz, H. L. E. (Border, Griq. W. & OFS) b Feb. 23, 1904, d Sept. 7, 1983

*Pullar, G. (Lancs & Glos; *CY 1960*) b Aug. 1, 1935

*Puna, N. (N. Dist.) b Oct. 28, 1929, d June 7, 1996

*Punjabi, P. H. (Sind & Guj.) b Sept. 20, 1921

*Pushpakumara, K. R. (NCC) b July 21, 1975

*Pycroft, A. J. (Zimb.) b June 6, 1956

Pydanna, M. R. (Guyana) b Jan. 27, 1950

*Qasim Omar (Kar. & MCB) b Feb. 9, 1957

Quaife, B. W. (Warwicks & Worcs) b Nov. 24, 1899, d Nov. 28, 1984

Quaife, Walter (Sussex & Warwicks) b April 1, 1864, d Jan. 18, 1943

*Quaife, William (W. G.) (Warwicks & Griq. W.; *CY 1902*) b March 17, 1872, d Oct. 13, 1951

*Quinn, N. A. (Griq. W. & Tvl) b Feb. 21, 1908, d Aug. 5, 1934

*Rabone, G. O. (Wgtn & Auck.) b Nov. 6, 1921

*Rackemann, C. G. (Qld & Surrey) b June 3, 1960

Radcliffe, Sir Everard J. Bt (Yorks) b Jan. 27, 1884, d Nov. 23, 1969

*Radford, N. V. (Lancs, Tvl & Worcs; *CY 1986*) b June 7, 1957

*Radley, C. T. (Middx; *CY 1979*) b May 13, 1944

*Rae, A. F. (Jam.) b Sept. 30, 1922

Raees Mohammad (Kar.) b Dec. 24, 1932

*Rai Singh, K. (S. Punjab & Ind. Serv.) b Feb. 24, 1922

Rait Kerr, Col. R. S. (Eur.; Sec. MCC 1936-52) b April 13, 1891, d April 2, 1961

Rajadurai, B. E. A. (SSC) b Aug. 24, 1965

*Rajinarnath, V. (N. Ind., U. Prov., S. Punjab, Bihar & E. Punjab) b Jan. 7, 1928, d Nov. 22, 1989

*Rajinder Pal (Delhi, S. Punjab & Punjab) b Nov. 18, 1937

*Rajput, L. S. (Bombay & Vidarbha) b Dec. 18, 1961

*Raju, S. L. V. (H'bad) b July 9, 1969

Ralph, L. H. R. (Essex) b May 22, 1920

*Ramadhin, S. (T/T & Lancs; *CY 1951*) b May 1, 1929

*Raman, W. V. (TN) b May 23, 1965

*Ramanayake, C. P. H. (TU) b Jan. 8, 1965

*Ramaswami, C. (Madras) b June 18, 1896, presumed dead.

*Ramchand, G. S. (Sind, Bombay & Raja.) b July 26, 1927

*Ramiz Raja (Lahore, Allied Bank, PNSC & I'bad) b Aug. 14, 1962

*Ramji, L. (W. Ind.) b Oct. 2, 1902, d Dec. 20, 1948

*Ramprakash, M. R. (Middx) b Sept. 5, 1969

*Ranasinghe, A. N. (BRC) b Oct. 13, 1956

Ranasinghe, S. K. (SL) b July 4, 1962

*Ranatunga, A. (SSC) b Dec. 1, 1963

*Ranatunga, D. (SSC) b Oct. 12, 1962

*Ranatunga, S. (NCC) b April 25, 1969

*Ranchod, U. (Mash.) b May 17, 1969

*Randall, D. W. (Notts; *CY 1980*) b Feb. 24, 1951

Randhir Singh (Orissa & Bihar) b Aug. 16, 1957

*Rangachari, C. R. (Madras) b April 14, 1916, d Oct. 9, 1993

*Rangnekar, K. M. (M'tra, Bombay & †M. Pradesh) b June 27, 1917, d Oct. 11, 1984

*Ranjane, V. B. (M'tra & Ind. Rlwys) b July 22, 1937

*Ranjitsinhji, K. S., (later H. H. the Jam Sahib of Nawanagar) (CU & Sussex; *CY 1897*) b Sept. 10, 1872, d April 2, 1933

*Ransford, V. S. (Vic.; *CY 1910*) b March 20, 1885, d March 19, 1958

*Rashid Khan (PWD, Kar. & PIA) b Dec. 15, 1959

*Rashid Latif (Kar., UBL & Allied Bank) b Oct. 14, 1968

*Rathore, V. (Punjab) b March 26, 1969

Ratnayake, N. L. K. (SSC) b Nov. 22, 1968

*Ratnayake, R. J. (NCC) b Jan. 2, 1964

*Ratnayeke, J. R. (NCC) b May 2, 1960

Rawlin, J. T. (Yorks & Middx) b Nov. 10, 1856, d Jan. 19, 1924

Rawson, P. W. E. (Zimb. & Natal) b May 25, 1957

Rayment, A. W. H. (Hants) b May 29, 1928

*Razdan, V. (Delhi) b Aug. 25, 1969

*Read, H. D. (Surrey & Essex) b Jan. 28, 1910

*Read, J. M. (Surrey; *CY 1890*) b Feb. 9, 1859, d Feb. 17, 1929

*Read, W. W. (Surrey; *CY 1893*) b Nov. 23, 1855, d Jan. 6, 1907

*Reddy, B. (TN) b Nov. 12, 1954

*Redmond, R. E. (Wgtn & Auck.) b Dec. 29, 1944

*Redpath, I. R. MBE (Vic.) b May 11, 1941

Reed, B. L. (Hants) b Sept. 17, 1937

*Reedman, J. C. (S. Aust.) b Oct. 9, 1865, d March 25, 1924

Rees, A. (Glam) b Feb. 17, 1938

*Reeve, D. A. OBE (Sussex & Warwicks; *CY 1996*) b April 2, 1963

Reeves, W. (Essex; Test umpire) b Jan. 22, 1875, d March 22, 1944

*Rege, M. R. (M'tra) b March 18, 1924

*Rehman, S. F. (Punjab, Pak. Us & Lahore) b June 11, 1935

*Reid, B. A. (W. Aust.) b March 14, 1963

*Reid, J. F. (Auck.) b March 3, 1956

*Reid, J. R. OBE (Wgtn & Otago; *CY 1959*) b June 3, 1928

*Reid, N. (W. Prov.) b Dec. 26, 1890, d June 6, 1947

Reid, R. B. (Wgtn & Auck.) b Dec. 3, 1958

Reidy, B. W. (Lancs) b Sept. 18, 1953

*Reifer, F. L. (B'dos) b July 23, 1972

*Reiffel, P. R. (Vic.) b April 19, 1966

*Relf, A. E. (Sussex & Auck.; *CY 1914*) b June 26, 1874, d March 26, 1937

Relf, R. R. (Sussex) b Sept. 1, 1883, d April 28, 1965

*Renneburg, D. A. (NSW) b Sept. 23, 1942

*Rennie, J. A. (Mat.) b July 29, 1970

Revill, A. C. (Derbys & Leics) b March 27, 1923

Reynolds, B. L. (Northants) b June 10, 1932

Rhodes, A. E. G. (Derbys; Test umpire) b Oct. 10, 1916, d Oct. 18, 1983

*Rhodes, H. J. (Derbys) b July 22, 1936

*Rhodes, J. N. (Natal) b July 26, 1969

*Rhodes, S. J. (Yorks & Worcs; *CY 1995*) b June 17, 1964

*Rhodes, W. (Yorks; *CY 1899*) b Oct. 29, 1877, d July 8, 1973

Rice, C. E. B. (Tvl & Notts; *CY 1981*) b July 23, 1949

Rice, J. M. (Hants) b Oct. 23, 1949

*Richards, A. R. (W. Prov.) b Dec. 14, 1867, d Jan. 9, 1904

*Richards, B. A. (Natal, Glos, Hants & S. Aust.; *CY 1969*) b July 21, 1945

*Richards, C. J. (Surrey & OFS) b Aug. 10, 1958

Richards, D. L. (Chief Exec. ICC 1993-) b July 28, 1946

Richards, G. (Glam) b Nov. 29, 1951

*Richards, I. V. A. OBE (Comb. Is., Leewards, Som, Qld & Glam; *CY 1977*) b March 7, 1952

*Richards, W. H. (SA) b March 26, 1862, d Jan. 4, 1903

*Richardson, A. J. (S. Aust.) b July 24, 1888, d Dec. 23, 1973

Richardson, A. W. (Derbys) b March 4, 1907, d July 29, 1983

*Richardson, D. J. (E. Prov. & N. Tvl) b Sept. 16, 1959

Richardson, D. W. (Worcs) b Nov. 3, 1934

*Richardson, P. E. (Worcs & Kent; *CY 1957*) b July 4, 1931

*Richardson, R. B. (Leewards, Yorks and N. Tvl; *CY 1992*) b Jan. 12, 1962

*Richardson, T. (Surrey & Som; *CY 1897*) b Aug. 11, 1870, d July 2, 1912

*Richardson, V. Y. (S. Aust.) b Sept. 7, 1894, d Oct. 29, 1969

Riches, N. V. H. (Glam) b June 9, 1883, d Nov. 6, 1975

*Richmond, T. L. (Notts) b June 23, 1890, d Dec. 29, 1957

*Rickards, K. R. (Jam. & Essex) b Aug. 23, 1923, d Aug. 21, 1995

Riddington, A. (Leics) b Dec. 22, 1911

Ridgway, F. (Kent) b Aug. 10, 1923

*Rigg, K. E. (Vic.) b May 21, 1906, d Feb. 28, 1995

*Ring, D. T. (Vic.) b Oct. 14, 1918

*Ritchie, G. M. (Qld) b Jan. 23, 1960

*Rixon, S. J. (NSW) b Feb. 25, 1954

*Rizwan-uz-Zaman (Kar. & PIA) b Sept. 4, 1962

*Roach, C. A. (T/T) b March 13, 1904, d April 16, 1988

*Roberts, A. D. G. (N. Dist.) b May 6, 1947, d Oct. 26, 1989

*Roberts, A. M. E. CBE (Comb. Is., Leewards, Hants, NSW & Leics; *CY 1975*) b Jan. 29, 1951

*Roberts, A. T. (Windwards & T/T) b Sept. 18, 1937, d July 24, 1996

*Roberts, A. W. (Cant. & Otago) b Aug. 20, 1909, d May 13, 1978

Roberts, B. (Tvl & Derbys) b May 30, 1962

Roberts, The Hon. Sir Denys (Pres. MCC 1989-90) b Jan. 19, 1923

*Roberts, F. G. (Glos) b April 1, 1862, d April 7, 1936

Roberts, S. J. (Cant.) b March 22, 1965

Roberts, W. B. (Lancs & Victory Tests) b Sept. 27, 1914, d Aug. 24, 1951

*Robertson, G. K. (C. Dist.) b July 15, 1960

Robertson, G. R. (NSW) b May 28, 1966

*Robertson, J. B. (W. Prov.) b June 5, 1906, d July 5, 1985

*Robertson, J. D. (Middx; *CY 1948*) b Feb. 22, 1917, d Oct. 12, 1996

*Robertson, W. R. (Vic.) b Oct. 6, 1861, d June 24, 1938

Robertson-Glasgow, R. C. (OU & Som; writer) b July 15, 1901, d March 4, 1965

Robins, D. H. (Warwicks) b June 26, 1914

*Robins, R. W. V. (CU & Middx; *CY 1930*) b June 3, 1906, d Dec. 12, 1968

Robinson, D. C. (Glos & Essex) b April 20, 1884, d July 29, 1963

Robinson, E. (Yorks) b Nov. 16, 1883, d Nov. 17, 1969

Robinson, E. P. (Yorks & Som) b Aug. 10, 1911

Robinson, Sir Foster G. (Glos) b Sept. 19, 1880, d Oct. 31, 1967

Robinson, P. E. (Yorks & Leics) b Aug. 3, 1963

Robinson, P. J. (Worcs & Som) b Feb. 9, 1943

*Robinson, R. D. (Vic.) b June 8, 1946

*Robinson, R. H. (NSW, S. Aust. & Otago) b March 26, 1914, d Aug. 10, 1965

*Robinson, R. T. (Notts; *CY 1986*) b Nov. 21, 1958

Robson, C. (Hants) b June 20, 1859, d Sept. 27, 1943

Robson, E. (Som) b May 1, 1870, d May 23, 1924

*Rodriguez, W. V. (T/T) b June 25, 1934

Roe, B. (Som) b Jan. 27, 1939

Roebuck, P. M. (CU & Som; *CY 1988*) b March 6, 1956

Rogers, N. H. (Hants) b March 9, 1918

Rogers, S. S. (Eur. & Som) b March 18, 1923, d Nov. 6, 1969

Romaines, P. W. (Northants, Glos & Griq. W.) b Dec. 25, 1955

*Roope, G. R. J. (Surrey & Griq. W.) b July 12, 1946

*Root, C. F. (Derbys & Worcs) b April 16, 1890, d Jan. 20, 1954

*Rorke, G. F. (NSW) b June 27, 1938

*Rose, B. C. (Som; *CY 1980*) b June 4, 1950

*Rose, F. A. (Jam.) b Feb. 1, 1972

*Rose-Innes, A. (Kimberley & Tvl) b Feb. 16, 1868, d Nov. 22, 1946

Rotherham, G. A. (Rugby, CU, Warwicks & Wgtn.; *CY 1918*) b May 28, 1899, d Jan. 31, 1985

Rouse, S. J. (Warwicks) b Jan. 20, 1949

*Routledge, T. W. (W. Prov. & Tvl) b April 18, 1867, d May 9, 1927

*Rowan, A. M. B. (Tvl) b Feb. 7, 1921

*Rowan, E. A. B. (Tvl; *CY 1952*) b July 20, 1909, d April 30, 1993

Rowbotham, J. (Yorks; Test umpire) b July 8, 1831, d Dec. 22, 1899

*Rowe, C. G. (Wgtn & C. Dist.) b June 30, 1915, d June 9, 1995

Rowe, C. J. C. (Kent & Glam) b Nov. 11, 1951

Rowe, E. J. (Notts) b July 21, 1920, d Dec. 17, 1989

*Rowe, G. A. (W. Prov.) b June 15, 1874, d Jan. 8, 1950

*Rowe, L. G. (Jam. & Derbys) b Jan. 8, 1949

*Roy, A. (Bengal) b June 5, 1945, d Sept. 19, 1997

*Roy, Pankaj (Bengal) b May 31, 1928

*Roy, Pranab (Bengal) b Feb. 10, 1957

*Royle, Rev. V. P. F. A. (OU & Lancs) b Jan. 29, 1854, d May 21, 1929

*Rumsey, F. E. (Worcs, Som & Derbys) b Dec. 4, 1935

Rushby, T. (Surrey) b Sept. 6, 1880, d July 13, 1962

*Rushmere, M. W. (E. Prov. & Tvl) b Jan. 7, 1965

*Russell, A. C. (Essex; *CY 1923*) b Oct. 7, 1887, d March 23, 1961

Russell, P. E. (Derbys) b May 9, 1944

*Russell, R. C. MBE (Glos; *CY 1990*) b Aug. 15, 1963

Russell, S. E. J. (Middx & Glos) b Oct. 4, 1937, d June 18, 1994

*Russell, W. E. (Middx) b July 3, 1936

*Rutherford, J. W. (W. Aust.) b Sept. 25, 1929

*Rutherford, K. R. (Otago & Tvl) b Oct. 26, 1965

Ryan, F. (Hants & Glam) b Nov. 14, 1888, d Jan. 5, 1954

Ryan, M. (Yorks) b June 23, 1933

*Ryder, J. (Vic.) b Aug. 8, 1889, d April 3, 1977

Saadat Ali (Lahore, UBL & HBFC) b Feb. 6, 1955

*Sadiq Mohammad (Kar., PIA, Tas., Essex, Glos & UBL) b May 3, 1945

*Saeed Ahmed (Punjab, Pak. Us, Lahore, PIA, Kar., PWD & Sind) b Oct. 1, 1937

*Saeed Anwar (Kar., UBL & ADBP; *CY 1997*) b Sept. 6, 1968

*Saggers, R. A. (NSW) b May 15, 1917, d March 17, 1987

Sainsbury, P. J. (Hants; *CY 1974*) b June 13, 1934

*St Hill, E. L. (T/T) b March 9, 1904, d May 21, 1957

*St Hill, W. H. (T/T) b July 6, 1893, d *circa* 1957

*Salah-ud-Din (Kar., PIA & Pak. Us) b Feb. 14, 1947

*Saleem Altaf (Lahore & PIA) b April 19, 1944

*Saleem Jaffer (Kar. & UBL) b Nov. 19, 1962

*Salim Elahi (Lahore & UBL) b Nov. 21, 1976

*Salim Malik (Lahore, HBL & Essex; *CY 1988*) b April 16, 1963

Salim Pervez (NBP) b Sept. 9, 1947

*Salim Yousuf (Sind, Kar., IDBP, Allied Bank & Customs) b Dec. 7, 1959

*Salisbury, I. D. K. (Sussex & Surrey; *CY 1993*) b Jan. 21, 1970

Samaranayake, A. D. A. (SL) b Feb. 25, 1962

*Samarasekera, M. A. R. (CCC) b Aug. 5, 1961

*Samaraweera, D. P. (Colts) b Feb. 12, 1972

Sampson, H. (Yorks & All-England) b March 13, 1813, d March 29, 1885

*Samuels, R. G. (Jam.) b March 13, 1971

*Samuelson, S. V. (Natal) b Nov. 21, 1883, d Nov. 18, 1958

*Sandham, A. (Surrey; *CY 1923*) b July 6, 1890, d April 20, 1982

*Sandhu, B. S. (Bombay) b Aug. 3, 1956

Santall, F. R. (Warwicks) b July 12, 1903, d Nov. 3, 1950

Santall, S. (Warwicks) b June 10, 1873, d March 19, 1957

*Saqlain Mushtaq (I'bad, PIA & Surrey) b Nov. 27, 1976

*Sardesai, D. N. (Bombay) b Aug. 8, 1940

*Sarfraz Nawaz (Lahore, Punjab, Northants, Pak. Rlwys & UBL) b Dec. 1, 1948

*Sarwate, C. T. (CP & B, M'tra, Bombay & †M. Pradesh) b June 22, 1920

*Saunders, J. V. (Vic. & Wgtn) b March 21, 1876, d Dec. 21, 1927

Savage, J. S. (Leics & Lancs) b March 3, 1929

Savill, L. A. (Essex) b June 30, 1935

Saville, G. J. (Essex) b Feb. 5, 1944

Saxelby, K. (Notts) b Feb. 23, 1959

*Saxena, R. C. (Delhi & Bihar) b Sept. 20, 1944

Sayer, D. M. (OU & Kent) b Sept. 19, 1936

*Scarlett, R. O. (Jam.) b Aug. 15, 1934

*Schultz, B. N. (E. Prov. & W. Prov.) b Aug. 26, 1970

*Schultz, S. S. (CU & Lancs) b Aug. 29, 1857, d Dec. 18, 1937

*Schwarz, R. O. (Middx & Natal; *CY 1908*) b May 4, 1875, d Nov. 18, 1918

*Scott, A. P. H. (Jam.) b July 29, 1934

Scott, C. J. (Glos) b May 1, 1919, d Nov. 22, 1992

Scott, C. W. (Notts & Durham) b Jan. 23, 1964

*Scott, H. J. H. (Vic.) b Dec. 26, 1858, d Sept. 23, 1910

Scott, M. E. (Northants) b May 8, 1936

*Scott, O. C. (Jam.) b Aug. 14, 1893, d June 15, 1961

*Scott, R. H. (Cant.) b March 6, 1917

Scott, S. W. (Middx; *CY 1893*) b March 24, 1854, d Dec. 8, 1933

*Scott, V. J. (Auck.) b July 31, 1916, d Aug. 2, 1980

*Scotton, W. H. (Notts) b Jan. 15, 1856, d July 9, 1893

*Sealey, B. J. (T/T) b Aug. 12, 1899, d Sept. 12, 1963

*Sealy, J. E. D. (B'dos & T/T) b Sept. 11, 1912, d Jan. 3, 1982

*Seccull, A. W. (Kimberley, W. Prov. & Tvl) b Sept. 14, 1868, d July 20, 1945

*Sekar, T. A. P. (TN) b March 28, 1955

*Selby, J. (Notts) b July 1, 1849, d March 11, 1894

Sellers, A. B. MBE (Yorks; *CY 1940*) b March 5, 1907, d Feb. 20, 1981

*Sellers, R. H. D. (S. Aust.) b Aug. 20, 1940

*Selvey, M. W. W. (CU, Surrey, Middx, Glam & OFS; writer) b April 25, 1948

*Sen, P. (Bengal) b May 31, 1926, d Jan. 27, 1970

*Sen Gupta, A. K. (Ind. Serv.) b Aug. 3, 1939

*Senanayake, C. P. (CCC) b Dec. 19, 1962

*Serjeant, C. S. (W. Aust.) b Nov. 1, 1951

Seymour, James (Kent) b Oct. 25, 1879, d Sept. 30, 1930

*Seymour, M. A. (W. Prov.) b June 5, 1936

*Shackleton, D. (Hants; *CY 1959*) b Aug. 12, 1924

*Shadab Kabir (Kar.) b Nov. 12, 1977

*Shafiq Ahmed (Lahore, Punjab, NBP & UBL) b March 28, 1949

*Shafqat Rana (Lahore & PIA) b Aug. 10, 1943

*Shah, A. H. (Mash.) b Aug. 7, 1959

*Shahid Israr (Kar. & Sind) b March 1, 1950

*Shahid Mahboob (Kar., Quetta, R'pindi, I'bad, PACO & Allied Bank) b Aug. 25, 1962

*Shahid Mahmoud (Kar., Pak. Us & PWD) b March 17, 1939

*Shahid Nazir (F'bad & NBP) b Dec. 4, 1977

*Shahid Saeed (HBFC, Lahore & PACO) b Jan. 6, 1966

*Shakeel Ahmed (B'pur, HBL, R'pindi & Peshawar) b Nov. 12, 1971

*Shalders, W. A. (Griq. W. & Tvl) b Feb. 12, 1880, d March 18, 1917

*Sharma, Ajay (Delhi) b April 3, 1964

*Sharma, Chetan (Haryana & Bengal) b Jan. 3, 1966
*Sharma, Gopal (U. Pradesh) b Aug. 3, 1960
*Sharma, P. (Raja.) b Jan. 5, 1948
Sharma, Sanjeev (Delhi & H. Pradesh) b Aug. 25, 1965
Sharp, G. (Northants; Test umpire) b March 12, 1950
Sharp, H. P. (Middx) b Oct. 6, 1917, d Jan. 15, 1995
*Sharp, J. (Lancs) b Feb. 15, 1878, d Jan. 28, 1938
Sharp, K. (Yorks & Griq. W.) b April 6, 1959
*Sharpe, D. (Punjab, Pak. Rlwys, Lahore & S. Aust.) b Aug. 3, 1937
*Sharpe, J. W. (Surrey & Notts; *CY 1892*) b Dec. 9, 1866, d June 19, 1936
*Sharpe, P. J. (Yorks & Derbys; *CY 1963*) b Dec. 27, 1936
*Shastri, R. J. (Bombay & Glam) b May 27, 1962
*Shaw, Alfred (Notts & Sussex) b Aug. 29, 1842, d Jan. 16, 1907
*Sheahan, A. P. (Vic.) b Sept. 30, 1946
Sheffield, J. R. (Essex & Wgtn) b Nov. 19, 1906, d Nov. 16, 1997
*Shepherd, B. K. (W. Aust.) b April 23, 1937
Shepherd, D. J. (Glam; *CY 1970*) b Aug. 12, 1927
Shepherd, D. R. MBE (Glos; Test umpire) b Dec. 27, 1940
*Shepherd, J. N. (B'dos, Kent, Rhod. & Glos; *CY 1979*) b Nov. 9, 1943
Shepherd, T. F. (Surrey) b Dec. 5, 1889, d Feb. 13, 1957
*Sheppard, Rt Rev. D. S. (Bishop of Liverpool; later Baron Sheppard) (CU & Sussex; *CY 1953*) b March 6, 1929
*Shepstone, G. H. (Tvl) b April 9, 1876, d July 3, 1940
*Sherwell, P. W. (Tvl) b Aug. 17, 1880, d April 17, 1948
*Sherwin, M. (Notts; *CY 1891*) b Feb. 26, 1851, d July 3, 1910
Shields, J. (Leics) b Feb. 1, 1882, d May 11, 1960
*Shillingford, G. C. (Comb. Is. & Windwards) b Sept. 25, 1944
*Shillingford, I. T. (Comb. Is. & Windwards) b April 18, 1944
*Shinde, S. G. (Baroda, M'tra & Bombay) b Aug. 18, 1923, d June 22, 1955
Shipman, A. W. (Leics) b March 7, 1901, d Dec. 12, 1979
Shirreff, A. C. (CU, Hants, Kent & Som) b Feb. 12, 1919
*Shivnarine, S. (Guyana) b May 13, 1952
*Shoaib Mohammad (Kar. & PIA) b Jan. 8, 1961
*Shodhan, R. H. (Guj. & Baroda) b Oct. 18, 1928

*Shrewsbury, A. (Notts; *CY 1890*) b April 11, 1856, d May 19, 1903
*Shrimpton, M. J. F. (C. Dist. & N. Dist.) b June 23, 1940
*Shuja-ud-Din, Col. (N. Ind., Pak. Us, Pak. Serv., B'pur & R'pindi) b April 10, 1930
*Shukla, R. C. (Bihar & Delhi) b Feb. 4, 1948
*Shuter, J. (Kent & Surrey) b Feb. 9, 1855, d July 5, 1920
*Shuttleworth, K. (Lancs & Leics) b Nov. 13, 1944
Sibbles, F. M. (Lancs) b March 15, 1904, d July 20, 1973
*Sidebottom, A. (Yorks & OFS) b April 1, 1954
*Sidhu, N. S. (Punjab) b Oct. 20, 1963
Sidwell, T. E. (Leics) b Jan. 30, 1888, d Dec. 8, 1958
*Siedle, I. J. (Natal) b Jan. 11, 1903, d Aug. 24, 1982
*Sievers, M. W. (Vic.) b April 13, 1912, d May 10, 1968
*Sikander Bakht (PWD, PIA, Sind, Kar. & UBL) b Aug. 25, 1957
Silk, D. R. W. CBE (CU & Som; Pres. MCC 1992-94; Chairman TCCB 1994-96) b Oct. 8, 1931
*Silva, K. J. (Bloom.) b June 2, 1973
*Silva, S. A. R. (NCC) b Dec. 12, 1960
*Silverwood, C. E. W. (Yorks) b March 5, 1975
Sime, W. A. MBE (OU & Notts) b Feb. 8, 1909, d May 5, 1993
Simmons, J. MBE (Lancs & Tas.; *CY 1985*) b March 28, 1941
*Simmons, P. V. (T/T, Border, Leics & Easterns; *CY 1997*) b April 18, 1963
*Simpson, R. B. (NSW & W. Aust.; *CY 1965*) b Feb. 3, 1936
*Simpson, R. T. (Sind & Notts; *CY 1950*) b Feb. 27, 1920
*Simpson-Hayward, G. H. (Worcs) b June 7, 1875 d Oct. 2, 1936
Sims, Sir Arthur (Cant.) b July 22, 1877, d April 27, 1969
*Sims, J. M. (Middx) b May 13, 1903, d April 27, 1973
*Sinclair, B. W. (Wgtn) b Oct. 23, 1936
*Sinclair, I. M. (Cant.) b June 1, 1933
*Sinclair, J. H. (Tvl) b Oct. 16, 1876, d Feb. 23, 1913
*Sincock, D. J. (S. Aust.) b Feb. 1, 1942
*Sinfield, R. A. (Glos) b Dec. 24, 1900, d March 17, 1988
*Singh, Charan K. (T/T) b Nov. 27, 1935
Singleton, A. P. (OU, Worcs & Rhod.) b Aug. 5, 1914
Sivaramakrishnan, L. (TN) b Dec. 31, 1965
Skelding, A. (Leics; umpire) b Sept. 5, 1886, d April 17, 1960

*Slack, W. N. (Middx & Windwards) b Dec. 12, 1954, d Jan. 15, 1989

Slade, D. N. F. (Worcs) b Aug. 24, 1940

Slater, A. G. (Derbys) b Nov. 22, 1890, d July 22, 1949

*Slater, K. N. (W. Aust.) b March 12, 1935

*Slater, M. J. (NSW) b Feb. 21, 1970

*Sleep, P. R. (S. Aust.) b May 4, 1957

*Slight, J. (Vic.) b Oct. 20, 1855, d Dec. 9, 1930

Slocombe, P. A. (Som) b Sept. 6, 1954

*Smailes, T. F. (Yorks) b March 27, 1910, d Dec. 1, 1970

Smales, K. (Yorks & Notts) b Sept. 15, 1927

*Small, G. C. (Warwicks & S. Aust.) b Oct. 18, 1961

Small, John, sen. (Hants & All-England) b April 19, 1737, d Dec. 31, 1826

*Small, J. A. (T/T) b Nov. 3, 1892, d April 26, 1958

*Small, M. A. (B'dos) b Feb. 12, 1964

Smart, C. C. (Warwicks & Glam) b July 23, 1898, d May 21, 1975

Smart, J. A. (Warwicks) b April 12, 1891, d Oct. 3, 1979

Smedley, M. J. (Notts) b Oct. 28, 1941

*Smith, A. C. CBE (OU & Warwicks; Chief Exec. TCCB 1987-96) b Oct. 25, 1936

*Smith, A. M. (Glos) b Oct. 1, 1967

*Smith, Sir C. Aubrey (OU, Sussex & Tvl) b July 21, 1863, d Dec. 20, 1948

*Smith, C. I. J. (Middx; *CY 1935*) b Aug. 25, 1906, d Feb. 9, 1979

*Smith, C. J. E. (Tvl) b Dec. 25, 1872, d March 27, 1947

*Smith, C. L. (Natal, Glam & Hants; *CY 1984*) b Oct. 15, 1958

Smith, C. L. A. (Sussex) b Jan. 1, 1879, d Nov. 22, 1949

Smith, C. S. (later Sir Colin Stansfield-) (CU & Lancs) b Oct. 1, 1932

*Smith, C. W. (B'dos) b July 29, 1933

*Smith, Denis (Derbys; *CY 1936*) b Jan. 24, 1907, d Sept. 12, 1979

*Smith, D. B. M. (Vic.) b Sept. 14, 1884, d July 29, 1963

Smith, D. H. K. (Derbys & OFS) b June 29, 1940

*Smith, D. M. (Surrey, Worcs & Sussex) b Jan. 9, 1956

*Smith, D. R. (Glos) b Oct. 5, 1934

*Smith, D. V. (Sussex) b June 14, 1923

Smith, Edwin (Derbys) b Jan. 2, 1934

Smith, Ernest (OU & Yorks) b Oct. 19, 1869, d April 9, 1945

*Smith, E. J. (Warwicks) b Feb. 6, 1886, d Aug. 31, 1979

*Smith, F. B. (Cant.) b March 13, 1922, d July 6, 1997

*Smith, F. W. (Tvl) b unknown, d 1913

Smith, G. J. (Essex) b April 2, 1935

*Smith, Harry (Glos) b May 21, 1890, d Nov. 12, 1937

Smith, H. A. (Leics) b March 29, 1901, d Aug. 7, 1948

*Smith, H. D. (Otago & Cant.) b Jan. 8, 1913, d Jan. 25, 1986

*Smith, I. D. S. MBE (C. Dist. & Auck.) b Feb. 28, 1957

Smith, K. D. (Warwicks) b July 9, 1956

Smith, M. J. (Middx) b Jan. 4, 1942

*Smith, M. J. K. OBE (Leics, OU & Warwicks; *CY 1960*) b June 30, 1933

Smith, N. (Yorks & Essex) b April 1, 1949

*Smith, O. G. ("Collie") (Jam.; *CY 1958*) b May 5, 1933, d Sept. 9, 1959

Smith, P. A. (Warwicks) b April 5, 1964

Smith, Ray (Essex) b Aug. 10, 1914, d Feb. 21, 1996

Smith, Roy (Som) b April 14, 1930

*Smith, R. A. (Natal & Hants; *CY 1990*) b Sept. 13, 1963

Smith, R. C. (Leics) b Aug. 3, 1935

*Smith, S. B. (NSW & Tvl) b Oct. 18, 1961

*Smith, S. G. (T/T, Northants & Auck.; *CY 1915*) b Jan. 15, 1881, d Oct. 25, 1963

*Smith, T. P. B. (Essex; *CY 1947*) b Oct. 30, 1908, d Aug. 4, 1967

*Smith, V. I. (Natal) b Feb. 23, 1925

Smith, W. A. (Surrey) b Sept. 15, 1937

Smith, W. C. (Surrey; *CY 1911*) b Oct. 4, 1877, d July 16, 1946

*Smithson, G. A. (Yorks & Leics) b Nov. 1, 1926, d Sept. 6, 1970

*Snedden, C. A. (Auck.) b Jan. 7, 1918, d May 19, 1993

*Snedden, M. C. (Auck.) b Nov. 23, 1958

*Snell, R. P. (Natal, Tvl & Som) b Sept. 12, 1968

Snellgrove, K. L. (Lancs) b Nov. 12, 1941

*Snooke, S. D. (W. Prov. & Tvl) b Nov. 11, 1878, d April 6, 1959

*Snooke, S. J. (Border, W. Prov. & Tvl) b Feb. 1, 1881, d Aug. 14, 1966

*Snow, J. A. (Sussex; *CY 1973*) b Oct. 13, 1941

*Sobers, Sir Garfield S. (B'dos, S. Aust. & Notts; *CY 1964*) b July 28, 1936

*Sohoni, S. W. (M'tra, Baroda & Bombay) b March 5, 1918, d May 19, 1993

*Solkar, E. D. (Bombay & Sussex) b March 18, 1948

*Solomon, J. S. (BG) b Aug. 26, 1930

*Solomon, W. R. (Tvl & E. Prov.) b April 23, 1872, d July 12, 1964

*Sood, M. M. (Delhi) b July 6, 1939

Southern, J. W. (Hants) b Sept. 2, 1952

*Southerton, James (Surrey, Hants & Sussex) b Nov. 16, 1827, d June 16, 1880

Southerton, S. J. (Editor of *Wisden* 1934-35) b July 7, 1874, d March 12, 1935

*Sparling, J. T. (Auck.) b July 24, 1938

*Spearman, C. M. (Auck. & C. Dist.) b July 4, 1972

Spencer, C. T. (Leics) b Aug. 18, 1931

Spencer, J. (CU & Sussex) b Oct. 6, 1949

Spencer, T. W. OBE (Kent; Test umpire) b March 22, 1914

Sperry, J. (Leics) b March 19, 1910, d April 21, 1997

*Spofforth, F. R. (NSW & Vic.) b Sept. 9, 1853, d June 4, 1926

*Spooner, R. H. (Lancs; *CY 1905*) b Oct. 21, 1880, d Oct. 2, 1961

*Spooner, R. T. (Warwicks) b Dec. 30, 1919, d Dec. 20, 1997

Springall, J. D. (Notts) b Sept. 19, 1932

Sprot, E. M. (Hants) b Feb. 4, 1872, d Oct. 8, 1945

Squires, H. S. (Surrey) b Feb. 22, 1909, d Jan. 24, 1950

*Srikkanth, K. (TN) b Dec. 21, 1959

*Srinath, J. (Karn. & Glos) b Aug. 31, 1969

*Srinivasan, T. E. (TN) b Oct. 26, 1950

*Stackpole, K. R. MBE (Vic.; *CY 1973*) b July 10, 1940

Standen, J. A. (Worcs) b May 30, 1935

*Stanyforth, Lt-Col. R. T. (Yorks) b May 30, 1892, d Feb. 20, 1964

Staples, A. (Notts) b Feb. 4, 1899, d Sept. 9, 1965

*Staples, S. J. (Notts; *CY 1929*) b Sept. 18, 1892, d June 4, 1950

*Statham, J. B. CBE (Lancs; *CY 1955*) b June 17, 1930

*Stayers, S. C. (†Guyana & Bombay) b June 9, 1937

Stead, B. (Yorks, Essex, Notts & N. Tvl) b June 21, 1939, d April 15, 1980

*Steel, A. G. (CU & Lancs; Pres. MCC 1902) b Sept. 24, 1858, d June 15, 1914

*Steele, D. S. OBE (Northants & Derbys; *CY 1976*) b Sept. 29, 1941

Steele, J. F. (Leics, Natal & Glam) b July 23, 1946

Stephens, E. J. (Glos) b March 23, 1909, d April 3, 1983

Stephenson, F. D. (B'dos, Glos, Tas., Notts, Sussex & †FS; *CY 1989*) b April 8, 1959

Stephenson, G. R. (Derbys & Hants) b Nov. 19, 1942

Stephenson, H. H. (Surrey & All-England) b May 3, 1832, d Dec. 17, 1896

Stephenson, H. W. (Som) b July 18, 1920

*Stephenson, J. P. (Essex, Boland & Hants) b March 14, 1965

Stephenson, Lt-Col. J. R. CBE (Sec. MCC 1987-93) b Feb. 25, 1931

Stephenson, Lt-Col. J. W. A. (Essex, Worcs, Army, Europeans & Victory Tests) b Aug. 1, 1907, d May 20, 1982

Stevens, Edward ("Lumpy") (Hants) b *circa* 1735, d Sept. 7, 1819

*Stevens, G. B. (S. Aust.) b Feb. 29, 1932

*Stevens, G. T. S. (UCS, OU & Middx; *CY 1918*) b Jan. 7, 1901, d Sept. 19, 1970

*Stevenson, G. B. (Yorks & Northants) b Dec. 16, 1955

Stevenson, K. (Derbys & Hants) b Oct. 6, 1950

*Stewart, A. J. (Surrey; *CY 1993*) b April 8, 1963

*Stewart, M. J. OBE (Surrey; *CY 1958*) b Sept. 16, 1932

*Stewart, R. B. (SA) b Sept. 3, 1856, d Sept. 12, 1913

Stewart, W. J. (Warwicks & Northants) b Oct. 31, 1934

*Steyn, P. J. R. (Griq. W., OFS & Natal) b June 30, 1967

*Stirling, D. A. (C. Dist.) b Oct. 5, 1961

Stocks, F. W. (Notts) b Nov. 6, 1918, d Feb. 23, 1996

*Stoddart, A. E. (Middx; *CY 1893*) b March 11, 1863, d April 3, 1915

*Stollmeyer, J. B. (T/T) b April 11, 1921, d Sept. 10, 1989

*Stollmeyer, V. H. (T/T) b Jan. 24, 1916

Stone, J. (Hants & Glam) b Nov. 29, 1876, d Nov. 15, 1942

Storer, H. jun. (Derbys) b Feb. 2, 1898, d Sept. 1, 1967

*Storer, W. (Derbys; *CY 1899*) b Jan. 25, 1867, d Feb. 28, 1912

Storey, S. J. (Surrey & Sussex) b Jan. 6, 1941

Stott, L. W. (Auck.) b Dec. 8, 1946

Stott, W. B. (Yorks) b July 18, 1934

Stovold, A. W. (Glos & OFS) b March 19, 1953

*Strang, B. C. (Mash.) b June 9, 1972

*Strang, P. A. (Mash. & Kent) b July 28, 1970

*Streak, H. H. (Mat. & Hants) b March 16, 1974

*Street, G. B. (Sussex) b Dec. 6, 1889, d April 24, 1924

*Stricker, L. A. (Tvl) b May 26, 1884, d Feb. 5, 1960

*Strudwick, H. (Surrey; *CY 1912*) b Jan. 28, 1880, d Feb. 14, 1970

*Studd, C. T. (CU & Middx) b Dec. 2, 1860, d July 16, 1931

*Studd, G. B. (CU & Middx) b Oct. 20, 1859, d Feb. 13, 1945

Studd, Sir J. E. Kynaston (Middx & CU; Pres. MCC 1930) b July 26, 1858, d Jan. 14, 1944

*Su'a, M. L. (N. Dist. & Auck.) b Nov. 7, 1966

*Subba Row, R. CBE (CU, Surrey & Northants; *CY 1961*) b Jan. 29, 1932

*Subramanya, V. (Mysore) b July 16, 1936

*Such, P. M. (Notts, Leics & Essex) b June 12, 1964

Sudhakar Rao, R. (Karn.) b Aug. 8, 1952

Sueter, T. (Hants & Surrey) b *circa* 1749, d Feb. 17, 1827

*Sugg, F. H. (Yorks, Derbys & Lancs; *CY 1890*) b Jan. 11, 1862, d May 29, 1933

Sullivan, J. (Lancs) b Feb. 5, 1945

Sully, H. (Som & Northants) b Nov. 1, 1939

*Sunderram, G. (Bombay & Raja.) b March 29, 1930

*Surendranath, R. (Ind. Serv.) b Jan. 4, 1937

Surridge, W. S. (Surrey; *CY 1953*) b Sept. 3, 1917, d April 13, 1992

*Surti, R. F. (Guj., Raja., & Qld) b May 25, 1936

*Susskind, M. J. (CU, Middx & Tvl) b June 8, 1891, d July 9, 1957

*Sutcliffe, B. MBE (Auck., Otago & N. Dist.; *CY 1950*) b Nov. 17, 1923

*Sutcliffe, H. (Yorks; *CY 1920*) b Nov. 24, 1894, d Jan. 22, 1978

Sutcliffe, W. H. H. (Yorks) b Oct. 10, 1926

Suttle, K. G. (Sussex) b Aug. 25, 1928

*Swamy, V. N. (Ind. Serv.) b May 23, 1924, d May 1, 1983

Swanton, E. W. CBE (Middx; writer & broadcaster) b Feb. 11, 1907

Swarbrook, F. W. (Derbys, Griq. W. & OFS) b Dec. 17, 1950

Swart, P. D. (Rhod., W. Prov., Glam & Boland) b April 27, 1946

*Swetman, R. (Surrey, Notts & Glos) b Oct. 25, 1933

Sydenham, D. A. D. (Surrey) b April 6, 1934

*Symcox, P. L. (Griq. W., Natal & N. Tvl) b April 14, 1960

*Taber, H. B. (NSW) b April 29, 1940

*Taberer, H. M. (OU & Natal) b Oct. 7, 1870, d June 5, 1932

*Tahir Naqqash (Servis Ind., MCB, Punjab & Lahore) b July 6, 1959

*Talat Ali (Lahore, PIA & UBL) b May 29, 1950

*Tallon, D. (Qld; *CY 1949*) b Feb. 17, 1916, d Sept. 7, 1984

*Tamhane, N. S. (Bombay) b Aug. 4, 1931

*Tancred, A. B. (Kimberley, Griq. W. & Tvl) b Aug. 20, 1865, d Nov. 23, 1911

*Tancred, L. J. (Tvl) b Oct. 7, 1876, d July 28, 1934

*Tancred, V. M. (Tvl) b July 7, 1875, d June 3, 1904

Tanvir Mehdi (Lahore & UBL) b Nov. 7, 1972

*Tapscott, G. L. (Griq. W.) b Nov. 7, 1889, d Dec. 13, 1940

*Tapscott, L. E. (Griq. W.) b March 18, 1894, d July 7, 1934

*Tarapore, K. K. (Bombay) b Dec. 17, 1910, d June 15, 1986

Tarbox, C. V. (Worcs) b July 2, 1891, d June 15, 1978

Tarrant, F. A. (Vic., Middx & Patiala; *CY 1908*) b Dec. 11, 1880, d Jan. 29, 1951

Tarrant, G. F. (Cambs. & All-England) b Dec. 7, 1838, d July 2, 1870

*Taslim Arif (Kar., Sind & NBP) b May 1, 1954

*Tate, F. W. (Sussex) b July 24, 1867, d Feb. 24, 1943

*Tate, M. W. (Sussex; *CY 1924*) b May 30, 1895, d May 18, 1956

*Tattersall, R. (Lancs) b Aug. 17, 1922

*Tauseef Ahmed (PWD, UBL & Kar.) b May 10, 1958

*Tavaré, C. J. (OU, Kent & Som) b Oct. 27, 1954

*Tayfield, H. J. (Natal, Rhod. & Tvl; *CY 1956*) b Jan. 30, 1929, d Feb. 25, 1994

Taylor, A. I. (Tvl) b July 25, 1925

Taylor, B. (Essex; *CY 1972*) b June 19, 1932

*Taylor, B. R. (Cant. & Wgtn) b July 12, 1943

Taylor, C. G. (CU & Sussex) b Nov. 21, 1816, d Sept. 10, 1869

*Taylor, Daniel (Natal) b Jan. 9, 1887, d Jan. 24, 1957

*Taylor, D. D. (Auck. & Warwicks) b March 2, 1923, d Dec. 5, 1980

Taylor, D. J. S. (Surrey, Som & Griq. W.) b Nov. 12, 1942

*Taylor, H. W. (Natal, Tvl & W. Prov.; *CY 1925*) b May 5, 1889, d Feb. 8, 1973

*Taylor, J. (T/T) b Jan. 3, 1932

*Taylor, J. M. (NSW) b Oct. 10, 1895, d May 12, 1971

*Taylor, J. P. (Derbys & Northants) b Aug. 8, 1964

*Taylor, K. (Yorks & Auck.) b Aug. 21, 1935

*Taylor, L. B. (Leics & Natal) b Oct. 25, 1953

*Taylor, M. A. (NSW; *CY 1990*) b Oct. 27, 1964

Taylor, M. N. S. (Notts & Hants) b Nov. 12, 1942

*Taylor, P. L. (NSW & Qld) b Aug. 22, 1956

Taylor, R. M. (Essex) b Nov. 30, 1909, d Jan. 7, 1984

*Taylor, R. W. MBE (Derbys; *CY 1977*) b July 17, 1941

Taylor, T. L. (CU & Yorks; *CY 1901*) b May 25, 1878, d March 16, 1960

*Tendulkar, S. R. (†Mumbai & Yorks; *CY 1997*) b April 24, 1973

Tennekoon, A. P. B. (SL) b Oct. 29, 1946

*Tennyson, 3rd Lord (Hon. L. H.) (Hants; *CY 1914*) b Nov. 7, 1889, d June 6, 1951

*Terry, V. P. (Hants) b Jan. 14, 1959

*Theunissen, N. H. (W. Prov.) b May 4, 1867, d Nov. 9, 1929

Thomas, A. E. (Northants) b June 7, 1893, d March 21, 1965

Thomas, D. J. (Surrey, N. Tvl, Natal & Glos) b June 30, 1959

*Thomas, G. (NSW) b March 21, 1938

*Thomas, J. G. (Glam, Border, E. Prov. & Northants) b Aug. 12, 1960

Thompson, A. (Middx) b April 17, 1916

*Thompson, G. J. (Northants; Test umpire; *CY 1906*) b Oct. 27, 1877, d March 3, 1943

Thompson, R. G. (Warwicks) b Sept. 26, 1932

*Thoms, G. R. (Vic.) b March 22, 1927

*Thomson, A. L. (Vic.) b Dec. 2, 1945

*Thomson, J. R. (NSW, Qld & Middx) b Aug. 16, 1950

*Thomson, K. (Cant.) b Feb. 26, 1941

*Thomson, N. F. D. (NSW) b May 29, 1839, d Sept. 2, 1896

*Thomson, N. I. (Sussex) b Jan. 23, 1929

*Thomson, P. I. C. (B'dos) b Sept. 26, 1971

*Thomson, S. A. (N. Dist.) b Jan. 27, 1969

Thornton, C. I. (CU, Kent & Middx) b March 20, 1850, d Dec. 10, 1929

*Thornton, Dr P. G. (Yorks, Middx & SA) b Dec. 24, 1867, d Jan. 31, 1939

*Thorpe, G. P. (Surrey; *CY 1998*) b Aug. 1, 1969

*Thurlow, H. M. (Qld) b Jan. 10, 1903, d Dec. 3, 1975

*Tillekeratne, H. P. (NCC) b July 14, 1967

Timms, B. S. V. (Hants & Warwicks) b Dec. 17, 1940

Timms, J. E. (Northants) b Nov. 3, 1906, d May 18, 1980

Tindall, R. A. E. (Surrey) b Sept. 23, 1935

*Tindill, E. W. T. (Wgtn) b Dec. 18, 1910

Tissera, M. H. (SL) b March 23, 1939

*Titmus, F. J. MBE (Middx, Surrey & OFS; *CY 1963*) b Nov. 24, 1932

Todd, L. J. (Kent) b June 19, 1907, d Aug. 20, 1967

Todd, P. A. (Notts & Glam) b March 12, 1953

*Tolchard, R. W. (Leics) b June 15, 1946

Tomlins, K. P. (Middx & Glos) b Oct. 23, 1957

*Tomlinson, D. S. (Rhod. & Border) b Sept. 4, 1910, d July 11, 1993

Tompkin, M. (Leics) b Feb. 17, 1919, d Sept. 27, 1956

*Toohey, P. M. (NSW) b April 20, 1954

Topley, T. D. (Surrey, Essex & Griq. W.) b Feb. 25, 1964

*Toshack, E. R. H. (NSW) b Dec. 15, 1914

Townsend, A. (Warwicks) b Aug. 26, 1921

Townsend, A. F. (Derbys) b March 29, 1912, d Feb. 26, 1994

*Townsend, C. L. (Glos; *CY 1899*) b Nov. 7, 1876, d Oct. 17, 1958

*Townsend, D. C. H. (OU) b April 20, 1912, d Jan. 27, 1997

*Townsend, L. F. (Derbys & Auck.; *CY 1934*) b June 8, 1903, d Feb. 17, 1993

**Traicos, A. J. (Rhod. & Mash.) b May 17, 1947

*Travers, J. P. F. (S. Aust.) b Jan. 10, 1871, d Sept. 15, 1942

*Tremlett, M. F. (Som & C. Dist.) b July 5, 1923, d July 30, 1984

Tremlett, T. M. (Hants) b July 26, 1956

*Tribe, G. E. (Vic. & Northants; *CY 1955*) b Oct. 4, 1920

*Trim, J. (BG) b Jan. 25, 1915, d Nov. 12, 1960

Trimble, G. S. (Qld) b Jan. 1, 1963

*Trimborn, P. H. J. (Natal) b May 18, 1940

**Trott, A. E. (Vic., Middx & Hawkes Bay; *CY 1899*) b Feb. 6, 1873, d July 30, 1914

*Trott, G. H. S. (Vic.; *CY 1894*) b Aug. 5, 1866, d Nov. 10, 1917

Troughton, L. H. W. (Kent) b May 17, 1879, d Aug. 31, 1933

*Troup, G. B. (Auck.) b Oct. 3, 1952

*Trueman, F. S. OBE (Yorks; *CY 1953*) b Feb. 6, 1931

*Trumble, H. (Vic.; *CY 1897*) b May 12, 1867, d Aug. 14, 1938

*Trumble, J. W. (Vic.) b Sept. 16, 1863, d Aug. 17, 1944

*Trumper, V. T. (NSW; *CY 1903*) b Nov. 2, 1877, d June 28, 1915

*Truscott, P. B. (Wgtn) b Aug. 14, 1941

*Tuckett, L. (OFS) b Feb. 6, 1919

*Tuckett, L. R. (Natal & OFS) b April 19, 1885, d April 8, 1963

*Tufnell, N. C. (CU & Surrey) b June 13, 1887, d Aug. 3, 1951

*Tufnell, P. C. R. (Middx) b April 29, 1966

Tuke, Sir Anthony (Pres. MCC 1982-83) b Aug. 22, 1920

Tunnicliffe, C. J. (Derbys) b Aug. 11, 1951

*Tunnicliffe, J. (Yorks; *CY 1901*) b Aug. 26, 1866, d July 11, 1948

*Turnbull, M. J. (CU & Glam; *CY 1931*) b March 16, 1906, d Aug. 5, 1944

*Turner, A. (NSW) b July 23, 1950

Turner, C. (Yorks) b Jan. 11, 1902, d Nov. 19, 1968

*Turner, C. T. B. (NSW; *CY 1889*) b Nov. 16, 1862, d Jan. 1, 1944

Turner, D. R. (Hants & W. Prov.) b Feb. 5, 1949

Turner, F. M. MBE (Leics) b Aug. 8, 1934

*Turner, G. M. (Otago, N. Dist. & Worcs; *CY 1971*) b May 26, 1947

Turner, S. (Essex & Natal) b July 18, 1943

*Twentyman-Jones, P. S. (W. Prov.) b Sept. 13, 1876, d March 8, 1954

Twining, R. H. (OU & Middx; Pres. MCC 1964-65) b Nov. 3, 1889, d Jan. 3, 1979

*Twose, R. G. (Warwicks, N. Dist., C. Dist. & Wgtn) b April 17, 1968

*Tyldesley, E. (Lancs; *CY 1920*) b Feb. 5, 1889, d May 5, 1962

*Tyldesley, J. T. (Lancs; *CY 1902*) b Nov. 22, 1873, d Nov. 27, 1930

*Tyldesley, R. K. (Lancs; *CY 1925*) b March 11, 1897, d Sept. 17, 1943

*Tylecote, E. F. S. (OU & Kent) b June 23, 1849, d March 15, 1938

*Tyler, E. J. (Som) b Oct. 13, 1864, d Jan. 25, 1917

*Tyson, F. H. (Northants; *CY 1956*) b June 6, 1930

Ufton, D. G. (Kent) b May 31, 1928

*Ulyett, G. (Yorks) b Oct. 21, 1851, d June 18, 1898

*Umrigar, P. R. (Bombay & Guj.) b March 28, 1926

*Underwood, D. L. MBE (Kent; *CY 1969*) b June 8, 1945

*Vaas, W. P. U. J. C. (Colts) b Jan. 27, 1975

Vaidya, P. S. (Bengal) b Sept. 23, 1967

*Valentine, A. L. (Jam.; *CY 1951*) b April 29, 1930

*Valentine, B. H. (CU & Kent) b Jan. 17, 1908, d Feb. 2, 1983

*Valentine, V. A. (Jam.) b April 4, 1908, d July 6, 1972

*Vance, R. H. (Wgtn) b March 31, 1955

*van der Bijl, P. G. (W. Prov. & OU) b Oct. 21, 1907, d Feb. 16, 1973

van der Bijl, V. A. P. (Natal, Middx & Tvl; *CY 1981*) b March 19, 1948

*Van der Merwe, E. A. (Tvl) b Nov. 9, 1904, d Feb. 26, 1971

*Van der Merwe, P. L. (W. Prov. & E. Prov.) b March 14, 1937

van Geloven, J. (Yorks & Leics) b Jan. 4, 1934

*Van Ryneveld, C. B. (W. Prov. & OU) b March 19, 1928

van Zyl, C. J. P. G. (OFS & Glam) b Oct. 1, 1961

*Varnals, G. D. (E. Prov., Tvl & Natal) b July 24, 1935

*Vaughan, J. T. C. (Auck.) b Aug. 30, 1967

*Veivers, T. R. (Qld) b April 6, 1937

*Veletta, M. R. J. (W. Aust.) b Oct. 30, 1963

*Vengsarkar, D. B. (Bombay; *CY 1987*) b April 6, 1956

*Venkataraghavan, S. (†TN & Derbys; Test umpire) b April 21, 1946

*Venkataramana, M. (TN) b April 24, 1966

*Verity, H. (Yorks; *CY 1932*) b May 18, 1905, d July 31, 1943

*Vernon, G. F. (Middx) b June 20, 1856, d Aug. 10, 1902

*Vettori, D. L. (N. Dist.) b Jan. 27, 1979

Vials, G. A. T. (Northants) b March 18, 1887, d April 26, 1974

Vigar, F. H. (Essex) b July 7, 1917

*Viljoen, K. G. (Griq. W., OFS & Tvl) b May 14, 1910, d Jan. 21, 1974

*Vincent, C. L. (Tvl) b Feb. 16, 1902, d Aug. 24, 1968

*Vine, J. (Sussex; *CY 1906*) b May 15, 1875, d April 25, 1946

*Vintcent, C. H. (Tvl & Griq. W.) b Sept. 2, 1866, d Sept. 28, 1943

Virgin, R. T. (Som, Northants & W. Prov.; *CY 1971*) b Aug. 26, 1939

*Viswanath, G. R. (†Karn.) b Feb. 12, 1949

*Viswanath, S. (Karn.) b Nov. 29, 1962

*Vivian, G. E. (Auck.) b Feb. 28, 1946

*Vivian, H. G. (Auck.) b Nov. 4, 1912, d Aug. 12, 1983

*Vizianagram, Maharaj Kumar of, Sir Vijay A., (U. Prov.) b Dec. 28, 1905, d Dec. 2, 1965

*Voce, W. (Notts; *CY 1933*) b Aug. 8, 1909, d June 6, 1984

*Vogler, A. E. E. (Middx, Natal, Tvl & E. Prov.; *CY 1908*) b Nov. 28, 1876, d Aug. 9, 1946

Vonhagt, D. M. (Moors) b March 31, 1965

*Waddington, A. (Yorks) b Feb. 4, 1893, d Oct. 28, 1959

*Wade, H. F. (Natal) b Sept. 14, 1905, d Nov. 23, 1980

Wade, T. H. (Essex) b Nov. 24, 1910, d July 25, 1987

*Wade, W. W. (Natal) b June 18, 1914

*Wadekar, A. L. (Bombay) b April 1, 1941

*Wadsworth, K. J. (C. Dist. & Cant.) b Nov. 30, 1946, d Aug. 19, 1976

*Wainwright, E. (Yorks; *CY 1894*) b April 8, 1865, d Oct. 28, 1919

*Waite, J. H. B. (E. Prov. & Tvl) b Jan. 19, 1930

*Waite, M. G. (S. Aust.) b Jan. 7, 1911, d Dec. 16, 1985

*Walcott, Sir Clyde L. (B'dos & BG; *CY 1958*) b Jan. 17, 1926

*Walcott, L. A. (B'dos) b Jan. 18, 1894, d Feb. 27, 1984

Walden, F. (Northants; Test umpire) b March 1, 1888, d May 3, 1949

*Walker, C. (Yorks & Hants) b June 27, 1919, d Dec. 3, 1992

Walker, I. D. (Middx) b Jan. 8, 1844, d July 6, 1898

*Walker, M. H. N. (Vic.) b Sept. 12, 1948

*Walker, P. M. (Glam, Tvl & W. Prov.) b Feb. 17, 1936

Walker, V. E. (Middx) b April 20, 1837, d Jan. 3, 1906

Walker, W. (Notts) b Nov. 24, 1892, d Dec. 3, 1991

*Wall, T. W. (S. Aust.) b May 13, 1904, d March 25, 1981

Wallace, P. A. (B'dos) b Aug. 2, 1970

*Wallace, W. M. (Auck.) b Dec. 19, 1916

*Waller, A. C. (Mash.) b Sept. 25, 1959

Waller, C. E. (Surrey & Sussex) b Oct. 3, 1948

*Walmsley, K. P. (Auck.) b Aug. 23, 1973

*Walsh, C. A. (Jam. & Glos; *CY 1987*) b Oct. 30, 1962

Walsh, J. E. (NSW & Leics) b Dec. 4, 1912, d May 20, 1980

*Walter, K. A. (Tvl) b Nov. 5, 1939

*Walters, C. F. (Glam & Worcs; *CY 1934*) b Aug. 28, 1905, d Dec. 23, 1992

*Walters, F. H. (Vic. & NSW) b Feb. 9, 1860, d June 1, 1922

*Walters, K. D. MBE (NSW) b Dec. 21, 1945

*Waqar Hassan (Pak. Us, Punjab, Pak. Serv. & Kar.) b Sept. 12, 1932

*Waqar Younis (Multan, UBL, Surrey & Glam; *CY 1992*) b Nov. 16, 1971

*Ward, Alan (Derbys, Leics & Border) b Aug. 10, 1947

*Ward, Albert (Yorks & Lancs; *CY 1890*) b Nov. 21, 1865, d Jan. 6, 1939

Ward, B. (Essex) b Feb. 28, 1944

Ward, D. (Glam) b Aug. 30, 1934

Ward, D. M. (Surrey) b Feb. 10, 1961

*Ward, F. A. (S. Aust.) b Feb. 23, 1906, d March 25, 1974

*Ward, J. T. (Cant.) b March 11, 1937

*Ward, T. A. (Tvl) b Aug. 2, 1887, d Feb. 16, 1936

Ward, William (MCC & Hants) b July 24, 1787, d June 30, 1849

*Wardle, J. H. (Yorks; *CY 1954*) b Jan. 8, 1923, d July 23, 1985

*Warnapura, B. (SL) b March 1, 1953

*Warnaweera, K. P. J. (Galle & Singha) b Nov. 23, 1960

*Warne, S. K. (Vic.; *CY 1994*) b Sept. 13, 1969

Warner, A. E. (Worcs & Derbys) b May 12, 1959

*Warner, Sir Pelham F. (OU & Middx; *CY 1904, special portrait 1921*; Pres. MCC 1950-51) b Oct. 2, 1873, d Jan. 30, 1963

*Warr, J. J. (CU & Middx; Pres. MCC 1987-88) b July 16, 1927

*Warren, A. R. (Derbys) b April 2, 1875, d Sept. 3, 1951

*Washbrook, C. CBE (Lancs; *CY 1947*) b Dec. 6, 1914

*Wasim Akram (Lahore, PACO, PNSC, PIA & Lancs; *CY 1993*) b June 3, 1966

*Wasim Bari (Kar., PIA & Sind) b March 23, 1948

*Wasim Raja (Lahore, Sargodha, Pak. Us, PIA, Punjab & NBP) b July 3, 1952

Wass, T. G. (Notts; *CY 1908*) b Dec. 26, 1873, d Oct. 27, 1953

*Wassan, A. S. (Delhi) b March 23, 1968

Wassell, A. (Hants) b April 15, 1940

*Watkin, S. L. (Glam; *CY 1994*) b Sept. 15, 1964

*Watkins, A. J. (Glam) b April 21, 1922

*Watkins, J. C. (Natal) b April 10, 1923

*Watkins, J. R. (NSW) b April 16, 1943

*Watkinson, M. (Lancs) b Aug. 1, 1961

Watson, A. (Lancs) b Nov. 4, 1844, d Oct. 26, 1920

*Watson, C. (Jam. & Delhi) b July 1, 1938

Watson, F. (Lancs) b Sept. 17, 1898, d Feb. 1, 1976

*Watson, G. D. (Vic., W. Aust. & NSW) b March 8, 1945

Watson, G. S. (Kent & Leics) b April 10, 1907, d April 1, 1974

*Watson, W. (Yorks & Leics; *CY 1954*) b March 7, 1920

*Watson, W. (Auck.) b Aug. 31, 1965

*Watson, W. J. (NSW) b Jan. 31, 1931

Watt, A. E. (Kent) b June 19, 1907, d Feb. 3, 1974

*Watt, L. (Otago) b Sept. 17, 1924, d Nov. 15, 1996

Watts, E. A. (Surrey) b Aug. 1, 1911, d May 2, 1982

Watts, P. D. (Northants & Notts) b March 31, 1938

Watts, P. J. (Northants) b June 16, 1940

*Waugh, M. E. (NSW & Essex; *CY 1991*) b June 2, 1965

*Waugh, S. R. (NSW & Som; *CY 1989*) b June 2, 1965

*Wazir, Ali, S. (C. Ind., S. Punjab & Patiala) b Sept. 15, 1903, d June 17, 1950

*Wazir Mohammad (B'pur & Kar.) b Dec. 22, 1929

*Webb, M. G. (Otago & Cant.) b June 22, 1947

*Webb, P. N. (Auck.) b July 14, 1957

Webb, R. J. (Otago) b Sept. 15, 1952

Webb, R. T. (Sussex) b July 11, 1922

*Webbe, A. J. (OU & Middx) b Jan. 16, 1855, d Feb. 19, 1941

Webster, W. H. (CU & Middx; Pres. MCC 1976-77) b Feb. 22, 1910, d June 19, 1986

*Weekes, Sir Everton D. (B'dos; *CY 1951*) b Feb. 26, 1925

*Weekes, K. H. (Jam.) b Jan. 24, 1912

Weeks, R. T. (Warwicks) b April 30, 1930

Weerakkody, A. P. (NCC) b Oct. 1, 1970

*Weerasinghe, C. D. U. S. (TU & NCC) b March 1, 1968

Weigall, G. J. V. (CU & Kent) b Oct. 19, 1870, d May 17, 1944

*Weir, G. L. (Auck.) b June 2, 1908

*Wellard, A. W. (Som; *CY 1936*) b April 8, 1902, d Dec. 31, 1980

*Wellham, D. M. (NSW, Tas. & Qld) b March 13, 1959

*Wells, A. P. (Sussex, Kent & Border) b Oct. 2, 1961

Wells, B. D. (Glos & Notts) b July 27, 1930

Wells, C. M. (Sussex, Border, W. Prov. & Derbys) b March 3, 1960

Wells, W. (Northants) b March 14, 1881, d March 18, 1939

Wenman, E. G. (Kent & England) b Aug. 18, 1803, d Dec. 31, 1879

Wensley, A. F. (Sussex, Auck., Naw. & Eur.) b May 23, 1898, d June 17, 1970

*Wesley, C. (Natal) b Sept. 5, 1937

**Wessels, K. C. (OFS, W. Prov., N. Tvl, Sussex, Qld & E. Prov.; *CY 1995*) b Sept. 14, 1957

West, G. H. (Editor of *Wisden* 1880-86) b 1851, d Oct. 6, 1896

*Westcott, R. J. (W. Prov.) b Sept. 19, 1927

Weston, M. J. (Worcs) b April 8, 1959

*Wettimuny, M. D. (SL) b June 11, 1951

*Wettimuny, S. (SL; *CY 1985*) b Aug. 12, 1956

Wettimuny, S. R. de S. (SL) b Feb. 7, 1949

*Wharton, A. (Lancs & Leics) b April 30, 1923, d Aug. 26, 1993

*Whatmore, D. F. (Vic.) b March 16, 1954

Wheatley, O. S. CBE (CU, Warwicks & Glam; *CY 1969*) b May 28, 1935

Whitaker, Haddon OBE (Editor of *Wisden* 1940-43) b Aug. 30, 1908, d Jan. 5, 1982

*Whitaker, J. J. (Leics; *CY 1987*) b May 5, 1962

White, A. F. T. (CU, Warwicks & Worcs) b Sept. 5, 1915, d March 16, 1993

White, Sir Archibald W. 4th Bt (Yorks) b Oct. 14, 1877, d Dec. 16, 1945

*White, C. (Vic. & Yorks) b Dec. 16, 1969

*White, D. J. (N. Dist.) b June 26, 1961

*White, D. W. (Hants & Glam) b Dec. 14, 1935

*White, G. C. (Tvl) b Feb. 5, 1882, d Oct. 17, 1918

*White, J. C. (Som; *CY 1929*) b Feb. 19, 1891, d May 2, 1961

White, Hon. L. R. (5th Lord Annaly) (Middx & Victory Test) b March 15, 1927, d Sept. 30, 1990

White, R. A. (Middx & Notts) b Oct. 6, 1936

White, R. C. (CU, Glos & Tvl) b Jan. 29, 1941

*White, W. A. (B'dos) b Nov. 20, 1938

Whitehead, A. G. T. (Som; Test umpire) b Oct. 28, 1940

Whitehead, H. (Leics) b Sept. 19, 1874, d Sept. 14, 1944

Whitehouse, J. (Warwicks) b April 8, 1949

*Whitelaw, P. E. (Auck.) b Feb. 10, 1910, d Aug. 28, 1988

Whiteside, J. P. (Lancs & Leics) b June 11, 1861, d March 8, 1946

Whitfield, E. W. (Surrey & Northants) b May 31, 1911, d Aug. 10, 1996

Whitington, R. S. (S. Aust. & Victory Tests; writer) b June 30, 1912, d March 13, 1984

*Whitney, M. R. (NSW & Glos) b Feb. 24, 1959

Whittaker, G. J. (Surrey) b May 29, 1916, d April 20, 1997

*Whittall, A. R. (CU & Mat.) b March 28, 1973

*Whittall, G. J. (Mat.) b Sept. 5, 1972

Whitticase, P. (Leics) b March 15, 1965

Whittingham, N. B. (Notts) b Oct. 22, 1940

*Whitty, W. J. (S. Aust.) b Aug. 15, 1886, d Jan. 30, 1974

*Whysall, W. W. (Notts; *CY 1925*) b Oct. 31, 1887, d Nov. 11, 1930

Wickremaratne, R. P. A. H. (SSC) b Feb. 21, 1971

*Wickremasinghe, A. G. D. (NCC) b Dec. 27, 1965

*Wickremasinghe, G. P. (BRC & SSC) b Aug. 14, 1971

*Wiener, J. M. (Vic.) b May 1, 1955

*Wight, C. V. (BG) b July 28, 1902, d Oct. 4, 1969

*Wight, G. L. (BG) b May 28, 1929

Wight, P. B. (BG, Som & Cant.) b June 25, 1930

*Wijegunawardene, K. I. W. (CCC) b Nov. 23, 1964

*Wijesuriya, R. G. C. E. (Mor. & Colts) b Feb. 18, 1960

*Wijetunge, P. K. (SSC) b Aug. 6, 1971

Wilcox, D. R. (Essex & CU) b June 4, 1910, d Feb. 6, 1953

Wild, D. J. (Northants) b Nov. 28, 1962

*Wiles, C. A. (B'dos & T/T) b Aug. 11, 1892, d Nov. 4, 1957

Wilkins, C. P. (Derbys, Border, E. Prov. & Natal) b July 31, 1944

Wilkinson, C. T. A. (Surrey) b Oct. 4, 1884, d Dec. 16, 1970

*Wilkinson, L. L. (Lancs) b Nov. 5, 1916

Willatt, G. L. (CU, Notts & Derbys) b May 7, 1918

*Willett, E. T. (Comb. Is. & Leewards) b May 1, 1953

Willett, M. D. (Surrey) b April 21, 1933

*Willey, P. (Northants, E. Prov. & Leics; Test umpire) b Dec. 6, 1949

*Williams, A. B. (Jam.) b Nov. 21, 1949

*Williams, D. (T/T) b Nov. 4, 1963

Williams, D. L. (Glam) b Nov. 20, 1946

*Williams, E. A. V. (B'dos) b April 10, 1914, d April 13, 1997

*Williams, N. F. (Middx, Windwards, Tas. & Essex) b July 2, 1962

Williams, R. G. (Northants) b Aug. 10, 1957

*Williams, S. C. (Leewards) b Aug. 12, 1969

*Willis, R. G. D. MBE (Surrey, Warwicks & N. Tvl; *CY 1978*) b May 30, 1949

*Willoughby, J. T. (SA) b Nov. 7, 1874, d March 11, 1952

Willsher, E. (Kent & All-England) b Nov. 22, 1828, d Oct. 7, 1885

Wilson, A. (Lancs) b April 24, 1921

Wilson, A. E. (Middx & Glos) b May 18, 1910

*Wilson, Rev. C. E. M. (CU & Yorks) b May 15, 1875, d Feb. 8, 1944
*Wilson, D. (Yorks) b Aug. 7, 1937
*Wilson, E. R. (CU & Yorks) b March 25, 1879, d July 21, 1957
Wilson, G. (CU & Yorks) b Aug. 21, 1895, d Nov. 29, 1960
Wilson, H. L. (Sussex) b June 27, 1881, d March 15, 1937
Wilson, J. V. (Yorks; *CY 1961*) b Jan. 17, 1921
*Wilson, J. W. (Vic. & S. Aust.) b Aug. 20, 1921, d Oct. 13, 1985
Wilson, R. C. (Kent) b Feb. 18, 1928
*Wimble, C. S. (Tvl) b April 22, 1861, d Jan. 28, 1930
Windows, A. R. (Glos & CU) b Sept. 25, 1942
Winfield, H. M. (Notts) b June 13, 1933
Winrow, H. F. (Notts) b Jan. 17, 1916, d Aug. 19, 1973
*Winslow, P. L. (Sussex, Tvl & Rhod.) b May 21, 1929
Wisden, John (Sussex; founder John Wisden & Co and *Wisden's Cricketers' Almanack*) b Sept. 5, 1826, d April 5, 1884
*Wishart, C. B. (Mash.) b Jan. 9, 1974
*Wishart, K. L. (BG) b Nov. 28, 1908, d Oct. 18, 1972
Wolton, A. V. (Warwicks) b June 12, 1919, d Sept. 9, 1990
*Wood, A. (Yorks; *CY 1939*) b Aug. 25, 1898, d April 1, 1973
*Wood, B. (Yorks, Lancs, Derbys & E. Prov.) b Dec. 26, 1942
Wood, C. J. B. (Leics) b Nov. 21, 1875, d June 5, 1960
Wood, D. J. (Sussex) b May 19, 1914, d March 12, 1989
*Wood, G. E. C. (CU & Kent) b Aug. 22, 1893, d March 18, 1971
*Wood, G. M. (W. Aust.) b Nov. 6, 1956
*Wood, H. (Kent & Surrey; *CY 1891*) b Dec. 14, 1854, d April 30, 1919
*Wood, R. (Lancs & Vic.) b March 7, 1860, d Jan. 6, 1915
*Woodcock, A. J. (S. Aust.) b Feb. 27, 1948
Woodcock, John C. OBE (Writer; Editor of *Wisden* 1981-86) b Aug. 7, 1926
*Woodfull, W. M. OBE (Vic.; *CY 1927*) b Aug. 22, 1897, d Aug. 11, 1965
Woodhead, F. G. (Notts) b Oct. 30, 1912, d May 24, 1991
**Woods, S. M. J. (CU & Som; *CY 1889*) b April 13, 1867, d April 30, 1931
Wooller, W. (CU & Glam) b Nov. 20, 1912, d March 10, 1997
Woolley, C. N. (Glos & Northants) b May 5, 1886, d Nov. 3, 1962
*Woolley, F. E. (Kent; *CY 1911*) b May 27, 1887, d Oct. 18, 1978

*Woolley, R. D. (Tas.) b Sept. 16, 1954
*Woolmer, R. A. (Kent, Natal & W. Prov.; *CY 1976*) b May 14, 1948
*Worrall, J. (Vic.) b June 21, 1861, d Nov. 17, 1937
*Worrell, Sir Frank M. M. (B'dos & Jam.; *CY 1951*) b Aug. 1, 1924, d March 13, 1967
Worsley, D. R. (OU & Lancs) b July 18, 1941
Worsley, Sir W. A. 4th Bt (Yorks; Pres. MCC 1961-62) b April 5, 1890, d Dec. 4, 1973
*Worthington, T. S. (Derbys; *CY 1937*) b Aug. 21, 1905, d Aug. 31, 1973
Wrathall, H. (Glos) b Feb. 1, 1869, d June 1, 1944
Wright, A. C. (Kent) b April 4, 1895, d May 26, 1959
*Wright, C. W. (CU & Notts) b May 27, 1863, d Jan. 10, 1936
*Wright, D. V. P. (Kent; *CY 1940*) b Aug. 21, 1914
Wright, Graeme A. (Editor of *Wisden* 1987-92) b April 23, 1943
*Wright, J. G. MBE (N. Dist., Derbys, Cant. & Auck.) b July 5, 1954
*Wright, K. J. (W. Aust. & S. Aust.) b Dec. 27, 1953
Wright, L. G. (Derbys; *CY 1906*) b June 15, 1862, d Jan. 11, 1953
Wright, W. (Notts & Kent) b Feb. 29, 1856, d March 22, 1940
*Wyatt, R. E. S. (Warwicks & Worcs; *CY 1930*) b May 2, 1901, d April 20, 1995
*Wynne, O. E. (Tvl & W. Prov.) b June 1, 1919, d July 13, 1975
*Wynyard, E. G. (Hants) b April 1, 1861, d Oct. 30, 1936

Yachad, M. (Tvl) b Nov. 17, 1960
*Yadav, N. S. (H'bad) b Jan. 26, 1957
*Yadav, V. S. (Haryana) b March 14, 1967
*Yajurvindra Singh (M'tra & S'tra) b Aug. 1, 1952
*Yallop, G. N. (Vic.) b Oct. 7, 1952
*Yardley, B. (W. Aust.) b Sept. 5, 1947
*Yardley, N. W. D. (CU & Yorks; *CY 1948*) b March 19, 1915, d Oct. 4, 1989
Yardley, T. J. (Worcs & Northants) b Oct. 27, 1946
Yarnold, H. (Worcs) b July 6, 1917, d Aug. 13, 1974
*Yashpal Sharma (Punjab) b Aug. 11, 1954
Yawar Saeed (Som & Punjab) b Jan. 22, 1935
*Yograj Singh (Haryana & Punjab) b March 25, 1958
Young, A. (Som) b Nov. 6, 1890, d April 2, 1936
*Young, B. A. (N. Dist.) b Nov. 3, 1964
Young, D. M. (Worcs & Glos) b April 15, 1924, d June 18, 1993

*Young, H. I. (Essex) b Feb. 5, 1876, d Dec. 12, 1964

*Young, J. A. (Middx) b Oct. 14, 1912, d Feb. 5, 1993

*Young, R. A. (CU & Sussex) b Sept. 16, 1885, d July 1, 1968

*Young, S. (Tas. & Glos) b June 13, 1970

*Younis Ahmed (Lahore, Kar., Surrey, PIA, S. Aust., Worcs & Glam) b Oct. 20, 1947

*Yuile, B. W. (C. Dist.) b Oct. 29, 1941

*Zaheer Abbas (Kar., Glos, PWD, Dawood Ind., Sind & PIA; *CY 1972*) b July 24, 1947

*Zahid Fazal (PACO, PIA & Lahore) b Nov. 10, 1973

*Zahoor Elahi (ADBP, Multan, R'pindi & Lahore) b March 1, 1971

*Zakir Khan (Sind, Peshawar & ADBP) b April 3, 1963

Zesers, A. K. (S. Aust.) b March 11, 1967

*Zoehrer, T. J. (W. Aust.) b Sept. 25, 1961

*Zoysa, D. N. T. (SSC) b May 13, 1978

*Zulch, J. W. (Tvl) b Jan. 2, 1886, d May 19, 1924

*Zulfiqar Ahmed (B'pur & PIA) b Nov. 22, 1926

*Zulqarnain (Pak. Rlwys, Lahore, HBFC & PACO) b May 25, 1962

PRESIDENTS OF MCC SINCE 1946

1946	General Sir Ronald Adam, Bart
1947	Captain Lord Cornwallis
1948	Brig.-Gen. The Earl of Gowrie
1949	HRH The Duke of Edinburgh
1950	Sir Pelham Warner
1951-52	W. Findlay
1952-53	The Duke of Beaufort
1953-54	The Earl of Rosebery
1954-55	Viscount Cobham
1955-56	Field Marshal Earl Alexander of Tunis
1956-57	Viscount Monckton of Brenchley
1957-58	The Duke of Norfolk
1958-59	Marshal of the RAF Viscount Portal of Hungerford
1959-60	H. S. Altham
1960-61	Sir Hubert Ashton
1961-62	Col. Sir William Worsley, Bart
1962-63	Lt-Col. Lord Nugent
1963-64	G. O. B. Allen
1964-65	R. H. Twining
1965-66	Lt-Gen. Sir Oliver Leese, Bart
1966-67	Sir Alec Douglas-Home
1967-68	A. E. R. Gilligan
1968-69	R. Aird
1969-70	M. J. C. Allom
1970-71	Sir Cyril Hawker
1971-72	F. R. Brown
1972-73	A. M. Crawley
1973-74	Lord Caccia
1974-75	HRH The Duke of Edinburgh
1975-76	C. G. A. Paris
1976-77	W. H. Webster
1977-78	D. G. Clark
1978-79	C. H. Palmer
1979-80	S. C. Griffith
1980-81	P. B. H. May
1981-82	G. H. G. Doggart
1982-83	Sir Anthony Tuke
1983-84	A. H. A. Dibbs
1984-85	F. G. Mann
1985-86	J. G. W. Davies
1986-87	M. C. Cowdrey
1987-88	J. J. Warr
1988-89	Field Marshal The Lord Bramhall
1989-90	The Hon. Sir Denys Roberts
1990-91	The Rt Hon. The Lord Griffiths
1991-92	M. E. L. Melluish
1992-94	D. R. W. Silk
1994-96	The Hon. Sir Oliver Popplewell
1996-	A. C. D. Ingleby-Mackenzie

Since 1951, Presidents of MCC have taken office on October 1. Previously they took office immediately after the annual general meeting at the start of the season. Since 1992, Presidents have been eligible for two consecutive years of office.

REGISTER OF PLAYERS

The qualifications for inclusion are as follows:

1. All players who appeared in Tests or one-day internationals for a Test-playing country in 1996-97 or 1997.

2. All players who appeared in the County Championship in 1997.

3. All players who appeared in the Sheffield Shield, Supersport Series, Red Stripe Cup and Duleep Trophy in 1996-97.

4. All players who appeared in first-class domestic cricket in New Zealand, Pakistan, Sri Lanka and Zimbabwe in 1996-97, who have also played in Tests or one-day international cricket.

Notes: The forename by which the player is known is underlined if it is not his first name.

Teams are those played for in 1996-97 and/or 1997, or the last domestic team for which that player appeared.

Countries are those for which players are qualified.

The country of birth is given if it is not the one for which a player is qualified. It is also given to differentiate between nations in the Leeward and Windward Islands, and where it is essential for clarity.

* *Denotes Test player.*

	Team	Country	Born	Birthplace
Aamer Hanif	Karachi/Allied Bank	P	4.10.71	*Karachi*
***Aamir Nazir**	Lahore/Allied Bank	P	2.1.71	*Lahore*
***Aamir Sohail**	Allied Bank	P	14.9.66	*Lahore*
Abdur Razzaq	Lahore	P	2.12.79	*Lahore*
Ackerman Hylton Deon	Western Province	SA	14.2.73	*Cape Town*
Ackerman Sean	Boland	SA	6.6.77	*Cape Town*
Adams Christopher John	Derbyshire	E	6.5.70	*Whitwell*
Adams Fabian Alex	Leeward Islands	WI	7.1.75	*The Valley, Anguilla*
***Adams** James Clive	Jamaica	WI	9.1.68	*Port Maria*
***Adams** Paul Regan	Western Province	SA	20.1.77	*Cape Town*
Afzaal Usman	Nottinghamshire	E	9.6.77	*Rawalpindi, Pakistan*
***Akram Raza**	Faisalabad/Habib Bank	P	22.11.64	*Lahore*
Albanie James Daniel	Boland	SA	1.5.68	*Touwsrivier*
Aldred Paul	Derbyshire	E	4.2.69	*Chellaston*
Allen Jeremy Michael	Western Australia	A	11.6.71	*Subiaco*
Alley Phillip John Sydney	New South Wales	A	26.7.70	*Orange*
Alleyne Mark Wayne	Gloucestershire	E	23.5.68	*Tottenham*
***Allott** Geoffrey Ian	Canterbury	NZ	24.12.71	*Christchurch*
Altree Darren Anthony	Warwickshire	E	30.9.74	*Rugby*
***Ambrose** Curtly Elconn Lynwall	Leeward Islands	WI	21.9.63	*Swetes Village, Antigua*
Amin Rupesh Mahesh	Surrey	E	20.8.77	*London*
Amm Philip Geoffrey	Eastern Province	SA	2.4.64	*Grahamstown*
***Amre** Pravin Kalyan	Bengal	I	14.8.68	*Bombay*
Andrew Stephen Jon Walter	Essex	E	27.1.66	*London*
***Angel** Jo	Western Australia	A	22.4.68	*Mount Lawley*
***Ankola** Salil Ashok	Mumbai	I	1.3.68	*Sholapur*
Anthony Hamish Arbeb Gervais	Leeward Islands	WI	16.1.71	*Urlings Village, Antigua*
Antoine Eugene Clifford	Trinidad & Tobago	WI	8.4.67	*Trinidad*
***Anurasiri** Sangarange Don	Panadura	SL	25.2.66	*Panadura*
***Aqib Javed**	Islamabad/Allied Bank	P	5.8.72	*Sheikhupura*
Archer Graeme Francis	Nottinghamshire	E	26.9.70	*Carlisle*
Armstrong Sean Hussain	Barbados	WI	11.5.73	*Barbados*
Arnberger Jason Lee	New South Wales	A	18.11.72	*Penrith*
***Arnold** Russel Premakumaran	Nondescripts	SL	25.10.73	*Colombo*
Arshad Khan	Peshawar/Allied Bank	P	22.3.71	*Peshawar*
Arthur John Michael	Griqualand West	SA	17.5.68	*Johannesburg*
***Arthurton** Keith Lloyd Thomas	Leeward Islands	WI	21.2.65	*Charlestown, Nevis*
***Asif Mujtaba**	Karachi/PIA	P	4.11.67	*Karachi*

	Team	Country	Born	Birthplace
*Astle Nathan John	Canterbury/Notts	NZ	15.9.71	Christchurch
*Atapattu Marvan Samson	Sinhalese	SL	22.11.70	Kalutara
*Ata-ur-Rehman	Lahore/Allied Bank	P	28.3.75	Lahore
*Atherton Michael Andrew	Lancashire	E	23.3.68	Manchester
*Athey Charles William Jeffrey	Sussex	E	27.9.57	Middlesbrough
*Atif Rauf	ADBP	P	3.3.64	Lahore
Atkinson Mark Neville	Tasmania	A	11.2.69	Sydney
Atkinson Mark Peter	Western Australia	A	27.11.70	Bentley
Austin Ian David	Lancashire	E	30.5.66	Haslingden
Averis James Maxwell Michael	Glos/Oxford U.	E	28.5.74	Bristol
Aymes Adrian Nigel	Hampshire	E	4.6.64	Southampton
Ayres Warren Geoffrey	Victoria	A	25.10.65	Moorabbin
*Azam Khan	Karachi/Customs	P	1.3.69	Karachi
*Azeem Hafeez	PIA	P	29.7.63	Jhelum
Azhar Mahmood	Islamabad/United Bank	P	28.2.75	Rawalpindi
*Azharuddin Mohammad	Hyderabad	I	8.2.63	Hyderabad
*Bacher Adam Marc	Transvaal	SA	29.10.73	Johannesburg
Badenhorst Alan	Eastern Province	SA	10.7.70	Cape Town
Baguley Bryan Charles	Boland	SA	25.3.71	Cape Town
Bahutule Sairaj Vasant	Mumbai	I	6.1.73	Bombay
*Bailey Robert John	Northamptonshire	E	28.10.63	Biddulph
Baker Robert Michael	Western Australia	A	24.7.75	Osborne Park
Bakker Jason Richard	Victoria	A	12.11.67	Geelong
Bakkes Herman Charles	Free State	SA	24.12.69	Port Elizabeth
Ball Martyn Charles John	Gloucestershire	E	26.4.70	Bristol
Balliram Anil	Trinidad & Tobago	WI	27.2.74	Trinidad
*Banerjee Subroto Tara	Bengal	I	13.2.69	Patna
Bangar Sanjay Bapusaheb	Railways	I	11.10.72	Beed
*Baptiste Eldine Ashworth Elderfield	Eastern Province	WI	12.3.60	Liberta, Antigua
Barnard Pieter Hendrik	Griqualand West	SA	8.5.70	Nelspruit
*Barnett Kim John	Derbyshire	E	17.7.60	Stoke-on-Trent
Barsby Trevor John	Queensland	A	16.1.64	Herston
Basdeo Amarnath	Trinidad & Tobago	WI	13.4.77	Trinidad
*Basit Ali	Karachi/United Bank	P	13.12.70	Karachi
Bates Justin Jonathan	Sussex	E	9.4.76	Farnborough, Hants
Bates Richard Terry	Nottinghamshire	E	17.6.72	Stamford
Batty Jonathan Neil	Surrey	E	18.4.74	Chesterfield
Beamish Michael Gwynne	Eastern Province	SA	30.7.69	King William's Town
Bedade Atul Chandrakant	Baroda	I	24.9.66	Bombay
Bell Michael Anthony Vincent	Warwickshire	E	19.12.66	Birmingham
Benfield Mark Rowland	Transvaal	SA	3.12.76	Potgietersrus
*Benjamin Joseph Emmanuel	Surrey	E	2.2.61	Christ Church, St Kitts
*Benjamin Kenneth Charlie Griffith	Leeward Islands	WI	8.4.67	St John's, Antigua
Benkenstein Brett Norman	Griqualand West	SA	14.4.71	Salisbury, Rhodesia
Benkenstein Dale Martin	Natal	SA	9.6.74	Salisbury, Rhodesia
Berry Darren Shane	Victoria	A	10.12.69	Melbourne
Betts Melvyn Morris	Durham	E	26.3.75	Sacriston
*Bevan Michael Gwyl	New South Wales	A	8.5.70	Belconnen
Bhave Surendra Shriram	Maharashtra	I	30.3.66	Poona
*Bichel Andrew John	Queensland	A	27.8.70	Laidley
Bicknell Darren John	Surrey	E	24.6.67	Guildford
*Bicknell Martin Paul	Surrey	E	14.1.69	Guildford
Birrell Adrian Victor	Eastern Province	SA	8.12.60	Grahamstown
*Bishop Ian Raphael	Trinidad & Tobago	WI	24.10.67	Port-of-Spain
Black Marlon Ian	Trinidad & Tobago	WI	7.6.75	Trinidad
Blackwell Ian David	Derbyshire	E	10.6.78	Chesterfield

	Team	Country	Born	Birthplace
Blain John Angus Rae	Northamptonshire	E	4.1.79	Edinburgh, Scotland
*****Blakey** Richard John	Yorkshire	E	15.1.67	Huddersfield
*****Blewett** Gregory Scott	South Australia	A	29.10.71	Adelaide
Bloomfield Timothy Francis	Middlesex	E	31.5.73	Ashford, Middlesex
Bodoe Mahadeo	Trinidad & Tobago	WI	3.12.66	Chaguanas
Boiling James	Durham	E	8.4.68	New Delhi, India
Boje Nico	Free State	SA	20.3.73	Bloemfontein
*****Boon** David Clarence	Tasmania/Durham	A	29.12.60	Launceston
*****Bosch** Tertius	Natal	SA	14.3.66	Vereeniging
Bossenger Wendell	Griqualand West	SA	23.10.76	Cape Town
Boswell Scott Antony John	Northamptonshire	E	11.9.74	Fulford
Botha Anthony Greyvensteyn	Natal	SA	17.11.76	Pretoria
Botha Henk	Free State	SA	16.1.76	Bloemfontein
Botha Lodewikus Daniel	Eastern Province	SA	11.4.68	Elsburg
Botha Peterus Johannes	Border	SA	28.9.66	Vereeniging
Boucher Mark Verdon	Border	SA	3.12.76	East London
Bovill James Noel Bruce	Hampshire	E	2.6.71	High Wycombe
Bowen Mark Nicholas	Nottinghamshire	E	6.12.67	Redcar
Bowler Peter Duncan	Somerset	E	30.7.63	Plymouth
*****Bradburn** Grant Eric	Northern Districts	NZ	26.5.66	Hamilton
Bradfield Carl Crispin	Eastern Province	SA	18.1.75	Grahamstown
*****Brandes** Eddo Andre	Mashonaland	Z	5.3.63	Port Shepstone, SA
Brayshaw James Antony	South Australia	A	11.5.67	Subiaco
Breese Gareth Rohan	Jamaica	WI	9.1.76	Montego Bay
Brent Gary Bazil	Mashonaland	Z	13.1.76	Sinoia
Brimson Matthew Thomas	Leicestershire	E	1.12.70	Plumstead
Brink Mechiel Matthys	Boland	SA	10.6.75	Baberton
Brooker Finley Clint	Griqualand West	SA	26.12.72	Kimberley
Brown Alistair Duncan	Surrey	E	11.2.70	Beckenham
Brown Douglas Robert	Warwickshire	E	29.10.69	Stirling, Scotland
Brown Jason Fred	Northamptonshire	E	10.10.74	Newcastle-under-Lyme
Brown Keith Robert	Middlesex	E	18.3.63	Edmonton
*****Brown** Simon John Emmerson	Durham	E	29.6.69	Cleadon
Browne Barrington St Aubyn	Guyana	WI	16.9.67	Georgetown
*****Browne** Courtney Oswald	Barbados	WI	7.12.70	London, England
Bruyns Mark Lloyd	Natal	SA	8.11.73	Pietermaritzburg
Bryan Henderson Ricardo	Barbados	WI	21.3.70	Barbados
Bryson Rudi Edwin	Northern Transvaal	SA	25.7.68	Springs
Buch Valmik Nalinkant	Baroda	I	29.8.75	Rajkot
Burns Michael	Somerset	E	2.6.69	Barrow-in-Furness
Butcher Gary Paul	Glamorgan	E	11.3.75	Clapham
*****Butcher** Mark Alan	Surrey	E	23.8.72	Croydon
Byam Denis F. A.	Windward Islands	WI		St Vincent
Byas David	Yorkshire	E	26.8.63	Kilham
*****Caddick** Andrew Richard	Somerset	E	21.11.68	Christchurch, NZ
*****Cairns** Christopher Lance	Canterbury	NZ	13.6.70	Picton
Callaghan David John	Eastern Province	SA	1.2.65	Queenstown
*****Campbell** Alistair Douglas Ross	Mashonaland	Z	23.9.72	Salisbury
Campbell Colin Lockley	Durham	E	11.8.77	Newcastle-upon-Tyne
Campbell Ryan John	Western Australia	A	7.2.72	Osborne Park
*****Campbell** Sherwin Legay	Barbados	WI	1.11.70	Bridgetown
*****Capel** David John	Northamptonshire	E	6.2.63	Northampton
*****Carlisle** Stuart Vance	Mashonaland	Z	10.5.72	Salisbury
Carpenter James Robert	Sussex	E	20.10.75	Birkenhead
Cary Sean Ross	Western Australia	A	10.3.71	Subiaco
Cassar Matthew Edward	Derbyshire	E	16.10.72	Sydney, Australia

	Team	Country	Born	Birthplace
Chandana Umagiliya Durage Upul	Tamil Union	SL	7.5.72	*Galle*
*****Chanderpaul** Shivnarine	Guyana	WI	18.8.74	*Unity Village*
Chandrasekhar Vakkadai Biksheswaran	Goa	I	21.8.61	*Madras*
Chapple Glen	Lancashire	E	23.1.74	*Skipton*
Chatterjee Utpal	Bengal	I	13.7.64	*Calcutta*
*****Chauhan** Rajesh Kumar	Madhya Pradesh	I	19.12.66	*Ranchi*
Chilton Mark James	Lancashire	E	2.10.76	*Sheffield*
Chinsammy Michael Nathaniel	Guyana	WI	25.9.74	*Guyana*
Church Matthew John	Gloucestershire	E	26.7.72	*Guildford*
Cilliers Sarel Arnold	Free State	SA	6.6.71	*Klerksdorp*
Clarke Vincent Paul	Derbyshire	E	11.11.71	*Liverpool*
Collingwood Paul David	Durham	E	26.5.76	*Shotley Bridge*
Collins Pedro Tyrone	Barbados	WI	12.8.76	*Boscobelle*
*****Commins** John Brian	Western Province	SA	19.2.65	*East London*
Connor Cardigan Adolphus	Hampshire	E	24.3.61	*The Valley, Anguilla*
Corbett Troy Frederick	Victoria	A	11.10.72	*Ouyen*
*****Cork** Dominic Gerald	Derbyshire	E	7.8.71	*Newcastle-under-Lyme*
Cosker Dean Andrew	Glamorgan	E	7.1.78	*Weymouth*
Cottey Phillip *Anthony*	Glamorgan	E	2.6.66	*Swansea*
Cowan Ashley Preston	Essex	E	7.5.75	*Hitchin*
Cowdrey Graham Robert	Kent	E	27.6.64	*Farnborough, Kent*
Cox David Mathew	Durham	E	2.3.72	*Southall*
Cox Jamie	Tasmania	A	15.10.69	*Burnie*
Craig Shawn Andrew Jacob	Victoria	A	23.6.73	*Carlton*
Craven Christiaan Frans	Free State	SA	6.12.70	*Dundee*
*****Crawley** John Paul	Lancashire	E	21.9.71	*Maldon*
Creevey Brendan Neville	Queensland	A	18.2.70	*Charleville*
*****Croft** Robert Damien Bale	Glamorgan	E	25.5.70	*Morriston*
Cronje Frans *Johannes* Cornelius	Border	SA	15.5.67	*Bloemfontein*
*****Cronje** Wessel *Johannes* (Hansie)	Free State	SA	25.9.69	*Bloemfontein*
Crookes Derek Norman	Natal	SA	5.3.69	*Mariannhill*
Cuff Wayne Everton	Jamaica	WI	26.12.71	*Kingston*
*****Cuffy** Cameron Eustace	Windward Islands	WI	8.2.70	*South Rivers, St Vincent*
*****Cullinan** Daryll John	Transvaal	SA	4.3.67	*Kimberley*
Cunliffe Robert John	Gloucestershire	E	8.11.73	*Oxford*
Curran Kevin Malcolm	Northamptonshire	E	7.9.59	*Rusape, Rhodesia*
*****Curtis** Timothy Stephen	Worcestershire	E	15.1.60	*Chislehurst*
Dahiya Vijay	Delhi	I	10.5.73	*Delhi*
Dakin Jonathan Michael	Leicestershire	E	28.2.73	*Hitchin*
Dale Adam Craig	Queensland	A	30.12.68	*Ivanhoe*
Dale Adrian	Glamorgan	E	24.10.68	*Germiston, South Africa*
Daley James Arthur	Durham	E	24.9.73	*Sunderland*
Daly Anthony John	Tasmania	A	25.7.69	*Newcastle*
Darlington Kevin Godfrey	Guyana	WI	26.4.72	*Guyana*
Das Shiv Sunder	Orissa	I	5.11.77	*Bhubaneshwar*
*****Dassanayake** Pubudu Bathiya	Bloomfield	SL	11.7.70	*Kandy*
David Noel	Hyderabad	I	26.2.71	*Hyderabad*
Davids Faiek	Western Province	SA	1.9.64	*Cape Town*
Davies Michael Kenton	Northamptonshire	E	17.7.76	*Ashby-de-la-Zouch*
Davis Casper Andre	Windward Islands	WI	14.3.66	*St Vincent*
*****Davis** Heath Te-Ihi-O-Te-Rangi	Wellington	NZ	30.11.71	*Lower Hutt*
Davis Mark Jeffrey Gronow	Northern Transvaal	SA	10.10.71	*Port Elizabeth*
Davis Richard Peter	Gloucestershire	E	18.3.66	*Margate*
Davison Rodney John	New South Wales	A	26.6.69	*Kogarah*
Dawson Alan Charles	Western Province	SA	27.11.69	*Cape Town*

	Team	Country	Born	Birthplace
Dawson Robert Ian	Gloucestershire	E	29.3.70	*Exmouth*
Dean Kevin James	Derbyshire	E	16.10.75	*Derby*
de Bruyn Zander	Transvaal	SA	5.7.75	*Johannesburg*
*****DeFreitas** Phillip Anthony Jason	Derbyshire	E	18.2.66	*Scotts Head, Dominica*
De Groot Nicholas Alexander	Guyana	WI	22.10.75	*Guyana*
*****Dekker** Mark Hamilton	Matabeleland	Z	5.12.69	*Gatooma*
*****de Silva** Ashley Matthew	Colombo	SL	3.12.63	*Colombo*
*****de Silva** Ellawalakankanamge Asoka Ranjit	Nondescripts	SL	28.3.56	*Kalutara*
*****de Silva** Karunakalage Sajeewa Chanaka	Nondescripts	SL	11.1.71	*Kalutara*
*****de Silva** Pinnaduwage Aravinda	Nondescripts	SL	17.10.65	*Colombo*
de Silva Sanjeewa Kumara Lanka	Kurunegala Youth	SL	29.7.75	*Kurunegala*
*****de Villiers** Petrus Stephanus	Northern Transvaal	SA	13.10.64	*Vereeniging*
de Vos Dirk Johannes Jacobus	Northern Transvaal	SA	15.6.75	*Pretoria*
*****Dhanraj** Rajindra	Trinidad & Tobago	WI	6.2.69	*Barrackpore*
Dharmani Pankaj	Punjab	I	27.9.74	*Delhi*
*****Dharmasena** Handunnettige Deepthi Priyantha Kumara	Bloomfield	SL	24.4.71	*Colombo*
Dighe Samir Sudhakar	Mumbai	I	8.10.68	*Bombay*
*****Dillon** Mervyn	Trinidad & Tobago	WI	5.6.74	*Toco*
Dimond Matthew	Somerset	E	24.9.75	*Taunton*
Dippenaar Hendrik Human	Free State	SA	14.6.77	*Kimberley*
Di Venuto Michael James	Tasmania	A	12.12.73	*Hobart*
Dixon Troy James	Queensland	A	22.12.69	*Geelong*
*****Dodemaide** Anthony Ian Christopher	Victoria	A	5.10.63	*Williamstown*
*****Donald** Allan Anthony	Free State/Warwicks	SA	20.10.66	*Bloemfontein*
*****Doull** Simon Blair	Northern Districts	NZ	6.8.69	*Pukekohe*
Dowlin Travis Montague	Guyana	WI	24.2.77	*Georgetown*
Dowman Mathew Peter	Nottinghamshire	E	10.5.74	*Grantham*
Drakes Vasbert Conniel	Barbados/Sussex/Border	WI	5.8.69	*St James*
*****Dravid** Rahul	Karnataka	I	11.1.73	*Indore*
Dros Gerald	Northern Transvaal	SA	2.4.73	*Pretoria*
Dry Willem Moolman	Griqualand West	SA	9.1.71	*Vryburg*
*****Dunusinghe** Chamara Iroshan	Nondescripts	SL	19.10.70	*Colombo*
du Plessis Petrus Bouwer	Border	SA	13.10.69	*Somerset East*
Dutch Keith Philip	Middlesex	E	21.3.73	*Harrow*
*****Ealham** Mark Alan	Kent	E	27.8.69	*Willesborough*
Ecclestone Simon Charles	Somerset	E	16.7.71	*Great Dunmow*
Edmond Michael Denis	Warwickshire	E	30.7.69	*Barrow-in-Furness*
Edwards Alexander David	Sussex	E	2.8.75	*Cuckfield*
Eime Andrew Barry	South Australia	A	3.7.71	*North Adelaide*
*****Eksteen** Clive Edward	Transvaal	SA	2.12.66	*Johannesburg*
*****Elliott** Matthew Thomas Gray	Victoria	A	28.9.71	*Chelsea*
Elworthy Steven	Northern Transvaal	SA	23.2.65	*Bulawayo, Rhodesia*
*****Emburey** John Ernest	Northamptonshire	E	20.8.52	*Peckham*
*****Emery** Philip Allen	New South Wales	A	25.6.64	*St Ives*
Emslie Peter Arthur Norman	Border	SA	21.10.68	*Grahamstown*
English Cedric Vaughan	Griqualand West	SA	13.9.73	*Kimberley*
Erasmus Marais	Boland	SA	27.2.64	*George*
Evans Alun Wyn	Glamorgan	E	20.8.75	*Glanamman*
*****Evans** Craig Neil	Mashonaland	Z	29.11.69	*Salisbury*
Evans Kevin Paul	Nottinghamshire	E	10.9.63	*Calverton*
*****Fairbrother** Neil Harvey	Lancashire	E	9.9.63	*Warrington*
Faull Martin Peter	South Australia	A	10.5.68	*Darwin*

	Team	Country	Born	Birthplace
Felix Brian	Windward Islands	WI		*Dominica*
Fernando Ungamandalige Nisal Kumudusiri	Sinhalese	SL	10.3.70	*Colombo*
Ferreira Lloyd Douglas	Boland	SA	6.5.74	*Johannesburg*
Ferreira Quentin	Eastern Province	SA	28.12.72	*East London*
Fisher Ian Douglas	Yorkshire	E	31.5.76	*Bradford*
Fitzgerald David Andrew	South Australia	A	30.11.72	*Osborne Park*
Flanagan Ian Nicholas	Essex	E	5.6.80	*Colchester*
*****Fleming** Damien William	Victoria	A	24.4.70	*Bentley*
Fleming Matthew Valentine	Kent	E	12.12.64	*Macclesfield*
*****Fleming** Stephen Paul	Canterbury	NZ	1.4.73	*Christchurch*
Flintoff Andrew	Lancashire	E	6.12.77	*Preston*
*****Flower** Andrew	Mashonaland	Z	28.4.68	*Cape Town, SA*
*****Flower** Grant William	Mashonaland	Z	20.12.70	*Salisbury*
Foley Geoffrey Ian	Queensland	A	11.10.67	*Jandowae*
Follett David	Northamptonshire	E	14.10.68	*Newcastle-under-Lyme*
Ford Shane George Bancroft	Jamaica	WI	8.9.69	*Kingston*
Forde Keith Adrian	Natal	SA	12.7.69	*Pietermaritzburg*
Fordham Alan	Northamptonshire	E	9.11.64	*Bedford*
Foster Michael James	Durham	E	17.9.72	*Leeds*
Foster Michael Robert	Victoria	A	5.3.73	*East Melbourne*
Fourie Brenden Craig	Border	SA	13.4.70	*East London*
Fourie Shaun Eddie	Border	SA	28.8.73	*East London*
Francis Nigel Bernard	Trinidad & Tobago	WI	6.9.71	*Trinidad*
Francis Simon Richard George	Hampshire	E	15.8.78	*Bromley*
*****Fraser** Angus Robert Charles	Middlesex	E	8.8.65	*Billinge*
Freedman David Andrew	New South Wales	A	19.6.64	*Sydney*
Frost Tony	Warwickshire	E	17.11.75	*Stoke-on-Trent*
Fulton David Paul	Kent	E	15.11.71	*Lewisham*
Gain Douglas Robert	Transvaal	SA	29.12.76	*Johannesburg*
*****Gallian** Jason Edward Riche	Lancashire	E	25.6.71	*Sydney, Australia*
Gamage Janak Champika	Galle	SL	17.4.64	*Matara*
Gandhe Ulhas Vithal	Vidarbha	I	5.10.74	*Nagpur*
Gandhi Devang	Bengal	I	6.9.71	*Bhavnagar*
*****Ganesh** Doddanarasiah	Karnataka	I	30.6.73	*Bangalore*
Ganga Darren	Trinidad & Tobago	WI	14.1.79	*Trinidad*
*****Ganguly** Sourav Chandidas	Bengal	I	8.7.72	*Calcutta*
Garnaut Matthew Stuart	Western Australia	A	7.11.73	*Subiaco*
Garrick Leon Vivian	Jamaica	WI	11.11.76	*St Ann*
*****Gatting** Michael William	Middlesex	E	6.6.57	*Kingsbury*
Gavaskar Rohan Sunil	Bengal	I	20.2.76	*Kanpur*
George Shane Peter	South Australia	A	20.10.70	*Adelaide*
*****Germon** Lee Kenneth	Canterbury	NZ	4.11.68	*Christchurch*
Ghayas Feroze	Delhi	I	3.5.73	*Delhi*
Ghulam Ali	Karachi/PIA	P	8.9.66	*Karachi*
*****Gibbs** Herschelle Herman	Western Province	SA	23.2.74	*Cape Town*
*****Gibson** Ottis Delroy	Barbados	WI	16.3.69	*Sion Hill*
Gidley Martyn Ian	Griqualand West	SA	30.9.68	*Leicester, England*
Gie Noel Addison	Nottinghamshire	E	12.4.77	*Pretoria, South Africa*
Gilchrist Adam Craig	Western Australia	A	14.11.71	*Bellingen*
Gilder Gary Michael	Natal	SA	6.7.74	*Salisbury, Rhodesia*
Giles Ashley Fraser	Warwickshire	E	19.3.73	*Chertsey*
*****Gillespie** Jason Neil	South Australia	A	19.4.75	*Darlinghurst*
Gokulkrishnan Jayaraman	Goa	I	4.1.73	*Madras*
*****Gooch** Graham Alan	Essex	E	23.7.53	*Leytonstone*
Goodwin Murray William	Western Australia	Z	11.12.72	*Salisbury, Rhodesia*

	Team	Country	Born	Birthplace
***Gough** Darren	Yorkshire	E	18.9.70	*Barnsley*
Grayson Adrian <u>Paul</u>	Essex	E	31.3.71	*Ripon*
***Greatbatch** Mark John	Central Districts	NZ	11.12.63	*Auckland*
Green Richard James	Lancashire	E	13.3.76	*Warrington*
Greenfield Keith	Sussex	E	6.12.68	*Brighton*
***Griffith** Adrian Frank Gordon	Barbados	WI	19.11.71	*Barbados*
Gunawardene Aruna Alwis Wijesiri	Sinhalese	SL	31.3.69	*Colombo*
Gupta Ashwini	Jammu and Kashmir	I	13.11.67	*Jammu*
***Gurusinha** Asanka Pradeep	Sinhalese	SL	16.9.66	*Colombo*
Habib Aftab	Leicestershire	E	7.2.72	*Reading*
Hall Andrew James	Transvaal	SA	31.7.75	*Johannesburg*
Hamilton Gavin Mark	Yorkshire	E	16.9.74	*Broxburn, Scotland*
Hancock Timothy Harold Coulter	Gloucestershire	E	20.4.72	*Reading*
Haniff Azeemul	Guyana	WI	24.10.77	*Guyana*
Haniff Zaheer Abbass	Guyana	WI	13.4.74	*Guyana*
Hansen Thomas Munkholt	Hampshire	Den	25.3.76	*Glostrup, Denmark*
Harden Richard John	Somerset	E	16.8.65	*Bridgwater*
Harper Laurence Damien	Victoria	A	10.12.70	*Deniliquin*
Harris Andrew James	Derbyshire	E	26.6.73	*Ashton-under-Lyne*
***Harris** Chris Zinzan	Canterbury	NZ	20.11.69	*Christchurch*
Harrity Mark Andrew	South Australia	A	9.3.74	*Semaphore*
***Hart** Matthew Norman	Northern Districts	NZ	16.5.72	*Hamilton*
***Hartland** Blair Robert	Canterbury	NZ	22.10.66	*Christchurch*
Hartley Peter John	Yorkshire	E	18.4.60	*Keighley*
Harvey Ian Joseph	Victoria	A	10.4.72	*Wonthaggi*
Harvey Kade Murray	Western Australia	A	7.10.75	*Subiaco*
Harvey Mark Edward	Lancashire	E	26.6.74	*Burnley*
***Hasan Raza**	Karachi	P	11.3.82	*Karachi*
***Haslam** Mark James	Auckland	NZ	26.9.72	*Bury, England*
***Hathurusinghe** Upul <u>Chandika</u>	Tamil Union	SL	13.9.68	*Colombo*
***Hayden** Matthew Lawrence	Queensland/Hampshire	A	29.10.71	*Kingaroy*
Hayhurst Andrew Neil	Derbyshire	E	23.11.62	*Manchester*
***Haynes** Desmond Leo	Western Province	WI	15.2.56	*Holders Hill, Barbados*
Haynes Gavin Richard	Worcestershire	E	29.9.69	*Stourbridge*
Haynes Jamie Jonathan	Lancashire	E	5.7.74	*Bristol*
Hayward Mornantau	Eastern Province	SA	6.3.77	*Uitenhage*
***Headley** Dean Warren	Kent	E	27.1.70	*Stourbridge*
***Healy** Ian Andrew	Queensland	A	30.4.64	*Spring Hill*
Hegg Warren Kevin	Lancashire	E	23.2.68	*Whitefield*
Hemp David Lloyd	Warwickshire	E	8.11.70	*Hamilton, Bermuda*
Henderson Claude William	Boland	SA	14.6.72	*Worcester*
Herzberg Steven	Somerset	E	25.5.67	*Carshalton*
Hewitt James Peter	Middlesex	E	26.2.76	*Southwark*
Hewson Dominic Robert	Gloucestershire	E	3.10.74	*Cheltenham*
***Hick** Graeme Ashley	Worcestershire	E	23.5.66	*Salisbury, Rhodesia*
Hills Dene Fleetwood	Tasmania	A	27.8.70	*Wynyard*
Hinds Wavell Wayne	Jamaica	WI	7.9.76	*Kingston*
Hindson James Edward	Nottinghamshire	E	13.9.73	*Huddersfield*
***Hirwani** Narendra Deepchand	Bengal	I	18.10.68	*Gorakhpur*
Hodge Bradley John	Victoria	A	29.12.74	*Sandringham*
Hodgson Timothy Philip	Essex	E	27.3.75	*Guildford*
***Hogg** George <u>Bradley</u>	Western Australia	A	6.2.71	*Narrogin*
***Holder** Roland Irwin Christopher	Barbados	WI	22.12.67	*Port-of-Spain, Trinidad*
***Hollioake** Adam John	Surrey	E	5.9.71	*Melbourne, Australia*
***Hollioake** Benjamin Caine	Surrey	E	11.11.77	*Melbourne, Australia*
Holloway Piran Charles Laity	Somerset	E	1.10.70	*Helston*
***Hooper** Carl Llewellyn	Guyana	WI	15.12.66	*Georgetown*

	Team	Country	Born	Birthplace
Horan Brendan Patrick	Border	SA	17.9.74	*Cape Town*
*****Horne** Matthew Jeffery	Otago	NZ	5.2.70	*Takapuna*
*****Houghton** David Laud	Mashonaland	Z	23.6.57	*Bulawayo*
House William John	Kent/Cambridge U.	E	16.3.76	*Sheffield*
Howell Ian Lester	Border	SA	20.5.58	*Port Elizabeth*
Hoyte Ricardo Lawrence	Barbados	WI	15.10.69	*Bridgetown*
*****Hudson** Andrew Charles	Natal	SA	17.3.65	*Eshowe*
Hughes John Gareth	Northamptonshire	E	3.5.71	*Wellingborough*
Hurley Ryan O'Neal	Barbados	WI	13.9.75	*Barbados*
*****Hussain** Nasser	Essex	E	28.3.68	*Madras, India*
Hussey Michael Edward	Western Australia	A	27.5.75	*Morley*
Hutchison Paul James	Tasmania	A	17.2.68	*Glen Innes*
Hutchison Paul Michael	Yorkshire	E	9.6.77	*Leeds*
Hutton Stewart	Durham	E	30.11.69	*Stockton-on-Tees*
Hyam Barry James	Essex	E	9.9.75	*Romford*
*****Igglesden** Alan Paul	Kent	E	8.10.64	*Farnborough, Kent*
*****Ijaz Ahmed**, sen.	Habib Bank	P	20.9.68	*Sialkot*
*****Ijaz Ahmed**, jun.	Faisalabad/Allied Bank	P	2.2.69	*Lyallpur*
*****Illingworth** Richard Keith	Worcestershire	E	23.8.63	*Bradford*
*****Ilott** Mark Christopher	Essex	E	27.8.70	*Watford*
*****Inzamam-ul-Haq**	Faisalabad/United Bank	P	3.3.70	*Multan*
Iqbal Sikandar	Karachi	P	19.12.58	*Karachi*
*****Irani** Ronald Charles	Essex	E	26.10.71	*Leigh*
Irfan Bhatti	Rawalpindi	P	28.9.64	*Peshawar*
Irish Lesroy	Leeward Islands	WI		*Montserrat*
*****Jack** Steven Douglas	Transvaal	SA	4.8.70	*Durban*
Jackson Kenneth Charles	Boland	SA	16.8.64	*Kitwe, Zambia*
Jackson Paul William	Queensland	A	1.11.61	*East Melbourne*
Jacobs Ridley Detamore	Leeward Islands	WI	26.11.67	*Antigua*
Jacobs Stefan	Transvaal	SA	11.3.66	*Virginia*
*****Jadeja** Ajaysinhji	Haryana	I	1.2.71	*Jamnagar*
James Kevan David	Hampshire	E	18.3.61	*Lambeth*
James Stephen Peter	Glamorgan	E	7.9.67	*Lydney*
*****James** Wayne Robert	Matabeleland	Z	27.8.65	*Bulawayo*
*****Jarvis** Paul William	Sussex	E	29.6.65	*Redcar*
Javed Qadir	Karachi/PIA	P	25.8.76	*Karachi*
*****Jayasuriya** Sanath Teran	Bloomfield	SL	30.6.69	*Matara*
*****Jayawardene** Denagamage Proboth Mahela	Sinhalese	SL	27.5.77	*Colombo*
Jitender Singh	Haryana	I	10.1.76	*Rohtak*
Johnson Benjamin Andrew	South Australia	A	1.8.73	*Naracoorte*
*****Johnson** David Jude	Karnataka	I	16.10.71	*Arasikere*
Johnson Neil Clarkson	Natal/Leicestershire	SA	24.1.70	*Salisbury, Rhodesia*
Johnson Paul	Nottinghamshire	E	24.4.65	*Newark*
Johnson Richard Leonard	Middlesex	E	29.12.74	*Chertsey*
*****Jones** Dean Mervyn	Victoria/Derbyshire	A	24.3.61	*Coburg*
Jones Philip Steffan	Somerset/Cambridge U.	E	9.2.74	*Llanelli*
Jordaan Deon	Free State	SA	3.12.70	*Bloemfontein*
Joseph David Rolston Emmanuel	Leeward Islands	WI	15.11.69	*Antigua*
Joseph Dawnley Alister	Windward Islands	WI	20.8.66	*Stubbs, St Vincent*
Joseph Jenson Eugene Simon	Leeward Islands	WI	7.10.66	*Antigua*
Joseph Sylvester Cleofoster	Leeward Islands	WI	5.9.78	*St John's, Antigua*
*****Joshi** Sunil Bandacharya	Karnataka	I	6.6.69	*Gadag*
Joubert Pierre	Northern Transvaal	SA	2.5.78	*Pretoria*
*****Julian** Brendon Paul	Western Australia	A	10.8.70	*Hamilton, New Zealand*

	Team	Country	Born	Birthplace
*Kabir Khan	Peshawar/Habib Bank	P	12.4.74	*Peshawar*
Kale Abhijit Vasant	Maharashtra	I	3.7.73	*Ahmednagar*
*Kallis Jacques Henry	W. Province/Middlesex	SA	16.10.75	*Cape Town*
*Kalpage Ruwan Senani	Bloomfield	SL	19.2.70	*Kandy*
*Kaluwitharana Romesh Shantha	Colts	SL	24.11.69	*Colombo*
*Kambli Vinod Ganpat	Mumbai	I	18.1.72	*Bombay*
Kanitkar Hrishikesh Hemant	Maharashtra	I	14.11.74	*Poona*
*Kapoor Aashish Rakesh	Punjab	I	25.3.71	*Madras*
Karim Syed Saba	Bengal	I	14.11.67	*Patna*
*Kasprowicz Michael Scott	Queensland	A	10.2.72	*South Brisbane*
Katich Simon Mathew	Western Australia	A	21.8.75	*Middle Swan*
Keech Matthew	Hampshire	E	21.10.70	*Hampstead*
Keedy Gary	Lancashire	E	27.11.74	*Wakefield*
Kendall William Salwey	Hampshire	E	18.12.73	*Wimbledon*
*Kennedy Robert John	Otago	NZ	3.6.72	*Dunedin*
Kennis Gregor John	Surrey	E	9.3.74	*Yokohama, Japan*
Kenway Derek Anthony	Hampshire	E	12.6.78	*Fareham*
Kerr Jason Ian Douglas	Somerset	E	7.4.74	*Bolton*
Kettleborough Richard Allan	Yorkshire	E	15.3.73	*Sheffield*
Khan Amer Ali	Sussex	E	5.11.69	*Lahore, Pakistan*
Khan Gul Abbass	Derbyshire	E	31.12.73	*Gujrat, Pakistan*
Khan Wasim Gulzar	Warwickshire	E	26.2.71	*Birmingham*
Khoda Gagan Kishanlal	Rajasthan	I	24.10.74	*Barmer*
Khurasia Amay Ramsevak	Madhya Pradesh	I	18.5.72	*Jabalpur*
Kidwell Errol Wayne	Transvaal	SA	6.6.75	*Vereeniging*
Killeen Neil	Durham	E	17.10.75	*Shotley Bridge*
Kimber Adam Patrick	South Australia	A	30.9.69	*North Adelaide*
King Reon Dane	Guyana	WI	6.10.75	*Guyana*
*Kirsten Gary	Western Province	SA	23.11.67	*Cape Town*
Kirsten Paul	Western Province	SA	30.10.69	*Cape Town*
*Kirsten Peter Noel	Border	SA	14.5.55	*Pietermaritzburg*
Kirtley Robert James	Sussex/Mashonaland	E	10.1.75	*Eastbourne*
*Klusener Lance	Natal	SA	4.9.71	*Durban*
*Knight Nicholas Verity	Warwickshire	E	28.11.69	*Watford*
Knott James Alan	Surrey	E	14.6.75	*Canterbury*
Koen Louis Johannes	Eastern Province	SA	28.3.67	*Paarl*
Koenig Sven Gaetan	Western Province	SA	9.12.73	*Durban*
Koortzen Pieter Petrus Johannes	Griqualand West	SA	24.9.79	*Kimberley*
Koster Ralph Alexander	Griqualand West	SA	21.10.68	*Beaufort West*
Krikken Karl Matthew	Derbyshire	E	9.4.69	*Bolton*
Krishnakumar Pudiyangum	Rajasthan	I	1.1.74	*Palghat*
Kruis Gideon Jacobus	Northern Transvaal	SA	9.5.74	*Pretoria*
*Kuiper Adrian Paul	Boland	SA	24.8.59	*Johannesburg*
*Kulkarni Nilesh Moreshwar	Mumbai	I	3.4.73	*Dombivili*
Kumar Avinash	Bihar	I	14.12.62	*Patna*
*Kumble Anil	Karnataka	I	17.10.70	*Bangalore*
*Kuruvilla Abey	Mumbai	I	8.8.68	*Mannar*
Lacey Simon James	Derbyshire	E	9.3.75	*Nottingham*
Laing Dean Ralph	Transvaal	SA	18.9.70	*Durban*
*Lamba Raman	Delhi	I	2.1.60	*Meerut*
*Lambert Clayton Benjamin	Guyana	WI	10.2.62	*New Amsterdam*
Lampitt Stuart Richard	Worcestershire	E	29.7.66	*Wolverhampton*
Laney Jason Scott	Hampshire	E	27.4.73	*Winchester*
*Langer Justin Lee	Western Australia	A	21.11.70	*Perth*
*Lara Brian Charles	Trinidad & Tobago	WI	2.5.69	*Santa Cruz*
Larkin Rohan Patrick	Victoria	A	19.10.69	*Seymour*
*Larsen Gavin Rolf	Wellington	NZ	27.9.62	*Wellington*
*Lathwell Mark Nicholas	Somerset	E	26.12.71	*Bletchley*
Lavender Mark Philip	Western Australia	A	28.8.67	*Madras, India*

	Team	Country	Born	Birthplace
Law Danny Richard	Essex	E	15.7.75	London
*****Law** Stuart Grant	Queensland/Essex	A	18.10.68	Herston
Lawrence Andre	Trinidad & Tobago	WI	4.5.69	Trinidad
*****Lawrence** Dave Valentine	Gloucestershire	E	28.1.64	Gloucester
*****Laxman** Vangipurappu Venkata Sai	Hyderabad	I	1.11.74	Hyderabad
Leatherdale David Antony	Worcestershire	E	26.11.67	Bradford
Lee Shane	New South Wales	A	8.8.73	Wollongong
Lehmann Darren Scott	South Australia	A	5.2.70	Gawler
Lenham Neil John	Sussex	E	17.12.65	Worthing
*****Lewis** Clairmonte Christopher	Surrey	E	14.2.68	Georgetown, Guyana
Lewis Jonathan	Gloucestershire	E	26.8.75	Aylesbury
Lewis Jonathan James Benjamin	Durham	E	21.5.70	Isleworth
Lewis Rawl Nicholas	Windward Islands	WI	5.9.74	Grenada
Liburd Merlin Dave	Leeward Islands	WI	15.12.69	Nevis
Liebenberg Elmar	Boland	SA	28.3.73	Paarl
Liebenberg Gerhardus Frederick Johannes	Free State	SA	7.4.72	Upington
Light Craig	Griqualand West	SA	23.9.72	Randburg
*****Liyanage** Dulip Kapila	Colts	SL	6.6.72	Kalutara
Llong Nigel James	Kent	E	11.2.69	Ashford, Kent
Lloyd Graham David	Lancashire	E	1.7.69	Accrington
*****Lock** Alan Charles Ingram	Mashonaland	Z	10.9.62	Marondellas
Lodding Brent Andrew	Victoria	A	20.3.73	Upper Ferntree Gully
Love Geoff Terry	Eastern Province	SA	19.9.76	Port Elizabeth
Love Martin Lloyd	Queensland	A	30.3.74	Mundubbera
*****Loveridge** Greg Riaka	Central Districts	NZ	15.1.75	Palmerston North
Loye Malachy Bernard	Northamptonshire	E	27.9.72	Northampton
Lugsden Steven	Durham	E	10.7.76	Gateshead
Lyle Rowan Andrew	Transvaal	SA	1.12.68	Kokstad
Lynch Monte Alan	Gloucestershire	E	21.5.58	Georgetown, Brit. Guiana
*****McCague** Martin John	Kent	E	24.5.69	Larne, Northern Ireland
McGarrell Neil Christopher	Guyana	WI	12.7.72	Guyana
MacGill Stuart Charles Glyndwr	NSW/Somerset	A	25.2.71	Mount Lawley
McGinty Adam David	Victoria	A	24.3.71	Melbourne
McGrath Anthony	Yorkshire	E	6.10.75	Bradford
*****McGrath** Glenn Donald	New South Wales	A	9.2.70	Dubbo
MacHelm Dean Quinton	Western Province	SA	18.4.71	Kuils River
*****McIntyre** Peter Edward	South Australia	A	27.4.66	Gisborne
McKenzie Denville St Delmo	Jamaica	WI	4.12.75	Little London
McKenzie Neil Douglas	Transvaal	SA	24.11.75	Johannesburg
McKeown Patrick Christopher	Lancashire	E	1.6.76	Liverpool
McLean Nixon Alexei McNamara	Windward Islands	WI	28.7.73	St Vincent
*****McMillan** Brian Mervin	Western Province	SA	22.12.63	Welkom
McMillan Craig Douglas	Canterbury	NZ	13.9.76	Christchurch
Macmillan Gregor Innes	Leicestershire	E	7.8.69	Guildford
McNamara Bradley Edward	New South Wales	A	30.12.65	Sydney
Maddy Darren Lee	Leicestershire	E	23.5.74	Leicester
*****Madurasinghe** Arachchige Wijaysiri Raniith	Kurunegala Youth	SL	30.1.61	Kurunegala
*****Mahanama** Roshan Siriwardene	Bloomfield	SL	31.5.66	Colombo
Maher James Patrick	Queensland	A	27.2.74	Innistail
Mahmood Hamid	Karachi/PIA	P	19.1.69	Karachi
*****Malcolm** Devon Eugene	Derbyshire	E	22.2.63	Kingston, Jamaica
Manack Hussein Ahmed	Transvaal	SA	10.4.68	Pretoria
*****Manjrekar** Sanjay Vijay	Mumbai	I	12.7.65	Mangalore
*****Mansoor Akhtar**	United Bank	P	25.12.57	Karachi
Mansoor Rana	Lahore/ADBP	P	27.12.62	Lahore
*****Manzoor Elahi**	Lahore/ADBP	P	15.4.63	Sahiwal

	Team	Country	Born	Birthplace
Maqsood Rana	Lahore/National Bank	P	1.8.72	Lahore
Maron Ryan	Western Province	SA	24.2.75	Cape Town
Marquet Joshua Phillip	Tasmania	A	3.12.69	Melbourne
Marsh Daniel James	Tasmania	A	14.6.73	Subiaco
Marsh Steven Andrew	Kent	E	27.1.61	London
Marshall Dave Kerwin	Barbados	WI	24.5.72	Barbados
Marshall Roy Ashworth	Windward Islands	WI	1.4.65	St Joseph, Dominica
Martin Kenroy	Windward Islands	WI		St Vincent
Martin Nico	Northern Transvaal	SA	4.2.72	Umtali, Rhodesia
*****Martin** Peter James	Lancashire	E	15.11.68	Accrington
Martin-Jenkins Robin Simon Christopher	Sussex	E	28.10.75	Guildford
Martyn Aubrey	Western Province	SA	23.6.72	Pretoria
*****Martyn** Damien Richard	Western Australia	A	21.10.71	Darwin
Maru Rajesh Jamandass	Hampshire	E	28.10.62	Nairobi, Kenya
Mascarenhas Adrian Dimitri	Hampshire	E	30.10.77	London
Masikazana Lulama	Eastern Province	SA	6.2.73	Port Elizabeth
Mason Keno	Trinidad & Tobago	WI	13.11.72	Trinidad
Mason Matthew Sean	Western Australia	A	20.3.74	Claremont
*****Masood Anwar**	Faisalabad/U. Bank	P	12.12.67	Khanewal
*****Matambanadzo** Everton	Mashonaland	Z	13.4.76	Salisbury
Matthews Craig Russell	Western Province	SA	15.2.65	Cape Town
*****Matthews** Gregory Richard John	New South Wales	A	15.12.59	Newcastle
May Michael Robert	Derbyshire	E	22.7.71	Chesterfield
Maynard John Carl	Leeward Islands	WI	18.5.69	Nevis
*****Maynard** Matthew Peter	Glamorgan	E	21.3.66	Oldham
*****Mbangwa** Mpumelelo	Matabeleland	Z	26.6.76	Plumtree
Mendis Chaminda	Colts	SL	28.12.68	Galle
Metcalfe Ashley Anthony	Nottinghamshire	E	25.12.63	Horsforth
*****Mhambrey** Paras Laxmikant	Mumbai	I	20.6.72	Bombay
Milburn Stuart Mark	Hampshire	E	29.9.72	Harrogate
Miller Colin Reid	Tasmania	A	6.2.64	Footscray
Millns David James	Leicestershire/Boland	E	27.2.65	Clipstone
Mills Michael	Leeward Islands	WI		Nevis
Mirza Maneer Mohammed	Worcestershire	E	1.4.78	Birmingham
Mitchum Junie	Leeward Islands	WI	22.11.73	St Kitts
Moffat Scott Park	Middlesex	E	1.2.73	Germiston, South Africa
*****Mohammad Akram**	Rawalpindi/Allied Bank/Northants	P	10.9.74	Islamabad
Mohammad Aslam	Rajasthan	I	7.8.74	Jaipur
*****Mohammad Hussain**	Lahore/United Bank	P	8.10.76	Lahore
*****Mohammad Wasim**	Rawalpindi	P	8.8.77	Rawalpindi
*****Mohammad Zahid**	PIA	P	2.8.76	Gaggu Mandi
*****Mohanty** Debasis Sarbeswar	Orissa	I	20.7.76	Bhubaneshwar
Mohapatra Prasanta Raghunath	Orissa	I	1.9.73	Bhubaneshwar
*****Mohsin Kamal**	PNSC	P	16.6.63	Lyallpur
*****Moin Khan**	Karachi	P	23.9.71	Rawalpindi
Moin-ul-Atiq	Karachi/Habib Bank	P	5.8.64	Karachi
Moles Andrew James	Warwickshire	E	12.2.61	Solihull
*****Mongia** Nayan Ramlal	Baroda	I	19.12.69	Baroda
Montgomerie Richard Robert	Northamptonshire	E	3.7.71	Rugby
*****Moody** Thomas Masson	W. Australia/Worcs	A	2.10.65	Adelaide
Moores Peter	Sussex	E	18.12.62	Macclesfield
*****More** Kiran Shankar	Baroda	I	4.9.62	Baroda
Morgan Delroy Simeon	Jamaica	WI	4.3.67	Rollington Town
Morgan Grant	Eastern Province	SA	19.5.71	Port Elizabeth
Morgan McNeil Junior	Windward Islands	WI	18.10.70	St Vincent
Morris Alexander Corfield	Yorkshire	E	4.10.76	Barnsley
*****Morris** Hugh	Glamorgan	E	5.10.63	Cardiff

	Team	Country	Born	Birthplace
*Morris John Edward	Durham	E	1.4.64	Crewe
*Morrison Daniel Kyle	Auckland	NZ	3.2.66	Auckland
Morton Runako Shaku	Leeward Islands	WI	22.7.78	Nevis
Mott Matthew Peter	Queensland	A	3.10.73	Charleville
*Moxon Martyn Douglas	Yorkshire	E	4.5.60	Barnsley
Mujahid Jamshed	Lahore/Habib Bank	P	1.12.71	Muredke
Mulder Bret	Western Australia	A	6.2.64	Subiaco
*Mullally Alan David	Leicestershire	E	12.7.69	Southend-on-Sea
Muller Scott Andrew	Queensland	A	11.7.71	Herston
*Muralitharan Muttiah	Tamil Union	SL	17.4.72	Kandy
Murphy Brian Samuel	Jamaica	WI	7.4.73	Jamaica
*Murray Darrin James	Canterbury	NZ	4.9.67	Christchurch
*Murray Junior Randalph	Windward Islands	WI	20.1.68	St Georges, Grenada
*Mushtaq Ahmed	Lahore/Somerset	P	28.6.70	Sahiwal
Muzumdar Amol Anil	Mumbai	I	11.11.74	Bombay
Myers Jodi Henre	Griqualand West	SA	6.9.73	Cape Town
*Nadeem Abbasi	Rawalpindi	P	15.4.64	Rawalpindi
*Nadeem Ghauri	Habib Bank	P	12.10.62	Lahore
*Nadeem Khan	Karachi/PIA	P	10.12.69	Rawalpindi
Naeem Ashraf	Lahore/National Bank	P	10.11.72	Lahore
Nagamootoo Mahendra Veeren	Guyana	WI	9.10.75	Guyana
Nagamootoo Vishal	Guyana	WI	7.1.77	Guyana
Napier Graham Richard	Essex	E	6.1.80	Colchester
Nash David Charles	Middlesex	E	19.1.78	Chertsey
*Nash Dion Joseph	Northern Districts	NZ	20.11.71	Auckland
*Naved Anjum	Habib Bank	P	27.7.63	Lahore
Nayyar Rajiv	Himachal Pradesh	I	28.3.70	Delhi
Neblett Jermaine Cleavon	Guyana	WI	15.9.74	Guyana
Nedd Gavin Hilton	Guyana	WI	21.7.72	Guyana
Newell Keith	Sussex	E	25.3.72	Crawley
Newell Mark	Sussex	E	19.12.73	Crawley
*Newport Philip John	Worcestershire	E	11.10.62	High Wycombe
Nicholson Matthew James	Western Australia	A	2.10.74	St Leonards
Nielsen Timothy John	South Australia	A	5.5.68	Forest Gate, England
Nikitaras Steven	New South Wales	A	31.8.70	Port Kembla
Nixon Paul Andrew	Leicestershire	E	21.10.70	Carlisle
Noon Wayne Michael	Nottinghamshire	E	5.2.71	Grimsby
Ntini Makhaya	Border	SA	6.7.77	Zwelitsha
Obaid Kamal	Uttar Pradesh	I	4.9.72	Allahabad
O'Connor Shayne Barry	Otago	NZ	15.11.73	Hastings
*Olonga Henry Khaaba	Matabeleland	Z	3.7.76	Lusaka, Zambia
Oosthuizen Riaan Carel	Boland	SA	3.5.72	Cape Town
Oram Andrew Richard	Nottinghamshire	E	7.3.75	Northampton
Ormond James	Leicestershire	E	20.8.77	Walsgrave
Ostler Dominic Piers	Warwickshire	E	15.7.70	Solihull
Owen John Edward	Derbyshire	E	7.8.71	Derby
Padmanabhan K. Narayanaiyer Anantha	Kerala	I	8.9.69	Trivandrum
Palframan Steven John	Border	SA	12.5.70	East London
*Pandit Chandrakant Sitaram	Madhya Pradesh	I	30.9.61	Bombay
Parker Bradley	Yorkshire	E	30.1.66	Mirfield
Parker Geoffrey Ross	South Australia	A	31.3.68	Malvern
*Parore Adam Craig	Auckland	NZ	23.1.71	Auckland
Parsana Hitesh Jayarambhai	Saurashtra	I	20.2.70	Rajkot
Parsons Gordon James	Leicestershire	E	17.10.59	Slough
Parsons Keith Alan	Somerset	E	2.5.73	Taunton

	Team	Country	Born	Birthplace
Patel Chetan	Hampshire/Oxford U.	E	12.4.72	London
*****Patel** Dipak Narshibhai	Auckland	NZ	25.10.58	Nairobi, Kenya
*****Patel** Minal Mahesh	Kent	E	7.7.70	Bombay, India
*****Patel** Rashid	Baroda	I	1.6.64	Sabarkantha
Pathak Amit	Andhra	I	30.11.72	Vishakhapatnam
Pearson Richard Michael	Surrey	E	27.1.72	Batley
Peirce Michael <u>Toby</u> Edward	Sussex	E	14.6.73	Maidenhead
Penberthy Anthony Leonard	Northamptonshire	E	1.9.69	Troon, Cornwall
Penn Andrew Jonathan	Central Districts	NZ	27.7.74	Wanganui
Penney Trevor Lionel	Warwickshire	E	12.6.68	Salisbury, Rhodesia
Percival Andre Ricardo	Guyana	WI	5.1.75	New Amsterdam
Perera Kahawelage <u>Gamini</u>	Antonians	SL	22.5.64	Colombo
Perry Nehemiah Odolphus	Jamaica	WI	16.6.68	Jamaica
Persad Mukesh	Trinidad & Tobago	WI	1.5.70	Trinidad
Peters Stephen David	Essex	E	10.12.78	Harold Wood
Petrie Richard George	Wellington	NZ	23.8.67	Christchurch
Phillip Warrington Dexter	Leeward Islands	WI	23.7.68	Nevis
Phillips Ben James	Kent	E	30.9.74	Lewisham
Phillips Nicholas Charles	Sussex	E	10.5.74	Pembury
Pick Robert <u>Andrew</u>	Nottinghamshire	E	19.11.63	Nottingham
Pienaar Roy Francois	Northern Transvaal	SA	17.7.61	Johannesburg
Pierre Andrew Jones	Windward Islands	WI	5.10.63	Goodwill, Dominica
Pierson Adrian Roger Kirshaw	Leicestershire	E	21.7.63	Enfield, Middlesex
Piper Keith John	Warwickshire	E	18.12.69	Leicester
Pistorius Ivan	Northern Transvaal	SA	8.7.70	Durban
Player Bradley Thomas	Free State	SA	18.1.67	Benoni
*****Pocock** Blair Andrew	Northern Districts	NZ	18.6.71	Papakura
Pollard Paul Raymond	Nottinghamshire	E	24.9.68	Nottingham
*****Pollock** Shaun Maclean	Natal	SA	16.7.73	Port Elizabeth
*****Ponting** Ricky Thomas	Tasmania	A	19.12.74	Launceston
Pooley Jason Calvin	Middlesex	E	8.8.69	Hammersmith
Pope Steven Charles	Border	SA	15.11.72	East London
Pope Uzzah	Windward Islands	WI	3.1.71	St Vincent
Pothas Nic	Transvaal	SA	18.11.73	Johannesburg
Powell Jonathan Christopher	Essex	E	13.6.79	Harold Wood
Powell Michael John	Glamorgan	E	3.2.77	Abergavenny
Powell Ronald Malcolm	Leeward Islands	WI	5.3.68	Nevis
Powell Tony Orlando	Jamaica	WI	22.12.72	Jamaica
*****Prabhakar** Manoj	Delhi	I	15.4.63	Ghaziabad
*****Prasad** Bapu Krishnarao Venkatesh	Karnataka	I	5.8.69	Bangalore
Prasad Mannava Sri Kanth	Andhra	I	24.4.75	Guntur
Pretorius Nicolaas Willem	Free State	SA	8.3.69	Ventersdorp
Prichard Paul John	Essex	E	7.1.65	Billericay
*****Priest** Mark Wellings	Canterbury	NZ	12.8.61	Greymouth
Prince Ashwell Gavin	Eastern Province	SA	28.5.77	Port Elizabeth
*****Pringle** Meyrick Wayne	Western Province	SA	22.6.66	Adelaide
Proverbs Stanton Nathaniel	Barbados	WI	6.3.68	Barbados
*****Pushpakumara** Karuppiahyage Ravindra	Nondescripts	SL	21.7.75	Panadura
Quinn Whitmoore <u>Kenneth</u> Lyndon	Leeward Islands	WI	30.5.71	All Saints, Antigua
Radford Toby Alexander	Sussex	E	31.12.71	Caerphilly
Radley Philip Johannes Lourens	Free State	SA	7.2.69	Bloemfontein
Ragoonath Suruj	Trinidad & Tobago	WI	22.3.68	Trinidad
*****Rajput** Lalchand Sitaram	Vidarbha	I	18.12.61	Bombay
*****Raju** Sagi Lakshmi Venkatapathy	Hyderabad	I	9.7.69	Hyderabad

	Team	Country	Born	Birthplace
*Raman Woorkeri Venkat	Tamil Nadu	I	23.5.65	Madras
Ramesh Sandagoppan	Tamil Nadu	I	16.10.75	Madras
*Ramiz Raja	Allied Bank	P	14.8.62	Lyallpur
Ramkishen Hanumara	Andhra	I	29.7.71	Vijayawada
Ramnarine Dinanth	Trinidad & Tobago	WI	4.6.75	Trinidad
Rampersad Denis	Trinidad & Tobago	WI	22.9.74	Trinidad
Ramprakash Bhaskaran	Kerala	I	18.12.66	Madras
*Ramprakash Mark Ravin	Middlesex	E	5.9.69	Bushey
*Ranatunga Arjuna	Sinhalese	SL	1.12.63	Colombo
Ranatunga Nishantha	Colts	SL	22.1.66	Gampaha
*Ranatunga Sanjeeva	Nondescripts	SL	25.4.69	Colombo
Rao Rajesh Krishnakant	Sussex	E	9.12.74	Park Royal
*Rashid Latif	Karachi/Allied Bank	P	14.10.68	Karachi
Ratcliffe Jason David	Surrey	E	19.6.69	Solihull
*Rathore Vikram	Punjab	I	26.3.69	Jullundur
Raul Sanjay	Orissa	I	6.10.76	Cuttack
Rawnsley Matthew James	Worcestershire	E	8.6.76	Birmingham
Reid Winston Emmerson	Barbados	WI	29.9.62	Bank Hall
*Reifer Floyd Lamonte	Barbados	WI	23.7.72	Parish Land
*Reiffel Paul Ronald	Victoria	A	19.4.66	Box Hill
Rennie Gavin James	Mashonaland	Z	12.1.76	Fort Victoria
*Rennie John Alexander	Matabeleland	Z	29.7.70	Fort Victoria
Renshaw Simon John	Hampshire	E	6.3.74	Bebington
*Rhodes Jonathan Neil	Natal	SA	26.7.69	Pietermaritzburg
*Rhodes Steven John	Worcestershire	E	17.6.64	Bradford
Ricci Brendan Paul	Victoria	A	24.4.65	Fitzroy
Richards Corey John	New South Wales	A	25.8.75	Camden
*Richardson David John	Eastern Province	SA	16.9.59	Johannesburg
*Richardson Richard Benjamin	Northern Transvaal	WI	12.1.62	Five Islands, Antigua
Ridgway Mark William	Tasmania	A	21.5.63	Warragul
Ridgway Paul Matthew	Lancashire	E	13.2.77	Airedale
Rindel Michael John Raymond	Northern Transvaal	SA	9.2.63	Durban
Ripley David	Northamptonshire	E	13.9.66	Leeds
*Rizwan-uz-Zaman	PIA	P	4.9.61	Karachi
Roberts David James	Northamptonshire	E	29.12.76	Truro
Roberts Glenn Martin	Derbyshire	E	4.11.73	Huddersfield
Roberts Kevin Joseph	New South Wales	A	25.7.72	North Sydney
Roberts Lincoln Abraham	Trinidad & Tobago	WI	4.9.74	Tobago
Robinson Darren David John	Essex	E	2.3.73	Braintree
Robinson Mark Andrew	Sussex	E	23.11.66	Hull
*Robinson Robert Timothy	Nottinghamshire	E	21.11.58	Sutton-in-Ashfield
Roe Garth Anthony	Griqualand West	SA	9.7.73	Port Elizabeth
Rollins Adrian Stewart	Derbyshire	E	8.2.72	Barking
Rollins Robert John	Essex	E	30.1.74	Plaistow
Rollock Terry Euclyn	Barbados	WI	25.9.69	Barbados
*Rose Franklyn Albert	Jamaica	WI	1.2.72	St Ann's Bay
Rose Graham David	Somerset	E	12.4.64	Tottenham
Roseberry Michael Anthony	Durham	E	28.11.66	Sunderland
Rundle David Bryan	Western Province	SA	25.9.65	Cape Town
*Rushmere Mark Weir	Eastern Province	SA	7.1.65	Port Elizabeth
*Russell Robert Charles	Gloucestershire	E	15.8.63	Stroud
*Rutherford Kenneth Robert	Transvaal	NZ	26.10.65	Dunedin
Saballus Andrew William	Tasmania	A	1.6.69	Hobart
*Saeed Anwar	ADBP	P	6.9.68	Karachi
Saeed Azad	Karachi/National Bank	P	14.8.66	Karachi
Saggers Martin John	Durham	E	23.5.72	King's Lynn
Saint John Michael	Tasmania	A	31.1.69	Auburn

	Team	Country	Born	Birthplace
Sajid Ali	Karachi/National Bank	P	1.7.63	*Karachi*
Sajjad Akbar	PNSC	P	1.3.61	*Lahore*
*****Saker** David James	Victoria	A	29.5.66	*Oakleigh*
*****Saleem Yousuf**	Customs	P	7.12.59	*Karachi*
Sales David John	Northamptonshire	E	3.12.77	*Carshalton*
*****Salim Elahi**	United Bank	P	21.11.76	*Sahiwal*
*****Salim Malik**	Habib Bank	P	16.4.63	*Lahore*
*****Salisbury** Ian David Kenneth	Surrey	E	21.1.70	*Northampton*
*****Samaraweera** Dulip Prasanna	Colts	SL	12.2.72	*Colombo*
Samaroo Avidesh	Trinidad & Tobago	WI	22.1.78	*Trinidad*
Samuels Marlon Nathaniel	Jamaica	WI	5.1.81	*Kingston*
*****Samuels** Robert George	Jamaica	WI	13.3.71	*Jamaica*
Sanford Adam	Windward Islands	WI	12.7.76	*Dominica*
Sanghvi Rahul	Delhi	I	3.9.74	*Surat*
Sapru Rahul Vijay	Uttar Pradesh	I	13.6.64	*Kanpur*
*****Saqlain Mushtaq**	Surrey	P	27.11.76	*Lahore*
Sarkar Arindam	Bengal	I	12.8.73	*Calcutta*
Sarwan Ramnaresh	Guyana	WI	23.6.80	*Guyana*
Savident Lee	Hampshire	E	22.10.76	*Guernsey*
Schonegevel Wayne Edward	Griqualand West	SA	25.8.62	*Bloemfontein*
*****Schultz** Brett Nolan	Western Province	SA	26.8.70	*East London*
Scuderi Joseph Charles	South Australia	A	24.12.68	*Ingham*
Seccombe Wade Anthony	Queensland	A	30.10.71	*Murgon*
Semple Keith Fitzpatrick	Guyana	WI	21.8.70	*Georgetown*
Seymore Andre Johan	Northern Transvaal	SA	16.2.75	*Rustenburg*
*****Shadab Kabir**	Karachi	P	12.11.77	*Karachi*
Shadford Darren James	Lancashire	E	4.3.75	*Oldham*
*****Shah** Ali Hassimshah	Mashonaland	Z	7.8.59	*Salisbury*
Shah Owais Alam	Middlesex	E	22.10.78	*Karachi, Pakistan*
Shahid Nadeem	Surrey	E	23.4.69	*Karachi, Pakistan*
Shahid Afridi	Karachi	P	1.3.80	*Kohat*
Shahid Anwar	Lahore/National Bank	P	5.7.68	*Multan*
*****Shahid Mahboob**	Karachi	P	25.8.62	*Karachi*
*****Shahid Nazir**	Faisalabad	P	4.12.77	*Faisalabad*
*****Shahid Saeed**	Lahore	P	6.1.66	*Lahore*
*****Shakeel Ahmed**	Peshawar/Habib Bank	P	12.11.71	*Daska*
Shakeel Khan	Habib Bank	P	28.5.68	*Lahore*
Shamshad Rizwan	Uttar Pradesh	I	19.11.72	*Aligarh*
Sharath Sridharan	Madras	I	31.10.72	*Madras*
*****Sharma** Ajay	Delhi	I	3.4.64	*Delhi*
*****Sharma** Chetan	Bengal	I	3.1.66	*Ludhiana*
Sharma Sandeep	Punjab	I	14.2.74	*Jullundur*
Shaw Adrian David	Glamorgan	E	17.2.72	*Neath*
*****Shaw** Timothy Gower	Eastern Province	SA	5.7.59	*Empangeni*
Sheeraz Kamran Pasha	Gloucestershire	E	28.12.73	*Wellington, Shropshire*
Sheikh Mohamed Avez	Warwickshire	E	2.7.73	*Birmingham*
Sheriyar Alamgir	Worcestershire	E	15.11.73	*Birmingham*
Shine Kevin James	Somerset	E	22.2.69	*Bracknell*
*****Shoaib Mohammad**	Karachi/PIA	P	8.1.61	*Karachi*
Siddons James Darren	South Australia	A	25.4.64	*Robinvale*
Sidebottom Ryan Jay	Yorkshire	E	15.6.78	*Huddersfield*
*****Sidhu** Navjot Singh	Punjab	I	20.10.63	*Patiala*
*****Silva** Kelaniyage Jayantha	Sinhalese	SL	2.6.73	*Kalutara*
*****Silverwood** Christopher Eric Wilfred	Yorkshire	E	5.3.75	*Pontefract*
*****Simmons** Philip Verant	T & T/Easterns	WI	18.4.63	*Arima*
Simons Eric Owen	Western Province	SA	9.3.62	*Cape Town*
Singh Anurag	Warwicks/Camb. U.	E	9.9.75	*Kanpur, India*
Singh Rabindra Ramanarayan	Tamil Nadu	I	14.9.63	*Princes Town, Trinidad*

	Team	Country	Born	Birthplace
***Slater** Michael Jonathon	New South Wales	A	21.2.70	Wagga Wagga
***Small** Gladstone Cleophas	Warwickshire	E	18.10.61	St George, Barbados
Smith Adam Matthew	Victoria	A	6.4.76	Greensborough
***Smith** Andrew Michael	Gloucestershire	E	1.10.67	Dewsbury
Smith Benjamin Francis	Leicestershire	E	3.4.72	Corby
Smith Edward Thomas	Kent/Cambridge U.	E	19.7.77	Pembury
Smith Gregory James	Northern Transvaal	SA	30.10.71	Pretoria
Smith Neil Michael Knight	Warwickshire	E	27.7.67	Birmingham
Smith Richard Andrew Mortimer	Trinidad & Tobago	WI	17.7.71	Trinidad
***Smith** Robin Arnold	Hampshire	E	13.9.63	Durban, South Africa
Smith Trevor	Derbyshire	E	18.1.77	Derby
Snape Jeremy Nicholas	Northamptonshire	E	27.4.73	Stoke-on-Trent
Sodhi Harvinder Singh	Madhya Pradesh	I	17.10.71	Agra
Sohail Fazal	Habib Bank	P	11.11.67	Lahore
Solanki Vikram Singh	Worcestershire	E	1.4.76	Udaipur, India
Somasunder Sujith	Karnataka	I	2.12.72	Bangalore
Sommerville Blaise Justin	Northern Transvaal	SA	25.5.67	Pretoria
Speak Nicholas Jason	Durham	E	21.11.66	Manchester
***Spearman** Craig Murray	Central Districts	NZ	4.7.72	Auckland
Speight Martin Peter	Durham	E	24.10.67	Walsall
Spendlove Benjamin Lee	Derbyshire	E	4.11.78	Belper
Spiring Karl Reuben	Worcestershire	E	13.11.74	Southport
Sridhar Maruti Venkat	Hyderabad	I	2.8.65	Vijayawada
***Srinath** Javagal	Karnataka	I	31.8.69	Mysore
Stacey Bradley John	Victoria	A	11.6.72	Geelong
Stelling William Frederick	Boland	SA	30.6.69	Johannesburg
Stemp Richard David	Yorkshire	E	11.12.67	Birmingham
Stephen Lee	Windward Islands	WI	29.10.75	St Lucia
Stephenson Franklyn Dacosta	Free State	WI	8.4.59	St James, Barbados
***Stephenson** John Patrick	Hampshire	E	14.3.65	Stebbing
Stevens Darren Ian	Leicestershire	E	30.4.76	Leicester
***Stewart** Alec James	Surrey	E	8.4.63	Merton
Stewart Errol Leslie Rae	Natal	SA	30.7.69	Durban
***Steyn** Philippus Jeremia Rudolf	Natal	SA	30.6.67	Kimberley
Storey Keith Graham	Natal	SA	25.1.69	Salisbury, Rhodesia
***Strang** Bryan Colin	Mashonaland	Z	9.6.72	Bulawayo
***Strang** Paul Andrew	Mashonaland/Kent	Z	28.7.70	Bulawayo
***Streak** Heath Hilton	Matabeleland	Z	16.3.74	Bulawayo
Strydom Pieter Coenraad	Border	SA	10.6.69	Somerset East
Stuart Anthony Mark	New South Wales	A	2.1.70	Newcastle
Stuart Colin Ellsworth Laurie	Guyana	WI	28.9.73	Guyana
Stubbings Stephen David	Derbyshire	E	31.3.78	Huddersfield
***Such** Peter Mark	Essex	E	12.6.64	Helensburgh, Scotland
Sugden Craig Brian	Natal	SA	7.3.74	Durban
Suresh Kumar Mani	Railways	I	19.4.73	Alleppey
Sutcliffe Iain John	Leicestershire	E	20.12.74	Leeds
Swanepoel Adriaan Johannes	Griqualand West	SA	19.3.72	Kimberley
Swann Alec James	Northamptonshire	E	26.10.76	Northampton
Sylvester John Anthony Rodney	Windward Islands	WI	6.10.69	Grenada
Sylvester Kester Kenneth	Windward Islands	WI	5.12.73	Grenada
***Symcox** Patrick Leonard	Natal	SA	14.4.60	Kimberley
Symonds Andrew	Queensland	A	9.6.75	Birmingham, England
Taljard Dion	Border	SA	7.1.70	East London
***Tauseef Ahmed**	United Bank	P	10.5.60	Karachi
***Taylor** Jonathan Paul	Northamptonshire	E	8.8.64	Ashby-de-la-Zouch
***Taylor** Mark Anthony	New South Wales	A	27.10.64	Leeton
Taylor Neil Royston	Sussex	E	21.7.59	Orpington

	Team	Country	Born	Birthplace
Telemachus Roger	Boland	SA	27.3.73	*Stellenbosch*
***Tendulkar** Sachin Ramesh	Mumbai	I	24.4.73	*Bombay*
Thomas Dennison	Windward Islands	WI	3.3.68	*Grenada*
Thomas P.	Windward Islands	WI		
Thomas Stuart <u>Darren</u>	Glamorgan	E	25.1.75	*Morriston*
Thompson Julian Barton DeCourcy	Kent	E	28.10.68	*Cape Town, SA*
***Thompson** Patterson Ian Chesterfield	Barbados	WI	26.9.71	*Barbados*
Thompson Scott Michael	New South Wales	A	4.5.72	*Bankstown*
***Thomson** Shane Alexander	Northern Districts	NZ	27.1.69	*Hamilton*
***Thorpe** Graham Paul	Surrey	E	1.8.69	*Farnham*
Thursfield Martin John	Sussex	E	14.12.71	*South Shields*
***Tillekeratne** Hashan Prasantha	Nondescripts	SL	14.7.67	*Colombo*
Titchard Stephen Paul	Lancashire	E	17.12.67	*Warrington*
Tolley Christopher Mark	Nottinghamshire	E	30.12.67	*Kidderminster*
Trainor Nicholas James	Gloucestershire	E	29.6.75	*Gateshead*
Trescothick Marcus Edward	Somerset	E	25.12.75	*Keynsham*
Trott Benjamin James	Somerset	E	14.3.75	*Wellington, Somerset*
Truter Wayne Stoney	Boland	SA	27.6.65	*Cape Town*
Tuckett Carl McArthur	Leeward Islands	WI	18.5.70	*Nevis*
Tudor Alex Jeremy	Surrey	E	23.10.77	*Kensington*
***Tufnell** Philip Charles Roderick	Middlesex	E	29.4.66	*Barnet*
Turner Robert Julian	Somerset	E	25.11.67	*Malvern*
Tweats Timothy Andrew	Derbyshire	E	18.4.74	*Stoke-on-Trent*
***Twose** Roger Graham	Wellington	NZ	17.4.68	*Torquay, England*
Udal Shaun David	Hampshire	E	18.3.69	*Farnborough, Hants*
Upashantha Kalutarage <u>Eric</u> Amila	Colts	SL	10.6.72	*Kurunegala*
***Vaas** Warnakulasooriya Patabendige Ushantha Joseph <u>Chaminda</u>	Colts	SL	27.1.74	*Mattumagala*
van der Merwe Casparus Cornelius	Free State	SA	11.7.73	*Johannesburg*
Vandrau Matthew James	Derbyshire	E	22.7.69	*Epsom*
van Jaarsveld Martin	Northern Transvaal	SA	18.6.74	*Klerksdorp*
van Rensburg Petrus	Free State	SA	28.3.77	*Virginia*
van Troost Adrianus Petrus	Somerset	Hol	2.10.72	*Schiedam, Netherlands*
van Wyk Morne Nico	Free State	SA	20.3.79	*Bloemfontein*
van Zyl Daniel Jacobus	Northern Transvaal	SA	8.1.71	*Pretoria*
Vaughan Jeffrey Mark	South Australia	A	26.3.74	*Blacktown*
***Vaughan** Justin Thomas Caldwell	Auckland	NZ	30.8.67	*Hereford, England*
Vaughan Michael Paul	Yorkshire	E	29.10.74	*Manchester*
Veenstra Ross Edward	Transvaal	SA	22.4.72	*Estcourt*
***Venkataramana** Margashayam	Tamil Nadu	I	24.4.66	*Secunderabad*
Venter Jacobus Francois	Free State	SA	1.10.69	*Bloemfontein*
Ventura Mario Dimitri	Jamaica	WI	21.4.74	*Jamaica*
***Vettori** Daniel Luca	Northern Districts	NZ	27.1.79	*Auckland*
Victor Gavin Charles	Eastern Province	SA	11.8.66	*Port Elizabeth*
Vij Bharati	Punjab	I	9.1.67	*Ludhiana*
Vijay Raghvendrarao	Karnataka	I	15.8.75	*Bangalore*
Viljoen Dirk Peter	Mashonaland	Z	11.3.77	*Salisbury*
Vimpani Graeme Ronald	Victoria	A	27.1.72	*Herston*
Vorster Christiaan Jakobus	Boland	SA	17.8.76	*Paarl*
Wagh Mark Anant	Warwicks/Oxford U.	E	20.10.76	*Birmingham*
Waldron Earl	Leeward Islands	WI	31.8.66	*All Saints, Antigua*
Wallace Philo Alphonso	Barbados	WI	2.8.70	*Around-the-town*
Walker Alan	Durham	E	7.7.62	*Emley*
Walker Lyndsay Nicholas Paton	Nottinghamshire	E	22.6.74	*Armidale, Australia*

	Team	Country	Born	Birthplace
Walker Matthew Jonathan	Kent	E	2.1.74	*Gravesend*
*****Waller** Andrew Christopher	Mashonaland	Z	25.9.59	*Salisbury*
*****Walmsley** Kerry Peter	Auckland	NZ	23.8.73	*Dunedin*
*****Walsh** Courtney Andrew	Jamaica	WI	30.10.62	*Kingston*
Walsh Vaughn Anthony	Griqualand West	WI	2.12.64	*Liberta, Antigua*
Walton Timothy Charles	Northamptonshire	E	8.11.72	*Low Head*
*****Waqar Younis**	Glamorgan	P	16.11.71	*Vehari*
Ward Ian James	Surrey	E	30.9.72	*Plymouth*
Ward Trevor Robert	Kent	E	18.1.68	*Farningham*
*****Warnaweera** Kahakatchchi Patabandige <u>Jayananda</u>	Singha	SL	23.11.60	*Matara*
*****Warne** Shane Keith	Victoria	A	13.9.69	*Ferntree Gully*
Warren Russell John	Northamptonshire	E	10.9.71	*Northampton*
*****Wasim Akram**	Lancashire	P	3.6.66	*Lahore*
Wasim Haider	Faisalabad/PIA	P	6.6.67	*Lyallpur*
*****Wassan** Atul Satish	Delhi	I	23.3.68	*Delhi*
*****Watkin** Steven Llewellyn	Glamorgan	E	15.9.64	*Maesteg*
*****Watkinson** Michael	Lancashire	E	1.8.61	*Westhoughton*
Watson Douglas James	Natal	SA	15.5.73	*Pietermaritzburg*
Watt Balthazar Michael	Windward Islands	WI	12.4.75	*Dominica*
*****Waugh** Mark Edward	New South Wales	A	2.6.65	*Sydney*
*****Waugh** Stephen Rodger	New South Wales	A	2.6.65	*Sydney*
Webber Darren Scott	South Australia	A	18.8.71	*Barnside*
Webster Trevor Craig	Transvaal	SA	4.10.69	*Johannesburg*
Weekes Lesroy Charlesworth	Leeward Islands	WI	19.7.71	*Montserrat*
Weekes Paul Nicholas	Middlesex	E	8.7.69	*Hackney*
*****Weerasinghe** Colombage Don Udesh <u>Sanjeewa</u>	Nondescripts	SL	1.3.68	*Colombo*
Welch Graeme	Warwickshire	E	21.3.72	*Durham*
Wellings Peter Edward	Middlesex	E	5.3.70	*Wolverhampton*
*****Wells** Alan Peter	Kent	E	2.10.61	*Newhaven*
Wells Vincent John	Leicestershire	E	6.8.65	*Dartford*
Welton Guy Edward	Nottinghamshire	E	4.5.78	*Grimsby*
Wessels Andrew	Boland	SA	13.5.74	*Pietermaritzburg*
*****Wessels** Kepler Christoffel	Eastern Province	SA	14.9.57	*Bloemfontein*
Weston Robin Michael Swann	Durham	E	7.6.75	*Durham*
Weston William <u>Philip</u> Christopher	Worcestershire	E	16.6.73	*Durham*
Wharf Alexander George	Yorkshire	E	4.6.75	*Bradford*
*****Whitaker** John James	Leicestershire	E	5.5.62	*Skipton*
Whitaker Paul Robert	Hampshire	E	28.6.73	*Keighley*
White Brad Middleton	Border	SA	15.5.70	*Johannesburg*
*****White** Craig	Yorkshire	E	16.12.69	*Morley*
White Giles William	Hampshire	E	23.3.72	*Barnstaple*
*****Whittall** Andrew Richard	Matabeleland	Z	28.3.73	*Mutare*
*****Whittall** Guy James	Matabeleland	Z	5.9.72	*Chipinga*
Wickremaratne Ranasinghe Pattikirikoralalage Aruna <u>Hemantha</u>	Sinhalese	SL	21.2.71	*Colombo*
*****Wickremasinghe** Gallage <u>Pramodya</u>	Sinhalese	SL	14.8.71	*Matara*
Wigney Bradley Neil	South Australia	A	30.6.65	*Leongatha*
Wilkinson Louis Johannes	Free State	SA	19.11.66	*Vereeniging*
Williams Brad Andrew	Victoria	A	20.11.74	*Frankston*
Williams David	Trinidad & Tobago	WI	4.11.63	*San Fernando*
Williams Elton Charl	Boland	SA	19.9.73	*Stellenbosch*
Williams Henry Smith	Boland	SA	11.6.67	*Stellenbosch*
Williams Laurie Rohan	Jamaica	WI	12.12.68	*Jamaica*
*****Williams** Neil FitzGerald	Essex	E	2.7.62	*Hope Well, St Vincent*
*****Williams** Stuart Clayton	Leeward Islands	WI	12.8.69	*Government Road, Nevis*

	Team	Country	Born	Birthplace
Williamson Dominic	Leicestershire	E	15.11.75	*Durham*
Willoughby Charl Myles	Boland	SA	3.12.74	*Cape Town*
Wilson Craig Rhys	Border	SA	24.3.74	*Cradock*
Wilson Jeffrey William	Otago	NZ	24.10.73	*Invercargill*
Wilson Paul	South Australia	A	12.1.72	*Newcastle*
Windows Matthew Guy Norman	Gloucestershire	E	5.4.73	*Bristol*
*****Wishart** Craig Brian	Mashonaland	Z	9.1.74	*Salisbury*
Wong Kenneth Arthur	Guyana	WI	22.5.73	*Guyana*
Wood John	Durham	E	22.7.70	*Crofton*
Wood Nathan Theodore	Lancashire	E	4.10.74	*Thornhill Edge*
Wright Anthony John	Gloucestershire	E	27.6.62	*Stevenage*
Wylie Andrew Robert	Boland	SA	31.12.71	*Pietermaritzburg*
Yadav Jai Prakash	Madhya Pradesh	I	7.8.74	*Bhopal*
*****Yadav** Vijay Singh	Haryana	I	14.3.67	*Gonda*
Yates Gary	Lancashire	E	20.9.67	*Ashton-under-Lyne*
Young Bradley Evan	South Australia	A	23.2.73	*Semaphore*
*****Young** Bryan Andrew	Northern Districts	NZ	3.11.64	*Whangarei*
*****Young** Shaun	Tasmania/Glos	A	13.6.70	*Burnie*
Zafar Iqbal	Karachi/Nat. Bank	P	6.3.69	*Karachi*
Zahid Ahmed	PIA	P	15.11.61	*Karachi*
*****Zahid Fazal**	PIA	P	10.11.73	*Sialkot*
*****Zahoor Elahi**	Lahore	P	1.3.71	*Sahiwal*
Zakir Hussain	Railways	I	26.1.76	*Bikaner*
*****Zoysa** Demuni <u>Nuwan</u> Tharanga	Sinhalese	SL	13.5.78	*Colombo*

I ZINGARI RESULTS, 1997

Matches 24: Won 5, Lost 8, Drawn 11.

April 22	Eton College	Drawn
May 11	Hampshire Hogs	Drawn
May 17	Eton Ramblers	Lost by five wickets
May 18	Stragglers of Asia	Lost by seven wickets
May 19	Harrow School	Won by six wickets
May 31	Royal Armoured Corps	Drawn
June 8	Bradfield Waifs	Drawn
June 8	Earl of Carnarvon's XI	Won by two wickets
June 14	Charterhouse	Lost by eight wickets
June 15	Sandhurst Wanderers	Drawn
June 21	Guards CC	Drawn
June 29	J. Paul Getty's XI	Lost by six wickets
July 1	Winchester College	Drawn
July 6	Hagley CC	Lost by 30 runs
July 12	Green Jackets Club	Lost by seven wickets
July 13	Rickling Green CC	Drawn
July 19	Lord Stafford's XI	Lost by 136 runs
July 20	Earl of Arundel's XI	Drawn
July 20	Sir John Starkey's XI	Won by 29 runs
July 26	Hurlingham CC	Drawn
August 3	Band of Brothers	Won by 12 runs
August 9, 10	South Wales Hunts XI	Won by 60 runs
August 31	Willow Warblers	Drawn
September 7	J. H. Pawle's XI	Lost by four wickets

WISDEN'S CRICKETERS OF THE YEAR, 1889-1998

1889	*Six Great Bowlers of the Year:* J. Briggs, J. J. Ferris, G. A. Lohmann, R. Peel, C. T. B. Turner, S. M. J. Woods.
1890	*Nine Great Batsmen of the Year:* R. Abel, W. Barnes, W. Gunn, L. Hall, R. Henderson, J. M. Read, A. Shrewsbury, F. H. Sugg, A. Ward.
1891	*Five Great Wicket-Keepers:* J. McC. Blackham, G. MacGregor, R. Pilling, M. Sherwin, H. Wood.
1892	*Five Great Bowlers:* W. Attewell, J. T. Hearne, F. Martin, A. W. Mold, J. W. Sharpe.
1893	*Five Batsmen of the Year:* H. T. Hewett, L. C. H. Palairet, W. W. Read, S. W. Scott, A. E. Stoddart.
1894	*Five All-Round Cricketers:* G. Giffen, A. Hearne, F. S. Jackson, G. H. S. Trott, E. Wainwright.
1895	*Five Young Batsmen of the Season:* W. Brockwell, J. T. Brown, C. B. Fry, T. W. Hayward, A. C. MacLaren.
1896	W. G. Grace.
1897	*Five Cricketers of the Season:* S. E. Gregory, A. A. Lilley, K. S. Ranjitsinhji, T. Richardson, H. Trumble.
1898	*Five Cricketers of the Year:* F. G. Bull, W. R. Cuttell, N. F. Druce, G. L. Jessop, J. R. Mason.
1899	*Five Great Players of the Season:* W. H. Lockwood, W. Rhodes, W. Storer, C. L. Townsend, A. E. Trott.
1900	*Five Cricketers of the Season:* J. Darling, C. Hill, A. O. Jones, M. A. Noble, Major R. M. Poore.
1901	*Mr R. E. Foster and Four Yorkshiremen:* R. E. Foster, S. Haigh, G. H. Hirst, T. L. Taylor, J. Tunnicliffe.
1902	L. C. Braund, C. P. McGahey, F. Mitchell, W. G. Quaife, J. T. Tyldesley.
1903	W. W. Armstrong, C. J. Burnup, J. Iremonger, J. J. Kelly, V. T. Trumper.
1904	C. Blythe, J. Gunn, A. E. Knight, W. Mead, P. F. Warner.
1905	B. J. T. Bosanquet, E. A. Halliwell, J. Hallows, P. A. Perrin, R. H. Spooner.
1906	D. Denton, W. S. Lees, G. J. Thompson, J. Vine, L. G. Wright.
1907	J. N. Crawford, A. Fielder, E. G. Hayes, K. L. Hutchings, N. A. Knox.
1908	A. W. Hallam, R. O. Schwarz, F. A. Tarrant, A. E. E. Vogler, T. G. Wass.
1909	*Lord Hawke and Four Cricketers of the Year:* W. Brearley, Lord Hawke, J. B. Hobbs, A. Marshal, J. T. Newstead.
1910	W. Bardsley, S. F. Barnes, D. W. Carr, A. P. Day, V. S. Ransford.
1911	H. K. Foster, A. Hartley, C. B. Llewellyn, W. C. Smith, F. E. Woolley.
1912	*Five Members of the MCC's Team in Australia:* F. R. Foster, J. W. Hearne, S. P. Kinneir, C. P. Mead, H. Strudwick.
1913	John Wisden: Personal Recollections.
1914	M. W. Booth, G. Gunn, J. W. Hitch, A. E. Relf, Hon. L. H. Tennyson.
1915	J. W. H. T. Douglas, P. G. H. Fender, H. T. W. Hardinge, D. J. Knight, S. G. Smith.
1916-17	No portraits appeared.
1918	*School Bowlers of the Year:* H. L. Calder, J. E. D'E. Firth, C. H. Gibson, G. A. Rotherham, G. T. S. Stevens.
1919	*Five Public School Cricketers of the Year:* P. W. Adams, A. P. F. Chapman, A. C. Gore, L. P. Hedges, N. E. Partridge.
1920	*Five Batsmen of the Year:* A. Ducat, E. H. Hendren, P. Holmes, H. Sutcliffe, E. Tyldesley.
1921	P. F. Warner.
1922	H. Ashton, J. L. Bryan, J. M. Gregory, C. G. Macartney, E. A. McDonald.
1923	A. W. Carr, A. P. Freeman, C. W. L. Parker, A. C. Russell, A. Sandham.
1924	*Five Bowlers of the Year:* A. E. R. Gilligan, R. Kilner, G. G. Macaulay, C. H. Parkin, M. W. Tate.
1925	R. H. Catterall, J. C. W. MacBryan, H. W. Taylor, R. K. Tyldesley, W. W. Whysall.
1926	J. B. Hobbs.

1927	G. Geary, H. Larwood, J. Mercer, W. A. Oldfield, W. M. Woodfull.
1928	R. C. Blunt, C. Hallows, W. R. Hammond, D. R. Jardine, V. W. C. Jupp.
1929	L. E. G. Ames, G. Duckworth, M. Leyland, S. J. Staples, J. C. White.
1930	E. H. Bowley, K. S. Duleepsinhji, H. G. Owen-Smith, R. W. V. Robins, R. E. S. Wyatt.
1931	D. G. Bradman, C. V. Grimmett, B. H. Lyon, I. A. R. Peebles, M. J. Turnbull.
1932	W. E. Bowes, C. S. Dempster, James Langridge, Nawab of Pataudi sen., H. Verity.
1933	W. E. Astill, F. R. Brown, A. S. Kennedy, C. K. Nayudu, W. Voce.
1934	A. H. Bakewell, G. A. Headley, M. S. Nichols, L. F. Townsend, C. F. Walters.
1935	S. J. McCabe, W. J. O'Reilly, G. A. E. Paine, W. H. Ponsford, C. I. J. Smith.
1936	H. B. Cameron, E. R. T. Holmes, B. Mitchell, D. Smith, A. W. Wellard.
1937	C. J. Barnett, W. H. Copson, A. R. Gover, V. M. Merchant, T. S. Worthington.
1938	T. W. J. Goddard, J. Hardstaff jun., L. Hutton, J. H. Parks, E. Paynter.
1939	H. T. Bartlett, W. A. Brown, D. C. S. Compton, K. Farnes, A. Wood.
1940	L. N. Constantine, W. J. Edrich, W. W. Keeton, A. B. Sellers, D. V. P. Wright.
1941-46	No portraits appeared.
1947	A. V. Bedser, L. B. Fishlock, V. (M. H.) Mankad, T. P. B. Smith, C. Washbrook.
1948	M. P. Donnelly, A. Melville, A. D. Nourse, J. D. Robertson, N. W. D. Yardley.
1949	A. L. Hassett, W. A. Johnston, R. R. Lindwall, A. R. Morris, D. Tallon.
1950	T. E. Bailey, R. O. Jenkins, John Langridge, R. T. Simpson, B. Sutcliffe.
1951	T. G. Evans, S. Ramadhin, A. L. Valentine, E. D. Weekes, F. M. M. Worrell.
1952	R. Appleyard, H. E. Dollery, J. C. Laker, P. B. H. May, E. A. B. Rowan.
1953	H. Gimblett, T. W. Graveney, D. S. Sheppard, W. S. Surridge, F. S. Trueman.
1954	R. N. Harvey, G. A. R. Lock, K. R. Miller, J. H. Wardle, W. Watson.
1955	B. Dooland, Fazal Mahmood, W. E. Hollies, J. B. Statham, G. E. Tribe.
1956	M. C. Cowdrey, D. J. Insole, D. J. McGlew, H. J. Tayfield, F. H. Tyson.
1957	D. Brookes, J. W. Burke, M. J. Hilton, G. R. A. Langley, P. E. Richardson.
1958	P. J. Loader, A. J. McIntyre, O. G. Smith, M. J. Stewart, C. L. Walcott.
1959	H. L. Jackson, R. E. Marshall, C. A. Milton, J. R. Reid, D. Shackleton.
1960	K. F. Barrington, D. B. Carr, R. Illingworth, G. Pullar, M. J. K. Smith.
1961	N. A. T. Adcock, E. R. Dexter, R. A. McLean, R. Subba Row, J. V. Wilson.
1962	W. E. Alley, R. Benaud, A. K. Davidson, W. M. Lawry, N. C. O'Neill.
1963	D. Kenyon, Mushtaq Mohammad, P. H. Parfitt, P. J. Sharpe, F. J. Titmus.
1964	D. B. Close, C. C. Griffith, C. C. Hunte, R. B. Kanhai, G. S. Sobers.
1965	G. Boycott, P. J. Burge, J. A. Flavell, G. D. McKenzie, R. B. Simpson.
1966	K. C. Bland, J. H. Edrich, R. C. Motz, P. M. Pollock, R. G. Pollock.
1967	R. W. Barber, B. L. D'Oliveira, C. Milburn, J. T. Murray, S. M. Nurse.
1968	Asif Iqbal, Hanif Mohammad, K. Higgs, J. M. Parks, Nawab of Pataudi jun.
1969	J. G. Binks, D. M. Green, B. A. Richards, D. L. Underwood, O. S. Wheatley.
1970	B. F. Butcher, A. P. E. Knott, Majid Khan, M. J. Procter, D. J. Shepherd.
1971	J. D. Bond, C. H. Lloyd, B. W. Luckhurst, G. M. Turner, R. T. Virgin.
1972	G. G. Arnold, B. S. Chandrasekhar, L. R. Gibbs, B. Taylor, Zaheer Abbas.
1973	G. S. Chappell, D. K. Lillee, R. A. L. Massie, J. A. Snow, K. R. Stackpole.
1974	K. D. Boyce, B. E. Congdon, K. W. R. Fletcher, R. C. Fredericks, P. J. Sainsbury.
1975	D. L. Amiss, M. H. Denness, N. Gifford, A. W. Greig, A. M. E. Roberts.
1976	I. M. Chappell, P. G. Lee, R. B. McCosker, D. S. Steele, R. A. Woolmer.
1977	J. M. Brearley, C. G. Greenidge, M. A. Holding, I. V. A. Richards, R. W. Taylor.
1978	I. T. Botham, M. Hendrick, A. Jones, K. S. McEwan, R. G. D. Willis.
1979	D. I. Gower, J. K. Lever, C. M. Old, C. T. Radley, J. N. Shepherd.
1980	J. Garner, S. M. Gavaskar, G. A. Gooch, D. W. Randall, B. C. Rose.
1981	K. J. Hughes, R. D. Jackman, A. J. Lamb, C. E. B. Rice, V. A. P. van der Bijl.
1982	T. M. Alderman, A. R. Border, R. J. Hadlee, Javed Miandad, R. W. Marsh.
1983	Imran Khan, T. E. Jesty, A. I. Kallicharran, Kapil Dev, M. D. Marshall.
1984	M. Amarnath, J. V. Coney, J. E. Emburey, M. W. Gatting, C. L. Smith.
1985	M. D. Crowe, H. A. Gomes, G. W. Humpage, J. Simmons, S. Wettimuny.
1986	P. Bainbridge, R. M. Ellison, C. J. McDermott, N. V. Radford, R. T. Robinson.
1987	J. H. Childs, G. A. Hick, D. B. Vengsarkar, C. A. Walsh, J. J. Whitaker.
1988	J. P. Agnew, N. A. Foster, D. P. Hughes, P. M. Roebuck, Salim Malik.
1989	K. J. Barnett, P. J. L. Dujon, P. A. Neale, F. D. Stephenson, S. R. Waugh.

1990	S. J. Cook, D. M. Jones, R. C. Russell, R. A. Smith, M. A. Taylor.
1991	M. A. Atherton, M. Azharuddin, A. R. Butcher, D. L. Haynes, M. E. Waugh.
1992	C. E. L. Ambrose, P. A. J. DeFreitas, A. A. Donald, R. B. Richardson, Waqar Younis.
1993	N. E. Briers, M. D. Moxon, I. D. K. Salisbury, A. J. Stewart, Wasim Akram.
1994	D. C. Boon, I. A. Healy, M. G. Hughes, S. K. Warne, S. L. Watkin.
1995	B. C. Lara, D. E. Malcolm, T. A. Munton, S. J. Rhodes, K. C. Wessels.
1996	D. G. Cork, P. A. de Silva, A. R. C. Fraser, A. Kumble, D. A. Reeve.
1997	S. T. Jayasuriya, Mushtaq Ahmed, Saeed Anwar, P. V. Simmons, S. R. Tendulkar.
1998	M. T. G. Elliott, S. G. Law, G. D. McGrath, M. P. Maynard, G. P. Thorpe.

POST-WAR CRICKETERS OF THE YEAR

The five players chosen to be Cricketers of the Year for 1998 bring the number chosen since selection resumed in 1947 after the wartime hiatus to 260. The 260 have been chosen from 26 different teams as follows:

Derbyshire	7	Lancashire	12	Sussex	8	South Africans	11
Durham	–	Leicestershire	5	Warwickshire	13	West Indians	21
Essex	13	Middlesex	11	Worcestershire	13	New Zealanders	5
Glamorgan	8	Northants	9	Yorkshire	13	Indians	9
Gloucestershire	7	Nottinghamshire	7	Oxford Univ.	1	Pakistanis	10
Hampshire	9	Somerset	10	Cambridge Univ.	2	Sri Lankans	2
Kent	10	Surrey	16	Australians	35	Zimbabweans	–

Note: The total of sides comes to 265 because five players played regularly for two teams (England excluded) in the year for which they were chosen: K. D. Boyce (Essex and West Indians), Imran Khan (Sussex and Pakistanis), Kapil Dev (Northamptonshire and Indians), P. B. H. May (Surrey and Cambridge University) and D. S. Sheppard (Sussex and Cambridge University).

S. T. Jayasuriya of Sri Lanka, in 1997, was the first player to be chosen who did not play in England the previous season.

Types of players

Of the 260 Cricketers of the Year, 144 are best classified as batsmen, 74 as bowlers, 26 as all-rounders and 16 as wicket-keepers.

Nationalities

At the time they were chosen, 131 (50.38 per cent) were qualified to play for England, 41 for Australia, 33 West Indies, 19 South Africa, 13 Pakistan, 10 India, 9 New Zealand, 3 Sri Lanka and 1 Zimbabwe.

A. J. Lamb (1981) and G. A. Hick (1987) were chosen when they were regarded as South African and Zimbabwean respectively, though they subsequently played Test cricket for England.

No England-qualified players were chosen in 1949, 1962, 1982 and 1997.

Non-Test players

The following post-war Cricketers of the Year never appeared in Test cricket: W. E. Alley (1962), P. Bainbridge (1986), J. D. Bond (1971), N. E. Briers (1993), D. M. Green (1969), D. P. Hughes (1988), G. W. Humpage (1985), T. E. Jesty (1983), A. Jones (1978), John Langridge (1950), P. G. Lee (1976), K. S. McEwan (1978), P. A. Neale (1989), C. E. B. Rice (1981), P. M. Roebuck (1988), P. J. Sainsbury (1974), D. J. Shepherd (1970), J. Simmons (1985), F. D. Stephenson (1989), W. S. Surridge (1953), B. Taylor (1972), V. A. P. van der Bijl (1981), R. T. Virgin (1971), O. S. Wheatley (1969), J. Wilson (1961).

All the above were England-qualified except for Alley (Australian), McEwan, Rice and van der Bijl (South African) and Stephenson (West Indian).

PART THREE: RECORDS

CRICKET RECORDS

Test match and first-class records amended by BILL FRINDALL to end of the 1997 season in England

Updated Test records can be found on Wisden's web site, www.wisden.com

Unless stated to be of a minor character, all records apply only to first-class cricket. This is traditionally considered to have started in 1815, after the Napoleonic War.

* Denotes not out or an unbroken partnership.

(A), (SA), (WI), (NZ), (I), (P), (SL) or (Z) indicates either the nationality of the player, or the country in which the record was made.

FIRST-CLASS RECORDS

BATTING RECORDS

ALL-ROUND RECORDS

WICKET-KEEPING RECORDS

FIELDING RECORDS

TEAM RECORDS

TEST MATCH RECORDS

BATTING RECORDS

BOWLING RECORDS

ALL-ROUND RECORDS

WICKET-KEEPING RECORDS

FIELDING RECORDS

TEAM RECORDS

CAPTAINCY

UMPIRING

TEST SERIES

LIMITED-OVERS INTERNATIONAL RECORDS

MISCELLANEOUS

FIRST-CLASS RECORDS

BATTING RECORDS

HIGHEST INDIVIDUAL SCORES

501*	B. C. Lara	Warwickshire v Durham at Birmingham	1994
499	Hanif Mohammad	Karachi v Bahawalpur at Karachi	1958-59
452*	D. G. Bradman	NSW v Queensland at Sydney	1929-30

443*	B. B. Nimbalkar	Maharashtra v Kathiawar at Poona	1948-49
437	W. H. Ponsford	Victoria v Queensland at Melbourne	1927-28
429	W. H. Ponsford	Victoria v Tasmania at Melbourne	1922-23
428	Aftab Baloch	Sind v Baluchistan at Karachi	1973-74
424	A. C. MacLaren	Lancashire v Somerset at Taunton	1895
405*	G. A. Hick	Worcestershire v Somerset at Taunton	1988
385	B. Sutcliffe	Otago v Canterbury at Christchurch	1952-53
383	C. W. Gregory	NSW v Queensland at Brisbane	1906-07
377	S. V. Manjrekar	Bombay v Hyderabad at Bombay	1990-91
375	B. C. Lara	West Indies v England at St John's	1993-94
369	D. G. Bradman	South Australia v Tasmania at Adelaide	1935-36
366	N. H. Fairbrother	Lancashire v Surrey at The Oval	1990
366	M. V. Sridhar	Hyderabad v Andhra at Secunderabad	1993-94
365*	C. Hill	South Australia v NSW at Adelaide	1900-01
365*	G. S. Sobers	West Indies v Pakistan at Kingston	1957-58
364	L. Hutton	England v Australia at The Oval	1938
359*	V. M. Merchant	Bombay v Maharashtra at Bombay	1943-44
359	R. B. Simpson	NSW v Queensland at Brisbane	1963-64
357*	R. Abel	Surrey v Somerset at The Oval	1899
357	D. G. Bradman	South Australia v Victoria at Melbourne	1935-36
356	B. A. Richards	South Australia v Western Australia at Perth	1970-71
355*	G. R. Marsh	Western Australia v South Australia at Perth	1989-90
355	B. Sutcliffe	Otago v Auckland at Dunedin	1949-50
352	W. H. Ponsford	Victoria v NSW at Melbourne	1926-27
350	Rashid Israr	Habib Bank v National Bank at Lahore	1976-77
345	C. G. Macartney	Australians v Nottinghamshire at Nottingham	1921
344*	G. A. Headley	Jamaica v Lord Tennyson's XI at Kingston	1931-32
344	W. G. Grace	MCC v Kent at Canterbury	1876
343*	P. A. Perrin	Essex v Derbyshire at Chesterfield	1904
341	G. H. Hirst	Yorkshire v Leicestershire at Leicester	1905
340*	D. G. Bradman	NSW v Victoria at Sydney	1928-29
340	S. M. Gavaskar	Bombay v Bengal at Bombay	1981-82
340	S. T. Jayasuriya	Sri Lanka v India at Colombo	1997-98
338*	R. C. Blunt	Otago v Canterbury at Christchurch	1931-32
338	W. W. Read	Surrey v Oxford University at The Oval	1888
337*	Pervez Akhtar	Railways v Dera Ismail Khan at Lahore	1964-65
337*	D. J. Cullinan	Transvaal v Northern Transvaal at Johannesburg	1993-94
337†	Hanif Mohammad	Pakistan v West Indies at Bridgetown	1957-58
336*	W. R. Hammond	England v New Zealand at Auckland	1932-33
336	W. H. Ponsford	Victoria v South Australia at Melbourne	1927-28
334	D. G. Bradman	Australia v England at Leeds	1930
333	K. S. Duleepsinhji	Sussex v Northamptonshire at Hove	1930
333	G. A. Gooch	England v India at Lord's	1990
332	W. H. Ashdown	Kent v Essex at Brentwood	1934
331*	J. D. Robertson	Middlesex v Worcestershire at Worcester	1949
325*	H. L. Hendry	Victoria v New Zealanders at Melbourne	1925-26
325	A. Sandham	England v West Indies at Kingston	1929-30
325	C. L. Badcock	South Australia v Victoria at Adelaide	1935-36
324*	D. M. Jones	Victoria v South Australia at Melbourne	1994-95
324	J. B. Stollmeyer	Trinidad v British Guiana at Port-of-Spain	1946-47
324	Waheed Mirza	Karachi Whites v Quetta at Karachi	1976-77
323	A. L. Wadekar	Bombay v Mysore at Bombay	1966-67
322	E. Paynter	Lancashire v Sussex at Hove	1937
322	I. V. A. Richards	Somerset v Warwickshire at Taunton	1985
321	W. L. Murdoch	NSW v Victoria at Sydney	1881-82
320	R. Lamba	North Zone v West Zone at Bhilai	1987-88
319	Gul Mahomed	Baroda v Holkar at Baroda	1946-47
318*	W. G. Grace	Gloucestershire v Yorkshire at Cheltenham	1876
317	W. R. Hammond	Gloucestershire v Nottinghamshire at Gloucester	1936
317	K. R. Rutherford	New Zealanders v D. B. Close's XI at Scarborough	1986

316*	J. B. Hobbs	Surrey v Middlesex at Lord's	1926
316*	V. S. Hazare	Maharashtra v Baroda at Poona	1939-40
316	R. H. Moore	Hampshire v Warwickshire at Bournemouth	1937
315*	T. W. Hayward	Surrey v Lancashire at The Oval	1898
315*	P. Holmes	Yorkshire v Middlesex at Lord's	1925
315*	A. F. Kippax	NSW v Queensland at Sydney	1927-28
314*	C. L. Walcott	Barbados v Trinidad at Port-of-Spain	1945-46
314*	Wasim Jaffer	Mumbai v Saurashtra at Rajkot....................	1996-97
313*	S. J. Cook	Somerset v Glamorgan at Cardiff	1990
313	H. Sutcliffe	Yorkshire v Essex at Leyton	1932
313	W. V. Raman	Tamil Nadu v Goa at Panjim	1988-89
312*	W. W. Keeton	Nottinghamshire v Middlesex at The Oval‡..........	1939
312*	J. M. Brearley	MCC Under-25 v North Zone at Peshawar	1966-67
312	R. Lamba	Delhi v Himachal Pradesh at Delhi	1994-95
312	J. E. R. Gallian	Lancashire v Derbyshire at Manchester	1996
311*	G. M. Turner	Worcestershire v Warwickshire at Worcester........	1982
311	J. T. Brown	Yorkshire v Sussex at Sheffield....................	1897
311	R. B. Simpson	Australia v England at Manchester	1964
311	Javed Miandad	Karachi Whites v National Bank at Karachi	1974-75
310*	J. H. Edrich	England v New Zealand at Leeds	1965
310	H. Gimblett	Somerset v Sussex at Eastbourne	1948
309	V. S. Hazare	The Rest v Hindus at Bombay	1943-44
308*	F. M. M. Worrell	Barbados v Trinidad at Bridgetown	1943-44
307*	T. N. Lazard	Boland v W. Province at Worcester, Cape Province ...	1993-94
307	M. C. Cowdrey	MCC v South Australia at Adelaide	1962-63
307	R. M. Cowper	Australia v England at Melbourne	1965-66
306*	A. Ducat	Surrey v Oxford University at The Oval	1919
306*	E. A. B. Rowan	Transvaal v Natal at Johannesburg	1939-40
306*	D. W. Hookes	South Australia v Tasmania at Adelaide	1986-87
305*	F. E. Woolley	MCC v Tasmania at Hobart	1911-12
305*	F. R. Foster	Warwickshire v Worcestershire at Dudley	1914
305*	W. H. Ashdown	Kent v Derbyshire at Dover	1935
304*	A. W. Nourse	Natal v Transvaal at Johannesburg	1919-20
304*	P. H. Tarilton	Barbados v Trinidad at Bridgetown	1919-20
304*	E. D. Weekes	West Indians v Cambridge University at Cambridge...	1950
304	R. M. Poore	Hampshire v Somerset at Taunton	1899
304	D. G. Bradman	Australia v England at Leeds	1934
303*	W. W. Armstrong	Australians v Somerset at Bath	1905
303*	Mushtaq Mohammad	Karachi Blues v Karachi University at Karachi	1967-68
303*	Abdul Azeem	Hyderabad v Tamil Nadu at Hyderabad	1986-87
303*	S. Chanderpaul	Guyana v Jamaica at Kingston	1995-96
303*	G. A. Hick	Worcestershire v Hampshire at Southampton	1997
302*	P. Holmes	Yorkshire v Hampshire at Portsmouth	1920
302*	W. R. Hammond	Gloucestershire v Glamorgan at Bristol	1934
302*	Arjan Kripal Singh	Tamil Nadu v Goa at Panjim	1988-89
302	W. R. Hammond	Gloucestershire v Glamorgan at Newport	1939
302	L. G. Rowe	West Indies v England at Bridgetown	1973-74
301*	E. H. Hendren	Middlesex v Worcestershire at Dudley	1933
301	W. G. Grace	Gloucestershire v Sussex at Bristol................	1896
300*	V. T. Trumper	Australians v Sussex at Hove	1899
300*	F. B. Watson	Lancashire v Surrey at Manchester	1928
300*	Imtiaz Ahmed	PM's XI v Commonwealth XI at Bombay	1950-51
300	J. T. Brown	Yorkshire v Derbyshire at Chesterfield.............	1898
300	D. C. S. Compton	MCC v N. E. Transvaal at Benoni	1948-49
300	R. Subba Row	Northamptonshire v Surrey at The Oval............	1958
300	Ramiz Raja	Allied Bank v Habib Bank at Lahore	1994-95

† *Hanif Mohammad batted for 16 hours 10 minutes – the longest innings in first-class cricket.*

‡ *Played at The Oval because Lord's was required for Eton v Harrow.*

Note: W. V. Raman (313) and Arjan Kripal Singh (302*) provide the only instance of two triple-hundreds in the same innings.

DOUBLE-HUNDRED ON DEBUT

227	T. Marsden	Sheffield & Leicester v Nottingham at Sheffield	1826
207	N. F. Callaway†	New South Wales v Queensland at Sydney	1914-15
240	W. F. E. Marx	Transvaal v Griqualand West at Johannesburg	1920-21
200*	A. Maynard	Trinidad v MCC at Port-of-Spain	1934-35
232*	S. J. E. Loxton	Victoria v Queensland at Melbourne	1946-47
215*	G. H. G. Doggart	Cambridge University v Lancashire at Cambridge ..	1948
202	J. Hallebone	Victoria v Tasmania at Melbourne	1951-52
230	G. R. Viswanath	Mysore v Andhra at Vijayawada	1967-68
260	A. A. Muzumdar	Bombay v Haryana at Faridabad	1993-94
209*	A. Pandey	Madhya Pradesh v Uttar Pradesh at Bhilai	1995-96
210*	D. J. Sales	Northants v Worcestershire at Kidderminster	1996
200*	M. J. Powell	Glamorgan v Oxford University at Oxford	1997

† *In his only first-class innings. He was killed in action in France in 1917.*

TWO SEPARATE HUNDREDS ON DEBUT

148	and 111	A. R. Morris	New South Wales v Queensland at Sydney	1940-41
152	and 102*	N. J. Contractor	Gujarat v Baroda at Baroda	1952-53
132*	and 110	Aamer Malik	Lahore "A" v Railways at Lahore	1979-80

Notes: J. S. Solomon, British Guiana, scored a hundred in each of his first three innings in first-class cricket: 114* v Jamaica; 108 v Barbados in 1956-57; 121 v Pakistanis in 1957-58.

R. Watson-Smith, Border, scored 310 runs before he was dismissed in first-class cricket, including not-out centuries in his first two innings: 183* v Orange Free State and 125* v Griqualand West in 1969-70.

G. R. Viswanath and D. M. Wellham alone have scored a hundred on their debut in both first-class cricket and Test cricket. Viswanath scored 230 for Mysore v Andhra in 1967-68 and 137 for India v Australia in 1969-70. Wellham scored 100 for New South Wales v Victoria in 1980-81 and 103 for Australia v England in 1981.

HUNDRED ON DEBUT IN BRITAIN

(The following list does not include instances of players who have previously appeared in first-class cricket outside the British Isles or who performed the feat before 1965. Full lists of earlier instances are in *Wisdens* prior to 1984.)

108	D. R. Shepherd	Gloucestershire v Oxford University at Oxford	1965
110*	A. J. Harvey-Walker†	Derbyshire v Oxford University at Burton upon Trent .	1971
173	J. Whitehouse	Warwickshire v Oxford University at Oxford.........	1971
106	J. B. Turner	Minor Counties v Pakistanis at Jesmond..............	1974
112	J. A. Claughton†	Oxford University v Gloucestershire at Oxford	1976
100*	A. W. Lilley†	Essex v Nottinghamshire at Nottingham	1978
146*	J. S. Johnson	Minor Counties v Indians at Wellington	1979
110	N. R. Taylor	Kent v Sri Lankans at Canterbury	1979
146*	D. G. Aslett	Kent v Hampshire at Bournemouth	1981
116	M. D. Moxon†	Yorkshire v Essex at Leeds	1981
100	D. A. Banks	Worcestershire v Oxford University at Oxford........	1983
122	A. A. Metcalfe	Yorkshire v Nottinghamshire at Bradford	1983
117*	K. T. Medlycott† ⎱		
101*	N. J. Falkner‡ ⎰	Surrey v Cambridge University at Banstead	1984
106	A. C. Storie†	Northamptonshire v Hampshire at Northampton	1985
102	M. P. Maynard	Glamorgan v Yorkshire at Swansea..................	1985
117*	R. J. Bartlett	Somerset v Oxford University at Oxford	1986
100*	P. D. Bowler	Leicestershire v Hampshire at Leicester	1986
145	I. L. Philip	Scotland v Ireland at Glasgow.....................	1986
114*	P. D. Atkins	Surrey v Cambridge University at The Oval	1988
100	B. M. W. Patterson	Scotland v Ireland at Dumfries	1988

116*	J. J. B. Lewis	Essex v Surrey at The Oval	1990
117	J. D. Glendenen	Durham v Oxford University at Oxford	1992
109	J. R. Wileman	Nottinghamshire v Cambridge U. at Nottingham	1992
123	A. J. Hollioake†	Surrey v Derbyshire at Ilkeston	1993
101	E. T. Smith	Cambridge University v Glamorgan at Cambridge	1996
110	S. D. Peters	Essex v Cambridge University at Cambridge	1996
210*	D. J. Sales†	Northamptonshire v Worcestershire at Kidderminster	1996
200*	M. J. Powell	Glamorgan v Oxford University at Oxford	1997

† *In his second innings.*

‡ *The only instance in England of two players performing the feat in the same match.*

TWO DOUBLE-HUNDREDS IN A MATCH

| A. E. Fagg | 244 | 202* | Kent v Essex at Colchester | 1938 |

TRIPLE-HUNDRED AND HUNDRED IN A MATCH

| G. A. Gooch | 333 | 123 | England v India at Lord's | 1990 |

DOUBLE-HUNDRED AND HUNDRED IN A MATCH

C. B. Fry	125	229	Sussex v Surrey at Hove	1900
W. W. Armstrong	157*	245	Victoria v South Australia at Melbourne	1920-21
H. T. W. Hardinge	207	102*	Kent v Surrey at Blackheath	1921
C. P. Mead	113	224	Hampshire v Sussex at Horsham	1921
K. S. Duleepsinhji	115	246	Sussex v Kent at Hastings	1929
D. G. Bradman	124	225	Woodfull's XI v Ryder's XI at Sydney	1929-30
B. Sutcliffe	243	100*	New Zealanders v Essex at Southend	1949
M. R. Hallam	210*	157	Leicestershire v Glamorgan at Leicester	1959
M. R. Hallam	203*	143*	Leicestershire v Sussex at Worthing	1961
Hanumant Singh	109	213*	Rajasthan v Bombay at Bombay	1966-67
Salah-ud-Din	256	102*	Karachi v East Pakistan at Karachi	1968-69
K. D. Walters	242	103	Australia v West Indies at Sydney	1968-69
S. M. Gavaskar	124	220	India v West Indies at Port-of-Spain	1970-71
L. G. Rowe	214	100*	West Indies v New Zealand at Kingston	1971-72
G. S. Chappell	247*	133	Australia v New Zealand at Wellington	1973-74
L. Baichan	216*	102	Berbice v Demerara at Georgetown	1973-74
Zaheer Abbas	216*	156*	Gloucestershire v Surrey at The Oval	1976
Zaheer Abbas	230*	104*	Gloucestershire v Kent at Canterbury	1976
Zaheer Abbas	205*	108*	Gloucestershire v Sussex at Cheltenham	1977
Saadat Ali	141	222	Income Tax v Multan at Multan	1977-78
Talat Ali	214*	104	PIA v Punjab at Lahore	1978-79
Shafiq Ahmad	129	217*	National Bank v MCB at Karachi	1978-79
D. W. Randall	209	146	Notts. v Middlesex at Nottingham	1979
Zaheer Abbas	215*	150*	Gloucestershire v Somerset at Bath	1981
Qasim Omar	210*	110	MCB v Lahore at Lahore	1982-83
A. I. Kallicharran	200*	117*	Warwicks. v Northants at Birmingham	1984
Rizwan-uz-Zaman	139	217*	PIA v PACO at Lahore	1989-90
G. A. Hick	252*	100*	Worcs. v Glamorgan at Abergavenny	1990
N. R. Taylor	204	142	Kent v Surrey at Canterbury	1990
N. R. Taylor	111	203*	Kent v Sussex at Hove	1991
W. V. Raman	226	120	Tamil Nadu v Haryana at Faridabad	1991-92
A. J. Lamb	209	107	Northants v Warwicks. at Northampton	1992
G. A. Gooch	101	205	Essex v Worcestershire at Worcester	1994
P. A. de Silva	255	116	Kent v Derbyshire at Maidstone	1995
M. C. Mendis	111	200*	Colts CC v Singha SC at Colombo	1995-96
A. M. Bacher	210	112*	Transvaal v Griqualand West at Kimberley	1996-97
H. H. Gibbs	200*	171	South Africans v India at Nagpur	1996-97
M. L. Hayden	235*	119	Hampshire v Warwickshire at Southampton	1997

TWO SEPARATE HUNDREDS IN A MATCH

Eight times: Zaheer Abbas.
Seven times: W. R. Hammond.
Six times: J. B. Hobbs, G. M. Turner.
Five times: C. B. Fry, G. A. Gooch.
Four times: D. G. Bradman, G. S. Chappell, J. H. Edrich, L. B. Fishlock, T. W. Graveney, C. G. Greenidge, H. T. W. Hardinge, E. H. Hendren, Javed Miandad, G. L. Jessop, H. Morris, P. A. Perrin, B. Sutcliffe, H. Sutcliffe.
Three times: Agha Zahid, L. E. G. Ames, Basit Ali, G. Boycott, I. M. Chappell, D. C. S. Compton, S. J. Cook, M. C. Cowdrey, D. Denton, P. A. de Silva, K. S. Duleepsinhji, R. E. Foster, R. C. Fredericks, S. M. Gavaskar, W. G. Grace, G. Gunn, M. R. Hallam, Hanif Mohammad, M. J. Harris, M. L. Hayden, T. W. Hayward, V. S. Hazare, D. W. Hookes, L. Hutton, A. Jones, D. M. Jones, P. N. Kirsten, R. B. McCosker, P. B. H. May, C. P. Mead, T. M. Moody, M. H. Parmar, R. T. Ponting, Rizwan-uz-Zaman, R. T. Robinson, A. C. Russell, Sadiq Mohammad, J. T. Tyldesley, K. C. Wessels.
Twice: Ali Zia, D. L. Amiss, C. W. J. Athey, L. Baichan, D. C. Boon, A. R. Border, B. J. T. Bosanquet, R. J. Boyd-Moss, A. R. Butcher, J. Cox, M. D. Crowe, C. C. Dacre, G. M. Emmett, A. E. Fagg, L. E. Favell, H. Gimblett, C. Hallows, R. A. Hamence, A. L. Hassett, D. L. Haynes, G. A. Headley, G. A. Hick, A. I. Kallicharran, J. H. King, A. F. Kippax, A. J. Lamb, J. G. Langridge, S. G. Law, H. W. Lee, E. Lester, C. B. Llewellyn, C. G. Macartney, M. P. Maynard, C. A. Milton, A. R. Morris, P. H. Parfitt, Nawab of Pataudi jun., E. Paynter, C. Pinch, R. G. Pollock, R. M. Prideaux, Qasim Omar, M. R. Ramprakash, W. Rhodes, B. A. Richards, I. V. A. Richards, Pankaj Roy, Salim Malik, James Seymour, Shafiq Ahmad, R. B. Simpson, C. L. Smith, G. S. Sobers, M. V. Sridhar, M. A. Taylor, N. R. Taylor, E. Tyldesley, C. L. Walcott, T. R. Ward, W. W. Whysall, G. N. Yallop.

Notes: W. Lambert scored 107 and 157 for Sussex v Epsom at Lord's in 1817 and it was not until W. G. Grace made 130 and 102* for South of the Thames v North of the Thames at Canterbury in 1868 that the feat was repeated.

C. J. B. Wood, 107* and 117* for Leicestershire v Yorkshire at Bradford in 1911, and S. J. Cook, 120* and 131* for Somerset v Nottinghamshire at Nottingham in 1989, are alone in carrying their bats and scoring hundreds in each innings.

FOUR HUNDREDS OR MORE IN SUCCESSION

Six in succession: D. G. Bradman 1938-39; C. B. Fry 1901; M. J. Procter 1970-71.
Five in succession: B. C. Lara 1993-94/1994; E. D. Weekes 1955-56.
Four in succession: C. W. J. Athey 1987; M. Azharuddin 1984-85; M. G. Bevan 1990-91; A. R. Border 1985; D. G. Bradman 1931-32, 1948/1948-49; D. C. S. Compton 1946-47; N. J. Contractor 1957-58; S. J. Cook 1989; K. S. Duleepsinhji 1931; C. B. Fry 1911; C. G. Greenidge 1986; W. R. Hammond 1936-37, 1945/1946; H. T. W. Hardinge 1913; T. W. Hayward 1906; J. B. Hobbs 1920, 1925; D. W. Hookes 1976-77; Ijaz Ahmed, jun. 1994-95; R. S. Kaluwitharana 1996-97; P. N. Kirsten 1976-77; J. G. Langridge 1949; C. G. Macartney 1921; K. S. McEwan 1977; P. B. H. May 1956-57; V. M. Merchant 1941-42; A. Mitchell 1933; Nawab of Pataudi sen. 1931; Rizwan-uz-Zaman 1989-90; L. G. Rowe 1971-72; Pankaj Roy 1962-63; Sadiq Mohammad 1976; Saeed Ahmed 1961-62; M. V. Sridhar 1990-91/1991-92; H. Sutcliffe 1931, 1939; S. R. Tendulkar 1994-95; E. Tyldesley 1926; W. W. Whysall 1930; F. E. Woolley 1929; Zaheer Abbas 1970-71, 1982-83.

Notes: T. W. Hayward (Surrey v Nottinghamshire and Leicestershire) and D. W. Hookes (South Australia v Queensland and New South Wales) are the only players listed above to score two hundreds in two successive matches. Hayward scored his in six days, June 4-9, 1906.

The most fifties in consecutive innings is ten – by E. Tyldesley in 1926, by D. G. Bradman in the 1947-48 and 1948 seasons and by R. S. Kaluwitharana in 1994-95.

MOST HUNDREDS IN A SEASON

Eighteen: D. C. S. Compton 1947.
Sixteen: J. B. Hobbs 1925.
Fifteen: W. R. Hammond 1938.
Fourteen: H. Sutcliffe 1932.
Thirteen: G. Boycott 1971, D. G. Bradman 1938, C. B. Fry 1901, W. R. Hammond 1933 and 1937, T. W. Hayward 1906, E. H. Hendren 1923, 1927 and 1928, C. P. Mead 1928, H. Sutcliffe 1928 and 1931.

Since 1969 (excluding G. Boycott – above)

Twelve: G. A. Gooch 1990.
Eleven: S. J. Cook 1991, Zaheer Abbas 1976.
Ten: G. A. Hick 1988, H. Morris 1990, M. R. Ramprakash 1995, G. M. Turner 1970, Zaheer Abbas 1981.

MOST DOUBLE-HUNDREDS IN A SEASON

Six: D. G. Bradman 1930.
Five: K. S. Ranjitsinhji 1900; E. D. Weekes 1950.
Four: Arun Lal 1986-87; C. B. Fry 1901; W. R. Hammond 1933, 1934; E. H. Hendren 1929-30; V. M. Merchant 1944-45; G. M. Turner 1971-72.
Three: L. E. G. Ames 1933; Arshad Pervez 1977-78; D. G. Bradman 1930-31, 1931-32, 1934, 1935-36, 1936-37, 1938, 1939-40; W. J. Edrich 1947; C. B. Fry 1903, 1904; M. W. Gatting 1994; G. A. Gooch 1994; W. R. Hammond 1928, 1928-29, 1932-33, 1938; J. Hardstaff jun. 1937, 1947; V. S. Hazare 1943-44; E. H. Hendren 1925; J. B. Hobbs 1914, 1926; L. Hutton 1949; D. M. Jones 1991-92; A. I. Kallicharran 1982; V. G. Kambli 1992-93; P. N. Kirsten 1980; R. S. Modi 1944-45; Nawab of Pataudi sen. 1933; W. H. Ponsford 1927-28, 1934; W. V. Raman 1988-89; M. R. Ramprakash 1995; K. S. Ranjitsinhji 1901; I. V. A. Richards 1977; R. B. Simpson 1963-64; P. R. Umrigar 1952, 1959; F. B. Watson 1928.

MOST HUNDREDS IN A CAREER

(35 or more)

		100s	Total Inns	100th 100 Season	Inns	400+	300+	200+
1	J. B. Hobbs	197	1,315	1923	821	0	1	16
2	E. H. Hendren	170	1,300	1928-29	740	0	1	22
3	W. R. Hammond	167	1,005	1935	679	0	4	36
4	C. P. Mead	153	1,340	1927	892	0	0	13
5	G. Boycott	151	1,014	1977	645	0	0	10
6	H. Sutcliffe	149	1,088	1932	700	0	1	17
7	F. E. Woolley	145	1,532	1929	1,031	0	1	9
8	L. Hutton	129	814	1951	619	0	1	11
9	**G. A. Gooch**	**128**	**988**	**1992-93**	**820**	**0**	**1**	**13**
10	W. G. Grace	126	1,493	1895	1,113	0	3	13
11	D. C. S. Compton	123	839	1952	552	0	1	9
12	T. W. Graveney	122	1,223	1964	940	0	0	7
13	D. G. Bradman	117	338	1947-48	295	1	6	37
14	I. V. A. Richards	114	796	1988-89	658	0	1	10
15	Zaheer Abbas	108	768	1982-83	658	0	0	10
16	A. Sandham	107	1,000	1935	871	0	1	11
	M. C. Cowdrey	107	1,130	1973	1,035	0	1	3

		100s	Total Inns	100th 100 Season	Inns	400+	300+	200+
18	T. W. Hayward	104	1,138	1913	1,076	0	1	8
19	J. H. Edrich	103	979	1977	945	0	1	4
	G. M. Turner	103	792	1982	779	0	1	10
	L. E. G. Ames	102	951	1950	915	0	0	9
21	E. Tyldesley	102	961	1934	919	0	0	7
	D. L. Amiss	102	1,139	1986	1,081	0	0	3

E. H. Hendren, D. G. Bradman and I. V. A. Richards scored their 100th hundreds in Australia, G. A. Gooch scored his in India. His record includes his century in South Africa in 1981-82, which is no longer accepted by ICC. Zaheer Abbas scored his in Pakistan. Zaheer Abbas and G. Boycott did so in Test matches.

Most double-hundreds scored by batsmen not included in the above list:

Sixteen: C. B. Fry.

Fourteen: C. G. Greenidge, K. S. Ranjitsinhji.

Thirteen: W. H. Ponsford (including two 400s and two 300s), J. T. Tyldesley.

Twelve: P. Holmes, Javed Miandad, R. B. Simpson.

Eleven: J. W. Hearne, G. A. Hick, V. M. Merchant.

Ten: S. M. Gavaskar, J. Hardstaff, jun., V. S. Hazare, A. Shrewsbury, R. T. Simpson.

J. W. Hearne ... 96	R. E. Marshall ... 68	W. W. Keeton ... 54
G. A. Hick ... **96**	R. N. Harvey ... 67	W. Bardsley ... 53
C. B. Fry ... 94	P. Holmes ... 67	B. F. Davison ... 53
M. W. Gatting ... **92**	J. D. Robertson ... 67	A. E. Dipper ... 53
C. G. Greenidge ... 92	P. A. Perrin ... 66	D. I. Gower ... 53
A. J. Lamb ... 89	S. J. Cook ... 64	G. L. Jessop ... 53
A. I. Kallicharran ... 87	R. G. Pollock ... 64	**H. Morris** ... **53**
W. J. Edrich ... 86	R. T. Simpson ... 64	James Seymour ... 53
G. S. Sobers ... 86	**M. E. Waugh** ... **64**	Shafiq Ahmad ... 53
J. T. Tyldesley ... 86	**D. C. Boon** ... **63**	**R. A. Smith** ... **53**
P. B. H. May ... 85	K. W. R. Fletcher ... 63	**K. J. Barnett** ... **52**
R. E. S. Wyatt ... 85	G. Gunn ... 62	E. H. Bowley ... 52
J. Hardstaff, jun. ... 83	**R. T. Robinson** ... **62**	D. B. Close ... 52
R. B. Kanhai ... 83	**K. C. Wessels** ... **62**	A. Ducat ... 52
S. M. Gavaskar ... 81	**D. L. Haynes** ... **61**	**D. M. Jones** ... **52**
Javed Miandad ... 80	V. S. Hazare ... 60	D. W. Randall ... 52
M. Leyland ... 80	G. H. Hirst ... 60	E. R. Dexter ... 51
B. A. Richards ... 80	R. B. Simpson ... 60	J. M. Parks ... 51
C. H. Lloyd ... 79	P. F. Warner ... 60	W. W. Whysall ... 51
K. F. Barrington ... 76	I. M. Chappell ... 59	B. C. Broad ... 50
J. G. Langridge ... 76	A. L. Hassett ... 59	G. Cox, jun. ... 50
C. Washbrook ... 76	W. Larkins ... 59	H. E. Dollery ... 50
H. T. W. Hardinge ... 75	A. Shrewsbury ... 59	K. S. Duleepsinhji ... 50
R. Abel ... 74	J. G. Wright ... 59	H. Gimblett ... 50
G. S. Chappell ... 74	A. E. Fagg ... 58	W. M. Lawry ... 50
D. Kenyon ... 74	P. H. Parfitt ... 58	Sadiq Mohammad ... 50
K. S. McEwan ... 74	W. Rhodes ... 58	F. B. Watson ... 50
Majid Khan ... 73	**P. N. Kirsten** ... **57**	**M. Azharuddin** ... **49**
Mushtaq Mohammad ... 72	L. B. Fishlock ... 56	C. G. Macartney ... 49
J. O'Connor ... 72	A. Jones ... 56	M. J. Stewart ... 49
W. G. Quaife ... 72	C. A. Milton ... 56	K. G. Suttle ... 49
K. S. Ranjitsinhji ... 72	**T. M. Moody** ... **56**	P. R. Umrigar ... 49
D. Brookes ... 71	**C. W. J. Athey** ... **55**	W. M. Woodfull ... 49
M. D. Crowe ... 71	C. Hallows ... 55	C. J. Barnett ... 48
A. C. Russell ... 71	Hanif Mohammad ... 55	M. R. Benson ... 48
A. R. Border ... 70	D. B. Vengsarkar ... 55	W. Gunn ... 48
D. Denton ... 69	W. Watson ... 55	E. G. Hayes ... 48
M. J. K. Smith ... 69	D. J. Insole ... 54	B. W. Luckhurst ... 48

M. J. Procter	48	A. F. Kippax	43	D. Lloyd	38
C. E. B. Rice	48	J. W. H. Makepeace	43	V. L. Manjrekar	38
C. J. Tavaré	48	**M. P. Maynard**	**43**	A. W. Nourse	38
A. C. MacLaren	47	**R. J. Bailey**	**42**	N. Oldfield	38
P. W. G. Parker	47	James Langridge	42	Rev. J. H. Parsons	38
W. H. Ponsford	47	Mudassar Nazar	42	W. W. Read	38
C. L. Smith	47	H. W. Parks	42	**Rizwan-uz-Zaman**	**38**
A. R. Butcher	46	T. F. Shepherd	42	J. Sharp	38
J. Iddon	46	V. T. Trumper	42	V. P. Terry	38
A. R. Morris	46	M. J. Harris	41	L. J. Todd	38
C. T. Radley	46	G. D. Mendis	41	**J. J. Whitaker**	**38**
Younis Ahmed	46	K. R. Miller	41	J. Arnold	37
W. W. Armstrong	45	A. D. Nourse	41	**Asif Mujtaba**	**37**
Asif Iqbal	45	J. H. Parks	41	G. Brown	37
L. G. Berry	45	R. M. Prideaux	41	G. Cook	37
J. M. Brearley	45	G. Pullar	41	G. M. Emmett	37
A. W. Carr	45	W. E. Russell	41	**N. H. Fairbrother**	**37**
C. Hill	45	**A. J. Stewart**	**41**	**C. L. Hooper**	**37**
M. D. Moxon	**45**	R. C. Fredericks	40	H. W. Lee	37
N. C. O'Neill	45	J. Gunn	40	M. A. Noble	37
E. Paynter	45	**Salim Malik**	**40**	B. P. Patel	37
Rev. D. S. Sheppard	45	M. J. Smith	40	**R. B. Richardson**	**37**
N. R. Taylor	**45**	C. L. Walcott	40	H. S. Squires	37
K. D. Walters	45	D. M. Young	40	R. T. Virgin	37
S. R. Waugh	**45**	Arshad Pervez	39	C. J. B. Wood	37
M. A. Atherton	**44**	W. H. Ashdown	39	N. F. Armstrong	36
H. H. Gibbons	44	J. B. Bolus	39	G. Fowler	36
V. M. Merchant	44	W. A. Brown	39	Mr. C. J. Nicholas	36
A. Mitchell	44	R. J. Gregory	39	E. Oldroyd	36
J. E. Morris	**44**	**M. A. Lynch**	**39**	W. Place	36
P. E. Richardson	44	W. R. D. Payton	39	**M. A. Taylor**	**36**
B. Sutcliffe	44	**M. R. Ramprakash**	**39**	A. L. Wadekar	36
G. R. Viswanath	44	J. R. Reid	39	E. D. Weekes	36
A. P. Wells	**44**	F. M. M. Worrell	39	C. S. Dempster	35
P. Willey	44	I. T. Botham	38	**N. Hussain**	**35**
E. J. Barlow	43	F. L. Bowley	38	D. R. Jardine	35
T. S. Curtis	**43**	P. J. Burge	38	T. E. Jesty	35
B. L. D'Oliveira	43	J. F. Crapp	38	B. H. Valentine	35
J. H. Hampshire	43			G. M. Wood	35

Bold type denotes those who played in 1996-97 and 1997 seasons.

3,000 RUNS IN A SEASON

	Season	I	NO	R	HS	100s	Avge
D. C. S. Compton	1947	50	8	3,816	246	18	90.85
W. J. Edrich	1947	52	8	3,539	267*	12	80.43
T. W. Hayward	1906	61	8	3,518	219	13	66.37
L. Hutton	1949	56	6	3,429	269*	12	68.58
F. E. Woolley	1928	59	4	3,352	198	12	60.94
H. Sutcliffe	1932	52	7	3,336	313	14	74.13
W. R. Hammond	1933	54	5	3,323	264	13	67.81
E. H. Hendren	1928	54	7	3,311	209*	13	70.44
R. Abel	1901	68	8	3,309	247	7	55.15
W. R. Hammond	1937	55	5	3,252	217	13	65.04
M. J. K. Smith	1959	67	11	3,245	200*	8	57.94
E. H. Hendren	1933	65	9	3,186	301*	11	56.89
C. P. Mead	1921	52	6	3,179	280*	10	69.10
T. W. Hayward	1904	63	5	3,170	203	11	54.65
K. S. Ranjitsinhji	1899	58	8	3,159	197	8	63.18
C. B. Fry	1901	43	3	3,147	244	13	78.67

	Season	I	NO	R	HS	100s	Avge
K. S. Ranjitsinhji........	1900	40	5	3,065	275	11	87.57
L. E. G. Ames..........	1933	57	5	3,058	295	9	58.80
J. T. Tyldesley..........	1901	60	5	3,041	221	9	55.29
C. P. Mead.............	1928	50	10	3,027	180	13	75.67
J. B. Hobbs	1925	48	5	3,024	266*	16	70.32
E. Tyldesley............	1928	48	10	3,024	242	10	79.57
W. E. Alley	1961	64	11	3,019	221*	11	56.96
W. R. Hammond	1938	42	2	3,011	271	15	75.27
E. H. Hendren	1923	51	12	3,010	200*	13	77.17
H. Sutcliffe.............	1931	42	11	3,006	230	13	96.96
J. H. Parks.............	1937	63	4	3,003	168	11	50.89
H. Sutcliffe.............	1928	44	5	3,002	228	13	76.97

Notes: W. G. Grace scored 2,739 runs in 1871 – the first batsman to reach 2,000 runs in a season. He made ten hundreds and twice exceeded 200, with an average of 78.25 in all first-class matches.

The highest aggregate in a season since the reduction of County Championship matches in 1969 is 2,755 by S. J. Cook (42 innings) in 1991.

2,000 RUNS IN A SEASON

Since Reduction of Championship Matches in 1969

Five times: G. A. Gooch 2,746 (1990), 2,559 (1984), 2,324 (1988), 2,208 (1985), 2,023 (1993).

Three times: D. L. Amiss 2,239 (1984), 2,110 (1976), 2,030 (1978); S. J. Cook 2,755 (1991), 2,608 (1990), 2,241 (1989); M. W. Gatting 2,257 (1984), 2,057 (1991), 2,000 (1992); G. A. Hick 2,713 (1988), 2,347 (1990), 2,004 (1986); G. M. Turner 2,416 (1973), 2,379 (1970), 2,101 (1981).

Twice: G. Boycott 2,503 (1971), 2,051 (1970); J. H. Edrich 2,238 (1969), 2,031 (1971); A. I. Kallicharran 2,301 (1984), 2,120 (1982); Zaheer Abbas 2,554 (1976), 2,306 (1981).

Once: M. Azharuddin 2,016 (1991); J. B. Bolus 2,143 (1970); P. D. Bowler 2,044 (1992); B. C. Broad 2,226 (1990); A. R. Butcher 2,116 (1990); C. G. Greenidge 2,035 (1986); M. J. Harris 2,238 (1971); D. L. Haynes 2,346 (1990); Javed Miandad 2,083 (1981); A. J. Lamb 2,049 (1981); B. C. Lara 2,066 (1994); K. S. McEwan 2,176 (1983); Majid Khan 2,074 (1972); A. A. Metcalfe 2,047 (1990); H. Morris 2,276 (1990); M. R. Ramprakash 2,258 (1995); D. W. Randall 2,151 (1990); I. V. A. Richards 2,161 (1977); R. T. Robinson 2,032 (1984); M. A. Roseberry 2,044 (1992); C. L. Smith 2,000 (1985); R. T. Virgin 2,223 (1970); D. M. Ward 2,072 (1990); M. E. Waugh 2,072 (1990).

1,000 RUNS IN A SEASON MOST TIMES

(Includes Overseas Tours and Seasons)

28 times: W. G. Grace 2,000 (6); F. E. Woolley 3,000 (1), 2,000 (12).

27 times: M. C. Cowdrey 2,000 (2); C. P. Mead 3,000 (2), 2,000 (9).

26 times: G. Boycott 2,000 (3); J. B. Hobbs 3,000 (1), 2,000 (16).

25 times: E. H. Hendren 3,000 (3), 2,000 (12).

24 times: D. L. Amiss 2,000 (1); W. G. Quaife 2,000 (1); H. Sutcliffe 3,000 (3), 2,000 (12).

23 times: A. Jones.

22 times: T. W. Graveney 2,000 (7); W. R. Hammond 3,000 (3), 2,000 (9).

21 times: D. Denton 2,000 (5); J. H. Edrich 2,000 (6); G. A. Gooch 2,000 (5); W. Rhodes 2,000 (2).

20 times: D. B. Close; K. W. R. Fletcher; G. Gunn; T. W. Hayward 3,000 (2), 2,000 (8); James Langridge 2,000 (1); J. M. Parks 2,000 (3); A. Sandham 2,000 (8); M. J. K. Smith 3,000 (1), 2,000 (5); C. Washbrook 2,000 (2).

19 times: M. W. Gatting 2,000 (3); J. W. Hearne 2,000 (4); G. H. Hirst 2,000 (3); D. Kenyon 2,000 (7); E. Tyldesley 3,000 (1), 2,000 (5); J. T. Tyldesley 3,000 (1), 2,000 (4).

18 times: L. G. Berry 2,000 (1); H. T. W. Hardinge 2,000 (5); R. E. Marshall 2,000 (6); P. A. Perrin; G. M. Turner 2,000 (3); R. E. S. Wyatt 2,000 (5).

17 times: L. E. G. Ames 3,000 (1), 2,000 (5); T. E. Bailey 2,000 (1); D. Brookes 2,000 (6); D. C. S. Compton 3,000 (1), 2,000 (5); C. G. Greenidge 2,000 (1); L. Hutton 3,000 (1), 2,000 (8); J. G. Langridge 2,000 (11); M. Leyland 2,000 (3); I. V. A. Richards 2,000 (1); K. G. Suttle 2,000 (1); Zaheer Abbas 2,000 (2).

16 times: D. G. Bradman 2,000 (4); D. E. Davies 2,000 (1); E. G. Hayes 2,000 (2); C. A. Milton 2,000 (1); J. O'Connor 2,000 (1); C. T. Radley; James Seymour 2,000 (1); C. J. Tavaré.

15 times: G. Barker; K. F. Barrington 2,000 (3); E. H. Bowley 2,000 (4); M. H. Denness; A. E. Dipper 2,000 (5); H. E. Dollery 2,000 (2); W. J. Edrich 3,000 (1), 2,000 (8); J. H. Hampshire; P. Holmes 2,000 (7); Mushtaq Mohammad; R. B. Nicholls 2,000 (1); P. H. Parfitt 2,000 (3); W. G. A. Parkhouse 2,000 (1); B. A. Richards 2,000 (1); J. D. Robertson 2,000 (9); G. S. Sobers; M. J. Stewart 2,000 (1).

Notes: F. E. Woolley reached 1,000 runs in 28 consecutive seasons (1907-1938), C. P. Mead in 27 (1906-1936).

Outside England, 1,000 runs in a season has been reached most times by D. G. Bradman (in 12 seasons in Australia).

Three batsmen have scored 1,000 runs in a season in each of four different countries: G. S. Sobers in West Indies, England, India and Australia; M. C. Cowdrey and G. Boycott in England, South Africa, West Indies and Australia.

HIGHEST AGGREGATES OUTSIDE ENGLAND

	Season	I	NO	R	HS	100s	Avge
In Australia D. G. Bradman	1928-29	24	6	1,690	340*	7	93.88
In South Africa J. R. Reid	1961-62	30	2	1,915	203	7	68.39
In West Indies E. H. Hendren	1929-30	18	5	1,765	254*	6	135.76
In New Zealand M. D. Crowe	1986-87	21	3	1,676	175*	8	93.11
In India C. G. Borde	1964-65	28	3	1,604	168	6	64.16
In Pakistan Saadat Ali	1983-84	27	1	1,649	208	4	63.42
In Sri Lanka R. P. Arnold	1995-96	24	3	1,475	217*	5	70.23
In Zimbabwe G. W. Flower	1994-95	20	3	983	201*	4	57.82

Note: In more than one country, the following aggregates of over 2,000 runs have been recorded:

M. Amarnath (P/I/WI)	1982-83	34	6	2,234	207	9	79.78
J. R. Reid (SA/A/NZ)	1961-62	40	2	2,188	203	7	57.57
S. M. Gavaskar (I/P)	1978-79	30	6	2,121	205	10	88.37
R. B. Simpson (I/P/A/WI)	1964-65	34	4	2,063	201	8	68.76

LEADING BATSMEN IN AN ENGLISH SEASON

(Qualification: 8 completed innings)

Season	Leading scorer	Runs	Avge	Top of averages	Runs	Avge
1946	D. C. S. Compton	2,403	61.61	W. R. Hammond	1,783	84.90
1947	D. C. S. Compton	3,816	90.85	D. C. S. Compton	3,816	90.85
1948	L. Hutton	2,654	64.73	D. G. Bradman	2,428	89.92
1949	L. Hutton	3,429	68.58	J. Hardstaff	2,251	72.61

Season	Leading scorer	Runs	Avge	Top of averages	Runs	Avge
1950	R. T. Simpson	2,576	62.82	E. Weekes	2,310	79.65
1951	J. D. Robertson	2,917	56.09	P. B. H. May	2,339	68.79
1952	L. Hutton	2,567	61.11	D. S. Sheppard	2,262	64.62
1953	W. J. Edrich	2,557	47.35	R. N. Harvey	2,040	65.80
1954	D. Kenyon	2,636	51.68	D. C. S. Compton	1,524	58.61
1955	D. J. Insole	2,427	42.57	D. J. McGlew	1,871	58.46
1956	T. W. Graveney	2,397	49.93	K. Mackay	1,103	52.52
1957	T. W. Graveney	2,361	49.18	P. B. H. May	2,347	61.76
1958	P. B. H. May	2,231	63.74	P. B. H. May	2,231	63.74
1959	M. J. K. Smith	3,245	57.94	V. L. Manjrekar	755	68.63
1960	M. J. K. Smith	2,551	45.55	R. Subba Row	1,503	55.66
1961	W. E. Alley	3,019	56.96	W. M. Lawry	2,019	61.18
1962	J. H. Edrich	2,482	51.70	R. T. Simpson	867	54.18
1963	J. B. Bolus	2,190	41.32	G. S. Sobers	1,333	47.60
1964	T. W. Graveney	2,385	54.20	K. F. Barrington	1,872	62.40
1965	J. H. Edrich	2,319	62.67	M. C. Cowdrey	2,093	63.42
1966	A. R. Lewis	2,198	41.47	G. S. Sobers	1,349	61.31
1967	C. A. Milton	2,089	46.42	K. F. Barrington	2,059	68.63
1968	B. A. Richards	2,395	47.90	G. Boycott	1,487	64.65
1969	J. H. Edrich	2,238	69.93	J. H. Edrich	2,238	69.93
1970	G. M. Turner	2,379	61.00	G. S. Sobers	1,742	75.73
1971	G. Boycott	2,503	100.12	G. Boycott	2,503	100.12
1972	Majid Khan	2,074	61.00	G. Boycott	1,230	72.35
1973	G. M. Turner	2,416	67.11	G. M. Turner	2,416	67.11
1974	R. T. Virgin	1,936	56.94	C. H. Lloyd	1,458	63.39
1975	G. Boycott	1,915	73.65	R. B. Kanhai	1,073	82.53
1976	Zaheer Abbas	2,554	75.11	Zaheer Abbas	2,554	75.11
1977	I. V. A. Richards	2,161	65.48	G. Boycott	1,701	68.04
1978	D. L. Amiss	2,030	53.42	C. E. B. Rice	1,871	66.82
1979	K. C. Wessels	1,800	52.94	G. Boycott	1,538	102.53
1980	P. N. Kirsten	1,895	63.16	A. J. Lamb	1,797	66.55
1981	Zaheer Abbas	2,306	88.69	Zaheer Abbas	2,306	88.69
1982	A. I. Kallicharran	2,120	66.25	G. M. Turner	1,171	90.07
1983	K. S. McEwan	2,176	64.00	I. V. A. Richards	1,204	75.25
1984	G. A. Gooch	2,559	67.34	C. G. Greenidge	1,069	82.23
1985	G. A. Gooch	2,208	71.22	I. V. A. Richards	1,836	76.50
1986	C. G. Greenidge	2,035	67.83	C. G. Greenidge	2,035	67.83
1987	G. A. Hick	1,879	52.19	M. D. Crowe	1,627	67.79
1988	G. A. Hick	2,713	77.51	R. A. Harper	622	77.75
1989	S. J. Cook	2,241	60.56	D. M. Jones	1,510	88.82
1990	G. A. Gooch	2,746	101.70	G. A. Gooch	2,746	101.70
1991	S. J. Cook	2,755	81.02	C. L. Hooper	1,501	93.81
1992	{ P. D. Bowler	2,044	65.93	Salim Malik	1,184	78.93
	{ M. A. Roseberry	2,044	56.77			
1993	G. A. Gooch	2,023	63.21	D. C. Boon	1,437	75.63
1994	B. C. Lara	2,066	89.82	J. D. Carr	1,543	90.76
1995	M. R. Ramprakash	2,258	77.86	M. R. Ramprakash	2,258	77.86
1996	G. A. Gooch	1,944	67.03	S. C. Ganguly	762	95.25
1997	S. P. James	1,775	68.26	G. A. Hick	1,524	69.27

Notes: The highest average recorded in an English season was 115.66 (2,429 runs, 26 innings) by D. G. Bradman in 1938.

In 1953 W. A. Johnston averaged 102.00 from 17 innings, 16 not out.

25,000 RUNS IN A CAREER

Dates in italics denote the first half of an overseas season; i.e. *1945* denotes the 1945-46 season.

		Career	R	I	NO	HS	100s	Avge
1	J. B. Hobbs	1905-34	61,237	1,315	106	316*	197	50.65
2	F. E. Woolley	1906-38	58,969	1,532	85	305*	145	40.75
3	E. H. Hendren	1907-38	57,611	1,300	166	301*	170	50.80

		Career	R	I	NO	HS	100s	Avge
4	C. P. Mead	1905-36	55,061	1,340	185	280*	153	47.67
5	W. G. Grace	1865-1908	54,896	1,493	105	344	126	39.55
6	W. R. Hammond	1920-51	50,551	1,005	104	336*	167	56.10
7	H. Sutcliffe	1919-45	50,138	1,088	123	313	149	51.95
8	G. Boycott	1962-86	48,426	1,014	162	261*	151	56.83
9	T. W. Graveney	1948-71	47,793	1,223	159	258	122	44.91
10	**G. A. Gooch**	**1973-97**	**44,841**	**988**	**75**	**333**	**128**	**49.11**
11	T. W. Hayward	1893-1914	43,551	1,138	96	315*	104	41.79
12	D. L. Amiss	1960-87	43,423	1,139	126	262*	102	42.86
13	M. C. Cowdrey	1950-76	42,719	1,130	134	307	107	42.89
14	A. Sandham	1911-37	41,284	1,000	79	325	107	44.82
15	L. Hutton	1934-60	40,140	814	91	364	129	55.51
16	M. J. K. Smith	1951-75	39,832	1,091	139	204	69	41.84
17	W. Rhodes	1898-1930	39,802	1,528	237	267*	58	30.83
18	J. H. Edrich	1956-78	39,790	979	104	310*	103	45.47
19	R. E. S. Wyatt	1923-57	39,405	1,141	157	232	85	40.04
20	D. C. S. Compton	1936-64	38,942	839	88	300	123	51.85
21	E. Tyldesley	1909-36	38,874	961	106	256*	102	45.46
22	J. T. Tyldesley	1895-1923	37,897	994	62	295*	86	40.66
23	K. W. R. Fletcher	1962-88	37,665	1,167	170	228*	63	37.77
24	C. G. Greenidge	1970-92	37,354	889	75	273*	92	45.88
25	J. W. Hearne	1909-36	37,252	1,025	116	285*	96	40.98
26	L. E. G. Ames	1926-51	37,248	951	95	295	102	43.51
27	D. Kenyon	1946-67	37,002	1,159	59	259	74	33.63
28	W. J. Edrich	1934-58	36,965	964	92	267*	86	42.39
29	J. M. Parks	1949-76	36,673	1,227	172	205*	51	34.76
30	D. Denton	1894-1920	36,479	1,163	70	221	69	33.37
31	G. H. Hirst	1891-1929	36,323	1,215	151	341	60	34.13
32	I. V. A. Richards	1971-93	36,212	796	63	322	114	49.40
33	A. Jones	1957-83	36,049	1,168	72	204*	56	32.89
34	W. G. Quaife	1894-1928	36,012	1,203	185	255*	72	35.37
35	R. E. Marshall	1945-72	35,725	1,053	59	228*	68	35.94
36	**M. W. Gatting**	**1975-97**	**35,410**	**832**	**120**	**258**	**92**	**49.73**
37	G. Gunn	1902-32	35,208	1,061	82	220	62	35.96
38	D. B. Close	1949-86	34,994	1,225	173	198	52	33.26
39	Zaheer Abbas	1965-86	34,843	768	92	274	108	51.54
40	J. G. Langridge	1928-55	34,380	984	66	250*	76	37.45
41	G. M. Turner	1964-82	34,346	792	101	311*	103	49.70
42	C. Washbrook	1933-64	34,101	906	107	251*	76	42.67
43	M. Leyland	1920-48	33,660	932	101	263	80	40.50
44	H. T. W. Hardinge	1902-33	33,519	1,021	103	263*	75	36.51
45	R. Abel	1881-1904	33,124	1,007	73	357*	74	35.46
46	A. I. Kallicharran	1966-90	32,650	834	86	243*	87	43.64
47	A. J. Lamb	1972-95	32,502	772	108	294	89	48.94
48	C. A. Milton	1948-74	32,150	1,078	125	170	56	33.73
49	J. D. Robertson	1937-59	31,914	897	46	331*	67	37.50
50	J. Hardstaff, jun	1930-55	31,847	812	94	266	83	44.35
51	James Langridge	1924-53	31,716	1,058	157	167	42	35.20
52	K. F. Barrington	1953-68	31,714	831	136	256	76	45.63
53	C. H. Lloyd	1963-86	31,232	730	96	242*	79	49.26
54	Mushtaq Mohammad	1956-85	31,091	843	104	303*	72	42.07
55	C. B. Fry	1892-1921	30,886	658	43	258*	94	50.22
56	D. Brookes	1934-59	30,874	925	70	257	71	36.10
57	P. Holmes	1913-35	30,573	810	84	315*	67	42.11
58	R. T. Simpson	1944-63	30,546	852	55	259	64	38.32
59	{ L. G. Berry	1924-51	30,225	1,056	57	232	45	30.25
	{ K. G. Suttle	1949-71	30,225	1,064	92	204*	49	31.09
61	P. A. Perrin	1896-1928	29,709	918	91	343*	66	35.92

		Career	R	I	NO	HS	100s	Avge
62	P. F. Warner	1894-1929	29,028	875	75	244	60	36.28
63	R. B. Kanhai	*1954-81*	28,774	669	82	256	83	49.01
64	J. O'Connor	1921-39	28,764	903	79	248	72	34.90
65	Javed Miandad	*1973-93*	28,647	631	95	311	80	53.44
66	T. E. Bailey	1945-67	28,641	1,072	215	205	28	33.42
67	**G. A. Hick**	***1983-97***	**28,473**	**565**	**59**	**405***	**96**	**56.27**
68	D. W. Randall	1972-93	28,456	827	81	237	52	38.14
69	E. H. Bowley	1912-34	28,378	859	47	283	52	34.94
70	B. A. Richards	*1964-82*	28,358	576	58	356	80	54.74
71	G. S. Sobers	*1952-74*	28,315	609	93	365*	86	54.87
72	A. E. Dipper	1908-32	28,075	865	69	252*	53	35.27
73	D. G. Bradman	*1927-48*	28,067	338	43	452*	117	95.14
74	J. H. Hampshire	1961-84	28,059	924	112	183*	43	34.55
75	P. B. H. May	1948-63	27,592	618	77	285*	85	51.00
76	B. F. Davison	*1967-87*	27,453	766	79	189	53	39.96
77	Majid Khan	*1961-84*	27,444	700	62	241	73	43.01
78	A. C. Russell	1908-30	27,358	717	59	273	71	41.57
79	E. G. Hayes	1896-1926	27,318	896	48	276	48	32.21
80	A. E. Fagg	1932-57	27,291	803	46	269*	58	36.05
81	James Seymour	1900-26	27,237	911	62	218*	53	32.08
82	W. Larkins	1972-95	27,142	842	54	252	59	34.44
83	A. R. Border	*1976-95*	27,131	625	97	205	70	51.38
84	P. H. Parfitt	1956-*73*	26,924	845	104	200*	58	36.33
85	G. L. Jessop	1894-1914	26,698	855	37	286	53	32.63
86	K. S. McEwan	*1972-91*	26,628	705	67	218	74	41.73
87	D. E. Davies	1924-54	26,564	1,032	80	287*	32	27.90
88	A. Shrewsbury	1875-1902	26,505	813	90	267	59	36.65
89	**R. T. Robinson**	**1978-97**	**26,493**	**699**	**82**	**220***	**62**	**42.93**
90	M. J. Stewart	1954-72	26,492	898	93	227*	49	32.90
91	C. T. Radley	1964-87	26,441	880	134	200	46	35.44
92	D. I. Gower	1975-93	26,339	727	70	228	53	40.08
93	C. E. B. Rice	*1969-93*	26,331	766	123	246	48	40.95
94	Younis Ahmed	*1961-86*	26,073	762	118	221*	46	40.48
95	P. E. Richardson	1949-65	26,055	794	41	185	44	34.60
96	**D. L. Haynes**	**1976-96**	**26,030**	**639**	**72**	**255***	**61**	**45.90**
97	M. H. Denness	1959-80	25,886	838	65	195	33	33.48
98	S. M. Gavaskar	*1966-87*	25,834	563	61	340	81	51.46
99	J. W. H. Makepeace	1906-30	25,799	778	66	203	43	36.23
100	W. Gunn	1880-1904	25,691	850	72	273	48	33.02
101	W. Watson	1939-64	25,670	753	109	257	55	39.86
102	G. Brown	1908-33	25,649	1,012	52	232*	37	26.71
103	G. M. Emmett	1936-59	25,602	865	50	188	37	31.41
104	J. B. Bolus	1956-75	25,598	833	81	202*	39	34.03
105	W. E. Russell	1956-72	25,525	796	64	193	41	34.87
106	**C. W. J. Athey**	**1976-97**	**25,453**	**784**	**71**	**184**	**55**	**35.69**
107	C. J. Barnett	1927-*53*	25,389	821	45	259	48	32.71
108	L. B. Fishlock	1931-52	25,376	699	54	253	56	39.34
109	D. J. Insole	1947-63	25,241	743	72	219*	54	37.61
110	J. M. Brearley	1961-83	25,185	768	102	312*	45	37.81
111	J. Vine	1896-1922	25,171	920	79	202	34	29.92
112	R. M. Prideaux	1958-*74*	25,136	808	75	202*	41	34.29
113	J. H. King	1895-1925	25,122	988	69	227*	34	27.33
114	J. G. Wright	*1975-92*	25,073	636	44	192	59	42.35

Bold type denotes those who played in 1996-97 and 1997 seasons.

Note: Some works of reference provide career figures which differ from those in this list, owing to the exclusion or inclusion of matches recognised or not recognised as first-class by *Wisden*.

Current Players with 20,000 Runs

	Career	R	I	NO	HS	100s	Avge
K. J. Barnett	1979-97	24,327	670	62	239*	52	40.01
K. C. Wessels	1973-96	23,493	512	46	254	62	50.41
P. N. Kirsten........	1973-96	22,635	568	59	271	57	44.46
R. A. Smith.........	1980-97	21,645	568	78	209*	53	44.17
M. D. Moxon	1981-97	21,161	541	47	274*	45	42.83
T. S. Curtis	1979-97	20,832	579	67	248	43	40.68
D. C. Boon	1978-97	20,583	496	44	227	63	45.53

CAREER AVERAGE OVER 50

(Qualification: 10,000 runs)

Avge		Career	I	NO	R	HS	100s
95.14	D. G. Bradman	1927-48	338	43	28,067	452*	117
71.22	V. M. Merchant	1929-51	229	43	13,248	359*	44
65.18	W. H. Ponsford	1920-34	235	23	13,819	437	47
64.99	W. M. Woodfull	1921-34	245	39	13,388	284	49
58.24	A. L. Hassett	1932-53	322	32	16,890	232	59
58.19	V. S. Hazare	1934-66	365	45	18,621	316*	60
57.22	A. F. Kippax	1918-35	256	33	12,762	315*	43
56.83	G. Boycott	1962-86	1,014	162	48,426	261*	151
56.55	C. L. Walcott	1941-63	238	29	11,820	314*	40
56.37	K. S. Ranjitsinhji	1893-1920	500	62	24,692	285*	72
56.27	**G. A. Hick**	**1983-97**	**565**	**59**	**28,473**	**405***	**96**
56.22	R. B. Simpson	1952-77	436	62	21,029	359	60
56.10	W. R. Hammond	1920-51	1,005	104	50,551	336*	167
56.02	M. D. Crowe	1979-95	412	62	19,608	299	71
55.51	L. Hutton	1934-60	814	91	40,140	364	129
55.34	E. D. Weekes	1944-64	241	24	12,010	304*	36
54.87	G. S. Sobers	1952-74	609	93	28,315	365*	86
54.74	B. A. Richards	1964-82	576	58	28,358	356	80
54.67	R. G. Pollock	1960-86	437	54	20,940	274	64
54.24	F. M. M. Worrell	1941-64	326	49	15,025	308*	39
54.07	**B. C. Lara**	**1987-96**	**209**	**6**	**10,978**	**501***	**31**
54.07	**M. E. Waugh**	**1985-97**	**419**	**52**	**19,846**	**229***	**64**
53.78	R. M. Cowper	1959-69	228	31	10,595	307	26
53.67	A. R. Morris	1940-63	250	15	12,614	290	46
53.44	Javed Miandad	1973-93	631	95	28,647	311	80
52.86	D. B. Vengsarkar	1975-91	390	52	17,868	284	55
52.32	Hanif Mohammad	1951-75	371	45	17,059	499	55
52.27	P. R. Umrigar	1944-67	350	41	16,154	252*	49
52.20	G. S. Chappell	1966-83	542	72	24,535	247*	74
51.95	H. Sutcliffe	1919-45	1,088	123	50,138	313	149
51.89	**S. R. Waugh**	**1984-97**	**361**	**61**	**15,568**	**216***	**45**
51.85	D. C. S. Compton	1936-64	839	88	38,942	300	123
51.83	**M. Azharuddin**	**1981-96**	**300**	**33**	**13,840**	**226**	**49**
51.81	**D. M. Jones**	**1981-97**	**394**	**41**	**18,292**	**324***	**52**
51.54	Zaheer Abbas	1965-86	768	92	34,843	274	108
51.53	A. D. Nourse	1931-52	269	27	12,472	260*	41
51.46	S. M. Gavaskar	1966-87	563	61	25,834	340	81
51.44	W. A. Brown	1932-49	284	15	13,838	265*	39
51.38	A. R. Border	1976-95	625	97	27,131	205	70
51.00	P. B. H. May	1948-63	618	77	27,592	285*	85
50.95	N. C. O'Neill	1955-67	306	34	13,859	284	45
50.93	R. N. Harvey	1946-62	461	35	21,699	231*	67
50.90	W. M. Lawry	1955-71	417	49	18,734	266	50

Avge		Career	I	NO	R	HS	100s
50.90	A. V. Mankad	1963-82	326	71	12,980	265	31
50.80	E. H. Hendren	1907-38	1,300	166	57,611	301*	170
50.65	J. B. Hobbs	1905-34	1,315	106	61,237	316*	197
50.58	S. J. Cook	1972-94	475	57	21,143	313*	64
50.22	C. B. Fry	1892-1921	658	43	30,886	258*	94
50.41	**K. C. Wessels**	**1973-96**	**512**	**46**	**23,493**	**254**	**62**
50.06	**Asif Mujtaba**	**1984-96**	**309**	**60**	**12,465**	**208**	**37**
50.01	Shafiq Ahmad	1967-90	449	58	19,555	217*	53

Note: G. A. Headley (*1927-1954*) scored 9,921 runs, average 69.86.

Bold type denotes those who played in 1996-97 and 1997 seasons.

FASTEST FIFTIES

Minutes

11	C. I. J. Smith (66)	Middlesex v Gloucestershire at Bristol	1938
14	S. J. Pegler (50)	South Africans v Tasmania at Launceston	1910-11
14	F. T. Mann (53)	Middlesex v Nottinghamshire at Lord's	1921
14	H. B. Cameron (56)	Transvaal v Orange Free State at Johannesburg ...	1934-35
14	C. I. J. Smith (52)	Middlesex v Kent at Maidstone	1935

Note: The following fast fifties were scored in contrived circumstances when runs were given from full tosses and long hops to expedite a declaration: C. C. Inman (8 minutes), Leicestershire v Nottinghamshire at Nottingham, 1965; G. Chapple (10 minutes), Lancashire v Glamorgan at Manchester, 1993; T. M. Moody (11 minutes), Warwickshire v Glamorgan at Swansea, 1990; A. J. Stewart (14 minutes), Surrey v Kent at Dartford, 1986; M. P. Maynard (14 minutes), Glamorgan v Yorkshire at Cardiff, 1987.

FASTEST HUNDREDS

Minutes

35	P. G. H. Fender (113*)	Surrey v Northamptonshire at Northampton	1920
40	G. L. Jessop (101)	Gloucestershire v Yorkshire at Harrogate	1897
40	Ahsan-ul-Haq (100*)	Muslims v Sikhs at Lahore	1923-24
42	G. L. Jessop (191)	Gentlemen of South v Players of South at Hastings	1907
43	A. H. Hornby (106)	Lancashire v Somerset at Manchester	1905
43	D. W. Hookes (107)	South Australia v Victoria at Adelaide	1982-83
44	R. N. S. Hobbs (100)	Essex v Australians at Chelmsford	1975

Notes: The fastest recorded authentic hundred in terms of balls received was scored off 34 balls by D. W. Hookes (above).

Research of the scorebook has shown that P. G. H. Fender scored his hundred from between 40 and 46 balls. He contributed 113 to an unfinished sixth-wicket partnership of 171 in 42 minutes with H. A. Peach.

E. B. Alletson (Nottinghamshire) scored 189 out of 227 runs in 90 minutes against Sussex at Hove in 1911. It has been estimated that his last 139 runs took 37 minutes.

The following fast hundreds were scored in contrived circumstances when runs were given from full tosses and long hops to expedite a declaration: G. Chapple (21 minutes), Lancashire v Glamorgan at Manchester, 1993; T. M. Moody (26 minutes), Warwickshire v Glamorgan at Swansea, 1990; S. J. O'Shaughnessy (35 minutes), Lancashire v Leicestershire at Manchester, 1983; C. M. Old (37 minutes), Yorkshire v Warwickshire at Birmingham, 1977; N. F. M. Popplewell (41 minutes), Somerset v Gloucestershire at Bath, 1983.

FASTEST DOUBLE-HUNDREDS

Minutes
113	R. J. Shastri (200*)	Bombay v Baroda at Bombay	1984-85
120	G. L. Jessop (286)	Gloucestershire v Sussex at Hove	1903
120	C. H. Lloyd (201*)	West Indians v Glamorgan at Swansea	1976
130	G. L. Jessop (234)	Gloucestershire v Somerset at Bristol	1905
131	V. T. Trumper (293)	Australians v Canterbury at Christchurch	1913-14

FASTEST TRIPLE-HUNDREDS

Minutes
181	D. C. S. Compton (300)	MCC v N. E. Transvaal at Benoni	1948-49
205	F. E. Woolley (305*)	MCC v Tasmania at Hobart	1911-12
205	C. G. Macartney (345)	Australians v Nottinghamshire at Nottingham	1921
213	D. G. Bradman (369)	South Australia v Tasmania at Adelaide	1935-36

300 RUNS IN ONE DAY

390*	B. C. Lara	Warwickshire v Durham at Birmingham	1994
345	C. G. Macartney	Australians v Nottinghamshire at Nottingham	1921
334	W. H. Ponsford	Victoria v New South Wales at Melbourne	1926-27
333	K. S. Duleepsinhji	Sussex v Northamptonshire at Hove	1930
331*	J. D. Robertson	Middlesex v Worcestershire at Worcester	1949
325*	B. A. Richards	S. Australia v W. Australia at Perth	1970-71
322†	E. Paynter	Lancashire v Sussex at Hove	1937
322	I. V. A. Richards	Somerset v Warwickshire at Taunton	1985
318	C. W. Gregory	New South Wales v Queensland at Brisbane	1906-07
317	K. R. Rutherford	New Zealanders v D. B. Close's XI at Scarborough .	1986
316†	R. H. Moore	Hampshire v Warwickshire at Bournemouth........	1937
315*	R. C. Blunt	Otago v Canterbury at Christchurch	1931-32
312*	J. M. Brearley	MCC Under-25 v North Zone at Peshawar........	1966-67
311*	G. M. Turner	Worcestershire v Warwickshire at Worcester	1982
311*	N. H. Fairbrother	Lancashire v Surrey at The Oval.................	1990
309*	D. G. Bradman	Australia v England at Leeds....................	1930
307*	W. H. Ashdown	Kent v Essex at Brentwood	1934
306*	A. Ducat	Surrey v Oxford University at The Oval...........	1919
305*	F. R. Foster	Warwickshire v Worcestershire at Dudley	1914

† *E. Paynter's 322 and R. H. Moore's 316 were scored on the same day: July 28, 1937.*

These scores do not necessarily represent the complete innings. See pages 179-181.

1,000 RUNS IN MAY

	Runs	Avge
W. G. Grace, May 9 to May 30, 1895 (22 days):		
13, 103, 18, 25, 288, 52, 257, 73*, 18, 169	1,016	112.88
Grace was within two months of completing his 47th year.		
W. R. Hammond, May 7 to May 31, 1927 (25 days):		
27, 135, 108, 128, 17, 11, 99, 187, 4, 30, 83, 7, 192, 14	1,042	74.42
Hammond scored his 1,000th run on May 28, thus equalling		
Grace's record of 22 days.		
C. Hallows, May 5 to May 31, 1928 (27 days):		
100, 101, 51*, 123, 101*, 22, 74, 104, 58, 34*, 232.................	1,000	125.00

1,000 RUNS IN APRIL AND MAY

	Runs	*Avge*

T. W. Hayward, April 16 to May 31, 1900:
120*, 55, 108, 131*, 55, 193, 120, 5, 6, 3, 40, 146, 92 1,074   97.63

D. G. Bradman, April 30 to May 31, 1930:
236, 185*, 78, 9, 48*, 66, 4, 44, 252*, 32, 47* 1,001   143.00
    On April 30 Bradman was 75 not out.

D. G. Bradman, April 30 to May 31, 1938:
258, 58, 137, 278, 2, 143, 145*, 5, 30* 1,056   150.85
    Bradman scored 258 on April 30, and his 1,000th run on May 27.

W. J. Edrich, April 30 to May 31, 1938:
104, 37, 115, 63, 20*, 182, 71, 31, 53*, 45, 15, 245, 0, 9, 20* 1,010   84.16
    Edrich was 21 not out on April 30. All his runs were scored at Lord's.

G. M. Turner, April 24 to May 31, 1973:
41, 151*, 143, 85, 7, 8, 17*, 81, 13, 53, 44, 153*, 3, 2, 66*, 30, 10*,
111 1,018   78.30

G. A. Hick, April 17 to May 29, 1988:
61, 37, 212, 86, 14, 405*, 8, 11, 6, 7, 172 1,019   101.90
    Hick scored a record 410 runs in April, and his 1,000th run on May 28.

1,000 RUNS IN TWO SEPARATE MONTHS

Only four batsmen, C. B. Fry, K. S. Ranjitsinhji, H. Sutcliffe and L. Hutton, have scored over 1,000 runs in each of two months in the same season. L. Hutton, by scoring 1,294 in June 1949, made more runs in a single month than anyone else. He also made 1,050 in August 1949.

MOST RUNS SCORED OFF ONE OVER

(All instances refer to six-ball overs)

36	G. S. Sobers	off M. A. Nash, Nottinghamshire v Glamorgan at Swansea (six sixes)	1968
36	R. J. Shastri	off Tilak Raj, Bombay v Baroda at Bombay (six sixes)	1984-85
34	E. B. Alletson	off E. H. Killick, Nottinghamshire v Sussex at Hove (46604446; including two no-balls)	1911
34	F. C. Hayes	off M. A. Nash, Lancashire v Glamorgan at Swansea (646666)	1977
32	I. T. Botham	off I. R. Snook, England XI v Central Districts at Palmerston North (466466)	1983-84
32	P. W. G. Parker	off A. I. Kallicharran, Sussex v Warwickshire at Birmingham (466664)	1982
32	I. R. Redpath	off N. Rosendorff, Australians v Orange Free State at Bloemfontein (666644)	1969-70
32	C. C. Smart	off G. Hill, Glamorgan v Hampshire at Cardiff (664664)	1935

Notes: The following instances have been excluded from the above table because of the bowlers' compliance: 34 – M. P. Maynard off S. A. Marsh, Glamorgan v Kent at Swansea, 1992; 34 – G. Chapple off P. A. Cottey, Lancashire v Glamorgan at Manchester, 1993; 32 – C. C. Inman off N. W. Hill, Leicestershire v Nottinghamshire at Nottingham, 1965; 32 – T. E. Jesty off R. J. Boyd-Moss, Hampshire v Northamptonshire at Southampton, 1984; 32 – G. Chapple off P. A. Cottey, Lancashire v Glamorgan at Manchester, 1993. Chapple's 34 and 32 came off successive overs from Cottey.

There were 35 runs off an over received by A. T. Reinholds off H. T. Davis, Auckland v Wellington at Auckland 1995-96, but this included six no-balls (counting as two runs each), four byes and only 19 off the bat.

The greatest number of runs scored off an eight-ball over is 34 (40446664) by R. M. Edwards off M. C. Carew, Governor-General's XI v West Indians at Auckland, 1968-69.

In a Shell Trophy match against Canterbury at Christchurch in 1989-90, R. H. Vance (Wellington), acting on the instructions of his captain, deliberately conceded 77 runs in an over of full tosses which contained 17 no-balls and, owing to the umpire's understandable miscalculation, only five legitimate deliveries.

MOST SIXES IN AN INNINGS

16	A. Symonds (254*)	Gloucestershire v Glamorgan at Abergavenny	1995
15	J. R. Reid (296)	Wellington v N. Districts at Wellington	1962-63
14	Shakti Singh (128)	Himachal Pradesh v Haryana at Dharmsala	1990-91
13	Majid Khan (147*)	Pakistanis v Glamorgan at Swansea	1967
13	C. G. Greenidge (273*)	D. H. Robins' XI v Pakistanis at Eastbourne	1974
13	C. G. Greenidge (259)	Hampshire v Sussex at Southampton	1975
13	G. W. Humpage (254)	Warwickshire v Lancashire at Southport	1982
13	R. J. Shastri (200*)	Bombay v Baroda at Bombay	1984-85
12	Gulfraz Khan (207)	Railways v Universities at Lahore	1976-77
12	I. T. Botham (138*)	Somerset v Warwickshire at Birmingham	1985
12	R. A. Harper (234)	Northamptonshire v Gloucestershire at Northampton ..	1986
12	D. M. Jones (248)	Australians v Warwickshire at Birmingham	1989
12	D. N. Patel (204)	Auckland v Northern Districts at Auckland	1991-92
12	W. V. Raman (206)	Tamil Nadu v Kerala at Madras	1991-92
12	G. D. Lloyd (241)	Lancashire v Essex at Chelmsford	1996
12	Wasim Akram (257*)	Pakistan v Zimbabwe at Sheikhupura	1996-97
11	C. K. Nayudu (153)	Hindus v MCC at Bombay	1926-27
11	C. J. Barnett (194)	Gloucestershire v Somerset at Bath	1934
11	R. Benaud (135)	Australians v T. N. Pearce's XI at Scarborough......	1953
11	R. Bora (126)	Assam v Tripura at Gauhati	1987-88
11	G. A. Hick (405*)	Worcestershire v Somerset at Taunton	1988

MOST SIXES IN A MATCH

20	A. Symonds (254*, 76)	Gloucestershire v Glamorgan at Abergavenny	1995
17	W. J. Stewart (155, 125)	Warwickshire v Lancashire at Blackpool	1959

MOST SIXES IN A SEASON

80	I. T. Botham	1985	49	I. V. A. Richards	1985
66	A. W. Wellard.................	1935	48	A. W. Carr	1925
57	A. W. Wellard.................	1936	48	J. H. Edrich	1965
57	A. W. Wellard.................	1938	48	A. Symonds	1995
51	A. W. Wellard.................	1933			

MOST BOUNDARIES IN AN INNINGS

	4s/6s			
72	62/10	B. C. Lara (501*)	Warwickshire v Durham at Birmingham ..	1994
68	68/–	P. A. Perrin (343*)	Essex v Derbyshire at Chesterfield.......	1904
64	64/–	Hanif Mohammad (499)	Karachi v Bahawalpur at Karachi	1958-59
63	62/1	A. C. MacLaren (424)	Lancashire v Somerset at Taunton	1895
57	52/5	J. H. Edrich (310*)	England v New Zealand at Leeds	1965
55	55/–	C. W. Gregory (383)	NSW v Queensland at Brisbane	1906-07
55	53/2	G. R. Marsh (355*)	W. Australia v S. Australia at Perth	1989-90
54	53/1	G. H. Hirst (341)	Yorkshire v Leicestershire at Leicester ...	1905
54	51/2†	S. V. Manjrekar (377)	Bombay v Hyderabad at Bombay	1990-91
53	53/–	A. W. Nourse (304*)	Natal v Transvaal at Johannesburg.......	1919-20
53	45/8	K. R. Rutherford (317)	New Zealanders v D. B. Close's XI at	
			Scarborough	1986
52	47/5	N. H. Fairbrother (366)	Lancashire v Surrey at The Oval	1990
51	47/4	C. G. Macartney (345)	Australians v Notts at Nottingham......	1921
51	50/1	B. B. Nimbalkar (443*)	Maharashtra v Kathiawar at Poona	1948-49
50	46/4	D. G. Bradman (369)	S. Australia v Tasmania at Adelaide	1935-36
50	47/–‡	A. Ducat (306*)	Surrey v Oxford U. at The Oval	1919
50	35/15	J. R. Reid (296)	Wellington v N. Districts at Wellington ...	1962-63
50	42/8	I. V. A. Richards (322)	Somerset v Warwickshire at Taunton	1985

† Plus one five.

‡ Plus three fives.

HIGHEST PARTNERSHIPS

577	V. S. Hazare (288) and Gul Mahomed (319), fourth wicket, Baroda v Holkar at Baroda.	1946-47
576	S. T. Jayasuriya (340) and R. S. Mahanama (225), second wicket, Sri Lanka v India at Colombo	1997-98
574*	F. M. M. Worrell (255*) and C. L. Walcott (314*), fourth wicket, Barbados v Trinidad at Port-of-Spain	1945-46
561	Waheed Mirza (324) and Mansoor Akhtar (224*), first wicket, Karachi Whites v Quetta at Karachi.	1976-77
555	P. Holmes (224*) and H. Sutcliffe (313), first wicket, Yorkshire v Essex at Leyton.	1932
554	J. T. Brown (300) and J. Tunnicliffe (243), first wicket, Yorkshire v Derbyshire at Chesterfield.	1898
502*	F. M. M. Worrell (308*) and J. D. C. Goddard (218*), fourth wicket, Barbados v Trinidad at Bridgetown	1943-44
490	E. H. Bowley (283) and J. G. Langridge (195), first wicket, Sussex v Middlesex at Hove	1933
487*	G. A. Headley (344*) and C. C. Passailaigue (261*), sixth wicket, Jamaica v Lord Tennyson's XI at Kingston	1931-32
475	Zahir Alam (257) and L. S. Rajput (239), second wicket, Assam v Tripura at Gauhati	1991-92

HIGHEST PARTNERSHIPS FOR EACH WICKET

The following lists include all stands above 400; otherwise the top ten for each wicket.

First Wicket

561	Waheed Mirza and Mansoor Akhtar, Karachi Whites v Quetta at Karachi	1976-77
555	P. Holmes and H. Sutcliffe, Yorkshire v Essex at Leyton	1932
554	J. T. Brown and J. Tunnicliffe, Yorkshire v Derbyshire at Chesterfield	1898
490	E. H. Bowley and J. G. Langridge, Sussex v Middlesex at Hove	1933
464	R. Sehgal and R. Lamba, Delhi v Himachal Pradesh at Delhi	1994-95
459	Wasim Jaffer and S. K. Kulkarni, Mumbai v Saurashtra at Rajkot	1996-97
456	E. R. Mayne and W. H. Ponsford, Victoria v Queensland at Melbourne	1923-24
451*	S. Desai and R. M. H. Binny, Karnataka v Kerala at Chikmagalur.	1977-78
431	M. R. J. Veletta and G. R. Marsh, Western Australia v South Australia at Perth	1989-90
428	J. B. Hobbs and A. Sandham, Surrey v Oxford University at The Oval	1926
424	I. J. Siedle and J. F. W. Nicolson, Natal v Orange Free State at Bloemfontein . .	1926-27
421	S. M. Gavaskar and G. A. Parkar, Bombay v Bengal at Bombay	1981-82
418	Kamal Najamuddin and Khalid Alvi, Karachi v Railways at Karachi	1980-81
413	V. Mankad and Pankaj Roy, India v New Zealand at Madras	1955-56
405	C. P. S. Chauhan and M. S. Gupte, Maharashtra v Vidarbha at Poona.	1972-73

Second Wicket

576	S. T. Jayasuriya and R. S. Mahanama, Sri Lanka v India at Colombo	1997-98
475	Zahir Alam and L. S. Rajput, Assam v Tripura at Gauhati	1991-92
465*	J. A. Jameson and R. B. Kanhai, Warwicks v Gloucestershire at Birmingham . .	1974
455	K. V. Bhandarkar and B. B. Nimbalkar, Maharashtra v Kathiawar at Poona	1948-49
451	W. H. Ponsford and D. G. Bradman, Australia v England at The Oval	1934
446	C. C. Hunte and G. S. Sobers, West Indies v Pakistan at Kingston	1957-58
429*	J. G. Dewes and G. H. G. Doggart, Cambridge U. v Essex at Cambridge	1949
426	Arshad Pervez and Mohsin Khan, Habib Bank v Income Tax at Lahore	1977-78
417†	K. J. Barnett and T. A. Tweats, Derbyshire v Yorkshire at Derby	1997

415   A. D. Jadeja and S. V. Manjrekar, Indians v Bowl XI at Springs   1992-93
403   G. A. Gooch and P. J. Prichard, Essex v Leicestershire at Chelmsford   1990

Third Wicket

467   A. H. Jones and M. D. Crowe, New Zealand v Sri Lanka at Wellington   1990-91
456   Khalid Irtiza and Aslam Ali, United Bank v Multan at Karachi   1975-76
451   Mudassar Nazar and Javed Miandad, Pakistan v India at Hyderabad   1982-83
445   P. E. Whitelaw and W. N. Carson, Auckland v Otago at Dunedin   1936-37
438*† G. A. Hick and T. M. Moody, Worcestershire v Hampshire at Southampton . .   1997
434   J. B. Stollmeyer and G. E. Gomez, Trinidad v British Guiana at Port-of-Spain . .   1946-47
424* W. J. Edrich and D. C. S. Compton, Middlesex v Somerset at Lord's   1948
413   D. J. Bicknell and D. M. Ward, Surrey v Kent at Canterbury   1990
410* R. S. Modi and L. Amarnath, India in England v The Rest at Calcutta   1946-47
405   A. D. Jadeja and A. S. Kaypee, Haryana v Services at Faridabad   1991-92

Fourth Wicket

577   V. S. Hazare and Gul Mahomed, Baroda v Holkar at Baroda   1946-47
574* C. L. Walcott and F. M. M. Worrell, Barbados v Trinidad at Port-of-Spain   1945-46
502* F. M. M. Worrell and J. D. C. Goddard, Barbados v Trinidad at Bridgetown . . .   1943-44
470   A. I. Kallicharran and G. W. Humpage, Warwicks v Lancs at Southport   1982
462* D. W. Hookes and W. B. Phillips, South Australia v Tasmania at Adelaide   1986-87
448   R. Abel and T. W. Hayward, Surrey v Yorkshire at The Oval   1899
425*† A. Dale and I. V. A. Richards, Glamorgan v Middlesex at Cardiff   1993
424   I. S. Lee and S. O. Quin, Victoria v Tasmania at Melbourne   1933-34
411   P. B. H. May and M. C. Cowdrey, England v West Indies at Birmingham   1957
410   G. Abraham and P. Balan Pandit, Kerala v Andhra at Palghat   1959-60
402   W. Watson and T. W. Graveney, MCC v British Guiana at Georgetown   1953-54
402   R. B. Kanhai and K. Ibadulla, Warwicks v Notts at Nottingham   1968

Fifth Wicket

464*† M. E. Waugh and S. R. Waugh, New South Wales v Western Australia at Perth   1990-91
405   S. G. Barnes and D. G. Bradman, Australia v England at Sydney   1946-47
397   W. Bardsley and C. Kelleway, New South Wales v South Australia at Sydney. .   1920-21
393   E. G. Arnold and W. B. Burns, Worcestershire v Warwickshire at Birmingham .   1909
391   A. Malhotra and S. Dogra, Delhi v Services at Delhi.   1995-96
385   S. R. Waugh and G. S. Blewett, Australia v South Africa at Johannesburg   1996-97
360   U. M. Merchant and M. N. Raiji, Bombay v Hyderabad at Bombay   1947-48
355   Altaf Shah and Tariq Bashir, HBFC v Multan at Multan   1976-77
355   A. J. Lamb and J. J. Strydom, OFS v Eastern Province at Bloemfontein   1987-88
347   D. Brookes and D. W. Barrick, Northamptonshire v Essex at Northampton   1952

Sixth Wicket

487* G. A. Headley and C. C. Passailaigue, Jamaica v Lord Tennyson's XI at Kingston   1931-32
428   W. W. Armstrong and M. A. Noble, Australians v Sussex at Hove   1902
411   R. M. Poore and E. G. Wynyard, Hampshire v Somerset at Taunton   1899
376   R. Subba Row and A. Lightfoot, Northamptonshire v Surrey at The Oval   1958
371   V. M. Merchant and R. S. Modi, Bombay v Maharashtra at Bombay   1943-44
356   W. V. Raman and A. Kripal Singh, Tamil Nadu v Goa at Panjim   1988-89
353   Salah-ud-Din and Zaheer Abbas, Karachi v East Pakistan at Karachi   1968-69
346   J. H. W. Fingleton and D. G. Bradman, Australia v England at Melbourne   1936-37
337† R. R. Montgomerie and D. J. Capel, Northamptonshire v Kent at Canterbury . . .   1995
332   N. G. Marks and G. Thomas, New South Wales v South Australia at Sydney . .   1958-59

Seventh Wicket

460	Bhupinder Singh, jun. and P. Dharmani, Punjab v Delhi at Delhi	1994-95
347	D. St E. Atkinson and C. C. Depeiza, West Indies v Australia at Bridgetown	1954-55
344	K. S. Ranjitsinhji and W. Newham, Sussex v Essex at Leyton	1902
340	K. J. Key and H. Philipson, Oxford University v Middlesex at Chiswick Park	1887
336	F. C. W. Newman and C. R. N. Maxwell, Sir J. Cahn's XI v Leicestershire at Nottingham	1935
335	C. W. Andrews and E. C. Bensted, Queensland v New South Wales at Sydney	1934-35
325	G. Brown and C. H. Abercrombie, Hampshire v Essex at Leyton	1913
323	E. H. Hendren and L. F. Townsend, MCC v Barbados at Bridgetown	1929-30
308	Waqar Hassan and Imtiaz Ahmed, Pakistan v New Zealand at Lahore	1955-56
301	C. C. Lewis and B. N. French, Nottinghamshire v Durham at Chester-le-Street	1993

Eighth Wicket

433	V. T. Trumper and A. Sims, A. Sims' Aust. XI v Canterbury at Christchurch	1913-14
313	Wasim Akram and Saqlain Mushtaq, Pakistan v Zimbabwe at Sheikhupura	1996-97
292	R. Peel and Lord Hawke, Yorkshire v Warwickshire at Birmingham	1896
270	V. T. Trumper and E. P. Barbour, New South Wales v Victoria at Sydney	1912-13
263	D. R. Wilcox and R. M. Taylor, Essex v Warwickshire at Southend	1946
255	E. A. V. Williams and E. A. Martindale, Barbados v Trinidad at Bridgetown	1935-36
249*	Shaukat Mirza and Akram Raza, Habib Bank v PNSC at Lahore	1993-94
246	L. E. G. Ames and G. O. B. Allen, England v New Zealand at Lord's	1931
243	R. J. Hartigan and C. Hill, Australia v England at Adelaide	1907-08
242*	T. J. Zoehrer and K. H. MacLeay, W. Australia v New South Wales at Perth	1990-91

Ninth Wicket

283	J. Chapman and A. Warren, Derbyshire v Warwickshire at Blackwell	1910
268	J. B. Commins and N. Boje, South Africa A v Mashonaland at Harare	1994-95
251	J. W. H. T. Douglas and S. N. Hare, Essex v Derbyshire at Leyton	1921
245	V. S. Hazare and N. D. Nagarwalla, Maharashtra v Baroda at Poona	1939-40
244*	Arshad Ayub and M. V. Ramanamurthy, Hyderabad v Bihar at Hyderabad	1986-87
239	H. B. Cave and I. B. Leggat, Central Districts v Otago at Dunedin	1952-53
232	C. Hill and E. Walkley, South Australia v New South Wales at Adelaide	1900-01
231	P. Sen and J. Mitter, Bengal v Bihar at Jamshedpur	1950-51
230	D. A. Livingstone and A. T. Castell, Hampshire v Surrey at Southampton	1962
226	C. Kelleway and W. A. Oldfield, New South Wales v Victoria at Melbourne	1925-26

Tenth Wicket

307	A. F. Kippax and J. E. H. Hooker, New South Wales v Victoria at Melbourne	1928-29
249	C. T. Sarwate and S. N. Banerjee, Indians v Surrey at The Oval	1946
235	F. E. Woolley and A. Fielder, Kent v Worcestershire at Stourbridge	1909
233	Ajay Sharma and Maninder Singh, Delhi v Bombay at Bombay	1991-92
230	R. W. Nicholls and W. Roche, Middlesex v Kent at Lord's	1899
228	R. Illingworth and K. Higgs, Leicestershire v Northamptonshire at Leicester	1977
218	F. H. Vigar and T. P. B. Smith, Essex v Derbyshire at Chesterfield	1947
211	M. Ellis and T. J. Hastings, Victoria v South Australia at Melbourne	1902-03
196*	Nadim Yousuf and Maqsood Kundi, MCB v National Bank at Lahore	1981-82
192	H. A. W. Bowell and W. H. Livsey, Hampshire v Worcs at Bournemouth	1921

† Partnerships affected by ECB or ACB regulations governing no-balls and wides.

UNUSUAL DISMISSALS

Handled the Ball

J. Grundy	MCC v Kent at Lord's	1857
G. Bennett	Kent v Sussex at Hove	1872
W. H. Scotton	Smokers v Non-Smokers at East Melbourne	1886-87
C. W. Wright	Nottinghamshire v Gloucestershire at Bristol	1893
E. Jones	South Australia v Victoria at Melbourne	1894-95
A. W. Nourse	South Africans v Sussex at Hove	1907
E. T. Benson	MCC v Auckland at Auckland	1929-30
A. W. Gilbertson	Otago v Auckland at Auckland	1952-53
W. R. Endean	South Africa v England at Cape Town	1956-57
P. J. Burge	Queensland v New South Wales at Sydney	1958-59
Dildar Awan	Services v Lahore at Lahore	1959-60
M. Mehra	Railways v Delhi at Delhi	1959-60
Mahmood-ul-Hasan	Karachi University v Railways-Quetta at Karachi	1960-61
Ali Raza	Karachi Greens v Hyderabad at Karachi	1961-62
Mohammad Yusuf	Rawalpindi v Peshawar at Peshawar	1962-63
A. Rees	Glamorgan v Middlesex at Lord's	1965
Pervez Akhtar	Multan v Karachi Greens at Sahiwal	1971-72
Javed Mirza	Railways v Punjab at Lahore	1972-73
R. G. Pollock	Eastern Province v Western Province at Cape Town	1973-74
C. I. Dey	Northern Transvaal v Orange Free State at Bloemfontein	1973-74
Nasir Valika	Karachi Whites v National Bank at Karachi	1974-75
Haji Yousuf	National Bank v Railways at Lahore	1974-75
Masood-ul-Hasan	PIA v National Bank B at Lyallpur	1975-76
D. K. Pearse	Natal v Western Province at Cape Town	1978-79
A. M. J. Hilditch	Australia v Pakistan at Perth	1978-79
Musleh-ud-Din	Railways v Lahore at Lahore	1979-80
Jalal-ud-Din	IDBP v Habib Bank at Bahawalpur	1981-82
Mohsin Khan	Pakistan v Australia at Karachi	1982-83
D. L. Haynes	West Indies v India at Bombay	1983-84
K. Azad	Delhi v Punjab at Amritsar	1983-84
Athar A. Khan	Allied Bank v HBFC at Sialkot	1983-84
A. N. Pandya	Saurashtra v Baroda at Baroda	1984-85
G. L. Linton	Barbados v Windward Islands at Bridgetown	1985-86
R. B. Gartrell	Tasmania v Victoria at Melbourne	1986-87
R. Nayyar	Himachal Pradesh v Punjab at Una	1988-89
R. Weerawardene	Moratuwa v Nomads SC at Colombo	1988-89
A. M. Kane	Vidarbha v Railways at Nagpur	1989-90
P. Bali	Jammu and Kashmir v Services at Delhi	1991-92
M. J. Davis	Northern Transvaal B v OFS B at Bloemfontein	1991-92
J. T. C. Vaughan	Emerging Players v England XI at Hamilton	1991-92
G. A. Gooch	England v Australia at Manchester	1993
A. C. Waller	Mashonaland CD v Mashonaland Under-24 at Harare	1994-95
K. M. Krikken	Derbyshire v Indians at Derby	1996

Obstructing the Field

C. A. Absolom	Cambridge University v Surrey at The Oval	1868
T. Straw	Worcestershire v Warwickshire at Worcester	1899
T. Straw	Worcestershire v Warwickshire at Birmingham	1901
J. P. Whiteside	Leicestershire v Lancashire at Leicester	1901
L. Hutton	England v South Africa at The Oval	1951
J. A. Hayes	Canterbury v Central Districts at Christchurch	1954-55
D. D. Deshpande	Madhya Pradesh v Uttar Pradesh at Benares	1956-57
K. Ibadulla	Warwickshire v Hampshire at Coventry	1963
Qaiser Khan	Dera Ismail Khan v Railways at Lahore	1964-65
Ijaz Ahmed	Lahore Greens v Lahore Blues at Lahore	1973-74

Qasim Feroze	Bahawalpur v Universities at Lahore	1974-75
T. Quirk	Northern Transvaal v Border at East London	1978-79
Mahmood Rashid	United Bank v Muslim Commercial Bank at Bahawalpur . .	1981-82
Arshad Ali	Sukkur v Quetta at Quetta	1983-84
H. R. Wasu	Vidarbha v Rajasthan at Akola	1984-85
Khalid Javed	Railways v Lahore at Lahore	1985-86
C. Binduhewa	Singha SC v Sinhalese SC at Colombo	1990-91
S. J. Kalyani	Bengal v Orissa at Calcutta	1994-95

Hit the Ball Twice

H. E. Bull	MCC v Oxford University at Lord's	1864
H. R. J. Charlwood	Sussex v Surrey at Hove	1872
R. G. Barlow	North v South at Lord's	1878
P. S. Wimble	Transvaal v Griqualand West at Kimberley	1892-93
G. B. Nicholls	Somerset v Gloucestershire at Bristol	1896
A. A. Lilley	Warwickshire v Yorkshire at Birmingham	1897
J. H. King	Leicestershire v Surrey at The Oval	1906
A. P. Binns	Jamaica v British Guiana at Georgetown	1956-57
K. Bhavanna	Andhra v Mysore at Guntur	1963-64
Zaheer Abbas	PIA v Karachi Blues at Karachi	1969-70
Anwar Miandad	IDBP v United Bank at Lahore	1979-80
Anwar Iqbal	Hyderabad v Sukkur at Hyderabad	1983-84
Iqtidar Ali	Allied Bank v Muslim Commercial Bank at Lahore	1983-84
Aziz Malik	Lahore Division v Faisalabad at Sialkot	1984-85
Javed Mohammad	Multan v Karachi Whites at Sahiwal	1986-87
Shahid Pervez	Jammu and Kashmir v Punjab at Srinagar	1986-87

BOWLING RECORDS

TEN WICKETS IN AN INNINGS

	O	M	R		
E. Hinkly (Kent)				v England at Lord's	1848
*J. Wisden (North)				v South at Lord's	1850
V. E. Walker (England)	43	17	74	v Surrey at The Oval	1859
V. E. Walker (Middlesex)	44.2	5	104	v Lancashire at Manchester	1865
G. Wootton (All England)	31.3	9	54	v Yorkshire at Sheffield	1865
W. Hickton (Lancashire).	36.2	19	46	v Hampshire at Manchester	1870
S. E. Butler (Oxford)	24.1	11	38	v Cambridge at Lord's	1871
James Lillywhite (South)	60.2	22	129	v North at Canterbury.	1872
A. Shaw (MCC)	36.2	8	73	v North at Lord's	1874
E. Barratt (Players)	29	11	43	v Australians at The Oval	1878
G. Giffen (Australian XI)	26	10	66	v The Rest at Sydney	1883-84
W. G. Grace (MCC)	36.2	17	49	v Oxford University at Oxford. .	1886
G. Burton (Middlesex)	52.3	25	59	v Surrey at The Oval	1888
†A. E. Moss (Canterbury)	21.3	10	28	v Wellington at Christchurch . . .	1889-90
S. M. J. Woods (Cambridge U.) .	31	6	69	v Thornton's XI at Cambridge . .	1890
T. Richardson (Surrey)	15.3	3	45	v Essex at The Oval	1894
H. Pickett (Essex)	27	11	32	v Leicestershire at Leyton	1895
E. J. Tyler (Somerset).	34.3	15	49	v Surrey at Taunton	1895
W. P. Howell (Australians)	23.2	14	28	v Surrey at The Oval	1899
C. H. G. Bland (Sussex).	25.2	10	48	v Kent at Tonbridge	1899
J. Briggs (Lancashire).	28.5	7	55	v Worcestershire at Manchester .	1900
A. E. Trott (Middlesex)	14.2	5	42	v Somerset at Taunton	1900
A. Fielder (Players).	24.5	1	90	v Gentlemen at Lord's	1906
E. G. Dennett (Gloucestershire) .	19.4	7	40	v Essex at Bristol	1906
A. E. E. Vogler (E. Province) . .	12	2	26	v Griqualand W. at Johannesburg	1906-07

	O	M	R		
C. Blythe (Kent)	16	7	30	v Northants at Northampton	1907
A. Drake (Yorkshire)	8.5	0	35	v Somerset at Weston-s-Mare	1914
W. Bestwick (Derbyshire)	19	2	40	v Glamorgan at Cardiff	1921
A. A. Mailey (Australians)	28.4	5	66	v Gloucestershire at Cheltenham	1921
C. W. L. Parker (Glos.)	40.3	13	79	v Somerset at Bristol	1921
T. Rushby (Surrey)	17.5	4	43	v Somerset at Taunton	1921
J. C. White (Somerset)	42.2	11	76	v Worcestershire at Worcester	1921
G. C. Collins (Kent)	19.3	4	65	v Nottinghamshire at Dover	1922
H. Howell (Warwickshire)	25.1	5	51	v Yorkshire at Birmingham	1923
A. S. Kennedy (Players)	22.4	10	37	v Gentlemen at The Oval	1927
G. O. B. Allen (Middlesex)	25.3	10	40	v Lancashire at Lord's	1929
A. P. Freeman (Kent)	42	9	131	v Lancashire at Maidstone	1929
G. Geary (Leicestershire)	16.2	8	18	v Glamorgan at Pontypridd	1929
C. V. Grimmett (Australians)	22.3	8	37	v Yorkshire at Sheffield	1930
A. P. Freeman (Kent)	30.4	8	53	v Essex at Southend	1930
H. Verity (Yorkshire)	18.4	6	36	v Warwickshire at Leeds	1931
A. P. Freeman (Kent)	36.1	9	79	v Lancashire at Manchester	1931
V. W. C. Jupp (Northants)	39	6	127	v Kent at Tunbridge Wells	1932
H. Verity (Yorkshire)	19.4	16	10	v Nottinghamshire at Leeds	1932
T. W. Wall (South Australia)	12.4	2	36	v New South Wales at Sydney	1932-33
T. B. Mitchell (Derbyshire)	19.1	4	64	v Leicestershire at Leicester	1935
J. Mercer (Glamorgan)	26	10	51	v Worcestershire at Worcester	1936
T. W. J. Goddard (Glos.)	28.4	4	113	v Worcestershire at Cheltenham	1937
T. F. Smailes (Yorkshire)	17.1	5	47	v Derbyshire at Sheffield	1939
E. A. Watts (Surrey)	24.1	8	67	v Warwickshire at Birmingham	1939
*W. E. Hollies (Warwickshire)	20.4	4	49	v Notts at Birmingham	1946
J. M. Sims (East)	18.4	2	90	v West at Kingston	1948
T. E. Bailey (Essex)	39.4	9	90	v Lancashire at Clacton	1949
J. K. Graveney (Glos.)	18.4	2	66	v Derbyshire at Chesterfield	1949
R. Berry (Lancashire)	36.2	9	102	v Worcestershire at Blackpool	1953
S. P. Gupte (President's XI)	24.2	7	78	v Combined XI at Bombay	1954-55
J. C. Laker (Surrey)	46	18	88	v Australians at The Oval	1956
J. C. Laker (England)	51.2	23	53	v Australia at Manchester	1956
G. A. R. Lock (Surrey)	29.1	18	54	v Kent at Blackheath	1956
K. Smales (Nottinghamshire)	41.3	20	66	v Gloucestershire at Stroud	1956
P. M. Chatterjee (Bengal)	19	11	20	v Assam at Jorhat	1956-57
J. D. Bannister (Warwickshire)	23.3	11	41	v Comb. Services at Birmingham‡	1959
A. J. G. Pearson (Cambridge U.)	30.3	8	78	v Leics at Loughborough	1961
N. I. Thomson (Sussex)	34.2	19	49	v Warwickshire at Worthing	1964
P. J. Allan (Queensland)	15.6	3	61	v Victoria at Melbourne	1965-66
I. J. Brayshaw (W. Australia)	17.6	4	44	v Victoria at Perth	1967-68
Shahid Mahmood (Karachi Whites)	25	5	58	v Khairpur at Karachi	1969-70
E. E. Hemmings (International XI)	49.3	14	175	v West Indies XI at Kingston	1982-83
P. Sunderam (Rajasthan)	22	5	78	v Vidarbha at Jodhpur	1985-86
S. T. Jefferies (W. Province)	22.5	7	59	v Orange Free State at Cape Town	1987-88
Imran Adil (Bahawalpur)	22.5	3	92	v Faisalabad at Faisalabad	1989-90
G. P. Wickremasinghe (Sinhalese SC)	19.2	5	41	v Kalutara at Colombo (SSC)	1991-92
R. L. Johnson (Middlesex)	18.5	6	45	v Derbyshire at Derby	1994
Naeem Akhtar (Rawalpindi B)	21.3	10	28	v Peshawar at Peshawar	1995-96

Note: The following instances were achieved in 12-a-side matches:

	O	M	R		
E. M. Grace (MCC)	32.2	7	69	v Gents of Kent at Canterbury	1862
W. G. Grace (MCC)	46.1	15	92	v Kent at Canterbury	1873
†D. C. S. Hinds (A. B. St Hill's XII)	19.1	6	36	v Trinidad at Port-of-Spain	1900-01

* J. Wisden and W. E. Hollies achieved the feat without the direct assistance of a fielder. Wisden's ten were all bowled; Hollies bowled seven and had three lbw.

† On debut in first-class cricket.   ‡ Mitchells & Butlers Ground.

OUTSTANDING ANALYSES

	O	M	R	W		
H. Verity (Yorkshire)	19.4	16	10	10	v Nottinghamshire at Leeds	1932
G. Elliott (Victoria)	19	17	2	9	v Tasmania at Launceston	1857-58
Ahad Khan (Railways)	6.3	4	7	9	v Dera Ismail Khan at Lahore	1964-65
J. C. Laker (England)	14	12	2	8	v The Rest at Bradford	1950
D. Shackleton (Hampshire)	11.1	7	4	8	v Somerset at Weston-s-Mare	1955
E. Peate (Yorkshire)	16	11	5	8	v Surrey at Holbeck	1883
F. R. Spofforth (Australians)	8.3	6	3	7	v England XI at Birmingham	1884
W. A. Henderson (N.E. Transvaal)	9.3	7	4	7	v Orange Free State at Bloemfontein	1937-38
Rajinder Goel (Haryana)	7	4	7	7	v Jammu and Kashmir at Chandigarh	1977-78
V. I. Smith (South Africans)	4.5	3	1	6	v Derbyshire at Derby	1947
S. Cosstick (Victoria)	21.1	20	1	6	v Tasmania at Melbourne	1868-69
Israr Ali (Bahawalpur)	11	10	1	6	v Dacca U. at Bahawalpur	1957-58
A. D. Pougher (MCC)	3	3	0	5	v Australians at Lord's	1896
G. R. Cox (Sussex)	6	6	0	5	v Somerset at Weston-s-Mare	1921
R. K. Tyldesley (Lancashire)	5	5	0	5	v Leicestershire at Manchester	1924
P. T. Mills (Gloucestershire)	6.4	6	0	5	v Somerset at Bristol	1928

MOST WICKETS IN A MATCH

19-90	J. C. Laker	England v Australia at Manchester	1956
17-48	C. Blythe	Kent v Northamptonshire at Northampton	1907
17-50	C. T. B. Turner	Australians v England XI at Hastings	1888
17-54	W. P. Howell	Australians v Western Province at Cape Town	1902-03
17-56	C. W. L. Parker	Gloucestershire v Essex at Gloucester	1925
17-67	A. P. Freeman	Kent v Sussex at Hove	1922
17-89	W. G. Grace	Gloucestershire v Nottinghamshire at Cheltenham	1877
17-89	F. C. L. Matthews	Nottinghamshire v Northants at Nottingham	1923
17-91	H. Dean	Lancashire v Yorkshire at Liverpool	1913
17-91	H. Verity	Yorkshire v Essex at Leyton	1933
17-92	A. P. Freeman	Kent v Warwickshire at Folkestone	1932
17-103	W. Mycroft	Derbyshire v Hampshire at Southampton	1876
17-106	G. R. Cox	Sussex v Warwickshire at Horsham	1926
17-106	T. W. J. Goddard	Gloucestershire v Kent at Bristol	1939
17-119	W. Mead	Essex v Hampshire at Southampton	1895
17-137	W. Brearley	Lancashire v Somerset at Manchester	1905
17-159	S. F. Barnes	England v South Africa at Johannesburg	1913-14
17-201	G. Giffen	South Australia v Victoria at Adelaide	1885-86
17-212	J. C. Clay	Glamorgan v Worcestershire at Swansea	1937

SIXTEEN OR MORE WICKETS IN A DAY

17-48	C. Blythe	Kent v Northamptonshire at Northampton	1907
17-91	H. Verity	Yorkshire v Essex at Leyton	1933
17-106	T. W. J. Goddard	Gloucestershire v Kent at Bristol	1939
16-38	T. Emmett	Yorkshire v Cambridgeshire at Hunslet	1869
16-52	J. Southerton	South v North at Lord's	1875
16-69	T. G. Wass	Nottinghamshire v Lancashire at Liverpool	1906
16-38	A. E. E. Vogler	E. Province v Griqualand West at Johannesburg	1906-07
16-103	T. G. Wass	Nottinghamshire v Essex at Nottingham	1908
16-83	J. C. White	Somerset v Worcestershire at Bath	1919

FOUR WICKETS WITH CONSECUTIVE BALLS

J. Wells	Kent v Sussex at Brighton	1862
G. Ulyett	Lord Harris's XI v New South Wales at Sydney	1878-79
G. Nash	Lancashire v Somerset at Manchester	1882
J. B. Hide	Sussex v MCC and Ground at Lord's	1890
F. J. Shacklock	Nottinghamshire v Somerset at Nottingham	1893
A. D. Downes	Otago v Auckland at Dunedin	1893-94
F. Martin	MCC and Ground v Derbyshire at Lord's	1895
A. W. Mold	Lancashire v Nottinghamshire at Nottingham	1895
W. Brearley†	Lancashire v Somerset at Manchester	1905
S. Haigh	MCC v Army XI at Pretoria	1905-06
A. E. Trott‡	Middlesex v Somerset at Lord's	1907
F. A. Tarrant	Middlesex v Gloucestershire at Bristol	1907
A. Drake	Yorkshire v Derbyshire at Chesterfield	1914
S. G. Smith	Northamptonshire v Warwickshire at Birmingham	1914
H. A. Peach	Surrey v Sussex at The Oval	1924
A. F. Borland	Natal v Griqualand West at Kimberley	1926-27
J. E. H. Hooker†	New South Wales v Victoria at Sydney	1928-29
R. K. Tyldesley†	Lancashire v Derbyshire at Derby	1929
R. J. Crisp	Western Province v Griqualand West at Johannesburg	1931-32
R. J. Crisp	Western Province v Natal at Durban	1933-34
A. R. Gover	Surrey v Worcestershire at Worcester	1935
W. H. Copson	Derbyshire v Warwickshire at Derby	1937
W. A. Henderson	N.E. Transvaal v Orange Free State at Bloemfontein	1937-38
F. Ridgway	Kent v Derbyshire at Folkestone	1951
A. K. Walker§	Nottinghamshire v Leicestershire at Leicester	1956
S. N. Mohol	President's XI v Combined XI at Poona	1965-66
P. I. Pocock	Surrey v Sussex at Eastbourne	1972
S. S. Saini†	Delhi v Himachal Pradesh at Delhi	1988-89
D. Dias	W. Province (Suburbs) v Central Province at Colombo	1990-91
Ali Gauhar	Karachi Blues v United Bank at Peshawar	1994-95
K. D. James**	Hampshire v Indians at Southampton	1996

† *Not all in the same innings.*

‡ *Trott achieved another hat-trick in the same innings of this, his benefit match.*

§ *Having bowled Firth with the last ball of the first innings, Walker achieved a unique feat by dismissing Lester, Tompkin and Smithson with the first three balls of the second.*

** *James also scored a century, a unique double.*

Notes: In their match with England at The Oval in 1863, Surrey lost four wickets in the course of a four-ball over from G. Bennett.

Sussex lost five wickets in the course of the final (six-ball) over of their match with Surrey at Eastbourne in 1972. P. I. Pocock, who had taken three wickets in his previous over, captured four more, taking in all seven wickets with 11 balls, a feat unique in first-class matches. (The eighth wicket fell to a run-out.)

HAT-TRICKS

Double Hat-Trick

Besides Trott's performance, which is given in the preceding section, the following instances are recorded of players having performed the hat-trick twice in the same match, Rao doing so in the same innings.

A. Shaw	Nottinghamshire v Gloucestershire at Nottingham	1884
T. J. Matthews	Australia v South Africa at Manchester	1912
C. W. L. Parker	Gloucestershire v Middlesex at Bristol	1924
R. O. Jenkins	Worcestershire v Surrey at Worcester	1949
J. S. Rao	Services v Northern Punjab at Amritsar	1963-64
Amin Lakhani	Combined XI v Indians at Multan	1978-79

Five Wickets in Six Balls

W. H. Copson	Derbyshire v Warwickshire at Derby	1937
W. A. Henderson	N.E. Transvaal v Orange Free State at Bloemfontein	1937-38
P. I. Pocock	Surrey v Sussex at Eastbourne..........................	1972

Most Hat-Tricks

Seven times: D. V. P. Wright.

Six times: T. W. J. Goddard, C. W. L. Parker.

Five times: S. Haigh, V. W. C. Jupp, A. E. G. Rhodes, F. A. Tarrant.

Four times: R. G. Barlow, J. T. Hearne, J. C. Laker, G. A. R. Lock, G. G. Macaulay, T. J. Matthews, M. J. Procter, T. Richardson, F. R. Spofforth, F. S. Trueman.

Three times: W. M. Bradley, H. J. Butler, S. T. Clarke, W. H. Copson, R. J. Crisp, J. W. H. T. Douglas, J. A. Flavell, A. P. Freeman, G. Giffen, D. W. Headley, K. Higgs, A. Hill, W. A. Humphreys, R. D. Jackman, R. O. Jenkins, A. S. Kennedy, W. H. Lockwood, E. A. McDonald, T. L. Pritchard, J. S. Rao, A. Shaw, J. B. Statham, M. W. Tate, H. Trumble, D. Wilson, G. A. Wilson.

Twice (current players only): D. G. Cork.

HAT-TRICK ON DEBUT

H. Hay	South Australia v Lord Hawke's XI at Unley, Adelaide ..	1902-03
H. A. Sedgwick	Yorkshire v Worcestershire at Hull	1906
J. C. Treanor	New South Wales v Queensland at Brisbane	1954-55
V. B. Ranjane	Maharashtra v Saurashtra at Poona	1956-57
N. Frederick	Ceylon v Madras at Colombo	1963-64
J. S. Rao.........	Services v Jammu & Kashmir at Delhi	1963-64
Mehboodullah......	Uttar Pradesh v Madhya Pradesh at Lucknow	1971-72
R. O. Estwick......	Barbados v Guyana at Bridgetown	1982-83
S. A. Ankola	Maharashtra v Gujarat at Poona	1988-89
J. Srinath	Karnataka v Hyderabad at Secunderabad	1989-90
S. P. Mukherjee ...	Bengal v Hyderabad at Secunderabad	1989-90

Notes: R. R. Phillips (Border) took a hat-trick in his first over in first-class cricket (v Eastern Province at Port Elizabeth, 1939-40) having previously played in four matches without bowling.

J. S. Rao took two more hat-tricks in his next match.

250 WICKETS IN A SEASON

	Season	O	M	R	W	Avge
A. P. Freeman	1928	1,976.1	423	5,489	304	18.05
A. P. Freeman	1933	2,039	651	4,549	298	15.26
T. Richardson	1895‡	1,690.1	463	4,170	290	14.37
C. T. B. Turner**	1888†	2,427.2	1,127	3,307	283	11.68
A. P. Freeman	1931	1,618	360	4,307	276	15.60
A. P. Freeman	1930	1,914.3	472	4,632	275	16.84
T. Richardson	1897‡	1,603.4	495	3,945	273	14.45
A. P. Freeman	1929	1,670.5	381	4,879	267	18.27
W. Rhodes.............	1900	1,553	455	3,606	261	13.81
J. T. Hearne............	1896	2,003.1	818	3,670	257	14.28
A. P. Freeman	1932	1,565.5	404	4,149	253	16.39
W. Rhodes.............	1901	1,565	505	3,797	251	15.12

† Indicates 4-ball overs; ‡ 5-ball overs.

** Exclusive of matches not reckoned as first-class.

Notes: In four consecutive seasons (1928-31), A. P. Freeman took 1,122 wickets, and in eight consecutive seasons (1928-35), 2,090 wickets. In each of these eight seasons he took over 200 wickets.

T. Richardson took 1,005 wickets in four consecutive seasons (1894-97).

In 1896, J. T. Hearne took his 100th wicket as early as June 12. In 1931, C. W. L. Parker did the same and A. P. Freeman obtained his 100th wicket a day later.

LEADING BOWLERS IN AN ENGLISH SEASON

(Qualification: 10 wickets in 10 innings)

Season	Leading wicket-taker	Wkts	Avge	Top of averages	Wkts	Avge
1946	W. E. Hollies	184	15.60	A. Booth	111	11.61
1947	T. W. J. Goddard	238	17.30	J. C. Clay	65	16.44
1948	J. E. Walsh	174	19.56	J. C. Clay	41	14.17
1949	R. O. Jenkins	183	21.19	T. W. J. Goddard	160	19.18
1950	R. Tattersall	193	13.59	R. Tattersall	193	13.59
1951	R. Appleyard	200	14.14	R. Appleyard	200	14.14
1952	J. H. Wardle	177	19.54	F. S. Trueman	61	13.78
1953	B. Dooland	172	16.58	C. J. Knott	38	13.71
1954	B. Dooland	196	15.48	J. B. Statham	92	14.13
1955	G. A. R. Lock	216	14.49	R. Appleyard	85	13.01
1956	D. J. Shepherd	177	15.36	G. A. R. Lock	155	12.46
1957	G. A. R. Lock	212	12.02	G. A. R. Lock	212	12.02
1958	G. A. R. Lock	170	12.08	H. L. Jackson	143	10.99
1959	D. Shackleton	148	21.55	J. B. Statham	139	15.01
1960	F. S. Trueman	175	13.98	J. B. Statham	135	12.31
1961	J. A. Flavell	171	17.79	J. A. Flavell	171	17.79
1962	D. Shackleton	172	20.15	C. Cook	58	17.13
1963	D. Shackleton	146	16.75	C. C. Griffith	119	12.83
1964	D. Shackleton	142	20.40	J. A. Standen	64	13.00
1965	D. Shackleton	144	16.08	H. J. Rhodes	119	11.04
1966	D. L. Underwood	157	13.80	D. L. Underwood	157	13.80
1967	T. W. Cartwright	147	15.52	D. L. Underwood	136	12.39
1968	R. Illingworth	131	14.36	O. S. Wheatley	82	12.95
1969	R. M. H. Cottam	109	21.04	A. Ward	69	14.82
1970	D. J. Shepherd	106	19.16	Majid Khan	11	18.81
1971	L. R. Gibbs	131	18.89	G. G. Arnold	83	17.12
1972	{ T. W. Cartwright	98	18.64	I. M. Chappell	10	10.60
	{ B. Stead	98	20.38			
1973	B. S. Bedi	105	17.94	T. W. Cartwright	89	15.84
1974	A. M. E. Roberts	119	13.62	A. M. E. Roberts	119	13.62
1975	P. G. Lee	112	18.45	A. M. E. Roberts	57	15.80
1976	G. A. Cope	93	24.13	M. A. Holding	55	14.38
1977	M. J. Procter	109	18.04	R. A. Woolmer	19	15.21
1978	D. L. Underwood	110	14.49	D. L. Underwood	110	14.49
1979	{ D. L. Underwood	106	14.85	J. Garner	55	13.83
	{ J. K. Lever	106	17.30			
1980	R. D. Jackman	121	15.40	J. Garner	49	13.93
1981	R. J. Hadlee	105	14.89	R. J. Hadlee	105	14.89
1982	M. D. Marshall	134	15.73	R. J. Hadlee	61	14.57
1983	{ J. K. Lever	106	16.28	Imran Khan	12	7.16
	{ D. L. Underwood	106	19.28			
1984	R. J. Hadlee	117	14.05	R. J. Hadlee	117	14.05
1985	N. V. Radford	101	24.68	R. M. Ellison	65	17.20
1986	C. A. Walsh	118	18.17	M. D. Marshall	100	15.08
1987	N. V. Radford	109	20.81	R. J. Hadlee	97	12.64
1988	F. D. Stephenson	125	18.31	M. D. Marshall	42	13.16
1989	{ D. R. Pringle	94	14.85	T. M. Alderman	70	15.64
	{ S. L. Watkin	94	25.09			
1990	N. A. Foster	94	26.61	I. R. Bishop	59	19.05
1991	Waqar Younis	113	14.65	Waqar Younis	113	14.65
1992	C. A. Walsh	92	15.96	C. A. Walsh	92	15.96
1993	S. L. Watkin	92	22.80	Wasim Akram	59	19.27
1994	M. M. Patel	90	22.86	C. E. L. Ambrose	77	14.45
1995	A. Kumble	105	20.40	A. A. Donald	89	16.07
1996	C. A. Walsh	85	16.84	C. E. L. Ambrose	43	16.67
1997	A. M. Smith	83	17.63	A. A. Donald	60	15.63

100 WICKETS IN A SEASON

Since Reduction of Championship Matches in 1969

Five times: D. L. Underwood 110 (1978), 106 (1979), 106 (1983), 102 (1971), 101 (1969).
Four times: J. K. Lever 116 (1984), 106 (1978), 106 (1979), 106 (1983).
Twice: B. S. Bedi 112 (1974), 105 (1973); T. W. Cartwright 108 (1969), 104 (1971); N. A. Foster 105 (1986), 102 (1991); N. Gifford 105 (1970), 104 (1983); R. J. Hadlee 117 (1984), 105 (1981); P. G. Lee 112 (1975), 101 (1973); M. D. Marshall 134 (1982), 100 (1986); M. J. Procter 109 (1977), 108 (1969); N. V. Radford 109 (1987), 101 (1985); F. J. Titmus 105 (1970), 104 (1971).
Once: J. P. Agnew 101 (1987); I. T. Botham 100 (1978); K. E. Cooper 101 (1988); R. M. H. Cottam 109 (1969); D. R. Doshi 101 (1980); J. E. Emburey 103 (1983); L. R. Gibbs 131 (1971); R. N. S. Hobbs 102 (1970); Intikhab Alam 104 (1971); R. D. Jackman 121 (1980); A. Kumble 105 (1995); A. M. E. Roberts 119 (1974); P. J. Sainsbury 107 (1971); Sarfraz Nawaz 101 (1975); M. W. W. Selvey 101 (1978); D. J. Shepherd 106 (1970); F. D. Stephenson 125 (1988); C. A. Walsh 118 (1986); Waqar Younis 113 (1991); D. Wilson 102 (1969).

100 WICKETS IN A SEASON MOST TIMES

(Includes Overseas Tours and Seasons)

23 times: W. Rhodes 200 wkts (3).
20 times: D. Shackleton (In successive seasons – 1949 to 1968 inclusive).
17 times: A. P. Freeman 300 wkts (1), 200 wkts (7).
16 times: T. W. J. Goddard 200 wkts (4), C. W. L. Parker 200 wkts (5), R. T. D. Perks, F. J. Titmus.
15 times: J. T. Hearne 200 wkts (3), G. H. Hirst 200 wkts (1), A. S. Kennedy 200 wkts (1).
14 times: C. Blythe 200 wkts (1), W. E. Hollies, G. A. R. Lock 200 wkts (2), M. W. Tate 200 wkts (3), J. C. White.
13 times: J. B. Statham.
12 times: J. Briggs, E. G. Dennett 200 wkts (1), C. Gladwin, D. J. Shepherd, N. I. Thomson, F. S. Trueman.
11 times: A. V. Bedser, G. Geary, S. Haigh, J. C. Laker, M. S. Nichols, A. E. Relf.
10 times: W. Attewell, W. G. Grace, R. Illingworth, H. L. Jackson, V. W. C. Jupp, G. G. Macaulay 200 wkts (1), W. Mead, T. B. Mitchell, T. Richardson 200 wkts (3), J. Southerton 200 wkts (1), R. K. Tyldesley, D. L. Underwood, J. H. Wardle, T. G. Wass, D. V. P. Wright.
9 times: W. E. Astill, T. E. Bailey, W. E. Bowes, C. Cook, R. Howorth, J. Mercer, A. W. Mold 200 wkts (2), J. A. Newman, C. F. Root 200 wkts (1), A. Shaw 200 wkts (1), H. Verity 200 wkts (3).
8 times: T. W. Cartwright, H. Dean, J. A. Flavell, A. R. Gover 200 wkts (2), H. Larwood, G. A. Lohmann 200 wkts (3), R. Peel, J. M. Sims, F. A. Tarrant, R. Tattersall, G. J. Thompson, G. E. Tribe, A. W. Wellard, F. E. Woolley, J. A. Young.

100 WICKETS IN A SEASON OUTSIDE ENGLAND

W		Season	Country	R	Avge
116	M. W. Tate	1926-27	India/Ceylon	1,599	13.78
107	Ijaz Faqih	1985-86	Pakistan	1,719	16.06
106	C. T. B. Turner	1887-88	Australia	1,441	13.59
106	R. Benaud	1957-58	South Africa	2,056	19.39
105	Murtaza Hussain	1995-96	Pakistan	1,882	17.92
104	S. F. Barnes..........	1913-14	South Africa	1,117	10.74
104	Sajjad Akbar	1989-90	Pakistan	2,328	22.38
103	Abdul Qadir..........	1982-83	Pakistan	2,367	22.98

1,500 WICKETS IN A CAREER

Dates in italics denote the first half of an overseas season; i.e. *1970* denotes the 1970-71 season.

		Career	W	R	Avge
1	W. Rhodes	1898-1930	4,187	69,993	16.71
2	A. P. Freeman	1914-36	3,776	69,577	18.42
3	C. W. L. Parker.........	1903-35	3,278	63,817	19.46
4	J. T. Hearne	1888-1923	3,061	54,352	17.75
5	T. W. J. Goddard........	1922-52	2,979	59,116	19.84
6	W. G. Grace.............	1865-1908	2,876	51,545	17.92
7	A. S. Kennedy	1907-36	2,874	61,034	21.23
8	D. Shackleton...........	1948-69	2,857	53,303	18.65
9	G. A. R. Lock	1946-*70*	2,844	54,709	19.23
10	F. J. Titmus	1949-82	2,830	63,313	22.37
11	M. W. Tate	1912-37	2,784	50,571	18.16
12	G. H. Hirst.............	1891-1929	2,739	51,282	18.72
13	C. Blythe	1899-1914	2,506	42,136	16.81
14	D. L. Underwood........	1963-87	2,465	49,993	20.28
15	W. E. Astill	1906-39	2,431	57,783	23.76
16	J. C. White.............	1909-37	2,356	43,759	18.57
17	W. E. Hollies...........	1932-57	2,323	48,656	20.94
18	F. S. Trueman	1949-69	2,304	42,154	18.29
19	J. B. Statham	1950-68	2,260	36,999	16.37
20	R. T. D. Perks	1930-55	2,233	53,770	24.07
21	J. Briggs	1879-1900	2,221	35,431	15.95
22	D. J. Shepherd	1950-72	2,218	47,302	21.32
23	E. G. Dennett...........	1903-26	2,147	42,571	19.82
24	T. Richardson..........	1892-1905	2,104	38,794	18.43
25	T. E. Bailey	1945-67	2,082	48,170	23.13
26	R. Illingworth...........	1951-83	2,072	42,023	20.28
27 ⎰	N. Gifford.............	1960-88	2,068	48,731	23.56
⎱	F. E. Woolley	1906-38	2,068	41,066	19.85
29	G. Geary	1912-38	2,063	41,339	20.03
30	D. V. P. Wright	1932-57	2,056	49,307	23.98
31	J. A. Newman	1906-30	2,032	51,111	25.15
32	†A. Shaw	1864-97	2,027	24,580	12.12
33	S. Haigh	1895-1913	2,012	32,091	15.94
34	H. Verity	1930-39	1,956	29,146	14.90
35	W. Attewell	1881-1900	1,951	29,896	15.32
36	J. C. Laker	1946-*64*	1,944	35,791	18.41
37	A. V. Bedser	1939-60	1,924	39,279	20.41
38	W. Mead	1892-1913	1,916	36,388	18.99
39	A. E. Relf.............	1900-21	1,897	39,724	20.94
40	P. G. H. Fender	1910-36	1,894	47,458	25.05
41	J. W. H. T. Douglas	1901-30	1,893	44,159	23.32
42	J. H. Wardle............	1946-*67*	1,846	35,027	18.97
43	G. R. Cox..............	1895-1928	1,843	42,136	22.86
44	G. A. Lohmann	1884-*97*	1,841	25,295	13.73
45	J. W. Hearne	1909-36	1,839	44,926	24.42
46	G. G. Macaulay	1920-35	1,837	32,440	17.65
47	M. S. Nichols...........	1924-39	1,833	39,666	21.63
48	J. B. Mortimore	1950-75	1,807	41,904	23.18
49	C. Cook	1946-64	1,782	36,578	20.52
50	R. Peel	1882-99	1,752	28,442	16.23
51	H. L. Jackson...........	1947-63	1,733	30,101	17.36
52	J. K. Lever.............	1967-89	1,722	41,772	24.25
53	T. P. B. Smith	1929-52	1,697	45,059	26.55
54	J. Southerton	1854-79	1,681	24,290	14.44
55	A. E. Trott	*1892*-1911	1,674	35,317	21.09
56	A. W. Mold	1889-1901	1,673	26,010	15.54

		Career	W	R	Avge
57	T. G. Wass..............	1896-1920	1,666	34,092	20.46
58	V. W. C. Jupp	1909-38	1,658	38,166	23.01
59	C. Gladwin..............	1939-58	1,653	30,265	18.30
60	M. D. Marshall	1977-95	1,651	31,548	19.10
61	W. E. Bowes	1928-47	1,639	27,470	16.76
62	A. W. Wellard	1927-50	1,614	39,302	24.35
63	**J. E. Emburey**	**1973-97**	**1,608**	**41,958**	**26.09**
64	P. I. Pocock	1964-86	1,607	42,648	26.53
65	N. I. Thomson	1952-72	1,597	32,867	20.58
66	J. Mercer	1919-47	1,591	37,210	23.38
	G. J. Thompson	1897-1922	1,591	30,058	18.89
68	J. M. Sims	1929-53	1,581	39,401	24.92
69	T. Emmett	1866-88	1,571	21,314	13.56
	Intikhab Alam	1957-82	1,571	43,474	27.67
71	B. S. Bedi	1961-81	1,560	33,843	21.69
72	W. Voce	1927-52	1,558	35,961	23.08
73	A. R. Gover	1928-48	1,555	36,753	23.63
74	T. W. Cartwright	1952-77	1,536	29,357	19.11
	K. Higgs...............	1958-86	1,536	36,267	23.61
76	James Langridge	1924-53	1,530	34,524	22.56
77	J. A. Flavell	1949-67	1,529	32,847	21.48
78	E. E. Hemmings	1966-95	1,515	44,403	29.30
79	C. F. Root	1910-33	1,512	31,933	21.11
	F. A. Tarrant	1898-1936	1,512	26,450	17.49
81	R. K. Tyldesley	1919-35	1,509	25,980	17.21

Bold type denotes those who played in 1996-97 and 1997 seasons.

† *The figures for A. Shaw exclude one wicket for which no analysis is available.*

Note: Some works of reference provide career figures which differ from those in this list, owing to the exclusion or inclusion of matches recognised or not recognised as first-class by *Wisden*.

Current Player with 1,000 Wickets

	Career	W	R	Avge
C. A. Walsh	1981-96	1,465	32,593	22.24

ALL-ROUND RECORDS

HUNDRED AND TEN WICKETS IN AN INNINGS

V. E. Walker, England v Surrey at The Oval; 20*, 108, ten for 74, and four for 17 .. 1859
W. G. Grace, MCC v Oxford University at Oxford; 104, two for 60, and ten for 49 .. 1886

Note: E. M. Grace, for MCC v Gentlemen of Kent in a 12-a-side match at Canterbury in 1862, scored 192* and took five for 77 and ten for 69.

TWO HUNDRED RUNS AND SIXTEEN WICKETS

G. Giffen, South Australia v Victoria at Adelaide; 271, nine for 96, and seven for 70.   1891-92

HUNDRED IN EACH INNINGS AND FIVE WICKETS TWICE

G. H. Hirst, Yorkshire v Somerset at Bath; 111, 117*, six for 70, and five for 45.... 1906

HUNDRED IN EACH INNINGS AND TEN WICKETS

B. J. T. Bosanquet, Middlesex v Sussex at Lord's; 103, 100*, three for 75, and eight for 53	1905
F. D. Stephenson, Nottinghamshire v Yorkshire at Nottingham; 111, 117, four for 105, and seven for 117	1988

HUNDRED AND FOUR WICKETS WITH CONSECUTIVE BALLS

K. D. James, Hampshire v Indians at Southampton; 103 and five for 74 including four wickets with consecutive balls	1996

HUNDRED AND HAT-TRICK

G. Giffen, Australians v Lancashire at Manchester; 13, 113, and six for 55 including hat-trick	1884
W. E. Roller, Surrey v Sussex at The Oval; 204, four for 28 including hat-trick, and two for 16. (Unique instance of 200 and hat-trick.)	1885
W. B. Burns, Worcestershire v Gloucestershire at Worcester; 102*, three for 56 including hat-trick, and two for 21	1913
V. W. C. Jupp, Sussex v Essex at Colchester; 102, six for 61 including hat-trick, and six for 78	1921
R. E. S. Wyatt, MCC v Ceylon at Colombo; 124 and five for 39 including hat-trick ..	1926-27
L. N. Constantine, West Indians v Northamptonshire at Northampton; seven for 45 including hat-trick, 107, and six for 67	1928
D. E. Davies, Glamorgan v Leicestershire at Leicester; 139, four for 27, and three for 31 including hat-trick	1937
V. M. Merchant, Dr C. R. Pereira's XI v Sir Homi Mehta's XI at Bombay; 1, 142, three for 31 including hat-trick, and no wicket for 17	1946-47
M. J. Procter, Gloucestershire v Essex at Westcliff-on-Sea; 51, 102, three for 43, and five for 30 including hat-trick (all lbw)	1972
M. J. Procter, Gloucestershire v Leicestershire at Bristol; 122, no wkt for 32, and seven for 26 including hat-trick	1979

Note: W. G. Grace, for MCC v Kent in a 12-a-side match at Canterbury in 1874, scored 123 and took five for 82 and six for 47 including a hat-trick.

SEASON DOUBLES

2,000 Runs and 200 Wickets

1906	G. H. Hirst	2,385 runs and 208 wickets

3,000 Runs and 100 Wickets

1937	J. H. Parks	3,003 runs and 101 wickets

2,000 Runs and 100 Wickets

	Season	R	W		Season	R	W
W. G. Grace	1873	2,139	106	F. E. Woolley	1914	2,272	125
W. G. Grace	1876	2,622	129	J. W. Hearne	1920	2,148	142
C. L. Townsend	1899	2,440	101	V. W. C. Jupp	1921	2,169	121
G. L. Jessop	1900	2,210	104	F. E. Woolley	1921	2,101	167
G. H. Hirst	1904	2,501	132	F. E. Woolley	1922	2,022	163
G. H. Hirst	1905	2,266	110	F. E. Woolley	1923	2,091	101
W. Rhodes	1909	2,094	141	L. F. Townsend	1933	2,268	100
W. Rhodes	1911	2,261	117	D. E. Davies	1937	2,012	103
F. A. Tarrant	1911	2,030	111	James Langridge	1937	2,082	101
J. W. Hearne	1913	2,036	124	T. E Bailey	1959	2,011	100
J. W. Hearne	1914	2,116	123				

1,000 Runs and 200 Wickets

	Season	R	W		Season	R	W
A. E. Trott	1899	1,175	239	M. W. Tate	1923	1,168	219
A. E. Trott	1900	1,337	211	M. W. Tate	1924	1,419	205
A. S. Kennedy	1922	1,129	205	M. W. Tate	1925	1,290	228

1,000 Runs and 100 Wickets

Sixteen times: W. Rhodes.
Fourteen times: G. H. Hirst.
Ten times: V. W. C. Jupp.
Nine times: W. E. Astill.
Eight times: T. E. Bailey, W. G. Grace, M. S. Nichols, A. E. Relf, F. A. Tarrant, M. W. Tate†, F. J. Titmus, F. E. Woolley.
Seven times: G. E. Tribe.
Six times: P. G. H. Fender, R. Illingworth, James Langridge.
Five times: J. W. H. T. Douglas, J. W. Hearne, A. S. Kennedy, J. A. Newman.
Four times: E. G. Arnold, J. Gunn, R. Kilner, B. R. Knight.
Three times: W. W. Armstrong (Australians), L. C. Braund, G. Giffen (Australians), N. E. Haig, R. Howorth, C. B. Llewellyn, J. B. Mortimore, Ray Smith, S. G. Smith, L. F. Townsend, A. W. Wellard.

† M. W. Tate also scored 1,193 runs and took 116 wickets for MCC in first-class matches on the 1926-27 MCC tour of India and Ceylon.

Note: R. J. Hadlee (1984) and F. D. Stephenson (1988) are the only players to perform the feat since the reduction of County Championship matches. A complete list of those performing the feat before then will be found on p. 202 of the 1982 *Wisden*.

Wicket-Keeper's Double

	Season	R	D
L. E. G. Ames.....................	1928	1,919	122
L. E. G. Ames.....................	1929	1,795	128
L. E. G. Ames.....................	1932	2,482	104
J. T. Murray	1957	1,025	104

20,000 RUNS AND 2,000 WICKETS IN A CAREER

	Career	R	Avge	W	Avge	Doubles
W. E. Astill	1906-39	22,731	22.55	2,431	23.76	9
T. E. Bailey	1945-67	28,641	33.42	2,082	23.13	8
W. G. Grace	1865-1908	54,896	39.55	2,876	17.92	8
G. H. Hirst..........	1891-1929	36,323	34.13	2,739	18.72	14
R. Illingworth	1951-83	24,134	28.06	2,072	20.28	6
W. Rhodes...........	1898-1930	39,802	30.83	4,187	16.71	16
M. W. Tate	1912-37	21,717	25.01	2,784	18.16	8
F. J. Titmus	1949-82	21,588	23.11	2,830	22.37	8
F. E. Woolley	1906-38	58,969	40.75	2,068	19.85	8

WICKET-KEEPING RECORDS

MOST DISMISSALS IN AN INNINGS

9 (8ct, 1st)	Tahir Rashid	Habib Bank v PACO at Gujranwala	1992-93
9 (7ct, 2st)	W. R. James*	Matabeleland v Mashonaland CD at Bulawayo	1995-96
8 (all ct)	A. T. W. Grout	Queensland v Western Australia at Brisbane	1959-60
8 (all ct)†	D. E. East	Essex v Somerset at Taunton.	1985
8 (all ct)	S. A. Marsh‡	Kent v Middlesex at Lord's	1991
8 (6ct, 2st)	T. J. Zoehrer	Australians v Surrey at The Oval	1993
8 (7ct, 1st)	D. S. Berry	Victoria v South Australia at Melbourne	1996-97
7 (4ct, 3st)	E. J. Smith	Warwickshire v Derbyshire at Birmingham	1926
7 (6ct, 1st)	W. Farrimond	Lancashire v Kent at Manchester	1930
7 (all ct)	W. F. F. Price	Middlesex v Yorkshire at Lord's.	1937
7 (3ct, 4st)	D. Tallon	Queensland v Victoria at Brisbane	1938-39
7 (all ct)	R. A. Saggers	New South Wales v Combined XI at Brisbane	1940-41
7 (1ct, 6st)	H. Yarnold	Worcestershire v Scotland at Dundee	1951
7 (4ct, 3st)	J. Brown	Scotland v Ireland at Dublin	1957
7 (6ct, 1st)	N. Kirsten	Border v Rhodesia at East London	1959-60
7 (all ct)	M. S. Smith	Natal v Border at East London	1959-60
7 (all ct)	K. V. Andrew	Northamptonshire v Lancashire at Manchester.	1962
7 (all ct)	A. Long	Surrey v Sussex at Hove	1964
7 (all ct)	R. M. Schofield	Central Districts v Wellington at Wellington	1964-65
7 (all ct)	R. W. Taylor	Derbyshire v Glamorgan at Derby	1966
7 (6ct, 1st)	H. B. Taber	New South Wales v South Australia at Adelaide. . . .	1968-69
7 (6ct, 1st)	E. W. Jones	Glamorgan v Cambridge University at Cambridge . .	1970
7 (6ct, 1st)	S. Benjamin	Central Zone v North Zone at Bombay	1973-74
7 (all ct)	R. W. Taylor	Derbyshire v Yorkshire at Chesterfield	1975
7 (6ct, 1st)	Shahid Israr	Karachi Whites v Quetta at Karachi	1976-77
7 (4ct, 3st)	Wasim Bari	PIA v Sind at Lahore	1977-78
7 (all ct)	J. A. Maclean	Queensland v Victoria at Melbourne.	1977-78
7 (5ct, 2st)	Taslim Arif	National Bank v Punjab at Lahore	1978-79
7 (all ct)	Wasim Bari	Pakistan v New Zealand at Auckland	1978-79
7 (all ct)	R. W. Taylor	England v India at Bombay	1979-80
7 (all ct)	D. L. Bairstow	Yorkshire v Derbyshire at Scarborough	1982
7 (6ct, 1st)	R. B. Phillips	Queensland v New Zealanders at Bundaberg	1982-83
7 (3ct, 4st)	Masood Iqbal	Habib Bank v Lahore at Lahore	1982-83
7 (3ct, 4st)	Arif-ud-Din	United Bank v PACO at Sahiwal	1983-84
7 (6ct, 1st)	R. J. East	OFS v Western Province B at Cape Town.	1984-85
7 (all ct)	B. A. Young	Northern Districts v Canterbury at Christchurch	1986-87
7 (all ct)	D. J. Richardson	Eastern Province v OFS at Bloemfontein	1988-89
7 (6ct, 1st)	Dildar Malik	Multan v Faisalabad at Sahiwal.	1988-89
7 (all ct)	W. K. Hegg	Lancashire v Derbyshire at Chesterfield	1989
7 (all ct)	Imran Zia	Bahawalpur v Faisalabad at Faisalabad.	1989-90
7 (all ct)	I. D. S. Smith	New Zealand v Sri Lanka at Hamilton	1990-91
7 (all ct)	J. F. Holyman	Tasmania v Western Australia at Hobart	1990-91
7 (all ct)	P. J. L. Radley	OFS v Western Province at Cape Town	1990-91
7 (all ct)	C. P. Metson	Glamorgan v Derbyshire at Chesterfield	1991
7 (all ct)	H. M. de Vos	W. Transvaal v E. Transvaal at Potchefstroom	1993-94
7 (all ct)	P. Kirsten	Griqualand West v W. Transvaal at Potchefstroom . .	1993-94
7 (6ct, 1st)	S. A. Marsh	Kent v Durham at Canterbury	1994
7 (all ct)	K. J. Piper	Warwickshire v Essex at Birmingham	1994
7 (6ct, 1st)	K. J. Piper	Warwickshire v Derbyshire at Chesterfield.	1994
7 (all ct)	H. H. Devapriya	Colts CC v Sinhalese SC at Colombo	1995-96
7 (all ct)	D. J. R. Campbell	Mashonaland CD v Matabeleland at Bulawayo	1995-96
7 (all ct)	A. C. Gilchrist	Western Australia v South Australia at Perth.	1995-96
7 (all ct)	C. W. Scott	Durham v Yorkshire at Chester-le-Street	1996

* W. R. James also scored 99 and 99 not out. † The first eight wickets to fall. ‡ S. A. Marsh also scored 108 not out.

WICKET-KEEPERS' HAT-TRICKS

W. H. Brain, Gloucestershire v Somerset at Cheltenham, 1893 – three stumpings off successive balls from C. L. Townsend.

G. O. Dawkes, Derbyshire v Worcestershire at Kidderminster, 1958 – three catches off successive balls from H. L. Jackson.

R. C. Russell, Gloucestershire v Surrey at The Oval, 1986 – three catches off successive balls from C. A. Walsh and D. V. Lawrence (2).

MOST DISMISSALS IN A MATCH

13 (11ct, 2st)	W. R. James*	Matabeleland v Mashonaland CD at Bulawayo.	1995-96
12 (8ct, 4st)	E. Pooley	Surrey v Sussex at The Oval	1868
12 (9ct, 3st)	D. Tallon	Queensland v New South Wales at Sydney	1938-39
12 (9ct, 3st)	H. B. Taber	New South Wales v South Australia at Adelaide	1968-69
11 (all ct)	A. Long	Surrey v Sussex at Hove	1964
11 (all ct)	R. W. Marsh	Western Australia v Victoria at Perth	1975-76
11 (all ct)	D. L. Bairstow	Yorkshire v Derbyshire at Scarborough	1982
11 (all ct)	W. K. Hegg	Lancashire v Derbyshire at Chesterfield	1989
11 (all ct)	A. J. Stewart	Surrey v Leicestershire at Leicester	1989
11 (all ct)	T. J. Nielsen	South Australia v Western Australia at Perth . .	1990-91
11 (10ct, 1st)	I. A. Healy	Australians v N. Transvaal at Verwoerdburg . . .	1993-94
11 (10ct, 1st)	K. J. Piper	Warwickshire v Derbyshire at Chesterfield	1994
11 (all ct)	D. S. Berry	Victoria v Pakistanis at Melbourne	1995-96
11 (10ct, 1st)	W. A. Seccombe	Queensland v Western Australia at Brisbane . . .	1995-96
11 (all ct)	R. C. Russell	England v South Africa (Second Test) at Johannesburg	1995-96
11 (10ct, 1st)	D. S. Berry	Victoria v South Australia at Melbourne	1996-97

* W. R. James also scored 99 and 99 not out.

MOST DISMISSALS IN A SEASON

128 (79ct, 49st)	L. E. G. Ames	Kent	1929
122 (70ct, 52st)	L. E. G. Ames	Kent	1928
110 (63ct, 47st)	H. Yarnold	Worcestershire	1949
107 (77ct, 30st)	G. Duckworth	Lancashire	1928
107 (96ct, 11st)	J. G. Binks	Yorkshire	1960
104 (40ct, 64st)	L. E. G. Ames	Kent	1932
104 (82ct, 22st)	J. T. Murray	Middlesex	1957
102 (69ct, 33st)	F. H. Huish	Kent	1913
102 (95ct, 7st)	J. T. Murray	Middlesex	1960
101 (62ct, 39st)	F. H. Huish	Kent	1911
101 (85ct, 16st)	R. Booth	Worcestershire	1960
100 (91ct, 9st)	R. Booth	Worcestershire	1964

MOST DISMISSALS IN A CAREER

Dates in italics denote the first half of an overseas season; i.e. *1914* denotes the 1914-15 season.

		Career	M	Ct	St	Total
1	R. W. Taylor	1960-88	639	1,473	176	1,649
2	J. T. Murray	1952-75	635	1,270	257	1,527
3	H. Strudwick	1902-27	675	1,242	255	1,497
4	A. P. E. Knott	1964-85	511	1,211	133	1,344
5	F. H. Huish	1895-1914	497	933	377	1,310
6	B. Taylor	1949-73	572	1,083	211	1,294
7	D. Hunter	1889-1909	548	906	347	1,253

		Career	M	Ct	St	Total
8	H. R. Butt	1890-1912	550	953	275	1,228
9	J. H. Board	1891-*1914*	525	852	355	1,207
10	H. Elliott	1920-47	532	904	302	1,206
11	J. M. Parks	1949-76	739	1,088	93	1,181
12	R. Booth	1951-70	468	948	178	1,126
13	L. E. G. Ames	1926-51	593	703	418†	1,121
14	D. L. Bairstow	1970-90	459	961	138	1,099
15	G. Duckworth	1923-47	504	753	343	1,096
16	H. W. Stephenson	1948-64	462	748	334	1,082
17	J. G. Binks...........	1955-75	502	895	176	1,071
18	T. G. Evans	1939-69	465	816	250	1,066
19	A. Long	1960-80	452	922	124	1,046
20	G. O. Dawkes	1937-61	482	895	148	1,043
21	R. W. Tolchard	1965-83	483	912	125	1,037
22	W. L. Cornford	1921-47	496	675	342	1,017
23	**R. C. Russell**	**1981-97**	**367**	**893**	**109**	**1,002**

Bold type denotes those who played in 1996-97 and 1997 seasons.

† Record.

Current Players with 500 Dismissals

	Career	M	Ct	St	Total
S. J. Rhodes	1981-97	328	821	108	929
S. A. Marsh	1982-97	260	618	50	668
I. A. Healy	*1986-97*	183	566	49	615
C. P. Metson	1981-97	231	560	51	611
W. K. Hegg	1986-97	223	536	63	599
D. Ripley	1984-97	247	525	74	599
D. J. Richardson	*1977-96*	189	549	36	585
R. J. Blakey	1985-97	258	517	46	563
P. Moores..........	1983-97	228	500	44	544

FIELDING RECORDS

(Excluding wicket-keepers)

MOST CATCHES IN AN INNINGS

7	M. J. Stewart	Surrey v Northamptonshire at Northampton........	1957
7	A. S. Brown	Gloucestershire v Nottinghamshire at Nottingham...	1966

MOST CATCHES IN A MATCH

10	W. R. Hammond†	Gloucestershire v Surrey at Cheltenham...........	1928
8	W. B. Burns	Worcestershire v Yorkshire at Bradford	1907
8	F. G. Travers	Europeans v Parsees at Bombay	1923-24
8	A. H. Bakewell	Northamptonshire v Essex at Leyton	1928
8	W. R. Hammond	Gloucestershire v Worcestershire at Cheltenham	1932
8	K. J. Grieves	Lancashire v Sussex at Manchester...............	1951
8	C. A. Milton	Gloucestershire v Sussex at Hove	1952
8	G. A. R. Lock	Surrey v Warwickshire at The Oval	1957
8	J. M. Prodger	Kent v Gloucestershire at Cheltenham	1961
8	P. M. Walker	Glamorgan v Derbyshire at Swansea	1970
8	Masood Anwar	Rawalpindi v Lahore Division at Rawalpindi	1983-84
8	M. C. J. Ball	Gloucestershire v Yorkshire at Cheltenham	1994
8	J. D. Carr	Middlesex v Warwickshire at Birmingham	1995

† Hammond also scored a hundred in each innings.

MOST CATCHES IN A SEASON

78	W. R. Hammond	1928		65	D. W. Richardson	1961
77	M. J. Stewart	1957		64	K. F. Barrington	1957
73	P. M. Walker	1961		64	G. A. R. Lock	1957
71	P. J. Sharpe	1962		63	J. Tunnicliffe	1896
70	J. Tunnicliffe	1901		63	J. Tunnicliffe	1904
69	J. G. Langridge	1955		63	K. J. Grieves	1950
69	P. M. Walker	1960		63	C. A. Milton	1956
66	J. Tunnicliffe	1895		61	J. V. Wilson	1955
65	W. R. Hammond	1925		61	M. J. Stewart	1958
65	P. M. Walker	1959				

Note: The most catches by a fielder since the reduction of County Championship matches in 1969 is 49 by C. J. Tavaré in 1978.

MOST CATCHES IN A CAREER

Dates in italics denote the first half of an overseas season; i.e. *1970* denotes the 1970-71 season.

1,018	F. E. Woolley (1906-38)		784	J. G. Langridge (1928-55)
887	W. G. Grace (1865-1908)		764	W. Rhodes (1898-1930)
830	G. A. R. Lock (1946-*70*)		758	C. A. Milton (1948-74)
819	W. R. Hammond (1920-51)		754	E. H. Hendren (1907-38)
813	D. B. Close (1949-86)			

Most Catches by Current Players

555	G. A. Gooch (1973-97)		429	C. W. J. Athey (1976-97)
459	J. E. Emburey (1973-97)		417	G. A. Hick (*1983*-97)
474	M. W. Gatting (1975-97)			

TEAM RECORDS

HIGHEST TOTALS

1,107	Victoria v New South Wales at Melbourne	1926-27
1,059	Victoria v Tasmania at Melbourne	1922-23
952-6 dec.	Sri Lanka v India at Colombo	1997-98
951-7 dec.	Sind v Baluchistan at Karachi	1973-74
944-6 dec.	Hyderabad v Andhra at Secunderabad	1993-94
918	New South Wales v South Australia at Sydney	1900-01
912-8 dec.	Holkar v Mysore at Indore	1945-46
912-6 dec.†	Tamil Nadu v Goa at Panjim	1988-89
910-6 dec.	Railways v Dera Ismail Khan at Lahore	1964-65
903-7 dec.	England v Australia at The Oval	1938
887	Yorkshire v Warwickshire at Birmingham	1896
868†	North Zone v West Zone at Bhilai	1987-88
863	Lancashire v Surrey at The Oval	1990
855-6 dec.†	Bombay v Hyderabad at Bombay	1990-91
849	England v West Indies at Kingston	1929-30
843	Australians v Oxford & Cambridge U P & P at Portsmouth	1893
839	New South Wales v Tasmania at Sydney	1898-99
826-4	Maharashtra v Kathiawar at Poona	1948-49
824	Lahore Greens v Bahawalpur at Lahore	1965-66
821-7 dec.	South Australia v Queensland at Adelaide	1939-40
815	New South Wales v Victoria at Sydney	1908-09

811	Surrey v Somerset at The Oval	1899
810-4 dec.	Warwickshire v Durham at Birmingham	1994
807	New South Wales v South Australia at Adelaide	1899-1900
805	New South Wales v Victoria at Melbourne.....................	1905-06
803-4 dec.	Kent v Essex at Brentwood	1934
803	Non-Smokers v Smokers at East Melbourne	1886-87
802-8 dec.	Karachi Blues v Lahore City at Peshawar	1994-95
802	New South Wales v South Australia at Sydney	1920-21
801	Lancashire v Somerset at Taunton	1895
798	Maharashtra v Northern India at Poona	1940-41
793	Victoria v Queensland at Melbourne	1927-28
791-6 dec.	Karnataka v Bengal at Calcutta	1990-91
790-3 dec.	West Indies v Pakistan at Kingston	1957-58
786	New South Wales v South Australia at Adelaide	1922-23
784	Baroda v Holkar at Baroda	1946-47
783-8 dec.	Hyderabad v Bihar at Secunderabad..........................	1986-87
781-7 dec.	Northamptonshire v Nottinghamshire at Northampton	1995
780-8	Punjab v Delhi at Delhi....................................	1994-95
777	Canterbury v Otago at Christchurch.........................	1996-97
775	New South Wales v Victoria at Sydney.......................	1881-82
774-7 dec.	Australians v Gloucestershire at Bristol	1948
774	Lahore v Sargodha at Lahore	1968-69
772-7 dec.	Karachi v Bahawalpur at Karachi............................	1958-59
770	New South Wales v South Australia at Adelaide	1920-21
769	A. C. MacLaren's XI v New South Wales at Sydney	1901-02
764	Bombay v Holkar at Bombay	1944-45
763	New South Wales v Queensland at Brisbane...................	1906-07
762	Karachi Whites v Karachi Blues at Karachi	1956-57
761-6 dec.	Essex v Leicestershire at Chelmsford	1990
761-8 dec.	New South Wales v Queensland at Sydney.....................	1929-30
760	Bengal v Assam at Calcutta	1951-52
758-7 dec.†	Bengal v Tripura at Calcutta...............................	1990-91
758-8 dec.	Australia v West Indies at Kingston........................	1954-55
757-7 dec.	Maharashtra v Bihar at Poona	1991-92
757	Holkar v Hyderabad at Indore	1950-51
753	Barbados v Jamaica at Bridgetown...........................	1951-52
752-8 dec.	New South Wales v Otago at Dunedin	1923-24
750-7 dec.	Bengal v Bihar at Calcutta	1996-97
750-8 dec.	Trinidad v British Guiana at Port-of-Spain	1946-47

† *Tamil Nadu's total of 912-6 dec. included 52 penalty runs from their opponents' failure to meet the required bowling rate. North Zone's total of 868 included 68, Bombay's total of 855-6 dec. included 48, and Bengal's total of 758-7 dec. included 60.*

LOWEST TOTALS

12	Oxford University v MCC and Ground at Oxford	†1877
12	Northamptonshire v Gloucestershire at Gloucester.....................	1907
13	Auckland v Canterbury at Auckland	1877-78
13	Nottinghamshire v Yorkshire at Nottingham............................	1901
14	Surrey v Essex at Chelmsford	1983
15	MCC v Surrey at Lord's	1839
15	Victoria v MCC at Melbourne..	†1903-04
15	Northamptonshire v Yorkshire at Northampton	†1908
15	Hampshire v Warwickshire at Birmingham	1922
	(Following on, Hampshire scored 521 and won by 155 runs.)	
16	MCC and Ground v Surrey at Lord's	1872
16	Derbyshire v Nottinghamshire at Nottingham...........................	1879
16	Surrey v Nottinghamshire at The Oval	1880
16	Warwickshire v Kent at Tonbridge	1913

16	Trinidad v Barbados at Bridgetown.....................................	1942-43
16	Border v Natal at East London (first innings)	1959-60
17	Gentlemen of Kent v Gentlemen of England at Lord's	1850
17	Gloucestershire v Australians at Cheltenham	1896
18	The Bs v England at Lord's..	1831
18	Kent v Sussex at Gravesend...	†1867
18	Tasmania v Victoria at Melbourne	1868-69
18	Australians v MCC and Ground at Lord's	†1896
18	Border v Natal at East London (second innings)	1959-60
19	Sussex v Surrey at Godalming...	1830
19	Sussex v Nottinghamshire at Hove	†1873
19	MCC and Ground v Australians at Lord's	1878
19	Wellington v Nelson at Nelson	1885-86

† *Signifies that one man was absent.*

Note: At Lord's in 1810, The Bs, with one man absent, were dismissed by England for 6.

LOWEST TOTAL IN A MATCH

| 34 | (16 and 18) Border v Natal at East London .... | 1959-60 |
| 42 | (27 and 15) Northamptonshire v Yorkshire at Northampton .... | 1908 |

Note: Northamptonshire batted one man short in each innings.

HIGHEST MATCH AGGREGATES

2,376 for 37 wickets	Maharashtra v Bombay at Poona.....................	1948-49
2,078 for 40 wickets	Bombay v Holkar at Bombay........................	1944-45
1,981 for 35 wickets	England v South Africa at Durban..................	1938-39
1,945 for 18 wickets	Canterbury v Wellington at Christchurch............	1994-95
1,929 for 39 wickets	New South Wales v South Australia at Sydney	1925-26
1,911 for 34 wickets	New South Wales v Victoria at Sydney	1908-09
1,905 for 40 wickets	Otago v Wellington at Dunedin.....................	1923-24

In Britain

1,808 for 20 wickets	Sussex v Essex at Hove	1993
1,723 for 31 wickets	England v Australia at Leeds......................	1948
1,706 for 23 wickets	Hampshire v Warwickshire at Southampton	1997
1,650 for 19 wickets	Surrey v Lancashire at The Oval...................	1990
1,642 for 29 wickets	Nottinghamshire v Kent at Nottingham...............	1995
1,641 for 16 wickets	Glamorgan v Worcestershire at Abergavenny..........	1990
1,614 for 30 wickets	England v India at Manchester.....................	1990
1,606 for 34 wickets	Somerset v Derbyshire at Taunton..................	1996
1,603 for 28 wickets	England v India at Lord's.........................	1990
1,601 for 29 wickets	England v Australia at Lord's.....................	1930
1,601 for 35 wickets	Kent v Surrey at Canterbury.......................	1995

LOWEST AGGREGATE IN A COMPLETED MATCH

| 105 for 31 wickets | MCC v Australians at Lord's....................... | 1878 |

Note: The lowest aggregate since 1900 is 157 for 22 wickets, Surrey v Worcestershire at The Oval, 1954.

HIGHEST FOURTH-INNINGS TOTALS

(Unless otherwise stated, the side making the runs won the match.)

654-5	England v South Africa at Durban....................................	1938-39
	(After being set 696 to win. The match was left drawn on the tenth day	
604	Maharashtra v Bombay at Poona	1948-49
	(After being set 959 to win.)	
576-8	Trinidad v Barbados at Port-of-Spain................................	1945-46
	(After being set 672 to win. Match drawn on fifth day.)	
572	New South Wales v South Australia at Sydney.........................	1907-08
	(After being set 593 to win.)	
529-9	Combined XI v South Africans at Perth...............................	1963-64
	(After being set 579 to win. Match drawn on fourth day.)	
518	Victoria v Queensland at Brisbane	1926-27
	(After being set 753 to win.)	
507-7	Cambridge University v MCC and Ground at Lord's....................	1896
506-6	South Australia v Queensland at Adelaide..............................	1991-92
502-6	Middlesex v Nottinghamshire at Nottingham...........................	1925
	(Game won by an unfinished stand of 271; a county record.)	
502-8	Players v Gentlemen at Lord's	1900
500-7	South African Universities v Western Province at Stellenbosch.............	1978-79

LARGEST VICTORIES

Largest Innings Victories

Inns and 851 runs:	Railways (910-6 dec.) v Dera Ismail Khan (Lahore)	1964-65
Inns and 666 runs:	Victoria (1,059) v Tasmania (Melbourne)..................	1922-23
Inns and 656 runs:	Victoria (1,107) v New South Wales (Melbourne)...........	1926-27
Inns and 605 runs:	New South Wales (918) v South Australia (Sydney).........	1900-01
Inns and 579 runs:	England (903-7 dec.) v Australia (The Oval)	1938
Inns and 575 runs:	Sind (951-7 dec.) v Baluchistan (Karachi)	1973-74
Inns and 527 runs:	New South Wales (713) v South Australia (Adelaide)	1908-09
Inns and 517 runs:	Australians (675) v Nottinghamshire (Nottingham)	1921

Largest Victories by Runs Margin

685 runs:	New South Wales (235 and 761-8 dec.) v Queensland (Sydney).......	1929-30
675 runs:	England (521 and 342-8 dec.) v Australia (Brisbane).................	1928-29
638 runs:	New South Wales (304 and 770) v South Australia (Adelaide).........	1920-21
625 runs:	Sargodha (376 and 416) v Lahore Municipal Corporation (Faisalabad)...	1978-79
609 runs:	Muslim Commercial Bank (575 and 282-0 dec.) v WAPDA (Lahore) ...	1977-78
573 runs:	Sinhalese SC (395-7 dec. and 350-2 dec.) v Sebastianites C and AC (63 and 109) at Colombo	1990-91
571 runs:	Victoria (304 and 649) v South Australia (Adelaide)	1926-27
562 runs:	Australia (701 and 327) v England (The Oval)	1934

Victory Without Losing a Wicket

Lancashire (166-0 dec. and 66-0) beat Leicestershire by ten wickets (Manchester) ...	1956
Karachi A (277-0 dec.) beat Sind A by an innings and 77 runs (Karachi)	1957-58
Railways (236-0 dec. and 16-0) beat Jammu and Kashmir by ten wickets (Srinagar) .	1960-61
Karnataka (451-0 dec.) beat Kerala by an innings and 186 runs (Chikmagalur)......	1977-78

TIED MATCHES IN FIRST-CLASS CRICKET

Since 1948 a tie has been recognised only when the scores are level with all the wickets down in the fourth innings.

The following are the instances since then:

D. G. Bradman's XI v A. L. Hassett's XI at Melbourne	1948-49
Hampshire v Kent at Southampton	1950
Sussex v Warwickshire at Hove	1952
Essex v Lancashire at Brentwood	1952
Northamptonshire v Middlesex at Peterborough	1953
Yorkshire v Leicestershire at Huddersfield	1954
Sussex v Hampshire at Eastbourne	1955
Victoria v New South Wales at Melbourne	1956-57
T. N. Pearce's XI v New Zealanders at Scarborough	1958
Essex v Gloucestershire at Leyton	1959
Australia v West Indies (First Test) at Brisbane	1960-61
Bahawalpur v Lahore B at Bahawalpur	1961-62
Hampshire v Middlesex at Portsmouth	1967
England XI v England Under-25 XI at Scarborough	1968
Yorkshire v Middlesex at Bradford	1973
Sussex v Essex at Hove	1974
South Australia v Queensland at Adelaide	1976-77
Central Districts v England XI at New Plymouth	1977-78
Victoria v New Zealanders at Melbourne	1982-83
Muslim Commercial Bank v Railways at Sialkot	1983-84
Sussex v Kent at Hastings	1984
Northamptonshire v Kent at Northampton	1984
Eastern Province B v Boland at Albany SC, Port Elizabeth	1985-86
Natal B v Eastern Province B at Pietermaritzburg	1985-86
India v Australia (First Test) at Madras	1986-87
Gloucestershire v Derbyshire at Bristol	1987
Bahawalpur v Peshawar at Bahawalpur	1988-89
Wellington v Canterbury at Wellington	1988-89
Sussex v Kent at Hove	†1991
Nottinghamshire v Worcestershire at Nottingham	1993

† *Sussex (436) scored the highest total to tie a first-class match.*

MATCHES BEGUN AND FINISHED ON FIRST DAY

Since 1900. A fuller list may be found in the Wisden *of 1981 and preceding editions.*

Yorkshire v Worcestershire at Bradford, May 7	1900
MCC and Ground v London County at Lord's, May 20	1903
Transvaal v Orange Free State at Johannesburg, December 30	1906
Middlesex v Gentlemen of Philadelphia at Lord's, July 20	1908
Gloucestershire v Middlesex at Bristol, August 26	1909
Eastern Province v Orange Free State at Port Elizabeth, December 26	1912
Kent v Sussex at Tonbridge, June 21	1919
Lancashire v Somerset at Manchester, May 21	1925
Madras v Mysore at Madras, November 4	1934
Ireland v New Zealanders at Dublin, September 11	1937
Derbyshire v Somerset at Chesterfield, June 11	1947
Lancashire v Sussex at Manchester, July 12	1950
Surrey v Warwickshire at The Oval, May 16	1953
Somerset v Lancashire at Bath, June 6 (H. F. T. Buse's benefit)	1953
Kent v Worcestershire at Tunbridge Wells, June 15	1960

TEST MATCH RECORDS

Note: This section covers all Tests up to August 23, 1997.

BATTING RECORDS

HIGHEST INDIVIDUAL INNINGS

375	B. C. Lara	West Indies v England at St John's	1993-94
365*	G. S. Sobers	West Indies v Pakistan at Kingston	1957-58
364	L. Hutton	England v Australia at The Oval	1938
340	S. T. Jayasuriya	Sri Lanka v India at Colombo (RPS)	1997-98
337	Hanif Mohammad	Pakistan v West Indies at Bridgetown	1957-58
336*	W. R. Hammond	England v New Zealand at Auckland	1932-33
334	D. G. Bradman	Australia v England at Leeds	1930
333	G. A. Gooch	England v India at Lord's	1990
325	A. Sandham	England v West Indies at Kingston	1929-30
311	R. B. Simpson	Australia v England at Manchester	1964
310*	J. H. Edrich	England v New Zealand at Leeds	1965
307	R. M. Cowper	Australia v England at Melbourne	1965-66
304	D. G. Bradman	Australia v England at Leeds	1934
302	L. G. Rowe	West Indies v England at Bridgetown	1973-74
299*	D. G. Bradman	Australia v South Africa at Adelaide	1931-32
299	M. D. Crowe	New Zealand v Sri Lanka at Wellington	1990-91
291	I. V. A. Richards	West Indies v England at The Oval	1976
287	R. E. Foster	England v Australia at Sydney	1903-04
285*	P. B. H. May	England v West Indies at Birmingham	1957
280*	Javed Miandad	Pakistan v India at Hyderabad	1982-83
278	D. C. S. Compton	England v Pakistan at Nottingham	1954
277	B. C. Lara	West Indies v Australia at Sydney	1992-93
274	R. G. Pollock	South Africa v Australia at Durban	1969-70
274	Zaheer Abbas	Pakistan v England at Birmingham	1971
271	Javed Miandad	Pakistan v New Zealand at Auckland	1988-89
270*	G. A. Headley	West Indies v England at Kingston	1934-35
270	D. G. Bradman	Australia v England at Melbourne	1936-37
268	G. N. Yallop	Australia v Pakistan at Melbourne	1983-84
267*	B. A. Young	New Zealand v Sri Lanka at Dunedin	1996-97
267	P. A. de Silva	Sri Lanka v New Zealand at Wellington	1990-91
266	W. H. Ponsford	Australia v England at The Oval	1934
266	D. L. Houghton	Zimbabwe v Sri Lanka at Bulawayo	1994-95
262*	D. L. Amiss	England v West Indies at Kingston	1973-74
261	F. M. M. Worrell	West Indies v England at Nottingham	1950
260	C. C. Hunte	West Indies v Pakistan at Kingston	1957-58
260	Javed Miandad	Pakistan v England at The Oval	1987
259	G. M. Turner	New Zealand v West Indies at Georgetown	1971-72
258	T. W. Graveney	England v West Indies at Nottingham	1957
258	S. M. Nurse	West Indies v New Zealand at Christchurch	1968-69
257*	Wasim Akram	Pakistan v Zimbabwe at Sheikhupura	1996-97
256	R. B. Kanhai	West Indies v India at Calcutta	1958-59
256	K. F. Barrington	England v Australia at Manchester	1964
255*	D. J. McGlew	South Africa v New Zealand at Wellington	1952-53
254	D. G. Bradman	Australia v England at Lord's	1930
251	W. R. Hammond	England v Australia at Sydney	1928-29
250	K. D. Walters	Australia v New Zealand at Christchurch	1976-77
250	S. F. A. F. Bacchus	West Indies v India at Kanpur	1978-79

The highest individual innings for India is:

236*	S. M. Gavaskar	India v West Indies at Madras	1983-84

HUNDRED ON TEST DEBUT

C. Bannerman (165*)	Australia v England at Melbourne	1876-77
W. G. Grace (152)..........	England v Australia at The Oval	1880
H. Graham (107)	Australia v England at Lord's..............	1893
†K. S. Ranjitsinhji (154*)	England v Australia at Manchester	1896
†P. F. Warner (132*).......	England v South Africa at Johannesburg.......	1898-99
†R. A. Duff (104)	Australia v England at Melbourne	1901-02
R. E. Foster (287)	England v Australia at Sydney	1903-04
G. Gunn (119)	England v Australia at Sydney	1907-08
†R. J. Hartigan (116).........	Australia v England at Adelaide	1907-08
†H. L. Collins (104)	Australia v England at Sydney	1920-21
W. H. Ponsford (110)	Australia v England at Sydney	1924-25
A. A. Jackson (164).........	Australia v England at Adelaide	1928-29
†G. A. Headley (176)	West Indies v England at Bridgetown	1929-30
J. E. Mills (117)............	New Zealand v England at Wellington	1929-30
Nawab of Pataudi sen. (102) ..	England v Australia at Sydney	1932-33
B. H. Valentine (136)	England v India at Bombay	1933-34
†L. Amarnath (118)..........	India v England at Bombay	1933-34
†P. A. Gibb (106)	England v South Africa at Johannesburg	1938-39
S. C. Griffith (140)	England v West Indies at Port-of-Spain	1947-48
A. G. Ganteaume (112)	West Indies v England at Port-of-Spain	1947-48
†J. W. Burke (101*)	Australia v England at Adelaide	1950-51
P. B. H. May (138)	England v South Africa at Leeds	1951
R. H. Shodhan (110)	India v Pakistan at Calcutta	1952-53
B. H. Pairaudeau (115)	West Indies v India at Port-of-Spain	1952-53
†O. G. Smith (104)	West Indies v Australia at Kingston	1954-55
A. G. Kripal Singh (100*) ...	India v New Zealand at Hyderabad	1955-56
C. C. Hunte (142)	West Indies v Pakistan at Bridgetown	1957-58
C. A. Milton (104*).........	England v New Zealand at Leeds	1958
†A. A. Baig (112)	India v England at Manchester	1959
Hanumant Singh (105).......	India v England at Delhi	1963-64
Khalid Ibadulla (166).......	Pakistan v Australia at Karachi	1964-65
B. R. Taylor (105)..........	New Zealand v India at Calcutta	1964-65
K. D. Walters (155).........	Australia v England at Brisbane	1965-66
J. H. Hampshire (107)	England v West Indies at Lord's	1969
†G. R. Viswanath (137)	India v Australia at Kanpur	1969-70
G. S. Chappell (108)	Australia v England at Perth	1970-71
‡L. G. Rowe (214, 100*)	West Indies v New Zealand at Kingston	1971-72
A. I. Kallicharran (100*).....	West Indies v New Zealand at Georgetown	1971-72
R. E. Redmond (107)	New Zealand v Pakistan at Auckland	1972-73
†F. C. Hayes (106*)	England v West Indies at The Oval	1973
†C. G. Greenidge (107).......	West Indies v India at Bangalore	1974-75
†L. Baichan (105*)	West Indies v Pakistan at Lahore	1974-75
G. J. Cosier (109)	Australia v West Indies at Melbourne	1975-76
S. Amarnath (124)	India v New Zealand at Auckland	1975-76
Javed Miandad (163)........	Pakistan v New Zealand at Lahore	1976-77
†A. B. Williams (100)........	West Indies v Australia at Georgetown	1977-78
†D. M. Wellham (103)........	Australia v England at The Oval	1981
†Salim Malik (100*)	Pakistan v Sri Lanka at Karachi	1981-82
K. C. Wessels (162)	Australia v England at Brisbane.............	1982-83
W. B. Phillips (159)	Australia v Pakistan at Perth.............	1983-84
§M. Azharuddin (110)........	India v England at Calcutta	1984-85
D. S. B. P. Kuruppu (201*) ..	Sri Lanka v New Zealand at Colombo (CCC) ..	1986-87
†M. J. Greatbatch (107*)	New Zealand v England at Auckland	1987-88
M. E. Waugh (138)	Australia v England at Adelaide	1990-91
A. C. Hudson (163)..........	South Africa v West Indies at Bridgetown	1991-92
R. S. Kaluwitharana (132*)...	Sri Lanka v Australia at Colombo (SSC)	1992-93
D. L. Houghton (121)	Zimbabwe v India at Harare	1992-93
P. K. Amre (103)............	India v South Africa at Durban	1992-93

†G. P. Thorpe (114*) .... England v Australia at Nottingham 1993
G. S. Blewett (102*) .... Australia v England at Adelaide 1994-95
S. C. Ganguly (131) .... India v England at Lord's 1996
†Mohammad Wasim (109*) ... Pakistan v New Zealand at Lahore 1996-97

† *In his second innings of the match.*

‡ *L. G. Rowe is the only batsman to score a hundred in each innings on debut.*

§ *M. Azharuddin is the only batsman to score hundreds in each of his first three Tests.*

Notes: L. Amarnath and S. Amarnath were father and son.

In 1997-98, after the deadline for inclusion in this section, Ali Naqvi scored 115 and Azhar Mahmood 128* on debut for Pakistan v South Africa at Rawalpindi. It was the first time two debutants had achieved the feat in the same innings.

300 RUNS IN FIRST TEST

314 L. G. Rowe (214, 100*) West Indies v New Zealand at Kingston 1971-72
306 R. E. Foster (287, 19) England v Australia at Sydney 1903-04

TWO SEPARATE HUNDREDS IN A TEST

Three times: S. M. Gavaskar v West Indies (1970-71), v Pakistan (1978-79), v West Indies (1978-79).

Twice in one series: C. L. Walcott v Australia (1954-55).

Twice: H. Sutcliffe v Australia (1924-25), v South Africa (1929); G. A. Headley v England (1929-30 and 1939); G. S. Chappell v New Zealand (1973-74), v West Indies (1975-76); ‡A. R. Border v Pakistan (1979-80), v New Zealand (1985-86); §P. A. de Silva v Pakistan (1996-97), v India (1997-98).

Once: W. Bardsley v England (1909); A. C. Russell v South Africa (1922-23); W. R. Hammond v Australia (1928-29); E. Paynter v South Africa (1938-39); D. C. S. Compton v Australia (1946-47); A. R. Morris v England (1946-47); A. Melville v England (1947); B. Mitchell v England (1947); D. G. Bradman v India (1947-48); V. S. Hazare v Australia (1947-48); E. D. Weekes v India (1948-49); J. Moroney v South Africa (1949-50); G. S. Sobers v Pakistan (1957-58); R. B. Kanhai v Australia (1960-61); Hanif Mohammad v England (1961-62); R. B. Simpson v Pakistan (1964-65); K. D. Walters v West Indies (1968-69); †L. G. Rowe v New Zealand (1971-72); I. M. Chappell v New Zealand (1973-74); G. M. Turner v Australia (1973-74); C. G. Greenidge v England (1976); G. P. Howarth v England (1977-78); L. R. D. Mendis v India (1982-83); Javed Miandad v New Zealand (1984-85); D. M. Jones v Pakistan (1989-90); G. A. Gooch v India (1990); A. H. Jones v Sri Lanka (1990-91); A. P. Gurusinha v New Zealand (1990-91); A. J. Stewart v West Indies (1993-94); G. Kirsten v India (1996-97); S. R. Waugh v England (1997).

† *L. G. Rowe's two hundreds were on his Test debut.*

‡ *A. R. Border scored 150* and 153 against Pakistan to become the first to score 150 in each innings of a Test match.*

§ *P. A. de Silva scored 138* and 103* against Pakistan to become the first to score two not out hundreds in a Test match.*

TRIPLE-HUNDRED AND HUNDRED IN SAME TEST

G. A. Gooch (England) 333 and 123 v India at Lord's 1990

The only instance in first-class cricket.

DOUBLE-HUNDRED AND HUNDRED IN SAME TEST

K. D. Walters (Australia)	242 and 103 v West Indies at Sydney	1968-69
S. M. Gavaskar (India)	124 and 220 v West Indies at Port-of-Spain	1970-71
†L. G. Rowe (West Indies)	214 and 100* v New Zealand at Kingston	1971-72
G. S. Chappell (Australia)	247* and 133 v New Zealand at Wellington	1973-74

 † *On Test debut.*

MOST RUNS IN A SERIES

	T	I	NO	R	HS	100s	Avge		
D. G. Bradman	5	7	0	974	334	4	139.14	A v E	1930
W. R. Hammond	5	9	1	905	251	4	113.12	E v A	1928-29
M. A. Taylor	6	11	1	839	219	2	83.90	A v E	1989
R. N. Harvey	5	9	0	834	205	4	92.66	A v SA	1952-53
I. V. A. Richards.....	4	7	0	829	291	3	118.42	WI v E	1976
C. L. Walcott........	5	10	0	827	155	5	82.70	WI v A	1954-55
G. S. Sobers	5	8	2	824	365*	3	137.33	WI v P	1957-58
D. G. Bradman	5	9	0	810	270	3	90.00	A v E	1936-37
D. G. Bradman	5	5	1	806	299*	4	201.50	A v SA	1931-32
B. C. Lara	5	8	0	798	375	2	99.75	WI v E	1993-94
E. D. Weekes	5	7	0	779	194	4	111.28	WI v I	1948-49
†S. M. Gavaskar	4	8	3	774	220	4	154.80	I v WI	1970-71
B. C. Lara	6	10	1	765	179	3	85.00	WI v E	1995
Mudassar Nazar......	6	8	2	761	231	4	126.83	P v I	1982-83
D. G. Bradman	5	8	0	758	304	2	94.75	A v E	1934
D. C. S. Compton	5	8	0	753	208	4	94.12	E v SA	1947
‡G. A. Gooch	3	6	0	752	333	3	125.33	E v I	1990

 † *Gavaskar's aggregate was achieved in his first Test series.*
 ‡ *G. A. Gooch is alone in scoring 1,000 runs in Test cricket during an English season with 1,058 runs in 11 innings against New Zealand and India in 1990.*

MOST RUNS IN A CALENDAR YEAR

	T	I	NO	R	HS	100s	Avge	Year
I. V. A. Richards (WI)	11	19	0	1,710	291	7	90.00	1976
S. M. Gavaskar (I)	18	27	1	1,555	221	5	59.80	1979
G. R. Viswanath (I)	17	26	3	1,388	179	5	60.34	1979
R. B. Simpson (A)	14	26	3	1,381	311	3	60.04	1964
D. L. Amiss (E)	13	22	2	1,379	262*	5	68.95	1974
S. M. Gavaskar (I)	18	32	4	1,310	236*	5	46.78	1983
G. A. Gooch (E)..............	9	17	1	1,264	333	4	79.00	1990
D. C. Boon (A)...............	16	25	5	1,241	164*	4	62.05	1993
B. C. Lara (WI)	12	20	2	1,222	179	4	67.88	1995
M. A. Taylor (A)	11	20	1	1,219	219	4	64.15	1989†

 † *The year of his debut.*

Notes: M. Amarnath reached 1,000 runs in 1983 on May 3.
 The only batsman to score 1,000 runs in a year before World War II was C. Hill of Australia: 1,061 in 1902.

MOST RUNS IN A CAREER

(Qualification: 2,000 runs)

ENGLAND

		T	I	NO	R	HS	100s	Avge
1	G. A. Gooch	118	215	6	8,900	333	20	42.58
2	D. I. Gower	117	204	18	8,231	215	18	44.25
3	G. Boycott	108	193	23	8,114	246*	22	47.72
4	M. C. Cowdrey	114	188	15	7,624	182	22	44.06
5	W. R. Hammond	85	140	16	7,249	336*	22	58.45
6	L. Hutton	79	138	15	6,971	364	19	56.67
7	K. F. Barrington	82	131	15	6,806	256	20	58.67
8	D. C. S. Compton	78	131	15	5,807	278	17	50.06
9	J. B. Hobbs	61	102	7	5,410	211	15	56.94
10	**M. A. Atherton**	**73**	**134**	**5**	**5,243**	**185***	**11**	**40.64**
11	I. T. Botham	102	161	6	5,200	208	14	33.54
12	J. H. Edrich	77	127	9	5,138	310*	12	43.54
13	T. W. Graveney...........	79	123	13	4,882	258	11	44.38
14	**A. J. Stewart**	**69**	**123**	**8**	**4,701**	**190**	**10**	**40.87**
15	A. J. Lamb...............	79	139	10	4,656	142	14	36.09
16	H. Sutcliffe..............	54	84	9	4,555	194	16	60.73
17	P. B. H. May............	66	106	9	4,537	285*	13	46.77
18	E. R. Dexter	62	102	8	4,502	205	9	47.89
19	M. W. Gatting............	79	138	14	4,409	207	10	35.55
20	A. P. E. Knott	95	149	15	4,389	135	5	32.75
21	R. A. Smith	62	112	15	4,236	175	9	43.67
22	D. L. Amiss.............	50	88	10	3,612	262*	11	46.30
23	A. W. Greig.............	58	93	4	3,599	148	8	40.43
24	E. H. Hendren	51	83	9	3,525	205*	7	47.63
25	F. E. Woolley	64	98	7	3,283	154	5	36.07
26	K. W. R. Fletcher	59	96	14	3,272	216	7	39.90
27	**G. P. Thorpe**	**43**	**78**	**8**	**2,964**	**138**	**5**	**42.34**
28	M. Leyland	41	65	5	2,764	187	9	46.06
29	G. A. Hick..............	46	80	6	2,672	178	4	36.10
30	C. Washbrook...........	37	66	6	2,569	195	6	42.81
31	B. L. D'Oliveira	44	70	8	2,484	158	5	40.06
32	D. W. Randall	47	79	5	2,470	174	7	33.37
33	W. J. Edrich	39	63	2	2,440	219	6	40.00
34	T. G. Evans	91	133	14	2,439	104	2	20.49
35	L. E. G. Ames...........	47	72	12	2,434	149	8	40.56
36	W. Rhodes...............	58	98	21	2,325	179	2	30.19
37	T. E. Bailey.............	61	91	14	2,290	134*	1	29.74
38	M. J. K. Smith	50	78	6	2,278	121	3	31.63
39	P. E. Richardson	34	56	1	2,061	126	5	37.47

AUSTRALIA

		T	I	NO	R	HS	100s	Avge
1	A. R. Border	156	265	44	11,174	205	27	50.56
2	D. C. Boon	107	190	20	7,422	200	21	43.65
3	G. S. Chappell...........	87	151	19	7,110	247*	24	53.86
4	D. G. Bradman	52	80	10	6,996	334	29	99.94
5	R. N. Harvey............	79	137	10	6,149	205	21	48.41
6	**M. A. Taylor**	**87**	**155**	**9**	**6,116**	**219**	**15**	**41.89**
7	**S. R. Waugh**............	**95**	**148**	**28**	**5,960**	**200**	**14**	**49.66**
8	K. D. Walters	74	125	14	5,357	250	15	48.26
9	I. M. Chappell...........	75	136	10	5,345	196	14	42.42
10	W. M. Lawry............	67	123	12	5,234	210	13	47.15
11	R. B. Simpson...........	62	111	7	4,869	311	10	46.81

		T	I	NO	R	HS	100s	Avge
12	I. R. Redpath	66	120	11	4,737	171	8	43.45
13	**M. E. Waugh**	**69**	**112**	**4**	**4,464**	**140**	**11**	**41.33**
14	K. J. Hughes	70	124	6	4,415	213	9	37.41
15	R. W. Marsh	96	150	13	3,633	132	3	26.51
16	D. M. Jones	52	89	11	3,631	216	11	46.55
17	A. R. Morris	46	79	3	3,533	206	12	46.48
18	**I. A. Healy**	**94**	**143**	**19**	**3,470**	**161***	**3**	**27.98**
19	C. Hill	49	89	2	3,412	191	7	39.21
20	G. M. Wood	59	112	6	3,374	172	9	31.83
21	V. T. Trumper	48	89	8	3,163	214*	8	39.04
22	C. C. McDonald	47	83	4	3,107	170	5	39.32
23	A. L. Hassett	43	69	3	3,073	198*	10	46.56
24	K. R. Miller	55	87	7	2,958	147	7	36.97
25	W. W. Armstrong	50	84	10	2,863	159*	6	38.68
26	G. R. Marsh	50	93	7	2,854	138	4	33.18
27	K. R. Stackpole	43	80	5	2,807	207	7	37.42
28	N. C. O'Neill	42	69	8	2,779	181	6	45.55
29	G. N. Yallop	39	70	3	2,756	268	8	41.13
30	S. J. McCabe	39	62	5	2,748	232	6	48.21
31	**M. J. Slater**	**34**	**59**	**3**	**2,655**	**219**	**7**	**47.41**
32	W. Bardsley	41	66	5	2,469	193*	6	40.47
33	W. M. Woodfull	35	54	4	2,300	161	7	46.00
34	P. J. Burge	42	68	8	2,290	181	4	38.16
35	S. E. Gregory	58	100	7	2,282	201	4	24.53
36	R. Benaud	63	97	7	2,201	122	3	24.45
37	C. G. Macartney	35	55	4	2,131	170	7	41.78
38	W. H. Ponsford	29	48	4	2,122	266	7	48.22
39	R. M. Cowper	27	46	2	2,061	307	5	46.84

SOUTH AFRICA

		T	I	NO	R	HS	100s	Avge
1	B. Mitchell	42	80	9	3,471	189*	8	48.88
2	A. D. Nourse	34	62	7	2,960	231	9	53.81
3	H. W. Taylor	42	76	4	2,936	176	7	40.77
4	{ E. J. Barlow	30	57	2	2,516	201	6	45.74
	{ T. L. Goddard	41	78	5	2,516	112	1	34.46
6	D. J. McGlew	34	64	6	2,440	255*	7	42.06
7	J. H. B. Waite	50	86	7	2,405	134	4	30.44
8	R. G. Pollock	23	41	4	2,256	274	7	60.97
9	A. W. Nourse	45	83	8	2,234	111	1	29.78
10	R. A. McLean	40	73	3	2,120	142	5	30.28
11	**W. J. Cronje**	**36**	**63**	**7**	**2,012**	**135**	**5**	**35.92**

K. C. Wessels scored 2,788 runs in 40 Tests: 1,761 (average 42.95) in 24 Tests for Australia, and 1,027 (average 38.03) in 16 Tests for South Africa.

WEST INDIES

		T	I	NO	R	HS	100s	Avge
1	I. V. A. Richards	121	182	12	8,540	291	24	50.23
2	G. S. Sobers	93	160	21	8,032	365*	26	57.78
3	C. G. Greenidge	108	185	16	7,558	226	19	44.72
4	C. H. Lloyd	110	175	14	7,515	242*	19	46.67
5	D. L. Haynes	116	202	25	7,487	184	18	42.29
6	R. B. Kanhai	79	137	6	6,227	256	15	47.53

		T	I	NO	R	HS	100s	Avge
7	R. B. Richardson	86	146	12	5,949	194	16	44.39
8	E. D. Weekes	48	81	5	4,455	207	15	58.61
9	A. I. Kallicharran	66	109	10	4,399	187	12	44.43
10	R. C. Fredericks	59	109	7	4,334	169	8	42.49
11	**B. C. Lara**	**45**	**76**	**2**	**4,004**	**375**	**10**	**54.10**
12	F. M. M. Worrell	51	87	9	3,860	261	9	49.48
13	C. L. Walcott	44	74	7	3,798	220	15	56.68
14	P. J. L. Dujon	81	115	11	3,322	139	5	31.94
15	**C. L. Hooper**	**64**	**108**	**10**	**3,303**	**178***	**7**	**33.70**
16	C. C. Hunte	44	78	6	3,245	260	8	45.06
17	H. A. Gomes	60	91	11	3,171	143	9	39.63
18	B. F. Butcher	44	78	6	3,104	209*	7	43.11
19	S. M. Nurse	29	54	1	2,523	258	6	47.60
20	A. L. Logie	52	78	9	2,470	130	2	35.79
21	G. A. Headley	22	40	4	2,190	270*	10	60.83
22	J. B. Stollmeyer	32	56	5	2,159	160	4	42.33
23	L. G. Rowe	30	49	2	2,047	302	7	43.55

NEW ZEALAND

		T	I	NO	R	HS	100s	Avge
1	M. D. Crowe	77	131	11	5,444	299	17	45.36
2	J. G. Wright	82	148	7	5,334	185	12	37.82
3	B. E. Congdon	61	114	7	3,448	176	7	32.22
4	J. R. Reid	58	108	5	3,428	142	6	33.28
5	R. J. Hadlee	86	134	19	3,124	151*	2	27.16
6	G. M. Turner	41	73	6	2,991	259	7	44.64
7	A. H. Jones	39	74	8	2,922	186	7	44.27
8	B. Sutcliffe	42	76	8	2,727	230*	5	40.10
9	M. G. Burgess	50	92	6	2,684	119*	5	31.20
10	J. V. Coney	52	85	14	2,668	174*	3	37.57
11	G. P. Howarth	47	83	5	2,531	147	6	32.44
12	K. R. Rutherford	56	99	8	2,465	107*	3	27.08
13	G. T. Dowling	39	77	3	2,306	239	3	31.16
14	**M. J. Greatbatch**	**41**	**71**	**5**	**2,021**	**146***	**3**	**30.62**

INDIA

		T	I	NO	R	HS	100s	Avge
1	S. M. Gavaskar	125	214	16	10,122	236*	34	51.12
2	D. B. Vengsarkar	116	185	22	6,868	166	17	42.13
3	G. R. Viswanath	91	155	10	6,080	222	14	41.93
4	**M. Azharuddin**	**85**	**123**	**7**	**5,267**	**199**	**19**	**45.40**
5	Kapil Dev	131	184	15	5,248	163	8	31.05
6	M. Amarnath	69	113	10	4,378	138	11	42.50
7	**S. R. Tendulkar**	**55**	**83**	**8**	**3,907**	**179**	**13**	**52.09**
8	R. J. Shastri	80	121	14	3,830	206	11	35.79
9	P. R. Umrigar	59	94	8	3,631	223	12	42.22
10	V. L. Manjrekar	55	92	10	3,208	189*	7	39.12
11	C. G. Borde	55	97	11	3,061	177*	5	35.59
12	Nawab of Pataudi jun.	46	83	3	2,793	203*	6	34.91
13	S. M. H. Kirmani	88	124	22	2,759	102	2	27.04
14	F. M. Engineer	46	87	3	2,611	121	2	31.08
15	**N. S. Sidhu**	**42**	**63**	**2**	**2,519**	**201**	**8**	**41.29**
16	Pankaj Roy	43	79	4	2,442	173	5	32.56
17	V. S. Hazare	30	52	6	2,192	164*	7	47.65

		T	I	NO	R	HS	100s	Avge
18	A. L. Wadekar............	37	71	3	2,113	143	1	31.07
19	V. Mankad...............	44	72	5	2,109	231	5	31.47
20	C. P. S. Chauhan.........	40	68	2	2,084	97	0	31.57
21	K. Srikkanth.............	43	72	3	2,062	123	2	29.88
22	M. L. Jaisimha...........	39	71	4	2,056	129	3	30.68
23	**S. V. Manjrekar**	**37**	**61**	**6**	**2,043**	**218**	**4**	**37.14**
24	D. N. Sardesai............	30	55	4	2,001	212	5	39.23

PAKISTAN

		T	I	NO	R	HS	100s	Avge
1	Javed Miandad	124	189	21	8,832	280*	23	52.57
2	**Salim Malik**	**96**	**142**	**21**	**5,528**	**237**	**15**	**45.68**
3	Zaheer Abbas	78	124	11	5,062	274	12	44.79
4	Mudassar Nazar..........	76	116	8	4,114	231	10	38.09
5	Majid Khan	63	106	5	3,931	167	8	38.92
6	Hanif Mohammad	55	97	8	3,915	337	12	43.98
7	Imran Khan	88	126	25	3,807	136	6	37.69
8	Mushtaq Mohammad	57	100	7	3,643	201	10	39.17
9	Asif Iqbal................	58	99	7	3,575	175	11	38.85
10	Saeed Ahmed	41	78	4	2,991	172	5	40.41
11	**Ramiz Raja**	**57**	**94**	**5**	**2,833**	**122**	**2**	**31.83**
12	Wasim Raja..............	57	92	14	2,821	125	4	36.16
13	Mohsin Khan	48	79	6	2,709	200	7	37.10
14	Shoaib Mohammad	45	68	7	2,705	203*	7	44.34
15	Sadiq Mohammad	41	74	2	2,579	166	5	35.81
16	**Inzamam-ul-Haq**	**37**	**63**	**8**	**2,491**	**148**	**5**	**45.29**
17	**Aamir Sohail**	**34**	**62**	**3**	**2,103**	**205**	**2**	**35.64**
18	Imtiaz Ahmed	41	72	1	2,079	209	3	29.28
19	**Ijaz Ahmed, sen.**	**36**	**54**	**2**	**2,034**	**141**	**7**	**39.11**

SRI LANKA

		T	I	NO	R	HS	100s	Avge
1	P. A. de Silva	63	110	6	4,220	267	14	40.57
2	**A. Ranatunga**	**71**	**121**	**7**	**4,034**	**135***	**4**	**35.38**
3	H. P. Tillekeratne	43	72	12	2,579	126*	6	42.98
4	A. P. Gurusinha..........	41	70	7	2,452	143	7	38.92
5	R. S. Mahanama	45	77	1	2,383	225	4	31.35

ZIMBABWE: The highest aggregate is 1,396, average 46.53, by **D. L. Houghton** in 20 Tests.

Bold type denotes those who played Test cricket in 1996-97 and 1997 seasons.

HIGHEST CAREER AVERAGES

(Qualification: 20 innings)

Avge		T	I	NO	R	HS	100s
99.94	D. G. Bradman (A)..........	52	80	10	6,996	334	29
60.97	R. G. Pollock (SA)..........	23	41	4	2,256	274	7
60.83	G. A. Headley (WI)	22	40	4	2,190	270*	10
60.73	H. Sutcliffe (E)	54	84	9	4,555	194	16
59.23	E. Paynter (E)	20	31	5	1,540	243	4
58.67	K. F. Barrington (E).........	82	131	15	6,806	256	20
58.61	E. D. Weekes (WI)	48	81	5	4,455	207	15
58.45	W. R. Hammond (E)	85	140	16	7,249	336*	22

Avge		T	I	NO	R	HS	100s
57.78	G. S. Sobers (WI)	93	160	21	8,032	365*	26
56.94	J. B. Hobbs (E)	61	102	7	5,410	211	15
56.88	**J. C. Adams (WI)**	**29**	**46**	**11**	**1,991**	**208***	**5**
56.68	C. L. Walcott (WI)	44	74	7	3,798	220	15
56.67	L. Hutton (E)...............	79	138	15	6,971	364	19
55.00	E. Tyldesley (E)	14	20	2	990	122	3
54.20	C. A. Davis (WI)	15	29	5	1,301	183	4
54.20	V. G. Kambli (I)............	17	21	1	1,084	227	4
54.10	**B. C. Lara (WI)**.........	**45**	**76**	**2**	**4,004**	**375**	**10**
53.86	G. S. Chappell (A)	87	151	19	7,110	247*	24
53.85	**S. Chanderpaul (WI)**	**21**	**33**	**6**	**1,454**	**137***	**1**
53.81	A. D. Nourse (SA)	34	62	7	2,960	231	9
52.57	Javed Miandad (P)	124	189	21	8,832	280*	23
52.09	**S. R. Tendulkar (I)**	**55**	**83**	**8**	**3,907**	**179**	**13**
51.62	J. Ryder (A)	20	32	5	1,394	201*	3
51.12	S. M. Gavaskar (I)	125	214	16	10,122	236*	34
50.56	A. R. Border (A)...........	156	265	44	11,174	205	27
50.23	I. V. A. Richards (WI)	121	182	12	8,540	291	24
50.06	D. C. S. Compton (E)........	78	131	15	5,807	278	17

Bold type denotes those who played Test cricket in 1996-97 and 1997 seasons.

MOST HUNDREDS

							Opponents					
	Total	200+	Inns	E	A	SA	WI	NZ	I	P	SL	Z
S. M. Gavaskar (I)...	34	4	214	4	8	–	13	2	–	5	2	–
D. G. Bradman (A) ..	29	12	80	19	–	4	2	–	4	–	–	–
A. R. Border (A)	27	2	265	8	–	0	3	5	4	6	1	–
G. S. Sobers (WI) ...	26	2	160	10	4	–	–	1	8	3	–	–
G. S. Chappell (A) ..	24	4	151	9	–	–	5	3	1	6	0	–
I. V. A. Richards (WI)	24	3	182	8	5	–	–	1	8	2	–	–
Javed Miandad (P)...	23	6	189	2	6	–	2	7	5	–	1	–
G. Boycott (E)	22	1	193	–	7	1	5	2	4	3	–	–
M. C. Cowdrey (E) ..	22	0	188	–	5	3	6	2	3	3	–	–
W. R. Hammond (E)	22	7	140	–	9	6	1	4	2	–	–	–
D. C. Boon (A)	21	1	190	7	–	–	3	3	6	1	1	–
R. N. Harvey (A)....	21	2	137	6	–	8	3	–	4	0	–	–
K. F. Barrington (E) .	20	1	131	–	5	2	3	3	3	4	–	–
G. A. Gooch (E)	20	2	215	–	4	–	5	4	5	1	1	–
M. Azharuddin (I) ..	**19**	**0**	**123**	**6**	**1**	**3**	**0**	**1**	**–**	**3**	**5**	**0**
C. G. Greenidge (WI)	19	4	185	7	4	–	–	2	5	1	–	–
L. Hutton (E)	19	4	138	–	5	4	5	3	2	0	–	–
C. H. Lloyd (WI)....	19	1	175	5	6	–	–	0	7	1	–	–
D. I. Gower (E)	18	2	204	–	9	–	1	4	2	2	0	–
D. L. Haynes (WI) ..	18	0	202	5	5	0	–	3	2	3	–	–
D. C. S. Compton (E)	17	2	131	–	5	7	2	2	0	1	–	–
M. D. Crowe (NZ) ..	17	1	131	5	3	–	3	–	1	2	2	1
D. B. Vengsarkar (I) .	17	0	185	5	2	–	6	0	–	2	2	–
R. B. Richardson (WI)	16	0	146	4	9	0	–	1	2	0	–	–
H. Sutcliffe (E)	16	0	84	–	8	6	0	2	0	–	–	–
J. B. Hobbs (E)	15	1	102	–	12	2	1	–	–	–	–	–
R. B. Kanhai (WI)...	15	2	137	5	5	–	–	–	4	1	–	–
Salim Malik (P)	**15**	**1**	**142**	**4**	**2**	**0**	**1**	**2**	**3**	**–**	**3**	**0**
M. A. Taylor (A) ...	**15**	**1**	**155**	**6**	**–**	**1**	**1**	**1**	**1**	**3**	**2**	**–**

	Total	200+	Inns	E	A	SA	WI	NZ	I	P	SL	Z
C. L. Walcott (WI) ..	15	1	74	4	5	–	–	1	4	1	–	–
K. D. Walters (A) ...	15	2	125	4	–	0	6	3	1	1	–	–
E. D. Weekes (WI) ..	15	2	81	3	1	–	–	3	7	1	–	–

Opponents (column group heading above E A SA WI NZ I P SL Z)

Notes: The most hundreds for South Africa is 9 by A. D. Nourse in 62 innings, for Sri Lanka is 14 by **P. A. de Silva** in 110 innings and for Zimbabwe 4 by **D. L. Houghton** in 32 innings.

The most double-hundreds by batsmen not qualifying for the above list is four by Zaheer Abbas (12 hundreds for Pakistan) and three by R. B. Simpson (10 hundreds for Australia).

Bold type denotes those who played Test cricket in 1996-97 and 1997 seasons. Dashes indicate that a player did not play against the country concerned.

CARRYING BAT THROUGH TEST INNINGS

(Figures in brackets show side's total)

A. B. Tancred	26*	(47)	South Africa v England at Cape Town.....	1888-89
J. E. Barrett	67*	(176)	Australia v England at Lord's	1890
R. Abel............	132*	(307)	England v Australia at Sydney	1891-92
P. F. Warner	132*	(237)	England v South Africa at Johannesburg ..	1898-99
W. W. Armstrong ..	159*	(309)	Australia v South Africa at Johannesburg ..	1902-03
J. W. Zulch	43*	(103)	South Africa v England at Cape Town.....	1909-10
W. Bardsley.......	193*	(383)	Australia v England at Lord's	1926
W. M. Woodfull ...	30*	(66)‡	Australia v England at Brisbane	1928-29
W. M. Woodfull ...	73*	(193)†	Australia v England at Adelaide	1932-33
W. A. Brown......	206*	(422)	Australia v England at Lord's	1938
L. Hutton	202*	(344)	England v West Indies at The Oval	1950
L. Hutton	156*	(272)	England v Australia at Adelaide	1950-51
Nazar Mohammad ..	124*	(331)	Pakistan v India at Lucknow	1952-53
F. M. M. Worrell ..	191*	(372)	West Indies v England at Nottingham	1957
T. L. Goddard	56*	(99)	South Africa v Australia at Cape Town	1957-58
D. J. McGlew	127*	(292)	South Africa v New Zealand at Durban ...	1961-62
C. C. Hunte	60*	(131)	West Indies v Australia at Port-of-Spain ..	1964-65
G. M. Turner	43*	(131)	New Zealand v England at Lord's	1969
W. M. Lawry......	49*	(107)	Australia v India at Delhi	1969-70
W. M. Lawry......	60*	(116)†	Australia v England at Sydney	1970-71
G. M. Turner	223*	(386)	New Zealand v West Indies at Kingston ...	1971-72
I. R. Redpath......	159*	(346)	Australia v New Zealand at Auckland	1973-74
G. Boycott	99*	(215)	England v Australia at Perth	1979-80
S. M. Gavaskar	127*	(286)	India v Pakistan at Faisalabad	1982-83
Mudassar Nazar	152*	(323)	Pakistan v India at Lahore...............	1982-83
S. Wettimuny......	63*	(144)	Sri Lanka v New Zealand at Christchurch ..	1982-83
D. C. Boon	58*	(103)	Australia v New Zealand at Auckland	1985-86
D. L. Haynes	88*	(211)	West Indies v Pakistan at Karachi	1986-87
G. A. Gooch	154*	(252)	England v West Indies at Leeds	1991
D. L. Haynes	75*	(176)	West Indies v England at The Oval	1991
A. J. Stewart	69*	(175)	England v Pakistan at Lord's	1992
D. L. Haynes	143*	(382)	West Indies v Pakistan at Port-of-Spain ...	1992-93
M. H. Dekker	68*	(187)	Zimbabwe v Pakistan at Rawalpindi.......	1993-94
M. A. Atherton	94*	(228)	England v New Zealand at Christchurch ...	1996-97

† *One man absent.*   ‡ *Two men absent.*

Notes: G. M. Turner (223*) holds the record for the highest score by a player carrying his bat through a Test innings. He is also the youngest player to do so, being 22 years 63 days old when he first achieved the feat (1969).

G. A. Gooch (61.11%) holds the record for the highest percentage of a side's total by anyone carrying his bat throughout a Test innings.

Nazar Mohammad and Mudassar Nazar were father and son.

D. L. Haynes, who is alone in achieving this feat on three occasions, also opened the batting and was last man out in each innings for West Indies v New Zealand at Dunedin, 1979-80.

FASTEST FIFTIES

Minutes

28	J. T. Brown	England v Australia at Melbourne	1894-95
29	S. A. Durani	India v England at Kanpur	1963-64
30	E. A. V. Williams ...	West Indies v England at Bridgetown	1947-48
30	B. R. Taylor	New Zealand v West Indies at Auckland	1968-69
33	C. A. Roach	West Indies v England at The Oval	1933
34	C. R. Browne	West Indies v England at Georgetown	1929-30

The fastest fifties in terms of balls received (where recorded) are:

Balls

30	Kapil Dev	India v Pakistan at Karachi (2nd Test)	1982-83
32	I. V. A. Richards....	West Indies v India at Kingston	1982-83
32	I. T. Botham	England v New Zealand at The Oval	1986
33	R. C. Fredericks	West Indies v Australia at Perth	1975-76
33	Kapil Dev	India v Pakistan at Karachi	1978-79
33	Kapil Dev	India v England at Manchester	1982
33	A. J. Lamb.........	England v New Zealand at Auckland	1991-92

FASTEST HUNDREDS

Minutes

70	J. M. Gregory	Australia v South Africa at Johannesburg........	1921-22
75	G. L. Jessop........	England v Australia at The Oval	1902
78	R. Benaud	Australia v West Indies at Kingston	1954-55
80	J. H. Sinclair	South Africa v Australia at Cape Town	1902-03
81	I. V. A. Richards....	West Indies v England at St John's.............	1985-86
86	B. R. Taylor	New Zealand v West Indies at Auckland	1968-69

The fastest hundreds in terms of balls received (where recorded) are:

Balls

56	I. V. A. Richards....	West Indies v England at St John's.............	1985-86
67	J. M. Gregory	Australia v South Africa at Johannesburg........	1921-22
71	R. C. Fredericks	West Indies v Australia at Perth	1975-76
74	M. Azharuddin	India v South Africa at Calcutta	1996-97
74	Majid Khan	Pakistan v New Zealand at Karachi	1976-77
74	Kapil Dev	India v Sri Lanka at Kanpur	1986-87
76	G. L. Jessop........	England v Australia at The Oval	1902

FASTEST DOUBLE-HUNDREDS

Minutes

214	D. G. Bradman	Australia v England at Leeds..................	1930
223	S. J. McCabe.......	Australia v England at Nottingham	1938
226	V. T. Trumper......	Australia v South Africa at Adelaide	1910-11
234	D. G. Bradman	Australia v England at Lord's	1930
240	W. R. Hammond....	England v New Zealand at Auckland	1932-33
241	S. E. Gregory	Australia v England at Sydney.................	1894-95
245	D. C. S. Compton ...	England v Pakistan at Nottingham..............	1954

The fastest double-hundreds in terms of balls received (where recorded) are:

Balls

220	I. T. Botham	England v India at The Oval	1982
232	C. G. Greenidge	West Indies v England at Lord's	1984
240	C. H. Lloyd	West Indies v India at Bombay	1974-75
241	Zaheer Abbas	Pakistan v India at Lahore	1982-83
242	D. G. Bradman	Australia v England at The Oval	1934
242	I. V. A. Richards....	West Indies v Australia at Melbourne...........	1984-85

FASTEST TRIPLE-HUNDREDS

Minutes

288	W. R. Hammond	England v New Zealand at Auckland	1932-33
336	D. G. Bradman	Australia v England at Leeds	1930

MOST RUNS IN A DAY BY A BATSMAN

309	D. G. Bradman	Australia v England at Leeds	1930
295	W. R. Hammond	England v New Zealand at Auckland	1932-33
273	D. C. S. Compton ...	England v Pakistan at Nottingham	1954
271	D. G. Bradman	Australia v England at Leeds	1934

SLOWEST INDIVIDUAL BATTING

2* in 81 minutes	P. C. R. Tufnell, England v India at Bombay	1992-93
3* in 100 minutes	J. T. Murray, England v Australia at Sydney	1962-63
5 in 102 minutes	Nawab of Pataudi jun., India v England at Bombay	1972-73
6 in 106 minutes	D. R. Martyn, Australia v South Africa at Sydney	1993-94
7 in 123 minutes	G. Miller, England v Australia at Melbourne	1978-79
9 in 132 minutes	R. K. Chauhan, India v Sri Lanka at Ahmedabad	1993-94
10* in 133 minutes	T. G. Evans, England v Australia at Adelaide	1946-47
16* in 147 minutes	D. B. Vengsarkar, India v Pakistan at Kanpur	1979-80
17* in 166 minutes	G. M. Ritchie, Australia v India at Sydney	1985-86
18 in 194 minutes	W. R. Playle, New Zealand v England at Leeds	1958
19 in 217 minutes	M. D. Crowe, New Zealand v Sri Lanka at Moratuwa	1983-84
25 in 242 minutes	D. K. Morrison, New Zealand v Pakistan at Faisalabad	1990-91
28* in 250 minutes	J. W. Burke, Australia v England at Brisbane	1958-59
29* in 277 minutes	R. C. Russell, England v South Africa at Johannesburg	1995-96
35 in 332 minutes	C. J. Tavaré, England v India at Madras	1981-82
55 in 336 minutes	B. A. Edgar, New Zealand v Australia at Wellington	1981-82
57 in 346 minutes	G. S. Camacho, West Indies v England at Bridgetown	1967-68
58 in 367 minutes	Ijaz Butt, Pakistan v Australia at Karachi	1959-60
60 in 390 minutes	D. N. Sardesai, India v West Indies at Bridgetown	1961-62
62 in 408 minutes	Ramiz Raja, Pakistan v West Indies at Karachi	1986-87
68 in 458 minutes	T. E. Bailey, England v Australia at Brisbane	1958-59
86 in 474 minutes	Shoaib Mohammad, Pakistan v West Indies at Karachi.....	1990-91
99 in 505 minutes	M. L. Jaisimha, India v Pakistan at Kanpur	1960-61
105 in 575 minutes	D. J. McGlew, South Africa v Australia at Durban	1957-58
114 in 591 minutes	Mudassar Nazar, Pakistan v England at Lahore	1977-78
120* in 609 minutes	J. J. Crowe, New Zealand v Sri Lanka, Colombo (CCC) ...	1986-87
146* in 655 minutes	M. J. Greatbatch, New Zealand v Australia at Perth	1989-90
163 in 720 minutes	Shoaib Mohammad, Pakistan v New Zealand at Wellington .	1988-89
201* in 777 minutes	D. S. B. P. Kuruppu, Sri Lanka v New Zealand at Colombo	
	(CCC)	1986-87
337 in 970 minutes	Hanif Mohammad, Pakistan v West Indies at Bridgetown ..	1957-58

Note: The longest any batsman in all first-class innings has taken to score his first run is 97 minutes by T. G. Evans for England against Australia at Adelaide, 1946-47.

SLOWEST HUNDREDS

557 minutes	Mudassar Nazar, Pakistan v England at Lahore	1977-78
545 minutes	D. J. McGlew, South Africa v Australia at Durban	1957-58
535 minutes	A. P. Gurusinha, Sri Lanka v Zimbabwe at Harare	1994-95
516 minutes	J. J. Crowe, New Zealand v Sri Lanka at Colombo (CCC)	1986-87
500 minutes	S. V. Manjrekar, India v Zimbabwe at Harare	1992-93
488 minutes	P. E. Richardson, England v South Africa at Johannesburg	1956-57

Notes: The slowest hundred for any Test in England is 458 minutes (329 balls) by K. W. R. Fletcher, England v Pakistan, The Oval, 1974.

The slowest double-hundred in a Test was scored in 777 minutes (548 balls) by D. S. B. P. Kuruppu for Sri Lanka v New Zealand at Colombo (CCC), 1986-87, on his debut. It is also the slowest-ever first-class double-hundred.

HIGHEST PARTNERSHIPS FOR EACH WICKET

413 for 1st	V. Mankad (231)/Pankaj Roy (173)	I v NZ	Madras	1955-56
576 for 2nd	S. T. Jayasuriya (340)/R. S. Mahanama (225) ..	SL v I	Colombo (RPS)	1997-98
467 for 3rd	A. H. Jones (186)/M. D. Crowe (299)	NZ v SL	Wellington	1990-91
411 for 4th	P. B. H. May (285*)/M. C. Cowdrey (154)	E v WI	Birmingham	1957
405 for 5th	S. G. Barnes (234)/D. G. Bradman (234)	A v E	Sydney	1946-47
346 for 6th	J. H. W. Fingleton (136)/D. G. Bradman (270) .	A v E	Melbourne	1936-37
347 for 7th	D. St E. Atkinson (219)/C. C. Depeiza (122)...	WI v A	Bridgetown	1954-55
313 for 8th	Wasim Akram (257*)/Saqlain Mushtaq (79)....	P v Z	Sheikhupura	1996-97
190 for 9th	Asif Iqbal (146)/Intikhab Alam (51)	P v E	The Oval	1967
151 for 10th	B. F. Hastings (110)/R. O. Collinge (68*)	NZ v P	Auckland	1972-73

PARTNERSHIPS OF 300 AND OVER

576	for 2nd	S. T. Jayasuriya (340)/R. S. Mahanama (225) ..	SL v I	Colombo (RPS)	1997-98
467	for 3rd	A. H. Jones (186)/M. D. Crowe (299)	NZ v SL	Wellington	1990-91
451	for 2nd	W. H. Ponsford (266)/D. G. Bradman (244)....	A v E	The Oval	1934
451	for 3rd	Mudassar Nazar (231)/Javed Miandad (280*)...	P v I	Hyderabad	1982-83
446	for 2nd	C. C. Hunte (260)/G. S. Sobers (365*)........	WI v P	Kingston	1957-58
413	for 1st	V. Mankad (231)/Pankaj Roy (173)	I v NZ	Madras	1955-56
411	for 4th	P. B. H. May (285*)/M. C. Cowdrey (154)	E v WI	Birmingham	1957
405	for 5th	S. G. Barnes (234)/D. G. Bradman (234)	A v E	Sydney	1946-47
399	for 4th	G. S. Sobers (226)/F. M. M. Worrell (197*) ...	WI v E	Bridgetown	1959-60
397	for 3rd	Qasim Omar (206)/Javed Miandad (203*)	P v SL	Faisalabad	1985-86
388	for 4th	W. H. Ponsford (181)/D. G. Bradman (304)....	A v E	Leeds	1934
387	for 1st	G. M. Turner (259)/T. W. Jarvis (182)	NZ v WI	Georgetown	1971-72
385	for 5th	S. R. Waugh (160)/G. S. Blewett (214)	A v SA	Johannesburg	1996-97
382	for 2nd	L. Hutton (364)/M. Leyland (187).............	E v A	The Oval	1938
382	for 1st	W. M. Lawry (210)/R. B. Simpson (201).......	A v WI	Bridgetown	1964-65
370	for 3rd	W. J. Edrich (189)/D. C. S. Compton (208)....	E v SA	Lord's	1947
369	for 2nd	J. H. Edrich (310*)/K. F. Barrington (163).....	E v NZ	Leeds	1965
359	for 1st	L. Hutton (158)/C. Washbrook (195)	E v SA	Johannesburg	1948-49
351	for 2nd	G. A. Gooch (196)/D. I. Gower (157).........	E v A	The Oval	1985
350	for 4th	Mushtaq Mohammad (201)/Asif Iqbal (175)...	P v NZ	Dunedin	1972-73
347	for 7th	D. St E. Atkinson (219)/C. C. Depeiza (122)...	WI v A	Bridgetown	1954-55
346	for 6th	J. H. Fingleton (136)/D. G. Bradman (270) ...	A v E	Melbourne	1936-37
344*	for 2nd	S. M. Gavaskar (182*)/D. B. Vengsarkar (157*)	I v WI	Calcutta	1978-79
341	for 3rd	E. J. Barlow (201)/R. G. Pollock (175)........	SA v A	Adelaide	1963-64
338	for 3rd	E. D. Weekes (206)/F. M. M. Worrell (167) ...	WI v E	Port-of-Spain	1953-54
336	for 4th	W. M. Lawry (151)/K. D. Walters (242)	A v WI	Sydney	1968-69
332*	for 5th	A. R. Border (200*)/S. R. Waugh (157*)......	A v E	Leeds	1993
331	for 2nd	R. T. Robinson (148)/D. I. Gower (215).......	E v A	Birmingham	1985
329	for 1st	G. R. Marsh (138)/M. A. Taylor (219)	A v E	Nottingham	1989
323	for 1st	J. B. Hobbs (178)/W. Rhodes (179)	E v A	Melbourne	1911-12
322	for 4th	Javed Miandad (153*)/Salim Malik (165)......	P v E	Birmingham	1992
319	for 3rd	A. Melville (189)/A. D. Nourse (149)..........	SA v E	Nottingham	1947
316†	for 3rd	G. R. Viswanath (222)/Yashpal Sharma (140) .	I v E	Madras	1981-82
313	for 8th	Wasim Akram (257*)/Saqlain Mushtaq (79)....	P v Z	Sheikhupura	1996-97
308	for 7th	Waqar Hassan (189)/Imtiaz Ahmed (209)......	P v NZ	Lahore	1955-56
308	for 3rd	R. B. Richardson (154)/I. V. A. Richards (178).	WI v A	St John's	1983-84
308	for 3rd	G. A. Gooch (333)/A. J. Lamb (139)	E v I	Lord's	1990
303	for 3rd	I. V. A. Richards (232)/A. I. Kallicharran (97) .	WI v E	Nottingham	1976
303	for 3rd	M. A. Atherton (135)/R. A. Smith (175)	E v WI	St John's	1993-94
301	for 2nd	A. R. Morris (182)/D. G. Bradman (173*).....	A v E	Leeds	1948

† 415 runs were scored for this wicket in two separate partnerships: D. B. Vengsarkar retired hurt when he and Viswanath had added 99 runs.

BOWLING RECORDS

MOST WICKETS IN AN INNINGS

10-53	J. C. Laker.........	England v Australia at Manchester..............	1956
9-28	G. A. Lohmann.....	England v South Africa at Johannesburg........	1895-96
9-37	J. C. Laker........	England v Australia at Manchester.............	1956
9-52	R. J. Hadlee......	New Zealand v Australia at Brisbane...........	1985-86
9-56	Abdul Qadir......	Pakistan v England at Lahore.................	1987-88
9-57	D. E. Malcolm......	England v South Africa at The Oval............	1994
9-69	J. M. Patel	India v Australia at Kanpur...................	1959-60
9-83	Kapil Dev	India v West Indies at Ahmedabad.............	1983-84
9-86	Sarfraz Nawaz	Pakistan v Australia at Melbourne.............	1978-79
9-95	J. M. Noreiga	West Indies v India at Port-of-Spain...........	1970-71
9-102	S. P. Gupte	India v West Indies at Kanpur.................	1958-59
9-103	S. F. Barnes.......	England v South Africa at Johannesburg........	1913-14
9-113	H. J. Tayfield......	South Africa v England at Johannesburg........	1956-57
9-121	A. A. Mailey......	Australia v England at Melbourne..............	1920-21
8-7	G. A. Lohmann	England v South Africa at Port Elizabeth........	1895-96
8-11	J. Briggs.........	England v South Africa at Cape Town.........	1888-89
8-29	S. F. Barnes.......	England v South Africa at The Oval...........	1912
8-29	C. E. H. Croft	West Indies v Pakistan at Port-of-Spain........	1976-77
8-31	F. Laver	Australia v England at Manchester.............	1909
8-31	F. S. Trueman	England v India at Manchester	1952
8-34	I. T. Botham	England v Pakistan at Lord's.................	1978
8-35	G. A. Lohmann	England v Australia at Sydney.................	1886-87
8-38	L. R. Gibbs	West Indies v India at Bridgetown	1961-62
8-38	G. D. McGrath	Australia v England at Lord's	1997
8-43†	A. E. Trott.........	Australia v England at Adelaide	1894-95
8-43	H. Verity	England v Australia at Lord's	1934
8-43	R. G. D. Willis	Australia v England at Leeds.................	1981
8-45	C. E. L. Ambrose ...	West Indies v England at Bridgetown...........	1989-90
8-51	D. L. Underwood ...	England v Pakistan at Lord's	1974
8-52	V. Mankad........	India v Pakistan at Delhi	1952-53
8-53	G. B. Lawrence.....	South Africa v New Zealand at Johannesburg	1961-62
8-53†	R. A. L. Massie.....	Australia v England at Lord's	1972
8-55	V. Mankad........	India v England at Madras	1951-52
8-56	S. F. Barnes.......	England v South Africa at Johannesburg........	1913-14
8-58	G. A. Lohmann	England v Australia at Sydney.................	1891-92
8-58	Imran Khan	Pakistan v Sri Lanka at Lahore	1981-82
8-59	C. Blythe.........	England v South Africa at Leeds..............	1907
8-59	A. A. Mallett.......	Australia v Pakistan at Adelaide	1972-73
8-60	Imran Khan	Pakistan v India at Karachi	1982-83
8-61†	N. D. Hirwani	India v West Indies at Madras.................	1987-88
8-64†	L. Klusener	South Africa v India at Calcutta	1996-97
8-65	H. Trumble	Australia v England at The Oval	1902
8-68	W. Rhodes.........	England v Australia at Melbourne..............	1903-04
8-69	H. J. Tayfield......	South Africa v England at Durban	1956-57
8-69	Sikander Bakht	Pakistan v India at Delhi	1979-80
8-70	S. J. Snooke........	South Africa v England at Johannesburg........	1905-06
8-71	G. D. McKenzie	Australia v West Indies at Melbourne...........	1968-69
8-71	S. K. Warne	Australia v England at Brisbane	1994-95
8-71	A. A. Donald.......	South Africa v Zimbabwe at Harare	1995-96
8-72	S. Venkataraghavan..	India v New Zealand at Delhi	1964-65
8-75†	N. D. Hirwani	India v West Indies at Madras.................	1987-88
8-75	A. R. C. Fraser	England v West Indies at Bridgetown...........	1993-94
8-76	E. A. S. Prasanna ...	India v New Zealand at Auckland	1975-76
8-79	B. S. Chandrasekhar .	India v England at Delhi	1972-73
8-81	L. C. Braund	England v Australia at Melbourne..............	1903-04
8-83	J. R. Ratnayeke	Sri Lanka v Pakistan at Sialkot	1985-86
8-84†	R. A. L. Massie.....	Australia v England at Lord's	1972
8-85	Kapil Dev	India v Pakistan at Lahore	1982-83

8-86	A. W. Greig.......	England v West Indies at Port-of-Spain	1973-74
8-87	M. G. Hughes......	Australia v West Indies at Perth	1988-89
8-92	M. A. Holding......	West Indies v England at The Oval	1976
8-94	T. Richardson......	England v Australia at Sydney.................	1897-98
8-97	C. J. McDermott	Australia v England at Perth	1990-91
8-103	I. T. Botham	England v West Indies at Lord's	1984
8-104†	A. L. Valentine	West Indies v England at Manchester	1950
8-106	Kapil Dev	India v Australia at Adelaide	1985-86
8-107	B. J. T. Bosanquet ..	England v Australia at Nottingham	1905
8-107	N. A. Foster.......	England v Pakistan at Leeds	1987
8-112	G. F. Lawson.......	Australia v West Indies at Adelaide	1984-85
8-126	J. C. White	England v Australia at Adelaide	1928-29
8-141	C. J. McDermott	Australia v England at Manchester	1985
8-143	M. H. N. Walker....	Australia v England at Melbourne	1974-75

† *On Test debut.*
Note: The best for Zimbabwe is 6-90 by **H. H. Streak** against Pakistan at Harare in 1994-95.

OUTSTANDING ANALYSES

	O	*M*	*R*	*W*		
J. C. Laker (E)	51.2	23	53	10	v Australia at Manchester	1956
G. A. Lohmann (E)	14.2	6	28	9	v South Africa at Johannesburg ...	1895-96
J. C. Laker (E)	16.4	4	37	9	v Australia at Manchester	1956
G. A. Lohmann (E)	9.4	5	7	8	v South Africa at Port Elizabeth ...	1895-96
J. Briggs (E)	14.2	5	11	8	v South Africa at Cape Town	1888-89
J. Briggs (E)	19.1	11	17	7	v South Africa at Cape Town	1888-89
M. A. Noble (A)	7.4	2	17	7	v England at Melbourne..........	1901-02
W. Rhodes (E)	11	3	17	7	v Australia at Birmingham........	1902
A. E. R. Gilligan (E)	6.3	4	7	6	v South Africa at Birmingham	1924
S. Haigh (E)	11.4	6	11	6	v South Africa at Cape Town	1898-99
D. L. Underwood (E)	11.6	7	12	6	v New Zealand at Christchurch....	1970-71
S. L. V. Raju (I)	17.5	13	12	6	v Sri Lanka at Chandigarh........	1990-91
H. J. Tayfield (SA)	14	7	13	6	v New Zealand at Johannesburg ...	1953-54
C. T. B. Turner (A)	18	11	15	6	v England at Sydney	1886-87
M. H. N. Walker (A)	16	8	15	6	v Pakistan at Sydney	1972-73
E. R. H. Toshack (A)	2.3	1	2	5	v India at Brisbane..............	1947-48
H. Ironmonger (A)	7.2	5	6	5	v South Africa at Melbourne......	1931-32
T. B. A. May (A)	6.5	3	9	5	v West Indies at Adelaide	1992-93
Pervez Sajjad (P)	12	8	5	4	v New Zealand at Rawalpindi	1964-65
K. Higgs (E)	9	7	5	4	v New Zealand at Christchurch....	1965-66
P. H. Edmonds (E)	8	6	6	4	v Pakistan at Lord's	1978
J. C. White (E)	6.3	2	7	4	v Australia at Brisbane..........	1928-29
J. H. Wardle (E)	5	2	7	4	v Australia at Manchester	1953
R. Appleyard (E)	6	3	7	4	v New Zealand at Auckland	1954-55
R. Benaud (A)	3.4	3	0	3	v India at Delhi	1959-60

MOST WICKETS IN A MATCH

19-90	J. C. Laker..........	England v Australia at Manchester	1956
17-159	S. F. Barnes.........	England v South Africa at Johannesburg	1913-14
16-136†	N. D. Hirwani	India v West Indies at Madras	1987-88
16-137†	R. A. L. Massie.......	Australia v England at Lord's	1972
15-28	J. Briggs............	England v South Africa at Cape Town	1888-89
15-45	G. A. Lohmann	England v South Africa at Port Elizabeth	1895-96
15-99	C. Blythe	England v South Africa at Leeds..............	1907
15-104	H. Verity	England v Australia at Lord's	1934
15-123	R. J. Hadlee.........	New Zealand v Australia at Brisbane	1985-86
15-124	W. Rhodes...........	England v Australia at Melbourne	1903-04
14-90	F. R. Spofforth........	Australia v England at The Oval	1882

14-99	A. V. Bedser	England v Australia at Nottingham	1953
14-102	W. Bates	England v Australia at Melbourne	1882-83
14-116	Imran Khan	Pakistan v Sri Lanka at Lahore	1981-82
14-124	J. M. Patel	India v Australia at Kanpur	1959-60
14-144	S. F. Barnes.........	England v South Africa at Durban	1913-14
14-149	M. A. Holding........	West Indies v England at The Oval	1976
14-199	C. V. Grimmett	Australia v South Africa at Adelaide	1931-32

† *On Test debut.*

Notes: The best for South Africa is 13-165 by H. J. Tayfield against Australia at Melbourne, 1952-53; for Sri Lanka 10-90 by W. P. U. J. C. Vaas against New Zealand at Napier, 1994-95; for Zimbabwe 9-105 by H. H. Streak against Pakistan at Harare, 1994-95.

MOST WICKETS IN A SERIES

	T	R	W	Avge		
S. F. Barnes............	4	536	49	10.93	England v South Africa...	1913-14
J. C. Laker.............	5	442	46	9.60	England v Australia......	1956
C. V. Grimmett	5	642	44	14.59	Australia v South Africa ..	1935-36
T. M. Alderman	6	893	42	21.26	Australia v England......	1981
R. M. Hogg	6	527	41	12.85	Australia v England......	1978-79
T. M. Alderman	6	712	41	17.36	Australia v England......	1989
Imran Khan	6	558	40	13.95	Pakistan v India.........	1982-83
A. V. Bedser	5	682	39	17.48	England v Australia......	1953
D. K. Lillee	6	870	39	22.30	Australia v England......	1981
M. W. Tate	5	881	38	23.18	England v Australia......	1924-25
W. J. Whitty	5	632	37	17.08	Australia v South Africa ..	1910-11
H. J. Tayfield	5	636	37	17.18	South Africa v England...	1956-57
A. E. E. Vogler........	5	783	36	21.75	South Africa v England...	1909-10
A. A. Mailey..........	5	946	36	26.27	Australia v England......	1920-21
G. D. McGrath	6	701	36	19.47	Australia v England......	1997
G. A. Lohmann.......	3	203	35	5.80	England v South Africa...	1895-96
B. S. Chandrasekhar	5	662	35	18.91	India v England	1972-73
M. D. Marshall	5	443	35	12.65	West Indies v England ...	1988

Notes: The most for New Zealand is 33 by R. J. Hadlee against Australia in 1985-86, for Sri Lanka 20 by R. J. Ratnayake against India in 1985-86, and for Zimbabwe 22 by H. H. Streak against Pakistan in 1994-95.

MOST WICKETS IN A CALENDAR YEAR

	T	R	W	Avge	5W/i	10W/m	Year
D. K. Lillee (A)........	13	1,781	85	20.95	5	2	1981
J. Garner (WI)	15	1,604	77	20.83	4	–	1984
Kapil Dev (I)	18	1,739	75	23.18	5	1	1983
Kapil Dev (I)	18	1,720	74	23.24	5	–	1979
M. D. Marshall (WI)	13	1,471	73	20.15	9	1	1984
S. K. Warne (A)	16	1,697	72	23.56	2	–	1993
G. D. McKenzie (A)	14	1,737	71	24.46	4	1	1964
S. K. Warne (A)	10	1,274	70	18.20	6	2	1994

MOST WICKETS IN A CAREER

(Qualification: 100 wickets)

ENGLAND

		T	Balls	R	W	Avge	5W/i	10W/m
1	I. T. Botham	102	21,815	10,878	383	28.40	27	4
2	R. G. D. Willis	90	17,357	8,190	325	25.20	16	—
3	F. S. Trueman	67	15,178	6,625	307	21.57	17	3
4	D. L. Underwood	86	21,862	7,674	297	25.83	17	6
5	J. B. Statham	70	16,056	6,261	252	24.84	9	1
6	A. V. Bedser	51	15,918	5,876	236	24.89	15	5
7	J. A. Snow	49	12,021	5,387	202	26.66	8	1
8	J. C. Laker	46	12,027	4,101	193	21.24	9	3
9	S. F. Barnes	27	7,873	3,106	189	16.43	24	7
10	G. A. R. Lock	49	13,147	4,451	174	25.58	9	3
11	M. W. Tate	39	12,523	4,055	155	26.16	7	1
12	F. J. Titmus	53	15,118	4,931	153	32.22	7	—
13	J. E. Emburey	64	15,391	5,646	147	38.40	6	—
14	H. Verity	40	11,173	3,510	144	24.37	5	2
15	C. M. Old	46	8,858	4,020	143	28.11	4	—
16	A. W. Greig	58	9,802	4,541	141	32.20	6	2
17	P. A. J. DeFreitas	44	9,838	4,700	140	33.57	4	—
18	G. R. Dilley	41	8,192	4,107	138	29.76	6	—
19	T. E. Bailey	61	9,712	3,856	132	29.21	5	1
20	**D. E. Malcolm ......**	**40**	**8,480**	**4,748**	**128**	**37.09**	**5**	**2**
21	W. Rhodes	58	8,231	3,425	127	26.96	6	1
22	P. H. Edmonds	51	12,028	4,273	125	34.18	2	—
23	{D. A. Allen	39	11,297	3,779	122	30.97	4	—
	{R. Illingworth	61	11,934	3,807	122	31.20	3	—
25	A. R. C. Fraser	32	7,967	3,509	119	29.48	8	—
26	J. Briggs	33	5,332	2,095	118	17.75	9	4
27	G. G. Arnold	34	7,650	3,254	115	28.29	6	—
28	G. A. Lohmann	18	3,821	1,205	112	10.75	9	5
29	D. V. P. Wright	34	8,135	4,224	108	39.11	6	1
30	J. H. Wardle	28	6,597	2,080	102	20.39	5	1
31	R. Peel	20	5,216	1,715	101	16.98	5	1
32	C. Blythe	19	4,546	1,863	100	18.63	9	4

AUSTRALIA

		T	Balls	R	W	Avge	5W/i	10W/m
1	D. K. Lillee	70	18,467	8,493	355	23.92	23	7
2	C. J. McDermott	71	16,586	8,332	291	28.63	14	2
3	**S. K. Warne ....**	**58**	**16,642**	**6,323**	**264**	**23.95**	**11**	**3**
4	R. Benaud	63	19,108	6,704	248	27.03	16	1
5	G. D. McKenzie	60	17,681	7,328	246	29.78	16	3
6	R. R. Lindwall	61	13,650	5,251	228	23.03	12	—
7	C. V. Grimmett	37	14,513	5,231	216	24.21	21	7
8	M. G. Hughes	53	12,285	6,017	212	28.38	7	1
9	J. R. Thomson	51	10,535	5,601	200	28.00	8	—
10	A. K. Davidson	44	11,587	3,819	186	20.53	14	2
11	G. F. Lawson	46	11,118	5,501	180	30.56	11	2
12	{K. R. Miller	55	10,461	3,906	170	22.97	7	1
	{T. M. Alderman	41	10,181	4,616	170	27.15	14	1

		T	Balls	R	W	Avge	5W/i	10W/m
14	W. A. Johnston	40	11,048	3,826	160	23.91	7	—
15	**G. D. McGrath**	**34**	**8,133**	**3,636**	**155**	**23.45**	**8**	**—**
16	W. J. O'Reilly........	27	10,024	3,254	144	22.59	11	3
17	H. Trumble	32	8,099	3,072	141	21.78	9	3
18	M. H. N. Walker......	34	10,094	3,792	138	27.47	6	—
19	A. A. Mallett	38	9,990	3,940	132	29.84	6	1
20	B. Yardley	33	8,909	3,986	126	31.63	6	1
21	R. M. Hogg	38	7,633	3,503	123	28.47	6	2
22	M. A. Noble	42	7,159	3,025	121	25.00	9	2
23	B. A. Reid	27	6,244	2,784	113	24.63	5	2
24	I. W. Johnson	45	8,780	3,182	109	29.19	3	—
25	G. Giffen	31	6,457	2,791	103	27.09	7	1
26	A. N. Connolly	29	7,818	2,981	102	29.22	4	—
27	C. T. B. Turner.......	17	5,179	1,670	101	16.53	11	2

SOUTH AFRICA

		T	Balls	R	W	Avge	5W/i	10W/m
1	H. J. Tayfield........	37	13,568	4,405	170	25.91	14	2
2	**A. A. Donald**	**33**	**7,609**	**3,621**	**155**	**23.36**	**8**	**2**
3	T. L. Goddard	41	11,736	3,226	123	26.22	5	—
4	P. M. Pollock	28	6,522	2,806	116	24.18	9	1
5	N. A. T. Adcock	26	6,391	2,195	104	21.10	5	—

WEST INDIES

		T	Balls	R	W	Avge	5W/i	10W/m
1	M. D. Marshall	81	17,584	7,876	376	20.94	22	4
2	**C. A. Walsh**	**93**	**19,851**	**8,798**	**339**	**25.95**	**13**	**2**
3	L. R. Gibbs	79	27,115	8,989	309	29.09	18	2
4	**C. E. L. Ambrose**	**72**	**16,489**	**6,566**	**306**	**21.45**	**18**	**3**
5	J. Garner	58	13,169	5,433	259	20.97	7	—
6	M. A. Holding........	60	12,680	5,898	249	23.68	13	2
7	G. S. Sobers	93	21,599	7,999	235	34.03	6	—
8	A. M. E. Roberts......	47	11,136	5,174	202	25.61	11	2
9	W. W. Hall	48	10,421	5,066	192	26.38	9	1
10	S. Ramadhin	43	13,939	4,579	158	28.98	10	1
11	**I. R. Bishop**	**37**	**7,759**	**3,522**	**154**	**22.87**	**6**	**—**
12	A. L. Valentine	36	12,953	4,215	139	30.32	8	2
13	C. E. H. Croft	27	6,165	2,913	125	23.30	3	—
14	V. A. Holder	40	9,095	3,627	109	33.27	3	—

NEW ZEALAND

		T	Balls	R	W	Avge	5W/i	10W/m
1	R. J. Hadlee..........	86	21,918	9,612	431	22.29	36	9
2	**D. K. Morrison**	**48**	**10,064**	**5,549**	**160**	**34.68**	**10**	**—**
3	B. L. Cairns..........	43	10,628	4,280	130	32.92	6	1
4	E. J. Chatfield	43	10,360	3,958	123	32.17	3	1
5	R. O. Collinge	35	7,689	3,392	116	29.24	3	—
6	B. R. Taylor	30	6,334	2,953	111	26.60	4	—
7	J. G. Bracewell	41	8,403	3,653	102	35.81	4	1
8	R. C. Motz...........	32	7,034	3,148	100	31.48	5	—

INDIA

		T	Balls	R	W	Avge	5W/i	10W/m
1	Kapil Dev	131	27,740	12,867	434	29.64	23	2
2	B. S. Bedi	67	21,364	7,637	266	28.71	14	1
3	B. S. Chandrasekhar	58	15,963	7,199	242	29.74	16	2
4	E. A. S. Prasanna	49	14,353	5,742	189	30.38	10	2
5	**A. Kumble**	**40**	**12,106**	**4,903**	**168**	**29.18**	**9**	**1**
6	V. Mankad	44	14,686	5,236	162	32.32	8	2
7	S. Venkataraghavan.......	57	14,877	5,634	156	36.11	3	1
8	R. J. Shastri..............	80	15,751	6,185	151	40.96	2	—
9	S. P. Gupte	36	11,284	4,403	149	29.55	12	1
10	D. R. Doshi	33	9,322	3,502	114	30.71	6	—
11	K. D. Ghavri	39	7,042	3,656	109	33.54	4	—
12	N. S. Yadav..............	35	8,349	3,580	102	35.09	3	—

PAKISTAN

		T	Balls	R	W	Avge	5W/i	10W/m
1	Imran Khan	88	19,458	8,258	362	22.81	23	6
2	**Wasim Akram**	**72**	**16,464**	**7,054**	**311**	**22.68**	**21**	**4**
3	Abdul Qadir..............	67	17,126	7,742	236	32.80	15	5
4	**Waqar Younis**	**44**	**9,071**	**4,844**	**227**	**21.33**	**19**	**4**
5	Sarfraz Nawaz	55	13,927	5,798	177	32.75	4	1
6	Iqbal Qasim..............	50	13,019	4,807	171	28.11	8	2
7	Fazal Mahmood.........	34	9,834	3,434	139	24.70	13	4
8	Intikhab Alam	47	10,474	4,494	125	35.95	5	2
9	**Mushtaq Ahmed**	**28**	**7,172**	**3,309**	**117**	**28.28**	**7**	**2**

SRI LANKA

		T	Balls	R	W	Avge	5W/i	10W/m
1	**M. Muralitharan**	**32**	**9,012**	**3,895**	**132**	**29.50**	**9**	**—**

ZIMBABWE: The highest aggregate is 69 wickets, average 22.47, by **H. H. Streak** in 15 Tests.

Bold type denotes those who played Test cricket in 1996-97 and 1997 seasons.

WICKET WITH FIRST BALL IN TEST CRICKET

	Batsman dismissed			
A. Coningham	A. C. MacLaren	A v E.......	Melbourne	1894-95
W. M. Bradley	F. Laver	E v A......	Manchester......	1899
E. G. Arnold	V. T. Trumper	E v A......	Sydney..........	1903-04
G. G. Macaulay	G. A. L. Hearne	E v SA......	Cape Town	1922-23
M. W. Tate	M. J. Susskind	E v SA......	Birmingham	1924
M. Henderson	E. W. Dawson	NZ v E......	Christchurch.....	1929-30
H. D. Smith	E. Paynter	NZ v E......	Christchurch.....	1932-33
T. F. Johnson	W. W. Keeton	WI v E......	The Oval	1939
R. Howorth	D. V. Dyer	E v SA......	The Oval	1947
Intikhab Alam	C. C. McDonald	P v A......	Karachi........	1959-60
R. K. Illingworth	P. V. Simmons	E v WI......	Nottingham	1991
N. M. Kulkarni	M. S. Atapattu	I v SL	Colombo (RPS)..	1997-98

HAT-TRICKS

F. R. Spofforth......	Australia v England at Melbourne........................	1878-79
W. Bates	England v Australia at Melbourne....................	1882-83
J. Briggs..........	England v Australia at Sydney.....................	1891-92
G. A. Lohmann	England v South Africa at Port Elizabeth................	1895-96
J. T. Hearne........	England v Australia at Leeds	1899
H. Trumble	Australia v England at Melbourne..................	1901-02
H. Trumble	Australia v England at Melbourne..................	1903-04
T. J. Matthews†..... } T. J. Matthews†..... }	Australia v South Africa at Manchester	1912
M. J. C. Allom‡	England v New Zealand at Christchurch..............	1929-30
T. W. J. Goddard ...	England v South Africa at Johannesburg	1938-39
P. J. Loader.......	England v West Indies at Leeds	1957
L. F. Kline........	Australia v South Africa at Cape Town	1957-58
W. W. Hall	West Indies v Pakistan at Lahore	1958-59
G. M. Griffin	South Africa v England at Lord's	1960
L. R. Gibbs	West Indies v Australia at Adelaide	1960-61
P. J. Petherick‡	New Zealand v Pakistan at Lahore	1976-77
C. A. Walsh§.......	West Indies v Australia at Brisbane	1988-89
M. G. Hughes§	Australia v West Indies at Perth	1988-89
D. W. Fleming‡	Australia v Pakistan at Rawalpindi	1994-95
S. K. Warne........	Australia v England at Melbourne..................	1994-95
D. G. Cork.........	England v West Indies at Manchester	1995

  † *T. J. Matthews did the hat-trick in each innings of the same match.*
  ‡ *On Test debut.*
  § *Not all in the same innings.*

FOUR WICKETS IN FIVE BALLS

M. J. C. Allom	England v New Zealand at Christchurch..................	1929-30
	On debut, in his eighth over: W-WWW	
C. M. Old	England v Pakistan at Birmingham	1978
	Sequence interrupted by a no-ball: WW-WW	
Wasim Akram	Pakistan v West Indies at Lahore (WW-WW)..............	1990-91

MOST BALLS BOWLED IN A TEST

S. Ramadhin (West Indies) sent down 774 balls in 129 overs against England at Birmingham, 1957. It was the most delivered by any bowler in a Test, beating H. Verity's 766 for England against South Africa at Durban, 1938-39. In this match Ramadhin also bowled the most balls (588) in any single first-class innings, including Tests.

ALL-ROUND RECORDS

100 RUNS AND FIVE WICKETS IN AN INNINGS

England

A. W. Greig	148	6-164	v West Indies	Bridgetown	1973-74
I. T. Botham	103	5-73	v New Zealand	Christchurch	1977-78
I. T. Botham	108	8-34	v Pakistan	Lord's	1978
I. T. Botham	114	6-58 } 7-48 }	v India	Bombay	1979-80
I. T. Botham	149*	6-95	v Australia	Leeds	1981
I. T. Botham	138	5-59	v New Zealand	Wellington	1983-84

Australia

C. Kelleway	114	5-33	v South Africa	Manchester	1912
J. M. Gregory	100	7-69	v England	Melbourne	1920-21
K. R. Miller	109	6-107	v West Indies	Kingston	1954-55
R. Benaud	100	5-84	v South Africa	Johannesburg	1957-58

South Africa

J. H. Sinclair	106	6-26	v England	Cape Town	1898-99
G. A. Faulkner	123	5-120	v England	Johannesburg	1909-10

West Indies

D. St E. Atkinson	219	5-56	v Australia	Bridgetown	1954-55
O. G. Smith	100	5-90	v India	Delhi	1958-59
G. S. Sobers	104	5-63	v India	Kingston	1961-62
G. S. Sobers	174	5-41	v England	Leeds	1966

New Zealand

B. R. Taylor†	105	5-86	v India	Calcutta	1964-65

India

V. Mankad	184	5-196	v England	Lord's	1952
P. R. Umrigar	172*	5-107	v West Indies	Port-of-Spain	1961-62

Pakistan

Mushtaq Mohammad	201	5-49	v New Zealand	Dunedin	1972-73
Mushtaq Mohammad	121	5-28	v West Indies	Port-of-Spain	1976-77
Imran Khan	117	6-98 } 5-82 }	v India	Faisalabad	1982-83
Wasim Akram	123	5-100	v Australia	Adelaide	1989-90

Zimbabwe

P. A. Strang	106*	5-212	v Pakistan	Sheikhupura	1996-97

† *On debut.*

100 RUNS AND FIVE DISMISSALS IN AN INNINGS

D. T. Lindsay	182	6ct	SA v A	Johannesburg	1966-67
I. D. S. Smith	113*	4ct, 1st	NZ v E	Auckland	1983-84
S. A. R. Silva	111	5ct	SL v I	Colombo (PSS)	1985-86

100 RUNS AND TEN WICKETS IN A TEST

A. K. Davidson	44 80	5-135 } 6-87 }	A v WI	Brisbane	1960-61
I. T. Botham	114	6-58 } 7-48 }	E v I	Bombay	1979-80
Imran Khan	117	6-98 } 5-82 }	P v I	Faisalabad	1982-83

1,000 RUNS AND 100 WICKETS IN A CAREER

	Tests	Runs	Wkts	Tests for Double
England				
T. E. Bailey	61	2,290	132	47
†I. T. Botham	102	5,200	383	21
J. E. Emburey	64	1,713	147	46
A. W. Greig	58	3,599	141	37
R. Illingworth	61	1,836	122	47
W. Rhodes	58	2,325	127	44
M. W. Tate	39	1,198	155	33
F. J. Titmus	53	1,449	153	40
Australia				
R. Benaud	63	2,201	248	32
A. K. Davidson	44	1,328	186	34
G. Giffen	31	1,238	103	30
M. G. Hughes	53	1,032	212	52
I. W. Johnson	45	1,000	109	45
R. R. Lindwall	61	1,502	228	38
K. R. Miller	55	2,958	170	33
M. A. Noble	42	1,997	121	27
S. K. Warne	**58**	**1,027**	**264**	**58**
South Africa				
T. L. Goddard	41	2,516	123	36
West Indies				
C. E. L. Ambrose	**72**	**1,064**	**306**	**69**
M. D. Marshall	81	1,810	376	49
†G. S. Sobers	93	8,032	235	48
New Zealand				
J. G. Bracewell	41	1,001	102	41
R. J. Hadlee	86	3,124	431	28
India				
Kapil Dev	131	5,248	434	25
V. Mankad	44	2,109	162	23
R. J. Shastri	80	3,830	151	44
Pakistan				
Abdul Qadir	67	1,029	236	62
Imran Khan	88	3,807	362	30
Intikhab Alam	47	1,493	125	41
Sarfraz Nawaz	55	1,045	177	55
Wasim Akram	**72**	**1,944**	**311**	**45**

Bold type denotes those who played Test cricket in 1996-97 and 1997 seasons.

† I. T. Botham (120 catches) and G. S. Sobers (109) are the only players to have achieved the treble of 1,000 runs, 100 wickets and 100 catches.

WICKET-KEEPING RECORDS

Most Dismissals in an Innings

7 (all ct)	Wasim Bari	Pakistan v New Zealand at Auckland	1978-79
7 (all ct)	R. W. Taylor	England v India at Bombay	1979-80
7 (all ct)	I. D. S. Smith	New Zealand v Sri Lanka at Hamilton	1990-91
6 (all ct)	A. T. W. Grout	Australia v South Africa at Johannesburg	1957-58
6 (all ct)	D. T. Lindsay	South Africa v Australia at Johannesburg	1966-67
6 (all ct)	J. T. Murray	England v India at Lord's	1967

6 (5ct, 1st)	S. M. H. Kirmani ...	India v New Zealand at Christchurch	1975-76
6 (all ct)	R. W. Marsh	Australia v England at Brisbane	1982-83
6 (all ct)	S. A. R. Silva	Sri Lanka v India at Colombo (SSC)	1985-86
6 (all ct)	R. C. Russell	England v Australia at Melbourne	1990-91
6 (all ct)	R. C. Russell	England v South Africa at Johannesburg ..	1995-96
6 (all ct)	I. A. Healy..........	Australia v England at Birmingham	1997
6 (all ct)	A. J. Stewart	England v Australia at Manchester	1997

Note: The most stumpings in an innings is 5 by K. S. More for India v West Indies at Madras in 1987-88.

Most Dismissals in a Test

11 (all ct)	R. C. Russell	England v South Africa at Johannesburg ...	1995-96
10 (all ct)	R. W. Taylor	England v India at Bombay	1979-80
9 (8ct, 1st)	G. R. A. Langley ...	Australia v England at Lord's	1956
9 (all ct)	D. A. Murray.......	West Indies v Australia at Melbourne	1981-82
9 (all ct)	R. W. Marsh	Australia v England at Brisbane	1982-83
9 (all ct)	S. A. R. Silva	Sri Lanka v India at Colombo (SSC)	1985-86
9 (8ct, 1st)	S. A. R. Silva	Sri Lanka v India at Colombo (PSS).......	1985-86
9 (all ct)	D. J. Richardson	South Africa v India at Port Elizabeth	1992-93
9 (all ct)	Rashid Latif........	Pakistan v New Zealand at Auckland	1993-94
9 (all ct)	I. A. Healy..........	Australia v England at Brisbane	1994-95
9 (all ct)	C. O. Browne	West Indies v England at Nottingham......	1995
9 (7ct, 2st)	R. C. Russell	England v South Africa at Port Elizabeth ...	1995-96

Notes: S. A. R. Silva made 18 dismissals in two successive Tests.

The most stumpings in a match is 6 by K. S. More for India v West Indies at Madras in 1987-88.

J. J. Kelly (8ct) for Australia v England in 1901-02 and L. E. G. Ames (6ct, 2st) for England v West Indies in 1933 were the only wicket-keepers to make eight dismissals in a Test before World War II.

Most Dismissals in a Series

(Played in 5 Tests unless otherwise stated)

28 (all ct)	R. W. Marsh	Australia v England	1982-83
27 (25ct, 2st)	R. C. Russell	England v South Africa	1995-96
27 (25ct, 2st)	I. A. Healy..........	Australia v England (6 Tests)	1997
26 (23ct, 3st)	J. H. B. Waite	South Africa v New Zealand	1961-62
26 (all ct)	R. W. Marsh	Australia v West Indies (6 Tests)	1975-76
26 (21ct, 5st)	I. A. Healy..........	Australia v England (6 Tests)	1993
25 (23ct, 2st)	I. A. Healy..........	Australia v England	1994-95
24 (22ct, 2st)	D. L. Murray	West Indies v England	1963
24 (all ct)	D. T. Lindsay	South Africa v Australia................	1966-67
24 (21ct, 3st)	A. P. E. Knott	England v Australia (6 Tests)	1970-71
24 (all ct)	I. A. Healy..........	Australia v England	1990-91
23 (16ct, 7st)	J. H. B. Waite	South Africa v New Zealand	1953-54
23 (22ct, 1st)	F. C. M. Alexander..	West Indies v England	1959-60
23 (20ct, 3st)	A. T. W. Grout	Australia v West Indies	1960-61
23 (21ct, 2st)	A. E. Dick	New Zealand v South Africa	1961-62
23 (21ct, 2st)	R. W. Marsh	Australia v England	1972
23 (22ct, 1st)	A. P. E. Knott	England v Australia (6 Tests)	1974-75
23 (all ct)	R. W. Marsh	Australia v England (6 Tests)	1981
23 (all ct)	P. J. L. Dujon	West Indies v Australia	1990-91
23 (19ct, 4st)	I. A. Healy..........	Australia v West Indies	1992-93
23 (all ct)	A. J. Stewart	England v Australia (6 Tests)	1997
22 (all ct)	S. J. Rixon.........	Australia v India	1977-78
22 (21ct, 1st)	S. A. R. Silva	Sri Lanka v India (3 Tests)	1985-86

Notes: G. R. A. Langley made 20 dismissals (16ct, 4st) in four Tests for Australia v West Indies in 1954-55.

H. Strudwick, with 21 (15ct, 6st) for England v South Africa in 1913-14, was the only wicket-keeper to make as many as 20 dismissals in a series before World War II.

Most Dismissals in a Career

		T	Ct	St	Total
1	R. W. Marsh (Australia)	96	343	12	355
2	**I. A. Healy (Australia)**	**94**	**307**	**22**	**329**
3	P. J. L. Dujon (West Indies)	81	267	5	272
4	A. P. E. Knott (England)	95	250	19	269
5	Wasim Bari (Pakistan)	81	201	27	228
6	T. G. Evans (England)	91	173	46	219
7	S. M. H. Kirmani (India)	88	160	38	198
8	D. L. Murray (West Indies)	62	181	8	189
9	A. T. W. Grout (Australia)	51	163	24	187
10	I. D. S. Smith (New Zealand)	63	168	8	176
11	R. W. Taylor (England)	57	167	7	174
12	R. C. Russell (England)	49	141	11	152
13	J. H. B. Waite (South Africa)	50	124	17	141
14	**D. J. Richardson (South Africa)**	**37**	**134**	**1**	**135**
15	⎰ K. S. More (India)	49	110	20	130
	⎱ W. A. S. Oldfield (Australia)	54	78	52	130
17	**A. J. Stewart (England)**	**69**	**112**	**7**	**119**
18	J. M. Parks (England)	46	103	11	114
19	Salim Yousuf (Pakistan)	32	91	13	104

Notes: The records for P. J. L. Dujon and J. M. Parks each include two catches taken when not keeping wicket in two and three Tests respectively. A. J. Stewart's record includes 27 catches taken in 41 Tests when not keeping wicket.

The most wicket-keeping dismissals for other countries are Sri Lanka 34 (S. A. R. Silva 33ct, 1st in 9 Tests; **R. S. Kaluwitharana** 31ct, 3st in 16 Tests) and Zimbabwe 49 (**A. Flower** 45ct, 4st in 18 Tests as wicket-keeper).

Bold type denotes those who played Test cricket in 1996-97 and 1997 seasons.

FIELDING RECORDS

(Excluding wicket-keepers)

Most Catches in an Innings

5	V. Y. Richardson	Australia v South Africa at Durban	1935-36
5	Yajurvindra Singh	India v England at Bangalore	1976-77
5	M. Azharuddin	India v Pakistan at Karachi	1989-90
5	K. Srikkanth	India v Australia at Perth	1991-92

Most Catches in a Test

7	G. S. Chappell	Australia v England at Perth	1974-75
7	Yajurvindra Singh	India v England at Bangalore	1976-77
7	H. P. Tillekeratne	Sri Lanka v New Zealand at Colombo (SSC)	1992-93
6	A. Shrewsbury	England v Australia at Sydney	1887-88
6	A. E. E. Vogler	South Africa v England at Durban	1909-10
6	F. E. Woolley	England v Australia at Sydney	1911-12
6	J. M. Gregory	Australia v England at Sydney	1920-21
6	B. Mitchell	South Africa v Australia at Melbourne	1931-32
6	V. Y. Richardson	Australia v South Africa at Durban	1935-36
6	R. N. Harvey	Australia v England at Sydney	1962-63
6	M. C. Cowdrey	England v West Indies at Lord's	1963
6	E. D. Solkar	India v West Indies at Port-of-Spain	1970-71
6	G. S. Sobers	West Indies v England at Lord's	1973
6	I. M. Chappell	Australia v New Zealand at Adelaide	1973-74
6	A. W. Greig	England v Pakistan at Leeds	1974
6	D. F. Whatmore	Australia v India at Kanpur	1979-80

6	A. J. Lamb	England v New Zealand at Lord's	1983
6	G. A. Hick	England v Pakistan at Leeds	1992
6	B. A. Young	New Zealand v Pakistan at Auckland	1993-94
6	J. C. Adams	West Indies v England at Kingston	1993-94

Most Catches in a Series

15	J. M. Gregory	Australia v England	1920-21
14	G. S. Chappell	Australia v England (6 Tests)	1974-75
13	R. B. Simpson	Australia v South Africa	1957-58
13	R. B. Simpson	Australia v West Indies	1960-61

Most Catches in a Career

A. R. Border (Australia)	156 in 156 matches
M. A. Taylor (Australia)	**123 in 87 matches**
G. S. Chappell (Australia)	122 in 87 matches
I. V. A. Richards (West Indies)	122 in 121 matches
I. T. Botham (England)	120 in 102 matches
M. C. Cowdrey (England)	120 in 114 matches
R. B. Simpson (Australia)	110 in 62 matches
W. R. Hammond (England)	110 in 85 matches
G. S. Sobers (West Indies)	109 in 93 matches
S. M. Gavaskar (India)	108 in 125 matches
I. M. Chappell (Australia)	105 in 75 matches
G. A. Gooch (England)	103 in 118 matches

The most catches in the field for other countries are South Africa 56 (B. Mitchell in 42 Tests); New Zealand 71 (M. D. Crowe in 77 Tests); Pakistan 93 (Javed Miandad in 124 Tests); Sri Lanka 46 (**R. S. Mahanama** in 45 Tests); Zimbabwe 17 (**A. D. R. Campbell** in 22 Tests).

Bold type denotes those who played Test cricket in 1996-97 and 1997 seasons.

TEAM RECORDS

HIGHEST INNINGS TOTALS

952-6 dec.	Sri Lanka v India at Colombo (RPS)	1997-98
903-7 dec.	England v Australia at The Oval	1938
849	England v West Indies at Kingston	1929-30
790-3 dec.	West Indies v Pakistan at Kingston	1957-58
758-8 dec.	Australia v West Indies at Kingston	1954-55
729-6 dec.	Australia v England at Lord's	1930
708	Pakistan v England at The Oval	1987
701	Australia v England at The Oval	1934
699-5	Pakistan v India at Lahore	1989-90
695	Australia v England at The Oval	1930
692-8 dec.	West Indies v England at The Oval	1995
687-8 dec.	West Indies v England at The Oval	1976
681-8 dec.	West Indies v England at Port-of-Spain	1953-54
676-7	India v Sri Lanka at Kanpur	1986-87
674-6	Pakistan v India at Faisalabad	1984-85
674	Australia v India at Adelaide	1947-48
671-4	New Zealand v Sri Lanka at Wellington	1990-91
668	Australia v West Indies at Bridgetown	1954-55
660-5 dec.	West Indies v New Zealand at Wellington	1994-95

659-8 dec.	Australia v England at Sydney	1946-47
658-8 dec.	England v Australia at Nottingham	1938
657-8 dec.	Pakistan v West Indies at Bridgetown	1957-58
656-8 dec.	Australia v England at Manchester	1964
654-5	England v South Africa at Durban	1938-39
653-4 dec.	England v India at Lord's	1990
653-4 dec.	Australia v England at Leeds	1993
652-7 dec.	England v India at Madras	1984-85
652-8 dec.	West Indies v England at Lord's	1973
652	Pakistan v India at Faisalabad	1982-83
650-6 dec.	Australia v West Indies at Bridgetown	1964-65

The highest innings for the countries not mentioned above are:

622-9 dec.	South Africa v Australia at Durban	1969-70
544-4 dec.	Zimbabwe v Pakistan at Harare	1994-95

HIGHEST FOURTH-INNINGS TOTALS

To win

406-4	India (needing 403) v West Indies at Port-of-Spain	1975-76
404-3	Australia (needing 404) v England at Leeds	1948
362-7	Australia (needing 359) v West Indies at Georgetown	1977-78
348-5	West Indies (needing 345) v New Zealand at Auckland	1968-69
344-1	West Indies (needing 342) v England at Lord's	1984

To tie

347	India v Australia at Madras	1986-87

To draw

654-5	England (needing 696 to win) v South Africa at Durban	1938-39
429-8	India (needing 438 to win) v England at The Oval	1979
423-7	South Africa (needing 451 to win) v England at The Oval	1947
408-5	West Indies (needing 836 to win) v England at Kingston	1929-30

To lose

445	India (lost by 47 runs) v Australia at Adelaide	1977-78
440	New Zealand (lost by 38 runs) v England at Nottingham	1973
417	England (lost by 45 runs) v Australia at Melbourne	1976-77
411	England (lost by 193 runs) v Australia at Sydney	1924-25
402	Australia (lost by 103 runs) v England at Manchester	1981

MOST RUNS IN A DAY (BOTH SIDES)

588	England (398-6), India (190-0) at Manchester (2nd day)	1936
522	England (503-2), South Africa (19-0) at Lord's (2nd day)	1924
508	England (221-2), South Africa (287-6) at The Oval (3rd day)	1935

MOST RUNS IN A DAY (ONE SIDE)

503	England (503-2) v South Africa at Lord's (2nd day)...................... 1924
494	Australia (494-6) v South Africa at Sydney (1st day) 1910-11
475	Australia (475-2) v England at The Oval (1st day) 1934
471	England (471-8) v India at The Oval (1st day) 1936
458	Australia (458-3) v England at Leeds (1st day) 1930
455	Australia (455-1) v England at Leeds (2nd day) 1934

MOST WICKETS IN A DAY

27	England (18-3 to 53 out and 62) v Australia (60) at Lord's (2nd day) 1888
25	Australia (112 and 48-5) v England (61) at Melbourne (1st day)............. 1901-02

HIGHEST MATCH AGGREGATES

Runs	Wkts			Days played
1,981	35	South Africa v England at Durban	1938-39	10†
1,815	34	West Indies v England at Kingston	1929-30	9‡
1,764	39	Australia v West Indies at Adelaide	1968-69	5
1,753	40	Australia v England at Adelaide	1920-21	6
1,723	31	England v Australia at Leeds	1948	5
1,661	36	West Indies v Australia at Bridgetown	1954-55	6

† *No play on one day.*   ‡ *No play on two days.*

LOWEST INNINGS TOTALS

26	New Zealand v England at Auckland 1954-55
30	South Africa v England at Port Elizabeth............................. 1895-96
30	South Africa v England at Birmingham 1924
35	South Africa v England at Cape Town 1898-99
36	Australia v England at Birmingham 1902
36	South Africa v Australia at Melbourne 1931-32
42	Australia v England at Sydney....................................... 1887-88
42	New Zealand v Australia at Wellington 1945-46
42†	India v England at Lord's.. 1974
43	South Africa v England at Cape Town 1888-89
44	Australia v England at The Oval 1896
45	England v Australia at Sydney....................................... 1886-87
45	South Africa v Australia at Melbourne 1931-32
46	England v West Indies at Port-of-Spain 1993-94
47	South Africa v England at Cape Town 1888-89
47	New Zealand v England at Lord's.................................... 1958

The lowest innings for the countries not mentioned above are:

53	West Indies v Pakistan at Faisalabad 1986-87
62	Pakistan v Australia at Perth 1981-82
71	Sri Lanka v Pakistan at Kandy 1994-95
127	Zimbabwe v Sri Lanka at Colombo (RPS).............................. 1996-97

† *Batted one man short.*

FEWEST RUNS IN A FULL DAY'S PLAY

95   At Karachi, October 11, 1956. Australia 80 all out; Pakistan 15 for two (first day, $5\frac{1}{2}$ hours).

104 At Karachi, December 8, 1959. Pakistan 0 for no wicket to 104 for five v Australia (fourth day, $5\frac{1}{2}$ hours).

106 At Brisbane, December 9, 1958. England 92 for two to 198 all out v Australia (fourth day, 5 hours). *England were dismissed five minutes before the close of play, leaving no time for Australia to start their second innings.*

112 At Karachi, October 15, 1956. Australia 138 for six to 187 all out; Pakistan 63 for one (fourth day, $5\frac{1}{2}$ hours).

115 At Karachi, September 19, 1988. Australia 116 for seven to 165 all out and 66 for five following on v Pakistan (fourth day, $5\frac{1}{3}$ hours).

117 At Madras, October 19, 1956. India 117 for five v Australia (first day, $5\frac{1}{2}$ hours).

117 At Colombo (SSC), March 21, 1984. New Zealand 6 for no wicket to 123 for four (fifth day, 5 hours 47 minutes).

In England

151 At Lord's, August 26, 1978. England 175 for two to 289 all out; New Zealand 37 for seven (third day, 6 hours).

159 At Leeds, July 10, 1971. Pakistan 208 for four to 350 all out; England 17 for one (third day, 6 hours).

LOWEST MATCH AGGREGATES

(For a completed match)

Runs	Wkts			Days played
234	29	Australia v South Africa at Melbourne	1931-32	3†
291	40	England v Australia at Lord's	1888	2
295	28	New Zealand v Australia at Wellington	1945-46	2
309	29	West Indies v England at Bridgetown	1934-35	3
323	30	England v Australia at Manchester	1888	2

† *No play on one day.*

YOUNGEST TEST PLAYERS

Years	Days			
14	227†	Hasan Raza	Pakistan v Zimbabwe at Faisalabad	1996-97
15	124	Mushtaq Mohammad	Pakistan v West Indies at Lahore	1958-59
16	189	Aqib Javed	Pakistan v New Zealand at Wellington	1988-89
16	205	S. R. Tendulkar	India v Pakistan at Karachi	1989-90
16	221	Aftab Baloch	Pakistan v New Zealand at Dacca	1969-70
16	248	Nasim-ul-Ghani	Pakistan v West Indies at Bridgetown	1957-58
16	352	Khalid Hassan	Pakistan v England at Nottingham	1954
17	5	Zahid Fazal	Pakistan v West Indies at Karachi	1990-91

Years	Days			
17	69	Ata-ur-Rehman	Pakistan v England at Birmingham......	1992
17	118	L. Sivaramakrishnan......	India v West Indies at St John's........	1982-83
17	122	J. E. D. Sealy	West Indies v England at Bridgetown ...	1929-30
17	189	C. D. U. S. Weerasinghe ..	Sri Lanka v India at Colombo (PSS)	1985-86
17	193	Maninder Singh	India v Pakistan at Karachi	1982-83
17	239	I. D. Craig..............	Australia v South Africa at Melbourne...	1952-53
17	245	G. S. Sobers	West Indies v England at Kingston	1953-54
17	265	V. L. Mehra	India v New Zealand at Bombay	1955-56
17	300	Hanif Mohammad	Pakistan v India at Delhi	1952-53
17	341	Intikhab Alam...........	Pakistan v Australia at Karachi.........	1959-60
17	364	Waqar Younis	Pakistan v India at Karachi	1989-90

† Hasan Raza's age is in dispute and has been rejected by the Pakistan Cricket Board.
Note: The youngest Test players for countries not mentioned above are: England – D. B. Close, 18 years 149 days, v New Zealand at Manchester, 1949; New Zealand – D. L. Vettori, 18 years 10 days, v England at Wellington, 1996-97; South Africa – P. R. Adams, 18 years 340 days v England at Port Elizabeth, 1995-96; Zimbabwe – H. R. Olonga, 18 years 212 days, v Pakistan at Harare, 1994-95.

OLDEST PLAYERS ON TEST DEBUT

Years	Days			
49	119	J. Southerton	England v Australia at Melbourne	1876-77
47	284	Miran Bux..............	Pakistan v India at Lahore.............	1954-55
46	253	D. D. Blackie	Australia v England at Sydney	1928-29
46	237	H. Ironmonger	Australia v England at Brisbane	1928-29
42	242	N. Betancourt	West Indies v England at Port-of-Spain ..	1929-30
41	337	E. R. Wilson...........	England v Australia at Sydney	1920-21
41	27	R. J. D. Jamshedji	India v England at Bombay...........	1933-34
40	345	C. A. Wiles............	West Indies v England at Manchester ...	1933
40	295	O. Henry	South Africa v India at Durban........	1992-93
40	216	S. P. Kinneir...........	England v Australia at Sydney	1911-12
40	110	H. W. Lee.............	England v South Africa at Johannesburg .	1930-31
40	56	G. W. A. Chubb........	South Africa v England at Nottingham ..	1951
40	37	C. Ramaswami	India v England at Manchester	1936

Note: The oldest Test player on debut for New Zealand was H. M. McGirr, 38 years 101 days, v England at Auckland, 1929-30; for Sri Lanka, D. S. de Silva, 39 years 251 days, v England at Colombo (PSS), 1981-82; for Zimbabwe, A. C. Waller, 37 years 84 days, v England at Bulawayo, 1996-97. A. J. Traicos was 45 years 154 days old when he made his debut for Zimbabwe (v India at Harare, 1992-93) having played three Tests for South Africa in 1969-70.

OLDEST TEST PLAYERS

(Age on final day of their last Test match)

Years	Days			
52	165	W. Rhodes...........	England v West Indies at Kingston	1929-30
50	327	H. Ironmonger........	Australia v England at Sydney..........	1932-33
50	320	W. G. Grace	England v Australia at Nottingham	1899
50	303	G. Gunn..............	England v West Indies at Kingston	1929-30
49	139	J. Southerton	England v Australia at Melbourne.......	1876-77
47	302	Miran Bux	Pakistan v India at Peshawar	1954-55

Years	Days			
47	249	J. B. Hobbs	England v Australia at The Oval	1930
47	87	F. E. Woolley	England v Australia at The Oval	1934
46	309	D. D. Blackie	Australia v England at Adelaide	1928-29
46	206	A. W. Nourse	South Africa v England at The Oval	1924
46	202	H. Strudwick	England v Australia at The Oval	1926
46	41	E. H. Hendren	England v West Indies at Kingston	1934-35
45	304	A. J. Traicos	Zimbabwe v India at Delhi	1992-93
45	245	G. O. B. Allen........	England v West Indies at Kingston	1947-48
45	215	P. Holmes	England v India at Lord's	1932
45	140	D. B. Close	England v West Indies at Manchester	1976

MOST TEST APPEARANCES

156 A. R. Border (Australia)	116 D. B. Vengsarkar (India)
131 Kapil Dev (India)	114 M. C. Cowdrey (England)
125 S. M. Gavaskar (India)	110 C. H. Lloyd (West Indies)
124 Javed Miandad (Pakistan)	108 G. Boycott (England)
121 I. V. A. Richards (West Indies)	108 C. G. Greenidge (West Indies)
118 G. A. Gooch (England)	107 D. C. Boon (Australia)
117 D. I. Gower (England)	102 I. T. Botham (England)
116 D. L. Haynes (West Indies)	

The most appearances for New Zealand is 86 by R. J. Hadlee, for South Africa 50 by J. H. B. Waite, for Sri Lanka 71 by **A. Ranatunga** and for Zimbabwe 22 by **A. D. R. Campbell, A. Flower** and **G. W. Flower**.

Bold type denotes those who played Test cricket in 1996-97 and 1997 seasons.

MOST CONSECUTIVE TEST APPEARANCES

153	A. R. Border (Australia)..........	March 1979 to March 1994
106	S. M. Gavaskar (India)	January 1975 to February 1987
87	G. R. Viswanath (India)	March 1971 to February 1983
85	G. S. Sobers (West Indies).......	April 1955 to April 1972
72	D. L. Haynes (West Indies)	December 1979 to June 1988
71	I. M. Chappell (Australia)	January 1966 to February 1976
66	Kapil Dev (India)	October 1978 to December 1984
65	I. T. Botham (England)	February 1978 to March 1984
65	Kapil Dev (India)	January 1985 to March 1994
65	A. P. E. Knott (England)	March 1971 to August 1977

The most consecutive Test appearances for the countries not mentioned above are:

58†	J. R. Reid (New Zealand).........	July 1949 to July 1965
53	Javed Miandad (Pakistan).........	December 1977 to January 1984
45†	A. W. Nourse (South Africa)......	October 1902 to August 1924
35	P. A. de Silva (Sri Lanka)	February 1988 to March 1995

The most for Zimbabwe is 22 (as above).

  † *Indicates complete Test career.*

CAPTAINCY

MOST TESTS AS CAPTAIN

	P	W	L	D		P	W	L	D
A. R. Border (A)	93	32	22	38*	M. Azharuddin (I)	37	11	9	17
C. H. Lloyd (WI)	74	36	12	26	G. A. Gooch (E)	34	10	12	12
I. V. A. Richards (WI)	50	27	8	15	Javed Miandad (P)	34	14	6	14
G. S. Chappell (A)	48	21	13	14	Kapil Dev (I)	34	4	7	22*
Imran Khan (P)	48	14	8	26	J. R. Reid (NZ)	34	3	18	13
S. M. Gavaskar (I)	47	9	8	30	**M. A. Taylor (A)**	**33**	**18**	**10**	**5**
M. A. Atherton (E)	**46**	**12**	**16**	**18**	D. I. Gower (E)	32	5	18	9
A. Ranatunga (SL)	**44**	**7**	**16**	**21**	J. M. Brearley (E)	31	18	4	9
P. B. H. May (E)	41	20	10	11	R. Illingworth (E)	31	12	5	14
Nawab of Pataudi jun. (I)	40	9	19	12	I. M. Chappell (A)	30	15	5	10
R. B. Simpson (A)	39	12	12	15	E. R. Dexter (E)	30	9	7	14
G. S. Sobers (WI)	39	9	10	20	G. P. Howarth (NZ)	30	11	7	12

* One match tied.

Most Tests as captain of countries not mentioned above:

	P	W	L	D
H. W. Taylor (SA)	18	1	10	7
A. Flower (Z)	12	1	5	6

Notes: A. R. Border captained Australia in 93 consecutive Tests.

W. W. Armstrong (Australia) captained his country in the most Tests without being defeated: ten matches with eight wins and two draws.

I. T. Botham (England) captained his country in the most Tests without ever winning: 12 matches with eight draws and four defeats.

Bold type denotes those who were captains in 1996-97 and 1997 seasons.

UMPIRING

MOST TEST MATCHES

		First Test	Last Test
66	H. D. Bird (England)	1973	1996
48	F. Chester (England)	1924	1955
42	C. S. Elliott (England)	1957	1974
36	D. J. Constant (England)	1971	1988
36	**D. R. Shepherd (England)**	**1985**	**1997**
34	**Khizar Hayat (Pakistan)**	**1979-80**	**1996-97**
33	J. S. Buller (England)	1956	1969
33	A. R. Crafter (Australia)	1978-79	1991-92
32	R. W. Crockett (Australia)	1901-02	1924-25
31	D. Sang Hue (West Indies)	1961-62	1980-81
30	**S. A. Bucknor (West Indies)**	**1988-89**	**1997**
30	**S. G. Randell (Australia)**	**1984-85**	**1997-98**

Bold type indicates an umpire who stood in 1996-97 or 1997 seasons.

SUMMARY OF ALL TEST MATCHES

To August 23, 1997

	Opponents	Tests	Won by									Tied	Drawn
			E	A	SA	WI	NZ	I	P	SL	Z		
England	Australia	291	92	114	–	–	–	–	–	–	–	–	85
	South Africa	110	47	–	20	–	–	–	–	–	–	–	43
	West Indies	115	27	–	–	48	–	–	–	–	–	–	40
	New Zealand	78	36	–	–	–	4	–	–	–	–	–	38
	India	84	32	–	–	–	–	14	–	–	–	–	38
	Pakistan	55	14	–	–	–	–	–	9	–	–	–	32
	Sri Lanka	5	3	–	–	–	–	–	–	1	–	–	1
	Zimbabwe	2	0	–	–	–	–	–	–	–	0	–	2
Australia	South Africa	62	–	33	14	–	–	–	–	–	–	–	15
	West Indies	86	–	35	–	29	–	–	–	–	–	1	21
	New Zealand	32	–	13	–	–	7	–	–	–	–	–	12
	India	51	–	24	–	–	–	9	–	–	–	1	17
	Pakistan	40	–	14	–	–	–	–	11	–	–	–	15
	Sri Lanka	10	–	7	–	–	–	–	–	0	–	–	3
South Africa	West Indies	1	–	–	0	1	–	–	–	–	–	–	0
	New Zealand	21	–	–	12	–	3	–	–	–	–	–	6
	India	10	–	–	4	–	–	2	–	–	–	–	4
	Pakistan	1	–	–	1	–	–	–	0	–	–	–	0
	Sri Lanka	3	–	–	1	–	–	–	–	0	–	–	2
	Zimbabwe	1	–	–	1	–	–	–	–	–	0	–	0
West Indies	New Zealand	28	–	–	–	10	4	–	–	–	–	–	14
	India	70	–	–	–	28	–	7	–	–	–	–	35
	Pakistan	31	–	–	–	12	–	–	7	–	–	–	12
	Sri Lanka	3	–	–	–	1	–	–	–	0	–	–	2
New Zealand	India	35	–	–	–	–	6	13	–	–	–	–	16
	Pakistan	39	–	–	–	–	5	–	18	–	–	–	16
	Sri Lanka	15	–	–	–	–	6	–	–	2	–	–	7
	Zimbabwe	4	–	–	–	–	1	–	–	–	0	–	3
India	Pakistan	44	–	–	–	–	–	4	7	–	–	–	33
	Sri Lanka	16	–	–	–	–	–	7	–	1	–	–	8
	Zimbabwe	2	–	–	–	–	–	1	–	–	0	–	1
Pakistan	Sri Lanka	19	–	–	–	–	–	–	9	3	–	–	7
	Zimbabwe	8	–	–	–	–	–	–	5	–	1	–	2
Sri Lanka	Zimbabwe	5	–	–	–	–	–	–	–	2	0	–	3
		1,377	251	240	53	129	36	57	66	9	1	2	533

	Tests	Won	Lost	Drawn	Tied	Toss Won
England	740	251	210	279	–	362
Australia	572	240	162	168	2	287
South Africa	209	53	86	70	–	100
West Indies	334	129	80	124	1	174
New Zealand	252	36	104	112	–	128
India	312	57	102	152	1	159
Pakistan	237	66	54	117	–	116
Sri Lanka	76	9	34	33	–	38
Zimbabwe	22	1	10	11	–	13

ENGLAND v AUSTRALIA

Season	England	*Captains* Australia	T	E	A	D
1876-77	James Lillywhite	D. W. Gregory	2	1	1	0
1878-79	Lord Harris	D. W. Gregory	1	0	1	0
1880	Lord Harris	W. L. Murdoch	1	1	0	0
1881-82	A. Shaw	W. L. Murdoch	4	0	2	2
1882	A. N. Hornby	W. L. Murdoch	1	0	1	0

THE ASHES

Season	England	*Captains* Australia	T	E	A	D	Held by
1882-83	Hon. Ivo Bligh	W. L. Murdoch	4*	2	2	0	E
1884	Lord Harris[1]	W. L. Murdoch	3	1	0	2	E
1884-85	A. Shrewsbury	T. P. Horan[2]	5	3	2	0	E
1886	A. G. Steel	H. J. H. Scott	3	3	0	0	E

Captains

Season	England	Australia	T	E	A	D	Held by
1886-87	A. Shrewsbury	P. S. McDonnell	2	2	0	0	E
1887-88	W. W. Read	P. S. McDonnell	1	1	0	0	E
1888	W. G. Grace[3]	P. S. McDonnell	3	2	1	0	E
1890†	W. G. Grace	W. L. Murdoch	2	2	0	0	E
1891-92	W. G. Grace	J. McC. Blackham	3	1	2	0	A
1893	W. G. Grace[4]	J. McC. Blackham	3	1	0	2	E
1894-95	A. E. Stoddart	G. Giffen[5]	5	3	2	0	E
1896	W. G. Grace	G. H. S. Trott	3	2	1	0	E
1897-98	A. E. Stoddart[6]	G. H. S. Trott	5	1	4	0	A
1899	A. C. MacLaren[7]	J. Darling	5	0	1	4	A
1901-02	A. C. MacLaren	J. Darling[8]	5	1	4	0	A
1902	A. C. MacLaren	J. Darling	5	1	2	2	A
1903-04	P. F. Warner	M. A. Noble	5	3	2	0	E
1905	Hon. F. S. Jackson	J. Darling	5	2	0	3	E
1907-08	A. O. Jones[9]	M. A. Noble	5	1	4	0	A
1909	A. C. MacLaren	M. A. Noble	5	1	2	2	A
1911-12	J. W. H. T. Douglas	C. Hill	5	4	1	0	E
1912	C. B. Fry	S. E. Gregory	3	1	0	2	E
1920-21	J. W. H. T. Douglas	W. W. Armstrong	5	0	5	0	A
1921	Hon. L. H. Tennyson[10]	W. W. Armstrong	5	0	3	2	A
1924-25	A. E. R. Gilligan	H. L. Collins	5	1	4	0	A
1926	A. W. Carr[11]	H. L. Collins[12]	5	1	0	4	E
1928-29	A. P. F. Chapman[13]	J. Ryder	5	4	1	0	E
1930	A. P. F. Chapman[14]	W. M. Woodfull	5	1	2	2	A
1932-33	D. R. Jardine	W. M. Woodfull	5	4	1	0	E
1934	R. E. S. Wyatt[15]	W. M. Woodfull	5	1	2	2	A
1936-37	G. O. B. Allen	D. G. Bradman	5	2	3	0	A
1938†	W. R. Hammond	D. G. Bradman	4	1	1	2	A
1946-47	W. R. Hammond[16]	D. G. Bradman	5	0	3	2	A
1948	N. W. D. Yardley	D. G. Bradman	5	0	4	1	A
1950-51	F. R. Brown	A. L. Hassett	5	1	4	0	A
1953	L. Hutton	A. L. Hassett	5	1	0	4	E
1954-55	L. Hutton	I. W. Johnson[17]	5	3	1	1	E
1956	P. B. H. May	I. W. Johnson	5	2	1	2	E
1958-59	P. B. H. May	R. Benaud	5	0	4	1	A
1961	P. B. H. May[18]	R. Benaud[19]	5	1	2	2	A
1962-63	E. R. Dexter	R. Benaud	5	1	1	3	A
1964	E. R. Dexter	R. B. Simpson	5	0	1	4	A
1965-66	M. J. K. Smith	R. B. Simpson[20]	5	1	1	3	A
1968	M. C. Cowdrey[21]	W. M. Lawry[22]	5	1	1	3	A
1970-71†	R. Illingworth	W. M. Lawry[23]	6	2	0	4	E
1972	R. Illingworth	I. M. Chappell	5	2	2	1	E
1974-75	M. H. Denness[24]	I. M. Chappell	6	1	4	1	A
1975	A. W. Greig[25]	I. M. Chappell	4	0	1	3	A
1976-77‡	A. W. Greig	G. S. Chappell	1	0	1	0	—
1977	J. M. Brearley	G. S. Chappell	5	3	0	2	E
1978-79	J. M. Brearley	G. N. Yallop	6	5	1	0	E
1979-80‡	J. M. Brearley	G. S. Chappell	3	0	3	0	—
1980‡	I. T. Botham	G. S. Chappell	1	0	0	1	—
1981	J. M. Brearley[26]	K. J. Hughes	6	3	1	2	E
1982-83	R. G. D. Willis	G. S. Chappell	5	1	2	2	A
1985	D. I. Gower	A. R. Border	6	3	1	2	E
1986-87	M. W. Gatting	A. R. Border	5	2	1	2	E
1987-88‡	M. W. Gatting	A. R. Border	1	0	0	1	—
1989	D. I. Gower	A. R. Border	6	0	4	2	A
1990-91	G. A. Gooch[27]	A. R. Border	5	0	3	2	A
1993	G. A. Gooch[28]	A. R. Border	6	1	4	1	A
1994-95	M. A. Atherton	M. A. Taylor	5	1	3	1	A
1997	M. A. Atherton	M. A. Taylor	6	2	3	1	A

			T	E	A	D	
In Australia			150	52	73	25	
In England			141	40	41	60	
Totals			291	92	114	85	

* The Ashes were awarded in 1882-83 after a series of three matches which England won 2-1. A fourth match was played and this was won by Australia.

† The matches at Manchester in 1890 and 1938 and at Melbourne (Third Test) in 1970-71 were abandoned without a ball being bowled and are excluded.

‡ The Ashes were not at stake in these series.

Notes: The following deputised for the official touring captain or were appointed by the home authority for only a minor proportion of the series:
[1]A. N. Hornby (First). [2]W. L. Murdoch (First), H. H. Massie (Third), J. McC. Blackham (Fourth). [3]A. G. Steel (First). [4]A. E. Stoddart (First). [5]J. McC. Blackham (First). [6]A. C. MacLaren (First, Second and Fifth). [7]W. G. Grace (First). [8]H. Trumble (Fourth and Fifth). [9]F. L. Fane (First, Second and Third). [10]J. W. H. T. Douglas (First and Second). [11]A. P. F. Chapman (Fifth). [12]W. Bardsley (Third and Fourth). [13]J. C. White (Fifth). [14]R. E. S. Wyatt (Fifth). [15]C. F. Walters (First). [16]N. W. D. Yardley (Fifth). [17]A. R. Morris (Second). [18]M. C. Cowdrey (First and Second). [19]R. N. Harvey (Second). [20]B. C. Booth (First and Third). [21]T. W. Graveney (Fourth). [22]B. N. Jarman (Fourth). [23]I. M. Chappell (Seventh). [24]J. H. Edrich (Fourth). [25]M. H. Denness (First). [26]I. T. Botham (First and Second). [27]A. J. Lamb (First). [28]M. A. Atherton (Fifth and Sixth).

HIGHEST INNINGS TOTALS

For England in England: 903-7 dec. at The Oval 1938
in Australia: 636 at Sydney 1928-29

For Australia in England: 729-6 dec. at Lord's 1930
in Australia: 659-8 dec. at Sydney................................ 1946-47

LOWEST INNINGS TOTALS

For England in England: 52 at The Oval 1948
in Australia: 45 at Sydney 1886-87

For Australia in England: 36 at Birmingham 1902
in Australia: 42 at Sydney 1887-88

INDIVIDUAL HUNDREDS

For England (204)

R. Abel (1)			102	Adelaide.... 1965-66	**J. Briggs** (1)
132*‡	Sydney 1891-92		115	Melbourne .. 1965-66	121 Melbourne .. 1884-85
L. E. G. Ames (1)			**I. T. Botham** (4)		**B. C. Broad** (4)
120	Lord's...... 1934		119* Melbourne .. 1979-80		162 Perth....... 1986-87
M. A. Atherton (1)			149* Leeds 1981		116 Adelaide.... 1986-87
105	Sydney 1990-91		118 Manchester.. 1981		112 Melbourne .. 1986-87
R. W. Barber (1)			138 Brisbane.... 1986-87		139 Sydney 1987-88
185	Sydney 1965-66		**G. Boycott** (7)		**J. T. Brown** (1)
W. Barnes (1)			113 The Oval ... 1964		140 Melbourne .. 1894-95
134	Adelaide.... 1884-85		142* Sydney 1970-71		**A. P. F. Chapman** (1)
C. J. Barnett (2)			119* Adelaide.... 1970-71		121 Lord's...... 1930
129	Adelaide.... 1936-37		107 Nottingham . 1977		**D. C. S. Compton** (5)
126	Nottingham . 1938		191 Leeds 1977		102† Nottingham . 1938
K. F. Barrington (5)			128* Lord's...... 1980		147 } Adelaide.... 1946-47
132*	Adelaide.... 1962-63		137 The Oval ... 1981		103*}
101	Sydney 1962-63		**L. C. Braund** (2)		184 Nottingham . 1948
256	Manchester.. 1964		103* Adelaide.... 1901-02		145* Manchester.. 1948
			102 Sydney 1903-04		

M. C. Cowdrey (5)
102 Melbourne .. 1954-55
100* Sydney 1958-59
113 Melbourne .. 1962-63
104 Melbourne .. 1965-66
104 Birmingham. 1968
M. H. Denness (1)
188 Melbourne .. 1974-75
E. R. Dexter (2)
180 Birmingham. 1961
174 Manchester.. 1964
B. L. D'Oliveira (2)
158 The Oval ... 1968
117 Melbourne .. 1970-71
K. S. Duleepsinhji (1)
173† Lord's...... 1930
J. H. Edrich (7)
120† Lord's...... 1964
109 Melbourne .. 1965-66
103 Sydney 1965-66
164 The Oval ... 1968
115* Perth....... 1970-71
130 Adelaide.... 1970-71
175 Lord's...... 1975
W. J. Edrich (2)
119 Sydney 1946-47
111 Leeds 1948
K. W. R. Fletcher (1)
146 Melbourne .. 1974-75
R. E. Foster (1)
287† Sydney 1903-04
C. B. Fry (1)
144 The Oval ... 1905
M. W. Gatting (4)
160 Manchester.. 1985
100* Birmingham. 1985
100 Adelaide.... 1986-87
117 Adelaide.... 1994-95
G. A. Gooch (4)
196 The Oval ... 1985
117 Adelaide.... 1990-91
133 Manchester.. 1993
120 Nottingham . 1993
D. I. Gower (9)
102 Perth....... 1978-79
114 Adelaide.... 1982-83
166 Nottingham . 1985
215 Birmingham. 1985
157 The Oval ... 1985
136 Perth....... 1986-87
106 Lord's...... 1989
100 Melbourne .. 1990-91
123 Sydney 1990-91
W. G. Grace (2)
152† The Oval ... 1880
170 The Oval ... 1886
T. W. Graveney (1)
111 Sydney 1954-55
A. W. Greig (1)
110 Brisbane 1974-75
G. Gunn (2)
119† Sydney 1907-08
122* Sydney 1907-08
W. Gunn (1)
102* Manchester.. 1893

W. R. Hammond (9)
251 Sydney 1928-29
200 Melbourne .. 1928-29
119*}
177 } Adelaide.... 1928-29
113 Leeds 1930
112 Sydney 1932-33
101 Sydney 1932-33
231* Sydney 1936-37
240 Lord's...... 1938
J. Hardstaff jun. (1)
169* The Oval ... 1938
T. W. Hayward (2)
130 Manchester.. 1899
137 The Oval ... 1899
J. W. Hearne (1)
114 Melbourne .. 1911-12
E. H. Hendren (3)
127* Lord's...... 1926
169 Brisbane 1928-29
132 Manchester.. 1934
J. B. Hobbs (12)
126* Melbourne .. 1911-12
187 Adelaide.... 1911-12
178 Melbourne .. 1911-12
107 Lord's...... 1912
122 Melbourne .. 1920-21
123 Adelaide.... 1920-21
115 Sydney 1924-25
154 Melbourne .. 1924-25
119 Adelaide.... 1924-25
119 Lord's...... 1926
100 The Oval ... 1926
142 Melbourne .. 1928-29
N. Hussain (2)
207 Birmingham. 1997
105 Leeds 1997
K. L. Hutchings (1)
126 Melbourne .. 1907-08
L. Hutton (5)
100† Nottingham . 1938
364 The Oval ... 1938
122* Sydney 1946-47
156*‡ Adelaide.... 1950-51
145 Lord's...... 1953
Hon. F. S. Jackson (5)
103 The Oval ... 1893
118 The Oval ... 1899
128 Manchester.. 1902
144* Leeds 1905
113 Manchester.. 1905
G. L. Jessop (1)
104 The Oval ... 1902
A. P. E. Knott (2)
106* Adelaide.... 1974-75
135 Nottingham . 1977
A. J. Lamb (1)
125 Leeds 1989
M. Leyland (7)
137† Melbourne .. 1928-29
109 Lord's...... 1934
153 Manchester.. 1934
110 The Oval ... 1934

126 Brisbane 1936-37
111* Melbourne .. 1936-37
187 The Oval ... 1938
B. W. Luckhurst (2)
131 Perth....... 1970-71
109 Melbourne .. 1970-71
A. C. MacLaren (5)
120 Melbourne .. 1894-95
109 Sydney 1897-98
124 Adelaide.... 1897-98
116 Sydney 1901-02
140 Nottingham . 1905
J. W. H. Makepeace (1)
117 Melbourne .. 1920-21
P. B. H. May (3)
104 Sydney 1954-55
101 Leeds 1956
113 Melbourne .. 1958-59
C. P. Mead (1)
182* The Oval ... 1921
Nawab of Pataudi sen. (1)
102† Sydney 1932-33
E. Paynter (1)
216* Nottingham . 1938
D. W. Randall (3)
174† Melbourne .. 1976-77
150 Sydney 1978-79
115 Perth....... 1982-83
K. S. Ranjitsinhji (2)
154*† Manchester.. 1896
175 Sydney 1897-98
W. W. Read (1)
117 The Oval ... 1884
W. Rhodes (1)
179 Melbourne .. 1911-12
C. J. Richards (1)
133 Perth....... 1986-87
P. E. Richardson (1)
104 Manchester.. 1956
R. T. Robinson (2)
175† Leeds 1985
148 Birmingham. 1985
A. C. Russell (3)
135* Adelaide.... 1920-21
101 Manchester.. 1921
102* The Oval ... 1921
R. C. Russell (1)
128* Manchester.. 1989
J. Sharp (1)
105 The Oval ... 1909
Rev. D. S. Sheppard (2)
113 Manchester.. 1956
113 Melbourne .. 1962-63
A. Shrewsbury (3)
105* Melbourne .. 1884-85
164 Lord's...... 1886
106 Lord's...... 1893
R. T. Simpson (1)
156* Melbourne .. 1950-51
R. A. Smith (2)
143 Manchester.. 1989
101 Nottingham . 1989

A. G. Steel (2)
135*	Sydney	1882-83
148	Lord's......	1884

A. E. Stoddart (2)
134	Adelaide	1891-92
173	Melbourne ..	1894-95

R. Subba Row (2)
112†	Birmingham.	1961
137	The Oval ...	1961

H. Sutcliffe (8)
115†	Sydney	1924-25
176 } 127 }	Melbourne ..	1924-25
143	Melbourne ..	1924-25

161	The Oval ...	1926
135	Melbourne ..	1928-29
161	The Oval ...	1930
194	Sydney	1932-33

G. P. Thorpe (3)
114*†	Nottingham .	1993
123	Perth.......	1994-95
138	Birmingham.	1997

J. T. Tyldesley (3)
138	Birmingham.	1902
100	Leeds	1905
112*	The Oval ...	1905

G. Ulyett (1)
149	Melbourne ..	1881-82

A. Ward (1)
117	Sydney	1894-95

C. Washbrook (2)
112	Melbourne ..	1946-47
143	Leeds	1948

W. Watson (1)
109†	Lord's......	1953

F. E. Woolley (2)
133*	Sydney	1911-12
123	Sydney	1924-25

R. A. Woolmer (3)
149	The Oval ...	1975
120	Lord's......	1977
137	Manchester..	1977

† *Signifies hundred on first appearance in England–Australia Tests.*
‡ *Carried his bat.*

For Australia (239)

W. W. Armstrong (4)
133*	Melbourne ..	1907-08
158	Sydney	1920-21
121	Adelaide....	1920-21
123*	Melbourne ..	1920-21

C. L. Badcock (1)
118	Melbourne ..	1936-37

C. Bannerman (1)
165*†	Melbourne ..	1876-77

W. Bardsley (3)
136 } 130 }	The Oval ...	1909
193*‡	Lord's......	1926

S. G. Barnes (2)
234	Sydney	1946-47
141	Lord's......	1948

G. S. Blewett (3)
102*†	Adelaide ..	1994-95
115	Perth.......	1994-95
125	Birmingham.	1997

G. J. Bonnor (1)
128	Sydney	1884-85

D. C. Boon (7)
103	Adelaide....	1986-87
184*	Sydney	1987-88
121	Adelaide....	1990-91
164*	Lord's......	1993
101	Nottingham .	1993
107	Leeds	1993
131	Melbourne ..	1994-95

B. C. Booth (2)
112	Brisbane....	1962-63
103	Melbourne ..	1962-63

A. R. Border (8)
115	Perth.......	1979-80
123*	Manchester..	1981
106*	The Oval ...	1981
196	Lord's......	1985
146*	Manchester..	1985
125	Perth.......	1986-87
100*	Adelaide....	1986-87
200*	Leeds	1993

D. G. Bradman (19)
112	Melbourne ..	1928-29
123	Melbourne ..	1928-29
131	Nottingham .	1930
254	Lord's......	1930
334	Leeds	1930
232	The Oval ...	1930
103*	Melbourne ..	1932-33
304	Leeds	1934
244	The Oval ...	1934
270	Melbourne ..	1936-37
212	Adelaide....	1936-37
169	Melbourne ..	1936-37
144*	Nottingham .	1938
102*	Lord's......	1938
103	Leeds	1938
187	Brisbane....	1946-47
234	Sydney	1946-47
138	Nottingham .	1948
173*	Leeds	1948

W. A. Brown (3)
105	Lord's......	1934
133	Nottingham .	1938
206*‡	Lord's......	1938

P. J. Burge (4)
181	The Oval ...	1961
103	Sydney	1962-63
160	Leeds	1964
120	Melbourne ..	1965-66

J. W. Burke (1)
101*†	Adelaide....	1950-51

G. S. Chappell (9)
108†	Perth.......	1970-71
131	Lord's......	1972
113	The Oval ...	1972
144	Sydney	1974-75
102	Melbourne ..	1974-75
112	Manchester..	1977
114	Melbourne ..	1979-80
117	Perth.......	1982-83
115	Adelaide....	1982-83

I. M. Chappell (4)
111	Melbourne ..	1970-71
104	Adelaide....	1970-71
118	The Oval ...	1972
192	The Oval ...	1975

H. L. Collins (3)
104†	Sydney	1920-21
162	Adelaide....	1920-21
114	Sydney	1924-25

R. M. Cowper (1)
307	Melbourne ..	1965-66

J. Darling (3)
101	Sydney	1897-98
178	Adelaide....	1897-98
160	Sydney	1897-98

R. A. Duff (2)
104†	Melbourne ..	1901-02
146	The Oval ...	1905

J. Dyson (1)
102	Leeds	1981

R. Edwards (2)
170*	Nottingham .	1972
115	Perth.......	1974-75

M. T. G. Elliott (2)
112	Lord's......	1997
199	Leeds	1997

J. H. Fingleton (2)
100	Brisbane....	1936-37
136	Melbourne ..	1936-37

G. Giffen (1)
161	Sydney	1894-95

H. Graham (2)
107†	Lord's......	1893
105	Sydney	1894-95

J. M. Gregory (1)
100	Melbourne ..	1920-21

S. E. Gregory (4)
201	Sydney	1894-95
103	Lord's......	1896
117	The Oval ...	1899
112	Adelaide....	1903-04

R. J. Hartigan (1)
116†	Adelaide....	1907-08

R. N. Harvey (6)

112†	Leeds	1948
122	Manchester..	1953
162	Brisbane	1954-55
167	Melbourne ..	1958-59
114	Birmingham.	1961
154	Adelaide....	1962-63

A. L. Hassett (4)

128	Brisbane	1946-47
137	Nottingham .	1948
115	Nottingham .	1953
104	Lord's......	1953

I. A. Healy (1)

102*	Manchester..	1993

H. L. Hendry (1)

112	Sydney	1928-29

A. M. J. Hilditch (1)

119	Leeds	1985

C. Hill (4)

188	Melbourne ..	1897-98
135	Lord's......	1899
119	Sheffield	1902
160	Adelaide....	1907-08

T. P. Horan (1)

124	Melbourne ..	1881-82

K. J. Hughes (3)

129	Brisbane	1978-79
117	Lord's......	1980
137	Sydney	1982-83

F. A. Iredale (2)

140	Adelaide....	1894-95
108	Manchester..	1896

A. A. Jackson (1)

164†	Adelaide....	1928-29

D. M. Jones (3)

184*	Sydney	1986-87
157	Birmingham.	1989
122	The Oval ...	1989

C. Kelleway (1)

147	Adelaide....	1920-21

A. F. Kippax (1)

100	Melbourne ..	1928-29

W. M. Lawry (7)

130	Lord's......	1961
102	Manchester..	1961
106	Manchester..	1964
166	Brisbane	1965-66
119	Adelaide....	1965-66
108	Melbourne ..	1965-66
135	The Oval ...	1968

R. R. Lindwall (1)

100	Melbourne ..	1946-47

J. J. Lyons (1)

134	Sydney	1891-92

C. G. Macartney (5)

170	Sydney	1920-21
115	Leeds	1921
133*	Lord's......	1926
151	Leeds	1926
109	Manchester..	1926

S. J. McCabe (4)

187*	Sydney	1932-33
137	Manchester..	1934
112	Melbourne ..	1936-37
232	Nottingham .	1938

C. L. McCool (1)

104*	Melbourne ..	1946-47

R. B. McCosker (2)

127	The Oval ...	1975
107	Nottingham .	1977

C. C. McDonald (2)

170	Adelaide....	1958-59
133	Melbourne ..	1958-59

P. S. McDonnell (3)

147	Sydney	1881-82
103	The Oval ...	1884
124	Adelaide....	1884-85

C. E. McLeod (1)

112	Melbourne ..	1897-98

G. R. Marsh (2)

110†	Brisbane	1986-87
138	Nottingham .	1989

R. W. Marsh (1)

110*	Melbourne ..	1976-77

G. R. J. Matthews (1)

128	Sydney	1990-91

K. R. Miller (3)

141*	Adelaide....	1946-47
145*	Sydney	1950-51
109	Lord's......	1953

A. R. Morris (8)

155	Melbourne ..	1946-47
122 }	Adelaide....	1946-47
124* }		
105	Lord's......	1948
182	Leeds	1948
196	The Oval ...	1948
206	Adelaide....	1950-51
153	Brisbane	1954-55

W. L. Murdoch (2)

153*	The Oval ...	1880
211	The Oval ...	1884

M. A. Noble (1)

133	Sydney	1903-04

N. C. O'Neill (2)

117	The Oval ...	1961
100	Adelaide....	1962-63

C. E. Pellew (2)

116	Melbourne ..	1920-21
104	Adelaide....	1920-21

W. H. Ponsford (5)

110†	Sydney	1924-25
128	Melbourne ..	1924-25
110	The Oval ...	1930
181	Leeds	1934
266	The Oval ...	1934

R. T. Ponting (1)

127†	Leeds	1997

V. S. Ransford (1)

143*	Lord's......	1909

I. R. Redpath (2)

171	Perth.......	1970-71
105	Sydney	1974-75

A. J. Richardson (1)

100	Leeds	1926

V. Y. Richardson (1)

138	Melbourne ..	1924-25

G. M. Ritchie (1)

146	Nottingham .	1985

J. Ryder (2)

201*	Adelaide....	1924-25
112	Melbourne ..	1928-29

H. J. H. Scott (1)

102	The Oval ...	1884

R. B. Simpson (2)

311	Manchester..	1964
225	Adelaide....	1965-66

M. J. Slater (4)

152	Lord's......	1993
176	Brisbane	1994-95
103	Sydney	1994-95
124	Perth.......	1994-95

K. R. Stackpole (3)

207	Brisbane	1970-71
136	Adelaide....	1970-71
114	Nottingham .	1972

J. M. Taylor (1)

108	Sydney	1924-25

M. A. Taylor (6)

136†	Leeds	1989
219	Nottingham .	1989
124	Manchester..	1993
111	Lord's......	1993
113	Sydney	1994-95
129	Birmingham.	1997

G. H. S. Trott (1)

143	Lord's......	1896

V. T. Trumper (6)

135*	Lord's......	1899
104	Manchester..	1902
185*	Sydney	1903-04
113	Adelaide....	1903-04
166	Sydney	1907-08
113	Sydney	1911-12

K. D. Walters (4)

155†	Brisbane	1965-66
115	Melbourne ..	1965-66
112	Brisbane	1970-71
103	Perth.......	1974-75

M. E. Waugh (3)

138†	Adelaide....	1990-91
137	Birmingham.	1993
140	Brisbane	1994-95

S. R. Waugh (5)

177*	Leeds	1989
152*	Lord's......	1989
157*	Leeds	1993
108 }	Manchester..	1997
116 }		

D. M. Wellham (1)

103†	The Oval ...	1981

K. C. Wessels (1)

162†	Brisbane	1982-83

G. M. Wood (3)

100	Melbourne ..	1978-79
112	Lord's......	1980
172	Nottingham .	1985

W. M. Woodfull (6)					107	Melbourne ..	1928-29	**G. N. Yallop** (3)		
141	Leeds	1926		102		Melbourne ..	1928-29	102†	Brisbane....	1978-79
117	Manchester..	1926						121	Sydney	1978-79
111	Sydney	1928-29		155	Lord's......		1930	114	Manchester..	1981

† *Signifies hundred on first appearance in England–Australia Tests.*
‡ *Carried his bat.*

RECORD PARTNERSHIPS FOR EACH WICKET

For England

323 for 1st	J. B. Hobbs and W. Rhodes at Melbourne	1911-12
382 for 2nd†	L. Hutton and M. Leyland at The Oval	1938
262 for 3rd	W. R. Hammond and D. R. Jardine at Adelaide	1928-29
288 for 4th	N. Hussain and G. P. Thorpe at Birmingham..............	1997
206 for 5th	E. Paynter and D. C. S. Compton at Nottingham..............	1938
215 for 6th	{ L. Hutton and J. Hardstaff jun. at The Oval	1938
	{ G. Boycott and A. P. E. Knott at Nottingham	1977
143 for 7th	F. E. Woolley and J. Vine at Sydney	1911-12
124 for 8th	E. H. Hendren and H. Larwood at Brisbane..............	1928-29
151 for 9th	W. H. Scotton and W. W. Read at The Oval..............	1884
130 for 10th†	R. E. Foster and W. Rhodes at Sydney..............	1903-04

For Australia

329 for 1st	G. R. Marsh and M. A. Taylor at Nottingham	1989
451 for 2nd†	W. H. Ponsford and D. G. Bradman at The Oval	1934
276 for 3rd	D. G. Bradman and A. L. Hassett at Brisbane	1946-47
388 for 4th†	W. H. Ponsford and D. G. Bradman at Leeds	1934
405 for 5th†	S. G. Barnes and D. G. Bradman at Sydney	1946-47
346 for 6th†	J. H. Fingleton and D. G. Bradman at Melbourne..............	1936-37
165 for 7th	C. Hill and H. Trumble at Melbourne..............	1897-98
243 for 8th†	R. J. Hartigan and C. Hill at Adelaide	1907-08
154 for 9th†	S. E. Gregory and J. McC. Blackham at Sydney	1894-95
127 for 10th†	J. M. Taylor and A. A. Mailey at Sydney	1924-25

† *Denotes record partnership against all countries.*

MOST RUNS IN A SERIES

England in England	732 (average 81.33)	D. I. Gower	1985
England in Australia	905 (average 113.12)	W. R. Hammond ...	1928-29
Australia in England	974 (average 139.14)	D. G. Bradman	1930
Australia in Australia	810 (average 90.00)	D. G. Bradman	1936-37

TEN WICKETS OR MORE IN A MATCH

For England (37)

13-163 (6-42, 7-121)	S. F. Barnes, Melbourne................................	1901-02
14-102 (7-28, 7-74)	W. Bates, Melbourne	1882-83
10-105 (5-46, 5-59)	A. V. Bedser, Melbourne	1950-51
14-99 (7-55, 7-44)	A. V. Bedser, Nottingham	1953

11-102 (6-44, 5-58)	C. Blythe, Birmingham.............................	1909
11-176 (6-78, 5-98)	I. T. Botham, Perth	1979-80
10-253 (6-125, 4-128)	I. T. Botham, The Oval	1981
11-74 (5-29, 6-45)	J. Briggs, Lord's	1886
12-136 (6-49, 6-87)	J. Briggs, Adelaide	1891-92
10-148 (5-34, 5-114)	J. Briggs, The Oval..............................	1893
10-104 (6-77, 4-27)†	R. M. Ellison, Birmingham	1985
10-179 (5-102, 5-77)†	K. Farnes, Nottingham	1934
10-60 (6-41, 4-19)	J. T. Hearne, The Oval	1896
11-113 (5-58, 6-55)	J. C. Laker, Leeds	1956
19-90 (9-37, 10-53)	J. C. Laker, Manchester	1956
10-124 (5-96, 5-28)	H. Larwood, Sydney..............................	1932-33
11-76 (6-48, 5-28)	W. H. Lockwood, Manchester	1902
12-104 (7-36, 5-68)	G. A. Lohmann, The Oval	1886
10-87 (8-35, 2-52)	G. A. Lohmann, Sydney	1886-87
10-142 (8-58, 2-84)	G. A. Lohmann, Sydney	1891-92
12-102 (6-50, 6-52)†	F. Martin, The Oval	1890
11-68 (7-31, 4-37)	R. Peel, Manchester	1888
15-124 (7-56, 8-68)	W. Rhodes, Melbourne	1903-04
10-156 (5-49, 5-107)†	T. Richardson, Manchester........................	1893
11-173 (6-39, 5-134)	T. Richardson, Lord's	1896
13-244 (7-168, 6-76)	T. Richardson, Manchester........................	1896
10-204 (8-94, 2-110)	T. Richardson, Sydney	1897-98
11-228 (6-130, 5-98)†	M. W. Tate, Sydney	1924-25
11-88 (5-58, 6-30)	F. S. Trueman, Leeds	1961
11-93 (7-66, 4-27)	P. C. R. Tufnell, The Oval........................	1997
10-130 (4-45, 6-85)	F. H. Tyson, Sydney..............................	1954-55
10-82 (4-37, 6-45)	D. L. Underwood, Leeds	1972
11-215 (7-113, 4-102)	D. L. Underwood, Adelaide	1974-75
15-104 (7-61, 8-43)	H. Verity, Lord's	1934
10-57 (6-41, 4-16)	W. Voce, Brisbane	1936-37
13-256 (5-130, 8-126)	J. C. White, Adelaide	1928-29
10-49 (5-29, 5-20)	F. E. Woolley, The Oval	1912

For Australia (39)

10-151 (5-107, 5-44)	T. M. Alderman, Leeds	1989
10-239 (4-129, 6-110)	L. O'B. Fleetwood-Smith, Adelaide	1936-37
10-160 (4-88, 6-72)	G. Giffen, Sydney	1891-92
11-82 (5-45, 6-37)†	C. V. Grimmett, Sydney...........................	1924-25
10-201 (5-107, 5-94)	C. V. Grimmett, Nottingham	1930
10-122 (5-65, 5-57)	R. M. Hogg, Perth	1978-79
10-66 (5-30, 5-36)	R. M. Hogg, Melbourne	1978-79
12-175 (5-85, 7-90)†	H. V. Hordern, Sydney	1911-12
10-161 (5-95, 5-66)	H. V. Hordern, Sydney	1911-12
10-164 (7-88, 3-76)	E. Jones, Lord's	1899
11-134 (6-47, 5-87)	G. F. Lawson, Brisbane	1982-83
10-181 (5-58, 5-123)	D. K. Lillee, The Oval	1972
11-165 (6-26, 5-139)	D. K. Lillee, Melbourne	1976-77
11-138 (6-60, 5-78)	D. K. Lillee, Melbourne	1979-80
11-159 (7-89, 4-70)	D. K. Lillee, The Oval	1981
11-85 (7-58, 4-27)	C. G. Macartney, Leeds	1909
11-157 (8-97, 3-60)	C. J. McDermott, Perth...........................	1990-91
10-302 (5-160, 5-142)	A. A. Mailey, Adelaide	1920-21
13-236 (4-115, 9-121)	A. A. Mailey, Melbourne	1920-21
16-137 (8-84, 8-53)†	R. A. L. Massie, Lord's	1972
10-152 (5-72, 5-80)	K. R. Miller, Lord's	1956
13-77 (7-17, 6-60)	M. A. Noble, Melbourne	1901-02
11-103 (5-51, 6-52)	M. A. Noble, Sheffield	1902
10-129 (5-63, 5-66)	W. J. O'Reilly, Melbourne	1932-33
11-129 (4-75, 7-54)	W. J. O'Reilly, Nottingham	1934

10-122 (5-66, 5-56)	W. J. O'Reilly, Leeds	1938
11-165 (7-68, 4-97)	G. E. Palmer, Sydney	1881-82
10-126 (7-65, 3-61)	G. E. Palmer, Melbourne	1882-83
13-148 (6-97, 7-51)	B. A. Reid, Melbourne	1990-91
13-110 (6-48, 7-62)	F. R. Spofforth, Melbourne	1878-79
14-90 (7-46, 7-44)	F. R. Spofforth, The Oval	1882
11-117 (4-73, 7-44)	F. R. Spofforth, Sydney	1882-83
10-144 (4-54, 6-90)	F. R. Spofforth, Sydney	1884-85
12-89 (6-59, 6-30)	H. Trumble, The Oval	1896
10-128 (4-75, 6-53)	H. Trumble, Manchester	1902
12-173 (8-65, 4-108)	H. Trumble, The Oval	1902
12-87 (5-44, 7-43)	C. T. B. Turner, Sydney	1887-88
10-63 (5-27, 5-36)	C. T. B. Turner, Lord's	1888
11-110 (3-39, 8-71)	S. K. Warne, Brisbane	1994-95

† *Signifies ten wickets or more on first appearance in England–Australia Tests.*

Note: J. Briggs, J. C. Laker, T. Richardson in 1896, R. M. Hogg, A. A. Mailey, H. Trumble and
C. T. B. Turner took ten wickets or more in successive Tests. J. Briggs was omitted, however,
from the England team for the first Test match in 1893.

MOST WICKETS IN A SERIES

England in England	46 (average 9.60)	J. C. Laker	1956
England in Australia	38 (average 23.18)	M. W. Tate	1924-25
Australia in England	42 (average 21.26)	T. M. Alderman (6 Tests)	1981
Australia in Australia	41 (average 12.85)	R. M. Hogg (6 Tests)	1978-79

WICKET-KEEPING – MOST DISMISSALS

	M	Ct	St	Total
†R. W. Marsh (Australia)	42	141	7	148
I. A. Healy (Australia)	28	107	9	116
A. P. E. Knott (England)	34	97	8	105
†W. A. Oldfield (Australia)	38	59	31	90
A. A. Lilley (England)	32	65	19	84
A. T. W. Grout (Australia)	22	69	7	76
T. G. Evans (England)	31	63	12	75

† *The number of catches by R. W. Marsh (141) and stumpings by W. A. Oldfield (31) are
respective records in England–Australia Tests.*

SCORERS OF OVER 2,000 RUNS

	T		I		NO		R		HS		Avge
D. G. Bradman	37	..	63	..	7	..	5,028	..	334	..	89.78
J. B. Hobbs	41	..	71	..	4	..	3,636	..	187	..	54.26
A. R. Border	47	..	82	..	19	..	3,548	..	200*	..	56.31
D. I. Gower	42	..	77	..	4	..	3,269	..	215	..	44.78
G. Boycott	38	..	71	..	9	..	2,945	..	191	..	47.50
W. R. Hammond	33	..	58	..	3	..	2,852	..	251	..	51.85
H. Sutcliffe	27	..	46	..	5	..	2,741	..	194	..	66.85
C. Hill	41	..	76	..	1	..	2,660	..	188	..	35.46
J. H. Edrich	32	..	57	..	3	..	2,644	..	175	..	48.96
G. A. Gooch	42	..	79	..	0	..	2,632	..	196	..	33.31
G. S. Chappell	35	..	65	..	8	..	2,619	..	144	..	45.94
M. C. Cowdrey	43	..	75	..	4	..	2,433	..	113	..	34.26
L. Hutton	27	..	49	..	6	..	2,428	..	364	..	56.46

	T		I		NO		R		HS		Avge
R. N. Harvey	37	..	68	..	5	..	2,416	..	167	..	38.34
M. A. Taylor	28	..	51	..	2	..	2,268	..	219	..	46.28
V. T. Trumper	40	..	74	..	5	..	2,263	..	185*	..	32.79
D. C. Boon	31	..	57	..	8	..	2,237	..	184	..	45.65
W. M. Lawry	29	..	51	..	5	..	2,233	..	166	..	48.54
S. E. Gregory	52	..	92	..	7	..	2,193	..	201	..	25.80
W. W. Armstrong	42	..	71	..	9	..	2,172	..	158	..	35.03
I. M. Chappell	30	..	56	..	4	..	2,138	..	192	..	41.11
K. F. Barrington	23	..	39	..	6	..	2,111	..	256	..	63.96
A. R. Morris	24	..	43	..	2	..	2,080	..	206	..	50.73
S. E. Waugh	32	..	50	..	12	..	2,076	..	177*	..	54.63

BOWLERS WITH 100 WICKETS

	T		Balls		R		W		5W/i		Avge
D. K. Lillee	29	..	8,516	..	3,507	..	167	..	11	..	21.00
I. T. Botham	36	..	8,479	..	4,093	..	148	..	9	..	27.65
H. Trumble	31	..	7,895	..	2,945	..	141	..	9	..	20.88
R. G. D. Willis	35	..	7,294	..	3,346	..	128	..	7	..	26.14
M. A. Noble	39	..	6,845	..	2,860	..	115	..	9	..	24.86
R. R. Lindwall	29	..	6,728	..	2,559	..	114	..	6	..	22.44
W. Rhodes	41	..	5,791	..	2,616	..	109	..	6	..	24.00
S. F. Barnes	20	..	5,749	..	2,288	..	106	..	12	..	21.58
C. V. Grimmett	22	..	9,224	..	3,439	..	106	..	11	..	32.44
D. L. Underwood	29	..	8,000	..	2,770	..	105	..	4	..	26.38
A. V. Bedser	21	..	7,065	..	2,859	..	104	..	7	..	27.49
G. Giffen	31	..	6,457	..	2,791	..	103	..	7	..	27.09
W. J. O'Reilly	19	..	7,864	..	2,587	..	102	..	8	..	25.36
R. Peel	20	..	5,216	..	1,715	..	101	..	5	..	16.98
C. T. B. Turner	17	..	5,195	..	1,670	..	101	..	11	..	16.53
T. M. Alderman	17	..	4,717	..	2,117	..	100	..	11	..	21.17
J. R. Thomson	21	..	4,951	..	2,418	..	100	..	5	..	24.18

RESULTS ON EACH GROUND

In England

THE OVAL (32)
England (15) 1880, 1886, 1888, 1890, 1893, 1896, 1902, 1912, 1926, 1938, 1953, 1968, 1985, 1993, 1997.
Australia (5) 1882, 1930, 1934, 1948, 1972.
Drawn (12) 1884, 1899, 1905, 1909, 1921, 1956, 1961, 1964, 1975, 1977, 1981, 1989.

MANCHESTER (27)
England (7) 1886, 1888, 1905, 1956, 1972, 1977, 1981.
Australia (7) 1896, 1902, 1961, 1968, 1989, 1993, 1997.
Drawn (13) 1884, 1893, 1899, 1909, 1912, 1921, 1926, 1930, 1934, 1948, 1953, 1964, 1985.

The scheduled matches in 1890 and 1938 were abandoned without a ball bowled and are excluded.

LORD'S (31)
England (5) 1884, 1886, 1890, 1896, 1934.
Australia (12) 1888, 1899, 1909, 1921, 1930, 1948, 1956, 1961, 1972, 1985, 1989, 1993.
Drawn (14) 1893, 1902, 1905, 1912, 1926, 1938, 1953, 1964, 1968, 1975, 1977, 1980, 1981, 1997.

NOTTINGHAM (18)
England (3) 1905, 1930, 1977.
Australia (6) 1921, 1934, 1948, 1981, 1989, 1997.
Drawn (9) 1899, 1926, 1938, 1953, 1956, 1964, 1972, 1985, 1993.

LEEDS (22)

England (6)	1956, 1961, 1972, 1977, 1981, 1985.
Australia (8)	1909, 1921, 1938, 1948, 1964, 1989, 1993, 1997.
Drawn (8)	1899, 1905, 1926, 1930, 1934, 1953, 1968, 1975.

BIRMINGHAM (10)

England (4)	1909, 1981, 1985, 1997.
Australia (2)	1975, 1993.
Drawn (4)	1902, 1961, 1968, 1989.

SHEFFIELD (1)

Australia (1)	1902.

In Australia

MELBOURNE (50)

England (18)	*1876, 1882, 1884*(2), *1894*(2), *1903, 1907, 1911*(2), *1924, 1928, 1950, 1954, 1962, 1974, 1982, 1986.*
Australia (25)	*1876, 1878, 1882, 1891, 1897*(2), *1901*(2), *1903, 1907, 1920*(2), *1924, 1928, 1932, 1936*(2), *1950, 1958*(2), *1976, 1978, 1979, 1990, 1994.*
Drawn (7)	*1881*(2), *1946, 1965*(2), *1970, 1974.*

One scheduled match in 1970-71 was abandoned without a ball bowled and is excluded.

SYDNEY (50)

England (20)	*1882, 1886*(2), *1887, 1894, 1897, 1901, 1903*(2), *1911, 1928, 1932*(2), *1936, 1954, 1965, 1970*(2), *1978*(2).
Australia (23)	*1881*(2), *1882, 1884*(2), *1891, 1894, 1897, 1901, 1907*(2), *1911, 1920*(2), *1924*(2), *1946*(2), *1950, 1962, 1974, 1979, 1986.*
Drawn (7)	*1954, 1958, 1962, 1982, 1987, 1990, 1994.*

ADELAIDE (26)

England (8)	*1884, 1891, 1911, 1928, 1932, 1954, 1978, 1994.*
Australia (13)	*1894, 1897, 1901, 1903, 1907, 1920, 1924, 1936, 1950, 1958, 1965, 1974, 1982.*
Drawn (5)	*1946, 1962, 1970, 1986, 1990.*

BRISBANE Exhibition Ground (1)

England (1)	*1928.*

BRISBANE Woolloongabba (15)

England (4)	*1932, 1936, 1978, 1986.*
Australia (8)	*1946, 1950, 1954, 1958, 1974, 1982, 1990, 1994.*
Drawn (3)	*1962, 1965, 1970.*

PERTH (8)

England (1)	*1978.*
Australia (4)	*1974, 1979, 1990, 1994.*
Drawn (3)	*1970, 1982, 1986.*

For Tests in Australia the first year of the season is given in italics; i.e. *1876* denotes the 1876-77 season.

ENGLAND v SOUTH AFRICA

	Captains					
Season	*England*	*South Africa*	*T*	*E*	*SA*	*D*
1888-89	C. A. Smith[1]	O. R. Dunell[2]	2	2	0	0
1891-92	W. W. Read	W. H. Milton	1	1	0	0
1895-96	Lord Hawke[3]	E. A. Halliwell[4]	3	3	0	0
1898-99	Lord Hawke	M. Bisset	2	2	0	0
1905-06	P. F. Warner	P. W. Sherwell	5	1	4	0
1907	R. E. Foster	P. W. Sherwell	3	1	0	2
1909-10	H. D. G. Leveson Gower[5]	S. J. Snooke	5	2	3	0
1912	C. B. Fry	F. Mitchell[6]	3	3	0	0
1913-14	J. W. H. T. Douglas	H. W. Taylor	5	4	0	1
1922-23	F. T. Mann	H. W. Taylor	5	2	1	2
1924	A. E. R. Gilligan[7]	H. W. Taylor	5	3	0	2
1927-28	R. T. Stanyforth[8]	H. G. Deane	5	2	2	1
1929	J. C. White[9]	H. G. Deane	5	2	0	3
1930-31	A. P. F. Chapman	H. G. Deane[10]	5	0	1	4
1935	R. E. S. Wyatt	H. F. Wade	5	0	1	4
1938-39	W. R. Hammond	A. Melville	5	1	0	4
1947	N. W. D. Yardley	A. Melville	5	3	0	2
1948-49	F. G. Mann	A. D. Nourse	5	2	0	3
1951	F. R. Brown	A. D. Nourse	5	3	1	1
1955	P. B. H. May	J. E. Cheetham[11]	5	3	2	0
1956-57	P. B. H. May	C. B. van Ryneveld[12]	5	2	2	1
1960	M. C. Cowdrey	D. J. McGlew	5	3	0	2
1964-65	M. J. K. Smith	T. L. Goddard	5	1	0	4
1965	M. J. K. Smith	P. L. van der Merwe	3	0	1	2
1994	M. A. Atherton	K. C. Wessels	3	1	1	1
1995-96	M. A. Atherton	W. J. Cronje	5	0	1	4
	In South Africa		63	25	14	24
	In England		47	22	6	19
	Totals		110	47	20	43

Notes: The following deputised for the official touring captain or were appointed by the home authority for only a minor proportion of the series:

[1]M. P. Bowden (Second). [2]W. H. Milton (Second). [3]Sir T. C. O'Brien (First). [4]A. R. Richards (Third). [5]F. L. Fane (Fourth and Fifth). [6]L. J. Tancred (Second and Third). [7]J. W. H. T. Douglas (Fourth). [8]G. T. S. Stevens (Fifth). [9]A. W. Carr (Fourth and Fifth). [10]E. P. Nupen (First), H. B. Cameron (Fourth and Fifth). [11]D. J. McGlew (Third and Fourth). [12]D. J. McGlew (Second).

HIGHEST INNINGS TOTALS

For England in England: 554-8 dec. at Lord's 1947
             in South Africa: 654-5 at Durban 1938-39

For South Africa in England: 538 at Leeds 1951
               in South Africa: 530 at Durban 1938-39

LOWEST INNINGS TOTALS

For England in England: 76 at Leeds   1907
         in South Africa: 92 at Cape Town.   1898-99

For South Africa in England: 30 at Birmingham   1924
         in South Africa: 30 at Port Elizabeth.   1895-96

INDIVIDUAL HUNDREDS

For England (90)

R. Abel (1)		181 Cape Town. . 1938-39	**W. Rhodes** (1)
120 Cape Town. . 1888-89		120 Durban 1938-39	152 Johannesburg 1913-14
L. E. G. Ames (2)		140 Durban 1938-39	**P. E. Richardson** (1)
148* The Oval . . . 1935		**T. W. Hayward** (1)	117† Johannesburg 1956-57
115 Cape Town. . 1938-39		122 Johannesburg 1895-96	**R. W. V. Robins** (1)
M. A. Atherton (1)		**E. H. Hendren** (2)	108 Manchester. . 1935
185* Johannesburg 1995-96		132 Leeds 1924	**A. C. Russell** (2)
K. F. Barrington (2)		142 The Oval . . . 1924	140 ⎫
148* Durban 1964-65		**G. A. Hick** (2)	111 ⎬ Durban 1922-23
121 Johannesburg 1964-65		110 Leeds 1994	**R. T. Simpson** (1)
G. Boycott (1)		141 Centurion . . . 1995-96	137 Nottingham . 1951
117 Port Elizabeth 1964-65		**A. J. L. Hill** (1)	**M. J. K. Smith** (1)
L. C. Braund (1)		124 Cape Town. . 1895-96	121 Cape Town. . 1964-65
104† Lord's. 1907		**J. B. Hobbs** (2)	**R. H. Spooner** (1)
D. C. S. Compton (7)		187 Cape Town. . 1909-10	119† Lord's. 1912
163† Nottingham . 1947		211 Lord's. 1924	**H. Sutcliffe** (6)
208 Lord's. 1947		**L. Hutton** (4)	122 Lord's. 1924
115 Manchester. . 1947		100 Leeds 1947	102 Johannesburg 1927-28
113 The Oval . . . 1947		158 Johannesburg 1948-49	114 Birmingham . 1929
114 Johannesburg 1948-49		123 Johannesburg 1948-49	100 Lord's. 1929
112 Nottingham . 1951		100 Leeds 1951	104 ⎫
158 Manchester. . 1955		**D. J. Insole** (1)	109*⎬ The Oval . . . 1929
M. C. Cowdrey (3)		110* Durban 1956-57	**M. W. Tate** (1)
101 Cape Town. . 1956-57		**M. Leyland** (2)	100* Lord's. 1929
155 The Oval . . . 1960		102 Lord's. 1929	**E. Tyldesley** (2)
105 Nottingham . 1965		161 The Oval . . . 1935	122 Johannesburg 1927-28
D. Denton (1)		**F. G. Mann** (1)	100 Durban 1927-28
104 Johannesburg 1909-10		136* Port Elizabeth 1948-49	**J. T. Tyldesley** (1)
E. R. Dexter (1)		**P. B. H. May** (3)	112 Cape Town. . 1898-99
172 Johannesburg 1964-65		138† Leeds 1951	**B. H. Valentine** (1)
J. W. H. T. Douglas (1)		112 Lord's. 1955	112 Cape Town. . 1938-39
119† Durban 1913-14		117 Manchester. . 1955	**P. F. Warner** (1)
W. J. Edrich (3)		**C. P. Mead** (3)	132*†‡Johannesburg 1898-99
219 Durban 1938-39		102 Johannesburg 1913-14	**C. Washbrook** (1)
189 Lord's. 1947		117 Port Elizabeth 1913-14	195 Johannesburg 1948-49
191 Manchester. . 1947		181 Durban 1922-23	**A. J. Watkins** (1)
F. L. Fane (1)		**P. H. Parfitt** (1)	111 Johannesburg 1948-49
143 Johannesburg 1905-06		122* Johannesburg 1964-65	**H. Wood** (1)
C. B. Fry (1)		**J. M. Parks** (1)	134* Cape Town. . 1891-92
129 The Oval . . . 1907		108* Durban 1964-65	**F. E. Woolley** (3)
P. A. Gibb (2)		**E. Paynter** (3)	115* Johannesburg 1922-23
106† Johannesburg 1938-39		117 ⎫	134* Lord's. 1924
120 Durban 1938-39		100 ⎬†Johannesburg 1938-39	154 Manchester. . 1929
W. R. Hammond (6)		243 Durban 1938-39	**R. E. S. Wyatt** (2)
138* Birmingham . 1929		**G. Pullar** (1)	113 Manchester. . 1929
101* The Oval . . . 1929		175 The Oval . . . 1960	149 Nottingham . 1935
136* Durban 1930-31			

For South Africa (62)

E. J. Barlow (1)			**B. M. McMillan** (1)			**E. A. B. Rowan** (2)		
100*	Cape Town..	1964-65	100*	Johannesburg	1995-96	156*	Johannesburg	1948-49
K. C. Bland (2)			**A. Melville** (4)			236	Leeds	1951
144*	Johannesburg	1964-65	103	Durban	1938-39	**P. W. Sherwell** (1)		
127	The Oval ...	1965	189 ⎫			115	Lord's......	1907
R. H. Catterall (3)			104* ⎬	Nottingham .	1947	**I. J. Siedle** (1)		
120	Birmingham.	1924	117	Lord's......	1947	141	Cape Town..	1930-31
120	Lord's......	1924	**B. Mitchell** (7)			**J. H. Sinclair** (1)		
119	Durban	1927-28	123	Cape Town..	1930-31	106	Cape Town..	1898-99
E. L. Dalton (2)			164*	Lord's......	1935	**H. W. Taylor** (7)		
117	The Oval ...	1935	128	The Oval ...	1935	109	Durban	1913-14
102	Johannesburg	1938-39	109	Durban	1938-39	176	Johannesburg	1922-23
W. R. Endean (1)			120 ⎫			101	Johannesburg	1922-23
116*	Leeds	1955	189* ⎬	The Oval ...	1947	102	Durban	1922-23
G. A. Faulkner (1)			120	Cape Town..	1948-49	101	Johannesburg	1927-28
123	Johannesburg	1909-10	**A. D. Nourse** (7)			121	The Oval ...	1929
T. L. Goddard (1)			120	Cape Town..	1938-39	117	Cape Town..	1930-31
112	Johannesburg	1964-65	103	Durban	1938-39	**P. G. V. van der Bijl** (1)		
C. M. H. Hathorn (1)			149	Nottingham .	1947	125	Durban	1938-39
102	Johannesburg	1905-06	115	Manchester..	1947	**K. G. Viljoen** (1)		
G. Kirsten (1)			112	Cape Town..	1948-49	124	Manchester..	1935
110	Johannesburg	1995-96	129*	Johannesburg	1948-49	**W. W. Wade** (1)		
P. N. Kirsten (1)			208	Nottingham .	1951	125	Port Elizabeth	1948-49
104	Leeds	1994	**H. G. Owen-Smith** (1)			**J. H. B. Waite** (1)		
D. J. McGlew (2)			129	Leeds	1929	113	Manchester..	1955
104*	Manchester..	1955	**A. J. Pithey** (1)			**K. C. Wessels** (1)		
133	Leeds	1955	154	Cape Town..	1964-65	105†	Lord's.....	1994
R. A. McLean (3)			**R. G. Pollock** (2)			**G. C. White** (2)		
142	Lord's......	1955	137	Port Elizabeth	1964-65	147	Johannesburg	1905-06
100	Durban	1956-57	125	Nottingham .	1965	118	Durban	1909-10
109	Manchester..	1960				**P. L. Winslow** (1)		
						108	Manchester..	1955

† *Signifies hundred on first appearance in England–South Africa Tests. K. C. Wessels had earlier scored 162 on his Test debut for Australia against England at Brisbane in 1982-83.*

‡ *P. F. Warner carried his bat through the second innings.*

A. Melville's four hundreds were made in successive Test innings.

H. Wood scored the only hundred of his career in a Test match.

RECORD PARTNERSHIP FOR EACH WICKET

For England

359	for 1st†	L. Hutton and C. Washbrook at Johannesburg	1948-49
280	for 2nd	P. A. Gibb and W. J. Edrich at Durban	1938-39
370	for 3rd†	W. J. Edrich and D. C. S. Compton at Lord's	1947
197	for 4th	W. R. Hammond and L. E. G. Ames at Cape Town	1938-39
237	for 5th	D. C. S. Compton and N. W. D. Yardley at Nottingham	1947
206*	for 6th	K. F. Barrington and J. M. Parks at Durban.....................	1964-65
115	for 7th	J. W. H. T. Douglas and M. C. Bird at Durban...................	1913-14
154	for 8th	C. W. Wright and H. R. Bromley-Davenport at Johannesburg	1895-96
71	for 9th	H. Wood and J. T. Hearne at Cape Town	1891-92
92	for 10th	A. C. Russell and A. E. R. Gilligan at Durban	1922-23

For South Africa

260	for 1st†	B. Mitchell and I. J. Siedle at Cape Town	1930-31
198	for 2nd	E. A. B. Rowan and C. B. van Ryneveld at Leeds	1951
319	for 3rd	A. Melville and A. D. Nourse at Nottingham....................	1947
214	for 4th†	H. W. Taylor and H. G. Deane at The Oval	1929
157	for 5th†	A. J. Pithey and J. H. B. Waite at Johannesburg	1964-65
171	for 6th	J. H. B. Waite and P. L. Winslow at Manchester	1955
123	for 7th	H. G. Deane and E. P. Nupen at Durban	1927-28

109*	for 8th	B. Mitchell and L. Tuckett at The Oval	1947
137	for 9th†	E. L. Dalton and A. B. C. Langton at The Oval	1935
103	for 10th†	H. G. Owen-Smith and A. J. Bell at Leeds	1929

† *Denotes record partnership against all countries.*

MOST RUNS IN A SERIES

England in England	753 (average 94.12)	D. C. S. Compton	1947
England in South Africa	653 (average 81.62)	E. Paynter	1938-39
South Africa in England	621 (average 69.00)	A. D. Nourse	1947
South Africa in South Africa	582 (average 64.66)	H. W. Taylor	1922-23

TEN WICKETS OR MORE IN A MATCH

For England (24)

11-110 (5-25, 6-85)†	S. F. Barnes, Lord's	1912
10-115 (6-52, 4-63)	S. F. Barnes, Lord's	1912
13-57 (5-28, 8-29)	S. F. Barnes, The Oval	1912
10-105 (5-57, 5-48)	S. F. Barnes, Durban	1913-14
17-159 (8-56, 9-103)	S. F. Barnes, Johannesburg	1913-14
14-144 (7-56, 7-88)	S. F. Barnes, Durban	1913-14
12-112 (7-58, 5-54)	A. V. Bedser, Manchester	1951
11-118 (6-68, 5-50)	C. Blythe, Cape Town	1905-06
15-99 (8-59, 7-40)	C. Blythe, Leeds	1907
10-104 (7-46, 3-58)	C. Blythe, Cape Town	1909-10
15-28 (7-17, 8-11)	J. Briggs, Cape Town	1888-89
13-91 (6-54, 7-37)†	J. J. Ferris, Cape Town	1891-92
10-207 (7-115, 3-92)	A. P. Freeman, Leeds	1929
12-171 (7-71, 5-100)	A. P. Freeman, Manchester	1929
12-130 (7-70, 5-60)	G. Geary, Johannesburg	1927-28
11-90 (6-7, 5-83)	A. E. R. Gilligan, Birmingham	1924
10-119 (4-64, 6-55)	J. C. Laker, The Oval	1951
15-45 (7-38, 8-7)†	G. A. Lohmann, Port Elizabeth	1895-96
12-71 (9-28, 3-43)	G. A. Lohmann, Johannesburg	1895-96
10-138 (1-81, 9-57)	D. E. Malcolm, The Oval	1994
11-97 (6-63, 5-34)	J. B. Statham, Lord's	1960
12-101 (7-52, 5-49)	R. Tattersall, Lord's	1951
12-89 (5-53, 7-36)	J. H. Wardle, Cape Town	1956-57
10-175 (5-95, 5-80)	D. V. P. Wright, Lord's	1947

For South Africa (6)

11-112 (4-49, 7-63)†	A. E. Hall, Cape Town	1922-23
11-150 (5-63, 6-87)	E. P. Nupen, Johannesburg	1930-31
10-87 (5-53, 5-34)	P. M. Pollock, Nottingham	1965
12-127 (4-57, 8-70)	S. J. Snooke, Johannesburg	1905-06
13-192 (4-79, 9-113)	H. J. Tayfield, Johannesburg	1956-57
12-181 (5-87, 7-94)	A. E. E. Vogler, Johannesburg	1909-10

† *Signifies ten wickets or more on first appearance in England–South Africa Tests.*

Note: S. F. Barnes took ten wickets or more in his first five Tests v South Africa and in six of his seven Tests v South Africa. A. P. Freeman and G. A. Lohmann took ten wickets or more in successive matches.

MOST WICKETS IN A SERIES

England in England	34 (average 8.29)	S. F. Barnes	1912
England in South Africa	49 (average 10.93)	S. F. Barnes	1913-14
South Africa in England	26 (average 21.84)	H. J. Tayfield	1955
South Africa in England	26 (average 22.57)	N. A. T. Adcock	1960
South Africa in South Africa	37 (average 17.18)	H. J. Tayfield	1956-57

ENGLAND v WEST INDIES

Captains

Season	England	West Indies	T	E	WI	D
1928	A. P. F. Chapman	R. K. Nunes	3	3	0	0
1929-30	Hon. F. S. G. Calthorpe	E. L. G. Hoad[1]	4	1	1	2
1933	D. R. Jardine[2]	G. C. Grant	3	2	0	1
1934-35	R. E. S. Wyatt	G. C. Grant	4	1	2	1
1939	W. R. Hammond	R. S. Grant	3	1	0	2
1947-48	G. O. B. Allen[3]	J. D. C. Goddard[4]	4	0	2	2
1950	N. W. D. Yardley[5]	J. D. C. Goddard	4	1	3	0
1953-54	L. Hutton	J. B. Stollmeyer	5	2	2	1
1957	P. B. H. May	J. D. C. Goddard	5	3	0	2
1959-60	P. B. H. May[6]	F. C. M. Alexander	5	1	0	4

THE WISDEN TROPHY

Captains

Season	England	West Indies	T	E	WI	D	Held by
1963	E. R. Dexter	F. M. M. Worrell	5	1	3	1	WI
1966	M. C. Cowdrey[7]	G. S. Sobers	5	1	3	1	WI
1967-68	M. C. Cowdrey	G. S. Sobers	5	1	0	4	E
1969	R. Illingworth	G. S. Sobers	3	2	0	1	E
1973	R. Illingworth	R. B. Kanhai	3	0	2	1	WI
1973-74	M. H. Denness	R. B. Kanhai	5	1	1	3	WI
1976	A. W. Greig	C. H. Lloyd	5	0	3	2	WI
1980	I. T. Botham	C. H. Lloyd[8]	5	0	1	4	WI
1980-81†	I. T. Botham	C. H. Lloyd	4	0	2	2	WI
1984	D. I. Gower	C. H. Lloyd	5	0	5	0	WI
1985-86	D. I. Gower	I. V. A. Richards	5	0	5	0	WI
1988	J. E. Emburey[9]	I. V. A. Richards	5	0	4	1	WI
1989-90‡	G. A. Gooch[10]	I. V. A. Richards[11]	4	1	2	1	WI
1991	G. A. Gooch	I. V. A. Richards	5	2	2	1	WI
1993-94	M. A. Atherton	R. B. Richardson[12]	5	1	3	1	WI
1995	M. A. Atherton	R. B. Richardson	6	2	2	2	WI

In England			65	18	28	19
In West Indies			50	9	20	21
Totals			115	27	48	40

† *The Second Test, at Georgetown, was cancelled owing to political pressure and is excluded.*
‡ *The Second Test, at Georgetown, was abandoned without a ball being bowled and is excluded.*

Notes: The following deputised for the official touring captain or were appointed by the home authority for only a minor proportion of the series:
[1]N. Betancourt (Second), M. P. Fernandes (Third), R. K. Nunes (Fourth). [2]R. E. S. Wyatt (Third). [3]K. Cranston (First). [4]G. A. Headley (First), G. E. Gomez (Second). [5]F. R. Brown (Fourth). [6]M. C. Cowdrey (Fourth and Fifth). [7]M. J. K. Smith (First), D. B. Close (Fifth). [8]I. V. A. Richards (Fifth). [9]M. W. Gatting (First), C. S. Cowdrey (Fourth), G. A. Gooch (Fifth). [10]A. J. Lamb (Fourth and Fifth). [11]D. L. Haynes (Third). [12]C. A. Walsh (Fifth).

HIGHEST INNINGS TOTALS

For England in England: 619-6 dec. at Nottingham	1957
in West Indies: 849 at Kingston	1929-30
For West Indies in England: 692-8 dec. at The Oval	1995
in West Indies: 681-8 dec. at Port-of-Spain	1953-54

LOWEST INNINGS TOTALS

For England in England: 71 at Manchester 1976
    in West Indies: 46 at Port-of-Spain 1993-94

For West Indies in England: 86 at The Oval 1957
    in West Indies: 102 at Bridgetown 1934-35

INDIVIDUAL HUNDREDS

For England (95)

L. E. G. Ames (3)			**G. A. Gooch** (5)			100*	Manchester..	1984
105	Port-of-Spain	1929-30	123	Lord's......	1980	113	Lord's......	1988
149	Kingston ...	1929-30	116	Bridgetown .	1980-81	132	Kingston ...	1989-90
126	Kingston ...	1934-35	153	Kingston ...	1980-81	119	Bridgetown .	1989-90
D. L. Amiss (4)			146	Nottingham .	1988	**P. B. H. May** (3)		
174	Port-of-Spain	1973-74	154*‡	Leeds	1991	135	Port-of-Spain	1953-54
262*	Kingston ...	1973-74	**D. I. Gower** (1)			285*	Birmingham .	1957
118	Georgetown .	1973-74	154*	Kingston ...	1980-81	104	Nottingham .	1957
203	The Oval ...	1976	**T. W. Graveney** (5)			**C. Milburn** (1)		
M. A. Atherton (3)			258	Nottingham .	1957	126*	Lord's......	1966
144	Georgetown .	1993-94	164	The Oval ...	1957	**J. T. Murray** (1)		
135	St John's ...	1993-94	109	Nottingham .	1966	112†	The Oval ...	1966
113	Nottingham .	1995	165	The Oval ...	1966	**J. M. Parks** (1)		
A. H. Bakewell (1)			118	Port-of-Spain	1967-68	101*†	Port-of-Spain	1959-60
107†	The Oval ...	1933	**A. W. Greig** (3)			**W. Place** (1)		
K. F. Barrington (3)			148	Bridgetown .	1973-74	107	Kingston ...	1947-48
128†	Bridgetown .	1959-60	121	Georgetown .	1973-74	**P. E. Richardson** (2)		
121	Port-of-Spain	1959-60	116	Leeds	1976	126	Nottingham .	1957
143	Port-of-Spain	1967-68	**S. C. Griffith** (1)			107	The Oval ...	1957
G. Boycott (5)			140†	Port-of-Spain	1947-48	**J. D. Robertson** (1)		
116	Georgetown .	1967-68	**W. R. Hammond** (1)			133	Port-of-Spain	1947-48
128	Manchester..	1969	138	The Oval ...	1939	**A. Sandham** (2)		
106	Lord's......	1969	**J. H. Hampshire** (1)			152†	Bridgetown .	1929-30
112	Port-of-Spain	1973-74	107†	Lord's......	1969	325	Kingston ...	1929-30
104*	St John's ...	1980-81	**F. C. Hayes** (1)			**M. J. K. Smith** (1)		
D. C. S. Compton (2)			106*†	The Oval ...	1973	108	Port-of-Spain	1959-60
120†	Lord's......	1939	**E. H. Hendren** (2)			**R. A. Smith** (3)		
133	Port-of-Spain	1953-54	205*	Port-of-Spain	1929-30	148*	Lord's......	1991
M. C. Cowdrey (6)			123	Georgetown .	1929-30	109	The Oval ...	1991
154†	Birmingham .	1957	**G. A. Hick** (1)			175	St John's ...	1993-94
152	Lord's......	1957	118*	Nottingham .	1995	**D. S. Steele** (1)		
114	Kingston ...	1959-60	**J. B. Hobbs** (1)			106†	Nottingham .	1976
119	Port-of-Spain	1959-60	159	The Oval ...	1928	**A. J. Stewart** (2)		
101	Kingston ...	1967-68	**L. Hutton** (5)			118 ⎱	Bridgetown .	1993-94
148	Port-of-Spain	1967-68	196†	Lord's......	1939	143 ⎰		
E. R. Dexter (2)			165*	The Oval ...	1939	**R. Subba Row** (1)		
136*†	Bridgetown .	1959-60	202*‡	The Oval ...	1950	100†	Georgetown .	1959-60
110	Georgetown .	1959-60	169	Georgetown .	1953-54	**E. Tyldesley** (1)		
J. H. Edrich (1)			205	Kingston ...	1953-54	122†	Lord's......	1928
146	Bridgetown .	1967-68	**R. Illingworth** (1)			**C. Washbrook** (2)		
T. G. Evans (1)			113	Lord's......	1969	114†	Lord's......	1950
104	Manchester..	1950	**D. R. Jardine** (1)			102	Nottingham .	1950
K. W. R. Fletcher (1)			127	Manchester..	1933	**W. Watson** (1)		
129*	Bridgetown .	1973-74	**A. P. E. Knott** (1)			116†	Kingston ...	1953-54
G. Fowler (1)			116	Leeds	1976	**P. Willey** (2)		
106	Lord's......	1984	**A. J. Lamb** (6)			100*	The Oval ...	1980
			110	Lord's......	1984	102*	St John's ...	1980-81
			100	Leeds	1984			

For West Indies (107)

J. C. Adams (1)			106	} Lord's......	1939	114	St John's ...	1980-81
137	Georgetown .	1993-94	107			117	Birmingham .	1984
K. L. T. Arthurton (1)			**D. A. J. Holford** (1)			110*	St John's ...	1985-86
126	Kingston ...	1993-94	105*	Lord's......	1966	**R. B. Richardson** (4)		
I. Barrow (1)			**J. K. Holt** (1)			102	Port-of-Spain	1985-86
105	Manchester..	1933	166	Bridgetown .	1953-54	160	Bridgetown .	1985-86
C. A. Best (1)			**C. L. Hooper** (2)			104	Birmingham .	1991
164	Bridgetown .	1989-90	111	Lord's......	1991	121	The Oval ...	1991
B. F. Butcher (2)			127	The Oval ...	1995	**C. A. Roach** (2)		
133	Lord's......	1963	**C. C. Hunte** (3)			122	Bridgetown .	1929-30
209*	Nottingham .	1966	182	Manchester..	1963	209	Georgetown .	1929-30
G. M. Carew (1)			108*	The Oval ...	1963	**L. G. Rowe** (3)		
107	Port-of-Spain	1947-48	135	Manchester..	1966	120	Kingston ...	1973-74
C. A. Davis (1)			**B. D. Julien** (1)			302	Bridgetown .	1973-74
103	Lord's......	1969	121	Lord's......	1973	123	Port-of-Spain	1973-74
P. J. L. Dujon (1)			**A. I. Kallicharran** (2)			**O. G. Smith** (2)		
101	Manchester..	1984	158	Port-of-Spain	1973-74	161†	Birmingham .	1957
R. C. Fredericks (3)			119	Bridgetown .	1973-74	168	Nottingham .	1957
150	Birmingham .	1973	**R. B. Kanhai** (5)			**G. S. Sobers** (10)		
138	Lord's......	1976	110	Port-of-Spain	1959-60	226	Bridgetown .	1959-60
109	Leeds	1976	104	The Oval ...	1966	147	Kingston ...	1959-60
A. G. Ganteaume (1)			153	Port-of-Spain	1967-68	145	Georgetown .	1959-60
112†	Port-of-Spain	1947-48	150	Georgetown .	1967-68	102	Leeds	1963
H. A. Gomes (2)			157	Lord's......	1973	161	Manchester..	1966
143	Birmingham .	1984	**B. C. Lara** (5)			163*	Lord's......	1966
104*	Leeds	1984	167	Georgetown .	1993-94	174	Leeds	1966
C. G. Greenidge (7)			375	St John's ...	1993-94	113*	Kingston ...	1967-68
134	} Manchester..	1976	145	Manchester..	1995	152	Georgetown .	1967-68
101			152	Nottingham .	1995	150*	Lord's......	1973
115	Leeds	1976	179	The Oval ...	1995	**C. L. Walcott** (4)		
214*	Lord's......	1984	**C. H. Lloyd** (5)			168*	Lord's......	1950
223	Manchester..	1984	118†	Port-of-Spain	1967-68	220	Bridgetown .	1953-54
103	Lord's......	1988	113*	Bridgetown .	1967-68	124	Port-of-Spain	1953-54
149	St John's ...	1989-90	132	The Oval ...	1973	116	Kingston ...	1953-54
D. L. Haynes (5)			101	Manchester..	1980	**E. D. Weekes** (3)		
184	Lord's......	1980	100	Bridgetown .	1980-81	141	Kingston ...	1947-48
125	The Oval ...	1984	**S. M. Nurse** (2)			129	Nottingham .	1950
131	St John's ...	1985-86	137	Leeds	1966	206	Port-of-Spain	1953-54
109	Bridgetown .	1989-90	136	Port-of-Spain	1967-68	**K. H. Weekes** (1)		
167	St John's ...	1989-90	**A. F. Rae** (2)			137	The Oval ...	1939
G. A. Headley (8)			106	Lord's......	1950	**F. M. M. Worrell** (6)		
176†	Bridgetown .	1929-30	109	The Oval ...	1950	131*	Georgetown .	1947-48
114	} Georgetown .	1929-30	**I. V. A. Richards** (8)			261	Nottingham .	1950
112			232†	Nottingham .	1976	138	The Oval ...	1950
223	Kingston ...	1929-30	135	Manchester..	1976	167	Port-of-Spain	1953-54
169*	Manchester..	1933	291	The Oval ...	1976	191*‡	Nottingham .	1957
270*	Kingston ...	1934-35	145	Lord's......	1980	197*	Bridgetown .	1959-60
			182*	Bridgetown .	1980-81			

† *Signifies hundred on first appearance in England–West Indies Tests. S. C. Griffith provides the only instance for England of a player hitting his maiden century in first-class cricket in his first Test.*

‡ *Carried his bat.*

RECORD PARTNERSHIPS FOR EACH WICKET

For England

212	for 1st	C. Washbrook and R. T. Simpson at Nottingham	1950
266	for 2nd	P. E. Richardson and T. W. Graveney at Nottingham	1957
303	for 3rd	M. A. Atherton and R. A. Smith at St John's	1993-94

411	for 4th†	P. B. H. May and M. C. Cowdrey at Birmingham	1957
150	for 5th	A. J. Stewart and G. P. Thorpe at Bridgetown	1993-94
163	for 6th	A. W. Greig and A. P. E. Knott at Bridgetown	1973-74
197	for 7th†	M. J. K. Smith and J. M. Parks at Port-of-Spain	1959-60
217	for 8th	T. W. Graveney and J. T. Murray at The Oval	1966
109	for 9th	G. A. R. Lock and P. I. Pocock at Georgetown	1967-68
128	for 10th	K. Higgs and J. A. Snow at The Oval	1966

For West Indies

298	for 1st†	C. G. Greenidge and D. L. Haynes at St John's	1989-90
287*	for 2nd	C. G. Greenidge and H. A. Gomes at Lord's	1984
338	for 3rd†	E. D. Weekes and F. M. M. Worrell at Port-of-Spain	1953-54
399	for 4th†	G. S. Sobers and F. M. M. Worrell at Bridgetown	1959-60
265	for 5th‡	S. M. Nurse and G. S. Sobers at Leeds	1966
274*	for 6th†	G. S. Sobers and D. A. J. Holford at Lord's	1966
155*	for 7th‡	G. S. Sobers and B. D. Julien at Lord's	1973
99	for 8th	C. A. McWatt and J. K. Holt at Georgetown	1953-54
150	for 9th	E. A. E. Baptiste and M. A. Holding at Birmingham	1984
67*	for 10th	M. A. Holding and C. E. H. Croft at St John's	1980-81

† *Denotes record partnership against all countries.*

‡ *231 runs were added for this wicket in two separate partnerships: G. S. Sobers retired ill and was replaced by K. D. Boyce when 155 had been added.*

TEN WICKETS OR MORE IN A MATCH

For England (11)

11-98 (7-44, 4-54)	T. E. Bailey, Lord's	1957
10-93 (5-54, 5-39)	A. P. Freeman, Manchester	1928
13-156 (8-86, 5-70)	A. W. Greig, Port-of-Spain	1973-74
11-48 (5-28, 6-20)	G. A. R. Lock, The Oval	1957
10-137 (4-60, 6-77)	D. E. Malcolm, Port-of-Spain	1989-90
11-96 (5-37, 6-59)†	C. S. Marriott, The Oval	1933
10-142 (4-82, 6-60)	J. A. Snow, Georgetown	1967-68
10-195 (5-105, 5-90)†	G. T. S. Stevens, Bridgetown	1929-30
11-152 (6-100, 5-52)	F. S. Trueman, Lord's	1963
12-119 (5-75, 7-44)	F. S. Trueman, Birmingham	1963
11-149 (4-79, 7-70)	W. Voce, Port-of-Spain	1929-30

For West Indies (14)

10-127 (2-82, 8-45)	C. E. L. Ambrose, Bridgetown	1989-90
11-84 (5-60, 6-24)	C. E. L. Ambrose, Port-of-Spain	1993-94
10-174 (5-105, 5-69)	K. C. G. Benjamin, Nottingham	1995
11-147 (5-70, 6-77)†	K. D. Boyce, The Oval	1973
11-229 (5-137, 6-92)	W. Ferguson, Port-of-Spain	1947-48
11-157 (5-59, 6-98)†	L. R. Gibbs, Manchester	1963
10-106 (5-37, 5-69)	L. R. Gibbs, Manchester	1966
14-149 (8-92, 6-57)	M. A. Holding, The Oval	1976
10-96 (5-41, 5-55)†	H. H. H. Johnson, Kingston	1947-48
10-92 (6-32, 4-60)	M. D. Marshall, Lord's	1988
11-152 (5-66, 6-86)	S. Ramadhin, Lord's	1950
10-123 (5-60, 5-63)	A. M. E. Roberts, Lord's	1976
11-204 (8-104, 3-100)†	A. L. Valentine, Manchester	1950
10-160 (4-121, 6-39)	A. L. Valentine, The Oval	1950

† *Signifies ten wickets or more on first appearance in England–West Indies Tests.*

Note: F. S. Trueman took ten wickets or more in successive matches.

ENGLAND v NEW ZEALAND

Captains

Season	England	New Zealand	T	E	NZ	D
1929-30	A. H. H. Gilligan	T. C. Lowry	4	1	0	3
1931	D. R. Jardine	T. C. Lowry	3	1	0	2
1932-33	D. R. Jardine[1]	M. L. Page	2	0	0	2
1937	R. W. V. Robins	M. L. Page	3	1	0	2
1946-47	W. R. Hammond	W. A. Hadlee	1	0	0	1
1949	F. G. Mann[2]	W. A. Hadlee	4	0	0	4
1950-51	F. R. Brown	W. A. Hadlee	2	1	0	1
1954-55	L. Hutton	G. O. Rabone	2	2	0	0
1958	P. B. H. May	J. R. Reid	5	4	0	1
1958-59	P. B. H. May	J. R. Reid	2	1	0	1
1962-63	E. R. Dexter	J. R. Reid	3	3	0	0
1965	M. J. K. Smith	J. R. Reid	3	3	0	0
1965-66	M. J. K. Smith	B. W. Sinclair[3]	3	0	0	3
1969	R. Illingworth	G. T. Dowling	3	2	0	1
1970-71	R. Illingworth	G. T. Dowling	2	1	0	1
1973	R. Illingworth	B. E. Congdon	3	2	0	1
1974-75	M. H. Denness	B. E. Congdon	2	1	0	1
1977-78	G. Boycott	M. G. Burgess	3	1	1	1
1978	J. M. Brearley	M. G. Burgess	3	3	0	0
1983	R. G. D. Willis	G. P. Howarth	4	3	1	0
1983-84	R. G. D. Willis	G. P. Howarth	3	0	1	2
1986	M. W. Gatting	J. V. Coney	3	0	1	2
1987-88	M. W. Gatting	J. J. Crowe[4]	3	0	0	3
1990	G. A. Gooch	J. G. Wright	3	1	0	2
1991-92	G. A. Gooch	M. D. Crowe	3	2	0	1
1994	M. A. Atherton	K. R. Rutherford	3	1	0	2
1996-97	M. A. Atherton	L. K. Germon[5]	3	2	0	1
In New Zealand			38	15	2	21
In England			40	21	2	17
Totals			78	36	4	38

Notes: The following deputised for the official touring captain or were appointed by the home authority for only a minor proportion of the series:

[1]R. E. S. Wyatt (Second). [2]F. R. Brown (Third and Fourth). [3]M. E. Chapple (First). [4]J. G. Wright (Third). [5]S. P. Fleming (Third).

HIGHEST INNINGS TOTALS

For England in England: 567-8 dec. at Nottingham	1994
in New Zealand: 593-6 dec. at Auckland	1974-75
For New Zealand in England: 551-9 dec. at Lord's	1973
in New Zealand: 537 at Wellington	1983-84

LOWEST INNINGS TOTALS

For England in England: 158 at Birmingham...................................	1990
in New Zealand: 64 at Wellington	1977-78
For New Zealand in England: 47 at Lord's	1958
in New Zealand: 26 at Auckland	1954-55

INDIVIDUAL HUNDREDS

For England (83)

G. O. B. Allen (1)
122† Lord's 1931

L. E. G. Ames (2)
137† Lord's 1931
103 Christchurch. 1932-33

D. L. Amiss (2)
138*† Nottingham . 1973
164* Christchurch. 1974-75

M. A. Atherton (4)
151† Nottingham . 1990
101 Nottingham . 1994
111 Manchester. . 1994
118 Christchurch. 1996-97

T. E. Bailey (1)
134* Christchurch. 1950-51

K. F. Barrington (3)
126† Auckland . . . 1962-63
137 Birmingham . 1965
163 Leeds 1965

I. T. Botham (3)
103 Christchurch. 1977-78
103 Nottingham . 1983
138 Wellington . . 1983-84

E. H. Bowley (1)
109 Auckland . . . 1929-30

G. Boycott (2)
115 Leeds 1973
131 Nottingham . 1978

B. C. Broad (1)
114† Christchurch. 1987-88

D. C. S. Compton (2)
114 Leeds 1949
116 Lord's 1949

M. C. Cowdrey (2)
128* Wellington . . 1962-63
119 Lord's 1965

M. H. Denness (1)
181 Auckland . . . 1974-75

E. R. Dexter (1)
141 Christchurch. 1958-59

B. L. D'Oliveira (1)
100 Christchurch. 1970-71

K. S. Duleepsinhji (2)
117 Auckland . . . 1929-30
109 The Oval . . . 1931

J. H. Edrich (3)
310*† Leeds 1965
115 Lord's 1969
155 Nottingham . 1969

W. J. Edrich (1)
100 The Oval . . . 1949

K. W. R. Fletcher (2)
178 Lord's 1973
216 Auckland . . . 1974-75

G. Fowler (1)
105† The Oval . . . 1983

M. W. Gatting (1)
121 The Oval . . . 1986

G. A. Gooch (4)
183 Lord's 1986
154 Birmingham . 1990
114 Auckland . . . 1991-92
210 Nottingham . 1994

D. I. Gower (4)
111† The Oval . . . 1978
112* Leeds 1983
108 Lord's 1983
131 The Oval . . . 1986

A. W. Greig (1)
139*† Nottingham . 1973

W. R. Hammond (4)
100* The Oval . . . 1931
227 Christchurch. 1932-33
336* Auckland . . . 1932-33
140 Lord's 1937

J. Hardstaff jun. (2)
114† Lord's 1937
103 The Oval . . . 1937

L. Hutton (3)
100 Manchester. . 1937
101 Leeds 1949
206 The Oval . . . 1949

B. R. Knight (1)
125† Auckland . . . 1962-63

A. P. E. Knott (1)
101 Auckland . . . 1970-71

A. J. Lamb (3)
102*† The Oval . . . 1983
137* Nottingham . 1983
142 Wellington . . 1991-92

G. B. Legge (1)
196 Auckland . . . 1929-30

P. B. H. May (3)
113* Leeds 1958
101 Manchester. . 1958
124* Auckland . . . 1958-59

C. A. Milton (1)
104*† Leeds 1958

P. H. Parfitt (1)
131*† Auckland . . . 1962-63

C. T. Radley (1)
158 Auckland . . . 1977-78

D. W. Randall (2)
164 Wellington . . 1983-84
104 Auckland . . . 1983-84

P. E. Richardson (1)
100† Birmingham . 1958

J. D. Robertson (1)
121† Lord's 1949

P. J. Sharpe (1)
111 Nottingham . 1969

R. T. Simpson (1)
103† Manchester. . 1949

A. J. Stewart (4)
148 Christchurch. 1991-92
107 Wellington . . 1991-92
119 Lord's 1994
173 Auckland . . . 1996-97

H. Sutcliffe (2)
117† The Oval . . . 1931
109* Manchester. . 1931

C. J. Tavaré (1)
109† The Oval . . . 1983

G. P. Thorpe (2)
119† Auckland . . . 1996-97
108 Wellington . . 1996-97

C. Washbrook (1)
103* Leeds 1949

For New Zealand (40)

N. J. Astle (1)
102*† Auckland . . . 1996-97

J. G. Bracewell (1)
110 Nottingham . 1986

M. G. Burgess (2)
104 Auckland . . . 1970-71
105 Lord's 1973

J. V. Coney (1)
174* Wellington . . 1983-84

B. E. Congdon (3)
104 Christchurch. 1965-66
176 Nottingham . 1973
175 Lord's 1973

J. J. Crowe (1)
128 Auckland . . . 1983-84

M. D. Crowe (5)
100 Wellington . . 1983-84
106 Lord's 1986
143 Wellington . . 1987-88
142 Lord's 1994
115 Manchester. . 1994

C. S. Dempster (2)
136 Wellington . . 1929-30
120 Lord's 1931

M. P. Donnelly (1)
206 Lord's 1949

S. P. Fleming (1)
129 Auckland . . . 1996-97

T. J. Franklin (1)
101 Lord's 1990

M. J. Greatbatch (1)
107*† Auckland . . . 1987-88

W. A. Hadlee (1)
116 Christchurch. 1946-47

G. P. Howarth (3)
122
102 } Auckland . . . 1977-78
123 Lord's 1978

A. H. Jones (1)
143 Wellington . . 1991-92

J. E. Mills (1)	**J. R. Reid** (1)		**B. Sutcliffe** (2)
117† Wellington .. 1929-30	100 Christchurch. 1962-63		101 Manchester.. 1949
M. L. Page (1)	**K. R. Rutherford** (1)		116 Christchurch. 1950-51
104 Lord's..... 1931	107* Wellington .. 1987-88		**J. G. Wright** (4)
J. M. Parker (1)	**B. W. Sinclair** (1)		130 Auckland ... 1983-84
121 Auckland ... 1974-75	114 Auckland ... 1965-66		119 The Oval 1986
V. Pollard (2)	**I. D. S. Smith** (1)		103 Auckland ... 1987-88
116 Nottingham .. 1973	113* Auckland ... 1983-84		116 Wellington .. 1991-92
105* Lord's...... 1973			

† *Signifies hundred on first appearance in England–New Zealand Tests.*

RECORD PARTNERSHIPS FOR EACH WICKET

For England

223	for 1st	G. Fowler and C. J. Tavaré at The Oval	1983
369	for 2nd	J. H. Edrich and K. F. Barrington at Leeds	1965
245	for 3rd	J. Hardstaff jun. and W. R. Hammond at Lord's	1937
266	for 4th	M. H. Denness and K. W. R. Fletcher at Auckland..............	1974-75
242	for 5th	W. R. Hammond and L. E. G. Ames at Christchurch	1932-33
240	for 6th†	P. H. Parfitt and B. R. Knight at Auckland	1962-63
149	for 7th	A. P. E. Knott and P. Lever at Auckland	1970-71
246	for 8th†	L. E. G. Ames and G. O. B. Allen at Lord's..................	1931
163*	for 9th†	M. C. Cowdrey and A. C. Smith at Wellington	1962-63
59	for 10th	A. P. E. Knott and N. Gifford at Nottingham.................	1973

For New Zealand

276	for 1st	C. S. Dempster and J. E. Mills at Wellington	1929-30
241	for 2nd†	J. G. Wright and A. H. Jones at Wellington.................	1991-92
210	for 3rd	B. A. Edgar and M. D. Crowe at Lord's	1986
155	for 4th	M. D. Crowe and M. J. Greatbatch at Wellington	1987-88
180	for 5th	M. D. Crowe and S. A. Thomson at Lord's	1994
141	for 6th	M. D. Crowe and A. C. Parore at Manchester	1994
117	for 7th	D. N. Patel and C. L. Cairns at Christchurch	1991-92
104	for 8th	D. A. R. Moloney and A. W. Roberts at Lord's	1937
118	for 9th	J. V. Coney and B. L. Cairns at Wellington.................	1983-84
106*	for 10th	N. J. Astle and D. K. Morrison at Auckland	1996-97

† *Denotes record partnership against all countries.*

TEN WICKETS OR MORE IN A MATCH

For England (8)

11-140 (6-101, 5-39)	I. T. Botham, Lord's.................................	1978
10-149 (5-98, 5-51)	A. W. Greig, Auckland...............................	1974-75
11-65 (4-14, 7-51)	G. A. R. Lock, Leeds	1958
11-84 (5-31, 6-53)	G. A. R. Lock, Christchurch	1958-59
11-147 (4-100, 7-47)†	P. C. R. Tufnell, Christchurch	1991-92
11-70 (4-38, 7-32)†	D. L. Underwood, Lord's..............................	1969
12-101 (6-41, 6-60)	D. L. Underwood, The Oval	1969
12-97 (6-12, 6-85)	D. L. Underwood, Christchurch	1970-71

For New Zealand (5)

10-144 (7-74, 3-70)	B. L. Cairns, Leeds.................................	1983
10-140 (4-73, 6-67)	J. Cowie, Manchester	1937
10-100 (4-74, 6-26)	R. J. Hadlee, Wellington	1977-78
10-140 (6-80, 4-60)	R. J. Hadlee, Nottingham	1986
11-169 (6-76, 5-93)	D. J. Nash, Lord's..................................	1994

† *Signifies ten wickets or more on first appearance in England–New Zealand Tests.*

Note: D. L. Underwood took 12 wickets in successive matches against New Zealand in 1969 and 1970-71.

HAT-TRICK AND FOUR WICKETS IN FIVE BALLS

M. J. C. Allom, in his first Test match, v New Zealand at Christchurch in 1929-30, dismissed C. S. Dempster, T. C. Lowry, K. C. James, and F. T. Badcock to take four wickets in five balls (w-www).

ENGLAND v INDIA

Captains

Season	England	India	T	E	I	D
1932	D. R. Jardine	C. K. Nayudu	1	1	0	0
1933-34	D. R. Jardine	C. K. Nayudu	3	2	0	1
1936	G. O. B. Allen	Maharaj of Vizianagram	3	2	0	1
1946	W. R. Hammond	Nawab of Pataudi sen.	3	1	0	2
1951-52	N. D. Howard[1]	V. S. Hazare	5	1	1	3
1952	L. Hutton	V. S. Hazare	4	3	0	1
1959	P. B. H. May[2]	D. K. Gaekwad[3]	5	5	0	0
1961-62	E. R. Dexter	N. J. Contractor	5	0	2	3
1963-64	M. J. K. Smith	Nawab of Pataudi jun.	5	0	0	5
1967	D. B. Close	Nawab of Pataudi jun.	3	3	0	0
1971	R. Illingworth	A. L. Wadekar	3	0	1	2
1972-73	A. R. Lewis	A. L. Wadekar	5	1	2	2
1974	M. H. Denness	A. L. Wadekar	3	3	0	0
1976-77	A. W. Greig	B. S. Bedi	5	3	1	1
1979	J. M. Brearley	S. Venkataraghavan	4	1	0	3
1979-80	J. M. Brearley	G. R. Viswanath	1	1	0	0
1981-82	K. W. R. Fletcher	S. M. Gavaskar	6	0	1	5
1982	R. G. D. Willis	S. M. Gavaskar	3	1	0	2
1984-85	D. I. Gower	S. M. Gavaskar	5	2	1	2
1986	M. W. Gatting[4]	Kapil Dev	3	0	2	1
1990	G. A. Gooch	M. Azharuddin	3	1	0	2
1992-93	G. A. Gooch[5]	M. Azharuddin	3	0	3	0
1996	M. A. Atherton	M. Azharuddin	3	1	0	2
	In England		41	22	3	16
	In India..........................		43	10	11	22
	Totals		84	32	14	38

Notes: The 1932 Indian touring team was captained by the Maharaj of Porbandar but he did not play in the Test match.

The following deputised for the official touring captain or were appointed by the home authority for only a minor proportion of the series:

[1]D. B. Carr (Fifth). [2]M. C. Cowdrey (Fourth and Fifth). [3]Pankaj Roy (Second). [4]D. I. Gower (First). [5]A. J. Stewart (Second).

HIGHEST INNINGS TOTALS

For England in England: 653-4 dec. at Lord's.................................	1990
in India: 652-7 dec. at Madras...................................	1984-85
For India in England: 606-9 dec. at The Oval	1990
in India: 591 at Bombay	1992-93

LOWEST INNINGS TOTALS

For England in England: 101 at The Oval	1971
in India: 102 at Bombay	1981-82
For India in England: 42 at Lord's	1974
in India: 83 at Madras	1976-77

INDIVIDUAL HUNDREDS

For England (76)

D. L. Amiss (2)
188	Lord's	1974
179	Delhi	1976-77

M. A. Atherton (2)
131	Manchester	1990
160	Nottingham	1996

K. F. Barrington (3)
151*	Bombay	1961-62
172	Kanpur	1961-62
113*	Delhi	1961-62

I. T. Botham (5)
137	Leeds	1979
114	Bombay	1979-80
142	Kanpur	1981-82
128	Manchester	1982
208	The Oval	1982

G. Boycott (4)
246*†	Leeds	1967
155	Birmingham	1979
125	The Oval	1979
105	Delhi	1981-82

M. C. Cowdrey (3)
160	Leeds	1959
107	Calcutta	1963-64
151	Delhi	1963-64

M. H. Denness (2)
118	Lord's	1974
100	Birmingham	1974

E. R. Dexter (1)
126*	Kanpur	1961-62

B. L. D'Oliveira (1)
109†	Leeds	1967

J. H. Edrich (1)
100*	Manchester	1974

T. G. Evans (1)
104	Lord's	1952

K. W. R. Fletcher (2)
113	Bombay	1972-73
123*	Manchester	1974

G. Fowler (1)
201	Madras	1984-85

M. W. Gatting (3)
136	Bombay	1984-85
207	Madras	1984-85
183*	Birmingham	1986

G. A. Gooch (5)
127	Madras	1981-82
114	Lord's	1986
333 }	Lord's	1990
123 }		
116	Manchester	1990

D. I. Gower (2)
200*†	Birmingham	1979
157*	The Oval	1990

T. W. Graveney (2)
175†	Bombay	1951-52
151	Lord's	1967

A. W. Greig (3)
148	Bombay	1972-73
106	Lord's	1974
103	Calcutta	1976-77

W. R. Hammond (2)
167	Manchester	1936
217	The Oval	1936

J. Hardstaff jun. (1)
205*	Lord's	1946

G. A. Hick (1)
178	Bombay	1992-93

N. Hussain (2)
128†	Birmingham	1996
107*	Nottingham	1996

L. Hutton (2)
150	Lord's	1952
104	Manchester	1952

R. Illingworth (1)
107	Manchester	1971

B. R. Knight (1)
127	Kanpur	1963-64

A. J. Lamb (3)
107	The Oval	1982

139	Lord's	1990
109	Manchester	1990

A. R. Lewis (1)
125	Kanpur	1972-73

C. C. Lewis (1)
117	Madras	1992-93

D. Lloyd (1)
214*	Birmingham	1974

B. W. Luckhurst (1)
101	Manchester	1971

P. B. H. May (1)
106	Nottingham	1959

P. H. Parfitt (1)
121	Kanpur	1963-64

G. Pullar (2)
131	Manchester	1959
119	Kanpur	1961-62

D. W. Randall (1)
126	Lord's	1982

R. T. Robinson (1)
160	Delhi	1984-85

R. C. Russell (1)
124	Lord's	1996

D. S. Sheppard (1)
119	The Oval	1952

M. J. K. Smith (1)
100†	Manchester	1959

R. A. Smith (2)
100*†	Lord's	1990
121*	Manchester	1990

C. J. Tavaré (1)
149	Delhi	1981-82

B. H. Valentine (1)
136†	Bombay	1933-34

C. F. Walters (1)
102	Madras	1933-34

A. J. Watkins (1)
137*†	Delhi	1951-52

T. S. Worthington (1)
128	The Oval	1936

For India (64)

L. Amarnath (1)
118†	Bombay	1933-34

M. Azharuddin (6)
110†	Calcutta	1984-85
105	Madras	1984-85
122	Kanpur	1984-85
121	Lord's	1990
179	Manchester	1990
182	Calcutta	1992-93

A. A. Baig (1)
112†	Manchester	1959

F. M. Engineer (1)
121	Bombay	1972-73

S. C. Ganguly (2)
131†	Lord's	1996
136	Nottingham	1996

S. M. Gavaskar (4)
101	Manchester	1974
108	Bombay	1976-77
221	The Oval	1979
172	Bangalore	1981-82

Hanumant Singh (1)
105†	Delhi	1963-64

V. S. Hazare (2)
164*	Delhi	1951-52
155	Bombay	1951-52

M. L. Jaisimha (2)
127	Delhi	1961-62
129	Calcutta	1963-64

V. G. Kambli (1)
224	Bombay	1992-93

Kapil Dev (2)
116	Kanpur	1981-82
110	The Oval	1990

S. M. H. Kirmani (1)
102	Bombay	1984-85

B. K. Kunderan (2)
192	Madras	1963-64
100	Delhi	1963-64

V. L. Manjrekar (3)		
133	Leeds	1952
189*	Delhi	1961-62
108	Madras	1963-64

V. Mankad (1)		
184	Lord's	1952

V. M. Merchant (3)		
114	Manchester	1936
128	The Oval	1946
154	Delhi	1951-52

Mushtaq Ali (1)		
112	Manchester	1936

R. G. Nadkarni (1)		
122*	Kanpur	1963-64

Nawab of Pataudi jun. (3)		
103	Madras	1961-62
203*	Delhi	1963-64
148	Leeds	1967

S. M. Patil (1)		
129*	Manchester	1982

D. G. Phadkar (1)		
115	Calcutta	1951-52

Pankaj Roy (2)		
140	Bombay	1951-52
111	Madras	1951-52

R. J. Shastri (4)		
142	Bombay	1984-85
111	Calcutta	1984-85
100	Lord's	1990
187	The Oval	1990

N. S. Sidhu (1)		
106	Madras	1992-93

S. R. Tendulkar (4)		
119*	Manchester	1990
165	Madras	1992-93
122	Birmingham	1996
177	Nottingham	1996

P. R. Umrigar (3)		
130*	Madras	1951-52
118	Manchester	1959
147*	Kanpur	1961-62

D. B. Vengsarkar (5)		
103	Lord's	1979
157	Lord's	1982
137	Kanpur	1984-85
126*	Lord's	1986
102*	Leeds	1986

G. R. Viswanath (4)		
113	Bombay	1972-73
113	Lord's	1979
107	Delhi	1981-82
222	Madras	1981-82

Yashpal Sharma (1)		
140	Madras	1981-82

† *Signifies hundred on first appearance in England–India Tests.*

Notes: G. A. Gooch's match aggregate of 456 (333 and 123) for England at Lord's in 1990 is the record in Test matches and provides the only instance of a batsman scoring a triple-hundred and a hundred in the same first-class match. His 333 is the highest innings in any match at Lord's.

M. Azharuddin scored hundreds in each of his first three Tests.

RECORD PARTNERSHIPS FOR EACH WICKET

For England

225 for 1st	G. A. Gooch and M. A. Atherton at Manchester	1990
241 for 2nd	G. Fowler and M. W. Gatting at Madras	1984-85
308 for 3rd	G. A. Gooch and A. J. Lamb at Lord's	1990
266 for 4th	W. R. Hammond and T. S. Worthington at The Oval	1936
254 for 5th†	K. W. R. Fletcher and A. W. Greig at Bombay	1972-73
171 for 6th	I. T. Botham and R. W. Taylor at Bombay	1979-80
125 for 7th	D. W. Randall and P. H. Edmonds at Lord's	1982
168 for 8th	R. Illingworth and P. Lever at Manchester	1971
83 for 9th	K. W. R. Fletcher and N. Gifford at Madras	1972-73
70 for 10th	P. J. W. Allott and R. G. D. Willis at Lord's	1982

For India

213 for 1st	S. M. Gavaskar and C. P. S. Chauhan at The Oval	1979
192 for 2nd	F. M. Engineer and A. L. Wadekar at Bombay	1972-73
316 for 3rd†‡	G. R. Viswanath and Yashpal Sharma at Madras	1981-82
222 for 4th†	V. S. Hazare and V. L. Manjrekar at Leeds	1952
214 for 5th†	M. Azharuddin and R. J. Shastri at Calcutta	1984-85
130 for 6th	S. M. H. Kirmani and Kapil Dev at The Oval	1982
235 for 7th†	R. J. Shastri and S. M. H. Kirmani at Bombay	1984-85
128 for 8th	R. J. Shastri and S. M. H. Kirmani at Delhi	1981-82
104 for 9th	R. J. Shastri and Madan Lal at Delhi	1981-82
51 for 10th	{ R. G. Nadkarni and B. S. Chandrasekhar at Calcutta	1963-64
	{ S. M. H. Kirmani and Chetan Sharma at Madras	1984-85

† *Denotes record partnership against all countries.*

‡ *415 runs were added between the fall of the 2nd and 3rd wickets: D. B. Vengsarkar retired hurt when he and Viswanath had added 99 runs.*

TEN WICKETS OR MORE IN A MATCH

For England (7)

10-78 (5-35, 5-43)†	G. O. B. Allen, Lord's	1936
11-145 (7-49, 4-96)†	A. V. Bedser, Lord's	1946
11-93 (4-41, 7-52)	A. V. Bedser, Manchester	1946
13-106 (6-58, 7-48)	I. T. Botham, Bombay	1979-80
11-163 (6-104, 5-59)†	N. A. Foster, Madras	1984-85
10-70 (7-46, 3-24)†	J. K. Lever, Delhi	1976-77
11-153 (7-49, 4-104)	H. Verity, Madras	1933-34

For India (4)

10-177 (6-105, 4-72)	S. A. Durani, Madras	1961-62
12-108 (8-55, 4-53)	V. Mankad, Madras	1951-52
10-188 (4-130, 6-58)	Chetan Sharma, Birmingham	1986
12-181 (6-64, 6-117)†	L. Sivaramakrishnan, Bombay	1984-85

† *Signifies ten wickets or more on first appearance in England–India Tests.*

Note: A. V. Bedser took 11 wickets in a match in each of the first two Tests of his career.

ENGLAND v PAKISTAN

Captains

Season	England	Pakistan	T	E	P	D
1954	L. Hutton[1]	A. H. Kardar	4	1	1	2
1961-62	E. R. Dexter	Imtiaz Ahmed	3	1	0	2
1962	E. R. Dexter[2]	Javed Burki	5	4	0	1
1967	D. B. Close	Hanif Mohammad	3	2	0	1
1968-69	M. C. Cowdrey	Saeed Ahmed	3	0	0	3
1971	R. Illingworth	Intikhab Alam	3	1	0	2
1972-73	A. R. Lewis	Majid Khan	3	0	0	3
1974	M. H. Denness	Intikhab Alam	3	0	0	3
1977-78	J. M. Brearley[3]	Wasim Bari	3	0	0	3
1978	J. M. Brearley	Wasim Bari	3	2	0	1
1982	R. G. D. Willis[4]	Imran Khan	3	2	1	0
1983-84	R. G. D. Willis[5]	Zaheer Abbas	3	0	1	2
1987	M. W. Gatting	Imran Khan	5	0	1	4
1987-88	M. W. Gatting	Javed Miandad	3	0	1	2
1992	G. A. Gooch	Javed Miandad	5	1	2	2
1996	M. A. Atherton	Wasim Akram	3	0	2	1
	In England		37	13	7	17
	In Pakistan		18	1	2	15
	Totals		55	14	9	32

Notes: The following deputised for the official touring captain or were appointed by the home authority for only a minor proportion of the series:
[1]D. S. Sheppard (Second and Third). [2]M. C. Cowdrey (Third). [3]G. Boycott (Third). [4]D. I. Gower (Second). [5]D. I. Gower (Second and Third).

HIGHEST INNINGS TOTALS

For England in England: 558-6 dec. at Nottingham		1954
in Pakistan: 546-8 dec. at Faisalabad		1983-84
For Pakistan in England: 708 at The Oval		1987
in Pakistan: 569-9 dec. at Hyderabad		1972-73

LOWEST INNINGS TOTALS

For England in England: 130 at The Oval	1954
in Pakistan: 130 at Lahore	1987-88
For Pakistan in England: 87 at Lord's	1954
in Pakistan: 191 at Faisalabad	1987-88

INDIVIDUAL HUNDREDS

For England (47)

D. L. Amiss (3)			**J. P. Crawley** (1)			**B. W. Luckhurst** (1)		
112	Lahore	1972-73	106	The Oval ...	1996	108*†	Birmingham.	1971
158	Hyderabad ..	1972-73	**E. R. Dexter** (2)			**C. Milburn** (1)		
183	The Oval ...	1974	205	Karachi.....	1961-62	139	Karachi.....	1968-69
C. W. J. Athey (1)			172	The Oval ...	1962	**P. H. Parfitt** (4)		
123	Lord's......	1987	**B. L. D'Oliveira** (1)			111	Karachi.....	1961-62
K. F. Barrington (4)			114*	Dacca	1968-69	101*	Birmingham.	1962
139†	Lahore	1961-62	**K. W. R. Fletcher** (1)			119	Leeds	1962
148	Lord's......	1967	122	The Oval ...	1974	101*	Nottingham .	1962
109*	Nottingham .	1967	**M. W. Gatting** (2)			**G. Pullar** (1)		
142	The Oval ...	1967	124	Birmingham.	1987	165	Dacca	1961-62
I. T. Botham (2)			150*	The Oval ...	1987	**C. T. Radley** (1)		
100†	Birmingham.	1978	**G. A. Gooch** (1)			106†	Birmingham.	1978
108	Lord's......	1978	135	Leeds	1992	**D. W. Randall** (1)		
G. Boycott (3)			**D. I. Gower** (2)			105	Birmingham.	1982
121*	Lord's......	1971	152	Faisalabad ..	1983-84	**R. T. Robinson** (1)		
112	Leeds	1971	173*	Lahore	1983-84	166†	Manchester.	1987
100*	Hyderabad ..	1977-78	**T. W. Graveney** (3)			**R. T. Simpson** (1)		
B. C. Broad (1)			153	Lord's......	1962	101	Nottingham .	1954
116	Faisalabad ..	1987-88	114	Nottingham .	1962	**R. A. Smith** (1)		
D. C. S. Compton (1)			105	Karachi.....	1968-69	127†	Birmingham.	1992
278	Nottingham .	1954	**N. V. Knight** (1)			**A. J. Stewart** (2)		
M. C. Cowdrey (3)			113	Leeds	1996	190†	Birmingham.	1992
159†	Birmingham.	1962	**A. P. E. Knott** (1)			170	Leeds	1996
182	The Oval ...	1962	116	Birmingham.	1971			
100	Lahore	1968-69						

For Pakistan (38)

Aamir Sohail (1)			**Ijaz Ahmed, sen.** (1)			**Mohsin Khan** (2)		
205	Manchester..	1992	141	Leeds	1996	200	Lord's......	1982
Alim-ud-Din (1)			**Imran Khan** (1)			104	Lahore	1983-84
109	Karachi.....	1961-62	118	The Oval ...	1987	**Moin Khan** (1)		
Asif Iqbal (3)			**Intikhab Alam** (1)			105	Leeds	1996
146	The Oval ...	1967	138	Hyderabad ..	1972-73	**Mudassar Nazar** (3)		
104*	Birmingham.	1971	**Inzamam-ul-Haq** (1)			114†	Lahore	1977-78
102	Lahore	1972-73	148	Lord's......	1996	124	Birmingham.	1987
Hanif Mohammad (3)			**Javed Burki** (3)			120	Lahore	1987-88
111 }	Dacca	1961-62	138†	Lahore	1961-62	**Mushtaq Mohammad** (3)		
104 }			140	Dacca	1961-62	100*	Nottingham .	1962
187*	Lord's......	1967	101	Lord's......	1962	100	Birmingham.	1971
Haroon Rashid (2)			**Javed Miandad** (2)			157	Hyderabad ..	1972-73
122†	Lahore	1977-78	260	The Oval ...	1987	**Nasim-ul-Ghani** (1)		
108	Hyderabad ..	1977-78	153*	Birmingham.	1992	101	Lord's......	1962

Sadiq Mohammad (1)		102	The Oval ...		1987	**Zaheer Abbas** (2)		
119 Lahore	1972-73	165	Birmingham.		1992	274† Birmingham.	1971	
Saeed Anwar (1)		100*	The Oval ...		1996	240 The Oval ...	1974	
176 The Oval ...	1996							
Salim Malik (4)		**Wasim Raja** (1)						
116 Faisalabad ..	1983-84	112	Faisalabad ..	1983-84				

† *Signifies hundred on first appearance in England–Pakistan Tests.*

Note: Three batsmen – Majid Khan, Mushtaq Mohammad and D. L. Amiss – were dismissed for 99 at Karachi, 1972-73: the only instance in Test matches.

RECORD PARTNERSHIPS FOR EACH WICKET

For England

198	for 1st	G. Pullar and R. W. Barber at Dacca	1961-62
248	for 2nd	M. C. Cowdrey and E. R. Dexter at The Oval	1962
227	for 3rd	A. J. Stewart and R. A. Smith at Birmingham	1992
188	for 4th	E. R. Dexter and P. H. Parfitt at Karachi	1961-62
192	for 5th	D. C. S. Compton and T. E. Bailey at Nottingham	1954
153*	for 6th	P. H. Parfitt and D. A. Allen at Birmingham	1962
167	for 7th	D. I. Gower and V. J. Marks at Faisalabad	1983-84
99	for 8th	P. H. Parfitt and D. A. Allen at Leeds	1962
76	for 9th	T. W. Graveney and F. S. Trueman at Lord's	1962
79	for 10th	R. W. Taylor and R. G. D. Willis at Birmingham	1982

For Pakistan

173	for 1st	Mohsin Khan and Shoaib Mohammad at Lahore	1983-84
291	for 2nd†	Zaheer Abbas and Mushtaq Mohammad at Birmingham	1971
180	for 3rd	Mudassar Nazar and Haroon Rashid at Lahore	1977-78
322	for 4th	Javed Miandad and Salim Malik at Birmingham	1992
197	for 5th	Javed Burki and Nasim-ul-Ghani at Lord's	1962
145	for 6th	Mushtaq Mohammad and Intikhab Alam at Hyderabad...........	1972-73
112	for 7th	Asif Mujtaba and Moin Khan at Leeds.......................	1996
130	for 8th	Hanif Mohammad and Asif Iqbal at Lord's	1967
190	for 9th†	Asif Iqbal and Intikhab Alam at The Oval	1967
62	for 10th	Sarfraz Nawaz and Asif Masood at Leeds	1974

† *Denotes record partnership against all countries.*

TEN WICKETS OR MORE IN A MATCH

For England (2)

11-83 (6-65, 5-18)†	N. G. B. Cook, Karachi	1983-84
13-71 (5-20, 8-51)	D. L. Underwood, Lord's..............................	1974

For Pakistan (6)

10-194 (5-84, 5-110)	Abdul Qadir, Lahore..............................	1983-84
10-211 (7-96, 3-115)	Abdul Qadir, The Oval............................	1987
13-101 (9-56, 4-45)	Abdul Qadir, Lahore.............................	1987-88
10-186 (5-88, 5-98)	Abdul Qadir, Karachi............................	1987-88
12-99 (6-53, 6-46)	Fazal Mahmood, The Oval..........................	1954
10-77 (3-37, 7-40)	Imran Khan, Leeds	1987

† *Signifies ten wickets or more on first appearance in England–Pakistan Tests.*

FOUR WICKETS IN FIVE BALLS

C. M. Old, v Pakistan at Birmingham in 1978, dismissed Wasim Raja, Wasim Bari, Iqbal Qasim and Sikander Bakht to take four wickets in five balls (ww-ww).

ENGLAND v SRI LANKA

Captains

Season	England	Sri Lanka	T	E	SL	D
1981-82	K. W. R. Fletcher	B. Warnapura	1	1	0	0
1984	D. I. Gower	L. R. D. Mendis	1	0	0	1
1988	G. A. Gooch	R. S. Madugalle	1	1	0	0
1991	G. A. Gooch	P. A. de Silva	1	1	0	0
1992-93	A. J. Stewart	A. Ranatunga	1	0	1	0
	In England		3	2	0	1
	In Sri Lanka		2	1	1	0
	Totals		5	3	1	1

HIGHEST INNINGS TOTALS

For England in England: 429 at Lord's 1988
    in Sri Lanka: 380 at Colombo (SSC) 1992-93

For Sri Lanka in England: 491-7 dec. at Lord's 1984
    in Sri Lanka: 469 at Colombo (SSC) 1992-93

LOWEST INNINGS TOTALS

For England in England: 282 at Lord's 1991
    in Sri Lanka: 223 at Colombo (PSS) 1981-82

For Sri Lanka in England: 194 at Lord's 1988
    in Sri Lanka: 175 at Colombo (PSS) 1981-82

INDIVIDUAL HUNDREDS

For England (4)

G. A. Gooch (1)
174 Lord's...... 1991

A. J. Lamb (1)
107† Lord's...... 1984

R. A. Smith (1)
128 Colombo (SSC) 1992-93

A. J. Stewart (1)
113*† Lord's...... 1991

For Sri Lanka (3)

L. R. D. Mendis (1)
111 Lord's...... 1984

S. A. R. Silva (1)
102*† Lord's...... 1984

S. Wettimuny (1)
190 Lord's...... 1984

 † *Signifies hundred on first appearance in England–Sri Lanka Tests.*

BEST BOWLING

Best bowling in an innings for England: 7-70 by P. A. J. DeFreitas at Lord's 1991
    for Sri Lanka: 5-69 by R. J. Ratnayake at Lord's 1991

RECORD PARTNERSHIPS FOR EACH WICKET

For England

78 for 1st	G. A. Gooch and H. Morris at Lord's..........................	1991
139 for 2nd	G. A. Gooch and A. J. Stewart at Lord's......................	1991
112 for 3rd	R. A. Smith and G. A. Hick at Colombo (SSC)	1992-93
122 for 4th	R. A. Smith and A. J. Stewart at Colombo (SSC)...............	1992-93

40 for 5th	A. J. Stewart and I. T. Botham at Lord's	1991
87 for 6th	A. J. Lamb and R. M. Ellison at Lord's	1984
63 for 7th	A. J. Stewart and R. C. Russell at Lord's......................	1991
20 for 8th	J. E. Emburey and P. W. Jarvis at Colombo (SSC).............	1992-93
37 for 9th	P. J. Newport and N. A. Foster at Lord's......................	1988
40 for 10th	J. E. Emburey and D. E. Malcolm at Colombo (SSC)	1992-93

For Sri Lanka

99 for 1st	R. S. Mahanama and U. C. Hathurusinghe at Colombo (SSC).....	1992-93
83 for 2nd	B. Warnapura and R. L. Dias at Colombo (PSS)................	1981-82
101 for 3rd	S. Wettimuny and R. L. Dias at Lord's	1984
148 for 4th	S. Wettimuny and A. Ranatunga at Lord's......................	1984
150 for 5th†	S. Wettimuny and L. R. D. Mendis at Lord's	1984
138 for 6th	S. A. R. Silva and L. R. D. Mendis at Lord's..................	1984
74 for 7th	U. C. Hathurusinghe and R. J. Ratnayake at Lord's	1991
29 for 8th	R. J. Ratnayake and C. P. H. Ramanayake at Lord's	1991
83 for 9th†	H. P. Tillekeratne and M. Muralitharan at Colombo (SSC)	1992-93
64 for 10th†	J. R. Ratnayeke and G. F. Labrooy at Lord's.................	1988

† *Denotes record partnership against all countries.*

ENGLAND v ZIMBABWE

Season	England	*Captains* Zimbabwe	T	E	Z	D
1996-97	M. A. Atherton	A. D. R. Campbell	2	0	0	2

HIGHEST INNINGS TOTALS

For England: 406 at Bulawayo 1996-97

For Zimbabwe: 376 at Bulawayo 1996-97

INDIVIDUAL HUNDREDS

For England (3)

J. P. Crawley (1)	**N. Hussain** (1)	**A. J. Stewart** (1)
112† Bulawayo... 1996-97	113† Bulawayo... 1996-97	101* Harare 1996-97

For Zimbabwe (1)

A. Flower (1)
112† Bulawayo... 1996-97

† *Signifies hundred on first appearance in England–Zimbabwe Tests.*

HUNDRED PARTNERSHIPS

For England

137 for 2nd	N. V. Knight and A. J. Stewart at Bulawayo.....................	1996-97
106* for 4th	A. J. Stewart and G. P. Thorpe at Harare........................	1996-97
148 for 5th	N. Hussain and J. P. Crawley at Bulawayo	1996-97

For Zimbabwe

127 for 2nd   G. W. Flower and A. D. R. Campbell at Bulawayo 1996-97

BEST MATCH BOWLING ANALYSES

For England

6-137 (2-76, 4-61)†   P. C. R. Tufnell, Bulawayo 1996-97

For Zimbabwe

7-186 (5-123, 2-63)†   P. A. Strang, Bulawayo 1996-97

† *Signifies on first appearance in England–Zimbabwe Tests.*

AUSTRALIA v SOUTH AFRICA

		Captains				
Season	*Australia*	*South Africa*	*T*	*A*	*SA*	*D*
1902-03S	J. Darling	H. M. Taberer[1]	3	2	0	1
1910-11A	C. Hill	P. W. Sherwell	5	4	1	0
1912E	S. E. Gregory	F. Mitchell[2]	3	2	0	1
1921-22S	H. L. Collins	H. W. Taylor	3	1	0	2
1931-32A	W. M. Woodfull	H. B. Cameron	5	5	0	0
1935-36S	V. Y. Richardson	H. F. Wade	5	4	0	1
1949-50S	A. L. Hassett	A. D. Nourse	5	4	0	1
1952-53A	A. L. Hassett	J. E. Cheetham	5	2	2	1
1957-58S	I. D. Craig	C. B. van Ryneveld[3]	5	3	0	2
1963-64A	R. B. Simpson[4]	T. L. Goddard	5	1	1	3
1966-67S	R. B. Simpson	P. L. van der Merwe	5	1	3	1
1969-70S	W. M. Lawry	A. Bacher	4	0	4	0
1993-94A	A. R. Border	K. C. Wessels[5]	3	1	1	1
1993-94S	A. R. Border	K. C. Wessels	3	1	1	1
1996-97S	M. A. Taylor	W. J. Cronje	3	2	1	0
	In South Africa		36	18	9	9
	In Australia		23	13	5	5
	In England		3	2	0	1
	Totals		62	33	14	15

S Played in South Africa.   A Played in Australia.   E Played in England.

Notes: The following deputised for the official touring captain or were appointed by the home authority for only a minor proportion of the series:
[1]J. H. Anderson (Second), E. A. Halliwell (Third). [2]L. J. Tancred (Third). [3]D. J. McGlew (First). [4]R. Benaud (First). [5]W. J. Cronje (Third).

HIGHEST INNINGS TOTALS

For Australia in Australia: 578 at Melbourne.................................... 1910-11
                in South Africa: 628-8 dec. at Johannesburg........................ 1996-97

For South Africa in Australia: 595 at Adelaide 1963-64
                in South Africa: 622-9 dec. at Durban 1969-70

LOWEST INNINGS TOTALS

For Australia in Australia: 111 at Sydney 1993-94
in South Africa: 75 at Durban 1949-50

For South Africa in Australia: 36† at Melbourne 1931-32
in South Africa: 85‡ at Johannesburg 1902-03
85‡ at Cape Town............................. 1902-03

† *Scored 45 in the second innings giving the smallest aggregate of 81 (12 extras) in Test cricket.*
‡ *In successive innings.*

INDIVIDUAL HUNDREDS

For Australia (61)

W. W. Armstrong (2)
159*‡ Johannesburg 1902-03
132 Melbourne .. 1910-11
W. Bardsley (3)
132† Sydney 1910-11
121 Manchester.. 1912
164 Lord's...... 1912
R. Benaud (2)
122 Johannesburg 1957-58
100 Johannesburg 1957-58
G. S. Blewett (1)
214† Johannesburg 1996-97
B. C. Booth (2)
169† Brisbane 1963-64
102* Sydney 1963-64
D. G. Bradman (4)
226† Brisbane 1931-32
112 Sydney 1931-32
167 Melbourne .. 1931-32
299* Adelaide.... 1931-32
W. A. Brown (1)
121 Cape Town.. 1935-36
J. W. Burke (1)
189 Cape Town.. 1957-58
A. G. Chipperfield (1)
109† Durban 1935-36
H. L. Collins (1)
203 Johannesburg 1921-22
J. H. Fingleton (3)
112 Cape Town.. 1935-36
108 Johannesburg 1935-36

118 Durban 1935-36
J. M. Gregory (1)
119 Johannesburg 1921-22
R. N. Harvey (8)
178 Cape Town.. 1949-50
151* Durban 1949-50
100 Johannesburg 1949-50
116 Port Elizabeth 1949-50
109 Brisbane 1952-53
190 Sydney 1952-53
116 Adelaide.... 1952-53
205 Melbourne .. 1952-53
A. L. Hassett (3)
112† Johannesburg 1949-50
167 Port Elizabeth 1949-50
163 Adelaide.... 1952-53
C. Hill (3)
142† Johannesburg 1902-03
191 Sydney 1910-11
100 Melbourne .. 1910-11
C. Kelleway (2)
114 Manchester.. 1912
102 Lord's...... 1912
W. M. Lawry (1)
157 Melbourne .. 1963-64
S. J. E. Loxton (1)
101† Johannesburg 1949-50
C. G. Macartney (2)
137 Sydney 1910-11
116 Durban 1921-22

S. J. McCabe (2)
149 Durban 1935-36
189* Johannesburg 1935-36
C. C. McDonald (1)
154 Adelaide.... 1952-53
J. Moroney (2)
118 } Johannesburg 1949-50
101*}
A. R. Morris (2)
111 Johannesburg 1949-50
157 Port Elizabeth 1949-50
K. E. Rigg (1)
127† Sydney 1931-32
J. Ryder (1)
142 Cape Town.. 1921-22
R. B. Simpson (1)
153 Cape Town.. 1966-67
K. R. Stackpole (1)
134 Cape Town.. 1966-67
M. A. Taylor (1)
170† Melbourne .. 1993-94
V. T. Trumper (2)
159 Melbourne .. 1910-11
214* Adelaide.... 1910-11
M. E. Waugh (2)
113* Durban 1993-94
116 Port Elizabeth 1996-97
S. R. Waugh (2)
164† Adelaide.... 1993-94
160 Johannesburg 1996-97
W. M. Woodfull (1)
161 Melbourne .. 1931-32

For South Africa (38)

E. J. Barlow (5)
114† Brisbane 1963-64
109 Melbourne .. 1963-64
201 Adelaide.... 1963-64
127 Cape Town.. 1969-70
110 Johannesburg 1969-70
K. C. Bland (1)
126 Sydney 1963-64
W. J. Cronje (1)
122 Johannesburg 1993-94
W. R. Endean (1)
162* Melbourne .. 1952-53
G. A. Faulkner (3)
204 Melbourne .. 1910-11

115 Adelaide.... 1910-11
122* Manchester.. 1912
C. N. Frank (1)
152 Johannesburg 1921-22
A. C. Hudson (1)
102 Cape Town.. 1993-94
B. L. Irvine (1)
102 Port Elizabeth 1969-70
D. T. Lindsay (3)
182 Johannesburg 1966-67
137 Durban 1966-67
131 Johannesburg 1966-67
D. J. McGlew (2)
108 Johannesburg 1957-58

105 Durban 1957-58
A. D. Nourse (2)
231 Johannesburg 1935-36
114 Cape Town.. 1949-50
A. W. Nourse (1)
111 Johannesburg 1921-22
R. G. Pollock (5)
122 Sydney 1963-64
175 Adelaide.... 1963-64
209 Cape Town.. 1966-67
105 Port Elizabeth 1966-67
274 Durban 1969-70

B. A. Richards (2)		104	Cape Town..	1902-03	134	Durban	1957-58
140	Durban 1969-70	**S. J. Snooke** (1)			**J. W. Zulch** (2)		
126	Port Elizabeth 1969-70	103	Adelaide	1910-11	105	Adelaide	1910-11
E. A. B. Rowan (1)		**K. G. Viljoen** (1)			150	Sydney	1910-11
143	Durban 1949-50	111	Melbourne . .	1931-32			
J. H. Sinclair (2)		**J. H. B. Waite** (2)					
101	Johannesburg 1902-03	115	Johannesburg	1957-58			

† *Signifies hundred on first appearance in Australia–South Africa Tests.*
‡ *Carried his bat.*

RECORD PARTNERSHIPS FOR EACH WICKET

For Australia

233 for 1st	J. H. Fingleton and W. A. Brown at Cape Town	1935-36
275 for 2nd	C. C. McDonald and A. L. Hassett at Adelaide	1952-53
242 for 3rd	C. Kelleway and W. Bardsley at Lord's	1912
169 for 4th	M. A. Taylor and M. E. Waugh at Melbourne	1993-94
385 for 5th	S. R. Waugh and G. S. Blewett at Johannesburg	1996-97
108 for 6th	S. R. Waugh and I. A. Healy at Cape Town	1993-94
160 for 7th	R. Benaud and G. D. McKenzie at Sydney	1963-64
83 for 8th	A. G. Chipperfield and C. V. Grimmett at Durban	1935-36
78 for 9th	⎰ D. G. Bradman and W. J. O'Reilly at Adelaide	1931-32
	⎱ K. D. Mackay and I. Meckiff at Johannesburg	1957-58
82 for 10th	V. S. Ransford and W. J. Whitty at Melbourne	1910-11

For South Africa

176 for 1st	D. J. McGlew and T. L. Goddard at Johannesburg	1957-58
173 for 2nd	L. J. Tancred and C. B. Llewellyn at Johannesburg	1902-03
341 for 3rd†	E. J. Barlow and R. G. Pollock at Adelaide	1963-64
206 for 4th	C. N. Frank and A. W. Nourse at Johannesburg	1921-22
129 for 5th	J. H. B. Waite and W. R. Endean at Johannesburg	1957-58
200 for 6th†	R. G. Pollock and H. R. Lance at Durban	1969-70
221 for 7th	D. T. Lindsay and P. L. van der Merwe at Johannesburg	1966-67
124 for 8th	A. W. Nourse and E. A. Halliwell at Johannesburg	1902-03
85 for 9th	R. G. Pollock and P. M. Pollock at Cape Town	1966-67
53 for 10th	L. A. Stricker and S. J. Pegler at Adelaide	1910-11

† *Denotes record partnership against all countries.*

TEN WICKETS OR MORE IN A MATCH

For Australia (6)

14-199 (7-116, 7-83)	C. V. Grimmett, Adelaide	1931-32
10-88 (5-32, 5-56)	C. V. Grimmett, Cape Town	1935-36
10-110 (3-70, 7-40)	C. V. Grimmett, Johannesburg	1935-36
13-173 (7-100, 6-73)	C. V. Grimmett, Durban	1935-36
11-24 (5-6, 6-18)	H. Ironmonger, Melbourne	1931-32
12-128 (7-56, 5-72)	S. K. Warne, Sydney	1993-94

For South Africa (3)

10-123 (4-80, 6-43)	P. S. de Villiers, Sydney	1993-94
10-116 (5-43, 5-73)	C. B. Llewellyn, Johannesburg	1902-03
13-165 (6-84, 7-81)	H. J. Tayfield, Melbourne	1952-53

Note: C. V. Grimmett took ten wickets or more in three consecutive matches in 1935-36.

AUSTRALIA v WEST INDIES

Captains

Season	Australia	West Indies	T	A	WI	T	D
1930-31*A*	W. M. Woodfull	G. C. Grant	5	4	1	0	0
1951-52*A*	A. L. Hassett[1]	J. D. C. Goddard[2]	5	4	1	0	0
1954-55*W*	I. W. Johnson	D. St E. Atkinson[3]	5	3	0	0	2

THE FRANK WORRELL TROPHY

Captains

Season	Australia	West Indies	T	A	WI	T	D	Held by
1960-61*A*	R. Benaud	F. M. M. Worrell	5	2	1	1	1	A
1964-65*W*	R. B. Simpson	G. S. Sobers	5	1	2	0	2	WI
1968-69*A*	W. M. Lawry	G. S. Sobers	5	3	1	0	1	A
1972-73*W*	I. M. Chappell	R. B. Kanhai	5	2	0	0	3	A
1975-76*A*	G. S. Chappell	C. H. Lloyd	6	5	1	0	0	A
1977-78*W*	R. B. Simpson	A. I. Kallicharran[4]	5	1	3	0	1	WI
1979-80*A*	G. S. Chappell	C. H. Lloyd[5]	3	0	2	0	1	WI
1981-82*A*	G. S. Chappell	C. H. Lloyd	3	1	1	0	1	WI
1983-84*W*	K. J. Hughes	C. H. Lloyd[6]	5	0	3	0	2	WI
1984-85*A*	A. R. Border[7]	C. H. Lloyd	5	1	3	0	1	WI
1988-89*A*	A. R. Border	I. V. A. Richards	5	1	3	0	1	WI
1990-91*W*	A. R. Border	I. V. A. Richards	5	1	2	0	2	WI
1992-93*A*	A. R. Border	R. B. Richardson	5	1	2	0	2	WI
1994-95*W*	M. A. Taylor	R. B. Richardson	4	2	1	0	1	A
1996-97*A*	M. A. Taylor	C. A. Walsh	5	3	2	0	0	A
	In Australia		52	25	18	1	8	
	In West Indies		34	10	11	0	13	
	Totals		86	35	29	1	21	

A Played in Australia. W Played in West Indies.

Notes: The following deputised for the official touring captain or were appointed by the home authority for only a minor proportion of the series:
[1]A. R. Morris (Third). [2]J. B. Stollmeyer (Fifth). [3]J. B. Stollmeyer (Second and Third). [4]C. H. Lloyd (First and Second). [5]D. L. Murray (First). [6]I. V. A. Richards (Second). [7]K. J. Hughes (First and Second).

HIGHEST INNINGS TOTALS

For Australia in Australia: 619 at Sydney	1968-69
in West Indies: 758-8 dec. at Kingston	1954-55
For West Indies in Australia: 616 at Adelaide	1968-69
in West Indies: 573 at Bridgetown	1964-65

LOWEST INNINGS TOTALS

For Australia in Australia: 76 at Perth	1984-85
in West Indies: 90 at Port-of-Spain	1977-78
For West Indies in Australia: 78 at Sydney	1951-52
in West Indies: 109 at Georgetown	1972-73

INDIVIDUAL HUNDREDS

For Australia (78)

R. G. Archer (1)
128   Kingston ...   1954-55

R. Benaud (1)
121   Kingston ...   1954-55

D. C. Boon (3)
149   Sydney   1988-89
109*   Kingston ...   1990-91
111   Brisbane....   1992-93

B. C. Booth (1)
117   Port-of-Spain   1964-65

A. R. Border (3)
126   Adelaide....   1981-82

| 100* | Port-of-Spain | 1983-84 |
| 110 | Melbourne .. | 1992-93 |

D. G. Bradman (2)
223   Brisbane....   1930-31
152   Melbourne ..   1930-31

G. S. Chappell (5)
106   Bridgetown .   1972-73
123 }
109*} ‡Brisbane ...   1975-76
182*   Sydney   1975-76
124   Brisbane....   1979-80

I. M. Chappell (5)
117†   Brisbane....   1968-69
165   Melbourne ..   1968-69
106*   Bridgetown .   1972-73
109   Georgetown .   1972-73
156   Perth.......   1975-76

G. J. Cosier (1)
109†   Melbourne ..   1975-76

R. M. Cowper (2)
143   Port-of-Spain   1964-65
102   Bridgetown .   1964-65

J. Dyson (1)

127*†	Sydney	1981-82

R. N. Harvey (3)

133	Kingston	1954-55
133	Port-of-Spain	1954-55
204	Kingston	1954-55

A. L. Hassett (2)

| 132 | Sydney | 1951-52 |
| 102 | Melbourne | 1951-52 |

M. L. Hayden (1)

| 125 | Adelaide | 1996-97 |

I. A. Healy (1)

| 161* | Brisbane | 1996-97 |

A. M. J. Hilditch (1)

| 113† | Melbourne | 1984-85 |

K. J. Hughes (2)

| 130*† | Brisbane | 1979-80 |
| 100* | Melbourne | 1981-82 |

D. M. Jones (1)

| 216 | Adelaide | 1988-89 |

A. F. Kippax (1)

| 146† | Adelaide | 1930-31 |

W. M. Lawry (4)

210	Bridgetown	1964-65
105	Brisbane	1968-69
205	Melbourne	1968-69
151	Sydney	1968-69

R. R. Lindwall (1)

| 118 | Bridgetown | 1954-55 |

R. B. McCosker (1)

| 109* | Melbourne | 1975-76 |

C. C. McDonald (2)

| 110 | Port-of-Spain | 1954-55 |
| 127 | Kingston | 1954-55 |

K. R. Miller (4)

129	Sydney	1951-52
147	Kingston	1954-55
137	Bridgetown	1954-55
109	Kingston	1954-55

A. R. Morris (1)

| 111 | Port-of-Spain | 1954-55 |

N. C. O'Neill (1)

| 181† | Brisbane | 1960-61 |

W. B. Phillips (1)

| 120 | Bridgetown | 1983-84 |

W. H. Ponsford (2)

| 183 | Sydney | 1930-31 |
| 109 | Brisbane | 1930-31 |

I. R. Redpath (4)

132	Sydney	1968-69
102	Melbourne	1975-76
103	Adelaide	1975-76
101	Melbourne	1975-76

C. S. Serjeant (1)

| 124 | Georgetown | 1977-78 |

R. B. Simpson (1)

| 201 | Bridgetown | 1964-65 |

K. R. Stackpole (1)

| 142 | Kingston | 1972-73 |

M. A. Taylor (1)

| 144 | St John's | 1990-91 |

P. M. Toohey (1)

| 122 | Kingston | 1977-78 |

A. Turner (1)

| 136 | Adelaide | 1975-76 |

K. D. Walters (6)

118	Sydney	1968-69
110	Adelaide	1968-69
242 }		
103 }	Sydney	1968-69
102*	Bridgetown	1972-73
112	Port-of-Spain	1972-73

M. E. Waugh (3)

139*	St John's	1990-91
112	Melbourne	1992-93
126	Kingston	1994-95

S. R. Waugh (2)

| 100 | Sydney | 1992-93 |
| 200 | Kingston | 1994-95 |

K. C. Wessels (1)

| 173 | Sydney | 1984-85 |

G. M. Wood (2)

| 126 | Georgetown | 1977-78 |
| 111 | Perth | 1988-89 |

For West Indies (81)

F. C. M. Alexander (1)

| 108 | Sydney | 1960-61 |

K. L. T. Arthurton (1)

| 157*† | Brisbane | 1992-93 |

D. St E. Atkinson (1)

| 219 | Bridgetown | 1954-55 |

B. F. Butcher (3)

117	Port-of-Spain	1964-65
101	Sydney	1968-69
118	Adelaide	1968-69

S. L. Campbell (1)

| 113 | Brisbane | 1996-97 |

C. C. Depeiza (1)

| 122 | Bridgetown | 1954-55 |

P. J. L. Dujon (2)

| 130 | Port-of-Spain | 1983-84 |
| 139 | Perth | 1984-85 |

M. L. C. Foster (1)

| 125† | Kingston | 1972-73 |

R. C. Fredericks (1)

| 169 | Perth | 1975-76 |

H. A. Gomes (6)

101†	Georgetown	1977-78
115	Kingston	1977-78
126	Sydney	1981-82
124*	Adelaide	1981-82
127	Perth	1984-85
120*	Adelaide	1984-85

C. G. Greenidge (4)

120*	Georgetown	1983-84
127	Kingston	1983-84
104	Adelaide	1988-89
226	Bridgetown	1990-91

D. L. Haynes (5)

103*	Georgetown	1983-84
145	Bridgetown	1983-84
100	Perth	1988-89
143	Sydney	1988-89
111	Georgetown	1990-91

G. A. Headley (2)

| 102* | Brisbane | 1930-31 |
| 105 | Sydney | 1930-31 |

C. L. Hooper (1)

| 102 | Brisbane | 1996-97 |

C. C. Hunte (1)

| 110 | Melbourne | 1960-61 |

A. I. Kallicharran (4)

101	Brisbane	1975-76
127	Port-of-Spain	1977-78
126	Kingston	1977-78
106	Adelaide	1979-80

R. B. Kanhai (5)

117 }		
115 }	Adelaide	1960-61
129	Bridgetown	1964-65
121	Port-of-Spain	1964-65
105	Bridgetown	1972-73

B. C. Lara (2)

| 277 | Sydney | 1992-93 |
| 132 | Perth | 1996-97 |

C. H. Lloyd (6)

129†	Brisbane	1968-69
178	Georgetown	1972-73
149	Perth	1975-76
102	Melbourne	1975-76
121	Adelaide	1979-80
114	Brisbane	1984-85

F. R. Martin (1)

| 123* | Sydney | 1930-31 |

S. M. Nurse (2)

| 201 | Bridgetown | 1964-65 |
| 137 | Sydney | 1968-69 |

I. V. A. Richards (5)

101	Adelaide	1975-76
140	Brisbane	1979-80
178	St John's	1983-84
208	Melbourne	1984-85
146	Perth	1988-89

R. B. Richardson (9)

131*	Bridgetown	1983-84
154	St John's	1983-84
138	Brisbane	1984-85
122	Melbourne	1988-89
106	Adelaide	1988-89
104*	Kingston	1990-91

182	Georgetown .	1990-91	**G. S. Sobers** (4)		126	Port-of-Spain	1954-55

182	Georgetown .	1990-91
109	Sydney	1992-93
100	Kingston . . .	1994-95
L. G. Rowe (1)		
107	Brisbane	1975-76
P. V. Simmons (1)		
110	Melbourne . .	1992-93
O. G. Smith (1)		
104†	Kingston . . .	1954-55

G. S. Sobers (4)		
132	Brisbane	1960-61
168	Sydney	1960-61
110	Adelaide	1968-69
113	Sydney	1968-69
J. B. Stollmeyer (1)		
104	Sydney	1951-52
C. L. Walcott (5)		
108	Kingston . . .	1954-55

126 } 110 }	Port-of-Spain	1954-55
155 } 110 }	Kingston . . .	1954-55
E. D. Weekes (1)		
139	Port-of-Spain	1954-55
A. B. Williams (1)		
100†	Georgetown .	1977-78
F. M. M. Worrell (1)		
108	Melbourne . .	1951-52

† *Signifies hundred on first appearance in Australia–West Indies Tests.*

‡ *G. S. Chappell is the only player to score hundreds in both innings of his first Test as captain.*

Note: F. C. M. Alexander and C. C. Depeiza scored the only hundreds of their first-class careers in a Test match.

RECORD PARTNERSHIPS FOR EACH WICKET

For Australia

382 for 1st†	W. M. Lawry and R. B. Simpson at Bridgetown	1964-65
298 for 2nd	W. M. Lawry and I. M. Chappell at Melbourne	1968-69
295 for 3rd†	C. C. McDonald and R. N. Harvey at Kingston.	1954-55
336 for 4th	W. M. Lawry and K. D. Walters at Sydney	1968-69
220 for 5th	K. R. Miller and R. G. Archer at Kingston	1954-55
206 for 6th	K. R. Miller and R. G. Archer at Bridgetown	1954-55
134 for 7th	A. K. Davidson and R. Benaud at Brisbane	1960-61
137 for 8th	R. Benaud and I. W. Johnson at Kingston	1954-55
114 for 9th	D. M. Jones and M. G. Hughes at Adelaide.	1988-89
97 for 10th	T. G. Hogan and R. M. Hogg at Georgetown	1983-84

For West Indies

250* for 1st	C. G. Greenidge and D. L. Haynes at Georgetown	1983-84
297 for 2nd	D. L. Haynes and R. B. Richardson at Georgetown	1990-91
308 for 3rd	R. B. Richardson and I. V. A. Richards at St John's	1983-84
198 for 4th	L. G. Rowe and A. I. Kallicharran at Brisbane	1975-76
210 for 5th	R. B. Kanhai and M. L. C. Foster at Kingston	1972-73
165 for 6th	R. B. Kanhai and D. L. Murray at Bridgetown	1972-73
347 for 7th†‡	D. St E. Atkinson and C. C. Depeiza at Bridgetown	1954-55
87 for 8th	P. J. L. Dujon and C. E. L. Ambrose at Port-of-Spain	1990-91
122 for 9th	D. A. J. Holford and J. L. Hendriks at Adelaide	1968-69
56 for 10th	J. Garner and C. E. H. Croft at Brisbane	1979-80

† *Denotes record partnership against all countries.*

‡ *Record seventh-wicket partnership in first-class cricket.*

TEN WICKETS OR MORE IN A MATCH

For Australia (12)

10-113 (4-31, 6-82)	M. G. Bevan, Adelaide	1996-97
11-96 (7-46, 4-50)	A. R. Border, Sydney	1988-89
11-222 (5-135, 6-87)†	A. K. Davidson, Brisbane.	1960-61
11-183 (7-87, 4-96)†	C. V. Grimmett, Adelaide	1930-31
10-115 (6-72, 4-43)	N. J. N. Hawke, Georgetown	1964-65
10-144 (6-54, 4-90)	R. G. Holland, Sydney	1984-85
13-217 (5-130, 8-87)	M. G. Hughes, Perth	1988-89
11-79 (7-23, 4-56)	H. Ironmonger, Melbourne	1930-31
11-181 (8-112, 3-69)	G. F. Lawson, Adelaide	1984-85
10-127 (7-83, 3-44)	D. K. Lillee, Melbourne	1981-82
10-159 (8-71, 2-88)	G. D. McKenzie, Melbourne	1968-69
10-185 (3-87, 7-98)	B. Yardley, Sydney	1981-82

For West Indies (4)

10-120 (6-74, 4-46)	C. E. L. Ambrose, Adelaide	1992-93
10-113 (7-55, 3-58)	G. E. Gomez, Sydney	1951-52
11-107 (5-45, 6-62)	M. A. Holding, Melbourne	1981-82
10-107 (5-69, 5-38)	M. D. Marshall, Adelaide	1984-85

† *Signifies ten wickets or more on first appearance in Australia–West Indies Tests.*

AUSTRALIA v NEW ZEALAND

		Captains					
Season	*Australia*		*New Zealand*	*T*	*A*	*NZ*	*D*
1945-46*N*	W. A. Brown		W. A. Hadlee	1	1	0	0
1973-74*A*	I. M. Chappell		B. E. Congdon	3	2	0	1
1973-74*N*	I. M. Chappell		B. E. Congdon	3	1	1	1
1976-77*N*	G. S. Chappell		G. M. Turner	2	1	0	1
1980-81*A*	G. S. Chappell		G. P. Howarth[1]	3	2	0	1
1981-82*N*	G. S. Chappell		G. P. Howarth	3	1	1	1

TRANS-TASMAN TROPHY

		Captains						
Season	*Australia*		*New Zealand*	*T*	*A*	*NZ*	*D*	*Held by*
1985-86*A*	A. R. Border		J. V. Coney	3	1	2	0	NZ
1985-86*N*	A. R. Border		J. V. Coney	3	0	1	2	NZ
1987-88*A*	A. R. Border		J. J. Crowe	3	1	0	2	A
1989-90*A*	A. R. Border		J. G. Wright	1	0	0	1	A
1989-90*N*	A. R. Border		J. G. Wright	1	0	1	0	NZ
1992-93*N*	A. R. Border		M. D. Crowe	3	1	1	1	NZ
1993-94*A*	A. R. Border		M. D. Crowe[2]	3	2	0	1	A
		In Australia		16	8	2	6	
		In New Zealand		16	5	5	6	
		Totals		32	13	7	12	

A Played in Australia.   N Played in New Zealand.

Note: The following deputised for the official touring captain: [1]M. G. Burgess (Second). [2]K. R. Rutherford (Second and Third).

HIGHEST INNINGS TOTALS

For Australia in Australia: 607-6 dec. at Brisbane		1993-94
in New Zealand: 552 at Christchurch		1976-77
For New Zealand in Australia: 553-7 dec. at Brisbane		1985-86
in New Zealand: 484 at Wellington		1973-74

LOWEST INNINGS TOTALS

For Australia in Australia: 162 at Sydney		1973-74
in New Zealand: 103 at Auckland		1985-86
For New Zealand in Australia: 121 at Perth		1980-81
in New Zealand: 42 at Wellington		1945-46

INDIVIDUAL HUNDREDS

For Australia (30)

D. C. Boon (3)
143   Brisbane....   1987-88
200   Perth.......   1989-90
106   Hobart   1993-94

A. R. Border (5)
152*   Brisbane....   1985-86
140 }
114* }   Christchurch.   1985-86
205   Adelaide....   1987-88
105   Brisbane....   1993-94

G. S. Chappell (3)
247* }
133 }   Wellington ..   1973-74
176   Christchurch.   1981-82

I. M. Chappell (2)
145 }
121 }   Wellington ..   1973-74

G. J. Gilmour (1)
101   Christchurch.   1976-77

I. A. Healy (1)
113*   Perth.......   1993-94

G. R. Marsh (1)
118   Auckland ...   1985-86

R. W. Marsh (1)
132   Adelaide....   1973-74

G. R. J. Matthews (2)
115†   Brisbane....   1985-86
130   Wellington ..   1985-86

I. R. Redpath (1)
159*‡   Auckland ...   1973-74

M. J. Slater (1)
168   Hobart   1993-94

K. R. Stackpole (1)
122†   Melbourne ..   1973-74

M. A. Taylor (1)
142*   Perth.......   1993-94

K. D. Walters (3)
104*   Auckland ...   1973-74
250   Christchurch.   1976-77
107   Melbourne ..   1980-81

M. E. Waugh (1)
111   Hobart   1993-94

S. R. Waugh (1)
147*   Brisbane....   1993-94

G. M. Wood (2)
111†   Brisbane....   1980-81
100   Auckland ...   1981-82

For New Zealand (19)

J. V. Coney (1)
101*   Wellington ..   1985-86

B. E. Congdon (2)
132   Wellington ..   1973-74
107*   Christchurch.   1976-77

M. D. Crowe (3)
188   Brisbane....   1985-86
137   Christchurch.   1985-86
137   Adelaide....   1987-88

B. A. Edgar (1)
161   Auckland ...   1981-82

M. J. Greatbatch (1)
146*†   Perth.......   1989-90

B. F. Hastings (1)
101   Wellington ..   1973-74

A. H. Jones (2)
150   Adelaide....   1987-88
143   Perth.......   1993-94

J. F. M. Morrison (1)
117   Sydney   1973-74

J. M. Parker (1)
108   Sydney   1973-74

J. F. Reid (1)
108†   Brisbane....   1985-86

K. R. Rutherford (1)
102   Christchurch.   1992-93

G. M. Turner (2)
101 }
110*} Christchurch.   1973-74

J. G. Wright (2)
141   Christchurch.   1981-82
117*   Wellington ..   1989-90

† *Signifies hundred on first appearance in Australia–New Zealand Tests.*
‡ *Carried his bat.*

Notes: G. S. and I. M. Chappell at Wellington in 1973-74 provide the only instance in Test matches of brothers both scoring a hundred in each innings and in the same Test.

RECORD PARTNERSHIPS FOR EACH WICKET

For Australia

198 for 1st	M. J. Slater and M. A. Taylor at Perth............................	1993-94
235 for 2nd	M. J. Slater and D. C. Boon at Hobart............................	1993-94
264 for 3rd	I. M. Chappell and G. S. Chappell at Wellington	1973-74
150 for 4th	M. E. Waugh and A. R. Border at Hobart	1993-94
213 for 5th	G. M. Ritchie and G. R. J. Matthews at Wellington	1985-86
197 for 6th	A. R. Border and G. R. J. Matthews at Brisbane.................	1985-86
217 for 7th†	K. D. Walters and G. J. Gilmour at Christchurch	1976-77
93 for 8th	G. J. Gilmour and K. J. O'Keeffe at Auckland	1976-77
69 for 9th	I. A. Healy and C. J. McDermott at Perth	1993-94
60 for 10th	K. D. Walters and J. D. Higgs at Melbourne	1980-81

For New Zealand

111	for 1st	M. J. Greatbatch and J. G. Wright at Wellington	1992-93
128*	for 2nd	J. G. Wright and A. H. Jones at Wellington	1989-90
224	for 3rd	J. F. Reid and M. D. Crowe at Brisbane	1985-86
229	for 4th†	B. E. Congdon and B. F. Hastings at Wellington	1973-74
88	for 5th	J. V. Coney and M. G. Burgess at Perth	1980-81
109	for 6th	K. R. Rutherford and J. V. Coney at Wellington	1985-86
132*	for 7th	J. V. Coney and R. J. Hadlee at Wellington	1985-86
88*	for 8th	M. J. Greatbatch and M. C. Snedden at Perth	1989-90
73	for 9th	H. J. Howarth and D. R. Hadlee at Christchurch	1976-77
124	for 10th	J. G. Bracewell and S. L. Boock at Sydney	1985-86

† *Denotes record partnership against all countries.*

TEN WICKETS OR MORE IN A MATCH

For Australia (2)

10-174 (6-106, 4-68)	R. G. Holland, Sydney	1985-86
11-123 (5-51, 6-72)	D. K. Lillee, Auckland	1976-77

For New Zealand (4)

10-106 (4-74, 6-32)	J. G. Bracewell, Auckland	1985-86
15-123 (9-52, 6-71)	R. J. Hadlee, Brisbane	1985-86
11-155 (5-65, 6-90)	R. J. Hadlee, Perth	1985-86
10-176 (5-109, 5-67)	R. J. Hadlee, Melbourne	1987-88

AUSTRALIA v INDIA

Captains

Season	Australia	India	T	A	I	T	D
1947-48 *A*	D. G. Bradman	L. Amarnath	5	4	0	0	1
1956-57 *I*	I. W. Johnson[1]	P. R. Umrigar	3	2	0	0	1
1959-60 *I*	R. Benaud	G. S. Ramchand	5	2	1	0	2
1964-65 *I*	R. B. Simpson	Nawab of Pataudi jun.	3	1	1	0	1
1967-68 *A*	R. B. Simpson[2]	Nawab of Pataudi jun.[3]	4	4	0	0	0
1969-70 *I*	W. M. Lawry	Nawab of Pataudi jun.	5	3	1	0	1
1977-78 *A*	R. B. Simpson	B. S. Bedi	5	3	2	0	0
1979-80 *I*	K. J. Hughes	S. M. Gavaskar	6	0	2	0	4
1980-81 *A*	G. S. Chappell	S. M. Gavaskar	3	1	1	0	1
1985-86 *A*	A. R. Border	Kapil Dev	3	0	0	0	3
1986-87 *I*	A. R. Border	Kapil Dev	3	0	0	1	2
1991-92 *A*	A. R. Border	M. Azharuddin	5	4	0	0	1
1996-97 *I*	M. A. Taylor	S. R. Tendulkar	1	0	1	0	0
	In Australia		25	16	3	0	6
	In India		26	8	6	1	11
	Totals		51	24	9	1	17

A Played in Australia. I Played in India.

Notes: The following deputised for the official touring captain or were appointed by the home authority for only a minor proportion of the series:
[1]R. R. Lindwall (Second). [2]W. M. Lawry (Third and Fourth). [3]C. G. Borde (First).

HIGHEST INNINGS TOTALS

For Australia in Australia: 674 at Adelaide	1947-48
in India: 574-7 dec. at Madras	1986-87
For India in Australia: 600-4 dec. at Sydney	1985-86
in India: 517-5 dec. at Bombay	1986-87

LOWEST INNINGS TOTALS

For Australia in Australia: 83 at Melbourne..................................	1980-81
in India: 105 at Kanpur..................................	1959-60
For India in Australia: 58 at Brisbane	1947-48
in India: 135 at Delhi	1959-60

INDIVIDUAL HUNDREDS

For Australia (51)

S. G. Barnes (1)
112	Adelaide	1947-48

D. C. Boon (6)
123†	Adelaide	1985-86
131	Sydney	1985-86
122	Madras	1986-87
129*	Sydney	1991-92
135	Adelaide	1991-92
107	Perth	1991-92

A. R. Border (4)
162†	Madras	1979-80
124	Melbourne ..	1980-81
163	Melbourne ..	1985-86
106	Madras	1986-87

D. G. Bradman (4)
185†	Brisbane	1947-48
132 } 127* }	Melbourne ..	1947-48
201	Adelaide	1947-48

J. W. Burke (1)
161	Bombay	1956-57

G. S. Chappell (1)
204†	Sydney	1980-81

I. M. Chappell (2)
151	Melbourne ..	1967-68
138	Delhi	1969-70

R. M. Cowper (2)
108	Adelaide	1967-68
165	Sydney	1967-68

L. E. Favell (1)
101	Madras	1959-60

R. N. Harvey (4)
153	Melbourne ..	1947-48
140	Bombay	1956-57
114	Delhi	1959-60
102	Bombay	1959-60

A. L. Hassett (1)
198*	Adelaide	1947-48

K. J. Hughes (2)
100	Madras	1979-80
213	Adelaide	1980-81

D. M. Jones (2)
210†	Madras	1986-87
150*	Perth	1991-92

W. M. Lawry (1)
100	Melbourne ..	1967-68

A. L. Mann (1)
105	Perth	1977-78

G. R. Marsh (1)
101	Bombay	1986-87

G. R. J. Matthews (1)
100*	Melbourne ..	1985-86

T. M. Moody (1)
101†	Perth	1991-92

A. R. Morris (1)
100*	Melbourne ..	1947-48

N. C. O'Neill (2)
163	Bombay	1959-60
113	Calcutta	1959-60

G. M. Ritchie (1)
128†	Adelaide	1985-86

A. P. Sheahan (1)
114	Kanpur	1969-70

R. B. Simpson (4)
103	Adelaide	1967-68
109	Melbourne ..	1967-68
176	Perth	1977-78
100	Adelaide	1977-78

K. R. Stackpole (1)
103†	Bombay	1969-70

M. A. Taylor (1)
100	Adelaide	1991-92

K. D. Walters (1)
102	Madras	1969-70

G. M. Wood (1)
125	Adelaide	1980-81

G. N. Yallop (2)
121†	Adelaide	1977-78
167	Calcutta	1979-80

For India (36)

M. Amarnath (2)			**M. L. Jaisimha** (1)			**R. J. Shastri** (2)		
100	Perth.......	1977-78	101	Brisbane....	1967-68	121*	Bombay	1986-87
138	Sydney	1985-86	**Kapil Dev** (1)			206	Sydney	1991-92
M. Azharuddin (1)			119	Madras.....	1986-87	**K. Srikkanth** (1)		
106	Adelaide...	1991-92	**S. M. H. Kirmani** (1)			116	Sydney	1985-86
N. J. Contractor (1)			101*	Bombay	1979-80	**S. R. Tendulkar** (2)		
108	Bombay	1959-60	**V. Mankad** (2)			148*	Sydney	1991-92
S. M. Gavaskar (8)			116	Melbourne ..	1947-48	114	Perth.......	1991-92
113†	Brisbane....	1977-78	111	Melbourne ..	1947-48	**D. B. Vengsarkar** (2)		
127	Perth.......	1977-78	**N. R. Mongia** (1)			112	Bangalore...	1979-80
118	Melbourne ..	1977-78	152†	Delhi	1996-97	164*	Bombay	1986-87
115	Delhi	1979-80	**Nawab of Pataudi jun.** (1)			**G. R. Viswanath** (4)		
123	Bombay	1979-80	128*†	Madras	1964-65	137†	Kanpur	1969-70
166*	Adelaide....	1985-86	**S. M. Patil** (1)			161*	Bangalore...	1979-80
172	Sydney	1985-86	174	Adelaide....	1980-81	131	Delhi	1979-80
103	Bombay	1986-87	**D. G. Phadkar** (1)			114	Melbourne ..	1980-81
V. S. Hazare (2)			123	Adelaide....	1947-48	**Yashpal Sharma** (1)		
116			**G. S. Ramchand** (1)			100*	Delhi	1979-80
145 }	Adelaide....	1947-48	109	Bombay	1956-57			

† *Signifies hundred on first appearance in Australia–India Tests.*

RECORD PARTNERSHIPS FOR EACH WICKET

For Australia

217	for 1st	D. C. Boon and G. R. Marsh at Sydney...........................	1985-86
236	for 2nd	S. G. Barnes and D. G. Bradman at Adelaide	1947-48
222	for 3rd	A. R. Border and K. J. Hughes at Madras	1979-80
178	for 4th	D. M. Jones and A. R. Border at Madras	1986-87
223*	for 5th	A. R. Morris and D. G. Bradman at Melbourne..................	1947-48
151	for 6th	T. R. Veivers and B. N. Jarman at Bombay	1964-65
66	for 7th	G. R. J. Matthews and R. J. Bright at Melbourne	1985-86
73	for 8th	T. R. Veivers and G. D. McKenzie at Madras	1964-65
87	for 9th	I. W. Johnson and W. P. A. Crawford at Madras	1956-57
77	for 10th	A. R. Border and D. R. Gilbert at Melbourne	1985-86

For India

192	for 1st	S. M. Gavaskar and C. P. S. Chauhan at Bombay................	1979-80
224	for 2nd	S. M. Gavaskar and M. Amarnath at Sydney....................	1985-86
159	for 3rd	S. M. Gavaskar and G. R. Viswanath at Delhi..................	1979-80
159	for 4th	D. B. Vengsarkar and G. R. Viswanath at Bangalore	1979-80
196	for 5th	R. J. Shastri and S. R. Tendulkar at Sydney	1991-92
298*	for 6th†	D. B. Vengsarkar and R. J. Shastri at Bombay	1986-87
132	for 7th	V. S. Hazare and H. R. Adhikari at Adelaide	1947-48
127	for 8th	S. M. H. Kirmani and K. D. Ghavri at Bombay	1979-80
81	for 9th	S. R. Tendulkar and K. S. More at Perth	1991-92
94	for 10th	S. M. Gavaskar and N. S. Yadav at Adelaide	1985-86

† *Denotes record partnership against all countries.*

TEN WICKETS OR MORE IN A MATCH

For Australia (11)

11-105 (6-52, 5-53)	R. Benaud, Calcutta	1956-57
12-124 (5-31, 7-93)	A. K. Davidson, Kanpur................................	1959-60

12-166 (5-99, 7-67)	G. Dymock, Kanpur	1979-80
10-168 (5-76, 5-92)	C. J. McDermott, Adelaide	1991-92
10-91 (6-58, 4-33)†	G. D. McKenzie, Madras	1964-65
10-151 (7-66, 3-85)	G. D. McKenzie, Melbourne	1967-68
10-144 (5-91, 5-53)	A. A. Mallett, Madras	1969-70
10-249 (5-103, 5-146)	G. R. J. Matthews, Madras	1986-87
12-126 (6-66, 6-60)	B. A. Reid, Melbourne	1991-92
11-31 (5-2, 6-29)†	E. R. H. Toshack, Brisbane	1947-48
11-95 (4-68, 7-27)	M. R. Whitney, Perth	1991-92

For India (6)

10-194 (5-89, 5-105)	B. S. Bedi, Perth	1977-78
12-104 (6-52, 6-52)	B. S. Chandrasekhar, Melbourne	1977-78
10-130 (7-49, 3-81)	Ghulam Ahmed, Calcutta	1956-57
11-122 (5-31, 6-91)	R. G. Nadkarni, Madras	1964-65
14-124 (9-69, 5-55)	J. M. Patel, Kanpur	1959-60
10-174 (4-100, 6-74)	E. A. S. Prasanna, Madras	1969-70

† *Signifies ten wickets or more on first appearance in Australia–India Tests.*

AUSTRALIA v PAKISTAN

Captains

Season	Australia	Pakistan	T	A	P	D
1956-57 *P*	I. W. Johnson	A. H. Kardar	1	0	1	0
1959-60 *P*	R. Benaud	Fazal Mahmood[1]	3	2	0	1
1964-65 *P*	R. B. Simpson	Hanif Mohammad	1	0	0	1
1964-65 *A*	R. B. Simpson	Hanif Mohammad	1	0	0	1
1972-73 *P*	I. M. Chappell	Intikhab Alam	3	3	0	0
1976-77 *A*	G. S. Chappell	Mushtaq Mohammad	3	1	1	1
1978-79 *A*	G. N. Yallop[2]	Mushtaq Mohammad	2	1	1	0
1979-80 *P*	G. S. Chappell	Javed Miandad	3	0	1	2
1981-82 *A*	G. S. Chappell	Javed Miandad	3	2	1	0
1982-83 *P*	K. J. Hughes	Imran Khan	3	0	3	0
1983-84 *A*	K. J. Hughes	Imran Khan[3]	5	2	0	3
1988-89 *P*	A. R. Border	Javed Miandad	3	0	1	2
1989-90 *A*	A. R. Border	Imran Khan	3	1	0	2
1994-95 *P*	M. A. Taylor	Salim Malik	3	0	1	2
1995-96 *A*	M. A. Taylor	Wasim Akram	3	2	1	0
	In Pakistan		17	2	7	8
	In Australia		23	12	4	7
	Totals		40	14	11	15

A Played in Australia. P Played in Pakistan.

Notes: The following deputised for the official touring captain or were appointed by the home authority for only a minor proportion of the series:

[1]Imtiaz Ahmed (Second). [2]K. J. Hughes (Second). [3]Zaheer Abbas (First, Second and Third).

HIGHEST INNINGS TOTALS

For Australia in Australia: 585 at Adelaide	1972-73
in Pakistan: 617 at Faisalabad	1979-80
For Pakistan in Australia: 624 at Adelaide	1983-84
in Pakistan: 537 at Rawalpindi	1994-95

LOWEST INNINGS TOTALS

For Australia in Australia: 125 at Melbourne	1981-82
in Pakistan: 80 at Karachi	1956-57

For Pakistan in Australia: 62 at Perth	1981-82
in Pakistan: 134 at Dacca	1959-60

INDIVIDUAL HUNDREDS

For Australia (42)

J. Benaud (1)
142   Melbourne . .   1972-73

D. C. Boon (1)
114*   Karachi.   1994-95

A. R. Border (6)
105†   Melbourne . .   1978-79
150* } Lahore   1979-80
153 }
118   Brisbane   1983-84
117*   Adelaide   1983-84
113*   Faisalabad . .   1988-89

G. S. Chappell (6)
116*   Melbourne . .   1972-73
121   Melbourne . .   1976-77
235   Faisalabad . .   1979-80
201   Brisbane   1981-82
150*   Brisbane   1983-84
182   Sydney   1983-84

I. M. Chappell (1)
196   Adelaide   1972-73

G. J. Cosier (1)
168   Melbourne . .   1976-77

I. C. Davis (1)
105†   Adelaide   1976-77

K. J. Hughes (2)
106   Perth   1981-82
106   Adelaide   1983-84

D. M. Jones (2)
116 } Adelaide   1989-90
121* }

R. B. McCosker (1)
105   Melbourne . .   1976-77

R. W. Marsh (1)
118†   Adelaide   1972-73

N. C. O'Neill (1)
134   Lahore.   1959-60

W. B. Phillips (1)
159†   Perth   1983-84

I. R. Redpath (1)
135   Melbourne . .   1972-73

G. M. Ritchie (1)
106*   Faisalabad . .   1982-83

A. P. Sheahan (1)
127   Melbourne . .   1972-73

R. B. Simpson (2)
153 } †Karachi.   1964-65
115 }

M. J. Slater (1)
110   Rawalpindi . .   1994-95

M. A. Taylor (3)
101†   Melbourne . .   1989-90
101*   Sydney   1989-90
123   Hobart   1995-96

K. D. Walters (1)
107   Adelaide   1976-77

M. E. Waugh (1)
116   Sydney   1995-96

S. R. Waugh (1)
112*   Brisbane   1995-96

K. C. Wessels (1)
179   Adelaide   1983-84

G. M. Wood (1)
100   Melbourne . .   1981-82

G. N. Yallop (3)
172   Faisalabad . .   1979-80
141   Perth   1983-84
268   Melbourne . .   1983-84

For Pakistan (36)

Aamir Sohail (1)
105   Lahore   1994-95

Asif Iqbal (3)
152*   Adelaide   1976-77
120   Sydney   1976-77
134*   Perth   1978-79

Hanif Mohammad (2)
101*   Karachi.   1959-60
104   Melbourne . .   1964-65

Ijaz Ahmed, sen. (3)
122   Faisalabad . .   1988-89
121   Melbourne . .   1989-90
137   Sydney   1995-96

Imran Khan (1)
136   Adelaide   . . .   1989-90

Javed Miandad (6)
129*   Perth.   1978-79
106*   Faisalabad . .   1979-80
138   Lahore   1982-83

131   Adelaide   1983-84
211   Karachi.   1988-89
107   Faisalabad . .   1988-89

Khalid Ibadulla (1)
166†   Karachi.   1964-65

Majid Khan (3)
158   Melbourne . .   1972-73
108   Melbourne . .   1978-79
110*   Lahore   1979-80

Mansoor Akhtar (1)
111   Faisalabad . .   1982-83

Mohsin Khan (3)
135   Lahore   1982-83
149   Adelaide   1983-84
152   Melbourne . .   1983-84

Moin Khan (1)
115*†   Lahore   1994-95

Mushtaq Mohammad (1)
121   Sydney   1972-73

Qasim Omar (1)
113   Adelaide   1983-84

Sadiq Mohammad (2)
137   Melbourne . .   1972-73
105   Melbourne . .   1976-77

Saeed Ahmed (1)
166   Lahore   1959-60

Salim Malik (2)
237   Rawalpindi . .   1994-95
143   Lahore   1994-95

Taslim Arif (1)
210*   Faisalabad . .   1979-80

Wasim Akram (1)
123   Adelaide   1989-90

Zaheer Abbas (2)
101   Adelaide   1976-77
126   Faisalabad . .   1982-83

† *Signifies hundred on first appearance in Australia–Pakistan Tests.*

RECORD PARTNERSHIPS FOR EACH WICKET

For Australia

176 for 1st	M. A. Taylor and M. J. Slater at Rawalpindi	1994-95
259 for 2nd	W. B. Phillips and G. N. Yallop at Perth	1983-84
203 for 3rd	G. N. Yallop and K. J. Hughes at Melbourne	1983-84
217 for 4th	G. S. Chappell and G. N. Yallop at Faisalabad	1979-80
171 for 5th	{ G. S. Chappell and G. J. Cosier at Melbourne	1976-77
	{ A. R. Border and G. S. Chappell at Brisbane	1983-84
139 for 6th	R. M. Cowper and T. R. Veivers at Melbourne	1964-65
185 for 7th	G. N. Yallop and G. R. J. Matthews at Melbourne	1983-84
117 for 8th	G. J. Cosier and K. J. O'Keeffe at Melbourne	1976-77
83 for 9th	J. R. Watkins and R. A. L. Massie at Sydney	1972-73
52 for 10th	{ D. K. Lillee and M. H. N. Walker at Sydney	1976-77
	{ G. F. Lawson and T. M. Alderman at Lahore	1982-83

For Pakistan

249	for 1st†	Khalid Ibadulla and Abdul Kadir at Karachi	1964-65
233	for 2nd	Mohsin Khan and Qasim Omar at Adelaide	1983-84
223*	for 3rd	Taslim Arif and Javed Miandad at Faisalabad	1979-80
155	for 4th	Mansoor Akhtar and Zaheer Abbas at Faisalabad	1982-83
186	for 5th	Javed Miandad and Salim Malik at Adelaide	1983-84
196	for 6th	Salim Malik and Aamir Sohail at Lahore	1994-95
104	for 7th	Intikhab Alam and Wasim Bari at Adelaide	1972-73
111	for 8th	Majid Khan and Imran Khan at Lahore	1979-80
56	for 9th	Intikhab Alam and Afaq Hussain at Melbourne	1964-65
87	for 10th	Asif Iqbal and Iqbal Qasim at Adelaide	1976-77

   † *Denotes record partnership against all countries.*

TEN WICKETS OR MORE IN A MATCH

For Australia (4)

10-111 (7-87, 3-24)†	R. J. Bright, Karachi	1979-80
10-135 (6-82, 4-53)	D. K. Lillee, Melbourne	1976-77
11-118 (5-32, 6-86)†	C. G. Rackemann, Perth	1983-84
11-77 (7-23, 4-54)	S. K. Warne, Brisbane	1995-96

For Pakistan (6)

11-218 (4-76, 7-142)	Abdul Qadir, Faisalabad	1982-83
13-114 (6-34, 7-80)†	Fazal Mahmood, Karachi	1956-57
12-165 (6-102, 6-63)	Imran Khan, Sydney	1976-77
11-118 (4-69, 7-49)	Iqbal Qasim, Karachi	1979-80
11-125 (2-39, 9-86)	Sarfraz Nawaz, Melbourne	1978-79
11-160 (6-62, 5-98)†	Wasim Akram, Melbourne	1989-90

   † *Signifies ten wickets or more on first appearance in Australia–Pakistan Tests.*

AUSTRALIA v SRI LANKA

		Captains				
Season	Australia	Sri Lanka	T	A	SL	D
1982-83S	G. S. Chappell	L. R. D. Mendis	1	1	0	0
1987-88A	A. R. Border	R. S. Madugalle	1	1	0	0
1989-90A	A. R. Border	A. Ranatunga	2	1	0	1
1992-93S	A. R. Border	A. Ranatunga	3	1	0	2
1995-96A	M. A. Taylor	A. Ranatunga[1]	3	3	0	0
	In Australia		6	5	0	1
	In Sri Lanka......................		4	2	0	2
	Totals		10	7	0	3

A Played in Australia. S Played in Sri Lanka.

Note: The following deputised for the official touring captain:
[1]P. A. de Silva (Third).

HIGHEST INNINGS TOTALS

For Australia in Australia: 617-5 dec. at Perth 1995-96
in Sri Lanka: 514-4 dec. at Kandy 1982-83

For Sri Lanka in Australia: 418 in Brisbane 1989-90
in Sri Lanka: 547-8 dec. at Colombo (SSC) 1992-93

LOWEST INNINGS TOTALS

For Australia in Australia: 224 at Hobart 1989-90
in Sri Lanka: 247 at Colombo (KS) 1992-93

For Sri Lanka in Australia: 153 at Perth 1987-88
in Sri Lanka: 164 at Colombo (SSC)............................ 1992-93

INDIVIDUAL HUNDREDS

For Australia (15)

D. C. Boon (1)
110   Melbourne .. 1995-96
A. R. Border (1)
106   Moratuwa... 1992-93
D. W. Hookes (1)
143*† Kandy...... 1982-83
D. M. Jones (3)
102† Perth....... 1987-88
118* Hobart 1989-90

100* Colombo (KS) 1992-93
T. M. Moody (1)
106† Brisbane 1989-90
M. J. Slater (1)
219† Perth....... 1995-96
M. A. Taylor (2)
164† Brisbane 1989-90
108   Hobart 1989-90

M. E. Waugh (1)
111   Perth....... 1995-96
S. R. Waugh (3)
134* Hobart 1989-90
131* Melbourne .. 1995-96
170   Adelaide.... 1995-96
K. C. Wessels (1)
141† Kandy...... 1982-83

For Sri Lanka (7)

P. A. de Silva (1)
167   Brisbane 1989-90
A. P. Gurusinha (2)
137   Colombo(SSC) 1992-93
143   Melbourne .. 1995-96

S. T. Jayasuriya (1)
112   Adelaide.... 1995-96
R. S. Kaluwitharana (1)
132*† Colombo(SSC) 1992-93

A. Ranatunga (1)
127   Colombo(SSC) 1992-93
H. P. Tillekeratne (1)
119   Perth....... 1995-96

† *Signifies hundred on first appearance in Australia–Sri Lanka Tests.*

RECORD PARTNERSHIPS FOR EACH WICKET

For Australia

228	for 1st	M. J. Slater and M. A. Taylor at Perth	1995-96
170	for 2nd	K. C. Wessels and G. N. Yallop at Kandy	1982-83
158	for 3rd	T. M. Moody and A. R. Border at Brisbane	1989-90
163	for 4th	M. A. Taylor and A. R. Border at Hobart	1989-90
155*	for 5th	D. W. Hookes and A. R. Border at Kandy	1982-83
260*	for 6th	D. M. Jones and S. R. Waugh at Hobart	1989-90
129	for 7th	G. R. J. Matthews and I. A. Healy at Moratuwa	1992-93
56	for 8th	G. R. J. Matthews and C. J. McDermott at Colombo (SSC)	1992-93
45	for 9th	I. A. Healy and S. K. Warne at Colombo (SSC)	1992-93
49	for 10th	I. A. Healy and M. R. Whitney at Colombo (SSC)	1992-93

For Sri Lanka

110	for 1st	R. S. Mahanama and U. C. Hathurusinghe at Colombo (KS)	1992-93
92	for 2nd	R. S. Mahanama and A. P. Gurusinha at Colombo (SSC)	1992-93
125	for 3rd	S. T. Jayasuriya and S. Ranatunga at Adelaide	1995-96
230	for 4th	A. P. Gurusinha and A. Ranatunga at Colombo (SSC)	1992-93
116	for 5th	H. P. Tillekeratne and A. Ranatunga at Moratuwa	1992-93
96	for 6th	A. P. Gurusinha and R. S. Kaluwitharana at Colombo (SSC)	1992-93
144	for 7th†	P. A. de Silva and J. R. Ratnayeke at Brisbane	1989-90
33	for 8th	A. Ranatunga and C. P. H. Ramanayake at Perth	1987-88
46	for 9th	H. D. P. K. Dharmasena and G. P. Wickremasinghe at Perth	1995-96
27	for 10th	P. A. de Silva and C. P. H. Ramanayake at Brisbane	1989-90

† *Denotes record partnership against all countries.*

BEST MATCH BOWLING ANALYSES

For Australia

8-156 (3-68, 5-88) M. G. Hughes, Hobart 1989-90

For Sri Lanka

8-157 (5-82, 3-75) C. P. H. Ramanayake, Moratuwa 1992-93

SOUTH AFRICA v WEST INDIES

		Captains					
Season	*South Africa*		*West Indies*	*T*	*SA*	*WI*	*D*
1991-92 *W*	K. C. Wessels		R. B. Richardson	1	0	1	0

W Played in West Indies.

HIGHEST INNINGS TOTALS

For South Africa: 345 at Bridgetown 1991-92

For West Indies: 283 at Bridgetown 1991-92

INDIVIDUAL HUNDREDS
For South Africa (1)

A. C. Hudson (1)
163† Bridgetown . 1991-92

Highest score for West Indies: 79* at Bridgetown 1991-92 by J. C. Adams.

† *Signifies hundred on first appearance in South Africa–West Indies Tests.*

HIGHEST PARTNERSHIPS
For South Africa

125 for 2nd   A. C. Hudson and K. C. Wessels at Bridgetown.................. 1991-92

For West Indies

99 for 1st   D. L. Haynes and P. V. Simmons at Bridgetown 1991-92

BEST MATCH BOWLING ANALYSES
For South Africa

8-158 (4-84, 4-74)   R. P. Snell, Bridgetown 1991-92

For West Indies

8-81 (2-47, 6-34)   C. E. L. Ambrose, Bridgetown 1991-92

SOUTH AFRICA v NEW ZEALAND

Season	South Africa	*Captains* New Zealand	T	SA	NZ	D
1931-32*N*	H. B. Cameron	M. L. Page	2	2	0	0
1952-53*N*	J. E. Cheetham	W. M. Wallace	2	1	0	1
1953-54*S*	J. E. Cheetham	G. O. Rabone[1]	5	4	0	1
1961-62*S*	D. J. McGlew	J. R. Reid	5	2	2	1
1963-64*N*	T. L. Goddard	J. R. Reid	3	0	0	3
1994-95*S*	W. J. Cronje	K. R. Rutherford	3	2	1	0
1994-95*N*	W. J. Cronje	K. R. Rutherford	1	1	0	0
	In New Zealand		8	4	0	4
	In South Africa		13	8	3	2
	Totals		21	12	3	6

N Played in New Zealand.   S Played in South Africa.

Note: The following deputised for the official touring captain:
[1]B. Sutcliffe (Fourth and Fifth).

HIGHEST INNINGS TOTALS

For South Africa in South Africa: 464 at Johannesburg 1961-62
                in New Zealand: 524-8 at Wellington 1952-53

For New Zealand in South Africa: 505 at Cape Town 1953-54
                in New Zealand: 364 at Wellington 1931-32

LOWEST INNINGS TOTALS

For South Africa in South Africa: 148 at Johannesburg 1953-54
in New Zealand: 223 at Dunedin 1963-64

For New Zealand in South Africa: 79 at Johannesburg 1953-54
in New Zealand: 138 at Dunedin 1963-64

INDIVIDUAL HUNDREDS

For South Africa (14)

X. C. Balaskas (1)
122* Wellington . . 1931-32
J. A. J. Christy (1)
103† Christchurch. 1931-32
W. J. Cronje (2)
112 Cape Town . . 1994-95
101 Auckland . . . 1994-95
W. R. Endean (1)
116 Auckland . . . 1952-53

D. J. McGlew (3)
255*† Wellington . . 1952-53
127*‡ Durban 1961-62
120 Johannesburg 1961-62
R. A. McLean (2)
101 Durban 1953-54
113 Cape Town . . 1961-62
B. Mitchell (1)
113† Christchurch. 1931-32

A. R. A. Murray (1)
109† Wellington . . 1952-53
D. J. Richardson (1)
109 Cape Town . 1994-95
J. H. B. Waite (1)
101 Johannesburg 1961-62

For New Zealand (7)

P. T. Barton (1)
109 Port Elizabeth 1961-62
P. G. Z. Harris (1)
101 Cape Town. . 1961-62

G. O. Rabone (1)
107 Durban 1953-54
J. R. Reid (2)
135 Cape Town. . 1953-54
142 Johannesburg 1961-62

B. W. Sinclair (1)
138 Auckland . . . 1963-64
H. G. Vivian (1)
100† Wellington . . 1931-32

† *Signifies hundred on first appearance in South Africa–New Zealand Tests.*
‡ *Carried his bat.*

RECORD PARTNERSHIPS FOR EACH WICKET

For South Africa

196 for 1st	J. A. J. Christy and B. Mitchell at Christchurch	1931-32
97 for 2nd	G. Kirsten and J. B. Commins at Durban	1994-95
112 for 3rd	D. J. McGlew and R. A. McLean at Johannesburg	1961-62
135 for 4th	K. J. Funston and R. A. McLean at Durban	1953-54
130 for 5th	W. R. Endean and J. E. Cheetham at Auckland	1952-53
83 for 6th	K. C. Bland and D. T. Lindsay at Auckland	1963-64
246 for 7th†	D. J. McGlew and A. R. A. Murray at Wellington	1952-53
95 for 8th	J. E. Cheetham and H. J. Tayfield at Cape Town	1953-54
60 for 9th	P. M. Pollock and N. A. T. Adcock at Port Elizabeth	1961-62
47 for 10th	D. J. McGlew and H. D. Bromfield at Port Elizabeth	1961-62

For New Zealand

126 for 1st	G. O. Rabone and M. E. Chapple at Cape Town..................	1953-54
72 for 2nd	D. J. Murray and S. P. Fleming at Johannesburg.................	1994-95
94 for 3rd	M. B. Poore and B. Sutcliffe at Cape Town.....................	1953-54
171 for 4th	B. W. Sinclair and S. N. McGregor at Auckland.................	1963-64
174 for 5th	J. R. Reid and J. E. F. Beck at Cape Town	1953-54
100 for 6th	H. G. Vivian and F. T. Badcock at Wellington	1931-32
84 for 7th	J. R. Reid and G. A. Bartlett at Johannesburg	1961-62
74 for 8th	S. A. Thomson and D. J. Nash at Johannesburg	1994-95
69 for 9th	C. F. W. Allcott and I. B. Cromb at Wellington	1931-32
57 for 10th	S. B. Doull and R. P. de Groen at Johannesburg................	1994-95

† *Denotes record partnership against all countries.*

TEN WICKETS OR MORE IN A MATCH

For South Africa (1)

11-196 (6-128, 5-68)†   S. F. Burke, Cape Town................................   1961-62

† *Signifies ten wickets or more on first appearance in South Africa–New Zealand Tests.*

Note: The best match figures by a New Zealand bowler are 8-134 (3-57, 5-77), M. N. Hart at Johannesburg, 1994-95.

SOUTH AFRICA v INDIA

		Captains					
Season	*South Africa*		*India*	*T*	*SA*	*I*	*D*
1992-93*S*	K. C. Wessels		M. Azharuddin	4	1	0	3
1996-97*I*	W. J. Cronje		S. R. Tendulkar	3	1	2	0
1996-97*S*	W. J. Cronje		S. R. Tendulkar	3	2	0	1
	In South Africa			7	3	0	4
	In India.........................			3	1	2	0
	Totals			10	4	2	4

S Played in South Africa.   I Played in India.

HIGHEST INNINGS TOTALS

For South Africa in South Africa: 529-7 dec. at Cape Town   1996-97
　　　　　　　　　　in India: 428 at Calcutta   1996-97

For India in South Africa: 410 at Johannesburg   1996-97
　　　　　　　in India: 400-7 dec. at Kanpur   1996-97

LOWEST INNINGS TOTALS

For South Africa in South Africa: 235 at Durban   1996-97
　　　　　　　　　　in India: 105 at Ahmedabad   1996-97

For India in South Africa: 66 at Durban   1996-97
　　　　　　　in India: 137 at Calcutta   1996-97

INDIVIDUAL HUNDREDS

For South Africa (10)

W. J. Cronje (1)
135   Port Elizabeth 1992-93
D. J. Cullinan (2)
153*   Calcutta 1996-97
122*   Johannesburg 1996-97

A. C. Hudson (1)
146   Calcutta   1996-97
G. Kirsten (3)
102 ⎫
133 ⎬ Calcutta   1996-97
103   Cape Town .   1996-97

L. Klusener (1)
102*   Cape Town .   1996-97
B. M. McMillan (1)
103*   Cape Town .   1996-97
K. C. Wessels (1)
118†   Durban   1992-93

For India (8)

P. K. Amre (1)		163*	Kanpur 1996-97
103†	Durban 1992-93	115	Cape Town . 1996-97
M. Azharuddin (3)		**R. Dravid** (1)	
109	Calcutta 1996-97	148	Johannesburg 1996-97

Kapil Dev (1)		
129	Port Elizabeth	1992-93
S. R. Tendulkar (2)		
111	Johannesburg	1992-93
169	Cape Town .	1996-97

† *Signifies hundred on first appearance in South Africa–India Tests.*

RECORD PARTNERSHIPS FOR EACH WICKET

For South Africa

236	for 1st	A. C. Hudson and G. Kirsten at Calcutta	1996-97
212	for 2nd†	G. Kirsten and D. J. Cullinan at Calcutta	1996-97
114	for 3rd	G. Kirsten and D. J. Cullinan at Cape Town	1996-97
94	for 4th	A. C. Hudson and D. J. Cullinan at Cape Town	1996-97
99	for 5th	D. J. Cullinan and J. N. Rhodes at Cape Town	1992-93
112	for 6th	B. M. McMillan and S. M. Pollock at Johannesburg	1996-97
101*	for 7th	B. M. McMillan and S. M. Pollock at Cape Town	1996-97
147*	for 8th†	B. M. McMillan and L. Klusener at Cape Town	1996-97
60	for 9th	P. S. de Villiers and A. A. Donald at Ahmedabad	1996-97
74	for 10th	B. M. McMillan and A. A. Donald at Durban	1996-97

For India

90	for 1st	V. Rathore and N. R. Mongia at Johannesburg	1996-97
85	for 2nd	M. Prabhakar and S. V. Manjrekar at Cape Town	1992-93
54	for 3rd	R. Dravid and S. R. Tendulkar at Johannesburg	1996-97
145	for 4th	R. Dravid and S. C. Ganguly at Johannesburg	1996-97
87	for 5th	M. Azharuddin and P. K. Amre at Durban	1992-93
222	for 6th	S. R. Tendulkar and M. Azharuddin at Cape Town	1996-97
76	for 7th	R. Dravid and J. Srinath at Johannesburg	1996-97
161	for 8th†	M. Azharuddin and A. Kumble at Calcutta	1996-97
77	for 9th	Kapil Dev and A. Kumble at Port Elizabeth	1992-93
19	for 10th	S. R. Tendulkar and D. Ganesh at Cape Town	1996-97

† *Denotes record partnership against all countries.*

TEN WICKETS OR MORE IN A MATCH

For South Africa (1)

12-139 (5-55, 7-84)	A. A. Donald, Port Elizabeth	1992-93

For India (1)

10-153 (5-60, 5-93)	B. K. V. Prasad, Durban	1996-97

SOUTH AFRICA v PAKISTAN

		Captains					
Season	*South Africa*		*Pakistan*	*T*	*SA*	*P*	*D*
1994-95*S*	W. J. Cronje		Salim Malik	1	1	0	0

S Played in South Africa.

HIGHEST INNINGS TOTALS

For South Africa: 460 at Johannesburg... 1994-95

For Pakistan: 230 at Johannesburg 1994-95

INDIVIDUAL HUNDREDS

For South Africa (1)

B. M. McMillan (1)
113†   Johannesburg 1994-95

Highest score for Pakistan: 99 by Salim Malik at Johannesburg 1994-95.

† Signifies hundred on first appearance in South Africa–Pakistan Tests.

HUNDRED PARTNERSHIP

For South Africa

157 for 6th   J. N. Rhodes and B. M. McMillan at Johannesburg 1994-95

Note: The highest partnership for Pakistan is 93 for the 4th wicket between Asif Mujtaba and Inzamam-ul-Haq at Johannesburg, 1994-95.

TEN WICKETS OR MORE IN A MATCH

For South Africa (1)

10-108 (6-81, 4-27)†   P. S. de Villiers, Johannesburg 1994-95

Note: The best match figures for Pakistan are 5-184 (3-102, 2-82), Aqib Javed at Johannesburg, 1994-95.

† Signifies ten wickets or more on first appearance in South Africa–Pakistan Tests.

SOUTH AFRICA v SRI LANKA

		Captains					
Season	*South Africa*		*Sri Lanka*	*T*	*SA*	*SL*	*D*
1993-94*SL*	K. C. Wessels		A. Ranatunga	3	1	0	2

SL Played in Sri Lanka.

HIGHEST INNINGS TOTALS

For South Africa: 495 at Colombo (SSC) 1993-94

For Sri Lanka: 331 at Moratuwa... 1993-94

INDIVIDUAL HUNDREDS

For South Africa (3)

W. J. Cronje (1) | **D. J. Cullinan** (1) | **J. N. Rhodes** (1)
122   Colombo (SSC) 1993-94 | 102   Colombo (PSS) 1993-94 | 101*† Moratuwa... 1993-94

For Sri Lanka (1)

A. Ranatunga (1)
131†   Moratuwa... 1993-94

† *Signifies hundred on first appearance in South Africa–Sri Lanka Tests.*

HUNDRED PARTNERSHIPS

For South Africa

137 for 1st	K. C. Wessels and A. C. Hudson at Colombo (SSC)	1993-94
122 for 6th	D. J. Cullinan and D. J. Richardson at Colombo (PSS)	1993-94
105 for 3rd	W. J. Cronje and D. J. Cullinan at Colombo (SSC)	1993-94
104 for 1st	K. C. Wessels and A. C. Hudson at Moratuwa	1993-94

For Sri Lanka

121 for 5th	P. A. de Silva and A. Ranatunga at Moratuwa	1993-94
103 for 6th	A. Ranatunga and H. P. Tillekeratne at Moratuwa...............	1993-94
101 for 4th	P. A. de Silva and A. Ranatunga at Colombo (PSS).............	1993-94

BEST MATCH BOWLING ANALYSES

For South Africa

9-106 (5-48, 4-58)   B. N. Schultz, Colombo (SSC) 1993-94

For Sri Lanka

6-152 (5-104, 1-48)   M. Muralitharan, Moratuwa 1993-94

SOUTH AFRICA v ZIMBABWE

		Captains				
Season	South Africa		Zimbabwe	T	SA	Z	D
1995-96Z	W. J. Cronje		A. Flower	1	1	0	0

Z Played in Zimbabwe.

HIGHEST INNINGS TOTALS

For South Africa: 346 at Harare 1995-96

For Zimbabwe: 283 at Harare 1995-96

INDIVIDUAL HUNDREDS

For South Africa (1)

A. C. Hudson (1)
135†   Harare 1995-96

Highest score for Zimbabwe: 63 by A. Flower at Harare 1995-96.

† *Signifies hundred on first appearance in South Africa–Zimbabwe Tests.*

HUNDRED PARTNERSHIP

For South Africa

101 for 6th   A. C. Hudson and B. M. McMillan at Harare 1995-96

Note: The highest partnership for Zimbabwe is 97 for the 5th wicket between A. Flower and G. J. Whittall at Harare, 1995-96.

TEN WICKETS OR MORE IN A MATCH

For South Africa (1)

11-113 (3-42, 8-71)†   A. A. Donald, Harare   1995-96

Note: The best match figures for Zimbabwe are 5-105 (3-68, 2-37) by A. C. I. Lock at Harare, 1995-96.

  † *Signifies ten wickets or more on first appearance in South Africa–Zimbabwe Tests.*

WEST INDIES v NEW ZEALAND

		Captains				
Season	*West Indies*	*New Zealand*	*T*	*WI*	*NZ*	*D*
1951-52*N*	J. D. C. Goddard	B. Sutcliffe	2	1	0	1
1955-56*N*	D. St E. Atkinson	J. R. Reid[1]	4	3	1	0
1968-69*N*	G. S. Sobers	G. T. Dowling	3	1	1	1
1971-72*W*	G. S. Sobers	G. T. Dowling[2]	5	0	0	5
1979-80*N*	C. H. Lloyd	G. P. Howarth	3	0	1	2
1984-85*W*	I. V. A. Richards	G. P. Howarth	4	2	0	2
1986-87*N*	I. V. A. Richards	J. V. Coney	3	1	1	1
1993-94*N*	C. A. Walsh	K. R. Rutherford	2	1	0	1
1995-96*W*	C. A. Walsh	L. K. Germon	2	1	0	1
	In New Zealand		17	7	4	6
	In West Indies		11	3	0	8
	Totals		28	10	4	14

N Played in New Zealand.   W Played in West Indies.

Notes: The following deputised for the official touring captain or were appointed by the home authority for only a minor proportion of the series:
  [1]H. B. Cave (First). [2]B. E. Congdon (Third, Fourth and Fifth).

HIGHEST INNINGS TOTALS

For West Indies in West Indies: 564-8 at Bridgetown   1971-72
in New Zealand: 660-5 dec. at Wellington   1994-95

For New Zealand in West Indies: 543-3 dec. at Georgetown   1971-72
in New Zealand: 460 at Christchurch   1979-80

LOWEST INNINGS TOTALS

For West Indies in West Indies: 133 at Bridgetown   1971-72
in New Zealand: 77 at Auckland   1955-56

For New Zealand in West Indies: 94 at Bridgetown   1984-85
in New Zealand: 74 at Dunedin   1955-56

INDIVIDUAL HUNDREDS

By West Indies (31)

J. C. Adams (2)			121	Wellington ..	1986-87	**L. G. Rowe** (3)		
151	Wellington ..	1994-95	**A. I. Kallicharran** (2)			214 }		
208*	St John's ...	1995-96	100*†	Georgetown .	1971-72	100*}	†Kingston ..	1971-72
S. L. Campbell (1)			101	Port-of-Spain	1971-72	100	Christchurch.	1979-80
208	Bridgetown .	1995-96	**C. L. King** (1)			**R. G. Samuels** (1)		
M. C. Carew (1)			100*	Christchurch.	1979-80	125	St John's ...	1995-96
109†	Auckland ...	1968-69	**B. C. Lara** (1)			**G. S. Sobers** (1)		
C. A. Davis (1)			147	Wellington ..	1994-95	142	Bridgetown .	1971-72
183	Bridgetown .	1971-72	**J. R. Murray** (1)			**J. B. Stollmeyer** (1)		
R. C. Fredericks (1)			101*	Wellington ..	1994-95	152	Auckland ...	1951-52
163	Kingston ...	1971-72	**S. M. Nurse** (2)			**C. L. Walcott** (1)		
C. G. Greenidge (2)			168†	Auckland ...	1968-69	115	Auckland ...	1951-52
100	Port-of-Spain	1984-85	258	Christchurch.	1968-69	**E. D. Weekes** (3)		
213	Auckland ...	1986-87	**I. V. A. Richards** (1)			123	Dunedin	1955-56
D. L. Haynes (3)			105	Bridgetown .	1984-85	103	Christchurch.	1955-56
105†	Dunedin	1979-80	**R. B. Richardson** (1)			156	Wellington ..	1955-56
122	Christchurch.	1979-80	185	Georgetown .	1984-85	**F. M. M. Worrell** (1)		
						100	Auckland ...	1951-52

By New Zealand (20)

N. J. Astle (2)			119	Wellington ..	1986-87	**T. W. Jarvis** (1)		
125†	Bridgetown .	1995-96	104	Auckland ...	1986-87	182	Georgetown .	1971-72
103	St John's ...	1995-96	**B. A. Edgar** (1)			**A. C. Parore** (1)		
M. G. Burgess (1)			127	Auckland ...	1979-80	100*†	Christchurch.	1994-95
101	Kingston ...	1971-72	**R. J. Hadlee** (1)			**B. R. Taylor** (1)		
B. E. Congdon (2)			103	Christchurch.	1979-80	124†	Auckland ...	1968-69
166*	Port-of-Spain	1971-72	**B. F. Hastings** (2)			**G. M. Turner** (2)		
126	Bridgetown .	1971-72	117*	Christchurch.	1968-69	223*‡	Kingston....	1971-72
J. J. Crowe (1)			105	Bridgetown .	1971-72	259	Georgetown .	1971-72
112	Kingston ...	1984-85	**G. P. Howarth** (1)			**J. G. Wright** (1)		
M. D. Crowe (3)			147	Christchurch.	1979-80	138	Wellington ..	1986-87
188	Georgetown .	1984-85						

† *Signifies hundred on first appearance in West Indies–New Zealand Tests.*
‡ *Carried his bat.*

Notes: E. D. Weekes in 1955-56 made three hundreds in consecutive innings.

L. G. Rowe and A. I. Kallicharran each scored hundreds in their first two innings in Test cricket, Rowe being the only batsman to do so in his first match.

RECORD PARTNERSHIPS FOR EACH WICKET

For West Indies

225 for 1st	C. G. Greenidge and D. L. Haynes at Christchurch...............	1979-80
269 for 2nd	R. C. Fredericks and L. G. Rowe at Kingston	1971-72
221 for 3rd	B. C. Lara and J. C. Adams at Wellington......................	1994-95
162 for 4th	{ E. D. Weekes and O. G. Smith at Dunedin	1955-56
	{ C. G. Greenidge and A. I. Kallicharran at Christchurch	1979-80
189 for 5th	F. M. M. Worrell and C. L. Walcott at Auckland	1951-52
254 for 6th	C. A. Davis and G. S. Sobers at Bridgetown	1971-72
143 for 7th	D. St E. Atkinson and J. D. C. Goddard at Christchurch	1955-56
83 for 8th	I. V. A. Richards and M. D. Marshall at Bridgetown	1984-85
70 for 9th	M. D. Marshall and J. Garner at Bridgetown	1984-85
31 for 10th	T. M. Findlay and G. C. Shillingford at Bridgetown.............	1971-72

For New Zealand

387	for 1st†	G. M. Turner and T. W. Jarvis at Georgetown	1971-72
210	for 2nd	G. P. Howarth and J. J. Crowe at Kingston	1984-85
241	for 3rd	J. G. Wright and M. D. Crowe at Wellington	1986-87
175	for 4th	B. E. Congdon and B. F. Hastings at Bridgetown	1971-72
144	for 5th	N. J. Astle and J. T. C. Vaughan at Bridgetown	1995-96
220	for 6th	G. M. Turner and K. J. Wadsworth at Kingston	1971-72
143	for 7th	M. D. Crowe and I. D. S. Smith at Georgetown	1984-85
136	for 8th†	B. E. Congdon and R. S. Cunis at Port-of-Spain	1971-72
62*	for 9th	V. Pollard and R. S. Cunis at Auckland	1968-69
45	for 10th	D. K. Morrison and R. J. Kennedy at Bridgetown................	1995-96

† *Denotes record partnership against all countries.*

TEN WICKETS OR MORE IN A MATCH

For West Indies (2)

11-120 (4-40, 7-80)	M. D. Marshall, Bridgetown	1984-85
13-55 (7-37, 6-18)	C. A. Walsh, Wellington	1994-95

For New Zealand (3)

10-124 (4-51, 6-73)†	E. J. Chatfield, Port-of-Spain	1984-85
11-102 (5-34, 6-68)†	R. J. Hadlee, Dunedin................................	1979-80
10-166 (4-71, 6-95)	G. B. Troup, Auckland................................	1979-80

† *Signifies ten wickets or more on first appearance in West Indies–New Zealand Tests.*

WEST INDIES v INDIA

Captains

Season	West Indies	India	T	WI	I	D
1948-49*I*	J. D. C. Goddard	L. Amarnath	5	1	0	4
1952-53*W*	J. B. Stollmeyer	V. S. Hazare	5	1	0	4
1958-59*I*	F. C. M. Alexander	Ghulam Ahmed[1]	5	3	0	2
1961-62*W*	F. M. M. Worrell	N. J. Contractor[2]	5	5	0	0
1966-67*I*	G. S. Sobers	Nawab of Pataudi jun.	3	2	0	1
1970-71*W*	G. S. Sobers	A. L. Wadekar	5	0	1	4
1974-75*I*	C. H. Lloyd	Nawab of Pataudi jun.[3]	5	3	2	0
1975-76*W*	C. H. Lloyd	B. S. Bedi	4	2	1	1
1978-79*I*	A. I. Kallicharran	S. M. Gavaskar	6	0	1	5
1982-83*W*	C. H. Lloyd	Kapil Dev	5	2	0	3
1983-84*I*	C. H. Lloyd	Kapil Dev	6	3	0	3
1987-88*I*	I. V. A. Richards	D. B. Vengsarkar[4]	4	1	1	2
1988-89*W*	I. V. A. Richards	D. B. Vengsarkar	4	3	0	1
1994-95*I*	C. A. Walsh	M. Azharuddin	3	1	1	1
1996-97*W*	C. A. Walsh[5]	S. R. Tendulkar	5	1	0	4
	In India...........................		37	14	5	18
	In West Indies		33	14	2	17
	Totals		70	28	7	35

I Played in India. W Played in West Indies.

Notes: The following deputised for the official touring captain or were appointed by the home authority for only a minor proportion of the series:
[1]P. R. Umrigar (First), V. Mankad (Fourth), H. R. Adhikari (Fifth). [2]Nawab of Pataudi jun. (Third, Fourth and Fifth). [3]S. Venkataraghavan (Second). [4]R. J. Shastri (Fourth). [5]B. C. Lara (Third).

HIGHEST INNINGS TOTALS

For West Indies in West Indies: 631-8 dec. at Kingston 1961-62
           in India: 644-8 dec. at Delhi 1958-59

For India in West Indies: 469-7 at Port-of-Spain 1982-83
           in India: 644-7 dec. at Kanpur 1978-79

LOWEST INNINGS TOTALS

For West Indies in West Indies: 140 at Bridgetown 1996-97
           in India: 127 at Delhi 1987-88

For India in West Indies: 81 at Bridgetown 1996-97
           in India: 75 at Delhi 1987-88

INDIVIDUAL HUNDREDS

For West Indies (82)

J. C. Adams (2)
125* Nagpur 1994-95
174* Mohali 1994-95
S. F. A. F. Bacchus (1)
250   Kanpur 1978-79
B. F. Butcher (2)
103   Calcutta 1958-59
142   Madras 1958-59
S. Chanderpaul (1)
137* Bridgetown . 1996-97
R. J. Christiani (1)
107† Delhi 1948-49
C. A. Davis (2)
125* Georgetown . 1970-71
105   Port-of-Spain 1970-71
P. J. L. Dujon (1)
110   St John's ... 1982-83
R. C. Fredericks (2)
100   Calcutta 1974-75
104   Bombay 1974-75
H. A. Gomes (1)
123   Port-of-Spain 1982-83
G. E. Gomez (1)
101† Delhi 1948-49
C. G. Greenidge (5)
107† Bangalore .. 1974-75
154* St John's ... 1982-83
194   Kanpur 1983-84
141   Calcutta 1987-88
117   Bridgetown . 1988-89
D. L. Haynes (2)
136   St John's ... 1982-83
112* Bridgetown . 1988-89
J. K. Holt (1)
123   Delhi 1958-59
C. L. Hooper (2)
100* Calcutta 1987-88
129   Kingston ... 1996-97
C. C. Hunte (1)
101   Bombay 1966-67

A. I. Kallicharran (3)
124† Bangalore .. 1974-75
103* Port-of-Spain 1975-76
187   Bombay 1978-79
R. B. Kanhai (4)
256   Calcutta 1958-59
138   Kingston ... 1961-62
139   Port-of-Spain 1961-62
158* Kingston ... 1970-71
B. C. Lara (1)
103   St John's ... 1996-97
C. H. Lloyd (7)
163   Bangalore .. 1974-75
242* Bombay 1974-75
102   Bridgetown . 1975-76
143   Port-of-Spain 1982-83
106   St John's ... 1982-83
103   Delhi 1983-84
161* Calcutta 1983-84
A. L. Logie (2)
130   Bridgetown . 1982-83
101   Calcutta 1987-88
E. D. A. McMorris (1)
125† Kingston ... 1961-62
B. H. Pairaudeau (1)
115† Port-of-Spain 1952-53
A. F. Rae (2)
104   Bombay 1948-49
109   Madras 1948-49
I. V. A. Richards (8)
192* Delhi 1974-75
142   Bridgetown . 1975-76
130   Port-of-Spain 1975-76
177   Port-of-Spain 1975-76
109   Georgetown . 1982-83
120   Bombay 1983-84
109* Delhi 1987-88
110   Kingston ... 1988-89

R. B. Richardson (2)
194   Georgetown . 1988-89
156   Kingston ... 1988-89
O. G. Smith (1)
100   Delhi 1958-59
G. S. Sobers (8)
142*† Bombay 1958-59
198   Kanpur 1958-59
106* Calcutta 1958-59
153   Kingston ... 1961-62
104   Kingston ... 1961-62
108* Georgetown . 1970-71
178* Bridgetown . 1970-71
132   Port-of-Spain 1970-71
J. S. Solomon (1)
100* Delhi 1958-59
J. B. Stollmeyer (2)
160   Madras 1948-49
104* Port-of-Spain 1952-53
C. L. Walcott (4)
152† Delhi 1948-49
108   Calcutta 1948-49
125   Georgetown . 1952-53
118   Kingston ... 1952-53
E. D. Weekes (7)
128† Delhi 1948-49
194   Bombay 1948-49
162 } Calcutta 1948-49
101 }
207   Port-of-Spain 1952-53
161   Port-of-Spain 1952-53
109   Kingston ... 1952-53
A. B. Williams (1)
111   Calcutta 1978-79
S. C. Williams (1)
128   Port-of-Spain 1996-97
F. M. M. Worrell (1)
237   Kingston ... 1952-53

For India (59)

H. R. Adhikari (1)			120	Delhi	1978-79	150	Bridgetown .	1970-71
114*†	Delhi	1948-49	147*	Georgetown .	1982-83	**R. J. Shastri** (2)		
M. Amarnath (3)			121	Delhi	1983-84	102	St John's ...	1982-83
101*	Kanpur	1978-79	236*	Madras	1983-84	107	Bridgetown	1988-89
117	Port-of-Spain	1982-83	**V. S. Hazare** (2)			**N. S. Sidhu** (3)		
116	St John's ...	1982-83	134*	Bombay	1948-49	116	Kingston ...	1988-89
M. L. Apte (1)			122	Bombay	1948-49	107	Nagpur	1994-95
163*	Port-of-Spain	1952-53	**Kapil Dev** (3)			201	Port-of-Spain	1996-97
C. G. Borde (3)			126*	Delhi	1978-79	**E. D. Solkar** (1)		
109	Delhi	1958-59	100*	Port-of-Spain	1982-83	102	Bombay	1974-75
121	Bombay	1966-67	109	Madras	1987-88	**S. R. Tendulkar** (1)		
125	Madras	1966-67	**S. V. Manjrekar** (1)			179	Nagpur	1994-95
S. A. Durani (1)			108	Bridgetown .	1988-89	**P. R. Umrigar** (3)		
104	Port-of-Spain	1961-62	**V. L. Manjrekar** (1)			130	Port-of-Spain	1952-53
F. M. Engineer (1)			118	Kingston ...	1952-53	117	Kingston ...	1952-53
109	Madras	1966-67	**R. S. Modi** (1)			172*	Port-of-Spain	1961-62
A. D. Gaekwad (1)			112	Bombay	1948-49	**D. B. Vengsarkar** (6)		
102	Kanpur	1978-79	**Mushtaq Ali** (1)			157*	Calcutta	1978-79
S. M. Gavaskar (13)			106†	Calcutta	1948-49	109	Delhi	1978-79
116	Georgetown .	1970-71	**B. P. Patel** (1)			159	Delhi	1983-84
117*	Bridgetown .	1970-71	115*	Port-of-Spain	1975-76	100	Bombay	1983-84
124 }	Port-of-Spain	1970-71	**M. Prabhakar** (1)			102	Delhi	1987-88
220 }			120	Mohali	1994-95	102*	Calcutta	1987-88
156	Port-of-Spain	1975-76	**Pankaj Roy** (1)			**G. R. Viswanath** (4)		
102	Port-of-Spain	1975-76	150	Kingston ...	1952-53	139	Calcutta	1974-75
205	Bombay	1978-79	**D. N. Sardesai** (3)			112	Port-of-Spain	1975-76
107 }	Calcutta	1978-79	212	Kingston ...	1970-71	124	Madras	1978-79
182* }			112	Port-of-Spain	1970-71	179	Kanpur	1978-79

† *Signifies hundred on first appearance in West Indies–India Tests.*

RECORD PARTNERSHIPS FOR EACH WICKET

For West Indies

296	for 1st	C. G. Greenidge and D. L. Haynes at St John's	1982-83
255	for 2nd	E. D. A. McMorris and R. B. Kanhai at Kingston	1961-62
220	for 3rd	I. V. A. Richards and A. I. Kallicharran at Bridgetown	1975-76
267	for 4th	C. L. Walcott and G. E. Gomez at Delhi	1948-49
219	for 5th	E. D. Weekes and B. H. Pairaudeau at Port-of-Spain	1952-53
250	for 6th	C. H. Lloyd and D. L. Murray at Bombay	1974-75
130	for 7th	C. G. Greenidge and M. D. Marshall at Kanpur	1983-84
124	for 8th†	I. V. A. Richards and K. D. Boyce at Delhi	1974-75
161	for 9th†	C. H. Lloyd and A. M. E. Roberts at Calcutta	1983-84
98*	for 10th	F. M. M. Worrell and W. W. Hall at Port-of-Spain	1961-62

For India

153	for 1st	S. M. Gavaskar and C. P. S. Chauhan at Bombay	1978-79
344*	for 2nd†	S. M. Gavaskar and D. B. Vengsarkar at Calcutta	1978-79
177	for 3rd	N. S. Sidhu and S. R. Tendulkar at Nagpur	1994-95
172	for 4th	G. R. Viswanath and A. D. Gaekwad at Kanpur	1978-79
204	for 5th	S. M. Gavaskar and B. P. Patel at Port-of-Spain	1975-76
170	for 6th	S. M. Gavaskar and R. J. Shastri at Madras	1983-84
186	for 7th	D. N. Sardesai and E. D. Solkar at Bridgetown	1970-71
107	for 8th	Yashpal Sharma and B. S. Sandhu at Kingston	1982-83
143*	for 9th	S. M. Gavaskar and S. M. H. Kirmani at Madras	1983-84
64	for 10th	J. Srinath and S. L. V. Raju at Mohali	1994-95

† *Denotes record partnership against all countries.*

TEN WICKETS OR MORE IN A MATCH

For West Indies (4)

11-126 (6-50, 5-76)	W. W. Hall, Kanpur	1958-59
11-89 (5-34, 6-55)	M. D. Marshall, Port-of-Spain	1988-89
12-121 (7-64, 5-57)	A. M. E. Roberts, Madras	1974-75
10-101 (6-62, 4-39)	C. A. Walsh, Kingston	1988-89

For India (4)

11-235 (7-157, 4-78)†	B. S. Chandrasekhar, Bombay	1966-67
10-223 (9-102, 1-121)	S. P. Gupte, Kanpur	1958-59
16-136 (8-61, 8-75)†	N. D. Hirwani, Madras	1987-88
10-135 (1-52, 9-83)	Kapil Dev, Ahmedabad	1983-84

† *Signifies ten wickets or more on first appearance in West Indies–India Tests.*

WEST INDIES v PAKISTAN

Season	West Indies	Captains Pakistan	T	WI	P	D
1957-58W	F. C. M. Alexander	A. H. Kardar	5	3	1	1
1958-59P	F. C. M. Alexander	Fazal Mahmood	3	1	2	0
1974-75P	C. H. Lloyd	Intikhab Alam	2	0	0	2
1976-77W	C. H. Lloyd	Mushtaq Mohammad	5	2	1	2
1980-81P	C. H. Lloyd	Javed Miandad	4	1	0	3
1986-87P	I. V. A. Richards	Imran Khan	3	1	1	1
1987-88W	I. V. A. Richards[1]	Imran Khan	3	1	1	1
1990-91P	D. L. Haynes	Imran Khan	3	1	1	1
1992-93W	R. B. Richardson	Wasim Akram	3	2	0	1
	In West Indies		16	8	3	5
	In Pakistan		15	4	4	7
	Totals		31	12	7	12

P Played in Pakistan. W Played in West Indies.

Note: The following was appointed by the home authority for only a minor proportion of the series:

[1]C. G. Greenidge (First).

HIGHEST INNINGS TOTALS

For West Indies in West Indies: 790-3 dec. at Kingston		1957-58
in Pakistan: 493 at Karachi		1974-75
For Pakistan in West Indies: 657-8 dec. at Bridgetown		1957-58
in Pakistan: 406-8 dec. at Karachi		1974-75

LOWEST INNINGS TOTALS

For West Indies in West Indies: 127 at Port-of-Spain		1992-93
in Pakistan: 53 at Faisalabad		1986-87
For Pakistan in West Indies: 106 at Bridgetown		1957-58
in Pakistan: 77 at Lahore		1986-87

INDIVIDUAL HUNDREDS

For West Indies (24)

L. Baichan (1)
105*† Lahore 1974-75

P. J. L. Dujon (1)
106* Port-of-Spain 1987-88

R. C. Fredericks (1)
120 Port-of-Spain 1976-77

C. G. Greenidge (1)
100 Kingston ... 1976-77

D. L. Haynes (3)
117 Karachi..... 1990-91
143*‡ Port-of-Spain 1992-93
125 Bridgetown . 1992-93

C. L. Hooper (2)
134 Lahore 1990-91
178* St John's ... 1992-93

C. C. Hunte (3)
142† Bridgetown . 1957-58
260 Kingston 1957-58
114 Georgetown . 1957-58

B. D. Julien (1)
101 Karachi..... 1974-75

A. I. Kallicharran (1)
115 Karachi..... 1974-75

R. B. Kanhai (1)
217 Lahore 1958-59

C. H. Lloyd (1)
157 Bridgetown . 1976-77

I. V. A. Richards (2)
120* Multan 1980-81
123 Port-of-Spain 1987-88

I. T. Shillingford (1)
120 Georgetown . 1976-77

G. S. Sobers (3)
365* Kingston ... 1957-58
125 }
109*} Georgetown . 1957-58

C. L. Walcott (1)
145 Georgetown . 1957-58

E. D. Weekes (1)
197† Bridgetown . 1957-58

For Pakistan (18)

Asif Iqbal (1)
135 Kingston ... 1976-77

Hanif Mohammad (2)
337† Bridgetown . 1957-58
103 Karachi..... 1958-59

Imtiaz Ahmed (1)
122 Kingston ... 1957-58

Imran Khan (1)
123 Lahore 1980-81

Inzamam-ul-Haq (1)
123 St John's ... 1992-93

Javed Miandad (2)
114 Georgetown . 1987-88
102 Port-of-Spain 1987-88

Majid Khan (2)
100 Karachi..... 1974-75
167 Georgetown . 1976-77

Mushtaq Mohammad (2)
123 Lahore 1974-75
121 Port-of-Spain 1976-77

Saeed Ahmed (1)
150 Georgetown . 1957-58

Salim Malik (1)
102 Karachi..... 1990-91

Wasim Raja (2)
107* Karachi..... 1974-75
117* Bridgetown . 1976-77

Wazir Mohammad (2)
106 Kingston ... 1957-58
189 Port-of-Spain 1957-58

† *Signifies hundred on first appearance in West Indies–Pakistan Tests.*
‡ *Carried his bat.*

RECORD PARTNERSHIPS FOR EACH WICKET

For West Indies

182	for 1st	R. C. Fredericks and C. G. Greenidge at Kingston	1976-77
446	for 2nd†	C. C. Hunte and G. S. Sobers at Kingston	1957-58
169	for 3rd	D. L. Haynes and B. C. Lara at Port-of-Spain	1992-93
188*	for 4th	G. S. Sobers and C. L. Walcott at Kingston	1957-58
185	for 5th	E. D. Weekes and O. G. Smith at Bridgetown....................	1957-58
151	for 6th	C. H. Lloyd and D. L. Murray at Bridgetown	1976-77
70	for 7th	C. H. Lloyd and J. Garner at Bridgetown......................	1976-77
60	for 8th	C. L. Hooper and A. C. Cummins at St John's	1992-93
61*	for 9th	P. J. L. Dujon and W. K. M. Benjamin at Bridgetown	1987-88
106	for 10th†	C. L. Hooper and C. A. Walsh at St John's.....................	1992-93

For Pakistan

159	for 1st[1]	Majid Khan and Zaheer Abbas at Georgetown....................	1976-77
178	for 2nd	Hanif Mohammad and Saeed Ahmed at Karachi	1958-59
169	for 3rd	Saeed Ahmed and Wazir Mohammad at Port-of-Spain	1957-58
174	for 4th	Shoaib Mohammad and Salim Malik at Karachi	1990-91

88 for 5th	Basit Ali and Inzamam-ul-Haq at St John's	1992-93
166 for 6th	Wazir Mohammad and A. H. Kardar at Kingston	1957-58
128 for 7th[2]	Wasim Raja and Wasim Bari at Karachi	1974-75
94 for 8th	Salim Malik and Salim Yousuf at Port-of-Spain	1987-88
96 for 9th	Inzamam-ul-Haq and Nadeem Khan at St John's..................	1992-93
133 for 10th†	Wasim Raja and Wasim Bari at Bridgetown	1976-77

† *Denotes record partnership against all countries.*

[1] *219 runs were added for this wicket in two separate partnerships: Sadiq Mohammad retired hurt and was replaced by Zaheer Abbas when 60 had been added. The highest partnership by two opening batsmen is 152 by Hanif Mohammad and Imtiaz Ahmed at Bridgetown, 1957-58.*

[2] *Although the seventh wicket added 168 runs against West Indies at Lahore in 1980-81, this comprised two partnerships with Imran Khan adding 72* with Abdul Qadir (retired hurt) and a further 96 with Sarfraz Nawaz.*

TEN WICKETS OR MORE IN A MATCH

For Pakistan (2)

| 12-100 (6-34, 6-66) | Fazal Mahmood, Dacca .... | 1958-59 |
| 11-121 (7-80, 4-41) | Imran Khan, Georgetown .... | 1987-88 |

Note: The best match figures by a West Indian bowler are 9-95 (8-29, 1-66) by C. E. H. Croft at Port-of-Spain, 1976-77.

WEST INDIES v SRI LANKA

		Captains				
Season	*West Indies*	*Sri Lanka*	*T*	*WI*	*SL*	*D*
1993-94 *S*	R. B. Richardson	A. Ranatunga	1	0	0	1
1996-97 *W*	C. A. Walsh	A. Ranatunga	2	1	0	1
	In West Indies		2	1	0	1
	In Sri Lanka......................		1	0	0	1
	Totals		3	1	0	2

W Played in West Indies.   S Played in Sri Lanka.

HIGHEST INNINGS TOTALS

| For West Indies: 343 at St Vincent... | 1996-97 |
| For Sri Lanka: 233-8 at St Vincent .... | 1996-97 |

LOWEST INNINGS TOTALS

| For West Indies: 147 at St Vincent .... | 1996-97 |
| For Sri Lanka: 152 at St John's... | 1996-97 |

INDIVIDUAL HUNDREDS

For West Indies (1)

B. C. Lara (1)
115   St Vincent . . 1996-97

Highest score for Sri Lanka: 90 by S. T. Jayasuriya at St Vincent   1996-97

HUNDRED PARTNERSHIPS

For West Indies

160   for 1st   S. L. Campbell and S. C. Williams at St John's   1996-97

For Sri Lanka

110   for 4th   S. T. Jayasuriya and A. Ranatunga at St John's...................   1996-97

BEST MATCH BOWLING ANALYSES

For West Indies

8-78 (5-37, 3-41)   C. E. L. Ambrose, St John's   1996-97

For Sri Lanka

8-106 (5-34, 3-72)   M. Muralitharan, St John's............................   1996-97

NEW ZEALAND v INDIA

Captains

Season	New Zealand	India	T	NZ	I	D
1955-56 *I*	H. B. Cave	P. R. Umrigar[1]	5	0	2	3
1964-65 *I*	J. R. Reid	Nawab of Pataudi jun.	4	0	1	3
1967-68 *N*	G. T. Dowling[2]	Nawab of Pataudi jun.	4	1	3	0
1969-70 *I*	G. T. Dowling	Nawab of Pataudi jun.	3	1	1	1
1975-76 *N*	G. M. Turner	B. S. Bedi[3]	3	1	1	1
1976-77 *I*	G. M. Turner	B. S. Bedi	3	0	2	1
1980-81 *N*	G. P. Howarth	S. M. Gavaskar	3	1	0	2
1988-89 *I*	J. G. Wright	D. B. Vengsarkar	3	1	2	0
1989-90 *N*	J. G. Wright	M. Azharuddin	3	1	0	2
1993-94 *N*	K. R. Rutherford	M. Azharuddin	1	0	0	1
1995-96 *I*	L. K. Germon	M. Azharuddin	3	0	1	2
	In India..........................		21	2	9	10
	In New Zealand		14	4	4	6
	Totals		35	6	13	16

I Played in India.   N Played in New Zealand.

Notes: The following deputised for the official touring captain or were appointed by the home
authority for a minor proportion of the series:
   [1]Ghulam Ahmed (First). [2]B. W. Sinclair (First). [3]S. M. Gavaskar (First).

HIGHEST INNINGS TOTALS

For New Zealand in New Zealand: 502 at Christchurch   1967-68
      in India: 462-9 dec. at Calcutta   1964-65

For India in New Zealand: 482 at Auckland   1989-90
    in India: 537-3 dec. at Madras   1955-56

LOWEST INNINGS TOTALS

For New Zealand in New Zealand: 100 at Wellington   1980-81
      in India: 124 at Hyderabad   1988-89

For India in New Zealand: 81 at Wellington   1975-76
    in India: 88 at Bombay   1964-65

INDIVIDUAL HUNDREDS

For New Zealand (21)

M. D. Crowe (1)		**J. M. Parker** (1)		230* Delhi	1955-56
113 Auckland	1989-90	104 Bombay	1976-77	151* Calcutta	1964-65
G. T. Dowling (3)		**J. F. Reid** (1)		**B. R. Taylor** (1)	
129 Bombay	1964-65	123* Christchurch	1980-81	105† Calcutta	1964-65
143 Dunedin	1967-68	**J. R. Reid** (2)		**G. M. Turner** (2)	
239 Christchurch	1967-68	119* Delhi	1955-56	117 Christchurch	1975-76
J. W. Guy (1)		120 Calcutta	1955-56	113 Kanpur	1976-77
102† Hyderabad	1955-56	**I. D. S. Smith** (1)		**J. G. Wright** (3)	
G. P. Howarth (1)		173 Auckland	1989-90	110 Auckland	1980-81
137* Wellington	1980-81	**B. Sutcliffe** (3)		185 Christchurch	1989-90
A. H. Jones (1)		137*† Hyderabad	1955-56	113* Napier	1989-90
170* Auckland	1989-90				

For India (22)

S. Amarnath (1)		177 Delhi	1955-56	**D. N. Sardesai** (2)	
124† Auckland	1975-76	102* Madras	1964-65	200* Bombay	1964-65
M. Azharuddin (1)		**V. Mankad** (2)		106 Delhi	1964-65
192 Auckland	1989-90	223 Bombay	1955-56	**N. S. Sidhu** (1)	
C. G. Borde (1)		231 Madras	1955-56	116† Bangalore	1988-89
109 Bombay	1964-65	**Nawab of Pataudi jun.** (2)		**P. R. Umrigar** (1)	
S. M. Gavaskar (2)		153 Calcutta	1964-65	223† Hyderabad	1955-56
116† Auckland	1975-76	113 Delhi	1964-65	**G. R. Viswanath** (1)	
119 Bombay	1976-77	**G. S. Ramchand** (1)		103* Kanpur	1976-77
A. G. Kripal Singh (1)		106* Calcutta	1955-56	**A. L. Wadekar** (1)	
100*† Hyderabad	1955-56	**Pankaj Roy** (2)		143 Wellington	1967-68
V. L. Manjrekar (3)		100 Calcutta	1955-56		
118† Hyderabad	1955-56	173 Madras	1955-56		

† Signifies hundred on first appearance in New Zealand–India Tests. B. R. Taylor provides the only instance for New Zealand of a player scoring his maiden hundred in first-class cricket in his first Test.

RECORD PARTNERSHIPS FOR EACH WICKET

For New Zealand

149	for 1st	T. J. Franklin and J. G. Wright at Napier............................	1989-90
155	for 2nd	G. T. Dowling and B. E. Congdon at Dunedin	1967-68
222*	for 3rd	B. Sutcliffe and J. R. Reid at Delhi..............................	1955-56
125	for 4th	J. G. Wright and M. J. Greatbatch at Christchurch	1989-90
119	for 5th	G. T. Dowling and K. Thomson at Christchurch	1967-68
87	for 6th	J. W. Guy and A. R. MacGibbon at Hyderabad...................	1955-56
163	for 7th	B. Sutcliffe and B. R. Taylor at Calcutta	1964-65
103	for 8th	R. J. Hadlee and I. D. S. Smith at Auckland	1989-90
136	for 9th†	I. D. S. Smith and M. C. Snedden at Auckland	1989-90
61	for 10th	J. T. Ward and R. O. Collinge at Madras........................	1964-65

For India

413	for 1st†	V. Mankad and Pankaj Roy at Madras	1955-56
204	for 2nd	S. M. Gavaskar and S. Amarnath at Auckland	1975-76
238	for 3rd	P. R. Umrigar and V. L. Manjrekar at Hyderabad................	1955-56
171	for 4th	P. R. Umrigar and A. G. Kripal Singh at Hyderabad	1955-56
127	for 5th	V. L. Manjrekar and G. S. Ramchand at Delhi	1955-56
193*	for 6th	D. N. Sardesai and Hanumant Singh at Bombay	1964-65
128	for 7th	S. R. Tendulkar and K. S. More at Napier	1989-90
143	for 8th	R. G. Nadkarni and F. M. Engineer at Madras	1964-65
105	for 9th	{ S. M. H. Kirmani and B. S. Bedi at Bombay.....................	1976-77
		{ S. M. H. Kirmani and N. S. Yadav at Auckland	1980-81
57	for 10th	R. B. Desai and B. S. Bedi at Dunedin	1967-68

† *Denotes record partnership against all countries.*

TEN WICKETS OR MORE IN A MATCH

For New Zealand (2)

11-58 (4-35, 7-23)	R. J. Hadlee, Wellington	1975-76
10-88 (6-49, 4-39)	R. J. Hadlee, Bombay...................................	1988-89

For India (2)

11-140 (3-64, 8-76)	E. A. S. Prasanna, Auckland	1975-76
12-152 (8-72, 4-80)	S. Venkataraghavan, Delhi	1964-65

NEW ZEALAND v PAKISTAN

		Captains				
Season	New Zealand	Pakistan	T	NZ	P	D
1955-56*P*	H. B. Cave	A. H. Kardar	3	0	2	1
1964-65*N*	J. R. Reid	Hanif Mohammad	3	0	0	3
1964-65*P*	J. R. Reid	Hanif Mohammad	3	0	2	1
1969-70*P*	G. T. Dowling	Intikhab Alam	3	1	0	2
1972-73*N*	B. E. Congdon	Intikhab Alam	3	0	1	2
1976-77*P*	G. M. Turner[1]	Mushtaq Mohammad	3	0	2	1
1978-79*N*	M. G. Burgess	Mushtaq Mohammad	3	0	1	2
1984-85*P*	J. V. Coney	Zaheer Abbas	3	0	2	1

Captains

Season	New Zealand	Pakistan	T	NZ	P	D
1984-85*N*	G. P. Howarth	Javed Miandad	3	2	0	1
1988-89*N* †	J. G. Wright	Imran Khan	2	0	0	2
1990-91*P*	M. D. Crowe	Javed Miandad	3	0	3	0
1992-93*N*	K. R. Rutherford	Javed Miandad	1	0	1	0
1993-94*N*	K. R. Rutherford	Salim Malik	3	1	2	0
1995-96*N*	L. K. Germon	Wasim Akram	1	0	1	0
1996-97*P*	L. K. Germon	Saeed Anwar	2	1	1	0
	In Pakistan		20	2	12	6
	In New Zealand		19	3	6	10
	Totals		39	5	18	16

N Played in New Zealand.   P Played in Pakistan.
   † *The First Test at Dunedin was abandoned without a ball being bowled and is excluded.*

Note: The following deputised for the official touring captain:
   ¹J. M. Parker (Third).

HIGHEST INNINGS TOTALS

For New Zealand in New Zealand: 492 at Wellington 1984-85
                in Pakistan: 482-6 dec. at Lahore 1964-65

For Pakistan in New Zealand: 616-5 dec. at Auckland 1988-89
                in Pakistan: 565-9 dec. at Karachi 1976-77

LOWEST INNINGS TOTALS

For New Zealand in New Zealand: 93 at Hamilton........................... 1992-93
                in Pakistan: 70 at Dacca 1955-56

For Pakistan in New Zealand: 169 at Auckland............................ 1984-85
                in Pakistan: 102 at Faisalabad 1990-91

INDIVIDUAL HUNDREDS

For New Zealand (21)

M. G. Burgess (2)
119* Dacca 1969-70
111   Lahore 1976-77
J. V. Coney (1)
111* Dunedin 1984-85
M. D. Crowe (2)
174   Wellington .. 1988-89
108* Lahore 1990-91
B. A. Edgar (1)
129† Christchurch. 1978-79
M. J. Greatbatch (1)
133   Hamilton .. 1992-93
B. F. Hastings (1)
110   Auckland ... 1972-73

G. P. Howarth (1)
114   Napier 1978-79
W. K. Lees (1)
152   Karachi..... 1976-77
S. N. McGregor (1)
111   Lahore 1955-56
R. E. Redmond (1)
107† Auckland ... 1972-73
J. F. Reid (3)
106   Hyderabad .. 1984-85
148   Wellington .. 1984-85
158* Auckland ... 1984-85
J. R. Reid (1)
128   Karachi..... 1964-65

B. W. Sinclair (1)
130   Lahore 1964-65
S. A. Thomson (1)
120* Christchurch. 1993-94
G. M. Turner (1)
110† Dacca 1969-70
J. G. Wright (1)
107   Karachi..... 1984-85
B. A. Young (1)
120   Christchurch. 1993-94

For Pakistan (41)

Asif Iqbal (3)			160*	Christchurch.	1978-79	103*	Hyderabad ..	1976-77
175	Dunedin	1972-73	104 }	Hyderabad ..	1984-85	**Saeed Ahmed** (1)		
166	Lahore	1976-77	103*}			172	Karachi.....	1964-65
104	Napier	1978-79	118	Wellington ..	1988-89	**Saeed Anwar** (2)		
Basit Ali (1)			271	Auckland ...	1988-89	169	Wellington ..	1993-94
103	Christchurch.	1993-94	**Majid Khan** (3)			149	Rawalpindi..	1996-97
Hanif Mohammad (3)			110	Auckland ...	1972-73	**Salim Malik** (2)		
103	Dacca	1955-56	112	Karachi.....	1976-77	119*	Karachi.....	1984-85
100*	Christchurch.	1964-65	119*	Napier	1978-79	140	Wellington ..	1993-94
203*	Lahore	1964-65	**Mohammad Ilyas** (1)			**Shoaib Mohammad** (5)		
Ijaz Ahmed, sen. (2)			126	Karachi.....	1964-65	163	Wellington ..	1988-89
103	Christchurch.	1995-96	**Mohammad Wasim** (1)			112	Auckland ...	1988-89
125	Rawalpindi..	1996-97	109*†	Lahore	1996-97	203*	Karachi.....	1990-91
Imtiaz Ahmed (1)			**Mudassar Nazar** (1)			105	Lahore	1990-91
209	Lahore	1955-56	106	Hyderabad ..	1984-85	142	Faisalabad ..	1990-91
Inzamam-ul-Haq (1)			**Mushtaq Mohammad** (3)			**Waqar Hassan** (1)		
135*	Wellington ..	1993-94	201	Dunedin	1972-73	189	Lahore	1955-56
Javed Miandad (7)			101	Hyderabad ..	1976-77	**Zaheer Abbas** (1)		
163†	Lahore	1976-77	107	Karachi.....	1976-77	135	Auckland ...	1978-79
206	Karachi.....	1976-77	**Sadiq Mohammad** (2)					
			166	Wellington ..	1972-73			

† *Signifies hundred on first appearance in New Zealand–Pakistan Tests.*

Notes: Mushtaq and Sadiq Mohammad, at Hyderabad in 1976-77, provide the fourth instance in Test matches, after the Chappells (thrice), of brothers each scoring hundreds in the same innings.

RECORD PARTNERSHIPS FOR EACH WICKET

For New Zealand

159 for 1st	R. E. Redmond and G. M. Turner at Auckland	1972-73
195 for 2nd	J. G. Wright and G. P. Howarth at Napier	1978-79
178 for 3rd	B. W. Sinclair and J. R. Reid at Lahore	1964-65
128 for 4th	B. F. Hastings and M. G. Burgess at Wellington.................	1972-73
183 for 5th†	M. G. Burgess and R. W. Anderson at Lahore	1976-77
145 for 6th	J. F. Reid and R. J. Hadlee at Wellington	1984-85
186 for 7th†	W. K. Lees and R. J. Hadlee at Karachi......................	1976-77
100 for 8th	B. W. Yuile and D. R. Hadlee at Karachi	1969-70
96 for 9th	M. G. Burgess and R. S. Cunis at Dacca	1969-70
151 for 10th†	B. F. Hastings and R. O. Collinge at Auckland	1972-73

For Pakistan

172 for 1st	Ramiz Raja and Shoaib Mohammad at Karachi.................	1990-91
262 for 2nd	Saeed Anwar and Ijaz Ahmed, sen. at Rawalpindi	1996-97
248 for 3rd	Shoaib Mohammad and Javed Miandad at Auckland..............	1988-89
350 for 4th†	Mushtaq Mohammad and Asif Iqbal at Dunedin	1972-73
281 for 5th†	Javed Miandad and Asif Iqbal at Lahore	1976-77
217 for 6th†	Hanif Mohammad and Majid Khan at Lahore	1964-65
308 for 7th†	Waqar Hassan and Imtiaz Ahmed at Lahore	1955-56
89 for 8th	Anil Dalpat and Iqbal Qasim at Karachi......................	1984-85
52 for 9th	Intikhab Alam and Arif Butt at Auckland.....................	1964-65
65 for 10th	Salah-ud-Din and Mohammad Farooq at Rawalpindi..............	1964-65

† *Denotes record partnership against all countries.*

TEN WICKETS OR MORE IN A MATCH

For New Zealand (1)

11-152 (7-52, 4-100)	C. Pringle, Faisalabad	1990-91

For Pakistan (10)

10-182 (5-91, 5-91)	Intikhab Alam, Dacca	1969-70
11-130 (7-52, 4-78)	Intikhab Alam, Dunedin	1972-73
11-130 (4-64, 7-66)†	Mohammad Zahid, Rawalpindi	1996-97
10-171 (3-115, 7-56)	Mushtaq Ahmed, Christchurch	1995-96
10-143 (4-59, 6-84)	Mushtaq Ahmed, Lahore	1996-97
10-106 (3-20, 7-86)	Waqar Younis, Lahore	1990-91
12-130 (7-76, 5-54)	Waqar Younis, Faisalabad	1990-91
10-128 (5-56, 5-72)	Wasim Akram, Dunedin	1984-85
11-179 (4-60, 7-119)	Wasim Akram, Wellington	1993-94
11-79 (5-37, 6-42)†	Zulfiqar Ahmed, Karachi	1955-56

† *Signifies ten wickets or more on first appearance in New Zealand–Pakistan Tests.*

Note: Waqar Younis's performances were in successive matches.

NEW ZEALAND v SRI LANKA

Season	New Zealand	*Captains* Sri Lanka	T	NZ	SL	D
1982-83*N*	G. P. Howarth	D. S. de Silva	2	2	0	0
1983-84*S*	G. P. Howarth	L. R. D. Mendis	3	2	0	1
1986-87*S*†	J. J. Crowe	L. R. D. Mendis	1	0	0	1
1990-91*N*	M. D. Crowe[1]	A. Ranatunga	3	0	0	3
1992-93*S*	M. D. Crowe	A. Ranatunga	2	0	1	1
1994-95*N*	K. R. Rutherford	A. Ranatunga	2	0	1	1
1996-97*N*	S. P. Fleming	A. Ranatunga	2	2	0	0
	In New Zealand		9	4	1	4
	In Sri Lanka		6	2	1	3
	Totals		15	6	2	7

N Played in New Zealand. S Played in Sri Lanka.

† *The Second and Third Tests were cancelled owing to civil disturbances.*

Note: The following was appointed by the home authority for only a minor proportion of the series:

[1]I. D. S. Smith (Third).

HIGHEST INNINGS TOTALS

For New Zealand in New Zealand: 671-4 at Wellington 1990-91
         in Sri Lanka: 459 at Colombo (CCC)...................... 1983-84

For Sri Lanka in New Zealand: 497 at Wellington 1990-91
         in Sri Lanka: 397-9 dec. at Colombo (CCC).................... 1986-87

LOWEST INNINGS TOTALS

For New Zealand in New Zealand: 109 at Napier............................ 1994-95
         in Sri Lanka: 102 at Colombo (SSC) 1992-93

For Sri Lanka in New Zealand: 93 at Wellington 1982-83
         in Sri Lanka: 97 at Kandy................................ 1983-84

INDIVIDUAL HUNDREDS

For New Zealand (11)

J. J. Crowe (1)	**A. H. Jones** (3)	**K. R. Rutherford** (1)
120* Colombo (CCC) 1986-87	186 Wellington .. 1990-91	105 Moratuwa ... 1992-93
M. D. Crowe (2)	122 ⎫ Hamilton.... 1990-91	**J. G. Wright** (1)
299 Wellington.... 1990-91	100* ⎭	101 Hamilton.... 1990-91
107 Colombo (SSC) 1992-93	**J. F. Reid** (1)	**B. A. Young** (1)
R. J. Hadlee (1)	180 Colombo (CCC) 1983-84	267* Dunedin 1996-97
151* Colombo (CCC) 1986-87		

For Sri Lanka (11)

P. A. de Silva (2)	127 Dunedin 1994-95	**H. P. Tillekeratne** (1)
267† Wellington .. 1990-91	**R. S. Kaluwitharana** (1)	108 Dunedin 1994-95
123 Auckland ... 1990-91	103† Dunedin 1996-97	
R. L. Dias (1)	**D. S. B. P. Kuruppu** (1)	
108† Colombo (SSC) 1983-84	201*† Colombo (CCC) 1986-87	
A. P. Gurusinha (3)	**R. S. Mahanama** (2)	
119 ⎫ Hamilton.... 1990-91	153 Moratuwa ... 1992-93	
102 ⎭	109 Colombo (SSC) 1992-93	

† *Signifies hundred on first appearance in New Zealand–Sri Lanka Tests.*

Note: A. P. Gurusinha and A. H. Jones at Hamilton in 1990-91 provided the second instance of a player on each side hitting two separate hundreds in a Test match.

RECORD PARTNERSHIPS FOR EACH WICKET

For New Zealand

161	for 1st	T. J. Franklin and J. G. Wright at Hamilton	1990-91
140	for 2nd	B. A. Young and M. J. Horne at Dunedin......................	1996-97
467	for 3rd†‡	A. H. Jones and M. D. Crowe at Wellington....................	1990-91
82	for 4th	J. F. Reid and S. L. Boock at Colombo (CCC)..................	1983-84
151	for 5th	K. R. Rutherford and C. Z. Harris at Moratuwa	1992-93
246*	for 6th†	J. J. Crowe and R. J. Hadlee at Colombo (CCC)	1986-87
47	for 7th	D. N. Patel and M. L. Su'a at Dunedin.......................	1994-95
79	for 8th	J. V. Coney and W. K. Lees at Christchurch...................	1982-83
42	for 9th	W. K. Lees and M. C. Snedden at Christchurch	1982-83
52	for 10th	W. K. Lees and E. J. Chatfield at Christchurch................	1982-83

For Sri Lanka

102	for 1st	R. S. Mahanama and U. C. Hathurusinghe at Colombo (SSC)	1992-93
138	for 2nd	R. S. Mahanama and A. P. Gurusinha at Moratuwa	1992-93
159*	for 3rd[1]	S. Wettimuny and R. L. Dias at Colombo (SSC)	1983-84
192	for 4th	A. P. Gurusinha and H. P. Tillekeratne at Dunedin	1994-95
130	for 5th	R. S. Madugalle and D. S. de Silva at Wellington	1982-83
109*	for 6th[2]	R. S. Madugalle and A. Ranatunga at Colombo (CCC)	1983-84
137	for 7th	R. S. Kaluwitharana and W. P. U. J. C. Vaas at Dunedin	1996-97
73	for 8th	H. P. Tillekeratne and G. P. Wickremasinghe at Dunedin	1996-97
31	for 9th	⎧ G. F. Labrooy and R. J. Ratnayake at Auckland................ ⎩ S. T. Jayasuriya and R. J. Ratnayake at Auckland	1990-91 1990-91
60	for 10th	V. B. John and A. M. J. G. Amerasinghe at Kandy	1983-84

† *Denotes record partnership against all countries.*

‡ *Record third-wicket partnership in first-class cricket.*

[1] *163 runs were added for this wicket in two separate partnerships: S. Wettimuny retired hurt and was replaced by J. R. Ratnayeke when 159 had been added.*

[2] *119 runs were added for this wicket in two separate partnerships: R. S. Madugalle retired hurt and was replaced by D. S. de Silva when 109 had been added.*

TEN WICKETS OR MORE IN A MATCH

For New Zealand (1)

10-102 (5-73, 5-29)   R. J. Hadlee, Colombo (CCC) 1983-84

For Sri Lanka (1)

10-90 (5-47, 5-43)†   W. P. U. J. C. Vaas, Napier........................... 1994-95

† *Signifies ten wickets or more on first appearance in New Zealand–Sri Lanka Tests.*

NEW ZEALAND v ZIMBABWE

Season	New Zealand	Captains Zimbabwe	T	NZ	Z	D
1992-93Z	M. D. Crowe	D. L. Houghton	2	1	0	1
1995-96N	L. K. Germon	A. Flower	2	0	0	2
	In New Zealand		2	0	0	2
	In Zimbabwe		2	1	0	1
	Totals		4	1	0	3

NZ Played in New Zealand.   Z Played in Zimbabwe.

HIGHEST INNINGS TOTALS

For New Zealand in New Zealand: 441-5 dec. at Auckland...................... 1995-96
                    in Zimbabwe: 335 at Harare 1992-93

For Zimbabwe in New Zealand: 326 at Auckland........................... 1995-96
                  in Zimbabwe: 283-9 dec. at Harare 1992-93

LOWEST INNINGS TOTALS

For New Zealand in New Zealand: 251 at Auckland 1995-96
                    in Zimbabwe: 335 at Harare 1992-93

For Zimbabwe in New Zealand: 196 at Hamilton 1995-96
                  in Zimbabwe: 137 at Harare 1992-93

INDIVIDUAL HUNDREDS

For New Zealand (4)

C. L. Cairns (1)
120   Auckland ... 1995-96
M. D. Crowe (1)
140   Harare 1992-93

R. T. Latham (1)
119†   Bulawayo... 1992-93
C. M. Spearman (1)
112   Auckland ... 1995-96

For Zimbabwe (2)

K. J. Arnott (1)
101*† Bulawayo... 1992-93

D. L. Houghton (1)
104*   Auckland ... 1995-96

† *Signifies hundred on first appearance in New Zealand–Zimbabwe Tests.*

HUNDRED PARTNERSHIPS

For New Zealand

214 for 1st	C. M. Spearman and R. G. Twose at Auckland	1995-96
116 for 1st	M. J. Greatbatch and R. T. Latham at Bulawayo.................	1992-93
102 for 1st	M. J. Greatbatch and R. T. Latham at Bulawayo.................	1992-93
127 for 2nd	R. T. Latham and A. H. Jones at Bulawayo......................	1992-93
168 for 4th	M. D. Crowe and K. R. Rutherford at Harare	1992-93
166 for 5th	A. C. Parore and C. L. Cairns at Auckland	1995-96
130 for 5th	K. R. Rutherford and D. N. Patel at Harare	1992-93

For Zimbabwe

120 for 1st†	G. W. Flower and S. V. Carlisle at Auckland	1995-96
107 for 2nd	K. J. Arnott and A. D. R. Campbell at Harare..................	1992-93
105* for 2nd	K. J. Arnott and A. D. R. Campbell at Bulawayo	1992-93

† *Denotes record partnership against all countries.*

BEST MATCH BOWLING ANALYSES

For New Zealand

8-131 (2-81, 6-50) D. N. Patel, Harare 1992-93

For Zimbabwe

7-160 (3-50, 4-110) H. H. Streak, Auckland 1995-96

INDIA v PAKISTAN

Season	*India*	*Captains* *Pakistan*	*T*	*I*	*P*	*D*
1952-53*I*	L. Amarnath	A. H. Kardar	5	2	1	2
1954-55*P*	V. Mankad	A. H. Kardar	5	0	0	5
1960-61*I*	N. J. Contractor	Fazal Mahmood	5	0	0	5
1978-79*P*	B. S. Bedi	Mushtaq Mohammad	3	0	2	1
1979-80*I*	S. M. Gavaskar[1]	Asif Iqbal	6	2	0	4
1982-83*P*	S. M. Gavaskar	Imran Khan	6	0	3	3
1983-84*I*	Kapil Dev	Zaheer Abbas	3	0	0	3
1984-85*P*	S. M. Gavaskar	Zaheer Abbas	2	0	0	2
1986-87*I*	Kapil Dev	Imran Khan	5	0	1	4
1989-90*P*	K. Srikkanth	Imran Khan	4	0	0	4
	In India............................		24	4	2	18
	In Pakistan		20	0	5	15
	Totals		44	4	7	33

I Played in India. P Played in Pakistan.

Note: The following was appointed by the home authority for only a minor proportion of the series:

[1]G. R. Viswanath (Sixth).

HIGHEST INNINGS TOTALS

For India in India: 539-9 dec. at Madras		1960-61
in Pakistan: 509 at Lahore		1989-90
For Pakistan in India: 487-9 dec. at Madras		1986-87
in Pakistan: 699-5 at Lahore		1989-90

LOWEST INNINGS TOTALS

For India in India: 106 at Lucknow   1952-53
        in Pakistan: 145 at Karachi   1954-55

For Pakistan in India: 116 at Bangalore   1986-87
          in Pakistan: 158 at Dacca   1954-55

INDIVIDUAL HUNDREDS

For India (31)

M. Amarnath (4)
109* Lahore 1982-83
120   Lahore 1982-83
103* Karachi 1982-83
101* Lahore 1984-85
M. Azharuddin (3)
141   Calcutta 1986-87
110   Jaipur 1986-87
109   Faisalabad . . 1989-90
C. G. Borde (1)
177* Madras 1960-61
A. D. Gaekwad (1)
201   Jullundur . . . 1983-84
S. M. Gavaskar (5)
111 }
137 } Karachi 1978-79

166   Madras 1979-80
127*‡ Faisalabad . . 1982-83
103* Bangalore . . 1983-84
V. S. Hazare (1)
146* Bombay 1952-53
S. V. Manjrekar (2)
113*† Karachi 1989-90
218   Lahore 1989-90
S. M. Patil (1)
127   Faisalabad . . 1984-85
R. J. Shastri (3)
128   Karachi 1982-83
139   Faisalabad . . 1984-85
125   Jaipur 1986-87
R. H. Shodhan (1)
110† Calcutta 1952-53

K. Srikkanth (1)
123   Madras 1986-87
P. R. Umrigar (5)
102   Bombay 1952-53
108   Peshawar . . . 1954-55
115   Kanpur 1960-61
117   Madras 1960-61
112   Delhi 1960-61
D. B. Vengsarkar (2)
146* Delhi 1979-80
109   Ahmedabad . 1986-87
G. R. Viswanath (1)
145† Faisalabad . . 1978-79

For Pakistan (41)

Aamer Malik (2)
117   Faisalabad . . 1989-90
113   Lahore 1989-90
Alim-ud-Din (1)
103* Karachi 1954-55
Asif Iqbal (1)
104† Faisalabad . . 1978-79
Hanif Mohammad (2)
142   Bahawalpur . 1954-55
160   Bombay 1960-61
Ijaz Faqih (1)
105† Ahmedabad . 1986-87
Imtiaz Ahmed (1)
135   Madras 1960-61
Imran Khan (3)
117   Faisalabad . . 1982-83
135* Madras 1986-87
109* Karachi 1989-90
Javed Miandad (5)
154*† Faisalabad . . 1978-79
100   Karachi 1978-79

126   Faisalabad . . 1982-83
280* Hyderabad . . 1982-83
145   Lahore 1989-90
Mohsin Khan (1)
101*† Lahore 1982-83
Mudassar Nazar (6)
126   Bangalore . . 1979-80
119   Karachi 1982-83
231   Hyderabad . . 1982-83
152*‡ Lahore 1982-83
152   Karachi 1982-83
199   Faisalabad . . 1984-85
Mushtaq Mohammad (1)
101   Delhi 1960-61
Nazar Mohammad (1)
124*‡ Lucknow . . . 1952-53
Qasim Omar (1)
210   Faisalabad . . 1984-85
Ramiz Raja (1)
114   Jaipur 1986-87

Saeed Ahmed (2)
121† Bombay 1960-61
103   Madras 1960-61
Salim Malik (3)
107   Faisalabad . . 1982-83
102* Faisalabad . . 1984-85
102* Karachi 1989-90
Shoaib Mohammad (2)
101   Madras 1986-87
203* Lahore 1989-90
Wasim Raja (1)
125   Jullundur . . . 1983-84
Zaheer Abbas (6)
176† Faisalabad . . 1978-79
235* Lahore 1978-79
215   Lahore 1982-83
186   Karachi 1982-83
168   Faisalabad . . 1982-83
168* Lahore 1984-85

† *Signifies hundred on first appearance in India–Pakistan Tests.*
‡ *Carried his bat.*

RECORD PARTNERSHIPS FOR EACH WICKET

For India

200 for 1st	S. M. Gavaskar and K. Srikkanth at Madras	1986-87
135 for 2nd	N. S. Sidhu and S. V. Manjrekar at Karachi	1989-90
190 for 3rd	M. Amarnath and Yashpal Sharma at Lahore.....................	1982-83
186 for 4th	S. V. Manjrekar and R. J. Shastri at Lahore.....................	1989-90
200 for 5th	S. M. Patil and R. J. Shastri at Faisalabad	1984-85
143 for 6th	M. Azharuddin and Kapil Dev at Calcutta	1986-87
155 for 7th	R. M. H. Binny and Madan Lal at Bangalore	1983-84
122 for 8th	S. M. H. Kirmani and Madan Lal at Faisalabad	1982-83
149 for 9th†	P. G. Joshi and R. B. Desai at Bombay	1960-61
109 for 10th†	H. R. Adhikari and Ghulam Ahmed at Delhi....................	1952-53

For Pakistan

162 for 1st	Hanif Mohammad and Imtiaz Ahmed at Madras	1960-61
250 for 2nd	Mudassar Nazar and Qasim Omar at Faisalabad	1984-85
451 for 3rd†	Mudassar Nazar and Javed Miandad at Hyderabad	1982-83
287 for 4th	Javed Miandad and Zaheer Abbas at Faisalabad	1982-83
213 for 5th	Zaheer Abbas and Mudassar Nazar at Karachi...................	1982-83
207 for 6th	Salim Malik and Imran Khan at Faisalabad	1982-83
154 for 7th	Imran Khan and Ijaz Faqih at Ahmedabad	1986-87
112 for 8th	Imran Khan and Wasim Akram at Madras	1986-87
60 for 9th	Wasim Bari and Iqbal Qasim at Bangalore......................	1979-80
104 for 10th	Zulfiqar Ahmed and Amir Elahi at Madras	1952-53

† *Denotes record partnership against all countries.*

TEN WICKETS OR MORE IN A MATCH

For India (3)

11-146 (4-90, 7-56)	Kapil Dev, Madras	1979-80
10-126 (7-27, 3-99)	Maninder Singh, Bangalore	1986-87
13-131 (8-52, 5-79)†	V. Mankad, Delhi	1952-53

For Pakistan (5)

12-94 (5-52, 7-42)	Fazal Mahmood, Lucknow..............................	1952-53
11-79 (3-19, 8-60)	Imran Khan, Karachi	1982-83
11-180 (6-98, 5-82)	Imran Khan, Faisalabad	1982-83
10-175 (4-135, 6-40)	Iqbal Qasim, Bombay...................................	1979-80
11-190 (8-69, 3-121)	Sikander Bakht, Delhi..................................	1979-80

† *Signifies ten wickets or more on first appearance in India–Pakistan Tests.*

INDIA v SRI LANKA

		Captains				
Season	India	Sri Lanka	T	I	SL	D
1982-83*I*	S. M. Gavaskar	B. Warnapura	1	0	0	1
1985-86*S*	Kapil Dev	L. R. D. Mendis	3	0	1	2
1986-87*I*	Kapil Dev	L. R. D. Mendis	3	2	0	1
1990-91*I*	M. Azharuddin	A. Ranatunga	1	1	0	0
1993-94*S*	M. Azharuddin	A. Ranatunga	3	1	0	2
1993-94*I*	M. Azharuddin	A. Ranatunga	3	3	0	0
1997-98*S*	S. R. Tendulkar	A. Ranatunga	2	0	0	2
	In India............................		8	6	0	2
	In Sri Lanka.......................		8	1	1	6
	Totals		16	7	1	8

I Played in India. S Played in Sri Lanka.

HIGHEST INNINGS TOTALS

For India in India: 676-7 at Kanpur   1986-87
        in Sri Lanka: 537-8 dec. at Colombo (RPS)   1997-98

For Sri Lanka in India: 420 at Kanpur   1986-87
        in Sri Lanka: 952-6 dec. at Colombo (RPS)   1997-98

LOWEST INNINGS TOTALS

For India in India: 288 at Chandigarh   1990-91
        in Sri Lanka: 198 at Colombo (PSS)   1985-86

For Sri Lanka in India: 82 at Chandigarh   1990-91
        in Sri Lanka: 198 at Kandy   1985-86

INDIVIDUAL HUNDREDS

For India (23)

M. Amarnath (2)			**S. M. Gavaskar** (2)			**N. S. Sidhu** (3)		
116*	Kandy	1985-86	155†	Madras	1982-83	104	Colombo (SSC)	1993-94
131	Nagpur	1986-87	176	Kanpur	1986-87	124	Lucknow . . .	1993-94
M. Azharuddin (5)			**V. G. Kambli** (2)			111	Colombo (RPS)	1997-98
199	Kanpur	1986-87	125	Colombo (SSC)	1993-94	**S. R. Tendulkar** (4)		
108	Bangalore . . .	1993-94	120	Colombo (PSS)	1993-94	104*	Colombo (SSC)	1993-94
152	Ahmedabad .	1993-94	**Kapil Dev** (1)			142	Lucknow . . .	1993-94
126	Colombo (RPS)	1997-98	163	Kanpur	1986-87	143	Colombo (RPS)	1997-98
108*	Colombo (SSC)	1997-98	**S. M. Patil** (1)			139	Colombo (SSC)	1997-98
S. C. Ganguly (1)			114*†	Madras	1982-83	**D. B. Vengsarkar** (2)		
147	Colombo (SSC)	1997-98				153	Nagpur	1986-87
						166	Cuttack	1986-87

For Sri Lanka (15)

P. A. de Silva (4)			**S. T. Jayasuriya** (2)			**L. R. D. Mendis** (3)		
148	Colombo (PSS)	1993-94	340	Colombo (RPS)	1997-98	105 ⎫		
126	Colombo (RPS)	1997-98	199	Colombo (SSC)	1997-98	105 ⎬†Madras		1982-83
146 ⎫			**R. S. Madugalle** (1)			124	Kandy	1985-86
120 ⎬	Colombo (SSC)	1997-98	103	Colombo (SSC)	1985-86	**A. Ranatunga** (1)		
R. L. Dias (1)			**R. S. Mahanama** (2)			111	Colombo (SSC)	1985-86
106	Kandy	1985-86	151	Colombo (PSS)	1993-94	**S. A. R. Silva** (1)		
			225	Colombo (RPS)	1997-98	111	Colombo (PSS)	1985-86

† *Signifies hundred on first appearance in India–Sri Lanka Tests.*

RECORD PARTNERSHIPS FOR EACH WICKET

For India

171	for 1st	M. Prabhakar and N. S. Sidhu at Colombo (SSC)	1993-94
173	for 2nd	S. M. Gavaskar and D. B. Vengsarkar at Madras	1982-83
173	for 3rd	M. Amarnath and D. B. Vengsarkar at Nagpur	1986-87
221	for 4th	S. R. Tendulkar and M. Azharuddin at Colombo (RPS)	1997-98
150	for 5th	S. R. Tendulkar and S. C. Ganguly at Colombo (SSC)	1997-98
272	for 6th	M. Azharuddin and Kapil Dev at Kanpur	1986-87
78*	for 7th	S. M. Patil and Madan Lal at Madras	1982-83
70	for 8th	Kapil Dev and L. Sivaramakrishnan at Colombo (PSS)	1985-86
67	for 9th	M. Azharuddin and R. K. Chauhan at Ahmedabad	1993-94
29	for 10th	Kapil Dev and Chetan Sharma at Colombo (PSS)	1985-86

For Sri Lanka

159	for 1st†	S. Wettimuny and J. R. Ratnayeke at Kanpur	1986-87
576	for 2nd†	S. T. Jayasuriya and R. S. Mahanama at Colombo (RPS)..........	1997-98
218	for 3rd†	S. T. Jayasuriya and P. A. de Silva at Colombo (SSC)............	1997-98
216	for 4th	R. L. Dias and L. R. D. Mendis at Kandy	1985-86
144	for 5th	R. S. Madugalle and A. Ranatunga at Colombo (SSC)	1985-86
89	for 6th	L. R. D. Mendis and A. N. Ranasinghe at Madras	1982-83
77	for 7th	R. S. Madugalle and D. S. de Silva at Madras	1982-83
48	for 8th	P. A. de Silva and M. Muralitharan at Colombo (SSC)	1997-98
60	for 9th	H. P. Tillekeratne and A. W. R. Madurasinghe at Chandigarh	1990-91
44	for 10th	R. J. Ratnayake and E. A. R. de Silva at Nagpur	1986-87

† *Denotes record partnership against all countries.*

TEN WICKETS OR MORE IN A MATCH

For India (3)

11-128 (4-69, 7-59)	A. Kumble, Lucknow	1993-94
10-107 (3-56, 7-51)	Maninder Singh, Nagpur	1986-87
11-125 (5-38, 6-87)	S. L. V. Raju, Ahmedabad..........................	1993-94

Note: The best match figures by a Sri Lankan bowler are 9-125 (4-76, 5-49) by R. J. Ratnayake against India at Colombo (PSS), 1985-86.

INDIA v ZIMBABWE

Season	India	Captains Zimbabwe	T	I	Z	D
1992-93Z	M. Azharuddin	D. L. Houghton	1	0	0	1
1992-93I	M. Azharuddin	D. L. Houghton	1	1	0	0
	In India...........................		1	1	0	0
	In Zimbabwe		1	0	0	1
	Totals		2	1	0	1

I Played in India. Z Played in Zimbabwe.

HIGHEST INNINGS TOTALS

For India: 536-7 dec. at Delhi 1992-93

For Zimbabwe: 456 at Harare 1992-93

INDIVIDUAL HUNDREDS

For India (2)

V. G. Kambli (1)
227† Delhi 1992-93

S. V. Manjrekar (1)
104† Harare 1992-93

For Zimbabwe (2)

A. Flower (1)
115 Delhi 1992-93

D. L. Houghton (1)
121† Harare 1992-93

† *Signifies hundred on first appearance in India–Zimbabwe Tests.*

HUNDRED PARTNERSHIPS

For India

107 for 2nd	N. S. Sidhu and V. G. Kambli at Delhi	1992-93
137 for 3rd	V. G. Kambli and S. R. Tendulkar at Delhi	1992-93
107 for 4th	V. G. Kambli and M. Azharuddin at Delhi	1992-93

For Zimbabwe

100 for 1st	K. J. Arnott and G. W. Flower at Harare	1992-93
192 for 4th	G. W. Flower and A. Flower at Delhi	1992-93
165 for 6th†	D. L. Houghton and A. Flower at Harare	1992-93

† *Denotes record partnership against all countries.*

BEST MATCH BOWLING ANALYSES

For India

8-160 (3-90, 5-70)	A. Kumble, Delhi	1992-93

For Zimbabwe

5-86 (5-86)	A. J. Traicos, Harare	1992-93

PAKISTAN v SRI LANKA

		Captains					
Season	*Pakistan*	*Sri Lanka*	*T*	*P*	*SL*	*D*
1981-82*P*	Javed Miandad	B. Warnapura[1]	3	2	0	1
1985-86*P*	Javed Miandad	L. R. D. Mendis	3	2	0	1
1985-86*S*	Imran Khan	L. R. D. Mendis	3	1	1	1
1991-92*P*	Imran Khan	P. A. de Silva	3	1	0	2
1994-95*S*†	Salim Malik	A. Ranatunga	2	2	0	0
1995-96*P*	Ramiz Raja	A. Ranatunga	3	1	2	0
1996-97*S*	Ramiz Raja	A. Ranatunga	2	0	0	2
	In Pakistan		12	6	2	4
	In Sri Lanka		7	3	1	3
	Totals		19	9	3	7

P Played in Pakistan.   S Played in Sri Lanka.

† *One Test was cancelled owing to the threat of civil disturbances following a general election.*
Note: The following deputised for the official touring captain:
[1]L. R. D. Mendis (Second).

HIGHEST INNINGS TOTALS

For Pakistan in Pakistan: 555-3 at Faisalabad	1985-86
in Sri Lanka: 390 at Colombo (PSS)	1994-95
For Sri Lanka in Pakistan: 479 at Faisalabad	1985-86
in Sri Lanka: 423-8 dec. at Colombo (RPS)	1996-97

LOWEST INNINGS TOTALS

For Pakistan in Pakistan: 209 at Faisalabad	1995-96
in Sri Lanka: 132 at Colombo (CCC)	1985-86
For Sri Lanka in Pakistan: 149 at Karachi	1981-82
in Sri Lanka: 71 at Kandy	1994-95

INDIVIDUAL HUNDREDS

For Pakistan (13)

Haroon Rashid (1)	**Mohsin Khan** (1)	**Saeed Anwar** (1)
153† Karachi..... 1981-82	129 Lahore 1981-82	136† Colombo (PSS) 1994-95
Ijaz Ahmed, sen. (1)	**Moin Khan** (1)	**Salim Malik** (3)
113† Colombo (RPS) 1996-97	117* Sialkot 1995-96	100*† Karachi..... 1981-82
Inzamam-ul-Haq (1)	**Qasim Omar** (1)	101 Sialkot 1991-92
100* Kandy...... 1994-95	206† Faisalabad .. 1985-86	155 Colombo (SSC) 1996-97
Javed Miandad (1)	**Ramiz Raja** (1)	**Zaheer Abbas** (1)
203* Faisalabad .. 1985-86	122 Colombo (PSS) 1985-86	134† Lahore 1981-82

For Sri Lanka (14)

P. A. de Silva (7)	**R. L. Dias** (2)	**H. P. Tillekeratne** (2)
122† Faisalabad .. 1985-86	109 Lahore 1981-82	115 Faisalabad .. 1995-96
105 Karachi..... 1985-86	**A. P. Gurusinha** (1)	103 Colombo (RPS) 1996-97
127 Colombo (PSS) 1994-95	116* Colombo (PSS) 1985-86	**S. Wettimuny** (1)
105 Faisalabad .. 1995-96	**S. T. Jayasuriya** (1)	157 Faisalabad .. 1981-82
168 Colombo (RPS) 1996-97	113 Colombo (SSC) 1996-97	
138*} Colombo (SSC) 1996-97	**A. Ranatunga** (1)	
103*}	135* Colombo (PSS) 1985-86	

† *Signifies hundred on first appearance in Pakistan–Sri Lanka Tests.*

RECORD PARTNERSHIPS FOR EACH WICKET

For Pakistan

128 for 1st {	Ramiz Raja and Shoaib Mohammad at Sialkot	1991-92
{	Saeed Anwar and Aamir Sohail at Colombo (PSS)	1994-95
151 for 2nd	Mohsin Khan and Majid Khan at Lahore	1981-82
397 for 3rd	Qasim Omar and Javed Miandad at Faisalabad	1985-86
162 for 4th	Salim Malik and Javed Miandad at Karachi.....................	1981-82
132 for 5th	Salim Malik and Imran Khan at Sialkot	1991-92
100 for 6th	Zaheer Abbas and Imran Khan at Lahore	1981-82
104 for 7th	Haroon Rashid and Tahir Naqqash at Karachi	1981-82
38 for 8th	Saqlain Mushtaq and Mushtaq Ahmed at Colombo (RPS)	1996-97
127 for 9th	Haroon Rashid and Rashid Khan at Karachi	1981-82
65 for 10th	Moin Khan and Aamir Nazir at Sialkot	1995-96

For Sri Lanka

157 for 1st	S. T. Jayasuriya and R. P. Arnold at Colombo (SSC)	1996-97
217 for 2nd	S. Wettimuny and R. L. Dias at Faisalabad	1981-82
176 for 3rd	U. C. Hathurusinghe and P. A. de Silva at Faisalabad	1995-96
240* for 4th†	A. P. Gurusinha and A. Ranatunga at Colombo (PSS)	1985-86
125 for 5th	A. Ranatunga and H. P. Tillekeratne at Peshawar	1995-96
121 for 6th	A. Ranatunga and P. A. de Silva at Faisalabad	1985-86
131 for 7th	H. P. Tillekeratne and R. S. Kalpage at Kandy	1994-95
106 for 8th†	P. A. de Silva and W. P. U. J. C. Vaas at Colombo (SSC)	1996-97
52 for 9th	P. A. de Silva and R. J. Ratnayake at Faisalabad	1985-86
36 for 10th	R. J. Ratnayake and R. G. C. E. Wijesuriya at Faisalabad	1985-86

† *Denotes record partnership against all countries.*

TEN WICKETS OR MORE IN A MATCH

For Pakistan (2)

14-116 (8-58, 6-58)	Imran Khan, Lahore	1981-82
11-119 (6-34, 5-85)	Waqar Younis, Kandy	1994-95

Note: The best match figures by a Sri Lankan bowler are 9-162 (4-103, 5-59), D. S. de Silva at Faisalabad, 1981-82.

PAKISTAN v ZIMBABWE

		Captains				
Season	Pakistan	Zimbabwe	T	P	Z	D
1993-94*P*	Wasim Akram[1]	A. Flower	3	2	0	1
1994-95*Z*	Salim Malik	A. Flower	3	2	1	0
1996-97*P*	Wasim Akram	A. D. R. Campbell	2	1	0	1
	In Pakistan		5	3	0	2
	In Zimbabwe		3	2	1	0
	Totals		8	5	1	2

P Played in Pakistan.   Z Played in Zimbabwe.

Note: The following was appointed by the home authority for only a minor proportion of the series:
[1]Waqar Younis (First).

HIGHEST INNINGS TOTALS

For Pakistan in Pakistan: 553 at Sheikhupura	1996-97
in Zimbabwe: 322 at Harare	1994-95
For Zimbabwe in Pakistan: 375 at Sheikhupura............................	1996-97
in Zimbabwe: 544-4 dec. at Harare	1994-95

LOWEST INNINGS TOTALS

For Pakistan in Pakistan: 147 at Lahore	1993-94
in Zimbabwe: 158 at Harare	1994-95
For Zimbabwe in Pakistan: 133 at Faisalabad	1996-97
in Zimbabwe: 139 at Harare	1994-95

INDIVIDUAL HUNDREDS

For Pakistan (2)

Inzamam-ul-Haq (1)	**Wasim Akram** (1)
101 Harare 1994-95	257* Sheikhupura . 1996-97

For Zimbabwe (5)

A. Flower (1)	**P. A. Strang** (1)
156 Harare 1994-95	106* Sheikhupura . 1996-97
G. W. Flower (2)	**G. J. Whittall** (1)
201* Harare 1994-95	113* Harare 1994-95
110 Sheikhupura . 1996-97	

RECORD PARTNERSHIPS FOR EACH WICKET

For Pakistan

95	for 1st	Aamir Sohail and Shoaib Mohammad at Karachi (DS)	1993-94
118*	for 2nd	Shoaib Mohammad and Asif Mujtaba at Lahore	1993-94
83	for 3rd	Shoaib Mohammad and Javed Miandad at Karachi (DS)	1993-94
116	for 4th	Inzamam-ul-Haq and Ijaz Ahmed, sen. at Harare.	1994-95
76	for 5th	Ijaz Ahmed, sen. and Inzamam-ul-Haq at Harare.	1994-95
96	for 6th	Inzamam-ul-Haq and Rashid Latif at Harare	1994-95
120	for 7th	Ijaz Ahmed, sen. and Inzamam-ul-Haq at Harare	1994-95
313	for 8th†	Wasim Akram and Saqlain Mushtaq at Sheikhupura	1996-97
60*	for 9th	Rashid Latif and Tausif Ahmed at Karachi (DS)	1993-94
27	for 10th	Inzamam-ul-Haq and Aamir Nazir at Harare	1994-95

For Zimbabwe

33	for 1st	G. W. Flower and M. H. Dekker at Sheikhupura.	1996-97
135	for 2nd†	M. H. Dekker and A. D. R. Campbell at Rawalpindi	1993-94
84	for 3rd	G. W. Flower and D. L. Houghton at Sheikhupura	1996-97
269	for 4th†	G. W. Flower and A. Flower at Harare	1994-95
233*	for 5th†	G. W. Flower and G. J. Whittall at Harare.	1994-95
72	for 6th	M. H. Dekker and G. J. Whittall at Rawalpindi	1993-94
131	for 7th†	G. W. Flower and P. A. Strang at Sheikhupura	1996-97
46	for 8th	A. Flower and D. H. Brain at Lahore	1993-94
87	for 9th†	P. A. Strang and B. C. Strang at Sheikhupura	1996-97
29	for 10th	E. A. Brandes and S. G. Peall at Rawalpindi	1993-94

† *Denotes record partnership against all countries.*

TEN WICKETS OR MORE IN A MATCH

For Pakistan (2)

13-135 (7-91, 6-44)†	Waqar Younis, Karachi (DS)	1993-94
10-106 (6-48, 4-58)	Wasim Akram, Faisalabad	1996-97

Note: The best match figures for Zimbabwe are 9-105 (6-90, 3-15) by H. H. Streak at Harare, 1994-95.

† *Signifies ten wickets or more on first appearance in Pakistan–Zimbabwe Tests.*

SRI LANKA v ZIMBABWE

		Captains				
Season	Sri Lanka	Zimbabwe	T	SL	Z	D
1994-95*Z*	A. Ranatunga	A. Flower	3	0	0	3
1996-97*S*	A. Ranatunga	A. D. R. Campbell	2	2	0	0
	In Sri Lanka		2	2	0	0
	In Zimbabwe		3	0	0	3
	Totals		5	2	0	3

S Played in Sri Lanka.   Z Played in Zimbabwe.

HIGHEST INNINGS TOTALS

For Sri Lanka: 402 at Harare.	1994-95
For Zimbabwe: 462-9 dec. at Bulawayo.	1994-95

LOWEST INNINGS TOTALS

For Sri Lanka: 218 at Bulawayo 1994-95
For Zimbabwe: 127 at Colombo (RPS) 1996-97

INDIVIDUAL HUNDREDS

For Sri Lanka (5)

A. P. Gurusinha (1)	**S. Ranatunga** (2)		**H. P. Tillekeratne** (2)	
128† Harare 1994-95	118† Harare 1994-95		116 Harare 1994-95	
	100* Bulawayo... 1994-95		126* Colombo (SSC) 1996-97	

For Zimbabwe (2)

D. L. Houghton (2)
266   Bulawayo... 1994-95
142   Harare 1994-95

† *Signifies hundred on first appearance in Sri Lanka–Zimbabwe Tests.*

HUNDRED PARTNERSHIPS

For Sri Lanka

217 for 2nd†	A. P. Gurusinha and S. Ranatunga at Harare	1994-95
114 for 5th	A. P. Gurusinha and H. P. Tillekeratne at Colombo (SSC).	1996-97
143 for 6th†	A. Ranatunga and R. S. Kaluwitharana at Colombo (RPS).	1996-97

For Zimbabwe

113 for 1st	G. W. Flower and M. H. Dekker at Harare	1994-95
194 for 3rd†	A. D. R. Campbell and D. L. Houghton at Harare	1994-95
121 for 4th	D. L. Houghton and A. Flower at Bulawayo	1994-95
100 for 6th	D. L. Houghton and W. R. James at Bulawayo	1994-95

† *Denotes record partnership against all countries.*

BEST MATCH BOWLING ANALYSES

For Sri Lanka

7-35 (3-10, 4-25)†   K. J. Silva, Colombo (RPS) 1996-97

For Zimbabwe

5-106 (5-106)   P. A. Strang, Colombo (RPS) 1996-97

† *Signifies on first appearance in Sri Lanka–Zimbabwe Tests.*

TEST MATCH GROUNDS

In Chronological Sequence

City and Ground	*First Test Match*		*Tests*
1 Melbourne, Melbourne Cricket Ground	March 15, 1877	A v E	89
2 London, Kennington Oval	September 6, 1880	E v A	80
3 Sydney, Sydney Cricket Ground (No. 1)	February 17, 1882	A v E	83
4 Manchester, Old Trafford	July 11, 1884	E v A	63

	City and Ground	*First Test Match*		*Tests*
5	London, Lord's	July 21, 1884	E v A	96
6	Adelaide, Adelaide Oval	December 12, 1884	A v E	55
7	Port Elizabeth, St George's Park	March 12, 1889	SA v E	15
8	Cape Town, Newlands	March 25, 1889	SA v E	29
9	Johannesburg, Old Wanderers	March 2, 1896	SA v E	22
	Now the site of Johannesburg Railway Station.			
10	Nottingham, Trent Bridge	June 1, 1899	E v A	45
11	Leeds, Headingley	June 29, 1899	E v A	59
12	Birmingham, Edgbaston	May 29, 1902	E v A	33
13	Sheffield, Bramall Lane	July 3, 1902	E v A	1
	Sheffield United Football Club have built a stand over the cricket pitch.			
14	Durban, Lord's	January 21, 1910	SA v E	4
	Ground destroyed and built on.			
15	Durban, Kingsmead	January 18, 1923	SA v E	24
16	Brisbane, Exhibition Ground	November 30, 1928	A v E	2
	No longer used for cricket.			
17	Christchurch, Lancaster Park	January 10, 1930	NZ v E	35
18	Bridgetown, Kensington Oval	January 11, 1930	WI v E	33
19	Wellington, Basin Reserve	January 24, 1930	NZ v E	31
20	Port-of-Spain, Queen's Park Oval	February 1, 1930	WI v E	45
21	Auckland, Eden Park	February 17, 1930	NZ v E	39
22	Georgetown, Bourda	February 21, 1930	WI v E	24
23	Kingston, Sabina Park	April 3, 1930	WI v E	32
24	Brisbane, Woolloongabba	November 27, 1931	A v SA	39
25	Bombay, Gymkhana Ground	December 15, 1933	I v E	1
	No longer used for first-class cricket.			
26	Calcutta, Eden Gardens	January 5, 1934	I v E	28
27	Madras, Chepauk (Chidambaram Stadium)	February 10, 1934	I v E	22
28	Delhi, Feroz Shah Kotla	November 10, 1948	I v WI	24
29	Bombay, Brabourne Stadium	December 9, 1948	I v WI	17
	Rarely used for first-class cricket.			
30	Johannesburg, Ellis Park	December 27, 1948	SA v E	6
	Mainly a rugby stadium, no longer used for cricket.			
31	Kanpur, Green Park (Modi Stadium)	January 12, 1952	I v E	17
32	Lucknow, University Ground	October 25, 1952	I v P	1
	Ground destroyed, now partly under a river bed.			
33	Dacca, Dacca Stadium	January 1, 1955	P v I	7
	Ceased staging Tests after East Pakistan seceded and became Bangladesh.			
34	Bahawalpur, Dring (now Bahawal) Stadium	January 15, 1955	P v I	1
	Still used for first-class cricket.			
35	Lahore, Lawrence Gardens (Bagh-i-Jinnah)	January 29, 1955	P v I	3
	Still used for club and occasional first-class matches.			
36	Peshawar, Services Ground	February 13, 1955	P v I	1
	Superseded by new stadium.			
37	Karachi, National Stadium	February 26, 1955	P v I	30
38	Dunedin, Carisbrook	March 11, 1955	NZ v E	10
39	Hyderabad, Fateh Maidan (Lal Bahadur Stadium)	November 19, 1955	I v NZ	3
40	Madras, Corporation Stadium	January 6, 1956	I v NZ	9
	Superseded by rebuilt Chepauk Stadium.			
41	Johannesburg, Wanderers	December 24, 1956	SA v E	18
42	Lahore, Gaddafi Stadium	November 21, 1959	P v A	28
43	Rawalpindi, Pindi Club Ground	March 27, 1965	P v NZ	1
	Superseded by new stadium.			
44	Nagpur, Vidarbha C.A. Ground	October 3, 1969	I v NZ	4
45	Perth, Western Australian C.A. Ground	December 11, 1970	A v E	24
46	Hyderabad, Niaz Stadium	March 16, 1973	P v E	5
47	Bangalore, Karnataka State C.A. Ground (Chinnaswamy Stadium)	November 22, 1974	I v WI	11
48	Bombay, Wankhede Stadium	January 23, 1975	I v WI	15

City and Ground	First Test Match		Tests
49 Faisalabad, Iqbal Stadium	October 16, 1978	P v I	18
50 Napier, McLean Park	February 16, 1979	NZ v P	3
51 Multan, Ibn-e-Qasim Bagh Stadium	December 30, 1980	P v WI	1
52 St John's (Antigua), Recreation Ground	March 27, 1981	WI v E	12
53 Colombo, P. Saravanamuttu Stadium	February 17, 1982	SL v E	6
54 Kandy, Asgiriya Stadium	April 22, 1983	SL v A	6
55 Jullundur, Burlton Park	September 24, 1983	I v P	1
56 Ahmedabad, Gujarat Stadium	November 12, 1983	I v WI	4
57 Colombo, Sinhalese Sports Club Ground	March 16, 1984	SL v NZ	10
58 Colombo, Colombo Cricket Club Ground	March 24, 1984	SL v NZ	3
59 Sialkot, Jinnah Stadium	October 27, 1985	P v SL	4
60 Cuttack, Barabati Stadium	January 4, 1987	I v SL	2
61 Jaipur, Sawai Mansingh Stadium	February 21, 1987	I v P	1
62 Hobart, Bellerive Oval	December 16, 1989	A v SL	3
63 Chandigarh, Sector 16 Stadium	November 23, 1990	I v SL	1
Superseded by Mohali ground			
64 Hamilton, Trust Bank (Seddon) Park	February 22, 1991	NZ v SL	5
65 Gujranwala, Municipal Stadium	December 20, 1991	P v SL	1
66 Colombo, R. Premadasa (Khettarama) Stadium	August 28, 1992	SL v A	4
67 Moratuwa, Tyronne Fernando Stadium	September 8, 1992	SL v A	4
68 Harare, Harare Sports Club	October 18, 1992	Z v I	8
69 Bulawayo, Bulawayo Athletic Club	November 1, 1992	Z v NZ	1
Superseded by Queens Sports Club ground.			
70 Karachi, Defence Stadium	December 1, 1993	P v Z	1
71 Rawalpindi, Rawalpindi Cricket Stadium	December 9, 1993	P v Z	3
72 Lucknow, K. D. "Babu" Singh Stadium	January 18, 1994	I v SL	1
73 Bulawayo, Queens Sports Club	October 20, 1994	Z v SL	3
74 Mohali, Punjab Cricket Association Stadium	December 10, 1994	I v WI	1
75 Peshawar, Arbab Niaz Stadium	September 8, 1995	P v SL	1
76 Centurion (*formerly Verwoerdburg*), Centurion Park	November 16, 1995	SA v E	2
77 Sheikhupura, Municipal Stadium	October 17, 1996	P v Z	1
78 St Vincent, Arnos Vale	June 20, 1997	WI v SL	1

FAMILIES IN TEST CRICKET

GRANDFATHER, FATHER AND SON

G. A. Headley (West Indies, 22 Tests, 1929-30–1953-54), R. G. A. Headley (West Indies, 2 Tests, 1973) and D. W. Headley (England, 3 Tests, 1997).

FATHERS AND SONS

England

A. R. Butcher (1 Test, 1979) and M. A. Butcher (5 Tests, 1997).
M. C. Cowdrey (114 Tests, 1954-55–1974-75) and C. S. Cowdrey (6 Tests, 1984-85–1988).
J. Hardstaff (5 Tests, 1907-08) and J. Hardstaff jun. (23 Tests, 1935–1948).
L. Hutton (79 Tests, 1937–1954-55) and R. A. Hutton (5 Tests, 1971).
F. T. Mann (5 Tests, 1922-23) and F. G. Mann (7 Tests, 1948-49–1949).
J. H. Parks (1 Test, 1937) and J. M. Parks (46 Tests, 1954–1967-68).
M. J. Stewart (8 Tests, 1962–1963-64) and A. J. Stewart (69 Tests, 1989-90–1997).
F. W. Tate (1 Test, 1902) and M. W. Tate (39 Tests, 1924–1935).
C. L. Townsend (2 Tests, 1899) and D. C. H. Townsend (3 Tests, 1934-35).

Australia

E. J. Gregory (1 Test, 1876-77) and S. E. Gregory (58 Tests, 1890–1912).

South Africa

F. Hearne (4 Tests, 1891-92–1895-96) and G. A. L. Hearne (3 Tests, 1922-23–1924).
  F. Hearne also played 2 Tests for England in 1888-89.
J. D. Lindsay (3 Tests, 1947) and D. T. Lindsay (19 Tests, 1963-64–1969-70).
A. W. Nourse (45 Tests, 1902-03–1924) and A. D. Nourse (34 Tests, 1935-1951).
P. M. Pollock (28 Tests, 1961-62–1969-70) and S. M. Pollock (10 Tests, 1995-96–1996-97).
L. R. Tuckett (1 Test, 1913-14) and L. Tuckett (9 Tests, 1947–1948-49).

West Indies

O. C. Scott (8 Tests, 1928–1930-31) and A. P. H. Scott (1 Test, 1952-53).

New Zealand

W. M. Anderson (1 Test, 1945-46) and R. W. Anderson (9 Tests, 1976-77–1978).
W. P. Bradburn (2 Tests, 1963-64) and G. E. Bradburn (4 Tests, 1990-91).
B. L. Cairns (43 Tests, 1973-74–1985-86) and C. L. Cairns (23 Tests, 1989-90–1996-97).
W. A. Hadlee (11 Tests, 1937–1950-51) and D. R. Hadlee (26 Tests, 1969–1977-78); R. J.
  Hadlee (86 Tests, 1972-73–1990).
P. G. Z. Harris (9 Tests, 1955-56–1964-65) and C. Z. Harris (9 Tests, 1993-94–1996-97).
H. G. Vivian (7 Tests, 1931–1937) and G. E. Vivian (5 Tests, 1964-65–1971-72).

India

L. Amarnath (24 Tests, 1933-34–1952-53) and M. Amarnath (69 Tests, 1969-70–1987-88);
  S. Amarnath (10 Tests, 1975-76–1978-79).
D. K. Gaekwad (11 Tests, 1952–1960-61) and A. D. Gaekwad (40 Tests, 1974-75–1984-85).
Nawab of Pataudi (Iftikhar Ali Khan) (3 Tests, 1946) and Nawab of Pataudi (Mansur Ali
  Khan) (46 Tests, 1961-62–1974-75).
  Nawab of Pataudi sen. also played 3 Tests for England, 1932-33–1934.
V. L. Manjrekar (55 Tests, 1951-52–1964-65) and S. V. Manjrekar (37 Tests, 1987-88–1996-97).
V. Mankad (44 Tests, 1946–1958-59) and A. V. Mankad (22 Tests, 1969-70–1977-78).
Pankaj Roy (43 Tests, 1951-52–1960-61) and Pranab Roy (2 Tests, 1981-82).

India and Pakistan

M. Jahangir Khan (4 Tests, 1932–1936) and Majid Khan (63 Tests, 1964-65–1982-83).
S. Wazir Ali (7 Tests, 1932–1936) and Khalid Wazir (2 Tests, 1954).

Pakistan

Hanif Mohammad (55 Tests, 1954–1969-70) and Shoaib Mohammad (45 Tests, 1983-84–1995-96).
Nazar Mohammad (5 Tests, 1952-53) and Mudassar Nazar (76 Tests, 1976-77–1988-89).

GRANDFATHERS AND GRANDSONS

Australia

V. Y. Richardson (19 Tests, 1924-25–1935-36) and G. S. Chappell (87 Tests, 1970-71–1983-84);
  I. M. Chappell (75 Tests, 1964-65–1979-80); T. M. Chappell (3 Tests, 1981).

GREAT-GRANDFATHER AND GREAT-GRANDSON

Australia

W. H. Cooper (2 Tests, 1881-82 and 1884-85) and A. P. Sheahan (31 Tests, 1967-68–1973-74).

BROTHERS IN SAME TEST TEAM

England

E. M., G. F. and W. G. Grace: 1 Test, 1880; C. T. and G. B. Studd: 4 Tests, 1882-83; A. and G. G. Hearne: 1 Test, 1891-92. *F. Hearne, their brother, played in this match for South Africa;* D. W. and P. E. Richardson: 1 Test, 1957; A. J. and B. C. Hollioake: 1 Test, 1997.

Australia

E. J. and D. W. Gregory: 1 Test, 1876-77; C. and A. C. Bannerman: 1 Test, 1878-79; G. and W. F. Giffen: 2 Tests, 1891-92; G. H. S. and A. E. Trott: 3 Tests, 1894-95; I. M. and G. S. Chappell: 43 Tests, 1970-71–1979-80; S. R. and M. E. Waugh: 52 Tests, 1990-91–1996-97 – the only instance of twins appearing together.

South Africa

S. J. and S. D. Snooke: 1 Test, 1907; D. and H. W. Taylor: 2 Tests, 1913-14; R. H. M. and P. A. M. Hands: 1 Test, 1913-14; E. A. B. and A. M. B. Rowan: 9 Tests, 1948-49–1951; P. M. and R. G. Pollock: 23 Tests, 1963-64–1969-70; A. J. and D. B. Pithey: 5 Tests, 1963-64; P. N. and G. Kirsten: 7 Tests, 1993-94–1994.

West Indies

G. C. and R. S. Grant: 4 Tests, 1934-35; J. B. and V. H. Stollmeyer: 1 Test, 1939; D. St E. and E. St E. Atkinson: 1 Test, 1957-58.

New Zealand

D. R. and R. J. Hadlee: 10 Tests, 1973–1977-78; H. J. and G. P. Howarth: 4 Tests, 1974-75–1976-77; J. M. and N. M. Parker: 3 Tests, 1976-77; B. P. and J. G. Bracewell: 1 Test, 1980-81; J. J. and M. D. Crowe: 34 Tests, 1983–1989-90.

India

S. Wazir Ali and S. Nazir Ali: 2 Tests, 1932–1933-34; L. Ramji and Amar Singh: 1 Test, 1933-34; C. K. and C. S. Nayudu: 4 Tests, 1933-34–1936; A. G. Kripal Singh and A. G. Milkha Singh: 1 Test, 1961-62; S. and M. Amarnath: 8 Tests, 1975-76–1978-79.

Pakistan

Wazir and Hanif Mohammad: 18 Tests, 1952-53–1959-60; Wazir and Mushtaq Mohammad: 1 Test, 1958-59; Hanif and Mushtaq Mohammad: 19 Tests, 1960-61–1969-70; Hanif, Mushtaq and Sadiq Mohammad: 1 Test, 1969-70; Mushtaq and Sadiq Mohammad: 26 Tests, 1969-70–1978-79; Wasim and Ramiz Raja: 2 Tests, 1983-84.

Sri Lanka

M. D. and S. Wettimuny: 2 Tests, 1982-83; A. and D. Ranatunga: 2 Tests, 1989-90; A. and S. Ranatunga: 8 Tests, 1994-95–1996-97.

Zimbabwe

A. and G. W. Flower: 22 Tests, 1992-93–1996-97; P. A. and B. C. Strang: 9 Tests, 1994-95–1996-97.

LIMITED-OVERS INTERNATIONAL RECORDS

Amended by PHILIP BAILEY to end of the 1997 season in England

Note: Limited-overs international matches do not have first-class status.

SUMMARY OF ALL LIMITED-OVERS INTERNATIONALS

1970-71 to September 21, 1997

	Opponents	Matches	_____ Won by _____										Tied	NR
			E	A	SA	WI	NZ	I	P	SL	Z	Ass		
England	Australia	60	29	29	–	–	–	–	–	–	–	–	1	1
	South Africa	12	5	–	7	–	–	–	–	–	–	–	–	–
	West Indies	51	22	–	–	27	–	–	–	–	–	–	–	2
	New Zealand	47	23	–	–	–	20	–	–	–	–	–	1	3
	India	32	18	–	–	–	–	13	–	–	–	–	–	1
	Pakistan	40	25	–	–	–	–	–	14	–	–	–	–	1
	Sri Lanka	12	8	–	–	–	–	–	–	4	–	–	–	–
	Zimbabwe	6	1	–	–	–	–	–	–	–	5	–	–	–
	Associates	4	4	–	–	–	–	–	–	–	–	0	–	–
Australia	South Africa	30	–	16	14	–	–	–	–	–	–	–	–	–
	West Indies	84	–	33	–	49	–	–	–	–	–	–	1	1
	New Zealand	63	–	44	–	–	17	–	–	–	–	–	–	2
	India	47	–	26	–	–	–	18	–	–	–	–	–	3
	Pakistan	46	–	22	–	–	–	–	21	–	–	–	1	2
	Sri Lanka	35	–	22	–	–	–	–	–	11	–	–	–	2
	Zimbabwe	9	–	8	–	–	–	–	–	–	1	–	–	–
	Associates	3	–	3	–	–	–	–	–	–	–	0	–	–
South Africa	West Indies	9	–	–	4	5	–	–	–	–	–	–	–	–
	New Zealand	8	–	–	4	–	4	–	–	–	–	–	–	–
	India	27	–	–	18	–	–	8	–	–	–	–	–	1
	Pakistan	16	–	–	9	–	–	–	7	–	–	–	–	–
	Sri Lanka	8	–	–	3	–	–	–	–	4	–	–	–	1
	Zimbabwe	7	–	–	6	–	–	–	–	–	0	–	–	1
	Associates	3	–	–	3	–	–	–	–	–	–	0	–	–
West Indies	New Zealand	24	–	–	–	18	4	–	–	–	–	–	–	2
	India	55	–	–	–	35	–	19	–	–	–	–	1	–
	Pakistan	81	–	–	–	54	–	–	25	–	–	–	2	–
	Sri Lanka	28	–	–	–	20	–	–	–	7	–	–	–	1
	Zimbabwe	5	–	–	–	5	–	–	–	–	0	–	–	–
	Associates	1	–	–	–	0	–	–	–	–	–	1*	–	–
New Zealand	India	42	–	–	–	–	18	24	–	–	–	–	–	–
	Pakistan	48	–	–	–	–	18	–	28	–	–	–	1	1
	Sri Lanka	37	–	–	–	–	24	–	–	10	–	–	1	2
	Zimbabwe	8	–	–	–	–	7	–	–	–	1	–	–	–
	Associates	4	–	–	–	–	4	–	–	–	–	0	–	–
India	Pakistan	58	–	–	–	–	–	20	34	–	–	–	–	4
	Sri Lanka	49	–	–	–	–	–	25	–	20	–	–	–	4
	Zimbabwe	16	–	–	–	–	–	12	–	–	2	–	2	–
	Associates	7	–	–	–	–	–	7	–	–	–	0	–	–
Pakistan	Sri Lanka	67	–	–	–	–	–	–	44	21	–	–	–	2
	Zimbabwe	14	–	–	–	–	–	–	12	–	1	–	1	–
	Associates	9	–	–	–	–	–	–	9	–	–	0	–	–
Sri Lanka	Zimbabwe	10	–	–	–	–	–	–	–	9	1	–	–	–
	Associates	7	–	–	–	–	–	–	–	7	–	0	–	–
Zimbabwe	Associates	2	–	–	–	–	–	–	–	–	1	0	–	1
Associate	Associates	1	–	–	–	–	–	–	–	–	–	1†	–	–
		1,232	135	203	68	213	116	146	194	93	12	2	12	38

* *Kenya beat West Indies in the 1996 World Cup.*
† *United Arab Emirates beat Holland in the 1996 World Cup.*

Note: Current Associate Members of ICC who have played one-day internationals are Bangladesh, Canada, East Africa, Holland, Kenya and United Arab Emirates. Sri Lanka and Zimbabwe also played one-day internationals before being given Test status; these are not included among the Associates' results.

RESULTS SUMMARY OF ALL LIMITED-OVERS INTERNATIONALS

1970-71 to September 21, 1997 (1,232 matches)

	Matches	Won	Lost	Tied	No Result	% Won (excl. NR)
West Indies	338	213	115	4	6	64.15
South Africa	120	68	49	–	3	58.11
Australia	377	203	160	3	11	55.46
England	264	135	119	2	8	52.73
Pakistan	379	194	170	5	10	52.57
India	333	146	171	3	13	45.62
New Zealand	281	116	152	3	10	42.80
Sri Lanka	253	93	147	1	12	38.58
Zimbabwe	77	12	60	3	2	16.00
United Arab Emirates	7	1	6	–	–	14.28
Kenya	9	1	7	–	1	12.50
Canada	3	–	3	–	–	–
East Africa	3	–	3	–	–	–
Holland	5	–	5	–	–	–
Bangladesh	15	–	15	–	–	–

Note: ICC has ruled that matches abandoned and started again should now count as official internationals in their own right, contrary to its previous ruling.

MOST RUNS

	M	I	NO	R	HS	100s	Avge
D. L. Haynes (West Indies)	238	237	28	8,648	152*	17	41.37
Javed Miandad (Pakistan)	233	218	41	7,381	119*	8	41.70
M. Azharuddin (India)	259	239	46	7,294	111*	4	37.79
Salim Malik (Pakistan)	268	242	37	6,883	102	5	33.57
P. A. de Silva (Sri Lanka)	218	212	22	6,874	145	9	36.17
I. V. A. Richards (West Indies)	187	167	24	6,721	189*	11	47.00
A. R. Border (Australia)	273	252	39	6,524	127*	3	30.62
R. B. Richardson (West Indies)	224	217	30	6,249	122	5	33.41
A. Ranatunga (Sri Lanka)	221	209	41	6,074	131*	3	36.15
D. M. Jones (Australia)	164	161	25	6,068	145	7	44.61
D. C. Boon (Australia)	181	177	16	5,964	122	5	37.04
Ramiz Raja (Pakistan)	198	197	15	5,841	119*	9	32.09
S. R. Tendulkar (India)	164	159	15	5,621	137	12	39.03
C. G. Greenidge (West Indies)	128	127	13	5,134	133*	11	45.03
S. R. Waugh (Australia)	221	201	43	5,092	102*	1	32.22
B. C. Lara (West Indies)	118	116	12	4,881	169	11	46.93
M. D. Crowe (New Zealand)	143	140	18	4,704	107*	4	38.55
Saeed Anwar (Pakistan)	131	130	12	4,659	194	12	39.48
M. E. Waugh (Australia)	135	130	11	4,542	130	10	38.16
Inzamam-ul-Haq (Pakistan)	143	137	18	4,446	137*	4	37.36
Ijaz Ahmed, sen. (Pakistan)	181	165	23	4,416	124*	5	31.09
R. S. Mahanama (Sri Lanka)	176	163	19	4,360	119*	4	30.27
G. R. Marsh (Australia)	117	115	6	4,357	126*	9	39.97
G. A. Gooch (England)	125	122	6	4,290	142	8	36.98
K. Srikkanth (India)	146	145	4	4,092	123	4	29.02
A. J. Lamb (England)	122	118	16	4,010	118	4	39.31

Leading aggregates for other Test-playing countries:

	M	I	NO	R	HS	100s	Avge
W. J. Cronje (South Africa)	115	107	20	3,473	112	2	39.91
A. Flower (Zimbabwe)	65	63	4	1,711	115*	1	29.00

HIGHEST INDIVIDUAL SCORES

194	Saeed Anwar	Pakistan v India at Chennai	1996-97
189*	I. V. A. Richards	West Indies v England at Manchester	1984
188*	G. Kirsten	South Africa v UAE at Rawalpindi	1995-96
181	I. V. A. Richards	West Indies v Sri Lanka at Karachi	1987-88
175*	Kapil Dev	India v Zimbabwe at Tunbridge Wells	1983
171*	G. M. Turner	New Zealand v East Africa at Birmingham	1975
169*	D. J. Callaghan	South Africa v New Zealand at Verwoerdburg	1994-95
169	B. C. Lara	West Indies v Sri Lanka at Sharjah	1995-96
167*	R. A. Smith	England v Australia at Birmingham	1993
161	A. C. Hudson	South Africa v Holland at Rawalpindi	1995-96
158	D. I. Gower	England v New Zealand at Brisbane	1982-83
153*	I. V. A. Richards	West Indies v Australia at Melbourne	1979-80
153	B. C. Lara	West Indies v Pakistan at Sharjah	1993-94
152*	D. L. Haynes	West Indies v India at Georgetown	1988-89
151*	S. T. Jayasuriya	Sri Lanka v India at Mumbai	1996-97

Highest individual scores for other Test-playing countries:

145	D. M. Jones	Australia v England at Brisbane	1990-91
142	D. L. Houghton	Zimbabwe v New Zealand at Hyderabad, India	1987-88

MOST HUNDREDS

Total		E	A	SA	WI	NZ	I	P	SL	Z	Ass
17	D. L. Haynes (West Indies)	2	6	0	–	2	2	4	1	0	–
12	Saeed Anwar (Pakistan)	0	1	0	1	2	1	–	6	1	0
12	S. R. Tendulkar (India)	0	1	1	1	2	–	2	3	1	1
11	C. G. Greenidge (West Indies) . . .	0	1	–	–	3	3	2	1	1	–
11	B. C. Lara (West Indies)	0	2	2	–	2	0	4	1	0	0
11	I. V. A. Richards (West Indies) . .	3	3	–	–	1	3	0	1	0	–
10	M. E. Waugh (Australia)	1	–	2	1	2	1	1	1	0	1
9	P. A. de Silva (Sri Lanka)	0	2	0	0	0	2	2	–	2	1
9	G. R. Marsh (Australia)	1	–	0	2	2	3	1	0	0	–
9	Ramiz Raja (Pakistan)	1	0	0	2	3	0	–	3	0	0
8	G. A. Gooch (England)	–	4	0	1	1	1	1	0	0	0
8	Javed Miandad (Pakistan)	1	0	1	1	0	3	–	2	0	0
7	D. I. Gower (England)	–	2	–	0	3	0	1	1	–	0
7	D. M. Jones (Australia)	3	–	0	0	2	0	1	1	0	0
7	G. Kirsten (South Africa)	1	2	–	0	0	2	1	0	0	1
7	Zaheer Abbas (Pakistan)	0	2	–	0	1	3	–	1	–	0

Note: Ass = Associate Members.

HIGHEST PARTNERSHIP FOR EACH WICKET

212	for 1st	G. R. Marsh and D. C. Boon	A v I	Jaipur	1986-87
263	for 2nd	Aamir Sohail and Inzamam-ul-Haq	P v NZ	Sharjah	1993-94
224*	for 3rd	D. M. Jones and A. R. Border	A v SL	Adelaide	1984-85
232	for 4th	D. J. Cullinan and J. N. Rhodes	SA v P	Nairobi (Gymkhana)	1996-97
223	for 5th	M. Azharuddin and A. Jadeja	I v SL	Colombo (RPS)	1997-98
154	for 6th	R. B. Richardson and P. J. L. Dujon	WI v P	Sharjah	1991-92
115	for 7th	{ P. J. L. Dujon and M. D. Marshall	WI v P	Gujranwala	1986-87
		{ A. C. Parore and L. K. Germon	NZ v P	Sharjah	1996-97
119	for 8th	P. R. Reiffel and S. K. Warne	A v SA	Port Elizabeth	1993-94
126*	for 9th	Kapil Dev and S. M. H. Kirmani	I v Z	Tunbridge Wells	1983
106*	for 10th	I. V. A. Richards and M. A. Holding	WI v E	Manchester	1984

MOST WICKETS

	M	Balls	R	W	BB	4W/i	Avge
Wasim Akram (Pakistan)	232	11,954	7,517	333	5-15	18	22.57
Waqar Younis (Pakistan)..........	156	7,707	5,762	265	6-26	20	21.74
Kapil Dev (India)................	225	11,202	6,945	253	5-43	4	27.45
C. J. McDermott (Australia)	138	7,461	5,018	203	5-44	5	24.71
C. E. L. Ambrose (West Indies)....	146	7,805	4,518	200	5-17	10	22.59
C. A. Walsh (West Indies)	176	9,288	5,936	196	5-1	6	30.28
Imran Khan (Pakistan)............	175	7,461	4,845	182	6-14	4	26.62
S. R. Waugh (Australia)	221	7,860	5,877	172	4-33	2	34.16
A. Kumble (India)	126	6,739	4,600	169	6-12	7	27.21
Aqib Javed (Pakistan)	148	7,299	5,148	164	7-37	5	31.39
R. J. Hadlee (New Zealand)	115	6,182	3,407	158	5-25	6	21.56
J. Srinath (India)	123	6,387	4,577	158	5-24	2	28.96
M. D. Marshall (West Indies)......	136	7,175	4,233	157	4-18	6	26.96
M. Prabhakar (India)	130	6,360	4,535	157	5-33	6	28.88
A. A. Donald (South Africa)	87	4,710	3,211	147	6-23	7	21.84
J. Garner (West Indies)	98	5,330	2,752	146	5-31	5	18.84
I. T. Botham (England)	116	6,271	4,139	145	4-31	3	28.54
M. A. Holding (West Indies)	102	5,473	3,034	142	5-26	6	21.36
Mushtaq Ahmed (Pakistan)........	124	6,431	4,638	141	5-36	3	32.89
E. J. Chatfield (New Zealand)	114	6,065	3,618	140	5-34	4	25.84
C. L. Hooper (West Indies)	155	6,263	4,536	134	4-34	1	33.85
Abdul Qadir (Pakistan)	104	5,100	3,453	132	5-44	6	26.15
S. K. Warne (Australia)	76	4,260	2,859	129	5-33	10	22.16
R. J. Shastri (India)	150	6,613	4,650	129	5-15	3	36.04
D. K. Morrison (New Zealand)	96	4,586	3,470	126	5-34	3	27.53
Saqlain Mushtaq (Pakistan)........	65	3,346	2,390	123	5-29	8	19.43
S. T. Jayasuriya (Sri Lanka)	141	4,986	4,037	121	6-29	5	33.36
I. V. A. Richards (West Indies)	187	5,644	4,228	118	6-41	3	35.83
I. R. Bishop (West Indies)	83	4,302	3,085	117	5-25	9	26.36
P. A. J. DeFreitas (England).......	103	5,712	3,775	115	4-35	1	32.82
M. C. Snedden (New Zealand)	93	4,525	3,237	114	4-34	1	28.39
Mudassar Nazar (Pakistan)	122	4,855	3,432	111	5-28	2	30.91
S. P. O'Donnell (Australia)........	87	4,350	3,102	108	5-13	6	28.72
D. K. Lillee (Australia)	63	3,593	2,145	103	5-34	6	20.82
C. Pringle (New Zealand)	64	3,314	2,455	103	5-45	3	23.83
M. Muralitharan (Sri Lanka)	77	4,212	2,924	101	4-18	3	28.95
W. K. M. Benjamin (West Indies) ..	85	4,442	3,079	100	5-22	1	30.79
R. A. Harper (West Indies)........	105	5,175	3,431	100·	4-40	3	34.31

Leading aggregate for Zimbabwe:

	M	Balls	R	W	BB	4W/i	Avge
E. A. Brandes.................	44	2,190	1,755	59	5-28	3	29.74

BEST ANALYSES

7-37	Aqib Javed	Pakistan v India at Sharjah......................	1991-92
7-51	W. W. Davis	West Indies v Australia at Leeds................	1983
6-12	A. Kumble	India v West Indies at Calcutta	1993-94
6-14	G. J. Gilmour	Australia v England at Leeds....................	1975
6-14	Imran Khan	Pakistan v India at Sharjah.....................	1984-85
6-15	C. E. H. Croft	West Indies v England at St Vincent	1980-81
6-23	A. A. Donald	South Africa v Kenya at Nairobi (Gymkhana)	1996-97
6-26	Waqar Younis	Pakistan v Sri Lanka at Sharjah................	1989-90
6-29	B. P. Patterson	West Indies v India at Nagpur..................	1987-88
6-29	S. T. Jayasuriya	Sri Lanka v England at Moratuwa...............	1992-93
6-30	Waqar Younis	Pakistan v New Zealand at Auckland	1993-94
6-39	K. H. MacLeay	Australia v India at Nottingham................	1983
6-41	I. V. A. Richards	West Indies v India at Delhi	1989-90
6-44	Waqar Younis	Pakistan v New Zealand at Sharjah	1996-97
6-50	A. H. Gray	West Indies v Australia at Port-of-Spain..........	1990-91

Best analyses for other Test-playing countries:

5-20	V. J. Marks	England v New Zealand at Wellington	1983-84
5-21	P. A. Strang	Zimbabwe v Kenya at Patna	1995-96
5-22	M. N. Hart	New Zealand v West Indies at Margao...........	1994-95

HAT-TRICKS

Jalal-ud-Din	Pakistan v Australia at Hyderabad......................	1982-83
B. A. Reid	Australia v New Zealand at Sydney	1985-86
Chetan Sharma	India v New Zealand at Nagpur	1987-88
Wasim Akram	Pakistan v West Indies at Sharjah	1989-90
Wasim Akram	Pakistan v Australia at Sharjah	1989-90
Kapil Dev	India v Sri Lanka at Calcutta...........................	1990-91
Aqib Javed	Pakistan v India at Sharjah.............................	1991-92
D. K. Morrison	New Zealand v India at Napier	1993-94
Waqar Younis	Pakistan v New Zealand at East London	1994-95
Saqlain Mushtaq†	Pakistan v England at Peshawar........................	1996-97
E. A. Brandes	Zimbabwe v England at Harare	1996-97
A. M. Stuart	Australia v Pakistan at Melbourne......................	1996-97

† *Four wickets in five balls.*

MOST DISMISSALS IN AN INNINGS

5 (all ct)	R. W. Marsh	Australia v England at Leeds	1981
5 (all ct)	R. G. de Alwis	Sri Lanka v Australia at Colombo (PSS).......	1982-83
5 (all ct)	S. M. H. Kirmani ...	India v Zimbabwe at Leicester	1983
5 (3ct, 2st)	S. Viswanath	India v England at Sydney	1984-85
5 (3ct, 2st)	K. S. More.........	India v New Zealand at Sharjah...............	1987-88
5 (all ct)	H. P. Tillekeratne ...	Sri Lanka v Pakistan at Sharjah	1990-91
5 (3ct, 2st)	N. R. Mongia	India v New Zealand at Auckland	1993-94
5 (3ct, 2st)	A. C. Parore	New Zealand v West Indies at Margao	1994-95
5 (all ct)	D. J. Richardson	South Africa v Pakistan at Johannesburg.......	1994-95
5 (all ct)	Moin Khan	Pakistan v Zimbabwe at Harare	1994-95
5 (4ct, 1st)	R. S. Kaluwitharana .	Sri Lanka v Pakistan at Sharjah	1994-95
5 (all ct)	D. J. Richardson	South Africa v Zimbabwe at Harare	1995-96
5 (all ct)	A. Flower..........	Zimbabwe v South Africa at Harare	1995-96
5 (all ct)	C. O. Browne	West Indies v Sri Lanka at Brisbane	1995-96
5 (4 ct, 1 st)	J. C. Adams........	West Indies v Kenya at Pune	1995-96
5 (4 ct, 1 st)	Rashid Latif	Pakistan v New Zealand at Lahore	1995-96
5 (3 ct, 2 st)	N. R. Mongia	India v Pakistan at Toronto	1996
5 (all ct)	A. Flower..........	Zimbabwe v England at Harare	1996-97

MOST DISMISSALS IN A CAREER

	M	Ct	St	Total
I. A. Healy (Australia)	168	195	39	234
P. J. L. Dujon (West Indies)	169	183	21	204
D. J. Richardson (South Africa)	108	131	15	146
R. W. Marsh (Australia)	92	120	4	124
Moin Khan (Pakistan)	91	86	35	121
Rashid Latif (Pakistan)	84	81	22	103
Salim Yousuf (Pakistan)	86	81	22	103

MOST CATCHES IN AN INNINGS

(Excluding wicket-keepers)

5	J. N. Rhodes	South Africa v West Indies at Bombay	1993-94
4	Salim Malik	Pakistan v New Zealand at Sialkot	1984-85
4	S. M. Gavaskar	India v Pakistan at Sharjah	1984-85
4	R. B. Richardson	West Indies v England at Birmingham	1991
4	K. C. Wessels	South Africa v West Indies at Kingston	1991-92
4	M. A. Taylor	Australia v West Indies at Sydney	1992-93
4	C. L. Hooper	West Indies v Pakistan at Durban	1992-93
4	K. R. Rutherford	New Zealand v India at Napier	1994-95
4	P. V. Simmons	West Indies v Sri Lanka at Sharjah	1995-96
4	R. A. Harper	West Indies v New Zealand at Georgetown	1995-96

Note: While fielding as substitute, J. G. Bracewell held 4 catches for New Zealand v Australia at Adelaide, 1980-81.

MOST CATCHES IN A CAREER

	M	Ct
A. R. Border (Australia)	273	127
M. Azharuddin (India)	259	117
I. V. A. Richards (West Indies)	187	101
R. S. Mahanama (Sri Lanka)	176	93
S. R. Waugh (Australia)	221	79
C. L. Hooper (West Indies)	155	76
Salim Malik (Pakistan)	268	76
R. B. Richardson (West Indies)	224	75
Kapil Dev (India)	225	71
Ijaz Ahmed, sen. (Pakistan)	181	70

ALL-ROUND

1,000 Runs and 100 Wickets

	M	R	W
I. T. Botham (England)	116	2,113	145
R. J. Hadlee (New Zealand)	115	1,751	158
C. L. Hooper (West Indies)	155	3,600	134
Imran Khan (Pakistan)	175	3,709	182
S. T. Jayasuriya (Sri Lanka)	141	3,592	121
Kapil Dev (India)	225	3,783	253
Mudassar Nazar (Pakistan)	122	2,653	111

	M	R	W
S. P. O'Donnell (Australia)	87	1,242	108
M. Prabhakar (India)..............	130	1,858	157
I. V. A. Richards (West Indies)......	187	6,721	118
R. J. Shastri (India)...............	150	3,108	129
Wasim Akram (Pakistan)	232	2,180	333
S. R. Waugh (Australia)...........	221	5,092	172

1,000 Runs and 100 Dismissals

	M	R	D
P. J. L. Dujon (West Indies)	169	1,945	204
I. A. Healy (Australia)	168	1,764	234
R. W. Marsh (Australia)............	92	1,225	124
Moin Khan (Pakistan)..............	91	1,127	121

TEAM RECORDS

HIGHEST INNINGS TOTALS

398-5	(50 overs)	Sri Lanka v Kenya at Kandy	1995-96
371-9	(50 overs)	Pakistan v Sri Lanka at Nairobi (Gymkhana)...........	1996-97
363-7	(55 overs)	England v Pakistan at Nottingham....................	1992
360-4	(50 overs)	West Indies v Sri Lanka at Karachi	1987-88
349-9	(50 overs)	Sri Lanka v Pakistan at Singapore....................	1995-96
348-8	(50 overs)	New Zealand v India at Nagpur	1995-96
339-4	(50 overs)	Sri Lanka v Pakistan at Mohali	1996-97
338-4	(50 overs)	New Zealand v Bangladesh at Sharjah	1989-90
338-5	(60 overs)	Pakistan v Sri Lanka at Swansea	1983
334-4	(60 overs)	England v India at Lord's	1975
333-7	(50 overs)	West Indies v Sri Lanka at Sharjah...................	1995-96
333-8	(45 overs)	West Indies v India at Jamshedpur	1983-84
333-9	(60 overs)	England v Sri Lanka at Taunton	1983
332-3	(50 overs)	Australia v Sri Lanka at Sharjah	1989-90
330-6	(60 overs)	Pakistan v Sri Lanka at Nottingham	1975

Highest totals by other Test-playing countries:

328-3	(50 overs)	South Africa v Holland at Rawalpindi	1995-96
312-4	(50 overs)	Zimbabwe v Sri Lanka at New Plymouth..............	1991-92
305-5	(50 overs)	India v Pakistan at Sharjah..........................	1995-96

HIGHEST TOTALS BATTING SECOND

329	(49.3 overs)	Sri Lanka v West Indies at Sharjah...................	1995-96
		(Lost by 4 runs)	
315	(49.4 overs)	Pakistan v Sri Lanka at Singapore....................	1995-96
		(Lost by 34 runs)	
313-7	(49.2 overs)	Sri Lanka v Zimbabwe at New Plymouth..............	1991-92
		(Won by 3 wickets)	
300-7	(50 overs)	India v Sri Lanka at Colombo (SSC)	1997-98
		(Lost by 2 runs)	

HIGHEST MATCH AGGREGATES

664-19	(99.4 overs)	Pakistan v Sri Lanka at Singapore....................	1995-96
662-17	(99.3 overs)	Sri Lanka v West Indies at Sharjah...................	1995-96
660-19	(99.5 overs)	Pakistan v Sri Lanka at Nairobi (Gymkhana)...........	1996-97
652-12	(100 overs)	Sri Lanka v Kenya at Kandy	1995-96
626-14	(120 overs)	Pakistan v Sri Lanka at Swansea	1983
625-11	(99.2 overs)	Sri Lanka v Zimbabwe at New Plymouth..............	1991-92

LOWEST INNINGS TOTALS

43	(19.5 overs)	Pakistan v West Indies at Cape Town..................	1992-93
45	(40.3 overs)	Canada v England at Manchester......................	1979
55	(28.3 overs)	Sri Lanka v West Indies at Sharjah....................	1986-87
63	(25.5 overs)	India v Australia at Sydney	1980-81
64	(35.5 overs)	New Zealand v Pakistan at Sharjah....................	1985-86
69	(28 overs)	South Africa v Australia at Sydney....................	1993-94
70	(25.2 overs)	Australia v England at Birmingham	1977
70	(26.3 overs)	Australia v New Zealand at Adelaide	1985-86

Note: This section does not take into account those matches in which the number of overs was reduced.

Lowest totals by other Test-playing countries:

87	(29.3 overs)	West Indies v Australia at Sydney	1992-93
93	(36.2 overs)	England v Australia at Leeds	1975
94	(31.4 overs)	Zimbabwe v Pakistan at Sharjah	1996-97

LARGEST VICTORIES

232 runs	Australia (323-2 in 50 overs) v Sri Lanka (91 in 35.5 overs) at Adelaide..	1984-85
206 runs	New Zealand (276-7 in 50 overs) v Australia (70 in 26.3 overs) at Adelaide..	1985-86
202 runs	England (334-4 in 60 overs) v India (132-3 in 60 overs) at Lord's	1975

By ten wickets: There have been ten instances of victory by ten wickets.

TIED MATCHES

West Indies 222-5 (50 overs) v Australia 222-9 (50 overs) at Melbourne	1983-84
England 226-5 (55 overs) v Australia 226-8 (55 overs) at Nottingham	1989
West Indies 186-5 (39 overs) v Pakistan 186-9 (39 overs) at Lahore	1991-92
India 126 (47.4 overs) v West Indies 126 (41 overs) at Perth	1991-92
Australia 228-7 (50 overs) v Pakistan 228-9 (50 overs) at Hobart	1992-93
Pakistan 244-6 (50 overs) v West Indies 244-5 (50 overs) at Georgetown	1992-93
India 248-5 (50 overs) v Zimbabwe 248 (50 overs) at Indore	1993-94
Pakistan 161-9 (50 overs) v New Zealand 161 (49.4 overs) at Auckland	1993-94
Zimbabwe 219-9 (50 overs) v Pakistan 219 (49.5 overs) at Harare	1994-95
New Zealand 169-8 (50 overs) v Sri Lanka 169 (48 overs) at Sharjah	1996-97
Zimbabwe 236-8 (50 overs) v India 236 (49.5 overs) at Paarl	1996-97
New Zealand 237 (49.4 overs) v England 237-8 (50 overs) at Napier.............	1996-97

MOST APPEARANCES

(200 or more)

	Total	E	A	SA	WI	NZ	I	P	SL	Z	Ass
A. R. Border (A)	273	43	–	15	61	52	38	34	23	5	2
Salim Malik (P)	268	24	24	16	45	42	45	–	53	13	6
M. Azharuddin (I).....	259	21	35	26	41	29	–	44	43	14	6
D. L. Haynes (WI)	238	35	64	8	–	13	36	65	14	3	–
Javed Miandad (P)	233	27	35	3	64	24	35	–	35	6	4
Wasim Akram (P)......	232	24	29	11	52	26	33	–	37	14	6
Kapil Dev (I)	225	23	41	13	42	29	–	32	34	9	2

	Total	E	A	SA	WI	NZ	I	P	SL	Z	Ass
R. B. Richardson (WI) ..	224	35	51	9	–	11	32	61	21	3	1
A. Ranatunga (SL)	221	10	28	8	21	32	45	61	–	10	6
S. R. Waugh (A).......	221	26	–	28	39	40	33	28	20	5	2
P. A. de Silva (SL).....	218	8	29	8	24	28	43	61	–	10	7

Most appearances for other Test-playing countries:

J. G. Wright (NZ)......	149	30	42	–	11	–	21	18	24	2	1
G. A. Gooch (E).......	125	–	32	1	32	16	18	16	6	3	1
W. J. Cronje (SA)......	115	12	30	–	8	8	25	15	7	7	3
A. Flower (Z)	65	6	5	7	3	6	12	14	10	–	2

WORLD CUP FINALS

1975	WEST INDIES (291-8) beat Australia (274) by 17 runs.............	Lord's
1979	WEST INDIES (286-9) beat England (194) by 92 runs	Lord's
1983	INDIA (183) beat West Indies (140) by 43 runs	Lord's
1987-88	AUSTRALIA (253-5) beat England (246-8) by seven runs	Calcutta
1991-92	PAKISTAN (249-6) beat England (227) by 22 runs	Melbourne
1995-96	SRI LANKA (245-3) beat Australia (241-7) by seven wickets.......	Lahore

Other World Cup records may be found in Wisden 1997.

CAPTAINCY

LIMITED-OVERS INTERNATIONAL CAPTAINS

England (264 matches; 20 captains)

G. A. Gooch 50; M. A. Atherton 43; M. W. Gatting 37; R. G. D. Willis 29; J. M. Brearley 25; D. I. Gower 24; M. H. Denness 12; I. T. Botham 9; A. J. Stewart 7; K. W. R. Fletcher 5; J. E. Emburey 4; A. J. Lamb 4; D. B. Close 3; R. Illingworth 3; G. Boycott 2; N. Gifford 2; A. W. Greig 2; J. H. Edrich 1; N. Hussain 1; A. P. E. Knott 1.

Australia (377 matches; 13 captains)

A. R. Border 178; M. A. Taylor 67; G. S. Chappell 49; K. J. Hughes 49; I. M. Chappell 11; I. A. Healy 8; G. R. Marsh 4; G. N. Yallop 4; R. B. Simpson 2; S. R. Waugh 2; R. J. Bright 1; D. W. Hookes 1; W. M. Lawry 1.

South Africa (120 matches; 3 captains)

W. J. Cronje 65; K. C. Wessels 52; C. E. B. Rice 3.

West Indies (338 matches; 13 captains)

I. V. A. Richards 108; R. B. Richardson 87; C. H. Lloyd 81; C. A. Walsh 36; C. G. Greenidge 8; D. L. Haynes 7; M. A. Holding 2; R. B. Kanhai 2; B. C. Lara 2; D. L. Murray 2; P. J. L. Dujon 1; C. L. Hooper 1; A. I. Kallicharran 1.

New Zealand (281 matches; 13 captains)

G. P. Howarth 60; M. D. Crowe 44; K. R. Rutherford 37; L. K. Germon 36; J. G. Wright 31; J. V. Coney 25; J. J. Crowe 16; M. G. Burgess 8; G. M. Turner 8; B. E. Congdon 6; S. P. Fleming 5; G. R. Larsen 3; A. H. Jones 2.

India (333 matches; 13 captains)

M. Azharuddin 119; Kapil Dev 74; S. R. Tendulkar 45; S. M. Gavaskar 37; D. B. Vengsarkar 18; K. Srikkanth 13; R. J. Shastri 11; S. Venkataraghavan 7; B. S. Bedi 4; A. L. Wadekar 2; M. Amarnath 1; S. M. H. Kirmani 1; G. R. Viswanath 1.

Pakistan (379 matches; 17 captains)

Imran Khan 139; Wasim Akram 66; Javed Miandad 62; Salim Malik 34; Ramiz Raja 22; Zaheer Abbas 13; Aamir Sohail 9; Asif Iqbal 6; Abdul Qadir 5; Saeed Anwar 5; Wasim Bari 5; Mushtaq Mohammad 4; Intikhab Alam 3; Majid Khan 2; Moin Khan 2; Sarfraz Nawaz 1; Waqar Younis 1.

Sri Lanka (253 matches; 9 captains)

A. Ranatunga 145; L. R. D. Mendis 61; P. A. de Silva 18; R. S. Madugalle 13; B. Warnapura 8; A. P. B. Tennekoon 4; R. S. Mahanama 2; D. S. de Silva 1; J. R. Ratnayeke 1.

Zimbabwe (77 matches; 5 captains)

A. Flower 28; A. D. R. Campbell 20; D. L. Houghton 17; D. A. G. Fletcher 6; A. J. Traicos 6.

Associate Members (42 matches; 9 captains)

M. Odumbe (Kenya) 9; Gazi Ashraf (Bangladesh) 7; Sultan M. Zarawani (UAE) 7; Akram Khan (Bangladesh) 6; S. W. Lubbers (Holland) 4; B. M. Mauricette (Canada) 3; Harilal R. Shah (East Africa) 3; Minhaz-ul-Abedin (Bangladesh) 2; R. P. Lefebvre (Holland) 1.

MISCELLANEOUS

LARGE ATTENDANCES

Test Series

943,000	Australia v England (5 Tests)	1936-37
In England		
549,650	England v Australia (5 Tests)	1953

Test Matches

†350,534	Australia v England, Melbourne (Third Test)...............	1936-37
325,000+	India v England, Calcutta (Second Test)..................	1972-73
In England		
158,000+	England v Australia, Leeds (Fourth Test).................	1948
137,915	England v Australia, Lord's (Second Test)................	1953

Test Match Day

| 90,800 | Australia v West Indies, Melbourne (Fifth Test, 2nd day) .... | 1960-61 |

Other First-Class Matches in England

93,000	England v Australia, Lord's (Fourth Victory Match, 3 days)	1945
80,000+	Surrey v Yorkshire, The Oval (3 days)........................	1906
78,792	Yorkshire v Lancashire, Leeds (3 days)	1904
76,617	Lancashire v Yorkshire, Manchester (3 days).................	1926

Limited-Overs Internationals

‡100,000	India v South Africa, Calcutta	1993-94
‡100,000	India v West Indies, Calcutta.............................	1993-94
‡100,000	India v West Indies, Calcutta.............................	1994-95
‡100,000	India v Sri Lanka, Calcutta (World Cup semi-final)	1995-96
‡90,000	India v Pakistan, Calcutta.................................	1986-87
‡90,000	India v South Africa, Calcutta.............................	1991-92
87,182	England v Pakistan, Melbourne (World Cup final)	1991-92
86,133	Australia v West Indies, Melbourne	1983-84

† *Although no official figures are available, the attendance at the Fourth Test between India and England at Calcutta, 1981-82, was thought to have exceeded this figure.*

‡ *No official attendance figures were issued for these games, but capacity is believed to have reached 100,000 following rebuilding in 1993.*

LORD'S CRICKET GROUND

Lord's and the Marylebone Cricket Club were founded in 1787. The Club has enjoyed an uninterrupted career since that date, but there have been three grounds known as Lord's. The first (1787-1810) was situated where Dorset Square now is; the second (1809-13), at North Bank, had to be abandoned owing to the cutting of the Regent's Canal; and the third, opened in 1814, is the present one at St John's Wood. It was not until 1866 that the freehold of Lord's was secured by MCC. The present pavilion was erected in 1890 at a cost of £21,000.

HIGHEST INDIVIDUAL SCORES MADE AT LORD'S

333	G. A. Gooch .... England v India.........................	1990
316*	J. B. Hobbs .... Surrey v Middlesex	1926
315*	P. Holmes .... Yorkshire v Middlesex	1925

Note: The longest innings in a first-class match at Lord's was played by S. Wettimuny (636 minutes, 190 runs) for Sri Lanka v England, 1984.

HIGHEST TOTALS AT LORD'S

First-Class Matches

729-6 dec.	Australia v England	1930
665	West Indians v Middlesex	1939
653-4 dec.	England v India...	1990
652-8 dec.	West Indies v England	1973

Minor Match

735-9 dec.   MCC and Ground v Wiltshire   1888

BIGGEST HIT AT LORD'S

The only known instance of a batsman hitting a ball over the present pavilion at Lord's occurred when A. E. Trott, appearing for MCC against Australians on July 31, August 1, 2, 1899, drove M. A. Noble so far and high that the ball struck a chimney pot and fell behind the building.

MINOR CRICKET

HIGHEST INDIVIDUAL SCORES

628* A. E. J. Collins, Clark's House v North Town at Clifton College.
      (A Junior House match. His innings of 6 hours 50 minutes was spread over
      four afternoons.)   1899
566 C. J. Eady, Break-o'-Day v Wellington at Hobart   1901-02
515 D. R. Havewalla, B.B. and C.I. Rly v St Xavier's at Bombay   1933-34
506* J. C. Sharp, Melbourne GS v Geelong College at Melbourne   1914-15
502* Chaman Lal, Mehandra Coll., Patiala v Government Coll., Rupar at Patiala   1956-57
485 A. E. Stoddart, Hampstead v Stoics at Hampstead   1886
475* Mohammad Iqbal, Muslim Model HS v Islamia HS, Sialkot at Lahore   1958-59
466* G. T. S. Stevens, Beta v Lambda (University College School House match) at
      Neasden   1919
459 J. A. Prout, Wesley College v Geelong College at Geelong   1908-09

Note: The highest score in a Minor County match is 323* by F. E. Lacey for Hampshire v Norfolk at Southampton in 1887; the highest in the Minor Counties Championship is 282 by E. Garnett for Berkshire v Wiltshire at Reading in 1908.

HIGHEST PARTNERSHIP

664* for 3rd   V. G. Kambli and S. R. Tendulkar, Sharadashram Vidyamandir School
             v St Xavier's High School at Bombay   1987-88

RECORD HIT

The Rev. W. Fellows, while at practice on the Christ Church ground at Oxford in 1856, drove a ball bowled by Charles Rogers 175 yards from hit to pitch.

THROWING THE CRICKET BALL

140 yards 2 feet, Robert Percival, on the Durham Sands racecourse, Co. Durham .....   c 1882
140 yards 9 inches, Ross Mackenzie, at Toronto   1872
140 yards, "King Billy" the Aborigine at Clermont, Queensland   1872

Note: Extensive research by David Rayvern Allen has shown that these traditional records are probably authentic, if not necessarily wholly accurate. Modern competitions have failed to produce similar distances although Ian Pont, the Essex all-rounder who also played baseball, was reported to have thrown 138 yards in Cape Town in 1981. There have been speculative reports attributing throws of 150 yards or more to figures as diverse as the South African Test player Colin Bland, the Latvian javelin thrower Janis Lusis, who won a gold medal for the Soviet Union in the 1968 Olympics, and the British sprinter Charley Ransome. The definitive record is still awaited.

DATES OF FORMATION OF FIRST-CLASS COUNTIES

County	First known organisation	Present Club Original date	Reorganisation, if substantial	First-class status from
Derbyshire	1870	1870	—	1871
Durham	1874	1882	1991	1992
Essex	By 1790	1876	—	1895
Glamorgan	1861	1888	—	1921
Gloucestershire	1863	1871	—	1870
Hampshire	1849	1863	1879	1864
Kent	1842	1859	1870	1864
Lancashire	1864	1864	—	1865
Leicestershire	By 1820	1879	—	1895
Middlesex	1863	1864	—	1864
Northamptonshire ..	1820†	1878	—	1905
Nottinghamshire ...	1841	1841	1866	1864
Somerset	1864	1875	—	1882
Surrey............	1845	1845	—	1864
Sussex	1836	1839	1857	1864
Warwickshire......	1826	1882	—	1895
Worcestershire	1844	1865	—	1899
Yorkshire	1861	1863	1891	1864

Note: Derbyshire lost first-class status from 1888 to 1894, Hampshire between 1886 and 1894 and Somerset between 1886 and 1890.

† *Town club.*

DATES OF FORMATION OF CLUBS IN THE CURRENT MINOR COUNTIES CHAMPIONSHIP

County	First known organisation	Present Club
Bedfordshire.............	1847	1899
Berkshire	By 1841	1895
Buckinghamshire	1864	1891
Cambridgeshire	1844	1891
Cheshire	1819	1908
Cornwall...............	1813	1894
Cumberland	1884	1948
Devon.................	1824	1899
Dorset.................	1862 or 1871	1896
Herefordshire	1836	1991
Hertfordshire	1838	1876
Lincolnshire	1853	1906
Norfolk................	1827	1876
Northumberland	1834	1895
Oxfordshire	1787	1921
Shropshire	1819 or 1829	1956
Staffordshire............	1871	1871
Suffolk	1864	1932
Wales Minor Counties	1988	1988
Wiltshire...............	1881	1893

CONSTITUTION OF COUNTY CHAMPIONSHIP

At least four possible dates have been given for the start of county cricket in England. The first, patchy, references began in 1825. The earliest mention in any cricket publication is in 1864 and eight counties have come to be regarded as first-class from that date, including Cambridgeshire, who dropped out after 1871. For many years, the County Championship was considered to have started in 1873, when regulations governing qualification first applied; indeed, a special commemorative stamp was issued by the Post Office in 1973. However, the Championship was not formally organised until 1890 and before then champions were proclaimed by the press; sometimes publications differed in their views and no definitive list of champions can start before that date. Eight teams contested the 1890 competition – Gloucestershire, Kent, Lancashire, Middlesex, Nottinghamshire, Surrey, Sussex and Yorkshire. Somerset joined in the following year, and in 1895 the Championship began to acquire something of its modern shape when Derbyshire, Essex, Hampshire, Leicestershire and Warwickshire were added. At that point MCC officially recognised the competition's existence. Worcestershire, Northamptonshire and Glamorgan were admitted to the Championship in 1899, 1905 and 1921 respectively and are regarded as first-class from these dates. An invitation in 1921 to Buckinghamshire to enter the Championship was declined, owing to the lack of necessary playing facilities, and an application by Devon in 1948 was unsuccessful. Durham were admitted to the Championship in 1992 and were granted first-class status prior to their pre-season tour of Zimbabwe.

MOST COUNTY CHAMPIONSHIP APPEARANCES

762	W. Rhodes	Yorkshire	1898-1930
707	F. E. Woolley	Kent	1906-38
668	C. P. Mead	Hampshire	1906-36
617	N. Gifford	Worcestershire (484), Warwickshire (133)	1960-88
611	W. G. Quaife	Warwickshire	1895-1928
601	G. H. Hirst	Yorkshire	1891-1921

The most appearances for counties not mentioned singly above are:

594	F. J. Titmus	Middlesex	1949-82
591	W. E. Astill	Leicestershire	1906-39
589	D. J. Shepherd	Glamorgan	1950-72
571	C. W. L. Parker	Gloucestershire	1905-35
561	J. Langridge	Sussex	1924-53
544	G. Gunn	Nottinghamshire	1902-32
538	D. Kenyon	Worcestershire	1946-67
536	J. B. Hobbs	Surrey	1905-34
529	K. W. R. Fletcher	Essex	1962-88
526	E. Tyldesley	Lancashire	1909-36
506	D. C. Morgan	Derbyshire	1950-69
479	B. A. Langford	Somerset	1953-74
464	D. Brookes	Northamptonshire	1934-59
97	S. J. E. Brown	Durham	1992-97

Notes: F. J. Titmus also played one match for Surrey (1978). The most appearances by a captain is 407 by Lord Hawke for Yorkshire (1883-1909), by a wicket-keeper 506 by H. Strudwick for Surrey (1902-27) and by an amateur 496 by P. A. Perrin for Essex (1896-1928).

MOST CONSECUTIVE COUNTY CHAMPIONSHIP APPEARANCES

423	K. G. Suttle	Sussex	1954-69
412	J. G. Binks	Yorkshire	1955-69
399	J. Vine	Sussex	1899-1914
344	E. H. Killick	Sussex	1898-1912
326	C. N. Woolley	Northamptonshire	1913-31
305	A. H. Dyson	Glamorgan	1930-47
301	B. Taylor	Essex	1961-72

Notes: J. Vine made 417 consecutive appearances for Sussex in all first-class matches between July 1900 and September 1914.

J. G. Binks did not miss a Championship match for Yorkshire between making his debut in June 1955 and retiring at the end of the 1969 season.

UMPIRES

MOST COUNTY CHAMPIONSHIP APPEARANCES

569	T. W. Spencer	1950-1980
533	F. Chester	1922-1955
516	H. G. Baldwin	1932-1962
481	P. B. Wight	1966-1995
457	A. Skelding	1931-1958

MOST SEASONS ON FIRST-CLASS LIST

31	T. W. Spencer	1950-1980
30	P. B. Wight	1966-1995
29	**D. J. Constant**	**1969-1997**
28	**H. D. Bird**	**1970-1997**
28	F. Chester	1922-1955
28	**A. G. T. Whitehead**	**1970-1997**
27	J. Moss	1899-1929
26	**R. Julian**	**1972-1997**
26	**K. E. Palmer**	**1972-1997**
26	W. A. J. West	1896-1925
25	H. G. Baldwin	1932-1962
25	A. Jepson	1960-1984
25	J. G. Langridge	1956-1980
25	**B. J. Meyer**	**1973-1997**

Bold type denotes umpires who stood in the 1997 season.

UMPIRES FOR 1998

FIRST-CLASS UMPIRES

J. C. Balderstone, H. D. Bird, G. I. Burgess, A. Clarkson, D. J. Constant, B. Dudleston, J. H. Hampshire, J. H. Harris, M. J. Harris, J. W. Holder, V. A. Holder, T. E. Jesty, A. A. Jones, R. Julian, M. J. Kitchen, B. Leadbeater, J. W. Lloyds, K. E. Palmer, R. Palmer, N. T. Plews, G. Sharp, D. R. Shepherd, J. F. Steele, R. A. White, A. G. T. Whitehead and P. Willey. *Reserves:* P. Adams, M. R. Benson, P. Carrick, N. G. Cowley, K. J. Lyons, N. A. Mallender, M. K. Reed and K. Shuttleworth.

MINOR COUNTIES UMPIRES

P. Adams, S. F. Bishopp, P. Brown, A. R. Bundy, D. L. Burden, P. D. Clubb, K. Coburn, J. H. Evans, A. J. Hardy, J. Ilott, M. A. Johnson, C. S. Kelly, P. W. Kingston-Davey, S. W. Kuhlmann, D. Lea, G. Lowden, G. I. McLean, M. P. Moran, D. Norton, C. T. Puckett, G. P. Randall-Johnson, J. G. Reed, M. K. Reed, G. Ripley, K. S. Shenton, W. E. Smith, C. Stone, J. M. Tythcott, B. H. Willey, T. G. Wilson and R. Wood. *Reserves:* N. Bainton, A. E. Bayley, P. G. Burrows, D. R. M. Crowson, M. Dixon, C. J. Edwards, P. D. Fisher, F. D. Fowler, J. H. James, N. L. Jones, C. Megennis, W. Morgan, C. A. W. Revell, T. R. Riley, R. M. Sutton, K. J. Timpson and D. J. Warnford.

PART FOUR: ENGLISH CRICKET IN 1997

FEATURES OF 1997

Double-Hundreds (17)

303*	G. A. Hick...............	Worcestershire v Hampshire at Southampton.
271*	A. J. Stewart	Surrey v Yorkshire at The Oval.
237	S. Young	Gloucestershire v Derbyshire at Cheltenham.
235*	M. L. Hayden	Hampshire v Warwickshire at Southampton.
233*	H. Morris................	Glamorgan v Warwickshire at Cardiff.
229	Salim Elahi	Pakistan A v Worcestershire at Worcester.
225	G. D. Lloyd..............	Lancashire v Yorkshire at Leeds.
224	P. J. Prichard............	Essex v Kent at Canterbury:
224	V. J. Wells...............	Leicestershire v Middlesex at Lord's.
222	G. P. Thorpe	Surrey v Glamorgan at The Oval.
210*	K. J. Barnett	Derbyshire v Yorkshire at Derby.
210*†	J. J. B. Lewis	Durham v Oxford University at Oxford.
210	A. S. Rollins	Derbyshire v Hampshire at Chesterfield.
207	N. Hussain...............	England v Australia (First Test) at Birmingham.
205	W. P. C. Weston..........	Worcestershire v Northamptonshire at Northampton.
200*	K. L. T. Arthurton	MCC v Pakistan A at Shenley Park.
200*	M. J. Powell	Glamorgan v Oxford University at Oxford.

† *County record.*

Hundred on First-Class Debut

200*	M. J. Powell	Glamorgan v Oxford University at Oxford.

Three Hundreds in Successive Innings

S. P. James (Glamorgan) .... 130 v Worcestershire at Worcester,
103 and 113 v Northamptonshire at Abergavenny.

Hundred in Each Innings of a Match

M. L. Hayden	235*	119	Hampshire v Warwickshire at Southampton.
D. L. Hemp	138	114*†	Warwickshire v Hampshire at Southampton.
S. P. James	103	113	Glamorgan v Northamptonshire at Abergavenny.
M. A. Wagh	116	101	Oxford University v Glamorgan at Oxford.
S. R. Waugh	108	116	Australia v England (Third Test) at Manchester.

† *In contrived circumstances.*

Fastest Authentic Hundred

G. D. Lloyd............. 73 balls Lancashire v Leicestershire at Leicester.

Hundred Before Lunch

C. J. Adams.........	107*	Derbyshire v Durham at Chester-le-Street (1st day).
K. J. Barnett	105*	Derbyshire v Leicestershire at Leicester (3rd day).
D. L. Hemp.........	114*†	Warwickshire v Hampshire at Southampton (4th day).
S. P. James	109*	Glamorgan v Durham at Cardiff (1st day).
N. V. Knight	119*†	Warwickshire v Hampshire at Southampton (4th day).
G. D. Lloyd.........	100*	Lancashire v Leicestershire at Leicester (4th day).
A. S. Rollins	108*	Derbyshire v Glamorgan at Chesterfield (1st day).

† *In contrived circumstances.*

First to 1,000 Runs

S. P. James (Glamorgan) on July 18.

2,000 Runs

No batsman scored 2,000 runs. The highest aggregate was 1,775 by S. P. James (Glamorgan).

Carrying Bat Through Completed Innings

J. J. B. Lewis.........	158*	Durham (251) v Kent at Darlington.
M. R. Ramprakash.....	113*	Middlesex (256) v Kent at Lord's.

First-Wicket Partnerships of 100 in Each Innings

110	213	J. S. Laney/M. L. Hayden, Hampshire v Derbyshire at Chesterfield.
144	153	V. J. Wells/D. L. Maddy, Leicestershire v Derbyshire at Leicester.

Other Notable Partnerships

First Wicket

290	J. J. B. Lewis/P. D. Collingwood, Durham v Oxford University at Oxford.
259	N. T. Wood/M. A. Atherton, Lancashire v Surrey at The Oval.

Second Wicket

417†	K. J. Barnett/T. A. Tweats, Derbyshire v Yorkshire at Derby.
317*	J. H. Kallis/M. R. Ramprakash, Middlesex v Worcestershire at Kidderminster.
257*	P. E. Wellings/M. W. Gatting, Middlesex v Cambridge University at Cambridge.

Third Wicket

438*†	G. A. Hick/T. M. Moody, Worcestershire v Hampshire at Southampton.
317	N. Hussain/S. G. Law, Essex v Leicestershire at Colchester.
316*†	A. S. Rollins/K. J. Barnett, Derbyshire v Leicestershire at Leicester.

Fourth Wicket

288	N. Hussain/G. P. Thorpe, England v Australia (First Test) at Birmingham.
204†	J. J. B. Lewis/J. Boiling, Durham v Derbyshire at Chester-le-Street.

Fifth Wicket

268	M. T. G. Elliott/R. T. Ponting, Australia v England (Fourth Test) at Leeds.
244	S. Young/M. W. Alleyne, Gloucestershire v Derbyshire at Cheltenham.
241	W. P. C. Weston/D. A. Leatherdale, Worcestershire v Northamptonshire at Northampton.
225*	N. C. Johnson/B. F. Smith, Leicestershire v Kent at Canterbury.

Seventh Wicket

279†	R. J. Harden/G. D. Rose,	Somerset v Sussex at Taunton.
248†	G. D. Lloyd/I. D. Austin,	Lancashire v Yorkshire at Leeds.
205*	M. L. Hayden/S. D. Udal,	Hampshire v Warwickshire at Southampton.
205	J. M. Dakin/D. J. Millns,	Leicestershire v Northamptonshire at Northampton.

Eighth Wicket

186	N. M. K. Smith/D. R. Brown,	Warwickshire v Gloucestershire at Birmingham.

Ninth Wicket

171†	M. A. Ealham/P. A. Strang,	Kent v Nottinghamshire at Nottingham.

Tenth Wicket

183	S. A. Marsh/B. J. Phillips,	Kent v Sussex at Horsham.
146	G. Chapple/P. J. Martin,	Lancashire v Durham at Manchester.
101	P. A. Nixon/J. Ormond,	Leicestershire v Gloucestershire at Leicester.
100*	J. O. Davy/P. McCrum,	Ireland v Scotland at Dublin.

* Unbroken partnership.   † County record for that wicket.

Eight or More Wickets in an Innings (6)

9-64†	M. M. Betts	Durham v Northamptonshire at Northampton.
8-17	Waqar Younis	Glamorgan v Sussex at Swansea.
8-32	P. J. Martin	Lancashire v Middlesex at Uxbridge.
8-38	G. D. McGrath	Australia v England (Second Test) at Lord's.
8-49	K. D. James	Hampshire v Somerset at Basingstoke.
8-89	D. R. Brown	First-Class Counties Select XI v Pakistan A at Chelmsford.

† County record.

Twelve or More Wickets in a Match (4)

13-79	P. J. Martin	Lancashire v Middlesex at Uxbridge.
13-93	K. D. James	Hampshire v Somerset at Basingstoke.
13-143	M. M. Betts	Durham v Northamptonshire at Northampton.
12-148	C. E. W. Silverwood	Yorkshire v Kent at Leeds.

Hat-Tricks

P. J. Franks	Nottinghamshire v Warwickshire at Nottingham.
C. Patel	Oxford University v Warwickshire at Oxford.
Saqlain Mushtaq	Surrey v Middlesex at Lord's.
C. M. Tolley	Nottinghamshire v Leicestershire at Leicester.
Waqar Younis	Glamorgan v Lancashire at Liverpool.

100 Wickets

No bowler took 100 wickets. The highest aggregate was 83 by A. M. Smith (Gloucestershire and England).

Most Overs Bowled in an Innings

86–49–94–4	P. M. Such	Essex v Leicestershire at Colchester.

Championship record.

Six or More Wicket-Keeping Dismissals in an Innings

6 ct... I. A. Healy   Australia v England (First Test) at Birmingham.
6 ct... S. A. Marsh   Kent v Nottinghamshire at Nottingham.
6 ct... W. M. Noon   Nottinghamshire v Derbyshire at Nottingham.
6 ct... A. J. Stewart   England v Australia (Third Test) at Manchester.

Nine or More Wicket-Keeping Dismissals in a Match

9 ct.... Javed Qadir   Pakistan A v Nottinghamshire at Nottingham.
9 ct.... P. A. Nixon   Leicestershire v Nottinghamshire at Leicester.

No Byes Conceded in Total of 500 or More

P. Moores ..... Sussex v Lancashire (561-8 dec.) at Manchester.
D. Ripley ...... Northamptonshire v Middlesex (531) at Lord's.
R. J. Turner .... Somerset v Glamorgan (527) at Taunton.
A. N. Aymes... Hampshire v Derbyshire (523) at Chesterfield.
S. J. Rhodes.... Worcestershire v Yorkshire (501-7 dec.) at Leeds.
A. N. Aymes... Hampshire v Yorkshire (501-8 dec.) at Portsmouth.

Highest Innings Totals

631-7 dec. ..... Warwickshire v Hampshire at Southampton.
597-8 dec.† .... Glamorgan v Durham at Cardiff.
592-4 dec. ..... Lancashire v Surrey at The Oval.
581-7 dec. ..... Surrey v Northamptonshire at Northampton.
569-8 dec. ..... Lancashire v Hampshire at Southampton.
561-8 dec. ..... Lancashire v Sussex at Manchester.
557 .... Leicestershire v Northamptonshire at Northampton.
554-8 dec. ..... Worcestershire v Derbyshire at Worcester.
551-3 dec. ..... Glamorgan v Warwickshire at Cardiff.
551 .... Worcestershire v Northamptonshire at Northampton.

   † *County record.*

Lowest Innings Totals

31 .... Glamorgan v Middlesex at Cardiff.
51 .... Lancashire v Glamorgan at Liverpool.
54 .... Sussex v Glamorgan (1st innings) at Swansea.
63 .... Sussex v Warwickshire at Birmingham.
67 .... Sussex v Glamorgan (2nd innings) at Swansea.
69 .... Leicestershire v Worcestershire at Worcester.
71 .... Sussex v Worcestershire at Arundel.
77 .... England v Australia (Second Test) at Lord's.
86 .... Derbyshire v Essex at Southend.
86 .... Durham v Gloucestershire at Cheltenham.
88 .... Lancashire v Somerset at Taunton.
97 .... Hampshire v Middlesex at Lord's.
99† .... Derbyshire v Middlesex at Lord's.
99† .... Gloucestershire v Middlesex at Bristol.

   † *One batsman absent/retired hurt.*

Match Aggregates of 1,500 Runs

Runs	Wkts	
1,706	23	.... Hampshire v Warwickshire at Southampton.
1,545	32	.... Northamptonshire v Worcestershire at Northampton.
1,513	30	.... Leicestershire v Lancashire at Leicester.

60 Extras in an Innings

	b	l-b	w	n-b	
86†	10	16	8	52	Somerset (463) v Surrey at The Oval.
72	17	13	0	42	Yorkshire (378) v Pakistan A at Leeds.
71	6	27	2	36	Glamorgan (551-3 dec.) v Warwickshire at Cardiff.
71	1	26	28	16	Nottinghamshire (263) v Lancashire at Manchester.
64	6	6	14	38	Hampshire (549-6 dec.) v Warwickshire at Southampton.
60	16	8	16	20	Hampshire (415-5 dec.) v Oxford University at Oxford.

Under ECB regulations (Test matches excluded), two extras were scored for every no-ball, in addition to any runs scored off that ball, and, for the first time, two extras were also scored for every wide. There were 16 further instances of 50 or more extras in an innings.

† *World record.*

Career Aggregate Milestones

35,000 runs	M. W. Gatting.
25,000 runs	C. W. J. Athey.
20,000 runs	D. C. Boon.
15,000 runs	A. J. Moles, S. R. Waugh.
10,000 runs	M. W. Alleyne, D. Byas, J. P. Crawley, S. P. James, N. J. Lenham, M. Watkinson.
500 wickets	G. D. Rose.
1,000 dismissals	R. C. Russell.

HONOURS' LIST, 1997-98

In 1997-98, the following were decorated for their services to cricket:

Queen's Birthday Honours, 1997: M. A. Atherton (England) OBE, M. C. Cowdrey (England) Life Baron, J. C. Malfait (services to cricket in Northamptonshire) MBE, D. R. Shepherd (Gloucestershire; umpire) MBE.

Queen's Birthday Honours (Australia), 1997: P. J. Burge (Australia; ICC referee) AM, B. N. Jarman (Australia; ICC referee) OAM.

New Year's Honours, 1998: A. R. Gover (England) MBE, C. Griffiths (services to Bridgend Town CC) MBE, A. J. M. Mansell (services to Ealing CC and to youth cricket in Middlesex) MBE, Rt Rev. D. S. Sheppard (England; lately Bishop of Liverpool) Life Baron.

FIRST-CLASS AVERAGES, 1997

BATTING

(Qualification: 8 completed innings)

* Signifies not out.   *† Denotes a left-handed batsman.*

		M	I	NO	R	HS	100s	50s	Avge
1	G. A. Hick (*Worcs*)	18	28	6	1,524	303*	6	4	69.27
2	S. P. James (*Glam*)	18	30	4	1,775	162	7	8	68.26
3	M. P. Maynard (*Glam*)	18	25	7	1,170	161*	3	7	65.00
4	R. T. Ponting (*Australians*)	8	12	3	571	127	2	2	63.44
5	†D. S. Lehmann (*Yorks*)	17	27	2	1,575	182	4	10	63.00
	†N. C. Johnson (*Leics*)	12	18	5	819	150	2	5	63.00
7	†G. P. Thorpe (*Surrey*)	14	23	4	1,160	222	3	6	61.05
8	†M. T. G. Elliott (*Australians*)	12	19	0	1,091	199	4	5	57.42
9	S. G. Law (*Essex*)	17	28	2	1,482	175	5	8	57.00
10	M. R. Ramprakash (*Middx*)	19	30	4	1,453	190	6	7	55.88
11	S. R. Waugh (*Australians*)	13	17	0	924	154	4	4	54.35
12	T. A. Tweats (*Derbys*)	7	13	2	590	189	1	1	53.63
13	†M. L. Hayden (*Hants*)	17	30	3	1,446	235*	4	7	53.55
14	M. A. Ealham (*Kent*)	18	30	10	1,055	139	3	6	52.75
15	†H. Morris (*Glam*)	17	28	4	1,262	233*	4	3	52.58
16	D. A. Leatherdale (*Worcs*)........	17	25	8	886	129	2	5	52.11
17	R. J. Turner (*Somerset*)	17	28	7	1,069	144	1	7	50.90
18	K. J. Barnett (*Derbys*)	15	24	3	1,055	210*	3	5	50.23
19	G. D. Rose (*Somerset*)	18	26	9	852	191	2	3	50.11
20	J. P. Crawley (*Lancs*)............	16	25	2	1,141	133	3	7	49.60
21	†W. P. C. Weston (*Worcs*)	17	29	5	1,190	205	4	3	49.58
22	†N. V. Knight (*Warwicks*)	11	17	3	689	119*	2	3	49.21
23	G. D. Lloyd (*Lancs*).............	16	24	2	1,073	225	4	5	48.77
24	T. M. Moody (*Worcs*)	14	21	1	973	180*	3	4	48.65
25	Salim Elahi (*Pakistan A*)	8	13	0	625	229	1	3	48.07
26	P. J. Prichard (*Essex*)............	17	27	2	1,184	224	3	9	47.36
27	J. H. Kallis (*Middx*)	16	25	3	1,034	172*	4	4	47.00
28	K. M. Curran (*Northants*)	15	26	4	1,032	159	2	6	46.90
29	†R. C. Russell (*Glos*)............	19	29	6	1,049	103*	1	8	45.60
30	†D. Byas (*Yorks*)	20	33	4	1,319	128	3	9	45.48
31	G. W. White (*Hants*)	10	17	2	681	145	1	4	45.40
32	†S. C. Ecclestone (*Somerset*).......	13	23	2	951	133	3	4	45.28
33	A. Fordham (*Northants*)..........	9	17	2	673	85*	0	7	44.86
34	J. J. B. Lewis (*Durham*)	18	32	4	1,252	210*	3	5	44.71
35	B. F. Smith (*Leics*)	13	19	5	624	131*	2	2	44.57
36	V. J. Wells (*Leics*)	18	27	0	1,200	224	3	6	44.44
37	R. J. Warren (*Northants*)	10	17	2	664	174*	1	4	44.26
38	†P. A. Nixon (*Leics*)	19	25	9	708	96	0	4	44.25
39	A. S. Rollins (*Derbys*)	17	29	3	1,142	210	3	6	43.92
40	R. J. Harden (*Somerset*)..........	7	11	2	395	136*	2	1	43.88
41	M. E. Waugh (*Australians*)	13	20	3	746	173	2	3	43.88
42	J. J. Whitaker (*Leics*)	16	23	2	919	133*	3	4	43.76
43	M. Keech (*Hants*)...............	10	16	4	518	127	2	1	43.16
44	R. J. Bailey (*Northants*)..........	17	30	5	1,078	117*	3	5	43.12
45	E. T. Smith (*CU & Kent*)	18	30	3	1,163	190	2	6	43.07
46	D. Ripley (*Northants*)	17	24	6	772	92	0	4	42.88
47	P. Johnson (*Notts*)	16	27	5	942	96*	0	8	42.81
48	A. D. Brown (*Surrey*)	14	21	1	848	170*	3	2	42.40
49	D. C. Boon (*Durham*)	18	30	3	1,144	117	3	8	42.37

		M	I	NO	R	HS	100s	50s	Avge
50	R. A. Smith (*Hants*)	14	23	1	918	154	2	4	41.72
51	D. M. Jones (*Derbys*)	7	12	1	458	99*	0	5	41.63
52	A. J. Stewart (*Surrey*)	15	26	2	994	271*	2	3	41.41
53	T. L. Penney (*Warwicks*)	16	24	5	784	99	0	6	41.26
54	†D. L. Hemp (*Warwicks*)	18	31	4	1,107	138	3	5	41.00
55	A. P. Grayson (*Essex*)	19	28	3	1,022	105	1	6	40.88
56	M. W. Alleyne (*Glos*)	19	30	4	1,059	169	1	8	40.73
57	†I. J. Sutcliffe (*Leics*)	13	20	2	727	130	2	3	40.38
58	G. S. Blewett (*Australians*)	12	18	1	686	125	2	4	40.35
59	†N. H. Fairbrother (*Lancs*)	16	24	2	887	132	2	4	40.31
60	N. J. Astle (*Notts*)	10	16	0	644	100	2	3	40.25
61	†P. R. Pollard (*Notts*)	10	17	5	480	115*	1	1	40.00
62	M. A. Wagh (*OU & Warwicks*)	18	31	2	1,156	125*	4	5	39.86
63	S. A. Marsh (*Kent*)	18	27	6	837	142	1	3	39.85
64	A. Habib (*Leics*)	9	14	4	397	175*	1	1	39.70
65	†D. J. Bicknell (*Surrey*)	9	15	0	594	162	2	1	39.60
66	†I. D. Austin (*Lancs*)	17	25	4	825	95	0	8	39.28
67	M. R. May (*Derbys*)	9	17	2	588	116	2	3	39.20
68	O. A. Shah (*Middx*)	11	16	2	548	104*	1	2	39.14
69 {	M. W. Gatting (*Middx*)	19	29	2	1,053	160*	2	4	39.00
	A. F. Giles (*Warwicks*)	16	20	4	624	97	0	5	39.00
71	N. Hussain (*Essex*)	16	28	0	1,081	207	4	3	38.60
72	N. R. Taylor (*Sussex*)	16	28	1	1,033	127	3	5	38.25
73	R. J. Blakey (*Yorks*)	18	24	6	680	92	0	6	37.77
74	A. Dale (*Glam*)	19	27	4	860	142*	2	5	37.39
75	A. P. Wells (*Kent*)	18	31	1	1,120	109	1	9	37.33
76	A. J. Hollioake (*Surrey*)	16	25	1	891	182	1	6	37.12
77	T. S. Curtis (*Worcs*)	13	21	1	742	160	4	1	37.10
78	D. P. Fulton (*Kent*)	16	29	3	953	110	1	4	36.65
79	†S. Young (*Glos & Australians*)	19	31	4	985	237	2	5	36.48
80	K. A. Parsons (*Somerset*)	10	15	3	437	74	0	3	36.41
81	R. O. Jones (*CU*)	8	11	2	325	60	0	3	36.11
82	D. L. Maddy (*Leics*)	19	30	1	1,047	103	3	5	36.10
83	G. R. Haynes (*Worcs*)	17	25	3	794	70	0	6	36.09
84	†N. T. Wood (*Lancs*)	10	15	2	469	155	1	2	36.07
85	C. W. J. Athey (*Sussex*)	12	21	2	682	138*	1	5	35.89
86	†M. A. Taylor (*Australians*)	12	19	0	680	129	2	4	35.78
87	†M. G. Bevan (*Australians*)	11	16	3	463	104*	1	3	35.61
88	V. P. Clarke (*Derbys*)	19	30	6	847	99	0	5	35.29
89	K. R. Spiring (*Worcs*)	17	28	3	876	150	1	4	35.04
90	D. D. J. Robinson (*Essex*)	14	22	1	735	148	2	3	35.00
91	Hasan Raza (*Pakistan A*)	6	10	0	349	96	0	4	34.90
92	J. E. Morris (*Durham*)	17	30	1	1,009	149	2	4	34.79
93	A. McGrath (*Yorks*)	15	25	1	832	141	2	3	34.66
94	†D. J. Millns (*Leics*)	15	15	2	449	121	2	1	34.53
95	R. C. Irani (*Essex*)	16	24	1	793	123*	3	3	34.47
96	S. J. Rhodes (*Worcs*)	18	23	6	584	78	0	4	34.35
97	M. B. Loye (*Northants*)	8	15	3	412	86	0	2	34.33
98	†M. P. Dowman (*Notts*)	19	33	1	1,091	149	3	5	34.09
99	J. P. Stephenson (*Hants*)	17	26	3	784	140	2	1	34.08
100	T. R. Ward (*Kent*)	18	32	2	1,018	161*	1	8	33.93
101	I. A. Healy (*Australians*)	12	16	4	407	63	0	1	33.91
102	N. M. K. Smith (*Warwicks*)	15	22	3	642	148	1	3	33.78
103	R. R. Montgomerie (*Northants*)	10	18	3	504	73	0	4	33.60
104	M. P. Vaughan (*Yorks*)	15	27	2	839	161	3	2	33.56
105	A. J. Moles (*Warwicks*)	12	22	3	635	168	1	2	33.42
106	G. P. Butcher (*Glam*)	11	11	2	296	101*	1	1	32.88
107	M. A. Atherton (*Lancs*)	16	28	2	853	149	2	5	32.80
108	M. D. Moxon (*Yorks*)	12	18	0	589	155	1	3	32.72
109	J. S. Laney (*Hants*)	15	27	1	848	95	0	6	32.61

		M	I	NO	R	HS	100s	50s	Avge
110	R. T. Robinson (*Notts*)	17	29	4	812	143*	1	5	32.48
111	†M. A. Butcher (*Surrey*)	19	34	1	1,068	153	1	7	32.36
112	B. Parker (*Yorks*)	19	30	5	806	138*	1	4	32.24
113	C. J. Adams (*Derbys*)	15	25	1	767	108	2	3	31.95
114	J. D. Ratcliffe (*Surrey*)	15	26	2	759	135	1	4	31.62
115	Azhar Mahmood (*Pakistan A*)	8	13	1	379	92	0	3	31.58
116	T. H. C. Hancock (*Glos*)	19	31	3	854	100*	1	5	30.50
117	A. Flintoff (*Lancs*)	5	8	0	243	117	1	1	30.37
118	†P. C. L. Holloway (*Somerset*)	19	34	4	905	106	1	5	30.16
119	K. R. Brown (*Middx*)	19	29	9	601	144*	1	2	30.05
120	J. E. R. Gallian (*Lancs*)	11	19	2	506	106	1	3	29.76
121	D. J. Roberts (*Northants*)	7	13	0	385	117	1	0	29.61
122	G. R. Cowdrey (*Kent*)	9	15	0	442	101	1	1	29.46
123	M. V. Fleming (*Kent*)	18	31	4	790	138	1	4	29.25
124	C. White (*Yorks*)	17	24	2	639	172*	1	2	29.04
125	M. Watkinson (*Lancs*)	12	19	1	520	135	1	2	28.88
126	S. D. Udal (*Hants*)	18	24	3	600	117*	1	4	28.57
127	K. Newell (*Sussex*)	17	31	2	827	112	2	3	28.51
128	V. S. Solanki (*Worcs*)	14	18	1	478	128*	1	2	28.11
129	P. A. Cottey (*Glam*)	17	21	4	475	83	0	2	27.94
130	Ali Naqvi (*Pakistan A*)	8	13	0	362	114	1	1	27.84
131	S. R. Lampitt (*Worcs*)	15	17	7	277	52	0	1	27.70
132	M. N. Lathwell (*Somerset*)	20	34	1	912	95	0	6	27.63
133	†K. D. James (*Hants*)	10	15	2	359	85	0	5	27.61
134	D. J. Sales (*Northants*)	14	21	1	548	103	1	2	27.40
135	A. Singh (*CU & Warwicks*)	10	14	1	355	134	1	1	27.30
136	G. E. Welton (*Notts*)	6	11	0	295	95	0	1	26.81
137	†U. Afzaal (*Notts*)	17	29	2	720	80	0	5	26.66
	Rana Qayyum (*Pakistan A*)	8	13	1	320	97	0	2	26.66
139	P. D. Bowler (*Somerset*)	16	26	1	666	123	1	5	26.64
140	B. C. Hollioake (*Surrey*)	14	22	1	559	76	0	3	26.61
141	C. M. Tolley (*Notts*)	12	22	4	479	73*	0	3	26.61
142	P. D. Collingwood (*Durham*)	8	13	1	316	107	1	1	26.33
143	†A. L. Penberthy (*Northants*)	13	19	0	499	96	0	3	26.26
144	P. G. Morgan (*OU*)	10	18	1	444	63	0	2	26.11
145	R. D. B. Croft (*Glam*)	18	26	1	652	86	0	4	26.08
146	Mohammad Wasim (*Pakistan A*)	9	15	0	390	155	1	1	26.00
147	M. A. Lynch (*Glos*)	12	19	1	465	64	0	3	25.83
148	W. M. Noon (*Notts*)	18	25	4	542	83	0	3	25.80
149	T. C. Walton (*Northants*)	7	10	1	231	60	0	2	25.66
150	M. Burns (*Somerset*)	14	21	1	510	82	0	4	25.50
151	†W. J. House (*CU & Kent*)	10	14	1	331	94	0	2	25.46
152	W. K. Hegg (*Lancs*)	17	23	5	456	77*	0	5	25.33
153	Javed Qadir (*Pakistan A*)	9	15	4	277	61	0	2	25.18
154	R. J. Rollins (*Essex*)	13	19	1	452	82	0	4	25.11
155	J. M. M. Averis (*OU & Glos*)	10	15	4	276	42	0	0	25.09
156	B. J. Phillips (*Kent*)	13	19	4	376	100*	1	1	25.06
157	†M. T. E. Peirce (*Sussex*)	12	23	0	576	104	1	3	25.04
158	†C. Patel (*OU & Hants*)	12	22	5	420	63*	0	3	24.70
159	M. G. N. Windows (*Glos*)	8	15	0	369	84	0	2	24.60
160	P. A. Strang (*Kent*)	17	26	2	590	82	0	5	24.58
161	M. C. J. Ball (*Glos*)	18	27	3	587	50	0	1	24.45
162	J. Ratledge (*CU*)	8	12	1	268	100*	1	0	24.36
163	A. D. Shaw (*Glam*)	18	21	5	389	53*	0	1	24.31
164	W. S. Kendall (*Hants*)	12	19	2	413	76	0	1	24.29
165	K. M. Krikken (*Derbys*)	19	27	4	558	72	0	3	24.26
166	N. J. Lenham (*Sussex*)	7	12	0	290	93	0	2	24.16
167	D. R. Brown (*Warwicks*)	17	24	3	504	79	0	4	24.00
	D. G. Cork (*Derbys*)	6	9	1	192	55*	0	2	24.00
169	M. J. Foster (*Durham*)	14	24	0	575	129	1	3	23.95

		M	I	NO	R	HS	100s	50s	Avge
170	A. A. Metcalfe (*Notts*)	9	12	1	262	79	0	2	23.81
171	†J. A. G. Fulton (*OU*)	10	19	0	451	78	0	4	23.73
172	G. Chapple (*Lancs*)	11	14	4	237	66	0	2	23.70
173	N. J. Speak (*Durham*)	12	21	3	426	124*	1	1	23.66
174	J. N. Snape (*Northants*)	11	16	3	306	66	0	3	23.53
175	R. I. Dawson (*Glos*)	8	14	0	329	100	1	1	23.50
176	P. W. Jarvis (*Sussex*)	11	18	2	374	64	0	4	23.37
177	A. N. Aymes (*Hants*)	18	23	4	442	96*	0	1	23.26
178	G. A. Gooch (*Essex*)	10	17	1	369	56	0	2	23.06
179	†J. C. Pooley (*Middx*)	18	28	1	619	98	0	3	22.92
180	M. P. Speight (*Durham*)	17	28	3	573	73*	0	3	22.92
181	C. C. Lewis (*Surrey*)	13	19	2	389	76	0	1	22.88
182	G. Welch (*Warwicks*)	18	26	6	455	75	0	2	22.75
183	M. Newell (*Sussex*)	12	22	1	471	100	1	3	22.42
184	S. J. Renshaw (*Hants*)	13	19	7	269	56	0	1	22.41
185	A. P. Cowan (*Essex*)	16	26	6	447	77	0	1	22.35
186	Farhan Adil (*Pakistan A*)	5	9	0	198	50	0	1	22.00
187	A. J. Wright (*Glos*)	13	22	3	416	79	0	1	21.89
188	†Q. J. Hughes (*CU*)	8	12	3	197	47*	0	0	21.88
189	†M. E. Trescothick (*Somerset*)	13	19	1	390	83*	0	4	21.66
190	†P. J. Franks (*Notts*)	14	19	6	280	50	0	1	21.53
191	{†S. D. Thomas (*Glam*)	18	19	5	301	75*	0	1	21.50
	{†S. Hutton (*Durham*)	7	13	1	258	95	0	1	21.50
193	C. E. W. Silverwood (*Yorks*)	18	23	6	365	58	0	1	21.47
194	P. Moores (*Sussex*)	17	31	4	571	102*	1	2	21.14
195	A. P. Scrini (*OU*)	11	18	6	253	58*	0	1	21.08
196	P. A. J. DeFreitas (*Derbys*)	19	24	1	484	96	0	2	21.04
197	R. J. Cunliffe (*Glos*)	9	14	1	273	61	0	1	21.00
198	M. P. Bicknell (*Surrey*)	15	20	5	305	74	0	2	20.33
199	N. J. Trainor (*Glos*)	14	25	1	484	121	1	1	20.16
200	S. P. Titchard (*Lancs*)	6	9	0	180	79	0	1	20.00
201	D. P. Ostler (*Warwicks*)	15	22	1	419	65	0	3	19.95
202	M. J. Slater (*Australians*)	5	8	0	159	47	0	0	19.87
203	R. K. Rao (*Sussex*)	11	20	1	375	89	0	3	19.73
204	†M. J. Walker (*Kent*)	10	19	0	369	62	0	2	19.42
205	G. Yates (*Lancs*)	11	13	3	194	39	0	0	19.40
206	†M. C. Ilott (*Essex*)	13	20	5	290	47	0	0	19.33
207	G. F. Archer (*Notts*)	12	22	2	375	81	0	2	18.75
208	P. J. Martin (*Lancs*)	17	19	4	281	78*	0	1	18.73
209	S. K. Warne (*Australians*)	12	17	1	293	53	0	1	18.31
210	†P. N. Weekes (*Middx*)	15	24	0	439	101	1	0	18.29
211	†N. J. Llong (*Kent*)	8	14	0	256	99	0	2	18.28
212	{†C. G. R. Lightfoot (*OU*)	9	16	0	289	61	0	1	18.06
	{Waqar Younis (*Glam*)	16	17	1	289	47	0	0	18.06
214	N. Shahid (*Surrey*)	7	11	0	198	34	0	0	18.00
215	A. R. Caddick (*Somerset*)	18	22	4	321	56*	0	1	17.83
216	K. Greenfield (*Sussex*)	11	21	0	372	108	1	0	17.71
217	B. W. Byrne (*OU*)	11	20	0	354	49	0	0	17.70
218	T. Frost (*Warwicks*)	9	11	2	158	56	0	1	17.55
219	J. Lewis (*Glos*)	15	19	8	193	30	0	0	17.54
220	M. J. McCague (*Kent*)	11	17	6	190	53*	0	1	17.27
221	†G. M. Hamilton (*Yorks*)	11	16	2	240	49	0	0	17.14
222	R. M. S. Weston (*Durham*)	5	8	0	137	36	0	0	17.12
223	D. R. Law (*Essex*)	19	29	0	492	81	0	2	16.96
224	J. E. Benjamin (*Surrey*)	11	15	6	152	35	0	0	16.88
225	L. G. Buchanan (*OU*)	8	14	4	168	43*	0	0	16.80
226	A. R. K. Pierson (*Leics*)	16	16	0	266	59	0	1	16.62
227	†J. P. Hewitt (*Middx*)	18	21	4	264	75	0	1	15.52
228	Mujahid Jamshed (*Pakistan A*)	9	15	0	230	59	0	1	15.33
229	A. A. Khan (*Sussex*)	15	24	5	291	52	0	1	15.31

		M	I	NO	R	HS	100s	50s	Avge
230	J. Boiling (*Durham*)	17	26	4	334	62	0	1	15.18
231	A. R. C. Fraser (*Middx*)	19	23	6	244	35	0	0	14.35
232	P. S. Jones (*CU & Somerset*)	10	13	3	142	36	0	0	14.20
233	R. L. Johnson (*Middx*)	18	24	1	320	39	0	0	13.91
234	K. J. Piper (*Warwicks*)	8	11	3	111	34*	0	0	13.87
235	D. W. Headley (*Kent*)	12	17	5	166	40	0	0	13.83
236	S. A. J. Boswell (*Northants*)	9	12	3	122	35	0	0	13.55
237	D. Gough (*Yorks*)	12	16	1	196	58	0	1	13.06
238 {	V. C. Drakes (*Sussex*)	10	18	1	221	48	0	0	13.00
	†A. C. Morris (*Yorks*)	7	9	0	117	37	0	0	13.00
240	†J. P. Taylor (*Northants*)	16	21	4	216	36	0	0	12.70
241	Mushtaq Ahmed (*Somerset*)	14	16	2	174	33	0	0	12.42
242	K. P. Evans (*Notts*)	15	18	1	208	47	0	0	12.23
243	P. J. Hartley (*Yorks*)	9	10	0	121	39	0	0	12.10
244	M. M. Betts (*Durham*)	13	19	1	207	35	0	0	11.50
245	R. P. Davis (*Glos*)	9	12	0	135	39	0	0	11.25
246	R. D. Hudson (*OU*)	11	20	2	202	62	0	1	11.22
247	M. N. Bowen (*Notts*)	15	19	6	145	32	0	0	11.15
248	R. D. Stemp (*Yorks*)	17	20	6	154	33*	0	0	11.00
249	S. L. Watkin (*Glam*)	17	16	3	138	39	0	0	10.61
250	I. D. K. Salisbury (*Surrey*)	13	17	2	159	30*	0	0	10.60
251	A. Sheriyar (*Worcs*)	18	13	4	94	21	0	0	10.44
252	B. J. Hyam (*Essex*)	7	10	2	79	26	0	0	9.87
253	A. M. Smith (*Glos*)	18	26	9	165	41*	0	0	9.70
254	Mohammad Akram (*Northants*)	11	14	2	116	28	0	0	9.66
255	A. J. Harris (*Derbys*)	18	24	4	171	36	0	0	8.55
256	A. D. Edwards (*Sussex*)	6	10	2	66	20	0	0	8.25
257	†A. Walker (*Durham*)	12	20	8	92	16	0	0	7.66
258	M. A. Robinson (*Sussex*)	17	25	9	114	27	0	0	7.12
259	J. Ormond (*Leics*)	13	12	2	69	35	0	0	6.90
260	P. C. R. Tufnell (*Middx*)	17	21	6	101	21	0	0	6.73
261	Ali Hussain Rizvi (*Pakistan A*)	8	13	1	77	28	0	0	6.41
262	K. J. Shine (*Somerset*)	18	20	5	96	18	0	0	6.40
263	S. J. E. Brown (*Durham*)	17	24	5	121	30	0	0	6.36
264	D. E. Malcolm (*Derbys*)	19	24	9	92	21*	0	0	6.13
265	P. M. Such (*Essex*)	21	22	11	63	14	0	0	5.72
266	R. J. Kirtley (*Sussex*)	11	16	7	49	15*	0	0	5.44

BOWLING

(Qualification: 10 wickets in 10 innings)

† *Denotes a left-arm bowler.*

		O	M	R	W	BB	5W/i	Avge
1	A. A. Donald (*Warwicks*)	387.5	123	938	60	6-55	3	15.63
2	†A. M. Smith (*Glos*)	512.2	125	1,464	83	6-45	5	17.63
3	P. R. Reiffel (*Australians*)	188.4	49	520	28	5-49	2	18.57
4	†K. D. James (*Hants*)	161.1	37	504	27	8-49	2	18.66
5	Saqlain Mushtaq (*Surrey*)	254.5	75	617	32	5-17	4	19.28
6	D. R. Brown (*Warwicks*)	522.3	135	1,569	81	8-89	4	19.37
7	B. J. Phillips (*Kent*)	282.1	73	877	44	5-47	2	19.93
8	†P. M. Hutchison (*Yorks*)	233.1	56	741	37	7-38	3	20.02
9	S. K. Warne (*Australians*)	433.4	112	1,154	57	7-103	4	20.24
10	J. H. Kallis (*Middx*)	234.3	61	655	32	5-54	1	20.46
11	G. D. McGrath (*Australians*)	363.4	104	1,012	49	8-38	2	20.65
12	Azhar Mahmood (*Pakistan A*)	290.5	66	829	40	5-66	1	20.72

		O	M	R	W	BB	5Wi	Avge
13	†P. C. R. Tufnell (*Middx*)	561.5	174	1,205	55	7-66	3	21.90
14	†M. C. Ilott (*Essex*)	332	91	946	43	7-59	1	22.00
15	M. M. Betts (*Durham*)	329	77	1,085	49	9-64	3	22.14
16	Waqar Younis (*Glam*)	441.4	83	1,551	68	8-17	3	22.80
17	S. L. Watkin (*Glam*)	508.2	143	1,393	61	7-41	2	22.83
18	A. D. Edwards (*Sussex*)	103.2	19	389	17	5-34	1	22.88
19	P. J. Hartley (*Yorks*)	170	39	532	23	5-34	1	23.13
20	P. J. Martin (*Lancs*)	474.2	136	1,342	58	8-32	3	23.13
21	J. P. Hewitt (*Middx*)	437	96	1,389	60	6-14	2	23.15
22	P. J. Newport (*Worcs*)	177.2	56	444	19	7-37	1	23.36
23	M. J. McCague (*Kent*)	312.4	55	1,125	48	7-50	4	23.43
24	D. E. Malcolm (*Derbys*)	526.1	81	1,761	75	6-23	5	23.48
25	J. N. Gillespie (*Australians*)	198.4	43	692	29	7-37	2	23.86
26	N. J. Astle (*Notts*)	209	44	525	22	5-46	1	23.86
27	G. D. Rose (*Somerset*)	488.5	124	1,563	63	5-53	1	24.80
28	G. Welch (*Warwicks*)	540.5	151	1,625	65	6-115	3	25.00
29	†A. Sheriyar (*Worcs*)	446.1	94	1,575	62	6-19	3	25.40
30	A. P. Cowan (*Essex*)	420	106	1,334	52	5-45	3	25.65
31	M. S. Kasprowicz (*Australians*)	267.2	50	1,010	39	7-36	1	25.89
32	J. Lewis (*Glos*)	418.5	98	1,401	54	6-50	3	25.94
33	M. W. Alleyne (*Glos*)	360.1	89	1,148	44	6-64	3	26.09
34	A. R. Oram (*Notts*)	226.4	55	684	26	4-53	0	26.30
35	P. M. Such (*Essex*)	725.1	219	1,739	66	6-55	6	26.34
36	C. E. W. Silverwood (*Yorks*)	478.4	108	1,531	58	7-93	4	26.39
37	J. Ormond (*Leics*)	345.3	72	1,162	44	6-54	3	26.40
38	A. R. Caddick (*Somerset*)	702.4	139	2,156	81	6-65	6	26.61
39	M. P. Bicknell (*Surrey*)	385.2	94	1,174	44	5-34	1	26.68
40	D. Gough (*Yorks*)	334.4	70	1,149	43	5-56	3	26.72
41	P. A. J. DeFreitas (*Derbys*)	574.1	132	1,810	67	7-64	5	27.01
42	I. D. Austin (*Lancs*)	448.4	130	1,218	45	4-44	0	27.06
43	S. D. Thomas (*Glam*)	405.3	58	1,444	53	5-24	3	27.24
44	D. J. Millns (*Leics*)	408.4	87	1,341	49	6-61	2	27.36
45	R. D. B. Croft (*Glam*)	666.1	159	1,698	62	5-33	1	27.38
46	J. J. Bates (*Sussex*)	227.2	71	525	19	5-89	1	27.63
47	†S. J. E. Brown (*Durham*)	590.3	126	1,855	67	5-58	4	27.68
48	Mushtaq Ahmed (*Somerset*)	513	146	1,407	50	6-70	3	28.14
49	G. R. Haynes (*Worcs*)	287.1	68	875	31	3-46	0	28.22
50	†J. P. Taylor (*Northants*)	455.4	81	1,532	54	7-87	3	28.37
51	K. P. Evans (*Notts*)	457.5	103	1,277	45	6-40	2	28.37
52	D. A. Leatherdale (*Worcs*)	219.3	46	742	26	5-56	1	28.53
53	R. L. Johnson (*Middx*)	429.2	80	1,429	50	4-26	0	28.58
54	J. B. D. Thompson (*Kent*)	223.2	30	890	31	5-89	1	28.70
55	†C. M. Tolley (*Notts*)	363	87	1,005	35	6-61	1	28.71
56	†K. J. Dean (*Derbys*)	234.4	47	811	28	4-39	0	28.96
57	†M. K. Davies (*Northants*)	234.2	71	674	23	5-46	1	29.30
58	C. C. Lewis (*Surrey*)	291.4	66	970	33	5-42	1	29.39
59	M. A. Robinson (*Sussex*)	448.2	87	1,426	48	6-78	2	29.70
60	K. M. Curran (*Northants*)	215.2	57	715	24	4-32	0	29.79
61	Shoaib Akhtar (*Pakistan A*)	194.3	29	747	25	5-62	2	29.88
62	A. P. Igglesden (*Kent*)	152	23	538	18	4-67	0	29.88
63	C. White (*Yorks*)	353.4	58	1,236	41	5-31	3	30.14
64	K. J. Shine (*Somerset*)	443.3	89	1,678	55	7-43	3	30.50
65	A. J. Hollioake (*Surrey*)	132.4	23	458	15	4-22	0	30.53
66	P. A. Strang (*Kent*)	733.1	211	1,929	63	7-118	4	30.61
67	D. W. Headley (*Kent*)	425.2	75	1,419	46	5-92	1	30.84
68	M. V. Fleming (*Kent*)	398.2	97	1,145	37	5-51	2	30.94
69	M. A. Ealham (*Kent*)	407.4	80	1,238	40	4-47	0	30.95
70	A. R. C. Fraser (*Middx*)	571.5	155	1,460	47	6-77	2	31.06
71	I. D. K. Salisbury (*Surrey*)	314.1	65	936	30	6-19	2	31.20
72	D. R. Law (*Essex*)	270.3	51	969	31	5-93	1	31.25

		O	M	R	W	BB	5Wi	Avge
73	P. S. Jones (*CU & Somerset*)	207.5	37	739	23	6-67	1	32.13
74	A. Walker (*Durham*)	341.1	87	1,063	33	7-56	2	32.21
75	†A. F. Giles (*Warwicks*)	506.1	155	1,225	38	4-54	0	32.23
76	J. F. Brown (*Northants*)	203.4	39	651	20	4-50	0	32.55
77	M. M. Mirza (*Worcs*)	152.4	25	620	19	4-51	0	32.63
78	Abdur Razzaq (*Pakistan A*)	187.2	29	753	23	5-106	1	32.73
79	†R. D. Stemp (*Yorks*)	473	111	1,379	42	6-77	1	32.83
80	G. Yates (*Lancs*)	302.4	57	963	29	5-59	1	33.20
81	G. Chapple (*Lancs*)	275.5	45	900	27	4-80	0	33.33
82	G. M. Hamilton (*Yorks*)	241	53	907	27	5-89	1	33.59
83	V. C. Drakes (*Sussex*)	300	63	1,043	31	4-55	0	33.64
84	†G. Keedy (*Lancs*)	292.4	60	917	27	6-79	1	33.96
85	M. N. Bowen (*Notts*)	467.2	107	1,394	41	7-75	3	34.00
	B. C. Hollioake (*Surrey*)	214.2	42	782	23	4-54	0	34.00
87	M. J. Foster (*Durham*)	275.4	55	1,027	30	4-58	0	34.23
88	Ali Hussain Rizvi (*Pakistan A*)	306	70	822	24	5-68	1	34.25
89	S. Young (*Glos & Australians*)	396.3	111	1,104	32	4-26	0	34.50
90	S. J. Renshaw (*Hants*)	356.3	62	1,278	37	5-110	1	34.54
91	†A. D. Mullally (*Leics*)	383.1	89	1,302	37	5-52	4	35.18
92	R. J. Kirtley (*Sussex*)	276.3	48	1,094	31	6-60	1	35.29
93	A. J. Tudor (*Surrey*)	160.3	27	607	17	6-101	1	35.70
	†R. P. Davis (*Glos*)	241	76	607	17	4-35	0	35.70
95	†A. P. Grayson (*Essex*)	394.5	112	1,009	28	4-53	0	36.03
96	P. W. Jarvis (*Sussex*)	318.5	46	1,091	30	5-44	2	36.36
97	R. J. Bailey (*Northants*)	112.3	19	367	10	4-10	0	36.70
98	S. R. Lampitt (*Worcs*)	334.4	70	1,302	35	5-39	1	37.20
99	Mohammad Akram (*Northants*)	287	43	1,135	30	5-72	2	37.83
	P. Aldred (*Derbys*)	181	52	454	12	3-28	0	37.83
101	†D. A. Cosker (*Glam*)	375.2	92	1,100	29	4-64	0	37.93
102	G. J. Parsons (*Leics*)	182.2	48	500	13	4-22	0	38.46
103	P. J. Franks (*Notts*)	372.4	63	1,158	30	4-47	0	38.60
104	R. C. Irani (*Essex*)	261.5	73	695	18	3-51	0	38.61
105	G. P. Butcher (*Glam*)	114.1	21	466	12	3-87	0	38.83
106	A. R. K. Pierson (*Leics*)	499.1	104	1,478	38	6-56	1	38.89
107	J. N. B. Bovill (*Hants*)	233.4	37	902	23	4-62	0	39.21
108	V. J. Wells (*Leics*)	204	47	671	17	2-8	0	39.47
109	K. Newell (*Sussex*)	138.1	35	436	11	4-61	0	39.63
110	J. P. Stephenson (*Hants*)	428.5	68	1,480	37	6-54	1	40.00
111	M. Watkinson (*Lancs*)	231.4	41	805	20	3-35	0	40.25
112	N. M. K. Smith (*Warwicks*)	318.2	77	930	23	4-32	0	40.43
113	†M. T. Brimson (*Leics*)	170.5	48	451	11	3-49	0	41.00
114	D. J. Shadford (*Lancs*)	149	8	786	19	5-80	1	41.36
115	A. A. Khan (*Sussex*)	444.3	100	1,397	33	5-137	1	42.33
116	T. M. Moody (*Worcs*)	213.4	42	829	19	5-148	1	43.63
117	M. C. J. Ball (*Glos*)	479.2	129	1,271	29	5-66	1	43.82
118	J. Boiling (*Durham*)	336	98	925	21	3-21	0	44.04
119	J. N. Snape (*Northants*)	253.1	60	724	15	4-46	0	48.26
120	A. J. Harris (*Derbys*)	481.3	98	1,694	35	3-66	0	48.40
121	C. Patel (*OU & Hants*)	327	51	1,326	27	6-110	1	49.11
122	†U. Afzaal (*Notts*)	199.1	40	689	14	3-79	0	49.21
123	S. M. Milburn (*Hants*)	332	56	1,127	22	4-38	0	51.22
124	S. A. J. Boswell (*Northants*)	185.5	26	769	15	5-94	1	51.26
125	R. T. Bates (*Notts*)	225.4	51	576	11	3-89	0	52.36
126	S. D. Udal (*Hants*)	627.1	153	1,810	34	4-17	0	53.23
127	†M. G. Bevan (*Australians*)	152.4	23	606	11	3-73	0	55.09
128	J. W. O. Freeth (*CU*)	149	16	609	11	4-101	0	55.36
129	C. M. Battarbee (*OU*)	150.4	21	627	11	2-56	0	57.00
130	†E. J. How (*CU*)	193.4	41	685	12	5-59	1	57.08
131	J. E. Benjamin (*Surrey*)	211	39	759	13	3-52	0	58.38
132	V. P. Clarke (*Derbys*)	223.5	48	835	13	3-47	0	64.23
133	J. M. M. Averis (*OU & Glos*)	272.3	40	1,104	16	5-98	1	69.00

The following bowlers took ten wickets but bowled in fewer than ten innings:

	O	M	R	W	BB	5W/i	Avge
H. A. G. Anthony (*MCC*)	42	11	113	10	6-34	1	11.30
T. F. Bloomfield (*Middx*)	85	17	258	13	5-77	1	19.84
†R. K. Illingworth (*Worcs*)	206	75	442	18	7-79	1	24.55
N. F. Williams (*Essex*)	101	16	336	13	5-55	1	25.84
†J. E. Hindson (*Notts*)	96.4	24	287	11	4-28	0	26.09
Shoaib Malik (*Pakistan A*)	123	24	333	12	3-49	0	27.75
S. Herzberg (*Somerset*)	102	25	281	10	3-100	0	28.10
C. A. Connor (*Hants*)	122.5	18	430	13	7-46	1	33.07
R. J. Chapman (*Worcs*)	103.3	18	468	13	3-26	0	36.00
J. I. D. Kerr (*Somerset*)	103	20	374	10	4-83	0	37.40
D. G. Cork (*Derbys*)	132	28	457	11	4-48	0	41.54
J. Wood (*Durham*)	112	14	541	11	4-73	0	49.18

FIELDING IN 1997

(Qualification: 20 dismissals)

63	S. A. Marsh (61 ct, 2 st)	30	T. R. Ward
61	P. A. Nixon (57 ct, 4 st)	29	T. Frost (27 ct, 2 st)
57	R. C. Russell (52 ct, 5 st)	29	D. P. Ostler
55	K. M. Krikken (53 ct, 2 st)	28	†M. A. Butcher
54	A. D. Shaw (52 ct, 2 st)	27	Javed Qadir (26 ct, 1 st)
54	M. P. Speight	26	R. J. Rollins (24 ct, 2 st)
53	R. J. Blakey (49 ct, 4 st)	25	K. J. Piper (24 ct, 1 st)
53	R. J. Turner (51 ct, 2 st)	24	M. C. J. Ball
50	K. R. Brown (47 ct, 3 st)	24	D. Byas
47	S. J. Rhodes (44 ct, 3 st)	23	D. P. Fulton
43	I. A. Healy (39 ct, 4 st)	23	†M. W. Gatting
42	A. N. Aymes (35 ct, 7 st)	21	M. P. Maynard
39	W. K. Hegg (37 ct, 2 st)	21	J. C. Pooley
39	A. J. Stewart	20	P. D. Bowler
38	W. M. Noon (34 ct, 4 st)	20	A. P. Grayson
36	P. Moores	20	G. A. Hick
36	D. Ripley (29 ct, 7 st)		

† *M. A. Butcher took two catches as wicket-keeper and M. W. Gatting took four.*

INDIVIDUAL SCORES OF 100 AND OVER

There were 263 three-figure innings in 196 first-class matches in 1997, 72 fewer than in 1996 when 204 matches were played. Of these, 17 were double-hundreds, compared with 24 in 1996. The list includes 196 hundreds hit in the County Championship, compared with 247 in 1996.

Signifies not out.

S. P. James (7)
109	Glam v Yorks, Leeds
153	Glam v Durham, Cardiff
152*	Glam v Lancs, Liverpool
162	Glam v Notts, Colwyn Bay
130	Glam v Worcs, Worcester
103 103 113	Glam v Northants, Abergavenny

G. A. Hick (6)
164*	Worcs v Oxford U., Oxford
137	Worcs v Glos, Bristol
144	Worcs v Pakistan A, Worcester
107*	Worcs v Essex, Chelmsford
122	Worcs v Warwicks, Birmingham
303*	Worcs v Hants, Southampton

M. R. Ramprakash (6)
108*	The Rest v England A, Birmingham
145	Middx v Sussex, Lord's
111	Middx v Northants, Lord's
113*	Middx v Kent, Lord's
190	Middx v Hants, Lord's
123*	Middx v Worcs, Kidderminster

S. G. Law (5)
118*	Essex v Durham, Chelmsford
157	Essex v Derbys, Southend
175	Essex v Leics, Colchester
115	Essex v Notts, Worksop
155	Essex v Lancs, Manchester

T. S. Curtis (4)
113	Worcs v Notts, Nottingham
101	Worcs v Somerset, Worcester
137	Worcs v Glos, Bristol
160	Worcs v Glam, Worcester

M. T. G. Elliott (4)
124	Australians v Glos, Bristol
127	Australians v Notts, Nottingham
112	Australia v England, Lord's
199	Australia v England, Leeds

M. L. Hayden (4)
235* 119	Hants v Warwicks, Southampton
136*	Hants v Derbys, Chesterfield
150	Hants v Northants, Northampton

N. Hussain (4)
207	England v Australia, Birmingham
105	England v Australia, Leeds
128	Essex v Leics, Colchester
104	Essex v Middx, Chelmsford

J. H. Kallis (4)
121	Middx v Northants, Lord's
102*	Middx v Hants, Lord's
172*	Middx v Worcs, Kidderminster
100	Middx v Somerset, Taunton

D. S. Lehmann (4)
177	Yorks v Somerset, Taunton
100	Yorks v Surrey, The Oval
163*	Yorks v Leics, Leicester
182	Yorks v Hants, Portsmouth

G. D. Lloyd (4)
225	Lancs v Yorks, Leeds
102	Lancs v Durham, Manchester
100*	Lancs v Leics, Leicester
122	Lancs v Kent, Manchester

H. Morris (4)
233*	Glam v Warwicks, Cardiff
135	Glam v Durham, Cardiff
173	Glam v Glos, Swansea
165	Glam v Somerset, Taunton

M. A. Wagh (4)
116 101	Oxford U. v Glam, Oxford
125*	Oxford U. v Somerset, Taunton
124	Warwicks v Durham, Chester-le-Street

S. R. Waugh (4)
115	Australians v Notts, Nottingham
108 116	Australia v England, Manchester
154	Australians v Kent, Canterbury

W. P. C. Weston (4)
119	Worcs v Oxford U., Oxford
205	Worcs v Northants, Northampton
114	Worcs v Glam, Worcester
188	Worcs v Derbys, Worcester

R. J. Bailey (3)
105   Northants v Cambridge U., Cambridge
117*   Northants v Notts, Northampton
115   Northants v Worcs, Northampton

K. J. Barnett (3)
101   Derbys v Hants, Chesterfield
147*   Derbys v Leics, Leicester
210*   Derbys v Yorks, Derby

D. C. Boon (3)
105*   Durham v Cambridge U., Cambridge
110   Durham v Middx, Chester-le-Street
117   Durham v Northants, Northampton

A. D. Brown (3)
109   Surrey v Essex, The Oval
121   Surrey v Worcs, Worcester
170*   Surrey v Northants, Northampton

D. Byas (3)
126*   Yorks v Oxford U., Oxford
103*   Yorks v Somerset, Taunton
128   Yorks v Notts, Nottingham

J. P. Crawley (3)
101   Lancs v Notts, Manchester
112   Lancs v Sussex, Manchester
133   Lancs v Derbys, Derby

M. P. Dowman (3)
111   Notts v Northants, Northampton
149   Notts v Leics, Leicester
124   Notts v Somerset, Nottingham

M. A. Ealham (3)
122   Kent v Notts, Nottingham
139   Kent v Leics, Canterbury
105   Kent v Somerset, Taunton

S. C. Ecclestone (3)
133   Somerset v Oxford U., Taunton
102   Somerset v Pakistan A, Taunton
123   Somerset v Kent, Taunton

D. L. Hemp (3)
138 } Warwicks v Hants, Southampton
114*
117   Warwicks v Kent, Tunbridge Wells

R. C. Irani (3)
123*   Essex v Hants, Chelmsford
100   Essex v Yorks, Ilford
110   Essex v Sussex, Hove

J. J. B. Lewis (3)
210*   Durham v Oxford U., Oxford
158*   Durham v Kent, Darlington
160*   Durham v Derbys, Chester-le-Street

D. L. Maddy (3)
103   Leics v Surrey, Leicester
103   Leics v Middx, Lord's
103   Leics v Notts, Leicester

M. P. Maynard (3)
134*   Glam v Durham, Cardiff
161*   Glam v Worcs, Worcester
142   Glam v Somerset, Taunton

T. M. Moody (3)
108   Worcs v Warwicks, Birmingham
101   Worcs v Derbys, Worcester
180*   Worcs v Hants, Southampton

P. J. Prichard (3)
106   Essex v Derbys, Southend
120   Essex v Worcs, Chelmsford
224   Essex v Kent, Canterbury

A. S. Rollins (3)
210   Derbys v Hants, Chesterfield
148   Derbys v Glam, Chesterfield
171*   Derbys v Leics, Leicester

N. R. Taylor (3)
127   Sussex v Northants, Hove
109   Sussex v Durham, Chester-le-Street
122*   Sussex v Leics, Eastbourne

G. P. Thorpe (3)
138   England v Australia, Birmingham
106*   Surrey v Sussex, Hove
222   Surrey v Glam, The Oval

M. P. Vaughan (3)
109   Yorks v Oxford U., Oxford
161   Yorks v Essex, Ilford
105   Yorks v Lancs, Manchester

V. J. Wells (3)
107   Leics v Lancs, Leicester
224   Leics v Middx, Lord's
190   Leics v Derbys, Leicester

J. J. Whitaker (3)
100*   Leics v Cambridge U., Cambridge
110   Leics v Middx, Lord's
133*   Leics v Somerset, Bath

C. J. Adams (2)
108   Derbys v Kent, Canterbury
107   Derbys v Durham, Chester-le-Street

N. J. Astle (2)
100   Notts v Warwicks, Nottingham
100   Notts v Essex, Worksop

M. A. Atherton (2)
108   Lancs v Leics, Leicester
149   Lancs v Surrey, The Oval

D. J. Bicknell (2)
162 Surrey v Northants, Northampton
130 Surrey v Kent, Canterbury

G. S. Blewett (2)
121 Australians v Derbys, Derby
125 Australia v England, Birmingham

K. M. Curran (2)
108 Northants v Lancs, Manchester
159 Northants v Glam, Abergavenny

J. M. Dakin (2)
103* Leics v Cambridge U., Cambridge
190 Leics v Northants, Northampton

A. Dale (2)
106 Glam v Warwicks, Cardiff
142* Glam v Derbys, Chesterfield

N. H. Fairbrother (2)
132 Lancs v Sussex, Manchester
112* Lancs v Surrey, The Oval

M. W. Gatting (2)
160* Middx v Cambridge U., Cambridge
108 Middx v Northants, Lord's

R. J. Harden (2)
136* Somerset v Surrey, The Oval
103 Somerset v Sussex, Taunton

N. C. Johnson (2)
150 Leics v Lancs, Leicester
117* Leics v Kent, Canterbury

M. Keech (2)
127 Hants v Oxford U., Oxford
101* Hants v Lancs, Southampton

N. V. Knight (2)
119* Warwicks v Hants, Southampton
116* Warwicks v Worcs, Birmingham

D. A. Leatherdale (2)
129 Worcs v Kent, Worcester
110 Worcs v Northants, Northampton

A. McGrath (2)
105* Yorks v Oxford U., Oxford
141 Yorks v Worcs, Leeds

M. R. May (2)
107* Derbys v Pakistan A, Derby
116 Derbys v Glam, Chesterfield

D. J. Millns (2)
114* Leics v Hants, Southampton
121 Leics v Northants, Northampton

J. E. Morris (2)
149 Durham v Glam, Cardiff
124 Durham v Sussex, Chester-le-Street

K. Newell (2)
107* Sussex v Northants, Hove
112 Sussex v Kent, Horsham

R. T. Ponting (2)
126* Australians v Glam, Cardiff
127 Australia v England, Leeds

D. D. J. Robinson (2)
148 Essex v Worcs, Chelmsford
134 Essex v Middx, Chelmsford

G. D. Rose (2)
109* Somerset v Northants, Northampton
191 Somerset v Sussex, Taunton

B. F. Smith (2)
121* Leics v Kent, Canterbury
131* Leics v Essex, Colchester

E. T. Smith (2)
190 Cambridge U. v Leics, Cambridge
102 Kent v Hants, Portsmouth

R. A. Smith (2)
154 Hants v Derbys, Chesterfield
110 Hants v Yorks, Portsmouth

J. P. Stephenson (2)
140 Hants v Oxford U., Oxford
114 Hants v Yorks, Portsmouth

A. J. Stewart (2)
271* Surrey v Yorks, The Oval
170 Surrey v Kent, Canterbury

I. J. Sutcliffe (2)
112 Leics v Somerset, Bath
130 Leics v Essex, Colchester

M. A. Taylor (2)
129 Australia v England, Birmingham
109 Australians v Hants, Southampton

M. E. Waugh (2)
173 Australians v Hants, Southampton
142* Australians v Middx, Lord's

S. Young (2)
237 Glos v Derbys, Cheltenham
100 Glos v Lancs, Bristol

The following each played one three-figure innings:

Ali Naqvi, 114, Pakistan A v MCC, Shenley Park; M. W. Alleyne, 169, Glos v Durham, Cheltenham; K. L. T. Arthurton, 200*, MCC v Pakistan A, Shenley Park; C. W. J. Athey, 138*, Sussex v Somerset, Taunton.

M. G. Bevan, 104*, Australians v Derbys, Derby; P. D. Bowler, 123, Somerset v Oxford U., Taunton; K. R. Brown, 144*, Middx v Sussex, Lord's; G. P. Butcher, 101*, Glam v Oxford U., Oxford; M. A. Butcher, 153, England A v The Rest, Birmingham.

P. D. Collingwood, 107, Durham v Oxford U., Oxford; G. R. Cowdrey, 101, Kent v Somerset, Taunton.

R. I. Dawson, 100, Glos v Kent, Canterbury.

M. V. Fleming, 138, Kent v Essex, Canterbury; A. Flintoff, 117, Lancs v Hants, Southampton; M. J. Foster, 129, Durham v Glam, Cardiff; D. P. Fulton, 110, Kent v Surrey, Canterbury.

J. E. R. Gallian, 106, England A v The Rest, Birmingham; A. P. Grayson, 105, Essex v Surrey, The Oval; K. Greenfield, 108, Sussex v Pakistan A, Hove.

A. Habib, 175*, Leics v Cambridge U., Cambridge; T. H. C. Hancock, 100*, Glos v Somerset, Taunton; A. J. Hollioake, 182, Surrey v Middx, Lord's; P. C. L. Holloway, 106, Somerset v Warwicks, Birmingham.

R. K. Illingworth, 112, Worcs v Warwicks, Birmingham.

J. L. Langer, 152*, Australians v Glos, Bristol.

S. A. Marsh, 142, Kent v Sussex, Horsham; Mohammad Wasim, 155, Pakistan A v Yorks, Leeds; A. J. Moles, 168, Warwicks v Hants, Southampton; P. Moores, 102*, Sussex v Notts, Hove; M. D. Moxon, 155, Yorks v Pakistan A, Leeds.

D. C. Nash, 100, Middx v Essex, Chelmsford; M. Newell, 100, Sussex v Notts, Hove.

B. Parker, 138*, Yorks v Oxford U., Oxford; M. T. E. Peirce, 104, Sussex v Hants, Southampton; S. D. Peters, 102*, Essex v Cambridge U., Cambridge; B. J. Phillips, 100*, Kent v Lancs, Manchester; P. R. Pollard, 115*, Notts v Oxford U., Oxford; M. J. Powell, 200*, Glam v Oxford U., Oxford.

J. D. Ratcliffe, 135, Surrey v Worcs, Worcester; J. Ratledge, 100*, Cambridge U. v Oxford U., Lord's; D. J. Roberts, 117, Northants v Essex, Northampton; R. T. Robinson, 143*, Notts v Essex, Worksop; R. C. Russell, 103*, Glos v Durham, Cheltenham.

D. J. Sales, 103, Northants v Glam, Abergavenny; Salim Elahi, 229, Pakistan A v Worcs, Worcester; O. A. Shah, 104*, Middx v Notts, Lord's; A. Singh, 134, Cambridge U. v Essex, Cambridge; N. M. K. Smith, 148, Warwicks v Glos, Birmingham; V. S. Solanki, 128*, Worcs v Oxford U., Oxford; N. J. Speak, 124*, Durham v Cambridge U., Cambridge; K. R. Spiring, 150, Worcs v Essex, Chelmsford; A. J. Swann, 136, Northants v Warwicks, Birmingham.

N. J. Trainor, 121, Glos v Australians, Bristol; R. J. Turner, 144, Somerset v Kent, Taunton; T. A. Tweats, 189, Derbys v Yorks, Derby.

S. D. Udal, 117*, Hants v Warwicks, Southampton.

T. R. Ward, 161*, Kent v Glos, Canterbury; R. J. Warren, 174*, Northants v Worcs, Northampton; M. Watkinson, 135, Lancs v Hants, Southampton; P. N. Weekes, 101, Middx v Cambridge U., Cambridge; P. E. Wellings, 128*, Middx v Cambridge U., Cambridge; A. P. Wells, 109, Kent v Essex, Canterbury; C. White, 172*, Yorks v Worcs, Leeds; G. W. White, 145, Hants v Yorks, Portsmouth; N. T. Wood, 155, Lancs v Surrey, The Oval.

TEN WICKETS IN A MATCH

There were 30 instances of bowlers taking ten or more wickets in a match in first-class cricket in 1997, one more than in 1996. The list includes 26 in the County Championship. Two bowlers achieved the feat in the same match, when S. J. E. Brown took ten wickets for Durham and D. J. Millns ten for Leicestershire at Leicester.

A. M. Smith (3)
10-106, Glos v Hants, Bristol; 10-132, Glos v Yorks, Leeds; 10-106, Glos v Derbys, Cheltenham.

P. A. J. DeFreitas (2)
10-99, Derbys v Kent, Canterbury; 10-172, Derbys v Yorks, Derby.

D. E. Malcolm (2)
11-125, Derbys v Middx, Lord's; 10-65, Derbys v Lancs, Derby.

Saqlain Mushtaq (2)
10-128, Surrey v Durham, The Oval; 10-116, Surrey v Middx, Lord's.

The following each took ten wickets in a match on one occasion:

H. A. G. Anthony, 10-113, MCC v Pakistan A, Shenley Park.
M. M. Betts, 13-143, Durham v Northants, Northampton; M. N. Bowen, 11-109, Notts v Derbys,
   Nottingham; D. R. Brown, 11-154, First-Class Counties Select XI v Pakistan A, Chelmsford;
   S. J. E. Brown, 10-141, Durham v Leics, Leicester.
A. A. Donald, 10-119, Warwicks v Surrey, Birmingham.
P. M. Hutchison, 11-102, Yorks v Pakistan A, Leeds.
R. K. Illingworth, 10-147, Worcs v Hants, Southampton.
K. D. James, 13-93, Hants v Somerset, Basingstoke.
G. Keedy, 10-173, Lancs v Surrey, The Oval.
P. J. Martin, 13-79, Lancs v Middx, Uxbridge; D. J. Millns, 10-130, Leics v Durham, Leicester.
A. Sheriyar, 10-63, Worcs v Sussex, Arundel; K. J. Shine, 11-97, Somerset v Lancs, Taunton;
   C. E. W. Silverwood, 12-148, Yorks v Kent, Leeds; P. A. Strang, 11-186, Kent v Lancs,
   Manchester; P. M. Such, 11-215, Essex v Yorks, Ilford.
J. P. Taylor, 10-141, Northants v Notts, Northampton; P. C. R. Tufnell, 11-93, England v
   Australia, The Oval.
Waqar Younis, 10-134, Glam v Northants, Abergavenny; G. Welch, 11-140, Warwicks v Lancs,
   Blackpool.

THE ASHES

''In affectionate remembrance of English cricket which died at The Oval, 29th August, 1882.
Deeply lamented by a large circle of sorrowing friends and acquaintances, R.I.P.
N.B. The body will be cremated and the Ashes taken to Australia.''

Australia's first victory on English soil over the full strength of England, on August 29, 1882,
inspired a young London journalist, Reginald Shirley Brooks, to write this mock ''obituary''. It
appeared in the *Sporting Times*.
   Before England's defeat at The Oval, by seven runs, arrangements had already been made for
the Hon. Ivo Bligh, afterwards Lord Darnley, to lead a team to Australia. Three weeks later they
set out, now with the popular objective of recovering the Ashes. In the event, Australia won the
First Test by nine wickets, but with England winning the next two it became generally accepted
that they brought back the Ashes.
   It was long accepted that the real Ashes – a small urn believed to contain the ashes of a bail
used in the third match – were presented to Bligh by a group of Melbourne women. At the time
of the 1982 centenary of The Oval Test match, however, evidence was produced which suggested
that these ashes were the remains of a ball and that they were given to the England captain by Sir
William Clarke, the presentation taking place before the Test matches in Australia in 1883. The
certain origin of the Ashes, therefore, is the subject of some dispute.
   After Lord Darnley's death in 1927, the urn was given to MCC by Lord Darnley's Australian-
born widow, Florence. It can be seen in the cricket museum at Lord's, together with a red and
gold velvet bag, made specially for it, and the scorecard of the 1882 match.

THE AUSTRALIANS IN ENGLAND, 1997

The best skyline in English cricket is the one you see from the top of The Oval pavilion, encompassing the gasometer, Big Ben, the incongruous gaudiness of the MI5 headquarters, and, on a clear day, half of London. In 1997, there was an extra attraction: "The World's First Tethered Balloon Ride", in the Harleyford Road. Every so often, a hot-air balloon would rise behind the sightscreen at the Vauxhall End, dangle for a few minutes, and return to earth.

It could have been put there to represent England's summer. They started so commandingly, in the one-day internationals and the First Test, that the nation became more excited about the team's performance than it had been at any time since Kingston 1989-90, arguably since Headingley 1981. But the Australians, undisputed world champions for the first time in many years, dug deep into their reserves of skill and will power. After having the better of a rainy stalemate at Lord's, they needed only three Test matches to draw level, pull ahead, and then secure both the Ashes and the series. At The Oval, England finished as they had begun, with a pulsating victory. It was too late. The balloon had been tethered all along.

Of all the possible scorelines, 3-2 was the one most likely to satisfy both sides. For Australia, it was a third major victory in nine months, following the series against West Indies and South Africa, and a fifth consecutive series win over England – a sequence they had never achieved in 115 years of the Ashes. And they had overcome, if not the odds, then a powerful conspiracy of circumstances.

Their captain, Mark Taylor, was so out of form that he dropped himself from the one-day team for the second time in two months. Their administrators allowed them only nine days' play against the counties before the First Test, about half as much as in 1993 (17 days). Their acclimatisation was made harder still by the climate: if it was not actually raining, it was grey and dank. They were tired: leading players such as Ian Healy and the Waugh brothers had flown 70,000 miles since October 1996. And for once, steps were taken – unofficially, but unmistakably – to fix the pitches in England's favour. Only one Test out of six was played on a flat track. Taylor was disappointed to miss out on the 4-1 victory that looked certain the night before the series ended; but given all of this, he would have settled for a victory of any kind.

For England, 2-3 was less than they had dreamed of after going 1-0 up, but more than they had had any right to expect in advance. In the 28 months since the teams had last met, Australia had beaten West Indies away and home, as well as Pakistan, Sri Lanka and South Africa. They had discovered one great fast bowler (Glenn McGrath), and possibly a second (Jason Gillespie). England had drawn with West Indies and Zimbabwe and lost to Pakistan and South Africa; their only victories had come over India, at home, and New Zealand, away. They had discovered a very good medium-fast bowler, Dominic Cork, but had already lost him to injury (a scenario that was to replay itself in this series, first with the reborn Darren Gough, then with Dean Headley). If there were two divisions in Test cricket, England would be in the lower one, as the Wisden World Championship shows.

The Ashes remain freighted with history and resonance, but in the 1990s their most fervent admirer could not describe them as a clash of the giants. Australia had won the previous four series with cruel ease: 4-0, 3-0, 4-1 and 3-1. In the

THE AUSTRALIAN TOURING PARTY

[*Professional Sport*

Back row: E. L. Alcott (*physiotherapist*), D. S. Berry, G. S. Blewett, M. S. Kasprowicz, B. P. Julian, G. D. McGrath, M. T. G. Elliott, M. G. Bevan, J. N. Gillespie, M. K. Walsh (*scorer*), S. A. Smith (*fitness adviser*). *Front row:* R. T. Ponting, S. K. Warne, M. E. Waugh, I. A. Healy, G. R. Marsh (*coach*), M. A. Taylor (*captain*), A. B. Crompton (*manager*), S. R. Waugh, M. J. Slater, P. R. Reiffel, J. L. Langer.

context of 17-4, 3-2 wasn't bad. And although the victory was convincing, it was never insulting. Steve Waugh, the only member of the touring side who had experienced an Ashes defeat, noticed the difference at Trent Bridge, when the clock threatened to turn all the way back to 1989: flat pitch, Australia win toss, 302 for three at the close. Next morning, instead of supinely ushering them to 600, England bowled them out for 427. "That was the best England played in the whole series," Waugh said. "I don't think they would have done that on the two previous tours."

There were two critical differences between the sides. The first, as widely predicted, was the Australian bowlers – though, as not predicted at all, it was the bowlers' batting that really stood out. In McGrath and Shane Warne, Australia had far and away the best bowlers, yet the two top orders performed identically – each team's first five wickets raised, on average, 186 runs. The second half of the order was another story: England's remaining wickets added an average of 60, Australia's 117.

Behind the figures lay a deeper truth. These tail-end runs, always worth double in the currency of the mind, were largely scored by Ian Healy, Warne and Paul Reiffel – three senior players with battle-hardened temperaments. There was a gulf between the sides not just in talent and success, but in experience and self-belief. Australia had five players with more than 50 Tests behind them – Taylor, Healy, the Waughs and Warne. England had two – Mike Atherton and Alec Stewart. Atherton was targeted, with chilling efficiency, by McGrath, who dismissed him seven times out of 11. Stewart was a victim of friendly fire: asked to keep wicket as well as go in at No. 3, he batted, as he always had done in this situation against good teams, like a mere wicket-keeper. By the end of the series, he had played 19 Ashes Tests without once making a century. Of the five 50-cap Australians, only Mark Waugh failed to make a telling contribution. (This may have been nemesis: Waugh was the man who had written England off in a magazine article as lacking the toughness or the hunger required to win Test series.) It was less a black mark against Atherton and Stewart than a sign of a team at a different stage of its development. England were at the point where Australia, under Allan Border, had been nine years earlier: inching towards respectability.

As entertainment, the series was all the better for not being played on what are conventionally termed good pitches. Both England's victories were famous ones; all three of Australia's displayed the attacking flair that had propelled them to the top of the world. Even the one drawn Test, shrunk by the rain to a fraction over two days' play, was riveting: not until the final session did a result become impossible. If lost time was a recurring motif, the way the teams played made up for it. Spanning only 1,750 overs, or 20 full days, the series was short, but near-perfectly formed.

And packed with sub-plots. Uneasy lay the heads that wore the crown: the series began with Taylor under intense pressure to resign, and ended with Atherton under intense pressure to resign. (Neither did.) And there was a whole dynasty of prodigal sons. Devon Malcolm was welcomed back, and played in both England's victories: but he kept bowling fast and well without reward, and was dropped for the middle two Tests. Phil Tufnell had the surely unprecedented experience of being 12th or 13th man for five Tests and the match-winner in the Sixth (no wonder that end-of-season drugs test slipped his mind – it must still have been boggling). Mark Ramprakash earned his umpteenth recall at The Oval, did his familiar impression of a frightened horse, came in again with England in effect 12 for four, and coolly helped Graham Thorpe compile the partnership of the match (79). Andy Caddick, who had made his debut in 1993 and finished that series with five wickets from four Tests, took five on the first day this time, and 24 in all: why he didn't play in the pivotal Fourth Test, only the selectors knew. As McGrath was to Atherton, so Caddick was to Steve Waugh, dismissing him five times in nine innings.

Michael Slater, the swashbuckling opener who had been a huge influence in 1993, was yet another player summoned from the wilderness. He appeared in a couple of one-day internationals, in the middle order, and was not seen again. He went home without a single first-class fifty to his name. Almost as wretched was Michael Bevan, Australia's Man of the Series in the Texaco Trophy, who was picked as a Test all-rounder, but managed only 43 runs and two wickets, one of which was a freak – a leg-side full toss to Mark Butcher, which the irrepressible Healy somehow finessed into a stumping.

The summer began, as it ended, with a bang. England, the underdogs, won the one-day series 3-0. On a green pitch at Headingley, chasing 171, they slithered to 40 for four. Thorpe, who was used to this sort of thing, was joined by Adam Hollioake, who was not: in both his previous one-day internationals, Hollioake had come in at No. 7 in a non-crisis. He was at sea against Warne, and made only seven from his first 25 balls. But he battled through and eventually took command, adding another 59 at a run a ball and stealing the match award from Thorpe. England's confidence grew and in the second match at The Oval Hollioake did it again, in less testing conditions, making an undefeated 53 as Atherton completed only his second one-day international hundred. At Lord's the next day, England were cocky enough to give Ben Hollioake, straight out of the Under-19s, a senior debut, and put him in at No. 3; Australia were worried enough to leave out Taylor, who had twice failed. Ben Hollioake made a breezily brilliant 63 in 48 balls, and England won in style. Atherton, often discounted as a one-day player, completed a magnificent set: Texaco Trophy victories over all the other six nations who had been permitted to take part.

The one-day game is far from Test cricket, as both teams were soon to acknowledge by openly mooting separate captains for the two. But sometimes one game can colour the other. England were now on a roll, and so were their supporters, who gathered in front of the Lord's pavilion to borrow the football team's theme tune and sing ''Ashes Coming Home''. To watch video footage of the First Test at Edgbaston is to hear a strange sound: a steady roar, like a motorway. ''No Test crowd had had a better effect on England since Edgbaston 1981,'' wrote Scyld Berry. The first ball set the tone: Gough, acutely aware of past failures in this department, ordered himself to put it on the spot, Taylor played and missed, and the crowd oohed. Australia, so often dominant on the first day of an Ashes series, staggered to 54 for eight. When Warne rallied them with a fearless 47, it was a hint of things to come. When England in turn were 50 for three, it looked like the old, old story. But Thorpe, again, and Nasser Hussain hauled their team to supremacy. By the close of an unforgettable day, they were already 82 runs ahead.

Hussain went all the way to 207, the innings of his life, and his team's: no member of his England generation had reached 200 in a Test before. Australia fought back, with hundreds from Taylor, on the very brink of oblivion, and Greg Blewett. But England had only to hold their nerve, and the bowlers did so. Needing 118 – roughly the score that would prove beyond Australia at The Oval – England knocked them off in 21.3 overs on a sunlit Sunday evening. Atherton played more shots than he had in his one-day hundred. Euphoria became cause as well as effect: by his own admission, he and Stewart were carried along on the crowd's adrenalin.

Next day, while England basked in their first Ashes lead since 1986-87, one central figure went back on to the deserted stage. McGrath had taken two for 149 in the match, bowling persistently short and wide. Out on the Edgbaston square, Taylor and Geoff Marsh, the coach, drilled into him the difference between an Australian length and an English one. Next time he smelt the blood of an Englishman, he finished with eight for 38. A quick bowler is one thing, a quick learner quite another.

McGrath was helped by the arrival of Reiffel, the parsimonious veteran of the 1993 series. The Australian selectors left him out of this party, on the grounds that he was not fully fit. Thanks to an injury to Andy Bichel, they were able to have the best of both worlds: Reiffel rested and with a point to prove. His batting was more obviously successful than his bowling but, as in 1993, he played a crucial role, keeping it endlessly tight, showing the way, taking wickets for the man at the other end. The two Tests he missed were the two Australia lost.

Lord's restored Australia's equilibrium, but again England failed to fold when they might have been expected to – sent back in on the final morning, 136 behind, largely thanks to a horror-film sequence of dropped or missed catches. Three times the guilty man had been Butcher, playing only his second Test. When Taylor returned the favour, dropping him after he had made only two, Butcher had the gumption to build on his mixed fortune, and he helped Atherton add 162 to save the game.

At Old Trafford, you didn't have to be the ECB Inspector of Pitches to see a result coming. For Australia, it was do or die: a comeback from 0-2 would be close to impossible. The elders of the side rose to the occasion. Taylor, fearlessly, elected to bat, thinking that the bare patches might assist Warne in the fourth innings. Steve Waugh, whose highest score in six international outings had been a lugubrious 33 at Edgbaston, came in at 42 for three. "The way he prepared himself," said the reserve wicket-keeper Adam Gilchrist, "you just knew something special was going to happen." Waugh took a calculated decision to seize the initiative, and was the only man on either side to score at more than a run every two balls in the first innings. He made 108; Australia had a first-innings lead of 73, even though it was England, with the better of the conditions, who lasted longer. At 74 for one, England had been ahead on points, but then another of the elders, Warne, took six wickets. When Australia were 39 for three, England had another glimpse of Nirvana. Waugh snuffed it out, becoming the first man in 50 years to make two centuries in an Ashes Test, content this time to drop anchor while Healy, Warne and Reiffel enjoyed themselves. The tide had turned.

At Headingley, England again had their openings. After being put in on an up-and-down pitch, they reached 103 for two, thanks to what looked like being one of Atherton's defensive epics. When he allowed McGrath to tempt him into a mis-hook, the rest surrendered to a single hostile spell from Gillespie. Steve Waugh thought Australia now had the best attack in the world; certainly they had variety, penetration, hunger, and that indefinable quality which ensures that at least one bowler is on fire at any time.

England's seamers sometimes kept pace and they opened another chink of hope at Headingley by reducing Australia to 50 for four. If Thorpe had caught Matthew Elliott – a routine slip chance off the hapless debutant Mike Smith – they might have been 50 for five. Instead Elliott, never entirely secure but formidably good at punishing the bad ball, combined with the nonchalant Ricky Ponting to do what Thorpe and Hussain had done at Edgbaston.

Now that they were behind, the new England selectors reverted to old ways, to chop and change, and the curious business of picking a radically different team when a match has to be won. In, by popular demand, came the Hollioake brothers: Adam on merit, Ben on the wildest hunch since the Aussies picked Peter Taylor at Sydney ten years earlier. It was an interesting time for an experiment. The brothers totalled 77 in four innings. They also took four wickets, held three catches, and did nothing to disgrace themselves; but Ben was a boy among men and, although he was retained in the squad for The Oval, he never looked like making the final eleven.

At Trent Bridge, yet again, England had their moment of equality. Stewart, pushed up to open, lasted two hours for the only time in the series, and batted with the spirit of a 19-year-old. England reached 106 for nought and, thanks to Thorpe and Adam Hollioake, 243 for four. Having conceded a lead of 114, they clawed their way back as Caddick and Headley removed the top five in the second innings for 171. Healy saw the urgency of the situation, launched a gleeful counter-attack, put England out of the game, and deservedly won the Man of the Match award. Requiring 451, England spontaneously combusted.

It was a good-natured series, by modern standards. The match referees were not heard from once, and the stump microphones seldom picked up anything more colourful than Healy's mantra of "Bowlin', Warney!" (occasionally subject, like Warne's bowling itself, to a guileful variation, such as "Bowled, Shane!"). McGrath huffed and puffed, as if unable to see that his performances were doing enough talking. Healy won applause from umpire Shepherd at Lord's for coming clean about a catch that may have been a half-volley. The Australians sledged Hussain long and loud after he had claimed a similar catch at Old Trafford to dismiss Blewett; he reacted with England's only hundred of the last five Tests.

Away from the spotlight, the Australians generally beat the counties when the rain gave them enough time. They suffered two defeats: two obscure medium-pacers, Gavin Haynes and David Leatherdale, had the time of their lives in a one-day warm-up at Worcester, and then Dean Jones, in one of his last appearances for Derbyshire, orchestrated a run-chase that was exciting even on Ceefax.

The Australians found time for exhibition matches, slotting in a visit to Ireland and a private fixture against J. Paul Getty's XI at Wormsley as well as the traditional opener at Arundel. They were warmly received everywhere except, mysteriously, Taunton. Steve Waugh, leading the tourists against his old county, complained to the umpires about the taunting of Warne. Justin Langer, one of several forgotten men on the tour, wrote home about it: "I would shudder if my daughter, my wife, my mum or my grandmother had to listen to the disgusting and thoughtless rubbish coming from the stands at Taunton." If the sentiments were old-fashioned, the medium was not: Langer was corresponding by e-mail. Things change and, unfortunately for England, they stay the same. – TIM DE LISLE.

Tim de Lisle is editor of Wisden Cricket Monthly.

AUSTRALIAN TOURING PARTY

M. A. Taylor (New South Wales) (*captain*), S. R. Waugh (New South Wales) (*vice-captain*), M. G. Bevan (New South Wales), A. J. Bichel (Queensland), G. S. Blewett (South Australia), M. T. G. Elliott (Victoria), A. C. Gilchrist (Western Australia), J. N. Gillespie (South Australia), I. A. Healy (Queensland), B. P. Julian (Western Australia), M. S. Kasprowicz (Queensland), J. L. Langer (Western Australia), G. D. McGrath (New South Wales), R. T. Ponting (Tasmania), M. J. Slater (New South Wales), S. K. Warne (Victoria), M. E. Waugh (New South Wales).

P. R. Reiffel (Victoria) replaced Bichel when he went home injured. D. S. Berry (Victoria) replaced Gilchrist as reserve wicket-keeper when he was hurt playing football. S. Lee (New South Wales) was called up from the Lancashire League and S. Young (Tasmania) from his county, Gloucestershire, after Gillespie was injured and Reiffel returned home for the birth of his child.

Manager: A. B. Crompton.   *Coach:* G. R. Marsh.

AUSTRALIAN TOUR RESULTS

Test matches – Played 6: Won 3, Lost 2, Drawn 1.
First-class matches – Played 15: Won 6, Lost 3, Drawn 6. Abandoned 1.
Wins – England (3), Leicestershire, Hampshire, Kent.
Losses – England (2), Derbyshire.
Draws – England, Gloucestershire, Nottinghamshire, Glamorgan, Middlesex, Somerset.
Abandoned – British Universities.
One-day internationals – Played 3: Lost 3.
Other non-first-class matches – Played 6: Won 4, Lost 1, No result 1. Abandoned 1. *Wins* – Duke of Norfolk's XI, Northamptonshire, Minor Counties, Ireland. *Loss* – Worcestershire. *No result* – Scotland. *Abandoned* – Durham.

TEST MATCH AVERAGES

ENGLAND – BATTING

	T	I	NO	R	HS	100s	Avge	Ct
G. P. Thorpe	6	11	2	453	138	1	50.33	8
N. Hussain	6	11	0	431	207	2	39.18	8
M. A. Ealham . . .	4	6	3	105	53*	0	35.00	3
J. P. Crawley . . .	5	9	1	243	83	0	30.37	3
M. A. Butcher . . .	5	10	0	254	87	0	25.40	8
A. J. Stewart	6	12	1	268	87	0	24.36	23
M. A. Atherton . .	6	12	1	257	77	0	23.36	2
A. J. Hollioake . .	2	4	0	51	45	0	12.75	4
A. R. Caddick . . .	5	8	2	59	26*	0	9.83	1
D. W. Headley . .	3	6	2	39	22	0	9.75	1
R. D. B. Croft . . .	5	8	0	75	24	0	9.37	1
D. E. Malcolm . .	4	5	1	12	12	0	3.00	2
D. Gough	4	6	0	17	10	0	2.83	0

Played in one Test: B. C. Hollioake 28, 2 (1 ct); P. J. Martin 20, 3 (1 ct); M. R. Ramprakash 4, 48; A. M. Smith 0, 4*; P. C. R. Tufnell 1, 0.

* Signifies not out.

BOWLING

	O	M	R	W	BB	5W/i	Avge
P. C. R. Tufnell	47.4	22	93	11	7-66	1	8.45
M. A. Ealham	58.4	11	191	8	3-60	0	23.87
A. R. Caddick	179.5	27	634	24	5-42	2	26.41
D. W. Headley.....	131.2	20	444	16	4-72	0	27.75
D. Gough	142	27	511	16	5-149	1	31.93
D. E. Malcolm	93	19	307	6	3-100	0	51.16
R. D. B. Croft	161.5	41	439	8	3-125	0	54.87

Also bowled: M. A. Butcher 2–0–14–0; A. J. Hollioake 19–2–55–2; B. C. Hollioake 15–2–83–2; P. J. Martin 19–5–51–0; A. M. Smith 23–2–89–0.

AUSTRALIA – BATTING

	T	I	NO	R	HS	100s	Avge	Ct/St
P. R. Reiffel	4	6	3	179	54*	0	59.66	1
M. T. G. Elliott......	6	10	0	556	199	2	55.60	4
R. T. Ponting	3	5	0	241	127	1	48.20	1
S. R. Waugh	6	10	0	390	116	2	39.00	4
G. S. Blewett	6	10	0	381	125	1	38.10	9
M. A. Taylor........	6	10	0	317	129	1	31.70	6
I. A. Healy	6	10	1	225	63	0	25.00	25/2
M. E. Waugh	6	10	0	209	68	0	20.90	6
S. K. Warne	6	10	0	188	53	0	18.80	2
G. D. McGrath	6	8	6	25	20*	0	12.50	2
J. N. Gillespie	4	7	2	57	28*	0	11.40	3
M. G. Bevan	3	5	0	43	24	0	8.60	1
M. S. Kasprowicz....	3	4	0	21	17	0	5.25	2

Played in one Test: S. Young 0, 4*.

* *Signifies not out.*

BOWLING

	O	M	R	W	BB	5W/i	Avge
G. D. McGrath	249.5	67	701	36	8-38	2	19.47
J. N. Gillespie	91.4	20	332	16	7-37	1	20.75
M. S. Kasprowicz....	93.3	19	310	14	7-36	1	22.14
S. K. Warne	237.1	69	577	24	6-48	1	24.04
P. R. Reiffel	112.1	28	293	11	5-49	1	26.63

Also bowled: M. G. Bevan 34.4–6–121–2; G. S. Blewett 3–0–17–0; M. E. Waugh 7–3–16–1; S. R. Waugh 20–3–76–0; S. Young 8–3–13–0.

AUSTRALIAN TOUR AVERAGES – FIRST-CLASS AVERAGES

BATTING

	M	I	NO	R	HS	100s	Avge	Ct/St
R. T. Ponting	8	12	3	571	127	2	63.44	7
M. T. G. Elliott......	12	19	0	1,091	199	4	57.42	7
S. R. Waugh	13	17	0	924	154	4	54.35	9
P. R. Reiffel	8	9	4	242	56	0	48.40	2

	M	I	NO	R	HS	100s	Avge	Ct/St
J. L. Langer	6	10	3	312	152*	1	44.57	5
M. E. Waugh	13	20	3	746	173	2	43.88	11
B. P. Julian	5	5	1	162	71	0	40.50	4
G. S. Blewett	12	18	1	686	125	2	40.35	17
M. A. Taylor	12	19	0	680	129	2	35.78	8
M. G. Bevan	11	16	3	463	104*	1	35.61	6
I. A. Healy	12	16	4	407	63	0	33.91	39/4
M. J. Slater	5	8	0	159	47	0	19.87	3
S. K. Warne	12	17	1	293	53	0	18.31	5
M. S. Kasprowicz	10	8	3	56	17	0	11.20	8
J. N. Gillespie	8	9	2	67	28*	0	9.57	5
G. D. McGrath	11	10	6	25	20*	0	6.25	4

Played in two matches: D. S. Berry 9, 12 (9 ct, 1 st); S. Young 0, 0, 4*. Played in one match: A. C. Gilchrist 9* (3 ct); S. Lee 1 (1 ct); A. J. Bichel did not bat.

* Signifies not out.

BOWLING

	O	M	R	W	BB	5W/i	Avge
S. Lee	35.3	11	113	8	4-27	0	14.12
P. R. Reiffel	188.4	49	520	28	5-49	2	18.57
S. K. Warne	433.4	112	1,154	57	7-103	4	20.24
G. D. McGrath	363.4	104	1,012	49	8-38	2	20.65
J. N. Gillespie	198.4	43	692	29	7-37	2	23.86
M. S. Kasprowicz	267.2	50	1,010	39	7-36	1	25.89
B. P. Julian	108	17	455	9	3-88	0	50.55
M. G. Bevan	152.4	23	606	11	3-73	0	55.09

Also bowled: A. J. Bichel 5–1–28–0; G. S. Blewett 20–4–93–0; M. T. G. Elliott 9–0–43–0; R. T. Ponting 3–0–9–0; M. E. Waugh 47–10–150–4; S. R. Waugh 26–5–97–1; S. Young 34–13–99–2.

Note: Matches in this section which were not first-class are signified by a dagger.

†DUKE OF NORFOLK'S XI v AUSTRALIANS

At Arundel, May 15. Australians won by 113 runs. Australians batted first by agreement.

The Australians eased themselves into the tour by thrashing a weaker team than is normally fielded on this occasion. With all 18 counties engaged in first-class cricket, the Duke's star player was 44-year-old Emburey, who conceded only 2.5 an over and then rescued his side from a miserable 59 for eight. He and Radford doubled the score after the upper order crashed to Kasprowicz and Gillespie; six of the top seven managed 15 runs between them. They lost with 15 overs to spare, barely halfway to an Australian total of 235. Taking the chance of batting practice, Taylor and Mark Waugh had put on 101 and Slater hit three sixes off Grant Flower.

Australians

M. E. Waugh c Ward b Whittall 46	†I. A. Healy not out 15
*M. A. Taylor b Emburey 45	
S. R. Waugh st A. Flower b G. W. Flower 27	B 8, l-b 3, w 5, n-b 1 17
R. T. Ponting b Emburey 13	
J. L. Langer c Ward b Radford 22	1/101 2/107 3/143 (5 wkts, 50 overs) 235
M. J. Slater not out 50	4/143 5/190

B. P. Julian, J. N. Gillespie, M. S. Kasprowicz and G. D. McGrath did not bat.

Bowling: Radford 10–0–52–1; Foster 7–0–26–0; Whittall 10–0–45–1; Capel 4–0–21–0; Emburey 10–2–25–2; G. W. Flower 9–1–55–1.

Duke of Norfolk's XI

G. W. Flower c Langer b Julian	26	D. J. Capel c Langer b Gillespie	5	
J. W. Hall b Kasprowicz	4	N. V. Radford not out	30	
T. S. Curtis c Healy b Kasprowicz	2	N. A. Foster c Healy b Julian	1	
†A. Flower b Gillespie	2	L-b 4, w 11, n-b 1	16	
T. C. Walton c and b Kasprowicz	3		—	
D. M. Ward c Healy b Gillespie	2	1/19 2/31 3/39	(34.5 overs) 122	
A. R. Whittall lbw b Gillespie	2	4/43 5/45 6/47		
*J. E. Emburey c Gillespie b M. E. Waugh	29	7/51 8/59 9/119		

Bowling: McGrath 10–1–37–0; Kasprowicz 7–0–17–3; Julian 7.5–1–20–2; Gillespie 6–2–21–4; M. E. Waugh 4–0–23–1.

Umpires: A. Clarkson and R. Palmer.

†NORTHAMPTONSHIRE v AUSTRALIANS

At Northampton, May 17. Australians won by 17 runs (D/L method). Toss: Australians.

As they entered their first county game, Australian minds were much occupied by the form of their captain, Taylor. He did something to ease the pressure after a painful run of low scores, making 76 – not the most influential of innings, but the biggest of the match. His team-mates looked rusty, and batted without much concentration. Northamptonshire's innings was punctuated by rain and finally ground to a halt after 35 overs. With Loye going well, they might have won, even with Warne in full flight. But the shroud of Duckworth/Lewis closed over the proceedings, and the Australians were pronounced victors.

Australians

*M. A. Taylor lbw b Curran	76	S. K. Warne c Bailey b Penberthy	1	
M. J. Slater b Taylor	33	M. S. Kasprowicz c Taylor b Curran	1	
M. T. G. Elliott c Snape b Taylor	4	J. N. Gillespie not out	1	
M. E. Waugh c Curran b Snape	38	L-b 4, w 10, n-b 1	15	
R. T. Ponting b Penberthy	2		—	
J. L. Langer c Sales b Hughes	20	1/43 2/47 3/126	(47.4 overs) 232	
†A. C. Gilchrist c Bailey b Taylor	40	4/130 5/168 6/204		
B. P. Julian run out	1	7/209 8/210 9/227		

Bowling: Taylor 8.4–0–44–3; Hughes 7–0–57–1; Curran 9–2–34–2; Penberthy 10–0–39–2; Snape 10–0–37–1; Bailey 3–0–17–0.

Northamptonshire

A. Fordham c Gilchrist b Gillespie	2	D. J. Sales not out	11	
M. B. Loye not out	65			
*R. J. Bailey c and b Julian	10	L-b 4, w 9	13	
K. M. Curran c Gilchrist b Julian	12		—	
A. L. Penberthy c Waugh b Warne	19	1/14 2/40 3/55	(5 wkts, 35 overs) 134	
T. C. Walton st Gilchrist b Warne	2	4/108 5/113		

J. N. Snape, †D. Ripley, J. G. Hughes and J. P. Taylor did not bat.

Bowling: Gillespie 6–0–16–1; Kasprowicz 7–2–15–0; Julian 6–0–27–2; Ponting 4–0–22–0; Waugh 6–0–29–0; Warne 6–0–21–2.

Umpires: M. J. Kitchen and P. Willey.

†WORCESTERSHIRE v AUSTRALIANS

At Worcester, May 18. Worcestershire won by five wickets. Toss: Worcestershire.

Worcestershire had been deprived of their traditional opening first-class fixture with the tourists, but had the best of a one-day encounter, winning with 11 overs to spare in front of a 4,500 capacity crowd. They were lucky to get fine weather: a lorry was needed to tow the

Australians' coach out of axle-deep mud. The Australian batsmen, however, were unable to extricate themselves as Worcestershire's seamers exploited a damp pitch and overcast conditions. Haynes removed the top four and then Leatherdale returned his best-ever analysis, five for ten, as the tourists were routed for 121 in only 35 overs. An opening stand of 58 between Western Australian Moody and Weston assured Worcestershire of victory, although Kasprowicz moved the ball sharply.

Australians

*M. A. Taylor c Rhodes b Haynes	14	S. K. Warne c Rhodes b Leatherdale	....	3
G. S. Blewett b Haynes	22	M. S. Kasprowicz c Lampitt b Leatherdale		2
S. R. Waugh c Rhodes b Haynes	21	G. D. McGrath c Rhodes b Leatherdale	..	2
M. G. Bevan c Rhodes b Haynes	8	L-b 4, w 6, n-b 4		14
J. L. Langer lbw b Leatherdale	15			
A. C. Gilchrist lbw b Lampitt	10	1/33 2/53 3/64	(35 overs)	121
†I. A. Healy not out	9	4/78 5/104 6/104		
B. P. Julian c Moody b Leatherdale	1	7/105 8/109 9/113		

Bowling: Newport 6–0–18–0; Haynes 10–1–40–4; Sheriyar 7–0–29–0; Lampitt 7–0–20–1; Leatherdale 5–1–10–5.

Worcestershire

*T. M. Moody c Warne b Kasprowicz	32	D. A. Leatherdale not out	....	8
W. P. C. Weston c Julian b Warne	12			
G. A. Hick c Warne b Blewett	35	B 5, l-b 1, w 11, n-b 4	....	21
G. R. Haynes c Warne b Kasprowicz	0			
V. S. Solanki c Gilchrist b Warne	6	1/58 2/65 3/65	(5 wkts, 38.5 overs)	123
K. R. Spiring not out	9	4/87 5/114		

†S. J. Rhodes, P. J. Newport, A. Sheriyar and S. R. Lampitt did not bat.

Bowling: McGrath 10–1–32–0; Kasprowicz 10–3–13–2; Julian 6–3–13–0; Warne 10–1–36–2; Blewett 2.5–0–23–1.

Umpires: R. Julian and D. R. Shepherd.

†DURHAM v AUSTRALIANS

At Chester-le-Street, May 20. Abandoned.

The match was called off at 10 a.m. because of heavy rain overnight, to the intense disappointment of Durham chairman Don Robson, who thought the decision premature. Members had to be content with watching Kevin Keegan, the former manager of Newcastle United FC, opening the new County Stand and Members Lounge; the Australians turned down his offer of a football match.

†ENGLAND v AUSTRALIA

First One-Day International

At Leeds, May 22. England won by six wickets. Toss: England.

England set the tone for the early part of the summer, overwhelming an under-prepared Australian side with a vibrant all-round performance. Even the announcement of the squad caused excitement; it included both Hollioake brothers, though 19-year-old Ben was omitted from this match, along with Crawley, Giles and Silverwood. When the game started, on a gloomy Yorkshire morning, they seized the initiative at once through a menacing opening spell by Gough. Then Ealham and Croft, who conceded only 16 in ten overs, turned the screw with the help of some outstanding fielding – Atherton and Ealham held spectacular one-handed catches, while Bevan, Australia's top scorer with 30, was efficiently run out by Thorpe. Chasing 171 to win, England's upper order did their best to fritter the advantage away by collapsing to 40 for four. But Thorpe was more composed; he built a commanding, unbeaten partnership of 135 with Hollioake, who finished the match with a pulled six off Gillespie.

Man of the Match: A. J. Hollioake.   *Attendance:* 16,141; *receipts* £460,013.

Australia

*M. A. Taylor c Stewart b Gough	7	M. S. Kasprowicz not out	17
M. E. Waugh b Headley	11	J. N. Gillespie not out	3
S. R. Waugh lbw b Ealham	19	L-b 7, w 9, n-b 1	17
M. G. Bevan run out	30		—
G. S. Blewett b Gough	28	1/8 (1) 2/39 (2) (8 wkts, 50 overs) 170	
M. J. Slater c and b Ealham	17	3/43 (3) 4/106 (4)	
†I. A. Healy c Atherton b Hollioake	17	5/106 (5) 6/140 (7)	
S. K. Warne c Thorpe b Hollioake	4	7/140 (6) 8/157 (8) Score at 15 overs: 39-2	

G. D. McGrath did not bat.

Bowling: DeFreitas 9–1–35–0; Gough 10–2–33–2; Ealham 8–3–21–2; Headley 8–0–36–1; Croft 10–1–16–0; Hollioake 5–0–22–2.

England

N. V. Knight lbw b McGrath	12	A. J. Hollioake not out	66
*M. A. Atherton c Healy b Kasprowicz	4	B 1, w 6, n-b 4	11
†A. J. Stewart lbw b McGrath	7		
G. P. Thorpe not out	75	1/18 (2) 2/20 (1) (4 wkts, 40.1 overs) 175	
G. D. Lloyd run out	0	3/32 (3) 4/40 (5) Score at 15 overs: 42-4	

M. A. Ealham, P. A. J. DeFreitas, R. D. B. Croft, D. Gough and D. W. Headley did not bat.

Bowling: McGrath 10–2–34–2; Kasprowicz 7–0–27–1; Gillespie 8.1–1–39–0; Warne 10–0–46–0; M. E. Waugh 2–0–16–0; Blewett 3–0–12–0.

Umpires: R. Julian and P. Willey.   Referee: R. S. Madugalle (Sri Lanka).

†ENGLAND v AUSTRALIA

Second One-Day International

At The Oval, May 24. England won by six wickets. Toss: England.

England were dominant in the field once again, restricting Australia to 249 for six on a first-rate batting track. Four of those wickets fell to run-outs, including that of Mark Waugh, who had looked in ominous form as he scored 25 at a run a ball. Waugh had also run out Taylor, to add to the captain's problems with the bat. Bevan and Gilchrist resisted the lemming instinct in a fifth-wicket stand of 113, but they could not score quickly enough; Bevan found the boundary only six times in his unbeaten 108. After Knight's early demise, Stewart kick-started England's innings by charging at Warne's leg-spin. He eventually became Warne's only victim of the series, but Atherton was on hand to guide his team home with a century, only his second in one-day internationals.

Man of the Match: M. A. Atherton.   *Attendance:* 16,066; *receipts* £486,106.

Australia

M. E. Waugh run out	25	S. K. Warne not out	11
*M. A. Taylor run out	11		
S. R. Waugh b Croft	24	L-b 8, w 1	9
M. G. Bevan not out	108		—
M. J. Slater run out	1	1/35 (2) 2/37 (1) (6 wkts, 50 overs) 249	
A. C. Gilchrist lbw b Hollioake	53	3/94 (3) 4/98 (5)	
†I. A. Healy run out	7	5/211 (6) 6/226 (7) Score at 15 overs: 57-2	

M. S. Kasprowicz, J. N. Gillespie and G. D. McGrath did not bat.

Bowling: DeFreitas 8–0–47–0; Gough 10–3–42–0; Ealham 9–2–40–0; Giles 9–0–48–0; Croft 10–2–39–1; Hollioake 4–0–25–1.

England

N. V. Knight lbw b Kasprowicz	4	A. J. Hollioake not out	53
*M. A. Atherton not out	113	L-b 5, w 8, n-b 1	14
†A. J. Stewart b Warne	40		
G. P. Thorpe c S. R. Waugh b Bevan	7	1/6 (1) 2/77 (3) (4 wkts, 48.2 overs)	253
G. D. Lloyd c Warne b McGrath	22	3/104 (4) 4/158 (5) Score at 15 overs: 78-2	

M. A. Ealham, P. A. J. DeFreitas, R. D. B. Croft, D. Gough and A. F. Giles did not bat.

Bowling: McGrath 9–1–46–1; Kasprowicz 9.2–0–58–1; Gillespie 8–1–42–0; Warne 10–0–39–1; Bevan 9–0–43–1; S. R. Waugh 3–0–20–0.

Umpires: J. H. Hampshire and D. R. Shepherd.   Referee: R. S. Madugalle (Sri Lanka).

†ENGLAND v AUSTRALIA

Third One-Day International

At Lord's, May 25. England won by six wickets. Toss: England. International debut: B. C. Hollioake.

England made a clean sweep of the series with their third consecutive six-wicket victory. Every match began with Atherton winning the toss and ended with a stroke from Adam Hollioake. But it was Adam's 19-year-old brother Ben who stole the show here, on his debut, as he thrilled Lord's with an audacious half-century. Australia, captained by Steve Waugh because Taylor had dropped himself, had set England 270, their most demanding target yet, despite a five-wicket haul by Gough. Hollioake junior made his entrance when the reply stood at 21 for one, and drove his third ball back past McGrath for four. He lasted just 45 more balls, but some glorious strokes – including a swept six off Warne – and some streaky edges had already taken him to 63, with another ten fours. England still needed 157 when he fell, but the run-rate was down to five an over. Stewart, Crawley and Thorpe cruised along with few alarms.

Man of the Match: D. Gough.   *Attendance:* 24,951; *receipts* £874,236.

Men of the Series: A. J. Hollioake and M. G. Bevan.

Australia

M. T. G. Elliott c A. J. Hollioake b Gough	1	J. N. Gillespie c Thorpe b Gough	6
M. E. Waugh lbw b Gough	95	G. D. McGrath st Stewart	
*S. R. Waugh c Thorpe b Gough	17	b A. J. Hollioake	1
M. G. Bevan c sub (N. V. Knight)		B 2, l-b 10, w 5, n-b 2	19
b Gough	8		
J. L. Langer run out	29	1/2 (1) 2/52 (3) 3/63 (4) (49.2 overs)	269
A. C. Gilchrist lbw b Ealham	33	4/142 (5) 5/184 (2)	
†I. A. Healy c Lloyd b Croft	27	6/218 (6) 7/228 (8)	
S. K. Warne c Stewart b Ealham	5	8/242 (7) 9/268 (10)	
M. S. Kasprowicz not out	28	10/269 (11) Score at 15 overs: 88-3	

Bowling: Gough 10–0–44–5; Silverwood 6–0–44–0; Ealham 10–0–47–2; Croft 10–0–51–1; B. C. Hollioake 7–0–36–0; A. J. Hollioake 6.2–0–35–1.

England

*M. A. Atherton lbw b Kasprowicz	1	A. J. Hollioake not out	4
†A. J. Stewart c Langer b M. E. Waugh	79	L-b 9, w 13, n-b 4	26
B. C. Hollioake c S. R. Waugh b Gillespie	63		
J. P. Crawley run out	52	1/21 (1) 2/113 (3) (4 wkts, 49 overs)	270
G. P. Thorpe not out	45	3/193 (2) 4/253 (4) Score at 15 overs: 72-1	

G. D. Lloyd, M. A. Ealham, R. D. B. Croft, D. Gough and C. E. W. Silverwood did not bat.

Bowling: McGrath 9–2–45–0; Kasprowicz 8–1–40–1; Warne 9–0–44–0; Gillespie 10–0–55–1; Bevan 3–0–27–0; S. R. Waugh 4–0–22–0; M. E. Waugh 6–0–28–1.

Umpires: M. J. Kitchen and G. Sharp.   Referee: R. S. Madugalle (Sri Lanka).

GLOUCESTERSHIRE v AUSTRALIANS

At Bristol, May 27, 28, 29. Drawn. Toss: Australians.

A fortnight into the tour and only nine days before the Edgbaston Test, the Australians played their opening first-class match. In five overs, they were 21 for three. The torment of Taylor, hunting for runs and confidence, worsened: he was caught behind after four balls, and had to endure being presented with a giant bat as a newspaper stunt. Russell quickly collected two more left-handers, Elliott and Langer, off the bowling of Lewis, and the Australians managed only 249. They appeared tentative, at times technically imprudent, and lacking the assurance expected of them; they leaned heavily on the Waughs, who responded attractively. The second innings was more reassuring. Taylor lasted almost two hours, and Elliott and Langer had some invaluable batting practice, adding 152. Alleyne used nine bowlers, including Russell, bowling round-arm in dark glasses. Trainor's maiden hundred was the innings of the match, though. He had just scored three ducks in a row, but batted here for five hours, sharing a solid stand of 140 with Cunliffe. It was a diligent, even unassuming, innings, applauded generously by the tourists. Gloucestershire's biggest shock came after the match: the boundary rope was stolen.

Close of play: First day, Gloucestershire 55-1 (N. J. Trainor 36*, R. P. Davis 0*); Second day, Australians 43-0 (M. T. G. Elliott 21*, M. A. Taylor 19*).

Australians

*M. A. Taylor c Russell b Smith	0	– (2) lbw b Ball	30
M. T. G. Elliott c Russell b Lewis	6	– (1) lbw b Smith	124
J. L. Langer c Russell b Lewis	6	– not out	152
M. E. Waugh c Smith b Davis	66	– (6) not out	32
S. R. Waugh b Smith	92		
M. G. Bevan c Wright b Lewis	18		
†I. A. Healy not out	30		
S. K. Warne c Young b Lewis	5	– (4) b Smith	0
M. S. Kasprowicz b Ball	16		
J. N. Gillespie c Hancock b Ball	3	– (5) c Russell b Lewis	7
G. D. McGrath st Russell b Ball	0		
L-b 3, n-b 4	7	B 6, l-b 2, w 1	9
	249	(4 wkts dec.)	**354**

1/0 2/10 3/21 4/117 5/184 6/205 7/217 8/241 9/249

1/62 2/254 3/262 4/269

Bowling: *First Innings*—Smith 11–3–26–2; Lewis 21–9–39–4; Alleyne 7–2–26–0; Hancock 8–1–29–0; Davis 11–3–20–1; Ball 17.4–3–56–3. *Second Innings*—Smith 13–5–18–2; Davis 29–6–101–0; Lewis 18–5–59–1; Ball 28–9–89–1; Alleyne 8–2–25–0; Trainor 3–2–8–0; Hancock 5–0–26–0; Russell 3–0–15–0; Young 2–0–5–0.

Gloucestershire

A. J. Wright lbw b Gillespie	16	M. C. J. Ball c and b Kasprowicz	25
N. J. Trainor c Kasprowicz b McGrath	121	A. M. Smith c Gillespie b Warne	4
R. P. Davis lbw b Warne	30	J. Lewis not out	7
R. J. Cunliffe c Kasprowicz b Warne	61		
T. H. C. Hancock lbw b Kasprowicz	15	B 4, l-b 6, n-b 20	30
S. Young c Healy b Kasprowicz	1		
*M. W. Alleyne c and b Gillespie	20	1/52 2/103 3/243 4/250 5/257	**350**
†R. C. Russell c Bevan b Warne	20	6/286 7/288 8/339 9/339	

Bowling: McGrath 19–11–31–1; Kasprowicz 21–2–101–3; Warne 35.2–10–97–4; Gillespie 20–4–66–2; Bevan 12–1–45–0.

Umpires: P. Adams and G. I. Burgess.

DERBYSHIRE v AUSTRALIANS

At Derby, May 31, June 1, 2. Derbyshire won by one wicket. Toss: Australians. First-class debut: I. D. Blackwell.

Derbyshire achieved their first victory over an Australian team since beating the Imperial Forces in 1919. It was a particularly satisfying win for Jones – exiled from the Australian Test scene – but it was to be his last hurrah before his resignation from Derbyshire turned quiet turmoil there into open warfare. The pursuit of 371 from 69 overs was led by Adams, who scored a vivid 91 from 76 balls. It compensated for his behaviour when given lbw to Warne in the first innings, in what replays suggested was a faulty decision: he argued with umpire Holder and, later, with a £750 fine from the club. He was to fall to Warne again in the second innings, one of his seven wickets. But Warne was expensive, and Julian's inaccuracy cost six an over. Derbyshire's last pair reached the target – Derbyshire's highest ever fourth-innings score – with three balls to spare. On the eve of the match, the England selectors had asked for Malcolm to be withdrawn, a strong hint he would play in the First Test. Blewett booked his own Test place by scoring 121 on a bland pitch. But after mutual declarations and another comfortable century, by Bevan, Derbyshire were to provide another setback for Australia.

Close of play: First day, Derbyshire 68-1 (M. R. May 27*, P. Aldred 4*); Second day, Australians 148-2 (M. A. Taylor 59*, M. G. Bevan 58*).

Australians

*M. A. Taylor c Aldred b DeFreitas	5	– (2) c Krikken b Aldred 63
M. T. G. Elliott c Adams b Dean	67	– (1) b Harris 4
J. L. Langer lbw b DeFreitas	1	– lbw b Dean 12
G. S. Blewett b Harris	121	
S. R. Waugh c DeFreitas b Blackwell	43	
M. G. Bevan b DeFreitas	56	– (4) not out 104
†I. A. Healy not out	40	
B. P. Julian not out	12	– (5) c Jones b Dean 62
S. K. Warne (did not bat)		– (6) not out 2
B 5, l-b 2, n-b 10	17	B 2, l-b 4, n-b 12 18

1/10 2/16 3/147 4/246   (6 wkts dec.) 362   1/5 2/35   (4 wkts dec.) 265
5/260 6/335   3/159 4/260

A. J. Bichel and J. N. Gillespie did not bat.

Bowling: *First Innings*—DeFreitas 14–2–61–3; Harris 18–2–70–1; Dean 16–1–76–1; Aldred 12–3–26–0; Clarke 6–0–45–0; Blackwell 15–1–57–1; Jones 4–0–20–0. *Second Innings*—DeFreitas 10–3–31–0; Harris 16–3–49–1; Blackwell 9–1–49–0; Dean 10–0–45–2; Aldred 15–1–65–1; Rollins 2–0–12–0; Clarke 4–1–8–0.

Derbyshire

A. S. Rollins lbw b Julian	15	– lbw b Warne 66
M. R. May c Waugh b Julian	67	– c Waugh b Julian 27
P. Aldred b Gillespie	8	– (9) not out 14
C. J. Adams lbw b Warne	7	– (3) c sub (G. D. McGrath)
		b Warne . 91
*D. M. Jones b Warne	31	– (4) c Healy b Julian 57
I. D. Blackwell c Blewett b Julian	0	– (5) c and b Warne 5
V. P. Clarke c and b Bevan	20	– (6) c Julian b Warne 28
†K. M. Krikken c sub (M. J. Slater) b Gillespie	6	– (7) c Bevan b Warne 21
P. A. J. DeFreitas b Bevan	6	– (8) c sub (M. E. Waugh) b Warne. 26
A. J. Harris not out	26	– lbw b Warne 5
K. J. Dean not out	21	– not out 9
B 7, l-b 6, w 3, n-b 34	50	L-b 4, w 2, n-b 16 22

1/55 2/77 3/114 4/158 5/168   (9 wkts dec.) 257   1/49 2/191 3/197   (9 wkts) 371
6/168 7/198 8/204 9/206   4/213 5/251 6/291
           7/339 8/343 9/360

Bowling: *First Innings*—Bichel 5–1–28–0; Julian 20–6–88–3; Gillespie 17–3–62–2; Warne 14–3–45–2; Bevan 9–4–21–2. *Second Innings*—Gillespie 5–0–35–0; Julian 21.3–1–126–2; Waugh 1–0–8–0; Warne 23–2–103–7; Bevan 10–0–60–0; Elliott 8–0–35–0.

Umpires: V. A. Holder and R. A. White.

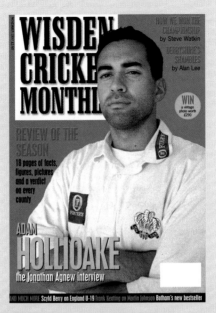

ENGLAND v AUSTRALIA

First Cornhill Test

At Birmingham, June 5, 6, 7, 8. England won by nine wickets. Toss: Australia. Test debut: M. A. Butcher.

The ripples of patriotic optimism which followed England's 3-0 victory in the one-day internationals had become a tidal wave of emotion and euphoria by the end of this extraordinary match. There were reasons to think England might perform well – their growing confidence in New Zealand, the whitewash in the one-day internationals, Taylor's personal purgatory, Australia's injuries and general lack of form – but nothing had prepared a disbelieving public for what actually happened.

The game had everything as far as England were concerned: Australia's collapse to 54 for eight on the opening morning, magnificent innings by Hussain and Thorpe, a heroic century by Taylor and a suitably dramatic finale. England won at 6.52 p.m. on Sunday evening, when Stewart cracked Warne to the extra cover boundary. They passed their target of 118 in just 21.3 overs and the crowd, close to a fourth successive full house, engulfed the field. "They're coming home, they're coming home, Ashes coming home," they sang, to the tune made famous in the Euro 96 soccer championships. Not even the most hard-bitten realists dared argue: the electric, jingoistic atmosphere was a feature of the grand occasion.

England fielded eight of the team which had gained back-to-back Test victories in Wellington and Christchurch in February. Cork was injured, Tufnell left out of the final eleven and Knight dropped. Malcolm was recalled for the first time since his falling out with Ray Illingworth in South Africa, Ealham also returned and Surrey's Mark Butcher made his debut. In a ceremony unashamedly pinched from the Australians to emphasise the team's sense of patriotism, he was ceremoniously presented with his cap on the outfield by Atherton. Adam Hollioake, like Tufnell, was omitted from the original 13; Alex Tudor, the 19-year-old Surrey quick bowler, also joined in practice on Tuesday "for experience". Australia departed from the strategy of two front-line seamers and seven batsmen used against West Indies and stuck to in South Africa, reverting to a more normal three plus six.

Taylor chose to bat and, by 12.36 on the first day, Australia were 54 for eight from 20 overs. The sheer drama of it all scrambled the senses. Gough's last ball fizzed past Taylor's outside edge – by contrast, the opening delivery of the previous Ashes series, at Brisbane in November 1994, was a long hop from Phil DeFreitas which Michael Slater square cut for four. Gough, bowling with pace, rhythm and confidence, made the initial thrusts, removing three of the top four, while Malcolm persuaded Taylor to chase a wide one and disturbed Bevan with lift. Caddick then swept through the middle and lower order. Only a flurry from Warne took Australia beyond three figures.

Edgbaston's future as a Test venue was already threatened, because the matches of 1995 and 1996 finished well inside three and four days respectively. Ten wickets in two and a half hours scarcely calmed the demeanour of Dennis Amiss, Warwickshire's chief executive, or Steve Rouse, the groundsman. But Australia's collapse had little to do with demons in the pitch. There was some uneven bounce and lateral movement, certainly, but it was swing and self-destructive shots which undermined their batsmen.

Mutterings about the pitch continued as England's top three succumbed in an hour. But they were silenced when Hussain and Thorpe put on 288, which surpassed 222, by Wally Hammond and Eddie Paynter, at Lord's in 1938, as England's highest fourth-wicket partnership against Australia. Here were two friends, once part of the so-called Bat Pack of aggressive young England players, demoralising the ultimate foe and the best side in the world. Hussain was touched by genius during a truly great innings. When Warne dropped short, he cut with power and precision. When the quick bowlers over-pitched, he drove with skill and certainty. In all, he batted for 440 minutes and 337 balls; 38 fours peppered his maiden double-hundred in any cricket, and England's first against Australia since David Gower scored 215 on the same ground in 1985. Left-hander Thorpe was Hussain's equal; indeed, he probably displayed superior range and execution of shot on the first day, when they added 150 in 169 minutes. It was Thorpe's third century in four Tests, and his cutting and sweeping of Warne were crucial in seizing the initiative.

Warne was ineffective, partly because his sore shoulder reduced the rip he could impart and partly because Hussain and Thorpe never allowed him to settle. McGrath bowled where he would do in Australia, rather than the fuller length required in England, and Gillespie retired with a hamstring strain. Kasprowicz, who had failed to take a wicket in his previous two Tests, sustained his hostility and was easily their best bowler. Healy took six catches, equalling the Australian Test record.

THE ENGLAND TEAM FOR THE EDGBASTON TEST

[*Patrick Eagar*

Back row: M. A. Ealham, R. D. B. Croft, A. R. Caddick, J. P. Crawley, M. A. Butcher, D. Gough. *Front row*: D. E. Malcolm, N. Hussain, M. A. Atherton (*captain*), A. J. Stewart, G. P. Thorpe.

Facing a first-innings deficit of 360, Taylor knew failure could mean the end of his international career. He had not reached fifty in his previous 21 Test innings and he was being castigated, it seemed, by every old Test player with a platform. His batting was a monument to courage and determination – if not technique, because he was still susceptible around off stump. He reached his first century since November 1995 on Saturday evening, sharing stands of 133 with Elliott and 194 with Blewett. Blewett's cover driving on the up was dazzling: he became the first man to score centuries in his first three Ashes Tests. Shortly before lunch on the fourth day, Australia were 327 for one – just 33 adrift. But once Croft had winkled out the top three, Gough, in another inspired burst, removed the heart of their innings in seven overs. Ealham finished them off with three for nought in ten balls.

Suddenly, England knew they could win with a day to spare. They required 118 and had a possible 32 overs (24 plus eight in the extra half-hour). They did it in style. Butcher set the tempo, striking 14 in ten balls, and then Atherton and Stewart blazed away. "The adrenalin was flowing so much," said Atherton, "that I couldn't stop myself playing attacking shots." He scored 57 in 65 balls, passing 5,000 Test runs on the way. Victory brought an outpouring of elation, in front of the pavilion and across the country; people suddenly felt the little urn could, indeed, be recaptured. – JOHN ETHERIDGE.

Man of the Match: N. Hussain.　　　*Attendance:* 72,693; *receipts* £1,588,593.

Close of play: First day, England 200-3 (N. Hussain 80*, G. P. Thorpe 83*); Second day, England 449-6 (M. A. Ealham 32*, R. D. B. Croft 18*); Third day, Australia 256-1 (M. A. Taylor 108*, G. S. Blewett 61*).

Australia

*M. A. Taylor c Butcher b Malcolm	7	– (2) c and b Croft	129
M. T. G. Elliott b Gough	6	– (1) b Croft	66
G. S. Blewett c Hussain b Gough	7	– c Butcher b Croft	125
M. E. Waugh b Gough	5	– (6) c Stewart b Gough	1
S. R. Waugh c Stewart b Caddick	12	– (4) lbw b Gough	33
M. G. Bevan c Ealham b Malcolm	8	– (5) c Hussain b Gough	24
†I. A. Healy c Stewart b Caddick	0	– c Atherton b Ealham	30
J. N. Gillespie lbw b Caddick	4	– (10) run out	0
S. K. Warne c Malcolm b Caddick	47	– (8) c and b Ealham	32
M. S. Kasprowicz c Butcher b Caddick	17	– (9) c Butcher b Ealham	0
G. D. McGrath not out	1	– not out	0
W 2, n-b 2	4	B 18, l-b 12, w 2, n-b 5	37

1/11 (2) 2/15 (1) 3/26 (4) 4/28 (3) 　　118 　　1/133 (1) 2/327 (2) 3/354 (3)　　477
5/48 (5) 6/48 (7) 7/48 (6) 　　　　　　　　4/393 (5) 5/399 (6) 6/431 (4)
8/54 (8) 9/110 (10) 10/118 (9) 　　　　　　7/465 (7) 8/465 (9)
　　　　　　　　　　　　　　　　　　　　9/477 (10) 10/477 (8)

Bowling: First Innings—Gough 10–1–43–3; Malcolm 10–2–25–2; Caddick 11.5–1–50–5. *Second Innings*—Gough 35–7–123–3; Malcolm 21–6–52–0; Croft 43–10–125–3; Caddick 30–6–87–0; Ealham 15.4–3–60–3.

England

M. A. Butcher c Healy b Kasprowicz	8	– lbw b Kasprowicz	14
*M. A. Atherton c Healy b McGrath	2	– not out	57
†A. J. Stewart c Elliott b Gillespie	18	– not out	40
N. Hussain c Healy b Warne	207		
G. P. Thorpe c Bevan b McGrath	138		
J. P. Crawley c Healy b Kasprowicz	1		
M. A. Ealham not out	53		
R. D. B. Croft c Healy b Kasprowicz	24		
D. Gough c Healy b Kasprowicz	0		
A. R. Caddick lbw b Bevan	0		
B 4, l-b 7, w 1, n-b 15	27	B 4, l-b 4	8

1/8 (2) 2/16 (1) 3/50 (3) 　　(9 wkts dec.) 478 　　1/29 (1)　　　　(1 wkt) 119
4/338 (5) 5/345 (6) 6/416 (4)
7/460 (8) 8/463 (9) 9/478 (10)

D. E. Malcolm did not bat.

Bowling: *First Innings*—McGrath 32–8–107–2; Kasprowicz 39–8–113–4; Gillespie 10–1–48–1; Warne 35–8–110–1; Bevan 10.4–0–44–1; S. R. Waugh 12–2–45–0. *Second Innings*—McGrath 7–1–42–0; Kasprowicz 7–0–42–1; Warne 7.3–0–27–0.

Umpires: S. A. Bucknor (West Indies) and P. Willey.   Referee: R. S. Madugalle (Sri Lanka).

NOTTINGHAMSHIRE v AUSTRALIANS

At Nottingham, June 11, 12, 13. Drawn. Toss: Australians. First-class debut: A. R. Oram.

Despite a first-day washout, the Australians were encouraged by the play that did take place, especially the performance of Reiffel. Summoned from Melbourne when Andy Bichel was forced out of the tour by back problems, he was picked just 24 hours after landing. With the rain allowing him an extra day to recover from jet lag, he bowled with impressive accuracy to claim three for 15 in ten overs. The only batsman to master the attack was New Zealander Astle, who hit 16 fours in 109 balls, square-driving frequently and dishing out some severe treatment to Julian; he fell one short of a maiden hundred for his new county. With more showers forecast on the final day, the tourists settled for batting practice. Steve Waugh shared century stands with Elliott, who reached his hundred with a six, and Bevan, who hit a ball from Afzaal on to the roof of a hospitality box.

Close of play: First day, No play; Second day, Australians 51-1 (M. T. G. Elliott 20*, R. T. Ponting 15*).

Nottinghamshire

G. E. Welton c Gilchrist b Julian	16	P. J. Franks c Gilchrist b McGrath		1
M. P. Dowman c Julian b Reiffel	22	R. A. Pick b McGrath		7
U. Afzaal lbw b Kasprowicz	34	A. R. Oram not out		0
N. J. Astle c Elliott b McGrath	99			
†L. N. P. Walker c Bevan b Reiffel	5	B 1, l-b 4, w 1, n-b 22		28
*P. Johnson c Elliott b Reiffel	6			—
W. M. Noon c Gilchrist b Julian	0	1/39 2/44 3/121 4/148 5/156		239
K. P. Evans c M. E. Waugh b McGrath	21	6/173 7/203 8/221 9/236		

Bowling: McGrath 18.1–4–63–4; Kasprowicz 17–4–54–1; Reiffel 10–3–15–3; Julian 18–1–70–2; Bevan 7–1–32–0.

Australians

M. T. G. Elliott b Afzaal	127	M. G. Bevan not out		75
M. J. Slater lbw b Evans	14	†A. C. Gilchrist not out		9
R. T. Ponting lbw b Pick	19	B 3, l-b 3, w 4		10
M. E. Waugh c Astle b Dowman	29			—
*S. R. Waugh c Afzaal b Dowman	115	1/29 2/55 3/133 4/250 5/382 (5 wkts)		398

B. P. Julian, P. R. Reiffel, M. S. Kasprowicz and G. D. McGrath did not bat.

Bowling: Franks 18–3–54–0; Pick 13–0–62–1; Evans 15–1–51–1; Oram 5–1–14–0; Astle 13–1–37–0; Dowman 16–0–78–2; Afzaal 15.2–1–96–1.

Umpires: J. D. Bond and B. J. Meyer.

LEICESTERSHIRE v AUSTRALIANS

At Leicester, June 14, 15, 16. Australians won by 84 runs. Toss: Leicestershire.

The Australians warmed up for the Second Test with their opening first-class win of the tour. They owed some thanks, though, to the generosity of the umpires and their opponents, as the match was badly hit by the weather. Three declarations were necessary before Taylor set a target of 264, and Leicestershire were 158 for seven when bad light and rain forced a halt. Several Australians ostentatiously remained on the field to practise. The umpires swiftly did an about turn, to the delight of Warne, who finished with five for 42, and Reiffel, who took three in each innings to confirm his fast-track return to the Test side. However, the best figures belonged to Leicestershire's 19-year-old pace bowler James Ormond, who took a career-best six for 54 on the opening day. Often, he swung the ball too much, and Nixon conceded 23 byes.

Close of play: First day, Australians 220-8 (J. L. Langer 9*, P. R. Reiffel 6*); Second day, Leicestershire 62-4 (A. Habib 11*, P. A. Nixon 2*).

Australians

M. J. Slater c Sutcliffe b Ormond	16	– (2) b Ormond	17
*M. A. Taylor b Ormond	1	– (1) c Macmillan b Mason	57
R. T. Ponting b Ormond	64		
M. G. Bevan c Sutcliffe b Wells	11	– c and b Mason	13
†I. A. Healy b Ormond	34		
M. E. Waugh lbw b Ormond	6	– (3) not out	16
J. L. Langer not out	9		
B. P. Julian c Maddy b Ormond	5		
S. K. Warne lbw b Pierson	20		
P. R. Reiffel not out	6		
B 23, l-b 14, w 7, n-b 4	48	L-b 2	2

1/10 2/29 3/83 4/158 5/167   (8 wkts dec.) 220   1/39 2/83 3/105   (3 wkts dec.) 105
6/176 7/182 8/212

G. D. McGrath did not bat.

Bowling: *First Innings*—Mullally 14-1-55-0; Ormond 20-7-54-6; Wells 9-3-24-1; Pierson 10-3-34-1; Maddy 7-1-15-0; Mason 1-0-1-0. *Second Innings*—Ormond 8-0-36-1; Maddy 7-1-13-0; Mason 4.4-0-21-2; Pierson 4-0-33-0.

Leicestershire

D. L. Maddy b Reiffel	1	– lbw b Reiffel	7
I. J. Sutcliffe c Healy b Reiffel	3	– c Healy b McGrath	31
G. I. Macmillan c Bevan b Warne	34	– c Slater b Julian	25
*J. J. Whitaker c Langer b Reiffel	1	– lbw b Warne	21
A. Habib not out	11	– c Ponting b Warne	13
†P. A. Nixon not out	2	– st Healy b Warne	24
V. J. Wells (did not bat)		– c Ponting b Reiffel	38
J. Ormond (did not bat)		– b Warne	1
T. J. Mason (did not bat)		– c Julian b Reiffel	4
A. R. K. Pierson (did not bat)		– c Langer b Warne	0
A. D. Mullally (did not bat)		– not out	2
B 2, l-b 2, n-b 6	10	B 1, l-b 1, w 1, n-b 10	13

1/1 2/24 3/30 4/59   (4 wkts dec.) 62   1/21 2/66 3/68 4/92 5/118   179
                                           6/155 7/157 8/168 9/177

Bowling: *First Innings*—McGrath 12-4-24-0; Reiffel 10-6-12-3; Warne 5-1-20-1; Julian 3.3-2-2-0. *Second Innings*—McGrath 14-5-40-1; Reiffel 12-3-49-3; Julian 8-1-35-1; Warne 16.4-2-42-5; Bevan 1-0-11-0.

Umpires: D. J. Constant and J. H. Harris.

ENGLAND v AUSTRALIA

Second Cornhill Test

At Lord's, June 19, 20, 21, 22, 23. Drawn. Toss: Australia.

Rain prevented a conclusive result to the Second Test, ending Australia's run of 18 Tests without a draw. But there was never a chance of England ending their melancholy sequence of failure against Australia at Lord's; their 1934 victory will remain their only success in 23 Tests in the 20th century. By the end, they were not remotely concerned about that; having been humiliated for 77, they were grateful that the weather enabled them to cling on to their 1-0 lead in the series. Atherton lost an important toss on his 42nd appearance as England captain (surpassing Peter May's record of 41). This time, Taylor put England in, and bowled them out for even less than Australia had managed after choosing to bat in not dissimilar conditions at Edgbaston.

No play had been possible on the scheduled first day, and there was only an hour and a half on the second. In that time, England, fielding an unchanged eleven for the first time in home Tests since June 1991, lost Butcher, Atherton and Stewart – who left an off-cutter – all to McGrath, on a pitch of uneven bounce. Thorpe almost went too, before he had scored, but wicket-keeper Healy was uncertain about his "catch" and told the umpires so, prompting a burst of applause from umpire Shepherd.

At that stage, England's supporters were still more concerned about the ruin of the great occasion. On the Saturday, the cricket became more of a concern. The rest of England's wickets toppled before lunch next day while they scraped together just 39. The tall McGrath, continuing from the Pavilion End, adopted a fuller length than at Edgbaston and bowled with pace, lift, movement off the seam and unwavering accuracy to pick up five more wickets. The batsmen had found no relief at the other end, for Reiffel, flown in to reinforce the ranks because of Bichel's injury, bowled a tight line and moved the ball away dangerously. He found the edge of Thorpe's bat for a catch via the pad and later deceived Ealham into playing early. The rigid England batsmen could scarcely score a run an over off him. McGrath swept away the rest: Crawley played especially limply, probably with Stewart's fatal "leave-alone" in mind. When Caddick was lbw, McGrath had taken eight for 38, the best analysis in the 31 England–Australia Tests staged at Lord's, the second-best bowling for Australia in England (behind Frank Laver's eight for 31 at Old Trafford in 1909), and the third-best by an Australian bowler in any Test (behind also Arthur Mailey's nine for 121 at Melbourne against England in 1920-21). England's 77 was their lowest in any Test on this ground since 1888; only nine times in 287 Tests against Australia had they fared worse. The national spirit of self-confidence which followed victory at Edgbaston had been both drenched and deflated.

The stunned atmosphere was relieved a touch by the early dismissal of Australia's captain when they began their reply. Gough, rested by Yorkshire before this Test, bounded in and, in his third over, Taylor deflected a widish delivery into his stumps. Blewett soon saw a looping edge off Caddick fall safely as Butcher and Thorpe froze, but settled to play some resonant strokes before edging Croft to slip. It was by no means the end of England's maladroitness, however. In a bizarre spell of play in the late-afternoon dankness, Elliott was missed three times as he reached 55 – twice by Butcher at slip and, in between, by Malcolm at long leg. Meanwhile, Mark Waugh gave a sharp chance to Hussain at slip and a difficult leg-side stumping opportunity to Crawley (deputising as wicket-keeper for Stewart, who had suffered a back spasm), both off Croft. England were suddenly unrecognisable from the competent unit of a fortnight earlier.

Impatient to level the series, Australia were frustrated again on the fourth day, when only 17.4 overs were bowled as shower after shower sprayed Lord's. From 131 for two they progressed to 213 for seven, the pace resembling that of a one-day match. Waugh slashed a catch to third man and brother Steve went back to his first ball and was lbw. In between, Warne, promoted to No. 5, had wafted a high off-side catch. And all this happened with the score on 147. Undeterred, Elliott still sought to score from every delivery, and ran to his first Test century from his 171st ball. He fell soon afterwards to his favoured stroke, the hook, having loaded his 112 with 20 fours, an exceptional proportion.

Declaring overnight in the hope of cashing in a lead of 136, Australia were favoured with clearer weather at last, but the pitch had calmed. Prepared for a gruelling final day with their backs to the wall, England firmly reclaimed their poise, though only after Taylor, at slip, had spared Butcher – the fielder who had been so generous to the Australian batsmen – when he was two. But at lunch England were 70 without loss, and they eased to a lead of 26 before Atherton accidentally kicked his off stump as he played to leg. When light rain forced a slightly early tea-break at 169 for one, the only remaining interest was whether Butcher, seeming more and more comfortable, might reach a hundred. But his hopes were dashed by a well-flighted ball from Warne that spun out of the rough. Warne was looking more like his old self. From there, England batted it out: chastened but still one up. – DAVID FRITH.

Man of the Match: G. D. McGrath.   *Attendance:* 105,901; *receipts* £2,679,340.

Close of play: First day, No play; Second day, England 38-3 (N. Hussain 10*, G. P. Thorpe 13*); Third day, Australia 131-2 (M. T. G. Elliott 55*, M. E. Waugh 26*); Fourth day, Australia 213-7 (I. A. Healy 13*, P. R. Reiffel 1*).

England

M. A. Butcher c Blewett b McGrath	5	– b Warne	87
*M. A. Atherton c Taylor b McGrath	1	– hit wkt b Kasprowicz	77
†A. J. Stewart b McGrath	1	– c Kasprowicz b McGrath	13
N. Hussain lbw b McGrath	19	– c and b Warne	0
G. P. Thorpe c Blewett b Reiffel	21	– not out	30
J. P. Crawley c Healy b McGrath	1	– not out	29
M. A. Ealham c Elliott b Reiffel	7		
R. D. B. Croft c Healy b McGrath	2		
D. Gough c Healy b McGrath	10		
A. R. Caddick lbw b McGrath	1		
D. E. Malcolm not out	0		
B 4, n-b 5	9	B 8, l-b 14, w 1, n-b 7	30

1/11 (1) 2/12 (2) 3/13 (3) 4/47 (5)   77   1/162 (2) 2/189 (3) (4 wkts dec.) 266
5/56 (6) 6/62 (4) 7/66 (8)   3/197 (4) 4/202 (1)
8/76 (9) 9/77 (7) 10/77 (10)

Bowling: First Innings—McGrath 20.3–8–38–8; Reiffel 15–9–17–2; Kasprowicz 5–1–9–0; Warne 2–0–9–0. *Second Innings*—McGrath 20–5–65–1; Reiffel 13–5–29–0; Kasprowicz 15–3–54–1; Warne 19–4–47–2; Bevan 8–1–29–0; S. R. Waugh 4–0–20–0.

Australia

*M. A. Taylor b Gough	1	†I. A. Healy not out	13
M. T. G. Elliott c Crawley b Caddick	112	P. R. Reiffel not out	1
G. S. Blewett c Hussain b Croft	45	B 1, l-b 3	4
M. E. Waugh c Malcolm b Caddick	33		
S. K. Warne c Hussain b Gough	0	1/4 (1) 2/73 (3) 3/147 (4) (7 wkts dec.) 213	
S. R. Waugh lbw b Caddick	0	4/147 (5) 5/147 (6)	
M. G. Bevan c Stewart b Caddick	4	6/159 (7) 7/212 (2)	

M. S. Kasprowicz and G. D. McGrath did not bat.

Bowling: Gough 20–4–82–2; Caddick 22–6–71–4; Malcolm 7–1–26–0; Croft 12–5–30–1.

Umpires: S. Venkataraghavan (India) and D. R. Shepherd.
Referee: R. S. Madugalle (Sri Lanka).

BRITISH UNIVERSITIES v AUSTRALIANS

At Oxford, June 25, 26, 27. Abandoned.
The heavy rain sweeping the whole of the country caused the match to be given up – a disappointment not only for the students, but also for those of the tourists' fringe players hoping to put their case for selection at Old Trafford.

HAMPSHIRE v AUSTRALIANS

At Southampton, June 28, 29, 30. Australians won by an innings and 133 runs. Toss: Hampshire.
Stephenson's attempt to deny the Australians much-needed time at the crease by batting first backfired. The forecast storms did not materialise and, after ten days of rain, just 11 overs were lost, to bad light. The tourists' crushing win was an ideal preparation for Old Trafford. Hampshire's brittle batting offered ample opportunities to the seamers contesting Test places; and the in-form Hayden failed twice in his attempt to make the Australian selectors regret overlooking him. The pitch offered movement, but a total of 156 looked even more paltry as Taylor eased his worries with a painstaking century, and Mark Waugh struck three sixes and 23

fours in a riotous 173 from 199 balls. With Hampshire needing 309 to avoid an innings defeat, Hayden shouldered arms and was bowled by his second ball, a devastating psychological blow for him, even more than for his team. Smith could only delay the inevitable, and Gillespie, back in form after injury, and Kasprowicz completed victory after lunch on the final day.

Close of play: First day, Australians 157-2 (M. A. Taylor 61*, M. E. Waugh 25*); Second day, Hampshire 71-2 (J. S. Laney 27*, R. A. Smith 31*).

Hampshire

J. S. Laney lbw b Kasprowicz	6	– c Healy b Reiffel	30
M. L. Hayden c Blewett b Kasprowicz	6	– b Gillespie	2
M. Keech c and b Reiffel	17	– c Kasprowicz b Gillespie	6
R. A. Smith c Healy b Warne	22	– c Warne b Gillespie	44
W. S. Kendall c M. E. Waugh b Reiffel	0	– lbw b Gillespie	18
*J. P. Stephenson c Taylor b Gillespie	0	– b Gillespie	0
†A. N. Aymes not out	31	– c Blewett b Kasprowicz	18
S. D. Udal c Healy b Warne	2	– b Kasprowicz	21
S. J. Renshaw lbw b Warne	4	– not out	13
J. N. B. Bovill lbw b Gillespie	9	– c Healy b Kasprowicz	1
S. M. Milburn b Kasprowicz	23	– b Kasprowicz	3
B 1, l-b 10, w 1, n-b 24	36	L-b 6, n-b 14	20

1/9 2/30 3/45 4/57 5/79   156   1/4 2/14 3/91 4/111 5/111   176
6/83 7/85 8/93 9/112   6/114 7/143 8/159 9/160

Bowling: *First Innings*—Kasprowicz 11.1–2–33–3; Gillespie 16–2–65–2; Reiffel 7–1–17–2; Warne 15–4–30–3. *Second Innings*—Kasprowicz 14.4–1–69–3; Gillespie 13–6–33–5; Warne 19–3–26–1; Reiffel 8–1–27–1; Bevan 7–3–15–0.

Australians

M. T. G. Elliott c Keech b Udal	61	P. R. Reiffel lbw b Renshaw	1
*M. A. Taylor c Bovill b Stephenson	109	M. S. Kasprowicz not out	6
G. S. Blewett run out	2		
M. E. Waugh c Hayden b Renshaw	173	L-b 8, w 1, n-b 2	11
S. R. Waugh c Udal b Renshaw	11		
M. G. Bevan b Renshaw	24	1/95 2/118 3/275	(8 wkts dec.) 465
†I. A. Healy not out	29	4/294 5/377 6/404	
S. K. Warne lbw b Stephenson	38	7/446 8/447	

J. N. Gillespie did not bat.

Bowling: Renshaw 27–5–107–4; Bovill 26–7–87–0; Milburn 21–3–96–0; Stephenson 27–3–82–2; Udal 20–1–85–1.

Umpires: H. D. Bird and B. Leadbeater.

ENGLAND v AUSTRALIA

Third Cornhill Test

At Manchester, July 3, 4, 5, 6, 7. Australia won by 268 runs. Toss: Australia. Test debut: D. W. Headley.

The slumbering giant, aroused by the unaccustomed situation of trailing in a Test series, awoke, flexed its not inconsiderable muscle and demolished the opposition with brutal efficiency. Australia's emphatic triumph put them back on track after a stuttering start and weeks of depressing grey skies and rain. Suddenly, the weather resembled something vaguely like summer, but England's first defeat in eight Tests dampened the optimism springing from their resounding victories in the one-day series and the First Test. The contest had high achievement and occasional drama, but, from the moment Steve Waugh put his stamp on it, the whip hand was

[Patrick Eagar   *[Patrick Eagar*

Steve Waugh (*right*) scored twin hundreds at Old Trafford, combining with Shane Warne (*left*) to wrest the initiative from England.

held by Australia. Waugh became the first batsman to score twin Ashes hundreds for 50 years; backed up by Warne, who convincingly returned to his best form, he well and truly wrested the initiative from England.

Australia had reinforced McGrath's intimidating pace with Gillespie, who replaced Kasprowicz after proving his recovery from a hamstring strain. England gave Dean Headley a historic debut: he was the third generation of his family to play Test cricket, following his grandfather George and his father Ron, who both represented West Indies. Malcolm was dropped, and Tufnell and the Gloucestershire left-armer Mike Smith were also omitted from a squad of 14.

Headley was straight into the action, striking Taylor on the helmet as he ducked into a bouncer in his opening over. England had hardly concealed their joy when Taylor chose to bat on a moist, green pitch with bare patches at either end. It seemed a foolish gamble; it proved a brave and calculated decision – one made easier for a captain with Warne's genius at his disposal. But Taylor was the first sufferer. Headley pressed home the advantage in his third over, squaring him up with a fiery delivery which was edged to first slip. Taylor's headache worsened as Australia declined to 42 for three. That was when Steve Waugh entered the fray, but he got little support from the middle order. The total was a miserable 160 for seven when Reiffel joined him, just before tea.

Their luck changed, shortly after a break for bad light, when Reiffel was dropped on 13 by Stewart, off Headley. This could be construed as the turning point of the entire season. Reiffel contributed 31 to a tremendously important stand of 70 before he finally fell next morning, to Gough's trademark in-swinging yorker. By then, Waugh had completed a century of enormous skill and character. With his lucky red handkerchief poking from his trouser pocket like a matador's cape, he faced the charging attack for four hours, and later called it his finest Test innings. When he was ninth out, edging Gough's delivery on to his middle stump, he had seen Australia to 235, an admirable total in testing conditions. Headley ensured his fourth wicket, thanks to Stewart, whose sixth catch equalled England's record for an innings against Australia; later, he added two more to break the record for a match. His opposite number, Healy, soon retaliated. A brilliant leg-side stumping off a full toss from Bevan removed Butcher and provided Healy's 100th dismissal in 25 England–Australia Tests. Only Rod Marsh (148 in 42 games) and Alan Knott (105 in 34) had previously reached this landmark.

Healy's 99th victim had been Atherton, who, for the third time in three Tests, went cheaply in the first innings to McGrath. This time, he gloved a seemingly erratic leg-side delivery. But Butcher, possibly sensing his last chance to justify his place, and his brother-in-law Stewart steered England serenely to 74. Then Warne made his first telling impact and sent shivers of apprehension through the home camp. Recalling his "ball from hell" to dismiss Mike Gatting here four years earlier, he bowled a sharply spinning leg-break; Stewart, nonplussed, jabbed desperately and jerked his head back to see Taylor fling himself sideways at slip and snaffle a superb low catch. Now Warne was ready to put Australia in charge, and he had just the pitch to encourage him. The green demon of the previous day had been transformed into a brown strip, already scarred by footmarks. Flighting the ball cleverly and getting some vicious spin, he dismissed Thorpe, Hussain and Crawley for one run in a magical spell of 26 balls, as the baffled Englishmen slumped to 111 for six with barely a whimper. He and McGrath mopped up the final two wickets in 22 balls of the third morning, and England were all out for 162. Warne finished with six for 48 from 30 overs, his first haul of five or more since he took seven for 23 against Pakistan at Brisbane in November 1995.

Australia led by 73, but Headley and Croft removed their top three for 39 by the 14th over. Controversy enveloped the second wicket: Hussain, at slip, lunged forward as Blewett drove at Croft, and the ball bounced out of his right hand before he clasped it with his left. Umpire Venkataraghavan was unsure whether the edge had carried and consulted George Sharp before giving Blewett out. But the Waughs combined to guide Australia into safer waters. Mark played a sublime two-hour 55, with seven fours and a six, while the flint-eyed Steve, often wincing in pain as he snatched a badly bruised right hand away from his bat, held firm for more than six hours. In that time, he became the third Australian to score a century in each innings against England in 288 Tests, and the first right-hander, joining Warren Bardsley, at The Oval in 1909, and Arthur Morris, at Adelaide in 1946-47. Though Bevan failed again, the lower order did themselves proud. Taylor finally declared 20 minutes after Sunday lunch.

He left England a theoretical target of 469 in a minimum of 141 overs – 63 more than any Test team had made to win. The pressure was overwhelming and England buckled. Butcher and Atherton opened aggressively, Atherton hooking Gillespie for six; the angry bowler struck back by trapping him lbw as he snapped up three for five in 19 balls. Warne and McGrath completed the rout. On bowling Stewart, Warne became the third Australian bowler, after Dennis Lillee and Craig McDermott, to take 250 Test wickets, in his 55th match; his legend was further enhanced when Healy put on a helmet, complete with grille, to keep to him. Only Crawley resisted, but he emulated Atherton at Lord's by treading on his wicket when in sight of a century. England were all out for 200 at 12.30 on the final day. Australia's champagne celebrations were in stark contrast to the glum atmosphere in the home camp; the series was level at 1-1, but the momentum now was all one-way. – KEN CASELLAS.

Man of the Match: S. R. Waugh.   *Attendance:* 87,829; *receipts* £1,621,959.

Close of play: First day, Australia 224-7 (S. R. Waugh 102*, P. R. Reiffel 26*); Second day, England 161-8 (M. A. Ealham 23*, A. R. Caddick 15*); Third day, Australia 262-6 (S. R. Waugh 82*, S. K. Warne 33*); Fourth day, England 130-5 (J. P. Crawley 53*, M. A. Ealham 5*).

Australia

*M. A. Taylor c Thorpe b Headley	2	– (2) c Butcher b Headley	1
M. T. G. Elliott c Stewart b Headley	40	– (1) c Butcher b Headley	11
G. S. Blewett b Gough	8	– c Hussain b Croft	19
M. E. Waugh c Stewart b Ealham	12	– b Ealham	55
S. R. Waugh b Gough	108	– c Stewart b Headley	116
M. G. Bevan c Stewart b Headley	7	– c Atherton b Headley	0
†I. A. Healy c Stewart b Caddick	9	– c Butcher b Croft	47
S. K. Warne c Stewart b Ealham	3	– c Stewart b Caddick	53
P. R. Reiffel b Gough	31	– not out	45
J. N. Gillespie c Stewart b Headley	0	– not out	28
G. D. McGrath not out	0		
B 8, l-b 4, n-b 3	15	B 1, l-b 13, n-b 6	20

1/9 (1) 2/22 (3) 3/42 (4) 4/85 (2)　　　235　　1/5 (2) 2/33 (3)　　(8 wkts dec.) 395
5/113 (6) 6/150 (7) 7/160 (8)　　　　　　　　3/39 (1) 4/131 (4)
8/230 (9) 9/235 (5) 10/235 (10)　　　　　　　5/132 (6) 6/210 (7)
　　　　　　　　　　　　　　　　　　　　　　7/298 (8) 8/333 (5)

Bowling: *First Innings*—Gough 21–7–52–3; Headley 27.3–4–72–4; Caddick 14–2–52–1; Ealham 11–2–34–2; Croft 4–0–13–0. *Second Innings*—Gough 20–3–62–0; Headley 29–4–104–4; Croft 39–12–105–2; Ealham 13–3–41–1; Caddick 21–0–69–1.

England

M. A. Butcher st Healy b Bevan	51	– c McGrath b Gillespie	28
*M. A. Atherton c Healy b McGrath	5	– lbw b Gillespie	21
†A. J. Stewart c Taylor b Warne	30	– b Warne	1
N. Hussain c Healy b Warne	13	– lbw b Gillespie	1
G. P. Thorpe c Taylor b Warne	3	– c Healy b Warne	7
J. P. Crawley c Healy b Warne	4	– hit wkt b McGrath	83
M. A. Ealham not out	24	– c Healy b McGrath	9
R. D. B. Croft c S. R. Waugh b McGrath	7	– c Reiffel b McGrath	7
D. Gough lbw b Warne	1	– b McGrath	6
A. R. Caddick c M. E. Waugh b Warne	15	– c Gillespie b Warne	17
D. W. Headley b McGrath	0	– not out	0
B 4, l-b 3, n-b 2	9	B 14, l-b 4, w 1, n-b 1	20
	162		**200**

1/8 (2) 2/74 (3) 3/94 (1) 4/101 (5) 1/44 (2) 2/45 (3) 3/50 (4)
5/110 (4) 6/111 (6) 7/122 (8)   4/55 (1) 5/84 (5) 6/158 (7)
8/123 (9) 9/161 (10) 10/162 (11)   7/170 (8) 8/177 (6)
              9/188 (9) 10/200 (10)

Bowling: *First Innings*—McGrath 23.4–9–40–3; Reiffel 9–3–14–0; Warne 30–14–48–6; Gillespie 14–3–39–0; Bevan 8–3–14–1. *Second Innings*—McGrath 21–4–46–4; Gillespie 12–4–31–3; Reiffel 2–0–8–0; Warne 30.4–8–63–3; Bevan 8–2–34–0.

Umpires: S. Venkataraghavan (India) and G. Sharp.
Referee: R. S. Madugalle (Sri Lanka).

†MINOR COUNTIES v AUSTRALIANS

At Jesmond, July 8. Australians won by nine runs. Toss: Australians.

 The Minor Counties gave the tourists a good run for their money, falling only nine short with one wicket left. Marcus Sharp of Cumberland struck twice early on as the Australians made a shaky start; they were 53 for three before Julian, promoted to No. 4, came to the rescue. He hit a century from 79 deliveries, with nine fours and eight sixes, six of them in his concluding ten-ball assault. Dean launched the Minor Counties in an opening stand of 61, but their captain, Cockbain, was the mainstay, falling in the closing stages for 82.

Australians

M. J. Slater c Fell b Sharp	27	M. T. G. Elliott not out	35
J. L. Langer c Humphries b Richardson	12	M. S. Kasprowicz not out	7
R. T. Ponting lbw b Sharp	1	B 4, l-b 15, w 14	33
B. P. Julian b Oakes	106		
M. G. Bevan st Humphries b Dalton	32	1/35 2/36 3/53 (7 wkts, 50 overs) 290
G. S. Blewett c Cockbain b Oakes	3	4/146 5/202	
†D. S. Berry b Richardson	34	6/205 7/256	

*S. R. Waugh and P. R. Reiffel did not bat.

 Bowling: Oakes 10–0–43–2; Sharp 10–2–29–2; Richardson 10–0–51–2; Dalton 9–0–63–1; Fielding 4–0–45–0; Myles 7–0–40–0.

Minor Counties

S. J. Dean c and b Julian 38	M. A. Sharp c Slater b Ponting 0
G. W. Ecclestone b Reiffel 21	S. Oakes not out 15
M. A. Fell c Berry b Reiffel 20	A. Richardson not out 0
S. D. Myles c Julian b Bevan 27	B 4, l-b 6, w 10, n-b 16 36
*I. Cockbain c Bevan b Langer 82	—
R. N. Dalton c Kasprowicz 33	1/61 2/92 3/104 (9 wkts, 50 overs) 281
†M. I. Humphries c and b Ponting 5	4/150 5/218 6/241
J. M. Fielding c Reiffel b Slater 4	7/249 8/254 9/267

Bowling: Kasprowicz 10–0–58–1; Julian 7–1–34–1; Blewett 2–0–7–0; Reiffel 6–0–16–2; Bevan 10–0–39–1; Elliott 6–0–49–0; Ponting 7–0–42–2; Slater 1–0–7–1; Langer 1–0–19–1.

Umpires: D. L. Burden and J. M. Tythcott.

†SCOTLAND v AUSTRALIANS

At Raeburn Place, Edinburgh, July 12. No result. Toss: Scotland.

A crowd of 7,000 assembled at the Grange Cricket Club ground and saw Slater hit 95 in 80 balls, with 12 fours and three sixes, out of an opening stand of 143. But slow left-armer Keith Sheridan took revenge for the mauling by snatching four wickets in eight balls, including the Waugh twins. Some fine fielding also helped to keep the Australians down to 50 from their last ten overs. In reply, the Scots were struggling against the Test attack, nearly half their total of 95 for six being contributed by Extras, when a thunderstorm ended proceedings at 5 p.m.

Australians

M. J. Slater c Lockhart b Stanger 95	J. N. Gillespie b Williamson 4
J. L. Langer c Salmond b Beven 46	M. S. Kasprowicz not out 15
R. T. Ponting c Salmond b Williamson . . 33	G. D. McGrath not out 7
G. S. Blewett c Steindl b Sheridan 30	L-b 2, w 6, n-b 20 28
M. E. Waugh c Steindl b Sheridan 11	—
*S. R. Waugh b Sheridan 2	1/143 2/174 3/226 (9 wkts, 50 overs) 278
B. P. Julian c Salmond b Sheridan 5	4/235 5/239 6/250
†I. A. Healy c Stanger b Sheridan 2	7/250 8/252 9/261

Bowling: Steindl 6–0–43–0; Thomson 9–0–29–0; Stanger 8–0–48–1; Williamson 7–0–47–2; Beven 10–0–44–1; Sheridan 10–0–65–5.

Scotland

B. M. W. Patterson c Healy b Kasprowicz 14	I. M. Stanger not out 10
I. L. Philip b McGrath 3	P. D. Steindl not out 0
M. J. Smith c S. R. Waugh b Julian 15	L-b 5, w 17, n-b 24 46
*G. Salmond c Healy b Kasprowicz 0	—
J. G. Williamson c Julian b Kasprowicz . . 2	1/31 2/31 3/32 (6 wkts, 21.5 overs) 95
†D. R. Lockhart c Julian b Gillespie 5	4/39 5/69 6/95

I. R. Beven, K. L. P. Sheridan and K. Thomson did not bat.

Bowling: McGrath 6–2–17–1; Kasprowicz 6–0–28–3; Julian 5–0–32–1; Gillespie 4.5–0–13–1.

Umpires: J. Breslin and D. M. Potter.

†At Wormsley, July 14. Drawn. Toss: Australians. Australians 267 for five dec. (M. T. G. Elliott 95, R. T. Ponting 36, M. G. Bevan 54, M. A. Taylor 38 not out); J. Paul Getty's XI 237 for four (R. A. Smith 57, M. D. Crowe 115 not out; M. G. Bevan four for 85).

This match was not part of the official tour schedule.

GLAMORGAN v AUSTRALIANS

At Cardiff, July 16, 17, 18. Drawn. Toss: Glamorgan.

The tourists were disgruntled not to be able to test themselves against the Championship leaders' front-line attack: Watkin was injured, Croft withdrawn at the selectors' request, and Waqar Younis predictably rested. On an easy-paced pitch, Ponting made an unbeaten 126. It was only his third first-class innings of the tour, but earned him a Test place after Bevan flopped yet again with the bat. Glamorgan had a brief sniff of a win, when the Australians juggled their batting order in their second innings and slid to 42 for five. Reiffel put them back on course and Taylor delayed his declaration until the final afternoon. Set 333 in 59 overs, James and Morris opened with 96 from 26, but there was little real prospect of a result. James, who had just missed his hundred on the second day, became the first batsman to reach 1,000 runs for the season – unusually late for the landmark, because of all the rain.

Close of play: First day, Glamorgan 30-0 (S. P. James 16*, H. Morris 5*); Second day, Australians 100-5 (P. R. Reiffel 35*, M. T. G. Elliott 22*).

Australians

*M. A. Taylor c Morris b Cosker	71			
M. T. G. Elliott c Maynard b Butcher	26	– (7) st Metson b Cosker	37
G. S. Blewett b Butcher	54	– (8) not out	50
R. T. Ponting not out	126	– (9) not out	28
M. J. Slater c Metson b Cosker	26	– (1) lbw b Thomas	7
J. L. Langer not out	50	– (2) b Parkin	10
M. G. Bevan (did not bat)		– (3) c Metson b Thomas	1
B. P. Julian (did not bat)		– (4) c and b Parkin	12
†D. S. Berry (did not bat)		– (5) c Metson b Parkin	9
P. R. Reiffel (did not bat)		– (6) b Thomas	56
B 4, l-b 8, w 2, n-b 2	16	B 1, l-b 4, n-b 2	7

1/72 2/132 3/197 4/246   (4 wkts dec.) 369   1/14 2/18 3/26   (7 wkts dec.) 217
4/37 5/42
6/122 7/147

M. S. Kasprowicz did not bat.

Bowling: *First Innings*—Thomas 16–1–73–0; Parkin 19–4–78–0; Dale 13–2–49–0; Butcher 13–1–52–2; Cosker 24–5–95–2; Maynard 3–0–10–0. *Second Innings*—Thomas 14–3–42–3; Parkin 15–3–38–3; Cosker 17–3–36–1; Butcher 10–1–36–0; Dale 9–1–43–0; Maynard 4–0–17–0.

Glamorgan

S. P. James c Kasprowicz b Bevan	91	– c Julian b Bevan	79
H. Morris lbw b Bevan	13	– c Berry b Kasprowicz	42
A. Dale c Blewett b Bevan	0	– (5) not out	20
*M. P. Maynard c Berry b Kasprowicz	19	– not out	45
M. J. Powell lbw b Kasprowicz	24		
G. P. Butcher c Blewett b Reiffel	23		
P. A. Cottey c Berry b Reiffel	22		
S. D. Thomas c Taylor b Reiffel	10	– (3) st Berry b Bevan	15
†C. P. Metson b Reiffel	0		
D. A. Cosker b Reiffel	2		
O. T. Parkin not out	0		
B 4, l-b 17, w 5, n-b 24	50	L-b 2, n-b 8	10

1/88 2/88 3/127 4/178 5/182   254   1/96 2/139 3/160   (3 wkts) 211
6/218 7/233 8/237 9/249

Bowling: *First Innings*—Reiffel 18.3–5–61–5; Kasprowicz 18–5–56–2; Bevan 20–2–73–3; Julian 9–2–34–0; Ponting 3–0–9–0. *Second Innings*—Kasprowicz 15–2–63–1; Reiffel 11–2–46–0; Julian 9–1–26–0; Bevan 16–1–74–2.

Umpires: J. C. Balderstone and T. E. Jesty.

MIDDLESEX v AUSTRALIANS

At Lord's, July 19, 20, 21. Drawn. Toss: Middlesex.

The Australians fielded ten of their eventual Test side at Headingley, whereas Middlesex, like Glamorgan, rested their overseas player, Kallis. Apart from Ramprakash and Gatting, the county batsmen had problems against an international attack. Ramprakash, unused to captaincy in three-day cricket, prolonged the innings unduly: Middlesex took a full day to score 305. The Australians made 351 in the same time, with the Waughs adding 103 in 110 minutes, and Mark Waugh reached his first century at Lord's off the last ball of the evening. Taylor declared 80 minutes into the final morning, apparently too late for a result. Then Warne removed Middlesex's top three in seven overs, and Shah, who had just finished his A-levels, fell one run later, leaving them 72 for four. But Gatting stood firm, adding 84 with Brown, and the match drifted towards the draw.

Close of play: First day, Middlesex 305; Second day, Australians 351-6 (M. E. Waugh 100*, S. K. Warne 5*).

Middlesex

P. N. Weekes run out	19	– c and b Warne	28
J. C. Pooley c S. R. Waugh b McGrath	17	– b Warne	20
*M. R. Ramprakash c Healy b Gillespie	76	– c Healy b Warne	16
M. W. Gatting b McGrath	85	– lbw b S. R. Waugh	47
O. A. Shah c M. E. Waugh b Warne	28	– lbw b Kasprowicz	0
†K. R. Brown c Healy b Kasprowicz	18	– not out	48
K. P. Dutch c Healy b Gillespie	10	– b M. E. Waugh	4
R. L. Johnson c Blewett b Kasprowicz	1	– not out	27
A. R. C. Fraser c Elliott b McGrath	15		
P. C. R. Tufnell not out	11		
T. F. Bloomfield c Healy b McGrath	4		
L-b 6, w 3, n-b 12	21	B 4, l-b 5, n-b 2	11

1/23 2/49 3/169 4/241 5/243   305   1/45 2/50 3/71   (6 wkts) 201
6/268 7/275 8/280 9/295   4/72 5/156 6/163

Bowling: *First Innings*—Gillespie 23–2–67–2; McGrath 21.4–7–61–4; Warne 23–4–76–1; Blewett 5–1–12–0; Kasprowicz 13–2–47–2; M. E. Waugh 12–0–36–0. *Second Innings*—McGrath 11–3–37–0; Gillespie 13–6–32–0; Warne 16–4–55–3; Kasprowicz 6–1–10–1; M. E. Waugh 7–1–37–1; S. R. Waugh 5–2–13–1; Elliott 1–0–8–0.

Australians

M. T. G. Elliott st Brown b Dutch	83	S. K. Warne c Pooley b Dutch	39
*M. A. Taylor b Dutch	27		
G. S. Blewett b Tufnell	40	B 2, l-b 10, w 1, n-b 10	23
M. E. Waugh not out	142		
S. R. Waugh c Gatting b Johnson	57	1/75 2/154 3/168 (7 wkts dec.) 432
R. T. Ponting c Shah b Tufnell	5	4/271 5/299	
†I. A. Healy c Pooley b Bloomfield	16	6/341 7/432	

J. N. Gillespie, G. D. McGrath and M. S. Kasprowicz did not bat.

Bowling: Fraser 29–6–115–0; Bloomfield 17–1–57–1; Johnson 17–2–63–1; Tufnell 38–8–106–2; Dutch 15–3–79–3.

Umpires: A. A. Jones and A. G. T. Whitehead.

ENGLAND v AUSTRALIA

Fourth Cornhill Test

At Leeds, July 24, 25, 26, 27, 28. Australia won by an innings and 61 runs. Toss: Australia. Test debut: A. M. Smith.

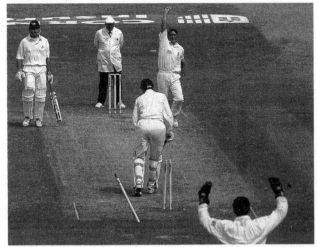

[*Patrick Eagar*

Darren Gough's yorker dismisses Matthew Elliott one short of a double-century.

In the Third Test, Australia had levelled the series through fine work from some of their senior players. The most notable aspect of Australia's comprehensive win in the Fourth Test, which gave them the lead for the first time, was that the protagonists were young players in their first Ashes series. Elliott, aged 25, and Ponting, aged 22, scored centuries to lead Australia out of trouble and into an unbeatable position, after the 22-year-old Gillespie had destroyed England's first innings with seven for 37, the best figures by an Australian in a Headingley Test. England returned to their old ways, bowling and fielding poorly to concede a huge first-innings score, and batting with minimal application under sustained pressure. But the Australians were back to their best, combining tightly disciplined play with just the right amount of risk-taking.

Before the start of play on the first morning, Australia announced that they had lodged a formal complaint about the alleged role of England chairman of selectors David Graveney in the decision to switch pitches less than two weeks before the game. The Australians cried foul, though the ECB claimed Graveney was merely kept informed of developments. In the end, the protest appeared to have been lodged more to spark Australian pride than to right any grievous wrong. If motivation was the aim, the plan worked perfectly.

England had announced the day after their defeat at Old Trafford that they would retain the same eleven, plus Phil Tufnell, for Headingley. A few days before the game, they added Gloucestershire's swing bowler, Mike Smith, to the squad, and he made his debut in place of Caddick, while Tufnell was sent away again. Smith was to take no wickets on a pitch of uneven bounce. Australia's one change, Ponting for the out-of-form Bevan, was far more successful.

Having won his fourth consecutive toss, Taylor chose to bowl on a green pitch. Rain restricted the first day's play to 36 overs, which Atherton survived unbeaten on 34, with England 106 for three. The apparent solidity of that start crumbled to dust the next day when Gillespie produced a spell of genuine speed and outstanding control. After he had caught Atherton at long leg, out to McGrath yet again, Gillespie took the last five wickets as England added just 18 runs in nine overs. They were all out for 172.

That fragility with the bat was to be mirrored by a sloppy performance in the field. Not for the first time, they made a fine start, on a pitch offering England's seam attack more than enough assistance. Australia were in some strife at 50 for four in the 18th over. That brought their two most inexperienced batsmen, Elliott and Ponting, together. They promptly accepted the challenge by counter-attacking with courage, common sense and, in Elliott's case, a little luck. As in his century at Lord's, the left-handed Elliott was dropped three times. Yet, in between those lapses, he drove, hooked and cut with impressive assurance and deceptive power. The first miss, when Elliott was on 29 and Australia still only 50, was a relatively easy chance to Thorpe at first slip off the bowling of Smith. It was deemed by many observers to be the sort of dropped catch that costs a Test series. Although that is too simplistic, Thorpe's lapse was typical of England's poor play. Elliott went on to bat for seven and a half hours and 351 balls, hitting three sixes and 23 fours, before being bowled, one short of a double-hundred, by a superb swinging yorker from England's best bowler, Gough. Meanwhile, Ponting's chanceless maiden Test century, on his Ashes debut, was as near perfection as could be expected from a young player returning to the team; he had missed the previous eight Tests through a selection decision that still seemed harsh some seven months later. From the start, he drove and pulled superbly, to gather 19 fours and a six. Together, Elliott and Ponting added 268 for the fifth wicket in 263 minutes, and Elliott shared further half-century partnerships with Healy and Reiffel.

When Taylor declared at lunch on the fourth day, Australia had reached 501, a lead of 329. But England played well over the next two sessions. By stumps, they were 212 for four. Hussain had completed his second century of the series and had put on 123 with Crawley. Any hopes of a draw inspired by their stand were dashed early on the final morning, however, when Warne took his only wicket of the match (he bowled one solitary over in the first innings): he deceived Hussain in flight for a simple catch to Gillespie at mid-off. Crawley went on to 72, but the end came quickly enough. England were bowled out for 268 to lose by an innings, with Reiffel adding five more wickets to his 54 not out. It was Gillespie, though, who won Ian Botham's vote as Man of the Match for setting up Australia's winning position in England's first innings.

Gillespie had bowled down the hill from the Kirkstall Lane End to excellent effect, something none of the England bowlers seemed able to do. In hindsight, the decision to omit Caddick in favour of Smith looked a disaster: uneven bounce was more relevant than swing, and Caddick should have been able to exploit that far better.

Once again, there was tension between the fierce Headingley stewards and the sometimes raucous spectators in the Western Terrace, especially those keen on the fashion for attending Tests in fancy dress. Two men dressed in a pantomime-cow costume cavorted round the boundary, and were crash-tackled by officials after play: the man playing the rear end, Branco Risek, needed treatment in hospital. Brian Cheesman, a university lecturer dressed as a carrot, was frogmarched from the ground for "drunken and abusive behaviour". He vehemently denied the allegations. Mr Cheesman has been attending Headingley Tests in fancy dress since 1982. – MARK RAY.

Man of the Match: J. N. Gillespie.   *Attendance:* 66,694; *receipts* £1,310,200.

Close of play: First day, England 106-3 (M. A. Atherton 34*, D. W. Headley 0*); Second day, Australia 258-4 (M. T. G. Elliott 134*, R. T. Ponting 86*); Third day, Australia 373-5 (M. T. G. Elliott 164*, I. A. Healy 27*); Fourth day, England 212-4 (N. Hussain 101*, J. P. Crawley 48*).

England

M. A. Butcher c Blewett b Reiffel	24	– c Healy b McGrath	19
*M. A. Atherton c Gillespie b McGrath	41	– c Warne b McGrath	2
†A. J. Stewart c Blewett b Gillespie	7	– b Reiffel	16
N. Hussain c Taylor b McGrath	26	– c Gillespie b Warne	105
D. W. Headley c S. R. Waugh b Gillespie	22	– (8) lbw b Reiffel	3
G. P. Thorpe b Gillespie	15	– (5) c M. E. Waugh b Gillespie	15
J. P. Crawley c Blewett b Gillespie	2	– (6) b Reiffel	72
M. A. Ealham not out	8	– (7) c M. E. Waugh b Reiffel	4
R. D. B. Croft c Ponting b Gillespie	6	– c Healy b Reiffel	5
D. Gough b Gillespie	0	– c M. E. Waugh b Gillespie	0
A. M. Smith b Gillespie	0	– not out	4
B 4, l-b 4, w 1, n-b 12	21	B 6, l-b 4, n-b 13	23

1/43 (1) 2/58 (3) 3/103 (4) 4/138 (5)   172   1/23 (1) 2/28 (2) 3/57 (3)   268
5/154 (2) 6/154 (6) 7/163 (7)   4/89 (5) 5/222 (4) 6/252 (7)
8/172 (9) 9/172 (10) 10/172 (11)   7/256 (6) 8/263 (8)
                                                             9/264 (10) 10/268 (9)

Bowling: *First Innings*—McGrath 22–5–67–2; Reiffel 20–4–41–1; Gillespie 13.4–1–37–7; Blewett 3–0–17–0; Warne 1–0–2–0. *Second Innings*—McGrath 22–5–80–2; Reiffel 21.1–2–49–5; Gillespie 23–8–65–2; Warne 21–6–53–1; S. R. Waugh 4–1–11–0.

Australia

*M. A. Taylor c Stewart b Gough 0	J. N. Gillespie b Gough 3
M. T. G. Elliott b Gough 199	G. D. McGrath not out 20
G. S. Blewett c Stewart b Gough 1	
M. E. Waugh c and b Headley 8	B 9, l-b 10, n-b 35 54
S. R. Waugh c Crawley b Headley 4	
R. T. Ponting c Ealham b Gough 127	1/0 (1) 2/16 (3) 3/43 (4) (9 wkts dec.) 501
†I. A. Healy b Ealham 31	4/50 (5) 5/318 (6)
S. K. Warne c Thorpe b Ealham 0	6/382 (7) 7/383 (8)
P. R. Reiffel not out 54	8/444 (2) 9/461 (10)

Bowling: Gough 36–5–149–5; Headley 25–2–125–2; Smith 23–2–89–0; Ealham 19–3–56–2; Croft 18–1–49–0; Butcher 2–0–14–0.

Umpires: C. J. Mitchley (South Africa) and M. J. Kitchen.   Referee: C. W. Smith (West Indies).

SOMERSET v AUSTRALIANS

At Taunton, August 1, 2, 3, 4. Drawn. Toss: Somerset.

The tourists' only scheduled four-day match was terminated by rain after two days. Those days attracted large crowds, a small number of whom were ejected by the police for abusing Warne. Somerset made an electrifying start: Parsons, promoted to open, raced to 50 in 39 balls. The score was 95 from 17 overs when his partner, Holloway, fell for 11. But Warne and McGrath restored order, and the only other fifties came from Turner and Extras. When the Australians replied, Caddick bowled steadily for five wickets and a Test recall. But van Troost was extraordinarily profligate, conceding 132 at 8.5 an over. The Waughs were in the vanguard, then Julian scored 71 in 60 balls to dominate a 106-run stand in 18 overs with Healy. Once Jones dismissed them both, van Troost swiftly ended the innings: the last four wickets fell for six. There was time for Turner – another new opener, after Parsons was injured fielding – to score a second half-century before the rain.

Close of play: First day, Australians 182-4 (S. R. Waugh 51*, M. G. Bevan 12*); Second day, Somerset 147-3 (R. J. Turner 65*, P. S. Jones 5*); Third day, No play.

Somerset

K. A. Parsons c Blewett b Kasprowicz 71		
P. C. L. Holloway c Healy b McGrath 11	– c Langer b McGrath	17
*S. C. Ecclestone lbw b Warne 12	– c McGrath b M. E. Waugh	47
M. N. Lathwell c M. E. Waugh b Warne 18	– st Healy b Warne	11
M. E. Trescothick b Warne 8		
†R. J. Turner c Slater b Julian 58	– (1) not out	65
G. D. Rose c Slater b McGrath 4		
S. Herzberg b Kasprowicz 18		
A. R. Caddick c McGrath b Warne 16		
A. P. van Troost not out 12		
P. S. Jones lbw b Warne 4	– (5) not out	5
B 10, n-b 42 52	N-b 2	2

1/95 2/122 3/122 4/143 5/154	284	1/33 2/118 3/138 (3 wkts) 147
6/167 7/240 8/258 9/262		

Bowling: *First Innings*—Kasprowicz 14–2–95–2; Julian 14–2–52–1; McGrath 11–2–31–2; Warne 18.3–7–57–5; Bevan 8–2–39–0. *Second Innings*—Kasprowicz 5–2–11–0; Julian 5–1–22–0; McGrath 7–1–24–1; Blewett 4–0–33–0; Warne 11–3–26–1; M. E. Waugh 9–1–31–1.

Australians

M. J. Slater c Turner b Caddick	18	S. K. Warne c Rose b van Troost	1
J. L. Langer b Caddick	30	M. S. Kasprowicz not out	1
G. S. Blewett b Caddick	20	G. D. McGrath lbw b van Troost	0
M. E. Waugh c Turner b Rose	37		
*S. R. Waugh c Lathwell b Caddick	62	L-b 2, n-b 32	34
M. G. Bevan c Turner b Caddick	16		
†I. A. Healy c Trescothick b Jones	33	1/40 2/63 3/82 4/145 5/188	323
B. P. Julian c Turner b Jones	71	6/211 7/317 8/320 9/320	

Bowling: Caddick 16–2–54–5; van Troost 15.3–0–132–2; Jones 5–1–32–2; Rose 14–3–50–1; Parsons 2–0–4–0; Herzberg 5–0–36–0; Trescothick 2–0–13–0.

Umpires: N. T. Plews and J. F. Steele.

ENGLAND v AUSTRALIA

Fifth Cornhill Test

At Nottingham, August 7, 8, 9, 10. Australia won by 264 runs. Toss: Australia. Test debuts: A. J. Hollioake, B. C. Hollioake.

Crushing defeat cost England the series and the Ashes but not, this time, their captain. Mike Atherton withstood all the demands that he follow the example of his predecessor, Graham Gooch, who had fallen on his sword in similar circumstances four years earlier. But the public debate about his future did nothing to ease the pressure on Atherton. By the start of the third day, when all hope of the essential victory had gone, the ECB issued an official communiqué denying a newspaper report that he had offered to resign on the eve of the match. Appointed for the series, Atherton insisted he would "see it through", a phrase grim enough to capture the mood of a man and a team faced by overwhelming odds.

There were times when England's out-cricket was impeccable – disciplined, athletic and enthusiastic. Yet it seemed only to incite the Australians to lift their game, to emphasise that the series had, since the upset at Edgbaston, been an unequal contest between honest endeavour and pure talent.

Accepting that, the England selectors revoked their vow after the Old Trafford defeat to stand by their men, left out those useful tradesmen Butcher, Ealham and Smith, and went instead for action heroes. Pace bowlers Malcolm and Caddick were restored and the brothers Adam and Ben Hollioake, left to bask in the public's adulation since their Texaco Trophy heroics, were asked to give the side some of their Australian-bred self-confidence. Adam, seen by many as a serious candidate for the captaincy, needed to prove his ability as a Test batsman. Ben, at 19 years 269 days, was the youngest England Test debutant since Brian Close, aged 18 years 149 days, played against New Zealand in 1949. The Hollioakes were only the fifth set of brothers to play a Test for England, and the first since Worcestershire's Peter and Dick Richardson in 1957. Tufnell, meanwhile, was chosen and sent away yet again.

The Hollioakes' inclusion was a gamble, but not the only one forced upon England. Conscious that Stewart's role as wicket-keeper/batsman was crucial, yet aware that he was desperately out of touch, the selectors tried some daring alternative medicine. Instead of keeping him back at No. 3, they asked him to open again. It was a temporary and seemingly unfair expedient – but it inspired his finest innings of the series. By the time Stewart made those spectacular runs, though, two unpredictable factors had given Australia – who retained their triumphant team from Headingley – a command they never relaxed. First, Gough, England's most successful bowler, failed a fitness test on an inflamed knee. Then, Atherton lost the toss for the fifth successive time.

Given first use of the only flawless pitch of the series, Australia used it entertainingly but mercilessly. Headley, Caddick and Malcolm bowled with speed, devotion and some accuracy under a relentless sun. England's ground fielding was superb. Yet, on that decisive opening day, the first four Australian batsmen made half-centuries, each different in style but all tinged with an air of inevitability, as they advanced to 302 for three. Headley eventually broke the opening stand of 117 when he had Elliott, who had completed 1,000 first-class runs on the tour, taken behind off a dubious inside edge. Taylor was bowled by Caddick after becoming the sixth Australian to pass 6,000 Test runs, and Ben Hollioake claimed his first Test wicket, Blewett, with his 38th delivery. Hollioake minor was carefully nursed by Atherton and allowed to bowl only eight overs of bland medium-pace. But it was a painful learning experience, as he went for five an over. He and Adam shared another moment of history by bowling in tandem – brothers against brothers – at the Waugh twins, Mark and Steve. The Waughs took their stand to 86 and Steve added the fifth fifty of the innings next morning, but Australia lost their last seven for 116 as the England bowlers were finally rewarded for their hard labour.

Australia's 427 left them virtually fireproof. Yet they were singed by Stewart's 87. He made the runs with his old, instinctive timing off only 107 balls, hitting 14 fours. He and Atherton had reached 106 in 27 overs and were promising England an honourable retreat when Warne turned in another of his hugely influential spells, removing both of them, plus Hussain, in 40 deliveries. England rallied again on the third day to reach 313, a deficit of 114. Thorpe reached his first Test fifty since Edgbaston, supported by Adam Hollioake in a stand of 102, and Ben hit a few fearless shots in his 28. But, by the close, Australia had stretched their lead to 281. And on the fourth day, England totally lost the plot.

Some wildly off-line bowling gave Healy the chance to show he is still the game's supreme and toughest wicket-keeper/batsman. Together with Ponting, he thrashed 105 in 104 minutes, and hit nine fours in his 63 in 78 balls, as Australia went through one of their familiar spirit-crushing routines.

Left to get 451 or to survive for more than eight hours, England lasted just 48.5 overs. From the moment Atherton glanced a jaw-threatening bouncer from McGrath into Healy's gloves, it was an innings with no visible plan, a strange mix of strokeless submission and devil-may-care defiance. Only Thorpe, with an unbeaten 82, looked sure of what he was doing and why. But even he could not stop the rampant Australian attack and their hawk-like fielders from picking off the stragglers. His last six companions contributed 14 as he scored 68.

Australia claimed the extra half-hour at 173 for eight and one of the more lifeless and misguided England innings of a dark decade passed quietly into history with seven balls to spare. Warne led Australia's cavortings in front of the pavilion as they claimed the Ashes for the fifth time in a row. Atherton resolutely declined journalists' invitations to resign at once, though his wording suggested to many that he would answer differently when the series was over. – PETER JOHNSON.

Man of the Match: I. A. Healy.   *Attendance:* 48,581; *receipts* £1,110,135.

Close of play: First day, Australia 302-3 (M. E. Waugh 60*, S. R. Waugh 38*); Second day, England 188-4 (G. P. Thorpe 30*, A. J. Hollioake 15*); Third day, Australia 167-4 (S. R. Waugh 10*, R. T. Ponting 5*).

Australia

M. T. G. Elliott c Stewart b Headley	69	– (2) c Crawley b Caddick	37
*M. A. Taylor b Caddick	76	– (1) c Hussain b B. C. Hollioake	45
G. S. Blewett c Stewart b B. C. Hollioake	50	– c Stewart b Caddick	60
M. E. Waugh lbw b Caddick	68	– lbw b Headley	7
S. R. Waugh b Malcolm	75	– c A. J. Hollioake b Caddick	14
R. T. Ponting b Headley	9	– c Stewart b A. J. Hollioake	45
†I. A. Healy c A. J. Hollioake b Malcolm	16	– c Stewart b A. J. Hollioake	63
S. K. Warne c Thorpe b Malcolm	0	– c Thorpe b Croft	20
P. R. Reiffel c Thorpe b Headley	26	– c B. C. Hollioake b Croft	22
J. N. Gillespie not out	18	– c Thorpe b Headley	4
G. D. McGrath b Headley	1	– not out	1
B 4, l-b 10, w 1, n-b 4	19	B 1, l-b 11, n-b 6	18

1/117 (1) 2/160 (2) 3/225 (3) 4/311 (4) 427   1/51 (2) 2/105 (1) 3/134 (4) 336
5/325 (6) 6/355 (7) 7/363 (8)   4/156 (3) 5/171 (5) 6/276 (7)
8/386 (5) 9/419 (9) 10/427 (11)   7/292 (6) 8/314 (8)
                                             9/326 (10) 10/336 (9)

Bowling: *First Innings*—Malcolm 25-4-100-3; Headley 30.5-7-87-4; Caddick 30-4-102-2; B. C. Hollioake 10-1-57-1; Croft 19-7-43-0; A. J. Hollioake 7-0-24-0. *Second Innings*—Malcolm 16-4-52-0; Headley 19-3-56-2; Croft 26.5-6-74-2; Caddick 20-2-85-3; B. C. Hollioake 5-1-26-1; A. J. Hollioake 12-2-31-2.

England

*M. A. Atherton c Healy b Warne	27	– c Healy b McGrath	8
†A. J. Stewart c Healy b Warne	87	– c S. R. Waugh b Reiffel	16
J. P. Crawley c Healy b McGrath	18	– c Healy b Gillespie	33
N. Hussain b Warne	2	– b Gillespie	21
G. P. Thorpe c Blewett b Warne	53	– not out	82
A. J. Hollioake c Taylor b Reiffel	45	– lbw b Gillespie	2
B. C. Hollioake c M. E. Waugh b Reiffel	28	– lbw b Warne	2
R. D. B. Croft c Blewett b McGrath	18	– c McGrath b Warne	6
A. R. Caddick c Healy b McGrath	0	– lbw b Warne	0
D. W. Headley not out	10	– c Healy b McGrath	4
D. E. Malcolm b McGrath	12	– c M. E. Waugh b McGrath	0
B 2, l-b 6, n-b 5	13	B 6, l-b 2, n-b 4	12

1/106 (1) 2/129 (2) 3/135 (4) 4/141 (3)   313   1/25 (1) 2/25 (2) 3/78 (4)   186
5/243 (6) 6/243 (5) 7/272 (8)   4/99 (3) 5/121 (6) 6/144 (7)
8/290 (7) 9/290 (9) 10/313 (11)   7/150 (8) 8/166 (9)
                                                            9/186 (10) 10/186 (11)

Bowling: *First Innings*—McGrath 29.5–9–71–4; Reiffel 21–2–101–2; Gillespie 11–3–47–0; Warne 32–8–86–4. *Second Innings*—McGrath 13.5–4–36–3; Reiffel 11–3–34–1; Gillespie 8–0–65–3; Warne 16–4–43–3.

Umpires: C. J. Mitchley (South Africa) and D. R. Shepherd.
Referee: C. W. Smith (West Indies).

†At Eglinton, August 14. Australians won by 139 runs. Toss: Australians. Australians 303 for seven (50 overs) (G. S. Blewett 44, M. E. Waugh 32, J. L. Langer 57, R. T. Ponting 117 not out); Ireland 164 (45.3 overs) (W. K. McCallan 64 not out; R. T. Ponting three for 14).

Ponting, whose grandmother emigrated from Ulster in 1938, met her sisters, who live in Belfast, before hitting 117 not out, including six sixes and ten fours, in 89 balls and taking three wickets.

KENT v AUSTRALIANS

At Canterbury, August 16, 17, 18. Australians won by six wickets. Toss: Kent.

With Gillespie returning home injured, and Reiffel for the birth of his child, the Australians called up all-rounders Shaun Young from Gloucestershire, and Shane Lee from Lancashire League cricket. Lee had the more successful match, with eight for 113, but Young was picked for the Oval Test. A burst of three wickets from Kasprowicz put Kent firmly on the back foot. But Fleming hit 67, including 14 fours, and added a valuable 90 with Marsh. Then Lee took four for nought in 15 balls to produce a symmetrical conclusion to Kent's innings: their top three and bottom three batsmen all made ducks. Igglesden had the tourists in trouble at 40 for four, before Steve Waugh and Bevan added 158 for the sixth wicket: Waugh's 154 was his fourth and biggest hundred of the tour. Kent's top order cleared a deficit of 114 and Ealham scored a fine 85, with 14 fours, before he was last out. The Australians needed 230 to win, and they reached the target in comfort, thanks to an undefeated stand of 90 between Ponting and Bevan.

Close of play: First day, Australians 207-5 (S. R. Waugh 94*, M. G. Bevan 37*); Second day, Kent 234-5 (M. A. Ealham 17*).

Kent

T. R. Ward c Berry b Kasprowicz	0	– c Blewett b Bevan	68
E. T. Smith c Lee b Kasprowicz	0	– lbw b M. E. Waugh	46
A. P. Wells c Berry b Kasprowicz	0	– c Berry b Young	65
W. J. House c Langer b Kasprowicz	16	– b Lee	20
B. J. Phillips c M. E. Waugh b Young	25	– (6) c S. R. Waugh b Kasprowicz	0
M. A. Ealham c S. R. Waugh b Bevan	30	– (5) c Ponting b Kasprowicz	85
M. V. Fleming c Berry b Lee	67	– c Berry b Lee	29
*†S. A. Marsh not out	35	– c Kasprowicz b Lee	5
P. A. Strang c Langer b Lee	0	– c Ponting b Lee	2
J. B. D. Thompson c Ponting b Lee	0	– c Ponting b Kasprowicz	3
A. P. Igglesden c Berry b Lee	0	– not out	2
L-b 2, n-b 26	28	B 4, l-b 2, n-b 12	18

1/2 2/6 3/15 4/46 5/77   201   1/99 2/159 3/200 4/233 5/234   343
6/107 7/197 8/201 9/201   6/285 7/303 8/307 9/318

Bowling: *First Innings*—Kasprowicz 15–4–72–4; Young 11–3–46–1; Lee 10.3–4–27–4; Bevan 11–1–49–1; Blewett 3–1–5–0. *Second Innings*—Kasprowicz 24.4–4–89–3; Young 15–7–40–1; Lee 25–7–86–4; Blewett 5–2–26–0; M. E. Waugh 12–5–30–1; Bevan 17–2–66–1.

Australians

M. J. Slater lbw b Igglesden	14	– (2) b Fleming	47
J. L. Langer c Marsh b Igglesden	20	– (1) c Marsh b Thompson	22
G. S. Blewett run out	0	– c Marsh b Thompson	18
M. E. Waugh c Marsh b Igglesden	1	– c Smith b Strang	35
*S. R. Waugh c Marsh b Strang	154		
R. T. Ponting b Ealham	32	– (5) not out	56
M. G. Bevan c Ward b Phillips	55	– (6) not out	47
S. Young c Marsh b Phillips	0		
S. Lee c Marsh b Phillips	1		
†D. S. Berry c House b Thompson	12		
M. S. Kasprowicz not out	12		
B 7, w 1, n-b 6	14	L-b 2, n-b 4	6

1/29 2/31 3/35 4/40 5/106   315   1/67 2/91 3/95 4/141   (4 wkts) 231
6/264 7/266 8/268 9/288

Bowling: *First Innings*—Igglesden 16–2–56–3; Phillips 15–1–57–3; Ealham 14–3–63–1; Thompson 11–1–61–1; Strang 20.1–4–44–1; Fleming 5–0–27–0. *Second Innings*—Igglesden 5–0–28–0; Ealham 5–1–19–0; Phillips 6–2–36–0; Thompson 12–3–58–2; Fleming 11–2–22–1; Strang 10–0–42–1; House 2.5–0–24–0.

Umpires: M. J. Harris and J. W. Holder.

ENGLAND v AUSTRALIA

Sixth Cornhill Test

At The Oval, August 21, 22, 23. England won by 19 runs. Toss: England. Test debut: S. Young.
Too late to rescue the Ashes, but not too late to rescue their self-respect, England won a sensational victory after a contest fit to rank with the great games of Ashes history. The match was over at 5.24 p.m. on the third day, but the cricket that did take place was amazing, and the climax utterly riveting. Australia, needing only 124 to win, were bowled out for just 104. The Oval crowd celebrated England's triumph in a manner not seen at least since the Edgbaston win, 11 weeks earlier – but that seemed like an awfully long time ago.

[*Patrick Eagar*

Glenn McGrath, caught Thorpe bowled Tufnell (*centre*) – and England win the Sixth Test at The Oval.

Australia's collapse maintained their reputation for vulnerability in a run-chase, and for flunking the Tests that matter least. It was the third time in 1997 they had lost the last match of a series they had already won. It did not much dent their reputation as one of the great Ashes teams. The result meant far more to England. In advance, they would have settled for losing the series 3-2, a result that suggested tangible progress after all the bleak years. And though the ECB had to refund £400,000 to ticket-holders for Sunday (a 16,500 sell-out, like the first three days), the gain was incalculable. The English public had grown weary of failure.

Like so many great matches, this came about thanks to what is conventionally known as a bad pitch. It was too dry, and by the second day it was crumbling. This came as a surprise to just about everyone. When England were all out on the first day, it was assumed to be yet another pathetic batting failure, and perhaps a terminal one for Atherton's captaincy. The first assumption was correct, because the pitch was still mild and there was no excuse at all for their collapse from 128 for three to 132 for seven.

But for once the luck favoured England in this contest. After five successes in a row, Taylor's habit of shouting his nickname – "tails" – at the toss let him down. England were able to bat first and hoped to give Australia the runaround in steamy, Brisbane-like heat. They must have fancied 500; even afterwards, Atherton thought 350 was par; they made 180, a useful total only at darts.

No one had imagined two spinners would be of much value; Croft, his declining reputation further dented after an on-pitch shoving match at the NatWest semi-final, was told not to bother turning up. He had been in the 14-man squad along with Headley, who was ruled out injured, and Ben Hollioake, who was left out. Crawley failed to make the party at all, and the final eleven had four changes from Trent Bridge: Butcher was quickly recalled, along with the in-form Ramprakash and Martin, plus Tufnell, in the squad but not the team for the previous five Tests. Australia made two changes: Gillespie and Reiffel had flown home, so Kasprowicz came back in, along with Young, who had been making heaps of runs for Gloucestershire but seemed like a potential weak link in a four-man attack.

On Day One it made no difference. After the openers were out cheaply, Stewart, Hussain and Thorpe gave England hope of a decent score. But McGrath once again was both insistent and persistent, and the middle order suddenly crumpled in a sort of cataleptic fit. Hussain, who had been unconvincing even against Young, drove to mid-on, and the rest of the flock followed. Caddick and Martin each hit a six, which was something, but England were all out before tea. McGrath finished with seven for 76, including England's top six; he did little more than bowl fast and straight.

Tufnell removed Australia's openers in the evening session, but even so England's position looked dire, and direr still when Australia were 94 for two. But then the game changed. Over the years, Tufnell had displayed more than his share of the slow left-armer's traditional eccentricity; now he displayed the breed's quieter virtues. He kept his line and his patience and, in the afternoon, as the pitch began to wear visibly, he reaped his reward. Bowling unchanged for 35 overs, he worked his way through the Australian batting. He, too, finished with seven and, until Warne began slogging him, he conceded hardly more than a run an over.

And so, after tea, England were in again, their hopes renewed. But the first three batsmen were gone before they had even wiped off their narrow deficit. And Saturday began with two blows. Firstly, Australia's first-innings lead was recalculated from 38 to 40 because a four hit by Blewett was ruled a six after the third umpire, Ken Palmer, had pored over the TV evidence. And in this game every run mattered. Then, to the third ball of the morning, Hussain toe-ended a cut straight to Elliott. England were effectively 12 for four.

But the luck had turned. England supporters had long since assumed that injuries happened only to their side. However, Warne had been struggling on the second night, and now it was obvious he had a nasty groin strain. He was only able to lope in off three paces, and it seemed to curb his variety. That did not stop him turning the ball viciously out of the rough, and could not save the likes of Hussain, bent on doing something daft. But the next pair avoided the daft, and put on 79.

Thorpe, not for the first time, failed to convert a fifty into a century but, since he scored the only fifty of the match, that was wholly forgivable. It was an innings of exceptional quality and tenacity. Ramprakash made 48, which was worth at least double, and began at long last to bat for England with the certainty he showed for Middlesex.

At the time it still did not look enough. The England tail was useless yet again – the last four wickets fell for three – and Kasprowicz followed McGrath and Tufnell in taking seven in an innings; three bowlers had never done this in the same Test. Australia needed just 124 to win. But there was a sense that the situation was not hopeless. The crowd roared Malcolm in as he took the new ball, and he responded by straightening his fourth delivery to dismiss Elliott.

Tufnell bowled over the wicket to turn the ball from the crumbling pitch rather than the footmarks, and applied enough pressure to help the bowler at the other end. The beneficiary was Caddick, who removed Taylor and Blewett, given out caught behind, though TV replays suggested this was a quaint decision – by no means his first – by umpire Barker. The Waughs soon followed. Australia were 54 for five and suddenly all England was agog, even if it was the first day of the league football season.

Ponting and Healy battled back, with a stand of 34. But Tufnell finally trapped Ponting on the back pad, and Caddick took a return catch from Healy, juggled with it one-handed twice, and then clung on. Warne, batting with a runner, tried to lash out again. This time Martin got underneath his first big hit. Since Martin's fielding is willing rather than athletic, and he had dropped Warne badly 24 hours earlier, he seemed a plausible candidate to be the modern answer to Fred Tate. But he took it easily. England were confident now. The last act was Thorpe catching McGrath at mid-off – Tufnell's 11th victim – and his sunglasses falling off as he did so.

This was the first three-day Test at The Oval since 1957. On the Saturday evening Mark Taylor received a replica Ashes urn from the master of ceremonies David Gower, who had waved around a similar copy 12 years earlier. But this was greeted with only casual applause. It was a moment for England, and not just for the team. For the administrators, desperate to keep the game alive in the hearts of the public in difficult times, it was a priceless victory. – MATTHEW ENGEL.

Man of the Match: P. C. R. Tufnell.   *Attendance:* 60,123; receipts £1,595,945.

Close of play: First day, Australia 77-2 (G. S. Blewett 10*, M. E. Waugh 13*); Second day, England 52-3 (N. Hussain 2*, G. P. Thorpe 22*).

England

M. A. Butcher b McGrath	5	– lbw b M. E. Waugh 13
*M. A. Atherton c Healy b McGrath	8	– c S. R. Waugh b Kasprowicz 8
†A. J. Stewart lbw b McGrath	36	– lbw b McGrath 3
N. Hussain c Elliott b McGrath	35	– c Elliott b Warne 2
G. P. Thorpe b McGrath	27	– c Taylor b Kasprowicz 62
M. R. Ramprakash b Blewett b McGrath	4	– st Healy b Warne 48
A. J. Hollioake b Warne	0	– lbw b Kasprowicz 4
A. R. Caddick not out	26	– not out 0
P. J. Martin b McGrath	20	– c and b Kasprowicz 3
P. C. R. Tufnell c Blewett b Warne	1	– c Healy b Kasprowicz 0
D. E. Malcolm lbw b Kasprowicz	0	– b Kasprowicz 0
B 2, l-b 6, n-b 10	18	B 6, l-b 10, n-b 4 20

1/18 (1) 2/24 (2) 3/97 (3) 4/128 (4)   180   1/20 (2) 2/24 (3) 3/26 (1)   163
5/131 (5) 6/132 (7) 7/132 (6)   4/52 (4) 5/131 (5) 6/138 (7)
8/158 (9) 9/175 (10) 10/180 (11)   7/160 (6) 8/163 (9)
                                           9/163 (10) 10/163 (11)

Bowling: *First Innings*—McGrath 21–4–76–7; Kasprowicz 11.4–2–56–1; Warne 17–8–32–2; Young 7–3–8–0. *Second Innings*—McGrath 17–5–33–0; Kasprowicz 15.5–5–36–7; Warne 26–9–57–2; M. E. Waugh 7–3–16–1; Young 1–0–5–0.

Australia

M. T. G. Elliott b Tufnell	12	– (2) lbw b Malcolm 4
*M. A. Taylor c Hollioake b Tufnell	38	– (1) lbw b Caddick........... 18
G. S. Blewett c Stewart b Tufnell	47	– c Stewart b Caddick 19
M. E. Waugh c Butcher b Tufnell	19	– c Hussain b Tufnell 1
S. R. Waugh lbw b Caddick	22	– c Thorpe b Caddick 6
R. T. Ponting c Hussain b Tufnell	40	– lbw b Tufnell 20
†I. A. Healy c Stewart b Tufnell	2	– c and b Caddick 14
S. Young c Stewart b Tufnell	0	– not out 4
S. K. Warne b Caddick	30	– c Martin b Tufnell 3
M. S. Kasprowicz lbw b Caddick	0	– c Hollioake b Caddick 4
G. D. McGrath not out	1	– c Thorpe b Tufnell 1
L-b 3, w 1, n-b 5	9	B 3, l-b 4, w 1, n-b 2 10

1/49 (1) 2/54 (2) 3/94 (4) 4/140 (5)   220   1/5 (2) 2/36 (1) 3/42 (4)   104
5/150 (3) 6/164 (7) 7/164 (8)   4/49 (3) 5/54 (5) 6/88 (6)
8/205 (9) 9/205 (10) 10/220 (6)   7/92 (7) 8/95 (9)
                                           9/99 (10) 10/104 (11)

Bowling: *First Innings*—Malcolm 11–2–37–0; Martin 15–5–38–0; Caddick 19–4–76–3; Tufnell 34.3–16–66–7. *Second Innings*—Malcolm 3–0–15–1; Martin 4–0–13–0; Tufnell 13.1–6–27–4; Caddick 12–2–42–5.

Umpires: L. H. Barker (West Indies) and P. Willey. Referee: C. W. Smith (West Indies).

COOPERS & LYBRAND AWARDS

The Coopers & Lybrand International Test Player of the Year Trophy was retained in April 1997 by Steve Waugh of Australia, for his all-round performances against West Indies and South Africa. Waugh was also voted Test Player of the Year again in a Coopers & Lybrand poll carried out on the Internet, gaining 39 per cent of the vote – the same as in 1996. The award for the England player who had made the biggest impact in the Coopers & Lybrand Ratings in the 12 months to April 1997 was won by Alec Stewart, who had climbed to fifth in the world rankings for batsmen.

CORNHILL INSURANCE ENGLAND PLAYER OF THE YEAR

The Cornhill Insurance England Player of the Year Award was won in April 1997 by Alec Stewart of Surrey. He received £8,000.

PAKISTAN A IN ENGLAND, 1997

Pakistan sent an inexperienced team to England in July 1997, and they were rewarded with mixed results. They won only one of their nine first-class matches, against Somerset, and lost four. But they did win three out of four one-day games. Their coach, Agha Zahid, was not too concerned by their poor first-class record: he believed that the tour had been useful preparation for would-be internationals. "This is a very young team – the average age is under 20 – so it has been good for them to experience the conditions here, and also the daily diet of cricket," he said. "They are all going home better cricketers, and that is enough for me."

With three players reported to be 15 years old – there was still controversy over the precise age of Hasan Raza, who had made his Test debut against Zimbabwe the previous October – it was certainly a youthful party. Shoaib Malik and Irfan Fazil were the other 15-year-olds. Mujahid Jamshed, at 25, and Ali Hussain Rizvi, 23, were much the eldest present. Three of the 15 tourists had played Test cricket: their captain, Mohammad Wasim, who had made a century on debut against New Zealand in November 1996, Raza and Salim Elahi. Four others had appeared in one-day internationals: Abdur Razzaq, Azhar Mahmood, Javed Qadir and Jamshed. A few more experienced players might have been fitted in had the tour not coincided with the Asia Cup in Sri Lanka. Raza was actually summoned to Colombo to reinforce the senior squad halfway through the trip; but he was not required to play there, and eventually returned to England.

Elahi was the best-established of the international players, and demonstrated it by heading the batting averages: he scored 625 runs, 235 more than anyone else, at an average of 48.07. Much of this he owed to one innings, a double-hundred against Worcestershire, though he underlined his consistency with three more half-centuries. Raza passed 50 four times in his ten innings without ever reaching three figures, whereas Wasim leaned heavily on one performance, a forceful 155 at Headingley. Opener Ali Naqvi made the other century of the tour, 114 in a losing cause against MCC. One of the most reliable contributors was all-rounder Azhar Mahmood, who scored 379 at 31.58, and also led the bowling averages, with 40 wickets at 20.72. But the bowling find of the tour was Shoaib Akhtar, whose lively pace (if not his overlong run-up) impressed many observers, and he gathered 25 wickets at 29.88. He was partnered by Razzaq, who took 23 wickets, and leg-spinner Rizvi, with 24. Wicket-keeper Qadir's finest moments came when he collected nine catches in the opening match with Nottinghamshire.

Zahid's hopes that more of his charges would make the leap to Test cricket were soon fulfilled: Naqvi and Mahmood were selected to play South Africa a couple of months later, and distinguished themselves by scoring Test debut centuries in the same innings. But, as on similar tours in recent years, England had failed to offer their guests an intermediate step between the first-class game and full internationals. Whereas England A had played three unofficial Tests and three one-day games against Pakistan A when they toured in 1995-96, there was only one representative match at the conclusion of this programme. A First-Class Counties Select XI, drawing only on those counties who were not taking part in the County Championship or playing the Australians, indicated the low priority the authorities continue to attach to visiting A teams. Pakistan A lost to this slightly random selection of Englishmen, after fielding a weakened team; Akhtar, Naqvi and Rana Qayyum were omitted, apparently exhausted after six weeks of touring. Zahid said that the attraction of a representative series might have motivated his players to maintain their enthusiasm to the end.

For most of the trip, the Pakistanis played with abundant enthusiasm; indeed, their frequent appeals in the field were often described as excessive. Home scorers also complained that they had not brought their own scorer with them causing problems of identification for both them and the spectators. Then again, it should perhaps be remembered that England A have never taken a scorer on their overseas trips either.

PAKISTAN A TOURING PARTY

Mohammad Wasim (Rawalpindi) (*captain*), Mujahid Jamshed (Lahore/Habib Bank) (*vice-captain*), Abdur Razzaq (Lahore), Ali Hussain Rizvi (Karachi/Pakistan Customs), Ali Naqvi (Karachi/HBFC), Azhar Mahmood (Islamabad/United Bank), Farhan Adil (Karachi), Fazal-e-Akbar (Peshawar), Hasan Raza (Karachi), Irfan Fazil, Javed Qadir (Karachi/PIA), Rana Qayyum (Gujranwala), Salim Elahi (United Bank), Shoaib Akhtar (Rawalpindi/ADBP), Shoaib Malik (Gujranwala).

Manager: Ijaz Yousuf. *Coach:* Agha Zahid.

PAKISTAN A TOUR RESULTS

First-class matches – Played 9: Won 1, Lost 4, Drawn 4.
Win – Somerset.
Losses – Derbyshire, MCC, Yorkshire, First-Class Counties Select XI.
Draws – Nottinghamshire, Worcestershire, Sussex, Gloucestershire.
Non-first-class matches – Played 4: Won 3, Lost 1. *Wins* – ECB XI, Gloucestershire, Hampshire.
  Loss – Northamptonshire.

PAKISTAN A TOUR AVERAGES – FIRST-CLASS MATCHES

BATTING

	M	I	NO	R	HS	100s	Avge	Ct/St
Salim Elahi	8	13	0	625	229	1	48.07	6
Hasan Raza	6	10	0	349	96	0	34.90	3
Azhar Mahmood	8	13	1	379	92	0	31.58	2
Abdur Razzaq	6	9	2	216	62	0	30.85	0
Ali Naqvi	8	13	0	362	114	1	27.84	4
Rana Qayyum	8	13	1	320	97	0	26.66	0
Mohammad Wasim	9	15	0	390	155	1	26.00	17
Javed Qadir	9	15	4	277	61	0	25.18	26/1
Farhan Adil	5	9	0	198	50	0	22.00	3
Mujahid Jamshed	9	15	0	230	59	0	15.33	3
Irfan Fazil	3	5	2	43	19	0	14.33	0
Ali Hussain Rizvi	8	13	1	77	28	0	6.41	5
Shoaib Akhtar	7	10	4	32	10	0	5.33	6
Shoaib Malik	3	4	0	18	9	0	4.50	0

Played in two matches: Fazal-e-Akbar 6, 4, 1*.

* *Signifies not out.*

BOWLING

	O	M	R	W	BB	5Wfi	Avge
Azhar Mahmood	290.5	66	829	40	5-66	1	20.72
Shoaib Malik	123	24	333	12	3-49	0	27.75
Shoaib Akhtar	194.3	29	747	25	5-62	2	29.88
Abdur Razzaq	187.2	29	753	23	5-106	1	32.73
Irfan Fazil	56	12	234	7	3-51	0	33.42
Ali Hussain Rizvi ...	306	70	822	24	5-68	1	34.25

Also bowled: Ali Naqvi 6–1–20–1; Fazal-e-Akbar 45–10–181–4; Hasan Raza 19–4–50–1; Mohammad Wasim 7–2–21–0; Mujahid Jamshed 3.1–0–18–0.

Note: Matches in this section which were not first-class are signified by a dagger.

NOTTINGHAMSHIRE v PAKISTAN A

At Nottingham, July 2, 3, 4. Drawn. Toss: Pakistan A.

The Pakistanis' tour got off to a mixed start, typified by Shoaib Akhtar's first over, which took 11 minutes. He made two false starts, bowled four no-balls, conceded 17 runs and dismissed Pollard. In all, there were 52 extras, all but six from no-balls, during the innings, dragging the over-rate down to twelve and a half hour. Archer ended a lean spell by batting three hours for 81, with ten fours and a six. Only 34 overs were bowled on a rainy second day, in which time Tolley reduced the tourists to 71 for five. They lost their ninth wicket still eight short of saving the follow-on, but Azhar Mahmood, who scored a rousing fifty, just saw them to safety. Then he picked up three wickets as Nottinghamshire collapsed in turn. Wicket-keeper Javed Qadir made nine dismissals in the match.

Close of play: First day, Nottinghamshire 298-9 (P. J. Franks 29*, M. N. Bowen 0*); Second day, Pakistan A 71-5 (Rana Qayyum 1*, Azhar Mahmood 2*).

Nottinghamshire

P. R. Pollard c Javed Qadir b Shoaib Akhtar	10	– c Javed Qadir b Shoaib Akhtar	15
*R. T. Robinson c Javed Qadir b Abdur Razzaq	18	– b Shoaib Akhtar	4
G. F. Archer c Javed Qadir b Azhar Mahmood	81	– c Mohammad Wasim b Azhar Mahmood	1
A. A. Metcalfe c Ali Naqvi b Shoaib Akhtar	39		
M. P. Dowman c Javed Qadir b Azhar Mahmood	3	– (4) c Ali Naqvi b Azhar Mahmood	3
U. Afzaal c Mohammad Wasim b Shoaib Akhtar	17	– (5) c Javed Qadir b Shoaib Malik	31
C. M. Tolley lbw b Abdur Razzaq	2	– (6) c Javed Qadir b Azhar Mahmood	19
†L. N. P. Walker lbw b Shoaib Akhtar	34	– (7) not out	12
R. T. Bates c Javed Qadir b Azhar Mahmood	13	– (8) b Abdur Razzaq	1
P. J. Franks not out	29	– (9) c Javed Qadir b Shoaib Malik	5
M. N. Bowen not out	0	– (10) not out	0
B 2, l-b 4, n-b 46	52	L-b 3, w 1, n-b 12	16

1/23 2/59 3/155 4/164 5/193   (9 wkts dec.) 298   1/24 2/29 3/31   (8 wkts dec.) 107
6/202 7/237 8/256 9/279   4/49 5/87 6/97
7/98 8/107

Bowling: *First Innings*—Abdur Razzaq 18.1–3–80–2; Shoaib Akhtar 15–2–71–4; Azhar Mahmood 26–5–69–3; Shoaib Malik 14–1–61–0; Mujahid Jamshed 1–0–11–0. *Second Innings*—Shoaib Akhtar 8–2–22–2; Abdur Razzaq 7–2–28–1; Azhar Mahmood 14–4–33–3; Shoaib Malik 13–3–21–2.

Pakistan A

Ali Naqvi b Dowman	29	Abdur Razzaq lbw b Dowman	0
Salim Elahi c Afzaal b Tolley	23	Shoaib Malik run out	1
*Mohammad Wasim lbw b Tolley	12	Shoaib Akhtar run out	4
Mujahid Jamshed lbw b Bates	1		
Hasan Raza b Tolley	0		
Rana Qayyum b Franks	2	B 2, l-b 2, n-b 2	6
Azhar Mahmood not out	56		
†Javed Qadir c Robinson b Dowman	16	1/45 2/59 3/68 4/68 5/68	150
		6/74 7/140 8/140 9/141	

Bowling: Franks 15–3–32–1; Bowen 16–3–49–0; Tolley 16–6–32–3; Dowman 10–4–10–3; Bates 11–3–23–1.

Umpires: N. G. Cowley and B. Dudleston.

DERBYSHIRE v PAKISTAN A

At Derby, July 5, 6, 7. Derbyshire won by seven wickets. Toss: Derbyshire. First-class debut: B. L. Spendlove.

Only Hasan Raza and Rollins settled on the first two days, during which 30 wickets fell. Raza showed a range of strokes and the poise to be unruffled by lack of support; he scored the only fifty of the first innings and narrowly missed a century in the second. In between, Rollins made 51, while Derbyshire's next-highest score came, improbably, from Malcolm. Striking firmly, Malcolm limited the first-innings deficit to 21, and followed up with two early wickets. Derbyshire had just over a day to score 223 for their first victory over a Pakistani team since they beat the Eaglets in 1963. Shoaib Akhtar, the tourists' liveliest bowler, was hampered by a shoulder injury, and an opening partnership of 154 put the county in control. May guided them home with a five-hour maiden century. It earned him a run in the Championship; four of his five first-class games to date had been against touring teams. None of those teams had appealed as often or as irrelevantly as the Pakistanis.

Close of play: First day, Derbyshire 116-7 (A. S. Rollins 51*, S. J. Lacey 3*); Second day, Derbyshire 19-0 (A. S. Rollins 10*, M. R. May 8*).

Pakistan A

Ali Naqvi run out		2 – lbw b DeFreitas	4
Mujahid Jamshed c Aldred b DeFreitas	5	– c Clarke b Malcolm	4
*Mohammad Wasim lbw b Dean	33	– c Griffiths b Malcolm	1
Hasan Raza c Griffiths b Aldred	56	– lbw b Dean	96
Farhan Adil lbw b Dean	0	– (6) b Clarke	28
Rana Qayyum c Dean b DeFreitas	12	– (5) c Griffiths b DeFreitas	32
Azhar Mahmood c Spendlove b Dean	19	– b Dean	4
†Javed Qadir not out	12	– not out	11
Ali Hussain Rizvi b Malcolm	0	– b Dean	0
Fazal-e-Akbar b Malcolm	6	– (11) b DeFreitas	4
Shoaib Akhtar c Aldred b Clarke	1	– (10) b Malcolm	10
B 10, l-b 4, w 1, n-b 8	23	B 1, l-b 2, n-b 4	7

1/8 2/12 3/63 4/63 5/123		169	1/4 2/12 3/12 4/83 5/142	201
6/129 7/153 8/155 9/167			6/157 7/182 8/182 9/194	

Bowling: *First Innings*—Malcolm 17–2–49–2; DeFreitas 18–8–37–2; Aldred 13–1–29–1; Dean 14–4–40–3; Clarke 5.1–5–0–1. *Second Innings*—DeFreitas 21–8–33–3; Malcolm 12–4–30–3; Aldred 18–9–43–0; Dean 18–7–48–3; Clarke 14–2–44–1.

Derbyshire

A. S. Rollins c Mujahid Jamshed b Fazal-e-Akbar .	51	– c Shoaib Akhtar	
		b Ali Hussain Rizvi .	77
M. R. May b Shoaib Akhtar	4	– not out	107
B. L. Spendlove b Shoaib Akhtar	0	– c Ali Hussain Rizvi	
		b Azhar Mahmood .	12
G. A. Khan lbw b Azhar Mahmood	14	– c Javed Qadir b Azhar Mahmood .	4
V. P. Clarke b Azhar Mahmood	9	– not out	5
*P. A. J. DeFreitas c Mohammad Wasim			
b Azhar Mahmood .	13		
P. Aldred c Javed Qadir b Ali Hussain Rizvi	0		
†S. P. Griffiths b Ali Hussain Rizvi	1		
S. J. Lacey not out	3		
D. E. Malcolm c Ali Hussain Rizvi			
b Azhar Mahmood .	19		
K. J. Dean lbw b Ali Hussain Rizvi	8		
B 1, l-b 11, n-b 14	26	B 2, l-b 8, n-b 8	18

1/7 2/7 3/56 4/72 5/86   148   1/154 2/203 3/217   (3 wkts) 223
6/87 7/93 8/116 9/139

Bowling: *First Innings*—Shoaib Akhtar 8–0–35–2; Fazal-e-Akbar 8–0–44–1; Azhar Mahmood 13–1–34–4; Ali Hussain Rizvi 12.1–3–21–3; Mohammad Wasim 1–0–2–0. *Second Innings*—Shoaib Akhtar 6–0–25–0; Fazal-e-Akbar 17–6–43–0; Ali Hussain Rizvi 28–6–65–1; Azhar Mahmood 22.3–6–61–2; Mohammad Wasim 6–2–19–0.

Umpires: T. E. Jesty and M. K. Reed.

MCC v PAKISTAN A

At Shenley Park, July 9, 10, 11. MCC won by ten wickets. Toss: Pakistan A. First-class debut: Irfan Fazil.

MCC eased to their first victory in a first-class game since 1984, thanks to two Leeward Islanders. Hamish Anthony took ten in a match for the first time, while Keith Arthurton scored a maiden double-century. Pakistan A's first innings lasted 43 overs, with Anthony claiming three wickets in each of his two spells. Salim Elahi batted nearly three hours for 53; only two of his colleagues managed double figures. The Australian Mark Lavender fell first ball in MCC's reply. But Arthurton and Grant Flower shared a stand of 186 in the next 34 overs. Arthurton was in danger twice: he was run out but reprieved because the umpire had mistakenly signalled four, and later caught off a no-ball. He remained unbeaten after 373 minutes and 269 balls, striking 23 fours and two sixes to reach his double-hundred before Shoaib Akhtar finished off MCC with four in ten balls. Resuming 243 behind, Ali Naqvi fought back with a six-hour century. But MCC needed only 15 to win, and got there before lunch on the final day.

Close of play: First day, MCC 276-5 (K. L. T. Arthurton 138*, M. P. W. Jeh 16*); Second day, Pakistan A 187-5 (Ali Naqvi 95*).

Pakistan A

Ali Naqvi lbw b Anthony	13	– c G. W. Flower b Badenhorst	114
Salim Elahi c Lavender b Jeh	53	– c Francis b Jeh	34
Rana Qayyum c Garaway b Anthony	1	– lbw b Anthony	1
Hasan Raza c Garaway b Anthony	3	– b Badenhorst	15
*Mohammad Wasim b Badenhorst	0	– lbw b Anthony	10
Mujahid Jamshed lbw b Badenhorst	19	– c Lavender b Jeh	12
Azhar Mahmood c Foley b Anthony	0	– (8) c Lavender b Anthony	31
†Javed Qadir c Garaway b Anthony	1	– (7) lbw b Jeh	0
Irfan Fazil not out	3	– c Garaway b Anthony	11
Ali Hussain Rizvi c Garaway b Anthony	1	– c Anthony b Badenhorst	5
Shoaib Akhtar c Arthurton b Jeh	8	– not out	2
L-b 1, w 2, n-b 14	17	B 1, l-b 4, w 1, n-b 16	22

1/23 2/29 3/38 4/41 5/71   119   1/82 2/96 3/134 4/158 5/187   257
6/78 7/85 8/103 9/108   6/187 7/231 8/239 9/253

Bowling: *First Innings*—Francis 8–0–36–0; Anthony 17–5–34–6; Badenhorst 11–4–24–2; Jeh 6.5–1–24–2. *Second Innings*—Francis 10–2–20–0; Anthony 25–6–79–4; Badenhorst 20–6–48–3; Foley 19–5–53–0; Jeh 12–3–37–3; Arthurton 3–1–5–0; G. W. Flower 5–1–10–0.

MCC

M. P. Lavender lbw b Shoaib Akhtar	0	– (2) not out	6
G. W. Flower c Javed Qadir b Azhar Mahmood	78		
K. L. T. Arthurton not out	200		
G. I. Foley c Mohammad Wasim b Azhar Mahmood	4		
*A. Flower c Javed Qadir b Azhar Mahmood	14		
Asif Din lbw b Azhar Mahmood	4	– (1) not out	12
M. P. W. Jeh b Irfan Fazil	30		
†M. Garaway hit wkt b Shoaib Akhtar	5		
H. A. G. Anthony b Shoaib Akhtar	0		
A. Badenhorst b Shoaib Akhtar	0		
N. B. Francis c Mohammad Wasim b Shoaib Akhtar	1		
B 2, l-b 5, w 1, n-b 18	26		

1/0 2/186 3/194 4/224 5/240   362   (no wkt) 18
6/324 7/355 8/355 9/359

Bowling: *First Innings*—Shoaib Akhtar 17.2–0–64–5; Irfan Fazil 15–2–87–1; Ali Hussain Rizvi 24–0–114–0; Azhar Mahmood 30–1–90–4. *Second Innings*—Shoaib Akhtar 1.3–0–12–0; Azhar Mahmood 1–0–6–0.

Umpires: M. R. Benson and P. Willey.

†At Walsall, July 13. Pakistan A won by ten wickets. Toss: Pakistan A. ECB XI 145 (47.1 overs) (S. J. Foster 49; Shoaib Akhtar three for 30, Abdur Razzaq three for 34); Pakistan A 147 for no wkt (30.3 overs) (Ali Naqvi 80 not out, Salim Elahi 58 not out).

WORCESTERSHIRE v PAKISTAN A

At Worcester, July 16, 17, 18. Drawn. Toss: Pakistan A. First-class debut: M. M. Mirza.

Hick captained Worcestershire in a first-class match for the first time and his 93rd century thwarted Pakistan A, who led by 224 on first innings. There was plenty to encourage the tourists. Leg-spinnner Ali Hussain Rizvi survived a first-day assault from Hick – who smashed 55 in 48 balls – to return five for 68. Then Salim Elahi scored a maiden first-class hundred (he had already scored one in a limited-overs international). He converted it into 229, with 35 fours and two sixes in 451 minutes and 335 balls, and figured in three successive century partnerships. For Worcestershire, Maneer Mirza, the brother of fast bowler Parvaz who died in 1995, picked up three wickets on first-class debut – at a cost. On the final day, Hick hit 20 fours and five sixes and added 171 with Haynes to make the game safe. There were casualties: the fiery Shoaib Akhtar struck Weston on the instep, and Leatherdale in the mouth – and limped off himself after trying to stop a drive from Hick with his foot.

Close of play: First day, Pakistan A 166-3 (Salim Elahi 78*, Farhan Adil 32*); Second day, Worcestershire 35-0 (V. S. Solanki 21*, W. P. C. Weston 9*).

Worcestershire

V. S. Solanki c Javed Qadir b Abdur Razzaq	 6	– lbw b Shoaib Akhtar	 38
W. P. C. Weston c Javed Qadir b Ali Hussain Rizvi	8	– retired hurt	 20
*G. A. Hick c Shoaib Akhtar b Ali Hussain Rizvi	. 55	– c sub b Azhar Mahmood	144
K. R. Spiring lbw b Abdur Razzaq	 35	– c Farhan Adil b Azhar Mahmood	. 13
G. R. Haynes c and b Ali Hussain Rizvi	 65	– c sub b Azhar Mahmood	 48
D. A. Leatherdale lbw b Azhar Mahmood	 6	– retired hurt	 9
†I. Dawood lbw b Azhar Mahmood	 0	– not out	 10
M. J. Rawnsley b Azhar Mahmood	 16	– not out	 13
A. Sheriyar st Javed Qadir b Ali Hussain Rizvi	. . . 21		
P. A. Thomas not out	 16		
M. M. Mirza c Azhar Mahmood			
b Ali Hussain Rizvi	. 6		
B 5, l-b 7, w 1, n-b 18	 31	B 10, l-b 18, w 2, n-b 13	. . 43

1/15 2/54 3/95 4/141 5/176   265   1/60 2/114   (4 wkts) 338
6/176 7/206 8/242 9/247   3/285 4/292

In the second innings W. P. C. Weston retired hurt at 69 and D. A. Leatherdale retired hurt at 302.

Bowling: *First Innings—*Shoaib Akhtar 10–0–57–0; Abdur Razzaq 10.1–1–33–2; Azhar Mahmood 25–8–89–3; Ali Hussain Rizvi 18.2–7–68–5; Mujahid Jamshed 2–0–6–0. *Second Innings—*Shoaib Akhtar 30–5–125–1; Abdur Razzaq 20–4–81–0; Azhar Mahmood 24–6–64–3; Mujahid Jamshed 0.1–0–1–0; Ali Hussain Rizvi 13–4–39–0.

Pakistan A

Ali Naqvi lbw b Sheriyar 36	Abdur Razzaq not out 36
Salim Elahi c Leatherdale b Rawnsley . . .229	Ali Hussain Rizvi st Dawood b Rawnsley 1
Mujahid Jamshed lbw b Sheriyar 4	
Rana Qayyum lbw b Mirza 12	B 1, l-b 4, w 3 8
Farhan Adil c Weston b Sheriyar 50	
†Javed Qadir st Dawood b Rawnsley 40	1/50 2/66 3/93 (9 wkts dec.) 489
*Mohammad Wasim c Solanki b Mirza . . 64	4/208 5/319 6/439
Azhar Mahmood c Dawood b Mirza 9	7/452 8/452 9/489

Shoaib Akhtar did not bat.

Bowling: Sheriyar 17–0–80–3; Thomas 17–2–87–0; Mirza 27–2–136–3; Leatherdale 17–2–53–0; Rawnsley 31.4–10–67–3; Solanki 13–3–61–0.

Umpires: J. D. Bond and N. A. Mallender.

SOMERSET v PAKISTAN A

At Taunton, July 19, 20, 21. Pakistan A won by five wickets. Toss: Somerset. First-class debuts: N. R. Boulton, L. D. Sutton. County debuts: P. S. Jones, S. C. G. MacGill.

Ali Naqvi set up Pakistan A's only first-class win of the tour. He hit 18 fours in 101 balls and was looking for a 19th to bring up his hundred when he was caught at cover. Victory arrived 50 minutes after lunch, with Rana Qayyum scoring 47 in 49 balls. It had been an entertaining contest on a good pitch in ideal weather. Ecclestone scored a powerful hundred on the opening day, supported by Bowler, but Somerset's middle order crumbled as Irfan Fazil took three for seven in 17 balls. Oddly enough, both first innings saw a second-wicket century stand followed by the fall of nine wickets for 99 runs; in Pakistan A's response, Salim Elahi and Mujahid Jamshed put on 122 and Shine collected six wickets. Lathwell helped Somerset leave a target of 231 in just over a day, which set the stage for Naqvi.

Close of play: First day, Pakistan A 136-3 (Shoaib Malik 2*); Second day, Pakistan A 35-0 (Ali Naqvi 22*, Salim Elahi 9*).

Somerset

*P. D. Bowler c Salim Elahi b Shoaib Malik	30	– c Mohammad Wasim	
		b Fazal-e-Akbar .	26
P. C. L. Holloway b Fazal-e-Akbar	0	– lbw b Fazal-e-Akbar	2
S. C. Ecclestone c Javed Qadir b Shoaib Malik	102	– lbw b Ali Hussain Rizvi	49
M. N. Lathwell c Mohammad Wasim b Irfan Fazil	0	– c Ali Naqvi b Irfan Fazil	60
K. A. Parsons lbw b Irfan Fazil	1	– lbw b Ali Hussain Rizvi	36
N. R. Boulton lbw b Irfan Fazil	1	– b Ali Hussain Rizvi	14
J. I. D. Kerr lbw b Ali Hussain Rizvi	35	– b Irfan Fazil	18
†L. D. Sutton not out	11	– b Shoaib Malik	6
P. S. Jones b Ali Hussain Rizvi	4	– c Salim Elahi b Shoaib Malik	0
S. C. G. MacGill c Salim Elahi b Shoaib Malik	7	– c Farhan Adil b Shoaib Malik	25
K. J. Shine c Mohammad Wasim			
b Ali Hussain Rizvi .	4	– not out	0
L-b 9, w 1, n-b 8	18	N-b 8	8

1/1 2/114 3/115 4/117 5/125   213   1/22 2/47 3/115 4/163 5/194   244
6/179 7/189 8/195 9/206   6/195 7/210 8/212 9/238

Bowling: *First Innings*—Fazal-e-Akbar 11–3–47–1; Irfan Fazil 13–4–51–3; Shoaib Malik 24–6–49–3; Ali Hussain Rizvi 16.3–0–57–3. *Second Innings*—Irfan Fazil 12–0–53–2; Fazal-e-Akbar 9–1–47–2; Shoaib Malik 20–2–66–3; Ali Hussain Rizvi 23–6–78–3.

Pakistan A

Ali Naqvi c Jones b Shine	4	– c Jones b MacGill	96
Salim Elahi lbw b Shine	70	– b Jones	14
Mujahid Jamshed c Ecclestone b MacGill	59	– b Shine	5
Shoaib Malik c Sutton b Shine	7		
Farhan Adil c Holloway b Kerr	43	– (4) b Lathwell b Shine	9
*Mohammad Wasim lbw b Shine	0	– (5) c Sutton b MacGill	40
Rana Qayyum c Sutton b Shine	18	– (6) not out	47
†Javed Qadir c Sutton b Shine	1	– (7) not out	13
Irfan Fazil c Bowler b MacGill	19		
Ali Hussain Rizvi c Sutton b Kerr	0		
Fazal-e-Akbar not out	1		
B 1, l-b 4	5	L-b 2, w 1, n-b 4	7

1/6 2/128 3/136 4/150 5/150   227   1/41 2/72 3/100   (5 wkts) 231
6/182 7/194 8/225 9/225   4/164 5/175

Bowling: *First Innings*—Shine 24–3–74–6; Jones 14–1–66–0; Kerr 10–3–33–2; MacGill 17–8–49–2. *Second Innings*—Shine 20.5–5–57–2; Kerr 8–1–46–0; MacGill 19–3–74–2; Jones 3–1–18–1; Parsons 4–0–23–0; Bowler 0.5–0–11–0.

Umpires: P. Adams and J. C. Balderstone.

†At Cheltenham, July 22. Pakistan A won by 49 runs. Toss: Gloucestershire. Pakistan A 279 for seven (50 overs) (Ali Naqvi 46, Salim Elahi 66, Rana Qayyum 56, Azhar Mahmood 48); Gloucestershire 230 (47.1 overs) (M. G. N. Windows 45, M. J. Church 49, R. C. J. Williams 38, Extras 34; Azhar Mahmood three for 24).
Church, formerly of Worcestershire, was making his first-team debut for Gloucestershire.

SUSSEX v PAKISTAN A

At Hove, July 24, 25, 26, 27. Drawn. Toss: Sussex.
Sussex's eighth-wicket pair, Bates and Khan, held firm for four overs to secure the draw. But Pakistan A had delayed their declaration far too long. They finally set a target of 224 in just 28 overs. Shoaib Akhtar and Azhar Mahmood then found enough life in a hitherto moribund surface to grab three wickets in nine balls. Sussex subsided to 60 for seven, and a few more overs might

have finished them off. Earlier in the match, which was cut back from four days to three by rain, neither side could wrest the initiative. Sussex took a 25-run lead, thanks to a ninth-wicket stand of 100 between Greenfield, who scored a fluent century, and Khan. Pakistan A were just 81 ahead when they lost their first wicket, but Rana Qayyum, their top scorer on the opening day, turned the innings round and almost reached his hundred. Edwards bowled at a lively pace to collect his first five-wicket haul.

Close of play: First day, Sussex 2-0 (R. K. Rao 0*, M. T. E. Peirce 2*); Second day, Pakistan A 43-2 (Mujahid Jamshed 15*, Abdur Razzaq 9*); Third day, No play.

Pakistan A

Ali Naqvi c Peirce b Edwards	46	– lbw b Kirtley	0
Salim Elahi c Edwards b Martin-Jenkins	27	– lbw b Edwards	17
Mujahid Jamshed c Humphries b Kirtley	7	– c Rao b Bates	15
Farhan Adil b Martin-Jenkins	3	– (5) c Bates b Edwards	5
*Mohammad Wasim c Taylor b Kirtley	9	– (6) c Martin-Jenkins b Khan	23
Rana Qayyum c Khan b Bates	75	– (7) c Humphries b Edwards	97
Azhar Mahmood c Humphries b Martin-Jenkins	63	– (8) lbw b Bates	1
†Javed Qadir c Greenfield b Khan	26	– (9) not out	6
Abdur Razzaq c Peirce b Khan	14	– (4) c Greenfield b Bates	62
Ali Hussain Rizvi c Humphries b Edwards	28	– c Greenfield b Edwards	17
Shoaib Akhtar not out	6	– c sub (N. C. Phillips) b Edwards	0
B 1, l-b 1	2	B 1, l-b 2, n-b 2	5

1/58 2/76 3/83 4/85 5/94   306   1/0 2/28 3/43 4/50 5/106   248
6/187 7/258 8/258 9/287   6/162 7/174 8/230 9/248

Bowling: *First Innings*—Kirtley 18–2–99–2; Edwards 15–3–71–2; Bates 18–10–20–1; Martin-Jenkins 13–3–26–3; Khan 28.2–12–88–2. *Second Innings*—Kirtley 20–2–80–1; Martin-Jenkins 8–0–31–0; Edwards 13–3–34–5; Bates 20–9–35–3; Khan 18–3–65–1.

Sussex

R. K. Rao c Mohammad Wasim b Abdur Razzaq	71	– c Salim Elahi b Abdur Razzaq	1
M. T. E. Peirce run out	37	– lbw b Shoaib Akhtar	0
N. R. Taylor lbw b Ali Hussain Rizvi	37		
M. Newell lbw b Azhar Mahmood	4	– (3) c Javed Qadir b Shoaib Akhtar	0
*K. Greenfield c Shoaib Akhtar		– (4) c Mohammad Wasim	
b Azhar Mahmood	108	b Azhar Mahmood	16
R. S. C. Martin-Jenkins b Abdur Razzaq	0	– (5) c and b Azhar Mahmood	9
†S. Humphries c Javed Qadir b Ali Hussain Rizvi	4	– (6) b Shoaib Akhtar	7
A. D. Edwards lbw b Ali Hussain Rizvi	4	– (7) lbw b Azhar Mahmood	13
J. J. Bates c and b Shoaib Akhtar	3	– (8) not out	15
A. A. Khan not out	33	– (9) not out	17
R. J. Kirtley b Shoaib Akhtar	0		
B 5, l-b 6, w 1, n-b 18	30	N-b 12	12

1/72 2/118 3/129 4/171 5/171   331   1/1 2/1 3/5 4/30   (7 wkts) 90
6/182 7/204 8/231 9/331   5/39 6/49 7/60

Bowling: *First Innings*—Shoaib Akhtar 19.4–4–72–2; Abdur Razzaq 24–3–101–2; Azhar Mahmood 23–4–79–2; Ali Hussain Rizvi 26–8–68–3. *Second Innings*—Shoaib Akhtar 14–3–58–3; Abdur Razzaq 5–0–17–1; Azhar Mahmood 9–4–15–3.

Umpires: B. J. Meyer and J. F. Steele.

†At Southampton, July 29. Pakistan A won by six wickets. Toss: Hampshire. Hampshire 167 (47.1 overs) (S. D. Udal 35; Azhar Mahmood three for 31); Pakistan A 168 for four (44.5 overs) (Mohammad Wasim 42, Rana Qayyum 47 not out).

GLOUCESTERSHIRE v PAKISTAN A

At Bristol, August 1, 2, 3, 4. Drawn. Toss: Pakistan A.

Gloucestershire had already lost to Pakistan A in a one-day match, and were soon in trouble again. Despite leading the Championship, they showed little technique against the pacy Shoaib Akhtar and Abdur Razzaq, and were 23 for five after 11 overs. But Hancock and Ball, who sometimes looks a better late-order batsman than off-spinner, scored fifties, and the tourists were five down themselves by the close. Smith dismissed Ali Naqvi in eight balls, slight consolation for a wicketless Test debut at Leeds — and his imminent exclusion from the next Test. But Hasan Raza and Javed Qadir built a modest lead. Trainor and Church, the newcomer from Worcestershire, made useful runs before rain washed out the final two days.

Close of play: First day, Pakistan A 113-5 (Hasan Raza 39*, Javed Qadir 5*); Second day, Gloucestershire 204-5 (M. W. Alleyne 22*, R. C. Russell 4*); Third day, No play.

Gloucestershire

N. J. Trainor b Shoaib Akhtar		6 – c Mohammad Wasim b Ali Naqvi	69
M. G. N. Windows lbw b Abdur Razzaq	1	– b Azhar Mahmood	34
T. H. C. Hancock c Mohammad Wasim b Shoaib Akhtar	50	– b Azhar Mahmood	2
M. J. Church c Mohammad Wasim b Abdur Razzaq	0	– lbw b Abdur Razzaq	53
R. I. Dawson c Salim Elahi b Shoaib Akhtar	7	– b Azhar Mahmood	8
*M. W. Alleyne c Hasan Raza b Shoaib Akhtar	0	– not out	22
†R. C. Russell c Ali Naqvi b Ali Hussain Rizvi	26	– not out	4
M. C. J. Ball c Salim Elahi b Abdur Razzaq	50		
R. P. Davis c Javed Qadir b Abdur Razzaq	12		
A. M. Smith c and b Shoaib Akhtar	5		
J. Lewis not out	0		
L-b 6, n-b 4	10	B 1, l-b 4, w 1, n-b 6	12

1/8 2/8 3/8 4/23 5/23   167   1/57 2/63 3/139   (5 wkts) 204
6/86 7/114 8/159 9/164   4/171 5/180

Bowling: *First Innings*—Shoaib Akhtar 17-3-62-5; Abdur Razzaq 11.2-3-33-4; Azhar Mahmood 13-4-35-0; Ali Naqvi 2-0-9-0; Ali Hussain Rizvi 8-2-22-1. *Second Innings*—Shoaib Akhtar 8-1-23-0; Abdur Razzaq 21-2-71-1; Azhar Mahmood 20-6-45-3; Ali Hussain Rizvi 19-2-49-0; Ali Naqvi 4-1-11-1.

Pakistan A

Ali Naqvi lbw b Smith	0	Abdur Razzaq lbw b Alleyne	0
Salim Elahi c Russell b Lewis	21	Ali Hussain Rizvi c Windows b Alleyne	2
Mujahid Jamshed c Russell b Ball	35	Shoaib Akhtar not out	0
Hasan Raza c Davis b Alleyne	63		
*Mohammad Wasim c Alleyne b Ball	0	L-b 3, n-b 4	7
Rana Qayyum c Russell b Hancock	7		
†Javed Qadir c Davis b Alleyne	61	1/8 2/47 3/75 4/79 5/90	220
Azhar Mahmood c Russell b Ball	24	6/190 7/199 8/199 9/215	

Bowling: Smith 15.4-4-50-1; Lewis 16-5-42-1; Alleyne 16-5-46-4; Ball 14.5-3-44-3; Hancock 10-4-31-1; Windows 1-0-4-0.

Umpires: M. J. Kitchen and R. Palmer.

YORKSHIRE v PAKISTAN A

At Leeds, August 7, 8, 9, 10. Yorkshire won by 69 runs. Toss: Yorkshire.

Bowlers on both sides had trouble with the worn footholds of a pitch already used against Northamptonshire; Pakistan A said they would complain about conditions to the International Cricket Council. But it was their batsmen who lost the match, collapsing to Hutchison's left-arm seam. Hutchison, who was on a hat-trick twice, finished with seven for 38 and 11 for 102 in all. It was his first-class county debut in England; he had appeared for Yorkshire in Zimbabwe and for The Rest against England A in 1996 before injury ended his season. On the first day, Shoaib Akhtar had achieved impressive pace but little reward as Yorkshire batted patchily. But Pakistan

A struggled until Mohammad Wasim, on his 20th birthday, played a captain's innings of great character. He added 178 with Javed Qadir, during which he scored 71 of the 75 runs between 146 and 221, the other four being extras. Moxon replied with an identical score of 155 and, helped by 72 extras, set a target of 257 in 86 overs. Hutchison did the rest.

Close of play: First day, Pakistan A 81-3 (Mujahid Jamshed 28*, Mohammad Wasim 19*); Second day, Yorkshire 37-0 (M. D. Moxon 16*, M. P. Vaughan 15*); Third day, Yorkshire 352-6 (C. A. Chapman 22*, G. M. Hamilton 5*).

Yorkshire

M. D. Moxon c Javed Qadir b Abdur Razzaq	6	– c Mujahid Jamshed b Hasan Raza	155
M. P. Vaughan b Shoaib Akhtar	1	– c Mohammad Wasim b Azhar Mahmood	31
*D. Byas c Javed Qadir b Azhar Mahmood	84	– (6) b Ali Hussain Rizvi	11
B. Parker c Mohammad Wasim b Ali Hussain Rizvi	8	– b Abdur Razzaq	43
A. McGrath b Azhar Mahmood	39	– (3) c Hasan Raza b Abdur Razzaq	5
†C. A. Chapman b Azhar Mahmood	2	– (7) run out	22
A. C. Morris lbw b Ali Hussain Rizvi	37	– (5) c and b Ali Hussain Rizvi	13
G. M. Hamilton c Mujahid Jamshed b Azhar Mahmood	13	– c Ali Hussain Rizvi b Abdur Razzaq	14
I. D. Fisher b Azhar Mahmood	3	– c Shoaib Akhtar b Abdur Razzaq	10
C. E. W. Silverwood b Abdur Razzaq	20	– b Abdur Razzaq	1
P. M. Hutchison not out	1	– not out	1
B 11, l-b 6, w 2, n-b 10	29	B 17, l-b 13, n-b 42	72
	243		**378**

1/3 2/20 3/73 4/161 5/166 6/167 7/195 8/201 9/231

1/89 2/94 3/179 4/204 5/254 6/340 7/360 8/366 9/377

Bowling: *First Innings*—Shoaib Akhtar 17-4-61-1; Abdur Razzaq 12.4-2-41-2; Azhar Mahmood 16-3-66-5; Ali Hussain Rizvi 26-10-44-2; Hasan Raza 7-1-14-0. *Second Innings*—Shoaib Akhtar 23-5-60-0; Abdur Razzaq 28.5-5-106-5; Ali Hussain Rizvi 46-12-91-2; Azhar Mahmood 15-1-55-1; Hasan Raza 12-3-36-1.

Pakistan A

Ali Naqvi c Chapman b Silverwood	5	– (3) c Chapman b Hamilton	13
Salim Elahi lbw b Hutchison	13	– (1) c Morris b Hutchison	89
Mujahid Jamshed b Hamilton	28	– (2) lbw b Hamilton	0
Hasan Raza lbw b Hutchison	5	– lbw b Hutchison	7
*Mohammad Wasim lbw b Hutchison	155	– b Hutchison	12
Rana Qayyum b Hamilton	16	– lbw b Hutchison	0
Azhar Mahmood c Vaughan b Hamilton	8	– (8) c Parker b Fisher	35
†Javed Qadir c Hamilton b Silverwood	61	– (7) c Chapman b Hutchison	0
Abdur Razzaq b Hamilton	29	– not out	20
Ali Hussain Rizvi c Parker b Hutchison	15	– c Byas b Hutchison	0
Shoaib Akhtar not out	1	– c Byas b Hutchison	0
B 11, l-b 2, w 4, n-b 12	29	L-b 6, w 3, n-b 2	11
	365		**187**

1/14 2/35 3/45 4/87 5/117 6/129 7/307 8/347 9/353

1/4 2/22 3/31 4/57 5/57 6/63 7/136 8/183 9/187

Bowling: *First Innings*—Silverwood 27-8-73-2; Hamilton 26-8-95-4; Hutchison 23.2-5-64-4; Fisher 12-2-38-0; Vaughan 17-4-53-0; Morris 9-2-29-0. *Second Innings*—Silverwood 10-3-24-0; Hamilton 12-4-52-2; Hutchison 12.3-4-38-7; Vaughan 10-1-41-0; Fisher 6-0-26-1.

Umpires: G. I. Burgess and J. W. Lloyds.

†At Northampton, August 12. Northamptonshire won by 60 runs. Toss: Pakistan A. Northamptonshire 300 for five (50 overs) (R. R. Montgomerie 81, R. J. Bailey 153 not out; Abdur Razzaq three for 55); Pakistan A 240 (39.2 overs) (Salim Elahi 41, Mohammad Wasim 59, Rana Qayyum 31).

Bailey scored his 153 not out in 113 balls, with 15 fours and five sixes.

FIRST-CLASS COUNTIES SELECT XI v PAKISTAN A

At Chelmsford, August 15, 16, 17, 18. First-Class Counties Select XI won by five wickets. Toss: Pakistan A.

Pakistan A's tour ended with another defeat, at the hands of a Select XI drawn from the five first-class counties not otherwise engaged. Brown of Warwickshire took a career-best eight for 89, which gave him 11 for 154 in the match. It seemed the tourists would succumb in three days when they lost their sixth second-innings wicket, still 75 behind. But Azhar Mahmood played some exciting strokes, hitting six sixes and five fours, to reach 92 and push the match into another day. The home side were made to fight for their win; they lost five batsmen before passing a target of 107 early on the final afternoon. Pakistan A struggled on the opening day, when Such took five wickets in an unchanged 22-over spell. The Counties' reply was consistent, rather than spectacular. They owed much of their first-innings lead of 212 to Giles, who scored 81 as the last three wickets put on 130.

Close of play: First day, First-Class Counties Select XI 114-2 (D. L. Hemp 51*, A. P. Grayson 34*); Second day, First-Class Counties Select XI 431-9 (A. F. Giles 75*, P. M. Such 3*); Third day, Pakistan A 311-9 (Irfan Fazil 4*, Ali Hussain Rizvi 1*).

Pakistan A

Mujahid Jamshed c Nixon b Welch	16	– c Giles b Brown 20
Salim Elahi c Nixon b Such	27	– c Nixon b Brown 8
*Mohammad Wasim c Grayson b Such	31	– c Maddy b Brown.......... 0
Hasan Raza c Grayson b Such	47	– c Nixon b Brown 57
Farhan Adil b Welch	17	– c Grayson b Such 43
Azhar Mahmood b Brown	37	– (7) c Nixon b Brown 92
†Javed Qadir c Giles b Such	24	– (6) c Maddy b Brown.......... 5
Abdur Razzaq b Brown	0	– c Grayson b Giles 55
Shoaib Malik st Nixon b Such	1	– b Brown 9
Irfan Fazil c Nixon b Brown	5	– not out 5
Ali Hussain Rizvi not out	1	– c Nixon b Brown 7
B 4, l-b 1, w 2, n-b 14	21	B 12, l-b 1, n-b 4 17

1/25 2/81 3/84 4/131 5/167   227   1/25 2/25 3/34 4/98 5/130   318
6/197 7/197 8/198 9/225   6/137 7/221 8/264 9/310

Bowling: *First Innings*—Ormond 8–1–34–0; Welch 14–3–36–2; Brown 16–3–65–3; Giles 6–3–13–0; Such 22–6–74–5. *Second Innings*—Welch 15–8–34–0; Brown 21.5–1–89–8; Ormond 12–0–67–0; Such 17–4–60–1; Giles 22–7–55–1.

First-Class Counties Select XI

J. J. B. Lewis b Abdur Razzaq	4	– lbw b Azhar Mahmood 4
D. L. Maddy c Javed Qadir b Abdur Razzaq	17	– c Javed Qadir b Abdur Razzaq ... 0
D. L. Hemp run out	53	– c Mohammad Wasim
		b Shoaib Malik . 41
*A. P. Grayson lbw b Shoaib Malik	77	– c Mohammad Wasim
		b Ali Hussain Rizvi . 31
D. J. Sales c Javed Qadir b Irfan Fazil	25	– c Hasan Raza b Shoaib Malik 3
†P. A. Nixon c Javed Qadir b Azhar Mahmood	42	– not out 10
D. R. Brown c Farhan Adil b Azhar Mahmood	43	– not out 13
G. Welch run out	62	
A. F. Giles c Javed Qadir b Azhar Mahmood	81	
J. Ormond b Shoaib Malik	4	
P. M. Such not out	5	
B 6, l-b 4, n-b 16	26	B 1, l-b 2, n-b 4 7

1/6 2/39 3/117 4/169 5/207   439   1/3 2/11 3/74   (5 wkts) 109
6/268 7/309 8/377 9/389   4/81 5/88

Bowling: *First Innings*—Abdur Razzaq 24–3–128–2; Irfan Fazil 16–6–43–1; Azhar Mahmood 30.5–11–64–3; Shoaib Malik 42–9–115–2; Ali Hussain Rizvi 34–7–79–0. *Second Innings*—Abdur Razzaq 6–1–34–1; Azhar Mahmood 8.3–2–24–1; Ali Hussain Rizvi 12–3–27–1; Shoaib Malik 10–3–21–2.

Umpires: H. D. Bird and D. R. Shepherd.

BRITANNIC ASSURANCE
COUNTY CHAMPIONSHIP, 1997

Steve James

One of county cricket's most regular set of under-achievers came good and won the 1997 County Championship. Glamorgan took the title for the third time when they steamrollered Somerset on the last Saturday of the season in front of a large crowd of Welsh supporters who had crossed the Severn Bridge to go down to Taunton.

In a damp summer, it was even more unexpected than usual that a team from one of the rainier counties should take the title. But Glamorgan dodged the showers when it mattered most and, above all, dodged the injuries. They fielded a settled team that changed little except to accommodate Robert Croft's departures to play for England. They had a balanced attack, fearsomely headed by Waqar Younis,

Continued overleaf

BRITANNIC ASSURANCE CHAMPIONSHIP

Win = 16 pts Draw = 3 pts	Played	Won	Lost	Drawn	Batting	Bowling	Points
					Bonus points		
1 – Glamorgan (10)...........	17	8	2	7	50	57	256
2 – Kent (4).................	17	8	4	5	44	60	252†
3 – Worcestershire (7)........	17	6	3	8	49	54	228†
4 { Middlesex (9)	17	7	4	6	33	56	219
{ Warwickshire (8)	17	7	2	8*	32	51	219
6 – Yorkshire (6).............	17	6	3	8	41	54	215
7 – Gloucestershire (13)	17	6	6	5	35	60	206
8 { Essex (5)	17	5	6	6	39	55	192
{ Surrey (3)	17	5	5	7	39	52	192
10 – Leicestershire (1)	17	4	1	12*	37	54	191
11 – Lancashire (15)..........	17	5	6	6	34	54	186
12 – Somerset (11)	17	3	3	11	38	64	183
13 – Nottinghamshire (17)	17	4	3	10	26	55	175
14 – Hampshire (14)..........	17	3	5	9*	42	41	158
15 – Northamptonshire (16)	17	3	5	9	33	48	156
16 – Derbyshire (2)...........	17	2	9	6	32	59	141
17 – Durham (18)	17	2	8	7*	22	56	131
18 – Sussex (12)	17	1	10	6	24	57	115

1996 positions are shown in brackets.

† *The totals for Kent and Worcestershire include 8 points for levelling the scores while batting second in drawn games.*

* *The following matches were abandoned: June 26, 27, 28, 30 – Leicestershire v Warwickshire at Leicester; July 2, 3, 4, 5 – Durham v Hampshire at Chester-le-Street.*

and a batting line-up – led by the season's top scorer, Steve James – which was rarely less than steady, and often devastating.

Glamorgan were bowled out for just 31 by Middlesex at Cardiff in mid-June, the lowest total by anyone in the Championship for 14 years. But that seemed to galvanise them. The next three times they fielded, they got rid of the opposition for 51, 54 and 67, won three matches in a row and marched to top place. They won only one game in the next two months, but no one else could seize the initiative either, and victory in the last two matches left them four points clear.

Kent were their closest challengers. After their wooden-spoon year in 1995, they confirmed their return as a team of serious players in serious cricket. Having lost to Glamorgan early on, they won four consecutive matches and remained leading contenders throughout. Their lower order often bailed them out after the batting had failed. But Kent could not quite bring the same determination to bear in close finishes, and two near-misses looked crucial in retrospect: they finished one run short of victory against Somerset, and went down to a one-wicket defeat against Northamptonshire at Maidstone. They did, however, win one of the summer's epics: by four runs, against Middlesex. With two games to go, Kent were ahead. But they failed to force a victory in the penultimate game at Headingley, and Glamorgan went into the final round of matches with a precious one-point lead.

Worcestershire surprised themselves by finishing third, suffering badly from the weather but less so from what looked an inadequate attack. This was as much a comment on the muddled season and, arguably, the general low standard as anything else. They were nine points clear of two of the pre-season favourites, Warwickshire and Middlesex. Warwickshire, swapping captains due to injuries almost weekly, found form too late to get in a serious blow. Middlesex changed captains seamlessly – from Mike Gatting to Mark Ramprakash – in mid-season. But they were inconsistent, and produced some shocking performances to go with their good ones.

Yorkshire finished sixth for the second year running, clear of Gloucestershire, who for the second year out of three surpassed expectations. After two innings wins at Cheltenham, they were top of the table, and were there again in the second half of August, but they faded badly after that, to the disappointment of their supporters but not their surprise.

Essex and Surrey came joint eighth, a situation that cannot be repeated in 1998, when the top eight are supposed to go into a new one-day knockout. They got there from different directions. Essex challenged for the leadership early on, but won only once after June. It was nearly July before Surrey's multi-talented team – with ten internationals at full-strength – won at all. Then they surged and won five out of seven. But they lost their impetus, and some of their perspective, in a bad-tempered draw against Glamorgan, and were beaten horribly in their last two games.

The 1996 champions Leicestershire never got going at all. Bad luck, bad weather, bad injuries – all the things they had avoided the previous year – dogged them at every turn, and they came tenth. Lancashire started appallingly, and were second-bottom on Midsummer's Day. Four wins out of five briefly put them near the contenders, before they settled back to 11th. Somerset had a colourless year and came 12th, ahead of Nottinghamshire, who had three early wins then did next to nothing.

Hampshire, with few resources, were 14th, ahead of Northamptonshire, who had heaps of talent but no direction. Derbyshire, almost champions in 1996, were the crisis team of the summer. Dean Jones, their captain, walked out and from then on they spent so much time bickering it was a wonder they got on to the field at all. Durham were the only team in the bottom five not to change captain: David Boon led them to two wins and 17th which, for them, was a mild relief. Sussex had their crisis in advance: they lost almost half the team and their committee was driven out. They were not surprised to be last.

Sixty-six of the 153 Championship matches were drawn, and two abandoned. This was the highest proportion of draws since the advent of the completely four-day competition in 1993 and can be explained by the bad weather, especially in June, and the three points for a draw introduced in 1996. Of the 85 games with a result, 28 were over inside three days, and two of these inside two – both defeats for Lancashire.

Pre-season betting (William Hill) 9-2 Surrey and Warwickshire; 5-1 Essex; 6-1 Middlesex; 8-1 Lancashire; 9-1 Leicestershire and Yorkshire; 11-1 Kent; 12-1 Derbyshire; 16-1 Worcestershire; 20-1 GLAMORGAN and Somerset; 25-1 Northamptonshire; 50-1 Gloucestershire and Nottinghamshire; 66-1 Hampshire; 150-1 Durham and Sussex.

Leaders: from May 10 Gloucestershire; June 2 Glamorgan; June 7 Gloucestershire; June 16 Kent; June 21 Middlesex; July 5 Glamorgan; July 26 Gloucestershire; August 4 Glamorgan; August 9 Kent; August 18 Gloucestershire; August 23 Glamorgan; August 30 Glamorgan and Kent; September 5 Kent; September 13 Glamorgan. Glamorgan became champions on September 20.

Bottom place: May 10 Warwickshire; May 17 Kent, Lancashire and Yorkshire; May 24 Lancashire; June 2 Derbyshire, Northamptonshire and Surrey; June 7 Northamptonshire; July 5 Derbyshire; August 4 Sussex; August 9 Derbyshire; August 23 Sussex.

Prize money

First (Glamorgan)	£70,000
Second (Kent)	£32,000
Third (Worcestershire)	£16,000
Joint Fourth { (Middlesex)	£10,500
{ (Warwickshire)	£10,500
Sixth (Yorkshire)	£9,000
Seventh (Gloucestershire)	£8,000
Joint Eighth { (Essex)	£6,500
{ (Surrey)	£6,500
Winner of each match	£1,000

Scoring of Points

(a) For a win, 16 points plus any points scored in the first innings.

(b) In a tie, each side scores eight points, plus any points scored in the first innings.

(c) In a drawn match, each side scores three points, plus any points scored in the first innings (see also paragraph (f)).

(d) If the scores are equal in a drawn match, the side batting in the fourth innings scores eight points, plus any points scored in the first innings, and the opposing side scores three points plus any points scored in the first innings.

(e) First-innings points (awarded only for performances in the first 120 overs of each first innings and retained whatever the result of the match).

(i) A maximum of four batting points to be available: 200 to 249 runs – 1 point; 250 to 299 runs – 2 points; 300 to 349 – 3 points; 350 runs or over – 4 points.

(ii) A maximum of four bowling points to be available: 3 or 4 wickets taken – 1 point; 5 or 6 wickets taken – 2 points; 7 or 8 wickets taken – 3 points; 9 or 10 wickets taken – 4 points.

(f) If play starts when less than eight hours' playing time remains and a one-innings match is played, no first-innings points shall be scored. The side winning on the one innings scores 12 points. In a tie, each side scores six points. In a drawn match, each side scores three points. If the scores are equal in a drawn match, the side batting in the second innings scores six points and the opposing side scores three points.

(g) If a match is abandoned without a ball being bowled, each side scores three points.

(h) A county which is adjudged to have prepared a pitch unsuitable for first-class cricket shall be liable to have 25 points deducted. In addition, a penalty of 10 or 15 points may in certain circumstances be imposed on a county in respect of a poor pitch.

(*i*) The side which has the highest aggregate of points shall be the Champion County. Should any sides in the Championship table be equal on points, the side with most wins will have priority.

Under ECB playing conditions, two extras were scored for every no-ball and wide bowled whether scored off or not. Any runs scored off the bat were credited to the batsman, while byes and leg-byes were counted as no-balls or wides, as appropriate, in accordance with Law 24.9, in addition to the initial penalty.

COUNTY CHAMPIONS

The Championship was not formally organised until 1890. Champions before that date were decided by the sporting press, which was not always unanimous. In 1963, *Wisden* formally accepted the list of champions "most generally selected" by contemporaries, as researched by the late Rowland Bowen (See *Wisden* 1959, pp 91-98). This appears to be the most accurate available list but has no official status. The county champions from 1864 to 1890 were, according to Bowen:

1864 Surrey; 1865 Nottinghamshire; 1866 Middlesex; 1867 Yorkshire; 1868 Nottinghamshire; 1869 Nottinghamshire and Yorkshire; 1870 Yorkshire; 1871 Nottinghamshire; 1872 Nottinghamshire; 1873 Gloucestershire and Nottinghamshire; 1874 Gloucestershire; 1875 Nottinghamshire; 1876 Gloucestershire; 1877 Gloucestershire; 1878 undecided; 1879 Lancashire and Nottinghamshire; 1880 Nottinghamshire; 1881 Lancashire; 1882 Lancashire and Nottinghamshire; 1883 Nottinghamshire; 1884 Nottinghamshire; 1885 Nottinghamshire; 1886 Nottinghamshire; 1887 Surrey; 1888 Surrey; 1889 Lancashire, Nottinghamshire and Surrey.

Official champions					
1890	Surrey	1927	Lancashire	1965	Worcestershire
1891	Surrey	1928	Lancashire	1966	Yorkshire
1892	Surrey	1929	Nottinghamshire	1967	Yorkshire
1893	Yorkshire	1930	Lancashire	1968	Yorkshire
1894	Surrey	1931	Yorkshire	1969	Glamorgan
1895	Surrey	1932	Yorkshire	1970	Kent
1896	Yorkshire	1933	Yorkshire	1971	Surrey
1897	Lancashire	1934	Lancashire	1972	Warwickshire
1898	Yorkshire	1935	Yorkshire	1973	Hampshire
1899	Surrey	1936	Derbyshire	1974	Worcestershire
1900	Yorkshire	1937	Yorkshire	1975	Leicestershire
1901	Yorkshire	1938	Yorkshire	1976	Middlesex
1902	Yorkshire	1939	Yorkshire	1977 {	Middlesex
1903	Middlesex	1946	Yorkshire	{	Kent
1904	Lancashire	1947	Middlesex	1978	Kent
1905	Yorkshire	1948	Glamorgan	1979	Essex
1906	Kent	1949 {	Middlesex	1980	Middlesex
1907	Nottinghamshire	{	Yorkshire	1981	Nottinghamshire
1908	Yorkshire	1950 {	Lancashire	1982	Middlesex
1909	Kent	{	Surrey	1983	Essex
1910	Kent	1951	Warwickshire	1984	Essex
1911	Warwickshire	1952	Surrey	1985	Middlesex
1912	Yorkshire	1953	Surrey	1986	Essex
1913	Kent	1954	Surrey	1987	Nottinghamshire
1914	Surrey	1955	Surrey	1988	Worcestershire
1919	Yorkshire	1956	Surrey	1989	Worcestershire
1920	Middlesex	1957	Surrey	1990	Middlesex
1921	Middlesex	1958	Surrey	1991	Essex
1922	Yorkshire	1959	Yorkshire	1992	Essex
1923	Yorkshire	1960	Yorkshire	1993	Middlesex
1924	Yorkshire	1961	Hampshire	1994	Warwickshire
1925	Yorkshire	1962	Yorkshire	1995	Warwickshire
1926	Lancashire	1963	Yorkshire	1996	Leicestershire
		1964	Worcestershire	1997	Glamorgan

Notes: Since the championship was constituted in 1890 it has been won outright as follows: Yorkshire 29 times, Surrey 15, Middlesex 10, Lancashire 7, Essex and Kent 6, Warwickshire and Worcestershire 5, Nottinghamshire 4, Glamorgan 3, Hampshire and Leicestershire 2, Derbyshire 1.

The title has been shared three times since 1890, involving Middlesex twice, Kent, Lancashire, Surrey and Yorkshire.

Wooden Spoons: Since the major expansion of the Championship from nine teams to 14 in 1895, the counties have finished outright bottom as follows: Derbyshire, Northamptonshire and Somerset 11; Glamorgan 9; Nottinghamshire 8; Leicestershire and Sussex 7; Gloucestershire and Worcestershire 6; Hampshire 5; Durham and Warwickshire 3; Kent 2; Essex and Yorkshire 1. Lancashire, Middlesex and Surrey have never finished bottom. Leicestershire have also shared bottom place twice, once with Hampshire and once with Somerset.

From 1977 to 1983 the Championship was sponsored by Schweppes and since 1984 by Britannic Assurance.

BRITANNIC ASSURANCE CHAMPIONSHIP STATISTICS FOR 1997

County	For			Against		
	Runs	Wickets	Avge	Runs	Wickets	Avge
Derbyshire	7,393	233	31.72	7,560	213	35.49
Durham	6,622	265	24.98	7,115	224	31.76
Essex	8,578	265	32.36	7,519	238	31.59
Glamorgan	7,672	189	40.59	6,870	259	26.52
Gloucestershire	7,424	254	29.22	7,254	251	28.90
Hampshire	7,846	217	36.15	8,810	198	44.49
Kent	8,544	257	33.24	8,439	291	29.00
Lancashire	7,696	222	34.66	7,654	227	33.71
Leicestershire	7,407	193	38.37	7,474	213	35.08
Middlesex	6,887	228	30.20	6,867	255	26.92
Northamptonshire ...	8,211	248	33.10	8,153	210	38.82
Nottinghamshire	7,439	246	30.23	7,858	228	34.46
Somerset	7,350	233	31.54	7,752	253	30.64
Surrey	7,825	240	32.60	7,056	219	32.21
Sussex	6,801	285	23.86	7,530	204	36.91
Warwickshire	6,920	217	31.88	7,078	254	27.86
Worcestershire	8,380	199	42.11	8,032	244	32.91
Yorkshire	7,605	232	32.78	7,579	242	31.31
	136,600	4,223	32.34	136,600	4,223	32.34

MATCH RESULTS, 1864-1997

County	Years of Play	Played	Won	Lost	Tied	Drawn
Derbyshire.........	1871-87; 1895-1997	2,241	556	818	1	866
Durham	1992-1997	106	14	63	0	29
Essex	1895-1997	2,203	639	638	5	921
Glamorgan	1921-1997	1,738	384	591	0	763
Gloucestershire	1870-1997	2,477	732	918	2	825
Hampshire.........	1864-85; 1895-1997	2,312	600	797	4	911
Kent..............	1864-1997	2,601	942	784	5	870
Lancashire	1865-1997	2,679	990	562	3	1,124
Leicestershire	1895-1997	2,170	486	798	1	885
Middlesex	1864-1997	2,381	894	598	5	884
Northamptonshire ...	1905-1997	1,938	476	676	3	783
Nottinghamshire	1864-1997	2,510	761	665	1	1,083
Somerset	1882-85; 1891-1997	2,211	522	888	3	798
Surrey	1864-1997	2,758	1,086	615	4	1,053
Sussex	1864-1997	2,650	735	918	6	991
Warwickshire	1895-1997	2,183	595	634	1	953
Worcestershire	1899-1997	2,125	533	735	2	855
Yorkshire	1864-1997	2,778	1,232	479	2	1,065
Cambridgeshire.....	1864-69; 1871	19	8	8	0	3
		20,040	12,185	12,185	24	7,831

Notes: Matches abandoned without a ball bowled are wholly excluded.

Counties participated in the years shown, except that there were no matches in the years 1915-18 and 1940-45; Hampshire did not play inter-county matches in 1868-69, 1871-74 and 1879; Worcestershire did not take part in the Championship in 1919.

OVERS BOWLED AND RUNS SCORED IN THE BRITANNIC ASSURANCE CHAMPIONSHIP, 1997

County	Over-rate per hour	Run-rate/ 100 balls
*Derbyshire (16)	15.76	57.48
*Durham (17)	15.68	48.07
Essex (8=)	16.06	58.57
*Glamorgan (1)	15.73	63.62
Gloucestershire (7)	16.11	54.98
Hampshire (14)	16.18	53.75
*Kent (2)	15.93	56.94
*Lancashire (11)	15.91	60.17
Leicestershire (10)	16.06	54.12
*Middlesex (4=)	15.70	53.70
Northamptonshire (15)	16.12	51.04
Nottinghamshire (13)	16.02	48.24
†Somerset (12)	15.02	57.17
*Surrey (8=)	15.54	59.31
Sussex (18)	16.30	46.65
*Warwickshire (4=)	15.60	57.63
Worcestershire (3)	16.09	53.33
*Yorkshire (6)	15.76	61.73
1997 average rate	15.87	55.36

1997 Championship positions are shown in brackets.
* £4,000 fine.   † £6,000 fine.

SUMMARY OF RESULTS, 1997

	Derbyshire	Durham	Essex	Glamorgan	Gloucestershire	Hampshire	Kent	Lancashire	Leicestershire	Middlesex	Northamptonshire	Nottinghamshire	Somerset	Surrey	Sussex	Warwickshire	Worcestershire	Yorkshire
Derbyshire	—	L	L	D	L	L	D	W	L	L	L	L	D	D	D	D	L	W
Durham	W	—	L	L	L	A	W	D	L	D	D	D	L	L	D	L	D	L
Essex	W	W	—	L	D	D	L	W	D	D	L	D	L	W	W	L	D	L
Glamorgan	D	W	W	—	W	D	W	W	D	L	W	D	W	D	W	D	L	D
Gloucestershire	W	W	D	L	—	W	L	D	D	L	D	L	D	W	W	L	L	W
Hampshire	W	A	D	D	L	—	D	D	L	D	D	W	L	W	D	L	D	L
Kent	D	L	W	L	W	D	—	W	L	W	L	W	D	W	W	W	D	D
Lancashire	L	D	L	L	D	D	L	—	D	W	D	L	L	W	W	W	W	D
Leicestershire	W	W	D	D	D	W	W	D	—	D	D	D	D	L	A	D	D	D
Middlesex	W	D	D	W	W	W	L	L	D	—	W	W	D	L	D	L	W	D
Northamptonshire	W	D	W	L	D	D	W	D	D	L	—	D	L	D	D	D	L	L
Nottinghamshire	W	D	D	D	W	D	L	W	D	L	W	—	D	L	D	D	D	D
Somerset	D	W	W	L	D	L	D	W	D	D	D	D	—	D	D	D	D	L
Surrey	D	W	L	D	L	W	L	L	D	W	D	D	W	—	W	L	D	D
Sussex	D	D	L	L	L	L	L	L	W	D	D	D	D	L	—	L	L	L
Warwickshire	D	W	W	D	W	W	L	L	A	W	D	D	D	W	W	—	D	W
Worcestershire	W	D	D	W	W	W	D	L	D	L	W	D	W	D	W	D	—	L
Yorkshire	L	W	W	D	L	D	D	D	D	D	W	D	W	D	W	L	W	—

Home games in bold, away games in italics. W = Won, L = Lost, D = Drawn, A = Abandoned.

COUNTY CHAMPIONSHIP – FINAL POSITIONS, 1890-1997

	Derbyshire	Essex	Glamorgan	Gloucestershire	Hampshire	Kent	Lancashire	Leicestershire	Middlesex	Northamptonshire	Nottinghamshire	Somerset	Surrey	Sussex	Warwickshire	Worcestershire	Yorkshire
1890	—	—	—	6	—	3	2	—	7	—	5	—	1	8	—	—	3
1891	—	—	—	9	—	5	2	—	3	—	4	5	1	7	—	—	8
1892	—	—	—	7	—	7	4	—	5	—	2	3	1	9	—	—	6
1893	—	—	—	9	—	4	2	—	3	—	6	8	5	7	—	—	1
1894	—	—	—	9	—	4	4	—	3	—	7	6	1	8	—	—	2
1895	5	9	—	4	10	14	2	12	6	—	12	8	1	11	6	—	3
1896	7	5	—	10	8	9	2	13	3	—	6	11	4	14	12	—	1
1897	14	3	—	5	9	12	1	13	8	—	10	11	2	6	7	—	4
1898	9	5	—	3	12	7	6	13	2	—	8	13	4	9	9	—	1
1899	15	6	—	9	10	8	4	13	2	—	10	13	1	5	7	12	3
1900	13	10	—	7	15	3	2	14	7	—	5	11	7	3	6	12	1
1901	15	10	—	14	7	7	3	12	2	—	9	12	6	4	5	11	1
1902	10	13	—	14	15	7	5	11	12	—	3	7	4	2	6	9	1
1903	12	8	—	13	14	8	4	14	1	—	5	10	11	2	7	6	3
1904	10	14	—	9	15	3	1	7	4	—	5	12	11	6	7	13	2
1905	14	12	—	8	16	6	2	5	11	13	10	15	4	3	7	8	1
1906	16	7	—	9	8	1	4	15	11	11	5	11	3	10	6	14	2
1907	16	7	—	10	12	8	6	11	5	15	1	14	4	13	9	2	2
1908	14	11	—	10	9	2	7	13	4	15	8	16	3	5	12	6	1
1909	15	14	—	16	8	1	2	13	6	7	10	11	5	4	12	8	3
1910	15	11	—	12	6	1	4	10	3	9	5	16	2	7	14	13	8
1911	14	6	—	12	11	2	4	15	3	10	8	16	5	13	1	9	7
1912	12	15	—	11	6	3	4	13	5	2	8	14	7	10	9	16	1
1913	13	15	—	9	10	1	8	14	6	4	5	16	3	7	11	12	2
1914	12	8	—	16	5	3	11	13	2	9	10	15	1	6	7	14	4
1919	9	14	—	8	7	2	5	9	13	12	3	5	4	11	15	—	1
1920	16	9	—	8	11	5	2	13	1	14	7	10	3	6	12	15	4
1921	12	15	17	7	6	4	5	11	1	13	8	10	2	9	16	14	3
1922	11	8	16	13	6	4	5	14	7	15	2	10	3	9	12	17	1
1923	10	13	16	11	7	5	3	14	8	17	2	9	4	6	12	15	1
1924	17	15	13	6	12	5	4	11	2	16	6	8	3	10	9	14	1
1925	14	7	17	10	9	5	3	12	6	11	4	15	2	13	8	16	1
1926	11	9	8	15	7	3	1	13	6	16	4	14	5	10	12	17	2
1927	5	8	15	12	13	4	1	7	9	16	2	14	6	10	11	17	3
1928	10	16	15	5	12	2	1	9	8	13	3	14	6	7	11	17	4
1929	7	12	17	4	11	8	2	9	6	13	1	15	10	4	14	16	2
1930	9	6	11	2	13	5	1	12	16	17	4	13	8	7	15	10	3
1931	7	10	15	2	12	3	6	16	11	17	5	13	8	4	9	14	1
1932	10	14	15	13	8	3	6	12	10	16	4	7	5	2	9	17	1
1933	6	4	16	10	14	3	5	17	12	13	8	11	9	2	7	15	1
1934	3	8	13	7	14	5	1	12	10	17	9	15	11	2	4	16	5
1935	2	9	13	15	16	10	4	6	3	17	5	14	11	7	8	12	1
1936	1	9	16	4	10	8	11	15	2	17	5	7	6	14	13	12	3
1937	3	6	7	4	14	12	9	16	2	17	10	13	8	5	11	15	1
1938	5	6	16	10	14	9	4	15	2	17	12	7	3	8	13	11	1
1939	9	4	13	3	15	5	6	17	2	16	12	14	8	10	11	7	1
1946	15	8	6	5	10	6	3	11	2	16	13	4	11	17	14	8	1
1947	5	11	9	2	16	4	3	14	1	17	11	11	6	9	15	7	7
1948	6	13	1	8	9	15	5	11	3	17	14	12	2	16	7	10	4
1949	15	9	8	7	16	13	11	17	1	6	11	9	5	13	4	3	1

	Derbyshire	Durham	Essex	Glamorgan	Gloucestershire	Hampshire	Kent	Lancashire	Leicestershire	Middlesex	Northamptonshire	Nottinghamshire	Somerset	Surrey	Sussex	Warwickshire	Worcestershire	Yorkshire
1950	5	—	17	11	7	12	9	1	16	14	10	15	7	1	13	4	6	3
1951	11	—	8	5	12	9	16	3	15	7	13	17	14	6	10	1	4	2
1952	4	—	10	7	9	12	15	3	6	5	8	16	17	1	13	10	14	2
1953	6	—	12	10	6	14	16	3	3	5	11	8	17	1	2	9	15	12
1954	3	—	15	4	13	14	11	10	16	7	7	5	17	1	9	6	11	2
1955	8	—	14	16	12	3	13	9	6	5	7	11	17	1	4	9	15	2
1956	12	—	11	13	3	6	16	2	17	5	4	8	15	1	9	14	9	7
1957	4	—	5	9	12	13	14	6	17	7	2	15	8	1	9	11	16	3
1958	5	—	6	15	14	2	8	7	12	10	4	17	3	1	13	16	9	11
1959	7	—	9	6	2	8	13	5	16	10	11	17	12	3	15	4	14	1
1960	5	—	6	11	8	12	10	2	17	3	9	16	14	7	4	15	13	1
1961	7	—	6	14	5	1	11	13	9	3	16	17	10	15	8	12	4	2
1962	7	—	9	14	4	10	11	16	17	13	8	15	6	5	12	3	2	1
1963	17	—	12	2	8	10	13	15	16	6	7	9	3	11	4	4	14	1
1964	12	—	10	11	17	12	7	14	16	6	3	15	8	4	9	2	1	5
1965	9	—	15	3	10	12	5	13	14	6	2	17	7	8	16	11	1	4
1966	9	—	16	14	15	11	4	12	8	12	5	17	3	7	10	6	2	1
1967	6	—	15	14	17	12	2	11	2	7	9	15	8	4	13	10	5	1
1968	8	—	14	3	16	5	2	6	9	10	13	4	12	15	17	11	7	1
1969	16	—	6	1	2	5	10	15	14	11	9	8	17	3	7	4	12	13
1970	7	—	12	2	17	10	1	3	15	16	14	11	13	5	9	7	6	4
1971	17	—	10	16	8	9	4	3	5	6	14	12	7	1	11	2	15	13
1972	17	—	5	13	3	9	2	15	6	8	4	14	11	12	16	1	7	10
1973	16	—	8	11	5	1	4	12	9	13	3	17	10	2	15	7	6	14
1974	17	—	12	16	14	2	10	8	4	6	3	15	5	7	13	9	1	11
1975	15	—	7	9	16	3	5	4	1	11	8	13	12	6	17	14	10	2
1976	15	—	6	17	3	12	14	16	4	1	2	13	7	9	10	5	11	8
1977	7	—	6	14	3	11	1	16	5	1	9	17	4	14	8	10	13	12
1978	14	—	2	13	10	8	1	12	6	3	17	7	5	16	9	11	15	4
1979	16	—	1	17	10	12	5	13	6	14	11	9	8	3	4	15	2	7
1980	9	—	8	13	7	17	16	15	10	1	12	3	5	2	4	14	11	6
1981	12	—	5	14	13	7	9	16	8	4	15	1	3	6	2	17	11	10
1982	11	—	7	16	15	3	13	12	2	1	9	4	6	5	8	17	14	10
1983	9	—	1	15	12	3	7	12	4	2	6	14	10	8	11	5	16	17
1984	12	—	1	13	17	15	5	16	4	3	11	2	7	8	6	9	10	14
1985	13	—	4	12	3	2	9	14	16	1	10	8	17	6	7	15	5	11
1986	11	—	1	17	2	6	8	15	7	12	9	4	16	3	14	12	5	10
1987	6	—	12	13	10	5	14	2	3	16	7	1	11	4	17	15	9	8
1988	14	—	3	17	10	15	2	9	8	7	12	5	11	4	16	6	1	13
1989	6	—	2	17	9	6	15	4	13	3	5	11	14	12	10	8	1	16
1990	12	—	2	8	13	3	16	6	7	1	11	13	15	9	17	5	4	10
1991	3	—	1	12	13	9	6	8	16	15	10	4	17	5	11	2	6	14
1992	5	18	1	14	10	15	2	12	8	11	3	4	9	13	7	6	17	16
1993	15	18	11	3	17	13	8	13	9	1	4	7	5	6	10	16	2	12
1994	17	16	6	18	12	13	9	10	2	4	5	3	11	7	8	1	15	13
1995	14	17	5	16	6	13	18	4	7	2	3	11	9	12	15	1	10	8
1996	2	18	5	10	13	14	4	15	1	9	16	17	11	3	12	8	7	6
1997	16	17	8	1	7	14	2	11	10	4	13	13	12	8	18	4	3	6

Note: From 1969 onwards, positions have been given in accordance with the Championship regulations which state that "Should *any* sides in the table be equal on points the side with most wins will have priority".

ECB COUNTY PITCHES TABLE OF MERIT

First-Class Matches

		Points	Matches	Average in 1997	Average in 1996
1	Somerset (1)	114	11	5.18	5.00
2	Surrey (1)	99	10	4.95	5.00
3	Northamptonshire (10)	87	9	4.83	4.56
4	Essex (14)	106	11	4.81	4.41
5	Kent (11)	104	11	4.72	4.45
6	Leicestershire (7)	84	9	4.66	4.65
7	Sussex (4)	83	9	4.61	4.82
8	Durham (15)	73	8	4.56	4.35
9	Derbyshire (3)	91	10	4.55	4.91
10	Lancashire (18)	90	10	4.50	4.00
	Nottinghamshire (11)	99	11	4.50	4.45
12	Gloucestershire (5)	88	10	4.40	4.80
13	Hampshire (7)	79	9	4.38	4.65
	Worcestershire (16)	78	9	4.38	4.33
15	Yorkshire (11)	95	11	4.31	4.45
16	Middlesex (9)	103	12	4.29	4.64
17	Warwickshire (17)	84	10	4.20	4.20
18	Glamorgan (5)	80	10	4.00	4.80
	Oxford University	71	8	4.43	4.50
	Cambridge University	53	6	4.41	4.14

One-Day Matches

		Points	Matches	Average in 1997	Average in 1996
1	Leicestershire (9)	113	11	5.13	4.75
2	Somerset (1)	112	11	5.09	5.19
3	Derbyshire (3)	97	10	4.85	5.08
4	Surrey (4)	145	15	4.83	4.94
	Sussex (2)	116	12	4.83	5.14
6	Essex (6)	135	14	4.82	4.89
	Warwickshire (15)	135	14	4.82	4.19
8	Gloucestershire (10)	115	12	4.79	4.70
9	Worcestershire (5)	114	12	4.75	4.90
10	Hampshire (13)	113	12	4.70	4.41
11	Kent (8)	122	13	4.69	4.88
12	Nottinghamshire (12)	103	11	4.68	4.58
13	Lancashire (14)	102	11	4.63	4.33
14	Northamptonshire (11)	110	12	4.58	4.62
15	Yorkshire (16)	106	12	4.41	3.93
16	Durham (17)	88	10	4.40	3.88
17	Middlesex (7)	141	17	4.14	4.88
18	Glamorgan (18)	105	13	4.03	3.64
	Oxford University	10	1	5.00	6.00
	Cambridge University	21	2	5.25	4.50

In both tables 1996 positions are shown in brackets. Each umpire in a game marks the pitch on the following scale of merit: 6 – very good; 5 – good; 4 – above average; 3 – below average; 2 – poor; 1 – unfit.

The tables, provided by the ECB, cover all major matches, including Tests etc., played on grounds under the county's jurisdiction. Middlesex pitches at Lord's are the responsibility of MCC.

The ECB points out that the tables of merit are not a direct assessment of the groundsmen's ability. Marks may be affected by many factors including weather, soil conditions and the resources available.

DERBYSHIRE

Adrian Rollins

President: J. W. Moss

Chairman: V. L. Brownett

Chairman, Cricket Committee: V. L. Brownett

Secretary/General Manager: J. Smedley

Captain: 1997 – D. M. Jones/P. A. J. DeFreitas

1998 – D. G. Cork

Director of Cricket: A. N. Hayhurst

Head Groundsman: B. Marsh

Scorer: S. W. Tacey

As Derbyshire rounded off their season on a lovely September afternoon with a decisive victory over Yorkshire, it was almost possible to believe that all was well. The list of the disappeared at the County Ground told a different story. During an extraordinary four months, starting with defeat by Hampshire at Chesterfield, Derbyshire contrived to lose their captain, coach, cricket chairman, chairman, secretary and commercial manager. After the season, two of their most gifted players went too. It was a horrible summer for the long-suffering membership – one which had begun with such optimism after Derbyshire were Championship runners-up in 1996.

Even in May, Derbyshire were wasting the opportunities they had seized so regularly the previous year, as when they finished one Warwickshire wicket away from the Benson and Hedges Cup quarter-finals. Mutterings from the dressing-room were increasingly audible, but the scale of the crisis in early June came as a complete surprise. After Hampshire won on his declaration, Dean Jones resigned as captain and overseas player, promptly returning to Australia. He issued a statement, through the club, in which he criticised the attitude of senior players.

Chairman Mike Horton and cricket chairman Ian Buxton warned the players not to comment to the media but, during the next match, against Warwickshire at Edgbaston, Kim Barnett went on Radio Derby to say that their case should be heard and that there were questions to be answered. A statement issued in the same way as Jones's, through the club, would have saved much turmoil. At this stage, Les Stillman, the Australian coach who joined Derbyshire with Jones, ceased to have a role with the first team. Before long, he was removed from contact with all players.

With Jones's departure not satisfactorily explained, Derbyshire now embroiled themselves in the Barnett affair. Barnett was fined £500 for "a blatant and deliberate disregard of club policy" and there was a further suspended fine of £1,000. He immediately missed a session of the Sussex game at Derby to frame a reply, gave notice of appeal and said that nine of the other ten involved in the match had offered to contribute financially. This isolated Chris Adams, already desperate to leave and a strong supporter of the Australian pair. The suspended fine came into play but, if some members of the committee were keen to take Barnett on, they were doing so on the wrong battlefield. ECB regulations give players the right to comment, with certain provisos. Horton returned from a two-month combined holiday and business trip to the United States to find that Barnett had been vindicated, and he resigned soon afterwards, citing lack of committee support.

Phillip DeFreitas replaced Jones as captain but, towards the end of the season, was told he would not be considered for 1998 because results were not good enough. Andy Hayhurst, acting-coach during the same period, became director of cricket, with Dominic Cork appointed captain and Karl Krikken vice-captain. John Smedley was promoted to secretary at the age of 26, the county's youngest since Will Taylor began a 51-year reign, when he was 23, in 1908. Even setting aside Derbyshire's propensity for factionalism, Smedley is unlikely to match that record.

Adams was, finally, granted his release with a year remaining on his contract, and became captain of Sussex. He had worked hard to distance himself from the club, but, though officials tried to force him to stick to the letter of his contract, they never gave him reasons why he should want to stay. Adams joins an illustrious list of departed batsmen which also includes John Morris and Peter Bowler.

In the circumstances, it is hardly surprising that so much of Derbyshire's cricket was poor, although there were handsome Championship wins over Lancashire, in two days, and Yorkshire. Jones, so influential in 1996, enjoyed one last triumph with victory over an Australian team, Derbyshire's first since they beat the Imperial Forces in 1919.

Jones's resignation deprived Derbyshire of their overseas player and they were also without Cork for three months. His injury against Kent in April necessitated a hernia operation and ruled him out of contention for the Ashes series. Devon Malcolm, who regained an England place in his benefit year, and DeFreitas carried the bowling, while Andrew Harris plugged away without equalling the form that had earned him an England A tour.

One remarkable feature was Barnett's ability to concentrate on his batting while conducting a political campaign. He passed 1,000 for the 14th time and shared two county-record partnerships, an unbroken 316 for the third wicket with Adrian Rollins against Leicestershire, and 417 for the second wicket, the highest stand in Derbyshire's history, with Tim Tweats against Yorkshire. Tweats, who made his debut in 1992, thrived on greater responsibility late in the season and his maiden century showed much promise, as did two centuries from Michael May, an effective rather than an elegant opener. Australian-born Matthew Cassar, in his first year after qualifying residentially, was unfortunate to damage ankle ligaments in April while practising with his wife Jane, the England women's team wicket-keeper. Not until late August was he fit enough to confirm his potential. The most consistent batsman was Rollins, who reached 50 nine times. Simon Lacey also offered encouragement for the future.

More bad news emerged in December, when Malcolm also jumped ship and signed for Northamptonshire. And what seemed like the best news for 1998 – the signing of Saeed Anwar as overseas player – acquired a tinge of doubt as the club began to realise the extent to which his commitments for Pakistan would eat into their season. If a regeneration process has begun at all at the County Ground, it has a long distance to travel. – GERALD MORTIMER.

432

DERBYSHIRE 1997

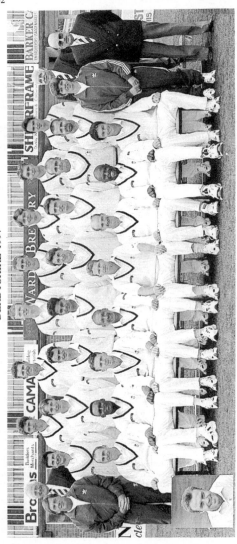

[Bill Smith]

Back row: J. D. Brown *(youth coach).* A. N. Hayhurst, V. P. Clarke, K. J. Dean, T. A. Tweats, T. Smith, B. L. Spendlove, S. P. Griffiths, S. W. Tacey *(scorer). Middle row:* W. L. Stillman *(coach),* M. E. Cassar, I. D. Blackwell, J. E. Owen, G. A. Khan, P. Aldred, G. M. Roberts, S. J. Lacey, M. R. May, A. Brentnall *(physiotherapist),* S. Edwards *(secretary/general manager). Front row:* K. M. Krikken, D. E. Malcolm, D. G. Cork, P. A. J. DeFreitas, D. M. Jones *(captain),* K. J. Barnett, A. S. Rollins, M. J. Vandrau. *Inset:* C. J. Adams.

DERBYSHIRE RESULTS

All first-class matches – Played 20: Won 5, Lost 9, Drawn 6.

County Championship matches – Played 17: Won 2, Lost 9, Drawn 6.

Competition placings – Britannic Assurance County Championship, 16th;
NatWest Trophy, q-f; Benson and Hedges Cup, 3rd in Group A;
AXA Life League, 14th.

COUNTY CHAMPIONSHIP AVERAGES

BATTING

Cap		M	I	NO	R	HS	100s	50s	Avge	Ct/St
	T. A. Tweats........	7	13	2	590	189	1	1	53.63	7
1982	K. J. Barnett	15	24	3	1,055	210*	3	5	50.23	3
1995	A. S. Rollins........	14	24	3	854	210	3	2	40.66	10
1996	D. M. Jones§	5	9	1	312	99*	0	3	39.00	6
	V. P. Clarke	16	25	5	728	99	0	4	36.40	8
	M. E. Cassar	7	8	1	227	78	0	2	32.42	2
	M. R. May†	7	13	1	383	116	1	2	31.91	2
	S. J. Lacey	5	7	3	126	50	0	1	31.50	1
1992	C. J. Adams†	12	21	1	611	108	2	2	30.55	14
	M. J. Vandrau.......	4	7	1	168	54	0	1	28.00	1
	P. Aldred†	6	5	1	111	83	0	1	27.75	4
1993	D. G. Cork	6	9	1	192	55*	0	2	24.00	4
1992	K. M. Krikken	17	24	3	492	72	0	3	23.42	51/2
1994	P. A. J. DeFreitas	16	20	1	417	96	0	2	21.94	4
	J. E. Owen†	4	6	0	83	22	0	0	13.83	3
1996	A. J. Harris........	16	22	3	140	36	0	0	7.36	9
	K. J. Dean†........	7	9	3	41	16	0	0	6.83	1
1989	D. E. Malcolm	13	18	8	61	21*	0	0	6.10	0

Also batted: I. D. Blackwell† (3 matches) 2, 42, 2; A. N. Hayhurst (1 match) 6 (1 ct); G. A. Khan (2 matches) 62*, 4, 11; G. M. Roberts (1 match) 2, 13; B. L. Spendlove† (1 match) 15* (1 ct); S. D. Stubbings (1 match) 5, 22. T. Smith† (1 match) did not bat (1 ct).

* Signifies not out.   *† Born in Derbyshire.*   *§ Overseas player.*

BOWLING

	O	M	R	W	BB	5W/i	Avge
D. E. Malcolm	373.3	52	1,262	60	6-23	5	21.03
P. Aldred	123	38	291	10	3-28	0	29.10
P. A. J. DeFreitas	486.1	104	1,574	54	7-64	5	29.14
K. J. Dean	158.4	32	541	14	3-21	0	38.64
D. G. Cork	132	28	457	11	4-48	0	41.54
A. J. Harris...........	434.3	89	1,531	33	3-66	0	46.39

Also bowled: C. J. Adams 2.5–0–16–0; I. D. Blackwell 28–8–121–1; M. E. Cassar 52.1–6–224–8; V. P. Clarke 171.4–35–668–7; D. M. Jones 2–2–0–0; S. J. Lacey 94–19–291–7; M. R. May 4.1–0–50–0; G. M. Roberts 6–1–8–0; A. S. Rollins 1–0–9–0; T. Smith 18–6–51–1; M. J. Vandrau 44–6–182–4.

COUNTY RECORDS

Highest score for:	274	G. Davidson v Lancashire at Manchester	1896
Highest score against:	343*	P. A. Perrin (Essex) at Chesterfield	1904
Best bowling for:	10-40	W. Bestwick v Glamorgan at Cardiff............	1921
Best bowling against:	10-45	R. L. Johnson (Middlesex) at Derby	1994
Highest total for:	645	v Hampshire at Derby.......................	1898
Highest total against:	662	by Yorkshire at Chesterfield	1898
Lowest total for:	16	v Nottinghamshire at Nottingham	1879
Lowest total against:	23	by Hampshire at Burton upon Trent	1958

At Cambridge, April 15, 16, 17. DERBYSHIRE beat CAMBRIDGE UNIVERSITY by an innings and 12 runs.

At Canterbury, April 23, 24, 25, 26. DERBYSHIRE drew with KENT.

DERBYSHIRE v SURREY

At Derby, May 7, 8, 9, 10. Drawn. Derbyshire 7 pts, Surrey 6 pts. Toss: Surrey. Championship debut: M. E. Cassar.

Bad weather severely curtailed the match and persuaded England coach David Lloyd, who was watching, that he needed an overcoat. Play did not begin until the third day, when Surrey were held together first by Thorpe, then by Martin Bicknell. The pitch was receptive to bowlers and Malcolm maintained his early form with four wickets, reducing Surrey to 134 for seven. But, under Bicknell's supervision, the score was all but doubled. For Derbyshire, Khan scored his first Championship half-century before a storm ended play 50 minutes into the final day. It was severe enough to put paid to the Sunday League game next day.

Close of play: First day, No play; Second day, No play; Third day, Derbyshire 113-2 (G. A. Khan 35*, D. M. Jones 36*).

Surrey

D. J. Bicknell c Krikken b Malcolm	4	M. P. Bicknell c Adams b Dean		74
M. A. Butcher lbw b DeFreitas	0	A. J. Tudor c Adams b Dean		17
†A. J. Stewart lbw b Malcolm	12	J. E. Benjamin not out		1
G. P. Thorpe lbw b Clarke	83			
N. Shahid lbw b Harris	32	B 2, l-b 9, w 2, n-b 2		15
*A. J. Hollioake c Rollins b Dean	22			—
C. C. Lewis c Harris b Malcolm	6	1/4 2/12 3/16 4/80 5/117		267
I. D. K. Salisbury lbw b Malcolm	1	6/130 7/134 8/208 9/266		

Bonus points – Surrey 2, Derbyshire 4.

Bowling: Malcolm 21–1–95–4; DeFreitas 16–4–53–1; Harris 16–3–73–1; Dean 12.5–4–21–3; Clarke 10–4–14–1.

Derbyshire

A. S. Rollins c Lewis b M. P. Bicknell	0	V. P. Clarke not out		10
G. A. Khan not out	62	L-b 11, n-b 18		29
C. J. Adams lbw b M. P. Bicknell	14			—
*D. M. Jones c Thorpe b Benjamin	43	1/0 2/24 3/141	(3 wkts)	158

M. E. Cassar, †K. M. Krikken, P. A. J. DeFreitas, K. J. Dean, A. J. Harris and D. E. Malcolm did not bat.

Bonus point – Surrey 1.

Bowling: M. P. Bicknell 8–1–38–2; Lewis 6–0–25–0; Tudor 2–0–20–0; Hollioake 3–0–12–0; Benjamin 11.4–3–29–1; Salisbury 9–2–23–0.

Umpires: J. C. Balderstone and A. A. Jones.

At Lord's, May 14, 15, 16. DERBYSHIRE lost to MIDDLESEX by 131 runs.

At Nottingham, May 21, 22, 23, 24. DERBYSHIRE lost to NOTTINGHAMSHIRE by two wickets.

At Derby, May 31, June 1, 2. DERBYSHIRE beat AUSTRALIANS by one wicket (See Australian tour section).

DERBYSHIRE v HAMPSHIRE

At Chesterfield, June 4, 5, 6, 7. Hampshire won by seven wickets. Hampshire 23 pts, Derbyshire 6 pts. Toss: Hampshire.

Hampshire's first victory of the season was the catalyst which helped plunge Derbyshire into crisis. Dressing-room tensions boiled over and, within a week, their captain and overseas player Dean Jones had walked out. Derbyshire began the game well. On a lifeless pitch, Rollins batted with authority for 585 minutes and 443 balls for 210, his highest score, which included 29 fours – but, as with his previous double-century, at Bristol two years earlier, he finished on the losing side. Derbyshire's first innings saw two other career-best performances: Aldred made a maiden half-century and Renshaw persevered for five wickets. Smith hit 23 fours and two sixes with great power to help Hampshire avoid the follow-on. Then Barnett scored his 50th first-class century as Derbyshire looked for a declaration. Jones offered Hampshire 310 in 65 overs which rain cut to 59. In the conditions, it seemed absurdly generous. The openers put on 213 and Hayden scored his third century in four Championship innings. Hampshire cantered home, and Derbyshire began squabbling.

Close of play: First day, Derbyshire 361-7 (A. S. Rollins 151*, P. Aldred 0*); Second day, Hampshire 166-2 (K. D. James 25*, R. A. Smith 31*); Third day, Derbyshire 56-0 (K. J. Barnett 28*, A. S. Rollins 22*).

Derbyshire

K. J. Barnett c Aymes b Bovill	4	– run out	101
A. S. Rollins b Renshaw	210	– c Aymes b Renshaw	51
C. J. Adams c Hayden b Renshaw	79	– c Hayden b Renshaw	15
*D. M. Jones lbw b Renshaw	4	– st Aymes b Udal	5
M. E. Cassar c Aymes b James	4		
V. P. Clarke b Renshaw	33	– (5) not out	18
†K. M. Krikken b James	23		
P. A. J. DeFreitas c Aymes b Stephenson	40	– (6) not out	0
P. Aldred b Stephenson	83		
A. J. Harris b Renshaw	10		
K. J. Dean not out	0		
L-b 13, w 4, n-b 16	33	B 5, l-b 3, w 6, n-b 4	18

1/6 2/130 3/146 4/175 5/248   523   1/106 2/147   (4 wkts dec.) 208
6/297 7/360 8/509 9/515   3/166 4/200

Bonus points – Derbyshire 4, Hampshire 3 (Score at 120 overs: 421-7).

Bowling: *First Innings*—Bovill 22–3–76–1; Renshaw 32–6–110–5; Mascarenhas 20–1–96–0; Stephenson 28–4–99–2; Udal 35–14–71–0; James 18–5–58–2. *Second Innings*—Renshaw 17–1–80–2; Stephenson 6–0–34–0; Udal 15–1–63–1; Bovill 6–0–23–0.

Hampshire

J. S. Laney lbw b Harris	61	– b Harris	93
M. L. Hayden c Adams b Harris	46	– not out	136
K. D. James c and b Aldred	51	– (5) not out	1
R. A. Smith c Adams b Dean	154	– (3) c Jones b Dean	52
W. S. Kendall c Krikken b Aldred	25		
*J. P. Stephenson lbw b Aldred	31		
†A. N. Aymes c Adams b Clarke	20		
S. D. Udal not out	23	– (4) c Rollins b Dean	4
A. D. Mascarenhas not out	4		
L-b 3, n-b 4	7	L-b 8, w 2, n-b 14	24

1/110 2/111 3/220 4/258   (7 wkts dec.) 422   1/213 2/301 3/309   (3 wkts) 310
5/366 6/382 7/418

S. J. Renshaw and J. N. B. Bovill did not bat.

Bonus points – Hampshire 4, Derbyshire 2 (Score at 120 overs: 418-6).

Bowling: *First Innings*—DeFreitas 22–4–76–0; Harris 29–5–95–2; Dean 18–2–86–1; Clarke 26–5–100–1; Jones 2–2–0–0; Aldred 18–5–40–3; Cassar 6–0–22–0. *Second Innings*—DeFreitas 18–1–76–0; Harris 12–0–81–1; Dean 15.5–0–86–2; Clarke 6–0–43–0; Aldred 4–0–16–0.

Umpires: K. E. Palmer and G. Sharp.

At Birmingham, June 12, 13, 14, 16. DERBYSHIRE drew with WARWICKSHIRE.

DERBYSHIRE v SUSSEX

At Derby, June 18, 19, 20, 21. Drawn. Derbyshire 8 pts, Sussex 8 pts. Toss: Sussex.

Rain intervened to wipe out most of the last two days. Nothing could stop Derbyshire's descent into open warfare after Jones's departure. Adams did not field at slip because he said he was unable to concentrate, and Barnett did not field at all on the first evening. The club had already fined him for speaking to the media about the crisis. Now he was preparing a response, which incurred him a further £1,000 suspended fine. The cricket was mundane. Derbyshire constricted the Sussex batsmen, with Rao scoring just 16 in the 135 minutes before lunch. Taylor hit seven fours, and his colleagues just seven between them. However, Moores was enterprising enough to declare after gaining a batting point, and was rewarded with two quick wickets before the close. Next day Adams and Clarke led a recovery.

Close of play: First day, Derbyshire 3–2 (T. A. Tweats 1*); Second day, Derbyshire 209–8 (V. P. Clarke 48*, P. Aldred 0*); Third day, Derbyshire 233–9 (V. P. Clarke 65*, A. J. Harris 7*).

Sussex

N. J. Lenham lbw b Dean	7	A. A. Khan b Dean		6
R. K. Rao lbw b Harris	16	M. A. Robinson not out		0
N. R. Taylor c Tweats b Aldred	49	R. J. Kirtley not out		3
C. W. J. Athey c Adams b DeFreitas	6			
K. Newell c Krikken b Clarke	14	B 9, l-b 19, w 2, n-b 12		42
M. Newell c Clarke b DeFreitas	13			
*†P. Moores c DeFreitas b Harris	32	1/15 2/59 3/89 4/91 5/125 (9 wkts dec.)		200
V. C. Drakes c Harris b DeFreitas	12	6/135 7/162 8/187 9/191		

Bonus points – Sussex 1, Derbyshire 4.

Bowling: DeFreitas 28–5–63–3; Harris 25–9–40–2; Aldred 15.5–9–10–1; Dean 25–11–49–2; Clarke 10–6–10–1.

Derbyshire

A. S. Rollins c and b Drakes	0	*P. A. J. DeFreitas c M. Newell b Kirtley		9
T. A. Tweats b Drakes	9	P. Aldred c Moores b Kirtley		0
K. J. Dean lbw b Kirtley	0	A. J. Harris not out		7
K. J. Barnett b Drakes	24			
C. J. Adams c K. Newell b Robinson	53	B 4, l-b 13, w 2, n-b 16		35
J. E. Owen lbw b Kirtley	14			
V. P. Clarke not out	65	1/0 2/3 3/27 4/42 5/82 (9 wkts)		233
†K. M. Krikken lbw b Drakes	17	6/141 7/198 8/209 9/209		

Bonus points – Derbyshire 1, Sussex 4.

Bowling: Drakes 22–6–55–4; Kirtley 20.1–4–98–4; Robinson 11–3–41–1; K. Newell 6–1–22–0.

Umpires: A. Clarkson and T. E. Jesty.

At Southend, June 26, 27, 28. DERBYSHIRE lost to ESSEX by an innings and 145 runs.

At Derby, July 5, 6, 7. DERBYSHIRE beat PAKISTAN A by seven wickets (See Pakistan A tour section).

At Cheltenham, July 16, 17, 18. DERBYSHIRE lost to GLOUCESTERSHIRE by an innings and 35 runs.

DERBYSHIRE v GLAMORGAN

At Chesterfield, July 23, 24, 25, 26. Drawn. Derbyshire 10 pts, Glamorgan 9 pts. Toss: Glamorgan.

Glamorgan came into this match on a three-game winning streak, but hopes of making it four were quickly dampened by Rollins, who hit a century before lunch. May scored his first Championship hundred at the other end as the pair put on 247, Derbyshire's fourth-highest opening stand and the foundation for what became their largest total against Glamorgan. After rain had wiped out the better part of the second day, Derbyshire found the going harder with the ball. Dale averted the follow-on with a composed innings, and at one point DeFreitas, frustrated by the blandness of the pitch, was bowling to Butcher with all nine fielders on the off side. The rain returned on the fourth day, limiting play to just 13 balls and ruling out a contrived finish.

Close of play: First day, Derbyshire 379-4 (M. J. Vandrau 11*, A. J. Harris 6*); Second day, Glamorgan 39-1 (H. Morris 7*, S. D. Thomas 5*); Third day, Derbyshire 28-0 (A. S. Rollins 19*, M. R. May 6*).

Derbyshire

A. S. Rollins c James b Cosker	148 – not out	24
M. R. May c James b Watkin	116 – not out	8
C. J. Adams b Waqar Younis	46	
K. J. Barnett c Shaw b Waqar Younis	29	
M. J. Vandrau c Maynard b Watkin	30	
A. J. Harris c Shaw b Watkin	11	
V. P. Clarke not out	76	
†K. M. Krikken not out	30	
B 1, l-b 9, w 8, n-b 9	27	L-b 3 3

1/247 2/324 3/345 4/372 (6 wkts dec.) 513
5/391 6/429

(no wkt) 35

*P. A. J. DeFreitas, P. Aldred and D. E. Malcolm did not bat.

Bonus points – Derbyshire 4, Glamorgan 2 (Score at 120 overs: 442-6).

Bowling: *First Innings*—Waqar Younis 28-3-132-2; Watkin 33-5-131-3; Butcher 9-3-36-0; Thomas 15-2-84-0; Dale 8-2-33-0; Cosker 38-14-79-1; Maynard 2-0-8-0. *Second Innings*—Waqar Younis 5-0-17-0; Watkin 6-2-11-0; Cosker 3.1-1-4-0.

Glamorgan

S. P. James lbw b DeFreitas	25	†A. D. Shaw b Malcolm	38
H. Morris lbw b DeFreitas	11	Waqar Younis c Barnett b Harris	8
S. D. Thomas c Vandrau b Harris	31	S. L. Watkin not out	10
A. Dale not out	142	B 2, l-b 8, n-b 10	20
*M. P. Maynard c Rollins b Vandrau	43		
P. A. Cottey run out	14	1/31 2/54 3/88 4/151	(8 wkts dec.) 364
G. P. Butcher c Clarke b DeFreitas	22	5/175 6/222 7/312 8/343	

D. A. Cosker did not bat.

Bonus points – Glamorgan 4, Derbyshire 3.

Bowling: Malcolm 23-2-84-1; DeFreitas 24-3-86-3; Vandrau 21-5-68-1; Harris 17.5-4-61-2; Aldred 10-3-30-0; Clarke 5-0-25-0.

Umpires: J. D. Bond and V. A. Holder.

At Chester-le-Street, July 31, August 1, 2. DERBYSHIRE lost to DURHAM by six wickets.

DERBYSHIRE v LANCASHIRE

At Derby, August 15, 16. Derbyshire won by an innings and 37 runs. Derbyshire 24 pts, Lancashire 4 pts. Toss: Lancashire.

After nearly four months, Derbyshire needed only two days to complete their first Championship win of the summer. Barnett, whose £1,500 fine for discussing the departure of Dean Jones on local radio had been revoked the previous week, initiated a recovery from 123 for five, which was maintained by Krikken, and DeFreitas went on the attack with 96 from 80 balls. Then Lancashire batted dreadfully to be bowled out twice on the second day, the first time in just 27.3 overs. Malcolm set the tone with an opening spell of 8–2–15–5 and finished with match figures of ten for 65; he twice dismissed Atherton, who attracted vocal criticism from some Lancashire supporters. Crawley drew out the second innings with a glittering 133, including 26 fours, but eventually he became one of four victims for Cork, who was making his Championship comeback after a four-month lay-off. During the match, Derbyshire entered talks with Saeed Anwar, the Pakistan opener who eventually agreed to become their overseas player for 1998. After it, Mike Horton resigned as chairman.

Close of play: First day, Derbyshire 408-9 (A. J. Harris 12*, D. E. Malcolm 0*).

Derbyshire

A. S. Rollins c Atherton b Martin	0	*P. A. J. DeFreitas c Crawley b Shadford	96
M. R. May c Crawley b Martin	23	A. J. Harris lbw b Martin	12
D. G. Cork c Hegg b Green	13	D. E. Malcolm not out	3
K. J. Barnett c Hegg b Martin	86		
J. E. Owen b Austin	22	B 1, l-b 10, n-b 16	27
V. P. Clarke b Austin	15		
†K. M. Krikken run out	72	1/14 2/25 3/46 4/99 5/123	411
I. D. Blackwell c Crawley b Gallian	42	6/189 7/248 8/372 9/402	

Bonus points – Derbyshire 4, Lancashire 4.

Bowling: Martin 21–6–77–4; Austin 24–7–71–2; Shadford 15–0–108–1; Green 20–6–46–1; Gallian 7–0–29–1; Watkinson 18–1–69–0.

Lancashire

M. A. Atherton c Krikken b Malcolm	4	– lbw b Malcolm	5
J. E. R. Gallian lbw b DeFreitas	9	– c Krikken b Malcolm	15
J. P. Crawley lbw b Cork	18	– c May b Cork	133
G. D. Lloyd b Malcolm	0	– c and b Cork	17
A. Flintoff b Malcolm	0	– c Krikken b Cork	0
*M. Watkinson lbw b Malcolm	3	– c Krikken b Blackwell	31
I. D. Austin not out	47	– c Krikken b Harris	15
†W. K. Hegg b Malcolm	0	– lbw b Cork	10
R. J. Green b DeFreitas	13	– b Malcolm	1
P. J. Martin c Harris b DeFreitas	6	– not out	13
D. J. Shadford c Clarke b Malcolm	0	– c Krikken b Malcolm	12
B 4, l-b 2, n-b 12	18	L-b 4	4

1/19 2/19 3/20 4/24 5/42	118	1/20 2/21 3/74 4/74 5/145	256
6/44 7/44 8/105 9/117		6/170 7/210 8/215 9/241	

Bonus points – Derbyshire 4.

Bowling: *First Innings*—DeFreitas 9–2–28–3; Malcolm 9.3–2–23–6; Cork 5–0–35–1; Harris 4–0–26–0. *Second Innings*—DeFreitas 10–0–57–0; Malcolm 12.4–2–42–4; Cork 13–4–48–4; Harris 9–0–59–1; Clarke 2–0–19–0; Blackwell 7–2–27–1.

Umpires: M. J. Kitchen and J. F. Steele.

At Leicester, August 20, 21, 22, 23. DERBYSHIRE lost to LEICESTERSHIRE by 163 runs.

DERBYSHIRE v SOMERSET

At Derby, August 27, 28, 29, 30. Drawn. Derbyshire 8 pts, Somerset 9 pts. Toss: Somerset.

The fall-out from the resignation of Dean Jones continued to dog Derbyshire. Adams, one of Jones's few supporters at the club, was omitted by the authorities on the grounds that he had tonsillitis, but the player later said he had been fit and available. On the field, Rollins suffered a more genuine affliction: he involuntarily moved his left pad with his bat as he played forward to Shine and the ball struck his unprotected kneecap. The resulting fracture ended his season, although he did return in this innings to bat with a runner. Derbyshire's lower-order batting helped them out of a spot at 113 for five. DeFreitas hit fiercely, and both Cassar and Lacey improved on their highest scores; Lacey was pleased to discover he had reached a maiden 50 as the scoreboard was still showing 49 when he was dismissed. Somerset declared behind, but the last day was washed out.

Close of play: First day, Derbyshire 73-2 (A. J. Harris 5*, K. J. Barnett 0*); Second day, Somerset 24-0 (R. J. Turner 12*, P. C. L. Holloway 2*); Third day, Derbyshire 97-2 (D. G. Cork 55*, A. J. Harris 7*).

Derbyshire

A. S. Rollins not out	13		
M. R. May c Turner b Rose	25	– c Turner b Shine	1
T. A. Tweats lbw b Caddick	26	– c Mushtaq Ahmed b Rose	26
A. J. Harris b Caddick	13	– not out	7
K. J. Barnett b Rose	16		
D. G. Cork c Trescothick b Caddick	13	– (1) not out	55
M. E. Cassar c Turner b Herzberg	78		
†K. M. Krikken b Shine	14		
*P. A. J. DeFreitas c Turner b Rose	58		
S. J. Lacey c Turner b Caddick	50		
D. E. Malcolm b Shine	0		
L-b 7, w 4, n-b 6	17	B 1, l-b 3, w 4	8
	323	**(2 wkts) 97**	

1/67 2/71 3/96 4/108 5/113   1/8 2/81
6/153 7/256 8/293 9/295

Bonus points – Derbyshire 3, Somerset 4.

In the first innings A. S. Rollins, when 12, retired hurt at 20 and resumed at 295.

Bowling: *First Innings*—Caddick 36–11–96–4; Shine 22–5–80–2; Rose 22–5–79–3; Mushtaq Ahmed 11–4–23–0; Burns 8–3–36–0; Herzberg 1–0–2–1. *Second Innings*—Caddick 8–0–19–0; Shine 8–0–48–1; Rose 5–1–23–1; Mushtaq Ahmed 5–3–3–0.

Somerset

†R. J. Turner c Krikken b Cork	23	M. Burns b Lacey	50
P. C. L. Holloway c Krikken b Cork	8	G. D. Rose not out	28
*S. C. Ecclestone st Krikken b Lacey	24	B 2, l-b 12, n-b 10	24
M. N. Lathwell lbw b Harris	11		
M. E. Trescothick not out	83	1/36 2/41 3/60 4/85 5/187 (5 wkts dec.) 251	

S. Herzberg, A. R. Caddick, Mushtaq Ahmed and K. J. Shine did not bat.

Bonus points – Somerset 2, Derbyshire 2.

Bowling: Malcolm 10–1–31–0; DeFreitas 11–3–44–0; Harris 10–1–27–1; Cork 9–1–37–2; Lacey 14.4–2–76–2; Cassar 4–0–22–0.

Umpires: R. Julian and B. Leadbeater.

DERBYSHIRE v NORTHAMPTONSHIRE

At Derby, September 2, 3, 4, 5. Northamptonshire won by nine wickets. Northamptonshire 23 pts, Derbyshire 4 pts. Toss: Northamptonshire.

Club politics still dominated the agenda at Derby; the home players found it impossible to give their full concentration to the match, and they lost to Northamptonshire for the sixth year running. Inserted on a pitch dampened by weekend storms, they disintegrated rapidly to be all out before tea. Northamptonshire's workmanlike reply began with a stand of 89 – the county's highest opening partnership of the season to date – and ended with a lead of 142. Considering that the second day was lost to rain, Derbyshire should have saved the game, but their second innings was lamentable. Young spinners Brown and Davies, who claimed his first five-wicket haul, took eight wickets between them. Meanwhile, Derbyshire appointed Hayhurst, the acting-coach, as the new director of cricket, finally granted Adams's umpteenth request to leave, and told DeFreitas that he would not be considered as captain for 1998.

Close of play: First day, Northamptonshire 104-1 (A. Fordham 59*, R. J. Bailey 7*); Second day, No play; Third day, Derbyshire 59-1 (D. G. Cork 37*, T. A. Tweats 20*).

Derbyshire

D. G. Cork b Taylor	11	– st Ripley b Davies	53
M. R. May c Curran b Mohammad Akram	1	– lbw b Taylor	0
T. A. Tweats c Ripley b Curran	43	– lbw b Curran	43
K. J. Barnett b Penberthy	21	– c Curran b Davies	12
V. P. Clarke c Ripley b Taylor	45	– c Sales b Brown	42
M. E. Cassar c Fordham b Taylor	16	– b Brown	8
†K. M. Krikken c Sales b Mohammad Akram	13	– c Curran b Davies	1
*P. A. J. DeFreitas c Penberthy b Mohammad Akram	27	– c Fordham b Davies	4
S. J. Lacey not out	9	– c Ripley b Davies	16
A. J. Harris c Ripley b Davies	0	– lbw b Brown	3
D. E. Malcolm lbw b Davies	4	– not out	0
L-b 2	2	L-b 7	7

1/3 2/13 3/53 4/121 5/123   192   1/8 2/99 3/107 4/125 5/148   189
6/147 7/151 8/186 9/188   6/151 7/159 8/178 9/187

Bonus points – Northamptonshire 4.

Bowling: *First Innings*—Mohammad Akram 16–2–60–3; Taylor 17–4–50–3; Curran 13–5–34–1; Penberthy 11–2–31–1; Brown 3–1–11–0; Davies 0.5–0–4–2. *Second Innings*—Mohammad Akram 11–0–51–0; Taylor 13–5–31–1; Davies 22.2–8–46–5; Penberthy 4–1–5–0; Bailey 1–0–1–0; Curran 8–2–25–1; Brown 12–4–23–3.

Northamptonshire

A. Fordham c Tweats b Malcolm	72	– c Tweats b Malcolm	0
R. R. Montgomerie c Cork b DeFreitas	31	– not out	25
*R. J. Bailey c Krikken b Cork	25	– not out	20
K. M. Curran c Krikken b Malcolm	86		
D. J. Sales c Lacey b Harris	34		
A. L. Penberthy c Krikken b Cassar	14		
†D. Ripley c Clarke b Cassar	30		
J. P. Taylor c Tweats b Cassar	7		
Mohammad Akram c DeFreitas b Malcolm	4		
M. K. Davies c Krikken b Malcolm	4		
J. F. Brown not out	0		
B 4, l-b 5, w 4, n-b 14	27	L-b 4, w 2	6

1/89 2/124 3/156 4/213 5/249   334   1/2   (1 wkt) 51
6/310 7/318 8/326 9/334

Bonus points – Northamptonshire 3, Derbyshire 4 (Score at 120 overs: 334-9).

Bowling: *First Innings*—Malcolm 23.4–2–82–4; DeFreitas 23–6–39–1; Cork 11–1–38–1; Harris 25–4–75–1; Lacey 23–8–34–0; Clarke 4–0–26–0; Cassar 11–2–31–3. *Second Innings*—Malcolm 4–0–18–1; Harris 4–0–12–0; DeFreitas 3–0–7–0; Lacey 2.4–1–10–0.

Umpires: H. D. Bird and D. J. Constant.

At Worcester, September 10, 11, 12, 13. DERBYSHIRE lost to WORCESTERSHIRE by ten wickets.

DERBYSHIRE v YORKSHIRE

At Derby, September 18, 19, 20, 21. Derbyshire won by nine wickets. Derbyshire 24 pts, Yorkshire 3 pts. Toss: Yorkshire. First-class debut: T. Smith.

Derbyshire's sorry season ended on an upbeat note as they crushed Yorkshire, losing only four wickets in the process, thus climbing to third-bottom a year after they were almost champions. The chief architects of victory were Barnett and Tweats, who built a massive stand of 417, the highest in the county's history, while DeFreitas offered valuable assistance with ten wickets in his last match before losing the captaincy. After an undistinguished batting performance from Yorkshire on the first day, Barnett and Tweats came together on the second afternoon when

HIGHEST PARTNERSHIPS FOR DERBYSHIRE

417	**K. J. Barnett and T. A. Tweats v Yorkshire at Derby, second wicket**	**1997**
349	C. S. Elliott and J. D. Eggar v Nottinghamshire at Nottingham, second wicket ..	1947
328	P. Vaulkhard and D. Smith v Nottinghamshire at Nottingham, fourth wicket	1946
322	H. Storer, jun., and J. Bowden v Essex at Derby, first wicket	1929
321*	J. G. Wright and P. N. Kirsten v Lancashire at Manchester, first wicket	1980
316*	**A. S. Rollins and K. J. Barnett v Leicestershire at Leicester, third wicket** ..	**1997**
308	G. A. Davidson and W. Storer v Lancashire at Manchester, fourth wicket	1896
302*†	J. E. Morris and D. G. Cork v Gloucestershire at Cheltenham, fifth wicket	1993

* Denotes an unbroken partnership.

† 346 runs in all were added for this wicket by Morris, Cork and M. J. Vandrau, who came in after Cork retired hurt.

Krikken was out quickly. They stayed there for the next 105 overs, easily beating the 349-run county record, also for the second wicket, established by Charlie Elliott and John Eggar at Trent Bridge in 1947. Barnett's fourth double-century took him past 1,000 runs for the 14th time, and he also became the first Derbyshire player to remain on the field throughout a completed match. Tweats made his maiden first-class hundred. The best stand of Yorkshire's second innings, by contrast, was 62 between Silverwood and Fisher. Charlie Elliott, aged 85, attended on the final day to offer congratulations.

Close of play: First day, Derbyshire 0-0 (K. J. Barnett 0*, K. M. Krikken 0*); Second day, Derbyshire 30-1 (K. J. Barnett 16*, T. A. Tweats 2*); Third day, Derbyshire 473-3 (K. J. Barnett 210*, B. L. Spendlove 15*).

Yorkshire

A. McGrath run out	19	– (7) c Aldred b DeFreitas	21
M. P. Vaughan c Smith b DeFreitas	17	– c Cassar b Harris	4
*D. Byas c Barnett b Cassar	56	– (1) b DeFreitas	13
D. S. Lehmann b DeFreitas	2	– (3) c Spendlove b Cassar	45
A. C. Morris lbw b DeFreitas	0	– (4) c sub b DeFreitas	0
B. Parker c Krikken b Smith	6	– (5) c Cassar b DeFreitas	73
†R. J. Blakey c Tweats b Aldred	76	– (6) c Aldred b Harris	5
G. M. Hamilton b DeFreitas	17	– c Krikken b DeFreitas	13
C. E. W. Silverwood c Krikken b Harris	11	– c sub b DeFreitas	40
I. D. Fisher c DeFreitas b Cassar	25	– c Tweats b Harris	37
P. M. Hutchison not out	15	– not out	3
B 5, l-b 16, w 2	23	B 4, l-b 7, n-b 2	13
	267		**267**

1/31 2/37 3/43 4/43 5/58 6/176 7/187 8/207 9/221

1/6 2/42 3/42 4/78 5/91 6/139 7/186 8/187 9/249

Bonus points – Yorkshire 2, Derbyshire 4.

Bowling: *First Innings*—DeFreitas 27–9–74–4; Harris 23–7–56–1; Smith 11–4–27–1; Aldred 15–3–50–1; Cassar 6.1–0–31–2; Clarke 2–0–8–0. *Second Innings*—DeFreitas 22–5–98–6; Harris 16.4–3–66–3; Cassar 10–1–68–1; Smith 7–2–24–0; Clarke 1–1–0–0.

Derbyshire

K. J. Barnett not out	210	– not out	25
†K. M. Krikken c Blakey b Silverwood	6	– c Blakey b Silverwood	17
T. A. Tweats c Lehmann b Hutchison	189	– not out	21
V. P. Clarke c Blakey b Hutchison	8		
B. L. Spendlove not out	15		
B 10, l-b 25, w 2, n-b 8	45	L-b 1	1
	(3 wkts dec.) 473		**(1 wkt) 64**

1/13 2/430 3/452

1/19

T. Smith, M. E. Cassar, *P. A. J. DeFreitas, P. Aldred, S. J. Lacey and A. J. Harris did not bat.

Bonus points – Derbyshire 4, Yorkshire 1.

Bowling: *First Innings*—Silverwood 21–3–77–1; Hutchison 27–4–130–2; Fisher 20–4–39–0; Hamilton 14–3–67–0; Morris 15–3–56–0; Vaughan 14–3–48–0; Lehmann 6–0–21–0. *Second Innings*—Silverwood 5–0–28–1; Hutchison 4–0–23–0; Lehmann 1.2–0–12–0; Fisher 1–1–0–0.

Umpires: A. Clarkson and D. J. Constant.

BIGGEST FALLS IN THE COUNTY CHAMPIONSHIP

15 places	Gloucestershire	second to 17th	1970
	Glamorgan	third to 18th	1994
14 places	Glamorgan	second to 16th	1971
	Middlesex	first to 15th	1991
	Derbyshire	second to 16th	1997
13 places	Middlesex	first equal to 14th	1950
	Leicestershire	third equal to 16th	1954
	Kent	second to 15th	1989
	Worcestershire	second to 15th	1994
	Northamptonshire	third to 16th	1996

DURHAM

Melvyn Betts

Patrons: Sir Donald Bradman and A. W. Austin
President: D. W. Midgley
Chairman: J. D. Robson
Cricket Executive: G. Cook
Chief Executive: M. Candlish
Coach: N. Gifford
Captain: D. C. Boon
Head Groundsman: T. Flintoft
Scorer: B. Hunt

The general feeling was that Durham progressed under David Boon in 1997 rather more than results suggested. Finishing with only Sussex below them in the Championship and the Sunday League – a rise of one place in both cases – and making early exits from the other competitions simply confirmed the size of the task Boon inherited after their disastrous 1996. Before returning to Tasmania, he said: "The improvement is in the way we have competed in terms of commitment, demeanour and attitude. There wasn't a county we played against who didn't remark on the vast improvement in the team."

Boon proved a quiet and undemonstrative leader, who invested much time in instilling self-belief and fighting qualities in his players. But there was little room for flair and experimentation, and the Durham ethos of providing first-class opportunities for local youngsters appeared to have been put into cold storage. Darren Blenkiron, scorer of three centuries in 33 first-class innings, was frozen out altogether. With no opportunity to impress Boon, he lost patience: in mid-August, he was told that he did not appear to get on with the club and was released. Another young bat, Robin Weston, was the only other player let go, but there was the threat of an outcry at the end of the season when the members' favourite home-bred batsman, Jimmy Daley, had to be dissuaded from taking up an offer from another county. Durham's final match, at Leicester, was his only Championship appearance.

The need to fit four new signings, including Boon, into the top six inevitably created a difficult situation. Daley, Blenkiron, Weston, Mike Roseberry and Stewart Hutton all felt the squeeze. Of the newcomers, opener Jon Lewis struck gold from his debut – a double-hundred against Oxford – onwards, but Nick Speak struggled for form and Martin Speight was only a partial success as batsman/wicket-keeper, averaging 21.72 in the Championship. That was, however, good enough to earn him fifth place in the averages. Despite investing heavily in bolstering the batting, Durham matched the previous season's tally of 22 batting points – fewer than any other county.

The Chester-le-Street pitches could not be blamed. They were certainly not as difficult as in 1996, and batsmen no longer rushed to blame the ground for their failings. The club certainly had every confidence in the groundsman, Tom Flintoft. They awarded him a testimonial in 1998, and decided to play all but one of their home games at the Riverside.

It was not easy to know where responsibility did lie. With nine boys enlisted in an academy, Geoff Cook took up more of a youth development role, under the title of cricket executive instead of director of cricket. The coach, Norman Gifford, was at home in Sussex for much of the winter – he was unaware of at least one of the signings – but he felt obliged to get them all into the team before Boon's arrival. He also wanted Paul Collingwood in the side and installed him as an opening batsman, where the talented youngster survived until just before a finger injury ended his season in early July.

Boon tended to stick with the team selected for him for the early Benson and Hedges Cup matches. Consequently, Alan Walker's early success and whole-hearted efforts were rewarded with a regular place and a new contract, though he was already 35, while the young pace bowlers, Steve Lugsden, Colin Campbell and Martin Saggers, made only four Championship appearances between them. Similarly, James Boiling became the first-choice spinner again, taking 17 Championship wickets at 49.94, while the previous season's big find, David Cox, played only twice.

Two Championship wins were two more than in 1996, and Durham could argue that they would have beaten Nottinghamshire and Northamptonshire but for the weather. Rain also interfered with winning opportunities against Sussex and Middlesex and prevented any play at all in the home match against Hampshire. But, while Durham remained unbeaten at home until September, they went through a second successive season without beating county opposition away from home in any form of cricket.

Lewis played the decisive innings in both Championship victories, carrying his bat for 158 against Kent and hitting 160 not out against Derbyshire. Other batting improvements stemmed from Boon shoring up the middle order, while John Morris returned to something like his best form, although both narrowly failed to join Lewis in reaching 1,000 Championship runs. Mike Foster made encouraging strides as the team's all-rounder, winning a memorable battle with Waqar Younis at Cardiff to score his maiden century, while Melvyn Betts produced two superb performances with the ball which must have put him in the running for an England A tour. When everything clicked into place, he bowled his away-swing at high pace, destroying Kent with seven for 29 and recording the season's best figures for any team with nine for 64 at Northampton. He helped to take the weight off Simon Brown, who, in contrast to previous years, appeared to be finding his best form at the end of the season, taking ten wickets in the final match at Leicester. Durham had lost their previous four encounters with Leicestershire by an innings, but this time they were beaten by only 17 runs.

"So near, yet so far," said Boon, as that last match appeared to sum up the summer. He gave all the players written instructions detailing improvements they could make in fitness and technique during the winter. After his first season of assessment, it was to be hoped that the real benefits would be felt in the second year of his contract. He himself was in no doubt of it. – TIM WELLOCK.

445

DURHAM 1997

Standing: D. G. C. Ligertwood, D. A. Blenkiron, P. D. Collingwood, M. M. Betts, R. M. S. Weston, N. Killeen, M. J. Saggers, J. Boiling, J. Wood, C. L. Campbell, S. Lugsden, M. J. Foster, A. Pratt, D. M. Cox, J. A. Daley, J. J. B. Lewis, J. P. Searle.
Seated: S. Hutton, J. E. Morris, S. J. E. Brown, D. C. Boon (*captain*), M. A. Roseberry, N. J. Speak, M. P. Speight, A. Walker.

DURHAM RESULTS

All first-class matches – Played 19: Won 3, Lost 8, Drawn 7, Abandoned 1.

County Championship matches – Played 17: Won 2, Lost 8, Drawn 6, Abandoned 1.

Competition placings – Britannic Assurance County Championship, 17th;
NatWest Trophy, 1st round; Benson and Hedges Cup, 3rd in Group B;
AXA Life League, 17th.

COUNTY CHAMPIONSHIP AVERAGES

BATTING

	M	I	NO	R	HS	100s	50s	Avge	Ct
J. J. B. Lewis	16	29	3	1,034	160*	2	5	39.76	10
D. C. Boon§	16	28	2	981	117	2	7	37.73	18
J. E. Morris	16	28	1	972	149	2	4	36.00	6
M. J. Foster	14	24	0	575	129	1	3	23.95	2
M. P. Speight	16	27	2	543	73*	0	3	21.72	50
S. Hutton†	7	13	1	258	95	0	1	21.50	1
J. Wood	5	8	4	72	21*	0	0	18.00	4
R. M. S. Weston†	5	8	0	137	36	0	0	17.12	5
P. D. Collingwood†	6	10	0	169	62	0	1	16.90	7
N. J. Speak	10	18	1	274	93	0	1	16.11	6
J. Boiling	15	26	4	334	62	0	1	15.18	13
M. A. Roseberry†	3	6	0	69	45	0	0	11.50	3
M. M. Betts†	11	18	0	201	35	0	0	11.16	1
A. Walker	12	20	8	92	16	0	0	7.66	0
M. J. Saggers	2	4	2	14	10*	0	0	7.00	2
S. J. E. Brown†	15	24	5	121	30	0	0	6.36	2

Also batted: D. M. Cox (2 matches) 24, 0, 22 (1 ct); J. A. Daley† (1 match) 7, 39 (1 ct); N. Killeen† (2 matches) 9*, 15, 0* (1 ct); S. Lugsden† (1 match) 4, 0*. C. L. Campbell (1 match) did not bat.

* *Signifies not out.* † *Born in Durham.* § *Overseas player.*
Durham have awarded all playing staff caps.

BOWLING

	O	M	R	W	BB	5W/i	Avge
M. M. Betts	276.3	63	939	43	9-64	2	21.83
S. J. E. Brown	513.4	103	1,667	57	5-58	4	29.24
A. Walker	341.1	87	1,063	33	7-56	2	32.21
M. J. Foster	275.4	55	1,027	30	4-58	0	34.23
J. Wood	102	13	476	11	4-73	0	43.27
J. Boiling	280.5	76	849	17	3-72	0	49.94

Also bowled: D. C. Boon 12.2–3–39–2; C. L. Campbell 12–0–92–1; P. D. Collingwood 42–4–177–5; D. M. Cox 44.3–8–132–4; N. Killeen 44–9–139–6; S. Lugsden 16.5–2–88–1; J. E. Morris 1–0–1–0; M. J. Saggers 58–13–160–7; R. M. S. Weston 1–0–5–0.

COUNTY RECORDS

Highest score for:	210*	J. J. B. Lewis v Oxford University at Oxford.	1997
Highest score against:	501*	B. C. Lara (Warwickshire) at Birmingham ...	1994
Best bowling for:	9-64	M. M. Betts v Northants at Northampton	1997
Best bowling against:	8-22	D. Follett (Middlesex) at Lord's............	1996
Highest total for:	625-6 dec.	v Derbyshire at Chesterfield	1994
Highest total against:	810-4 dec.	by Warwickshire at Birmingham	1994
Lowest total for:	67	v Middlesex at Lord's...................	1996
Lowest total against:	73	by Oxford University at Oxford............	1994

At Oxford, April 15, 16, 17. DURHAM beat OXFORD UNIVERSITY by 97 runs.

At Manchester, April 23, 24, 25, 26. DURHAM drew with LANCASHIRE.

DURHAM v NOTTINGHAMSHIRE

At Hartlepool, May 7, 8, 9, 10. Drawn. Durham 10 pts, Nottinghamshire 7 pts. Toss: Nottinghamshire.

In with a chance of their first Championship win since beating Nottinghamshire in the last match of 1995, Durham were foiled by the weather. With one day already lost, rain returned at 2.40 p.m. on the final day when Nottinghamshire were only 39 ahead with four wickets standing. On the first day, they were dismissed for 170, with Walker taking seven for 56 – quite an achievement after his previous season's Championship figures of two for 277. "It was a plug-away wicket and that's what I did," he explained. Then Speak led Durham to a lead of 161, grafting patiently for 93, though it was to be a false dawn in an otherwise gloomy start with his new county. Nottinghamshire's best performer, with both bat and ball, was Tolley. After his first-innings 54, he took three wickets and returned to the crease with his side still 11 behind to dominate an unbroken stand of 50 with Noon.

Close of play: First day, Durham 115-3 (N. J. Speak 20*, D. C. Boon 20*); Second day, No play; Third day, Nottinghamshire 68-2 (R. T. Robinson 32*, M. N. Bowen 7*).

Nottinghamshire

P. R. Pollard lbw b Walker	28	– c Boiling b Killeen	5
R. T. Robinson c Lewis b Walker	15	– c Boiling b Walker	69
G. F. Archer c Speight b Walker	6	– lbw b Boiling	20
M. P. Dowman c Collingwood b Foster	19	– (5) c Boon b Foster	10
*P. Johnson b Walker	10	– (6) c Lewis b Boiling	34
C. M. Tolley c Speight b Walker	54	– (7) not out	37
†W. M. Noon lbw b Brown	11	– (8) not out	13
K. P. Evans c Killeen b Walker	0		
R. T. Bates lbw b Walker	0		
M. N. Bowen lbw b Brown	4	– (4) c Boon b Brown	7
P. J. Franks not out	0		
L-b 13, w 6, n-b 4	23	L-b 3, n-b 2	5

1/46 2/52 3/63 4/85 5/99   170   1/11 2/60 3/68   (6 wkts) 200
6/150 7/151 8/151 9/166   4/106 5/150 6/150

Bonus points – Durham 4.

Bowling: *First Innings*—Brown 19–5–61–2; Killeen 6–3–8–0; Walker 17–5–56–7; Foster 6–0–32–1; Boiling 1–1–0–0. *Second Innings*—Brown 22–7–57–1; Killeen 13–2–24–1; Walker 10–2–50–1; Boiling 21.1–12–32–2; Boon 3–1–7–0; Foster 5–0–21–1; Collingwood 1–0–6–0.

Durham

J. J. B. Lewis lbw b Bowen	26	S. J. E. Brown b Bowen	30
P. D. Collingwood b Franks	6	N. Killeen not out	9
J. E. Morris c Robinson b Tolley	27	A. Walker c Tolley b Evans	0
N. J. Speak run out	93		
*D. C. Boon c Robinson b Bates	68	B 1, l-b 12, w 12, n-b 10	35
†M. P. Speight run out	26		
M. J. Foster lbw b Tolley	11	1/18 2/66 3/70 4/205 5/265	331
J. Boiling c Noon b Tolley	0	6/281 7/281 8/314 9/330	

Bonus points – Durham 3, Nottinghamshire 4 (Score at 120 overs: 330-9).

Bowling: Evans 29.2–5–81–1; Franks 20–3–62–1; Bowen 22–9–62–2; Tolley 29–6–80–3; Bates 20–5–33–1.

Umpires: R. Julian and J. F. Steele.

At Chelmsford, May 14, 15, 16, 17. DURHAM lost to ESSEX by 125 runs.

At Chester-le-Street, May 20. DURHAM v AUSTRALIANS. Abandoned (See Australian tour section).

DURHAM v WORCESTERSHIRE

At Chester-le-Street, May 21, 22, 23, 24. Drawn. Durham 5 pts, Worcestershire 16 pts. Toss: Durham.

Worcestershire were awarded eight points as the side batting last when the scores finished level. They needed 114 to win in 25 overs when they dismissed Durham for 332 after enforcing the follow-on. It should have been a stroll, but Saggers and Walker bowled their hearts out to make up for Durham's dreadfully wayward bowling in the first innings, when Lugsden alone contributed nine wides. Saggers took five for 57, but the target was just two off three balls when Weston heaved across the line and was bowled by Walker for 42. Two run-outs followed, though Rhodes scrambled another single. After the first day was lost to rain, Worcestershire had collected maximum bonus points and given Durham a lesson in how to exploit seaming conditions: Sheriyar had match figures of nine for 107. Foster made his maiden Championship fifty for Durham.

Close of play: First day, No play; Second day, Worcestershire 345-6 (D. A. Leatherdale 44*, S. J. Rhodes 13*); Third day, Durham 125-1 (J. J. B. Lewis 47*, J. E. Morris 39*).

Worcestershire

T. S. Curtis c Collingwood b Walker	43	– b Saggers	9
W. P. C. Weston c Collingwood b Walker	6	– b Walker	42
G. A. Hick c Speight b Lugsden	39	– c Morris b Saggers	8
K. R. Spiring b Foster	32	– (6) c Speight b Saggers	9
*T. M. Moody b Saggers	61	– (4) c Speight b Saggers	5
G. R. Haynes c Lewis b Collingwood	67	– (7) run out	18
D. A. Leatherdale not out	47	– (8) not out	0
†S. J. Rhodes not out	14	– (9) run out	1
S. R. Lampitt (did not bat)		– (5) c Boiling b Saggers	7
B 2, l-b 12, w 24, n-b 4	42	L-b 8, w 6	14

1/24 2/107 3/142 4/180 5/249	(6 wkts dec.) 351	1/21 2/39 3/52 4/66 (8 wkts) 113
6/317		5/82 6/112 7/112 8/113

P. J. Newport and A. Sheriyar did not bat.

Bonus points – Worcestershire 4, Durham 2.

Bowling: *First Innings*—Lugsden 16.5–2–88–1; Saggers 14–3–28–1; Walker 25–8–61–2; Foster 19–3–69–1; Boiling 23–3–62–0; Boon 1–0–3–0; Collingwood 6–1–26–1. *Second Innings*—Walker 13–1–48–1; Saggers 12–2–57–5.

Durham

J. J. B. Lewis b Sheriyar	7	– c Rhodes b Lampitt	52
P. D. Collingwood c Curtis b Sheriyar	13	– lbw b Leatherdale	21
J. E. Morris lbw b Haynes	19	– c Hick b Sheriyar	48
N. J. Speak c Weston b Sheriyar	12	– b Sheriyar	3
*D. C. Boon lbw b Lampitt	24	– lbw b Sheriyar	57
†M. P. Speight c Curtis b Newport	15	– c Moody b Haynes	29
M. J. Foster b Newport	0	– b Sheriyar	58
J. Boiling lbw b Sheriyar	0	– b Newport	18
M. J. Saggers not out	1	– c Rhodes b Lampitt	2
A. Walker b Newport	0	– lbw b Newport	1
S. Lugsden b Newport	4	– not out	0
B 4, l-b 7, n-b 26	37	B 7, l-b 3, n-b 33	43
	132		**332**

1/22 2/25 3/45 4/67 5/115   132   1/42 2/142 3/142 4/148 5/211   332
6/115 7/120 8/127 9/128   6/299 7/320 8/328 9/329

Bonus points – Worcestershire 4.

Bowling: *First Innings*—Newport 15.2–4–33–4; Sheriyar 17–5–53–4; Haynes 7–2–21–1; Lampitt 6–2–13–1; Leatherdale 1–0–1–0. *Second Innings*—Newport 21.4–6–48–2; Sheriyar 25–9–54–5; Haynes 17–4–44–1; Lampitt 18–4–69–1; Hick 15–6–30–0; Leatherdale 19–5–62–1; Moody 2–1–5–0; Curtis 1–0–10–0.

Umpires: A. Clarkson and N. T. Plews.

At Cardiff, May 29, 30, 31, June 2. DURHAM lost to GLAMORGAN by an innings and eight runs.

DURHAM v SUSSEX

At Chester-le-Street, June 4, 5, 6, 7. Drawn. Durham 10 pts, Sussex 11 pts. Toss: Sussex.

Two sets of strugglers desperately needed a win but were thwarted by rain. A shower took away three overs when Durham needed another 63 to win off 13.3 overs with three wickets left. On resuming, the batsmen struggled to pick up the tempo and required 54 off eight when Morris was caught on the mid-wicket boundary for a magnificent 124. Saggers and Brown then hung on for the draw. The sparring of two uncertain sides produced a good deal of mediocrity, but the final day was absorbing from start to finish. Durham did themselves no favours, returning to their obsession with an all-seam attack at the Riverside and bowling badly on the first day. Victory looked beyond them after Taylor's languid strokeplay brought him a second-innings century. But Walker bowled manfully into a stiff wind to take six wickets, leaving a target of 307. With Jarvis suffering from an Achilles tendon injury, leg-spinner Khan bowled 37 overs unchanged into the wind; Morris was the last of his three well-deserved victims.

Close of play: First day, Sussex 314-7 (P. Moores 34*, P. W. Jarvis 10*); Second day, Durham 309-9 (S. J. E. Brown 6*, A. Walker 7*); Third day, Sussex 243-8 (P. Moores 23*, A. A. Khan 1*).

Sussex

N. J. Lenham lbw b Brown	93	– c Boon b Walker	6
K. Greenfield c and b Foster	22	– c Speight b Brown	0
N. R. Taylor c Speight b Walker	29	– c Speight b Walker	109
C. W. J. Athey c Speight b Betts	40	– lbw b Brown	50
K. Newell b Saggers	13	– c Speak b Betts	28
M. Newell lbw b Brown	29	– c Roseberry b Walker	6
V. C. Drakes c Speight b Foster	10	– (8) lbw b Walker	2
*†P. Moores c Roseberry b Brown	60	– (7) c Speight b Walker	26
P. W. Jarvis c Boon b Brown	29	– c Saggers b Brown	10
A. A. Khan c Speight b Brown	3	– c Saggers b Walker	20
M. A. Robinson not out	7	– not out	0
L-b 16, w 18, n-b 4	38	B 1, l-b 3, w 6, n-b 4	14

1/96 2/153 3/177 4/202 5/250   373   1/3 2/19 3/161 4/178 5/206   271
6/265 7/281 8/344 9/348   6/206 7/208 8/235 9/270

Bonus points – Sussex 4, Durham 4 (Score at 120 overs: 359-9).

Bowling: *First Innings*—Brown 37.5–5–115–5; Betts 15–0–51–1; Saggers 24–5–56–1; Walker 27–8–82–1; Foster 18–8–53–2. *Second Innings*—Brown 23–2–76–3; Betts 18–2–61–1; Walker 26.3–4–68–6; Foster 8–1–43–0; Saggers 8–3–19–0.

Durham

J. J. B. Lewis c Moores b Jarvis	89	– b Drakes	14
M. A. Roseberry lbw b Drakes	0	– lbw b Drakes	1
J. E. Morris b Drakes	44	– c Drakes b Khan	124
N. J. Speak b Drakes	0	– b Khan	9
*D. C. Boon lbw b Drakes	3	– lbw b Robinson	26
†M. P. Speight c Greenfield b Robinson	49	– run out	29
M. J. Foster b Robinson	56	– b Khan	7
M. M. Betts c Moores b Robinson	13	– c Moores b Drakes	3
M. J. Saggers c and b Jarvis	1	– not out	10
S. J. E. Brown c Robinson b Khan	24	– not out	4
A. Walker not out	14		
B 6, l-b 11, n-b 24	41	B 1, l-b 11, n-b 30	42

1/6 2/101 3/101 4/107 5/184   338   1/9 2/38 3/77 4/134   (8 wkts) 269
6/244 7/286 8/295 9/297   5/210 6/230 7/241 8/253

Bonus points – Durham 3, Sussex 4.

Bowling: *First Innings*—Jarvis 28–7–97–2; Drakes 27–5–90–4; Robinson 14–2–46–3; Khan 20–3–54–1; K. Newell 9–1–34–0. *Second Innings*—Drakes 26–4–93–3; Robinson 19.5–4–47–1; Khan 37–6–117–3.

Umpires: J. C. Balderstone and D. J. Constant.

At Cambridge, June 14, 15, 16. DURHAM drew with CAMBRIDGE UNIVERSITY.

DURHAM v KENT

At Darlington, June 18, 19, 20, 21. Durham won by 135 runs. Durham 22 pts, Kent 4 pts. Toss: Durham.

Durham secured their first win in 24 Championship matches since the end of 1995, against the side who began the match leading the table. Durham's captain Boon, bowling his rarely-used off-spin only because of poor light, dismissed McCague with 5.4 overs remaining. The foundation for their victory was laid by Lewis, who became the second player after Wayne Larkins to carry his bat for Durham. Coincidentally, both scored 158. Lewis batted ten minutes short of seven hours and shared a vital eighth-wicket stand of 110 with Boiling, who also put on 92 in the second innings with Speight. Betts finally produced the performance he had often promised, swinging the ball away at high speed to wreck Kent with a career-best seven for 29. But the weather looked likely to foil Durham once more when the final morning was lost, forcing them to declare and set a target of 268 in 64 overs. Their hopes revived when Betts and Brown bowled superbly to reduce Kent to 41 for five. For the visitors, Headley was out of luck on his return from injury, though Fleming took nine in a match for the first time.

Close of play: First day, Durham 215-7 (J. J. B. Lewis 129*, J. Boiling 24*); Second day, Kent 138-4 (N. J. Llong 15*, M. V. Fleming 29*); Third day, Durham 183-8 (M. P. Speight 73*, S. J. E. Brown 9*).

Durham

J. J. B. Lewis not out	158	– c Wells b Fleming	30
P. D. Collingwood c Llong b Phillips	8	– lbw b Headley	1
J. E. Morris c Fulton b Strang	7	– b Fleming	21
N. J. Speak b Strang	0	– c Llong b Fleming	5
*D. C. Boon c Llong b McCague	0	– lbw b Strang	1
†M. P. Speight c Strang b Headley	9	– not out	73
M. J. Foster c Wells b Fleming	26	– c Marsh b Strang	4
M. M. Betts c and b Fleming	6	– b Fleming	0
J. Boiling b Fleming	28	– b Phillips	20
S. J. E. Brown c Marsh b Fleming	2	– not out	9
A. Walker c Strang b Fleming	1		
B 4, l-b 2	6	L-b 17, w 2	19
	251	(8 wkts dec.)	**183**

1/32 2/57 3/57 4/58 5/76 6/115 7/127 8/237 9/245

1/4 2/52 3/65 4/66 5/66 6/76 7/77 8/169

Bonus points – Durham 2, Kent 4.

Bowling: *First Innings*—McCague 19–3–45–1; Headley 26–7–60–1; Fleming 23–4–55–5; Phillips 16–6–37–1; Strang 31–10–48–2. *Second Innings*—McCague 9–1–35–0; Headley 11–1–27–1; Phillips 6–1–21–1; Fleming 19–5–34–4; Strang 24–11–45–2; Llong 4–2–4–0.

Kent

D. P. Fulton b Foster	31	– b Betts	8
M. J. Walker lbw b Betts	6	– lbw b Betts	1
T. R. Ward c Speight b Betts	7	– c Speight b Brown	0
A. P. Wells c Speight b Walker	16	– c Speight b Brown	27
N. J. Llong b Betts	17	– c Collingwood b Brown	3
M. V. Fleming not out	43	– c Lewis b Boiling	14
B. J. Phillips c Speight b Betts	1	– (9) b Brown	4
P. A. Strang c Speight b Betts	5	– (7) b Boiling	47
*†S. A. Marsh c Boon b Betts	0	– (8) c Speak b Boon	2
M. J. McCague c Speight b Betts	0	– c Morris b Boon	12
D. W. Headley b Brown	0	– not out	0
B 1, l-b 9, w 12, n-b 19	41	B 4, l-b 2, n-b 8	14
	167		**132**

1/20 2/42 3/77 4/77 5/140 6/146 7/160 8/160 9/160

1/2 2/5 3/21 4/24 5/41 6/93 7/116 8/116 9/123

Bonus points – Durham 4.

Bowling: *First Innings*—Brown 18–2–85–1; Betts 16–7–29–7; Walker 13–6–18–1; Foster 6–4–16–1; Collingwood 2–0–6–0; Boiling 2–1–3–0. *Second Innings*—Brown 22–8–57–4; Betts 12–3–25–2; Walker 8–3–16–0; Boiling 11–8–10–2; Boon 5.2–2–18–2.

Umpires: B. Leadbeater and A. G. T. Whitehead.

DURHAM v HAMPSHIRE

At Chester-le-Street, July 2, 3, 4, 5. Abandoned. Durham 3 pts, Hampshire 3 pts.

Prolonged rain left the outfield so wet that the match had to be abandoned on the final day. It was the first time Durham had suffered a Championship washout. "I feel very sorry for the groundsman," said their captain David Boon. "He has worked his socks off."

At Scarborough, July 16, 17, 18. DURHAM lost to YORKSHIRE by an innings and 56 runs.

At Cheltenham, July 23, 24, 25, 26. DURHAM lost to GLOUCESTERSHIRE by an innings and 28 runs.

DURHAM v DERBYSHIRE

At Chester-le-Street, July 31, August 1, 2. Durham won by six wickets. Durham 20 pts, Derbyshire 6 pts. Toss: Durham.

After 33 wickets fell in two days, Durham began the third on a precarious 48 for three, needing another 209. But they lost only one more batsman, night-watchman Boiling, and that was after he had put on 204 with Lewis, a county fourth-wicket record. Poor bowling at the start allowed Lewis to come swiftly out of the blocks. He combined vigilance with superb strokeplay, profiting hugely from his square cut and hitting 25 fours in an unbeaten 160, which took him past 1,000 runs for the first time. Pitches at the Riverside have much improved, but this one showed early signs of variable bounce, prompting batsmen to go for their shots in the belief that survival would be short lived. Adams seemed to have given Derbyshire the advantage with a 107-ball century before lunch on the first day. But Brown took nine wickets in his 100th match for Durham, whereas DeFreitas failed to follow up his five wickets in the first innings and was largely responsible for giving Lewis his flying start on the third day.

Close of play: First day, Durham 109-6 (M. J. Foster 37*, M. M. Betts 5*); Second day, Durham 48-3 (J. J. B. Lewis 28*, J. Boiling 9*).

Derbyshire

A. S. Rollins c Morris b Wood	12	– run out		1
M. R. May b Wood	4	– (3) c Boiling b Foster		64
C. J. Adams c Wood b Brown	107	– (5) lbw b Brown		1
K. J. Barnett c Speight b Foster	23	– (2) c Lewis b Brown		5
M. J. Vandrau b Brown	47	– (4) c Boiling b Wood		14
V. P. Clarke b Brown	33	– c Speak b Betts		25
†K. M. Krikken c Boiling b Betts	1	– not out		36
*P. A. J. DeFreitas b Betts	0	– b Brown		12
A. J. Harris lbw b Brown	1	– lbw b Brown		0
K. J. Dean run out	3	– c Speak b Brown		5
D. E. Malcolm not out	0	– b Foster		9
L-b 4, n-b 19	23	L-b 4		4

1/4 2/37 3/119 4/172 5/232		254	1/3 2/20 3/49 4/50 5/93	176
6/233 7/233 8/234 9/254			6/134 7/151 8/151 9/157	

Bonus points – Derbyshire 2, Durham 4.

Bowling: *First Innings*—Brown 20.1–2–63–4; Wood 14–1–77–2; Betts 10–0–48–2; Foster 7–0–42–1; Boiling 3–0–20–0. *Second Innings*—Brown 15–5–58–5; Wood 12–2–42–1; Betts 9–2–20–1; Foster 11.4–3–33–2; Boiling 8–3–19–0.

Durham

J. J. B. Lewis lbw b DeFreitas	36	– not out	160
S. Hutton lbw b Harris	8	– lbw b Malcolm	0
J. E. Morris b Malcolm	2	– c Krikken b Malcolm	6
N. J. Speak c DeFreitas b Harris	6	– c Rollins b Harris	1
*M. D. C. Boon b Harris	0	– (6) not out	5
†M. P. Speight c Krikken b DeFreitas	9		
M. J. Foster c Adams b Malcolm	37		
M. M. Betts c Harris b DeFreitas	23		
J. Boiling lbw b DeFreitas	17	– (5) c Rollins b Harris	62
J. Wood not out	21		
S. J. E. Brown c Krikken b DeFreitas	5		
L-b 4, w 2, n-b 4	10	L-b 9, n-b 14	23

1/20 2/29 3/38 4/38 5/63	174	1/9 2/25 3/28 4/232 (4 wkts) 257
6/82 7/109 8/146 9/146		

Bonus points – Derbyshire 4.

Bowling: *First Innings*—Malcolm 14–3–30–2; Harris 21–1–72–3; DeFreitas 15–3–37–5; Dean 7–0–31–0. *Second Innings*—Malcolm 21–3–55–2; Harris 24–4–89–2; DeFreitas 15–2–56–0; Dean 8–0–20–0; Clarke 3–1–7–0; Vandrau 3–0–19–0; May 0.1–0–2–0.

Umpires: A. A. Jones and P. Willey.

At The Oval, August 6, 7, 8, 9. DURHAM lost to SURREY by nine wickets.

DURHAM v MIDDLESEX

At Chester-le-Street, August 20, 21, 22, 23. Drawn. Durham 10 pts, Middlesex 9 pts. Toss: Durham. Championship debut: D. C. Nash.

Durham's fourth first-class captain, Boon, became the first to score a Championship century while in office. He blamed self-imposed pressure for a lean run in which his Championship average had slipped to 29 but, after Hewitt dropped him at long leg on 42, he played with a relaxed authority. In the 27 minutes' play possible on the second day, Foster boosted Durham further by racing from 22 to 54. When he was last out on the third, they were only seven short of a maximum four batting points, having earned none at all for two months. Foster also relished extra responsibility with the ball when a knuckle injury prevented Brown bowling; he helped reduce Middlesex to 133 for seven. Even though Nash displayed nimble footwork in scoring 94 on his Championship debut, Durham led by 92. Rain washed out their hopes, however, permitting only nine overs of declaration bowling on the final day.

Close of play: First day, Durham 285-6 (M. J. Foster 22*, M. M. Betts 11*); Second day, Durham 321-7 (M. J. Foster 54*, J. Boiling 4*); Third day, Durham 28-0 (J. J. B. Lewis 14*, S. Hutton 10*).

Durham

J. J. B. Lewis lbw b Kallis	38	– not out	45
S. Hutton c Brown b Johnson	29	– not out	28
J. E. Morris c Gatting b Johnson	0		
*D. C. Boon c Weekes b Kallis	110		
†M. P. Speight c Gatting b Kallis	9		
R. M. S. Weston c Gatting b Kallis	36		
M. J. Foster c Kallis b Johnson	70		
M. M. Betts c Shah b Dutch	11		
J. Boiling c Brown b Fraser	7		
S. J. E. Brown b Fraser	1		
A. Walker not out	0		
B 7, l-b 5, w 2, n-b 18	32	B 1, w 4	5

1/65 2/68 3/131 4/153 5/239	343	(no wkt) 78
6/260 7/285 8/329 9/339		

Bonus points – Durham 3, Middlesex 4.

Bowling: *First Innings*—Fraser 26–7–56–2; Hewitt 15–2–69–0; Kallis 21–6–98–4; Johnson 21.3–4–53–3; Dutch 16–2–34–1; Weekes 9–3–21–0. *Second Innings*—Fraser 7–2–8–0; Johnson 4–0–20–0; Dutch 3–0–19–0; Shah 2–0–19–0; Nash 2–0–11–0.

Middlesex

J. C. Pooley b Betts	0	R. L. Johnson c Weston b Boiling	39
J. H. Kallis c Boon b Foster	31	J. P. Hewitt c Speight b Foster	4
M. W. Gatting b Betts	7	A. R. C. Fraser not out	5
O. A. Shah c sub b Foster	14		
*†K. R. Brown c Speight b Foster	11	B 4, l-b 9, w 6, n-b 16	35
D. C. Nash c Lewis b Boiling	94		—
P. N. Weekes b Walker	1	1/0 2/18 3/52 4/79 5/94	251
K. P. Dutch c Morris b Boiling	10	6/101 7/133 8/211 9/228	

Bonus points – Middlesex 2, Durham 4.

Bowling: Betts 21–10–51–2; Foster 19–4–58–4; Walker 18–6–48–1; Boiling 21.5–3–72–3; Boon 2–0–9–0.

Umpires: B. Dudleston and M. J. Kitchen.

At Northampton, August 27, 28, 29, 30. DURHAM drew with NORTHAMPTONSHIRE.

DURHAM v WARWICKSHIRE

At Chester-le-Street, September 2, 3, 4, 5. Warwickshire won by an innings and 99 runs. Warwickshire 23 pts, Durham 3 pts. Toss: Durham.

The first day seemed like a throwback to the Riverside's inaugural first-class match in May 1995, when Warwickshire put on 172 for the first wicket. That had survived as the record opening stand on the ground until Knight and Wagh put on 206 in this match. Both were dropped at slip by Boon, shortly after he returned from having three stitches in a mouth wound, but Wagh blossomed after an edgy start to complete his maiden Championship century. Though only three brief sessions were possible next day, Warwickshire's disciplined bowling, supported by excellent catching by Piper, quickly made up for lost time against feeble batting. Following on 294 behind, Durham subsided to their first home defeat of the season, with only Boon resisting. A 10.15 start had been arranged each day to allow Warwickshire an early getaway on the final day for the NatWest Trophy final; in the event, they had time for a round of golf before leaving.

Close of play: First day, Warwickshire 338-5 (N. M. K. Smith 22*, K. J. Piper 2*); Second day, Durham 12-0 (J. J. B. Lewis 4*, S. Hutton 6*); Third day, Durham 120-5 (D. C. Boon 48*, M. J. Foster 8*).

Warwickshire

*N. V. Knight c Speight b Brown	92	G. Welch lbw b Brown	0
M. A. Wagh b Boiling	124	A. F. Giles c Boiling b Walker	7
D. L. Hemp b Betts	13	A. A. Donald b Brown	29
D. P. Ostler c Speight b Foster	18	B 4, l-b 23, w 2, n-b 2	31
T. L. Penney lbw b Foster	40		—
N. M. K. Smith lbw b Walker	23	1/206 2/234 3/246	412
†K. J. Piper not out	34	4/280 5/334 6/339	
D. R. Brown b Brown	1	7/342 8/342 9/357	

Bonus points – Warwickshire 3, Durham 3 (Score at 120 overs: 349-8).

Bowling: Brown 40.2–5–135–4; Betts 20–6–43–1; Walker 32–11–52–2; Boiling 27–7–70–1; Foster 21–4–85–2.

Durham

	First Innings		Second Innings	
J. J. B. Lewis	c Donald b Brown	4	c Piper b Brown	3
S. Hutton	c Ostler b Giles	20	c Ostler b Brown	0
J. E. Morris	lbw b Brown	3	c Penney b Giles	28
*D. C. Boon	b Welch	16	c Piper b Donald	81
†M. P. Speight	c Piper b Brown	1	lbw b Donald	14
R. M. S. Weston	lbw b Giles	8	run out	0
M. J. Foster	st Piper b Giles	29	b Brown	22
M. M. Betts	b Donald	3	b Brown	6
J. Boiling	c Piper b Donald	0	b Donald	8
S. J. E. Brown	c Piper b Donald	1	not out	10
A. Walker	not out	15	c Brown b Smith	1
	B 3, l-b 9, w 4, n-b 2	18	B 4, l-b 6, n-b 12	22
		118		**195**

1/13 2/21 3/45 4/52 5/60   118
6/75 7/92 8/92 9/102

1/2 2/7 3/40 4/93 5/97   195
6/142 7/163 8/183 9/184

Bonus points – Warwickshire 4.

Bowling: *First Innings*—Donald 14.4–7–33–3; Brown 10–3–28–3; Welch 9–4–16–1; Giles 13–5–29–3. *Second Innings*—Donald 20–10–38–3; Brown 23–9–39–4; Welch 6–2–22–0; Giles 22–6–29–1; Smith 20.3–5–57–1.

Umpires: B. Leadbeater and G. Sharp.

DURHAM v SOMERSET

At Chester-le-Street, September 10, 11, 12. Somerset won by eight wickets. Somerset 21 pts, Durham 5 pts. Toss: Durham.

World-class bowling by Caddick and Mushtaq Ahmed tipped a match of wonderful ebb and flow in Somerset's favour. In 64 overs, Durham went from likely winners to dispirited losers. At 66 without loss in their second innings, they led by 79 and, with Shine unable to bowl because of back trouble, Somerset looked threadbare. But Rose made the breakthrough – his 500th first-class wicket – and it was ruthlessly exploited by Caddick and Mushtaq, who mesmerised Durham with three for four in 13 overs. They collapsed for 135 and Somerset swept home. The visitors could not have envisaged such an easy victory when they collapsed themselves the previous day. Their first innings sank from 130 for one to 217 all out as sublime conditions, matched by Durham's batting, gave way to thickening cloud cover. Boon caught last man Shine behind the stumps; he was deputising for Speight, who had been hit on the finger while batting.

Close of play: First day, Somerset 75-1 (P. C. L. Holloway 17*, M. N. Lathwell 29*); Second day, Durham 132-7 (M. J. Foster 27*, J. Boiling 0*).

Durham

	First Innings		Second Innings	
J. J. B. Lewis	c Turner b Caddick	0	c Turner b Mushtaq Ahmed	50
S. Hutton	b Shine	14	c Turner b Rose	20
J. E. Morris	lbw b Rose	79	c Turner b Caddick	7
*D. C. Boon	c Turner b Rose	15	lbw b Caddick	10
†M. P. Speight	retired hurt	16	(6) lbw b Mushtaq Ahmed	1
R. M. S. Weston	lbw b Bowler	29	(5) c Ecclestone b Caddick	1
M. J. Foster	lbw b Mushtaq Ahmed	6	c Trescothick b Caddick	27
M. M. Betts	lbw b Burns	11	lbw b Mushtaq Ahmed	1
J. Boiling	c Turner b Rose	19	not out	0
S. J. E. Brown	c Turner b Mushtaq Ahmed	1	lbw b Rose	1
A. Walker	not out	0	lbw b Rose	0
	L-b 8, w 6, n-b 10	24	B 4, l-b 7, n-b 6	17
		230		**135**

1/0 2/32 3/82 4/146 5/155   230
6/176 7/192 8/226 9/230

1/66 2/81 3/99 4/99 5/101   135
6/101 7/108 8/132 9/135

Bonus points – Durham 1, Somerset 4.

In the first innings M. P. Speight, when 14, retired hurt at 117 and resumed at 176; when 16, he retired again at 185.

Bowling: *First Innings*—Caddick 22–2–83–1; Shine 6–0–26–1; Rose 15.4–4–40–3; Burns 9–1–24–1; Mushtaq Ahmed 21–4–49–2; Bowler 1–1–0–1. *Second Innings*—Caddick 21–7–60–4; Rose 13.5–2–43–3; Mushtaq Ahmed 13–10–4–3; Bowler 6–3–17–0.

Somerset

†R. J. Turner b Foster	21	– c Lewis b Foster	41
P. C. L. Holloway lbw b Foster	46	– c Speight b Foster	33
M. N. Lathwell lbw b Walker	57	– (4) not out	20
M. E. Trescothick c Weston b Walker	4		
*P. D. Bowler lbw b Brown	23		
M. Burns lbw b Brown	7		
S. C. Ecclestone b Betts	12	– (3) not out	54
G. D. Rose not out	15		
A. R. Caddick lbw b Betts	0		
Mushtaq Ahmed run out	8		
K. J. Shine c Boon b Brown	0		
B 3, l-b 14, w 5, n-b 2	24	L-b 4	4

1/35 2/130 3/140 4/146 5/168   217   1/76 2/87   (2 wkts) 152
6/185 7/197 8/197 9/217

Bonus points – Somerset 1, Durham 4.

Bowling: *First Innings*—Brown 27.1–6–69–3; Betts 19–6–56–2; Foster 14–3–37–2; Walker 13–4–28–2; Boiling 4–1–10–0. *Second Innings*—Brown 10–0–52–0; Betts 5–1–21–0; Foster 11–1–48–2; Walker 6–1–24–0; Boiling 1–0–2–0; Morris 1–0–1–0.

Umpires: J. D. Bond and J. W. Holder.

At Leicester, September 18, 19, 20, 21. DURHAM lost to LEICESTERSHIRE by 14 runs.

COUNTY MEMBERSHIP

	1987	1996	1997
Derbyshire	1,500	2,555	2,504
Durham	—	5,876	6,438
Essex	9,006	7,237	7,402
Glamorgan	2,926	10,812	11,217
Gloucestershire	4,136	5,339	5,480
Hampshire	4,499	4,394	4,174
Kent	5,186	5,960	5,972
Lancashire	11,276	14,044	13,942
Leicestershire	3,622	4,591	5,363
Middlesex	8,270	8,810	8,957
Northamptonshire	1,971	4,121	4,066
Nottinghamshire	1,950	5,145	5,057
Somerset	5,192	5,736	6,013
Surrey	6,084	7,051	7,533
Sussex	4,961	6,629	6,153
Warwickshire	8,366	15,081	14,333
Worcestershire	5,545	5,869	5,601
Yorkshire	10,531	9,201	9,298
MCC	19,794	19,860	19,851
Total	114,815	148,311	149,354

Note: All the first-class countries except three quote their membership in terms of the total number of individuals affiliated to their clubs. Only Derbyshire, Kent and Yorkshire continue to register corporate or joint membership as representing one person.

ESSEX

Peter Such

President: D. J. Insole

Chairman: D. L. Acfield

Chairman, Cricket Committee: G. J. Saville

Secretary/General Manager: P. J. Edwards

Captain: P. J. Prichard

Head Groundsman: S. Kerrison

Scorer: C. F. Driver

Two events dominated Essex cricket in 1997. After five years without any kind of title, and 12 without a one-day trophy, Paul Prichard lifted the NatWest Trophy at Lord's in September, a triumph which redeemed their disastrous performance there a year earlier.

And, for the first time in the club's history, it was a competition won without Graham Gooch. After a miraculous 1996, when he was the leading run-scorer in England, Gooch found it impossible in 1997 to live up to the high standards by which he measured himself. He managed only two half-centuries before announcing in July that he was calling it a day. The only sour note, as far as the county's hierarchy was concerned, was that he chose to tell the *News of the World* before he told them.

But as he began his final match, on his 44th birthday, everyone remembered that no one had committed himself so resolutely to Essex's cause. He made his debut for Essex in 1973, when they had never won anything, but since breaking their duck the county had claimed six Championships and five one-day tournaments, the best record of the modern era. It would have been impossible without Gooch's unique blend of destructiveness and consistency. He is ninth on the list of all-time century-makers, the tenth-highest run-scorer in the history of first-class cricket, and as the 1998 *Wisden* shows (see pages 19–22), the greatest run-scorer of all, taking one-day cricket into account.

Instead of Gooch, Essex's rock was the mighty talent of Stuart Law, who destroyed the Warwickshire attack, including Allan Donald, in the NatWest final, with an unbeaten 80 to claim the match award. In five Trophy matches, he scored 333 runs at an average of 83.25, but he unleashed his exciting, impertinent strokeplay in all the competitions. Law scored 1,482 Championship runs at 57, including five centuries, and reached 50 in 12 of his 17 games.

Prichard shared the major batting honours with Law, discovering a fluency of stroke which had been conspicuous by its absence in 1996. There were three centuries and nine fifties in his 1,184 first-class runs. But putting their limited-overs exploits aside, Prichard will have been disappointed by his side's decline in the second half of the season. Victory over Derbyshire at Southend in the final week of June had lifted them to second in the Championship table with a game in hand, and in the same week they reached the summit of the Sunday League. Significantly, two of their three other first-class victories up to that point came against Durham and Sussex, who finished 17th and 18th respectively. Thereafter, success against Lancashire was the sole cause for celebration in the last ten Championship games as Essex drifted down to eighth equal. It was much the same story on Sunday: they won only twice in the last nine games after winning seven of the first eight, and had to settle for seventh.

Injuries did not help. Mark Ilott was nearing peak form in early July, with 33 first-class wickets at an average of 18. Then a heel injury ruled him out for the next four matches and, on his return, he was unable to recapture his earlier control. Ashley Cowan claimed five for 49 in the opening game against Hampshire, and by mid-June he had picked up further five-fors against Surrey and Sussex. Soon afterwards, however, he developed a niggling shoulder problem which, although not serious enough to keep him out of the side, robbed him of his cutting edge. Still, Cowan was to confirm his promise with an impressive display in the NatWest Trophy final and cement his place on England's tour to the West Indies.

As one has come to expect, off-spinner Peter Such was a model of consistency. He took 66 first-class wickets, easily surpassing the rest of the Essex bowlers and – as at Colchester where he bowled 86 overs in an innings – bore the burden unflinchingly. The disappointment was the form of Danny Law, the young all-rounder recruited from Sussex. He struggled on both fronts. His bowling so lacked rhythm and accuracy that he collected a mere 31 wickets – and five of those came against Cambridge University. His batting produced fewer than 500 runs at an average of 16.96.

In between injections for a painful tennis elbow, Nasser Hussain reserved his best performances for England against Australia. He waited until the beginning of August before scoring the first of his two centuries for Essex. Ronnie Irani's best was seen in the opening weeks, as he collected three centuries in the first half-dozen matches, but an intercostal muscle injury prevented him from bowling in the last few Championship matches.

Paul Grayson, meanwhile, continued to enhance his reputation, displaying fighting qualities to go with a sound temperament as he completed 1,000 runs for the first time since joining the county. His composure in the heat of battle was a quality which occasionally deserted others, particularly in the county's thrilling one-wicket victory over Glamorgan in the NatWest Trophy semi-final at Chelmsford. Millions of TV viewers witnessed a shoving match between Ilott and Robert Croft which saw both men receive a £1,000 fine from their respective counties and a suspended two-match ban from the ECB. In the same tie, Stuart Law was seen to verbally abuse Darren Thomas after his finger was broken by a beamer, an offence for which he was later fined £300 by Essex, while Irani was warned as to his future conduct for uttering an expletive on his way back to the pavilion after being dismissed.

In the months ahead, the county will be hoping Darren Robinson grasps the opportunity afforded by Gooch's retirement. He scored 148 in Gooch's final match when batting at No. 3, an effort which won him his cap, but although he was immediately promoted to opener for the last seven matches, he topped 50 only once more.

More pressure is likely to be applied next season by a posse of promising teenage batsmen, among them Graham Napier, Ian Flanagan and Stephen Peters. All three have played for England Under-19, as has off-spinner Jonathan Powell who, with only one first-class match behind him, was a shock choice when the England A winter touring party was announced. Less surprising was the county's decision to release seamer Steve Andrew, who was never able to hold down a regular place in the side after moving from Hampshire in 1989. – NIGEL FULLER.

459

ESSEX 1997

[Bill Smith]

Back row: J. C. Powell, D. D. J. Robinson, B. J. Hyam, J. O. Grove, I. N. Flanagan, D. G. Wilson, S. D. Peters, T. P. Hodgson. *Middle row:* J. S. W. Davis (*physiotherapist*), A. I. E. Hibbert, N. F. Williams, D. M. Cousins, S. J. W. Andrew, A. P. Cowan, D. R. Law, A. P. Grayson, G. J. A. Goodwin, A. R. Butcher (*coach*). *Front row:* R. J. Rollins, P. M. Such, G. A. Gooch, P. J. Prichard (*captain*), N. Hussain, M. C. Ilott, R. C. Irani. *Insets:* S. G. Law, W. Ritzema.

ESSEX RESULTS

All first-class matches – Played 19: Won 5, Lost 6, Drawn 8.

County Championship matches – Played 17: Won 5, Lost 6, Drawn 6.

*Competition placings – Britannic Assurance County Championship, 8th equal;
NatWest Trophy, winners; Benson and Hedges Cup, q-f;
AXA Life League, 7th.*

COUNTY CHAMPIONSHIP AVERAGES

BATTING

Cap		M	I	NO	R	HS	100s	50s	Avge	Ct/St
1996	S. G. Law§	17	28	2	1,482	175	5	8	57.00	19
1986	P. J. Prichard†	15	25	1	1,098	224	3	8	45.75	9
1996	A. P. Grayson	16	25	3	876	105	1	5	39.81	16
1989	N. Hussain	10	17	0	650	128	2	3	38.23	9
1994	R. C. Irani..........	15	24	1	793	123*	3	3	34.47	4
1997	D. D. J. Robinson† ...	12	20	0	664	148	2	2	33.20	12
1995	R. J. Rollins†	12	19	1	452	82	0	4	25.11	24/2
1975	G. A. Gooch†	10	17	1	369	56	0	2	23.06	12
1997	A. P. Cowan	16	26	6	447	77	0	1	22.35	7
1993	M. C. Ilott..........	12	20	5	290	47	0	0	19.33	1
	T. P. Hodgson.......	3	6	0	101	44	0	0	16.83	0
1996	N. F. Williams	3	5	1	66	23	0	0	16.50	3
	D. R. Law..........	17	28	0	411	59	0	1	14.67	10
	B. J. Hyam†	5	9	1	60	26	0	0	7.50	8
1991	P. M. Such..........	17	21	10	58	14	0	0	5.27	5

Also batted: S. J. W. Andrew (2 matches) 24, 0, 3; I. N. Flanagan† (2 matches) 16*, 16, 40;
G. R. Napier† (1 match) 35*, 4*; S. D. Peters† (1 match) 33, 0 (1 ct); J. C. Powell† (1 match)
4*.

* Signifies not out.　　† Born in Essex.　　§ Overseas player.

BOWLING

	O	M	R	W	BB	5W/i	Avge
M. C. Ilott	317	85	924	40	7-59	1	23.10
A. P. Cowan...........	420	106	1,334	52	5-45	3	25.65
P. M. Such	627.1	186	1,492	56	6-55	5	26.64
D. R. Law	239.4	47	854	24	4-69	0	35.58
A. P. Grayson	371.5	102	972	27	4-53	0	36.00
R. C. Irani	256.5	71	682	18	3-51	0	37.88

Also bowled: S. J. W. Andrew 46–14–131–3; G. A. Gooch 2–1–3–0; S. G. Law
116–30–356–5; G. R. Napier 8–3–40–1; J. C. Powell 39–5–109–1; N. F. Williams 83–11–281–8.

COUNTY RECORDS

Highest score for:	343*	P. A. Perrin v Derbyshire at Chesterfield	1904
Highest score against:	332	W. H. Ashdown (Kent) at Brentwood	1934
Best bowling for:	10-32	H. Pickett v Leicestershire at Leyton........	1895
Best bowling against:	10-40	E. G. Dennett (Gloucestershire) at Bristol	1906
Highest total for:	761-6 dec.	v Leicestershire at Chelmsford	1990
Highest total against:	803-4 dec.	by Kent at Brentwood....................	1934
Lowest total for:	30	v Yorkshire at Leyton	1901
Lowest total against:	14	by Surrey at Chelmsford.................	1983

ESSEX v HAMPSHIRE

At Chelmsford, April 23, 24, 25, 26. Drawn. Essex 8 pts, Hampshire 7 pts. Toss: Hampshire. County debuts: D. R. Law; M. L. Hayden.

Rain washed out all but 35 overs of the last two days to ruin Essex's hopes of victory. On the opening day, Connor, obtaining sharp movement off the pitch, had bowled superbly to undermine them with seven wickets. But Cowan retaliated, discovering more bounce than most, and claimed a career-best five for 49 as Hampshire finished 85 adrift on first innings. Prichard then scored his second fifty of the game and Stuart Law a robust 78 from 89 balls to provide the springboard for a big advantage, which Irani carried through by making 123 not out, his highest innings yet. Left with a target of 528 – or, more significantly, just over five sessions to survive – Hampshire were grateful for the weather.

Close of play: First day, Hampshire 103-7 (A. N. Aymes 9*, A. D. Mascarenhas 4*); Second day, Essex 373-7 (R. C. Irani 95*, M. C. Ilott 34*); Third day, Hampshire 3-0 (J. S. Laney 3*, M. L. Hayden 0*).

Essex

G. A. Gooch lbw b Connor	11	– lbw b Stephenson	34
*P. J. Prichard lbw b Connor	65	– b James	56
N. Hussain b Connor	45	– lbw b James	22
S. G. Law lbw b Mascarenhas	27	– c Aymes b Stephenson	78
R. C. Irani c James b Connor	49	– not out	123
D. D. J. Robinson c Aymes b Connor	3	– c Keech b James	0
D. R. Law c Keech b Stephenson	2	– c Keech b Mascarenhas	13
†B. J. Hyam lbw b Stephenson	1	– c Laney b Stephenson	1
M. C. Ilott c Hayden b Connor	17	– b Udal	42
A. P. Cowan c Hayden b Connor	6	– not out	29
P. M. Such not out	1		
L-b 15, n-b 4	19	B 2, 1-b 16, w 2, n-b 24	44

1/32 2/129 3/134 4/180 5/211 246   1/65 2/126 3/139 (8 wkts dec.) 442
6/214 7/214 8/227 9/245   4/267 5/276 6/300
   7/307 8/398

Bonus points – Essex 1, Hampshire 4.

Bowling: *First Innings*—Connor 18-4-46-7; Milburn 11-1-51-0; James 14-2-40-0; Mascarenhas 11-0-53-1; Udal 3-0-20-0; Stephenson 5-0-21-2. *Second Innings*—Connor 12-0-66-0; Milburn 11-0-75-0; Stephenson 20-3-74-3; James 22-0-106-3; Mascarenhas 15-2-48-1; Udal 16-2-55-1.

Hampshire

M. L. Hayden c Hyam b Cowan	18	– (2) not out	35
J. S. Laney c S. G. Law b Cowan	3	– (1) b Ilott	4
*J. P. Stephenson c Robinson b Irani	11	– lbw b Irani	20
M. Keech b Gooch b Cowan	21	– not out	0
W. S. Kendall lbw b D. R. Law	9		
K. D. James b Irani	4		
†A. N. Aymes not out	33		
S. D. Udal b Cowan	13		
A. D. Mascarenhas c Hyam b Cowan	13		
S. M. Milburn c Hyam b Ilott	7		
C. A. Connor lbw b Ilott	11		
B 2, 1-b 8, n-b 8	18	L-b 1, n-b 4	5

1/22 2/27 3/51 4/73 5/73 161   1/6 2/60 (2 wkts) 64
6/81 7/94 8/122 9/139

Bonus points – Essex 4.

Bowling: *First Innings*—Ilott 15.1-2-37-2; Cowan 21-6-49-5; Irani 15-7-23-2; D. R. Law 9-2-42-1. *Second Innings*—Ilott 8-3-13-1; Cowan 7-0-27-0; D. R. Law 4-1-13-0; Irani 3-1-10-1.

Umpires: J. C. Balderstone and V. A. Holder.

At Cambridge, May 7, 8, 9. ESSEX drew with CAMBRIDGE UNIVERSITY.

ESSEX v DURHAM

At Chelmsford, May 14, 15, 16, 17. Essex won by 125 runs. Essex 21 pts, Durham 6 pts. Toss: Essex.

Such spun Essex to victory, which arrived in the eighth over of the final hour after Speight had resisted doggedly for two and a half hours. Essex recovered from the depths of 27 for four on the opening day, as Grayson shared stands of 95 with each of the Laws, but half-centuries from Collingwood and Speight helped Durham carve out a first-innings lead of 54. Prichard and Hussain both scored freely when Essex went in again but it was Stuart Law who played the innings of the match, an unbeaten 118 in 139 balls with 17 fours and a six. Durham were left fighting a battle for survival when Such breached Morris's defences after he had hit 76 from 88 balls, and quickly followed up by having Boon taken at short leg. Morris's innings was his first Championship fifty in his last 16 attempts.

Close of play: First day, Durham 122-3 (J. E. Morris 10*, D. C. Boon 1*); Second day, Durham 236-5 (M. P. Speight 47*, M. J. Foster 11*); Third day, Essex 309-5 (S. G. Law 81*, D. R. Law 12*).

Essex

G. A. Gooch c Lewis b Killeen	4	– b Foster	31
*P. J. Prichard c Speight b Brown	5	– b Boiling	80
N. Hussain lbw b Brown	4	– c sub b Foster	67
S. G. Law c Speight b Walker	63	– not out	118
R. C. Irani b Brown	9	– c Boon b Boiling	1
A. P. Grayson c Speight b Killeen	76	– c Speight b Killeen	26
D. R. Law c Foster b Walker	41	– run out	14
†B. J. Hyam c Speight b Killeen	0	– (10) c Boon b Walker	4
M. C. Ilott c Boiling b Killeen	0	– b Foster	2
A. P. Cowan lbw b Brown	18	– (8) c Speight b Foster	5
P. M. Such not out	2		
L-b 7, w 2, n-b 6	15	B 5, l-b 4, n-b 9	18

1/9 2/9 3/13 4/27 5/122   237   1/77 2/158 3/203   (9 wkts dec.) 366
6/217 7/217 8/217 9/222   4/212 5/285 6/313
                                          7/347 8/349 9/366

Bonus points – Essex 1, Durham 4.

Bowling: *First Innings*—Brown 17.1–1–54–4; Killeen 12–2–50–4; Foster 13–5–43–0; Walker 15–4–51–2; Collingwood 6–0–24–0; Boiling 1–0–8–0. *Second Innings*—Brown 9–1–35–0; Killeen 13–2–57–1; Foster 22–2–94–4; Walker 17.3–4–73–1; Collingwood 4–0–18–0; Boiling 23–5–80–2.

Durham

J. J. B. Lewis c Gooch b D. R. Law	19	– c Hyam b Ilott	1
P. D. Collingwood c Hyam b Cowan	62	– b Such	27
J. E. Morris c Gooch b Cowan	11	– b Such	76
N. J. Speak c Hussain b Cowan	0	– lbw b Irani	12
*D. C. Boon c Grayson b Irani	45	– c Grayson b Such	3
†M. P. Speight c S. G. Law b Cowan	53	– b Such	36
M. J. Foster c Prichard b D. R. Law	31	– b Such	1
J. Boiling lbw b Ilott	1	– c S. G. Law b Ilott	15
S. J. E. Brown c Hussain b D. R. Law	0	– (10) c Grayson b Such	1
N. Killeen c S. G. Law b Ilott	15	– (11) not out	0
A. Walker not out	9	– (9) c Gooch b Cowan	1
B 5, l-b 13, w 4, n-b 23	45	B 4, l-b 6, n-b 4	14

1/89 2/107 3/107 4/130 5/214   291   1/10 2/85 3/126 4/126 5/132   187
6/254 7/263 8/263 9/265   6/138 7/182 8/185 9/187

Bonus points – Durham 2, Essex 4.

Bowling: *First Innings*—Ilott 25.3–10–53–2; Cowan 33–14–73–4; Irani 22–7–52–1; D. R. Law 18–3–81–3; Such 9–4–14–0. *Second Innings*—Ilott 19–7–48–2; Cowan 17.5–9–33–1; Irani 9–3–25–1; D. R. Law 2–0–8–0; Such 29–15–55–6; S. G. Law 3–0–8–0.

Umpires: K. E. Palmer and A. G. T. Whitehead.

At Gloucester, May 21, 22, 23, 24. ESSEX drew with GLOUCESTERSHIRE.

ESSEX v YORKSHIRE

At Ilford, May 29, 30, 31, June 2. Yorkshire won by two wickets. Yorkshire 23 pts, Essex 6 pts. Toss: Essex.

A fluctuating contest – described by Byas as the finest he had played in – ended when Gough cut the eighth ball of the final day for four. Such was the luckless bowler, although he had the consolation of figures of 11 for 215. Despite too many of their batsmen wasting good starts, Essex had been in firm control as they reduced Yorkshire's first innings to 67 for five on a pitch offering bounce and some turn. But Vaughan, who scored 161 including 23 fours and a six, and Blakey revived them with a magnificent stand of 188. A spirited 76 from Stuart Law and a very responsible century from Irani, his second of the season, left Yorkshire a target of 276. Following a shaky start, they recovered thanks to a 139-run stand between Byas and Lehmann. Then Such removed the middle order. The extra half-hour was taken in an attempt to force a result on Saturday; Gough's nerve saw Yorkshire through it and swiftly sealed victory on the fourth morning.

Close of play: First day, Yorkshire 158-5 (M. P. Vaughan 92*, R. J. Blakey 41*); Second day, Essex 215-4 (R. C. Irani 35*, D. R. Law 23*); Third day, Yorkshire 270-8 (D. Gough 21*, C. E. W. Silverwood 2*).

Essex

G. A. Gooch b White	34	– c Blakey b Silverwood	4
*P. J. Prichard b Gough	0	– (8) c Byas b White	1
N. Hussain c Byas b Stemp	42	– c Blakey b White	38
R. C. Irani c Blakey b Gough	36	– (5) c Blakey b Stemp	100
S. G. Law c Lehmann b Stemp	30	– (4) c Byas b White	76
A. P. Grayson b Gough	0	– (2) c Byas b Stemp	27
D. R. Law lbw b Gough	10	– (6) lbw b Stemp	33
†R. J. Rollins c Blakey b White	60	– (7) c Lehmann b Stemp	0
M. C. Ilott c White b Stemp	7	– c Lehmann b Stemp	11
A. P. Cowan not out	43	– c Byas b Stemp	2
P. M. Such b Gough	12	– not out	2
L-b 11, n-b 12	23	L-b 4, n-b 14	18

1/11 2/71 3/97 4/149 5/151 6/151 7/161 8/184 9/268 **297**

1/11 2/63 3/89 4/180 5/235 6/239 7/242 8/293 9/297 **312**

Bonus points – Essex 2, Yorkshire 4.

Bowling: *First Innings*—Gough 15.5–3–74–5; Silverwood 6–0–33–0; Hartley 4–0–26–0; Stemp 22–4–79–3; White 11–3–54–2; Vaughan 4–0–20–0. *Second Innings*—Gough 18–1–78–0; Silverwood 5–0–12–1; Stemp 31.2–8–77–6; Hartley 2–0–15–0; White 16–1–82–3; Vaughan 8–0–44–0; Lehmann 1–1–0–0.

Yorkshire

M. D. Moxon b Ilott	1	– c Rollins b Ilott	16
M. P. Vaughan c S. G. Law b Grayson	161	– b Ilott	0
*D. Byas c and b Such	5	– lbw b Such	89
D. S. Lehmann c Prichard b Ilott	8	– lbw b Such	81
B. Parker run out	0	– c Rollins b Such	33
C. White c Grayson b Such	0	– (7) c sub b Such	2
†R. J. Blakey b Such	92	– (8) lbw b Such	0
P. J. Hartley c and b Such	5	– (6) c D. R. Law b Grayson	1
D. Gough c D. R. Law b Such	1	– not out	26
C. E. W. Silverwood c Grayson b Such	7	– not out	4
R. D. Stemp not out	33		
B 1, l-b 6, w 4, n-b 10	21	B 4, l-b 17, w 4	25

1/2 2/45 3/58 4/58 5/67   334   1/1 2/26 3/165 4/229   (8 wkts) 277
6/255 7/266 8/268 9/280   5/232 6/235 7/235 8/266

Bonus points – Yorkshire 3, Essex 4.

Bowling: *First Innings*—Ilott 19–6–69–2; Cowan 9–0–35–0; Such 37.2–7–121–6; Grayson 24–2–65–1; Irani 2–0–23–0; S. G. Law 4–0–14–0. *Second Innings*—Ilott 10–3–30–2; Cowan 6–1–30–0; Such 34.2–7–94–5; Grayson 22–0–79–1; S. G. Law 5–0–23–0.

Umpires: G. Sharp and J. F. Steele.

At The Oval, June 4, 5, 6, 7. ESSEX beat SURREY by 147 runs.

At Hove, June 12, 13, 14. ESSEX beat SUSSEX by ten wickets.

ESSEX v OXFORD UNIVERSITY

At Chelmsford, June 20, 21, 22. Drawn. Toss: Oxford University. First-class debut: J. R. Cockcroft.

Rain was the only winner in this match, the first meeting between the two sides since 1972. Less than four and a half hours' play was possible in three days, but that was time enough for the students to collapse against an accurate seam attack. Only Morgan and Buchanan batted with any semblance of authority.

Close of play: First day, Oxford University 65-5 (R. D. Hudson 6*, L. G. Buchanan 2*); Second day, Oxford University 90-7 (L. G. Buchanan 13*, A. P. Scrini 12*).

Oxford University

N. G. Pirihi lbw b Ilott	0	†A. P. Scrini c Robinson b Williams	18
B. W. Byrne lbw b Ilott	8	J. R. Cockcroft c Irani b Law	1
*M. A. Wagh c Law b Williams	2	C. M. Battarbee not out	0
C. G. R. Lightfoot c Hyam b Williams	16		
P. G. Morgan b Hyam b Law	30	L-b 1	1
R. D. Hudson c Hyam b Ilott	7		
L. G. Buchanan c Hyam b Williams	36	1/0 2/9 3/15 4/40 5/58	120
C. Patel c Peters b Williams	1	6/67 7/68 8/119 9/120	

Bowling: Ilott 15–6–22–3; Williams 18–5–55–5; Irani 5–2–13–0; Law 11.5–3–22–2; Such 8–5–7–0.

Essex

*P. J. Prichard not out	....	14
D. D. J. Robinson not out	....	12
W 4, n-b 4	....	8

(no wkt) 34

A. P. Grayson, R. C. Irani, S. D. Peters, R. J. Rollins, D. R. Law, †B. J. Hyam, M. C. Ilott, N. F. Williams and P. M. Such did not bat.

Bowling: Patel 3–0–15–0; Battarbee 3–0–19–0.

Umpires: M. R. Benson and B. J. Meyer.

ESSEX v DERBYSHIRE

At Southend, June 26, 27, 28. Essex won by an innings and 145 runs. Essex 24 pts, Derbyshire 3 pts. Toss: Derbyshire. First-class debut: S. J. Lacey.

Essex achieved their third consecutive Championship win, which effectively took only two days; the second day was completely washed out. Derbyshire's performance throughout illustrated the turmoil inside the club. And in the second innings their batsmen pushed and prodded against Such to score just 86 all out in 52 overs. The pitch was slow and blameless, and Derbyshire collapsed the first time against the in-swing of Ilott, who finished with seven for 59. Stuart Law surpassed Derbyshire on his own, and put on 199 with Prichard. His 157 came off 174 balls, with 19 fours and three sixes. Malcolm bowled only eight overs, having suffered a bruised foot while batting.

Close of play: First day, Essex 157-2 (P. J. Prichard 71*, S. G. Law 69*); Second day, No play.

Derbyshire

A. S. Rollins c Rollins b Cowan	....	35	– c S. G. Law b Ilott	....	6
M. J. Vandrau lbw b Ilott	....	5	– c Robinson b Such	....	17
C. J. Adams c Rollins b Ilott	....	0	– c Prichard b Ilott	....	6
T. A. Tweats lbw b Ilott	....	19	– c Robinson b Such	....	8
J. E. Owen c Gooch b Cowan	....	19	– b Grayson	....	10
V. P. Clarke lbw b Ilott	....	2	– c Grayson b Such	....	9
†K. M. Krikken b Ilott	....	5	– b Grayson	....	9
*P. A. J. DeFreitas b Cowan	....	38	– c Rollins b Such	....	3
S. J. Lacey b Ilott	....	4	– not out	....	2
A. J. Harris lbw b Ilott	....	0	– c Prichard b Grayson	....	0
D. E. Malcolm not out	....	5	– c D. R. Law b Such	....	1
B 1, l-b 5, w 2, n-b 2	....	10	B 7, l-b 8	....	15

1/9 2/9 3/57 4/65 5/67   142   1/8 2/16 3/35 4/56 5/56   86
6/81 7/95 8/114 9/114   6/71 7/83 8/83 9/83

Bonus points – Essex 4.

Bowling: *First Innings*—Ilott 19–5–59–7; Cowan 18.4–5–46–3; Irani 5–0–18–0; Such 5–0–13–0. *Second Innings*—Ilott 9–1–16–2; Cowan 5–2–8–0; Such 20.5–7–27–5; Grayson 17–9–20–3.

Essex

G. A. Gooch c Krikken b Harris	....	7	†R. J. Rollins c Rollins b Vandrau	 6
*P. J. Prichard lbw b Lacey	....	106	M. C. Ilott not out	 11
D. D. J. Robinson c Krikken b Harris	...	4	A. P. Cowan not out	 11
S. G. Law c Harris b Lacey	....	157	W 2, n-b 8	 10
R. C. Irani c Owen b Lacey	....	23	
A. P. Grayson b Vandrau	....	7	1/19 2/31 3/230 4/280 (8 wkts dec.) 373
D. R. Law b Vandrau	....	31	5/289 6/315 7/327 8/357

P. M. Such did not bat.

Bonus points – Essex 4, Derbyshire 3.

Bowling: DeFreitas 15–1–55–0; Harris 22–5–87–2; Clarke 5–0–20–0; Lacey 21–0–97–3; Malcolm 8–0–36–0; Vandrau 13–0–78–3.

Umpires: J. H. Harris and B. J. Meyer.

ESSEX v SOMERSET

At Chelmsford, July 2, 3, 4. Somerset won by ten wickets. Somerset 24 pts, Essex 6 pts. Toss: Somerset.

Somerset's attack – skilfully spearheaded by Shine – needed just 37.3 overs to dismantle Essex's second innings and set up victory with a day to spare. It was their first victory at Chelmsford since 1948. Only Stuart Law, whose 55 came from 57 balls, and Gooch passed double figures. It had all looked much rosier on the first day for Essex, who came into the match as powerful Championship contenders on the back of three successive wins. After a resolute 78 from Robinson and an entertaining half-century from Prichard, Ilott removed Bowler and Ecclestone with the first two balls of the Somerset innings. But Holloway and Lathwell wrested the initiative, each recording their highest scores of the season thus far. Turner added an unbeaten 80 and the wagging tail left the bowlers a lead of 109 to work with. Despite Caddick's absence through Test duty, they were well up to the task.

Close of play: First day, Somerset 42-2 (P. C. L. Holloway 10*, M. N. Lathwell 30*); Second day, Somerset 249-6 (R. J. Turner 11*, G. D. Rose 6*).

Essex

G. A. Gooch c Parsons b Shine	4	– lbw b Shine	23
*P. J. Prichard c Ecclestone b Rose	51	– c Turner b Shine	0
D. D. J. Robinson c and b Shine	78	– (8) c Turner b Shine	4
S. G. Law b Kerr	5	– c Bowler b Kerr	55
R. C. Irani c Herzberg b Kerr	14	– c Shine b Kerr	6
A. P. Grayson lbw b Rose	8	– (3) c Holloway b Rose	6
D. R. Law lbw b Rose	8	– (6) c Parsons b Shine	4
†R. J. Rollins lbw b Kerr	27	– (7) b Shine	0
M. C. Ilott lbw b Kerr	0	– (10) not out	1
A. P. Cowan not out	46	– (9) c Bowler b Rose	8
P. M. Such c Turner b Shine	14	– lbw b Rose	1
B 4, l-b 13, w 8	25	L-b 1, w 6, n-b 14	21

1/14 2/73 3/78 4/122 5/143   280   1/5 2/14 3/61 4/76 5/104   129
6/165 7/210 8/210 9/214   6/104 7/106 8/117 9/127

Bonus points – Essex 2, Somerset 4.

Bowling: *First Innings*—Shine 23.4–8–73–3; Rose 24–8–79–3; Kerr 23–4–83–4; Parsons 13–3–27–0; Herzberg 1–0–1–0. *Second Innings*—Shine 19–5–72–5; Rose 10.3–3–22–5; Kerr 8–3–34–2.

Somerset

*P. D. Bowler lbw b Ilott	0		
P. C. L. Holloway c Gooch b Grayson	90	– not out	5
S. C. Ecclestone c Gooch b Ilott	0		
M. N. Lathwell c Cowan b D. R. Law	87		
K. A. Parsons c Rollins b Cowan	31		
†R. J. Turner not out	80		
M. Burns c Rollins b Grayson	4	– (1) not out	15
G. D. Rose c Grayson b Cowan	36		
J. I. D. Kerr b D. R. Law	26		
S. Herzberg c Grayson b D. R. Law	4		
K. J. Shine lbw b Ilott	12		
B 4, l-b 5, w 4, n-b 6	19	W 2	2

1/0 2/0 3/147 4/207 5/219   389   (no wkt) 22
6/233 7/308 8/348 9/360

Bonus points – Somerset 4, Essex 4 (Score at 120 overs: 375-9).

Bowling: *First Innings*—Ilott 22.4–7–70–3; Cowan 22–3–99–2; Such 27–9–56–0; Grayson 19–7–42–2; Irani 18–5–41–0; D. R. Law 19–1–72–3. *Second Innings*—Ilott 2.4–0–13–0; Cowan 2–0–9–0.

Umpires: R. Julian and M. J. Kitchen.

At Northampton, July 16, 17, 18, 19. ESSEX lost to NORTHAMPTONSHIRE by 15 runs.

ESSEX v WORCESTERSHIRE

At Chelmsford, July 23, 24, 25, 26. Drawn. Essex 8 pts, Worcestershire 8 pts. Toss: Worcestershire.

Graham Gooch had chosen this as the final match of his grand career. It began on his 44th birthday, but he failed to sign off in style. The MP for Colchester, Bob Russell, tabled a Commons motion listing Gooch's achievements, and the Chelmsford town crier rang a bell, but Gooch's leg stump was uprooted by the 26th ball he received, bowled by Sheriyar. The next man in was Robinson, the player earmarked to replace Gooch in the side, who was playing only because Hussain was with England. He responded with a career-best 148, shared a stand of 182 with Prichard, and won his county cap. Worcestershire conceded an advantage of 57, despite a lengthy first-innings vigil from Spiring, which had lasted six hours and 20 minutes. By the close of the third day they were only 42 ahead with five wickets remaining, but next morning Hick, who scored his 94th first-class century, and Leatherdale would not be budged. Rain arrived during the lunch break and prevented any play until after tea, when Worcestershire resumed their innings. Visiting captain Moody had offered to declare to allow one of the game's greats a last, sentimental visit to the crease, but Gooch declined, preferring to crack open the champagne on the pavilion balcony.

Close of play: First day, Worcestershire 328-6 (K. R. Spiring 119*, M. J. Rawnsley 7*); Second day, Essex 230-3 (D. D. J. Robinson 81*, R. J. Rollins 3*); Third day, Worcestershire 99-5 (G. A. Hick 29*).

Worcestershire

*T. M. Moody lbw b Such	45	– c Rollins b Andrew	41
T. S. Curtis c Cowan b Andrew	33	– c Prichard b Such	2
G. A. Hick lbw b S. G. Law	14	– not out	107
K. R. Spiring c S. G. Law b Grayson	150	– b Such	14
G. R. Haynes c S. G. Law b Such	4	– (6) c D. R. Law b S. G. Law	0
D. A. Leatherdale c Rollins b Such	21	– (7) not out	59
V. S. Solanki c Gooch b S. G. Law	60		
M. J. Rawnsley c Grayson b S. G. Law	26		
†S. J. Rhodes not out	5	– (5) c Rollins b S. G. Law	4
S. R. Lampitt lbw b Grayson	4		
A. Sheriyar b Irani	0		
L-b 12, w 4, n-b 16	32	B 4, l-b 9, w 6, n-b 4	23

1/53 2/98 3/128 4/138 5/166	394	1/23 2/51 3/88 (5 wkts dec.) 250
6/317 7/375 8/389 9/393		4/99 5/99

Bonus points – Worcestershire 4, Essex 2 (Score at 120 overs: 358-6).

Bowling: *First Innings*—Cowan 9–0–49–0; D. R. Law 21–6–54–0; Andrew 18–7–26–1; Irani 22–2–69–1; Such 36–9–103–3; S. G. Law 12–4–27–3; Grayson 20–5–54–2. *Second Innings*—Cowan 8–0–40–0; Irani 11–4–20–0; Such 35–11–70–2; Andrew 5–0–18–1; S. G. Law 11–1–56–2; Grayson 13–4–30–0; Gooch 2–1–3–0.

Essex

G. A. Gooch b Sheriyar	11	A. P. Cowan b Haynes	0
*P. J. Prichard c and b Solanki	120	P. M. Such c Rhodes b Lampitt	0
D. D. J. Robinson b Haynes	148	S. J. W. Andrew st Rhodes b Rawnsley	24
S. G. Law c Curtis b Sheriyar	1		
†R. J. Rollins c Leatherdale b Rawnsley	44	B 2, 1-b 7, n-b 22	31
R. C. Irani b Moody	20		
A. P. Grayson not out	45	1/36 2/218 3/223 4/303 5/359	451
D. R. Law c Rhodes b Moody	7	6/367 7/390 8/393 9/398	

Bonus points – Essex 3, Worcestershire 1 (Score at 120 overs: 337-4).

Bowling: Sheriyar 11–2–28–2; Haynes 20–5–53–2; Lampitt 14–4–54–1; Hick 34–9–79–0; Moody 12–2–50–2; Rawnsley 19–8–45–2; Solanki 31–6–98–1; Leatherdale 7–1–35–0.

Umpires: G. I. Burgess and J. W. Holder.

ESSEX v LEICESTERSHIRE

At Colchester, July 31, August 1, 2, 4. Drawn. Essex 9 pts, Leicestershire 7 pts. Toss: Essex. First-class debut: J. C. Powell.

Peter Such bowled himself into the record books in this inconclusive run rampage. After Essex had declared at 533 for eight, there was every hope that Such might bowl Essex to victory and back to a place among the Championship leaders. Instead, the Castle Park pitch – rather than wearing in its customary fashion – simply got flatter, and Such made unexpected history as the game became meaningless in every other respect. He found himself bowling 86 overs, the most six-ball overs anyone has ever bowled in a Championship innings, adding up to a record 516 balls. Alfred Shaw bowled 100.1 five-ball overs in 1895. Shaw, it should be noted, was 52 at the time; Such was 33. He failed to threaten the world record of 588 balls in an innings, set in the 1957 Edgbaston Test by Sonny Ramadhin, and equalled by Arshad Ayub of Hyderabad in the

MOST BALLS BOWLED IN A COUNTY CHAMPIONSHIP INNINGS

516	P. M. Such (4-94), Essex v Leicestershire at Colchester	1997
501	A. Shaw (4-168), Sussex v Nottinghamshire at Nottingham	1895
490	F. Martin (4-151), Kent v Nottinghamshire at Nottingham	1891
486	J. H. Wardle (3-172), Yorkshire v Derbyshire at Bradford	1949

Research by Robert Brooke

1991-92 Ranji Trophy. There are 18 other instances of more than 516 balls in an innings in Tests or overseas, mostly on the subcontinent. Leicestershire were content simply to survive against Such, and he conceded only just above a run an over. Essex's innings was based on a third-wicket stand of 317 between Stuart Law, who scored 110 of his runs in boundaries, and Hussain, whose century was his first of the summer for the county. Leicestershire lost their fourth wicket with only 100 up, but their middle order held firm for nearly two full days.

Close of play: First day, Essex 204-2 (N. Hussain 52*, S. G. Law 124*); Second day, Leicestershire 18-2 (A. R. K. Pierson 4*, I. J. Sutcliffe 1*); Third day, Leicestershire 316-6 (B. F. Smith 28*, P. A. Nixon 3*).

Essex

*P. J. Prichard c and b Mullally	2	†R. J. Rollins c Millns b Pierson	15
D. D. J. Robinson c Pierson b Millns	4	J. C. Powell not out	4
N. Hussain c Whitaker b Brimson	128	A. P. Cowan not out	0
S. G. Law st Nixon b Brimson	175	B 1, l-b 15, w 6, n-b 22	44
R. C. Irani c Wells b Pierson	76		
A. P. Grayson b Pierson	81	1/9 2/9 3/326 4/363 5/506 (8 wkts dec.) 533	
D. R. Law b Nixon b Millns	4	6/509 7/527 8/529	

P. M. Such did not bat.

Bonus points – Essex 4, Leicestershire 1 (Score at 120 overs: 466-4).

Bowling: Millns 28–8–97–2; Mullally 33–7–114–1; Johnson 7–1–38–0; Wells 7–2–35–0; Brimson 32–5–124–2; Pierson 29–2–109–3.

Leicestershire

V. J. Wells c Rollins b Cowan	6	D. J. Millns c Rollins b Powell	55
D. L. Maddy c Robinson b Such	1	M. T. Brimson lbw b Grayson	0
A. R. K. Pierson c Robinson b Such	17	A. D. Mullally not out	13
I. J. Sutcliffe b Irani	130		
*J. J. Whitaker b Such	16	B 17, l-b 10, n-b 14	41
N. C. Johnson c S. G. Law b Such	91		
B. F. Smith not out	131	1/6 2/11 3/66 4/100 5/270 (9 wkts dec.) 515	
†P. A. Nixon c Hussain b Grayson	14	6/303 7/330 8/469 9/470	

Bonus points – Leicestershire 3, Essex 2 (Score at 120 overs: 315-6).

Bowling: Cowan 14–2–59–1; Irani 9–1–25–1; Such 86–49–94–4; Powell 39–5–109–1; Grayson 38–16–81–2; D. R. Law 17–1–94–0; S. G. Law 7–0–26–0.

Umpires: T. E. Jesty and B. Leadbeater.

At Canterbury, August 6, 7, 8, 9. ESSEX lost to KENT by an innings and eight runs.

At Worksop, August 20, 21, 22, 23. ESSEX drew with NOTTINGHAMSHIRE.

ESSEX v WARWICKSHIRE

At Chelmsford, August 27, 28, 29. Warwickshire won by eight wickets. Warwickshire 21 pts, Essex 4 pts. Toss: Essex. First-class debut: I. N. Flanagan.

A week before they were scheduled to meet Warwickshire in the NatWest final, Essex were brushed aside by the same opponents with a day to spare, despite the loss of more than 100 overs to the weather. With the exception of Stuart Law, who played well in the first innings, they batted recklessly on a pitch which offered only slight assistance to the bowlers. Penney was more resilient, taking three and a half hours over his unbeaten 77, and even though Such claimed his sixth five-wicket haul of the season, Warwickshire still led by 59. Essex immediately lost three wickets for one run, and the game was up. Donald collected eight wickets in the match and became the 19th bowler to take 500 for Warwickshire, but Moles ruptured his Achilles tendon going for a quick single. The injury would put an end to his season.

Close of play: First day, Essex 107-3 (S. G. Law 30*, M. C. Ilott 0*); Second day, Warwickshire 136-5 (T. L. Penney 35*, K. J. Piper 0*).

Essex

D. D. J. Robinson c Donald b Welch	38	– lbw b Brown	0
T. P. Hodgson c Piper b Welch	12	– c Piper b Donald	1
*N. Hussain lbw b Brown	21	– lbw b Welch	7
S. G. Law c Knight b Giles	54	– c Piper b Brown	0
M. C. Ilott c Piper b Donald	4	– (10) not out	1
A. P. Grayson c Piper b Donald	5	– (5) c Donald b Smith	20
I. N. Flanagan not out	16	– (6) b Giles	16
D. R. Law c Ostler b Donald	0	– (7) lbw b Giles	7
†R. J. Rollins c Piper b Giles	0	– (8) c Brown b Giles	29
A. P. Cowan c Piper b Donald	14	– (9) c Hemp b Donald	15
P. M. Such lbw b Donald	2	– c Welch b Donald	1
B 1, l-b 9, n-b 2	12	L-b 2, n-b 2	4

1/29 2/76 3/93 4/117 5/141   178   1/1 2/1 3/1 4/13 5/33   101
6/142 7/142 8/145 9/166   6/42 7/69 8/99 9/99

Bonus points – Warwickshire 4.

Bowling: *First Innings*—Donald 23.1–9–50–5; Brown 19–3–60–1; Welch 10–5–15–2; Giles 14–6–43–2. *Second Innings*—Donald 7.4–4–7–3; Brown 10–2–30–2; Welch 5–1–8–1; Smith 8–1–30–1; Giles 10–6–24–3.

Warwickshire

*N. V. Knight lbw b Such	48	– not out	20
A. J. Moles c Hussain b Ilott	0	– retired hurt	20
D. L. Hemp b Cowan	18	– c Grayson b Such	0
D. P. Ostler c Rollins b Such	2	– b Such	0
T. L. Penney not out	77	– not out	0
N. M. K. Smith b Cowan	17		
†K. J. Piper lbw b Such	21		
D. R. Brown b Such	0		
G. Welch c Ilott b Such	0		
A. F. Giles lbw b Such	14		
A. A. Donald c Cowan b Grayson	19		
B 7, l-b 6, n-b 8	21	L-b 1, n-b 2	3

1/2 2/31 3/56 4/93 5/132   237   1/40 2/40   (2 wkts) 43
6/169 7/169 8/169 9/191

Bonus points – Warwickshire 1, Essex 4.

In the second innings A. J. Moles retired hurt at 40-0.

Bowling: *First Innings*—Cowan 20–1–76–2; Ilott 14–4–42–1; Such 30–4–94–6; Grayson 5.5–1–12–1. *Second Innings*—Cowan 4–1–21–0; Ilott 3–0–19–0; Such 1–1–0–2; Grayson 0.4–0–2–0.

Umpires: J. D. Bond and J. F. Steele.

At Manchester, September 2, 3, 4, 5. ESSEX beat LANCASHIRE by 26 runs.

At Cardiff, September 10, 11, 12, 13. ESSEX lost to GLAMORGAN by seven wickets.

ESSEX v MIDDLESEX

At Chelmsford, September 18, 19, 20, 21. Drawn. Essex 9 pts, Middlesex 10 pts. Toss: Middlesex.

Set a target of 267 in a minimum of 50 overs, Middlesex shut up shop after losing three wickets in the first three overs. Shah steered them to safety on a docile pitch and the extra half-hour was not claimed, even though a win would have lifted Middlesex to third in the table and £16,000 in prize money. Instead they earned £10,500 for finishing joint fourth. Stuart Law, who had top-scored in the first innings of Essex's last four games, extricated them from yet another batting collapse on the first morning, and then Cowan struck a career-best 77 as he and Ilott shared a century ninth-wicket stand. A maiden century by Nash and Hewitt's first Championship fifty provided the backbone of Middlesex's reply, and Nash's game improved still further when he took the wicket of Ilott with his first ball. By that stage Essex were sacrificing wickets for quick runs, trying to add to the lead established by Robinson and Hussain, who had both made their second Championship hundreds of the season. But expectations of a tight finish were soon frustrated.

Close of play: First day, Middlesex 30-1 (M. R. Ramprakash 2*, R. L. Johnson 0*); Second day, Middlesex 174-6 (D. C. Nash 34*, J. P. Hewitt 21*); Third day, Essex 170-1 (D. D. J. Robinson 73*, N. Hussain 85*).

Essex

*P. J. Prichard c Brown b Bloomfield	25	– c Brown b Hewitt	3
D. D. J. Robinson c Weekes b Hewitt	3	– c Shah b Johnson	134
N. Hussain c Brown b Fraser	0	– c Brown b Hewitt	104
S. G. Law c Johnson b Fraser	63	– c Brown b Hewitt	1
R. C. Irani b Bloomfield	5	– c Weekes b Hewitt	0
A. P. Grayson b Bloomfield	0	– (10) not out	7
D. R. Law run out	34	– (6) c Johnson b Tufnell	26
†B. J. Hyam c Shah b Johnson	10	– (9) not out	2
M. C. Ilott c Gatting b Bloomfield	47	– (8) c Shah b Nash	2
A. P. Cowan c Weekes b Bloomfield	77	– (7) c Weekes b Tufnell	1
P. M. Such not out	1		
L-b 2, n-b 4	6	B 5, l-b 4, w 10, n-b 2	21
	271	**(8 wkts dec.)**	**301**

1/18 2/29 3/31 4/63 5/63
6/117 7/137 8/145 9/258

1/3 2/216 3/218
4/220 5/283 6/288
7/290 8/293

Bonus points – Essex 2, Middlesex 4.

Bowling: *First Innings*—Fraser 25-4-69-2; Hewitt 13-3-50-1; Bloomfield 21-5-77-5; Johnson 13-2-37-1; Tufnell 12-1-36-0. *Second Innings*—Fraser 20-5-52-0; Hewitt 12-2-31-4; Bloomfield 6-1-23-0; Tufnell 29-6-63-2; Weekes 11-0-53-0; Johnson 18-1-62-1; Nash 1-0-8-1.

Middlesex

*M. R. Ramprakash c Robinson b Ilott	2	– (3) c Robinson b Ilott	3
P. N. Weekes lbw b D. R. Law	26	– c Hyam b Cowan	0
R. L. Johnson c Hyam b Cowan	15	– (1) b Ilott	12
M. W. Gatting b Ilott	14	– b Grayson	27
O. A. Shah b Such	37	– not out	54
D. C. Nash c Irani b Ilott	100	– b D. R. Law	23
†K. R. Brown c Irani b Such	8	– not out	6
J. P. Hewitt c Robinson b Ilott	75		
A. R. C. Fraser c Hussain b Cowan	5		
P. C. R. Tufnell c S. G. Law b Cowan	0		
T. F. Bloomfield not out	0		
B 7, l-b 13, w 2, n-b 2	24	B 4, l-b 6, w 4	14
	306	**(5 wkts)**	**139**

1/30 2/34 3/50 4/86 5/112
6/128 7/297 8/306 9/306

1/10 2/14 3/21
4/67 5/128

Bonus points – Middlesex 3, Essex 4.

Bowling: *First Innings*—Ilott 28-8-63-4; Cowan 26.1-5-84-3; D. R. Law 13-5-31-1; S. G. Law 5-4-1-0; Such 23-2-65-2; Grayson 18-2-42-0. *Second Innings*—Ilott 11-1-37-2; Cowan 5-0-20-1; Grayson 9-5-20-1; Such 9-3-16-0; S. G. Law 8-2-32-0; D. R. Law 2-1-4-1.

Umpires: R. Palmer and N. T. Plews.

GLAMORGAN

Darren Thomas

Patron: HRH The Prince of Wales
President: G. Craven
Chairman: F. D. Morgan
Chairman, Cricket Committee: H. D. Davies
Secretary: M. J. Fatkin
Captain: M. P. Maynard
Director of Coaching: A. Jones
First Eleven Coach: 1997 – D. A. G. Fletcher
Grounds Supervisor: L. A. Smith
Scorer: B. T. Denning

When Steve James struck Graham Rose to the fine-leg boundary at 6.18 on the penultimate evening of the season, Glamorgan started to celebrate their third County Championship title, and their first for 28 years. The tenacity and self-belief which characterised their play throughout the season was present in abundance in that final game at Taunton, where they thoroughly outplayed Somerset. They began it one point ahead of Kent, needing maximum points to make sure of the title. From the moment Matthew Maynard won the toss and inserted the opposition, his team assumed complete control.

After Pakistan Test star Waqar Younis signed a two-year contract, Maynard had described the signing as "probably the best the club has ever made". But, although Waqar made a huge impact, Glamorgan's success was a collective effort. The team was complemented by their coach, former Zimbabwe captain Duncan Fletcher, whose efficiency, technique and ability improved the standards of the younger players. Maynard's captaincy was another significant contribution. Not only did he inspire self-belief with his imaginative leadership, he was also prepared to gamble in pursuit of victory.

They won eight of their 17 matches – only Middlesex, with eight wins out of 16 in 1903 and eight out of 24 in 1985, had won the Championship with so few since it was formally organised in 1890. But rain intervened in almost every game. Glamorgan lost more than 2,000 overs during the summer; only defending champions Leicestershire lost more. The pattern was set in the opening match, when only 90 minutes' play was possible over the last two days and Warwickshire were 323 short of avoiding an innings defeat.

Glamorgan were a settled, well-balanced team, who suffered few injuries. Apart from Alun Evans, who played just one Championship game, they relied on 13 players – as did Leicestershire the previous season and, coincidentally, the Glamorgan squad of 1969. Maynard, James, Adrian Dale, Adrian Shaw and Steve Watkin were ever-present.

Waqar, who arrived in April with a foot injury, missed the opening game but then repaid the money invested in him by playing in the remaining 16 and heading the bowling averages with 68 wickets at 22.80. He produced two match-winning performances, against Lancashire and Sussex, taking 15 wickets for 42 in successive innings. Watkin, who for many years had to be both spearhead and workhorse, was rejuvenated by the reduced burden, while Darren Thomas improved greatly to take 50 first-class wickets in a season for the first time and earn his county cap. Until 1996, Thomas's bowling had been loose and erratic, but a summer with his new coach and advice from Waqar transformed him into a seamer of considerable potential, and sometimes Waqar-like pace. He achieved a career-best five for 24 against Sussex and bowled magnificently, when Waqar failed, in Somerset's crucial second innings at Taunton.

The three-man pace attack was complemented by the spin of Robert Croft and 19-year-old left-armer Dean Cosker, who was rewarded with selection for the England A tour of Kenya and Sri Lanka. These five key bowlers responded well to every type of pitch.

Glamorgan gained 50 batting points, more than any other county, thanks mainly to James, who had a phenomenal season. He amassed 1,775 first-class runs, nine more than in 1996, but from 30 innings, rather than 38, and out-scored his nearest challenger, Darren Lehmann of Yorkshire, by 200 runs, striking seven centuries and eight fifties. The Professional Cricketers' Association voted him their player of the year, and his disappointment at not being picked for England's party to the West Indies was tempered by being named vice-captain of the A tour. The dependable Hugh Morris was his perfect opening partner. He started the season with a career-best 233 against Warwickshire, and finished it with 165 against Somerset, his 52nd century for the county, equalling Alan Jones's record. But it proved to have been his final appearance for Glamorgan before he retired, after being appointed the ECB's technical director in succession to Micky Stewart. He ended his career, which began in 1981, with 19,785 first-class runs at 40.29. Fletcher, the coach, also decided against returning in 1998.

Maynard flourished, after a quiet start, with two particularly memorable innings. He scored an unbeaten 161 in 145 balls at Worcester, though it was in a losing cause. And he effectively settled the Championship when he demolished Somerset in the final game. His glorious strokeplay, as he hit 142 in 117 balls in dreadful light, evoked memories of Ian Botham and Viv Richards in their Taunton prime. He averaged 65 to James's 68. Dale played some useful innings – his undefeated 142 at Chesterfield averted the threat of following on – but Tony Cottey, after several productive summers, had a wretched season, averaging under 25 in the Championship, although he played a vital innings in the last home game against Essex. Colin Metson was kept out completely by wicket-keeper/batsman Shaw, and announced in October that he was leaving.

In one-day cricket, Glamorgan failed to qualify for the Benson and Hedges quarter-finals, hardly threatened in the Sunday League, but did reach the NatWest semi-final for the third time in five years. They lost an acrimonious encounter against Essex at Chelmsford, after which Croft was fined £1,000 by the club for a shoving incident with Mark Ilott.

There was little opportunity in the first team for the younger players, but Michael Powell, who celebrated his first-class debut at Oxford University with an undefeated double-century, scored 1,210 runs for the Second Eleven, a county record.

The future looked bright for Glamorgan. They expected their success to attract new sponsorship and, after taking control of Sophia Gardens at the end of the season, started work on developing their Cardiff headquarters, ready to host a World Cup game in 1999. Since the establishment of the Cricket Board of Wales, with Peter Walker as its first director of cricket development, coaches have been appointed throughout the principality. Many young cricketers will hope to emulate the Championship team of 1997, which included eight former Welsh Schools players. – EDWARD BEVAN.

GLAMORGAN 1997

[Bill Smith

Back row: A. W. Evans, S. C. B. Tomlinson, A. P. Davies, S. P. Jones, O. T. Parkin, M. J. Powell, W. L. Law. *Middle row:* B. T. Denning *(First Eleven scorer),* J. Derrick *(coach),* D. A. G. Fletcher *(First Eleven coach),* S. D. Thomas, A. D. Shaw, G. P. Butcher, A. Jones *(director of coaching),* G. N. Lewis *(Second Eleven scorer).* *Front row:* S. P. James, R. D. B. Croft, H. Morris, P. A. Cottey, M. P. Maynard *(captain),* S. L. Watkin, C. P. Metson, A. Dale. *Inset:* Waqar Younis.

GLAMORGAN RESULTS

All first-class matches – Played 19: Won 8, Lost 3, Drawn 8.

County Championship matches – Played 17: Won 8, Lost 2, Drawn 7.

Competition placings – Britannic Assurance County Championship, winners; NatWest Trophy, s-f; Benson and Hedges Cup, 3rd in Group D; AXA Life League, 13th.

COUNTY CHAMPIONSHIP AVERAGES

BATTING

Cap		M	I	NO	R	HS	100s	50s	Avge	Ct/St
1992	S. P. James	17	28	4	1,605	162	7	6	66.87	14
1987	M. P. Maynard	17	23	6	1,106	161*	3	7	65.05	20
1986	H. Morris†	16	26	4	1,207	233*	4	3	54.86	13
1992	A. Dale	17	25	3	840	142*	2	5	38.18	5
1992	R. D. B. Croft†......	13	18	1	577	86	0	4	33.94	13
1992	P. A. Cottey†	15	19	4	370	76*	0	1	24.66	15
	A. D. Shaw†	17	20	5	352	53*	0	1	23.46	49/2
1997	S. D. Thomas†	16	16	4	259	75*	0	1	21.58	7
	G. P. Butcher	9	9	1	172	58	0	1	21.50	1
1997	Waqar Younis§	16	17	1	289	47	0	0	18.06	3
	M. J. Powell†	3	6	2	62	41*	0	0	15.50	1
1989	S. L. Watkin†	17	16	3	138	39	0	0	10.61	3
	D. A. Cosker........	13	8	5	14	7	0	0	4.66	4

Also batted: A. W. Evans† (1 match) 31 (1 ct).

* *Signifies not out.* † *Born in Wales.* § *Overseas player.*

BOWLING

	O	M	R	W	BB	5W/i	Avge
Waqar Younis..........	441.4	83	1,551	68	8-17	3	22.80
S. L. Watkin...........	508.2	143	1,393	61	7-41	2	22.83
R. D. B. Croft	504.2	118	1,259	54	5-33	1	23.31
S. D. Thomas..........	330.3	49	1,160	44	5-24	2	26.36
D. A. Cosker	255.3	62	736	20	4-64	0	36.80

Also bowled: G. P. Butcher 65.4–14–270–8; P. A. Cottey 3.3–1–19–0; A. Dale 49.1–11–169–0; M. P. Maynard 6.5–0–39–0; M. J. Powell 1–0–3–0.

COUNTY RECORDS

Highest score for:	287*	D. E. Davies v Gloucestershire at Newport ..	1939
Highest score against:	313*	S. J. Cook (Somerset) at Cardiff	1990
Best bowling for:	10-51	J. Mercer v Worcestershire at Worcester.....	1936
Best bowling against:	10-18	G. Geary (Leicestershire) at Pontypridd	1929
Highest total for:	597-8 dec.	v Durham at Cardiff	1997
Highest total against:	657-7 dec.	by Warwickshire at Birmingham	1994
Lowest total for:	22	v Lancashire at Liverpool	1924
Lowest total against:	33	by Leicestershire at Ebbw Vale	1965

GLAMORGAN v WARWICKSHIRE

At Cardiff, April 23, 24, 25, 26. Drawn. Glamorgan 11 pts, Warwickshire 3 pts. Toss: Warwickshire. County debut: D. L. Hemp.

An amazingly one-sided match did not end in the win Glamorgan deserved because rain allowed less than two hours' play on the last two days. Warwickshire had been 400 behind on first innings when Glamorgan spared them further torment by declaring with only three wickets down. Warwickshire failed to earn a single bonus point, the first time this has happened to them in a game where the first innings was completed since the system was introduced in 1968. It made for a traumatic return to Cardiff for their new recruit, Hemp, who had switched counties in the close season. After choosing to bat, Warwickshire were undone by early moisture in the pitch, but they then saw it flatten out beautifully as Morris shared huge stands with both James and Dale. Morris had reached 233, his 50th and highest first-class hundred, when Donald found some residual life and hit him behind the ear. Morris had to be stretchered off the ground and was taken to hospital. It was the third-highest innings in England to end with the batsman retiring; Andrew Sandham retired ill on 282, playing for Surrey at Old Trafford in 1928, and Stan Worthington collapsed with cramp when on 238 for Derbyshire v Sussex in 1937.

Close of play: First day, Glamorgan 195-1 (H. Morris 78*, S. L. Watkin 0*); Second day, Warwickshire 15-1 (A. J. Moles 9*, G. Welch 6*); Third day, Warwickshire 77-3 (A. J. Moles 40*).

Warwickshire

*A. J. Moles c Shaw b Thomas	9	– not out	40
W. G. Khan c Shaw b Watkin	6	– b Thomas	0
D. L. Hemp c and b Croft	9		
D. P. Ostler c and b Croft	14		
T. L. Penney c Shaw b Thomas	16		
†K. J. Piper c James b Watkin	1		
N. M. K. Smith c Shaw b Thomas	36		
G. Welch c James b Thomas	3	– (3) c Dale b Croft	35
A. F. Giles c Shaw b Watkin	29		
A. A. Donald not out	20	– (4) c Shaw b Thomas	0
G. C. Small c Maynard b Butcher	0		
L-b 4, w 2, n-b 2	8	N-b 2	2

1/9 2/19 3/35 4/42 5/43   151   1/6 2/74 3/77   (3 wkts) 77
6/80 7/96 8/97 9/148

Bonus points – Glamorgan 4.

Bowling: *First Innings*—Watkin 11–4–32–3; Thomas 12–1–62–4; Croft 13–2–37–2; Dale 1–0–2–0; Butcher 2.4–0–14–1. *Second Innings*—Watkin 12–3–15–0; Thomas 12.5–3–31–2; Croft 7–4–10–1; Butcher 3–0–21–0.

Glamorgan

S. P. James b Donald	83	P. A. Cottey not out	20
H. Morris retired hurt	233		
S. L. Watkin c Small b Giles	18	B 6, l-b 27, w 2, n-b 36	71
A. Dale c Ostler b Welch	106		
*M. P. Maynard not out	20	1/190 2/249 3/491 (3 wkts dec.) 551

G. P. Butcher, †A. D. Shaw, R. D. B. Croft, S. D. Thomas and D. A. Cosker did not bat.

Bonus points – Glamorgan 4 (Score at 120 overs: 388-2).

H. Morris retired hurt at 514.

Bowling: Donald 33–12–62–1; Small 22–3–80–0; Welch 33–8–135–1; Giles 38–11–116–1; Smith 26–3–97–0; Hemp 2–0–28–0.

Umpires: D. J. Constant and M. J. Kitchen.

At Leeds, May 7, 8, 9, 10. GLAMORGAN drew with YORKSHIRE.

At Canterbury, May 14, 15, 16, 17. GLAMORGAN beat KENT by 87 runs.

GLAMORGAN v HAMPSHIRE

At Cardiff, May 21, 22, 23, 24. Drawn. Glamorgan 4 pts, Hampshire 6 pts. Toss: Glamorgan.

Glamorgan's fourth Championship game was disrupted by rain, like the previous three, taking their total of days lost to five and a half. The captains set up a run chase, with reciprocal forfeits, but Glamorgan eventually called off their hunt for 310 in 78 overs. Hampshire's innings, spread over three days, was dominated by a stand of 144 between Smith and Kevan James: both were dismissed short of their centuries by 19-year-old slow left-armer Cosker. Steve James gave Glamorgan a sound start, and Butcher and Shaw consolidated. But they were out in successive overs and, when Waqar Younis was run out, Glamorgan gave up.

Close of play: First day, Hampshire 94-1 (M. L. Hayden 54*, K. D. James 23*); Second day, Hampshire 232-2 (K. D. James 76*, R. A. Smith 81*); Third day, No play.

Hampshire

G. W. White c James b Waqar Younis	6	*J. P. Stephenson not out	25
M. L. Hayden lbw b Watkin	57	B 7, l-b 7, w 2, n-b 2	18
K. D. James b Cosker	85		—
R. A. Smith b Cosker	94	1/20 2/100 (4 wkts dec.)	309
W. S. Kendall not out	24	3/244 4/259	

†A. N. Aymes, S. D. Udal, J. N. B. Bovill, S. M. Milburn and C. A. Connor did not bat.

Bonus points – Hampshire 3, Glamorgan 1.

Bowling: Waqar Younis 16–5–39–1; Watkin 24–2–70–1; Thomas 12–0–52–0; Cosker 20–1–61–2; Dale 6.1–2–10–0; Butcher 5–2–16–0; Maynard 3.5–0–30–0; Cottey 1.3–0–17–0.

Hampshire forfeited their second innings.

Glamorgan

Glamorgan forfeited their first innings.

S. P. James c Aymes b Bovill	76	S. D. Thomas not out	2
H. Morris c Aymes b Stephenson	21	Waqar Younis run out	1
A. Dale c Aymes b Bovill	1	S. L. Watkin not out	0
*M. P. Maynard c White b Bovill	34	B 1, l-b 10, n-b 14	25
P. A. Cottey b James	34		
G. P. Butcher b Stephenson	58	1/39 2/44 3/100 4/169 (8 wkts)	287
†A. D. Shaw b Connor	35	5/190 6/279 7/285 8/286	

D. A. Cosker did not bat.

Bowling: Connor 21.5–4–58–1; Milburn 11–1–47–0; Udal 13–4–31–0; Stephenson 12–0–55–2; Bovill 17–3–65–3; James 3–0–20–1.

Umpires: J. H. Harris and R. Palmer.

GLAMORGAN v DURHAM

At Cardiff, May 29, 30, 31, June 2. Glamorgan won by an innings and eight runs. Glamorgan 24 pts, Durham 4 pts. Toss: Glamorgan.

Glamorgan went top of the Championship when they won just before lunch on the final day. The foundation for victory was the club's highest total in first-class cricket, beating by ten their score against Derbyshire at the Arms Park in 1951. Maynard declared at lunch on the second day at 597 for eight; that still left Glamorgan as the only county never to reach 600. They had started at a gallop with James scoring a century in the first session. He shared an opening stand of 229 with Hugh Morris, and Maynard became the third centurion, from only 108 balls. Durham lurched to 81 for five before Boon and Foster put on 140, and Foster, hitting the ball without inhibitions or too much footwork, reached a maiden hundred. Durham still had to follow on, and this time only John Morris resisted. He scored his first century since 1995, more than 60 per cent of the runs, and hit 22 fours before being last man out.

Close of play: First day, Glamorgan 433-3 (M. P. Maynard 47*, P. A. Cottey 9*); Second day, Durham 230-6 (M. J. Foster 66*, D. M. Cox 8*); Third day, Durham 142-4 (J. E. Morris 84*, J. Boiling 0*).

Glamorgan

S. P. James c and b Boiling	153	Waqar Younis c Collingwood b Cox	7
H. Morris c Morris b Collingwood	135	S. D. Thomas c Boon b Cox	0
A. Dale lbw b Walker	73	B 3, l-b 7, w 2, n-b 6	18
*M. P. Maynard not out	134		
P. A. Cottey c Collingwood b Brown	15	1/229 2/348 3/408 (8 wkts dec.) 597
R. D. B. Croft c Collingwood b Foster	29	4/458 5/509 6/584
†A. D. Shaw lbw b Cox	33	7/594 8/597

S. L. Watkin and D. A. Cosker did not bat.

Bonus points – Glamorgan 4, Durham 1 (Score at 120 overs: 509-4).

Bowling: Brown 33–4–113–1; Foster 22–4–122–1; Walker 26–4–112–1; Boiling 33–5–117–1; Collingwood 11–1–51–1; Cox 15.3–2–72–3.

Durham

J. J. B. Lewis c Maynard b Watkin	21	– lbw b Watkin	5
P. D. Collingwood c Croft b Waqar Younis	17	– lbw b Waqar Younis	1
J. E. Morris b Watkin	20	– c Cottey b Waqar Younis	149
N. J. Speak c Shaw b Waqar Younis	10	– b Thomas	25
*D. C. Boon b Waqar Younis	66	– lbw b Waqar Younis	15
†M. P. Speight b Thomas	5	– (7) b Waqar Younis	1
M. J. Foster lbw b Croft	129	– (8) c Shaw b Watkin	11
D. M. Cox b Thomas	24	– (9) c Maynard b Watkin	0
J. Boiling not out	10	– (6) c Cottey b Croft	4
S. J. E. Brown c and b Watkin	1	– c Cottey b Croft	5
A. Walker b Watkin	16	– not out	10
B 4, l-b 14, w 2, n-b 6	26	B 5, l-b 7, n-b 6	18

1/23 2/58 3/59 4/76 5/81	345	1/5 2/13 3/97 4/141 5/152	244
6/221 7/259 8/328 9/329		6/165 7/195 8/195 9/202

Bonus points – Durham 3, Glamorgan 4.

Bowling: *First Innings*—Waqar Younis 22–4–98–3; Watkin 28.2–10–73–4; Thomas 20–7–59–2; Croft 25–8–51–1; Cosker 12–4–41–0; Dale 3–2–5–0. *Second Innings*—Waqar Younis 20–7–56–4; Watkin 18–7–31–3; Croft 33–10–81–2; Thomas 9–1–28–1; Dale 5–2–10–0; Cosker 8–2–26–0.

Umpires: A. A. Jones and B. J. Meyer.

At Oxford, June 5, 6, 7. GLAMORGAN lost to OXFORD UNIVERSITY by five wickets.

GLAMORGAN v MIDDLESEX

At Cardiff, June 12, 13, 14. Middlesex won by an innings and seven runs. Middlesex 23 pts, Glamorgan 6 pts. Toss: Glamorgan.

The Middlesex seamers, Hewitt and Fraser, needed just 16 overs to finish the game by dismissing Glamorgan for the fourth-lowest Championship score in their history. It was easily the nadir of Glamorgan's season. Hewitt achieved career-best figures on a pitch where the ball squatted after the heavy roller was used during the change of innings. Six batsmen were leg-before and, at 11 for six, Glamorgan threatened their all-time nadir, 22 against Lancashire in 1924. The result was even more remarkable than Middlesex's last Championship match at Cardiff, in 1993, when Tufnell transformed a high-scoring game with eight for 29. Glamorgan were struggling at 26 for three in their first innings but were rescued by Croft and Maynard who put on 84 together. Kallis, with superb strokeplay, and Ramprakash added 160 for Middlesex's second wicket, but accurate bowling from Thomas and Watkin restricted their first-innings lead to 38. Remarkably, that was enough to gain them an innings victory; Glamorgan disintegrated after lunch on the third day.

Close of play: First day, Glamorgan 272-9 (S. D. Thomas 10*, S. L. Watkin 0*); Second day, Middlesex 251-5 (A. R. C. Fraser 5*, K. R. Brown 4*).

Glamorgan

S. P. James c Brown b Fraser	3	– lbw b Fraser	2
H. Morris c Kallis b Hewitt	16	– lbw b Fraser	5
A. Dale c Kallis b Fraser	0	– c and b Hewitt	2
*M. P. Maynard c Brown b Hewitt	59	– lbw b Fraser	0
P. A. Cottey c Weekes b Johnson	19	– lbw b Hewitt	12
R. D. B. Croft c Brown b Fraser	82	– lbw b Hewitt	0
G. P. Butcher c Weekes b Hewitt	21	– b Hewitt	0
†A. D. Shaw b Fraser	0	– c Gatting b Hewitt	1
Waqar Younis c Fraser b Tufnell	26	– lbw b Fraser	2
S. D. Thomas not out	11	– not out	0
S. L. Watkin c Brown b Johnson	4	– c Brown b Hewitt	7
B 19, l-b 7, w 8, n-b 6	40		

1/10 2/26 3/26 4/64 5/148	281	1/2 2/7 3/7 4/11 5/11	31
6/216 7/217 8/240 9/269		6/11 7/21 8/24 9/24	

Bonus points – Glamorgan 2, Middlesex 4.

Bowling: *First Innings*—Fraser 24-4-68-4; Hewitt 23-3-88-3; Kallis 2-2-0-0; Johnson 20-5-55-2; Tufnell 14-4-31-1; Dutch 9-2-13-0. *Second Innings*—Fraser 8-2-17-4; Hewitt 8-4-14-6.

Middlesex

P. N. Weekes c Thomas b Watkin	3	R. L. Johnson c Maynard b Waqar Younis	6
J. H. Kallis c Maynard b Watkin	96	J. P. Hewitt not out	15
*M. R. Ramprakash c Shaw b Watkin	63	P. C. R. Tufnell b Thomas	21
M. W. Gatting c Shaw b Thomas	28		
J. C. Pooley lbw b Croft	40	L-b 15, w 4, n-b 4	23
A. R. C. Fraser c Shaw b Watkin	8		
†K. R. Brown lbw b Thomas	12	1/5 2/165 3/172 4/237 5/243	319
K. P. Dutch c Shaw b Thomas	4	6/259 7/265 8/272 9/278	

Bonus points – Middlesex 3, Glamorgan 4.

Bowling: Waqar Younis 22-2-89-1; Watkin 27-12-43-4; Thomas 21.2-5-52-4; Croft 27-3-90-1; Butcher 5-1-21-0; Dale 3-1-9-0.

Umpires: T. E. Jesty and R. A. White.

At Liverpool, June 18, 19, 20, 21. GLAMORGAN beat LANCASHIRE by 221 runs.

GLAMORGAN v SUSSEX

At Swansea, June 26, 27, 28. Glamorgan won by 234 runs. Glamorgan 20 pts, Sussex 4 pts. Toss: Sussex.

Glamorgan continued their extraordinary sequence of low-scoring matches and won before lunch on the third day. Since being bowled out themselves for 31 two weeks earlier, they had dismissed the opposition in three consecutive innings for a combined total of 172. Waqar Younis made his figures in his last two innings 15 for 42 as Sussex crumpled to 54 all out, 118 behind Glamorgan. With damp air and a damp pitch, Waqar was unplayable. James and Maynard then put on 119 for the third wicket, a remarkable effort given that no one else scored double figures. Maynard left Sussex 302 to win, and they crashed again, this time to Thomas and Croft. For the third successive Saturday afternoon, Glamorgan were able to forget cricket and watch the Lions' rugby fixture on TV. The umpires marked the pitch "below average", but heavy rain had hampered preparations, and Moores, the Sussex captain, offered no excuses. He said the pitch was the same for both teams and added: "We were thoroughly outplayed."

Close of play: First day, Glamorgan 114-5 (R. D. B. Croft 22*, A. D. Shaw 4*); Second day, Sussex 10-0 (M. T. E. Peirce 1*, K. Greenfield 9*).

Glamorgan

S. P. James c Moores b Kirtley	48	– not out	82
H. Morris lbw b Kirtley	11	– b Drakes	3
A. Dale c Moores b Kirtley	0	– c M. Newell b Drakes	6
*M. P. Maynard c Moores b Robinson	15	– run out	61
P. A. Cottey lbw b Robinson	0	– c Moores b Robinson	0
R. D. B. Croft c Athey b Robinson	24	– lbw b Robinson	6
†A. D. Shaw not out	34	– lbw b Khan	0
Waqar Younis c and b Kirtley	7	– c Drakes b Khan	5
S. D. Thomas b Kirtley	0	– b Robinson	0
S. L. Watkin c Greenfield b Drakes	10	– lbw b Robinson	3
D. A. Cosker b Kirtley	1	– not out	0
L-b 2, w 2, n-b 18	22	L-b 3, w 2, n-b 12	17

1/30 2/30 3/52 4/52 5/98   172   1/11 2/29 3/148   (9 wkts dec.) 183
6/127 7/138 8/140 9/171   4/150 5/168 6/171
7/177 8/178 9/182

Bonus points – Sussex 4.

Bowling: *First Innings*—Drakes 16–3–56–1; Kirtley 22.5–4–60–6; Robinson 15–0–54–3. *Second Innings*—Drakes 11–2–47–2; Kirtley 9–1–37–0; Robinson 15.4–4–42–4; Khan 12–2–44–2; K. Newell 1–0–10–0.

Sussex

M. T. E. Peirce lbw b Croft	6	– lbw b Croft	16
K. Greenfield c Croft b Waqar Younis	0	– c Cottey b Watkin	14
N. R. Taylor c Shaw b Waqar Younis	0	– lbw b Watkin	0
C. W. J. Athey lbw b Croft	7	– lbw b Thomas	7
K. Newell b Waqar Younis	11	– c Croft b Thomas	3
M. Newell b Waqar Younis	2	– b Croft	2
*†P. Moores c Croft b Waqar Younis	3	– lbw b Croft	1
V. C. Drakes c Croft b Waqar Younis	0	– c Maynard b Thomas	9
A. A. Khan lbw b Waqar Younis	0	– c Cottey b Thomas	6
M. A. Robinson not out	15	– b Thomas	0
R. J. Kirtley lbw b Waqar Younis	2	– not out	1
L-b 8	8	L-b 4, w 4	8

1/5 2/5 3/11 4/16 5/19   54   1/18 2/18 3/45 4/45 5/49   67
6/31 7/31 8/35 9/42   6/51 7/60 8/60 9/66

Bonus points – Glamorgan 4.

Bowling: *First Innings*—Waqar Younis 11.5–4–17–8; Watkin 3–2–4–0; Croft 8–2–25–2. *Second Innings*—Waqar Younis 7–2–17–0; Watkin 8–2–13–2; Thomas 9.4–3–24–5; Croft 8–5–9–3.

Umpires: J. W. Holder and P. Willey.

GLAMORGAN v GLOUCESTERSHIRE

At Swansea, July 2, 3, 4, 5. Glamorgan won by ten wickets. Glamorgan 24 pts, Gloucestershire 3 pts. Toss: Gloucestershire.

Despite a swelling chorus of complaints about worsening facilities at the ground, Glamorgan had no grumbles on the field at Swansea, and they beat the rain to secure their second win of the festival. After four sessions in which only seven overs could be bowled, their batsmen took over; Maynard hit 17 fours in his 98 and shared a stand of 223 with Morris, who ground his way to 173 in five and three-quarter hours. Then Gloucestershire offered limited resistance against accurate bowling on a two-paced pitch. The follow-on was enforced, and Cosker took four wickets in the second innings to finish with seven in the match. Needing only 48 in 21 overs, Glamorgan won with 25 balls to spare when James hit a six into the members' enclosure, striking a spectator on the head. He needed hospital treatment.

Close of play: First day, Glamorgan 19-0 (S. P. James 6*, H. Morris 10*); Second day, Glamorgan 319-3 (H. Morris 158*, P. A. Cottey 26*); Third day, Gloucestershire 54-1 (N. J. Trainor 20*, R. P. Davis 2*).

Glamorgan

S. P. James c Lynch b Lewis	8	– not out	26
H. Morris lbw b Lewis	173	– not out	24
A. Dale c Russell b Lewis	0		
*M. P. Maynard c and b Young	98		
P. A. Cottey not out	76		
G. P. Butcher c Ball b Alleyne	0		
†A. D. Shaw not out	16		
B 4, l-b 3, w 12, n-b 10	29	W 2	2

1/28 2/40 3/263 4/347 5/350   (5 wkts dec.) 400   (no wkt) 52

Waqar Younis, S. D. Thomas, S. L. Watkin and D. A. Cosker did not bat.

Bonus points – Glamorgan 4, Gloucestershire 2.

Bowling: *First Innings*—Lewis 26–3–87–3; Young 18–4–59–1; Sheeraz 7–0–40–0; Ball 19–1–76–0; Alleyne 17–1–61–1; Davis 15.3–0–70–0. *Second Innings*—Lewis 4–1–12–0; Young 5–1–18–0; Davis 4.5–1–18–0; Ball 3–2–4–0.

Gloucestershire

A. J. Wright c Butcher b Cosker	32	– c Cottey b Cosker	28
N. J. Trainor c James b Waqar Younis	6	– c Shaw b Thomas	37
T. H. C. Hancock c Shaw b Watkin	21	– (4) b Thomas	1
M. A. Lynch c Maynard b Watkin	38	– (5) lbw b Cosker	8
S. Young lbw b Waqar Younis	38	– (6) c Maynard b Cosker	3
*M. W. Alleyne c Cottey b Cosker	0	– (7) lbw b Watkin	42
†R. C. Russell c Cottey b Cosker	22	– (8) c Maynard b Cosker	27
M. C. J. Ball c Thomas b Watkin	12	– (9) b Waqar Younis	41
R. P. Davis lbw b Waqar Younis	2	– (3) c Morris b Thomas	15
J. Lewis c Shaw b Thomas	20	– b Waqar Younis	10
K. P. Sheeraz not out	12	– not out	3
L-b 11	11	B 4, l-b 5, w 5, n-b 4	18

1/19 2/46 3/93 4/101 5/102   214   1/43 2/84 3/89 4/94 5/102   233
6/162 7/170 8/182 9/182   6/103 7/169 8/183 9/222

Bonus points – Gloucestershire 1, Glamorgan 4.

Bowling: *First Innings*—Waqar Younis 15–2–55–3; Watkin 17–5–61–3; Cosker 18–1–59–3; Thomas 7.4–1–26–1; Cottey 1–0–2–0. *Second Innings*—Waqar Younis 16.1–3–40–2; Watkin 22–8–46–1; Thomas 18–4–40–3; Cosker 27–8–87–4; Butcher 1–0–2–0; Dale 4–1–9–0; Cottey 1–1–0–0.

Umpires: A. Clarkson and A. G. T. Whitehead.

At Cardiff, July 16, 17, 18. GLAMORGAN drew with AUSTRALIANS (See Australian tour section).

At Chesterfield, July 23, 24, 25, 26. GLAMORGAN drew with DERBYSHIRE.

GLAMORGAN v NOTTINGHAMSHIRE

At Colwyn Bay, July 31, August 1, 2, 4. Drawn. Glamorgan 11 pts, Nottinghamshire 6 pts. Toss: Nottinghamshire.

An unbroken ninth-wicket partnership of 80 between Tolley and Hindson thwarted Glamorgan's bid to open up a 23-point lead at the top of the Championship table. The first day and a half were lost to rain, but Glamorgan had gained a first-innings lead of 151 and maximum bonus points by the end of the third day. James struck 162, the highest first-class century on the ground and his third in successive seasons against Nottinghamshire. On the final day, Croft, who had been helicoptered in after his induction into the Bardic Circle at the National Eisteddfod, captured two early wickets. But Tolley, who batted for three and a half hours, and Hindson were less obliging. Philip North, the left-arm spinner who captains the Wales Minor Counties team, was called up by Glamorgan for the first time in eight years, but he was dropped again after arriving at the ground late. He said his wake-up call had not come through.

Close of play: First day, No play; Second day, Nottinghamshire 165-9 (W. M. Noon 14*, M. N. Bowen 1*); Third day, Nottinghamshire 6-0 (M. P. Dowman 5*, R. T. Robinson 1*).

Nottinghamshire

M. P. Dowman c Dale b Waqar Younis	62	– lbw b Waqar Younis	6
R. T. Robinson b Waqar Younis	8	– b Croft	4
N. J. Astle c Shaw b Watkin	47	– c Morris b Watkin	13
*P. Johnson lbw b Watkin	1	– c Maynard b Croft	6
G. F. Archer c and b Croft	10	– c Dale b Croft	40
U. Afzaal c Cottey b Croft	3	– b Thomas	10
C. M. Tolley b Thomas	10	– not out	73
†W. M. Noon not out	29	– lbw b Butcher	17
K. P. Evans lbw b Croft	1	– b Butcher	0
J. E. Hindson b Waqar Younis	0	– not out	42
M. N. Bowen c Shaw b Thomas	19		
B 1, l-b 6, n-b 5	12	B 14, l-b 10, w 2, n-b 2	28

1/21 2/71 3/79 4/108 5/112   202   1/8 2/14 3/26 4/32   (8 wkts) 239
6/131 7/158 8/160 9/163   5/74 6/110 7/159 8/159

Bonus points – Nottinghamshire 1, Glamorgan 4.

Bowling: *First Innings*—Waqar Younis 18–3–66–3; Watkin 12–3–46–2; Croft 24–8–46–3; Thomas 11.1–2–37–2. *Second Innings*—Waqar Younis 19–3–62–1; Croft 30–5–52–3; Watkin 18–8–27–1; Thomas 15–2–55–1; Butcher 9–2–18–2; Maynard 1–0–1–0.

Glamorgan

S. P. James c Hindson b Evans	162	G. P. Butcher not out	48
H. Morris c Evans b Hindson	12	†A. D. Shaw not out	31
A. Dale lbw b Astle	20	B 14, l-b 12, w 4, n-b 6	36
*M. P. Maynard c Robinson b Afzaal	13		
P. A. Cottey lbw b Astle	0	1/57 2/112 3/139 (6 wkts dec.) 353	
R. D. B. Croft b Evans	31	4/140 5/236 6/287	

Waqar Younis, S. D. Thomas and S. L. Watkin did not bat.

Bonus points – Glamorgan 4, Nottinghamshire 2.

Bowling: Evans 17–1–52–2; Bowen 10–1–48–0; Tolley 13–3–44–0; Hindson 20–0–101–1; Astle 10–1–39–2; Afzaal 13–4–43–1.

Umpires: H. D. Bird and G. Sharp.

At Worcester, August 15, 16, 17, 18. GLAMORGAN lost to WORCESTERSHIRE by 54 runs.

GLAMORGAN v NORTHAMPTONSHIRE

At Abergavenny, August 20, 21, 22, 23. Glamorgan won by six wickets. Glamorgan 24 pts, Northamptonshire 5 pts. Toss: Northamptonshire.

Glamorgan returned to the top of the table with the help of the prolific James, who became the 11th player from the county to score two centuries in a Championship game. Morris had turned an ankle in pre-match practice, and Cosker and Evans were summoned from a Second Eleven match as cover. But the umpires led the players from the field after just two overs of play. They had noticed that the stumps were four inches out of line, and 27 minutes were added at the end of the day to make up for the time spent re-aligning the creases. When play resumed, Curran dominated the opening exchanges with his career-best 159, but James gave Glamorgan the lead, and then Waqar burst through with three wickets in eight balls. At 61 for five, Northamptonshire were in danger of losing in three days. Sales and Ripley managed to hang on till the next morning and gave their bowlers a glimmer of hope, but James's disciplined 113 saved Maynard, who had dislocated a finger, and Evans, suffering from a back spasm, from having to bat.

Close of play: First day, Northamptonshire 302-8 (K. M. Curran 159*, M. K. Davies 0*); Second day, Glamorgan 232-3 (S. D. Thomas 11*); Third day, Northamptonshire 146-5 (D. J. Sales 56*, D. Ripley 36*).

Northamptonshire

D. J. Roberts lbw b Waqar Younis	14	– (2) c Cosker b Watkin	11
R. J. Warren c Shaw b Watkin	4	– (1) c Maynard b Waqar Younis	12
A. Fordham c Maynard b Thomas	22	– c Evans b Watkin	25
*R. J. Bailey c James b Croft	20	– c Shaw b Waqar Younis	2
K. M. Curran b Croft	159	– c James b Waqar Younis	2
D. J. Sales c Maynard b Waqar Younis	22	– c sub b Waqar Younis	103
†D. Ripley c Shaw b Waqar Younis	5	– lbw b Croft	58
J. P. Taylor c Shaw b Croft	28	– c Shaw b Waqar Younis	0
Mohammad Akram run out	22	– c Waqar Younis b Croft	1
M. K. Davies lbw b Waqar Younis	17	– not out	1
J. F. Brown not out	8	– b Waqar Younis	0
L-b 7, n-b 2	9	L-b 4	4

1/18 2/18 3/51 4/123 5/176	330	1/24 2/31 3/33 4/35 5/61	219
6/182 7/261 8/298 9/302		6/192 7/193 8/198 9/218	

Bonus points – Northamptonshire 3, Glamorgan 4.

Bowling: *First Innings*—Waqar Younis 22.2–6–78–4; Watkin 22–6–49–1; Croft 28–5–68–3; Thomas 15–1–80–1; Dale 4–0–17–0; Cosker 15–5–31–0. *Second Innings*—Waqar Younis 22.2–4–56–6; Watkin 21–6–41–2; Croft 21–5–54–2; Thomas 4–0–24–0; Cosker 11–4–40–0.

Glamorgan

S. P. James run out	103	– lbw b Brown	113
A. W. Evans c Curran b Davies	31		
A. Dale c Bailey b Brown	71	– c Warren b Davies	36
S. D. Thomas c Bailey b Davies	19		
M. J. Powell not out	41	– not out	10
*M. P. Maynard c Fordham b Bailey	58		
R. D. B. Croft c Fordham b Bailey	15	– (6) not out	8
†A. D. Shaw (did not bat)		– (2) c Bailey b Brown	11
Waqar Younis (did not bat)		– (4) c Brown b Davies	9
B 1, l-b 13, w 2	16	B 1, l-b 2, w 5, n-b 2	10

1/84 2/200 3/232 4/246   (6 wkts dec.) 354   1/40 2/163 3/179 4/183   (4 wkts) 197
5/332 6/354

S. L. Watkin and D. A. Cosker did not bat.

Bonus points – Glamorgan 4, Northamptonshire 2.

Bowling: *First Innings*—Mohammad Akram 12–1–57–0; Taylor 13–1–49–0; Curran 9–4–17–0; Davies 29–5–109–2; Brown 24–3–90–1; Bailey 2.2–0–18–2. *Second Innings*—Mohammad Akram 11–2–46–0; Taylor 6–0–21–0; Brown 18–3–68–2; Davies 13.1–0–59–2.

Umpires: G. I. Burgess and A. Clarkson.

At Leicester, August 27, 28, 29, 30. GLAMORGAN drew with LEICESTERSHIRE.

At The Oval, September 2, 3, 4, 5. GLAMORGAN drew with SURREY.

GLAMORGAN v ESSEX

At Cardiff, September 10, 11, 12, 13. Glamorgan won by seven wickets. Glamorgan 24 pts, Essex 4 pts. Toss: Glamorgan.

Glamorgan took maximum points and regained the Championship lead from Kent, who drew with Yorkshire. Needing 149 to win, they stumbled to 26 for three, but Maynard and Cottey took command, and settled the nerves of a tense Saturday afternoon crowd and an even tenser dressing-room. Glamorgan picked up maximum batting points after substantial partnerships for the second and fourth wickets, and then dismissed Essex in only 43.2 overs. Stuart Law struck a rapid 85 from 63 balls but Essex, who were 192 runs adrift in the first innings, followed on after tea on the second day. They applied themselves far better in the second innings with four of the first six batsmen scoring half-centuries. Grayson resisted for nearly five hours but ran out of partners as Watkin, armed with the second new ball, took the last two wickets on the fourth morning to finish with five.

Close of play: First day, Glamorgan 307-7 (S. D. Thomas 4*, Waqar Younis 1*); Second day, Essex 59-1 (P. J. Prichard 31*, N. Hussain 23*); Third day, Essex 320-8 (A. P. Grayson 83*, A. P. Cowan 13*).

Glamorgan

S. P. James c Robinson b Ilott	2	– b Cowan	4
H. Morris lbw b Ilott	82	– c Hyam b Cowan	0
A. Dale b Ilott	49	– b Such	12
*M. P. Maynard c and b D. R. Law	71	– not out	75
P. A. Cottey c Prichard b D. R. Law	46	– not out	35
R. D. B. Croft c Hussain b Grayson	16		
†A. D. Shaw c Cowan b Grayson	6		
S. D. Thomas b D. R. Law	39		
Waqar Younis c S. G. Law b D. R. Law	17		
S. L. Watkin run out	3		
D. A. Cosker not out	0		
B 5, l-b 14, w 5, n-b 6	30	B 4, l-b 12, n-b 8	24

1/8 2/146 3/149 4/276 5/277   361   1/4 2/13 3/26   (3 wkts) 150
6/286 7/301 8/337 9/356

Bonus points – Glamorgan 4, Essex 4.

Bowling: *First Innings*—Ilott 22–4–65–3; Cowan 5–1–26–0; D. R. Law 24.4–6–69–4; Grayson 33–7–84–2; Such 31–6–82–0; S. G. Law 4–0–16–0. *Second Innings*—Ilott 13.1–2–43–0; Cowan 11–4–14–2; Such 12–2–35–1; D. R. Law 4–0–19–0; Grayson 4–0–23–0.

Essex

*P. J. Prichard c James b Waqar Younis	6	– c James b Croft	51
D. D. J. Robinson c Shaw b Watkin	12	– c Maynard b Watkin	0
N. Hussain c Cottey b Waqar Younis	0	– b Watkin	53
S. G. Law c Dale b Watkin	85	– c Shaw b Watkin	9
R. C. Irani lbw b Thomas	7	– b Waqar Younis	50
A. P. Grayson lbw b Thomas	0	– not out	98
D. R. Law c Morris b Watkin	15	– b Waqar Younis	1
†B. J. Hyam run out	10	– lbw b Thomas	26
M. C. Ilott not out	26	– b Croft	7
A. P. Cowan b Waqar Younis	0	– c Shaw b Watkin	13
P. M. Such c sub b Croft	0	– c Croft b Watkin	5
B 1, l-b 7	8	B 9, l-b 16, n-b 2	27

1/6 2/6 3/70 4/79 5/79   169   1/2 2/104 3/123 4/130 5/211   340
6/122 7/133 8/156 9/156   6/215 7/277 8/292 9/320

Bonus points – Glamorgan 4.

Bowling: *First Innings*—Waqar Younis 11–2–31–3; Watkin 14–2–68–3; Croft 8.2–2–10–1; Thomas 8–0–48–2; Cosker 2–1–4–0. *Second Innings*—Waqar Younis 22–2–82–2; Watkin 26.4–9–68–5; Croft 31–6–86–2; Cosker 11–3–25–0; Thomas 18–0–54–1.

Umpires: J. H. Harris and R. Julian.

At Taunton, September 18, 19, 20. GLAMORGAN beat SOMERSET by ten wickets.

PROFESSIONAL CRICKETERS' ASSOCIATION AWARDS

The Professional Cricketers' Association chose Steve James of Glamorgan as the winner of the Reg Hayter Cup for Player of the Year in 1997. The John Arlott Cup for Young Player of the Year went to Ben Hollioake of Surrey. Alistair Brown of Surrey won the Slazenger Sheer Instinct Individual Performance Award, for his 203 against Hampshire in the AXA Life League. Peter Willey was awarded the Harold Goldblatt Umpires' Cup. Lord Cowdrey was given the Waterford Crystal PCA Special Merit Award for his achievements in the game.

GLOUCESTERSHIRE

Mike Smith

Patron: Lord Vestey
President: J. A. Horne
Chairman: J. C. Higson
Chief Executive: C. L. Sexstone
Cricket Secretary: P. G. M. August
Captain: M. W. Alleyne
Coach: A. W. Stovold
Head Groundsman: D. Bridle
Scorer: K. T. Gerrish

It is rather too facile just to offer a Gloucestershire groan at the county's final seventh position in the table, the lowest place they occupied all season, and share Nevil Road angst over the way the team had trifled with local emotions.

The fact was that Gloucestershire intermittently headed an exciting, open race for the pennant. This they did without their best batsman and bowler from the previous year, Andrew Symonds and Courtney Walsh. It was a thoroughly unlikely accomplishment by a side that, at least theoretically, possessed modest skills and suspect balance. No one really gave them much chance of making any kind of impact in 1997. The pundits dismissed them; the bookies were generous at their expense.

Gloucestershire did not win anything after their visit to Hove in mid-August. Otherwise, in a genuine conflict with logic and almost every prediction, the Championship could well have been theirs. So, ignoring the end-of-season decline, what were the club's unscheduled virtues? With an attack which leaned unashamedly on Mike Smith – there had seemed at the outset of the summer a worrying, unproven back-up for him – the county ended with the same number of bowling points as Kent, and more than anyone else apart from Somerset.

Smith, seemingly frail of frame, took more wickets than any other bowler in the country. He was second in the national averages. His fleeting Test appearance came at Headingley where, dispassionate observers said, dressing-room psychology worked against him. He had a vital catch dropped, and prejudice in some quarters appeared to imply he was no more than a useful county swing bowler. Yet much of his form over the season, including three ten-wicket hauls, against Hampshire, Yorkshire and Derbyshire, afforded a different judgment.

There was at times admirable support for him. Jon Lewis sustained his progress, worthy of the new ball and 54 wickets. Mark Alleyne came next, using himself wisely and effectively, entrapping the over-confident batsman by the technique of accurate medium-pace which he has conscientiously refined over recent years. The slow bowling was nondescript in a season singularly unhelpful to the spinners. Martyn Ball and Richard Davis had their best match at Hove, where they briefly spun their county back to the top position. Overall, there were meagre rewards, though Ball compensated with nearly 600 runs, often brightly made, from down the order.

Gloucestershire were too often let down by their batsmen. Too rarely was there a formidable early stand or two to send them confidently on their way. Indeed, Jack Russell topped the averages. He scored runs, stubbornly or breezily according to the needs of the team, with the physical contortions at the crease that garnish the appeal of his endeavour. For the first time, he passed 1,000 runs. He kept wicket as efficiently as he has ever done. Some of his catches were breathtakingly agile, but the essentials of his game were his intuition and intense concentration. It would have been unthinkable if he had not been named again for the winter tour. And he emphasised the point in his final game by making the England captain, Mike Atherton, the 1,000th victim of his career.

The recall of Courtney Walsh, absent in 1997 because of West Indies commitments, as next year's overseas player was understandable. Even at 35, he was still seen as a match-winner. But it was not easy for the committee. The Australian left-hander, Shaun Young, was keen to come back. He was only just short of 1,000 runs in his maiden season. His double-hundred at Cheltenham was a truly superb innings to live in memory with some of the timeless ones on the College ground. Then he rounded off his English summer with the most proficient of centuries against Lancashire. His lively medium-paced bowling could be, as at The Oval and Leeds, a distinct bonus.

Captaincy was one of the strengths of the county's year. Alleyne knew he had not been the first choice. He accepted with boyish enthusiasm when he was invited to be the leader, after Russell had demanded an unprecedented degree of control, a condition the club rejected. Alleyne did the job with quiet authority, as well as a tactical sense that grew as the summer went on. He was not afraid to consult others, but mostly the decisions were his own. Again, he played beautifully at Cheltenham; again, he proved himself one of English cricket's most reliable all-rounders. There was surely a case for some kind of national recognition when the tour teams were announced.

He experimented, not always successfully, with the top-order batsmen. Tim Hancock held down a place, was capable of playing an attractive innings, and yet should still have scored more runs. Less successful were the majority of the others with whom he competed for selection. Rob Cunliffe receded as the year went on. Nick Trainor did not live up to his late-May century against the Australians. Matt Windows and Bobby Dawson played in no more than eight matches each. Monte Lynch disappeared from the county scene after a career laced with appealing but inherently fallible strokeplay.

The Bristol headquarters, inclined to be maligned for its sombre countenance, demonstrated several times that it could put on its finery and create a tingling, nostalgic atmosphere. Drama and rebukes were introduced during the match with Middlesex in June, when 25 wickets fell in a day and the "pitch jury" arrived at the bidding of Harry Brind to administer a suspended sentence.

Despite the paucity of points in the closing weeks, everyone seemed to agree that Gloucestershire had done better than expected. Team spirit remained visibly strong. This was evident, for instance, when David Lawrence made his four appearances, two in May and the others at the end of the season. His eight wickets earned him the encouragement and acclaim of a goal scorer at Wembley. The knee, so seriously injured in New Zealand, did not noticeably trouble him. But there were other aches and strains. His county return was a sentimental one and no more than a qualified success. As one knew, there was absolutely nothing wrong with his heart. – DAVID FOOT.

GLOUCESTERSHIRE 1997

[*Bill Smith*]

Back row: R. C. J. Williams, J. Lewis, R. P. Davis, M. J. Cawdron, N. J. Trainor, R. J. Cunliffe, M. G. N. Windows. *Middle row:* A. Jenkins (*Second Eleven scorer*), M. C. J. Ball, D. R. Hewson, C. M. W. Read, K. P. Sheeraz, T. H. C. Hancock, R. I. Dawson, M. A. Lynch, S. Young, K. T. Gerrish (*First Eleven scorer*). *Front row:* R. C. Russell, A. J. Wright, M. W. Alleyne (*captain*), D. V. Lawrence, A. W. Stovold (*director of coaching*), A. M. Smith. *Inset:* M. J. Church.

GLOUCESTERSHIRE RESULTS

All first-class matches – Played 19: Won 6, Lost 6, Drawn 7.
County Championship matches – Played 17: Won 6, Lost 6, Drawn 5.
Competition placings – Britannic Assurance County Championship, 7th;
NatWest Trophy, 2nd round; Benson and Hedges Cup, 3rd in Group C;
AXA Life League, 11th.

COUNTY CHAMPIONSHIP AVERAGES

BATTING

Cap		M	I	NO	R	HS	100s	50s	Avge	Ct/St
1985	R. C. Russell†.......	17	26	5	999	103*	1	8	47.57	44/4
1990	M. W. Alleyne	17	27	3	1,017	169	1	8	42.37	13
1997	S. Young§...........	16	27	3	980	237	2	5	40.83	9
	T. H. C. Hancock	17	28	3	787	100*	1	4	31.48	9
	R. I. Dawson........	7	12	0	314	100	1	1	26.16	3
1995	M. A. Lynch	12	19	1	465	64	0	3	25.83	9
	M. G. N. Windows†..	7	13	0	334	84	0	2	25.69	6
1996	M. C. J. Ball†.......	16	25	3	512	41	0	0	23.27	24
1987	A. J. Wright	12	21	3	400	79	0	1	22.22	10
	R. J. Cunliffe........	8	13	1	212	49	0	0	17.66	4
	J. Lewis............	13	17	6	186	30	0	0	16.90	2
	D. R. Hewson†......	3	4	0	56	42	0	0	14.00	3
	N. J. Trainor	12	22	1	288	40	0	0	13.71	3
1995	A. M. Smith	15	22	8	152	41*	0	0	10.85	3
1985	D. V. Lawrence†	4	6	3	32	23*	0	0	10.66	1
	R. P. Davis	7	10	0	93	39	0	0	9.30	7

Also batted: M. J. Church (1 match) 4, 16; K. P. Sheeraz (2 matches) 12*, 3*. J. M. M. Averis† (1 match) did not bat (1 ct).

* *Signifies not out.* † *Born in Gloucestershire.* § *Overseas player.*

BOWLING

	O	M	R	W	BB	5W/i	Avge
A. M. Smith	450.2	111	1,281	78	6-45	5	16.42
J. Lewis	365.5	86	1,211	48	6-50	3	25.22
M. W. Alleyne	329.1	80	1,051	40	6-64	3	26.27
R. P. Davis	201	67	486	16	4-35	0	30.37
S. Young	360.3	98	1,000	30	4-26	0	33.33
M. C. J. Ball	418.5	114	1,082	22	5-66	1	49.18

Also bowled: J. M. M. Averis 17–4–76–0; R. I. Dawson 3–0–22–0; T. H. C. Hancock 76.5–17–300–4; D. V. Lawrence 86–9–359–8; K. P. Sheeraz 7–0–40–0; N. J. Trainor 18–5–81–0; M. G. N. Windows 6–1–47–0.

COUNTY RECORDS

Highest score for:	318*	W. G. Grace v Yorkshire at Cheltenham	1876
Highest score against:	296	A. O. Jones (Nottinghamshire) at Nottingham .	1903
Best bowling for:	10-40	E. G. Dennett v Essex at Bristol	1906
Best bowling against:	10-66	A. A. Mailey (Australians) at Cheltenham ...	1921
Highest total for:	653-6 dec.	v Glamorgan at Bristol	1928
Highest total against:	774-7 dec.	by Australians at Bristol	1948
Lowest total for:	17	v Australians at Cheltenham	1896
Lowest total against:	12	by Northamptonshire at Gloucester	1907

At Leicester, April 23, 24, 25, 26. GLOUCESTERSHIRE drew with LEICESTERSHIRE.

GLOUCESTERSHIRE v HAMPSHIRE

At Bristol, May 7, 8, 9, 10. Gloucestershire won by six wickets. Gloucestershire 24 pts, Hampshire 6 pts. Toss: Hampshire.

The match was special because of the return of David Lawrence, defying medical opinion and playing in a major fixture for the first time since February 10, 1992, when he smashed his kneecap playing for England in the Wellington Test. He was as optimistic and as endearingly unco-ordinated as ever, and found life in a placid pitch. Used sparingly, he hit Kendall on the helmet and took a wicket in each innings. In terms of achievement, he was outshone by the other Gloucestershire seamers, the Tasmanian Shaun Young, who made an immediate impact on his home debut, and Mike Smith, who took a career-best ten for 106 in the match. Hampshire offered modest opposition and their cause was not helped when Keech dislocated his thumb. They were 87 behind on first innings, and then collapsed for 145 in 67 overs. Gloucestershire were left a token 59 to win, losing four wickets as they competed with the ominous rain clouds, and went top of the embryonic county table.

Close of play: First day, Hampshire 221-6 (W. S. Kendall 33*, S. D. Udal 13*); Second day, Gloucestershire 143-2 (R. J. Cunliffe 43*, M. A. Lynch 54*); Third day, Hampshire 46-3 (R. A. Smith 20*, W. S. Kendall 8*).

Hampshire

M. L. Hayden lbw b Smith	23	– (2) c Ball b Smith	0
J. S. Laney c Hancock b Lawrence	19	– (1) lbw b Smith	9
*J. P. Stephenson c Russell b Smith	19	– c Hancock b Ball	8
R. A. Smith lbw b Young	52	– c Russell b Alleyne	36
M. Keech c Russell b Hancock	46	– absent hurt	
W. S. Kendall lbw b Alleyne	47	– (5) c Russell b Lawrence	20
†A. N. Aymes lbw b Smith	8	– (6) lbw b Smith	10
S. D. Udal c and b Young	58	– (7) lbw b Smith	14
A. D. Mascarenhas c Hancock b Smith	1	– (8) c Alleyne b Smith	21
S. J. Renshaw c Russell b Young	14	– (9) lbw b Smith	7
C. A. Connor not out	12	– (10) not out	11
L-b 9, w 2, n-b 6	17	B 5, l-b 2, n-b 2	9

1/41 2/63 3/64 4/147 5/169   316   1/5 2/12 3/21 4/72 5/80   145
6/195 7/272 8/283 9/297   6/102 7/113 8/132 9/145

Bonus points – Hampshire 3, Gloucestershire 4.

Bowling: *First Innings*—Smith 28–8–61–4; Lawrence 18–1–78–1; Young 26.3–11–43–3; Ball 22–8–39–0; Alleyne 14–4–47–1; Hancock 10–2–39–1. *Second Innings*—Smith 22–5–45–6; Lawrence 8–3–15–1; Young 21–8–48–0; Ball 8–3–16–1; Alleyne 8–2–14–1.

Gloucestershire

A. J. Wright b Mascarenhas	34	– c Aymes b Renshaw	10
N. J. Trainor c Laney b Renshaw	12	– lbw b Renshaw	26
R. J. Cunliffe b Renshaw	49		
M. A. Lynch c Keech b Connor	62	– lbw b Renshaw	10
S. Young lbw b Stephenson	73	– (6) not out	4
*M. W. Alleyne lbw b Connor	62	– (5) not out	3
†R. C. Russell b Stephenson	66		
T. H. C. Hancock c sub b Connor	4	– (3) b Renshaw	5
M. C. J. Ball lbw b Stephenson	25		
A. M. Smith not out	3		
D. V. Lawrence b Stephenson	1		
B 2, l-b 2, w 6, n-b 2	12	L-b 1	1

1/28 2/72 3/151 4/175 5/273   403   1/15 2/23 3/51 4/54   (4 wkts) 59
6/331 7/341 8/386 9/401

Bonus points – Gloucestershire 4, Hampshire 3 (Score at 120 overs: 394-8).

Bowling: *First Innings*—Connor 28–4–93–3; Renshaw 25–2–73–2; Mascarenhas 20–2–65–1; Udal 19–2–59–0; Stephenson 23.1–3–81–4; Hayden 8–0–28–0. *Second Innings*—Hayden 5–0–20–0; Renshaw 6–0–30–4; Mascarenhas 1.4–0–8–0.

Umpires: G. I. Burgess and R. A. White.

At The Oval, May 14, 15, 16. GLOUCESTERSHIRE beat SURREY by nine wickets.

GLOUCESTERSHIRE v ESSEX

At Gloucester, May 21, 22, 23, 24. Drawn. Gloucestershire 9 pts, Essex 10 pts. Toss: Essex.

Essex captain Prichard was blamed for letting the match tail away into a meaningless draw, and he was not the most popular figure among those boys from King's School who had returned in search of a last-day result. A few of them had already sacrificed the blankets from their dormitories, in what has become an annual ritual at this rain-tormented fixture, to assist with the mopping-up. But the ground was not popular with Prichard either. Essex claimed that adequate covering would have allowed a prompt start; as it was, there was no play on the first day, and none until 4 p.m. on the second. After that, Gloucestershire were put in to bat and immediately ran into trouble. By the close of play they were 84 for seven; in just ten overs, Ilott had taken four for 17. This was followed by a notable recovery. Gloucestershire nearly reached 300 and Russell was set for a typical fighting hundred before he ran out of partners. He and Hancock, though both dropped, compounded Essex's frustrations. The best of the Essex batting came from Stuart Law, with Grayson a stubborn partner.

Close of play: First day, No play; Second day, Gloucestershire 84-7 (R. C. Russell 0*); Third day, Essex 136-4 (S. G. Law 60*, A. P. Grayson 15*).

Gloucestershire

A. J. Wright c Gooch b Irani	26	– not out	24
N. J. Trainor c D. R. Law b Ilott	0	– lbw b Ilott	0
R. J. Cunliffe b Ilott	0	– lbw b Ilott	0
M. A. Lynch c Gooch b Irani	15	– c Grayson b Such	20
S. Young lbw b Cowan	27	– not out	14
*M. W. Alleyne c Grayson b Ilott	16		
R. P. Davis lbw b Ilott	0		
†R. C. Russell not out	91		
T. H. C. Hancock c Grayson b Cowan	62		
M. C. J. Ball c Prichard b D. R. Law	38		
A. M. Smith lbw b D. R. Law	0		
B 1, l-b 10, w 2, n-b 2	15	L-b 2, n-b 4	6

1/3 2/3 3/30 4/43 5/80   290   1/15 2/15 3/42   (3 wkts) 64
6/80 7/84 8/192 9/290

Bonus points – Gloucestershire 2, Essex 4.

Bowling: *First Innings*—Ilott 27–7–82–4; Cowan 25–9–47–2; Irani 20–7–49–2; Such 23–5–57–0; D. R. Law 5.3–0–34–2; Grayson 3–0–10–0. *Second Innings*—Ilott 7–4–22–2; Cowan 6–6–0–0; Such 5–0–7–1; D. R. Law 5–2–29–0; S. G. Law 3–2–1–0; Grayson 3–2–3–0.

Essex

G. A. Gooch lbw b Smith	20	M. C. Ilott b Smith	16
*P. J. Prichard lbw b Young	1	A. P. Cowan b Hancock	34
N. Hussain c Russell b Smith	8	P. M. Such not out	2
S. G. Law c Cunliffe b Davis	84		
R. C. Irani b Alleyne	21	B 4, l-b 7, n-b 2	13
A. P. Grayson st Russell b Alleyne	81		
D. R. Law st Russell b Davis	24	1/10 2/25 3/36 4/72 5/177	310
†B. J. Hyam run out	6	6/217 7/236 8/263 9/298	

Bonus points – Essex 3, Gloucestershire 4.

Bowling: Smith 22–3–68–3; Young 16–4–34–1; Hancock 6.5–0–28–1; Alleyne 13–4–41–2; Ball 28–3–65–0; Davis 22–8–63–2.

Umpires: D. J. Constant and B. Leadbeater.

At Bristol, May 27, 28, 29. GLOUCESTERSHIRE drew with AUSTRALIANS (See Australian tour section).

At Leeds, June 4, 5, 6, 7. GLOUCESTERSHIRE beat YORKSHIRE by 164 runs.

GLOUCESTERSHIRE v WORCESTERSHIRE

At Bristol, June 12, 13, 14, 16. Worcestershire won by 95 runs. Worcestershire 22 pts, Gloucestershire 5 pts. Toss: Worcestershire.

Hick's first Championship hundred of 1997 brought about Worcestershire's first win. Both Hick and Curtis scored 137, leaving a demanding target of 372. Gloucestershire were let down by misjudgment, and even an air of resignation. It hardly helped when Wright was out to the first ball of the final day, and Young was recklessly run out the last ball before lunch. Lynch hit nine fours in his 37 and Russell manned the ramparts, but they could not make enough. Worcestershire's stand-in captain Rhodes appeared to miscalculate when he chose to bat first, but vindicated himself with the win, and seven catches. Both sets of batsmen struggled at first in swing bowlers' weather and Alleyne took five first-innings wickets, the last three for nought in 12 balls. Gloucestershire's reply was not that of a team temporarily leading the table, though Cunliffe drove attractively through the off side, and the last pair, Ball and Lewis, added a defiant 67.

Close of play: First day, Worcestershire 243-8 (S. R. Lampitt 51*); Second day, Worcestershire 36-0 (T. S. Curtis 23*, W. P. C. Weston 13*); Third day, Gloucestershire 9-1 (A. J. Wright 8*, J. Lewis 1*).

Worcestershire

T. S. Curtis c Wright b Lewis	1	– c Ball b Young	137
W. P. C. Weston c Lynch b Smith	0	– c Russell b Smith	14
G. A. Hick lbw b Lewis	12	– c Trainor b Ball	137
K. R. Spiring b Smith	52	– not out	33
G. R. Haynes b Young	24	– lbw b Young	0
D. A. Leatherdale c Lynch b Alleyne	5	– not out	12
V. S. Solanki c Smith b Alleyne	0		
*†S. J. Rhodes b Alleyne	78		
S. R. Lampitt c Russell b Alleyne	52		
A. Sheriyar not out	6		
R. J. Chapman c Russell b Alleyne	0		
B 4, l-b 4, w 6, n-b 6	20	B 1, l-b 12, w 2, n-b 2	17

1/1 2/5 3/19 4/60 5/65	250	1/45 2/272 (4 wkts dec.)	350
6/65 7/119 8/243 9/244		3/316 4/316	

Bonus points – Worcestershire 2, Gloucestershire 4.

Bowling: *First Innings*—Smith 20–1–46–2; Lewis 22–5–68–2; Young 18–4–55–1; Alleyne 20.5–7–41–5; Ball 15.5–5–32–0. *Second Innings*—Smith 13–4–34–1; Lewis 22–10–49–0; Young 24–6–65–2; Alleyne 21–6–55–0; Ball 28–3–111–1; Hancock 9–2–23–0.

Gloucestershire

A. J. Wright c and b Haynes	15	– c Hick b Chapman	8
N. J. Trainor c Rhodes b Lampitt	20	– lbw b Chapman	0
R. J. Cunliffe c Rhodes b Sheriyar	48	– (4) b Lampitt	14
M. A. Lynch b Chapman	31	– (5) c Rhodes b Leatherdale	37
S. Young b Leatherdale	0	– (6) run out	38
*M. W. Alleyne c Rhodes b Chapman	6	– (7) b Haynes	32
†R. C. Russell c Rhodes b Lampitt	6	– (8) c Weston b Lampitt	65
T. H. C. Hancock lbw b Haynes	13	– (9) c and b Lampitt	45
M. C. J. Ball not out	40	– (10) c Rhodes b Leatherdale	3
A. M. Smith b Lampitt	1	– (11) not out	0
J. Lewis c Rhodes b Leatherdale	30	– (3) c and b Chapman	12
B 2, l-b 1, n-b 16	19	B 4, l-b 6, w 2, n-b 10	22
	229		**276**

1/34 2/49 3/94 4/99 5/124   1/8 2/9 3/38 4/38 5/101
6/137 7/137 8/161 9/162   6/132 7/189 8/259 9/268

Bonus points – Gloucestershire 1, Worcestershire 4.

Bowling: *First Innings*—Chapman 16–2–69–2; Sheriyar 15–5–28–1; Solanki 1–0–7–0; Lampitt 18–6–53–3; Haynes 12–4–19–2; Leatherdale 14–3–50–2. *Second Innings*—Sheriyar 16–3–62–0; Chapman 14–2–67–3; Lampitt 16–2–63–3; Leatherdale 9–2–28–2; Haynes 10–2–24–1; Solanki 3–0–15–0; Hick 6–2–7–0.

Umpires: B. Dudleston and J. F. Steele.

GLOUCESTERSHIRE v MIDDLESEX

At Bristol, June 18, 19, 20, 21. Middlesex won by 44 runs. Middlesex 21 pts, Gloucestershire 4 pts. Toss: Gloucestershire. First-class debut: T. F. Bloomfield.

Twenty-five wickets fell in a day and a half and several players were struck – Dutch three times – on a strip of unpredictable bounce. The umpires summoned the ECB adviser on pitches, Harry Brind, who was followed by his four-man back-up team. Apart from one Second Eleven match, it was the first time that the track, relaid in 1994, had been used. There was less variable bounce by the fourth day but the visiting jury marked the pitch "poor" and imposed a suspended ten-point deduction, to be invoked if Gloucestershire produced another poor pitch within 12 months. Put in to bat, Middlesex were soon 47 for five. Ramprakash and Dutch extricated them, helped by Hewitt's late support. Smith, shortly to be named in the Old Trafford Test squad, took five for 50, but Gloucestershire's batting was grim: Wright alone held firm as they were all out for 99 in 46 overs. After the third day was washed out, Smith's partner Lewis took six for 50, but Middlesex were able to declare and set a target of 263 that was well beyond Gloucestershire on this pitch. Only Alleyne was a threat, though Smith, with a flurry of adventurous boundaries, gave Middlesex a final fright before Gatting hung on to a difficult slip catch off the persevering Johnson.

Close of play: First day, Gloucestershire 57-3 (A. J. Wright 27*, J. Lewis 0*); Second day, Middlesex 78-6 (A. R. C. Fraser 0*); Third day, No play.

Middlesex

P. N. Weekes lbw b Lewis	7	– c Russell b Lewis	10
J. H. Kallis lbw b Smith	0	– c Cunliffe b Smith	15
*M. R. Ramprakash lbw b Alleyne	75	– b Lewis	24
M. W. Gatting b Smith	6	– lbw b Lewis	4
J. C. Pooley c Russell b Smith	0	– c Alleyne b Young	11
†K. R. Brown c Alleyne b Young	3	– c Wright b Lewis	13
K. P. Dutch b Smith	79	– (8) not out	6
R. L. Johnson c and b Alleyne	13	– (9) c Wright b Lewis	31
J. P. Hewitt c Russell b Smith	38		
A. R. C. Fraser run out	0	– (7) b Lewis	6
T. F. Bloomfield not out	0		
B 8, l-b 4, n-b 4	16	L-b 2, w 2	4
	237		**124**

1/7 2/7 3/27 4/27 5/47   1/15 2/37 3/51 4/58 (8 wkts dec.) 124
6/133 7/157 8/233 9/237   5/78 6/78 7/92 8/124

Bonus points – Middlesex 1, Gloucestershire 4.

Bowling: *First Innings*—Smith 17.5–9–23–5; Lewis 16–0–72–1; Alleyne 16–7–37–2; Young 13–1–49–1; Hancock 9–2–30–0; Ball 5–1–14–0. *Second Innings*—Smith 10–2–42–1; Lewis 12.5–1–50–6; Young 8–0–26–1; Alleyne 1–0–4–0.

Gloucestershire

A. J. Wright c and b Bloomfield	40	– c Weekes b Johnson	0
N. J. Trainor c Brown b Johnson	6	– lbw b Johnson	14
R. J. Cunliffe c Brown b Fraser	5	– b Fraser	11
M. A. Lynch retired hurt	10	– (7) c and b Hewitt	2
S. Young c Weekes b Fraser	0	– c Brown b Hewitt	1
J. Lewis c Dutch b Johnson	2	– (11) c Gatting b Johnson	12
*M. W. Alleyne c Brown b Johnson	4	– (4) b Fraser	75
†R. C. Russell c Bloomfield b Johnson	2	– (6) c Ramprakash b Hewitt	20
T. H. C. Hancock b Bloomfield	0	– (8) b Bloomfield	8
M. C. J. Ball not out	8	– (9) b Bloomfield	20
A. M. Smith run out	2	– (10) not out	41
B 3, l-b 7, w 8, n-b 2	20	B 4, l-b 2, n-b 8	14

1/25 2/39 3/55 4/62 5/74   99 1/1 2/27 3/55 4/60 5/128 218
6/78 7/80 8/82 9/99   6/128 7/134 8/160 9/169

Bonus points – Middlesex 4.

In the first innings M. A. Lynch, when 5, retired hurt at 44 and resumed at 82; when 10, he retired again at 96.

Bowling: *First Innings*—Fraser 10–3–18–2; Hewitt 12–2–31–0; Johnson 17.2–6–27–4; Bloomfield 7–2–13–2. *Second Innings*—Hewitt 17–6–28–3; Johnson 22.2–5–88–3; Bloomfield 13–1–43–2; Fraser 25–11–40–2; Weekes 5–0–13–0.

Umpires: R. Julian and P. Willey.

At Luton, June 26, 27, 28, 30. GLOUCESTERSHIRE drew with NORTHAMPTONSHIRE.

At Swansea, July 2, 3, 4, 5. GLOUCESTERSHIRE lost to GLAMORGAN by ten wickets.

GLOUCESTERSHIRE v DERBYSHIRE

At Cheltenham, July 16, 17, 18. Gloucestershire won by an innings and 35 runs. Gloucestershire 24 pts, Derbyshire 4 pts. Toss: Derbyshire.

Smith, about to win an England call-up, and Young, the Tasmanian all-rounder, swept Gloucestershire to victory inside three days. Derbyshire's troubles grew: their first innings lasted only 28 overs, a pulsating, partisan start to the Cheltenham festival. They seldom looked like coping with Smith's late in-swing and bounce. He took six in the innings and – for the third time in 1997 – ten in the match, having on the first day become the first to take 50 wickets in 1997. Barnett alone knew how to play him; he scored almost half Derbyshire's first-innings total and later added an unavailing 94, sharing a century stand with Vandrau, who had been hit on the jaw on the opening day. For Gloucestershire, Young was a revelation, converting his maiden Championship hundred into 237, the highest first-class score on the College ground since W. G. Grace's 318 not out in 1876. It also equalled the county's best against Derbyshire, by Wally Hammond in 1938. Young hit 39 fours and two sixes in 350 minutes and 312 balls and added 244 with Alleyne as the bowlers struggled to find a full length. This posed Gloucestershire a problem, as home supporters began to wonder if he might return as overseas player instead of Courtney Walsh in 1998.

Close of play: First day, Gloucestershire 306-4 (S. Young 156*, M. W. Alleyne 63*); Second day, Derbyshire 174-3 (K. J. Barnett 51*, M. J. Vandrau 33*).

Derbyshire

A. S. Rollins lbw b Smith	6	– c Lynch b Alleyne	44
M. R. May c Russell b Smith	5	– lbw b Smith	46
C. J. Adams b Smith	0	– c Russell b Alleyne	0
K. J. Barnett c Russell b Lewis	58	– c Russell b Young	94
M. J. Vandrau retired hurt	1	– c Lynch b Young	54
V. P. Clarke c Young b Smith	9	– c Lewis b Young	0
†K. M. Krikken c Ball b Young	0	– c Ball b Lewis	37
*P. A. J. DeFreitas c Russell b Smith	9	– c Russell b Smith	45
A. J. Harris b Smith	0	– c Wright b Smith	2
K. J. Dean c Wright b Lewis	16	– not out	2
D. E. Malcolm not out	1	– b Smith	0
L-b 7, w 2, n-b 6	15	L-b 3, n-b 2	5

1/10 2/10 3/21 4/41 5/45   120   1/71 2/73 3/119 4/240 5/240   329
6/74 7/74 8/119 9/120   6/251 7/325 8/325 9/329

Bonus points – Gloucestershire 4.

In the first innings M. J. Vandrau retired hurt at 29.

Bowling: *First Innings*—Smith 12–1–47–6; Lewis 7–0–36–2; Young 7–1–19–1; Alleyne 2–0–11–0. *Second Innings*—Smith 21.4–5–59–4; Lewis 20–4–57–1; Alleyne 18–4–70–2; Young 12–4–25–3; Ball 29–5–80–0; Trainor 5–1–27–0; Hancock 1–0–8–0.

Gloucestershire

A. J. Wright c Adams b Malcolm	2	M. C. J. Ball c Krikken b Harris	30
N. J. Trainor c Krikken b Malcolm	0	A. M. Smith b Malcolm	1
T. H. C. Hancock c Rollins b DeFreitas	54	J. Lewis not out	0
M. A. Lynch c Dean b Malcolm	8		
S. Young lbw b DeFreitas	237	B 1, l-b 8, n-b 22	31
*M. W. Alleyne c Adams b DeFreitas	97		
†R. C. Russell c Krikken b Harris	24	1/1 2/2 3/16 4/155 5/399	484
R. I. Dawson c Krikken b Harris	0	6/434 7/439 8/483 9/484	

Bonus points – Gloucestershire 4, Derbyshire 4.

Bowling: Malcolm 28.3–2–102–4; Dean 17–1–73–0; DeFreitas 28–5–99–3; Harris 24–4–124–3; Vandrau 7–1–17–0; Clarke 10–1–60–0.

Umpires: D. R. Shepherd and J. F. Steele.

At Cheltenham, July 22. GLOUCESTERSHIRE lost to PAKISTAN A by 49 runs (See Pakistan A tour section).

GLOUCESTERSHIRE v DURHAM

At Cheltenham, July 23, 24, 25, 26. Gloucestershire won by an innings and 28 runs. Gloucestershire 24 pts, Durham 2 pts. Toss: Durham. Championship debut: J. M. M. Averis.

As so often, Cheltenham proved the highlight of Gloucestershire's season. Big crowds saw them take 48 points out of 48 and this win took them back to the top of the Championship table. Durham, dismissed inside 36 overs after choosing to bat, managed to take play into a fourth day. Gloucestershire then captured the final three wickets just before heavy rain. Once again, Alleyne played as though Cheltenham was his personal preserve. With Smith absent at the Leeds Test, he bowled with deceptive skill to take nine wickets and scored a composed 169, putting on 205 with Russell. Six of Alleyne's 13 first-class centuries have come at this ground. Despite Durham's first-day collapse, nothing much was wrong with the pitch, as Lewis and Boon showed at their second attempt. It was a frustrating debut for Oxford seamer James Averis, son of *The Guardian* sports editor: he had Roseberry walking for a catch at slip, only for umpire Balderstone to rule "not out", and had Speight caught off a no-ball.

Close of play: First day, Gloucestershire 253-5 (M. W. Alleyne 77*, R. C. Russell 17*); Second day, Durham 3-0 (J. J. B. Lewis 1*, M. A. Roseberry 2*); Third day, Durham 321-7 (N. J. Speak 13*, J. Boiling 0*).

Durham

J. J. B. Lewis lbw b Young	81	1 – b Ball	81
M. A. Roseberry c Davis b Young	9	– b Alleyne	45
J. E. Morris c Davis b Alleyne	32	– c Davis b Young	37
N. J. Speak c Wright b Alleyne	22	– (8) not out	31
*D. C. Boon c Russell b Alleyne	0	– (4) lbw b Young	66
†M. P. Speight c Ball b Lewis	0	– (5) c Russell b Lewis	44
M. J. Foster c Ball b Young	6	– (6) c Russell b Alleyne	15
J. Boiling lbw b Lewis	0	– (9) lbw b Young	7
J. Wood c Davis b Alleyne	9	– (10) c Lewis b Alleyne	6
S. J. E. Brown c Averis b Alleyne	0	– (11) c Russell b Alleyne	4
A. Walker not out	1	– (7) c Wright b Davis	10
L-b 6	6	L-b 3, w 2, n-b 6	11
	86		357

1/2 2/21 3/61 4/65 5/70   86   1/92 2/139 3/193 4/263 5/296   357
6/70 7/70 8/85 9/85   6/296 7/310 8/330 9/341

Bonus points – Gloucestershire 4.

Bowling: *First Innings*—Young 10–4–9–3; Lewis 12–4–35–2; Averis 5–2–22–0; Alleyne 8.2–2–14–5. *Second Innings*—Young 30–8–91–3; Lewis 19–5–51–1; Davis 27–11–31–1; Alleyne 22.2–6–69–4; Averis 12–2–54–0; Ball 28–9–58–1; Windows 1–1–0–0.

Gloucestershire

A. J. Wright lbw b Brown	0	†R. C. Russell not out	103
M. G. N. Windows c Speight b Brown	75	M. C. J. Ball not out	36
T. H. C. Hancock c and b Wood	7	L-b 12, w 2, n-b 14	28
M. A. Lynch lbw b Brown	1		
S. Young c Speight b Brown	52		471
*M. W. Alleyne c Roseberry b Walker	169	(6 wkts dec.)	

1/0 2/23 3/28   (6 wkts dec.) 471
4/144 5/185 6/390

J. Lewis, J. M. M. Averis and R. P. Davis did not bat.

Bonus points – Gloucestershire 4, Durham 2.

Bowling: Brown 29–7–120–4; Wood 25–7–97–1; Foster 11–1–53–0; Walker 27.1–7–109–1; Boiling 19–3–78–0; Boon 1–0–2–0.

Umpires: J. C. Balderstone and K. E. Palmer.

At Bristol, August 1, 2, 3, 4. GLOUCESTERSHIRE drew with PAKISTAN A (See Pakistan A tour section).

At Taunton, August 6, 7, 8, 9. GLOUCESTERSHIRE drew with SOMERSET.

At Hove, August 15, 16, 17, 18. GLOUCESTERSHIRE beat SUSSEX by 166 runs.

GLOUCESTERSHIRE v NOTTINGHAMSHIRE

At Bristol, August 27, 28, 29, 30. Nottinghamshire won by 21 runs. Nottinghamshire 22 pts, Gloucestershire 6 pts. Toss: Gloucestershire.

Gloucestershire started the match eight points behind Championship leaders Glamorgan so they opted, after rain and last-day negotiations, to go all out for a win which would have put them back on top. After some donated runs, Johnson declared gracefully, four short of a cheap hundred and leaving a target of 261 in 60 overs. Despite an encouraging start, Gloucestershire were all out with nine balls left. Astle was Nottinghamshire's hero. In his farewell appearance before joining New Zealand for their African tour, he took a career-best nine for 86 in the match with his accurate medium-paced swing, including four in 18 balls in the run-chase. In between, he paraded a succession of straight-driven boundaries. Nottinghamshire had been put in on a pitch which played easier than it looked. But, after Dowman and Robinson had gone for confident fifties, only Noon and the tailenders prospered as Smith had his fifth five-wicket haul of the season. Lawrence made his third appearance of 1997: his two wickets were greeted with special enthusiasm.

Close of play: First day, Nottinghamshire 255-8 (K. P. Evans 20*, M. N. Bowen 0*); Second day, Gloucestershire 84-4 (S. Young 8*, M. W. Alleyne 2*); Third day, Nottinghamshire 134-5 (P. Johnson 44*, C. M. Tolley 12*).

Nottinghamshire

M. P. Dowman c Young b Alleyne	52	– lbw b Lewis	1
R. T. Robinson c Russell b Smith	56	– c Trainor b Lewis	6
N. J. Astle lbw b Smith	0	– c Trainor b Lewis	39
*P. Johnson c and b Alleyne	6	– (6) not out	96
A. A. Metcalfe lbw b Smith	11	– c Russell b Lawrence	14
U. Afzaal c Ball b Smith	23	– (4) c Alleyne b Lawrence	14
C. M. Tolley c Russell b Lewis	0	– not out	52
†W. M. Noon c Russell b Lewis	60		
K. P. Evans lbw b Smith	23		
M. N. Bowen not out	31		
A. R. Oram b Smith	5		
B 4, l-b 11, w 6, n-b 6	27	W 4, n-b 2	6

1/101 2/102 3/109 4/132 5/141 294   1/1 2/18 3/49 (5 wkts dec.) 228
6/148 7/226 8/248 9/276   4/67 5/92

Bonus points – Nottinghamshire 2, Gloucestershire 4.

Bowling: *First Innings*—Smith 25.3–4–83–6; Lawrence 13–2–42–0; Lewis 21–4–63–2; Young 13–1–43–0; Alleyne 13–2–42–2; Ball 9–5–6–0. *Second Innings*—Smith 8–1–18–0; Lewis 10–4–42–3; Lawrence 6–0–28–2; Young 5–2–13–0; Alleyne 4–1–14–0; Trainor 6–1–38–0; Ball 5–3–7–0; Windows 5–0–47–0; Dawson 2–0–21–0.

Gloucestershire

N. J. Trainor lbw b Bowen	0	– (8) b Astle	4
M. G. N. Windows b Bowen	2	– (1) c Afzaal b Tolley	34
T. H. C. Hancock c Noon b Evans	32	– (2) c Noon b Oram	68
R. I. Dawson c Noon b Oram	25	– c Astle b Oram	17
S. Young c Bowen b Astle	56	– (3) c Johnson b Evans	14
*M. W. Alleyne b Astle	71	– (5) not out	36
†R. C. Russell lbw b Astle	9	– (6) st Noon b Astle	35
M. C. J. Ball c Astle b Evans	32	– (7) b Evans	16
A. M. Smith b Astle	3	– (10) b Astle	1
J. Lewis c Oram b Astle	12	– (9) c Dowman b Evans	1
D. V. Lawrence not out	0	– lbw b Astle	0
B 2, l-b 10, w 2, n-b 6	20	B 2, l-b 7, w 4	13

1/0 2/21 3/70 4/74 5/169 262   1/73 2/104 3/136 4/137 5/204 239
6/203 7/228 8/234 9/262   6/229 7/234 8/237 9/239

Bonus points – Gloucestershire 2, Nottinghamshire 4.

Bowling: *First Innings*—Bowen 22–7–45–2; Oram 17–4–55–1; Tolley 12–4–45–0; Evans 18–3–59–2; Astle 20.3–4–46–5. *Second Innings*—Bowen 14–1–65–0; Oram 12–2–29–2; Evans 15–2–67–3; Tolley 7–0–29–1; Astle 10.3–0–40–4.

Umpires: T. E. Jesty and D. R. Shepherd.

At Canterbury, September 2, 3, 4, 5. GLOUCESTERSHIRE lost to KENT by 272 runs.

At Birmingham, September 10, 11, 12. GLOUCESTERSHIRE lost to WARWICKSHIRE by an innings and 81 runs.

GLOUCESTERSHIRE v LANCASHIRE

At Bristol, September 18, 19, 20, 21. Drawn. Gloucestershire 9 pts, Lancashire 8 pts. Toss: Gloucestershire.

Gloucestershire had ended their agonising by re-engaging Courtney Walsh for 1998, rather than Young, who responded with a valedictory hundred. His vigilant, good-looking innings was much needed after his side lost their top three to Austin by the tenth over. But, despite earning a 59-run lead, the home batting was patchy to the end. Their second innings was a wretched 97 for seven before Alleyne and Davis, adding 119, set Lancashire a challenging 288 in 72 overs. Crawley led the way in making that look possible, but their last pair had to survive two overs for the draw. Russell, still wearing his black armband in memory of Diana, Princess of Wales (his county's former patron), three weeks after her death, made his 1,000th dismissal when he caught Atherton on the third day, while Lewis's five wickets carried him past 50 in the season for the first time. Umpires Barrie Meyer and Jack Bond were standing in their final match; with a welcome touch of sentimentality, they had been asked to supervise their old counties and were guests of honour at a farewell dinner.

Close of play: First day, Lancashire 24-2 (M. A. Atherton 17*); Second day, No play; Third day, Gloucestershire 115-7 (M. W. Alleyne 12*, R. P. Davis 6*).

Gloucestershire

D. R. Hewson c Hegg b Austin	5	– b Watkinson	42
M. G. N. Windows lbw b Austin	10	– c Hegg b Chapple	0
T. H. C. Hancock c Fairbrother b Austin	0	– c Chapple b Keedy	24
R. I. Dawson c Crawley b Shadford	26	– c Atherton b Keedy	18
S. Young c Watkinson b Chapple	100	– c and b Watkinson	7
*M. W. Alleyne c Fairbrother b Austin	11	– not out	82
†R. C. Russell b Keedy	38	– c Wood b Keedy	3
M. C. J. Ball c Shadford b Chapple	5	– c and b Watkinson	1
R. P. Davis lbw b Shadford	17	– c Hegg b Shadford	39
J. Lewis lbw b Keedy	27	– not out	5
A. M. Smith not out	0		
B 4, l-b 6, w 13	23	B 1, l-b 6	7

1/9 2/9 3/20 4/105 5/127   262   1/1 2/39 3/84   (8 wkts dec.) 228
6/189 7/205 8/214 9/254   4/92 5/93 6/96
                                       7/97 8/216

Bonus points – Gloucestershire 2, Lancashire 4.

Bowling: *First Innings*—Chapple 22–4–50–2; Austin 22–9–44–4; Shadford 7–0–50–2; Watkinson 18–7–40–0; Keedy 25.4–5–68–2. *Second Innings*—Chapple 14–1–40–1; Austin 12–6–14–0; Keedy 21–0–101–3; Shadford 7–0–31–1; Watkinson 10–2–35–3.

Lancashire

N. T. Wood c Ball b Smith	3	– c Ball b Davis	24
M. A. Atherton c Russell b Lewis	69	– b Smith	3
D. J. Shadford lbw b Smith	3	– (10) st Russell b Ball	1
J. P. Crawley lbw b Smith	9	– (3) lbw b Lewis	78
N. H. Fairbrother b Davis	61	– (4) c Dawson b Davis	43
M. E. Harvey c Russell b Alleyne	25	– (5) run out	1
*M. Watkinson b Lewis	4	– (6) run out	1
I. D. Austin c Young b Lewis	0	– (7) c Ball b Davis	53
†W. K. Hegg c Hancock b Lewis	8	– (8) c Ball b Smith	21
G. Chapple c Young b Lewis	12	– (9) not out	6
G. Keedy not out	0	– not out	0
B 2, l-b 7	9	L-b 10, n-b 4	14

1/20 2/24 3/43 4/139 5/171	203	1/15 2/64 3/146	(9 wkts) 245
6/179 7/179 8/189 9/199		4/154 5/155 6/191	
		7/232 8/243 9/244	

Bonus points – Lancashire 1, Gloucestershire 4.

Bowling: *First Innings*—Smith 20–7–35–3; Lewis 22.3–9–55–5; Ball 15–5–33–0; Alleyne 6–2–17–1; Hancock 5–2–16–0; Davis 10–1–38–1. *Second Innings*—Smith 12–4–41–2; Lewis 14–4–45–1; Davis 19–6–59–3; Ball 21–5–68–1; Alleyne 5–0–21–0; Dawson 1–0–1–0.

Umpires: J. D. Bond and B. J. Meyer.

THE WHYTE & MACKAY RANKINGS

Mark Ramprakash of Middlesex and Andrew Caddick of Somerset won £10,000 each after finishing top of the Whyte & Mackay Rankings in 1997, their third year.

Players were given a mark for their performance in each match, adjusted to take account of the strength of the opposition and the nature of the pitch. Prizes down to £1,000 were given to the top 20 in both batting and bowling. In addition, Steve James of Glamorgan won £6,000 as Cricketer of the Year, while Mark Alleyne and Jack Russell, both of Gloucestershire, took £4,000 each as Best All-Rounder and Best Wicket-Keeper/Batsman respectively; Russell won for the second year running.

Mathew Dowman of Nottinghamshire and Jamie Hewitt of Middlesex won £1,500 each as the leading batsman and bowler who had not been capped by April 1, 1997. Only England-qualified players were eligible, but special £1,000 awards were made to the leading overseas batsman and bowler.

Batting: 1 M. R. Ramprakash 496 pts; **2** G. P. Thorpe 487; **3** S. P. James 482; **4** N. Hussain 404; **5** M. P. Maynard 402; **6** J. P. Crawley 396; **7** A. J. Stewart 384; **8** D. L. Hemp 366; **9** D. Byas 365; **10** A. P. Wells 362. **Overseas award:** D. S. Lehmann 532.

Bowling: 1 A. R. Caddick 540 pts; **2** A. M. Smith 537; **3** D. R. Brown 529; **4** R. D. B. Croft 484; **5** S. L. Watkin 477; **6** G. D. Rose 463; **7** P. M. Such 455; **8** A. R. C. Fraser 429; **9** P. J. Martin 423; **10** J. P. Hewitt 419. **Overseas award:** A. A. Donald 443.

RIDLEY WICKET

No bowler took 100 first-class wickets in 1997 to claim the Ridley Wicket, a silver stump, but the Ridley Plate was awarded to Mike Smith of Gloucestershire, the leading wicket-taker with 83. He received £1,000.

HAMPSHIRE

Matthew Hayden

President: W. J. Weld
Chairman: B. G. Ford
Chairman, Cricket Committee: J. R. Gray
Chief Executive: A. F. Baker
Captain: 1997 – J. P. Stephenson
        1998 – R. A. Smith
Director of Cricket: T. M. Tremlett
Coach: M. D. Marshall
Head Groundsman: N. Gray
Scorer: V. H Isaacs

On the face of it, Hampshire marked time in 1997. They finished 14th in the County Championship and 15th in the Sunday League – the same as the previous year. But statistics can create an illusion. This was a summer of regression and bitter disappointment. Hampshire had not really expected any trophies – the club is still in transition. But they had believed some youngsters would make the leap from pretender to recognised player.

They had also hoped not to have to cope with a crisis over the captaincy. Hampshire have had only eight captains in 52 seasons since 1945. All except one of John Stephenson's post-war predecessors – his namesake Bob in 1979 – had served at least three years. Stephenson, captain since 1996, asked an enormous amount of himself: only Shaun Udal bowled more overs.

But there were times when his frustration at having to cajole the youngsters was painfully obvious. Perhaps he tried to do too much: he would have batted and bowled at both ends if he could. He certainly found it difficult to communicate what he wanted. And it was hardly a shock when he resigned at the end of the season. The fact remains that Stephenson's inheritance was a threadbare one. And there is no reason to suppose that his successor, Robin Smith, will find life any easier.

There was no lack of opportunity for batsmen. The decision to cut Paul Terry adrift had left Smith as the last of the men whose runs carried the club through the late 1980s and early 1990s, when they won four one-day titles in seven seasons. Opener Matthew Hayden was recruited from Queensland, but that left at least three places up for grabs, and at least four players – Giles White, Matthew Keech, Will Kendall and Paul Whitaker – in contention. It was also hoped that Jason Laney would fulfil the promise he displayed in the closing stages of the 1996 campaign.

Hayden's signing had been controversial. Most agreed there was a greater need for a proven strike bowler. But the club's response, when the rank and file manifested their unease at a meeting in July, was to ask, "Which bowler should we have signed?" In the end, the rebels had to concede that there was no obvious candidate, given that Waqar Younis, the initial target, had priced himself well above the limits of the county's modest purse. Hampshire managed to stop the disaffection turning into a full scale *coup d'état*, as happened next door at Sussex. Indeed, by the time the trouble surfaced, Hayden had also gone a long way towards softening the opposition. In three weeks, he made four centuries in seven innings, and led the race to reach 1,000 first-class runs. He was pipped by Glamorgan's Steve James after a washout at Chester-le-Street deprived him of two potential innings. Hayden finished with 1,446 at 53.55, and picked up £5,000 as the leading run-scorer in the Sunday League, where he confounded critics of his one-day technique by gathering 654. His aggregate in all cricket was 2,426.

If Hayden exceeded expectations, few others did. Smith was the only other batsman to approach 1,000 runs, but was 82 short. Laney periodically threatened a major innings, but was too often undone by over-ambition. The rest wasted their opportunities until White, the diffident Devonian, suggested he had finally kicked open the door. His run began in August at Lord's, where he scored 62. The next match, against Yorkshire at Portsmouth, saw him play the innings which could be his turning point. Hampshire had followed on 220 behind and faced defeat; White, supported by Stephenson, killed that threat with a mature, disciplined, maiden Championship century. From then on, he showed a new belief in his batting, and completed three more fifties. Before August, he had scored 127 runs in four matches; his last six brought him 554.

Ironically, though the batting was often frail and lacking in confidence, it earned Hampshire 42 bonus points: only the top three bettered that. But the bowlers managed only 41, fewer than any other county, and carried the bulk of the blame for the inability to improve on 1996's three Championship victories. The failure to recruit a cutting edge from overseas had left their resources slender – and, before the first Championship match, at Chelmsford, ended, they looked even slimmer. By then, the club knew pace bowler Cardigan Connor's suspect knee had not been healed by autumn surgery and winter rest and rehab. He took seven wickets in Essex's first innings, but the knee blew up in the second. The ever enthusiastic Connor played only three more Championship matches, taking four more wickets. Later, seamer James Bovill was forced to leave because of a bad back. Dimitri Mascarenhas, so successful at the end of 1996, almost disappeared from view. Too much was expected of those left to cope; by the final match, when Worcestershire visited Southampton, an attack so inexperienced it contained two debutants took just three wickets in 166 overs.

Yet, in the main, those asked to shoulder the load responded manfully, none more than Simon Renshaw, a powerfully built young man from the Wirral. Forced into the role of strike bowler, he bowled 356 overs and finished with 37 first-class wickets, to tie with Stephenson as leading wicket-taker. It was not earth-shattering – in fact, it was the lowest highest aggregate in Hampshire's history – but, provided he can find support, the experience should stand Renshaw in good stead. In the short term, the acquisition of 38-year-old Peter Hartley from Yorkshire ought to help. Off-spinner Udal had his second successive poor summer, with his 34 wickets costing more than 53 apiece, though he scored a maiden hundred in the high-scoring match against Warwickshire.

That was a prelude to Hampshire's most successful fortnight of 1997. They beat Derbyshire after Dean Jones's challenge to score 310 in 65 overs coincided with the one occasion when the Hayden–Laney opening partnership lived up to its potential – they put on 213. In the next match, Somerset ran into Kevan James at his deadliest: his left-arm swing claimed a career-best 13 for 93. That was at Basingstoke in mid-June; Hampshire waited another nine matches and three months before they won again, seeing off struggling Sussex at Southampton.

The other competitions proved even more disappointing. There were few tears when the curtain came down on the season, but it was not obvious why 1998 should be any better. – MIKE NEASOM.

HAMPSHIRE 1997

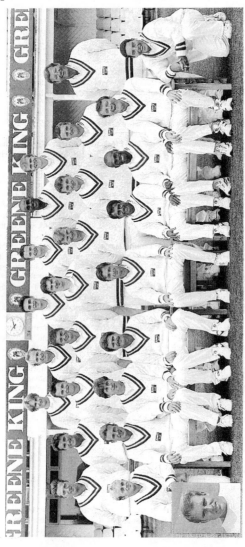

[Bill Smith]

Back row: G. R. Treagus, W. S. Kendall, S. R. G. Francis, A. D. Mascarenhas, R. R. Dibden. *Middle row:* M. Keech, G. W. White, J. N. B. Bovill, S. J. Renshaw, L. Savident, S. M. Milburn, D. A. Kenway, J. S. Laney, T. M. Tremlett (*coach*). *Front row:* P. R. Whitaker, A. N. Aymes, K. D. James, R. A. Smith, J. P. Stephenson (*captain*), R. J. Maru, C. A. Connor, S. D. Udal, M. Garaway. *Inset:* M. L. Hayden.

HAMPSHIRE RESULTS

All first-class matches – Played 19: Won 3, Lost 6, Drawn 9, Abandoned 1.
County Championship matches – Played 17: Won 3, Lost 5, Drawn 8, Abandoned 1.

Competition placings – Britannic Assurance County Championship, 14th;
NatWest Trophy, 2nd round; Benson and Hedges Cup, 5th in Group C;
AXA Life League, 15th.

COUNTY CHAMPIONSHIP AVERAGES

BATTING

Cap		M	I	NO	R	HS	100s	50s	Avge	Ct/St
1997	M. L. Hayden§	16	28	3	1,438	235*	4	7	57.52	12
	G. W. White	9	16	2	667	145	1	4	47.64	6
1985	R. A. Smith.........	13	21	1	852	154	2	4	42.60	4
	M. Keech	8	13	4	368	101*	1	1	40.88	9
1996	J. S. Laney†	13	23	0	808	95	0	6	35.13	6
	P. R. Whitaker	2	4	0	131	73	0	1	32.75	0
1995	J. P. Stephenson	15	23	3	644	114	1	1	32.20	6
1992	S. D. Udal†	16	22	3	577	117*	1	4	30.36	2
	W. S. Kendall	10	16	2	375	76	0	1	26.78	5
1989	K. D. James	9	14	2	306	85	0	4	25.50	5
	S. J. Renshaw	12	17	6	252	56	0	1	22.90	3
1986	R. J. Maru..........	4	4	1	67	36*	0	0	22.33	6
1991	A. N. Aymes†.......	16	21	3	393	96*	0	1	21.83	33/7
1988	C. A. Connor	4	4	2	34	12*	0	0	17.00	0
	S. M. Milburn	9	6	2	64	19	0	0	16.00	1
	J. N. B. Bovill	8	7	2	55	27	0	0	11.00	4
	A. D. Mascarenhas ...	5	7	1	50	21	0	0	8.33	0
	L. Savident	3	4	1	15	6	0	0	5.00	1

Also batted: S. R. G. Francis (1 match) 4, 4; T. M. Hansen (1 match) 12*, 19; D. A. Kenway† (1 match) 2, 20* (1 ct); C. Patel (1 match) 6, 3*.

* Signifies not out.   † Born in Hampshire.   § Overseas player.

BOWLING

	O	M	R	W	BB	5W/i	Avge
K. D. James	132.1	29	443	23	8-49	2	19.26
C. A. Connor	102.5	15	364	11	7-46	1	33.09
J. N. B. Bovill	207.4	30	815	23	4-62	0	35.43
S. J. Renshaw..........	329.3	57	1,171	33	5-110	1	35.48
J. P. Stephenson........	386.5	62	1,356	35	6-54	1	38.74
S. D. Udal	564.1	131	1,666	32	4-17	0	52.06
S. M. Milburn	277	41	972	18	4-38	0	54.00

Also bowled: A. N. Aymes 9–0–76–0; S. R. G. Francis 19–1–97–0; T. M. Hansen 26–10–75–0; M. L. Hayden 33–0–166–3; M. Keech 12–1–51–1; W. S. Kendall 5–0–46–0; D. A. Kenway 9–2–58–2; J. S. Laney 5–2–19–0; R. J. Maru 127–35–336–3; A. D. Mascarenhas 93.4–16–319–3; C. Patel 18–3–65–0; L. Savident 56–9–247–4; R. A. Smith 5.1–0–75–0; P. R. Whitaker 22–3–73–1; G. W. White 10.5–0–49–0.

COUNTY RECORDS

Highest score for:	316	R. H. Moore v Warwickshire at Bournemouth.	1937
Highest score against:	303*	G. A. Hick (Worcestershire) at Southampton .	1997
Best bowling for:	9-25	R. M. H. Cottam v Lancashire at Manchester .	1965
Best bowling against:	10-46	W. Hickton (Lancashire) at Manchester	1870
Highest total for:	672-7 dec.	v Somerset at Taunton....................	1899
Highest total against:	742	by Surrey at The Oval....................	1909
Lowest total for:	15	v Warwickshire at Birmingham	1922
Lowest total against:	23	by Yorkshire at Middlesbrough.............	1965

At Oxford, April 18, 19, 21. HAMPSHIRE drew with OXFORD UNIVERSITY.

At Chelmsford, April 23, 24, 25, 26. HAMPSHIRE drew with ESSEX.

At Bristol, May 7, 8, 9, 10. HAMPSHIRE lost to GLOUCESTERSHIRE by six wickets.

HAMPSHIRE v LEICESTERSHIRE

At Southampton, May 14, 15, 16, 17. Leicestershire won by five wickets. Leicestershire 23 pts, Hampshire 6 pts. Toss: Hampshire.

Leicestershire's opening bowler, Millns, scored his second first-class century to turn the course of the match. He came in with the champions in deep trouble at 157 for seven, pursuing Hampshire's 285. But, after offering a difficult chance on one, he batted impressively and added 96 with Habib and 75 for the last wicket with Brimson. His career-best 114 included two sixes and nine fours, and established a lead of 64. Hampshire had also owed much to a late stand, 66 for the eighth wicket between James and Maru. James and Extras were joint top-scorers with 56 each in Hampshire's first innings; in the second, Extras were unchallenged on 41 as the humans folded against the off-spin of Pierson on a pitch taking increasing turn. Hampshire responded by opening with an all-spin attack, but Leicestershire needed only 119 and completed victory before lunch on the final day.

Close of play: First day, Leicestershire 2-0 (A. R. K. Pierson 0*, D. L. Maddy 0*); Second day, Leicestershire 326-9 (D. J. Millns 101*, M. T. Brimson 16*); Third day, Leicestershire 31-0 (V. J. Wells 7*, D. L. Maddy 24*).

Hampshire

G. W. White c Johnson b Pierson	45	– c Nixon b Wells	24
M. L. Hayden c Wells b Mullally	15	– lbw b Millns	15
*J. P. Stephenson c Nixon b Mullally	10	– c and b Pierson	14
R. A. Smith c Johnson b Millns	46	– c Johnson b Pierson	11
W. S. Kendall lbw b Mullally	21	– c Habib b Pierson	11
K. D. James not out	56	– c Nixon b Pierson	7
†A. N. Aymes c Nixon b Mullally	1	– lbw b Millns	8
S. D. Udal c and b Johnson	13	– c Nixon b Millns	0
R. J. Maru c Maddy b Millns	27	– not out	36
S. J. Renshaw lbw b Millns	0	– lbw b Mullally	15
J. N. B. Bovill c Pierson b Brimson	8	– c Johnson b Brimson	0
B 20, l-b 4, w 2, n-b 30	56	B 14, l-b 9, w 6, n-b 12	41
	285		**182**

1/2 2/18 3/104 4/144 5/150   **285**   1/31 2/76 3/88 4/95 5/104   **182**
6/158 7/198 8/264 9/266   6/123 7/124 8/137 9/181

Bonus points – Hampshire 2, Leicestershire 4.

Bowling: *First Innings*—Millns 23–4–38–3; Mullally 23–8–69–4; Wells 7–2–16–0; Johnson 14–2–59–1; Pierson 21–4–56–1; Brimson 12.5–3–23–1. *Second Innings*—Millns 14–4–34–3; Mullally 16–5–44–1; Pierson 26–7–58–4; Wells 8–2–19–1; Brimson 2–0–4–1.

Leicestershire

A. R. K. Pierson c Bovill b Udal	35	
D. L. Maddy c Maru b Udal	32	– st Aymes b Udal 26
V. J. Wells b Maru	3	– (1) c and b Stephenson 8
*J. J. Whitaker lbw b Maru	0	– (3) b Bovill 37
N. C. Johnson c Aymes b Udal	38	– (4) lbw b Stephenson 6
B. F. Smith lbw b James	16	– (5) c Stephenson b Bovill 21
A. Habib c White b Bovill	77	– (6) not out 12
†P. A. Nixon st Aymes b James	0	– (7) not out 1
D. J. Millns not out	114	
A. D. Mullally b Udal	2	
M. T. Brimson lbw b Bovill	25	
B 2, l-b 5	7	B 4, l-b 4 8

1/57 2/68 3/68 4/111 5/114	349	1/37 2/41 3/64	(5 wkts) 119
6/157 7/157 8/253 9/274		4/95 5/108	

Bonus points – Leicestershire 3, Hampshire 4 (Score at 120 overs: 325-9).

Bowling: *First Innings*—Udal 48–12–118–4; Renshaw 16–3–53–0; Bovill 18.3–0–61–2; Maru 29–13–60–2; Stephenson 8–1–25–0; James 8–2–25–2. *Second Innings*—Udal 23–7–52–1; Maru 8–7–1–0; White 1–0–4–0; Stephenson 9–3–24–2; Bovill 7–1–30–2.

Umpires: D. J. Constant and G. Sharp.

At Cardiff, May 21, 22, 23, 24. HAMPSHIRE drew with GLAMORGAN.

HAMPSHIRE v WARWICKSHIRE

At Southampton, May 29, 30, 31, June 2. Drawn. Hampshire 7 pts, Warwickshire 9 pts. Toss: Warwickshire. First-class debut: D. A. Kenway.

A flat, true Northlands Road pitch produced a dreadful match for bowlers, but a memorable one for Australian opener Matthew Hayden. After scoring only 150 in his first seven Championship innings, he stayed 535 minutes and 414 balls for a career-best unbeaten 235, including one six and 30 fours, Hampshire's biggest ever maiden century. In the second innings, he became only the second player to score a double-hundred and a hundred for Hampshire in the same match, following Phil Mead in 1921. In between, he scored 118 in the Sunday game. Hampshire needed 482 just to avoid following on, after centuries from Moles and Hemp – his first for Warwickshire – had carried the visitors to 631; no one in the top five scored less than 75. But Hayden put on 206 with Kendall and 205 with Udal, who reached his own maiden hundred. On the final day, Knight and Hemp were fed meaningless centuries to set up a target of 335 in what became 72 overs. Hayden set off in determined pursuit, but no one could follow his lead. The last pair, debutant Derek Kenway and Bovill, had to survive seven overs to deny Warwickshire. An aggregate of 1,706 runs was the third-highest in English cricket, but artificially boosted by Warwickshire's farcical second innings.

Close of play: First day, Warwickshire 351-2 (D. L. Hemp 76*, G. Welch 6*); Second day, Hampshire 172-3 (M. L. Hayden 81*, W. S. Kendall 29*); Third day, Hampshire 549-6 (M. L. Hayden 235*, S. D. Udal 117*).

Warwickshire

*N. V. Knight c Aymes b Bovill	81	– not out	119
A. J. Moles c Hayden b Kenway	168	– c Aymes b Kenway	8
D. L. Hemp lbw b Bovill	138	– not out	114
G. Welch c Kenway b James	75		
T. L. Penney not out	86		
N. M. K. Smith c Kendall b Bovill	6		
D. P. Ostler c White b Udal	36		
D. R. Brown c Aymes b Udal	8		
A. F. Giles not out	2		
B 4, l-b 11, w 8, n-b 8	31	B 4, l-b 1, w 2, n-b 4	11

1/154 2/338 3/438 4/524   (7 wkts dec.) 631   1/21   (1 wkt dec.) 252
5/530 6/595 7/619

†T. Frost and D. A. Altree did not bat.

Bonus points – Warwickshire 4 (Score at 120 overs: 420-2).

Bowling: *First Innings*—Connor 23–3–101–0; Bovill 33–4–154–3; James 18–5–52–1; Hayden 3–0–19–0; Maru 42–3–137–0; Udal 42–9–132–2; White 5–0–16–0; Kenway 1–0–5–1. *Second Innings*—Kenway 8–2–53–1; Kendall 5–0–46–0; Aymes 9–0–76–0; Smith 3–0–36–0; Hayden 2–0–36–0.

Hampshire

G. W. White c Frost b Welch	1	– lbw b Brown	37
M. L. Hayden not out	235	– c Brown b Giles	119
K. D. James c Knight b Altree	0	– c Hemp b Brown	0
*R. A. Smith c Penney b Altree	35	– lbw b Brown	4
W. S. Kendall c Moles b Welch	76	– c Moles b Brown	44
D. A. Kenway b Welch	2	– (7) not out	20
†A. N. Aymes c Moles b Welch	19	– (8) lbw b Giles	1
S. D. Udal not out	117	– (6) c Penney b Brown	15
R. J. Maru (did not bat)		– c Hemp b Welch	0
C. A. Connor (did not bat)		– b Welch	0
J. N. B. Bovill (did not bat)		– not out	8
B 6, l-b 6, w 14, n-b 38	64	B 4, l-b 6, w 2, n-b 14	26

1/3 2/8 3/76 4/282 5/284   (6 wkts dec.) 549   1/89 2/91 3/101   (9 wkts) 274
6/344   4/201 5/225 6/248
                                       7/254 8/260 9/260

Bonus points – Hampshire 4, Warwickshire 2 (Score at 120 overs: 404-6).

Bowling: *First Innings*—Altree 22–3–108–2; Welch 31–6–119–4; Giles 44–10–112–0; Smith 30–3–120–0; Brown 18–4–54–0; Hemp 3–0–24–0. *Second Innings*—Welch 15–6–58–2; Altree 3–0–11–0; Brown 22–3–106–5; Smith 10–3–25–0; Giles 22–7–64–2.

Umpires: J. W. Holder and A. G. T. Whitehead.

At Chesterfield, June 4, 5, 6, 7. HAMPSHIRE beat DERBYSHIRE by seven wickets.

HAMPSHIRE v SOMERSET

At Basingstoke, June 12, 13, 14. Hampshire won by nine runs. Hampshire 21 pts, Somerset 4 pts. Toss: Somerset.

Kevan James had one of his occasional magically inspired games and returned the best figures of his career – eight for 49 in the final innings, and 13 for 93 in all – to give Hampshire a narrow win on the third afternoon. Ball dominated bat throughout on a pitch of unpredictable but never dangerous bounce. Thirty wickets fell in the first two days, but the umpires considered the surface quite adequate. Hampshire looked comfortable as Somerset crumbled to 59 for six in reply to their 204. Next morning, however, Holloway and Caddick put on 57 for the ninth wicket, reducing the deficit to 45. With Hayden making up for a first-ball dismissal in the first innings, Hampshire advanced steadily to 157 for four – then collapsed to the seam of Rose and the pace of their old boy, Shine. Somerset were left with two days to score 235. Again, Holloway batted obstinately, adding 112 with Parsons. But, once James dismissed Parsons, Somerset imploded. Holloway, unbeaten first time round, was last out.

Close of play: First day, Somerset 79-6 (P. C. L. Holloway 43*, Mushtaq Ahmed 12*); Second day, Hampshire 189.

Hampshire

J. S. Laney lbw b Rose	40	– lbw b Rose	28
M. L. Hayden lbw b van Troost		– c Bowler b Parsons	63
K. D. James c Bowler b Caddick	6	– c Turner b Rose	2
R. A. Smith b Rose	17	– lbw b Mushtaq Ahmed	29
W. S. Kendall c Turner b Caddick		– c Bowler b Shine	21
*J. P. Stephenson b Shine	16	– c Turner b Shine	18
†A. N. Aymes lbw b Mushtaq Ahmed	28	– not out	12
S. D. Udal lbw b Parsons	1	– c Bowler b Shine	0
A. D. Mascarenhas c Caddick b Mushtaq Ahmed	9	– lbw b Rose	2
S. J. Renshaw not out	7	– lbw b Rose	0
J. N. B. Bovill c Caddick b Rose	27	– b Rose	5
L-b 14, w 13, n-b 20	47	L-b 7, n-b 2	9

1/10 2/66 3/66 4/88 5/92	**204**	1/73 2/85 3/102 4/131 5/157	**189**
6/120 7/121 8/162 9/163		6/172 7/172 8/177 9/183	

Bonus points – Hampshire 1, Somerset 4.

Bowling: *First Innings*—Shine 10–3–41–1; van Troost 6–1–43–1; Rose 15–7–26–3; Caddick 21–10–42–2; Parsons 7–3–10–1; Mushtaq Ahmed 11–3–28–2. *Second Innings*—Caddick 13–3–36–0; Shine 19–8–37–3; Rose 21.1–8–53–5; Mushtaq Ahmed 17–5–46–1; Parsons 3–0–10–1.

Somerset

M. N. Lathwell c Udal b James	18	– lbw b James	33
*P. D. Bowler lbw b Renshaw	3	– b Bovill	3
P. C. L. Holloway not out	73	– c Aymes b James	59
R. J. Harden lbw b Renshaw	1	– b James	2
K. A. Parsons lbw b James	1	– c Stephenson b James	74
†R. J. Turner st Aymes b James	4	– c James b Udal	6
G. D. Rose b Stephenson	1	– c Bovill b James	1
Mushtaq Ahmed b James	17	– (9) c Laney b James	4
A. P. van Troost b James	5	– (8) st Aymes b James	0
A. R. Caddick lbw b Stephenson	38	– c Bovill b James	8
K. J. Shine lbw b Stephenson	0	– not out	0
L-b 2	2	B 12, l-b 19, n-b 4	35

1/6 2/34 3/39 4/48 5/48	**159**	1/18 2/59 3/63 4/175 5/188	**225**
6/59 7/88 8/102 9/159		6/195 7/195 8/207 9/219	

Bonus points – Hampshire 4.

Bowling: *First Innings*—Bovill 5–2–23–0; Renshaw 17–3–36–2; James 18–5–44–5; Stephenson 7.4–1–27–3; Udal 2–0–15–0; Mascarenhas 4–2–12–0. *Second Innings*—Renshaw 9–0–34–0; Bovill 11–2–40–1; Udal 12–4–27–1; James 22.1–9–49–8; Stephenson 16–6–42–0; Mascarenhas 3–2–2–0.

Umpires: A. Clarkson and A. A. Jones.

At Northampton, June 18, 19, 20, 21. HAMPSHIRE drew with NORTHAMPTONSHIRE.

At Southampton, June 28, 29, 30. HAMPSHIRE lost to AUSTRALIANS by an innings and 133 runs (See Australian tour section).

At Chester-le-Street, July 2, 3, 4, 5. DURHAM v HAMPSHIRE. Abandoned.

At Guildford, July 16, 17, 18, 19. HAMPSHIRE lost to SURREY by nine wickets.

HAMPSHIRE v LANCASHIRE

At Southampton, July 23, 24, 25, 26. Drawn. Hampshire 10 pts, Lancashire 8 pts. Toss: Lancashire.

The intrusion of rain on the fourth day made sure a batsman's match would peter out into a draw. The highlight was a maiden Championship century by England Under-19 captain Flintoff, an innings of considerable maturity even allowing for Hampshire's toothless attack and the amiability of the pitch. Flintoff hit one six and 22 fours and put on 214 in 43 overs with Watkinson, who scored 135. Hayden and Laney gave Hampshire a solid 200-run start but both fell in their nineties: the home side then faltered until a hundred from Keech allowed Stephenson to declare 157 behind. They even had hopes of a win when Lancashire slumped to 107 for seven. But Hegg, supported by Yates and Shadford, steered them to a lead of 412 before the weather intervened. Before the start of the last day, Hampshire officials held a forum for 200 members disgruntled by the team's poor form, and talked them out of plans for a special general meeting.

Close of play: First day, Lancashire 423-5 (M. Watkinson 102*, D. J. Shadford 5*); Second day, Hampshire 171-0 (J. S. Laney 67*, M. L. Hayden 90*); Third day, Lancashire 103-5 (M. Watkinson 24*, I. D. Austin 25*).

Lancashire

J. E. R. Gallian lbw b Bovill	10 – c Keech b Milburn	1
N. T. Wood c Smith b Udal	82 – c Aymes b Bovill	7
N. H. Fairbrother run out	5 – b Stephenson	18
G. D. Lloyd c Smith b Udal	90 – c Aymes b Milburn	1
A. Flintoff c and b Stephenson	117 – c Maru b Bovill	19
*M. Watkinson run out	135 – c Aymes b Bovill	24
D. J. Shadford b Milburn	30 – (11) not out	28
I. D. Austin not out	69 – (7) b Bovill	29
†W. K. Hegg c Maru b Milburn	5 – (8) not out	77
G. Yates not out	10 – (9) st Aymes b Maru	39
P. J. Martin (did not bat)	– (10) run out	4
B 5, l-b 9, n-b 2	16	L-b 6, w 2	8

1/24 2/33 3/191 4/194 5/408   (8 wkts. dec.) 569   1/2 2/10 3/11   (9 wkts. dec.) 255
6/467 7/488 8/502   4/51 5/53 6/106
     7/107 8/175 9/184

Bonus points – Lancashire 4, Hampshire 3 (Score at 120 overs: 492-7).

Bowling: *First Innings*—Bovill 28–5–106–1; Milburn 36–7–135–2; Stephenson 33–7–103–1; Udal 24–3–142–2; Maru 10–2–52–0; Keech 2–0–17–0. *Second Innings*—Milburn 20–4–35–2; Bovill 17–2–62–4; Stephenson 13–3–30–1; Udal 12–2–47–0; Maru 17–4–56–1; Laney 5–2–19–0.

Hampshire

J. S. Laney lbw b Martin	95	*J. P. Stephenson not out	37
M. L. Hayden c Hegg b Yates	94		
K. D. James c Austin b Watkinson	30	B 4, l-b 4, n-b 12	20
R. A. Smith lbw b Gallian	35		
M. Keech not out	101	1/200 2/208 3/252 4/327 (4 wkts. dec.) 412	

†A. N. Aymes, S. D. Udal, R. J. Maru, S. M. Milburn and J. N. B. Bovill did not bat.

Bonus points – Hampshire 4, Lancashire 1.

Bowling: Martin 14–5–41–1; Shadford 13–2–80–0; Austin 17–5–61–0; Watkinson 19–2–99–1; Yates 31–6–84–1; Gallian 9–1–39–1.

Umpires: D. R. Shepherd and P. Willey.

At Southampton, July 29. HAMPSHIRE lost to PAKISTAN A by six wickets (See Pakistan A tour section).

At Lord's, August 6, 7, 8, 9. HAMPSHIRE lost to MIDDLESEX by 217 runs.

HAMPSHIRE v YORKSHIRE

At Portsmouth, August 15, 16, 17, 18. Drawn. Hampshire 8 pts, Yorkshire 11 pts. Toss: Yorkshire. First-class debut: L. Savident. Championship debuts: C. Patel; P. M. Hutchison.

Hampshire had waited four years for Giles White to come good, but he picked a helpful moment to score his maiden century for the county. Stephenson's first Championship hundred for two years was equally timely; mixing violence and application, he hit six sixes and ten fours. Together, they put on 173 in 155 minutes to avert what had looked like being a heavy defeat. Yorkshire had cruised past 500 on the back of a superb 182 from the Australian Lehmann, his biggest score of the season. Hampshire's own Australian, Hayden, and Smith replied with a solid stand of 184. But left-arm pace bowler Paul Hutchison followed up his 11 wickets against Pakistan A by rolling up the innings with seven for 50 on his Championship debut. The home side followed on 220 behind and slipped to 202 for four before White and Stephenson punctured Yorkshire's hopes.

Close of play: First day, Yorkshire 389-6 (R. J. Blakey 29*, A. C. Morris 4*); Second day, Hampshire 264-8 (L. Savident 5*, S. J. Renshaw 1*); Third day, Hampshire 173-3 (G. W. White 58*, M. Keech 17*).

Yorkshire

M. D. Moxon c Aymes b Renshaw	0	G. M. Hamilton not out	24
M. P. Vaughan c Aymes b Savident	74	R. D. Stemp not out	7
*D. Byas c Keech b Savident	26		
D. S. Lehmann c Stephenson b Udal	182	L-b 6, w 6, n-b 16	28
C. White b Udal	30		
B. Parker lbw b Stephenson	20	1/0 2/39 3/155	(8 wkts dec.) 501
†R. J. Blakey c Smith b Udal	75	4/206 5/266	
A. C. Morris c Hayden b Stephenson	35	6/379 7/447 8/484	

P. M. Hutchison did not bat.

Bonus points – Yorkshire 4, Hampshire 3 (Score at 120 overs: 447-7).

Bowling: Renshaw 23–4–101–1; Patel 18–3–65–0; Savident 23–7–86–2; Udal 41–10–134–3; Stephenson 25–5–98–2; Hayden 2–0–11–0.

Hampshire

J. S. Laney lbw b Hutchison	3	– lbw b Hamilton ... 81
M. L. Hayden c White b Hutchison	88	– c Blakey b Hutchison ... 4
G. W. White lbw b Hutchison	3	– lbw b Hamilton ... 145
R. A. Smith b Morris	110	– c Parker b Hamilton ... 0
M. Keech c Blakey b Hutchison	17	– c Morris b White ... 25
*J. P. Stephenson b Hutchison	0	– b Hamilton ... 114
†A. N. Aymes lbw b Hutchison	4	– lbw b Hutchison ... 3
S. D. Udal b White	14	– st Blakey b Lehmann ... 37
L. Savident c Blakey b Hutchison	6	– c Stemp b Hamilton ... 5
S. J. Renshaw not out	11	– not out ... 16
C. Patel b White	6	– not out ... 3
L-b 5, w 8, n-b 6	19	B 4, l-b 12, w 8, n-b 14 ... 38

1/7 2/15 3/199 4/240 5/240	281	1/26 2/149 3/149 (9 wkts dec.) 471
6/241 7/248 8/260 9/266		4/202 5/375 6/400
		7/404 8/410 9/464

Bonus points – Hampshire 2, Yorkshire 4.

Bowling: *First Innings*—Hamilton 11–1–49–0; Hutchison 20–4–50–7; White 16.2–2–51–2; Stemp 13–2–45–0; Vaughan 11–0–49–0; Lehmann 3–1–14–0; Morris 6–1–18–1. *Second Innings*—Hamilton 27–5–89–5; Hutchison 30–6–95–2; White 21–5–65–1; Stemp 30–10–81–0; Morris 13–4–24–0; Vaughan 16–0–92–0; Lehmann 5–1–6–1; Parker 1–0–3–0.

Umpires: J. D. Bond and B. Dudleston.

HAMPSHIRE v KENT

At Portsmouth, August 27, 28, 29, 30. Drawn. Hampshire 9 pts, Kent 10 pts. Toss: Kent.

In the end, Kent were grateful for small mercies – to be precise, a fourth batting point, which put them level with Glamorgan at the top of the Championship table. Persistent heavy showers claimed more than ten hours' play, and Hampshire's first innings stretched into the third afternoon. Kent, who had put them in, still hoped for a positive return at 279 for eight, but Udal, racing from 50 to 91 in 24 balls, and Renshaw frustrated them by adding 113 in 20 overs. When Kent finally replied, Ed Smith scored his maiden Championship century, including 16 fours, out of a first-wicket stand of 170 with Fulton. Kent began the fourth day on 182 for one, but rain claimed the first three hours and, once they did get going, they suddenly wobbled; it took Marsh's steady nerves to see them to 350 and maximum batting points with two wickets and four overs remaining.

Close of play: First day, Hampshire 111-2 (G. W. White 35*, R. A. Smith 19*); Second day, Hampshire 210-5 (J. P. Stephenson 54*, A. N. Aymes 11*); Third day, Kent 182-1 (D. P. Fulton 64*, T. R. Ward 5*).

Hampshire

J. S. Laney b Ealham	24	L. Savident c Ealham b Headley	4
M. L. Hayden c Headley b Ealham	26	S. J. Renshaw not out	35
G. W. White c Marsh b Headley	44	S. M. Milburn c Strang b Phillips	7
R. A. Smith lbw b Headley	42		
M. Keech c Ward b Headley	2	B 10, l-b 9, n-b 8	27
*J. P. Stephenson c Marsh b Phillips	76		
†A. N. Aymes b Phillips	28	1/48 2/81 3/121 4/127 5/190	406
S. D. Udal c Wells b Phillips	91	6/236 7/267 8/279 9/392	

Bonus points – Hampshire 3, Kent 3 (Score at 120 overs: 323-8).

Bowling: Headley 36–9–105–4; Phillips 24.5–7–64–4; Ealham 26–11–50–2; Fleming 24–4–86–0; Strang 22–4–82–0.

Kent

D. P. Fulton c Aymes b Stephenson	75	P. A. Strang c Hayden b Udal	0
E. T. Smith c and b Renshaw	102	B. J. Phillips not out	4
T. R. Ward c Aymes b Savident	66		
A. P. Wells c sub b Udal	20	L-b 7, n-b 14	21
G. R. Cowdrey c sub b Renshaw	11		
M. A. Ealham c Aymes b Renshaw	8	1/170 2/201 3/276	(8 wkts dec.) 350
M. V. Fleming c White b Renshaw	0	4/285 5/297 6/297	
*†S. A. Marsh not out	43	7/316 8/317	

D. W. Headley did not bat.

Bonus points – Kent 4, Hampshire 3.

Bowling: Milburn 10–0–44–0; Renshaw 19–3–61–4; Udal 41–14–96–2; Stephenson 12–0–61–1; Savident 10–0–64–1; White 1.5–0–17–0.

Umpires: A. Clarkson and D. J. Constant.

At Nottingham, September 2, 3, 4, 5. HAMPSHIRE drew with NOTTINGHAMSHIRE.

HAMPSHIRE v SUSSEX

At Southampton, September 10, 11, 12, 13. Hampshire won by seven wickets. Hampshire 21 pts, Sussex 4 pts. Toss: Sussex.

When the first day ended, Hampshire already led bottom-placed Sussex by 71, with eight wickets in hand, and day four appeared redundant. Instead, it was not until the penultimate session that they completed their third victory of the summer. Sussex had folded against the seam of Milburn and Udal's off-breaks. But another seam-spin pairing, Kirtley and leg-spinner Khan, inflicted a similar collapse on Hampshire; once Khan ended a 125-run stand between White and Whitaker, the last eight fell for 49 in 20 overs. Sussex's batsmen displayed greater steel second time round. Left-hander Peirce ground out a maiden century in five and a half hours, while Carpenter and Khan scored their first fifties. Still, Hampshire needed only 260. Laney set them on their way with a belligerent 76, and White applied himself to steer them home.

Close of play: First day, Hampshire 185-2 (G. W. White 68*, P. R. Whitaker 68*); Second day, Sussex 201-3 (M. T. E. Peirce 81*, K. Newell 30*); Third day, Hampshire 37-0 (J. S. Laney 24*, M. L. Hayden 10*).

Sussex

M. T. E. Peirce c Maru b Milburn	7	– lbw b Renshaw	104
*†P. Moores c Aymes b Renshaw	0	– lbw b Milburn	21
N. R. Taylor lbw b Milburn	4	– c Aymes b Renshaw	52
K. Greenfield b Udal	17	– c Maru b Milburn	11
K. Newell c Laney b Milburn	4	– c Hayden b Renshaw	44
J. R. Carpenter lbw b Stephenson	21	– c Kendall b Hayden	63
P. W. Jarvis c Hayden b Udal	22	– c White b Milburn	6
J. J. Bates b Milburn	16	– c Maru b Stephenson	12
A. A. Khan lbw b Udal	4	– run out	52
M. A. Robinson not out	6	– lbw b Hayden	3
R. J. Kirtley c Renshaw b Udal	5	– not out	7
L-b 2, n-b 6	8	B 4, l-b 5, w 2, n-b 4	15

1/2 2/12 3/15 4/19 5/49   114   1/35 2/114 3/142 4/236 5/245   390
6/73 7/83 8/101 9/103   6/252 7/287 8/336 9/348

Bonus points – Hampshire 4.

Bowling: First Innings—Milburn 17–4–38–4; Renshaw 5–2–8–1; Stephenson 10–2–49–1; Udal 15.1–7–17–4. *Second Innings*—Milburn 32–3–106–3; Renshaw 27.3–10–52–3; Udal 44–12–98–0; Maru 21–6–30–0; Stephenson 25–5–78–1; Hayden 6–0–17–2.

Hampshire

J. S. Laney c Moores b Kirtley	7	– c Kirtley b Khan	76
M. L. Hayden c Jarvis b Bates	25	– c Moores b Robinson	10
G. W. White b Khan	80	– not out	75
P. R. Whitaker b Khan	73	– c Greenfield b Bates	24
W. S. Kendall c Jarvis b Khan	15	– not out	42
*J. P. Stephenson lbw b Kirtley	1		
†A. N. Aymes lbw b Kirtley	0		
S. D. Udal b Kirtley	5		
S. J. Renshaw b Jarvis	11		
R. J. Maru c Carpenter b Khan	4		
S. M. Milburn not out	4		
L-b 6, n-b 14	20	B 4, l-b 3, w 6, n-b 20	33

1/15 2/71 3/196 4/205 5/206   245   1/40 2/112 3/169   (3 wkts) 260
6/206 7/212 8/230 9/239

Bonus points – Hampshire 1, Sussex 4.

Bowling: *First Innings*—Jarvis 16–1–71–1; Kirtley 15–3–41–4; Robinson 10–4–17–0; Bates 15–6–31–1; Khan 27.4–6–79–4. *Second Innings*—Jarvis 13–2–32–0; Kirtley 14–4–34–0; Khan 28–6–89–1; Robinson 12–1–41–1; Bates 11–3–38–1; Carpenter 3–0–13–0; Peirce 1.1–0–6–0.

Umpires: J. C. Balderstone and R. A. White.

HAMPSHIRE v WORCESTERSHIRE

At Southampton, September 18, 19, 20, 21. Worcestershire won by nine wickets. Worcestershire 24 pts, Hampshire 3 pts. Toss: Worcestershire. First-class debuts: S. R. G. Francis, T. M. Hansen.

Worcestershire sprang to third place in the final Championship table on the back of a record-breaking partnership between Hick and Moody. Andrew Jones and Martin Crowe retained the biggest third-wicket stand in cricket history – but it was a close call. If rain had not cut the last two sessions of the second day, their 467 for New Zealand against Sri Lanka in 1990-91 might have been eclipsed. As it was, Moody declared overnight at 538 for two – when he and Hick had added 438 in 112 overs, overhauling the County Championship third-wicket record, held by Bill Edrich and Denis Compton, with an unbroken stand of 424 against Somerset, since 1948. It was

HIGHEST PARTNERSHIPS IN THE COUNTY CHAMPIONSHIP

555	P. Holmes and H. Sutcliffe, Yorkshire v Essex at Leyton, first wicket	1932
554	J. T. Brown and J. Tunnicliffe, Yorkshire v Derbyshire at Chesterfield, first wicket	1898
490	E. H. Bowley and J. G. Langridge, Sussex v Middlesex at Hove, first wicket	1933
470	A. I. Kallicharran and G. W. Humpage, Warwickshire v Lancashire at Southport, fourth wicket	1982
465*	J. A. Jameson and R. B. Kanhai, Warwickshire v Gloucestershire at Birmingham, second wicket	1974
448	R. Abel and T. W. Hayward, Surrey v Yorkshire at The Oval, fourth wicket	1899
438*	**G. A. Hick and T. M. Moody, Worcestershire v Hampshire at Southampton, third wicket**	**1997**
425*	A. Dale and I. V. A. Richards, Glamorgan v Middlesex at Cardiff, fourth wicket .	1993
424*	W. J. Edrich and D. C. S. Compton, Middlesex v Somerset at Lord's, third wicket	1948

HIGHEST PARTNERSHIPS FOR WORCESTERSHIRE

438*	**G. A. Hick and T. M. Moody v Hampshire at Southampton, third wicket**	**1997**
393	E. G. Arnold and W. B. Burns v Warwickshire at Birmingham, fifth wicket	1909
314	M. J. Horton and T. W. Graveney v Somerset at Worcester, third wicket	1962
309	H. K. Foster and F. L. Bowley v Derbyshire at Derby, first wicket.............	1901
306	F. L. Bowley and F. A. Pearson v Gloucestershire at Worcester, first wicket.....	1913
306	L. G. Crawley and W. V. Fox v Northamptonshire at Worcester, third wicket....	1923
303	H. K. Foster and R. E. Foster v Kent at Worcester, third wicket...............	,1907

the fifth-highest third-wicket stand in cricket history, and the seventh-highest for any wicket in the Championship. Moody finished on 180; Hick was unbeaten on 303, the highest innings of the season, after all but a minute of eight hours' laser-sharp concentration, in which he faced 393 balls. It was the latest triple-century ever scored in an English season – the only other September 300 was scored by Ken Rutherford on September 1, at the 1986 Scarborough festival. Hick took three sixes and 45 fours off an inexperienced attack – Hampshire fielded two debutants, including Danish fast bowler Thomas Hansen, who maintained their spirits bravely. Home ambitions did not extend beyond the draw, but Hampshire soon capitulated to Illingworth's spin. He forced them to follow on with seven for 79 – the best Championship return of his career. Their second innings also lacked conviction, and Worcestershire knocked off 88 to win in 30 overs. Hick was still there, and still unbeaten; his 28 runs were just enough to push him to the top of the national averages, after a season generally thought indifferent by his high standards.

Close of play: First day, Worcestershire 428-2 (G. A. Hick 253*, T. M. Moody 120*); Second day, Worcestershire 538-2 (G. A. Hick 303*, T. M. Moody 180*); Third day, Hampshire 127-1 (M. L. Hayden 57*, G. W. White 20*).

Worcestershire

W. P. C. Weston c Hayden b Renshaw	4	– not out	34
K. R. Spiring lbw b Udal	42	– b Whitaker	24
G. A. Hick not out	303	– not out	28
*T. M. Moody not out	180		
B 3, l-b 4, w 2	9	L-b 2	2

1/20 2/100   (2 wkts dec.) 538   1/37   (1 wkt) 88

G. R. Haynes, D. A. Leatherdale, R. J. Chapman, †S. J. Rhodes, S. R. Lampitt, R. K. Illingworth and A. Sheriyar did not bat.

Bonus points – Worcestershire 4 (Score at 120 overs: 470-2).

Bowling: *First Innings*—Renshaw 29-3-106-1; Francis 19-1-97-0; Hansen 24-10-61-0; Udal 31-4-125-1; Stephenson 18-1-76-0; Hayden 3-0-12-0; Whitaker 9-1-42-0; White 3-0-12-0. *Second Innings*—Hansen 2-0-14-0; Udal 12-1-32-0; Whitaker 13-2-31-1; Stephenson 3-0-9-0.

Hampshire

J. S. Laney b Lampitt	45	– b Lampitt	46
M. L. Hayden c Leatherdale b Illingworth	25	– c Haynes b Hick	77
G. W. White c Hick b Moody	62	– lbw b Hick	45
P. R. Whitaker c Sheriyar b Illingworth	20	– b Hick	14
W. S. Kendall c Leatherdale b Illingworth	7	– lbw b Illingworth	7
*J. P. Stephenson c and b Illingworth	18	– lbw b Moody	39
†A. N. Aymes c Leatherdale b Hick	26	– c Leatherdale b Illingworth	12
S. D. Udal st Rhodes b Illingworth	66	– c Moody b Illingworth	5
S. J. Renshaw c Chapman b Illingworth	14	– not out	34
T. M. Hansen not out	12	– c Rhodes b Sheriyar	19
S. R. G. Francis lbw b Illingworth	4	– b Sheriyar	4
B 4, l-b 1, w 2, n-b 6	13	B 4, l-b 7	11

1/75 2/75 3/109 4/119 5/145   312   1/67 2/161 3/184 4/189 5/227   313
6/203 7/243 8/289 9/294   6/239 7/250 8/259 9/287

Bonus points – Hampshire 3, Worcestershire 4.

Bowling: *First Innings*—Sheriyar 11-1-44-0; Haynes 5-1-17-0; Illingworth 42.2-14-79-7; Lampitt 8-2-27-1; Hick 25-3-94-1; Moody 9-1-46-1. *Second Innings*—Sheriyar 6.3-0-39-2; Chapman 3-0-21-0; Illingworth 42-21-68-3; Lampitt 4-1-14-1; Hick 24-6-90-3; Moody 16-2-70-1.

Umpires: J. H. Hampshire and R. Julian.

KENT

Mark Ealham

Patron: HRH The Duke of Kent
President: P. Edgley
Chairman: D. S. Kemp
Chairman, Cricket Committee: D. G. Ufton
Secretary: S. T. W. Anderson
Captain: S. A. Marsh
Coach: J. G. Wright
Cricket Administrator: Ms L. Walters
Head Groundsman: M. Grantham
Scorer: J. C. Foley

Nobody remembers who comes second in sport – victors celebrate while the vanquished slip away. In 1997, Kent turned coming second into an art form, finishing runners-up three times. A poor performance in the Benson and Hedges Cup final in July saw them lose to Surrey. But they put that behind them to mount concerted challenges for the Championship and the Sunday League. On September 9, with 12 days of the season to go, they led in both.

They faltered at Headingley. First, they drew their penultimate Championship game, allowing Glamorgan to take a one-point lead. Then, they lost their final League game by seven wickets to Yorkshire, and their biggest one-day foes, Warwickshire, pipped them to the Sunday title. The following weekend, a five-wicket victory over Surrey was not enough to claim the Championship, as Glamorgan achieved a ten-wicket success against Somerset on the same evening.

It was difficult to know whether such a season should be celebrated or mourned. And questions were directed at coach John Wright and captain Steve Marsh: why had the county yet again been bridesmaids? But the problem predates Wright and Marsh. In 19 seasons Kent have come second 12 times in the four main competitions, and won just one – the 1995 Sunday League.

The feeling was that the appointment of Wright, the former New Zealand captain, to succeed Daryl Foster was an inspired decision. Like Marsh, he is quiet, but approachable and an excellent communicator. Both were deeply hurt by the club's lack of silverware, and pledged that the side would learn from the experience. Marsh displayed a positive, aggressive approach throughout, which rubbed off on his squad. Kent won eight Championship and 18 one-day games. They would have had a ninth Championship win, which would have secured the title, had they scored one more run against Somerset in August; instead, they finished with the scores level. They collected 60 bowling points – no other county managed more. And this was despite injuries and Test calls which deprived them of several key players – Dean Headley, Martin McCague, Mark Ealham, Graham Cowdrey and Min Patel – at different but critical times of the season.

Patel, the former England left-arm spinner, figured in only one Championship match, the opening fixture against Derbyshire. He had been injured while teaching PE at his old school, Dartford Grammar, but decided to try to play on without surgery. Unfortunately, he broke down batting in a club match and an operation put him out for the season. He planned to spend the winter in South

Africa in the hope of returning in 1998 fully fit. McCague spearheaded the seam attack with relish until he sustained a lower back injury, and Headley's elevation to the Test arena meant that Kent rarely had the luxury of the pair operating together. There were, however, occasional appearances from Alan Igglesden, who had missed the whole of 1996. Ealham played in four Tests and was then dropped by England. Kent were upset for him but delighted to see him back; he finished top of the county batting averages and 14th in the national list. Cowdrey, however, pulled a hamstring batting in the Sunday League against Nottinghamshire, and missed most of the next two months – though he did appear in the Benson and Hedges Cup final.

As well as a new coach and captain, Kent employed a new overseas player. They selected Zimbabwe's leg-spinner, Paul Strang, as a one-season replacement for West Indian Carl Hooper, who was unavailable because of Test commitments. Strang proved an ideal choice, as popular and successful as Aravinda de Silva in 1995. He made an all-round contribution to Kent's success, scoring 590 first-class runs and claiming 63 wickets, including seven for 118, and 11 in the match, against Lancashire. Hooper returns in 1998, while Strang moves on to Nottinghamshire.

Overall, Kent's success was built on collective performances rather than individuals. With extraordinary regularity, the lower order scored more than the established batsmen and got the team out of trouble. In successive matches, Marsh and Ben Phillips put on 183 for the last wicket against Sussex, Ealham and Strang added 171 – a county ninth-wicket record – against Nottinghamshire, and Julian Thompson and Phillips added 109, also for the ninth wicket, against Warwickshire. Kent won all three games, plus the next one against Lancashire, when Phillips scored a maiden hundred.

Phillips, better known as a seam bowler, benefited from an extended run in the senior side; he headed the bowling averages with 44 first-class wickets at 19.93, which put him seventh in the national list. But batsmen Matthew Walker and Nigel Llong had disappointing Championship seasons. When Ed Smith arrived, after completing his second year at Cambridge, he was swiftly installed as David Fulton's opening partner. Smith, 20 in mid-season, is tipped for a bright future, and made his first Championship hundred against Hampshire at Portsmouth. He was also intent on improving his fielding, and two catches in Middlesex's run-chase at Lord's were crucial to a dramatic four-run win.

Alan Wells took time to settle after his move from Sussex. He was under pressure, with some Kent members still questioning the decision to sign him and dispense with Neil Taylor, who went the other way. But Wells did come good in time, scoring a hundred in the victory over Essex and passing 1,000 runs for the season.

Tim Wren and Nick Preston were released and Kent also said goodbye to head groundsman Brian Fitch, who retired after 28 years with the county. His last game at the St Lawrence Ground, the Championship match against Surrey, was an eventful one: after 19 wickets fell on the opening day, the umpires reported the pitch as under-prepared. The ECB imposed a ten-point suspended penalty.

Headley and Ealham were both called up for the England winter squads. There was also international recognition for Matthew Fleming. Having been named Player of the Tournament in the Hong Kong Sixes in October, he replaced Darren Gough in the one-day squad for England's trip to Sharjah. The challenge for 1998 is for Kent to play as well as they did day-in, day-out in 1997, and end the suggestions that they lack that elusive quality: "bottle". – ANDREW GIDLEY.

KENT 1997

[Bill Smith]

Back row: E. J. Stanford, R. W. T. Key, B. J. Phillips, S. C. Willis, M. J. Walker. Middle row: J. C. Foley (scorer), F. Errington (physiotherapist), D. P. Fulton, J. B. D. Thompson, T. N. Wren, N. W. Preston, A. P. Wells, J. G. Wright (First Eleven coach), A. G. E. Ealham (Second Eleven coach). Front row: N. J. Llong, M. V. Fleming, P. A. Strang, G. R. Cowdrey, S. A. Marsh (captain), T. R. Ward, A. P. Igglesden, M. J. McCague, M. M. Patel. Insets: D. W. Headley, M. A. Ealham, W. J. House, E. T. Smith.

KENT RESULTS

All first-class matches – Played 19: Won 8, Lost 5, Drawn 6.
County Championship matches – Played 17: Won 8, Lost 4, Drawn 5.
Competition placings – Britannic Assurance County Championship, 2nd;
NatWest Trophy, 1st round; Benson and Hedges Cup, finalists;
AXA Life League, 2nd.

COUNTY CHAMPIONSHIP AVERAGES

BATTING

Cap		M	I	NO	R	HS	100s	50s	Avge	Ct/St
1992	M. A. Ealham†	12	20	6	809	139	3	4	57.78	9
1986	S. A. Marsh	17	25	5	797	142	1	3	39.85	54/2
1997	A. P. Wells	17	29	1	1,055	109	1	8	37.67	16
	D. P. Fulton	15	27	3	885	110	1	3	36.87	22
1989	T. R. Ward†	16	28	2	895	161*	1	7	34.42	29
	B. J. Phillips	11	15	4	343	100*	1	1	31.18	5
1988	G. R. Cowdrey†	9	15	0	442	101	1	1	29.46	7
	E. T. Smith†	9	16	1	434	102	1	1	28.93	4
1990	M. V. Fleming	17	29	4	694	138	1	3	27.76	5
1997	P. A. Strang§	16	24	2	588	82	0	5	26.72	17
	J. B. D. Thompson . . .	7	7	3	103	59*	0	1	25.75	3
	M. J. Walker†	9	17	0	298	51	0	1	17.52	4
1992	M. J. McCague	11	17	6	190	53*	0	1	17.27	3
1993	D. W. Headley	7	9	3	99	40	0	0	16.50	2
1993	N. J. Llong†	7	12	0	140	57	0	1	11.66	9
1989	A. P. Igglesden†	5	6	2	4	3	0	0	1.00	1

Also batted: W. J. House (1 match) 2; (cap 1994) M. M. Patel (1 match) 8, 30 (1 ct).

* Signifies not out.   † Born in Kent.   § Overseas player.

BOWLING

	O	M	R	W	BB	5W/i	Avge
B. J. Phillips	254.1	67	773	41	5-47	2	18.85
M. J. McCague	312.4	55	1,125	48	7-50	4	23.43
J. B. D. Thompson	186.2	24	713	24	5-89	1	29.70
M. A. Ealham	317	62	928	31	4-47	0	29.93
P. A. Strang	703	207	1,843	61	7-118	4	30.21
A. P. Igglesden	131	21	454	15	4-67	0	30.26
M. V. Fleming	382.2	95	1,096	36	5-51	2	30.44
D. W. Headley	253	44	841	26	5-92	1	32.34

Also bowled: G. R. Cowdrey 5–0–31–0; N. J. Llong 52.3–11–200–4; M. M. Patel 3–0–12–0; E. T. Smith 2–0–22–0; T. R. Ward 5–0–34–0; A. P. Wells 18–6–55–0.

COUNTY RECORDS

Highest score for:	332	W. H. Ashdown v Essex at Brentwood	1934
Highest score against:	344	W. G. Grace (MCC) at Canterbury	1876
Best bowling for:	10-30	C. Blythe v Northamptonshire at Northampton	1907
Best bowling against:	10-48	C. H. G. Bland (Sussex) at Tonbridge	1899
Highest total for:	803-4 dec.	v Essex at Brentwood	1934
Highest total against:	676	by Australians at Canterbury	1921
Lowest total for:	18	v Sussex at Gravesend	1867
Lowest total against:	16	by Warwickshire at Tonbridge	1913

KENT v DERBYSHIRE

At Canterbury, April 23, 24, 25, 26. Drawn. Kent 9 pts, Derbyshire 8 pts. Toss: Kent. County debuts: P. A. Strang, A. P. Wells.

Derbyshire's quest for a victory at the first attempt was foiled by the weather, which forced the contest to be abandoned while they were chasing hard for their target of 337. The game began in bizarre fashion when the visitors took the field with the wrong side. Kent captain Steve Marsh was under the impression that Matthew Vandrau was in the Derbyshire eleven until the sixth over, when left-arm seamer Dean came on to bowl. Secretary Stuart Anderson walked out on to the pitch, followed by Marsh, and they spent several minutes talking to Derbyshire skipper Jones and the umpires, complaining that Law 1.2 had been broken. In the end it was announced that Derbyshire had made a "genuine error" when they named their team, and Dean was allowed to stay. It was an eventful match in many respects with five players suffering injuries over the four days: Kent's Fulton (broken finger) and Headley (back) were joined in the treatment room by Hayhurst (torn cartilage), DeFreitas (groin) and Cork, whose groin injury was to wreck his season. Adams's hundred was the 20th of his first-class career and he shared a third-wicket stand of 202 with Jones before play was called off after the second interruption on the final day.

Close of play: First day, Derbyshire 35-4 (V. P. Clarke 4*, A. N. Hayhurst 1*); Second day, Kent 174-5 (T. R. Ward 95*, P. A. Strang 29*); Third day, Derbyshire 59-2 (C. J. Adams 33*, D. M. Jones 19*).

Kent

D. P. Fulton c Jones b Cork	43	– lbw b DeFreitas		29
N. J. Llong b Malcolm	5	– c Jones b DeFreitas		12
T. R. Ward b Malcolm	6	– b DeFreitas		96
A. P. Wells c Adams b DeFreitas	36	– lbw b DeFreitas		0
M. V. Fleming b DeFreitas	1	– lbw b DeFreitas		0
M. A. Ealham not out	72	– c Cork b Dean		8
P. A. Strang c Krikken b Malcolm	0	– c Rollins b DeFreitas		69
*†S. A. Marsh c Krikken b Malcolm	57	– lbw b DeFreitas		12
M. J. McCague lbw b DeFreitas	1	– not out		53
D. W. Headley c Krikken b Malcolm	5	– c Krikken b Dean		22
M. M. Patel c Hayhurst b Malcolm	8	– c Rollins b Malcolm		30
B 4, l-b 7, n-b 6	17	L-b 2		2

1/7 2/23 3/78 4/79 5/104   251   1/55 2/79 3/79 4/79 5/120   333
6/105 7/199 8/200 9/209   6/180 7/218 8/227 9/293

Bonus points – Kent 2, Derbyshire 4.

Bowling: *First Innings*—Malcolm 27-4-74-6; Cork 21-6-52-1; Dean 12-2-44-0; DeFreitas 21-10-35-3; Clarke 8-2-35-0. *Second Innings*—Cork 19-5-50-0; Malcolm 20.4-0-112-1; DeFreitas 20-5-64-7; Dean 11-1-43-2; Clarke 6-0-53-0; Rollins 1-0-9-0.

Derbyshire

K. J. Barnett c Marsh b McCague	9	– c Llong b Headley		6
A. S. Rollins c Llong b McCague	1	– c Ealham b Headley		0
C. J. Adams b McCague	10	– c Llong b McCague		108
*D. M. Jones c Fulton b Headley	5	– not out		99
V. P. Clarke c Ward b Headley	40	– not out		18
A. N. Hayhurst c Ward b McCague	6			
D. G. Cork c Patel b Headley	32			
†K. M. Krikken run out	61			
P. A. J. DeFreitas b Headley	24			
K. J. Dean c Marsh b McCague	14			
D. E. Malcolm not out	21			
B 4, l-b 9, n-b 12	25	B 4, l-b 9, n-b 4		17

1/5 2/21 3/30 4/30 5/44   248   1/5 2/14 3/216   (3 wkts) 248
6/109 7/138 8/204 9/217

Bonus points – Derbyshire 1, Kent 4.

Bowling: *First Innings*—McCague 20.1–2–75–5; Headley 26–3–81–4; Ealham 3–0–20–0; Strang 15–7–37–0; Fleming 7–0–22–0. *Second Innings*—Headley 8–1–26–2; McCague 18–2–91–1; Ealham 14–1–45–0; Strang 11–0–50–0; Fleming 4–0–11–0; Patel 3–0–12–0.

Umpires: K. E. Palmer and P. Willey.

KENT v GLAMORGAN

At Canterbury, May 14, 15, 16, 17. Glamorgan won by 87 runs. Glamorgan 22 pts, Kent 4 pts. Toss: Glamorgan.

A match of multiple collapses and recoveries, which would assume far greater importance in retrospect, finished just before lunch on the final day when Kent, needing 319 to win, were bowled out for 231. Overnight, the game was poised, but Wells was out in the second over of the day, and Glamorgan hurried to victory. The damage was done by the spinners, Cosker and Croft, who completed a fine all-round match. He began Glamorgan's first-innings revival, from 108 for six to 279, then took five for 33 as Kent fell from 68 for two to 154 all out. Next, Glamorgan themselves crashed from 109 for one to 193, but they had enough runs in the bank. They collected 22 points; four months later they would be champions, just four points ahead of Kent.

Close of play: First day, Kent 67-2 (A. P. Wells 31*, G. R. Cowdrey 5*); Second day, Kent 154; Third day, Kent 156-3 (A. P. Wells 84*, S. A. Marsh 1*).

Glamorgan

S. P. James b McCague	46	– b Fleming	54
H. Morris b McCague	18	– (6) c McCague b Fleming	25
A. Dale c Strang b McCague	0	– lbw b Strang	6
*M. P. Maynard lbw b Headley	12	– c Marsh b Strang	5
P. A. Cottey c Marsh b McCague	17	– lbw b Strang	0
R. D. B. Croft c Fulton b Ealham	39	– (7) c Walker b Fleming	29
†A. D. Shaw lbw b Strang	0	– (2) b McCague	30
Waqar Younis c Marsh b McCague	47	– lbw b Fleming	10
S. D. Thomas c Marsh b Headley	46	– run out	8
S. L. Watkin c Strang b McCague	39	– c Marsh b Strang	0
D. A. Cosker not out	0	– not out	5
B 1, l-b 4, n-b 10	15	L-b 9, n-b 12	21

1/37 2/37 3/71 4/88 5/105   279   1/100 2/109 3/109 4/109 5/114   193
6/108 7/171 8/191 9/249   6/161 7/176 8/181 9/186

Bonus points – Glamorgan 2, Kent 4.

Bowling: *First Innings*—McCague 20.4–5–75–6; Headley 25–7–74–2; Ealham 15–5–64–1; Strang 21–6–51–1; Fleming 3–0–10–0. *Second Innings*—McCague 12–2–54–1; Headley 7–1–31–0; Ealham 5–3–12–0; Strang 23.5–5–59–4; Fleming 14–4–28–4.

Kent

D. P. Fulton c Thomas b Waqar Younis	19	– b Waqar Younis	6
M. J. Walker c Croft b Watkin	9	– b Cosker	35
A. P. Wells lbw b Croft	31	– c Cottey b Cosker	85
G. R. Cowdrey c Maynard b Croft	36	– c Shaw b Cosker	29
N. J. Llong lbw b Croft	4	– (6) b Cosker	15
M. A. Ealham c Cosker b Thomas	15	– (7) not out	20
M. V. Fleming c and b Croft	1	– (8) b Croft	14
P. A. Strang c Cosker b Thomas	1	– (9) c Watkin b Croft	3
*†S. A. Marsh lbw b Thomas	7	– (5) c Shaw b Croft	15
M. J. McCague c Thomas b Croft	12	– c Cottey b Waqar Younis	4
D. W. Headley not out	4	– lbw b Waqar Younis	2
B 4, l-b 9, n-b 2	15	B 1, l-b 2	3

1/20 2/33 3/68 4/78 5/111   154   1/8 2/90 3/154 4/161 5/185   231
6/113 7/126 8/135 9/144   6/195 7/221 8/225 9/229

Bonus points – Glamorgan 4.

Bowling: *First Innings*—Waqar Younis 10–3–49–1; Watkin 14–5–46–1; Thomas 11–4–13–3; Croft 18.4–5–33–5. *Second Innings*—Waqar Younis 14.1–0–52–3; Watkin 9–1–35–0; Thomas 7–1–23–0; Croft 18–4–54–3; Cosker 25–4–64–4.

Umpires: J. C. Balderstone and J. F. Steele.

At Horsham, May 21, 22, 23, 24. KENT beat SUSSEX by 104 runs.

At Nottingham, May 29, 30, 31. KENT beat NOTTINGHAMSHIRE by an innings and 105 runs.

KENT v WARWICKSHIRE

At Tunbridge Wells, June 4, 5, 6, 7. Kent won by four wickets. Kent 23 pts, Warwickshire 6 pts. Toss: Warwickshire.

Kent's cricketing doctor, Julian Thompson, chose the perfect match to emerge from the shadows with an excellent all-round display at The Nevill, his home ground. McCague retired on the first morning with a sore hip, but Thompson – playing his first Championship match for over a year – picked up the second five-wicket haul of his career and saved Kent's reply in a ninth-wicket stand of 109 with Phillips, to give Kent a first-innings lead of 65. Hemp then made his third Championship hundred in four innings, including 17 fours and one six, but he departed early on the final morning as Thompson finished off the Warwickshire tail. Kent were left needing 216 to win in a minimum of 72 overs, and the game reached a tense climax. Kent were outsiders when the score was 158 for six, but Wells and Marsh inched them towards their third win in a row. Warwickshire, already without Donald and Munton, lost Small with a groin strain, and Moles also retired to the dressing-room with a damaged Achilles tendon. When Smith dismissed Strang, his first-class wicket of the season in his 99th over, he kissed the ground in relief.

Close of play: First day, Kent 30–0 (D. P. Fulton 15*, M. J. Walker 11*); Second day, Kent 319–8 (J. B. D. Thompson 27*, B. J. Phillips 38*); Third day, Warwickshire 237–6 (D. L. Hemp 113*, G. Welch 15*).

Warwickshire

*N. V. Knight c Wells b Thompson	36	– c Fulton b Phillips	30
A. J. Moles b Fleming	42	– (7) c Fulton b Fleming	12
D. L. Hemp b Thompson	2	– c Llong b Strang	117
T. L. Penney c Phillips b Llong	84	– c Strang b Phillips	9
D. P. Ostler c Ward b Thompson	38	– c Marsh b Strang	19
D. R. Brown c Marsh b Strang	6	– c Llong b Thompson	0
G. Welch lbw b Llong	27	– (8) c Ward b Strang	40
N. M. K. Smith lbw b Phillips	15	– (2) b Phillips	14
†T. Frost not out	14	– c Marsh b Thompson	2
M. D. Edmond c Wells b Thompson	21	– c Fulton b Thompson	9
G. C. Small c Wells b Thompson	11	– not out	2
B 4, l-b 10, n-b 4	18	B 8, l-b 8, w 10	26

1/73 2/77 3/95 4/182 5/191   314   1/24 2/100 3/118 4/175 5/176   280
6/245 7/266 8/266 9/294   6/212 7/250 8/254 9/266

Bonus points – Warwickshire 3, Kent 4.

Bowling: *First Innings*—McCague 5–0–20–0; Phillips 16–5–49–1; Thompson 22.2–4–89–5; Strang 34–11–65–1; Fleming 14.5–5–44–1; Llong 8–3–33–2. *Second Innings*—Thompson 25–6–48–3; Phillips 12–2–48–3; Fleming 20–7–43–1; Strang 38.2–10–109–3; Llong 4–2–16–0.

Kent

D. P. Fulton c Frost b Brown	73	– c Ostler b Edmond 46
M. J. Walker c Frost b Small	11	– c Penney b Smith 14
T. R. Ward lbw b Brown	33	– b Smith 11
A. P. Wells b Edmond	70	– not out 62
N. J. Llong b Small	13	– c Knight b Welch 5
M. V. Fleming c Penney b Small	5	– b Smith 33
P. A. Strang b Smith	12	– c Edmond b Smith 1
*†S. A. Marsh lbw b Brown	5	– not out 34
J. B. D. Thompson not out	59	
B. J. Phillips c and b Welch	41	
M. J. McCague c Penney b Smith	16	
B 2, l-b 9, w 10, n-b 20	41	L-b 4, n-b 6 10

1/30 2/99 3/147 4/181 5/193	379	1/43 2/63 3/81	(6 wkts) 216
6/235 7/237 8/243 9/352		4/101 5/150 6/158	

Bonus points – Kent 3, Warwickshire 3 (Score at 120 overs: 339-8).

Bowling: *First Innings*—Welch 39–8–136–1; Small 19–7–51–3; Smith 30.2–8–68–2; Brown 25–5–73–3; Edmond 18–7–40–1. *Second Innings*—Brown 6–1–34–0; Welch 19–2–67–1; Smith 27.5–5–68–4; Edmond 10–0–43–1.

Umpires: B. Dudleston and R. Julian.

At Manchester, June 12, 13, 14, 16. KENT beat LANCASHIRE by 58 runs.

At Darlington, June 18, 19, 20, 21. KENT lost to DURHAM by 135 runs.

KENT v CAMBRIDGE UNIVERSITY

At Canterbury, June 28, 29, 30. Drawn. Toss: Kent.

Left-arm seamer How got among the wickets on the first day to give Cambridge a little encouragement before the Varsity match; this was the only time either university bowled out a county side all season. However, a Kent side with eight uncapped players was still good enough to get first-innings lead, and even Cambridge's batting successes could have pleased both sides: the two top scorers, Smith and House, were Kent players. Llong and Fulton built on Kent's lead, but rain washed out the final day.

Close of play: First day, Cambridge University 84-4 (W. J. House 9*, A. N. Janisch 3*); Second day, Kent 195-5 (S. C. Willis 18*).

Kent

D. P. Fulton c Churton b How	11	– c and b Freeth 57
M. J. Walker b Freeth	62	– b P. S. Jones 9
*T. R. Ward c Churton b Janisch	49	– (4) c Singh b Freeth 6
N. J. Llong c House b How	17	– (3) c House b P. S. Jones 99
B. J. Phillips c Churton b How	8	– b R. O. Jones 0
†S. C. Willis c Churton b P. S. Jones	19	– not out 18
D. W. Headley b How	5	
J. B. D. Thompson lbw b How	0	
N. W. Preston c Churton b Janisch	8	
E. J. Stanford c Singh b R. O. Jones	32	
T. N. Wren not out	11	
B 7, l-b 4, w 2, n-b 10	23	B 1, l-b 5 6

1/45 2/135 3/149 4/155 5/170	245	1/23 2/90 3/120	(5 wkts) 195
6/180 7/180 8/188 9/210		4/127 5/195	

Bowling: *First Innings*—P. S. Jones 19–0–87–1; How 15–3–59–5; House 3–2–12–0; Janisch 13–4–43–2; Freeth 9–4–21–1; R. O. Jones 2.3–0–12–1. *Second Innings*—P. S. Jones 16.3–4–45–2; How 13–3–36–0; Janisch 5–1–17–0; House 3–0–11–0; R. O. Jones 10–1–47–1; Freeth 8–2–28–2; Hughes 1–0–5–0.

Cambridge University

J. Ratledge lbw b Thompson	2
E. T. Smith c Fulton b Stanford	54
*A. Singh b Thompson	0
R. O. Jones b Thompson	8
W. J. House lbw b Preston	42
A. N. Janisch c Phillips b Headley	11
Q. J. Hughes c Willis b Thompson	13
†D. R. H. Churton run out	22

P. S. Jones not out	23
J. W. O. Freeth b Wren	0
E. J. How b Wren	0
L-b 2, n-b 10	12

1/27 2/27 3/57 4/80 5/103   187
6/120 7/149 8/176 9/181

Bowling: Headley 14–2–63–1; Thompson 14–2–58–4; Wren 8.4–1–22–2; Stanford 5–2–10–1; Phillips 7–3–11–0; Preston 8–2–21–1.

Umpires: M. K. Reed and D. R. Shepherd.

KENT v NORTHAMPTONSHIRE

At Maidstone, July 2, 3, 4, 5. Northamptonshire won by one wicket. Northamptonshire 20 pts, Kent 3 pts. Toss: Northamptonshire.

Northamptonshire secured their first Championship victory of 1997 off the last ball of the match, when Snape clipped Phillips to the fine-leg boundary. Snape scored 32 in 34 balls to win the day, after his team lost their eighth and ninth wickets with 15 still required from two overs. Kent had started badly, losing their top three for 31 before Llong scored what was to be his one Championship fifty of the season; it was only thanks to Strang and Phillips that they passed 300. More than 150 overs were lost to rain on the second and third days. But two engineered declarations set up a run-chase of 322 from 96 overs. Warren and Bailey gave Northamptonshire a solid platform by adding 137 in 46 overs; Warren eventually gave Marsh his 50th first-class stumping, but there were no wickets for Igglesden, making his come-back in the Championship after missing the 1996 season.

Close of play: First day, Kent 306; Second day, Northamptonshire 41-0 (M. B. Loye 27*, R. J. Warren 10*); Third day, Kent 99-2 dec.

Kent

D. P. Fulton lbw b Taylor	14	– not out	35
M. J. Walker c Warren b Taylor	6	– c Loye b Snape	23
T. R. Ward c Ripley b Mohammad Akram	9	– (4) not out	31
A. P. Wells b Mohammad Akram	26		
N. J. Llong c Bailey b Taylor	57		
M. V. Fleming c Taylor b Curran	12	– (3) b Bailey	8
P. A. Strang c Boswell b Snape	55		
*†S. A. Marsh c Snape b Mohammad Akram	32		
B. J. Phillips b Mohammad Akram	47		
J. B. D. Thompson b Snape	11		
A. P. Igglesden not out	0		
B 4, l-b 6, w 3, n-b 24	37	N-b 2	2

1/10 2/31 3/31 4/125 5/141   306   1/49 2/58   (2 wkts dec.) 99
6/149 7/215 8/248 9/274

Bonus points – Kent 3, Northamptonshire 4.

Bowling: *First Innings*—Mohammad Akram 21.3–6–56–4; Taylor 26–2–95–3; Boswell 16–0–66–0; Curran 15–6–32–1; Snape 23–8–47–2. *Second Innings*—Mohammad Akram 3–1–3–0; Boswell 2–1–3–0; Bailey 10–0–48–1; Snape 9–0–45–1.

Northamptonshire

M. B. Loye not out	48	– lbw b Thompson		10
R. J. Warren not out	31	– st Marsh b Llong		74
*R. J. Bailey (did not bat)		– b Strang		83
K. M. Curran (did not bat)		– c Fulton b Strang		14
T. C. Walton (did not bat)		– lbw b Thompson		11
D. J. Sales (did not bat)		– c and b Strang		59
†D. Ripley (did not bat)		– run out		9
J. N. Snape (did not bat)		– not out		32
J. P. Taylor (did not bat)		– c Fulton b Phillips		4
Mohammad Akram (did not bat)		– run out		0
S. A. J. Boswell (did not bat)		– not out		3
L-b 1, n-b 4	5	B 5, l-b 10, n-b 8		23

(no wkt dec.) 84   1/13 2/150 3/173   (9 wkts) 322
4/196 5/236 6/271
7/300 8/307 9/307

Bowling: *First Innings*—Igglesden 10–5–18–0; Thompson 10–2–28–0; Strang 3–1–11–0; Phillips 2–1–5–0; Llong 5–1–19–0; Wells 3–2–2–0. *Second Innings*—Igglesden 12–0–42–0; Thompson 15–1–65–2; Phillips 8–1–32–1; Fleming 13–3–36–0; Strang 36–9–84–3; Llong 12–2–48–1.

Umpires: H. D. Bird and V. A. Holder.

KENT v LEICESTERSHIRE

At Canterbury, July 16, 17, 18, 19. Leicestershire won by six wickets. Leicestershire 19 pts, Kent 5 pts. Toss: Kent.

For the second time running, Kent were beaten after setting a contrived target in a rain-affected contest. Leicestershire had now lost nearly 1,500 overs to the rain, which had allowed them only one win so far in defence of their title. But Johnson and Ben Smith enjoyed the sun on their backs during an unbroken match-winning stand of 225. For Kent, Ealham had spent five and a half hours over a career-best 139. He added 145 with Strang, who made his highest Championship score, and 146 with Marsh. When rain arrived just before lunch on the second day, Marsh needed two for his century and for Kent's 500. But the innings never resumed. Swift declarations left Leicestershire a seemingly difficult challenge of 365 in just over a day. However, Smith, scoring his second century in four Championship innings against Kent, and Johnson saw them home with four overs to spare.

Close of play: First day, Kent 356-7 (M. A. Ealham 96*, S. A. Marsh 16*); Second day, Kent 498-9 (S. A. Marsh 98*, M. J. McCague 14*); Third day, Leicestershire 20-0 (V. J. Wells 7*, D. L. Maddy 13*).

Kent

D. P. Fulton lbw b Mullally	26	– not out	19
E. T. Smith c Nixon b Ormond	31	– not out	5
T. R. Ward c and b Pierson	51		
A. P. Wells c Nixon b Ormond	5		
N. J. Llong lbw b Ormond	0		
M. A. Ealham b Ormond	139		
M. V. Fleming c Nixon b Pierson	16		
P. A. Strang b Millns	82		
*†S. A. Marsh not out	98		
J. B. D. Thompson b Ormond	0		
M. J. McCague not out	14		
B 8, l-b 12, w 8, n-b 8	36	W 2	2

1/63 2/71 3/108 4/108 5/126   (9 wkts dec.) 498   (no wkt dec.) 26
6/162 7/307 8/453 9/453

Bonus points – Kent 4, Leicestershire 3 (Score at 120 overs: 384-7).

Bowling: *First Innings*—Millns 30–5–106–1; Mullally 30–5–116–1; Ormond 28–4–107–5; Pierson 32–11–79–2; Johnson 20–6–56–0; Wells 3–0–14–0. *Second Innings*—Ormond 3–0–13–0; Wells 1–0–9–0; Smith 1–0–4–0.

Leicestershire

V. J. Wells c Strang b Thompson	15	– b Strang	39
D. L. Maddy b Thompson	24	– c Marsh b McCague	18
I. J. Sutcliffe b Fleming	0	– c Marsh b Fleming	41
*J. J. Whitaker c Fulton b Thompson	47	– b Llong	19
N. C. Johnson not out	72	– not out	117
B. F. Smith not out	0	– not out	121
N-b 2	2	B 2, l-b 8, n-b 2	12

1/38 2/39 3/39 4/138   (4 wkts dec.) 160   1/39 2/72 3/103 4/142   (4 wkts) 367

†P. A. Nixon, A. R. K. Pierson, D. J. Millns, A. D. Mullally and J. Ormond did not bat.

Bonus point – Kent 1.

Bowling: *First Innings*—McCague 8–2–26–0; Thompson 15–3–54–3; Fleming 6–1–22–1; Strang 3–1–16–0; Ealham 10–0–42–0. *Second Innings*—McCague 11–1–62–1; Thompson 11–1–52–0; Fleming 16–5–50–1; Strang 39–9–103–1; Ealham 12–0–43–0; Llong 11.3–0–47–1.

Umpires: B. J. Meyer and K. E. Palmer.

At Lord's, July 23, 24, 25. KENT beat MIDDLESEX by four runs.

At Worcester, July 31, August 1, 2, 4. KENT drew with WORCESTERSHIRE.

KENT v ESSEX

At Canterbury, August 6, 7, 8, 9. Kent won by an innings and eight runs. Kent 24 pts, Essex 2 pts. Toss: Kent. First-class debut: T. P. Hodgson. Championship debut: W. J. House.

A fine double-hundred from Prichard could not deny Kent a comprehensive victory before lunch on the final day. Maximum points took them back to the top of the table. Prichard needed a runner after pulling a hamstring, but batted throughout Essex's second innings; he was last out, after six and a half hours, for 224. He struck 34 boundaries – moving from 76 to 100 with six fours – and made nearly two-thirds of his side's runs off the bat. But it was too late to save them. Kent had amassed 525, their biggest total of the season, thanks to centuries from Wells and Fleming. Wells's 109 was his first hundred since moving from Sussex – he thought he had been trying too hard in the early weeks – and Fleming's 138 was his highest score. Then Essex collapsed, losing their last five for three runs as Thompson struck three times in seven balls, and followed on 369 behind. On the final morning, Strang took four wickets in ten overs, before McCague claimed the new ball to end Prichard's single-handed defiance.

Close of play: First day, Kent 203-4 (A. P. Wells 102*); Second day, Essex 80-5 (R. C. Irani 26*, A. P. Grayson 2*); Third day, Essex 277-5 (P. J. Prichard 171*, D. R. Law 4*).

Kent

T. R. Ward lbw b Andrew	35	P. A. Strang c Rollins b D. R. Law	55
E. T. Smith c Robinson b Williams	5	M. J. McCague not out	7
A. P. Wells c S. G. Law b Irani	109		
G. R. Cowdrey lbw b Irani	53	B 1, l-b 5, w 6, n-b 4	16
W. J. House c and b Such	2		
M. A. Ealham lbw b Such	58	1/23 2/52 3/190 (9 wkts dec.) 525
M. V. Fleming c Irani b D. R. Law	138	4/203 5/211 6/349
*†S. A. Marsh c Robinson b Grayson	47	7/424 8/516 9/525

J. B. D. Thompson did not bat.

Bonus points – Kent 4, Essex 2 (Score at 120 overs: 368-6).

Bowling: Williams 13–0–65–1; Irani 28–6–80–2; Andrew 23–7–87–1; S. G. Law 18–7–49–0; D. R. Law 25.2–6–77–2; Such 26–5–117–2; Grayson 9–1–44–1.

Essex

*P. J. Prichard b McCague	3	– c Ealham b McCague	224
D. D. J. Robinson lbw b McCague	20	– c and b Thompson	23
T. P. Hodgson c Ward b Ealham	8	– c Ward b Strang	15
S. G. Law c Wells b McCague	2	– b Fleming	1
R. C. Irani c Ward b Thompson	50	– c Strang b McCague	9
N. F. Williams c Thompson b McCague	10	– (9) c Ward b Strang	10
A. P. Grayson c Strang b Thompson	48	– (6) lbw b Ealham	38
D. R. Law c Marsh b Ealham	1	– (7) c Ward b Strang	8
†R. J. Rollins c Marsh b Thompson	0	– (8) c Ward b Strang	4
S. J. W. Andrew c Marsh b Ealham	0	– c Thompson b Strang	3
P. M. Such not out	2	– not out	5
B 4, l-b 2, w 2, n-b 4	12	L-b 9, w 4, n-b 8	21

1/10 2/39 3/42 4/59 5/73	156	1/73 2/116 3/121 4/157 5/250 361
6/153 7/154 8/154 9/154		6/290 7/302 8/340 9/352

Bonus points – Kent 4.

Bowling: *First Innings*—McCague 17–0–81–4; Thompson 9–0–23–3; Ealham 8.3–2–14–3; Strang 11–2–32–0. *Second Innings*—McCague 13.5–2–54–2; Ealham 18–4–49–1; Thompson 25–3–105–1; Strang 36–13–119–5; Fleming 10–6–25–1.

Umpires: J. C. Balderstone and P. Willey.

At Canterbury, August 16, 17, 18. KENT lost to AUSTRALIANS by six wickets (See Australian tour section).

At Taunton, August 20, 21, 22, 23. KENT drew with SOMERSET.

At Portsmouth, August 27, 28, 29, 30. KENT drew with HAMPSHIRE.

KENT v GLOUCESTERSHIRE

At Canterbury, September 2, 3, 4, 5. Kent won by 272 runs. Kent 23 pts, Gloucestershire 6 pts. Toss: Kent.

Kent's conclusive victory, halfway through the final day, over third-placed Gloucestershire made them clear Championship leaders and the favourites, 12 points ahead with two games to go. They made another shaky start but Wells hit 77, all but nine of them in fours, and Walker, recalled because Cowdrey had a back injury, helped him add 117. A watchful innings from Ealham and a cavalier one from Fleming saw Kent to 305. Phillips soon had Gloucestershire in trouble, at 61 for five, but Dawson, coming in on a hat-trick, scored his first hundred since May 1995, and the deficit was only 49. Kent hit back, with Ward, who was dropped on six, adding 193 with Wells – the first to pass a thousand runs for Kent in 1997 – and 76 with Walker. The declaration set Gloucestershire an unlikely 482. In 20 overs on the third evening, they had already lost four wickets. Windows batted bravely until after lunch, and Alleyne stayed for two hours before he was last out, giving Headley a fifth wicket.

Close of play: First day, Gloucestershire 12-0 (D. R. Hewson 6*, M. G. N. Windows 4*); Second day, Kent 21-0 (D. P. Fulton 8*, E. T. Smith 8*); Third day, Gloucestershire 59-4 (M. G. N. Windows 42*, D. V. Lawrence 0*).

Kent

D. P. Fulton b Smith	7	– c Alleyne b Ball	44
E. T. Smith lbw b Smith	11	– c Windows b Ball	29
T. R. Ward c Young b Alleyne	14	– not out	161
A. P. Wells c Russell b Alleyne	77	– c Alleyne b Hancock	94
M. J. Walker c Russell b Ball	38	– c Lawrence b Ball	51
M. A. Ealham c Hewson b Davis	31	– not out	16
M. V. Fleming c Hancock b Young	46		
*†S. A. Marsh c Hewson b Smith	28		
P. A. Strang c Alleyne b Ball	14		
B. J. Phillips c and b Ball	7		
D. W. Headley not out	1		
B 1, l-b 10, w 2, n-b 18	31	B 11, l-b 5, n-b 21	37

	305		(4 wkts dec.) 432

1/23 2/28 3/51 4/168 5/174   305   1/66 2/111   (4 wkts dec.) 432
6/240 7/271 8/289 9/304   3/304 4/380

Bonus points – Kent 3, Gloucestershire 4.

Bowling: *First Innings*—Smith 20–7–46–3; Lawrence 15–2–50–0; Young 21–8–59–1; Alleyne 12–2–48–2; Hancock 3–1–19–0; Ball 10.5–0–43–3; Davis 18–8–29–1. *Second Innings*—Smith 9–2–35–0; Lawrence 6–0–53–0; Ball 27–2–126–3; Young 8–3–43–0; Davis 26–9–86–0; Alleyne 6–1–42–0; Hancock 4–0–31–1.

Gloucestershire

D. R. Hewson c Marsh b Phillips	8	– c Marsh b Headley	1
M. G. N. Windows c Wells b Phillips	8	– lbw b Phillips	84
T. H. C. Hancock c Marsh b Phillips	8	– c Strang b Headley	8
R. I. Dawson c Headley b Strang	100	– c Ward b Strang	0
S. Young b Phillips	2	– (7) lbw b Ealham	22
*M. W. Alleyne b Ealham	0	– (8) lbw b Headley	42
†R. C. Russell lbw b Ealham	55	– (9) b Strang	12
M. C. J. Ball c Walker b Headley	34	– (10) c Marsh b Headley	5
R. P. Davis c Fulton b Strang	5	– (5) c Fulton b Strang	0
A. M. Smith run out	9	– (11) not out	1
D. V. Lawrence not out	0	– (6) c Marsh b Headley	8
L-b 5, w 2, n-b 20	27	B 4, l-b 4, n-b 18	26

1/20 2/20 3/58 4/60 5/61   256   1/18 2/40 3/49 4/55 5/80   209
6/177 7/226 8/242 9/251   6/113 7/165 8/193 9/208

Bonus points – Gloucestershire 2, Kent 4.

Bowling: *First Innings*—Headley 25–3–72–1; Strang 25.2–6–50–2; Phillips 14–5–44–4; Ealham 18–4–43–2; Fleming 13–3–42–0. *Second Innings*—Headley 23.4–4–92–5; Phillips 12–3–46–1; Strang 28–14–40–3; Ealham 11–5–23–1.

Umpires: V. A. Holder and A. A. Jones.

At Leeds, September 10, 11, 12, 13. KENT drew with YORKSHIRE.

KENT v SURREY

At Canterbury, September 18, 19, 20. Kent won by five wickets. Kent 21 pts, Surrey 4 pts. Toss: Kent.

Kent won a roller-coaster match in three days, but could not clinch their first County Championship since 1978. They started one point behind Glamorgan, but failed to pick up vital batting points on a pitch which was under-prepared and earned the club a suspended ten-point penalty. Minutes after their victory, it became immaterial; Glamorgan beat Somerset with maximum points. Three days of excitement and controversy ended in muted champagne celebrations for the nearly men of 1997 – Kent finished runners-up in three competitions. "We seem to be perennial bridesmaids," said Matthew Fleming, "but at least we're at the wedding."

With Strang back in Zimbabwe, Kent had to rely on an all-seam attack. But even without their preferred spearheads, the injured Headley and McCague, they dismissed Surrey – also missing three internationals in Adam Hollioake, Thorpe and Martin Bicknell – before lunch. Kent found batting no easier, however, losing Fulton first ball and another eight wickets by the first-day close. That meant a call to Lord's and a visit from an ECB delegation, who eventually pronounced the pitch "poor". Kent were all out within two overs next morning, and they owed their single batting point to the determination of Wells and Ealham. But, in Surrey's second innings, the match suddenly changed course. Stewart, coming in on an Ealham hat-trick, batted beautifully to reach a century in 90 balls. He and Darren Bicknell put on 219 and the home bowlers suddenly looked below par. They displayed more determination on the third morning, however; Surrey's last seven wickets added only 83, with Stewart last out for 170. Kent needed 276, a task made easy by a maiden and long-awaited Championship hundred from Fulton; Fleming completed the win with 41 in 26 balls, but by then they knew it would be unavailing.

Close of play: First day, Kent 217-9 (B. J. Phillips 19*, A. P. Igglesden 1*); Second day, Surrey 288-3 (A. J. Stewart 122*, A. D. Brown 0*).

Surrey

D. J. Bicknell c Ward b Thompson	0	– b Phillips	130
M. A. Butcher c Marsh b Phillips	38	– c and b Ealham	30
J. D. Ratcliffe lbw b Thompson	0	– c Ward b Ealham	0
*†A. J. Stewart c Fulton b Igglesden	4	– c Marsh b Fleming	170
A. D. Brown c Wells b Thompson	0	– c Marsh b Phillips	4
N. Shahid b Igglesden	0	– c Marsh b Phillips	8
B. C. Hollioake c Smith b Thompson	2	– c Marsh b Thompson	2
C. C. Lewis c Fleming b Phillips	27	– lbw b Thompson	0
I. D. K. Salisbury c Marsh b Ealham	8	– c Phillips b Thompson	15
J. E. Benjamin not out	17	– c Ward b Igglesden	0
R. M. Amin b Fleming	4	– not out	1
B 4, l-b 8, w 2, n-b 10	24	B 1, l-b 10	11
	124		**371**

1/9 2/9 3/22 4/29 5/29   124   1/69 2/69 3/288 4/292 5/316   371
6/40 7/74 8/101 9/105   6/327 7/328 8/358 9/359

Bonus points – Kent 4.

Bowling: *First Innings*—Igglesden 10-4-17-2; Thompson 8-1-33-4; Ealham 5-0-28-1; Phillips 2-0-19-2; Fleming 2-0-15-1. *Second Innings*—Igglesden 18-2-81-1; Thompson 23-1-112-3; Ealham 12-2-39-2; Fleming 14.3-1-59-1; Phillips 18-2-58-3; Wells 2-0-11-0.

Kent

D. P. Fulton c Butcher b Lewis	0	– c and b Butcher	110
E. T. Smith lbw b Benjamin	26	– c Salisbury b Benjamin	16
T. R. Ward c Shahid b Hollioake	14	– c Lewis b Butcher	9
A. P. Wells c Lewis b Butcher	48	– c and b Salisbury	12
G. R. Cowdrey c Salisbury b Butcher	7	– c Stewart b Butcher	33
M. A. Ealham c Butcher b Hollioake	52	– not out	18
M. V. Fleming lbw b Hollioake	0	– not out	41
*†S. A. Marsh c Hollioake b Amin	16		
B. J. Phillips not out	22		
J. B. D. Thompson c Stewart b Butcher	0		
A. P. Igglesden c and b Hollioake	1		
B 1, l-b 3, n-b 30	34	B 8, w 6, n-b 23	37
	220	(5 wkts)	**276**

1/0 2/27 3/87 4/110 5/125   220   1/36 2/63 3/116   (5 wkts) 276
6/126 7/162 8/213 9/213   4/201 5/210

Bonus points – Kent 1, Surrey 4.

Bowling: *First Innings*—Lewis 8-0-54-1; Hollioake 18.2-5-54-4; Benjamin 17-3-45-1; Butcher 16-6-24-3; Ratcliffe 3-0-18-0; Amin 12-5-21-1. *Second Innings*—Lewis 13.2-0-79-0; Benjamin 13-2-56-1; Hollioake 8-1-38-0; Butcher 13-1-26-3; Salisbury 14-2-38-1; Amin 11-1-31-0.

Umpires: T. E. Jesty and A. G. T. Whitehead.

LANCASHIRE

Peter Martin

Patron: HM The Queen
President: J. B. Statham
Chairman: J. Simmons
Chairman, Cricket Committee: G. Ogden
Chief Executive: J. Cumbes
Cricket Secretary: D. M. R. Edmundson
Captain: 1997 – M. Watkinson
          1998 – Wasim Akram
Head Coach: D. F. Whatmore
Head Groundsman: P. Marron
Scorer: A. West

Lancashire finished outside the top eight of the County Championship for the 20th time in 30 years, and without the compensation of the traditional day out at Lord's. Late in the summer, a muddled patch off the field and a muddy patch on it caused turmoil and controversy. There were mitigating factors, notably the avalanche of injuries which forced Lancashire to use 23 players in the Championship and four captains – with a fifth in one-day cricket. And there was some cause for optimism, with Australian coach Dav Whatmore determined to use the lessons he learned from a tough introduction to county cricket. But most at Old Trafford were glad to see the back of this particular summer. It ended with a wide-ranging change of personnel among the club officials, although the committee refused to acknowledge the word "crisis".

Whatmore's task was difficult from the start. England call-ups meant Mike Atherton and John Crawley played only 21 Championship games between them, and injuries to overseas star Wasim Akram and captain Mike Watkinson badly affected the quality and balance of the side. Wasim missed virtually the entire campaign and, although Watkinson fought his way back, he was never at his best. Lancashire had hoped that, with Wasim's return, they could win the Championship. Yet, by late June, they were without a win. They had been embarrassed in two days at Taunton, and devastated in 14 overs at Liverpool, where Waqar Younis took seven for 25.

After that humiliation by Glamorgan, however, Lancashire produced five victories in their last ten Championship games. The catalyst was success in a contrived finish at rain-hit Worcester, with England Under-19 captain Andy Flintoff playing a key role. The powerfully built Flintoff went on to his maiden first-class century at Southampton and earned a place on the England A tour. Flintoff headed a string of promising youngsters – others included left-handed opener Nathan Wood, son of Barry, who also chalked up a maiden century, and left-arm spinner Gary Keedy, who took ten wickets in the penultimate match against Surrey.

Lancashire's revival, coupled with Yorkshire's outside challenge for the Championship, put extra spice into the Roses match at Old Trafford at the end of August. But it turned into a bizarre, unhappy week. Chairman Bob Bennett, shouldering increased England responsibilities, had just announced he was stepping down after 11 years. Then, in an unrelated move, chief executive John Bower suddenly departed, citing differences on "issues of philosophy" with some committee members. On the field, Lancashire were struggling; Jason Gallian vented his frustration by knocking out two stumps with his bat, for which he was fined. Already unhappy with the terms of a new contract, which eventually he refused, Gallian finished his Old Trafford career in the Second Eleven. He later joined Nottinghamshire. The previous year, he had set a ground record with 312 against Derbyshire; it was sad to see such a good player leaving.

But the Gallian incident was not the last act of the Roses drama. That came in perfect weather on the final morning, when play was abandoned without a ball bowled because overnight rain had leaked on to the pitch. Lancashire claimed they had taken every precaution, but Yorkshire were seething. The row also fuelled their feud in the Second Eleven Championship, which Lancashire won despite forfeiting 24 points for fielding two overseas players against Yorkshire.

Lancashire's senior team did end their Championship campaign on a brighter note. There was a vain but gallant run-chase against Essex, an easy win over Surrey, and a defiant draw with Gloucestershire, on a last, balmy day at Bristol.

With the line-up constantly shuffled to accommodate injuries and Test duties, Lancashire's Championship form was an odd mix. Yet they figured in a lot of positive cricket, particularly when set challenging targets by Kent and Essex at Old Trafford – though they lost both. Other matches might have gone their way but for the weather, which loomed large from the opening game, against Durham, when a promising position came to naught with the last two days washed out. But they still had to face the accusation that they under-achieved. Inconsistent batting, the lack of a match-winning spinner – until Keedy's performance at The Oval – and Wasim's absence were all too evident.

Peter Martin and Ian Austin were the outstanding individuals. Martin, disappointed at being left out by England, responded with his best ever season, taking 58 first-class wickets at 23.13. He briefly regained his Test place at the end of the summer. Although he did not do enough to join Atherton and Crawley on the trip to the West Indies, he was picked for the one-day party to Sharjah. Austin scored 825 first-class runs, took 45 wickets and missed only one match; he was the supporters' choice for Player of the Season. Graham Lloyd started the season with a double-century in the "friendly" against Yorkshire, when he shared a seventh-wicket stand of 248 with Austin, a county record. Three times he reached a hundred inside 80 balls and, though his form tailed off, he was the only player to pass 1,000 first-class runs for Lancashire. Crawley did it when his Test runs were thrown in, and averaged nearly 60 in the county games he did play.

In previous years, Lancashire's Championship problems were partly forgotten along the road to one-day glory. Not this time. The Benson and Hedges Cup/ NatWest Trophy double of 1996 was quickly wiped out. Out of sorts in the Benson and Hedges group games – they even struggled against Minor Counties in the swirling sleet of Walsall – Lancashire failed to qualify, and they were the victims of a NatWest upset in the second round against Sussex. The Sunday League remained their best hope; but they suffered a crucial home defeat by eventual winners Warwickshire in early August, and finished third.

As the season drew to a close, Jack Simmons was voted in as the new chairman, and in October Jim Cumbes became chief executive, forming a partnership with a deep cricketing background. Simmons's career as the Old Trafford off-spinner stretched over 22 years and Cumbes had played for four counties, including two spells with Lancashire. Mike Watkinson then stepped down as captain and, in November, Wasim was asked to take over, with Crawley as his deputy, for 1998. Lancashire also broke new ground by putting their players on full-time rather than summer-only contracts. – COLIN EVANS.

530

LANCASHIRE 1997

[*Bill Smith*]

Back row: L. Brown (*physiotherapist*), P. R. Sleep (*Second Eleven captain/coach*), N. T. Wood, C. Brown, M. J. Chilton, A. Flintoff, P. M. Ridgway, D. J. Shadford, P. C. McKeown, J. J. Haynes, G. Keedy, R. J. Green, M. E. Harvey, D. F. Whatmore (*coach*). *Front row:* S. P. Titchard, G. Yates, P. J. Martin, G. D. Lloyd, N. H. Fairbrother, M. Watkinson (*captain*), M. A. Atherton, J. P. Crawley, W. K. Hegg, J. E. R. Gallian, I. D. Austin, G. Chapple. *Inset:* Wasim Akram.

LANCASHIRE RESULTS

All first-class matches – Played 18: Won 6, Lost 6, Drawn 6.

County Championship matches – Played 17: Won 5, Lost 6, Drawn 6.

Competition placings – Britannic Assurance County Championship, 11th; NatWest Trophy, 2nd round; Benson and Hedges Cup, 4th in Group A; AXA Life League, 3rd.

COUNTY CHAMPIONSHIP AVERAGES

BATTING

Cap		M	I	NO	R	HS	100s	50s	Avge	Ct/St
1994	J. P. Crawley	11	16	1	898	133	3	5	59.86	8
1992	G. D. Lloyd†	15	22	2	831	122	3	5	41.55	16
1985	N. H. Fairbrother† ...	15	22	1	855	132	2	4	40.71	17
1989	M. A. Atherton†	10	16	1	596	149	2	3	39.73	6
1990	I. D. Austin†	16	24	4	742	95	0	7	37.10	5
	N. T. Wood	10	15	2	469	155	1	2	36.07	3
	A. Flintoff†	4	6	0	216	117	1	1	36.00	3
1987	M. Watkinson†	11	17	0	473	135	1	2	27.82	5
	R. J. Green†	3	4	1	81	51	0	1	27.00	0
1989	W. K. Hegg†	16	22	5	455	77*	0	5	26.76	36/2
1994	J. E. R. Gallian	10	17	2	394	99	0	3	26.26	11
1995	S. P. Titchard†	5	7	0	155	79	0	1	22.14	2
1994	P. J. Martin†	15	16	4	258	78*	0	1	21.50	3
1994	G. Chapple	10	13	3	214	66	0	2	21.40	2
1994	G. Yates†	10	12	3	192	39	0	0	21.33	7
	P. C. McKeown†	3	4	0	68	46	0	0	17.00	2
	D. J. Shadford†	8	10	3	106	30	0	0	15.14	5
	M. E. Harvey†	2	4	0	49	25	0	0	12.25	1
	G. Keedy	8	8	7	11	6*	0	0	11.00	1

Also batted: M. J. Chilton (1 match) 9; J. J. Haynes (1 match) 18, 2 (7 ct); P. M. Ridgway (2 matches) 0, 0*; (cap 1989) Wasim Akram§ (1 match) 13, 3 (1 ct).

* Signifies not out. † Born in Lancashire. § Overseas player.

BOWLING

	O	M	R	W	BB	5W/i	Avge
P. J. Martin	408	119	1,180	52	8-32	3	22.69
I. D. Austin	409.1	119	1,083	41	4-44	0	26.41
G. Chapple	255.2	39	816	25	4-80	0	32.64
G. Keedy	292.4	60	917	27	6-79	1	33.96
G. Yates	274.4	51	876	25	5-59	1	35.04
D. J. Shadford	149	8	786	19	5-80	1	41.36
M. Watkinson	204.4	35	735	17	3-35	0	43.23

Also bowled: M. A. Atherton 1–0–7–0; M. J. Chilton 4–0–23–0; J. E. R. Gallian 79.2–12–357–7; R. J. Green 60.2–15–172–4; G. D. Lloyd 11.5–0–101–0; P. M. Ridgway 39–6–163–2; S. P. Titchard 13–1–44–3; Wasim Akram 36–10–86–3; N. T. Wood 4.1–0–38–0.

COUNTY RECORDS

Highest score for:	424	A. C. MacLaren v Somerset at Taunton	1895
Highest score against:	315*	T. W. Hayward (Surrey) at The Oval	1898
Best bowling for:	10-46	W. Hickton v Hampshire at Manchester	1870
Best bowling against:	10-40	G. O. B. Allen (Middlesex) at Lord's	1929
Highest total for:	863	v Surrey at The Oval	1990
Highest total against:	707-9 dec.	by Surrey at The Oval	1990
Lowest total for:	25	v Derbyshire at Manchester	1871
Lowest total against:	22	by Glamorgan at Liverpool...............	1924

At Leeds, April 16, 17, 18, 19. LANCASHIRE beat YORKSHIRE by six wickets (Non-Championship fixture).

LANCASHIRE v DURHAM

At Manchester, April 23, 24, 25, 26. Drawn. Lancashire 9 pts, Durham 8 pts. Toss: Lancashire. Championship debut: D. C. Boon.

Appropriately, at the start of an Ashes summer, there was a heavy Australian influence on this game, as Dav Whatmore, Lancashire's new coach, welcomed David Boon, Durham's new captain. The sense of adventure which pervaded the first day was encouraging: Boon maintained attacking fields and Lancashire raced along, with 213 runs in the afternoon session. Lloyd hit 102 in 80 balls and then, just when Durham thought it was over at 360 for nine, Chapple and Martin combined to add 134 in the last 19 overs of the day. Next morning, they extended that to 146, Lancashire's best last-wicket stand since 1885. Needing 357 to avoid the follow-on, Durham struggled although Boon gave them backbone with an unbeaten 85. It all ended in frustration, anyway, with the last two days washed out. Morris retired twice with a split thumb and Lancashire captain Watkinson suffered an arm injury which was to trouble him for a lengthy period.

Close of play: First day, Lancashire 494-9 (G. Chapple 65*, P. J. Martin 67*); Second day, Durham 201-6 (D. C. Boon 85*, J. Wood 13*); Third day, No play.

Lancashire

J. E. R. Gallian c Speight b Brown	78	G. Yates b Boiling	6
M. A. Atherton c Speight b Wood	15	G. Chapple c Lewis b Betts	66
J. P. Crawley lbw b Betts	19	P. J. Martin not out	78
N. H. Fairbrother c Boiling b Brown	21		
G. D. Lloyd c Wood b Collingwood	102	B 2, l-b 7, n-b 10	19
*M. Watkinson c Wood b Campbell	51		
I. D. Austin b Collingwood	29	1/38 2/97 3/118 4/155 5/245	506
†W. K. Hegg c Speak b Campbell	22	6/315 7/328 8/353 9/360	

Bonus points – Lancashire 4, Durham 4.

Bowling: Brown 26–5–93–2; Betts 20.2–2–114–2; Wood 13–1–70–1; Campbell 12–0–92–1; Boiling 17–3–82–1; Collingwood 12–2–46–3.

Durham

J. J. B. Lewis b Chapple	44	J. Boiling c Lloyd b Martin	5
P. D. Collingwood lbw b Austin	13	J. Wood not out	13
J. E. Morris retired hurt	8		
N. J. Speak c Fairbrother b Watkinson	21	B 5, l-b 1, n-b 2	8
*D. C. Boon not out	85		
†M. P. Speight c Hegg b Yates	3	1/57 2/61 3/115	(6 wkts) 201
M. M. Betts b Chapple	1	4/143 5/146 6/168	

S. J. E. Brown and C. L. Campbell did not bat.

Bonus points – Durham 1, Lancashire 2.

J. E. Morris, when 7, retired hurt at 71 and resumed at 146; he retired again at 147.

Bowling: Chapple 23.2–2–95–2; Martin 20–9–31–1; Austin 14.1–5–28–1; Gallian 2–0–12–0; Watkinson 4.5–1–10–1; Yates 10–4–19–1.

Umpires: G. I. Burgess and R. Palmer.

LANCASHIRE v NOTTINGHAMSHIRE

At Manchester, May 14, 15, 16, 17. Nottinghamshire won by six wickets. Nottinghamshire 22 pts, Lancashire 4 pts. Toss: Nottinghamshire.

Lancashire collapsed at once to 52 for nine on a green pitch against the bowling of Evans, who took a career-best six for 40. And though they had another successful last-wicket stand –

Crawley and Martin – they were to go down to a deserved defeat. Nottinghamshire also owed much to the batting of Afzaal and Johnson, who shared two century stands, and Johnson's adept captaincy. Nineteen-year-old left-hander Afzaal, born in Rawalpindi but educated in Nottingham, improved his highest score twice with 70 and 77, both not out, after being called up from the Second Eleven. Lancashire had their chances, notably on the third day, when they were 142 ahead with six wickets left, and when Martin reduced Nottinghamshire to 63 for four on the final morning. They were handicapped by the fact that Wasim Akram bowled only nine overs in the second innings because of a shoulder strain, which kept him out for the rest of the season. But there were no excuses for the profusion of wides which helped hand Nottinghamshire 71 first-innings extras.

Close of play: First day, Nottinghamshire 128-4 (P. Johnson 52*, U. Afzaal 25*); Second day, Lancashire 133-1 (M. A. Atherton 48*, J. P. Crawley 64*); Third day, Nottinghamshire 30-0 (P. R. Pollard 4*, C. M. Tolley 24*).

Lancashire

J. E. R. Gallian c Archer b Evans	0	– c Noon b Evans	0
M. A. Atherton c Pollard b Evans	1	– run out	68
J. P. Crawley not out	51	– c Noon b Franks	101
N. H. Fairbrother c Johnson b Evans	0	– (6) c Franks b Bowen	37
G. D. Lloyd c Noon b Evans	1	– (4) c Afzaal b Archer	62
*M. Watkinson c Evans b Tolley	9	– (5) lbw b Franks	1
I. D. Austin c Evans b Tolley	0	– b Afzaal	13
Wasim Akram c Archer b Tolley	13	– st Noon b Afzaal	3
†W. K. Hegg c Archer b Evans	5	– c Noon b Bowen	5
G. Chapple c Archer b Evans	0	– (11) not out	17
P. J. Martin c Gie b Franks	32	– (10) c Franks b Afzaal	9
L-b 5, w 2, n-b 6	13	L-b 9, w 8, n-b 24	41

1/0 2/1 3/11 4/14 5/33   125   1/0 2/178 3/238 4/240 5/280   357
6/33 7/47 8/52 9/52   6/316 7/324 8/328 9/331

Bonus points – Nottinghamshire 4.

Bowling: *First Innings*—Evans 16–6–40–6; Franks 10–0–37–1; Tolley 8–0–35–3; Bowen 2–0–8–0. *Second Innings*—Evans 26–9–63–1; Franks 25–3–86–2; Bowen 31–8–70–2; Tolley 11–5–26–0; Afzaal 21.5–3–79–3; Archer 6–1–24–1.

Nottinghamshire

P. R. Pollard b Chapple	2	– lbw b Martin	15
R. T. Robinson lbw b Wasim Akram	7		
G. F. Archer lbw b Wasim Akram	0	– c Gallian b Martin	4
N. A. Gie b Wasim Akram	4	– c Hegg b Austin	8
*P. Johnson b Chapple	66	– not out	87
U. Afzaal not out	70	– not out	77
C. M. Tolley c Hegg b Austin	15	– (2) c Gallian b Martin	25
†W. M. Noon c Hegg b Austin	5		
K. P. Evans c Wasim Akram b Chapple	11		
M. N. Bowen c Hegg b Austin	9		
P. J. Franks c Lloyd b Austin	3		
B 1, l-b 26, w 28, n-b 16	71	B 1, l-b 2, n-b 4	7

1/13 2/13 3/13 4/37 5/157   263   1/32 2/36 3/49 4/63   (4 wkts) 223
6/182 7/194 8/218 9/245

Bonus points – Nottinghamshire 2, Lancashire 4.

Bowling: *First Innings*—Wasim Akram 27–6–74–3; Martin 21–8–44–0; Chapple 21–6–49–3; Austin 22–6–44–4; Gallian 1–0–8–0; Watkinson 5–1–17–0. *Second Innings*—Wasim Akram 9–4–12–0; Chapple 14–0–47–0; Austin 17–4–38–1; Martin 14–3–52–3; Watkinson 10–2–35–0; Gallian 6.1–2–36–0.

Umpires: V. A. Holder and A. A. Jones.

LANCASHIRE v NORTHAMPTONSHIRE

At Manchester, May 21, 22, 23, 24. Drawn. Lancashire 6 pts, Northamptonshire 7 pts. Toss: Northamptonshire.

Injuries and England duties were beginning to bite into Lancashire's resources. Watkinson and Wasim Akram were under treatment while Atherton, Crawley and Lloyd were playing in the one-day internationals. Fairbrother returned to the captaincy and even put on the keeper's gloves when Hegg suffered a back spasm. On a pitch with early turn, off-spinner Yates and left-armer Keedy made Northamptonshire work hard; by 3.35 p.m. on the second day, they had crawled to 479 off 171.4 overs. Lancashire's reply, only marginally quicker, featured a duel between Fairbrother and Embury, whose first 22 overs yielded just eight runs. But the entertainment value was dwindling, and it touched zero on the last day.

Close of play: First day, Northamptonshire 281-4 (K. M. Curran 91*, D. J. Capel 8*); Second day, Lancashire 89-2 (S. P. Titchard 20*, N. H. Fairbrother 3*); Third day, Lancashire 410-8 (I. D. Austin 93*, G. Chapple 13*).

Northamptonshire

R. R. Montgomerie c Gallian b Keedy	49	– c McKeown b Martin	11
M. B. Loye c Hegg b Martin	31	– c Gallian b Yates	61
*R. J. Bailey c McKeown b Keedy	58	– b Yates	63
K. M. Curran c Titchard b Chapple	108	– b Titchard	10
A. L. Penberthy c Yates b Titchard	32	– c Hegg b Keedy	28
D. J. Capel lbw b Chapple	15	– c and b Yates	1
T. C. Walton c Austin b Keedy	60	– not out	50
J. N. Snape hit wkt b Yates	8	– not out	1
†D. Ripley not out	79		
J. E. Embury b Chapple	0		
J. P. Taylor lbw b Yates	18		
B 10, l-b 11	21	L-b 5, w 2	7

1/49 2/140 3/147 4/257 5/301   479   1/21 2/93 3/113   (6 wkts dec.) 232
6/306 7/319 8/434 9/434   4/162 5/163 6/202

Bonus points – Northamptonshire 2, Lancashire 1 (Score at 120 overs: 299-4).

Bowling: *First Innings*—Chapple 29–3–77–3; Martin 25–8–81–1; Keedy 57–13–149–3; Austin 21–6–43–0; Yates 32.4–5–86–2; Titchard 5–1–11–1; Gallian 2–0–11–0. *Second Innings*—Chapple 4–1–13–0; Martin 6–2–10–1; Gallian 4–0–27–0; Yates 16–2–70–3; Keedy 20–4–85–1; Titchard 4–0–22–1.

Lancashire

J. E. R. Gallian c Bailey b Embury	49	– (2) not out	56
N. T. Wood c Ripley b Penberthy	7	– (1) not out	48
S. P. Titchard c Ripley b Taylor	25		
*N. H. Fairbrother c Taylor b Penberthy	83		
P. C. McKeown c Curran b Taylor	46		
G. Yates b Taylor	25		
I. D. Austin lbw b Snape	95		
†W. K. Hegg c Bailey b Taylor	33		
P. J. Martin lbw b Capel	17		
G. Chapple not out	14		
B 1, l-b 4, w 2, n-b 14	21	L-b 10	10

1/12 2/84 3/99 4/178 5/218   (9 wkts dec.) 415   (no wkt) 114
6/263 7/320 8/386 9/415

G. Keedy did not bat.

Bonus points – Lancashire 2, Northamptonshire 2 (Score at 120 overs: 299-6).

Bowling: *First Innings*—Taylor 36–9–101–4; Penberthy 15–3–52–2; EmbUrey 49–18–115–1; Snape 36.1–7–99–1; Walton 2–0–7–0; Bailey 2–0–14–0; Capel 6–0–22–1. *Second Innings*—Taylor 3–2–9–0; Penberthy 3–1–10–0; Emburey 1–0–2–0; Snape 12–3–40–0; Curran 7–0–27–0; Capel 4–0–16–0.

Umpires: K. E. Palmer and J. F. Steele.

At Leicester, May 29, 30, 31, June 2. LANCASHIRE drew with LEICESTERSHIRE.

At Taunton, June 4, 5. LANCASHIRE lost to SOMERSET by seven wickets.

LANCASHIRE v KENT

At Manchester, June 12, 13, 14, 16. Kent won by 58 runs. Kent 24 pts, Lancashire 6 pts. Toss: Lancashire. First-class debut: P. M. Ridgway.

Kent went to the top of the table, winning with only seven balls left, but Lancashire could take heart, both from the way they kept going for a win and from the performances of two young seamers, Darren Shadford and Paul Ridgway. Kent took the initiative, thanks to a maiden century from night-watchman Phillips. Lancashire then had to cope with beautiful leg-spin bowling from Strang, who had match figures of 11 for 186. Shadford also had a game to remember. After helping Lloyd save the follow-on, he grabbed three wickets in a lively spell on the third evening. But Kent set a target of 306 and Crawley's masterly 91 was not quite enough. On the Saturday, Atherton was awarded the OBE, an honour he knew was coming but which had slipped his mind until he spotted an unusual number of cameras at the ground.

Close of play: First day, Kent 151-5 (A. P. Wells 31*, B. J. Phillips 3*); Second day, Lancashire 113-5 (G. D. Lloyd 13*, J. J. Haynes 1*); Third day, Kent 81-4 (M. V. Fleming 12*, M. A. Ealham 4*).

Kent

D. P. Fulton c Fairbrother b Chapple	19	– lbw b Shadford	22
M. J. Walker c Lloyd b Shadford	45	– c Haynes b Ridgway	26
T. R. Ward c Haynes b Shadford	16	– c Crawley b Shadford	9
A. P. Wells c Fairbrother b Shadford	65	– c Lloyd b Shadford	0
M. V. Fleming c Haynes b Austin	0	– c Haynes b Shadford	19
M. A. Ealham c Lloyd b Chapple	15	– c Haynes b Austin	10
B. J. Phillips not out	100	– (9) c Haynes b Chapple	18
P. A. Strang lbw b Austin	43	– (7) c Atherton b Chapple	25
*†S. A. Marsh c Haynes b Chapple	24	– (8) lbw b Ridgway	35
J. B. D. Thompson c Atherton b Titchard	3	– not out	23
M. J. McCague b Austin	5	– not out	8
B 8, l-b 6, w 12, n-b 12	38	L-b 10, n-b 12	22

1/44 2/76 3/87 4/92 5/135   373   1/50 2/60 3/60   (9 wkts dec.) 217
6/198 7/283 8/326 9/356   4/71 5/94 6/98
                                         7/154 8/160 9/205

Bonus points – Kent 4, Lancashire 4.

Bowling: *First Innings*—Chapple 28–7–86–3; Shadford 20–1–110–3; Austin 24.3–7–58–3; Ridgway 19–4–73–0; Watkinson 4–1–21–0; Titchard 4–0–11–1. *Second Innings*—Chapple 15–2–44–2; Austin 16–4–50–1; Shadford 12–0–67–4; Ridgway 13–1–46–2.

Lancashire

S. P. Titchard st Marsh b Strang	18	– (2) lbw b Phillips	8
M. A. Atherton c Marsh b McCague	5	– (1) c Ward b McCague	28
J. P. Crawley c Marsh b Strang	44	– lbw b Phillips	91
N. H. Fairbrother c Walker b Phillips	20	– c Fulton b Fleming	22
G. D. Lloyd c Ward b Strang	122	– c Phillips b Strang	17
*M. Watkinson b Strang	3	– c sub b Strang	29
†J. J. Haynes c Walker b Strang	18	– (10) b McCague	2
I. D. Austin b Strang	20	– (7) b Strang	14
G. Chapple c Wells b Ealham	0	– (8) c Fulton b McCague	21
D. J. Shadford not out	22	– (9) c Fulton b Strang	1
P. M. Ridgway c Ward b Strang	0	– not out	0
B 3, l-b 2, n-b 8	13	B 4, l-b 5, w 3, n-b 2	14

1/13 2/53 3/86 4/90 5/104	285	1/12 2/79 3/132 4/159 5/203	247
6/174 7/204 8/207 9/277		6/207 7/242 8/244 9/245	

Bonus points – Lancashire 2, Kent 4.

Bowling: *First Innings*—McCague 21–4–70–1; Thompson 10–2–33–0; Ealham 12–0–38–1; Strang 37–12–118–7; Phillips 8–4–21–1. *Second Innings*—McCague 15.5–4–61–3; Phillips 10–1–47–2; Thompson 4–0–15–0; Ealham 4–0–16–0; Strang 17–6–68–4; Fleming 6–0–31–1.

Umpires: J. W. Holder and G. Sharp.

LANCASHIRE v GLAMORGAN

At Liverpool, June 18, 19, 20, 21. Glamorgan won by 221 runs. Glamorgan 18 pts. Toss: Glamorgan. First-class debut: M. J. Chilton.

Waqar Younis led Glamorgan to a spectacular victory, annihilating Lancashire for 51 in just 14 overs. It was a swift reversal of their own collapse, for 31 in 16 overs against Middlesex, a week earlier. Waqar was unplayable, returning career-best figures of 7–1–25–7. He almost took a hat-trick in his first over – when Fairbrother survived a confident lbw appeal – and did complete one with the second ball of his seventh. Though it should take nothing away from Waqar's performance, Lancashire were weakened by Test calls and injuries. Waqar's Pakistan bowling partner, Wasim Akram, had hoped to lead the team, but failed another fitness test on his shoulder and, visibly upset, left the ground. Lancashire introduced Mark Chilton, their latest recruit from Manchester Grammar; he became the 20th player to appear for them in the 1997 Championship. Rain cut the first day to 50 overs, in which James reached 99. After the loss of eight sessions, some declaration bowling helped him to 152, and double forfeits set Lancashire 273 in 60 overs. Waqar and Watkin inflicted their third successive Championship defeat, in 69 minutes. Nearly all Glamorgan's travelling supporters missed their team's triumph; expecting further bad weather, they went sightseeing instead.

Close of play: First day, Glamorgan 173-1 (S. P. James 99*, A. Dale 34*); Second day, No play; Third day, No play.

Glamorgan

S. P. James not out	152	
H. Morris c Hegg b Austin	24	
A. Dale not out	78	
B 8, l-b 6, w 2, n-b 2	18	

1/62	(1 wkt dec.) 272

*M. P. Maynard, P. A. Cottey, G. P. Butcher, †A. D. Shaw, Waqar Younis, S. D. Thomas, D. A. Cosker and S. L. Watkin did not bat.

Bonus points – Glamorgan 2.

Bowling: Martin 14–3–32–0; Chapple 12–2–31–0; Austin 15–7–41–1; Keedy 5–1–26–0; Chilton 4–0–23–0; Yates 1–0–8–0; Lloyd 5–0–59–0; Wood 4.1–0–38–0.

Glamorgan forfeited their second innings.

Lancashire

Lancashire forfeited their first innings.

N. T. Wood lbw b Waqar Younis	0	G. Yates b Waqar Younis	0
S. P. Titchard lbw b Waqar Younis	5	P. J. Martin lbw b Watkin	1
G. Chapple b Waqar Younis	0	G. Keedy c Waqar Younis b Watkin	0
*N. H. Fairbrother b Watkin	5		
G. D. Lloyd c Shaw b Waqar Younis	7	B 4, l-b 1, n-b 2	7
M. J. Chilton c Shaw b Waqar Younis	9		
I. D. Austin not out	17	1/4 2/4 3/13 4/17 5/27	51
†W. K. Hegg b Waqar Younis	0	6/38 7/50 8/50 9/51	

Bowling: Waqar Younis 7–1–25–7; Watkin 7–3–21–3.

Umpires: J. H. Hampshire and V. A. Holder (A. A. Jones deputised for V. A. Holder on the 1st day).

At Worcester, June 26, 27, 28, 30. LANCASHIRE beat WORCESTERSHIRE by three wickets.

At Uxbridge, July 2, 3, 4, 5. LANCASHIRE beat MIDDLESEX by an innings and 54 runs.

LANCASHIRE v SUSSEX

At Manchester, July 16, 17, 18, 19. Lancashire won by an innings and 18 runs. Lancashire 24 pts, Sussex 5 pts. Toss: Sussex.

Lancashire's first Championship win at Old Trafford for just over two years was hard-earned, despite the convincing margin. After putting Lancashire in on a relaid pitch and in damp, overcast conditions, Sussex might have caused problems as they did in their shock NatWest Trophy win the previous week. However, Crawley was dropped at slip before scoring, and Sussex paid dearly for that: Crawley and Fairbrother added 243 in 58 overs. On the second day, Watkinson and Austin scored freely, and Lancashire declared at 561 for eight. It was a monumental task for Sussex's vulnerable batting. But they produced unexpected resistance, mainly through Taylor and Newell, although even Robinson, a notoriously unsuccessful batsman, was difficult to dislodge. He was rewarded for a career-best 27 with promotion to night-watchman in the follow-on. However, the pitch was offering increasing help to the spinners, Watkinson and Yates, and Lancashire secured their third Championship victory on the trot early on the final afternoon.

Close of play: First day, Lancashire 380-5 (M. Watkinson 25*, I. D. Austin 12*); Second day, Sussex 156-5 (K. Newell 21*, P. Moores 4*); Third day, Sussex 150-4 (K. Greenfield 21*, M. A. Robinson 4*).

Lancashire

M. A. Atherton lbw b Kirtley	33	G. Yates b Jarvis	8
J. E. R. Gallian b Robinson	25	P. J. Martin not out	37
J. P. Crawley c Moores b Robinson	112		
N. H. Fairbrother c Greenfield b Kirtley	132	L-b 15, w 2, n-b 32	49
G. D. Lloyd c Athey b Robinson	3		
*M. Watkinson lbw b Jarvis	75	1/57 2/67 3/310 (8 wkts dec.)	561
I. D. Austin not out	78	4/334 5/338 6/457	
†W. K. Hegg lbw b Drakes	9	7/486 8/499	

D. J. Shadford did not bat.

Bonus points – Lancashire 4, Sussex 2 (Score at 120 overs: 468-6).

Bowling: Drakes 30–6–114–1; Jarvis 28–2–104–2; Robinson 32–4–142–3; Kirtley 30–6–125–2; Newell 8–1–25–0; Greenfield 4–1–18–0; Rao 7–1–18–0.

Sussex

N. J. Lenham lbw b Martin	5	– c Hegg b Watkinson	14
R. K. Rao lbw b Martin	18	– c Hegg b Gallian	24
N. R. Taylor c Shadford b Yates	82	– b Yates	26
C. W. J. Athey c Fairbrother b Austin	6	– b Yates	53
K. Greenfield b Austin	0	– lbw b Austin	36
K. Newell c Yates b Austin	74	– (7) c and b Austin	6
*†P. Moores c Crawley b Watkinson	22	– (8) c Atherton b Yates	20
V. C. Drakes c Shadford b Watkinson	27	– (9) c Gallian b Yates	22
P. W. Jarvis lbw b Martin	11	– (10) c Lloyd b Yates	0
M. A. Robinson c Martin b Watkinson	27	– (6) lbw b Austin	17
R. J. Kirtley not out	7	– not out	7
B 9, l-b 11, n-b 8	28	L-b 11	11

1/9 2/41 3/65 4/65 5/137　　　　　　　　307　　1/38 2/38 3/82 4/145 5/178　　　236
6/194 7/261 8/265 9/285　　　　　　　　　　　6/179 7/190 8/223 9/225

Bonus points – Sussex 3, Lancashire 4.

Bowling: *First Innings*—Shadford 15–1–54–0; Martin 23–7–61–3; Austin 18–6–36–3; Watkinson 19.5–3–79–3; Yates 18–4–57–1. *Second Innings*—Shadford 6–1–17–0; Martin 12–3–25–0; Austin 18–7–34–3; Watkinson 32–8–73–1; Gallian 5–2–10–1; Yates 30.5–8–59–5; Atherton 1–0–7–0.

Umpires: D. J. Constant and R. Julian.

At Southampton, July 23, 24, 25, 26. LANCASHIRE drew with HAMPSHIRE.

LANCASHIRE v WARWICKSHIRE

At Blackpool, August 6, 7, 8. Lancashire won by three wickets. Lancashire 24 pts, Warwickshire 4 pts. Toss: Warwickshire.

As Warwickshire were only 18 ahead with two wickets standing, admission for the third day was free. A thousand spectators took advantage – and were rewarded with a day of nerve-tingling cricket. Warwickshire made a game of it thanks to Giles and Frost, who stretched their ninth-wicket stand to 107 in 17 overs. Lancashire needed 88 and were made to sweat by Welch, who took a career-best 11 for 140 in the match, and Donald. They slumped to 45 for six before the stoical youngster, Wood, and their experienced later order steered them home. Smith, leading Warwickshire for the first time in the Championship, had decided to bat, only to be trapped in conditions ideal for Martin, who claimed six for 46. After conceding a lead of 223, Warwickshire staggered to 98 for six, with promising pace bowler Shadford grabbing three in ten balls on the way to his first five-wicket haul. It looked like being over in two days – until Giles and Frost turned free-fall into free for all.

Close of play: First day, Lancashire 194-3 (G. D. Lloyd 70*, M. E. Harvey 13*); Second day, Warwickshire 241-8 (A. F. Giles 34*, T. Frost 9*).

Warwickshire

D. P. Ostler c Gallian b Martin	8	– b Shadford	11
M. A. Wagh lbw b Austin	6	– b Austin	4
D. L. Hemp c Hegg b Martin	15	– c Gallian b Shadford	35
A. Singh lbw b Martin	1	– b Shadford	0
T. L. Penney c Fairbrother b Austin	20	– c Watkinson b Martin	12
*N. M. K. Smith b Martin	2	– b Austin	24
D. R. Brown c Harvey b Martin	42	– c Fairbrother b Martin	53
G. Welch c Yates b Austin	27	– c Hegg b Shadford	38
A. F. Giles c Gallian b Martin	6	– c Yates b Austin	72
†T. Frost not out	6	– c and b Shadford	40
A. A. Donald c Hegg b Austin	1	– not out	0
L-b 1, n-b 4	5	L-b 7, w 2, n-b 12	21

1/8 2/20 3/21 4/36 5/44   139   1/8 2/54 3/54 4/59 5/98   310
6/76 7/112 8/132 9/132   6/98 7/179 8/203 9/310

Bonus points – Lancashire 4.

Bowling: *First Innings*—Martin 19–5–46–6; Austin 18.4–3–45–4; Shadford 4–0–17–0; Gallian 8–2–30–0. *Second Innings*—Martin 26–7–110–2; Austin 23.2–5–78–3; Gallian 6–2–24–0; Shadford 11–1–80–5; Watkinson 3–0–11–0.

Lancashire

J. E. R. Gallian c Ostler b Welch	22	– b Welch	2
N. T. Wood c Brown b Donald	4	– c Wagh b Brown	26
N. H. Fairbrother c Frost b Brown	60	– b Welch	4
G. D. Lloyd c Ostler b Brown	75	– c Wagh b Welch	1
M. E. Harvey c Wagh b Donald	14	– c Frost b Donald	9
*M. Watkinson c Frost b Welch	22	– b Welch	6
I. D. Austin c Frost b Welch	68	– c Frost b Welch	1
†W. K. Hegg c Frost b Welch	0	– not out	16
G. Yates c Penney b Welch	32	– not out	14
P. J. Martin b Smith b Welch	6		
D. J. Shadford not out	0		
B 9, l-b 13, w 7, n-b 30	59	L-b 4, w 6, n-b 2	12

1/9 2/42 3/169 4/199 5/205   362   1/3 2/13 3/17 4/28   (7 wkts) 91
6/274 7/274 8/351 9/362   5/39 6/45 7/67

Bonus points – Lancashire 4, Warwickshire 4.

Bowling: *First Innings*—Donald 25–7–52–2; Welch 30.1–7–115–6; Brown 29–3–106–2; Giles 6–2–21–0; Hemp 8–1–46–0. *Second Innings*—Donald 16–6–40–1; Welch 17–7–25–5; Brown 7.1–2–22–1.

Umpires: H. D. Bird and J. H. Harris.

At Derby, August 15, 16. LANCASHIRE lost to DERBYSHIRE by an innings and 37 runs.

LANCASHIRE v YORKSHIRE

At Manchester, August 27, 28, 29, 30. Drawn. Lancashire 9 pts, Yorkshire 10 pts. Toss: Yorkshire.

On a sunny Saturday morning, relations between the Roses rivals acquired an edge of genuine ill-feeling when the final day was abandoned. Heavy overnight rain had crept over a board holding the covering in place, and on to the pitch. "If this costs us the Championship we will be distraught," said Yorkshire captain David Byas. But groundsman Peter Marron said he had taken every precaution. "My conscience is clear." Yorkshire, already 318 ahead, had planned to bat for a few more overs and leave Lancashire a challenging target. They had controlled the match from the start, with Vaughan leading a solid effort from their top order. Only a fifty from Hegg saved Lancashire from following on. Gallian, when bowled by Hutchison, knocked out two stumps with an exasperated flick of his bat. He apologised but was fined £250, reprimanded and warned about his conduct by the club.

Close of play: First day, Yorkshire 247-3 (D. S. Lehmann 17*, C. E. W. Silverwood 8*); Second day, Lancashire 135-3 (N. H. Fairbrother 39*, G. D. Lloyd 35*); Third day, Yorkshire 176-5 (C. White 23*).

Yorkshire

A. McGrath c Lloyd b Yates	33	– c Hegg b Watkinson	76
M. P. Vaughan b Gallian	105	– b Watkinson	47
*D. Byas c Martin b Green	61	– c Gallian b Yates	4
D. S. Lehmann c Hegg b Martin	40	– b Yates	13
C. E. W. Silverwood c Martin b Watkinson	58		
C. White c Lloyd b Green	52	– (5) not out	23
B. Parker c Hegg b Austin	16	– (6) st Hegg b Yates	5
†R. J. Blakey c Hegg b Austin	10		
G. M. Hamilton c Yates b Green	3		
R. D. Stemp not out	10		
P. M. Hutchison not out	3		
B 5, l-b 5, n-b 18	28	L-b 6, n-b 2	8

1/69 2/216 3/222 4/292 5/354   (9 wkts dec.) 419   1/82 2/109 3/136   (5 wkts) 176
6/386 7/402 8/406 9/410   4/148 5/176

Bonus points – Yorkshire 4, Lancashire 4.

Bowling: *First Innings*—Martin 25–6–69–1; Austin 23–4–77–2; Green 25.2–7–66–3; Yates 21–1–89–1; Watkinson 13–0–60–1; Gallian 7–0–48–1. *Second Innings*—Martin 5–0–38–0; Austin 6–0–39–0; Yates 5.1–0–45–3; Watkinson 4–0–48–2.

Lancashire

J. E. R. Gallian b Hutchison	10	†W. K. Hegg not out	50
N. T. Wood c Blakey b Hutchison	20	G. Yates b Stemp	18
J. P. Crawley c Blakey b Stemp	28	R. J. Green not out	16
N. H. Fairbrother c Blakey b White	44	B 1, l-b 9, n-b 4	14
G. D. Lloyd b Hutchison	44		
*M. Watkinson c Byas b Hamilton	18	1/21 2/42 3/84 4/153 5/157 (8 wkts dec.) 277
I. D. Austin c McGrath b Silverwood	15	6/183 7/189 8/222

P. J. Martin did not bat.

Bonus points – Lancashire 2, Yorkshire 3.

Bowling: Silverwood 14.3–1–47–1; Hutchison 21–5–67–3; Hamilton 11–2–35–1; Stemp 13–2–44–2; Vaughan 7–0–42–0; White 12–3–32–1.

Umpires: N. T. Plews and A. G. T. Whitehead.

LANCASHIRE v ESSEX

At Manchester, September 2, 3, 4, 5. Essex won by 26 runs. Essex 20 pts, Lancashire 4 pts. Toss: Essex.

Stuart Law produced an exhilarating innings, 155 in 131 balls, out of 199 while he was in. He hit three sixes off Keedy's left-arm spin. But Keedy, given his chance when Watkinson left himself out, refused to be overawed and bowled with composure for four wickets. Playing hours had been adjusted to allow Essex an early departure for the NatWest final, and another rain-hit match led to another contrived finish, but the cricket was of a high calibre. Eventually,

Lancashire had to chase 351 in 135 overs. Spinners Such and Grayson were soon bowling in harness, and to great effect, despite a welcome 56 from Atherton. Lancashire's cause seemed hopeless, until Hegg and Green, who chalked up a maiden fifty, revived them with an eighth-wicket stand of 97. But when Prichard brought back Cowan, his fifth ball pinned Green, and Such and Grayson then completed Essex's first Championship win since June.

Close of play: First day, Essex 389; Second day, No play; Third day, Lancashire 213-6 (W. K. Hegg 11*, G. Yates 6*).

Essex

*P. J. Prichard c Hegg b Austin	15	A. P. Cowan c Crawley b Keedy	5
D. D. J. Robinson c Hegg b Keedy	32	M. C. Ilott c Austin b Martin	22
I. N. Flanagan c Hegg b Austin	40	P. M. Such run out	1
S. G. Law c Yates b Martin	155		
R. C. Irani c Fairbrother b Yates	2	B 1, l-b 1, w 2, n-b 6	10
A. P. Grayson c and b Keedy	44		
D. R. Law c Hegg b Keedy	3	1/31 2/68 3/173 4/184 5/267	389
†R. J. Rollins not out	60	6/277 7/328 8/340 9/388	

Bonus points – Essex 4, Lancashire 4.

Bowling: Martin 16–1–63–2; Austin 17–2–81–2; Green 15–2–60–0; Keedy 34–6–98–4; Yates 29–4–85–1.

Essex forfeited their second innings.

Lancashire

M. A. Atherton not out	24	– c Prichard b Such	56
N. T. Wood not out	7	– c Rollins b D. R. Law	16
*J. P. Crawley (did not bat)		– c S. G. Law b Such	35
N. H. Fairbrother (did not bat)		– lbw b Grayson	6
G. D. Lloyd (did not bat)		– b Such	8
I. D. Austin (did not bat)		– c S. G. Law b Grayson	50
†W. K. Hegg (did not bat)		– b Such	55
G. Yates (did not bat)		– c S. G. Law b Grayson	9
R. J. Green (did not bat)		– lbw b Cowan	51
P. J. Martin (did not bat)		– c Irani b Grayson	2
G. Keedy (did not bat)		– not out	0
L-b 2, n-b 6	8	B 6, l-b 8, w 18, n-b 4	36

(no wkt dec.) 39   1/48 2/107 3/114 4/129 5/166   324
6/202 7/220 8/317 9/324

Bowling: *First Innings*—Ilott 4–2–9–0; D. R. Law 4–2–8–0; Grayson 4–0–17–0; Such 3–1–3–0. *Second Innings*—Ilott 8–1–25–0; Cowan 8–1–22–1; Such 42–15–103–4; D. R. Law 4–1–17–1; Grayson 38.2–12–143–4.

Umpires: B. Dudleston and R. A. White.

At The Oval, September 10, 11, 12. LANCASHIRE beat SURREY by an innings and 55 runs.

At Bristol, September 18, 19, 20, 21. LANCASHIRE drew with GLOUCESTERSHIRE.

WALTER LAWRENCE TROPHY

The Walter Lawrence Trophy for the fastest first-class century in 1997 was won, for the second year running, by Graham Lloyd of Lancashire, who reached 100 in 73 balls against Leicestershire. He received £1,000.

LEICESTERSHIRE

David Millns

President: B. A. F. Smith

Chairman: R. Goadby

Chairman, Cricket Committee: P. R. Haywood

Chief Executive: D. G. Collier

Captain: J. J. Whitaker

Cricket Manager: J. Birkenshaw

Head Groundsman: S. Wright

Scorer: G. A. York

After the summer of 1997, Leicestershire captain James Whitaker could have auditioned for Noah. His team's defence of the County Championship sank without trace in one of the wettest summers of modern times. And it seemed to be wettest wherever Leicestershire were playing. Rain cost them 2,260 overs, which equates to 22 days, five and a half matches, or, more starkly, nearly one third of the season.

Their game against Warwickshire was washed out without a ball bowled – the first time that a four-day Championship match had been abandoned. The only rain-free match was against Lancashire – they still drew. When they went to Eastbourne to play Championship rabbits Sussex, whose form suggested they were not a safe bet to beat a local school team, the south coast was lashed by storms and the match reduced to one innings. Sussex won by 38 runs, their only win of the season and Leicestershire's only defeat.

None of this implies that, with better weather, Leicestershire would have retained the Championship pennant. Glamorgan were second in the rain-table but managed to rise to a famous triumph. Still, the chances are Leicestershire would have won a few more than their four victories, lost one or two more and finished perhaps in the top four. As it was, they had to settle for tenth, their lowest position since 1991.

Their difficulties illustrated the law of averages: in 1996, they hardly saw a black cloud and enjoyed such freedom from injury that they used only 13 players. In 1997, they used 18, and several key men spent time on the treatment table. There were occasions when Leicestershire played well, but they never reached the standards of their Championship season. Whitaker was unsure whether to blame the players or the weather for destroying their rhythm. Probably they share the responsibility.

Only one batsman, Vince Wells, topped 1,000 runs for the county, against four in 1996; not one bowler took 50 wickets, whereas two, David Millns and Phil Simmons, sailed past that the year before.

It took Whitaker a while to realise that, without Simmons, their West Indian all-rounder and talisman, Leicestershire could not steamroller the opposition. That was rammed home in the match against Yorkshire, whose captain, David Byas, criticised him for letting the match drift. Whitaker took the lesson on board, but he still could not fill the huge gap left by Simmons, who had set up so many wins by ripping out the middle order. As a result, killing teams off, even when Leicestershire had their foot on their opponents' throats, proved a problem, especially as fast bowlers Millns and Alan Mullally were in less than rampaging form.

Leicestershire decided against waiting for Simmons, who was hoping to be selected for West Indies' late series against India and Sri Lanka. He missed out, but it proved a wise decision; when Simmons visited Grace Road in mid-season, he had an elbow injury. His replacement, South African Neil Johnson, half-filled Simmons's shoes. He topped the batting averages with 819 at 63, which put him joint fifth nationally, but bowled only 116 overs for eight wickets because of an Achilles tendon injury. It upset the whole balance of the side.

If Leicestershire's Championship campaign was disappointing, they gained some encouragement from the one-day competitions. They moved up eight places in the Sunday League to fourth – their highest finish for 15 years – and reached the semi-finals of the Benson and Hedges Cup. That said, they were lucky to overcome Somerset in the quarter-finals, after being skittled for 197 in 46.2 overs, and they crashed to a 130-run defeat against Surrey in the semis. Yorkshire walloped them by 128 runs in the NatWest second round.

Perhaps the most encouraging feature of the season was the development of talented youngsters like batsmen Iain Sutcliffe and Darren Maddy and fast bowler James Ormond. Sutcliffe, rated by former captain Nigel Briers as a future England certainty, was a mite unlucky not to make the England A tour. But the other two did. Maddy scored three Championship centuries – 103 every time – and averaged 40.79; he made 1,047 in all first-class cricket. He had the technique and the dedication; time will tell whether he goes all the way. The cavalier Ormond's dedication was a moot point, but he was probably the most gifted young fast bowler on the circuit. Aged 19, he burst upon national consciousness in June by taking six in an innings against the Australians, with the sort of swing they usually see from a boomerang, and finished with 44 first-class victims at 26.40. Ormond, a strapping 6ft 3in with a hint of Fred Trueman about him, is also rapid, as Nottinghamshire discovered when he bowled one of the quickest sustained spells at Grace Road for some time – uphill too.

Ormond and co will be joined in 1998 by a prodigal son, Chris Lewis, England's sometime all-rounder, who agreed in November to return to his first county, which he left in 1991 to go wandering round the circuit. The prospect of being groomed to succeed Whitaker as captain apparently reconciled Lewis to his original employers.

Sadly, though, it was the end for two stalwarts, wicket-keeper Phil Whitticase and Gordon Parsons, who were released. Parsons was still the most accurate bowler at the club at the age of 37, and had hoped to play on for another year; Grace Road won't seem the same without "Bullhead", steam emanating from both ears, doing a double teapot in the middle of the pitch. – CHRIS GODDARD.

LEICESTERSHIRE 1997

[*Bill Smith*]

Back row: T. J. Mason, C. D. Crowe, I. J. Sutcliffe, A. Thomas, D. I. Stevens, P. E. Robinson (*Second Eleven captain*), D. Williamson. *Middle row:* C. Mortimer (*physiotherapist*), B. F. Smith, M. T. Brimson, J. Ormond, J. M. Dakin, G. I. Macmillan, A. Habib, D. L. Maddy, G. A. York (*scorer*). *Front row:* V. J. Wells, G. J. Parsons, D. J. Millns, J. M. Josephs (*chairman*), J. Birkenshaw (*cricket manager*), B. A. F. Smith (*president*), J. J. Whitaker (*captain*), A. O. Norman (*chief executive*), P. A. Nixon, A. R. K. Pierson, P. Whitticase. *Insets:* A. D. Mullally, N. C. Johnson.

LEICESTERSHIRE RESULTS

All first-class matches – Played 19: Won 4, Lost 2, Drawn 12, Abandoned 1.

County Championship matches – Played 17: Won 4, Lost 1, Drawn 11, Abandoned 1.

Competition placings – Britannic Assurance County Championship, 10th;
NatWest Trophy, 2nd round; Benson and Hedges Cup, s-f;
AXA Life League, 4th.

COUNTY CHAMPIONSHIP AVERAGES

BATTING

Cap		M	I	NO	R	HS	100s	50s	Avge	Ct/St
1997	N. C. Johnson§	12	18	5	819	150	2	5	63.00	13
	J. M. Dakin	3	4	0	208	190	1	0	52.00	2
1994	P. A. Nixon	16	20	7	595	96	0	4	45.76	49/3
1995	B. F. Smith	13	19	5	624	131*	2	2	44.57	3
1994	V. J. Wells	16	24	0	1,061	224	3	5	44.20	10
1986	J. J. Whitaker	14	20	1	797	133*	2	4	41.94	5
1996	D. L. Maddy†	16	24	0	979	103	3	5	40.79	14
1997	I. J. Sutcliffe	11	16	1	582	130	2	2	38.80	3
1991	D. J. Millns	14	15	2	449	121	2	1	34.53	2
1984	G. J. Parsons	5	6	1	113	69*	0	1	22.60	1
	A. Habib	7	11	2	198	77	0	1	22.00	4
1995	A. R. K. Pierson	15	15	0	266	59	0	1	17.73	8
	M. T. Brimson	6	7	2	59	30*	0	0	11.80	3
	G. I. Macmillan	4	5	1	40	19	0	0	10.00	2
	J. Ormond	10	10	2	64	35	0	0	8.00	2
1993	A. D. Mullally	12	11	5	41	13*	0	0	6.83	2

Also batted: D. I. Stevens† (1 match) 8 (1 ct); D. Williamson (1 match) 3.

* Signifies not out. † Born in Leicestershire. § Overseas player.

BOWLING

	O	M	R	W	BB	5W/i	Avge
J. Ormond	269.3	58	906	35	6-68	2	25.88
D. J. Millns	395.4	84	1,286	48	6-61	2	26.79
A. D. Mullally	369.1	88	1,247	37	5-52	4	33.70
A. R. K. Pierson	485.1	101	1,411	37	6-56	1	38.13
G. J. Parsons	161.2	43	425	11	4-22	0	38.63
V. J. Wells	187	43	621	16	2-8	0	38.81

Also bowled: M. T. Brimson 131.5–34–357–9; J. M. Dakin 52–12–152–4; A. Habib 4–0–37–0; N. C. Johnson 116–18–420–8; G. I. Macmillan 11–1–41–0; D. L. Maddy 33.2–8–94–2; P. A. Nixon 2–0–4–0; B. F. Smith 1–0–4–0; D. I. Stevens 2–1–5–1; I. J. Sutcliffe 1–0–12–0; J. J. Whitaker 0.2–0–0–0; D. Williamson 17.5–5–40–4.

COUNTY RECORDS

Highest score for:	261	P. V. Simmons v Northants at Leicester	1994
Highest score against:	341	G. H. Hirst (Yorkshire) at Leicester	1905
Best bowling for:	10-18	G. Geary v Glamorgan at Pontypridd	1929
Best bowling against:	10-32	H. Pickett (Essex) at Leyton	1895
Highest total for:	701-4 dec.	v Worcestershire at Worcester	1906
Highest total against:	761-6 dec.	by Essex at Chelmsford	1990
Lowest total for:	25	v Kent at Leicester	1912
Lowest total against:	{ 24	by Glamorgan at Leicester	1971
	24	by Oxford University at Oxford	1985

At Cambridge, April 18, 19, 20. LEICESTERSHIRE drew with CAMBRIDGE UNIVERSITY.

LEICESTERSHIRE v GLOUCESTERSHIRE

At Leicester, April 23, 24, 25, 26. Drawn. Leicestershire 10 pts, Gloucestershire 8 pts. Toss: Gloucestershire. County debut: S. Young. Championship debut: J. Ormond.

A match full of fluctuations was cut short after only two days by rain. Mullally, anxious for brownie points after a disappointing winter with England in Zimbabwe and New Zealand, got the perfect start by taking five wickets in front of the national coach, David Lloyd. It was time Mullally had some good news; while on tour, he also picked up a nasty dose of psoriasis and was fined £8,000 by an Australian court for a car accident some three years previously. Gloucestershire were in severe trouble at 84 for five, but recovered to 245, thanks to Russell and the newly arrived Tasmanian all-rounder Shaun Young. They looked set for first-innings lead when Leicestershire were nine down for 206, but the Coventry-born fast bowler James Ormond marked his Championship debut by sharing a last-wicket stand of 101 with Nixon.

Close of play: First day, Leicestershire 99-3 (D. L. Maddy 42*, A. R. K. Pierson 0*); Second day, Gloucestershire 8-0 (N. J. Trainor 4*, A. J. Wright 4*); Third day, No play.

Gloucestershire

N. J. Trainor c Nixon b Mullally	2	– not out		4
A. J. Wright c Macmillan b Mullally	23	– not out		4
R. J. Cunliffe lbw b Millns	3			
M. A. Lynch c Nixon b Mullally	36			
S. Young c Macmillan b Millns	59			
*M. W. Alleyne lbw b Ormond	0			
†R. C. Russell b Millns	57			
T. H. C. Hancock not out	38			
M. C. J. Ball c Pierson b Wells	1			
A. M. Smith c Nixon b Mullally	1			
J. Lewis c Pierson b Mullally	3			
B 3, l-b 11, w 2, n-b 6	22			

1/3 2/6 3/68 4/73 5/84   245   (no wkt)   8
6/196 7/203 8/204 9/206

Bonus points – Gloucestershire 1, Leicestershire 4.

Bowling: *First Innings*—Millns 15–2–47–3; Mullally 20.5–9–52–5; Ormond 15–3–61–1; Wells 15–5–46–1; Pierson 7–0–25–0. *Second Innings*—Millns 1.1–0–5–0; Mullally 1–0–3–0.

Leicestershire

V. J. Wells lbw b Smith	2	D. J. Millns lbw b Ball		15
D. L. Maddy c Lynch b Lewis	80	A. D. Mullally c Wright b Ball		4
I. J. Sutcliffe lbw b Alleyne	37	J. Ormond lbw b Smith		35
A. Habib lbw b Alleyne	5			
A. R. K. Pierson c Ball b Lewis	6	B 12, l-b 11, n-b 4		27
*J. J. Whitaker b Alleyne	19			
G. I. Macmillan c Russell b Hancock	0	1/6 2/71 3/95 4/115 5/156		307
†P. A. Nixon not out	77	6/157 7/170 8/202 9/206		

Bonus points – Leicestershire 3, Gloucestershire 4.

Bowling: Smith 24.1–8–62–2; Lewis 23–3–76–2; Young 20–5–56–0; Ball 17–4–36–2; Alleyne 20–11–29–3; Hancock 5–1–24–1; Trainor 3–2–1–0.

Umpires: J. D. Bond and J. H. Hampshire.

At Worcester, May 7, 8, 9, 10. LEICESTERSHIRE drew with WORCESTERSHIRE.

At Southampton, May 14, 15, 16, 17. LEICESTERSHIRE beat HAMPSHIRE by five wickets.

LEICESTERSHIRE v SURREY

At Leicester, May 21, 22, 23, 24. Drawn. Leicestershire 10 pts, Surrey 9 pts. Toss: Leicestershire. Championship debut: J. A. Knott.

Surrey, with four players away at the one-day internationals, seemed mostly interested in
avoiding defeat. The match, played on a flat pitch, ended in a hopelessly dull draw. Despite the
loss of the first day because of a wet run-up, Surrey dawdled to 278, using up 108 overs. Maddy
led Leicestershire to 340 in 106 overs, but there was too little time left to force a result. Surrey's
acting-captain Lewis scored an unbeaten 47 to follow his four for 64 against one of his old clubs.

Close of play: First day, No play; Second day, Surrey 235-8 (M. P. Bicknell 5*, R. M. Pearson
0*); Third day, Leicestershire 305-6 (P. A. Nixon 53*, D. J. Millns 9*).

Surrey

D. J. Bicknell lbw b Millns	18	– c Habib b Pierson	24
M. A. Butcher lbw b Millns	59	– lbw b Millns	0
J. D. Ratcliffe c Maddy b Johnson	36	– b Mullally	19
N. Shahid c Habib b Pierson	31	– lbw b Parsons	14
A. D. Brown b Pierson	21	– b Parsons	40
*C. C. Lewis c Habib b Pierson	22	– not out	47
†J. A. Knott b Pierson	14	– not out	6
M. P. Bicknell not out	34		
A. J. Tudor run out	1		
R. M. Pearson lbw b Millns	1		
J. E. Benjamin c Wells b Millns	5		
B 3, l-b 15, w 6, n-b 12	36	B 6, l-b 6, w 2, n-b 2	16

1/45 2/96 3/151 4/173 5/190   278   1/5 2/47 3/53   (5 wkts) 166
6/220 7/227 8/234 9/236   4/92 5/154

Bonus points – Surrey 2, Leicestershire 4.

Bowling: *First Innings*—Millns 26–7–64–4; Mullally 19–3–75–0; Parsons 22–9–38–0; Wells
4–0–17–0; Pierson 30–14–47–4; Johnson 7–1–19–1. *Second Innings*—Millns 7–0–17–1; Parsons
14–6–27–2; Mullally 14–2–48–1; Pierson 27–5–62–1; Wells 1–1–0–0.

Leicestershire

V. J. Wells c Butcher b Pearson	56	G. J. Parsons c M. P. Bicknell b Lewis	6
D. L. Maddy c Brown b M. P. Bicknell	103	A. R. K. Pierson b Lewis	16
*J. J. Whitaker c Butcher b Pearson	1	A. D. Mullally c Pearson b Lewis	0
N. C. Johnson b Tudor	24		
B. F. Smith lbw b Lewis	4	B 7, l-b 1, w 8, n-b 40	56
A. Habib c Butcher b Tudor	1		
†P. A. Nixon not out	64	1/131 2/147 3/188 4/197 5/204	340
D. J. Millns lbw b Tudor	9	6/271 7/305 8/314 9/336	

Bonus points – Leicestershire 3, Surrey 4.

Bowling: M. P. Bicknell 19–2–58–1; Lewis 20–4–64–4; Tudor 18–4–62–3; Benjamin
16–4–35–0; Pearson 26–4–90–2; D. J. Bicknell 5–1–13–0; Butcher 2–0–10–0.

Umpires: G. I. Burgess and B. J. Meyer.

LEICESTERSHIRE v LANCASHIRE

At Leicester, May 29, 30, 31, June 2. Drawn. Leicestershire 11 pts, Lancashire 10 pts. Toss: Lancashire.

Again, Leicestershire had to settle for a draw, though this time they could not blame the rain. Set 331 to win in what became 71 overs, they finished well short on 247 for five. Although Wells scored a century and just missed two in the match, no one really came to terms with the spin of Yates and Keedy, and Leicestershire were always behind the asking-rate. It was a disappointing end to a match which the batsmen dominated on a bland pitch. Lloyd smacked a scintillating 82 in Lancashire's first innings and an unbeaten hundred from 73 balls in the second; it was the third time he had reached three figures in under 80 balls in 1997, and it remained the fastest century of the season. The game's other centurions were the England captain Atherton, leading Lancashire for once and responding with his first Championship century since 1995, and Leicestershire's new overseas player, Neil Johnson from Natal, who made a splendid 150. Gallian, who put on 169 with Atherton, was out for 99.

Close of play: First day, Lancashire 365-9 (G. Chapple 57*, G. Keedy 0*); Second day, Leicestershire 380-5 (N. C. Johnson 134*, P. A. Nixon 68*); Third day, Lancashire 279-2 (M. A. Atherton 100*).

Lancashire

J. E. R. Gallian c Johnson b Millns	12	– lbw b Parsons	99
*M. A. Atherton b Mullally	24	– c Maddy b Pierson	108
J. P. Crawley c Nixon b Johnson	41	– lbw b Parsons	61
N. H. Fairbrother c Whitaker b Johnson	35	– c Whitaker b Pierson	20
G. D. Lloyd st Nixon b Harvie	82	– not out	100
I. D. Austin c Johnson b Mullally	9	– st Nixon b Pierson	5
G. Yates c Wells b Mullally	0		
†W. K. Hegg b Parsons	58	– (7) not out	8
P. J. Martin c Nixon b Mullally	4		
G. Chapple c Smith b Mullally	63		
G. Keedy not out	0		
B 6, l-b 5, w 2, n-b 32	45	L-b 12, n-b 12	24

1/12 2/83 3/111 4/158 5/179	373	1/169 2/279 3/293 (5 wkts dec.) 425
6/179 7/246 8/264 9/349		4/342 5/381

Bonus points – Lancashire 4, Leicestershire 4.

Bowling: *First Innings*—Millns 19–2–75–1; Mullally 24.3–5–79–5; Parsons 24–4–76–1; Pierson 18–4–34–1; Johnson 16–0–76–2; Wells 6–0–22–0. *Second Innings*—Millns 8–3–32–0; Mullally 8–3–26–0; Parsons 33–4–125–2; Pierson 39.3–3–159–3; Wells 3–0–17–0; Johnson 8–0–25–0; Maddy 5–0–29–0.

Leicestershire

V. J. Wells c Fairbrother b Gallian	95	– b Yates	107
D. L. Maddy c Lloyd b Chapple	0	– c Fairbrother b Keedy	11
B. F. Smith lbw b Austin	31	– st Hegg b Keedy	34
*J. J. Whitaker lbw b Yates	6	– (5) c Austin b Keedy	20
N. C. Johnson lbw b Austin	150	– (4) c Lloyd b Yates	29
A. Habib b Martin	38	– not out	21
†P. A. Nixon lbw b Gallian	96	– not out	10
D. J. Millns b Chapple	11		
G. J. Parsons c Atherton b Gallian	16		
A. R. K. Pierson b Chapple	12		
A. D. Mullally not out	1		
L-b 6, w 6	12	B 8, l-b 7	15

1/0 2/57 3/97 4/170 5/215	468	1/44 2/135 3/181 (5 wkts) 247
6/414 7/437 8/437 9/462		4/202 5/217

Bonus points – Leicestershire 4, Lancashire 3 (Score at 120 overs: 448-8).

Bowling: *First Innings*—Martin 23–6–84–1; Chapple 20–4–79–3; Austin 23–7–65–2; Yates 28–5–93–1; Keedy 17–2–90–0; Gallian 14.1–3–51–3. *Second Innings*—Martin 9–3–34–0; Austin 6–2–15–0; Yates 21–4–92–2; Keedy 26–7–66–3; Chapple 4–0–15–0; Gallian 2–0–10–0.

Umpires: B. Leadbeater and R. Palmer.

At Lord's, June 4, 5, 6, 7. LEICESTERSHIRE drew with MIDDLESEX.

At Leicester, June 14, 15, 16. LEICESTERSHIRE lost to AUSTRALIANS by 84 runs (See Australian tour section).

At Bath, June 18, 19, 20, 21. LEICESTERSHIRE drew with SOMERSET.

LEICESTERSHIRE v WARWICKSHIRE

At Leicester, June 26, 27, 28, 30. Abandoned. Leicestershire 3 pts, Warwickshire 3 pts.

Rain prevented any play, for the first time in a four-day Championship match; the last Championship game to be washed out had been Worcestershire v Gloucestershire on May 29, 30, June 1, 1992, at Worcester.

LEICESTERSHIRE v YORKSHIRE

At Leicester, July 2, 3, 4, 5. Drawn. Leicestershire 11 pts, Yorkshire 8 pts. Toss: Yorkshire. First-class debut: R. J. Sidebottom.

Leicestershire were again hit by the weather: they lost another 139 overs, taking their total for the season to 1,339. Only one of their first nine Championship matches had reached a positive conclusion. Play did not start until 2.15 on the first afternoon because of a wet run-up and it was washed out on day two after lunch. Even so, Leicestershire constructed a possible winning position which crumbled. They bowled Yorkshire out for 268, with Mullally taking his third five-wicket haul of the season; then Whitaker and Maddy raced along, adding 150 for the third wicket. But both of them, plus Johnson, fell at the same score, costing vital momentum. Leicestershire had to bat on 35 minutes into the final day for a lead of 138. Byas criticised Whitaker for not declaring overnight and inviting him to set a target; Whitaker said he had wanted to win properly. The match drifted towards a draw, but Lehmann gave the crowd something to cheer, with a brilliant unbeaten 163 off 146 balls, including five sixes and nine fours.

Close of play: First day, Yorkshire 149-5 (D. Byas 66*, R. J. Blakey 0*); Second day, Leicestershire 5-1 (D. L. Maddy 0*); Third day, Leicestershire 363-6 (P. A. Nixon 52*, D. J. Millns 25*).

Yorkshire

M. D. Moxon b Mullally	21	– lbw b Ormond	63
A. McGrath lbw b Ormond	28	– lbw b Ormond	25
*D. Byas c Johnson b Mullally	88	– c Johnson b Wells	9
D. S. Lehmann c Maddy b Wells	3	– not out	163
B. Parker lbw b Wells	0	– not out	15
C. White b Pierson	17		
†R. J. Blakey c Nixon b Mullally	39		
P. J. Hartley b Mullally	33		
C. E. W. Silverwood c Nixon b Mullally	0		
R. D. Stemp c Maddy b Pierson	0		
R. J. Sidebottom not out	2		
B 5, l-b 6, w 6, n-b 20	37	B 9, l-b 5, w 4, n-b 16	34

1/41 2/67 3/86 4/86 5/146   268   1/62 2/77 3/149   (3 wkts dec.) 309
6/208 7/247 8/247 9/250

Bonus points – Yorkshire 2, Leicestershire 4.

Bowling: *First Innings*—Millns 15–1–60–0; Mullally 25.5–8–103–5; Pierson 14–6–30–2; Ormond 6–2–19–1; Wells 8–0–45–2. *Second Innings*—Millns 8–0–45–0; Mullally 14–1–57–0; Pierson 19–2–109–0; Ormond 19–7–45–2; Wells 9–1–29–1; Maddy 3–1–10–0; Whitaker 0.2–0–0–0.

Leicestershire

V. J. Wells b Hartley	4	D. J. Millns c White b Sidebottom	40
D. L. Maddy c Byas b Stemp	94	J. Ormond b Sidebottom	0
I. J. Sutcliffe lbw b Sidebottom	33	B 2, l-b 14, w 4, n-b 10	30
*J. J. Whitaker c Blakey b Hartley	87		
N. C. Johnson b Hartley	0	1/5 2/86 3/236 (8 wkts dec.)	406
B. F. Smith c Blakey b White	41	4/236 5/236 6/310	
†P. A. Nixon not out	77	7/402 8/406	

A. R. K. Pierson and A. D. Mullally did not bat.

Bonus points – Leicestershire 4, Yorkshire 3.

Bowling: Silverwood 27–4–86–0; Hartley 22–7–63–3; White 15–0–70–1; Stemp 33–11–90–1; Sidebottom 16.4–4–71–3; McGrath 3–0–10–0.

Umpires: N. T. Plews and P. Willey.

At Canterbury, July 16, 17, 18, 19. LEICESTERSHIRE beat KENT by six wickets.

LEICESTERSHIRE v NOTTINGHAMSHIRE

At Leicester, July 23, 24, 25, 26. Drawn. Leicestershire 9 pts, Nottinghamshire 10 pts. Toss: Leicestershire.

This match summed up Leicestershire's season: more rain, and some dreadful own goals. Whitaker thought the uneven bounce of a relaid pitch made the game "a lottery", but also owned up to bad bowling and dropped catches. The home side conceded 52 extras and dropped Dowman five times; he batted more than seven hours for his highest score, 149. Nottinghamshire passed 300 for only the third time in the 1997 Championship, raising their total of batting points to eight. The reply leaned heavily on Johnson and Maddy, who fell for his third score of 103 this season when he was the first victim in a hat-trick for Tolley, which soon became a career-best six for 61. Leicestershire bowled better at their second attempt, with five wickets for Mullally and five catches for Nixon. Their target was 258 in just over a day. But rain cut 28 overs and, ultimately, their last pair had to keep out 13 balls.

Close of play: First day, Nottinghamshire 296-9 (M. P. Dowman 125*, A. R. Oram 0*); Second day, Leicestershire 143-3 (D. L. Maddy 75*, N. C. Johnson 20*); Third day, Leicestershire 5-0 (A. R. K. Pierson 4*, D. L. Maddy 0*).

Nottinghamshire

G. E. Welton c Nixon b Millns	0	– c Nixon b Ormond	21
*R. T. Robinson c Nixon b Wells	32	– c Nixon b Mullally	13
M. P. Dowman c Wells b Ormond	149	– b Mullally	19
N. J. Astle c Smith b Mullally	13	– c Johnson b Mullally	38
G. F. Archer c Nixon b Johnson	30	– c Smith b Ormond	35
U. Afzaal c Nixon b Millns	22	– c Nixon b Mullally	0
C. M. Tolley c Pierson b Ormond	26	– c Nixon b Ormond	10
†W. M. Noon lbw b Pierson	3	– lbw b Mullally	7
P. J. Franks b Ormond	6	– (10) not out	10
M. N. Bowen b Mullally	4	– (9) c Nixon b Mullally	0
A. R. Oram not out	5	– b Millns	0
B 9, l-b 13, w 6, n-b 24	52	B 13, l-b 6, n-b 10	29

1/10 2/51 3/67 4/131 5/206 342   1/29 2/41 3/91 4/122 5/122   182
6/244 7/251 8/273 9/294   6/160 7/160 8/161 9/182

Bonus points – Nottinghamshire 3, Leicestershire 4 (Score at 120 overs: 338-9).

Bowling: *First Innings*—Millns 22–3–91–2; Mullally 34–10–99–2; Wells 9–4–16–1; Ormond 24.5–8–61–3; Pierson 27–11–36–1; Johnson 6–3–17–1. *Second Innings*—Mullally 19–7–62–5; Ormond 20–1–55–3; Millns 7.4–2–21–2; Wells 5–1–24–0; Pierson 1–0–1–0.

Leicestershire

V. J. Wells c Noon b Tolley	17	– (3) c Astle b Oram 59
D. L. Maddy lbw b Tolley	103	– c Astle b Bowen 2
I. J. Sutcliffe lbw b Astle	11	– (4) lbw b Astle 35
*J. J. Whitaker lbw b Astle	14	– (5) c Robinson b Oram 1
N. C. Johnson not out	76	– (6) b Astle 14
B. F. Smith c Noon b Tolley	0	– (7) c Archer b Oram.......... 0
†P. A. Nixon c Astle b Tolley	0	– (8) c Bowen b Tolley.......... 42
J. Ormond c Tolley b Oram	6	– (10) not out 11
D. J. Millns lbw b Tolley	12	– b Oram 24
A. R. K. Pierson b Oram	4	– (1) lbw b Tolley 6
A. D. Mullally c Archer b Tolley	3	– not out 0
B 8, l-b 3, n-b 10	21	B 12, l-b 7, n-b 4 23

1/52 2/91 3/109 4/201 5/201	267	1/8 2/16 3/107 (9 wkts) 217
6/201 7/217 8/247 9/260		4/108 5/119 6/119
		7/143 8/198 9/212

Bonus points – Leicestershire 2, Nottinghamshire 4.

Bowling: *First Innings*—Franks 5–2–9–0; Oram 20–8–49–2; Bowen 20–1–80–0; Tolley 25–8–61–6; Astle 20–2–50–2; Afzaal 3–1–7–0. *Second Innings*—Tolley 21–6–40–2; Astle 16–6–27–2; Bowen 16–4–44–1; Oram 16–2–69–4; Afzaal 2–0–18–0.

Umpires: A. A. Jones and R. A. White.

At Colchester, July 31, August 1, 2, 4. LEICESTERSHIRE drew with ESSEX.

At Eastbourne, August 6, 7, 8, 9. LEICESTERSHIRE lost to SUSSEX by 38 runs.

LEICESTERSHIRE v DERBYSHIRE

At Leicester, August 20, 21, 22, 23. Leicestershire won by 163 runs. Leicestershire 20 pts, Derbyshire 8 pts. Toss: Leicestershire.

Leicestershire's third win of the 1997 Championship owed plenty to Derbyshire hitting the self-destruct button. Set 402 to win in a minimum of 88 overs, Derbyshire collapsed from a promising 161 for one to 238 all out, off-spinner Pierson doing the damage with six for 56. Though the pitch was taking spin, it was hardly vicious; the previous day, 547 runs had been scored for the fall of just three wickets. Batsmen had been filling their boots from the start. Leicestershire opener Wells scored a six-hour 190, passing 1,000 runs, and then a second-innings 93, sharing opening stands of 144 and 153 with Maddy. Parsons had joined in with an unbeaten 69 on his final Championship appearance, while Rollins and Barnett, who reached a century before lunch on the third day, put on 316, a Derbyshire third-wicket record, in their first innings.

Close of play: First day, Leicestershire 373-7 (P. A. Nixon 34*); Second day, Derbyshire 48-1 (A. S. Rollins 23*, C. J. Adams 9*); Third day, Leicestershire 229-2 (I. J. Sutcliffe 33*, B. F. Smith 31*).

Leicestershire

V. J. Wells b DeFreitas	190	– c Harris b Clarke	93
D. L. Maddy c Harris b DeFreitas	33	– lbw b DeFreitas	66
I. J. Sutcliffe c and c Cork	2	– not out	59
*J. J. Whitaker c Krikken b Harris	61		
B. F. Smith c Clarke b Harris	8	– (4) not out	55
A. Habib c May b DeFreitas	5		
†P. A. Nixon c Krikken b Aldred	40		
D. J. Millns st Krikken b DeFreitas	1		
J. Ormond c Krikken b DeFreitas	4		
G. J. Parsons not out	69		
A. R. K. Pierson c Krikken b Harris	20		
B 4, l-b 17, n-b 32	53	W 2, n-b 6	8

1/144 2/175 3/264 4/280 5/310   486   1/153 2/171   (2 wkts dec.) 281
6/367 7/373 8/379 9/405

Bonus points – Leicestershire 4, Derbyshire 4 (Score at 120 overs: 428-9).

Bowling: *First Innings*—DeFreitas 41–16–120–5; Cork 25–3–120–1; Aldred 23–6–83–1; Harris 24.3–5–98–3; Blackwell 9–4–24–0; Clarke 11–5–20–0. *Second Innings*—Cork 6–0–14–0; Harris 6–0–44–0; DeFreitas 16–1–69–1; Blackwell 6–0–57–0; Clarke 8–1–33–1; May 4–0–48–0; Adams 2.5–0–16–0.

Derbyshire

A. S. Rollins not out	171	– c Nixon b Ormond	23
M. R. May c Nixon b Millns	2	– c Nixon b Wells	88
C. J. Adams c and b Ormond	9	– c Nixon b Pierson	41
K. J. Barnett not out	147	– c Maddy b Wells	13
I. D. Blackwell (did not bat)		– c Whitaker b Pierson	2
V. P. Clarke (did not bat)		– c Nixon b Ormond	10
D. G. Cork (did not bat)		– lbw b Pierson	6
†K. M. Krikken (did not bat)		– b Pierson	6
*P. A. J. DeFreitas (did not bat)		– b Pierson	5
P. Aldred (did not bat)		– not out	10
A. J. Harris (did not bat)		– lbw b Pierson	5
B 8, l-b 7, w 16, n-b 6	37	B 4, l-b 17, w 4, n-b 4	29

1/9 2/50   (2 wkts dec.) 366   1/44 2/161 3/177 4/184 5/193   238
6/210 7/210 8/215 9/228

Bonus points – Derbyshire 4.

Bowling: *First Innings*—Millns 11–1–64–1; Ormond 17–0–110–1; Parsons 14–2–53–0; Pierson 17–0–52–0; Wells 12–4–18–0; Maddy 4–0–17–0; Habib 4–0–37–0. *Second Innings*—Millns 13–2–41–0; Ormond 10–1–40–2; Parsons 17–5–41–0; Wells 8–1–39–2; Pierson 15.4–2–56–6.

Umpires: J. H. Hampshire and G. Sharp.

LEICESTERSHIRE v GLAMORGAN

At Leicester, August 27, 28, 29, 30. Drawn. Leicestershire 7 pts, Glamorgan 8 pts. Toss: Leicestershire. Championship debut: D. Williamson.

Championship contenders Glamorgan left Grace Road in angry mood, complaining that the decision to leave a large area of the square uncovered overnight had cost them a possible victory. Leicestershire blamed poor drainage and an over-optimistic weather forecast: they had left off the covers to help one muddy area dry out. In the event, it poured down and the last day was washed out, like the first. Between showers, Glamorgan generally had the upper hand. Though they stumbled to 126 for six, the last four wickets added 100, thanks to some mighty hitting from Croft and Waqar Younis. Then Watkin took seven for 41 to skittle Leicestershire, his first five-wicket haul since May 1995. By the close of the third day, Glamorgan were 118 ahead, with seven wickets left.

Close of play: First day, No play; Second day, Glamorgan 180-7 (R. D. B. Croft 10*, Waqar Younis 18*); Third day, Glamorgan 67-3 (H. Morris 23*, P. A. Cottey 6*).

Glamorgan

S. P. James c Nixon b Millns	14	– c Johnson b Williamson	21
H. Morris b Millns	8	– not out	23
A. Dale lbw b Wells	69	– b Wells	13
M. J. Powell c Nixon b Ormond	3	– lbw b Wells	0
*M. P. Maynard b Ormond	0		
P. A. Cottey c Nixon b Williamson	25	– (5) not out	6
†A. D. Shaw b Williamson	0		
R. D. B. Croft c Wells b Williamson	35		
Waqar Younis c Sutcliffe b Wells	28		
S. L. Watkin c Nixon b Millns	1		
D. A. Cosker not out	1		
B 2, l-b 8, w 10, n-b 22	42	L-b 2, n-b 2	4

1/32 2/33 3/65 4/71 5/126   226   1/35 2/61 3/61   (3 wkts) 67
6/126 7/159 8/205 9/216

Bonus points – Glamorgan 1, Leicestershire 4.

Bowling: *First Innings*—Millns 16–3–58–3; Ormond 15–4–64–2; Pierson 5–0–23–0; Williamson 9.5–3–19–3; Wells 12–2–52–2. *Second Innings*—Millns 6–2–20–0; Williamson 8–2–21–1; Ormond 6–3–16–0; Wells 4–1–8–2; Maddy 0.2–0–0–0.

Leicestershire

V. J. Wells c Shaw b Watkin	3	D. Williamson b Watkin	3
D. L. Maddy c Shaw b Waqar Younis	20	J. Ormond c Morris b Watkin	7
I. J. Sutcliffe b Watkin	19	A. R. K. Pierson c Morris b Watkin	2
*J. J. Whitaker lbw b Croft	62		
N. C. Johnson b Watkin	6	L-b 5	5
B. F. Smith b Watkin	0		
†P. A. Nixon not out	47	1/7 2/39 3/62 4/78 5/78	175
D. J. Millns c Shaw b Croft	1	6/135 7/141 8/145 9/167	

Bonus points – Glamorgan 4.

Bowling: Waqar Younis 13–3–53–1; Watkin 19.4–6–41–7; Dale 3–0–23–0; Croft 16–5–35–2; Cosker 11–5–18–0.

Umpires: H. D. Bird and B. Dudleston.

At Northampton, September 10, 11, 12, 13. LEICESTERSHIRE drew with NORTHAMPTON-SHIRE.

LEICESTERSHIRE v DURHAM

At Leicester, September 18, 19, 20, 21. Leicestershire won by 17 runs. Leicestershire 21 pts, Durham 4 pts. Toss: Leicestershire.

Millns preserved Leicestershire's unbeaten home record in the Championship, which stretched back to August 1995, when he claimed Durham's last three wickets in 14 balls. A pitch which had favoured the seamers flattened out by the last day. And chasing 328, Durham had high hopes of beating Leicestershire for the first time when Morris and Boon whacked 59 in the first nine overs on the final morning. Eventually, Millns got rid of both, but Durham were still well placed at 302 for seven. Then he took the new ball. Before long it was all over; Durham were still looking for their first away win for more than two years and Millns had match figures of ten for 130. Brown had also taken ten, including three of the game's 12 lbws, and passed 400 first-class wickets in the process. The second-day washout meant that Grace Road had lost ten full Championship days to the weather in 1997.

Close of play: First day, Durham 66-4 (D. C. Boon 7*, M. P. Speight 5*); Second day, No play; Third day, Durham 88-2 (J. E. Morris 41*, D. C. Boon 22*).

Leicestershire

V. J. Wells lbw b Brown	2	– lbw b Betts	4
D. L. Maddy c Speight b Betts	27	– c Speight b Brown	9
I. J. Sutcliffe lbw b Betts	11	– b Brown	22
*J. J. Whitaker b Betts	93	– lbw b Brown	30
B. F. Smith c Boiling b Walker	32	– c Boon b Brown	3
J. M. Dakin b Betts	0	– b Wood	18
†P. A. Nixon c Speight b Brown	6	– c Speight b Betts	38
D. J. Millns c Speight b Brown	41	– c Speight b Wood	0
A. R. K. Pierson c Betts b Brown	27	– c Boiling b Brown	59
J. Ormond not out	1	– c Daley b Walker	0
M. T. Brimson lbw b Brown	0	– not out	30
L-b 1	1	B 1, l-b 3, n-b 2	6

1/4 2/23 3/61 4/166 5/166   241   1/9 2/17 3/40 4/48 5/87   219
6/166 7/180 8/232 9/241   6/87 7/87 8/154 9/155

Bonus points – Leicestershire 1, Durham 4.

Bowling: *First Innings*—Brown 21.3–5–67–5; Betts 18–3–68–4; Wood 11–1–66–0; Walker 13–4–35–1; Boiling 1–0–4–0. *Second Innings*—Brown 20–2–74–5; Betts 19.5–5–71–2; Wood 8–1–35–2; Walker 8–0–35–1.

Durham

J. J. B. Lewis c Maddy b Millns	6	– lbw b Ormond	5
S. Hutton c Nixon b Wells	13	– c Maddy b Millns	8
J. E. Morris c Wells b Dakin	19	– lbw b Millns	84
*D. C. Boon b Millns	17	– c Nixon b Millns	93
J. A. Daley lbw b Dakin	7	– b Maddy	39
†M. P. Speight lbw b Millns	12	– c Whitaker b Dakin	0
M. M. Betts lbw b Wells	21	– lbw b Wells	4
J. Boiling c Maddy b Ormond	16	– c Nixon b Millns	20
J. Wood b Millns	0	– not out	20
S. J. E. Brown not out	2	– c Pierson b Millns	1
A. Walker c Maddy b Ormond	0	– lbw b Millns	1
B 4, l-b 10, w 4, n-b 2	20	B 5, l-b 14, w 8, n-b 8	35

1/8 2/34 3/50 4/59 5/88   133   1/17 2/35 3/149 4/232 5/235   310
6/111 7/125 8/125 9/133   6/246 7/260 8/302 9/304

Bonus points – Leicestershire 4.

Bowling: *First Innings*—Millns 11–1–49–4; Ormond 8.5–0–31–2; Dakin 5–1–12–2; Wells 7–0–27–2. *Second Innings*—Millns 33–13–81–6; Ormond 13–6–33–1; Wells 16–7–38–1; Dakin 30–8–109–1; Brimson 8–3–12–0; Pierson 3–0–7–0; Maddy 8–4–11–1.

Umpires: V. A. Holder and D. R. Shepherd.

MIDDLESEX

Mark Ramprakash

Patron: HRH The Duke of Edinburgh
President: M. P. Murray
Chairman: A. E. Moss
Chairman, Cricket Committee: R. A. Gale
Secretary: V. J. Codrington
Captain: M. R. Ramprakash
Head Coach: I. J. Gould
First-team Coach: J. M. Buchanan
Scorer: M. J. Smith

For most counties, jumping from ninth to joint fourth place in the Championship would represent a successful season. But Middlesex regarded it as a missed opportunity. They had led the table in June, won seven matches to champions Glamorgan's eight, and lost a nail-biter to Kent by only four runs.

It was, however, a watershed year, which saw a change of captain and the end of Don Bennett's 29 years as coach. Mike Gatting, captain since 1983, already intended to step down in favour of Mark Ramprakash. But at the end of May, with new responsibilities as an England selector, he decided to do it immediately. In contrast with bloody coups at other counties, the handover could not have been smoother. The continuity was emphasised in Ramprakash's first match in charge, against Northamptonshire: both players scored hundreds to set up an innings win. Ramprakash maintained his splendid form, scoring six first-class hundreds and 1,453 runs, and Gatting and his fellow-selectors recalled him to the England team for the final Test. But Gatting himself – who had his 40th birthday in mid-season – endured another disappointing year. He scored no further centuries, remaining eight short of a hundred hundreds, and made only 761 Championship runs – the same as 1996, when he missed three games.

Several other batsmen under-performed and the team managed maximum batting points in only four games, even worse than in 1996. Middlesex stuck by their players, though. Nine were ever-present in the first 11 matches, and it could have been ten had Philip Tufnell not missed a couple that clashed with Tests for which he was not, ultimately, required. Loyalty is to be applauded, but sticking with Paul Weekes, who was averaging 13 with the bat, seemed perverse. His poor form and, less seriously, that of Jason Pooley, who opened when Weekes dropped out, meant that the innings often lacked a launching pad.

Their opening partner, however, was anything but a disappointment. South African all-rounder Jacques Kallis was a late replacement for Greg Blewett, who was picked for the Australian tour. After the dismal failure of Dion Nash, Middlesex supporters warmed rapidly to a high-quality overseas player who delivered. Kallis scored four Championship centuries, averaging 47, while his lively fast-medium bowling brought 32 wickets, and he took some stunning catches. He also inspired victory over Gloucestershire in the NatWest Trophy second round with four wickets and a hundred. That was a rare one-day win for Middlesex. They lost all their Benson and Hedges group matches, starting with Ireland, who had never beaten a first-class county before. They did better in the

NatWest Trophy, with a surprise win over Kent – runners-up in three other competitions – as well as Gloucestershire, before going out to Warwickshire in the quarter-finals. But the Sunday League was an embarrassment. They went 12 matches before reaching 200. After winning two of their first three games, Middlesex did not win again until their final fixture, when they beat Nottinghamshire by one run. Limited-overs cricket is a problem the new regime needs to tackle, particularly with the new two-division league coming in 1999.

There was encouragement in the talent coming up through the club, especially teenagers Owais Shah and David Nash. Once he had completed his A-levels, Shah became a regular; he made his maiden first-class hundred, against Nottinghamshire, in the penultimate match, and Nash followed suit in the final game at Chelmsford. Both were selected for the England A tour to Kenya and Sri Lanka. Jamie Hewitt, aged 21, played in every Championship match and took 57 wickets; Tim Bloomfield, making his debut a little later, aged 24, bowled with genuine pace. Again, off-spinner Keith Dutch had limited opportunities but Weekes's bad form extended to his off-breaks and, if that continues in 1998, Dutch might get his chance.

Perhaps it was the distraction of his benefit year, but Angus Fraser rarely showed real menace; he took five or more in an innings only twice. However, his reliability earned him a place on England's tour of the West Indies, along with Ramprakash and Tufnell. Richard Johnson started well and missed only one game, though it was still unclear whether he would ever regain the rhythm and consistency he had before his back injury. Tufnell had bowled only 186 overs by the end of June – restricted by rain and phantom England call-ups – and seldom found conditions to suit him early on. He did finish with 55 wickets, thanks to his match-winning 11 in the final Test at The Oval. Then his reviving international career was threatened when he was called to account for missing a drug test. But a fine and a suspended ban left him free to go to the Caribbean.

Middlesex could be forgiven for some ambivalence about 1998, with a newish captain, new overseas player, new coach and also a new secretary – Joe Hardstaff retired after nine years in the post, to be succeeded by Vinny Codrington, who moved from Richmond Rugby Club. But they were looking to Australia for help. With South Africa touring in 1998, Kallis was ruled out. Though Blewett was still under contract, he was reported to be troubled by a knee injury. In November, Middlesex secured Western Australian batsman Justin Langer, but planned to play on for another year or so. While Gatting's old team-mate Ian Gould stepped up to head coach, John Buchanan, famous for coaching Queensland to their first ever Sheffield Shield title, was engaged to run the First Eleven.

Bennett's retirement ended nearly half a century's service to Middlesex. He made his debut for them in 1950, retired in 1968, and became coach the following year. His low-key approach was just right for the club, complemented as it was by the positive captaincy of Mike Brearley and Gatting. Perhaps his most important contribution derived from his ability to spot talent, including Gatting himself, Gould and John Emburey.

Looking back over his coaching career, Bennett picked out that year in the mid-1970s when Gatting and Gould burst upon the scene and there was an immediate lifting of spirits in the dressing-room. That, allied to their abundant talent, brought about an upsurge in the county's fortunes and a clutch of trophies. Bennett thought that something similar could be on the horizon with the advent of Shah and Nash. – NORMAN DE MESQUITA.

557

MIDDLESEX 1997

[Bill Smith]

Back row: K. P. Dutch, S. P. Moffat, P. E. Wellings, M. R. Evans, A. W. Laraman, A. J. Strauss, N. D. Martin. *Middle row:* S. Shepard (*physiotherapist*), D. Bennett (*coach*), D. C. Nash, D. F. Lye, J. M. de la Pena, J. P. Hewitt, R. A. Fay, J. C. Harrison, I. N. Blanchett, D. J. Goodchild, U. B. A. Rashid, O. A. Shah, I. J. Gould (*assistant coach*). A. Jones (*Second Eleven scorer*). *Front row:* J. C. Pooley, P. C. R. Tufnell, A. R. C. Fraser, M. W. Gatting, M. R. Ramprakash (*captain*), K. R. Brown, R. L. Johnson, P. N. Weekes.
Insets: M. J. Smith (*First Eleven scorer*), J. H. Kallis, T. F. Bloomfield.

MIDDLESEX RESULTS

All first-class matches – Played 19; Won 7, Lost 4, Drawn 8.
County Championship matches – Played 17; Won 7, Lost 4, Drawn 6.
Competition placings – Britannic Assurance County Championship, 4th equal;
NatWest Trophy, q-f; Benson and Hedges Cup, 5th in Group D;
AXA Life League, 16th.

COUNTY CHAMPIONSHIP AVERAGES

BATTING

Cap		M	I	NO	R	HS	100s	50s	Avge	Ct/St
	D. C. Nash	5	7	2	311	100	1	1	62.20	3
1990	M. R. Ramprakash ...	16	25	3	1,201	190	5	6	54.59	8
1997	J. H. Kallis§	16	25	3	1,034	172*	4	4	47.00	15
	O. A. Shah	10	14	2	520	104*	1	2	43.33	13
1977	M. W. Gatting†	17	26	1	761	108	1	3	30.44	22
1990	K. R. Brown†	17	25	6	515	144*	1	2	27.10	46/2
	K. P. Dutch†	5	7	2	124	79	0	1	24.80	2
	S. P. Moffat........	4	6	1	122	47	0	0	24.40	2
1995	J. C. Pooley†	16	24	0	549	98	0	3	22.87	16
	J. P. Hewitt........	17	21	4	264	75	0	1	15.52	5
1988	A. R. C. Fraser	17	22	6	229	35	0	0	14.31	4
1995	R. L. Johnson	16	22	0	292	39	0	0	13.27	6
1993	P. N. Weekes	13	20	0	261	44	0	0	13.05	18
1990	P. C. R. Tufnell	14	18	5	89	21	0	0	6.84	2

Also batted: T. F. Bloomfield (3 matches) 0*, 0* (2 ct); P. E. Wellings (1 match) 13 (1 ct).

* Signifies not out.   † Born in Middlesex.   § Overseas player.

BOWLING

	O	M	R	W	BB	5W/i	Avge
T. F. Bloomfield	68	16	201	12	5-77	1	16.75
J. H. Kallis.............	234.3	61	655	32	5-54	1	20.46
J. P. Hewitt	424	90	1,351	57	6-14	2	23.70
P. C. R. Tufnell	474.1	143	1,000	41	5-61	2	24.39
R. L. Johnson.........	395.2	77	1,277	47	4-26	0	27.17
A. R. C. Fraser	531.5	147	1,308	47	6-77	2	27.82

Also bowled: K. P. Dutch 69–10–207–4; M. W. Gatting 7–1–46–1; D. C. Nash 3–0–19–1;
M. R. Ramprakash 35.2–10–126–2; O. A. Shah 2–0–19–0; P. N. Weekes 128–16–397–4.

COUNTY RECORDS

Highest score for:	331*	J. D. Robertson v Worcestershire at Worcester ..	1949
Highest score against:	316*	J. B. Hobbs (Surrey) at Lord's	1926
Best bowling for:	10-40	G. O. B. Allen v Lancashire at Lord's	1929
Best bowling against:	9-38	R. C. Robertson-Glasgow (Somerset) at Lord's..	1924
Highest total for:	642-3 dec.	v Hampshire at Southampton	1923
Highest total against:	665	by West Indians at Lord's	1939
Lowest total for:	20	v MCC at Lord's	1864
Lowest total against:	{ 31	by Gloucestershire at Bristol	1924
	{ 31	by Glamorgan at Cardiff	1997

At Cambridge, April 23, 24, 25. MIDDLESEX drew with CAMBRIDGE UNIVERSITY.

MIDDLESEX v SUSSEX

At Lord's, May 7, 8, 9, 10. Drawn. Middlesex 11 pts, Sussex 5 pts. Toss: Sussex. Championship debut: J. H. Kallis.

For the third time in three Championship visits to Lord's, Sussex won the toss only to regret their decision. This time, they avoided defeat, thanks to rain and bad light which wiped out some 140 overs during the last three days. Moores tried nine bowlers as Middlesex, put in, amassed 490. Ramprakash scored his second successive century, following his 108 for The Rest, and the new overseas player, South African Jacques Kallis, looked briefly impressive. But the main support for Ramprakash came, as so often, from Brown, who completed his own century just before lunch on the second day. Leg-spinner Khan, once on Middlesex's books, took five wickets for the first time. The Sussex batting then collapsed and they followed on 303 behind. Middlesex had a glimmer of hope of beating the weather when Hewitt, improving his career-best figures for the second time running, took three for nought in 13 balls, but Newell and Moores held out. On the second day, a small fire forced the evacuation of the Warner Stand. The previous night MCC members had voted to ban smoking in the Long Room.

Close of play: First day, Middlesex 337-5 (K. R. Brown 72*, P. E. Wellings 4*); Second day, Sussex 44-3 (C. W. J. Athey 13*, R. K. Rao 4*); Third day, Sussex 6-0 (M. T. E. Peirce 2*, K. Greenfield 0*).

Middlesex

P. N. Weekes lbw b Jarvis	7	J. P. Hewitt c Greenfield b Khan	0
J. H. Kallis c sub b Newell	31	A. R. C. Fraser b Khan	35
M. R. Ramprakash c Moores b Rao	145	P. C. R. Tufnell not out	12
*M. W. Gatting b Khan	23	B 6, l-b 10, w 6, n-b 10	32
J. C. Pooley b Robinson	30		
†K. R. Brown not out	144		(9 wkts dec.) 490
P. E. Wellings c Drakes b Khan	13	1/24 2/53 3/96	4/185 5/321 6/363
R. L. Johnson c Drakes b Khan	18	7/389 8/390 9/468	

Bonus points – Middlesex 4, Sussex 2 (Score at 120 overs: 389-6).

Bowling: Jarvis 39.5–8–126–1; Drakes 6–1–21–0; Robinson 30–7–87–1; Newell 9–2–35–1; Khan 37–5–137–5; Greenfield 1–0–15–0; Athey 6–0–17–0; Peirce 7–0–22–0; Rao 5–1–14–1.

Sussex

M. T. E. Peirce c Tufnell b Hewitt	10	– c Brown b Tufnell	28
K. Greenfield lbw b Hewitt	11	– b Hewitt	0
N. R. Taylor c Brown b Hewitt	6	– c Wellings b Tufnell	14
C. W. J. Athey not out	60	– b Hewitt	31
R. K. Rao b Johnson	10	– (6) c Brown b Hewitt	0
V. C. Drakes c Gatting b Hewitt	1	– (7) c Weekes b Hewitt	0
K. Newell lbw b Johnson	7	– (5) not out	23
*†P. Moores c Weekes b Kallis	15	– not out	7
P. W. Jarvis c Kallis b Johnson	22		
A. A. Khan c Johnson b Fraser	29		
M. A. Robinson b Kallis	0		
B 1, l-b 1, w 2, n-b 12	16	B 4, l-b 6, w 4, n-b 2	16

1/16 2/26 3/31 4/54 5/55		187	1/10 2/38 3/73	(6 wkts) 119
6/74 7/105 8/140 9/187			4/97 5/97 6/97	

Bonus points – Middlesex 4.

Bowling: *First Innings*—Fraser 19–5–53–1; Hewitt 17–4–60–4; Johnson 14–1–56–3; Kallis 10.3–5–16–2. *Second Innings*—Kallis 6–2–15–0; Hewitt 15–5–24–4; Johnson 9–2–24–0; Fraser 11.3–2–33–0; Tufnell 15–10–8–2; Weekes 1–0–5–0.

Umpires: J. H. Hampshire and V. A. Holder.

MIDDLESEX v DERBYSHIRE

At Lord's, May 14, 15, 16. Middlesex won by 131 runs. Middlesex 20 pts, Derbyshire 4 pts. Toss: Middlesex. Championship debut: S. P. Moffat.

The bowlers were on top from the start, when Middlesex quickly sank to two for two, and the match ended in three days as Derbyshire folded for 99. Earlier, Malcolm had seized his chance to impress the selectors. Their chairman, David Graveney, was in the pavilion, as was his co-selector Gatting, who had been better placed to assess Malcolm's effectiveness . . . he was dismissed by him twice, the second time first ball. Malcolm split the first-innings wickets with DeFreitas and picked up six more in the second, when keeper Krikken took five catches. Their good work was squandered by the batsmen, however; their performance was woeful, even allowing for the injured knee that prevented Barnett from batting. For Middlesex, 32 behind after the low-scoring first innings, Brown was the saviour: his 76 left Derbyshire a reasonably taxing target of 231. Some dreadful-looking shots – notably Khan's charge down the pitch to Weekes – saw them bundled out inside 36 overs by Johnson and Kallis, who bowled with unexpected pace.

Close of play: First day, Derbyshire 123-5 (D. M. Jones 42*, A. J. Harris 4*); Second day, Middlesex 108-3 (J. H. Kallis 52*, J. C. Pooley 8*).

Middlesex

P. N. Weekes c Krikken b DeFreitas	44	– b Malcolm	18
J. H. Kallis c Adams b DeFreitas	0	– c Krikken b Malcolm	52
M. R. Ramprakash c Jones b DeFreitas	1	– lbw b Malcolm	26
*M. W. Gatting c Jones b Malcolm	39	– c Krikken b Malcolm	0
J. C. Pooley lbw b DeFreitas	13	– c Krikken b Harris	46
†K. R. Brown c Harris b Malcolm	8	– c Krikken b Malcolm	76
S. P. Moffat not out	21	– c Krikken b Harris	3
R. L. Johnson b Malcolm	4	– lbw b DeFreitas	0
J. P. Hewitt lbw b Malcolm	0	– c Clarke b Malcolm	8
A. R. C. Fraser c Adams b Malcolm	4	– c Adams b Clarke	7
P. C. R. Tufnell c Clarke b DeFreitas	3	– not out	2
L-b 1, w 8	9	L-b 14, w 2, n-b 8	24

1/0 2/2 3/81 4/103 5/112   146   1/26 2/91 3/99 4/112 5/169   262
6/116 7/133 8/133 9/139   6/181 7/182 8/219 9/254

Bonus points – Derbyshire 4.

Bowling: *First Innings*—Malcolm 19–6–50–5; DeFreitas 19.1–6–46–5; Clarke 5–1–18–0; Harris 6–2–23–0; Roberts 6–1–8–0. *Second Innings*—Malcolm 22.3–5–75–6; DeFreitas 25–4–88–1; Harris 24–5–72–2; Clarke 4–0–13–1.

Derbyshire

A. S. Rollins c Pooley b Weekes	5	– run out	15
G. A. Khan c Brown b Fraser	4	– st Brown b Weekes	11
C. J. Adams c Brown b Fraser	7	– c Gatting b Johnson	16
*D. M. Jones c Kallis b Hewitt	53	– lbw b Kallis	14
V. P. Clarke lbw b Tufnell	44	– c Brown b Kallis	9
G. M. Roberts c Fraser b Johnson	2	– (8) c Brown b Johnson	13
A. J. Harris b Hewitt	17	– (9) not out	4
†K. M. Krikken not out	10	– (6) c Pooley b Johnson	1
P. A. J. DeFreitas b Johnson	15	– (7) c Pooley b Kallis	3
D. E. Malcolm b Johnson	0	– b Johnson	0
K. J. Barnett absent hurt		– absent hurt	
B 3, l-b 4, w 8, n-b 6	21	L-b 5, w 6, n-b 2	13

1/6 2/18 3/23 4/102 5/113   178   1/28 2/48 3/52 4/71 5/78   99
6/137 7/152 8/178 9/178   6/80 7/85 8/99 9/99

Bonus points – Middlesex 4.

Bowling: *First Innings*—Hewitt 19–5–52–2; Fraser 20–6–45–2; Weekes 1–0–2–1; Johnson 12.4–3–39–3; Kallis 9–3–14–0; Tufnell 6–1–19–1. *Second Innings*—Fraser 7–1–12–0; Hewitt 4–0–13–0; Weekes 5–2–17–1; Tufnell 1–1–0–0; Kallis 10–2–26–3; Johnson 8.4–1–26–4.

Umpires: G. I. Burgess and B. Dudleston.

At Birmingham, May 21, 22, 23, 24. MIDDLESEX lost to WARWICKSHIRE by eight wickets.

MIDDLESEX v NORTHAMPTONSHIRE

At Lord's, May 29, 30, 31, June 2. Middlesex won by an innings and 57 runs. Middlesex 24 pts, Northamptonshire 3 pts. Toss: Middlesex.

Two days earlier, Gatting had announced the end of his 14 years as Middlesex captain, in order to concentrate on his duties as a Test selector. He handed the reins to Ramprakash, and they celebrated the changeover by sharing a partnership of 187. Both scored centuries, as did Kallis, whose 121 was his maiden hundred for Middlesex and took only 116 balls. Facing a total of 531, Northamptonshire followed on, 315 behind, before lunch on the third day. Curran, in his usual forthright way, prolonged the first innings with an unbeaten 89 and Ripley showed defiance and good technique in the second. But Middlesex just had too many runs to play with. Hewitt took five in an innings for the first time and Tufnell tidied up in the closing stages. He ended the match by dismissing former team-mate Follett, who was making his Championship debut for the visitors.

Close of play: First day, Middlesex 400-2 (M. R. Ramprakash 109*, M. W. Gatting 102*); Second day, Northamptonshire 165-4 (K. M. Curran 57*, J. P. Taylor 7*); Third day, Northamptonshire 168-6 (D. J. Capel 23*, J. N. Snape 19*).

Middlesex

J. H. Kallis c Snape b Curran 121	J. P. Hewitt lbw b Penberthy 0
P. N. Weekes c Snape b Curran 41	A. R. C. Fraser c Curran b Taylor 20
*M. R. Ramprakash lbw b Follett 111	P. C. R. Tufnell c Montgomerie b Follett. 0
M. W. Gatting b Taylor 108	
J. C. Pooley lbw b Taylor 2	L-b 12, w 12, n-b 14 38
†K. R. Brown not out 61	
S. P. Moffat lbw b Taylor 0	1/107 2/219 3/406 4/412 5/412 531
R. L. Johnson run out................. 29	6/412 7/476 8/477 9/529

Bonus points – Middlesex 4, Northamptonshire 2 (Score at 120 overs: 435-6).

Bowling: Taylor 41–13–99–4; Follett 24.3–1–123–2; Capel 9–1–62–0; Curran 23–5–67–2; Penberthy 24–3–80–1; Snape 15–2–60–0; Bailey 7–0–28–0.

Northamptonshire

D. J. Roberts c Moffat b Tufnell 21	– c Brown b Kallis 42
R. R. Montgomerie lbw b Hewitt 0	– lbw b Johnson 14
*R. J. Bailey c Moffat b Tufnell 44	– c Weekes b Kallis 23
K. M. Curran not out 89	– c Kallis b Tufnell 23
A. L. Penberthy c Brown b Hewitt 27	– c Kallis b Tufnell 8
J. P. Taylor c Weekes b Hewitt 7	– (10) c Brown b Johnson 6
D. J. Capel c Gatting b Hewitt 4	– (6) c Weekes b Hewitt 42
T. C. Walton lbw b Hewitt 8	– (7) lbw b Tufnell 4
J. N. Snape c Gatting b Johnson 2	– (8) c Brown b Fraser 24
†D. Ripley lbw b Johnson 0	– (9) not out 51
D. Follett b Johnson 0	– st Brown b Tufnell 3
L-b 2, w 10, n-b 2 14	B 3, l-b 11, n-b 4 18

1/6 2/63 3/72 4/146 5/169	216	1/39 2/82 3/93 4/121 5/130 258
6/185 7/195 8/204 9/208		6/134 7/186 8/224 9/239

Bonus points – Northamptonshire 1, Middlesex 4.

Bowling: *First Innings*—Fraser 15–6–30–0; Hewitt 20–5–59–5; Johnson 22–5–70–3; Weekes 8–2–33–0; Tufnell 14–4–22–2. *Second Innings*—Fraser 21–6–35–1; Hewitt 12–3–33–1; Weekes 16–2–37–0; Tufnell 39.5–16–64–4; Johnson 20–8–55–2; Kallis 9–3–20–2.

Umpires: J. D. Bond and R. Julian.

MIDDLESEX v LEICESTERSHIRE

At Lord's, June 4, 5, 6, 7. Drawn. Middlesex 11 pts, Leicestershire 9 pts. Toss: Leicestershire.

Strokeplay was never easy on a cracked pitch, but no one bowled well enough to take full advantage. Fraser did take six for 77, his best Championship return since he took seven, also against Leicestershire, four years earlier, but three of his victims were tailenders. The visitors scored only two and a half an over in their first innings, and Whitaker spent nearly four and a half hours over his century. When Middlesex finally opened their reply, Ramprakash and Gatting again supplied the backbone, adding 178 in 49 overs to help make up some of the lost time. Both fell in the nineties, but Middlesex built a lead of 115. Inadequate covering and the ground staff's apparent reluctance to aid the drying process saw the final morning lost, and there was too little time to engineer a result. Instead, Wells completed a career-best 224 in 480 minutes and 400 balls, with two sixes and 28 fours – his third double-hundred in 12 months – against unchallenging bowling.

Close of play: First day, Leicestershire 267-7 (J. J. Whitaker 108*, A. D. Mullally 6*); Second day, Middlesex 298-4 (J. C. Pooley 28*, K. R. Brown 5*); Third day, Leicestershire 236-3 (V. J. Wells 76*, A. R. K. Pierson 9*).

Leicestershire

V. J. Wells c Ramprakash b Hewitt	39	– c Ramprakash b Tufnell	224
D. L. Maddy b Fraser	23	– c Ramprakash b Tufnell	103
B. F. Smith not out	23		
*J. J. Whitaker b Fraser	110	– (6) c Brown b Gatting	41
N. C. Johnson c Johnson b Fraser	12	– (4) lbw b Hewitt	17
A. Habib c and b Weekes	18	– (3) c Kallis b Tufnell	13
†P. A. Nixon b Tufnell	7	– not out	19
G. J. Parsons b Fraser	5	– c Brown b Ramprakash	0
A. R. K. Pierson b Fraser	13	– (5) b Johnson	9
A. D. Mullally b Fraser	10	– (9) not out	0
M. T. Brimson lbw b Hewitt	0		
B 1, l-b 7, w 6, n-b 6	20	B 10, l-b 12, w 12, n-b 2	36

1/66 2/72 3/153 4/175 5/194   280   1/173 2/191 3/220   (7 wkts dec.) 462
6/223 7/255 8/273 9/274   4/236 5/337
                                       6/462 7/462

Bonus points – Leicestershire 2, Middlesex 4.

In the first innings B. F. Smith, when 23, retired hurt at 104 and resumed at 274.

Bowling: *First Innings*—Fraser 31.2–7–77–6; Hewitt 27–8–63–2; Johnson 18–2–84–0; Weekes 10–2–16–1; Tufnell 26–13–32–1. *Second Innings*—Fraser 23–6–60–0; Hewitt 17–2–64–1; Weekes 24–0–97–0; Tufnell 46–15–92–3; Johnson 12–2–51–1; Ramprakash 6.2–1–30–1; Gatting 7–1–46–1.

Middlesex

P. N. Weekes b Pierson	23		J. P. Hewitt b Parsons	0
J. H. Kallis c Nixon b Mullally	23		A. R. C. Fraser not out	4
*M. R. Ramprakash c sub b Mullally	97		P. C. R. Tufnell c and b Parsons	2
M. W. Gatting b Pierson	94			
J. C. Pooley c and b Brimson	55		B 11, l-b 16, n-b 16	43
†K. R. Brown lbw b Wells	5			
S. P. Moffat lbw b Parsons	36		1/35 2/55 3/233 4/287 5/298	395
R. L. Johnson b Parsons	13		6/343 7/382 8/382 9/391	

Bonus points – Middlesex 4, Leicestershire 4.

Bowling: Mullally 23–7–75–2; Parsons 13.2–5–22–4; Johnson 12–1–48–0; Pierson 33–3–115–2; Wells 8–0–46–1; Brimson 16–1–62–1.

Umpires: A. Clarkson and V. A. Holder.

At Cardiff, June 12, 13, 14. MIDDLESEX beat GLAMORGAN by an innings and seven runs.

At Bristol, June 18, 19, 20, 21. MIDDLESEX beat GLOUCESTERSHIRE by 44 runs.

At Leeds, June 26, 27, 28, 30. MIDDLESEX drew with YORKSHIRE.

MIDDLESEX v LANCASHIRE

At Uxbridge, July 2, 3, 4, 5. Lancashire won by an innings and 54 runs. Lancashire 23 pts, Middlesex 1 pt. Toss: Lancashire.

Uxbridge pitches have often been criticised for offering no help to the bowlers; this one was different. Fairbrother, the acting Lancashire captain, had no hesitation putting Middlesex in, but he could hardly have expected to reduce them to 42 for seven. Martin bowled the spell of his life, taking five for eight in his first seven overs. He was helped by a great deal of movement, through the air and off the seam. By the close of the first day, the Lancashire openers had already overtaken Middlesex's feeble 118 – Wood reaching a maiden fifty. With time on their side, Lancashire had no need to hurry; and as conditions eased, they established a lead of 299 before declaring early on the third afternoon. The main question was whether Middlesex would last into the final day. They did – just – thanks mostly to Kallis. Martin's match analysis was 13 for 79, by far the best of his career.

Close of play: First day, Lancashire 126-0 (S. P. Titchard 49*, N. T. Wood 67*); Second day, Lancashire 309-4 (N. H. Fairbrother 82*, I. D. Austin 35*); Third day, Middlesex 198-6 (O. A. Shah 20*, R. L. Johnson 0*).

Middlesex

P. N. Weekes c Wood b Martin	9	– c Fairbrother b Yates	31
J. H. Kallis c Fairbrother b Austin	14	– c Flintoff b Yates	62
*M. R. Ramprakash c Hegg b Martin	0	– lbw b Yates	2
M. W. Gatting c Flintoff b Martin	0	– c sub b Martin	7
J. C. Pooley c Hegg b Martin	1	– lbw b Keedy	24
†K. R. Brown c Flintoff b Martin	0	– c Lloyd b Martin	31
O. A. Shah lbw b Martin	32	– b Yates	27
R. L. Johnson b Austin	0	– c Fairbrother b Martin	9
J. P. Hewitt c Titchard b Martin	28	– c Hegg b Martin	7
A. R. C. Fraser c Lloyd b Martin	7	– not out	14
P. C. R. Tufnell not out	11	– b Martin	3
L-b 2, n-b 14	16	B 8, l-b 4, w 2, n-b 14	28

1/16 2/16 3/20 4/32 5/36   118   1/79 2/85 3/112 4/112 5/166   245
6/36 7/42 8/96 9/101   6/196 7/210 8/220 9/237

Bonus points – Lancashire 4.

Bowling: *First Innings*—Martin 14.5–4–32–8; Shadford 7–0–43–0; Austin 12–4–36–2; Keedy 5–3–5–0; Yates 1–1–0–0. *Second Innings*—Martin 23.2–9–47–5; Shadford 11–0–47–0; Austin 1–0–10–0; Yates 30–7–89–4; Keedy 15–2–40–1.

Lancashire

S. P. Titchard c Pooley b Tufnell	79	P. J. Martin c Gatting b Tufnell	2
N. T. Wood c Gatting b Tufnell	67	D. J. Shadford b Kallis	9
*N. H. Fairbrother c and b Hewitt	97	G. Keedy not out	6
G. D. Lloyd b Tufnell	8	B 5, l-b 7, w 12, n-b 10	34
A. Flintoff lbw b Fraser	10		
I. D. Austin c Johnson b Tufnell	69	1/126 2/193 3/215	(9 wkts dec.) 417
†W. K. Hegg c Gatting b Hewitt	5	4/244 5/334 6/348	
G. Yates not out	31	7/369 8/373 9/405	

Bonus points – Lancashire 3, Middlesex 1 (Score at 120 overs: 312-4).

Bowling: Hewitt 35–8–79–2; Fraser 30–5–105–1; Tufnell 41–10–90–5; Johnson 24–6–64–0; Kallis 17–6–51–1; Weekes 8–2–16–0.

Umpires: J. C. Balderstone and J. W. Holder.

At Lord's, July 19, 20, 21. MIDDLESEX drew with AUSTRALIANS (See Australian tour section).

MIDDLESEX v KENT

At Lord's, July 23, 24, 25. Kent won by four runs. Kent 21 pts, Middlesex 4 pts. Toss: Kent.

Some indifferent batting on an indifferent pitch led to a most intriguing match; few could recall one with a more enthralling conclusion. Middlesex began the third day needing 127 to win with five wickets left. Their best hope lay in Ramprakash and Kallis, batting down the order because he had a migraine. But Kallis fell to McCague, and Brown, who had a cracked finger, was caught sweeping his first ball, from Strang. That left Middlesex wanting 104, with only three wickets standing. Johnson batted impressively to help Ramprakash add 57; but he, too, fell to Strang. Fraser shared a stand of 22, and finally last man Tufnell came in with 25 required. When they broke for lunch, it was down to 11. But with just five runs to go, Tufnell hit a catch to silly mid-off. Ramprakash had carried his bat for 113, and can rarely have displayed such class and concentration. In the end, however, the perseverance of Strang won the day, with six wickets in the innings (plus two catches). Nineteen wickets had fallen on the first day and 16 on the second. Poor shots were responsible, as much as the pitch; Wells and Gatting showed what experience and technique could achieve. McCague took seven wickets to dismiss Middlesex 103 behind, but Kallis revived their hopes, taking five for the first time in the Championship. Gatting made four catches, deputising for Brown behind the stumps; his dive to the left to remove Walker was unexpectedly agile.

Close of play: First day, Middlesex 103-9 (J. P. Hewitt 3*); Second day, Middlesex 134-5 (M. R. Ramprakash 69*, J. H. Kallis 5*).

Kent

D. P. Fulton c Hewitt b Fraser	4	– c Hewitt b Kallis	45
E. T. Smith b Fraser	10	– lbw b Fraser	2
T. R. Ward c Brown b Hewitt	0	– lbw b Kallis	14
A. P. Wells c Pooley b Tufnell	63	– b Kallis	2
M. J. Walker c Brown b Fraser	8	– c Gatting b Kallis	4
M. V. Fleming c Shah b Johnson	44	– lbw b Fraser	21
P. A. Strang c Weekes b Hewitt	12	– c Gatting b Kallis	17
*†S. A. Marsh c Shah b Tufnell	40	– not out	32
B. J. Phillips c Kallis b Weekes	12	– c Gatting b Tufnell	0
M. J. McCague b Tufnell	3	– c Gatting b Johnson	15
A. P. Igglesden not out	0	– c Shah b Johnson	0
L-b 4, w 4, n-b 4	12	B 2, l-b 3	5

1/13 2/16 3/16 4/24 5/86	**208**	1/9 2/40 3/42 4/46 5/85	**157**
6/102 7/187 8/202 9/206		6/103 7/118 8/118 9/149	

Bonus points – Kent 1, Middlesex 4.

Bowling: *First Innings*—Fraser 14–2–45–3; Hewitt 13–4–41–2; Kallis 12–2–40–0; Johnson 12–3–29–1; Tufnell 12.5–5–21–3; Weekes 9.3–0–28–1. *Second Innings*—Fraser 12–3–30–2; Hewitt 5–0–22–0; Kallis 16–3–54–5; Johnson 8.5–2–26–2; Tufnell 13–6–20–1.

Middlesex

P. N. Weekes b Igglesden		12 – c Strang b McCague		7
J. H. Kallis c Wells b Igglesden		10 – (7) lbw b McCague		22
*M. R. Ramprakash lbw b McCague	5	– (2) not out		113
M. W. Gatting b McCague	41	– c Strang b Igglesden		0
J. C. Pooley b McCague	1	– (3) c Phillips b Igglesden		17
O. A. Shah lbw b Phillips	13	– (5) lbw b Strang		21
A. R. C. Fraser c Strang b McCague	0	– (10) c Smith b Strang		13
†K. R. Brown c Strang b McCague	0	– c Smith b Strang		0
R. L. Johnson c Strang b McCague	0	– lbw b Strang		33
J. P. Hewitt not out	5	– (6) b Strang		11
P. C. R. Tufnell c Ward b McCague	0	– c Ward b Strang		8
B 12, l-b 4, w 2	18	L-b 8, w 3		11

1/18 2/27 3/33 4/56 5/82		105
6/84 7/84 8/84 9/103		

1/8 2/41 3/41 4/111 5/125		256
6/156 7/157 8/214 9/236		

Bonus points – Kent 4.

Bowling: *First Innings*—McCague 15.3–4–50–7; Igglesden 7–0–23–2; Phillips 4–2–8–1; Strang 6–2–8–0. *Second Innings*—McCague 21–4–72–2; Igglesden 14–3–47–2; Phillips 7–0–31–0; Strang 27.2–2–88–6; Fleming 6–3–10–0.

Umpires: D. J. Constant and J. H. Hampshire.

MIDDLESEX v HAMPSHIRE

At Lord's, August 6, 7, 8, 9. Middlesex won by 217 runs. Middlesex 22 pts, Hampshire 5 pts. Toss: Middlesex.

Salvos from Fraser and Hewitt wrecked Hampshire's pursuit of 315 in 77 overs. Fraser opened with four for five in ten balls, and added Keech after lunch; then Hewitt took three in four balls, as the last five fell for 11 runs. Ramprakash dominated the opening stages, scoring 190, his third century against Hampshire in as many years. He put on 128 with his predecessor, Gatting, and the county's future was on show on the second day, when Shah joined him to make a career-best 77 in a stand of 185. A total of 442 put the pressure on Hampshire. Middlesex old boy Keech did most to enable them to declare, 136 behind. Kallis hit a fluent century, to set the challenge which Hampshire failed so dismally.

Close of play: First day, Middlesex 212-3 (M. R. Ramprakash 99*, O. A. Shah 11*); Second day, Hampshire 69-2 (G. W. White 8*, S. J. Renshaw 0*); Third day, Middlesex 91-1 (J. H. Kallis 49*, M. W. Gatting 37*).

Middlesex

P. N. Weekes c Aymes b Renshaw	7	– c White b Renshaw		1
J. H. Kallis c Aymes b Milburn	39	– not out		102
*M. R. Ramprakash c Stephenson b Udal	190			
M. W. Gatting c Smith b Hayden	47	– (3) not out		69
O. A. Shah c Keech b Udal	77			
†K. R. Brown lbw b Stephenson	1			
J. C. Pooley c Aymes b Milburn	28			
K. P. Dutch not out	19			
R. L. Johnson c Aymes b Milburn	2			
B 7, l-b 11, w 8, n-b 6	32	B 4, l-b 2		6

1/13 2/66 3/194 4/379 5/382	(8 wkts dec.) 442	1/5
6/390 7/434 8/442		

(1 wkt dec.) 178

J. P. Hewitt and A. R. C. Fraser did not bat.

Bonus points – Middlesex 4, Hampshire 2 (Score at 120 overs: 390-5).

Bowling: *First Innings*—Milburn 34.3–6–112–3; Renshaw 28–8–98–1; Mascarenhas 19–7–35–0; Stephenson 25–4–84–1; Udal 20–1–72–2; Hayden 4–0–23–1; Keech 1–1–0–0. *Second Innings*—Milburn 6–2–16–0; Renshaw 13–2–55–1; Stephenson 12–1–35–0; Udal 13–1–44–0; Keech 5–0–22–0.

Hampshire

J. S. Laney c Pooley b Hewitt	23	– c Brown b Fraser	4
M. L. Hayden lbw b Dutch	36	– c and b Fraser	1
G. W. White c Shah b Dutch	62	– c Shah b Fraser	8
S. J. Renshaw c Gatting b Hewitt	14	– (10) b Johnson	0
R. A. Smith b Kallis	27	– (4) lbw b Fraser	8
M. Keech not out	78	– (5) c Brown b Fraser	14
*J. P. Stephenson not out	48	– (6) c Pooley b Hewitt	35
†A. N. Aymes (did not bat)		– (7) c Kallis b Johnson	11
S. D. Udal (did not bat)		– (8) lbw b Hewitt	0
A. D. Mascarenhas (did not bat)		– (9) c Brown b Hewitt	0
S. M. Milburn (did not bat)		– not out	11
L-b 10, n-b 8	18	L-b 3, w 2	5

1/41 2/69 3/100 4/148 5/206   (5 wkts dec.) 306   1/4 2/13 3/18 4/21 5/50   97
6/86 7/86 8/86 9/86

Bonus points – Hampshire 3, Middlesex 2.

Bowling: *First Innings*—Fraser 15–2–38–0; Hewitt 17–2–70–2; Johnson 13–1–36–0; Kallis 12–3–22–1; Dutch 29–6–94–2; Weekes 16–3–36–0. *Second Innings*—Fraser 10–1–38–5; Hewitt 7–1–27–3; Kallis 6–1–19–0; Johnson 3.3–1–10–2.

Umpires: T. E. Jesty and J. F. Steele.

MIDDLESEX v SURREY

At Lord's, August 15, 16, 17. Surrey won by an innings and 125 runs. Surrey 24 pts, Middlesex 4 pts. Toss: Middlesex.

This was Middlesex's worst performance of the season, and probably Surrey's best. It ended any lingering hopes Middlesex had of the Championship, while Surrey leaped six places to fifth. Saqlain Mushtaq took ten wickets for the second match running, including a hat-trick on the first day, when Middlesex wilted from 142 for two to 162 for nine. Only Fraser, hitting Saqlain for three sixes, got them a batting point. A brilliant 182 from Adam Hollioake pressed home Surrey's advantage. He hit 20 fours and four sixes and added 143 in 26 overs with his brother, who confirmed the appreciation of Lord's he had shown in his two high-profile one-day appearances; both made career-bests. Middlesex needed 326 to make Surrey bat again. But when they resumed on Sunday, which was for once preserved for first-class cricket, their form was no better than it had been on most other Sundays. Only Pooley and Keith Brown offered resistance: the spinners finished them off with four sessions in hand.

Close of play: First day, Surrey 123-2 (M. A. Butcher 56*, A. J. Hollioake 14*); Second day, Middlesex 24-1 (J. C. Pooley 1*, R. L. Johnson 10*).

Middlesex

J. C. Pooley c Butcher b B. C. Hollioake	10	– b Amin	72
J. H. Kallis c Batty b B. C. Hollioake	23	– c Batty b Bicknell	9
M. W. Gatting c Brown b Amin	54	– (5) c Ratcliffe b Saqlain Mushtaq	7
O. A. Shah c Amin b B. C. Hollioake	44	– (6) c Batty b Lewis	25
*M. R. Ramprakash c A. J. Hollioake b Saqlain Mushtaq	8	– (4) c and b Saqlain Mushtaq	0
†K. R. Brown c Bicknell b Saqlain Mushtaq	7	– (7) c Ratcliffe b Saqlain Mushtaq	35
K. P. Dutch c Brown b Saqlain Mushtaq	0	– (8) c Butcher b Saqlain Mushtaq	6
R. L. Johnson c Amin b Saqlain Mushtaq	0	– (3) run out	27
J. P. Hewitt c A. J. Hollioake b Saqlain Mushtaq	0	– c B. C. Hollioake b Amin	8
A. R. C. Fraser not out	30	– st Batty b Saqlain Mushtaq	6
P. C. R. Tufnell c Batty b A. J. Hollioake	7	– not out	2
B 3, l-b 7, n-b 12	22	B 4	4
	205		**201**

1/37 2/38 3/142 4/142 5/159
6/159 7/162 8/162 9/162

1/10 2/67 3/80 4/96 5/120
6/175 7/184 8/189 9/199

Bonus points – Middlesex 1, Surrey 4.

Bowling: *First Innings*—Bicknell 11–2–33–0; Lewis 12–1–44–0; B. C. Hollioake 13–4–23–3; A. J. Hollioake 6.5–1–24–1; Saqlain Mushtaq 14–2–50–5; Amin 12–4–21–1. *Second Innings*—Lewis 14–2–43–1; Bicknell 7–3–14–1; Saqlain Mushtaq 27–6–66–5; B. C. Hollioake 3–0–14–0; Amin 18.3–5–55–2; Thorpe 1–0–5–0.

Surrey

M. A. Butcher c Gatting b Johnson	79	M. P. Bicknell c Pooley b Tufnell	1
J. D. Ratcliffe c Dutch b Fraser	13	Saqlain Mushtaq c Brown b Johnson	9
G. P. Thorpe c Ramprakash b Dutch	32	R. M. Amin not out	0
*A. J. Hollioake lbw b Fraser	182	B 3, l-b 18, w 4, n-b 6	31
A. D. Brown c Gatting b Johnson	70		
B. C. Hollioake lbw b Fraser	76		**(9 wkts dec.) 531**
C. C. Lewis c Kallis b Tufnell	15		
†J. N. Batty not out	23		

1/17 2/99 3/168
4/318 5/461 6/496
7/502 8/512 9/531

Bonus points – Surrey 4, Middlesex 3 (Score at 120 overs: 508-7).

Bowling: Fraser 26–5–106–2; Hewitt 21–0–126–1; Kallis 8–0–31–0; Johnson 22–2–79–3; Tufnell 36.3–6–106–2; Dutch 12–0–47–1; Ramprakash 4–0–15–0.

Umpires: J. C. Balderstone and G. Sharp.

At Chester-le-Street, August 20, 21, 22, 23. MIDDLESEX drew with DURHAM.

At Kidderminster, August 27, 28, 29, 20. MIDDLESEX beat WORCESTERSHIRE by 169 runs.

At Taunton, September 2, 3, 4, 5. MIDDLESEX drew with SOMERSET.

MIDDLESEX v NOTTINGHAMSHIRE

At Lord's, September 10, 11, 12, 13. Middlesex won by ten wickets. Middlesex 23 pts, Nottinghamshire 3 pts. Toss: Middlesex.

Middlesex ended their home programme with a resounding win. They could not quite beat Nottinghamshire by an innings, but, with only nine required, Fraser was sent in and hit Noon – who had given up his keeper's pads – for three fours. On the opening day, Pooley scored only his third half-century of 1997, showing the technique and concentration he had often lacked. This added to the disappointment when he danced down the pitch trying to reach his hundred and was stumped. Shah was determined not to make such a mistake as he approached his maiden century. He took an hour to advance from 81 to 96 in singles. But, apart from that attack of nerves, he confirmed his abundant gifts. After Tufnell and Kallis made Nottinghamshire follow on, Welton defied the home bowlers for nearly three hours. He was finally bowled by the young seamer Tim Bloomfield, whose three top-order wickets suggested great promise.

Close of play: First day, Middlesex 283-5 (O. A. Shah 21*, K. R. Brown 0*); Second day, Nottinghamshire 116-4 (U. Afzaal 8*, C. M. Tolley 23*); Third day, Nottinghamshire 93-2 (G. E. Welton 33*, P. Johnson 18*).

Middlesex

J. C. Pooley st Noon b Bates	98		
J. H. Kallis lbw b Tolley	34		
*M. R. Ramprakash run out	55		
M. W. Gatting b Franks	33		
O. A. Shah not out	104		
D. C. Nash b Bowen	6		
†K. R. Brown c Tolley b Evans	14		
J. P. Hewitt c Johnson b Afzaal	13	– (2) not out	0
A. R. C. Fraser st Noon b Afzaal	27	– (1) not out	12
P. C. R. Tufnell not out	7		
B 5, l-b 6, n-b 28	39		

1/66 2/184 3/225 4/269 5/283   (8 wkts dec.) 430   (no wkt) 12
6/319 7/376 8/410

T. F. Bloomfield did not bat.

Bonus points – Middlesex 3, Nottinghamshire 2 (Score at 120 overs: 321-6).

Bowling: *First Innings*—Bowen 25-4-75-1; Franks 25-3-95-1; Tolley 23-4-70-1; Evans 33-10-70-1; Bates 42-11-80-1; Afzaal 12-2-29-2. *Second Innings*—Noon 1-0-12-0.

Nottinghamshire

M. P. Dowman lbw b Tufnell	28	– c Brown b Tufnell	13
R. T. Robinson c Brown b Tufnell	35	– lbw b Bloomfield	19
G. E. Welton c Brown b Tufnell	14	– b Bloomfield	47
*P. Johnson c Pooley b Kallis	1	– lbw b Bloomfield	44
U. Afzaal b Kallis	14	– run out	21
C. M. Tolley c Brown b Kallis	42	– lbw b Fraser	2
†W. M. Noon run out	39	– b Kallis	7
P. J. Franks c Gatting b Kallis	1	– c Shah b Kallis	19
K. P. Evans c Shah b Tufnell	13	– lbw b Kallis	14
R. T. Bates not out	8	– not out	6
M. N. Bowen c Nash b Tufnell	3	– retired hurt	3
L-b 8, n-b 4	12	B 7, l-b 12, w 2, n-b 12	33

1/69 2/72 3/73 4/91 5/123   210   1/30 2/47 3/129 4/136 5/148   228
6/148 7/152 8/179 9/207   6/168 7/184 8/200 9/221

Bonus points – Nottinghamshire 1, Middlesex 4.

In the second innings M. N. Bowen retired hurt at 228.

Bowling: *First Innings*—Fraser 14-7-24-0; Hewitt 17-5-48-0; Tufnell 32.1-6-61-5; Kallis 18-5-39-4; Bloomfield 4-1-12-0; Ramprakash 6-3-18-0. *Second Innings*—Fraser 20-10-34-1; Hewitt 7-1-25-0; Bloomfield 17-6-33-3; Kallis 25-6-58-3; Tufnell 40-15-57-1; Ramprakash 6-4-2-0.

Umpires: G. I. Burgess and B. Leadbeater.

At Chelmsford, September 18, 19, 20, 21. MIDDLESEX drew with ESSEX.

NORTHAMPTONSHIRE

Kevin Curran

Patrons: The Earl of Dalkeith and
    The Earl Spencer
President: A. P. Arnold
Chairman: L. A. Wilson
Chairman, Cricket Committee: R. T. Virgin
Chief Executive: S. P. Coverdale
Captain: 1997 – R. J. Bailey
    1998 – K. M. Curran
Coach: J. E. Emburey
Head Groundsman: D. Bates
Scorer: A. C. Kingston

It was an abysmal season for Northamptonshire. And the occupants of the West Stand, lugubrious at the best of times, became downright grumpy: how could a county nurturing so much talent perform so woefully? As one local put it: "They're like battery chickens – nice, plump birds, but not a lot of flavour."

The excess of talent seemed to be part of the problem. Twenty-three players were used in the Championship, partly because of an abnormal number of injuries and partly because no one seemed sure what the real first team should be – the understudies were generally as successful as those they replaced. Thirteen members of the 1997 staff had first-class centuries to their name. On the other hand, they had very little help from their overseas player, Mohammad Akram, who fulfilled none of the promise of his tour with Pakistan the previous year. If Northamptonshire had expected Akram to turn into a Wasim or a Waqar they were sadly disappointed.

The effect was that the county again hovered near the foot of the Championship, eventually settling fourth from bottom with just three victories: narrow wins over Kent and Essex plus a sixth successive demolition job on Derbyshire. However, Derbyshire knocked them out of the NatWest; they performed indifferently in the Sunday League; and, after they were beaten by Kent in the semi-finals of the Benson and Hedges, there was very little to play for.

In this situation, politics inevitably began to take over. Talk quickly centred on the captain, Rob Bailey, whose two years in charge had seen the team slump from Championship contenders to no-hopers. An ill-timed leak about negotiations with Shane Warne, who had allegedly been offered the captaincy as well as a huge contract, did not help. Bailey commands respect from all quarters both as a man and as a cricketer, but the rumours inevitably affected his form: against Essex, he suffered the indignity of a pair. None the less, he was the leading scorer with 1,078 runs, and often held the innings together, while other senior batsmen played as though gully, first slip and third man presented the best scoring opportunities.

In October, he was deprived of the captaincy – a decision he accepted with his customary dignity – and Kevin Curran replaced him a month later. Curran was the only other batsman to pass 1,000, and he played several inspired innings. But his batting retained its annoying mixture of high quality and village blacksmith shots. His supporters say "that's the way he plays". Given his new responsibilities, it might be better for the team if he played otherwise.

Most of the other batsmen were inconsistent, and it may be that seeing so many batsmen make runs in the Second Eleven had an unsettling effect on those in the First. Richard Montgomerie scored 68 at the first attempt, but could not reach 50 in his next ten first-class innings. He gave way to Russell Warren, returning after a broken finger. When he did regain his place, Montgomerie showed some improvement. Warren himself was unable to settle, although his unbeaten 174 against Worcestershire was a reminder of his immense talent.

Warren was happy to cede his role of wicket-keeper/batsman, and David Ripley returned to a regular place, showing efficiency behind the stumps and very often more guts and determination in front of them than many of the top-order players.

Mal Loye did not return after his back seized up against Essex in July. David Sales did not progress as rapidly as hoped, and perhaps needs to ally more work ethic to his natural ability. One of the few players to make the most of his talent was Tony Penberthy and, some of the time, he had a fellow-Cornishman for company: David Roberts, who scored a wonderfully mature century against Essex, but never quite sustained that form. In the last match of the season, Alec Swann, like Roberts a 20-year-old, scored 136 on his fifth first-class appearance.

The bowling was less rich. With Akram contributing so sparsely, the burden fell on Paul Taylor, who shrugged off illness and injury to capture 54 wickets. He took ten against Nottinghamshire, and a magnificent six for 45 in the first innings against Yorkshire, but both games ended in defeat. David Capel had one glorious highlight in the Benson and Hedges quarter-final at Headingley, when he took five for 51 and hit a whizz-bang 67. But he was plagued by injury, and played just four Championship matches, which left the seam attack dangerously dependent on youngsters, though Scott Boswell showed improvement.

John Emburey gradually withdrew from the side to concentrate on his coaching duties, and eventually announced his retirement after 25 years in the game, and 1,608 first-class wickets. This left the field clear for two young spin bowlers, with some very gratifying results. Slow left-armer Michael Davies, 21, and 22-year-old off-spinner Jason Brown bowled long spells with maturity and growing self-confidence.

That is one hopeful sign for 1998. Another could be the arrival of the Australian Paul Reiffel, an overseas player with a record which should make him a more effective successor to Curtly Ambrose and Anil Kumble than Akram was. Northamptonshire also won the race for Devon Malcolm, who had grown disaffected at Derby. At 35, he is hardly a long-term bet. But if Bailey had had these fast-bowling resources he would probably still be in office. The county have lost Alan Fordham, who retired to become cricket operations manager for the ECB. But they remain heavily staffed, and the club are not making the best of their resources. The green shoots of a Northamptonshire revival are there; the club's problem is deciding which of them they think will grow best. – IAN DAVIES.

NORTHAMPTONSHIRE 1997

[*Bill Smith*]

Back row: J. A. R. Blain, D. J. Roberts, D. J. Sales, S. A. J. Boswell, A. J. Swann, K. J. Innes, M. V. Steele, A. M. Dobson.
Middle row: N. A. Foster (*development coach*), M. K. Davies, J. F. Brown, R. R. Montgomerie, D. Follett, J. G. Hughes, Mohammad Akram, M. B. Loye, R. J. Warren, A. L. Penberthy, T. C. Walton, J. N. Snape, K. Russell (*physiotherapist*).
Front row: J. E. Emburey (*coach*), J. P. Taylor, D. Ripley, R. J. Bailey (*captain*), D. J. Capel, A. Fordham, K. M. Curran, N. G. B. Cook.
Insets: T. M. B. Bailey, G. P. Swann, R. J. Logan.

NORTHAMPTONSHIRE RESULTS

All first-class matches – Played 18: Won 3, Lost 5, Drawn 10.

County Championship matches – Played 17: Won 3, Lost 5, Drawn 9.

Competition placings – Britannic Assurance County Championship, 15th;
NatWest Trophy, 2nd round; Benson and Hedges Cup, s-f;
AXA Life League, 9th.

COUNTY CHAMPIONSHIP AVERAGES

BATTING

Cap		M	I	NO	R	HS	100s	50s	Avge	Ct/St
1992	K. M. Curran	15	26	4	1,032	159	2	6	46.90	8
1990	A. Fordham	8	16	2	629	85*	0	6	44.92	8
1995	R. J. Warren†	9	16	2	614	174*	1	3	43.85	10/1
1987	D. Ripley	16	23	6	728	92	0	4	42.82	27/6
1985	R. J. Bailey	16	29	5	973	117*	2	5	40.54	19
1994	M. B. Loye†	8	15	3	412	86	0	2	34.33	2
1995	R. R. Montgomerie...	9	17	3	476	73	0	4	34.00	6
	D. J. Roberts........	6	12	0	367	117	1	0	30.58	0
	D. J. Sales..........	12	18	1	510	103	1	2	30.00	4
	T. C. Walton	7	10	1	231	60	0	2	25.66	1
1994	A. L. Penberthy	12	18	0	443	96	0	2	24.61	7
	J. N. Snape	10	15	3	286	66	0	3	23.83	9
1986	D. J. Capel†	4	7	0	140	57	0	1	20.00	1
	S. A. J. Boswell	9	12	3	122	35	0	0	13.55	2
1992	J. P. Taylor	16	21	4	216	36	0	0	12.70	7
	M. K. Davies	4	9	4	49	17	0	0	9.80	2
	Mohammad Akram§..	11	14	2	116	28	0	0	9.66	1
	J. F. Brown	5	8	4	25	16*	0	0	6.25	2

Also batted: J. A. R. Blain (1 match) 0 (1 ct); J. E. Emburey (3 matches) 0, 0, 39 (1 ct);
D. Follett (1 match) 0, 3; J. G. Hughes† (1 match) 5*; A. J. Swann† (2 matches) 1, 25, 136.

* Signifies not out.   † Born in Northamptonshire.   § Overseas player.

BOWLING

	O	M	R	W	BB	5W/i	Avge
J. P. Taylor............	455.4	81	1,532	54	7-87	3	28.37
M. K. Davies	234.2	71	674	23	5-46	1	29.30
K. M. Curran	215.2	57	715	24	4-32	0	29.79
J. F. Brown	178.2	32	583	16	3-23	0	36.43
R. J. Bailey	112.3	19	367	10	4-10	0	36.70
Mohammad Akram	287	43	1,135	30	5-72	2	37.83
S. A. J. Boswell........	185.5	26	769	15	5-94	1	51.26
J. N. Snape............	225.1	47	681	11	4-46	0	61.90

Also bowled: J. A. R. Blain 30–8–105–2; D. J. Capel 39.4–4–180–2; J. E. Emburey
110.3–39–259–4; D. Follett 24.3–1–123–2; A. Fordham 2.3–0–7–0; J. G. Hughes 22–6–66–1;
A. L. Penberthy 175–27–647–9; D. J. Sales 3–0–16–0; T. C. Walton 8–0–45–0.

COUNTY RECORDS

Highest score for:	300	R. Subba Row v Surrey at The Oval........	1958
Highest score against:	333	K. S. Duleepsinhji (Sussex) at Hove	1930
Best bowling for:	10-127	V. W. C. Jupp v Kent at Tunbridge Wells ...	1932
Best bowling against:	10-30	C. Blythe (Kent) at Northampton............	1907
Highest total for:	781-7 dec.	v Nottinghamshire at Northampton	1995
Highest total against:	670-9 dec.	by Sussex at Hove........................	1921
Lowest total for:	12	v Gloucestershire at Gloucester	1907
Lowest total against:	33	by Lancashire at Northampton	1977

At Hove, April 23, 24, 25, 26. NORTHAMPTONSHIRE drew with SUSSEX.

NORTHAMPTONSHIRE v SOMERSET

At Northampton, May 7, 8, 9, 10. Drawn. Northamptonshire 7 pts, Somerset 9 pts. Toss: Northamptonshire.

Some fine pace bowling on both sides illuminated this rain-affected match, which also saw snow on the first day. Caddick bowled with menace, movement and pace on a helpful pitch, and deserved his figures of six for 65. His only real opposition came from Curran, in a cavalier 73 including ten fours. Somerset found the going just as difficult against Northamptonshire's Mohammad Akram, making his home Championship debut. His lively pace, helped by a little movement in the air, brought him five wickets in spite of some sloppy slip fielding. Rose and Burns took advantage of their luck in this regard to put on 170 for the eighth wicket, just two short of the county record. Burns scored a career-best 82 and Rose completed his century as the visitors took a lead of 105. Hopes of a Somerset win flickered on the last day – Northamptonshire were only 13 ahead when their fifth wicket fell – but they were inevitably extinguished by the rain.

Close of play: First day, Northamptonshire 126-4 (K. M. Curran 65*, D. J. Capel 7*); Second day, Somerset 23-3 (P. D. Bowler 11*, A. R. Caddick 3*); Third day, Northamptonshire 104-3 (R. R. Montgomerie 33*, A. L. Penberthy 26*).

Northamptonshire

R. R. Montgomerie c Trescothick b Shine	0	– not out	33
M. B. Loye c Bowler b Caddick	18	– c Kerr b Shine	10
*R. J. Bailey c Turner b Shine	8	– lbw b Rose	7
K. M. Curran c Caddick b Rose	73	– b Caddick	18
A. L. Penberthy b Caddick	19	– c Turner b Caddick	37
D. J. Capel b Caddick	20	– c Lathwell b Rose	1
J. N. Snape lbw b Caddick	3	– not out	4
†D. Ripley lbw b Rose	0		
J. P. Taylor b Caddick	7		
S. A. J. Boswell lbw b Caddick	2		
Mohammad Akram not out	20		
B 4, l-b 6, n-b 5	15	B 4, l-b 4, n-b 4	12
	185	**(5 wkts)**	**122**

1/11 2/25 3/64 4/116 5/134
6/155 7/156 8/156 9/158

1/18 2/38 3/65
4/115 5/118

Bonus points – Somerset 4.

Bowling: *First Innings*—Caddick 24.2–6–65–6; Shine 7–2–29–2; Rose 20–5–60–2; Mushtaq Ahmed 4–1–21–0. *Second Innings*—Caddick 17–2–70–2; Shine 6–2–8–1; Rose 10–4–17–2; Mushtaq Ahmed 4–2–9–0; Kerr 4–1–10–0.

Somerset

M. N. Lathwell c Montgomerie b Mohammad Akram	5	
M. E. Trescothick c Capel b Mohammad Akram	4	
*P. D. Bowler c Bailey b Mohammad Akram	15	
J. I. D. Kerr b Mohammad Akram	0	
A. R. Caddick lbw b Taylor	16	
P. C. L. Holloway lbw b Taylor	3	
M. Burns c Loye b Snape	82	
†R. J. Turner b Taylor	10	
G. D. Rose not out	109	
Mushtaq Ahmed c Snape b Boswell	8	
K. J. Shine b Mohammad Akram	17	
L-b 7, n-b 14	21	
	290	

1/8 2/13 3/19 4/42 5/42
6/55 7/73 8/243 9/253

Bonus points – Somerset 2, Northamptonshire 4.

Bowling: Mohammad Akram 20.4–3–72–5; Taylor 22–3–71–3; Boswell 14–1–83–1; Penberthy 4–1–13–0; Capel 7–2–23–0; Snape 9–1–21–1.

Umpires: T. E. Jesty and B. J. Meyer.

At Cambridge, May 14, 15, 16. NORTHAMPTONSHIRE drew with CAMBRIDGE UNIVERSITY.

At Northampton, May 17. NORTHAMPTONSHIRE lost to AUSTRALIANS by 17 runs (See Australian tour section).

At Manchester, May 21, 22, 23, 24. NORTHAMPTONSHIRE drew with LANCASHIRE.

At Lord's, May 29, 30, 31, June 2. NORTHAMPTONSHIRE lost to MIDDLESEX by an innings and 57 runs.

NORTHAMPTONSHIRE v NOTTINGHAMSHIRE

At Northampton, June 4, 5, 6, 7. Nottinghamshire won by three wickets. Nottinghamshire 22 pts, Northamptonshire 5 pts. Toss: Northamptonshire. First-class debut: G. E. Welton. County debut: N. J. Astle.

Three days of aimless endeavour were redeemed on an eventful final day that produced an exciting finish in the last over. The two first innings followed similar plots. Inept batting against steady bowling brought meagre scores, but both sides were rescued by their wicket-keepers, Ripley and Noon. Trailing by 37, Northamptonshire set about their second innings with purpose. A solid century from Bailey, including 17 fours and a six, with able support from Snape, set Nottinghamshire 301 in 77 overs. After two early wickets, Dowman and the New Zealander Nathan Astle, in his first county match, shared a stand of 156. Both fell within two overs: Dowman for 111, with 20 fours, and Astle for 64, after a first-innings duck. But then Johnson sealed the win with a hard-hit 57. The stoical Taylor took all seven second-innings wickets but, despite match figures of ten for 141, finished a loser. John Emburey later announced his retirement from first-class cricket to concentrate on coaching Northamptonshire.

Close of play: First day, Northamptonshire 226-9 (J. P. Taylor 8*, Mohammad Akram 2*); Second day, Nottinghamshire 259-9 (M. N. Bowen 26*, R. A. Pick 5*); Third day, Northamptonshire 253-5 (R. J. Bailey 78*, J. N. Snape 61*).

Northamptonshire

R. R. Montgomerie c Bates b Bowen	2	– c Archer b Astle	14
M. B. Loye lbw b Bowen	3	– b Astle	26
*R. J. Bailey lbw b Bowen	33	– not out	117
K. M. Curran c Bates b Tolley	22	– c Astle b Bowen	23
T. C. Walton b Bowen	6	– c Tolley b Bowen	42
D. J. Sales c Bates b Astle	25	– b Bowen	0
J. N. Snape c Welton b Tolley	0	– c and b Bowen	66
†D. Ripley c Noon b Pick	77	– not out	39
J. E. Emburey b Bowen	39		
J. P. Taylor not out	12		
Mohammad Akram c Afzaal b Pick	7		
B 5, l-b 4	9	B 4, l-b 4, n-b 2	10

	235	(6 wkts dec.) 337

1/4 2/9 3/61 4/67 5/68   235   1/39 2/40 3/88   (6 wkts dec.) 337
6/69 7/128 8/213 9/217   4/144 5/144 6/264

Bonus points – Northamptonshire 1, Nottinghamshire 4.

Bowling: *First Innings*—Bowen 33–11–57–5; Pick 21.2–6–55–2; Tolley 27–9–46–2; Bates 8–2–29–0; Astle 13–7–19–1; Dowman 2–1–8–0; Afzaal 2–1–3–0; Archer 2–1–9–0. *Second Innings*—Bowen 25.3–2–128–4; Pick 23–4–85–0; Astle 16–4–33–2; Tolley 11–0–47–0; Bates 6–0–22–0; Afzaal 5–0–14–0.

Nottinghamshire

G. E. Welton lbw b Curran	3	– c Ripley b Taylor	0
M. P. Dowman b Curran	21	– b Taylor	111
U. Afzaal b Curran	4	– c Montgomerie b Taylor	11
N. J. Astle c Bailey b Mohammad Akram	0	– c Ripley b Taylor	64
*P. Johnson b Emburey	41	– c Walton b Taylor	57
G. F. Archer c Ripley b Emburey	11	– c Snape b Taylor	4
C. M. Tolley lbw b Taylor	12	– c and b Taylor	20
†W. M. Noon c Emburey b Taylor	83	– not out	9
R. T. Bates c Ripley b Curran	21	– not out	2
M. N. Bowen c Bailey b Taylor	32		
R. A. Pick not out	8		
B 4, l-b 14, w 2, n-b 16	36	B 4, l-b 11, w 4, n-b 4	23

1/8 2/14 3/19 4/79 5/81	272	1/1 2/43 3/199 4/200	(7 wkts) 301
6/91 7/130 8/183 9/246		5/204 6/256 7/297	

Bonus points – Nottinghamshire 2, Northamptonshire 4.

Bowling: *First Innings*—Mohammad Akram 20–3–79–1; Taylor 20.4–2–54–3; Curran 23–9–61–4; Emburey 25–11–36–2; Snape 13–5–24–0. *Second Innings*—Mohammad Akram 16–4–66–0; Taylor 25–5–87–7; Emburey 21.3–8–67–0; Curran 6–1–32–0; Snape 8–0–34–0.

Umpires: G. I. Burgess and J. H. Harris.

NORTHAMPTONSHIRE v HAMPSHIRE

At Northampton, June 18, 19, 20, 21. Drawn. Northamptonshire 5 pts, Hampshire 7 pts. Toss: Northamptonshire.

Two performances will endure from this rain-scarred match. The first-day century of Hayden, after Bailey surprisingly put Hampshire in to bat, was one of the best seen on the ground in recent years. Starting slowly, without the semblance of a rash stroke, Hayden accelerated to reach 150 in 226 balls with 27 fours, a chanceless innings and his fourth century in four matches. Meanwhile, a laborious spell from Taylor – six for 91 off 32.4 overs – gave him his 29th wicket of the season, out of his county's total of 61. Thirteen overs on the second day and 18.4 on the third forced contrivance between the teams. Northamptonshire were set to chase 320 in 90 overs, reduced to 66 by rain. Led by Loye, they made a genuine attempt but, after the loss of five wickets in 39 balls, the last pair had to survive the final three overs.

Close of play: First day, Hampshire 335-4 (R. A. Smith 71*, J. P. Stephenson 24*); Second day, Hampshire 373-6 (A. N. Aymes 1*); Third day, Northamptonshire 40-2 (R. J. Bailey 14*, K. M. Curran 4*).

Hampshire

J. S. Laney lbw b Boswell	4		S. D. Udal b Taylor	18
M. L. Hayden c Bailey b Taylor	150		S. J. Renshaw not out	2
K. D. James b Taylor	56		B 8, l-b 10, w 14, n-b 15	47
R. A. Smith b Hughes	74			
W. S. Kendall lbw b Taylor	0		1/5 2/194 3/273	(8 wkts dec.) 405
*J. P. Stephenson c Ripley b Taylor	49		4/273 5/367 6/373	
†A. N. Aymes c Bailey b Taylor	5		7/396 8/405	

S. M. Milburn and J. N. B. Bovill did not bat.

Bonus points – Hampshire 4, Northamptonshire 2 (Score at 120 overs: 396-6).

Bowling: Taylor 32.4–7–91–6; Boswell 21–3–101–1; Hughes 22–6–66–1; Curran 16–7–49–0; Snape 21–5–44–0; Bailey 6–0–13–0; Walton 4–0–23–0.

Hampshire forfeited their second innings.

Northamptonshire

M. B. Loye c Kendall b Renshaw	13	– c Hayden b Bovill	86
R. J. Warren c James b Renshaw	8	– b James	31
*R. J. Bailey not out	20	– (4) c James b Bovill	31
K. M. Curran not out	43	– (3) lbw b Bovill	28
T. C. Walton (did not bat)		– c Kendall b Renshaw	39
D. J. Sales (did not bat)		– c Kendall b Udal	36
†D. Ripley (did not bat)		– c Laney b Udal	10
J. N. Snape (did not bat)		– c Laney b Udal	10
J. G. Hughes (did not bat)		– not out	5
J. P. Taylor (did not bat)		– b Renshaw	1
S. A. J. Boswell (did not bat)		– not out	1
L-b 2	2	B 6, l-b 3, n-b 10	19

1/18 2/33   (2 wkts dec.) 86   1/55 2/104 3/188   (9 wkts) 297
4/199 5/255 6/270
7/281 8/292 9/296

Bowling: *First Innings*—Milburn 7–1–27–0; Renshaw 7–2–13–2; Smith 2–0–38–0; Stephenson 1–0–6–0. *Second Innings*—Milburn 9–2–42–0; Renshaw 14–2–55–2; James 9–1–49–1; Bovill 11–1–40–3; Stephenson 6–0–33–0; Udal 17–2–69–3.

Umpires: B. Dudleston and N. T. Plews.

NORTHAMPTONSHIRE v GLOUCESTERSHIRE

At Luton, June 26, 27, 28, 30. Drawn. Northamptonshire 3 pts, Gloucestershire 3 pts. Toss: Northamptonshire.

Three days' incessant rain frustrated the local organisers and turned the match into a single-innings affair with no bonus points. Gloucestershire were unlucky not to claim 12 points for a one-day win. Sent in, they found runs hard to get, particularly against the swing of Mohammad Akram. Young was their mainstay until he was run out by Curran, who also claimed four wickets. It was Curran who eventually had to save the game for Northamptonshire. Their target of 181 off 42 overs seemed very reasonable on this smallish ground, but Smith and Lewis – one of the many pace bowlers allowed to escape from Northamptonshire – ripped through the batting. Rain brought 85 minutes' respite at 26 for five; when play resumed, less than eight overs remained.

Close of play: First day, No play; Second day, No play; Third day, No play.

Gloucestershire

A. J. Wright c Penberthy b Mohammad Akram	9	*M. W. Alleyne c Ripley b Curran	21
N. J. Trainor c Penberthy b Mohammad Akram	20	†R. C. Russell not out	31
R. J. Cunliffe c Penberthy b Curran	2	T. H. C. Hancock not out	5
M. A. Lynch c Bailey b Curran	22	B 4, l-b 4, w 2, n-b 6	16
A. M. Smith b Curran	6		
S. Young run out	48	1/14 2/21 3/43 (7 wkts dec.) 180	
		4/49 5/75	
		6/120 7/168	

K. P. Sheeraz and J. Lewis did not bat.

Bowling: Mohammad Akram 14–4–30–2; Taylor 12–1–40–0; Curran 15–3–69–4; Boswell 10–5–14–0; Penberthy 3–0–19–0.

Northamptonshire

M. B. Loye lbw b Smith	1	A. L. Penberthy lbw b Smith	6
R. J. Warren b Lewis	0	†D. Ripley not out	2
*R. J. Bailey lbw b Smith	7	L-b 1, n-b 4	5
K. M. Curran not out	32		
T. C. Walton b Lewis	5	1/0 2/2 3/13 (6 wkts) 58	
D. J. Sales c Russell b Lewis	0	4/18 5/18 6/37	

J. P. Taylor, Mohammad Akram and S. A. J. Boswell did not bat.

Bowling: Smith 10–3–36–3; Lewis 9.3–6–21–3.

Umpires: R. Palmer and R. A. White.

At Maidstone, July 2, 3, 4, 5. NORTHAMPTONSHIRE beat KENT by one wicket.

NORTHAMPTONSHIRE v ESSEX

At Northampton, July 16, 17, 18, 19. Northamptonshire won by 15 runs. Northamptonshire 24 pts, Essex 6 pts. Toss: Northamptonshire.

The scorecard suggests a glorious match with a thrilling climax. But it hides warts and imperfections throughout the game, and on both sides. The match may go down in history as the one that finally convinced Gooch it was time to bow out. His 24 and 16 continued his run of low scores, and he announced his retirement in the *News of the World* the day after this game ended. A responsible maiden century by 20-year-old Roberts, who battled it out for four and a half hours while no one else reached 40, and a last-wicket stand of 70 enabled Northamptonshire to collect full batting points on a perfect strip. Essex were just as inconsistent against some wayward pace bowling; they leaned heavily on Hussain, but even he was out to a poor stroke. The pattern continued as poor batting and injuries saw Northamptonshire stutter – with a pair for their captain Bailey – and they were helped to 216 only by a sensible innings from another youngster, 19-year-old Sales. A target of 306 in 92 overs made Essex favourites. But more kamikaze strokes, plus Snape's off-spin, undid them.

Close of play: First day, Northamptonshire 354-9 (D. Ripley 33*, S. A. J. Boswell 27*); Second day, Northamptonshire 14-0 (D. J. Roberts 0*, R. J. Warren 12*); Third day, Northamptonshire 216-8 (K. M. Curran 40*, D. J. Sales 63*).

Northamptonshire

R. J. Warren c Rollins b D. R. Law	25	– (2) lbw b Williams	32
D. J. Roberts b Grayson	117	– (1) c Williams b Cowan	4
*R. J. Bailey c Rollins b D. R. Law	0	– c Rollins b Irani	0
M. B. Loye c Williams b Cowan	32	– not out	43
K. M. Curran b Cowan	36	– c Rollins b Cowan	40
D. J. Sales lbw b Such	31	– c Such b D. R. Law	63
J. N. Snape c D. R. Law b Grayson	23	– c D. R. Law b Grayson	1
†D. Ripley not out	39	– st Rollins b Grayson	5
J. P. Taylor b Grayson	1	– b Cowan	0
Mohammad Akram lbw b Grayson	7	– c Grayson b Cowan	1
S. A. J. Boswell c Hussain b Cowan	29	– b Williams	0
B 1, l-b 6, n-b 17	24	B 9, l-b 4, w 2, n-b 12	27

1/55 2/55 3/100 4/155 5/224   364   1/26 2/26 3/72 4/135 5/147   216
6/281 7/282 8/284 9/294   6/154 7/156 8/182 9/216

Bonus points – Northamptonshire 4, Essex 4.

In the second innings M. B. Loye, when 43, retired hurt at 120 and resumed at 216-9; K. M. Curran, when 28, retired hurt at 128 and resumed at 182.

Bowling: *First Innings*—Cowan 24–5–98–3; Williams 19–4–58–0; D. R. Law 23–5–70–2; Irani 16–4–37–0; Such 13–3–41–1; Grayson 19–6–53–4. *Second Innings*—Cowan 19–9–54–4; Williams 18–3–52–2; Such 3–2–1–0; Irani 16–6–44–1; D. R. Law 12.3–1–31–1; Grayson 23–11–21–2.

Essex

G. A. Gooch lbw b Mohammad Akram	24	– c Taylor b Boswell	16
*P. J. Prichard c Ripley b Curran	50	– c Ripley b Taylor	75
N. Hussain c Bailey b Curran	77	– c Ripley b Mohammad Akram	13
S. G. Law c and b Mohammad Akram	14	– c Snape b Taylor	45
R. C. Irani c Warren b Taylor	18	– c Ripley b Taylor	30
A. P. Grayson c and b Boswell	3	– run out	62
D. R. Law c Warren b Snape	33	– st Ripley b Snape	8
†R. J. Rollins c Bailey b Mohammad Akram	2	– c and b Snape	0
A. P. Cowan c Ripley b Curran	23	– lbw b Snape	0
N. F. Williams not out	6	– c Bailey b Snape	23
P. M. Such b Curran	0	– not out	0
L-b 5, w 8, n-b 12	25	B 4, l-b 8, w 2, n-b 4	18

1/44 2/94 3/123 4/160 5/167   275   1/37 2/92 3/154 4/183 5/192   290
6/212 7/217 8/256 9/271   6/221 7/221 8/225 9/277

Bonus points – Essex 2, Northamptonshire 4.

Bowling: *First Innings*—Mohammad Akram 19–2–91–3; Taylor 19–3–82–1; Boswell 14–2–41–1; Curran 11.2–2–32–4; Snape 3–0–23–1; Bailey 1–0–1–0. *Second Innings*—Mohammad Akram 16–3–72–1; Taylor 17.2–2–72–3; Boswell 13–3–55–1; Snape 19–6–46–4; Curran 7–1–33–0.

Umpires: J. H. Hampshire and P. Willey.

NORTHAMPTONSHIRE v SURREY

At Northampton, July 23, 24, 25, 26. Drawn. Northamptonshire 9 pts, Surrey 10 pts. Toss: Surrey. Championship debut: J. N. Batty.

Amid off-the-field speculation about Northamptonshire's next overseas player and the captaincy – Shane Warne had been linked to both jobs – the current incumbents struggled. Mohammad Akram's bowling was hammered as Surrey ground out a formidable 581 for seven and, though the club publicly backed Bailey's leadership, murmurings resumed after being stilled a little by two successive wins. For Surrey, Darren Bicknell scored a fine 162 on his come-back after several weeks in the seconds, while Brown followed up his Sunday double-hundred with 170 not out. In retrospect, perhaps, Surrey scored too many, and left too little time to dismiss the opposition twice on such a good pitch. Though Northamptonshire could not quite save the follow-on, several half-centuries – Penberthy missed a maiden Championship hundred by four – helped prolong their first innings into the third evening. They batted just as doggedly on the final day, anchored by Fordham, in his first Championship game of the season. Rain made their task a little easier, but in the end the winner was a perfect batting strip.

Close of play: First day, Surrey 386-4 (A. D. Brown 63*, B. C. Hollioake 18*); Second day, Northamptonshire 154-1 (R. J. Warren 56*, A. Fordham 69*); Third day, Northamptonshire 48-0 (D. J. Roberts 17*, R. J. Warren 22*).

Surrey

D. J. Bicknell c Taylor b Snape	162	†J. N. Batty run out	23
J. D. Ratcliffe c and b Taylor	31	M. P. Bicknell not out	2
I. J. Ward c Warren b Boswell	7	B 3, l-b 12, w 8, n-b 24	47
*A. J. Hollioake run out	81		
A. D. Brown not out	170	1/53 2/73 3/248 (7 wkts dec.) 581	
B. C. Hollioake c Fordham b Boswell	49	4/332 5/436	
C. C. Lewis c and b Penberthy	9	6/452 7/572	

I. D. K. Salisbury and J. E. Benjamin did not bat.

Bonus points – Surrey 4, Northamptonshire 2 (Score at 120 overs: 472-6).

Bowling: Mohammad Akram 25–2–112–0; Taylor 24–4–112–1; Penberthy 20–4–73–1; Boswell 23–2–107–2; Snape 35–4–133–1; Bailey 13–2–29–0.

Northamptonshire

R. J. Warren c B. C. Hollioake b M. P. Bicknell	..	72 – (2) b Benjamin	41
D. J. Roberts b Lewis		10 – (1) b Lewis	23
A. Fordham c A. J. Hollioake b Lewis		72 – not out	82
*R. J. Bailey c A. J. Hollioake b M. P. Bicknell	...	12 – not out	62
D. J. Sales c Batty b Salisbury		4	
A. L. Penberthy c M. P. Bicknell b Benjamin	.....	96	
J. N. Snape c Batty b B. C. Hollioake		52	
†D. Ripley b Salisbury		12	
J. P. Taylor c B. C. Hollioake b Lewis		7	
S. A. J. Boswell c Ward b Lewis		12	
Mohammad Akram not out		2	
B 3, l-b 7, n-b 40		50	B 4, l-b 5, w 12, n-b 12... 33

1/20 2/164 3/184 4/189 5/199   401   1/73 2/82   (2 wkts dec.) 241
6/322 7/345 8/381 9/399

Bonus points – Northamptonshire 4, Surrey 3 (Score at 120 overs: 381-8).

Bowling: *First Innings*—M. P. Bicknell 31–8–111–2; Lewis 25.3–7–82–4; Benjamin 16–6–41–1; Salisbury 32–4–85–2; B. C. Hollioake 10–1–31–1; A. J. Hollioake 9–1–36–0; Ratcliffe 2–0–5–0. *Second Innings*—M. P. Bicknell 13–4–43–0; Lewis 13–3–34–1; B. C. Hollioake 2–0–7–0; Benjamin 8–0–31–1; Salisbury 9–0–31–0; A. J. Hollioake 2–0–18–0; Ratcliffe 15–3–35–0; Brown 15–4–24–0; Batty 4–0–9–0.

Umpires: J. H. Harris and A. G. T. Whitehead (J. E. Emburey deputised for Harris on the 4th day).

At Leeds, July 31, August 1, 2, 4. NORTHAMPTONSHIRE lost to YORKSHIRE by 36 runs.

NORTHAMPTONSHIRE v WORCESTERSHIRE

At Northampton, August 6, 7, 8, 9. Worcestershire won by 101 runs. Worcestershire 22 pts, Northamptonshire 6 pts. Toss: Worcestershire. First-class debut: M. K. Davies. County debut: J. A. R. Blain.

For the second home match running, Northamptonshire conceded over 550 in their visitors' first innings – and, this time, they did not get away with it. They threw the match open by declaring 148 behind, but ended up chasing 421 in 90 overs, way beyond the county's best ever score to win. The fourth innings became a duel between the captains: Bailey scored a century while Moody, in blistering heat, abandoned seam for off-spin. He bowled unchanged from the ninth over and won the match with his fifth wicket - Bailey, caught at slip. Worcestershire's rather laboured 551 rested on centuries from Weston and Leatherdale. Weston, recalled because Hick was injured, converted his into a maiden double-hundred, with 30 fours and three sixes, batting 454 minutes and 386 balls. Boswell claimed a career-best five for 94 and Warren averted the follow-on with an unbeaten 174.

Close of play: First day, Worcestershire 433-5 (W. P. C. Weston 196*, V. S. Solanki 25*); Second day, Northamptonshire 208-3 (R. J. Warren 85*, R. J. Bailey 2*); Third day, Worcestershire 219-5 (D. A. Leatherdale 20*, V. S. Solanki 0*).

Worcestershire

*T. M. Moody lbw b Boswell	25	– (3) c Warren b Davies	26
T. S. Curtis b Blain	1	– (1) c Sales b Blain	5
W. P. C. Weston c Blain b Curran	205	– (2) c Warren b Bailey	31
K. R. Spiring run out	35	– st Ripley b Davies	84
G. R. Haynes lbw b Boswell	8	– c Warren b Davies	50
D. A. Leatherdale c Ripley b Penberthy	110	– not out	37
V. S. Solanki c Fordham b Boswell	47	– c Warren b Bailey	10
†S. J. Rhodes c Bailey b Boswell	55	– c Davies b Bailey	20
S. R. Lampitt b Curran	5	– not out	6
P. J. Newport c Ripley b Boswell	17		
A. Sheriyar not out	0		
B 8, l-b 7, n-b 28	43	L-b 1, n-b 2	3

1/2 2/35 3/98 4/127 5/368	551
6/467 7/473 8/485 9/542	

1/9 2/56 3/78	(7 wkts dec.) 272
4/179 5/218	
6/233 7/265	

Bonus points – Worcestershire 4, Northamptonshire 2 (Score at 120 overs: 457-5).

Bowling: *First Innings*—Boswell 26.5–3–94–5; Blain 24–5–87–1; Penberthy 24–3–126–1; Curran 17–4–52–2; Davies 28–9–89–0; Bailey 24–5–72–0; Sales 3–0–16–0. *Second Innings*—Boswell 5–0–16–0; Blain 6–3–18–1; Davies 37–10–95–3; Bailey 32–7–121–3; Curran 2–0–20–0; Fordham 1–0–1–0.

Northamptonshire

D. J. Roberts c Spiring b Haynes	40	– (2) c Weston b Lampitt	13
R. J. Warren not out	174	– (1) c and b Moody	67
A. Fordham c Haynes b Leatherdale	57	– lbw b Lampitt	13
S. A. J. Boswell c Moody b Leatherdale	0	– (9) b Haynes	0
*R. J. Bailey c Lampitt b Leatherdale	14	– (4) c Lampitt b Moody	115
K. M. Curran b Haynes	29	– (5) c Rhodes b Curtis	55
D. J. Sales not out	48	– (6) b Moody	0
A. L. Penberthy (did not bat)		– (7) c Lampitt b Moody	14
†D. Ripley (did not bat)		– (8) c Curtis b Moody	11
J. A. R. Blain (did not bat)		– c Rhodes b Haynes	0
M. K. Davies (did not bat)		– not out	0
B 4, l-b 7, w 2, n-b 28	41	B 4, l-b 1, w 6, n-b 20	31

1/79 2/198 3/198 4/230 5/289	(5 wkts dec.) 403

1/50 2/82 3/140 4/243 5/244	319
6/290 7/318 8/319 9/319	

Bonus points – Northamptonshire 4, Worcestershire 2.

Bowling: *First Innings*—Newport 14–5–43–0; Sheriyar 18–1–77–0; Haynes 20–7–58–2; Lampitt 17–1–97–0; Moody 19–7–67–0; Leatherdale 15–5–29–3; Weston 3–0–21–0. *Second Innings*—Newport 4–1–14–0; Sheriyar 6–1–23–0; Moody 34.4–3–148–5; Lampitt 8–0–44–2; Leatherdale 6–2–19–0; Curtis 11–1–55–1; Haynes 7–2–11–2.

Umpires: B. Leadbeater and G. Sharp.

At Northampton, August 12. NORTHAMPTONSHIRE beat PAKISTAN A by 60 runs (See Pakistan A tour section).

At Abergavenny, August 20, 21, 22, 23. NORTHAMPTONSHIRE lost to GLAMORGAN by six wickets.

NORTHAMPTONSHIRE v DURHAM

At Northampton, August 27, 28, 29, 30. Drawn. Northamptonshire 6 pts, Durham 11 pts. Toss: Northamptonshire.

After weather permitted only five overs on the first day, Betts's pace destroyed Northamptonshire's batting. His figures of nine for 64 were the best of 1997, and Durham's best as a first-class county. Though some of the batsmanship was a little wayward, it was a fine spell of unchanged bowling – especially as Betts twisted his ankle early on. Durham pursued their advantage by constructing a lead of 232. Left-hander Hutton batted sensibly for 95, but the real gem was Boon's second century in consecutive Championship matches. For nearly five hours, he provided an object lesson in how to build an innings calmly and cleverly. Simon Brown bowled eight maidens off the reel when Northamptonshire resumed on the third evening, but the home side, with no chance of winning, refused to collapse a second time. They saved the game with dignity, and a lead of 77.

Close of play: First day, Northamptonshire 4-0 (R. R. Montgomerie 1*, A. J. Swann 0*); Second day, Durham 118-2 (S. Hutton 46*, D. C. Boon 8*); Third day, Northamptonshire 52-0 (R. R. Montgomerie 35*, A. J. Swann 16*).

Northamptonshire

R. R. Montgomerie c Weston b Betts	5	– c and b Cox	73
A. J. Swann lbw b Brown	1	– c Boon b Brown	25
A. Fordham c Hutton b Betts	18	– c Boon b Foster	83
*R. J. Bailey c Boon b Betts	22	– c Speight b Betts	45
D. J. Sales c Morris b Betts	4	– c Weston b Boiling	15
A. L. Penberthy b Betts	9	– lbw b Betts	11
†D. Ripley b Betts	18	– c Speight b Brown	5
J. P. Taylor b Betts	1	– c Speight b Betts	6
Mohammad Akram c Speight b Betts	28	– c Brown b Betts	7
M. K. Davies c Speight b Betts	0	– not out	11
J. F. Brown not out	16	– not out	1
B 1, l-b 15, w 2, n-b 4	22	B 4, l-b 12, w 7, n-b 4	27

1/11 2/19 3/36 4/40 5/58	144	1/67 2/138 3/198 (9 wkts dec.) 309
6/92 7/94 8/97 9/97		4/221 5/275 6/280
		7/280 8/289 9/302

Bonus points – Durham 4.

Bowling: *First Innings*—Brown 13–5–43–1; Betts 22–7–64–9; Foster 8–1–18–0; Boiling 1–0–3–0. *Second Innings*—Brown 30–15–52–2; Betts 15–0–79–4; Boiling 32–16–67–1; Cox 29–6–60–1; Foster 8–1–30–1; Weston 1–0–5–0.

Durham

J. J. B. Lewis b Taylor	17	M. M. Betts lbw b Penberthy ... 8
S. Hutton lbw b Davies	95	J. Boiling not out ... 23
†M. P. Speight st Ripley b Brown	34	D. M. Cox c Ripley b Mohammad Akram 22
*D. C. Boon c Ripley		S. J. E. Brown b Mohammad Akram ... 0
b Mohammad Akram	.117	
J. E. Morris c Ripley b Brown	5	B 15, l-b 10, n-b 6 ... 31
R. M. S. Weston c Bailey		
b Mohammad Akram	. 24	1/21 2/103 3/206 4/234 5/292 376
M. J. Foster b Mohammad Akram	0	6/292 7/315 8/342 9/376

Bonus points – Durham 4, Northamptonshire 3 (Score at 120 overs: 352-8).

Bowling: Mohammad Akram 24.5–2–100–5; Taylor 31–4–96–1; Davies 34–14–68–1; Penberthy 16–4–40–1; Brown 18–1–47–2.

Umpires: J. H. Hampshire and R. A. White.

At Derby, September 2, 3, 4, 5. NORTHAMPTONSHIRE beat DERBYSHIRE by nine wickets.

NORTHAMPTONSHIRE v LEICESTERSHIRE

At Northampton, September 10, 11, 12, 13. Drawn. Northamptonshire 9 pts, Leicestershire 11 pts. Toss: Northamptonshire.

The 1996 champions' season of frustration continued when Leicestershire were unable to force home what looked like certain victory against their local rivals. Ripley, who had already rescued Northamptonshire in the first innings, was manning the ramparts again with his team only ten ahead and one wicket to fall. He was joined by Bailey, batting last because of a broken finger, and they survived 20 overs until a truce was called. Leicestershire were too slow to recall Ormond, who had taken six in the first innings, to replace Pierson's off-spin, and probably too slow to declare on the third evening. Their lead was 225, thanks to Dakin, in his second Championship game of 1997, and Millns. Both reached career-bests as they added 205. The home side's young spinners, left-armer Davies and off-spinner Brown, offered some hope; they bowled 87 overs between them, were never dominated, and took seven wickets.

Close of play: First day, Northamptonshire 310-7 (J. P. Taylor 30*, S. A. J. Boswell 0*); Second day, Leicestershire 380-6 (J. M. Dakin 135*, D. J. Millns 60*); Third day, Northamptonshire 36-1 (R. R. Montgomerie 19*, S. A. J. Boswell 2*).

Northamptonshire

A. Fordham c Nixon b Ormond	32	– lbw b Brimson	15
R. R. Montgomerie b Brimson	19	– b Pierson	56
*R. J. Bailey b Sutcliffe b Pierson	28	– (11) not out	16
K. M. Curran b Ormond	4	– c Wells b Brimson	13
D. J. Sales c Nixon b Millns	21	– c Brimson b Pierson	18
A. L. Penberthy c Nixon b Maddy	65	– c Maddy b Brimson	16
†D. Ripley c Nixon b Ormond	92	– not out	83
J. P. Taylor b Ormond	36	– b Pierson	13
S. A. J. Boswell c and b Ormond	9	– (3) b Dakin	35
M. K. Davies not out	2	– (9) c Nixon b Ormond	14
J. F. Brown b Ormond	0	– (10) lbw b Ormond	0
B 5, l-b 11, n-b 8	24	B 12, l-b 1, w 4, n-b 2	19

1/48 2/52 3/56 4/104 5/105   332   1/27 2/109 3/127   (9 wkts) 298
6/260 7/300 8/323 9/332   1/27 2/109 3/127
                                              4/131 5/161 6/171
                                              7/204 8/235 9/253

Bonus points – Northamptonshire 3, Leicestershire 4.

Bowling: *First Innings*—Millns 22–4–58–1; Ormond 24.5–5–68–6; Wells 10–0–32–0; Brimson 27–9–63–1; Pierson 27–6–84–1; Dakin 5–1–9–0; Maddy 3–2–2–1. *Second Innings*—Millns 11–1–45–0; Ormond 24–10–55–2; Pierson 41–8–118–3; Brimson 26–9–49–3; Dakin 6–1–14–1; Wells 4–3–4–0.

Leicestershire

V. J. Wells b Taylor	21	A. R. K. Pierson b Brown	40
D. L. Maddy c Bailey b Boswell	29	J. Ormond lbw b Davies	0
I. J. Sutcliffe c Curran b Brown	61	M. T. Brimson not out	4
*J. J. Whitaker c Ripley b Boswell	0		
B. F. Smith lbw b Brown	30	B 5, l-b 12, n-b 24	41
J. M. Dakin st Ripley b Davies	190		
†P. A. Nixon lbw b Davies	20	1/44 2/67 3/67 4/122 5/183	557
D. J. Millns c Ripley b Davies	121	6/271 7/476 8/531 9/531	

Bonus points – Leicestershire 4, Northamptonshire 3 (Score at 120 overs: 476-7).

Bowling: Taylor 17–0–82–1; Boswell 19–3–89–2; Brown 52.3–14–142–3; Davies 34–9–118–4; Penberthy 12–0–48–0; Bailey 3–0–12–0; Curran 7–0–49–0.

Umpires: M. J. Kitchen and R. Palmer.

At Birmingham, September 18, 19, 20, 21. NORTHAMPTONSHIRE drew with WARWICKSHIRE.

NOTTINGHAMSHIRE

Mathew Dowman

President: K. A. Taylor

Chairman: A. Wheelhouse

Chairman, Cricket Committee: S. Foster

Chief Executive: M. Arthur

Secretary: B. Robson

Captain: P. Johnson

Cricket Manager: J. A. Ormrod

Head Groundsman: S. Birks

Scorer: G. Stringfellow

Nottinghamshire planted seeds in 1997 that should help them to develop a much brighter future, even if the fruits of recovery were not yet apparent. There was only a modest improvement in their Championship position – from 17th to 13th – and they never looked like reproducing the Sunday League form that saw them pipped for the title on run-rate in 1996. A spirited NatWest Trophy campaign provided their best moments. They created an upset by defeating favourites Surrey at The Oval in the second round, and then pushed the eventual Trophy winners, Essex, hard before going down in the quarter-finals.

Their optimism for the future was founded on the encouraging progress made by several young players, the go-ahead for a magnificent £7.2 million development at Trent Bridge and some important winter signings. Nottinghamshire were one of several counties in determined pursuit of Shane Warne. That came to nothing, as Warne decided against playing county cricket. But, in November, they did sign another international leg-spinner, Zimbabwean Paul Strang, who had just had a successful season at Kent. Shortly afterwards, they also won the services of Test batsman Jason Gallian, who had left Lancashire.

The gloomy mood at Trent Bridge at the start of the season had been heightened by the unfortunately complicated saga of finding an overseas replacement for the injured Chris Cairns. After failing in their attempt to land South African all-rounder Lance Klusener, Nottinghamshire engaged Pakistani fast bowler Mohammad Zahid. But he never played, because of what turned out to be a stress fracture of the spine. They then terminated his contract and had to seek special clearance to sign a replacement. Six weeks into the season, New Zealand batsman Nathan Astle eventually arrived to solve their problems. It was an enormous relief that he settled in so quickly, and he proved to be a splendid influence.

His task was made easier by the fact that confidence had already risen before his arrival. Two marvellous Championship victories, against the odds, had lifted Nottinghamshire to second in the table at the end of May. Usman Afzaal, just short of his 20th birthday, showed great maturity in steering them home against Lancashire. But beating Derbyshire was even more satisfying, given that three front-line batsmen were injured. First, they managed to save the follow-on in the face of some hostile bowling from Devon Malcolm; then, they successfully chased a target of 245 on a difficult pitch. Again, Afzaal played a crucial part, as did another youngster, Paul Franks.

Invigorated by the energy and enthusiasm of the younger generation, Nottinghamshire discovered steel and character which resurfaced many times over the season, a refreshing change from the embarrassing decline in their Championship form which began in August 1995. All too often, though, they were fighting uphill battles as a direct result of the frailties of the first-innings batting. Their final Championship position could have been a lot higher than 13th had they won more than a meagre 26 batting points. The second innings could let them down, too; they failed to beat Somerset in a run-chase despite needing only 66 from the final 12 overs, with eight wickets standing.

The batting inadequacies were highlighted by the fact that only Mathew Dowman reached 1,000 first-class runs. In a prolific second half of the season, he finally found the self-belief to fulfil the promise of his 267 in an Under-19 Test against West Indies in 1993, an England record. For once, Tim Robinson missed out on his 1,000; he had a lean mid-season spell when bad weather disrupted his come-back after three weeks off with a broken hand. Captain Paul Johnson, who scored 942, also broke his hand, and Paul Pollard was out for half the season. But there was encouragement in the solid performances of Afzaal and, in the closing stages, 19-year-old Guy Welton made his mark, narrowly missing a hundred against Sussex.

Nottinghamshire had been seriously worried about the strength of their seam attack. But the successes in the early games made them less concerned, and the absence of established names created openings for the 18-year-old Franks, who seized his opportunities with both hands. Against Warwickshire, he became the third-youngest bowler in English cricket history to claim a hat-trick. Chris Tolley and Mark Bowen were determined to prove a point, not only to their former counties – Worcestershire and Northamptonshire respectively – but also to those who doubted Nottinghamshire's wisdom in signing them the previous season. They took 76 first-class wickets between them, and both earned their county caps. The surprise package, though, was Andy Oram. Having failed to break through at Northamptonshire, he had written to ask for a trial. He forced his way into the Championship side after some impressive Sunday League displays and he captured 26 victims in seven games, placing him second in the bowling averages.

All the seam bowlers were helped by the livelier Trent Bridge pitches prepared by new groundsman Steve Birks, who had switched from Derbyshire. But suddenly finding themselves with a variety of options to back up Kevin Evans, the leading wicket-taker, the club released the long-serving Andy Pick, as well as spinner Andy Afford and batsman Ashley Metcalfe.

The development work which has unearthed so much young talent will be fortified by the creation of a residential indoor cricket school. This was being built within the new 4,500-seater Radcliffe Road stand, an ambitious project made possible by National Lottery funding of over £4 million. It should establish Trent Bridge as a regional centre of excellence; the club hoped it would also establish the excellence needed on the field to end their lean years. – NICK LUCY.

NOTTINGHAMSHIRE 1997

[*Bill Smith*]

Back row: L. N. P. Walker, U. Afzaal, P. J. Franks, J. P. Hart, G. E. Welton, N. A. Gie, M. P. Dowman. *Middle row:* S. Ball (*physiotherapist*), C. M. Tolley, G. F. Archer, R. T. Bates, M. N. Bowen, J. E. Hindson, W. M. Noon, A. A. Metcalfe, G. Stringfellow (*First Eleven scorer*), B. Hewes (*Second Eleven scorer*). *Front row:* E. E. Hemmings (*coach*), J. A. Afford, K. P. Evans, R. T. Robinson, J. A. Ormrod (*cricket manager*), P. Johnson (*captain*), R. A. Pick, P. R. Pollard, M. Newell. *Insets:* A. R. Oram, N. J. Astle.

NOTTINGHAMSHIRE RESULTS

All first-class matches – Played 20: Won 4, Lost 3, Drawn 13.

County Championship matches – Played 17: Won 4, Lost 3, Drawn 10.

*Competition placings – Britannic Assurance County Championship, 13th;
NatWest Trophy, q-f; Benson and Hedges Cup, 4th in Group B;
AXA Life League, 12th.*

COUNTY CHAMPIONSHIP AVERAGES

BATTING

Cap		M	I	NO	R	HS	100s	50s	Avge	Ct/St
1986	P. Johnson†	15	26	5	936	96*	0	8	44.57	12
	M. P. Dowman	16	28	1	1,046	149	3	5	38.74	11
	N. J. Astle§	9	15	0	545	100	2	2	36.33	10
1992	P. R. Pollard†	8	14	4	340	81	0	1	34.00	8
1983	R. T. Robinson†	15	25	3	737	143*	1	4	33.50	5
1997	C. M. Tolley	11	20	4	458	73*	0	3	28.62	6
	G. E. Welton	5	10	0	279	95	0	1	27.90	1
1995	W. M. Noon	17	24	4	542	83	0	3	27.10	34/4
	U. Afzaal	15	26	2	638	80	0	5	26.58	7
	P. J. Franks†	11	16	5	245	50	0	1	22.27	7
	A. A. Metcalfe	7	10	1	145	79	0	1	16.11	3
1995	G. F. Archer	10	18	1	242	49	0	0	14.23	15
	R. T. Bates	6	9	5	51	21	0	0	12.75	6
1990	K. P. Evans†	14	17	1	187	47	0	0	11.68	6
1997	M. N. Bowen	14	17	4	145	32	0	0	11.15	5
	N. A. Gie	2	4	0	28	9	0	0	7.00	1
	A. R. Oram	7	8	4	14	5*	0	0	3.50	5

Also batted: J. E. Hindson (2 matches) 6, 0, 42* (2 ct); (cap 1987) R. A. Pick† (2 matches) 8*;
L. N. P. Walker (1 match) 4.

* Signifies not out.　　† Born in Nottinghamshire.　　§ Overseas player.

BOWLING

	O	M	R	W	BB	5W/i	Avge
N. J. Astle	196	43	488	22	5-46	1	22.18
A. R. Oram	221.4	54	670	26	4-53	0	25.76
K. P. Evans	442.5	102	1,226	44	6-40	2	27.86
C. M. Tolley	347	81	973	32	6-61	1	30.40
M. N. Bowen	451.2	104	1,345	41	7-75	3	32.80
P. J. Franks	315.4	48	1,038	26	4-47	0	39.92
U. Afzaal	183.5	39	593	13	3-79	0	45.61

Also bowled: G. F. Archer 50–9–173–4; R. T. Bates 167.4–36–442–8; M. P. Dowman
48–9–159–0; J. E. Hindson 44.2–9–162–3; P. Johnson 14–5–34–0; W. M. Noon 1–0–12–0; R. A.
Pick 62.2–13–193–2.

COUNTY RECORDS

Highest score for:	312*	W. W. Keeton v Middlesex at The Oval	1939
Highest score against:	345	C. G. Macartney (Australians) at Nottingham	1921
Best bowling for:	10-66	K. Smales v Gloucestershire at Stroud	1956
Best bowling against:	10-10	H. Verity (Yorkshire) at Leeds	1932
Highest total for:	739-7 dec.	v Leicestershire at Nottingham	1903
Highest total against:	781-7 dec.	by Northamptonshire at Northampton	1995
Lowest total for:	13	v Yorkshire at Nottingham	1901
Lowest total against:	{ 16	by Derbyshire at Nottingham	1879
	{ 16	by Surrey at The Oval	1880

NOTTINGHAMSHIRE v WORCESTERSHIRE

At Nottingham, April 23, 24, 25, 26. Drawn. Nottinghamshire 5 pts, Worcestershire 8 pts. Toss: Worcestershire.

Neither side had a clear advantage when heavy rain washed out the last two days. Worcestershire had built a substantial total, thanks largely to their former captain, Curtis, and his successor, Moody. Curtis, who had confirmed this would be his last season, reached his 40th first-class hundred in 102 overs; he batted nearly seven hours in all and struck 12 fours. Moody scored a more rapid 70, with nine fours, in 160 minutes. Both lost their middle stump to Bowen, who took four for 17 in 41 balls. Nottinghamshire's openers responded with 173; Pollard hit ten fours in a stylish 81. Then the rain arrived.

Close of play: First day, Worcestershire 286-3 (T. S. Curtis 100*, T. M. Moody 44*); Second day, Nottinghamshire 196-3 (R. T. Bates 6*, A. A. Metcalfe 6*); Third day, No play.

Worcestershire

T. S. Curtis b Bowen	113	P. J. Newport lbw b Bowen	2
W. P. C. Weston c Pollard b Bates	52	M. J. Rawnsley b Archer	9
G. A. Hick c Bates b Evans	4	A. Sheriyar c Noon b Bowen	21
K. R. Spiring c Pollard b Evans	48		
*T. M. Moody b Bowen	70	B 8, l-b 23, w 14, n-b 12	57
V. S. Solanki b Bowen	15		
†S. J. Rhodes c Dowman b Evans	0	1/87 2/101 3/203 4/314 5/333	417
S. R. Lampitt not out	26	6/336 7/353 8/355 9/380	

Bonus points – Worcestershire 4, Nottinghamshire 2 (Score at 120 overs: 353-6).

Bowling: Evans 38–11–89–3; Franks 30–7–77–0; Bowen 31.5–7–99–5; Archer 21–5–56–1; Bates 13–1–33–1; Dowman 11–2–32–0.

Nottinghamshire

P. R. Pollard lbw b Rawnsley	81	A. A. Metcalfe not out	6
R. T. Robinson c Rhodes b Sheriyar	80	B 4, l-b 3, w 6, n-b 6	19
G. F. Archer c Hick b Lampitt	4		
R. T. Bates not out	6	1/173 2/182 3/186 (3 wkts)	196

*P. Johnson, M. P. Dowman, †W. M. Noon, K. P. Evans, M. N. Bowen and P. J. Franks did not bat.

Bonus point – Worcestershire 1.

Bowling: Newport 12–1–40–0; Sheriyar 12–1–45–1; Moody 4–1–5–0; Lampitt 18–3–59–1; Rawnsley 13–1–40–1.

Umpires: T. E. Jesty and N. T. Plews.

At Hartlepool, May 7, 8, 9, 10. NOTTINGHAMSHIRE drew with DURHAM.

At Manchester, May 14, 15, 16, 17. NOTTINGHAMSHIRE beat LANCASHIRE by six wickets.

NOTTINGHAMSHIRE v DERBYSHIRE

At Nottingham, May 21, 22, 23, 24. Nottinghamshire won by two wickets. Nottinghamshire 20 pts, Derbyshire 7 pts. Toss: Nottinghamshire.

Nottinghamshire successfully pursued 245 to go second in the table despite having three injured batsmen. Robinson had broken his hand in the field, and Pollard while batting in the first innings; then Dowman had to retire with a badly bruised elbow. Pollard and Dowman did return to help their team to victory. But it was a gritty four-hour 63 from Noon and a maiden fifty from 18-year-old Franks which did most to rescue Nottinghamshire from 43 for four – effectively, they feared, 43 for seven. Franks had assisted a first-innings fightback too; after a fiery spell from Malcolm wrecked the top order, he came in at 128 for eight, still 42 short of saving the follow-on, and helped fellow teenager Afzaal add 64. Then Evans and Bowen dismissed Derbyshire cheaply to create an unlikely chance of victory. Bowen's match analysis was 11 for 109; in the first innings, he had claimed a career-best seven for 75, while Noon took six catches to equal the club record. Barnett became the first Derbyshire batsman to score 2,000 runs against another county.

Close of play: First day, Derbyshire 283-5 (D. M. Jones 71*, K. M. Krikken 7*); Second day, Derbyshire 2-1 (K. J. Barnett 0*, P. Aldred 2*); Third day, Nottinghamshire 122-5 (W. M. Noon 26*, P. J. Franks 8*).

Derbyshire

K. J. Barnett c Noon b Bowen	27	– c Metcalfe b Evans	1
A. S. Rollins c Noon b Archer	30	– lbw b Bowen	0
C. J. Adams c Johnson b Bowen	39	– (4) lbw b Bowen	28
*D. M. Jones lbw b Bowen	77	– (5) c Dowman b Evans	12
M. E. Cassar c Noon b Bowen	9	– (6) lbw b Bowen	28
V. P. Clarke c Noon b Evans	50	– (7) lbw b Franks	12
†K. M. Krikken c Noon b Bowen	11	– (8) c Archer b Franks	4
P. Aldred c Noon b Bowen	16	– (3) c Afzaal b Evans	2
A. J. Harris c Archer b Franks	3	– lbw b Bowen	7
K. J. Dean c and b Bowen	0	– not out	1
D. E. Malcolm not out	3	– c Archer b Evans	5
L-b 16, w 12, n-b 26	54	B 4, l-b 7, w 2, n-b 4	17
	319		**117**

1/53 2/100 3/136 4/158 5/270   319   1/0 2/3 3/10 4/45 5/61   117
6/294 7/295 8/314 9/316   6/80 7/90 8/105 9/112

Bonus points – Derbyshire 3, Nottinghamshire 4.

Bowling: *First Innings*—Evans 29–6–68–1; Franks 20–2–52–1; Bowen 28.4–6–75–7; Dowman 9–2–33–0; Archer 14–2–60–1; Afzaal 7–2–15–0. *Second Innings*—Evans 17.2–6–40–4; Bowen 20–9–34–4; Franks 14–2–28–2; Afzaal 1–0–4–0.

Nottinghamshire

P. R. Pollard c Krikken b Malcolm	5	– (9) not out	23
A. A. Metcalfe lbw b Malcolm	7	– (1) c Adams b Malcolm	7
G. F. Archer c Jones b Malcolm	0	– c Krikken b Malcolm	10
M. P. Dowman c Rollins b Dean	23	– (2) c Clarke b Malcolm	7
*P. Johnson b Dean	60	– (4) run out	3
U. Afzaal b Malcolm	52	– (5) c Krikken b Dean	5
†W. M. Noon b Dean	0	– c Aldred b Malcolm	63
K. P. Evans lbw b Aldred	5	– (6) b Clarke	47
M. N. Bowen c Krikken b Aldred	1	– (10) not out	5
P. J. Franks c Krikken b Aldred	20	– (8) lbw b Aldred	50
R. T. Robinson not out	0		
B 4, l-b 9, w 2, n-b 4	19	B 9, l-b 11, w 2, n-b 6	28
	192	**(8 wkts)**	**248**

1/12 2/12 3/31 4/84 5/111   192   1/8 2/19 3/26 4/43   (8 wkts) 248
6/113 7/126 8/128 9/192   5/103 6/197 7/211 8/220

Bonus points – Derbyshire 4.

In the second innings M. P. Dowman, when 2, retired hurt at 16 and resumed at 197.

Bowling: *First Innings*—Malcolm 23–7–42–4; Harris 21–5–55–0; Dean 16–5–51–3; Aldred 16.1–3–28–3; Clarke 1–0–3–0. *Second Innings*—Malcolm 30–4–91–4; Harris 17–7–32–0; Aldred 21–9–34–1; Dean 16–6–37–1; Clarke 13–3–34–1.

Umpires: J. D. Bond and A. G. T. Whitehead.

NOTTINGHAMSHIRE v KENT

At Nottingham, May 29, 30, 31. Kent won by an innings and 105 runs. Kent 24 pts, Nottingham-shire 4 pts. Toss: Nottinghamshire.

Kent won in three days, having taken charge from the start. Fleming took a career-best five for 51, including the last three in eight deliveries as he ended Afzaal's fourth half-century in five innings. Though Fulton just missed a maiden Championship century, Kent led by only 34 when their eighth wicket fell. Then, however, Nottinghamshire paid for dropping Ealham. He had made his maiden hundred here in 1995, and this time went one run better. He added 171 with Strang, beating by ten the Kent ninth-wicket record which had stood since 1949. Ealham hit 16 fours and a six in four and three-quarter hours and earned a call-up for the First Test. By lunch on the third day, Nottinghamshire were 24 for four, McCague having removed the top three; only Afzaal and Noon reached double figures as they slid to an innings defeat.

Close of play: First day, Kent 39-1 (D. P. Fulton 25*, B. J. Phillips 2*); Second day, Kent 376-8 (M. A. Ealham 100*, P. A. Strang 51*).

Nottinghamshire

A. A. Metcalfe c Marsh b Phillips	7	– c Ealham b McCague 8
M. P. Dowman c Marsh b Fleming	21	– lbw b McCague 7
G. F. Archer c Marsh b McCague	49	– c Cowdrey b McCague 0
N. A. Gie lbw b Ealham	9	– c Ward b Strang 7
*P. Johnson c Ward b Ealham	0	– c Marsh b Ealham 2
U. Afzaal c Marsh b Fleming	54	– c Fulton b Fleming 36
†W. M. Noon c Fulton b Fleming	14	– c Ealham b Phillips 30
K. P. Evans c Marsh b McCague	26	– c Ealham b McCague 5
P. J. Franks not out	21	– b Strang 6
R. T. Bates c Marsh b Fleming	0	– lbw b Phillips 8
M. N. Bowen b Fleming	0	– not out 4
B 1, l-b 10, w 2, n-b 2	15	B 2, l-b 2, w 2 6

1/13 2/57 3/86 4/86 5/98   216   1/12 2/12 3/17 4/20 5/62   119
6/122 7/180 8/214 9/216   6/72 7/78 8/87 9/112

Bonus points – Nottinghamshire 1, Kent 4.

Bowling: *First Innings*—McCague 16–3–46–2; Phillips 11–6–21–1; Fleming 28.5–9–51–5; Ealham 20–6–54–2; Strang 14–4–33–0. *Second Innings*—McCague 17–7–33–4; Phillips 6.5–1–9–2; Ealham 15–6–23–1; Fleming 10–4–29–1; Strang 21–11–21–2.

Kent

D. P. Fulton c Archer b Bowen	94	*†S. A. Marsh c Archer b Bates 6
M. J. Walker c Dowman b Bowen	8	P. A. Strang c Johnson b Evans 73
B. J. Phillips lbw b Evans	7	M. J. McCague not out 14
T. R. Ward c Bates b Bowen	7	
A. P. Wells b Franks b Evans	35	B 14, l-b 11, w 8, n-b 2 35
G. R. Cowdrey c Evans b Bates	28	
M. A. Ealham c Johnson b Franks	122	1/27 2/52 3/63 4/156 5/172 440
M. V. Fleming c Noon b Bates	11	6/215 7/240 8/250 9/421

Bonus points – Kent 4, Nottinghamshire 3 (Score at 120 overs: 382-8).

Bowling: Evans 35–4–115–3; Franks 29.4–4–94–1; Bowen 35–9–103–3; Bates 30–8–89–3; Dowman 3–0–14–0.

Umpires: A. Clarkson and D. R. Shepherd.

At Northampton, June 4, 5, 6, 7. NOTTINGHAMSHIRE beat NORTHAMPTONSHIRE by three wickets.

At Nottingham, June 11, 12, 13. NOTTINGHAMSHIRE drew with AUSTRALIANS (See Australian tour section).

At Oxford, June 14, 16, 17. NOTTINGHAMSHIRE drew with OXFORD UNIVERSITY.

NOTTINGHAMSHIRE v YORKSHIRE

At Nottingham, June 18, 19, 20, 21. Drawn. Nottinghamshire 7 pts, Yorkshire 10 pts. Toss: Nottinghamshire.

Yorkshire built up a strong position, only to see their chances of victory washed away. Rain permitted only 43.1 overs during the second and third days, and none on the fourth. Yorkshire were put in on a well-grassed pitch, but Byas exploited some wayward seam bowling to hit 14 fours and a six in a flawless century. He shared three-figure stands with Moxon and Lehmann, who reached 50 for the seventh time in 12 Championship innings. In reply, Nottinghamshire were in trouble against some fiery bowling from White, one of whose sharper deliveries broke the little finger on Johnson's left hand. When rain ended proceedings, Nottinghamshire still needed 67 to avoid the follow-on and, effectively, had only two wickets left.

Close of play: First day, Nottinghamshire 5-0 (M. N. Bowen 5*, R. T. Robinson 0*); Second day, Nottinghamshire 116-4 (N. J. Astle 28*, P. Johnson 11*); Third day, Nottinghamshire 148-7 (G. F. Archer 10*, K. P. Evans 5*).

Yorkshire

M. D. Moxon lbw b Evans	60	P. J. Hartley c Johnson b Bowen	8
R. A. Kettleborough lbw b Evans	3	C. E. W. Silverwood c Noon b Evans	19
*D. Byas c Johnson b Astle	128	R. D. Stemp c Pollard b Evans	1
D. S. Lehmann b Bowen	62		
B. Parker lbw b Archer	4	B 2, l-b 6, w 8, n-b 4	20
C. White c Pollard b Evans	15		
†R. J. Blakey not out	40	1/4 2/107 3/242 4/251 5/286	364
A. C. Morris c Dowman b Evans	4	6/290 7/300 8/317 9/360	

Bonus points – Yorkshire 4, Nottinghamshire 4.

Bowling: Pick 18–3–53–0; Evans 24.3–2–91–6; Bowen 22–5–84–2; Astle 20–5–58–1; Dowman 3–0–15–0; Afzaal 6–0–31–0; Archer 7–0–24–1.

Nottinghamshire

M. N. Bowen c Blakey b Silverwood	10	G. F. Archer not out	10
R. T. Robinson c Byas b White	18	†W. M. Noon b White	6
P. R. Pollard c Stemp b White	26	K. P. Evans not out	5
M. P. Dowman c Blakey b White	15	L-b 4, n-b 6	10
N. J. Astle c Kettleborough b Hartley	28		
*P. Johnson retired hurt	14	1/14 2/59 3/75 4/82 (7 wkts) 148	
U. Afzaal c Byas b Hartley	6	5/116 6/126 7/134	
R. A. Pick did not bat.			

Bonus points – Yorkshire 3.

P. Johnson retired hurt at 127.

Bowling: Silverwood 7–2–21–1; Hartley 15–5–40–2; Morris 9–3–32–0; White 13.1–5–51–4.

Umpires: J. W. Holder and R. Palmer.

At The Oval, June 27, 28, 29, 30. NOTTINGHAMSHIRE lost to SURREY by 131 runs.

At Nottingham, July 2, 3, 4. NOTTINGHAMSHIRE drew with PAKISTAN A (See Pakistan A tour section).

NOTTINGHAMSHIRE v WARWICKSHIRE

At Nottingham, July 16, 17, 18, 19. Drawn. Nottinghamshire 7 pts, Warwickshire 10 pts. Toss: Nottinghamshire. Championship debut: A. R. Oram. County debut: M. A. Wagh.

Despite having the worst of the first two days, Nottinghamshire rediscovered their fighting spirit to claim the draw. They even had wild hopes of victory in the final session, when Warwickshire, set 205 in a minimum 32 overs, slumped to eight for three. On the opening day, Hemp and Ostler scored half-centuries in difficult conditions, before Nottinghamshire's 18-year-old seamer Paul Franks claimed a hat-trick – Nottinghamshire's last was by Richard Hadlee ten years earlier. Only two younger players are believed to have achieved the feat in English first-class cricket: C. L. Townsend, who was a 16-year-old Clifton schoolboy when playing for Gloucestershire against Somerset in 1893, and Peter Cousens, who was a slightly younger 18-year-old than Franks when he took a hat-trick for Essex against Combined Services in 1950. Warwickshire recovered to reach a useful 344 and Brown ensured the home side would follow on. Pollard had already broken a finger, and soon Johnson was struck on the hand too. But Dowman turned the game round in a rousing stand of 170 with Astle, who reached his first hundred for Nottinghamshire in 112 balls. With contributions all down the order, Donald toiled long and hard for his 50th five-wicket haul, before his team's brief scare in the evening.

Close of play: First day, Warwickshire 328-9 (A. A. Donald 15*, M. A. V. Bell 21*); Second day, Nottinghamshire 93-7 (M. P. Dowman 7*, W. M. Noon 10*); Third day, Nottinghamshire 279-4 (U. Afzaal 19*, C. M. Tolley 20*).

Warwickshire

*A. J. Moles lbw b Oram	20	– b Oram 1
M. A. Wagh c Archer b Franks...............	25	
D. L. Hemp c Archer b Tolley	70	– c Johnson b Tolley 37
D. P. Ostler c Franks b Tolley	65	– b Oram 1
T. L. Penney c Noon b Franks	25	– not out 31
D. R. Brown b Franks	0	– (2) c Archer b Franks.......... 4
G. Welch b Franks	0	– (6) not out 13
A. F. Giles c Tolley b Oram	42	
†T. Frost c Dowman b Tolley	6	
A. A. Donald not out	22	
M. A. V. Bell lbw b Tolley	30	
B 7, l-b 10, w 14, n-b 8	39	L-b 6, n-b 2 8

1/25 2/98 3/160 4/225 5/225   344   1/5 2/5 3/8 4/68   (4 wkts) 95
6/225 7/265 8/275 9/293

Bonus points – Warwickshire 3, Nottinghamshire 4.

Bowling: *First Innings*—Franks 25-7-84-4; Oram 25-4-81-2; Tolley 33-10-92-4; Astle 18-4-47-0; Dowman 5-1-12-0; Afzaal 5-3-11-0. *Second Innings*—Franks 7-0-31-1; Oram 10-1-29-2; Tolley 6-1-17-1; Astle 3-0-12-0.

Nottinghamshire

P. R. Pollard c Ostler b Brown	29	– (11) not out	0
R. T. Robinson lbw b Brown	10	– (1) c Frost b Donald	4
*P. Johnson lbw b Brown	8	– c Bell b Donald	38
N. J. Astle b Welch	11	– c Ostler b Welch	100
G. F. Archer c Frost b Welch	3	– lbw b Bell	6
U. Afzaal c Frost b Donald	5	– c Ostler b Donald	21
M. P. Dowman c Hemp b Welch	19	– (2) lbw b Welch	96
C. M. Tolley c Penney b Brown	0	– (7) c Ostler b Brown	49
†W. M. Noon b Bell	21	– (8) b Brown	30
P. J. Franks lbw b Welch	7	– (9) c Frost b Donald	32
A. R. Oram not out	0	– (10) b Donald	4
B 2, l-b 4, w 6, n-b 8	20	B 16, l-b 7, w 6, n-b 6	35

1/22 2/34 3/53 4/61 5/69   133   1/14 2/209 3/228 4/240 5/283   415
6/79 7/79 8/119 9/133   6/325 7/373 8/409 9/410

Bonus points – Warwickshire 4.

In the second innings P. Johnson, when 16, retired hurt at 39 and resumed at 373.

Bowling: *First Innings*—Donald 19-4-52-1; Brown 23-13-37-4; Welch 12-4-26-4; Bell 8.3-3-12-1; Giles 1-1-0-0. *Second Innings*—Donald 37.4-11-98-5; Brown 32-9-95-2; Bell 21-3-49-1; Welch 27-4-95-2; Giles 25-5-55-0; Wagh 2-2-0-0.

Umpires: V. A. Holder and B. Leadbeater.

At Leicester, July 23, 24, 25, 26. NOTTINGHAMSHIRE drew with LEICESTERSHIRE.

At Colwyn Bay, July 31, August 1, 2, 4. NOTTINGHAMSHIRE drew with GLAMORGAN.

NOTTINGHAMSHIRE v SOMERSET

At Nottingham, August 15, 16, 17, 18. Drawn. Nottinghamshire 11 pts, Somerset 10 pts. Toss: Somerset.

Nottinghamshire blew a golden opportunity to claim a fourth Championship win. With 12 overs to go, they needed 66, with eight wickets in hand. But the last pair ended up playing out the final over after seven wickets fell for 51. The key loss was that of Dowman, whose third hundred of the season had steered them to 262 for three. But when he fell, after four and a quarter hours, panic set in. All along it had been a good contest between bat and ball. Burns initiated Somerset's lower-order revival after Oram reduced them to 136 for five, and Nottinghamshire then claimed maximum batting points for the first time in 1997 – at the 12th attempt. Trescothick made a welcome return to form, scoring 81 in two and a half hours as Somerset went for quick runs, setting up the home side's dramatic pursuit of 320 in 76 overs.

Close of play: First day, Somerset 290-6 (R. J. Turner 48*, G. D. Rose 28*); Second day, Nottinghamshire 231-6 (A. A. Metcalfe 40*, W. M. Noon 8*); Third day, Somerset 248-4 (M. E. Trescothick 70*, M. Burns 33*).

Somerset

*P. D. Bowler c Astle b Tolley	8	– c Noon b Oram	1
P. C. L. Holloway c Johnson b Astle	72	– c Astle b Tolley	23
S. C. Ecclestone c Afzaal b Oram	7	– b Afzaal	65
M. N. Lathwell lbw b Oram	34	– c Evans b Tolley	47
M. E. Trescothick c Noon b Oram	5	– c Noon b Franks	81
M. Burns c Noon b Oram	72	– c Noon b Tolley	33
†R. J. Turner c Afzaal b Franks	55	– not out	46
G. D. Rose lbw b Evans	40	– not out	33
Mushtaq Ahmed b Franks	2		
A. R. Caddick not out	22		
K. J. Shine c Dowman b Evans	3		
B 2, l-b 9, w 2, n-b 4	17	B 1, l-b 6, w 2	9

1/26 2/33 3/98 4/125 5/136   337   1/14 2/28 3/127   (6 wkts dec.) 338
6/228 7/305 8/311 9/318   4/161 5/248 6/278

Bonus points – Somerset 3, Nottinghamshire 4.

Bowling: *First Innings*—Franks 28–4–84–2; Oram 19–6–53–4; Tolley 21–6–48–1; Evans 27.4–7–70–2; Astle 14–2–35–1; Afzaal 8–1–36–0. *Second Innings*—Oram 15–4–46–1; Evans 15–3–70–0; Tolley 22–2–79–3; Franks 12–1–57–1; Afzaal 18–2–62–1; Astle 8–0–17–0.

Nottinghamshire

M. P. Dowman c Holloway b Mushtaq Ahmed	43	– b Rose	124
R. T. Robinson c Turner b Rose	32	– c Ecclestone b Shine	30
N. J. Astle b Caddick	21	– lbw b Mushtaq Ahmed	60
*P. Johnson run out	38	– b Mushtaq Ahmed	20
A. A. Metcalfe c Lathwell b Rose	79	– (6) c Caddick b Rose	2
U. Afzaal b Shine	5	– (7) run out	11
C. M. Tolley c Ecclestone b Caddick	19	– (5) c Rose b Mushtaq Ahmed	4
†W. M. Noon c Turner b Shine	17	– not out	21
P. J. Franks not out	42	– run out	0
K. P. Evans lbw b Mushtaq Ahmed	25	– lbw b Caddick	0
A. R. Oram c Bowler b Mushtaq Ahmed	0	– not out	0
B 2, l-b 17, w 10, n-b 6	35	B 14, l-b 13, w 2, n-b 4	33

1/95 2/95 3/152 4/162 5/176   356   1/87 2/220 3/254   (9 wkts) 305
6/218 7/262 8/304 9/356   4/262 5/264 6/272
                                    7/303 8/304 9/305

Bonus points – Nottinghamshire 4, Somerset 4.

Bowling: *First Innings*—Caddick 32–7–74–2; Shine 24–7–79–2; Mushtaq Ahmed 38.4–6–97–3; Rose 21–5–83–2; Burns 4–2–4–0. *Second Innings*—Caddick 20–5–57–1; Rose 16–0–67–2; Mushtaq Ahmed 29–3–88–3; Burns 2–0–7–0; Shine 9–0–59–1.

Umpires: J. H. Hampshire and J. H. Harris.

NOTTINGHAMSHIRE v ESSEX

At Worksop, August 20, 21, 22, 23. Drawn. Nottinghamshire 9 pts, Essex 8 pts. Toss: Essex. Championship debut: G. R. Napier.

Indifferent weather and a slow pitch condemned this match to a dull draw. Essex chose to bat out the final rain-interrupted day, even though Nottinghamshire attempted to set up a run-chase which would offer their opponents a faint chance of staying in the title race. On the opening day, Essex had made confident progress. Stuart Law provided their backbone; once he mastered the conditions, he scored his fourth hundred of the season. A forceful debut by 17-year-old Graham Napier, who hit five fours and a six in 41 balls, carried Essex to 440 for seven in the 36 overs possible next day. Nottinghamshire replied steadily, as Robinson emerged from a bad patch by batting for nearly six hours. He added 193 with Astle and was unbeaten on 143 when they collected their fourth batting point. Johnson declared behind, and bowled himself to encourage Essex to set a target. But they settled for the draw.

Close of play: First day, Essex 319-4 (A. P. Grayson 35*, D. R. Law 13*); Second day, Essex 440-7 (G. R. Napier 35*, A. P. Cowan 6*); Third day, Essex 10-1 (P. J. Prichard 6*, M. C. Ilott 1*).

Essex

*P. J. Prichard c Noon b Oram	46	– c Metcalfe b Astle	46
D. D. J. Robinson c Astle b Evans	40	– c Johnson b Oram	0
T. P. Hodgson lbw b Astle	44	– (4) c Oram b Tolley	21
S. G. Law c Noon b Afzaal	115	– (9) not out	4
A. P. Grayson c Metcalfe b Evans	44		
D. R. Law c Oram b Tolley	59	– (5) c Evans b Afzaal	0
†R. J. Rollins c Johnson b Tolley	19	– (6) c and b Tolley	42
G. R. Napier not out	35	– not out	4
A. P. Cowan not out	6	– (7) b Afzaal	15
M. C. Ilott (did not bat)		– (3) c Oram b Afzaal	33
B 14, l-b 8, w 4, n-b 6	32	B 4, l-b 4, w 6	18

1/94 2/101 3/194 4/288 5/329   (7 wkts dec.) 440   1/2 2/79 3/89   (7 wkts dec.) 183
6/380 7/421   4/90 5/120
                                                        6/171 7/173

P. M. Such did not bat.

Bonus points – Essex 4, Nottinghamshire 2 (Score at 120 overs: 373-5).

Bowling: *First Innings*—Oram 22–8–71–1; Evans 23–8–48–2; Tolley 30–7–102–2; Bowen 26–6–84–0; Astle 15–4–29–1; Afzaal 17–4–64–1; Dowman 4–0–20–0. *Second Innings*—Bowen 11–4–23–0; Oram 4–3–2–1; Johnson 13–5–32–0; Afzaal 30–10–83–3; Astle 7–3–10–1; Tolley 16–5–21–2.

Nottinghamshire

M. P. Dowman lbw b Napier	27	
R. T. Robinson not out	143	
N. J. Astle c D. R. Law b Cowan	100	
*P. Johnson c Grayson b Such	41	
B 4, l-b 12, w 14, n-b 10	40	

1/61 2/254 3/351   (3 wkts dec.) 351

A. A. Metcalfe, U. Afzaal, C. M. Tolley, †W. M. Noon, K. P. Evans, M. N. Bowen and A. R. Oram did not bat.

Bonus points – Nottinghamshire 4, Essex 1.

Bowling: Ilott 16–6–49–0; Cowan 13–3–59–1; Such 26.3–4–78–1; S. G. Law 10–3–28–0; Grayson 24–5–71–0; Napier 8–3–40–1; D. R. Law 2–0–10–0.

Umpires: D. J. Constant and J. W. Holder.

At Bristol, August 27, 28, 29, 30. NOTTINGHAMSHIRE beat GLOUCESTERSHIRE by 21 runs.

NOTTINGHAMSHIRE v HAMPSHIRE

At Nottingham, September 2, 3, 4, 5. Drawn. Nottinghamshire 7 pts, Hampshire 9 pts. Toss: Hampshire.

Rain, which wiped out most of the second day, returned during the run-chase to wash away hopes of a result. For the second game running, Johnson sacrificed a century in a bid to win; he hit 93 from 88 balls before asking Hampshire to score 285 from 61 overs. But with Smith nursing a broken hand, the odds were against them, and a half-hour interruption killed off their interest. Dowman's late-season form continued; two half-centuries made him the only Nottinghamshire batsman to reach 1,000 runs in 1997. He was still waiting for a county cap, though Tolley and Bowen got theirs on the third day. Stephenson had restricted Nottinghamshire to 291 with six wickets, five of them lbw – umpire Julian gave nine lbws in the match. Hampshire's middle order collapsed when they lost four for 32 and Smith was injured; a vibrant fifty by Udal revived them, but reciprocal declarations could not keep the contest alive.

Close of play: First day, Nottinghamshire 252-6 (U. Afzaal 26*, W. M. Noon 23*); Second day, Nottinghamshire 291; Third day, Nottinghamshire 94-2 (G. E. Welton 18*, P. Johnson 0*).

Nottinghamshire

M. P. Dowman c Savident b Udal	74	– c Milburn b Savident	62
R. T. Robinson c Aymes b Stephenson	32	– lbw b Renshaw	0
G. E. Welton lbw b Renshaw	12	– b Udal	40
*P. Johnson lbw b Stephenson	37	– not out	93
L. N. P. Walker b Udal	4		
U. Afzaal lbw b Stephenson	35	– (5) lbw b Udal	16
C. M. Tolley lbw b Stephenson	0	– (6) not out	8
†W. M. Noon lbw b Stephenson	25		
K. P. Evans lbw b Stephenson	0		
M. N. Bowen c Aymes b Milburn	13		
A. R. Oram not out	0		
B 1, l-b 20, w 26, n-b 12	59	L-b 10, w 4, n-b 20	34

1/84 2/126 3/160 4/168 5/216	291	1/8 2/92 (4 wkts dec.)	253
6/216 7/264 8/264 9/291		3/157 4/209	

Bonus points – Nottinghamshire 2, Hampshire 4 (Score at 120 overs: 291-9).

Bowling: *First Innings*—Renshaw 13–1–57–1; Milburn 31.3–7–78–1; Savident 15–2–43–0; Udal 34–15–38–2; Stephenson 27–11–54–6. *Second Innings*—Milburn 10–0–52–0; Renshaw 11–1–52–1; Stephenson 14–1–48–0; Savident 8–0–54–1; Udal 13–3–37–2.

Hampshire

J. S. Laney lbw b Oram	59	– b Oram	33
M. L. Hayden c Dowman b Bowen	74	– lbw b Evans	21
G. W. White lbw b Evans	5	– not out	25
R. A. Smith retired hurt	0		
M. Keech c Dowman b Tolley	17	– (4) not out	28
*J. P. Stephenson c Noon b Evans	11		
†A. N. Aymes c and b Oram	23		
S. D. Udal not out	54		
L. Savident not out	0		
B 4, l-b 9, w 2, n-b 2	17	L-b 7	7

1/108 2/146 3/146 4/168	(6 wkts dec.) 260	1/50 2/65 (2 wkts)	114
5/178 6/255			

S. J. Renshaw and S. M. Milburn did not bat.

Bonus points – Hampshire 2, Nottinghamshire 2.

In the first innings R. A. Smith retired hurt at 146-2.

Bowling: *First Innings*—Bowen 20–2–60–1; Oram 17.4–1–62–2; Tolley 18–3–58–1; Evans 17–2–56–2; Afzaal 5–1–11–0. *Second Innings*—Oram 8–1–24–1; Bowen 9–3–11–0; Tolley 14–2–33–0; Evans 5–2–13–1; Afzaal 10–3–13–0; Dowman 4–0–11–0; Johnson 1–0–2–0.

Umpires: R. Julian and A. G. T. Whitehead.

At Lord's, September 10, 11, 12, 13. NOTTINGHAMSHIRE lost to MIDDLESEX by ten wickets.

At Hove, September 18, 19, 20, 21. NOTTINGHAMSHIRE drew with SUSSEX.

SOMERSET

Graham Rose

President: M. F. Hill

Chairman: R. Parsons

Chairman, Cricket Committee: B. C. Rose

Chief Executive: P. W. Anderson

Captain: P. D. Bowler

Coach: D. A. Reeve

Head Groundsman: P. Frost

Scorer: D. A. Oldam

Somerset entered 1997 in optimistic mood, with the promise of Mushtaq Ahmed's return, Andy Caddick's encouraging form for England over the winter, and the appointment of Dermot Reeve, Warwickshire's highly successful captain, as coach. But their hopes gradually faded into disappointment. Mushtaq's heavy winter workload for Pakistan, and a bad knee which never quite healed, reduced his effectiveness; Caddick was frequently away for the Tests; other players suffered long-term injuries or struggled for form; and the new coaching regime had no obvious effect on Somerset's results. They fell one place in both the County Championship, to 12th, and the Sunday League, to sixth, while their achievements in the knockout competitions – one quarter-final – matched those of 1996.

Somerset won only three Championship matches, though all their victories were decisive. They beat Lancashire by seven wickets in two days; Essex by ten wickets in three days; and Durham by eight wickets, again in three days. They also lost three games, including a real thrashing in the final match, against Glamorgan, whose ten-wicket victory at Taunton secured the Championship. It was odd to recall that Somerset had won two resounding one-day victories over Glamorgan in the first two weeks of the season. They were close to winning up to three more Championship matches but, apart from the frequent intrusion of rain, there were several sharp examples of wasting excellent positions, in all forms of the game.

The county's players of the year were undoubtedly Graham Rose and Rob Turner. Rose had a wonderful benefit season. He never missed a Championship appearance, retrieved dangerous situations and set up favourable ones with both bat and ball, and headed both sets of Championship averages. Figures of 848 runs at 53.00 and 62 wickets at 24.40 brook no argument. Turner's wicket-keeping remained top-class, and he became a regular opening batsman. He was the only player to pass 1,000 first-class runs, and missed only one Championship game – after a horrid eye injury when the ball shattered his contact lens. He was back eight days later.

Against Leicestershire, Turner shared two classic match-saving partnerships with Keith Parsons on a bruising, spiteful pitch at Bath, which was aggravated by rain. But that pitch virtually ended Richard Harden's season, when Millns broke his finger. It was a severe blow to the county, as Harden had made a superb start. In his first 12 innings in three competitions, he scored 752 runs, including two centuries and seven fifties, at an average of 94. Parsons also disappeared after breaking his finger, in early August, by which time he had established himself as a fine all-rounder and slip fielder.

During the match at Bath, in mid-June, the county awarded caps to Kevin Shine and Andre van Troost. Many felt that rewarding van Troost devalued the honour. Even the award to Shine seemed a little premature. But he had recently won the match against Lancashire by taking 11 for 97, and in all he had claimed 58 Championship wickets in 17 matches since moving to Somerset the previous season. The Dutchman van Troost, whose pace numerous coaches had failed to harness, had come to the county in 1991. In six seasons, he had taken 103 Championship wickets in 51 matches at 39.33. Before the award of his cap, he added five for 149 in two matches. Afterwards, in four first-class games, he removed two Australian tailenders for 347 runs in 51.5 overs. He did not even find a place in the one-day side. But Reeve said that van Troost should be made to feel wanted, and he duly received his cap.

Shine's loss of form, van Troost's failure to find any, and injuries to Jason Kerr greatly added to the strain on Rose, Mushtaq and Caddick. Meanwhile, captain Peter Bowler was struggling with his own sketchy batting form and a niggling back injury, while the performances of Mark Lathwell and Marcus Trescothick remained unreliable. Piran Holloway did eventually establish himself as an opening batsman, without being completely convincing. Simon Ecclestone, who suggested a future in captaincy when he deputised for Bowler, confirmed that he was also a powerful batsman. His best performance was against Kent, when he scored 123 – despite a bad knee, which had earlier forced him to retire – and 94. It was just enough to prevent Kent from gaining the win which would, ultimately, have given them the Championship: they could only level the scores.

Curiously, off-spinner Harvey Trump played no first-class cricket and only five one-day games, although he fulfilled a fairly full Second Eleven programme. Anglo-Australian Steve Herzberg, also an off-spinner, made some useful contributions, but was not re-engaged. Another newcomer, Michael Burns, who arrived from Warwickshire as a wicket-keeper but turned himself into a successful one-day opening bat and occasional bowler, made a good impression.

There was plenty of cricket outside the main competitions to divert spectators. Taunton was visited by the Australians, the lively Pakistan A tourists and Oxford University, plus the England and South African women's teams, who impressed a large crowd with their skill and attitude during the second one-day international. But one of the most remarkable matches of the season was a four-day Second Eleven game between Somerset and Warwickshire in July. Warwickshire set a target of 612, but won by only six runs when Trescothick was last out for 322, out of 605. – ERIC HILL.

SOMERSET 1997

[*Bill Smith*]

Back row: P. C. L. Holloway, S. M. Trego, S. C. Ecclestone, K. J. Shine, B. J. Trott, K. A. Parsons, M. Dimond, H. J. Morgan. *Middle row*: C. M. Wells, L. D. Sutton, M. E. Trescothick, J. I. D. Kerr, S. Herzberg, M. Burns, I. E. Bishop, D. Veness (*physiotherapist*). *Front row*: R. J. Harden, M. N. Lathwell, A. R. Caddick, P. D. Bowler (*captain*), R. Parsons (*chairman*), D. A. Reeve (*director of cricket*), G. D. Rose, H. R. J. Trump, R. J. Turner. *Insets*: Mushtaq Ahmed, A. P. van Troost.

SOMERSET RESULTS

All first-class matches – Played 20: Won 4, Lost 4, Drawn 12.

County Championship matches – Played 17: Won 3, Lost 3, Drawn 11.

Competition placings – Britannic Assurance County Championship, 12th;
NatWest Trophy, 2nd round; Benson and Hedges Cup, q-f;
AXA Life League, 6th.

COUNTY CHAMPIONSHIP AVERAGES

BATTING

Cap		M	I	NO	R	HS	100s	50s	Avge	Ct/St
1988	G. D. Rose	17	25	9	848	191	2	3	53.00	6
1994	R. J. Turner.........	16	26	6	946	144	1	5	47.30	47/2
1989	R. J. Harden†	7	11	2	395	136*	2	1	43.88	3
	S. Herzberg	5	6	2	167	56	0	1	41.75	2
1997	S. C. Ecclestone	10	18	2	608	123	1	4	38.00	11
	K. A. Parsons†	7	11	3	281	74	0	2	35.12	9
1997	P. C. L. Holloway ...	16	29	4	855	106	1	5	34.20	9
1992	M. N. Lathwell......	17	29	1	802	95	0	5	28.64	8
	M. Burns...........	13	20	1	454	82	0	3	23.89	7/1
	M. E. Trescothick†...	11	17	1	379	83*	0	4	23.68	5
1992	A. R. Caddick.......	12	13	2	246	56*	0	1	22.36	4
1995	P. D. Bowler........	14	23	1	487	73	0	5	22.13	17
1993	Mushtaq Ahmed§	14	16	2	174	33	0	0	12.42	3
1997	K. J. Shine	17	18	4	92	18	0	0	6.57	5
1997	A. P. van Troost	5	7	2	8	5	0	0	1.60	1

Also batted: M. Dimond† (1 match) 4; P. S. Jones (1 match) 13 (1 ct); J. I. D. Kerr (3 matches) 0, 26, 26 (1 ct); B. J. Trott† (1 match) 1*, 0.

* Signifies not out.   † Born in Somerset.   § Overseas player.

BOWLING

	O	M	R	W	BB	5W/i	Avge
G. D. Rose	474.5	121	1,513	62	5-53	1	24.40
Mushtaq Ahmed	513	146	1,407	50	6-70	3	28.14
A. R. Caddick	506.5	110	1,468	52	6-65	3	28.23
K. J. Shine	399.3	81	1,547	47	7-43	2	32.91

Also bowled: P. D. Bowler 41.3–18–129–3; M. Burns 56–12–236–4; M. Dimond 11–3–30–0; S. C. Ecclestone 1–1–0–0; S. Herzberg 47–11–136–6; P. S. Jones 9–0–49–3; J. I. D. Kerr 59–12–217–7; M. N. Lathwell 5–0–60–1; K. A. Parsons 55–14–139–3; M. E. Trescothick 13–3–56–1; B. J. Trott 11–0–74–3; A. P. van Troost 63.2–5–364–5.

COUNTY RECORDS

Highest score for:	322	I. V. A. Richards v Warwickshire at Taunton.	1985
Highest score against:	424	A. C. MacLaren (Lancashire) at Taunton	1895
Best bowling for:	10-49	E. J. Tyler v Surrey at Taunton	1895
Best bowling against:	10-35	A. Drake (Yorkshire) at Weston-super-Mare..	1914
Highest total for:	675-9 dec.	v Hampshire at Bath	1924
Highest total against:	811	by Surrey at The Oval	1899
Lowest total for:	25	v Gloucestershire at Bristol	1947
Lowest total against:	22	by Gloucestershire at Bristol	1920

At The Oval, April 23, 24, 25, 26. SOMERSET drew with SURREY.

At Northampton, May 7, 8, 9, 10. SOMERSET drew with NORTHAMPTONSHIRE.

SOMERSET v SUSSEX

At Taunton, May 14, 15, 16, 17. Drawn. Somerset 11 pts, Sussex 8 pts. Toss: Somerset.

Somerset were frustrated by the weather and a stubborn century from Athey, which carried him past 25,000 first-class runs. It had been a fluctuating match, with Sussex apparently in charge early on. They had reached 149 for three before faltering against Mushtaq Ahmed, who took six, his first Championship wickets since 1995. Then Jarvis and Robinson reduced Somerset to 67 for six, 25 short of saving the follow-on. Rose responded with a career-best 191, hitting 28 fours in just 251 balls, and shared a stand of 279 in 73 overs with Harden, a Somerset seventh-wicket record, beating by one the partnership by Shane Lee and Rob Turner at Bath the previous year. That set up a lead of 168. Athey helped Sussex draw clear again but only 93.1 overs were possible on the last two days. On the final day, wicket-keeper Turner was hit in the eye by a googly from Mushtaq, which shattered his contact lens; he required hospital treatment.

Close of play: First day, Somerset 35-1 (M. E. Trescothick 16*, P. D. Bowler 4*); Second day, Sussex 6-0 (P. Moores 4*, C. W. J. Athey 2*); Third day, Sussex 142-3 (C. W. J. Athey 70*, K. Newell 10*).

Sussex

M. T. E. Peirce lbw b Rose	35	– (6) run out 8
K. Greenfield lbw b Mushtaq Ahmed	17	– (3) lbw b Rose 16
N. R. Taylor lbw b Mushtaq Ahmed	17	– (4) c Harden b Mushtaq Ahmed .. 28
C. W. J. Athey lbw b Parsons	39	– (2) not out 138
K. Newell c Parsons b Shine	35	– c Parsons b Caddick 21
*†P. Moores b Mushtaq Ahmed	24	– (1) c Turner b Shine 8
P. W. Jarvis c Turner b Shine	1	– not out 21
N. C. Phillips lbw b Mushtaq Ahmed	6	
M. J. Thursfield not out	32	
A. A. Khan b Mushtaq Ahmed	12	
M. A. Robinson c and b Mushtaq Ahmed	1	
L-b 10, n-b 12	22	L-b 9, n-b 10 19

1/38 2/71 3/86 4/149 5/161　　　　　　　241　　1/25 2/64 3/128　　　(5 wkts) 259
6/163 7/182 8/199 9/233　　　　　　　　　　　4/183 5/193

Bonus points – Sussex 1, Somerset 4.

Bowling: *First Innings*—Caddick 21–5–43–0; Shine 20–2–75–2; Mushtaq Ahmed 31–12–70–6; Rose 15–5–32–1; Parsons 4–0–11–1. *Second Innings*—Caddick 30–6–59–1; Mushtaq Ahmed 34.1–16–67–1; Shine 13–1–66–1; Parsons 5–2–12–0; Rose 13–3–41–1; Bowler 3–1–5–0.

Somerset

M. N. Lathwell lbw b Jarvis	8	Mushtaq Ahmed c Taylor b Khan 16
M. E. Trescothick lbw b Robinson	16	A. R. Caddick b Khan 13
*P. D. Bowler lbw b Robinson	4	K. J. Shine not out 1
R. J. Harden c Moores b Jarvis	103	
M. Burns c Khan b Jarvis	0	B 7, l-b 12, n-b 26 45
K. A. Parsons b Jarvis	1	
†R. J. Turner c Moores b Jarvis	10	1/10 2/35 3/40 4/41 5/45　　　409
G. D. Rose run out	191	6/67 7/346 8/372 9/404

Bonus points – Somerset 4, Sussex 4.

Bowling: Jarvis 31–1–122–5; Robinson 23–7–80–2; Khan 30–6–73–2; Newell 6–1–26–0; Phillips 10–2–39–0; Thursfield 3.3–0–38–0; Greenfield 5–1–12–0.

Umpires: B. Leadbeater and R. A. White.

SOMERSET v YORKSHIRE

At Taunton, May 21, 22, 23, 24. Yorkshire won by 140 runs. Yorkshire 21 pts, Somerset 5 pts.
Toss: Yorkshire.

Lehmann's maiden century for Yorkshire gave them a grip on the game which they converted into their first Championship win of the season. It was a remarkable innings – 177 from 228 balls, with 22 fours, in the alien surroundings of seamy pitch, low cloud, bitter breeze and his colleagues' failures. The next-best score came from Blakey, who made 33 out of their stand of 138. Only 58 overs were possible during the first two days so, after Ecclestone had led Somerset to one batting point, Bowler declared behind. On the final morning, Yorkshire were fed ten overs of declaration bowling to create a target of 341 from what would have been 80 overs. It looked impossible at 58 for four, after White had taken two wickets with successive balls. Ecclestone and Harden raised Somerset's hopes a little before Hartley took three wickets in four balls and Yorkshire won with 26 overs to spare.

Close of play: First day, Yorkshire 52-3 (D. S. Lehmann 24*, A. McGrath 5*); Second day, Yorkshire 183-5 (D. S. Lehmann 109*, R. J. Blakey 20*); Third day, Yorkshire 124-2 (D. Byas 51*, D. S. Lehmann 30*).

Yorkshire

M. D. Moxon c Bowler b Shine	0	– lbw b Mushtaq Ahmed	33
M. P. Vaughan c Burns b Caddick	1	– b Caddick	2
*D. Byas b Rose	18	– not out	103
D. S. Lehmann lbw b Mushtaq Ahmed	177	– c Burns b Rose	30
A. McGrath c Burns b Shine	11	– st Burns b Bowler	2
C. White b Caddick	11	– b Bowler	13
†R. J. Blakey c Holloway b Caddick	33	– (8) not out	4
P. J. Hartley b Caddick	16	– (7) c Harden b Lathwell	39
A. G. Wharf lbw b Caddick	0		
G. M. Hamilton c Holloway b Caddick	0		
R. D. Stemp not out	13		
B 5, l-b 13, n-b 8	26	B 3, l-b 4, n-b 4	11

1/1 2/3 3/39 4/79 5/122   306   1/11 2/65 3/124   (6 wkts dec.) 237
6/260 7/278 8/279 9/281   4/126 5/156 6/233

Bonus points – Yorkshire 3, Somerset 4.

Bowling: First Innings—Caddick 30.3–3–103–6; Shine 16–1–54–2; Rose 8–2–19–1; Mushtaq Ahmed 22–6–91–1; Parsons 4–0–21–0. *Second Innings*—Caddick 7–2–16–1; Shine 8–1–34–0; Mushtaq Ahmed 8–0–42–1; Rose 9–2–30–1; Bowler 5–1–48–2; Lathwell 5–0–60–1.

Somerset

M. N. Lathwell lbw b Hartley	0	– lbw b Hartley	0
*P. D. Bowler c Blakey b Hartley	14	– lbw b White	18
P. C. L. Holloway run out	14	– c Blakey b Hamilton	25
R. J. Harden lbw b Wharf	32	– (6) not out	50
S. C. Ecclestone not out	79	– (4) c Blakey b Hartley	33
†M. Burns c McGrath b Vaughan	40	– (5) b White	0
K. A. Parsons not out	10	– c Blakey b Hartley	5
G. D. Rose (did not bat)		– lbw b Hartley	0
A. R. Caddick (did not bat)		– lbw b Hartley	0
Mushtaq Ahmed (did not bat)		– lbw b Stemp	33
K. J. Shine (did not bat)		– b White	18
B 4, n-b 10	14	L-b 8, w 4, n-b 6	18

1/0 2/19 3/36 4/102 5/179   (5 wkts dec.) 203   1/0 2/54 3/58 4/58 5/116   200
                                       6/123 7/123 8/123 9/162

Bonus points – Somerset 1, Yorkshire 2.

Bowling: *First Innings*—Hartley 11–3–39–2; Hamilton 10–1–54–0; Stemp 11–4–36–0; White 6–2–16–0; Wharf 6–1–23–1; Vaughan 4–0–25–1; McGrath 0.5–0–6–0. *Second Innings*—Hartley 12–4–34–5; Wharf 12–1–34–0; Hamilton 10–1–44–1; Stemp 11–3–52–1; White 8.2–1–28–3.

Umpires: J. W. Holder and V. A. Holder.

At Worcester, May 29, 30, 31, June 2. SOMERSET drew with WORCESTERSHIRE.

SOMERSET v LANCASHIRE

At Taunton, June 4, 5. Somerset won by seven wickets. Somerset 20 pts, Lancashire 4 pts. Toss: Lancashire.

Lancashire maintained their habit of brief matches at Taunton, and of being bowled over by Kevin Shine. The game was over by 5.40 on the second day, despite the loss of the morning to rain; Lancashire had lost in two days here in 1993, then won on the third morning in 1995. Shine set up Somerset's victory by taking seven for 43 in the first session and 11 for 97 in the match. While with Hampshire, he took eight for 47 at Old Trafford in 1992. Shine was aided at first by a pitch slightly damp after early mist, but Watkinson had chosen to bat and the umpires made no complaint. Lancashire crumbled in 22.1 overs for 88 runs before lunch and Bowler and Holloway easily overtook them. But, as the weather grew hot and humid, Somerset's last nine wickets fell for 76, Martin and Chapple claiming four apiece. In a further 16 overs that evening, Lancashire lost Gallian to a broken finger and McKeown bowled by Rose. After rain destroyed the second morning, Shine and van Troost renewed the previous day's havoc under heavy cloud, helped by fine fielding, especially a racing boundary catch by Mushtaq Ahmed. Somerset lost three men reaching a target of 64.

Close of play: First day, Lancashire 40-1 (S. P. Titchard 11*, G. Chapple 2*).

Lancashire

J. E. R. Gallian c Burns b Shine	0	– retired hurt	6
S. P. Titchard lbw b Shine	4	– lbw b Shine	16
P. C. McKeown lbw b Shine	2	– b Rose	11
N. H. Fairbrother b Shine	15	– (5) c Parsons b Shine	15
G. D. Lloyd c Turner b van Troost	0	– (6) c Turner b van Troost	5
*M. Watkinson c van Troost b Rose	33	– (7) c Bowler b Shine	28
I. D. Austin c Parsons b Shine	0	– (8) b Mushtaq Ahmed	24
†W. K. Hegg c Bowler b Shine	9	– (9) c Bowler b van Troost	5
P. J. Martin c Holloway b Shine	12	– (10) c Mushtaq Ahmed b van Troost	11
G. Chapple c Turner b Rose	0	– (4) b Shine	10
G. Keedy not out	0	– not out	5
L-b 7, w 4, n-b 2	13	L-b 9, w 3, n-b 16	28

1/0 2/8 3/11 4/20 5/32	88	1/38 2/49 3/64 4/69 5/83	164
6/36 7/64 8/88 9/88		6/116 7/121 8/135 9/164

Bonus points – Somerset 4.

In the second innings J. E. R. Gallian retired hurt at 13.

Bowling: *First Innings*—Shine 11.1–3–43–7; van Troost 7–0–27–1; Rose 4–3–11–2. *Second Innings*—van Troost 14–1–79–3; Shine 17–2–54–4; Mushtaq Ahmed 7.3–6–7–1; Rose 5–0–15–1.

Somerset

M. N. Lathwell c Gallian b Martin	13	– c Hegg b Martin	18
*P. D. Bowler lbw b Chapple	53	– lbw b Martin	9
P. C. L. Holloway lbw b Martin	48	– not out	23
R. J. Harden lbw b Martin	0	– b Chapple	5
K. A. Parsons lbw b Austin	30		
†R. J. Turner lbw b Chapple	1		
M. Burns b Chapple	3		
G. D. Rose c Hegg b Chapple	0		
Mushtaq Ahmed c Chapple b Austin	29	– (5) not out	9
K. J. Shine c Gallian b Martin	1		
A. P. van Troost not out	0		
L-b 9, w 2	11	L-b 2	2

1/34 2/113 3/113 4/130 5/136   189   1/26 2/31 3/57   (3 wkts) 66
6/148 7/148 8/164 9/189

Bonus points – Lancashire 4.

Bowling: *First Innings*—Martin 16–5–29–4; Chapple 18–1–80–4; Austin 16.2–5–33–2; Gallian 6–0–22–0; Watkinson 3–0–10–0; Keedy 1–0–6–0. *Second Innings*—Martin 9–4–21–2; Chapple 4–0–17–1; Austin 7–1–16–0; Keedy 1.2–0–10–0.

Umpires: J. D. Bond and N. T. Plews.

At Basingstoke, June 12, 13, 14. SOMERSET lost to HAMPSHIRE by nine runs.

SOMERSET v LEICESTERSHIRE

At Bath, June 18, 19, 20, 21. Drawn. Somerset 7 pts, Leicestershire 11 pts. Toss: Leicestershire.
Leicestershire dominated the match, but were cheated by rain. Wells and Maddy had given them the ideal start, opening with 133 in 31 overs. Then Sutcliffe scored his maiden century for the county, hitting 19 fours and adding 192 in 63 overs with Whitaker. Somerset suffered further blows when van Troost – who, like Shine, was capped during the match – pulled a hamstring and Mushtaq Ahmed succumbed to knee trouble. Surprisingly, Whitaker kept on batting to add 105 in the 32 overs possible late on the second day. The following day saw only 21 overs and on the closing day Somerset had to stave off defeat. The pitch had now grown spiteful; Millns exploited it to take six wickets and also broke Harden's finger. Turner and Parsons put on 68 in 21 bruising overs, not enough to save the follow-on, but they did save the match in the second innings with their unbroken fourth-wicket partnership of 115.
Close of play: First day, Leicestershire 337-3 (J. J. Whitaker 78*, N. C. Johnson 0*); Second day, Leicestershire 442-6 (J. J. Whitaker 133*, D. J. Millns 4*); Third day, Somerset 72-2 (P. C. L. Holloway 9*, R. J. Harden 12*).

Leicestershire

V. J. Wells lbw b Mushtaq Ahmed	70	†P. A. Nixon c Parsons b Rose	8
D. L. Maddy c Rose b Kerr	58	D. J. Millns not out	4
I. J. Sutcliffe c Lathwell b Shine	112	L-b 15, w 4, n-b 14	33
*J. J. Whitaker not out	133		
N. C. Johnson c Shine b Rose	5	1/133 2/143 3/335 (6 wkts dec.) 442
G. I. Macmillan lbw b Rose	19	4/350 5/383 6/413

A. R. K. Pierson, A. D. Mullally and J. Ormond did not bat.

Bonus points – Leicestershire 4, Somerset 2 (Score at 120 overs: 406-5).

Bowling: Shine 26.4–4–92–1; van Troost 9.2–1–69–0; Rose 30–7–82–3; Mushtaq Ahmed 15.3–6–32–1; Kerr 24–4–90–1; Parsons 17–5–44–0; Bowler 9.3–3–18–0.

Somerset

M. N. Lathwell c Sutcliffe b Millns	6	– lbw b Millns	0
*P. D. Bowler lbw b Ormond	30	– c Wells b Millns	6
P. C. L. Holloway lbw b Millns	16	– c Maddy b Ormond	10
R. J. Harden b Ormond	33		
K. A. Parsons c Nixon b Ormond	25	– (4) not out	56
†R. J. Turner c Maddy b Millns	66	– (5) not out	46
G. D. Rose c Nixon b Mullally	8		
J. I. D. Kerr c Nixon b Millns	26		
Mushtaq Ahmed c Mullally b Millns	4		
K. J. Shine b Millns	6		
A. P. van Troost not out	0		
B 5, l-b 13, w 8, n-b 10	36	B 11, l-b 1, n-b 16	28

1/32 2/42 3/98 4/112 5/180	256	1/8 2/27 3/31 (3 wkts) 146
6/201 7/227 8/231 9/245		

Bonus points – Somerset 2, Leicestershire 4.

Bowling: *First Innings*—Millns 22.3–6–61–6; Mullally 20–3–90–1; Ormond 19–1–69–3; Pierson 2–2–0–0; Johnson 3–0–18–0. *Second Innings*—Millns 8–4–24–2; Mullally 10–1–39–0; Ormond 7–1–21–1; Wells 2–0–6–0; Pierson 9–1–29–0; Johnson 2–0–3–0; Sutcliffe 1–0–12–0.

Umpires: J. C. Balderstone and G. I. Burgess.

SOMERSET v OXFORD UNIVERSITY

At Taunton, June 28, 29, 30. Somerset won by an innings and 46 runs. Toss: Oxford University. First-class debut: B. J. Trott. County debut: R. W. Sladdin.

Needing to bat four hours to save the match, their last before Lord's, Oxford failed by 13 balls. Several batsmen settled in, only to play rash shots. The gentle turn of left-armer Sladdin and right-armer Herzberg was no real threat, as tailenders Buchanan and Scrini showed. Then Parsons yorked Scrini and removed the captain, Wagh, batting one-handed because of injury, next ball. Wagh dominated Oxford's first innings with a fine, career-best 125 not out; his last 75 came at a run a ball. But he split the webbing of his left hand trying to catch a fierce return drive from Ecclestone, who went on to score 133 in 112 balls, with two sixes and 20 fours, and put on 214 in 33 overs with Bowler.

Close of play: First day, Oxford University 147-7 (M. A. Wagh 49*, L. G. Buchanan 7*); Second day, Somerset 323-3 (M. N. Lathwell 18*, K. A. Parsons 14*).

Oxford University

C. G. R. Lightfoot c Parsons b Herzberg	2	– c Holloway b Sladdin	24
B. W. Byrne c Bowler b Trott	40	– lbw b Kerr	7
*M. A. Wagh not out	125	– (11) lbw b Parsons	0
P. G. Morgan c Sladdin b Parsons	25	– (3) lbw b Sladdin	17
J. A. G. Fulton b Sladdin	8	– c Burns b Sladdin	31
R. D. Hudson b Parsons	2	– (4) b Herzberg	2
C. Patel c Parsons b Burns	5	– (6) c Holloway b Sladdin	29
J. M. M. Averis c Trott b Herzberg	3	– (7) c Parsons b Herzberg	29
L. G. Buchanan c Lathwell b Trott	8	– (8) c Bowler b Sladdin	15
†A. P. Scrini not out	17	– (9) b Parsons	18
C. M. Battarbee (did not bat)		– (10) not out	2
L-b 2, w 4	6	L-b 6, n-b 6	12

1/19 2/51 3/93 4/101 5/104	(8 wkts dec.) 241	1/9 2/43 3/68 4/75 5/85 186
6/120 7/127 8/150		6/129 7/152 8/176 9/186

Bowling: *First Innings*—Kerr 12–1–37–0; Trott 13–3–40–2; Herzberg 27–8–48–2; Parsons 14–3–34–2; Sladdin 13–1–45–1; Burns 6–1–30–1; Bowler 2–0–5–0. *Second Innings*—Kerr 14–3–41–1; Trott 3–0–14–0; Herzberg 23–6–61–2; Sladdin 25–9–60–5; Parsons 3.5–1–4–2.

Somerset

*P. D. Bowler c Scrini b Patel 123
P. C. L. Holloway c Scrini b Wagh 20
S. C. Ecclestone c Lightfoot b Averis....133
M. N. Lathwell b Averis 21
K. A. Parsons c Scrini b Byrne 48
†M. Burns c Averis b Battarbee 56
M. E. Trescothick b Battarbee 3

J. I. D. Kerr not out 28
S. Herzberg not out 22
    B 7, l-b 6, n-b 6 19
                   —
1/57 2/271 3/292   (7 wkts dec.) 473
4/328 5/409
6/421 7/424

R. W. Sladdin and B. J. Trott did not bat.

Bowling: Averis 22–2–103–2; Patel 23–2–115–1; Wagh 6–1–24–1; Byrne 22–3–116–1; Battarbee 18–1–91–2; Lightfoot 1–0–11–0.

Umpires: J. W. Lloyds and K. E. Palmer.

At Chelmsford, July 2, 3, 4. SOMERSET beat ESSEX by ten wickets.

At Taunton, July 19, 20, 21. SOMERSET lost to PAKISTAN A by five wickets (See Pakistan A tour section).

At Birmingham, July 24, 25, 26, 27. SOMERSET drew with WARWICKSHIRE.

At Taunton, August 1, 2, 3, 4. SOMERSET drew with AUSTRALIANS (See Australian tour section).

SOMERSET v GLOUCESTERSHIRE

At Taunton, August 6, 7, 8, 9. Drawn. Somerset 8 pts, Gloucestershire 9 pts. Toss: Somerset. Championship debut: P. S. Jones.

A controlled two-and-a-half-hour innings from Rose granted Somerset a narrow escape. Set 277 in 45 overs, in excellent conditions, they had collapsed to 38 for six against Smith and Ball, who took three in four balls. But Mushtaq Ahmed, dropped by Wright, survived 23 overs, and last man Shine helped Rose last out the final 37 balls. After a blank first day, play was delayed until 4 p.m. on the second, partly because of a change of pitch. As the one originally chosen was still damp, Somerset had decided to play on one just used against the Australians. Gloucestershire objected to the same wicket being used for successive four-day games (even though the tourist match's last two days were washed out), and the ECB supported them, so Somerset had to switch back. Gloucestershire were put in and started well enough, until checked by three wickets from Rose. Next morning, Young and Alleyne took their stand to 140 in 27 overs against some wayward bowling. Bowler replied steadily, adding 133 with Lathwell, before declaring 98 behind. Cambridge seamer Steffan Jones picked up three wickets off mis-hooks, but Hancock hit a 90-ball 100 to create the target.

Close of play: First day, No play; Second day, Gloucestershire 119-4 (S. Young 10*, M. W. Alleyne 4*); Third day, Somerset 191-3 (M. N. Lathwell 68*, M. E. Trescothick 2*).

Gloucestershire

A. J. Wright c Turner b Rose	30	– c Turner b Jones	21
M. G. N. Windows lbw b Mushtaq Ahmed	44	– c Rose b Jones	12
T. H. C. Hancock c Turner b Rose	11	– not out	100
M. A. Lynch b Rose	8	– c Rose b Jones	0
S. Young c Turner b Trescothick	83	– not out	31
*M. W. Alleyne c Turner b Shine	70		
†R. C. Russell not out	37		
R. I. Dawson lbw b Shine	14		
M. C. J. Ball c Jones b Rose	18		
A. M. Smith not out	1		
B 4, l-b 2, w 4, n-b 24	34	B 4, l-b 4, w 4, n-b 2	14

1/61 2/91 3/105 4/105 5/245　　　　(8 wkts dec.) 350　　1/26 2/40 3/48　　　(3 wkts dec.) 178
6/282 7/310 8/342

J. Lewis did not bat.

Bonus points – Gloucestershire 4, Somerset 3.

Bowling: *First Innings*—Rose 22.3–8–55–4; Shine 15–3–79–2; van Troost 16–2–69–0; Mushtaq Ahmed 26–5–98–1; Bowler 5–3–6–0; Jones 2–0–19–0; Trescothick 3–0–18–1. *Second Innings*—Jones 7–0–30–3; Trescothick 6–2–20–0; Shine 2–1–4–0; Mushtaq Ahmed 7–1–31–0; Bowler 5–1–24–0; Rose 4.1–0–34–0; van Troost 4–0–27–0.

Somerset

*P. D. Bowler c Lynch b Lewis	73	– (7) c Hancock b Ball	1
P. C. L. Holloway lbw b Smith	11	– c Russell b Smith	0
S. C. Ecclestone lbw b Young	30	– c Lynch b Ball	6
M. N. Lathwell c Young b Smith	95	– c Windows b Lewis	13
M. E. Trescothick c Russell b Smith	2	– (6) c Alleyne b Ball	0
†R. J. Turner not out	26	– (1) c Russell b Smith	16
G. D. Rose not out	4	– (5) not out	67
Mushtaq Ahmed (did not bat)		– c Ball b Smith	16
P. S. Jones (did not bat)		– c Young b Ball	13
A. P. van Troost (did not bat)		– b Smith	0
K. J. Shine (did not bat)		– not out	0
L-b 3, n-b 8	11	N-b 6	6

1/23 2/54 3/187 4/206 5/243　　　(5 wkts dec.) 252　　1/5 2/16 3/31　　　(9 wkts) 138
　　　　　　　　　　　　　　　　　　　　　　　4/36 5/36 6/38
　　　　　　　　　　　　　　　　　　　　　　　7/103 8/130 9/133

Bonus points – Somerset 2, Gloucestershire 2.

Bowling: *First Innings*—Smith 17–5–60–3; Lewis 17–4–84–1; Young 9–1–32–1; Alleyne 10–2–43–0; Ball 10–3–30–0. *Second Innings*—Smith 15–4–60–4; Lewis 5–1–24–1; Ball 17–11–15–4; Young 5–1–15–0; Alleyne 3–0–24–0.

Umpires: A. Clarkson and B. Dudleston.

At Nottingham, August 15, 16, 17, 18. SOMERSET drew with NOTTINGHAMSHIRE.

SOMERSET v KENT

At Taunton, August 20, 21, 22, 23. Drawn. Somerset 11 pts, Kent 16 pts. Toss: Somerset.
　　Kent needed seven from the final over; they ran four singles before Turner caught Fleming, and Marsh managed two off the final ball. With the scores level, Kent took eight points as the side batting second, and finished the game two points behind leaders Glamorgan. As it turned out, one more run would have given them the Championship. The start had been equally dramatic.

In five overs, Phillips dismissed Holloway first ball, acting-captain Ecclestone retired with knee trouble, and umpire Whitehead ordered McCague to be taken off for bowling four bouncers and a beamer. Turner responded with a career-best 144, while Ecclestone resumed to score a maiden Championship century. Cowdrey and Ealham played similar roles for Kent, adding 183, and Fleming's fifty helped build a 74-run lead. Ecclestone fell six short of another hundred when he was caught at leg slip from a rebound off short leg, one of Strang's six wickets. But Herzberg scored enough to make a Kent win less than certain: a challenge of 161 in 26 overs. They still seemed to be in charge until Wells went with 16 needed from 11 balls, setting up the finale.

Close of play: First day, Somerset 336-6 (S. C. Ecclestone 103*, S. Herzberg 6*); Second day, Kent 99-3 (E. T. Smith 45*, G. R. Cowdrey 6*); Third day, Somerset 51-1 (P. C. L. Holloway 20*, S. C. Ecclestone 20*).

Somerset

†R. J. Turner c Cowdrey b Ealham	144	– c Marsh b Phillips	11
P. C. L. Holloway c Ward b Phillips	0	– c Cowdrey b Fleming	20
*S. C. Ecclestone lbw b Phillips	123	– c Wells b Strang	94
M. N. Lathwell c Ward b Ealham	26	– c Ward b Ealham	22
M. E. Trescothick c Marsh b Fleming	0	– c Fulton b Strang	3
M. Burns c Wells b Phillips	11	– lbw b Strang	13
G. D. Rose c Marsh b Fleming	35	– lbw b Phillips	13
S. Herzberg c Ward b Phillips	15	– not out	42
Mushtaq Ahmed c and b Ealham	0	– c Ward b Strang	0
A. P. van Troost c Cowdrey b Phillips	3	– c Phillips b Strang	0
K. J. Shine not out	0	– c Cowdrey b Strang	6
B 1, l-b 3, w 6, n-b 8	18	B 1, l-b 7, n-b 2	10
	375		**234**

1/14 2/73 3/76 4/93 5/148 6/319 7/360 8/365 9/368

1/18 2/51 3/92 4/127 5/163 6/175 7/197 8/202 9/214

Bonus points – Somerset 4, Kent 4.

In the first innings S. C. Ecclestone, when 3, retired hurt at 17 and resumed at 148.

Bowling: *First Innings*—McCague 2.1–0–22–0; Phillips 25.3–7–86–5; Ealham 29.5–4–84–3; Fleming 25–2–83–2; Strang 26–8–78–0; Wells 6–2–18–0. *Second Innings*—Phillips 19–4–47–2; Ealham 16–3–49–1; Strang 28.3–9–72–6; Fleming 21–11–54–1; Ward 1–0–4–0.

Kent

D. P. Fulton lbw b Rose	16		
E. T. Smith c Ecclestone b Mushtaq Ahmed	56	– run out	34
T. R. Ward b Rose	8	– (1) c Ecclestone b Mushtaq Ahmed	19
A. P. Wells lbw b Rose	1	– (3) c Lathwell b Mushtaq Ahmed	57
G. R. Cowdrey c Shine b Mushtaq Ahmed	101	– (4) st Turner b Mushtaq Ahmed	18
M. A. Ealham b Herzberg	105	– (5) c Lathwell b Burns	2
M. V. Fleming c Turner b Herzberg	53	– (6) c Turner b Burns	17
*†S. A. Marsh b Mushtaq Ahmed	18	– not out	2
P. A. Strang c Ecclestone b Mushtaq Ahmed	24	– (7) not out	3
B. J. Phillips b Herzberg	0		
M. J. McCague not out	20		
B 8, l-b 8, w 4, n-b 27	47	L-b 6, w 2	8
	449	(6 wkts)	**160**

1/65 2/77 3/79 4/121 5/304 6/342 7/373 8/423 9/425

1/54 2/79 3/126 4/131 5/145 6/158

Bonus points – Kent 4, Somerset 4.

Bowling: *First Innings*—Shine 12–0–70–0; van Troost 7–0–50–0; Rose 22–5–60–3; Mushtaq Ahmed 37.1–10–114–4; Herzberg 22–1–100–3; Burns 8–1–39–0. *Second Innings*—Shine 1–0–10–0; Rose 10–0–48–0; Mushtaq Ahmed 12–1–78–3; Burns 3–0–18–2.

Umpires: R. A. White and A. G. T. Whitehead.

At Derby, August 27, 28, 29, 30. SOMERSET drew with DERBYSHIRE.

SOMERSET v MIDDLESEX

At Taunton, September 2, 3, 4, 5. Drawn. Somerset 8 pts, Middlesex 8 pts. Toss: Somerset.

Kallis and Pooley started briskly in pursuit of 301 in 57 overs. But Middlesex ran into difficulties against Mushtaq Ahmed and, after Ramprakash fell at 98 in the 27th over, they quietly played out time. Despite knee problems, Mushtaq took nine in the match. Somerset had chosen to bat, but were reduced to 65 for four by the seamers before Turner and Burns combined to put on 80. Rose scored an unbeaten fifty as Tufnell went through the tail. Middlesex's innings took a similar course, Caddick clearing the top order and Mushtaq the bottom, with Kallis and Shah adding 96 in between. Kallis scored his fourth hundred of the season. Resuming, Somerset stumbled again, but Trescothick rescued them, with Burns's patient support, and the tail set up the final conundrum. Only five balls were bowled on the second day; no runs were scored or wickets taken.

Close of play: First day, Middlesex 80-3 (J. H. Kallis 27*, O. A. Shah 8*); Second day, Middlesex 80-3 (J. H. Kallis 27*, O. A. Shah 8*); Third day, Somerset 174-5 (M. Burns 34*, G. D. Rose 2*).

Somerset

†R. J. Turner c Brown b Kallis	71	– lbw b Fraser	6
P. C. L. Holloway lbw b Hewitt	11	– c Pooley b Johnson	37
*S. C. Ecclestone c Nash b Hewitt	0	– b Hewitt	8
M. N. Lathwell c Nash b Kallis	13	– run out	10
M. E. Trescothick c Brown b Johnson	7	– c Kallis b Tufnell	65
M. Burns c Johnson b Kallis	36	– b Johnson	34
G. D. Rose not out	56	– c and b Tufnell	27
S. Herzberg c Ramprakash b Tufnell	10	– not out	40
A. R. Caddick b Tufnell	12	– c Fraser b Ramprakash	39
Mushtaq Ahmed c Kallis b Tufnell	0	– not out	14
K. J. Shine c Shah b Tufnell	6		
B 8, l-b 5, w 2, n-b 4	19	L-b 5, w 2, n-b 2	15

1/20 2/20 3/48 4/65 5/145   241   1/22 2/33 3/46   (8 wkts dec.) 295
6/145 7/172 8/207 9/207   4/74 5/162 6/174
                                     7/224 8/281

Bonus points – Somerset 1, Middlesex 4.

Bowling: *First Innings*—Fraser 15-6-34-0; Hewitt 13-1-63-2; Kallis 13-5-34-3; Johnson 13-2-44-1; Tufnell 24.4-8-53-4; Ramprakash 1-1-0-0. *Second Innings*—Fraser 18-4-46-1; Hewitt 6-0-23-1; Johnson 17-3-52-2; Tufnell 30-9-90-2; Kallis 9-1-21-0; Ramprakash 11-1-58-1.

Middlesex

J. C. Pooley c Lathwell b Caddick	0	– c Turner b Shine	17
J. H. Kallis c Holloway b Caddick	100	– c Burns b Mushtaq Ahmed	52
*M. R. Ramprakash b Caddick	0	– c Turner b Mushtaq Ahmed	21
M. W. Gatting lbw b Caddick	31	– c Trescothick b Mushtaq Ahmed	21
O. A. Shah run out	27	– c Trescothick b Mushtaq Ahmed	23
D. C. Nash c Ecclestone b Mushtaq Ahmed	11	– not out	32
†K. R. Brown not out	30	– not out	7
R. L. Johnson c Turner b Mushtaq Ahmed	11		
J. P. Hewitt c Turner b Mushtaq Ahmed	1		
A. R. C. Fraser b Mushtaq Ahmed	3		
P. C. R. Tufnell lbw b Mushtaq Ahmed	5		
L-b 3, w 10, n-b 4	17	B 4, l-b 6, n-b 4	14

1/0 2/6 3/54 4/150 5/179   236   1/60 2/93 3/98   (5 wkts) 187
6/187 7/200 8/216 9/228   4/133 5/166

Bonus points – Middlesex 1, Somerset 4.

Bowling: *First Innings*—Caddick 23–4–71–4; Shine 12–2–64–0; Rose 12–2–26–0; Mushtaq Ahmed 19.4–2–66–5; Herzberg 2–0–6–0. *Second Innings*—Caddick 18–2–68–0; Rose 7–2–19–0; Mushtaq Ahmed 23.2–7–71–4; Shine 4–0–17–1; Herzberg 3–1–2–0; Ecclestone 1–1–0–0.

Umpires: B. J. Meyer and D. R. Shepherd.

At Chester-le-Street, September 10, 11, 12. SOMERSET beat DURHAM by eight wickets.

SOMERSET v GLAMORGAN

At Taunton, September 18, 19, 20. Glamorgan won by ten wickets. Glamorgan 24 pts, Somerset 6 pts. Toss: Glamorgan. Championship debut: B. J. Trott.

Batting of rare brilliance from their captain, Maynard, and Morris, his ideal partner, backed up by pointed seam bowling by Waqar Younis and Thomas, carried Glamorgan to victory and their first County Championship since 1969. Leading Kent by only one point as they entered the final round, they had to get the maximum 24 points to make sure of the title. Despite the handicap of rain, they did it in style, with a day to spare. Glamorgan's triumph came with a four to fine leg by James at 6.18 on the Saturday, with four scoreboard lights shining through the September gloom. They were watched by a crowd of almost 4,000, mostly Welsh. The only disappointment was that thousands more were planning to cross the Severn Bridge on the Sunday, the scheduled last day. In keeping with ancient Welsh tradition, it is possible that in years to come many will claim they really were there. Six members of the 1969 squad were definitely present: Alan and Eifion Jones, Don Shepherd, Peter Walker, Roger Davis and Kevin Lyons.

In lovely weather, Maynard put Somerset in and Waqar broke through almost at once, dismissing Holloway and Ecclestone for ducks. After going off because of the throat virus which afflicted him throughout the match, he took two more wickets to check the recovery. Bowler steered Somerset towards 252 and Caddick made two early strikes when Glamorgan replied. That brought in Maynard. He and Morris added 117 in 24 overs that evening. Next day, rain prevented any play before 3.50 p.m., when they resumed in wintry gloom – there were frequently five lights on. But Maynard and Morris hardly seemed to notice as they ran up another 118 in 17 overs. Maynard finally fell for 142 from 117 balls, with 28 fours and a six. Morris batted on into the third morning, scoring 165 from 244 balls, with 28 fours. It was his 52nd century for Glamorgan, equalling Alan Jones's county record, and it was to be his last before retiring on being appointed the ECB's technical director a month later. Croft and Shaw contributed attacking fifties and Glamorgan soared to a lead of 275. When Somerset resumed, Waqar was beginning to struggle: he conceded 38 in three overs. But Thomas – bowling at something close to Waqar's pace – stepped up to take five wickets, and Glamorgan looked likely to win by an innings when the score was 166 for seven. Rose and Caddick added a defiant 95 in 14 overs to make them bat again. They needed only 11, and did it in eight balls when James hit the winning boundary to wild acclaim.

Close of play: First day, Glamorgan 159-2 (H. Morris 49*, M. P. Maynard 76*); Second day, Glamorgan 353-4 (H. Morris 136*, R. D. B. Croft 18*).

Somerset

†R. J. Turner c Thomas b Watkin	40	– b Thomas	38
P. C. L. Holloway b Waqar Younis	0	– c Shaw b Thomas	25
S. C. Ecclestone c Morris b Waqar Younis	0	– c Morris b Watkin	10
M. N. Lathwell b Waqar Younis	62	– b Thomas	47
M. E. Trescothick c Maynard b Croft	20	– c James b Croft	16
M. Burns b Waqar Younis	28	– c Shaw b Thomas	18
*P. D. Bowler c Morris b Watkin	63	– lbw b Thomas	3
G. D. Rose lbw b Cosker	13	– c Shaw b Watkin	67
A. R. Caddick c Croft b Cosker	11	– not out	56
K. J. Shine c Morris b Watkin	6	– c James b Watkin	0
B. J. Trott not out	1	– lbw b Cosker	0
L-b 6, n-b 2	8	L-b 3, n-b 2	5

1/17 2/17 3/72 4/113 5/155   252   1/60 2/67 3/88 4/133 5/145   285
6/156 7/197 8/217 9/251   6/153 7/166 8/261 9/273

Bonus points – Somerset 2, Glamorgan 4.

Bowling: *First Innings*—Waqar Younis 12–3–41–4; Watkin 13.4–2–61–3; Thomas 16–2–53–0; Cosker 14–3–42–2; Croft 13–1–49–1. *Second Innings*—Waqar Younis 11–0–84–0; Watkin 15–1–75–3; Thomas 15–2–38–5; Cosker 11.4–3–34–1; Croft 18–5–51–1.

Glamorgan

S. P. James lbw b Caddick	8	– not out	9
H. Morris b Caddick	165	– not out	1
A. Dale c Bowler b Caddick	8		
*M. P. Maynard c Bowler b Shine	142		
P. A. Cottey c Bowler b Shine	13		
R. D. B. Croft lbw b Rose	86		
†A. D. Shaw not out	53		
S. D. Thomas c Ecclestone b Trott	0		
Waqar Younis c Ecclestone b Trott	5		
S. L. Watkin c Shine b Trott	5		
D. A. Cosker b Caddick	7		
L-b 7, w 12, n-b 16	35	L-b 1	1

1/12 2/42 3/277 4/293 5/404   527   (no wkt) 11
6/475 7/476 8/482 9/495

Bonus points – Glamorgan 4, Somerset 4.

Bowling: *First Innings*—Caddick 34.4–5–132–4; Shine 17–3–88–2; Rose 29–3–152–1; Trott 11–0–74–3; Burns 7–0–65–0; Bowler 1–0–9–0. *Second Innings*—Caddick 1–0–5–0; Rose 0.2–0–5–0.

Umpires: G. Sharp and P. Willey.

THE CHAMPIONS

The dates on which the County Championship has been settled since 1979 are as follows:

			Final margin
1979	Essex	August 21	77 pts
1980	Middlesex	September 2	13 pts
1981	Nottinghamshire	September 14	2 pts
1982	Middlesex	September 11	39 pts
1983	Essex	September 13	16 pts
1984	Essex	September 11	14 pts
1985	Middlesex	September 17	18 pts
1986	Essex	September 10	28 pts
1987	Nottinghamshire	September 14	4 pts
1988	Worcestershire	September 16	1 pt
1989	Worcestershire	August 31	6 pts
1990	Middlesex	September 20	31 pts
1991	Essex	September 19	13 pts
1992	Essex	September 3	41 pts
1993	Middlesex	August 30	36 pts
1994	Warwickshire	September 2	42 pts
1995	Warwickshire	September 16	32 pts
1996	Leicestershire	September 21	27 pts
1997	Glamorgan	September 20	4 pts

Note: The earliest date on which the Championship has been won since it was expanded in 1895 was August 12, 1910, by Kent.

SURREY

Saqlain Mushtaq

Patron: HM The Queen
President: M. J. Stewart
Chairman: M. J. Soper
Chief Executive: P. J. S. Sheldon
Captain: A. J. Hollioake
Cricket Manager: K. T. Medlycott
Director of Cricket Development: M. J. Edwards
Head Groundsman: P. D. Brind
Scorer: K. R. Booth

Dave Gilbert's all-too-brief tenure as Surrey coach came to an end after two years in which a great deal was achieved at The Oval. Most obviously, Surrey won two titles – the Sunday League crown of 1996, their first success since 1982, was followed by the Benson and Hedges Cup in 1997. But Gilbert made his presence felt in other areas too: tearing down dressing-room barriers between capped and uncapped players, organising Surrey's first day/night match – which, disappointingly, was washed out – and making some valuable additions to the county's already enviably talented playing staff.

In 1997, Surrey took the season's first trophy when they crushed Kent by eight wickets in the final, but such was the pre-season level of expectation that their year went down as only a heavily qualified success. Many counties would have been delighted with joint eighth place in the Championship and fifth in the Sunday League, but not a side which – once Ben Hollioake had been blooded by England – could boast ten internationals. When they were eliminated from the NatWest Trophy in the second round, bowled out for 154 by a modest Nottinghamshire attack, accusations of complacency were quickly levelled.

Perhaps more could have been done to unite the powerful personalities in the squad, but cohesion was hindered by the two-edged sword of England calls. Adam and Ben Hollioake joined Alec Stewart and Graham Thorpe for the one-day internationals in May – and all four, plus Mark Butcher, were required at various times for Test matches. That may have accounted for an appalling start, which saw Surrey lose two games and draw five before claiming their first victory against Nottinghamshire in the last week of June. Surrey were 15th in the table after seven games. Almost inevitably, there was a late surge. Three consecutive victories in August took Surrey to the fringes of the title race, but a bad-tempered draw against Glamorgan saw them out of contention.

It took some time for Adam Hollioake to come to terms with full-time captaincy. No other side had so many egos crammed into one basket. But he handled them well and knew how to turn the screw on the opposition; you had only to see the fielders clustered around the bat in the Nottinghamshire match to appreciate that. His personal form fell away, however, after the all-conquering performances of 1996, and he finished the season with 15 first-class wickets and just one century, against Middlesex.

Surrey's biggest problem was that none of their batsmen came anywhere near scoring 1,000 runs for the club, although Thorpe's impressive England performances lifted him to 1,160 at 61.05 overall. Alistair Brown, who made a delayed entry into the side, was the most productive with 848 runs and three centuries. He also produced some thundering one-day innings – a Surrey-record 157 not out in a Sunday game against Leicestershire, which he soon surpassed with 203 against Hampshire, the first double-century in the competition's 29 seasons. But Brown's first-class opportunities came partly at the expense of the slower-scoring Darren Bicknell, who spent almost half his season piling up runs for the Second Eleven. When Bicknell did get a chance in the Championship, he was his usual reliable self, maintaining his high career average with 594 runs at 39.60. He seemed to be one of Gilbert's rare blind spots. And his ill luck continued in the winter with a back injury which threatened to ruin his 1998 season as well.

The tragic death of the popular Graham Kersey the previous winter left an aching void in the dressing-room and a decided problem behind the stumps whenever Stewart was away. Stewart hit a superb 271 not out against Yorkshire, his first Championship hundred since June 1995, as well as keeping wicket. But then he joined the Ashes campaign and left Surrey with a dilemma they could not resolve: James Knott had his father Alan's genes but not his flypaper gloves – in 1998 he plans to switch to leg-spin – and Jonathan Batty, though promising, needs to work on his game.

Among the bowlers, only Saqlain Mushtaq excelled. He finished fifth in the first-class averages – higher than any other spinner – with 32 wickets at 19.28, and would have taken more if his season had not been interrupted by one-day appearances for Pakistan. He was signed late and missed Surrey's final two matches, both of which they lost, as well as a fortnight in mid-season. Nevertheless, he made enough of an impression to win a new one-year contract, even though Pakistan are unlikely to free him for the whole of the 1998 season either. With Ian Salisbury sewing up a couple of victories in his first season at The Oval, and Rupesh Amin emerging as an orthodox left-armer, there is suddenly no shortage of slow-bowling talent.

Ironically, it is the seam attack, Surrey's area of greatest strength over the last few years, that is now showing cracks. Chris Lewis finished his two-year contract and opted to return to Leicestershire, his first county. He picked up 33 wickets during the season at just under 30, a disappointing return – although the leadership qualities he showed in the absence of Hollioake and Stewart must have caught Leicestershire's eye. Martin Bicknell threatened to have an injury-free season until normal service was resumed in the penultimate match against Lancashire and he tore knee ligaments. But his new-ball partner of old, Joey Benjamin, has surrendered a yard of pace to his advancing years. As for the young guns, Alex Tudor was ineffectual, and Ben Hollioake still has much to learn about bowling in the first-class game, let alone Test matches.

Gilbert's high-profile signings had promised to turn Surrey into the cricketing equivalent of Manchester United but, as he departed for an administrative post at Sussex, the job was clearly left half finished. Surrey were forced to cast around for a coach who could cope with the inflated ambitions of both players and supporters. They opted for Keith Medlycott, who had built up a strong reputation within the club, without being anything like as well known as many of the cricketers he must now control. – DAVID LLEWELLYN.

613

SURREY 1997

[Bill Smith]

Back row: J. N. Batty, I. D. K. Salisbury, A. J. Tudor, R. M. Pearson, I. J. Ward. Middle row: D. Naylor (physiotherapist), N. Shahid, G. J. Kennis, J. D. Ratcliffe, B. C. Hollioake, R. W. Nowell, J. A. Knott, D. R. Gilbert (cricket manager). Front row: C. C. Lewis, A. D. Brown, J. E. Benjamin, A. J. Stewart, A. J. Hollioake (captain), M. P. Bicknell, G. P. Thorpe, D. J. Bicknell, M. A. Butcher.
Insets: Saqlain Mushtaq, R. M. Amin.

SURREY RESULTS

All first-class matches – Played 17: Won 5, Lost 5, Drawn 7.
County Championship matches – Played 17: Won 5, Lost 5, Drawn 7.

Competition placings – Britannic Assurance County Championship, 8th equal;
NatWest Trophy, 2nd round; Benson and Hedges Cup, winners;
AXA Life League, 5th.

COUNTY CHAMPIONSHIP AVERAGES

BATTING

Cap		M	I	NO	R	HS	100s	50s	Avge	Ct/St
1991	G. P. Thorpe†	8	12	2	707	222	2	3	70.70	9
1985	A. J. Stewart†	9	14	1	726	271*	2	2	55.84	16
1994	A. D. Brown	14	21	1	848	170*	3	2	42.40	11
1990	D. J. Bicknell†	9	15	0	594	162	2	1	39.60	1
1995	A. J. Hollioake	13	19	0	731	182	1	5	38.47	10
	J. D. Ratcliffe	15	26	2	759	135	1	4	31.62	3
1996	M. A. Butcher†	13	22	1	659	79	0	5	31.38	19
	I. J. Ward	3	4	0	102	56	0	1	25.50	6
	B. C. Hollioake	12	19	0	483	76	0	3	25.42	10
	Saqlain Mushtaq§	8	10	4	149	41*	0	0	24.83	1
1996	C. C. Lewis	13	19	2	389	76	0	1	22.88	10
	A. J. Tudor	8	11	6	109	35*	0	0	21.80	0
1989	M. P. Bicknell†	15	20	5	305	74	0	2	20.33	8
	J. A. Knott	5	9	3	118	27*	0	0	19.66	8/1
	N. Shahid	7	11	0	198	34	0	0	18.00	4
1993	J. E. Benjamin	11	15	6	152	35	0	0	16.88	0
	I. D. K. Salisbury	13	17	2	159	30*	0	0	10.60	7
	G. J. Kennis	3	5	0	49	24	0	0	9.80	4
	R. M. Amin†	4	6	3	11	4*	0	0	3.66	2

Also batted: J. N. Batty (3 matches) 23, 8, 23* (7 ct, 1 st); R. M. Pearson (1 match) 1 (1 ct).

* Signifies not out.   † Born in Surrey.   § Overseas player.

BOWLING

	O	M	R	W	BB	5W/i	Avge
Saqlain Mushtaq	254.5	75	617	32	5-17	4	19.28
M. P. Bicknell	385.2	94	1,174	44	5-34	1	26.68
C. C. Lewis	291.4	66	970	33	5-42	1	29.39
A. J. Hollioake	108.4	19	388	13	4-22	0	29.84
I. D. K. Salisbury	314.1	65	936	30	6-19	2	31.20
A. J. Tudor	127.3	17	526	16	6-101	1	32.87
B. C. Hollioake	169.2	34	594	17	4-54	0	34.94
J. E. Benjamin	211	39	759	13	3-52	0	58.38

Also bowled: R. M. Amin 134.3–35–348–8; J. N. Batty 4–0–9–0; D. J. Bicknell 12–1–38–1;
A. D. Brown 16–4–37–0; M. A. Butcher 39–8–83–7; G. J. Kennis 1–0–4–0; R. M. Pearson
26–4–90–2; J. D. Ratcliffe 58–10–177–1; N. Shahid 5–0–14–0; G. P. Thorpe 4–0–13–0.

COUNTY RECORDS

Highest score for:	357*	R. Abel v Somerset at The Oval	1899
Highest score against:	366	N. H. Fairbrother (Lancashire) at The Oval	1990
Best bowling for:	10-43	T. Rushby v Somerset at Taunton	1921
Best bowling against:	10-28	W. P. Howell (Australians) at The Oval	1899
Highest total for:	811	v Somerset at The Oval	1899
Highest total against:	863	by Lancashire at The Oval	1990
Lowest total for:	14	v Essex at Chelmsford	1983
Lowest total against:	16	by MCC at Lord's	1872

SURREY v SOMERSET

At The Oval, April 23, 24, 25, 26. Drawn. Surrey 7 pts, Somerset 10 pts. Toss: Somerset. County debuts: I. D. K. Salisbury; M. Burns, S. Herzberg.

The season opened with a minute's silence for Surrey's late wicket-keeper, Graham Kersey, who died on New Year's Day, and Denis Compton, whose death had been announced that morning. Somerset dominated what cricket there was, but only 16 overs were possible on the last two days. Surrey's attack – which used nine bowlers – seemed determined to oblige the batsmen, especially Harden, who punished short and overpitched deliveries alike and remained unbeaten after seven hours and 48 minutes. Herzberg, now with his third county, joined him in a 109-run stand for the ninth wicket. Meanwhile, Surrey conceded a world record 86 extras. Under ECB regulations, no-balls and wides both counted for two each, plus any runs scored off them, but, even without that rule, it would have been a hefty 56. Lewis was the main contributor, bowling 11 actual no-balls, followed by Tudor, with eight. Surrey's much vaunted batting was just as ineffectual. After a promising start from the openers, Rose removed three prime wickets in nine balls. One of them was Stewart and, during his short innings, there were four recognised wicket-keepers on the field: Somerset played Burns and Holloway – both migrants from Warwickshire – alongside Turner.

Close of play: First day, Somerset 311-5 (R. J. Harden 81*, R. J. Turner 16*); Second day, Surrey 172-7 (I. D. K. Salisbury 16*); Third day, Surrey 209-8 (I. D. K. Salisbury 30*, A. J. Tudor 3*).

Somerset

M. N. Lathwell b Salisbury	50	G. D. Rose c Stewart b Lewis	10
M. E. Trescothick c Lewis		A. R. Caddick c Stewart b Tudor	11
b M. P. Bicknell	10	S. Herzberg c Butcher b Salisbury	56
*P. D. Bowler lbw b Tudor	63	K. J. Shine b Salisbury	1
R. J. Harden not out	136	B 10, l-b 16, w 8, n-b 52	86
P. C. L. Holloway c Stewart b Holloioake	22		
M. Burns lbw b Holloioake	0	1/37 2/105 3/215 4/280 5/280	463
†R. J. Turner b Lewis	18	6/315 7/327 8/347 9/456	

Bonus points – Somerset 4, Surrey 3 (Score at 120 overs: 356-8).

Bowling: M. P. Bicknell 25-8-61-1; Lewis 28.4-3-109-2; Tudor 24-3-83-2; Benjamin 6.2-1-28-0; Salisbury 34.3-10-107-3; Hol-lioake 20-8-30-2; Shahid 3-0-9-0; Thorpe 3-0-8-0; D. J. Bicknell 1-0-2-0.

Surrey

D. J. Bicknell c and b Herzberg	48	I. D. K. Salisbury not out	30
M. A. Butcher st Turner b Herzberg	46	M. P. Bicknell c Turner b Caddick	13
†A. J. Stewart lbw b Rose	6	A. J. Tudor not out	3
G. P. Thorpe lbw b Rose	8	B 2, l-b 9, w 4, n-b 8	23
N. Shahid c Turner b Shine	29		
*A. J. Hollioake c and b Rose	0	1/94 2/109 3/120 4/121 5/121 (8 wkts) 209	
C. C. Lewis c Holloway b Caddick	3	6/143 7/172 8/206	

J. E. Benjamin did not bat.

Bonus points – Surrey 1, Somerset 3.

Bowling: Caddick 26-2-94-2; Shine 9-2-41-1; Rose 18-7-35-3; Herzberg 18-9-25-2; Burns 5-3-3-0.

Umpires: B. Dudleston and J. H. Harris.

At Derby, May 7, 8, 9, 10. SURREY drew with DERBYSHIRE.

SURREY v GLOUCESTERSHIRE

At The Oval, May 14, 15, 16. Gloucestershire won by nine wickets. Gloucestershire 24 pts, Surrey 4 pts. Toss: Surrey.

A couple of quick one-twos at the start of each innings from the heavyweight Lawrence, continuing his comeback, provided some bright spots in a patchy match. Again, Surrey's batting was brittle, crumbling inside 39 overs on the first day. Tudor, their young pretender to English fast bowling's crown, took six for 101, his best figures yet, but had no back-up, and a dogged fifty from Russell – his eighth in ten Championship innings – helped set up a Gloucestershire lead of 256. Then their captain Alleyne turned in a career-best six for 64 to ensure that, despite a shortened second day, the match barely crept past tea on the third. Only Thorpe, who batted 72 overs for 81, resisted for long. Surrey's coterie of Chelsea fans were able to watch their team win the FA Cup on what should have been the fourth day. More importantly, Gloucestershire confirmed their position as early Championship leaders.

Close of play: First day, Gloucestershire 190-5 (M. W. Alleyne 30*, R. C. Russell 4*); Second day, Surrey 59-3 (G. P. Thorpe 10*, N. Shahid 13*).

Surrey

D. J. Bicknell lbw b Young	24	– c Wright b Lawrence	8
M. A. Butcher c Smith b Lawrence	1	– c Russell b Lawrence	15
†A. J. Stewart c Russell b Lawrence	0	– b Smith	11
G. P. Thorpe lbw b Alleyne	15	– c Ball b Alleyne	81
N. Shahid c Lynch b Young	9	– c Russell b Alleyne	34
*A. J. Hollioake c Ball b Young	8	– lbw b Alleyne	4
B. C. Hollioake c Wright b Smith	29	– (8) c Ball b Alleyne	19
J. D. Ratcliffe c Ball b Young	1	– (7) st Russell b Ball	45
M. P. Bicknell b Smith	16	– c Cunliffe b Alleyne	16
A. J. Tudor lbw b Smith	0	– lbw b Alleyne	10
J. E. Benjamin not out	3	– not out	1
B 1, w 8	9	B 2, l-b 9, w 6, n-b 8	25
	115		**269**

1/4 2/11 3/46 4/46 5/58   115   1/15 2/34 3/34 4/114 5/124   269
6/63 7/65 8/94 9/94   6/207 7/242 8/243 9/262

Bonus points – Gloucestershire 4.

Bowling: *First Innings*—Smith 12.5–4–35–3; Lawrence 7–0–35–2; Young 12–4–26–4; Alleyne 7–2–18–1. *Second Innings*—Smith 20–5–44–1; Lawrence 13–1–58–2; Young 15–5–26–0; Ball 16–7–35–1; Trainor 2–0–11–0; Alleyne 16.4–3–64–6; Hancock 4–0–20–0.

Gloucestershire

A. J. Wright lbw b M. P. Bicknell	0	– (2) not out	6
N. J. Trainor c Thorpe b Tudor	37	– (1) c Shahid b M. P. Bicknell	0
R. J. Cunliffe c Stewart b Tudor	47	– not out	9
M. A. Lynch c M. P. Bicknell b Tudor	33		
S. Young lbw b A. J. Hollioake	12		
*M. W. Alleyne c Stewart b M. P. Bicknell	31		
†R. C. Russell c Stewart b Tudor	59		
T. H. C. Hancock c Shahid b Tudor	49		
M. C. J. Ball lbw b A. J. Hollioake	5		
A. M. Smith c M. P. Bicknell b Tudor	35		
D. V. Lawrence not out	23		
L-b 6, n-b 34	40		
	371		**(1 wkt) 15**

1/4 2/82 3/128 4/135 5/175   371   1/0   (1 wkt) 15
6/214 7/295 8/302 9/332

Bonus points – Gloucestershire 4, Surrey 4.

Bowling: *First Innings*—M. P. Bicknell 24–6–65–2; Benjamin 23–5–72–0; B. C. Hollioake 18–6–45–0; Tudor 23.3–2–101–6; A. J. Hollioake 11–1–57–2; Shahid 1–0–1–0; D. J. Bicknell 2–0–11–0; Ratcliffe 3–0–13–0. *Second Innings*—M. P. Bicknell 2–0–7–1; Tudor 2–0–8–0.

Umpires: H. D. Bird and J. W. Holder.

At Leicester, May 21, 22, 23, 24. SURREY drew with LEICESTERSHIRE.

SURREY v ESSEX

At The Oval, June 4, 5, 6, 7. Essex won by 147 runs. Essex 23 pts, Surrey 6 pts. Toss: Essex.

Missing several England players, Surrey were all too easily cut down. On the opening day, they dropped Robinson twice and he almost reached his first hundred since July 1995; next morning, Cowan reduced Surrey to 36 for four. Then Brown, without a first-class century for almost as long as Robinson, rescued them, though a sharp delivery from Danny Law fractured his right hand. Brown defiantly still reached three figures in what was, for him, a sedate 135 balls, with two of his customary big sixes plus 15 fours. But he did not bat second time around. By then, Essex had slipped the leash and hared away. Gooch scored his first fifty of the season in any competition and Grayson added a century. Cowan, who took eight in the match, and Irani did the rest: Surrey, chasing 370, fell woefully short, despite 72 from the junior Hollioake, his maiden first-class fifty, though he had scored one a fortnight earlier in the one-day international at Lord's.

Close of play: First day, Surrey 0-0 (D. J. Bicknell 0*, I. D. K. Salisbury 0*); Second day, Essex 40-0 (G. A. Gooch 16*, D. D. J. Robinson 22*); Third day, Surrey 70-2 (J. D. Ratcliffe 30*, J. A. Knott 5*).

Essex

*G. A. Gooch b Tudor	26	– c Hollioake b Salisbury	56
D. D. J. Robinson c Knott b Tudor	98	– c Lewis b Benjamin	23
A. P. Grayson c Brown b Benjamin	4	– c Knott b Salisbury	105
S. G. Law c Brown b Lewis	27	– c sub b Lewis	10
R. C. Irani b Hollioake	24	– c Kennis b Hollioake	10
S. D. Peters lbw b Salisbury	33	– lbw b Hollioake	0
D. R. Law c Knott b Ratcliffe	7	– b Salisbury	1
†R. J. Rollins lbw b Salisbury	56	– c Bicknell b Benjamin	6
M. C. Ilott lbw b Benjamin	21	– not out	20
A. P. Cowan c Shahid b Lewis	38	– c Kennis b Hollioake	29
P. M. Such not out	1	– b Lewis	0
L-b 12, w 4, n-b 16	32	B 2, l-b 12, w 2, n-b 9	25

1/44 2/51 3/64 4/103 5/206   347   1/47 2/133 3/197 4/222 5/228   302
6/218 7/239 8/295 9/346   6/229 7/244 8/250 9/301

Bonus points – Essex 3, Surrey 4.

Bowling: *First Innings*—Tudor 21–3–77–2; Lewis 17–4–57–1; Benjamin 16–4–52–3; Hollioake 18–5–53–1; Salisbury 22–5–78–2; Kennis 1–0–4–0; Ratcliffe 5–2–14–1. *Second Innings*—Tudor 6–2–18–0; Benjamin 17–6–60–2; Ratcliffe 11–1–35–0; Lewis 13.1–3–39–2; Salisbury 24–4–79–3; Hollioake 14–3–53–3; Shahid 1–0–4–0.

Surrey

D. J. Bicknell c Cowan b Ilott	5	– c Rollins b Irani	34
I. D. K. Salisbury b Cowan	5	– (8) st Rollins b Such	6
G. J. Kennis c Gooch b Cowan	0	– (2) c Robinson b Cowan	0
J. D. Ratcliffe c S. G. Law b Such	31	– (3) c Cowan b D. R. Law	53
N. Shahid c Grayson b Cowan	12	– lbw b Irani	11
A. D. Brown b Cowan	109	– absent hurt	
B. C. Hollioake c Rollins b Cowan	17	– (6) c Rollins b Such	72
*C. C. Lewis c Rollins b Irani	40	– (7) c Peters b Cowan	6
†J. A. Knott not out	27	– (4) c S. G. Law b Cowan	6
A. J. Tudor lbw b Such	1	– (9) not out	7
J. E. Benjamin b D. R. Law	22	– (10) c S. G. Law b Irani	9
L-b 9, n-b 2	11	B 5, l-b 9, w 2, n-b 2	18

1/6 2/12 3/14 4/36 5/82   280   1/0 2/61 3/77 4/95 5/150   222
6/107 7/192 8/248 9/249   6/164 7/200 8/203 9/222

Bonus points – Surrey 2, Essex 4.

Bowling: *First Innings*—Ilott 11.5–1–58–1; Cowan 20–4–58–5; Irani 11–0–49–1; Such 19.1–3–66–2; D. R. Law 9.4–1–40–1. *Second Innings*—Ilott 2–1–2–0; Cowan 18–2–75–3; D. R. Law 11–3–20–1; Irani 23.2–8–51–3; Such 18–3–40–2; S. G. Law 7–2–20–0.

Umpires: A. A. Jones and D. R. Shepherd.

SURREY v YORKSHIRE

At The Oval, June 12, 13, 14, 16. Drawn. Surrey 11 pts, Yorkshire 10 pts. Toss: Surrey. Championship debut: Saqlain Mushtaq.

In a masterful display of batsmanship, Stewart converted his 40th first-class century into his second double-hundred by the close of the opening day, and then advanced to a career-best unbeaten 271. He batted for 399 minutes and 315 balls, and struck three sixes and 36 fours, overtaking his father Micky's best, 227 not out, en route. Surrey piled up 549 as Stewart shared three-figure stands with both Hollioakes and concluded by adding 54 with last man Benjamin. A largely ineffectual Yorkshire attack found it impossible to stem the flow of runs. And though Lehmann led them to 387, this was not enough to avoid the follow-on. Adam Hollioake chose not to enforce it, but his batsmen then returned to their old inconsistency, and were bowled out for 153 with Silverwood claiming a Championship-best five for 49. Rain closed in at lunch on the final day, leaving Surrey still without a Championship win.

Close of play: First day, Surrey 426-6 (A. J. Stewart 200*, I. D. K. Salisbury 2*); Second day, Yorkshire 226-4 (D. S. Lehmann 61*, C. White 13*); Third day, Yorkshire 19-0 (M. D. Moxon 11*, R. A. Kettleborough 8*).

Surrey

J. D. Ratcliffe c Byas b Stemp	43	– (7) b Silverwood	8
M. A. Butcher c Byas b Morris	45	– c Lehmann b Hartley	0
†A. J. Stewart not out	271	– (6) c Hartley b Stemp	32
B. C. Hollioake c Byas b Stemp	53	– c Byas b Stemp	10
A. D. Brown lbw b White	0	– lbw b Stemp	35
*A. J. Hollioake lbw b Morris	69	– (3) b Hartley	25
C. C. Lewis c Moxon b Stemp	6	– (1) c Byas b Silverwood	11
I. D. K. Salisbury c Lehmann b Silverwood	2	– lbw b Silverwood	0
M. P. Bicknell c Blakey b Hartley	15	– c White b Silverwood	0
Saqlain Mushtaq c and b Hartley	4	– not out	9
J. E. Benjamin b White	21	– c White b Silverwood	10
B 8, l-b 8, w 4	20	L-b 11, n-b 2	13
	549		**153**

1/78 2/92 3/233 4/234 5/366   1/1 2/35 3/49 4/49 5/94
6/404 7/429 8/483 9/495   6/123 7/129 8/129 9/129

Bonus points – Surrey 4, Yorkshire 3 (Score at 120 overs: 482-7).

Bowling: *First Innings*—Hartley 27-4-103-2; Silverwood 23-7-83-1; White 27.5-2-137-2; Stemp 46-8-148-3; Morris 12-3-62-2. *Second Innings*—Hartley 8-0-36-2; Silverwood 13.1-2-49-5; Stemp 17-3-44-3; White 8-2-13-0.

Yorkshire

M. D. Moxon c Lewis b Saqlain Mushtaq	57	– c Salisbury b Bicknell	19
R. A. Kettleborough b Bicknell	10	– b Bicknell	8
*D. Byas c Lewis b Saqlain Mushtaq	59	– lbw b Bicknell	0
D. S. Lehmann b Salisbury	100	– not out	57
B. Parker c Butcher b Saqlain Mushtaq	0	– b Saqlain Mushtaq	19
C. White c Brown b Saqlain Mushtaq	36		
†R. J. Blakey not out	53		
A. C. Morris b A. J. Hollioake	17		
P. J. Hartley b A. J. Hollioake	5		
C. E. W. Silverwood c Butcher b A. J. Hollioake	7		
R. D. Stemp b A. J. Hollioake	4		
L-b 7, w 2, n-b 30	39	B 2, l-b 6, n-b 4	12
	387	**(4 wkts)**	**115**

1/37 2/107 3/195 4/195 5/286   1/19 2/19 3/34 4/115
6/306 7/350 8/358 9/366

Bonus points – Yorkshire 4, Surrey 4.

Bowling: *First Innings*—Bicknell 20–7–67–1; Lewis 8–2–22–0; Saqlain Mushtaq 45–11–118–4; Benjamin 8–0–49–0; Salisbury 22–4–83–1; B. C. Hollioake 3–0–19–0; A. J. Hollioake 4.5–1–22–4. *Second Innings*—Lewis 10–8–7–0; Bicknell 11–3–32–3; Saqlain Mushtaq 6.1–2–16–1; Salisbury 1–0–6–0; Benjamin 3–0–14–0; B. C. Hollioake 4–0–26–0; A. J. Hollioake 2–0–6–0.

Umpires: R. Julian and A. G. T. Whitehead.

At Worcester, June 18, 19, 20, 21. SURREY drew with WORCESTERSHIRE.

SURREY v NOTTINGHAMSHIRE

At The Oval, June 27, 28, 29, 30. Surrey won by 131 runs. Surrey 17 pts, Nottinghamshire 4 pts. Toss: Surrey.

On the final day of the wettest June in decades, Surrey completed a Championship win at last. After their first attempt at floodlit Sunday League cricket had been washed out on the Thursday, they had to wait another two days before play finally began on Sunday. Though the finish required collusion between the captains and contrived declarations, there was no tacky bowling and the match had a thrilling conclusion. The pavilion clock showed half a minute remaining when Salisbury began the final over – and he immediately found Bowen's edge. Shades of Laker and Lock had haunted the ground as fielders crowded the nervy batsmen and Surrey's newly signed spinners Salisbury and Saqlain Mushtaq wheeled away, bewitching, bothering and bewildering. Salisbury took six for 19 in just 18.1 overs, by far his best figures for his new county, and Saqlain two for 34 in 26 overs.

Close of play: First day, No play; Second day, No play; Third day, Nottinghamshire 73-1 (P. R. Pollard 37*, M. P. Dowman 24*).

Surrey

J. D. Ratcliffe c Afzaal b Franks	9	– (2) c Dowman b Evans	11
M. A. Butcher c Astle b Franks	7	– (1) c Pollard b Franks	10
G. P. Thorpe c Noon b Evans	3	– c Franks b Bowen	34
*A. J. Hollioake c Noon b Evans	2	– c Hindson b Evans	7
A. D. Brown c Noon b Bowen	27	– c Robinson b Franks	1
B. C. Hollioake c Bowen b Franks	44	– c Noon b Hindson	10
C. C. Lewis run out	48	– not out	33
†J. A. Knott c Noon b Hindson	10	– not out	7
I. D. K. Salisbury c and b Franks	12		
M. P. Bicknell not out	21		
Saqlain Mushtaq not out	7		
B 3, l-b 4, n-b 4	11	B 8, w 2	10

1/12 2/15 3/19 4/21 5/67 (9 wkts dec.) 201   1/13 2/27 3/41 (6 wkts dec.) 123
6/103 7/145 8/169 9/178   4/50 5/66 6/98

Bonus points – Surrey 1, Nottinghamshire 4.

Bowling: *First Innings*—Evans 21–9–35–2; Franks 18.4–4–47–4; Bowen 18–4–56–1; Astle 5–1–26–0; Hindson 16.2–6–30–1. *Second Innings*—Evans 8–0–20–2; Franks 9–3–30–2; Bowen 9.2–1–34–1; Hindson 8–3–31–1.

Nottinghamshire

P. R. Pollard not out	37	– c Salisbury b Saqlain Mushtaq	...	33
*R. T. Robinson c Bicknell b Lewis	7	– c Bicknell b Lewis		10
M. P. Dowman not out	24	– lbw b Bicknell		11
N. J. Astle (did not bat)		– c Thorpe b Salisbury		11
A. A. Metcalfe (did not bat)		– c Thorpe b Salisbury		4
U. Afzaal (did not bat)		– b Salisbury		12
†W. M. Noon (did not bat)		– c Thorpe b Salisbury		7
K. P. Evans (did not bat)		– c Butcher b Salisbury		4
J. E. Hindson (did not bat)		– lbw b Saqlain Mushtaq		6
P. J. Franks (did not bat)		– not out		1
M. N. Bowen (did not bat)		– c Knott b Salisbury		0
L-b 1, n-b 4	5	B 12, l-b 5, n-b 4		21

1/14		(1 wkt dec.) 73	1/14 2/48 3/78 4/79 5/88
			6/95 7/101 8/117 9/120

(second innings total) 120

Bowling: *First Innings*—Bicknell 5–1–10–0; Lewis 7–2–20–1; Saqlain Mushtaq 8–2–15–0; A. J. Hollioake 4–1–7–0; Salisbury 4–1–19–0; Ratcliffe 1–0–1–0. *Second Innings*—Bicknell 11–3–30–1; Lewis 7–1–20–1; Saqlain Mushtaq 26–13–34–2; Salisbury 18.1–11–19–6; A. J. Hollioake 1–1–0–0.

Umpires: J. H. Hampshire and N. T. Plews.

At Birmingham, July 2, 3, 4, 5. SURREY lost to WARWICKSHIRE by five wickets.

SURREY v HAMPSHIRE

At Guildford, July 16, 17, 18, 19. Surrey won by nine wickets. Surrey 24 pts, Hampshire 7 pts. Toss: Surrey.

Surrey looked like winning in three days when Hampshire followed on 174 behind and collapsed to 71 for seven. But Aymes and Renshaw prolonged the game with a stand of 123. Renshaw scored a maiden fifty and Aymes missed a deserved hundred when his last partner became Bicknell's fifth wicket of the innings and ninth of the match; it was a rare occasion in 1997 when Bicknell delivered the figures to match his form. Surrey knocked off their target on the final afternoon. Their first innings had featured five half-centuries, some of which could and should have been hundreds; Stewart and Thorpe got very close, and Adam Hollioake scored 75 in 69 balls. Lewis scored his only fifty of the season and added 62 with last man Tudor, which proved crucial in enforcing the follow-on. It was unreasonable to expect Hayden to score his fifth Championship century in as many matches. He did get halfway before Bicknell bowled him, but there was little support. Stewart was hit under the eye keeping wicket on the third morning; Butcher took over while he had stitches.

Close of play: First day, Surrey 457-9 (C. C. Lewis 66*, A. J. Tudor 27*); Second day, Hampshire 200-5 (J. P. Stephenson 18*, A. N. Aymes 20*); Third day, Hampshire 227-8 (A. N. Aymes 83*, S. M. Milburn 12*).

Surrey

J. D. Ratcliffe c Keech b Milburn	1	– (2) not out	29
M. A. Butcher c Keech b Stephenson	69	– (1) c Bovill b Udal	20
†A. J. Stewart c Aymes b Milburn	98		
G. P. Thorpe c Aymes b Bovill	84	– (3) not out	26
A. D. Brown c Renshaw b Stephenson	7		
*A. J. Hollioake st Aymes b Keech	75		
B. C. Hollioake c James b Milburn	0		
C. C. Lewis c Udal b Bovill	76		
M. P. Bicknell b Stephenson	0		
I. D. K. Salisbury c Hayden b Bovill	11		
A. J. Tudor not out	35		
B 3, l-b 10, w 4, n-b 4	21	L-b 1, w 2	3

1/3 2/177 3/183 4/203 5/327   477   1/42   (1 wkt) 78
6/328 7/367 8/368 9/415

Bonus points – Surrey 4, Hampshire 4.

Bowling: First Innings—Bovill 24.1–4–116–3; Milburn 26–1–97–3; Renshaw 15–3–86–0; Udal 13–1–43–0; Stephenson 28–1–110–3; Keech 4–0–12–1. *Second Innings*—Milburn 5–2–17–0; Bovill 8–3–19–0; Udal 6–0–29–1; Renshaw 3–1–11–0; Smith 0.1–0–1–0.

Hampshire

J. S. Laney lbw b B. C. Hollioake	41	– b Bicknell	10
M. L. Hayden b Bicknell	58	– lbw b Bicknell	0
K. D. James c Brown b Bicknell	8	– lbw b Bicknell	0
R. A. Smith c Salisbury b Lewis	25	– lbw b Lewis	1
M. Keech hit wkt b Lewis	12	– lbw b Bicknell	7
*J. P. Stephenson c Thorpe b Salisbury	18	– c sub b Tudor	26
†A. N. Aymes c B. C. Hollioake b Salisbury	45	– not out	96
S. D. Udal c Stewart b Bicknell	29	– c A. J. Hollioake b B. C. Hollioake	0
S. J. Renshaw c A. J. Hollioake b Bicknell	16	– lbw b A. J. Hollioake	56
S. M. Milburn c Butcher b Salisbury	19	– run out	16
J. N. B. Bovill not out	1	– c Butcher b Bicknell	6
B 7, l-b 6, w 6, n-b 12	31	B 15, l-b 7, w 2, n-b 9	33

1/76 2/114 3/125 4/153 5/158   303   1/1 2/13 3/16 4/22 5/24   251
6/204 7/251 8/279 9/293   6/70 7/71 8/194 9/233

Bonus points – Hampshire 3, Surrey 4.

Bowling: First Innings—Bicknell 30–5–88–4; Lewis 15–5–31–2; Tudor 8–0–46–0; A. J. Hollioake 2–0–7–0; Salisbury 32.3–7–83–3; B. C. Hollioake 5–1–11–1; Ratcliffe 9–2–24–0. *Second Innings*—Bicknell 18.3–10–34–5; Lewis 14–2–66–1; B. C. Hollioake 5–2–14–1; Tudor 6–0–44–1; Salisbury 16–0–40–0; A. J. Hollioake 6–1–31–1.

Umpires: J. W. Holder and M. J. Kitchen.

At Northampton, July 23, 24, 25, 26. SURREY drew with NORTHAMPTONSHIRE.

SURREY v DURHAM

At The Oval, August 6, 7, 8, 9. Surrey won by nine wickets. Surrey 24 pts, Durham 4 pts. Toss: Surrey. First-class debut: R. M. Amin.

The Oval has become a whipping post for Durham – on their two previous visits, they lost by an innings. In fact, they had lost all their five first-class and six one-day games against Surrey, and a spineless collapse maintained that record. On a drying pitch (half the opening day had been lost to rain), Saqlain Mushtaq took his first five-wicket haul for Surrey and added a second when Durham followed on. He was supported by 19-year-old slow left-armer Rupesh Amin, who replaced the injured Salisbury. It was Martin Bicknell and Benjamin who started the rot, however, after Durham's first innings reached 67 for one. Their remaining wickets barely doubled that. They improved second time round, but Surrey passed 61 to win on the final morning. Despite losing four players to the Nottingham Test, their first-innings batting was as solid and evenly spread as concrete, led by Ratcliffe and Ian Ward, who made a maiden fifty. Saqlain made his best county score before taking control with the ball.

Close of play: First day, Surrey 164-2 (J. D. Ratcliffe 54*, I. J. Ward 34*); Second day, Durham 120-6 (R. M. S. Weston 18*, M. M. Betts 4*); Third day, Durham 241-7 (M. M. Betts 0*).

Surrey

D. J. Bicknell c Speight b Betts	33	– c Boon b Boiling	29
M. A. Butcher b Foster	24	– not out	27
J. D. Ratcliffe c Boon b Foster	76	– not out	6
I. J. Ward lbw b Wood	56		
A. D. Brown c Boon b Wood	7		
*C. C. Lewis c Boon b Boiling	24		
†J. N. Batty c Brown b Wood	8		
M. P. Bicknell b Wood	5		
Saqlain Mushtaq not out	41		
J. E. Benjamin c Weston b Foster	35		
R. M. Amin not out	4		
B 4, l-b 17, w 10, n-b 6	37	B 1, l-b 1	2

1/63 2/67 3/215 4/224 5/235 (9 wkts dec.) 350   1/58 (1 wkt) 64
6/253 7/263 8/266 9/327

Bonus points – Surrey 4, Durham 4.

Bowling: *First Innings*—Brown 30.3–4–101–0; Wood 17–0–73–4; Betts 22–8–58–1; Foster 20–7–52–3; Boiling 11–2–45–1. *Second Innings*—Brown 7–2–17–0; Betts 5–0–22–0; Wood 2–0–16–0; Boiling 0.5–0–7–1.

Durham

J. J. B. Lewis c Lewis b Benjamin	29	– c Batty b M. P. Bicknell	39
S. Hutton lbw b M. P. Bicknell	4	– c Brown b Saqlain Mushtaq	19
J. E. Morris lbw b Benjamin	30	– b Amin	53
*D. C. Boon c Ward b Saqlain Mushtaq	10	– c Ward b Saqlain Mushtaq	34
†M. P. Speight c Brown b Saqlain Mushtaq	14	– lbw b Benjamin	51
R. M. S. Weston b Saqlain Mushtaq	21	– c Butcher b Saqlain Mushtaq	18
M. J. Foster c Ward b Saqlain Mushtaq	0	– c Butcher b Amin	9
M. M. Betts c Lewis b M. P. Bicknell	12	– c Lewis b Saqlain Mushtaq	20
J. Boiling c Ward b Saqlain Mushtaq	0	– c Butcher b Amin	3
J. Wood not out	0	– b Saqlain Mushtaq	3
S. J. E. Brown c Brown b M. P. Bicknell	0	– not out	0
B 3, l-b 7, n-b 6	16	B 11, l-b 8, n-b 6	25

1/21 2/67 3/70 4/96 5/109 136   1/36 2/116 3/118 4/209 5/215 274
6/109 7/130 8/130 9/132 6/239 7/241 8/260 9/274

Bonus points – Surrey 4.

Bowling: *First Innings*—M. P. Bicknell 14–5–37–3; Lewis 6–1–23–0; Amin 17–4–27–0; Benjamin 7–1–22–2; Saqlain Mushtaq 14–6–17–5. *Second Innings*—M. P. Bicknell 10–4–24–1; Benjamin 10–1–34–1; Lewis 6–2–17–0; Saqlain Mushtaq 43.2–14–111–5; Amin 36–11–58–3; Ratcliffe 2–0–11–0.

Umpires: V. A. Holder and R. Palmer.

At Lord's, August 15, 16, 17. SURREY beat MIDDLESEX by an innings and 125 runs.

At Hove, August 28, 29, 30. SURREY beat SUSSEX by an innings and 101 runs.

SURREY v GLAMORGAN

At The Oval, September 2, 3, 4, 5. Drawn. Surrey 8 pts, Glamorgan 11 pts. Toss: Surrey.

A tense match turned to open bitterness when Maynard accepted an offer of bad light to end the game. Glamorgan had shown little interest in pursuing 254 in 46 overs after losing three wickets, preferring the certainty of three points for a draw; they were justified by events when they took the Championship by four points a fortnight later. But Surrey, 20 points behind at the start, had still harboured hopes themselves. Their captain Adam Hollioake threw the ball down in disgust. And Dave Gilbert, their coach, called Glamorgan's decision "outrageous". He was quoted as saying that they could expect no favours when Surrey played the other title contenders Kent in the final match, adding later that Kent deserved to be champions. Some Welshmen took this to mean that Surrey might not try, and the bad blood lasted for the rest of the season. Surrey had been outplayed for most of the match. Having chosen to bat, their team of ten international players succumbed for 204, and Glamorgan built a lead of 234 against indifferent bowling. Surrey did fight back, thanks to Thorpe, who played the kind of innings modern England batsmen ought to play in county cricket but rarely do. He was both fluent and determined, and took total control to score an almost chanceless career-best 222, in 438 minutes and 305 balls, with 21 fours. He was eighth out, and there was no declaration, which made Surrey's subsequent accusations rather childish.

Close of play: First day, Glamorgan 133-2 (A. Dale 28*, M. P. Maynard 56*); Second day, Glamorgan 363-7 (S. D. Thomas 25*, Waqar Younis 12*); Third day, Surrey 324-6 (G. P. Thorpe 140*, Saqlain Mushtaq 11*).

Surrey

M. A. Butcher lbw b Watkin	20	– c Cosker b Watkin		7
†A. J. Stewart c Shaw b Waqar Younis	6	– c Shaw b Waqar Younis		2
J. D. Ratcliffe c Morris b Croft	9	– c Cottey b Croft		14
G. P. Thorpe c Shaw b Thomas	13	– c Watkin b Cosker		222
A. D. Brown c Shaw b Watkin	60	– run out		41
*A. J. Hollioake lbw b Croft	22	– lbw b Waqar Younis		65
B. C. Hollioake lbw b Croft	14	– b Thomas		31
Saqlain Mushtaq c Shaw b Thomas	21	– c Morris b Croft		17
M. P. Bicknell c James b Waqar Younis	17	– st Shaw b Cosker		53
I. D. K. Salisbury not out	8	– c Cottey b Cosker		14
J. E. Benjamin c Shaw b Thomas	3	– not out		1
B 1, l-b 2, w 6, n-b 2	11	B 5, l-b 11, w 4		20

1/11 2/36 3/49 4/60 5/96   204   1/5 2/9 3/32 4/95 5/215   487
6/138 7/154 8/186 9/196   6/264 7/341 8/451 9/482

Bonus points – Surrey 1, Glamorgan 4.

Bowling: *First Innings*—Waqar Younis 16–3–55–2; Watkin 16–6–42–2; Thomas 11.2–3–36–3; Croft 23–5–54–3; Cosker 5–1–14–0. *Second Innings*—Waqar Younis 23–4–79–2; Watkin 22–1–78–1; Croft 37–4–128–2; Cosker 23.4–2–107–3; Thomas 24–3–79–1.

Glamorgan

S. P. James lbw b Bicknell	23	– c Stewart b Salisbury	28
H. Morris c Stewart b Saqlain Mushtaq	16	– c Stewart b Bicknell	9
A. Dale c Stewart b B. C. Hollioake	72		
*M. P. Maynard c and b Bicknell	76	– (5) not out	26
P. A. Cottey c Stewart b B. C. Hollioake	34		
R. D. B. Croft lbw b B. C. Hollioake	53	– (4) c A. J. Hollioake b Salisbury	7
†A. D. Shaw lbw b Salisbury	8	– (3) not out	36
S. D. Thomas not out	75		
Waqar Younis c Butcher b Saqlain Mushtaq	15		
S. L. Watkin lbw b A. J. Hollioake	19		
D. A. Cosker lbw b A. J. Hollioake	0		
B 8, l-b 15, w 4, n-b 20	47	L-b 1	1

1/30 2/50 3/172 4/229 5/264   **438**   1/21 2/55 3/65   (3 wkts) 107
6/305 7/337 8/366 9/438

Bonus points – Glamorgan 4, Surrey 4.

Bowling: *First Innings*—Bicknell 30–4–93–2; Benjamin 13–0–72–0; Saqlain Mushtaq 31–8–96–2; B. C. Hollioake 25–3–91–3; A. J. Hollioake 2–0–12–2; Salisbury 14–1–51–1. *Second Innings*—Bicknell 11–1–32–1; Benjamin 4–0–22–0; Saqlain Mushtaq 5–0–19–0; Salisbury 11–2–31–2; A. J. Hollioake 1–0–2–0.

Umpires: G. I. Burgess and J. F. Steele.

SURREY v LANCASHIRE

At The Oval, September 10, 11, 12. Lancashire won by an innings and 55 runs. Lancashire 24 pts, Surrey 3 pts. Toss: Lancashire.

There were shades of Lancashire's visit to The Oval in 1990 – the time they scored 863. Had they batted on, they might have challenged that. Instead they declared, and demolished Surrey, who still seemed distracted by their quarrel with Glamorgan, in three days. Atherton dominated an opening stand of 259, a first-wicket record in this fixture; his 149 was his highest for Lancashire since May 1995, and his partner, Wood, converted a maiden century into 155. Fairbrother added another hundred, while Crawley and Lloyd chipped in with sixties. The home bowlers – all ten of them – failed to master the basics of line and length and were duly punished. Youngsters Amin and Ben Hollioake each conceded over 100; Atherton hit one Hollioake over for 18. Surrey's batsmen fared little better. Without Thorpe, resting a bad shoulder, they folded to the spin of Watkinson and Keedy, and followed on 322 behind. Keedy completed the win with a career-best six for 79, which gave him ten in the match.

Close of play: First day, Lancashire 459-4 (N. H. Fairbrother 53*); Second day, Surrey 254-7 (I. D. K. Salisbury 1*, J. E. Benjamin 0*).

Lancashire

N. T. Wood c B. C. Hollioake b Butcher	.155	G. Chapple c B. C. Hollioake b D. J. Bicknell	5
M. A. Atherton c Stewart b A. J. Hollioake	.149	G. D. Lloyd not out	65
J. P. Crawley b Amin	64	B 4, l-b 2, w 12, n-b 24	42
N. H. Fairbrother not out	.112	1/259 2/373 3/446 4/459 (4 wkts dec.)	592

*M. Watkinson, P. M. Ridgway, †W. K. Hegg, P. J. Martin and G. Keedy did not bat.

Bonus points – Lancashire 4, Surrey 1 (Score at 120 overs: 516-4).

Bowling: M. P. Bicknell 14–3–56–0; Benjamin 22–3–97–0; A. J. Hollioake 17–2–61–1; B. C. Hollioake 18–2–101–0; Salisbury 20–2–77–0; Amin 28–5–135–1; Ratcliffe 3–1–11–0; Brown 1–0–13–0; D. J. Bicknell 4–0–12–1; Butcher 8–1–23–1.

Surrey

	First Innings		Second Innings	
D. J. Bicknell lbw b Watkinson	74	– lbw b Martin	1
M. A. Butcher c Fairbrother b Watkinson	49	– lbw b Watkinson	52
J. D. Ratcliffe c Watkinson b Keedy	12	– b Keedy	90
†A. J. Stewart c Hegg b Keedy	73	– lbw b Watkinson	7
A. D. Brown b Watkinson	0	– c Lloyd b Keedy	47
*A. J. Hollioake c Lloyd b Keedy	4	– b Chapple	8
B. C. Hollioake c Wood b Keedy	18	– c Fairbrother b Keedy	8
I. D. K. Salisbury b Martin	1	– c Lloyd b Keedy	12
J. E. Benjamin c Fairbrother b Martin	0	– (10) not out	24
R. M. Amin c Hegg b Martin	2	– (11) lbw b Keedy	0
M. P. Bicknell not out	14	– (9) lbw b Keedy	3
B 5, l-b 6, n-b 2	13	B 3, l-b 12	15

1/103 2/118 3/171 4/171 5/204   270   1/8 2/89 3/97 4/173 5/184   267
6/245 7/254 8/254 9/255   6/212 7/239 8/242 9/257

Bonus points – Surrey 2, Lancashire 4.

Bowling: *First Innings*—Martin 12.5–4–42–3; Chapple 7–2–18–0; Ridgway 5–1–30–0; Keedy 35–11–94–4; Watkinson 25–7–75–3. *Second Innings*—Martin 13–3–58–1; Chapple 11–1–48–1; Keedy 29.4–6–79–6; Watkinson 16–0–53–2; Ridgway 2–0–14–0.

Umpires: A. Clarkson and P. Willey.

At Canterbury, September 18, 19, 20. SURREY lost to KENT by five wickets.

YOUNG CRICKETER OF THE YEAR

(Elected by the Cricket Writers' Club)

1950	R. Tattersall	1975	A. Kennedy
1951	P. B. H. May	1976	G. Miller
1952	F. S. Trueman	1977	I. T. Botham
1953	M. C. Cowdrey	1978	D. I. Gower
1954	P. J. Loader	1979	P. W. G. Parker
1955	K. F. Barrington	1980	G. R. Dilley
1956	B. Taylor	1981	M. W. Gatting
1957	M. J. Stewart	1982	N. G. Cowans
1958	A. C. D. Ingleby-Mackenzie	1983	N. A. Foster
1959	G. Pullar	1984	R. J. Bailey
1960	D. A. Allen	1985	D. V. Lawrence
1961	P. H. Parfitt	1986 {	A. A. Metcalfe
1962	P. J. Sharpe		J. J. Whitaker
1963	G. Boycott	1987	R. J. Blakey
1964	J. M. Brearley	1988	M. P. Maynard
1965	A. P. E. Knott	1989	N. Hussain
1966	D. L. Underwood	1990	M. A. Atherton
1967	A. W. Greig	1991	M. R. Ramprakash
1968	R. M. H. Cottam	1992	I. D. K. Salisbury
1969	A. Ward	1993	M. N. Lathwell
1970	C. M. Old	1994	J. P. Crawley
1971	J. Whitehouse	1995	A. Symonds
1972	D. R. Owen-Thomas	1996	C. E. W. Silverwood
1973	M. Hendrick	1997	B. C. Hollioake
1974	P. H. Edmonds		

An additional award, in memory of Norman Preston, Editor of *Wisden* from 1951 to 1980, was made to C. W. J. Athey in 1980.

SUSSEX

Mark Robinson

President: The Duke of Richmond and Gordon

Chairman: R. G. Marlar

Chief Executive: A. C. S. Pigott

Captain: 1997 – P. Moores
1998 – C. J. Adams

Player-coach: P. Moores

Director of Cricket: D. R. Gilbert

Head Groundsman: P. Eaton

Scorer: L. V. Chandler

It was no surprise that 1997 was a struggle for Sussex; six capped players, including Alan Wells, last year's captain, had left amid confusion and bitterness. It turned out even worse than they feared: one of the most difficult seasons in their 158-year history. The county suffered a dismal double, wooden spoons in both County Championship and Sunday League, lost to the British Universities in the Benson and Hedges Cup, and found solace only in the NatWest Trophy, where two startling wins galvanised the club's supporters and distracted attention from day-to-day reality.

These successes helped members believe that Sussex were well placed to recover, as a new, forward-thinking, regime got into its stride. Nothing on the field could quite match the drama that preceded the season, when a members' revolt forced out the old committee at the annual general meeting. A fortnight earlier, chairman Alan Caffyn had resigned, following criticism of the club management. His successor, Ken Hopkins, was also challenged by the Sussex 2000 group, headed by Tony Pigott, the club's former opening bowler.

They tabled a motion of no confidence for a special general meeting. But the AGM made that unnecessary. A thousand members packed into Brighton's Grand Hotel, and the insurgents came to power almost by acclamation. Jim May, who had just been elected to the committee, proposed the rejection of the annual report. To loud applause, he labelled the management style of the committee "aloof, arrogant and autocratic". He said the team had fallen apart because of poor man-management and communication; the committee could no longer be trusted. They bowed to overwhelming opposition and resigned. The secretary, Nigel Bett, followed soon afterwards.

Former captain Robin Marlar, a management consultant and for many years cricket correspondent of the *Sunday Times*, was elected chairman, having been an outspoken critic of the Hove authorities for years. Pigott left his coaching post at Surrey and was installed as chief executive and director of cricket. They promised a change of atmosphere, and there was a sense that Hove, instead of being a backwater, was now a place open to new ideas and new developments in the game. Sussex were one of three counties to experiment by staging a Sunday League game under floodlights in midweek (it was fairly successful), and they played around with start times in the Championship to try and increase attendances.

Above all, Sussex tried to make big-name signings, including perhaps the biggest name of all: Australian leg-spin wizard Shane Warne. He decided not to come, despite rumours of large financial inducements. But Sussex did beat off the competition to sign former Derbyshire batsman Chris Adams, who was given the captaincy and a jumbo-sized contract. They also engaged New South Wales batsman Michael Bevan, who was keen to find a county after Yorkshire opted to keep his stand-in, Darren Lehmann.

Another Australian signing was quite a coup: Dave Gilbert was hired as director of cricket. Gilbert had spent two rewarding years at Surrey, coaching them to one trophy each year. But he hankered to be involved in the day-to-day running of a club. His brief was to work closely with Pigott and to link administration and players. Peter Moores lost the captaincy, but was named player-coach for 1998, his benefit year, and assured that he had a long-term role. "Peter's motivation, enthusiasm and general management of the cricket side have been outstanding," said Pigott. Moores had had to struggle on without a coach and vice-captain in the closing stages, after Desmond Haynes left, and Bill Athey retired – so he had effectively started his new job already.

Haynes's days were numbered once Pigott assumed greater control of team selection. The news that he was to be axed with a year of his contract to go came in early August, ten days before Sussex's NatWest semi-final with Warwickshire, and less than a week after a quarter-final thriller at Derby. Set 328 – a record to win in this competition – Sussex got home with four balls to spare, led by Rajesh Rao, whose 158 was their highest ever one-day innings. Earlier, they had knocked out holders Lancashire in one of the biggest upsets of the entire season. On this occasion, another unsung player, Keith Greenfield, played the hero.

Generally, batting was even more of a weakness than it had been in previous years. In 1997, Sussex were bowled out for under 200 in 13 of their 31 Championship innings. From late June, when Glamorgan dismissed them for 54 and 67, they lost eight out of their last ten games, three by an innings and two by nine wickets. There was just one win in the Championship, plus two in the Sunday League and two in the Benson and Hedges Cup.

But for Neil Taylor, Sussex would have plumbed even greater depths. The 37-year-old Taylor had joined from Kent, effectively a swap with Alan Wells. He had not had a first-class match since July 1995, but was the only batsman to make 1,000 runs. Greenfield was unable to transfer his one-day form to the longer game; Neil Lenham was often injured and eventually retired to become marketing manager. Former England batsman Athey also called it a day after a career spanning three counties, 22 seasons and 25,453 runs at 35.69. He moved to coach Worcestershire. It was difficult for the youngsters to shine, but the Newells, Keith and Mark, suggested their potential and Toby Peirce could develop into a sound opening batsman. Sussex took on another opener, Wasim Khan from Warwickshire, for 1998.

With Ed Giddins banned for drug use and sacked from the club, Ian Salisbury gone to Surrey, and Jason Lewry sidelined by a back operation, Sussex paraded a much-changed attack. Yet they gained 57 bowling points, as many as champions Glamorgan. Mark Robinson, signed from Yorkshire, played all 17 Championship games and took 48 wickets – it would have been more but for his team's propensity for innings defeats. But it was an under-achieving summer for Paul Jarvis, who was injured for several games, and Vasbert Drakes, who was not retained as overseas player. James Kirtley missed most of the first seven weeks with a side strain and was wayward on his return, but his later control confirmed a genuine fast bowling prospect. New leg-spinner Amer Khan stepped into Salisbury's footsteps and off-spinner Justin Bates looked promising.

Pigott remained anxious to push the cause of Sussex on and off the field. The next couple of seasons may not bring immediate success, but they are unlikely to be dull. – ANDY ARLIDGE.

SUSSEX 1997

[Bill Smith]

Back row: T. A. Radford, A. D. Edwards, G. R. Haywood, J. J. Bates, R. S. C. Martin-Jenkins, M. J. Thursfield, M. R. Strong, J. P. Pyemont, A. A. Khan, R. K. Rao. Middle row: L. V. Chandler (First Eleven scorer), S. M. B. Robertson (physiotherapist), N. C. Phillips, K. Newell, N. R. Taylor, M. A. Robinson, R. J. Kirtley, M. Newell, S. Humphries, M. T. E. Peirce, J. Hartridge (Second Eleven scorer). Front row: K. Greenfield, V. C. Drakes, C. W. J. Athey, C. E. Waller (coach), P. Moores (captain), D. L. Haynes (First Eleven coach), N. J. Lenham, P. W. Jarvis, J. D. Lewry.

SUSSEX RESULTS

All first-class matches – Played 19: Won 2, Lost 10, Drawn 7.

County Championship matches – Played 17: Won 1, Lost 10, Drawn 6.

Competition placings – Britannic Assurance County Championship, 18th; NatWest Trophy, s-f; Benson and Hedges Cup, 4th in Group C; AXA Life League, 18th.

COUNTY CHAMPIONSHIP AVERAGES

BATTING

Cap		M	I	NO	R	HS	100s	50s	Avge	Ct
1997	N. R. Taylor...........	15	27	1	996	127	3	5	38.30	2
1993	C. W. J. Athey.........	12	21	2	682	138*	1	5	35.89	9
	K. Newell†	17	31	2	827	112	2	3	28.51	2
	M. T. E. Peirce	11	21	0	539	104	1	3	25.66	8
	J. R. Carpenter.........	3	6	0	153	63	0	1	25.50	2
1990	N. J. Lenham†	6	10	0	245	93	0	2	24.50	1
	M. Newell†	10	19	1	435	100	1	3	24.16	8
1994	P. W. Jarvis	11	18	2	374	64	0	4	23.37	5
	R. S. C. Martin-Jenkins..	2	4	1	68	36*	0	0	22.66	1
1989	P. Moores.............	17	31	4	571	102*	1	2	21.14	36
	J. J. Bates.............	5	7	1	95	47	0	0	15.83	3
1996	K. Greenfield†	10	19	0	248	37	0	0	13.05	9
1996	V. C. Drakes§	10	18	1	221	48	0	0	13.00	7
	R. K. Rao	9	16	0	207	89	0	1	12.93	2
	A. A. Khan	14	22	3	241	52	0	1	12.68	3
	A. D. Edwards†	5	8	2	49	20	0	0	8.16	4
1997	M. A. Robinson........	17	25	9	114	27	0	0	7.12	4
	R. J. Kirtley†	9	15	7	49	15*	0	0	6.12	4

Also batted: N. C. Phillips (2 matches) 1*, 6; T. A. Radford (1 match) 4, 0 (2 ct); M. J. Thursfield (1 match) 32*.

* Signifies not out. † *Born in Sussex.* § *Overseas player.*

BOWLING

	O	M	R	W	BB	5W/i	Avge
A. D. Edwards	75.2	13	284	10	4-94	0	28.40
M. A. Robinson	448.2	87	1,426	48	6-78	2	29.70
V. C. Drakes	300	60	1,043	31	4-55	0	33.64
R. J. Kirtley	227.3	41	881	26	6-60	1	33.88
P. W. Jarvis	318.5	46	1,091	30	5-44	2	36.36
J. J. Bates	152	42	373	10	5-89	1	37.30
K. Newell	138.1	35	436	11	4-61	0	39.63
A. A. Khan............	398.1	85	1,244	30	5-137	1	41.46

Also bowled: C. W. J. Athey 7–0–21–0; J. R. Carpenter 21.3–5–81–1; K. Greenfield 10–2–45–0; R. S. C. Martin-Jenkins 36.7–7–127–2; M. T. E. Peirce 20.1–2–76–0; N. C. Phillips 13–2–52–0; R. K. Rao 14–2–46–1; M. J. Thursfield 3.3–0–38–0.

COUNTY RECORDS

Highest score for:	333	K. S. Duleepsinhji v Northamptonshire at Hove...	1930
Highest score against:	322	E. Paynter (Lancashire) at Hove	1937
Best bowling for:	10-48	C. H. G. Bland v Kent at Tonbridge............	1899
Best bowling against:	9-11	A. P. Freeman (Kent) at Hove	1922
Highest total for:	705-8 dec.	v Surrey at Hastings........................	1902
Highest total against:	726	by Nottinghamshire at Nottingham	1895
Lowest total for:	{ 19	v Surrey at Godalming	1830
	{ 19	v Nottinghamshire at Hove....................	1873
Lowest total against:	18	by Kent at Gravesend	1867

SUSSEX v NORTHAMPTONSHIRE

At Hove, April 23, 24, 25, 26. Drawn. Sussex 11 pts, Northamptonshire 9 pts. Toss: Northamptonshire. County debuts: A. A. Khan, M. A. Robinson, N. R. Taylor; Mohammad Akram.

After a traumatic winter, reconstituted Sussex made a much better start than expected, and controlled the game until rain wrecked most of the last two days. Indeed, when they quickly earned a bowling point on the first day of the season, Sussex chairman Robin Marlar was heard to cry "We're top of the table!" He was actually wrong, but he did have cause for encouragement from two of his debutants. First, Mark Robinson maintained an accurate off-stump line and took six for 78 against his former county. Then Neil Taylor, who had scored a century on debut for Kent, repeated the feat 18 years on with a flawless 127, full of on-side strength. He became Sussex's first century-maker on debut since Hugh Bartlett in 1937. Keith Newell, the older of the county's latest set of brothers, drove his way to an unbeaten 107. A rapid 64 from Jarvis, and an outbreak of no-balls from Northamptonshire's new Pakistani fast bowler, Mohammad Akram, helped build a handy lead before the rain set in.

Close of play: First day, Northamptonshire 288-9 (J. N. Snape 39*, J. P. Taylor 7*); Second day, Sussex 344-6 (K. Newell 91*, P. W. Jarvis 19*); Third day, Sussex 411-7 (K. Newell 107*, N. C. Phillips 1*).

Northamptonshire

R. R. Montgomerie lbw b Jarvis	68	– not out	18
M. B. Loye lbw b Jarvis	11	– not out	19
*R. J. Bailey lbw b Jarvis	12		
K. M. Curran lbw b Robinson	5		
A. L. Penberthy lbw b Robinson	43		
†R. J. Warren c Greenfield b Newell	16		
D. J. Capel b Robinson	57		
J. N. Snape c Greenfield b Robinson	55		
J. E. Emburey c Athey b Robinson	0		
Mohammad Akram c Moores b Robinson	1		
J. P. Taylor not out	15		
B 4, l-b 13, n-b 15	32	L-b 4	4
	315	(no wkt)	**41**

1/18 2/55 3/62 4/146 5/164
6/219 7/254 8/254 9/260

Bonus points – Northamptonshire 3, Sussex 4.

Bowling: *First Innings*—Drakes 26–5–88–0; Jarvis 22–5–51–3; Robinson 29.5–8–78–6; Khan 19–7–27–0; Newell 14–6–41–1; Phillips 3–0–13–0. *Second Innings*—Drakes 5–0–21–0; Jarvis 4–0–16–0.

Sussex

N. J. Lenham lbw b Taylor	0	P. W. Jarvis lbw b Mohammad Akram . . . 64
K. Greenfield c Montgomerie		N. C. Phillips not out 1
b Mohammad Akram .	4	
N. R. Taylor c Snape b Capel	127	B 2, l-b 7, n-b 30 39
C. W. J. Athey lbw b Mohammad Akram	50	
K. Newell not out	107	1/5 2/15 3/137 (7 wkts dec.) 411
V. C. Drakes c Snape b Taylor	14	4/263 5/288
*†P. Moores st Warren b Emburey	5	6/303 7/410

A. A. Khan and M. A. Robinson did not bat.

Bonus points – Sussex 4, Northamptonshire 3.

Bowling: Mohammad Akram 22–2–118–3; Taylor 20–7–52–2; Curran 9–3–32–0; Snape 16–4–55–0; Emburey 14–2–39–1; Capel 13–1–57–1; Penberthy 11–1–49–0.

Umpires: A. Clarkson and A. G. T. Whitehead.

At Lord's, May 7, 8, 9, 10. SUSSEX drew with MIDDLESEX.

At Taunton, May 14, 15, 16, 17. SUSSEX drew with SOMERSET.

SUSSEX v KENT

At Horsham, May 21, 22, 23, 24. Kent won by 104 runs. Kent 21 pts, Sussex 6 pts. Toss: Kent.
Kent's first match at Horsham for 70 years gave them a memorable victory, secured by an extraordinary last-wicket partnership of 183 between Marsh and Phillips. They came together in the second innings with Kent's lead still a precarious 238, though Sussex had just been irritated by a ninth-wicket stand of 60 between Marsh and Strang. That soon paled into insignificance, as the next pair racked up the 12th-highest last-wicket stand in first-class history (behind the top ten, as listed in Cricket Records, and the 184 by R. C. Blunt and W. Hawksworth for Otago v Canterbury at Christchurch in 1931-32). It did not, however, beat the 88-year-old Kent record of 235. The eighth wicket fell at 11.40 on the third day; the last at 5.22. Sussex were still not totally out of the game. Forced to chase 422, they recovered their morale sufficiently to reach 289 for four after a stand of 138 between the Newell brothers. But Strang broke the partnership and McCague then burst through the breach with the new ball. The match had been eventful from the start: Jarvis put Fulton in hospital when the second ball struck his elbow, and Kent decided to hit their way out of trouble, with Ward leading the way. Mark Newell and Jarvis gave Sussex a narrow first-innings lead, despite five for 47 from Phillips, who managed to make the most of conditions, both then and when they changed to favour the bat.
Close of play: First day, Sussex 102-4 (K. Newell 19*, A. A. Khan 0*); Second day, Kent 154-4 (T. R. Ward 79*, G. R. Cowdrey 24*); Third day, Sussex 31-1 (K. Greenfield 17*, N. J. Lenham 14*).

Kent

D. P. Fulton not out	35	– c Athey b Robinson	34
M. J. Walker b Jarvis	12	– lbw b Jarvis	1
T. R. Ward c Moores b K. Newell	67	– c and b Khan	83
A. P. Wells c Radford b K. Newell	20	– c Moores b Drakes	3
N. J. Llong b Jarvis	9	– b Drakes	0
G. R. Cowdrey c Robinson b Jarvis	28	– c M. Newell b Drakes	40
M. V. Fleming lbw b Drakes	14	– c Jarvis b Robinson	20
*†S. A. Marsh c Moores b Drakes	1	– c Radford b K. Newell	142
M. J. McCague c Jarvis b Drakes	6	– c Greenfield b Drakes	0
P. A. Strang c Lenham b K. Newell	1	– c Greenfield b Robinson	17
B. J. Phillips c Robinson b K. Newell	15	– not out	65
B 1, l-b 8, w 4, n-b 24	37	B 8, l-b 11, w 10, n-b 6	35

1/51 2/119 3/128 4/156 5/175   245   1/5 2/69 3/84 4/86 5/158   440
6/199 7/203 8/215 9/216   6/188 7/197 8/197 9/257

Bonus points – Kent 1, Sussex 4.

In the first innings D. P. Fulton, when 0, retired hurt at 0 and resumed at 156.

Bowling: *First Innings*—Jarvis 17–3–61–3; Drakes 21–5–69–3; Robinson 12–2–45–0; K. Newell 15.3–4–61–4. *Second Innings*—Jarvis 24–3–75–1; Drakes 39–4–152–4; Robinson 32–11–82–3; Khan 26–8–62–1; K. Newell 12.4–2–46–1; Athey 1–0–4–0.

Sussex

T. A. Radford lbw b Phillips	4	– c Marsh b McCague	0
K. Greenfield c Fulton b Strang	37	– c Marsh b McCague	29
N. J. Lenham c McCague b Phillips	8	– lbw b Phillips	49
C. W. J. Athey b Strang	17	– lbw b McCague	37
K. Newell c Marsh b McCague	25	– c Ward b Strang	112
A. A. Khan c Fleming b Phillips	29	– (10) not out	0
M. Newell c Llong b Phillips	56	– (6) c Strang b McCague	57
V. C. Drakes c Fleming b Phillips	0	– (7) lbw b McCague	1
*†P. Moores c McCague b Strang	3	– (8) b McCague	4
P. W. Jarvis c Fulton b Fleming	55	– (9) c Fulton b Strang	5
M. A. Robinson not out	3	– b McCague	4
B 5, l-b 8, w 10, n-b 4	27	L-b 9, w 2, n-b 8	19

1/7 2/36 3/77 4/90 5/124   264   1/14 2/55 3/96 4/151 5/289   317
6/147 7/147 8/154 9/246   6/294 7/300 8/305 9/309

Bonus points – Sussex 2, Kent 4.

Bowling: *First Innings*—McCague 23–1–71–1; Phillips 19–5–47–5; Fleming 17–4–42–1; Strang 32–9–91–3. *Second Innings*—McCague 27.3–8–82–7; Phillips 13–4–33–1; Strang 42–14–102–2; Fleming 15–4–41–0; Llong 8–1–33–0; Wells 3–0–17–0.

Umpires: T. E. Jesty and A. A. Jones.

At Oxford, May 30, 31, June 2. SUSSEX beat OXFORD UNIVERSITY by nine wickets.

At Chester-le-Street, June 4, 5, 6, 7. SUSSEX drew with DURHAM.

SUSSEX v ESSEX

At Hove, June 12, 13, 14. Essex won by ten wickets. Essex 24 pts, Sussex 4 pts. Toss: Essex.

Essex won a crucial toss and were able to dictate terms on a pitch offering early movement off the pitch and through the air. Williams, in his first Championship appearance of the season, reduced Sussex to 17 for four with a burst of three for ten, and then Cowan ran through the middle and late order. Athey took four superb slip catches, including a sprawling effort to remove former team-mate Danny Law, but batting looked a much easier proposition when Essex replied. Irani, dropped on 50, completed his third hundred of the season, and a solid 82 from Rollins helped Essex to a first-innings lead of 244. An opening stand of 116 between Rao and Lenham at least ensured that Sussex went down with a fight. Rao, driving confidently off front and back foot, compiled a career-best while Essex waited for the batsmen to make mistakes. But Cowan returned impressively to pick up four more wickets. Sussex had 26 of their former players back for a reunion on the third day and they were obliged to watch while Prichard and Gooch, who made his second fifty of the season, knocked off the runs with the minimum of fuss. As an experiment, Sussex scheduled 12 noon starts in the hope of getting more spectators late in the day. The poor weather kept attendances down anyway, but the move was considered enough of a success to be worth trying again in 1998; indeed, the club were keen on 1 p.m. starts in midsummer if opponents would agree. At the end of the second day, umpire Bird was locked in his dressing-room; he was rescued after yelling for help.

Close of play: First day, Essex 232-5 (R. C. Irani 79*, D. R. Law 15*); Second day, Sussex 220-5 (K. Newell 16*, M. Newell 0*).

Sussex

N. J. Lenham lbw b Williams	3	– run out	60
R. K. Rao c S. G. Law b Williams	0	– c Gooch b Cowan	89
N. R. Taylor b Cowan	11	– c Cowan b Such	37
C. W. J. Athey c Prichard b Williams	33	– lbw b Grayson	1
K. Newell lbw b Williams	1	– c Hussain b Williams	35
M. Newell c Williams b Cowan	8	– (7) b Cowan	29
*†P. Moores c Such b D. R. Law	19	– (8) b Cowan	4
V. C. Drakes c Rollins b Cowan	18	– (9) b Irani	48
A. A. Khan c sub b Cowan	18	– (10) c D. R. Law b Irani	12
R. J. Kirtley b Cowan	0	– (6) c Hussain b Cowan	0
M. A. Robinson not out	5	– not out	0
B 5, l-b 1, w 2, n-b 16	24	B 6, l-b 7, w 10, n-b 18	41

1/3 2/8 3/14 4/17 5/51   140   1/116 2/181 3/182 4/218 5/218   356
6/84 7/90 8/133 9/133   6/267 7/276 8/283 9/346

Bonus points – Essex 4.

Bowling: *First Innings*—Cowan 14.2–2–45–5; Williams 11–2–29–4; Irani 7–3–16–0; S. G. Law 7–4–13–0; D. R. Law 4–0–31–1. *Second Innings*—Cowan 29–11–78–4; Williams 22–2–77–1; Irani 19.3–7–50–2; Such 23–9–40–1; S. G. Law 12–1–42–0; Grayson 25–7–56–1.

Essex

G. A. Gooch c Moores b Robinson	13	– not out	51
*P. J. Prichard b Kirtley	13	– not out	54
N. Hussain lbw b Drakes	21		
S. G. Law b Kirtley	31		
R. C. Irani c Athey b Khan	110		
A. P. Grayson run out	41		
D. R. Law c Athey b Robinson	17		
†R. J. Rollins c Athey b Khan	82		
A. P. Cowan c Kirtley b Drakes	9		
N. F. Williams c Athey b Robinson	17		
P. M. Such not out	6		
B 3, n-b 21	24	L-b 2, w 6, n-b 2	10

1/20 2/38 3/68 4/98 5/192   384   (no wkt) 115
6/238 7/303 8/332 9/370

Bonus points – Essex 4, Sussex 4.

Bowling: *First Innings*—Drakes 22–6–86–2; Kirtley 20–2–112–2; Robinson 25–2–101–3; Khan 21–5–70–2; K. Newell 5–3–12–0. *Second Innings*—Drakes 8–0–34–0; Kirtley 6–0–28–0; Khan 5.2–1–28–0; Robinson 3–0–16–0; Rao 1–0–7–0.

Umpires: H. D. Bird and G. I. Burgess.

At Derby, June 18, 19, 20, 21. SUSSEX drew with DERBYSHIRE.

At Swansea, June 26, 27, 28. SUSSEX lost to GLAMORGAN by 234 runs.

SUSSEX v WORCESTERSHIRE

At Arundel, July 2, 3, 4. Worcestershire won by an innings and 35 runs. Worcestershire 22 pts, Sussex 4 pts. Toss: Worcestershire.

A season of struggle for Sussex got worse when they were dismissed for under 75 for the third successive innings. Their destroyer on this occasion was left-arm seamer Sheriyar, who completed match figures of ten for 63 when Sussex lost 17 wickets on the third day. Though the batsmen at least totalled three figures when they followed on, Worcestershire claimed the extra half-hour to finish the match a day early. Overcast conditions and a damp pitch, a legacy of record rainfall in the days leading up to the festival, gave seam and swing bowlers conditions which would have troubled less brittle batting sides than Sussex. Worcestershire's decision to bat first had looked a risky one, especially when Drakes blew away the top order, but, when he went off with a back injury, Rhodes took advantage, completing an unbeaten half-century. Sheriyar then got to work, bagging six for 19 as Sussex were dismissed for 71. Only opener Peirce defied him, but he was facing the music again half an hour after being eighth out in the first innings. This time, Athey held out for a while, but Sheriyar and Lampitt swept up.

Close of play: First day, Worcestershire 185-8 (S. J. Rhodes 20*, P. J. Newport 14*); Second day, Sussex 23-3 (M. T. E. Peirce 7*, M. A. Robinson 0*).

Worcestershire

T. S. Curtis lbw b Drakes	3	S. R. Lampitt b K. Newell 5
W. P. C. Weston lbw b Drakes	8	P. J. Newport c Moores b Martin-Jenkins. 45
G. A. Hick c Martin-Jenkins b Drakes ...	4	A. Sheriyar c M. Newell b Martin-Jenkins 0
K. R. Spiring c Khan b Kirtley	36	
*T. M. Moody c Moores b Kirtley	43	L-b 11, w 4, n-b 2 17
G. R. Haynes c Moores b Robinson	2	
D. A. Leatherdale c Drakes b K. Newell	34	1/10 2/19 3/34 4/102 5/105 255
†S. J. Rhodes not out	58	6/111 7/154 8/168 9/255

Bonus points – Worcestershire 2, Sussex 4.

Bowling: Drakes 20–8–33–3; Kirtley 24–9–59–2; Robinson 22–5–48–1; Martin-Jenkins 14–3–51–2; Khan 11–2–33–0; K. Newell 12–4–20–2.

Sussex

C. W. J. Athey b Newport	1	– (4) c Curtis b Sheriyar 32
M. T. E. Peirce b Leatherdale	29	– c and b Sheriyar 2
N. R. Taylor lbw b Sheriyar	7	– b Leatherdale 4
A. A. Khan c Rhodes b Sheriyar	3	– (9) lbw b Lampitt 10
M. A. Robinson c Hick b Sheriyar	0	– (10) b Lampitt 3
K. Newell c Rhodes b Sheriyar	3	– (5) b Lampitt 16
M. Newell lbw b Sheriyar	10	– (6) lbw b Lampitt 24
R. S. C. Martin-Jenkins b Sheriyar	0	– (7) c Moody b Lampitt......... 26
*†P. Moores not out	3	– (1) c Lampitt b Sheriyar...... 15
V. C. Drakes c Rhodes b Leatherdale	0	– (8) b Lampitt 0
R. J. Kirtley c sub b Leatherdale	0	– not out 0
B 2, l-b 1, n-b 12	15	B 1, l-b 8, n-b 8 17

1/8 2/15 3/23 4/27 5/37	71	1/4 2/23 3/25 4/61 5/87 149
6/53 7/53 8/65 9/69		6/124 7/124 8/146 9/149

Bonus points – Worcestershire 4.

Bowling: *First Innings*—Newport 14–7–22–1; Sheriyar 16–9–19–6; Leatherdale 6.2–4–12–3; Lampitt 4–0–15–0. *Second Innings*—Newport 8–2–21–0; Sheriyar 14.3–3–44–4; Leatherdale 12–4–32–1; Lampitt 15–5–39–5; Moody 3–2–4–0.

Umpires: A. A. Jones and R. Palmer.

At Manchester, July 16, 17, 18, 19. SUSSEX lost to LANCASHIRE by an innings and 18 runs.

At Hove, July 24, 25, 26, 27. SUSSEX drew with PAKISTAN A (See Pakistan A tour section).

At Birmingham, July 31, August 1, 2. SUSSEX lost to WARWICKSHIRE by nine wickets.

SUSSEX v LEICESTERSHIRE

At Eastbourne, August 6, 7, 8, 9. Sussex won by 38 runs. Sussex 19 pts, Leicestershire 2 pts. Toss: Leicestershire. Championship debut: J. J. Bates.

Sussex finally secured their first and only Championship win of the season in a one-innings game against the reigning champions. It was Leicestershire's only defeat of the summer. The result marked the centenary of Championship cricket at The Saffrons more satisfactorily than Sussex might have expected, especially after persistent rain meant that the match could not begin until the third day. The outfield was soggy but the pitch was true enough for Taylor to score his third hundred for Sussex and build a stand of 143 with Newell. After a declaration and a double forfeiture, Leicestershire were left a day to score 331. Smith and Maddy added 126 for the third wicket before they fell to the spinners, and Johnson shared half-century stands with Nixon and Parsons. But Jarvis returned at the Sea End with a burst of pace reminiscent of his younger days, and the last four wickets were swept away for nine runs. Leicestershire coach Jack Birkenshaw said it was one of the best displays of fast bowling he had seen in a long while.

Close of play: First day, No play; Second day, No play; Third day, Sussex 330-6 dec.

Sussex

M. T. E. Peirce c Johnson b Pierson	31	P. W. Jarvis c Wells b Stevens	55
R. K. Rao b Pierson	10	A. A. Khan not out	9
N. R. Taylor not out	122	B 8, l-b 7, w 8, n-b 4	27
C. W. J. Athey c Nixon b Pierson	7		
K. Newell c Johnson b Parsons	64	1/24 2/63 3/79 (6 wkts dec.)	330
*†P. Moores c Stevens b Parsons	5	4/222 5/228 6/317	

J. J. Bates, A. D. Edwards and M. A. Robinson did not bat.

Bonus points – Sussex 3, Leicestershire 2.

Bowling: Mullally 6–1–10–0; Ormond 9–2–38–0; Pierson 42–10–122–3; Parsons 24–8–43–2; Macmillan 11–1–41–0; Wells 12–4–32–0; Maddy 9–1–20–0; Stevens 2–1–5–1; Nixon 2–0–4–0.

Sussex forfeited their second innings.

Leicestershire

Leicestershire forfeited their first innings.

*V. J. Wells lbw b Jarvis	4	J. Ormond b Jarvis	0
D. L. Maddy c Moores b Bates	61	A. R. K. Pierson b Jarvis	0
G. I. Macmillan c Moores b Jarvis	3	A. D. Mullally c Peirce b Bates	1
B. F. Smith c Peirce b Khan	74		
N. C. Johnson not out	74	B 16, l-b 10, n-b 2	28
D. I. Stevens b Khan	8		
†P. A. Nixon lbw b Khan	22	1/4 2/10 3/136 4/161 5/169	292
G. J. Parsons c Moores b Jarvis	17	6/226 7/283 8/283 9/287	

Bowling: Jarvis 17–2–44–5; Edwards 4–1–9–0; Khan 36–8–108–3; Robinson 9–2–29–0; Bates 30.2–8–75–2; Newell 1–0–1–0.

Umpires: M. J. Kitchen and N. T. Plews.

SUSSEX v GLOUCESTERSHIRE

At Hove, August 15, 16, 17, 18. Gloucestershire won by 166 runs. Gloucestershire 23 pts, Sussex 7 pts. Toss: Gloucestershire.

Sussex matched their Championship-chasing opponents until halfway through the final day, when they capitulated to spinners Ball and Davis, crumpling embarrassingly from 109 for one to 161 all out. Gloucestershire were in trouble early on and, although Dawson and Russell pulled them round from 119 for five, Robinson finished off the lower order by bowling a superb off-stump line in hot conditions. Two big stands – including one of 104 for the eighth wicket between Moores and 21-year-old Justin Bates – gave Sussex parity, and a declaration left them 328 in a minimum 82 overs to win. Taylor and Peirce had a century stand for the second time in the match but, as the final hour approached, Sussex fell to pieces in all-too-familiar fashion. Gloucestershire returned to the top of the table.

Close of play: First day, Gloucestershire 291-8 (R. P. Davis 1*, A. M. Smith 0*); Second day, Sussex 255-7 (P. Moores 34*, J. J. Bates 18*); Third day, Gloucestershire 271-6 (R. C. Russell 37*, M. C. J. Ball 11*).

Gloucestershire

N. J. Trainor c Moores b Khan	30	– lbw b Jarvis		0
M. G. N. Windows b Edwards	14	– b Khan		31
T. H. C. Hancock c Bates b Edwards	36	– b K. Newell		84
M. J. Church c Edwards b Khan	4	– c Edwards b Khan		16
R. I. Dawson c Taylor b Khan	98	– c Peirce b Khan		1
*M. W. Alleyne b Robinson	0	– lbw b Jarvis		77
†R. C. Russell lbw b Robinson	48	– not out		69
M. C. J. Ball lbw b Robinson	29	– c Peirce b Robinson		25
R. P. Davis c Moores b Robinson	10			
A. M. Smith b Robinson	14	– (9) not out		2
J. Lewis not out	6			
L-b 5, w 4, n-b 22	31	B 9, l-b 5, n-b 12		26
	320	(7 wkts dec.)		**331**

1/32 2/56 3/76 4/114 5/119   1/0 2/69 3/93   (7 wkts dec.)
6/239 7/282 8/289 9/311   4/101 5/179
                                    6/257 7/322

Bonus points – Gloucestershire 3, Sussex 4.

Bowling: *First Innings*—Jarvis 25.4–88–0; Edwards 19–3–55–2; Robinson 29.2–9–66–5; Khan 17–5–59–3; Bates 13–3–29–0; K. Newell 8–3–11–0; Rao 1–0–7–0. *Second Innings*—Jarvis 11–1–42–2; Edwards 10–1–39–0; Bates 15–1–48–0; Khan 37.4–8–126–3; Robinson 20–5–53–1; K. Newell 7–3–9–1.

Sussex

M. T. E. Peirce c Davis b Lewis	73	– c Dawson b Ball		54
R. K. Rao lbw b Lewis	14	– c Ball b Lewis		0
N. R. Taylor c and b Davis	74	– c Windows b Ball		62
M. Newell c Russell b Davis	0	– c Hancock b Davis		5
K. Newell c Windows b Smith	14	– c Windows b Davis		4
*†P. Moores b Davis	65	– not out		17
P. W. Jarvis lbw b Smith	4	– c Alleyne b Ball		4
A. A. Khan lbw b Lewis	9	– c Hancock b Davis		0
J. J. Bates c Smith b Alleyne	47	– lbw b Ball		6
A. D. Edwards not out	2	– c Alleyne b Ball		0
M. A. Robinson c Dawson b Davis	0	– b Davis		0
B 1, l-b 5, n-b 16	22	B 2, l-b 3, n-b 4		9
	324			**161**

1/22 2/157 3/157 4/183 5/187   1/2 2/109 3/128 4/130 5/135   **161**
6/195 7/218 8/322 9/322   6/142 7/147 8/156 9/160

Bonus points – Sussex 3, Gloucestershire 4 (Score at 120 overs: 324-9).

Bowling: *First Innings*—Smith 22–3–88–2; Lewis 24–4–81–3; Davis 23.4–10–35–4; Alleyne 25–3–80–1; Hancock 10–4–17–0; Ball 16–10–17–0. *Second Innings*—Smith 5–1–11–0; Lewis 8–2–34–1; Davis 29–13–35–4; Ball 30–7–66–5; Alleyne 5–3–10–0.

Umpires: B. Leadbeater and K. E. Palmer.

At Scarborough, August 20, 21, 22. SUSSEX lost to YORKSHIRE by nine wickets.

SUSSEX v SURREY

At Hove, August 28, 29, 30. Surrey won by an innings and 101 runs. Surrey 24 pts, Sussex 3 pts.
Toss: Sussex. First-class debut: J. R. Carpenter.

Surrey, suddenly sensing a late run for the Championship, won their third game in a row and
Sussex's season plumbed new depths in this embarrassingly one-sided derby. The match was put
back a day to allow for a floodlit Sunday League game, but Surrey did not need the final day
anyway, and an indefinite postponement might have been preferable for Sussex, who slumped to
137 all out. The openers could not manage a run between them, and two hostile spells down the
slope from Lewis earned him figures of five for 42. Surrey's batsmen deflected any criticism of
the pitch, reaching 400 with ease, thanks to a stand of 142 between Thorpe and Adam Hol010ake,
who slammed three sixes and 11 fours in his 87 from 58 balls. Sussex were soon up against it
again as Salisbury mesmerised his former team-mates in fading light. James Carpenter, a 21-year-
old left-hander from Liverpool, showed impressive application for 33, Sussex's highest score of
the match, but it was all over shortly after lunch on the third day.

Close of play: First day, Sussex 102-7 (P. Moores 28*, A. A. Khan 8*); Second day, Sussex
20-4 (R. K. Rao 6*).

Sussex

M. T. E. Peirce lbw b Bicknell	0	– lbw b Salisbury	11
R. K. Rao c A. J. Hol010ake b Bicknell	0	– b Salisbury	15
N. R. Taylor b Lewis	3	– lbw b Salisbury	2
K. Greenfield b Lewis	1	– (6) b Bicknell	20
K. Newell lbw b Bicknell	5	– (7) c B. C. Hol010ake b Bicknell	28
J. R. Carpenter b Salisbury	19	– (8) c Salisbury b Lewis	33
*†P. Moores lbw b Lewis	30	– (9) b Lewis	31
A. D. Edwards c Ratcliffe b Lewis	20	– (4) c Butcher b Salisbury	0
A. A. Khan c Stewart b Lewis	15	– (10) not out	0
M. A. Robinson c Thorpe b Saqlain Mushtaq	4	– (11) c Thorpe b Saqlain Mushtaq	0
R. J. Kirtley not out	15	– (5) c Thorpe b Salisbury	0
B 2, l-b 2, w 2, n-b 19	25	B 4, l-b 4, n-b 14	22

1/0 2/5 3/5 4/13 5/23   137   1/16 2/20 3/20 4/20 5/41   162
6/47 7/85 8/104 9/113   6/73 7/90 8/160 9/161

Bonus points – Surrey 4.

Bowling: *First Innings*—Bicknell 21–6–53–3; Lewis 20–8–42–5; A. J. Hol010ake 3–1–3–0;
Saqlain Mushtaq 8.1–1–15–1; Salisbury 8–2–20–1. *Second Innings*—Bicknell 9–4–24–2; Saqlain
Mushtaq 12.3–7–18–1; Salisbury 23–8–66–5; Lewis 8–2–43–2; B. C. Hol010ake 2–1–3–0.

Surrey

M. A. Butcher c Newell b Edwards	61	C. C. Lewis lbw b Edwards	7
J. D. Ratcliffe lbw b Robinson	19	M. P. Bicknell not out	2
†A. J. Stewart c Edwards b Kirtley	34	B 6, l-b 6, w 2, n-b 14	28
G. P. Thorpe not out	106		
A. D. Brown c Moores b Robinson	37	1/48 2/116 3/157	(7 wkts dec.) 400
*A. J. Hol010ake c Moores b Edwards	87	4/217 5/359	
B. C. Hol010ake c Carpenter b Edwards	19	6/383 7/393	

I. D. K. Salisbury and Saqlain Mushtaq did not bat.

Bonus points – Surrey 4, Sussex 3.

Bowling: Kirtley 19–3–89–1; Edwards 15–1–94–4; Robinson 19–3–80–2; Newell 7–0–35–0;
Khan 15–0–90–0.

Umpires: B. J. Meyer and R. Palmer.

At Southampton, September 10, 11, 12, 13. SUSSEX lost to HAMPSHIRE by seven wickets.

SUSSEX v NOTTINGHAMSHIRE

At Hove, September 18, 19, 20, 21. Drawn. Sussex 8 pts, Nottinghamshire 9 pts. Toss: Nottinghamshire.

Derbyshire's win over Yorkshire had consigned Sussex to their third wooden spoon in 11 years, and they were unable to gain a consolation victory from a fourth-day run-chase here. A typical Hove belter had worked to the batsmen's advantage before that; Welton came close to a maiden hundred, but Mark Newell reached his when Sussex replied, and Moores made his first century of the season. Nottinghamshire were fed cheap runs to set up a declaration on the final morning, and the agreed target was 356 in 82 overs. Peirce added 70 for the first wicket with Taylor and 95 for the third with Keith Newell, but momentum was lost when Afzaal ran him out, deflecting a drive on to his stumps at the non-striker's end. Pollard kept wicket in both Sussex innings after Noon injured his hand while batting.

Close of play: First day, Nottinghamshire 337-5 (U. Afzaal 26*, W. M. Noon 5*); Second day, Sussex 80-2 (M. Newell 30*, K. Newell 0*); Third day, Nottinghamshire 147-2 (U. Afzaal 14*, P. Johnson 21*).

Nottinghamshire

M. P. Dowman b Kirtley	0	– b Kirtley	2
R. T. Robinson c Peirce b Bates	63	– retired hurt	44
G. E. Welton lbw b Kirtley	95	– c and b Bates	47
*P. Johnson c Moores b Kirtley	74	– (5) not out	59
P. R. Pollard lbw b Jarvis	43	– (6) not out	13
U. Afzaal c Peirce b Bates	80	– (4) b Carpenter	31
†W. M. Noon c and b Bates	25		
P. J. Franks c Peirce b Bates	27		
K. P. Evans c Kirtley b Bates	8		
R. T. Bates not out	0		
L-b 10, w 2, n-b 27	39	L-b 9, n-b 10	19

1/0 2/169 3/189 4/287 5/327   (9 wkts dec.) 454   1/2 2/107 3/185   (3 wkts dec.) 215
6/383 7/445 8/453 9/454

A. R. Oram did not bat.

Bonus points – Nottinghamshire 4, Sussex 2 (Score at 120 overs: 383-6).

In the second innings R. T. Robinson retired hurt at 123.

Bowling: *First Innings*—Kirtley 30–4–115–3; Jarvis 19–3–67–1; Robinson 29–2–85–0; Martin-Jenkins 14–3–49–0; Bates 42.4–14–89–5; K. Newell 8–1–21–0; Carpenter 9–4–18–0. *Second Innings*—Kirtley 4.4–1–13–1; Jarvis 2–0–13–0; Martin-Jenkins 8–1–27–0; Robinson 8.2–1–32–0; Bates 11–4–23–1; Carpenter 9.3–1–50–1; Peirce 12–2–48–0.

Sussex

M. T. E. Peirce c sub b Bates	15	– (2) run out	90
N. R. Taylor lbw b Oram	18	– (1) c Pollard b Franks	42
M. Newell c sub b Bates	100	– c Pollard b Franks	6
K. Newell lbw b Oram	0	– run out	75
J. R. Carpenter c Bates b Franks	10	– c and b Oram	7
*†P. Moores not out	102	– c Franks b Afzaal	15
R. S. C. Martin-Jenkins not out	36	– c Dowman b Afzaal	6
P. W. Jarvis (did not bat)		– not out	13
J. J. Bates (did not bat)		– not out	3
L-b 5, w 2, n-b 26	33	L-b 12, w 2, n-b 16	30

1/33 2/77 3/88 4/112 5/250   (5 wkts dec.) 314   1/70 2/104 3/199 4/213   (7 wkts) 287
5/246 6/269 7/278

M. A. Robinson and R. J. Kirtley did not bat.

Bonus points – Sussex 3, Nottinghamshire 2.

Bowling: *First Innings*—Oram 17–5–48–2; Franks 20–0–102–1; Evans 16–3–45–0; Bates 30–8–77–2; Dowman 7–3–14–0; Afzaal 4–0–23–0. *Second Innings*—Oram 19–5–52–1; Evans 12–3–34–0; Franks 18–3–63–2; Afzaal 18.4–1–79–0; Bates 14–2–47–2.

Umpires: M. J. Kitchen and K. E. Palmer.

WARWICKSHIRE

Dougie Brown

President: The Earl of Aylesford

Chairman: M. J. K. Smith

Chairman, Cricket Committee: J. Whitehouse

Chief Executive: D. L. Amiss

Captain: 1997 – T. A. Munton

1998 – B. C. Lara

Director of Coaching: P. A. Neale

Head Groundsman: S. J. Rouse

Scorer: A. E. Davis

Warwickshire's strength in depth paid dividends in 1997. They won the Sunday League – their seventh trophy in five years – and reached the NatWest final. They also came joint fourth in the County Championship and lost the Benson and Hedges quarter-final, despite topping 300 at Canterbury.

Yet they ran into injury problems that other clubs would have found insuperable even before the opening game. Club captain Tim Munton broke down during pre-season training in the Cape, and missed the entire campaign. Wicket-keeper Keith Piper was unavailable for half the season, chiefly because of recurring Achilles tendon problems. Opening batsmen Nick Knight and Andy Moles and pace bowler Allan Donald missed 15 Championship matches between them. It says much for the various captains – Knight, Moles and Neil Smith – as well as youngsters such as deputy keeper Tony Frost and Mark Wagh, the Oxford captain, that the side challenged so strongly for three trophies.

The biggest advances were made by all-rounders Dougie Brown and Graeme Welch. But both derived enormous benefit from bowling with Donald, who was at his very best and headed the national averages. His 60 wickets at 15.63 apiece took him past 500 for Warwickshire, and he claimed a wicket on average every 39 balls. Had Donald not missed four games through injury, another which was abandoned, and the final match when he returned to South Africa, Warwickshire's Championship challenge would have been even stronger. He was not available for 1998, because of South Africa's tour of England, though he hoped to play in 1999 around his World Cup commitments. But there could be a competing claim. Brian Lara had been invited to return in 1998 – slightly surprisingly, as stories have seeped out about his behavioural problems during his record-breaking season in 1994. The club made clear their commitment to Lara by handing him the captaincy in place of Tim Munton, whose fitness was still considered in doubt. Munton thus ended his reign without having led the team once during that period.

Scottish-born Brown took 81 first-class wickets and earned an England call-up for December's one-day tournament in Sharjah, while Welch took 63 for the county to win his cap. Both were also hard-hitting batsmen; with spinners Smith and Ashley Giles, they formed a quartet of front-line bowlers all worth a place in the first eight. The other player capped was David Hemp, imported from Glamorgan. He had a shaky start, but twin hundreds against Hampshire – the second helped by contrivance – restored his confidence. He was the only batsman to reach 1,000 runs. Knight should have done, but broken fingers limited him to 17 innings, from which he scored 689 at 49.21. He was rewarded with the captaincy of the England A tour, for which Giles was also selected, and both went to Sharjah. With Trevor Penney and Wagh averaging around 40, the potent attack more often than not had sufficient runs to bowl against.

The Edgbaston pitches varied in quality; they were ranked 17th in the ECB table. They had been 17th the previous two seasons, and the club was fortunate that several early finishes brought low markings, rather than punishment. Five of their seven Championship wins were at home, and none of those lasted for as much as the equivalent of two and a half days. Donald's 34 wickets, out of 98 taken, explain some of these early finishes but, surely, not all. Away from Edgbaston, it was a different story. When Donald helped Warwickshire to the Championship in 1995, half their 14 wins came away from home. This time, only two did. But it was a home draw against Worcestershire which effectively ended their title hopes. Their final finish of joint fourth was tainted; one precious batting point in the last game was gifted by joke bowling from Northamptonshire, which was contrivance of the worst sort, as the handful of overs thus saved could not have made the difference between a deal and no deal.

The Sunday League title was well deserved. Warwickshire won 13 games (they were lucky to be the only team never washed out) through aggressive but well-paced batting and a varied pace and spin attack; bowling Donald and Small in mid-innings paid off. Smith proved an outstanding captain, despite being the fourth choice. Following M. J. K., he completed the first father and son pairing to captain Warwickshire. His success, particularly in limited overs, was such that he was put in charge in the NatWest final, even though Knight, the official vice-captain, was fit. But that match was a big disappointment. Essex won with embarrassing ease after winning the toss and bowling first in conditions perfect for swing. The pitch eased later but, had Warwickshire's attack bowled to their usual standard, they would surely not have lost by nine wickets. They had also bowled poorly against Kent in the Benson and Hedges quarter-final, wasting their batsmen's work in amassing 304. But they had the last laugh on Kent, who were triple runners-up; Warwickshire did win a trophy, and 27 competitive matches to Kent's 26.

A less happy feature of the year was the recurrent motif of drug abuse. Former player Paul Smith made lurid revelations about his lifestyle, and the club responded with a surprise test of their present squad. Piper tested positive, was fined £500 and suspended for one match. Warwickshire were praised for their swift action, but criticised for their arrangements with ex-Sussex fast bowler Ed Giddins. He had signed to join the county in April 1998, after serving a 20-month ban for taking cocaine, and they reportedly paid him to visit Birmingham for practice.

Warwickshire's hopes for 1998 rested heavily on Giddins justifying the confidence placed in him, on Munton recovering from his second serious back injury, and on Lara scoring the runs he made in 1994 without upsetting the dressing-room. The club administration was disappointed to lose the battle within the ECB for a two-division Championship. But, looking to the future, they staged the first Sunday League fixture under floodlights – an outstanding success. The attendance of over 15,000 almost doubled pre-match forecasts, and brought in a profit of £70,000. – JACK BANNISTER.

WARWICKSHIRE 1997

[Bill Smith]

Back row: N. V. Prabhu, T. Frost, S. McDonald, C. R. Howell, M. J. Powell, M. A. Sheikh, M. D. Edmond, D. A. Altree. *Middle row:* D. L. Amiss (*chief executive*), W. G. Khan, D. R. Brown, M. A. V. Bell, A. F. Giles, G. Welch, D. L. Hemp, S. Nottingham (*physiotherapist*). *Front row:* R. N. Abberley (*head coach*), K. J. Piper, T. L. Penney, N. M. K. Smith, A. A. Donald, M. J. K. Smith (*chairman*), T. A. Munton (*captain*), P. A. Neale (*director of coaching*), G. C. Small, A. J. Moles, D. P. Ostler. *Insets:* N. V. Knight, A. Singh, M. A. Wagh.

WARWICKSHIRE RESULTS

All first-class matches – Played 18: Won 8, Lost 2, Drawn 7, Abandoned 1.

County Championship matches – Played 17: Won 7, Lost 2, Drawn 7, Abandoned 1.

Competition placings – Britannic Assurance County Championship, 4th equal;
NatWest Trophy, finalists; Benson and Hedges Cup, q-f;
AXA Life League, winners.

COUNTY CHAMPIONSHIP AVERAGES

BATTING

Cap		M	I	NO	R	HS	100s	50s	Avge	Ct/St
1995	N. V. Knight........	10	16	3	677	119*	2	3	52.07	7
1997	D. L. Hemp.........	16	28	4	1,008	138	3	4	42.00	7
1994	T. L. Penney.......	16	24	5	784	99	0	6	41.26	11
	M. A. Wagh†	8	13	1	472	124	1	3	39.33	7
1987	A. J. Moles†	12	22	3	635	168	1	2	33.42	10
1996	A. F. Giles	14	18	3	474	97	0	3	31.60	2
1993	N. M. K. Smith†	14	21	2	587	148	1	2	30.89	7
1995	D. R. Brown	15	21	2	448	79	0	4	23.57	8
1997	G. Welch...........	16	24	6	393	75	0	1	21.83	3
1989	A. A. Donald§	11	13	6	140	29	0	0	20.00	5
1991	D. P. Ostler†	14	21	1	368	65	0	2	18.40	27
	T. Frost	8	11	2	158	56	0	1	17.55	25/1
	W. G. Khan†	2	4	0	59	29	0	0	14.75	1
1992	K. J. Piper.........	8	11	3	111	34*	0	0	13.87	24/1
1982	G. C. Small.........	3	4	1	13	11	0	0	4.33	1

Also batted: M. A. V. Bell† (3 matches) 30, 0 (1 ct); M. D. Edmond (2 matches) 21, 9, 5* (1 ct); M. A. Sheikh† (1 match) 24; A. Singh (2 matches) 0, 1, 0 (2 ct); D. A. Altree† (1 match) did not bat.

* Signifies not out.   † Born in Warwickshire.   § Overseas player.

BOWLING

	O	M	R	W	BB	5W/i	Avge
A. A. Donald	387.5	123	938	60	6-55	3	15.63
D. R. Brown...........	462.1	123	1,382	64	5-62	3	21.59
G. Welch	487.2	133	1,501	56	6-115	3	26.80
A. F. Giles	436.1	126	1,086	32	4-54	0	33.93
N. M. K. Smith	307.2	74	907	23	4-32	0	39.43

Also bowled: D. A. Altree 25–3–119–2; M. A. V. Bell 79.3–14–232–3; M. D. Edmond 43–9–135–2; D. L. Hemp 23–4–120–0; N. V. Knight 6–0–71–0; D. P. Ostler 6–0–66–0; M. A. Sheikh 14.3–7–24–3; G. C. Small 50–12–158–3; M. A. Wagh 3–3–0–0.

COUNTY RECORDS

Highest score for:	501*	B. C. Lara v Durham at Birmingham..............	1994
Highest score against:	322	I. V. A. Richards (Somerset) at Taunton	1985
Best bowling for:	10-41	J. D. Bannister v Combined Services at Birmingham.	1959
Best bowling against:	10-36	H. Verity (Yorkshire) at Leeds	1931
Highest total for:	810-4 dec.	v Durham at Birmingham	1994
Highest total against:	887	by Yorkshire at Birmingham.....................	1896
Lowest total for:	16	v Kent at Tonbridge...........................	1913
Lowest total against:	15	by Hampshire at Birmingham	1922

At Cardiff, April 23, 24, 25, 26. WARWICKSHIRE drew with GLAMORGAN.

At Oxford, May 7, 8, 9. WARWICKSHIRE beat OXFORD UNIVERSITY by an innings and 53 runs.

WARWICKSHIRE v YORKSHIRE

At Birmingham, May 14, 15, 16. Warwickshire won by four wickets. Warwickshire 20 pts, Yorkshire 5 pts. Toss: Warwickshire. Championship debut: T. Frost.

Warwickshire's stronger and more varied attack, plus determined batting at the end from Brown, won a low-scoring game in two and a half days. On a pitch of inconsistent bounce which aided the faster bowlers, Yorkshire led by 93 on first innings, after taking Warwickshire's last five for two runs in 20 balls. Resuming, however, Yorkshire succumbed in 49 overs. Donald was well supported by Brown and Giles; in contrast, Yorkshire's spearhead Gough, who took four in each innings, had little back-up. Even so, his fiery spell of 9–5–12–3 reduced Warwickshire's final innings to 94 for five, chasing 248. A recovery launched by Penney and Brown was halted when Penney was struck on the finger and forced to retire. But an attacking partnership of 68 in 16 overs between Brown – defying blows to his hand and elbow – and Giles carried them to victory.

Close of play: First day, Warwickshire 64-4 (T. L. Penney 28*, D. R. Brown 11*); Second day, Warwickshire 76-3 (D. L. Hemp 26*, D. P. Ostler 0*).

Yorkshire

A. McGrath c Frost b Donald	0	– b Donald	0
M. P. Vaughan c Frost b Donald	56	– c Ostler b Donald	7
*D. Byas b Donald	8	– c Frost b Brown	19
D. S. Lehmann b Brown	62	– c Giles b Brown	43
B. Parker lbw b Giles	10	– lbw b Giles	41
C. White c Frost b Giles	0	– c Frost b Brown	0
†R. J. Blakey not out	25	– b Giles	13
D. Gough c Frost b Brown	4	– c Moles b Welch	0
G. M. Hamilton b Donald	13	– c Donald b Giles	4
C. E. W. Silverwood c Welch b Giles	21	– not out	10
R. D. Stemp b Giles	0	– b Donald	0
B 17, l-b 11, n-b 6	34	B 11, l-b 4, n-b 2	17

1/10 2/40 3/113 4/154 5/154   233   1/0 2/21 3/38 4/87 5/91   154
6/170 7/176 8/200 9/233   6/127 7/128 8/138 9/149

Bonus points – Yorkshire 1, Warwickshire 4.

Bowling: *First Innings*—Donald 19–5–55–4; Welch 16–4–46–0; Small 9–2–27–0; Giles 24–6–54–4; Brown 10–4–23–2. *Second Innings*—Donald 13.3–3–33–3; Welch 9–1–25–1; Giles 17–4–45–3; Brown 9–2–36–3.

Warwickshire

*N. V. Knight lbw b Gough	8	– c Blakey b Stemp	9
A. J. Moles lbw b Silverwood	6	– b Gough	33
D. L. Hemp lbw b Gough	0	– c Blakey b Gough	37
D. P. Ostler lbw b Gough	1	– (5) b Gough	2
T. L. Penney lbw b Stemp	67	– (6) retired hurt	26
D. R. Brown b Gough	26	– (7) not out	65
G. Welch c McGrath b Hamilton	15	– (8) b White	17
A. F. Giles c Blakey b Stemp	0	– (9) not out	38
†T. Frost lbw b Hamilton	0	– (4) c Blakey b Gough	4
A. A. Donald not out	2		
G. C. Small c White b Hamilton	0		
B 2, l-b 7, w 6	15	L-b 16, w 2	18

1/8 2/12 3/16 4/22 5/104   140   1/27 2/61 3/75   (6 wkts) 249
6/138 7/138 8/138 9/138   4/79 5/94 6/181

Bonus points – Yorkshire 4.

In the second innings T. L. Penney retired hurt at 148.

Bowling: *First Innings*—Gough 17–5–62–4; Silverwood 8–3–28–1; Hamilton 10.5–5–23–3; Stemp 9–2–18–2. *Second Innings*—Gough 24–7–65–4; Silverwood 16.4–4–53–0; Hamilton 7–1–18–0; Stemp 19–5–57–1; Vaughan 4–2–3–0; White 11–1–37–1.

Umpires: J. H. Harris and B. J. Meyer.

WARWICKSHIRE v MIDDLESEX

At Birmingham, May 21, 22, 23, 24. Warwickshire won by eight wickets. Warwickshire 20 pts, Middlesex 5 pts. Toss: Warwickshire. First-class debut: M. A. Sheikh.

For the second game running, Warwickshire triumphed despite a substantial first-innings deficit in a low-scoring match; they had yet to score a batting point in 1997. With the first day and nearly half the second lost to rain, the match lasted only 240.2 overs – effectively seven sessions. Seam and swing bowlers held sway, only two wickets falling to spin. Both sets of batsmen started shakily: Middlesex were 97 for five, Warwickshire 97 for four. But thanks to Moffat, playing his second Championship match, Middlesex's last five added 124, whereas Warwickshire's last six managed only 61. On the third day, however, the tide turned. Superb swing bowling by Welch earned him career-best figures as the visitors lost their last nine for 84. That left a target of 196 in 57 overs; Smith reached 50 in 61 balls, with two sixes and six fours, and Moles, unbeaten on 67, completed victory with ten overs to spare.

Close of play: First day, No play; Second day, Middlesex 161-7 (S. P. Moffat 18*, J. P. Hewitt 10*); Third day, Middlesex 21-1 (M. R. Ramprakash 10*, M. W. Gatting 2*).

Middlesex

P. N. Weekes c Frost b Brown	7	– lbw b Brown	3
J. H. Kallis lbw b Brown	18	– (7) b Sheikh	1
M. R. Ramprakash c Khan b Brown	2	– (2) b Welch	50
*M. W. Gatting c Moles b Donald	38	– (3) c Ostler b Welch	13
J. C. Pooley c Frost b Donald	8	– (4) b Brown	1
†K. R. Brown c Ostler b Welch	13	– (5) b Welch	1
S. P. Moffat c Frost b Welch	47	– (6) b Sheikh	15
R. L. Johnson c Moles b Welch	7	– c Penney b Welch	14
J. P. Hewitt run out	27	– not out	14
A. R. C. Fraser not out	2	– c Donald b Welch	6
P. C. R. Tufnell c sub b Sheikh	1	– c Frost b Donald	5
B 17, l-b 16, w 2, n-b 16	51	B 1, l-b 4, n-b 4	9

1/31 2/35 3/50 4/77 5/97   221   1/7 2/48 3/49 4/50 5/85   132
6/130 7/150 8/214 9/218   6/91 7/91 8/117 9/123

Bonus points – Middlesex 1, Warwickshire 4.

Bowling: *First Innings*—Donald 22–4–38–2; Welch 22–4–75–3; Brown 28–9–54–3; Sheikh 9.3–5–10–1; Smith 5–0–11–0. *Second Innings*—Donald 14.1–5–24–1; Brown 15–4–43–2; Welch 16–5–46–5; Sheikh 5–2–14–2.

Warwickshire

*A. J. Moles b Johnson	1	– (3) not out	67
W. G. Khan c Brown b Tufnell	24	– (1) c Brown b Johnson	29
D. L. Hemp lbw b Fraser	37	– (4) not out	29
T. L. Penney c Weekes b Hewitt	9		
D. P. Ostler b Hewitt	18		
D. R. Brown c Weekes b Fraser	2		
N. M. K. Smith c Ramprakash b Johnson	9	– (2) b Johnson	60
G. Welch c Gatting b Hewitt	4		
M. A. Sheikh run out	24		
†T. Frost c Pooley b Tufnell	8		
A. A. Donald not out	3		
B 1, l-b 5, w 2, n-b 11	19	L-b 7, n-b 6	13

1/8 2/66 3/74 4/97 5/104   158   1/67 2/135   (2 wkts) 198
6/106 7/110 8/120 9/155

Bonus points – Middlesex 4.

Bowling: *First Innings*—Fraser 12–5–30–2; Hewitt 17–4–38–3; Johnson 16.1–6–40–2; Tufnell 11–1–44–2. *Second Innings*—Fraser 15–5–34–0; Hewitt 5–1–26–0; Johnson 12–0–66–2; Tufnell 11–1–42–0; Weekes 4.3–0–23–0.

Umpires: G. Sharp and R. A. White.

At Southampton, May 29, 30, 31, June 2. WARWICKSHIRE drew with HAMPSHIRE.

At Tunbridge Wells, June 4, 5, 6, 7. WARWICKSHIRE lost to KENT by four wickets.

WARWICKSHIRE v DERBYSHIRE

At Birmingham, June 12, 13, 14, 16. Drawn. Warwickshire 10 pts, Derbyshire 8 pts. Toss: Derbyshire. Championship debut: I. D. Blackwell.

The game began with the news that Dean Jones had resigned Derbyshire's captaincy, citing differences with leading players; by the end, his fellow-Victorian, coach Les Stillman, had been asked to keep out of the dressing-room. DeFreitas took over as acting-captain. His side were soon in trouble, when Brown reduced them to 16 for four. But Clarke – English-born, Australian-bred – came to the rescue. He was one short of a maiden century when he was last out at 200. Warwickshire lost only three wickets overtaking that, with Moles and Hemp adding 124, and they eased to a lead of 140, despite Malcolm taking five. Barnett and Rollins were much steadier in the second innings and, with Donald missing the game through injury and a day and a half lost to rain, that was enough to ensure a draw.

Close of play: First day, Warwickshire 4-0 (N. V. Knight 0*, A. J. Moles 0*); Second day, Warwickshire 209-3 (D. P. Ostler 30*, T. L. Penney 10*); Third day, Warwickshire 321-7 (T. L. Penney 72*, N. M. K. Smith 21*).

Derbyshire

K. J. Barnett c Knight b Brown	3	– b Welch	54
A. S. Rollins c Smith b Brown	0	– c Brown b Welch	59
C. J. Adams lbw b Brown	1	– (5) not out	31
T. A. Tweats b Smith	36	– (3) not out	45
J. E. Owen c Giles b Brown	8	– (4) lbw b Giles	10
V. P. Clarke c Piper b Giles	99		
†K. M. Krikken c Piper b Smith	5		
I. D. Blackwell b Giles	2		
*P. A. J. DeFreitas c Penney b Smith	24		
A. J. Harris c Ostler b Smith	0		
D. E. Malcolm not out	8		
B 2, l-b 2, n-b 10	14	B 4, l-b 6, w 2, n-b 18	30

1/3 2/4 3/4 4/16 5/124   200   1/113 2/138 3/162   (3 wkts dec.) 229
6/140 7/145 8/180 9/180

Bonus points – Derbyshire 1, Warwickshire 4.

Bowling: *First Innings*—Welch 9–3–22–0; Brown 9–2–33–4; Giles 23.2–5–86–2; Edmond 6–1–18–0; Smith 20–9–37–4. *Second Innings*—Brown 5–2–14–0; Welch 14–2–50–2; Giles 26–12–47–1; Smith 29–10–61–0; Edmond 9–1–34–0; Hemp 5–2–13–0.

Warwickshire

*N. V. Knight c Krikken b Malcolm	13	N. M. K. Smith c Owen b Malcolm	26
A. J. Moles c Krikken b DeFreitas	83	A. F. Giles c Barnett b Harris	8
D. L. Hemp c Krikken b DeFreitas	60	M. D. Edmond not out	5
D. P. Ostler b Malcolm	33		
T. L. Penney lbw b Harris	73	B 7, l-b 9	16
D. R. Brown c Owen b Malcolm	2		
†K. J. Piper c Krikken b Malcolm	12	1/26 2/150 3/177 4/216 5/218	340
G. Welch lbw b Clarke	9	6/254 7/269 8/326 9/328	

Bonus points – Warwickshire 3, Derbyshire 4.

Bowling: Malcolm 29–5–85–5; Harris 36.3–11–109–2; DeFreitas 31–6–88–2; Clarke 13–2–29–1; Blackwell 6–2–13–0.

Umpires: R. Palmer and N. T. Plews.

At Leicester, June 26, 27, 28, 30. LEICESTERSHIRE v WARWICKSHIRE. Abandoned.

WARWICKSHIRE v SURREY

At Birmingham, July 2, 3, 4, 5. Warwickshire won by five wickets. Warwickshire 23 pts, Surrey 4 pts. Toss: Warwickshire.

Once again, spectators got short rations: rain wiped out more than a day's playing time, but the game finished 11 balls into the final day. Warwickshire needed only 32 to win but, tantalisingly for Surrey, lost five wickets. Surrey's irresolute batsmen had been overwhelmed by Donald, returning after a muscle strain to take ten for 119. He comfortably outbowled the visitors' attack, which conceded a lead of 113. Surrey missed at least six chances. "It was unprofessional," said their coach, Dave Gilbert, "and everyone should feel embarrassed." Penney profited with 99, while Brown and Smith hit attacking sixties. Then Surrey's second innings fell apart, the last nine going for 57. Lewis lasted three balls against Donald and, on the way off, kicked and damaged the pavilion gate. Acting-captain Knight suffered more serious damage; he broke his finger catching Lewis and was out for seven weeks, wrecking his hopes of a chance in the Ashes series.

Close of play: First day, Surrey 157-6 (J. A. Knott 2*, M. P. Bicknell 11*); Second day, Warwickshire 159-4 (T. L. Penney 47*, D. R. Brown 57*); Third day, Warwickshire 23-4 (D. P. Ostler 5*, D. R. Brown 0*).

Surrey

J. D. Ratcliffe lbw b Welch	9	– c Hemp b Donald	59
G. J. Kennis b Welch	16	– lbw b Brown	9
I. J. Ward c Frost b Donald	18	– b Donald	21
*A. J. Hollioake lbw b Brown	31	– c Frost b Donald	5
A. D. Brown c Ostler b Donald	46	– lbw b Donald	5
C. C. Lewis c Hemp b Welch	9	– c Knight b Donald	0
†J. A. Knott run out	21	– c Ostler b Welch	1
M. P. Bicknell b Donald	11	– c Ostler b Brown	4
I. D. K. Salisbury c Ostler b Welch	1	– b Donald	24
Saqlain Mushtaq c Moles b Donald	7	– c and b Smith	10
A. J. Tudor not out	1	– not out	3
B 4, l-b 5, n-b 14	23	B 2, l-b 1	3

1/25 2/26 3/51 4/95 5/144   193   1/16 2/87 3/93 4/99 5/99   144
6/144 7/162 8/163 9/192   6/102 7/103 8/107 9/122

Bonus points – Warwickshire 4.

Bowling: *First Innings*—Donald 23–5–64–4; Welch 28–13–62–4; Giles 2–0–8–0; Brown 13–6–40–1; Smith 1–0–10–0. *Second Innings*—Donald 17.4–4–55–6; Welch 14–4–22–1; Brown 15–3–39–2; Smith 8–2–25–1.

Warwickshire

*N. V. Knight lbw b Bicknell	2		
A. J. Moles lbw b Bicknell	9	– (1) c Knott b Bicknell	0
D. L. Hemp c Knott b Bicknell	14	– b Bicknell	8
D. P. Ostler c Ward b Tudor	10	– not out	9
T. L. Penney lbw b Lewis	99	– lbw b Lewis	5
D. R. Brown b Bicknell	66	– c Brown b Bicknell	7
G. Welch c Knott b Tudor	6	– not out	0
N. M. K. Smith not out	69	– (2) c Hollioake b Lewis	0
†T. Frost c Kennis b Lewis	0		
A. F. Giles c Hollioake b Lewis	0		
A. A. Donald st Knott b Saqlain Mushtaq	2		
B 5, l-b 12, w 2, n-b 10	29	L-b 1, n-b 4	5

1/2 2/26 3/37 4/55 5/186   306   1/0 2/0 3/8   (5 wkts) 34
6/203 7/287 8/291 9/303   4/21 5/30

Bonus points – Warwickshire 3, Surrey 4.

Bowling: *First Innings*—Bicknell 30–3–96–4; Lewis 15–3–40–3; Tudor 11–1–49–2; Hollioake 14–1–60–0; Ratcliffe 4–1–10–0; Saqlain Mushtaq 13.4–3–34–1. *Second Innings*—Bicknell 5.5–1–24–3; Lewis 5–3–9–2.

Umpires: D. J. Constant and K. E. Palmer.

At Nottingham, July 16, 17, 18, 19. WARWICKSHIRE drew with NOTTINGHAMSHIRE.

WARWICKSHIRE v SOMERSET

At Birmingham, July 24, 25, 26, 27. Drawn. Warwickshire 8 pts, Somerset 10 pts. Toss: Warwickshire.

Both sides seemed a little off-key after their floodlit match on the Wednesday – though the delayed start on Thursday, to compensate for a near-midnight finish, became irrelevant when rain prevented play until 5.15 p.m. On the final afternoon, Warwickshire challenged Somerset to score 231 in 47 overs, and were rewarded when they slipped to 82 for six. Parsons and Rose held firm

to make the game safe. On the second day, Mushtaq Ahmed's wrist-spin had reduced Warwickshire to 157 for eight, on a bland pitch. Then Giles and Frost put on 141, a county ninth-wicket
record against Somerset. Frost scored a maiden fifty, and Giles just missed a hundred when
Caddick yorked him. Former Warwickshire player Holloway hit 106, with 19 fours and a six,
and Somerset declared on collecting three batting points. Wagh then scored 57 in his second
Championship game, and the prolific Hemp helped to set the target.

Close of play: First day, Warwickshire 2-0 (A. J. Moles 0*, M. A. Wagh 2*); Second day,
Somerset 8-0 (P. D. Bowler 0*, P. C. L. Holloway 8*); Third day, Warwickshire 0-0 (T. Frost
0*, A. J. Moles 0*).

Warwickshire

*A. J. Moles lbw b Caddick	38	– (2) b Rose	22
M. A. Wagh c Parsons b Caddick	23	– (3) lbw b Rose	57
D. L. Hemp c Parsons b Mushtaq Ahmed	49	– (4) not out	65
D. P. Ostler c Ecclestone b Mushtaq Ahmed	4		
T. L. Penney c Turner b Rose	22		
N. M. K. Smith b Mushtaq Ahmed	0	– (5) c Holloway b Rose	3
D. R. Brown b Mushtaq Ahmed	0		
G. Welch b Mushtaq Ahmed	2	– (7) not out	12
A. F. Giles b Caddick	97	– (6) c and b Rose	8
†T. Frost c Turner b Rose	56	– (1) b Caddick	22
A. A. Donald not out	19		
B 4, l-b 10, w 2, n-b 10	26	L-b 5, n-b 4	9

1/31 2/112 3/120 4/125 5/131   336   1/44 2/52 3/124   (5 wkts dec.) 198
6/131 7/137 8/157 9/298   4/134 5/159

Bonus points – Warwickshire 3, Somerset 4.

Bowling: *First Innings*—Caddick 30–8–92–3; Shine 23–6–61–0; Rose 19.4–8–81–2; Mushtaq
Ahmed 31–9–66–5; Parsons 2–1–4–0; Trescothick 4–1–18–0. *Second Innings*—Mushtaq Ahmed
16–4–43–0; Shine 6–0–42–0; Caddick 11–4–33–1; Rose 15–1–75–4.

Somerset

*P. D. Bowler lbw b Brown	2	– c Penney b Donald	9
P. C. L. Holloway c Smith b Brown	106	– c Moles b Brown	0
S. C. Ecclestone b Giles	28	– c Smith b Giles	35
M. N. Lathwell c Ostler b Giles	21	– lbw b Smith	17
M. E. Trescothick st Frost b Giles	57	– c Ostler b Smith	6
†R. J. Turner not out	37	– (7) lbw b Donald	4
K. A. Parsons c Smith b Brown	2	– (6) not out	45
G. D. Rose not out	46	– not out	11
L-b 5	5	B 1, l-b 4, n-b 2	7

1/15 2/72 3/136 4/188 5/234   (6 wkts dec.) 304   1/2 2/16 3/51   (6 wkts) 134
6/237   4/67 5/73 6/82

A. R. Caddick, Mushtaq Ahmed and K. J. Shine did not bat.

Bonus points – Somerset 3, Warwickshire 2.

Bowling: *First Innings*—Donald 16–4–47–0; Giles 32.5–4–113–3; Brown 15–1–65–3; Welch
12–3–38–0; Smith 9–2–36–0. *Second Innings*—Donald 14–1–52–2; Brown 9–3–31–1; Smith
11–7–14–2; Giles 11–2–32–1; Wagh 1–1–0–0.

Umpires: T. E. Jesty and R. Palmer.

WARWICKSHIRE v SUSSEX

At Birmingham, July 31, August 1, 2. Warwickshire won by nine wickets. Warwickshire 21 pts,
Sussex 4 pts. Toss: Warwickshire. Championship debut: A. D. Edwards.

Sussex were totally outclassed in a match occupying less than 150 overs. The pitch offered
Donald, in particular, extravagant bounce and pace. Only 16 overs were possible on the first day,

but the second saw 22 wickets go down in 74.2. The one significant event on the opening day occurred when Moles's finger was broken by Drakes. This made him the third Warwickshire captain, after Munton and Knight, to be sidelined by injury. But Moles did make a notable intervention: he returned, at 188 for nine, to hit 22 from 15 balls, earning a batting point and incidentally doubling the follow-on target from 39 to 78. Sussex were bowled out in two hours for 63. No batsman passed 17 and no partnership beat 15. Donald returned four for 11 and made that eight for 51 in the match, while Brown and Welch took five each. Athey held out for 51 overs second time round, and Drakes hit a whirlwind 42 in 33 balls to avert a third successive innings defeat. Sussex still sank to the bottom of the table.

Close of play: First day, Warwickshire 50-0 (M. A. Wagh 24*, D. L. Hemp 10*); Second day, Sussex 7-2 (A. D. Edwards 2*, M. A. Robinson 1*).

Warwickshire

*A. J. Moles c Rao b Robinson	31			
M. A. Wagh c Moores b Robinson	57	– not out		30
D. L. Hemp c Athey b Drakes	15	– not out		0
A. Singh c Drakes b Edwards	0			
T. L. Penney c Robinson b Drakes	1			
N. M. K. Smith c Moores b Robinson	38			
D. R. Brown c Moores b Edwards	6			
G. Welch b Drakes	12			
A. F. Giles b Robinson	4			
A. A. Donald c Edwards b Drakes	23			
†K. J. Piper not out	17	– (1) c Moores b Kirtley		10
L-b 3, w 2, n-b 18	23	L-b 1		1

1/56 2/59 3/60 4/130 5/145   227   1/22   (1 wkt) 41
6/149 7/154 8/185 9/188

Bonus points – Warwickshire 1, Sussex 4.

In the first innings A. J. Moles, when 9, retired hurt at 34 and resumed at 188.

Bowling: *First Innings*—Drakes 21–5–84–4; Kirtley 10–0–50–0; Edwards 14–4–37–2; Robinson 14–0–53–4. *Second Innings*—Kirtley 2.5–0–20–1; Edwards 2–0–20–0.

Sussex

R. K. Rao run out	3	– c Piper b Donald		4
M. T. E. Peirce c Piper b Donald	10	– lbw b Brown		0
C. W. J. Athey b Donald	0	– (5) c Piper b Donald		67
M. Newell c Wagh b Brown	7	– (6) c Wagh b Donald		12
K. Greenfield c sub b Welch	4	– (7) c sub b Donald		9
K. Newell lbw b Brown	17	– (8) b Welch		25
*†P. Moores c Singh b Brown	0	– (9) c sub b Brown		7
V. C. Drakes c Brown b Welch	15	– (10) not out		42
A. D. Edwards b Donald	0	– (3) c Brown b Welch		16
M. A. Robinson not out	0	– (4) c Singh b Welch		1
R. J. Kirtley b Donald	1	– run out		1
W 6	6	L-b 13, n-b 6		19

1/13 2/13 3/13 4/20 5/26   63   1/0 2/4 3/11 4/38 5/60   203
6/26 7/41 8/56 9/56   6/72 7/126 8/149 9/185

Bonus points – Warwickshire 4.

Bowling: *First Innings*—Donald 10.2–5–11–4; Welch 12–7–22–2; Brown 4–0–30–3. *Second Innings*—Donald 16.1–7–40–4; Brown 14–4–58–2; Welch 15–2–63–3; Hemp 5–1–9–0; Giles 9–4–20–0.

Umpires: B. Dudleston and J. H. Hampshire.

At Blackpool, August 6, 7, 8. **WARWICKSHIRE** lost to **LANCASHIRE** by three wickets.

WARWICKSHIRE v WORCESTERSHIRE

At Birmingham, August 20, 21, 22, 23. Drawn. Warwickshire 7 pts, Worcestershire 10 pts. Toss: Warwickshire.

Rain trimmed 87 overs from the first two days, and there was little prospect of contrivance between the local rivals. Instead, Moody decided to bat Warwickshire out of the game and hope he could bowl them out again as cheaply as Mirza and Sheriyar had on the opening day. Thanks to centuries from night-watchman Illingworth, Hick, and Moody himself, the first part of the plan succeeded; Worcestershire took a lead of 196. It was Illingworth's fourth first-class hundred – his second against Warwickshire – in his first Championship match of 1997, putting on 239 with Hick. The home attack badly missed the injured Donald, though Brown picked up five wickets. Worcestershire then reduced Warwickshire to 53 for four, and scented a third successive win, which would have lifted them to third place. But Knight, returning after seven weeks off with a broken finger, thwarted them. His century secured the draw on another rain-shortened day.

Close of play: First day, Worcestershire 20-2 (R. K. Illingworth 5*, G. A. Hick 7*); Second day, Worcestershire 133-2 (R. K. Illingworth 76*, G. A. Hick 40*); Third day, Warwickshire 8-1 (N. V. Knight 6*, K. J. Piper 2*).

Warwickshire

*N. V. Knight c Rhodes b Sheriyar	20	– not out	116
A. J. Moles c Rhodes b Sheriyar	25	– c Leatherdale b Moody	0
D. L. Hemp c Illingworth b Mirza	25	– (4) c and b Moody	9
M. A. Wagh c Moody b Mirza	32	– (5) c Leatherdale b Illingworth	16
T. L. Penney c Curtis b Lampitt	0	– (6) c Mirza b Moody	42
N. M. K. Smith c Rhodes b Moody	40	– (7) not out	21
D. R. Brown c Rhodes b Sheriyar	8		
G. Welch b Mirza	38		
A. F. Giles lbw b Lampitt	20		
†K. J. Piper not out	4	– (3) c Sheriyar b Mirza	4
M. A. V. Bell lbw b Mirza	0		
B 4, l-b 8, w 8, n-b 20	40	B 5, l-b 3, w 10, n-b 15	33

1/48 2/53 3/111 4/115 5/133   252   1/2 2/10 3/29   (5 wkts dec.) 241
6/146 7/197 8/238 9/246   4/53 5/185

Bonus points – Warwickshire 2, Worcestershire 4.

Bowling: *First Innings*—Sheriyar 15–3–48–3; Mirza 16–4–51–4; Moody 16–4–56–1; Lampitt 17–3–60–2; Illingworth 3–0–12–0; Leatherdale 2–0–13–0. *Second Innings*—Illingworth 17–4–34–1; Moody 21–5–57–3; Mirza 11–2–58–1; Sheriyar 13–6–47–0; Hick 1–0–2–0; Lampitt 8–1–21–0; Leatherdale 4–0–14–0.

Worcestershire

T. S. Curtis lbw b Brown	6	S. R. Lampitt b Brown	7
W. P. C. Weston c Moles b Brown	2	A. Sheriyar lbw b Giles	3
R. K. Illingworth c Piper b Giles	112	M. M. Mirza not out	10
G. A. Hick c Hemp b Giles	122		
*T. M. Moody c Piper b Welch	108	B 2, l-b 10, w 6, n-b 2	20
D. A. Leatherdale c Moles b Welch	16		
V. S. Solanki c Wagh b Brown	1	1/8 2/9 3/248 4/257 5/296	448
†S. J. Rhodes lbw b Brown	41	6/300 7/383 8/405 9/414	

Bonus points – Worcestershire 3, Warwickshire 2 (Score at 120 overs: 339-6).

Bowling: Welch 34.1–9–96–2; Brown 38–7–118–5; Giles 38–10–77–3; Bell 27–4–101–0; Smith 11–2–44–0.

Umpires: J. C. Balderstone and B. J. Meyer.

At Chelmsford, August 27, 28, 29. WARWICKSHIRE beat ESSEX by eight wickets.

At Chester-le-Street, September 2, 3, 4, 5. WARWICKSHIRE beat DURHAM by an innings and 99 runs.

WARWICKSHIRE v GLOUCESTERSHIRE

At Birmingham, September 10, 11, 12. Warwickshire won by an innings and 81 runs. Warwickshire 24 pts, Gloucestershire 4 pts. Toss: Warwickshire.

Neil Smith took a stranglehold on this match with his first hundred for eight years and his best bowling in 1997. After penetrative seam bowling by Lewis had reduced Warwickshire to 167 for five, Smith came in to score 148 at nearly a run a ball, with 25 fours and a six. He added 186 with Brown, a county eighth-wicket record against Gloucestershire. Then he took four for 32, helping dismiss the visitors for a paltry 113, which was 305 behind. Donald's extra pace, supported by Giles's spin, won the match before lunch on the third day. It lasted that long only because Russell, who had been concussed by a blow from Brown, returned to reach 67 and pass 1,000 in a season for the first time. Gloucestershire's frail batting surrendered twice in 109 overs on a dry pitch, which might have had inconsistent bounce but was never unplayable. Their third successive defeat was the third successive win for Warwickshire, who climbed above them in the table.

Close of play: First day, Warwickshire 407-7 (N. M. K. Smith 145*, D. R. Brown 74*); Second day, Gloucestershire 186-5 (M. C. J. Ball 19*, R. P. Davis 3*).

Warwickshire

*N. V. Knight c Hewson b Smith	71	D. R. Brown c Davis b Smith	79
M. A. Wagh b Lewis	10	G. Welch not out	1
D. L. Hemp c Ball b Lewis	66	A. A. Donald c Ball b Smith	0
D. P. Ostler c Russell b Smith	1		
T. L. Penney lbw b Lewis	13	L-b 8, n-b 10	18
†K. J. Piper c Ball b Lewis	2		
N. M. K. Smith lbw b Lewis	148	1/18 2/148 3/156 4/165 5/167	418
A. F. Giles c Windows b Lewis	9	6/204 7/226 8/412 9/418	

Bonus points – Warwickshire 4, Gloucestershire 4.

Bowling: Smith 20.3–2–70–4; Lewis 24–5–89–6; Ball 29–10–69–0; Young 12–0–70–0; Alleyne 17–3–69–0; Davis 6–0–22–0; Hancock 4–1–21–0.

Gloucestershire

M. G. N. Windows c Piper b Donald	0	– c Piper b Welch	20
T. H. C. Hancock b Smith	35	– b Giles	41
R. I. Dawson c Ostler b Brown	10	– c Ostler b Smith	5
S. Young c Piper b Welch	9	– c Ostler b Giles	25
*M. W. Alleyne c Ostler b Welch	5	– b Smith	4
†R. C. Russell c Wagh b Donald	10	– c Piper b Donald	67
M. C. J. Ball c Ostler b Smith	10	– c Knight b Donald	23
R. P. Davis lbw b Smith	2	– c sub b Donald	3
J. Lewis not out	9	– not out	8
A. M. Smith b Smith	15	– b Donald	2
D. R. Hewson absent ill		– absent ill	
N-b 8	8	B 13, l-b 8, w 2, n-b 8	26
1/0 2/25 3/44 4/62 5/70	113	1/34 2/71 3/73 4/77 5/154	224
6/83 7/89 8/89 9/113		6/186 7/191 8/222 9/224	

Bonus points – Warwickshire 4.

In the second innings R. C. Russell, when 44, retired hurt at 158 and resumed at 186.

Bowling: *First Innings*—Donald 10–4–24–2; Brown 9–5–20–1; Welch 10–2–37–2; Smith 11–3–32–4. *Second Innings*—Donald 15.5–6–63–4; Brown 16–7–23–0; Welch 4–1–17–1; Giles 19–6–48–2; Smith 14–2–57–2.

Umpires: N. T. Plews and G. Sharp.

WARWICKSHIRE v NORTHAMPTONSHIRE

At Birmingham, September 18, 19, 20, 21. Drawn. Warwickshire 7 pts, Northamptonshire 9 pts. Toss: Northamptonshire.

Warwickshire started 20 points behind Glamorgan, with a very faint chance of the title if other results and the weather fell the right way. But the return of Donald to South Africa, losing the toss, stubborn Northamptonshire batting and a second-day washout all worked against them. They were lucky to share fourth place with Middlesex; friendly bowling had donated them an extra batting point. In return, Northamptonshire accepted 150 easy runs – including a parting gift of 85 not out for Fordham before he joined the ECB – setting Warwickshire 271 in 64 overs. But, with the pitch turning, they lost too many wickets to threaten that. On the opening day, the home side had clashed with umpire Jones, who objected to the slips moving up at a signal for Bell's slower ball. It did not trouble Swann, who scored a maiden hundred and displayed unwavering concentration for more than seven hours and 112 overs. He steered Northamptonshire towards 371. Their young spinners, Jason Brown and Davies, then reduced Warwickshire to 215 for eight on the final morning before the captains agreed to contrivance.

Close of play: First day, Northamptonshire 215-5 (A. J. Swann 73*, A. L. Penberthy 2*); Second day, No play; Third day, Warwickshire 157-6 (M. A. Wagh 64*, A. F. Giles 4*).

Northamptonshire

A. Fordham c Knight b Bell	35	– not out 85
R. R. Montgomerie c Smith b Brown	58	
A. J. Swann c Brown b Smith	136	
*K. M. Curran c Piper b Brown	0	– (2) not out 57
D. J. Sales c Ostler b Giles	27	
T. C. Walton run out	6	
A. L. Penberthy lbw b Brown	14	
†D. Ripley lbw b Brown	48	
J. P. Taylor not out	27	
M. K. Davies c Piper b Brown	0	
J. F. Brown b Smith	0	
B 6, l-b 12, n-b 2	20	B 3, l-b 1, w 4 8

1/58 2/133 3/133 4/200 5/212   371   (no wkt dec.) 150
6/253 7/333 8/369 9/370

Bonus points – Northamptonshire 3, Warwickshire 2 (Score at 120 overs: 313-6).

Bowling: *First Innings*—Welch 19-9-43-0; Brown 28-7-62-5; Giles 39-14-63-1; Bell 23-4-70-1; Smith 35.4-9-115-2. *Second Innings*—Ostler 6-0-66-0; Knight 6-0-71-0; Brown 1-0-9-0.

Warwickshire

*N. V. Knight c Penberthy b Taylor	9	– b Taylor 3
N. M. K. Smith c Sales b Taylor	35	– b Curran 1
M. A. Wagh c Davies b Brown	70	– c Fordham b Penberthy 18
D. L. Hemp b Curran	11	– lbw b Taylor 15
D. P. Ostler c Montgomerie b Davies	20	– b Davies 58
T. L. Penney c Curran b Davies	0	– c Montgomerie b Davies 27
†K. J. Piper c and b Brown	6	– b Brown 0
A. F. Giles b Brown	45	– not out 73
D. R. Brown not out	28	– st Ripley b Brown 45
G. Welch not out	19	– not out 0
L-b 4, n-b 4	8	L-b 4, n-b 2 6

1/26 2/65 3/84 4/135 5/137   (8 wkts dec.) 251   1/4 2/4 3/23 4/54   (8 wkts) 246
6/146 7/183 8/215   5/119 6/124 7/126 8/246

M. A. V. Bell did not bat.

Bonus points – Warwickshire 2, Northamptonshire 3.

Bowling: *First Innings*—Taylor 14-0-68-2; Penberthy 5-0-35-0; Brown 26-4-79-3; Curran 4-0-15-1; Davies 21-13-29-2; Walton 2-0-6-0; Fordham 1.3-0-6-0. *Second Innings*—Taylor 12-3-27-2; Curran 6-2-25-1; Davies 15-3-57-2; Brown 24.5-2-123-2; Penberthy 6-2-10-1.

Umpires: J. C. Balderstone and A. A. Jones.

WORCESTERSHIRE

Alamgir Sheriyar

Patron: The Duke of Westminster

President: T. W. Graveney

Chairman: C. D. Fearnley

Chairman, Cricket Committee: J. E. Chadd

Secretary: The Rev. M. D. Vockins

Captain: T. M. Moody

Coach: C. W. J. Athey

Head Groundsman: R. McLaren

David Houghton signed off as Worcestershire coach with third place in the Championship. This was not merely the best finish of his four-year reign but represented a process of continuous improvement for a team that was 15th in 1994, tenth in 1995 and seventh in 1996. It was a remarkable performance since there were thought to be short of attacking penetration even before the loss of their two most experienced bowlers, Phil Newport and Richard Illingworth, to long-term injuries. And Houghton deserves much of the credit for generating the self-belief that made it possible.

Most of Worcestershire's running was made in the second half of the season: they won four of their last seven games. They could have moved into a position to challenge for the title if they had not begun their campaign with four consecutive draws – three of which were rain-affected. As it was, they never threatened to overtake Glamorgan or Kent, who contested the leadership of the table for the last month, and it was something of a surprise when their win against Hampshire enabled them to leapfrog from sixth to third on the last day of the season.

In a year when no one escaped the attentions of the weather, Worcestershire were particularly unfortunate; they dominated matches against Leicestershire and Warwickshire, but on both occasions enough time was lost on the final day to prevent a result. The match against Durham was drawn with scores level after a first-day washout. As Tom Moody, the captain, commented: "You expect rain in an English season, and it normally saves you on some occasions and frustrates you on others. But in 1997, hand on heart, I can say we were denied several times and not once were rescued." In all, 1,851 overs and over 115 hours of play in the Championship were lost – the equivalent of nearly 18 days' cricket.

When they did make it on to the field, Worcestershire were a handful for most sides. The man who came through in the absence of Newport and Illingworth was left-arm seamer Alamgir Sheriyar, who prospered with the new ball, and took 62 first-class wickets at 25.40. Sheriyar bowled with improved control at a probing length, and reliably made the ball duck back into the right-hander, having obviously benefited from a winter's coaching by Newport.

There was also surprisingly effective support from medium-pacers David Leatherdale and Gavin Haynes, who made the headlines when they took nine wickets between them in a one-day victory over the Australians at New Road in May. Leatherdale, who had previously tended to be brought on as a last resort, claimed five for ten and never looked back, ending the season with 53 wickets in all competitions. Haynes was not far behind with 48 – an encouraging return for a player who missed the whole of the 1996 season with a knee injury.

But it was the batting that really distinguished itself. Worcestershire scored 18 Championship centuries, the most by any county, and only Glamorgan beat their total of 49 batting points. At the heart of it was Graeme Hick, who came top of the national batting averages, one of the few statistical successes that had previously eluded him. But it was a mixed season for Hick. After his first long winter break for seven years, he had hoped to return refreshed and push his claims for a place in the Ashes series through weight of runs. But for the first month and a half it was often a struggle even to reach double figures. England decided to get by without him. Slowly but surely he regained his form, with six centuries taking him to a career figure of 96. His average was heavily influenced by two innings: an opportunistic 164 not out milked off Oxford University in May and the end-of-season fiesta when he took an unbeaten 303 off a Hampshire attack that included two debutant bowlers.

Moody failed to pass 1,000 runs for only the second time in six seasons at New Road, but made up for it in that final game at Southampton. He scored 180 out of an unbroken stand of 438 with Hick – the highest third-wicket partnership in the history of the Championship, and an all-wicket record for Worcestershire. Hick now has a share in four of Worcestershire's record stands, more than any other man, past or present, can currently claim for any county.

Among the supporting players, Phil Weston bounced back strongly after a poor start saw him lose his place in the side, and was rewarded with 1,190 runs at a shade under fifty. Leatherdale also came on as a batsman. Often guilty of under-achievement during a nine-year Worcestershire career, he found new consistency in 1997, and his 863 Championship runs at 57.53, plus his startling progress with the ball, were enough for him to sweep the board in the club's individual honours awards. He was chosen as Clubman of the Year and voted Player of the Year by both full and junior members.

For all Worcestershire's batting depth, it will be difficult to replace opener Tim Curtis, who retired after 19 seasons, five England caps, 43 centuries and 20,832 runs to take up a full-time teaching post at Worcester Royal Grammar School. Curtis never achieved the sort of accolades handed out to his former England opening partner Graham Gooch on his retirement. His fondness for grinding out six-hour hundreds endeared him to only the most committed spectators, but during Phil Neale's successful years as Worcestershire captain Curtis was the rock on which many an opposing attack foundered. And he was no slouch in the one-day game either, finishing his career with 6,423 Sunday League runs at an average of 40.65.

Against most expectations, Worcestershire were less effective in limited-overs cricket than the first-class game in 1997. They failed in the knockouts and had to settle for retaining eighth place in the Sunday League, despite a period in late August when they were on the fringes of the title race.

New coach Bill Athey may look for stronger one-day performances from all-rounders such as Vikram Solanki and Stuart Lampitt next season but, if he is to continue Worcestershire's progress up the Championship table, he needs Newport, the beneficiary, to stay fit.

One familiar face will be missing from New Road next year. Jim Sewter, the county's scorer since 1979, died in October at the age of 81. He had officially retired at the end of the season, after recording Hick and Moody's mammoth stand at Southampton. – JOHN CURTIS.

WORCESTERSHIRE 1997

[Bill Smith]

Back row: B. E. A. Preece, I. Dawood, M. J. Rawnsley. *Middle row:* P. A. Thomas, R. J. Chapman, K. R. Spiring, D. A. Leatherdale, W. P. C. Weston, G. R. Haynes, V. S. Solanki, A. Sheriyar, J. E. Brinkley. *Front row:* D. B. D'Oliveira (*Second Eleven captain/assistant coach*), S. R. Lampitt, R. K. Illingworth, T. S. Curtis, T. M. Moody (*captain*), S. J. Rhodes, G. A. Hick, P. J. Newport, D. L. Houghton (*coach*).

WORCESTERSHIRE RESULTS

All first-class matches – Played 19: Won 6, Lost 3, Drawn 10.

County Championship matches – Played 17: Won 6, Lost 3, Drawn 8.

Competition placings – Britannic Assurance County Championship, 3rd; NatWest Trophy, 2nd round; Benson and Hedges Cup, 5th in Group A; AXA Life League, 8th.

COUNTY CHAMPIONSHIP AVERAGES

BATTING

Cap		M	I	NO	R	HS	100s	50s	Avge	Ct/St
1986	R. K. Illingworth	5	4	2	157	112	1	0	78.50	3
1986	G. A. Hick	16	25	5	1,161	303*	4	3	58.05	18
1994	D. A. Leatherdale	15	22	7	863	129	2	5	57.53	14
1995	W. P. C. Weston ...	15	25	4	1,029	205	3	3	49.00	6
1991	T. M. Moody§	14	21	1	973	180*	3	4	48.65	14
1984	T. S. Curtis	13	21	1	742	160	4	1	37.10	9
1997	K. R. Spiring	15	24	2	800	150	1	4	36.36	7
1986	S. J. Rhodes	17	22	6	581	78	0	4	36.31	39/3
1994	G. R. Haynes†	15	22	3	657	70	0	5	34.57	3
1989	S. R. Lampitt	15	17	7	277	52	0	1	27.70	16
	V. S. Solanki	11	13	0	279	61	0	2	21.46	8
1986	P. J. Newport	8	6	0	91	45	0	0	15.16	0
1997	A. Sheriyar	16	12	4	73	21	0	0	9.12	4
	M. M. Mirza........	5	6	4	11	10*	0	0	5.50	1

Also batted: R. J. Chapman (5 matches) 3, 0, 0 (2 ct); M. J. Rawnsley (2 matches) 9, 26.

* Signifies not out.   † Born in Worcestershire.   § Overseas player.

BOWLING

	O	M	R	W	BB	5W/i	Avge
P. J. Newport	177.2	56	444	19	7-37	1	23.36
R. K. Illingworth	206	75	442	18	7-79	1	24.55
A. Sheriyar............	404.1	87	1,438	56	6-19	3	25.67
D. A. Leatherdale	195.3	43	674	25	5-56	1	26.96
G. R. Haynes	270.1	63	826	29	3-46	0	28.48
M. M. Mirza	125.4	23	484	16	4-51	0	30.25
S. R. Lampitt	334.4	70	1,302	35	5-39	1	37.20
T. M. Moody	213.4	42	829	19	5-148	1	43.63

Also bowled: R. J. Chapman 78.4–13–388–8; T. S. Curtis 12–1–65–1; G. A. Hick 187–45–603–9; M. J. Rawnsley 32–9–85–3; V. S. Solanki 44–8–152–1; K. R. Spiring 2–0–10–0; W. P. C. Weston 7–0–57–0.

COUNTY RECORDS

Highest score for:	405*	G. A. Hick v Somerset at Taunton	1988
Highest score against:	331*	J. D. Robertson (Middlesex) at Worcester....	1949
Best bowling for:	9-23	C. F. Root v Lancashire at Worcester	1931
Best bowling against:	10-51	J. Mercer (Glamorgan) at Worcester	1936
Highest total for:	670-7 dec.	v Somerset at Worcester...................	1995
Highest total against:	701-4 dec.	by Leicestershire at Worcester	1906
Lowest total for:	24	v Yorkshire at Huddersfield	1903
Lowest total against:	30	by Hampshire at Worcester	1903

At Nottingham, April 23, 24, 25, 26. WORCESTERSHIRE drew with NOTTINGHAMSHIRE.

WORCESTERSHIRE v LEICESTERSHIRE

At Worcester, May 7, 8, 9, 10. Drawn. Worcestershire 9 pts, Leicestershire 7 pts. Toss: Worcestershire. Championship debut: N. C. Johnson.

High-class swing bowling from Newport produced his best Championship figures for nine seasons, but it was to no avail. After three rain-shortened days, a final-day washout denied Worcestershire victory against the county champions. Leicestershire initially held the upper hand, reducing the home side to 60 for four. A half-century by Spiring and a gutsy, unbeaten 47 from Haynes, who missed the previous season with a knee injury, redressed the balance. Newport had been another long-term absentee in 1996, with Achilles tendon trouble. Now, he superbly exploited the overcast conditions to take seven for 37, which carried him past 800 first-class wickets. Leicestershire were routed for 69 and subsided to 14 for three following on. A three-day finish might have been achieved had Natal all-rounder Neil Johnson, Leicestershire's replacement for Phil Simmons, been held at slip off Haynes when seven. He survived to dominate a stand of 118 with Maddy, which delayed Worcestershire long enough for the weather to have the final say.

Close of play: First day, Worcestershire 199-6 (G. R. Haynes 16*, S. J. Rhodes 37*); Second day, Leicestershire 42-5 (G. I. Macmillan 5*, P. A. Nixon 5*); Third day, Leicestershire 141-4 (N. C. Johnson 87*, G. I. Macmillan 0*).

Worcestershire

T. S. Curtis lbw b Millns	4	P. J. Newport b Mullally	4
W. P. C. Weston c Millns b Mullally	11	R. J. Chapman c Dakin b Mullally	3
G. A. Hick lbw b Millns	9	A. Sheriyar c Dakin b Millns	13
K. R. Spiring c Maddy b Johnson	55		
*T. M. Moody c Nixon b Johnson	8	B 6, l-b 8, w 6, n-b 20	40
V. S. Solanki c Brimson b Mullally	24		
G. R. Haynes not out	47	1/4 2/22 3/36 4/60 5/109	257
†S. J. Rhodes c Nixon b Johnson	39	6/131 7/207 8/232 9/236	

Bonus points – Worcestershire 2, Leicestershire 4.

Bowling: Millns 18.2–6–53–3; Mullally 28–3–86–4; Brimson 8–4–20–0; Johnson 21–4–61–3; Wells 6–3–10–0; Dakin 6–1–8–0; Maddy 1–0–5–0.

Leicestershire

D. L. Maddy c Hick b Sheriyar	20	– c Rhodes b Chapman	36
I. J. Sutcliffe lbw b Newport	6	– c Hick b Newport	3
A. Habib c Hick b Newport	3	– c Rhodes b Haynes	5
*V. J. Wells c Rhodes b Newport	0	– c Rhodes b Haynes	0
N. C. Johnson lbw b Newport	1	– not out	87
G. I. Macmillan b Sheriyar	18	– not out	0
†P. A. Nixon c Spiring b Newport	7		
J. M. Dakin lbw b Sheriyar	0		
D. J. Millns lbw b Newport	1		
A. D. Mullally not out	7		
M. T. Brimson c Moody b Newport	0		
L-b 6	6	B 2, l-b 4, w 2, n-b 2	10
1/13 2/21 3/21 4/27 5/33	69	1/3 2/14 3/14 4/132 (4 wkts)	141
6/44 7/45 8/46 9/68			

Bonus points – Worcestershire 4.

Bowling: *First Innings*—Newport 17.2–5–37–7; Sheriyar 17–5–26–3. *Second Innings*—Newport 11–6–20–1; Sheriyar 9–1–30–0; Chapman 9.4–2–42–1; Haynes 11–1–43–2.

Umpires: J. W. Holder and K. E. Palmer.

At Oxford, May 14, 15, 16. WORCESTERSHIRE drew with OXFORD UNIVERSITY.

At Worcester, May 18. WORCESTERSHIRE beat AUSTRALIANS by five wickets (See Australian tour section).

At Chester-le-Street, May 21, 22, 23, 24. WORCESTERSHIRE drew with DURHAM.

WORCESTERSHIRE v SOMERSET

At Worcester, May 29, 30, 31, June 2. Drawn. Worcestershire 10 pts, Somerset 10 pts. Toss: Worcestershire.

The contest spluttered out of second gear only when Somerset were asked to score 277 in 55 overs – almost twice the game's going rate. They looked as if they would win easily, racing to 82 for one in 12 overs against an attack missing the injured Newport. But, with the hard work seemingly done, some helter-skelter batting saw three wickets lost in 11 balls to kill their ambitions. On a wearing, uneven pitch, Curtis had applied himself for six hours in the face of probing bowling by Caddick. Haynes kept Curtis company, putting on 129 in 49 overs. Somerset's reply was equally plodding, apart from an enterprising 61 from Holloway. Leatherdale registered his first five-wicket haul but Turner shepherded the tail so effectively that the last two wickets added 87. Caddick again bowled aggressively but disciplined fifties from Haynes and Leatherdale steered Worcestershire out of trouble.

Close of play: First day, Worcestershire 270-6 (V. S. Solanki 16*, S. J. Rhodes 4*); Second day, Somerset 256-8 (R. J. Turner 37*); Third day, Worcestershire 186-4 (G. R. Haynes 16*, D. A. Leatherdale 35*).

Worcestershire

T. S. Curtis c Harden b Rose	101	– c Turner b Caddick	1
W. P. C. Weston c Bowler b Rose	13	– c Turner b Caddick	65
G. A. Hick c Lathwell b Caddick	14	– lbw b Caddick	17
K. R. Spiring c Lathwell b Burns	24	– lbw b Shine	37
G. R. Haynes b Rose	70	– c Bowler b Mushtaq Ahmed	52
D. A. Leatherdale lbw b Caddick	6	– c Burns b Mushtaq Ahmed	57
V. S. Solanki lbw b Shine	28	– c Turner b Mushtaq Ahmed	0
*†S. J. Rhodes c Turner b Caddick	8	– not out	41
S. R. Lampitt c Burns b Caddick	9	– not out	27
P. J. Newport c Turner b Caddick	0		
A. Sheriyar not out	7		
L-b 21, n-b 2	23	B 4, l-b 7, w 8	19

1/35 2/61 3/101 4/230 5/245   303   1/12 2/40 3/129   (7 wkts dec.) 316
6/254 7/284 8/292 9/292   4/136 5/234
                                    6/236 7/261

Bonus points – Worcestershire 3, Somerset 4.

Bowling: *First Innings*—Caddick 29.2–10–64–5; Shine 19–6–42–1; Dimond 9–2–26–0; Rose 20–6–44–3; Mushtaq Ahmed 27–10–66–0; Burns 10–2–40–1; Bowler 2–2–0–0. *Second Innings*—Caddick 31–6–86–3; Shine 14–4–59–1; Mushtaq Ahmed 42–10–97–3; Rose 17–5–57–0; Bowler 4–3–2–0; Dimond 2–1–4–0.

Somerset

M. N. Lathwell lbw b Lampitt	42	– c Rhodes b Haynes	27
*P. D. Bowler c Hick b Lampitt	25	– (5) not out	61
P. C. L. Holloway c Rhodes b Sheriyar	61	– (7) not out	14
R. J. Harden lbw b Leatherdale	15	– (6) b Leatherdale	18
M. Burns c Rhodes b Leatherdale	0	– (2) b Sheriyar	8
G. D. Rose c Hick b Leatherdale	37	– (4) c Lampitt b Haynes	0
†R. J. Turner not out	83	– (3) lbw b Lampitt	47
M. Dimond c Lampitt b Leatherdale	4		
Mushtaq Ahmed c Rhodes b Sheriyar	14		
A. R. Caddick lbw b Leatherdale	20		
K. J. Shine lbw b Lampitt	15		
B 2, l-b 5, w 4, n-b 16	27	N-b 10	10

1/63 2/108 3/135 4/143 5/168	343	1/11 2/82 3/82	(5 wkts) 185
6/227 7/237 8/256 9/296		4/82 5/119	

Bonus points – Somerset 3, Worcestershire 4 (Score at 120 overs: 341-9).

Bowling: *First Innings*—Newport 15–8–22–0; Sheriyar 29–9–90–2; Haynes 19–4–54–0; Lampitt 28.4–11–80–3; Leatherdale 20–5–56–5; Solanki 5–1–22–0; Hick 5–2–12–0. *Second Innings*—Sheriyar 9–0–57–1; Lampitt 13–4–55–1; Haynes 11–2–33–2; Leatherdale 10–1–30–1; Solanki 4–1–10–0.

Umpires: H. D. Bird and D. J. Constant.

At Bristol, June 12, 13, 14, 16. WORCESTERSHIRE beat GLOUCESTERSHIRE by 95 runs.

WORCESTERSHIRE v SURREY

At Worcester, June 18, 19, 20, 21. Drawn. Worcestershire 7 pts, Surrey 7 pts. Toss: Surrey.

With Surrey's Test batsmen at Lord's, Ratcliffe was promoted to his preferred position as opener and responded with his first century since joining from Warwickshire in 1995. He scored a career-best 135, with 22 fours and a six, on the eve of his 28th birthday. But the most exhilarating batting came from Brown, who raced to a run-a-ball 121 containing 18 fours and three sixes, one onto the roof of the Ladies' Pavilion. He and Ratcliffe added 179 in 38 overs. A last-wicket stand of 59 between Saqlain Mushtaq and Tudor took Surrey past 450 before rain wiped out most of the second day. When Worcestershire did get in, Curtis was out first ball. Hick, with ten fours, finally hit back, but persistent rain wiped out the final two days.

Close of play: First day, Surrey 382-7 (J. A. Knott 17*, M. P. Bicknell 2*); Second day, Worcestershire 81-1 (W. P. C. Weston 17*, G. A. Hick 48*); Third day, No play.

Surrey

J. D. Ratcliffe c Leatherdale b Sheriyar	135	M. P. Bicknell c Rhodes b Lampitt	4
G. J. Kennis c Hick b Lampitt	24	Saqlain Mushtaq not out	24
N. Shahid c Hick b Lampitt	18	A. J. Tudor not out	31
B. C. Hollioake c Leatherdale b Sheriyar	10	B 5, l-b 9, n-b 12	26
A. D. Brown c Hick b Sheriyar	121		
*A. J. Hollioake lbw b Haynes	24	1/61 2/105 3/125 (9 wkts dec.)	452
†J. A. Knott c Solanki b Lampitt	26	4/304 5/347 6/353	
I. D. K. Salisbury c Spiring b Chapman	9	7/368 8/392 9/393	

Bonus points – Surrey 4, Worcestershire 4.

Bowling: Sheriyar 27–2–118–3; Chapman 17–5–72–1; Haynes 24.1–10–46–1; Lampitt 28–7–104–4; Leatherdale 20–4–78–0; Hick 3–0–20–0.

Worcestershire

T. S. Curtis c Knott b Bicknell	....	0
W. P. C. Weston not out	....	17
G. A. Hick not out	....	48
N-b 16	....	16

1/0   (1 wkt) 81

K. R. Spiring, V. S. Solanki, G. R. Haynes, D. A. Leatherdale, *†S. J. Rhodes, S. R. Lampitt, A. Sheriyar and R. J. Chapman did not bat.

Bowling: Bicknell 5–0–44–1; Tudor 6–2–18–0; B. C. Hollioake 3–0–11–0; Saqlain Mushtaq 1–0–8–0.

Umpires: J. D. Bond and R. A. White.

WORCESTERSHIRE v LANCASHIRE

At Worcester, June 26, 27, 28, 30. Lancashire won by three wickets. Lancashire 19 pts. Toss: Lancashire.

With Watkinson injured, Atherton led Lancashire to their first Championship win – after three successive defeats – in another rain-ravaged fixture at New Road. He made only four, but saw England Under-19 captain Flintoff take charge with the bat. Lancashire were set 236 from 64 overs, and fine seam bowling reduced them to 64 for five. But Flintoff, in his fourth first-class match, played with great composure in making 70, his maiden half-century, with ten fours and a six. His stand of 98 with Hegg turned the game, but he was trapped lbw when Lancashire still needed 33. Hegg saw them home with 12 overs to spare. The first three days contained only 46.1 overs and Worcestershire struggled in seamer-friendly conditions. Two declarations and a forfeit set up the final run-chase.

Close of play: First day, No play; Second day, Worcestershire 58-4 (T. M. Moody 26*, G. R. Haynes 14*); Third day, Worcestershire 100-7 (G. R. Haynes 38*, S. R. Lampitt 0*).

Worcestershire

T. S. Curtis c and b Shadford	....	0	– not out	 77
W. P. C. Weston c Hegg b Martin	....	11	– not out	 46
G. A. Hick lbw b Martin	....	2		
K. R. Spiring lbw b Shadford	....	1		
*T. M. Moody c Hegg b Shadford	....	26		
G. R. Haynes not out	....	38		
D. A. Leatherdale c Crawley b Martin	....	13		
†S. J. Rhodes c Lloyd b Austin	....	2		
S. R. Lampitt not out	....	0		
L-b 1, w 4, n-b 2	....	7	B 1, l-b 3, w 4, n-b 4	 12

1/0 2/11 3/14 4/18 5/58   (7 wkts. dec.) 100   (no wkt dec.) 135
6/89 7/96

P. J. Newport and A. Sheriyar did not bat.

Bonus points – Lancashire 3.

Bowling: *First Innings*—Shadford 13–1–31–3; Martin 17–7–30–3; Chapple 9–3–27–0; Austin 7.1–4–11–1. *Second Innings*—Shadford 8–1–51–0; Martin 9–1–23–0; Austin 8–3–15–0; Lloyd 6.5–0–42–0.

Lancashire

Lancashire forfeited their first innings.

N. T. Wood c Lampitt b Newport	3	†W. K. Hegg not out 54
*M. A. Atherton c Rhodes b Sheriyar ...	4	P. J. Martin not out 24
J. P. Crawley lbw b Newport	13	
G. D. Lloyd b Lampitt	21	L-b 1, w 4, n-b 12 17
P. C. McKeown b Leatherdale..........	9	
A. Flintoff lbw b Leatherdale..........	70	1/8 2/14 3/52 4/52 (7 wkts) 237
I. D. Austin c and b Lampitt	22	5/64 6/105 7/203

G. Chapple and D. J. Shadford did not bat.

Bowling: Newport 15–3–53–2; Sheriyar 8–0–47–1; Lampitt 14–3–46–2; Leatherdale 11.1–0–70–2; Moody 4–0–20–0.

Umpires: V. A. Holder and T. E. Jesty.

At Arundel, July 2, 3, 4. WORCESTERSHIRE beat SUSSEX by an innings and 35 runs.

At Worcester, July 16, 17, 18. WORCESTERSHIRE drew with PAKISTAN A (See Pakistan A tour section).

At Chelmsford, July 23, 24, 25, 26. WORCESTERSHIRE drew with ESSEX.

WORCESTERSHIRE v KENT

At Worcester, July 31, August 1, 2, 4. Drawn. Worcestershire 11 pts, Kent 9 pts. Toss: Worcestershire. Championship debut: M. M. Mirza.

A potentially interesting finale was spoiled by rain, which washed out the last 32 overs and left Kent stranded on 158 for four in pursuit of 321. After a shortened first day, Worcestershire took the upper hand thanks to Leatherdale, who made his first century for 11 months. He was aided by Solanki, who curbed his attacking instincts to lend support in a sixth-wicket stand of 136. Kent were cruising at 193 for three in reply, but Leatherdale and Moody dealt with their middle-order engine room so effectively that they came within four runs of following on. Worcestershire then had to be fed cheap runs on the final morning to set up a declaration. Ward gave Kent a brisk start, hitting eight fours in his 52, but the dismissal of Wells put the contest back in the balance before the weather-intervened.

Close of play: First day, Worcestershire 58-0 (T. M. Moody 32*, T. S. Curtis 21*); Second day, Worcestershire 409-7 (D. A. Leatherdale 120*, P. J. Newport 23*); Third day, Worcestershire 82-3 (G. A. Hick 56*, G. R. Haynes 4*).

Worcestershire

*T. M. Moody lbw b Fleming	60	– c Marsh b Headley	0
T. S. Curtis c Marsh b Headley	25	– c Marsh b Ealham	10
G. A. Hick c Cowdrey b Fleming	46	– retired hurt	56
K. R. Spiring lbw b Fleming	5	– c Marsh b Ealham	5
G. R. Haynes c Marsh b Igglesden	35	– not out	38
D. A. Leatherdale c Cowdrey b Headley	129	– not out	51
V. S. Solanki c Wells b Headley	61		
†S. J. Rhodes c Wells b Igglesden	11		
P. J. Newport c Wells b Strang	23		
R. J. Chapman b Headley	0		
M. M. Mirza not out	0		
B 5, l-b 6, n-b 16	27	B 7, l-b 1, n-b 6	14

1/66 2/137 3/143 4/156 5/208　　　　　422　　1/4 2/62 3/70　　　(3 wkts dec.) 174
6/344 7/381 8/410 9/413

Bonus points – Worcestershire 4, Kent 4.

In the second innings G. A. Hick retired hurt at 82.

Bowling: *First Innings*—Headley 29.2–6–102–4; Igglesden 23–3–81–2; Strang 22–6–63–1; Ealham 22–4–60–0; Thompson 9–0–56–0; Fleming 14–2–49–3. *Second Innings*—Headley 6–0–21–1; Igglesden 4–1–23–0; Ealham 4–0–23–2; Fleming 3–0–14–0; Cowdrey 5–0–31–0; Wells 3–2–2–0; Ward 4–0–30–0; Smith 2–0–22–0.

Kent

T. R. Ward c Hick b Chapman	14	– b Mirza	52
E. T. Smith c Solanki b Haynes	45	– c sub b Newport	19
A. P. Wells c Moody b Newport	24	– c Moody b Haynes	43
G. R. Cowdrey c Curtis b Leatherdale	32	– c Solanki b Moody	21
M. A. Ealham c and b Moody	56	– not out	14
M. V. Fleming b Leatherdale	20	– not out	0
P. A. Strang c Curtis b Moody	0		
*†S. A. Marsh c Hick b Leatherdale	17		
D. W. Headley c Hick b Mirza	25		
J. B. D. Thompson not out	7		
A. P. Igglesden b Mirza	3		
B 1, n-b 32	33	L-b 1, n-b 8	9

1/35 2/88 3/100 4/193 5/197　　　　276　　1/27 2/88 3/133 4/158　　(4 wkts) 158
6/199 7/213 8/261 9/273

Bonus points – Kent 2, Worcestershire 4.

Bowling: *First Innings*—Newport 16–4–58–1; Chapman 14–2–87–1; Mirza 19.3–6–56–2; Haynes 11–6–17–1; Moody 8–1–32–2; Leatherdale 10–2–25–3. *Second Innings*—Newport 14–4–33–1; Chapman 5–0–30–0; Haynes 8–2–32–1; Mirza 9–2–22–1; Moody 12–3–40–1.

Umpires: J. D. Bond and J. H. Harris.

At Northampton, August 6, 7, 8, 9. WORCESTERSHIRE beat NORTHAMPTONSHIRE by 101 runs.

WORCESTERSHIRE v GLAMORGAN

At Worcester, August 15, 16, 17, 18. Worcestershire won by 54 runs. Worcestershire 24 pts, Glamorgan 6 pts. Toss: Worcestershire. Championship debut: M. J. Powell.

Worcestershire raised their game to beat the eventual champions in New Road's best match of the season. It was a triumph of the tortoises over the hares, which began with an appropriate farewell from Curtis, who hit his best score for two seasons – 160 in six hours with 26 fours – in what turned out to be his last home Championship match before retirement. After Worcestershire had taken ten hours to grind out 476, Glamorgan went off like an express train through James's 69 in 76 balls. At 155 for six, they had almost been derailed, but Maynard chose to defend with even more attack and hit an exhilarating 161 off 145 balls. Worcestershire's president Tom Graveney described it as one of the finest innings he had seen on the ground. Glamorgan finished with a total of 398, scored at a rate of 5.8 per over, and a deficit of 78 to make up. But now it was the turn of Worcestershire's other opener to frustrate them, as a cautious hundred from Weston allowed his side to build a position of strength. Chasing 374 in 81 overs, James made his fifth Championship hundred of the season, but Maynard was out first ball, and no one else provided substantial support. Even after James was seventh out at 269, Glamorgan went for victory; Waqar Younis raced to 44 before Mirza mopped up the rest of the tail.

Close of play: First day, Worcestershire 342-4 (T. M. Moody 29*, A. Sheriyar 2*); Second day, Glamorgan 355-8 (M. P. Maynard 140*, Waqar Younis 34*); Third day, Worcestershire 263-7 (W. P. C. Weston 106*, S. R. Lampitt 4*).

Worcestershire

T. S. Curtis b Croft	160	– c Shaw b Watkin 11
W. P. C. Weston lbw b Butcher	17	– c Shaw b Croft 114
G. A. Hick c Maynard b Croft	65	– c Dale b Croft 31
G. R. Haynes c Shaw b Waqar Younis	45	– lbw b Watkin 33
*T. M. Moody lbw b Butcher	42	– c Thomas b Croft 14
A. Sheriyar retired hurt	2	– (11) c Croft b Waqar Younis..... 9
D. A. Leatherdale c Morris b Butcher	23	– (6) lbw b Waqar Younis 2
V. S. Solanki c Maynard b Croft	8	– (7) c Powell b Croft 5
†S. J. Rhodes c Morris b Thomas	33	– (8) c Shaw b Waqar Younis 27
S. R. Lampitt c and b Thomas	49	– (9) not out 18
M. M. Mirza not out	1	– (10) run out 0
B 5, l-b 14, w 2, n-b 10	31	L-b 13, w 8, n-b 10 31

1/34 2/212 3/295 4/337 5/365   476   1/13 2/69 3/130 4/159 5/161   295
6/378 7/397 8/459 9/476   6/174 7/249 8/277 9/278

Bonus points – Worcestershire 4, Glamorgan 2 (Score at 120 overs: 379-6).

In the first innings A. Sheriyar retired hurt at 342.

Bowling: *First Innings*—Waqar Younis 25–7–86–1; Watkin 33–11–82–0; Butcher 20–4–87–3; Thomas 21.3–1–92–2; Croft 39–11–80–3; Dale 8–1–30–0. *Second Innings*—Waqar Younis 20.5–6–50–3; Watkin 24–7–49–2; Thomas 11–1–38–0; Butcher 6–1–44–0; Croft 42–10–98–4; Powell 1–0–3–0.

Glamorgan

S. P. James c Rhodes b Haynes	69	– c Curtis b Leatherdale 130
H. Morris c Solanki b Sheriyar	4	– run out 37
A. Dale b Haynes	9	– c Lampitt b Moody 13
M. J. Powell st Rhodes b Haynes	0	– c Solanki b Haynes 8
*M. P. Maynard not out	161	– c Rhodes b Haynes 0
G. P. Butcher c Solanki b Lampitt	5	– (7) c and b Moody 18
†A. D. Shaw lbw b Mirza	15	– (8) run out 5
R. D. B. Croft c and b Leatherdale	27	– (6) c Lampitt b Mirza 33
S. D. Thomas b Lampitt	25	– (10) lbw b Mirza 1
Waqar Younis c Weston b Mirza	46	– (9) not out 44
S. L. Watkin c Lampitt b Mirza	1	– c Lampitt b Mirza 0
L-b 12, w 2, n-b 22	36	B 11, l-b 7, w 4, n-b 8..... 30

1/43 2/72 3/78 4/107 5/124   398   1/115 2/135 3/152 4/152 5/230   319
6/155 7/218 8/294 9/394   6/269 7/269 8/300 9/309

Bonus points – Glamorgan 4, Worcestershire 4.

Bowling: *First Innings*—Sheriyar 11–3–72–1; Mirza 17.4–1–95–3; Haynes 11–1–46–3; Lampitt 11–0–82–2; Hick 5–0–27–0; Leatherdale 10–0–55–1; Moody 3–1–9–0. *Second Innings*—Sheriyar 6–2–12–0; Mirza 13.3–1–53–3; Hick 12–3–38–0; Moody 22–3–105–2; Lampitt 5–0–36–0; Haynes 12–1–34–2; Leatherdale 6–0–23–1.

Umpires: D. J. Constant and R. A. White.

At Birmingham, August 20, 21, 22, 23. WORCESTERSHIRE drew with WARWICKSHIRE.

WORCESTERSHIRE v MIDDLESEX

At Kidderminster, August 27, 28, 29, 30. Middlesex won by 169 runs. Middlesex 20 pts, Worcestershire 6 pts. Toss: Worcestershire.

Moody gambled and lost as Worcestershire suffered their first defeat in 11 matches at Chester Road since first-class cricket returned to the venue in 1987. Rain dogged the first two days, when conditions were less weighted in favour of the bat than is usual on this ground, and Sheriyar took advantage. The third day was more typical, with only two wickets falling; Leatherdale and Rhodes added an unbeaten 112 for Worcestershire's sixth wicket, but Moody opted to declare one run behind. Kallis and Ramprakash responded with an unbroken 317-run stand – a ground record for any wicket and Middlesex's highest second-wicket partnership against Worcestershire, although the last 111 runs of the partnership were fed them in 40 minutes to set up the declaration. A target of 319 in 78 overs became purely academic after Fraser and Hewitt reduced Worcestershire to 54 for five; Weston delayed Middlesex but not for long enough.

Close of play: First day, Middlesex 217-7 (D. C. Nash 33*, J. P. Hewitt 10*); Second day, Worcestershire 90-4 (G. R. Haynes 18*, D. A. Leatherdale 7*); Third day, Middlesex 206-1 (J. H. Kallis 115*, M. R. Ramprakash 72*).

Middlesex

J. C. Pooley c Sheriyar b Haynes	45	– c Leatherdale b Sheriyar	0
J. H. Kallis c Hick b Sheriyar	4	– not out	172
*M. R. Ramprakash c Rhodes b Mirza	9	– not out	123
M. W. Gatting c Spiring b Sheriyar	35		
O. A. Shah c Lampitt b Sheriyar	22		
D. C. Nash not out	45		
†K. R. Brown lbw b Haynes	14		
R. L. Johnson c Spiring b Haynes	9		
J. P. Hewitt c Rhodes b Lampitt	10		
A. R. C. Fraser b Sheriyar	15		
P. C. R. Tufnell b Sheriyar	0		
L-b 10, w 6, n-b 28	44	B 1, l-b 7, w 4, n-b 10	22

1/7 2/47 3/77 4/141 5/142   252   1/0   (1 wkt dec.) 317
6/175 7/191 8/219 9/252

Bonus points – Middlesex 2, Worcestershire 4.

Bowling: *First Innings*—Sheriyar 18–3–55–5; Mirza 18–4–70–1; Haynes 18–2–57–3; Moody 7–4–11–0; Lampitt 16.4–4–49–1. *Second Innings*—Sheriyar 11–2–34–1; Mirza 5–0–23–0; Lampitt 7–0–45–0; Illingworth 20–7–41–0; Haynes 9–1–43–0; Moody 9–2–40–0; Hick 6–1–37–0; Weston 4–0–36–0; Spiring 2–0–10–0.

Worcestershire

*T. M. Moody c Pooley b Kallis	32	– c Brown b Fraser	12
W. P. C. Weston lbw b Hewitt	4	– c Brown b Kallis	74
G. A. Hick c Shah b Fraser	0	– c Pooley b Hewitt	3
K. R. Spiring c Pooley b Fraser	23	– c Pooley b Hewitt	0
G. R. Haynes b Hewitt	29	– c Ramprakash b Hewitt	2
D. A. Leatherdale not out	88	– c Kallis b Fraser	8
†S. J. Rhodes not out	59	– c Pooley b Johnson	9
S. R. Lampitt (did not bat)		– lbw b Kallis	24
R. K. Illingworth (did not bat)		– c Kallis b Johnson	5
A. Sheriyar (did not bat)		– c Brown b Kallis	0
M. M. Mirza (did not bat)		– not out	0
L-b 6, w 6, n-b 4	16	B 4, l-b 2, w 6	12

1/8 2/13 3/56 4/70 5/139   (5 wkts dec.) 251   1/34 2/37 3/37 4/39 5/54   149
                                                         6/86 7/140 8/145 9/147

Bonus points – Worcestershire 2, Middlesex 2.

Bowling: *First Innings*—Fraser 26–8–55–2; Hewitt 17–8–36–2; Kallis 19–3–58–1; Johnson 14.5–4–51–0; Tufnell 13–2–42–0; Ramprakash 1–0–3–0. *Second Innings*—Fraser 12–7–16–2; Hewitt 13–1–48–3; Johnson 6.3–0–33–2; Kallis 12–3–39–3; Tufnell 7–3–7–0.

Umpires: J. H. Harris and K. E. Palmer.

At Leeds, September 2, 3, 4, 5. WORCESTERSHIRE lost to YORKSHIRE by 66 runs.

WORCESTERSHIRE v DERBYSHIRE

At Worcester, September 10, 11, 12, 13. Worcestershire won by ten wickets. Worcestershire 24 pts, Derbyshire 2 pts. Toss: Worcestershire. First-class debut: S. D. Stubbings.

Worcestershire overcame spirited second-innings resistance from their trouble-torn opponents, who announced before the game that Cork would replace DeFreitas as captain for 1998. Opener Weston, who had been dropped in mid-season, continued his prolific run with 188; he shared stands of 173 with Moody and 197 with Leatherdale. Sheriyar and Haynes quickly removed the Derbyshire top order and, despite resistance from Cassar, they followed on 331 runs behind. In the second innings, Barnett and Tweats got in practice for their record stand of the next match with a 156-run partnership for the fourth wicket, though Hick, who had taken his first Championship wicket of the season in the first innings, picked up four more. It took defiant resistance from Krikken and Lacey to take the game into the fourth day, and they eventually added 108 – the first century ninth-wicket stand for either county in the 98-year history of the fixture. Spiring hastened Worcestershire to their modest target with a 56-ball half-century.

Close of play: First day, Worcestershire 400-4 (W. P. C. Weston 145*, D. A. Leatherdale 63*); Second day, Derbyshire 223; Third day, Derbyshire 364-8 (K. M. Krikken 47*, S. J. Lacey 19*).

Worcestershire

K. R. Spiring b Harris	20	– (2) not out	50
W. P. C. Weston c Krikken b Cassar	188	– (1) not out	19
G. A. Hick b DeFreitas	31		
*T. M. Moody b Cassar	101		
G. R. Haynes b Cork	6		
D. A. Leatherdale b Malcolm	93		
V. S. Solanki c Harris b Lacey	20		
†S. J. Rhodes c Tweats b Lacey	24		
S. R. Lampitt not out	14		
R. K. Illingworth not out	7		
B 14, l-b 20, n-b 16	50	L-b 1, n-b 2	3

1/41 2/94 3/267 4/280 5/477   (8 wkts dec.) 554   (no wkt) 72
6/481 7/511 8/527

A. Sheriyar did not bat.

Bonus points – Worcestershire 4, Derbyshire 1 (Score at 120 overs: 464-4).

Bowling: *First Innings*—Malcolm 23–3–117–1; DeFreitas 22–3–85–1; Harris 13–3–47–1; Cork 23–8–63–1; Lacey 28–7–60–2; Clarke 18.4–3–98–0; Cassar 15–3–50–2. *Second Innings*—Malcolm 4–0–18–0; Harris 4–1–8–0; DeFreitas 5–0–31–0; Lacey 4.4–1–14–0.

Derbyshire

S. D. Stubbings c Rhodes b Haynes	5	– lbw b Sheriyar	22
D. G. Cork c Weston b Sheriyar	0	– (3) b Hick	9
T. A. Tweats run out	42	– (4) b Illingworth	83
K. J. Barnett c Rhodes b Sheriyar	1	– (5) c Leatherdale b Hick	86
V. P. Clarke c Moody b Haynes	19	– (6) c Leatherdale b Hick	37
M. E. Cassar not out	76	– (7) lbw b Hick	8
†K. M. Krikken b Illingworth	48	– (8) c Weston b Illingworth	65
*P. A. J. DeFreitas b Hick	4	– (9) c Lampitt b Sheriyar	1
S. J. Lacey lbw b Illingworth	11	– (10) not out	34
A. J. Harris c Solanki b Moody	2	– (2) c Illingworth b Sheriyar	36
D. E. Malcolm c Spiring b Illingworth	1	– b Sheriyar	0
B 7, l-b 5, w 2	14	B 4, l-b 3, w 4, n-b 10	21

1/3 2/11 3/12 4/51 5/84   223   1/62 2/71 3/73 4/229 5/283   402
6/155 7/170 8/209 9/222   6/284 7/293 8/294 9/402

Bonus points – Derbyshire 1, Worcestershire 4.

Bowling: *First Innings*—Sheriyar 8.1–1–36–3; Haynes 8–2–30–2; Lampitt 7–1–22–0; Hick 20–6–71–1; Illingworth 16.4–8–39–2; Moody 3–0–13–1. *Second Innings*—Lampitt 10–1–55–0; Haynes 9–1–63–0; Sheriyar 21.1–8–84–4; Hick 26–6–70–4; Illingworth 26–8–51–2; Moody 5–0–30–0; Leatherdale 13–5–42–0.

Umpires: D. R. Shepherd and A. G. T. Whitehead.

At Southampton, September 18, 19, 20, 21. WORCESTERSHIRE beat HAMPSHIRE by nine wickets.

Darren Lehmann

YORKSHIRE

Patron: HRH The Duchess of Kent

President: Sir Lawrence Byford

Chairman of Cricket: R. K. Platt

Chief Executive: C. D. Hassell

Captain: D. Byas

Head Groundsman: A. W. Fogarty

Scorer: J. T. Potter

At the start of 1998 Yorkshire found themselves back in one of those politics-dominated winters that characterised the club in the 1980s. After a disappointing season finished with a heavy defeat at Derby, they found themselves in disarray on three separate fronts.

First, the dream of moving to a site outside Wakefield was interrupted by reality. The club finally seemed resigned to the fact that they could not walk away from the 99-year lease that ties them to Headingley, and talks were starting with their landlords to see if the existing ground could be redeveloped. Then, in the committee room, Sir Lawrence Byford first announced his retirement as president and chairman, then said he would carry on as president – which led to the resignation of public relations chairman Sid Fielden.

Furthermore, there was open disagreement between captain David Byas and the committee over the decision to release experienced seamer Peter Hartley. The captain favoured the original plan which would have given Hartley a prominent role with the second team and the opportunity to provide cover for the senior side – and he said so, publicly and forcefully. The news of David Bairstow's tragic death also cast a pall over the county.

Meanwhile, supporters of the club found themselves asking: "Is this as good as it gets?" As ever, Yorkshire began the campaign with high hopes, but the best they managed was to retain sixth place in the Championship. In other areas, things took a definite turn for the worse. Yorkshire slipped from third to tenth in the Sunday League and disappeared at the quarter-final stage in both major knockout competitions.

On the credit side, they displayed considerable character in maintaining an outside challenge for the Championship throughout the closing stages of the summer, despite missing three leading players for much of that time. Opener Martyn Moxon, handicapped by a severe back problem, managed only one Championship innings – a duck – after mid-July, although he did score 155 against Pakistan A in August. Over the same period, Darren Gough, the leading strike bowler, took none for 106 in 29 overs. This owed something to England calls, but there was also knee trouble and a strained hamstring. Hartley required a hernia operation, and missed the last seven Championship games.

A heavy responsibility thus fell on the shoulders of Chris Silverwood, who had a season of two halves. At first, his action lacked any sort of rhythm, but he ran into the best form of his career in the last five fixtures, when he claimed 27 wickets at 18.40, including 12 for 148 against Kent. There was unexpected support from 20-year-old Paul Hutchison, who was marooned in the backwaters until Ryan Sidebottom – another young left-arm seamer who stood ahead of him in the pecking order – was required by England Under-19s. Hutchison announced his arrival with 11 for 102 against Pakistan A and then picked up another 23 wickets at 16.21 in his first four Championship appearances. Inevitably he came back down to earth, with three for 266 in his last two games, but his restriction of bad deliveries to an absolute minimum, even in difficult circumstances, was an encouraging sign.

Despite this welcome find, Yorkshire had good cause to wonder about the depth of their bowling resources. They depended too much on the deceptive medium-pace of Craig White, who did much steady work in defiance of a sore back which eventually forced him to miss the final game. Gavin Hamilton fell some way below expectations when called upon, while Richard Stemp endured a long, lean spell: he simply did not maintain the necessary accuracy, and lost his place at the end.

Undoubtedly the outstanding individual was Australian left-hander Darren Lehmann, whose Championship aggregate of 1,575 was the highest for the county since 1991, when Moxon managed 1,669. Ignoring his lack of experience in England, Lehmann adapted his approach to suit all conditions, and was just as happy to work the ball for ones and twos as he was to switch to the all-out attack mode. Either way, he rarely failed, reaching 40 in 18 out of 27 Championship innings. He also scored heavily on the one-day front and proved extremely popular in the dressing-room, so it was predictable that Yorkshire should re-engage him for 1998. Originally they had planned to go back to his fellow-countryman, Michael Bevan, who was unavailable in 1997 because he was on the Ashes tour – which was not an entirely happy experience for him.

The rest of the batting lacked conviction. Michael Vaughan matured as an opener, although he dropped out with a fractured bone in his hand for a lengthy spell. Byas was his usual, solidly professional self, but Anthony McGrath was guilty of too many unforced errors, and White made a terrible start, averaging only 20.76 from his first 17 Championship innings. He rallied to hit the county's record Sunday League score of 148 at Leicester, and also plundered an unbeaten 172 at the expense of Worcestershire in September. Yorkshire need more consistency from such a pivotal player, whose individual form significantly influences the shape of the team's performances. Bradley Parker did not do enough, even making allowances for the difficulties of batting down the order, and wicket-keeper/batsman Richard Blakey had to rescue the innings on a number of occasions.

Morale was not improved by a number of departures. Richard Kettleborough, after another season in the wilderness, asked for his release, as did former England Under-19 captain, Alex Morris. Several other promising youngsters – including two more Under-19 stars in Gareth Batty and Zac Morris – were also released, further undermining the practical value of the Academy project. Alex Wharf had already moved on to Nottinghamshire. The two Morrises joined Hartley in exile at Hampshire.

It all led to the impression that too much is being built on shifting sands. Yorkshire remain an enigma at all levels. They possess obvious strengths, yet they cannot fashion themselves into a unit effective enough to win trophies. The impression lingers, too, that they are vulnerable to pressure, which is why the present side seems most likely to flatter to deceive. – JOHN CALLAGHAN.

YORKSHIRE 1997

[*Bill Smith*]

Back row: C. A. Chapman, B. Parker, I. D. Fisher, R. Robinson, J. W. Hood, A. McGrath, R. A. Kettleborough. *Middle row:* D. E. V. Padgett (*coach*), M. J. Hoggard, A. G. Wharf, A. C. Morris, R. J. Sidebottom, P. M. Hutchison, G. M. Hamilton, M. J. Wood, G. J. Batty. *Front row:* R. D. Stemp, C. White, R. J. Blakey, P. J. Hartley, D. Byas (*captain*), M. D. Moxon, D. Gough, M. P. Vaughan, C. E. W. Silverwood. *Inset:* D. S. Lehmann.

YORKSHIRE RESULTS

All first-class matches – Played 20: Won 7, Lost 4, Drawn 9.

County Championship matches – Played 17: Won 6, Lost 3, Drawn 8.

Competition placings – Britannic Assurance County Championship, 6th;
NatWest Trophy, q-f; Benson and Hedges Cup, q-f;
AXA Life League, 10th.

COUNTY CHAMPIONSHIP AVERAGES

BATTING

Cap		M	I	NO	R	HS	100s	50s	Avge	Ct/St
1997	D. S. Lehmann§	17	27	2	1,575	182	4	10	63.00	9
1991	D. Byas†	17	28	3	1,044	128	2	8	41.76	20
1987	R. J. Blakey†	17	23	5	670	92	0	6	37.22	48/4
1995	M. P. Vaughan	12	21	2	667	161	2	2	35.10	2
1993	C. White†	16	23	2	633	172*	1	2	30.14	17
	A. McGrath†	12	20	0	575	141	1	2	28.75	4
	P. M. Hutchison†	6	6	5	27	15*	0	0	27.00	1
1984	M. D. Moxon†	9	13	0	342	63	0	4	26.30	2
	B. Parker†	16	25	3	496	74*	0	3	22.54	3
1996	C. E. W. Silverwood†	15	20	6	300	58	0	1	21.42	0
1993	D. Gough†	7	10	1	179	58	0	1	19.88	0
	G. M. Hamilton	9	12	2	159	45	0	0	15.90	2
1987	P. J. Hartley†	8	10	0	121	39	0	0	12.10	2
1996	R. D. Stemp	15	18	6	120	33*	0	0	10.00	6
	A. C. Morris†	6	7	0	67	35	0	0	9.57	3

Also batted: I. D. Fisher† (1 match) 25, 37; R. A. Kettleborough† (2 matches) 10, 8, 3 (1 ct); R. J. Sidebottom† (1 match) 2*; A. G. Wharf† (1 match) 0.

* Signifies not out.   † Born in Yorkshire.   § Overseas player.

BOWLING

	O	M	R	W	BB	5W/i	Avge
P. J. Hartley	163	38	511	23	5-34	1	22.21
D. Gough	181.4	42	598	25	5-56	2	23.92
C. E. W. Silverwood	394.3	87	1,272	53	7-93	4	24.00
P. M. Hutchison	197.2	47	639	26	7-50	2	24.57
C. White	349.4	57	1,222	40	5-31	1	30.55
G. M. Hamilton	180.2	36	654	18	5-89	1	36.33
R. D. Stemp	456	109	1,309	36	6-77	1	36.36

Also bowled: I. D. Fisher 21–5–39–0; D. S. Lehmann 20.3–3–71–2; A. McGrath 8.5–0–44–1; A. C. Morris 69–15–260–4; B. Parker 1–0–3–0; R. J. Sidebottom 16.4–4–71–3; M. P. Vaughan 118–11–522–3; A. G. Wharf 18–2–57–1.

COUNTY RECORDS

Highest score for:	341	G. H. Hirst v Leicestershire at Leicester	1905
Highest score against:	318*	W. G. Grace (Gloucestershire) at Cheltenham.	1876
Best bowling for:	10-10	H. Verity v Nottinghamshire at Leeds	1932
Best bowling against:	10-37	C. V. Grimmett (Australians) at Sheffield	1930
Highest total for:	887	v Warwickshire at Birmingham	1896
Highest total against:	681-7 dec.	by Leicestershire at Bradford	1996
Lowest total for:	23	v Hampshire at Middlesbrough	1965
Lowest total against:	13	by Nottinghamshire at Nottingham	1901

YORKSHIRE v LANCASHIRE

Non-Championship Match

At Leeds, April 16, 17, 18, 19. Lancashire won by six wickets. Toss: Lancashire. First-class debuts: G. J. Batty, M. J. Wood.

A remarkable double-hundred by Lloyd destroyed the morale of an inexperienced Yorkshire side. A slow, low pitch made timing the ball difficult and batsmen generally struggled. But Lloyd launched a furious assault to plunder 225 from only 151 balls. He reached 100 in 76 balls and hit ten sixes and 25 fours. Lloyd's seventh-wicket partnership of 248 in only 31 overs with Austin was a record for Lancashire – and the highest against Yorkshire by any side. Yorkshire surrendered a lead of 193, and could not recover. Of their two debutants, Matthew Wood had scored a promising 81, while off-spinner Gareth Batty met with mixed fortunes. Dismissed first ball on the opening day, he bowled Fairbrother with his third delivery, then conceded eight sixes in five overs – but no fours.

Close of play: First day, Lancashire 45-1 (P. C. McKeown 31*, J. J. Haynes 2*); Second day, Yorkshire 34-1 (M. J. Wood 21*, D. Byas 0*); Third day, Yorkshire 298.

Yorkshire

M. D. Moxon b Austin	23	– c Fairbrother b Flintoff	10
M. J. Wood lbw b Martin	81	– lbw b Martin	21
*D. Byas c Haynes b Watkinson	15	– c Haynes b Green	39
R. A. Kettleborough lbw b Watkinson	0	– lbw b Martin	1
B. Parker not out	85	– c Lloyd b Martin	36
†C. A. Chapman c and b Austin	35	– c Fairbrother b Martin	80
A. G. Wharf c Flintoff b Yates	14	– c Green b Watkinson	5
G. M. Hamilton c Haynes b Yates	5	– run out	49
G. J. Batty lbw b Yates	0	– b Austin	18
R. D. Stemp c Haynes b Yates	18	– b Martin	16
M. J. Hoggard c Haynes b Martin	1	– not out	1
B 3, l-b 3, n-b 6	12	B 2, l-b 14, w 4, n-b 2	22

1/31 2/108 3/120 4/136 5/203	**289**	1/32 2/39 3/47 4/79 5/127	**298**
6/220 7/234 8/234 9/282		6/144 7/238 8/280 9/282	

Bowling: *First Innings*—Martin 17.2–3–58–2; Green 18–2–71–0; Austin 14–3–70–2; Yates 14–2–46–4; Watkinson 17–3–38–2. *Second Innings*—Martin 30–9–53–4; Green 24–8–77–1; Flintoff 10–6–11–1; Austin 25.3–8–65–2; Watkinson 10–3–32–1; Yates 14–4–41–0; Titchard 2–0–3–0.

Lancashire

S. P. Titchard c Kettleborough b Hamilton	11	– (2) c Wood b Hoggard	14
P. C. McKeown b Hoggard	35	– (1) b Wharf	32
†J. J. Haynes b Kettleborough	21		
A. Flintoff b Wharf	9	– (3) c Wharf b Batty	18
N. H. Fairbrother b Batty	21	– (4) not out	11
G. D. Lloyd c Byas b Hamilton	225	– (5) b Wharf	17
*M. Watkinson c Moxon b Stemp	45	– (6) not out	2
I. D. Austin st Chapman b Stemp	83		
G. Yates lbw b Stemp	2		
R. J. Green not out	12		
P. J. Martin c Parker b Hamilton	0		
L-b 16, w 2	18	B 1, l-b 3, n-b 8	12

1/32 2/52 3/69 4/103 5/111	**482**	1/35 2/57 3/83 4/100	(4 wkts) **106**
6/173 7/421 8/445 9/482			

Bowling: *First Innings*—Hamilton 18.4–3–97–3; Wharf 15–2–61–1; Hoggard 20–4–110–1; Kettleborough 13–3–74–1; Batty 5–0–59–1; Stemp 13–1–65–3. *Second Innings*—Hamilton 4–2–9–0; Hoggard 7–0–45–1; Wharf 10–1–37–2; Batty 6–0–11–1.

Umpires: K. E. Palmer and R. A. White.

At Oxford, April 23, 24, 25. YORKSHIRE drew with OXFORD UNIVERSITY.

YORKSHIRE v GLAMORGAN

At Leeds, May 7, 8, 9, 10. Drawn. Yorkshire 8 pts, Glamorgan 10 pts. Toss: Glamorgan. Championship debut: D. S. Lehmann.

Rain, which wiped out the second day, also cut short the match at lunch on the last, when Yorkshire had been set 303 in 64 overs. The most interesting cricket was on the third day, when 18 wickets fell for 350. Glamorgan, who had resumed at 213 for one, thanks to an unbeaten century from James, were swept away by Gough. His burst of five for 11 in 33 balls included his 300th victim for Yorkshire. In reply, the home side sacrificed wickets in their attempts to score quickly. Australian Darren Lehmann, in his first Championship game, made 54 from 64 deliveries – 12 fours and six singles. But Croft's persistence induced a string of errors, though Waqar Younis took only one wicket on his first-class debut for Glamorgan. Morris completed his fourth successive half-century against Yorkshire and James his third before Maynard declared and the weather closed in.

Close of play: First day, Glamorgan 213-1 (S. P. James 101*, A. Dale 36*); Second day, No play; Third day, Glamorgan 27-0 (S. P. James 14*, H. Morris 11*).

Glamorgan

S. P. James run out	109	– b Stemp	52
H. Morris c Blakey b Silverwood	55	– b Vaughan	96
A. Dale c Blakey b Gough	44	– not out	10
*M. P. Maynard c Byas b Silverwood	3	– not out	0
P. A. Cottey c Blakey b Gough	4		
R. D. B. Croft st Blakey b Stemp	57		
G. P. Butcher lbw b Gough	0		
†A. D. Shaw lbw b Gough	0		
S. D. Thomas c Lehmann b Gough	2		
Waqar Younis lbw b Silverwood	12		
S. L. Watkin not out	18		
B 4, l-b 12, w 2, n-b 14	32	B 4, n-b 4	8

1/86 2/225 3/230 4/237 5/250   336   1/110 2/166   (2 wkts dec.) 166
6/250 7/250 8/252 9/285

Bonus points – Glamorgan 3, Yorkshire 4.

Bowling: *First Innings*—Gough 23–9–56–5; Silverwood 23.3–8–80–3; Hamilton 21–6–63–0; White 13–0–62–0; Stemp 16.4–2–44–1; Vaughan 4–2–6–0; McGrath 2–0–9–0. *Second Innings*—Gough 6–0–33–0; Stemp 16–5–35–1; Vaughan 10–1–50–1; Silverwood 5–0–27–0; Hamilton 3–0–17–0.

Yorkshire

A. McGrath c Shaw b Waqar Younis	14	G. M. Hamilton st Shaw b Croft	11
M. P. Vaughan c Shaw b Croft	25	C. E. W. Silverwood not out	11
*D. Byas lbw b Watkin	8	R. D. Stemp not out	1
D. S. Lehmann b Butcher	54		
B. Parker c James b Butcher	9	B 1, l-b 1, n-b 6	8
C. White lbw b Thomas	25		
†R. J. Blakey c Maynard b Croft	6	1/14 2/33 3/93 4/112 5/113 (9 wkts dec.) 200
D. Gough c Waqar Younis b Croft	28	6/130 7/172 8/184 9/192

Bonus points – Yorkshire 1, Glamorgan 4.

Bowling: Waqar Younis 12–1–42–1; Watkin 12–4–34–1; Thomas 5–0–32–1; Dale 4–0–21–0; Croft 16.2–3–58–4; Butcher 5–1–11–2.

Umpires: B. Leadbeater and D. R. Shepherd.

At Birmingham, May 14, 15, 16. YORKSHIRE lost to WARWICKSHIRE by four wickets.

At Taunton, May 21, 22, 23, 24. YORKSHIRE beat SOMERSET by 140 runs.

At Ilford, May 29, 30, 31, June 2. YORKSHIRE beat ESSEX by two wickets.

YORKSHIRE v GLOUCESTERSHIRE

At Leeds, June 4, 5, 6, 7. Gloucestershire won by 164 runs. Gloucestershire 21 pts, Yorkshire 4 pts. Toss: Gloucestershire.

Sixteen wickets fell for 332 on the first day, on a pitch offering exceptional bounce from a full length. ECB inspector Harry Brind had to be called, because more than 15 wickets had gone in a day, but by the time he arrived the wicket had eased and he took no action. Gloucestershire gained a first-innings lead of 22 through Lynch, who hit 13 fours in a storming 37-ball 60. Yorkshire's batting faltered as Smith claimed six wickets and broke a bone in Vaughan's left wrist with a ball that reared viciously. Only a patient unbeaten 51 by Blakey prevented a complete collapse. Next day Gloucestershire took command. Lynch was sedate by his standards – 64 from 72 balls – but further half-centuries from Wright and Alleyne left a target of 411, well out of Yorkshire's reach. The seamers won the game, supported by excellent fielding, notably from Cunliffe. Smith finished with ten for 132 and Gloucestershire returned to the top of the table.

Close of play: First day, Yorkshire 127-6 (R. J. Blakey 33*, G. M. Hamilton 1*); Second day, Gloucestershire 281-5 (M. W. Alleyne 49*, R. C. Russell 22*); Third day, Yorkshire 194-4 (C. White 27*, R. J. Blakey 0*).

Gloucestershire

A. J. Wright b White	9	– c Byas b Silverwood	79
N. J. Trainor lbw b Stemp	40	– c Blakey b Stemp	30
R. J. Cunliffe b Hamilton	2	– b Silverwood	22
M. A. Lynch c Lehmann b Hamilton	60	– b White	64
S. Young lbw b Hartley	15	– c and b Stemp	10
*M. W. Alleyne c Blakey b Hartley	9	– b White	52
†R. C. Russell run out	15	– st Blakey b Stemp	28
T. H. C. Hancock b Stemp	0	– c White b Silverwood	28
M. C. J. Ball c Blakey b White	35	– c sub b Hamilton	20
A. M. Smith b Silverwood	0	– not out	14
J. Lewis not out	4	– b Hamilton	25
B 9, l-b 7	16	B 1, l-b 3, w 10, n-b 2	16
	205		**388**

1/19 2/32 3/110 4/136 5/150   205   1/56 2/129 3/150 4/167 5/217   388
6/152 7/152 8/166 9/183   6/289 7/297 8/343 9/343

Bonus points – Gloucestershire 1, Yorkshire 4.

Bowling: *First Innings*—Silverwood 12–3–28–1; Hartley 11–4–22–2; White 14.5–6–50–2; Hamilton 8–2–48–2; Stemp 11–3–41–2; Vaughan 1–1–0–0. *Second Innings*—Silverwood 20–2–96–3; Hartley 11–2–31–0; Hamilton 16.4–3–56–2; White 25–2–88–2; Stemp 36–8–108–3; Lehmann 1–0–5–0.

Yorkshire

M. D. Moxon c Russell b Lewis	6	– lbw b Smith	63
M. P. Vaughan retired hurt	15	– absent hurt	
*D. Byas c Hancock b Smith	8	– (2) b Young	22
D. S. Lehmann c Ball b Smith	5	– (3) lbw b Young	10
B. Parker lbw b Smith	33	– (4) c Russell b Young	64
C. White c and b Alleyne	13	– (5) lbw b Smith	37
†R. J. Blakey not out	51	– (6) c Cunliffe b Young	11
P. J. Hartley b Lewis	2	– (7) b Smith	10
G. M. Hamilton lbw b Smith	14	– (8) not out	10
C. E. W. Silverwood b Smith	18	– (9) run out	2
R. D. Stemp c Russell b Smith	4	– (10) b Smith	6
B 4, l-b 2, w 4, n-b 4	14	L-b 5, w 4, n-b 2	11

1/21 2/38 3/38 4/66 5/111   183   1/48 2/90 3/104 4/194 5/212   246
6/114 7/151 8/179 9/183   6/224 7/232 8/238 9/246

Bonus points – Gloucestershire 4.

In the first innings M. P. Vaughan retired hurt at 21-1.

Bowling: *First Innings*—Smith 22.1–6–58–6; Lewis 18–4–58–2; Young 11–3–35–0; Alleyne 5–2–11–1; Hancock 3–0–11–0; Ball 1–0–4–0. *Second Innings*—Smith 20.4–7–74–4; Lewis 9–3–22–0; Young 21–9–41–4; Alleyne 13–0–55–0; Ball 10–2–32–0; Hancock 3–2–13–0; Trainor 2–1–4–0.

Umpires: J. H. Hampshire and T. E. Jesty.

At The Oval, June 12, 13, 14, 16. YORKSHIRE drew with SURREY.

At Nottingham, June 18, 19, 20, 21. YORKSHIRE drew with NOTTINGHAMSHIRE.

YORKSHIRE v MIDDLESEX

At Leeds, June 26, 27, 28, 30. Drawn. Yorkshire 4 pts, Middlesex 3 pts. Toss: Yorkshire.

Play was possible only on the second day because of heavy rain, and even then the weather permitted just 41 overs. Ramprakash, however, had time to demonstrate his liking for the Yorkshire bowling with some expansive strokeplay. He had reached fifty in all but one of his nine first-class matches.

Close of play: First day, No play; Second day, Middlesex 150-3 (M. R. Ramprakash 76*, K. R. Brown 15*); Third day, No play.

Middlesex

P. N. Weekes c Blakey b Silverwood	4	†K. R. Brown not out	15
J. H. Kallis retired hurt	3		
*M. R. Ramprakash not out	76	N-b 7	7
M. W. Gatting b White	15		
J. C. Pooley c White b Morris	30	1/11 2/50 3/125 (3 wkts) 150	

O. A. Shah, R. L. Johnson, J. P. Hewitt, A. R. C. Fraser and P. C. R. Tufnell did not bat.

Bonus point – Yorkshire 1.

J. H. Kallis retired hurt at 3.

Bowling: Gough 12–2–36–0; Silverwood 8–3–13–1; Hartley 10–1–39–0; White 6–0–44–1; Morris 5–0–18–1.

Yorkshire

M. D. Moxon, *D. Byas, D. S. Lehmann, A. McGrath, B. Parker, C. White, †R. J. Blakey, A. C. Morris, P. J. Hartley, D. Gough and C. E. W. Silverwood.

Umpires: M. J. Kitchen and J. F. Steele.

At Leicester, July 2, 3, 4, 5. YORKSHIRE drew with LEICESTERSHIRE.

YORKSHIRE v DURHAM

At Scarborough, July 16, 17, 18. Yorkshire won by an innings and 56 runs. Yorkshire 24 pts, Durham 4 pts. Toss: Durham.

Durham never came to terms with a pitch which was well grassed in the middle, but shaved at both ends. Boon later described it as "the most extraordinary I've seen". They were further unnerved by injury to Roseberry, who retired with double vision after being hit on the helmet by White when the total was 27 without loss. After he resumed, on 122 for six, he was given out caught behind first ball and then reported for showing dissent. Yorkshire made the most of some poor Durham bowling to build a decisive lead. White and McGrath both enjoyed two escapes as the visitors' fielding also fell well below the required standards. In sharp contrast, Yorkshire held some excellent catches – particularly White at first slip – and Durham collapsed a second time, bringing the game to a close before lunch on the third day.

Close of play: First day, Yorkshire 137-2 (A. McGrath 57*, D. S. Lehmann 27*); Second day, Durham 61-5 (M. P. Speight 2*, M. M. Betts 0*).

Durham

J. J. B. Lewis c White b Hartley	50	– b Silverwood	4
M. A. Roseberry c Blakey b Hartley	5	– (8) c Byas b Gough	9
J. E. Morris b White	12	– c White b Gough	17
N. J. Speak lbw b Gough	11	– c White b Hartley	13
*D. C. Boon lbw b Gough	5	– c Blakey b Silverwood	9
†M. P. Speight c Blakey b Silverwood	8	– c Blakey b Hartley	2
M. J. Foster c White b Hartley	6	– (2) c Blakey b Gough	14
M. M. Betts run out	0	– (7) b Silverwood	35
J. Boiling not out	11	– c Blakey b McGrath	40
S. J. E. Brown c White b Gough	0	– c Moxon b Lehmann	3
A. Walker b Gough	0	– not out	12
B 8, l-b 1, w 2, n-b 10	21	B 2, l-b 4	6

1/49 2/75 3/83 4/102 5/106   152   1/11 2/29 3/44 4/48 5/61   164
6/122 7/122 8/152 9/152   6/61 7/78 8/113 9/147

Bonus points – Yorkshire 4.

In the first innings M. A. Roseberry, when 5, retired hurt at 27 and resumed at 122-6.

Bowling: *First Innings*—Gough 18.5–7–37–4; Silverwood 17–7–32–1; White 12–2–42–1; Hartley 14–4–29–3; Stemp 3–1–3–0. *Second Innings*—Gough 18–4–51–3; Silverwood 13–4–40–3; Hartley 16–4–34–2; Stemp 3–3–0–0; White 5–2–14–0; McGrath 3–0–19–1; Lehmann 0.1–0–0–1.

Yorkshire

M. D. Moxon c Speight b Betts	3	D. Gough b Boiling	34
A. McGrath c Speight b Walker	57	C. E. W. Silverwood run out	15
*D. Byas b Walker	48	R. D. Stemp c Boiling b Betts	0
D. S. Lehmann b Foster	86		
C. White c Lewis b Brown	31	B 4, l-b 7	11
B. Parker not out	74		
†R. J. Blakey c Speight b Foster	11	1/9 2/97 3/147 4/232 5/232	372
P. J. Hartley c Speak b Boiling	2	6/270 7/273 8/317 9/369	

Bonus points – Yorkshire 4, Durham 4.

Bowling: Brown 23–5–70–1; Betts 10.1–1–58–2; Walker 26–5–97–2; Foster 26–3–78–2; Boiling 19–3–58–2.

Umpires: J. H. Harris and G. Sharp.

YORKSHIRE v NORTHAMPTONSHIRE

At Leeds, July 31, August 1, 2, 4. Yorkshire won by 36 runs. Yorkshire 20 pts, Northamptonshire 6 pts. Toss: Yorkshire.

Outplayed for the first three days, Yorkshire recovered to snatch the spoils as the pitch, which offered assistance to the bowlers throughout, became highly unreliable. Taylor's movement off the seam and extra bounce proved too much at first for Yorkshire, and Northamptonshire built a significant lead. But they bowled much too short in the second innings. The key moment came when Warren, at slip, dropped Blakey from a straightforward chance off Akram. Blakey went on to add 102 in 35 overs with White, who then produced county-best figures of five for 31 as Northamptonshire collapsed on the last day. Gareth Clough, an Academy boy fielding as a substitute for Gough, held a brilliant mid-wicket catch to remove the dangerous Curran. Gough did not bowl in Northamptonshire's second innings because of a sore knee, while Snape could not bat after breaking his right thumb in the field.

Close of play: First day, Yorkshire 163-9 (R. J. Blakey 24*, R. D. Stemp 2*); Second day, Yorkshire 74-0 (A. McGrath 39*, M. P. Vaughan 29*); Third day, Northamptonshire 78-1 (D. J. Roberts 18*, A. Fordham 14*).

Yorkshire

A. McGrath b Taylor	7	– lbw b Mohammad Akram	47
M. P. Vaughan lbw b Taylor	13	– lbw b Taylor	41
*D. Byas b Taylor	4	– lbw b Penberthy	27
D. S. Lehmann b Taylor	11	– lbw b Curran	48
C. White lbw b Mohammad Akram	22	– lbw b Bailey	67
B. Parker b Boswell	26	– c Penberthy b Curran	9
†R. J. Blakey lbw b Taylor	24	– c Taylor b Bailey	51
A. C. Morris c Fordham b Curran	4	– c Warren b Bailey	7
D. Gough c Ripley b Boswell	11	– c Bailey b Mohammad Akram	7
C. E. W. Silverwood c Ripley b Taylor	7	– not out	9
R. D. Stemp not out	5	– lbw b Bailey	9
L-b 8, w 6, n-b 18	32	B 5, n-b 14	19

1/28 2/29 3/44 4/51 5/99   166   1/90 2/110 3/154 4/181 5/205   332
6/117 7/132 8/145 9/155   6/307 7/310 8/323 9/323

Bonus points – Northamptonshire 4.

Bowling: *First Innings*—Mohammad Akram 14·5–28–1; Taylor 16·3–45–6; Boswell 9–1–45–2; Penberthy 6–2–18–0; Curran 7–2–22–1. *Second Innings*—Mohammad Akram 21–1–94–2; Taylor 18–1–98–1; Snape 6–2–10–0; Boswell 13–2–55–0; Penberthy 11–0–38–1; Curran 10–1–22–2; Bailey 11.1–5–10–4.

Northamptonshire

D. J. Roberts b White	45	– (2) lbw b White	27
R. J. Warren c Byas b Silverwood	0	– (1) b Vaughan	27
A. Fordham c Byas b Silverwood	0	– lbw b White	18
*R. J. Bailey c Morris b Silverwood	61	– c Blakey b Stemp	25
K. M. Curran lbw b Stemp	63	– c sub b White	0
A. L. Penberthy c and b White	2	– c Blakey b Stemp	2
J. N. Snape c Morris b Silverwood	5	– absent hurt	
†D. Ripley c White b Stemp	24	– (7) lbw b Silverwood	31
J. P. Taylor c and b Stemp	2	– (8) not out	18
S. A. J. Boswell not out	30	– (9) c Byas b White	1
Mohammad Akram c Blakey b White	16	– (10) c Lehmann b White	0
B 12, l-b 18, n-b 18	38	B 4, l-b 5, w 2, n-b 16	27

1/2 2/10 3/125 4/147 5/156   286   1/54 2/85 3/100 4/100 5/109   176
6/163 7/231 8/232 9/237   6/143 7/169 8/174 9/176

Bonus points – Northamptonshire 2, Yorkshire 4.

Bowling: *First Innings*—Gough 17–3–50–0; Silverwood 23–10–62–4; White 17.4–0–61–3; Morris 9–1–50–0; Stemp 15–3–43–3. *Second Innings*—Silverwood 14–3–32–1; White 12.3–1–31–5; Stemp 27–4–59–2; Vaughan 15–2–40–1; Lehmann 1–0–5–0.

Umpires: V. A. Holder and R. Julian.

At Leeds, August 7, 8, 9, 10. YORKSHIRE beat PAKISTAN A by 69 runs (See Pakistan A tour section).

At Portsmouth, August 15, 16, 17, 18. YORKSHIRE drew with HAMPSHIRE.

YORKSHIRE v SUSSEX

At Scarborough, August 20, 21, 22. Yorkshire won by nine wickets. Yorkshire 22 pts, Sussex 4 pts. Toss: Sussex.

Fifteen wickets fell for 331 runs on the first day, but neither the umpires nor Harry Brind, the ECB inspector who duly visited the ground on the second day, expressed any concern about the green-tinged pitch. Taylor hit 57 from 69 balls and Mark Newell contributed a more sedate half-century, but Sussex lost their last five wickets for seven runs in 15 balls. Hutchison, who had recorded a seven-for in each of his last two matches, picked up five. Yorkshire looked little more comfortable when their turn came, although Lehmann made the highest score of the match and Hamilton, despite a blow on the head from Jarvis when 20, hit out cheerfully. Sussex needed help from the rain to carry the contest into a third day. Jarvis struck some powerful blows against his former county, while Robinson, another exile, made a rare contribution with the bat. But Yorkshire still won with almost five sessions to spare.

Close of play: First day, Yorkshire 174-5 (D. S. Lehmann 63*, C. E. W. Silverwood 8*); Second day, Sussex 41-6 (P. W. Jarvis 6*, J. J. Bates 1*).

Sussex

M. T. E. Peirce lbw b Hutchison	2	– lbw b Hutchison		8
R. K. Rao lbw b Silverwood	0	– lbw b Silverwood		4
N. R. Taylor b White	57	– b Silverwood		14
M. Newell not out	62	– run out		7
K. Newell c Hamilton b Hutchison	13	– c White b Silverwood		0
*†P. Moores lbw b Silverwood	7	– lbw b Silverwood		0
P. W. Jarvis lbw b Silverwood	1	– lbw b White		51
J. J. Bates lbw b Hutchison	0	– lbw b Hutchison		11
A. A. Khan lbw b Hutchison	0	– c Hamilton b White		4
A. D. Edwards b Silverwood	1	– not out		10
M. A. Robinson b Hutchison	0	– b Silverwood		18
B 1, l-b 11, n-b 2	14	L-b 10		10

1/3 2/3 3/102 4/125 5/138   157   1/5 2/27 3/27 4/33 5/33   137
6/150 7/151 8/151 9/156   6/40 7/74 8/97 9/110

Bonus points – Yorkshire 4.

Bowling: *First Innings*—Silverwood 15–3–27–4; Hutchison 13.2–5–48–5; Hamilton 5–0–12–0; Stemp 12–3–38–0; White 6–0–20–1. *Second Innings*—Silverwood 13.4–2–59–5; Hutchison 13–1–44–2; Hamilton 2–1–2–0; White 9–1–18–2; Stemp 4–1–4–0.

Yorkshire

A. McGrath lbw b Robinson	33	– c Moores b Edwards	2
M. P. Vaughan c Peirce b Jarvis	9	– not out	8
*D. Byas c M. Newell b Jarvis	17	– not out	3
D. S. Lehmann c M. Newell b Robinson	67		
C. White c Moores b K. Newell	34		
B. Parker lbw b Robinson	0		
C. E. W. Silverwood c M. Newell b Robinson	14		
†R. J. Blakey b Jarvis	28		
G. M. Hamilton c M. Newell b Jarvis	45		
R. D. Stemp c Rao b Edwards	14		
P. M. Hutchison not out	2		
B 2, l-b 5, n-b 12	19		

1/23 2/45 3/72 4/154 5/158   282   1/2   (1 wkt) 13
6/181 7/188 8/257 9/274

Bonus points – Yorkshire 2, Sussex 4.

Bowling: *First Innings*—Jarvis 22-4-82-4; Edwards 7.2-1-24-1; Khan 15-5-41-0; Bates 14-3-40-0; Robinson 14-1-61-4; K. Newell 9-3-27-1. *Second Innings*—Edwards 4-2-6-1; Khan 3.3-2-7-0.

Umpires: J. D. Bond and D. R. Shepherd.

At Manchester, August 27, 28, 29, 30. YORKSHIRE drew with LANCASHIRE.

YORKSHIRE v WORCESTERSHIRE

At Leeds, September 2, 3, 4, 5. Yorkshire won by 66 runs. Yorkshire 22 pts, Worcestershire 5 pts. Toss: Yorkshire.

Two teams with an outside chance of the title both needed a win to stay in touch with the leaders, and Yorkshire got one thanks to their own risky declaration. Their first innings lasted into the third day, after rain had wiped out all but 11 overs of the second. McGrath batted almost six hours for a career-best, and White provided impetus with his unbeaten 172 from 167 balls, hitting Illingworth for 25 in one over (464641). Worcestershire, who dropped six catches, were also guilty of losing wickets to unforced errors, notably when Haynes found himself stumped in slow motion, apparently unaware he was out of his ground. After discussion between the captains, and a ten-over thrash from Yorkshire, Worcestershire were set the generous target of 272 in 71 overs. But Moody was the only batsman to come to terms with Yorkshire's in-form attack.

Close of play: First day, Yorkshire 369-5 (C. White 74*, R. J. Blakey 14*); Second day, Yorkshire 414-6 (C. White 110*, G. M. Hamilton 1*); Third day, Worcestershire 313-6 (S. J. Rhodes 46*, S. R. Lampitt 12*).

Yorkshire

A. McGrath b Illingworth	141	– c Leatherdale b Sheriyar	12
M. P. Vaughan c Hick b Mirza	14	– c Lampitt b Sheriyar	3
*D. Byas b Illingworth	53	– not out	35
D. S. Lehmann c Moody b Haynes	51	– c Spiring b Lampitt	20
C. White not out	172	– b Sheriyar	4
B. Parker run out	2	– not out	8
†R. J. Blakey b Rhodes b Sheriyar	19		
G. M. Hamilton lbw b Illingworth	5		
C. E. W. Silverwood not out	19		
L-b 15, n-b 10	25	L-b 1	1

1/42 2/158 3/243 4/301 5/323   (7 wkts dec.) 501   1/9 2/20   (4 wkts dec.) 83
6/379 7/422   3/58 4/67

R. D. Stemp and P. M. Hutchison did not bat.

Bonus points – Yorkshire 4, Worcestershire 2 (Score at 120 overs: 406-6).

Bowling: *First Innings*—Sheriyar 28.4–2–126–1; Mirza 16–3–56–1; Lampitt 19–5–58–0; Haynes 21–3–81–1; Illingworth 39–13–118–3; Moody 4–0–21–0; Hick 5–1–26–0. *Second Innings*—Sheriyar 5.1–0–40–3; Lampitt 5–0–42–1.

Worcestershire

*T. M. Moody c Blakey b Hutchison	7	– (5) c Stemp b Hutchison 67
W. P. C. Weston run out 48		– c Vaughan b Silverwood 4
G. A. Hick c Vaughan b Hamilton 57		– c Blakey b Silverwood 4
K. R. Spiring b Hamilton 11		– lbw b Hutchison 10
G. R. Haynes st Blakey b Stemp................. 62		– (6) b White 27
D. A. Leatherdale c Parker b Stemp 32		– (7) lbw b Silverwood 20
†S. J. Rhodes not out 46		– (1) b Hutchison 6
S. R. Lampitt not out 12		– c Parker b White............... 12
R. K. Illingworth (did not bat)		– not out 33
A. Sheriyar (did not bat)		– c Stemp b Hamilton 12
M. M. Mirza (did not bat)		– c Hutchison b Hamilton 0
B 8, l-b 4, n-b 26 38		B 1, l-b 3, n-b 6 10

1/19 2/110 3/132 4/137 5/231   (6 wkts dec.) 313   1/11 2/11 3/20 4/26 5/87   205
6/244   6/142 7/150 8/174 9/204

Bonus points – Worcestershire 3, Yorkshire 2.

Bowling: *First Innings*—Silverwood 16–3–50–0; Hutchison 9–3–31–1; Hamilton 15–3–50–2; White 17–2–55–0; Stemp 25–6–74–2; Vaughan 8–0–33–0; Lehmann 2–0–8–0. *Second Innings*—Silverwood 17–4–61–3; Hutchison 12–1–38–3; Hamilton 8.5–2–27–2; White 13–5–36–2; Stemp 9–1–39–0.

Umpires: J. C. Balderstone and A. Clarkson.

YORKSHIRE v KENT

At Leeds, September 10, 11, 12, 13. Drawn. Yorkshire 10 pts, Kent 11 pts. Toss: Yorkshire.

Leaders Kent and third-placed Yorkshire could not engineer a result from a closely fought encounter that was seriously affected by injuries. Headley barely managed to achieve medium-pace because of a back problem which eventually forced him out of the match, while Gough also struggled to achieve any sort of rhythm before retiring with a strained left hamstring. Kent started poorly, their bowlers failing to take advantage of early movement in a pitch that became slower and lower, and their batsmen seemingly determined to get out playing across the line. But Marsh made light of a painful blow on the thumb to oversee the addition of 172 for the last three wickets. Lehmann hit 68 in Yorkshire's second innings to underline his standing as the most accomplished batsman on either side, but despite his efforts and those of Byas, Kent required only 240 in 89 overs. Once again, however, the top half of their batting order proved vulnerable to Silverwood, who bowled with genuine pace to achieve a career-best match return of 12 for 148. Fleming and Ealham, concentrating entirely on survival, had to battle their way through 48 overs to draw. The real winners were Glamorgan, whose victory over Essex restored them to first place with one match to go.

Close of play: First day, Kent 79-1 (D. P. Fulton 21*, D. W. Headley 4*); Second day, Kent 374; Third day, Yorkshire 290-8 (C. E. W. Silverwood 1*, R. D. Stemp 3*).

Yorkshire

A. McGrath lbw b Igglesden	15	– lbw b Igglesden	32
M. P. Vaughan c Marsh b Fleming	23	– c and b Ealham	42
*D. Byas lbw b Ealham	59	– c Smith b Strang	74
D. S. Lehmann c Marsh b Ealham	87	– c and b Fleming	68
C. White c Marsh b Igglesden	18	– b Igglesden	11
B. Parker lbw b Igglesden	0	– c Igglesden b Ealham	29
†R. J. Blakey c Fulton b Headley	0	– lbw b Ealham	4
D. Gough b Ealham	58	– b Ealham	10
C. E. W. Silverwood lbw b Ealham	31	– not out	6
R. D. Stemp b Igglesden	4	– b Strang	9
P. M. Hutchison not out	4	– c Ward b Strang	0
L-b 1, w 2, n-b 10	13	B 5, l-b 11	16

1/21 2/97 3/101 4/134 5/134   312   1/53 2/90 3/205 4/222 5/260   301
6/137 7/254 8/283 9/297   6/266 7/272 8/286 9/301

Bonus points – Yorkshire 3, Kent 4.

Bowling: *First Innings*—Headley 17–1–83–1; Igglesden 19–3–67–4; Strang 12–2–45–0; Ealham 20.4–2–62–4; Fleming 16–3–54–1. *Second Innings*—Headley 13–1–67–0; Igglesden 14–0–55–2; Fleming 18–5–56–1; Ealham 16–0–47–4; Strang 16.4–3–55–3; Wells 1–0–5–0.

Kent

D. P. Fulton c Blakey b Silverwood	21	– b Silverwood	10
E. T. Smith c McGrath b Silverwood	36	– c Blakey b Silverwood	7
D. W. Headley run out	40		
T. R. Ward b White	56	– (3) lbw b Silverwood	7
A. P. Wells lbw b Silverwood	10	– (4) lbw b Silverwood	14
G. R. Cowdrey c Blakey b Silverwood	4	– (5) lbw b Silverwood	1
M. A. Ealham b Silverwood	4	– (6) not out	44
M. V. Fleming c White b Silverwood	53	– (7) not out	50
*†S. A. Marsh b Hutchison	84		
P. A. Strang not out	29		
A. P. Igglesden b Silverwood	0		
B 2, l-b 13, w 2, n-b 20	37	L-b 4, n-b 10	14

1/71 2/82 3/169 4/193 5/195   374   1/15 2/18 3/29   (5 wkts) 147
6/199 7/202 8/285 9/371   4/31 5/48

Bonus points – Kent 4, Yorkshire 4.

Bowling: *First Innings*—Gough 12–1–56–0; Hutchison 28–8–91–1; Silverwood 29.3–8–93–7; White 20.4–4–52–1; Stemp 10–1–32–0; Vaughan 5–0–35–0. *Second Innings*—Silverwood 22–6–55–5; Hutchison 20–10–22–0; Stemp 13–6–18–0; White 13–5–13–0; Vaughan 7–0–35–0.

Umpires: H. D. Bird and B. J. Meyer.

At Derby, September 18, 19, 20, 21. YORKSHIRE lost to DERBYSHIRE by nine wickets.

PETER SMITH MEMORIAL AWARD, 1997

The Peter Smith Memorial Award, given by the Cricket Writers' Club in memory of its former chairman for services to the presentation of cricket to the public, was won in 1997 by the umpire Dickie Bird. The award was instituted in 1992. Previous winners were David Gower, John Woodcock, Brian Lara, Mark Taylor and the Sri Lankan World Cup squad.

NATWEST TROPHY, 1997

Paul Prichard

Essex, fall guys in the 1996 NatWest final, made triumphant amends with a blistering victory over Warwickshire to take their first one-day trophy in 12 years. Again, they won the toss but this time the match followed the conventions of the occasion: Warwickshire's batsmen struggled in difficult September morning conditions, and Stuart Law and Paul Prichard raced to victory in the afternoon sunshine. Essex passed their 1996 all out total of 57 in just six overs. The game had been postponed 24 hours because of the funeral of Diana, Princess of Wales.

On handicap, the team of the tournament was Sussex. Struggling in every other competition, their young side were given no hope of reaching the quarter-finals before journeyman Keith Greenfield swept holders Lancashire away. In the next round, Rajesh Rao, in the side only as a last-minute replacement, led them past a Derbyshire total of 327. Their score of 329 was the highest ever by a team batting second in this competition and winning.

Sussex lost in the semi-finals to Warwickshire. Glamorgan also reached the last four, for the third time in five years, but completed their 20th successive season without reaching a Lord's final after a finish against Essex so tense that Robert Croft and Mark Ilott started pushing each other in a row over the light. The umpires took the players off with Essex needing six to win, and two wickets standing. Croft and Ilott were both fined £1,000.

The non-Championship teams made as little impact as ever, though Warwickshire's run at the trophy might have been over before it started: they were 25 for six against Norfolk before order was restored.

Prize money

£45,000 for winners: ESSEX.
£22,500 for runners-up: WARWICKSHIRE.
£11,250 for losing semi-finalists: GLAMORGAN and SUSSEX.
£5,500 for losing quarter-finalists: DERBYSHIRE, MIDDLESEX, NOTTINGHAMSHIRE and YORKSHIRE.

Man of the Match award winners received £1,000 in the final, £450 in the semi-finals, £400 in the quarter-finals, £350 in the second round and £275 in the first round. The prize money was increased from £115,450 in the 1996 tournament to £122,700.

FIRST ROUND

BUCKINGHAMSHIRE v ESSEX

At Beaconsfield, June 24. Essex won by 89 runs. Toss: Buckinghamshire.

The bucolic surroundings of Wilton Park witnessed a violent innings by Rollins. He slammed seven sixes and three fours in his unbeaten 67 from 26 balls, endangering cars on the nearby Oxford Road. Earlier, Hussain and Prichard had compiled a more watchful stand of 123. West Indian all-rounder Arthurton took four wickets for Buckinghamshire, and a fifty from Burns, once of Essex and Somerset, helped them to 238, their biggest NatWest total.

Man of the Match: R. J. Rollins.

Essex

*P. J. Prichard c Scriven b Percy	58	†R. J. Rollins not out	67
D. D. J. Robinson c Burns b Owen	0	A. P. Cowan not out	3
N. Hussain c Owen b Arthurton	78	L-b 3, w 14	17
S. G. Law c Stanway b Clarke	14		
R. C. Irani c Burns b Arthurton	28	1/7 2/130 3/159	(7 wkts, 60 overs) 327
A. P. Grayson c and b Arthurton	56	4/172 5/220	
D. R. Law c Hurd b Arthurton	6	6/232 7/297	

M. C. Ilott and P. M. Such did not bat.

Bowling: Stanway 6–2–27–0; Owen 12–0–81–1; Scriven 12–2–58–0; Percy 7–0–35–1; Clarke 11–1–70–1; Arthurton 12–1–53–4.

Buckinghamshire

R. B. Hurd c Prichard b Such	18	A. R. Clarke c Rollins b Irani	0
M. Bowyer c Cowan b Grayson	43	*T. J. A. Scriven not out	3
†N. D. Burns b S. G. Law	51	L-b 10, w 14, n-b 4	28
K. L. T. Arthurton c Hussain b Grayson	18		
B. S. Percy c Hussain b Grayson	17	1/43 2/117 3/127	(7 wkts, 60 overs) 238
P. Sawyer not out	32	4/166 5/166	
C. M. Jaggard c Grayson b Cowan	28	6/213 7/215	

D. M. Owen and S. F. Stanway did not bat.

Bowling: Ilott 12–1–34–0; Cowan 10–1–35–1; Irani 7–0–31–1; Such 12–1–56–1; Grayson 11–0–40–3; S. G. Law 8–1–32–1.

Umpires: A. Clarkson and J. H. Hampshire.

CAMBRIDGESHIRE v HAMPSHIRE

At Wisbech, June 24. Hampshire won by 239 runs. Toss: Hampshire.

Cambridgeshire paid dearly for dropping Robin Smith on two. He went on to make 126 off 134 balls, forging a partnership of 176 with Hayden. The frustrated bowler was Tim Smith, a left-arm spinner who breeds llamas and ostriches for a living; he conceded a creditable 44 from his 12 overs. Stephenson then took five for 34, his best one-day figures, as Cambridgeshire suffered the heaviest defeat in runs of the round.

Man of the Match: R. A. Smith.

Hampshire

J. S. Laney c Akhtar b Ralfs	40	W. S. Kendall not out	0
M. L. Hayden c and b Whyborn	90	B 8, l-b 9, w 15, n-b 2	34
R. A. Smith b Ralfs	126		
M. Keech run out	25	1/77 2/253	(4 wkts, 60 overs) 321
S. D. Udal not out	6	3/297 4/315	

*J. P. Stephenson, R. J. Maru, †A. N. Aymes, C. A. Connor and S. J. Renshaw did not bat.

Bowling: Whyborn 11–0–62–1; Akhtar 11–3–44–0; Smith 12–2–44–0; Ralfs 12–1–69–2; Donelan 7–0–44–0; Gadsby 7–0–41–0.

Cambridgeshire

R. P. Merriman c Aymes b Connor	11	D. F. Ralfs not out		14
S. A. Kellett lbw b Stephenson	10	C. M. Whyborn b Stephenson		7
G. W. Ecclestone run out	0	†C. D. Durant lbw b Stephenson		1
S. Mohammed b Stephenson	7	L-b 7, w 3, n-b 4		14
*N. T. Gadsby lbw b Udal	1			
B. T. P. Donelan c Stephenson b Udal	3	1/19 2/19 3/32	(38.2 overs)	82
A. Akhtar c and b Stephenson	5	4/33 5/33 6/43		
T. S. Smith c Renshaw b Udal	9	7/47 8/60 9/80		

Bowling: Connor 8–3–11–1; Renshaw 7–1–17–0; Udal 12–7–13–3; Stephenson 11.2–3–34–5.

Umpires: M. R. Benson and R. A. White.

CUMBERLAND v NORTHAMPTONSHIRE

At Barrow, June 24. Northamptonshire won by 36 runs. Toss: Cumberland.

Northamptonshire were in trouble at 68 for five before Penberthy and Sales got their heads down and eked out 84, the largest stand of the game. Andrew Mawson, a 22-year-old opener from Workington, scored 77 for Cumberland, but had too little support. Penberthy added five wickets to make sure of the match award.

Man of the Match: A. L. Penberthy.

Northamptonshire

M. B. Loye lbw b Sharp	19	K. J. Innes c Dutton b Pennett		25
†R. J. Warren c Dutton b Sharp	3	J. E. Emburey b Pennett		1
*R. J. Bailey c Mawson b Pennett	10	J. P. Taylor not out		3
K. M. Curran c Clarke b Beech	21	L-b 9, w 11		20
A. L. Penberthy c Pearson b Kippax	57			
T. C. Walton c Dutton b Scothern	6	1/22 2/33 3/33	(56.4 overs)	223
D. J. Sales c Kippax b Fielding	53	4/50 5/68 6/152		
J. N. Snape c Knox b Kippax	5	7/182 8/210 9/218		

Bowling: Pennett 9.4–1–42–3; Sharp 9–1–27–2; Scothern 12–1–50–1; Beech 5–0–21–1; Fielding 12–3–24–1; Kippax 9–0–50–2.

Cumberland

D. J. Pearson b Curran	3	D. B. Pennett c Snape b Penberthy		1
A. D. Mawson c Warren b Penberthy	77	M. G. Scothern not out		23
S. T. Knox c Warren b Penberthy	0	M. A. Sharp not out		7
G. J. Clarke c Bailey b Penberthy	9	B 2, l-b 2, w 6, n-b 4		14
*†S. M. Dutton c Bailey b Snape	38			
P. Beech c Walton b Curran	5	1/14 2/20 3/34	(9 wkts, 60 overs)	187
S. A. J. Kippax c and b Penberthy	5	4/100 5/106 6/114		
J. M. Fielding run out	5	7/125 8/126 9/169		

Bowling: Taylor 10–1–40–0; Curran 12–4–31–2; Penberthy 11–2–56–5; Emburey 12–3–22–0; Bailey 3–0–12–0; Snape 12–4–22–1.

Umpires: B. Leadbeater and M. Johnson.

DEVON v LEICESTERSHIRE

At Exmouth, June 24. Leicestershire won by 53 runs. Toss: Leicestershire.

Minor Counties champions Devon shook their first-class counterparts in a low-scoring game. Leicestershire were 99 for six, with Sutcliffe the only recognised batsman remaining, but he stayed – with help from Mason – and scored his maiden one-day century for the county. After an early flurry from Townsend, Devon's reply was smothered by accurate bowling from Wells and the spinners.

Man of the Match: I. J. Sutcliffe.

Leicestershire

V. J. Wells b Warren	0	G. J. Parsons c Folland b Pugh	9
D. L. Maddy b Roebuck	15	D. J. Millns not out	6
I. J. Sutcliffe not out	103		
*J. J. Whitaker lbw b Roebuck	12	B 10, l-b 17, w 10, n-b 2	39
N. C. Johnson st Read b MacGill	4		
J. M. Dakin lbw b Donohue	6	1/3 2/43 3/73 (8 wkts, 60 overs) 225
†P. A. Nixon c Read b Donohue	1	4/78 5/96 6/99
T. J. Mason c and b Pugh	30	7/166 8/181

M. T. Brimson did not bat.

Bowling: Donohue 12–2–44–2; Warren 6–1–24–1; Pugh 6–0–32–2; Roebuck 12–2–27–2; MacGill 12–2–30–1; Cottam 12–1–41–0.

Devon

N. R. Gaywood lbw b Millns	5	K. Donohue b Wells	5
G. T. J. Townsend b Wells	37	A. C. Cottam not out	22
N. A. Folland c Maddy b Mason	17	P. M. Warren not out	12
*P. M. Roebuck c Nixon b Wells	6	B 5, l-b 14, w 8	27
R. J. Baggs b Brimson	5		
A. J. Pugh st Nixon b Brimson	29	1/27 2/58 3/78 (9 wkts, 60 overs) 172
†C. M. W. Read lbw b Mason	3	4/86 5/97 6/101
S. C. G. MacGill b Mason	4	7/115 8/132 9/149

Bowling: Parsons 12–3–34–0; Millns 7–1–25–1; Wells 12–1–30–3; Mason 12–1–29–3; Brimson 12–4–16–2; Maddy 4–0–15–0; Johnson 1–0–4–0.

Umpires: N. Mallender and G. Sharp.

GLAMORGAN v BEDFORDSHIRE

At Cardiff, June 24. Glamorgan won by seven wickets. Toss: Bedfordshire.

Bedfordshire's decision to bat under cloud never looked like paying off, though they received a late fillip from a ninth-wicket stand of 38 between Young and Sandford, who gamely declined to wear a helmet against Waqar Younis. The donation of 49 extras, including 35 in wides and no-balls, also helped them. Croft, who conceded only 14 in his 12 overs, then hit 64 from 58 balls, and Glamorgan won with almost 30 overs to spare.

Man of the Match: R. D. B. Croft.

Bedfordshire

W. Larkins lbw b Watkin	1	B. J. Young not out	30
R. N. Dalton b Waqar Younis	8	†G. D. Sandford c Maynard b Cottey	16
N. A. Stanley lbw b Butcher	29	M. R. White not out	6
A. R. Roberts lbw b Watkin	7	B 1, l-b 13, w 21, n-b 14	49
C. K. Bullen lbw b Watkin	2		
*P. D. B. Hoare lbw b Butcher	12	1/5 2/9 3/18 (9 wkts, 60 overs) 179
A. J. Trott c Morris b Croft	14	4/32 5/74 6/93
Z. A. Sher b Waqar Younis	5	7/111 8/111 9/149

Bowling: Waqar Younis 10–3–35–2; Watkin 11–3–23–3; Thomas 12–1–38–0; Dale 2–0–5–0; Butcher 7–0–33–2; Croft 12–5–14–1; Cottey 3–0–9–1; Maynard 3–0–8–0.

Glamorgan

R. D. B. Croft c Stanley b Dalton	64	P. A. Cottey not out	26
H. Morris c Larkins b Sher	13	L-b 2, w 15, n-b 2	19
†A. D. Shaw c Roberts b Dalton	19		
*M. P. Maynard not out	41	1/40 2/106 3/114 (3 wkts, 30.2 overs) 182

S. P. James, A. Dale, G. P. Butcher, S. D. Thomas, Waqar Younis and S. L. Watkin did not bat.

Bowling: White 9.2–0–46–0; Sher 3–0–42–1; Roberts 9–0–40–0; Dalton 6–0–32–2; Bullen 2–0–9–0; Trott 1–0–11–0.

Umpires: N. Cowley and V. A. Holder.

GLOUCESTERSHIRE v SCOTLAND

At Bristol, June 24. Gloucestershire won by 101 runs. Toss: Gloucestershire.

A stand of 311 between Gloucestershire openers Wright and Trainor broke the all-wicket tournament record set by Tim Curtis and Tom Moody, who put on 309 for Worcestershire's third wicket in their 1994 semi-final against Surrey. A total of 351 and Wright's 177, from 188 balls with 19 fours and a six, were Gloucestershire's best in any one-day competition. Responding to a mountain of runs, Patterson and Smith mustered a worthy stand of 135, which led to Scotland's highest total yet in this competition. Both fell to Hancock, whose occasional medium-pace claimed six wickets.

Man of the Match: A. J. Wright.

Gloucestershire

A. J. Wright c Kennedy b Williamson . . .	177
N. J. Trainor c Patterson b Steindl	143
S. Young not out.	14
M. A. Lynch not out.	0
L-b 3, w 10, n-b 4	17

1/311 2/348   (2 wkts, 60 overs) 351

R. J. Cunliffe, *M. W. Alleyne, †R. C. Russell, T. H. C. Hancock, M. C. J. Ball, K. P. Sheeraz and J. Lewis did not bat.

Bowling: Steindl 12–2–67–1; Thomson 12–1–53–0; Stanger 10–0–69–0; Williamson 4–0–28–1; Sheridan 12–0–69–0; Kennedy 10–0–62–0.

Scotland

B. M. W. Patterson c Russell b Hancock .	77	P. D. Steindl b Hancock.	7
I. L. Philip c Ball b Young	21	K. L. P. Sheridan c and b Trainor.	0
M. J. Smith st Russell b Hancock	73	K. Thomson not out	1
*G. Salmond c Russell b Hancock	1	L-b 3, w 14, n-b 2	19
J. G. Williamson c Lewis b Hancock	7		
I. M. Stanger b Hancock	21	1/33 2/168 3/183 (9 wkts, 60 overs) 250
†A. G. Davies c Lynch b Trainor	16	4/187 5/202 6/234
S. R. Kennedy not out	7	7/236 8/245 9/249

Bowling: Lewis 9–0–38–0; Young 6–0–20–1; Alleyne 6–0–28–0; Sheeraz 10–1–30–0; Ball 12–1–48–0; Hancock 12–0–58–6; Trainor 5–0–25–2.

Umpires: J. W. Holder and M. K. Reed.

LANCASHIRE v BERKSHIRE

At Manchester, June 24. Lancashire won by 169 runs. Toss: Berkshire.

Berkshire's hopes were raised when Atherton and Crawley, just back from the Lord's Test, were out early, having scored just 19 runs between them. But they were dashed again as Lloyd and 22-year-old Mark Harvey put on 176 in 28 overs for the fourth wicket. Hodgson's painstaking fifty was little consolation.

Man of the Match: M. E. Harvey.

Lancashire

P. C. McKeown c Hodgson b Kendrick . .	42	G. Yates not out	34
*M. A. Atherton c Seymour b Barrow . . .	8	G. Chapple not out	2
J. P. Crawley lbw b Marc	11	B 2, l-b 10, w 11, n-b 10.	33
G. D. Lloyd b Sylvester	96		
M. E. Harvey b Myles	86	1/30 2/58 3/88 (7 wkts, 60 overs) 351
I. D. Austin b Myles.	2	4/264 5/267
†W. K. Hegg st Lane b Sylvester	37	6/285 7/337

P. J. Martin and D. J. Shadford did not bat.

Bowling: Marc 9–0–61–1; Barrow 9–0–32–1; Kendrick 12–0–46–1; Myles 12–0–77–2; Hartley 9–0–64–0; Sylvester 9–0–59–2.

Berkshire

G. E. Loveday c Hegg b Martin	11	†M. G. Lane not out	18
*J. P. J. Sylvester c Atherton b Chapple	22		
S. A. Seymour b Yates	17	L-b 5, w 12, n-b 2	19
S. D. Myles c Hegg b Yates	25		—
J. Hodgson not out	53	1/37 2/37 3/79 (5 wkts, 60 overs) 182	
H. M. Hall c Harvey b Austin	17	4/82 5/147	

N. M. Kendrick, K. Marc, D. J. B. Hartley and J. K. Barrow did not bat.

Bowling: Austin 12–5–22–1; Martin 10–3–14–1; Chapple 6–0–28–1; Shadford 7–0–31–0; Yates 12–3–15–2; Lloyd 2–0–12–0; McKeown 10–0–51–0; Crawley 1–0–4–0.

Umpires: H. D. Bird and A. G. T. Whitehead.

LINCOLNSHIRE v DERBYSHIRE

At Lincoln Lindum, June 24. Derbyshire won by eight wickets. Toss: Derbyshire.

DeFreitas, newly confirmed as Derbyshire's captain for the rest of the season, found Lincolnshire in obliging mood. They managed only one partnership of substance – 50 for the eighth wicket between Gouldstone and Bradford – and their bowlers had no answer to Adams's adventurous strokeplay. He made 71 not out from 44 balls and led Derbyshire past the target in the 19th over with his fourth six.

Man of the Match: C. J. Adams.

Lincolnshire

J. R. Wileman b Malcolm	1	S. A. Bradford not out	15
S. G. Plumb b Malcolm	8	D. A. Christmas b Aldred	0
M. R. Gouldstone b Aldred	37	S. Oakes c Clarke b Aldred	4
R. J. Evans c Aldred b DeFreitas	3	B 2, l-b 2, w 14, n-b 5	23
*M. A. Fell lbw b Aldred	17		—
P. A. Rawden run out	0	1/2 2/11 3/14 (50.2 overs) 116	
L. C. Weekes c Krikken b Harris	8	4/40 5/40 6/53	
†P. Trend lbw b Harris	0	7/61 8/111 9/111	

Bowling: Malcolm 12–2–27–2; DeFreitas 11–4–20–1; Aldred 10.2–2–30–4; Harris 8–2–12–2; Clarke 6–1–12–0; Barnett 3–0–11–0.

Derbyshire

A. S. Rollins c Gouldstone b Bradford	21
J. E. Owen c Trend b Oakes	10
C. J. Adams not out	71
T. A. Tweats not out	5
W 4, n-b 10	14

1/24 2/87 (2 wkts, 19 overs) 121

K. J. Barnett, V. P. Clarke, †K. M. Krikken, *P. A. J. DeFreitas, P. Aldred, A. J. Harris and D. E. Malcolm did not bat.

Bowling: Weekes 6–1–39–0; Oakes 5–0–34–1; Christmas 4–0–30–0; Bradford 4–1–18–1.

Umpires: P. Adams and N. T. Plews.

MIDDLESEX v KENT

At Lord's, June 24. Middlesex won by three wickets. Toss: Kent.

Kent, who challenged for honours in the other county competitions in 1997, fell at the first fence in this one. They held the advantage when Ramprakash was out for 72, leaving Middlesex 148 for four in the 44th over, still 78 short. But the early withdrawal of McCague with a strained hamstring left the attack short of firepower, and Shah and Hewitt guided Middlesex home with four balls to spare. Kent had recovered from 64 for four – all caught behind – thanks to a stand of 97 between Llong and Ealham, and 41 in 27 balls from Fleming, including three successive sixes off Hewitt. Johnson picked up three wickets in his last over. The game was played on the strip used for the rain-affected Lord's Test, which had finished the previous day.

Man of the Match: M. R. Ramprakash.

Kent

D. P. Fulton c Brown b Fraser	9	*†S. A. Marsh b Johnson	0
M. J. Walker c Brown b Fraser	13	M. J. McCague not out	4
T. R. Ward c Brown b Hewitt	0	D. W. Headley lbw b Weekes	1
A. P. Wells c Brown b Bloomfield	9	L-b 12, w 14, n-b 2	28
N. J. Llong c Brown b Johnson	68		
M. A. Ealham c Fraser b Johnson	46	1/11 2/21 3/33	(60 overs) 225
M. V. Fleming c Ramprakash b Johnson	41	4/64 5/161 6/173	
P. A. Strang c Ramprakash b Johnson	6	7/217 8/217 9/218	

Bowling: Fraser 12–4–22–2; Hewitt 8–0–41–1; Bloomfield 8–2–25–1; Johnson 12–1–50–5; Weekes 12–0–47–1; Ramprakash 8–0–28–0.

Middlesex

P. N. Weekes b Llong	34	R. L. Johnson b Headley	8
J. H. Kallis c Marsh b Headley	4	J. P. Hewitt not out	14
*M. R. Ramprakash b Fleming	72	B 2, l-b 8, w 6	16
M. W. Gatting b Ealham	20		
J. C. Pooley c sub b Llong	12	1/5 2/86 3/142	(7 wkts, 59.2 overs) 227
†K. R. Brown lbw b Headley	20	4/148 5/169	
O. A. Shah not out	27	6/183 7/195	

A. R. C. Fraser and T. F. Bloomfield did not bat.

Bowling: Headley 12–1–31–3; McCague 2–0–8–0; Fleming 12–3–22–1; Ealham 12–0–45–1; Llong 9.2–0–49–2; Strang 12–0–62–0.

Umpires: G. I. Burgess and B. J. Meyer.

NOTTINGHAMSHIRE v STAFFORDSHIRE

At Nottingham, June 24. Nottinghamshire won by ten wickets. Toss: Nottinghamshire.

The top score in Staffordshire's measly total of 95 was Potter's 19, with Pick and Astle taking three cheap wickets each. The Nottinghamshire openers took a leisurely 32 overs to complete the county's first ten-wicket win in this competition.

Man of the Match: N. J. Astle.

Staffordshire

*S. J. Dean b Evans	4	D. J. Brock b Pick	3
I. W. E. Stokes c Afzaal b Franks	18	A. Richardson lbw b Pick	0
L. Potter c Archer b Astle	19	S. D. Horsfall run out	0
D. K. Pashley b Astle	5	L-b 7, w 7	14
P. F. Shaw c Franks b Archer	18		
D. R. Womble lbw b Astle	6	1/13 2/48 3/48	(45.3 overs) 95
†M. I. Humphries c Archer b Pick	2	4/73 5/76 6/86	
C. G. Feltham not out	6	7/90 8/95 9/95	

Bowling: Pick 9–1–17–3; Evans 7.3–4–3–1; Franks 9–5–14–1; Bowen 5–0–17–0; Astle 10–2–20–3; Archer 5–1–17–1.

Nottinghamshire

P. R. Pollard not out.................. 42
*R. T. Robinson not out.............. 41
      L-b 1, w 8, n-b 4 13

          (no wkt, 31.5 overs) 96

U. Afzaal, N. J. Astle, A. A. Metcalfe, G. F. Archer, †W. M. Noon, K. P. Evans, M. N. Bowen, R. A. Pick and P. J. Franks did not bat.

Bowling: Richardson 9–2–26–0; Horsfall 6–1–15–0; Brock 8–1–31–0; Womble 4–0–17–0; Potter 4–1–5–0; Feltham 0.5–0–1–0.

Umpires: J. C. Balderstone and M. J. Kitchen.

SOMERSET v HEREFORDSHIRE

At Taunton, June 24. Somerset won by 231 runs. Toss: Somerset.

Holloway and Bowler put on 166 to get Somerset started, then Ecclestone, with a 60-ball hundred, and Lathwell added 128 to carry them to 367 for five, the highest total of the round. Herefordshire started brightly through Hall and Barlow, but Mushtaq Ahmed halted them with four wickets.

Man of the Match: S. C. Ecclestone.

Somerset

M. Burns c Cooper b Radford	6	K. A. Parsons not out.................	0
P. C. L. Holloway c and b Skyrme	90		
*P. D. Bowler c Cooper b Skyrme	87	B 7, l-b 10, w 10	27
S. C. Ecclestone b Radford	101		
M. N. Lathwell c Skyrme b Fowles	42	1/27 2/193 3/223 (5 wkts, 60 overs)	367
†R. J. Turner not out	14	4/351 5/361	

G. D. Rose, J. I. D. Kerr, A. R. Caddick and Mushtaq Ahmed did not bat.

Bowling: Radford 12–1–64–2; Cooper 12–0–63–0; Harding 12–0–53–0; Fowles 10–0–73–1; Blakemore 2–0–19–0; Skyrme 12–0–78–2.

Herefordshire

H. V. Patel b Rose	3	M. G. Fowles b Kerr	0
R. Hall b Mushtaq Ahmed	29	R. J. Harding c Lathwell b Rose	17
R. G. R. Barlow b Mushtaq Ahmed ...	15	K. E. Cooper b Caddick..............	4
I. P. C. Blakemore c Bowler b Kerr	7		
D. A. Graham b Kerr	2	L-b 4, w 11, n-b 4	19
*R. P. Skyrme c Bowler			
b Mushtaq Ahmed .	7	1/8 2/60 3/65 (37.4 overs)	136
†S. R. Bevins c Rose b Mushtaq Ahmed .	8	4/68 5/72 6/83	
N. V. Radford not out	25	7/99 8/100 9/131	

Bowling: Caddick 8.4–1–30–1; Rose 9–0–43–2; Mushtaq Ahmed 12–2–27–4; Kerr 8–0–32–3.

Umpires: D. J. Constant and K. J. Lyons.

SURREY v DURHAM

At The Oval, June 24. Surrey won by five wickets. Toss: Surrey.

Durham's 247 was never going to be easy to defend on a back-breaking Oval pitch and, once Stewart had settled in, Surrey were clearly in control. Morris and Boon had given Durham a chance with a third-wicket stand of 117, and Foster then hit an unbeaten 56 from 40 balls. But Surrey needed little more than four an over, and they won in comfort.

Man of the Match: A. J. Stewart.

Durham

J. J. B. Lewis c B. C. Holliaoke b Bicknell	1
N. J. Speak c Butcher b Lewis	4
J. E. Morris c Stewart b Lewis	75
*D. C. Boon b Salisbury	57
†M. P. Speight b Salisbury	9
P. D. Collingwood c Brown b Saqlain Mushtaq	15
M. J. Foster not out	56

M. M. Betts c Lewis b Salisbury	3
J. Boiling not out	6
B 2, 1-b 7, w 12	21
	—

1/5 2/26 3/143   (7 wkts, 60 overs) 247
4/165 5/172
6/196 7/208

S. J. E. Brown and A. Walker did not bat.

Bowling: Bicknell 10–2–25–1; Lewis 11–1–37–2; A. J. Holliaoke 8–0–46–0; B. C. Holliaoke 7–1–31–0; Saqlain Mushtaq 12–1–63–1; Salisbury 12–0–36–3.

Surrey

J. D. Ratcliffe c Boon b Foster	39
M. A. Butcher c Speight b Brown	0
†A. J. Stewart not out	90
G. P. Thorpe c Speight b Foster	0
A. D. Brown c Morris b Betts	44
*A. J. Holliaoke b Brown	34

C. C. Lewis not out	3
L-b 13, w 12, n-b 16	41
	—

1/16 2/102 3/102   (5 wkts, 48.5 overs) 251
4/180 5/231

B. C. Holliaoke, M. P. Bicknell, I. D. K. Salisbury and Saqlain Mushtaq did not bat.

Bowling: Brown 10–0–42–2; Betts 9–0–73–1; Walker 9.5–1–32–0; Foster 8–1–37–2; Boiling 12–0–54–0.

Umpires: T. E. Jesty and R. Palmer.

SUSSEX v SHROPSHIRE

At Hove, June 24. Sussex won by ten wickets. Toss: Sussex.

Put in to bat on a seaming wicket, Shropshire passed 100 only through a last-wicket stand of 37. The damage was done by Kirtley, who took five wickets, among them former Warwickshire batsman Asif Din. Greenfield found the amateur bowlers less challenging, but Athey did his best to prolong the agony, failing to score a run between the 23rd and 44th overs. The man of the match was chosen by the former England women's captain, Rachael Heyhoe-Flint, the first time a woman had made the adjudication.

Man of the Match: R. J. Kirtley.

Shropshire

J. V. Anders c Moores b Drakes	8
K. Sharp lbw b Kirtley	3
J. B. R. Jones c Moores b Robinson	14
Asif Din b Kirtley	1
*M. R. Davies lbw b Robinson	9
A. N. Johnson c Moores b Kirtley	15
A. B. Byram b Khan	5
G. J. Byram lbw b Kirtley	0

†A. N. Mackelworth b Kirtley	0
D. L. Bowett not out	11
A. M. Shimmons run out	14
L-b 15, w 13, n-b 8	36
	—

1/5 2/23 3/25   (47.5 overs) 116
4/39 5/54 6/79
7/79 8/79 9/79

Bowling: Kirtley 12–2–39–5; Drakes 7–4–13–1; K. Newell 9–4–8–0; Robinson 11.5–4–28–2; Khan 8–2–13–1.

Sussex

K. Greenfield not out	89
C. W. J. Athey not out	18
B 4, w 2, n-b 6	12

(no wkt, 45.4 overs) 119

N. R. Taylor, M. Newell, K. Newell, *†P. Moores, V. C. Drakes, M. J. Thursfield, A. A. Khan, M. A. Robinson and R. J. Kirtley did not bat.

Bowling: Shimmons 4–0–27–0; G. J. Byram 7–1–22–0; Asif Din 12–7–20–0; A. B. Byram 12–4–29–0; Bowett 7–2–15–0; Anders 3.4–2–2–0.

Umpires: R. Julian and J. W. Lloyds.

WARWICKSHIRE v NORFOLK

At Birmingham, June 24. Warwickshire won by 80 runs. Toss: Norfolk.

Warwickshire found themselves staring at possible humiliation after barely an hour when Norfolk's opening bowlers had reduced them to 25 for six. But Moles and Giles added 137, and Small took the total past 200. Paul Newman, who was in the Derbyshire team which won the trophy in 1981, still finished with figures of 12–2–23–4. But Giles came on early and capped him with 12–8–21–5, and Donald stopped any thought of a revival.

Man of the Match: A. F. Giles.

Warwickshire

*N. V. Knight c Amos b Newman	0	†T. Frost c Boyden b D. R. Thomas	0
N. M. K. Smith c Amos b Newman	4	G. C. Small not out	32
D. L. Hemp c Rogers b Newman	0	A. A. Donald c Newman b Bradshaw	1
T. L. Penney run out	0	B 1, l-b 5, w 15, n-b 10	31
A. J. Moles b Newman	64		
D. R. Brown c Rogers b Bradshaw	1	1/0 2/5 3/5	(59.3 overs) 207
G. Welch b Bradshaw	5	4/6 5/15 6/25	
A. F. Giles lbw b D. R. Thomas	69	7/162 8/162 9/202	

Bowling: Newman 12–2–23–4; Bradshaw 11.3–1–42–3; Goldsmith 6–1–13–0; M. W. Thomas 12–0–50–0; Adams 3–0–13–0; D. R. Thomas 10–1–38–2; Fox 5–0–22–0.

Norfolk

C. J. Rogers b Giles	13	M. W. Thomas st Frost b Giles	6
C. Amos c Knight b Welch	13	P. J. Bradshaw c Hemp b Donald	0
T. J. Boon lbw b Giles	12	†M. K. L. Boyden not out	8
D. R. Thomas c Moles b Giles	4	B 1, l-b 13, w 7, n-b 2	23
N. J. Adams b Giles	0		
S. C. Goldsmith c Frost b Donald	22	1/22 2/46 3/49	(48.2 overs) 127
*P. G. Newman c Frost b Donald	5	4/53 5/53 6/83	
N. Fox lbw b Small	21	7/84 8/91 9/96	

Bowling: Donald 12–4–36–3; Welch 8–1–18–1; Brown 12–4–22–0; Giles 12–8–21–5; Smith 4–0–16–0; Small 0.2–0–0–1.

Umpires: J. H. Harris and A. A. Jones.

WORCESTERSHIRE v HOLLAND

At Worcester, June 24. Worcestershire won by 111 runs. Toss: Holland.

Worcestershire won comfortably, thanks to an untroubled century from Moody, but 20-year-old Dutch student Bas Zuiderent won a standing ovation. He had made a half-century against England in the 1996 World Cup, and so nearly reached three figures here, hitting ten fours and two sixes, before a reckless single to Spring at mid-wicket was his downfall.

Man of the Match: B. Zuiderent.

Worcestershire

*T. M. Moody c Lefebvre b Dulfer	108	S. R. Lampitt not out	28
T. S. Curtis b van Dijk	28	†S. J. Rhodes not out	0
G. A. Hick c de Leede b Goodwin	7	L-b 8, w 20, n-b 10	38
G. R. Haynes run out	32		
K. R. Spiring c de Leede b Lefebvre	53	1/81 2/109 3/199	(6 wkts, 60 overs) 336
D. A. Leatherdale c Dulfer b de Leede	42	4/206 5/292 6/330	

P. J. Newport, A. Sheriyar and M. J. Rawnsley did not bat.

Bowling: Khan 12–2–59–0; Lefebvre 12–0–42–1; van Dijk 12–0–68–1; Dulfer 10–0–62–1; de Leede 8–0–49–1; Goodwin 5–1–28–1; Zulfiqar 1–0–20–0.

Holland

R. F. van Oosterom c Hick b Newport	2		R. P. Lefebvre b Rawnsley	4	
B. Zuiderent run out	99		S. van Dijk not out	8	
M. W. Goodwin c Rhodes b Haynes	4		E. Dulfer lbw b Hick	3	
K. J. van Noortwijk run out	25		L-b 3, w 9, n-b 22	34	
*T. B. M. de Leede c Spring b Sheriyar	10				
A. Zulfiqar b Newport	21		1/6 2/26 3/122		(54.2 overs) 225
†M. Schewe c Haynes b Rawnsley	10		4/139 5/181 6/195		
A. Khan c Newport b Hick	5		7/205 8/209 9/217		

Bowling: Newport 12–0–52–2; Haynes 9–2–18–1; Lampitt 5–0–28–0; Rawnsley 11–2–50–2; Sheriyar 7–0–35–1; Leatherdale 6–0–25–0; Hick 4.2–0–14–2.

Umpires: J. F. Steele and P. Willey.

YORKSHIRE v IRELAND

At Leeds, June 24. Yorkshire won by 196 runs. Toss: Ireland.

Yorkshire were rattled by McCrum and Eagleson, whose early inroads left them 55 for six. Then Hartley arrived, to share stands of 100 with White and 79 with Gough. Gough's best moments were still to come; he bagged seven for 27, finished the match with a hat-trick, and received the match award from Fred Trueman, whose tournament record for Yorkshire (six for 15 at Taunton in 1965) he had just eclipsed.

Man of the Match: D. Gough.

Yorkshire

M. D. Moxon c Rutherford b McCrum	0		D. Gough run out	46	
A. McGrath c Rutherford b Eagleson	0		C. E. W. Silverwood c Lewis b Heasley	3	
*D. Byas b Eagleson	10		R. D. Stemp not out	0	
D. S. Lehmann b Heasley	17		L-b 1, w 23	24	
B. Parker c Molins b McCrum	0				
C. White lbw b Benson	63		1/4 2/16 3/23		(59.4 overs) 249
†R. J. Blakey c Patterson b McCrum	3		4/31 5/45 6/55		
P. J. Hartley c Benson b Heasley	83		7/155 8/234 9/239		

Bowling: McCrum 12–5–26–3; Eagleson 10–2–40–2; Heasley 9.4–1–41–3; Molins 8–0–39–0; Benson 11–1–55–1; Lewis 3–0–23–0; Curry 6–0–24–0.

Ireland

J. D. Curry lbw b Gough	4		†A. T. Rutherford not out	4	
W. K. McCallan c Blakey b Gough	2		G. L. Molins lbw b Gough	0	
D. A. Lewis c Byas b Silverwood	0		P. McCrum lbw b Gough	0	
*J. D. R. Benson lbw b Silverwood	0		L-b 2, w 6, n-b 2	10	
A. D. Patterson b Silverwood	0				
A. R. Dunlop lbw b Gough	5		1/5 2/7 3/11		(18.5 overs) 53
D. Heasley b Gough	18		4/12 5/12 6/24		
R. L. Eagleson c Byas b Gough	10		7/39 8/53 9/53		

Bowling: Gough 9.5–1–27–7; Silverwood 8–2–24–3; Hartley 1–1–0–0.

Umpires: J. D. Bond and M. J. Harris.

SECOND ROUND

DERBYSHIRE v NORTHAMPTONSHIRE

At Derby, July 9. Derbyshire won by 144 runs. Toss: Northamptonshire.

When Malcolm followed a major partnership between Adams and Barnett with an opening spell of 8–1–27–5, the tie was effectively decided. Penberthy and Snape worked hard to rescue Northamptonshire's innings but they were beaten with nearly 12 overs to spare. Malcolm, often regarded as too inaccurate for one-day cricket, came back to finish with seven for 35. Derbyshire lost two early wickets, but their opponents donated 17 wides in the first 15 overs. Then Adams got going: his century came from 112 balls and he dominated a stand of 183 in 39 overs, Derbyshire's best for the third wicket in the competition. Barnett maintained the momentum in their highest total against a first-class county.

Man of the Match: D. E. Malcolm.

Derbyshire

A. S. Rollins c Sales b Taylor	6	†K. M. Krikken c Loye b Bailey	1
M. R. May c Warren b Mohammad Akram	5	P. Aldred not out	0
C. J. Adams st Warren b Bailey	101	B 5, l-b 7, w 21	33
K. J. Barnett c Loye b Emburey	111		—
G. A. Khan c Penberthy b Taylor	19	1/18 2/25 3/208 (7 wkts, 60 overs) 324	
*P. A. J. DeFreitas c Loye b Bailey	24	4/254 5/294	
V. P. Clarke not out	24	6/301 7/319	

K. J. Dean and D. E. Malcolm did not bat.

Bowling: Mohammad Akram 12–2–42–1; Taylor 9–0–58–2; Curran 4–0–23–0; Penberthy 2–0–23–0; Emburey 12–0–61–1; Snape 12–0–50–0; Bailey 9–0–55–3.

Northamptonshire

M. B. Loye c Clarke b Malcolm	2	J. E. Emburey b Clarke	1
†R. J. Warren b Malcolm	0	J. P. Taylor b Malcolm	6
*R. J. Bailey lbw b Dean	23	Mohammad Akram not out	0
K. M. Curran b Malcolm	9	L-b 10, w 13	23
D. J. Sales c DeFreitas b Malcolm	0		—
T. C. Walton lbw b Malcolm	0	1/1 2/8 3/24 (48.1 overs) 180	
A. L. Penberthy lbw b Malcolm	62	4/29 5/29 6/52	
J. N. Snape b DeFreitas	54	7/149 8/160 9/179	

Bowling: Malcolm 10.1–1–35–7; DeFreitas 12–0–39–1; Dean 9–2–24–1; Aldred 7–0–34–0; Clarke 10–1–38–1.

Umpires: A. Clarkson and J. W. Holder.

ESSEX v WORCESTERSHIRE

At Chelmsford, July 9. Essex won by seven wickets. Toss: Worcestershire.

Stuart Law pointed Essex towards victory after they had lost two wickets in their first five overs. He scored 100 in 91 balls, and then Grayson took up the chase with a run-a-ball 82. But it was Irani, their anchor during successive century stands, who won Trevor Bailey's vote for the match award, for 79 runs spanning 161 deliveries, plus two wickets. Another candidate would have been Hick, who had assaulted the Essex attack with a thrilling 146 from 157 balls, helping himself to ten fours and five sixes, one of which hit a spectator named Doris Day through the open window of the pavilion. Hick struck 26 off one over of Grayson's left-arm spin. Worcestershire failed to cash in, though, losing six for 17 in their final three overs.

Man of the Match: R. C. Irani.

Worcestershire

*T. M. Moody lbw b Williams	6
T. S. Curtis b Such	41
G. A. Hick c Grayson b Cowan	146
K. R. Spiring lbw b Grayson	47
D. A. Leatherdale b Irani	9
V. S. Solanki c Williams b Cowan	6
S. R. Lampitt b Irani	0
†S. J. Rhodes not out	7
P. J. Newport run out	2
A. Sheriyar run out	0
L-b 12, w 4, n-b 6	22

1/11 2/102 3/223   (9 wkts, 60 overs) 286
4/269 5/275 6/275
7/280 8/286 9/286

R. J. Chapman did not bat.

Bowling: Williams 12–4–41–1; Cowan 12–0–50–2; S. G. Law 4–0–19–0; Irani 12–1–61–2; Such 10–1–27–1; Grayson 10–0–76–1.

Essex

*P. J. Prichard c Rhodes b Sheriyar	1
S. G. Law c Lampitt b Solanki	100
N. Hussain c Spiring b Newport	1
R. C. Irani not out	79
A. P. Grayson not out	82
L-b 10, w 8, n-b 6	24

1/10 2/19 3/151   (3 wkts, 57.3 overs) 287

D. D. J. Robinson, D. R. Law, †R. J. Rollins, A. P. Cowan, N. F. Williams and P. M. Such did not bat.

Bowling: Newport 6–0–32–1; Sheriyar 8–0–39–1; Moody 8–0–35–0; Lampitt 7–0–44–0; Hick 12–0–40–0; Leatherdale 6–0–36–0; Solanki 10.3–0–51–1.

Umpires: B. Leadbeater and R. A. White.

HAMPSHIRE v GLAMORGAN

At Southampton, July 9. Glamorgan won by two wickets. Toss: Glamorgan.
Robin Smith scored his seventh century in this competition, to equal the record held by his elder brother, Chris. But he was left empty-handed as Glamorgan squeezed through with two balls to spare. Smith hit one six and 14 fours, and enabled Hampshire to reach an imposing 302. Morris and Dale launched the reply with 128, but the match hinged on an incident in the 53rd over when Glamorgan were 241 for six, with James running short of partners: Shaw was given run out but then recalled by umpire Julian after Udal indicated he had not had the ball in his hand as he broke the wicket. Shaw and James put on 76 in ten overs, and Shaw was still there as Glamorgan crossed the finishing line.
Man of the Match: S. P. James.

Hampshire

J. S. Laney c James b Dale	35
M. L. Hayden lbw b Thomas	20
R. A. Smith c Maynard b Thomas	119
M. Keech c Morris b Waqar Younis	34
W. S. Kendall c Cottey b Watkin	16
*J. P. Stephenson lbw b Croft	1
S. D. Udal not out	39
†A. N. Aymes not out	11
B 3, l-b 10, w 14	27

1/45 2/101 3/149   (6 wkts, 60 overs) 302
4/193 5/194 6/277

R. J. Maru, S. J. Renshaw and C. A. Connor did not bat.

Bowling: Waqar Younis 12–0–62–1; Watkin 12–1–44–1; Thomas 11–0–70–2; Croft 12–1–30–1; Dale 9–0–61–1; Cottey 4–0–22–0.

Glamorgan

R. D. B. Croft c Laney b Renshaw	0	S. D. Thomas c Udal b Renshaw	1
H. Morris run out	53	Waqar Younis not out	8
A. Dale c Aymes b Connor	71		
*M. P. Maynard c Keech b Stephenson	30	L-b 12, w 10	22
P. A. Cottey c Hayden b Stephenson	5		
S. P. James c Aymes b Connor	69	1/0 2/128 3/132 (8 wkts, 59.4 overs) 304	
G. P. Butcher c Aymes b Stephenson	11	4/144 5/192 6/215	
†A. D. Shaw not out	34	7/291 8/292	

S. L. Watkin did not bat.

Bowling: Renshaw 12–1–71–2; Connor 11.4–1–55–2; Maru 11–0–55–0; Stephenson 12–1–49–3; Udal 12–0–56–0; Keech 1–0–6–0.

Umpires: R. Julian and B. J. Meyer.

LEICESTERSHIRE v YORKSHIRE

At Leicester, July 9. Yorkshire won by 128 runs. Toss: Yorkshire.

White had recently claimed he was so out of form he did not know which end of the bat to hold. That all changed at Grace Road; he followed up 148 on Sunday with 96 not out to set up this easy win. White and Parker put Leicestershire to the sword with a scintillating stand of 129 in 15 overs, and the last ten overs yielded 100. Parker's 69 came off just 49 balls. Once Gough and Silverwood had ripped out three of Leicestershire's top four, their target of 311 was virtually impossible. Sutcliffe's 90 was excellent but token.

Man of the Match: C. White.

Yorkshire

M. D. Moxon c Smith b Parsons	74	†R. J. Blakey not out	0
A. McGrath c Nixon b Parsons	24		
*D. Byas b Parsons	2	L-b 9, w 18, n-b 8	35
D. S. Lehmann c Johnson b Wells	10		
C. White not out	96	1/66 2/68 3/83 (5 wkts, 60 overs) 310	
B. Parker run out	69	4/177 5/306	

P. J. Hartley, D. Gough, C. E. W. Silverwood and R. D. Stemp did not bat.

Bowling: Mullally 12–0–59–0; Millns 12–4–56–0; Wells 10–1–40–1; Parsons 12–1–68–3; Mason 12–0–63–0; Johnson 2–0–15–0.

Leicestershire

V. J. Wells b Gough	0	G. J. Parsons run out	8
D. L. Maddy b Silverwood	0	D. J. Millns run out	3
I. J. Sutcliffe b Stemp	90	A. D. Mullally not out	0
*J. J. Whitaker lbw b Gough	5	L-b 3, w 4	7
N. C. Johnson c Blakey b Stemp	15		
B. F. Smith c Hartley b Stemp	4	1/0 2/5 3/14 (47.2 overs) 182	
†P. A. Nixon lbw b Stemp	14	4/43 5/51 6/75	
T. J. Mason b Hartley	36	7/162 8/173 9/181	

Bowling: Gough 9–1–22–2; Silverwood 9.2–2–35–1; Hartley 9–0–32–1; White 8–0–36–0; Stemp 12–0–54–4.

Umpires: A. A. Jones and A. G. T. Whitehead.

MIDDLESEX v GLOUCESTERSHIRE

At Uxbridge, July 9. Middlesex won by four wickets. Toss: Gloucestershire.

This was a match of two centuries, from Lynch and Kallis. Both scored exactly 100 and both were out next ball. But Kallis had the edge, as he also took four wickets (including that of

Lynch) and helped to restrict Gloucestershire to only 26 runs off their last five overs. It was Middlesex who reached the quarter-finals. Lynch batted as usual: with minimal footwork, but the straightest of bats and tremendous power. Kallis, in contrast, was mostly classical, except when he hit two remarkable sixes with reverse sweeps which cleared the cover-point boundary. His partnership with Pooley added 96 in 20 overs and took Middlesex within sight of victory, clinched by Pooley in the final over.

Man of the Match: J. H. Kallis.

Gloucestershire

A. J. Wright c Weekes b Hewitt	1	M. C. J. Ball not out	9
N. J. Trainor c Brown b Kallis	29	A. M. Smith b Kallis	4
R. J. Cunliffe c Ramprakash b Dutch	33	R. P. Davis not out	1
M. A. Lynch c Dutch b Kallis	100	L-b 19, w 12, n-b 2	33
S. Young c Brown b Kallis	0		
*M. W. Alleyne c Hewitt b Weekes	43	1/2 2/65 3/75	(9 wkts, 60 overs) 277
†R. C. Russell c Shah b Johnson	20	4/76 5/192 6/251	
T. H. C. Hancock lbw b Johnson	4	7/262 8/263 9/272	

Bowling: Fraser 11–2–50–0; Hewitt 9–1–37–1; Kallis 11–1–47–4; Dutch 10–1–24–1; Weekes 10–1–54–1; Ramprakash 5–0–17–0; Johnson 4–0–29–2.

Middlesex

P. N. Weekes c Wright b Smith	4	O. A. Shah c Ball b Smith	8
J. H. Kallis c Russell b Alleyne	100	K. P. Dutch not out	6
*M. R. Ramprakash b Ball	42	L-b 9, w 4, n-b 4	17
M. W. Gatting b Alleyne	6		
J. C. Pooley not out	79	1/10 2/87 3/104	(6 wkts, 59.3 overs) 280
†K. R. Brown c Russell b Alleyne	18	4/200 5/232 6/248	

R. L. Johnson, J. P. Hewitt and A. R. C. Fraser did not bat.

Bowling: Smith 12–0–62–2; Young 8.3–1–43–0; Davis 12–0–44–0; Alleyne 12–0–47–3; Ball 12–0–51–1; Trainor 3–0–24–0.

Umpires: K. E. Palmer and R. Palmer.

SURREY v NOTTINGHAMSHIRE

At The Oval, July 9. Nottinghamshire won by 22 runs. Toss: Surrey.

Defiant batting and miserly bowling earned Astle his second award in as many NatWest matches, and gave Nottinghamshire a win few expected: Surrey were fielding ten international players, Nottinghamshire two. They were ten for three with the match barely started, and then Astle was dropped by Butcher at slip on nought. He hung around to score 56, though this hardly seemed enough as Butcher and Stewart, both just recovering from the misery of losing the Old Trafford Test, took Surrey to 72 for one. But the ball was swinging, despite the sunshine, and the pitch Surrey chose – in a late change of mind – turned out to be two-paced when they had been expecting help for the spinners. Thereafter, Nottinghamshire's unregarded attack proved unhittable, with Astle, the sixth bowler used, conceding just 12 in ten overs. In response, the batting self-destructed.

Man of the Match: N. J. Astle.

Nottinghamshire

P. R. Pollard c Stewart b Bicknell	2	P. J. Franks run out	4
R. T. Robinson lbw b Bicknell	1	R. T. Bates c Butcher b Saqlain Mushtaq	11
*P. Johnson c Thorpe b Lewis	4	M. N. Bowen not out	8
N. J. Astle c Thorpe b Salisbury	56	B 5, l-b 10, w 13, n-b 2	30
G. F. Archer c Butcher b B. C. Hollioake	12		
C. M. Tolley c Stewart b Salisbury	18	1/5 2/10 3/10	(55.1 overs) 176
†W. M. Noon c Thorpe b Saqlain Mushtaq	19	4/41 5/109 6/120	
K. P. Evans lbw b Saqlain Mushtaq	11	7/150 8/151 9/159	

Bowling: Bicknell 12–3–28–2; Lewis 9–1–12–1; A. J. Hollioake 5–0–20–0; B. C. Hollioake 9–1–39–1; Salisbury 12–1–32–2; Saqlain Mushtaq 8.1–0–30–3.

Surrey

M. A. Butcher lbw b Tolley 35	M. P. Bicknell b Evans 24
J. D. Ratcliffe lbw b Bowen............ 3	I. D. K. Salisbury c Noon b Bowen 5
†A. J. Stewart c Johnson b Franks 26	Saqlain Mushtaq not out.............. 6
G. P. Thorpe c Bates b Tolley......... 0	B 2, w 10, n-b 2 14
A. D. Brown c Noon b Tolley.......... 19	
*A. J. Hollioake c Bates b Evans 7	1/12 2/72 3/73 (55.5 overs) 154
C. C. Lewis c Pollard b Bowen........ 15	4/80 5/100 6/113
B. C. Hollioake lbw b Astle 0	7/114 8/124 9/132

Bowling: Bowen 10–0–38–3; Franks 6–1–21–1; Bates 9–0–38–0; Evans 11.5–4–22–2; Tolley 9–0–21–3; Astle 10–5–12–1.

Umpires: B. Dudleston and T. E. Jesty.

SUSSEX v LANCASHIRE

At Hove, July 9. Sussex won by seven wickets. Toss: Lancashire.

Though these teams are ancient rivals, this result was probably the shock of the domestic season. Before the match it was possible to get odds of 150-1 against Sussex winning the trophy, yet they knocked out the holders with extraordinary ease. The architect of victory was Greenfield, who scored 129, by far his most dramatic performance in 11 years of county cricket. This was more than the whole team had scored in three of their last four Championship innings. With Drakes swinging the new ball, Sussex had quickly reduced Lancashire's powerful batting to 38 for four. But Crawley eased the team out of trouble, and the second half of the innings consisted of a stand of 178, a tournament sixth-wicket record, between Crawley and Austin, which ended when Austin tried to reach his hundred with a six off the last ball. Sussex might have been overawed. However, the batsmen were helped when Chapple went off with a stomach strain, and Greenfield quickly began to strike the ball imperiously on both sides of the wicket. His chief ally was Mark Newell, who in the end was joined by Lenham to speed Sussex to a stunning win.

Man of the Match: K. Greenfield.

Lancashire

M. A. Atherton c Greenfield b Drakes ... 2	I. D. Austin c K. Newell b Kirtley 97
J. E. R. Gallian c Greenfield b Kirtley ... 1	
J. P. Crawley not out 113	L-b 6, w 14, n-b 8 28
G. D. Lloyd b Robinson............... 4	
A. Flintoff c Athey b Drakes 2	1/3 2/22 3/33 (6 wkts, 60 overs) 283
*M. Watkinson c Khan b K. Newell..... 36	4/38 5/105 6/283

†W. K. Hegg, G. Yates, P. J. Martin and G. Chapple did not bat.

Bowling: Drakes 12–4–35–2; Kirtley 12–1–61–2; Robinson 12–1–54–1; Khan 12–1–66–0; K. Newell 12–0–61–1.

Sussex

K. Greenfield b Watkinson............129	N. J. Lenham not out 28
C. W. J. Athey b Austin.............. 27	L-b 5, w 10, n-b 4 19
N. R. Taylor lbw b Austin 8	
M. Newell not out................... 75	1/85 2/105 3/233 (3 wkts, 56.3 overs) 286

K. Newell, *†P. Moores, V. C. Drakes, A. A. Khan, M. A. Robinson and R. J. Kirtley did not bat.

Bowling: Chapple 4.1–0–18–0; Martin 11.3–2–46–0; Flintoff 5.5–0–21–0; Austin 11–0–45–2; Yates 10–0–73–0; Watkinson 7–0–41–1; Gallian 7–0–37–0.

Umpires: J. H. Harris and J. F. Steele.

WARWICKSHIRE v SOMERSET

At Birmingham, July 9. Warwickshire won by 11 runs. Toss: Warwickshire.

Dermot Reeve, at the centre of so many improbable Warwickshire one-day wins, returned to his old home in the role of Somerset coach but could do nothing as a spell of intelligent bowling from Small pulled back a game that was heading Somerset's way. Warwickshire had been bowled out for only 220, and Donald and Small struggled to control the new ball. Somerset eased to 135 for two before Small took three in 21 balls. Ecclestone survived and, with Rose, gave Somerset a slight edge again. The tension was ended by Donald, whose extra pace polished off the innings.

Man of the Match: S. C. Ecclestone.

Warwickshire

A. J. Moles lbw b Rose	21	†K. J. Piper lbw b Caddick	13
*N. M. K. Smith b Rose	4	G. C. Small c Mushtaq Ahmed b Kerr	4
D. L. Hemp c Turner b Kerr	29	A. A. Donald not out	0
D. P. Ostler b Parsons	54	L-b 12, w 17, n-b 2	31
T. L. Penney b Mushtaq Ahmed	25		
D. R. Brown c Turner b Parsons	6	1/27 2/38 3/96	(58.1 overs) 220
G. Welch c Holloway b Mushtaq Ahmed	20	4/146 5/156 6/156	
A. F. Giles c Turner b Parsons	13	7/187 8/206 9/219	

Bowling: Caddick 10.1–2–27–1; Rose 12–1–45–2; Burns 6–0–27–0; Kerr 7–0–41–2; Mushtaq Ahmed 12–1–34–2; Parsons 11–1–34–3.

Somerset

M. Burns c Ostler b Welch	3	J. I. D. Kerr b Donald	0
P. C. L. Holloway c Piper b Small	38	Mushtaq Ahmed not out	10
*P. D. Bowler lbw b Donald	14	A. R. Caddick b Giles	5
S. C. Ecclestone c Smith b Donald	87	B 6, l-b 5, w 12, n-b 8	31
M. N. Lathwell b Small	1		
†R. J. Turner c Donald b Brown	1	1/12 2/47 3/135	(58.3 overs) 209
K. A. Parsons c Piper b Small	1	4/137 5/146 6/153	
G. D. Rose c Piper b Donald	18	7/184 8/184 9/193	

Bowling: Donald 12–1–54–4; Welch 12–1–27–1; Small 12–1–22–3; Brown 11–0–49–1; Giles 9.3–0–35–1; Smith 2–0–11–0.

Umpires: N. T. Plews and D. R. Shepherd.

QUARTER-FINALS

DERBYSHIRE v SUSSEX

At Derby, July 29. Sussex won by five wickets. Toss: Derbyshire.

For the second round running, struggling Sussex conjured up an extraordinary victory. This time they made the highest score by a chasing team in the competition, surpassing the total with which Warwickshire beat them in the famous 1993 final. Once again they had an unsung hero: this time it was 22-year-old Rajesh Rao, a last-minute selection when Lenham pulled out injured. He had to face the fourth ball of the innings after the star of the previous round, Greenfield, was out for a duck. Rao had never made a hundred for Sussex but started with utter assurance, striking a series of leg-side boundaries against Malcolm, and went on to dominate the innings with 158 off 165 balls, including 18 fours. He was out 50 short of the target, but Sussex were touched by magic and Moores hit the winning boundary with four balls to spare. For Derbyshire, this was a bitter defeat. Adams had given them every reason to feel confident with his fifth one-day century of the season, a mature and controlled 129 not out. For the second round running, they made their highest total in this competition against a first-class county. But even that was not enough to ensure victory.

Man of the Match: R. K. Rao.

Derbyshire

A. S. Rollins lbw b Drakes	40
D. G. Cork b Drakes	16
C. J. Adams not out	129
†K. M. Krikken st Moores b Khan	38
K. J. Barnett c and b Robinson	18
G. A. Khan b Robinson	0
V. P. Clarke c Taylor b Robinson	11
*P. A. J. DeFreitas c Rao b Drakes	26

P. Aldred c Moores b Drakes	4
A. J. Harris not out	5
L-b 21, w 9, n-b 10	40
	—
1/38 2/74 3/138	(8 wkts, 60 overs) 327
4/201 5/203 6/249	
7/298 8/316	

D. E. Malcolm did not bat.

Bowling: Drakes 12–0–62–4; Jarvis 9–0–53–0; Khan 12–1–48–1; Robinson 11–0–59–3; K. Newell 4–0–17–0; Greenfield 12–0–67–0.

Sussex

K. Greenfield b Malcolm	0
C. W. J. Athey b Clarke	30
R. K. Rao c Khan b Harris	158
M. Newell run out	32
N. R. Taylor c Barnett b Cork	48
K. Newell not out	29

*†P. Moores not out	19
L-b 5, w 2, n-b 6	13
	—
1/0 2/101 3/168	(5 wkts, 59.2 overs) 329
4/278 5/289	

V. C. Drakes, P. W. Jarvis, A. A. Khan and M. A. Robinson did not bat.

Bowling: Malcolm 6–0–33–1; DeFreitas 8–1–43–0; Aldred 6–0–35–0; Cork 11.2–0–67–1; Clarke 11–0–42–1; Barnett 7–0–37–0; Harris 10–0–67–1.

Umpires: H. D. Bird and G. Sharp.

GLAMORGAN v YORKSHIRE

At Cardiff, July 29. Glamorgan won by one wicket. Toss: Yorkshire.

Waqar Younis won this tie for Glamorgan in the unexpected role of batsman. With 47 wanted and two wickets left, Glamorgan looked beaten. And 28 were still needed when Waqar was joined at the crease by the teenage No. 11, Cosker. Waqar farmed the bowling and took Glamorgan to within ten of victory with two overs left. Gough, who had bowled magnificently until then, conceded nine, and Silverwood bowled a wide at the start of the final over to send a large Welsh crowd delirious. The Glamorgan captain Maynard was not able to play a full part in the celebrations: he was suffering from chicken-pox and, though he played, was isolated in a separate dressing-room. Yorkshire started well, suffered a mini-collapse to Cosker, and then were carried through to a reasonable score by the Australian Lehmann, who scored 105 off 103 balls. The suffering Maynard, together with Croft, put Glamorgan in control, but Gough removed them both, and tilted the game Yorkshire's way before Waqar – whose bowling had been treated with unusual disdain – came good in the taut climax.

Man of the Match: Waqar Younis.

Yorkshire

M. D. Moxon c Shaw b Cosker	34
M. P. Vaughan b Cosker	22
P. J. Hartley c Morris b Cosker	3
*D. Byas lbw b Croft	5
D. S. Lehmann c James b Waqar Younis	105
C. White c Shaw b Watkin	21
A. McGrath lbw b Croft	11

†R. J. Blakey not out	20
D. Gough b Thomas	4
L-b 6, w 5	11
	—
1/57 2/61 3/66	(8 wkts, 60 overs) 236
4/72 5/127 6/176	
7/229 8/236	

C. E. W. Silverwood and R. D. Stemp did not bat.

Bowling: Waqar Younis 12–1–58–1; Watkin 12–2–38–1; Thomas 8–0–44–1; Croft 12–0–45–2; Cosker 12–3–26–3; Cottey 1–0–6–0; Dale 3–0–13–0.

Glamorgan

R. D. B. Croft b Gough	55	Waqar Younis not out	34
H. Morris lbw b Hartley	7	S. L. Watkin b Gough	1
A. Dale c Byas b Hartley	6	D. A. Cosker not out	3
*M. P. Maynard c White b Gough	62	B 1, l-b 15, w 11, n-b 14	41
P. A. Cottey run out	5		—
S. P. James lbw b Gough	0	1/28 2/38 3/140 (9 wkts, 59 overs) 237	
†A. D. Shaw lbw b White	10	4/155 5/155 6/174	
S. D. Thomas lbw b Vaughan	13	7/177 8/190 9/209	

Bowling: Gough 12–3–36–4; Silverwood 5–0–36–0; Hartley 12–0–49–2; Stemp 12–4–35–0; Vaughan 5–0–17–1; White 12–0–43–1; Lehmann 1–0–5–0.

Umpires: B. Dudleston and T. E. Jesty.

MIDDLESEX v WARWICKSHIRE

At Lord's, July 29. Warwickshire won by 28 runs. Toss: Middlesex.

Ill-disciplined bowling by Middlesex can be blamed for their defeat: they gave away 31 in no-balls and wides, while Warwickshire bowled no no-balls at all. Despite losing Smith in the first over of the match, the visitors' innings quickly gained momentum. It was anchored by an outstanding century from Hemp, and Ostler, caught off a no-ball on 14, helped him add 130. A target of 287 was far from unreasonable, but the poor form of Weekes and Gatting put too much pressure on Ramprakash. He made a fine 98, but had little support from the other end until Brown arrived. They put on 101 in 15 overs, Brown disregarding a broken finger to score 50 off 55 balls. Once he was out, Giles took three wickets in an over to kill off the chase.

Man of the Match: D. L. Hemp.

Warwickshire

A. J. Moles lbw b Kallis	18	G. Welch not out	11
*N. M. K. Smith c Brown b Fraser	0		
D. L. Hemp c Kallis b Johnson	112	L-b 16, w 20, n-b 11	47
D. P. Ostler run out	51		—
T. L. Penney c Gatting b Weekes	45	1/1 2/49 3/179 (6 wkts, 60 overs) 286	
D. R. Brown run out	2	4/261 5/274 6/286	

A. F. Giles, †K. J. Piper, A. A. Donald and G. C. Small did not bat.

Bowling: Fraser 12–2–31–1; Hewitt 8–0–39–0; Kallis 12–0–60–1; Johnson 10–0–51–1; Dutch 12–0–54–0; Weekes 6–0–35–1.

Middlesex

P. N. Weekes c Ostler b Brown	8	R. L. Johnson c Penney b Giles	0
J. H. Kallis lbw b Brown	12	J. P. Hewitt not out	4
*M. R. Ramprakash c Penney b Giles	98	A. R. C. Fraser not out	9
M. W. Gatting b Donald	4	L-b 13, w 12	25
J. C. Pooley b Small	34		—
O. A. Shah run out	11	1/20 2/26 3/55 (9 wkts, 60 overs) 258	
†K. R. Brown c Piper b Donald	50	4/117 5/140 6/241	
K. P. Dutch b Giles	3	7/245 8/245 9/246	

Bowling: Brown 12–2–34–2; Welch 12–1–67–0; Small 12–0–35–1; Donald 12–0–60–2; Giles 12–0–49–3.

Umpires: G. I. Burgess and D. R. Shepherd.

NOTTINGHAMSHIRE v ESSEX

At Nottingham, July 29. Essex won by three wickets. Toss: Essex.

Hussain dropped three early catches but still ended up as Man of the Match. He put down Johnson twice and Robinson once. The pair survived to take Nottinghamshire to 126 for one in the 27th over. But, though Johnson went on to a century, in 123 balls, Hussain began his rehabilitation by running out Astle with a direct hit, and the innings faltered. Stuart Law threatened to make light work of the target, hammering 11 fours in 49 from 33 balls. Nottinghamshire chipped away at the middle order, however, and the game was in the balance when Johnson disclaimed a tumbling catch at mid-on which would have left Essex 274 for eight. The reprieved batsman, Cowan, applauded this sportsmanship, and remained to help Hussain complete victory with ten balls to spare.

Man of the Match: N. Hussain.

Nottinghamshire

M. P. Dowman b Irani	14	†W. M. Noon not out	13
R. T. Robinson b Grayson	52		
*P. Johnson b S. G. Law	106	L-b 7, w 14, n-b 10	31
N. J. Astle run out	27		—
G. F. Archer c Grayson b S. G. Law	33	1/35 2/126 3/198 (5 wkts, 60 overs) 288	
C. M. Tolley not out	12	4/248 5/267	

K. P. Evans, P. J. Franks, J. E. Hindson and A. R. Oram did not bat.

Bowling: Cowan 10–3–44–0; Irani 12–1–57–1; D. R. Law 3–0–18–0; S. G. Law 8–0–54–2; Grayson 12–1–40–1; Such 12–1–40–0; Cousins 3–0–28–0.

Essex

*P. J. Prichard b Oram	40	†R. J. Rollins b Franks	16
S. G. Law c Johnson b Franks	49	A. P. Cowan not out	17
N. Hussain not out	89	L-b 5, w 9, n-b 6	20
R. C. Irani lbw b Evans	10		—
A. P. Grayson c Franks b Evans	19	1/81 2/115 3/143 (7 wkts, 58.2 overs) 289	
D. R. Law c Johnson b Tolley	17	4/171 5/211	
D. D. J. Robinson c Robinson b Franks	12	6/237 7/255	

D. M. Cousins and P. M. Such did not bat.

Bowling: Evans 11.2–1–53–2; Oram 11–2–51–1; Franks 12–0–80–3; Tolley 12–1–34–1; Hindson 5–0–37–0; Astle 7–0–29–0.

Umpires: J. D. Bond and V. A. Holder.

SEMI-FINALS

ESSEX v GLAMORGAN

At Chelmsford, August 12, 13. Essex won by one wicket. Toss: Essex.

A pulsating cricket match achieved notoriety when a live, prime-time BBC audience watched Ilott and Croft start shoving each other during an angry exchange as Ilott appealed against the light. The two players are good friends from tours together with England A, and their wives were watching alongside each other at the time. Next day the men embraced in the morning calm after Essex had come back to eke out victory. Both suffered the consequences: £1,000 fines from their clubs. The umpires agreed it was too dark to continue at 8.10 p.m., when Essex needed six from seven overs, but had only two wickets left, with Waqar Younis bowling. In the morning Essex lost a ninth wicket to Thomas – his fifth victim – but last man Such drove Thomas to the boundary to win. A day earlier, James had scored a rock-solid 109 to set up a target of 302.

Stuart Law and Robinson responded by opening with 150 in 24 overs. But bad feeling surfaced when Thomas struck Law's hand with a beamer. After sharp words, Law resumed a brilliant innings of 90 from 73 balls. Then Irani, on pain-killers for a rib injury, saw Essex past 250 with only three wickets down. He also clashed with Thomas, when the bowler accidentally struck him in the face while celebrating his dismissal. It was one of a flurry of wickets which left the result in doubt until the last shot.

Man of the Match: S. G. Law.

Close of play: Essex 296-8 (53.1 overs) (T. P. Hodgson 0*, M. C. Ilott 0*).

Glamorgan

S. P. James c Robinson b Grayson	109	†A. D. Shaw run out	1
H. Morris c S. G. Law b Cowan	6	S. D. Thomas c S. G. Law b Cowan	1
A. Dale c Cowan b Grayson	45	L-b 9, w 10, n-b 6	25
*M. P. Maynard run out	26		
P. A. Cottey c Grayson b Ilott	56	1/13 2/115 3/165 (8 wkts, 60 overs)	301
R. D. B. Croft not out	14	4/251 5/276 6/291	
G. P. Butcher not out	18	7/294 8/301	

Waqar Younis and S. L. Watkin did not bat.

Bowling: Ilott 12–2–50–1; Cowan 12–0–62–2; Irani 9.2–0–36–0; S. G. Law 5.4–0–37–0; Such 12–0–56–0; Grayson 9–0–51–2.

Essex

D. D. J. Robinson c Cottey b Watkin	62	T. P. Hodgson c Shaw b Thomas	2
S. G. Law c Waqar Younis b Butcher	90	M. C. Ilott not out	1
*N. Hussain c Maynard b Watkin	28	P. M. Such not out	4
R. C. Irani lbw b Thomas	51	B 4, l-b 6, w 6, n-b 6	22
A. P. Grayson c Shaw b Thomas	22		
D. R. Law b Thomas	17	1/150 2/194 3/195 (9 wkts, 55 overs)	303
†R. J. Rollins c James b Thomas	2	4/256 5/280 6/286	
A. P. Cowan run out	2	7/295 8/295 9/299	

Bowling: Watkin 12–1–64–2; Waqar Younis 9–1–48–0; Thomas 12–0–74–5; Croft 12–0–47–0; Butcher 7–0–39–1; Dale 3–0–21–0.

Umpires: J. C. Balderstone and D. J. Constant.

WARWICKSHIRE v SUSSEX

At Birmingham, August 13, 14. Warwickshire won by 105 runs. Toss: Sussex.

Sussex's improbable sequence of NatWest wins finally came to a halt as Warwickshire reached the final for the fourth time in five years. It was their 100th game in the competition and their tenth final in all, both records. Sussex had been record-breakers a fortnight earlier, when they scored 329 to win; here they needed 343, and it was too much. For the first time, the NatWest semi-finals were scheduled for consecutive days to allow the BBC to cover both. Erratic bowling, particularly from Jarvis, helped Moles and Smith, who scored a run-a-ball 72, open with 130 in 29 overs. Then came a blazing century from Hemp, his second in successive NatWest matches: his first fifty took 54 balls, his second 34, and he finished unbeaten on 111 from 93, with five sixes and seven fours. He and Ostler added 142 in 22 overs, and the final ten overs yielded 105 – the eventual winning margin. Sussex lost Greenfield and Rao, their match-winners of the last two rounds, in the play rain permitted that evening. Next day, Donald was irresistible. He soon bowled Athey, who later announced his retirement, ended Mark Newell's fighting 79, and wound up with five wickets. He had just enough time to fly home to receive South Africa's highest sporting honour, the Gold Medal of Merit, from President Mandela.

Man of the Match: D. L. Hemp.

Close of play: Sussex 43-2 (11 overs) (C. W. J. Athey 18*, M. Newell 16*).

Warwickshire

A. J. Moles lbw b Drakes	56	T. L. Penney not out	25
*N. M. K. Smith c Rao b K. Newell	72	L-b 9, w 11	20
D. L. Hemp not out	111		
D. P. Ostler b Drakes	58	1/130 2/150 3/292 (3 wkts, 60 overs) 342

D. R. Brown, G. Welch, A. F. Giles, †K. J. Piper, G. C. Small and A. A. Donald did not bat.

Bowling: Drakes 12–5–38–2; Jarvis 10–0–76–0; Robinson 12–1–34–0; K. Newell 10–0–62–1; Khan 8–0–69–0; Greenfield 8–0–54–0.

Sussex

K. Greenfield run out	5	P. W. Jarvis lbw b Donald	16
C. W. J. Athey b Donald	20	A. A. Khan c Smith b Donald	4
R. K. Rao c Ostler b Welch	0	M. A. Robinson not out	3
M. Newell b Donald	79	B 2, l-b 3, w 10	15
N. R. Taylor run out	12		
K. Newell b Giles	23	1/6 2/12 3/53 (53.1 overs) 237
V. C. Drakes c Hemp b Smith	15	4/73 5/122 6/147
*†P. Moores b Donald	45	7/193 8/221 9/233

Bowling: Welch 10–1–45–1; Brown 8–0–29–0; Giles 12–0–70–1; Donald 10.1–1–37–5; Small 6–0–21–0; Smith 7–0–30–1.

Umpires: J. H. Hampshire and K. E. Palmer.

FINAL

ESSEX v WARWICKSHIRE

At Lord's, September 7. Essex won by nine wickets. Toss: Essex.

Essex made up for their wretched performance in the 1996 final by beating Warwickshire in even shorter order than Lancashire had beaten them. This game lasted just 86.3 overs, five balls fewer than the previous year. Then, the entire team managed only 57. This time they passed that score in just six overs. But, with the team batting first beaten for the 11th time in 12 years, neutrals in the crowd again went home dissatisfied with the consequences of starting a final at 10.30 on a September morning.

The match was played a day later than scheduled, owing to the funeral of Diana, Princess of Wales – killed in a car crash a week earlier – in Westminster Abbey on the Saturday, and a minute's silence was observed before play.

As usual, the toss was perceived to be crucial. Prichard won it for the second year running and chose to disregard the aberration of 1996. The ball duly moved around extravagantly in the morning and the match followed a familiar pattern. Warwickshire's captain, Smith, said afterwards that his side did well to survive the full quota of overs and score 170. The Essex bowlers caused problems from the first over, when Cowan seamed his third ball a long way into the left-handed Knight for a formality of an lbw. Hemp, who had made hundreds in the quarter-final and semi-final, was run out by Grayson's under-arm shy after hesitation with Ostler.' As Warwickshire's innings spluttered along, the highest score proved to be 37 from Brown. Essex's seam bowling was accurate and intelligent, especially that of Cowan and Irani, who had recovered sooner than expected from a torn intercostal muscle. He had been to Munich earlier in the week for vitamin injections by a German specialist. Warwickshire were slipping beyond salvation, by injection or any other means.

Conditions eased during the afternoon, and Prichard and Law tucked into Warwickshire's bowling. By any standards their batting was stunning. They passed 100 in 13 overs when Prichard swung Giles over mid-wicket for six. Even Donald, the South African fast bowler, looked powerless. At tea, Essex's score stood at 152 off 25 overs for the loss of Prichard, who had made 57 in 45 balls, and Essex's first NatWest Trophy since 1985 was already assured.

As though to dispel any possible doubt, Law hooked Brown's second ball after the interval for six, in an over costing 15. Law finished with 80 not out off 71 balls. There had been one earlier nine-wicket victory in the final, also over Warwickshire, by Surrey in 1982, but this win, with almost 34 overs to spare, stood out on its own. It was Essex's first ever trophy achieved without the assistance of Gooch, who did not play in any of the games. – CHARLES RANDALL.

Man of the Match: S. G. Law.   *Attendance:* 23,713; *receipts* £776,195.

Warwickshire

N. V. Knight lbw b Cowan	0	†K. J. Piper not out	15
*N. M. K. Smith c S. G. Law b Cowan	5	A. A. Donald not out	3
D. L. Hemp run out	21	B 5, l-b 15, w 5, n-b 2	27
D. P. Ostler c D. R. Law b Irani	34		
T. L. Penney c Rollins b Cowan	5	1/1 (1) 2/12 (2)	(8 wkts, 60 overs) 170
D. R. Brown c D. R. Law b Ilott	37	3/45 (3) 4/75 (5)	
G. Welch c and b Such	2	5/90 (4) 6/96 (7)	
A. F. Giles run out	21	7/147 (8) 8/156 (6)	

G. C. Small did not bat.

Bowling: Cowan 12–3–29–3; Ilott 12–3–29–1; Irani 12–4–22–1; S. G. Law 12–4–38–0; Such 12–1–32–1.

Essex

*P. J. Prichard lbw b Donald	57
S. G. Law not out	80
N. Hussain not out	25
B 1, l-b 4, w 4	9

1/109 (1)   (1 wkt, 26.3 overs) 171

R. C. Irani, D. D. J. Robinson, A. P. Grayson, D. R. Law, †R. J. Rollins, A. P. Cowan, M. C. Ilott and P. M. Such did not bat.

Bowling: Welch 5–0–34–0; Brown 4–0–29–0; Small 7–0–43–0; Donald 6–0–36–1; Giles 4–1–20–0; Penney 0.3–0–4–0.

Umpires: M. J. Kitchen and P. Willey.

NATWEST TROPHY RECORDS

(Including Gillette Cup, 1963-80)

Batting

Highest individual scores: 206, A. I. Kallicharran, Warwickshire v Oxfordshire, Birmingham, 1984; 201, V. J. Wells, Leicestershire v Berkshire, Leicester, 1996; 180*, T. M. Moody, Worcestershire v Surrey, The Oval, 1994; 177, C. G. Greenidge, Hampshire v Glamorgan, Southampton, 1975; 177, A. J. Wright, Gloucestershire v Scotland, Bristol, 1997; 172*, G. A. Hick, Worcestershire v Devon, Worcester, 1987; 165*, V. P. Terry, Hampshire v Berkshire, Southampton, 1985; 162*, C. J. Tavaré, Somerset v Devon, Torquay, 1990; 162*, I. V. A. Richards, Glamorgan v Oxfordshire, Swansea, 1993; 159, C. L. Smith, Hampshire v Cheshire, Chester, 1989; 158, Zaheer Abbas, Gloucestershire v Leicestershire, Leicester, 1983; 158, G. D. Barlow, Middlesex v Lancashire, Lord's, 1984; 158, R. A. Smith, Hampshire v Worcestershire, Worcester, 1996; 158, R. K. Rao, Sussex v Derbyshire, Derby, 1997; 156, D. I. Gower, Leicestershire v Derbyshire, Leicester, 1984; 155, J. J. Whitaker, Leicestershire v Wiltshire, Swindon, 1984; 154*, H. Morris, Glamorgan v Staffordshire, Cardiff, 1989; 154, P. Willey, Leicestershire v Hampshire, Leicester, 1987; 153, A. Hill, Derbyshire v Cornwall, Derby, 1986; 153, J. S. Laney, Hampshire v Norfolk, Southampton, 1996; 151*, M. P. Maynard, Glamorgan v Durham, Darlington, 1991; 151, N. V. Knight, Warwickshire v Somerset, Birmingham, 1995. *In the final:* 146, G. Boycott, Yorkshire v Surrey, 1965. (93 hundreds were scored in the Gillette Cup; 216 hundreds have been scored in the NatWest Bank Trophy. The most hundreds in one season is 22 in 1997.)

Most runs: 2,547, G. A. Gooch; 2,113, M. W. Gatting; 1,998, A. J. Lamb; 1,954, R. A. Smith; 1,950, D. L. Amiss.

Fastest hundred: G. D. Rose off 36 balls, Somerset v Devon, Torquay, 1990.

Most hundreds: 7, C. L. Smith and R. A. Smith; 6, G. A. Gooch; 5, D. I. Gower, I. V. A. Richards and G. M. Turner.

Highest totals (off 60 overs): 413 for four, Somerset v Devon, Torquay, 1990; 406 for five, Leicestershire v Berkshire, Leicester, 1996; 404 for three, Worcestershire v Devon, Worcester, 1987; 392 for five, Warwickshire v Oxfordshire, Birmingham, 1984; 386 for five, Essex v Wiltshire, Chelmsford, 1988; 384 for six, Kent v Berkshire, Finchampstead, 1994; 384 for nine, Sussex v Ireland, Belfast, 1996; 372 for five, Lancashire v Gloucestershire, Manchester, 1990; 371 for four, Hampshire v Glamorgan, Southampton, 1975; 367 for five, Somerset v Herefordshire, Taunton, 1997; 365 for three, Derbyshire v Cornwall, Derby, 1986; 361 for eight, Essex v Cumberland, Chelmsford, 1992; 361 for eight, Warwickshire v Bedfordshire, Birmingham, 1994; 361 for seven, Essex v Durham, Chelmsford, 1996; 360 for two, Northamptonshire v Staffordshire, Northampton, 1990. *In the final:* 322 for five, Warwickshire v Sussex, Lord's, 1993.

Highest total by a minor county: 305 for nine, Durham v Glamorgan, Darlington, 1991.

Highest total by a side batting first and losing: 327 for eight (60 overs), Derbyshire v Sussex, Derby, 1997. *In the final:* 321 for six (60 overs), Sussex v Warwickshire, 1993.

Highest totals by a side batting second: 350 (59.5 overs), Surrey lost to Worcestershire, The Oval, 1994; 339 for nine (60 overs), Somerset lost to Warwickshire, Birmingham, 1995; 329 for five (59.2 overs), Sussex beat Derbyshire, Derby, 1997; 326 for nine (60 overs), Hampshire lost to Leicestershire, Leicester, 1987; 322 for five (60 overs), Warwickshire beat Sussex, Lord's, 1993 (*in the final*); 319 for nine (59.5 overs), Essex beat Lancashire, Chelmsford, 1992; 314 for eight (60 overs), Nottinghamshire lost to Northamptonshire, Nottingham, 1995; 307 for five (60 overs), Hampshire beat Essex, Chelmsford, 1990; 306 for six (59.3 overs), Gloucestershire beat Leicestershire, Leicester, 1983; 305 for nine (60 overs), Durham lost to Glamorgan, Darlington, 1991; 304 for eight (59.4 overs), Glamorgan beat Hampshire, Southampton, 1997; 303 for nine (55 overs), Essex beat Glamorgan, Chelmsford, 1997; 300 for six (60 overs), Berkshire lost to Leicestershire, Leicester, 1996.

Lowest completed totals: 39 (26.4 overs), Ireland v Sussex, Hove, 1985; 41 (20 overs), Cambridgeshire v Buckinghamshire, Cambridge, 1972; 41 (19.4 overs), Middlesex v Essex, Westcliff, 1972; 41 (36.1 overs), Shropshire v Essex, Wellington, 1974. *In the final:* 57 (27.2 overs), Essex v Lancashire, 1996.

Lowest total by a side batting first and winning: 98 (56.2 overs), Worcestershire v Durham, Chester-le-Street, 1968.

Shortest innings: 10.1 overs (60 for one), Worcestershire v Lancashire, Worcester, 1963.

Matches re-arranged on a reduced number of overs are excluded from the above.

Record partnerships for each wicket

311	for 1st	A. J. Wright and N. J. Trainor, Gloucestershire v Scotland at Bristol ...	1997
286	for 2nd	I. S. Anderson and A. Hill, Derbyshire v Cornwall at Derby	1986
309*	for 3rd	T. S. Curtis and T. M. Moody, Worcestershire v Surrey at The Oval ...	1994
234*	for 4th	D. Lloyd and C. H. Lloyd, Lancashire v Gloucestershire at Manchester .	1978
166	for 5th	M. A. Lynch and G. R. J. Roope, Surrey v Durham at The Oval	1982
178	for 6th	J. P. Crawley and I. D. Austin, Lancashire v Sussex at Hove	1997
160*	for 7th	C. J. Richards and I. R. Payne, Surrey v Lincolnshire at Sleaford	1983
112	for 8th	A. L. Penberthy and J. E. Emburey, Northamptonshire v Lancashire at Manchester	1996
87	for 9th	M. A. Nash and A. E. Cordle, Glamorgan v Lincolnshire at Swansea ...	1974
81	for 10th	S. Turner and R. E. East, Essex v Yorkshire at Leeds	1982

Bowling

Most wickets: 81, G. G. Arnold; 79, J. Simmons.

Best bowling (12 overs unless stated): eight for 21 (10.1 overs), M. A. Holding, Derbyshire v Sussex, Hove, 1988; eight for 31 (11.1 overs), D. L. Underwood, Kent v Scotland, Edinburgh, 1987; seven for 15, A. L. Dixon, Kent v Surrey, The Oval, 1967; seven for 15 (9.3 overs),

R. P. Lefebvre, Somerset v Devon, Torquay, 1990; seven for 19, N. V. Radford, Worcestershire v Bedfordshire, Bedford, 1991; seven for 27 (9.5 overs), D. Gough, Yorkshire v Ireland, Leeds, 1997; seven for 30, P. J. Sainsbury, Hampshire v Norfolk, Southampton, 1965; seven for 32, S. P. Davis, Durham v Lancashire, Chester-le-Street, 1983; seven for 33, R. D. Jackman, Surrey v Yorkshire, Harrogate, 1970; seven for 35 (10.1 overs), D. E. Malcolm, Derbyshire v Northamptonshire, Derby, 1997; seven for 37, N. A. Mallender, Northamptonshire v Worcestershire, Northampton, 1984. *In the final:* six for 18 (6.2 overs), G. Chapple, Lancashire v Essex, 1996.

Most economical analysis: 12–9–3–1, J. Simmons, Lancashire v Suffolk, Bury St Edmunds, 1985.

Most expensive analysis: 12–0–107–2, C. C. Lovell, Cornwall v Warwickshire, St Austell, 1996.

Hat-tricks (11): J. D. F. Larter, Northamptonshire v Sussex, Northampton, 1963; D. A. D. Sydenham, Surrey v Cheshire, Hoylake, 1964; R. N. S. Hobbs, Essex v Middlesex, Lord's, 1968; N. M. McVicker, Warwickshire v Lincolnshire, Birmingham, 1971; G. S. le Roux, Sussex v Ireland, Hove, 1985; M. Jean-Jacques, Derbyshire v Nottinghamshire, Derby, 1987; J. F. M. O'Brien, Cheshire v Derbyshire, Chester, 1988; R. A. Pick, Nottinghamshire v Scotland, Nottingham, 1995; J. E. Emburey, Northamptonshire v Cheshire, Northampton, 1996; A. R. Caddick, Somerset v Gloucestershire, Taunton, 1996; D. Gough, Yorkshire v Ireland, Leeds, 1997.

Four wickets in five balls: D. A. D. Sydenham, Surrey v Cheshire, Hoylake, 1964.

Wicket-keeping and Fielding

Most dismissals: 66 (58 ct, 8 st), R. W. Taylor; 65 (59 ct, 6 st), A. P. E. Knott.

Most dismissals in an innings: 7 (all ct), A. J. Stewart, Surrey v Glamorgan, Swansea, 1994.

Most catches by a fielder: 27, J. Simmons; 26, G. A. Gooch; 25, G. Cook and M. W. Gatting; 24, P. J. Sharpe.

Most catches by a fielder in an innings: 4 – A. S. Brown, Gloucestershire v Middlesex, Bristol, 1963; G. Cook, Northamptonshire v Glamorgan, Northampton, 1972; C. G. Greenidge, Hampshire v Cheshire, Southampton, 1981; D. C. Jackson, Durham v Northamptonshire, Darlington, 1984; T. S. Smith, Hertfordshire v Somerset, St Albans, 1984; H. Morris, Glamorgan v Scotland, Edinburgh, 1988; C. C. Lewis, Nottinghamshire v Worcestershire, Nottingham, 1992.

Results

Largest victories in runs: Somerset by 346 runs v Devon, Torquay, 1990; Sussex by 304 runs v Ireland, Belfast, 1996; Worcestershire by 299 runs v Devon, Worcester, 1987; Essex by 291 runs v Wiltshire, Chelmsford, 1988; Sussex by 244 runs v Ireland, Hove, 1985; Lancashire by 241 runs v Gloucestershire, Manchester, 1990; Hampshire by 239 runs v Cambridgeshire, Wisbech, 1997; Somerset by 231 runs v Herefordshire, Taunton, 1997; Nottinghamshire by 228 runs v Northumberland, Jesmond, 1994; Warwickshire by 227 runs v Oxfordshire, Birmingham, 1984; Essex by 226 runs v Oxfordshire, Chelmsford, 1985; Durham by 207 runs v Herefordshire, Chester-le-Street, 1995; Yorkshire by 205 runs v Nottinghamshire, Leeds, 1996.

Victories by ten wickets (15): By Glamorgan, Hampshire (twice), Middlesex, Northamptonshire, Nottinghamshire, Surrey, Sussex (twice), Warwickshire (twice), Yorkshire (four times).

Earliest finishes: both at 2.20 p.m. Worcestershire beat Lancashire by nine wickets at Worcester, 1963; Essex beat Middlesex by eight wickets at Westcliff, 1972.

Scores level (10): Nottinghamshire 215, Somerset 215 for nine at Taunton, 1964; Surrey 196, Sussex 196 for eight at The Oval, 1970; Somerset 287 for six, Essex 287 at Taunton, 1978; Surrey 195 for seven, Essex 195 at Chelmsford, 1980; Essex 149, Derbyshire 149 for eight at Derby, 1981; Northamptonshire 235 for nine, Derbyshire 235 for six at Lord's, 1981 (*in the final*); Middlesex 222 for nine, Somerset 222 for eight at Lord's, 1983; Hampshire 224 for eight, Essex 224 for seven at Southampton, 1985; Essex 307 for six, Hampshire 307 for five at Chelmsford, 1990; Hampshire 204 for nine, Leicestershire 204 for nine at Leicester, 1995.

Note: Under the rules the side which lost fewer wickets won; at Leicester in 1995, Leicestershire won by virtue of their higher total after 30 overs.

Match Awards

Most awards: 9, G. A. Gooch; 8, C. H. Lloyd, C. L. Smith and R. A. Smith.

WINNERS 1963-97

Gillette Cup

		Man of the Match
1963	SUSSEX* beat Worcestershire by 14 runs.	N. Gifford†
1964	SUSSEX beat Warwickshire* by eight wickets.	N. I. Thomson
1965	YORKSHIRE beat Surrey* by 175 runs.	G. Boycott
1966	WARWICKSHIRE* beat Worcestershire by five wickets.	R. W. Barber
1967	KENT* beat Somerset by 32 runs.	M. H. Denness
1968	WARWICKSHIRE beat Sussex* by four wickets.	A. C. Smith
1969	YORKSHIRE beat Derbyshire* by 69 runs.	B. Leadbeater
1970	LANCASHIRE* beat Sussex by six wickets.	H. Pilling
1971	LANCASHIRE* beat Kent by 24 runs.	Asif Iqbal†
1972	LANCASHIRE* beat Warwickshire by four wickets.	C. H. Lloyd
1973	GLOUCESTERSHIRE* beat Sussex by 40 runs.	A. S. Brown
1974	KENT* beat Lancashire by four wickets.	A. P. E. Knott
1975	LANCASHIRE* beat Middlesex by seven wickets.	C. H. Lloyd
1976	NORTHAMPTONSHIRE* beat Lancashire by four wickets.	P. Willey
1977	MIDDLESEX* beat Glamorgan by five wickets.	C. T. Radley
1978	SUSSEX* beat Somerset by five wickets.	P. W. G. Parker
1979	SOMERSET beat Northamptonshire* by 45 runs.	I. V. A. Richards
1980	MIDDLESEX* beat Surrey by seven wickets.	J. M. Brearley

NatWest Trophy

1981	DERBYSHIRE* beat Northamptonshire by losing fewer wickets with the scores level.	G. Cook†
1982	SURREY* beat Warwickshire by nine wickets.	D. J. Thomas
1983	SOMERSET beat Kent* by 24 runs.	V. J. Marks
1984	MIDDLESEX beat Kent* by four wickets.	C. T. Radley
1985	ESSEX* beat Nottinghamshire* by one run.	B. R. Hardie
1986	SUSSEX* beat Lancashire by seven wickets.	D. A. Reeve
1987	NOTTINGHAMSHIRE* beat Northamptonshire by three wickets.	R. J. Hadlee
1988	MIDDLESEX* beat Worcestershire by three wickets.	M. R. Ramprakash
1989	WARWICKSHIRE beat Middlesex* by four wickets.	D. A. Reeve
1990	LANCASHIRE* beat Northamptonshire by seven wickets.	P. A. J. DeFreitas
1991	HAMPSHIRE* beat Surrey by four wickets.	R. A. Smith
1992	NORTHAMPTONSHIRE* beat Leicestershire by eight wickets.	A. Fordham
1993	WARWICKSHIRE* beat Sussex by five wickets.	Asif Din
1994	WORCESTERSHIRE* beat Warwickshire by eight wickets.	T. M. Moody
1995	WARWICKSHIRE beat Northamptonshire* by four wickets.	D. A. Reeve
1996	LANCASHIRE beat Essex* by 129 runs.	G. Chapple
1997	ESSEX* beat Warwickshire by nine wickets.	S. G. Law

* *Won toss.* † *On losing side.*

TEAM RECORDS 1963-97

	Rounds reached				Matches		
	W	F	SF	QF	P	W	L
Derbyshire..........	1	2	3	12	70*	36	34
Durham	0	0	0	1	39	12	27
Essex	2	3	6	15	79	46	33
Glamorgan	0	1	4	14	74	39	35
Gloucestershire	1	1	5	14	72	38	34
Hampshire..........	1	1	8	20	88	54	34
Kent...............	2	5	7	14	80	47	33
Lancashire..........	6	9	14	19	98	69	29
Leicestershire	0	1	3	14	71	36	35
Middlesex	4	6	13	19	95	64	31
Northamptonshire	2	7	10	19	90	57	33
Nottinghamshire	1	2	3	12	73	39	34
Somerset	2	4	9	17	84	51	33
Surrey	1	4	10	20	88*	54	34
Sussex	4	8	13	19	92	61	31
Warwickshire	5	10	16	20	101	71	30
Worcestershire	1	4	10	14	80	46	34
Yorkshire	2	2	6	16	75	42	33

* Derbyshire and Surrey totals each include a bowling contest after their first-round matches were abandoned in 1991; Derbyshire lost to Hertfordshire and Surrey beat Oxfordshire.

MINOR COUNTY RECORDS

From 1964 to 1979 the previous season's top five Minor Counties were invited to take part in the competition. In 1980 these were joined by Ireland, and in 1983 the competition was expanded to embrace 13 Minor Counties, Ireland and Scotland. The number of Minor Counties dropped to 12 in 1992 when Durham attained first-class status, and 11 in 1995 when Holland were admitted to the competition.

Between 1964 and 1991 Durham qualified 21 times, including 15 years in succession from 1977-91. They reached the second round a record six times.

Including the 1998 tournament, Staffordshire have qualified most among the remaining Minor Counties, 20 times, followed by Devon 19, Cambridgeshire, Hertfordshire and Oxfordshire 18, Berkshire, Buckinghamshire, Cheshire and Norfolk 17, Suffolk 16, Shropshire 13, Bedfordshire, Cumberland, Dorset, Lincolnshire and Wiltshire 12, Northumberland 8, Cornwall 7, Herefordshire and Wales Minor Counties 3.

Only Hertfordshire have reached the quarter-finals, beating Berkshire and then Essex in 1976.

Wins by a minor county over a first-class county (8): Durham v Yorkshire (by five wickets), Harrogate, 1973; Lincolnshire v Glamorgan (by six wickets), Swansea, 1974; Hertfordshire v Essex (by 33 runs), 2nd round, Hitchin, 1976; Shropshire v Yorkshire (by 37 runs), Telford, 1984; Durham v Derbyshire (by seven wickets), Derby, 1985; Buckinghamshire v Somerset (by seven runs), High Wycombe, 1987; Cheshire v Northamptonshire (by one wicket), Chester, 1988; Hertfordshire v Derbyshire (2-1 in a bowling contest after the match was abandoned), Bishop's Stortford, 1991.

BENSON AND HEDGES CUP, 1997

Ben Hollioake

Surrey and Kent collided in the final of the 1997 Benson and Hedges Cup – another step on their return to their traditional positions of power after years of under-achievement. It should have been a resounding battle. Instead, the contest was more like most recent NatWest Trophy finals. The Kent batsmen were caught on a swing bowlers' morning, and looked beaten by lunchtime. The game was settled by a marvellous 98 from England's teenage prodigy Ben Hollioake, and his brother Adam lifted the trophy, the first Surrey captain to do so since John Edrich in 1974. But Kent could blame no one but themselves: they chose to bat, and batted badly.

Kent did maintain their record as the most consistent side in the tournament. It was their eighth final in the event's 26 years, following their 13th semi-final. There, they overcame Northamptonshire in a game notable for what happened afterwards: a punch-up involving about a hundred rival supporters outside, after the game. Alcohol was blamed, and Kent subsequently strengthened controls on spectators bringing drink into the ground. In their semi-final, Surrey beat Leicestershire without any trouble at all. They lost only one game of their eight: to Kent, right at the start.

The flops of the competition were Lancashire, winners twice running and unbeaten in 16 matches since May 1994. Before April was out, they had gone down twice and were unable to recover.

The most dramatic contest was a zonal game at Derby, where Warwickshire needed six to win with two balls to go, and the winners of the match would reach the quarter-finals. Gladstone Small smashed the six off Devon Malcolm. Rather more zonal games baffled spectators instead of enthralling them. This included an earlier game at Derby, where Yorkshire were declared the winners because they had scored more runs in the first 25 overs though, since it was a league game, there was no reason for it not to be a tie.

The non-Championship teams had one of their better years: Ireland, marshalled by the captain of South Africa, Hansie Cronje, beat Middlesex, and the Universities beat Sussex. Graham Gooch retired with a competition record of 22 Gold Awards, twice as many as anyone else, 15 centuries – his nearest rivals have scored seven – and 5,176 runs, when no one else has passed 3,000. The tournament is due to end in 1998, owing to an anticipated clampdown on tobacco advertising and the reorganisation of the county season, so it may be assumed that these records will stand forever.

Prize money

£42,000 for winners: SURREY.
£21,000 for runners-up: KENT.
£10,500 for losing semi-finalists: LEICESTERSHIRE and NORTHAMPTONSHIRE.
£5,250 for losing quarter-finalists: ESSEX, SOMERSET, WARWICKSHIRE and YORKSHIRE.

There was also £800 each for the winners of group matches. Gold Award winners received £900 in the final, £425 in the semi-finals, £375 in the quarter-finals, £250 in the group matches. The prize money was increased from £154,300 in the 1996 tournament to £160,750; the total sponsorship rose from £800,000 to £824,457.

FINAL GROUP TABLE

	Played	Won	Lost	No result	Points	Net run-rate
Group A						
YORKSHIRE.............	5	4	1	0	8	16.13
WARWICKSHIRE	5	3	2	0	6	15.21
Derbyshire	5	3	2	0	6	2.68
Lancashire	5	3	2	0	6	−1.50
Worcestershire	5	2	3	0	4	−3.90
Minor Counties	5	0	5	0	0	−28.56
Group B						
LEICESTERSHIRE.........	4	3	1	0	6	18.15
NORTHAMPTONSHIRE	4	3	1	0	6	9.20
Durham	4	2	2	0	4	14.74
Nottinghamshire...........	4	1	2	1	3	−13.07
Scotland	4	0	3	1	1	−51.27
Group C						
KENT....................	5	4	0	1	9	9.84
SURREY	5	4	1	0	8	21.19
Gloucestershire	5	2	2	1	5	7.06
Sussex	5	2	3	0	4	−0.51
Hampshire	5	1	4	0	2	−15.50
British Universities	5	1	4	0	2	−18.57
Group D						
ESSEX	4	3	0	1	7	8.54
SOMERSET...............	4	3	1	0	6	29.88
Glamorgan	4	2	2	0	4	−6.83
Ireland	4	1	2	1	3	−32.62
Middlesex................	4	0	4	0	0	−6.75

Net run-rate was calculated by subtracting runs conceded per 100 balls from runs scored per 100 balls, revising figures in shortened matches and discounting those not played to a result.

GROUP A

The Minor Counties' squad for the competition was: I. Cockbain (Cheshire) (*captain*), R. N. Dalton (Bedfordshire), S. J. Dean (Staffordshire), G. W. Ecclestone (Cambridgeshire), M. A. Fell (Lincolnshire), J. M. Fielding (Cumberland), N. R. Gaywood (Devon), W. Larkins (Bedfordshire), S. V. Laudat (Oxfordshire), A. J. Murphy (Cheshire), P. J. Nicholson (Northumberland), S. Oakes (Lincolnshire), N. V. Radford (Herefordshire), M. A. Sharp (Cumberland), J. P. J. Sylvester (Berkshire).

LANCASHIRE v YORKSHIRE

At Manchester, April 28, 29. Yorkshire won by 49 runs. Toss: Lancashire.

Attacking bowling from Silverwood, Gough and Hartley allowed Yorkshire to defend a slight total of 203 and avenge their two cup defeats at Old Trafford in 1996. It was the first time Lancashire had lost in this competition since May 1994, following 15 wins and one no-result. Fairbrother was the only man to reach fifty in the match, but he hit just two fours in his 98-ball innings of 64 and received little support. Chapple did not bat after breaking a knuckle while fielding.

Gold Award: C. E. W. Silverwood.

Close of play: Yorkshire 43-0 (10.5 overs) (D. Byas 15*, M. D. Moxon 20*).

Yorkshire

*D. Byas c Atherton b Martin	32	D. Gough c Austin b Green	0
M. D. Moxon b Martin	28	C. E. W. Silverwood c and b Martin	0
M. P. Vaughan c Atherton b Austin	45	R. D. Stemp run out	2
P. J. Hartley lbw b Yates	6	B 2, l-b 7, w 11	20
A. McGrath c Austin b Yates	13		
B. Parker c Lloyd b Austin	15	1/69 2/77 3/90	(48 overs) 203
C. White c Crawley b Green	26	4/114 5/143 6/165	
†R. J. Blakey not out	16	7/198 8/199 9/201	

Bowling: Martin 9-2-31-3; Austin 9-0-27-2; Chapple 5-1-23-0; Yates 10-0-36-2; Green 10-0-45-2; Gallian 5-0-32-0.

Lancashire

J. E. R. Gallian lbw b Hartley	7	R. J. Green b Gough	7
*M. A. Atherton c White b Silverwood	15	P. J. Martin b Hartley	0
J. P. Crawley c Gough b Hartley	0	G. Chapple absent hurt	
N. H. Fairbrother not out	64	L-b 6, w 8, n-b 6	20
G. D. Lloyd b Gough	6		
I. D. Austin c Blakey b Silverwood	30	1/20 2/24 3/44	(45.4 overs) 154
†W. K. Hegg c Blakey b Silverwood	1	4/57 5/124 6/133	
G. Yates b Stemp	4	7/140 8/153 9/154	

Bowling: Gough 8-0-23-2; Silverwood 10-2-22-3; White 8-1-28-0; Hartley 9.4-1-31-3; Stemp 8-1-34-1; Vaughan 2-0-10-0.

Umpires: R. Julian and R. A. White.

MINOR COUNTIES v DERBYSHIRE

At Lakenham, April 28, 29. Derbyshire won by six wickets. Toss: Derbyshire.

Minor Counties fell only 17 runs short of their competition record, set against Sussex in 1990 when innings were five overs longer. They owed much to a stand of 76 in ten overs between Mark Fell and Richard Dalton, a leading indoor cricketer. Derbyshire responded by sending Malcolm in at No. 3 as a pinch-hitter (he scored every run of a brief second-wicket stand of 13) but it was Adams who saved their bacon with 138 off 123 balls, including 14 fours and six sixes.

Gold Award: C. J. Adams.

Close of play: Derbyshire 166-2 (32 overs) (C. J. Adams 95*, D. M. Jones 20*).

Minor Counties

S. J. Dean c Krikken b Malcolm	7	J. M. Fielding c Clarke b Roberts		1
W. Larkins c Jones b Malcolm	0	N. V. Radford not out		10
J. P. J. Sylvester b DeFreitas	7	L-b 4, w 11		15
*I. Cockbain b Dean	30			
M. A. Fell b Roberts	67	1/8 2/9 3/31	(7 wkts, 50 overs)	256
R. N. Dalton b Harris	76	4/97 5/173		
S. V. Laudat not out	43	6/229 7/232		

M. A. Sharp and †P. J. Nicholson did not bat.

Bowling: DeFreitas 10–2–25–1; Malcolm 10–2–42–2; Harris 10–0–65–1; Dean 8–0–57–1; Roberts 10–1–50–2; Clarke 2–0–13–0.

Derbyshire

K. J. Barnett c Nicholson b Fell	28	V. P. Clarke not out		17
C. J. Adams c Nicholson b Laudat	138	L-b 6, w 10		16
D. E. Malcolm c Larkins b Fielding	13			
*D. M. Jones run out	35	1/99 2/112	(4 wkts, 48.1 overs)	260
G. A. Khan not out	13	3/214 4/237		

P. A. J. DeFreitas, †K. M. Krikken, G. M. Roberts, A. J. Harris and K. J. Dean did not bat.

Bowling: Radford 10–0–31–0; Sharp 10–1–48–0; Dalton 6.1–0–53–0; Fielding 10–0–57–1; Fell 4–0–19–1; Laudat 8–0–46–1.

Umpires: B. Leadbeater and B. J. Meyer.

WORCESTERSHIRE v WARWICKSHIRE

At Worcester, April 28. Warwickshire won by six wickets. Toss: Warwickshire.

Despite featuring two first-class sides, the entire match lasted only 67.4 overs. A slow, seaming wicket proved ideal for Warwickshire's medium-pacers, particularly Brown, who took a one-day best of five for 31. Worcestershire were 56 for nine before a last-wicket stand carried them to 96 all out but, when Warwickshire slumped in turn, to 36 for four, the match hung in the balance. Ostler and Penney fought back with an unbroken stand of 61 to settle the issue.

Gold Award: D. R. Brown.

Worcestershire

W. P. C. Weston c Ostler b Brown	6	S. R. Lampitt c Donald b Giles		23
†S. J. Rhodes b Brown	7	R. J. Chapman b Small		0
G. A. Hick c Giles b Welch	8	P. J. Newport not out		15
*T. M. Moody b Brown	7	L-b 2, w 4		6
K. R. Spiring lbw b Brown	0			
V. S. Solanki c Giles b Small	14	1/13 2/20 3/28	(37.2 overs)	96
D. A. Leatherdale c Piper b Brown	0	4/28 5/32 6/33		
G. R. Haynes c Small b Small	10	7/52 8/56 9/56		

Bowling: Donald 10–4–20–0; Brown 10–0–31–5; Welch 8–2–18–1; Small 6–0–19–3; Giles 2.2–0–5–1; Smith 1–0–1–0.

Warwickshire

D. R. Brown c Moody b Newport	3	T. L. Penney not out		33
N. M. K. Smith c Rhodes b Lampitt	11	W 6, n-b 2		8
*A. J. Moles b Lampitt	5			
D. L. Hemp b Newport	0	1/8 2/18	(4 wkts, 30.2 overs)	97
D. P. Ostler not out	37	3/19 4/36		

G. Welch, †K. J. Piper, A. F. Giles, G. C. Small and A. A. Donald did not bat.

Bowling: Newport 8–2–23–2; Chapman 6–0–27–0; Lampitt 7–3–17–2; Haynes 6–1–18–0; Leatherdale 3.2–1–12–0.

Umpires: J. H. Hampshire and D. R. Shepherd.

LANCASHIRE v DERBYSHIRE

At Manchester, April 30. Derbyshire won by six wickets. Toss: Lancashire. First-team debut:
I. D. Blackwell.

Once-invincible Lancashire suffered their second defeat in two days under Atherton's
captaincy. They slumped to 29 for four, and inexperienced left-arm spinner Glenn Roberts then
picked up three wickets, as the reshuffle of the batting order which moved the in-form Lloyd to
No. 7 backfired. Barnett's 136-ball hundred – his fourth in the competition – emphasised the
inadequacy of Lancashire's total.

Gold Award: K. J. Barnett.

Lancashire

*M. A. Atherton c Adams b DeFreitas ...	16	G. Yates b Dean 14
A. Flintoff c Krikken b DeFreitas	0	P. J. Martin not out................... 10
†W. K. Hegg lbw b Harris..............	0	R. J. Green run out................... 0
J. P. Crawley run out	2	B 1, l-b 3, w 9, n-b 6......... 19
J. E. R. Gallian b Roberts	52	
N. H. Fairbrother lbw b Roberts	45	1/1 2/4 3/7 (44 overs) 223
G. D. Lloyd b Harris	36	4/29 5/122 6/138
I. D. Austin lbw b Roberts.............	29	7/180 8/209 9/217

Bowling: DeFreitas 10–1–43–2; Harris 9–0–42–2; Clarke 5–0–28–0; Blackwell 5–0–38–0;
Dean 7–1–23–1; Roberts 8–0–45–3.

Derbyshire

K. J. Barnett not out................112		†K. M. Krikken not out 42
C. J. Adams lbw b Austin 29		L-b 7, w 5............... 12
*D. M. Jones c Hegg b Green 12		
G. A. Khan c and b Gallian........... 14		1/68 2/87 (4 wkts, 48.3 overs) 225
V. P. Clarke run out 4		3/130 4/137

I. D. Blackwell, P. A. J. DeFreitas, K. J. Dean, A. J. Harris and G. M. Roberts did not bat.

Bowling: Martin 9.3–0–49–0; Green 9–0–59–1; Austin 10–1–29–1; Yates 10–1–43–0; Lloyd
2–0–8–0; Gallian 4–0–13–1; Flintoff 4–0–17–0.

Umpires: T. E. Jesty and R. Julian.

WARWICKSHIRE v MINOR COUNTIES

At Birmingham, April 30. Warwickshire won by 155 runs. Toss: Warwickshire. First-team debut:
T. Frost.

Small's best figures in the competition brought him his first Gold Award in 18 seasons with
Warwickshire. He took five wickets in 14 balls, despite an inauspicious start when Dean pulled
his first ball for six, and only Fell was able to keep him out for long.

Gold Award: G. C. Small.

Warwickshire

*A. J. Moles b Fielding 60		G. Welch not out 13
N. M. K. Smith lbw b Radford 2		†T. Frost not out..................... 10
D. R. Brown c Fielding b Dalton 62		B 5, l-b 7, w 8, n-b 6......... 26
D. L. Hemp c Nicholson b Dalton 21		
D. P. Ostler c and b Dalton 2		1/6 2/91 3/144 (7 wkts, 50 overs) 261
T. L. Penney b Fell.................. 36		4/152 5/169
A. F. Giles b Fell 29		6/221 7/236

G. C. Small and A. A. Donald did not bat.

Bowling: Radford 9–0–50–1; Sharp 10–1–22–0; Laudat 10–1–41–0; Fielding 8–0–53–1;
Dalton 4–0–28–3; Fell 9–0–55–2.

Minor Counties

S. J. Dean lbw b Small	22	J. M. Fielding b Giles	14
W. Larkins b Donald	1	N. V. Radford b Giles	6
J. P. J. Sylvester run out	0	M. A. Sharp run out	14
*I. Cockbain c Ostler b Small	4	L-b 3, w 5, n-b 4	12
M. A. Fell not out	33		—
S. V. Laudat b Small	0	1/10 2/10 3/27	(32.4 overs) 106
†P. J. Nicholson b Small	0	4/37 5/41 6/41	
R. N. Dalton c Moles b Small	0	7/41 8/71 9/87	

Bowling: Donald 6–1–28–1; Brown 6–2–11–0; Small 7–4–23–5; Giles 10–3–26–2; Smith 3.4–0–15–0.

Umpires: V. A. Holder and J. F. Steele.

YORKSHIRE v WORCESTERSHIRE

At Leeds, April 30. Worcestershire won by 12 runs. Toss: Yorkshire. County debut: D. S. Lehmann.

Newport's four wickets settled a slow-scoring match in which no batsman reached 50. The 19 runs that Brinkley and Lampitt took from the last over of the Worcestershire innings, bowled by White, turned out to be decisive.

Gold Award: P. J. Newport.

Worcestershire

W. P. C. Weston c Blakey b Hartley	16	S. R. Lampitt not out	14
†S. J. Rhodes lbw b Gough	0	P. J. Newport b White	3
G. A. Hick b Silverwood	2	J. E. Brinkley not out	7
*T. M. Moody c Hartley b Stemp	33	L-b 14, w 2, n-b 4	20
K. R. Spiring b Vaughan	33		—
V. S. Solanki c Gough b White	21	1/1 2/8 3/50	(9 wkts, 50 overs) 199
D. A. Leatherdale b White	25	4/80 5/111 6/122	
G. R. Haynes lbw b Silverwood	25	7/167 8/171 9/179	

Bowling: Gough 10–1–25–2; Silverwood 10–1–43–2; White 10–2–37–2; Hartley 6–0–35–1; Stemp 10–0–30–1; Vaughan 4–0–15–1.

Yorkshire

*D. Byas c Rhodes b Haynes	8	P. J. Hartley not out	11
M. D. Moxon b Newport	17	D. Gough not out	22
D. S. Lehmann b Newport	9	L-b 1, w 3, n-b 4	8
M. P. Vaughan b Brinkley	46		—
A. McGrath c Moody b Brinkley	38	1/19 2/31 3/40	(7 wkts, 50 overs) 187
C. White c and b Newport	17	4/120 5/125	
†R. J. Blakey b Moody b Newport	11	6/146 7/152	

C. E. W. Silverwood and R. D. Stemp did not bat.

Bowling: Newport 10–1–37–4; Haynes 10–3–25–1; Hick 5–0–22–0; Lampitt 9–0–40–0; Brinkley 10–0–35–2; Leatherdale 6–0–27–0.

Umpires: G. I. Burgess and G. Sharp.

DERBYSHIRE v YORKSHIRE

At Derby, May 2. Yorkshire won by virtue of their higher score after 25 overs. Toss: Yorkshire.

The last over, bowled by Silverwood, yielded ten, leaving the sides level on runs and wickets and the spectators perplexed. Eventually, the public announcer explained that Yorkshire won on countback to the 25-over mark, when they had scored 116 to Derbyshire's 103. No one explained why a tie could not be allowed in a non-knockout game. Needing a six from the last ball to win, DeFreitas had forced a high full toss away for two, but it had reached him above waist height and was declared a no-ball, making four in all and giving him another chance. He picked up only one, however, to draw Derbyshire level. Stemp earned the match award for a tight spell which removed Barnett, the top scorer.

Gold Award: R. D. Stemp.

Yorkshire

*D. Byas lbw b DeFreitas	19	†R. J. Blakey c Roberts b Barnett		6
M. D. Moxon lbw b Clarke	52	D. Gough not out		0
M. P. Vaughan c and b Roberts	46	B 4, l-b 6, w 8, n-b 2		20
D. S. Lehmann b Barnett	26			
P. J. Hartley b Roberts	12	1/35 2/106 3/150	(7 wkts, 50 overs)	260
A. McGrath c Khan b Barnett	43	4/162 5/170		
C. White not out	36	6/239 7/255		

C. E. W. Silverwood and R. D. Stemp did not bat.

Bowling: DeFreitas 10–1–38–1; Harris 9–0–56–0; Dean 8–1–40–0; Roberts 10–0–47–2; Clarke 3–0–17–1; Barnett 10–1–52–3.

Derbyshire

K. J. Barnett c Gough b Stemp	88	P. A. J. DeFreitas not out		32
C. J. Adams lbw b Hartley	23	G. M. Roberts not out		1
*D. M. Jones b Stemp	20	L-b 3, w 9, n-b 12		24
G. A. Khan c White b Silverwood	33			
V. P. Clarke run out	7	1/62 2/97 3/175	(7 wkts, 50 overs)	260
A. S. Rollins lbw b Silverwood	0	4/183 5/183		
†K. M. Krikken b Silverwood	32	6/202 7/252		

K. J. Dean and A. J. Harris did not bat.

Bowling: Gough 10–0–52–0; Silverwood 7–0–47–3; White 9–0–55–0; Hartley 10–1–32–1; Stemp 9–1–35–2; Vaughan 2–0–14–0; Lehmann 3–0–22–0.

Umpires: D. J. Constant and V. A. Holder.

WARWICKSHIRE v LANCASHIRE

At Birmingham, May 2. Lancashire won by virtue of losing fewer wickets. Toss: Lancashire.

Lancashire held their nerve brilliantly at the death when Warwickshire needed only six to win from two overs. Wasim Akram's last over cost just one run; then Austin bowled Donald and his final ball confounded Small, who was stranded well out of his ground as he went for a second run to win. Wasim collected the Gold Award both for that over and for a stylish half-century, but Donald was unlucky that his devastating return of five for 25 went unrewarded.

Gold Award: Wasim Akram.

Lancashire

J. E. R. Gallian c Penney b Donald	33	G. Yates lbw b Donald		5
M. A. Atherton c Ostler b Donald	24	R. J. Green not out		6
J. P. Crawley b Donald	0			
N. H. Fairbrother b Giles	0	L-b 9, w 8, n-b 4		21
G. D. Lloyd lbw b Small	13			
I. D. Austin c Frost b Donald	35	1/58 2/58 3/59	(8 wkts, 50 overs)	208
*Wasim Akram not out	52	4/70 5/96 6/139		
†W. K. Hegg b Small	19	7/177 8/196		

P. J. Martin did not bat.

Bowling: Welch 5–1–17–0; Brown 6–0–33–0; Donald 10–3–25–5; Giles 9–0–42–1; Small 10–0–35–2; Smith 10–1–47–0.

Warwickshire

*A. J. Moles lbw b Martin	3		†T. Frost b Austin	1
N. M. K. Smith b Wasim Akram	0		A. A. Donald b Austin	0
D. R. Brown c and b Yates	41		G. C. Small run out	1
D. L. Hemp b Martin	6		B 1, l-b 8, w 6, n-b 4	19
D. P. Ostler lbw b Green	17			
T. L. Penney b Wasim Akram	55		1/5 2/10 3/26	(50 overs) 208
A. F. Giles c Austin b Yates	10		4/71 5/71 6/88	
G. Welch not out	55		7/192 8/203 9/207	

Bowling: Wasim Akram 10–0–54–2; Martin 10–4–20–2; Austin 10–3–41–2; Green 10–1–41–1; Yates 10–0–43–2.

Umpires: J. D. Bond and T. E. Jesty.

WORCESTERSHIRE v MINOR COUNTIES

At Worcester, May 2. Worcestershire won by four wickets. Toss: Minor Counties.

Dalton enlivened the part-timers' innings with 69 off 47 balls, including 19 off one over from Brinkley. Until then it had been slow going – Newport bowled an opening spell of 7–5–7–0. When Worcestershire batted, Moody was able to take them most of the way to victory, scoring 50 before he became one of Dalton's three victims.

Gold Award: R. N. Dalton.

Minor Counties

S. J. Dean c Moody b Haynes	0		N. V. Radford c Weston b Leatherdale	7
W. Larkins c Rhodes b Lampitt	16		M. A. Sharp run out	5
J. P. J. Sylvester lbw b Brinkley	9		A. J. Murphy not out	1
*I. Cockbain c Rhodes b Leatherdale	16		L-b 15, w 19	34
M. A. Fell c Moody b Leatherdale	4			
R. N. Dalton c Spiring b Hick	69		1/1 2/33 3/65	(45.5 overs) 177
S. V. Laudat c Rhodes b Newport	2		4/65 5/73 6/102	
†P. J. Nicholson c Rhodes b Leatherdale	14		7/149 8/168 9/174	

Bowling: Newport 10–5–20–1; Haynes 10–3–15–1; Lampitt 8–1–33–1; Brinkley 8.5–0–55–1; Leatherdale 6–1–13–4; Hick 3–0–26–1.

Worcestershire

*T. M. Moody b Dalton	50		D. A. Leatherdale not out	17
W. P. C. Weston c Radford b Sharp	8		S. R. Lampitt not out	4
G. A. Hick c Sharp b Murphy	28		L-b 10, w 16	26
G. R. Haynes b Dalton	25			
V. S. Solanki c and b Dalton	16		1/26 2/95 3/116	(6 wkts, 42.4 overs) 181
K. R. Spiring c Cockbain b Murphy	7		4/138 5/160 6/160	

†S. J. Rhodes, P. J. Newport and J. E. Brinkley did not bat.

Bowling: Radford 10–2–23–0; Sharp 7–1–31–1; Murphy 10–0–39–2; Laudat 6.4–0–45–0; Dalton 9–1–33–3.

Umpires: A. Clarkson and R. Julian.

DERBYSHIRE v WORCESTERSHIRE

At Derby, May 5, 6. Derbyshire won by 20 runs. Toss: Worcestershire.

Clarke produced the most spectacular innings, 52 from 39 balls with six fours and a six. But his captain, Jones, played an even more crucial role, sharing a second-wicket stand of 85 with Barnett – who passed 2,500 runs in this competition – and outwitting Worcestershire's best batsmen, Moody and Hick, with expert field placements.

Gold Award: V. P. Clarke.

Close of play: Derbyshire 32-0 (7.3 overs) (K. J. Barnett 18*, C. J. Adams 4*).

Derbyshire

K. J. Barnett b Hick	59	A. J. Harris b Leatherdale	2
C. J. Adams lbw b Newport	9	D. E. Malcolm c Solanki b Newport	3
*D. M. Jones lbw b Leatherdale	35	K. J. Dean run out	6
G. A. Khan b Leatherdale	2	B 4, l-b 12, w 21, n-b 4	41
V. P. Clarke c Weston b Haynes	52		
†K. M. Krikken not out	20	1/37 2/122 3/131 (49.4 overs) 231	
P. A. J. DeFreitas b Solanki	0	4/157 5/209 6/209	
G. M. Roberts lbw b Leatherdale	2	7/212 8/214 9/220	

Bowling: Newport 10–1–36–2; Haynes 10–1–47–1; Lampitt 5–0–19–0; Brinkley 2–0–14–0; Hick 10–0–49–1; Leatherdale 9.4–0–33–4; Solanki 3–0–17–1.

Worcestershire

*T. M. Moody c Jones b Roberts	77	P. J. Newport c Krikken b DeFreitas	12
W. P. C. Weston b Malcolm	1	S. R. Lampitt c Jones b Harris	16
G. A. Hick c Jones b Malcolm	11	J. E. Brinkley not out	0
G. R. Haynes lbw b Dean	13	L-b 7, w 4, n-b 2	13
V. S. Solanki b Clarke	19		
K. R. Spring b Roberts	10	1/8 2/36 3/78 (48.5 overs) 211	
D. A. Leatherdale b Clarke	2	4/122 5/130 6/143	
†S. J. Rhodes b Harris	37	7/143 8/178 9/209	

Bowling: DeFreitas 9–1–33–1; Malcolm 10–1–38–2; Harris 9.5–1–30–2; Dean 4–0–16–1; Roberts 8–0–52–2; Clarke 8–0–35–2.

Umpires: J. F. Steele and R. A. White.

MINOR COUNTIES v LANCASHIRE

At Walsall, May 5, 6. Lancashire won by 35 runs. Toss: Lancashire.

Lancashire stumbled to 41 for five before Fairbrother and Hegg performed a rescue operation with a seventh-wicket stand of 101. Rain interrupted the Minor Counties' reply after one over. Then, on the reserve day, Dean and Larkins – with a brief reminder of his Northamptonshire heyday – bludgeoned an opening stand of 60 in less than nine overs. Austin conceded 28 in three overs, but his second spell of 6–3–4–3 ended any chance of an upset.

Gold Award: N. H. Fairbrother.

Close of play: Minor Counties 1-0 (1 over) (S. J. Dean 0*, W. Larkins 0*).

Lancashire

J. E. R. Gallian c Larkins b Radford	0	†W. K. Hegg not out	54
P. C. McKeown b Sharp	10	G. Yates not out	9
J. P. Crawley c Fielding b Sharp	0		
I. D. Austin c Nicholson b Radford	19	B 12, l-b 4, w 6, n-b 2	24
N. H. Fairbrother c Ecclestone b Fielding	62		
G. D. Lloyd c Gaywood b Radford	4	1/0 2/7 3/12 4/37 (7 wkts, 50 overs) 210	
*Wasim Akram c Sharp b Fielding	28	5/41 6/98 7/199	

R. J. Green and P. J. Martin did not bat.

Bowling: Radford 10–1–52–3; Sharp 10–2–17–2; Murphy 10–0–50–0; Dalton 10–0–28–0; Fielding 10–1–47–2.

Minor Counties

S. J. Dean c Hegg b Green	41	J. M. Fielding lbw b Austin	0
W. Larkins c Crawley b Yates	26	M. A. Sharp not out	16
N. R. Gaywood c Hegg b Austin	18	A. J. Murphy b Green	1
*I. Cockbain c Fairbrother b Martin	4	B 7, l-b 5, w 11, n-b 6	29
G. W. Ecclestone lbw b Martin	0		
R. N. Dalton c Crawley b Wasim Akram	25	1/60 2/91 3/102 (43.3 overs) 175	
†P. J. Nicholson lbw b Austin	1	4/102 5/133 6/134	
N. V. Radford b Martin	14	7/135 8/142 9/172	

Bowling: Wasim Akram 8–1–35–1; Austin 10–3–33–3; Green 5.3–0–33–2; Martin 10–1–41–3; Yates 10–3–21–1.

Umpires: J. C. Balderstone and J. H. Hampshire.

WARWICKSHIRE v YORKSHIRE

At Birmingham, May 5, 6. Yorkshire won by five wickets. Toss: Warwickshire.
    Yorkshire benefited from the rain which halted their reply after five overs on an overcast first day. The next morning was bright and there was no sign of swing in the air, allowing Vaughan and Lehmann to compile a match-winning second-wicket partnership of 117 in 22 overs. Ostler kept wicket for Warwickshire because Piper had back trouble.
    Gold Award: M. P. Vaughan.
    Close of play: Yorkshire 14-0 (5 overs) (D. Byas 5*, M. P. Vaughan 6*).

Warwickshire

*A. J. Moles b Gough	4	A. F. Giles not out	25
N. M. K. Smith c McGrath b Silverwood	57	A. A. Donald not out	17
D. R. Brown c Byas b White	2		
D. L. Hemp b Vaughan	23	L-b 10, w 5, n-b 4	19
D. P. Ostler lbw b Gough	26		
T. L. Penney st Blakey b Stemp	34	1/30 2/38 3/94 (8 wkts, 50 overs) 233	
†K. J. Piper st Blakey b Stemp	7	4/96 5/156 6/162	
G. Welch c Blakey b Gough	19	7/177 8/194	

G. C. Small did not bat.

Bowling: Gough 10–0–38–3; Silverwood 8–0–39–1; White 8–1–40–1; Hartley 10–0–59–0; Stemp 10–0–29–2; Vaughan 4–0–18–1.

Yorkshire

*D. Byas b Brown	7	†R. J. Blakey not out	0
M. P. Vaughan b Smith	88		
D. S. Lehmann c Brown b Giles	67	B 7, l-b 8, w 6, n-b 4	25
P. J. Hartley b Smith	22		
A. McGrath c Giles b Brown	20	1/17 2/134 3/173 (5 wkts, 46.3 overs) 237	
C. White not out	8	4/224 5/227	

B. Parker, D. Gough, C. E. W. Silverwood and R. D. Stemp did not bat.

Bowling: Donald 10–3–38–0; Welch 6–0–27–0; Brown 7.3–1–40–2; Giles 10–0–49–1; Small 4–1–26–0; Smith 9–0–42–2.

Umpires: G. I. Burgess and P. Willey.

DERBYSHIRE v WARWICKSHIRE

At Derby, May 12, 13. Warwickshire won by one wicket. Toss: Warwickshire.
    Needing six runs to win off the penultimate ball, with one wicket in hand and a quarter-final place at stake for both sides, Small drove Malcolm into the crowd at long-off. Earlier, three

wickets from Small had counteracted Adams's flamboyant 61 from 68 balls and earned him his second award in a fortnight after 17 blank years. A target of 217 had looked in easy reach when Knight and Brown put on 96 for the second wicket. But four wickets from Clarke's leg-breaks set up the cliffhanger finale. Rain had prevented any play on the first day.

Gold Award: G. C. Small.

Derbyshire

K. J. Barnett c Piper b Giles	38	D. E. Malcolm b Donald	0
C. J. Adams lbw b Small	61	A. J. Harris not out	4
*D. M. Jones b Small	3		
G. A. Khan c Piper b Small	26	B 1, l-b 13, w 8, n-b 8	30
V. P. Clarke run out	1		
†K. M. Krikken not out	29	1/114 2/114 3/130 (8 wkts, 50 overs)	216
P. A. J. DeFreitas c Penney b Smith	12	4/141 5/150 6/174	
G. M. Roberts b Donald	12	7/201 8/201	

K. J. Dean did not bat.

Bowling: Donald 10–0–32–2; Brown 10–1–38–0; Welch 5–0–34–0; Giles 10–0–37–1; Small 10–1–41–3; Smith 5–0–20–1.

Warwickshire

*N. V. Knight c and b Clarke	69	†K. J. Piper run out	1
N. M. K. Smith b Malcolm	17	A. A. Donald not out	10
D. R. Brown lbw b Clarke	58	G. C. Small not out	14
D. L. Hemp b Clarke	1	L-b 12, w 2	14
D. P. Ostler b Clarke	6		
T. L. Penney c DeFreitas b Harris	10	1/28 2/124 3/126 (9 wkts, 49.5 overs)	217
G. Welch c Jones b Harris	16	4/152 5/163 6/191	
A. F. Giles b Harris	1	7/191 8/193 9/193	

Bowling: DeFreitas 10–2–32–0; Malcolm 6.5–0–36–1; Harris 10–0–41–3; Dean 3–0–13–0; Roberts 10–0–34–0; Clarke 10–0–49–4.

Umpires: V. A. Holder and B. Leadbeater.

LANCASHIRE v WORCESTERSHIRE

At Manchester, May 12. Lancashire won by virtue of losing fewer wickets. Toss: Lancashire.

Newport holed out from the last ball, bowled by Wasim Akram, to hand Lancashire their second victory on tied scores in 11 days, but it was not enough to see them into the next round. Fairbrother's deft innings of 75, featuring only one four before he lifted Leatherdale for two sixes in the last over, contrasted with Moody's disdainful 92, which included 11 fours and two sixes.

Gold Award: T. M. Moody.

Lancashire

J. E. R. Gallian lbw b Hick	59	*Wasim Akram b Newport	4
M. A. Atherton c Weston b Newport	6	†W. K. Hegg not out	9
J. P. Crawley c Moody b Leatherdale	37	L-b 8, w 15, n-b 4	27
N. H. Fairbrother not out	75		
G. D. Lloyd b Sheriyar	32	1/20 2/100 3/124 (6 wkts, 50 overs)	274
I. D. Austin run out	25	4/193 5/237 6/247	

P. J. Martin, G. Yates and R. J. Green did not bat.

Bowling: Newport 9–1–45–2; Haynes 10–1–55–0; Sheriyar 10–0–65–1; Brinkley 2–0–18–0; Hick 9–0–42–1; Leatherdale 10–0–41–1.

Worcestershire

*T. M. Moody c Yates b Martin	92	†S. J. Rhodes lbw b Austin	0
W. P. C. Weston c Hegg b Wasim Akram	6	P. J. Newport c Green b Wasim Akram	12
G. A. Hick c Hegg b Martin	40	L-b 6, w 14, n-b 6	26
G. R. Haynes c Atherton b Martin	39		
V. S. Solanki lbw b Yates	20	1/25 2/156 3/156 (8 wkts, 50 overs) 274	
K. R. Spiring not out	32	4/196 5/235 6/245	
D. A. Leatherdale run out	7	7/248 8/274	

J. E. Brinkley and A. Sheriyar did not bat.

Bowling: Wasim Akram 10–1–31–2; Austin 10–0–42–1; Martin 10–0–56–3; Green 7–0–53–0; Yates 10–0–71–1; Gallian 3–1–15–0.

Umpires: B. J. Meyer and P. Willey.

YORKSHIRE v MINOR COUNTIES

At Leeds, May 12. Yorkshire won by 184 runs. Toss: Yorkshire.

Yorkshire's total, based around McGrath's maiden one-day hundred, an unbeaten 109 from 85 balls, would have been even stronger but for Oakes's spell of 10–1–37–3. Dean and Larkins built an opening partnership of 63 in 12 overs for the Minor Counties, but then they lost all ten wickets for 62, including the last five for just two runs. Yorkshire finished top of the group.

Gold Award: A. McGrath.

Yorkshire

*D. Byas c and b Oakes	72	†R. J. Blakey not out	23
M. P. Vaughan b Oakes	15		
D. S. Lehmann c Larkins b Laudat	34	B 1, l-b 8, w 17, n-b 6	32
P. J. Hartley c Nicholson b Oakes	0		
A. McGrath not out	109	1/70 2/128 3/128 (5 wkts, 50 overs) 309	
C. White c Gaywood b Sharp	24	4/136 5/197	

B. Parker, D. Gough, C. E. W. Silverwood and R. D. Stemp did not bat.

Bowling: Murphy 10–0–60–0; Sharp 10–0–53–1; Dalton 10–0–80–0; Oakes 10–1–37–3; Laudat 10–0–70–1.

Minor Counties

S. J. Dean b White	56	M. A. Sharp c Gough b Stemp	1
W. Larkins b White	15	S. Oakes lbw b Silverwood	0
N. R. Gaywood c McGrath b Vaughan	30	A. J. Murphy not out	0
*I. Cockbain b White	0	L-b 2, w 5, n-b 6	13
J. P. J. Sylvester b Stemp	6		
R. N. Dalton c Lehmann b Stemp	0	1/63 2/77 3/77 (33.3 overs) 125	
S. V. Laudat b Hartley	4	4/105 5/105 6/123	
†P. J. Nicholson lbw b Hartley	0	7/123 8/124 9/125	

Bowling: Gough 6–0–25–0; Silverwood 5–0–26–1; White 7–1–22–3; Hartley 6–0–28–2; Stemp 9–3–22–3; Vaughan 0.3–0–0–1.

Umpires: A. A. Jones and M. J. Kitchen.

GROUP B

LEICESTERSHIRE v SCOTLAND

At Leicester, April 28. Leicestershire won by 178 runs. Toss: Scotland.

Leicestershire ran up the second-highest total ever made in the Benson and Hedges Cup – the highest was 388 by Essex, also against Scotland – and the biggest since innings were reduced to 50 overs a side in 1996. The foundation was an opening stand of 159 in 25 overs between Maddy and Sutcliffe, and all the later batsmen contributed to a final tally of 36 fours and eight sixes. Scotland's opening bowler, Blain, went for 82 in six overs. When they came to bat, Scotland felt unable even to attempt such a vast target, and Patterson and Philip put on 76 for the first wicket in 19 overs of batting practice.

Gold Award: D. L. Maddy.

Leicestershire

D. L. Maddy c Hurlbatt b Williamson	97	†P. A. Nixon not out		11
I. J. Sutcliffe c Davies b Williamson	59	G. I. Macmillan not out		16
*J. J. Whitaker b Blain	51	L-b 4, w 5, n-b 28		37
V. J. Wells b Steindl	19			
A. Habib c Smith b Blain	53			—
J. M. Dakin c Lockhart b Hurlbatt	28	1/159 2/182 3/229	(6 wkts, 50 overs)	371
		4/283 5/338 6/339		

D. J. Millns, M. T. Brimson and A. D. Mullally did not bat.

Bowling: Blain 6–0–82–2; Hurlbatt 10–1–76–1; Steindl 9–0–61–1; Gourlay 5–0–34–0; Williamson 10–0–61–2; Govan 10–0–53–0.

Scotland

*I. L. Philip c Maddy b Wells	35	†A. G. Davies not out		35
B. M. W. Patterson b Dakin	36	J. W. Govan not out		22
D. R. Lockhart b Dakin	7	L-b 11, w 11, n-b 4		26
M. J. Smith b Wells	6			
J. G. Williamson c Nixon b Wells	10			—
S. Gourlay lbw b Maddy	16	1/76 2/91 3/97	(6 wkts, 50 overs)	193
		4/102 5/123 6/135		

G. P. Hurlbatt, P. D. Steindl and J. A. R. Blain did not bat.

Bowling: Mullally 8–1–29–0; Millns 7–1–25–0; Wells 10–1–35–3; Dakin 5–0–16–2; Brimson 10–1–26–0; Maddy 7–1–23–1; Macmillan 3–0–28–0.

Umpires: J. H. Harris and T. E. Jesty.

NOTTINGHAMSHIRE v DURHAM

At Nottingham, April 28, 29. Nottinghamshire won by five wickets. Toss: Durham.

Boon's third half-century in four innings since joining Durham left his team well positioned when play was suspended on the first day, with Nottinghamshire an unpromising 94 for three. They still needed 34 from the last four overs, but Archer, who made 111 from 125 balls, his maiden one-day century, struck Walker for six on his way to victory. Earlier, Robinson had reached 2,500 runs in the competition when five.

Gold Award: G. F. Archer.

Close of play: Nottinghamshire 94-3 (26 overs) (G. F. Archer 34*, P. R. Pollard 10*).

Durham

J. J. B. Lewis lbw b Archer	38	M. M. Betts not out		5
P. D. Collingwood b Bates	49			
M. A. Roseberry st Noon b Bates	22	L-b 8, w 6		14
*D. C. Boon not out	64			—
N. J. Speak c Noon b Pick	31	1/82 2/96 3/122	(5 wkts, 50 overs)	230
†M. P. Speight b Evans	7	4/207 5/219		

J. Boiling, N. Killeen, S. J. E. Brown and A. Walker did not bat.

Bowling: Evans 10–1–40–1; Pick 8–1–43–1; Tolley 9–0–40–0; Dowman 5–0–25–0; Bates 10–0–40–2; Archer 8–1–34–1.

Nottinghamshire

M. P. Dowman c Speight b Killeen 16	C. M. Tolley not out.................	23
R. T. Robinson c Speight b Betts 10		
G. F. Archer not out.................111	L-b 5, w 2.................	7
*P. D. Johnson b Boiling................. 21		—
P. R. Pollard c Boiling b Collingwood ... 38	1/13 2/39 3/78 (5 wkts, 49.3 overs) 234	
N. A. Gie run out 8	4/161 5/185	

†W. M. Noon, K. P. Evans, R. T. Bates and R. A. Pick did not bat.

Bowling: Brown 8.3–0–38–0; Betts 9–3–44–1; Killeen 10–0–43–1; Boiling 9–0–40–1; Walker 10–0–52–0; Collingwood 3–0–12–1.

Umpires: J. C. Balderstone and H. D. Bird.

DURHAM v NORTHAMPTONSHIRE

At Chester-le-Street, April 30. Durham won by 64 runs. Toss: Northamptonshire.

Brown bowled Durham to their second victory against first-class opposition since the end of the 1995 season, taking Northamptonshire's first three wickets in four balls on his way to figures of six for 30, his best in one-day cricket. For Brown, it was an even rarer success than for his team-mates: he had missed the Sunday League win over Essex in 1996 because he was in the England team that lost the Lord's Test to Pakistan, so had not been in a winning side in a major game since 1995. Earlier, Boon had scored his first century for Durham, another fine captain's innings; he added a stately 103 with Lewis and a more urgent 95 with Speight.

Gold Award: S. J. E. Brown.

Durham

J. J. B. Lewis c and b Capel 47	M. M. Betts c Taylor b Emburey	1
P. D. Collingwood b Mohammad Akram . 6		
M. A. Roseberry hit wkt b Taylor....... 1	L-b 6, w 7, n-b 12	25
*D. C. Boon b Emburey................103		—
†M. P. Speight not out 42	1/17 2/25 3/128 (6 wkts, 50 overs) 225	
N. J. Speak st Ripley b Emburey 0	4/223 5/223 6/225	

J. Boiling, N. Killeen, S. J. E. Brown and A. Walker did not bat.

Bowling: Mohammad Akram 9–1–34–1; Taylor 10–0–31–1; Penberthy 7–0–36–0; Curran 6–0–26–0; Emburey 8–0–34–3; Snape 5–0–24–0; Capel 5–0–34–1.

Northamptonshire

D. J. Capel c Boiling b Brown 2	J. E. Emburey c Brown b Boiling	1
M. B. Loye lbw b Brown.............. 0	J. P. Taylor run out.................	6
*R. J. Bailey b Brown 62	Mohammad Akram c and b Brown	4
K. M. Curran b Brown................ 0	L-b 9, w 11, n-b 2	22
A. L. Penberthy c Speight b Walker 14		—
T. C. Walton c Brown b Collingwood ... 28	1/2 2/3 3/3 (42.5 overs) 161	
J. N. Snape c Collingwood b Brown..... 11	4/53 5/95 6/138	
†D. Ripley not out 11	7/139 8/141 9/152	

Bowling: Brown 9.5–1–30–6; Betts 5–0–21–0; Killeen 6–2–16–0; Walker 7–1–21–1; Boiling 10–1–46–1; Collingwood 5–0–18–1.

Umpires: N. T. Plews and R. A. White.

LEICESTERSHIRE v NOTTINGHAMSHIRE

At Leicester, April 30. Leicestershire won by 77 runs. Toss: Nottinghamshire. County debut: N. C. Johnson.

Leicestershire made the highest total of the day for the second time in three days, and Maddy collected his second consecutive Gold Award, for his first century in the competition, scored off only 93 balls. Once Nottinghamshire had lost their first two wickets for seven there was no contest. Neil Johnson, Leicestershire's new all-rounder from Natal, managed two wickets despite having arrived in the country at 7 a.m. that morning.

Gold Award: D. L. Maddy.

Leicestershire

D. L. Maddy b Dowman	101	D. J. Millns run out		12
I. J. Sutcliffe c and b Evans	18	A. D. Mullally not out		0
*J. J. Whitaker retired hurt	1			
V. J. Wells c Archer b Evans	70	L-b 9, w 10		19
N. C. Johnson b Evans	1			
A. Habib run out	15	1/50 2/190 3/202	(7 wkts, 50 overs)	295
†P. A. Nixon b Dowman	13	4/215 5/231		
J. M. Dakin not out	45	6/235 7/292		

M. T. Brimson did not bat.

J. J. Whitaker retired hurt at 68.

Bowling: Evans 10–0–61–3; Pick 9–0–51–0; Tolley 10–2–31–0; Archer 4–0–35–0; Bates 10–0–62–0; Dowman 7–0–46–2.

Nottinghamshire

M. P. Dowman c Dakin b Johnson	43	K. P. Evans c Nixon b Dakin		13
R. T. Robinson c Nixon b Millns	7	R. T. Bates not out		4
G. F. Archer b Mullally	0	R. A. Pick c Habib b Wells		2
*P. Johnson c Dakin b Johnson	34	B 1, l-b 2, w 11, n-b 4		18
P. R. Pollard run out	14			
N. A. Gie b Dakin	47	1/6 2/7 3/86	(47.4 overs)	218
C. M. Tolley c Dakin b Wells	18	4/95 5/105 6/134		
†W. M. Noon lbw b Millns	24	7/185 8/209 9/214		

Bowling: Mullally 8–1–40–1; Millns 10–3–45–2; Dakin 6–0–35–2; Johnson 8–0–38–2; Brimson 10–1–34–0; Wells 5.4–0–23–2.

Umpires: H. D. Bird and B. Dudleston.

NOTTINGHAMSHIRE v NORTHAMPTONSHIRE

At Nottingham, May 2. Northamptonshire won by eight wickets. Toss: Northamptonshire.

One Pakistani fast bowler, Nottinghamshire's new recruit Mohammad Zahid, arrived at Trent Bridge just too late to see another, Mohammad Akram, taking four important wickets for the visitors. It could have been five if Dowman had not been dropped by Ripley when 25; he fell only eight short of a maiden hundred in the competition. For Northamptonshire, Capel made 68 from 69 balls and Bailey an unbeaten 73 in 71.

Gold Award: D. J. Capel.

Nottinghamshire

M. P. Dowman st Ripley b Emburey	92	†W. M. Noon not out		7
*P. Johnson c Curran		K. P. Evans c Ripley b Mohammad Akram		7
b Mohammad Akram	5	R. T. Bates b Taylor		4
G. F. Archer c Ripley		R. A. Pick not out		1
b Mohammad Akram	14	L-b 10, w 8		18
R. T. Robinson b Snape	25			
P. R. Pollard lbw b Taylor	18	1/18 2/50 3/108	(9 wkts, 50 overs)	218
N. A. Gie c Capel b Snape	6	4/149 5/161 6/195		
C. M. Tolley b Mohammad Akram	21	7/199 8/210 9/216		

Bowling: Mohammad Akram 10–0–47–4; Taylor 10–1–40–2; Capel 6–0–25–0; Emburey 10–0–43–1; Snape 10–1–37–2; Bailey 4–0–16–0.

Northamptonshire

D. J. Capel b Dowman 68
M. B. Loye c Evans b Tolley 24
*R. J. Bailey not out 73
K. M. Curran not out 49
      L-b 2, w 3, n-b 2 7

1/65 2/114   (2 wkts, 41.5 overs) 221

A. L. Penberthy, T. C. Walton, J. N. Snape, †D. Ripley, J. E. Emburey, J. P. Taylor and Mohammad Akram did not bat.

Bowling: Evans 7–1–26–0; Pick 8–0–59–0; Tolley 7–0–33–1; Dowman 9–0–44–1; Archer 1–0–4–0; Bates 9.5–2–53–0.

Umpires: G. I. Burgess and A. A. Jones.

SCOTLAND v DURHAM

At Forfar, May 2. Durham won by eight wickets. Toss: Durham.

A fourth-wicket stand of 73 between Smith and Williamson provided the only substance in the Scottish innings. Foster made as many on his own from 57 balls; Durham cruised to victory, using just under half their overs, when he hit a six out of the ground.

Gold Award: M. J. Smith.

Scotland

B. M. W. Patterson b Foster 2
*I. L. Philip lbw b Brown 11
D. R. Lockhart c Speight b Walker 6
M. J. Smith run out 55
J. G. Williamson b Boiling 24
S. Gourlay lbw b Boiling 0
†A. G. Davies b Brown 3
J. W. Govan c Boon b Walker 11

G. P. Hurlbatt not out 12
P. D. Steindl not out 9

      L-b 7, w 10 17

1/18 2/22 3/28   (8 wkts, 50 overs) 150
4/101 5/101 6/110
7/120 8/136

K. Thomson did not bat.

Bowling: Brown 10–2–13–2; Killeen 10–1–28–0; Foster 7–1–27–1; Walker 10–1–32–2; Boiling 10–2–26–2; Collingwood 3–0–17–0.

Durham

J. J. B. Lewis c Williamson b Thomson . . 16
P. D. Collingwood c and b Gourlay 32
M. J. Foster not out 73
M. A. Roseberry not out 27
      L-b 2, w 4 6

1/36 2/68   (2 wkts, 24.3 overs) 154

*D. C. Boon, N. J. Speak, †M. P. Speight, J. Boiling, N. Killeen, S. J. E. Brown and A. Walker did not bat.

Bowling: Thomson 6–1–28–1; Hurlbatt 4–0–19–0; Williamson 2–0–19–0; Gourlay 6.3–0–37–1; Steindl 3–0–21–0; Govan 2–0–24–0; Smith 1–0–4–0.

Umpires: B. Leadbeater and B. J. Meyer.

DURHAM v LEICESTERSHIRE

At Chester-le-Street, May 5, 6. Leicestershire won by 19 runs (D/L method). Toss: Durham.

Habib, scoring a maiden one-day century from 117 balls, and Wells built a third-wicket stand of 221, leaving Foster with the most expensive figures for Durham in the competition. After flurries of snow, Durham's target was reduced to 282 in 48 overs in line with the Duckworth/Lewis system (under ECB rules, the winning margin in these situations is the difference between target and total). No play was possible on the opening day.

Gold Award: A. Habib.

Leicestershire

D. L. Maddy c Lewis b Brown	11	N. C. Johnson not out		8
I. J. Sutcliffe c Boiling b Brown	8	B 1, l-b 10, w 19		30
A. Habib c Speak b Walker	111			
*V. J. Wells lbw b Walker	90	1/18 2/22	(4 wkts, 50 overs)	287
J. M. Dakin not out	29	3/243 4/261		

G. I. Macmillan, †P. A. Nixon, D. J. Millns, A. D. Mullally and M. T. Brimson did not bat.

Bowling: Brown 10–0–49–2; Killeen 10–0–52–0; Walker 10–0–54–2; Foster 9–0–64–0; Boiling 8–0–40–0; Collingwood 3–0–17–0.

Durham

J. J. B. Lewis c Dakin b Mullally	18	N. Killeen run out		3
P. D. Collingwood c Macmillan b Brimson	36	S. J. E. Brown not out		8
J. E. Morris c Habib b Brimson	62	A. Walker not out		3
M. J. Foster c Nixon b Dakin	1	L-b 5, w 10, n-b 10		25
*D. C. Boon c Nixon b Dakin	4			
†M. P. Speight c Habib b Mullally	33	1/38 2/109 3/113	(9 wkts, 48 overs)	263
N. J. Speak c Dakin b Wells	59	4/141 5/141 6/204		
J. Boiling c Brimson b Mullally	11	7/225 8/251 9/258		

Bowling: Mullally 10–0–53–3; Millns 7–3–23–0; Wells 8–0–50–1; Johnson 5–0–38–0; Brimson 9–0–41–2; Dakin 9–0–53–2.

Umpires: D. J. Constant and A. A. Jones.

NORTHAMPTONSHIRE v SCOTLAND

At Northampton, May 5, 6. Northamptonshire won by five wickets. Toss: Northamptonshire.

Northamptonshire restricted Scotland to 160 on a green pitch, although Embury, their player-coach, said afterwards that it should have been no more than 100; they dropped five catches and Loye was knocked out when one chance rebounded off his cheekbone. At first the home side's batting was as uncertain as their fielding, and they were 94 for five before Loye and Snape rescued them with an unbroken stand of 70.

Gold Award: M. B. Loye.

Close of play: Northamptonshire 126-5 (26.1 overs) (M. B. Loye 32*, J. N. Snape 9*).

Scotland

B. M. W. Patterson c Walton b Taylor	12	J. W. Govan not out		14
I. L. Philip c Walton b Follett	20	S. Gourlay c Ripley b Capel		4
D. R. Lockhart c Capel b Follett	0	K. Thomson not out		1
M. J. Smith c Snape b Capel	22	L-b 9, w 12, n-b 4		25
*G. Salmond b Capel	5			
J. G. Williamson c Bailey b Follett	26	1/35 2/35 3/42	(9 wkts, 50 overs)	160
G. P. Hurlbatt b Follett	28	4/65 5/70 6/133		
†A. G. Davies run out	3	7/134 8/141 9/158		

Bowling: Taylor 10–1–29–1; Follett 10–1–39–4; Capel 8–2–25–3; Curran 8–0–22–0; Embury 10–3–14–0; Penberthy 4–0–22–0.

Northamptonshire

D. J. Capel c Govan b Thomson	19	J. N. Snape not out	27
A. L. Penberthy c Salmond b Thomson	7		
*R. J. Bailey c Gourlay b Thomson	15	L-b 4, w 12, n-b 4	20
K. M. Curran c Davies b Hurlbatt	8		
T. C. Walton c Thomson b Govan	23	1/20 2/33 3/49 (5 wkts, 32.4 overs)	164
M. B. Loye not out	45	4/55 5/94	

J. E. Emburey, †D. Ripley, J. P. Taylor and D. Follett did not bat.

Bowling: Thomson 10–0–45–3; Gourlay 4–1–24–0; Hurlbatt 5–0–28–1; Govan 5–0–17–1; Williamson 8.4–0–46–0.

Umpires: A. Clarkson and D. R. Shepherd.

NORTHAMPTONSHIRE v LEICESTERSHIRE

At Northampton, May 12. Northamptonshire won by 52 runs. Toss: Leicestershire.

Both sides were 127 for three in the 32nd over and both failed to capitalise on their position. But while Walton sustained some sort of momentum for Northamptonshire – who benefited from 17 wides – Snape's five wickets, his best one-day figures, ensured that Leicestershire tailed off sharply. The teams tied on points in the group, however, and both advanced to the knockout.

Gold Award: J. N. Snape.

Northamptonshire

D. J. Capel c Maddy b Johnson	26	J. E. Emburey c Millns b Johnson	13
M. B. Loye c Nixon b Millns	47	Mohammad Akram not out	0
*R. J. Bailey c Parsons b Brimson	29		
K. M. Curran c and b Parsons	0	B 7, l-b 13, w 17, n-b 2	39
A. L. Penberthy c Maddy b Mullally	38		
T. C. Walton not out	35	1/73 2/106 3/107 (8 wkts, 50 overs)	238
J. N. Snape run out	2	4/152 5/178 6/186	
†D. Ripley st Nixon b Brimson	9	7/201 8/233	

J. P. Taylor did not bat.

Bowling: Mullally 10–2–27–1; Millns 10–1–44–1; Johnson 10–0–51–2; Parsons 10–0–39–1; Brimson 9–0–49–2; Maddy 1–0–8–0.

Leicestershire

D. L. Maddy c Bailey b Emburey	42	D. J. Millns not out	3
G. I. Macmillan c Ripley b Capel	12	A. D. Mullally not out	0
A. Habib c Emburey b Snape	25		
N. C. Johnson c Walton b Snape	58	L-b 10, w 9, n-b 2	21
B. F. Smith c and b Snape	11		
†P. A. Nixon c and b Snape	10	1/66 2/68 3/127 (8 wkts, 50 overs)	186
*J. J. Whitaker c Curran b Snape	0	4/150 5/172 6/178	
G. J. Parsons c Ripley b Bailey	4	7/178 8/185	

M. T. Brimson did not bat.

Bowling: Mohammad Akram 8–1–34–0; Taylor 9–1–17–0; Capel 6–0–19–1; Emburey 10–1–32–1; Snape 10–1–32–5; Curran 6–0–41–0; Bailey 1–0–1–1.

Umpires: J. C. Balderstone and D. R. Shepherd.

SCOTLAND v NOTTINGHAMSHIRE

At Raeburn Place, Edinburgh, May 12, 13. No result (abandoned).

The match was originally scheduled to take place at Titwood in Glasgow; it was moved to Edinburgh in an attempt to escape the rain, but the fixture proved to be doomed. By the second day, neither side could qualify anyway.

GROUP C

The British Universities' squad for the competition was: A. Singh (Cambridge) (*captain*), T. M. B. Bailey (Loughborough), S. A. J. Boswell (Wolverhampton), M. J. Chilton (Durham), M. K. Davies (Loughborough), A. D. Edwards (Loughborough), J. A. Ford (Durham), T. P. Hodgson (Durham), W. J. House (Cambridge), P. S. Jones (Cambridge), R. S. C. Martin-Jenkins (Durham), U. B. A. Rashid (South Bank), E. T. Smith (Cambridge), A. J. Strauss (Durham), M. A. Wagh (Oxford).

GLOUCESTERSHIRE v BRITISH UNIVERSITIES

At Bristol, April 28. Gloucestershire won by 122 runs. Toss: British Universities.

Mike Smith and Ball took seven wickets between them as the students' batting failed to match a disciplined bowling performance. All eyes were on Russell, whose imminent autobiography was going under the microscope at the ECB, but his four catches and 28 not out from 15 balls were not enough to steal the Gold Award from his county's Tasmanian all-rounder Young, who shared a stand of 62 with Alleyne.

Gold Award: S. Young.

Gloucestershire

N. J. Trainor b Martin-Jenkins	62	†R. C. Russell not out	28
M. A. Lynch c Smith b Jones	15	T. H. C. Hancock not out	24
A. J. Wright c Bailey b Martin-Jenkins	27	B 3, l-b 5, w 5, n-b 4	17
S. Young c Ford b Martin-Jenkins	52		
R. J. Cunliffe b Rashid	24	1/40 2/103 3/124 (6 wkts, 50 overs)	281
*M. W. Alleyne b Martin-Jenkins	32	4/167 5/229 6/230	

M. C. J. Ball, A. M. Smith and R. P. Davis did not bat.

Bowling: Martin-Jenkins 10–0–57–4; Jones 10–0–57–1; Boswell 10–1–62–0; Rashid 10–0–45–1; Chilton 5–0–25–0; Ford 5–0–27–0.

British Universities

T. P. Hodgson c Alleyne b Ball	23	R. S. C. Martin-Jenkins run out	10
E. T. Smith c Russell b Hancock	0	P. S. Jones not out	5
*A. Singh c Russell b Smith	0	S. A. J. Boswell c Russell b Hancock	3
M. J. Chilton c Cunliffe b Ball	13	B 5, l-b 4, w 3, n-b 2	14
W. J. House lbw b Ball	1		
J. A. Ford b Ball	7	1/3 2/8 3/38 (49.1 overs)	159
†T. M. B. Bailey c Russell b Smith	52	4/43 5/44 6/63	
U. B. A. Rashid c Trainor b Smith	31	7/117 8/141 9/154	

Bowling: Hancock 9.1–2–34–2; Smith 10.2–2–24–3; Young 4–0–8–0; Ball 10–3–23–4; Davis 10–2–35–0; Trainor 6–0–26–0.

Umpires: D. J. Constant and J. F. Steele.

SURREY v KENT

At The Oval, April 28. Kent won by four wickets. Toss: Kent.

Kent needed just one run to win when Ealham lifted the last ball of the match, from Ben Holioake, for six over mid-wicket. Surrey had threatened to score many more than 257 when they were 108 for one in the 13th over, but the tactic of using Salisbury as a pinch-hitter was unsuccessful, and Thorpe and Adam Holioake were left to rescue the innings when they came together at 135 for six. Fleming took the last two wickets to finish with five, his best one-day return.

Gold Award: M. V. Fleming.

Surrey

A. D. Brown c Ealham b Fleming	26	C. C. Lewis c Ward b Fleming		33
†A. J. Stewart run out	51	M. P. Bicknell c Marsh b Fleming		13
B. C. Hollioake b Fleming	30	J. E. Benjamin not out		0
I. D. K. Salisbury st Marsh b Strang	14	B 1, l-b 8, w 2, n-b 6		17
G. P. Thorpe c Wells b Ealham	47			
M. A. Butcher c Strang b Fleming	1	1/68 2/108 3/126	(49.5 overs)	257
N. Shahid b Strang	3	4/126 5/128 6/135		
*A. J. Hollioake c Marsh b Headley	22	7/191 8/222 9/257		

Bowling: McCague 10–0–61–0; Headley 10–1–47–1; Ealham 10–0–59–1; Fleming 9.5–1–54–5; Strang 10–2–27–2.

Kent

M. V. Fleming c Stewart b Lewis	19	N. J. Llong b A. J. Hollioake		6
M. J. Walker c and b Salisbury	56	P. A. Strang not out		3
T. R. Ward lbw b Benjamin	42			
A. P. Wells c Stewart b Benjamin	40	L-b 10, w 4, n-b 16		30
G. R. Cowdrey c A. J. Hollioake b Benjamin	47	1/44 2/134 3/136	(6 wkts, 50 overs)	262
M. A. Ealham not out	19	4/232 5/241 6/250		

*†S. A. Marsh, M. J. McCague and D. W. Headley did not bat.

Bowling: Bicknell 7–1–55–0; Lewis 5–0–31–1; B. C. Hollioake 9–0–50–0; A. J. Hollioake 9–0–37–1; Salisbury 10–1–31–1; Benjamin 10–0–48–3.

Umpires: J. D. Bond and V. A. Holder.

SUSSEX v HAMPSHIRE

At Hove, April 28. Sussex won by 49 runs. Toss: Hampshire.

Three Yorkshire exiles masterminded a comprehensive victory for unfancied Sussex. Athey was their top scorer with 66, receiving sterling support from Jarvis, who helped him add 87 for the seventh wicket in 11 overs. Then Jarvis shot out Laney and Smith and new recruit Mark Robinson compounded the pressure by conceding only 19 runs from his ten overs. Stephenson's 65 was no more than a face-saving exercise.

Gold Award: P. W. Jarvis.

Sussex

K. Greenfield lbw b Udal	39	P. W. Jarvis not out		42
V. C. Drakes c Aymes b Connor	12	N. C. Phillips not out		0
N. R. Taylor b Stephenson	22	B 2, l-b 14, w 9, n-b 4		29
N. J. Lenham b Stephenson	0			
C. W. J. Athey run out	66	1/22 2/60 3/60	(7 wkts, 50 overs)	232
K. Newell lbw b Udal	6	4/99 5/117		
*†P. Moores run out	16	6/144 7/231		

A. A. Khan and M. A. Robinson did not bat.

Bowling: Connor 10–0–61–1; Renshaw 10–0–47–0; James 10–0–46–0; Stephenson 10–1–34–2; Udal 10–1–28–2.

Hampshire

J. S. Laney b Jarvis	13
M. L. Hayden c Robinson b Phillips	44
R. A. Smith c Moores b Jarvis	2
M. Keech c Taylor b Robinson	11
S. D. Udal run out	0
W. S. Kendall b Khan	2
*J. P. Stephenson run out	65
†A. N. Aymes b Khan	15
K. D. James lbw b Khan	10
C. A. Connor b Jarvis	2
S. J. Renshaw not out	2
B 1, l-b 8, w 6, n-b 2	17

1/14 2/22 3/52   (47.3 overs) 183
4/53 5/59 6/119
7/159 8/173 9/179

Bowling: Jarvis 9–3–30–3; Drakes 8.3–0–31–0; Robinson 10–1–19–1; Khan 10–1–31–3; Newell 3–0–22–0; Phillips 7–0–41–1.

Umpires: A. Clarkson and K. E. Palmer.

BRITISH UNIVERSITIES v SUSSEX

At Cambridge, April 30. British Universities won by 19 runs. Toss: British Universities.

Sussex's thin batting line-up disintegrated to give the Universities their first win in the competition since 1990, and their fourth since they began to recruit from outside Oxford and Cambridge in 1987. Durham University medium-pacer Mark Chilton took five for 26 but it was Steffan Jones of Cambridge who was singled out for special praise by his coach, Derek Randall. Jones conceded just 22 in his ten overs. The students' modest total of 217 for six was built around contributions from most of the top order, but few observers expected them to defend it so stoutly. Athey passed 2,500 runs in the Benson and Hedges Cup.

Gold Award: M. J. Chilton.

British Universities

T. P. Hodgson c Newell b Robinson	41
E. T. Smith b Drakes	43
*A. Singh c Moores b Jarvis	14
M. J. Chilton b Drakes	34
W. J. House c Taylor b Newell	24
U. B. A. Rashid c Lenham b Drakes	35
M. A. Wagh not out	7
B 7, l-b 5, w 3, n-b 4	19

1/87 2/102 3/108   (6 wkts, 50 overs) 217
4/162 5/178 6/217

†T. M. B. Bailey, S. A. J. Boswell, R. S. C. Martin-Jenkins and P. S. Jones did not bat.

Bowling: Jarvis 10–1–41–1; Drakes 10–1–46–3; Khan 9–0–39–0; Robinson 10–0–24–1; Phillips 4–0–20–0; Newell 7–0–35–1.

Sussex

K. Greenfield b Jones	37
V. C. Drakes c Jones b Rashid	58
N. R. Taylor c Smith b Wagh	15
N. J. Lenham run out	6
C. W. J. Athey c Bailey b Chilton	12
K. Newell lbw b Chilton	34
*†P. Moores c Rashid b Chilton	12
P. W. Jarvis c Smith b Chilton	6
N. C. Phillips b Martin-Jenkins	0
A. A. Khan c Rashid b Chilton	5
M. A. Robinson not out	0
B 1, l-b 2, w 2, n-b 8	13

1/87 2/110 3/124   (48.3 overs) 198
4/126 5/167 6/176
7/186 8/192 9/198

Bowling: Boswell 6–1–29–0; Martin-Jenkins 9–0–46–1; Rashid 8–0–33–1; Jones 10–4–22–1; Wagh 9–0–39–1; Chilton 6.3–0–26–5.

Umpires: J. C. Balderstone and J. D. Bond.

GLOUCESTERSHIRE v SURREY

At Bristol, April 30. Surrey won by three wickets. Toss: Gloucestershire.

A brace of injuries – one to Stewart's left little finger, the other to Butcher's groin – were not enough to check Surrey's progress. Cunliffe's second Benson and Hedges century in successive seasons against Surrey formed the basis of a solid Gloucestershire total and a county record third-wicket stand of 169 with Young, but rumbustious innings from Brown and both Hollioakes took Surrey to victory with four balls to spare. The pavilion was evacuated and fire engines arrived after the alarm system went off twice; there was a fault rather than a fire.

Gold Award: R. J. Cunliffe.

Gloucestershire

N. J. Trainor c Stewart b Bicknell	10	R. I. Dawson run out		11
M. A. Lynch lbw b Lewis	1			
R. J. Cunliffe run out	113	B 15, l-b 10, w 10, n-b 2		37
S. Young b B. C. Hollioake	67			
†R. C. Russell c Lewis b A. J. Hollioake	23	1/5 2/27 3/196	(7 wkts, 50 overs)	280
*M. W. Alleyne not out	6	4/239 5/242		
T. H. C. Hancock b A. J. Hollioake	12	6/265 7/280		

M. C. J. Ball, A. M. Smith and J. Lewis did not bat.

Bowling: Bicknell 10–0–41–1; Lewis 10–1–54–1; Benjamin 8–0–32–0; Salisbury 10–0–44–0; A. J. Hollioake 7–0–52–2; B. C. Hollioake 5–0–32–1.

Surrey

A. D. Brown b Ball	66	M. A. Butcher c sub b Young		14
†A. J. Stewart c Alleyne b Lewis	7	I. D. K. Salisbury not out		4
B. C. Hollioake st Russell b Alleyne	69	B 4, l-b 6, w 6, n-b 2		18
G. P. Thorpe b Alleyne	2			
N. Shahid b Young	24	1/48 2/119 3/130	(7 wkts, 49.2 overs)	282
*A. J. Hollioake run out	43	4/155 5/198		
C. C. Lewis not out	35	6/241 7/278		

M. P. Bicknell and J. E. Benjamin did not bat.

Bowling: Lewis 9–0–74–1; Smith 10–1–50–0; Young 9.2–0–54–2; Alleyne 10–1–39–2; Ball 9–1–46–1; Hancock 2–0–9–0.

Umpires: D. J. Constant and P. Willey.

KENT v HAMPSHIRE

At Canterbury, April 30. Kent won by two wickets. Toss: Hampshire.

Fleming took five wickets, improved on his best limited-overs analysis and collected the Gold Award, all for the second time in three days, as Hampshire failed to set a worthy target. But Kent were wobbling at 116 for five before a sixth-wicket stand of 72 between Walker and Llong re-established their supremacy. Strang hit the winning runs with 26 balls to spare.

Gold Award: M. V. Fleming.

Hampshire

M. L. Hayden lbw b Strang	48	S. D. Udal b McCague		6
J. S. Laney b McCague	17	S. M. Milburn c Ealham b Fleming		1
R. A. Smith lbw b Fleming	20	S. J. Renshaw run out		0
*J. P. Stephenson b Fleming	1	B 1, l-b 5, w 7, n-b 15		28
W. S. Kendall c Llong b Fleming	26			
P. R. Whitaker b Fleming	28	1/43 2/80 3/84	(49.5 overs)	207
†A. N. Aymes c and b Ealham	19	4/124 5/140 6/185		
K. D. James not out	13	7/185 8/195 9/206		

Bowling: McCague 8–1–35–2; Headley 10–0–62–0; Strang 10–3–22–1; Llong 2–0–16–0; Fleming 9.5–1–27–5; Ealham 10–0–39–1.

Kent

M. V. Fleming c Laney b Renshaw	13	*†S. A. Marsh c Hayden b James	1
M. J. Walker b Renshaw	83	M. J. McCague not out	5
T. R. Ward b Renshaw	13		
A. P. Wells st Aymes b Stephenson	11	B 1, l-b 2, w 7	10
G. R. Cowdrey b Udal	5		
M. A. Ealham c Udal b Stephenson	0	1/13 2/74 3/104 (8 wkts, 45.4 overs) 211	
N. J. Llong b Milburn	55	4/111 5/116 6/188	
P. A. Strang not out	15	7/192 8/195	

D. W. Headley did not bat.

Bowling: Milburn 5.4–1–32–1; Renshaw 10–3–34–3; James 7–1–48–1; Stephenson 10–0–40–2; Udal 10–0–37–1; Whitaker 3–0–17–0.

Umpires: M. J. Kitchen and A. G. T. Whitehead.

HAMPSHIRE v GLOUCESTERSHIRE

At Southampton, May 2. Gloucestershire won by two runs. Toss: Gloucestershire.

Smith's valiant 92 from 104 balls was nearly enough to bring Hampshire their first win, but it was Lynch's even more dynamic 87 which proved the decisive innings. Lynch took just 80 balls and hit three sixes and seven fours.

Gold Award: M. A. Lynch.

Gloucestershire

N. J. Trainor st Aymes b Udal	26	M. C. J. Ball c and b Stephenson	28
M. A. Lynch c Keech b Maru	87	A. M. Smith not out	3
S. Young c Aymes b Maru	18		
†R. C. Russell c Hayden b Stephenson	26	L-b 8, w 10	18
*M. W. Alleyne c Aymes b Renshaw	17		
T. H. C. Hancock c Hayden b Renshaw	22	1/70 2/126 3/154 (9 wkts, 50 overs) 263	
R. J. Cunliffe run out	15	4/179 5/199 6/215	
R. I. Dawson lbw b Udal	3	7/228 8/232 9/263	

R. P. Davis did not bat.

Bowling: Mascarenhas 10–1–52–0; Renshaw 10–1–42–2; Maru 10–0–51–2; Udal 10–1–31–2; Stephenson 10–0–79–2.

Hampshire

J. S. Laney b Smith	4	A. D. Mascarenhas c Ball b Young	20
M. L. Hayden lbw b Young	0	S. J. Renshaw c Davis b Young	0
S. D. Udal b Ball	34	R. J. Maru not out	9
R. A. Smith c Ball b Alleyne	92	L-b 7, w 5, n-b 5	17
M. Keech c Lynch b Smith	32		
W. S. Kendall c and b Davis	19	1/6 2/6 3/86 (9 wkts, 50 overs) 261	
*J. P. Stephenson c Davis b Young	12	4/149 5/193 6/199	
†A. N. Aymes not out	22	7/214 8/245 9/247	

Bowling: Smith 10–2–35–2; Young 10–1–54–4; Alleyne 9–0–67–1; Ball 10–0–40–1; Hancock 1–0–10–0; Davis 10–0–48–1.

Umpires: R. Palmer and P. Willey.

KENT v SUSSEX

At Canterbury, May 2. Kent won by six wickets. Toss: Sussex.

Headley and Strang showed their international class for Kent with spells of 10–5–14–2 and 8.3–3–27–4 respectively. Only Jarvis resisted, scoring 63 in 61 balls, his first limited-overs fifty in his 17th season. Then Walker led Kent's reply confidently with his fourth fifty in as many innings, all within six days.

Gold Award: D. W. Headley.

Sussex

K. Greenfield c Wells b McCague	0	N. C. Phillips c Ward b Ealham	11
V. C. Drakes b Headley	5	A. A. Khan lbw b Ealham	8
N. R. Taylor lbw b Strang	30	M. A. Robinson not out	0
N. J. Lenham c Marsh b Headley	0	B 1, l-b 5, w 2	8
C. W. J. Athey c Marsh b Fleming	23		
K. Newell c Ealham b Strang	5	1/0 2/12 3/18	(47.3 overs) 153
*†P. Moores c Ward b Strang	0	4/57 5/60 6/60	
P. W. Jarvis c Headley b Strang	63	7/82 8/105 9/144	

Bowling: McCague 10–2–39–1; Headley 10–5–14–2; Fleming 10–1–36–1; Strang 8.3–3–27–4; Ealham 9–0–31–2.

Kent

M. V. Fleming b Jarvis	14	M. A. Ealham not out	0
M. J. Walker not out	69	L-b 3, w 7, n-b 10	20
T. R. Ward b Khan	20		
A. P. Wells c Phillips b Jarvis	16	1/23 2/94	(4 wkts, 37.1 overs) 154
G. R. Cowdrey st Moores b Phillips	15	3/120 4/152	

N. J. Llong, P. A. Strang, *†S. A. Marsh, M. J. McCague and D. W. Headley did not bat.

Bowling: Jarvis 10–1–42–2; Drakes 6–1–24–0; Robinson 7–0–42–0; Khan 10–1–36–1; Phillips 3.1–1–6–1; Newell 1–0–1–0.

Umpires: J. H. Harris and J. W. Holder.

SURREY v BRITISH UNIVERSITIES

At The Oval, May 2. Surrey won by six wickets. Toss: British Universities.

This match achieved unexpected publicity when John Major, resigning as Prime Minister after losing the previous day's general election, announced that he was going straight to The Oval. At least his cricket team did not let him down. He had lunch and watched for a while as Surrey cantered to victory. Only 93 by House kept the contest going at all. His partnership with Ford – both players were on Kent's books – realised 88 of the Universities' 198 runs, in 15 overs. Surrey's opening batsmen, Brown and Stewart, who passed 2,000 runs in the competition, hastened the end by reaching 98 in 11 overs.

Gold Award: W. J. House.

British Universities

T. P. Hodgson c Knott b Lewis	0	U. B. A. Rashid b A. J. Hollioake	0
E. T. Smith c Lewis b Bicknell	10	P. S. Jones c Brown b A. J. Hollioake	12
M. J. Chilton c Thorpe b B. C. Hollioake	8	M. K. Davies not out	1
*A. Singh c Knott b Benjamin	8		
W. J. House c Stewart b B. C. Hollioake	93	B 1, l-b 10, w 6	17
J. A. Ford c Thorpe b Bicknell	38		
†T. M. B. Bailey c Knott b Lewis	1	1/1 2/14 3/30	(49.5 overs) 198
R. S. C. Martin-Jenkins c Brown		4/30 5/118 6/123	
b A. J. Hollioake	10	7/185 8/185 9/188	

Bowling: Bicknell 10–4–27–2; Lewis 8–5–6–2; Benjamin 10–2–25–1; B. C. Hollioake 10–1–51–2; Salisbury 5–0–38–0; A. J. Hollioake 6.5–0–40–3.

Surrey

A. D. Brown c Ford b Chilton	47	N. Shahid not out	20
A. J. Stewart not out	86	B 2, l-b 1, w 2, n-b 4	9
B. C. Hollioake st Bailey b Chilton	8		
G. P. Thorpe b Davies	28	1/98 2/108	(4 wkts, 25.2 overs) 199
*A. J. Hollioake st Bailey b Rashid	1	3/163 4/164	

C. C. Lewis, I. D. K. Salisbury, †J. A. Knott, M. P. Bicknell and J. E. Benjamin did not bat.

Bowling: Rashid 7–0–53–1; Martin-Jenkins 4–0–37–0; Jones 3–0–29–0; Davies 8.2–1–69–1; Chilton 3–0–8–2.

Umpires: D. R. Shepherd and A. G. T. Whitehead.

HAMPSHIRE v SURREY

At Southampton, May 5. Surrey won by 165 runs. Toss: Surrey.

Adam Hollioake made 80 and shared a crucial partnership of 138 with Shahid after Surrey had reached a nadir of 22 for four. But Hampshire's start was worse: they were 19 for four, and there was to be no recovery as Benjamin cleaned up the middle and late order. Hampshire's final total of 63 was not quite their lowest ever – they made just 50 at Headingley in 1991. Their brightest moments came from Renshaw, whose return of six for 25 was the best by any Hampshire bowler in this competition.

Gold Award: A. J. Hollioake.

Surrey

A. D. Brown c Whitaker b Renshaw	0	I. D. K. Salisbury c Udal b Renshaw	8
A. J. Stewart b Maru	6	M. P. Bicknell not out	10
B. C. Hollioake c Udal b Renshaw	12	J. E. Benjamin not out	5
G. P. Thorpe c Aymes b Renshaw	3	L-b 17, w 3	20
N. Shahid run out	52		
*A. J. Hollioake c Stephenson b Renshaw	80	1/0 2/18 3/22 (9 wkts, 50 overs)	228
C. C. Lewis c and b Renshaw	22	4/22 5/160 6/175	
†J. A. Knott c Maru b Udal	10	7/201 8/206 9/215	

Bowling: Renshaw 10–2–25–6; Maru 10–1–28–1; Mascarenhas 7–0–40–0; Udal 10–0–48–1; Stephenson 9–0–52–0; Whitaker 4–0–18–0.

Hampshire

J. S. Laney c Salisbury b Bicknell	5	A. D. Mascarenhas c B. C. Hollioake b Benjamin	1
M. L. Hayden c Knott b Bicknell	4	R. J. Maru not out	10
S. D. Udal b Bicknell	0	S. J. Renshaw c Brown b B. C. Hollioake	1
R. A. Smith c Salisbury b Lewis	7	B 1, n-b 2	3
M. Keech b B. C. Hollioake	20		
P. R. Whitaker c Knott b Benjamin	0	1/9 2/9 3/11 4/19 5/23 (30.3 overs)	63
*J. P. Stephenson c Knott b Benjamin	11	6/45 7/48 8/51 9/54	
†A. N. Aymes c Lewis b Benjamin	1		

Bowling: Bicknell 10–2–20–3; Lewis 5–2–8–1; Benjamin 10–1–19–4; B. C. Hollioake 5.3–0–15–2.

Umpires: J. D. Bond and B. Dudleston.

KENT v BRITISH UNIVERSITIES

At Canterbury, May 5. Kent won by four wickets. Toss: Kent.

A stand of 122 between Ealham and Llong, who hit 75 in 65 balls, rescued Kent from the depths of 99 for five and possible defeat at the hands of the students. Instead, they made sure of a place in the quarter-finals. Solid batting had set a target of 224, which looked defensible during accurate early spells from Boswell and Jones.

Gold Award: N. J. Llong.

British Universities

T. P. Hodgson c Marsh b McCague	60	U. B. A. Rashid c Cowdrey b McCague	2
E. T. Smith c Llong b Headley	8	P. S. Jones not out	9
M. J. Chilton c Fleming b McCague	43		
*A. Singh not out	53	L-b 8, w 3, n-b 8	19
W. J. House c Wells b McCague	0		
J. A. Ford lbw b Headley	12	1/24 2/110 3/128 (8 wkts, 50 overs) 223	
†T. M. B. Bailey b Ealham	8	4/128 5/154 6/173	
A. D. Edwards c and b Ealham	9	7/199 8/204	

S. A. J. Boswell did not bat.

Bowling: McCague 10–1–41–4; Headley 10–1–30–2; Fleming 5–0–23–0; Ealham 10–0–50–2; Strang 10–1–43–0; Llong 5–0–28–0.

Kent

M. V. Fleming b Boswell	63	N. J. Llong c Jones b Boswell	75
M. J. Walker run out	0	P. A. Strang not out	4
T. R. Ward c Bailey b Boswell	8	L-b 5, w 4, n-b 2	11
A. P. Wells c Hodgson b Jones	14		
G. R. Cowdrey b Rashid	9	1/3 2/72 3/76 (6 wkts, 45 overs) 225	
M. A. Ealham not out	41	4/95 5/99 6/221	

*†S. A. Marsh, M. J. McCague and D. W. Headley did not bat.

Bowling: Boswell 9–1–39–3; Edwards 10–1–53–0; Jones 10–2–29–1; Chilton 5–0–35–0; Rashid 8–0–50–1; House 3–0–14–0.

Umpires: J. H. Harris and N. T. Plews.

SUSSEX v GLOUCESTERSHIRE

At Hove, May 5. Sussex won by 34 runs. Toss: Sussex.

Taylor, scoring his sixth tournament hundred, and Mark Newell, a late replacement for his flu-ridden brother Keith, rewrote Sussex's records with a partnership of 208 for the third wicket. The county's all-wicket best in the competition hitherto was 167 by Tony Greig and Peter Graves, against Cambridge, in 1974. Gloucestershire never really threatened.

Gold Award: N. R. Taylor.

Sussex

K. Greenfield c Alleyne b Smith	3	P. W. Jarvis not out	16
R. K. Rao b Young	15	B 4, l-b 5, w 4, n-b 2	15
N. R. Taylor run out	116		
M. Newell c Cunliffe b Smith	87	1/10 2/23 (4 wkts, 50 overs) 273	
*†P. Moores not out	21	3/231 4/236	

C. W. J. Athey, V. C. Drakes, N. C. Phillips, A. A. Khan and M. A. Robinson did not bat.

Bowling: Smith 10–2–39–2; Young 10–2–32–1; Hancock 6–0–23–0; Alleyne 10–0–76–0; Davis 10–0–59–0; Ball 4–0–35–0.

Gloucestershire

A. J. Wright c Moores b Robinson	41	M. C. J. Ball c Rao b Khan	9
M. A. Lynch run out	0	A. M. Smith c and b Khan	2
R. J. Cunliffe c Robinson b Khan	27	R. P. Davis not out	8
S. Young c Moores b Robinson	3	B 4, l-b 9, w 4, n-b 12	29
*M. W. Alleyne b Phillips	19		
†R. C. Russell c Moores b Drakes	66	1/8 2/61 3/73 (47.3 overs) 239	
T. H. C. Hancock b Phillips	11	4/87 5/116 6/135	
R. I. Dawson c Greenfield b Phillips	24	7/183 8/199 9/213	

Bowling: Jarvis 9–0–48–0; Drakes 6.3–0–45–1; Robinson 10–0–34–2; Khan 10–0–41–3; Phillips 10–0–48–3; Greenfield 2–0–10–0.

Umpires: H. D. Bird and M. J. Kitchen.

BRITISH UNIVERSITIES v HAMPSHIRE

At Oxford, May 12. Hampshire won by seven wickets. Toss: British Universities.

An ideal wicket for batting produced two fine centuries – one from Hodgson, a Durham University student affiliated to Essex, who put on 168 with Rashid, and one from Hayden, whose first hundred it was for Hampshire. It was the county's first win of the season. But the teams finished tied on points at the bottom of the group.

Gold Award: M. L. Hayden.

British Universities

T. P. Hodgson c Udal b Stephenson	113	†T. M. B. Bailey run out	13
A. J. Strauss lbw b Renshaw	1	A. D. Edwards not out	0
U. B. A. Rashid c Aymes b Hayden	82	L-b 15, w 8	23
*A. Singh lbw b Hayden	3		
W. J. House c James b Udal	37	1/6 2/174 3/191 (8 wkts, 50 overs) 284	
M. J. Chilton c Aymes b Stephenson	6	4/244 5/257 6/266	
J. A. Ford c Udal b Renshaw	6	7/272 8/284	

P. S. Jones and S. A. J. Boswell did not bat.

Bowling: Renshaw 9–0–54–2; Maru 10–1–35–0; Stephenson 10–0–47–2; James 3–0–18–0; Udal 8–0–55–1; Whitaker 1–0–15–0; Hayden 9–0–45–2.

Hampshire

G. W. White st Bailey b Jones	56	*J. P. Stephenson not out	35
M. L. Hayden not out	120	L-b 6, w 3, n-b 2	11
R. A. Smith c Hodgson b Chilton	45		
W. S. Kendall lbw b Jones	20	1/95 2/193 3/224 (3 wkts, 48.3 overs) 287	

P. R. Whitaker, †A. N. Aymes, K. D. James, S. D. Udal, R. J. Maru and S. J. Renshaw did not bat.

Bowling: Boswell 9.3–0–47–0; Edwards 10–0–56–0; Jones 10–1–51–2; Chilton 9–0–65–1; Rashid 10–0–62–0.

Umpires: J. H. Hampshire and J. W. Holder.

GLOUCESTERSHIRE v KENT

At Bristol, May 12, 13. No result. Toss: Kent.

Rain stopped play for good on the second day just as Lynch threatened to take another attack apart. For Kent, Cowdrey's experience showed through in a measured 77, his highest score in the competition.

Close of play: Gloucestershire 25-0 (4.2 overs) (M. A. Lynch 17*, A. J. Wright 4*).

Kent

T. R. Ward b Smith	2	*†S. A. Marsh b Young	27
M. V. Fleming c Alleyne b Young	4	M. J. McCague not out	7
A. P. Wells c Lynch b Alleyne	12	L-b 11, w 4	15
G. R. Cowdrey st Russell b Davis	77		
N. J. Llong run out	49	1/6 2/6 3/39 (7 wkts, 50 overs) 239	
M. A. Ealham b Davis	8	4/141 5/151	
P. A. Strang not out	38	6/168 7/228	

T. N. Wren and D. W. Headley did not bat.

Bowling: Smith 10–3–32–1; Young 9–0–48–2; Davis 10–1–48–2; Alleyne 6–0–24–1; Hancock 5–0–23–0; Ball 10–0–53–0.

Gloucestershire

M. A. Lynch not out	30
A. J. Wright b Fleming	8
R. J. Cunliffe not out	2
L-b 8, w 2	10

1/45   (1 wkt, 9 overs) 50

S. Young, *M. W. Alleyne, R. I. Dawson, †R. C. Russell, T. H. C. Hancock, M. C. J. Ball, A. M. Smith and R. P. Davis did not bat.

Bowling: McCague 3–0–12–0; Headley 2–0–10–0; Fleming 2–0–10–1; Ealham 2–0–10–0.

Umpires: B. Dudleston and G. Sharp.

SURREY v SUSSEX

At The Oval, May 12. Surrey won by 11 runs. Toss: Sussex. County debut: M. J. Thursfield.

Salisbury wrecked his old county's hopes of a surprise win by taking four in six balls in the 46th and 48th overs. Although Jarvis then hit 15 off four balls of the penultimate over, bowled by Ben Hollioake, Robinson was promptly run out to give Surrey their win and a place in the last eight. Their innings was based on two century stands – 101 in 17 overs between Brown and Stewart, and 112 between Thorpe and Butcher. But Sussex's top order had scored equally freely and were 268 for three before Salisbury struck.

Gold Award: I. D. K. Salisbury.

Surrey

A. D. Brown c Taylor b Thursfield	40		N. Shahid not out	20
†A. J. Stewart c Phillips b Thursfield	72		M. P. Bicknell not out	2
G. P. Thorpe c Thursfield b Greenfield	78			
M. A. Butcher c Moores b Jarvis	48		B 1, l-b 13, w 9	23
*A. J. Hollioake lbw b Jarvis	8			
B. C. Hollioake c Moores b Jarvis	16		1/101 2/135 3/247 (8 wkts, 50 overs) 310	
J. D. Ratcliffe c and b Khan	0		4/260 5/267 6/270	
I. D. K. Salisbury lbw b Jarvis	3		7/273 8/300	

J. E. Benjamin did not bat.

Bowling: Jarvis 10–1–60–4; Khan 10–0–70–1; Robinson 9–0–54–0; Thursfield 8–0–49–2; Phillips 10–0–46–0; Greenfield 3–0–17–1.

Sussex

K. Greenfield run out	44		A. A. Khan lbw b Salisbury	2
R. K. Rao b Ratcliffe	61		M. J. Thursfield run out	2
N. R. Taylor c Butcher b Ratcliffe	67		M. A. Robinson run out	0
M. Newell b Salisbury	60		L-b 10, w 3, n-b 8	21
C. W. J. Athey b Salisbury	20			
*†P. Moores b Benjamin	5		1/93 2/151 3/206 (48.5 overs) 299	
P. W. Jarvis not out	17		4/268 5/275 6/277	
N. C. Phillips b Salisbury	0		7/277 8/279 9/283	

Bowling: Bicknell 10–0–59–0; Benjamin 10–0–60–1; B. C. Hollioake 4.5–0–43–0; A. J. Hollioake 6–0–32–0; Salisbury 10–0–53–4; Ratcliffe 8–0–42–2.

Umpires: G. I. Burgess and K. E. Palmer.

GROUP D

ESSEX v GLAMORGAN

At Chelmsford, April 28. Essex won by five wickets. Toss: Essex.

Irani continued in his early-season vein of form, masterminding Essex's run-chase with an unbeaten 82 from 97 balls. Morris and Maynard had built a firm platform for Glamorgan at 141 for two, but one fell to Such and the other to Irani (who picked up three for 42) as the last eight went down for 69. Hussain did not bat after ricking his neck badly in the field.

Gold Award: R. C. Irani.

Glamorgan

S. P. James c Rollins b Ilott	15	S. D. Thomas not out	13
H. Morris c S. G. Law b Such	67	S. L. Watkin c Rollins b Ilott	1
A. Dale c Grayson b Irani	17	O. T. Parkin st Rollins b Grayson	7
*M. P. Maynard c Hussain b Irani	44	L-b 3, w 4	7
P. A. Cottey c Prichard b Grayson	9		
G. P. Butcher c Rollins b Irani	4	1/22 2/68 3/141 (49.3 overs) 210	
†A. D. Shaw c Grayson b Ilott	15	4/146 5/155 6/161	
R. D. B. Croft b Rollins b Grayson	11	7/180 8/195 9/196	

Bowling: Ilott 10–1–38–3; Cowan 10–1–55–0; Irani 10–0–42–3; Such 10–1–33–1; Grayson 9.3–0–39–3.

Essex

G. A. Gooch c James b Parkin	16	†R. J. Rollins not out	18
*P. J. Prichard c Shaw b Thomas	28		
S. G. Law c Shaw b Thomas	20	L-b 4, w 1, n-b 2	7
R. C. Irani not out	82		
A. P. Grayson c Maynard b Dale	12	1/29 2/62 3/71 (5 wkts, 43.1 overs) 211	
D. R. Law c Shaw b Watkin	28	4/95 5/157	

N. Hussain, M. C. Ilott, A. P. Cowan and P. M. Such did not bat.

Bowling: Watkin 10–2–27–1; Parkin 5–0–31–1; Dale 8–0–37–1; Thomas 6–0–60–2; Croft 10–0–33–0; Butcher 3.1–0–13–0; Maynard 1–0–6–0.

Umpires: B. Dudleston and A. G. T. Whitehead.

IRELAND v MIDDLESEX

At Castle Avenue, Dublin, April 28, 29. Ireland won by 46 runs. Toss: Middlesex. First-team debut: S. J. Cook.

Ireland claimed their first win over a first-class county and their biggest scalp since they famously beat the 1969 West Indian tourists. It provided some consolation for their failure to qualify for the World Cup. Their South African pro, Hansie Cronje, played a crucial role, scoring 94 not out and claiming three wickets, including Ramprakash, Middlesex's top scorer, but it was the Londonderry abattoir worker, "Decker" Curry, who took the Gold Award for his innings of 75. The input of Ireland's coach, Mike Hendrick, was reflected in some fine outfielding, especially Gillespie's 30-yard dash and dive to catch Brown.

Gold Award: J. D. Curry.

Close of play: Middlesex 134-6 (32.2 overs) (K. R. Brown 2*).

Ireland

J. D. Curry b Weekes	75	†A. D. Patterson not out	24
W. K. McCallan c Brown b Fraser	17	L-b 10, w 3, n-b 4	17
D. A. Lewis b Tufnell	34		
W. J. Cronje not out	94	1/72 2/117 (4 wkts, 50 overs) 281	
*J. D. R. Benson b Hewitt	20	3/165 4/234	

A. R. Dunlop, D. Heasley, P. G. Gillespie, G. L. Molins and P. McCrum did not bat.

Bowling: Fraser 10–3–34–1; Cook 9–0–71–0; Hewitt 10–0–53–1; Weekes 10–0–47–1; Tufnell 6–0–37–1; Dutch 5–0–29–0.

Middlesex

P. N. Weekes c Gillespie b Heasley	24	A. R. C. Fraser not out	30
P. E. Wellings lbw b Cronje	23	P. C. R. Tufnell b Cronje	10
M. R. Ramprakash lbw b Cronje	34	S. J. Cook b Heasley	6
*M. W. Gatting c and b Benson	23	B 3, l-b 14, w 15	32
J. C. Pooley b Benson	11		
†K. R. Brown c Gillespie b Molins	27	1/46 2/69 3/104 (46.4 overs) 235	
K. P. Dutch st Patterson b Molins	1	4/126 5/133 6/134	
J. P. Hewitt c Curry b Benson	14	7/175 8/180 9/227	

Bowling: Gillespie 8–0–40–0; McCrum 6–0–21–0; Heasley 5.4–0–30–2; Cronje 8–0–38–3; Molins 10–0–44–2; Benson 9–0–45–3.

Umpires: J. W. Holder and A. A. Jones.

MIDDLESEX v ESSEX

At Lord's, April 30. Essex won by one wicket. Toss: Essex. First-team debut: I. N. Blanchett.

Cowan took two match-winning runs from the last ball when Middlesex debutant Ian Blanchett failed to field cleanly. Victory should have been a formality for Essex after Ilott, collecting three wickets, restricted their target to 227; their batsmen progressed to 194 for three with little fuss, but some ill-judged running between the wickets produced a tense finish.

Gold Award: M. C. Ilott.

Middlesex

S. P. Moffat lbw b Ilott	2	J. P. Hewitt b Ilott	2
P. N. Weekes c Prichard b Such	39	A. R. C. Fraser not out	1
K. P. Dutch c Prichard b Cowan	5		
M. R. Ramprakash lbw b Grayson	77	L-b 11, w 6	17
*M. W. Gatting lbw b Such	15		
J. C. Pooley not out	50	1/5 2/23 3/107 (8 wkts, 50 overs) 226	
†K. R. Brown b Ilott	13	4/135 5/154 6/187	
R. L. Johnson c Rollins b Cowan	5	7/194 8/211	

I. N. Blanchett did not bat.

Bowling: Ilott 10–2–28–3; Cowan 10–1–35–2; Irani 10–0–63–0; Such 10–0–34–2; Grayson 10–0–55–1.

Essex

G. A. Gooch c Brown b Blanchett	40	M. C. Ilott run out	4
*P. J. Prichard b Fraser	19	A. P. Cowan not out	2
S. G. Law lbw b Hewitt	53	P. M. Such not out	0
R. C. Irani c Ramprakash b Dutch	45	B 3, l-b 6, w 19, n-b 6	34
A. P. Grayson c Ramprakash b Johnson	9		
D. R. Law c Brown b Johnson	0	1/43 2/105 3/163 (9 wkts, 50 overs) 227	
D. D. J. Robinson c Gatting b Dutch	8	4/194 5/194 6/205	
†R. J. Rollins run out	13	7/210 8/222 9/225	

Bowling: Fraser 10–2–30–1; Hewitt 10–0–53–1; Blanchett 6–0–44–1; Johnson 10–0–50–2; Weekes 10–1–27–0; Dutch 4–0–14–2.

Umpires: A. Clarkson and J. H. Harris.

SOMERSET v GLAMORGAN

At Taunton, April 30. Somerset won by 141 runs. Toss: Glamorgan.

A rash of dropped catches allowed Somerset to achieve a reasonable total, based mainly on a stand of 133 between Lathwell and Harden. Then Glamorgan's batting was no more impressive than their fielding; Rose, Caddick and Burns, better known as a wicket-keeper but bowling medium-pace here, picked up three cheap wickets each.

Gold Award: M. N. Lathwell.

Somerset

G. D. Rose b Watkin	0	J. I. D. Kerr c Shaw b Dale	12	
M. Burns c James b Parkin	30	A. R. Caddick not out	8	
*P. D. Bowler c Shaw b Watkin	12	H. R. J. Trump not out	2	
S. C. Ecclestone lbw b Dale	16	B 1, l-b 7, w 14	22	
M. N. Lathwell c Watkin b Cosker	77			
R. J. Harden c Dale b Parkin	68	1/0 2/41 3/48	(9 wkts, 50 overs) 258	
†R. J. Turner b Croft	1	4/68 5/201 6/202		
K. A. Parsons lbw b Parkin	10	7/224 8/245 9/252		

Bowling: Watkin 10–1–38–2; Parkin 10–0–42–3; Dale 10–0–61–2; Butcher 4–0–20–0; Croft 10–0–51–1; Cosker 6–0–38–1.

Glamorgan

S. P. James c and b Caddick	3	D. A. Cosker lbw b Burns	0	
H. Morris b Rose	2	S. L. Watkin not out	10	
A. Dale c Trump b Kerr	37	O. T. Parkin c Harden b Rose	8	
*M. P. Maynard c Turner b Caddick	11	L-b 4, w 14	18	
P. A. Cottey c Turner b Caddick	0			
G. P. Butcher c Harden b Burns	17	1/5 2/5 3/37	(30.4 overs) 117	
†A. D. Shaw lbw b Rose	9	4/37 5/74 6/77		
R. D. B. Croft c Turner b Burns	2	7/84 8/84 9/96		

Bowling: Rose 9.4–2–31–3; Caddick 9–0–43–3; Burns 6–0–18–3; Kerr 6–0–21–1.

Umpires: J. H. Hampshire and R. Palmer.

GLAMORGAN v MIDDLESEX

At Cardiff, May 2. Glamorgan won by seven runs. Toss: Glamorgan. County debut: J. H. Kallis.

Middlesex's new overseas player, South African all-rounder Jacques Kallis, announced his presence with a powerful 72, but it was Dale who turned in the performance of the match, notching up his first century in the competition and collecting Middlesex's last three wickets in the space of six balls.

Gold Award: A. Dale.

Glamorgan

S. P. James c Brown b Fraser	7	†A. D. Shaw b Dutch	2	
H. Morris st Brown b Tufnell	76	S. D. Thomas not out	1	
A. Dale st Brown b Dutch	100	L-b 4, w 5, n-b 2	11	
*M. P. Maynard c Brown b Johnson	1			
P. A. Cottey c Ramprakash b Dutch	15	1/26 2/138 3/143	(7 wkts, 50 overs) 252	
R. D. B. Croft c Ramprakash b Dutch	33	4/181 5/238		
G. P. Butcher not out	6	6/249 7/251		

S. L. Watkin and O. T. Parkin did not bat.

Bowling: Fraser 7–1–27–1; Hewitt 5–0–23–0; Weekes 4–0–37–0; Kallis 8–1–30–0; Tufnell 10–0–35–1; Johnson 9–0–54–1; Dutch 7–0–42–4.

Middlesex

P. N. Weekes lbw b Watkin	18	R. L. Johnson b Dale	15
J. H. Kallis st Shaw b Croft	72	A. R. C. Fraser c Maynard b Dale	0
K. P. Dutch c Croft b Watkin	4	P. C. R. Tufnell c Maynard b Dale	2
M. R. Ramprakash lbw b Croft	44	L-b 13, w 6, n-b 4	23
*M. W. Gatting b Thomas	8		
J. C. Pooley run out	17	1/37 2/43 3/150 (49.2 overs) 245	
†K. R. Brown not out	42	4/151 5/175 6/186	
J. P. Hewitt lbw b Thomas	0	7/188 8/239 9/239	

Bowling: Watkin 10–0–43–2; Parkin 10–1–51–0; Thomas 10–0–47–2; Dale 6.2–0–30–3; Croft 10–0–38–2; Butcher 3–0–23–0.

Umpires: H. D. Bird and K. E. Palmer.

SOMERSET v IRELAND

At Taunton, May 2. Somerset won by 221 runs. Toss: Somerset.

Ireland's euphoric win over Middlesex was swiftly forgotten as Ecclestone took their bowling to task with 92 from 83 balls. A total of 349 was Somerset's highest in this competition. Then Mushtaq Ahmed weighed in with seven for 24, the third-best bowling return by any bowler in Benson and Hedges cricket, less than 24 hours after flying in from Sri Lanka. It added up to the third-biggest winning margin, though Somerset had done better, beating the same victims by 233 two years earlier.

Gold Award: Mushtaq Ahmed.

Somerset

G. D. Rose c Eagleson b Cronje	24	K. A. Parsons not out	22
M. Burns b Benson	50		
S. C. Ecclestone c Patterson b McCrum	92	B 2, l-b 8, w 16, n-b 6	32
M. N. Lathwell b Cronje	8		
R. J. Harden c Molins b McCrum	37	1/87 2/91 3/126 (7 wkts, 50 overs) 349	
*P. D. Bowler c Molins b Heasley	42	4/216 5/256	
†R. J. Turner lbw b Cooke	42	6/311 7/349	

J. I. D. Kerr, A. R. Caddick and Mushtaq Ahmed did not bat.

Bowling: Eagleson 7–0–50–0; Cooke 10–0–76–1; McCrum 9–0–58–2; Cronje 9–1–60–2; Benson 4–0–29–1; Heasley 8–0–43–1; Molins 3–0–23–0.

Ireland

W. K. McCallan b Caddick	0	G. L. Molins b Mushtaq Ahmed	0
†A. D. Patterson c Bowler b Mushtaq Ahmed	50	G. Cooke not out	12
		P. McCrum c Rose b Mushtaq Ahmed	5
D. A. Lewis c Lathwell b Rose	10		
W. J. Cronje lbw b Mushtaq Ahmed	1	L-b 6, w 9, n-b 6	21
*J. D. R. Benson b Mushtaq Ahmed	8		
A. R. Dunlop c Harden b Mushtaq Ahmed	0	1/6 2/40 3/51 (27.2 overs) 128	
D. Heasley b Mushtaq Ahmed	12	4/71 5/72 6/85	
R. L. Eagleson c Parsons b Caddick	9	7/99 8/107 9/109	

Bowling: Rose 6–0–39–1; Caddick 10–1–53–2; Mushtaq Ahmed 9.2–2–24–7; Kerr 2–0–6–0.

Umpires: J. H. Hampshire and J. F. Steele.

ESSEX v SOMERSET

At Chelmsford, May 5. Essex won by eight wickets. Toss: Somerset.

Somerset's total of 269 – set up by Burns, continuing his success as an experimental opener – looked imposing enough. But then Prichard and Law built a first-wicket stand of 204. They treated their visitors' international bowlers with little respect – Caddick went for 60 in ten overs and Mushtaq Ahmed withdrew from the attack, complaining of a knee niggle, after his three overs had cost 31.

Gold Award: P. R. Prichard.

Somerset

G. D. Rose c Rollins b Cowan 6	†R. J. Turner not out 26
M. Burns lbw b Grayson 91	A. R. Caddick not out 1
S. C. Ecclestone c Such b Ilott 5	
J. I. D. Kerr c S. G. Law b Irani 17	B 1, l-b 1, w 6, n-b 2 10
M. N. Lathwell c Hussain b Irani 17	
Mushtaq Ahmed c D. R. Law b Cowan .. 31	1/9 2/32 3/78 (8 wkts, 50 overs) 269
R. J. Harden c Cowan b Grayson 64	4/109 5/152 6/205
*P. D. Bowler c Hussain b Irani 1	7/208 8/261

H. R. J. Trump did not bat.

Bowling: Cowan 10–1–60–2; Ilott 9–0–56–1; Irani 10–2–48–3; Such 4–0–22–0; S. G. Law 8–0–43–0; Grayson 9–0–38–2.

Essex

*P. J. Prichard c Turner b Kerr 114	
S. G. Law c Lathwell b Caddick 88	
N. Hussain not out 32	
G. A. Gooch not out 14	
L-b 3, w 13, n-b 6 22	

1/204 2/234   (2 wkts, 42.4 overs) 270

R. C. Irani, A. P. Grayson, D. R. Law, †R. J. Rollins, M. C. Ilott, A. P. Cowan and P. M. Such did not bat.

Bowling: Rose 7–0–41–0; Caddick 10–0–60–1; Mushtaq Ahmed 3–0–31–0; Kerr 9–0–57–1; Trump 4–0–29–0; Burns 9.4–0–49–0.

Umpires: V. A. Holder and G. Sharp.

GLAMORGAN v IRELAND

At Cardiff, May 5, 6. Glamorgan won by six wickets. Toss: Ireland. County debut: Waqar Younis.

Cronje hit three sixes off Croft in an accomplished 85 but, in his role as pinch-hitter, Croft retaliated by lifting Cronje four sixes in an opening stand of 73 in nine overs. Glamorgan were worried less about the result than improving their run-rate enough to give themselves a chance of qualifying for the quarter-finals. They needed Middlesex to annihilate Somerset a week later, to let them in the back door, but form was against that.

Gold Award: W. J. Cronje.

Close of play: Ireland 74-3 (20.5 overs) (W. J. Cronje 30*, J. D. R. Benson 4*).

Ireland

G. Cooke lbw b Parkin 7	P. G. Gillespie lbw b Watkin 4
†A. D. Patterson c Parkin b Watkin 1	G. L. Molins c Maynard b Waqar Younis 10
D. A. Lewis lbw b Butcher 20	P. McCrum not out 1
W. J. Cronje c and b Dale 85	L-b 12, w 8 20
*J. D. R. Benson c and b Watkin 23	
A. R. Dunlop not out 31	1/2 2/16 3/70 (9 wkts, 50 overs) 202
D. Heasley lbw b Croft 0	4/134 5/161 6/162
D. M. P. Moore b Dale 0	7/163 8/172 9/194

Bowling: Waqar Younis 10–0–42–1; Watkin 10–1–26–3; Parkin 7–1–25–1; Butcher 4–0–20–1; Croft 10–0–50–1; Dale 9–1–27–2.

Glamorgan

R. D. B. Croft c Patterson b Cronje	43	S. P. James not out	5
H. Morris b McCrum	24	B 2, l-b 3, w 6, n-b 4	15
A. Dale c Patterson b Molins	45		
*M. P. Maynard c Heasley b Benson	50	1/73 2/73	(4 wkts, 30.3 overs) 203
P. A. Cottey not out	21	3/164 4/190	

G. P. Butcher, †A. D. Shaw, Waqar Younis, S. L. Watkin and O. T. Parkin did not bat.

Bowling: Gillespie 4–0–24–0; Cooke 2–0–25–0; Cronje 5–0–36–1; McCrum 7–0–35–1; Heasley 2–0–16–0; Molins 6–0–40–1; Benson 4.3–0–22–1.

Umpires: T. E. Jesty and K. E. Palmer.

IRELAND v ESSEX

At Downpatrick, May 12, 13. No result (abandoned).

MIDDLESEX v SOMERSET

At Lord's, May 12, 13. Somerset won by 27 runs. Toss: Middlesex.

Another impressive batting performance from Somerset condemned Middlesex to their first whitewash in the zonal games since 1974. Somerset were 172 for four when rain curtailed the first day's play, and Bowler and Harden helped them add 115 in 12 overs next morning. With Ramprakash sidelined by injury, Middlesex relied too heavily on Weekes, who holed out after a strident 77, and the inexperienced Moffat.

Gold Award: P. D. Bowler.

Close of play: Somerset 172-4 (38 overs) (P. D. Bowler 54*, R. J. Harden 17*).

Somerset

M. N. Lathwell c Weekes b Hewitt	0	†R. J. Turner not out	30
M. Burns c Moffat b Fraser	54	K. A. Parsons not out	0
S. C. Ecclestone b Hewitt	9	B 6, l-b 15, w 17, n-b 2	40
*P. D. Bowler c Hewitt b Kallis	79		
G. D. Rose c Gatting b Kallis	9	1/0 2/17 3/125	(6 wkts, 50 overs) 287
R. J. Harden c Weekes b Fay	66	4/145 5/246 6/269	

J. I. D. Kerr, S. Herzberg and A. R. Caddick did not bat.

Bowling: Hewitt 10–1–49–2; Fay 10–0–63–1; Fraser 10–1–23–1; Johnson 10–0–50–0; Kallis 7–0–49–2; Weekes 3–0–32–0.

Middlesex

P. N. Weekes c Rose b Burns	77	A. R. C. Fraser b Kerr	4
J. H. Kallis c Turner b Rose	10	J. P. Hewitt b Caddick	6
*M. W. Gatting c Turner b Kerr	16	R. A. Fay not out	3
J. C. Pooley lbw b Rose	4	L-b 13, w 17, n-b 2	32
†K. R. Brown lbw b Burns	9		
S. P. Moffat c Turner b Caddick	60	1/24 2/95 3/118	(48.1 overs) 260
K. P. Dutch c Ecclestone b Parsons	20	4/127 5/143 6/197	
R. L. Johnson c Bowler b Kerr	19	7/231 8/240 9/253	

Bowling: Caddick 9.1–1–25–2; Rose 10–0–66–2; Parsons 10–0–74–1; Kerr 10–1–34–3; Burns 6–0–28–2; Herzberg 3–0–20–0.

Umpires: D. J. Constant and A. G. T. Whitehead.

QUARTER-FINALS

ESSEX v SURREY

At Chelmsford, May 27. Surrey won by six wickets. Toss: Surrey.

Essex had not yet lost a match in 1997. But they never recovered from the shock of losing Prichard, Stuart Law and Gooch in 16 deliveries which left them floundering at 37 for three. Hussain, who twice pulled Bicknell for six, and Irani hinted at a substantial recovery, but it never materialised; Bicknell was swinging the ball dangerously and Grayson was left stranded on 49 in the 46th over. Surrey began uncertainly, losing two wickets in five overs, while Thorpe was dropped twice in single figures. He made good his escape by helping Brown, whose belligerent 71 came from 78 balls, put on 110. Thorpe departed ten short of victory, leaving Butcher and Shahid – who pulled a leg muscle before facing a ball – to take Surrey into the semi-finals with 7.3 overs to spare. This proved to be Gooch's last game in the competition before retiring, having made his debut in its second season, 1973; despite finishing with a duck, he remained way ahead of all other batsmen with 5,176 runs and 15 centuries. His 22 Gold Awards and 68 catches were also records.

Gold Award: M. P. Bicknell.

Essex

*P. J. Prichard c Stewart b Lewis	12	M. C. Ilott b A. J. Hollioake		0
S. G. Law c Stewart b Bicknell	20	A. P. Cowan c A. J. Hollioake b Lewis		8
N. Hussain c Stewart b Bicknell	52	P. M. Such run out		3
G. A. Gooch b Lewis	0			
R. C. Irani c Shahid b Benjamin	38	L-b 6, w 4		10
A. P. Grayson not out	49			
D. R. Law c Stewart b Bicknell	10	1/34 2/36 3/37	(45.5 overs)	214
†R. J. Rollins c Salisbury		4/108 5/141 6/164		
b A. J. Hollioake	12	7/190 8/190 9/207		

Bowling: Bicknell 10–0–40–3; Lewis 9–1–51–3; Salisbury 8.5–0–39–0; Benjamin 10–1–44–1; B. C. Hollioake 6–0–28–0; A. J. Hollioake 2–1–6–2.

Surrey

A. D. Brown b Grayson	71	N. Shahid not out		3
†A. J. Stewart c S. G. Law b Ilott	0	B 4, l-b 3, w 3		10
B. C. Hollioake lbw b Cowan	17			
G. P. Thorpe b Ilott	73	1/6 2/25	(4 wkts, 42.3 overs)	215
M. A. Butcher not out	41	3/135 4/205		

*A. J. Hollioake, C. C. Lewis, I. D. K. Salisbury, M. P. Bicknell and J. E. Benjamin did not bat.

Bowling: Cowan 7–0–46–1; Ilott 10–1–60–2; Irani 2–0–16–0; S. G. Law 4–0–15–0; Such 10–1–37–0; Grayson 9.3–0–34–1.

Umpires: J. H. Harris and M. J. Kitchen.

KENT v WARWICKSHIRE

At Canterbury, May 27. Kent won by four wickets. Toss: Warwickshire.

Kent recorded an impressive victory in a high-scoring game to reach the semi-finals for the 13th time in the tournament's 26 years. A blistering opening from Warwickshire had threatened to bat them out of contention. The visitors reached 100 in 14 overs and Smith made 125 in 119 balls, his best limited-overs score, with 13 fours and three sixes. Welch and Giles added 61 in eight overs to pass 300. But Warwickshire suffered a blow when Donald retired with a back strain, after bowling five wides – three of which ran to the boundary – in two overs. Walker survived a chance on seven to proceed to his maiden one-day hundred. He also faced 119 balls and hit 12 fours and three sixes. When Cowdrey joined Ealham, Kent needed 60 from eight overs; the pair added 53 and Cowdrey went on to make the winning hit.

Gold Award: M. J. Walker.

Warwickshire

*N. V. Knight b McCague	5	
N. M. K. Smith c Strang b Ealham	125	
D. R. Brown b Fleming	28	
D. L. Hemp c Walker b Fleming	8	
D. P. Ostler b Strang	44	
T. L. Penney c Fleming b Ealham	14	
G. Welch c Walker b Fleming	26	
A. F. Giles not out	28	

†K. J. Piper b Fleming 0
A. A. Donald not out 1

B 2, l-b 7, w 8, n-b 8 25

1/6 2/72 3/103   (8 wkts, 50 overs) 304
4/206 5/242 6/242
7/303 8/303

G. C. Small did not bat.

Bowling: McCague 8–0–63–1; Headley 7–0–42–0; Ealham 10–0–53–2; Fleming 10–0–58–4; Strang 10–0–43–1; Llong 5–0–36–0.

Kent

M. V. Fleming run out	41	
M. J. Walker b Giles	117	
N. J. Llong b Small	39	
T. R. Ward b Small	4	
A. P. Wells c Giles b Welch	11	
M. A. Ealham c Penney b Brown	24	

G. R. Cowdrey not out 39
P. A. Strang not out 1
L-b 8, w 20, n-b 2 30

1/84 2/158 3/179   (6 wkts, 49.3 overs) 306
4/227 5/245 6/298

*†S. A. Marsh, M. J. McCague and D. W. Headley did not bat.

Bowling: Donald 2–0–16–0; Welch 10–1–60–1; Brown 10–0–63–1; Giles 10–1–52–1; Small 10–1–51–2; Smith 7.3–0–56–0.

Umpires: G. Sharp and A. G. T. Whitehead.

LEICESTERSHIRE v SOMERSET

At Leicester, May 27. Leicestershire won by 20 runs. Toss: Somerset.

Leicestershire owed victory to the pace duo of Millns and Mullally, who skittled Somerset for 177 after they had collapsed themselves for 197. Millns, in particular, bowled with real fire and hostility; Somerset's top five were ripped out for 57. They rallied, thanks largely to a ninth-wicket stand of 60 between Caddick and Turner. But Mullally returned to have Caddick caught behind for 38, the top score of the innings. Somerset's batsmen let down their bowlers, particularly Rose, who had bowled superbly when Bowler chose to field on a typically slow Grace Road pitch. He swung the ball and struck in each of his first three overs. Although Whitaker and Smith put on 102, the batsmen were always struggling and off-spinner Trump ran through the middle order with four for 51.

Gold Award: D. J. Millns.

Leicestershire

V. J. Wells lbw b Rose	0	
D. L. Maddy b Rose	0	
*J. J. Whitaker c and b Trump	51	
N. C. Johnson c Lathwell b Rose	6	
B. F. Smith b Trump	61	
A. Habib not out	43	
†P. A. Nixon b Trump	11	
J. M. Dakin b Trump	6	

D. J. Millns c Lathwell b Bowler 2
A. D. Mullally run out 2
M. T. Brimson b Caddick 0
L-b 6, w 5, n-b 4 15

1/1 2/8 3/14   (46.2 overs) 197
4/116 5/139 6/167
7/185 8/190 9/196

Bowling: Rose 8–0–37–3; Caddick 8.2–1–33–1; Mushtaq Ahmed 10–1–26–0; Kerr 4–0–20–0; Trump 10–0–51–4; Bowler 6–1–24–1.

Somerset

J. I. D. Kerr b Millns	2	Mushtaq Ahmed c Johnson b Brimson	10
M. Burns c Nixon b Millns	31	A. R. Caddick c Nixon b Mullally	38
S. C. Ecclestone b Mullally	8	H. R. J. Trump not out	1
M. N. Lathwell b Mullally	1	L-b 10, w 12, n-b 2	24
R. J. Harden lbw b Millns	0		
*P. D. Bowler c Nixon b Dakin	25	1/3 2/27 3/42 (47.5 overs)	177
G. D. Rose c Millns b Wells	7	4/48 5/57 6/73	
†R. J. Turner c Smith b Brimson	30	7/100 8/115 9/175	

Bowling: Mullally 9–1–33–3; Millns 10–0–36–3; Wells 10–3–24–1; Johnson 6–0–20–0; Brimson 9.5–0–36–2; Dakin 3–0–18–1.

Umpires: B. Leadbeater and R. A. White.

YORKSHIRE v NORTHAMPTONSHIRE

At Leeds, May 27. Northamptonshire won by seven wickets. Toss: Northamptonshire.

A splendid all-round performance from Capel overpowered Yorkshire, who made too many mistakes. Capel took four for three in nine balls to prevent Yorkshire capitalising on a sound start. Despite a stand of 115 from 24 overs between Vaughan and Parker, Northamptonshire never lost their grip. Capel completed his best one-day figures and followed up by opening the batting and hammering 67 from 59 balls, with nine fours and two sixes. He was particularly severe on Gough, who went for 60 in nine overs. With Yorkshire dropping three catches, the visitors cruised to victory under the calm influence of Bailey, whose unbeaten 70 was made from 84 deliveries and took him past 2,500 runs in the competition. During Northamptonshire's innings, Gough rugby-tackled a streaker, irritating his employers who said he was putting himself at risk.

Gold Award: D. J. Capel.

Yorkshire

*D. Byas b Mohammad Akram	4	D. Gough not out	18
M. P. Vaughan c Emburey b Taylor	85	C. E. W. Silverwood run out	8
D. S. Lehmann c Ripley b Capel	30		
A. McGrath lbw b Capel	0	B 3, l-b 9, w 16, n-b 4	32
C. White c Snape b Capel	0		
†R. J. Blakey c Bailey b Capel	4	1/12 2/81 3/81 (9 wkts, 50 overs)	253
B. Parker lbw b Snape	58	4/81 5/89 6/204	
P. J. Hartley c Ripley b Capel	14	7/220 8/229 9/253	

R. D. Stemp did not bat.

Bowling: Mohammad Akram 10–2–43–1; Taylor 8–0–47–1; Capel 10–1–51–5; Penberthy 2–0–20–0; Curran 6–0–21–0; Emburey 7–0–29–0; Snape 7–0–30–1.

Northamptonshire

D. J. Capel b White	67	A. L. Penberthy not out	30
R. R. Montgomerie run out	39	L-b 3, w 7, n-b 4	14
*R. J. Bailey not out	70		
K. M. Curran c Blakey b Hartley	34	1/90 2/140 3/192 (3 wkts, 46 overs)	254

†D. Ripley, T. C. Walton, J. N. Snape, J. P. Taylor, Mohammad Akram and J. E. Emburey did not bat.

Bowling: Silverwood 10–0–48–0; Gough 9–0–60–0; Hartley 8–0–54–1; White 10–1–44–1; Stemp 9–0–45–0.

Umpires: B. J. Meyer and N. T. Plews.

SEMI-FINALS

KENT v NORTHAMPTONSHIRE

At Canterbury, June 10. Kent won by 66 runs. Toss: Northamptonshire.

Kent earned a place in their eighth Benson and Hedges final through a fine display of bowling and fielding. They struggled early on, and were 63 for four. Then Ward and Ealham launched a recovery with a century stand. But the next four wickets fell for seven runs before Marsh and McCague ran up 34 in the last five overs. When Northamptonshire replied, Headley put them under immediate pressure, taking three wickets in 26 balls. Their hopes of a second successive trip to Lord's were effectively dead when Bailey was out at 79 for five. Kent's fielding was excellent, especially Walker's diving catch to dismiss Curran, with the close catching also impressive. Strang picked up four late wickets and took the catch that completed the victory with four overs left. After the game, what was described as "a mass brawl" involving about 100 rival supporters broke out by the Bat and Ball pub outside the ground. One police officer was injured. Stuart Anderson, the Kent secretary, said: "Large volumes of alcohol are the problem. There were no problems inside the ground. The crowd were good-humoured, noisy but fun." Subsequently, Kent began to monitor the amount of drink spectators brought in to one-day games.

Gold Award: D. W. Headley.

Kent

M. V. Fleming c Walton b Follett	6		*†S. A. Marsh not out	27
M. J. Walker c Warren b Follett	4		M. J. McCague not out	12
D. P. Fulton c Emburey b Taylor	17			
T. R. Ward run out	78		L-b 9, w 7, n-b 2	18
A. P. Wells c Warren b Penberthy	1			
M. A. Ealham b Emburey	41		1/11 2/13 3/56	(8 wkts, 50 overs) 206
N. J. Llong run out	0		4/63 5/163 6/163	
P. A. Strang c sub b Taylor	2		7/164 8/170	

D. W. Headley did not bat.

Bowling: Taylor 10–1–31–2; Follett 5–0–30–2; Curran 5–0–27–0; Penberthy 10–1–34–1; Emburey 10–1–35–1; Snape 10–0–40–0.

Northamptonshire

†R. J. Warren b Headley	4		J. E. Emburey not out	19
M. B. Loye lbw b Headley	4		J. P. Taylor c Fulton b Strang	7
*R. J. Bailey c Marsh b McCague	33		D. Follett c Strang b Ealham	4
K. M. Curran c Walker b Headley	5		L-b 3, w 3, n-b 6	12
A. L. Penberthy c Wells b Fleming	13			
T. C. Walton c Fulton b Strang	19		1/5 2/24 3/34	(46 overs) 140
D. J. Sales c Wells b Strang	15		4/59 5/79 6/94	
J. N. Snape c Llong b Strang	5		7/107 8/109 9/120	

Bowling: McCague 10–0–30–1; Headley 10–0–36–3; Fleming 8–1–20–1; Ealham 5–2–11–1; Strang 10–2–29–4; Llong 3–0–11–0.

Umpires: A. A. Jones and R. Palmer.

SURREY v LEICESTERSHIRE

At The Oval, June 10. Surrey won by 130 runs. Toss: Leicestershire.

First, Surrey's England batsmen, Stewart, Thorpe and Adam Hollioake, made batting look easy; then their former Test bowler Bicknell made it look next to impossible. He bowled his ten overs straight through for his best figures in the competition, leaving Leicestershire 68 for six as they edged their way towards one of the heaviest semi-final defeats. Surrey had begun badly themselves at 15 for two. Stewart and Thorpe were in commanding form, however, adding 158, a Surrey record for the third wicket in this competition. Adam Hollioake sped them on their way to 300 as he spanked the wayward bowling for 63 in 40 balls.

Gold Award: M. P. Bicknell.

Surrey

A. D. Brown c Nixon b Mullally	4	I. D. K. Salisbury c Nixon b Johnson	2
†A. J. Stewart st Nixon b Mason	87	M. P. Bicknell not out	1
B. C. Hollioake c Whitaker b Mullally	9		
G. P. Thorpe b Wells	79	L-b 7, w 11	18
*A. J. Hollioake c Millns b Johnson	63		
C. C. Lewis run out	12	1/4 2/15 3/173 (8 wkts, 50 overs) 308	
M. A. Butcher run out	20	4/210 5/228 6/290	
J. D. Ratcliffe not out	13	7/291 8/297	

Saqlain Mushtaq did not bat.

Bowling: Mullally 10–0–53–2; Millns 7–0–43–0; Wells 8–0–38–1; Johnson 7–0–58–2; Mason 10–0–55–1; Dakin 8–0–54–0.

Leicestershire

V. J. Wells b Bicknell	32	A. D. Mullally c Thorpe b B. C. Hollioake	4
D. L. Maddy c Stewart b Bicknell	2	T. J. Mason c Thorpe b A. J. Hollioake	30
*J. J. Whitaker b Bicknell	12	D. J. Millns not out	6
N. C. Johnson c Stewart b Lewis	0	L-b 6, w 7, n-b 2	15
A. Habib c Thorpe b Bicknell	2		
G. I. Macmillan lbw b Salisbury	15	1/9 2/28 3/29 (45.3 overs) 178	
†P. A. Nixon c Thorpe b A. J. Hollioake	53	4/32 5/68 6/68	
J. M. Dakin c Ratcliffe b Salisbury	7	7/84 8/96 9/171	

Bowling: Bicknell 10–2–41–4; Lewis 10–0–28–1; Salisbury 10–0–47–2; B. C. Hollioake 5–0–24–1; Saqlain Mushtaq 8–1–21–0; A. J. Hollioake 2.3–0–11–2.

Umpires: J. W. Holder and R. Julian.

FINAL

KENT v SURREY

At Lord's, July 12. Surrey won by eight wickets. Toss: Kent.

An innings of innocent near-genius from Ben Hollioake – a reprise of his international debut on the same ground in May – created a one-sided victory for Surrey. This was a disappointment for most but a relief for some: the malfunctioning main scoreboard looked incapable of coping with a close finish. It was Kent's sixth consecutive defeat in a Lord's final. They had produced some memorable performances in previous appearances, such as Aravinda de Silva's mesmerising century against Lancashire two years before; this time, on the admission of their captain, Marsh, they failed to compete. If there was a pivotal moment, it came early in Hollioake's innings. He had struck three carefree fours when he got a leading edge and the ball looped just short of Ealham at mid-on. Unsettled for the first and last time, he was immediately almost run out by McCague. But he survived, and so did Surrey.

Marsh soon had cause to regret batting. On a clammy morning, the ball swung for Surrey's spirited bowlers and Kent's fragile top order was quickly exposed. Though they made a good start, with 15 on the board in three overs, by the seventh they were 23 for three. Walker was the first to go, dragging on a wide half-volley from Bicknell, but it was Lewis, in one of his more determined moods, who caused most damage. Bowling with vigour, he had Fleming lbw with a ball which might have bounced over leg stump and added the wickets of Cowdrey, bowled by a delivery of full length, and Ealham, with a full toss. By then, Ward had fallen lbw to the elder Holllioake. And Wells, whose 16 years at Sussex had given him only limited experience of the big occasion, had gone the same way, diffidently half-forward to Bicknell, looking as nervous as he did on his sole Test appearance. Ealham batted intelligently for 52, although the responsibility on his shoulders gave him little opportunity to show his skills as a clean hitter, and Llong also looked assured before a late flurry from Marsh and Strang. Kent still looked about 30 short.

Surrey's batting suggested no total was beyond them. Though they lost Brown in the first over, to a fine reflex catch by Fleming at cover point from a full-blooded square cut, Ben Holllioake and Stewart then carried the match away from Kent. Holllioake's only previous appearance at Lord's had produced a half-century for England; this time, he almost completed a whole one.

Upright and poised and driving the ball from the top of its bounce, he made 98 from 112 balls, with 15 fours. When he was second out, at 161, Surrey were 51 short of Kent's total, and Stewart, who made 75 not out, emerged from Hollioake's long shadow to see his side home. The team dedicated what was only their second Benson and Hedges Cup to the memory of their late colleague, Graham Kersey. – PAUL WEAVER

Gold Award: B. C. Hollioake. *Attendance:* 24,150; *receipts* £788,001.

Kent

M. V. Fleming lbw b Lewis	7	M. J. McCague c Thorpe	
M. J. Walker b Bicknell	6	b Saqlain Mushtaq	0
T. R. Ward lbw b A. J. Hollioake	15	D. W. Headley not out	3
A. P. Wells lbw b Bicknell	5	B 1, l-b 7, w 17, n-b 2	27
N. J. Llong c Butcher			
b Saqlain Mushtaq	42	1/15 (2) 2/15 (1) (9 wkts, 50 overs)	212
M. A. Ealham c Brown b Lewis	52	3/23 (4) 4/68 (3)	
G. R. Cowdrey b Lewis	8	5/106 (5) 6/135 (7)	
P. A. Strang b Salisbury	23	7/170 (8) 8/194 (6)	
*†S. A. Marsh not out	24	9/198 (10)	

Bowling: Bicknell 8–0–33–2; Lewis 10–3–39–3; A. J. Hollioake 7–0–31–1; B. C. Hollioake 6–0–28–0; Saqlain Mushtaq 9–1–33–2; Salisbury 10–0–40–1.

Surrey

A. D. Brown c Fleming b McCague	2
†A. J. Stewart not out	75
B. C. Hollioake c Strang b Ealham	98
G. P. Thorpe not out	17
L-b 11, w 6, n-b 6	23

1/2 (1) 2/161 (3) (2 wkts, 45 overs) 215

*A. J. Hollioake, M. A. Butcher, C. C. Lewis, J. D. Ratcliffe, M. P. Bicknell, I. D. K. Salisbury and Saqlain Mushtaq did not bat.

Bowling: McCague 8–0–45–1; Headley 10–0–53–0; Fleming 7–1–29–0; Ealham 6–0–31–1; Strang 10–1–31–0; Llong 4–0–15–0.

Umpires: G. Sharp and D. R. Shepherd.

BENSON AND HEDGES CUP RECORDS

55 overs available in all games 1972-95, 50 overs in 1996-97.

Batting

Highest individual scores: 198*, G. A. Gooch, Essex v Sussex, Hove, 1982; 177, S. J. Cook, Somerset v Sussex, Hove, 1990; 173*, C. G. Greenidge, Hampshire v Minor Counties (South), Amersham, 1973; 167*, A. J. Stewart, Surrey v Somerset, The Oval, 1994; 160, A. J. Stewart, Surrey v Hampshire, The Oval, 1996; 158*, B. F. Davison, Leicestershire v Warwickshire, Coventry, 1972; 158, W. J. Cronje, Leicestershire v Lancashire, Manchester, 1995; 155*, M. D. Crowe, Somerset v Hampshire, Southampton, 1987; 155*, R. A. Smith, Hampshire v Glamorgan, Southampton, 1989; 154*, M. J. Procter, Gloucestershire v Somerset, Taunton, 1972; 154*, C. L. Smith, Hampshire v Combined Universities, Southampton, 1990; 151*, M. P. Maynard, Glamorgan v Middlesex, Lord's, 1996. *In the final:* 132*, I. V. A. Richards, Somerset v Surrey, 1981. (298 hundreds have been scored in the competition. The most hundreds in one season is 26 in 1996.)

Most runs: 5,176, G. A. Gooch; 2,921, M. W. Gatting; 2,761, C. J. Tavaré; 2,718, W. Larkins; 2,663, D. W. Randall; 2,636, A. J. Lamb; 2,595, K. J. Barnett; 2,589, G. A. Hick; 2,551, C. W. J. Athey; 2,538, R. J. Bailey; 2,531, R. T. Robinson.

Fastest hundred: M. A. Nash in 62 minutes, Glamorgan v Hampshire at Swansea, 1976.

Most hundreds: 15, G. A. Gooch; 7, G. A. Hick and W. Larkins; 6, N. R. Taylor; 5, C. G. Greenidge, A. J. Lamb and R. A. Smith.

Highest totals: 388 for seven, Essex v Scotland, Chelmsford, 1992; 371 for six, Leicestershire v Scotland, Leicester, 1997; 369 for eight, Warwickshire v Minor Counties, Jesmond, 1996; 366 for four, Derbyshire v Combined Universities, Oxford, 1991; 353 for seven, Lancashire v Nottinghamshire, Manchester, 1995; 350 for three, Essex v Oxford & Cambridge Univs, Chelmsford, 1979; 349 for seven, Somerset v Ireland, Taunton, 1997; 338 for six, Kent v Somerset, Maidstone, 1996; 333 for four, Essex v Oxford & Cambridge Univs, Chelmsford, 1985; 333 for six, Surrey v Hampshire, The Oval, 1996; 331 for five, Surrey v Hampshire, The Oval, 1990; 331 for five, Essex v British Univs, Chelmsford, 1996; 330 for four, Lancashire v Sussex, Manchester, 1991. *In the final:* 290 for six, Essex v Surrey, 1979.

Highest total by a side batting second and winning: 318 for five (54.3 overs), Lancashire v Leicestershire (312 for five), Manchester, 1995. *In the final:* 244 for six (55 overs), Yorkshire v Northamptonshire (244 for seven), 1987; 244 for seven (55 overs), Nottinghamshire v Essex (243 for seven), 1989.

Highest total by a side batting second and losing: 303 for seven (55 overs), Derbyshire v Somerset (310 for three), Taunton, 1990. *In the final:* 255 (51.4 overs), Surrey v Essex (290 for six), 1979.

Highest match aggregates: 631 for 15 wickets, Kent (338 for six) v Somerset (293 for nine), Maidstone, 1996; 630 for ten wickets, Leicestershire (312 for five) v Lancashire (318 for five), Manchester, 1995; 629 for 14 wickets, Lancashire (353 for seven) v Nottinghamshire (276 for seven), Manchester, 1995; 628 for 15 wickets, Warwickshire (312 for six) v Lancashire (316 for nine), Manchester, 1996; 626 for ten wickets, British Univs (312 for eight) v Glamorgan (314 for two), Cambridge, 1996; 615 for 11 wickets, Gloucestershire (307 for four) v Surrey (308 for seven), The Oval, 1996; 613 for ten wickets, Somerset (310 for three) v Derbyshire (303 for seven), Taunton, 1990; 610 for ten wickets, Sussex (303 for six) v Kent (307 for two), Hove, 1995; 610 for 14 wickets, Warwickshire (304 for eight) v Kent (306 for six), Canterbury, 1997.

Lowest totals: 50 in 27.2 overs, Hampshire v Yorkshire, Leeds, 1991; 56 in 26.2 overs, Leicestershire v Minor Counties, Wellington, 1982; 59 in 34 overs, Oxford & Cambridge Univs v Glamorgan, Cambridge, 1983; 60 in 26 overs, Sussex v Middlesex, Hove, 1978; 61 in 25.3 overs, Essex v Lancashire, Chelmsford, 1992; 62 in 26.5 overs, Gloucestershire v Hampshire, Bristol, 1975. *In the final:* 117 in 46.3 overs, Derbyshire v Hampshire, 1988.

Shortest completed innings: 21.4 overs (156), Surrey v Sussex, Hove, 1988.

Record partnership for each wicket

252 for 1st	V. P. Terry and C. L. Smith, Hampshire v Combined Universities at Southampton	1990
285* for 2nd	C. G. Greenidge and D. R. Turner, Hampshire v Minor Counties (South) at Amersham	1973
269* for 3rd	P. M. Roebuck and M. D. Crowe, Somerset v Hampshire at Southampton	1987
184* for 4th	D. Lloyd and B. W. Reidy, Lancashire v Derbyshire at Chesterfield	1980
160 for 5th	A. J. Lamb and D. J. Capel, Northamptonshire v Leicestershire at Northampton	1986
167* for 6th	M. G. Bevan and R. J. Blakey, Yorkshire v Lancashire at Manchester . .	1996
149* for 7th	J. D. Love and C. M. Old, Yorkshire v Scotland at Bradford	1981
109 for 8th	R. E. East and N. Smith, Essex v Northamptonshire at Chelmsford	1977
83 for 9th	P. G. Newman and M. A. Holding, Derbyshire v Nottinghamshire at Nottingham	1985
80* for 10th	D. L. Bairstow and M. Johnson, Yorkshire v Derbyshire at Derby	1981

Bowling

Most wickets: 149, J. K. Lever; 132, I. T. Botham.

Best bowling: seven for 12, W. W. Daniel, Middlesex v Minor Counties (East), Ipswich, 1978; seven for 22, J. R. Thomson, Middlesex v Hampshire, Lord's, 1981; seven for 24, Mushtaq Ahmed, Somerset v Ireland, Taunton, 1997; seven for 32, R. G. D. Willis, Warwickshire v Yorkshire, Birmingham, 1981. *In the final:* five for 13, S. T. Jefferies, Hampshire v Derbyshire, 1988.

Hat-tricks (11): G. D. McKenzie, Leicestershire v Worcestershire, Worcester, 1972; K. Higgs, Leicestershire v Surrey in the final, Lord's, 1974; A. A. Jones, Middlesex v Essex, Lord's, 1977; M. J. Procter, Gloucestershire v Hampshire, Southampton, 1977; W. Larkins, Northamptonshire v Oxford & Cambridge Univs, Northampton, 1980; E. A. Moseley, Glamorgan v Kent, Cardiff, 1981; G. C. Small, Warwickshire v Leicestershire, Leicester, 1984; N. A. Mallender, Somerset v Combined Universities, Taunton, 1987; W. K. M. Benjamin, Leicestershire v Nottinghamshire, Leicester, 1987; A. R. C. Fraser, Middlesex v Sussex, Lord's, 1988; S. M. Pollock (four in four balls), Warwickshire v Leicestershire, Birmingham, 1996.

Wicket-keeping and Fielding

Most dismissals: 122 (117 ct, 5 st), D. L. Bairstow.

Most dismissals in an innings: 8 (all ct), D. J. S. Taylor, Somerset v Oxford & Cambridge Univs, Taunton, 1982.

Most catches by a fielder: 68, G. A. Gooch; 55, C. J. Tavaré; 53, I. T. Botham.

Most catches by a fielder in an innings: 5, V. J. Marks, Oxford & Cambridge Univs v Kent, Oxford, 1976.

Results

Largest victories in runs: Essex by 272 runs v Scotland, Chelmsford, 1992; Somerset by 233 runs v Ireland, Eglinton, 1995; Somerset by 221 runs v Ireland, Taunton, 1997; Glamorgan by 217 runs v Combined Universities, Cardiff, 1995; Essex by 214 runs v Oxford & Cambridge Univs, Chelmsford, 1979; Derbyshire by 206 runs v Combined Universities, Oxford, 1991; Warwickshire by 195 runs v Minor Counties, Jesmond, 1996.

Victories by ten wickets (19): By Derbyshire, Essex (twice), Glamorgan, Hampshire, Kent (twice), Lancashire, Leicestershire (twice), Middlesex, Northamptonshire, Somerset, Warwickshire, Worcestershire (twice), Yorkshire (three times).

Gold Awards

Most awards: 22, G. A. Gooch; 11, K. J. Barnett, M. W. Gatting, G. A. Hick, T. E. Jesty and B. Wood.

WINNERS 1972-97

		Gold Award
1972	LEICESTERSHIRE* beat Yorkshire by five wickets.	J. C. Balderstone
1973	KENT* beat Worcestershire by 39 runs.	Asif Iqbal
1974	SURREY* beat Leicestershire by 27 runs.	J. H. Edrich
1975	LEICESTERSHIRE beat Middlesex* by five wickets.	N. M. McVicker
1976	KENT* beat Worcestershire by 43 runs.	G. W. Johnson
1977	GLOUCESTERSHIRE* beat Kent by 64 runs.	A. W. Stovold
1978	KENT beat Derbyshire* by six wickets.	R. A. Woolmer

		Gold Award
1979	ESSEX beat Surrey* by 35 runs.	G. A. Gooch
1980	NORTHAMPTONSHIRE* beat Essex by six runs.	A. J. Lamb
1981	SOMERSET* beat Surrey by seven wickets.	I. V. A. Richards
1982	SOMERSET* beat Nottinghamshire by nine wickets.	V. J. Marks
1983	MIDDLESEX beat Essex* by four runs.	C. T. Radley
1984	LANCASHIRE* beat Warwickshire by six wickets.	J. Abrahams
1985	LEICESTERSHIRE* beat Essex by five wickets.	P. Willey
1986	MIDDLESEX beat Kent* by two runs.	J. E. Emburey
1987	YORKSHIRE* beat Northamptonshire, having taken more wickets with the scores tied.	J. D. Love
1988	HAMPSHIRE* beat Derbyshire by seven wickets.	S. T. Jefferies
1989	NOTTINGHAMSHIRE beat Essex* by three wickets.	R. T. Robinson
1990	LANCASHIRE beat Worcestershire* by 69 runs.	M. Watkinson
1991	WORCESTERSHIRE beat Lancashire* by 65 runs.	G. A. Hick
1992	HAMPSHIRE beat Kent* by 41 runs.	R. A. Smith
1993	DERBYSHIRE beat Lancashire* by six runs.	D. G. Cork
1994	WARWICKSHIRE* beat Worcestershire by six wickets.	P. A. Smith
1995	LANCASHIRE beat Kent* by 35 runs.	P. A. de Silva†
1996	LANCASHIRE* beat Northamptonshire by 31 runs.	I. D. Austin
1997	SURREY beat Kent* by eight wickets.	B. C. Hollioake

* Won toss. † On losing side.

WINS BY NON-CHAMPIONSHIP TEAMS

1973	OXFORD beat Northamptonshire at Northampton by two wickets.
1975	{ OXFORD & CAMBRIDGE beat Worcestershire at Cambridge by 66 runs.
	{ OXFORD & CAMBRIDGE beat Northamptonshire at Oxford by three wickets.
1976	OXFORD & CAMBRIDGE beat Yorkshire at Barnsley by seven wickets.
1980	MINOR COUNTIES beat Gloucestershire at Chippenham by three runs.
1981	MINOR COUNTIES beat Hampshire at Southampton by three runs.
1982	MINOR COUNTIES beat Leicestershire at Wellington by 131 runs.
1984	OXFORD & CAMBRIDGE beat Gloucestershire at Bristol by 27 runs.
1986	SCOTLAND beat Lancashire at Perth by three runs.
1987	MINOR COUNTIES beat Glamorgan at Oxford (Christ Church) by seven wickets.
1989	{ COMBINED UNIVERSITIES beat Surrey at Cambridge by nine runs.
	{ COMBINED UNIVERSITIES beat Worcestershire at Worcester by five wickets.
1990	{ COMBINED UNIVERSITIES beat Yorkshire at Leeds by two wickets.
	{ SCOTLAND beat Northamptonshire at Northampton by two wickets.
1992	MINOR COUNTIES beat Sussex at Marlow by 19 runs.
1995	MINOR COUNTIES beat Leicestershire at Leicester by 26 runs.
1997	{ IRELAND beat Middlesex at Dublin (Castle Avenue) by 46 runs.
	{ BRITISH UNIVERSITIES beat Sussex at Cambridge by 19 runs.

TEAM RECORDS 1972-97

	Rounds reached					Matches		
	W	F	SF	QF	P	W	L	NR
Derbyshire	1	3	4	9	117	62	47	8
Durham	0	0	0	0	21	8	11	2
Essex	1	5	8	15	129	79	47	3
Glamorgan	0	0	1	8	110	49	57	4
Gloucestershire	1	1	2	7	111	54	53	4
Hampshire	2	2	5	12	120	61	54	5
Kent	3	8	13	18	139	90	46	3
Lancashire	4	6	10	16	134	86	41	7
Leicestershire	3	4	7	10	123	67	49	7

	Rounds reached					Matches		
	W	F	SF	QF	P	W	L	NR
Middlesex	2	3	5	14	124	63	53	8
Northamptonshire	1	3	6	11	118	57	53	8
Nottinghamshire	1	2	5	13	120	69	44	7
Somerset	2	2	8	13	122	67	53	2
Surrey	2	4	8	12	125	71	50	4
Sussex	0	0	1	9	111	54	56	1
Warwickshire	1	2	7	14	124	68	49	7
Worcestershire	1	5	8	15	127	66	57	4
Yorkshire	1	2	6	11	118	63	48	7
Cambridge University	0	0	0	0	8	0	8	0
Oxford University	0	0	0	0	4	1	3	0
Oxford & Cambridge Universities	0	0	0	0	48	4	42	2
Combined/British Universities	0	0	0	1	42	4	37	1
Minor Counties	0	0	0	0	70	6	60	4
Minor Counties (North)	0	0	0	0	20	0	20	0
Minor Counties (South)	0	0	0	0	20	0	19	1
Minor Counties (East)	0	0	0	0	12	0	12	0
Minor Counties (West)	0	0	0	0	12	0	12	0
Scotland	0	0	0	0	66	2	60	4
Ireland	0	0	0	0	13	1	11	1

Middlesex beat Gloucestershire on the toss of a coin in their quarter-final in 1983. Derbyshire, Kent, Somerset and Warwickshire totals each include a bowling contest; Derbyshire beat Somerset and Warwickshire beat Kent when their quarter-finals, in 1993 and 1994 respectively, were abandoned.

COUNTY CAPS AWARDED IN 1997

Essex	A. P. Cowan, D. D. J. Robinson.
Glamorgan	S. D. Thomas, Waqar Younis.
Gloucestershire	S. Young.
Hampshire	M. L. Hayden.
Kent	P. A. Strang, A. P. Wells.
Leicestershire	N. C. Johnson, I. J. Sutcliffe.
Middlesex	J. H. Kallis.
Nottinghamshire	M. N. Bowen, C. M. Tolley.
Somerset	S. C. Ecclestone, P. C. L. Holloway, K. J. Shine, A. P. van Troost.
Sussex	M. A. Robinson, N. R. Taylor.
Warwickshire	D. L. Hemp, G. Welch.
Worcestershire	A. Sheriyar, K. R. Spiring.
Yorkshire	D. S. Lehmann.

No caps were awarded by Derbyshire, Lancashire, Northamptonshire or Surrey. Durham give caps to all their playing staff.

COUNTY BENEFITS AWARDED FOR 1998

Durham	T. Flintoft, head groundsman (testimonial).
Essex	Essex CCC Benefit Association Fund.
Glamorgan	S. L. Watkin.
Gloucestershire	C. A. Walsh (testimonial).
Hampshire	R. J. Maru.
Kent	A. P. Igglesden (testimonial).
Lancashire	Wasim Akram.
Middlesex	K. R. Brown.
Northamptonshire	A. Fordham (testimonial).
Nottinghamshire	K. P. Evans.
Somerset	Somerset CCC.
Sussex	P. Moores.
Warwickshire	T. A. Munton.
Worcestershire	P. J. Newport.
Yorkshire	R. J. Blakey.

No benefit was awarded by Derbyshire, Leicestershire or Surrey.

AXA LIFE LEAGUE, 1997

Allan Donald

The Sunday League, under its seventh name in 29 seasons, had one of its tighter finishes when Kent fell at the final fence and handed the title to Warwickshire. Kent needed to win their last match, at Headingley, but the batsmen folded under pressure while Warwickshire were cantering home against Gloucestershire. It was their third Sunday triumph, and their second in four seasons.

Kent finished second, ahead of Lancashire, who began the season with five successive wins before faltering. Leicestershire, unbeaten in July and August, came fourth, ahead of the 1996 champions Surrey, who were distracted by England calls and never looked like retaining their title. They may also have been distracted by the gimmickry introduced to The Oval at Sunday matches to try and entice younger spectators. This included renaming the team ''the Surrey Lions'', with a mascot called Roary. Surrey said their attendances rose 15 per cent compared to a national downturn of five per cent.

Three matches were moved away from Sundays to be played on week-nights under floodlights. Surrey's game against Nottinghamshire was scheduled to make history as the first game under lights in a major English competition – but the weather was appalling, and the game was abandoned long before nightfall.

Instead, the honour fell to Warwickshire, whose match against Somerset was a sensation: on one of the warmest evenings of the year, a crowd of 15,000 turned up, prompting the club to speculate about putting in permanent lights rather than mobile ones. Warwickshire's win that night also began their sequence of six on the trot that led to them overhauling Kent. The Sussex–Surrey match at Hove, played in more middling English conditions, attracted almost 5,000.

The other innovation of the year was altogether less popular. The Duckworth/Lewis system for deciding rain-affected matches was generally recognised to be fairer than other methods, but baffled everyone except its inventors with its mathematical complexities. In a damp summer, it was called on 21 times: a further 19 matches failed to finish, of which 15 did not even start.

AXA Life League, 1997

AXA LIFE LEAGUE

	M	W	L	T	NR	Pts	Net run-rate
1 – Warwickshire (4)	17	13	4	0	0	52	14.14
2 – Kent (10).................	17	12	4	0	1	50	7.70
3 – Lancashire (9).............	17	10	4	1	2	46	1.89
4 – Leicestershire (12)	17	9	5	1	2	42	7.11
5 – Surrey (1)	17	9	5	0	3	42	1.06
6 – Somerset (5)...............	17	9	6	0	2	40	4.31
7 – Essex (17).................	17	9	6	1	1	40	−2.38
8 – Worcestershire (8)	17	8	6	1	2	38	6.87
9 – Northamptonshire (6).......	17	8	6	0	3	38	2.78
10 – Yorkshire (3)	17	8	7	1	1	36	5.24
11 – Gloucestershire (16)	17	7	6	0	4	36	1.01
12 – Nottinghamshire (2)	17	7	7	0	3	34	−0.19
13 – Glamorgan (13)	17	5	9	0	3	26	−4.01
14 – Derbyshire (11).............	17	4	9	0	4	24	−3.04
15 – Hampshire (15).............	17	5	11	0	1	22	−4.73
16 – Middlesex (7).............	17	3	10	1	3	20	−8.28
17 – Durham (18)..............	17	3	13	0	1	14	−12.27
18 – Sussex (14)...............	17	2	13	0	2	12	−16.72

1996 positions are shown in brackets.

When two or more counties finish with an equal number of points, the positions are decided by a) most wins, b) higher net run-rate (runs scored per 100 balls minus runs conceded per 100 balls).

Leading run-scorers: M. L. Hayden 654 (£5,000 individual award), D. S. Lehmann 643, S. G. Law 574, T. R. Ward 566, A. D. Brown 558, G. A. Hick 549, N. H. Fairbrother 546, N. M. K. Smith 532, T. M. Moody 529, D. L. Maddy 515.

Leading wicket-takers: P. J. Martin 31 (£5,000 individual award), A. A. Donald 30, S. D. Udal 29, M. V. Fleming 26, G. D. Rose and J. P. Stephenson 24, A. P. Cowan 23, S. J. Renshaw 22.

Most economical bowlers (runs per over, minimum 100 overs): D. W. Headley 3.72, G. D. Rose 3.84, Mushtaq Ahmed 3.90, A. A. Donald 3.92, A. R. C. Fraser 3.98, M. A. Robinson 4.05, P. J. Martin 4.07, I. D. Austin 4.09.

Leading wicket-keepers: W. K. Hegg 26 (18 ct, 8 st) (£2,000 individual award), S. J. Rhodes 24 (20 ct, 4 st), R. J. Blakey 22 (18 ct, 4 st), A. N. Aymes 20 (14 ct, 6 st), R. J. Rollins 16 (9 ct, 7 st).

Leading fielders: W. S. Kendall 15, M. W. Alleyne, N. M. K. Smith and A. P. Wells 10.

Prize money

£42,000 for winners: WARWICKSHIRE.
£21,000 for runners-up: KENT.
£10,500 for third place: LANCASHIRE.
£5,250 for fourth place: LEICESTERSHIRE.
£500 for the winners of each match, shared if tied or no result.

SUMMARY OF RESULTS, 1997

	Derbyshire	Durham	Essex	Glamorgan	Gloucestershire	Hampshire	Kent	Lancashire	Leicestershire	Middlesex	Northamptonshire	Nottinghamshire	Somerset	Surrey	Sussex	Warwickshire	Worcestershire	Yorkshire
Derbyshire	—	L	L	W	L	W	L	L	N	L	L	L	N	N	N	L	W	W
Durham	W	—	L	L	L	L	L	L	L	N	L	L	N	L	W	W	L	T	L
Essex	W	W	—	W	W	W	W	L	L	L	W	W	N	N	W	W	L	L
Glamorgan	L	W	L	—	L	W	L	N	N	W	N	L	L	L	W	W	L	L
Gloucestershire	W	W	L	W	—	N	L	N	W	W	N	L	L	L	L	L	W	W
Hampshire	L	W	L	L	N	—	L	L	L	W	L	L	L	W	W	W	L	L
Kent	W	W	W	W	W	W	—	L	L	W	W	W	W	W	L	W	N	L
Lancashire	W	W	W	N	N	W	W	—	W	T	W	W	L	L	W	L	L	W
Leicestershire	N	W	W	N	L	W	W	L	—	W	L	W	W	L	W	L	W	T
Middlesex	W	N	L	L	L	L	L	T	L	—	L	W	L	N	W	L	L	L
Northamptonshire	W	W	L	N	W	N	L	L	W	W	—	W	N	W	W	L	L	L
Nottinghamshire	W	W	N	N	N	W	L	L	L	L	L	—	L	N	W	W	L	W
Somerset	N	W	W	W	W	W	L	W	L	N	W	N	—	L	W	L	L	W
Surrey	N	W	L	W	W	W	L	W	W	N	L	N	W	—	W	L	L	L
Sussex	N	L	L	L	W	L	W	L	L	L	L	L	L	—	L	L	W	N
Warwickshire	W	W	W	L	L	W	L	L	W	W	W	W	W	W	W	—	W	W
Worcestershire	L	L	T	W	L	L	L	N	W	L	N	W	W	W	L	L	—	W
Yorkshire	L	W	W	W	L	W	W	L	T	W	W	L	W	L	N	L	L	—

Home games in bold, away games in italics. W = Won, L = Lost, T = Tied, N = No result.

DERBYSHIRE

At Canterbury, April 27. DERBYSHIRE lost to KENT by six wickets.

DERBYSHIRE v LANCASHIRE

At Derby, May 4. Lancashire won by 35 runs (D/L method). Toss: Lancashire.

A fourth-wicket stand of 128 in 18 overs between Lloyd and Fairbrother was decisive, regardless of a rainstorm that reduced Derbyshire's target to 252 from 38 overs. Atherton strained his groin early in the match and was run out without leaving the crease, when his runner went walkabout at square leg. The culprit, Yates, later redeemed himself with figures of three for 29.

Lancashire

M. A. Atherton run out	7	†W. K. Hegg run out	1
J. E. R. Gallian c DeFreitas b Malcolm	37	G. Yates not out	7
J. P. Crawley c Krikken b Harris	36	L-b 2, w 13	15
G. D. Lloyd c Dean b Harris	81		
N. H. Fairbrother c Krikken b Harris	74	1/39 2/51 3/106 (7 wkts, 40 overs) 262
I. D. Austin not out	3	4/234 5/250
*Wasim Akram b Adams	1	6/253 7/254

R. J. Green and P. J. Martin did not bat.

Bowling: Malcolm 8–0–51–1; Dean 7–0–40–0; Harris 8–0–42–3; Roberts 6–0–40–0; Rollins 2–0–15–0; Adams 7–0–49–1; Jones 2–0–23–0.

Derbyshire

A. S. Rollins c Crawley b Austin	29	A. J. Harris not out	10
C. J. Adams b Martin	14	D. E. Malcolm b Wasim Akram	3
*D. M. Jones b Green	58	K. J. Dean not out	1
G. A. Khan b Yates	13	B 3, l-b 19, w 6, n-b 8	36
V. P. Clarke c and b Yates	3		
P. A. J. DeFreitas c Martin b Yates	5	1/31 2/86 3/125 (9 wkts, 38 overs) 217
†K. M. Krikken b Wasim Akram	36	4/138 5/138 6/164
G. M. Roberts b Wasim Akram	9	7/188 8/203 9/211

Bowling: Wasim Akram 8–1–39–3; Martin 8–2–25–1; Austin 7–0–53–1; Green 8–0–49–1; Yates 7–0–29–3.

Umpires: A. Clarkson and R. A. White.

DERBYSHIRE v SURREY

At Derby, May 11. No result (abandoned).

At Lord's, May 18. DERBYSHIRE lost to MIDDLESEX by four wickets.

At Nottingham, May 25. DERBYSHIRE lost to NOTTINGHAMSHIRE by 32 runs.

DERBYSHIRE v HAMPSHIRE

At Chesterfield, June 8. Derbyshire won by four wickets (D/L method). Toss: Derbyshire.

The Duckworth/Lewis system required Derbyshire to score 181 in 33 overs in response to Hampshire's stuttering 170. They faltered after a second-wicket stand of 65 between Barnett and Jones, but Blackwell and Rollins put on 58 in nine overs to repair the damage.

Hampshire

G. W. White c Adams b DeFreitas	22	A. D. Mascarenhas b Harris	7
J. S. Laney c Adams b DeFreitas	22	S. J. Renshaw not out	19
R. A. Smith c Krikken b Aldred	11	B 2, l-b 5, w 12	19
M. Keech c Krikken b Aldred	19		
W. S. Kendall lbw b Clarke	7	1/48 2/51 3/76 (7 wkts, 33 overs) 170
*J. P. Stephenson not out	38	4/92 5/96
S. D. Udal c Roberts b Aldred	6	6/114 7/123

†A. N. Aymes and C. A. Connor did not bat.

Bowling: Harris 8–1–45–1; DeFreitas 8–0–27–2; Aldred 7–0–40–3; Clarke 6–0–23–1; Roberts 4–0–28–0.

Derbyshire

K. J. Barnett lbw b Udal	48	†K. M. Krikken run out	2
C. J. Adams c Mascarenhas b Renshaw	14	P. A. J. DeFreitas not out	5
*D. M. Jones c Udal b Keech	33	B 5, l-b 8, w 2, n-b 4	19
V. P. Clarke c Stephenson b Keech	6		
A. S. Rollins not out	26	1/38 2/103 3/105 (6 wkts, 32.1 overs) 182
I. D. Blackwell b Renshaw	29	4/111 5/169 6/176

G. M. Roberts, A. J. Harris and P. Aldred did not bat.

Bowling: Stephenson 5–0–28–0; Renshaw 6.1–0–26–2; Connor 7–0–39–0; Mascarenhas 2–0–16–0; Keech 5–0–29–2; Udal 7–0–31–1.

Umpires: K. E. Palmer and G. Sharp.

At Birmingham, June 15. DERBYSHIRE lost to WARWICKSHIRE by 108 runs.

DERBYSHIRE v SUSSEX

At Derby, June 22. No result (abandoned).

At Southend, June 29. DERBYSHIRE lost to ESSEX by one run (D/L method).

DERBYSHIRE v YORKSHIRE

At Derby, July 13. Derbyshire won by 114 runs. Toss: Yorkshire.

Derbyshire, who started the match next to bottom in the league, collected their second Sunday win to dash Yorkshire's hopes of staying in touch with the leaders. It was a hefty win too: Adams scored 109 in 110 balls and shared an unbroken third-wicket stand of 158 with Clarke to steer Derbyshire to a total that beat their previous highest league total against Yorkshire by 52. Then DeFreitas took the initiative in reducing Yorkshire to 39 for four, and McGrath's short stand with Lehmann was no more than an exercise in damage limitation.

Derbyshire

A. S. Rollins c Byas b Hartley	....	36
C. J. Adams not out	....	109
G. A. Khan c White b Stemp	....	6
V. P. Clarke not out	....	77
L-b 16, w 13, n-b 2	....	31

1/91 2/101   (2 wkts, 40 overs) 259

M. J. Vandrau, K. J. Barnett, †K. M. Krikken, *P. A. J. DeFreitas, P. Aldred, K. J. Dean and A. J. Harris did not bat.

Bowling: Gough 8–0–65–0; Silverwood 6–0–43–0; Stemp 8–0–34–1; Hartley 8–1–27–1; White 2–0–15–0; Morris 4–0–30–0; Lehmann 4–0–29–0.

Yorkshire

*D. Byas c Khan b Dean	....	4	D. Gough b Harris	....	10
C. White c Krikken b DeFreitas	....	8	C. E. W. Silverwood b Harris	....	1
D. S. Lehmann b Clarke	....	30	R. D. Stemp b Harris	....	1
†R. J. Blakey c Krikken b DeFreitas	.....	9	L-b 8, w 8	....	16
B. Parker b DeFreitas	....	0			
A. McGrath c Barnett b Clarke	....	40	1/11 2/16 3/39	(32.2 overs)	145
A. C. Morris c Krikken b Harris	....	17	4/39 5/84 6/115		
P. J. Hartley not out	....	9	7/124 8/139 9/141		

Bowling: DeFreitas 8–1–39–3; Dean 8–0–25–1; Clarke 8–1–28–2; Aldred 4–0–23–0; Harris 4.2–0–22–4.

Umpires: M. J. Kitchen and R. A. White.

At Cheltenham, July 20. DERBYSHIRE lost to GLOUCESTERSHIRE by seven wickets.

DERBYSHIRE v GLAMORGAN

At Chesterfield, July 27. Derbyshire won by eight wickets. Toss: Glamorgan.

Cork made a dramatic return to first-team cricket after being laid off since April through injury. He easily beat his previous best Sunday figures with six for 21, as Glamorgan were hustled out in only 27 overs. Then he opened the batting and scored 33 – though he was understandably tiring and he needed 16 of the 19 overs Derbyshire used up in cruising to a target of 104.

Glamorgan

A. W. Evans c Rollins b DeFreitas	0	S. L. Watkin c DeFreitas b Cork	0
H. Morris c Griffiths b DeFreitas	4	D. A. Cosker b Cork	5
A. Dale c Rollins b Harris	23	O. T. Parkin lbw b Cork	0
S. P. James b DeFreitas	0	L-b 5, w 4, n-b 2	11
*P. A. Cottey c DeFreitas b Cork	26		
G. P. Butcher b Cork	17	1/2 2/8 3/18	(27 overs) 103
†A. D. Shaw lbw b Cork	6	4/52 5/60 6/83	
Waqar Younis not out	11	7/87 8/87 9/103	

Bowling: DeFreitas 6–2–19–3; Dean 4–0–26–0; Harris 6–0–21–1; Cork 8–1–21–6; Clarke 3–0–11–0.

Derbyshire

D. G. Cork c James b Parkin	33
C. J. Adams lbw b Cosker	29
A. S. Rollins not out	35
V. P. Clarke not out	6
W 1, n-b 2	3

1/38 2/84   (2 wkts, 19.1 overs) 106

J. E. Owen, G. A. Khan, P. Aldred, *P. A. J. DeFreitas, †S. P. Griffiths, A. J. Harris and K. J. Dean did not bat.

Bowling: Waqar Younis 2–0–13–0; Watkin 4–0–27–0; Cosker 5–0–22–1; Parkin 5.1–0–24–1; Dale 0.2–0–1–0; Butcher 2.4–0–19–0.

Umpires: J. D. Bond and V. A. Holder.

At Chester-le-Street, August 3. DERBYSHIRE lost to DURHAM by five wickets.

At Leicester, August 24. LEICESTERSHIRE v DERBYSHIRE. No result (abandoned).

DERBYSHIRE v SOMERSET

At Derby, August 31. No result (abandoned).

DERBYSHIRE v NORTHAMPTONSHIRE

At Derby, September 7. Northamptonshire won by seven wickets. Toss: Derbyshire.

In their first match since the announcement that DeFreitas would not continue as club captain in 1998, Derbyshire were brushed aside by a more committed Northamptonshire team. Scotland fast bowler John Blain, making his Sunday debut, removed DeFreitas for a duck on his way to five wickets.

Derbyshire

D. G. Cork b Blain	21	P. Aldred not out	16
*P. A. J. DeFreitas c Walton b Blain	0	S. J. Lacey b Taylor	9
T. A. Tweats b Blain	4	A. J. Harris run out	3
K. J. Barnett b Swann	45	L-b 9, w 9	18
V. P. Clarke c T. M. B. Bailey b Blain	5		
M. E. Cassar b Blain	0	1/3 2/26 3/39	(9 wkts, 40 overs) 145
†K. M. Krikken c Montgomerie		4/54 5/54 6/110	
b Penberthy	24	7/122 8/141 9/145	

K. J. Dean did not bat.

Bowling: Taylor 8–1–27–1; Blain 8–0–24–5; Penberthy 8–0–25–1; Curran 8–0–22–0; Swann 8–1–38–1.

Northamptonshire

R. R. Montgomerie c Tweats b Lacey	20	*R. J. Bailey not out	5
A. L. Penberthy b Harris	28	B 4, l-b 3, w 8, n-b 4	19
K. M. Curran c Cassar b Aldred	32		
D. J. Sales not out	42	1/40 2/77 3/134	(3 wkts, 27.5 overs) 146

T. C. Walton, G. P. Swann, J. P. Taylor, †T. M. B. Bailey, K. J. Innes and J. A. R. Blain did not bat.

Bowling: DeFreitas 4–2–9–0; Dean 5.5–0–37–0; Cork 2–0–15–0; Lacey 6–0–38–1; Harris 4–0–15–1; Aldred 4–1–7–1; Cassar 2–0–18–0.

Umpires: H. D. Bird and J. F. Steele.

At Worcester, September 14. DERBYSHIRE beat WORCESTERSHIRE by five wickets.

DURHAM

At Manchester, April 27. DURHAM lost to LANCASHIRE by 57 runs.

DURHAM v NOTTINGHAMSHIRE

At Hartlepool, May 11. Nottinghamshire won by nine wickets (D/L method). Toss: Nottinghamshire.

Durham totalled 155 for eight in an innings reduced to 23 overs by rain, but Duckworth/Lewis set Nottinghamshire 154 to win. That discrepancy was irrelevant in the face of Johnson's vicious 74 from 42 balls, which won the match for his side with 4.2 overs in hand.

Durham

J. E. Morris c Bates b Evans	2	J. Boiling not out	4
†M. P. Speight c Pollard b Bates	42	N. Killeen not out	1
*D. C. Boon run out	27		
M. J. Foster c Noon b Tolley	1	B 4, l-b 7, w 12	23
N. J. Speak c Gie b Bowen	32		
J. J. B. Lewis run out	4	1/8 2/45 3/58	(8 wkts, 23 overs) 155
P. D. Collingwood c Johnson b Evans	19	4/104 5/111 6/136	
S. J. E. Brown c Noon b Bowen	0	7/137 8/147	

A. Walker did not bat.

Bowling: Evans 5–0–28–2; Tolley 5–0–26–1; Bowen 5–0–35–2; Bates 4–0–22–1; Dowman 4–0–33–0.

Nottinghamshire

M. P. Dowman c and b Brown 26
R. T. Robinson not out 46
*P. Johnson not out 74
    L-b 3, w 4, n-b 4 11

1/56   (1 wkt, 18.4 overs) 157

G. F. Archer, P. R. Pollard, N. A. Gie, C. M. Tolley, K. P. Evans, †W. M. Noon, R. T. Bates and M. N. Bowen did not bat.

Bowling: Brown 5–0–37–1; Killeen 3–0–36–0; Walker 4–0–28–0; Boiling 3–0–21–0; Foster 3–0–28–0; Collingwood 0.4–0–4–0.

Umpires: R. Julian and J. F. Steele.

At Chelmsford, May 18. DURHAM lost to ESSEX by two wickets.

DURHAM v WORCESTERSHIRE

At Chester-le-Street, May 25. Durham won by seven wickets. Toss: Worcestershire.

Worcestershire were largely ineffectual with both bat and ball, reaching the boundary just twice in the first 35 overs of their innings and then donating 25 runs to Durham in wides and no-balls. Speight shared half-century stands with Morris and Boon, who completed an easy win with Lewis's help. It was only Durham's second Sunday League win since August 1995, and followed seven successive defeats since their victory over Essex in July 1996.

Worcestershire

*T. M. Moody c Speight b Killeen	6		K. R. Spiring c Speight b Foster	18
W. P. C. Weston c Speak b Saggers	8		S. R. Lampitt not out	24
G. A. Hick run out	18		L-b 9, w 7	16
G. R. Haynes c Collingwood b Boiling	30			
V. S. Solanki lbw b Boiling	4		1/13 2/24 3/62 (6 wkts, 40 overs)	177
D. A. Leatherdale not out	53		4/76 5/83 6/112	

†S. J. Rhodes, P. J. Newport and A. Sheriyar did not bat.

Bowling: Killeen 8–1–36–1; Saggers 8–0–29–1; Walker 8–0–39–0; Foster 6–0–20–1; Boiling 7–0–32–2; Collingwood 3–0–12–0.

Durham

J. E. Morris c Spiring b Moody	18		J. J. B. Lewis not out	19
†M. P. Speight c Weston b Hick	61		B 2, l-b 4, w 9, n-b 16	31
*D. C. Boon not out	49			
N. J. Speak run out	2		1/58 2/108 3/110 (3 wkts, 34.4 overs)	180

P. D. Collingwood, M. J. Foster, J. Boiling, N. Killeen, M. J. Saggers and A. Walker did not bat.

Bowling: Newport 6–1–32–0; Haynes 3–1–24–0; Moody 4–1–20–1; Lampitt 6–0–31–0; Sheriyar 5–0–20–0; Leatherdale 5–0–22–0; Hick 5.4–0–25–1.

Umpires: A. Clarkson and N. T. Plews.

At Pontypridd, June 1. DURHAM lost to GLAMORGAN by six wickets.

DURHAM v SUSSEX

At Chester-le-Street, June 8. Durham won by 62 runs (D/L method). Toss: Sussex.

The new formula for rain-affected matches did Sussex no favours. Their innings was interrupted with the total standing at 39 for four from ten overs and, on resuming, they were asked to score another 80 in four overs to win. Under the old run-rate system, they would have needed only 37 more runs. To add to their difficulties, the rain was still falling. Moores registered his protest by blocking out the last over. Earlier, Durham had reached 216, their highest Sunday total at Chester-le-Street. Both Boon and Lewis made their best scores yet in this competition.

Durham

J. E. Morris b K. Newell	29	M. J. Foster b Drakes	4
†M. P. Speight c Moores b Kirtley	12	M. M. Betts not out	0
*D. C. Boon c Kirtley b Khan	76	L-b 7, w 6, n-b 2	15
N. J. Speak run out	2		
J. J. B. Lewis not out	69	1/27 2/55 3/60 (6 wkts, 40 overs) 216	
P. D. Collingwood b Drakes	9	4/176 5/205 6/209	

J. Boiling, S. J. E. Brown and A. Walker did not bat.

Bowling: Drakes 8–0–44–2; K. Newell 8–1–22–1; Kirtley 8–0–53–1; Khan 8–0–54–1; Robinson 8–0–36–0.

Sussex

R. K. Rao c Speight b Collingwood	13	*†P. Moores not out	11
C. W. J. Athey run out	1	L-b 2, w 2, n-b 2	6
N. R. Taylor c Speak b Brown	0		
K. Greenfield c Speak b Boiling	19	1/9 2/12 (4 wkts, 14 overs) 57	
M. Newell not out	7	3/21 4/39	

K. Newell, R. J. Kirtley, V. C. Drakes, A. A. Khan and M. A. Robinson did not bat.

Bowling: Brown 5–1–24–1; Betts 3–0–8–0; Boiling 3–0–13–1; Collingwood 1–0–2–1; Boon 1–0–7–0; Morris 1–0–1–0.

Umpires: J. C. Balderstone and D. J. Constant.

DURHAM v KENT

At Darlington, June 22. Kent won by 16 runs. Toss: Kent.

Casual batting by Kent gave Durham an excellent chance of following up their Championship victory of the day before, and at 104 for four they looked likely to pass 141 with ease. But McCague yorked Lewis for 34, and the last five wickets clattered for seven runs.

Kent

D. P. Fulton b Wood	5	M. J. McCague c Walker b Wood	0
T. R. Ward lbw b Walker	18	D. W. Headley not out	1
A. P. Wells b Walker	4	J. B. D. Thompson c and b Walker	4
M. J. Walker c Wood b Walker	21	L-b 9, w 13, n-b 4	26
G. R. Cowdrey c Speight b Wood	46		
M. V. Fleming lbw b Foster	5	1/16 2/24 3/59 (39.5 overs) 141	
P. A. Strang b Collingwood	6	4/59 5/80 6/113	
*†S. A. Marsh c Morris b Wood	5	7/127 8/134 9/134	

Bowling: Brown 8–0–27–0; Wood 8–2–17–4; Walker 7.5–1–18–4; Foster 6–0–39–1; Boiling 7–0–20–0; Collingwood 3–0–11–1.

Durham

J. E. Morris c Strang b Headley	47	J. Wood b Fleming	4
†M. P. Speight c Wells b Headley	6	S. J. E. Brown lbw b Fleming	0
*D. C. Boon b McCague	3	A. Walker not out	1
N. J. Speak lbw b Headley	0	B 1, l-b 2, w 2, n-b 2	7
J. J. B. Lewis b McCague	34		
P. D. Collingwood run out	11	1/32 2/58 3/58	(34.2 overs) 125
M. J. Foster b Fleming	10	4/63 5/104 6/118	
J. Boiling run out	2	7/118 8/124 9/124	

Bowling: Headley 8–1–30–3; Thompson 5–0–30–0; Strang 8–1–17–0; McCague 7.2–0–20–2; Fleming 6–1–25–3.

Umpires: B. Leadbeater and A. G. T. Whitehead.

DURHAM v HAMPSHIRE

At Chester-le-Street, July 6. Hampshire won by six wickets. Toss: Hampshire.
Durham's bowlers looked rusty after 11 days without a match – rain had washed out the Championship game – and contributed 33 of Hampshire's 41 extras in wides and no-balls. Although the in-form Lewis made the only fifty of the match, Stephenson's four wickets and 38 unbeaten runs helped to lift Hampshire to their second Sunday win of the season.

Durham

J. E. Morris c Aymes b Stephenson	33	J. Boiling b Connor	6
†M. P. Speight c Aymes b Stephenson	13	S. J. E. Brown b Renshaw	1
*D. C. Boon st Aymes b James	3	A. Walker not out	3
M. A. Roseberry lbw b Stephenson	1	L-b 4, w 12, n-b 6	22
J. J. B. Lewis not out	51		
P. D. Collingwood c Kendall b James	3	1/47 2/59 3/60	(9 wkts, 40 overs) 162
M. J. Foster c Aymes b James	5	4/62 5/67 6/82	
M. M. Betts b Stephenson	21	7/124 8/143 9/147	

Bowling: Connor 8–1–23–1; Renshaw 8–0–41–1; Stephenson 8–2–28–4; James 8–0–33–3; Udal 8–1–33–0.

Hampshire

J. S. Laney b Brown	15	*J. P. Stephenson not out	38
M. L. Hayden run out	25	B 1, l-b 7, w 11, n-b 22	41
R. A. Smith c Speight b Foster	11		
M. Keech not out	33	1/55 2/79	(4 wkts, 37 overs) 163
W. S. Kendall lbw b Walker	0	3/86 4/88	

K. D. James, †A. N. Aymes, S. D. Udal, S. J. Renshaw and C. A. Connor did not bat.

Bowling: Brown 7–0–36–1; Betts 6–1–29–0; Foster 8–0–32–1; Walker 7–1–19–1; Boiling 7–0–31–0; Collingwood 2–0–8–0.

Umpires: G. I. Burgess and J. F. Steele.

DURHAM v WARWICKSHIRE

At Chester-le-Street, July 13. Warwickshire won by five wickets (D/L method). Toss: Durham.
In a match shortened by two heavy showers, Hemp's 20-ball 50 helped Warwickshire to an unlikely win. Hutton and Speight had batted well enough to allow Durham to set a target of 137 in just 17 overs, and then Singh wasted 28 balls in scoring 14. The required run-rate was more than ten an over when Hemp arrived, but his clean hitting allowed Warwickshire to go top of the table on net run-rate. During Durham's innings, Small was removed from the attack for running down the pitch.

Durham

J. E. Morris run out	14
S. Hutton c Frost b Smith	57
†M. P. Speight not out	64
*D. C. Boon not out	26
B 3, l-b 3, w 3, n-b 4	13

1/41 2/103   (2 wkts, 27.4 overs) 174

M. A. Roseberry, J. J. B. Lewis, M. J. Foster, J. Boiling, J. Wood, S. J. E. Brown and A. Walker did not bat.

Bowling: Brown 4–1–15–0; Welch 3.5–0–27–0; Donald 5–0–38–0; Giles 5–0–33–0; Small 4.5–0–25–0; Smith 5–0–30–1.

Warwickshire

A. Singh b Boiling	14	T. L. Penney not out	4
*N. M. K. Smith c Walker b Brown	9		
D. R. Brown c Hutton b Walker	19	B 4, l-b 4, w 2, n-b 2	12
D. L. Hemp c Brown b Walker	50		
D. P. Ostler not out	24	1/14 2/37 3/81 (5 wkts, 16.3 overs) 137
G. Welch lbw b Walker	5	4/117 5/133

A. F. Giles, †T. Frost, G. C. Small and A. A. Donald did not bat.

Bowling: Brown 3–0–14–1; Wood 4–0–21–0; Boiling 3–0–30–1; Foster 3–0–25–0; Walker 3.3–0–39–3.

Umpires: H. D. Bird and G. I. Burgess.

At Scarborough, July 20. DURHAM lost to YORKSHIRE by 138 runs.

At Cheltenham, July 27. DURHAM lost to GLOUCESTERSHIRE by five wickets.

DURHAM v DERBYSHIRE

At Chester-le-Street, August 3. Durham won by five wickets. Toss: Durham.

Lewis, Durham's opening batsman and a centurion in their Championship win against Derbyshire the previous day, moved down to No. 5 for this match. When his side had reached 112 for two in pursuit of 182, it seemed he would not be needed. But Boon charged intemperately at Vandrau, and Lewis had to weigh in again: his stand of 61 with Roseberry levelled the scores and Betts hit the winning four.

Derbyshire

A. S. Rollins c Boiling b Betts	32	P. Aldred b Walker	4
C. J. Adams c Boon b Brown	17	A. J. Harris not out	5
V. P. Clarke c Betts b Brown	6	K. J. Dean not out	0
K. J. Barnett b Betts	30	B 1, l-b 13, w 4, n-b 2	20
G. A. Khan st Speight b Boiling	9		
†K. M. Krikken c Morris b Betts	3	1/35 2/45 3/75 (9 wkts, 40 overs) 181
*P. A. J. DeFreitas c Boon b Walker	45	4/93 5/107 6/113
M. J. Vandrau c and b Wood	10	7/128 8/157 9/180

Bowling: Brown 8–1–34–2; Wood 8–1–47–1; Betts 8–1–22–3; Boiling 8–0–25–1; Walker 8–1–39–2.

Durham

J. E. Morris lbw b Dean	5	M. M. Betts not out	4
S. Hutton c Adams b Dean	12		
†M. P. Speight c Dean b Vandrau	40	B 1, l-b 10, w 9, n-b 2	22
*D. C. Boon st Krikken b Vandrau	43		
J. J. B. Lewis c Vandrau b Aldred	36	1/11 2/24 3/112 (5 wkts, 38 overs)	185
M. A. Roseberry not out	23	4/120 5/181	

J. Boiling, J. Wood, A. Walker and S. J. E. Brown did not bat.

Bowling: DeFreitas 8–0–33–0; Dean 8–0–23–2; Harris 8–0–34–0; Aldred 7–0–52–1; Vandrau 7–0–32–2.

Umpires: A. A. Jones and P. Willey.

At The Oval, August 10. DURHAM lost to SURREY by seven wickets.

DURHAM v MIDDLESEX

At Chester-le-Street, August 24. No result (abandoned).

At Leicester, September 7. DURHAM lost to LEICESTERSHIRE by 106 runs.

At Northampton, September 8. DURHAM lost to NORTHAMPTONSHIRE by five wickets.

DURHAM v SOMERSET

At Chester-le-Street, September 14. Somerset won by seven wickets. Toss: Somerset.

Lewis was Durham's best batsman yet again, with 57 from 44 balls, but Lathwell, who shared an unbroken stand of 121 with Ecclestone, finished the match with a six. Durham were spared from retaining their wooden spoon when Sussex lost to Hampshire.

Durham

J. E. Morris c Holloway b Burns	7	J. Boiling not out	10
S. Hutton c Mushtaq Ahmed b Burns	1	N. Killeen c Lathwell b Caddick	0
†M. P. Speight lbw b Mushtaq Ahmed	50	S. J. E. Brown not out	4
*D. C. Boon c Turner b Trott	35	L-b 2, w 7, n-b 8	17
J. J. B. Lewis c Caddick			
b Mushtaq Ahmed	57	1/8 2/13 3/67 (8 wkts, 40 overs)	205
N. J. Speak run out	24	4/145 5/181 6/184	
J. Wood b Caddick	0	7/191 8/192	

A. Walker did not bat.

Bowling: Rose 8–0–35–0; Burns 8–0–35–2; Caddick 8–0–36–2; Trott 4–0–29–1; Trescothick 2–0–16–0; Mushtaq Ahmed 8–0–36–2; Bowler 2–0–16–0.

Somerset

M. Burns c Boiling b Brown	7	M. N. Lathwell not out	57
P. C. L. Holloway c Speight b Wood	2	B 2, l-b 15, w 7, n-b 6	30
S. C. Ecclestone not out	96		
*P. D. Bowler c Morris b Killeen	19	1/8 2/31 3/90 (3 wkts, 35.4 overs)	211

†R. J. Turner, M. E. Trescothick, G. D. Rose, A. R. Caddick, Mushtaq Ahmed and B. J. Trott did not bat.

Bowling: Brown 8–0–42–1; Wood 8–0–29–1; Killeen 6–0–38–1; Walker 6–2–20–0; Boiling 7.4–0–65–0.

Umpires: J. D. Bond and J. W. Holder.

ESSEX

ESSEX v HAMPSHIRE

At Chelmsford, April 27. Essex won by three wickets. Toss: Essex.

A fourth-wicket stand of 104 in 18 overs between Keech and Kendall boosted Hampshire's total. For Essex, Irani took three for 36 and then made 48 before falling to one of three middle-order run-outs. Playing a specialist batsman, Robinson, at No. 7 paid off when he guided them to victory in the last over.

Hampshire

M. L. Hayden lbw b Irani	27	†A. N. Aymes not out	21
J. S. Laney c Hussain b Irani	11		
R. A. Smith b Such	3	L-b 8, w 3, n-b 2	13
M. Keech b Grayson	52		
W. S. Kendall b Irani	55	1/34 2/42 3/56	(5 wkts, 40 overs) 198
*J. P. Stephenson not out	16	4/160 5/160	

K. D. James, S. D. Udal, S. J. Renshaw and C. A. Connor did not bat.

Bowling: Cowan 6–0–24–0; Ilott 8–0–54–0; Such 8–0–17–1; Irani 8–1–36–3; Grayson 8–0–33–1; D. R. Law 2–0–26–0.

Essex

*P. J. Prichard lbw b Stephenson	4	M. C. Ilott c Stephenson b James	12
S. G. Law c Aymes b Renshaw	14	A. P. Cowan not out	5
N. Hussain c Hayden b Udal	18	L-b 13, w 14, n-b 2	29
R. C. Irani run out	48		
A. P. Grayson run out	23	1/19 2/22 3/82	(7 wkts, 39.5 overs) 202
D. R. Law run out	23	4/120 5/129	
D. D. J. Robinson not out	26	6/162 7/184	

†B. J. Hyam and P. M. Such did not bat.

Bowling: Stephenson 8–1–37–1; Renshaw 8–1–23–1; Connor 7.5–0–47–0; Udal 8–0–33–1; James 8–0–49–1.

Umpires: J. C. Balderstone and V. A. Holder.

ESSEX v MIDDLESEX

At Chelmsford, May 4. Essex won by 66 runs. Toss: Middlesex.

Two good half-centuries from Essex's unrelated Laws, Stuart and Danny, set up a daunting score, before Middlesex lost four wickets in 18 balls. Hyam, Essex's reserve wicket-keeper, equalled the county's record for dismissals in a one-day match with five catches. With only two wickets left and still 154 behind, Middlesex were facing their heaviest Sunday defeat in terms of runs. But the tail did them proud, adding another 88 – and atoning in part for a slow over-rate which earned them a fine of £660. The match was played throughout to the sound of music from a nearby funfair.

Essex

*P. J. Prichard c Pooley b Fraser	25	A. P. Cowan c Pooley b Weekes	3
S. G. Law c Brown b Kallis	79	†B. J. Hyam c Hewitt b Weekes	3
N. Hussain c Brown b Hewitt	12	P. M. Such not out	1
R. C. Irani lbw b Fraser	5	L-b 10, w 12	22
A. P. Grayson c Wellings b Johnson	36		
D. R. Law b Weekes	55	1/60 2/80 3/95	(40 overs) 256
D. D. J. Robinson lbw b Weekes	12	4/175 5/176 6/231	
M. C. Ilott run out	3	7/238 8/242 9/254	

Bowling: Kallis 8–0–33–1; Hewitt 8–1–31–1; Fraser 8–0–42–2; Weekes 6–0–38–4; Dutch 2–0–19–0; Johnson 7–0–74–1; Wellings 1–0–9–0.

Middlesex

P. N. Weekes c S. G. Law b Ilott	5	R. L. Johnson run out	29
J. H. Kallis c Hyam b Irani	23	J. P. Hewitt not out	24
J. C. Pooley b Cowan	0	A. R. C. Fraser c S. G. Law b Robinson	33
*M. W. Gatting c Hyam b Ilott	1	L-b 9, w 14, n-b 10	33
†K. R. Brown b Cowan	0		
S. P. Moffat c Hyam b Cowan	29	1/14 2/15 3/20 (37.5 overs) 190	
P. E. Wellings c Hyam b Irani	12	4/22 5/57 6/82	
K. P. Dutch c Hyam b Cowan	1	7/90 8/102 9/144	

Bowling: Cowan 7–0–31–4; Ilott 4–0–10–2; Irani 6–0–17–2; D. R. Law 5–0–40–0; S. G. Law 8–0–31–0; Grayson 7–1–45–0; Robinson 0.5–0–7–1.

Umpires: M. J. Kitchen and D. R. Shepherd.

ESSEX v DURHAM

At Chelmsford, May 18. Essex won by two wickets. Toss: Durham.

Essex were the only county to lose to Durham in this competition in 1996 and, when they were 38 for four in pursuit of 209, they were favourites to do it again. But Danny Law produced his highest Sunday innings, 82 from 75 balls, to help them squeeze home. Earlier, Morris had reached a hundred in 90 balls.

Durham

J. E. Morris run out	110	J. Boiling not out	5
P. D. Collingwood c Robinson b Such	10	N. Killeen b Rollins b Grayson	0
*D. C. Boon st Rollins b Such	16	L-b 4, w 5	9
N. J. Speak c Rollins b Grayson	24		
†M. P. Speight run out	10	1/36 2/67 3/162 (8 wkts, 40 overs) 208	
J. J. B. Lewis st Rollins b Grayson	14	4/169 5/192 6/199	
M. J. Foster b Grayson	10	7/206 8/208	

M. J. Saggers and A. Walker did not bat.

Bowling: Cowan 8–0–34–0; Ilott 8–0–44–0; Such 8–0–41–2; Irani 8–0–22–0; Grayson 8–0–63–4.

Essex

*P. J. Prichard c Boiling b Saggers	2	M. C. Ilott not out	15
S. G. Law c Collingwood b Killeen	13	A. P. Cowan not out	15
N. Hussain c Speight b Killeen	12		
R. C. Irani c Boiling b Saggers	5	L-b 5, w 16	21
A. P. Grayson lbw b Foster	14		
D. R. Law c Foster b Killeen	82	1/4 2/29 3/37 (8 wkts, 38.4 overs) 210	
D. D. J. Robinson lbw b Saggers	27	4/38 5/91 6/152	
†R. J. Rollins c and b Saggers	4	7/161 8/185	

P. M. Such did not bat.

Bowling: Killeen 7.4–0–32–3; Saggers 8–0–35–4; Walker 7–0–28–0; Boiling 3–0–33–0; Foster 7–0–39–1; Collingwood 6–0–38–0.

Umpires: K. E. Palmer and A. G. T. Whitehead.

At Gloucester, May 25. ESSEX beat GLOUCESTERSHIRE by five wickets.

ESSEX v YORKSHIRE

At Ilford, June 1. Yorkshire won by four wickets. Toss: Essex.

Yorkshire scored at more than seven an over to pass a target of 263 with 19 balls in hand. Essex's first nine batsmen had all reached double figures, but twenties and thirties were not good enough on the small Valentine's Park ground, as an opening partnership of 146 in 17 overs between Byas and Vaughan made clear. It was Essex's first Sunday defeat of 1997, after a run of four wins out of four.

Essex

D. D. J. Robinson b Stemp	30	M. C. Ilott c Hartley b Gough	12
S. G. Law b White	47	A. P. Cowan not out	2
*N. Hussain c Blakey b Hartley	29	P. M. Such not out	2
R. C. Irani c Byas b Hamilton	36	L-b 8, w 7, n-b 2	17
A. P. Grayson c White b Vaughan	21		
S. D. Peters c Blakey b Vaughan	15	1/73 2/87 3/145	(9 wkts, 40 overs) 262
D. R. Law b Gough	19	4/156 5/186 6/193	
†R. J. Rollins c Silverwood b Vaughan	32	7/221 8/254 9/259	

Bowling: Silverwood 4–0–35–0; Gough 8–0–41–2; Stemp 8–0–52–1; White 8–0–31–1; Hartley 4–0–27–1; Hamilton 2–0–20–1; Vaughan 6–0–48–3.

Yorkshire

*D. Byas c Irani b Grayson	72	C. White b Grayson	14
M. P. Vaughan b Irani	66	D. Gough not out	13
D. S. Lehmann not out	58	B 5, l-b 9, w 4, n-b 8	26
P. J. Hartley b Irani	15		
†R. J. Blakey c Rollins b Irani	0	1/146 2/148 3/186	(6 wkts, 36.5 overs) 264
B. Parker run out	0	4/189 5/190 6/234	

G. M. Hamilton, C. E. W. Silverwood and R. D. Stemp did not bat.

Bowling: Ilott 8–0–37–0; Cowan 7.5–0–61–0; Such 3–0–31–0; S. G. Law 2–0–23–0; Irani 8–0–54–3; Grayson 8–0–44–2.

Umpires: G. Sharp and J. F. Steele.

At The Oval, June 8. ESSEX beat SURREY by six wickets (D/L method).

At Hove, June 15. ESSEX beat SUSSEX by eight wickets.

ESSEX v DERBYSHIRE

At Southend, June 29. Essex won by one run (D/L method). Toss: Essex.

Solid contributions from the lower middle order allowed Essex to recover from a shaky start, when Dean saw off Prichard, Stuart Law and Hussain in the first five overs. Derbyshire, by contrast, began confidently, Rollins and Adams putting on 79 for the first wicket as rain adjusted their target to 122 from 23 overs. But panic set in, and eight were needed from the last over. When Aldred was run out off the last ball they had mustered seven. Since the score they had to beat was actually 121.15, it was not a tie: Essex won – theoretically by 0.15 of a run – and returned to the top of the table.

Essex

*P. J. Prichard c Adams b Dean	0	†R. J. Rollins c and b Harris	0
S. G. Law c Krikken b Dean	7	A. P. Cowan not out	20
N. Hussain c Clarke b Dean	7	L-b 6, w 1	7
R. C. Irani c Adams b Clarke	52		
A. P. Grayson st Krikken b Clarke	37	1/0 2/14 3/15 (7 wkts, 40 overs) 205	
D. R. Law not out	39	4/96 5/113	
D. D. J. Robinson run out	36	6/166 7/168	

M. C. Ilott and P. M. Such did not bat.

Bowling: Dean 8–2–24–3; Harris 8–0–44–1; Aldred 8–0–43–0; DeFreitas 4–0–21–0; Lacey 5–0–24–0; Clarke 7–0–43–2.

Derbyshire

A. S. Rollins c Such b Irani	31	T. A. Tweats not out	1
C. J. Adams c Grayson b Such	40		
V. P. Clarke c Cowan b Grayson	14	B 1, l-b 9	10
*P. A. J. DeFreitas c D. R. Law b Irani	8		
A. N. Hayhurst st Rollins b S. G. Law	8	1/79 2/85 3/101 (7 wkts, 23 overs) 121	
†K. M. Krikken b Grayson	6	4/106 5/113	
P. Aldred run out	3	6/119 7/121	

S. J. Lacey, A. J. Harris and K. J. Dean did not bat.

Bowling: Ilott 5–0–18–1; Cowan 4–0–17–0; Such 5–0–14–1; Irani 5–0–32–1; Grayson 3–0–22–2; S. G. Law 1–0–8–1.

Umpires: J. H. Harris and B. J. Meyer.

ESSEX v SOMERSET

At Chelmsford, July 6. Somerset won by four wickets. Toss: Somerset.
Somerset were the sharper team in all departments as Mushtaq Ahmed picked up three wickets, Parsons took three catches and Burns opened the reply with an excellent 83 from 90 balls, including three straight-driven sixes off Such. Without a last-wicket stand of 28 in four overs between Ilott and Such, Essex would have presented even less of an obstacle.

Essex

*P. J. Prichard c Kerr b Rose	8	A. P. Cowan lbw b Mushtaq Ahmed	7
S. G. Law c Parsons b Mushtaq Ahmed	43	M. C. Ilott not out	13
D. D. J. Robinson lbw b Burns	33	P. M. Such not out	15
R. C. Irani c Parsons b Kerr	21	B 4, l-b 5, w 9	18
A. P. Grayson c Parsons b Burns	3		
D. R. Law c Turner b Kerr	8	1/20 2/74 3/109 (9 wkts, 40 overs) 209	
†R. J. Rollins c Bowler b Shine	38	4/113 5/120 6/133	
S. D. Peters b Mushtaq Ahmed	2	7/141 8/165 9/181	

Bowling: Parsons 4–0–23–0; Rose 8–0–33–1; Shine 7–0–40–1; Mushtaq Ahmed 8–0–36–3; Kerr 7–0–40–2; Burns 6–0–28–2.

Somerset

M. Burns c Rollins b Ilott	83	K. A. Parsons not out	21
P. C. L. Holloway lbw b S. G. Law	37	G. D. Rose not out	6
†R. J. Turner b Grayson	3	L-b 3, w 5	8
S. C. Ecclestone c D. R. Law b Grayson	15		
M. N. Lathwell c Grayson b Such	34	1/88 2/91 3/118 (6 wkts, 37.2 overs) 211	
*P. D. Bowler c S. G. Law b Such	4	4/178 5/182 6/198	

Mushtaq Ahmed, J. I. D. Kerr and K. J. Shine did not bat.

Bowling: Ilott 8–0–45–1; Cowan 4–0–19–0; Irani 3–0–18–0; Such 6.2–0–54–2; S. G. Law 8–0–36–1; Grayson 8–0–36–2.

Umpires: R. Julian and M. J. Kitchen.

At Northampton, July 20. ESSEX beat NORTHAMPTONSHIRE by two wickets.

ESSEX v WORCESTERSHIRE

At Chelmsford, July 27. Tied. Toss: Worcestershire.

Essex needed only four runs off the final over, bowled by Leatherdale, but they were down to their last-wicket pair. The penultimate delivery got through Cowan's guard, and the game was tied. Worcestershire's mainstays, as so often, were Moody and Hick, who passed 6,000 runs in the League; he was the youngest player to reach the landmark, at 31 years and 65 days, and had taken the fewest innings, 157. But Stuart Law, who took four for 37, had a hand in both their dismissals and then hit 42 off 29 balls. When Rhodes stumped Robinson, he collected his 258th Sunday dismissal and overtook David Bairstow's competition record.

Worcestershire

*T. M. Moody lbw b S. G. Law	59	†S. J. Rhodes c Prichard b S. G. Law ... 1
T. S. Curtis c Irani b S. G. Law	34	M. J. Rawnsley not out 1
G. A. Hick c S. G. Law b Cowan	48	R. J. Chapman run out 0
K. R. Spiring lbw b S. G. Law	8	L-b 7, w 6 13
D. A. Leatherdale c S. G. Law b Grayson	10	
V. S. Solanki c Such b Irani	33	1/92 2/103 3/113 (39.5 overs) 217
W. P. C. Weston c Powell b Cowan	9	4/137 5/177 6/208
S. R. Lampitt b Irani	1	7/213 8/215 9/217

Bowling: Irani 7–0–51–2; Cowan 8–0–33–2; Andrew 6–0–22–0; Such 3–0–28–0; Grayson 8–0–39–1; S. G. Law 7.5–0–37–4.

Essex

*P. J. Prichard c Rhodes b Rawnsley	40	J. C. Powell b Leatherdale 2
S. G. Law b Chapman	42	S. J. W. Andrew run out 7
D. D. J. Robinson st Rhodes b Rawnsley	27	P. M. Such not out 2
R. C. Irani run out	27	L-b 5, w 5 10
A. P. Grayson c and b Lampitt	1	
D. R. Law b Lampitt	12	1/81 2/105 3/136 (39.5 overs) 217
†R. J. Rollins c Curtis b Leatherdale	25	4/139 5/156 6/163
A. P. Cowan b Leatherdale	22	7/197 8/199 9/212

Bowling: Moody 8–0–52–0; Lampitt 8–0–49–2; Leatherdale 7.5–0–46–3; Chapman 8–1–36–1; Rawnsley 8–0–29–2.

Umpires: G. I. Burgess and J. W. Holder.

ESSEX v LEICESTERSHIRE

At Colchester, August 3. Leicestershire won by 35 runs. Toss: Leicestershire.

Both sides threw away decent starts recklessly, but Maddy's 75 at least provided some substance in the middle of Leicestershire's innings. He shared a stand of 69 in eight overs with Dakin, who put one six through the roof of the score-box. Maddy went on to pick up three tail-end wickets, though it was Ormond, bowling at some pace, who knocked over the top three. It was Leicestershire's first Sunday League win in Essex for 17 years.

Leicestershire

N. C. Johnson b Andrew	21	T. J. Mason c D. R. Law b Irani 5
V. J. Wells b Andrew	23	J. Ormond not out 7
B. F. Smith c Grayson b Andrew	18	D. Williamson not out 4
*J. J. Whitaker b Grayson	23	L-b 5, w 4, n-b 2 11
D. L. Maddy b Cowan	75	
D. I. Stevens b Cowan	6	1/46 2/51 3/78 (9 wkts, 40 overs) 225
J. M. Dakin c and b Such	28	4/99 5/119 6/188
†P. A. Nixon c Robinson b Cowan	4	7/198 8/211 9/212

Bowling: Cowan 8–1–49–3; Irani 8–0–56–1; Andrew 8–0–20–3; Such 8–0–37–1; Grayson 6–0–43–1; S. G. Law 2–0–15–0.

Essex

*P. J. Prichard c Williamson b Ormond ..	26	A. P. Cowan c Dakin b Maddy	11
S. G. Law b Ormond	15	S. J. W. Andrew not out	5
N. Hussain c Whitaker b Ormond	0	P. M. Such b Maddy	0
R. C. Irani c Nixon b Dakin	16	L-b 2, w 20, n-b 9	31
A. P. Grayson c and b Johnson	31		—
D. R. Law c Nixon b Johnson	12	1/54 2/58 3/68	(37.3 overs) 190
D. D. J. Robinson st Nixon b Maddy	38	4/96 5/115 6/140	
†R. J. Rollins c Stevens b Dakin.......	5	7/150 8/178 9/190	

Bowling: Ormond 8–0–30–3; Johnson 6–0–50–2; Wells 7–0–32–0; Dakin 6–0–34–2; Williamson 7–0–25–0; Maddy 3.3–0–17–3.

Umpires: T. E. Jesty and B. Leadbeater.

At Canterbury, August 10. ESSEX lost to KENT by 117 runs.

At Nottingham, August 24. NOTTINGHAMSHIRE v ESSEX. No result (abandoned).

ESSEX v WARWICKSHIRE

At Chelmsford, August 31. Warwickshire won by 147 runs. Toss: Essex.

Essex, who were due to play Warwickshire in the NatWest final a week later, were heavily beaten both in this match and the concurrent Championship fixture. Hemp continued his fine Sunday form with an unbeaten 70 from 64 balls, which included four sixes, one of them through the door of the pavilion bar. Then Welch got in on the act by taking 22 off the last over of the innings, bowled by Cowan. In reply, Essex were softened up by Small and finished off by Donald, who struck in each of five consecutive overs.

Warwickshire

N. V. Knight lbw b Cowan	12	G. Welch not out	27
*N. M. K. Smith c Cowan b Cousins	57		
D. R. Brown c Rollins b Such..........	35	B 4, l-b 6, w 3, n-b 2.........	15
D. L. Hemp not out	70		—
D. P. Ostler c and b Grayson	29	1/47 2/93 3/150	(5 wkts, 40 overs) 255
T. L. Penney c Rollins b Cowan	10	4/192 5/215	

A. F. Giles, †K. J. Piper, G. C. Small and A. A. Donald did not bat.

Bowling: Cowan 7–0–52–2; Ilott 7–0–53–0; Cousins 8–0–42–1; Grayson 6–0–40–1; Such 8–0–30–1; S. G. Law 4–0–28–0.

Essex

D. D. J. Robinson c Smith b Small......	29	M. C. Ilott lbw b Donald	0
S. G. Law b Welch..................	18	D. M. Cousins c Piper b Donald	1
*N. Hussain c Piper b Small	19	P. M. Such not out	0
A. P. Grayson c Smith b Small	9	W 5	5
†R. J. Rollins b Donald	11		—
D. R. Law b Donald.................	1	1/30 2/62 3/76	(28.5 overs) 108
T. P. Hodgson run out	12	4/79 5/83 6/92	
A. P. Cowan c Piper b Donald	3	7/98 8/102 9/108	

Bowling: Welch 6–0–19–1; Brown 5–0–24–0; Small 8–1–30–3; Giles 4–0–25–0; Donald 5.5–1–10–5.

Umpires: J. D. Bond and J. F. Steele.

At Manchester, September 9. ESSEX lost to LANCASHIRE by six wickets.

At Cardiff, September 14. ESSEX beat GLAMORGAN by six wickets.

GLAMORGAN

GLAMORGAN v WARWICKSHIRE

At Cardiff, April 27. Glamorgan won by 17 runs (D/L method). Toss: Warwickshire.

Watkin took three for seven in his first six overs for Glamorgan, whose batsmen were just beginning to surrender the advantage when they were saved by the rain which ended their innings. The Duckworth/Lewis system for settling the result of interrupted matches came into play for the first time in England. Glamorgan's par score for the 20 overs they had faced was calculated at 64.68, which they had beaten by 16.32. Although they were batting second, the ECB directed that this retrospective calculation should be listed as a 17-run win.

Warwickshire

D. P. Ostler b Watkin	0	A. F. Giles c Maynard b Watkin	6
N. M. K. Smith b Watkin	14	G. Welch not out	22
D. R. Brown b Dale	30	B 1, l-b 8, w 7	16
D. L. Hemp c Shaw b Watkin	3		—
*A. J. Moles c Parkin b Dale	19	1/3 2/22 3/28 (7 wkts, 40 overs)	147
T. L. Penney b Croft	8	4/75 5/75	
†K. J. Piper not out	29	6/89 7/112	

G. C. Small and A. A. Donald did not bat.

Bowling: Parkin 8–1–25–0; Watkin 8–0–15–4; Thomas 4–0–27–0; Dale 8–2–18–2; Croft 8–0–26–1; Butcher 4–0–27–0.

Glamorgan

A. Dale not out	27	G. P. Butcher not out	1
H. Morris run out	26	B 2, l-b 3, w 4, n-b 4	13
P. A. Cottey b Donald	1		—
*M. P. Maynard b Smith	13	1/42 2/46 3/80 (3 wkts, 20 overs)	81

A. W. Evans, †A. D. Shaw, R. D. B. Croft, S. D. Thomas, S. L. Watkin and O. T. Parkin did not bat.

Bowling: Welch 3–0–17–0; Brown 3–1–10–0; Small 7–0–24–0; Donald 5–0–22–1; Smith 2–0–3–1.

Umpires: M. J. Kitchen and D. R. Shepherd.

At Taunton, May 4. GLAMORGAN lost to SOMERSET by six wickets.

At Leeds, May 11. GLAMORGAN lost to YORKSHIRE by seven wickets (D/L method).

At Canterbury, May 18. GLAMORGAN lost to KENT by eight runs.

GLAMORGAN v HAMPSHIRE

At Cardiff, May 25. Glamorgan won by six wickets. Toss: Hampshire.

Glamorgan dominated this match from the start; it was Hampshire's 13th unsuccessful attempt out of 13 at beating another county since the start of the season. Waqar Younis took three in four balls to keep Hampshire's total down to 180, and then Dale and Maynard built a third-wicket stand of 87.

Hampshire

G. W. White lbw b Thomas	18	S. D. Udal b Waqar Younis 0
M. L. Hayden b Dale	45	R. J. Maru not out 6
R. A. Smith c Shaw b Dale	12	S. J. Renshaw not out............... 15
K. D. James c Cottey b Cosker	7	B 4, l-b 10, w 8 22
W. S. Kendall c James b Cottey	25	—
*J. P. Stephenson c Thomas		1/53 2/81 3/90 (8 wkts, 40 overs) 180
b Waqar Younis	26	4/100 5/133 6/155
†A. N. Aymes lbw b Waqar Younis	4	7/155 8/156

J. N. B. Bovill did not bat.

Bowling: Waqar Younis 8–1–25–3; Watkin 7–0–48–0; Thomas 4–0–16–1; Dale 8–4–20–2; Cosker 8–1–28–1; Cottey 5–0–29–1.

Glamorgan

S. D. Thomas lbw b Renshaw	8	S. P. James not out.................. 13
H. Morris c and b Udal	12	L-b 6, w 1 7
A. Dale c Stephenson b Udal	53	—
*M. P. Maynard st Aymes b Renshaw	47	1/18 2/22 (4 wkts, 38 overs) 181
P. A. Cottey not out	41	3/109 4/156

†A. D. Shaw, D. A. Cosker, Waqar Younis, S. L. Watkin and G. P. Butcher did not bat.

Bowling: Renshaw 8–0–32–2; Udal 8–0–30–2; Maru 8–0–26–0; Bovill 6–0–29–0; Stephenson 6–0–44–0; White 2–0–14–0.

Umpires: J. H. Harris and R. Palmer.

GLAMORGAN v DURHAM

At Pontypridd, June 1. Glamorgan won by six wickets. Toss: Glamorgan.

Only Speak, who made a bloody-minded 74, was able to cope with some incisive spells from the Glamorgan seamers. Croft went wicketless, but he smashed 46 from 33 balls when he opened the batting. Cottey and James finished the job off with nine overs to spare in an unbroken stand of 64.

Durham

J. E. Morris c Shaw b Waqar Younis	0	S. J. E. Brown c and b Watkin 5
†M. P. Speight c Shaw b Thomas	30	M. J. Saggers not out 5
*D. C. Boon lbw b Waqar Younis	17	
N. J. Speak not out	74	L-b 1, w 8, n-b 2 11
J. J. B. Lewis c Maynard b Thomas	8	—
P. D. Collingwood c Maynard b Butcher	11	1/0 2/27 3/61 (8 wkts, 40 overs) 183
M. J. Foster c Maynard b Butcher	18	4/87 5/107 6/139
J. Boiling b Watkin	4	7/160 8/172

A. Walker did not bat.

Bowling: Waqar Younis 7–1–28–2; Watkin 8–0–41–2; Thomas 8–0–31–2; Dale 4–0–15–0; Croft 8–0–39–0; Butcher 5–0–28–2.

Glamorgan

R. D. B. Croft c Speight b Brown....... 46	S. P. James not out.................. 45		
H. Morris c Speight b Brown 22	L-b 6, w 4, n-b 4 14		
A. Dale run out...................... 14	—		
*M. P. Maynard c Boiling b Foster...... 22	1/79 2/82	(4 wkts, 30.5 overs) 184	
P. A. Cottey not out 21	3/116 4/120		

G. P. Butcher, †A. D. Shaw, S. D. Thomas, Waqar Younis and S. L. Watkin did not bat.

Bowling: Brown 8–0–43–2; Saggers 7–0–52–0; Walker 6–0–25–0; Foster 4–0–26–1; Boiling 5.5–0–32–0.

Umpires: A. A. Jones and B. J. Meyer.

GLAMORGAN v MIDDLESEX

At Cardiff, June 15. Glamorgan won by six wickets. Toss: Middlesex.

Glamorgan's batting was rather more solid than it had been the previous day, when they were bowled out for 31 by the Middlesex seamers. Supported ably by Croft and James, Maynard guided them home with a 78-ball innings of 71.

Middlesex

P. N. Weekes b Watkin 16	K. P. Dutch not out 19		
J. H. Kallis c Shaw b Thomas.......... 15	A. R. C. Fraser not out.............. 2		
*M. R. Ramprakash c and b Cosker 47	L-b 7, w 9, n-b 2 18		
M. W. Gatting c Watkin b Cosker 23	—		
J. C. Pooley c Shaw b Thomas 35	1/30 2/43 3/108	(6 wkts, 40 overs) 185	
†K. R. Brown b Waqar Younis 10	4/115 5/148 6/179		

P. C. R. Tufnell, J. P. Hewitt and I. N. Blanchett did not bat.

Bowling: Waqar Younis 8–0–33–1; Watkin 6–0–24–1; Thomas 7–1–39–2; Dale 4–0–17–0; Croft 8–0–25–0; Cosker 7–0–40–2.

Glamorgan

R. D. B. Croft lbw b Dutch 44	S. P. James not out.................. 29		
H. Morris c Brown b Hewitt 1	L-b 1, w 3, n-b 5 9		
A. Dale c Pooley b Dutch 18	—		
*M. P. Maynard not out............... 71	1/7 2/60	(4 wkts, 35.3 overs) 186	
P. A. Cottey lbw b Weekes 14	3/75 4/106		

D. A. Cosker, †A. D. Shaw, Waqar Younis, S. D. Thomas and S. L. Watkin did not bat.

Bowling: Fraser 8–0–50–0; Hewitt 6–0–28–1; Tufnell 8–0–47–0; Dutch 8–0–41–2; Weekes 5–1–17–1; Ramprakash 0.3–0–2–0.

Umpires: T. E. Jesty and R. A. White.

At Manchester, June 22. LANCASHIRE v GLAMORGAN. No result (abandoned).

GLAMORGAN v SUSSEX

At Swansea, June 29. Glamorgan won by eight wickets. Toss: Sussex.

Sussex, who had been rolled over for just 54 and 67 in their Championship match here, collapsed again after a defiant third-wicket stand of 90 between Athey and Mark Newell. Morris finished the match in style with a six – and 12 overs to spare. Croft hit a six through the windscreen of a passing car, almost causing a serious accident.

Sussex

M. T. E. Peirce lbw b Waqar Younis	7	A. A. Khan lbw b Waqar Younis	0
C. W. J. Athey st Shaw b Croft	60	M. A. Robinson not out	2
K. Greenfield run out	4	R. J. Kirtley run out	0
M. Newell c Maynard b Dale	39	B 1, l-b 9, w 6	16
V. C. Drakes run out	0		
*†P. Moores b Waqar Younis	3	1/15 2/21 3/111 (37.3 overs) 135	
K. Newell c James b Dale	2	4/116 5/128 6/129	
J. J. Bates b Waqar Younis	2	7/131 8/133 9/134	

Bowling: Waqar Younis 7–1–14–4; Watkin 8–2–11–0; Cosker 8–2–27–0; Croft 8–0–41–1; Dale 6.3–0–32–2.

Glamorgan

R. D. B. Croft c Bates b Robinson	27
H. Morris not out	66
A. Dale c Greenfield b Khan	17
*M. P. Maynard not out	17
B 4, l-b 2, w 1, n-b 2	9

1/43 2/87   (2 wkts, 28 overs) 136

P. A. Cottey, S. P. James, G. P. Butcher, †A. D. Shaw, D. A. Cosker, Waqar Younis and S. L. Watkin did not bat.

Bowling: Kirtley 3–0–26–0; Drakes 5–2–13–0; Robinson 6–0–26–1; Khan 8–1–22–1; K. Newell 2–0–14–0; Bates 4–0–29–0.

Umpires: J. W. Holder and P. Willey.

GLAMORGAN v GLOUCESTERSHIRE

At Swansea, July 6. Gloucestershire won by 17 runs. Toss: Gloucestershire.

Gloucestershire took an early stranglehold on the game when Wright and Hancock put together an opening stand of 107 in 22 overs. Then the pitch began to take turn on a hot afternoon, and off-spinner Ball cleaned up Glamorgan's top order with figures of four for 26. James and Shaw dragged them back from 71 for five, staging a stand of 105, but they had too much to do.

Gloucestershire

A. J. Wright c Thomas b Waqar Younis .	69	M. C. J. Ball not out	0
T. H. C. Hancock c James b Dale	57		
S. Young c Morris b Watkin	30	L-b 10, w 8	18
M. A. Lynch b Dale	39		
†R. C. Russell b Waqar Younis	16	1/107 2/162 3/189 (7 wkts, 40 overs) 236	
*M. W. Alleyne b Waqar Younis	6	4/227 5/235	
R. I. Dawson run out	1	6/236 7/236	

R. P. Davis, J. Lewis and A. M. Smith did not bat.

Bowling: Waqar Younis 8–0–37–3; Watkin 8–0–42–1; Thomas 8–0–38–0; Dale 8–0–56–2; Cosker 8–0–53–0.

Glamorgan

G. P. Butcher b Ball	19	S. D. Thomas b Young...............	15
H. Morris c Wright b Ball	9	Waqar Younis not out	1
A. Dale c Young b Ball	8	L-b 10, w 6, n-b 2	18
*M. P. Maynard lbw b Young	20		
P. A. Cottey c Alleyne b Ball	6	1/28 2/46 3/47 (7 wkts, 40 overs) 219	
S. P. James not out	75	4/57 5/71	
†A. D. Shaw b Smith	48	6/176 7/218	

S. L. Watkin and D. A. Cosker did not bat.

Bowling: Smith 8–1–38–1; Lewis 6–0–34–0; Ball 8–0–26–4; Young 8–0–45–2; Davis 4–0–32–0; Alleyne 6–0–34–0.

Umpires: A. Clarkson and A. G. T. Whitehead.

At Worcester, July 20. GLAMORGAN lost to WORCESTERSHIRE by 45 runs.

At Chesterfield, July 27. GLAMORGAN lost to DERBYSHIRE by eight wickets.

GLAMORGAN v NOTTINGHAMSHIRE

At Colwyn Bay, August 3. Nottinghamshire won by 20 runs. Toss: Glamorgan.

Astle and Dowman took advantage of a weakened Glamorgan attack – Waqar Younis and Watkin were rested – to build a fourth-wicket stand of 129 in 20 overs. Dowman went on to claim a rare wicket with his medium-pace and, once Oram had sliced through the tail, Nottinghamshire were in the clear.

Nottinghamshire

G. E. Welton run out	9	K. P. Evans b Dale		2
L. N. P. Walker lbw b Thomas	22	J. E. Hindson not out		3
N. J. Astle c Dale b Parkin	63			
*P. Johnson b Butcher	8	L-b 12, w 5, n-b 6		23
M. P. Dowman c Cottey b Thomas	71			—
G. F. Archer b Thomas	4	1/24 2/46 3/62	(8 wkts, 40 overs)	228
C. M. Tolley not out	21	4/191 5/196 6/201		
†W. M. Noon run out	2	7/214 8/218		

A. R. Oram did not bat.

Bowling: Thomas 8–0–30–3; Parkin 8–1–43–1; Croft 8–1–17–0; Butcher 5–0–48–1; Dale 8–0–58–1; Cottey 3–0–20–0.

Glamorgan

R. D. B. Croft c and b Evans	21	†A. D. Shaw run out		2
A. Dale c Astle b Oram	1	S. D. Thomas b Oram		3
P. A. Cottey c Dowman b Tolley	26	O. T. Parkin not out		1
*M. P. Maynard c Welton b Dowman	24	L-b 16, w 5		21
G. P. Butcher lbw b Astle	44			—
S. P. James c Dowman b Tolley	8	1/3 2/35 3/64	(40 overs)	208
M. J. Powell b Oram	42	4/98 5/116 6/166		
A. W. Evans b Oram	15	7/193 8/202 9/205		

Bowling: Evans 8–1–41–1; Oram 8–0–45–4; Astle 8–0–35–1; Tolley 8–0–31–2; Dowman 8–0–40–1.

Umpires: H. D. Bird and G. Sharp.

GLAMORGAN v NORTHAMPTONSHIRE

At Cardiff, August 24. No result (abandoned).

At Leicester, August 31. LEICESTERSHIRE v GLAMORGAN. No result (abandoned).

At The Oval, September 7. GLAMORGAN lost to SURREY by two wickets.

AXA Life League, 1997

GLAMORGAN v ESSEX

At Cardiff, September 14. Essex won by six wickets. Toss: Glamorgan.

Essex had won only one match in eight since June, when they were top of the table, but then Glamorgan's form had been no better, and they stretched their winless sequence to eight. They did not appear unduly worried, having rested Croft, Maynard, Waqar Younis and Watkin for the following week's crucial Championship match. After all their batsmen except Dale and Cottey had failed, a second-string attack was not up to the task of constraining Stuart Law and Hussain. Such recorded the best Sunday bowling figures of his 15-year career.

Glamorgan

A. W. Evans c D. R. Law b Ilott	5	A. P. Davies b Such		3
W. L. Law b Ilott	8	D. A. Cosker c Prichard b Such		0
A. Dale c Napier b Such	62	O. T. Parkin not out		1
*P. A. Cottey c Hyam b D. R. Law	40	L-b 6, w 5		11
M. J. Powell b D. R. Law	20			
G. P. Butcher b Such	17			168
†A. D. Shaw run out	1	1/9 2/22 3/97	(38 overs)	
S. D. Thomas b Such	0	4/139 5/152 6/164		
		7/164 8/166 9/167		

Bowling: Cowan 6–0–16–0; Ilott 7–1–21–2; Such 7–0–29–5; Napier 4–0–31–0; Grayson 6–0–36–0; D. R. Law 8–0–29–2.

Essex

*P. J. Prichard b Thomas	31	D. R. Law not out		14
S. G. Law c Dale b Davies	59	L-b 2, w 7		9
N. Hussain not out	45			
R. C. Irani b Davies	2			169
A. P. Grayson b Cosker	9	1/78 2/106	(4 wkts, 32 overs)	
		3/112 4/127		

G. R. Napier, †B. J. Hyam, A. P. Cowan, M. C. Ilott and P. M. Such did not bat.

Bowling: Thomas 7–0–34–1; Parkin 5–0–45–0; Cosker 8–0–38–1; Davies 8–0–25–2; Butcher 4–0–25–0.

Umpires: J. H. Harris and R. Julian.

GLOUCESTERSHIRE

At Leicester, April 27. GLOUCESTERSHIRE beat LEICESTERSHIRE by 111 runs.

GLOUCESTERSHIRE v HAMPSHIRE

At Bristol, May 11. No result. Toss: Gloucestershire.

In a game reduced to 16 overs a side, Lynch scored 88 in 51 balls, with ten fours and two sixes; he put on 97 in nine overs with Alleyne. But rain returned to prevent Hampshire's reply.

Gloucestershire

M. A. Lynch not out	88	R. J. Cunliffe not out		0
A. J. Wright c Kendall b Stephenson	4			
S. Young c Maru b Stephenson	2	W 7, n-b 2		9
†R. C. Russell c Kendall b James	1			
*M. W. Alleyne c Hayden b Udal	33	1/9 2/17 3/18	(5 wkts, 16 overs)	139
T. H. C. Hancock c Hayden b Renshaw	2	4/115 5/123		

N. J. Trainor, M. C. J. Ball, A. M. Smith and K. P. Sheeraz did not bat.

Bowling: Renshaw 4–0–25–1; Stephenson 3–0–26–2; James 3–0–16–1; Mascarenhas 3–0–36–0; Udal 3–0–36–1.

Hampshire

M. L. Hayden, R. A. Smith, K. D. James, W. S. Kendall, *J. P. Stephenson, P. R. Whitaker, †A. N. Aymes, S. D. Udal, A. D. Mascarenhas, S. J. Renshaw and R. J. Maru.

Umpires: G. I. Burgess and R. A. White.

At The Oval, May 18. GLOUCESTERSHIRE lost to SURREY by five wickets.

GLOUCESTERSHIRE v ESSEX

At Gloucester, May 25. Essex won by five wickets. Toss: Gloucestershire.

None of Essex's six bowlers conceded runs readily, and Russell's 35 was the highest score in Gloucestershire's paltry 139. Essex maintained their 100 per cent league record with the help of Stuart Law's quick-fire fifty from 42 balls.

Gloucestershire

A. J. Wright lbw b Ilott	12	A. M. Smith b Irani	7
M. A. Lynch c Hussain b Cowan	7	R. P. Davis not out	4
R. J. Cunliffe st Rollins b Such	23	K. P. Sheeraz lbw b Irani	2
S. Young c S. G. Law b Cowan	2	B 5, l-b 13, w 5	23
†R. C. Russell b Grayson	35		
*M. W. Alleyne c Robinson b Grayson	7	1/19 2/26 3/38	(39.2 overs) 139
T. H. C. Hancock c Cowan b Irani	11	4/74 5/97 6/109	
M. C. J. Ball st Rollins b S. G. Law	6	7/124 8/126 9/135	

Bowling: Cowan 6–0–20–2; Ilott 6–0–23–1; Such 8–0–18–1; Irani 7.2–0–23–3; Grayson 6–0–20–2; S. G. Law 6–0–17–1.

Essex

*P. J. Prichard b Alleyne	29	D. D. J. Robinson not out	1
S. G. Law c and b Davis	58		
N. Hussain lbw b Alleyne	0	L-b 5, w 5, n-b 2	12
R. C. Irani not out	17		
A. P. Grayson c Davis b Alleyne	15	1/97 2/97 3/101	(5 wkts, 26.5 overs) 142
D. R. Law c Hancock b Davis	10	4/126 5/137	

†R. J. Rollins, M. C. Ilott, A. P. Cowan and P. M. Such did not bat.

Bowling: Smith 5–1–24–0; Sheeraz 2.5–0–16–0; Ball 4–0–26–0; Alleyne 8–4–24–3; Young 2–0–18–0; Davis 5–0–29–2.

Umpires: D. J. Constant and B. Leadbeater.

At Leeds, June 8. GLOUCESTERSHIRE beat YORKSHIRE by 44 runs (D/L method).

GLOUCESTERSHIRE v WORCESTERSHIRE

At Bristol, June 15. Gloucestershire won by one run. Toss: Worcestershire.

Worcestershire declined to 16 for four in pursuit of 178. They recovered with two good half-century partnerships but could not quite manage 12 from Young's last over.

Gloucestershire

A. J. Wright b Lampitt	19	A. M. Smith c Rhodes b Leatherdale	10
R. J. Cunliffe c Rhodes b Sheriyar	50	J. Lewis c Solanki b Leatherdale	8
S. Young c Leatherdale b Sheriyar	9	K. P. Sheeraz not out	7
M. A. Lynch lbw b Lampitt	11	B 2, l-b 9, w 10, n-b 4	25
*M. W. Alleyne b Haynes	16		—
†R. C. Russell b Lampitt	18	1/54 2/83 3/97 (38.3 overs) 177	
T. H. C. Hancock c Rhodes b Haynes	0	4/113 5/133 6/133	
M. C. J. Ball c Curtis b Lampitt	4	7/151 8/158 9/162	

Bowling: Chapman 8–0–24–0; Haynes 8–0–35–2; Lampitt 8–0–49–4; Sheriyar 7–1–31–2; Leatherdale 6.3–0–19–2; Hick 1–0–8–0.

Worcestershire

T. S. Curtis b Lewis	3	S. R. Lampitt not out	31
V. S. Solanki b Smith	1	*†S. J. Rhodes not out	0
G. A. Hick c Russell b Lewis	6	L-b 6, w 5	11
G. R. Haynes c Lynch b Young	45		
K. R. Spiring b Smith	0	1/5 2/7 3/15 (7 wkts, 40 overs) 176	
W. P. C. Weston c Lewis b Alleyne	28	4/16 5/79	
D. A. Leatherdale c Wright b Young	51	6/89 7/172	

R. J. Chapman and A. Sheriyar did not bat.

Bowling: Lewis 8–0–17–2; Smith 8–2–24–2; Young 8–0–43–2; Sheeraz 4–0–22–0; Alleyne 8–0–48–1; Ball 4–0–16–0.

Umpires: B. Dudleston and J. F. Steele.

GLOUCESTERSHIRE v MIDDLESEX

At Bristol, June 22. Gloucestershire won by 55 runs. Toss: Gloucestershire. First-team debut: N. D. Martin.

An inexperienced Middlesex attack was rattled by the assault of Young and Lynch, who put on 115 for the third wicket in 16 overs. But the real culprits were the senior batsmen: Kallis, Ramprakash and Gatting managed just 13 between them on a flat wicket and, although Shah made a fine 65 not out, it came too late to alter the result. To add to Middlesex's woes, they were fined £660 for a slow over-rate.

Gloucestershire

A. J. Wright lbw b Martin	15	T. H. C. Hancock st Brown b Weekes	1
R. J. Cunliffe c Brown b Bloomfield	0	M. C. J. Ball not out	8
S. Young not out	89	B 1, l-b 11, w 12, n-b 6	30
M. A. Lynch c Brown b Hewitt	53		—
*M. W. Alleyne b Bloomfield	28	1/2 2/27 3/142 (6 wkts, 40 overs) 232	
†R. C. Russell b Ramprakash	8	4/199 5/210 6/213	

A. M. Smith, K. P. Sheeraz and J. Lewis did not bat.

Bowling: Hewitt 8–0–29–1; Bloomfield 8–0–34–2; Martin 6–0–29–1; Blanchett 4–0–32–0; Weekes 8–0–41–1; Shah 2–0–29–0; Ramprakash 4–0–26–1.

Middlesex

P. N. Weekes c Russell b Sheeraz	28	O. A. Shah not out	65
J. H. Kallis c Russell b Lewis	7	J. P. Hewitt not out	32
*M. R. Ramprakash c Hancock b Lewis	2	L-b 2, w 9	11
M. W. Gatting c Russell b Lewis	4		—
J. C. Pooley c Alleyne b Sheeraz	14	1/16 2/20 3/43 (6 wkts, 38 overs) 177	
†K. R. Brown c Alleyne b Ball	14	4/53 5/66 6/101	

T. F. Bloomfield, I. N. Blanchett and N. D. Martin did not bat.

Bowling: Smith 8–1–32–0; Lewis 8–0–39–3; Sheeraz 8–1–34–2; Ball 8–0–43–1; Alleyne 6–0–27–0.

Umpires: R. Julian and P. Willey.

At Luton, June 29. NORTHAMPTONSHIRE v GLOUCESTERSHIRE. No result (abandoned).

At Swansea, July 6. GLOUCESTERSHIRE beat GLAMORGAN by 17 runs.

At Hove, July 13. GLOUCESTERSHIRE lost to SUSSEX by one wicket.

GLOUCESTERSHIRE v DERBYSHIRE

At Cheltenham, July 20. Gloucestershire won by seven wickets. Toss: Derbyshire.

Gloucestershire scored at seven and a half an over as they overhauled a useful Derbyshire total with seven overs to spare. Young had his foot on the accelerator during his 85 from 61 balls, which included five fours and seven sixes, and Lynch played a supporting role for once in a third-wicket stand of 140 in 17 overs.

Derbyshire

A. S. Rollins c Russell b Smith	20	M. J. Vandrau run out		6
C. J. Adams c Lynch b Lewis	21	A. J. Harris not out		0
G. A. Khan c Lynch b Alleyne	20			
K. J. Barnett c Hancock b Smith	99	L-b 1, w 4, n-b 3		8
V. P. Clarke c Hancock b Young	6			—
*P. A. J. DeFreitas c Lewis b Hancock	27	1/27 2/62 3/68	(9 wkts, 40 overs)	246
†K. M. Krikken c Alleyne b Young	39	4/83 5/124 6/206		
P. Aldred lbw b Young	0	7/207 8/246 9/246		

K. J. Dean did not bat.

Bowling: Lewis 8–0–33–1; Smith 8–0–51–2; Alleyne 7–0–55–1; Young 8–1–51–3; Ball 5–0–33–0; Hancock 4–0–22–1.

Gloucestershire

A. J. Wright c Rollins b Aldred	27	*M. W. Alleyne not out		15
T. H. C. Hancock c Adams b Harris	46	L-b 5, w 9, n-b 6		20
S. Young c and b Dean	85			
M. A. Lynch not out	54	1/72 2/83 3/223	(3 wkts, 32.4 overs)	247

R. I. Dawson, †R. C. Russell, M. C. J. Ball, M. G. N. Windows, A. M. Smith and J. Lewis did not bat.

Bowling: DeFreitas 6–0–54–0; Dean 6.4–0–55–1; Aldred 8–0–39–1; Harris 7–0–50–1; Vandrau 3–0–31–0; Clarke 2–0–13–0.

Umpires: D. R. Shepherd and J. F. Steele.

GLOUCESTERSHIRE v DURHAM

At Cheltenham, July 27. Gloucestershire won by five wickets. Toss: Gloucestershire.

Although Lewis gave Durham a promising start with his maiden Sunday hundred, which took 111 balls, no one could inject any real haste once he had gone. Gloucestershire faltered in mid-innings but finished on a high note: Russell made 59 from 41 balls and shared a match-winning partnership of 71 with Dawson.

Durham

J. E. Morris c Russell b Alleyne 32	J. Wood not out 11
J. J. B. Lewis c Wright b Alleyne 102	
†M. P. Speight c Hancock b Alleyne 8	L-b 8, w 2 10
*D. C. Boon c Hancock b Ball 23	—
N. J. Speak run out 15	1/54 2/84 3/136 (7 wkts, 40 overs) 226
R. M. S. Weston lbw b Averis 13	4/187 5/197
M. J. Foster b Averis 12	6/211 7/226

A. Walker, J. Boiling and S. J. E. Brown did not bat.

Bowling: Young 8–0–42–0; Lewis 8–0–45–0; Alleyne 8–0–47–3; Ball 8–0–41–1; Averis 8–0–43–2.

Gloucestershire

A. J. Wright b Wood 13	R. I. Dawson not out 28
T. H. C. Hancock c Weston b Foster 50	
S. Young c Lewis b Foster 41	B 1, l-b 7, w 5, n-b 2 15
M. A. Lynch b Foster 0	—
*M. W. Alleyne c Lewis b Brown 24	1/24 2/109 3/109 (5 wkts, 37.4 overs) 230
†R. C. Russell not out 59	4/116 5/159

M. G. N. Windows, M. C. J. Ball, J. M. M. Averis and J. Lewis did not bat.

Bowling: Brown 8–0–37–1; Wood 7–1–39–1; Foster 8–0–52–3; Walker 6.4–0–51–0; Boiling 8–0–43–0.

Umpires: J. C. Balderstone and K. E. Palmer.

At Taunton, August 10. GLOUCESTERSHIRE lost to SOMERSET by 73 runs.

GLOUCESTERSHIRE v LANCASHIRE

At Bristol, August 24. No result. Toss: Gloucestershire.

Play was possible in only three matches of this rain-affected round, each involving one of the top three. But third-placed Lancashire were denied the chance to keep up with Warwickshire and Kent, who both won. Ten overs were bowled before the rains came.

Lancashire

*M. Watkinson c Russell b Lewis 2	N. H. Fairbrother not out 0
J. E. R. Gallian b Smith 10	W 3 3
J. P. Crawley not out 16	—
G. D. Lloyd b Alleyne 10	1/11 2/20 3/41 (3 wkts, 10 overs) 41

G. Chapple, I. D. Austin, †W. K. Hegg, G. Yates, P. J. Martin and R. J. Green did not bat.

Bowling: Smith 4–0–13–1; Lewis 4–0–13–1; Averis 1–0–10–0; Alleyne 1–0–5–1.

Gloucestershire

R. I. Dawson, T. H. C. Hancock, *M. W. Alleyne, M. A. Lynch, M. G. N. Windows, D. R. Hewson, †R. C. Russell, M. C. J. Ball, J. Lewis, A. M. Smith and J. M. M. Averis.

Umpires: J. H. Harris and V. A. Holder.

GLOUCESTERSHIRE v NOTTINGHAMSHIRE

At Bristol, August 31. No result (abandoned).

At Canterbury, September 7. GLOUCESTERSHIRE lost to KENT by nine wickets.

At Birmingham, September 14. GLOUCESTERSHIRE lost to WARWICKSHIRE by 71 runs.

HAMPSHIRE

At Chelmsford, April 27. HAMPSHIRE lost to ESSEX by three wickets.

HAMPSHIRE v YORKSHIRE

At Southampton, May 4. Yorkshire won by 71 runs. Toss: Yorkshire.

Maru's best Sunday figures of four for 29 were not enough to restrict Yorkshire, for whom Lehmann played a strong hand with 75 from 65 balls on his first Sunday League appearance. Hampshire started steadily enough, but then lost their last nine wickets in seven overs, and their last three in five balls to Gough.

Yorkshire

*D. Byas lbw b Maru	19	D. Gough not out	23
M. P. Vaughan b Maru	38	C. E. W. Silverwood c Kendall b Renshaw	1
D. S. Lehmann b Maru	75	R. D. Stemp b Renshaw	2
P. J. Hartley c Kendall b Udal	11	L-b 2, w 6	8
†R. J. Blakey lbw b Udal	19		
A. McGrath b Stephenson	8	1/31 2/74 3/101 (39.3 overs) 227	
C. White c Kendall b Udal	22	4/160 5/173 6/179	
B. Parker c and b Maru	1	7/183 8/212 9/222	

Bowling: Mascarenhas 6–0–44–0; Stephenson 8–0–47–1; Maru 8–0–29–4; Renshaw 7.3–0–37–2; Udal 8–0–46–3; Kendall 2–0–22–0.

Hampshire

M. L. Hayden c Blakey b Silverwood	43	A. D. Mascarenhas b Gough	10
J. S. Laney c Byas b White	47	R. J. Maru b Gough	1
R. A. Smith b White	25	S. J. Renshaw not out	1
M. Keech c White b Stemp	3	L-b 4, w 7, n-b 2	13
W. S. Kendall c Hartley b Stemp	1		
*J. P. Stephenson c Hartley b Stemp	3	1/87 2/123 3/128 (35.5 overs) 156	
S. D. Udal c and b White	5	4/132 5/133 6/139	
†A. N. Aymes lbw b Gough	4	7/143 8/154 9/155	

Bowling: Silverwood 8–1–28–1; Gough 5.5–0–21–3; White 8–0–37–3; Hartley 6–0–37–0; Stemp 8–0–29–3.

Umpires: H. D. Bird and J. D. Bond.

At Bristol, May 11. GLOUCESTERSHIRE v HAMPSHIRE. No result.

HAMPSHIRE v LEICESTERSHIRE

At Southampton, May 18. Leicestershire won by 38 runs. Toss: Hampshire.

Solid scoring throughout the order allowed Leicestershire to reach 231 for six, and Hampshire required the unlikely figure of 103 from their last ten overs. Despite a late fifty from James, they fell well short.

Leicestershire

N. C. Johnson c Aymes b Maru	54	†P. A. Nixon run out	33
V. J. Wells c Maru b Hayden	31	J. M. Dakin not out	11
A. Habib c Stephenson b Hayden	23	B 1, l-b 5, w 7	13
D. L. Maddy c and b Udal	11		
B. F. Smith not out	51	1/89 2/92 3/120 (6 wkts, 40 overs) 231	
*J. J. Whitaker c Stephenson b Connor	4	4/138 5/145 6/199	

G. J. Parsons, M. T. Brimson and A. D. Mullally did not bat.

Bowling: Connor 8–0–43–1; Renshaw 7–0–48–0; James 2–0–17–0; Maru 8–0–38–1; Hayden 8–0–38–2; Udal 7–0–41–1.

Hampshire

M. L. Hayden c Whitaker b Wells	19	R. J. Maru b Mullally	6
G. W. White c Whitaker b Parsons	11	S. J. Renshaw not out	7
R. A. Smith c Wells b Mullally	0	C. A. Connor b Wells	0
W. S. Kendall lbw b Brimson	37	L-b 9, w 6, n-b 7	22
*J. P. Stephenson c Maddy b Johnson	6		
K. D. James run out	50	1/27 2/28 3/48 (39.5 overs) 193	
†A. N. Aymes c Dakin b Wells	30	4/59 5/104 6/157	
S. D. Udal c Brimson b Mullally	5	7/177 8/186 9/186	

Bowling: Mullally 8–0–36–3; Parsons 8–0–27–1; Wells 7.5–0–33–3; Johnson 8–0–38–1; Brimson 4–0–24–1; Dakin 4–0–26–0.

Umpires: D. J. Constant and G. Sharp.

At Cardiff, May 25. HAMPSHIRE lost to GLAMORGAN by six wickets.

HAMPSHIRE v WARWICKSHIRE

At Southampton, June 1. Hampshire won by 14 runs. Toss: Warwickshire.
In the Championship match the previous day, Hayden had scored an unbeaten 235. He followed it with 118, including 13 fours and three sixes, before he was run out when a straight drive was deflected on to the stumps at the bowler's end. He and White had put on 185 in the first 29 overs. Bovill's best Sunday figures helped Hampshire to close down the match, despite a late flurry by Giles. It was Hampshire's first win over another county in 25 matches since August 12 the previous year.

Hampshire

G. W. White c Hemp b Smith	67	S. J. Renshaw not out	0
M. L. Hayden run out	118	L-b 19, w 9, n-b 2	30
S. D. Udal not out	50		
*R. A. Smith c Welch b Edmond	11	1/185 2/217 (4 wkts, 40 overs) 278	
J. S. Laney run out	2	3/265 4/277	

K. D. James, W. S. Kendall, †A. N. Aymes, R. J. Maru and J. N. B. Bovill did not bat.

Bowling: Welch 4–0–28–0; Brown 6–0–14–0; Edmond 8–0–50–1; Small 8–0–50–0; Smith 8–0–68–1; Giles 6–0–49–0.

Warwickshire

*N. V. Knight c Smith b Bovill	22	M. D. Edmond c Renshaw b Maru	5
N. M. K. Smith c sub b Bovill	52	†T. Frost run out	0
D. R. Brown run out	3	G. C. Small not out	2
D. L. Hemp lbw b Bovill	3	L-b 2, w 2, n-b 2	6
D. P. Ostler st Aymes b Udal	70		
T. L. Penney c sub b Udal	32	1/72 2/76 3/81 (39.4 overs) 264	
G. Welch c Kendall b Bovill	12	4/88 5/184 6/199	
A. F. Giles c Hayden b Renshaw	57	7/201 8/215 9/242	

Bowling: Maru 9–0–78–1; Renshaw 6.4–0–43–1; Bovill 8–0–44–4; Udal 8–0–33–2; James 8–0–64–0.

Umpires: J. W. Holder and A. G. T. Whitehead.

At Chesterfield, June 8. HAMPSHIRE lost to DERBYSHIRE by four wickets (D/L method).

HAMPSHIRE v SOMERSET

At Basingstoke, June 15. Somerset won by six runs. Toss: Hampshire.
    Although he took only one wicket, it was Mushtaq Ahmed's spell of eight overs for 20 runs that won the match for Somerset. Hampshire were unable to accelerate on a slow pitch, although a 12-ball over from Caddick in the middle of the innings cost 16 runs.

Somerset

M. N. Lathwell lbw b Renshaw	0	J. I. D. Kerr c Smith b Renshaw	17
M. Burns lbw b Stephenson	0	A. R. Caddick c Aymes b Renshaw	8
†R. J. Turner c Hayden b James	35	Mushtaq Ahmed c Kendall b Connor	1
*P. D. Bowler b James	21	B 5, l-b 5, w 8	18
K. A. Parsons b James	6		—
P. C. L. Holloway b Stephenson	8	1/0 2/4 3/47	(40 overs) 175
R. J. Harden b Connor	24	4/65 5/74 6/86	
G. D. Rose not out	37	7/123 8/153 9/172	

Bowling: Renshaw 8–0–45–3; Stephenson 8–0–43–2; James 8–3–16–3; Connor 8–1–35–2; Udal 8–0–26–0.

Hampshire

J. S. Laney lbw b Rose	6	†A. N. Aymes run out	9
M. L. Hayden c Mushtaq Ahmed b Kerr	24	S. J. Renshaw not out	5
R. A. Smith b Rose	2	C. A. Connor not out	1
M. Keech c Holloway b Kerr	44	L-b 6, w 14, n-b 2	22
W. S. Kendall c Lathwell b Kerr	0		—
*J. P. Stephenson c Parsons b Rose	27	1/14 2/18 3/63	(9 wkts, 40 overs) 169
K. D. James lbw b Mushtaq Ahmed	0	4/72 5/116 6/117	
S. D. Udal c Parsons b Kerr	29	7/125 8/162 9/167	

Bowling: Rose 8–0–29–3; Parsons 6–0–25–0; Burns 3–0–10–0; Caddick 8–1–44–0; Kerr 6–0–28–4; Mushtaq Ahmed 8–1–20–1; Bowler 1–0–7–0.

Umpires: A. Clarkson and A. A. Jones.

At Northampton, June 22. HAMPSHIRE lost to NORTHAMPTONSHIRE by four wickets (D/L method).

At Chester-le-Street, July 6. HAMPSHIRE beat DURHAM by six wickets.

HAMPSHIRE v WORCESTERSHIRE

At Southampton, July 13. Hampshire won by 87 runs. Toss: Hampshire.
    Stephenson's best one-day bowling figures, six for 33, killed off Worcestershire's promising run-chase. Moody skied a catch off Udal, and then Stephenson took his wickets in a five-over burst, precipitating a rapid collapse from 100 for one to 145 all out. Udal had scored an unbeaten fifty during Hampshire's innings; his stand with Keech realised 98 from the last 11 overs.

Hampshire

J. S. Laney lbw b Moody............. 9	S. D. Udal not out 52
M. L. Hayden c Lampitt b Chapman 32	B 1, l-b 5, w 8, n-b 8......... 22
R. A. Smith c Rhodes b Chapman 49	
M. Keech not out 53	1/18 2/99 (4 wkts, 40 overs) 232
W. S. Kendall lbw b Chapman 15	3/108 4/134

*J. P. Stephenson, †A. N. Aymes, S. J. Renshaw, R. J. Maru and C. A. Connor did not bat.

Bowling: Moody 7–1–28–1; Hick 8–0–39–0; Lampitt 7–0–51–0; Sheriyar 6–0–44–0; Chapman 6–0–27–3; Leatherdale 4–0–28–0; Solanki 2–0–9–0.

Worcestershire

*T. M. Moody c Smith b Udal 49	†S. J. Rhodes not out 6
V. S. Solanki c Aymes b Connor 3	A. Sheriyar c Maru b Stephenson 1
G. A. Hick c Aymes b Stephenson 48	R. J. Chapman lbw b Stephenson 0
K. R. Spiring lbw b Stephenson 6	L-b 2, w 7.................. 9
D. A. Leatherdale c Aymes b Stephenson 12	
W. P. C. Weston b Udal 0	1/8 2/100 3/106 (30.3 overs) 145
I. Dawood c Aymes b Stephenson....... 1	4/124 5/125 6/126
S. R. Lampitt b Udal 10	7/127 8/144 9/145

Bowling: Connor 4–0–11–1; Renshaw 5–0–21–0; Maru 6–0–26–0; Stephenson 7.3–0–33–6; Udal 8–0–52–3.

Umpires: T. E. Jesty and B. J. Meyer.

At Guildford, July 20. HAMPSHIRE lost to SURREY by 68 runs.

HAMPSHIRE v LANCASHIRE

At Southampton, July 27. Lancashire won by four wickets. Toss: Hampshire.
Hampshire's challenge declined after medium-pacer Chilton had picked up the prize wickets of Hayden and Smith, who shared a stand of 70. Fairbrother's experience took Lancashire close to their target, and Austin hit three fours in five balls to beat it.

Hampshire

J. S. Laney c Hegg b Austin 12	†A. N. Aymes not out 12
M. L. Hayden c Yates b Chilton 55	S. M. Milburn b Austin 1
R. A. Smith b Chilton 39	R. J. Maru not out 2
M. Keech lbw b Gallian............... 22	L-b 5, w 6, n-b 2 13
W. S. Kendall lbw b Martin 15	
S. D. Udal st Hegg b Yates 3	1/27 2/97 3/135 (9 wkts, 40 overs) 210
*J. P. Stephenson c Austin b Martin..... 26	4/140 5/155 6/159
S. J. Renshaw c Watkinson b Martin 10	7/178 8/200 9/208

Bowling: Martin 8–0–38–3; Austin 8–1–35–2; Yates 8–0–29–1; Watkinson 3–0–22–0; Shadford 4–0–31–0; Chilton 5–0–27–2; Gallian 4–0–23–1.

Lancashire

*M. Watkinson c Udal b Renshaw 10	I. D. Austin not out 27
J. E. R. Gallian c and b Maru 15	†W. K. Hegg not out 4
N. H. Fairbrother b Milburn........... 88	L-b 14, w 7.................. 21
G. D. Lloyd lbw b Stephenson 33	
A. Flintoff c Kendall b Udal 8	1/21 2/49 3/115 (6 wkts, 39.3 overs) 214
M. J. Chilton st Aymes b Udal 8	4/143 5/163 6/192

P. J. Martin, G. Yates and D. J. Shadford did not bat.

Bowling: Milburn 8–0–45–1; Renshaw 7–0–30–1; Maru 7–0–44–1; Stephenson 8–0–39–1; Udal 8–0–32–2; Hayden 1.3–0–10–0.

Umpires: D. R. Shepherd and P. Willey.

At Lord's, August 10. HAMPSHIRE beat MIDDLESEX by 16 runs.

HAMPSHIRE v KENT

At Portsmouth, August 31. Kent won by six wickets. Toss: Hampshire.

Hampshire tailed off after Robin Smith had given them a bright start, and then missed three chances to dismiss Ed Smith, who batted throughout the Kent innings for an undefeated 72.

Hampshire

J. S. Laney c Smith b Ealham	29	†A. N. Aymes run out		2
M. L. Hayden c Wells b Fleming	18	L. Savident not out		7
R. A. Smith b Thompson	35	S. M. Milburn b Fleming		0
M. Keech run out	26	B 3, l-b 3, n-b 6		12
S. D. Udal lbw b Strang	7			—
*J. P. Stephenson c Headley b Strang	18	1/54 2/58 3/104	(39.2 overs)	175
G. W. White lbw b Fleming	19	4/123 5/125 6/162		
S. J. Renshaw c Smith b Ealham	2	7/165 8/165 9/169		

Bowling: Headley 8–0–33–0; Thompson 8–0–48–1; Fleming 7.2–1–14–3; Ealham 8–1–24–2; Strang 8–0–50–2.

Kent

T. R. Ward b Savident	21	M. V. Fleming not out		10
E. T. Smith not out	72	B 1, l-b 9, w 7, n-b 6		23
A. P. Wells c Laney b Udal	11			—
G. R. Cowdrey st Aymes b Udal	19	1/40 2/81	(4 wkts, 37.4 overs)	179
M. A. Ealham b Milburn	23	3/106 4/152		

P. A. Strang, *†S. A. Marsh, N. J. Llong, J. B. D. Thompson and D. W. Headley did not bat.

Bowling: Milburn 8–0–38–1; Renshaw 6.4–0–33–0; Savident 7–0–33–1; Stephenson 8–0–34–0; Udal 8–1–31–2.

Umpires: A. Clarkson and D. J. Constant.

At Nottingham, September 7. HAMPSHIRE lost to NOTTINGHAMSHIRE by three runs.

HAMPSHIRE v SUSSEX

At Southampton, September 14. Hampshire won by two wickets. Toss: Sussex. First-team debut: S. R. G. Francis.

Renshaw foiled Sussex's attempt to lift themselves off the foot of the table by clouting the last ball for four. Hampshire finished 15th, but had an extra interest in the match: Udal started it three wickets behind Lancashire's Peter Martin in the race for the £5,000 bowling prize, but he claimed only one. However, Hayden beat Yorkshire's Darren Lehmann to the batting prize, despite scoring just a single. Udal could take consolation from his innings of 70, which put Hampshire in a strong position; they needed 13 from the last three overs with four wickets in hand, before a sudden attack of nerves brought about the close finish.

Sussex

K. Greenfield c Kendall b Francis	35	J. J. Bates b Stephenson		1
*†P. Moores c Kendall b Francis	32	A. A. Khan run out		8
N. R. Taylor lbw b Stephenson	1	R. J. Kirtley not out		1
M. Newell c Laney b Stephenson	60			
K. Newell run out	7	L-b 9, w 5		14
J. R. Carpenter b Udal	18			—
R. S. C. Martin-Jenkins c Aymes b Milburn	3	1/66 2/68 3/82	(38.4 overs)	181
		4/104 5/147 6/165		
P. W. Jarvis lbw b Stephenson	1	7/165 8/169 9/171		

Bowling: Renshaw 4–0–25–0; Milburn 7–0–27–1; Francis 8–0–31–2; Stephenson 7.4–0–41–4; Udal 8–1–31–1; Whitaker 4–0–17–0.

Hampshire

J. S. Laney c Kirtley b K. Newell	15	†A. N. Aymes run out	4
M. L. Hayden lbw b Kirtley	1	S. M. Milburn not out	0
G. W. White c Taylor b Jarvis	17		
S. D. Udal c Moores b Khan	70	L-b 9, w 8, n-b 2	19
P. R. Whitaker c Moores b Jarvis	0		
W. S. Kendall lbw b Martin-Jenkins	33	1/18 2/20 3/65 (8 wkts, 40 overs)	184
*J. P. Stephenson b Jarvis	15	4/66 5/125 6/157	
S. J. Renshaw not out	10	7/170 8/180	

S. R. G. Francis did not bat.

Bowling: K. Newell 8–1–33–1; Kirtley 8–0–26–1; Martin-Jenkins 8–0–32–1; Jarvis 8–0–46–3; Khan 8–0–38–1.

Umpires: J. C. Balderstone and R. A. White.

KENT

KENT v DERBYSHIRE

At Canterbury, April 27. Kent won by six wickets. Toss: Kent.

Gul Khan, the former Essex and Oxford University batsman, did his best to hold the Derbyshire innings together, but they were hamstrung by four run-outs. Then Walker, who made his best Sunday score – 80 in 74 balls – shared a stand of 97 in 15 overs with Wells.

Derbyshire

K. J. Barnett run out	16	P. Aldred c Wren b Strang	13
C. J. Adams c Wells b Ealham	6	A. J. Harris not out	6
*D. M. Jones b McCague	31		
P. A. J. DeFreitas run out	2	B 1, l-b 8, w 8, n-b 2	19
G. A. Khan not out	71		
V. P. Clarke c Ealham b Strang	15	1/21 2/31 3/39 (8 wkts, 40 overs)	184
†K. M. Krikken run out	4	4/99 5/127 6/133	
G. M. Roberts run out	1	7/135 8/154	

K. J. Dean did not bat.

Bowling: Wren 8–0–32–0; Ealham 6–0–18–1; Fleming 6–0–31–0; McCague 7–1–36–1; Strang 8–0–34–2; Llong 5–0–24–0.

Kent

M. V. Fleming c Adams b Dean	40	M. A. Ealham not out	0
M. J. Walker c Clarke b Harris	80	L-b 3, w 3	6
T. R. Ward c and b Clarke	1		
A. P. Wells not out	56	1/67 2/75 (4 wkts, 31.3 overs)	185
G. R. Cowdrey lbw b Harris	2	3/172 4/184	

P. A. Strang, *†S. A. Marsh, M. J. McCague, N. J. Llong and T. N. Wren did not bat.

Bowling: Dean 8–1–45–1; Aldred 4–0–27–0; Harris 7–1–42–2; Clarke 8–1–44–1; Roberts 4.3–0–24–0.

Umpires: K. E. Palmer and P. Willey.

KENT v SURREY

At Canterbury, May 4. Kent won by 12 runs. Toss: Surrey.

In a match reduced to 25 overs a side, Adam Hollioake improved on the bowling form that was so instrumental in winning the competition for Surrey in 1996. He took five for 38, his best Sunday figures. But Cowdrey hit a devastating 82 from 46 balls – with five sixes and seven fours – and helped Kent to what might have been a possible 40-over total, 193 for eight. Free-scoring innings from Brown and Thorpe took Surrey close, but Headley chipped in with four timely wickets.

Kent

M. V. Fleming c Knott b Bicknell	0	M. J. McCague not out	2
M. J. Walker c Knott b A. J. Hollioake	7	D. W. Headley not out	7
T. R. Ward lbw b A. J. Hollioake	36		
A. P. Wells c Lewis b B. C. Hollioake	29		
G. R. Cowdrey c Thorpe b A. J. Hollioake	82	B 1, l-b 6, w 4, n-b 2	13
M. A. Ealham c A. J. Hollioake b Lewis	9		
P. A. Strang b A. J. Hollioake	5	1/2 2/44 3/63	(8 wkts, 25 overs) 193
*†S. A. Marsh c Salisbury		4/90 5/113 6/142	
b A. J. Hollioake	3	7/166 8/184	

A. P. Igglesden did not bat.

Bowling: Bicknell 3–0–23–1; Lewis 5–0–27–1; A. J. Hollioake 5–0–38–5; Salisbury 2–0–13–0; Benjamin 5–0–43–0; B. C. Hollioake 5–0–42–1.

Surrey

A. D. Brown c Strang b Headley	52	I. D. K. Salisbury not out	1
A. J. Stewart b Igglesden	7	M. P. Bicknell not out	8
G. P. Thorpe c Wells b McCague	33		
*A. J. Hollioake b Headley	7	L-b 12, w 4	16
†J. A. Knott b McCague	22		
C. C. Lewis c Marsh b Fleming	9	1/22 2/88 3/108	(8 wkts, 25 overs) 181
B. C. Hollioake c Marsh b Headley	16	4/137 5/137 6/158	
N. Shahid b Headley	10	7/170 8/172	

J. E. Benjamin did not bat.

Bowling: Igglesden 3–0–26–1; Ealham 5–0–26–0; Fleming 4–0–34–1; Headley 5–0–27–4; Strang 5–0–33–0; McCague 3–0–23–2.

Umpires: J. W. Holder and N. T. Plews.

KENT v GLAMORGAN

At Canterbury, May 18. Kent won by eight runs. Toss: Kent.

Ealham's last nine balls – split between spells – produced five wickets for one run to maintain Kent's unbeaten one-day record in 1997. Strong-arm batting from Croft, who was promoted to open and responded with 50 from 33 balls, and steady accumulation by Dale had left Glamorgan needing only 31 from the last four overs with six wickets in hand. But they were bowled out with four balls remaining. Ealham had earlier made 61 with the bat.

Kent

M. V. Fleming c Butcher b Watkin	33	*†S. A. Marsh not out	14
M. J. Walker b Dale	30	M. J. McCague run out	1
T. R. Ward c sub b Croft	24		
A. P. Wells c and b Croft	32	L-b 4, w 11	15
G. R. Cowdrey b Dale	2		
M. A. Ealham run out	61	1/44 2/94 3/99	(9 wkts, 40 overs) 238
N. J. Llong c Cottey b Butcher	4	4/101 5/161 6/172	
P. A. Strang c James b Waqar Younis	22	7/216 8/235 9/238	

T. N. Wren did not bat.

Bowling: Watkin 8–0–48–1; Waqar Younis 6–0–45–1; Parkin 1.5–0–14–0; Maynard 0.1–0–0–0; Dale 7–0–44–2; Croft 8–0–31–2; Butcher 5–0–31–1; Cottey 4–0–21–0.

Glamorgan

S. P. James b Llong	38	Waqar Younis b Ealham	0
R. D. B. Croft c Ealham b Strang	50	S. L. Watkin not out	5
A. Dale c and b McCague	65	O. T. Parkin b Ealham	0
G. P. Butcher b Fleming	24	B 2, l-b 11, w 4, n-b 3	20
*M. P. Maynard b Ealham	10		
P. A. Cottey run out	14	(39.2 overs) 230	
A. W. Evans b Ealham	3	1/65 2/129 3/170	
†A. D. Shaw lbw b Ealham	1	4/199 5/218 6/218	
		7/221 8/221 9/230	

Bowling: Wren 6–0–46–0; Ealham 7.2–0–41–5; McCague 8–0–38–1; Strang 8–0–39–1; Fleming 7–0–41–1; Llong 3–0–12–1.

Umpires: J. C. Balderstone and J. F. Steele.

At Horsham, May 25. KENT lost to SUSSEX by four wickets.

At Nottingham, June 1. KENT beat NOTTINGHAMSHIRE by 46 runs.

KENT v WARWICKSHIRE

At Tunbridge Wells, June 8. Kent won by 32 runs. Toss: Warwickshire.

A handy all-round performance from Strang sealed Kent's victory over a side that they had already beaten in the Championship and the Benson and Hedges Cup in the past fortnight. He made 40 from 33 balls, and then dismissed three batsmen, including the engine-room of Warwickshire's middle order, Ostler and Penney.

Kent

M. V. Fleming c Penney b Brown	19	M. J. McCague b Brown	11
M. J. Walker c Brown b Smith	4	D. W. Headley not out	1
T. R. Ward c Edmond b Welch	59	J. B. D. Thompson b Giles	1
A. P. Wells lbw b Brown	0	L-b 8, w 4, n-b 6	18
D. P. Fulton c Frost b Edmond	9		
*†S. A. Marsh c and b Welch	3	1/11 2/30 3/31	(39.1 overs) 177
N. J. Llong c Frost b Edmond	12	4/61 5/73 6/105	
P. A. Strang c Frost b Brown	40	7/124 8/173 9/176	

Bowling: Brown 8–0–42–4; Smith 8–0–26–1; Edmond 8–0–31–2; Welch 8–0–38–2; Giles 7.1–0–32–1.

Warwickshire

*N. V. Knight c Marsh b McCague	36	M. A. Sheikh c Wells b Strang	1
N. M. K. Smith c Strang b Thompson	11	M. D. Edmond c Fleming b Llong	19
D. R. Brown run out	7	†T. Frost not out	2
D. L. Hemp c Marsh b Fleming	23	B 4, l-b 6, w 1	11
D. P. Ostler st Marsh b Strang	7		
T. L. Penney c Ward b Strang	3	1/20 2/35 3/70	(36.3 overs) 145
G. Welch b Fleming	25	4/85 5/87 6/91	
A. F. Giles b McCague	0	7/98 8/99 9/142	

Bowling: Headley 8–1–23–0; Thompson 7–1–26–1; McCague 6–0–29–2; Fleming 6.3–1–24–2; Strang 8–0–31–3; Llong 1–0–2–1.

Umpires: B. Dudleston and R. Julian.

At Manchester, June 15. KENT lost to LANCASHIRE by 17 runs.

At Darlington, June 22. KENT beat DURHAM by 16 runs.

KENT v NORTHAMPTONSHIRE

At Maidstone, July 6. Kent won by two runs. Toss: Northamptonshire.

Kent once again went level on points at the top of the table, thanks to Marsh, who bludgeoned 39 from 26 balls at the end of their innings. Bailey, his opposite number, replied with the only fifty of the match. But, after he became one of McCague's three victims, Northamptonshire struggled. Even so, Sales almost snatched it at the death with another rapid 39, taking just 24 balls, while Snape hit 22 in 15.

Kent

T. R. Ward st Warren b Snape 40	M. J. McCague b Penberthy 5	
M. J. Walker c Penberthy b Emburey 40	J. B. D. Thompson not out 2	
A. P. Wells c Taylor b Bailey 39		
N. J. Llong c Warren b Penberthy 12	B 1, l-b 5, w 9, n-b 4 19	
M. V. Fleming run out 1		
W. J. House b Penberthy 0	1/86 2/96 3/128 (8 wkts, 40 overs) 209	
P. A. Strang run out 12	4/129 5/129 6/150	
*†S. A. Marsh not out 39	7/164 8/196	

A. P. Igglesden did not bat.

Bowling: Mohammad Akram 4–0–26–0; Taylor 6–0–34–0; Curran 3–0–25–0; Snape 8–0–30–1; Emburey 8–1–34–1; Penberthy 7–0–33–3; Bailey 4–0–21–1.

Northamptonshire

M. B. Loye c Walker b McCague 25	J. E. Emburey run out 3	
A. L. Penberthy lbw b Thompson 17	J. P. Taylor not out 4	
K. M. Curran c Ward b Igglesden 19	Mohammad Akram not out 0	
T. C. Walton c Marsh b McCague 6	B 1, l-b 6, w 1, n-b 5 13	
*R. J. Bailey lbw b McCague 54		
D. J. Sales b Fleming 39	1/46 2/46 3/55 (9 wkts, 40 overs) 207	
†R. J. Warren c Wells b Fleming 5	4/113 5/156 6/177	
J. N. Snape run out 22	7/177 8/188 9/207	

Bowling: Igglesden 8–0–41–1; Thompson 8–1–21–1; McCague 8–0–50–3; Fleming 8–0–33–2; Strang 8–0–55–0.

Umpires: H. D. Bird and V. A. Holder.

KENT v LEICESTERSHIRE

At Canterbury, July 20. Leicestershire won by 33 runs. Toss: Kent.

Wells and Whitaker, who made 60 from 58 balls, were the architects of Leicestershire's winning total. Kent's England bowler, Headley, who was struggling to be fit for the imminent Fourth Test, responded well, picking up three wickets in 14 balls in his second spell. But his team-mates could not get to grips with the run-chase.

Leicestershire

N. C. Johnson run out	3	†P. A. Nixon not out	23
V. J. Wells c McCague b Strang	69	T. J. Mason not out	17
I. J. Sutcliffe b Fleming	21	L-b 8, w 3, n-b 6	17
*J. J. Whitaker b Headley	60		
D. L. Maddy b Headley	11	1/12 2/81 3/145 (7 wkts, 40 overs) 258
B. F. Smith c Thompson b McCague	37	4/160 5/192
J. M. Dakin lbw b Headley	0	6/192 7/227

D. Williamson and J. Ormond did not bat.

Bowling: Thompson 4–0–20–0; Headley 8–0–44–3; Fleming 7–0–49–1; Ealham 6–0–38–0; Strang 8–1–41–1; McCague 7–0–58–1.

Kent

T. R. Ward b Wells	40	J. B. D. Thompson not out	18
M. J. Walker c Nixon b Ormond	19	M. J. McCague c Wells b Johnson	10
A. P. Wells b Ormond	2	D. W. Headley c Maddy b Johnson	3
M. A. Ealham run out	7	B 1, l-b 3, w 16, n-b 4	24
N. J. Llong b Johnson	52		
*†S. A. Marsh c Johnson b Mason	14	1/60 2/66 3/84 (38.2 overs) 225
P. A. Strang c Sutcliffe b Williamson	20	4/89 5/115 6/167
M. V. Fleming run out	16	7/181 8/195 9/212

Bowling: Ormond 8–0–30–2; Johnson 7.2–0–60–3; Wells 6–1–16–1; Williamson 8–0–40–1; Mason 4–0–35–1; Maddy 5–0–40–0.

Umpires: B. J. Meyer and K. E. Palmer.

At Lord's, July 27. KENT beat MIDDLESEX by eight wickets.

At Worcester, August 3. WORCESTERSHIRE v KENT. No result.

KENT v ESSEX

At Canterbury, August 10. Kent won by 117 runs. Toss: Kent.

Essex disintegrated alarmingly after the loss of their acting-captain Stuart Law, who was caught by Cowdrey in the fourth over. Cowdrey had already played a major role in the innings; he made the most of a missed stumping to score 80 from 79 balls. Most of the Kent bowlers finished with impressive figures, and particularly Igglesden, who took three for 29. The defeat effectively put Essex out of contention for the title.

Kent

T. R. Ward b S. G. Law	22	P. A. Strang not out	15
M. J. Walker lbw b Irani	13	*†S. A. Marsh not out	0
A. P. Wells st Rollins b S. G. Law	3	L-b 8, w 7, n-b 10	25
N. J. Llong lbw b Irani	1		
M. A. Ealham lbw b Such	50	1/44 2/44 3/45 (7 wkts, 40 overs) 223
G. R. Cowdrey c S. G. Law b Ilott	80	4/52 5/141
M. V. Fleming b Irani	14	6/189 7/221

J. B. D. Thompson and A. P. Igglesden did not bat.

Bowling: Cowan 7–2–42–0; Ilott 8–0–51–1; Irani 8–2–29–3; S. G. Law 8–0–44–2; Such 6–0–32–1; Powell 3–1–17–0.

Essex

D. D. J. Robinson c Ealham b Igglesden .	19	J. C. Powell c Strang b Fleming		2
*S. G. Law c Cowdrey b Thompson	7	M. C. Ilott b Llong		8
A. P. Grayson lbw b Igglesden	27	P. M. Such not out		5
R. C. Irani run out	0	B 4, w 4		8
†R. J. Rollins c Ward b Igglesden	2			—
D. R. Law c Fleming b Strang	0	1/24 2/33 3/33	(27.4 overs)	106
G. R. Napier c Wells b Fleming	12	4/50 5/51 6/60		
A. P. Cowan c Ward b Strang	16	7/81 8/88 9/88		

Bowling: Igglesden 8–0–29–3; Thompson 5–0–29–1; Strang 8–2–23–2; Fleming 6–1–20–2; Llong 0.4–0–1–1.

Umpires: J. C. Balderstone and P. Willey.

At Taunton, August 24. KENT beat SOMERSET by four wickets (D/L method).

At Portsmouth, August 31. KENT beat HAMPSHIRE by six wickets.

KENT v GLOUCESTERSHIRE

At Canterbury, September 7. Kent won by nine wickets. Toss: Gloucestershire.

Paul Strang led Kent out in his last home match before leaving the county. Gloucestershire did not present much of a challenge, scoring an inadequate 136. Ward, who hit three sixes, gave Kent a rousing launch. They demolished their target inside 28 overs to go top of the table, needing only to win their final match to be certain of the title.

Gloucestershire

R. I. Dawson b Ealham	27	R. P. Davis not out		12
T. H. C. Hancock c Cowdrey b Strang	30	A. M. Smith b Fleming		8
S. Young c Marsh b Igglesden	1	J. Lewis not out		1
M. A. Lynch run out	0	B 2, l-b 3, w 2		7
*M. W. Alleyne b Ealham	33			—
M. G. N. Windows lbw b Headley	8	1/52 2/55 3/55	(9 wkts, 40 overs)	136
M. C. J. Ball b Fleming	9	4/72 5/90 6/114		
†R. C. J. Williams b Fleming	0	7/114 8/114 9/135		

Bowling: Headley 8–1–18–1; Igglesden 8–0–37–1; Ealham 8–1–22–2; Fleming 8–1–19–3; Strang 8–1–35–1.

Kent

T. R. Ward b Alleyne	54
E. T. Smith not out	54
A. P. Wells not out	28
W 3	3

1/72   (1 wkt, 27.4 overs) 139

G. R. Cowdrey, M. A. Ealham, M. V. Fleming, N. J. Llong, P. A. Strang, *†S. A. Marsh, D. W. Headley and A. P. Igglesden did not bat.

Bowling: Smith 6–1–28–0; Lewis 5–2–23–0; Alleyne 6–1–23–1; Young 5–0–33–0; Ball 4–0–18–0; Hancock 1.4–0–14–0.

Umpires: G. I. Burgess and T. E. Jesty.

At Leeds, September 14. KENT lost to YORKSHIRE by seven wickets.

LANCASHIRE

LANCASHIRE v DURHAM

At Manchester, April 27. Lancashire won by 57 runs. Toss: Lancashire.

Graham Lloyd smashed a breakneck 134, from 85 balls with five sixes and 13 fours, and equalled Lancashire's Sunday record, 134 not out scored by his namesake Clive against Somerset in 1970. Together with Crawley, the young Lloyd put on 197 to break Lancashire's all-wicket record for the competition – 182, which Clive put on with Harry Pilling, in the same match. Durham could not get close to the required run-rate of nearly seven an over, but Roseberry saved them from humiliation.

Lancashire

J. E. R. Gallian c Collingwood b Killeen .	1	†W. K. Hegg not out 12
*M. A. Atherton c Roseberry		G. Yates not out 1
b Collingwood .	12	
J. P. Crawley b Betts	83	L-b 10, w 2 12
G. D. Lloyd c Boon b Walker 134		
N. H. Fairbrother c Lewis b Boiling	1	1/13 2/23 3/220 (6 wkts, 40 overs) 268
I. D. Austin run out	12	4/225 5/250 6/266

R. J. Green, G. Chapple and P. J. Martin did not bat.

Bowling: Killeen 8–1–40–1; Betts 7–0–45–1; Collingwood 5–0–29–1; Boiling 7–0–43–1; Foster 5–0–54–0; Walker 8–0–47–1.

Durham

P. D. Collingwood c Hegg b Martin	0	J. J. B. Lewis not out 41
†M. P. Speight c Lloyd b Austin........	9	
*D. C. Boon b Green	27	B 1, l-b 11, w 4, n-b 2 18
M. A. Roseberry not out	91	
N. J. Speak c Hegg b Chapple..........	19	1/2 2/23 3/56 (5 wkts, 40 overs) 211
M. J. Foster c Green b Yates...........	6	4/103 5/125

M. M. Betts, J. Boiling, N. Killeen and A. Walker did not bat.

Bowling: Austin 8–0–34–1; Martin 7–0–45–1; Green 8–0–36–1; Chapple 8–1–38–1; Yates 8–0–38–1; Gallian 1–0–8–0.

Umpires: G. I. Burgess and R. Palmer.

At Derby, May 4. LANCASHIRE beat DERBYSHIRE by 35 runs (D/L method).

LANCASHIRE v NOTTINGHAMSHIRE

At Manchester, May 18. Lancashire won by two wickets. Toss: Lancashire.

Nottinghamshire came surprisingly close to defending their 139 – a below-par total, even on a green pitch – when they reduced Lancashire to 104 for seven. But the phlegmatic Gallian applied himself to make the only fifty of the match.

Nottinghamshire

P. R. Pollard c Chapple b Martin	2	R. T. Bates run out 4
M. P. Dowman b Yates	20	R. A. Pick c Gallian b Martin 8
*P. Johnson c Hegg b Austin..........	2	M. N. Bowen not out 0
G. F. Archer c Hegg b Chapple.........	14	B 1, l-b 5, w 15 21
A. A. Metcalfe c Gallian b Watkinson ...	36	
N. A. Gie st Hegg b Watkinson	9	1/5 2/10 3/51 (39.4 overs) 139
†W. M. Noon c Watkinson b Yates	3	4/53 5/71 6/76
K. P. Evans st Hegg b Watkinson	20	7/127 8/127 9/135

Bowling: Austin 8–2–14–1; Martin 7.4–0–28–2; Gallian 2–0–14–0; Chapple 6–0–37–1; Yates 8–1–14–2; Watkinson 8–0–26–3.

Lancashire

*M. Watkinson c Pollard b Pick	5	G. Yates c Pollard b Evans	17
M. A. Atherton b Dowman	13	G. Chapple not out	4
J. E. R. Gallian not out	54		
J. P. Crawley c Noon b Bowen	9	L-b 3, w 5, n-b 2	10
G. D. Lloyd c Noon b Dowman	5		
N. H. Fairbrother lbw b Bowen	16	1/9 2/30 3/47 (8 wkts, 37.5 overs) 141
I. D. Austin c and b Bowen	0	4/54 5/87 6/87
†W. K. Hegg c Johnson b Bates	8	7/104 8/136

P. J. Martin did not bat.

Bowling: Evans 7–0–20–1; Pick 6.5–0–30–1; Dowman 8–0–31–2; Bowen 8–0–28–3; Bates 8–1–29–1.

Umpires: V. A. Holder and A. A. Jones.

LANCASHIRE v NORTHAMPTONSHIRE

At Manchester, May 25. Lancashire won by 75 runs. Toss: Northamptonshire.

Gallian scored his first Sunday hundred to set up an emphatic win for Lancashire. The margin could have been even larger if Bailey had not mounted a partial recovery from 27 for four, but Martin tied up Northamptonshire to finish with five for 21, his best one-day figures.

Lancashire

J. E. R. Gallian not out	101	†W. K. Hegg c Curran b Taylor	5
*M. Watkinson c Ripley b Follett	12	G. Yates not out	17
P. C. McKeown c and b Emburey	37	B 4, l-b 4, w 2, n-b 13	23
N. H. Fairbrother c Loye b Snape	14		
Wasim Akram c Follett b Snape	28	1/31 2/96 3/128 (6 wkts, 40 overs) 241
I. D. Austin c Follett b Snape	4	4/191 5/203 6/223

M. E. Harvey, G. Chapple and P. J. Martin did not bat.

Bowling: Taylor 7–0–26–1; Follett 8–0–35–1; Curran 4–0–28–0; Emburey 8–0–47–1; Capel 5–0–45–0; Snape 8–0–52–3.

Northamptonshire

M. B. Loye c Yates b Martin	5	J. E. Emburey b Wasim Akram	8
A. L. Penberthy run out	1	J. P. Taylor not out	6
K. M. Curran c Wasim Akram b Chapple	29	D. Follett b Martin	1
D. J. Capel c Hegg b Martin	2	L-b 3, w 2, n-b 4	9
T. C. Walton c Fairbrother b Martin	1		
*R. J. Bailey c Hegg b Martin	67	1/4 2/15 3/21 (39.4 overs) 166
J. N. Snape run out	33	4/27 5/53 6/125
†D. Ripley c Hegg b Austin	4	7/138 8/154 9/160

Bowling: Austin 8–0–20–1; Martin 7.4–1–21–5; Wasim Akram 8–0–32–1; Chapple 8–0–36–1; Yates 4–0–25–0; Watkinson 4–0–29–0.

Umpires: K. E. Palmer and J. F. Steele.

At Leicester, June 1. LANCASHIRE beat LEICESTERSHIRE by five wickets.

At Taunton, June 8. LANCASHIRE lost to SOMERSET by five wickets (D/L method).

LANCASHIRE v KENT

At Manchester, June 15. Lancashire won by 17 runs. Toss: Kent.

In his first innings since the announcement of his OBE, Atherton made an unbeaten 90, striking eight fours and one six over extra cover off the bowling of McCague. This answered the local joke that OBE stood for "Only Bats for England". Kent's best offering was a stand of 59 between Ward and Llong; they only got close to their target thanks to 37 extras. This was the first match to be broadcast on the Lancashire club's own radio station.

Lancashire

P. C. McKeown b Headley	1	N. H. Fairbrother not out	18
M. A. Atherton not out	90	B 1, l-b 1, w 2	4
†J. P. Crawley c Llong b Fleming	33		
G. D. Lloyd lbw b Ealham	26	1/2 2/68 3/132 (3 wkts, 35 overs)	172

*Wasim Akram, I. D. Austin, D. J. Shadford, G. Chapple, G. Yates and P. J. Martin did not bat.

Bowling: Headley 7–2–11–1; Thompson 7–0–22–0; McCague 6–0–46–0; Ealham 7–0–36–1; Fleming 6–0–35–1; Strang 2–0–20–0.

Kent

D. P. Fulton lbw b Martin	5	*†S. A. Marsh b Austin	7
M. J. Walker c Austin b Chapple	16	D. W. Headley b Austin	0
T. R. Ward b Chapple	53	J. B. D. Thompson not out	2
M. A. Ealham b Wasim Akram	1		
M. V. Fleming b Wasim Akram	0	B 2, l-b 18, w 14, n-b 3	37
N. J. Llong c Crawley b Shadford	26		
P. A. Strang c Fairbrother b Shadford	3	1/17 2/53 3/56 (34 overs)	155
M. J. McCague c Wasim Akram		4/56 5/115 6/123	
b Chapple	5	7/133 8/145 9/145	

Bowling: Austin 5–0–22–2; Martin 7–0–27–1; Wasim Akram 7–0–18–2; Chapple 7–1–22–3; Shadford 6–0–30–2; Yates 2–0–16–0.

Umpires: J. W. Holder and G. Sharp.

LANCASHIRE v GLAMORGAN

At Manchester, June 22. No result (abandoned). Two points put Lancashire on top of the table.

At Worcester, June 29. LANCASHIRE lost to WORCESTERSHIRE by 114 runs.

At Uxbridge, July 6. LANCASHIRE tied with MIDDLESEX.

LANCASHIRE v SUSSEX

At Manchester, July 20. Lancashire won by eight wickets. Toss: Lancashire.

The first ball of the match reared up to strike Greenfield on the glove, and Sussex never batted with any confidence. A stand of 69 between Rao and Taylor was their high point. Athey's three runs made him only the second player to reach 7,500 in the Sunday League. In reply, Atherton and Gallian batted with assurance for an opening stand of 103.

Sussex

K. Greenfield c Lloyd b Austin	4
C. W. J. Athey c Hegg b Martin	3
R. K. Rao c Martin b Yates	31
M. Newell b Shadford	10
N. R. Taylor b Yates	47
K. Newell c Hegg b Shadford	7
*†P. Moores c Gallian b Martin	15
V. C. Drakes b Shadford	11

P. W. Jarvis b Martin	4
M. A. Robinson not out	9
R. J. Kirtley not out	6
B 2, l-b 11, w 8, n-b 2	23

1/11 2/11 3/37   (9 wkts, 40 overs) 170
4/106 5/115 6/126
7/146 8/152 9/155

Bowling: Austin 8–1–14–1; Martin 8–0–26–3; Shadford 8–0–47–3; Gallian 8–1–26–0; Yates 8–0–44–2.

Lancashire

M. A. Atherton c Taylor b Robinson	36
J. E. R. Gallian not out	80
J. P. Crawley c Moores b Jarvis	9
N. H. Fairbrother not out	34
L-b 3, w 7, n-b 2	12

1/103 2/120   (2 wkts, 34.5 overs) 171

G. D. Lloyd, *M. Watkinson, I. D. Austin, †W. K. Hegg, G. Yates, P. J. Martin and D. J. Shadford did not bat.

Bowling: Drakes 8–2–11–0; Kirtley 5.5–0–51–0; Jarvis 8–1–30–1; Robinson 8–0–41–1; K. Newell 2–0–15–0; Rao 3–0–20–0.

Umpires: D. J. Constant and R. Julian.

At Southampton, July 27. LANCASHIRE beat HAMPSHIRE by four wickets.

LANCASHIRE v WARWICKSHIRE

At Manchester, August 10. Warwickshire won by 21 runs. Toss: Lancashire.

Warwickshire won the top-of-the-table battle, despite being undermined by an early burst from Martin. Ostler and Penney prevented total collapse. The target of 220 did not look too forbidding but the skies clouded over, and only Fairbrother could get going. A crowd of 8,000 watched, although both the Test and Manchester United were live on TV.

Warwickshire

A. Singh c Gallian b Martin	0
*N. M. K. Smith b Shadford	28
D. R. Brown c Watkinson b Martin	0
D. L. Hemp c Hegg b Austin	4
D. P. Ostler run out	53
T. L. Penney b Austin	57
G. Welch c Flintoff b Gallian	3
A. F. Giles b Martin	20

†K. J. Piper run out	9
G. C. Small not out	9
A. A. Donald not out	5
L-b 17, w 8, n-b 6	31

1/0 2/13 3/24   (9 wkts, 40 overs) 219
4/53 5/135 6/141
7/176 8/202 9/212

Bowling: Martin 8–1–32–3; Austin 8–1–32–2; Shadford 4–0–28–1; Yates 8–0–40–0; Chilton 3–0–18–0; Watkinson 4–0–29–0; Gallian 5–0–23–1.

Lancashire

*M. Watkinson lbw b Brown	10	G. Yates not out	11
J. E. R. Gallian c Donald b Welch	17	P. J. Martin run out	3
N. H. Fairbrother c Piper b Small	79	D. J. Shadford not out	0
G. D. Lloyd b Giles	24	B 6, l-b 3, w 2, n-b 2	13
A. Flintoff c Singh b Small	24		
M. J. Chilton b Brown	1	1/14 2/38 3/107 (9 wkts, 40 overs) 198
I. D. Austin run out	8	4/162 5/166 6/166
†W. K. Hegg c Smith b Brown	8	7/178 8/185 9/190

Bowling: Welch 8–0–28–1; Brown 8–0–43–3; Donald 8–0–33–0; Small 4–0–27–2; Giles 7–1–30–1; Smith 5–0–28–0.

Umpires: H. D. Bird and J. H. Harris.

At Bristol, August 24. GLOUCESTERSHIRE v LANCASHIRE. No result.

LANCASHIRE v YORKSHIRE

At Manchester, August 31. Lancashire won by 31 runs. Toss: Yorkshire.

The weather forced this Roses encounter to be cut back to ten overs per side – and some Yorkshire supporters wondered how the game had been possible at all when the previous day's play in the first-class match, which they needed to win to keep in touch with the Championship leaders, had been abandoned so quickly. Hegg's 13-ball 31 not out, with two fours and two sixes, was the major contribution in Lancashire's 93 for six. Then Green's first over cost 16, but he struck back with three wickets in four balls.

Lancashire

J. P. Crawley c and b White	17	M. A. Atherton b Hartley	7
N. H. Fairbrother c Blakey b Silverwood	7	G. Yates not out	6
G. D. Lloyd c Blakey b Morris	2	L-b 2, w 2, n-b 2	6
I. D. Austin c Blakey b Silverwood	6		
*M. Watkinson c McGrath b White	11	1/16 2/23 3/34 (6 wkts, 10 overs) 93
†W. K. Hegg not out	31	4/48 5/48 6/63

G. Chapple, P. J. Martin and R. J. Green did not bat.

Bowling: Hamilton 2–0–25–0; Silverwood 2–0–12–2; Morris 2–0–10–1; White 2–0–22–2; Hartley 2–0–22–1.

Yorkshire

M. P. Vaughan c Hegg b Chapple	16	P. J. Hartley b Martin	5
C. White b Austin	2	G. M. Hamilton not out	9
D. S. Lehmann c Chapple b Green	11		
*D. Byas st Hegg b Yates	0	L-b 3, w 5	8
A. McGrath c Atherton b Green	5		
B. Parker c Watkinson b Green	0	1/20 2/24 3/27 (8 wkts, 10 overs) 62
†R. J. Blakey st Hegg b Yates	2	4/41 5/41 6/42
A. C. Morris not out	4	7/43 8/50

C. E. W. Silverwood did not bat.

Bowling: Martin 2–0–12–1; Green 2–0–18–3; Chapple 2–0–14–1; Austin 2–0–9–1; Yates 2–0–6–2.

Umpires: N. T. Plews and A. G. T. Whitehead.

LANCASHIRE v ESSEX

At Manchester, September 9. Lancashire won by six wickets. Toss: Lancashire.

Martin beat Wasim Akram's club record of 29 Sunday wickets, set in 1995; the five he collected here took him to 31. For Essex, Prichard dominated a second-wicket stand of 119 with Hussain on his way to 103 in 100 balls. But there were runs from each of Lancashire's top four during an efficient chase, so it did not matter that they had been docked one over for getting through their own overs too slowly.

Essex

*P. J. Prichard c Lloyd b Green	103	M. C. Ilott not out	2
S. G. Law c Hegg b Martin	0	†B. J. Hyam not out	1
N. Hussain c Crawley b Watkinson	33		
R. C. Irani b Martin	16	L-b 6, w 10, n-b 2	18
A. P. Grayson c Hegg b Chapple	22		
D. D. J. Robinson b Martin	21	1/2 2/121 3/152 (8 wkts, 40 overs) 230	
G. R. Napier c Watkinson b Martin	5	4/169 5/205 6/215	
A. P. Cowan lbw b Martin	9	7/215 8/229	

P. M. Such did not bat.

Bowling: Austin 8–1–32–0; Martin 8–1–41–5; Green 8–0–47–1; Chapple 8–0–42–1; Yates 2–0–25–0; Watkinson 6–0–37–1.

Lancashire

*M. Watkinson c Robinson b Such	66	I. D. Austin not out	7
M. A. Atherton c Cowan b Such	41	L-b 8, w 4, n-b 2	14
J. P. Crawley c Robinson b Cowan	51		
G. D. Lloyd b Grayson	42	1/101 2/123 (4 wkts, 38 overs) 233	
N. H. Fairbrother not out	12	3/211 4/222	

†W. K. Hegg, G. Yates, G. Chapple, P. J. Martin and R. J. Green did not bat.

Bowling: Ilott 7–0–38–0; Cowan 8–0–56–1; Napier 7–0–48–0; Such 8–0–45–2; Grayson 8–0–38–1.

Umpires: K. E. Palmer and N. T. Plews.

At The Oval, September 14. LANCASHIRE lost to SURREY by five wickets.

LEICESTERSHIRE

LEICESTERSHIRE v GLOUCESTERSHIRE

At Leicester, April 27. Gloucestershire won by 111 runs. Toss: Leicestershire.

Gloucestershire rallied from an unpromising 139 for five to reach 236, as Alleyne masterminded the addition of 90 runs in the last ten overs. Parsons suffered the heaviest punishment, though he scored an unbeaten 41 while none of his team-mates passed 15 in a miserable Leicestershire reply.

Gloucestershire

N. J. Trainor c Whitaker b Ormond	22	M. C. J. Ball run out	0
M. A. Lynch c Nixon b Dakin	42	A. M. Smith not out	3
R. J. Cunliffe st Nixon b Brimson	36		
S. Young b Brimson	8	L-b 8, w 11, n-b 6	25
†R. C. Russell b Brimson	1		
*M. W. Alleyne not out	45	1/43 2/81 3/117 (8 wkts, 40 overs) 236	
A. J. Wright c Whitaker b Wells	18	4/119 5/139 6/172	
T. H. C. Hancock b Mullally	36	7/220 8/220	

J. Lewis did not bat.

Bowling: Mullally 8–0–37–1; Parsons 8–0–65–0; Ormond 4–0–24–1; Dakin 6–0–35–1; Brimson 8–0–37–3; Wells 6–0–30–1.

Leicestershire

V. J. Wells c Alleyne b Lewis	0	G. J. Parsons not out	41
D. L. Maddy run out	7	A. D. Mullally c sub b Ball	6
*J. J. Whitaker lbw b Smith	8	M. T. Brimson not out	12
A. Habib c Russell b Young	11	L-b 1, w 9	10
†P. A. Nixon c Lynch b Smith	1		—
G. I. Macmillan lbw b Lewis	15	1/0 2/17 3/17 (9 wkts, 40 overs) 125	
J. M. Dakin c Russell b Young	0	4/19 5/49 6/49	
J. Ormond c Trainor b Hancock	14	7/52 8/87 9/97	

Bowling: Lewis 8–0–33–2; Smith 6–2–14–2; Young 6–0–10–2; Ball 8–0–30–1; Hancock 8–0–25–1; Trainor 4–0–12–0.

Umpires: J. D. Bond and J. H. Hampshire.

At Worcester, May 11. LEICESTERSHIRE beat WORCESTERSHIRE by six runs.

At Southampton, May 18. LEICESTERSHIRE beat HAMPSHIRE by 38 runs.

LEICESTERSHIRE v SURREY

At Leicester, May 25. Surrey won by five wickets. Toss: Surrey.

Dakin took 19 off the last over of Leicestershire's innings, bowled by Salisbury, to lift Surrey's target to a demanding 235. But Brown returned to the form that took him into the England one-day side with a spectacular innings. He broke his own county record for the competition with 157 not out off 117 balls, striking three sixes and 15 fours as he ensured victory almost single-handedly: Surrey's next-highest score was 23.

Leicestershire

N. C. Johnson b Tudor	40	J. M. Dakin not out	41
V. J. Wells lbw b Benjamin	39	G. J. Parsons not out	12
*J. J. Whitaker b Salisbury	34	L-b 6, w 3	9
B. F. Smith b Salisbury	9		—
D. L. Maddy b Salisbury	21	1/75 2/90 3/101 (7 wkts, 40 overs) 234	
A. Habib c Butcher b Bicknell	20	4/129 5/169	
†P. A. Nixon lbw b Benjamin	9	6/169 7/187	

M. T. Brimson and A. D. Mullally did not bat.

Bowling: Bicknell 8–0–44–1; Lewis 8–0–46–0; Tudor 5–0–23–1; Benjamin 8–0–40–2; Salisbury 8–0–56–3; Ratcliffe 3–0–19–0.

Surrey

M. A. Butcher b Johnson	16	I. D. K. Salisbury not out	23
A. D. Brown not out	157		
J. D. Ratcliffe lbw b Johnson	7	L-b 4, w 9, n-b 6	19
N. Shahid lbw b Johnson	0		—
I. J. Ward lbw b Brimson	1	1/107 2/138 3/138 (5 wkts, 36.4 overs) 238	
*C. C. Lewis lbw b Parsons	15	4/139 5/175	

†J. A. Knott, M. P. Bicknell, J. E. Benjamin and A. J. Tudor did not bat.

Bowling: Mullally 8–0–43–0; Parsons 8–0–49–1; Brimson 6–0–42–1; Johnson 7.4–0–45–3; Dakin 5–0–33–0; Wells 2–0–22–0.

Umpires: G. I. Burgess and B. J. Meyer.

LEICESTERSHIRE v LANCASHIRE

At Leicester, June 1. Lancashire won by five wickets. Toss: Leicestershire.

Gallian's second century in consecutive Sunday League games gave Lancashire their fifth win out of five. The game should have ended with a no-ball from Johnson, which took their total to 259, but Fairbrother blocked another ball before pointing out the score to the umpires. For Leicestershire, Whitaker and Maddy had set up an apparently imposing 258 with a partnership of 144 in 19 overs, and Parsons claimed his 200th wicket in the competition on dismissing Atherton.

Leicestershire

N. C. Johnson c Fairbrother b Yates..... 31	†P. A. Nixon not out 5
V. J. Wells st Hegg b Gallian 34	
*J. J. Whitaker b Yates 74	L-b 9, w 6 15
D. L. Maddy c Martin b Austin........ 85	—
B. F. Smith b Chapple 3	1/57 2/71 3/215 (5 wkts, 40 overs) 258
A. Habib not out 11	4/223 5/249

A. R. K. Pierson, G. J. Parsons, M. T. Brimson and A. D. Mullally did not bat.

Bowling: Austin 8–0–54–1; Martin 7–0–31–0; Chapple 8–0–67–1; Yates 8–0–46–2; Gallian 5–0–24–1; Watkinson 4–0–27–0.

Lancashire

*M. Watkinson c Pierson b Mullally..... 18	I. D. Austin not out 1
M. A. Atherton c Whitaker b Parsons.... 17	
J. E. R. Gallian c and b Johnson........104	B 2, l-b 11, w 12, n-b 6....... 31
J. P. Crawley c Nixon b Parsons........ 0	—
G. D. Lloyd c Nixon b Brimson 38	1/20 2/50 3/50 (5 wkts, 38.4 overs) 259
N. H. Fairbrother not out 50	4/128 5/256

G. Chapple, †W. K. Hegg, G. Yates and P. J. Martin did not bat.

Bowling: Mullally 8–0–44–1; Parsons 8–0–27–2; Johnson 6.4–0–53–1; Brimson 5–0–44–1; Wells 7–0–45–0; Pierson 1–0–11–0; Maddy 3–0–22–0.

Umpires: B. Leadbeater and R. Palmer.

At Lord's, June 8. LEICESTERSHIRE beat MIDDLESEX by six wickets (D/L method).

At Bath, June 22. LEICESTERSHIRE beat SOMERSET by 17 runs (D/L method).

LEICESTERSHIRE v WARWICKSHIRE

At Leicester, June 29. Warwickshire won by eight wickets. Toss: Warwickshire.

Play was not possible until 5.15 p.m. because of a soggy pitch. Then the captains, Whitaker and Knight, agreed to play a 15-over match. Leicestershire made a good start, with Johnson and Wells running up 48 from the first six overs. But their innings tailed off, and Smith scored 46 from 21 balls to put Warwickshire on their way to victory.

Leicestershire

N. C. Johnson b Giles 33	I. J. Sutcliffe not out.................. 0
V. J. Wells b Small 26	T. J. Mason run out 1
D. L. Maddy c Penney b Small.......... 0	B 1, l-b 2, w 2 5
*J. J. Whitaker c Knight b Brown....... 22	—
J. M. Dakin c Giles b Brown........... 17	1/48 2/48 3/79 (8 wkts, 15 overs) 115
B. F. Smith b Giles................... 8	4/88 5/107 6/111
†P. A. Nixon run out 3	7/114 8/115

G. J. Parsons and A. D. Mullally did not bat.

Bowling: Welch 3–0–23–0; Donald 3–0–19–0; Small 3–0–23–2; Giles 3–0–26–2; Brown 3–0–21–2.

Warwickshire

*N. V. Knight c Nixon b Dakin	7
N. M. K. Smith c Parsons b Dakin	46
D. R. Brown not out	22
D. L. Hemp not out	36
L-b 2, w 2, n-b 2	6

1/55 2/56   (2 wkts, 13.4 overs) 117

T. L. Penney, D. P. Ostler, G. Welch, A. F. Giles, †T. Frost, G. C. Small and A. A. Donald did not bat.

Bowling: Mullally 3–0–23–0; Parsons 3–0–23–0; Wells 1–0–22–0; Dakin 3–0–19–2; Mason 3–0–23–0; Johnson 0.4–0–5–0.

Umpires: J. D. Bond and A. Clarkson.

LEICESTERSHIRE v YORKSHIRE

At Leicester, July 6. Tied. Toss: Yorkshire.

Yorkshire built their highest 40-over score, surpassing by two the 296 for eight they made against Surrey at The Oval in 1995. (They had reached 318 for seven, also against Leicestershire, when the competition was played in a 50-over format in 1993). White broke the club's individual record with his 114-ball 148, which included ten fours and five sixes. It would normally have been more than enough for victory, but Leicestershire had enjoyed a run-glut themselves, led by 70 in 45 balls from Maddy. Needing five to win off the last over, Yorkshire were suddenly frustrated by an over of careful placement by Parsons: three wickets fell and the match finished as a tie, the highest-scoring of the 46 in League history up to the end of 1997.

Leicestershire

N. C. Johnson c Blakey b Silverwood . . .	9	T. J. Mason not out	7
V. J. Wells c and b Morris	51	G. J. Parsons b White	2
I. J. Sutcliffe b Stemp	18	D. J. Millns not out	3
J. M. Dakin b Morris	27	B 9, l-b 10, w 14, n-b 7	40
*J. J. Whitaker c Hartley b Morris	66		
D. L. Maddy c McGrath b Morris	70	1/16 2/82 3/121 (9 wkts, 40 overs) 298
B. F. Smith b Hartley	3	4/141 5/258 6/280
†P. A. Nixon c Morris b White	2	7/283 8/287 9/294

Bowling: Silverwood 8–0–55–1; Sidebottom 6–1–44–0; Stemp 4–0–38–1; White 8–0–47–2; Hartley 8–0–46–1; Morris 6–0–49–4.

Yorkshire

*D. Byas lbw b Millns	8	C. E. W. Silverwood not out	1
C. White c Johnson b Wells 148		R. D. Stemp run out	1
D. S. Lehmann c Smith b Dakin	48		
P. J. Hartley c Mason b Dakin	6	L-b 7, w 7, n-b 4	18
†R. J. Blakey lbw b Mason	6		
B. Parker c Parsons b Wells	21	1/19 2/154 3/165 (9 wkts, 40 overs) 298
A. McGrath run out	33	4/179 5/246 6/258
A. C. Morris c Sutcliffe b Parsons	8	7/294 8/297 9/298

R. J. Sidebottom did not bat.

Bowling: Parsons 7–0–41–1; Millns 5–0–38–1; Dakin 8–0–64–2; Wells 8–0–60–2; Mason 8–0–48–1; Maddy 4–0–40–0.

Umpires: N. T. Plews and P. Willey.

At Canterbury, July 20. LEICESTERSHIRE beat KENT by 33 runs.

LEICESTERSHIRE v NOTTINGHAMSHIRE

At Leicester, July 27. Leicestershire won by 87 runs. Toss: Nottinghamshire.

Whitaker scored 73 in 80 balls and became the second Leicestershire batsman (after Nigel Briers) to reach 5,000 runs in Sunday cricket. He also gave his side something to bowl at and, despite a bland pitch, Nottinghamshire never looked like winners.

Leicestershire

V. J. Wells c Robinson b Oram........ 28	T. J. Mason not out 12
N. C. Johnson run out 6	J. Ormond c Bowen b Evans 18
I. J. Sutcliffe run out................ 26	D. Williamson not out 3
*J. J. Whitaker run out 73	L-b 12, w 9, n-b 4 25
D. L. Maddy c sub b Bowen 20	—
B. F. Smith c Astle b Bowen.......... 13	1/16 2/42 3/98 (9 wkts, 40 overs) 252
J. M. Dakin b Tolley 22	4/153 5/172 6/206
†P. A. Nixon b Tolley 6	7/213 8/220 9/247

Bowling: Evans 8–0–36–1; Oram 6–0–30–1; Tolley 8–0–52–2; Bowen 8–0–57–2; Astle 8–0–47–0; Bates 0.5–0–6–0; Dowman 1.1–0–12–0.

Nottinghamshire

M. P. Dowman c Smith b Ormond 16	R. T. Bates run out.................. 2
N. J. Astle c Wells b Johnson 0	M. N. Bowen b Dakin 2
R. T. Robinson b Williamson 37	A. R. Oram not out.................. 0
*P. Johnson c Whitaker b Williamson ... 18	B 1, l-b 15, w 13, n-b 4 33
G. F. Archer c Nixon b Wells 11	—
C. M. Tolley c Williamson b Johnson ... 28	1/6 2/51 3/74 (32.2 overs) 165
†W. M. Noon c Nixon b Johnson 6	4/92 5/125 6/140
K. P. Evans c Maddy b Mason 12	7/151 8/154 9/165

Bowling: Ormond 6–0–28–1; Johnson 6–0–37–3; Williamson 8–0–36–2; Wells 5–0–18–1; Mason 5.2–0–27–1; Dakin 2–0–3–1.

Umpires: A. A. Jones and R. A. White.

At Colchester, August 3. LEICESTERSHIRE beat ESSEX by 35 runs.

At Eastbourne, August 10. LEICESTERSHIRE beat SUSSEX by 44 runs.

LEICESTERSHIRE v DERBYSHIRE

At Leicester, August 24. No result (abandoned).

LEICESTERSHIRE v GLAMORGAN

At Leicester, August 31. No result (abandoned).

LEICESTERSHIRE v DURHAM

At Leicester, September 7. Leicestershire won by 106 runs. Toss: Leicestershire. First-team debut: M. J. Symington.

Gordon Parsons, who made his first appearance for Leicestershire in 1978, led the side out to a standing ovation in his farewell game. It was to be thoroughly one-sided. Sutcliffe and Maddy shared a stand of 86 for Leicestershire's fourth wicket, and Maddy went on to mop up Durham's tail for figures of 3.1–0–11–3. Leicestershire's eighth successive Sunday game without defeat lifted them to third in the table.

Leicestershire

V. J. Wells c Hutton b Killeen	2	G. J. Parsons not out	10	
I. J. Sutcliffe b Boiling	96	J. Ormond not out	0	
B. F. Smith c and b Brown	27			
*J. J. Whitaker b Symington	2	L-b 2, w 9, n-b 2	13	
D. L. Maddy c Symington b Killeen	70			
J. M. Dakin b Walker	15	1/4 2/72 3/84	(8 wkts, 40 overs) 252	
†P. A. Nixon c sub b Killeen	17	4/170 5/205 6/229		
T. J. Mason b Killeen	0	7/229 8/250		

M. T. Brimson did not bat.

Bowling: Brown 7–0–40–1; Killeen 8–1–46–4; Walker 7–0–45–1; Symington 7–0–51–1; Boiling 8–0–42–1; Boon 3–0–26–0.

Durham

J. E. Morris run out	42	N. Killeen b Maddy	1	
S. Hutton lbw b Wells	25	A. Walker c Ormond b Maddy	3	
†M. P. Speight run out	4	S. J. E. Brown b Maddy	6	
M. A. Roseberry c Brimson b Mason	13	B 5, l-b 7, w 1, n-b 4	17	
*D. C. Boon run out	7			
J. J. B. Lewis c Whitaker b Brimson	2	1/73 2/80 3/81	(36.1 overs) 146	
M. J. Symington c Parsons b Mason	7	4/92 5/97 6/107		
J. Boiling not out	19	7/116 8/120 9/128		

Bowling: Ormond 4–0–21–0; Parsons 8–0–31–0; Dakin 3–0–17–0; Wells 6–1–17–1; Brimson 8–2–22–1; Mason 4–0–15–2; Maddy 3.1–0–11–3.

Umpires: B. J. Meyer and R. A. White.

At Northampton, September 14. LEICESTERSHIRE lost to NORTHAMPTONSHIRE by five wickets.

MIDDLESEX

At Chelmsford, May 4. MIDDLESEX lost to ESSEX by 66 runs.

MIDDLESEX v SUSSEX

At Lord's, May 11. Middlesex won by seven wickets (D/L method). Toss: Middlesex.

Middlesex recorded their first win of the season in their seventh match when they passed a sorry Sussex total with 11 overs to spare. A brief shower had revised their target to 129 from 38 overs. Sussex's best stand was the 39 added by Khan and Robinson: this broke the county's last-wicket record, set in 1969, the first year of the competition.

Sussex

K. Greenfield c Kallis b Hewitt	13	A. A. Khan not out	22
R. K. Rao lbw b Fay	10	M. R. Strong b Kallis	1
N. R. Taylor b Fay	10	M. A. Robinson not out	9
M. Newell c Weekes b Kallis	21	L-b 15, w 16, n-b 2	33
J. P. Pyemont c Gatting b Weekes	1		
*†P. Moores b Fraser	4	1/29 2/44 3/54 (9 wkts, 40 overs)	131
P. W. Jarvis c Ramprakash b Fraser	4	4/58 5/71 6/84	
N. C. Phillips c Moffat b Fraser	3	7/87 8/90 9/92	

Bowling: Hewitt 6–0–24–1; Fay 8–1–23–2; Dutch 4–0–8–0; Weekes 8–0–32–1; Fraser 8–2–10–3; Kallis 6–0–19–2.

Middlesex

P. N. Weekes c Newell b Jarvis	4	J. C. Pooley not out	4
J. H. Kallis lbw b Robinson	10	L-b 2, w 15, n-b 6	23
M. R. Ramprakash not out	57		
*M. W. Gatting c Jarvis b Khan	34	1/9 2/20 3/115 (3 wkts, 27 overs)	132

†K. R. Brown, S. P. Moffat, K. P. Dutch, J. P. Hewitt, R. A. Fay and A. R. C. Fraser did not bat.

Bowling: Jarvis 7–0–35–1; Robinson 8–0–27–1; Phillips 3–0–14–0; Strong 3–0–23–0; Khan 6–0–31–1.

Umpires: J. H. Hampshire and V. A. Holder.

MIDDLESEX v DERBYSHIRE

At Lord's, May 18. Middlesex won by four wickets. Toss: Derbyshire.

A muscular 82 from 83 balls by Gatting enabled Middlesex to score the 79 runs they needed from the last ten overs. He was particularly severe on DeFreitas – just picked by a panel, which included Gatting, to play in the England one-day squad against the Australians.

Derbyshire

*D. M. Jones c Brown b Johnson	26	G. M. Roberts c Nash b Weekes	1
C. J. Adams c Kallis b Dutch	52	A. J. Harris lbw b Johnson	2
P. A. J. DeFreitas c Gatting b Hewitt	17	K. J. Dean lbw b Weekes	1
G. A. Khan lbw b Hewitt	5	B 1, l-b 11, w 8, n-b 2	22
I. D. Blackwell lbw b Dutch	3		
M. E. Cassar b Johnson	33	1/66 2/104 3/116 (39.4 overs)	178
V. P. Clarke b Fraser	7	4/121 5/127 6/159	
†K. M. Krikken not out	9	7/170 8/171 9/175	

Bowling: Fraser 8–0–30–1; Hewitt 8–0–36–2; Kallis 5–0–20–0; Johnson 7–0–39–3; Dutch 8–0–25–2; Weekes 3.4–1–16–2.

Middlesex

P. N. Weekes c Krikken b Dean	3	D. C. Nash b Harris	23
J. H. Kallis c Clarke b DeFreitas	10	K. P. Dutch not out	2
M. R. Ramprakash b Harris	28	L-b 10, w 4	14
*M. W. Gatting not out	82		
†K. R. Brown c Jones b Clarke	3	1/7 2/27 3/75 (6 wkts, 39.5 overs)	179
S. P. Moffat c Krikken b Cassar	14	4/84 5/103 6/165	

R. L. Johnson, J. P. Hewitt and A. R. C. Fraser did not bat.

Bowling: Dean 8–1–22–1; DeFreitas 7.5–1–34–1; Roberts 6–0–32–0; Harris 8–0–30–2; Clarke 7–0–36–1; Cassar 3–1–15–1.

Umpires: G. I. Burgess and B. Dudleston.

At Birmingham, May 25. MIDDLESEX lost to WARWICKSHIRE by 108 runs.

MIDDLESEX v NORTHAMPTONSHIRE

At Lord's, June 1. Northamptonshire won by 67 runs. Toss: Northamptonshire.

Both sets of bowlers struggled manfully with a fierce wind, which brought down part of the press-box ceiling. Most successful were Northamptonshire's opening pair – Taylor, who produced some hostile deliveries, and Follett, who had joined from Middlesex in the close season. Each took two wickets as Middlesex stumbled to 21 for four, and Pooley's defiant 55 was small consolation.

Northamptonshire

*R. J. Bailey b Hewitt 10	J. N. Snape not out 8
A. L. Penberthy b Dutch 53	J. E. Emburey not out 4
K. M. Curran b Blanchett 66	B 4, l-b 13, w 8 25
D. J. Capel lbw b Fraser 6	—
T. C. Walton b Fraser 1	1/30 2/122 3/137 (7 wkts, 40 overs) 198
D. J. Sales lbw b Weekes 13	4/139 5/165
†R. J. Warren c Gatting b Hewitt 12	6/184 7/187

D. Follett and J. P. Taylor did not bat.

Bowling: Fraser 8-1-28-2; Hewitt 8-0-31-2; Weekes 8-0-25-1; Dutch 8-0-46-1; Blanchett 8-0-51-1.

Middlesex

J. H. Kallis b Taylor 6	J. P. Hewitt run out 3
P. N. Weekes b Follett 6	A. R. C. Fraser c Bailey b Emburey 2
*M. R. Ramprakash lbw b Taylor 3	I. N. Blanchett not out 1
M. W. Gatting b Follett 0	L-b 14, w 4 18
J. C. Pooley lbw b Curran 55	—
†K. R. Brown c Warren b Curran 15	1/13 2/15 3/17 (33.5 overs) 131
S. P. Moffat b Curran 18	4/21 5/76 6/112
K. P. Dutch c Snape b Curran 4	7/119 8/123 9/130

Bowling: Taylor 6-1-13-2; Follett 8-0-28-2; Emburey 6.5-0-24-1; Curran 8-0-36-4; Snape 5-0-16-0.

Umpires: J. D. Bond and R. Julian.

MIDDLESEX v LEICESTERSHIRE

At Lord's, June 8. Leicestershire won by six wickets (D/L method). Toss: Middlesex.

An excellent stand of 135 from 21 overs between Johnson and Maddy took Leicestershire most of the way to their target, which had been variously calculated at 199 and 200 by the scorers before they contacted Frank Duckworth, joint inventor of the Duckworth/Lewis method, and the figure was brought down to 198. Once again, Pooley had been the pick of Middlesex's batsmen; he made 52 not out from 39 balls.

Middlesex

P. N. Weekes lbw b Dakin 45	†K. R. Brown not out 22
J. H. Kallis c Johnson b Dakin 24	B 2, l-b 8, w 13 23
*M. R. Ramprakash b Dakin 21	—
M. W. Gatting lbw b Mason 9	1/83 2/84 (4 wkts, 37 overs) 196
J. C. Pooley not out 52	3/103 4/131

K. P. Dutch, R. L. Johnson, J. P. Hewitt, A. R. C. Fraser and I. N. Blanchett did not bat.

Bowling: Parsons 8-0-34-0; Millns 8-0-20-0; Dakin 8-1-38-3; Mason 8-0-43-1; Wells 3-0-31-0; Johnson 2-0-20-0.

Leicestershire

N. C. Johnson not out	80	A. Habib not out		4
V. J. Wells c Brown b Fraser	7	B 2, l-b 13, w 4, n-b 2		21
*J. J. Whitaker b Fraser	4			—
D. L. Maddy c Pooley b Dutch	82	1/31 2/37	(4 wkts, 35.2 overs)	198
G. I. Macmillan c Hewitt b Weekes	0	3/172 4/178		

†P. A. Nixon, G. J. Parsons, D. J. Millns, J. M. Dakin and T. J. Mason did not bat.

Bowling: Fraser 8–1–33–2; Hewitt 7–0–33–0; Johnson 3–0–30–0; Blanchett 7–0–48–0; Dutch 8–0–31–1; Weekes 2.2–0–8–1.

Umpires: A. Clarkson and V. A. Holder.

At Cardiff, June 15. MIDDLESEX lost to GLAMORGAN by six wickets.

At Bristol, June 22. MIDDLESEX lost to GLOUCESTERSHIRE by 55 runs.

At Leeds, June 29. MIDDLESEX lost to YORKSHIRE by six wickets.

MIDDLESEX v LANCASHIRE

At Uxbridge, July 6. Tied. Toss: Middlesex.

Fine innings from Pooley and Fairbrother cancelled each other out as Lancashire were left needing 13 from the last over to win. Hegg hit Johnson's first two balls to the boundary, but two run-outs left Yates and Shadford needing two from the final delivery. They took a bye and levelled the scores. This ended a sequence of six successive Middlesex defeats.

Middlesex

P. N. Weekes c Hegg b Martin	6	R. L. Johnson not out		8
J. H. Kallis c Gallian b Shadford	19	A. R. C. Fraser c Shadford b Watkinson		26
*M. R. Ramprakash b Chilton	12	T. F. Bloomfield b Austin		1
O. A. Shah lbw b Shadford	0	L-b 4, w 10, n-b 6		20
J. C. Pooley lbw b Shadford	73			—
†K. R. Brown c Flintoff b Gallian	21	1/7 2/44 3/45	(39.5 overs)	197
S. P. Moffat st Hegg b Watkinson	10	4/45 5/103 6/155		
K. P. Dutch st Hegg b Watkinson	1	7/157 8/161 9/191		

Bowling: Austin 7.5–0–33–1; Martin 3–1–5–1; Shadford 8–2–30–3; Chilton 8–0–35–1; Yates 7–1–41–0; Gallian 3–0–26–1; Watkinson 3–0–23–3.

Lancashire

*M. Watkinson c Kallis b Fraser	8	G. Yates not out		0
J. E. R. Gallian c Brown b Fraser	5	P. J. Martin run out		1
N. H. Fairbrother c Weekes b Dutch	70	D. J. Shadford not out		1
G. D. Lloyd c Brown b Kallis	8	B 1, l-b 6, w 8, n-b 2		17
A. Flintoff c Ramprakash b Weekes	31			—
M. J. Chilton c Kallis b Dutch	22	1/14 2/20 3/40	(9 wkts, 40 overs)	197
I. D. Austin b Bloomfield	9	4/99 5/149 6/162		
†W. K. Hegg run out	25	7/182 8/194 9/195		

Bowling: Fraser 8–0–36–2; Bloomfield 8–1–27–1; Kallis 6–0–22–1; Johnson 8–0–52–0; Weekes 6–0–34–1; Dutch 4–0–19–2.

Umpires: J. C. Balderstone and J. W. Holder.

MIDDLESEX v KENT

At Lord's, July 27. Kent won by eight wickets. Toss: Middlesex. First team debut: A. J. Strauss.
   Gatting resumed the captaincy, as Ramprakash was injured. Middlesex made a poor fist of
their innings, despite a maiden one-day fifty from Dutch. For Kent, Ward and Wells paced
themselves expertly in a stand of 138.

Middlesex

P. N. Weekes st Willis b Strang	20	A. J. Strauss b Fleming	3
J. H. Kallis lbw b Igglesden	5	R. L. Johnson not out	8
*M. W. Gatting lbw b Igglesden	0	B 1, l-b 2, w 3, n-b 2	8
J. C. Pooley run out	17		
O. A. Shah c Ward b Thompson	18	1/11 2/11 3/42 (8 wkts, 40 overs) 151	
K. P. Dutch b Fleming	58	4/58 5/65 6/103	
†D. C. Nash b Fleming	14	7/113 8/151	

J. P. Hewitt and A. R. C. Fraser did not bat.

   Bowling: McCague 8–0–21–0; Igglesden 8–1–19–2; Strang 8–0–28–1; Thompson 8–0–49–1;
Fleming 8–0–31–3.

Kent

*T. R. Ward not out	68
M. J. Walker lbw b Hewitt	3
A. P. Wells c Fraser b Johnson	56
G. R. Cowdrey not out	1
L-b 12, w 5, n-b 7	24

1/11 2/149   (2 wkts, 39.2 overs) 152

M. V. Fleming, N. J. Llong, P. A. Strang, †S. C. Willis, M. J. McCague, J. B. D. Thompson and
A. P. Igglesden did not bat.

   Bowling: Fraser 5–0–11–0; Hewitt 8–0–31–1; Johnson 8–1–29–1; Dutch 7–0–32–0; Weekes
7–0–23–0; Kallis 4.2–0–14–0.

Umpires: D. J. Constant and J. H. Hampshire.

MIDDLESEX v SURREY

At Lord's, August 3. No result. Toss: Surrey.
   Middlesex missed out on the chance of a rare Sunday win when rain stopped play. Their
bowlers had made rapid inroads into Surrey's star-studded line-up, of whom only Lewis held
firm. Butcher, who had just heard that he was out of England's squad for Trent Bridge, flicked
his stumps in frustration after he was out.

Surrey

A. D. Brown lbw b Hewitt	1	I. J. Ward b Bloomfield	0
†A. J. Stewart c Nash b Fraser	0	M. P. Bicknell not out	4
C. C. Lewis not out	34	L-b 4, w 6	10
G. P. Thorpe c Gatting b Fraser	0		
M. A. Butcher c Nash b Hewitt	4	1/1 2/3 3/5 (7 wkts, 23 overs) 74	
*A. J. Hollioake b Kallis	16	4/12 5/51	
J. D. Ratcliffe c Nash b Bloomfield	5	6/62 7/62	

Saqlain Mushtaq and J. E. Benjamin did not bat.

   Bowling: Fraser 7–0–22–2; Hewitt 8–0–24–2; Kallis 5–1–16–1; Bloomfield 3–0–8–2.

Middlesex

P. N. Weekes, J. H. Kallis, *M. R. Ramprakash, M. W. Gatting, J. C. Pooley, †D. C. Nash, K. P. Dutch, T. F. Bloomfield, R. L. Johnson, J. P. Hewitt and A. R. C. Fraser.

Umpires: D. J. Constant and B. J. Meyer.

MIDDLESEX v HAMPSHIRE

At Lord's, August 10. Hampshire won by 16 runs. Toss: Hampshire. County debut: C. Patel. First-team debut: L. Savident.

With Ramprakash absent ill, Brown led Middlesex. At their 12th attempt in the 1997 competition, his team finally managed to reach 200. But they were unable to get the further 17 they needed to overhaul Hampshire. Hayden had completed 500 Sunday runs in 12 innings during his 89. Pooley surpassed him with an unbeaten 94 from 96 balls until Tufnell's dismissal left him stranded.

Hampshire

J. S. Laney c Shah b Tufnell	34
M. L. Hayden c Strauss b Johnson	89
R. A. Smith c Weekes b Johnson	16
M. Keech b Johnson	21
W. S. Kendall b Hewitt	13
S. D. Udal lbw b Hewitt	1
*J. P. Stephenson not out	16
S. J. Renshaw b Fraser	9
†A. N. Aymes not out	2
L-b 6, w 5, n-b 4	15

1/103 2/140 3/157 (7 wkts, 40 overs) 216
4/181 5/185
6/189 7/210

L. Savident and C. Patel did not bat.

Bowling: Fraser 8-0-42-1; Hewitt 8-0-35-2; Dutch 5-0-23-0; Johnson 8-0-35-3; Tufnell 8-0-56-1; Weekes 3-0-19-0.

Middlesex

O. A. Shah c Aymes b Renshaw	1
P. N. Weekes c Aymes b Stephenson	18
R. L. Johnson c Laney b Renshaw	21
J. C. Pooley not out	94
M. W. Gatting c Hayden b Udal	3
*†K. R. Brown lbw b Udal	14
K. P. Dutch st Aymes b Udal	12
A. J. Strauss c Udal b Savident	4
J. P. Hewitt c Hayden b Savident	7
A. R. C. Fraser c Patel b Renshaw	1
P. C. R. Tufnell b Savident	7
L-b 7, w 9, n-b 2	18

1/2 2/33 3/74 (38.1 overs) 200
4/79 5/106 6/124
7/140 8/173 9/177

Bowling: Renshaw 8-0-48-3; Patel 4-0-25-0; Savident 7.1-0-41-3; Stephenson 7-0-23-1; Udal 8-0-26-3; Hayden 4-0-30-0.

Umpires: T. E. Jesty and J. F. Steele.

At Chester-le-Street, August 24. DURHAM v MIDDLESEX. No result (abandoned).

At Worcester, August 31. WORCESTERSHIRE v MIDDLESEX. No result (abandoned).

At Taunton, September 7. MIDDLESEX lost to SOMERSET by 18 runs.

MIDDLESEX v NOTTINGHAMSHIRE

At Lord's, September 14. Middlesex won by one run. Toss: Middlesex.

Fresh from his maiden Championship hundred, Shah was Middlesex's top scorer in a close, but hardly tense, game with nothing at stake. Johnson shared a stand of 101 with Welton, but late wickets left Noon needing three to win from the last ball, bowled by Dutch; he managed only one. It was Middlesex's first Sunday win in four months, and 14 matches. MCC assistant secretary John Jameson stood as umpire in distressing circumstances. Barrie Leadbeater had returned home after his wife was killed, and his son injured, in a car accident.

Middlesex

P. N. Weekes c Evans b Franks	53	†K. R. Brown not out	9
*M. R. Ramprakash c Bates b Franks	52	L-b 11, w 5, n-b 4	20
O. A. Shah not out	66		—
J. C. Pooley c Johnson b Evans	29	1/104 2/125	(4 wkts, 40 overs) 231
D. C. Nash run out	2	3/199 4/204	

K. P. Dutch, J. P. Hewitt, A. R. C. Fraser, R. A. Fay and T. F. Bloomfield did not bat.

Bowling: Evans 8–0–40–1; Oram 8–0–36–0; Bates 8–0–37–0; Tolley 4–0–28–0; Franks 8–1–46–2; Afzaal 2–0–21–0; Dowman 2–0–12–0.

Nottinghamshire

G. E. Welton b Weekes	68	K. P. Evans b Weekes	0
U. Afzaal c Bloomfield b Fraser	9	R. T. Bates not out	3
M. P. Dowman b Fay	1	L-b 8, w 6	14
*P. Johnson c Fraser b Weekes	100		—
N. A. Gie b Weekes	24	1/27 2/48 3/149	(7 wkts, 40 overs) 230
C. M. Tolley run out	5	4/206 5/216	
†W. M. Noon not out	6	6/221 7/223	

P. J. Franks and A. R. Oram did not bat.

Bowling: Fraser 8–2–21–1; Fay 8–0–27–1; Dutch 4–0–36–0; Hewitt 4–0–25–0; Bloomfield 8–0–62–0; Weekes 8–0–51–4.

Umpires: G. I. Burgess and J. A. Jameson.

NORTHAMPTONSHIRE

At Hove, April 27. NORTHAMPTONSHIRE beat SUSSEX by nine wickets.

At Birmingham, May 4. NORTHAMPTONSHIRE lost to WARWICKSHIRE by five wickets (D/L method).

NORTHAMPTONSHIRE v SOMERSET

At Northampton, May 11. No result (abandoned).

At Manchester, May 25. NORTHAMPTONSHIRE lost to LANCASHIRE by 75 runs.

At Lord's, June 1. NORTHAMPTONSHIRE beat MIDDLESEX by 67 runs.

NORTHAMPTONSHIRE v NOTTINGHAMSHIRE

At Milton Keynes, June 8. Northamptonshire won by seven runs (D/L method). Toss: Nottinghamshire.

Northamptonshire returned to play in Buckinghamshire after a ten-year gap and deserted the old, unpopular Bletchley ground to stage the first county match at Campbell Park. Chasing an adjusted target of 211 from 27 overs, Nottinghamshire were kept in the hunt by a brave 75 from Astle; he struck five sixes in 61 balls on his Sunday League debut. But he was yorked by Emburey, who took command at the death, collecting four for 28. For Northamptonshire, Walton had hit 42 from 25 balls.

Northamptonshire

M. B. Loye run out	34	†R. J. Warren not out	16
A. L. Penberthy c Noon b Evans	9		
K. M. Curran c and b Bates	37	L-b 7, w 6, n-b 2	15
T. C. Walton c Evans b Astle	42		—
*R. J. Bailey not out	52	1/22 2/70 3/106 (5 wkts, 30 overs)	225
D. J. Sales c Archer b Bates	20	4/146 5/185	

J. N. Snape, J. E. Emburey, D. Follett and J. P. Taylor did not bat.

Bowling: Evans 6–1–16–1; Oram 6–0–28–0; Bowen 6–0–48–0; Astle 6–0–51–1; Bates 5–0–55–2; Dowman 1–0–20–0.

Nottinghamshire

M. P. Dowman b Follett	28	G. E. Welton b Emburey	4
N. J. Astle b Emburey	75	M. N. Bowen lbw b Taylor	13
*P. Johnson b Penberthy	32	A. R. Oram not out	0
G. F. Archer b Penberthy	4	B 3, l-b 8, w 7, n-b 2	20
N. A. Gie lbw b Emburey	2		—
†W. M. Noon not out	1	1/50 2/112 3/136 (9 wkts, 27 overs)	204
K. P. Evans b Emburey	17	4/139 5/164 6/179	
R. T. Bates c Sales b Curran	8	7/186 8/199 9/204	

W. M. Noon, when 0, retired hurt at 140 and resumed at 199.

Bowling: Taylor 6–0–39–1; Follett 5–0–50–1; Penberthy 6–0–23–2; Curran 5–0–53–1; Emburey 5–0–28–4.

Umpires: G. I. Burgess and J. H. Harris.

NORTHAMPTONSHIRE v HAMPSHIRE

At Northampton, June 22. Northamptonshire won by four wickets (D/L method). Toss: Northamptonshire.

Northamptonshire saved their best for last as Warren clouted two sixes and a four from the final over of the innings, bowled by Stephenson. That was enough to take them past their rain-adjusted target of 171 in 23 overs with two balls to spare.

Hampshire

J. S. Laney c Innes b Penberthy	53
M. L. Hayden c Warren b Penberthy	54
S. D. Udal not out	27
M. Keech not out	18
L-b 2, w 3, n-b 2	7
	—
1/105 2/117 (2 wkts, 23 overs)	159

J. N. B. Bovill, W. S. Kendall, *J. P. Stephenson, K. D. James, †A. N. Aymes, S. J. Renshaw and C. A. Connor did not bat.

Bowling: Taylor 4–0–19–0; Innes 3–0–22–0; Curran 4–0–36–0; Emburey 3–0–22–0; Penberthy 5–0–31–2; Snape 4–0–27–0.

Northamptonshire

M. B. Loye c Aymes b Renshaw	0	†R. J. Warren not out		43
A. L. Penberthy c Keech b Connor	1	J. N. Snape not out		6
K. M. Curran c Laney b Udal	41	B 1, l-b 11, n-b 2		14
T. C. Walton c Kendall b Udal	14			
*R. J. Bailey c Kendall b Bovill	50	1/0 2/4 3/49	(6 wkts, 22.4 overs)	174
D. J. Sales c Bovill b Renshaw	5	4/83 5/94 6/144		

K. J. Innes, J. E. Emburey and J. P. Taylor did not bat.

Bowling: Renshaw 5–0–38–2; Connor 5–0–21–1; Udal 5–0–27–2; Bovill 4–0–34–1; James 3–0–26–0; Stephenson 0.4–0–16–0.

Umpires: B. Dudleston and N. T. Plews.

NORTHAMPTONSHIRE v GLOUCESTERSHIRE

At Luton, June 29. No result (abandoned).

At Maidstone, July 6. NORTHAMPTONSHIRE lost to KENT by two runs.

NORTHAMPTONSHIRE v ESSEX

At Northampton, July 20. Essex won by two wickets. Toss: Essex.

Emburey conceded nine runs from the last over of the match and two from the last ball as Essex snatched victory. An unbeaten 69 in 51 balls by Grayson repaired the damage done by Hussain, who had run Stuart Law out before donating his own wicket with a reverse sweep. Almost two-thirds of Northamptonshire's runs had come from the longest-serving members of their team, Capel and Bailey.

Northamptonshire

R. R. Montgomerie run out	13	K. J. Innes not out		7
A. L. Penberthy c Rollins b Irani	6	J. E. Emburey not out		2
D. J. Capel c Rollins b Powell	54			
D. J. Sales lbw b Such	9	B 1, l-b 2, w 10, n-b 6		19
*R. J. Bailey b Irani	75			
T. C. Walton c Robinson b Powell	6	1/20 2/26 3/46	(8 wkts, 40 overs)	198
†R. J. Warren c Rollins b Cowan	4	4/168 5/172 6/182		
J. N. Snape b Cowan	3	7/182 8/187		

J. P. Taylor did not bat.

Bowling: Cowan 8–0–37–2; Irani 8–0–25–2; D. R. Law 3–0–15–0; Such 8–0–30–1; S. G. Law 8–0–43–0; Grayson 3–0–35–0; Powell 2–0–10–2.

Essex

*P. J. Prichard b Taylor	13	A. P. Cowan run out		0
S. G. Law run out	25	J. C. Powell not out		0
N. Hussain c Sales b Snape	20			
R. C. Irani c Warren b Capel	40	B 4, l-b 5, w 6		15
A. P. Grayson not out	69			
D. R. Law b Capel	9	1/22 2/53 3/83	(8 wkts, 40 overs)	199
D. D. J. Robinson b Emburey	1	4/155 5/170 6/175		
†R. J. Rollins c Capel b Penberthy	7	7/184 8/190		

P. M. Such did not bat.

Bowling: Penberthy 8–0–42–1; Taylor 8–1–29–1; Capel 8–0–42–2; Snape 8–1–31–1; Emburey 8–0–46–1.

Umpires: J. H. Hampshire and P. Willey.

NORTHAMPTONSHIRE v SURREY

At Northampton, July 27. Northamptonshire won by five wickets. Toss: Surrey.

Northamptonshire's injury-plagued fast bowler Mohammad Akram took his first Sunday wickets and finished with four for 19. Fordham and Penberthy then added 104 for the first wicket, and Penberthy steered his side home in the final over with an unbeaten 81 (one over having been docked for a slow over-rate).

Surrey

D. J. Bicknell c Warren b Mohammad Akram . 7	I. J. Ward not out 11
A. D. Brown c Emburey b Mohammad Akram . 6	†J. N. Batty b Mohammad Akram 1
B. C. Hollioake c Warren b Penberthy . . . 40	M. P. Bicknell not out 3
J. D. Ratcliffe b Mohammad Akram 82	L-b 19, w 7 26
*A. J. Hollioake run out 17	
C. C. Lewis run out 13	1/15 2/23 3/106 (7 wkts, 40 overs) 206

A. D. Brown c Emburey b Mohammad Akram . 6

4/157 5/185
6/194 7/199

J. E. Benjamin and Saqlain Mushtaq did not bat.

Bowling: Taylor 8–0–26–0; Mohammad Akram 8–0–19–4; Capel 7–0–36–0; Emburey 6–0–36–0; Snape 7–0–47–0; Penberthy 4–0–23–1.

Northamptonshire

A. Fordham c Ratcliffe b Saqlain Mushtaq . 43	T. C. Walton c Ratcliffe b Saqlain Mushtaq . 9
A. L. Penberthy not out 81	†R. J. Warren not out 10
D. J. Capel b A. J. Hollioake. 5	L-b 14, w 6, n-b 6 26
D. J. Sales c Brown b B. C. Hollioake . . . 19	
*R. J. Bailey c M. P. Bicknell b Saqlain Mushtaq . 15	1/104 2/113 3/136 (5 wkts, 38.3 overs) 208

4/156 5/177

Mohammad Akram, J. P. Taylor, J. E. Emburey and J. N. Snape did not bat.

Bowling: Lewis 7.3–1–31–0; M. P. Bicknell 6–0–30–0; Benjamin 6–0–33–0; Saqlain Mushtaq 8–0–31–3; A. J. Hollioake 4–0–28–1; B. C. Hollioake 7–0–41–1.

Umpires: J. H. Harris and A. G. T. Whitehead.

At Leeds, August 3. NORTHAMPTONSHIRE lost to YORKSHIRE by 38 runs.

NORTHAMPTONSHIRE v WORCESTERSHIRE

At Northampton, August 10. Worcestershire won by two wickets. Toss: Northamptonshire. First-team debut: G. P. Swann.

Batsmen failed to prosper on a slow turning pitch: no one managed 50, or a 50-run partnership, though Bailey got to 6,000 runs with a six over mid-wicket. But Lampitt, despite a rib injury, provided a thrilling finish, clubbing Emburey for 16 in five balls to win with a ball to spare. This was Emburey's final first-team appearance: he ended 23 seasons in the League with 368 wickets, second only to John Lever's 386. Another Northamptonshire off-spinner, England Under-19 player Graeme Swann, launched his career with two for 28.

Northamptonshire

A. Fordham b Lampitt	30	G. P. Swann run out	0
A. L. Penberthy c Rhodes b Haynes	9	J. E. Emburey c and b Leatherdale	4
K. M. Curran b Lampitt	17	Mohammad Akram not out	1
D. J. Sales c Solanki b Hick	17	L-b 7, w 9, n-b 13	29
*R. J. Bailey lbw b Leatherdale	21		
†R. J. Warren c Spiring b Mirza	44	1/20 2/69 3/73 (9 wkts, 40 overs) 207	
R. R. Montgomerie c Rhodes b Haynes	16	4/96 5/135 6/178	
K. J. Innes not out	19	7/184 8/190 9/200	

Bowling: Moody 4–0–17–0; Haynes 7–0–38–2; Mirza 4–0–31–1; Illingworth 8–0–19–0; Lampitt 4–0–20–2; Hick 8–0–44–1; Leatherdale 5–0–31–2.

Worcestershire

*T. M. Moody c Bailey b Penberthy	17	S. R. Lampitt not out	38
W. P. C. Weston c Montgomerie		†S. J. Rhodes b Mohammad Akram	19
b Mohammad Akram	4	R. K. Illingworth not out	2
G. A. Hick run out	16	B 1, l-b 18, w 3	22
G. R. Haynes st Warren b Emburey	22		
K. R. Spiring run out	30	1/11 2/27 3/66 (8 wkts, 39.5 overs) 208	
D. A. Leatherdale b Swann	8	4/68 5/85 6/134	
V. S. Solanki c Warren b Swann	30	7/151 8/190	

M. M. Mirza did not bat.

Bowling: Mohammad Akram 8–1–31–2; Penberthy 8–0–27–1; Emburey 7.5–0–35–1; Innes 1–0–14–0; Swann 8–0–28–2; Bailey 3–0–26–0; Curran 4–0–28–0.

Umpires: B. Leadbeater and G. Sharp.

At Cardiff, August 24. GLAMORGAN v NORTHAMPTONSHIRE. No result (abandoned).

At Derby, September 7. NORTHAMPTONSHIRE beat DERBYSHIRE by seven wickets.

NORTHAMPTONSHIRE v DURHAM

At Northampton, September 8 (Monday). Northamptonshire won by five wickets. Toss: Durham.
This match had been postponed from August 31 as a mark of respect for Diana, Princess of Wales, who had died that morning; she grew up near Northampton and her brother, Earl Spencer, is one of the club's patrons. Montgomerie led their run-chase, which ended successfully when he and Walton took 12 runs off Walker's last over; Walker kicked at the stumps in disappointment.

Durham

J. E. Morris b Blain	20	J. Wood run out	6
S. Hutton c T. M. B. Bailey b Swann	30	J. Boiling not out	1
†M. P. Speight b Curran	26		
*D. C. Boon not out	54	B 6, l-b 7, w 3	16
J. J. B. Lewis b Penberthy	26		
R. M. S. Weston c T. M. B. Bailey		1/28 2/80 3/86 (6 wkts, 40 overs) 185	
b Swann	6	4/135 5/156 6/181	

N. Killeen, M. J. Saggers and A. Walker did not bat.

Bowling: Blain 8–0–40–1; Taylor 8–1–38–0; Curran 5–0–25–1; Swann 8–0–29–2; Penberthy 7–0–24–1; R. J. Bailey 4–0–16–0.

Northamptonshire

R. R. Montgomerie not out	86		T. C. Walton not out	41
A. L. Penberthy b Wood	0			
K. M. Curran c Lewis b Killeen	16		B 3, l-b 7, w 3, n-b 2	15
D. J. Sales c Morris b Wood	3			—
*R. J. Bailey c Boiling b Saggers	10		1/1 2/26 3/41	(5 wkts, 39 overs) 186
A. Fordham c Speight b Walker	15		4/73 5/118	

J. P. Taylor, G. P. Swann, †T. M. B. Bailey and J. A. R. Blain did not bat.

Bowling: Wood 8–0–29–2; Killeen 7–0–31–1; Boiling 8–0–30–0; Saggers 5–0–25–1; Boon 3–0–13–0; Walker 8–0–48–1.

Umpires: D. J. Constant and R. Julian.

NORTHAMPTONSHIRE v LEICESTERSHIRE

At Northampton, September 14. Northamptonshire won by five wickets. Toss: Northamptonshire. Defeat cost Leicestershire the chance of third place. None of their batsmen could reach 40, and off-spinner Jason Brown made sure there would be no heroics from the tail with four for 26 on his Sunday debut. Acting-captain Curran made it easy for Northamptonshire, sharing a stand of 144 in 28 overs with Montgomerie.

Leicestershire

V. J. Wells c Taylor b Penberthy	38		T. J. Mason st Bailey b Brown	5
I. J. Sutcliffe c Bailey b Blain	0		J. Ormond not out	9
B. F. Smith c Blain b Curran	35			
*J. J. Whitaker b Penberthy	0		L-b 6, w 7	13
D. L. Maddy c Curran b Brown	34			—
J. M. Dakin c Fordham b Penberthy	7		1/1 2/60 3/61	(9 wkts, 40 overs) 179
†P. A. Nixon b Brown	21		4/82 5/99 6/140	
D. Williamson b Brown	17		7/146 8/156 9/179	

M. T. Brimson did not bat.

Bowling: Blain 8–0–46–1; Taylor 5–0–21–0; Curran 4–0–15–1; Penberthy 8–0–32–3; Swann 8–0–33–0; Brown 7–0–26–4.

Northamptonshire

A. Fordham c Smith b Wells	1		G. P. Swann not out	0
R. R. Montgomerie c Mason b Ormond	69			
*K. M. Curran not out	78		B 1, l-b 3, w 8, n-b 2	14
D. J. Sales c Nixon b Ormond	1			—
A. L. Penberthy b Mason	16		1/2 2/146 3/149	(5 wkts, 38.2 overs) 181
T. C. Walton b Maddy	2		4/170 5/177	

J. F. Brown, †T. M. B. Bailey, J. P. Taylor and J. A. R. Blain did not bat.

Bowling: Ormond 8–1–22–2; Wells 6–1–28–1; Dakin 8–0–40–0; Brimson 8–1–32–0; Mason 3.2–0–27–1; Williamson 2–0–14–0; Maddy 3–0–14–1.

Umpires: M. J. Kitchen and R. Palmer.

NOTTINGHAMSHIRE

NOTTINGHAMSHIRE v WORCESTERSHIRE

At Nottingham, April 27. Worcestershire won by seven wickets. Toss: Worcestershire. Worcestershire's old hands, Moody and Hick, made short work of an unexceptional Nottinghamshire total as they put on 102 for the second in 18 overs. Off-spinner Bates saw his five overs despatched for 50 runs.

Nottinghamshire

M. P. Dowman run out	7	K. P. Evans b Lampitt		4
R. T. Robinson c Rhodes b Lampitt	30	M. N. Bowen not out		5
G. F. Archer c Lampitt b Leatherdale	41			
*P. Johnson c Spiring b Chapman	3	B 4, l-b 9, w 13, n-b 8		34
P. R. Pollard c Rhodes b Haynes	34			
C. M. Tolley b Lampitt	20	1/20 2/67 3/81	(8 wkts, 40 overs)	183
R. T. Bates b Haynes	2	4/116 5/162 6/170		
†W. M. Noon not out	3	7/170 8/176		

R. A. Pick did not bat.

Bowling: Newport 8–1–20–0; Haynes 8–0–43–2; Chapman 8–0–36–1; Lampitt 8–0–29–3; Leatherdale 4–0–24–1; Hick 4–0–18–0.

Worcestershire

*T. M. Moody c Tolley b Dowman	89	V. S. Solanki not out		21
W. P. C. Weston run out	3	L-b 4, w 4		8
G. A. Hick b Tolley	32			
K. R. Spiring not out	31	1/8 2/110 3/146	(3 wkts, 38.4 overs)	184

D. A. Leatherdale, G. R. Haynes, †S. J. Rhodes, S. R. Lampitt, P. J. Newport and R. J. Chapman did not bat.

Bowling: Evans 7–0–31–0; Pick 8–1–19–0; Bowen 4–0–25–0; Tolley 8–0–26–1; Bates 5–0–50–0; Dowman 6.4–0–29–1.

Umpires: T. E. Jesty and N. T. Plews.

At Hove, May 4. NOTTINGHAMSHIRE beat SUSSEX by six wickets.

At Hartlepool, May 11. NOTTINGHAMSHIRE beat DURHAM by nine wickets (D/L method).

At Manchester, May 18. NOTTINGHAMSHIRE lost to LANCASHIRE by two wickets.

NOTTINGHAMSHIRE v DERBYSHIRE

At Nottingham, May 25. Nottinghamshire won by 32 runs. Toss: Derbyshire. First-team debuts: A. R. Oram; B. L. Spendlove.

A flat Trent Bridge pitch produced three centuries, and two in an innings for Nottinghamshire. Johnson and Archer added 200 in 28 overs, a county third-wicket record, and left Derbyshire needing to score at seven an over. Despite a fine opening stand of 117 between Adams and Jones, there were not enough runs down the order to keep them in touch.

Nottinghamshire

M. P. Dowman c Adams b Dean	8	†L. N. P. Walker b Harris		2
A. A. Metcalfe lbw b Harris	5	K. P. Evans not out		8
*P. Johnson c Krikken b Cassar	117	L-b 11, w 5, n-b 4		20
G. F. Archer not out	104			—
C. M. Tolley lbw b Hayhurst	16	1/8 2/17 3/217	(6 wkts, 40 overs)	280
N. A. Gie b Hayhurst	0	4/256 5/256 6/263		

R. T. Bates, M. N. Bowen and A. R. Oram did not bat.

Bowling: Dean 6–0–32–1; Harris 8–0–46–2; Roberts 8–0–42–0; Hayhurst 7–0–37–2; Clarke 3–0–29–0; Jones 2–0–22–0; Adams 3–0–36–0; Cassar 3–0–25–1.

Derbyshire

C. J. Adams b Bowen	121	B. L. Spendlove b Bowen		4
*D. M. Jones lbw b Bates	41	G. M. Roberts not out		5
A. N. Hayhurst c Johnson b Archer	12	L-b 4, w 5, n-b 2		11
I. D. Blackwell b Oram	13			—
V. P. Clarke c Archer b Bowen	20	1/117 2/152 3/192	(7 wkts, 40 overs)	248
†K. M. Krikken not out	18	4/219 5/219		
M. E. Cassar run out	3	6/227 7/238		

A. J. Harris and K. J. Dean did not bat.

Bowling: Evans 8–0–59–0; Oram 8–0–44–1; Bowen 8–0–59–3; Dowman 2–0–14–0; Archer 6–0–42–1; Bates 8–0–26–1.

Umpires: J. D. Bond and A. G. T. Whitehead.

NOTTINGHAMSHIRE v KENT

At Nottingham, June 1. Kent won by 46 runs. Toss: Nottinghamshire.

Nottinghamshire were left to regret dropping Cowdrey three times: his 81 not out from 43 balls lifted their target to 253. Despite a maiden one-day fifty by Gie, they never threatened to reach it.

Kent

M. V. Fleming c Archer b Oram	10	P. A. Strang run out		3
M. J. Walker c Tolley b Evans	78	*†S. A. Marsh not out		1
T. R. Ward c Gie b Bates	29	B 1, l-b 4, w 6		11
N. J. Llong c Archer b Bates	6			—
A. P. Wells c Gie b Bates	6	1/46 2/112 3/120	(7 wkts, 40 overs)	252
M. A. Ealham st Noon b Tolley	27	4/134 5/136		
G. R. Cowdrey not out	81	6/194 7/209		

M. J. McCague and J. B. D. Thompson did not bat.

Bowling: Tolley 6–0–50–1; Evans 8–0–66–1; Oram 8–0–36–1; Bowen 5–0–38–0; Bates 8–0–33–3; Dowman 5–0–24–0.

Nottinghamshire

M. P. Dowman b Thompson	0	R. T. Bates c Wells b Fleming		9
A. A. Metcalfe c Llong b Ealham	11	M. N. Bowen run out		14
*P. Johnson b Thompson	6			
G. F. Archer b Strang	31	L-b 10, w 5, n-b 6		21
N. A. Gie not out	75			—
C. M. Tolley lbw b Fleming	0	1/2 2/11 3/29	(9 wkts, 40 overs)	206
†W. M. Noon c Llong b Fleming	31	4/86 5/87 6/136		
K. P. Evans run out	8	7/163 8/180 9/206		

A. R. Oram did not bat.

Bowling: Thompson 8–0–23–2; Ealham 5–1–17–1; Strang 8–0–29–1; McCague 4–0–18–1; Fleming 8–0–60–2; Llong 7–0–49–0.

Umpires: A. Clarkson and N. T. Plews.

At Milton Keynes, June 8. NOTTINGHAMSHIRE lost to NORTHAMPTONSHIRE by seven
runs (D/L method).

NOTTINGHAMSHIRE v YORKSHIRE

At Nottingham, June 22. Nottinghamshire won by 13 runs (D/L method). Toss: Yorkshire. First-
team debut: R. J. Sidebottom.
Yorkshire's batting faded along with the light at the end of this weather-hit match. Their
innings had already been shortened once; then they lost four for seven and, when rain finally
ended play, they were 13 short of par for 15 overs. The Nottinghamshire innings was dominated
by 70 off 60 balls by Metcalfe, against his old county.

Nottinghamshire

M. P. Dowman c Blakey b Silverwood...	3	G. F. Archer not out.................	33
*R. T. Robinson c Blakey b Silverwood..	10	B 4, l-b 9, w 5, n-b 2........	20
N. J. Astle b Morris	32		
P. R. Pollard b Silverwood............	1	1/14 2/22 (4 wkts, 30 overs)	169
A. A. Metcalfe not out...............	70	3/30 4/85	

R. A. Pick, †W. M. Noon, R. T. Bates, M. N. Bowen and A. R. Oram did not bat.

Bowling: Silverwood 6–1–12–3; Sidebottom 6–1–18–0; White 6–0–37–0; Hartley 6–0–36–0;
Morris 6–0–53–1.

Yorkshire

*D. Byas c Noon b Astle..............	33	A. McGrath not out	2
C. White b Oram	4		
D. S. Lehmann c Pick b Bowen	19	L-b 3	3
†R. J. Blakey b Astle	5		
P. J. Hartley c Pollard b Bowen	0	1/18 2/57 3/61 (5 wkts, 15 overs)	78
B. Parker not out.....................	12	4/62 5/64	

A. C. Morris, R. J. Sidebottom, C. E. W. Silverwood and R. D. Stemp did not bat.

Bowling: Pick 3–0–18–0; Oram 3–0–7–1; Bowen 5–0–35–2; Astle 4–1–15–2.

Umpires: J. W. Holder and R. Palmer.

At The Oval, June 26. SURREY v NOTTINGHAMSHIRE. No result (abandoned).

NOTTINGHAMSHIRE v SOMERSET

At Nottingham, July 13. Somerset won by 30 runs. Toss: Nottinghamshire.
Parsons pulled Somerset out of a mid-innings slump with a late blast, scoring 52 from 30 balls
and adding 57 in the last four overs with Rose. For Nottinghamshire, Tolley took four wickets
and Pollard made 87, but too many of their team-mates failed to contribute, and they finished
well off the pace.

Somerset

M. Burns c Tolley b Astle	60	K. A. Parsons not out	52
P. C. L. Holloway b Tolley	35	G. D. Rose not out	13
†R. J. Turner c Johnson b Tolley	0	L-b 9, w 4, n-b 7	20
S. C. Ecclestone c Astle b Tolley	15		
M. N. Lathwell lbw b Tolley..........	2	1/67 2/67 3/87 (6 wkts, 40 overs)	227
*P. D. Bowler b Astle	30	4/96 5/149 6/170	

J. I. D. Kerr, Mushtaq Ahmed and A. R. Caddick did not bat.

Bowling: Evans 7–0–40–0; Franks 8–0–42–0; Oram 5.5–0–42–0; Johnson 0.1–0–1–0; Tolley
8–1–24–4; Bates 6–0–36–0; Astle 5–0–33–2.

Nottinghamshire

P. R. Pollard c Turner b Caddick	87	†W. M. Noon not out		6
A. A. Metcalfe c Turner b Rose	11	K. P. Evans not out		1
*P. Johnson c Bowler b Rose	14	B 1, l-b 6, w 1, n-b 2		10
N. J. Astle c Caddick b Mushtaq Ahmed	22			
R. T. Robinson c and b Mushtaq Ahmed	8	1/21 2/47 3/100	(7 wkts, 40 overs)	197
C. M. Tolley c Rose b Caddick	36	4/123 5/180		
R. T. Bates c Kerr b Caddick	2	6/190 7/190		

P. J. Franks and A. R. Oram did not bat.

Bowling: Rose 8–0–20–2; Parsons 8–0–50–0; Caddick 8–0–45–3; Mushtaq Ahmed 8–1–26–2; Kerr 8–0–49–0.

Umpires: J. H. Harris and P. Willey.

NOTTINGHAMSHIRE v WARWICKSHIRE

At Nottingham, July 20. Nottinghamshire won by 87 runs. Toss: Nottinghamshire.

Warwickshire's ragged fielding was the culprit as they succumbed to a heavy defeat to lose their place as joint leaders. Archer scored a run-a-ball 53 and added 94 with Robinson, who collected only two boundaries – one in the form of overthrows from Brown, the other via a dropped catch by Hemp. Brown made some amends with a fighting 68, but only one other batsman reached double figures as Astle took three wickets and Bowen four.

Nottinghamshire

M. P. Dowman c Hemp b Brown	20	R. T. Bates b Donald		1
G. E. Welton c Ostler b Brown	9	P. J. Franks not out		7
N. J. Astle run out	0	B 4, l-b 15, w 8, n-b 4		31
*R. T. Robinson c Welch b Small	58			
G. F. Archer b Welch	53	1/23 2/23 3/39	(8 wkts, 40 overs)	229
C. M. Tolley c Smith b Donald	43	4/133 5/192 6/210		
†W. M. Noon c Piper b Donald	7	7/214 8/229		

M. N. Bowen and A. R. Oram did not bat.

Bowling: Welch 8–0–38–1; Brown 8–0–34–2; Donald 8–1–36–3; Small 8–0–56–1; Giles 3–0–21–0; Smith 5–0–25–0.

Warwickshire

A. Singh b Oram	1	†K. J. Piper c Archer b Bowen		1
*N. M. K. Smith c Welton b Bowen	6	G. C. Small c Noon b Bowen		0
D. R. Brown st Noon b Astle	68	A. A. Donald not out		0
D. L. Hemp c Noon b Oram	0	L-b 14, w 6, n-b 2		22
D. P. Ostler c Tolley b Franks	26			
T. L. Penney c Noon b Astle	5	1/4 2/30 3/30	(28.2 overs)	142
G. Welch c Dowman b Bowen	7	4/94 5/104 6/127		
A. F. Giles lbw b Astle	6	7/135 8/136 9/136		

Bowling: Oram 6–0–15–2; Bowen 4.2–0–29–4; Tolley 4–0–22–0; Franks 6–0–40–1; Astle 8–2–22–3.

Umpires: V. A. Holder and B. Leadbeater.

At Leicester, July 27. NOTTINGHAMSHIRE lost to LEICESTERSHIRE by 87 runs.

At Colwyn Bay, August 3. NOTTINGHAMSHIRE beat GLAMORGAN by 20 runs.

NOTTINGHAMSHIRE v ESSEX

At Nottingham, August 24. No result (abandoned).

At Bristol, August 31. GLOUCESTERSHIRE v NOTTINGHAMSHIRE. No result (abandoned).

NOTTINGHAMSHIRE v HAMPSHIRE

At Nottingham, September 7. Nottinghamshire won by three runs. Toss: Nottinghamshire.
Hampshire self-destructed in extraordinary fashion. Laney and Hayden, who made a 119-ball hundred, shared a mammoth opening stand of 177 in 35 overs in pursuit of 210. But, after Hayden was bowled by Tolley at the start of the 38th over, six more wickets fell for 11 in 16 balls – three to run-outs and another three to Tolley. Savident could still have tied the match with a four off the last ball, but managed only one.

Nottinghamshire

G. E. Welton c Hayden b Milburn	6	P. J. Franks b Udal		8
U. Afzaal b Savident	20	K. P. Evans lbw b Stephenson		2
*P. Johnson lbw b Savident	33	M. N. Bowen not out		10
M. P. Dowman lbw b Udal	17	B 2, l-b 5, w 5, n-b 12		24
N. A. Gie c Kendall b Stephenson	39			—
C. M. Tolley c Stephenson b Renshaw	25	1/12 2/59 3/71	(9 wkts, 40 overs)	209
†W. M. Noon not out	24	4/114 5/151 6/162		
R. T. Bates c and b Whitaker	1	7/166 8/183 9/188		

Bowling: Milburn 4–0–27–1; Renshaw 7–0–38–1; Savident 5–0–30–2; Stephenson 8–0–45–2; Udal 8–1–25–2; Whitaker 8–0–37–1.

Hampshire

J. S. Laney b Franks	69	†A. N. Aymes not out		1
M. L. Hayden b Tolley	100	L. Savident not out		1
S. D. Udal st Noon b Tolley	9			
P. R. Whitaker st Noon b Tolley	6	L-b 3, w 8, n-b 6		17
G. W. White run out	0			—
*J. P. Stephenson b Tolley	2	1/177 2/194 3/196	(8 wkts, 40 overs)	206
W. S. Kendall run out	0	4/197 5/203 6/203		
S. J. Renshaw run out	1	7/204 8/205		

S. M. Milburn did not bat.

Bowling: Franks 5–0–35–1; Bowen 7–0–38–0; Evans 8–0–33–0; Tolley 7–0–39–4; Bates 8–0–27–0; Dowman 5–0–31–0.

Umpires: R. Palmer and G. Sharp.

At Lord's, September 14. NOTTINGHAMSHIRE lost to MIDDLESEX by one run.

SOMERSET

At The Oval, April 27. SOMERSET lost to SURREY by three wickets.

SOMERSET v GLAMORGAN

At Taunton, May 4. Somerset won by six wickets. Toss: Somerset.

Both teams had a mixed start. Somerset dismissed both openers for ducks, but a strong wind caused Kerr to bowl five wides in his opening over. Glamorgan mounted a minor recovery through Dale and Cottey. But Lathwell's 72 from 62 balls underpinned a more confident Somerset reply.

Glamorgan

S. P. James b Kerr	0	S. D. Thomas c Parsons b Caddick	12
H. Morris b Rose	0	S. L. Watkin run out	15
A. Dale b Parsons	47	O. T. Parkin not out	0
*M. P. Maynard lbw b Mushtaq Ahmed	26	L-b 14, w 11, n-b 2	27
P. A. Cottey b Caddick	61		
G. P. Butcher c Harden b Parsons	11	1/5 2/6 3/49	(40 overs) 207
†A. D. Shaw c Turner b Rose	2	4/121 5/143 6/161	
R. D. B. Croft c Turner b Caddick	6	7/173 8/182 9/197	

Bowling: Kerr 7–0–27–1; Rose 8–0–41–2; Mushtaq Ahmed 8–0–30–1; Caddick 8–0–46–3; Burns 5–0–31–0; Parsons 4–0–18–2.

Somerset

M. N. Lathwell c Maynard b Cottey	72	*P. D. Bowler not out	34
M. Burns c Croft b Watkin	9	B 1, l-b 6, w 3	10
S. C. Ecclestone run out	24		
G. D. Rose lbw b Croft	11	1/38 2/90	(4 wkts, 37.1 overs) 210
R. J. Harden not out	50	3/124 4/126	

†R. J. Turner, K. A. Parsons, J. I. D. Kerr, A. R. Caddick and Mushtaq Ahmed did not bat.

Bowling: Parkin 5–1–33–0; Watkin 8–0–36–1; Dale 3–0–26–0; Thomas 5.1–0–38–0; Croft 8–0–32–1; Cottey 8–0–38–1.

Umpires: R. Julian and R. Palmer.

At Northampton, May 11. NORTHAMPTONSHIRE v SOMERSET. No result (abandoned).

SOMERSET v SUSSEX

At Taunton, May 18. Somerset won by six wickets. Toss: Sussex.

Caddick, who was "breathing fire and thunder" after his omission from England's one-day international squad, according to Somerset's chief executive Peter Anderson, took four wickets as Sussex's batsmen failed again. Then their depleted attack could not cope with an assault from Lathwell, and Somerset won with almost 17 overs to spare.

Sussex

K. Greenfield b Parsons	14	N. C. Phillips c Burns b Caddick	7
R. K. Rao c Burns b Rose	4	A. A. Khan lbw b Caddick	0
N. R. Taylor not out	40	M. A. Robinson b Rose	1
M. Newell c Burns b Rose	13	B 4, w 9, n-b 2	15
K. Newell c Harden b Caddick	3		
J. P. Pyemont lbw b Kerr	3	1/16 2/26 3/51	(31.4 overs) 109
*†P. Moores lbw b Caddick	8	4/62 5/73 6/87	
P. W. Jarvis c Parsons b Mushtaq Ahmed	1	7/88 8/99 9/99	

Bowling: Parsons 4–0–22–1; Rose 7.4–0–29–3; Kerr 5–1–16–1; Caddick 8–1–19–4; Mushtaq Ahmed 7–0–19–1.

Somerset

M. N. Lathwell not out................ 53	R. J. Harden not out	8
†M. Burns c Pyemont b Robinson....... 12	L-b 2, w 4, n-b 2	8
S. C. Ecclestone c Moores b K. Newell .. 22		
M. E. Trescothick b Phillips 4	1/20 2/60 (4 wkts, 23.2 overs) 111	
G. D. Rose c Taylor b Khan 4	3/70 4/89	

*P. D. Bowler, K. A. Parsons, A. R. Caddick, J. I. D. Kerr and Mushtaq Ahmed did not bat.

Bowling: Jarvis 5–1–17–0; Robinson 4–0–18–1; Khan 7.2–0–30–1; K. Newell 1–0–13–1; Phillips 4–0–17–1; Rao 2–0–14–0.

Umpires: B. Leadbeater and R. A. White.

SOMERSET v YORKSHIRE

At Taunton, May 25. Yorkshire won by seven wickets. Toss: Yorkshire.

Yorkshire made short work of scoring 261. They won with almost four overs in hand, thanks to a stand of 134 in 18 overs between Vaughan and Lehmann, whose 76 took 66 balls. Harden had made an excellent 85 from 77 balls for Somerset and put on 133 with Bowler.

Somerset

M. N. Lathwell c Blakey b Hamilton 15	K. A. Parsons not out................	12
M. Burns run out 23	J. I. D. Kerr not out	1
S. C. Ecclestone b Hartley 16	B 1, l-b 8, w 12, n-b 4........	25
*P. D. Bowler b Hartley.............. 61		
R. J. Harden c Byas b Hartley.......... 85	1/49 2/50 3/73 (7 wkts, 40 overs) 260	
G. D. Rose b White 16	4/206 5/239	
†R. J. Turner b White................. 6	6/244 7/255	

Mushtaq Ahmed and A. R. Caddick did not bat.

Bowling: Hamilton 7–0–47–1; Wharf 3–0–34–0; White 7–0–34–2; Hartley 7–0–42–3; Stemp 8–0–39–0; Vaughan 8–0–55–0.

Yorkshire

*D. Byas lbw b Rose 15	†R. J. Blakey not out	36
M. P. Vaughan c Harden b Kerr 66	L-b 4, w 10, n-b 6	20
D. S. Lehmann c Parsons b Caddick..... 76		
P. J. Hartley not out 48	1/19 2/153 3/195 (3 wkts, 36.1 overs) 261	

A. G. Wharf, A. McGrath, C. White, B. Parker, G. M. Hamilton and R. D. Stemp did not bat.

Bowling: Rose 8–0–34–1; Parsons 4–0–23–0; Kerr 8–0–67–1; Caddick 7–0–60–1; Mushtaq Ahmed 7.1–0–53–0; Burns 2–0–20–0.

Umpires: J. W. Holder and V. A. Holder.

At Worcester, June 1. SOMERSET lost to WORCESTERSHIRE by 85 runs.

SOMERSET v LANCASHIRE

At Taunton, June 8. Somerset won by five wickets (D/L method). Toss: Lancashire.

Tentative batting by Lancashire saw them lose their 100 per cent record. Three wickets went down on 13, two to Rose, who finished with three for 15 in his benefit match. Somerset's requirement was altered by rain to 105 from 22 overs, but that made little difference, thanks to 42 from 32 balls by Turner.

Lancashire

*M. Watkinson b Parsons	5	G. Chapple not out	9
P. C. McKeown lbw b Rose	1	P. J. Martin not out	11
M. E. Harvey st Turner b Mushtaq Ahmed	8		
G. D. Lloyd c Turner b Rose	0	B 4, l-b 6, w 17, n-b 2	29
N. H. Fairbrother c Turner b Shine	29		
I. D. Austin c Harden b Rose	23	1/13 2/13 3/13 (8 wkts, 38.2 overs) 141
†W. K. Hegg c Burns b Shine	23	4/50 5/65 6/94
G. Yates b Kerr	3	7/115 8/119

D. J. Shadford did not bat.

Bowling: Rose 8–2–15–3; Parsons 8–0–24–1; Mushtaq Ahmed 8–2–24–1; Shine 7.2–0–25–2; Kerr 5–0–30–1; Burns 2–0–13–0.

Somerset

M. N. Lathwell lbw b Chapple	12	P. C. L. Holloway not out	4
M. Burns c McKeown b Martin	5		
†R. J. Turner c Lloyd b Shadford	42	L-b 4, w 2	6
*P. D. Bowler c Watkinson b Shadford	7		
R. J. Harden b Martin	11	1/17 2/40 3/55 (5 wkts, 21 overs) 107
G. D. Rose not out	20	4/76 5/87

K. A. Parsons, Mushtaq Ahmed, K. J. Shine and J. I. D. Kerr did not bat.

Bowling: Martin 5–0–12–2; Austin 4–0–20–0; Chapple 4–0–27–1; Yates 4–0–29–0; Shadford 4–0–15–2.

Umpires: J. D. Bond and N. T. Plews.

At Basingstoke, June 15. SOMERSET beat HAMPSHIRE by six runs.

SOMERSET v LEICESTERSHIRE

At Bath, June 22. Leicestershire won by 17 runs (D/L method). Toss: Somerset.

Bath evaded bad weather just long enough for a result to be possible – if the rain had arrived seven balls earlier, the points would have had to be shared. As it was, Duckworth/Lewis meant that Somerset needed 47 to be ahead after 11 overs, when rain did end play. Bowler gambled by putting Leicestershire in, and lost when Somerset could score nothing more than singles in their all-too-brief innings.

Leicestershire

N. C. Johnson b Parsons	12	D. J. Millns not out	3
V. J. Wells b Parsons	11	T. J. Mason not out	4
D. L. Maddy c Turner b Burns	10		
*J. J. Whitaker c Rose b Shine	26	L-b 4, w 6	10
J. M. Dakin c Turner b Shine	30		
†P. A. Nixon b Kerr	33	1/20 2/25 3/44 (8 wkts, 31 overs) 166
I. J. Sutcliffe run out	21	4/75 5/106 6/141
J. Ormond run out	6	7/152 8/158

G. J. Parsons did not bat.

Bowling: Rose 7–0–35–0; Parsons 6–0–24–2; Burns 4–0–20–1; Kerr 6–0–34–1; Shine 5–0–34–2; Trump 3–0–15–0.

Somerset

M. N. Lathwell b Millns	4
*P. D. Bowler not out	13
†R. J. Turner not out	11
L-b 1, w 1	2

1/9   (1 wkt, 11 overs) 30

M. Burns, P. C. L. Holloway, S. C. Ecclestone, K. A. Parsons, G. D. Rose, J. I. D. Kerr, K. J. Shine and H. R. J. Trump did not bat.

Bowling: Parsons 6–0–20–0; Millns 5–1–9–1.

Umpires: J. C. Balderstone and G. I. Burgess.

At Chelmsford, July 6. SOMERSET beat ESSEX by four wickets.

At Nottingham, July 13. SOMERSET beat NOTTINGHAMSHIRE by 30 runs.

At Birmingham, July 23. SOMERSET lost to WARWICKSHIRE by 35 runs.

SOMERSET v GLOUCESTERSHIRE

At Taunton, August 10. Somerset won by 73 runs. Toss: Somerset.

Holloway scored his first one-day century and shared a stand of 107 in 16 overs with Ecclestone; though Somerset did not quite capitalise, their final total of 267 was still far too good for Gloucestershire. Mushtaq Ahmed strangled the reply with a spell of 8–3–14–1, and Burns – the wicket-keeper turned opening bat and medium-pacer – picked up four wickets.

Somerset

M. Burns c Russell b Lewis	3	J. I. D. Kerr not out	6
P. C. L. Holloway c Alleyne b Davis	117	Mushtaq Ahmed not out	1
S. C. Ecclestone c Young b Alleyne	44		
*P. D. Bowler c Wright b Davis	46	L-b 6, w 3, n-b 6	15
†R. J. Turner c Dawson b Young	9		
M. N. Lathwell c Wright b Smith	16	1/5 2/112 3/202 (8 wkts, 40 overs) 267	
G. D. Rose c Lynch b Smith	4	4/230 5/235 6/248	
R. J. Harden c Young b Lewis	6	7/256 8/265	

K. J. Shine did not bat.

Bowling: Smith 7–0–39–2; Lewis 7–0–42–2; Ball 7–0–48–0; Young 8–0–55–1; Alleyne 5–0–35–1; Davis 6–0–42–2.

Gloucestershire

A. J. Wright c Harden b Mushtaq Ahmed	21	A. M. Smith c Harden b Bowler	3
T. H. C. Hancock c Holloway b Rose	33	R. P. Davis c Ecclestone b Shine	8
S. Young run out	22	J. Lewis not out	3
M. A. Lynch c Turner b Burns	13	B 5, l-b 6, w 11, n-b 2	24
*M. W. Alleyne c Bowler b Burns	18		
†R. C. Russell c Harden b Burns	0	1/64 2/66 3/96 (36.5 overs) 194	
R. I. Dawson lbw b Kerr	45	4/115 5/117 6/126	
M. C. J. Ball c Lathwell b Burns	4	7/136 8/141 9/186	

Bowling: Rose 8–0–23–1; Shine 3–0–20–1; Kerr 5.5–0–54–1; Mushtaq Ahmed 8–3–14–1; Burns 8–0–39–4; Bowler 4–0–33–1.

Umpires: A. Clarkson and B. Dudleston.

SOMERSET v KENT

At Taunton, August 24. Kent won by four wickets (D/L method). Toss: Kent.

This match got going at 4 p.m. as a 25-over affair; more showers cut it back still further. Somerset made heavy weather of batting, reaching 89 in 18 overs. Then Caddick, just back from the Oval Test, pegged Kent back to 11 for four. Five runs later, the skies opened again, revising the target to 78 in 13 overs; this meant no bowler was allowed more than three overs and Caddick was ruled out. Ward and Fleming shared a crucial stand of 57 and, with five needed off the last over, Fleming bashed Burns's first two balls to the on-side boundary. Somerset capped Ecclestone, their acting-captain, before the game.

Somerset

M. Burns c Wells b Phillips	13	Mushtaq Ahmed run out	0
P. C. L. Holloway c Phillips b Thompson	9		
*S. C. Ecclestone c Marsh b Thompson	1	L-b 11, w 2	13
M. N. Lathwell c Strang b Thompson	3		
†R. J. Turner c Marsh b Fleming	4	1/19 2/21 3/28 (7 wkts, 18 overs)	89
G. D. Rose c Walker b Llong	29	4/32 5/42	
M. E. Trescothick not out	17	6/83 7/89	

A. R. Caddick, S. Herzberg and P. S. Jones did not bat.

Bowling: Phillips 5–0–17–1; Thompson 5–0–17–3; Fleming 3–0–14–1; Strang 3–0–7–0; Ealham 1–0–12–0; Llong 1–0–11–1.

Kent

T. R. Ward c and b Burns	34	P. A. Strang c Caddick b Burns	0
M. J. Walker c Trescothick b Rose	3	*†S. A. Marsh not out	2
A. P. Wells b Caddick	0	B 1, l-b 8, w 7	16
G. R. Cowdrey c Jones b Caddick	1		
M. A. Ealham b Caddick	2	1/4 2/6 3/8 (6 wkts, 12.2 overs)	81
M. V. Fleming not out	23	4/11 5/68 6/68	

N. J. Llong, J. B. D. Thompson and B. J. Phillips did not bat.

Bowling: Caddick 3–0–8–3; Rose 3–0–7–1; Jones 2–0–19–0; Mushtaq Ahmed 3–0–27–0; Burns 1.2–0–11–2.

Umpires: R. A. White and A. G. T. Whitehead.

At Derby, August 31. DERBYSHIRE v SOMERSET. No result (abandoned).

SOMERSET v MIDDLESEX

At Taunton, September 7. Somerset won by 18 runs. Toss: Somerset.

Fraser gave Middlesex a fine start with a spell of 8–3–15–3, but two chances missed off Burns proved costly. Burns capitalised with his first one-day hundred, using only 108 balls in his unbeaten 115. Though Ramprakash and Shah took Middlesex to 183 for one, they could not save them from their tenth defeat and their 13th winless match in a row in the competition.

Somerset

M. Burns not out	115	M. E. Trescothick st Brown b Weekes	28
P. C. L. Holloway b Fraser	15	G. D. Rose not out	1
S. C. Ecclestone c Pooley b Fraser	1	B 1, l-b 12, w 5, n-b 2	20
*P. D. Bowler c Brown b Bloomfield	4		
M. N. Lathwell lbw b Fraser	9	1/19 2/29 3/43 (7 wkts, 40 overs)	237
†R. J. Turner c Ramprakash b Hewitt	33	4/61 5/154	
Mushtaq Ahmed b Dutch b Hewitt	6	6/166 7/226	

S. Herzberg and A. R. Caddick did not bat.

Bowling: Fraser 8–3–15–3; Hewitt 8–0–45–2; Bloomfield 8–0–52–1; Johnson 7–0–45–0; Dutch 5–0–32–0; Weekes 4–0–35–1.

Middlesex

P. N. Weekes c and b Herzberg	37	R. L. Johnson b Caddick		2
*M. R. Ramprakash c Caddick b Burns	90	K. P. Dutch not out		2
O. A. Shah c Lathwell b Rose	45	L-b 8, w 5, n-b 2		15
J. C. Pooley b Rose	4			
D. C. Nash c and b Rose	19	1/88 2/183 3/183	(6 wkts, 40 overs)	219
†K. R. Brown not out	5	4/201 5/214 6/216		

J. P. Hewitt, A. R. C. Fraser and T. F. Bloomfield did not bat.

Bowling: Rose 8–0–29–3; Burns 8–0–41–1; Caddick 8–0–46–1; Herzberg 5–0–37–1; Mushtaq Ahmed 8–1–34–0; Trescothick 3–0–24–0.

Umpires: D. R. Shepherd and A. G. T. Whitehead.

At Chester-le-Street, September 14. SOMERSET beat DURHAM by seven wickets.

SURREY

SURREY v SOMERSET

At The Oval, April 27. Surrey won by three wickets. Toss: Surrey.

Reinvented as the Surrey Lions, the home side boasted a master of ceremonies, a lion mascot named Roary, and a sound system that welcomed new batsmen with their own choice of music. On the field, the Lions recovered from a parlous 69 for five thanks to Lewis's unbeaten 68 from 64 balls, and won when the last ball, bowled by Burns, was declared a wide.

Somerset

M. Burns c Stewart b Bicknell	2	K. A. Parsons lbw b A. J. Hollioake		2
M. N. Lathwell c and b Tudor	22	J. I. D. Kerr not out		17
S. C. Ecclestone c Stewart b Lewis	0	A. R. Caddick c Tudor b Lewis		5
G. D. Rose c Butcher b Bicknell	23	L-b 9, w 6, n-b 8		23
R. J. Harden b B. C. Hollioake	53			
*P. D. Bowler b Salisbury	22	1/2 2/6 3/47	(37.4 overs)	180
M. E. Trescothick lbw b Salisbury	1	4/73 5/134 6/136		
†R. J. Turner b A. J. Hollioake	10	7/148 8/153 9/166		

Bowling: Bicknell 8–0–33–2; Lewis 6.4–0–27–2; Tudor 4–0–26–1; B. C. Hollioake 8–0–34–1; Salisbury 8–0–40–2; A. J. Hollioake 3–0–11–2.

Surrey

M. A. Butcher lbw b Rose	19	B. C. Hollioake c Trescothick b Burns		1
A. D. Brown c Turner b Kerr	15	I. D. K. Salisbury not out		9
†A. J. Stewart lbw b Rose	6	L-b 9, w 14		23
G. P. Thorpe b Caddick	14			
*A. J. Hollioake c Turner b Caddick	0	1/21 2/43 3/46	(7 wkts, 39.5 overs)	181
N. Shahid b Parsons	26	4/48 5/69		
C. C. Lewis not out	68	6/120 7/123		

M. P. Bicknell and A. J. Tudor did not bat.

Bowling: Kerr 8–0–36–1; Rose 8–2–28–2; Caddick 8–1–25–2; Parsons 8–0–31–1; Burns 5.5–0–40–1; Trescothick 2–0–12–0.

Umpires: B. Dudleston and J. H. Harris.

At Canterbury, May 4. SURREY lost to KENT by 12 runs.

At Derby, May 11. DERBYSHIRE v SURREY. No result (abandoned).

SURREY v GLOUCESTERSHIRE

At The Oval, May 18. Surrey won by five wickets. Toss: Surrey.

Surrey were set 177 to win, which should have presented no obstacle at The Oval, but nervous batting required Shahid to snatch victory off the last ball with a quick single. Adam Hollioake was the only man who found any fluency, hitting 30 off 20 balls. Earlier, Alleyne had rescued Gloucestershire from 87 for five.

Gloucestershire

N. J. Trainor b Bicknell	4	M. C. J. Ball c Butcher b Lewis	5
M. A. Lynch lbw b Bicknell	7	A. M. Smith not out	0
R. J. Cunliffe b A. J. Hollioake	42	K. P. Sheeraz not out	0
S. Young lbw b Bicknell	3		
†R. C. Russell b Benjamin	15	B 2, l-b 3, w 4, n-b 2	11
*M. W. Alleyne run out	58		
A. J. Wright c Thorpe b B. C. Hollioake	14	1/4 2/19 3/35 (9 wkts, 40 overs) 176	
T. H. C. Hancock c Stewart		4/71 5/87 6/119	
b A. J. Hollioake	17	7/156 8/174 9/175	

Bowling: Bicknell 8–0–24–3; Lewis 8–0–33–1; B. C. Hollioake 8–0–38–1; Benjamin 8–0–25–1; A. J. Hollioake 8–0–51–2.

Surrey

M. A. Butcher run out	26	C. C. Lewis not out	1
A. D. Brown b Sheeraz	0		
†A. J. Stewart c Russell b Young	26	B 1, l-b 8, w 9, n-b 4	22
G. P. Thorpe c Russell b Alleyne	38		
N. Shahid not out	34	1/2 2/53 3/75 (5 wkts, 40 overs) 177	
*A. J. Hollioake c Young b Smith	30	4/129 5/175	

B. C. Hollioake, J. D. Ratcliffe, M. P. Bicknell and J. E. Benjamin did not bat.

Bowling: Smith 7–1–39–1; Sheeraz 5–0–15–1; Ball 8–0–26–0; Young 7–0–35–1; Alleyne 8–0–34–1; Hancock 5–0–19–0.

Umpires: H. D. Bird and J. W. Holder.

At Leicester, May 25. SURREY beat LEICESTERSHIRE by five wickets.

SURREY v ESSEX

At The Oval, June 8. Essex won by six wickets (D/L method). Toss: Essex. County debut: Saqlain Mushtaq.

Gooch made one final Sunday League appearance (he had intended not to play again in the competition, but had to lead the team in the absence of Prichard and Hussain) and increased his record aggregate to 8,573 runs. Surrey were in a strong position at 139 for two, but their innings tailed off badly as Cowan picked up four wickets for 36. Then an unbroken stand of 88 in 12 overs between Danny Law and Irani passed a revised target of 184 from 35 overs to seal victory for Essex. After conceding the winning runs in the form of four wides, Lewis exchanged blows with an abusive member of the crowd, who was ejected. Surrey had offered spectators free cans of lager to take home – but this applied only if they won, so no one collected until the following week.

Surrey

J. D. Ratcliffe c Robinson b Cowan	69	M. P. Bicknell run out		4
I. J. Ward b Such	31	Saqlain Mushtaq b Cowan		3
N. Shahid b Grayson	5	J. E. Benjamin b Cowan		0
*A. J. Hollioake c Irani b Such	39	L-b 9, w 4, n-b 2		15
B. C. Hollioake lbw b Cowan	2			
C. C. Lewis b Grayson	5	1/79 2/92 3/139	(34.3 overs)	176
†J. A. Knott run out	0	4/146 5/164 6/165		
I. D. K. Salisbury not out	3	7/166 8/172 9/176		

Bowling: Irani 4–0–18–0; Cowan 6.3–0–36–4; D. R. Law 4–0–29–0; Such 7–0–22–2; Grayson 7–0–26–2; Powell 6–0–36–0.

Essex

D. D. J. Robinson b Lewis	0	D. R. Law not out		55
S. G. Law c Bicknell b Saqlain Mushtaq	24	B 8, l-b 5, w 15, n-b 2		30
*G. A. Gooch c Knott b A. J. Hollioake	28			
R. C. Irani not out	32	1/6 2/60	(4 wkts, 33.5 overs)	185
A. P. Grayson c Shahid b B. C. Hollioake	16	3/66 4/97		

S. D. Peters, †R. J. Rollins, J. C. Powell, A. P. Cowan and P. M. Such did not bat.

Bowling: Bicknell 3–0–18–0; Lewis 5.5–0–27–1; Saqlain Mushtaq 7–0–32–1; A. J. Hollioake 6–1–28–1; B. C. Hollioake 7–0–34–1; Salisbury 5–0–33–0.

Umpires: A. A. Jones and D. R. Shepherd.

SURREY v YORKSHIRE

At The Oval, June 15. Surrey won by five wickets. Toss: Surrey.

A twilit Oval saw Thorpe build a fine century and share a partnership of 103 in 93 balls with Ben Hollioake, which was enough to steer Surrey home. The match finished at 7.40 p.m. because the teams had been presented to the Duchess of Kent, Yorkshire's patron, during an extended tea interval.

Yorkshire

*D. Byas c A. J. Hollioake b Bicknell	6	C. E. W. Silverwood		
M. D. Moxon lbw b Bicknell	13	c and b Saqlain Mushtaq		2
D. S. Lehmann c Stewart b B. C. Hollioake	56	R. D. Stemp not out		0
†R. J. Blakey run out	25			
P. J. Hartley b A. J. Hollioake	21	B 1, l-b 6, w 9, n-b 2		18
B. Parker c Saqlain Mushtaq b Bicknell	11			
C. White lbw b A. J. Hollioake	11	1/11 2/33 3/107	(9 wkts, 40 overs)	198
A. C. Morris not out	29	4/112 5/131		
D. Gough c A. J. Hollioake b Saqlain Mushtaq	6	6/156 7/165		
		8/187 9/190		

Bowling: Bicknell 8–1–27–3; Benjamin 8–1–22–0; Saqlain Mushtaq 8–0–45–2; B. C. Hollioake 8–0–44–1; A. J. Hollioake 8–0–53–2.

Surrey

M. A. Butcher c Gough b Stemp	34	B. C. Hollioake not out		39
A. D. Brown c Stemp b Gough	7			
†A. J. Stewart b Silverwood	6	L-b 4, w 4		8
G. P. Thorpe not out	100			
*A. J. Hollioake c Byas b Stemp	4	1/16 2/25 3/83	(5 wkts, 38.3 overs)	199
J. D. Ratcliffe lbw b Hartley	1	4/93 5/96		

I. D. K. Salisbury, M. P. Bicknell, Saqlain Mushtaq and J. E. Benjamin did not bat.

Bowling: Gough 7.3–0–40–1; Silverwood 8–0–42–1; White 8–0–42–0; Hartley 7–0–38–1; Stemp 8–0–33–2.

Umpires: R. Julian and A. G. T. Whitehead.

At Worcester, June 22. SURREY lost to WORCESTERSHIRE by seven wickets.

SURREY v NOTTINGHAMSHIRE

At The Oval, June 26 (day/night). No result (abandoned).

What was scheduled to be the first day/night match in a major English competition was called off owing to torrential rain over the previous 24 hours. The temporary floodlights had already been positioned around the boundary, however, and the soggy turf was badly cut up as they were driven off in heavy lorries.

At Birmingham, July 6. SURREY lost to WARWICKSHIRE by 48 runs.

SURREY v HAMPSHIRE

At Guildford, July 20. Surrey won by 68 runs. Toss: Hampshire.

Stephenson put Surrey in at the small Woodbridge Road ground and then was powerless to stop Alistair Brown plundering the first double-century in the Sunday League. Brown's first hundred took 56 balls, his second 62, and he hit 19 fours and 11 sixes along the way. He struck the very next ball – his 119th – into Stephenson's hands at cover. The previous record score was 176 by Graham Gooch against Glamorgan in 1983. But Brown fell just short of the highest score in limited-overs matches in Britain – Alvin Kallicharran's 206 against Oxfordshire in the NatWest Trophy of 1984. Udal helped to limit the margin of defeat with his own display of big hitting; his 78 took 56 balls.

Surrey

A. D. Brown c Stephenson b Renshaw . . .203	M. A. Butcher not out 2
†A. J. Stewart b Udal 14	
B. C. Hollioake b Renshaw 17	L-b 4, w 10 14
G. P. Thorpe c Smith b Udal 40	
*A. J. Hollioake c Kendall b Udal 26	1/90 2/135 3/236 (5 wkts, 40 overs) 344
C. C. Lewis not out 28	4/300 5/340

J. D. Ratcliffe, M. P. Bicknell, I. D. K. Salisbury and J. E. Benjamin did not bat.

Bowling: Connor 8–0–81–0; Renshaw 8–0–58–2; Udal 8–0–57–3; Bovill 7–0–73–0; Stephenson 8–0–60–0; Keech 1–0–11–0.

Hampshire

J. S. Laney st Stewart b Salisbury 47	†A. N. Aymes c and b Lewis 18
M. L. Hayden c Stewart b Lewis 4	S. J. Renshaw c Butcher b B. C. Hollioake 25
R. A. Smith c Salisbury b Benjamin 15	J. N. B. Bovill c Stewart b B. C. Hollioake 2
M. Keech lbw b Salisbury 4	C. A. Connor not out 0
W. S. Kendall c B. C. Hollioake	B 4, l-b 11, w 10, n-b 4 29
b Bicknell . 34	
S. D. Udal lbw b B. C. Hollioake 78	1/6 2/70 3/76 (39 overs) 276
*J. P. Stephenson c Lewis	4/84 5/183 6/207
b A. J. Hollioake . 20	7/226 8/272 9/276

Bowling: Lewis 7–0–31–2; Bicknell 8–0–58–1; Benjamin 6–0–29–1; Salisbury 8–0–40–2; A. J. Hollioake 4–0–56–1; B. C. Hollioake 6–0–47–3.

Umpires: J. W. Holder and M. J. Kitchen.

At Northampton, July 27. SURREY lost to NORTHAMPTONSHIRE by five wickets.

At Lord's, August 3. MIDDLESEX v SURREY. No result.

SURREY v DURHAM

At The Oval, August 10. Surrey won by seven wickets. Toss: Surrey.

Martin Bicknell's four for 28 set the trend for this match, which Surrey won at a canter. Butcher took them close with 81 and Darren Bicknell made sure, finishing unbeaten on 49. Apart from Roseberry's stout 55 not out, the only good news for Boon, the Durham captain, was the announcement at 7 p.m. that Australia had retained the Ashes.

Durham

J. E. Morris c Ratcliffe b M. P. Bicknell . 11	J. Wood c Lewis b Saqlain Mushtaq..... 2
S. Hutton b M. P. Bicknell 17	S. J. E. Brown lbw b Lewis............ 8
†M. P. Speight c Lewis b Ratcliffe 25	A. Walker not out.................... 7
*D. C. Boon c Benjamin b Lewis 35	
J. J. B. Lewis c Batty b Benjamin....... 1	B 2, l-b 5, w 8, n-b 2......... 17
M. A. Roseberry not out 55	
M. M. Betts c D. J. Bicknell	1/35 2/39 3/90 (9 wkts, 40 overs) 189
b M. P. Bicknell . 8	4/91 5/130 6/150
J. Boiling b M. P. Bicknell 3	7/160 8/163 9/179

Bowling: M. P. Bicknell 8–0–28–4; Lewis 8–0–37–2; Ratcliffe 8–0–33–1; Benjamin 8–0–48–1; Saqlain Mushtaq 8–0–36–1.

Surrey

M. A. Butcher c Lewis b Walker 81	I. J. Ward not out 6
A. D. Brown c Hutton b Wood 8	L-b 9, w 8, n-b 2 19
J. D. Ratcliffe c and b Boiling 27	
D. J. Bicknell not out................. 49	1/20 2/97 3/148 (3 wkts, 38.3 overs) 190

*C. C. Lewis, †J. N. Batty, M. P. Bicknell, N. Shahid, Saqlain Mushtaq and J. E. Benjamin did not bat.

Bowling: Brown 7.3–1–32–0; Wood 7–0–41–1; Betts 8–0–30–0; Walker 8–0–41–1; Boiling 8–1–37–1.

Umpires: V. A. Holder and R. Palmer.

At Hove, August 27. SURREY beat SUSSEX by five wickets.

SURREY v GLAMORGAN

At The Oval, September 7. Surrey won by two wickets. Toss: Surrey.

Maynard made a magnificent 132 from just 75 balls, the highest individual score for Glamorgan in the competition. He hit seven sixes: one came within a whisker of hitting a sponsor's board, which would have earned him a bonus of £20,000. Glamorgan should have passed 300 easily, but the next-highest score was 25. Adam Hollioake and Ratcliffe added 115 in 15 overs, and Surrey's better team-work was rewarded in the end.

Glamorgan

A. W. Evans c Ward b Ratcliffe 25	†A. D. Shaw not out 0
W. L. Law c Salisbury b Saqlain Mushtaq 15	S. D. Thomas c Bicknell b B. C. Hollioake 0
P. A. Cottey b Saqlain Mushtaq 18	
*M. P. Maynard run out...............132	B 1, l-b 4, w 8, n-b 4......... 17
M. J. Powell c and b Bicknell 23	
G. P. Butcher run out................. 6	1/43 2/48 3/92 (8 wkts, 40 overs) 242
R. D. B. Croft c Salisbury	4/175 5/185 6/230
b A. J. Hollioake . 6	7/242 8/242

O. T. Parkin and D. A. Cosker did not bat.

Bowling: Bicknell 8–0–33–1; B. C. Hollioake 7–0–57–1; Saqlain Mushtaq 7–0–51–2; A. J. Hollioake 8–1–23–1; Ratcliffe 2–0–16–1; Salisbury 6–0–46–0; Butcher 2–0–11–0.

Surrey

M. A. Butcher c Shaw b Parkin	11	Saqlain Mushtaq c Thomas b Croft	0
A. D. Brown lbw b Butcher	64	M. P. Bicknell not out	0
B. C. Holliaoke c Croft b Parkin	9		
I. J. Ward c and b Cosker	15	B 1, l-b 5, w 10	16
*A. J. Holliaoke b Parkin	63		
J. D. Ratcliffe c Evans b Parkin	54	1/27 2/45 3/86 (8 wkts, 37 overs) 243	
N. Shahid c Law b Croft	5	4/115 5/230 6/231	
†J. N. Batty not out	6	7/236 8/236	

I. D. K. Salisbury did not bat.

Bowling: Parkin 8–0–45–4; Thomas 6–0–36–0; Croft 8–0–46–2; Cosker 8–0–42–1; Butcher 5–0–49–1; Cottey 2–0–19–0.

Umpires: J. C. Balderstone and V. A. Holder.

SURREY v LANCASHIRE

At The Oval, September 14. Surrey won by five wickets. Toss: Surrey.

Lancashire's hopes of capturing Surrey's Sunday crown were theoretical rather than practical, because of their poor net run-rate. Despite losing this game, they finished third, because Leicestershire also lost. Opening batsman Butcher gave Surrey an early lift when he produced an unexpected in-swinger to bowl Atherton. Fairbrother and Lloyd attempted a rescue mission with a stand of 80, but it was the 101-run partnership between Surrey's acting-captain Stewart and Ben Holliaoke, who made his first Sunday fifty, that was the more telling.

Lancashire

*M. Watkinson c Amin b Holliaoke	15	G. Chapple b Salisbury	0
M. A. Atherton b Butcher	30	P. J. Martin not out	1
J. P. Crawley c Butcher b Benjamin	2		
N. H. Fairbrother b Holliaoke	54	L-b 17, w 6, n-b 4	27
G. D. Lloyd c Butcher b Amin	41		
I. D. Austin c Ratcliffe b Amin	14	1/26 2/30 3/78 (8 wkts, 40 overs) 206	
†W. K. Hegg st Stewart b Salisbury	17	4/158 5/179 6/189	
G. Yates not out	5	7/205 8/205	

G. Keedy did not bat.

Bowling: Holliaoke 8–0–49–2; Benjamin 6–0–27–1; Ratcliffe 6–0–24–0; Butcher 6–0–24–1; Amin 8–0–43–2; Salisbury 6–0–22–2.

Surrey

M. A. Butcher lbw b Austin	0	N. Shahid not out	16
A. D. Brown c Yates b Austin	6		
B. C. Holliaoke run out	61	B 3, l-b 12, w 17	32
*†A. J. Stewart not out	67		
D. J. Bicknell c Hegg b Austin	21	1/1 2/32 3/133 (5 wkts, 37.1 overs) 210	
J. D. Ratcliffe b Watkinson	7	4/172 5/188	

I. J. Ward, J. E. Benjamin, I. D. K. Salisbury and R. M. Amin did not bat.

Bowling: Austin 8–1–25–3; Martin 2–0–16–0; Chapple 8–0–40–0; Keedy 5.1–0–47–0; Yates 8–0–36–0; Watkinson 6–0–31–1.

Umpires: A. Clarkson and P. Willey.

SUSSEX

SUSSEX v NORTHAMPTONSHIRE

At Hove, April 27. Northamptonshire won by nine wickets. Toss: Sussex. First-team debut: J. P. Pyemont.

Snape, who was celebrating his 24th birthday, took a Sunday-best four wickets in 12 balls as Sussex subsided from 107 for two to 160 all out. An opening stand of 149 between Loye and Penberthy helped Northamptonshire to reach their target with more than nine overs left.

Sussex

K. Greenfield c Loye b Capel	58	N. C. Phillips c Penberthy b Bailey	21
V. C. Drakes c Warren b Taylor	0	A. A. Khan not out	7
N. J. Lenham c sub b Emburey	41	M. A. Robinson run out	1
K. Newell c Capel b Snape	11	B 1, l-b 8, w 1, n-b 4	14
C. W. J. Athey b Snape	0		
J. P. Pyemont c and b Snape	1	1/6 2/85 3/107 (35.2 overs)	160
*†P. Moores b Snape	0	4/107 5/109 6/109	
P. W. Jarvis c Curran b Emburey	6	7/116 8/146 9/154	

Bowling: Mohammad Akram 6–2–21–0; Taylor 8–1–25–1; Snape 8–2–31–4; Emburey 6.2–1–28–2; Bailey 4–0–18–1; Capel 3–0–28–1.

Northamptonshire

M. B. Loye c Robinson b Khan	68
A. L. Penberthy not out	74
K. M. Curran not out	4
B 5, l-b 4, w 3, n-b 4	16

1/149   (1 wkt, 30.3 overs) 162

T. C. Walton, *R. J. Bailey, D. J. Capel, †R. J. Warren, J. N. Snape, J. E. Emburey, J. P. Taylor and Mohammad Akram did not bat.

Bowling: Drakes 6–0–25–0; Robinson 5–0–13–0; Khan 6.3–0–43–1; Jarvis 6–0–32–0; Phillips 6–1–33–0; Newell 1–0–7–0.

Umpires: G. Sharp and A. G. T. Whitehead.

SUSSEX v NOTTINGHAMSHIRE

At Hove, May 4. Nottinghamshire won by six wickets. Toss: Nottinghamshire.

Only Greenfield of the Sussex batsmen was able to capitalise on a decent batting track. Nottinghamshire's prolific pair, Robinson and Johnson, were well up to the chase in a rain-shortened match.

Sussex

V. C. Drakes c Johnson b Evans	6	N. C. Phillips lbw b Bowen	0
R. K. Rao b Evans	9	J. P. Pyemont not out	18
N. J. Lenham c Johnson b Archer	2	B 1, l-b 2, w 7	10
K. Greenfield not out	69		
M. Newell c and b Bates	19	1/16 2/17 3/20 (7 wkts, 28 overs)	160
*†P. Moores c Noon b Evans	26	4/66 5/115	
P. W. Jarvis c Robinson b Evans	1	6/118 7/118	

A. A. Khan and M. A. Robinson did not bat.

Bowling: Evans 6–0–26–4; Tolley 6–0–30–0; Archer 3–0–28–1; Bates 5–0–28–1; Bowen 6–0–37–1; Dowman 2–0–8–0.

Nottinghamshire

M. P. Dowman b Robinson	5	C. M. Tolley not out	2
R. T. Robinson b Jarvis	51	L-b 6, w 5, n-b 4	15
*P. Johnson lbw b Lenham	60		—
G. F. Archer not out	24	1/13 2/109 (4 wkts, 26.5 overs)	162
P. R. Pollard c Rao b Drakes	5	3/133 4/144	

N. A. Gie, †W. M. Noon, K. P. Evans, R. T. Bates and M. N. Bowen did not bat.

Bowling: Khan 6–0–39–0; Robinson 6–0–21–1; Jarvis 5.5–0–30–1; Drakes 4–0–37–1; Lenham 2–0–14–1; Phillips 3–0–15–0.

Umpires: B. Dudleston and G. Sharp.

At Lord's, May 11. SUSSEX lost to MIDDLESEX by seven wickets (D/L method).

At Taunton, May 18. SUSSEX lost to SOMERSET by six wickets.

SUSSEX v KENT

At Horsham, May 25. Sussex won by four wickets. Toss: Kent.

Kent had won three out of three Sunday matches, and Sussex lost four out of four. But Athey's staunch 109, his seventh League century, confounded the formbook and enabled Sussex to squeeze home with three balls to spare. Earlier, leg-spinner Khan had made up for dropping both Kent's openers by taking five for 40, his best figures in any competition.

Kent

T. R. Ward c Robinson b K. Newell	26	M. J. McCague c M. Newell b Khan	7
M. J. Walker b Khan	60	B. J. Phillips not out	1
A. P. Wells c K. Newell b Jarvis	45		
G. R. Cowdrey st Moores b Khan	39	L-b 8, w 6	14
M. V. Fleming b Drakes	13		—
N. J. Llong c Moores b Jarvis	9	1/49 2/135 3/159 (9 wkts, 40 overs)	220
*†S. A. Marsh c M. Newell b Khan	3	4/186 5/198 6/202	
P. A. Strang c Rao b Khan	3	7/211 8/217 9/220	

T. N. Wren did not bat.

Bowling: Drakes 8–0–48–1; K. Newell 8–0–27–1; Jarvis 8–0–41–2; Robinson 8–0–56–0; Khan 8–0–40–5.

Sussex

R. K. Rao lbw b Phillips	15	P. W. Jarvis c Phillips b Strang	6
C. W. J. Athey not out	109	V. C. Drakes not out	6
K. Greenfield b Llong	35	L-b 3, w 9	12
M. Newell c McCague b Cowdrey	16		—
K. Newell run out	15	1/32 2/132 3/151 (6 wkts, 39.3 overs)	224
*†P. Moores c Cowdrey	10	4/171 5/193 6/206	

N. C. Phillips, A. A. Khan and M. A. Robinson did not bat.

Bowling: Phillips 5–1–17–1; Wren 3–0–18–0; Fleming 6–0–41–0; McCague 3–0–18–0; Strang 7.3–0–49–1; Cowdrey 8–0–35–2; Llong 7–0–43–1.

Umpires: B. Dudleston and P. Willey.

At Chester-le-Street, June 8. SUSSEX lost to DURHAM by 62 runs (D/L method).

SUSSEX v ESSEX

At Hove, June 15. Essex won by eight wickets. Toss: Essex.

The ease with which Stuart Law compiled his 123 highlighted both the paucity of Sussex's bowling reserves and the shortcomings of their batsmen, who needed to make many more than 216 on a belter of a pitch. Law's innings lasted 94 balls and included 14 fours and three sixes; he had passed his hundred before his opening partner, Prichard, reached fifty.

Sussex

R. K. Rao c Prichard b Cowan	60	K. Newell c Hussain b Ilott		16
C. W. J. Athey c S. G. Law b Cowan	39	V. C. Drakes not out		12
N. R. Taylor c Rollins b Cowan	2	L-b 6, w 3		9
K. Greenfield not out	58			—
M. Newell c Cowan b S. G. Law	19	1/96 2/100 3/117	(6 wkts, 40 overs)	216
*†P. Moores b Such	1	4/165 5/169 6/201		

R. J. Kirtley, A. A. Khan and M. A. Robinson did not bat.

Bowling: Ilott 8–0–38–1; Cowan 8–1–33–3; Irani 8–0–40–0; Such 6–0–31–1; Grayson 8–0–52–0; S. G. Law 2–0–16–1.

Essex

*P. J. Prichard b Kirtley	68
S. G. Law c K. Newell b Kirtley	123
N. Hussain not out	11
R. C. Irani not out	4
B 1, l-b 1, w 4, n-b 8	14
1/199 2/216 (2 wkts, 30.2 overs)	220

J. C. Powell, M. C. Ilott, A. P. Grayson, D. R. Law, †R. J. Rollins, A. P. Cowan and P. M. Such did not bat.

Bowling: K. Newell 4–0–25–0; Kirtley 7.2–0–60–2; Khan 7–0–48–0; Drakes 6–0–49–0; Robinson 2–0–14–0; Greenfield 4–0–22–0.

Umpires: H. D. Bird and G. I. Burgess.

At Derby, June 22. DERBYSHIRE v SUSSEX. No result (abandoned).

At Swansea, June 29. SUSSEX lost to GLAMORGAN by eight wickets.

SUSSEX v WORCESTERSHIRE

At Arundel, July 6. Worcestershire won by 49 runs. Toss: Worcestershire.

Worcestershire's innings prospered after Spiring and Leatherdale came together at 96 for three. Both batsmen finished on 58, having added an unbeaten 111 together. Leatherdale went on to pick up three wickets, as did Newport, and Sussex rapidly lost their way.

Worcestershire

*T. M. Moody c Moores b Edwards	31	D. A. Leatherdale not out		58
V. S. Solanki b Kirtley	14	B 1, l-b 5, w 9, n-b 6		21
G. A. Hick b Robinson	25			—
K. R. Spiring not out	58	1/31 2/66 3/96	(3 wkts, 40 overs)	207

R. J. Chapman, W. P. C. Weston, S. R. Lampitt, †S. J. Rhodes, P. J. Newport and A. Sheriyar did not bat.

Bowling: Kirtley 8–0–48–1; K. Newell 6–0–24–0; Edwards 8–1–20–1; Robinson 8–0–41–1; Martin-Jenkins 8–0–58–0; Greenfield 2–0–10–0.

Sussex

R. K. Rao c Moody b Newport	4	A. D. Edwards c Rhodes b Leatherdale ..	0
C. W. J. Athey b Sheriyar	35	M. A. Robinson not out	8
K. Greenfield c Moody b Newport	9	R. J. Kirtley b Solanki	7
R. S. C. Martin-Jenkins c Moody b Newport	2		
K. Newell c Leatherdale b Lampitt	10	L-b 6, w 3, n-b 6	15
N. J. Lenham lbw b Leatherdale	21		
M. Newell c Sheriyar b Hick	39	1/4 2/22 3/24 (38 overs)	158
*†P. Moores b Leatherdale	8	4/56 5/80 6/100	
		7/121 8/121 9/143	

Bowling: Newport 6–1–18–3; Moody 6–0–13–0; Sheriyar 6–0–28–1; Lampitt 5–0–28–1; Leatherdale 6–1–22–3; Hick 7–0–34–1; Solanki 2–0–9–1.

Umpires: A. A. Jones and R. Palmer.

SUSSEX v GLOUCESTERSHIRE

At Hove, July 13. Sussex won by one wicket. Toss: Gloucestershire.

Greenfield made 62, nearly twice the next best in a low-scoring match, but almost saw his efforts wasted by a dramatic lower-order collapse. Sussex began the last over needing one to win with three wickets left; Keith Newell was bowled by Alleyne's first ball, then Robinson was stumped off the second, a wide. The dismissal stood, according to umpire Plews, because he gave the man out before umpire Jones signalled the wide.

Gloucestershire

R. J. Cunliffe b Kirtley	12	A. M. Smith not out	8
A. J. Wright c Rao b K. Newell	18	R. P. Davis lbw b Kirtley	0
S. Young c Khan b K. Newell	11	J. Lewis not out	3
M. A. Lynch lbw b Robinson	24	L-b 5, w 8, n-b 4	17
*M. W. Alleyne c Moores b Khan	13		
†R. C. Russell b Jarvis	3	1/38 2/42 3/71 (9 wkts, 40 overs)	141
T. H. C. Hancock c Rao b Jarvis	20	4/83 5/96 6/116	
M. C. J. Ball c Khan b Jarvis	12	7/125 8/131 9/131	

R. J. Cunliffe, when 7, retired hurt at 13-0 and resumed at 116.

Bowling: K. Newell 8–0–22–2; Kirtley 8–0–36–2; Robinson 8–2–22–1; Jarvis 8–0–32–3; Khan 8–1–24–1.

Sussex

K. Greenfield c Alleyne b Davis	62	A. A. Khan not out	6
C. W. J. Athey c Russell b Smith	1	M. A. Robinson st Russell b Alleyne	0
R. K. Rao b Smith	4		
M. Newell b Young	10	L-b 5, w 2, n-b 2	9
N. J. Lenham c and b Ball	7		
K. Newell b Alleyne	35	1/3 2/15 3/52 (9 wkts, 39.1 overs)	142
*†P. Moores c Smith b Young	8	4/73 5/114 6/127	
P. W. Jarvis b Young	0	7/127 8/141 9/142	

R. J. Kirtley did not bat.

Bowling: Smith 8–4–18–2; Lewis 7–1–23–0; Young 8–1–32–3; Ball 8–0–23–1; Alleyne 5.1–0–25–2; Davis 3–0–16–1.

Umpires: A. A. Jones and N. T. Plews.

At Manchester, July 20. SUSSEX lost to LANCASHIRE by eight wickets.

At Birmingham, August 3. SUSSEX lost to WARWICKSHIRE by 26 runs (D/L method).

SUSSEX v LEICESTERSHIRE

At Eastbourne, August 10. Leicestershire won by 44 runs. Toss: Leicestershire.

But for Smith's 71 in 72 balls, Leicestershire would have been shot out well inside their 40 overs. As it was, they used but one ball. In the field, they began disastrously with Ormond conceding 12 in the first over. But the medium-pacers proved more effective, and Williamson reaped the reward with five for 32 as Sussex tried and failed to get near the target.

Leicestershire

*V. J. Wells c M. Newell b Edwards	11	D. Williamson run out		4
D. I. Stevens lbw b Jarvis	1	J. Ormond not out		16
B. F. Smith lbw b Bates	71	G. J. Parsons run out		4
D. L. Maddy c and b K. Newell	5	L-b 2, w 4, n-b 4		10
G. I. Macmillan lbw b Robinson	9			
J. M. Dakin b Khan	26	1/6 2/30 3/37	(39.5 overs)	184
†P. A. Nixon run out	22	4/51 5/111 6/137		
T. J. Mason c Rao b Edwards	5	7/152 8/163 9/166		

Bowling: Jarvis 5–0–31–1; K. Newell 5–0–20–1; Edwards 7.5–0–44–2; Robinson 8–0–27–1; Khan 8–1–36–1; Bates 6–0–24–1.

Sussex

K. Greenfield c Smith b Wells	5	A. D. Edwards st Nixon b Wells		2
C. W. J. Athey b Williamson	4	J. J. Bates not out		5
R. K. Rao c Maddy b Mason	40	M. A. Robinson b Williamson		1
M. Newell lbw b Parsons	0	B 3, l-b 10, w 10, n-b 6		29
K. Newell c Nixon b Maddy	11			
*†P. Moores c Macmillan b Williamson	25	1/12 2/29 3/30	(35.4 overs)	140
P. W. Jarvis c and b Williamson	14	4/58 5/78 6/113		
A. A. Khan c Macmillan b Williamson	4	7/124 8/130 9/135		

Bowling: Ormond 1–0–12–0; Parsons 8–3–19–1; Wells 5–1–12–2; Williamson 7.4–0–32–5; Maddy 6–0–23–1; Mason 8–0–29–1.

Umpires: M. J. Kitchen and N. T. Plews.

At Scarborough, August 24. YORKSHIRE v SUSSEX. No result (abandoned).

SUSSEX v SURREY

At Hove, August 27 (day/night). Surrey won by five wickets. Toss: Sussex. First-team debut: J. R. Carpenter.

The Sunday League's second floodlit match pulled in a crowd close to 4,000 on an unappealing, damp evening – more than twice the normal Sunday attendance at Hove. But the so-called Sussex Tigers failed to make the occasion into a contest. Lewis topped and tailed their innings, finishing with four for 21, and Rao was fighting a lone battle with 58. Surrey reached their target of 152 with more than 12 overs in hand.

Sussex

V. C. Drakes c Lewis b Bicknell	11	A. A. Khan run out		0
K. Greenfield c Ratcliffe b Lewis	16	A. D. Edwards b Lewis		0
R. K. Rao c Salisbury b Lewis	58	M. A. Robinson b Lewis		3
N. R. Taylor c Stewart b B. C. Hollioake	12	L-b 9, w 5, n-b 2		16
K. Newell b Saqlain Mushtaq	7			
*†P. Moores lbw b Salisbury	8	1/32 2/34 3/56	(37.3 overs)	151
J. R. Carpenter not out	17	4/92 5/109 6/141		
P. W. Jarvis run out	3	7/145 8/146 9/146		

Bowling: Bicknell 6–0–29–1; Lewis 7.3–0–21–4; B. C. Hollioake 8–0–31–1; Salisbury 8–0–25–1; Saqlain Mushtaq 6–0–29–1; A. J. Hollioake 2–0–7–0.

Surrey

M. A. Butcher run out	34	C. C. Lewis not out		7
A. D. Brown c Greenfield b Khan	31			
B. C. Hollioake c Newell b Robinson	8	L-b 5, w 2, n-b 6		13
†A. J. Stewart c Edwards b Khan	15			
*A. J. Hollioake c Moores b Drakes	33	1/58 2/73 3/88	(5 wkts, 27.3 overs)	152
I. J. Ward not out	11	4/113 5/135		

J. D. Ratcliffe, M. P. Bicknell, Saqlain Mushtaq and I. D. K. Salisbury did not bat.

Bowling: Drakes 6–0–34–1; Jarvis 6.3–0–23–0; Robinson 6–0–15–1; Khan 8–0–60–2; Carpenter 1–0–15–0.

Umpires: B. J. Meyer and R. Palmer.

At Southampton, September 14. SUSSEX lost to HAMPSHIRE by two wickets.

WARWICKSHIRE

At Cardiff, April 27. WARWICKSHIRE lost to GLAMORGAN by 17 runs (D/L method).

WARWICKSHIRE v NORTHAMPTONSHIRE

At Birmingham, May 4. Warwickshire won by five wickets (D/L method). Toss: Warwickshire. County debut: D. Follett.

Neil Smith captained Warwickshire for the first time, and so he and M. J. K. Smith became the county's first father-and-son captains. After a rain interruption, Warwickshire's target was 145 from 30 overs.

Northamptonshire

M. B. Loye c Piper b Donald	19	J. E. Emburey run out		4
A. L. Penberthy run out	4	J. P. Taylor not out		3
K. M. Curran c Piper b Edmond	44	D. Follett not out		1
D. J. Capel c Piper b Edmond	11	B 4, l-b 10, w 2, n-b 6		22
*R. J. Bailey b Donald	0			
T. C. Walton run out	31	1/14 2/38 3/58	(9 wkts, 40 overs)	173
J. N. Snape c Hemp b Donald	23	4/59 5/112 6/134		
†D. Ripley st Piper b Giles	11	7/160 8/163 9/172		

Bowling: Brown 8–0–34–0; Welch 8–0–27–0; Donald 8–1–22–3; Edmond 8–0–43–2; Giles 8–0–33–1.

Warwickshire

D. R. Brown lbw b Capel	12	G. Welch not out		19
*N. M. K. Smith run out	30			
T. L. Penney lbw b Curran	22	B 1, l-b 5, w 3, n-b 4		13
D. L. Hemp c Penberthy b Follett	34			
D. P. Ostler not out	15	1/33 2/55 3/108	(5 wkts, 29.3 overs)	145
W. G. Khan lbw b Curran	0	4/110 5/112		

†K. J. Piper, A. F. Giles, M. D. Edmond and A. A. Donald did not bat.

Bowling: Taylor 6–0–26–0; Follett 5–0–25–1; Capel 5–0–20–1; Emburey 5.3–0–17–0; Snape 4–0–27–0; Curran 4–0–24–2.

Umpires: J. F. Steele and A. G. T. Whitehead.

WARWICKSHIRE v YORKSHIRE

At Birmingham, May 18. Warwickshire won by four wickets. Toss: Yorkshire.

Donald, who took six for 15 last time he played Yorkshire in the League, was on the mark again, with four for 32. His wickets included the match's top scorer, Parker. Although no one else reached 40, enough Warwickshire batsmen got into double figures to complete the win.

Yorkshire

M. P. Vaughan c Knight b Welch	6	D. Gough c Small b Donald	3
*D. Byas c Smith b Brown	20	C. E. W. Silverwood not out	5
D. S. Lehmann c Smith b Donald	22	R. D. Stemp not out	9
†R. J. Blakey b Giles	13	B 4, l-b 14, w 5, n-b 4	27
A. McGrath b Donald	9		
C. White lbw b Brown	15	1/10 2/39 3/71 (9 wkts, 40 overs) 185	
B. Parker b Donald	42	4/78 5/93 6/123	
P. J. Hartley b Giles	14	7/161 8/169 9/171	

Bowling: Welch 8–0–30–1; Brown 8–0–37–2; Donald 8–0–32–4; Giles 8–0–28–2; Small 6–0–27–0; Smith 2–0–13–0.

Warwickshire

*N. V. Knight c Vaughan b Gough	6	G. Welch not out	20
N. M. K. Smith c Parker b White	26	A. F. Giles not out	29
D. R. Brown b Stemp	36	L-b 4, w 2, n-b 2	8
D. L. Hemp c Blakey b White	8		
D. P. Ostler lbw b Stemp	36	1/15 2/42 3/60 (6 wkts, 37.4 overs) 186	
T. L. Penney b Stemp	17	4/89 5/135 6/140	

†T. Frost, A. A. Donald and G. C. Small did not bat.

Bowling: Silverwood 8–0–34–0; Gough 6.4–0–45–1; White 8–0–26–2; Hartley 7–1–38–0; Stemp 8–1–39–3.

Umpires: J. H. Harris and B. J. Meyer.

WARWICKSHIRE v MIDDLESEX

At Birmingham, May 25. Warwickshire won by 108 runs. Toss: Warwickshire.

In his 18th season, Small improved on his best Sunday figures, taking five for 26 as Middlesex were skittled for 114. Only Brown resisted for long. Warwickshire's more productive innings was dominated by a stand of 102 in 14 overs between Ostler and Penney.

Warwickshire

W. G. Khan c Blanchett b Hewitt	6	G. Welch not out	0
*N. M. K. Smith c Blanchett b Dutch	53		
D. R. Brown b Dutch	38	L-b 7, w 3, n-b 2	12
D. L. Hemp c Gatting b Johnson	3		
D. P. Ostler not out	68	1/27 2/95 3/109 (5 wkts, 40 overs) 222	
T. L. Penney c Nash b Johnson	42	4/117 5/219	

G. C. Small, †K. J. Piper, A. A. Donald and M. A. Sheikh did not bat.

Bowling: Fraser 8–0–60–0; Hewitt 8–0–34–1; Johnson 8–0–34–2; Dutch 8–0–34–2; Blanchett 8–0–53–0.

Middlesex

P. N. Weekes c Piper b Welch	12		J. P. Hewitt c Ostler b Small	3
M. R. Ramprakash lbw b Welch	7		I. N. Blanchett lbw b Donald	1
*M. W. Gatting run out	8		A. R. C. Fraser b Donald	0
S. P. Moffat c Donald b Small	6		B 1, l-b 4, w 10, n-b 2	17
†K. R. Brown not out	44			
D. C. Nash lbw b Small	11		1/22 2/29 3/37	(32.5 overs) 114
K. P. Dutch c Donald b Small	2		4/58 5/74 6/82	
R. L. Johnson c Piper b Small	3		7/89 8/108 9/114	

Bowling: Brown 5–1–15–0; Welch 8–0–33–2; Donald 3.5–0–6–2; Small 8–0–26–5; Smith 8–0–29–0.

Umpires: J. C. Balderstone and R. A. White.

At Southampton, June 1. WARWICKSHIRE lost to HAMPSHIRE by 14 runs.

At Tunbridge Wells, June 8. WARWICKSHIRE lost to KENT by 32 runs.

WARWICKSHIRE v DERBYSHIRE

At Birmingham, June 15. Warwickshire won by 108 runs. Toss: Derbyshire.

Disrupted off the field by the departure of their captain, Dean Jones, three days earlier, Derbyshire capitulated helplessly on it, handing Warwickshire their second 108-run walkover in consecutive home Sunday games. Smith had the starring role, smashing 60 from 34 balls in an opening partnership of 93 in 11 overs with Knight, and then picking up three wickets, although Brown's 57 from 23 balls was even more spectacular.

Warwickshire

*N. V. Knight b Aldred	43		D. L. Hemp not out	3
N. M. K. Smith c DeFreitas b Clarke	60		G. Welch not out	10
D. R. Brown c Aldred b DeFreitas	57		B 1, l-b 3, w 1	5
T. L. Penney c Harris b Barnett	12			
A. F. Giles c Adams b Harris	10		1/93 2/123 3/169	(6 wkts, 21 overs) 201
D. P. Ostler st Krikken b Barnett	1		4/187 5/188 6/191	

†K. J. Piper, M. D. Edmond and G. C. Small did not bat.

Bowling: Roberts 4–0–29–0; DeFreitas 4–0–42–1; Harris 4–0–43–1; Aldred 5–0–31–1; Clarke 2–0–32–1; Barnett 2–0–20–2.

Derbyshire

K. J. Barnett c Knight b Smith	18		P. Aldred b Edmond	17
C. J. Adams b Smith	4		G. M. Roberts not out	3
V. P. Clarke b Small	10		A. J. Harris b Edmond	1
J. E. Owen lbw b Small	5		B 3, l-b 8, w 3	14
*P. A. J. DeFreitas c Hemp b Smith	1			
†K. M. Krikken b Giles	1		1/14 2/34 3/36	(16.5 overs) 93
T. A. Tweats c Hemp b Giles	16		4/41 5/44 6/46	
A. S. Rollins b Giles	3		7/54 8/89 9/89	

Bowling: Brown 3–0–17–0; Smith 4–0–20–3; Small 4–0–23–2; Giles 4–0–18–3; Edmond 1.5–0–4–2.

Umpires: R. Palmer and N. T. Plews.

At Leicester, June 29. WARWICKSHIRE beat LEICESTERSHIRE by eight wickets.

WARWICKSHIRE v SURREY

At Birmingham, July 6. Warwickshire won by 48 runs. Toss: Surrey. County debut: J. N. Batty.

Warwickshire extended their 100 per cent home record to five matches, thanks mainly to some erratic Surrey bowling: Holliake's seven overs cost 57. Though he later bolstered his side with a 34-ball fifty, he received little assistance.

Warwickshire

W. G. Khan run out	27	G. Welch not out	32
*N. M. K. Smith b Lewis	19	M. D. Edmond not out	10
D. R. Brown c Lewis b Saqlain Mushtaq	8		
D. L. Hemp c D. J. Bicknell		B 7, l-b 7, w 2	16
b Saqlain Mushtaq	46		
D. P. Ostler c D. J. Bicknell b Holliake	58	1/24 2/56 3/62　(6 wkts, 40 overs)	231
T. L. Penney b Lewis	15	4/144 5/180 6/194	

†T. Frost, G. C. Small and A. A. Donald did not bat.

Bowling: M. P. Bicknell 5-0-23-0; Lewis 8-0-38-2; Benjamin 7-0-30-0; Saqlain Mushtaq 8-1-34-2; Holliake 7-0-57-1; Salisbury 5-0-35-0.

Surrey

D. J. Bicknell lbw b Brown	2	I. D. K. Salisbury b Edmond	7
A. D. Brown run out	8	Saqlain Mushtaq not out	29
J. D. Ratcliffe c Hemp b Welch	16	J. E. Benjamin not out	13
I. J. Ward run out	6	B 1, l-b 3, w 6, n-b 2	12
*A. J. Holliake c Penney b Edmond	50		
C. C. Lewis c Frost b Donald	1	1/10 2/13 3/34　(9 wkts, 40 overs)	183
†J. N. Batty b Donald	8	4/35 5/64 6/77	
M. P. Bicknell c Small b Brown	31	7/103 8/123 9/144	

Bowling: Brown 7-0-38-2; Welch 6-0-20-1; Small 8-0-45-0; Donald 7-0-31-2; Edmond 5-0-18-2; Smith 7-1-27-0.

Umpires: D. J. Constant and K. E. Palmer.

At Chester-le-Street, July 13. WARWICKSHIRE beat DURHAM by five wickets (D/L method).

At Nottingham, July 20. WARWICKSHIRE lost to NOTTINGHAMSHIRE by 87 runs.

WARWICKSHIRE v SOMERSET

At Birmingham, July 23 (day/night). Warwickshire won by 35 runs. Toss: Warwickshire.

This was the first Sunday League game to be staged under floodlights, Surrey's earlier attempt having been washed out, and it was a huge success. On perhaps the warmest evening of the year, 15,174 people watched Warwickshire's Wednesday night win, bringing in about £120,000 – a profit of £70,000, allowing for the cost of the lights. Crowd behaviour was impeccable, and the club were thrilled by their experiment. Smith chose to bat when the match began at 6.10 p.m. and shared an opening stand of 112 with Singh. Though Warwickshire's eventual total was only twice that, Somerset were soon in trouble under the lights. Brown and Small reduced them to 56 for five, which became 99 for seven before Bowler and Kerr put together a stand of 63. Donald ended the match when he bowled Shine at 11.38 p.m. Kerr was credited with five penalty runs after an incident that occurred in a corner unilluminated by the five pylons. Penney's cap dropped off when he was chasing the ball near the boundary, and the ball struck the cap. Ian Botham, commentating on TV, saw the incident and, after replaying it several times, alerted the third umpire, Barrie Leadbeater, who had the scores amended.

Warwickshire

A. Singh run out	86	G. Welch not out	0
*N. M. K. Smith c Rose b Kerr	59		
D. R. Brown run out	11	B 1, l-b 8, w 6	15
D. L. Hemp c sub b Rose	7		
D. P. Ostler c Rose b Kerr	42	1/112 2/135 3/155 (5 wkts, 40 overs) 224	
T. L. Penney run out	4	4/204 5/221	

A. F. Giles, †K. J. Piper, G. C. Small and A. A. Donald did not bat.

Bowling: Rose 8–0–40–1; Parsons 6–0–30–0; Shine 8–0–63–0; Mushtaq Ahmed 8–0–29–0; Burns 2–0–12–0; Kerr 8–0–41–2.

Somerset

M. Burns lbw b Brown	18	J. I. D. Kerr b Donald	33
P. C. L. Holloway run out	28	Mushtaq Ahmed not out	7
†R. J. Turner lbw b Brown	0	K. J. Shine b Donald	3
S. C. Ecclestone c Smith b Small	2	B 6, l-b 6, w 3	15
M. N. Lathwell lbw b Small	4		
*P. D. Bowler b Giles	57	1/41 2/41 3/44 (39.2 overs) 189	
K. A. Parsons c Brown b Smith	21	4/48 5/56 6/94	
G. D. Rose run out	1	7/99 8/162 9/178	

Bowling: Welch 8–0–48–0; Brown 8–0–31–2; Small 6–1–22–2; Donald 7.2–0–27–2; Giles 6–0–33–1; Smith 4–0–16–1.

Umpires: T. E. Jesty and R. Palmer.

WARWICKSHIRE v SUSSEX

At Birmingham, August 3. Warwickshire won by 26 runs (D/L method). Toss: Warwickshire.

Warwickshire held all the aces in a rehearsal for the NatWest semi-final ten days later. Donald and Small made a mess of Sussex's top order, and then Hemp led a reply that was well ahead of the required figure of 76.95 when the expected downpour materialised.

Sussex

K. Greenfield b Small	25	A. A. Khan lbw b Giles	1
R. K. Rao c Smith b Donald	18	A. D. Edwards not out	9
M. Newell c and b Small	5	M. A. Robinson not out	5
V. C. Drakes c Frost b Donald	2	L-b 3, w 5	8
N. R. Taylor b Giles	27		
K. Newell c Brown b Welch	28	1/38 2/50 3/53 (9 wkts, 40 overs) 162	
*†P. Moores c Frost b Donald	23	4/53 5/105 6/130	
P. W. Jarvis b Giles	11	7/134 8/135 9/151	

Bowling: Brown 6–1–25–0; Welch 8–0–30–1; Small 8–1–28–2; Donald 8–0–31–3; Smith 4–1–15–0; Giles 8–1–30–3.

Warwickshire

A. Singh c Moores b Drakes	11	D. P. Ostler not out	13
*N. M. K. Smith c Greenfield b Drakes	23	L-b 2, w 3	5
D. R. Brown run out	23		
D. L. Hemp not out	27	1/25 2/42 3/83 (3 wkts, 22 overs) 102	

T. L. Penney, G. Welch, A. F. Giles, †T. Frost, G. C. Small and A. A. Donald did not bat.

Bowling: Drakes 6–1–21–2; Edwards 2–0–18–0; Jarvis 6–0–38–0; Robinson 5–1–8–0; Khan 2–0–9–0; Greenfield 1–0–6–0.

Umpires: B. Dudleston and J. H. Hampshire.

At Manchester, August 10. WARWICKSHIRE beat LANCASHIRE by 21 runs.

At Worcester, August 24. WARWICKSHIRE beat WORCESTERSHIRE by eight runs (D/L method).

At Chelmsford, August 31. WARWICKSHIRE beat ESSEX by 147 runs.

WARWICKSHIRE v GLOUCESTERSHIRE

At Birmingham, September 14. Warwickshire won by 71 runs. Toss: Warwickshire. First-team debut: C. M. W. Read.

Warwickshire began the final round two points behind leaders Kent. But Kent's defeat at Headingley left the door open for them to take their third Sunday League title, and they barged through it with this crushing win – their 15th in 15 home league games since they lost to Leicestershire in May 1996. Knight made a steadying century as Gloucestershire were set a target of 222, but it was the bowling of Donald and Giles, who took four wickets each, that did the damage. Donald, described by acting-captain Neil Smith as "the best overseas player in England over the past ten years", received a replica of the trophy; the real one had been sent to Leeds.

Warwickshire

N. V. Knight run out	102	G. Welch c sub b Young	9
*N. M. K. Smith c and b Ball	39	A. F. Giles not out	4
D. R. Brown c Alleyne b Ball	1	B 2, l-b 7, w 5, n-b 4	18
D. L. Hemp c and b Alleyne	8		
D. P. Ostler c sub b Smith	24	(6 wkts, 40 overs)	221
T. L. Penney not out	16		

1/89 2/94 3/110 4/175 5/197 6/215

†K. J. Piper, A. A. Donald and G. C. Small did not bat.

Bowling: Smith 8–0–41–1; Lewis 8–0–48–0; Young 6–0–45–1; Ball 8–0–35–2; Alleyne 8–0–29–1; Hancock 2–0–14–0.

Gloucestershire

R. I. Dawson c Piper b Donald	15	†C. M. W. Read c Smith b Giles	0
T. H. C. Hancock c and b Smith	29	J. Lewis b Donald	1
S. Young c Ostler b Smith	8	A. M. Smith not out	7
M. J. Church b Giles	25	B 2, l-b 13, w 4	19
*M. W. Alleyne c Penney b Giles	29		
M. G. N. Windows b Giles	5	1/43 2/52 3/75 (36.5 overs)	150
M. C. J. Ball c Brown b Donald	6	4/102 5/122 6/129	
R. J. Cunliffe b Donald	6	7/136 8/136 9/139	

Bowling: Brown 3–0–17–0; Welch 3–0–15–0; Donald 7.5–1–24–4; Smith 8–0–29–2; Small 8–2–25–0; Giles 7–0–25–4.

Umpires: N. T. Plews and G. Sharp.

WORCESTERSHIRE

At Nottingham, April 27. WORCESTERSHIRE beat NOTTINGHAMSHIRE by seven wickets.

WORCESTERSHIRE v LEICESTERSHIRE

At Worcester, May 11. Leicestershire won by six runs. Toss: Worcestershire.

Rain delayed the start until 5.20 p.m., whereupon Leicestershire declined to 27 for six. But Habib played the best innings of the match – 45 from 43 balls – and Worcestershire could not push their run-rate above six per over.

Leicestershire

N. C. Johnson c Spiring b Newport 11	D. L. Maddy c Hick b Leatherdale 14
V. J. Wells b Newport 6	G. J. Parsons not out 1
J. M. Dakin run out 0	
†P. A. Nixon run out 2	L-b 4, w 2................. 6
A. Habib not out..................... 45	
B. F. Smith b Haynes................. 0	1/18 2/18 3/19 (8 wkts, 16 overs) 98
*J. J. Whitaker run out 4	4/20 5/23 6/27
G. I. Macmillan run out 9	7/44 8/84

A. D. Mullally did not bat.

Bowling: Newport 4–0–15–2; Haynes 3–0–9–1; Brinkley 3–0–26–0; Leatherdale 3–0–18–1; Sheriyar 3–0–26–0.

Worcestershire

*T. M. Moody c and b Mullally 2	P. J. Newport b Johnson............... 7
G. A. Hick c Johnson b Mullally 8	J. E. Brinkley run out................ 7
V. S. Solanki c Habib b Parsons 7	A. Sheriyar not out.................. 0
W. P. C. Weston c Dakin b Parsons 11	L-b 4, w 2, n-b 6 12
G. R. Haynes lbw b Dakin.............. 10	
D. A. Leatherdale c Habib b Dakin...... 8	1/6 2/11 3/33 (9 wkts, 16 overs) 92
K. R. Spiring not out 20	4/35 5/54 6/54
†S. J. Rhodes c Macmillan b Maddy 0	7/55 8/69 9/91

Bowling: Parsons 4–0–9–2; Mullally 3–0–24–2; Johnson 3–0–17–1; Maddy 3–0–17–1; Dakin 3–0–21–2.

Umpires: J. W. Holder and K. E. Palmer.

At Chester-le-Street, May 25. WORCESTERSHIRE lost to DURHAM by seven wickets.

WORCESTERSHIRE v SOMERSET

At Worcester, June 1. Worcestershire won by 85 runs. Toss: Worcestershire.

Hick scored his first competitive fifty of the season on the day that England announced their party for the First Test; it was the first time for seven years that they had started the Test summer without him. He soon went on to a hundred, in just 82 balls, and, after Somerset had been reduced to 27 for two, there was no way back for them.

Worcestershire

*T. M. Moody lbw b Caddick 23	W. P. C. Weston not out 11
V. S. Solanki b Kerr.................. 26	L-b 6, w 5, n-b 6 17
G. A. Hick not out 119	
G. R. Haynes c Trump b Rose 48	1/50 2/54 (4 wkts, 40 overs) 262
D. A. Leatherdale c Bowler b Caddick ... 18	3/152 4/204

K. R. Spiring, S. R. Lampitt, †S. J. Rhodes, R. J. Chapman and A. Sheriyar did not bat.

Bowling: Rose 8–1–38–1; Parsons 6–0–30–0; Caddick 8–0–46–2; Kerr 8–0–63–1; Burns 3–0–24–0; Trump 7–0–55–0.

Somerset

M. N. Lathwell run out	13	J. I. D. Kerr run out	1
M. Burns c Rhodes b Haynes	12	A. R. Caddick b Haynes	0
†R. J. Turner run out	67	H. R. J. Trump run out	0
G. D. Rose c Rhodes b Lampitt	16	L-b 3, w 5	8
R. J. Harden b Lampitt	7		
*P. D. Bowler b Sheriyar	30	1/17 2/27 3/73	(32.2 overs) 177
P. C. L. Holloway not out	12	4/93 5/152 6/155	
K. A. Parsons run out	11	7/168 8/176 9/176	

Bowling: Chapman 5–0–30–0; Haynes 7–0–29–2; Lampitt 8–0–32–2; Sheriyar 6–0–36–1; Hick 3–0–25–0; Leatherdale 3.2–0–22–0.

Umpires: H. D. Bird and D. J. Constant.

At Bristol, June 15. WORCESTERSHIRE lost to GLOUCESTERSHIRE by one run.

WORCESTERSHIRE v SURREY

At Worcester, June 22. Worcestershire won by seven wickets. Toss: Worcestershire.

Surrey got themselves into an almost irreparable position at 36 for seven and, despite an excellent ninth-wicket stand of 83 between Bicknell and Saqlain Mushtaq, they were well short of par on a decent pitch. Haynes and Spiring added 97 together to settle the match.

Surrey

A. D. Brown c Hick b Chapman	0	M. P. Bicknell not out	57
J. D. Ratcliffe lbw b Haynes	22	Saqlain Mushtaq c Lampitt b Sheriyar	29
I. J. Ward c Rhodes b Haynes	0	J. E. Benjamin c and b Leatherdale	5
*A. J. Hollioake c Rhodes b Haynes	3	L-b 3, w 3, n-b 4	10
N. Shahid run out	1		
C. C. Lewis c Rhodes b Haynes	1	1/0 2/0 3/15	(37 overs) 149
B. C. Hollioake c Lampitt b Sheriyar	20	4/30 5/32 6/35	
†J. A. Knott lbw b Leatherdale	1	7/36 8/59 9/142	

Bowling: Chapman 8–1–42–1; Haynes 8–2–13–4; Leatherdale 7–1–37–2; Lampitt 7–0–24–0; Sheriyar 7–0–30–2.

Worcestershire

*T. M. Moody c Knott b Bicknell	19	K. R. Spiring not out	43
V. S. Solanki c Knott b Lewis	7	B 1, l-b 11, w 10, n-b 2	24
G. A. Hick c Lewis b Benjamin	10		
G. R. Haynes not out	47	1/25 2/36 3/53	(3 wkts, 31.3 overs) 150

W. P. C. Weston, D. A. Leatherdale, S. R. Lampitt, †S. J. Rhodes, A. Sheriyar and R. J. Chapman did not bat.

Bowling: Lewis 8–0–27–1; Bicknell 5–0–19–1; Benjamin 7–0–24–1; B. C. Hollioake 5–0–27–0; A. J. Hollioake 3–0–23–0; Saqlain Mushtaq 3.3–0–18–0.

Umpires: J. D. Bond and R. A. White.

WORCESTERSHIRE v LANCASHIRE

At Worcester, June 29. Worcestershire won by 114 runs. Toss: Lancashire.

Worcestershire ended a sequence of four wins for Lancashire on Sunday visits to New Road. Solanki and Hick put together the decisive partnership of the match, 136 in just 21 overs. Needing almost six an over on a slow pitch, Lancashire succumbed quickly, with catches accounting for nine of their wickets.

Worcestershire

*T. M. Moody c McKeown b Martin	4
V. S. Solanki c Shadford b Austin	58
G. A. Hick c Chapple b Yates..........	86
G. R. Haynes b Yates.................	5
K. R. Spiring c Hegg b Martin	9
D. A. Leatherdale c Atherton b Martin...	18
W. P. C. Weston c Shadford b Austin ...	14

S. R. Lampitt not out	11
†S. J. Rhodes not out	7
L-b 6, w 17.................	23
	—
1/8 2/144 3/167 (7 wkts, 40 overs)	235
4/177 5/199	
6/211 7/217	

P. J. Newport and A. Sheriyar did not bat.

Bowling: Austin 8–0–35–2; Martin 8–2–33–3; Chapple 8–0–59–0; Shadford 8–0–65–0; Yates 8–0–37–2.

Lancashire

P. C. McKeown c Leatherdale b Newport	0
*M. A. Atherton c Moody b Newport.....	7
J. P. Crawley c Moody b Newport	11
G. D. Lloyd c Moody b Lampitt	17
A. Flintoff c Solanki b Hick	20
I. D. Austin c Rhodes b Hick	5
†W. K. Hegg c Rhodes b Lampitt.......	7
G. Yates c Spiring b Leatherdale........	18

G. Chapple not out	13
P. J. Martin lbw b Leatherdale	1
D. J. Shadford c Rhodes b Leatherdale...	2
L-b 3, w 3, n-b 14	20
	—
1/1 2/14 3/39 (28.1 overs)	121
4/46 5/65 6/76	
7/93 8/106 9/117	

Bowling: Newport 6–0–22–3; Haynes 8–0–25–0; Lampitt 6–0–33–2; Hick 6–0–25–2; Leatherdale 2.1–0–13–3.

Umpires: V. A. Holder and T. E. Jesty.

At Arundel, July 6. WORCESTERSHIRE beat SUSSEX by 49 runs.

At Southampton, July 13. WORCESTERSHIRE lost to HAMPSHIRE by 87 runs.

WORCESTERSHIRE v GLAMORGAN

At Worcester, July 20. Worcestershire won by 45 runs. Toss: Worcestershire.

Glamorgan escaped any penalty for their wretched over-rate (they bowled only 11 in the first hour and finished 15 minutes late), but were heavily punished by Curtis, who cut loose in uncharacteristic fashion. Only selected because of injuries, Curtis was steady on his way to 50 in 85 balls, then struck 43 more from 24 balls; he hit six fours and a six (back over Waqar Younis's head) in all. After the game, police arrested six spectators from the Cardiff area; they resorted to CS spray when an officer was punched.

Worcestershire

*T. M. Moody c Maynard b Thomas	12
T. S. Curtis c Morris b Dale	93
G. A. Hick c Watkin b Croft..........	37
G. R. Haynes not out	64

K. R. Spiring not out	12
L-b 8, w 16.................	24
	—
1/25 2/99 3/213 (3 wkts, 40 overs)	242

V. S. Solanki, †S. J. Rhodes, A. Sheriyar, S. R. Lampitt, M. J. Rawnsley and R. J. Chapman did not bat.

Bowling: Waqar Younis 8–0–61–0; Watkin 8–1–33–0; Thomas 5–1–18–1; Butcher 5–0–33–0; Croft 8–0–48–1; Dale 6–0–41–1.

Glamorgan

R. D. B. Croft c Haynes b Moody	1	S. D. Thomas c Solanki b Hick	15
H. Morris c Hick b Chapman	8	Waqar Younis c Curtis b Haynes	0
A. Dale st Rhodes b Rawnsley	47	S. L. Watkin c Solanki b Haynes	2
*M. P. Maynard b Lampitt	23	B 4, l-b 3, w 3, n-b 4	14
S. P. James b Lampitt	13		
G. P. Butcher lbw b Hick	47	1/10 2/21 3/52	(36 overs) 197
†A. D. Shaw c Hick b Rawnsley	5	4/85 5/133 6/141	
A. W. Evans not out	22	7/168 8/194 9/194	

Bowling: Moody 6–0–24–1; Chapman 6–0–19–1; Lampitt 6–0–36–2; Haynes 5–0–21–2; Rawnsley 7–0–54–2; Sheriyar 4–0–24–0; Hick 2–0–12–2.

Umpires: B. Dudleston and N. T. Plews.

At Chelmsford, July 27. WORCESTERSHIRE tied with ESSEX.

WORCESTERSHIRE v KENT

At Worcester, August 3. No result. Toss: Worcestershire.

The weather held off long enough for Moody to supersede Barry Richards as the fastest man to 4,000 Sunday League runs. Richards reached the mark in 1976 in 106 innings; Moody needed exactly 100.

Worcestershire

*T. M. Moody c Marsh b McCague	26	K. R. Spiring not out	0
T. S. Curtis run out	34	W 2, n-b 4	6
G. A. Hick not out	27		
G. R. Haynes c Wells b Strang	24	1/60 2/61 3/111	(3 wkts, 24 overs) 117

V. S. Solanki, D. A. Leatherdale, S. R. Lampitt, †S. J. Rhodes, A. Sheriyar and R. J. Chapman did not bat.

Bowling: Headley 7–1–34–0; Ealham 4–0–16–0; McCague 5–0–20–1; Fleming 5–0–25–0; Strang 3–0–22–1.

Kent

T. R. Ward, E. T. Smith, A. P. Wells, G. R. Cowdrey, M. V. Fleming, N. J. Llong, P. A. Strang, *†S. A. Marsh, M. J. McCague, D. W. Headley and M. A. Ealham.

Umpires: J. D. Bond and J. H. Harris.

At Northampton, August 10. WORCESTERSHIRE beat NORTHAMPTONSHIRE by two wickets.

WORCESTERSHIRE v WARWICKSHIRE

At Worcester, August 24. Warwickshire won by eight runs (D/L method). Toss: Worcestershire.

Knight and Hemp, who hit two sixes, constructed the only half-century stand of a rain-affected match, and gave Warwickshire the momentum that took them to 151 in their 25 overs. Then Welch and Small removed Worcestershire's top four for ten in three overs. They were behind the clock when the weather closed in again.

Warwickshire

N. V. Knight c Leatherdale b Illingworth	24	A. F. Giles not out	27
*N. M. K. Smith c Mirza b Moody	0	†K. J. Piper run out	14
D. R. Brown run out	4	B 1, l-b 5, w 6	12
D. L. Hemp b Sheriyar	45		
D. P. Ostler b Lampitt	0	1/1 2/18 3/74	(8 wkts, 25 overs) 151
T. L. Penney c Leatherdale b Moody	21	4/76 5/89 6/95	
G. Welch c Hick b Illingworth	4	7/129 8/151	

G. C. Small and A. A. Donald did not bat.

Bowling: Moody 5–0–29–2; Haynes 5–0–33–0; Mirza 3–0–23–0; Lampitt 5–0–16–1; Illingworth 5–0–29–2; Sheriyar 2–0–15–1.

Worcestershire

*T. M. Moody c Piper b Small	13	S. R. Lampitt not out	8
W. P. C. Weston c Piper b Welch	4		
G. A. Hick c Hemp b Welch	6	L-b 3, w 7	10
G. R. Haynes c Donald b Small	1		—
D. A. Leatherdale not out	27	1/17 2/24 3/26	(5 wkts, 16 overs) 87
V. S. Solanki c Giles b Donald	18	4/27 5/70	

†S. J. Rhodes, R. K. Illingworth, A. Sheriyar and M. M. Mirza did not bat.

Bowling: Welch 5–0–18–2; Brown 3–0–15–0; Small 5–0–31–2; Giles 2–0–15–0; Donald 1–0–5–1.

Umpires: J. C. Balderstone and B. J. Meyer.

WORCESTERSHIRE v MIDDLESEX

At Worcester, August 31. No result (abandoned).

At Leeds, September 7. WORCESTERSHIRE beat YORKSHIRE by 38 runs.

WORCESTERSHIRE v DERBYSHIRE

At Worcester, September 14. Derbyshire won by five wickets. Toss: Worcestershire.

Moody anchored Worcestershire's innings with 112, his tenth Sunday League hundred, removed both Derbyshire openers on his way to bowling figures of 8–0–29–2, and still saw his side lose. Clarke stole the initiative with an undefeated 69 in 61 balls.

Worcestershire

*T. M. Moody c Cassar b Harris	112	D. A. Leatherdale not out	0
T. S. Curtis b Clarke	31	B 4, l-b 3, w 7	14
G. A. Hick c Tweats b Harris	35		
G. R. Haynes not out	23	1/74 2/155 3/207	(3 wkts, 40 overs) 215

V. S. Solanki, S. R. Lampitt, †S. J. Rhodes, R. K. Illingworth, W. P. C. Weston and M. M. Mirza did not bat.

Bowling: DeFreitas 8–0–31–0; Aldred 8–0–28–0; Clarke 6–0–33–1; Cork 7–0–44–0; Harris 8–0–45–2; Cassar 3–0–27–0.

Derbyshire

D. G. Cork c Hick b Moody 13
*P. A. J. DeFreitas c Rhodes b Moody .. 30
T. A. Tweats st Rhodes b Illingworth 19
K. J. Barnett run out 41
V. P. Clarke not out 69
I. D. Blackwell lbw b Leatherdale 9

†K. M. Krikken not out 11

L-b 14, w 8, n-b 2 24

1/40 2/54 3/95   (5 wkts, 38.4 overs) 216
4/182 5/198

M. E. Cassar, S. J. Lacey, A. J. Harris and P. Aldred did not bat.

Bowling: Haynes 5–0–34–0; Mirza 7–0–42–0; Moody 8–0–29–2; Lampitt 8–0–34–0; Illingworth 6–0–30–1; Leatherdale 4.4–0–33–1.

Umpires: D. R. Shepherd and A. G. T. Whitehead.

YORKSHIRE

At Southampton, May 4. YORKSHIRE beat HAMPSHIRE by 71 runs.

YORKSHIRE v GLAMORGAN

At Leeds, May 11. Yorkshire won by seven wickets (D/L method). Toss: Yorkshire.

A stand of 83 in ten overs between Cottey and Croft helped to lift Glamorgan to a sizable total for an innings reduced by rain to 32 overs. Of the bowlers, Hartley suffered most, but as a pinch-hitter he contributed to a stand of 48 in seven overs with Byas. After that, Yorkshire were always ahead of the required rate – despite the application of Duckworth/Lewis, their target remained 193 from 32.

Glamorgan

S. P. James c White b Stemp 9
H. Morris c White b Stemp 32
A. Dale c Blakey b Hartley 18
*M. P. Maynard c Gough b Stemp 21
P. A. Cottey b Gough 59
R. D. B. Croft c and b Hartley 29

G. P. Butcher not out 6
†A. D. Shaw not out 8
L-b 5, w 3, n-b 2 10

1/21 2/52 3/84   (6 wkts, 32 overs) 192
4/86 5/169 6/180

Waqar Younis, S. L. Watkin and O. T. Parkin did not bat.

Bowling: Silverwood 6–0–38–0; Gough 7–0–33–1; Stemp 7–0–32–3; White 6–0–38–0; Hartley 6–1–46–2.

Yorkshire

*D. Byas c Morris b Dale 83
M. P. Vaughan b Parkin 37
P. J. Hartley c Morris b Butcher 23
D. S. Lehmann not out 33

†R. J. Blakey not out 3
L-b 5, w 5, n-b 4 14

1/84 2/132 3/177   (3 wkts, 26.3 overs) 193

B. Parker, A. McGrath, C. White, D. Gough, C. E. W. Silverwood and R. D. Stemp did not bat.

Bowling: Watkin 4–0–23–0; Waqar Younis 4–0–29–0; Croft 4–0–34–0; Parkin 5–0–33–1; Butcher 5–0–45–1; Dale 4–0–22–1; Maynard 0.3–0–2–0.

Umpires: B. Leadbeater and D. R. Shepherd.

At Birmingham, May 18. YORKSHIRE lost to WARWICKSHIRE by four wickets.

At Taunton, May 25. YORKSHIRE beat SOMERSET by seven wickets.

At Ilford, June 1. YORKSHIRE beat ESSEX by four wickets.

YORKSHIRE v GLOUCESTERSHIRE

At Leeds, June 8. Gloucestershire won by 44 runs (D/L method). Toss: Gloucestershire.

Having made 15 runs in his four previous Sunday innings, Young redressed the balance in a rumbustious 146 not out, compiled from 105 balls, with nine fours and nine sixes. It was the best score for Gloucestershire in the competition, eclipsing Alleyne's 134 in 1992. If rain had not stopped him with 32 balls left, Young could have threatened Gooch's then Sunday record of 176. Yorkshire did little to atone for dismal bowling, falling well short of a target of 250 from 30 overs, despite a stand of 77 in nine between Blakey and Hartley.

Gloucestershire

A. J. Wright b Silverwood	6	*M. W. Alleyne not out	14
R. J. Cunliffe b Silverwood	56	L-b 6, w 6	12
S. Young not out	146		
M. A. Lynch c Hartley b Stemp	18	1/10 2/170 3/203 (3 wkts, 34.4 overs)	252

T. H. C. Hancock, †R. C. Russell, M. C. J. Ball, A. M. Smith, R. P. Davis and J. Lewis did not bat.

Bowling: Silverwood 8–0–52–2; Hartley 5.4–1–34–0; Hamilton 8–0–75–0; White 5–0–32–0; Stemp 8–0–53–1.

Yorkshire

*D. Byas b Lewis	29	G. M. Hamilton not out	18
M. D. Moxon c Davis b Lewis	1	C. E. W. Silverwood not out	7
D. S. Lehmann c Hancock b Lewis	14		
B. Parker lbw b Smith	2	L-b 6, w 4	10
†R. J. Blakey c Hancock b Ball	56		
C. White c and b Ball	14	1/5 2/24 3/32 (8 wkts, 30 overs)	206
P. J. Hartley c and b Alleyne	46	4/56 5/82 6/159	
R. A. Kettleborough b Smith	9	7/179 8/183	

R. D. Stemp did not bat.

Bowling: Smith 6–0–25–2; Lewis 6–0–39–3; Young 6–0–35–0; Ball 6–0–37–2; Alleyne 5–0–44–1; Davis 1–0–20–0.

Umpires: J. H. Hampshire and T. E. Jesty.

At The Oval, June 15. YORKSHIRE lost to SURREY by five wickets.

At Nottingham, June 22. YORKSHIRE lost to NOTTINGHAMSHIRE by 13 runs (D/L method).

YORKSHIRE v MIDDLESEX

At Leeds, June 29. Yorkshire won by six wickets. Toss: Yorkshire.

Gough took his 100th wicket in the competition when Ramprakash was caught at backward point, and Middlesex's day scarcely improved from there. A stand of 91 between Pooley and Weekes raised their hopes briefly, but McGrath took Yorkshire to victory with four overs to spare, smiting an off-break from Dutch into the players' balcony.

Middlesex

*M. R. Ramprakash c Lehmann b Gough.	10	J. P. Hewitt b Gough	0
J. H. Kallis c White b Hartley	21	A. R. C. Fraser not out	1
R. L. Johnson c Hartley b Silverwood	1		
O. A. Shah c Byas b White	6	L-b 3, w 2	5
J. C. Pooley c Stemp b Morris	61		
†K. R. Brown c Blakey b White	2	1/15 2/16 3/33 (8 wkts, 40 overs) 173	
P. N. Weekes not out	53	4/41 5/50 6/141	
K. P. Dutch b Gough	13	7/167 8/167	

T. F. Bloomfield did not bat.

Bowling: Gough 8–0–30–3; Silverwood 8–1–16–1; White 8–0–46–2; Hartley 8–0–36–1; Stemp 5–0–29–0; Morris 3–0–13–1.

Yorkshire

*D. Byas c Brown b Fraser	28	A. McGrath not out	38
C. White b Johnson	41	B 1, l-b 13, w 5, n-b 2	21
D. S. Lehmann c Weekes b Johnson	12		
†R. J. Blakey not out	25	1/58 2/93 (4 wkts, 35.5 overs) 175	
B. Parker b Hewitt	10	3/104 4/119	

A. C. Morris, P. J. Hartley, D. Gough, C. E. W. Silverwood and R. D. Stemp did not bat.

Bowling: Hewitt 8–0–29–1; Bloomfield 4–0–15–0; Dutch 4.5–0–29–0; Fraser 8–0–30–1; Johnson 7–0–28–2; Weekes 4–0–30–0.

Umpires: M. J. Kitchen and J. F. Steele.

At Leicester, July 6. YORKSHIRE tied with LEICESTERSHIRE.

At Derby, July 13. YORKSHIRE lost to DERBYSHIRE by 114 runs.

YORKSHIRE v DURHAM

At Scarborough, July 20. Yorkshire won by 138 runs. Toss: Durham.

Durham's miserable batting form helped White to career-best figures of four for 18, while left-arm spinner Fisher took two for 24 on his Sunday debut. Yorkshire, by contrast, were overflowing with runs: Lehmann hit 77 from 60 balls and McGrath 51 from 26.

Yorkshire

*D. Byas c Boiling b Brown	10	A. C. Morris b Wood	1
C. White c Roseberry b Boiling	64	D. Gough not out	1
D. S. Lehmann c Roseberry b Boiling	77	B 4, l-b 3, w 1	8
P. J. Hartley c Brown b Boiling	2		
†R. J. Blakey c Walker b Betts	28	1/19 2/149 3/154 (7 wkts, 40 overs) 259	
B. Parker c Walker b Brown	17	4/158 5/192	
A. McGrath not out	51	6/252 7/254	

C. E. W. Silverwood and I. D. Fisher did not bat.

Bowling: Brown 8–0–54–2; Wood 8–1–55–1; Betts 8–0–59–1; Walker 8–0–51–0; Boiling 8–0–33–3.

Durham

J. E. Morris b Gough	6	J. Boiling b White	0
S. Hutton st Blakey b Fisher	46	S. J. E. Brown b White	1
†M. P. Speight c Blakey b Silverwood	7	A. Walker c McGrath b Lehmann	11
*D. C. Boon b Hartley	7	B 1, l-b 8, w 2, n-b 2	13
J. J. B. Lewis b White	5		—
M. A. Roseberry not out	19	1/8 2/34 3/53	(30.4 overs) 121
M. M. Betts st Blakey b Fisher	2	4/73 5/83 6/87	
J. Wood b White	4	7/100 8/100 9/104	

Bowling: Silverwood 6–1–21–1; Gough 4–1–16–1; Hartley 4–0–20–1; Fisher 8–0–24–2; White 7–0–18–4; Lehmann 1.4–0–13–1.

Umpires: J. H. Harris and G. Sharp.

YORKSHIRE v NORTHAMPTONSHIRE

At Leeds, August 3. Yorkshire won by 38 runs. Toss: Northamptonshire.

McGrath's dominant innings of 63 from 51 balls, including four off-side sixes, made the difference in the end. Yorkshire's innings had also been boosted by 57 from White and, though Curran made 57 for Northamptonshire, the visitors' lower order fell away. Lehmann's left-arm tweakers brought him figures of three for 43, his best in any cricket. The match was brought forward two hours to enable spectators to watch a rugby league match on the other side of the main stand afterwards.

Yorkshire

M. P. Vaughan lbw b Taylor	17	A. C. Morris c Warren b Emburey	35
C. White c Mohammad Akram		G. M. Hamilton not out	1
b Penberthy	57	C. E. W. Silverwood run out	1
D. S. Lehmann c Fordham b Emburey	9	B 1, l-b 4, w 5	10
*D. Byas b Capel	42		
†R. J. Blakey b Bailey	3	1/46 2/80 3/96	(9 wkts, 40 overs) 239
A. McGrath c Emburey b Taylor	63	4/102 5/148 6/149	
B. Parker run out	1	7/217 8/237 9/239	

R. D. Stemp did not bat.

Bowling: Mohammad Akram 8–0–44–0; Taylor 6–0–46–2; Emburey 8–0–33–2; Penberthy 8–1–47–1; Bailey 6–0–40–1; Capel 4–0–24–1.

Northamptonshire

A. L. Penberthy c Blakey b White	18	J. E. Emburey c Stemp b Vaughan	0
A. Fordham c Blakey b Stemp	25	J. P. Taylor lbw b White	20
K. M. Curran c and b Lehmann	57	Mohammad Akram not out	2
D. J. Capel c Vaughan b Stemp	1	L-b 7, w 7, n-b 2	16
*R. J. Bailey c and b Lehmann	22		
R. J. Warren lbw b Lehmann	10	1/48 2/50 3/51	(37.3 overs) 201
T. C. Walton c McGrath b Vaughan	10	4/110 5/128 6/159	
†D. Ripley b Silverwood	20	7/161 8/164 9/199	

Bowling: Hamilton 4–0–25–0; Silverwood 3.3–0–20–1; Stemp 8–0–23–2; White 7–0–37–2; Vaughan 8–0–46–2; Lehmann 7–0–43–3.

Umpires: V. A. Holder and R. Julian.

YORKSHIRE v SUSSEX

At Scarborough, August 24. No result (abandoned).

At Manchester, August 31. YORKSHIRE lost to LANCASHIRE by 31 runs.

YORKSHIRE v WORCESTERSHIRE

At Leeds, September 7. Worcestershire won by 38 runs. Toss: Worcestershire.

Moody made the only half-century of the match, but Worcestershire might have won by even more if he had resorted more quickly to his seventh bowler, Sheriyar – who recorded Sunday-best figures of four for 18. There was some cheer for Yorkshire in the form of Gough, who took two for 34 on his return from injury.

Worcestershire

*T. M. Moody c Silverwood b Vaughan . 67	S. R. Lampitt b Gough 7
W. P. C. Weston b Silverwood 1	†S. J. Rhodes not out 5
G. A. Hick b Gough 28	B 3, l-b 10, w 6, n-b 2 21
G. R. Haynes st Blakey b Stemp 36	
D. A. Leatherdale not out 38	1/4 2/53 3/129 (6 wkts, 40 overs) 220
V. S. Solanki lbw b Morris 17	4/163 5/192 6/204

R. K. Illingworth, A. Sheriyar and M. M. Mirza did not bat.

Bowling: Silverwood 8-0-44-1; Gough 8-0-34-2; Vaughan 8-0-59-1; Morris 8-0-34-1; Stemp 8-0-36-1.

Yorkshire

M. P. Vaughan run out 14	D. Gough c Moody b Sheriyar 13
C. White c Weston b Moody 8	C. E. W. Silverwood not out 3
B. Parker b Lampitt 37	R. D. Stemp b Sheriyar 0
D. S. Lehmann c Rhodes b Lampitt 25	L-b 6, w 4 10
*D. Byas st Rhodes b Hick 40	
A. McGrath c Hick b Sheriyar 23	1/11 2/36 3/83 (33.5 overs) 182
†R. J. Blakey c Leatherdale b Sheriyar . . . 1	4/100 5/144 6/145
A. C. Morris c Leatherdale b Hick 8	7/154 8/173 9/181

Bowling: Moody 5-1-29-1; Haynes 5-0-22-0; Lampitt 6-0-28-2; Illingworth 8-0-41-0; Mirza 2-0-17-0; Hick 4-0-21-2; Sheriyar 3.5-1-18-4.

Umpires: B. Dudleston and J. W. Holder.

YORKSHIRE v KENT

At Leeds, September 14. Yorkshire won by seven wickets. Toss: Kent.

League leaders Kent fell at the final hurdle once again. News from Edgbaston confirmed that they had finished as runners-up, just as they had in the Benson and Hedges Cup two months earlier. It did not augur well for their attempt to overhaul Glamorgan in the Championship. Their top order should have prospered against a Yorkshire attack missing Gough, Silverwood, White and Hutchison; instead, they stumbled to 124 for seven. A stand of 61 between Strang – his last contribution before returning to Zimbabwe – and Marsh was too little, too late. Vaughan and Lehmann, who made a superb 78 not out from 68 balls, rammed the point home, putting on 125 in 19 overs. Kent's captain Marsh later admitted: ''The issue of whether we freeze on the big occasion will be raised again, and rightly so.''

Kent

T. R. Ward c Blakey b Hamilton 41	P. A. Strang c Byas b Sidebottom 36
E. T. Smith c McGrath b Fisher 20	*†S. A. Marsh not out 16
A. P. Wells c Blakey b Hamilton 10	L-b 9, w 6, n-b 16 31
G. R. Cowdrey st Blakey b Fisher 1	
N. J. Llong c Lehmann b Hamilton 1	1/57 2/74 3/83 (8 wkts, 40 overs) 185
M. A. Ealham b Vaughan 21	4/88 5/93 6/122
M. V. Fleming c Sidebottom b Morris . . . 8	7/124 8/185

A. P. Igglesden and J. B. D. Thompson did not bat.

Bowling: Hartley 7-0-41-0; Sidebottom 7-0-41-1; Fisher 8-0-23-2; Hamilton 8-0-30-3; Vaughan 5-0-21-1; Morris 5-0-20-1.

Yorkshire

A. McGrath c Llong b Thompson	9	B. Parker not out		39
M. P. Vaughan lbw b Igglesden	49	B 2, l-b 3, w 7		12
D. S. Lehmann not out	78			—
*D. Byas c Marsh b Fleming	0	1/14 2/139 3/140	(3 wkts, 29.4 overs)	187

G. M. Hamilton, †R. J. Blakey, A. C. Morris, P. J. Hartley, R. J. Sidebottom and I. D. Fisher did not bat.

Bowling: Igglesden 8–0–43–1; Thompson 5.4–0–37–1; Ealham 5–0–30–0; Strang 3–0–18–0; Fleming 6–0–34–1; Llong 2–0–20–0.

Umpires: H. D. Bird and B. J. Meyer.

SUNDAY LEAGUE RECORDS

Batting

Highest individual score: 203, A. D. Brown, Surrey v Hampshire, Guildford, 1997.

Most runs: 8,573, G. A. Gooch; 7,504, C. W. J. Athey; 7,499, W. Larkins; 7,389, K. J. Barnett; 7,062, D. W. Randall; 7,040, D. L. Amiss; 6,671, M. W. Gatting; 6,650, C. T. Radley; 6,639, D. R. Turner; 6,568, R. T. Robinson. **In a season:** 917, T. M. Moody, Worcestershire, 1991.

Most hundreds: 14, W. Larkins; 12, G. A. Gooch; 11, C. G. Greenidge; 10, T. M. Moody; 9, K. S. McEwan, B. A. Richards and R. A. Smith. 578 hundreds have been scored in the League. The most in one season is 40 in 1990.

Most sixes in an innings: 13, I. T. Botham, Somerset v Northamptonshire, Wellingborough School, 1986. **By a team in an innings:** 18, Derbyshire v Worcestershire, Knypersley, 1985, and Surrey v Yorkshire, Scarborough, 1994. **In a season:** 26, I. V. A. Richards, Somerset, 1977.

Highest total: 375 for four, Surrey v Yorkshire, Scarborough, 1994. **By a side batting second:** 317 for six, Surrey v Nottinghamshire, The Oval, 1993 (50-overs match).

Highest match aggregate: 631 for 13 wickets, Nottinghamshire (314 for seven) v Surrey (317 for six), The Oval, 1993 (50-overs match).

Lowest total: 23 (19.4 overs), Middlesex v Yorkshire, Leeds, 1974.

Shortest completed innings: 16 overs (59), Northamptonshire v Middlesex, Tring, 1974.

Record partnerships for each wicket

239	for 1st	G. A. Gooch and B. R. Hardie, Essex v Nottinghamshire at Nottingham .	1985
273	for 2nd	G. A. Gooch and K. S. McEwan, Essex v Nottinghamshire at Nottingham	1983
223	for 3rd	S. J. Cook and D. C. Rose, Somerset v Glamorgan at Neath	1990
219	for 4th	C. G. Greenidge and C. L. Smith, Hampshire v Surrey at Southampton ..	1987
190	for 5th	R. J. Blakey and M. J. Foster, Yorkshire v Leicestershire at Leicester ...	1993
137	for 6th	M. P. Speight and I. D. K. Salisbury, Sussex v Surrey at Guildford	1996
132	for 7th	K. R. Brown and N. F. Williams, Middlesex v Somerset at Lord's	1988
110*	for 8th	C. L. Cairns and B. N. French, Nottinghamshire v Surrey at The Oval ..	1993
105	for 9th	D. G. Moir and R. W. Taylor, Derbyshire v Kent at Derby	1984
82	for 10th	G. Chapple and P. J. Martin, Lancashire v Worcestershire at Manchester .	1996

Bowling

Most wickets: 386, J. K. Lever; 368, J. E. Emburey; 346, D. L. Underwood; 307, J. Simmons; 303, S. Turner; 284, N. Gifford; 281, E. E. Hemmings; 267, J. N. Shepherd; 260, A. C. S. Pigott; 256, I. T. Botham; 249, T. E. Jesty; 240, G. C. Small. **In a season:** 39, A. J. Hollioake, Surrey, 1996.

Best bowling: eight for 26, K. D. Boyce, Essex v Lancashire, Manchester, 1971; seven for 15, R. A. Hutton, Yorkshire v Worcestershire, Leeds, 1969; seven for 39, A. Hodgson, Northamptonshire v Somerset, Northampton, 1976; seven for 41, A. N. Jones, Sussex v Nottinghamshire, Nottingham, 1986; six for six, R. W. Hooker, Middlesex v Surrey, Lord's, 1969; six for seven, M. Hendrick, Derbyshire v Nottinghamshire, Nottingham, 1972; six for nine, N. G. Cowans, Middlesex v Lancashire, Lord's, 1991.

Most economical analysis: 8–8–0–0, B. A. Langford, Somerset v Essex, Yeovil, 1969.

Most expensive analyses: 8–0–96–1, D. G. Cork, Derbyshire v Nottinghamshire, Nottingham, 1993; 8–0–94–2, P. N. Weekes, Middlesex v Leicestershire, Leicester, 1994; 7.5–0–89–3, G. Miller, Derbyshire v Gloucestershire, Gloucester, 1984; 8–0–88–1, E. E. Hemmings, Nottinghamshire v Somerset, Nottingham, 1983.

Hat-tricks: There have been 24 hat-tricks, four of them for Glamorgan.

Four wickets in four balls: A. Ward, Derbyshire v Sussex, Derby, 1970.

Wicket-keeping and Fielding

Most dismissals: 264 (206 ct, 58 st), S. J. Rhodes; 257 (234 ct, 23 st), D. L. Bairstow; 236 (187 ct, 49 st), R. W. Taylor; 223 (184 ct, 39 st), E. W. Jones. **In a season:** 29 (26 ct, 3 st), S. J. Rhodes, Worcestershire, 1988. **In an innings:** 7 (6 ct, 1 st), R. W. Taylor, Derbyshire v Lancashire, Manchester, 1975.

Most catches in an innings: 6, K. Goodwin, Lancashire v Worcestershire, Worcester, 1969; R. W. Taylor, Derbyshire v Lancashire, Manchester, 1975; K. M. Krikken, Derbyshire v Hampshire, Southampton, 1994; and P. A. Nixon, Leicestershire v Essex, Leicester, 1994.

Most stumpings in an innings: 4, S. J. Rhodes, Worcestershire v Warwickshire, Birmingham, 1986 and N. D. Burns, Somerset v Kent, Taunton, 1991.

Most catches by a fielder: 103, V. P. Terry; 101, J. F. Steele; 100, G. A. Gooch; 97, D. P. Hughes; 95, C. W. J. Athey†; 94, G. Cook and P. W. G. Parker. **In a season:** 16, J. M. Rice, Hampshire, 1978. **In an innings:** 5, J. M. Rice, Hampshire v Warwickshire, Southampton, 1978.

† C. W. J. Athey has also taken two catches as a wicket-keeper.

Results

Largest victory in runs: Somerset by 220 runs v Glamorgan, Neath, 1990.

Victories by ten wickets (32): By Derbyshire, Durham, Essex (four times), Glamorgan (twice), Hampshire (twice), Kent, Leicestershire (twice), Middlesex (twice), Northamptonshire, Nottinghamshire, Somerset (twice), Surrey (three times), Warwickshire, Worcestershire (six times) and Yorkshire (three times). This does not include those matches in which the side batting second was set a reduced target but does include matches where both sides faced a reduced number of overs.

Ties: There have been 46 tied matches. Worcestershire have tied ten times.

Shortest match: 1 hr 53 min (26.3 overs), Surrey v Leicestershire, The Oval, 1996.

CHAMPIONS 1969-97

John Player's County League
1969 Lancashire

John Player League
1970 Lancashire
1971 Worcestershire
1972 Kent
1973 Kent
1974 Leicestershire
1975 Hampshire
1976 Kent
1977 Leicestershire
1978 Hampshire
1979 Somerset
1980 Warwickshire
1981 Essex
1982 Sussex
1983 Yorkshire

John Player Special League
1984 Essex

1985 Essex
1986 Hampshire

Refuge Assurance League
1987 Worcestershire
1988 Worcestershire
1989 Lancashire
1990 Derbyshire
1991 Nottinghamshire

Sunday League
1992 Middlesex

AXA Equity & Law League
1993 Glamorgan
1994 Warwickshire
1995 Kent
1996 Surrey

AXA Life League
1997 Warwickshire

MATCH RESULTS 1969-97

	P	W	L	T	NR	1st	2nd	3rd
Derbyshire	470	198	219	4	49	1	0	1
Durham	102	29	58	2	13	0	0	0
Essex	470	243	180	8	39	3	5*	3
Glamorgan	470	166	248	4	52	1	0	0
Gloucestershire	470	161	248	4	57	0	1	1
Hampshire	470	223	200	7	40	3	1	3
Kent	470	256	165	6	43	4	4	4
Lancashire	470	239	171	9	51	3	2	3
Leicestershire	470	202	206	3	59	2	2*	2
Middlesex	470	210	203	7	50	1	1	3
Northamptonshire	470	184	232	5	49	0	0	1
Nottinghamshire	470	199	225	3	43	1	3	1
Somerset	470	222	199	2	47	1	6*	0
Surrey	470	212	203	4	51	1	0	1
Sussex	470	198	217	5	50	1	2*	1
Warwickshire	470	202	213	6	49	3	1	1
Worcestershire	470	230	188	10	42	3	3	2
Yorkshire	470	210	209	3	48	1	1	1

* *Includes one shared 2nd place in 1976.*

50+ COUNTY CHAMPIONSHIP

Middlesex beat Lancashire by three wickets at Ealing to win the ECB's competition for senior club players. Lancashire reached 87 for two, thanks to a hard-hitting second-wicket stand of 72 between Mike Bocarro and Paul Tatton. But Lancashire lost their last five wickets for five runs, and Ramesh Sethi, with 46 not out, was able to see Middlesex past their total of 136 with just two balls to spare.

THE UNIVERSITIES IN 1997

OXFORD

President: C. A. Fry (Trinity)
Hon. Treasurer: Dr S. R. Porter (St Cross College)

Captain: M. A. Wagh (King Edward's, Birmingham, and Keble)
Secretary: B. W. Byrne (Western Australia U. and Balliol)

Captain for 1998: J. A. G. Fulton (Eton and Brasenose)
Secretary: J. P. Barnes (Canford and Wycliffe Hall)

The 1997 season dawned with fresh personnel in several key areas. As well as a new captain, Mark Wagh, Oxford had a new coach, Zimbabwean Test keeper Andy Flower, and, for the first time, a cricket manager, Roger Newman, a former Devon player who had been involved in youth development at Warwickshire. On the playing front, the squad included only two Blues, Wagh (on the Warwickshire staff) and David Mather, though Mather was to play in just two out of 11 first-class matches. An inexperienced team faced a daunting summer.

Due to his commitments with Zimbabwe, Flower arrived midway through the opening first-class game, against Durham. He discovered Wagh missing, with a damaged finger, and Oxford plummeting towards defeat. Matters could only improve and a noticeable, if gradual, learning curve was soon evident. Wagh's enterprising captaincy was greatly influenced by Flower's coaching input and Newman's motivational skills. A talk from Johnny Giles, the former Ireland football manager, was one of several innovative ideas aimed at improving mental awareness.

None the less, results were mixed. Although Wagh led Oxford to their first victory over a first-class county since 1993, beating Glamorgan, the eventual county champions, there were four defeats – three in The Parks and one at Taunton – before they drew the Varsity Match.

In the absence of much early substance to their batting, Oxford relied heavily on the middle and late order. James Fulton, Peter Morgan, Chetan Patel, Alex Scrini and Charlie Lightfoot made polished first-class fifties, though they rarely had a healthy platform to build on. Byron Byrne, an Australian all-rounder from Sydney, and James Averis also played some useful innings, while Wagh's undoubted talent finally came to the fore against Glamorgan. That triumph owed much to the sporting captaincy of Tony Cottey, but hinged on the stylish Wagh's batting – he scored centuries in both innings. Wagh added 125 not out against Somerset and finished the term with 684 runs, the highest aggregate for Oxford since David Thorne scored 849 in 1985, the last time the University had played 11 matches. He was expected to be available again in 1998, though he handed over the captaincy to Fulton because of exams.

The bowling, so short of penetration in 1996, was bolstered by the arrival of seamers Patel, Averis and Chris Battarbee. Between them, they shouldered the bulk of the workload, and collected 54 wickets. Averis, on Gloucestershire's books and an Oxford rugby Blue, enjoyed a red-letter day when he took five wickets out of five against Hampshire, while Battarbee, whose pony-tail prompted much comment, also stood out for some lively swing bowling. But it was Patel who earned the most spectacular reward for his wholehearted efforts. Against Warwickshire – for whose Second Eleven he once played – he became the first bowler to perform a hat-trick for Oxford for 30 years. His final haul of 27 wickets was the best since medium-pace off-spinner Richard Savage claimed 29 in ten games in 1977. There was no Bradman scholar for 1997 or 1998 because the Bradman Trust was devoting its funds to the museum at Bowral.

As always, groundsman Richard Sula and his team kept the square in top condition, but one had to feel a pang of sympathy for both ground staff and administrator Simon Porter when the showpiece game of the season, between the British Universities and the Australians at the end of June, was abandoned without a ball bowled because of monsoon-like rain. – MIKE BERRY.

OXFORD UNIVERSITY RESULTS

First-class matches – Played 11: Won 1, Lost 4, Drawn 6.

FIRST-CLASS AVERAGES

BATTING AND FIELDING

	M	I	NO	R	HS	100s	50s	Avge	Ct
M. A. Wagh	10	18	1	684	125*	3	2	40.23	7
P. G. Morgan	10	18	1	444	63	0	2	26.11	4
C. Patel	11	20	4	411	63*	0	3	25.68	2
J. M. M. Averis	9	15	4	276	42	0	0	25.09	1
J. A. G. Fulton	10	19	0	451	78	0	4	23.73	6
A. P. Scrini	11	18	6	253	58*	0	1	21.08	13
C. G. R. Lightfoot	9	16	0	289	61	0	1	18.06	2
B. W. Byrne	11	20	0	354	49	0	0	17.70	2
L. G. Buchanan	8	14	4	168	43*	0	0	16.80	1
C. M. Battarbee	7	8	6	29	10*	0	0	14.50	1
J. J. Bull	3	5	1	49	30	0	0	12.25	0
R. D. Hudson	11	20	2	202	62	0	1	11.22	2
J. E. Haynes	2	4	0	13	9	0	0	3.25	0

Also batted: J. R. Cockcroft (1 match) 1; N. E. F. Laughton (1 match) 5, 1 (1 ct); D. P. Mather (2 matches) 4, 1, 5*; N. G. Pirihi (2 matches) 15, 0, 0; G. J. Wright (3 matches) 0, 0*.

* *Signifies not out.*

BOWLING

	O	M	R	W	BB	5W/i	Avge
C. Patel	309	48	1,261	27	6-110	1	46.70
C. M. Battarbee	150.4	21	627	11	2-56	0	57.00
J. M. M. Averis	255.3	36	1,028	16	5-98	1	64.25
M. A. Wagh	194	36	669	6	2-45	0	111.50

Also bowled: B. W. Byrne 98–11–439–3; J. A. G. Fulton 5–0–18–0; R. D. Hudson 41–5–184–0; C. G. R. Lightfoot 21–2–126–0; D. P. Mather 45–7–190–2; G. J. Wright 46–7–246–1.

Note: Matches in this section which were not first-class are signified by a dagger.

†At Oxford, April 11, 12. Oxford University won by five wickets. Loughborough Students batted first by mutual agreement. Loughborough Students 348 for eight (100 overs) (D. A. Ellis 38, A. Bourke 31, T. M. B. Bailey 125, P. Davies 35); Oxford University 349 for five (94.4 overs) (R. D. Hudson 91, J. E. Haynes 52, B. W. Byrne 92, J. J. Bull 35 not out).

OXFORD UNIVERSITY 1997

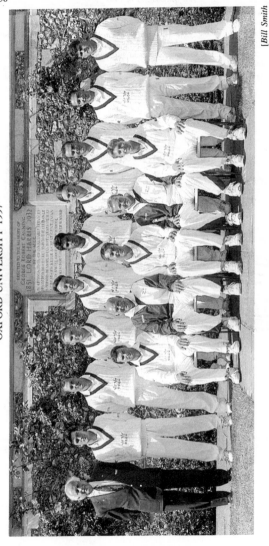

[*Bill Smith*

Back row: N. T. Harris (*scorer*), J. A. G. Fulton, J. M. M. Averis, L. G. Buchanan, R. D. Hudson, C. Patel, C. M. Batterbee, P. G. Morgan, A. P. Scrini, N. G. Pirihi. *Front row:* B. W. Byrne, R. J. Newman (*cricket manager*), M. A. Wagh (*captain*), A. Flower (*coach*), C. G. R. Lightfoot.

OXFORD UNIVERSITY v DURHAM

At Oxford, April 15, 16, 17. Durham won by 97 runs. Toss: Durham. First-class debuts: J. M. M. Averis, B. W. Byrne, J. A. G. Fulton, J. E. Haynes, R. D. Hudson, N. E. F. Laughton, C. Patel, A. P. Scrini. County debuts: D. C. Boon, J. J. B. Lewis, N. J. Speak, M. P. Speight.

David Boon began his reign at Durham by leading them to their first first-class win for 19 months. It was a welcome moment, even though Oxford fielded eight debutants, including Nigel Laughton, a former Black Watch soldier, who made his sole first-class appearance of the season to deputise for the injured Wagh as captain. The opening day was a disaster for his side, who replied to a total of 353 with 36 for six. Lewis became only the second player, following Peter Bowler, to score centuries on first-class debut for two counties (he had made 116 not out for Essex against Surrey in 1990). Neil Taylor of Kent and Sussex joined this select club a week later. Lewis out-did Bowler and Taylor by reaching an unbeaten 210, the highest innings yet for Durham, hitting 31 fours in 221 balls. His fellow-opener Collingwood, with a maiden hundred, helped him pile up 290 in 220 minutes. Then Brown and Betts wrecked the students' upper order. Although the last three wickets added 117, thanks to Fulton and Scrini, Oxford trailed by 200. Boon's second declaration left just over a day to score 345. Despite a better showing, it was too late to stave off defeat.

Close of play: First day, Oxford University 36-6 (J. A. G. Fulton 11*, C. Patel 1*); Second day, Oxford University 2-1 (J. E. Haynes 0*, C. G. R. Lightfoot 0*).

Durham

J. J. B. Lewis not out	210			
P. D. Collingwood b Patel	107			
J. E. Morris lbw b Patel	6	– (1) c Laughton b Mather	31
N. J. Speak not out	13	– (2) lbw b Patel	15
*D. C. Boon (did not bat)		– (3) c Scrini b Mather	58
†M. P. Speight (did not bat)		– (4) not out	30
M. M. Betts (did not bat)		– (5) not out	6
L-b 1, n-b 16	17	W 2, n-b 2	4

1/290 2/322	(2 wkts dec.) 353	1/24 2/71 3/122	(3 wkts dec.) 144	

J. Boiling, D. M. Cox, N. Killeen and S. J. E. Brown did not bat.

Bowling: *First Innings*—Patel 24–2–124–2; Averis 14–1–59–0; Mather 23–2–102–0; Byrne 8–0–52–0; Hudson 2–0–15–0. *Second Innings*—Averis 9–2–31–0; Patel 14–4–36–1; Byrne 7–0–27–0; Mather 13–4–38–2; Lightfoot 2–0–12–0.

Oxford University

R. D. Hudson c Speight b Brown	0	– lbw b Brown	0
J. E. Haynes c Speight b Betts	0	– lbw b Brown	4
C. G. R. Lightfoot c Collingwood b Betts	0	– c Speight b Collingwood	45
B. W. Byrne b Betts	3	– c Collingwood b Brown	36
J. J. Bull c Boon b Betts	9	– (11) not out	0
J. A. G. Fulton c Collingwood b Cox	54	– (5) b Brown	17
*N. E. F. Laughton lbw b Killeen	5	– (6) c Collingwood b Boiling	1
C. Patel c Speight b Brown	1	– (7) c Morris b Cox	50
†A. P. Scrini not out	58	– (8) run out	28
J. M. M. Averis b Betts	8	– (9) c Killeen b Boiling	42
D. P. Mather b Betts	4	– (10) lbw b Boiling	1
B 6, l-b 3, w 2	11	B 8, l-b 13, n-b 2	23

1/0 2/0 3/1 4/10 5/21	153	1/0 2/9 3/62 4/105 5/114	247
6/35 7/36 8/115 9/143		6/114 7/181 8/241 9/247	

Bowling: *First Innings*—Brown 15–5–33–2; Betts 17.3–5–51–6; Killeen 7–0–20–1; Boiling 11–3–28–0; Cox 8–4–12–1. *Second Innings*—Brown 22–9–35–4; Betts 21–7–43–0; Killeen 13–4–46–0; Collingwood 6–0–26–1; Boiling 20.1–8–21–3; Cox 11–5–41–1; Speak 4–0–14–0.

Umpires: J. H. Harris and N. A. Mallender.

OXFORD UNIVERSITY v HAMPSHIRE

At Oxford, April 18, 19, 21. Drawn. Toss: Oxford University. First-class debut: P. G. Morgan.

South African freshman Peter Morgan hit 60 on debut – with 12 fours and a six – after Wagh elected to bat. A sound 44 from Lightfoot laid the base for Oxford, and Patel helped Morgan add 99 in 38 overs. Then Stephenson steered his county towards a massive lead, adding 130 with James and 173 with Keech. He was dismissed in the last over of the day for 140, his biggest score for Hampshire, and Keech reached a career-best 127 in the morning. They finally declared on 415 for five – all five taken by Averis, who was rewarded with a bottle of champagne. Oxford then sank to 54 for four, 118 behind. But Byrne supervised a rearguard action and Patel and Scrini batted out the final 95 minutes.

Close of play: First day, Hampshire 9-0 (G. W. White 7*, J. P. Stephenson 0*); Second day, Hampshire 352-3 (M. Keech 93*).

Oxford University

R. D. Hudson lbw b Connor	9	– c White b Mascarenhas	19
J. E. Haynes lbw b Udal	9	– c Kendall b Milburn	0
C. G. R. Lightfoot lbw b Milburn	44	– c Stephenson b Mascarenhas	24
*M. A. Wagh b James	15	– b Mascarenhas	0
B. W. Byrne lbw b James	2	– c Aymes b Mascarenhas	49
J. A. G. Fulton c White b James	6	– c Aymes b James	15
P. G. Morgan c Whitaker b Connor	60	– lbw b Mascarenhas	5
C. Patel b Milburn	35	– not out	39
†A. P. Scrini not out	11	– not out	20
J. M. M. Averis b Milburn	6		
D. P. Mather not out	5		
B 7, l-b 18, w 12, n-b 4	41	B 1, l-b 9, w 8, n-b 4	22

1/10 2/60 3/83 4/95 5/105   (9 wkts dec.) 243   1/4 2/35 3/35 4/54   (7 wkts) 193
6/107 7/206 8/218 9/233   5/102 6/116 7/137

Bowling: *First Innings*—Connor 16-2-57-2; Milburn 18-8-35-3; Stephenson 10-2-29-0; Mascarenhas 13-3-35-0; Udal 18-11-26-1; James 16-6-36-3; Whitaker 1-1-0-0. *Second Innings*—Connor 4-1-9-0; Milburn 16-4-24-1; James 13-2-25-1; Mascarenhas 20-3-63-5; Udal 25-10-33-0; Stephenson 5-1-13-0; Whitaker 1.4-0-16-0.

Hampshire

G. W. White c Morgan b Averis	14	P. R. Whitaker not out ... 1
*J. P. Stephenson c Patel b Averis	140	B 16, l-b 8, w 16, n-b 20 ... 60
K. D. James c Lightfoot b Averis	53	
M. Keech c Wagh b Averis	127	1/49 2/179 3/352 (5 wkts dec.) 415
W. S. Kendall b Averis	20	4/410 5/415

†A. N. Aymes, S. D. Udal, A. D. Mascarenhas, C. A. Connor and S. M. Milburn did not bat.

Bowling: Averis 30.2-5-98-5; Patel 27-5-99-0; Hudson 21-5-62-0; Byrne 10-1-32-0; Wagh 23-5-50-0; Mather 9-1-50-0.

Umpires: J. H. Harris and N. A. Mallender.

OXFORD UNIVERSITY v YORKSHIRE

At Oxford, April 23, 24, 25. Drawn. Toss: Yorkshire. First-class debuts: C. M. Battarbee, L. G. Buchanan.

Yorkshire led Oxford by 496 when rain washed out the final day. The county's two innings followed a similar pattern: pairs of centuries following an early wicket from Battarbee, who dismissed Vaughan in his sixth first-class over, having already attained instant celebrity by going out with his hair tied up in Christmas wrapping tape. On the opening day, Byas and McGrath added 234, including 112 in 20 overs before tea; both had been given lives by the student fielders. Then, in the second innings, Vaughan, who hit 21 fours, and Parker, with 21 fours and a six, piled on the misery in a stand of 230. In between, Gough and Silverwood softened up the Oxford batsmen. They were hustled out for 114, though Byas did not enforce the follow-on. Blakey's catch to remove Wagh was the 500th dismissal of his Yorkshire career.

Close of play: First day, Oxford University 21-2 (M. A. Wagh 8*, B. W. Byrne 0*); Second day, Yorkshire 275-2 (B. Parker 138*, R. J. Blakey 10*).

Yorkshire

M. D. Moxon c Byrne b Wright	53			
M. P. Vaughan c Fulton b Battarbee	20	– c Scrini b Patel	109	
*D. Byas not out	126			
A. McGrath not out	105			
C. White (did not bat)		– (1) b Battarbee	6	
B. Parker (did not bat)		– (3) not out	138	
†R. J. Blakey (did not bat)		– (4) not out	10	
B 2, l-b 13, w 2, n-b 14	31	B 4, l-b 4, w 2, n-b 2	12	

1/45 2/101	(2 wkts dec.) 335	1/7 2/237	(2 wkts) 275

D. Gough, P. J. Hartley, C. E. W. Silverwood and R. D. Stemp did not bat.

Bowling: *First Innings*—Patel 18–3–67–0; Battarbee 21–8–52–1; Wright 14–3–60–1; Wagh 26–7–64–0; Byrne 7–2–23–0; Hudson 4–0–29–0; Lightfoot 4–0–25–0. *Second Innings*—Patel 22–5–63–1; Battarbee 11–0–48–1; Wright 9–0–57–0; Byrne 12–3–47–0; Wagh 8–1–17–0; Hudson 2–0–8–0; Lightfoot 5–0–27–0.

Oxford University

R. D. Hudson lbw b Gough	0	L. G. Buchanan c Stemp b White	0
*M. A. Wagh c Blakey b Stemp	35	G. J. Wright lbw b Vaughan	0
C. G. R. Lightfoot c Byas b Silverwood	11	C. M. Battarbee not out	10
B. W. Byrne b Silverwood	0		
J. A. G. Fulton b Gough	6	L-b 7, n-b 4	11
P. G. Morgan c Hartley b Stemp	28		
C. Patel b Stemp	0	1/0 2/17 3/21 4/44 5/83	114
†A. P. Scrini lbw b Vaughan	13	6/85 7/90 8/92 9/101	

Bowling: Gough 11–1–40–2; Silverwood 9–4–24–2; Hartley 7–1–21–0; Stemp 4–1–5–3; White 4–1–14–1; Vaughan 2.1–1–3–2.

Umpires: A. A. Jones and K. J. Lyons.

†At Oxford, April 29. Oxford University won by 72 runs. Toss: Oxford University. Oxford University 256 for nine (50 overs) (L. G. Buchanan 34, J. A. G. Fulton 50, P. G. Morgan 40 not out); Wiltshire 184 for nine (50 overs) (R. H. Wade 31; B. W. Byrne three for 26).

†At Oxford, May 6. Oxford University won by ten wickets. Toss: Hertfordshire. Hertfordshire 141 for eight (50 overs) (A. Burroughes 53; C. Patel four for 20); Oxford University 142 for no wkt (30.5 overs) (R. D. Hudson 33 not out, B. W. Byrne 84 not out).

OXFORD UNIVERSITY v WARWICKSHIRE

At Oxford, May 7, 8, 9. Warwickshire won by an innings and 53 runs. Toss: Oxford University. First-class debut: T. Frost.

Patel completed the first hat-trick for Oxford since John Easter did it against Northamptonshire in 1967. He removed Powell, lbw shouldering arms, with the final ball of one over, bowled Welch off his pads with the first ball of his next and then had Brown taken by Wagh in a fine two-handed catch at first slip. That reduced Warwickshire to 125 for six; Knight, making his first appearance since shattering a finger on England's tour of New Zealand, had fallen early to the swing of Battarbee. But Giles and Smith added a quickfire 123 in 13 overs. Oxford, bowled out inside 50 overs on a rain-shortened opening day, were soon in trouble again, 21 for three at the second-day close, and they quickly declined to 39 for six in the morning. Morgan and Patel could only delay a comprehensive innings defeat.

Close of play: First day, Oxford University 129; Second day, Oxford University 21-3 (B. W. Byrne 7*, A. P. Scrini 1*).

Oxford University

R. D. Hudson b Welch		5 – lbw b Brown		1
*M. A. Wagh c Ostler b Welch		4 – b Welch		0
C. G. R. Lightfoot b Welch		8 – c Knight b Brown		1
B. W. Byrne lbw b Brown		17 – c Ostler b Welch		8
J. A. G. Fulton st Frost b Giles		13 – (6) c Hemp b Giles		9
P. G. Morgan lbw b Brown		4 – (7) c Powell b Giles		21
C. Patel c Hemp b Giles		9 – (8) c Khan b Brown		25
†A. P. Scrini lbw b Edmond		1 – (5) lbw b Welch		1
L. G. Buchanan c Frost b Edmond		1 – c Powell b Giles		13
J. M. M. Averis not out		36 – not out		11
C. M. Battarbee c Brown b Welch		8 – c Frost b Brown		1
B 6, l-b 5, w 6, n-b 6		23	B 2, l-b 10, w 2, n-b 10	24

1/5 2/19 3/22 4/51 5/61   129   1/1 2/1 3/8 4/26 5/33   115
6/62 7/66 8/70 9/92   6/39 7/89 8/91 9/104

Bowling: *First Innings*—Welch 10.3–0–39–4; Brown 8–4–9–2; Giles 21–8–44–2; Edmond 9–2–26–2; Khan 1–1–0–0. *Second Innings*—Welch 14–7–15–3; Brown 14.3–4–24–4; Giles 21–11–27–3; Smith 11–3–23–0; Edmond 6–3–14–0.

Warwickshire

*N. V. Knight c Buchanan b Battarbee	12	A. F. Giles not out	69
W. G. Khan c Wagh b Averis	43	N. M. K. Smith not out	55
D. L. Hemp b Battarbee	5	B 9, l-b 9, w 2, n-b 22	42
D. P. Ostler lbw b Averis	51		
M. J. Powell lbw b Patel	20	1/39 2/57 3/71 (7 wkts dec.) 297
G. Welch b Patel	0	4/121 5/125
D. R. Brown c Wagh b Patel	0	6/125 7/174

†T. Frost and M. D. Edmond did not bat.

Bowling: Averis 22–5–97–2; Patel 19–2–78–3; Battarbee 19–4–72–2; Wagh 6–1–18–0; Hudson 2–0–14–0.

Umpires: A. G. T. Whitehead and P. Willey.

OXFORD UNIVERSITY v WORCESTERSHIRE

At Oxford, May 14, 15, 16. Drawn. Toss: Worcestershire.

Hick opted to search for form on a placid pitch at The Parks rather than join the Duke of Norfolk's XI against the Australians. He succeeded to the tune of 164 runs off 179 balls, with four sixes and 17 fours, and Weston contributed 119. They added 236 in 49 overs and Worcestershire declared at 359 for two. For once, Oxford were not daunted. Hudson and Byrne opened with a stand of 87 – previously in 1997, the first wicket had put on 0, 0, 10, 4, 0, 5 and 1 – and Wagh scored a fluent maiden half-century. Oxford were 212 for two before Thomas had Wagh caught at mid-wicket, and he struck twice more in seven balls. After Solanki made his first century, an unbeaten 128 off 133 balls, Oxford were challenged to score 271 in 56 overs. They had their backs to the wall at seven for three, but the later batsmen and rain rescued them.

Close of play: First day, Oxford University 36-0 (R. D. Hudson 14*, B. W. Byrne 17*); Second day, Worcestershire 38-0 (V. S. Solanki 16*, G. R. Haynes 18*).

Worcestershire

V. S. Solanki b Wagh	22	– not out	128
W. P. C. Weston c Scrini b Averis	119	– (6) c Scrini b Wagh	14
G. A. Hick not out	164		
K. R. Spiring not out	28	– lbw b Patel	0
G. R. Haynes (did not bat)		– (2) c Fulton b Averis	24
D. A. Leatherdale (did not bat)		– (3) lbw b Patel	8
**†S. J. Rhodes (did not bat)		– (5) c Wagh b Patel	3
P. A. Thomas (did not bat)		– (7) lbw b Wagh	0
R. J. Chapman (did not bat)		– (8) not out	7
L-b 3, w 6, n-b 17	26	L-b 6, n-b 2	8

1/38 2/274   (2 wkts dec.) 359   1/62 2/87 3/101   (6 wkts dec.) 192
                                              4/109 5/150 6/150

A. Sheriyar and M. J. Rawnsley did not bat.

Bowling: *First Innings*—Averis 19–3–79–1; Patel 22–5–97–0; Wright 6–0–35–0; Wagh 16–4–71–1; Lightfoot 9–2–51–0; Hudson 7–0–23–0. *Second Innings*—Averis 13–0–69–1; Patel 20–3–71–3; Wagh 9–3–45–2; Fulton 1–0–1–0.

Oxford University

R. D. Hudson lbw b Haynes	62	– c Rhodes b Sheriyar	4
B. W. Byrne c Haynes b Chapman	46	– c Rhodes b Sheriyar	6
*M. A. Wagh c Haynes b Thomas	64	– b Chapman	1
C. G. R. Lightfoot lbw b Thomas	24	– b Chapman	0
J. A. G. Fulton c Rhodes b Thomas	0	– c Hick b Haynes	36
C. Patel c Hick b Sheriyar	16	– (7) not out	33
P. G. Morgan not out	35	– (6) c Rhodes b Thomas	22
†A. P. Scrini lbw b Chapman	4	– c Rhodes b Chapman	12
L. G. Buchanan b Leatherdale	6	– not out	12
J. M. M. Averis not out	0		
L-b 10, w 6, n-b 8	24	L-b 3, n-b 6	9

1/87 2/154 3/212 4/212 5/217   (8 wkts dec.) 281   1/6 2/7 3/7 4/27   (7 wkts) 135
6/237 7/261 8/280   5/65 6/83 7/107

G. J. Wright did not bat.

Bowling: *First Innings*—Sheriyar 16–4–40–1; Chapman 14.5–3–54–2; Thomas 17–3–43–3; Rawnsley 20–4–55–0; Leatherdale 7–1–15–1; Hick 6–1–26–0; Weston 2–0–6–0; Haynes 8–4–17–1; Solanki 6–2–15–0. *Second Innings*—Sheriyar 9–3–17–2; Chapman 10–2–26–3; Thomas 9–1–36–1; Haynes 9–1–32–1; Rawnsley 2.5–0–11–0; Solanki 2–0–10–0.

Umpires: J. H. Hampshire and J. W. Lloyds.

At Cambridge, May 17. OXFORD UNIVERSITY lost to CAMBRIDGE UNIVERSITY.

†At Arundel, May 20. Earl of Arundel's XI v Oxford University. Abandoned.

†At Oxford, May 21. Drawn. Toss: Berkshire. Berkshire 193 (A. J. Johns 37, T. D. Fray 37; G. J. Wright five for 46); Oxford University 118 for nine (J. M. M. Averis 30 not out).

†At Oxford, May 22. Oxford University won by four wickets. Toss: Royal Navy. Royal Navy 175 (CPO P. Barsby 58, Lt D. Pinder 47; C. Patel six for 69, M. A. Wagh three for 37); Oxford University 176 for six (N. G. Pirihi 42).

†At Oxford, May 23. Oxford University won by seven wickets. Toss: Oxford University. Oxfordshire 234 for six dec. (S. V. Laudat 44, R. J. Williams 86); Oxford University 235 for three (R. D. Hudson 61, A. Flower 114 not out).

†At Oxford, May 24. Drawn. Toss: Oxford University. Oxford University 352 for three dec. (R. D. Hudson 100 retired out, B. W. Byrne 103 retired out, M. A. Wagh 75 not out); Free Foresters 140 for nine (P. McLarnon 31, S. Crisp 31; R. D. Hudson three for 17).

†At Oxford, May 26, 27, 28. Oxford University won by 47 runs. Toss: Oxford University. Oxford University 203 (R. D. Hudson 43, M. A. Wagh 49, J. M. M. Averis 63; A. J. Mackay five for 41) and 370 for five dec. (R. D. Hudson 56, B. W. Byrne 30, M. A. Wagh 112, J. A. G. Fulton 53, J. J. Bull 38 not out); MCC 269 (P. Bedford 32, P. J. Deakin 42, R. P. Gofton 56, A. R. Whittall 68; J. M. M. Averis four for 74, M. A. Wagh three for 82) and 257 (J. R. Boddington 46, R. P. Gofton 52, A. R. Whittall 65, N. Wilton 30; M. A. Wagh six for 70).

†At Oxford, May 29. Drawn. Toss: Harlequins. Harlequins 232 for four dec. (J. M. Attfield 113, J. O. D. Orders 48); Oxford University 210 for nine (N. G. Pirihi 34, J. J. Bull 79; S. D. Weale five for 65).

OXFORD UNIVERSITY v SUSSEX

At Oxford, May 30, 31, June 2. Sussex won by nine wickets. Toss: Oxford University. First-class debuts: J. J. Bates, C. J. Batt, J. P. Pyemont.

Oxford were strongly placed on the second evening, leading Sussex by 138 with eight second-innings wickets in hand. But they lost three of those before the close and three more early next morning. Only Averis, hitting 42 in 48 balls, and Scrini held Sussex up. County debutants Chris Batt, bowling a lively pace around off stump, and off-spinner Justin Bates collected four each. Sussex needed only 222 and won with an hour to spare as Rao knocked 64 off 57 balls after tea. Buchanan and Scrini had rescued Oxford's first innings with an unbroken ninth-wicket stand of 49, before Sussex ground their way to 203 for five, declaring 31 behind. Radford batted watchfully throughout their 58 overs for as many runs. Patel found some bounce on a flat wicket but marred another useful return by conceding 28 in no-balls.

Close of play: First day, Sussex 7-0 (N. J. Lenham 1*, T. A. Radford 2*); Second day, Oxford University 123-5 (J. J. Bull 2*, C. Patel 8*).

Oxford University

R. D. Hudson b Batt	2	– c Rao b Thursfield	6	
B. W. Byrne c Humphries b Kirtley	3	– b Thursfield	11	
*M. A. Wagh lbw b Kirtley	47	– b Bates	0	
J. A. G. Fulton c Thursfield b Batt	46	– c Lenham b Batt	50	
P. G. Morgan c Rao b Phillips	6	– c and b Batt	22	
J. J. Bull c Newell b Thursfield	6	– c Humphries b Batt	30	
C. Patel c Bates b Rao	10	– c Pyemont b Bates	15	
J. M. M. Averis c Pyemont b Bates	42	– c Rao b Bates	28	
L. G. Buchanan not out	3	– c Radford b Batt	43	
†A. P. Scrini not out	16	– c and b Bates	9	
G. J. Wright (did not bat)	0	– not out	–	
L-b 6, w 4, n-b 10	9	L-b 1, w 2, n-b 6	20	

1/15 2/19 3/21 4/55 5/119 (8 wkts dec.) 234   1/5 2/18 3/107 4/113 5/113 190
6/140 7/167 8/185   6/129 7/129 8/132 9/185

Bowling: *First Innings*—Kirtley 11–3–34–2; Batt 21–7–44–2; Phillips 10–0–47–1; Thursfield 15–2–34–1; Bates 21–7–50–1; Rao 8–1–19–1. *Second Innings*—Batt 19–4–56–4; Thursfield 11–3–36–2; Rao 6–0–35–0; Phillips 3–1–15–0; Bates 16.2–3–47–4.

Sussex

*N. J. Lenham c Fulton b Patel	1	– b Wagh	44
T. A. Radford not out	58	– not out	69
R. K. Rao c Scrini b Wagh	13	– not out	83
M. Newell lbw b Patel	32		
J. P. Pyemont c Wagh b Averis	22		
M. J. Thursfield lbw b Patel	0		
†S. Humphries not out	41		
L-b 4, n-b 32	36	B 1, l-b 7, w 6, n-b 12	26

1/7 2/39 3/92 4/142 5/146   (5 wkts dec.) 203   1/68   (1 wkt) 222

J. J. Bates, N. C. Phillips, C. J. Batt and R. J. Kirtley did not bat.

Bowling: *First Innings*—Averis 18–4–52–1; Patel 20–3–69–3; Wagh 13–2–39–1; Wright 7–1–39–0. *Second Innings*—Averis 14.4–2–40–0; Patel 8–0–34–0; Wright 10–3–55–0; Wagh 14–1–63–1; Fulton 3–0–12–0; Byrne 1–0–10–0.

Umpires: N. G. Cowley and N. T. Plews.

†At Wormsley, June 1. Oxford University won by six wickets. Toss: Oxford University. J. Paul Getty's XI 202 for five dec. (K. M. Wijesuriya 75, C. J. C. Rowe 42 not out; M. A. Wagh three for 72); Oxford University 205 for four (B. W. Byrne 82, J. A. G. Fulton 36 not out, P. G. Morgan 36 not out; N. A. Foster three for 50).

†At Oxford, June 3. Midlands Club Cricket Conference won by 17 runs. Toss: Midlands Club Cricket Conference. Midlands Club Cricket Conference 174 (H. V. Patel 47, G. Shephard 53); Oxford University 157 (R. D. Hudson 51, B. W. Byrne 39; S. Mahmood four for 69, A. Farooque five for 22).

†At Oxford, June 4. Oxford University won by six wickets. Toss: MCC Young Cricketers. MCC Young Cricketers 155 (R. A. Hawthorne 73; B. W. Byrne four for 22, C. T. Allen three for 37); Oxford University 156 for four (N. G. Pirihi 68 not out, J. A. G. Fulton 51).

OXFORD UNIVERSITY v GLAMORGAN

At Oxford, June 5, 6, 7. Oxford University won by five wickets. Toss: Glamorgan. First-class debuts: G. J. M. Edwards, W. L. Law, M. J. Powell, P. M. Warren.

Oxford scored a victory over a county for the first time since 1993. It was a curious win: Glamorgan fielded an especially weak team, lost only four wickets, and set a kindly target. That could not take the gloss off the occasion for the Oxford captain, Wagh, who became the first batsman to score a century in each innings for the University since Imran Khan in 1974. However, even he was overshadowed by Michael Powell, a 20-year-old from Abergavenny, who secured his place in the record books by becoming only the fourth batsman to score a double-hundred on first-class debut in an English season. He followed T. Marsden in 1826, Hubert Doggart in 1948 and David Sales in 1996. Powell needed only 213 balls, punishing some wayward bowling with 31 powerful fours and a six. Butcher's hundred was even more savage, taking just 64 balls: he moved from 45 to 100 in 23 deliveries. Oxford's first task was to reach 273 to avoid the follow-on. They did it with their last pair together, after Wagh scored the third maiden century of the match, with ten of his first 11 scoring shots racing to the boundary, to set up the University's biggest first-class total of the summer. Cottey set a sporting target of 276 in 58 overs. Wagh met the challenge with a second century – 101 off 116 balls – and Patel scored 63 in 61 balls. But it was Averis who drove the winning four with one ball to spare.

Close of play: First day, Oxford University 74-1 (B. W. Byrne 18*, M. A. Wagh 56*); Second day, Oxford University 284-9 (L. G. Buchanan 18*, C. M. Battarbee 5*).

Glamorgan

A. W. Evans c Scrini b Patel	14	– (2) c Morgan b Patel	16
M. J. Powell not out	200		
*P. A. Cottey c Fulton b Byrne	83		
G. P. Butcher not out	101		
†A. D. Shaw (did not bat)		– (1) c Fulton b Battarbee	37
W. L. Law (did not bat)		– (3) not out	38
S. D. Thomas (did not bat)		– (4) not out	17
L-b 4, w 4, n-b 16	24	B 2, l-b 9, w 18	29

1/33 2/251   (2 wkts dec.) 422   1/53 2/91   (2 wkts dec.) 137

A. Dale, D. A. Cosker, P. M. Warren and G. J. M. Edwards did not bat.

Bowling: *First Innings*—Averis 19–1–102–0; Patel 10–1–63–1; Battarbee 10–0–70–0; Wagh 18–1–103–0; Byrne 12–0–69–1; Hudson 1–0–11–0. *Second Innings*—Averis 6–2–19–0; Battarbee 15.4–1–57–1; Patel 4–0–26–1; Byrne 6–1–24–0.

Oxford University

R. D. Hudson b Thomas	0	– retired hurt	22
B. W. Byrne lbw b Thomas	28	– run out	15
*M. A. Wagh c sub b Thomas	116	– c Shaw b Thomas	101
J. A. G. Fulton c Shaw b Thomas	16	– c Thomas b Butcher	0
P. G. Morgan c Dale b Cosker	63	– c Warren b Cosker	25
J. J. Bull lbw b Thomas	4		
C. Patel c Shaw b Cosker	1	– (6) not out	63
J. M. M. Averis lbw b Cosker	14	– not out	16
L. G. Buchanan not out	18	– (7) lbw b Cosker	0
†A. P. Scrini lbw b Butcher	3		
C. M. Battarbee not out	5		
L-b 2, w 4, n-b 10	16	B 1, l-b 16, w 12, n-b 7	36

1/0 2/85 3/103 4/235 5/237   (9 wkts dec.) 284   1/42 2/81 3/159   (5 wkts) 278
6/238 7/240 8/256 9/268   4/237 5/238

In the second innings R. D. Hudson retired hurt at 81-1.

Bowling: *First Innings*—Thomas 25–4–95–5; Warren 14–5–45–0; Cosker 29–10–68–3; Butcher 14.3–3–56–1; Edwards 5–2–18–0. *Second Innings*—Thomas 20–1–74–1; Butcher 11–2–52–1; Cosker 17.5–4–89–2; Warren 5–2–15–0; Edwards 4–0–31–0.

Umpires: M. J. Kitchen and K. J. Lyons.

†At Oxford, June 10, 11, 12. Drawn. Toss: Oxford University. Oxford University 282 for nine dec. (N. G. Pirihi 44, J. A. G. Fulton 100, J. P. Barnes 51 not out, Extras 32; Capt P. D. O. Logan three for 59, LS S. Miles three for 64) and 209 for seven dec. (C. G. Lightfoot 47, J. A. G. Fulton 88 not out; Flt Lt P. Singleton three for 68); Combined Services 199 (SAC R. Beeston 61, Cpl A. Pick 46 not out; M. Mbangwa four for 65, C. M. Battarbee three for 48) and 213 for seven (Sgt G. S. Lumb 34, Capt C. H. G. St George 40, Cpl A. Pick 35; M. A. Wagh three for 65).

OXFORD UNIVERSITY v NOTTINGHAMSHIRE

At Oxford, June 14, 16, 17. Drawn. Toss: Oxford University. First-class debut: N. G. Pirihi.

The Parks' final match of the term saw a return to the bad old habits of early-season batting collapses. Slow left-armer Hindson, who had not played a first-class game since Nottingham-shire's previous visit in 1996, picked up four wickets in each innings. On the opening day, Pollard scored 115 before retiring at tea, and the county declared overnight. Oxford then slumped to 47 for five, though Morgan launched a mini-recovery. Even so, they conceded a deficit of 200.

Pick declined the follow-on for further batting practice and eventually left the University a daunting 367 to win. They were soon 93 for five. But one of the features of their season was runs from the lower order. Hudson, dropped down to No. 7 due to poor form, and Patel batted steadily; Nottinghamshire accepted the draw with nine overs remaining.

Close of play: First day, Nottinghamshire 324-4 dec.; Second day, Nottinghamshire 129-1 (R. T. Robinson 41*, N. A. Gie 45*).

Nottinghamshire

P. R. Pollard retired hurt	115		
R. T. Robinson b Averis	2	– not out	51
M. P. Dowman c Hudson b Patel	4	– (1) b Patel	13
A. A. Metcalfe c Wagh b Byrne	78		
G. F. Archer not out	50	– (4) c Wagh b Patel	1
N. A. Gie c Scrini b Averis	7	– (3) c Byrne b Averis	50
†L. N. P. Walker not out	42		
R. T. Bates (did not bat)		– (5) c Scrini b Averis	4
J. E. Hindson (did not bat)		– (6) not out	6
B 10, l-b 4, w 4, n-b 8	26	B 4, l-b 3, w 26, n-b 8	41

1/11 2/30 3/218 4/243   (4 wkts dec.) 324   1/29 2/139   (4 wkts dec.) 166
3/140 4/147

P. J. Franks and *R. A. Pick did not bat.

In the first innings P. R. Pollard retired hurt at 220.

Bowling: *First Innings*—Averis 18–2–74–2; Patel 21–3–63–1; Battarbee 20–3–91–0; Wagh 24–6–58–0; Byrne 8–0–19–1; Fulton 1–0–5–0. *Second Innings*—Averis 15–2–44–2; Patel 17–3–68–2; Battarbee 5–0–15–0; Byrne 5–1–20–0; Wagh 4–1–12–0.

Oxford University

N. G. Pirihi c Gie b Hindson	15	– lbw b Franks	0
B. W. Byrne c Walker b Pick	2	– lbw b Hindson	38
*M. A. Wagh b Dowman	11	– lbw b Hindson	34
C. G. R. Lightfoot b Franks	4	– b Hindson	17
P. G. Morgan lbw b Pick	41	– lbw b Bates	0
J. A. G. Fulton lbw b Hindson	0	– c Gie b Hindson	51
R. D. Hudson c Gie b Bates	10	– not out	45
C. Patel c Robinson b Hindson	12	– not out	51
J. M. M. Averis c Metcalfe b Hindson	13		
†A. P. Scrini b Franks	2		
C. M. Battarbee not out	0		
B 2, l-b 10, w 2	14	B 7, l-b 3, n-b 2	12

1/2 2/21 3/34 4/47 5/47   124   1/0 2/52 3/92   (6 wkts) 248
6/72 7/103 8/109 9/124   4/93 5/93 6/181

Bowling: *First Innings*—Franks 13–7–11–2; Pick 14–7–23–2; Dowman 7–2–13–1; Bates 15–6–37–1; Hindson 18.2–7–28–4. *Second Innings*—Franks 11–2–23–1; Pick 8–2–29–0; Archer 3–0–15–0; Bates 32–6–74–1; Hindson 34–8–97–4.

Umpires: K. E. Palmer and P. Willey.

At Chelmsford, June 20, 21, 22. OXFORD UNIVERSITY drew with ESSEX.

At Taunton, June 28, 29, 30. OXFORD UNIVERSITY lost to SOMERSET by an innings and 46 runs.

At Lord's, July 2, 3, 4. OXFORD UNIVERSITY drew with CAMBRIDGE UNIVERSITY.

CAMBRIDGE

President: Professor A. D. Buckingham (Pembroke)

Captain: A. Singh (King Edward's, Birmingham, and Gonville & Caius)
Secretary: W. J. House (Sevenoaks and Gonville & Caius)

Captain for 1998: A. Singh (King Edward's, Birmingham, and Gonville & Caius)
Secretary: Q. J. Hughes (Durham Johnston and St Edmund's)

Cambridge continued the progress that had marked 1996 – both on and off the field. Although the batting never reached the heights of the previous summer, Anurag Singh led a side that was competitive in most of its games against the first-class counties. At a time when the restructuring of English cricket put their position into the spotlight, the University advanced their case for retaining first-class status.

Ed Smith represented one powerful argument for the status quo. A young man who had scored a century on his debut as an 18-year-old the previous year, he completed the short Fenner's season leading the first-class averages with 683 runs at 68.30 – and still managed to obtain a first in his second-year history examinations. His 190 against Leicestershire was the highlight of the term; it was a pity that he squandered the chance of a double-century in the search for quick declaration runs, particularly when the champion county showed no signs of wanting to make a game of it. It seemed the uncompetitiveness in some of these games had as much to do with the attitude of county captains as any lack of student talent.

Singh led the side with great enthusiasm and some thought. Although he did not make the sheer volume of runs his first season had suggested, he did hit another century. Will House encountered similar difficulties and it was only at the end of the university season that he recaptured the form that had enabled him to top the batting averages as a freshman. All three batsmen remain in residence in 1998, when James Pyemont, who made his first-class debut for Sussex during 1997, should join them. However, the University will be without John Ratledge, who departed after four years studying law, but delighted Cambridge followers when he completed a maiden century at Lord's, in what was expected to be his final first-class match. Of the newcomers, Quentin Hughes showed promise as a left-hand batsman and some skill as the captain, as an off-spinner. He made runs in virtually every non-first-class match he played.

There was not such a happy tale to tell of the bowling, which, on paper at the start of the term, looked as strong as it had done for some summers. The addition of Steffan Jones, a seamer with a lot of pace for a student, was expected to make the attack more competitive. It did not. It was only in the Varsity Match, when he took six for 67 in the first innings and three more in the second, that he made the inroads expected of him. Ed How and Adam Janisch shared the seam attack while off-spinners Robin Jones and Jim Freeth toiled honestly without much success. Of the five front-line bowlers, only Janisch returns in 1998, a season that sees Cambridge celebrate 150 years of cricket at Fenner's. It is appropriate that, under groundsman John Moden, the ground is beginning to look and behave like its old self, ready for the planned celebrations. – DAVID HALLETT.

CAMBRIDGE UNIVERSITY RESULTS

First-class matches – Played 8: Lost 1, Drawn 7.

FIRST-CLASS AVERAGES

BATTING AND FIELDING

	M	I	NO	R	HS	100s	50s	Avge	Ct/St
E. T. Smith.............	8	12	2	683	190	1	5	68.30	2
R. O. Jones...........	8	11	2	325	60	0	3	36.11	4
A. Singh	8	11	1	354	134	1	1	35.40	3
D. R. H. Churton	7	7	1	177	44	0	0	29.50	9/1
W. J. House	8	11	1	293	94	0	2	29.30	10
J. Ratledge	8	12	1	268	100*	1	0	24.36	0
Q. J. Hughes..........	8	12	3	197	47*	0	0	21.88	1
P. S. Jones	7	8	2	116	36	0	0	19.33	1
M. W. Dawson........	4	7	0	35	23	0	0	5.00	1
J. W. O. Freeth	7	5	2	9	7*	0	0	3.00	2
E. J. How	8	4	1	0	0*	0	0	0.00	1

Also batted: M. R. K. Bailey (1 match) 6* (1 ct, 1 st); A. N. Janisch (4 matches) 3, 11, 4; I. Mohammed (1 match) 12; P. A. Schaffter (1 match) 0.

* Signifies not out.

BOWLING

	O	M	R	W	BB	5W/i	Avge
A. N. Janisch	79.5	10	299	9	4-71	0	33.22
P. S. Jones........	176.5	34	574	17	6-67	1	33.76
J. W. O. Freeth	149	16	609	11	4-101	0	55.36
E. J. How	193.4	41	685	12	5-59	1	57.08
R. O. Jones	148.4	17	580	9	3-116	0	64.44

Also bowled: M. W. Dawson 59.2–6–240–0; W. J. House 66–9–260–0; Q. J. Hughes 33–6–128–3; P. A. Schaffter 28–8–77–1; A. Singh 3–1–10–0.

Note: Matches in this section which were not first-class are signified by a dagger.

†At Cambridge, April 9. Cambridge University won by 13 runs. Toss: Cambridge University. Cambridge University 224 for six (50 overs) (J. Ratledge 40, E. T. Smith 99; A. Bourke three for 35); Loughborough Students 211 for six (50 overs) (A. Bourke 72, C. D. J. Bailey 62).

†At Cambridge, April 10. Cambridge University won by five wickets. Toss: Loughborough Students. Loughborough Students 212 for nine (50 overs) (N. Harvey 47, T. M. B. Bailey 51, B. T. P. Donelan 33; R. O. Jones three for 54); Cambridge University 213 for five (47.4 overs) (J. Ratledge 79, R. O. Jones 55, W. J. House 34; M. K. Davies three for 33).

†At Cambridge, April 12. Durham University won by four wickets. Toss: Cambridge University. Cambridge University 160 (43.5 overs) (A. Singh 46, E. T. Smith 31; J. D. Chaplin three for 20, D. Lewis five for 32); Durham University 161 for six (46.4 overs) (C. Clark 63 not out; E. J. How three for 21).

CAMBRIDGE UNIVERSITY 1997

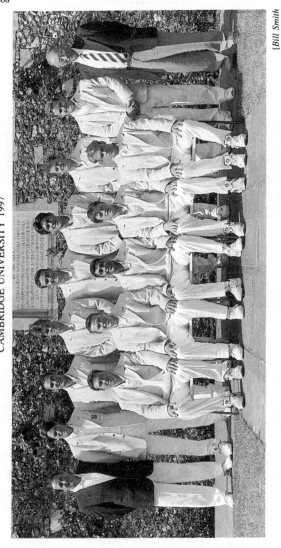

[*Bill Smith*]

Back row: D. W. Randall (*coach*), M. W. Dawson, E. J. How, E. T. Smith, P. S. Jones, A. N. Janisch, Q. J. Hughes, J. Ratledge, A. R. May (*scorer*). *Front row:* R. O. Jones, W. J. House, A. Singh (*captain*), D. R. H. Churton, J. W. O. Freeth.

†At Cambridge, April 13. Cambridge University won by five wickets. Toss: Durham University. Durham University 196 for six (50 overs) (T. P. Hodgson 33, M. J. Chilton 40, A. J. Strauss 35; M. W. Dawson three for 37); Cambridge University 199 for five (49.4 overs) (J. Ratledge 48, E. T. Smith 36, W. J. House 47 not out; J. D. Chaplin three for 33).

CAMBRIDGE UNIVERSITY v DERBYSHIRE

At Cambridge, April 15, 16, 17. Derbyshire won by an innings and 12 runs. Toss: Cambridge University. First-class debuts: M. W. Dawson, Q. J. Hughes, P. S. Jones. County debuts: V. P. Clarke, A. N. Hayhurst.

Cambridge paid for the positive decision to bat against a competitive Derbyshire side with what remained their only defeat of 1997. Smith carried on where he had left off in his debut season, but the top order found DeFreitas a handful, while the leg-spin of Clarke, on his Derbyshire debut, sank the lower order. Clarke followed up with a polished fifty after a century opening stand from Dean Jones and Rollins. Off-spinner Freeth claimed four wickets, although his overs cost nearly five apiece, before Jones declared, 168 ahead. It was a losing battle for Cambridge, prolonged by an unbeaten half-century from Robin Jones. Dean took three in six balls and Malcolm's late burst ensured the innings defeat, sealed when How walked, despite the umpire and opposing captain insisting he had not hit the last ball before lunch. Derbyshire brought a new sight to Fenner's: their physiotherapist regularly tossed drinking bottles on to the playing area.

Close of play: First day, Derbyshire 115-1 (A. S. Rollins 38*, C. J. Adams 5*); Second day, Cambridge University 104-6 (R. O. Jones 24*, D. R. H. Churton 15*).

Cambridge University

J. Ratledge c Hayhurst b DeFreitas	18	12 – lbw b DeFreitas	28
E. T. Smith c Krikken b DeFreitas	85	– b Dean	5
*A. Singh lbw b DeFreitas	9	– b Malcolm	13
W. J. House lbw b Hayhurst	8	– c Hayhurst b DeFreitas	57
R. O. Jones c Adams b Clarke	15	– not out	0
Q. J. Hughes c Adams b Clarke	4	– lbw b Dean	0
M. W. Dawson run out	23	– lbw b Dean	18
P. S. Jones lbw b Clarke	0	– (9) b Malcolm	15
†D. R. H. Churton lbw b Dean	28	– (8) c Jones b Dean	1
J. W. O. Freeth not out	7	– b Malcolm	0
E. J. How b Malcolm	0	– c Rollins b Clarke	1
L-b 2, n-b 2	4	L-b 1	

1/25 2/39 3/70 4/112 5/134	195	1/39 2/44 3/59 4/74 5/74	156
6/136 7/136 8/183 9/192		6/74 7/104 8/145 9/151	

Bowling: First Innings—Malcolm 14.4–1–59–1; DeFreitas 17–3–53–3; Dean 9–2–22–1; Hayhurst 4–1–12–1; Clarke 16–4–47–3. *Second Innings*—Malcolm 16–3–54–3; DeFreitas 8–4–21–2; Clarke 7–1–23–1; Dean 9–1–39–4; Vandrau 1–1–0–0; Hayhurst 5–1–18–0.

Derbyshire

*D. M. Jones c R. O. Jones b Freeth	58	P. A. J. DeFreitas c How b Freeth	22
A. S. Rollins run out	79	G. M. Roberts not out	30
C. J. Adams c Smith b Freeth	23	B 23, l-b 12, w 2	37
A. N. Hayhurst lbw b P. S. Jones	0		
V. P. Clarke lbw b Freeth	57	1/102 2/143 3/148 (7 wkts dec.) 363	
M. J. Vandrau c Dawson b R. O. Jones	18	4/197 5/261	
†K. M. Krikken not out	39	6/269 7/308	

K. J. Dean and D. E. Malcolm did not bat.

Bowling: P. S. Jones 27–3–76–1; How 11–1–43–0; Dawson 17–0–55–0; Freeth 22–1–101–4; House 5–1–14–0; R. O. Jones 14–3–39–1.

Umpires: M. R. Benson and R. Julian.

CAMBRIDGE UNIVERSITY v LEICESTERSHIRE

At Cambridge, April 18, 19, 20. Drawn. Toss: Cambridge University. First-class debut: D. I. Stevens.

Disappointingly, Leicestershire were interested only in practice. Their attitude was summed up at tea on the final day, when Whitaker declined to declare so that he could bat one ball afterwards to complete his hundred. It was one of four centuries in the match, and there would have been five had Sutcliffe not been bowled on 99, surprised by a leg-break from off-spinner Robin Jones. Habib, who had put on 168 with Sutcliffe, added another 173 with Dakin, and both reached three figures without trouble. But the biggest score came from Smith, who scored 190 of Cambridge's 333, hitting 27 fours in nearly seven hours, when the next-highest innings was Churton's 30. A double-century seemed certain until he surrendered his wicket in the search for quick runs. It was a gesture not reciprocated by Whitaker.

Close of play: First day, Leicestershire 430-3 (A. Habib 169*, J. M. Dakin 88*); Second day, Cambridge University 261-6 (E. T. Smith 142*, D. R. H. Churton 10*).

Leicestershire

V. J. Wells c House b P. S. Jones	27	– c and b R. O. Jones	74
I. J. Sutcliffe b R. O. Jones	99	– (4) not out	12
A. Habib not out	175		
D. I. Stevens lbw b How	27		
J. M. Dakin not out	103		
*J. J. Whitaker (did not bat)		– (2) not out	100
†P. A. Nixon (did not bat)		– (3) c House b Freeth	35
B 5, l-b 7, n-b 8	20	B 1	1

1/61 2/229 3/278   (3 wkts dec.) 451   1/142 2/196   (2 wkts dec.) 222

D. J. Millns, J. Ormond, M. T. Brimson and G. J. Parsons did not bat.

Bowling: *First Innings*—P. S. Jones 11.4-0-51-1; How 20-1-98-1; Dawson 12.2-1-64-0; Freeth 13-0-78-0; R. O. Jones 18-1-70-1; House 22-3-78-0. *Second Innings*—How 8-1-40-0; Dawson 3-0-24-0; Freeth 7-1-33-1; R. O. Jones 13.1-1-77-1; House 9-2-24-0; Hughes 4-0-23-0.

Cambridge University

J. Ratledge lbw b Brimson	23	– lbw b Brimson	12
E. T. Smith b Parsons	190		
*A. Singh c Nixon b Ormond	11	– not out	12
W. J. House lbw b Parsons	7		
R. O. Jones b Ormond	21		
Q. J. Hughes c Sutcliffe b Millns	19	– (2) not out	18
M. W. Dawson lbw b Dakin	12		
†D. R. H. Churton not out	30		
L-b 8, n-b 12	20	B 4, l-b 5	9

1/47 2/84 3/108 4/134 5/184   (7 wkts dec.) 333   1/37   (1 wkt) 51
6/246 7/333

P. S. Jones, J. W. O. Freeth and E. J. How did not bat.

Bowling: *First Innings*—Millns 13-3-55-1; Parsons 17-4-59-2; Brimson 36-12-93-1; Ormond 23-5-53-2; Dakin 10-1-39-1; Wells 8-1-26-0. *Second Innings*—Ormond 5-1-12-0; Dakin 6-4-13-0; Parsons 4-1-16-0; Brimson 3-2-1-1.

Umpires: M. R. Benson and R. Julian.

CAMBRIDGE UNIVERSITY v MIDDLESEX

At Cambridge, April 23, 24, 25. Drawn. Toss: Middlesex. First-class debuts: I. Mohammed, P. A. Schaffter; D. C. Nash.

The death of Denis Compton was marked by a minute's silence before the start of play and then by Gatting's 91st first-class century. After an uncertain start, he brought all his usual belligerence and a touch of Comptonesque insouciance to an innings of 160, hitting 23 fours and two sixes from 183 balls, before deciding at tea that sore hamstrings demanded a retirement. A maiden hundred from Wellings, who helped him add 257, was almost overlooked at the other end. Cambridge made a sturdy reply, with five batsmen getting to 30 – although none went on to 50. In his second innings, Weekes scored 101 in 113 balls, with 18 fours and a six, before falling in the last over of the second day; rain permitted only ten balls on the final day.

Close of play: First day, Cambridge University 61-2 (D. R. H. Churton 7*); Second day, Middlesex 154-2 (J. C. Pooley 28*).

Middlesex

P. N. Weekes c House b Schaffter	30	– c Jones b How 101
P. E. Wellings not out	128	
*M. W. Gatting retired hurt	160	
J. C. Pooley lbw b How	5	– (3) not out 28
†K. R. Brown not out	19	– (4) not out 1
D. C. Nash (did not bat)		– (2) c and b Freeth 21
B 4, l-b 5, w 8	17	B 5, l-b 2, w 2 9

1/49 2/314   (2 wkts dec.) 359   1/83 2/154   (2 wkts) 160

R. L. Johnson, J. P. Hewitt, K. P. Dutch, A. R. C. Fraser and P. C. R. Tufnell did not bat.

In the first innings M. W. Gatting retired hurt at 306.

Bowling: *First Innings*—How 18-5-70-1; Schaffter 20-5-58-1; House 10-0-61-0; Freeth 26-2-110-0; Jones 10-0-51-0. *Second Innings*—How 10.4-2-58-1; Schaffter 8-3-19-0; Freeth 8-0-31-1; House 3-0-20-0; Jones 7-2-25-0.

Cambridge University

J. Ratledge c Pooley b Johnson	12	J. W. O. Freeth c Hewitt b Dutch	1
E. T. Smith lbw b Tufnell	40	P. A. Schaffter c Nash b Hewitt	0
†D. R. H. Churton c Brown b Hewitt	38	E. J. How not out	0
*A. Singh c Tufnell b Weekes	30		
W. J. House c Pooley b Weekes	43	B 3, l-b 6, w 2, n-b 4	15
R. O. Jones c Pooley b Hewitt	41		
Q. J. Hughes lbw b Johnson	3	1/43 2/61 3/107 4/154 5/185	235
I. Mohammed c Tufnell b Dutch	12	6/200 7/227 8/235 9/235	

Bowling: Fraser 11-2-37-0; Johnson 17-1-89-2; Tufnell 2-1-6-1; Hewitt 13-6-38-3; Weekes 15-5-35-2; Wellings 3-0-18-0; Dutch 4.1-2-3-2.

Umpires: H. D. Bird and N. G. Cowley.

†At Cambridge, May 1. Cambridge University won by five wickets. Toss: Suffolk. Suffolk 274 for eight (50 overs) (D. W. Randall 39, S. M. Clements 36, K. M. Wijesuriya 38, I. D. Graham 36); Cambridge University 275 for five (49.1 overs) (R. O. Jones 92, Q. J. Hughes 109 not out).

†At Cambridge, May 5. Cambridge University won by 86 runs. Toss: Cambridge University. Cambridge University 298 for four (50 overs) (Q. J. Hughes 115 not out, I. Mohammed 119); Hertfordshire 212 for six (50 overs) (S. March 64, R. S. Jerome 38 not out; R. O. Jones three for 35).

CAMBRIDGE UNIVERSITY v ESSEX

At Cambridge, May 7, 8, 9. Drawn. Toss: Cambridge University. First-class debuts: G. R. Napier, D. G. Wilson.

As in their opening game, Singh elected to bat. This time he guarded against an innings defeat by making 134, with 12 fours. He put on 82 for the third wicket with Smith and, after Law took four for one in ten balls, 89 for the eighth with Steffan Jones to take his side to 285. Essex replied steadily, with most of the top order firing, but the highlight of a total of 403 was Peters's second successive century against the University. Prichard declared when Peters reached 102 in 103 balls, with 16 fours and two sixes. Resuming 118 behind, Cambridge were in grave danger at 70 for six. But opener Hughes held firm and Smith, batting at No. 8, helped to ensure the draw.

Close of play: First day, Essex 22-0 (P. J. Prichard 8*, D. D. J. Robinson 11*); Second day, Essex 222-3 (D. R. Law 39*, A. J. E. Hibbert 8*).

Cambridge University

J. Ratledge c Prichard b Such	12	– (5) c Hyam b Such	2
E. T. Smith b Law	72	– (4) not out	9
Q. J. Hughes c Hibbert b Such	8	– (1) not out	43
*A. Singh b Wilson	134	– (2) c Wilson b Napier	16
W. J. House c Hibbert b Law	5	– (2) b Wilson	1
R. O. Jones lbw b Law	0	– (3) c Hyam b Andrew	6
M. W. Dawson c Hibbert b Law	0	– b Such	0
†D. R. H. Churton lbw b Law	0		
P. S. Jones c Peters b Grayson	36	– (6) c Hyam b Napier	4
J. W. O. Freeth not out	0		
L-b 6, n-b 12	18	B 1, l-b 5, w 4	10

1/41 2/65 3/147 4/177 5/177 (9 wkts dec.) 285   1/12 2/21 3/55 (6 wkts) 91
6/177 7/179 8/268 9/285   4/60 5/65 6/70

E. J. How did not bat.

Bowling: *First Innings*—Law 19-1-93-5; Andrew 17-2-76-0; Such 28-12-41-2; Grayson 18-7-33-1; Wilson 4.3-0-36-1. *Second Innings*—Andrew 5-1-16-1; Wilson 11-2-31-1; Napier 9-3-25-2; Such 8-5-8-2; Grayson 5-3-4-0; Hibbert 1-0-1-0.

Essex

*P. J. Prichard c House b Hughes	72	†B. J. Hyam not out	19
D. D. J. Robinson c and b Hughes	59		
A. P. Grayson c House b Freeth	38	B 3, l-b 4, w 4, n-b 4	15
D. R. Law c Singh b Freeth	81		
A. J. E. Hibbert lbw b P. S. Jones	17	1/136 2/145 3/185 (5 wkts dec.) 403
S. D. Peters not out	102	4/253 5/322	

D. G. Wilson, G. R. Napier, S. J. W. Andrew and P. M. Such did not bat.

Bowling: P. S. Jones 16-3-49-1; How 13-5-25-0; Dawson 11-2-56-0; House 4-0-21-0; R. O. Jones 17-1-66-0; Freeth 27-3-101-2; Hughes 16-2-73-2; Singh 1-0-5-0.

Umpires: B. Dudleston and M. K. Reed.

†At Cambridge, May 11. Drawn. Toss: Cryptics. Cryptics 231 for three dec. (M. Williams 100 not out, P. Richardson 73); Cambridge University 17 for no wkt.

†At Cambridge, May 12. Cambridgeshire won by four wickets. Toss: Cambridge University. Cambridge University 164 for eight (50 overs) (Q. J. Hughes 36, J. Dahl 31 not out; T. S. Smith four for 20); Cambridgeshire 166 for six (46.4 overs) (T. S. Smith 38 not out).

CAMBRIDGE UNIVERSITY v NORTHAMPTONSHIRE

At Cambridge, May 14, 15, 16. Drawn. Toss: Cambridge University. First-class debut: M. R. K. Bailey.

Choosing to bat again, Cambridge prospered thanks to two century stands, the first between Smith and Robin Jones, the second between House and Hughes. That enabled Cambridge to declare on the first evening. Northamptonshire batted for most of the next two days, when showers permitted, led by their captain, Bailey, with a century containing eight fours and two sixes. When the declaration finally came, Cambridge batted out 27 overs. Smith took the opportunity to raise his batting average for the season to date to 85.83, but his team-mate Dawson completed his second pair in consecutive matches.

Close of play: First day, Northamptonshire 10-0 (D. J. Roberts 3*, R. R. Montgomerie 5*); Second day, Northamptonshire 191-3 (R. J. Bailey 88*, A. L. Penberthy 24*).

Cambridge University

J. Ratledge c Roberts b Hughes	16		
E. T. Smith run out	59	– not out	32
R. O. Jones c Fordham b Brown	60		
*A. Singh b Brown	0		
W. J. House b Brown	68	– not out	1
Q. J. Hughes c Penberthy b Snape	32	– (1) c Ripley b Hughes	6
M. W. Dawson c Fordham b Snape	0	– (3) c Montgomerie b Hughes	0
P. S. Jones lbw b Snape	10	– (4) c Ripley b Snape	20
A. N. Janisch st Ripley b Brown	3		
†M. R. K. Bailey not out	6		
B 9, l-b 8, w 2, n-b 4	23	W 2	2

1/26 2/129 3/144 4/144 5/255   (9 wkts dec.) 280   1/10 2/14 3/50   (3 wkts) 61
6/257 7/271 8/271 9/280

E. J. How did not bat.

Bowling: *First Innings*—Hughes 18–4–60–1; Innes 14–5–33–0; Penberthy 15–2–75–0; Sales 5–2–12–0; Snape 22–9–33–3; Brown 19.2–6–50–4. *Second Innings*—Hughes 6–1–15–2; Innes 6–1–16–0; Brown 6–1–18–0; Snape 6–4–10–1; Fordham 2–1–1–0; Montgomerie 1–0–1–0.

Northamptonshire

D. J. Roberts c Bailey b How	18	†D. Ripley b Janisch	44
R. R. Montgomerie c sub b Janisch	28	K. J. Innes not out	8
*R. J. Bailey st Bailey b R. O. Jones	105	B 6, l-b 14, w 6, n-b 8	34
D. J. Sales c and b R. O. Jones	10		
A. L. Penberthy c P. S. Jones b How	56	1/47 2/65 3/113 (8 wkts dec.) 367
A. Fordham c House b Hughes	44	4/227 5/266 6/299
J. N. Snape c Smith b R. O. Jones	20	7/338 8/367

J. G. Hughes and J. F. Brown did not bat.

Bowling: P. S. Jones 15–1–48–0; How 22–5–59–2; Dawson 16–3–41–0; Janisch 14.5–2–43–2; R. O. Jones 32–5–116–3; Hughes 6–3–18–1; House 6–1–17–0; Singh 2–1–5–0.

Umpires: M. J. Kitchen and N. A. Mallender.

†At Cambridge, May 17. Cambridge University won by 73 runs. Toss: Cambridge University. Cambridge University 297 for six (50 overs) (J. Ratledge 79, E. T. Smith 86, A. Singh 57); Oxford University 224 (48 overs) (R. D. Hudson 79, C. G. R. Lightfoot 58; R. O. Jones four for 57).

Cambridge took a 2-1 lead in the Johnson Fry limited-overs Varsity series.

†At Cambridge, May 18. Drawn. Toss: Cambridge University. Cambridge University 284 for four dec. (G. J. McCartney 58, R. O. Jones 135, I. Mohammed 42 not out); Free Foresters 282 for nine (G. W. Jones 61, C. J. Hollins 132; E. J. How three for 83, R. O. Jones four for 57).

†At Cambridge, June 8. Drawn. Toss: Quidnuncs. Cambridge University 163 for one (E. T. Smith 72 not out, Q. J. Hughes 54 not out) v Quidnuncs.

†At Arundel, June 10. Earl of Arundel's XI won by eight wickets. Toss: Cambridge University. Cambridge University 211 for five dec. (J. Ratledge 34, R. O. Jones 94, Q. J. Hughes 37 not out); Earl of Arundel's XI 213 for two (P. Carroll 38, T. J. G. O'Gorman 100 not out, G. W. Jones 58 not out).

†At Cambridge, June 11, 12, 13. MCC won by two wickets. Toss: Cambridge University. Cambridge University 145 for five dec. (E. T. Smith 67; A. J. Mackay three for 45) and 140 for six dec. (Q. J. Hughes 45 not out; G. A. Harris three for 37); MCC forfeited first innings and 288 for eight (R. J. Greatorex 86, D. Tallala 35, K. G. Sedgbeer 31, J. S. Brooks 31 not out; A. N. Janisch three for 55).

CAMBRIDGE UNIVERSITY v DURHAM

At Cambridge, June 14, 15, 16. Drawn. Toss: Cambridge University. First-class debut: A. Pratt.
  The short Fenner's season closed with Cambridge's first first-class encounter with Durham. Boon, the captain, and Speak, their new recruit from Lancashire, made maiden centuries for the county. Boon scored 105 in 174 balls, with 14 fours, and Speak 124 in 176; but he hit only seven fours and never looked totally convincing as he batted for four and a half hours. They added 203 together before declaring overnight. Batsmen stayed on top when Cambridge responded with an opening partnership of 132. Smith moved confidently towards a century, only to fall one short. Singh declared at once, but Durham's second innings had barely begun when rain ended the match.
  Close of play: First day, Durham 288-2 (N. J. Speak 124*, D. C. Boon 105*); Second day, Durham 9-0 (P. D. Collingwood 5*, M. A. Roseberry 2*).

Durham

P. D. Collingwood b P. S. Jones	32	– not out	8
M. A. Roseberry b P. S. Jones	6	– not out	22
N. J. Speak not out	124		
*D. C. Boon not out	105		
B 4, l-b 1, w 16	21	L-b 2	2

1/9 2/85   (2 wkts dec.) 288   (no wkt) 32

J. A. Daley, †A. Pratt, M. M. Betts, J. Boiling, D. M. Cox, J. Wood and M. J. Saggers did not bat.

  Bowling: *First Innings*—P. S. Jones 22–6–70–2; How 21–3–71–0; Janisch 16–0–46–0; Freeth 10–0–60–0; R. O. Jones 12–3–27–0; Hughes 6–1–9–0. *Second Innings*—How 7–4–10–0; Janisch 7–2–20–0.

Cambridge University

J. Ratledge lbw b Boiling	40
E. T. Smith c Daley b Cox	99
R. O. Jones not out	33
L-b 10, n-b 6	16

1/132 2/188   (2 wkts dec.) 188

Q. J. Hughes, W. J. House, *A. Singh, †D. R. H. Churton, P. S. Jones, A. N. Janisch, J. W. O. Freeth and E. J. How did not bat.

  Bowling: Betts 14–2–52–0; Wood 10–1–65–0; Saggers 6–2–17–0; Boiling 24–11–27–1; Cox 6–1–17–1.

Umpires: K. J. Lyons and B. J. Meyer.

†At Portsmouth, June 18, 19. Drawn. Toss: Cambridge University. Cambridge University 232 for five dec. (J. C. Hammill 65, T. P. Howland 61, Q. J. Hughes 36, Extras 30) and 134 for four (K. Jayarajasingham 36, Q. J. Hughes 61 not out); Combined Services 194 for one dec. (SAC M. Bray 103 not out, Sgt G. S. Lumb 60).

†At Cambridge, June 24. Queensland University won by eight wickets. Toss: Queensland University. Cambridge University 94 (39.4 overs) (I. Mohammed 32; T. Stallman three for 25); Queensland University 98 for two (25.1 overs) (P. Mackintosh 44 not out, D. Fleming 44 not out).

†At Cambridge, June 26. Cambridge University v Sydney University. Abandoned.

At Canterbury, June 28, 29, 30. CAMBRIDGE UNIVERSITY drew with KENT.

THE UNIVERSITY MATCH, 1997

OXFORD UNIVERSITY v CAMBRIDGE UNIVERSITY

At Lord's, July 2, 3, 4. Drawn. Toss: Cambridge University.

Oxford's ninth-wicket pair defied favourites Cambridge to earn a draw and prompt questions about whether sentiment had caused Singh to delay his declaration too long. He had chosen to bat on for 15 balls after lunch, allowing Ratledge to reach his maiden hundred – and leaving only 59 overs to dismiss Oxford again. They made a determined attempt on a target of 326, and reached 172 with only two down. But wickets fell regularly after that and the tail had to bat out time. Cambridge had taken the initiative from the start. Although their star batsman, Smith, went cheaply, on a pitch still damp after the previous week's torrential rain, Singh himself put on 138 with Robin Jones. Then, after they had gone, House hit 14 fours and a couple of sixes as he and Churton added another 124. Patel took six wickets for the first time, and next day his opposite number, Steffan Jones, did the same. Oxford's reply leaned heavily on a stand of 103 between their captain, Wagh, and Fulton. But the lower order for once failed to back them up. Jones finished off the innings to give Cambridge a lead of 86; after that, it was up to their batsmen to set up the fourth-innings chase. Both Varsity captains in this match, Wagh and Singh, came from the same school, King Edward's, Birmingham, the third such double. Harrow supplied Kenneth Carlisle and Eric Mann in 1905 and Manchester Grammar School provided Mark Crawley and Mike Atherton in 1989.

Close of play: First day, Oxford University 30-1 (B. W. Byrne 10*, A. P. Scrini 3*); Second day, Cambridge University 74-1 (J. Ratledge 30*, A. Singh 43*).

Cambridge University

J. Ratledge (*Bolton and St John's*) lbw b Battarbee	19 – not out	100
E. T. Smith (*Tonbridge and Peterhouse*) c Morgan b Patel	14 – b Patel	1
*A. Singh (*King Edward's, Birmingham, and Gonville & Caius*) c Battarbee b Patel	91 – c Scrini b Battarbee	43
R. O. Jones (*Millfield, Durham U. and Homerton*) c and b Patel	58 – c Fulton b Battarbee	26
W. J. House (*Sevenoaks and Gonville & Caius*) lbw b Patel	94 – c Scrini b Patel	11
Q. J. Hughes (*Durham Johnston and St Edmund's*) lbw b Patel	4 – not out	47
†D. R. H. Churton (*Wellington C. and St Catharine's*) c Hudson b Battarbee	44	
P. S. Jones (*Ysgol Gyfun Y Sterade, Loughborough U. and Homerton*) not out	5	
A. N. Janisch (*Abingdon and Trinity*) c Morgan b Patel	4	
B 2, l-b 11, w 8, n-b 4	25	L-b 11 ... 11

1/30 2/48 3/186 4/217 5/223   (8 wkts dec.) 358   1/16 2/74   (4 wkts dec.) 239
6/347 7/349 8/358   3/110 4/125

J. W. O. Freeth (*Sherborne and Pembroke*) and E. J. How (*Dr Challoner's GS and Hughes Hall*) did not bat.

Bowling: First Innings—Averis 18–1–88–0; Patel 23–3–110–6; Battarbee 16–4–56–2; Wagh 21–3–69–0; Hudson 2–0–22–0. *Second Innings*—Averis 17.3–4–73–0; Patel 14–4–63–2; Battarbee 12–0–56–2; Wagh 6–0–36–0.

Oxford University

C. G. R. Lightfoot (*Eton and Keble*)
c Churton b How . 8 – c Churton b How 61

B. W. Byrne (*Esperance, Perth, Western Australia U. and Balliol*) lbw b P. S. Jones 14 – b P. S. Jones 21

†A. P. Scrini (*Worksop C. and Hertford*) run out .. 14 – (10) not out 8

*M. A. Wagh (*King Edward's, Birmingham, and Keble*) b P. S. Jones 82 – (3) b Janisch 47

P. G. Morgan (*Hilton C., South Africa, Eton, Cape Town U. and Keble*) c House b Janisch 18 – (4) b Janisch 22

J. A. G. Fulton (*Eton and Brasenose*)
st Churton b R. O. Jones . 78 – (5) b P. S. Jones 15

R. D. Hudson (*Colmer's Farm and Keble*)
c Churton b P. S. Jones . 6 – (8) lbw b P. S. Jones 0

C. Patel (*Fortismere, Loughborough U. and Keble*)
lbw b P. S. Jones . 8 – (6) b Janisch 8

J. M. M. Averis (*Bristol Cathedral S., Portsmouth U. and St Cross*) c Churton b P. S. Jones . 5 – (7) c House b Janisch 23

L. G. Buchanan (*Latymer Upper and Keble*)
b P. S. Jones . 7 – (9) not out 6

C. M. Battarbee (*Colfe's S. and Keble*) not out 3
B 9, l-b 4, w 14, n-b 2 29   B 8, l-b 8, w 12, n-b 10 ... 38

1/25 2/37 3/54 4/87 5/190	272	1/81 2/121 3/172 (8 wkts) 249
6/221 7/252 8/253 9/261		4/189 5/197 6/205
		7/229 8/229

Bowling: *First Innings*—P. S. Jones 28.4–10–67–6; How 25–6–74–1; Janisch 9–0–59–1; Freeth 11–2–30–0; House 1–0–2–0; R. O. Jones 8–0–27–1. *Second Innings*—P. S. Jones 21–7–81–3; How 10–2–42–1; Janisch 15–1–71–4; Freeth 8–1–16–0; R. O. Jones 5–0–23–0.

Umpires: B. Leadbeater and D. R. Shepherd.

OXFORD v CAMBRIDGE, NOTES

The University Match dates back to 1827. Altogether there have been 152 official matches, Cambridge winning 55 and Oxford 48, with 49 drawn. Since the war Cambridge have won nine times (1949, 1953, 1957, 1958, 1972, 1979, 1982, 1986 and 1992) and Oxford nine (1946, 1948, 1951, 1959, 1966, 1976, 1984, 1993 and 1995). All other matches have been drawn; the 1988 fixture was abandoned without a ball being bowled.

One hundred and three three-figure innings have been played in the University matches, 55 for Oxford and 48 for Cambridge. For the fullest lists see the 1940 and 1993 *Wisdens*. There have been three double-centuries for Cambridge (211 by G. Goonesena in 1957, 201 by A. Ratcliffe in 1931 and 200 by Majid Khan in 1970) and two for Oxford (238* by Nawab of Pataudi, sen. in 1931 and 201* by M. J. K. Smith in 1954). Ratcliffe's score was a record for the match for only one day, before being beaten by Pataudi's. M. J. K. Smith and R. J. Boyd-Moss (Cambridge) are the only players to score three hundreds.

The highest totals in the fixture are 513 for six in 1996, 503 in 1900, 457 in 1947, 453 for eight in 1931 and 453 for nine in 1994, all by Oxford. Cambridge's highest is 432 for nine in 1936. The lowest totals are 32 by Oxford in 1878 and 39 by Cambridge in 1858.

F. C. Cobden, in the Oxford v Cambridge match in 1870, performed the hat-trick by taking the last three wickets and won an extraordinary game for Cambridge by two runs. Other hat-tricks, all for Cambridge, have been achieved by A. G. Steel (1879), P. H. Morton (1880), J. F. Ireland (1911) and R. G. H. Lowe (1926). S. E. Butler, in the 1871 match, took all ten wickets in the Cambridge first innings.

D. W. Jarrett (Oxford 1975, Cambridge 1976), S. M. Wookey (Cambridge 1975-76, Oxford 1978) and G. Pathmanathan (Oxford 1975-78, Cambridge 1983) gained Blues for both Universities.

A full list of Blues from 1837 may be found in Wisdens *published between 1923 and 1939. The lists thereafter were curtailed: Wisdens from 1948 to 1972 list Blues since 1880; from 1973 to 1983 since 1919; from 1984 to 1992 since 1946.*

THE HALIFAX BUSA CHAMPIONSHIP, 1997

By GRENVILLE HOLLAND

The universities participated in a new type of competition in 1997 – a two-tier affair designed by the British Universities Sports Association (BUSA) – but the result was familiar enough: Durham beat their chief rivals Loughborough in the final to win their eighth title in 12 years. The championship was contested by the 24 leading universities, divided into four regional leagues of six teams each, while other institutions played for the Halifax Shield in a separate competition.

There were few complaints about the new structure. The leading contenders were involved in a genuine competition, and those that did not make the grade – including Oxford, who fielded their second team – were relegated. There were teething problems, however: BUSA introduced a ''no replay'' rule in an attempt to streamline the competition, and many teams fell foul of endless rain in the early stages of the summer. Edinburgh, the Scottish champions of 1996, completed only one game out of five and found themselves in the relegation zone. Their appeal was accepted by BUSA, who granted them the escape route of a play-off against Glasgow in the spring.

Predictably, the northern league was the worst affected, with seven of the 15 scheduled matches failing to reach a conclusion. Durham were the major beneficiaries, as their well-protected wicket at the Racecourse Ground produced three results out of three. But defeat by Newcastle in the first of these fixtures meant that Durham needed to finish with three consecutive wins. They managed it, thanks to the reliable Tim Hodgson, who hit 39 not out and 42 not out in two low-scoring matches against Northumbria and Edinburgh respectively. Manchester, whose game with Durham was rained off, finished second in the group with two wins and three no-results.

There was little resistance to Loughborough in the Midlands group. They won all three of their completed games, and Chester squeaked in on run-rate after suffering three washouts. The recently created club at UWIC (University of Wales Institute, Cardiff) qualified from the west, alongside Exeter, and both teams ran up scores in excess of 240 against Oxford, whose attack was clearly inadequate.

In the south, Matthew Barham's left-arm spin was a feature in an outstanding season for Southampton, a side that had only just made it into the main competition. Barham took 18 wickets in the three games he was able to play, including five for 22 against Reading, who were bowled out for 38. London were disposed of almost as quickly, slumping to 43 all out. Southampton's final game was to be played at Cambridge but, despite a wealth of college pitches in the city, no ground could be made available. Southampton took the points by default and, after receiving compensation for their travel costs, proceeded to the quarter-finals in the company of runners-up Brighton.

The eight teams who were relegated were Bristol, Kent, Liverpool, Nottingham Trent, Oxford, Reading, Warwick and, provisionally, Edinburgh. When those are compared with the list of quarter-finalists, it is clear that tradition counts for little in the new competition. Several other unfamiliar names won promotion from the Halifax Shield, and will participate in the main tournament in 1998; the full list reads Birmingham, Brunel, Nottingham,

Sheffield, Southampton Institute, Sussex, Worcester and – if they can beat Edinburgh in their play-off – Glasgow.

The best of the quarter-finals featured a heroic performance from Chester's Alex Barr, who hit 69 out of their total of 234, and then took six for 90 as UWIC were restricted to 230 for nine. Elsewhere, Loughborough raced to 345 for three against Exeter (258 for nine) thanks to 78 from Toby Bailey and an unbeaten 102 from Andrew Bourke. Durham and Southampton won their games easily.

Barham was back to his best in Southampton's semi-final against Durham; he took all six wickets to fall for 39 runs, and accounted for Hodgson's only dismissal in the competition. But his batsmen had already let him down with a total of just 102. Only the captain, Sam Moss, showed any patience, and Durham won with time to spare. In the other semi-final, at The Parks in Oxford, Loughborough successfully defended a total of 210 against Chester; spinner Mike Davies collected seven for 54. The heavyweights of university cricket squared up for another duel.

Away from the playing fields, Lord MacLaurin's report, "Raising the Standard", recommended that centres of excellence should be established at several universities. Durham already has one, run by former England batsman Graeme Fowler, but although it has helped to reinforce Durham's status as a prime destination for keen cricketing students, it required £135,000 of funding. Such a scheme would have to be grafted on to institutions which are mostly already struggling financially to provide adequate facilities for their students and where admission policies could not necessarily be guaranteed to provide a steady stream of sporting talent. Frank Kemp, the ECB operations manager for the non-first-class game, said it was important that such initiatives should not exclude the vast majority of the population, and added that several universities were interested in the concept. "They must decide whether they can balance their academic and sporting requirements. We are still early in the discussion process."

SEMI-FINALS

At Abbeydale Park, Sheffield, June 9. Durham won by four wickets. Toss: Durham. Southampton 102; Durham 103 for six (M. J. Chilton 30; M. Barham six for 39).

At The Parks, Oxford, June 9. Loughborough won by 45 runs. Toss: Loughborough. Loughborough 210 (N. A. Bourke 92); Chester 165 (J. Gillson 58; M. K. Davies seven for 54).

FINAL

DURHAM v LOUGHBOROUGH

At Wardown Park, Luton, June 16. Durham won by eight wickets. Toss: Durham.

Once Luke Sutton had won the toss and asked Loughborough to bat on a damp wicket, Durham were always in command. The seamers bowled with pinpoint accuracy; Robin Martin-Jenkins conceded only ten runs from his 11 overs, while the outstanding medium-pacer Mark Chilton took two for 22 from 14. Despite an early contribution of 45 from Peter Davies, Loughborough were all out for 119. Conditions eased in the afternoon and Tim Hodgson, who made his Essex debut in 1996, was in a class of his own. His unbeaten 70 left him with a championship average of 255.

Loughborough

D. A. Ellis c Ford b Chilton 23	R. R. Dibden run out 0
N. P. Harvey b Lawrence 3	M. K. Davies lbw b Armstrong 0
P. G. T. Davies lbw b Armstrong 45	N. A. S. Smith not out 0
N. A. Bourke c Sutton b Hutton 3	B 6, l-b 1, n-b 11 18
C. D. J. Bailey c Sutton b Lawrence 0	
†T. M. B. Bailey c Ford b Chilton 4	1/9 2/38 3/53 (51 overs) 119
*M. R. Evans run out 11	4/54 5/74 6/107
A. D. Edwards c Hutton b Armstrong ... 12	7/107 8/112 9/119

Bowling: Martin-Jenkins 11–4–10–0; Lawrence 11–1–46–2; Chilton 14–2–22–2; Hutton 8–1–16–1; Armstrong 7–1–18–3.

Durham

*†L. D. Sutton b Smith 5	J. A. Ford not out 12
T. P. Hodgson not out 70	B 4, l-b 1 5
M. J. Chilton c T. M. B. Bailey	
b M. K. Davies . 30	1/13 2/80 (2 wkts, 31.1 overs) 122

A. J. Strauss, B. A. Hames, R. S. C. Martin-Jenkins, B. L. Hutton, J. D. Chaplin, J. R. G. Lawrence and N. J. Armstrong did not bat.

Bowling: Edwards 6–0–21–0; Smith 7.1–1–19–1; M. K. Davies 8–2–31–1; Evans 3–0–15–0; Dibden 4–1–13–0; Bourke 3–0–18–0.

Umpires: K. Hopley and D. J. A. Edwards.

WINNERS 1927-97

The UAU Championship was replaced by the BUSA Championship after 1994.

1927	Manchester	1956	Null and void	1977	Durham
1928	Manchester	1957	Loughborough Colls.	1978	Manchester
1929	Nottingham	1958	Null and void	1979	Manchester
1930	Sheffield	1959	Liverpool	1980	Exeter
1931	Liverpool	1960	Loughborough Colls.	1981	Durham
1932	Manchester	1961	Loughborough Colls.	1982	Exeter
1933	Manchester	1962	Manchester	1983	Exeter
1934	Leeds	1963	Loughborough Colls.	1984	Bristol
1935	Sheffield	1964	Loughborough Colls.	1985	Birmingham
1936	Sheffield	1965	Hull	1986	Durham
1937	Nottingham	1966 {	Newcastle	1987	Durham
1938	Durham		Southampton	1988	Swansea
1939	Durham	1967	Manchester	1989	Loughborough
1946	Not completed	1968	Southampton	1990	Durham
1947	Sheffield	1969	Southampton	1991	Durham
1948	Leeds	1970	Southampton	1992	Durham
1949	Leeds	1971	Loughborough Colls.	1993	Durham
1950	Manchester	1972	Durham	1994	Swansea
1951	Manchester	1973 {	Leicester	1995	Durham
1952	Loughborough Colls.		Loughborough Colls.	1996	Loughborough
1953	Durham	1974	Durham	1997	Durham
1954	Manchester	1975	Loughborough Colls.		
1955	Birmingham	1976	Loughborough		

OTHER FIRST-CLASS MATCHES, 1997

ENGLAND A v THE REST

At Birmingham, April 18, 19, 20, 21. Drawn. Toss: The Rest.

Bad light – perhaps not quite as bad as the umpires believed – interrupted the match on all four days and cut short The Rest's pursuit of 277 in 52 overs after just nine balls. Ramprakash asked England A to bat under overcast skies, and their openers kept warm by running up 237. Gallian fell just before tea, but Butcher continued into the next day, batting six hours in all for 153 runs. His team-mates advanced relentlessly onwards; among the bowlers only Tudor made much impression before Adam Hollioake finally chose to leave the crease with 453 on the board. The Rest lost Laney without a run scored, but most of their batsmen contributed, and Ramprakash shared century stands with Warren and Ben Hollioake. He declared 103 behind, and Brown removed England A's top three on the third evening. On the final day, Ben Hollioake took the eye again with three quick wickets, including his brother Adam, caught behind off his glove. But the weather defeated attempts to set up a result.

Close of play: First day, England A 272-2 (M. A. Butcher 129*, A. McGrath 1*); Second day, The Rest 73-2 (D. L. Maddy 24*, C. E. W. Silverwood 1*); Third day, England A 41-3 (A. McGrath 21*, A. J. Hollioake 4*).

England A

M. A. Butcher c Adams b Cosker	153	– lbw b Brown	2
J. E. R. Gallian c Hollioake b Silverwood	106	– c Warren b Brown	6
M. P. Vaughan b Tudor	10	– b Brown	1
A. McGrath c Solanki b Hollioake	46	– b Hollioake	62
*A. J. Hollioake not out	70	– c Warren b Hollioake	39
M. A. Ealham not out	24	– c Ramprakash b Hollioake	2
†W. K. Hegg (did not bat)		– c Maddy b Solanki	1
G. Chapple (did not bat)		– not out	23
D. W. Headley (did not bat)		– c Hollioake b Brown	23
B 7, l-b 20, w 2, n-b 15	44	B 2, l-b 6, w 4, n-b 2	14

1/237 2/271 3/323 4/383	(4 wkts dec.)	453

1/5 2/7 3/32	(8 wkts dec.)	173
4/109 5/122 6/123		
7/123 8/173		

P. M. Such and A. J. Harris did not bat.

Bowling: *First Innings*—Silverwood 25.1–5–100–1; Brown 24–6–70–0; Tudor 27–8–59–1; Hollioake 21–4–83–1; Solanki 12–3–38–0; Cosker 32–8–76–1. *Second Innings*—Silverwood 13–1–38–0; Brown 15.5–3–50–4; Tudor 6–2–22–0; Hollioake 9–2–22–3; Solanki 12–5–33–1.

The Rest

D. L. Maddy c Butcher b Headley	38	– not out	5
J. S. Laney c Hegg b Chapple	0	– not out	4
C. J. Adams c Gallian b Chapple	35		
C. E. W. Silverwood b Headley	44		
*M. R. Ramprakash not out	108		
†R. J. Warren c Hollioake b Gallian	50		
V. S. Solanki c McGrath b Headley	5		
B. C. Hollioake not out	46		
L-b 18, w 6	24		

1/0 2/71 3/121 4/138	(6 wkts dec.)	350
5/238 6/250		

(no wkt)	9

D. A. Cosker, A. J. Tudor and S. J. E. Brown did not bat.

Bowling: *First Innings*—Headley 26–9–63–3; Chapple 20–6–83–2; Harris 13–4–44–0; Such 15–1–57–0; Ealham 13–3–37–0; Hollioake 5–2–15–0; Gallian 4–0–18–1; McGrath 4–0–15–0. *Second Innings*—Headley 1–0–8–0; Chapple 0.3–0–1–0.

Umpires: H. D. Bird and R. Palmer.

IRELAND v SCOTLAND

At Malahide, Dublin, August 9, 10, 11. Drawn. Toss: Scotland. First-class debuts: J. E. Byrne, J. O. Davy, E. C. Joyce; N. Dyer, I. M. Stanger, C. M. Wright.

Scotland had victory in their sights when they needed only 83 from 15 overs, with Bruce Patterson and Salmond going strong. They had put on 144 together when Patterson was bowled and the innings began to crumble. Salmond was sixth out, going for a second run off a misfield, and eventually the last pair had to see out 15 balls to secure the draw. Rain delayed play until 2.30 p.m. on the opening day, when Scotland put Ireland in and reduced them to 165 for seven. After mist held up the second morning for 40 minutes, Wright added two more quick wickets. But Davy and McCrum put on 100 in 33 overs, an Irish tenth-wicket record, batting on into the afternoon. Scotland's batsmen stepped up the pace and then declared, and Ireland responded in kind to set a target of 274 in 61 overs.

Close of play: First day, Ireland 165-7 (A. T. Rutherford 17*, G. L. Molins 1*); Second day, Ireland 14-1 (W. K. McCallan 7*, J. O. Davy 1*).

Ireland

J. D. Curry c Salmond b Wright	3	– c Patterson b Thomson	6
W. K. McCallan b Dyer	65	– c Sheridan b Stanger	47
E. C. Joyce c Davies b Williamson	13	– (4) c Salmond b Williamson	43
A. D. Patterson b Sheridan	31	– (5) c Allingham b Dyer	12
*J. D. R. Benson b Sheridan	0	– (6) not out	61
J. E. Byrne c Dyer b Sheridan	7	– (7) not out	12
G. Cooke c Lockhart b Sheridan	0		
†A. T. Rutherford c Davies b Wright	19		
G. L. Molins c Sheridan b Wright	1		
J. O. Davy not out	51	– (3) b Thomson	2
P. McCrum not out	44		
B 3, l-b 9, w 4, n-b 20	36	L-b 2, w 3, n-b 4	9

1/7 2/61 3/117 4/117 5/129   (9 wkts dec.) 270   1/6 2/19 3/78   (5 wkts dec.) 192
6/129 7/163 8/165 9/170   4/94 5/158

Bowling: *First Innings*—Thomson 24–8–52–0; Wright 25.2–8–66–3; Stanger 3–0–23–0; Williamson 9–0–44–1; Dyer 16.4–4–30–1; Sheridan 30–12–43–4. *Second Innings*—Thomson 10–2–41–2; Wright 6–1–23–0; Sheridan 8–4–16–0; Williamson 12–3–40–1; Stanger 10–2–38–1; Dyer 5–0–29–1; Allingham 1–0–3–0.

Scotland

B. M. W. Patterson c Rutherford b McCrum	32	– b Benson	83
D. R. Lockhart not out	77	– c Joyce b Cooke	19
M. J. D. Allingham c Benson b Cooke	13	– run out	0
*G. Salmond b Benson	46	– run out	89
J. G. Williamson (did not bat)		– c Cooke b Benson	5
I. M. Stanger (did not bat)		– run out	8
†A. G. Davies (did not bat)		– c Patterson b Molins	10
C. M. Wright (did not bat)		– lbw b McCallan	0
K. L. P. Sheridan (did not bat)		– c McCallan b Molins	0
K. Thomson (did not bat)		– not out	9
N. Dyer (did not bat)		– not out	0
B 2, l-b 2, w 3, n-b 14	21	B 3, l-b 7, w 2, n-b 12	24

1/46 2/88 3/189   (3 wkts dec.) 189   1/44 2/47 3/191   (9 wkts) 247
                                            4/197 5/221 6/233
                                            7/233 8/236 9/247

Bowling: *First Innings*—McCrum 10–1–27–1; Davy 8–0–52–0; Cooke 8–1–31–1; McCallan 15–1–49–0; Benson 4.1–2–6–1; Joyce 2–0–20–0. *Second Innings*—McCrum 14–1–61–0; Davy 11–2–41–0; Cooke 9–4–32–1; Molins 17–2–55–2; Benson 5–0–38–2; McCallan 5–1–10–1.

Umpires: E. Cooke and P. L. O'Hara.

MCC MATCHES IN 1997

MCC's ever-expanding fixture list, which features games against school, club and representative teams, grew in 1997 to 396 – 375 matches within the British Isles and 21 on three tours abroad. This is believed to be a club record but, with tours planned to India, Austria, the Bahamas, East and Central Africa, Corfu, Italy and Japan, the 400 mark looks certain to be passed in 1998.

Not that all the matches scheduled in 1997 were played, or played to a conclusion. The dismal weather of May and June saw to that, and never more so than on June 25, when 19 of the club's 20 fixtures for the day were abandoned. The one game played to a finish was at Christ College, Brecon. From Co. Londonderry across to Co. Durham and all the way south and west to Dorset, rain otherwise dictated the day.

Among the 55 games abandoned in June was the meeting at Lord's of the two MCCs – Marylebone and Melbourne – and in all 96 games were abandoned in 1997. Of the remaining domestic fixtures, 131 were won, 83 were drawn and 61 lost. Four fixtures were cancelled. The weather was friendlier to MCC's cricketers on their tours to Fiji and Hong Kong in February and March (played 10, won 10), Germany in August (played 5, won 5) and Corfu in September (played 6, won 6).

Noteworthy performances for the club in 1997 included the unbeaten double-hundred by the West Indian Test batsman, Keith Arthurton, against Pakistan A at Shenley Park, and a hat-trick against Ireland at Lord's by the former Essex and England fast bowler, Neil Foster. Shenley again proved to be a popular setting for MCC's one first-class fixture and, with the need to relay more of the pitches at Lord's, Hertfordshire has provided MCC with a most attractive alternative. In addition to its first-class ground, which is named after Denis Compton, Shenley also boasts a nursery ground and generous net facilities. MCC Young Cricketers played most of their home games there in 1996 and 1997, and their traditional match against MCC was played there in 1997. – GRAEME WRIGHT.

Note: With the exception of the game against Pakistan A, matches in this section were not first-class.

At Shenley Park, May 1. MCC won by two wickets. MCC Young Cricketers batted first by agreement. MCC Young Cricketers 232 for seven dec. (N. J. Thurgood 38, R. Scragg 31, P. R. Shaw 47, O. Dawkins 35); MCC 233 for eight (C. J. Rogers 74, K. G. Sedgebeer 59 not out; B. S. Phelps four for 61).

At Lord's, May 4, 5. Drawn. Toss: Wales. MCC 240 for six dec. (D. M. Ward 53, T. Patel 36, R. M. Wight 69 not out; A. J. L. Barr three for 65) and 167 for seven dec. (K. C. Williams 30, R. J. Parks 52 not out; B. M. Morgan three for 55, A. D. Towse three for 25); Wales 154 for six dec. (T. J. Hemp 52 not out, P. D. North 33) and 243 for three (T. J. Hemp 81, M. J. Newbold 112).

At Southgate, May 20. Club Cricket Conference won by five wickets. Toss: MCC. MCC 193 for eight (C. M. Gupte 36, K. M. Wijesuriya 67; G. J. J. Sheen four for 70); Club Cricket Conference 196 for five (G. Martin 85 not out).

At Wolverhampton, May 21. Midlands Club Cricket Conference v MCC. Abandoned.

At Oxford, May 26, 27, 28. MCC lost to OXFORD UNIVERSITY by 47 runs (See The Universities section).

At Finchampstead, June 4. Drawn. Toss: National Association of Young Cricketers. MCC 263 for five (J. L. P. Meadows 82, N. J. C. Gandon 43, P. A. Cottey 78); National Association of Young Cricketers 249 for eight (C. P. R. Hodgson 40, I. C. Parkin 54, T. W. Hancock 42, Extras 35; P. A. Cottey three for 79).

At Cambridge, June 11, 12, 13. MCC beat CAMBRIDGE UNIVERSITY by two wickets (See The Universities section).

At Arundel, June 15. MCC won by seven wickets. Toss: Earl of Arundel's XI. Earl of Arundel's XI 234 for five dec. (R. M. Wight 45, T. J. G. O'Gorman 134 not out); MCC 235 for three (P. W. Romaines 32, P. W. G. Parker 106 not out, M. A. Crawley 52 not out).

At Durham, June 18, 19, 20. Drawn. Toss: MCC. MCC 377 for seven dec. (K. L. T. Arthurton 110, D. A. Banks 152 not out, A. R. Whittall 36; J. D. Chaplin five for 55) and 96 for three (M. P. W. Jeh 33 not out, K. C. Williams 36); Durham University 153 (A. J. Strauss 53, B. L. Hutton 38; N. B. Francis four for 20, A. R. Whittall four for 36).

At Lord's, June 26. MCC v Melbourne CC. Abandoned.

At Shenley Park, July 9, 10, 11. MCC beat PAKISTAN A by ten wickets (See Pakistan A tour section).

At Lord's, July 15. MCC Schools won by five wickets. Toss: MCC Schools. MCC 214 for six dec. (A. G. Lawson 95); MCC Schools 215 for five (A. J. Marsh 35, L. M. Hilton 60 not out).

At Aldershot, July 15. Combined Services won by one wicket. Toss: Combined Services. MCC 230 for eight dec. (M. D. Dale 105, D. C. Briance 40; POMEA D. Garbutt five for 49, Mne A. Proctor three for 105); Combined Services 231 for nine (SAC M. Bray 39, Lt Cdr P. H. G. Moore 75).

At Shenley Park, July 18. MCC won by 47 runs. Toss: MCC. MCC 131; Sydney University 84 (R. A. Flack three for 22, A. D. James four for 18).

At Wormsley, July 20. Drawn. Toss: J. Paul Getty's XI. MCC 271 for four dec. (G. W. Flower 145 not out, A. G. Lawson 32, D. M. Ward 80); J. Paul Getty's XI 258 for seven (C. M. Gupte 30, C. J. C. Rowe 46, M. A. Crawley 63, M. E. D. Jarrett 41, M. P. W. Jeh 31 not out).

At Hamilton Crescent, Glasgow, August 20, 21, 22. Drawn. Toss: MCC. MCC 323 for eight dec. (A. D. Hobson 59, A. P. Tarrant 47, N. A. Folland 107, K. C. Williams 56; K. Thomson three for 42) and 198 for four dec. (A. G. Lawson 73 not out, D. M. Ward 77, A. P. Tarrant 30); Scotland 179 (D. R. Lockhart 36, R. A. Parsons 40, K. Thomson 37; H. A. G. Anthony three for 15, M. C. J. Ball three for 71) and 310 for eight (I. L. Philip 134, I. M. Stanger 54; B. S. Phelps three for 45).

At Lord's, August 21, 22. MCC won by 61 runs. Toss: MCC. MCC 230 for six dec. (G. V. Palmer 58, J. Foster 57 not out, J. D. Ricketts 53 not out; W. K. McCallan three for 37) and 237 for four dec. (G. D. Hodgson 98, A. R. Whittall 60, C. M. Taylor 50); Ireland 185 for six dec. (E. C. Joyce 53, P. J. Davy 34) and 221 (J. A. M. Molins 51, W. K. McCallan 54, J. D. R. Benson 50; N. A. Foster three for 24, including a hat-trick, S. G. Kenlock four for 64).

OTHER MATCHES, 1997

Note: Matches in this section were not first-class.

HARROGATE FESTIVAL

Costcutter Cup

A 55-over competition contested by Yorkshire and three other invited teams.

At Harrogate, June 9. Gloucestershire won by five wickets. Toss: Yorkshire. Yorkshire 305 for four (55 overs) (D. Byas 82, C. White 72, R. A. Kettleborough 47 not out, D. S. Lehmann 63 not out); Gloucestershire 308 for five (52 overs) (N. J. Trainor 113, R. J. Cunliffe 32, M. A. Lynch 61, R. I. Dawson 49 not out; C. E. W. Silverwood three for 60).

Gloucestershire beat Yorkshire for the third time in three days, following victories in the Championship and Sunday League.

At Harrogate, June 10. Durham won by eight wickets. Toss: Scotland. Scotland 222 for seven (55 overs) (B. M. W. Patterson 97, I. L. Philip 41, G. Salmond 36); Durham 226 for two (50 overs) (J. J. B. Lewis 34, M. A. Roseberry 102 not out, P. D. Collingwood 64).

At Harrogate, June 11. **Final:** Durham v Gloucestershire. No result (abandoned).

Durham retained the Costcutter Cup on the toss of a coin, conditions being too wet even for a bowl-out.

SCARBOROUGH FESTIVAL

At Scarborough, July 12 (Northern Electric Trophy). Yorkshire won by five wickets. Toss: Durham. Durham 292 for seven (50 overs) (J. J. B. Lewis 100, J. E. Morris 31, N. J. Speak 51, M. P. Speight 30; G. M. Hamilton three for 51); Yorkshire 294 for five (49.3 overs) (M. D. Moxon 61, A. McGrath 67, D. Byas 63, C. White 56 not out).

At Scarborough, July 13 (McCain Challenge). Leicestershire won by one run. Toss: Leicestershire. Leicestershire 247 for four (40 overs) (D. L. Maddy 37, I. J. Sutcliffe 36, B. F. Smith 69, J. M. Dakin 50 not out); Essex 246 for six (40 overs) (S. G. Law 51, D. D. J. Robinson 93 not out, R. C. Irani 68; D. L. Maddy three for 28).

At Scarborough, July 14 (Tetley Bitter Festival Trophy). Yorkshire won by five wickets. Toss: President's XI. President's XI 168 for nine (50 overs) (D. C. Boon 59; C. E. W. Silverwood three for 28, R. J. Sidebottom five for 27); Yorkshire 169 for five (40.5 overs) (M. D. Moxon 51, A. McGrath 52; C. Z. Harris four for 26).

At Scarborough, July 15 (Boyes Store Challenge). Yorkshire won by 82 runs. Toss: Holland. Yorkshire 300 for seven (50 overs) (M. D. Moxon 43, A. McGrath 114, G. M. Hamilton 60, D. Byas 35; T. B. M. de Leede four for 53); Holland 218 for eight (50 overs) (K. J. van Noortwijk 82, E. Gouka 37, Extras 33).

FLOODLIT ROSES MATCH

At Manchester, July 21 (day/night). Lancashire won by 13 runs. Toss: Lancashire. Lancashire 239 for eight (50 overs) (M. Watkinson 35, N. H. Fairbrother 108 not out, G. D. Lloyd 41; D. S. Lehmann three for 43); Yorkshire 226 (45.1 overs) (D. S. Lehmann 63, C. White 55; D. J. Shadford three for 51).

This was the first floodlit 11-a-side county match. The game was split into "quarters", so that both teams could bat in daylight and under lights; Lancashire were 122 for two after their first 25 overs, after which Yorkshire scored 122 for three in theirs. The attendance was 5,343.

TRIPLE CROWN TOURNAMENT

At Old Hill, July 22. ECB XI won by 221 runs. Toss: ECB XI. ECB XI 351 for five (50 overs) (R. L. Robinson 45, S. J. Foster 130, J. D. Robinson 128; S. R. Barwick three for 57); Wales 130 (33.5 overs) (A. J. Jones 47, L. O. Jones 31; B. C. Usher three for 27).

Foster scored 130 in 127 balls, with 13 fours and four sixes; Jon Robinson scored 128 from only 94 balls, with 14 fours and six sixes. Together, they added 259 for the ECB XI's third wicket in 34 overs. Barwick took the last three wickets in five balls.

At West Bromwich Dartmouth, July 22. Scotland won by 19 runs. Toss: Ireland. Scotland 218 for six (50 overs) (B. M. W. Patterson 68, G. Salmond 69); Ireland 199 for nine (50 overs) (E. C. Joyce 60; I. M. Stanger three for 42).

At Stourbridge, July 23. ECB XI won by 19 runs. Toss: ECB XI. ECB XI 209 (49.2 overs) (J. D. Robinson 73, D. R. Clarke 44; J. O. Davy three for 23, J. D. R. Benson three for 45); Ireland 190 (48.2 overs) (A. D. Patterson 69; K. A. Arnold three for 40, A. J. Mackay three for 50).

At Wolverhampton, July 23. Scotland won by one run. Toss: Scotland. Scotland 245 for six (50 overs) (R. A. Parsons 41, B. M. W. Patterson 85, G. Salmond 51; L. O. Jones three for 59); Wales 244 for six (50 overs) (A. J. Dalton 86, S. W. Maddock 57, Extras 35; J. G. Williamson four for 42).

At Walsall, July 24. No result. Scotland won 3-2 in a bowling contest to take the Triple Crown. Toss: ECB XI. Scotland 70 for two (18.3 overs) (R. A. Parsons 36) v ECB XI.

At Moseley, July 24. No result. Ireland won 4-0 in a bowling contest. Toss: Wales. Wales 186 for nine (47 overs) (A. J. Dalton 68, S. W. Maddock 45; J. O. Davy four for 16) v Ireland.

D. A. Lewis made a record 119th appearance for Ireland. After the game was cut short by rain, a 20-over match was started, but also abandoned: Wales scored 44 for one (5.5 overs).

Final table

	Played	Won	Lost	Points
Scotland......................	3	3	0	6
England Cricket Board XI........	3	2	1	4
Ireland	3	1	2	2
Wales.........................	3	0	3	0

ECB RECREATIONAL COUNTY CHAMPIONSHIP

Surrey beat Lancashire by one wicket in a thrilling finale to the ECB Recreational County Championship at Southport on September 4. It had rained throughout the previous day when the game was originally due to be played and Lancashire struggled at once after being put in. David Hayes, with 29, led them away from 42 for five, but they were still all out for 124.

With the pitch playing easier in the afternoon, Surrey looked like comfortable winners, but Lancashire captain Roland Horridge rallied his team and Hayes had success with the ball, taking four for eight, as Surrey suddenly fell to 118 for nine. But Hayes also bowled six wides, and was taken off for the last over of the match: Gavin Piper then hit a four over mid-wicket with four balls left to settle the contest. The tournament involved 41 teams, comprising club players from all over England, Wales and Scotland.

THE MINOR COUNTIES IN 1997

By MICHAEL BERRY and ROBERT BROOKE

Devon made history by claiming an unprecedented fourth successive Minor Counties Championship. Their remarkable sequence under Peter Roebuck yielded their fifth Western Division crown in six seasons, and they confirmed their reputation as the modern juggernaut of the two-day game by defeating Bedfordshire, the Eastern Division winners, on superior run-rate in the play-off at Luton.

The two finalists possessed the two leading run-scorers in the Championship. For the second successive year, Nick Folland and Wayne Larkins were well ahead of the field; though the wet summer prevented them from reaching four figures, as they did in 1996, Larkins finished with 865 for Bedfordshire and left-hander Folland with 862 at 78.36 for Devon. Folland headed the main batting averages and collected the Wilfred Rhodes Trophy for the fourth time in six years, and the third season in a row. He missed out in 1993 and 1994 when he was playing first-class cricket with Somerset.

Norfolk, the previous season's Eastern champions, made up for losing the 1996 play-off to Devon by reaching the one-day MCC Trophy final, where they beat Shropshire comfortably in a rain-affected match.

The Minor Counties agreed with the ECB that in 1998 they would play some matches on the Australian "grade" model. This means they will be played primarily as single-innings two-day contests, though there is provision for them to become two-innings matches if there is time.

MINOR COUNTIES CHAMPIONSHIP, 1997

Eastern Division	M	W	L	D	NR	Bonus Points Batting	Bonus Points Bowling	Total Points
Bedfordshire[NW]	9	4	1	3	1	25	22	116
Staffordshire[NW]	9	3	1	2	3	15	20	98
Norfolk[NW]	9	3	2	4	0	23	26	97
Cumberland[NW]	9	3	0	5	1	15	19	87
Buckinghamshire[NW]	9	2	2	5	0	26	25	83
Cambridgeshire[NW]	9	2	0	6	1	20	23	80
Hertfordshire	9	2	3	4	0	22	15	69
Lincolnshire	9	1	5	3	0	21	15	52
Northumberland	9	1	4	3	1	9	21	51
Suffolk	9	0	3	5	1	9	19	33

Western Division	M	W	L	D	NR	Bonus Points Batting	Bonus Points Bowling	Total Points
Devon[NW]	9	4	3	1	1	22	27	118
Wales[NW]	9	4	1	3	1	12	17	98
Cheshire[NW]	9	3	2	3	1	17	20	90
Dorset[NW]	9	3	2	3	1	11	21	85
Herefordshire[NW]	9	2	2	4	1	16	22	75
Shropshire	9	2	0	6	1	13	15	65
Oxfordshire	9	2	3	3	1	12	15	64
Berkshire	9	2	2	5	0	9	21	62
Wiltshire	9	1	2	5	1	16	14	51
Cornwall	9	0	6	3	0	8	21	29

Final: Devon drew with Bedfordshire, but became champions by virtue of a superior run-rate.

Win = 16 pts. No result = 5 pts.
[NW] *Denotes qualified for NatWest Trophy in 1998.*

Devon won four of their nine Western Division games. Their triumph over Berkshire, in which they amassed 397 for eight, the biggest team total of the season, was their first victory by an innings since 1975. Folland, obviously, was the kingpin of the batting. Roebuck again proved his worth with the ball: his 40 wickets at 17.72 each were a major factor in their success. Keith Donohue was also a prominent figure, with 26 wickets, including three in a crucial spell in the final against Bedfordshire.

Wales celebrated Philip North's appointment as captain by finishing runners-up in the Western Division, their best ever placing. They got off on the right foot by defeating Devon in their opening fixture, and finished with four wins, as many as Devon, and only one defeat to the champions' three, but they trailed on bonus points. No batsman scaled 500 runs, but five passed 250. James Langworth's 143 not out against Cheshire equalled their highest individual score. North took 25 wickets and Steve Barwick 28, in his first season after leaving Glamorgan.

Ian Cockbain, captain of the Minor Counties representative side, had recovered from an eye complaint and was back to his best for **Cheshire**. He recorded unbeaten centuries in three of the first four games and finished with 540 runs at 67.50, while his rarely used slow left-arm bowling brought him a career-best five for 49 against Berkshire. Richard Hignett compiled a maiden Championship century against Herefordshire, on his way to 637 runs, while Tony Murphy pocketed 24 wickets. Left-arm spinner Steve Hampson returned match figures of ten for 64 against Dorset on debut. Engaging Jeremy Batty, formerly of Yorkshire and Somerset, as a professional was not a success, however; he played only two Championship games.

Dorset finished fourth in the division and reached the semi-finals of the MCC Trophy. Their medium-pacer, Julian Shackleton, headed the averages for bowlers with 20 wickets or more, taking 37 at 13.37 apiece to earn the Frank Edwards Trophy. His father, Derek, had won the same prize in 1972, after joining Dorset at the conclusion of his career for Hampshire and England. Leg-spinner Vyvian Pike was welcomed back to Dorset's ranks and collected 19 wickets in six appearances. Richard Scott, Jon Hardy and Stuart Rintoul all passed 450 runs; Scott and Alan Willows established a county second-wicket record of 187 in the win over Wales, in which Shackleton took 12 for 63.

Herefordshire used 32 players in the Championship, more than anyone else. Fourteen made just one appearance, and only three played in all nine. This lack of a settled side contributed to their mid-table position. Two of the ever-presents were the former first-class bowlers Kevin Cooper and Neal Radford. They had a personal duel for the title of the Championship's leading wicket-taker. Cooper had made a good start by taking 11 for 79 to set up their opening win against Dorset, and finished with five for 52 against Oxfordshire, which took him to 43, four ahead of Radford. Harshad Patel was top run-scorer with 398.

Despite a catalogue of behind-the-scenes turmoil, **Shropshire** were unbeaten in the Championship and ended the season at Lord's, reaching the MCC Trophy final, though they lost to Norfolk. They got there without their new professional, Paul Smith of Warwickshire, who made just one appearance in the knockout competition before he was banned by the England and Wales Cricket Board, having made lurid drugs and sex revelations in a tabloid newspaper. At the end of June, captain Mark Davies stood down for personal reasons. Ian Payne took over and led Shropshire to the knockout final. But Bryan Jones, who had returned to Minor Counties cricket after a self-imposed three-year absence, was appointed captain for 1998. Asif Din contributed 500 runs and 21 wickets; Adam Byram finished with 23 victims and Adam Shimmons 20. Former Yorkshire batsman Kevin Sharp announced his retirement.

Another captain who failed to see out the season was Rupert Evans of **Oxfordshire**, whose campaign came to a painful halt when he ruptured an Achilles tendon in a club game. As always, Keith Arnold and Ian Curtis were good value with the ball, taking 28 and 25 wickets respectively, while slow left-armer Arwyn Jones claimed 22. Stewart Laudat amassed 473 runs in only five appearances and both Bruce Ellison and Keith Mustow maintained their progress. Oxfordshire's two wins came back to back on their tour of Cornwall and Devon; Graham Savin hit 18 off the final over from Roebuck, including a last-ball six over extra cover, to clinch victory over the eventual champions.

Berkshire's success story was Neil Kendrick, the former Surrey and Glamorgan slow left-armer, who announced his arrival in Minor Counties cricket with 41 wickets. But Kendrick was also embroiled in controversy when Berkshire beat Cornwall off the last ball at Falmouth; he ran out last man Charlie Shreck, though Cornwall insisted Shreck had grounded his bat. Berkshire recruited Jamie Sylvester from Wales, but another newcomer, Stewart Seymour, stole the show with 461 runs, one behind Gary Loveday, the captain.

Steve Perrin started his first year as captain of **Wiltshire** with victory over Cheshire. But they never won again, although they came frustratingly close when Cornwall's last-wicket pair had to bat out 17.1 overs at Marlborough. Dwain Winter piled up 788 runs and became only the second Wiltshire player to score two centuries in a match, hitting 109 and 136 against Oxfordshire. The Taylor brothers weighed in with useful contributions, 423 runs from Jimmy and 23 from Billy, while seamer Roger Sillence took 11 for 145 against Herefordshire.

After their revival of the past three years, **Cornwall** hit freefall and were stranded once again at the foot of the Western Division. They lost six of their nine games and won none. Cornwall dispensed with one of their professionals, Mark Briers, in the winter and released the other, Adam Seymour, at the end of the season. Shreck, a promising quick bowler, earned 28 wickets in his first year, while consistent opener Gary Thomas gathered 572 runs.

Bedfordshire's triumph in heading the Eastern Division for the first time continued their renaissance following the previous year's run to the MCC Trophy final. Once again Larkins was integral to their success. Another former Northamptonshire player, Andy Roberts, was their star all-rounder, providing 648 runs, and 35 wickets with his leg-breaks. His match-winning 142 against Norfolk, which rescued Bedfordshire from 98 for five chasing 278, was probably the turning point of the season. That was one of four successive wins in July and August, after a disappointing start. David Clarke scored 479 runs, the most significant being the 23 he hammered in the last two overs to beat Hertfordshire; in another tight finish, Bobby Sher stroked ten off the final over in the last-ball conquest of Buckinghamshire. Neil Stanley hit 411 runs in just four appearances.

Like Bedfordshire, **Staffordshire** went four games without a win before rallying to challenge for the regional crown. After a sequence of three wins in four matches, a washout against Cumberland finally extinguished their hopes. Steve Dean, their captain, registered 553 runs, and former Derbyshire seamer Alan Richardson 20 wickets, seven of them in a memorable game at Stone, when he single-handedly reduced Northumberland to 72 for seven.

Norfolk, who undertook a short tour of South Africa in the spring, crowned another successful term with the MCC Trophy, and finished third in the Eastern Division after winning their last two matches. Carl Rogers, who compiled an unbeaten 119 in the knockout final at Lord's, hit 608 runs, Carl Amos stacked up eight half-centuries in his 712 and Steve Goldsmith made 614. Mark Thomas, who took 35 wickets, Goldsmith and Paul Newman led the attack. Wicket-keeper Matthew Boyden had a summer to savour, setting a Norfolk record with 36 victims (31 catches and five stumpings).

Cumberland's year was marred in October by the tragic death of secretary David Lamb, who died in France on a trip to see the Prix de l'Arc de Triomphe. One of only three counties who never suffered a Championship defeat, they were well served by Steve O'Shaughnessy and David Pennett. O'Shaughnessy scored 398 runs in only five games (six not outs in nine innings gave him an average of 132.66), while Pennett, picked up from Nottinghamshire, was the leading wicket-taker with 22 victims.

Neil Burns flayed 626 runs for **Buckinghamshire**, which included the highest individual total of the summer, a majestic 178 against Staffordshire. Jason Harrison, back from Middlesex, supported him with 565, while leg-spinner Andy Clarke secured 41 wickets, which raised his Championship aggregate to 157 in 32 matches. Neil Mallender, the former England bowler, started by taking 14 wickets in four games but then announced his retirement to concentrate on umpiring.

Nigel Gadsby stood down as captain of **Cambridgeshire** at the end of the season. His 11th and final year in charge saw the adoption of a policy of blooding young players. Eight up-and-coming newcomers were introduced: Jared Norman, who scored 494, looked the most promising. Two of the older guard led from the front, Simon Kellett making 626 runs and Ajaz Akhtar taking 23 wickets.

David Ward, the former Surrey batsman, scored 648 runs for **Hertfordshire**, who had a new captain in Nick Gilbert. Martin James scored 119 and 143 against Suffolk, on his way to 623 runs, while Andy Griffin made 519. Left-arm seamer Steve Sylvester, who had joined from Buckinghamshire, landed 21 wickets. Hertfordshire won two matches and lost three, but could have reversed that record had they not been bowled out with one ball left when they were three short of victory over Cumberland.

Mark Fell, the **Lincolnshire** captain, had a benefit in 1997. But it was not a profitable year for his team. They squeezed out only one win, over Northumberland. On a personal level, Steve Plumb moved into third place in the all-time list of run-scorers in Minor Counties cricket. He had passed 10,000 in his 18 years at Norfolk; his second season at Lincolnshire brought him another 502 and carried him to 10,954, a figure bettered only by Mike Nurton (12,713 for Oxfordshire, 1963-1990) and Michael Falcon (11,553 for Norfolk, 1906-1946). David Christmas, recovering from a fractured skull suffered in a street attack in Bourne, returned with 19 wickets.

Northumberland, led by new captain Phil Nicholson, began well, beating Buckinghamshire in thrilling fashion in both the MCC Trophy and the Championship in June. Matt Thompson thick-edged a boundary off the last ball to overhaul Buckinghamshire and reach 336, equalling the highest-ever score in the knockout cup. They won the Championship fixture by two runs. Thereafter the campaign went downhill, with four successive defeats. They were bowled out for 57, the lowest total of the year, by Cambridgeshire. Off-spinner Lee Crozier performed the county's first hat-trick for 20 years, against Norfolk. He finished with 20 wickets, while Andrew Golding, a slow left-armer recruited from Suffolk, took 29. Tim Adcock scored 603 runs.

Despite the county's own reputation for drought, **Suffolk's** season was literally a damp squib. They lost three successive days to bad weather on their tour of Lincolnshire and Northumberland, and finished bottom of the regional table for only the second time, failing to win a single match. But Phil Caley, their captain, ended the year on a personal high: he became the third batsman to score twin hundreds in the 1997 Championship when he made 103 and 126 in the final fixture against Cambridgeshire. Derek Randall passed 500 runs for the fourth successive season; since entering Minor Counties cricket in 1994, he has scored 2,760 at 50.18.

LEADING AVERAGES, 1997

BATTING

(Qualification: 8 innings, average 40.00)

	M	I	NO	R	HS	100s	Avge
S. J. O'Shaughnessy (*Cumberland*)	5	9	6	398	113	2	132.66
N. A. Folland (*Devon*)	9	15	4	862	116*	3	78.36
I. Cockbain (*Cheshire*)	8	13	5	540	103*	3	67.50
D. M. Ward (*Hertfordshire*)..........	6	12	2	648	123*	3	64.80
J. H. Langworth (*Wales*)	6	9	3	375	143*	1	62.50
P. M. Roebuck (*Devon*)	10	13	7	367	95*	0	61.16
J. R. Wileman (*Lincolnshire*)........	6	10	2	478	123*	2	59.75
S. V. Laudat (*Oxfordshire*)..........	5	10	2	473	133*	1	59.12
S. A. Kellett (*Cambridgeshire*)	9	14	3	626	121*	2	56.90
J. C. Harrison (*Buckinghamshire*)	8	15	5	565	107*	1	56.50
D. A. Winter (*Wiltshire*)............	9	15	1	788	136	3	56.28
A. N. Johnson (*Shropshire*)	9	13	8	267	73*	0	53.40
J. Hodgson (*Berkshire*).............	4	8	3	258	69*	0	51.60
I. R. Payne (*Shropshire*)............	8	11	3	412	107*	1	51.50

	M	I	NO	R	HS	100s	Avge
W. Larkins (*Bedfordshire*)	10	18	1	865	125	3	50.88
S. J. Dean (*Staffordshire*)	8	12	1	553	131	1	50.27
P. J. Caley (*Suffolk*)	8	13	3	498	126	2	49.80
J. S. G. Norman (*Cambridgeshire*) ...	7	11	1	494	107*	1	49.40
B. C. A. Ellison (*Oxfordshire*)	9	16	5	543	77*	0	49.36
D. W. Randall (*Suffolk*)	7	14	1	614	148	2	47.23
S. C. Goldsmith (*Norfolk*)	9	17	4	614	99*	0	47.23
A. D. Griffin (*Hertfordshire*)	8	16	5	519	138*	1	47.18
D. A. Christmas (*Lincolnshire*)	9	10	5	225	67	0	45.00
S. M. Dutton (*Cumberland*)	8	13	6	310	84*	0	44.28
D. R. Clarke (*Bedfordshire*)	7	12	1	479	114*	1	43.54
T. W. Adcock (*Northumberland*)	8	15	1	603	108*	1	43.07
J. J. E. Hardy (*Dorset*)	7	13	2	471	102	1	42.81
R. G. Hignett (*Cheshire*)	9	16	1	637	112	1	42.46
D. J. M. Mercer (*Bedfordshire*)	7	13	4	378	89	0	42.00
M. R. Davies (*Shropshire*)	8	13	3	417	80	0	41.70
R. J. Scott (*Dorset*)	7	14	2	492	108*	1	41.00
C. K. Bullen (*Bedfordshire*)	9	14	5	366	62	0	40.66
C. J. Rogers (*Norfolk*)	9	18	3	608	100*	1	40.53
R. B. Hurd (*Buckinghamshire*)	6	11	1	403	94	0	40.30
S. March (*Hertfordshire*)	8	14	3	442	70	0	40.18

* *Signifies not out.*

BOWLING

(Qualification: 10 wickets, average 24.00)

	O	M	R	W	BB	5W/i	Avge
S. Hampson (*Cheshire*)	56	18	125	11	6-18	1	11.36
N. A. Mallender (*Buckinghamshire*) ...	82.1	25	186	14	5-14	1	13.28
J. H. Shackleton (*Dorset*)	220.3	72	495	37	6-30	3	13.37
K. E. Cooper (*Herefordshire*)	310.3	102	652	43	7-46	3	15.16
M. W. Thomas (*Norfolk*)	160.1	28	535	35	4-35	0	15.28
S. C. Goldsmith (*Norfolk*)	144.1	41	398	24	4-35	0	16.58
P. M. Roebuck (*Devon*)	347.1	105	709	40	6-23	3	17.72
N. V. Radford (*Herefordshire*)	253.5	65	715	39	6-50	2	18.33
S. R. Barwick (*Wales*)	226.1	74	518	28	5-40	2	18.50
A. Akhtar (*Cambridgeshire*)	170.4	47	429	23	5-30	1	18.65
K. Donohue (*Devon*)	186.5	46	487	26	4-27	0	18.73
J. P. Kent (*Cornwall*)	62.5	16	218	11	4-33	0	19.81
N. M. Kendrick (*Berkshire*)	260.3	65	817	41	6-46	3	19.92
A. Jones (*Oxfordshire*)	154	38	458	22	5-15	1	20.81
S. D. Myles (*Berkshire*)	80	18	252	12	4-44	0	21.00
S. N. White (*Norfolk*)	112.3	18	392	18	4-65	0	21.77
A. K. Golding (*Northumberland*)	228.2	68	633	29	6-19	1	21.82
A. R. Clarke (*Buckinghamshire*)	286.3	73	913	41	8-60	3	22.26
C. G. Feltham (*Staffordshire*)	77.2	21	245	11	4-31	0	22.27
R. J. Catley (*Suffolk*)	53	3	274	12	4-57	0	22.83
D. Towse (*Wales*)	145.3	38	391	17	4-24	0	23.00
C. E. Dagnall (*Cumberland*)	129.1	35	369	16	4-37	0	23.06
A. M. Shimmons (*Shropshire*)	136	29	469	20	4-29	0	23.45
P. D. North (*Wales*)	179	41	588	25	7-72	2	23.52
C. E. Shreck (*Cornwall*)	135.2	20	664	28	5-63	1	23.71
S. R. Walbridge (*Dorset*)	104	26	357	15	4-46	0	23.80
J. M. Fielding (*Cumberland*)	114	30	336	14	4-22	0	24.00

Eastern Division

At Askam, May 25, 26. Drawn. Cumberland 194 for eight dec. and 215 for eight dec.; Bedfordshire 178 for eight dec. and 229 for seven. *Cumberland 4 pts, Bedfordshire 5 pts.*

At Sleaford, May 25, 26. Drawn. Hertfordshire 276 for two dec. (N. P. G. Wright 122*) and 305 for five dec.; Lincolnshire 231 for one dec. (J. R. Wileman 123*) and 171 for four. *Lincolnshire 4 pts, Hertfordshire 4 pts.*

At Beaconsfield, June 4, 5. Drawn. Buckinghamshire 226 for seven dec. and 354 for four dec. (N. D. Burns 178); Staffordshire 228 for three dec. and 260 for six. *Buckinghamshire 5 pts, Staffordshire 7 pts.*

At Dunstable, June 8, 9. Drawn. Bedfordshire 280 for three dec. (W. Larkins 124) and 307 for four dec. (N. A. Stanley 162); Suffolk 267 for six dec. and 223 for six. *Bedfordshire 6 pts, Suffolk 3 pts.*

At Bourne, June 8, 9. Buckinghamshire won by seven wickets. Lincolnshire 209 for eight dec. and 173 (A. R. Clarke eight for 60); Buckinghamshire 227 for six dec. and 156 for three. *Buckinghamshire 23 pts, Lincolnshire 4 pts.*

At Jesmond, June 8, 9. Drawn. Northumberland 202 for six dec. and 229; Norfolk 202 for six dec. and 175 for nine (L. J. Crozier six for 44, including a hat-trick). *Northumberland 5 pts, Norfolk 5 pts.*

At Bedford, June 15, 16. Drawn (no result). Staffordshire 200 for one dec.; Bedfordshire 105 for four. *Bedfordshire 5 pts, Staffordshire 5 pts.*

At Amersham, June 15, 16. Northumberland won by two runs. Northumberland 113 (N. A. Mallender five for 14) and 165 (A. R. Clarke five for 50); Buckinghamshire 167 and 109 (A. K. Golding six for 19). *Northumberland 20 pts, Buckinghamshire 4 pts.*

At Netherfield, June 16, 17. Cumberland won by eight wickets. Lincolnshire 223 for six dec. and 217 (P. A. Rawden 105); Cumberland 204 for six dec. and 237 for two (S. J. O'Shaughnessy 102*). *Cumberland 21 pts, Lincolnshire 5 pts.*

At St Albans, June 17, 18. Drawn. Northumberland 175 for seven dec. and 264 for six dec.; Hertfordshire 199 for five dec. and 132 for six. *Hertfordshire 5 pts, Northumberland 2 pts.*

At Saffron Walden, June 18, 19. Drawn. Norfolk 205 for seven dec. and 132 for one; Cambridgeshire 179 for seven dec. *Cambridgeshire 5 pts, Norfolk 6 pts.*

At Cleethorpes, June 29, 30. Drawn. Suffolk 185 for six dec and three for no wkt; Lincolnshire 225 for one dec. (S. G. Plumb 105). *Lincolnshire 6 pts.*

At Jesmond, July 1, 2. Northumberland v Suffolk. Abandoned (no result). *Northumberland 5 pts, Suffolk 5 pts.*

At Cannock, July 2, 3. Drawn (no result). Cambridgeshire 166 for eight v Staffordshire. *Staffordshire 5 pts, Cambridgeshire 5 pts.*

At Aylesbury, July 6, 7. Drawn. Cumberland 173 and 218 for three; Buckinghamshire 258 for nine dec. *Buckinghamshire 8 pts, Cumberland 4 pts.*

At Fenner's, Cambridge, July 8, 9. Cambridgeshire won by five runs. Cambridgeshire 217 for eight dec. and 219 (A. R. Roberts five for 73); Bedfordshire 237 for four dec. (W. Larkins 112) and 194. *Cambridgeshire 19 pts, Bedfordshire 7 pts.*

At Balls Park, Hertford, July 8, 9. Cumberland won by two runs. Cumberland 215 for four dec. and 117 for four dec.; Hertfordshire 35 for one dec. and 295. *Cumberland 18 pts, Hertfordshire 1 pt.*

At Southill Park, July 13, 14. Bedfordshire won by four wickets. Lincolnshire 220 for eight dec. and 252 (A. R. Roberts five for 69); Bedfordshire 226 for two dec. (N. A. Stanley 120*) and 249 for six. *Bedfordshire 23 pts, Lincolnshire 3 pts.*

At Radlett, July 13, 14. Norfolk won by 54 runs. Norfolk 227 for three dec. and 267 for three dec.; Hertfordshire 207 for seven dec. and 233. *Norfolk 23 pts, Hertfordshire 4 pts.*

At Tynemouth, July 13, 14. Cambridgeshire won by nine wickets. Northumberland 169 and 57 (C. M. Whyborn six for 33); Cambridgeshire 205 for nine dec. and 23 for one. *Cambridgeshire 23 pts, Northumberland 3 pts.*

At Carlisle, July 15, 16. Drawn. Cambridgeshire 101 and 262 for six (S. A. Kellett 121*); Cumberland 331 for four dec. (S. J. O'Shaughnessy 113). *Cumberland 7 pts, Cambridgeshire 2 pts.*

At Bishop's Stortford, July 24, 25. Hertfordshire won by six wickets. Staffordshire 190 for eight dec. and 261 for nine dec. (P. J. O'Reilly five for 67); Hertfordshire 188 for six dec. and 264 for four (D. M. Ward 110*). *Hertfordshire 21 pts, Staffordshire 4 pts.*

At Shenley Park, July 27, 28. Bedfordshire won by four wickets. Hertfordshire 224 for seven dec. and 246 for five dec. (D. M. Ward 107); Bedfordshire 194 for seven dec. and 277 for six (D. R. Clarke 114*). *Bedfordshire 21 pts, Hertfordshire 6 pts.*

At Lakenham, July 27, 28. Drawn. Cumberland 193 and 208; Norfolk 180 for seven dec. and 201 for seven. *Norfolk 6 pts, Cumberland 3 pts.*

At Ransomes, Ipswich, July 27, 28. Buckinghamshire won by two wickets. Suffolk 195 (A. W. Thomas eight for 83) and 270 for seven dec.; Buckinghamshire 201 for nine dec. and 266 for eight. *Buckinghamshire 23 pts, Suffolk 5 pts.*

At Stone, July 28, 29. Staffordshire won by eight wickets. Northumberland 152 and 168 (A. Richardson seven for 44); Staffordshire 226 for six dec. and 98 for two. *Staffordshire 24 pts, Northumberland 2 pts.*

At Lakenham, July 29, 30. Drawn. Norfolk 225 for four dec. and 228 (A. R. Clarke eight for 94); Buckinghamshire 221 for eight dec. and 151 for nine. *Norfolk 7 pts, Buckinghamshire 4 pts.*

At Mildenhall, July 29, 30. Drawn. Cumberland 281 (A. J. Bond five for 83) and 150 for four dec.; Suffolk 127 for six dec. and 287 for nine. *Suffolk 4 pts, Cumberland 5 pts.*

At Fenner's, Cambridge, July 30, 31. Drawn. Lincolnshire 220 for seven dec. (J. R. Wileman 102) and 17 for no wkt; Cambridgeshire 207 for five dec. *Cambridgeshire 6 pts, Lincolnshire 4 pts.*

At Lakenham, August 4, 5. Staffordshire won by seven wickets. Norfolk 197 and 112 (D. J. P. Boden six for 50); Staffordshire 178 for nine dec. and 134 for three. *Staffordshire 20 pts, Norfolk 6 pts.*

At March, August 6, 7. Drawn. Cambridgeshire 245 for three dec. (S. A. Kellett 105*) and 283 for seven dec. (J. D. R. Benson 100*); Hertfordshire 223 for five dec. and 206 for seven (A. D. Griffin 138*). *Cambridgeshire 6 pts, Hertfordshire 4 pts.*

At Lakenham, August 6, 7. Bedfordshire won by four wickets. Norfolk 169 (A. R. Roberts five for 49) and 274 for four dec. (C. J. Rogers 100*); Bedfordshire 166 for five dec. and 278 for six (A. R. Roberts 142). *Bedfordshire 21 pts, Norfolk 3 pts.*

At Bury St Edmunds, August 6, 7. Drawn. Suffolk 204 and 181 for two (D. W. Randall 138*); Staffordshire 396 for six dec. (S. J. Dean 131). *Suffolk 4 pts, Staffordshire 8 pts.*

At Slough, August 10, 11. Drawn. Buckinghamshire 142 (A. Akhtar five for 30) and 277 for three dec. (J. C. Harrison 107*); Cambridgeshire 178 for eight dec. and 222 for eight (J. C. Harrison six for 63). *Buckinghamshire 3 pts, Cambridgeshire 6 pts.*

At Lakenham, August 10, 11. Norfolk won by 143 runs. Norfolk 184 and 242 for four dec.; Suffolk 114 (P. J. Bradshaw five for 22) and 169. *Norfolk 22 pts, Suffolk 4 pts.*

At Jesmond, August 10, 11. Lincolnshire won by 36 runs. Lincolnshire 200 for eight dec. and 301 for nine dec.; Northumberland 225 for three dec. (T. W. Adcock 108*) and 240. *Lincolnshire 19 pts, Northumberland 7 pts.*

At Barrow, August 17, 18. Cumberland won by six wickets. Northumberland 208 for four dec. (P. J. Nicholson 100*) and 185; Cumberland 224 for seven dec. and 173 for four. *Cumberland 20 pts, Northumberland 5 pts.*

At Ipswich School, August 18, 19. Hertfordshire won by six wickets. Suffolk 227 for three dec. (D. W. Randall 148) and 321 for eight dec. (R. J. Catley 110); Hertfordshire 226 for three dec. (M. James 119) and 324 for four (M. James 143, D. M. Ward 123*). *Hertfordshire 21 pts, Suffolk 5 pts.*

At Brewood, August 19, 20. Staffordshire won by six wickets. Lincolnshire 194 for eight dec. and 149; Staffordshire 176 for nine dec. (D. A. Christmas five for 58) and 173 for four. *Staffordshire 20 pts, Lincolnshire 5 pts.*

At Wardown Park, Luton, August 24, 25. Bedfordshire won by two wickets. Buckinghamshire 228 (R. N. Dalton five for 70) and 252 for five dec.; Bedfordshire 231 for four dec. and 250 for eight (T. J. A. Scriven six for 64). *Bedfordshire 24 pts, Buckinghamshire 5 pts.*

At Marlow, August 31, September 1. Drawn. Hertfordshire 169 and 291 for nine dec.; Buckinghamshire 225 for six dec. and 215 for nine. *Buckinghamshire 8 pts, Hertfordshire 3 pts.*

At Lincoln Lindum, August 31, September 1. Norfolk won by 30 runs. Norfolk 176 for six dec. and 69 for one dec.; Lincolnshire 45 for three dec. and 170. *Norfolk 19 pts, Lincolnshire 2 pts.*

At Jesmond, August 31, September 1. Drawn. Bedfordshire 259 for three dec. (W. Larkins 125) and forfeited second innings; Northumberland forfeited first innings and 251 for eight. *Northumberland 1 pt, Bedfordshire 4 pts.*

At Longton, August 31, September 1. Staffordshire v Cumberland. Abandoned (no result). *Staffordshire 5 pts, Cumberland 5 pts.*

At Ransomes, Ipswich, August 31, September 1. Drawn. Suffolk 195 for nine dec. (P. J. Caley 103) and 313 for four dec. (P. J. Caley 126, S. M. Clements 100*); Cambridgeshire 229 for seven dec. and 244 for six (J. S. G. Norman 107*). *Suffolk 3 pts, Cambridgeshire 8 pts.*

Western Division

At Sidmouth, May 25, 26. Wales won by three wickets. Devon 210 and 236 for eight dec.; Wales 180 for seven dec. and 267 for seven. *Wales 21 pts, Devon 6 pts.*

At Sherborne School, May 25, 26. Herefordshire won by an innings and 32 runs. Dorset 105 (K. E. Cooper seven for 46) and 90 (N. V. Radford six for 50); Herefordshire 227 for four dec. *Herefordshire 24 pts, Dorset 1 pt.*

At Challow & Childrey, May 25, 26. Berkshire won by 21 runs. Berkshire 200 for six dec. and 174 (K. A. Arnold five for 68); Oxfordshire 201 for six dec. (S. V. Laudat 133*) and 152 (N. M. Kendrick five for 60). *Berkshire 19 pts, Oxfordshire 3 pts.*

At Neston, June 8, 9. Wiltshire won by six wickets. Cheshire 225 for two dec. and 274 for five dec. (I. Cockbain 101*); Wiltshire 204 for eight dec. and 298 for four (D. A. Winter 104). *Wiltshire 19 pts, Cheshire 7 pts.*

At Dean Park, Bournemouth, June 8, 9. Dorset won by nine wickets. Wales 149 for eight dec. (J. H. Shackleton six for 30) and 197 (J. H. Shackleton six for 33); Dorset 207 for three dec. and 141 for one. *Dorset 22 pts, Wales 1 pt.*

At Challow & Childrey, June 8, 9. Shropshire won by 133 runs. Shropshire 158 and 243 for two dec.; Oxfordshire 202 for four dec. and 66. *Shropshire 17 pts, Oxfordshire 7 pts.*

At Hurst, June 10, 11. Drawn. Berkshire 252 for six dec. (S. A. Seymour 102) and 197 for seven dec.; Shropshire 179 (N. M. Kendrick six for 46) and 77 for five. *Berkshire 7 pts, Shropshire 4 pts.*

At Swansea, June 15, 16. Drawn. Wales 184 and 169 for eight dec.; Oxfordshire 184 (P. D. North seven for 72) and 58 for three. *Wales 6 pts, Oxfordshire 4 pts.*

At Westbury, June 15, 16. Drawn. Herefordshire 177 (R. J. Sillence six for 69) and 262 for six dec. (R. J. Sillence five for 76); Wiltshire 155 and 78 for no wkt. *Wiltshire 5 pts, Herefordshire 5 pts.*

At New Brighton, June 16, 17. Cheshire won by four wickets. Cheshire 268 for eight dec. (I. Cockbain 103*) and 177 for six; Cornwall 135 (A. J. Murphy five for 44) and 306. *Cheshire 24 pts, Cornwall 3 pts.*

At Newport, June 18, 19. Drawn. Cornwall 226 for four dec. and 135 for two; Shropshire 225 for two dec. *Shropshire 5 pts, Cornwall 4 pts.*

At Dale's, Leominster, June 29, 30. Drawn. Herefordshire 241 for seven dec. and 12 for no wkt; Berkshire 113 (K. E. Cooper five for 38) and 191 (N. V. Radford six for 78). *Herefordshire 6 pts, Berkshire 3 pts.*

At Banbury, June 29, 30. Drawn (no result). Dorset 207 for six dec.; Oxfordshire 110 for five. *Oxfordshire 5 pts, Dorset 5 pts.*

At Bridgnorth, June 29, 30. Drawn. Devon 302 for nine dec. and 225 for two dec.; Shropshire 222 for seven dec. and 152 for four. *Shropshire 4 pts, Devon 6 pts.*

At Pontarddulais, June 29, 30. Wales won by ten wickets in a match reduced by the weather to one innings a side. Wiltshire 112 (S. R. Barwick five for 40); Wales 116 for no wkt. *Wales 16 pts.*

At Toft, July 1, 2. Drawn (no result). Cheshire 206 (J. G. Wyatt five for 25); Devon 73 for two. *Cheshire 5 pts, Devon 5 pts.*

At Reading, July 6, 7. Drawn. Dorset 202 for six dec. (R. J. Scott 108*) and 204 for seven dec.; Berkshire 173 for eight dec. and 212 for eight (V. J. Pike six for 75). *Berkshire 2 pts, Dorset 5 pts.*

At South Wilts CC, July 6, 7. Devon won by 186 runs. Devon 226 for one dec. (G. T. J. Townsend 102*, N. A. Folland 102*) and 311 for three dec. (A. J. Pugh 105); Wiltshire 206 for five dec. and 145 (P. M. Roebuck six for 23). *Devon 22 pts, Wiltshire 2 pts.*

At Oswestry, July 13, 14. Drawn. Shropshire 259 for five dec. and 303 for six dec.; Wales 249 for five dec. and 152 for nine. *Shropshire 5 pts, Wales 6 pts.*

At Marlborough, July 13, 14. Drawn. Wiltshire 259 for four dec. (M. J. Glasson 113) and 200 (A. C. H. Seymour five for 99); Cornwall 189 (B. V. Taylor six for 70) and 205 for nine. *Wiltshire 8 pts, Cornwall 3 pts.*

At Weymouth, July 15, 16. Dorset won by 13 runs. Dorset 160 for eight dec. and 193; Cornwall 148 and 192. *Dorset 20 pts, Cornwall 3 pts.*

At Brockhampton, July 22, 23. Cheshire won by two wickets. Herefordshire 225 for five dec. and 296 for nine dec. (N. D. Cross five for 58); Cheshire 209 for six dec. (I. Cockbain 102*) and 313 for eight (R. G. Hignett 112). *Cheshire 20 pts, Herefordshire 6 pts.*

At Torquay, July 27, 28. Devon won by an innings and 60 runs. Berkshire 117 (P. M. Warren five for 44) and 220; Devon 397 for eight dec. (I. Gompertz 131, K. A. O. Barrett 119). *Devon 23 pts, Berkshire 3 pts.*

At Colwall, July 27, 28. Drawn. Shropshire 205 for six dec. (I. R. Payne 107*) and 237 for nine dec.; Herefordshire 217 for four dec. (H. V. Patel 106*) and 202 for seven. *Herefordshire 5 pts, Shropshire 1 pt.*

At Thame, July 27, 28. Drawn. Wiltshire 221 for five dec. (D. A. Winter 109) and 301 for six dec. (D. A. Winter 136); Oxfordshire 226 for four dec. and 273 for nine. *Oxfordshire 6 pts, Wiltshire 4 pts.*

At Pontypridd, July 27, 28. Drawn. Wales 205 for five dec. and 271 for four dec. (J. H. Langworth 143*); Cheshire 194 for six dec. and 198 for eight (P. D. North six for 90). *Wales 3 pts, Cheshire 4 pts.*

At Falmouth, July 29, 30. Berkshire won by 44 runs. Berkshire 241 for eight dec. (S. D. Myles 105*) and 183 for eight dec. (C. E. Shreck five for 63); Cornwall 154 and 226. *Berkshire 22 pts, Cornwall 3 pts.*

At Rover, Cowley, August 3, 4. Drawn. Oxfordshire 183 for four dec. and 140 for three dec.; Cheshire 97 for two dec. and 152 for seven. *Oxfordshire 2 pts, Cheshire 1 pt.*

At Pontarddulais, August 3, 4. Drawn (no result). Wales 123 for six dec.; Herefordshire 107 for four. *Wales 5 pts, Herefordshire 5 pts.*

At Finchampstead, August 5, 6. Drawn. Cheshire 225 for five dec. and 142 for three; Berkshire 170 (I. Cockbain five for 49). *Berkshire 2 pts, Cheshire 8 pts.*

At Falkland, August 10, 11. Drawn. Berkshire 200 for six dec. and 292 for four dec.; Wiltshire 214 for four dec. and 196 for five. *Berkshire 4 pts, Wiltshire 5 pts.*

At St Austell, August 10, 11. Oxfordshire won by nine wickets. Cornwall 189 for four dec. and 164 (A. Jones five for 15); Oxfordshire 192 for nine dec. (A. C. H. Seymour seven for 62) and 162 for one. *Oxfordshire 19 pts, Cornwall 6 pts.*

At Wellington, August 10, 11. Drawn. Dorset 238 (A. B. Byram six for 76) and 207; Shropshire 234 for two dec. (J. B. R. Jones 105*) and 187 for seven (J. H. Shackleton five for 28). *Shropshire 8 pts, Dorset 1 pt.*

At Bowdon, August 12, 13. Cheshire won by nine wickets. Dorset 150 (S. Hampson six for 18) and 177; Cheshire 197 and 134 for one. *Cheshire 21 pts, Dorset 5 pts.*

At Bovey Tracey, August 12, 13. Oxfordshire won by three wickets. Devon 230 for six dec. and 169 for nine dec.; Oxfordshire 194 for nine dec. (P. M. Roebuck five for 46) and 209 for seven. *Oxfordshire 18 pts, Devon 7 pts.*

At Camborne, August 17, 18. Wales won by eight wickets. Wales 248 for nine dec. and 92 for two; Cornwall 89 and 247. *Wales 24 pts, Cornwall 4 pts.*

At Exmouth, August 17, 18. Devon won by 69 runs. Devon 243 and 214 for five dec.; Herefordshire 145 and 243 (P. M. Roebuck five for 52). *Devon 23 pts, Herefordshire 4 pts.*

At Truro, August 19, 20. Drawn. Cornwall 219 for six dec. and 232 for eight dec.; Herefordshire 333 for eight dec. (R. Hall 106). *Cornwall 3 pts, Herefordshire 4 pts.*

At Dean Park, Bournemouth, August 24, 25. Dorset won by seven wickets. Devon 231 for six dec. (N. A. Folland 105) and 128; Dorset 152 for seven dec. and 208 for three. *Dorset 18 pts, Devon 6 pts.*

At Westbury, August 24, 25. Drawn (no result). Shropshire 226 for four dec.; Wiltshire 76 for one. *Wiltshire 5 pts, Shropshire 5 pts.*

At Instow, August 31, September 1. Devon won by seven wickets. Cornwall 297 and 28 for no wkt dec.; Devon forfeited first innings and 327 for three (N. A. Folland 116*, K. A. O. Barrett 107). *Devon 20 pts.*

At Dean Park, Bournemouth, August 31, September 1. Drawn. Dorset 234 for eight dec. (J. J. E. Hardy 102) and 178 for seven; Wiltshire 128 and 304 for six dec. (J. L. Taylor 109*). *Dorset 8 pts, Wiltshire 3 pts.*

At Kington, August 31, September 1. Herefordshire won by 30 runs in a match reduced by the weather to one innings a side. Herefordshire 144; Oxfordshire 114 (K. E. Cooper five for 52). *Herefordshire 16 pts.*

At Shifnal, August 31, September 1. Shropshire won by three wickets in a match reduced by the weather to one innings a side. Cheshire 195 for eight dec. (Asif Din six for 51); Shropshire 199 for seven. *Shropshire 16 pts.*

At Colwyn Bay, August 31, September 1. Wales won by 32 runs in a match reduced by the weather to one innings a side. Wales 190 (N. M. Kendrick five for 54); Berkshire 158 (S. R. Barwick five for 61). *Wales 16 pts.*

FINAL

BEDFORDSHIRE v DEVON

At Wardown Park, Luton, September 7, 8. Devon won on superior run-rate. Toss: Bedfordshire. Devon dictated day one, thanks to fifties from Folland and Roebuck, and to Donohue, who exploited the pitch's movement and bounce to reduce Bedfordshire to 65 for five. But Devon were in grave danger of surrendering their supremacy on the second morning. A lead of 97 began to look inadequate when sloppy batting and Dalton's accuracy saw them lose six wickets for 51 in 19 overs. Donohue and Read salvaged them, adding 77. Set a challenging 278 to win in 67 overs, Bedfordshire did not capitalise on a solid start from Larkins and Roberts. They were 156 for one with 20 overs left, but spinners Roebuck and Coupe turned the screw, conceding only eight runs off six overs. Three wickets then fell in seven balls.

Close of play: Devon 27-0 (N. R. Gaywood 20*, K. A. O. Barrett 3*).

Devon

N. R. Gaywood run out	32	– lbw b Sher	34
K. A. O. Barrett b Dalton	27	– b Bullen	10
N. A. Folland c Bullen b Roberts	58	– c Bullen b Dalton	5
*P. M. Roebuck not out	56	– (5) c and b Dalton	4
G. T. J. Townsend c Roberts b Bullen	4	– (4) b Roberts	28
A. J. Pugh st Sandford b Roberts	23	– lbw b Dalton	7
†C. M. W. Read (did not bat)		– not out	30
K. Donohue (did not bat)		– b Dalton	45
P. M. Warren (did not bat)		– b Dalton	0
J. Rhodes (did not bat)		– not out	4
B 1, l-b 3, w 6, n-b 6	16	B 5, l-b 4, n-b 4	13

1/39 2/111 3/163 4/173   (5 wkts, 50 overs) 216   1/48 2/48 3/79   (8 wkts dec.) 180
5/216   4/87 5/99 6/99
     7/176 8/176

R. J. Coupe did not bat.

Bowling: *First Innings*—White 3–0–21–0; Sher 5–1–30–0; Dalton 13–4–39–1; Roberts 20–2–83–2; Bullen 9–0–39–1. *Second Innings*—Dalton 20–6–43–5; Sher 10–4–27–1; White 4–1–10–0; Bullen 16–4–51–1; Roberts 17–7–40–1.

Bedfordshire

W. Larkins c Read b Warren	11	– c Pugh b Rhodes	51
R. N. Dalton c Roebuck b Donohue	6	– (6) c Gaywood b Roebuck	0
A. R. Roberts c Read b Donohue	12	– (2) lbw b Roebuck	62
D. R. Clarke c Read b Donohue	0	– (3) c Gaywood b Coupe	36
D. J. M. Mercer lbw b Rhodes	9	– (4) c Warren b Rhodes	38
C. K. Bullen c Barrett b Coupe	36	– (5) c Pugh b Roebuck	19
*P. D. B. Hoare b Coupe	18	– not out	8
Z. A. Sher lbw b Roebuck	3	– not out	16
K. J. Wright lbw b Roebuck	2		
†G. D. Sandford not out	5		
M. R. White not out	9		
L-b 4, n-b 4	8	B 9, l-b 10, n-b 2	21

1/17 2/17 3/17 4/30 5/65   (9 wkts, 50 overs) 119   1/92 2/159 3/163   (6 wkts) 251
6/97 7/101 8/101 9/104   4/220 5/223 6/223

Bowling: *First Innings*—Donohue 8–2–17–3; Warren 4–1–13–1; Roebuck 16–4–27–2; Rhodes 6–1–20–1; Coupe 16–2–38–2. *Second Innings*—Donohue 9–1–38–0; Warren 4–0–21–0; Roebuck 27–4–67–3; Coupe 17–1–69–1; Pugh 2–0–7–0; Rhodes 8–0–30–2.

Umpires: P. Adams and M. P. Moran.

THE MINOR COUNTIES CHAMPIONS

1895	{ Norfolk	1928	Berkshire	1967	Cheshire
	{ Durham	1929	Oxfordshire	1968	Yorkshire II
	{ Worcestershire	1930	Durham	1969	Buckinghamshire
1896	Worcestershire	1931	Leicestershire II	1970	Bedfordshire
1897	Worcestershire	1932	Buckinghamshire	1971	Yorkshire II
1898	Worcestershire	1933	Undecided	1972	Bedfordshire
1899	{ Northamptonshire	1934	Lancashire II	1973	Shropshire
	{ Buckinghamshire	1935	Middlesex II	1974	Oxfordshire
1900	{ Glamorgan	1936	Hertfordshire	1975	Hertfordshire
	{ Durham	1937	Lancashire II	1976	Durham
	{ Northamptonshire	1938	Buckinghamshire	1977	Suffolk
1901	Durham	1939	Surrey II	1978	Devon
1902	Wiltshire	1946	Suffolk	1979	Suffolk
1903	Northamptonshire	1947	Yorkshire II	1980	Durham
1904	Northamptonshire	1948	Lancashire II	1981	Durham
1905	Norfolk	1949	Lancashire II	1982	Oxfordshire
1906	Staffordshire	1950	Surrey II	1983	Hertfordshire
1907	Lancashire II	1951	Kent II	1984	Durham
1908	Staffordshire	1952	Buckinghamshire	1985	Cheshire
1909	Wiltshire	1953	Berkshire	1986	Cumberland
1910	Norfolk	1954	Surrey II	1987	Buckinghamshire
1911	Staffordshire	1955	Surrey II	1988	Cheshire
1912	In abeyance	1956	Kent II	1989	Oxfordshire
1913	Norfolk	1957	Yorkshire II	1990	Hertfordshire
1914	Staffordshire†	1958	Yorkshire II	1991	Staffordshire
1920	Staffordshire	1959	Warwickshire II	1992	Staffordshire
1921	Staffordshire	1960	Lancashire II	1993	Staffordshire
1922	Buckinghamshire	1961	Somerset II	1994	Devon
1923	Buckinghamshire	1962	Warwickshire II	1995	Devon
1924	Berkshire	1963	Cambridgeshire	1996	Devon
1925	Buckinghamshire	1964	Lancashire II	1997	Devon
1926	Durham	1965	Somerset II		
1927	Staffordshire	1966	Lincolnshire		

† *Disputed. Some sources claim the Championship was never decided.*

MCC TROPHY FINAL

NORFOLK v SHROPSHIRE

At Lord's, August 27, 28. Norfolk won by 52 runs. Toss: Shropshire.

A stop-start first day ended with Norfolk in the ascendancy, after an unbeaten century from Carl Rogers. Well used to Lord's – he was a former MCC Young Professional – he kept his concentration through three rain interruptions to score 119 off 166 balls, with 13 fours. Rogers and Amos opened with 137 in 33 overs, and Newman helped to plunder 51 off the final 4.4 overs, with Shropshire guilty of some slovenly bowling and fielding. The weather forced the match into the reserve day, when play began at 2.45 p.m. with the pitch still damp. A burst of three wickets in four overs from Goldsmith had Shropshire plummeting to 148 for six with 15 overs left. Newman returned to help him polish off the tail.

Close of play: Shropshire 46-1 (15 overs) (J. B. R. Jones 8*, Asif Din 27*).

Norfolk

C. J. Rogers not out	119	*P. G. Newman not out	19
C. Amos c Johnson b A. B. Byram	56	B 4, l-b 19, w 26, n-b 4	53
S. C. Goldsmith b A. B. Byram	4		—
T. J. Boon c Mackelworth b G. J. Byram	13	1/137 2/151 (4 wkts, 55 overs)	279
D. R. Thomas c Johnson b Asif Din	15	3/179 4/228	

M. R. Tipping, N. Fox, M. W. Thomas, P. J. Bradshaw and †M. K. L. Boyden did not bat.

Bowling: G. J. Byram 11–0–59–1; Shimmons 11–0–40–0; Bowett 5–0–29–0; Asif Din 11–1–64–1; A. B. Byram 11–1–42–2; Payne 6–0–22–0.

Shropshire

J. V. Anders c Boyden b Goldsmith	0	G. J. Byram b Newman	18
J. B. R. Jones c Boyden b Goldsmith	31	D. J. Bowett not out	5
Asif Din c Amos b Bradshaw	37	A. M. Shimmons b Newman	8
M. R. Davies c Boon b Goldsmith	48		
*I. R. Payne b Goldsmith	9	L-b 14, w 23	37
A. N. Johnson c Rogers b Goldsmith	12		
A. B. Byram b Newman	4	1/3 2/70 3/102 (54.3 overs)	227
†A. N. Mackelworth c D. R. Thomas b Bradshaw	18	4/116 5/134 6/148 7/176 8/210 9/217	

Bowling: Goldsmith 10–1–42–5; Newman 10.3–1–33–3; M. W. Thomas 11–1–47–0; Bradshaw 11–1–31–2; D. R. Thomas 4–0–19–0; Rogers 8–0–41–0.

Umpires: C. S. Kelly and M. K. Reed.

WINNERS 1983-97

1983	Cheshire	1988	Dorset	1993	Staffordshire
1984	Hertfordshire	1989	Cumberland	1994	Devon
1985	Durham	1990	Buckinghamshire	1995	Cambridgeshire
1986	Norfolk	1991	Staffordshire	1996	Cheshire
1987	Cheshire	1992	Devon	1997	Norfolk

SECOND ELEVEN CHAMPIONSHIP, 1997

The ancient rivalry between Lancashire and Yorkshire came out in the unexpected surroundings of the Second Eleven Championship in 1997. Lancashire won the title but, even after the season finished, it was theoretically possible for the trophy to be taken away from them and given to Yorkshire because of a breach of rules.

The problem arose when Peter Sleep, Lancashire's Australian coach and captain, selected a team for the Yorkshire match at Bradford that included both himself and James Peterson, another Australian. Each team is allowed only one overseas player per match, but Sleep was under the misapprehension that Peterson, who is of British parentage, did not count as one because he has the right of residence in England. For cricketing purposes, however, Peterson would have to sign a declaration of intent, and live in England for four years, before he became English-qualified. Peterson scored 157 in that game out of a total of 458, and Lancashire won by an innings and 60 runs – a result which would have brought them 24 points. But those points were taken away again after a Yorkshire protest.

Sleep and Peterson turned out to have also appeared together two weeks earlier, in Lancashire's victory over Sussex. Sleep came into the team only because Andrew Flintoff was called up by the First Eleven during the match (Second Eleven rules allow for playing replacements, as opposed to substitutes, in that eventuality), and, since they were far from home at Middleton-on-Sea, there was no one else available. He neither batted nor bowled. Still, Lancashire

Continued over

SECOND ELEVEN CHAMPIONSHIP, 1997

Win = 16 points	M	W	L	D	A	Bonus points Batting	Bowling	Points
1 – Lancashire (5)	17	10	1	5	1	37	52	225*
2 – Yorkshire (4)	17	8	5	3	1	41	45	214
3 – Derbyshire (9)	17	7	2	6	2	43	47	202
4 – Warwickshire (1)	17	7	3	6	1	44	38	194
5 – Hampshire (15)	17	6	5	5	1	39	50	185
6 – Surrey (16)	17	5	3	8	1	44	53	177
7 – Northamptonshire (2)...	17	5	5	7	0	40	54	174
8 – Leicestershire (7)	17	6	3	7	1	39	38	173
9 – Sussex (16)	17	5	4	8	0	37	42	155†
10 – Glamorgan (13)	17	5	6	4	2	36	33	149
11 – Middlesex (3).........	17	4	4	8	1	35	50	149
12 – Gloucestershire (12)....	17	4	4	8	1	38	42	144
13 – Somerset (14).........	17	3	7	6	1	37	50	135
14 – Durham (8)...........	17	2	4	10	1	38	42	112
15 – Worcestershire (10)	17	2	7	7	1	36	43	111
16 – Kent (6)	17	2	5	10	0	34	39	105
17 – Essex (18)	17	1	10	5	1	29	45	90
18 – Nottinghamshire (11)...	17	0	4	11	2	42	41	83

1996 positions are shown in brackets.

* Lancashire had 24 points deducted, the total points gained, for fielding a second overseas player in their match against Yorkshire.

† The total for Sussex includes 12 points for a win in the match against Yorkshire which began when less than eight hours' playing time remained.

could – technically speaking – have lost more points. Yorkshire did not protest about this, however. "We wouldn't have wanted to win the title by default," said their cricket secretary, David Ryder.

Glamorgan's Michael Powell was named Second Eleven Player of the Year for scoring 1,210 runs in the Championship and 293 in the AON Trophy, both at an average of over 70. The Yorkshire pairing of Matthew Wood and Richard Kettleborough were the only men with higher aggregates. Lancashire's Gary Keedy was alone in passing fifty wickets, and did so at an unusually high strike rate for a spinner – a wicket every seven overs. Elsewhere, Somerset took the prize for heroic failure of the season. In an astounding game against Warwickshire, a triple-hundred by Marcus Trescothick took them to within seven runs of a fourth-innings target of 612 (*full scorecard page 903*).

Derbyshire's Second Eleven rose above club politics to finish third in the Championship, their highest placing in the 39-year history of the competition. Medium-pacer Paul Aldred got the ball rolling in May, taking eight for 73 against Nottinghamshire, and, in the Sussex fixture, Derbyshire accumulated a club-record total of 508 for four declared. Tim Tweats, who was to make a dramatic impact in the first team when he shared a stand of 417 in the last match of the season, scored 248 not out, and put on 176 for the fifth wicket with Matt Vandrau.

Durham slipped six places down the table, though there was nothing wrong with their batting. Twelve centuries, including three from former club captain Mike Roseberry and three from Robin Weston, made them difficult to beat, as ten draws demonstrated. But the bowling – with the honourable exception of Neil Killeen – was less effective. Normal service was resumed for bespectacled left-arm spinner David Cox; in 1996 he hit four Championship fifties to top the first team's averages, but nine second-team games in 1997 produced only 119 runs at 11.90.

Essex had a dreadful season, so it was something of a shock to find that five of their regulars – Stephen Peters, Jonathan Powell, Graham Napier, Ian Flanagan and Jamie Grove – were chosen for the England Under-19 tour of South Africa. Powell, an off-spinner, also went on the A tour of Kenya and Sri Lanka, even though his 36 wickets at 37.44 hardly represented an outstanding season. Essex suffered ten defeats, three more than any other county, and only avoided the wooden spoon thanks to Powell's best analysis of the summer – four for 46 – in a late win against Somerset.

Glamorgan were unable to emulate the feats of their first team, but Michael Powell's aggregate of 1,210 runs broke Alun Evans's year-old record. He hit 130 not out and 144 not out in the three-wicket win against Kent, and only Yorkshire's Richard Kettleborough and Surrey's Darren Bicknell matched his total of five centuries. Less encouragingly, Glamorgan finished as the only county without a single bowler past the 25-wicket mark.

Gloucestershire retained 12th place from the previous year, though they almost caused an upset against Surrey in the final of the AON Trophy. Matthew Windows and Robert Dawson defied an attack that included Joey Benjamin, Ian Salisbury and Alex Tudor to add 113 for the fourth wicket, but the bowlers narrowly failed to defend a total of 282. The highlight of their lacklustre Championship campaign was a county-record fourth-wicket stand of 284 between Matthew Church and Reggie Williams against Sussex.

Hampshire could boast few outstanding performers, but they functioned effectively enough as a unit to claim fifth place in the table. Eight batsmen averaged over 30, and seven scored centuries, while Dimitri Mascarenhas and Stuart Milburn both took twenty-plus wickets at an economical rate. Two other bowlers – Thomas Hansen from Denmark and Simon Francis – also impressed the first-team selectors, though it must be debatable whether they enjoyed their reward: a County Championship match against Worcestershire on a flat Southampton wicket. Hick and Moody put on an unbroken stand of 438 for Worcestershire's third wicket.

Kent, who had finished in the top six three times running, recorded only two wins in 1997 and fell to 16th. The release of Neil Taylor, their mainstay for the last couple of years, left the batting rather exposed, and only four centuries were scored. Robert Key, who averaged almost 43 with the bat from nine matches, might have improved matters if his availability had not been restricted by call-ups for England Under-18 and Under-19. Both James Hockley and David Masters showed enough promise to be offered contracts for the 1998 season.

Despite the ham-fisted mix-up over the status of their overseas players, **Lancashire** were worthy champions. Aggressive, penetrative bowling – especially from 22-year-old Gary Keedy – brought them ten wins, two more than second-placed Yorkshire. Keedy took 51 wickets at 14.80 with his left-arm spin, and carried his form over to the first team, claiming ten wickets against Surrey in September. Lancashire needed to win the equivalent Second Eleven fixture – their penultimate match – to keep one step ahead of Yorkshire, and they did so, thanks to an extraordinary match return of ten for 38 (six for 20 and four for 18) from Darren Shadford.

Just like their first team, **Leicestershire's** Second Eleven were hit by some of the country's worst weather. Only two of their 17 matches were unaffected, and Leicestershire won both of them on their way to a mid-season record of won five, drawn seven, abandoned one and lost none. But first-team calls and the introduction of several triallists led to three defeats in the remaining four games. However, opening batsman Darren Stevens improved as the summer went on; he made 96 runs at 8.72 from his first 12 innings, and still finished with 1,063 at 44.29, including four centuries.

Middlesex slid eight places to 11th and would have finished even lower but for three wins in their last four matches. The attack tended to be too one-paced, as seamers Simon Cook, Tim Bloomfield and Ricky Fay did most of the work. There were occasional appearances from off-spinning all-rounder Paul Weekes and 1996's Second Eleven Player of the Year, Keith Dutch, but the absence of a regular slow bowler was a disadvantage. Fifteen-year-old Matthew Creese showed great character in holding out for an unbeaten 14 as Middlesex beat Northamptonshire by one wicket.

Three wins in four matches in July raised **Northamptonshire's** hopes of at least equalling their second place of the previous year, but they tailed off after that. Tim Walton's 219 against Derbyshire was a highlight, and there were several successful bowlers, especially off-spinner Jason Brown and 18-year-old all-rounder Graeme Swann (whose older brother Alec also plays for the county). Northamptonshire finished with 54 bowling points, the most in the competition.

Winless **Nottinghamshire** took the wooden spoon for the second time in four years despite the efforts of Guy Welton, who made three centuries in his 898 runs. They lost only four matches, while second-placed Yorkshire lost five, but indifferent bowling and poor weather led to 11 draws, with another two matches abandoned. There was the small consolation of a county record stand, 130 for the ninth wicket, between Noel Gie and Mike Newell against Middlesex.

Somerset won three matches, but may have gained most satisfaction from the one that they lost, against Warwickshire. Somerset were set an apparently academic fourth-innings target of 612, but Marcus Trescothick smashed the record for the highest score in the competition with a brilliant 322, and took them to within seven runs of victory. In his one appearance, against Hampshire, Australian leg-spinner Stuart MacGill collected 13 wickets for 36. He went on to take a hat-trick for New South Wales against the New Zealanders early in the 1997-98 season.

The knock-on effect of international calls meant that **Surrey** were unable to field a settled side, though they remained in contention for the Championship until a run of three losses in their final three matches. But in the AON Trophy they were unstoppable, overcoming a committed Gloucestershire side in the final, thanks to fifties from Nadeem Shahid and Ben Hollioake. Another dominant performance came in the four-day game against Sussex at Hove, when Gregor

Kennis and Ian Ward both scored double-centuries and shared a mammoth second-wicket partnership of 392. Surrey's total, 678 for seven declared, was easily the highest in the history of the competition.

Sussex climbed seven places to ninth. James Kirtley bowled at high pace to top the bowling averages with 15 wickets from four matches, including a hat-trick against Hampshire. Among the batsmen, James Pyemont enjoyed a full complement of games in his last summer before going up to Cambridge University, and Rajesh Rao made the highest score – 199 against Derbyshire – though he was denied a double-century when he drove the ball into short leg's midriff. Later in the season, Rao would take revenge with 158 in Sussex's shock NatWest victory over the same opponents.

The 1996 champions **Warwickshire** came fourth and were again dependent on Australian-bred all-rounder Mike Edmond, who was prominent in both sets of averages. Just behind him in the batting table was Wasim Khan, who hit 215 against Glamorgan on his way to 1,158 runs in 13 matches, but asked to be released during the game against Somerset. He is likely to get more first-team cricket at Sussex next year. The most successful batsman of 1996, Michael Powell, had an indifferent season. He should not be confused with his record-breaking namesake at Glamorgan.

Worcestershire had a forgettable year, in which only two players really distinguished themselves. Vikram Solanki scored two centuries and averaged just over fifty, while Maneer Mirza, brother of the late Parvaz, was also promoted after five games in which he bowled with considerable pace.

Yorkshire climbed two places to second, and could have been champions if Lancashire had been penalised more than 24 points for fielding two overseas players on two separate occasions. Richard Kettleborough and Matthew Wood provided the foundation, scoring more than 2,500 runs between them, and Ian Fisher claimed 48 wickets with his orthodox left-arm spin. Only Lancashire's Keedy, another slow left-armer, took more. Kettleborough left the county at the end of the season, hoping to find greater first-team opportunity at Middlesex, while seamer Alex Wharf moved to Nottinghamshire soon after he was fined £100 and banned from one Second Eleven game for misbehaviour in a Bradford League match. Jamie Hood received a similar penalty after a bat-throwing incident – although his fine was only £50 – and was released by the county in September.

SOMERSET v WARWICKSHIRE

At Taunton, July 15, 16, 17, 18. Warwickshire won by six runs. Toss: Warwickshire.

Warwickshire's first four-day match in the Second Eleven Championship reached an extraordinary climax as Somerset, chasing a target of 612, were dismissed for 605. In their second innings, Trescothick entered at 50 for one and made 322 from 417 balls, striking 54 fours. It was the first triple-century in the history of the competition. But after he had shared a third-wicket stand of 154 with Burns, wickets were gradually winkled away at the other end, bringing Andrew Cottam, whose knuckle had been broken during the first innings, to the crease at 595 for nine. Trescothick tried to protect him, coming back for the second run after turning Edmond to the on side, but Howell's excellent throw ran him out by a foot. Trescothick had also boasted his county's best figures of the match – four for 41 out of Warwickshire's first-innings total of 296. Edmond hit back with six for 59 as Warwickshire took a 120-run lead, and then smashed 135 in just 66 minutes to set up the mammoth target.

Warwickshire

*W. G. Khan c Sutton b Jones	69	– c Bulbeck b Trescothick	29
M. J. Powell c Sutton b Jones	9	– c Sutton b Jones	14
A. Singh c Bulbeck b Burns	74	– lbw b Jones	129
C. R. Howell c Sutton b Trescothick	24	– lbw b Trescothick	93
N. V. Prabhu c Wells b Trescothick	13	– b Trego	72
M. D. Edmond c Wells b Burns	28	– c Herzberg b Trego	135
S. McDonald c Trego b Trescothick	0	– not out	2
†S. Platt c Sutton b Trescothick	17		
S. Vestergaard lbw b Cottam	14		
J. N. Webster not out	4		
K. Shah lbw b Burns	15		
B 2, l-b 15, n-b 12	29	L-b 13, n-b 4	17

1/15 2/139 3/171 4/193 5/200   296   1/19 2/72 3/233   (6 wkts dec.) 491
6/200 7/246 8/272 9/272   4/318 5/486 6/491

Bowling: *First Innings*—Jones 28-7-86-2; Burns 27.5-6-78-3; Bulbeck 6-0-39-0; Trescothick 17-3-41-4; Herzberg 7-0-31-0; Cottam 14-12-4-1. *Second Innings*—Jones 19-5-67-2; Burns 20-6-55-0; Trescothick 26-8-93-2; Morgan 37-7-156-0; Trego 22.3-6-107-2.

Somerset

H. J. Morgan c Platt b Edmond	0	– c Platt b Vestergaard	39
S. M. Trego lbw b Edmond	30	– c Platt b Webster	40
A. C. Cottam retired hurt	2	– (11) not out	0
L. A. Cooper lbw b Vestergaard	6	– (9) b Edmond	11
M. E. Trescothick lbw b Edmond	21	– (3) run out	322
M. Burns b Edmond	0	– (4) c Platt b Shah	68
S. Herzberg c Howell b Vestergaard	16	– (5) lbw b Prabhu	27
†L. D. Sutton c Platt b Edmond	4	– (6) lbw b Prabhu	34
P. S. Jones c Khan b McDonald	25	– (7) c Shah b McDonald	14
*C. M. Wells not out	49	– (8) lbw b Edmond	0
M. Bulbeck c Khan b Edmond	4	– (10) c Prabhu b Edmond	0
B 5, l-b 7, n-b 7	19	B 13, l-b 16, w 3, n-b 18	50

1/0 2/41 3/49 4/49 5/76   176   1/50 2/143 3/297 4/381 5/525   605
6/82 7/115 8/119 9/176   6/560 7/561 8/595 9/595

In the first innings A. C. Cottam retired hurt at 21.

Bowling: *First Innings*—Edmond 17.2-2-59-6; Vestergaard 14-2-65-2; Shah 7-3-15-0; McDonald 4-0-25-1. *Second Innings*—Vestergaard 26-7-106-1; Edmond 15.1-0-76-3; Shah 14-1-46-1; Webster 18-1-101-1; McDonald 36-5-143-1; Khan 3-0-17-0; Powell 26-11-64-0; Prabhu 9-2-23-2.

Umpires: B. Dudleston and B. Lucas.

DERBYSHIRE SECOND ELEVEN

Matches 17: Won – Durham, Essex, Hampshire, Nottinghamshire, Sussex, Warwickshire, Worcestershire. Lost – Lancashire, Northamptonshire. Drawn – Kent, Leicestershire, Middlesex, Somerset, Surrey, Yorkshire. Abandoned – Glamorgan, Gloucestershire.

Batting Averages

	M	I	NO	R	HS	100s	Avge
M. J. Vandrau	6	7	3	314	75*	0	78.50
G. A. Khan	11	13	2	670	114	2	60.90
I. D. Blackwell	8	10	2	434	102	1	54.25
S. D. Stubbings	9	13	2	568	146	1	51.63

	M	I	NO	R	HS	100s	Avge
*T. A. Tweats	7	11	1	504	248*	1	50.40
J. E. Owen	13	17	2	743	167	1	49.53
B. L. Spendlove	14	18	3	535	148	1	35.66
G. M. Roberts	10	6	3	100	54*	0	33.33
P. Aldred	7	5	1	129	75*	0	32.25
M. R. May	8	11	2	252	54	0	28.00
M. E. Cassar	5	7	0	175	70	0	25.00
†S. P. Griffiths	15	14	2	278	59	0	23.16

Played in 14 matches: T. Smith 4*, 0, 6, 7, 7*. Played in seven matches: K. J. Dean 2, 23, 58; A. N. Hayhurst 36*, 4*, 42*, 38*, 8, 84*, 6*, 29. Played in six matches: *A. M. Brown 4*, 0*. Played in five matches: S. J. Lacey 34, 0*, 15, 2. Played in two matches: D. Smit 7, 29. Played in one match: D. W. Ayres 3, 18; P. J. Clark 0; V. P. Clarke 86*; A. J. Harris 9; T. Lungley 4; A. P. Woolley 2*; J. Cornford, M. J. Deane, I. S. McDonnell, A. J. Marsh and N. D. Rimmer did not bat.

Bowling Averages

	O	M	R	W	BB	Avge
K. J. Dean	175.1	51	433	34	7-60	12.73
P. Aldred	264.5	70	762	41	8-73	18.58
S. J. Lacey	149.5	36	407	17	6-88	23.94
A. J. Harris	30.5	8	102	4	3-35	25.50
M. E. Cassar	87	13	360	13	4-100	27.69
I. D. Blackwell	190	53	576	18	4-21	32.00
M. J. Vandrau	181.4	37	534	16	4-62	33.37
T. Smith	345.4	72	1,210	36	5-37	33.61
G. M. Roberts	240	107	647	16	3-30	40.43
A. N. Hayhurst	73	16	203	4	2-78	50.75

Also bowled: D. W. Ayres 9–1–31–0; P. J. Clark 10–0–49–1; V. P. Clarke 27–3–103–1; J. Cornford 4–1–13–0; M. J. Deane 21–5–90–2; G. A. Khan 15–3–104–0; T. Lungley 9–3–21–0; A. J. Marsh 3–0–16–2; M. R. May 12–2–70–1; J. E. Owen 26.1–2–105–0; N. D. Rimmer 14–2–42–3; D. Smit 7–0–54–2; B. L. Spendlove 5–2–10–0; S. D. Stubbings 10.3–1–96–0; T. A. Tweats 10–2–62–0; A. P. Woolley 28–7–120–3.

DURHAM SECOND ELEVEN

Matches 17: Won – Essex, Worcestershire. Lost – Derbyshire, Leicestershire, Sussex, Yorkshire. Drawn – Glamorgan, Gloucestershire, Hampshire, Kent, Lancashire, Middlesex, Northamptonshire, Nottinghamshire, Somerset, Warwickshire. Abandoned – Surrey.

Batting Averages

	M	I	NO	R	HS	100s	Avge
†D. G. C. Ligertwood	6	9	4	550	147*	2	110.00
M. A. Roseberry	9	13	5	668	134	3	83.50
R. M. S. Weston	11	15	5	663	172*	3	66.30
Q. J. Hughes	3	5	0	279	168	1	55.80
S. Hutton	11	18	1	738	159	1	43.41
J. A. Daley	16	25	1	899	144	2	37.45
D. A. Blenkiron	8	10	1	308	86	0	34.22
P. L. Carlin	6	10	1	222	49	0	24.66
†A. Pratt	15	21	5	326	46	0	20.37
S. J. Birtwisle	4	7	0	116	54	0	16.57
N. Killeen	13	16	1	226	31	0	15.06
N. J. Speak	4	6	0	87	27	0	14.50
D. M. Cox	9	10	0	119	48	0	11.90

	M	I	NO	R	HS	100s	Avge
J. P. Searle	15	14	4	85	16*	0	8.50
C. L. Campbell	8	7	2	38	13*	0	7.60
S. Lugsden	10	8	3	32	24	0	6.40
M. J. Saggers	7	8	0	23	12	0	2.87

Played in three matches: J. Wood 27, 12*, 0. Played in two matches: P. D. Collingwood 32, 32; M. A. J. Gough 13, 0, 25; J. A. Graham 21, 10, 20; M. J. Symington 18, 4, 3. Played in one match: M. M. Betts 15, 0*; S. J. Harmison 0, 0; I. D. Hunter 15; C. G. Mason 18, 17; S. P. Naylor 4*; P. A. Spence 1, 40*; I. Jones, P. Lindsay, I. H. Shah and A. Walker did not bat.

Bowling Averages

	O	M	R	W	BB	Avge
I. Jones	20	8	48	4	3-22	12.00
J. Wood	75.2	18	236	13	4-65	18.15
M. J. Symington	29	6	115	5	3-89	23.00
N. Killeen............	360.4	92	999	42	7-57	23.78
D. M. Cox	329.2	119	742	28	5-109	26.50
S. Lugsden	170.2	23	759	28	5-41	27.10
M. J. Saggers	176.1	31	685	25	6-43	27.40
C. L. Campbell	148.3	36	504	12	4-50	42.00
J. P. Searle	357.3	76	1,135	20	3-50	56.75

Also bowled: M. M. Betts 42–13–95–3; D. A. Blenkiron 40.5–6–181–3; P. D. Collingwood 13–1–52–1; J. A. Daley 1–0–9–0; M. A. J. Gough 11–2–50–0; J. A. Graham 2–0–9–0; S. J. Harmison 5–0–27–0; I. D. Hunter 12–4–34–3; D. G. C. Ligertwood 2–0–19–0; P. Lindsay 11–1–50–0; C. G. Mason 5–1–24–1; S. P. Naylor 5–2–14–0; M. A. Roseberry 5.3–0–26–3; N. J. Speak 2–0–12–0; P. A. Spence 21–4–62–0; A. Walker 23–9–47–1; R. M. S. Weston 37.1–2–143–2.

ESSEX SECOND ELEVEN

Matches 17: Won – Somerset. Lost – Derbyshire, Durham, Glamorgan, Gloucestershire, Hampshire, Middlesex, Northamptonshire, Warwickshire, Worcestershire, Yorkshire. Drawn – Kent, Lancashire, Leicestershire, Surrey, Sussex. Abandoned – Nottinghamshire.

Batting Averages

	M	I	NO	R	HS	100s	Avge
D. D. J. Robinson	5	8	1	347	109	1	49.57
T. P. Hodgson	4	8	3	202	54	0	40.40
A. J. E. Hibbert	15	29	7	774	226*	1	35.18
*A. R. Butcher........	8	11	5	207	51*	0	34.50
G. R. Napier..........	8	14	2	318	70*	0	26.50
†W. Ritzema	10	18	1	429	106	1	25.23
†B. J. Hyam..........	10	16	1	319	79*	0	21.26
D. G. Wilson	13	22	4	379	57*	0	21.05
J. C. Powell	13	22	1	427	116	1	20.33
S. D. Peters	10	18	0	330	49	0	18.33
D. M. Cousins	6	6	1	80	26	0	16.00
I. N. Flanagan	12	22	1	334	56*	0	15.90
N. F. Williams	6	7	0	103	58	0	14.71
G. J. A. Goodwin	6	7	1	72	32*	0	12.00
S. J. W. Andrew	13	16	4	132	50	0	11.00
J. O. Grove..........	11	18	5	116	22	0	8.92

Played in three matches: M. Ismail 24, 2, 0, 15, 4; H. Sana 46, 5, 0*, 8, 23. Played in two matches: M. S. Ali 14, 1, 0; †R. J. Rollins 33, 48, 80, 31; P. R. Shaw 54, 8, 15. Played in one match: M. Asim 9, 9*, I. J. Boyton 24, 11; P. J. Clark 1, 0; D. J. Cowley 4, 13; J. G. Foster 0, 0; M. C. Ilott 53*, 11; G. S. Kandola 16*, 2; S. Mahmood 0; R. J. Mansfield 7, 1; T. J. Phillips 27; P. J. Pineo 1*, 9; A. Richardson 0*; J. Roberts 1*; I. Shah 2; C. J. Warn 34, 13.

Note: In the match v Northamptonshire at Northampton, N. F. Williams, called up for a first-team match, was replaced by D. G. Wilson.

Bowling Averages

	O	M	R	W	BB	Avge
M. C. Ilott	24	7	64	5	3-37	12.80
T. J. Phillips..........	28	12	58	4	2-18	14.50
D. M. Cousins	118	24	362	21	4-17	17.23
S. J. W. Andrew	264	67	728	38	5-18	19.15
H. Sana..............	69	13	237	12	6-72	19.75
D. J. Cowley	32	6	119	6	3-21	19.83
J. C. Powell	374.3	72	1,348	36	4-46	37.44
J. O. Grove...........	199.3	39	785	20	3-26	39.25
N. F. Williams	102.4	20	366	9	3-51	40.66
A. J. E. Hibbert	72	10	269	6	3-42	44.83
G. R. Napier..........	64	8	291	6	3-69	48.50
D. G. Wilson	156.2	28	593	10	2-50	59.30
G. J. A. Goodwin	108.3	21	365	6	3-95	60.83

Also bowled: M. Asim 19.2–2–76–1; A. R. Butcher 1–0–16–0; P. J. Clark 11–1–60–0; I. N. Flanagan 9–1–44–0; M. Ismail 17–1–128–2; G. S. Kandola 11–2–49–0; S. Mahmood 18–6–52–2; S. D. Peters 0.1–0–2–0; P. J. Pineo 18–4–44–2; A. Richardson 15–6–42–1; W. Ritzema 24–3–124–1; I. Shah 15–0–65–0.

GLAMORGAN SECOND ELEVEN

Matches 17: Won – Essex, Kent, Middlesex, Somerset, Yorkshire. Lost – Hampshire, Lancashire, Leicestershire, Surrey, Sussex, Warwickshire. Drawn – Durham, Gloucestershire, Northamptonshire, Nottinghamshire. Abandoned – Derbyshire, Worcestershire.

Batting Averages

	M	I	NO	R	HS	100s	Avge
M. J. Powell...........	11	20	4	1,210	152	5	75.62
R. V. Almond	4	8	2	389	149	1	64.83
I. J. Thomas	9	17	2	651	96*	0	43.40
A. W. Evans...........	12	22	1	775	124	2	36.90
*J. Derrick	15	21	6	538	66	0	35.86
W. L. Law	14	26	4	628	115*	1	28.54
A. P. Davies	6	11	1	218	62	0	21.80
M. D. O'Leary........	6	7	2	100	45*	0	20.00
C. W. Boroughs.......	4	8	0	127	47	0	15.87
O. T. Parkin	9	12	3	138	30	0	15.33
L. O. Jones	8	12	0	166	31	0	13.83
G. J. M. Edwards......	8	9	6	40	11*	0	13.33
P. S. George..........	4	6	0	57	30	0	9.50
†C. P. Metson	11	18	0	170	20	0	9.44
B. M. Morgan	6	7	2	46	23	0	9.20
D. L. Iniff............	7	8	3	38	28	0	7.60

Played in three matches: G. Arrowsmith 21, 2, 18, 2, 1, 58*; G. J. Hayne 36, 66*, 17, 53, 23; S. C. B. Tomlinson 13, 50*, 22*, 1, 12, 0. Played in two matches: G. P. Butcher 7, 12, 15, 2; D. A. Cosker 1*, 5*, 7; †R. E. Evans 54, 0, 6, 0; L. H. Nurse 5, 3, 13, 35; P. M. Warren 1, 2. Played in one match: I. Gompertz 0, 5; G. C. Hopkins 0, 0; J. Hughes 9, 4; S. P. Jones 0*; M. S. Leaf 35, 5; C. W. McDonnell 6, 12; M. K. Palmer 51, 4*; †W. Ritzema 6, 5; †M. A. Wallace 7; S. L. Chapman, M. D. Price and M. Taylor did not bat.

Bowling Averages

	O	M	R	W	BB	Avge
D. A. Cosker	68	26	128	11	6-65	11.63
P. M. Warren	51.3	15	144	7	5-43	20.57
G. P. Butcher	38.1	4	170	8	3-52	21.25
J. Derrick	165.3	41	524	19	5-105	27.57
D. L. Iniff............	139.1	23	585	16	6-96	36.56
P. S. George	71.1	14	235	6	2-18	39.16
O. T. Parkin	257.2	53	901	22	6-61	40.95
B. M. Morgan	124	14	563	13	5-87	43.30
L. O. Jones..........	167.5	38	580	13	5-124	44.61
A. P. Davies..........	159	32	559	12	4-70	46.58
M. D. O'Leary	86	17	342	7	2-36	48.85
G. J. M. Edwards......	231	42	891	10	2-54	89.10

Also bowled: G. Arrowsmith 31–7–114–2; C. W. Boroughs 59–11–176–1; S. L. Chapman 20–1–86–0; A. W. Evans 18–2–72–2; I. Gompertz 9–2–29–1; S. P. Jones 23–0–148–3; W. L. Law 19–2–82–0; M. J. Powell 5–0–30–0; M. D. Price 20.4–7–88–3; M. Taylor 32–6–101–1; S. C. B. Tomlinson 25–4–104–3.

GLOUCESTERSHIRE SECOND ELEVEN

Matches 17: Won – Essex, Hampshire, Lancashire, Somerset. Lost – Leicestershire, Sussex, Worcestershire, Yorkshire. Drawn – Durham, Glamorgan, Kent, Middlesex, Northamptonshire, Nottinghamshire, Surrey, Warwickshire. Abandoned – Derbyshire.

Batting Averages

	M	I	NO	R	HS	100s	Avge
M. A. Lynch	3	5	1	283	142	2	70.75
N. J. Trainor..........	5	8	2	422	191*	2	70.33
M. J. Church	11	17	5	682	137*	3	56.83
R. I. Dawson	7	11	1	477	105*	1	47.70
D. R. Hewson	14	23	3	853	139*	1	42.65
M. G. N. Windows	9	15	2	524	157*	1	40.30
M. A. Coombes	4	5	0	178	94	0	35.60
†R. C. J. Williams.....	13	17	3	468	132*	1	33.42
†C. M. W. Read	13	17	4	391	148*	1	30.07
C. M. Gupte	8	12	1	312	100*	1	28.36
M. P. Hunt	9	11	2	215	45	0	23.88
J. M. M. Averis	7	6	0	124	52	0	20.66
C. R. J. Budd.........	5	6	0	120	66	0	20.00
K. P. Sheeraz	12	13	3	173	31	0	17.30
R. J. Cunliffe	7	10	0	124	28	0	12.40
M. J. Cawdron	8	7	1	72	22	0	12.00
B. David	6	5	1	47	30	0	11.75
B. W. Gannon	7	7	3	35	13	0	8.75
R. Turnell	3	6	1	25	14	0	5.00
L. P. Collins.........	7	6	1	2	1*	0	0.40

Played in three matches: R. P. Davis 13, 40*; D. Forder 1*, 4*, 6*. Played in two matches: P. Fisher 0*; A. M. James 10, 5*, 2; P. S. Lazenbury 4, 5; C. G. Taylor 0, 0. Played in one match: B. W. Griffiths 2, 34; M. A. Hardinges 1; D. V. Lawrence 6; P. J. Morris 1, 1; L. J. Ratcliffe 0, 4; A. J. Wright 4.

Note: In the match v Nottinghamshire at Hatherley and Reddings, M. J. Cawdron and J. M. M. Averis, called up for a first-team match, were replaced by M. A. Coombes and M. A. Hardinges.

Bowling Averages

	O	M	R	W	BB	Avge
L. J. Ratcliffe	14.3	7	25	4	4-25	6.25
D. Forder	51.3	8	213	10	5-139	21.30
K. P. Sheeraz	346.2	75	1,074	46	5-43	23.34
R. P. Davis	78.3	25	177	7	3-93	25.28
M. P. Hunt	154	27	550	21	6-87	26.19
B. David	123.1	22	418	14	5-21	29.85
B. W. Gannon	154	29	630	21	3-45	30.00
J. M. M. Averis	138.2	30	443	13	5-73	34.07
M. J. Cawdron	172	40	547	15	3-39	36.46
M. G. N. Windows	78	18	288	7	3-33	41.14
R. Turnell	45.2	7	221	5	4-58	44.20
R. I. Dawson	78.2	7	321	7	4-73	45.85
P. Fisher	52	12	187	4	2-39	46.75
L. P. Collins	155.2	36	547	10	5-78	54.70
N. J. Trainor	70	6	269	4	3-101	67.25

Also bowled: C. R. J. Budd 13–2–60–1; M. J. Church 2–0–4–0; R. J. Cunliffe 1–0–1–0; M. A. Hardinges 6–1–28–1; D. R. Hewson 40–6–185–1; A. M. James 31–10–61–3; D. V. Lawrence 14–0–43–0; M. A. Lynch 10–3–32–0; P. J. Morris 13–2–38–0.

HAMPSHIRE SECOND ELEVEN

Matches 17: Won – Essex, Glamorgan, Kent, Middlesex, Nottinghamshire, Warwickshire. Lost – Derbyshire, Gloucestershire, Lancashire, Somerset, Yorkshire. Drawn – Durham, Northamptonshire, Surrey, Sussex, Worcestershire. Abandoned – Leicestershire.

Batting Averages

	M	I	NO	R	HS	100s	Avge
D. M. Lane	5	7	1	305	98	0	50.83
G. W. White	6	11	3	399	126	1	49.87
M. Keech	3	5	1	167	93	0	41.75
K. D. James	7	10	2	324	87	0	40.50
P. R. Whitaker	15	26	4	837	123	2	38.04
A. D. Mascarenhas	5	8	2	215	114*	1	35.83
†D. A. Kenway	12	18	1	592	112	1	34.82
*†M. Garaway	12	17	0	580	136	1	34.11
G. R. Treagus	16	28	1	795	105	1	29.44
W. S. Kendall	7	10	0	292	67	0	29.20
C. Patel	7	8	4	90	40*	0	22.50
L. Savident	9	13	3	193	43*	0	19.30
J. N. B. Bovill	3	5	1	76	29*	0	19.00
J. R. Carpenter	6	7	2	78	36	0	15.60
R. R. Dibden	9	7	3	54	41	0	13.50
S. R. G. Francis	7	7	2	48	26	0	9.60
M. Swarbrick	8	10	0	78	30	0	7.80
T. M. Hansen	5	6	0	46	29	0	7.66

Played in five matches: S. M. Milburn 14, 7*, 0, 4, 7*, 9*; B. V. Taylor 0*, 12*, 1*, 1, 1, 9. Played in three matches: N. J. Makin 0*, 0, 4, 10*. Played in two matches: J. S. Laney 5, 0, 180*, 44; R. D. McLaren 15, 33, 8; R. J. Maru 3. Played in one match: P. J. Bradshaw 2; A. P. Cole 33; J. A. G. Fulton 16, 11; N. D. Hughes 0; R. T. P. Miller 30, 5; S. J. Renshaw 24*; G. J. J. Sheen 21; B. Singh 0, 3; R. P. Taylor 20*; N. J. Thurgood 4, 9; C. G. Van der Gucht 2*; D. A. Walker 4; C. J. Warn 9; W. R. Coppin and A. M. Shimmons did not bat.

Bowling Averages

	O	M	R	W	BB	'Avge
J. N. B. Bovill	82	28	164	11	4-48	14.90
R. J. Maru	54	21	87	5	5-33	17.40
G. R. Treagus.........	45.5	9	182	10	5-56	18.20
A. D. Mascarenhas	152.4	39	474	24	6-82	19.75
S. M. Milburn	212.1	55	600	29	6-56	20.68
T. M. Hansen.........	102.4	27	294	12	4-52	24.50
N. J. Makin	34.5	2	175	6	3-33	29.16
C. Patel..............	152.1	26	593	20	5-88	29.65
P. R. Whitaker........	258.1	51	776	26	3-35	29.84
L. Savident...........	128.5	19	461	15	3-25	30.73
S. R. G. Francis.......	134.1	24	510	15	3-39	34.00
B. V. Taylor..........	76	17	266	5	1-23	53.20
R. R. Dibden	173.5	26	689	12	4-7	57.41
J. R. Carpenter........	111	19	359	6	2-45	59.83

Also bowled: P. J. Bradshaw 23–3–94–2; A. P. Cole 17.4–2–67–2; W. R. Coppin 12–4–40–1; N. D. Hughes 10–2–34–2; K. D. James 22–7–74–3; M. Keech 35–11–87–1; W. S. Kendall 8–0–57–1; D. A. Kenway 5–2–8–0; R. D. McLaren 27–4–114–2; R. T. P. Miller 9–0–31–0; S. J. Renshaw 34.1–8–78–1; A. M. Shimmons 31–8–92–3; M. Swarbrick 3–0–24–1; R. P. Taylor 7.4–3–14–1; C. G. Van der Gucht 5–3–6–0; D. A. Walker 9–2–53–1; G. W. White 8–1–46–0.

KENT SECOND ELEVEN

Matches 17: Won – Middlesex, Yorkshire. Lost – Glamorgan, Hampshire, Lancashire, Northamptonshire, Warwickshire. Drawn – Derbyshire, Durham, Essex, Gloucestershire, Leicestershire, Nottinghamshire, Somerset, Surrey, Sussex, Worcestershire.

Batting Averages

	M	I	NO	R	HS	100s	Avge
W. J. House	8	12	3	552	92*	0	61.33
M. J. Walker .....ç..	4	7	1	354	140*	1	59.00
J. H. Baldock	8	11	3	456	93	0	57.00
R. W. T. Key.........	9	12	3	386	139*	1	42.88
*N. J. Llong..........	8	13	2	455	151*	1	41.36
J. B. D. Thompson	4	5	1	147	61	0	36.75
C. D. Walsh	11	17	2	443	85	0	29.53
J. B. Hockley	10	11	0	286	69	0	26.00
B. J. Phillips..........	5	8	1	179	53	0	25.57
†S. C. Willis	16	20	1	452	87	0	23.78
D. A. Scott	15	13	4	211	68	0	23.44
J. A. Ford............	10	16	3	279	46	0	21.46
E. J. Stanford	16	17	4	262	47	0	20.15
N. W. Preston	12	14	2	225	62	0	18.75
T. N. Wren...........	15	15	1	163	83	0	11.64
D. D. Masters.........	16	15	5	109	53*	0	10.90
J. M. Golding.........	7	7	0	62	32	0	8.85

Played in three matches: S. J. Taylor 13, 0, 17, 25*. Played in two matches: A. P. Igglesden 0; R. Terry 0*, 4. Played in one match: †J. L. Hartley 0*; C. A. Holcomb 12; M. J. Ladbrook 35, 15; S. G. Milroy 7, 11*; M. M. Patel 3, 74; E. T. Smith 77, 102.

Bowling Averages

	O	M	R	W	BB	Avge
M. M. Patel	41.2	12	93	8	6-78	11.62
A. P. Igglesden	23	6	74	6	4-42	12.33
N. J. Llong	161.2	53	399	19	5-46	21.00
J. B. Hockley	55	12	186	8	3-22	23.25
D. A. Scott	250.1	71	689	26	6-26	26.50
N. W. Preston	210.3	51	575	21	3-50	27.38
E. J. Stanford	308	72	1,005	32	6-18	31.40
B. J. Phillips..........	109	32	326	10	3-46	32.60
W. J. House	58	11	200	5	4-61	40.00
T. N. Wren............	309.4	72	1,012	25	4-38	40.48
J. M. Golding.........	64.5	12	243	6	2-27	40.50
J. B. D. Thompson	73.5	19	250	6	4-80	41.66
D. D. Masters........	195	37	690	14	3-71	49.28
J. A. Ford	57.2	7	248	3	2-61	82.66

Also bowled: R. W. T. Key 5.4–1–25–2; S. G. Milroy 5–1–21–0; S. J. Taylor 6–1–23–0; R. Terry 23–4–131–0; M. J. Walker 3–1–2–0; C. D. Walsh 10–0–39–1.

LANCASHIRE SECOND ELEVEN

Matches 17: Won – Derbyshire, Glamorgan, Hampshire, Kent, Leicestershire, Nottinghamshire, Surrey, Sussex, Worcestershire, Yorkshire. Lost – Gloucestershire. Drawn – Durham, Essex, Middlesex, Northamptonshire, Warwickshire. Abandoned – Somerset.

Batting Averages

	M	I	NO	R	HS	100s	Avge
S. P. Titchard.........	6	8	3	262	72	0	52.40
M. J. Chilton	9	11	2	418	123	1	46.44
A. Flintoff............	8	9	2	312	187*	1	44.57
†J. J. Haynes	16	18	6	517	98	0	43.08
P. C. McKeown	15	21	1	810	107	3	40.50
G. Chapple	4	4	0	137	47	0	34.25
*P. R. Sleep	16	13	3	342	101*	1	34.20
M. E. Harvey	14	20	3	490	92	0	28.82
N. T. Wood	9	15	2	339	88*	0	26.07
C. P. Schofield	9	11	4	178	34	0	25.42
G. Keedy	9	8	3	122	33*	0	24.40
R. J. Green	6	8	0	189	53	0	23.62
G. Yates	3	4	0	85	60	0	21.25
A. J. Crozier..........	5	7	0	129	46	0	18.42
D. J. Shadford	8	7	0	118	46	0	16.85
P. M. Ridgway........	13	13	4	104	33*	0	11.55
C. Brown	10	12	3	99	32*	0	11.00

Played in three matches: L. J. Bones 0. Played in two matches: J. E. R. Gallian 55, 71, 49; S. C. Oddie 0*; J. C. Peterson 157, 43; †D. J. Pipe 3, 26. Played in one match: M. J. Brown 54, 9; K. Farooq 9*; J. R. G. Lawrence 0; G. D. Lloyd 228; A. D. MacLaren 0; S. Rashid 9*; A. Shadford 2; C. J. Hall did not bat.

Note: Owing to first-team calls, J. J. Haynes and P. M. Ridgway were replaced by A. J. Crozier and A. D. MacLaren in the match v Gloucestershire at Southport, and A. Flintoff was replaced by P. R. Sleep in the match v Sussex at Middleton-on-Sea, but Sleep did not bat or bowl.

Bowling Averages

	O	M	R	W	BB	Avge
G. Yates	131.4	64	200	22	7-49	9.09
G. Chapple	62.2	22	181	15	6-46	12.06
R. J. Green	60.1	19	157	11	6-43	14.27

	O	M	R	W	BB	Avge
S. P. Titchard	27	12	59	4	2-26	14.75
G. Keedy	362.2	115	755	51	7-74	14.80
D. J. Shadford	163.4	36	553	35	6-20	15.80
J. C. Peterson	41	14	87	4	2-25	21.75
P. R. Sleep	139	74	245	10	2-8	24.50
P. M. Ridgway	322.4	80	1,004	37	6-44	27.13
M. J. Chilton	50	17	145	5	2-13	29.00
C. Brown	272.2	78	725	24	5-36	30.20
C. P. Schofield	213.2	56	591	19	3-57	31.10

Also bowled: L. J. Bones 27–6–72–0; K. Farooq 9–2–41–1; A. Flintoff 5–1–25–0; J. E. R. Gallian 10–3–44–1; C. J. Hall 4–1–9–0; M. E. Harvey 4–3–1–0; J. R. G. Lawrence 21–4–57–0; A. D. MacLaren 6–2–10–0; P. C. McKeown 36–6–159–3; S. C. Oddie 26–4–92–1; S. Rashid 19–1–80–2; A. Shadford 20–6–64–3.

LEICESTERSHIRE SECOND ELEVEN

Matches 17: Won – Durham, Glamorgan, Gloucestershire, Northamptonshire, Nottinghamshire, Sussex. Lost – Lancashire, Warwickshire, Yorkshire. Drawn – Derbyshire, Essex, Kent, Middlesex, Somerset, Surrey, Worcestershire. Abandoned – Hampshire.

Batting Averages

	M	I	NO	R	HS	100s	Avge
*P. E. Robinson	11	10	4	341	103	1	56.83
G. I. Macmillan	3	4	0	201	129	1	50.25
D. I. Stevens	16	27	3	1,063	181	4	44.29
†I. J. Sutcliffe	4	7	0	291	128	1	41.57
D. Williamson	15	20	3	674	110	1	39.64
J. M. Dakin	9	14	1	477	100	1	36.69
T. J. Mason	14	18	7	401	57*	0	36.45
J. Ormond.	4	7	0	248	67	0	35.42
A. Habib.	4	7	0	205	64	0	29.28
C. D. Crowe.	16	25	3	555	63	0	25.22
G. A. White	2	4	1	74	45	0	24.66
A. S. Wright.	7	13	1	241	83*	0	20.08
S. A. Richardson	16	30	4	516	87	0	19.84
†P. Whitticase	6	6	2	63	28	0	15.75
A. Thomas	14	15	6	81	24*	0	9.00
S. Kirby	7	8	2	54	19*	0	9.00

Played in four matches: G. J. Parsons 21, 10*, 37. Played in three matches: †P. G. T. Davies 7, 39*, 5; P. Fisher 0*, 6, 0, 1*. Played in two matches: M. T. Brimson 23; †B. Moore 0, 2. Played in one match: †M. J. E. Bishop 15, 2; P. J. Bradshaw 8, 7; J. E. Brinkley 6, 11; S. M. Eustace 7*, 1; K. G. Howarth 4; D. J. Rock 0, 2; A. Sachdeva 0, 4; M. Sarfraz 0, 7; B. F. Smith 15*; †J. D. Smith 9; M. W. Thomas 12*, 34; †R. D. Whalley 8, 8; J. W. Cook and A. R. K. Pierson did not bat.

Bowling Averages

	O	M	R	W	BB	Avge
G. I. Macmillan	42.4	14	67	11	5-20	6.09
G. J. Parsons	85.5	33	163	9	3-62	18.11
M. T. Brimson	69	24	147	8	3-38	18.37
K. G. Howarth	29	7	80	4	2-32	20.00
D. Williamson	230.5	66	625	30	5-77	20.83
J. Ormond.	101	25	299	13	5-32	23.00
T. J. Mason	290	73	823	28	5-38	29.39

	O	M	R	W	BB	Avge
S. Kirby	102	16	392	13	4-41	30.15
C. D. Crowe	289.1	67	866	23	3-58	37.65
J. M. Dakin	116.5	31	388	10	2-11	38.80
A. Thomas	292.5	54	1,020	25	3-41	40.80

Also bowled: P. J. Bradshaw 16–4–68–0; J. E. Brinkley 15–3–67–0; P. Fisher 26.5–3–95–3; P. E. Robinson 4–1–11–0; A. Sachdeva 6–0–27–0; M. Sarfraz 9–0–36–0; D. I. Stevens 9.5–3–37–2; I. J. Sutcliffe 17–2–81–2; M. W. Thomas 13–2–55–0.

MIDDLESEX SECOND ELEVEN

Matches 17: Won – Essex, Northamptonshire, Somerset, Worcestershire. Lost – Glamorgan, Hampshire, Kent, Yorkshire. Drawn – Derbyshire, Durham, Gloucestershire, Lancashire, Leicestershire, Nottinghamshire, Surrey, Sussex. Abandoned – Warwickshire.

Batting Averages

	M	I	NO	R	HS	100s	Avge
P. N. Weekes	4	6	1	342	132	2	68.40
S. P. Moffat	8	14	3	489	117	1	44.45
D. J. Goodchild	9	15	0	563	145	2	37.53
P. E. Wellings	4	6	0	217	94	0	36.16
S. A. Selwood	4	6	1	175	88*	0	35.00
I. J. Gould	8	11	7	137	26*	0	34.25
P. R. Sawyer	3	5	0	171	57	0	34.20
J. C. Harrison	5	8	1	236	59*	0	33.71
†D. C. Nash	10	16	0	488	81	0	30.50
K. P. Dutch	5	7	1	181	65	0	30.16
A. W. Laraman	14	22	4	519	92*	0	28.83
†D. Alleyne	6	10	3	193	60*	0	27.57
B. L. Hutton	9	15	0	330	72	0	22.00
U. B. A. Rashid	5	7	1	128	43	0	21.33
I. N. Blanchett	10	14	3	231	108*	1	21.00
J. K. Maunders	5	9	1	153	41	0	19.12
M. R. Evans	3	5	1	69	28	0	17.25
A. J. Strauss	8	12	0	149	40	0	12.41
R. A. Fay	7	10	2	92	21	0	11.50
N. D. Martin	10	11	4	54	11*	0	7.71
T. F. Bloomfield	9	9	2	43	14	0	6.14
S. J. Cook	10	11	0	49	24	0	4.45

Played in three matches: C. P. Coleman 6, 22, 8. Played in two matches: M. L. Creese 0, 9, 14*; J. M. de la Pena 0, 1*; P. C. R. Tufnell 12*; A. A. Khan did not bat. Played in one match: M. W. Gatting 85; O. R. Hutton 10, 2; E. C. Joyce 23, 11*; R. P. Lane 62, 4; J. S. Norman 0, 17; S. Patel 0, 3; O. A. Shah 32, 9; R. W. Swetman 0, 0; R. C. Thelwell 20, 10.

Bowling Averages

	O	M	R	W	BB	Avge
R. P. Lane	19.1	8	42	4	4-42	10.50
K. P. Dutch	137	43	323	16	4-11	20.18
J. C. Harrison	108	24	275	13	4-66	21.15
P. N. Weekes	61	12	171	8	3-53	21.37
S. J. Cook	163.2	30	548	24	5-67	22.83
U. B. A. Rashid	122.1	34	391	17	4-84	23.00
T. F. Bloomfield	182	31	589	25	4-51	23.56

	O	M	R	W	BB	Avge
R. A. Fay	167.3	34	584	23	6-45	25.39
I. J. Gould	39.3	9	107	4	1-1	26.75
A. W. Laraman	124.1	30	402	14	3-48	28.71
N. D. Martin	131.5	29	417	14	4-25	29.78
I. N. Blanchett	152.2	18	571	13	3-53	43.92

Also bowled: M. L. Creese 27–8–93–2; J. M. de la Pena 57–5–283–3; M. R. Evans 20–1–79–1; D. J. Goodchild 26–3–84–1; B. L. Hutton 43–3–146–3; A. A. Khan 8–2–35–0; S. P. Moffat 5–1–21–0; S. Patel 11–3–32–0; A. J. Strauss 3–0–17–0; P. C. R. Tufnell 45–23–74–1; P. E. Wellings 19–1–79–2.

NORTHAMPTONSHIRE SECOND ELEVEN

Matches 17: Won – Derbyshire, Essex, Kent, Surrey, Worcestershire. Lost – Leicestershire, Middlesex, Somerset, Sussex, Warwickshire. Drawn – Durham, Glamorgan, Gloucestershire, Hampshire, Lancashire, Nottinghamshire, Yorkshire.

Batting Averages

	M	I	NO	R	HS	100s	Avge
T. C. Walton	8	13	2	745	219	1	67.72
R. R. Montgomerie	9	16	2	805	121	1	57.50
†R. J. Warren	4	6	0	333	151	1	55.50
J. G. Hughes	5	7	3	214	53	0	53.50
A. L. Penberthy	4	4	0	198	86	0	49.50
A. Fordham	10	17	3	617	105	1	44.07
K. J. Innes	16	23	4	830	194	1	43.68
A. J. Swann	15	24	3	747	162*	2	35.57
G. P. Swann	9	11	0	282	106	1	25.63
D. J. Roberts	9	13	1	299	51	0	24.91
†T. M. B. Bailey	12	15	1	263	57*	0	18.78
S. A. J. Boswell.......	4	5	0	83	36	0	16.60
N. G. B. Cook	7	7	1	81	27	0	13.50
M. V. Steele..........	7	9	0	101	24	0	11.22
J. A. R. Blain........	10	12	2	77	24	0	7.70
D. Follett	8	10	2	58	14*	0	7.25
J. F. Brown	13	12	5	37	16	0	5.28

Played in seven matches: M. K. Davies 30, 1, 0*, 2*. Played in three matches: D. J. Capel 111, 31*, 85, 28; M. B. Loye 16*, 6*, 15, 6, 6; D. J. Sales 8*, 58, 115*, 0, 140*; R. A. White 36*, 36, 0, 32. Played in two matches: A. M. Dobson 3, 6, 12; R. J. Logan 12, 19*, 1; A. Richardson 4*, 1*, P. A. Spence 7*; W. Stevens 0*, 1*, 0, 5*; P. A. Thomas 15, 13, 15. Played in one match: D. Culbard 5; J. E. Emburey 2*; J. M. Fielding 2*; B. S. Phelps 12*; M. J. Powell 0, 0; A. R. Roberts 17; A. Romaine 3; R. Turnell 4*.

Note: Owing to first-team calls, D. J. Roberts was replaced by G. P. Swann in the match v Worcestershire at Campbell Park, and A. L. Penberthy was replaced by R. A. White in the match v Middlesex at RAF Vine Lane, Uxbridge.

Bowling Averages

	O	M	R	W	BB	Avge
A. L. Penberthy	77	16	227	15	5-61	15.13
T. C. Walton	72	7	225	11	4-25	20.45
P. A. Spence	31	7	94	4	2-34	23.50
G. P. Swann..........	201.5	59	621	26	4-61	23.88
J. F. Brown	401.4	100	1,013	33	6-37	30.69
S. A. J. Boswell.......	95.1	14	338	11	4-56	30.72

	O	M	R	W	BB	Avge
K. J. Innes	253.3	46	898	28	4-48	32.07
M. V. Steele..........	76	6	334	9	3-47	37.11
D. J. Capel	61	11	225	6	3-50	37.50
M. K. Davies	168	51	490	13	2-25	37.69
J. A. R. Blain........	179	27	674	16	3-73	42.12
D. Follett	140.3	29	554	11	3-55	50.36
J. G. Hughes	140	30	387	7	2-70	55.28

Also bowled: T. M. B. Bailey 3–0–4–0; A. M. Dobson 10–2–50–1; J. E. Emburey 10–2–20–0; J. M. Fielding 22–4–72–2; R. J. Logan 14–0–65–0; M. J. Powell 7–3–26–1; A. Richardson 41–7–109–2; A. R. Roberts 33–10–83–2; D. J. Sales 4.3–0–15–2; W. Stevens 18–0–73–1; A. J. Swann 36–5–123–2; P. A. Thomas 43–8–158–3; R. Turnell 13–1–62–1.

NOTTINGHAMSHIRE SECOND ELEVEN

Matches 17: Lost – Derbyshire, Hampshire, Lancashire, Leicestershire. Drawn – Durham, Glamorgan, Gloucestershire, Kent, Middlesex, Northamptonshire, Somerset, Surrey, Sussex, Warwickshire, Worcestershire. Abandoned – Essex, Yorkshire.

Batting Averages

	M	I	NO	R	HS	100s	Avge
G. F. Archer..........	3	5	0	316	128	2	63.20
G. E. Welton	11	19	2	898	158	3	52.82
P. R. Pollard.........	3	5	0	255	77	0	51.00
A. G. Wharf..........	7	12	2	441	100*	1	44.10
R. G. Hignett	2	4	0	152	55	0	38.00
*†M. Newell	14	18	4	516	129*	1	36.85
†L. N. P. Walker	11	19	0	682	127	1	35.89
R. T. Bates	5	9	3	194	40*	0	32.33
R. W. J. Howitt	10	16	3	404	134	1	31.07
A. A. Metcalfe	8	13	2	335	182*	1	30.45
U. Afzaal	5	7	0	197	100	1	28.14
N. A. Gie	11	17	1	365	120*	1	22.81
D. S. Lucas	6	7	2	114	40	0	22.80
J. E. Hindson	13	18	1	363	102	1	21.35
J. Hemmings	8	11	6	81	29	0	16.20
J. W. Hood	4	6	2	45	25	0	11.25
A. R. Oram	6	10	1	94	43	0	10.44
R. A. Pick	7	10	2	78	26	0	9.75
S. J. Musgrove........	2	4	0	36	16	0	9.00
J. A. Afford	9	11	3	59	30*	0	7.37

Played in four matches: S. Rashid 1*. Played in three matches: S. J. Randall 11, 1, 0. Played in two matches: A. J. Crozier 41, 8, 2; K. S. Tate 49, 23, 7; †J. A. Wakeling 22, 2. Played in one match: S. J. Ali 3; †O. E. Burford 21, 4*; M. P. Dowman 1; C. Dunn 2, 0; P. J. Franks 25, 15; J. C. Harrison 25, 11; J. A. North 47, 0; A. Van der Berg 17, 0.

Note: In the match v Derbyshire at Trent Bridge, U. Afzaal, called up for a first-team match, was replaced by M. P. Dowman.

Bowling Averages

	O	M	R	W	BB	Avge
P. J. Franks	30	7	50	4	4-27	12.50
G. F. Archer..........	50	18	106	6	4-25	17.66
R. T. Bates	126	33	391	16	4-27	24.43
J. Hemmings	117.5	20	391	13	3-22	30.07
S. Rashid	74.2	16	285	9	3-46	31.66

	O	M	R	W	BB	Avge
J. W. Hood..........	102.2	20	367	11	4-51	33.36
R. A. Pick	165	31	470	14	3-75	33.57
J. A. Afford	187.1	53	512	14	3-9	36.57
A. R. Oram	194.2	53	500	13	5-82	38.46
J. E. Hindson	313.5	66	1,186	30	5-85	39.53
S. J. Randall.........	95	12	384	9	3-70	42.66
U. Afzaal	117.5	29	322	7	4-31	46.00
A. G. Wharf.........	101	13	388	8	3-96	48.50
D. S. Lucas	90.2	15	299	6	4-38	49.83

Also bowled: S. J. Ali 6–2–23–1; M. P. Dowman 21–4–68–2; N. A. Gie 1–0–4–0; R. G. Hignett 23–4–82–3; R. W. J. Howitt 10–1–40–0; M. Newell 18–0–133–0; A. Van der Berg 8–0–90–0; G. E. Welton 0.1–0–1–0.

SOMERSET SECOND ELEVEN

Matches 17: Won – Hampshire, Northamptonshire, Worcestershire. Lost – Essex, Glamorgan, Gloucestershire, Middlesex, Surrey, Warwickshire, Yorkshire. Drawn – Derbyshire, Durham, Kent, Leicestershire, Nottinghamshire, Sussex. Abandoned – Lancashire.

Batting Averages

	M	I	NO	R	HS	100s	Avge
K. A. Parsons.........	3	5	1	400	134*	2	100.00
M. E. Trescothick	7	10	0	523	322	1	52.30
S. C. Ecclestone.......	4	6	1	261	108	1	52.20
*C. M. Wells	13	22	8	701	86*	0	50.07
M. Burns	4	5	0	250	94	0	50.00
S. Herzberg	8	12	1	478	88	0	43.45
S. M. Trego	15	25	2	769	132*	1	33.43
J. I. D. Kerr	5	8	0	257	89	0	32.12
H. R. J. Trump........	12	18	5	392	56*	0	30.15
H. J. Morgan	14	23	1	648	112*	1	29.45
†L. D. Sutton	11	20	2	492	75	0	27.33
A. P. van Troost	6	9	0	205	59	0	22.77
P. S. Jones	7	10	0	226	70	0	22.60
M. Dimond...........	11	17	2	330	108*	1	22.00
A. N. Edwards........	2	4	0	67	38	0	16.75
I. E. Bishop	4	6	2	56	30*	0	14.00
A. C. Cottam	5	6	3	42	21	0	14.00
N. R. Boulton........	5	9	0	111	32	0	12.33
O. A. Dawkins........	2	4	0	40	22	0	10.00
R. W. Selway.........	4	4	1	21	12*	0	7.00
B. J. Trott	7	9	4	30	13*	0	6.00
L. A. Cooper	3	4	0	22	11	0	5.50
M. Bulbeck...........	5	6	0	25	18	0	4.16

Played in three matches: †S. P. Jenkins 1, 14. Played in two matches: R. W. Sladdin 25, 1; J. I. M. Smith 1, 1; P. D. Trego 15, 44. Played in one match: W. E. Fowlston 0, 0; R. J. Harden 4, 74; P. C. L. Holloway 57, 1; †J. M. Kerslake 0, 11; S. C. G. MacGill 10, 4; S. Seymour 6, 0; J. Tucker 11, 7*; P. M. Warren 1*; M. Wood 11, 5; †C. Durrant, V. Mehra and B. M. Wellington did not bat.

Note: Owing to first-team calls, P. S. Jones was replaced by R. W. Selway in the match v Yorkshire at Marske, and by S. Herzberg in the match v Nottinghamshire at Worksop College.

Bowling Averages

	O	M	R	W	BB	Avge
S. C. G. MacGill	36.4	25	36	13	7-21	2.76
K. A. Parsons	52.1	10	153	9	5-39	17.00
J. I. M. Smith	26.4	2	122	5	5-99	24.40
H. R. J. Trump	283.4	95	717	28	4-53	25.60
B. J. Trott	99.4	12	388	14	6-40	27.71
M. E. Trescothick	89	23	284	10	4-41	28.40
A. C. Cottam	51	13	122	4	2-70	30.50
O. A. Dawkins	56.5	8	158	5	3-94	31.60
M. Dimond	174	39	690	20	4-32	34.50
S. Herzberg	145	23	503	14	5-65	35.92
J. I. D. Kerr	118.5	17	428	11	4-41	38.90
A. P. van Troost	100.3	11	472	11	3-76	42.90
I. E. Bishop	102	14	400	9	3-39	44.44
M. Burns	108.3	21	386	8	3-78	48.25
M. Bulbeck	56.2	8	249	5	2-60	49.80
P. S. Jones	154	29	521	9	2-31	57.88

Also bowled: A. N. Edwards 9–1–31–0; W. E. Fowlston 3.5–0–11–0; H. J. Morgan 65–13–249–1; R. W. Selway 17–1–91–0; R. W. Sladdin 28–4–135–1; P. D. Trego 3.5–0–19–0; S. M. Trego 45.3–10–186–2; J. Tucker 7–0–45–1; P. M. Warren 16–2–50–0; B. M. Wellington 19–3–69–3.

SURREY SECOND ELEVEN

Matches 17: Won – Glamorgan, Somerset, Sussex, Worcestershire, Yorkshire. Lost – Lancashire, Northamptonshire, Warwickshire. Drawn – Derbyshire, Essex, Gloucestershire, Hampshire, Kent, Leicestershire, Middlesex, Nottinghamshire. Abandoned – Durham.

Batting Averages

	M	I	NO	R	HS	100s	Avge
*D. J. Bicknell	7	11	2	960	244	5	106.66
R. M. Pearson	10	11	6	339	79*	0	67.80
N. Shahid	10	18	2	973	200*	3	60.81
G. J. Kennis	7	13	1	618	210	1	51.50
I. J. Ward	13	24	3	969	217	2	46.14
R. W. Nowell	11	17	6	411	66	0	37.36
†J. N. Batty	13	21	2	636	105	2	33.47
†J. A. Knott	12	21	3	491	99	0	27.27
A. J. Tudor	4	6	0	155	77	0	25.83
*K. T. Medlycott	11	12	5	170	25*	0	24.28
M. W. Patterson	10	13	4	196	44	0	21.77
A. D. Patterson	4	7	0	127	63	0	18.14
R. Clinton	4	8	0	132	59	0	16.50
J. M. Stainer	7	12	2	164	63	0	16.40
A. Saleem	10	12	2	116	45	0	11.60
R. Johnson	3	5	3	22	12*	0	11.00
S. N. de Silva	4	7	0	73	52	0	10.42
R. M. Amin	6	4	2	17	9*	0	8.50
C. Greenidge	5	6	1	3	2	0	0.60

Played in two matches: M. Atkinson 0, 20, 0; G. A. Crawford 6, 11, 6, 1; C. P. R. Hodgson 2, 19; B. C. Hollioake 88, 12; M. Miller 1*; J. D. Ratcliffe 53, 116*, 4; P. R. Shaw 13, 13, 4, 44. Played in one match: A. J. Bailey 32, 20*; G. J. Batty 7, 23; J. E. Benjamin 0; A. D. Brown 89, 18*; S. Carter 2*, 3; M. Crocombe 0, 1*; M. Davis 13, 0; A. S. Down 3, 0; J. A. King 18; N. Millar 10, 27; S. A. Newman 0; B. O'Connell 22, 2; G. Puckle did not bat.

Note: In the match v Sussex at Hove, B. C. Hollioake and J. D. Ratcliffe, called up for a first-team match, were replaced by C. P. R. Hodgson and G. Puckle.

Bowling Averages

	O	M	R	W	BB	Avge
G. J. Kennis	12.4	2	34	4	3-27	8.50
M. Davis.	49	13	123	8	5-80	15.37
B. C. Hollioake	35.5	9	113	6	4-46	18.83
R. M. Amin	250.2	79	636	29	6-65	21.93
A. Saleem.	213	45	744	25	5-74	29.76
M. W. Patterson.	217.5	39	808	27	6-80	29.92
I. J. Ward	233	69	658	20	5-87	32.90
R. W. Nowell.	251.3	53	854	24	4-91	35.58
A. J. Tudor.	77.5	23	264	7	5-73	37.71
J. A. Knott	91	17	358	9	3-36	39.77
N. Shahid	102.4	19	359	9	2-28	39.88
R. M. Pearson	323	80	884	21	4-60	42.09
C. Greenidge	88	10	358	6	2-27	59.66

Also bowled: M. Atkinson 38–13–84–2; G. J. Batty 17–6–47–1; J. E. Benjamin 31–7–98–2; D. J. Bicknell 23–7–68–1; A. D. Brown 13–1–36–1; S. Carter 2–0–10–0; G. A. Crawford 14.5–5–36–0; R. Johnson 32–6–142–3; J. A. King 12–0–65–3; M. Miller 31–4–115–1; B. O'Connell 12.1–0–57–1; A. D. Patterson 4–2–11–0; G. Puckle 6–2–16–0; J. D. Ratcliffe 34–10–101–2.

SUSSEX SECOND ELEVEN

Matches 17: Won – Durham, Glamorgan, Gloucestershire, Northamptonshire, Yorkshire. Lost – Derbyshire, Lancashire, Leicestershire, Surrey. Drawn – Essex, Hampshire, Kent, Middlesex, Nottinghamshire, Somerset, Warwickshire, Worcestershire.

Batting Averages

	M	I	NO	R	HS	100s	Avge
M. T. E. Peirce	6	10	3	567	145*	2	81.00
A. J. Jones	3	6	2	278	152	1	69.50
R. K. Rao	5	10	0	513	199	2	51.30
J. D. Chaplin	4	7	3	205	72	0	51.25
M. Newell	7	12	2	501	128*	2	50.10
D. J. P. Bowden.	10	17	1	515	101	1	32.18
J. R. Carpenter	7	12	1	352	107*	1	32.00
M. J. Thursfield	7	9	1	251	60	0	31.37
J. J. Bates.	8	12	3	279	71	0	31.00
T. A. Radford	7	12	2	306	80	0	30.60
R. S. C. Martin-Jenkins.	7	9	1	231	53	0	28.87
G. R. Haywood	3	6	0	167	54	0	27.83
J. P. Pyemont	17	30	3	740	145	1	27.40
N. C. Phillips	10	10	3	176	65	0	25.14
*†S. Humphries	17	25	2	558	70*	0	24.26
R. N. Jackson	4	7	2	87	32*	0	17.40
C. J. Batt	10	12	4	133	54*	0	16.62
J. R. C. Hamblin	8	9	3	93	25	0	15.50
A. D. Edwards	4	5	0	73	25	0	14.60
R. G. Halsall	4	8	0	95	30	0	11.87
M. R. Strong	11	10	4	43	10	0	7.16

Played in six matches: R. S. G. Anderson 9*, 46, 2, 20. Played in four matches: K. Greenfield 25*, 12, 5, 14; R. J. Kirtley 0*, 18*, 9, 11. Played in two matches: P. G. Hudson 4, 6, 51; S. J. Jurgensen 13, 6, 16, 1*; J. D. Lewry 12, 0*, 6; C. M. Mole 1, 3. Played in one match: G. R. A. Campbell 1, 93; D. A. Clapp 14; L. W. Marshall 14, 12*; M. J. O'Sullivan 3*, 2; B. E. A. Preece 6*; M. J. Prior 12; S. Simmonds 0; M. H. Yardy 47.

Note: Owing to first-team calls, R. J. Kirtley was replaced by J. R. C. Hamblin in the match v Lancashire at Middleton-on-Sea, and M. Newell was replaced by R. S. C. Martin-Jenkins in the match v Worcestershire at Barnt Green.

Bowling Averages

	O	M	R	W	BB	Avge
R. J. Kirtley	79.1	10	268	15	4-27	17.86
R. S. C. Martin-Jenkins . .	134.3	22	397	17	4-61	23.35
N. C. Phillips	301.2	78	796	31	7-66	25.67
M. R. Strong	296.5	61	880	32	5-68	27.50
J. R. Carpenter	149	47	405	13	3-23	31.15
R. S. G. Anderson	86.5	13	335	9	3-21	37.22
A. D. Edwards	72.5	16	252	6	4-53	42.00
C. J. Batt	183.4	39	735	17	4-61	43.23
S. J. Jurgensen	60	10	209	4	1-6	52.25
M. J. Thursfield	117.2	21	449	8	3-36	56.12
J. R. C. Hamblin	139	20	635	10	4-36	63.50
J. J. Bates	252	52	805	8	2-111	100.62

Also bowled: D. J. P. Bowden 31-8-104-1; J. D. Chaplin 31.1-4-105-2; R. G. Halsall 22-5-89-2; G. R. Haywood 3-1-2-0; P. G. Hudson 48-11-159-1; R. N. Jackson 1-1-0-1; A. J. Jones 5-0-34-1; J. D. Lewry 45.5-13-96-2; M. Newell 6-1-45-1; M. J. O'Sullivan 42-10-121-2; B. E. A. Preece 5-0-26-2; J. P. Pyemont 12.2-0-106-1; R. K. Rao 14-3-50-2; S. Simmonds 7-0-27-0; M. H. Yardy 9-3-26-0.

WARWICKSHIRE SECOND ELEVEN

Matches 17: Won – Essex, Glamorgan, Kent, Leicestershire, Northamptonshire, Somerset, Surrey. Lost – Derbyshire, Hampshire, Yorkshire. Drawn – Durham, Gloucestershire, Lancashire, Nottinghamshire, Sussex, Worcestershire. Abandoned – Middlesex.

Batting Averages

	M	I	NO	R	HS	100s	Avge
M. D. Edmond	9	13	3	755	143*	4	75.50
W. G. Khan	13	22	1	1,158	215	2	55.14
M. A. Sheikh	12	17	2	700	186	2	46.66
†T. Frost	9	10	1	410	112	1	45.55
A. Singh	6	10	1	383	129	2	42.55
†S. Platt	4	6	2	141	48*	0	35.25
A. Hafeez	6	10	2	268	53*	0	33.50
M. J. Powell	15	25	3	682	155	1	31.00
D. A. T. Dalton	5	6	0	180	54	0	30.00
N. V. Prabhu	8	10	0	286	82	0	28.60
S. McDonald	13	18	6	325	52*	0	27.08
C. R. Howell	10	14	1	252	93	0	19.38
J. N. Webster	10	8	3	74	26*	0	14.80
S. Vestergaard	4	4	0	57	24	0	14.25
J. Troughton	3	5	0	63	21	0	12.60
M. A. V. Bell	11	12	3	112	38	0	12.44
D. A. Altree	10	7	4	19	7*	0	6.33
R. G. East	6	5	1	13	5*	0	3.25

Played in four matches: †S. M. Eustace 2, 1*, 0*, 12*; K. Shah 2*, 0, 11, 15. Played in two matches: G. D. Franklin 21*, 20*; H. R. Jones 32, 14; D. P. Ostler 124, 74*, 41, 23*, M. A. Wagh 0, 44, 57*. Played in one match: D. R. Maynard 0; D. R. Mudd 1; M. T. Pidgeon 5; G. A. Rollins 17*; D. J. Young 6; D. J. Ball and M. J. O'Sullivan did not bat.

Note: In the match v Gloucestershire at Solihull, T. Frost, called up for a first-team match, was replaced by S. M. Eustace.

Bowling Averages

	O	M	R	W	BB	Avge
D. R. Maynard........	19	4	52	4	4-52	13.00
M. D. Edmond........	213.3	37	762	34	6-59	22.41
M. A. V. Bell.........	256.5	59	829	36	6-58	23.02
D. A. Altree..........	224.4	46	746	30	5-34	24.86
S. Vestergaard	99	20	406	13	3-6	31.23
M. A. Sheikh	242.4	67	696	22	5-39	31.63
K. Shah..............	54	11	164	5	2-32	32.80
S. McDonald	286.1	82	851	19	4-29	44.78
J. N. Webster	145.2	27	561	12	3-65	46.75

Also bowled: D. J. Ball 10–2–40–0; D. A. T. Dalton 10–2–36–0; R. G. East 33–6–91–3; G. D. Franklin 38–13–112–3; A. Hafeez 5–1–31–0; W. G. Khan 35.4–9–119–1; D. R. Mudd 13–3–66–1; M. J. O'Sullivan 14–1–69–0; M. J. Powell 72–20–201–3; N. V. Prabhu 13–2–42–2; G. A. Rollins 15–4–58–1; J. Troughton 3.2–0–15–0.

WORCESTERSHIRE SECOND ELEVEN

Matches 17: Won – Essex, Gloucestershire. Lost – Derbyshire, Durham, Lancashire, Middlesex, Northamptonshire, Somerset, Surrey. Drawn – Hampshire, Kent, Leicestershire, Nottinghamshire, Sussex, Warwickshire, Yorkshire. Abandoned – Glamorgan.

Batting Averages

	M	I	NO	R	HS	100s	Avge
V. S. Solanki	6	8	0	404	138	2	50.50
R. K. Illingworth	4	5	1	198	90	0	49.50
S. W. K. Ellis	7	10	4	292	54	0	48.66
C. G. Mason..........	6	11	2	395	100	1	43.88
W. P. C. Weston	2	4	0	167	69	0	41.75
J. E. K. Schofield......	3	5	1	153	91	0	38.25
J. R. A. Williams	10	17	3	513	143	2	36.64
M. J. Rawnsley	13	14	3	358	122	1	32.54
R. C. Driver	3	6	1	143	60*	0	28.60
O. A. Dawkins........	4	7	0	198	83	0	28.28
†I. Dawood...........	15	22	1	587	90	0	27.95
*D. B. D'Oliveira	14	12	1	290	79	0	26.36
C. J. Schofield	8	13	1	262	60*	0	21.83
J. E. Brinkley	8	14	4	187	30	0	18.70
P. A. Thomas.........	9	11	2	144	42*	0	16.00
K. Afzaal	2	4	0	62	40	0	15.50
S. J. Price...........	4	6	0	79	32	0	13.16
M. R. J. Chapman	7	13	0	166	39	0	12.76
Naveed Din	2	4	0	50	41	0	12.50
R. J. Chapman	11	14	6	92	28*	0	11.50
B. E. A. Preece	5	5	1	35	32*	0	8.75

Played in five matches: M. M. Mirza 0, 5. Played in four matches: A. Wylie 4*, 2*, 4*. Played in three matches: C. Clark 0, 0, 62*, 4; N. D. Slade 0, 0*, 1, 0. Played in two matches: D. N. Catterall 23, 5, 8; A. Hafeez 33, 58, 11, 56*; D. A. Leatherdale 9, 1, 166; D. Patel 18*, 3, 0; D. J. Young 33*, 24*; 4, 0. Played in one match: †S. J. Adshead 1, 18; S. J. Ali 19*; C. W. Boroughs 29, 31; A. J. Dalton 37; N. Goodman 43; G. R. Haynes 6; T. S. Heyes 26*, 2*; D. L. Houghton 0; A. J. Marsh 0, 42; W. Ritzema 46; Z. A. Sher 7; K. R. Spiring 84, 75. .

Note: Owing to first-team calls, M. M. Mirza was replaced by P. A. Thomas in the match v Nottinghamshire at Nottingham High School, and V. S. Solanki was replaced by Z. A. Sher in the match v Northamptonshire at Milton Keynes, by O. A. Dawkins in the match v Surrey at Cheam and by D. J. Young in the match v Gloucestershire at Bristol.

Bowling Averages

	O	M	R	W	BB	Avge
M. M. Mirza	88	19	254	11	4-72	23.09
N. D. Slade	52	7	173	7	2-31	24.71
D. B. D'Oliveira	46.5	16	125	5	3-76	.25.00
C. G. Mason	35	7	114	4	4-50	28.50
R. J. Chapman	272.1	46	1,002	34	6-87	29.47
J. E. Brinkley	165	33	597	18	5-60	33.16
A. Wylie.............	75.3	9	338	10	4-29	33.80
M. J. Rawnsley	292.2	61	1,025	29	6-39	35.34
S. W. K. Ellis	87.2	15	332	8	5-42	41.50
P. A. Thomas	175	22	816	17	4-171	48.00
B. E. A. Preece	95	14	414	8	4-51	51.75
M. R. J. Chapman	44	5	249	4	1-32	62.25

Also bowled: S. J. Ali 19–3–72–1; C. W. Boroughs 21–6–66–1; D. N. Catterall 35–8–155–2; C. Clark 22.1–4–95–3; G. R. Haynes 13–2–38–2; T. S. Heyes 16–2–56–0; R. K. Illingworth 75.2–24–149–3; D. A. Leatherdale 12.3–1–52–2; Naveed Din 11–0–74–0; D. Patel 26–4–147–3; J. E. K. Schofield 29–7–108–1; Z. A. Sher 3–0–14–0; V. S. Solanki 52–11–172–3.

YORKSHIRE SECOND ELEVEN

Matches 17: Won – Durham, Essex, Gloucestershire, Hampshire, Leicestershire, Middlesex, Somerset, Warwickshire. Lost – Glamorgan, Kent, Lancashire, Surrey, Sussex. Drawn – Derbyshire, Northamptonshire, Worcestershire. Abandoned – Nottinghamshire.

Batting Averages

	M	I	NO	R	HS	100s	Avge
R. A. Kettleborough ...	14	25	2	1,261	173	5	54.82
M. J. Wood	16	29	1	1,279	168	2	45.67
A. McGrath	4	7	1	251	102*	1	41.83
R. Robinson	14	23	5	616	85	0	34.22
G. J. Batty	15	21	9	377	63*	0	31.41
N. G. Russell	11	19	1	545	136	1	30.27
G. M. Hamilton	7	9	1	234	64	0	29.25
†C. A. Chapman	13	22	2	539	68	0	26.95
J. D. Middlebrook	8	12	2	232	64	0	23.20
Z. C. Morris..........	3	5	1	89	57	0	22.25
G. M. Fellows	6	8	2	124	71	0	20.66
A. C. Morris..........	7	13	0	254	55	0	19.53
I. D. Fisher...........	12	13	3	164	55	0	16.40
J. W. Hood...........	5	7	0	108	29	0	15.42
P. M. Hutchison.......	9	9	2	66	29	0	9.42
M. J. Hoggard	10	10	2	32	12*	0	8.00
A. G. Wharf..........	7	8	0	37	14	0	4.62
R. J. Sidebottom	9	5	2	4	2	0	1.33

Played in three matches: †S. M. Guy 6, 0. Played in two matches: J. A. Smith 10, 20. Played in one match: P. J. Hartley 43, 52; M. D. Moxon 145; B. Parker 18, 13.

Note: Owing to first-team calls, G. M. Hamilton was replaced by G. M. Fellows in the match v Leicestershire at Oakham School, and by J. A. Smith in the match v Lancashire at Bradford.

Bowling Averages

	O	M	R	W	BB	Avge
A. G. Wharf	119.4	28	414	20	4-22	20.70
I. D. Fisher	426.1	134	1,034	48	5-47	21.54
G. M. Hamilton	153.1	22	484	22	5-65	22.00
A. C. Morris	122.5	36	339	13	4-35	26.07
M. J. Hoggard	255	55	760	28	6-59	27.14
G. J. Batty	363.4	98	1,035	37	6-49	27.97
R. J. Sidebottom	185	34	620	21	4-51	29.52
J. D. Middlebrook	124	28	434	14	4-60	31.00
G. M. Fellows	54	10	211	5	2-27	42.20
P. M. Hutchison	164.4	46	476	10	3-20	47.60

Also bowled: P. J. Hartley 8.1–0–43–0; J. W. Hood 20–5–71–2; Z. C. Morris 42–10–104–2; B. Parker 0.5–0–0–0; R. Robinson 27–10–85–0; J. A. Smith 17.2–0–87–1.

SECOND ELEVEN CHAMPIONS

1959	Gloucestershire	1973	Essex	1987	{ Kent
1960	Northamptonshire	1974	Middlesex		{ Yorkshire
1961	Kent	1975	Surrey	1988	Surrey
1962	Worcestershire	1976	Kent	1989	Middlesex
1963	Worcestershire	1977	Yorkshire	1990	Sussex
1964	Lancashire	1978	Sussex	1991	Yorkshire
1965	Glamorgan	1979	Warwickshire	1992	Surrey
1966	Surrey	1980	Glamorgan	1993	Middlesex
1967	Hampshire	1981	Hampshire	1994	Somerset
1968	Surrey	1982	Worcestershire	1995	Hampshire
1969	Kent	1983	Leicestershire	1996	Warwickshire
1970	Kent	1984	Yorkshire	1997	Lancashire
1971	Hampshire	1985	Nottinghamshire		
1972	Nottinghamshire	1986	Lancashire		

AON TROPHY, 1997

Counties were restricted to players qualified for England and for competitive county cricket, only two of whom could be capped players. The matches were of 50 overs per side.

North Zone	P	W	L	NR	Points	Net run-rate
Nottinghamshire	8	6	2	0	12	4.58
Durham	8	4	3	1	9	4.32
Lancashire	8	3	4	1	7	4.34
Yorkshire	8	2	4	2	6	−6.10
Derbyshire	8	2	4	2	6	−12.34

Central Zone	P	W	L	NR	Points	Net run-rate
Northamptonshire	8	5	2	1	11	10.79
Leicestershire	8	5	2	1	11	10.09
Middlesex	8	3	3	2	8	−7.51
Minor Counties	8	3	4	1	7	−5.05
Warwickshire	8	1	6	1	3	−9.58

South-West Zone	P	W	L	NR	Points	Net run-rate
Gloucestershire	8	5	2	1	11	19.44
Hampshire	8	4	2	2	10	10.70
Worcestershire	8	5	3	0	10	−6.57
Glamorgan	8	3	3	2	8	3.52
Somerset	8	0	7	1	1	−23.94

South-East Zone	P	W	L	NR	Points	Net run-rate
Surrey	8	6	1	1	13	20.61
Sussex	8	6	2	0	12	2.78
MCC Young Cricketers	8	4	4	0	8	−8.11
Kent..................	8	2	5	1	5	−8.94
Essex	8	1	7	0	2	−5.35

SEMI-FINALS

At Northampton, August 18. Surrey won by 30 runs. Toss: Surrey. Surrey 289 for five (50 overs) (D. J. Bicknell 107 not out, I. J. Ward 55, J. A. Knott 45); Northamptonshire 259 (46.3 overs) (A. Fordham 88, Extras 42; J. A. Knott three for 36).

At Bristol, August 19. Gloucestershire won by three wickets. Toss: Gloucestershire. Nottinghamshire 244 for nine (50 overs) (G. E. Welton 63, M. P. Dowman 33, J. E. Hindson 33; R. I. Dawson three for 32); Gloucestershire 245 for seven (48.1 overs) (D. R. Hewson 49, N. J. Trainor 47, T. H. C. Hancock 35, R. I. Dawson 30).

FINAL

GLOUCESTERSHIRE v SURREY

At Bristol, September 8. Surrey won by three wickets. Toss: Gloucestershire.
Man of the Match: N. Shahid.

Gloucestershire

D. R. Hewson c Hollioake b Benjamin...	3	†R. C. J. Williams not out	21
M. G. N. Windows run out	98	M. J. Cawdron not out	5
T. H. C. Hancock c Batty b Ratcliffe	7	L-b 6, w 5, n-b 18	29
R. J. Cunliffe b Ratcliffe...............	8		—
*R. I. Dawson c Shahid b Salisbury	61	1/4 2/53 3/69 (6 wkts, 50 overs) 282
M. J. Church c Ratcliffe b Benjamin.....	50	4/182 5/226 6/270

R. P. Davis, J. M. M. Averis and K. P. Sheeraz did not bat.

Bowling: Benjamin 10-2-52-2; Tudor 8-0-65-0; Ratcliffe 10-0-54-2; Amin 10-0-37-0; Salisbury 10-0-51-1; Shahid 2-0-17-0.

Surrey

N. Shahid c and b Davis	78	A. J. Tudor lbw b Sheeraz	0
I. J. Ward c Cunliffe b Hancock	42	I. D. K. Salisbury not out.............	14
B. C. Hollioake run out	63	L-b 8, w 4	12
*D. J. Bicknell c Dawson b Davis	8		—
J. D. Ratcliffe c Williams b Dawson.....	43	1/102 2/160 3/182 (7 wkts, 48.4 overs) 285
J. A. Knott lbw b Sheeraz	22	4/210 5/263
†J. N. Batty not out	3	6/269 7/269

R. M. Amin and J. E. Benjamin did not bat.

Bowling: Averis 5-0-42-0; Sheeraz 10-0-58-2; Windows 7-0-32-0; Hancock 8.4-0-49-1; Davis 10-0-53-2; Cawdron 3-0-22-0; Dawson 5-0-21-1.

Umpires: A. A. Jones and B. Leadbeater.

WINNERS 1986-97

1986	Northamptonshire	1990	Lancashire	1994	Yorkshire
1987	Derbyshire	1991	Nottinghamshire	1995	Leicestershire
1988	Yorkshire	1992	Surrey	1996	Leicestershire
1989	Middlesex	1993	Leicestershire	1997	Surrey

CAREER FIGURES

Players not expected to appear in county cricket in 1998

BATTING

	M	I	NO	R	HS	100s	Avge	1,000r/ season
J. A. Afford	170	167	72	398	22*	0	4.18	0
S. J. W. Andrew	132	112	42	499	35	0	7.12	0
C. W. J. Athey	467	784	71	25,453	184	55	35.69	13
G. J. Batty	1	2	0	18	18	0	9.00	0
D. A. Blenkiron	19	33	3	774	145	3	25.80	0
J. N. B. Bovill	38	49	16	324	31	0	9.81	0
J. E. Brinkley	14	16	4	89	29	0	7.41	0
T. S. Curtis	339	579	67	20,832	248	43	40.68	11
M. Dimond	5	5	1	71	26	0	17.75	0
G. J. M. Edwards	1	0	–	–	–	–	–	–
J. E. Emburey	513	644	130	12,021	133	7	23.38	0
A. Fordham	167	297	24	10,939	206*	25	40.06	5
G. A. Gooch	580	988	75	44,841	333	128	49.11	21†
J. C. Harrison	10	18	3	298	46*	0	19.86	0
S. Herzberg..........	21	26	8	394	57*	0	21.88	0
J. G. Hughes	20	26	2	128	17	0	5.33	0
G. J. Kennis	6	11	1	140	29	0	14.00	0
N. J. Lenham	192	332	29	10,135	222*	20	33.44	3
D. G. C. Ligertwood .	28	51	7	733	56	0	16.65	0
M. A. Lynch.........	359	585	64	18,325	172*	39	35.17	9
G. I. Macmillan	48	76	9	1,848	122	3	27.58	0
A. A. Metcalfe	216	369	21	11,938	216*	26	34.30	6
C. P. Metson	231	302	71	4,059	96	0	17.57	0
S. M. Milburn	27	28	6	292	54*	0	13.27	0
S. P. Moffat	5	7	1	122	47	0	20.33	0
H. Morris	314	544	53	19,785	233*	53	40.29	10
R. W. Nowell	12	22	3	162	28*	0	8.52	0
J. E. Owen	17	29	0	782	105	2	26.96	0
G. J. Parsons	338	449	100	6,763	76	0	19.37	0
R. M. Pearson	51	56	16	475	37	0	11.87	0
N. C. Phillips	19	26	10	450	53	0	28.12	0
R. A. Pick...........	195	206	56	2,259	65*	0	15.06	0
B. E. A. Preece	3	4	2	5	3*	0	2.50	0
N. W. Preston.......	9	12	4	71	17*	0	8.87	0
T. A. Radford.......	14	24	6	476	69*	0	26.44	0
P. A. Thomas	21	24	5	119	25	0	6.26	0
M. J. Thursfield	24	26	6	309	47	0	15.45	0
M. J. Vandrau	59	94	18	1,567	66	0	20.61	0
P. E. Wellings	6	10	2	378	128*	1	47.25	0
R. M. S. Weston	11	19	0	181	36	0	9.52	0
P. Whitticase	132	174	40	3,113	114*	1	23.23	0
R. C. J. Williams	35	44	8	640	90	0	17.77	0
T. N. Wren..........	30	34	13	141	23	0	6.71	0

* Signifies not out.
† Includes 1,363 runs scored overseas in India, Sri Lanka and South Africa in 1981-82.

BOWLING AND FIELDING

	R	W	BB	Avge	5W/i	10W/m	Ct/St
J. A. Afford	15,436	468	6-15	32.98	16	2	57
S. J. W. Andrew	10,679	317	7-47	33.68	7	0	26
C. W. J. Athey......	2,673	48	3-3	55.68	–	–	429/2
G. J. Batty	70	2	1-11	35.00	–	–	0
D. A. Blenkiron	187	6	4-43	31.16	–	–	7
J. N. B. Bovill	3,384	104	6-29	32.53	4	1	7
J. E. Brinkley	1,115	34	6-35	32.79	2	0	5
T. S. Curtis.........	813	14	2-17	58.07	–	–	192
M. Dimond.........	316	6	4-73	52.66	–	–	4
G. J. M. Edwards....	49	0	–	–	–	–	0
J. E. Emburey.......	41,958	1,608	8-40	26.09	72	12	459
A. Fordham	297	4	1-0	74.25	–	–	117
G. A. Gooch........	8,457	246	7-14	34.37	3	0	555
J. C. Harrison.......	–	–	–	–	–	–	12
S. Herzberg........	1,813	47	5-33	38.57	1	0	6
J. G. Hughes........	141	4	5-69	35.25	1	0	5
G. J. Kennis	4	0	–	–	–	–	6
N. J. Lenham	1,847	42	4-13	43.97	–	–	73
D. G. C. Ligertwood .	–	–	–	–	–	–	71/9
M. A. Lynch........	1,398	26	3-6	53.76	–	–	367
G. I. Macmillan	1,203	23	3-13	52.30	–	–	51
A. A. Metcalfe	362	4	2-18	90.50	–	–	82
C. P. Metson	0	0	–	–	–	–	560/51
S. M. Milburn	2,497	53	4-38	47.11	–	–	1
S. P. Moffat	–	–	–	–	–	–	2
H. Morris	380	2	1-6	190.00	–	–	197
R. W. Nowell	1,397	34	4-43	41.08	–	–	5
J. E. Owen	–	–	–	–	–	–	6
G. J. Parsons	24,509	809	9-72	30.29	19	1	147
R. M. Pearson	5,516	100	5-108	55.16	2	0	15
N. C. Phillips	1,581	26	3-39	60.80	–	–	9
R. A. Pick.........	16,454	495	7-128	33.24	16	3	50
B. E. A. Preece	388	8	4-79	48.50	–	–	1
N. W. Preston.......	373	12	4-68	31.08	–	–	3
T. A. Radford.......	0	1	1-0	0.00	–	–	13
P. A. Thomas	2,295	49	5-70	46.83	1	0	1
M. J. Thursfield	1,539	38	6-130	40.50	1	0	2
M. J. Vandrau	4,440	132	6-34	33.63	7	2	29
P. E. Wellings	18	0	–	–	–	–	2
R. M. S. Weston	81	1	1-41	81.00	–	–	11
P. Whitticase	7	0	–	–	–	–	309/14
R. C. J. Williams	–	–	–	–	–	–	94/14
T. N. Wren.........	2,416	66	6-48	36.60	3	0	12

Note: J. E. Emburey was the only bowler from this list to take 100 wickets in a season; he took 103 in 1983.

LEAGUE CRICKET IN ENGLAND AND WALES IN 1997

By GEOFFREY DEAN

In club cricket, the winter of 1997-98 was almost as hectic and uncertain as the summer had been. The whole structure of the league game was in turmoil as the game's ruling body, the ECB, tried to implement its planned reorganisation, under which the time-honoured patchwork of competition all over the country would be simplified with a top tier of about 20 premier leagues to provide excellence in amateur cricket.

Reactions to the planned changes ranged from enthusiasm to outright horror, with many leading players delighted at the idea of being involved in more testing, higher-standard cricket. However, it was clear that many traditions were likely to disappear in the process.

If leagues meet the Board's criteria for premier status, their clubs can expect annual grants of £1,000, plus help with administrative and other expenses. It was unclear whether any might get there in time for 1998, and there were many local obstacles – different in each part of the country – that made it questionable whether the structure would be securely in place for 1999. In a number of places, apparently simple processes were being delayed by personality clashes.

There were particular problems in Lancashire and Yorkshire, where the time-honoured set-up of tightly knit, small-community, local clubs playing hotly contested fixtures against their neighbours would have to be unravelled if the Board's plan was to work. And the Birmingham League, the world's oldest, reacted strongly against the idea of disbandment. But after protracted negotiations with Warwickshire, its future seemed guaranteed as the top tier of a new West Midlands structure.

Premier League clubs will be required to play all-day, non-limited-overs matches, and encouraged to adopt a two-day format, as in Australian grade cricket. The Yorkshire League became the first in the country to embrace the elongated game, scheduling four two-day matches within their 26-match programme for 1998. At the opposite end of the country, the Sussex League announced a significant change: all first-eleven fixtures in 1998 were scheduled to begin at 11 a.m., lengthening a day's play from five and a half hours to seven or more. The Middlesex League opted for 11.30 starts.

In "Raising the Standard", the ECB's document of proposals, the Board said it would seriously consider banning overseas cricketers (apart from EU citizens) from playing in Premier League cricket. But, as ever, players from foreign shores featured prominently in 1997. The New South Wales leg-spinner, Stuart MacGill, proved far too difficult a proposition for batsmen of the Devon League, taking 88 wickets for Tiverton Heathcote. He was left one short of the league record when he was banned for three matches for "bringing the game into disrepute". MacGill scored useful runs too, hitting 131 in his last match, against Hatherleigh, to complement a return of seven for 33, including a hat-trick.

Pakistani Test batsman Ijaz Ahmed scored a mountain of runs for Khalsa in the Leeds League. He finished with 1,075 at 97.72, and his 252 – out of a total of 306 – against Great Preston was the highest individual score in the league's history. But Ijaz had to return home before the final game; Khalsa lost at Woodhouse, allowing Esholt to become champions.

Numerous league records fell to home-grown players, too. Kevin Parsons became the first batsman to reach 1,000 in a season in the Somerset League, ending with 1,163 at 61. His side, Taunton St Andrews, finished third in their 50th anniversary year. In the neighbouring Western League, Keynsham's Marcus Trescothick took out his frustration at being dropped from Somerset's First Eleven by hammering 230 against Chippenham, the highest score in that league's history. Another county player, Derbyshire's Ian Blackwell, 19, equalled the Bassetlaw League individual record with 213 for Chesterfield against Bolsover – and followed up with 154 against Worksop.

Two amateurs performed the rare feat of taking all ten wickets in an innings. Coventry & North Warwicks spinner James Taplin was the first to do it in the Birmingham League for 29 years, returning figures of 18.3–3–60–10 against West Bromwich Dartmouth. Set 253 to win, Dartmouth reached 160 for four, with 12 overs remaining, before Taplin took the last six in five overs. Taplin had taken only three wickets before then in 1997, and never took another one. "I never really turned the ball," he admitted. Spectators thought the batsmen had played suicidally. Three weeks earlier, Taplin had achieved local headlines when he was given out for obstruction when he kicked the ball away. Not far away, Mick Kenley of Notts Alliance champions Kimberley Institute became the first bowler in that league's history to claim all ten, at a cost of just 45, against Long Eaton. Kimberley secured the title on the final day of the season when they beat Radcliffe-on-Trent by six wickets. The two sides had been level on points before the match.

Just three years after being accepted into the Birmingham League, Barnt Green of Worcestershire won it for the second time. Nothing appeared less likely at the end of May, when they were bottom of the 12-club table without a win. But by mid-August, they had climbed to the top – and stayed there. Remarkably, none of their batsmen scored a hundred and only two bowlers took as many as ten wickets: captain Gus Mackay, who claimed 50 at 17, and Scott Ellis, with 33.

There were several tight finishes and championships decided late on the final day. In the Middlesex League, Teddington lost their title when they failed to beat Finchley. Meanwhile, Ealing were cruising home against Enfield, which put them level on points with Teddington and gave them one more victory – enough to grab the title. In the Sussex League, Three Bridges had been top all season, but were held to a draw by Horsham on the final Saturday; Bexhill leapfrogged past them with victory over East Grinstead, to win their first championship.

Radlett won the Hertfordshire League for the third successive year, finishing level on points with Watford Town but with one more victory. Watford were left to rue their lack of covers, which led to their penultimate game, against Cheshunt, being abandoned. Both sides won their final game. In the Essex League, 52-year-old off-spinner Keith Goodman took 62 wickets, but it was not quite enough to help Chelmsford to the title; Wanstead pipped them by one point.

Among the most dominant champions in England or Wales were Havant, who won all 15 of their games to clinch the Southern League title by mid-August. Their wicket-keeper, Tim Roads, made 21 stumpings. They were matched by Lansdown, who won all 14 to become undisputed Western League champions. The fixture against Bath was started, rained off and, under League rules, erased from the records.

Torquay's run of 48 Devon League games without defeat was ended by newly promoted Budleigh Salterton early in the season, but they went on to retain their title. Hetton Lyons won the Durham County League for the first time since 1957. First-time champions included Sawley in the Derbyshire County League and Netherfield in the Northern League. Thanks to a remarkable unbeaten 115 off 42 balls from Heanor's Neil Sparham, the Derbyshire County League defeated the Tyneside Senior League in the final of the League Cricket Conference President's Trophy.

The wet June produced all kinds of odd results. In the Birmingham League, 23 Division One and 33 Division Two games were abandoned in the month. A hot spell followed and the top three in Division One were playing the bottom three on the same day. The bottom clubs won each time. Perhaps the most unjustly treated side of the season were Metropolitan Police of the Surrey League. Understandably, they could not field a side on the day of the funeral of Diana, Princess of Wales. But the Surrey Championship was one of the few leagues in the south-east not to postpone its programme that day. The Police had to concede their game, to fellow strugglers Limpsfield, as the league authorities refused to allow them to play a week later. The lost game ensured they were relegated.

LEAGUE WINNERS, 1997

League	Winners	League	Winners
Airedale & Wharfedale	Adel	Midlands Combined Counties	Kenilworth Wardens
Bassetlaw	Welbeck	Norfolk Alliance	Vauxhall Mallards
Birmingham	Barnt Green	Northants Championship	Northampton Saints
Bolton	Tonge	Northern	Netherfield
Bradford	Undercliffe	North Lancashire	Penrith
Central Yorkshire	Methley	North Staffs & South Cheshire	Moddershall
Cherwell	Bicester & North Oxon	Northumberland County	South Northumberland
Cheshire County	Bowdon	North Wales	Brymbo
Cornwall	Truro	North Yorks & South Durham	Normanby Hall
Derbyshire County	Sawley	Notts Alliance	Kimberley Institute
Devon	Torquay	Ribblesdale	Cherry Tree
Durham County	Hetton Lyons	Saddleworth	Shaw
Durham Senior	Felling	Shropshire	Ludlow
Essex	Wanstead	Somerset	Taunton
Hertfordshire	Radlett	Southern	Havant
Huddersfield	Meltham	South Wales Association	Ynysygerwn
Kent	Sevenoaks Vine	Surrey Championship	Wimbledon
Leeds	Esholt	Sussex	Bexhill
Leicestershire County	Barrow Town	Thames Valley	Beaconsfield
Lincolnshire	Caistow	Three Counties	Chepstow
Liverpool Competition	Bootle	Tyneside Senior	Blaydon
Manchester Association	Lytham	Western	Lansdown
Merseyside Competition	Caldy	West Wales Club Conference	Llanybydder
Middlesex	Ealing	Yorkshire	Harrogate
Midlands Club Conference	Knowle & Dorridge		

Note: To avoid confusion, traditional League names have been given in this list and sponsors' names omitted.

WOMBWELL CRICKET LOVERS' SOCIETY AWARDS, 1997

Steve James of Glamorgan was voted Cricketer of the Year by members of the Wombwell Cricket Lovers' Society. Other award-winners were: C. B. Fry Young Cricketer of the Year – Paul Hutchison; Brian Sellers County Captain of the Year – Matthew Maynard; J. M. Kilburn Cricket Writer of the Year – Mick Pope; Jack Fingleton Cricket Commentator of the Year – Jonathan Agnew.

THE LANCASHIRE LEAGUES, 1997

By CHRIS ASPIN

Plans for new premier leagues were received badly in Lancashire, where flourishing competitions still draw spectators who like to see local derbies. The clubs responded to the proposals from Old Trafford by setting up a new Federation of Lancashire Cricket Leagues.

It was not clear where this might ultimately lead, but in 1997 there was one piece of unprecedented co-operation. After more than a century of segregation, the 30 clubs in the Lancashire and Central Lancashire Leagues got together in a knockout competition. The final of the Lancashire Challenge Trophy, sponsored by the J. W. Lees Brewery, resulted in an all-CLL final, in which Littleborough beat Werneth by eight runs with just one ball to go.

Haslingden became Lancashire League champions for the eighth time in 14 years and, having beaten Burnley in the final of the Jennings Worsley Cup, achieved their first double. This was despite losing their Australian professional, Brad McNamara, who returned home with a shoulder injury after only seven games. Thereafter the club recruited eight substitutes, including, for the cup final, West Indian Hamish Anthony, who had helped Littleborough to win the CLL final a week earlier. He earned his second cup medal with five for 52, and, back with Littleborough, collected a third in the combined knockout. But Haslingden owed much to two non-professionals, wicket-keeper Jack Simpson and Steve Dearden, who were defectors from Ramsbottom. Both hit centuries in the cup final. In league games, Simpson scored 670 runs and made 30 dismissals, while Dearden scored 602 and took 43 wickets.

The player who made the greatest impact on the league in 1997 was South African slow left-arm bowler Corrie Jordaan, a last-minute signing by Lowerhouse. He took nine for 59 against Church in his first match, troubled batsmen throughout the season and finished with exactly 100 wickets at 9.27 each. New Zealander Chris Harris, playing for Ramsbottom, also took nine in an innings, at Accrington; his figures of 9.5–1–14–9 were the best in the league since Anton Ferreira took ten for 45 for Nelson (also against Accrington) in 1988.

Ben Johnson from South Australia was the leading scorer for the second year running, with 1,154 runs for Colne. Todmorden professional Frans Cronje – who scored 159 – and captain Brian Heywood shared an unbroken second-wicket stand of 230 at Rishton, a league record. The outstanding fielding performance came from Haslingden's captain, Mark Griffin, who took six catches at mid-off in a tied game with Burnley.

Rochdale won the Central Lancashire title, their 24th triumph and fifth in eight seasons, which owed much to their strong batting. Professional Robbie Baker from Western Australia and Peter Wilcock both passed 1,000 runs, with Wilcock the only amateur to do so.

Second-placed Littleborough lifted the Lees Wood Cup after beating Middleton in a low-scoring final. Littleborough squeezed past Middleton's 92 with two wickets in hand but, with Middleton spinner Lee Wolstenholme taking six for ten in nine overs, it was a close-run thing.

Former Lancashire player Dexter Fitton topped the batting averages with 1,251 for Milnrow at 62.55, and the Queenslander Mike Warden, who took 83 wickets at 11.98 for Stand, was first in the bowling. The best all-round performance came from Pakistan Test player Asif Mujtaba, who scored 772 runs and took 84 wickets for Norden. New Zealander Robert Kennedy, professional at Werneth, took most wickets, with 89 at 13.38. But amateur Les Whittle had an outstanding season for Crompton, capturing 87 at 13.83. Crompton, last season's wooden-spoonists, briefly headed the table, but finished sixth.

EW CARTONS LANCASHIRE LEAGUE

	P	W	L	NR	Bonus Pts	Pts	Professional	Runs	Avge	Wkts	Avge
Haslingden....	26	16	7	2	10	80*	‡B. E. McNamara ..	233	38.83	12	16.33
East Lancs. ...	26	17	8	1	8	78	W. F. Stelling	642	42.80	48	17.56
Enfield	26	15	8	2	11	77*	S. Lee	802	44.55	67	16.01
Lowerhouse ...	26	14	8	4	11	75	L. C. R. Jordaan ..	141	9.40	100	9.27
Ramsbottom...	26	14	8	3	11	75*	C. Z. Harris......	716	42.11	86	10.82
Colne	26	14	10	2	11	71	B. A. Johnson	1,154	54.95	49	21.08
Bacup	26	12	10	3	7	63*	J. Paterson	946	45.04	70	14.01
Todmorden....	26	12	12	2	8	60	F. J. C. Cronje ...	838	39.90	56	17.62
Nelson	26	11	12	3	6	56	A. C. Dawson	445	23.42	58	15.50
Rishton.......	26	9	13	4	7	51	M. W. Pringle	501	25.05	59	20.22
Accrington	26	8	13	4	5	47*	N. J. Astle	327	40.87	21	18.42
							P. R. Sleep	382	34.72	49	16.81
Burnley	26	8	15	2	7	45*	D. M. Benkenstein	1,036	74.00	10	15.30
Church	26	6	18	2	2	30	B. N. Creevey	528	29.33	66	16.40
Rawtenstall ...	26	4	18	2	3	27†	‡I. S. L. Hewett ...	237	14.81	32	22.68

Notes: Four points awarded for a win; two points for a no-result; one point for bowling out the opposition in a completed match.

* Includes two points for a tie; † includes four points for two ties.

‡ Did not play full season.

CENTRAL LANCASHIRE LEAGUE

	P	OW	LW	L	D	Pts	Professional	Runs	Avge	Wkts	Avge
Rochdale ...	30	11	12	4	3	109	R. M. Baker	1,114	39.78	57	17.33
Littleborough	30	13	5	7	5	95	H. A. G. Anthony ...	419	19.04	81	14.17
Middleton ..	30	10	8	7	5	92	J. D. Batty	984	35.14	73	19.10
Werneth	30	13	2	9	6	85	R. J. Kennedy	144	9.60	89	13.38
Milnrow	30	9	7	9	5	84*	J. D. Fitton	1,251	62.55	68	17.88
Crompton ...	30	9	5	8	8	82*	Zafar Iqbal	467	22.23	68	18.05
Norden	30	9	4	10	7	75	Asif Mujtaba	772	45.41	84	12.14
Heywood ...	30	9	3	11	7	71	A. Badenhorst	470	22.38	85	13.84
Walsden	30	8	4	12	6	68	A. Dykes	974	44.27	71	20.84
Royton	30	7	6	13	4	67	T. B. Arothe	1,060	44.16	52	19.05
Stockport ...	30	6	2	16	6	50	Jaffer Qureshi	701	30.47	71	18.52
Oldham	30	5	3	16	6	49	Sohail Jaffer.......	812	35.30	32	17.18
Stand	30	4	4	16	6	48	M. Warden	689	38.27	83	11.98
Unsworth ...	30	5	2	17	6	44	C. P. H. Ramanayake	637	26.54	75	16.78
Ashton	30	4	2	21	3	34	R. Burton..........	496	20.66	67	16.64
Radcliffe...	30	4	1	20	5	34	P. Skuse..........	858	29.58	60	25.88

Notes: Five points awarded for an outright win; four points for a limited win; two points for a draw. A team achieves an outright win by bowling out the opposition. CLL averages include cup games.

* Includes three points for a tie.

NATIONAL CLUB CHAMPIONSHIP, 1997

Eastbourne swept to their first Club Championship title with the help of a remarkable sequence of scores from Richard Halsall, the bar manager at their Saffrons ground. Halsall, a 28-year-old of Zimbabwean extraction, made 592 runs in the competition at an average of 148, culminating in a sequence of 79 not out in the quarter-final, against Brondesbury, 76 run out in the semi-final, against Exmouth, and 82 not out in the final. In both the last two games he won the Man of the Match award, which consisted of his own weight – 15 stone – in beer from the sponsors, Abbot Ale.

Eastbourne were lucky with the draw, which gave them home advantage in seven of their eight games before the Lord's final. In their one away tie, against four-time champions Old Hill, they were extended for the only time. Former captain Paul Tucker sliced the final ball away to third man to give them the narrowest of one-wicket victories. Eastbourne batted second in every match of their campaign, and won all of them – apart from the Old Hill game – by at least five wickets.

Harrogate were just as dominant on their way to the final. After making 313 for six in the first round, they completed a 278-run win by bowling Amaranth out for 35, and their narrowest margin of victory was a still-comfortable 17 runs against Pickering. Chorley, finalists for the previous three years, were knocked out in the fifth round by Fleetwood.

FINAL

EASTBOURNE v HARROGATE

At Lord's, August 29. Eastbourne won by nine wickets. Toss: Harrogate.

Harrogate's captain, Ian Houseman, failed to heed the lesson of countless NatWest finals when he won the toss and batted first at Lord's in late summer. Eastbourne's opening bowlers, Myall and Hacker, struck early blows on a moist wicket and, after 17 overs, Harrogate had limped to 37 for three. A recovery never really materialised, despite 41 from Kippax, and Halsall and Paul Stevens took Eastbourne to within 24 runs of victory before their opening partnership was broken. That brought Paul's brother Darren to the crease, but Eastbourne's other pair of Stevens brothers, Michael and Geoff, were not required.

Harrogate

J. Proud lbw b Hacker	0		A. Burton b Halsall	11
P. Hepworth b Hacker	3		M. Smart c and b Myall	4
D. Wyrill c and b Myall	13		*I. Houseman not out	4
D. Bates b G. Stevens	23		B 1, l-b 12, w 5	18
V. Craven b G. Stevens	15			
†D. J. Pipe st P. Stevens b G. Stevens	18		1/1 2/10 3/37	(44.2 overs) 158
S. A. J. Kippax b Halsall	41		4/49 5/81 6/84	
J. Henderson run out	8		7/94 8/143 9/154	

Bowling: Myall 8.2–0–22–2; Hacker 9–3–12–2; Hamblin 9–0–40–0; G. Stevens 9–1–25–3; Halliday 5–0–22–0; Halsall 4–0–24–2.

Eastbourne

R. G. Halsall not out 82
†P. Stevens c Wyrill b Kippax 63
D. Stevens not out 4
     L-b 2, w 8 10

1/135   (1 wkt, 30.5 overs) 159

*A. Halliday, M. Lyons, M. Stevens, D. Meacher, G. Stevens, J. R. C. Hamblin, R. Myall and P. Hacker did not bat.

Bowling: Burton 4–1–27–0; Houseman 9–0–52–0; Kippax 8.5–2–27–1; Smart 3–0–31–0; Hepworth 6–0–20–0.

Umpires: A. B. Bloodworth and K. Hopley.

WINNERS 1969-97

1969	Hampstead	1979	Scarborough	1989	Teddington
1970	Cheltenham	1980	Moseley	1990	Blackpool
1971	Blackheath	1981	Scarborough	1991	Teddington
1972	Scarborough	1982	Scarborough	1992	Optimists
1973	Wolverhampton	1983	Shrewsbury	1993	Old Hill
1974	Sunbury	1984	Old Hill	1994	Chorley
1975	York	1985	Old Hill	1995	Chorley
1976	Scarborough	1986	Stourbridge	1996	Walsall
1977	Southgate	1987	Old Hill	1997	Eastbourne
1978	Cheltenham	1988	Enfield		

NATIONAL VILLAGE CHAMPIONSHIP, 1997

Caldy, from the Wirral, retained the title in the National Village Championship – sponsored by Alliance and Leicester Giro – that they won for the first time in 1996. Their biggest scare came against Mawdesley in the third round, when they were set a target of only 137 to win. With a hundred on the board and only two out, they looked to have the game sewn up, but the loss of four quick wickets left them needing four runs to win off two balls. Jason Cooper hit the penultimate ball to the boundary, and Caldy were hardly troubled again. In a rain-shortened semi-final against Folkton & Flixton from Yorkshire, they slammed 142 for three off 15 overs to win by 38 runs.

In the other half of the draw, Shipton-under-Wychwood came through a semi-final against Milstead from Kent, who were making their debut in the competition. Shipton reached 216 for nine thanks to a late flurry from Sam Mendes, the well-known theatre director, who hit 48 from just 26 balls. Milstead replied with an opening stand of 70, but a weak performance from their middle order saw them bowled out for 146.

Woodhouse Grange, the champions in 1995, began encouragingly this year as well – slow left-armer Russell Bilton took nine for 38 in their first-round game against Harome. Those figures were the eighth-best in the history of the competition, but the club's campaign ended at the hands of Folkton & Flixton in the final of Group Five.

Moreton, in the Surrey and Berkshire group, were glad that Conservative candidate Robert Wilson failed to win the Bolton North East constituency. Wilson returned to take five for 37 in Round Two to deselect West Ilsley. But two weeks is a long time in village cricket, and Moreton lost heavily to Blackheath in the next round. – *Andrew Tong.*

FINAL

CALDY v SHIPTON-UNDER-WYCHWOOD

At Lord's, August 31. Caldy won by 56 runs. Toss: Shipton-under-Wychwood.

The final went ahead despite news of the death of Diana, Princess of Wales, in the early hours of the morning. A two-minute silence was observed. On the field, Caldy won a low-scoring game to become the third team – after Troon and St Fagans – to take the trophy in successive years. The covers had leaked on a length at one end and, without the patience of brothers Craig and Keith Findlay, Caldy would hardly have had anything to bowl at. Shipton's top three fell to Jason Cooper, the seamer ruled out of the 1996 final by a cycling accident, and his brother Byron took two spectacular catches. Saunders came on at the end to claim four wickets with his medium-paced dobbers for the second year running.

Caldy

B. M. Saunders c Macdonald b Snell	3	D. A. Aston b Humphreys	1	
P. M. Eymond b Snell	2	P. W. Urwin not out	2	
C. J. Findlay lbw b Panter	43	*†M. Rowan not out	1	
B. L. Cooper c Macdonald b Miller	28	B 1, l-b 11, w 7, n-b 1........	20	
C. M. Ruddock b Miller...............	3			
K. G. Findlay run out................	35	1/5 2/23 3/68 (9 wkts, 40 overs) 166		
P. I. Macdonald run out	27	4/75 5/94 6/153		
J. L. Cooper run out	1	7/157 8/161 9/163		

Bowling: Snell 9–3–28–2; Humphreys 9–0–33–1; Hartley 4–1–15–0; Panter 9–0–43–1; Miller 9–0–35–2.

Shipton-under-Wychwood

S. P. Gillette b J. L. Cooper	4	P. Snell b K. G. Findlay..............	1	
†P. N. Jennings c Rowan b J. L. Cooper .	3	*P. D. Humphreys c B. L. Cooper		
J. A. Senior c Saunders b J. L. Cooper...	9	b Saunders .	0	
F. O. S. Macdonald c Rowan b Aston ...	38			
J. S. Hartley c B. L. Cooper b Saunders..	1	L-b 5, w 10, n-b 1	16	
J. M. Constable c B. L. Cooper b Saunders	14			
S. A. Mendes b Urwin	8	1/6 2/20 3/28 (36 overs) 110		
S. Miller b Saunders.................	9	4/39 5/71 6/88		
C. P. Panter not out	7	7/93 8/104 9/107		

Bowling: K. G. Findlay 7–2–14–1; J. L. Cooper 9–0–25–3; Urwin 7–1–11–1; Saunders 9–0–26–4; Aston 4–0–29–1.

Umpires: B. Orton and T. Wilkins

WINNERS 1972-97

1972	Troon (Cornwall)	1985	Freuchie (Fife)
1973	Troon (Cornwall)	1986	Forge Valley (Yorkshire)
1974	Bomarsund (Northumberland)	1987	Longparish (Hampshire)
1975	Gowerton (Glamorgan)	1988	Goatacre (Wiltshire)
1976	Troon (Cornwall)	1989	Toft (Cheshire)
1977	Cookley (Worcestershire)	1990	Goatacre (Wiltshire)
1978	Linton Park (Kent)	1991	St Fagans (Glamorgan)
1979	East Bierley (Yorkshire)	1992	Hursley Park (Hampshire)
1980	Marchwiel (Clwyd)	1993	Kington (Herefordshire)
1981	St Fagans (Glamorgan)	1994	Elvaston (Derbyshire)
1982	St Fagans (Glamorgan)	1995	Woodhouse Grange (Yorkshire)
1983	Quarndon (Derbyshire)	1996	Caldy (Cheshire)
1984	Marchwiel (Clwyd)	1997	Caldy (Cheshire)

IRISH CRICKET IN 1997

By DEREK SCOTT

Ireland began the year with a major disappointment, losing to Scotland in the third-place play-off of the ICC Trophy when a win would have catapulted them into the 1999 World Cup. They lost far more than the simple kudos of being one of the 12 best national teams in the world: there would have been an injection of funds from ICC, government grants during the two years of preparation, and probably increased sponsorship as well. But it was not all gloom: fourth place in Malaysia was an improvement on their performance in the previous ICC tournament at Nairobi in 1994, when they failed at the quarter-final stage, and Ireland's new ranking moved the ICC Development Committee to schedule tours by Australia A in 1998 and South Africa A in 1999.

On the evidence of Kuala Lumpur, ICC named Ireland as one of the countries that could gain one-day international status in the next few years. The Irish were helped by a sponsorship deal – with Independent Newspapers – that allowed South African captain Hansie Cronje to join them for the beginning of the English season. The team responded brilliantly, picking themselves up off the ground to mount their most successful campaign in the Benson and Hedges Cup. The highlight was the victory over Middlesex at Dublin – Ireland's first victory over first-class county opposition in 27 attempts. Desmond Curry, an abattoir worker from Limavady, led the way with 75 off 93 balls, and Cronje followed with 94 not out. Another surprise win almost materialised in the first round of the NatWest Trophy when Ireland reduced Yorkshire to 55 for six, but the experience of the professionals came through.

Ireland lost their grip of the amateur Triple Crown tournament, which they won in 1996. Defeats against Scotland and England – both by 19 runs – might have been avoided by different tactics; Ireland are known to be poor chasers, but they insist on batting second when they win the toss. In the annual first-class game against Scotland, revenge was almost taken, but Ireland were stranded one wicket from victory. Australia were popular visitors to Eglinton, and a large crowd enjoyed an unbeaten century by Ricky Ponting, whose grandmother, Jean, came from Ulster.

Ireland's failure to qualify for the 1999 World Cup convinced the two most capped players in the country to call it a day. Garfield Harrison, who represented his country 118 times, did not begin the season. He scored 2,765 runs at 26.08 and took 140 wickets at 33.67 – only the great Alec O'Riordan had previously achieved the double of 2,000 runs and 100 wickets – but his record number of caps was surpassed during the year by Alan Lewis, who finished with 121. Lewis played his last game at Arundel, where he hit five successive sixes in one over. He made 3,579 runs at 28.63, and cricket's loss will be rugby refereeing's gain. There was, thankfully, an infusion of new blood in the shape of 18-year-old Edmund Joyce, who made 60 on debut against Scotland, and looks a player for the future: he stands very still at the crease and has time to make his shots.

Winners of Irish Leagues and Cups:
Royal Liver All Ireland Cup: Limavady; **Dublin Senior League:** Carlisle; **Munster League:** Cork County; **Munster Cup:** University College, Cork; **Northern Union:** Cliftonville; **Northern Union Cup:** Downpatrick; **North-West League:** Limavady; **North-West Cup:** Limavady.

SCOTTISH CRICKET IN 1997

By J. WATSON BLAIR

At the ICC Trophy in Malaysia, Scotland came through a crunch third-place play-off game against old rivals Ireland to qualify for the 1999 World Cup. Two fixtures will be played at Raeburn Place in Edinburgh, against Bangladesh and New Zealand. There is excitement in the Scottish cricket community, tempered by realism. The Scottish Cricket Union, which made a loss in 1997, will be grateful for the extra funds and exposure, though the team have work to do, as another series of heavy defeats in the Benson and Hedges Cup and NatWest Trophy showed.

Scotland's hold over Ireland extended to the annual Triple Crown tournament, which took place in the English Midlands in July. They won again there, this time by 19 runs, and also beat Wales by one run. Rain curtailed play against England, but Scotland won a sudden-death bowling contest, and with it the tournament. It was their third Triple Crown in four years. Ireland did make a better showing in the annual first-class fixture at Malahide, near Dublin. After a couple of sessions had been lost to rain and mist, Scotland's last-wicket pair of Thomson and Dyer had to bat out 15 balls to save the game.

Even the weather could not take the shine off the undoubted highlight of the international season: the visit of the Australians to Raeburn Place on July 12. Scotland did well to restrict the Australians to 278 for nine from their 50 overs. The batsmen were a little less successful, and their reply stood at 95 for six when a thunderstorm stopped play. None the less, a crowd of almost 7,000 enjoyed the cricket, and the three streakers.

Denmark also visited in July, meeting a trial Scottish XI, and then playing two full internationals. The first of the two was another washout, irritatingly for Scotland, who had reached 211 for five, thanks to 105 not out from opener Bruce Patterson. Denmark were 22 for two in reply. In the second game, Denmark's naturalised Pakistani Aftab Ahmed hit 74 to bring Scotland's 199 all out within range, and the visitors won by five wickets.

On the domestic front, Grange CC did the double by winning the first division of the Scottish League plus the Whyte and Mackay Scottish Cup, the country's biggest knockout competition. Ayr won the second division of the League in their first year since defecting from the Western Union, and won promotion. The Western Union itself was won by West of Scotland. However, a true national league is certain in 1998: the Scottish Cricket Union has voted to support a centrally controlled Scottish National Cricket League featuring 31 clubs, with conferences of equal status in 1998 and a divisional system in 1999.

Winners of other Scottish Leagues and Cups:
SCU Trophy: Watsonians; **West League Cup:** Greenock; **Border League:** Penicuik; **Small Clubs' Cup:** Buckie; **Rowan Cup:** West of Scotland; **Area Championship:** Edinburgh.

ZIMBABWE UNDER-19 IN ENGLAND, 1997

By GERALD HOWAT

During the winter, Zimbabwe's senior team had shown Mike Atherton's England that they were not to be trifled with. But their Under-19 cricketers had little success on the reverse trip. Their defeats in both one-day internationals and two of the three Tests were not unexpected, according to their coach, Andy Pycroft. Zimbabwe is short of skilled schoolmaster-coaches (though there is a strong schools cricketing tradition), financial resources for development and investment by business. Pycroft pointed out that most of the party were schoolboys who would be going home to finish their A-levels – and they certainly learned a lot in England. They had little experience of playing games of more than 50 overs a side but, by the end of the five-week tour, were growing more used to the longer game.

They had little time to adapt to the unfamiliar conditions, however. Because they waited for the end of the school term at home, they had only three days to acclimatise at Wellington College before embarking on the one-day inter-nationals. The Zimbabweans did win their opening game, a well-balanced match against ESCA, but then entered a run of eight successive defeats. That was ended by the drawn Second Test, in which their batsmen recovered some self-esteem with three centuries. In the final Test, there was a sustained spell when they matched their opponents, and even hinted they could force a win.

Their most successful players were Douglas Marillier and Mluleki Nkala. Marillier, the leading batsman, averaged 47.76 over the tour. He adapted quickly, learned to spend time at the crease and has professional ambitions. At 16, Nkala was the youngest tourist, and he could prove the most talented. He had already toured England as captain of the Under-15 team in the Lombard World Challenge in 1996. He could bat with authority, averaging 36.27; his bowling had swing and suggested the potential for pace, though his 14 wickets in all matches were expensive at 39.14. Both these two averaged over 50 in the Tests and scored centuries at Northampton, as did Mark Vermeulen. All-rounders Andre Hoffman and Aubrey Steyn would have done themselves more justice against representative schools' sides. Bertus Erasmus developed as a captain, keeping up team morale during the long stretch of failures, and he found his batting form in the final Test. Given the relatively small pool from which Zimbabwean cricket can draw, many from this party may appear in the full Test side in time.

England's pool was a strong one in a vintage year. Several of their players had appeared in first-class cricket for their counties; Ben Hollioake had already played a full one-day international. After the one-day series, in which he, Owais Shah and David Sales had been the dominant figures, he was withdrawn to play for the senior side against Australia at Nottingham, while Shah and Sales were restored to their counties. Further changes were made as the Test series continued, so that, by the end, England were fielding virtually their Second Eleven. Even Andrew Flintoff, the captain, who had made a commanding century at Birmingham, stepped down. There were also hundreds from opener Steve Peters, the leading run-scorer with 283 at 70.75, and Graeme Swann. Ryan Sidebottom, son of Arnie, was easily the most successful bowler on either side, with 16 at 13.56; he took ten, including an England record of seven for 30, in the First Test.

Manager John Abrahams regretted that his strongest side had not faced a more formidable challenge, and it did not help the case for removing the best youngsters from resentful counties who argued that first-team cricket was a better education. But it did enable the selectors to pursue a policy of introducing younger players, such as the England Under-17 captain, Robert Key, who averaged 46.75 as England's opener. They were able to stake a claim for the forthcoming tour of South Africa, which was to culminate in the 1998 Under-19 World Cup. Some of the players who appeared in the Zimbabwean series had already graduated; seven – Hollioake, Shah, Sales, Flintoff, Dean Cosker, Jonathan Powell and wicket-keeper Chris Read – were promoted to the England A tour of Kenya and Sri Lanka.

ZIMBABWE UNDER-19 TOURING PARTY

A. J. Erasmus (*captain*), C. Delport, I. A. Engelbrecht, N. A. Ferreira, A. P. Hoffman, B. D. McCoun, L. S. Malloch-Brown, T. Manoussis, D. A. Marillier, D. Mutendera, A. J. C. Neethling, M. L. Nkala, J. Oosthuizen, A. G. Steyn, M. A. Vermeulen.
Manager: P. Whalley.   *Coaches:* A. J. Pycroft and D. J. R. Campbell.

ZIMBABWE UNDER-19 TOUR RESULTS

Matches – Played 11: Won 1, Lost 9, Drawn 1.

Note: Matches in this section were not first-class.

At Wellington College, July 28. Zimbabwe Under-19 won by four runs. Toss: ESCA. Zimbabwe Under-19 232 for seven (50 overs) (D. A. Marillier 76, M. L. Nkala 45 not out, A. J. Erasmus 31); ESCA 228 for eight (50 overs) (C. R. J. Budd 70, A. J. Marsh 37, R. C. Driver 35; A. P. Hoffman five for 34, including a hat-trick).

At Wellington College, July 29. NAYC won by six wickets. Toss: Zimbabwe Under-19. Zimbabwe Under-19 159 for nine (50 overs) (D. A. Marillier 41, B. D. McCoun 51 not out; J. Frith four for 30); NAYC 160 for four (46.1 overs) (P. S. Lazenbury 71, R. Parker 31).

At Wellington College, July 30. ECB XI won by ten wickets. Toss: ECB XI. Zimbabwe Under-19 72 (30 overs) (D. Love four for 12); ECB XI 78 for no wkt (13.2 overs) (R. L. Robinson 52 not out).

At Hove, August 1. First unofficial one-day international: England Under-19 won by nine wickets. Toss: England Under-19. Zimbabwe Under-19 192 for seven (50 overs) (D. A. Marillier 35, A. J. Erasmus 31, C. Delport 45 not out, Extras 45); England Under-19 196 for one (27.3 overs) (O. A. Shah 57 not out, D. J. Sales 74, B. C. Hollioake 33 not out, Extras 32).

At Hove, August 2. Sussex Second XI won by 18 runs. Toss: Sussex Second XI. Sussex Second XI 254 (48 overs) (R. S. C. Martin-Jenkins 56, J. R. Carpenter 34, R. N. Jackson 56; M. L. Nkala four for 54, B. D. McCoun three for 40); Zimbabwe Under-19 236 (47.4 overs) (M. A. Vermeulen 37, D. A. Marillier 47, M. L. Nkala 42, T. Manoussis 40; N. C. Phillips three for 40).

At Southampton, August 4. Second unofficial one-day international. England Under-19 won by eight wickets. Toss: England Under-19. Zimbabwe Under-19 156 for nine (25 overs) (D. A. Marillier 41, L. S. Malloch-Brown 40; R. J. Sidebottom three for 33); England Under-19 157 for two (21.3 overs) (B. C. Hollioake 59 not out, A. Flintoff 72 not out).
   Hollioake had been named the previous day in the full England squad for the Nottingham Test, starting on August 7.

ENGLAND UNDER-19 v ZIMBABWE UNDER-19

First Unofficial Test

At Birmingham, August 7, 8, 9. England Under-19 won by an innings and 112 runs. Toss: Zimbabwe Under-19.

England completed an overwhelming victory with nearly five sessions to spare. Only Hoffman, with 70 on the second evening, and the 16-year-old Nkala, who made 71, delayed the end. But it had been inevitable since Sidebottom seized seven for 30, the best figures by an England Under-19 bowler, on the opening day. His left-arm swing and pace were too much for Zimbabwe, and he bowled six maidens before conceding a run. Then the captain, Flintoff, stepped up to score a commanding century, 116 from 86 balls, with 12 fours and seven sixes. England added 217 before lunch on the second day, when the temperature was in the eighties; even fielders used to Africa were wilting by tea, when Flintoff declared. Sidebottom took another three quick wickets that evening, but Hoffman and Nkala staved off a two-day defeat.

Close of play: First day, England Under-19 155-1 (S. D. Peters 85*, G. R. Haywood 14*); Second day, Zimbabwe Under-19 118-6 (M. L. Nkala 10*, C. Delport 0*).

Zimbabwe Under-19

N. A. Ferreira b Sidebottom	5 – c Cosker b Franks	5
L. S. Malloch-Brown c Cosker b Sidebottom	2 – lbw b Sidebottom	4
M. A. Vermuelen lbw b Sidebottom	50 – c Key b Sidebottom	0
D. A. Marillier c Peters b Tudor	30 – lbw b Tudor	4
A. P. Hoffman b Sidebottom	19 – c Key b Cosker	70
*A. J. Erasmus b Sidebottom	3 – c Morris b Sidebottom	2
M. L. Nkala lbw b Cosker	7 – b Batty	71
†C. Delport c Tudor b Sidebottom	3 – b Cosker	26
A. G. Steyn not out	32 – c Read b Batty	10
B. D. McCoun lbw b Sidebottom	0 – not out	10
I. A. Engelbrecht lbw b Tudor	5 – run out	1
B 8, l-b 20, n-b 24	52	B 12, l-b 7, w 2, n-b 8	29

1/15 2/20 3/77 4/117 5/137 208 1/6 2/6 3/13 4/43 5/60 232
6/154 7/160 8/160 9/161 6/118 7/162 8/214 9/227

Bowling: *First Innings*—Tudor 10.4–0–61–2; Sidebottom 18–9–30–7; Franks 15–7–30–0; Cosker 22–8–49–1; Batty 4–1–10–0. *Second Innings*—Tudor 6–3–14–1; Sidebottom 19–7–56–3; Franks 13–3–38–1; Cosker 27–8–79–2; Batty 12–4–26–2.

England Under-19

S. D. Peters c Ferreira b Steyn	85	P. J. Franks not out	49
R. W. T. Key c Erasmus b Engelbrecht	44	D. A. Cosker not out	27
G. R. Haywood c Erasmus b Steyn	16		
*A. Flintoff c Vermuelen b Steyn	116	B 6, l-b 7, w 4, n-b 2	19
Z. C. Morris c Erasmus b McCoun	13		
G. J. Batty b Steyn	64	1/94 2/155 3/162	(8 wkts dec.) 552
†C. M. W. Read c Delport b Nkala	78	4/211 5/320 6/361	
A. J. Tudor c Erasmus b McCoun	41	7/429 8/504	

R. J. Sidebottom did not bat.

Bowling: Nkala 25–2–140–1; Steyn 30–5–102–4; McCoun 13–1–93–2; Engelbrecht 12–1–69–1; Erasmus 2–0–12–0; Hoffman 9–0–53–0; Vermuelen 10–0–70–0.

Umpires: J. D. Bond and K. E. Palmer.

At Sleaford, August 12, 13, 14. ECB Under-18 XI won by an innings and 86 runs. Toss: Zimbabwe Under-19. Zimbabwe Under-19 155 (J. Oosthuizen 32, C. Delport 33; J. O. Grove four for 31) and 137 (M. L. Nkala 34; C. P. Schofield four for 43, R. J. Logan three for 14); ECB Under-18 XI 378 for five dec. (G. R. Napier 35, M. A. J. Gough 108 not out, G. P. Swann 142).

At Kimbolton, August 16, 17, 18. ECB Development XI won by three wickets. Toss: Zimbabwe Under-19. Zimbabwe Under-19 265 (D. A. Marillier 62, N. A. Ferreira 52 not out, A. G. Steyn 50; S. J. Randall three for 73, B. O'Connell four for 58) and 114 (B. O'Connell five for 24, S. J. Randall three for 30); ECB Development XI 200 for five dec. (B. L. Spendlove 76; I. A. Engelbrecht three for 52) and 183 for seven (J. W. Inglis 80, I. J. Thomas 31; M. A. Vermeulen three for 40).

ENGLAND UNDER-19 v ZIMBABWE UNDER-19

Second Unofficial Test

At Northampton, August 21, 22, 23, 24. Drawn. Toss: Zimbabwe Under-19.

Rain wiped out the fourth day, though the draw was already favourite after 1,102 runs and only 31 wickets. At last, Zimbabwe seemed capable of handling the opposition. Though Oosthuizen retired, struck in the groin, Marillier and Vermeulen added 268 on a flat pitch with a fast outfield, batting into the second morning and combining sound strokeplay with organised defence. Then Nkala quickened the rate with some dazzling shots, especially after hearing the declaration was due in seven overs. He completed Zimbabwe's third century just in time. England had made four changes, and an inexperienced attack struggled for line and length. But Zimbabwe's did no better, conceding 109 in 16 overs of long hops and full tosses. Next day, Peters and Key advanced to 198, Peters scoring a run-a-ball 145. Engelbrecht's left-arm spin claimed four victims, but Swann made a chanceless 156 on debut, at his home ground, lifting England to 563, their highest Under-19 total, before the rain came.

Close of play: First day, Zimbabwe Under-19 212-0 (D. A. Marillier 107*, M. A. Vermeulen 80*); Second day, England Under-19 109-0 (S. D. Peters 61*, R. W. T. Key 48*); Third day, England Under-19 563-8 (G. P. Swann 156*, R. J. Sidebottom 10*).

Zimbabwe Under-19

D. A. Marillier c Morris b Flintoff	150	A. G. Steyn c Morris b Powell	1
J. Oosthuizen retired hurt	6	†C. Delport not out	50
M. A. Vermeulen lbw b Haywood	134	B 4, l-b 11, w 18, n-b 14	47
A. P. Hoffman b Sidebottom	23		
M. L. Nkala not out	101	1/297 2/328 3/346 (5 wkts dec.) 539
*A. J. Erasmus c Read b Schofield	27	4/435 5/436

J. Oosthuizen retired hurt at 29.

N. A. Ferreira, I. A. Engelbrecht and D. Mutendera did not bat.

Bowling: Martin 17–1–76–0; Sidebottom 25–6–91–1; Haywood 16–6–39–1; Swann 12–5–19–0; Schofield 37.3–8–127–1; Powell 31–4–128–1; Morris 6–1–44–0; Flintoff 3–3–0–1.

England Under-19

S. D. Peters c Delport b Vermeulen	145	C. P. Schofield c Mutendera b Engelbrecht	35
R. W. T. Key c Nkala b Hoffman	81	R. J. Sidebottom not out	10
G. R. Haywood c Delport b Engelbrecht	5		
*A. Flintoff c Marillier b Engelbrecht	52	L-b 7, w 1, n-b 4	12
Z. C. Morris c Marillier b Engelbrecht	3		
J. C. Powell c Delport b Nkala	57	1/198 2/211 3/265 (8 wkts) 563
G. P. Swann not out	156	4/293 5/294 6/398
†C. M. W. Read b Steyn	5	7/425 8/523

N. D. Martin did not bat.

Bowling: Steyn 18–3–66–1; Mutendera 12–1–73–0; Engelbrecht 35–4–167–4; Vermeulen 11–0–53–1; Nkala 15–0–86–1; Hoffman 26–3–103–1; Erasmus 3–0–8–0.

Umpires: H. D. Bird and N. T. Plews.

ENGLAND UNDER-19 v ZIMBABWE UNDER-19

Third Unofficial Test

At Canterbury, August 28, 29, 30, 31. England Under-19 won by four wickets. Toss: Zimbabwe Under-19.

England made two more changes and the captaincy passed from Flintoff to Zac Morris, whose brother Alex had previously held the job. Their young team still took the series 2-0. Half the opening day was lost to rain, and Zimbabwe struggled against the seamers, especially Franks and Sidebottom, who broke through the later order with three for five in 25 balls. But next day, Zimbabwe put on their best all-round performance of the tour. They forced England on the defensive, after Peters and debutant Napier had made a spirited start at five an over. In both first innings, the last nine wickets fell for under 100. Zimbabwe resumed only 30 behind, and some excellent batting by Marillier and Nkala left the game finely balanced. They set England a target of 226 and reduced them to 123 for six, three of them to Nkala. But Laraman, another newcomer, hit 56 as he and Read shared a match-winning stand of 103.

Close of play: First day, Zimbabwe Under-19 118-8 (A. J. Erasmus 33*, D. Mutendera 0*); Second day, Zimbabwe Under-19 178-4 (M. L. Nkala 46*, A. G. Steyn 0*); Third day, England Under-19 19-1 (R. W. T. Key 12*, G. R. Napier 0*).

Zimbabwe Under-19

D. A. Marillier c Read b Franks	18	– lbw b Schofield	82
N. A. Ferreira c Read b Franks	0	– c Read b Laraman	0
M. A. Vermeulen not out	3	– (7) lbw b Sidebottom	0
A. P. Hoffman c Schofield b Laraman	24	– (3) c Laraman b Franks	7
M. L. Nkala c Peters b Napier	4	– b Sidebottom	48
*A. J. Erasmus b Franks	49	– (4) c Peters b Schofield	23
†C. Delport c Powell b Sidebottom	3	– (8) c and b Schofield	18
A. G. Steyn c Read b Sidebottom	4	– (6) c Swann b Schofield	34
B. D. McCoun c Laraman b Sidebottom	2	– b Franks	16
I. A. Engelbrecht c Powell b Franks	0	– not out	1
D. Mutendera b Franks	1	– b Franks	0
B 4, l-b 8, w 6, n-b 20	38	B 2, l-b 11, w 5, n-b 8	26
	146		**255**

1/1 2/52 3/56 4/72 5/80   1/0 2/23 3/76 4/178 5/181
6/87 7/109 8/117 9/132   6/183 7/228 8/251 9/255

In the first innings M. A. Vermeulen, when 0, retired hurt at 1-1 and resumed at 132.

Bowling: *First Innings*—Sidebottom 15–3–28–3; Franks 20.5–7–66–5; Laraman 15–6–25–1; Napier 5–0–10–1; Schofield 2–0–5–0. *Second Innings*—Franks 23–7–64–3; Laraman 8–1–36–1; Napier 6–0–24–0; Schofield 20–5–60–4; Powell 6–0–28–0; Swann 5–2–18–0; Sidebottom 13–8–12–2.

England Under-19

S. D. Peters c Steyn b Mutendera	46	– c Engelbrecht b Nkala	7
R. W. T. Key c Mutendera b Nkala	12	– c McCoun b Hoffman	50
G. R. Napier c Delport b Steyn	38	– c Delport b Nkala	9
G. P. Swann c McCoun b Mutendera	2	– c Hoffman b Mutendera	10
*Z. C. Morris b Mutendera	10	– lbw b Nkala	21
J. C. Powell c McCoun b Steyn	2	– c Engelbrecht b Hoffman	16
A. W. Laraman lbw b Hoffman	8	– not out	56
†C. M. W. Read c Delport b Hoffman	4	– not out	20
C. P. Schofield c Steyn b Mutendera	32		
P. J. Franks lbw b Steyn	7		
R. J. Sidebottom not out	6		
L-b 4, w 2, n-b 3	9	B 9, l-b 5, w 7, n-b 16	37
	176	(6 wkts)	**226**

1/24 2/77 3/94 4/106 5/114   1/15 2/41 3/54   (6 wkts)
6/114 7/119 8/131 9/166   4/83 5/117 6/123

Bowling: *First Innings*—Mutendera 19–5–51–4; Nkala 11–0–51–1; Steyn 13.5–5–42–3; Hoffman 6–2–28–2. *Second Innings*—Mutendera 16–4–49–3; Steyn 10.0–0–55–0; Hoffman 10–6–12–2; McCoun 2–0–9–0; Engelbrecht 5–1–13–0; Erasmus 2.2–0–17–0.

Umpires: G. Sharp and P. Willey.

NAYC UNDER-19 CRICKET, 1997

By PHILIP HOARE

The 1997 season saw the tangled strands of Under-19 county cricket sorting themselves out, as the National Association of Young Cricketers staged two major competitions. There was a two-day league, running from June to August, for 20 counties in four regional groups, whose winners advanced to a knockout. Matches featured one innings of 110 overs a side. This brought those counties who had left the NAYC festivals to concentrate on two-day cricket back into the fold; all the first-class counties except Durham played, plus three minors.

The inaugural winners were Leicestershire, who headed the Central Group. In the final, they drew with Sussex, the Southern leaders, but gained six bonus points to Sussex's five, thanks to a late century partnership between Jamie Hart and Karl Smith. Leicestershire had also drawn with Warwickshire in a rain-affected semi-final, but went through on a better group record; Sussex had beaten Glamorgan outright.

Meanwhile, the one-day competition was revised. Like the old festivals, it was held in August, but the 28 counties (11 first-class), in seven groups, were gathered in Somerset, Surrey and Northamptonshire, as well as the original centres, Oxford and Cambridge. Play-offs between the seven winners and the best runners-up produced the semi-finalists. A young Northamptonshire team were surprise winners when some fine pace bowling by Richard Logan defeated Surrey.

Their later order had fought back from 58 for five, and Logan's first spell reduced Surrey to 20 for four. Charles Hodgson and James McCulley added 83, but Logan dismissed both to settle the matter. Northamptonshire had won all three group matches, beaten Yorkshire after losing nine wickets to ten in a tied play-off, and defeated Kent by 27 runs in the semi-final. An efficient Surrey side also had a perfect record until the final, heading their group, then beating Lancashire in the play-off and Dorset in the semi-final, when Hodgson scored 123 not out. Northamptonshire also won the Hilda Overy Trophy, a one-day league overlapping with the one-day cup, in its final year.

Further changes were due in 1998. The ECB was to increase its funding from £27,000 to £100,000, to be spent on the two-day competition, which the NAYC was organising on their behalf. This would now feature all 18 first-class counties plus 11 minor counties. The one-day cup was to continue, based at Oxford and Cambridge as in previous years, but contested only by the minor counties and without direct ECB funding. It was expected to wither away, as all the minor counties were due to join the two-day competition in 1999.

NAYC ONE-DAY CUP FINAL

At Shenley Park, August 16. Northamptonshire won by 12 runs. Toss: Northamptonshire. Northamptonshire 169 for nine (50 overs) (A. M. Dobson 34; R. Johnson three for 19); Surrey 157 (47.3 overs) (C. P. R. Hodgson 32, J. J. McCulley 31; R. J. Logan five for 21, M. Dobson three for 20).

NAYC TWO-DAY CUP FINAL

LEICESTERSHIRE v SUSSEX

At Kimbolton School, August 28, 29. Leicestershire won on bonus points. Leicestershire 6 pts, Sussex 5 pts. Toss: Leicestershire.

A heroic stand of 123 between Jamie Hart and Karl Smith secured the inaugural NAYC Two-Day Cup for Leicestershire. An outright win was highly unlikely at 96 for seven. But Hart, fluently, and Smith, more carefully, kept them in the game. At 150, they achieved a first batting point, to pull level on five, and they took a second at 200. Hart and Smith then concentrated on preserving their wickets and one-point advantage. On a rain-affected first day, Sussex reached 202 for four. Richard Jackson and Michael Yardy extended their fifth-wicket stand to 104 in the morning. Then a hat-trick from Steve Kirby wrapped up the innings. Leicestershire's upper order crashed in reply, and the trophy was being given a final polish for Sussex until Hart and Smith joined forces.

Sussex

D. A. Clapp lbw b Pollard	27	A. Simmons not out		0
L. Schildkamp c and b Birchall	29	M. Nash lbw b Kirby		0
*†C. M. Mole c Wright b Birchall	34	C. W. Read b Kirby		0
G. R. A. Campbell c Hill b Pollard	0			
R. N. Jackson run out	81	B 7, l-b 14, w 1, n-b 7		29
M. H. Yardy c Hart b Birchall	38			
I. Ellis b Kirby	2	1/69 2/69 3/69 4/131 5/235		240
D. Shuttleworth b Kirby	0	6/238 7/239 8/240 9/240		

Bonus points – Sussex 2, Leicestershire 4.

Bowling: Kirby 19.4–7–23–4; Smith 5–2–10–0; Hart 8–2–33–0; Pollard 9–2–22–2; Birchall 40–8–93–3; Pullen 24–8–38–0.

Leicestershire

R. A. E. Martin b Ellis	1	J. Hart not out		70
O. Choudry c Campbell b Shuttleworth	8	K. Smith not out		56
J. Mason run out	20			
A. S. Wright lbw b Read	12	B 2, l-b 9, w 2, n-b 1		14
†E. Hill lbw b Yardy	0			
*N. Pullen c Schildkamp b Nash	16	1/5 2/13 3/38 4/38	(7 wkts)	219
L. Pollard b Jackson	22	5/44 6/69 7/96		

S. Kirby and W. Birchall did not bat.

Bonus points – Leicestershire 2, Sussex 3.

Bowling: Shuttleworth 13–3–40–1; Ellis 11–2–24–1; Read 23–9–36–1; Yardy 11–4–23–1; Nash 11–2–9–1; Jackson 20–8–47–1; Simmons 8–0–29–0.

Umpires: A. A. Jones and M. J. Kitchen.

CRICKET SOCIETY AWARDS, 1997

Ben Hollioake of Surrey won the Cricket Society's Most Promising Young Cricketer Award. The A. A. Thomson Fielding Prize, for the best schoolboy fielder, went to Christopher Budd of Ridings High School. The Sir John Hobbs Memorial Prize, for the outstanding Under-16 schoolboy, was won by Martyn Dobson of the Frederick Gough School, Bottesford. Society awards under the Wetherell bequest went to Graham Rose of Somerset as the outstanding all-rounder in the first-class game, and – for the second successive season – to Steven Tomlinson of the Oratory School, who was the outstanding all-rounder in schools cricket.

SCHOOLS CRICKET IN 1997

Nicholas Boulton of King's College, Taunton (left) and Lee Hilton of King Edward VII, Lytham, were two of the leading players at the MCC Schools Festival at Oxford and at Lord's.

The 14th MCC Schools Festival, held at Oxford from July 11–14, followed a new format in 1997. Four sides, each chosen from a squad of 12, all played each other in limited-overs games on the first three days, followed by a 12-a-side final trial match on the fourth day. As before, the squads were selected separately by the Headmasters' Conference (HMC) and the English Schools Cricket Association (ESCA). HMC North won all three of their matches on pitches which for the most part made batting difficult.

The outstanding player was Nicholas Boulton, a left-handed batsman and right-arm fast-medium bowler from King's, Taunton, who scored 159 runs for once out and took six wickets at 16.50. Ben Quick and Adrian Marsh both made hundreds on the best batting pitch of the tournament at St John's College, and the consistent Lee Hilton had two half-centuries in his 145 from three innings. Ian McCarter, who went on to captain MCC Schools at Lord's, was the other leading all-rounder, with 116 runs at 58.50 and six wickets at 19.83. Seven bowlers in all took six, but only James Schofield managed seven – at 17.42 off 27 overs. The best figures were Gavin Reynolds's four for 30 on the first day.

The four squads were:

HMC Northern Schools: I. J. W. McCarter (Shrewsbury) (*captain*), S. J. Birtwisle (Durham), D. N. Catterall (Queen Elizabeth GS, Blackburn), R. A. Harris (Stowe), L. M. Hilton (King Edward VII, Lytham), A. J. Marsh (Abbotsholme), P. R. Mouncey (Pocklington), T. J. Pearman (Haileybury), B. T. Quick (Ashville), J. A. Spires (Solihull), D. G. Weatherhead (King's, Tynemouth), R. A. White (Stowe).

HMC Southern Schools: H. J. H. Loudon (Eton) (*captain*), M. S. Ali (Chigwell), M. J. Banes (Tonbridge), N. R. Boulton (King's, Taunton), D. D. Cherry (Tonbridge), J. A. Claughton (King Edward VI, Southampton), A. N. Edwards (Millfield), C. J. Hellings (Millfield), S. J. Lamplough (Wellington C.), A. S. Owen (Prior Park), T. J. Phillips (Felsted), S. C. B. Tomlinson (Oratory).

ESCA North: R. J. Hall (Royal GS, Worcester; Worcs) (*captain*), M. Bamford (Shrewsbury SFC; Salop), S. M. Eustace (Birmingham CFE; Warwicks), T. A. Hicks (Lord Wandsworth; Dorset), C. Milward (Stafford CFE; Staffs), G. Reynolds (St Francis Xavier; Lancs), S. J. Price (Hereford Cathedral S.; Herefords), J. E. K. Schofield (Royal GS, Worcester; Worcs), K. S. Tate (Nottingham HS; Notts), J. Wagstaff (Worcester SFC; Worcs), G. White (Cockermouth; Cumbria), G. J. Wright (Smestow, Wolverhampton; Staffs).

ESCA South: T. W. M. Rose (Leighton Park; Berks) *(captain)*, R. A. Brook (Hinchingbrooke; Hunts), C. R. J. Budd (Ridings HS; Glos), R. D. Dorey (Millfield; Dorset), R. C. Driver (Redruth CS; Cornwall), T. Fray (East Berks SFC; Berks), S. Harrison (Bracknell SFC; Berks), J. E. Hartley (Rochester Maths; Kent), P. D. King (St Joseph's, Ipswich; Suffolk), M. J. Webb (Millfield; Devon), C. White (Forest; Essex).

At St Edward's School, July 11. HMC North won by three wickets. HMC South 205 for six (60 overs) (J. A. Claughton 45, M. S. Ali 70, N. R. Boulton 31 not out); HMC North 206 for seven (57.4 overs) (I. J. W. McCarter 32, P. R. Mouncey 40, R. A. White 46 not out, B. T. Quick 39 not out; N. R. Boulton three for 35).

At Wadham College, July 11. ESCA South won by 29 runs. ESCA South 246 for nine (60 overs) (C. R. J. Budd 50, T. Fray 37, R. D. Dorey 86 not out, Extras 32; G. Reynolds four for 30); ESCA North 217 for seven (60 overs) (R. J. Hall 69, J. E. K. Schofield 41).

At Wadham College, July 12. HMC South won by 85 runs. HMC South 256 for eight (60 overs) (A. N. Edwards 58, N. R. Boulton 92; R. D. Dorey three for 44); ESCA South 171 (46.1 overs) (R. C. Driver 38; T. J. Phillips four for 36).

At St Edward's School, July 12. HMC North won by 85 runs. HMC North 238 for seven (60 overs) (L. M. Hilton 70, D. G. Weatherhead 49, R. A. White 34, J. A. Spires 41 not out; T. A. Hicks three for 35); ESCA North 153 for eight (60 overs) (I. J. W. McCarter three for 21).

At St Edward's School, July 13. HMC South won by six wickets. ESCA North 187 for eight (55 overs) (R. J. Hall 46); HMC South 191 for four (M. J. Banes 57, J. A. Claughton 82 not out).

At St John's College, July 13. HMC North won by eight wickets. ESCA South 251 for seven (R. C. Driver 59, T. W. M. Rose 72, J. E. Hartley 62 not out; S. J. Birtwisle three for 42); HMC North 257 for two (45.2 overs) (A. J. Marsh 111 not out, B. T. Quick 103).

At Wadham College, July 14 (12-a-side). MCC Schools East won by two wickets. MCC Schools West 192 for ten dec. (L. M. Hilton 55 retired hurt, N. R. Boulton 36 retired hurt); MCC Schools East 193 for nine (I. J. W. McCarter 69 not out, S. C. B. Tomlinson 30; J. E. K. Schofield three for 17).

After this match, the following were selected to play for MCC Schools at Lord's: Muazam Ali, Matthew Banes, Nicholas Boulton, Chris Budd, Duncan Catterall, Ryan Driver, Andy Edwards, Stuart Eustace, Joe Hartley, Lee Hilton, Paul King, Ian McCarter, Adrian Marsh, Timothy Phillips and James Schofield.

MCC v MCC SCHOOLS

At Lord's, July 15. MCC Schools won by five wickets. Toss: MCC Schools. MCC 214 for six dec. (A. G. Lawson 95); MCC Schools 215 for five (A. J. Marsh 35, L. M. Hilton 60 not out).
   Andrew Lawson, of Eastern Province, narrowly missed a century at Lord's when he was run out through a deflection at the non-striker's end.

MCC SCHOOLS v NATIONAL ASSOCIATION OF YOUNG CRICKETERS

At Lord's, July 16. Drawn. Toss: MCC Schools. National Association of Young Cricketers 215 for eight dec. (C. P. R. Hodgson 74, P. S. Lazenbury 33; A. N. Edwards three for 66); MCC Schools 156 for eight (N. R. Boulton 72; D. Leather three for 48, I. C. Parkin three for 26).

ETON v HARROW

At Lord's, June 27. Abandoned, owing to rain, for the first time in the history of this fixture. The following teams were selected.

Eton

*H. J. H. Loudon, D. C. Kay-Shuttleworth, A. F. S. Leslie, J. R. S. Redmayne, D. R. Vassar-Smith, A. G. R. Loudon, J. T. A. Bruce, †R. F. Horne, O. R. A. Shuttleworth, L. J. Rankin and P. A. Norman-Butler.

Harrow

W. J. L. Matthews, †L. F. de Rougemont, *A. N. L. Cox, S. H. Stevens, J. R. W. Norris, D. R. Hepher, A. T. R. Titchener-Barrett, J. S. Weston-Simons, J. R. F. Cooke-Hurle, J. W. B. Neame and P. C. Bourke.

Of the 161 matches between the two schools since 1805, Eton have won 52, Harrow 44 and 65 have been drawn. Matches during the two world wars are excluded from the reckoning. The fixture was reduced from a two-day, two-innings-a-side match to one day in 1982. A full list of centuries since 1918 and results from 1950 can be found in Wisdens *prior to 1994.*

HIGHLIGHTS FROM THE SCHOOLS

In schools cricket, the season of 1997 is likely to be remembered more for the appalling weather than for broken records – except those concerning numbers of matches completely washed out or badly rain-affected. It will also be recalled for the disputatious match between Marlborough and Radley, which turned the question of sportsmanship in school cricket into national headlines (See "The End of Chivalry" by Andrew Longmore on pages 34-35). All the same, there were some notable performances with both bat and ball, and a number of players stood out. The most prolific batsman was A. R. Hemingway of Royal GS, Guildford, who scored 1,028 runs at 79.07 in 20 innings, followed by J. R. Lee of Manchester GS, the only other batsman to reach 1,000 runs, with 1,012 at 77.84 in five fewer innings.

Of the five others to pass 900 runs, R. Clinton of Colfe's accumulated 963 in 14 innings at an average of 107.00. His was the only three-figure average among those who scored 500 runs, the next best being 92.42 for 647 runs by A. J. Goode of Bromsgrove and 90.70 by N. R. Boulton of King's, Taunton, whose 907 came in just 12 innings. Boulton was alone in scoring five centuries, with four each from N. Pope of Plymouth (in 14 innings) and from M. J. Banes and J. J. McCulley, both of Tonbridge (17 innings each). There were no double-centuries, but nine scores above 150, the two highest being 166 by R. Dorey of Millfield and 163 from Hemingway. In general, batsmen had fewer opportunities than usual, but I. S. Pay of King's College, Wimbledon, and J. S. Oxborrow of Royal GS, Colchester both went to the wicket 23 times, scoring 440 and 366 runs respectively.

No bowler took 60 wickets and only two passed 50: T. W. Briggs of Reigate GS, who had 54 at 13.37 off 244.2 overs, and S. A. Musk of Royal GS, High Wycombe, whose 52 came at 13.32 off 231.2 overs. Of the four others to take 45, P. D. King of St Joseph's, Ipswich, bowled the fewest overs – 182. There were four single-figure averages among bowlers with 30 wickets. The most economical was S. Hayward of the Duke of York's Royal Military School, whose 30 came at only 5.03 apiece. Also economical were B. T. Quick of Ashville, whose 42 cost 8.52 each, G. Moore of Foyle and Londonderry with 32 at 8.75 and J. A. Spires of Solihull (44 at 9.79). N. G. Hatch of Barnard Castle finished with 21 wickets at 3.95 apiece.

The best return came from J. Cockburn of King Edward VI, Stourbridge, whose nine for 30 included a hat-trick, and there were five eight-wicket hauls. G. R. Saxton of Bradford GS also took a hat-trick, Felsted's T. J. Phillips returned seven for four. Far fewer overs were bowled than in 1996, and of the five who delivered more than 250, J. Rasheed of Merchant Taylors', Northwood, and M. B. McCreath of Loretto each sent down 271, taking 47 and 45 wickets respectively.

The Oratory School's Steven Tomlinson (left) had the best all-round averages for the second season running and Jonathan Lee of Manchester Grammar School was one of only two players to score a thousand runs in 1997.

The leading all-rounder in terms of quantity was Phillips, who had 649 runs at 59.00 and 41 wickets at 11.95, followed by R. Mutucumarana of Trinity (686 runs at 62.36 and 31 wickets at 20.48), R. E. Walker of Bradford GS (652 runs at 46.57 and 31 wickets at 15.61), M. Wright of Enfield GS (618 runs at 34.33 and 31 wickets at 16.41) and King, who collected 523 runs at 52.30 as well as his 46 wickets. In terms of averages the best among those with 500 runs and 30 wickets was S. C. B. Tomlinson of The Oratory, who achieved that distinction in 1996; in 1997 he scored 502 runs at 71.71 and took 30 wickets at 10.60, figures which earned him the Cricket Society's Wetherell Award for the second year running.

Of the 12 unbeaten schools, Tonbridge had the best winning percentage with 14 out of 16, and another six won at least half their matches – Cheltenham, Eton, King's (Rochester), The Leys, Portsmouth GS and Worksop. Still unbeaten but less successful were Lord Williams's (Thame), Manchester GS, St Joseph's (Ipswich), Sevenoaks and – especially – Radley, who won only one of their 11 matches. Two other sides worthy of mention were Richard Huish, who won six out of seven, and Royal GS, Worcester, with 16 out of 19. At the other end of the scale, Arnold, Clifton, Colston's, Dover College, Rydal and St Dunstan's all failed to achieve a single win. Rydal were particularly unfortunate, reporting six of their ten matches abandoned and losing all four that they played. Kingswood were also unable to start over half their scheduled matches, and many more in all parts of the country were severely curtailed by rain or appalling conditions. In contrast, King's College School, Wimbledon, Bangor GS, and King's, Worcester, managed to play 23 matches, and there were some schools who reported no completely abandoned games.

The five British Schools who participated in the 11th Sir Garfield Sobers Schools Cricket Festival, held in Barbados in July, were Bradfield College, King Edward's (Bath), St Ambrose College, Stamford School and Sutton Valence, who reached the semi-finals. There, they lost to Dominica Schools, who were eventual runners-up to Ellerslie School of Barbados.

Details of records broken, other outstanding performances and interesting features of the season may be found in the returns from the schools which follow.

THE SCHOOLS

(Qualification: Batting 150 runs; Bowling 15 wickets)

* On name indicates captain.   * On figures indicates not out.

Note: The line for batting reads Innings–Not Outs–Runs–Highest Score–100s–Average; that for bowling reads Overs–Maidens–Runs–Wickets–Best Bowling–Average.

ABINGDON SCHOOL   *Played 19: W 4, L 8, D 7. A 8*

Master i/c: A. M. Broadbent

Batting—J. R. C. Horton 15–2–465–78–0–35.76; G. A. O. Jones 10–3–241–61–0–34.42; E. J. K. Ryder 13–1–267–62–0–22.25; R. H. Smith 10–1–150–48–0–16.66; H. E. Dorling 13–2–156–24*–0–14.18; T. J. Evans 11–0–150–54–0–13.63.

Bowling—R. A. Pike 118–25–363–23–5/10–15.78; *T. W. Jones 146–18–511–20–3/19–25.55.

ALDENHAM SCHOOL   *Played 13: W 3, L 3, D 7*

Master i/c: S. D. Thomas

Batting—A. P. Meara 13–2–458–119–1–41.63; K. A. Habib 10–3–248–57–0–35.42; K. A. Worsnop 9–2–218–64–0–31.14; *A. P. Thrussell 13–1–293–91*–0–24.41; S. A. Bloom 9–2–151–38*–0–21.57.

Bowling—T. W. Smith 101–11–368–18–5/55–20.44; M. A. Tennant 160–33–533–24–5/69–22.20.

ALLEYN'S SCHOOL   *Played 17: W 6, L 8, D 3. A 5*

Master i/c: D. J. Tickner   Professional: P. H. Edwards

Batting—*S. Payne 15–4–435–115*–1–39.54; P. J. Mitchener 12–5–256–103*–1–36.57; P. M. B. Jenkins 13–1–264–56–0–22.00; D. J. Matthews 13–1–189–51–0–15.75.

Bowling—D. O. Tyler 74.4–7–342–18–4/9–19.00; S. McGill 124.4–16–434–20–6/17–21.70; M. J. Stringer 126.1–31–398–18–4/3–22.11.

AMPLEFORTH COLLEGE   *Played 11: W 2, L 2, D 7. A 1*

Master i/c: G. Thurman   Professional: D. Wilson

Batting—M. Wilkie 11–1–462–93*–0–46.20; A. G. M. Jenkins 11–2–296–78–0–32.88; *G. M. Denny 11–0–301–53–0–27.36; P. E. D. Cartwright-Taylor 11–0–243–60–0–22.09.

Bowling—H. F. P. Murphy 150.2–24–509–19–3/52–26.78; C. G. S. Shillington 153.4–17–588–21–5/47–28.00.

ARDINGLY COLLEGE   *Played 14: W 6, L 2, D 6. A 6*

Master i/c: G. Hart   Professional: D. Frame

Batting—M. Turner 9–2–335–108*–1–47.85; J. Chadburn 15–3–465–87*–0–38.75; D. Macaulay 9–2–173–53–0–24.71; *N. Strugnell 11–1–235–72*–0–23.50; N. Holloway 10–1–160–30–0–17.77; J. Fairbrother 14–2–213–80*–0–17.75.

Bowling—E. Smallman 83–19–228–25–4/15–9.12; J. Dower 120.4–25–344–26–6/35–13.23; J. Darby 90.3–11–319–20–5/58–15.95; D. Macaulay 126–27–329–19–5/27–17.31.

ARNOLD SCHOOL   *Played 12: W 0, L 7, D 5. A 3*

Master i/c: A. Crowther

Batting—J. Ingle 10–2–168–40*–0–21.00; *A. Rawlinson 12–1–172–29–0–15.63.

Bowling—M. Wand 106.4–21–316–18–4/32–17.55.

ASHVILLE COLLEGE   *Played 14: W 7, L 5, D 2. A 4*

Master i/c: J. S. Herrington

Batting—R. Rawlings 11–4–385–87*–0–55.00; B. T. Quick 10–2–373–78–0–46.62; M. Hughes 13–3–207–53*–0–20.70; M. Cousen 11–1–202–52–0–20.20.

Bowling—B. T. Quick 116.3–19–358–42–6/19–8.52; M. Grimson 90–24–316–21–6/43–15.04; R. Rawlings 80.2–14–280–16–3/13–17.50.

BABLAKE SCHOOL   *Played 10: W 5, L 3, D 2. A 3*

Master i/c: B. J. Sutton

A highlight was winning the Warwickshire Cup with a four-run victory over Solihull at Edgbaston. Stephen Byng was pre-eminent, scoring by far the most runs – including 118 against King Edward's, Birmingham, and 104 not out against Warwick School – and heading the bowling. He captained Warwickshire Under-17 as an under-16 player, while Adam Smyth represented Warwickshire in both age groups.

Batting—S. P. Byng 12–2–548–118–2–54.80; *H. W. Ayres 8–2–187–46*–0–31.16; A. C. Smyth 10–1–178–55–0–19.77.

Bowling—S. P. Byng 65–6–207–16–4/19–12.93.

BANCROFT'S SCHOOL   *Played 13: W 1, L 6, D 6. A 5*

Master i/c: J. G. Bromfield   Professional: J. K. Lever

As well as captaining the side astutely, James Davey scored three times more runs than anyone else and was the only bowler to take 15 wickets. With seven matches badly affected by rain, the side were unable to develop momentum, and it was only in the single victory over St Albans School that the batting and bowling performed well together.

Batting—*J. R. Davey 11–2–627–126*–1–69.66; B. Cooper 10–1–192–57–0–21.33; M. A. Cole 12–1–156–29–0–14.18.

Bowling—J. R. Davey 136.4–20–542–15–4/23–36.13.

BANGOR GRAMMAR SCHOOL   *Played 23: W 12, L 7, D 4. A 3*

Master i/c: C. C. J. Harte   Professional: G. Aldridge

The captain, Jonathan Harte, took his career tally to more than 100 wickets, a landmark narrowly missed by the Irish Under-19 player Mark Hutchinson, who had 41 in the season. These two were the leading all-rounders, although it was Harte's younger brother, Michael, who headed the batting. In the seven-wicket win at King's, Macclesfield, a ball hit out of the ground bounced on to a lorry, last seen heading towards Alderley Edge.

Batting—M. C. W. Harte 20–2–507–90–0–28.16; M. McBride 20–3–359–100*–1–21.11; M. K. Hutchinson 16–1–316–66–0–21.06; *J. C. W. Harte 19–0–388–95–0–20.42; A. D. Williamson 19–2–226–32–0–13.29.

Bowling—M. K. Hutchinson 124.4–13–446–41–6/9–10.87; A. D. Williamson 149–35–402–36–5/13–11.16; J. C. W. Harte 128.3–20–416–33–6/19–12.60; N. E. R. Boyd 128–22–405–27–4/38–15.00.

BARNARD CASTLE SCHOOL   *Played 10: W 2, L 4, D 4. A 7*

Master i/c: C. P. Johnson

Batting—N. G. Hatch 5–1–158–58*–0–39.50; S. C. Davies 10–1–276–65*–0–30.66; A. E. W. Haslam 8–2–151–63*–0–25.16.

Bowling—N. G. Hatch 52.4–12–83–21–7/17–3.95.

BEDFORD SCHOOL   *Played 14: W 4, L 4, D 6. A 2*

Master i/c: D. W. Jarrett   Professional: R. G. Caple

Fourteen-year-old Will Smith showed much promise as an opening bat and wicket-keeper, and the captain, Gareth Graham, had an encouraging season. Amir Gulzar closed his school career with 95 wickets.

Batting—*G. D. Graham 15–3–534–109–1–44.50; W. R. Smith 14–2–347–66–0–28.91; C. P. Stearn 14–0–293–70–0–20.92; T. W. J. Chapman 12–1–208–55–0–18.90; J. A. Shaw 13–2–206–61–0–18.72; M. R. G. Darbon 13–2–180–66–0–16.36.

Bowling—T. W. J. Chapman 117–24–400–15–3/23–26.66; A. Gulzar 165.3–31–547–20–3/26–27.35.

BEDFORD MODERN SCHOOL   *Played 19: W 12, L 1, D 6. A 1*

Master i/c: N. J. Chinneck

Batting—K. J. Locke 16–5–533–80–0–48.45; J. Wade 17–4–504–80–0–38.76; O. J. Clayson 17–3–530–75*–0–37.85; K. Patel 16–6–356–54*–0–35.60; *C. A. Ferguson 14–2–352–66–0–29.33; N. J. Packard 13–4–153–34–0–17.00.

Bowling—O. J. Clayson 149.5–28–521–30–5/26–17.36; M. S. R. Coles 116–24–369–19–3/3–19.42; S. E. P. Worthington 148–21–437–21–4/34–20.80; K. J. Locke 237.4–37–678–30–5/38–22.60.

BEECHEN CLIFF SCHOOL   *Played 9: W 3, L 2, D 4. A 6*

Master i/c: K. J. L. Mabe   Professional: G. Sheppard

The batting was headed by David Burton, who scored the side's only century – against Colston's Collegiate – while Mark Thorburn led by example with both bat and ball. Both represented Somerset Under-19.

Batting—D. A. Burton 6–3–302–109*–1–100.66; *M. Thorburn 8–2–190–54*–0–31.66.

Bowling—M. Thorburn 77–15–234–21–6/31–11.14; D. Towner 76.4–17–249–15–4/30–16.60.

BERKHAMSTED COLLEGIATE SCHOOL   *Played 12: W 3, L 6, D 3. A 5*

Master i/c: J. G. Tolchard   Professional: M. R. Herring

A highlight of the season, which was preceded by a tour to Barbados, was a record partnership of 217 for the first wicket against Brentwood between M. L. A. Davis (142) and S. D. Fan (58). Playing positively throughout, the side batted better than they bowled and all three wins came when batting second.

Batting—M. L. A. Davis 8–1–350–142–1–50.00; M. A. Bartholomew 11–2–391–73–0–43.44; G. H. Wallis 9–2–264–68*–0–37.71; S. D. Fan 11–1–280–58–0–28.00; S. N. Mayne 9–1–205–77–0–25.62; O. J. Matthews 8–0–167–67–0–20.87; *G. A. S. McHugh 10–0–190–42–0–19.00.

Bowling—No bowler took 15 wickets. The leading bowler was T. W. Hand 55–8–225–8–4/50–28.12.

BETHANY SCHOOL   *Played 12: W 4, L 7, D 1. A 1*

Master i/c: K. R. Daniel   Professional: P. Norgrove

Batting—R. Clark 6–0–243–81–0–40.50; R. Golds 9–1–217–48–0–27.12; *T. Golds 11–0–276–51–0–25.09; R. Cross 9–1–217–48–0–24.12; E. Streeton-Smith 7–0–150–54–0–21.42; D. Cheeseman 11–1–154–66*–0–15.40.

Bowling—R. Clark 63.3–27–174–20–4/6–8.70; O. Kelly 78–13–328–16–4/27–20.50.

BIRKENHEAD SCHOOL   *Played 20: W 13, L 4, D 3. A 4*

Master i/c: G. Prescott   Professional: H. L. Alleyne

Thirteen wins improved on the previous record set in 1991. Simon Marshall, who was by far the most successful bowler, played for ESCA Under-14.

Batting—I. S. Wilson 15–0–517–107–1–34.46; *M. R. Smathers 13–2–378–85–0–34.36; G. M. Cashin 19–3–456–67–0–28.50; S. J. Marshall 16–4–333–92*–0–27.75; R. A. Coventry 16–3–348– 62–0–26.76; O. J. Rule 18–1–422–64–0–24.82.

Bowling—*M. Cashin 132.1–34–301–24–4/17–12.54; S. J. Marshall 179.4–45–540– 41–6/49–13.17; C. M. Smylie 142–28–406–23–4/15–17.65.

BISHOP'S STORTFORD COLLEGE   *Played 13: W 2, L 7, D 4. A 6*

Master i/c: B. J. Cotton   Professional: C. S. Bannister

With the exception of Dominic O'Donnell, the batting was inconsistent and put undue pressure on an inexperienced attack, headed by James Bashford. However, progress during the season was reflected in two wins in the last week of term.

Batting—*D. O'Donnell 12–1–433–99*–0–39.36; P. J. H. Fishpool 11–2–209–55–0–23.22; J. R. Addison 13–1–243–58–0–20.25.

Bowling—J. Bashford 127–23–364–17–3/28–21.41.

BLOXHAM SCHOOL   *Played 9: W 6, L 1, D 2. A 5*

Master i/c: C. N. Boyns

Batting—*I. A. de Weymarn 9–3–491–91–0–81.83; J. E. Moore 9–1–155–54*–0–19.37.

Bowling—C. P. J. Stirling 79–21–219–18–4/40–12.16.

BLUNDELL'S SCHOOL   *Played 16: W 6, L 8, D 2. A 1*

Master i/c: N. A. Folland

Having lost their first four matches, the side improved dramatically after the introduction of some younger players. The mainstay of the batting was Mark Vaughan, whose superb century won the game against Downside, while 14-year-old Tom Wright took the most wickets with his away-swingers. Austin Smith captained the side ably, as well as batting and bowling with real enthusiasm.

Batting—M. Vaughan 16–1–556–113*–1–37.06; *A. Smith 15–2–332–53–0–25.53; A. Chambers 10–0–250–64–0–25.00; P. Arnold 15–1–301–69–0–21.50; T. Hooper 13–1–242–67–0–20.16.

Bowling—T. Wright 99–15–367–20–4/30–18.35.

BRADFIELD COLLEGE   *Played 21: W 3, L 9, D 9*

Master i/c: C. C. Ellison   Professional: J. F. Harvey

Batting—*R. J. Holland 20–2–705–107–2–39.16; J. R. Perkins 20–0–616–83–0–30.80; T. A. Campbell 11–0–308–97–0–28.00; A. J. P. Chubb 17–5–335–70–0–27.91; N. A. Denning 20–2–376–58–0–20.88; R. F. Pennock 12–2–157–40–0–15.70; R. D. Nevin 16–0–195–45–0–12.18.

Bowling—D. D. Ingram 94–9–353–23–5/33–15.34; N. A. Denning 237.4–54–694–39–4/53–17.79; N. A. C. Moore 141.2–29–413–21–4/8–19.66; C. A. K. Carpenter 116.5–37–573–27–4/42–21.22.

BRADFORD GRAMMAR SCHOOL   *Played 21: W 11, L 5, D 5. A 2*

Master i/c: A. G. Smith

A strong attack was headed by seam bowler Guy Saxton, whose 45 wickets included a hat-trick against Silcoates. R. E. Walker worked especially hard for his 652 runs on the slow, wet wickets, as well as taking 31 wickets with his off-spin. The season finished with a tour of the Netherlands, in which all three matches were won.

Batting—R. E. Walker 20–6–652–90–0–46.57; B. D. Cocker 20–2–486–100*–1–27.00; G. R. Saxton 16–6–230–54–0–23.00; *A. J. Modgill 17–1–362–73–0–22.62; C. H. Harper 20–3–319– 46*–0–18.76; A. R. Bates 19–3–235–53*–0–14.68; B. R. Graham 16–0–169–35–0–10.56.

Bowling—M. P. Donovan 91–23–204–17–5/58–12.00; G. R. Saxton 235.2–60–628– 45–7/12–13.95; R. E. Walker 142.3–32–484–31–5/95–15.61; N. R. Cockcroft 133.3–29–447– 22–5/27–20.31; K. D. A. Howes 154.4–27–588–28–5/64–21.00.

BRENTWOOD SCHOOL   *Played 14: W 4, L 4, D 6. A 4*

Master i/c: B. R. Hardie

Batting—E. Kirby 13–3–429–107*–1–42.90; G. R. Boyce 13–4–227–79*–0–25.22; *R. A. J. Wybrow 12–1–257–120–1–23.36.

Bowling—N. R. H. Taylor 165–27–573–21–5/40–27.28.

BRIGHTON COLLEGE   *Played 16: W 6, L 4, D 6. A 6*

Master i/c: J. Spencer   Professional: J. D. Morley

In a young side, Patrick Spencer, the son of the cricket master, led the way with 578 runs and 33 wickets, while 15-year-old Matthew Prior headed the batting. A tour of India was planned for the winter.

Batting—M. J. Prior 16–3–606–112*–1–46.61; P. J. S. Spencer 16–0–578–100–1–36.12; A. J. Nichol 15–2–467–71–0–35.92; J. B. James 16–1–414–77–0–27.60; C. D. Hopkinson 14–3–247–65–0–22.45.

Bowling—P. J. S. Spencer 198–39–626–33–5/45–18.96; J. T. Barr 119–25–345–16–4/50–21.56; M. S. Wilson 129–20–510–15–7/40–34.00.

BRISTOL GRAMMAR SCHOOL   *Played 12: W 1, L 1, D 10. A 4*

Master i/c: B. G. Blyth   Professional: N. Esterhuysen

Batting—N. Miller 6–1–199–47*–0–39.80; A. J. T. Winter 10–3–198–74*–0–28.28; D. R. Hayward 11–1–160–37*–0–16.00.

Bowling—No bowler took 15 wickets. The leading bowler was A. M. Lockyer 68–11–233–11–2/24–21.18.

BROMSGROVE SCHOOL   *Played 14: W 6, L 5, D 3. A 5*

Master i/c: P. G. Newman

Batting—A. J. Goode 13–6–647–97–0–92.42; N. W. Reade 11–1–251–70–0–25.10; A. N. Brown 12–2–206–36–0–20.60; E. H. Binham 11–0–214–78–0–19.45; B. R. Steer 13–1–219–47–0–18.25.

Bowling—E. H. Binham 107–12–376–21–4/32–17.90; A. J. Goode 147–23–479–21–4/25–22.80.

BRYANSTON SCHOOL   *Played 14: W 3, L 9, D 2*

Master i/c: T. J. Hill

Sam Denning, already considered one of the best off-spinners at this level, developed his batting and scored a fine, unbeaten century against Hilversum CC on an end-of-season tour of the Netherlands. In general, though, the batting was inconsistent, and the bowlers tended to be wayward, helping Clayesmore to victory by conceding 22 extras.

Batting—S. J. Denning 14–2–270–109*–1–22.50; *M. L. M. Davies 13–2–219–51–0–19.90; A. H. D. McArthur 11–1–165–51*–0–16.50; M. G. Buckland 14–4–162–29*–0–16.20; A. F. Lys 11–0–173–59–0–15.72; S. R. Brenchley 12–1–151–39–0–13.72.

Bowling—S. J. Denning 145.1–36–432–21–6/58–20.57; H. A. Fitch 116–12–457–16–3/23–28.56.

CAMPBELL COLLEGE   *Played 12: W 8, L 4, D 0*

Master i/c: B. F. Robinson   Professional: W. Haider

Batting—J. Rodgers 10–0–350–71–0–35.00; P. Wallace 11–1–295–85–0–29.50; R. Simpson 12–2–151–29–0–15.10.

Bowling—No bowler took 15 wickets. The leading bowler was C. Corlett 63.4–11–201–14–4/8–14.35.

CANFORD SCHOOL   *Played 9: W 6, L 2, D 1*

Master i/c: A. Copp

Professional: J. J. E. Hardy

Batting—*N. Makin 7–1–444–125–1–74.00; W. McClaren Clark 8–2–230–100*–1–38.33.

Bowling—N. Makin 68–17–225–20–6/28–11.25.

CATERHAM SCHOOL   *Played 10: W 1, L 3, D 6, A 7*

Master i/c: A. G. Tapp

Professional: Wasim Raja

Batting—R. N. Jackson 9–2–328–73–0–46.85; N. Alexander 8–2–266–73–0–44.33.

Bowling—R. N. Jackson 103–31–279–20–7/43–13.95.

CHARTERHOUSE   *Played 17: W 10, L 2, D 5*

Master i/c: P. Deakin

Professional: R. V. Lewis

Batting—*A. P. Hollingsworth 15–5–467–89–0–46.70; E. A. J. Breeze 13–1–457–76–0–38.08; T. N. G. Savage 11–2–328–66*–0–36.44; M. R. Gillespie 12–6–199–41–0–33.16; E. T. R. Bowes 15–1–409–76–0–29.21; A. D. W. Smith 11–2–254–89–0–28.22.

Bowling—A. P. Hollingsworth 137–15–471–21–3/37–22.42; M. R. Gillespie 132–33–386–16–3/24–24.12; A. D. W. Smith 146.3–23–521–21–5/19–24.80; B. J. O. Lewis 182.4–46–509–18–6/37–28.27.

CHELTENHAM COLLEGE   *Played 20: W 10, L 0, D 10. A 4*

Master i/c: M. W. Stovold

Professional: M. P. Briers

Batting—J. G. M. Smit 17–5–578–122*–1–48.16; T. F. G. Richardson 12–5–337–89*–0–48.14; S. T. J. Cowley 16–4–570–83*–0–47.50; T. A. O. Hughes 10–3–657–103–1–43.80; S. H. Fairbairn 15–6–253–45–0–28.11; R. T. J. Howell 11–2–184–39–0–20.44; S. A. A. Block 10–0–158–38–0–15.80.

Bowling—J. G. M. Smit 114–8–444–24–4/33–18.50; J. A. D. Brooker 180–12–724–36–5/54–20.11; S. J. C. Johnston 122.1–20–396–18–4/38–22.00.

CHIGWELL SCHOOL   *Played 12: W 3, L 4, D 5. A 3*

Master i/c: D. N. Morrison

Professional: F. A. Griffiths

Once again the season was notable for the performances of the captain, Muazam Ali, who dominated both batting and bowling. He played for Essex Second Eleven and MCC Schools, was selected for the England Under-17 Development Squad, received the Lord's Taverners' Young Cricketer of the Year award and was invited to join the Lord's ground staff for the summer.

Batting—*M. S. Ali 12–2–633–118–2–63.30; A. J. Wood 12–6–323–77–0–53.83; S. S. De 12–0–306–52–0–25.50; B. P. Richardson 11–0–197–42–0–17.90.

Bowling—M. S. Ali 161–28–553–21–4/56–26.33.

CHRIST COLLEGE, BRECON   *Played 12: W 7, L 1, D 4. A 7*

Master i/c: C. W. Kleiser

Professional: T. W. Higginson

Until their last innings of the season, the side looked set to equal their unbeaten record of 1979. Then, against the Australians, Geelong College, who had been dismissed for 91, some spineless batting saw them collapse for 77.

Batting—R. J. Chilman 11–4–348–74–0–49.71; R. J. W. Fish 11–3–244–56–0–30.50; B. G. John 9–2–177–91–0–25.28; J. R. Davies 12–1–254–38–0–23.09.

Bowling—D. H. Evans 79.5–20–194–17–4/11–11.41; C. M. P. Davenport 135–30–321–23–5/38–13.95; *R. H. Jones 102–26–255–17–6/23–15.00; T. R. Jay 117.1–27–320–21–5/36–15.23.

CHRIST'S COLLEGE, FINCHLEY   *Played 18: W 11, L 4, D 3*

Master i/c: S. S. Goldsmith

A young side, able to fight well under pressure, responded to the attacking captaincy of Rufus Johnstone by winning 11 of their first 15 games and finishing runners-up to John Lyon in the Middlesex Under-19 Schools Cup.

Batting—C. R. Depala 15–0–492–95–0–32.80; Z. L. Anwari 9–1–256–69–0–32.00; *R. Johnstone 18–0–398–69–0–22.11; R. Depala 10–3–154–25–0–22.00; C. C. Spanos 15–0–265–62–0–17.66; I. Azam 16–0–244–39–0–15.25; K. Hussain 15–0–156–44–0–10.40.

Bowling—M. Bukhari 98.2–16–357–29–6/18–12.31; R. Depala 62–12–237–19–5/8–12.47; C. R. Depala 131.2–26–434–32–5/23–13.56; I. Azam 126.4–16–478–27–4/14–17.70.

CHRIST'S HOSPITAL   *Played 9: W 1, L 3, D 5. A 6*

Master i/c: H. P. Holdsworth   Professionals: L. J. Lenham and K. G. Suttle

A sun-filled tour of South Africa in March contrasted sharply with the English season, in which the side were ahead in three of the rain-ruined draws.

Batting—F. Thomas 9–0–354–93–0–39.33; J. M. Gladding 9–1–261–133*–1–32.62; *P. J. Wilkins 9–0–164–39–0–18.22.

Bowling—E. Young 88–23–291–18–4/22–16.16.

CLAYESMORE SCHOOL   *Played 15: W 3, L 3, D 9. A 5*

Master i/c: D. I. Rimmer

Batting—M. Harris 15–0–517–102–1–34.46; T. Lack 6–1–159–99–0–31.80; T. Sharpe 11–3–223–89–0–27.87; *G. Tew 14–5–201–72*–0–22.33; R. Lack 14–3–223–44–0–20.27.

Bowling—C. Hull 118.2–22–388–25–5/52–15.52; R. Lack 146.5–30–417–22–4/13–18.95; G. Tew 170–38–496–23–4/61–21.56; M. Senior 139.4–25–416–18–3/10–23.11.

CLIFTON COLLEGE   *Played 12: W 0, L 7, D 5. A 7*

Master i/c: D. C. Henderson   Professional: P. W. Romaines

Although it was not a season for players' records, with more than half the matches curtailed by rain, Alex Turco completed five years as scorer without missing a first-team match.

Batting—*J. D. Walters 11–0–357–108–1–32.45; J. A. England 12–2–311–62*–0–31.10; E. H. Kenworthy 12–2–310–68–0–31.00.

Bowling—M. H. R. Bowden 121.5–11–496–17–6/63–29.17.

COLFE'S SCHOOL   *Played 20: W 10, L 2, D 8. A 4*

Master i/c: G. S. Clinton

Fifteen-year-old Richard Clinton, the cricket master's son, was an outstanding opening batsman, scoring three centuries in compiling 963 runs at a record average of 107, and going on to play for Surrey Second Eleven. The side won the Kent Schools Under-19 Cup and were optimistic for the future after also winning at Under-12 and Under-13 levels.

Batting—R. Clinton 14–5–963–134*–3–107.00; O. Chapman 11–2–365–111*–1–40.55; A. Jasquith 14–1–398–100–1–30.61; P. Burton 7–1–173–64–0–28.83; T. Allen 11–3–184–88*–0–23.00; P. Patel 10–3–152–56–0–21.71.

Bowling—*N. Campbell 160–25–494–33–6/20–14.96.

COLSTON'S COLLEGIATE SCHOOL   *Played 7: W 0, L 3, D 4. A 7*

Master i/c: H. W. Maddock

Batting—No batsman scored 150 runs. The leading batsman was B. Reeves 5–0–122–71–0–24.40.

Bowling—No bowler took 15 wickets. The leading bowler was *A. Holloway 44.2–3–186–11–4/23–16.90.

CRANBROOK SCHOOL   *Played 16: W 11, L 3, D 2. A 7*

Master i/c: Alex Presnell

School career records were broken by Dan Furnival (1,776 runs) and wicket-keeper James Harfoot (59 dismissals), and equalled by P. Wicken and T. Hinchliffe, with 65 wickets apiece.

Batting—*D. Furnival 13–2–434–79*–0–39.45; M. Knight 14–3–336–60–0–30.54; J. Harfoot 11–1–282–64*–0–28.20; O. Furnival 12–1–200–69–0–18.18.

Bowling—J. Agar 60–11–175–18–5/8–9.72; P. Wicken 68.5–10–201–16–7/51–12.56; M. Tregoning 82.4–15–266–20–5/36–13.30; T. Hinchliffe 140–28–439–28–6/24–15.67.

CRANLEIGH SCHOOL   *Played 13: W 2, L 6, D 5. A 5*

Master i/c: D. C. Williams

The batting was held together by Abeed Janmohamed, although he lacked consistent support as the side struggled for continuity. The attack relied heavily on the off-spin of I. D. Houston, backed by good-quality fielding.

Batting—A. M. T. Janmohamed 14–1–427–68–0–32.84; W. O. F. Howard 11–2–195–53*–0–21.66; M. J. S. Robinson-Moltke 14–0–294–75–0–21.00; *J. Bennett 14–1–253–38–0–19.46; I. D. Houston 14–2–226–50*–0–18.83; D. C. Scrase 11–2–160–63*–0–17.77.

Bowling—I. D. Houston 189.1–49–495–26–4/28–19.03; R. W. Russell 110.5–19–381–17–3/10–22.41; J. Bennett 103–19–343–15–3/42–22.86.

CULFORD SCHOOL   *Played 11: W 2, L 3, D 6. A 4*

Master i/c: R. P. Shepperson

Batting—R. J. R. Evans 11–2–327–106–1–36.33; D. S. Holliday 11–0–382–97–0–34.72; *S. F. Ornbo 10–0–332–92–0–33.20; J. R. Tarrant 10–0–212–46–0–21.20; D. J. Kemp 11–1–180–35–0–18.00.

Bowling—J. R. Tarrant 119–33–270–19–4/35–14.21; B. J. Unwin 78–17–253–15–4/48–16.86.

DARTFORD GRAMMAR SCHOOL   *Played 15: W 4, L 4, D 7*

Master i/c: S. R. D. de Winton

Batting—E. C. Tyler 9–1–390–76–0–48.75; *G. Siveyer 13–6–336–63*–0–48.00; G. J. Cook 12–1–301–77*–0–27.36; S. D. L. Henderson 14–1–272–82–0–20.92; S. J. Vanstone 12–4–163–45–0–20.37.

Bowling—G. J. Cook 130.4–14–550–37–7/44–14.86; T. R. Hazel 163.5–22–632–21–6/99–30.09.

DAUNTSEY'S SCHOOL   *Played 11: W 3, L 5, D 3. A 4*

Master i/c: D. C. R. Baker   Professional: P. Knowles

Batting—*D. Bell 10–2–238–60*–0–29.75; J. Hope 10–1–220–54–0–24.44; B. Darbyshire 11–1–199–63–0–19.90.

Bowling—D. Bell 109–27–277–19–6/25–14.57; C. Oldham 70–13–234–16–6/16–14.62.

DEAN CLOSE SCHOOL   *Played 13: W 4, L 4, D 5. A 3*

Master i/c: C. J. Townsend   Professional: S. Hansford

In an exciting season, with five matches decided in the final over, the captain, William Kinder, was the outstanding player with both bat and ball.

Batting—*W. M. Kinder 12–1–318–92–0–28.90; G. D. M. Lane 13–1–251–43–0–20.91; B. D. Mears 11–0–201–71–0–18.27.

Bowling—W. M. Kinder 118–27–317–25–4/10–12.68; A. D. Judge 72.3–13–219–15–4/42–14.60; G. D. M. Lane 58.3–6–257–15–3/16–17.13; N. G. E. Ball 83.3–10–315–18–4/35–17.50; O. E. Bretherton 121–25–395–19–4/30–20.78.

DENSTONE COLLEGE   *Played 17: W 11, L 1, D 5. A 5*

Master i/c: A. N. James

In their best season for 25 years, the side won 11 matches and lost only to Staffordshire Under-16. Phillip Cheadle and William Bagshawe shared three century opening partnerships, and Derbyshire Under-19 wicket-keeper Philip Davies was outstanding with 11 stumpings, all off the seam bowlers.

Batting—P. R. Davies 7–6–150–61*–0–150.00; *P. M. Cheadle 16–3–663–117–2–51.00; W. J. L. Bagshawe 16–3–572–106*–1–44.00; B. J. Brookes 9–3–161–51–0–26.83; J. A. Blackwell 14–4–220–75–0–22.00.

Bowling—W. E. Nicholls 168.2–51–407–32–5/30–12.71; C. J. Dexter 175.4–59–442–32–5/24–13.81; B. J. Brookes 87–12–326–21–4/8–15.52.

DOVER COLLEGE   *Played 10: W 0, L 5, D 5. A 4*

Master i/c: D. C. Butler

Batting—P. Karafillides 8–1–155–60*–0–22.14; *J. R. Telford 9–0–174–54–0–19.33.

Bowling—J. R. Telford 130.4–22–424–17–3/40–24.94.

DOWNSIDE SCHOOL   *Played 12: W 1, L 8, D 3*

Master i/c: A. P. Smerdon   Professional: J. Bird

Batting—P. D. Eke 10–0–208–48–0–20.80; W. Orr 12–0–225–46–0–18.75; *J. Acheson 12–1–162–65–0–14.72.

Bowling—S. Perkins 134–19–514–22–6/42–23.36; P. Moran 113–19–431–15–4/91–28.73.

DUKE OF YORK'S ROYAL MILITARY SCHOOL   *Played 10: W 2, L 2, D 6. A 6*

Master i/c: S. Salisbury   Professionals: C. Penn and S. B. Padgett

Inspired by a successful winter tour of Australia, the side played with flair and style, winning only twice but dominating the drawn matches. Stephan Hayward bowled with real pace, while Jeffrey Owen looked a real prospect as opening bat and wicket-keeper and Oliver Drummond-Smith batted with maturity.

Batting—O. C. Drummond-Smith 7–1–181–75–0–30.16; J. J. Owen 8–0–201–52–0–25.12.

Bowling—S.Hayward 68–13–151–30–7/9–5.03; R. Credland 60–17–145–15–4/51–9.66.

DULWICH COLLEGE   *Played 12: W 4, L 1, D 7. A 3*

Master i/c: S. R. Northcote-Green   Professionals: A. Ransom and W. Smith

Batting—V. Kumar 12–3–481–118–1–53.44; N. Martin 12–3–404–90–0–44.88; A. Moon 8–1–276–68–0–39.42; F. Hutton-Mills 8–1–150–38–0–21.42; R. Amlot 13–0–248–117–1–19.07.

Bowling—F. Hutton-Mills 130–26–294–15–3/12–19.60; A. Moon 176–68–504–21–5/37–24.00.

DURHAM SCHOOL   *Played 10: W 3, L 2, D 5. A 8*

Master i/c: M. Hirsch

Batting—A. Hedley 7–0–357–105–2–51.00; S. Birtwisle 5–0–182–91–0–36.40; A. Beales 13–1–371–144–1–30.91; I. Laidler 6–0–184–112–1–30.66; C. Wides 10–1–185–72–0–20.55.

Bowling—R. English 122–19–475–23–6/32–20.65; C. Wides 145–34–487–20–5/51–24.35.

EASTBOURNE COLLEGE   *Played 20: W 9, L 2, D 9. A 5*

Masters i/c: N. L. Wheeler and D. A. Stewart   Professional: J. N. Shepherd

In his innings of 154 not out against Sussex Martlets, Mark Lock hit five consecutive sixes and a four off one over. Headed by Lock and Hugo Southwell, the batting was strong, but lack of penetration in the bowling restricted them to nine wins.

Batting—M. J. Lock 16–5–719–154*–1–65.36; H. F. G. Southwell 18–1–673–104–2–39.58; *S. J. W. Whitton 16–1–451–69–0–30.06; A. J. Fyfe 18–1–493–78–0–29.00; A. D. Simcox 18–1–407–83–0–23.94; A. J. Firth 13–4–201–35–0–22.33.

Bowling—M. J. Kemp 71.1–11–284–20–4/23–14.20; N. S. Maclean 87–23–297–19–5/22–15.63; M. J. Lock 143.5–42–370–21–4/14–17.61; A. G. B. Waterlow 85.3–16–316–15–3/23–21.06; P. A. Baker 134–31–369–15–3/34–24.60; S. J. W. Whitton 201.2–39–701–21–4/48–33.38.

THE EDINBURGH ACADEMY   *Played 15: W 4, L 9, D 2. A 3*

Master i/c: G. R. Bowe

Batting—N. J. Hillyard 14–2–672–104–1–56.00; R. Murby 14–0–342–54–0–24.42; N. N. Pike 14–1–243–41–0–18.69.

Bowling—M. R. L. Blair 141–29–501–22–3/18–22.77; N. J. Hillyard 156–26–583–23–5/42–25.34; *A. J. Cowie 152–27–591–22–5/49–26.86.

ELIZABETH COLLEGE, GUERNSEY   *Played 22: W 5, L 8, D 9. A 1*

Master i/c: M. E. Kinder

After some early wins against local club sides, stronger opposition exposed inconsistent batting and a lack of penetration in the attack. Adrian Birkett opened both, while leg-spinner David Walder showed promise for the future.

Batting—C. J. Colclough 17–2–311–68*–0–20.73; S. D. Wilson 17–1–284–68–0–17.75; J. Rowland 15–1–230–55–0–16.42; *J. Barrett 17–0–275–56–0–16.17; A. Birkett 20–1–290–52–0–15.26; T. A. le Page 15–2–193–51–0–14.84; J. Chambers 14–2–154–26–0–12.83; G. J. le Prevost 18–2–180–45*–0–11.25.

Bowling—A. Birkett 174.1–46–481–26–4/9–18.50; A. G. P. Cooper 144.1–22–509–20–3/17–25.45; D. P. Walder 144.3–14–604–18–2/22–33.55.

ELLESMERE COLLEGE   *Played 8: W 2, L 2, D 4. A 7*

Master i/c: P. J. Hayes   Professional: R. G. Mapp

Batting—*H. A. Murphy 7–2–193–87*–0–38.60; J. P. Hedgecoe 7–0–161–99–0–23.00; P. J. Furniss 8–1–152–75–0–21.71.

Bowling—No bowler took 15 wickets. The leading bowler was J. P. Hedgecoe 49–15–105–11–5/5–9.54.

ELTHAM COLLEGE   *Played 16: W 8, L 4, D 4. A 1*

Masters i/c: P. C. McCartney and B. M. Withecombe   Professional: R. W. Hills

Positive cricket resulted in eight victories, most by emphatic margins, and just four draws. S. J. Whitehead was again a consistent and prolific batsman, while the 15-year-old S. J. Pereira showed promise as an all-rounder and headed the bowling with his off-spin.

Batting—S. J. Whitehead 15–2–671–105*–1–51.61; M. O. Bainbridge 13–2–363–121–1–33.00; M. N. Roche 14–2–348–70–0–29.00; A. J. Branchflower 14–3–304–66–0–27.63; T. J. Willis 13–5–215–104*–1–26.87; S. J. Pereira 9–2–162–38–0–23.14; B. J. Devon 10–1–196–82–0–21.77.

Bowling—S. J. Pereira 131.2–17–489–26–6/42–18.80; A. C. Buckley 84–11–336–16–5/39–21.00; *P. J. Fenn 174.3–39–605–26–7/17–23.26; B. J. Devon 110.4–6–439–16–3/34–27.43.

ENFIELD GRAMMAR SCHOOL   *Played 19: W 2, L 9, D 8. A 4*

Master i/c: M. Alder

Batting—M. Kapadia 17–1–560–117–1–35.00; M. Wright 18–0–618–86–0–34.33; J. Barber 18–3–372–61*–0–24.80; *B. Lyons 18–1–295–49–0–17.35; D. Rose 12–2–165–38–0–16.50; S. Sykes 15–2–177–39–0–13.61.

Bowling—M. Wright 181–45–509–31–6/24–16.41; J. Barber 161–36–501–25–7/26–20.04; J. Collard 84–21–321–15–3/25–21.40; M. Marston 86–33–342–15–3/30–22.80.

EPSOM COLLEGE   *Played 9: W 3, L 2, D 4. A 6*

Master i/c: G. A. Jones   Professional: G. W. Flower

Batting—C. M. Oatway 8–2–296–78*–0–49.33; *B. V. Patel 8–1–288–71–0–41.14; S. D. Price 4–0–151–63–0–37.75; R. A. Oram 8–0–291–119–1–36.37; J. R. Gill 6–0–192–53–0–32.00.

Bowling—S. D. Price 94–26–238–17–4/16–14.00; H. P. E. Kingham 131–27–427–18–6/46–23.72.

ETON COLLEGE   *Played 12: W 6, L 0, D 6. A 7*

Master i/c: S. J. G. Doggart   Professional: J. M. Rice

In another unbeaten season, Eton attributed their success to the prolific scoring of openers Hugo Loudon, the captain, and David Kay-Shuttleworth; the ten stands they shared included one of more than 200, two over 100 and six worth 50 or more. The bowling was always tight, but often less penetrative than it should have been.

Batting—*H. J. H. Loudon 12–3–807–154–2–89.66; D. C. Kay-Shuttleworth 10–3–499–117*–2–71.28; A. F. S. Leslie 11–2–377–74–0–41.88; J. R. S. Redmayne 11–5–234–77–0–39.00.

Bowling—L. J. Rankin 75–19–191–16–6/24–11.93; P. A. Norman-Butler 97–10–373–15–4/44–24.86.

EXETER SCHOOL   *Played 17: W 8, L 7, D 2. A 2*

Masters i/c: M. C. Wilcock and J. A. Lockwood

Highlights were the first and last matches, both played in glorious sunshine and both featuring individual hundreds for the eleven.

Batting—*I. P. Gamble 14–2–404–104*–1–33.66; J. D. Retter 8–1–234–101*–1–33.42; D. J. Oliver 10–1–250–55–0–27.77; P. J. Drought 13–3–268–54*–0–26.80; J. P. Cruft 14–1–336–90–0–25.84; J. W. Porter 7–0–168–76–0–24.00; C. J. Stead 15–2–310–50–0–23.84; M. W. Thornton 12–1–177–85*–0–16.09.

Bowling—P. M. Scoble 105–22–277–22–5/14–12.59; R. S. Wendover 136–12–527–32–5/72–16.46; I. P. Gamble 141–25–511–23–5/43–22.21.

FELSTED SCHOOL   *Played 13: W 7, L 1, D 5. A 4*

Master i/c: F. C. Hayes

The side were unbeaten in schools matches, winning seven out of ten. The most memorable of these featured the dismissal of Bishop's Stortford College for 11, with Timothy Phillips taking seven for four and George Finch three for five. Although everyone played a part during the season, Phillips was outstanding with 649 runs, including two centuries, and 41 wickets. He went on to play for MCC Schools and Essex Second Eleven.

Batting—T. J. Phillips 12–1–649–139–2–59.00; B. J. Tabor 11–1–321–70–0–32.10; C. J. A. Turtle 11–1–259–56–0–25.90; R. A. N. Perkins 9–2–170–48–0–24.28; L. M. G. Cooper 11–1–200–42–0–20.00.

Bowling—T. J. Phillips 231–84–490–41–7/4–11.95; G. E. M. Finch 138–33–363–16–4/14–22.68; L. M. G. Cooper 133.2–22–447–16–3/38–27.93.

FETTES COLLEGE *Played 11: W 3, L 3, D 5. A 4*

Master i/c: J. G. A. Frost   Professional: J. van Geloven

Neil Millar dominated with both bat and ball, going on to play for Scotland Under-19.

Batting—N. Millar 10–3–465–148–2–66.42; D. Leckie 7–1–196–77–0–32.66.

Bowling—N. Millar 144–39–254–22–5/51–11.54.

FOREST SCHOOL *Played 12: W 7, L 3, D 2. A 7*

Master i/c: S. Turner

The highlight of an excellent season was a one-wicket win off the last ball in a 40-overs contest against Eton Second Eleven. The side's success was an all-round team effort, although R. Marshall stood out with the bat, scoring two centuries. M. Patel played for England Under-15.

Batting—R. Marshall 12–1–454–125–2–41.27; J. Foster 12–4–309–66*–0–38.62; I. Rotsey 11–3–172–54*–0–21.50; *T. Cartwright 11–3–171–58–0–21.37.

Bowling—R. Smith 126.2–32–402–28–5/41–14.35; M. Orchard-Lisle 165.4–50–459–31–7/37–14.80; C. White 108.3–35–288–15–3/8–19.20.

FOYLE AND LONDONDERRY COLLEGE *Played 15: W 7, L 6, D 2. A 1*

Masters i/c: G. R. McCarter and I. McCracken

Batting—K. Dunn 15–4–287–81*–0–26.09; *A. Fleming 15–1–264–65–0–18.85; J. Winfield 15–1–160–30–0–11.42.

Bowling—G. Moore 123.1–35–280–32–7/19–8.75; A. Fleming 111.2–16–374–23–3/9–16.26; G. Brolly 93–18–319–19–3/17–16.78; K. Dunn 93–13–332–15–4/20–22.13.

FRAMLINGHAM COLLEGE *Played 12: W 7, L 2, D 3. A 2*

Master i/c: A. S. Griffiths   Professional: C. Rutterford

Batting—M. A. Truman 13–1–644–130–1–53.66; C. J. Goodfellow 8–1–312–87–0–44.57; G. Hames 13–1–417–118–1–34.75; M. Low 12–2–276–85–0–27.60.

Bowling—A. Tucker 117.4–6–460–25–5/30–18.40; M. Low 144.1–21–512–27–5/34–18.96.

GIGGLESWICK SCHOOL *Played 13: W 7, L 2, D 4. A 3*

Master i/c: N. Gemmell   Professional: A. G. Lawson

Batting—E. Baker 6–1–215–78*–0–43.00; *E. Smith 10–3–284–96*–0–40.57; C. Woolsey 13–3–281–79*–0–28.10; N. Harrison 13–4–160–48–0–17.77; C. Small 12–1–150–21–0–13.63.

Bowling—E. Smith 92–23–248–24–5/24–10.33; C. Woolsey 96–21–322–18–6/18–17.88; S. Langstaff 105–17–374–17–4/33–22.00.

GLENALMOND *Played 11: W 3, L 3, D 5. A 4*

Master i/c: J. D. Bassett

J. D. Burrowes was the most consistent batsman, although Alexander Monro, a colt, batted aggressively to score 116 in the last three games. Henry Smuts-Muller headed the fast bowling, which dismissed Merchiston for 49 and Fettes for 67, and was backed by outstanding fielding, notably that of M. Ruane.

Batting—J. D. Burrowes 11–1–302–51–0–30.20; J. Murray 8–0–208–51–0–26.00; *T. Stevenson 12–2–185–48*–0–18.50.

Bowling—H. Smuts-Muller 94.4–21–227–22–7/39–10.31; H. S. E. Monro 117.1–21–343–17–4/22–20.17.

GORDONSTOUN SCHOOL *Played 7: W 1, L 2, D 4. A 4*

Master i/c: C. J. Barton

A young side managed to show some of their potential, despite the dismal weather in June.

Batting—G. Jolly 5–1–212–104–1–53.00; *E. Lewis 7–1–173–85–0–28.83; J. Ridley 6–0–153–52–0–25.50.

Bowling—J. Ridley 90–11–307–15–5/19–20.46.

GRENVILLE COLLEGE *Played 9: W 4, L 3, D 2*

Master i/c: C. R. Beechey

Batting—J. Kirkham-Brown 9–4–413–116*–1–82.60; *A. Bott 7–2–184–54*–0–36.80; D. Watkins 6–1–150–38–0–30.00.

Bowling—A. Cork 53.2–5–220–19–7/38–11.57.

GRESHAM'S SCHOOL *Played 14: W 6, L 4, D 4. A 4*

Master i/c: A. M. Ponder

Highlights were a first win, by seven wickets, over the XL Club and J. P. Wyatt's record career tally of 1,958 runs.

Batting—*T. J. Hood 13–3–389–62*–0–38.90; J. P. Wyatt 12–2–383–113–1–38.30; J. N. Worby 11–2–305–77–0–33.88; D. L. Roper 11–1–318–65–0–31.80; G. M. J. Watson 8–1–152–44–0–21.71.

Bowling—J. N. Worby 185.2–68–379–34–5/11–11.14; R. D. MacNair 135–24–473–20–5/29–23.65; A. D. Horsley 105.3–7–421–17–6/34–24.76.

HABERDASHERS' ASKE'S SCHOOL *Played 20: W 7, L 2, D 11. A 5*

Masters i/c: S. D. Charlwood and D. I. Yeabsley

Undefeated by schools, the side concluded their season with a successful and enjoyable tour of Devon, the highlight of which was a victory over Devon Under-16.

Batting—D. B. Wilson 18–2–687–98–0–42.93; *A. M. Reid 15–7–306–58*–0–38.25; J. L. Moore 18–3–396–63*–0–26.40; D. M. J. Williams 16–4–288–68*–0–24.00; K. Pandit 17–2–263–56–0–17.53; J. Amin 10–0–157–56–0–15.70; C. C. K. Brown 16–2–213–39–0–15.21.

Bowling—J. Amin 207.2–49–612–37–5/12–16.54; A. K. Notaney 137.1–12–629–28–5/27–22.46; N. Rooban 227.1–47–767–33–4/46–23.24; D. B. Wilson 120.1–21–549–20–4/35–27.45.

HAILEYBURY *Played 16: W 3, L 3, D 10. A 4*

Master i/c: M. S. Seymour   Professional: J. W. Lloyds

Batting—C. J. Box 11–4–309–82*–0–44.14; J. S. Rixson 16–1–551–121*–2–36.73; M. H. Bradford 15–3–319–89*–0–26.58; R. J. Palmer 16–1–363–64–0–24.20; E. P. C. Mitchell 10–0–214–58–0–21.40; L. W. L. Molyneux 15–0–290–42–0–19.33; D. A. Raymond 13–2–173–33–0–15.72.

Bowling—M. K. M. Farmiloe 155–37–441–21–4/42–21.00; A. W. R. E. Okines 99–13–436–16–2/17–27.25; M. H. Bradford 117–13–415–15–4/28–27.66.

HAMPTON SCHOOL   *Played 18: W 8, L 2, D 8. A 3*

Master i/c: A. J. Cook   Professional: P. Farbrace

A spirited side was ably captained by Paul Frost, who led by example with both bat and ball. The only two defeats came at the hands of powerful Australian touring sides, and the Holmwood's six-a-side trophy was retained in July.

Batting—*P. J. Frost 18–3–715–108–1–47.66; R. T. H. Gaines 16–2–425–111–1–30.35; E. J. Martin 15–2–335–118*–1–25.76; G. J. Wilcock 16–2–254–62–0–18.14; P. C. K. Wood 16–2–249–72–0–17.78; G. E. Green 18–0–281–57–0–15.61.

Bowling—P. J. Frost 112–33–273–25–7/15–10.92; L. D. Meggitt 83.5–17–281–17–4/10–16.52; P. C. K. Wood 90.3–21–275–16–5/23–17.18; A. J. Evans 162–38–495–26–5/62–19.03.

HARROW SCHOOL   *Played 16: W 7, L 4, D 5. A 3*

Master i/c: C. M. B. Williams   Professional: R. K. Sethi

Benefiting from a winter tour to the Far East, the side recorded another successful season. The batting, strong in depth, was headed by Andrew Cox, whose century against Epsom was his sixth in all for the side. Although the bowling was tidy, with the most wickets falling to Jack Cooke-Hurle (in-swing) and leg-spinner Jasper Neame, it was not always incisive enough.

Batting—*A. N. L. Cox 14–1–599–141–1–46.07; J. R. W. Norris 13–2–308–54–0–28.00; D. R. Hepher 13–3–248–62–0–24.80; W. J. L. Matthews 13–1–278–82*–0–23.16; L. F. de Rougemont 9–0–154–55–0–17.11.

Bowling—J. R. F. Cooke-Hurle 167–33–485–27–5/24–17.96; J. W. B. Neame 115.3–13–555–27–5/90–20.55; D. R. Hepher 153.4–31–479–21–3/50–22.80.

THE HARVEY GRAMMAR SCHOOL   *Played 14: W 7, L 4, D 3. A 6*

Master i/c: P. J. Harding

Batting—A. Towse 14–4–465–101*–1–46.50; *K. Temple 14–2–381–103*–1–31.75; J. Hubbard 11–2–221–59*–0–24.55; W. Crumbie 12–2–151–46–0–15.10.

Bowling—S. Barlow 104.4–17–409–24–4/7–17.04; M. Ritchie 136.1–29–437–23–4/24–19.00; J. Hubbard 123–27–415–21–4/27–19.76; G. Bassant 92.3–8–483–15–3/31–32.20.

HEREFORD CATHEDRAL SCHOOL   *Played 14: W 5, L 4, D 5. A 6*

Master i/c: A. Connop

A highlight was the eight-wicket win over MCC, in which Owen Hewlett took eight for 33, five being caught by the wicket-keeper, Marc Norris.

Batting—*S. J. Price 13–4–637–106–3–70.77; A. Last 13–4–388–81–0–43.11; O. Hewlett 12–3–315–74*–0–35.00; R. Edwards 13–1–287–75–0–23.91.

Bowling—O. Hewlett 129.2–25–390–35–8/33–11.14; J. Layton 151.4–25–509–25–5/14–20.36.

HIGHGATE SCHOOL   *Played 13: W 3, L 3, D 6, T 1. A 2*

Master i/c: R. G. W. Marsh   Professional: R. E. Jones

Batting—*R. A. Swann 12–3–502–118*–2–55.77; D. C. Cohen 9–1–175–53–0–21.87; D. J. Miller 12–1–224–51–0–20.36.

Bowling—D. A. P. Gibberd 139–26–402–21–5/42–19.14.

HURSTPIERPOINT COLLEGE   *Played 8: W 2, L 2, D 4. A 3*

Master i/c: M. J. Mance   Professional: D. J. Semmence

Robert Redford was again the leading all-rounder in a season which saw the last seven matches washed out.

Batting—R. K. H. Redford 9–0–359–89–0–39.88; M. J. E. Imber 9–0–172–65–0–19.11; J. N. Cation 9–0–161–52–0–17.88.

Bowling—B. N. A. Firmin 99–15–319–19–4/17–16.78; R. K. H. Redford 122.3–24–326–15–3/41–21.73.

IPSWICH SCHOOL   *Played 15: W 3, L 4, D 8. A 3*

Master i/c: A. K. Golding   Professional: R. E. East

Batting—J. Achar 12–2–422–152*–1–42.20; T. Green 13–1–455–127–1–37.91; T. Jervis 14–0–291–46–0–20.78.

Bowling—*J. East 189–33–594–34–7/41–17.47; J. Bell 129–17–441–20–4/46–22.05; R. Leeburn 128–22–464–19–5/52–24.42.

THE JOHN LYON SCHOOL   *Played 18: W 9, L 1, D 8. A 5*

Master i/c: I. Parker

After losing their first match to Hampton, the side were unbeaten for the rest of the season; their nine wins included victory over Christ's College, Finchley, in the final of the Middlesex Under-19 Cup.

Batting—*M. Navaratnarajah 17–5–605–91*–0–50.41; N. D. Goh 17–2–677–111*–1–45.13; S. J. Thomas 14–3–287–70–0–26.09; N. J. Jago 15–2–226–32–0–17.38.

Bowling—R. Mehta 121.2–25–345–28–4/12–12.32; D. P. Connolly 111.4–20–341–24–3/15–14.20; L. W. Wijeratna 117–28–306–19–4/21–16.10; N. D. Goh 114–35–287–16–3/35–17.93.

KELLY COLLEGE   *Played 8: W 3, L 3, D 2. A 4*

Master i/c: T. Ryder

Highlights were an impressive win over the XL Club, and Crispin Procter's inspired spell of swing bowling against MCC, when he took four for eight in nine overs. Mark Anderson was a sound, positive captain.

Batting—S. James 7–2–222–74–0–44.40; R. Jones 8–1–219–54*–0–31.28; *M. Anderson 8–1–182–39–0–26.00.

Bowling—C. Procter 74.4–17–266–15–4/16–17.73; D. Nicholls 72.4–3–368–18–4/49–20.44.

KIMBOLTON SCHOOL   *Played 17: W 5, L 2, D 10. A 3*

Master i/c: R. P. Merriman   Professional: M. E. Latham

A balanced XI were challenged less by the opposition than by the weather, which affected all but three of their 17 matches. Oliver Bailey hit two excellent centuries, while Sam Moore showed promise with the bat. Slow left-armer Gary Woods was the leading wicket-taker, well supported by fast bowlers Chris Peel and William Follett, who has a contract with Gloucestershire.

Batting—O. T. Bailey 12–3–496–115–2–55.11; S. Moore 9–0–305–65–0–33.88; *M. D. Klein 14–3–370–79*–0–33.63; B. J. Klein 13–2–289–40–0–26.27; G. Woods 14–2–296–81–0–24.66; W. J. T. Follett 13–0–181–52–0–13.92; J. W. Caswell 15–2–172–42–0–13.23.

Bowling—G. Woods 161–40–465–30–5/11–15.50; W. J. T. Follett 138–23–368–22–5/46–16.72; C. M. V. Peel 145.4–32–384–21–4/29–18.28.

KING EDWARD VI COLLEGE, STOURBRIDGE   *Played 9: W 5, L 3, D 1. A 5*

Masters i/c: R. A. Williams and M. L. Ryan

Against Bishop Vesey's GS, J. Cockburn took a hat-trick and clean bowled the last five batsmen to return figures of 13.3-3-30-9.

Batting—*R. J. Perkins 7–3–246–75*–0–61.50; M. Foster 8–1–183–52*–0–26.14.

Bowling—J. Cockburn 75–20–186–18–9/30–10.33.

KING EDWARD VI SCHOOL, SOUTHAMPTON   *Played 19: W 13, L 2, D 4. A 4*

Master i/c: R. J. Putt

John Claughton completed his school career with more than 3,000 runs as he dominated the batting and captained the side to their most successful season ever. Luke Sully was the leading wicket-taker for the second season, and the wicket-keeper, Iain Brunnschweiler, was selected for England Under-17.

Batting—*J. A. Claughton 18–6–873–133*–2–72.75; J. D. Francis 11–4–316–69*–0–45.14; M. H. Tarry 13–3–324–57*–0–32.40; B. W. Craft 13–2–338–58–0–30.72; I. Brunnschweiler 8–0–190–74–0–23.75; N. P. Evans 12–1–185–70–0–16.81.

Bowling—B. W. Craft 140–27–335–31–5/36–10.80; L. D. Sully 197–65–463–41–5/36–11.29; P. S. Eyers 116–29–344–24–8/33–14.33; J. D. Francis 116–34–294–17–4/16–17.29; G. C. Douglas 127–34–348–18–3/22–19.33.

KING EDWARD VII SCHOOL, LYTHAM   *Played 21: W 8, L 4, D 9. A 2*

Master i/c: A. M. Weston   Professional: E. A. E. Baptiste

Opener Lee Hilton was outstanding with 916 runs, including a splendid 145 not out against UCS in the Lytham Festival. He went on to play for Lancashire and MCC Schools.

Batting—L. M. Hilton 20–6–916–145*–2–65.42; G. Evans 16–5–525–106*–2–47.72; A. Cairns 13–4–271–73–0–30.11; S. Long 14–0–398–80–0–28.42; B. Godfrey 16–3–284–60–0–21.84; J. Kok 17–2–315–49–0–21.00.

Bowling—*T. K. Brown 164.1–30–522–23–3/25–22.69; L. M. Hilton 117–24–404–17–2/7–23.76; G. Evans 111.2–21–406–17–4/39–23.88.

KING EDWARD'S SCHOOL, BIRMINGHAM   *Played 19: W 7, L 2, D 10. A 6*

Master i/c: M. D. Stead   Professional: J. Huband

Batting—R. J. McGuire 18–1–527–81–0–31.00; A. D. Treharne 18–2–431–84*–0–26.93; A. C. G. Brindley 10–2–193–40–0–24.12; N. Y. Khan 17–2–325–51–0–21.66; J. J. Child 17–2–231–59–0–15.40; R. J. Newman 15–2–152–37–0–11.69.

Bowling—G. A. Bhadri 84–8–263–16–6/39–16.43; A. D. Treharne 224.4–45–660–31–5/22–21.29; J. S. Ross 172–29–480–18–3/26–26.66.

KING HENRY VIII SCHOOL, COVENTRY   *Played 9: W 4, L 2, D 3. A 7*

Master i/c: A. M. Parker

Batting—A. Whitehall 7–4–153–66*–0–51.00; M. Goode 9–1–290–75*–0–36.25; G. Long 9–2–154–80–0–22.00.

Bowling—G. Long 62–7–182–15–3/2–12.13; B. Waghorn 81.2–12–287–15–4/48–19.13.

KING WILLIAM'S COLLEGE   *Played 11: W 3, L 5, D 3*

Master i/c: A. Maree   Professional: D. Mark

Batting—E. Zuiderent 11–1–318–70*–0–31.80; E. Lee 11–0–297–104–1–27.00; E. Craven 9–0–176–50–0–19.55.

Bowling—N. Hauser 84–17–219–19–5/21–11.52; E. Craven 68–5–265–15–5/15–17.66; E. Lee 81–11–305–16–3/2–19.06; J. Manuja 124–22–429–18–6/15–23.83.

KING'S COLLEGE, TAUNTON   *Played 14: W 8, L 2, D 4. A 1*

Master i/c: R. J. R. Yeates   Professional: D. Breakwell

An excellent season began with three victories – and a century in each from Nicholas Boulton. An inspiring captain and outstanding left-handed opener, he broke his own batting records of 1995 and

1996 with 910 runs and five centuries, passing 3,000 career runs for the eleven, with another year to go. He played for MCC Schools, and went on to score two centuries for Somerset Second Eleven before making his first-team debut against Pakistan A. He was joined in Somerset Second Eleven by B. J. Vickers.

Batting—*N. R. Boulton 12–2–907–151–5–90.70; B. J. Vickers 12–1–324–74–0–29.45; K. W. Albery 12–2–281–61–0–28.10; T. C. Gardiner 11–0–260–64–0–23.63.

Bowling—N. R. Boulton 93.1–19–233–20–4/21–11.65; P. K. Haworth 96–13–283–18–3/23–15.72; B. J. Vickers 107–22–291–17–4/26–17.11; C. P. Bostock 100.1–20–292–15–5/24–19.46.

KING'S COLLEGE SCHOOL, WIMBLEDON   *Played 23: W 13, L 2, D 8. A 1*

Master i/c: G. C. McGinn   Professional: A. Smith

In the Wimbledon Centenary year, the side were unbeaten in England, losing only to men's sides in Antigua and St Lucia on tour. The captain, Andrew Sleigh, again opened the batting prolifically and made a fine 125 in Antigua. Samir Sheikh retained his place at the top of the bowling and finished his career with 144 wickets in three seasons.

Batting—D. A. P. Bowen 19–6–530–78*–0–40.76; *A. P. Sleigh 22–0–842–125–1–38.27; S. M. Sheikh 18–6–399–55–0–33.25; I. S. Pay 23–3–440–75*–0–22.00; O. J. McGinn 21–2–402–53–0–21.15; C. P. Elliott 18–6–216–58*–0–18.00; R. W. Codd 17–2–204–25–0–13.60.

Bowling—S. M. Sheikh 178.2–39–576–37–6/41–15.56; J. C. Walsh 145.2–22–453–25–4/29–18.12; D. A. P. Bowen 173.2–25–617–33–7/25–18.69; J. E. Barker 147.4–27–493–23–7/41–21.43.

KING'S SCHOOL, BRUTON   *Played 13: W 7, L 5, D 1. A 2*

Master i/c: P. Platts-Martin

A programme of predominantly limited-overs matches provided some exciting cricket, in which Nicholas Price was particularly successful with bat and ball.

Batting—N. A. B. Price 13–3–402–97–0–40.20; R. W. Hastings 13–1–335–87–0–27.91; T. P. K. Rooke 11–1–232–75*–0–23.20; D. P. Weir 13–1–220–72*–0–18.33; *K. J. Pike 12–0–214–58–0–17.83.

Bowling—N. A. B. Price 128.2–37–351–33–7/14–10.63; A. P. Williams 77.1–19–242–16–3/8–15.12; E. W. Thomas 104.3–19–352–20–3/28–17.60.

THE KING'S SCHOOL, CANTERBURY   *Played 10: W 4, L 1, D 5. A 3*

Master i/c: A. W. Dyer   Professionals: A. G. E. Ealham and M. R. Benson

Disruption by poor weather prevented a potentially good side from developing into a really useful unit. A. Reynolds's 25 wickets included five in an innings four times.

Batting—G. J. R. Williams 9–3–374–100–1–62.33; *W. R. Bax 8–2–243–86*–0–40.50; S. R. Cleobury 8–1–158–36–0–22.57.

Bowling—A. C. Reynolds 143.1–41–301–25–5/25–12.04.

THE KING'S SCHOOL, CHESTER   *Played 13: W 6, L 6, D 1. A 4*

Master i/c: S. Neal

A young side produced their best cricket later in the season, culminating with victory at the Aldenham Festival. Twins Hugh and Simon Ratcliffe played; Simon was a dominant all-rounder, as was Under-19 Cheshire player David Reeves, who headed both sets of averages.

Batting—D. J. Reeves 13–0–402–83–0–30.92; C. S. Ratcliffe 12–0–223–71–0–18.58; J. C. Yates 12–1–155–37*–0–15.50; J. J. W. Fair 12–1–155–37–0–14.09.

Bowling—D. J. Reeves 65–7–255–20–4/18–12.75; C. S. Ratcliffe 102–21–378–18–4/13–21.00; *N. J. Bellamy 77.5–12–375–16–4/60–23.43.

THE KING'S SCHOOL, ELY   *Played 12: W 2, L 5, D 5. A 7*

Masters i/c: T. Firth and W. J. Marshall

The batsmen were often unable to press for victory, although the bowlers could make the opposition struggle. Ian Haigh captained by example: he scored the side's only century and his return of eight for 53 was the best for many years.

Batting—*I. P. N. Haigh 12–1–348–119*–1–31.63; C. A. Copping 11–2–272–99–0–30.22; D. M. Donaldson 11–3–166–57*–0–20.75; F. C. Thorogood 12–1–216–43–0–19.63; T. E. Mitzman 11–0–208–80–0–18.90.

Bowling—D. M. Donaldson 114.2–23–353–22–4/37–16.04; I. P. N. Haigh 100.4–22–323–18–8/53–17.94.

THE KING'S SCHOOL, MACCLESFIELD   *Played 20: W 9, L 2, D 9*

Master i/c: J. D. Nuttall   Professional: S. Moores

Highlights were Chris Buckley's 153 not out against Kelvinside Academy – the second-highest for the school – and the defeat of Nottingham HS, who were bowled out for 77, having been 53 for no wicket in pursuit of 118. The fielding was outstanding, with the bowling generally stronger than the batting.

Batting—C. J. Buckley 17–3–473–153*–1–33.78; *T. A. Jenkins 16–2–454–97–0–32.42; G. A. Emmett 14–0–384–66–0–27.42; D. P. Isherwood 17–1–363–79–0–22.68; T. A. N. Smith 11–1–222–77–0–22.20; L. E. G. Barnes 16–0–285–55–0–17.81.

Bowling—G. A. Emmett 187.4–50–492–30–5/18–16.40; S. O. Jones 259.3–79–706–42–6/8–16.80; R. R. O. Lees 129–18–476–27–5/27–17.62; M. S. Smethurst 118–16–386–18–6/27–21.44.

KING'S SCHOOL, ROCHESTER   *Played 15: W 9, L 0, D 6. A 1*

Master i/c: G. R. Williams

Batting—G. E. Davies 16–3–568–121*–1–43.69; G. J. E. Hunt 15–2–457–97–0–35.15; *S. P. A. Nicholls 12–2–323–119–1–32.30; C. K. Knight 10–4–176–35–0–29.33; S. D. R. Lapthorn 12–3–236–43–0–26.22; S. J. Pearce 11–1–153–54*–0–15.30.

Bowling—J. E. C. Shotter 87.3–15–279–20–4/27–13.95; M. A. Maurice 172–53–486–32–7/46–15.18; G. E. Davies 153.5–36–425–25–5/25–17.00; S. D. R. Lapthorn 163.4–43–474–24–4/18–19.75.

KING'S SCHOOL, WORCESTER   *Played 23: W 6, L 12, D 5. A 5*

Master i/c: D. P. Iddon   Professional: A. A. Gillgrass

Batting—D. A. Cullen 19–5–623–96*–0–44.50; E. M. Oliver 21–4–466–58*–0–27.41; L. A. Hinton 18–2–374–83–0–23.37; T. S. Heyes 15–3–263–62–0–21.91; C. J. B. Evans 16–2–255–76–0–18.21; R. A. S. Major 15–2–227–37*–0–17.46; J. D. Keegan 16–1–177–30–0–11.80.

Bowling—T. S. Heyes 191.1–39–664–36–4/32–18.44; A. T. C. Phillips 169.4–41–594–32–5/34–18.56; D. J. Kendrick 83.3–14–395–16–4/20–24.68; D. J. Harris 139.4–22–492–18–3/35–27.33.

KINGSTON GRAMMAR SCHOOL   *Played 9: W 4, L 2, D 3. A 5*

Master i/c: J. A. Royce   Professional: C. Mutucumarana

Batting—J. A. Smith 6–1–173–60–0–34.60; A. D. Evans 9–1–251–89*–0–31.37; *L. D. Garrard 9–1–248–53*–0–31.00.

Bowling—No bowler took 15 wickets. The leading bowler was M. W. Burns 73–12–234–9–2/29–26.00.

KINGSWOOD SCHOOL   Played 5: W 1, L 3, D 1. A 7

Master i/c: G. D. Opie

Batting—No batsman scored 150 runs. The leading batsman was U. Warmann 5–3–118–50*–0–59.00.

Bowling—No bowler took 15 wickets. The leading bowler was A. Pettifer 43–8–134–9–3/33–14.88.

LANCING COLLEGE   Played 12: W 8, L 3, D 1. A 6

Master i/c: M. P. Bentley   Professional: R. Davies

The captain, Giles Haywood, played for England Under-17 and England Under-19, and has a contract with Sussex. He completed five years in the eleven, as did George Campbell, who finished with more than 2,500 runs to his name. The first team for the festival included one set of twins and two other pairs of brothers.

Batting—G. R. A. Campbell 12–2–497–84*–0–49.70; H. N. E. Campbell 12–3–363–87–0–40.33; *G. R. Haywood 9–1–282–110*–1–35.25; R. D. D. Staves 11–4–244–55–0–34.85; G. D. Price 11–2–229–55*–0–25.44.

Bowling—G. R. Haywood 94–30–182–16–6/11–11.37; M. J. D. Stewart 112–29–306–21–5/30–14.57.

LANGLEY PARK SCHOOL   Played 8: W 3, L 3, D 2. A 5

Master i/c: C. H. Williams

After the successes of 1996, the poor weather combined with a weak attack to produce a disappointing season.

Batting—N. Buddell 5–1–162–82–0–40.50; R. Burgess 5–0–166–62–0–33.20; B. Simpson 6–0–185–56–0–30.83.

Bowling—No bowler took 15 wickets. The leading bowler was B. Norris 57–10–184–11–4/30–16.72.

LEEDS GRAMMAR SCHOOL   Played 11: W 2, L 1, D 8. A 6

Master i/c: R. Hill

Richard Wyn Griffith was the outstanding individual, although Adam Walton continued to show glimpses of his considerable potential.

Batting—*J. R. Wyn Griffith 11–0–466–123–1–42.36; A. N. Walton 8–0–230–97–0–28.75; A. R. Brown 11–1–252–59–0–25.20.

Bowling—J. R. Wyn Griffith 52–7–160–15–4/4–10.66.

LEIGHTON PARK SCHOOL   Played 8: W 4, L 2, D 2. A 4

Master i/c: M. Simmons

In one of many tight finishes, captain Tom Rose scored 158 on the way to a last-over victory against Oratory. He and fellow-opener Nick Head also compiled a record partnership of 158 against Reading School. The attack was spearheaded by Matthew Bloxham, well supported by David Bibby's left-arm spin.

Batting—*T. W. M. Rose 6–1–430–158*–2–86.00; N. J. Head 7–3–299–90–0–74.75.

Bowling—M. E. Bloxham 76.3–14–221–17–4/64–13.00; D. Bibby 67.1–8–272–17–4/37–16.00.

THE LEYS SCHOOL   Played 11: W 7, L 0, D 4

Master i/c: A. R. C. Batterham   Professional: D. Gibson

A highlight was an opening partnership of 199 against MCC by W. R. Graham and A. R. Newman.

Batting—W. R. Graham 11–3–590–131*–1–73.75; R. J. Bentley 11–4–261–80*–0–37.28; T. W. Nix 11–1–304–112*–1–30.40; *J. C. Welch 10–4–174–67–0–29.00; A. R. Newman 11–1–273–84–0–27.30.

Bowling—J. C. Welch 125.3–23–367–27–6/46–13.59; W. H. Spriggs 145.4–37–380–21–5/27–18.09.

LIVERPOOL COLLEGE   *Played 13: W 1, L 10, D 2. A 6*

Master i/c: A. Fox

Professional: S. Mukerjee

Batting—C. Irving 12–2–207–68–0–20.70.

Bowling—S. McNally 185–21–453–23–4/43–19.69; W. McCann 176–17–640–25–4/56–25.60.

LLANDOVERY COLLEGE   *Played 10: W 2, L 5, D 3. A 5*

Master i/c: T. G. Marks

Struggling for consistency, the side produced their best performances to defeat Rougemont and Ruthin Schools. Aled Leyshon bowled with pace and accuracy, ably supported by Emlyn Morton and Tom Walker. The batting was less memorable, but useful performances came from Morton, Jamie Roberts and Robert Coles, a promising wicket-keeper/batsman who was a member of the Welsh Schools Under-14 squad.

Batting—No batsman scored 150 runs. The leading batsman was E. Morton 8–0–120–36–0–15.00.

Bowling—A. Leyshon 78–17–233–29–6/29–8.03.

LORD WANDSWORTH COLLEGE   *Played 11: W 5, L 3, D 3. A 7*

Master i/c: M. C. Russell

In an experienced side, boosted by a successful winter tour to South Africa, Jonny Wilkinson continued his outstanding form, although his rugby commitments with England Under-18 and Newcastle prevented him from playing in more than seven games. He left the school with 85 wickets to his name. Tom Hicks, also restricted to seven matches, impressed with the bat, while Guy Hicks was the pick of the bowlers.

Batting—*J. P. Wilkinson 7–2–252–62*–0–50.40; T. A. Hicks 7–0–321–84–0–45.85; G. D. Hicks 9–3–154–33–0–25.66; S. A. Kent 8–0–157–34–0–19.62.

Bowling—G. D. Hicks 121.2–29–340–19–5/12–17.89.

LORD WILLIAMS'S SCHOOL   *Played 10: W 4, L 0, D 6. A 6*

Master i/c: J. E. Fulkes

The outstanding player was 16-year-old Robbie Eason, who headed both batting and bowling. The best win came in the last match of the season against a strong Old Boys' side.

Batting—R. Eason 8–2–382–93–0–63.66; A. Nicholas 8–3–159–43*–0–31.80; *A. Eason 8–0–177–81–0–22.12.

Bowling—No bowler took 15 wickets. The leading bowler was R. Eason 61–8–224–14–5/20–16.00.

LORETTO SCHOOL   *Played 16: W 7, L 8, D 1. A 2*

Master i/c: R. P. Whait

Batting—*W. A. Nicholson 13–2–248–42*–0–22.54; M. J. Ritchie 10–2–162–36–0–20.25; W. A. D. Oliver 13–2–217–45–0–19.72; M. B. McCreath 14–3–182–34–0–16.54; A. Jain 15–0–188–39–0–12.53; S. J. S. Smith 15–1–166–40–0–11.85.

Bowling—M. B. McCreath 270.4–67–695–45–7/39–15.44; W. A. D. Oliver 123.3–16–377–19–5/63–19.84.

LOUGHBOROUGH GRAMMAR SCHOOL　　　*Played 11: W 4, L 3, D 4. A 9*

Master i/c: J. S. Weitzel　　　　　　　　　　　　Professional: H. T. Tunnicliffe

Edward Woodcock's 134 not out included a record eight sixes and set up victory over the touring President's High School from Cape Town. That was the only game to be completed during the two-week end-of-term festival.

Batting—*M. J. Hayes 8–3–289–113*–1–57.80; E. O. Woodcock 9–1–306–134*–1–38.25; T. Emson 7–1–164–60–0–27.33; J. Carrington 10–1–191–47*–0–21.22.

Bowling—M. J. Hayes 104–13–360–15–4/40–24.00.

MAGDALEN COLLEGE SCHOOL　　　*Played 16: W 5, L 6, D 5. A 3*

Master i/c: P. Askew　　　　　　　　　　　　Professional: U. Mbangwa

A summer tour to British Columbia included a visit south to Seattle, where the side became the first English team to play at Fort Dent Park, home of Seattle CC.

Batting—B. J. Thompson 17–3–562–82–0–40.14; T. Jenkinson 12–2–261–45–0–26.10; P. Robinson 12–1–258–63–0–23.45; *C. Rees-Gay 16–1–327–56–0–21.80; D. Matheson 16–1–239–49–0–15.93.

Bowling—C. Rees-Gay 71–14–257–15–3/27–17.13; A. Hirtenstein 170–41–491–25–6/21–19.64; B. J. Thompson 99–20–374–16–7/28–23.37; J. Harrison 94.1–14–400–15–3/28–26.66.

MALVERN COLLEGE　　　*Played 18: W 5, L 6, D 7. A 6*

Master i/c: P. Goode　　　　　　　　　　　　Professional: R. W. Tolchard

In a season of rebuilding, Richard Neale emerged as a useful all-rounder and scored a century against Lancing. The attack was backed up admirably by Hugh Whitworth, who made an admirable job of stepping into the shoes of David Nash as wicket-keeper. For the third successive season the side reached the final of the Chesterton Cup, which was rained off.

Batting—R. Neale 17–2–521–109–1–34.73; H. Whitworth 14–1–311–97–0–23.92; *D. Hill 16–2–236–56–0–16.85; A. Griffiths 13–2–174–50–0–15.81.

Bowling—A. Arnold 107–22–287–26–5/58–11.03; D. Madden 111–22–307–24–5/28–12.79; R. Neale 104.3–12–336–24–4/11–14.00; W. Harrison 134.5–29–420–23–6/62–18.26.

MANCHESTER GRAMMAR SCHOOL　　　*Played 15: W 6, L 0, D 9. A 5*

Master i/c: D. Moss

Jonathan Lee continued to develop as a powerful batsman and became the fifth Manchester GS batsman to pass a thousand runs in a season, hitting three hundreds and seven fifties. However, the batting lacked fluency and, once Nick Garner tailed off after scoring centuries in the first two matches, too much depended on Lee. Richard Seddon, who often rescued the batting, also opened the bowling with pace, although the most wickets fell to two younger players: Rana Malook and leg-spinner Nick Murrills.

Batting—*J. R. Lee 15–2–1,012–148*–3–77.84; R. P. J. Seddon 9–2–300–65*–0–42.85; N. D. Garner 13–1–395–132*–2–32.91; N. P. Murrills 15–4–300–54*–0–27.27.

Bowling—N. P. Murrills 184–37–578–27–5/59–21.40; R. J. Malook 155.2–23–557–22–4/48–25.31.

MARLBOROUGH COLLEGE　　　*Played 11: W 1, L 2, D 8. A 3*

Master i/c: N. E. Briers　　　　　　　　　　　　Professional: R. M. Ratcliffe

Batting—M. A. L. Bickford 7–3–163–51–0–40.75; T. E. F. Burne 11–2–248–48–0–27.55; M. P. L. Bush 11–0–235–74–0–21.36; G. R. J. Comyn 9–1–163–34–0–20.37; A. J. R. Bird 10–1–165–64–0–18.33; P. M. Koronka 10–1–156–43*–0–17.33.

Bowling—No bowler took 15 wickets. The leading bowler was T. E. F. Burne 100.3–27–316–12–3/34–26.33.

MERCHANT TAYLORS' SCHOOL, CROSBY   *Played 12: W 8, L 1, D 3. A 6*

Master i/c: Rev D. A. Smith   Professional: B. C. Strang

Batting—C. J. Cheetham 12–4–551–102*–2–68.87; *J. N. C. Rees 8–5–161–56*–0–53.66; P. A. O'Leary 12–2–196–39–0–19.60.

Bowling—P. A. O'Leary 113.5–30–354–27–5/56–13.11; S. J. Nelson 93–15–325–24–6/54–13.54; D. R. Ball 112.1–24–336–21–3/30–16.00; J. N. C. Rees 80.5–14–321–16–4/27–20.06.

MERCHANT TAYLORS' SCHOOL, NORTHWOOD   *Played 18: W 8, L 1, D 9. A 4*

Master i/c: H. C. Latchman

In a season of rebuilding, the side were encouraged by victory in eight matches, including four out of five at the Cranleigh Festival, and lost only to MCC. Keith Fowler successfully combined the captaincy with keeping wicket and opening the batting, while Andrew Sharland scored freely throughout. Jawwad Rasheed's all-round contribution was crucial.

Batting—J. Rasheed 12–3–489–95–0–54.33; *K. G. W. Fowler 14–1–563–82*–0–43.30; A. S. J. S. Sharland 17–2–611–107*–1–40.73; T. A. Coleman 12–3–365–101*–1–40.55; P. K. Vandra 13–4–284–105–1–31.55; M. A. Howard 15–5–270–53*–0–27.00.

Bowling—J. Rasheed 270.5–49–858–47–5/16–18.25.

MERCHISTON CASTLE SCHOOL   *Played 10: W 6, L 3, D 1. A 9*

Master i/c: C. W. Swan

Batting—R. A. Swan 10–2–240–50*–0–30.00; D. M. Stewart 11–1–201–79*–0–20.10; J. A. C. Easton 12–0–235–53–0–19.58; J. C. Haslam-Jones 10–0–158–62–0–15.80.

Bowling—F. H. W. F. Sempill 87–14–264–15–4/8–17.60; A. R. Evans 110–19–334–16–3/9–20.87.

MILLFIELD SCHOOL   *Played 16: W 7, L 6, D 3. A 2*

Master i/c: R. M. Ellison   Professional: G. C. Wilson

Batting—R. D. Dorey 14–4–532–166–1–53.20; C. A. Sayers 15–1–556–120–1–39.71; *A. N. Edwards 15–1–357–75–0–25.50; L. J. De Souza 14–1–282–63*–0–21.69; H. T. P. Caines 15–2–271–73–0–20.84.

Bowling—H. T. P. Caines 208–39–687–36–7/32–19.08; M. J. Webb 147.4–34–446–22–8/47–20.27; S. P. Jones 165.2–26–520–23–4/28–22.60.

MILL HILL SCHOOL   *Played 11: W 2, L 3, D 6. A 4*

Master i/c: P. H. Edwards   Professional: I. C. F. Hutchinson

Batting—M. Dweck 11–2–465–83*–0–51.66; S. Bunyard 10–1–239–103*–1–26.55; M. Brandon 8–1–153–42–0–21.85.

Bowling—V. Bhinyiyani 68–20–195–15–6/49–13.00; J. Graves 95–23–256–19–4/35–13.47; E. Rashid 69–9–227–15–4/42–15.13.

MILTON ABBEY SCHOOL   *Played 12: W 2, L 5, D 5. A 3*

Master i/c: P. W. Wood

Batting—C. M. Gold 12–1–326–88–0–29.63; B. A. Clay 12–1–180–100*–1–16.36; J. Hook 11–0–174–39–0–15.81.

Bowling—T. Robertson 136.2–31–486–28–6/44–17.35; C. M. Gold 158–40–548–31–7/30–17.67; N. David 113.4–26–474–19–4/48–24.94.

MONKTON COMBE SCHOOL   *Played 9: W 6, L 2, D 1. A 5*

Master i/c: N. D. Botton

Batting—J. I. Solly 9–1–289–94*–0–36.12; T. E. Hankins 6–0–194–71–0–32.33.

Bowling—M. E. K. Rooke 74–20–202–19–4/14–10.63; C. A. Seccombe 55.4–7–183–15–5/25–12.20.

MONMOUTH SCHOOL   *Played 15: W 2, L 9, D 4. A 6*

Master i/c: A. Jones   Professional: G. I. Burgess

Batting—N. Jorgenson 13–1–397–106–1–33.08; T. Allan 13–1–292–46–0–24.33; *T. Ricks 13–2–201–63*–0–18.27; E. Barlow 14–0–236–61–0–16.85.

Bowling—G. Curtis 152.1–32–468–26–6/44–18.00; E. Barlow 100.2–23–399–17–7/60–23.47; N. Jorgenson 149–25–468–18–3/25–26.00.

NEWCASTLE-UNDER-LYME SCHOOL   *Played 11: W 2, L 4, D 5. A 7*

Master i/c: S. A. Robson   Professional: A. J. Dutton

Some aggressively co-ordinated out-cricket helped to compensate for the sacrificial ineptitude of the batting.

Batting—V. V. S. Handley 11–2–221–73–0–24.55; *J. A. Talathi 8–1–157–59*–0–22.42; P. J. Turnock 9–0–188–78–0–20.88.

Bowling—M. P. A. Emery 79–19–277–16–5/52–17.31.

NOTTINGHAM HIGH SCHOOL   *Played 12: W 4, L 4, D 4. A 8*

Master i/c: J. Lamb

Batting—M. J. Stewart 6–1–278–110–1–55.60; K. S. Tate 8–0–433–135–1–54.12; *A. J. Hunt 9–1–246–80*–0–30.75.

Bowling—K. S. Tate 88.4–20–236–19–5/18–12.42; A. J. Hunt 81.2–16–229–17–3/19–13.47; R. Kitching 127–17–435–24–5/35–18.12.

OAKHAM SCHOOL   *Played 12: W 2, L 2, D 8. A 7*

Master i/c: J. Wills   Professional: D. S. Steele

The captain, Richard Martin, scored 545 runs to finish his career in the eleven with a record 2,500 runs, including six centuries and a share in 15 century partnerships. He also played for Leicestershire Second Eleven and Cambridgeshire.

Batting—*R. A. E. Martin 10–1–545–115–2–60.55; M. A. Braddock 9–2–347–102*–1–49.57.

Bowling—S. Goode 143.1–34–425–15–5/34–28.33.

THE ORATORY SCHOOL   *Played 13: W 5, L 2, D 6. A 5*

Master i/c: P. L. Tomlinson   Professional: J. B. K. Howell

The cricket master's son, Steven Tomlinson, scored two hundreds, while David Allaway and Chris Clayton had one each. Tomlinson, captaining the side again, completed his career with a total of 3,118 runs at 72.51 and 170 wickets at 10.71 – all school records – and was awarded a three-year contract and university sports scholarship at Cardiff by Glamorgan.

Batting—*S. C. B. Tomlinson 10–3–502–110*–2–71.71; C. J. Clayton 9–1–508–100*–1–63.50; D. J. Allaway 11–2–550–156*–1–61.11; T. C. Wigley 12–0–186–40–0–15.50.

Bowling—S. C. B. Tomlinson 98–30–318–30–7/21–10.60; E. W. Orchard 140–36–462–32–6/36–14.43; S. J. Bird 80–8–340–16–4/36–21.25; T. C. Wigley 84–8–402–18–4/18–22.33.

OUNDLE SCHOOL   *Played 16: W 7, L 1, D 8. A 6*

Master i/c: J. R. Wake   Professional: T. Howorth

In a season of rebuilding, the side did well to win seven matches and remain unbeaten by schools. William Jefferson, the mainstay of the side with 689 runs and 23 wickets, went on to make his debut for Norfolk, while Michael Dobson, the leading wicket-taker, played for Northamptonshire Second Eleven, Under-17 and Under-19.

Batting—*D. Lowe 15–4–557–90*–0–50.63; W. I. Jefferson 15–1–689–143*–2–49.21; A. M. Dobson 10–4–210–54–0–35.00; J. Cope 12–4–217–46–0–27.12; S. J. Lowe 14–1–244–53–0–18.76.

Bowling—J. Cope 75–11–236–15–4/14–15.73; W. I. Jefferson 170.3–43–444–23–5/32–19.30; R. J. Lawson 84–16–290–15–3/13–19.33; A. M. Dobson 171.3–33–516–25–4/15–20.64; M. Simmonds 101.1–22–329–15–4/32–21.93.

THE PERSE SCHOOL   *Played 11: W 4, L 3, D 4. A 3*

Master i/c: A. C. Porter   Professional: D. C. Collard

Batting—M. Mayer 9–1–279–76*–0–34.87; M. Moffat 9–1–273–47*–0–34.12; C. Walker 10–1–262–90*–0–29.11; B. King 11–2–177–74*–0–19.66.

Bowling—A. Kay 116.4–15–437–20–5/38–21.85; C. Rodger 111–21–358–16–4/42–22.37.

PLYMOUTH COLLEGE   *Played 15: W 7, L 2, D 6. A 3*

Master i/c: T. J. Stevens

In a successful season, particularly good wins were achieved over Kelly College and Exeter School. The bowling and fielding were much improved, while the batsmen excelled with five centuries – four from the captain Nick Pope and one from Simon Hards.

Batting—*N. Pope 14–3–655–119*–4–59.54; S. Hards 13–2–436–102*–1–39.63; J. Newnham 12–1–337–63*–0–30.63; W. Andrews 14–5–219–56–0–24.33.

Bowling—L. Barnes 66–8–219–16–5/23–13.68; S. Hards 120–24–370–27–5/27–13.70; N. Pope 89–7–319–18–4/41–17.72; W. Andrews 139–35–392–19–5/29–20.63.

POCKLINGTON SCHOOL   *Played 17: W 2, L 5, D 10. A 3*

Master i/c: R. Smith

Batting—P. R. Mouncey 14–2–470–71–0–39.16; A. N. Mitchell 12–3–247–52*–0–27.44; *C. R. Rook 14–1–317–60–0–24.38; R. J. R. Poskitt 13–1–201–37*–0–16.75; R. J. Milne 13–0–217–77–0–16.69; E. D. Townend 15–1–159–54–0–11.35.

Bowling—C. R. Rook 87.4–20–202–15–4/45–13.46; P. R. Mouncey 186.3–47–555–30–4/40–18.50; S. T. Dodds 99.5–14–347–17–5/46–20.41.

PORTSMOUTH GRAMMAR SCHOOL   *Played 9: W 6, L 0, D 3. A 7*

Master i/c: G. D. Payne   Professional: R. J. Parks

Unbeaten and winning six out of nine matches, the side enjoyed their best season since 1985.

Batting—J. M. L. Tod 7–1–240–93–0–40.00; J. B. Grady 9–0–274–94–0–30.44; B. R. Pennells 9–0–241–80–0–26.77; S. R. Foulger 8–0–185–88–0–23.12.

Bowling—J. M. L. Tod 77–22–198–15–4/42–13.20; J. H. Stedman 73–12–237–15–6/71–15.80; B. R. Pennells 108–18–286–15–3/37–19.06.

PRIOR PARK COLLEGE   *Played 16: W 9, L 2, D 5. A 2*

Master i/c: D. R. Holland   Professional: R. Chambers

The side finished with a record number of wins, and Andrew Owen's 691 runs were also a record. Owen was the first from the college to be selected for the MCC Schools Festival at Oxford.

Batting—A. S. Owen 15–1–691–110*–1–49.35; N. Potter 11–6–201–59*–0–40.20; *A. Atkins 15–3–361–93–0–30.08; P. O'Dea 12–3–248–76*–0–27.55; S. Phillips 12–3–200–63–0–22.22; C. Wilson 12–2–177–62–0–17.70.

Bowling—D. Gadsden 133–23–367–33–7/14–11.12; S. Phillips 151–30–451–38–5/26–11.86.

QUEEN ELIZABETH GS, WAKEFIELD   *Played 9: W 5, L 2, D 2. A 5*

Master i/c: T. Barker   Professional: C. Jackson

Batting—M. J. Holding 8–1–270–77–0–38.57; D. A. Castle 9–1–261–65–0–32.62; R. A. Sykes 9–0–153–44–0–17.00.

Bowling—No bowler took 15 wickets. The leading bowler was A. J. Sharma 56.2–12–161–13–3/13–12.38.

QUEEN ELIZABETH'S HOSPITAL   *Played 10: W 3, L 1, D 6. A 4*

Master i/c: M. S. E. Broadley

Batting—G. P. J. Parker Jones 7–1–264–81*–0–44.00; W. H. Nash 8–3–166–87–0–33.20; J. H. Prosser 7–0–158–43–0–22.57; R. J. Gwyn 11–2–203–54–0–22.55; *P. A. Ross 11–1–221–71*–0–22.10; M. J. Penneycard 11–1–152–66*–0–15.20.

Bowling—No bowler took 15 wickets. The leading bowler was P. A. Ross 74.4–14–218–13–4/27–16.76.

QUEEN'S COLLEGE TAUNTON   *Played 11: W 6, L 4, D 1. A 3*

Master i/c: A. S. Free

Alex Bailey headed the batting and took his career aggregate to 1,141 runs, while his brother, Oliver, and Stephen Butt both showed promise. Matthew Gitsham and William Bates bowled well in tandem.

Batting—*A. Bailey 12–3–381–89*–0–42.33; S. Butt 6–1–165–65*–0–33.00; O. Bailey 7–2–160–57–0–32.00; T. Jones 10–2–187–68*–0–23.37; D. Bell 10–1–163–65–0–18.11; S. Gitsham 11–1–179–75*–0–17.90; O. Hobden 10–1–159–57–0–17.66.

Bowling—M. Gitsham 57.2–9–202–19–7/36–10.63; W. Bates 71.1–23–182–17–6/23–10.70.

RADLEY COLLEGE   *Played 11: W 1, L 0, D 10. A 5*

Master i/c: W. J. Wesson   Professionals: A. G. Robinson and A. R. Wagner

The most prolific batsman was Oliver Hutton – son of Richard Hutton and grandson of Sir Leonard. The captain, C. E. Pragnell, completed four seasons in the eleven and headed the averages, although the most wickets fell to Charlie Van der Gucht, grandson of former Gloucestershire wicket-keeper, Paul. Hutton and Van der Gucht went on to play in the Second Eleven Championship for Middlesex and Hampshire respectively.

Batting—*C. E. Pragnell 10–5–328–84*–0–65.60; O. R. Hutton 10–0–590–105–1–59.00; J. W. M. Dalrymple 9–2–258–86*–0–36.85; O. M. Broom 10–1–289–105*–1–32.11.

Bowling—C. E. Pragnell 90–18–258–15–4/16–17.20; C. G. Van der Gucht 115.5–20–379–18–5/24–21.05.

RATCLIFFE COLLEGE   *Played 12: W 5, L 1, D 6. A 4*

Master i/c: R. Hughes   Professional: C. Henderson

The Emeriti Trophy was retained in style after Karl Smith took six wickets to dismiss The Oratory for 65. Elliott Hill was again the leading batsman with two centuries.

Batting—J. Hart 10–4–391–106*–1–65.16; E. V. Hill 11–1–536–133*–2–53.60; K. Smith 9–1–170–59–0–21.25; B. N. Clarke 9–1–157–50–0–19.62.

Bowling—K. Smith 80.3–16–252–21–6/39–12.00; J. Hart 90–26–209–15–4/19–13.93; L. Buckby 77–13–299–18–5/12–16.61; W. J. Birchall 124–28–387–19–5/48–20.36.

READING SCHOOL   *Played 12: W 4, L 5, D 3*

Master i/c: S. A. Stevenson

Batting—D. Lowe 8–2–257–59–0–42.83; *I. Azuike 8–0–244–144–1–30.50; N. Singleton 11–2–265–101*–1–29.44; J. Taylor 10–2–164–66–0–20.50; J. Eatherley 9–0–152–56–0–16.88.

Bowling—No bowler took 15 wickets. The leading bowler was O. Mann 76–20–208–14–3/9–14.85.

REIGATE GRAMMAR SCHOOL   *Played 21: W 6, L 8, D 7. A 6*

Master i/c: D. C. R. Jones   Professional: H. Newton

Despite the abandonment of six successive games, the side managed to play more games than most schools and reported three record partnerships, including a thrilling 78 for the last wicket between Andrew Grave and John Eldred. Other highlights included Robbie Young's unbeaten hundred against Wallington GS and Toby Briggs's achievement in passing 50 wickets again.

Batting—A. J. Grave 11–6–158–44*–0–31.60; *R. C. G. Young 19–3–505–100*–1–31.56; S. A. Knight 12–3–232–64*–0–25.77; M. N. Cooper 20–2–460–85–0–25.55; T. W. Briggs 18–2–367–97–0–22.93; I. N. Bezodis 19–0–386–74–0–20.31; O. J. Jago 12–1–201–57–0–18.27; M. P. Ross 13–0–237–57–0–18.23; O. Bate 12–1–155–51–0–14.09.

Bowling—O. Bate 74–18–201–16–5/38–12.56; T. W. Briggs 244.2–56–722–54–7/40–13.37; A. J. Grave 134.3–21–435–20–3/11–21.75.

RENDCOMB COLLEGE   *Played 10: W 3, L 3, D 4. A 4*

Master i/c: J. P. Watson

Batting—C. P. E. Barton 7–4–219–120*–1–73.00.

Bowling—No bowler took 15 wickets. The leading bowler was J. R. F. Gibbs 82–18–292–10–4/43–29.20.

REPTON SCHOOL   *Played 10: W 2, L 3, D 5. A 5*

Master i/c: M. Stones   Professional: M. K. Kettle

Batting—T. A. Swerling 10–0–289–66–0–28.90; R. D. J. Probert 9–1–207–78*–0–25.87; C. H. M. Standage 8–1–172–57–0–24.57; A. J. Currie 10–1–213–62*–0–23.66; J. J. G. Fletcher 9–0–167–68–0–18.55.

Bowling—No bowler took 15 wickets. The leading bowler was J. L. Alsop 49–7–218–9–3/19–24.22.

RICHARD HUISH COLLEGE   *Played 7: W 6, L 1, D 0. A 6*

Master i/c: J. W. Davies

Losing only to Millfield, the side were particularly satisfied with their victories over Queen's (Taunton), Exeter University and Brighton GS from Australia.

Batting—A. Carter 6–1–226–101*–1–45.20.

Bowling—A. Mason 60–13–162–17–5/49–9.52.

ROSSALL SCHOOL   *Played 15: W 9, L 5, D 1*

Master i/c: A. D. Todd   Professional: K. Higgs

All-rounder Matthew Clapp, son of Somerset bowler Bob Clapp, opened the bowling to good effect as well as hitting 105 not out in 58 balls. James Atkins scored centuries on consecutive days at the Cranleigh Festival.

Batting—J. R. Atkins 14–4–456–124*–2–45.60; T. Slee 6–2–156–100*–1–39.00; M. D. Clapp 11–1–298–105*–1–29.80; S. J. Fraser-Cattenach 15–2–328–76*–0–25.23.

Bowling—M. D. Clapp 123–26–307–27–5/19–11.37; M. D. Dewhurst 141–24–441–23–5/27–19.17.

Andrew Hemingway (left) scored 1,028 runs for The Royal Grammar School, Guildford, and Sam Musk took 52 wickets for The Royal Grammar School, High Wycombe.

THE ROYAL GRAMMAR SCHOOL, COLCHESTER   *Played 22: W 3, L 12, D 7*

Master i/c: R. L. Bayes

Batting—M. Tyler 19–4–416–60–0–27.73; R. P. Burt 21–2–432–73*–0–22.73; P. B. Hazell 21–2–399–103*–1–21.00; J. S. Oxborrow 23–1–366–55–0–16.63; G. R. D. Gwyn-Jones 20–3–272–50–0–16.00; C. W. Norfolk 17–4–172–37*–0–13.23; P. J. Sadler 21–0–258–42–0–12.28; M. R. Perrin 17–4–156–36–0–12.00.

Bowling—P. J. Sadler 143.4–22–513–27–5/27–19.00; B. A. Pinkey 147–34–453–22–3/31–20.59; M. Tyler 252.4–33–799–34–7/59–23.50; C. W. Norfolk 179.1–32–655–27–3/2–24.25; M. J. E. Gittins 143–23–519–20–5/17–25.95.

THE ROYAL GRAMMAR SCHOOL, GUILDFORD   *Played 17: W 12, L 4, D 1. A 2*

Master i/c: S. B. R. Shore

Andrew Hemingway broke his own school batting record set in 1995 with a tally of 1,028 runs, including 163 against Tiffin (another record) and a match-winning 128 not out against Charterhouse. Another highlight was the victory over Trinity, who collapsed from 131 for three to 144 in reply to 155.

Batting—A. R. Hemingway 20–7–1,028–163–2–79.07; *R. C. Kitzinger 18–3–491–89–0–32.73; T. Hughes 11–3–213–56*–0–26.62; M. Copsey 14–2–312–70–0–26.00; J. Hartfield 15–5–257–78–0–25.70; J. A. Mitchell 12–0–160–62–0–13.33.

Bowling—J. A. Mitchell 180.4–36–502–36–5/49–13.94; M. Roberts 154–28–496–31–4/29–16.00; C. A. G. Cooper 153.2–28–519–28–6/52–18.53; W. B. Reep 112–14–380–15–2/44–25.33.

THE ROYAL GRAMMAR SCHOOL, HIGH WYCOMBE   *Played 19: W 10, L 3, D 6. A 5*

Master i/c: P. R. Miles

Sam Musk, an off-spinner and Buckinghamshire Under-19 representative, took 52 wickets. He made an outstanding all-round contribution against St Benedict's, scoring 60, taking seven for 20 and holding four catches.

Batting—A. Melrose 10–3–271–75–0–38.71; M. Honeyben 14–7–270–42*–0–38.57; D. Wilson 10–2–283–59–0–35.37; C. Dark 19–2–552–104*–1–32.47; S. A. Musk 11–3–208–60–0–26.00; A. Shaw 12–2–235–63–0–23.50; *A. Bentall 16–1–287–38–0–19.13.

Bowling—S. A. Musk 231.2–52–693–52–7/20–13.32; A. Bentall 187–34–538–30–4/20–17.93.

THE ROYAL GRAMMAR SCHOOL, NEWCASTLE   *Played 14: W 9, L 3, D 2. A 4*

Master i/c: D. W. Smith   Professional: C. Craven

Nicky Peng scored consistently to head the batting, going on to play for England at both Under-14 and Under-15 levels.

Batting—N. Peng 10–1–416–99–0–46.22; A. Kahn 7–3–162–46–0–40.50; C. Robson 10–1–322–71–0–35.77; I. Nairn 13–3–351–76–0–35.10.

Bowling—J. Harte 117–20–349–29–5/24–12.03; J. Gill 91–14–290–24–5/23–12.08; R. Munro 101–14–318–20–6/60–15.90.

THE ROYAL GRAMMAR SCHOOL, WORCESTER   *Played 19: W 16, L 2, D 1*

Master i/c: B. M. Rees   Professional: F. P. Watson

The season was notable for the batting of Richard Hall and James Schofield, both of whom played in the Oxford Festival, with Schofield going to represent MCC Schools and Worcestershire Second Eleven.

Batting—J. E. K. Schofield 10–3–561–122–3–80.14; R. J. Hall 14–4–762–139*–3–76.20; D. L. Andrews 11–4–203–42*–0–29.00; M. W. J. Wilkinson 16–2–393–80–0–28.07; N. S. A. Cockrell 16–2–366–69*–0–26.14; L. A. Clarke 12–2–240–58–0–24.00; T. M. Betts 11–3–182–67*–0–22.75; D. B. Rees 13–2–166–58–0–15.09.

Bowling—J. E. K. Schofield 66.5–19–173–22–5/18–7.86; J. Khalid 173–21–500–34–5/18–14.70; T. Mees 141.1–32–377–25–5/21–15.08.

RUGBY SCHOOL   *Played 13: W 1, L 4, D 8. A 4*

Master i/c: P. J. Rosser   Professional: L. Tennant

The two-day Marlborough match was abandoned without a ball bowled for the first time in the fixture's 130 years.

Batting—A. N. G. Beazley 12–1–352–66–0–32.00; H. Mobarak 12–2–248–73–0–24.80; D. J. Howe 12–0–282–63–0–23.50; T. J. T. Barton-Knott 12–1–214–52–0–19.45; M. C. R. Edward 12–0–209–52–0–17.41; A. Lockhart 12–1–184–65–0–16.72.

Bowling—B. H. B. Williams 136.4–42–473–20–6/50–23.65; T. J. T. Barton-Knott 105–19–390–15–4/44–26.00.

RYDAL SCHOOL   *Played 4: W 0, L 4, D 0. A 6*

Master i/c: M. T. Leach   Professional: R. W. C. Pitman

Rydal were particularly badly hit by the weather, with six of ten games completely washed out. The captain, Richard Binks, headed both batting and bowling and played for Glamorgan Under-19.

Batting—No batsman scored 150 runs. The leading batsman was R. J. Binks 4–0–97–42–0–24.25.

Bowling—No bowler took 15 wickets. The leading bowler was R. J. Binks 44–9–120–9–5/30–13.33.

ST ALBANS SCHOOL   *Played 13: W 4, L 5, D 4. A 7*

Master i/c: C. C. Hudson

At 14 years 6 months, Richard Little became the youngest player to captain the side, having in the previous four years captained Hertfordshire at each age level up to Under-16.

Batting—*R. J. Little 10–3–224–38–0–32.00; W. H. Hawling 10–2–209–54–0–26.12; M. Warren 10–1–231–77–0–25.66.

Bowling—A. S. Whitlow 77–7–363–15–4/63–24.20; A. S. Khan 116.1–15–399–15–4/56–26.60.

ST DUNSTAN'S COLLEGE   *Played 13: W 0, L 7, D 6. A 2*

Master i/c: O. T. Price   Professional: R. Chowdhary

James Vigus, the Great Britain Under-19 chess captain, scored his maiden century against Eltham, who won the match off the last ball. In a young side, Tim Edwards showed much promise.

Batting—R. M. J. Clark 11–2–288–77*–0–32.00; J. V. Patel 8–2–184–60*–0–30.66; J. E. Vigus 10–1–261–106–1–29.00; T. R. Edwards 11–1–172–33–0–17.20.

Bowling—T. S. Cole 134–17–523–18–5/55–29.05.

ST EDMUND'S COLLEGE, WARE   *Played 12: W 6, L 2, D 4. A 3*

Master i/c: J. D. T. Faithfull

Four of the six wins were achieved with the last pair at the wicket. The side attributed their ultimate success to a varied seven-man attack and the imaginative captaincy of Richard Gillham.

Batting—A. Bilimoria 6–1–249–95*–0–49.80; *R. Gillham 9–1–323–75*–0–40.37.

Bowling—A. Dowling 95.1–18–243–20–6/39–12.15.

ST EDMUND'S SCHOOL, CANTERBURY   *Played 11: W 1, L 7, D 3. A 6*

Master i/c: M. C. Dobson

Although the batsmen struggled to build an innings, Andrew Craig showed potential and determination.

Batting—W. D. Knight 10–0–242–55–0–24.20; A. S. Craig 9–2–161–53*–0–23.00; S. M. C. Narburgh 9–1–173–66*–0–21.62.

Bowling—No bowler took 15 wickets. The leading bowler was R. G. R. Dixon 80–8–299–13–3/41–23.00.

ST EDWARD'S SCHOOL, OXFORD   *Played 12: W 2, L 3, D 7. A 3*

Masters i/c: D. Drake-Brockman and M. I. Yeabsley   Professional: G. V. Palmer

Batting—O. D. Martin 12–1–351–74*–0–31.90; T. P. Leabitter 9–0–263–74–0–29.22; M. S. Cannon 12–1–262–61–0–23.81; J. A. Pigott 11–1–238–73–0–23.80; O. M. Wills 10–3–166–76–0–23.71; T. P. Sutton 12–0–204–76–0–17.00.

Bowling—O. M. Wills 180.4–27–521–30–5/40–17.36; N. J. Robbins 126–14–485–17–5/51–28.52.

ST GEORGE'S COLLEGE, WEYBRIDGE   *Played 14: W 3, L 8, D 3. A 1*

Master i/c: D. G. Ottley

Batting—*T. Clouston 11–1–334–68–0–33.40; A. Collin 10–0–233–58–0–23.30; C. Neill 13–0–219–46–0–16.84; J. Knox 13–0–178–54–0–13.69; N. Carlino 13–0–168–65–0–12.92.

Bowling—N. Carlino 172–23–557–25–5/24–22.28; J. Knox 192.2–44–603–25–5/49–24.12.

ST JOHN'S SCHOOL, LEATHERHEAD   *Played 12: W 4, L 4, D 4. A 5*

Master i/c: A. B. Gale

Batting—*J. M. A. Cook 12–2–410–101*–1–41.00; D. A. Bellenger 11–4–251–61*–0–35.85; G. R. Warren 12–0–245–72–0–20.41; J. S. Harvey 12–0–216–53–0–18.00.

Bowling—J. S. Harvey 143.1–34–364–25–4/0–14.56.

ST JOSEPH'S COLLEGE, IPSWICH   *Played 15: W 6, L 0, D 9*

Master i/c: M. Davey   Professional: K. Brooks

Paul King, who was outstanding with 523 runs and 46 wickets, played for MCC Schools.

Batting—C. Townrow 13–6–418–116*–2–59.71; P. D. King 14–4–523–80–0–52.30; A. J. Mallows 10–6–171–54–0–42.75; J. Debenham 12–1–440–117–1–40.00; J. Eaglesham 13–0–290–62–0–22.30; J. Regan 13–0–155–26–0–11.92.

Bowling—P. D. King 182–36–604–46–7/17–13.13; N. Jenkins 95–13–376–15–4/25–25.06; P. Living 129–21–473–18–4/33–26.27.

ST LAWRENCE COLLEGE, RAMSGATE   *Played 10: W 2, L 3, D 5. A 3*

Master i/c: N. O. S. Jones   Professional: A. P. E. Knott

Batting—A. R. Haines 9–3–362–100*–1–60.33; *A. J. Snell 8–4–230–97–0–57.50; J. R. W. Bolt 8–0–172–60–0–21.50.

Bowling—No bowler took 15 wickets. The leading bowler was J. E. Langman 68–8–253–13–4/22–19.46.

ST PAUL'S SCHOOL   *Played 10: W 2, L 1, D 7. A 6*

Master i/c: G. Hughes   Professional: M. Heath

In the six-wicket victory over Buccaneers CC, P. de Villiers and A. R. Duncan put on 163 for the fourth wicket.

Batting—P. de Villiers 9–3–317–98–0–52.83; A. R. Duncan 9–2–264–86–0–37.71; S. A. Hyman 7–2–178–71–0–35.60; *T. E. B. Etherton 9–0–217–73–0–24.11.

Bowling—W. J. McIntosh 87–29–252–15–4/24–16.80.

ST PETER'S SCHOOL, YORK   *Played 21: W 7, L 1, D 13. A 2*

Master i/c: D. Kirby   Professional: K. F. Mohan

Batting—N. J. C. Kay 17–1–799–109*–1–49.93; J. P. Hockin 14–4–288–52*–0–28.80; S. J. Leveson 18–2–445–68–0–27.81; C. J. Ellerbeck 15–5–267–60–0–26.70; J. P. G. Dougherty 17–2–357–87–0–23.80; E. D. Sykes 10–0–180–48–0–18.00.

Bowling—C. J. Ellerbeck 109–28–327–21–6/14–15.57; T. T. Bainbridge 222.1–64–689–39–6/29–17.66; J. P. G. Dougherty 195.5–56–592–28–4/53–21.14.

SEDBERGH SCHOOL   *Played 15: W 5, L 2, D 8. A 2*

Master i/c: N. A. Rollings   Professional: J. Potter

Simon Farnsworth again dominated the batting with 643 runs, as well as taking 23 wickets. Swing bowler James Hart, one of five to take 20 wickets, made a significant impression in his first season. Four of the five wins came in the second half of the season.

Batting—S. P. Farnsworth 15–1–643–85–0–45.92; *D. R. Scargill 14–3–336–89*–0–30.54; C. M. Jameson 15–4–174–28*–0–15.81.

Bowling—J. C. Hart 120–44–242–23–7/46–10.52; P. D. Thompson 139.2–46–262–20–5/43–13.10; J. D. Jameson 132–36–302–20–4/32–15.10; S. P. Farnsworth 147.4–34–387–23–6/38–16.82; J. M. Chapman 127–24–366–21–5/41–17.42.

SEVENOAKS SCHOOL   *Played 14: W 4, L 0, D 10. A 7*

Master i/c: I. J. B. Walker

Batting—M. Soulsby 11–4–406–76*–0–58.00; *H. Snuggs 10–2–343–54–0–42.87; E. Grant 11–0–419–74–0–38.09; S. Seldon 9–3–170–54–0–28.33; I. Jenkins 10–1–171–35–0–19.00.

Bowling—M. Soulsby 71–16–207–19–5/12–10.89; R. Walton 90.1–13–298–18–3/31–16.55; A. Miles 103–21–321–15–3/25–21.40.

SHEBBEAR COLLEGE   *Played 10: W 2, L 6, D 2. A 4*

Master i/c: A. Bryan   Professional: M. Clingeleffer

Batting—R. Knapman 9–2–197–46–0–28.14; *R. Bryan 9–1–215–75*–0–26.87; J. Marshall 10–2–151–46*–0–18.87.

Bowling—R. Knapman 75–12–212–20–4/11–10.60; G. Wilson 92–14–294–16–4/55–18.37.

SHERBORNE SCHOOL   *Played 10: W 4, L 2, D 4. A 3*

Master i/c: M. D. Nurton   Professional: A. Willows

Batting—J. Adams 13–1–459–83–0–38.25; J. Fradgley 12–1–313–66–0–28.45; B. Scott 11–2–229–65*–0–25.44; C. Warren 13–1–249–59–0–20.75; M. Shearer 11–0–207–67–0–18.81.

Bowling—J. Adams 63–19–151–18–6/14–8.38; W. Newbery 75.4–11–281–15–5/26–18.73; D. Reece-Smith 135–35–336–17–4/28–19.76.

SHREWSBURY SCHOOL   *Played 15: W 4, L 3, D 8. A 4*

Master i/c: M. J. Lascelles   Professional: A. P. Pridgeon

The captain and leading all-rounder, Ian McCarter, went on to captain MCC Schools and English Schools.

Batting—B. J. Champkin 10–3–260–53–0–37.14; S. T. Corbett 9–2–230–95*–0–32.85; *I. J. W. McCarter 13–1–381–76–0–31.75; A. S. Umpleby 9–1–214–63–0–26.75; M. C. H. Sanderson 8–1–153–65–0–21.85; R. G. Hillman 13–1–203–44–0–16.91.

Bowling—W. M. Lilley 78–13–219–18–3/2–12.16; I. J. W. McCarter 136–30–388–30–5/43–12.93.

SIMON LANGTON GRAMMAR SCHOOL   *Played 15: W 7, L 6, D 2*

Master i/c: R. H. Green

Although the side began the season with the smallest senior squad for many years, they finished with a creditable record and were runners-up in the Lemon (Kent) Cup.

Batting—T. Bilyard 14–3–428–137–2–38.90; D. Lloyd-James 7–1–184–71–0–30.66; *D. Patching 12–2–293–58*–0–29.30; J. Murphy 12–1–234–69–0–21.27; J. Uglow 10–0–177–55–0–17.70; C. Livesey 15–0–192–34–0–12.80.

Bowling—D. Patching 103.5–25–307–21–5/34–14.61; J. Murphy 111.2–23–344–22–5/14–15.63.

SIR ROGER MANWOOD'S SCHOOL   *Played 7: W 3, L 2, D 2. A 3*

Master i/c: J. F. Willmott

The Kent Under-15 representative, Lewis Jenkins, opened the batting with excellent technique and timing to lay the foundation for match-winning totals. James Hoople bowled with pace and penetration, but was handicapped by dropped catches.

Batting—L. Jenkins 6–0–177–73–0–29.50.

Bowling—No bowler took 15 wickets. The leading bowler was J. Hoople 47–3–195–9–5/25–21.66.

SOLIHULL SCHOOL   *Played 16: W 9, L 3, D 4. A 4*

Master i/c: S. A. Morgan   Professional: A. Farooque

Batting—J. A. Spires 15–4–462–85*–0–42.00; M. Travis 9–0–243–104*–1–27.00; W. Gilbert 10–2–162–73–0–20.25; N. Fowles 14–2–223–76–0–18.58; J. Hawkins 13–0–171–59–0–13.15; M. Hartley 14–0–171–33–0–12.21.

Bowling—J. A. Spires 152–27–431–44–5/16–9.79; C. Adams 78–11–291–15–2/34–19.40; M. Fent 81–13–334–17–3/24–19.64; *R. Robinson 117–16–450–18–3/20–25.00.

STAMFORD SCHOOL   *Played 12: W 1, L 6, D 5. A 6*

Master i/c: J. M. H. Beale

Batting—M. Shepard 10–1–286–94–0–31.77; G. Hawkins 12–3–269–73–0–29.88; *J. Fuller 11–1–205–54*–0–20.50; H. Wickham 12–0–173–51–0–14.41.

Bowling—D. McDonald 143.1–31–479–15–4/18–31.93.

STOCKPORT GRAMMAR SCHOOL   *Played 7: W 5, L 1, D 1. A 6*

Master i/c: A. Brett   Professional: D. J. Makinson

Batting—No batsman scored 150 runs. The leading batsman was S. Brown 4–0–113–77–0–28.25.

Bowling—No bowler took 15 wickets. The leading bowler was S. Wilkinson 58–12–195–12–5/35–16.25.

STOWE SCHOOL   *Played 10: W 2, L 1, D 7. A 4*

Master i/c: M. J. Harris

Batting—R. A. White 12–0–560–116–2–46.66; J. R. W. McDonagh 12–3–339–100*–1–37.66; *R. A. Harris 12–1–311–84–0–28.27; T. I. Pearce 12–0–237–61–0–19.75.

Bowling—R. A. Harris 134–20–369–19–5/35–19.42; R. A. White 157–26–412–19–5/70–21.68.

STRATHALLAN SCHOOL   *Played 10: W 4, L 1, D 5. A 6*

Master i/c: R. J. W. Proctor   Professional: I. L. Philip

Weather interruptions were particularly unwelcome to Strathallan's best team for years. There was some consolation in the all-round contribution of the captain, Robin Dicke, and a last-over win, chasing 219, against Edinburgh Academy.

Batting—C. A. Stevens 7–2–246–117*–1–49.20; *R. H. W. J. Dicke 9–3–231–60*–0–38.50; I. Stewart 9–1–275–83*–0–34.37; A. O. Sutherland 7–0–159–43–0–22.71; D. N. Mapleston 8–0–153–48–0–19.12.

Bowling—R. H. W. J. Dicke 123–30–311–18–3/18–17.27; D. N. Mapleston 142.5–41–406–22–5/29–18.45; I. Stewart 109–22–342–16–4/8–21.37; M. S. Elder 118–17–432–15–4/34–28.80.

SUTTON VALENCE SCHOOL   *Played 17: W 6, L 6, D 5. A 1*

Master i/c: J. H. Kittermaster   Professional: A. R. Day

In his first five innings, 16-year-old Matthew Day hit four consecutive fifties and in the win over the XL Club, became the youngest to score a hundred for the side. He was well supported with the bat by all-rounder Matthew Wooderson. As the smallest school playing in the Sir Garfield Sobers Tournament in Barbados, the side did especially well to reach the semi-finals.

Batting—M. J. A. Day 16–3–622–102*–1–47.84; M. G. J. Wooderson 15–1–420–81*–0–30.00; *T. Watts 12–2–225–65–0–22.50; G. H. Horton 16–2–304–74–0–21.71; F. Debney 13–3–150–34–0–15.00.

Bowling—M. G. J. Wooderson 132.3–11–518–27–4/28–19.18; J. Vincent 143.3–21–575–24–4/10–23.95; I. D. Harrison 123.4–22–443–18–2/12–24.61; T. Watts 140.2–14–476–16–3/36–29.75.

TAUNTON SCHOOL   *Played 9: W 3, L 2, D 4. A 3*

Master i/c: D. Baty   Professional: A. Kennedy

In the ten-wicket win over Clifton, L. Cooper and S. Rose (son of former Somerset captain Brian Rose) compiled an unbroken partnership of 153. Another highlight was the match against MCC, when past players and captains joined in celebrations of the school's 150th anniversary.

Batting—D. Law 8–5–272–110*–1–90.66; L. Cooper 7–2–206–74*–0–41.20; *R. Selway 7–1–244–79*–0–40.66; H. Tarr 6–1–168–37*–0–33.60.

Bowling—No bowler took 15 wickets. The leading bowler was M. Wood 62–8–181–12–4/18–15.08.

TIFFIN SCHOOL   *Played 14: W 1, L 5, D 8. A 5*

Master i/c: M. J. Williams

Batting—B. W. O'Connell 11–0–447–125–1–40.63; C. D. O'Connell 12–0–300–97–0–25.00; D. J. Procter 10–1–176–63–0–19.55; D. A. Urquhart 10–0–161–50–0–16.10; T. C. Aldred 13–1–185–34–0–15.41; I. J. Lulham 12–0–173–63–0–14.41.

Bowling—B. W. O'Connell 196.4–55–542–23–5/42–23.56.

TONBRIDGE SCHOOL   *Played 16: W 14, L 0, D 2. A 3*

Master i/c: P. B. Taylor   Professional: C. Stone

A Christmas tour to Australia was followed by the most successful season to date, in which the side were unbeaten and won 14 of their 16 games, bowling out the opposition 13 times. Ten centuries were scored in all, including four each from Matthew Banes and James McCulley. This exceptional opening pair shared four century partnerships, including 215 unbroken to beat the Band of Brothers. Off-spinner Robert Kemp bowled tirelessly for his 39 wickets. Banes played for MCC Schools, represented Kent and was a member of the England Under-17 development squad; McCulley played for Surrey Second Eleven and Dan Cherry for Glamorgan Second Eleven.

Batting—M. J. Banes 17–4–970–141*–4–74.61; *J. J. McCulley 17–3–965–125–4–68.92; J. G. C. Rowe 15–5–636–118*–1–63.60; D. D. Cherry 15–2–417–101–1–32.07; R. P. W. M. Hands 14–5–265–86–0–29.44.

Bowling—R. C. Kemp 252–59–661–39–5/58–16.94; D. D. Cherry 156.1–33–519–29–6/43–17.89; R. A. Brown 148.1–30–496–26–4/16–19.07; D. Hall 182.4–52–464–23–3/18–20.17.

TRENT COLLEGE   *Played 14: W 5, L 5, D 4. A 1*

Master i/c: Dr T. P. Woods   Professional: G. Miller

Determination and hard work brought the side four successive victories before half term. Although the batsmen struggled for consistency, the bowlers dominated. Two highlights were supplied by the Jordison brothers: David, the elder, took seven for 37 against Loughborough GS, and John – who had taken all ten for the Under-12 side in 1993 – returned seven for 23 against Wellingborough. No one had taken seven in an innings for the first team since 1988.

Batting—A. P. Siddall 14–3–385–63–0–35.00; *D. I. Jordison 14–1–380–74*–0–29.23; F. L. Larke 14–0–224–49–0–16.00.

Bowling—P. J. Kilburn 58.3–13–131–18–6/27–7.27; J. R. Jordison 138–35–296–25–7/23–11.84; R. B. Arnold 64–18–186–15–4/18–12.40; D. I. Jordison 168.1–49–408–25–7/37–16.32; A. P. Siddall 147.2–37–347–18–3/15–19.27.

TRINITY SCHOOL   *Played 13: W 5, L 5, D 3. A 5*

Master i/c: C. R. Burke

Batting—*R. Mutucumarana 13–2–686–138*–2–62.36; B. Cox 9–2–410–89*–0–58.57; M. Macaskill 10–2–311–61–0–38.87; A. Mutucumarana 9–2–259–106*–1–37.00.

Bowling—R. Mutucumarana 186–29–635–31–5/32–20.48; A. Yazoani 131–24–485–23–5/32–21.08; A. Hayes 133–20–427–16–3/38–26.68.

TRURO SCHOOL   *Played 13: W 5, L 6, D 2. A 5*

Master i/c: D. M. Phillips

Batting—L. Barrick 11–3–270–80–0–33.75; B. P. Price 11–0–293–116–1–26.63; P. J. Harris 10–1–170–50–0–18.88; *J. S. Price 11–0–188–58–0–17.09; M. J. Macmahon 12–0–164–46–0–13.66.

Bowling—No bowler took 15 wickets. The leading bowler was M. E. Phillips 65.2–17–177–13–4/6–13.61.

UNIVERSITY COLLEGE SCHOOL   *Played 12: W 3, L 5, D 4. A 5*

Master i/c: S. M. Bloomfield   Professional: W. G. Jones

Batting—*P. J. Durban 9–1–329–101–1–41.12; S. R. Nair 8–1–208–53*–0–29.71; D. M. Stewart 10–1–228–80*–0–25.33; M. K. Floyd 9–0–163–46–0–18.11.

Bowling—S. R. Nair 152.3–57–364–20–5/24–18.20; J. Rose 135–31–364–19–3/17–19.15.

UPPINGHAM SCHOOL   *Played 11: W 2, L 2, D 7. A 4*

Master i/c: I. E. W. Sanders   Professional: B. T. P. Donelan

The season's highlight was an unbroken second-wicket partnership of 216 between James Brydon and Edward Watts to beat Stamford by nine wickets. Both scored centuries. Nicholas Pont was selected to attend a two-week coaching course with Dennis Lillee in India.

Batting—J. W. M. Thomson 4–1–215–71–0–71.66; *J. A. Brydon 9–2–286–120*–1–40.85; R. E. C. Watts 11–2–362–104*–1–40.22; A. S. B. Lees 10–1–195–52–0–21.66.

Bowling—N. J. Pont 119.5–30–281–17–4/32–16.52.

VICTORIA COLLEGE, JERSEY   *Played 20: W 3, L 5, D 12. A 3*

Master i/c: D. A. R. Ferguson   Professional: C. McE. Minty

Batting—J. E. Mashiter 17–3–567–110–1–40.50; F. D. McInnes 13–2–381–68–0–34.63; R. O. Thompson 17–2–511–116*–1–34.06; A. M. B. Thomas 9–0–242–80–0–26.88; I. J. A. MacEacuern 16–1–393–89*–0–26.20; D. Mills 11–1–193–51–0–19.30; R. D. Minty 16–2–258–62*–0–18.42.

Bowling—N. S. Broughton 181–40–564–29–8/31–19.44; R. O. Thompson 216–55–712–32–5/43–22.25.

WARWICK SCHOOL   *Played 10: W 4, L 3, D 3. A 4*

Master i/c: G. A. Tedstone

Batting—*A. J. Preece 8–2–162–59*–0–27.00; J. M. Moffatt 8–1–182–75*–0–26.00.

Bowling—No bowler took 15 wickets. The leading bowler was J. D. Tickle 84.4–19–251–14–5/33–17.92.

WATFORD GRAMMAR SCHOOL   *Played 14: W 3, L 6, D 5. A 1*

Master i/c: R. W. Panter

Against Dr Challoner's, S. Farrell scored 106 not out and R. Hodgkinson took six for nine as the opposition were shot out for 29 in reply to 226 for three declared.

Batting—S. Farrell 13–2–502–106*–2–45.63; J. C. Phang 14–1–441–86–0–33.92; J. A. Rylett 14–1–327–78–0–25.15.

Bowling—J. A. Rylett 68–5–265–15–3/61–17.66; *R. L. Hodgkinson 131.5–25–447–25–6/9–17.88.

WELLINGBOROUGH SCHOOL   *Played 16: W 7, L 2, D 7. A 3*

Master i/c: M. H. Askham   Professional: J. C. J. Dye

Joss Lilley was the first 15-year-old to score a century for the first team.

Batting—L. L. Jones 12–1–539–112–1–49.00; J. P. Lilley 13–4–406–107*–1–45.11; T. C. Gee 10–5–184–68*–0–36.80; J. P. Phipps 9–3–206–60–0–34.33.

Bowling—K. A. C. Saville 213.2–44–667–39–5/45–17.10; R. Johnson 155.2–37–446–26–5/42–17.15.

WELLINGTON COLLEGE   *Played 16: W 1, L 8, D 7. A 2*

Masters i/c: C. M. St G. Potter and R. I. H. B. Dyer   Professional: P. J. Lewington

Jamie McDonald held 28 catches as wicket-keeper and led a side that was more competitive than the results suggest.

Batting—A. J. Clowes 18–3–472–89–0–31.46; J. A. Chicken 9–1–216–58–0–27.00; C. J. Ferguson-Davie 8–1–158–79–0–22.57; J. D. Clowes 17–0–346–64–0–20.35; J. L. Lewis 17–3–270–56–0–19.28; T. A. J. Acton 11–1–166–49–0–16.60; *J. J. McDonald 14–4–161–64*–0–16.10; S. J. Lamplough 13–3–151–31–0–15.10.

Bowling—P. C. Melville 180.1–31–461–29–5/44–15.89; S. J. Lamplough 179.2–35–540–31–5/20–17.41; S. F. Streatfeild 129.2–19–439–17–3/30–25.82.

WELLINGTON SCHOOL   *Played 18: W 5, L 6, D 6, T 1. A 2*

Master i/c: P. M. Pearce

The side recorded three close finishes: Exeter School won in the last over with the last pair at the wicket; Colston's were beaten by four runs with two overs to spare; and they tied with Torquay CC Midweek XI on a tour of Devon.

Batting—J. P. Derbyshire 17–1–530–100*–1–33.12; B. A. House 17–2–409–131*–1–27.26; *S. M. Gallagher 17–1–316–67–0–19.75; B. J. Rogers 15–1–264–64–0–18.85; T. R. C. Eve 16–2–198–45–0–14.14; L. J. Greany 16–1–181–32*–0–12.06.

Bowling—S. W. Turner 139–25–460–29–5/24–15.86; T. R. C. Eve 85.4–8–347–19–4/30–18.26; L. J. Greany 80–12–315–16–5/35–19.68; J. P. Derbyshire 79.4–9–367–15–4/12–24.46; J. C. McKenny 116–14–538–21–4/11–25.61.

WELLS CATHEDRAL SCHOOL   *Played 9: W 1, L 8, D 0*

Master i/c: M. Stringer

Batting—*B. Clements 9–0–352–66–0–39.11; M. Shercliff 9–0–174–38–0–19.33.

Bowling—No bowler took 15 wickets. The leading bowler was B. Clements 72–10–312–13–5/9–24.00.

WESTMINSTER SCHOOL   *Played 11: W 1, L 3, D 7. A 5*

Master i/c: G. P. A. Brown   Professional: R. Butcher

Batting—B. Gordon 6–0–285–115–1–47.50; J. Korgaonkar 11–0–359–92–0–32.63; R. Bamford 11–0–250–73–0–22.72.

Bowling—R. Bamford 87–9–334–15–4/18–22.26.

WHITGIFT SCHOOL   *Played 17: W 5, L 1, D 11. A 2*

Master i/c: P. C. Fladgate   Professional: D. M. Ward

Trevor Clarke dominated the batting with 722 runs, including a match-winning 111 not out against St John's, and also headed the bowling with his leg-spin. Nishil Patel again passed 500 runs, and James Furner scored 114 against Reigate GS. Fast-medium bowlers Andy Hooper and left-armer Kavel Patel both made excellent progress, and all age groups benefited from David Ward's contribution as coach.

Batting—T. Clarke 17–7–722–111*–1–72.20; N. A. Patel 15–3–526–92–0–43.83; *J. P. Furner 9–2–296–114–1–42.28; A. Goward 13–2–288–69*–0–26.18; D. G. N. Pawan 9–2–163–46–0–23.28.

Bowling—T. Clarke 153.2–30–430–24–5/25–17.91; A. Hooper 158.2–29–471–24–6/76–19.62; K. Patel 160–25–439–19–4/16–23.10.

WINCHESTER COLLEGE   *Played 11: W 3, L 3, D 5. A 8*

Master i/c: C. J. Good

Batting—T. Powell Jackson 11–2–433–122*–1–48.11; E. Witcomb 10–1–210–82–0–23.33; R. Okeeffe 10–2–170–55–0–21.25; J. Arnold-Curtis 8–0–157–46–0–19.62; S. McArthur 11–0–182–36–0–16.54.

Bowling—C. Foster 126–33–396–19–3/48–20.84; W. Close-Brooks 129–31–376–16–4/30–23.50.

WOODBRIDGE SCHOOL   *Played 9: W 3, L 3, D 3. A 3*

Master i/c: C. Seal

Batting—M. Johnston 7–0–209–73–0–29.85.

Bowling—No bowler took 15 wickets. The leading bowler was E. Parker 69–19–223–14–4/35–15.92.

WOODHOUSE GROVE SCHOOL   *Played 10: W 3, L 2, D 5. A 6*

Master i/c: R. I. Frost   Professional: G. R. J. Roope

Undefeated in the first eight matches, the side then lost the last two. Nick Smith played for Yorkshire Senior Schools and Nick Verity for Yorkshire Under-16. The school's first overseas cricket tour to Zimbabwe was planned for March.

Batting—G. M. Bennett 10–0–187–50–0–18.70; N. R. Smith 10–0–158–82–0–15.80.

Bowling—No bowler took 15 wickets. The leading bowler was N. Verity 38–6–143–13–5/41–11.00.

WORKSOP COLLEGE   *Played 14: W 7, L 0, D 7*

Master i/c: C. G. Paton   Professional: A. Kettleborough

The side was unbeaten and won half their matches in a season that saw some notable batting performances: R. Turner and B. W. Moore shared a record opening stand of 242 against Repton, and G. E. D. Harvey scored 104 in 84 minutes against Mount St Mary's. P. D. J. Chapman bowled with accuracy and guile to head the averages in his first season and H. E. Straw was selected for England Under-15.

Batting—G. E. D. Harvey 14–4–583–104*–1–58.30; R. Turner 14–2–568–122–1–47.33; B. W. Moore 14–0–446–114–1–31.85; H. E. Straw 13–3–300–78–0–30.00.

Bowling—P. D. J. Chapman 149–17–500–28–6/62–17.85; G. E. D. Harvey 141–30–410–20–5/11–20.50; R. Turner 115–25–481–18–4/45–26.72.

WREKIN COLLEGE   *Played 12: W 6, L 3, D 3. A 1*

Master i/c: M. de Weymarn   Professional: D. A. Banks

In an enjoyable season in which the batting was better than the bowling, Andrew Murison proved a useful all-rounder.

Batting—W. Merrick 8–2–316–78–0–52.66; *V. Padhaal 7–0–232–58–0–33.14; A. Murison 11–3–240–83*–0–30.00; P. Snodgrass 8–1–185–50–0–26.42.

Bowling—A. Murison 99–18–291–15–4/29–19.40.

WYCLIFFE COLLEGE   *Played 10: W 4, L 3, D 3. A 4*

Master i/c: C. R. C. Tetley   Professional: N. Martin

Batting—*L. Bowery 9–4–191–52*–0–38.20; G. Williams 9–1–203–60–0–25.37; A. Drury 8–1–173–58–0–24.71; A. Gidman 9–1–184–50*–0–23.00; A. Stait 9–1–181–60–0–22.62.

Bowling—A. Gidman 88.3–14–284–19–5/27–14.94; G. Williams 95–21–283–17–4/22–16.64.

WYGGESTON & QUEEN ELIZABETH I COLLEGE   *Played 9: W 4, L 4, D 1. A 3*

Master i/c: G. G. Wells

In a run-chase against Lawrence Sheriff GS, Matthew Ferns struck 11 fours in two overs, including nine in succession.

Batting—S. Patel 8–6–165–45*–0–82.50; M. Ferns 5–2–236–81*–0–78.66; *K. Jogia 9–0–182–49–0–20.22.

Bowling—No bowler took 15 wickets. The leading bowler was P. Shiva 75–14–277–11–3/52–25.18.

YOUTH CRICKET, 1997

UNDER-17 CRICKET

Northamptonshire staged a dramatic come-back to beat Hampshire in the final of the Texaco Under-17 County Championship. In a two-day match staged at New Road, Worcester, they were reduced to 92 for eight after being forced to bat first on a drying wicket. However, captain Mark Chatfield and tailender Mark Dobson steered the team to 162. Left-arm spinner Charlie Van der Gucht still finished with figures of four for 17 in 17.4 overs. Hampshire then collapsed to 45 for six and next morning crumpled to 66 all out. Dobson – whose unbeaten 36 was the highest score of the match – took three for 31 and his new-ball partner Richard Logan four for 20.

UNDER-16 CRICKET

Sussex won the Lord's Taverners Under-16 County Championship, beating Wales by eight wickets in the final at Finchampstead. In its second year, the Britvic Inner Cities Cup, organised by the Lord's Taverners, gained a preliminary qualifying round. Eight teams won through to the three-day final event at Arundel – Birmingham, Bristol, Glasgow, Leeds, Liverpool, London (North), Nottingham and Swansea – while Cardiff, Leicester, London (South), Manchester, Sheffield, Sunderland and Wolverhampton were eliminated. Bristol received a bye when Belfast's travel arrangements fell through, and went on to reach the final, where they lost to Birmingham by three wickets. For players to be eligible for the tournament, they must live within a ten-mile radius of their city centre – as defined by its postal code – and they must not have previously played cricket at national or county level.

UNDER-15 CRICKET

Despite winning only one of their three matches, the Midlands were overall champions at the annual Bunbury ESCA Festival. They beat the South and drew their other two games, while the South and the West both won one, drew one and lost one. The North failed to record any victories, but in Lee Rushworth they had the outstanding batsman of the tournament. Rushworth's 96 against the Midlands was the highest score of the week, and won him the Neil Lloyd Trophy.

Millfield were the predictable winners of the Lord's Taverners/*Cricketer* Colts Trophy for Schools, which they claimed for the third year running, and the eighth time in 12 years. They travelled to Trent Bridge for the final, but their opponents, Nottingham High School, hardly benefited from home advantage. Nottingham struggled to 93 for eight in their 40 overs, in response to Millfield's efficiently compiled 212 for six. The highlight of the competition came in a qualifying match between King's School, Tynemouth, and Durham's Parkside School. Gary Pratt of Parkside hit an unbeaten 158 out of their total of 207 for three, and then took four for 18 as King's were bowled out for 130.

Horsham failed to retain the Sun Life of Canada Under-15 Club Championship, but only by a hair's breadth. In the final, they set a target of 140 in 20 overs for their opponents, Cornwall's St Just, who mounted an expert run chase. Neil Curnow hit 67 from 55 balls before falling in the final over, and the players went off when the last ball, a wide signalled by Dickie Bird, brought the scores level. St Just won by virtue of losing two wickets to Horsham's five. In the ESCA/Lord's Taverners County Championship, Lancashire beat Norfolk by 99 runs in the semi-final, thanks to Craig Ferguson's 115, and then shaded Cornwall in the final. Lancashire could only set a target of 90, but Chris Barrow claimed figures of 7–2–8–5 as Cornwall were bowled out for 75.

UNDER-13 CRICKET

For the second year running, Oakham School played host to five days of finals for the Subaru Under-13 Club Championship. A total of 1,487 clubs entered the tournament and, after 39 county competitions and eight regional finals, eight teams went through to the finals week. Norfolk club Horsford came out on top after a round-robin, in which they won all seven of their games. Their captain, John Sutton, took five wickets for 12 runs against Cardiff, while Michael Pickett made 35 against Wolverhampton, and collected more runs and wickets in the game against Purley of Surrey, the runners-up.

The order in which the finalists finished was: Horsford, Purley, Hull (Yorkshire), Cardiff (Wales), Hetton Lyons (Durham), Wolverhampton (Staffordshire), Houghton on the Hill (Leicestershire), Weston-super-Mare (Somerset). Each team consists of eight players, who bat in pairs for five overs each, starting with a base score of 200 and conceding eight runs each time they lose a wicket. Horsford's squad comprised Sutton, Pickett, Lee Bowker, Shaun Burridge, Lee Cornfield, Jonathan Fudge, Edward Hopkins, Rory Lintott, John Spelman and George Walker.

Millfield won the Calypso Cup for schools, beating Lancaster Royal Grammar by eight wickets at Headingley. More than 1,000 schools took part.

UNDER-11 CRICKET

The sponsorship deal for the annual Hardball Competition fell through, but ESCA decided to continue the tournament's funding until a new sponsor could be found. Four of the 12 teams that made it through to the finals day came from state schools, and one of them – Gilmour Junior School, from Liverpool – won the title. Another state school, Dale Primary from Derby, finished third, while Town Close Prep School from Norwich were the runners-up.

Dale Primary did even better at the finals of the Wrigley Softball Cricket Tournament, held as usual at Edgbaston. They squeezed past King Alfred from Shaftesbury by seven runs in the semi-finals, and then beat Peny Gaer of Llanelli by a resounding 25 runs in the final. Dale Primary's squad comprised: Raza Hussain, Asad Hussain, Adnan Taj, Taieb Razaq, Mazher Qayyum, Muddasair Hussain, Manpreet Butoy and Nahman Khaliq. England players Mark Ramprakash and Robert Croft attended the event, and made presentations to the children. Both of these competitions follow an eight-a-side format, in which the teams begin with 200 runs and lose six of them every time a wicket falls, but the batsman stays in.

WOMEN'S CRICKET, 1997

By CAROL SALMON

SOUTH AFRICAN WOMEN IN ENGLAND, 1997

The South Africans' first tour of England provided useful preparation for the World Cup in December. There were no Tests, but England won the one-day internationals 2-1, and hoped to make it 4-1 until rain ruined the last two games. In the fourth, South Africa were in poor shape at 59 for five; the fifth was completely washed out. England had clearly learned from their disappointments in 1996, when New Zealand won all three one-day matches; their running between the wickets, in particular, was more aggressive.

England completed easy wins in the first and third games, slipping up only at Taunton. At Bristol, Charlotte Edwards and Helen Plimmer opened with a stand of 74 before vice-captain Sue Metcalfe scored an unbeaten 51; left-arm seamer Sue Redfern wrecked the reply with four wickets. The batting was even stronger at Taunton, where 17-year-old Edwards completed her maiden century for England, with 15 fours in 113 balls, and Jane Cassar (née Smit) hit a breezy fifty to reach 253 for five. But South Africa successfully promoted tailender Denise Reid as a pinch-hitter. Despite being dropped five times, she put on 105 for the first wicket with Linda Olivier. Even in the final over, with nine needed to win, England's woeful fielding let chances go begging, and South Africa scrambled home by two wickets. That encouraged the South Africans to bat first at Lord's, but this time Reid went cheaply. The target was a mere 135, which England reached with nearly ten overs in hand. Metcalfe took her series aggregate to 144 for once out, with WCA executive director Barbara Daniels adding fifty.

Press interest centred on England's break with tradition in adopting trousers instead of the divided skirts known as Mayfield Shorts. Some WCA members disapproved, but the players said trousers helped them to field more athletically, protecting them from grazed knees – not to mention intruding television cameras. They also wore the three lions emblem of the ECB, and were sponsored by Vodafone, like the men's team.

Metcalfe and Edwards, who averaged over 50, led the way with the bat; Redfern took nine wickets at 10.44 and captain Karen Smithies five, conceding only 2.55 an over. Olivier, who scored 176 at 58.66, and Helen Davies, with 141, were South Africa's biggest successes.

The South African coach, former West Indian Test player Conrad Hunte, was pleased with his team's progress; before the England series, they had played three one-day internationals against Ireland and won all of them. Hunte has played an important role in the rebirth of women's cricket in South Africa. They had been isolated since New Zealand toured the Republic in 1972, but the provincial tournament has quickly expanded to 11 sides, and the England Under-21s were invited to visit in 1998.

SOUTH AFRICAN TOURING PARTY

K. Price (Western Province) (*captain*), L. Olivier (Transvaal) (*vice-captain*), A. L. Bezuidenhout (North West), A. A. Burger (Northern Transvaal), H. A. Davies (Western Province), C. Eksteen (Free State), D. Hughes (Free State), L. Korkie (Free State), A. Kotze (Transvaal), A. Kuylaars (Western Province), K. A. Laing (Transvaal), D. J. Reid (Western Province), L. Sing (Natal), R. Stoop (Natal), D. Terblanche (Transvaal).
Manager: C. Roberts. *Coach:* C. C. Hunte.

[*WCA Archives*   [*Graham Chadwick*

The long and the short of it: Jackie Court and Hilary Dodds (left) wearing Mayfield Shorts, and Clare Connor with Karen Smithies (right) modelling the new-look trousers.

Note: Matches in this section were not first-class.

At Bristol, August 15. First one-day international: England won by 79 runs. Toss: South Africa. England 227 for six (50 overs) (C. M. Edwards 45, H. C. Plimmer 47, J. S. Metcalfe 51 not out); South Africa 148 for nine (50 overs) (H. A. Davies 64; S. Redfern four for 21).

At Taunton, August 17. Second one-day international: South Africa won by two wickets. Toss: England. England 253 for five (50 overs) (C. M. Edwards 102, J. S. Metcalfe 44, J. Cassar 50 not out); South Africa 254 for eight (50 overs) (L. Olivier 60, D. J. Reid 56, H. A. Davies 48).

At Lord's, August 20. Third one-day international: England won by seven wickets. Toss: South Africa. South Africa 134 (46.3 overs) (L. Olivier 57; K. Smithies three for 15); England 135 for three (40.3 overs) (B. A. Daniels 53, J. S. Metcalfe 49 not out).

At Hinckley, August 27. Fourth one-day international: No result. Toss: England. South Africa 59 for five (27 overs) (L. Olivier 34 not out) v England.

At Milton Keynes, August 30. Fifth one-day international: England v South Africa. Abandoned.

ENGLISH WOMEN'S CRICKET, 1997

The 1997 season was probably the last for the Women's Cricket Association in its present form. Negotiations were advancing inexorably towards amalgamation with the England and Wales Cricket Board, which was already involved on the marketing front and expected to take full control in 1998. The benefits of operating under the ECB umbrella were demonstrated when Vodafone's sponsorship of the England men's team was extended to the women, a tremendous boost, which permitted a full week's preparation for their series with South Africa.

At grassroots level, the biggest change will be that all local organisations must be aligned with men's county clubs, whether first-class or minor. Lancashire and Cheshire, which have traditionally played as one women's team, have already split at junior level; Thames Valley, Western Counties, West Midlands, East Midlands and East Anglia will follow. Other teams, such as Yorkshire, Surrey and Kent, have already forged links with their county boards.

The WCA will take an expanding membership into the ECB. Club affiliations have grown over three years from 53 to 90; they had 1,443 registered players. Development projects were launched in Dorset, Durham, Essex, Lancashire and Oxford, similar to those which advanced the game in Derbyshire and Hampshire, who both made their debut in the County Championship in July.

Unlike the men's version, this is already played in divisions, and Yorkshire have been champions for the past six years. Again, they won all their five matches. Thames Valley won the Second Division, to replace East Anglia, who were relegated despite two hundreds from the prolific Charlotte Edwards. Sussex went down to the Third, while Derbyshire, who won all their games, were promoted at their first attempt. But Sussex turned the tables on Yorkshire by beating them in the Under-21 Championship final. Captain Clare Connor conceded just 13 runs in eight overs and hit 59 to set up a four-wicket victory. At Under-17 level, The West won the representative territorial tournament and West Midlands the eight-a-side area championship. Surrey were Under-15 champions.

In the club competitions, Kent Invicta successfully defended their National League title, adding the National Knockout Plate, while Wakefield retained the National Club Knockout. Wakefield had hoped to avenge the previous year's defeat by Invicta in the National League, but a combination of steady bowling, rash shots and poor running between the wickets undid them again. They made no mistake the following week, in the Club Knockout final. Kathryn Leng led them to victory with three wickets in North Riding's innings and 53 in the run-chase. Invicta strolled home in the Plate final; Liz Whelan and Kate Brown opened with 193 but Bradford managed only 71 between them.

England failed in their attempt to defend the World Cup in India in December 1997, when they were beaten by New Zealand in the semi-final. Australia won the final by five wickets. A full report will appear in *Wisden* 1999. The new world champions were due to visit England in 1998, playing three Tests and five one-day internationals. Like the recent New Zealand and South African tours, this was to be televised by BSkyB, providing welcome publicity for the women's game.

ENGLAND WORLD CUP PARTY

K. Smithies (East Midlands) (*captain*), J. S. Metcalfe (Yorkshire) (*vice-captain*), J. A. Brittin (Surrey), J. Cassar (East Midlands), C. J. Connor (Sussex), B. A. Daniels (West Midlands), C. M. Edwards (East Anglia), K. M. Leng (Yorkshire), L. MacLeod (Lancashire and Cheshire), B. Nicholson (Yorkshire), H. C. Plimmer (Yorkshire), S. Redfern (Derbyshire), M. A. Reynard (Yorkshire), C. E. Taylor (Yorkshire).

Manager: S. Taylor. *Coach:* M. Lear.

Note: Matches in this section were not first-class.

COUNTY CHAMPIONSHIP

Division One

	Played	Won	Lost	Points
Yorkshire	5	5	0	101
West Midlands	5	3	2	68.5
Surrey	5	3	2	68
Western Counties	5	2	3	53.5
Kent	5	1	4	43.5
East Anglia	5	1	4	33.5

Division Two

	Played	Won	Lost	Points
Thames Valley	5	4	1	84
Lancashire and Cheshire.	5	3	2	75
East Midlands	5	3	2	71.5
Yorkshire Second XI	5	3	2	69
Middlesex	5	1	4	37.5
Sussex	5	1	4	36.5

Division Three

	Played	Won	Lost	Points
Derbyshire	3	3	0	57.5
Surrey Second XI	3	2	1	46
Hampshire	3	1	2	29.5
Sussex Second XI	3	0	3	10.5

NATIONAL LEAGUE FINAL

At Campbell Park, Milton Keynes, September 7. Kent Invicta won by 14 runs. Toss: Kent Invicta. Kent Invicta 134 for nine (49 overs) (B. A. Daniels 34); Wakefield 120 (46.1 overs) (B. Nicholson 49).

NATIONAL CLUB KNOCKOUT FINAL

At Wolverhampton Cricket Club, September 14. Wakefield won by eight wickets. Toss: Wakefield. North Riding 124 (40 overs) (J. S. Metcalfe 77; K. M. Leng three for 30); Wakefield 125 for two (36.5 overs) (K. M. Leng 53, J. Tedstone 50 not out).

NATIONAL KNOCKOUT PLATE FINAL

At Wolverhampton Cricket Club, September 14. Kent Invicta won by 129 runs. Toss: Kent Invicta. Kent Invicta 200 for one (40 overs) (L. Whelan 102, K. Brown 80 not out); Bradford 71 for six (40 overs) (P. Weeks four for 22).

PART FIVE: OVERSEAS CRICKET IN 1996-97

FEATURES OF 1996-97

Double-Hundreds (37)

314*†	Wasim Jaffer	Mumbai v Saurashtra at Rajkot.
274*	J. L. Langer	Western Australia v South Australia at Perth.
267*	B. A. Young	New Zealand v Sri Lanka (First Test) at Dunedin.
257*	Wasim Akram	Pakistan v Zimbabwe (First Test) at Sheikhupura.
255	D. S. Lehmann	South Australia v Queensland at Adelaide.
254	V. Rathore	Punjab v Jammu and Kashmir at Amritsar.
251*	C. Z. Harris§	Canterbury v Central Districts at Rangiora.
250	R. Lamba	Delhi v Punjab at Delhi.
243*	G. W. Flower	Mashonaland v Matebeleland at Harare.
239†	S. K. Kulkarni	Mumbai v Saurashtra at Rajkot.
230	Jitender Singh§	Haryana v Himachal Pradesh at Chamba.
229*	Jitender Singh§	Haryana v Uttar Pradesh at Faridabad.
224	M. L. Hayden	Australian XI v West Indians at Hobart.
220*	Ajay Sharma	Delhi v Railways at Delhi.
218	J. R. Murray	Windward Islands v Guyana at St George's.
215	A. Dani	Delhi v Himachal Pradesh at Delhi.
214*	A. A. Muzumdar	Mumbai v Gujarat at Mumbai.
214	G. S. Blewett	Australia v South Africa (First Test) at Johannesburg.
212	P. H. Barnard	Griqualand West v Northern Transvaal at Kimberley.
210	A. M. Bacher	Transvaal v Griqualand West at Kimberley.
209	A. R. Khurasia	Madhya Pradesh v Bengal at Indore.
207*	D. Mongia	Punjab v Services at Delhi.
207	Chinmoy Sharma	Services v Himachal Pradesh at Delhi.
207	Iqbal Saleem	Karachi Whites v Faisalabad at Karachi.
206	C. Z. Harris§	Canterbury v Central Districts at Blenheim.
205	H. H. Kanitkar	Maharashtra v Gujarat at Pune.
202*	D. L. Haynes	Western Province v Eastern Province at Port Elizabeth.
201*	M. J. Mitchley	Easterns v Western Province B at Cape Town.
201	N. S. Sidhu	India v West Indies (Second Test) at Port-of-Spain.
200*	J. B. Commins	Western Province v Griqualand West at Kimberley.
200*	H. H. Gibbs	South Africans v India A at Nagpur.
200*	A. Mehra	Punjab v Orissa at Mohali.
200*	A. Ranatunga	Sinhalese SC v Sebastianites C and AC at Colombo.
200*	D. J. Watson	Natal v Leicestershire at Durban.
200	J. Cox	Tasmania v Pakistanis at Hobart.
200	K. N. A. Padmanabhan	Kerala v Orissa at Cuttack.
200	F. L. Reifer	Barbados v Windward Islands at Bridgetown.

† Wasim Jaffer and S. K. Kulkarni scored double-hundreds in the same innings. Jaffer was playing his second first-class match.

§ C. Z. Harris and Jitender Singh scored two double-hundreds.

Hundred on First-Class Debut

111	D. Chakraborty	Bihar v Tripura at Jamshedpur.

Three or More Hundreds in Successive Innings

R. S. Kaluwitharana (Colts CC) (4)	149	v Antonians SC at Colombo
	179	v Kurunegala Youth CC at Colombo
	157	and 107 v Galle CC at Colombo.
P. A. de Silva (Sri Lanka)	168	v Pakistan (First Test) at Colombo
	138*	and 103* v Pakistan (Second Test) at Colombo.
Mujahid Jamshed (Lahore City/Habib Bank)	129	Lahore City v Islamabad at Lahore
	102	Habib Bank v PIA at Karachi
	120	Habib Bank v Pakistan Customs at Karachi.
R. T. Ponting (Tasmania)...............	126	and 145* v South Australia at Hobart
	159	v Queensland at Hobart.
J. N. Rhodes (Natal).................	156*	v Free State at Durban
	108	v Eastern Province at Port Elizabeth
	137	v Transvaal at Johannesburg.
Ajay Sharma (Delhi).................	128	v Tamil Nadu at Delhi
	220*	v Railways at Delhi
	118	v Baroda at Delhi.

Hundred in Each Innings of a Match

A. M. Bacher.........	210	112*	Transvaal v Griqualand West at Kimberley.
J. Cox...............	143	125	Tasmania v New South Wales at Sydney.
P. A. de Silva	138*	103*	Sri Lanka v Pakistan (Second Test) at Colombo.
H. H. Gibbs.........	200*	171	South Africans v India A at Nagpur.
D. P. M. Jayawardene..	100*	106*	Sinhalese SC v Colts CC at Colombo.
R. S. Kaluwitharana ...	157	107	Colts CC v Galle CC at Colombo.
G. Kirsten	102	133	South Africa v India (Second Test) at Calcutta.
R. Lamba............	192	101	Delhi v Maharashtra at Pune.
R. T. Ponting.........	126	145*	Tasmania v South Australia at Hobart.

Hundred Before Lunch

H. H. Gibbs..........	47* to 163*	Western Province v Natal at Cape Town (2nd day).
S. Lee...............	1* to 101*	New South Wales v Tasmania at Hobart (4th day).

Carrying Bat Through Completed Innings

M. A. Atherton	94*	England (228) v New Zealand (Third Test) at Christchurch.
R. V. C. Prasad.......	141*	Andhra (265) v Goa at Panaji.

First-Wicket Partnerships of 100 in Each Innings

214	192	V. Dahiya/R. Lamba, Delhi v Maharashtra at Pune.
125	151	M. J. Slater/R. J. Davison, New South Wales v Tasmania at Sydney.
112	152	D. F. Hills/J. Cox, Tasmania v Western Australia at Perth.
139	106	M. E. Hussey/R. J. Campbell, Western Australia v Tasmania at Hobart.
145	131	R. A. Lawson/C. B. Gaffaney, Otago v Wellington at Wellington.

Other Notable Partnerships

First Wicket

459	Wasim Jaffer/S. K. Kulkarni, Mumbai v Saurashtra at Rajkot.
323	M. L. Hayden/M. T. G. Elliott, Australian XI v West Indians at Hobart.
313	B. M. McMillan/H. H. Gibbs, South Africans v India A at Nagpur.
281	Zahoor Elahi/Mujahid Jamshed, Lahore City v Islamabad at Lahore.

Second Wicket

309	S. S. Sugwekar/H. H. Kanitkar, Maharashtra v Punjab at Pune.
294	A. Jadeja/N. R. Goel, Haryana v Delhi at Gurgaon.

Third Wicket

313	A. Dani/Ajay Sharma, Delhi v Mumbai at Gwalior.
300*	H. H. Dippenaar/L. J. Wilkinson, Free State v Western Province at Bloemfontein.
291	R. Lamba/A. Malhotra, Delhi v Punjab at Delhi.
290	K. N. A. Padmanabhan/S. Oasis, Kerala v Orissa at Cuttack.
279	H. H. Kanitkar/S. V. Jedhe, Maharashtra v Gujarat at Pune.
277	S. I. Fernando/R. S. Kaluwitharana, Colts CC v Galle CC at Colombo.
275	P. A. Wallace/F. L. Reifer, Barbados v Windward Islands at Bridgetown.

Fourth Wicket

301	Nasir Ali/Iqbal Saleem, Karachi Whites v Faisalabad at Karachi.

Fifth Wicket

385	S. R. Waugh/G. S. Blewett, Australia v South Africa (First Test) at Johannesburg.
317*†	A. Ranatunga/R. P. A. H. Wickremaratne, Sinhalese SC v Sebastianites C and AC at Colombo.
290	C. Z. Harris/G. R. Stead, Canterbury v Central Districts at Blenheim.

Sixth Wicket

290	M. T. G. Elliott/D. S. Berry, Victoria v New South Wales at Sydney.
260	D. S. Lehmann/T. J. Nielsen, South Australia v Queensland at Adelaide.
239*	A. Gunawardene/H. P. Tillekeratne, Nondescripts CC v Galle CC at Colombo.

Seventh Wicket

263	N. Bordoloi/Sukhbinder Singh, Assam v Tripura at Agartala.
218	P. Krishnakumar/N. Negi, Rajasthan v Railways at Jaipur.

Eighth Wicket

313†	Wasim Akram/Saqlain Mushtaq, Pakistan v Zimbabwe (First Test) at Sheikhupura.
230	A. A. Muzumdar/P. L. Mhambrey, Mumbai v Gujarat at Mumbai.
222†	D. Arnolda/S. Madanayake, Burgher RC v Galle CC at Galle.

Tenth Wicket

138*	B. E. McNamara/P. J. S. Alley, New South Wales v Tasmania at Hobart.
118	Mahmood Hamid/Ali Gauhar, Karachi Blues v Bahawalpur at Karachi.
106*	N. J. Astle/D. K. Morrison, New Zealand v England (First Test) at Auckland.
102	S. Attanayake/B. Perera, Colts CC v Sinhalese SC at Colombo.
100	Sukhbinder Singh/I. Hussain, Assam v Bengal at Gauhati.

* Unbroken partnership.   † National record for that wicket.

Eight or More Wickets in an Innings (17)

9-15	M. Villavarayan	Bloomfield C and AC v Police SC at Colombo.
9-29	A. D. B. Ranjith	Singha SC v Antonians SC at Colombo.
9-48	A. R. Tait	Northern Districts v Auckland at Hamilton.
9-51	Aqib Javed	Allied Bank v Habib Bank at Lahore.

8-25	B. Ramprakash	Kerala v Karnataka at Palghat.
8-27	J. T. C. Vaughan	Auckland v Otago at Alexandra.
8-29	U. C. Hathurusinghe	Tamil Union C and AC v Burgher RC at Colombo.
8-31	D. G. Sewell	Otago v Central Districts at Invercargill.
8-43	Manzoor Elahi	Lahore City v Karachi Whites at Lahore.
8-50	A. D. B. Ranjith	Singha SC v Galle CC at Galle.
8-59	V. C. Drakes	Border v Natal at Durban.
8-64	L. Klusener	South Africa v India (Second Test) at Calcutta.
8-66	P. J. Wiseman	Otago v Wellington at Wellington.
8-70	Kabir Khan	Peshawar v Islamabad at Islamabad.
8-77	C. D. U. S. Weerasinghe	Nondescripts CC v Colts CC at Colombo.
8-78	C. N. Bandaratilleke	Tamil Union C and AC v Galle CC at Colombo.
8-134	A. V. Birrell	Eastern Province B v Easterns at Port Elizabeth.

Twelve or More Wickets in a Match (13)

16-130	A. R. Tait	Northern Districts v Auckland at Hamilton.
15-98	A. D. B. Ranjith	Singha SC v Galle CC at Galle.
15-187	U. C. Hathurusinghe	Tamil Union C and AC v Burgher RC at Colombo.
14-77	B. Ramprakash	Kerala v Karnataka at Palghat.
13-130	A. D. B. Ranjith	Singha SC v Antonians SC at Colombo.
12-80	K. G. Perera	Antonians SC v Kalutara Town CC at Wattala.
12-94	R. K. Chauhan	Madhya Pradesh v Orissa at Cuttack.
12-113	R. S. Kalpage	Sri Lanka A v West Indies A at Colombo.
12-122	Manzoor Elahi	Lahore City v Karachi Whites at Lahore.
12-134	Aqib Javed	Allied Bank v Habib Bank at Lahore.
12-134	Sukhbinder Singh	Assam v Bihar at Gauhati.
12-151	P. Jain	Haryana v Bihar at Patna.
12-155	R. K. Chauhan	Madhya Pradesh v Rajasthan at Bhilai.

Hat-Tricks

Aqib Javed	Allied Bank v Habib Bank at Lahore.
S. J. Hotter	Wellington v Otago at Wellington.
M. Kartik	Railways v Vidarbha at Delhi.
R. J. Kirtley	Mashonaland v Matabeleland at Bulawayo.
Nadeem Ghauri	Habib Bank v Pakistan Customs at Karachi.
R. L. Perera	Bloomfield C and AC v Burgher RC at Colombo.
Zahid Ahmed	PIA v PNSC at Sahiwal.

Wicket with First Ball in First-Class Cricket

Khalid Butt	Bahawalpur v Islamabad at Islamabad.
P. P. J. Koortzen	Griqualand West v Western Province at Kimberley.
Rashid Hanif	Karachi Whites v Islamabad at Islamabad.

Outstanding Innings Analysis

11.1–6–15–9	M. Villavarayan	Bloomfield C and AC v Police SC at Colombo.
4.5–4–2–6	Shahid Anwar	National Bank v Pakistan Customs at Karachi.
6–4–2–5	B. Mulder	Western Australia v New South Wales at Perth.

Most Overs Bowled in an Innings

| 93.5–30–191–6 | R. K. Chauhan | Madhya Pradesh v Mumbai at Indore. |

Most Overs Bowled in a Match

107.2–23–226–9 .. Saqlain Mushtaq Pakistan v Sri Lanka (First Test) at Colombo.

Six or More Wicket-Keeping Dismissals in an Innings

7 ct, 1 st ..... D. S. Berry Victoria v South Australia at Melbourne.
5 ct, 1 st ..... D. S. Berry Victoria v Queensland at Brisbane.
4 ct, 2 st ..... V. Kamaruddin Kerala v Hyderabad at Secunderabad.
4 ct, 2 st ..... M. Kudagodage Police SC v Panadura SC at Panadura.
6 ct.......... S. K. Kulkarni Mumbai v Haryana at Mumbai.
6 ct.......... M. S. Mudgal Uttar Pradesh v Hyderabad at Secunderabad.
2 ct, 4 st ..... S. T. Perera Bloomfield C and AC v Antonians SC at Colombo.

Eleven Wicket-Keeping Dismissals in a Match

10 ct, 1 st .... D. S. Berry Victoria v South Australia at Melbourne.

Five Catches in an Innings in the Field

B. C. Lara† .... Trinidad & Tobago v Leeward Islands at Port-of-Spain.

 † *Equalling national record.*

Seven Catches in a Match in the Field

S. Abbas Ali .... Madhya Pradesh v Orissa at Cuttack.

Match Double (100 Runs and 10 Wickets)

Sukhbinder Singh .. 89, 11*; 5-35, 7-99 Assam v Bihar at Gauhati.
Sukhbinder Singh .. 167; 5-20, 5-41 Assam v Tripura at Agartala.

 In consecutive matches.

No Byes Conceded in Total of 500 or More

S. K. L. de Silva.... Sri Lanka A v West Indies A (523-9 dec.) at Matara.
S. S. Dighe .... West Zone v Central Zone (503) at Delhi.
R. S. Kaluwitharana .. Sri Lanka v New Zealand (586-7 dec.) (First Test) at Dunedin.
M. E. L. Lane .... Canterbury v Northern Districts (518-4 dec.) at Christchurch.
P. A. Nixon .... Leicestershire v Natal (503-5 dec.) at Durban.
K. K. Patel.......... Madhya Pradesh v Maharashtra (519-5 dec.) at Pune.

Highest Innings Totals

777† .... Canterbury v Otago at Christchurch.
750-7 dec. .... Bengal v Bihar at Calcutta.
656 .... Delhi v Maharashtra at Pune.
647-4 .... Mumbai v Saurashtra at Rajkot.
630 .... Mumbai v Delhi at Gwalior.
628-8 dec. .... Australia v South Africa (First Test) at Johannesburg.
604-9 dec. .... Delhi v Punjab at Delhi.

 † *National record.*

Lowest Innings Totals

32	Northern Districts v Auckland at Hamilton.
48	Karachi Whites v Bahawalpur at Bahawalpur.
53	Lahore City v Peshawar at Peshawar.
54	Antonians SC v Bloomfield C and AC at Colombo.
57	Police SC v Colts CC at Colombo.
61	Central Districts v Auckland at Auckland.
63	Police SC v Bloomfield C and AC at Colombo.
64†	Singha SC v Burgher RC at Colombo.
65	Tripura v Assam at Agartala.
66	India v South Africa (First Test) at Durban.
69	Northern Districts v England XI at Hamilton.
70†	Kurunegala Youth CC v Antonians SC at Wattala.
71	Kalutara Town CC v Antonians SC at Wattala.
74	Central Districts v Otago at Invercargill.
74	Kalutara Town CC v Sinhalese SC at Colombo.
74	Karnataka v Kerala at Palghat.

† Two batsmen absent.

Match Aggregates of 1,500 Runs

Runs	Wkts	
1,527	31	Central Zone v West Zone at Delhi.
1,507	26	New South Wales v Tasmania at Sydney.

Four Hundreds in an Innings

Central Zone (500-3 dec.) v West Zone at Delhi:
G. K. Khoda 124, A. R. Khurasia 126, Rizwan Shamshad 120*, R. V. Sapru 100*.

Saurashtra (595-4 dec.) v Mumbai at Rajkot:
S. S. Tanna 141, B. M. Jadeja 132*, P. J. Bhatt 123, H. J. Parsana 100*.

Seven Fifties in an Innings

Bengal (750-7 dec.) v Bihar at Calcutta:
A. Varma 98, N. Haldipur 113, R. S. Gavaskar 70, P. K. Amre 78, U. Chatterjee 120, H. Feroze 152*, S. T. Banerjee 50.

Canterbury (777) v Otago at Christchurch:
D. J. Murray 59, S. P. Fleming 66, C. Z. Harris 198, C. D. McMillan 94, N. J. Astle 160, C. L. Cairns 57, M. W. Priest 56.

60 Extras in an Innings

	b	l-b	w	n-b	
70	40	9	0	21	PIA (356) v ADBP at Rawalpindi.
66	26	12	0	28	Barbados (394) v Trinidad & Tobago at Port-of-Spain.

Career Aggregate Milestones

15,000 runs	Salim Malik.
10,000 runs	B. C. Lara, Mansoor Rana, Ramiz Raja, P. V. Simmons.
500 wickets	Akram Raza.

ENGLAND IN ZIMBABWE AND NEW ZEALAND, 1996-97

By DAVID LLOYD

After four barren winters, England at last came home in something close to triumph when they convincingly won their Test series in New Zealand. Victories in Wellington and Christchurch enabled them to quieten their critics, and end – for a few months, anyway – speculation about the continuation of Mike Atherton's captaincy.

Beating a weak New Zealand team did not necessarily seem like preparation for victory over all-conquering Australia, but it was possible to discern rays of hope, both in the team's overall approach and in individual performances.

It had been a long time coming, though. The English winter began gloomily in Zimbabwe, where the visitors could do no better than draw both Tests, and lost all three one-day internationals rather humiliatingly. Worse still, by the time they left Harare for Auckland in early January, few Zimbabweans were sorry to see the back of the England party. They had accomplished the rare double of failing to win a single match of significance while adopting an approach widely regarded as unfriendly, aloof and, thanks to one crass comment from coach David Lloyd, downright rude. It was hard to think how England could have made a bigger mess of their first senior tour to cricket's ninth and newest Test country.

Form, both on and off the field, improved considerably in New Zealand. There is little doubt that lectures delivered in Harare by Lord MacLaurin, the new ECB chairman, played a part. Like most good employers, Lord MacLaurin criticised behind closed doors and praised in public – but it was clear he had not come to Zimbabwe armed with Christmas presents. And there was no attempt to conceal his delight when he next caught up with England, during their Wellington Test victory. "I'm very proud of them," he said.

It was that sort of campaign . . . a real mixed bag right to the end, when Atherton's squad squandered a 2-0 lead in the one-day international series with New Zealand and had to share those particular spoils. They could have won both Tests in Zimbabwe, but managed neither, and should have whitewashed New Zealand 3-0, but failed to take the one last wicket needed on a frustrating final afternoon at Auckland. Overall, though, results fairly reflected England's seesawing performances.

To claim that they underestimated Zimbabwe is to invite argument from the tour management. The facts, however, support the prosecution. England, having already decided 15 players (rather than the usual 16) would be sufficient, declined to replace Dominic Cork, the Derbyshire bowler, when he withdrew from stage one to sort out his troubled personal life. Only four days were set aside to acclimatise to conditions, including the problems created by altitude, before the first match in Zimbabwe. And this was in late November, when most members of the squad had neither bowled nor batted for two months, net practice having been omitted at a training camp in Portugal. Zimbabwe were surprised and somewhat offended by England's apparently cavalier approach. They had gained Test status in 1992 despite English opposition. England had not rushed to play them, so they were more than normally pleased to ambush them.

England were thrashed in two early preparatory games, by the President's XI and Mashonaland, and suddenly began to find that their squad was on the thin side. Atherton, initially handicapped by his chronic back problem, and Graham

Thorpe both lost form completely. The management had decided Alec Stewart would be first-choice wicket-keeper, which meant Jack Russell was sent into internal exile; and neither Ronnie Irani nor Andy Caddick was pushing hard for inclusion.

Before long, Craig White was summoned from a holiday in Australia, following his successful A tour, and played a Test within 72 hours of landing in Harare. By that stage, the First Test, in Bulawayo, had been drawn (famously so, with scores level) and coach Lloyd was just about the most unpopular man in Zimbabwe. He told anyone who would listen, and a fair number of locals who did not want to, that "we flippin' murdered them", a claim based on England's almost successful fourth-innings run-chase and Zimbabwe's defensive tactics during the final afternoon, which included far-flung fields and deliberately negative bowling, both sides of the stumps. In an ideal world the umpires would have been stricter in their interpretation of wides. Then again, in an ideal world England's attack would not have squandered the new ball on the opening day. At least Zimbabwe's bowlers were landing the ball roughly where they intended and, if deliveries are not deemed wide in the first hour of a match, then those equally off line during the last should not be penalised, either.

England spent a dreary Christmas minus their families (another poor decision by the tour planners, unlikely to be repeated), but were set to finish the stronger side in the Second Test before rain washed out the final day. Another moral victory? Maybe. But does any Test team dismissed for 156 in its first innings deserve too much sympathy? Nothing but condemnation followed England's performances during the last two one-day internationals: one they lost from a position of power, the other ended in a rout after an inspired spell of swing bowling from Eddo Brandes, who claimed a hat-trick. Zimbabwe celebrated while England were more than happy to say their goodbyes, having underperformed as a unit throughout and failed in their wider obligations as cricketing tourists. "Lord MacLaurin and I were horrified by what we saw in Zimbabwe," ECB chief executive Tim Lamb confirmed later. "We were not happy with the way the England team presented themselves. Their demeanour was fairly negative and not particularly attractive."

There were some individual successes to build on. While Zimbabwe's impressive leg-spinner, Paul Strang, would have topped most polls for the outstanding performer of the series, England had their candidates. Stewart, given the wicket-keeping gloves full time and guaranteed a No. 3 batting spot, proved thoroughly reliable behind the stumps and top-quality in front of them. It was deeply satisfying for a man whose international career had been written off a few months earlier. John Crawley batted with great discipline at No. 6, fast bowler Darren Gough looked almost back to his best after two tough years and spinners Robert Croft and Phil Tufnell quickly developed into a useful double act.

No one, on the other hand, looked more out of sorts in Zimbabwe than Atherton: he managed just 196 runs from 13 innings in all cricket. That return, combined with his team's lack of success, prompted an English journalist to ask at the opening press conference in New Zealand: "When are you going to do the decent thing and resign?" He perhaps reached his nadir on the day he was caught by Emily Drumm of the New Zealand women's team in a benefit match. He was unable even to pretend that he saw the funny side. There is little doubt Atherton would have quit had England's fortunes not improved. Instead, after further personal flops in two warm-up matches, a lengthy session with a bowling machine at Hamilton somehow freed the captain's feet from concrete. Atherton was confident enough to predict a century for himself before the First Test in

Auckland. He failed, but by a mere 17 runs, and his return to form was the final piece in the jigsaw. From the moment they landed in New Zealand, England looked happier in conditions which, on and off the field, were much more like home and, although still capable of very bad sessions, generally dominated a three-Test series against disappointing opponents. The best contest by far was the last, at Christchurch, where all four results were possible for most of a riveting final day. England won, clinching the rubber 2-0, Atherton became a hero again, through his masterly innings of 94 not out and 118, and the captain axed when the tour ended was New Zealand's Lee Germon.

Thorpe had rescued his winter with back-to-back centuries at Auckland and Wellington, emulating Stewart, who hit successive hundreds at Harare and Auckland. Atherton finished the combined tours with an average of 51 from five Tests. Among the bowlers, Gough and Croft remained the outstanding performers – helped, it must be said, by the splendid close catching of Nick Knight and Nasser Hussain.

David Lloyd's reputation as coach was also enhanced by the end. There was no doubting Lloyd's passion for the job, nor his popularity with the players. It was perhaps a pity he did not have a more forceful character than John Barclay to keep him and his emotions in check when tensions were running high. Barclay, having been upgraded to tour manager after serving as Ray Illingworth's assistant the previous winter, showed few signs of managing decisively when it really mattered, particularly in Zimbabwe.

At least Lloyd and Barclay had proper jobs. With Lloyd running the nets, physiotherapist Wayne Morton never far from the action during some increasingly impressive fielding drills and fitness specialist Dean Riddle working on the players' speed and stamina, there often seemed little left for assistant coach John Emburey to tackle.

Overall, England finished the winter with something to build upon: time would tell whether the foundations were strong enough to withstand the gale due to blow in from Australia.

David Lloyd, who reported this tour for Wisden, *is the cricket correspondent of the* Evening Standard *and not the England coach.*

ENGLAND TOURING PARTY

M. A. Atherton (Lancashire) (*captain*), N. Hussain (Essex) (*vice-captain*), A. R. Caddick (Somerset), D. G. Cork (Derbyshire), J. P. Crawley (Lancashire), R. D. B. Croft (Glamorgan), D. Gough (Yorkshire), R. C. Irani (Essex), N. V. Knight (Warwickshire), A. D. Mullally (Leicestershire), R. C. Russell (Gloucestershire), C. E. W. Silverwood (Yorkshire), A. J. Stewart (Surrey), G. P. Thorpe (Surrey), P. C. R. Tufnell (Middlesex).

Cork did not join the tour until New Zealand. C. White (Yorkshire) joined the party in Zimbabwe after England A's tour of Australia.

Tour manager: J. R. T. Barclay. *Coach:* D. Lloyd. *Assistant coach:* J. E. Emburey (Northants). *Scorer:* M. N. Ashton. *Physiotherapist:* W. P. Morton (Yorkshire). *Fitness consultant:* D. Riddle.

ENGLAND TOUR RESULTS

Test matches – Played 5: Won 2, Drawn 3.
First-class matches – Played 10: Won 5, Lost 2, Drawn 3.
Wins – New Zealand (2), Matabeleland, New Zealand Selection XI, Northern Districts.

Losses – Mashonaland, New Zealand A.

Draws – Zimbabwe (2), New Zealand.

One-day internationals – Played 8: Won 2, Lost 5, Tied 1. *Wins* – New Zealand (2). *Losses* – Zimbabwe (3), New Zealand (2). *Tie* – New Zealand.

Other non-first-class matches – Played 4: Won 1, Lost 1, No result 2. *Win* – Matabeleland. *Loss* – Zimbabwe President's XI. *No results* – Zimbabwe Country Districts XI, New Zealand Cricket Academy XI.

TEST MATCH AVERAGES

ZIMBABWE – BATTING

	T	I	NO	R	HS	100s	Avge	Ct
P. A. Strang	2	3	1	104	47*	0	52.00	0
A. D. R. Campbell	2	3	0	135	84	0	45.00	7
A. Flower	2	3	0	132	112	1	44.00	3
G. W. Flower	2	3	0	116	73	0	38.66	3
D. L. Houghton	2	3	0	100	37	0	33.33	2
A. C. Waller	2	3	0	69	50	0	23.00	1
G. J. Whittall	2	3	0	64	56	0	21.33	1
H. H. Streak	2	3	1	34	19	0	17.00	0
H. K. Olonga	2	3	0	0	0	0	0.00	0

Played in one Test: E. A. Brandes 9; S. V. Carlisle 0, 4 (2 ct); M. H. Dekker 2 (1 ct); B. C. Strang 4*, 3 (1 ct).

* Signifies not out.

BOWLING

	O	M	R	W	BB	5W/i	Avge
G. J. Whittall	42	13	69	5	4-18	0	13.80
P. A. Strang	116.4	27	259	10	5-123	1	25.90
H. H. Streak.....	89.1	20	240	8	4-43	0	30.00
H. K. Olonga	41	3	160	5	3-90	0	32.00

Also bowled: E. A. Brandes 37–12–80–0; G. W. Flower 22–5–65–0; B. C. Strang 17–5–54–0.

ENGLAND – BATTING

	T	I	NO	R	HS	100s	Avge	Ct
J. P. Crawley ...	2	3	1	166	112	1	83.00	6
A. J. Stewart ...	2	4	1	241	101*	1	80.33	5
N. V. Knight ...	2	4	0	197	96	0	49.25	2
N. Hussain	2	4	0	130	113	1	32.50	2
G. P. Thorpe ...	2	4	1	70	50*	0	23.33	1
M. A. Atherton .	2	4	0	34	16	0	8.50	2
D. Gough	2	3	1	7	3*	0	3.50	1

Played in two Tests: R. D. B. Croft 7, 14 (2 ct); A. D. Mullally 4, 0 (1 ct); P. C. R. Tufnell 2*, 9 (1 ct). Played in one Test: C. E. W. Silverwood 0 (1 ct); C. White 9.

* Signifies not out.

BOWLING

	O	M	R	W	BB	5W/i	Avge
C. E. W. Silverwood	25	8	71	4	3-63	0	17.75
R. D. B. Croft	92	26	178	8	3-39	0	22.25
D. Gough	64	16	171	7	4-40	0	24.42
P. C. R. Tufnell	82.5	19	192	7	4-61	0	27.42
A. D. Mullally	64	16	150	3	1-32	0	50.00

Also bowled: C. White 16–4–41–1.

NEW ZEALAND – BATTING

	T	I	NO	R	HS	100s	Avge	Ct/St
D. L. Vettori	2	4	3	59	29*	0	59.00	1
S. P. Fleming	3	6	0	212	129	1	35.33	7
C. L. Cairns	3	6	0	208	67	0	34.66	0
N. J. Astle	3	6	1	172	102*	1	34.40	0
B. A. Pocock	3	6	0	182	70	0	30.33	1
B. A. Young	3	6	0	171	56	0	28.50	3
A. C. Parore	3	6	0	125	59	0	20.83	4
L. K. Germon ...	2	4	0	48	14	0	12.00	3/1
D. N. Patel	2	4	0	45	45	0	11.25	2
S. B. Doull	3	6	0	37	26	0	6.16	1
G. I. Allott	2	4	1	12	8*	0	4.00	1

Played in one Test: H. T. Davis 8, 1 (2 ct); M. J. Horne 42, 13; D. K. Morrison 6*, 14*; J. T. C. Vaughan 3, 2.

* Signifies not out.

BOWLING

	O	M	R	W	BB	5W/i	Avge
D. L. Vettori	103.3	32	208	7	4-97	0	29.71
S. B. Doull	105.4	31	299	9	5-75	1	33.22
N. J. Astle	67	20	134	4	2-26	0	33.50
D. K. Morrison	24.4	4	104	3	3-104	0	34.66
G. I. Allott	61.4	11	197	5	4-74	0	39.40
D. N. Patel	68	16	151	3	2-92	0	50.33

Also bowled: C. L. Cairns 52–11–146–2; H. T. Davis 36–8–93–1; B. A. Pocock 2–0–10–0; J. T. C. Vaughan 36–10–57–1.

ENGLAND – BATTING

	T	I	NO	R	HS	100s	Avge	Ct/St
M. A. Atherton	3	4	1	325	118	1	108.33	1
A. J. Stewart	3	4	0	257	173	1	64.25	14/2
G. P. Thorpe	3	4	0	247	119	2	61.75	1
D. G. Cork	3	4	1	121	59	0	40.33	3
P. C. R. Tufnell ...	3	3	2	38	19*	0	38.00	0
J. P. Crawley	3	4	1	111	56	0	37.00	1
N. Hussain	3	4	0	117	64	0	29.25	6
N. V. Knight......	3	4	0	56	29	0	14.00	9
A. R. Caddick	2	3	0	39	20	0	13.00	1
D. Gough	3	3	0	20	18	0	6.66	0

Played in two Tests: R. D. B. Croft 0, 31 (2 ct). Played in one Test: A. D. Mullally 21; C. White 0.

* Signifies not out.

BOWLING

	O	M	R	W	BB	5W/i	Avge
R. D. B. Croft	90.1	27	162	10	5-95	1	16.20
D. Gough	127.3	31	361	19	5-40	1	19.00
A. R. Caddick	87.5	25	174	8	4-45	0	21.75
A. D. Mullally	53	22	102	3	2-47	0	34.00
P. C. R. Tufnell	132	47	242	7	3-53	0	34.57
D. G. Cork	98.5	21	300	7	3-96	0	42.85

Also bowled: G. P. Thorpe 1–1–0–0; C. White 25–5–77–2.

ENGLAND TOUR AVERAGES – FIRST-CLASS MATCHES

BATTING

	M	I	NO	R	HS	100s	Avge	Ct/St
A. J. Stewart	9	14	2	774	173	3	64.50	30/3
J. P. Crawley	10	14	2	582	112	1	48.50	13
G. P. Thorpe	9	14	1	511	119	2	39.30	8
N. Hussain	10	16	0	583	139	2	36.43	13
D. G. Cork	5	6	2	128	59	0	32.00	4
N. V. Knight	10	17	1	508	114	1	31.75	18
M. A. Atherton	10	17	2	456	118	1	30.40	10
R. D. B. Croft	8	10	1	196	80*	0	21.77	4
R. C. Irani	2	4	1	59	40	0	19.66	1
A. R. Caddick	6	9	1	121	28	0	15.12	3
C. White..............	5	6	1	69	22*	0	13.80	1
P. C. R. Tufnell	9	10	5	69	19*	0	13.80	6
D. Gough	8	10	1	62	18	0	6.88	3
C. E. W. Silverwood	3	4	0	25	11	0	6.25	3
A. D. Mullally	5	6	0	32	21	0	5.33	2

Played in one match: R. C. Russell 0, 61* (3 ct).

* Signifies not out.

BOWLING

	O	M	R	W	BB	5W/i	Avge
C. E. W. Silverwood	88.2	23	242	15	6-44	1	16.13
D. Gough	276.3	63	802	44	6-64	3	18.22
C. White..............	90.4	18	273	14	4-15	0	19.50
R. D. B. Croft	306.3	82	652	28	5-95	1	23.28
P. C. R. Tufnell	356.3	110	785	29	5-58	2	27.06
A. R. Caddick	205.5	55	467	17	4-45	0	27.47
A. D. Mullally	164.4	52	370	13	4-52	0	28.46
D. G. Cork	147.5	34	441	14	3-18	0	31.50

Also bowled: R. C. Irani 22.1–4–67–2; G. P. Thorpe 5.4–1–12–1.

Note: Matches in this section which were not first-class are signified by a dagger.

†At Harare South Country Club, Harare, November 30. No result. Toss: England XI. Zimbabwe Country Districts XI 198 for nine (45.3 overs) (G. J. Whittall 58, G. J. Rennie 32; A. D. Mullally three for 35, R. C. Irani three for 46) v England XI.

†At Harare Sports Club, Harare, December 1. Zimbabwe President's XI won by five wickets. Toss: Zimbabwe President's XI. England XI 211 for five (50 overs) (A. J. Stewart 105, N. Hussain 50; E. A. Brandes three for 42); Zimbabwe President's XI 215 for five (45.5 overs) (D. N. Erasmus 67, A. D. R. Campbell 45, G. J. Whittall 36 not out).

MASHONALAND v ENGLAND XI

At Harare Sports Club, Harare, December 3, 4, 5. Mashonaland won by seven wickets. England XI batted first by agreement.

England could hardly have made a less encouraging start. Already well beaten on the same ground by the President's XI, in a limited-overs game, they lost their opening first-class fixture with a day to spare. Mashonaland thoroughly deserved their triumph and it was only a minor consolation for England that one of their conquerors hailed not from Harare but from Eastbourne. James Kirtley, a 21-year-old Sussex fast bowler wintering in Zimbabwe, dismissed Atherton in the third over and finished with seven wickets. Croft's sensible, unbeaten, 80 just about kept England afloat – they had been 27 for four. But no one could approach the authority of Houghton, Zimbabwe's former captain. He took only 144 balls to score 110 and his team's later collapse against the spinners mattered little once England were 29 for four second time around. Crawley attempted a rescue act but, with medium-pacer Brent and leg-spinner Paul Strang collecting four wickets apiece, the innings lasted just 71.1 overs, leaving Mashonaland a simple target of 98.

Close of play: First day, England XI 175-9 (R. D. B. Croft 66*, P. C. R. Tufnell 1*); Second day, Mashonaland 279-9 (D. Matambanadzo 2*, R. J. Kirtley 2*).

England XI

N. V. Knight run out	6	– c D. J. R. Campbell b Kirtley	3
*M. A. Atherton c D. J. R. Campbell b Kirtley	2	– c D. J. R. Campbell b Brent	7
†A. J. Stewart b B. C. Strang	1	– b Kirtley	0
N. Hussain b Kirtley	2	– lbw b P. A. Strang	39
G. P. Thorpe c Houghton b Matambanadzo	35	– c D. J. R. Campbell b Brent	2
J. P. Crawley run out	25	– c Matambanadzo b Brent	74
R. D. B. Croft not out	80	– b P. A. Strang	3
D. Gough c D. J. R. Campbell b Kirtley	2	– b P. A. Strang	12
A. R. Caddick c D. J. R. Campbell b Brent	19	– c A. D. R. Campbell b P. A. Strang	28
A. D. Mullally c Brent b Kirtley	3	– c and b Brent	2
P. C. R. Tufnell c D. J. R. Campbell b Kirtley	6	– not out	2
L-b 6, w 3, n-b 7	16	L-b 6, n-b 2	8

1/3 2/4 3/7 4/27 5/63   197   1/4 2/4 3/27 4/29 5/105   180
6/88 7/94 8/125 9/145   6/111 7/137 8/159 9/167

Bowling: *First Innings*—Kirtley 25.1–4–53–5; B. C. Strang 19–2–52–1; Brent 8–1–20–1; P. A. Strang 16–5–30–0; Matambanadzo 6–0–34–1; Flower 1–0–2–0. *Second Innings*—Kirtley 16–6–35–2; B. C. Strang 11–5–18–0; Brent 10–3–22–4; P. A. Strang 23.1–6–56–4; Flower 11–2–43–0.

Mashonaland

G. W. Flower lbw b Tufnell	28	– c Crawley b Mullally	2
S. V. Carlisle c and b Gough	9	– b Mullally	3
*A. D. R. Campbell c Hussain b Tufnell	55	– not out	53
D. L. Houghton c and b Tufnell	110	– c Gough b Thorpe	34
C. B. Wishart c Crawley b Croft	45	– not out	0
P. A. Strang c Crawley b Croft	6		
†D. J. R. Campbell c Hussain b Croft	8		
G. B. Brent lbw b Croft	1		
B. C. Strang lbw b Tufnell	0		
D. Matambanadzo not out	3		
R. J. Kirtley lbw b Tufnell	2		
L-b 6, n-b 7	13	L-b 5, n-b 1	6

1/22 2/80 3/142 4/258 5/266   280   1/6 2/11 3/95   (3 wkts) 98
6/267 7/274 8/275 9/275

Bowling: First Innings—Mullally 12–2–42–0; Gough 16–3–43–1; Caddick 10–2–46–0; Tufnell 25.4–7–78–5; Croft 22–4–65–4. *Second Innings*—Mullally 6–1–18–2; Gough 3–0–14–0; Tufnell 9–1–35–0; Croft 6.3–0–23–0; Thorpe 1–0–3–1.

Umpires: D. Kalan and K. Kanjee.

†At Bulawayo Athletic Club, Bulawayo, December 8. England XI won by 59 runs. Toss: Matabeleland. England XI 210 for nine (50 overs) (N. V. Knight 58, J. P. Crawley 30; A. R. Whittall three for 35, G. J. Whittall four for 45); Matabeleland 151 (43.3 overs) (G. J. Whittall 35, W. R. James 33, M. D. Abrams 33; R. D. B. Croft three for 42).

MATABELELAND v ENGLAND XI

At Bulawayo Athletic Club, Bulawayo, December 10, 11, 12, 13. England XI won by 115 runs. Toss: Matabeleland.

Bulawayo provided a memorable few days for Gough, who captured 11 wickets for the first time, as England started to acclimatise. When they were put in on a green, slightly damp, pitch and Atherton departed early again, a repeat of Mashonaland beckoned. Knight, however, refused to sell his wicket cheaply, made the most of two dropped catches after passing 50 and reached his hundred just before the close on a day limited to 54 overs by torrential rain. His five-hour innings ended early on the second day, when England lost their last seven for 135. Only Crawley showed the required resolution, but at least England had a total to bowl at. Gough, swinging the ball encouragingly, undid Matabeleland in three spells and then, to England's relief, both Atherton and Thorpe hinted at better form with half-centuries. Matabeleland bravely attacked a target of 377, Dekker and Streak adding 156 together, but Gough, well supported by Croft, secured victory with 11.1 overs remaining.

Close of play: First day, England XI 199-3 (N. V. Knight 100*, G. P. Thorpe 5*); Second day, Matabeleland 181-9 (H. K. Olonga 5*, M. Mbangwa 3*); Third day, Matabeleland 5-0 (G. J. Whittall 4*, M. H. Dekker 1*).

England XI

N. V. Knight c G. J. Whittall b Rennie	114	– lbw b Olonga		8
*M. A. Atherton b Olonga	4	– c G. J. Whittall b Vaghmaria		55
†A. J. Stewart c G. J. Whittall b Streak	39	– c G. J. Whittall b Vaghmaria		43
N. Hussain c James b Olonga	38	– st James b A. R. Whittall		40
G. P. Thorpe c James b Streak	15	– c G. J. Whittall b Vaghmaria		65
J. P. Crawley c James b Streak	63			
R. C. Irani c Olonga b Mbangwa	5	– (6) not out		10
R. D. B. Croft c G. J. Whittall b Rennie	8			
D. Gough lbw b G. J. Whittall	6			
A. R. Caddick not out	10			
P. C. R. Tufnell c James b G. J. Whittall	10			
B 5, l-b 5, w 4, n-b 8	22	B 5, w 1, n-b 3		9

1/14 2/100 3/185 4/215 5/240   334   1/10 2/88 3/121   (5 wkts dec.) 230
6/261 7/274 8/312 9/312   4/196 5/230

Bowling: *First Innings*—Olonga 14–3–63–2; Streak 19–3–65–3; G. J. Whittall 14–4–40–2; Mbangwa 19–3–60–1; Rennie 17–4–62–2; Vaghmaria 3–0–9–0; A. R. Whittall 6–1–25–0. *Second Innings*—Olonga 11–3–41–1; Mbangwa 11–2–35–0; Rennie 10–2–32–0; G. J. Whittall 3–0–17–0; Vaghmaria 16.3–3–58–3; A. R. Whittall 16–3–42–1.

Matabeleland

G. J. Whittall c Irani b Gough	19	– c Caddick b Gough		11
*J. A. Rennie c Tufnell b Caddick	0	– (7) not out		30
M. H. Dekker c Knight b Caddick	26	– (2) lbw b Croft		104
M. Ranchod c Stewart b Gough	0	– (3) lbw b Gough		0
†W. R. James c and b Tufnell	62	– c Crawley b Croft		7
M. D. Abrams c Stewart b Gough	15	– lbw b Gough		6
H. H. Streak c and b Tufnell	25	– (4) b Caddick		67
D. Vaghmaria b Gough	12	– c Stewart b Croft		0
A. R. Whittall b Gough	7	– b Gough		18
H. K. Olonga c Atherton b Gough	7	– b Gough		4
M. Mbangwa not out	7	– c Crawley b Croft		8
L-b 2, n-b 6	8	L-b 3, n-b 3		6

1/8 2/32 3/32 4/68 5/104   188   1/18 2/20 3/176 4/185 5/198   261
6/142 7/154 8/172 9/173   6/204 7/204 8/241 9/249

Bowling: *First Innings*—Gough 17.2–1–64–6; Caddick 12–1–38–2; Irani 7–3–26–0; Tufnell 20–5–40–2; Croft 9–3–18–0. *Second Innings*—Gough 24–6–75–5; Caddick 20–7–43–1; Tufnell 20–6–42–0; Irani 2.2–0–7–0; Thorpe 2.4–0–6–0; Croft 24.5–7–65–4.

Umpires: C. Coventry and R. B. Tiffin.

†ZIMBABWE v ENGLAND

First One-Day International

At Queens Sports Club, Bulawayo, December 15. Zimbabwe won by two wickets. Toss: Zimbabwe. International debut: C. E. W. Silverwood.

Zimbabwe overcame their own attack of nerves and the tourists' spirited fightback to record their eighth one-day international victory in their 64th match – and their third in four against England. While no one made batting look enjoyable on a slow but springy pitch, England's performance was woeful: they failed to survive into their final four overs. Only Hussain, whose

49 included 40 singles, showed sufficient patience as Rennie, a bespectacled medium-pacer, shared the honours with Streak. Chasing only three an over, Zimbabwe should have won more comfortably. But Silverwood, on his international debut, Gough and Mullally gnawed away at home confidence and, at 106 for seven, with 47 still needed, it was anyone's match. Campbell, batting down the order because of a hand injury, provided the common sense necessary to pass the winning post.

Man of the Match: A. D. R. Campbell.

England

N. V. Knight lbw b Streak	13	R. D. B. Croft c G. W. Flower b Streak..	0
†A. J. Stewart c A. Flower b Streak	26	D. Gough run out	9
*M. A. Atherton c sub (A. R. Whittall) b G. W. Flower	23	C. E. W. Silverwood c Houghton b Strang	1
		L-b 6, w 3, n-b 4	13
G. P. Thorpe b Brandes	1		
N. Hussain not out	49	1/28 (1) 2/41 (2) 3/47 (4) (45.5 overs) 152	
J. P. Crawley c Campbell b Rennie	10	4/96 (3) 5/124 (6) 6/134 (7)	
R. C. Irani c and b Rennie	7	7/134 (8) 8/135 (9) 9/150 (10)	
A. D. Mullally c and b Rennie	0	10/152 (11) Score at 15 overs: 49-3	

Bowling: Brandes 8-2-28-1; Rennie 8-1-27-3; Streak 9-1-30-3; Whittall 5-0-17-0; Strang 9.5-1-27-1; G. W. Flower 6-0-17-1.

Zimbabwe

G. W. Flower b Silverwood	14	H. H. Streak c and b Croft	11
A. C. Waller run out	48	E. A. Brandes not out	8
†A. Flower c Knight b Silverwood	10	L-b 9, w 4, n-b 1	14
D. L. Houghton c Crawley b Gough	2		
C. N. Evans c Stewart b Gough	1	1/33 (1) 2/58 (3) (8 wkts, 43.5 overs) 153	
G. J. Whittall c Stewart b Mullally	13	3/73 (4) 4/87 (5)	
*A. D. R. Campbell not out	32	5/97 (2) 6/106 (6)	
P. A. Strang c Stewart b Mullally	0	7/106 (8) 8/137 (9) Score at 15 overs: 48-1	

J. A. Rennie did not bat.

Bowling: Mullally 10-2-24-2; Gough 10-2-31-2; Silverwood 10-0-27-2; Croft 5-0-32-1; Irani 6.5-1-25-0; Thorpe 2-1-5-0.

Umpires: Q. J. Goosen and R. B. Tiffin.

ZIMBABWE v ENGLAND

First Test Match

At Queens Sports Club, Bulawayo, December 18, 19, 20, 21, 22. Drawn. Toss: Zimbabwe. Test debuts: A. C. Waller; C. E. W. Silverwood.

A gently smouldering match suddenly burst into full flame on the last afternoon when England were left to chase 205 from 37 overs. Often up with the rate but never sufficiently ahead to feel comfortable, they eventually needed three from Streak's final delivery. Knight managed two and this inaugural Test between the two countries earned another place in history: it was the first Test to be drawn with the scores level. Such excitement had seemed unlikely during the first four days, on a slow-turning pitch where both runs and wickets needed chiselling out. Zimbabwe won a useful toss, England swiftly hit back when Gough had Carlisle caught at short leg with his third delivery, and so it continued. First one side then the other put their noses in front, but neither could create a decisive advantage.

Zimbabwe's most commanding phase occurred while Grant Flower and Campbell were adding 127 in 145 minutes in the face of undemanding and often inaccurate bowling. Atherton treated his attack to a few home truths during lunch and the message got through. Silverwood, earning his first cap because of Caddick's unpromising form and Irani's back injury, launched the recovery when he had Flower well caught by the diving Hussain at third slip. Then Croft took charge. He had Campbell, 16 short of a maiden Test century, held off a sliced drive, but his best bowling followed tea, when he had a spell of 12–6–7–2, a performance of craft and control. With the new ball having accounted for Whittall before the close, England hoped to dismiss Zimbabwe for around 300. Instead, Andy Flower dug in to score a hundred and it took another three hours to wrap up the innings, which crept towards 400.

Atherton had broken Peter May's record by leading England in 36 consecutive Tests. He continued to struggle for runs; he was hit in front of his wicket when playing back to leg-spinner Paul Strang's 11th ball, the last before tea. Heavy rain wiped out the evening session, but the third day belonged to England. Initially, they were in trouble, with Knight missing a slow in-swinger from Olonga, Stewart losing a poor lbw decision and a horribly out-of-touch Thorpe charging out and being held at slip. Hussain and Crawley more than redressed the balance, however, and England were sitting pretty on 306 for four by the close. Hussain had survived a sharp chance, first ball, to Carlisle at short leg off Strang but, thereafter, advanced smoothly to his third century in six Tests, reaching it (in a shade over five hours) just before the close.

Now England hoped for a decisive lead. But it started to go wrong next morning, from the moment Hussain hooked Streak, and Bryan Strang stuck up a hand to hold a remarkable boundary catch, ending a stand of 148. England's suspect lower order failed to support Crawley and he was still ten short of his second century in consecutive Tests when joined by last man Tufnell. Had wicket-keeper Andy Flower held the chance Tufnell offered, Crawley would have been stranded on 96. Instead, they stole a single and Crawley pulled the next ball for six. He finally fell to Paul Strang who was good value for his five wickets. England's lead of 30 looked inconsequential but, by close of play, they entertained real hopes of victory: Zimbabwe were five down and only 77 ahead. Tufnell had already taken two and soon struck on the final morning as Bryan Strang slogged to mid-on. Once again, the tail showed it was made of stern stuff; it took England another 53 overs to capture the last four wickets.

And so the thrilling finale was set up. Atherton again departed quickly but Knight and, particularly, Stewart, who passed 4,000 Test runs as he scored 73 off 76 balls, gave the run-chase real impetus against increasingly negative bowling and far-flung fields. Stewart's exit, to a miscued pull, when England needed 51 from eight overs, was probably crucial. Three more wickets swiftly followed. Knight, though, brought fresh hope with a glorious square-leg six in Streak's final over and five runs were wanted from three deliveries. The next ball might have been called as a wide by the Zimbabwean umpire Robinson, whose decision-making was questioned several times. There was no signal, however, and Knight could not find the boundary again. Referee Hanumant Singh busied himself during and after the contest, reprimanding England for the "manner of their appealing", investigating but taking no action over coach David Lloyd's "we flippin' murdered them" outburst, and fining Streak 15 per cent of his match fee for "inferred criticism" of the umpires; Streak had said he was lucky not to have been called wide in that last over.

Man of the Match: N. V. Knight.

Close of play: First day, Zimbabwe 256-6 (A. Flower 58*, P. A. Strang 0*); Second day, England 48-1 (N. V. Knight 29*); Third day, England 306-4 (N. Hussain 101*, J. P. Crawley 51*); Fourth day, Zimbabwe 107-5 (A. C. Waller 14*, B. C. Strang 0*).

Zimbabwe

G. W. Flower c Hussain b Silverwood	43	– lbw b Gough	0
S. V. Carlisle c Crawley b Gough	0	– c Atherton b Mullally	4
*A. D. R. Campbell c Silverwood b Croft	84	– b Croft	29
D. L. Houghton c Stewart b Croft	34	– c Croft b Tufnell	37
†A. Flower c Stewart b Tufnell	112	– c Crawley b Tufnell	14
A. C. Waller c Crawley b Croft	15	– c Knight b Gough	50
G. J. Whittall c Atherton b Silverwood	7	– (8) c Croft b Tufnell	56
P. A. Strang c Tufnell b Silverwood	38	– (9) c Crawley b Croft	19
H. H. Streak b Mullally	19	– (10) not out	8
B. C. Strang not out	4	– (7) c Mullally b Tufnell	3
H. K. Olonga c Knight b Tufnell	0	– c Stewart b Silverwood	0
L-b 4, w 3, n-b 13	20	B 4, l-b 6, w 2, n-b 2	14

1/3 (2) 2/130 (1) 3/136 (3) 4/206 (4)   376   1/6 (2) 2/6 (1) 3/57 (3)   234
5/235 (6) 6/252 (7) 7/331 (8)   4/82 (5) 5/103 (4) 6/111 (7)
8/372 (9) 9/376 (5) 10/376 (11)   7/178 (6) 8/209 (9)
                                    9/233 (8) 10/234 (11)

Bowling: *First Innings*—Mullally 23–4–69–1; Gough 26–4–87–1; Silverwood 18–5–63–3; Croft 44–15–77–3; Tufnell 26.5–4–76–2. *Second Innings*—Gough 12–2–44–2; Mullally 18–5–49–1; Croft 33–9–62–2; Silverwood 7–3–8–1; Tufnell 31–12–61–4.

England

N. V. Knight lbw b Olonga	56	– run out	96
*M. A. Atherton lbw b P. A. Strang	16	– b Olonga	4
†A. J. Stewart lbw b P. A. Strang	48	– c Campbell b P. A. Strang	73
N. Hussain c B. C. Strang b Streak	113	– c Carlisle b P. A. Strang	0
G. P. Thorpe c Campbell b P. A. Strang	13	– (6) c Campbell b Streak	2
J. P. Crawley c A. Flower b P. A. Strang	112	– (5) c Carlisle b Whittall	7
R. D. B. Croft lbw b Olonga	7		
D. Gough c G. W. Flower b Olonga	2	– (7) not out	3
C. E. W. Silverwood c Houghton b P. A. Strang	0		
A. D. Mullally c Waller b Streak	4		
P. C. R. Tufnell not out	2		
B 4, l-b 4, w 1, n-b 24	33	B 2, l-b 13, w 3, n-b 1	19

1/48 (2) 2/92 (1) 3/160 (3) 4/180 (5)   406   1/17 (2) 2/154 (3)   (6 wkts) 204
5/328 (4) 6/340 (7) 7/344 (8)   3/156 (4) 4/178 (5)
8/353 (9) 9/378 (10) 10/406 (6)   5/182 (6) 6/204 (1)

Bowling: *First Innings*—Streak 36–8–86–2; B. C. Strang 17–5–54–0; P. A. Strang 58.4–14–123–5; Olonga 23–2–90–3; Whittall 10–2–25–0; G. W. Flower 7–3–20–0. *Second Innings*—Streak 11–0–64–1; Olonga 2–0–16–1; P. A. Strang 14–0–63–2; G. W. Flower 8–0–36–0; Whittall 2–0–10–1.

Umpires: R. S. Dunne (New Zealand) and I. D. Robinson.   Referee: Hanumant Singh (India).

ZIMBABWE v ENGLAND

Second Test Match

At Harare Sports Club, Harare, December 26, 27, 28, 29, 30. Drawn. Toss: Zimbabwe.

Torrential overnight rain and incomplete covering prevented any play on the last day, which might have produced a finish every bit as exciting as the one in Bulawayo a week earlier. England, 136 ahead with seven wickets in hand, seemed more likely to dictate terms; but talk of setting a target of 230 off 60 overs became irrelevant and this first, brief, series between the two countries ended 0-0.

Thoughts of an England win appeared ridiculous after their inept first-day batting. A slow pitch (and painfully slow outfield) demanded careful shot selection and plenty of patience, but England demonstrated neither: they plummeted to 137 before bad light halted play an hour early. Knight could be considered a little unlucky, glancing a catch down the leg side; Crawley showed what was possible; the rest surrendered to a succession of rash strokes, with medium-pacer Guy Whittall benefiting to the remarkable tune of 13–5–12–4.

The first real sign of danger came when Stewart drove loosely at Streak. Campbell dropped him in the slips, but a clear warning was ignored. Next over, Whittall's second, Campbell tried something similar without getting into position and, this time, Campbell made no mistake. Stewart followed without addition, edging Streak again, Thorpe clipped to short square leg and Hussain soon became Streak's third victim with another reckless drive. White, who had just flown in after a successful A tour of Australia and was picked ahead of Silverwood, snicked a half-volley, Croft fell in almost identical circumstances, Gough swung fatally across the line and Mullally prodded a slow off-break straight back to the delighted Whittall.

A further 19 runs on the second morning prevented England from recording the lowest Test total against Zimbabwe but did not begin to repair the damage, which looked more serious still when the home side reached 110 for two on the third afternoon. They had lost Dekker, recalled to replace Carlisle, with only five on the board and Campbell to an injudicious cut, but Grant Flower – perfectly suited to execute a no-risks policy – and Houghton, stifling his attacking instincts, added 64 in 38 overs. With only four balls after tea on the second day because of rain and two hours lost the following morning through a wet outfield, it took them longer than they wanted, but England seemed certain to face a substantial first-innings deficit. In fact, thanks mainly to Gough's swing bowling, it was just 59. He picked up four wickets for 27 during 15 top-quality overs, before Croft polished off the tail. Without an intelligently aggressive innings from Paul Strang, Zimbabwe would have struggled to reach 200.

England could not help but improve on their first effort. The signs were not too promising, however, when Atherton missed out again (he had now scored 153 in 11 tour innings), edging his third delivery. Strang, who was again impressive, then deceived Knight and Hussain with leg-breaks to leave Surrey colleagues Stewart and Thorpe under severe pressure, only 30 ahead. Neither wilted this time. Stewart, despite offering a half chance to short leg on 15, thoroughly earned his ninth Test century, which he reached in just over six hours. It was his first as a wicket-keeper/batsman and he ended 1996 as the world's leading Test run-maker for the year, with 793 runs, despite being dropped for one game in June. He should have received the match award, but somehow it found its way into Grant Flower's hands for a six-hour 73. Thorpe, completely out of touch before this innings, matched Stewart's determination and their undefeated stand of 106 deserved to set up something much better than a lunchtime abandonment.

Man of the Match: G. W. Flower.

Close of play: First day, England 137-9 (J. P. Crawley 37*, P. C. R. Tufnell 0*); Second day, Zimbabwe 93-2 (G. W. Flower 33*, D. L. Houghton 26*); Third day, England 17-1 (N. V. Knight 6*, A. J. Stewart 10*); Fourth day, England 195-3 (A. J. Stewart 101*, G. P. Thorpe 50*).

England

N. V. Knight c A. Flower b Olonga	15	– c Campbell b Strang	30
*M. A. Atherton c Campbell b Whittall	13	– c Campbell b Streak	1
†A. J. Stewart c G. W. Flower b Streak	19	– not out	101
N. Hussain c A. Flower b Streak	11	– c Houghton b Strang	6
G. P. Thorpe c Dekker b Streak	5	– not out	50
J. P. Crawley not out	47		
C. White c Campbell b Whittall	9		
R. D. B. Croft c G. W. Flower b Whittall	14		
D. Gough b Strang	2		
A. D. Mullally c and b Whittall	0		
P. C. R. Tufnell b Streak	9		
B 1, l-b 5, w 1, n-b 5	12	L-b 5, w 1, n-b 1	7

1/24 (1) 2/50 (2) 3/50 (3) 4/65 (5)   156   1/7 (2) 2/75 (1) 3/89 (4)   (3 wkts) 195
5/73 (4) 6/94 (7) 7/128 (8)
8/133 (9) 9/134 (10) 10/156 (11)

Bowling: *First Innings*—Streak 24.1–7–43–4; Brandes 16–6–35–0; Olonga 9–1–23–1; Whittall 16–5–18–4; Strang 18–7–31–1. *Second Innings*—Streak 18.5–5–47–1; Brandes 21–6–45–0; Olonga 7–0–31–0; Whittall 14–6–16–0; Strang 26–6–42–2; G. W. Flower 7–2–9–0.

Zimbabwe

G. W. Flower c Crawley b Gough	73	H. H. Streak c Crawley b Croft	7
M. H. Dekker c Stewart b Mullally	2	E. A. Brandes c Gough b Croft	9
*A. D. R. Campbell c Thorpe b White	22	H. K. Olonga c Hussain b Croft	0
D. L. Houghton c Stewart b Gough	29	L-b 8, w 1, n-b 6	15
†A. Flower lbw b Gough	6		
A. C. Waller lbw b Tufnell	4	1/5 (2) 2/46 (3) 3/110 (4) 4/131 (5)	215
G. J. Whittall b Gough	1	5/136 (6) 6/138 (7) 7/159 (1)	
P. A. Strang not out	47	8/197 (9) 9/211 (10) 10/215 (11)	

Bowling: Mullally 23–7–32–1; Gough 26–10–40–4; Croft 15–2–39–3; White 16–4–41–1; Tufnell 25–3–55–1.

Umpires: K. T. Francis (Sri Lanka) and R. B. Tiffin.   Referee: Hanumant Singh (India).

†ZIMBABWE v ENGLAND

Second One-Day International

At Harare Sports Club, Harare, January 1. Zimbabwe won by six runs, England's target having been revised to 186 from 42 overs. Toss: England.

A 2-0 lead gave Zimbabwe their first limited-overs series win and no one, least of all England's players, could deny that they deserved it. They were struggling at 38 for four and then hanging on grimly when England attacked a revised target, but Zimbabwe simply wanted the win more. Andy Flower, reprieved in the deep when Gough misjudged a catch off Croft's first delivery, masterminded their recovery, Evans and Streak gave excellent support, while gifts – ten wides and three no-balls – were gratefully received. Lunchtime rain allowed the newest recalculation system, the Duckworth/Lewis method, to get in on the act. The target should have been 186 in 42 overs, though it was mistakenly given as 185, an error which proved academic. The challenge looked comfortable enough while Stewart and Crawley were in full cry. Leg-spinner Strang turned the game, however, with three wickets in 17 balls and, when Streak conceded just three from the penultimate over, another little piece of cricket history was all but written. Campbell, Evans and Andy Flower were reprimanded by referee Hanumant Singh for excessive appealing.

Men of the Match: P. A. Strang and J. P. Crawley.

Zimbabwe

G. W. Flower c Hussain b Gough	4	E. A. Brandes c Atherton b Gough	0
A. C. Waller b Mullally	0	J. A. Rennie b Gough	0
*A. D. R. Campbell c Stewart b Gough	14	L-b 11, w 10, n-b 3	24
D. L. Houghton c Croft b Mullally	5		
†A. Flower c Stewart b Mullally	63	1/2 (2) 2/14 (1) 3/26 (4) (48.5 overs) 200	
C. N. Evans lbw b Croft	32	4/38 (3) 5/97 (6)	
G. J. Whittall run out	14	6/125 (7) 7/126 (8)	
P. A. Strang c Atherton b Croft	1	8/200 (5) 9/200 (10)	
H. H. Streak not out	43	10/200 (11) Score at 15 overs: 66-4	

Bowling: Mullally 9–1–29–3; Gough 8.5–1–43–4; Silverwood 6–0–30–0; White 10–1–39–0; Croft 10–2–33–2; Irani 5–0–15–0.

England

N. V. Knight c Houghton b Brandes	0	D. Gough not out	2
†A. J. Stewart c A. Flower b Whittall	41		
J. P. Crawley st A. Flower b Strang	73	B 2, l-b 5, w 5	12
N. Hussain lbw b Whittall	7		
*M. A. Atherton c Whittall b Strang	25	1/1 (1) 2/67 (2) (7 wkts, 42 overs) 179	
R. C. Irani st A. Flower b Strang	5	3/95 (4) 4/137 (5)	
C. White lbw b Streak	4	5/157 (3) 6/165 (6)	
R. D. B. Croft not out	10	7/169 (7) Score at 13 overs: 67-2	

A. D. Mullally and C. E. W. Silverwood did not bat.

Bowling: Brandes 6–2–25–1; Rennie 5–0–26–0; Streak 8–0–41–1; Whittall 8–0–30–2; Evans 2–0–6–0; Strang 9–0–24–3; G. W. Flower 4–0–20–0.

Umpires: G. R. Evans and I. D. Robinson.

†ZIMBABWE v ENGLAND

Third One-Day International

At Harare Sports Club, Harare, January 3. Zimbabwe won by 131 runs. Toss: England.

Zimbabwe completed a 3-0 whitewash in an emphatic manner with their biggest win in limited-overs internationals. Captain Campbell set a fine example by scoring a stylish and undefeated 80 but was dramatically upstaged by Brandes. Nearly five years earlier, Brandes had led his country to a shock World Cup win against England in Australia by taking four for 21. Here, during a wonderful exhibition of swing and seam bowling, he captured England's top five wickets, including a hat-trick, as they struggled to 54. Every British newspaper reported that the team had been humiliated by a chicken-farmer. England were already facing a stiff target of five an over, and that put them right out of contention. They failed to survive beyond 30 of their 50 overs, and only some late defiance from Croft and Mullally helped them into three figures. England still required a points victory in the drawn Test series, but Zimbabwe were one-day winners – by a knockout.

Man of the Match: E. A. Brandes.

Zimbabwe

G. W. Flower c Mullally b White	62	P. A. Strang run out	13
A. C. Waller run out	19	B 4, 1-b 5, w 8, n-b 2	19
*A. D. R. Campbell not out	80		
†A. Flower c Stewart b Irani	35		(7 wkts, 50 overs) 249
C. N. Evans c Stewart b Gough	1		

1/58 (2) 2/131 (1)   (7 wkts, 50 overs) 249
3/181 (4) 4/183 (5)
5/190 (6) 6/220 (7)

G. J. Whittall b Croft	1
D. L. Houghton c Stewart b Mullally	19

7/249 (8)   Score at 15 overs: 58-1

H. H. Streak, E. A. Brandes and J. A. Rennie did not bat.

Bowling: Mullally 10–3–39–1; Gough 10–1–42–1; Silverwood 5–0–27–0; White 7–0–39–1; Irani 10–0–39–1; Croft 8–0–54–1.

England

N. V. Knight c A. Flower b Brandes	3	A. D. Mullally b Whittall	20
†A. J. Stewart c A. Flower b Brandes	29	C. E. W. Silverwood c Evans b Whittall	0
J. P. Crawley lbw b Brandes	0	W 8, n-b 3	11
N. Hussain c A. Flower b Brandes	0		
*M. A. Atherton c A. Flower b Brandes	18	1/9 (1) 2/13 (3) 3/13 (4) (30 overs) 118
R. C. Irani c Whittall b Streak	0	4/45 (2) 5/54 (5)
C. White c A. Flower b Streak	0	6/55 (6) 7/63 (7)
R. D. B. Croft not out	30	8/77 (9) 9/118 (10)
D. Gough c Streak b Strang	7	10/118 (11) Score at 15 overs: 45-4

Bowling: Brandes 10–0–28–5; Rennie 3–0–11–0; Streak 10–0–50–2; Strang 5–0–18–1; Whittall 2–0–11–2.

Umpires: I. D. Robinson and R. B. Tiffin.   Series referee: Hanumant Singh (India).

†At New Plymouth, January 10. No result. Toss: England XI. New Zealand Cricket Academy XI 201 (40.4 overs) (C. D. McMillan 58, G. R. Loveridge 54; A. R. Caddick three for 44) v England XI.

Rain preceding Cyclone Drena shortened and then ended the match.

NEW ZEALAND SELECTION XI v ENGLAND XI

At Palmerston North, January 13, 14, 15, 16. England XI won by an innings and 113 runs. Toss: England XI.

Despite losing nearly seven hours to rain, England completed a crushing victory midway through the final day. Atherton's latest batting failure was their only real disappointment. First, England's seamers revelled in a pitch offering more pace and bounce than anything in Zimbabwe. White, who at times bowled faster than anyone before succumbing to a heavy cold, took the opening-day honours with four for 15, then Stewart and Hussain took charge. Stewart dominated from the start and struck two sixes and 20 fours in his 153 before a convenient hamstring twinge allowed other batsmen their turn. Hussain, having totalled 24 runs in his last five innings in Zimbabwe, began hesitantly but was flowing again by the time he miscued to cover for 139, including 19 fours. The home side, containing eight Test players, never threatened to bat out the final day. This time their chief tormentor was the spinner Tufnell, assisted by Silverwood and some splendid fielding.

Close of play: First day, England XI 106-3 (A. J. Stewart 40*, N. Hussain 0*); Second day, England XI 154-3 (A. J. Stewart 75*, N. Hussain 11*); Third day, New Zealand Selection XI 25-1 (B. A. Pocock 11*, A. C. Parore 8*).

New Zealand Selection XI

B. A. Pocock c Thorpe b Caddick	16	– (2) c Hussain b Tufnell 43
C. J. Spearman b White	41	– (1) c Atherton b Cork 6
†A. C. Parore c Atherton b Silverwood	0	– c Stewart b Silverwood 13
M. J. Horne c Silverwood b Cork	22	– c Knight b Tufnell 11
*M. J. Greatbatch c Cork b White	5	– run out 10
L. G. Howell c Caddick b Cork	10	– (7) c Tufnell b Silverwood 31
J. T. C. Vaughan b White	24	– (6) c Knight b Silverwood 1
P. J. Wiseman c Stewart b Silverwood	0	– lbw b Tufnell.................. 0
M. J. Haslam run out	8	– c Stewart b Tufnell 3
D. K. Morrison c Thorpe b White	4	– st Stewart b Tufnell 30
R. J. Kennedy not out	1	– not out 16
L-b 4, n-b 3	7	L-b 7, n-b 5 12

1/48 2/53 3/58 4/81 5/93	**138**	1/6 2/34 3/65 4/75 5/78	**176**
6/97 7/98 8/125 9/137		6/99 7/99 8/122 9/160	

Bowling: First Innings—Cork 17-7-42-2; Caddick 16-3-48-1; Silverwood 12-4-24-2; White 9.4-3-15-4; Tufnell 3-0-5-0. *Second Innings*—Cork 14-1-58-1; Caddick 18-8-24-0; Silverwood 14.1-5-29-3; Tufnell 24-8-58-5.

England XI

N. V. Knight c Parore b Morrison	46	D. G. Cork not out	0
*M. A. Atherton lbw b Kennedy	7	C. E. W. Silverwood c Vaughan	
†A. J. Stewart retired hurt	153	b Morrison .	4
A. R. Caddick c Parore b Morrison	7	L-b 9, w 4, n-b 7	20
N. Hussain c Horne b Wiseman	139		
G. P. Thorpe c Morrison b Kennedy	6	1/19 2/94 3/106	(8 wkts dec.) **427**
J. P. Crawley c Kennedy b Morrison	35	4/321 5/411 6/423	
C. White c Spearman b Wiseman	10	7/423 8/427	

P. C. R. Tufnell did not bat.

A. J. Stewart retired hurt at 312.

Bowling: Morrison 28.5-6-81-4; Kennedy 21-3-80-2; Vaughan 22-4-84-0; Wiseman 17-2-83-2; Haslam 25-7-90-0.

Umpires: R. S. Dunne and D. M. Quested.

NORTHERN DISTRICTS v ENGLAND XI

At Hamilton, January 18, 19, 20. England XI won by ten wickets. Toss: England XI. First-class debuts: D. R. T. Bennett, D. L. Vettori.

England could not quite manage another innings victory, but earned themselves a day off; however, a back injury to Cork, just when he seemed to be rediscovering his form, was cause for concern. Cork had responded to a damp, patchily grassed pitch by dismissing New Zealand openers Young and Pocock in his first three overs; by lunch, a badly embarrassed Northern Districts were all out for 69. Then Atherton failed again, which was another worry for England: he had only 208 in 15 innings on tour. Most of his colleagues made decent use of an easing pitch. Thorpe and Crawley added 125 before being undone by the new ball. Northerns started almost as badly second time around, with Young once more beaten by Cork's swing, but first Pocock and then Parlane showed some defiance. By now Cork had gone off for X-rays. Even without him, however, England needed only 35 for victory and the end came before tea on the third day.

Close of play: First day, England XI 166-4 (G. P. Thorpe 39*, J. P. Crawley 25*); Second day, Northern Districts 99-1 (B. A. Pocock 60*, M. D. Bell 35*).

Northern Districts

B. A. Young b Cork	4	– (2) c Stewart b Cork	2
*B. A. Pocock c Stewart b Cork	0	– (1) lbw b Gough	69
M. D. Bell b Mullally	5	– b Gough	35
M. D. Bailey c Thorpe b Cork	4	– c Thorpe b Mullally	26
M. E. Parlane c Stewart b White	9	– c and b Mullally	74
M. N. Hart c Thorpe b White	2	– c White b Mullally	1
†R. G. Hart c Thorpe b Gough	24	– b White	4
A. R. Tait b Gough	0	– c Atherton b White	20
S. B. Styris c Stewart b Gough	0	– b Mullally	13
D. L. Vettori c Stewart b White	5	– c Crawley b Gough	1
D. R. T. Bennett not out	4	– not out	4
L-b 5, n-b 7	12	B 3, l-b 3, n-b 4	10

1/4 2/5 3/13 4/17 5/32   69   1/9 2/99 3/114 4/156 5/164   259
6/53 7/54 8/54 9/65   6/171 7/212 8/243 9/255

Bowling: *First Innings*—Cork 9–2–18–3; Mullally 7–4–6–1; White 7–1–17–3; Gough 5.4–1–23–3. *Second Innings*—Cork 9–3–23–1; Mullally 22.4–7–52–4; White 17–3–61–2; Croft 23–5–63–0; Gough 19–5–51–3; Thorpe 1–0–3–0.

England XI

N. V. Knight c R. G. Hart b Styris	39	– not out	24
*M. A. Atherton lbw b Styris	5	– not out	12
†A. J. Stewart c Bennett b Tait	40		
N. Hussain c Young b Vettori	7		
G. P. Thorpe c R. G. Hart b Tait	71		
J. P. Crawley c R. G. Hart b Styris	65		
C. White not out	22		
R. D. B. Croft c Bell b Tait	2		
D. G. Cork c Pocock b Styris	7		
D. Gough b Tait	15		
A. D. Mullally b Tait	2		
L-b 7, w 1, n-b 11	19	W 1, n-b 1	2

1/12 2/89 3/93 4/116 5/241   294   (no wkt) 38
6/241 7/246 8/273 9/290

Bowling: *First Innings*—Styris 31–7–110–4; Bennett 12–0–31–0; Tait 36.5–12–96–5; Vettori 20–8–30–1; M. N. Hart 6–1–20–0. *Second Innings*—Styris 1–0–10–0; Bennett 4–1–17–0; Tait 3.1–1–11–0.

Umpires: D. B. Cowie and C. E. King.

NEW ZEALAND v ENGLAND

First Test Match

At Auckland, January 24, 25, 26, 27, 28. Drawn. Toss: England.

Cricket's ability to find new scripts and confound all logic was proved yet again as New Zealand's last pair, Astle and Morrison, remained undefeated for nearly three hours, thereby denying England a victory that seemed to be a certainty by lunch on the final day. Astle's reward was a third Test century, richly deserved. Morrison had to make do with 14 not out, the gratitude of his team-mates and, within the week, a few words of consolation from selectors who considered his bowling unworthy of retention for the next match.

England did themselves much credit by accepting a huge disappointment with stoicism and good grace. They played some dominating cricket which, with hindsight, could be seen as part of their rehabilitation process. But they had started the match as disastrously as they finished it. Atherton won what could have been a decisive toss but, not for the first time, saw his bowlers surrender the advantage by bowling hopelessly wide. Asked whether the green and slightly damp pitch had provided the assistance he expected, Atherton replied: "We'll never know."

With Cork recovered from a back strain, Croft was dropped and England fielded a four-pronged pace attack. Not one of them was up to standard before lunch, however, and the introduction of Tufnell's spin in the 11th over testified to Atherton's loss of faith in their accuracy. Wicket-keeper Stewart, diving right and left to intercept wayward deliveries, was in more danger than the batsmen and had a dislocated finger put back in place after one scrambling take. Mullally began to turn things round early in the afternoon, when he trapped Young, then Cork had Parore caught behind, flicking down the leg side. But the decision to field still looked like backfiring as New Zealand advanced to 193 for two.

It was just about level pegging by the close, though, with five men out. Indeed, if Gough had held a low chance at mid-off to remove Cairns, England might have been ahead on points. Cairns made them pay for that error, supplying 67 in a sixth-wicket stand of 118, and the second day belonged to his partner, Fleming. A tall, elegant left-hander, whose temperament appeared as solid as his technique, he finally reached a maiden Test century after hitting ten fifties in 22 Tests. Fleming had hit 18 fours and a six when he was last out, after six hours. His dismissal followed three quick wickets from Gough, but even so New Zealand finished on 390.

HIGHEST TEST LAST-WICKET PARTNERSHIPS

151	B. F. Hastings and R. O. Collinge	New Zealand v Pakistan at Auckland	1972-73
133	Wasim Raja and Wasim Bari	Pakistan v West Indies at Bridgetown	1976-77
130	R. E. Foster and W. Rhodes	England v Australia at Sydney	1903-04
128	K. Higgs and J. A. Snow	England v West Indies at The Oval	1966
127	J. M. Taylor and A. A. Mailey	Australia v England at Sydney	1924-25
124	J. G. Bracewell and S. L. Boock	New Zealand v Australia at Sydney	1985-86
120	R. A. Duff and W. W. Armstrong	Australia v England at Melbourne	1901-02
117*	P. Willey and R. G. D. Willis	England v West Indies at The Oval	1980
109	H. R. Adhikari and Ghulam Ahmed	India v Pakistan at Delhi	1952-53
106*	**N. J. Astle and D. K. Morrison**	**New Zealand v England at Auckland**	**1996-97**
106	C. L. Hooper and C. A. Walsh	West Indies v Pakistan at St John's	1992-93
104	Zulfiqar Ahmed and Amir Elahi	Pakistan v India at Madras	1952-53
103	H. G. Owen-Smith and A. J. Bell	South Africa v England at Leeds	1929

England moved rapidly to overhaul that. Knight went early, to Doull's in-swinger, but Atherton – finding form at last – and Stewart, maintaining his wonderful touch, added 105 in 28 overs before bad light ended play. Their partnership grew to 182 next day, with Stewart compiling a second consecutive Test century before Atherton drove Patel to Vaughan at short mid-on, who parried it for the bowler to complete a complex return catch. Hussain contributed only minimally, before Thorpe continued the fightback. England were past 300 by the time Stewart's splendid 173, spanning 364 minutes and including 23 fours and a six, was ended by Doull. Any lingering doubts about Stewart's ability to fill two key jobs had disappeared, along with Les Ames's name as holder of the highest Test score by an England wicket-keeper (149 at Kingston in 1929-30). Thorpe carelessly ran out Crawley before close of play and saw White removed, first ball, by Vaughan, but he kept going to reach his third Test century on the fourth morning in a stand of 114 with Cork which took England into the lead. Progress was slow but, after Thorpe went for 119, with 17 fours in 341 minutes, Cork's Test-best 59 plus a bonus last-wicket partnership of 43 between Mullally and Tufnell increased their total to 521, an advantage of 131.

Even so, a draw should have been within New Zealand's reach. Instead, they lost three wickets in 29 overs that evening and another five next morning: Parore induced panic by running out Germon and then offering a simple stumping. Doull helped Astle to avoid an innings defeat, but the afternoon session was only 37 minutes old and the home lead just 11 when he was ninth out, with his stumps uprooted by Gough's in-swinger. Enter Morrison, holder of a world record of 24 Test ducks. He was to negotiate 133 balls, exactly the same number as Astle during a remarkable stand of 106, and seldom looked like being dismissed. Atherton rotated his bowlers with increasing desperation on a pitch that suddenly seemed entirely bland, but nothing could shift the pair. After 165 minutes in tandem, Astle reached his hundred, and New Zealand's heroes left together, the draw secured.

Men of the Match: N. J. Astle and A. J. Stewart.

Close of play: First day, New Zealand 233-5 (S. P. Fleming 58*, C. L. Cairns 15*); Second day, England 123-1 (M. A. Atherton 48*, A. J. Stewart 67*); Third day, England 366-6 (G. P. Thorpe 57*, D. G. Cork 16*); Fourth day, New Zealand 56-3 (A. C. Parore 16*, L. K. Germon 4*).

New Zealand

B. A. Young lbw b Mullally	44	– (2) c Hussain b Cork	3
B. A. Pocock lbw b Gough	70	– (1) lbw b Gough	20
A. C. Parore c Stewart b Cork	6	– st Stewart b Tufnell	33
S. P. Fleming c and b Cork	129	– c Crawley b Tufnell	9
N. J. Astle c Stewart b White	10	– (6) not out	102
J. T. C. Vaughan lbw b Cork	3	– (7) lbw b Tufnell	2
C. L. Cairns c Stewart b White	67	– (8) b Mullally	7
*†L. K. Germon c Stewart b Gough	14	– (5) run out	13
D. N. Patel lbw b Gough	0	– lbw b Mullally	0
S. B. Doull c Knight b Gough	5	– b Gough	26
D. K. Morrison not out	6	– not out	14
B 5, l-b 12, w 2, n-b 17	36	L-b 11, n-b 8	19

1/85 (1) 2/114 (3) 3/193 (2) 4/210 (5) 390 1/17 (2) 2/28 (1) (9 wkts) 248
5/215 (6) 6/333 (7) 7/362 (8) 3/47 (4) 4/88 (5) 5/90 (3)
8/362 (9) 9/380 (10) 10/390 (4) 6/92 (7) 7/101 (8)
 8/105 (9) 9/142 (10)

Bowling: *First Innings*—Cork 32.5–8–96–3; Mullally 27–11–55–1; Gough 32.5–5–91–4; Tufnell 25–5–80–0; White 15–3–51–2. *Second Innings*—Cork 16–3–45–1; Mullally 26–11–47–2; White 10–2–26–0; Gough 22–3–66–2; Tufnell 40–18–53–3.

England

N. V. Knight lbw b Doull	5
*M. A. Atherton c and b Patel	83
†A. J. Stewart c and b Doull	173
N. Hussain c Fleming b Patel	8
G. P. Thorpe hit wkt b Cairns	119
J. P. Crawley run out	14
C. White lbw b Vaughan	0
D. G. Cork c Young b Morrison	59
D. Gough c Germon b Morrison	2
A. D. Mullally c Germon b Morrison	21
P. C. R. Tufnell not out	19
B 2, l-b 12, w 2, n-b 2	18

1/18 (1) 2/200 (2) 3/222 (4) 521
4/304 (3) 5/339 (6) 6/339 (7)
7/453 (5) 8/471 (9)
9/478 (8) 10/521 (10)

Bowling: Morrison 24.4–4–104–3; Doull 39–10–118–2; Cairns 30–3–103–1; Astle 14–3–33–0; Vaughan 36–10–57–1; Patel 44–10–92–2.

Umpires: S. A. Bucknor (West Indies) and R. S. Dunne. Referee: P. J. Burge (Australia).

NEW ZEALAND A v ENGLAND XI

At Wanganui, January 30, 31, February 1, 2. New Zealand A won by 90 runs. Toss: New Zealand A.

When England dismissed New Zealand A for a modest 181, with Silverwood returning a career-best six for 44, it looked as though they might agree with Wanganui's civic slogan: "Well worth a visit". Thereafter, however, they found little pleasure in visiting this delightful hilltop ground and were well beaten by lunch on the final day. They then antagonised the locals by making an over-hasty departure, rushing straight into the team bus with hardly a murmur of farewell. The left-arm pace bowler Geoff Allott dismissed Knight and Crawley in his first spell, and, after the innocuous bowling of New Zealand's attack at Auckland, it was no surprise when he was recalled to the Test squad even before completing a match haul of eight for 120. While both Allott and Davis were able to drag life out of the pitch with their extra pace, England had to work hard for wickets second time around and were left an unlikely target of 363. That they finished just 91 short was due mainly to Russell – in his only first-class game of the winter – and Croft.

Close of play: First day, England XI 30-3 (N. Hussain 5*, C. White 3*); Second day, New Zealand A 187-4 (C. Z. Harris 31*, L. G. Howell 51*); Third day, England XI 166-6 (R. C. Russell 19*, R. D. B. Croft 16*).

New Zealand A

C. M. Spearman c Hussain b Silverwood	0	– (2) c Knight b Irani	47
*D. J. Murray c Russell b Tufnell	49	– (1) c Caddick	12
P. J. B. Chandler lbw b Silverwood	3	– c Atherton b Croft	31
M. J. Horne b Silverwood	64	– lbw b Tufnell	8
C. Z. Harris c Knight b Silverwood	16	– c Knight b White	71
L. G. Howell c Russell b Silverwood	3	– lbw b Tufnell	66
†J. M. Mills not out	28	– c Silverwood b White	20
P. J. Wiseman b Caddick	8	– not out	12
H. T. Davis c Atherton b Caddick	0	– lbw b Caddick	0
R. J. Kennedy c Knight b Croft	3	– c Atherton b Caddick	11
G. I. Allott c Hussain b Silverwood	5	– c Russell b Irani	1
L-b 2	2	B 2, l-b 6, n-b 1	9
	181		**288**

1/0 2/12 3/109 4/121 5/134
6/139 7/159 8/161 9/164

1/28 2/84 3/101 4/101 5/218
6/253 7/266 8/267 9/281

Bowling: *First Innings*—Silverwood 20.1–5–44–6; Caddick 15–2–42–2; White 2–0–14–0; Croft 15–4–30–1; Tufnell 23–13–28–1; Irani 6–0–21–0. *Second Innings*—Silverwood 17–1–74–0; Caddick 27–7–52–3; Tufnell 17–4–45–2; Croft 24–6–48–1; Irani 6.5–1–13–2; White 14–2–48–2.

England XI

N. V. Knight c Chandler b Allott	11	– c Spearman b Allott	4
*M. A. Atherton c Mills b Davis	5	– lbw b Allott	0
N. Hussain c Harris b Davis	14	– c Allott b Davis	57
J. P. Crawley c Murray b Allott	5	– c Mills b Allott	38
C. White c Chandler b Allott	7	– c Chandler b Wiseman	21
R. C. Irani c Chandler b Allott	40	– b Allott	4
R. D. B. Croft c Horne b Davis	2	– (8) c Chandler b Wiseman	49
†R. C. Russell c Harris b Davis	0	– (7) not out	61
A. R. Caddick c and b Wiseman	6	– c Horne b Davis	12
C. E. W. Silverwood c Chandler b Wiseman	11	– run out	10
P. C. R. Tufnell not out	0	– c Kennedy b Harris	2
L-b 5, n-b 1	6	B 7, l-b 6, n-b 1	14
	107		**272**

1/16 2/17 3/23 4/39 5/51
6/57 7/57 8/79 9/107

1/3 2/6 3/72 4/126 5/126
6/143 7/216 8/241 9/266

Bowling: *First Innings*—Allott 15.3–6–44–4; Davis 14–8–22–4; Kennedy 7–2–23–0; Wiseman 8–2–13–2. *Second Innings*—Allott 16–1–76–4; Davis 18–3–63–2; Kennedy 10–2–32–0; Wiseman 30–6–84–2; Harris 2.4–1–4–1.

Umpires: B. F. Bowden and E. A. Watkin.

NEW ZEALAND v ENGLAND

Second Test Match

At Wellington, February 6, 7, 8, 9, 10. England won by an innings and 68 runs. Toss: New Zealand. Test debut: D. L. Vettori.

Having stalled on the winning line in Bulawayo and Auckland, England cruised over it here to record their first away Test victory for two years. The triumph was sealed early on the final afternoon but, in actual playing time, the contest lasted little more than three days, with the weather trying but failing to thwart England yet again.

England played consistently good cricket throughout the match and, after Croft and Caddick replaced White and the increasingly erratic Mullally, appeared at last to have found a combination that could stand them in good stead for more than one Test match.

For New Zealand, the match was a shambles on and off the field. They were struggling from the moment Germon opted to bat and soon found themselves with the kind of problem once associated with England. Four of the players were accused of being out on the town unacceptably late after the second day's play. New Zealand Cricket said three were back just after midnight, which was acceptable, and the other – reported to be Chris Cairns – had been dealt with. The incident was badly handled and the refusal to name names cast a shadow over the whole squad. Add the fact that Allott was accused by a TV commentator of seam-picking (an allegation rejected by referee Peter Burge) and this was a Test New Zealand wanted to forget – quickly.

However, their team changes worked well. Allott sharpened up their pace attack. And, most stunningly, Daniel Vettori, a shaggy-haired, bespectacled left-arm spinner with only two first-class matches behind him, also came in to be New Zealand's youngest ever Test cricketer. He was just 18 years and ten days – 187 days younger than Doug Freeman in 1932-33 – but had shown his ability to Northern Districts against England two weeks earlier, and performed with considerable maturity, more indeed than some of the senior players.

Rain and a wet outfield delayed play on the first day until after tea. Germon won a toss he would rather have lost and then saw his team crash to 56 for six in 30 overs. There was some movement off the seam but swing proved more deadly, particularly against batsmen who fenced at far too many deliveries. Pocock set the pattern with a limp shot outside off stump to give Caddick a welcome-back wicket. Caddick was perhaps the most deserving bowler but Gough was the most effective, and they more than made up for a disappointing performance by Cork. It took England less than 90 minutes next morning to put New Zealand out of their misery, with Gough completing his first five-wicket Test haul since Sydney, two years earlier.

Conditions were now just about ideal for batting and England did not waste them, securing a lead of 80 by the close with seven wickets in hand. Knight's lack of footwork gave a catch to gully, but New Zealand had to graft for further successes. Doull dislodged Atherton with a straight one, and a superb left-handed slip catch by Fleming stopped Stewart when he looked on course for a third successive Test century. Hussain and Thorpe combined effectively, however, until Vettori continued his meteoric rise to fame early on the third morning: he produced a little extra bounce to undo Hussain, and bowled throughout probingly and, so it seemed, nervelessly. But the seam attack was missing Cairns, who had a bruised finger, and Thorpe completed his second consecutive hundred during another century partnership, with Crawley.

At 331 for four, England already led by 207. Then Thorpe was stumped, after five and a half hours, and two more wickets fell at the same score. They added only 52 more as Doull picked up five wickets for the fourth time in his 15 Tests. The collapse did England no lasting harm but, after the near-misses of Bulawayo and Auckland, it was understandable if they felt uncomfortable when heavy rain (and second-rate equipment to combat it) prevented any play before late afternoon on day four and New Zealand then reached 89 without losing a wicket. Finally, the spinners broke through, and three wickets in 14 balls from Croft took England close to victory.

Pocock survived and reached fifty in 239 balls, the slowest in those Tests where balls received

[*Patrick Eagar*

Daniel Vettori in action during his impressive Test debut at Wellington.

have been recorded, though Trevor Bailey must have received more balls at Lord's in 1953. The dark clouds again threatened to put a dampener on England's final-day party. But the weather granted New Zealand only half an hour's respite and the new ball soon brought four wickets for Gough, two for Caddick and a knees-up for the Barmy Army, whose songs of triumph could be heard as Atherton gave a winner's press conference for the first time in ten overseas Tests since January 1995 in Adelaide.

Man of the Match: G. P. Thorpe.

Close of play: First day, New Zealand 56-6 (N. J. Astle 15*, D. N. Patel 5*); Second day, England 204-3 (N. Hussain 60*, G. P. Thorpe 47*); Third day, New Zealand 48-0 (B. A. Pocock 13*, B. A. Young 32*); Fourth day, New Zealand 125-4 (B. A. Pocock 45*, L. K. Germon 0*).

New Zealand

B. A. Young c Stewart b Gough	8	– (2) c Stewart b Tufnell	56
B. A. Pocock c Cork b Caddick	6	– (1) c Knight b Gough	64
A. C. Parore c Stewart b Gough	4	– lbw b Croft	15
S. P. Fleming c and b Caddick	1	– c and b Croft	0
N. J. Astle c Croft b Gough	36	– (7) c Stewart b Gough	4
C. L. Cairns c Hussain b Gough	3	– (8) c Knight b Caddick	22
*†L. K. Germon c Stewart b Caddick	10	– (6) b Gough	11
D. N. Patel c Cork b Caddick	45	– lbw b Croft	0
S. B. Doull c Stewart b Gough	0	– c Knight b Gough	0
G. I. Allott c Knight b Cork	1	– b Caddick	2
D. L. Vettori not out	3	– not out	2
L-b 5, n-b 2	7	B 5, l-b 4, n-b 6	15

1/14 (2) 2/18 (1) 3/19 (3) 4/19 (4)   124   1/89 (2) 2/125 (3) 3/125 (4)   191
5/23 (6) 6/48 (7) 7/85 (5)   4/125 (5) 5/161 (6) 6/164 (1)
8/85 (9) 9/106 (10) 10/124 (8)   7/175 (9) 8/175 (9)
                                    9/182 (10) 10/191 (8)

Bowling: First Innings—Cork 14–4–34–1; Caddick 18.3–5–45–4; Gough 16–6–40–5. *Second Innings*—Cork 10–1–42–0; Caddick 27.2–11–40–2; Croft 20–9–19–3; Gough 23–9–52–4; Tufnell 23–9–29–1.

England

N. V. Knight c Patel b Doull	8	A. R. Caddick c Allott b Vettori	20
*M. A. Atherton lbw b Doull	30	P. C. R. Tufnell not out	6
†A. J. Stewart c Fleming b Allott	52		
N. Hussain c Young b Vettori	64	B 3, l-b 9, n-b 2	14
G. P. Thorpe st Germon b Patel	108		
J. P. Crawley c Germon b Doull	56	1/10 (1) 2/80 (2) 3/106 (3)	383
D. G. Cork lbw b Astle	7	4/213 (4) 5/331 (5) 6/331 (6)
R. D. B. Croft c Fleming b Doull	0	7/331 (8) 8/357 (7)
D. Gough c Fleming b Doull	18	9/357 (9) 10/383 (10)

Bowling: Doull 28–10–75–5; Allott 31–6–91–1; Vettori 34.3–10–98–2; Cairns 4–2–8–0; Astle 14–5–30–1; Patel 24–6–59–1; Pocock 2–0–10–0.

Umpires: S. A. Bucknor (West Indies) and D. B. Cowie.   Referee: P. J. Burge (Australia).

NEW ZEALAND v ENGLAND

Third Test Match

At Christchurch, February 14, 15, 16, 17, 18. England won by four wickets. Toss: England. Test debut: M. J. Horne.

England successfully chased a target in excess of 300 for only the second time in their Test history; they won with 12.2 overs to spare, confirming their first overseas series triumph since their last visit to New Zealand, in 1991-92. Although a 2-0 scoreline accurately reflected the balance of power, it could have finished 1-1 but for an outstanding performance from England's captain Atherton. He carried his bat for 94 in the first innings, then took his team to within sight of victory by scoring 118; in all, he spent 12 hours and 24 minutes at the crease. If anything could upstage his undefeated 185 in Johannesburg 14 months earlier, this was it – another heroic effort but, this time, in a winning cause. Although disappointed, New Zealand regained some pride; they would win Tests in the future after playing worse cricket than this.

England went into the match unchanged, something they had not managed for 33 Tests. New Zealand gave a first cap to Otago batsman Matt Horne, summoned fast bowler Davis for his second, two and a half years after his debut at Nottingham, and hastily recalled Parore (initially dropped after Wellington) to keep wicket when Germon withdrew with a groin strain. Stephen Fleming took over the captaincy, becoming his country's youngest Test captain at 23 years 319 days.

[*Patrick Eagar*

Mike Atherton during his outstanding performance in the Third Test at Christchurch.

A well-grassed pitch persuaded Atherton to field first but, as at Auckland, the first-day dividends were modest; New Zealand reached 229 with half their wickets left. The off-spinner Croft demanded most respect, and took three of the wickets, including that of Fleming, who spoiled three and a half hours of sound example-setting by being stumped. New Zealand's other casualty, in more ways than one, was the newcomer Horne. Hit on the left hand by Gough, he soldiered on for another 30 runs before guiding the same bowler to slip; an X-ray revealed a broken bone. Croft went on to his first five-wicket haul in Tests but solid half-centuries from Parore and Cairns had given the home side a useful platform.

With a degree of confidence bordering on arrogance, England set out to cruise past New Zealand's total of 346. Instead, they nosedived to 104 for five, with only Atherton showing sufficient care. All had fallen to attacking strokes, most of them undermined by limited footwork, and the story continued next morning when Cork tried to pull Davis's fifth ball from well outside off stump and was caught behind. Croft gave decent support, but the rest followed all too quickly – leaving Atherton high and dry in the 90s and New Zealand 118 ahead.

Here, at last, was an opportunity for the home team to dominate, or, alternatively, for England to show they could attack from a position of weakness. And, after Cork and Gough began the process, the spinners, Croft and Tufnell, turned this day upside down by reducing New Zealand to 95 for six by close of play. England had some good fortune: Fleming appeared unlucky to lose a pad-bat decision, and Young stood in disbelief when umpire Hair ruled that Knight had got his hand underneath a prod at silly point. Young needed to be given out twice, although he claimed not to have seen the first signal. TV replays failed to prove whether the catch had carried but the batsman was fortunate that referee Peter Burge took no action, after "listening to his explanation and given his unblemished record".

Cairns and Vettori added 71 for the eighth wicket, however, and England faced a tantalising target of 305. A pitch still playing perfectly well offered them hope, even if history did not. But Vettori posed numerous problems by bowling his left-arm spin over the wicket and into footmarks outside the right-hander's leg stump. Knight succumbed, dragging a drive to mid-on,

HIGHEST FOURTH-INNINGS TOTALS TO WIN A TEST

406-4	India (needing 403) v West Indies at Port-of-Spain	1975-76
404-3	Australia (needing 404) v England at Leeds	1948
362-7	Australia (needing 359) v West Indies at Georgetown	1977-78
348-5	West Indies (needing 345) v New Zealand at Auckland...................	1968-69
344-1	West Indies (needing 342) v England at Lord's	1984
342-8	Australia (needing 339) v India at Perth	1977-78
336-5	Australia (needing 336) v South Africa at Durban	1949-50
332-7	England (needing 332) v Australia at Melbourne	1928-29
324-5	New Zealand (needing 324) v Pakistan at Christchurch	1993-94
317-2	West Indies (needing 317) v Pakistan at Georgetown	1957-58
315-6	Australia (needing 315) v England at Adelaide	1901-02
315-9	Pakistan (needing 314) v Australia at Karachi.........................	1994-95
307-6	**England (needing 305) v New Zealand at Christchurch**	**1996-97**

and Stewart, who scratched out 17 in nearly two hours, gave a catch to short leg when Vettori briefly tried his luck around the wicket. Next morning, England had some luck when a ball from Vettori jammed between the bat and pad of Caddick, the night-watchman. As it fell, Fleming grabbed it off the batsman's boot, but umpire Hair ruled not out under Law 23. Caddick gave important help to Atherton, who was in his element. He had seen out the fourth day and stayed for much of the fifth, completing his 11th Test century (and fourth against New Zealand), and looked set to finish the job until sheer fatigue, after 399 minutes of total concentration, saw him caught behind off Astle. Hussain, his partner during a vital stand of 80, followed him back in the next over, taken off pad and glove, and Vettori gave New Zealand further hope by adding Thorpe. Vettori was hugely impressive: he took four wickets and conceded only 97 in a marathon of 57 overs. He might just have been a winner, but a partnership of 76 between Crawley and Cork made sure Atherton's marvellous efforts would not be wasted.

Man of the Match: M. A. Atherton.

Close of play: First day, New Zealand 229-5 (A. C. Parore 38*, C. L. Cairns 10*); Second day, England 145-5 (M. A. Atherton 66*, D. G. Cork 16*); Third day, New Zealand 95-6 (C. L. Cairns 5*, M. J. Horne 4*); Fourth day, England 118-2 (M. A. Atherton 65*, A. R. Caddick 0*).

New Zealand

B. A. Young b Cork...........................	11	– (2) c Knight b Tufnell	49
B. A. Pocock c Atherton b Croft................	22	– (1) b Cork	0
M. J. Horne c Thorpe b Gough.................	42	– (8) c Stewart b Caddick	13
*S. P. Fleming st Stewart b Croft..............	62	– c Knight b Tufnell	11
N. J. Astle c Hussain b Croft..................	15	– c Hussain b Croft	5
†A. C. Parore c Hussain b Croft...............	59	– (3) c Stewart b Gough	8
C. L. Cairns c Stewart b Caddick..............	57	– (6) c Knight b Tufnell	52
S. B. Doull run out..........................	1	– (7) c Knight b Croft	5
D. L. Vettori run out	25	– not out	29
H. T. Davis c Hussain b Croft.................	8	– b Gough	1
G. I. Allott not out	8	– c Stewart b Gough	1
B 1, l-b 16, n-b 19	36	L-b 8, n-b 4.............	12

1/14 (1) 2/78 (2) 3/106 (3) 4/137 (5)	**346**	
5/201 (4) 6/283 (6) 7/288 (8)		1/0 (1) 2/42 (3) 3/61 (4) **186**
8/310 (7) 9/337 (9) 10/346 (10)		4/76 (5) 5/80 (2) 6/89 (7)
		7/107 (8) 8/178 (6)
		9/184 (10) 10/186 (11)

Bowling: *First Innings*—Cork 20–3–78–1; Caddick 32–8–64–1; Gough 21–3–70–1; Croft 39.1–5–95–5; Tufnell 16–6–22–0; Thorpe 1–1–0–0. *Second Innings*—Cork 6–2–5–1; Caddick 10–1–25–1; Croft 31–13–48–2; Gough 13.3–5–42–3; Tufnell 28–9–58–3.

England

N. V. Knight c Fleming b Allott	14	– c Davis b Vettori	29
*M. A. Atherton not out	94	– c Parore b Astle	118
†A. J. Stewart c sub (C. Z. Harris) b Allott	17	– c Pocock b Vettori	17
N. Hussain c Parore b Cairns	12	– (5) c Fleming b Vettori	33
G. P. Thorpe b Astle	18	– (6) c and b Vettori	2
J. P. Crawley c Parore b Allott	1	– (7) not out	40
D. G. Cork c Parore b Davis	16	– (8) not out	39
R. D. B. Croft c Davis b Astle	31		
D. Gough b Vettori	0		
A. R. Caddick c sub (C. Z. Harris) b Allott	4	– (4) c Fleming b Doull	15
P. C. R. Tufnell c Young b Doull	13		
L-b 4, w 1, n-b 5	10	B 2, l-b 8, w 1, n-b 3	14
	228		**(6 wkts) 307**

1/20 (1) 2/40 (3) 3/70 (4) 4/103 (5)   1/64 (1) 2/116 (3)   (6 wkts) 307
5/104 (6) 6/145 (7) 7/198 (8)   3/146 (4) 4/226 (2)
8/199 (9) 9/210 (10) 10/228 (11)   5/226 (5) 6/231 (6)

Bowling: *First Innings*—Allott 18–3–74–4; Doull 17.4–3–49–1; Davis 18–2–50–1; Vettori 12–4–13–1; Cairns 8–5–12–1; Astle 11–2–26–2. *Second Innings*—Allott 12.4–2–32–0; Davis 18–6–43–0; Doull 21–8–57–1; Vettori 57–18–97–4; Cairns 10–1–23–0; Astle 28–10–45–1.

Umpires: D. B. Hair (Australia) and R. S. Dunne.   Referee: P. J. Burge (Australia).

†NEW ZEALAND v ENGLAND

First One-Day International

At Christchurch, February 20 (day/night). England won by four wickets. Toss: New Zealand.

The mercurial Tufnell had a rapid change of fortunes and turned out the match-winner, even though England had planned to exclude him until they discovered they were to play on the worn Test match pitch. In his first one-day international for two years, he took four for 22, and a stand of 170 between Stewart and Thorpe then ensured victory. England had lost their last 12 one-day games overseas against Test-playing teams. A few days before the match Tufnell had been accused of smoking cannabis in the toilet at a Christchurch restaurant. No evidence was produced to support this claim, which began to look like a successful publicity stunt. New Zealand made a good start, thanks to Astle, but he was caught at mid-off from Tufnell's fourth ball and – despite an enterprising innings from Harris – England were not troubled again, although the novelty of the occasion, the first day-night international at Lancaster Park, made the atmosphere more than normally hysterical.

Man of the Match: P. C. R. Tufnell.

New Zealand

B. A. Young c Thorpe b Mullally	14	D. N. Patel not out	1
N. J. Astle c Thorpe b Tufnell	50		
A. C. Parore c and b Tufnell	26	L-b 9, w 4, n-b 2	15
S. P. Fleming st Stewart b Tufnell	34		
C. L. Cairns c Mullally b Tufnell	15	1/24 (1) 2/87 (2)	(6 wkts, 50 overs) 222
C. Z. Harris not out	48	3/100 (3) 4/134 (5)	
*†L. K. Germon b Cork	19	5/148 (4) 6/203 (7)	Score at 15 overs: 76-1

G. R. Larsen, S. B. Doull and H. T. Davis did not bat.

Bowling: Cork 9–0–52–1; Mullally 5–2–21–1; Croft 10–1–41–0; Gough 10–0–45–0; Tufnell 10–1–22–4; Thorpe 6–0–32–0.

England

N. V. Knight c Germon b Doull 8	R. D. B. Croft not out 8
*M. A. Atherton b Patel............... 19	
†A. J. Stewart c Astle b Davis 81	L-b 6, w 6 12
G. P. Thorpe b Davis 82	
N. Hussain not out 11	1/28 (2) 2/28 (1) (6 wkts, 48.5 overs) 226
J. P. Crawley b Doull................ 0	3/198 (4) 4/205 (3)
D. G. Cork c Young b Davis.......... 5	5/207 (6) 6/218 (7) Score at 15 overs: 77-2

D. Gough, A. D. Mullally and P. C. R. Tufnell did not bat.

Bowling: Doull 10–0–33–2; Patel 7–0–43–1; Astle 4–0–26–0; Cairns 4–0–25–0; Davis 8.5–0–44–3; Larsen 8–0–23–0; Harris 7–0–26–0.

Umpires: C. E. King and D. M. Quested.

A RECORD FOR EVERY BATSMAN

Players in the one-day internationals were asked to select a piece of music to be played as they went out to bat.

New Zealand

Nathan Astle	*Unbelievable* – EMF
Chris Cairns	*Back in Black* – AC/DC
Heath Davis	*Wild Thing* – The Troggs
Simon Doull	*No Second Prize* – Jimmy Barnes
Stephen Fleming	*Omen Theme (Carmina Burana)*
Lee Germon	*That's the Way (I Like It)* – KC and the Sunshine Band
Chris Harris	*Relax* – Frankie Goes To Hollywood
Matt Horne	*New Sensation* – INXS
Gavin Larsen	*Movin' On Up* – M People
Danny Morrison	*Start Me Up* – Rolling Stones
Adam Parore	*Danger Zone* – Kenny Loggins
Dipak Patel	*U R The Best Thing* – D:Ream
Blair Pocock	*Alive and Kicking* – Simple Minds
Craig Spearman	*Whatta Man* – Salt 'N' Pepa
Justin Vaughan	*Hit Me With Your Best Shot* – Pat Benatar
Bryan Young	*Start Me Up* – Rolling Stones

England

Mike Atherton	*Some Might Say* – Oasis
Nick Knight	*Some Might Say* – Oasis
Nasser Hussain	*Zombie* – The Cranberries
Graham Thorpe	*Swamp Thing* – The Grid
Alec Stewart	*Summer of '69* – Bryan Adams
John Crawley	*Wonderwall* – Oasis
Dominic Cork	*Return of the Mack* – Mark Morrison
Robert Croft	*Delilah* – Tom Jones
Darren Gough	*Walking on Sunshine* – Katrina and the Waves
Ronnie Irani	*Two Tribes* – Frankie Goes To Hollywood
Andrew Caddick	*I Feel Good* – James Brown
Chris Silverwood	*Supersonic* – Oasis
Alan Mullally	*Even Better than the Real Thing* – U2
Craig White	*Son of a Gun* – Jx
Jack Russell	*How Much is that Doggie in the Window?* – Lita Roza
Phil Tufnell	*Cigarettes & Alcohol* – Oasis

†NEW ZEALAND v ENGLAND

Second One-Day International

At Auckland, February 23. England won by six wickets, their target having been revised to 132 from 26 overs. Toss: New Zealand.

New Zealand paid for ignoring a threatening weather forecast, though the real losers were 24,000 spectators, who saw a potentially tight match turned into a cakewalk for England when old-fashioned average run-rate was used to set a revised target. With Mullally and Caddick hopelessly off line (ten wides between them in the first ten overs), New Zealand made a flying start. Irani and Croft restored some order, but Cairns raced to 79 off 74 balls to leave England needing five an over. With the promised rain closing in, Knight and Stewart were even more aggressive than usual. They took 47 from six overs before the heavens opened and, when play resumed, the required 85 off 20 – with no relaxation of the 15-over fielding restrictions – presented few problems and little excitement. At least Knight scored his first half-century since Bulawayo, while Hussain, deputising because Atherton had a bad back, tasted victory in his first outing as England captain.

Man of the Match: N. V. Knight.

New Zealand

B. A. Young c Stewart b Irani	46	G. R. Larsen not out	12
N. J. Astle c Stewart b Mullally	4		
A. C. Parore run out	2	L-b 9, w 16, n-b 4	29
S. P. Fleming c Caddick b Gough	42		
C. L. Cairns run out	79	1/24 (2) 2/44 (3) (8 wkts, 50 overs) 253	
C. Z. Harris c sub (C. White) b Caddick	14	3/96 (1) 4/138 (4)	
*†L. K. Germon b Caddick	1	5/189 (6) 6/202 (7)	
D. N. Patel run out	24	7/219 (5) 8/253 (8) Score at 15 overs: 81-2	

S. B. Doull and H. T. Davis did not bat.

Bowling: Cork 10–0–51–0; Mullally 7–0–36–1; Caddick 6–0–33–2; Gough 10–0–65–1; Irani 7–0–26–1; Croft 10–1–33–0.

England

N. V. Knight not out	84	*N. Hussain not out	9
†A. J. Stewart lbw b Davis	30	W 3	3
D. G. Cork c Young b Larsen	4		
R. C. Irani c Astle b Doull	0	1/86 (2) 2/91 (3) (4 wkts, 19.3 overs) 134	
G. P. Thorpe c and b Doull	4	3/92 (4) 4/100 (5) Score at 15 overs: 105-4	

J. P. Crawley, R. D. B. Croft, D. Gough, A. R. Caddick and A. D. Mullally did not bat.

Bowling: Davis 6–1–39–1; Doull 5–0–39–2; Larsen 5–0–31–1; Harris 2–0–8–0; Astle 1.3–0–17–0.

Umpires: B. F. Bowden and D. B. Cowie.

†NEW ZEALAND v ENGLAND

Third One-Day International

At Napier, February 26 (day/night). Tied. Toss: New Zealand.

Gough, needing two, missed Allott's last ball of the match. The batsmen scrambled a bye, so this seesawing contest finished all square – a fair result, which kept the series alive. New Zealand made another encouraging start, with Young to the fore, only to be frustrated by some disciplined bowling. Caddick's second spell, 5–2–10–2, put England back on track and then White, with career-best figures, scythed through the lower order. England, too, were quickly out of the blocks but were reduced to a crawl by Harris. Making the ball wobble alarmingly at slow-medium pace, he took three key wickets in 32 deliveries and conceded just 20 in his ten overs. Thorpe, though, stayed calm and White gave intelligent support to set up a nerve-tingling final over. England began it slight favourites at 230 for six. Although White was run out, four from Croft reduced the target to two from two. Then Allott, in his first one-day international, bowled Croft to set up the climax.

Man of the Match: C. Z. Harris.

New Zealand

B. A. Young b Caddick	53	H. T. Davis b White	1
N. J. Astle c Stewart b Gough	34	G. I. Allott not out	1
*†L. K. Germon st Stewart b Croft	22	L-b 11, w 4, n-b 4	19
S. P. Fleming run out	12		
C. L. Cairns c Cork b Caddick	11	1/50 (2) 2/103 (3) 3/125 (4) (49.4 overs) 237	
A. C. Parore c and b White	24	4/140 (5) 5/145 (1)	
C. Z. Harris c Stewart b White	19	6/178 (7) 7/191 (6)	
G. R. Larsen c Stewart b Gough	19	8/233 (8) 9/234 (10)	
S. B. Doull b White	22	10/237 (9) Score at 15 overs: 75-1	

Bowling: Cork 9–1–42–0; Caddick 10–2–43–2; Gough 10–0–34–2; Irani 5–0–28–0; Croft 10–0–42–1; White 5.4–0–37–4.

England

N. V. Knight c and b Allott	39	R. D. B. Croft b Allott	4
*M. A. Atherton b Harris	23	D. Gough not out	0
†A. J. Stewart b Harris	17	B 2, l-b 4, w 5, n-b 2	13
G. P. Thorpe c Germon b Doull	55		
N. Hussain b Harris	13	1/67 (1) 2/82 (2) (8 wkts, 50 overs) 237	
R. C. Irani c Doull b Larsen	4	3/87 (3) 4/114 (5)	
C. White run out	38	5/127 (6) 6/174 (4)	
D. G. Cork not out	31	7/232 (7) 8/236 (9) Score at 15 overs: 77-1	

A. R. Caddick did not bat.

Bowling: Doull 9–0–53–1; Allott 9–2–49–2; Davis 10–0–40–0; Harris 10–3–20–3; Larsen 10–0–50–1; Astle 2–0–19–0.

Umpires: C. E. King and D. M. Quested.

†NEW ZEALAND v ENGLAND

Fourth One-Day International

At Auckland, March 2. New Zealand won by nine runs. Toss: England.

After rain washed out play on the scheduled Saturday, New Zealand finally won a game, thanks to their medium-pacers, and despite a brave attempt by the one-handed Knight to see his team through. Bowling on a damp pitch — the match was reduced to 43 overs by further rain — England looked set to clinch the series when they took their hosts' last eight for just 40, with Croft, in particular, inducing false shots and crazy single-calling. Then Knight was hit by Davis's first ball and retired with a triple fracture of his left index finger. New Zealand defended their small total in tigerish fashion. Davis and Allott made inroads, but it was Astle who claimed the key wicket when he defeated Stewart's attempted clip to leg. Knight returned at the end of the 40th over, but faced only one ball as Silverwood hit 11 from eight at the other end, before being caught close to the fence, trying to drive Larsen for six.

Men of the Match: N. J. Astle and G. R. Larsen.

New Zealand

B. A. Young c and b White	16	H. T. Davis b Caddick	0
N. J. Astle c Stewart b Irani	51	G. I. Allott b Gough	3
*†L. K. Germon lbw b Gough	0	B 2, l-b 3, w 11	16
S. P. Fleming c Hussain b Croft	37		
C. L. Cairns not out	2	1/53 (1) 2/54 (3) 3/113 (2) (39.5 overs) 153	
A. C. Parore c Croft b Caddick	13	4/116 (5) 5/120 (4)	
C. Z. Harris c Hussain b Croft	0	6/120 (7) 7/129 (8)	
G. R. Larsen run out	2	8/136 (6) 9/141 (10)	
S. B. Doull not out	13	10/153 (11) Score at 12 overs: 59-2	

Bowling: Caddick 8–1–29–2; Silverwood 5–0–20–0; Gough 5.5–0–29–2; White 5–0–21–1; Croft 9–1–26–2; Irani 7–0–23–1.

England

N. V. Knight not out	1	A. R. Caddick b Larsen	0
*M. A. Atherton c Harris b Allott	9	C. E. W. Silverwood c Allott b Larsen	12
†A. J. Stewart b Astle	42	L-b 6, w 7	13
G. P. Thorpe c Parore b Allott	7		
N. Hussain b Davis	3	1/22 (2) 2/32 (4) 3/41 (5) (41.3 overs) 144	
R. C. Irani c Fleming b Davis	0	4/41 (6) 5/91 (3)	
C. White c Parore b Harris	32	6/113 (7) 7/132 (8)	
R. D. B. Croft run out	20	8/132 (9) 9/133 (10)	
D. Gough c and b Larsen	5	10/144 (11) Score at 12 overs: 53-4	

N. V. Knight, when 1, retired hurt at 1 and resumed at 133.

Bowling: Davis 6–0–32–2; Allott 5–1–21–2; Doull 6–1–15–0; Larsen 8.3–0–20–3; Harris 9–0–26–1; Astle 7–1–24–1.

Umpires: D. B. Cowie and R. S. Dunne.

†NEW ZEALAND v ENGLAND

Fifth One-Day International

At Wellington, March 4. New Zealand won by 28 runs. Toss: New Zealand.

New Zealand easily completed their comeback from 2-0 down to share the series. But it was a short-lived triumph for their captain, Germon. Before the day had ended, he had been dropped for the imminent series against Sri Lanka and succeeded by Fleming. The combination of Fleming's leadership and Parore's usefulness as a keeper-batsman had persuaded the selectors Germon was expendable. Once more, the home total fell away, after a splendid 94 from opener Astle, who struck ten fours. But this time it proved far too tall for England, who lacked New Zealand's hunger. Harris, again, offered them nothing to bat on, Larsen was only fractionally more generous and two wickets confirmed Astle as star of the show. Atherton tried to lead from the front, until run out by Harris, while Thorpe provided some middle-order substance, but New Zealand's victory would have been more emphatic still without a last-wicket stand of 27 between Gough and Caddick. Russell made his only international appearance of the 14-week tour. Ian Botham joined 30 New Zealand police officers and had his head shaved for charity during the interval. The stunt raised £50,000 for the Child Cancer foundation.

Man of the Match: N. J. Astle.

New Zealand

B. A. Young c Russell b Caddick	11	G. R. Larsen run out	0
N. J. Astle c Atherton b Caddick	94	H. T. Davis not out	7
S. P. Fleming b Croft	17	L-b 10, w 14, n-b 2	26
C. L. Cairns c Russell b White	1		
A. C. Parore lbw b Caddick	18	1/28 (1) 2/84 (3) (8 wkts, 50 overs) 228	
C. Z. Harris c Stewart b Gough	36	3/87 (4) 4/122 (5)	
*†L. K. Germon lbw b Silverwood	2	5/197 (2) 6/200 (7)	
D. N. Patel not out	16	7/206 (6) 8/208 (9) Score at 15 overs: 77-1	

G. I. Allott did not bat.

Bowling: Caddick 10–1–35–3; Silverwood 10–0–53–1; Gough 10–1–48–1; White 10–0–44–1; Croft 10–1–38–1.

England

*M. A. Atherton run out	43	D. Gough c Fleming b Davis	16
A. J. Stewart c Patel b Allott	18	A. R. Caddick not out	12
N. Hussain st Germon b Harris	20	L-b 8, w 8, n-b 1	17
G. P. Thorpe st Germon b Larsen	55		
C. E. W. Silverwood b Patel	4	1/43 (2) 2/77 (3) 3/107 (1) (47.5 overs) 200	
J. P. Crawley lbw b Larsen	11	4/119 (5) 5/136 (6)	
†R. C. Russell c Germon b Astle	2	6/139 (7) 7/139 (8)	
C. White c Germon b Astle	0	8/158 (9) 9/173 (4)	
R. D. B. Croft run out	2	10/200 (10) Score at 15 overs: 68-1	

Bowling: Allott 8–0–40–1; Davis 7.5–0–44–1; Larsen 10–0–31–2; Harris 10–2–22–1; Patel 7–0–29–1; Astle 5–0–26–2.

Umpires: R. S. Dunne and E. A. Watkin. Series referee: P. J. Burge (Australia).

INTERNATIONAL SCHEDULE, 1998-99

The following tours were arranged as at January 1998:

1998

August-September	Australians to Sri Lanka
August-September	Indians to Sri Lanka
September	Commonwealth Games
October	World tournament in Bangladesh
October	West Indians to Zimbabwe
October-November	Australians to Pakistan
November	Indians to Zimbabwe
November-December	Indians to Pakistan
November-December	Zimbabweans to Pakistan
November-January 1999	West Indians to South Africa
November-February 1999	England to Australia
December-January 1999	Sri Lankans to Australia
December-January 1999	Indians to New Zealand
1999	
January-March	Pakistanis to India
February-March	South Africans to New Zealand
February-April	Australians to the West Indies
May-June	WORLD CUP in England
June-August	New Zealanders to England

All fixtures subject to confirmation.

ENGLAND'S INTERNATIONAL SCHEDULE

Home		**Away**	
1998	Tests and one-day internationals v South Africa and Sri Lanka	1998-99	Tests and one-day internationals in Australia
1999	WORLD CUP Tests v New Zealand	1999-2000	Tests and one-day internationals in South Africa and Zimbabwe
2000	Tests and one-day internationals v West Indies and Zimbabwe	2000-01	Tests and one-day internationals in Pakistan and Sri Lanka
2001	Tests and one-day internationals v Australia	2001-02	Tests and one-day internationals in India and New Zealand
2002	Tests and one-day internationals v India and Sri Lanka	2002-03	Tests and one-day internationals in Australia
2003	Tests and one-day internationals v South Africa and New Zealand		WORLD CUP in South Africa

All fixtures subject to confirmation.

ENGLAND A IN AUSTRALIA, 1996-97

By RALPH DELLOR

It would be easy to be swept up in the euphoria of a tour which produced a highly satisfactory playing record, achieved by talented young cricketers who behaved in an exemplary manner on and off the field. England A, and their management, deserve the highest praise for their accomplishments in Australia, not the least of which was to restore some pride to English cricket. When they returned home in December, with six wins and only one defeat in ten matches, the senior team's trip to Zimbabwe was already beginning to turn sour; it was the fourth winter running that England A had shown up the Test side.

It came as a surprise to some Australians, conditioned to regard England cricketers as something of a soft option, to find that this team did not wilt at the first whiff of cordite. Instead, adversity gelled them into a spirited fighting unit. This was most clearly seen in Adelaide, where they played South Australia, the reigning Sheffield Shield champions: the kind of batting collapse which has bedevilled English teams was followed, less typically, by an inspired fightback. Similarly, in a one-day match against New South Wales, the last of the recognised batsmen was seventh out with 82 still needed from 15 overs. Yet England A won with three balls to spare.

Taking a pragmatic perspective, it has to be remembered that, to achieve these spectacular recoveries, the team had to be in trouble in the first place. However, plenty of English touring parties, especially in Australia, have dug holes without suggesting they could climb out.

The tour got off to a bad start with an embarrassing loss to a strong New South Wales Second Eleven. But they never lost again and won three out of their five remaining four-day matches. As on England A's previous tour of Australia four years earlier, there was no unofficial internationals, with the non-first-class Academy the closest thing to a representative Australian side.

Every player, apart from the twice-injured Jason Gallian, made significant contributions with either bat or ball at some stage. Mark Butcher was the outstanding batsman. Not only did he look a class above everyone else, but he scored consistently. His footwork was positive, either forward or back, and enabled him to make runs whatever the conditions. Dean Headley enjoyed a similar status among the bowlers. A thinking bowler, always ready to listen, he put theory into practice at a pace which bore comparison with any opponent. His great strength was an ability to make the batsmen play, and the pressure this created ensured regular rewards, including a career-best 11 for 98 against South Australia.

Wicket-keeper Warren Hegg demonstrated that he combined good hands and agility. He had plenty of chances to display his prowess standing up to the slow bowlers, and his batting was a bonus. The slow left-armer, Ashley Giles, responded well to his responsibilities and proved a more than useful lower-order batsman. Off-spinner Peter Such had fewer opportunities, but was reliability personified, with match figures of 79.3–44–102–8 in Canberra.

Of the other seamers, Andrew Harris will have learned much; Glen Chapple took time to overcome the fact that the ball would not swing for him, but was tireless in his efforts; Mark Ealham also suffered from a lack of swing, but batted usefully. However, he could not compete with Craig White, who suggested that he might fulfil his promise to become a genuine top-class all-rounder, and was called up to join the senior tour in late December. Yorkshire batsmen Anthony McGrath and Michael Vaughan were inconsistent, but McGrath did record the only century of the tour, against Australian Capital Territory in a non-first-class four-day game, and Vaughan was outstanding in the field. Owais Shah, who turned 18 a few days before setting out, scored 76 and 79 in the opening match, and looked to be the one batsman completely at home on turning pitches.

The captain, Adam Hollioake, set a fine example. His batting was attractive, and before suffering an ankle injury he proved to have a "golden arm", with a knack of taking important wickets. He directed the team with a sure touch and much cricketing sense, while imparting his own sense of enjoyment and creating a happy environment. English cricket will waste a genuine asset if his leadership is not employed again, possibly at a higher level. Along with manager David Graveney, Mike Gatting, in his first coaching role, and physiotherapist Dean Conway, Hollioake ensured that the touring party gave of its best.

This team spirit was a major strength, but the very nature of A tours means that these players are unlikely to feature again as a unit, and they will have to stand as individuals. Even so, the tour proved that it is possible to create an environment in which an English team can flourish. That alone justifies such an expedition, however many members of this side make a successful transition to Test cricket.

ENGLAND A TOURING PARTY

A. J. Hollioake (Surrey) (*captain*), M. A. Butcher (Surrey), G. Chapple (Lancashire), M. A. Ealham (Kent), J. E. R. Gallian (Lancashire), A. F. Giles (Warwickshire), A. J. Harris (Derbyshire), D. W. Headley (Kent), W. K. Hegg (Lancashire), A. McGrath (Yorkshire), O. A. Shah (Middlesex), P. M. Such (Essex), M. P. Vaughan (Yorkshire), C. White (Yorkshire).

Tour manager: D. A. Graveney.   *Cricket manager:* M. A. Gatting (Middlesex).

Physiotherapist: D. O. Conway (Glamorgan).

Gatting replaced G. A. Gooch, who withdrew because of family illness.

ENGLAND A TOUR RESULTS

First-class matches – Played 3: Won 2, Drawn 1.

Wins – South Australia, Victoria.

Draw – Queensland.

Other non-first-class matches – Played 7: Won 4, Lost 1, Drawn 1, No result 1. *Wins* – South Australia, Australian Cricket Academy (four days), Australian Capital Territory, New South Wales. *Loss* – New South Wales Second XI (four days). *Draw* – Australian Capital Territory (four days). *No result* – New South Wales.

ENGLAND A AVERAGES – FIRST-CLASS MATCHES

BATTING

	M	I	NO	R	HS	100s	Avge	Ct
M. A. Butcher	3	5	0	264	73	0	52.80	2
C. White	3	5	1	204	99	0	51.00	3
M. A. Ealham.....	3	4	0	137	78	0	34.25	0
D. W. Headley	3	4	1	71	28	0	23.66	0
W. K. Hegg	3	4	0	89	69	0	22.25	14
A. J. Hollioake	3	5	0	105	58	0	21.00	2
O. A. Shah	2	3	0	53	27	0	17.66	0
A. F. Giles	3	4	0	66	29	0	16.50	0
A. McGrath	3	5	0	52	19	0	10.40	0
M. P. Vaughan	3	5	0	35	27	0	7.00	3

Played in two matches: G. Chapple 27*, 16* (1 ct). Played in one match: J. E. R. Gallian 26, 12*; A. J. Harris 0, 4*.

* Signifies not out.

BOWLING

	O	M	R	W	BB	5W/i	Avge
C. White	74.2	15	178	11	6-66	1	16.18
D. W. Headley	102.1	31	230	14	6-60	2	16.42
G. Chapple	67.3	20	159	7	4-43	0	22.71
A. J. Hollioake	37	16	89	3	1-20	0	29.66
A. F. Giles	92.2	28	199	6	3-28	0	33.16

Also bowled: M. A. Butcher 6–3–8–0; M. A. Ealham 36–11–103–2; J. E. R. Gallian 14–3–33–0; A. J. Harris 15–0–54–0; A. McGrath 4–0–6–1; M. P. Vaughan 13–1–56–0.

Note: Matches in this section which were not first-class are signified by a dagger.

†At Tamworth, October 31, November 1, 2, 3. New South Wales Second XI won by nine wickets. Toss: England A. England A 155 (O. A. Shah 76, C. White 33; S. C. G. MacGill four for 43, D. A. Freedman three for 41) and 217 (M. A. Butcher 52, O. A. Shah 79; S. C. G. MacGill five for 84); New South Wales Second XI 330 (C. A. Glassock 84, S. M. Thompson 90, S. Clark 44; A. F. Giles five for 110) and 43 for one.

†At Adelaide (No. 2 Oval), November 6. England A won by six wickets. Toss: South Australia. South Australia 203 for seven (50 overs) (G. S. Blewett 45, D. S. Lehmann 61 not out, T. J. Nielsen 30; A. J. Hollioake three for 44); England A 204 for four (44.5 overs) (M. A. Butcher 76, A. McGrath 31, C. White 30 not out).

SOUTH AUSTRALIA v ENGLAND A

At Adelaide, November 8, 9, 10, 11. England A won by 12 runs. Toss: England A. First-class debut: B. E. Young.

Spirited bowling on the final day earned England A an exciting victory which their batting had hardly merited. They would have been 55 for five in the first innings if Butcher had been held at slip. But he survived to play responsibly in tandem with White, later supplemented by a tenth-wicket stand of 76 between Hegg and Headley. Then Headley bowled superbly for six wickets; only Siddons played with authority, going on to a three-hour hundred after being dropped on one. The tourists collapsed in their second innings, losing six for 11. Leg-spinner McIntyre had a spell of four for four in 21 balls. South Australia needed only 170, but Headley removed the top three on the final morning and returned to complete career-best figures of 11 for 98 in a thrilling win. Lehmann was absent in South Australia's second innings, having been called away to undertake promotional work for the Australian Cricket Board.

Close of play: First day, England A 232-9 (W. K. Hegg 21*, D. W. Headley 2*); Second day, South Australia 226-6 (T. J. Nielsen 2*, B. E. Young 4*); Third day, South Australia 6-0 (G. S. Blewett 2*, B. A. Johnson 4*).

England A

M. A. Butcher c sub (P. Wilson) b Scuderi	73	– lbw b Harrity	17
M. P. Vaughan c Nielsen b Harrity	2	– b Scuderi	27
A. McGrath c Nielsen b Blewett	5	– lbw b Scuderi	19
O. A. Shah c Siddons b Gillespie	9	– c Siddons b McIntyre	27
*A. J. Holliaoke c Nielsen b Harrity	28	– c Scuderi b Young	28
C. White c Scuderi b Young	61	– c Siddons b Young	9
M. A. Ealham c Nielsen b Scuderi	17	– b McIntyre	1
†W. K. Hegg b McIntyre	69	– c Siddons b McIntyre	0
A. F. Giles b Harrity	17	– c Siddons b McIntyre	0
A. J. Harris lbw b Harrity	0	– not out	4
D. W. Headley not out	15	– c Gillespie b Young	14
B 2, l-b 12, n-b 3	17	B 1, n-b 4	5
	294		**151**

1/2 2/18 3/27 4/46 5/154 6/174 7/191 8/216 9/218 (294)
1/24 2/65 3/66 4/122 5/127 6/131 7/131 8/133 9/133 (151)

Bowling: *First Innings*—Gillespie 23–10–40–1; Harrity 24–8–61–4; Blewett 13–1–50–1; McIntyre 31.4–12–63–1; Young 13–4–27–1; Scuderi 11–3–39–2. *Second Innings*—Gillespie 14–6–30–0; Harrity 11–4–24–1; Blewett 5–0–16–0; McIntyre 22–7–43–4; Scuderi 5–3–8–2; Young 10.4–2–29–3.

South Australia

B. A. Johnson c White b Holliaoke	39	– (2) c Holliaoke b Headley	17
G. S. Blewett c Hegg b Headley	0	– (1) c Hegg b Headley	2
*J. D. Siddons c Hegg b Headley	101	– lbw b Headley	18
D. S. Lehmann b Giles	26	– absent	
J. A. Brayshaw c Vaughan b Giles	22	– (4) run out	0
J. C. Scuderi c Hegg b White	16	– (5) not out	55
†T. J. Nielsen c Vaughan b Headley	37	– (6) c Hegg b Giles	11
B. E. Young c Hegg b Headley	8	– (7) c White b Giles	37
J. N. Gillespie c Butcher b Headley	10	– (8) b Headley	8
P. E. McIntyre lbw b Headley	0	– (9) lbw b Headley	0
M. A. Harrity not out	0	– (10) b Giles	0
B 1, l-b 9, n-b 7	17	B 3, l-b 2, n-b 4	9
	276		**157**

1/6 2/107 3/171 4/181 5/216 6/220 7/239 8/257 9/263 (276)
1/6 2/38 3/38 4/41 5/59 6/129 7/150 8/150 9/157 (157)

Bowling: *First Innings*—Headley 28.1–9–60–6; Harris 6–0–24–0; Ealham 7–0–28–0; White 14–1–41–1; Holliaoke 7–2–21–1; Giles 32–11–92–2. *Second Innings*—Headley 20–8–38–5; Harris 9–0–30–0; Ealham 6–0–18–0; Giles 14.2–3–28–3; White 8–3–12–0; Holliaoke 4–1–12–0; Vaughan 2–0–14–0.

Umpires: A. J. Hunter and R. G. Kinnear.

†At Mount Gambier, November 15, 16, 17, 18. England A won by seven wickets. Toss: England A. Australian Cricket Academy 258 (M. G. Dighton 72, S. A. J. Craig 61; A. F. Giles four for 63) and 175 (J. L. Cassell 69; A. J. Harris five for 61); England A 272 (M. A. Butcher 81, M. P. Vaughan 40, A. J. Holliaoke 62, Extras 32; D. A. Nash seven for 66) and 165 for three (M. P. Vaughan 70, O. A. Shah 43 not out).

VICTORIA v ENGLAND A

At Melbourne (Optus Oval), November 21, 22, 23, 24. England A won by an innings and eight runs. Toss: Victoria.

The tourists met Victoria at the Carlton grade team's ground, as the MCG was preparing for a Michael Jackson concert. Despite losing early wickets, England A built a considerable, if long-winded, total – 438 in nine and a half hours – thanks to a solid display from the middle and lower order. White, who had played twice for Victoria six years earlier, was within a single of becoming the first centurion of the tour when he drove at a wide ball, directly after a brief altercation with Saker, who had appeared to obstruct him during a run. In reply, Victoria were effectively 76 for six when Dodemaide broke a finger, and then Fleming injured his leg; neither batted in the follow-on. Still, the English bowlers had to work hard for victory; the state's last pair, Vimpani and Saker, added a stubborn 95 and held out for two hours. Only 11.4 overs remained when Chapple broke the stand.

Close of play: First day, England A 231-4 (C. White 92*, A. J. Hollioake 45*); Second day, Victoria 30-0 (W. G. Ayres 13*, B. J. Hodge 16*); Third day, Victoria 20-0 (W. G. Ayres 10*, B. J. Hodge 10*).

England A

M. A. Butcher st Roach b Hodge	55	A. F. Giles c Dodemaide b Hodge	29
M. P. Vaughan c Roach b Saker	5	G. Chapple not out	27
A. McGrath lbw b Fleming	9	D. W. Headley c Foster b Harvey	28
O. A. Shah c Foster b Dodemaide	17		
C. White c Harper b Fleming	99	B 2, l-b 7, w 1, n-b 6	16
*A. J. Hollioake c Stacey b Dodemaide	58		
M. A. Ealham run out	78	1/12 2/21 3/59 4/137 5/239	438
†W. K. Hegg c Hodge b Fleming	17	6/265 7/305 8/356 9/390	

Bowling: Fleming 32–10–56–3; Saker 30–7–83–1; Dodemaide 32–11–51–2; Harvey 21.4–5–63–1; Stacey 24–5–122–0; Hodge 15.3–3–41–2; Harper 3–0–13–0.

Victoria

W. G. Ayres lbw b Chapple	36	– lbw b Headley	42
B. J. Hodge b Headley	17	– c Butcher b Chapple	28
M. R. Foster lbw b Ealham	4	– b White	7
L. D. Harper lbw b Chapple	63	– c Hegg b Headley	0
G. R. Vimpani c and b White	2	– b Chapple	53
I. J. Harvey b White	0	– b White	3
*A. I. C. Dodemaide retired hurt	2	– absent hurt	
†P. J. Roach lbw b Giles	28	– (7) run out	12
B. J. Stacey c Hegg b Chapple	17	– (8) c Hegg b Hollioake	2
D. W. Fleming c Hegg b Chapple	7	– absent hurt	
D. J. Saker not out	11	– (9) not out	51
B 4, l-b 6, n-b 14	24	B 3, l-b 8, n-b 10	21
1/35 2/50 3/62 4/72 5/72	211	1/52 2/81 3/81 4/85 5/91	219
6/143 7/185 8/192 9/211		6/116 7/124 8/219	

In the first innings A. I. C. Dodemaide retired hurt at 76.

Bowling: *First Innings*—Headley 24–9–54–1; Chapple 21.1–5–43–4; Giles 15–1–32–1; Hollioake 6–2–7–0; Ealham 10–5–19–1; White 9–3–20–2; Vaughan 6–0–26–0. *Second Innings*—Headley 21–4–48–2; Chapple 23.2–8–57–2; Ealham 8–4–22–0; Giles 15–9–15–0; Hollioake 8–4–20–1; White 14–3–39–2; Vaughan 3–1–7–0.

Umpires: G. T. Morrow and R. W. Stratford.

---

†At Canberra, November 28. England A won by seven wickets. Toss: Australian Capital Territory. Australian Capital Territory 198 for seven (50 overs) (P. L. Evans 40, P. J. Solway 68, I. A. Garrity 31; A. J. Hollioake three for 32); England A 201 for three (42.3 overs) (M. A. Butcher 72, O. A. Shah 37, A. J. Hollioake 47 not out).

England A's fifth successive win.

†At Canberra, November 30, December 1, 2, 3. Drawn. Toss: Australian Capital Territory. Australian Capital Territory 216 (P. J. Solway 59, I. A. Garrity 49, D. J. Macdonald 33; P. M. Such five for 29) and 320 (P. L. Evans 47, M. R. J. Veletta 68, I. A. Garrity 90; P. M. Such three for 73, A. J. Hollioake four for 27); England A 408 (M. P. Vaughan 40, A. McGrath 108, C. White 53, A. J. Hollioake 31, G. Chapple 59 not out; B. J. Smith five for 91) and 123 for five (M. P. Vaughan 34 not out).

Veletta was banned for a month by the ACB for "dissent and denigration of umpires" when given out caught behind in the second innings. England A scored 123 in 15 overs chasing 129 to win.

†At Sydney, December 5. England A won by two wickets. Toss: England A. New South Wales 243 for six (50 overs) (C. J. Richards 55, S. Lee 113, K. J. Roberts 41); England A 244 for eight (49.3 overs) (A. McGrath 43, A. J. Hollioake 51, A. F. Giles 39 not out; G. R. Robertson four for 46).

England A recovered from 162 for seven to add 82 in the last 15 overs.

†At Wollongong, December 7. No result. Toss: England A. England A 154 for six (30.4 overs) (M. A. Ealham 70 not out; S. Lee four for 35) v New South Wales.

QUEENSLAND v ENGLAND A

At Brisbane, December 10, 11, 12, 13. Drawn. Toss: Queensland. First-class debuts: J. L. Cassell, B. N. Creevey.

Stoppages for bad light and torrential rain on the first three days rendered England A's final match a non-event. Butcher confirmed his class with his seventh fifty of the trip, though he was slightly upstaged by pace bowler Brendan Creevey, who marked his first-class debut, at the age of 26, with six wickets. White also took a career-best six wickets when Queensland replied, but Ealham fractured a finger attempting a return catch and Headley was absent for much of the game with an aggravated hip injury; coach Mike Gatting substituted. The occasion was marked by an end-of-term atmosphere. England A used ten bowlers and served fresh fruit and cakes from a makeshift picnic table in a seven-minute drinks interval. Earlier, during a break for bad light, Giles had entertained the meagre crowd with a mime act, including the antics of a heavyweight boxer, Olympic athlete, speed skater and gymnast.

Close of play: First day, England A 170-7 (M. A. Ealham 32*, A. F. Giles 1*); Second day, Queensland 154-4 (M. P. Mott 12*, J. L. Cassell 9*); Third day, Queensland 195-5 (M. P. Mott 29*, W. A. Seccombe 10*).

England A

M. A. Butcher c Cassell b Jackson	72	– hit wkt b Prestwidge 47
M. P. Vaughan c Barsby b Creevey	0	– c Maher b Muller 1
A. McGrath c Law b Muller	1	– c and b Muller 18
C. White c Seccombe b Creevey	24	– (6) not out 11
J. E. R. Gallian lbw b Creevey	26	– (4) not out 12
*A. J. Hollioake lbw b Prestwidge	0	– (5) lbw b Prestwidge 10
M. A. Ealham c Seccombe b Creevey	41	
†W. K. Hegg c Law b Creevey	3	
A. F. Giles c Seccombe b Creevey	20	
G. Chapple not out	16	
D. W. Headley b Muller	14	
L-b 7, n-b 6	13	B 1, l-b 4, n-b 2 7

1/8 2/9 3/39 4/99 5/114   230   1/13 2/59 3/68 4/82   (4 wkts) 106
6/147 7/164 8/198 9/201

Bowling: *First Innings*—Muller 18.3–6–42–2; Creevey 27–5–70–6; Prestwidge 12–2–45–1; Law 5–2–14–0; Jackson 21–8–52–1. *Second Innings*—Muller 9–3–28–2; Creevey 5–0–33–0; Maher 5–0–11–0; Prestwidge 5–0–16–2; Jackson 6–2–5–0; Mott 4–1–8–0; Seccombe 1–1–0–0.

Queensland

T. J. Dixon c Vaughan b White........ 62	B. N. Creevey c Hollioake b White 0
T. J. Barsby lbw b Ealham 29	P. W. Jackson lbw b McGrath.......... 4
J. P. Maher c Hegg b White 10	S. A. Muller b White 1
*S. G. Law c Chapple b Hollioake 19	
M. P. Mott c Hegg b White............ 73	L-b 10, w 1, n-b 22 33
J. L. Cassell c Hegg b Chapple 22	
†W. A. Seccombe c Hegg b White 23	1/62 2/81 3/130 4/132 5/176 298
S. A. Prestwidge not out 22	6/232 7/275 8/277 9/293

Bowling: Headley 9–1–30–0; Chapple 23–7–59–1; Ealham 5–2–16–1; Giles 16–4–32–0; White 29.2–5–66–6; Hollioake 12–7–29–1; Gallian 14–3–33–0; Vaughan 2–0–9–0; McGrath 4–0–6–1; Butcher 6–3–8–0.

Umpires: P. D. Parker and J. F. Torpey.

THE COOPERS & LYBRAND RATINGS

Introduced in 1987, the Coopers & Lybrand Ratings (formerly the Deloitte Ratings) rank Test cricketers on a scale up to 1,000 according to their performances in Test matches. The ratings take into account playing conditions, the quality of the opposition and the result of the matches. A player cannot get a full rating until he has played 30 innings or taken 70 wickets in Tests.

The leading 20 batsmen and bowlers in the Ratings after the 1997 series between England and Australia which ended on August 23 were:

	Batsmen	Rating		Bowlers	Rating
1.	S. R. Waugh (*Aus.*)	870	1.	C. E. L. Ambrose (*WI*)	876
2.	G. P. Thorpe (*Eng.*)	803	2.	G. D. McGrath (*Aus.*)	865
3.	S. R. Tendulkar (*Ind.*)	792	3.	A. A. Donald (*SA*)	838
4.	S. Chanderpaul (*WI*)	770	4.	S. K. Warne (*Aus.*)	800
5.	S. T. Jayasuriya (*SL*)	769	5.	Wasim Akram (*Pak.*)	784
6.	B. C. Lara (*WI*)	763	6.	H. H. Streak (*Zimb.*)	778†
7.	B. M. McMillan (*SA*)	736	7.	Mushtaq Ahmed (*Pak.*)	761
8.	R. Dravid (*Ind.*)	717*	8.	I. R. Bishop (*WI*)	722
9.	Saeed Anwar (*Pak.*)	711	9.	S. B. Doull (*NZ*)	706†
10.	D. J. Cullinan (*SA*)	709	10.	P. R. Reiffel (*Aus.*)	705
11. {	P. A. de Silva (*SL*)	705	11.	Waqar Younis (*Pak.*)	693
	Inzamam-ul-Haq (*Pak.*)	705	12.	J. N. Gillespie (*Aus.*)	692†
13.	M. T. G. Elliott (*Aus.*)	699*	13.	W. P. U. J. C. Vaas (*SL*)	675
14.	A. J. Stewart (*Eng.*)	688	14.	D. Gough (*Eng.*)	669
15.	G. S. Blewett (*Aus.*)	677	15.	C. A. Walsh (*WI*)	656
16. {	Ijaz Ahmed, sen. (*Pak.*)	669	16.	B. N. Schultz (*SA*)	650†
	Salim Malik (*Pak.*)	669	17.	P. S. de Villiers (*SA*)	634
18.	M. E. Waugh (*Aus.*)	666	18.	M. Muralitharan (*SL*)	632
19.	H. P. Tillekeratne (*SL*)	661	19.	A. Kumble (*Ind.*)	606
20.	B. A. Young (*NZ*)	647	20.	A. R. Caddick (*Eng.*)	600†

* *Signifies the batsman has played fewer than 30 Test innings.*

† *Signifies the bowler has taken fewer than 70 wickets.*

The following players have topped the ratings since they were launched on June 17, 1987. The date shown is that on which they first went top; those marked by an asterisk have done so more than once.

Batting: D. B. Vengsarkar, June 17, 1987; Javed Miandad*, February 28, 1989; R. B. Richardson*, November 20, 1989; M. A. Taylor, October 23, 1990; G. A. Gooch*, June 10, 1991; D. L. Haynes, May 6, 1993; B. C. Lara, April 21, 1994; S. R. Tendulkar, December 5, 1994; J. C. Adams, December 14, 1994; S. R. Waugh, May 3, 1995.

Bowling: R. J. Hadlee*, June 17, 1987; M. D. Marshall*, June 21, 1988; Waqar Younis*, December 17, 1991; C. E. L. Ambrose*, July 26, 1992; S. K. Warne*, November 29, 1994; G. D. McGrath*, December 3, 1996.

THE ZIMBABWEANS IN SRI LANKA, 1996-97

By SA'ADI THAWFEEQ

Zimbabwe's tour of Sri Lanka turned into a cricketing disaster for them. They lost all their games in the four-nation Singer World Series. Then, in the short Test series which followed, they were comprehensively beaten twice, both times well inside four days, by a confident Sri Lanka, fresh from victory over Australia in the Singer final.

Zimbabwe's weakness, especially against spin, surprised Sri Lankan captain Arjuna Ranatunga, who admitted at the end of the series that he had expected much stronger resistance. In the only previous Test series between the two countries, played in Zimbabwe two years earlier, Zimbabwe came out on top, even forcing Sri Lanka to follow on in the second match, although all three Tests ended in draws.

The loss of their best batsman, 39-year-old David Houghton, affected the tourists badly. He would have supplied a fine technique against spin, but he was unavailable for the tour because of his commitments as Worcestershire coach. In Houghton's absence, the captaincy passed from Andy Flower, who had decided that the combined pressures of wicket-keeping, batting in the top order and leading the side were too heavy, to the relatively inexperienced Alistair Campbell. Campbell proved no match for the astute and well-practised leadership of Ranatunga, and it was evident all too soon who was the master and who the pupil.

Zimbabwe's batsmen were undone by the spinners Muttiah Muralitharan and Jayantha Silva. Off-spinner Muralitharan took 14 wickets, and finished five short of becoming the first Sri Lankan bowler to take a century of wickets in Tests, while Silva proved an ideal foil, his left-arm leg-breaks claiming 13 wickets at just 7.69 apiece. Asanka Gurusinha and Hashan Tillekeratne were the most successful batsmen, but so weak was the opposition that Sri Lanka pulled off victories by an innings in the First Test and ten wickets in the Second without needing to score above 350. Ranatunga afterwards claimed that these wins, following Sri Lanka's triumphs in the World Cup and the recent Singer tournament, proved that his side were on course to become Test champions by the year 2000. But he needed firmer evidence than this to support his case.

Before the Tests began, Zimbabwe had a scare when life-savers had to rescue Campbell and fast bowler Henry Olonga after they were swept out to sea while swimming. A bodyguard who was with them had to be treated in hospital.

ZIMBABWEAN TOURING PARTY

A. D. R. Campbell (Mashonaland) (*captain*), A. Flower (Mashonaland) (*vice-captain*), E. A. Brandes (Mashonaland), M. H. Dekker (Matabeleland), C. N. Evans (Mashonaland), G. W. Flower (Mashonaland), W. R. James (Matabeleland), H. K. Olonga (Matabeleland), A. H. Shah (Mashonaland), B. C. Strang (Mashonaland), P. A. Strang (Mashonaland), H. H. Streak (Matabeleland), A. R. Whittall (Matabeleland), G. J. Whittall (Matabeleland), C. B. Wishart (Mashonaland).

Manager: M. P. Jarvis. *Assistant manager:* D. H. Streak.

ZIMBABWEAN TOUR RESULTS

Test matches – Played 2: Lost 2.
One-day internationals – Played 3: Lost 3. *Losses* – Australia, India, Sri Lanka.

Zimbabwe's matches v Australia, India and Sri Lanka in the Singer World Series (August 26–September 3) may be found in that section.

SRI LANKA v ZIMBABWE

First Test Match

At R. Premadasa Stadium, Colombo, September 11, 12, 13, 14. Sri Lanka won by an innings and 77 runs. Toss: Sri Lanka. Test debuts: C. N. Evans, A. R. Whittall.

The first Test between these countries on Sri Lankan soil was won by the host team in convincing manner. Sri Lanka achieved their eighth victory, and their first by an innings, in their 67 Tests on the fourth evening; but in fact the match lasted less than three days, with rain clipping more than seven hours' play.

The grassless pitch assisted spin from the first day, and Zimbabwe's batsmen had no answer to Muralitharan and Silva, who finished with seven wickets each. It was a welcome return for Muralitharan, whose career had been threatened during his last Test, in December at Melbourne, when he was no-balled for throwing by Australian umpire Darrell Hair.

Zimbabwe had every reason to be happy, however, when they reduced Sri Lanka to 128 for five on the first day. Ranatunga had decided to bat first but, by the seventh ball of the morning, Zimbabwe had sent back both their openers. Fresh from their latest one-day triumph, the Sri Lankan batsmen were guilty of many loose shots. Ranatunga and Kaluwitharana put some sense into the batting with a face-saving sixth-wicket stand of 142, but neither survived long enough to complete the centuries which were there for the taking. But Sri Lanka were eventually dismissed for 349 on the second morning. Leg-spinner Paul Strang ended a stubborn eighth-wicket stand of 74 between Dharmasena and Vaas by getting Vaas to play on, and made it three wickets in four balls to complete his first five-wicket haul in Test cricket.

Vaas, the only fast bowler in a side fielding three spinners, soon struck back by dismissing Grant Flower with the first delivery of the innings. His next victim, Campbell, who was caught at slip, was his fiftieth in only 13 Tests; he was the fifth Sri Lankan bowler to reach the landmark. Before long Zimbabwe were 45 for four. They needed 150 to save the follow-on and looked as if they might make it while Wishart was scoring a fighting 205-minute 51. But Silva finished the innings off, five short of the target, by removing Wishart and debutant Andrew Whittall with successive balls.

Play on the third day had been limited to the afternoon session, and the fourth morning was another blank. On resuming, however, Muralitharan and Silva swiftly wrapped up Zimbabwe's second innings, claiming nine wickets between them. After tea, Zimbabwe lost their last six wickets for 34 runs in 66 minutes, recording their lowest Test score, 127. Their previous low was 134 against Pakistan at Karachi in 1993-94.

Man of the Match: A. Ranatunga.

Close of play: First day, Sri Lanka 290-7 (H. D. P. K. Dharmasena 16*, W. P. U. J. C. Vaas 3*); Second day, Zimbabwe 105-6 (C. B. Wishart 31*, C. N. Evans 0*); Third day, Zimbabwe 20-0 (G. W. Flower 13*, M. H. Dekker 6*).

Sri Lanka

R. S. Mahanama lbw b Streak	4
S. T. Jayasuriya c Evans b Olonga	0
A. P. Gurusinha c Olonga b Strang	52
P. A. de Silva b Strang	35
H. P. Tillekeratne c A. Flower b Olonga	20
*A. Ranatunga lbw b Streak	75
†R. S. Kaluwitharana c and b Streak	71
H. D. P. K. Dharmasena not out	42
W. P. U. J. C. Vaas b Strang	34
M. Muralitharan b Strang	0
K. J. Silva c and b Strang	0
L-b 6, w 2, n-b 8	16

1/4 (1) 2/4 (2) 3/53 (4) 4/105 (5)   349
5/128 (3) 6/270 (6) 7/271 (7)
8/345 (9) 9/349 (10) 10/349 (11)

Bowling: Streak 20–6–54–3; Olonga 17–3–57–2; G. J. Whittall 12–1–43–0; Strang 34.3–3–106–5; A. R. Whittall 13–3–40–0; Evans 6–0–27–0; G. W. Flower 4–1–16–0.

Zimbabwe

G. W. Flower c Kaluwitharana b Vaas	0	– b Muralitharan	27
M. H. Dekker lbw b Vaas	10	– c Jayasuriya b Dharmasena	20
*A. D. R. Campbell c Mahanama b Vaas	12	– (4) c Mahanama b Muralitharan	26
†A. Flower c Ranatunga b Dharmasena	2	– (5) c Mahanama b Muralitharan	0
G. J. Whittall lbw b Silva	39	– (6) c Mahanama b Silva	13
C. B. Wishart c Vaas b Silva	51	– (3) b Silva	3
H. K. Olonga c Tillekeratne b Muralitharan	1	– (9) c Mahanama b Silva	0
C. N. Evans c Kaluwitharana b Vaas	9	– (7) lbw b Silva	1
P. A. Strang b Muralitharan	6	– (8) c Vaas b Muralitharan	8
A. R. Whittall c Dharmasena b Silva	1	– b Muralitharan	11
H. H. Streak not out	0	– not out	3
B 4, l-b 4, w 2, n-b 4	14	B 6, l-b 4, w 1, n-b 4	15
	145		**127**

1/0 (1) 2/15 (3) 3/21 (4) 4/45 (2) 5/103 (5) 6/105 (7) 7/123 (8) 8/138 (9) 9/145 (6) 10/145 (10)

1/35 (2) 2/42 (3) 3/65 (1) 4/65 (5) 5/98 (4) 6/99 (7) 7/102 (6) 8/102 (9) 9/113 (8) 10/127 (10)

Bowling: *First Innings*—Vaas 22–3–73–4; Gurusinha 3–1–3–0; Dharmasena 9–3–23–1; Muralitharan 24–9–28–2; Silva 14.5–9–10–3. *Second Innings*—Vaas 12–1–34–0; Gurusinha 2–0–4–0; de Silva 2–1–1–0; Dharmasena 14–7–19–1; Silva 19–12–25–4; Muralitharan 20.3–4–33–5; Jayasuriya 4–3–1–0.

Umpires: S. A. Bucknor (West Indies) and B. C. Cooray.
Referee: J. R. Reid (New Zealand).

SRI LANKA v ZIMBABWE

Second Test Match

At Sinhalese Sports Club, Colombo, September 18, 19, 20, 21. Sri Lanka won by ten wickets. Toss: Zimbabwe.

Zimbabwe did well to stave off a second successive innings defeat but could not prevent Sri Lanka from winning by ten wickets to make a clean sweep of the short series. Once more the tourists' batsmen showed their fallibility to spin and succumbed inside four days; this time Muralitharan and Silva took 13 wickets between them.

The SSC pitch was as grassless as the previous one, but it did offer bounce, so Sri Lanka picked a more balanced attack of two fast bowlers and two spinners. Zimbabwe suffered a big setback when their leading pace bowler, Streak, failed a fitness test on his injured groin; he was replaced by left-arm seamer Bryan Strang.

Having won the toss for the first time on the tour, Campbell showed no hesitation in batting first. His decision looked good when Zimbabwe reached 119 for two by mid-afternoon. He and Grant Flower batted as if they had shaken off the shackles imposed by the spinners. But then Campbell made a rash attempt to hit Silva out of the ground and was stumped. His dismissal triggered a remarkable collapse of eight wickets for 22 runs. Zimbabwe were all out by tea for 141 with Muralitharan and Silva collecting four wickets each.

Sri Lanka consolidated their position through left-handers Gurusinha and Tillekeratne. Gurusinha painstakingly compiled his second fifty of the series, taking almost five hours to score 88. Tillekeratne completed his fifth Test century, and his first at home, shortly before the close of the second day, and carried on the next day to remain undefeated on 126 – his highest score in Tests, occupying 409 minutes and 326 balls with 13 fours. Leg-spinner Paul Strang was again Zimbabwe's main strike bowler, claiming four wickets, with support from brother Bryan, who took three.

Ranatunga declared on 350, 209 ahead, and Zimbabwe made another a poor start, losing their first three wickets for 34. The 37-year-old left-hander Ali Shah steadied the innings, batting nearly five hours for a maiden Test fifty on his first appearance since Zimbabwe's debut season of 1992-93. But it was left to Paul Strang to make sure that Sri Lanka batted again. Coming in at No. 9 when Shah fell at the start of the fourth morning, Strang took over the responsibility of senior partner. Though Zimbabwe still trailed by eight when his brother was ninth out, Strang showed a sound technique and completed his own maiden Test fifty, before hitting a return catch to Vaas. By then, Zimbabwe had gained a slender lead of 26. Jayasuriya and Mahanama needed only 40 balls to knock the runs off.

Man of the Match: H. P. Tillekeratne. *Man of the Series:* M. Muralitharan.

Close of play: First day, Sri Lanka 86-3 (A. P. Gurusinha 22*, A. Ranatunga 0*); Second day, Sri Lanka 317-7 (H. P. Tillekeratne 100*, K. R. Pushpakumara 17*); Third day, Zimbabwe 162-6 (A. H. Shah 62*, A. R. Whittall 1*).

Zimbabwe

G. W. Flower c Mahanama b Muralitharan	52	– lbw b Silva	13
M. H. Dekker c Mahanama b Muralitharan	18	– lbw b Vaas	4
A. H. Shah c Kaluwitharana b Pushpakumara	1	– c Vaas b Pushpakumara	62
*A. D. R. Campbell st Kaluwitharana b Silva	36	– c sub (M. S. Atapattu) b Silva	4
†A. Flower run out	3	– c Gurusinha b Muralitharan	31
C. B. Wishart c Kaluwitharana b Silva	2	– c Kaluwitharana b Jayasuriya	25
G. J. Whittall c Silva b Muralitharan	0	– c Gurusinha b Jayasuriya	3
P. A. Strang not out	2	– (9) c and b Vaas	50
A. R. Whittall c Gurusinha b Muralitharan	3	– (8) b Muralitharan	12
B. C. Strang c de Silva b Silva	3	– b Muralitharan	2
H. K. Olonga c Mahanama b Silva	3	– not out	3
B 3, l-b 10, n-b 5	18	B 2, l-b 6, w 1, n-b 17	26

1/43 (2) 2/54 (3) 3/119 (4) 4/121 (1)   141   1/9 (2) 2/30 (1) 3/34 (4)   235
5/123 (5) 6/125 (7) 7/126 (6)   4/91 (5) 5/135 (6) 6/144 (7)
8/133 (9) 9/136 (10) 10/141 (11)   7/167 (3) 8/193 (8)
    9/201 (10) 10/235 (9)

Bowling: *First Innings*—Vaas 10–1–31–0; Pushpakumara 11–3–34–1; Muralitharan 20–5–40–4; Silva 10.1–4–16–4; de Silva 2–0–7–0. *Second Innings*—Vaas 26.3–11–34–2; Pushpakumara 8–0–24–1; Muralitharan 41–9–94–3; Silva 26–7–49–2; de Silva 5–1–10–0; Jayasuriya 7–3–16–2.

Sri Lanka

R. S. Mahanama c A. Flower b B. C. Strang	3	– (2) not out	12
S. T. Jayasuriya c A. R. Whittall b P. A. Strang	41	– (1) not out	18
A. P. Gurusinha c Wishart b B. C. Strang	88		
P. A. de Silva c and b P. A. Strang	16		
*A. Ranatunga c Wishart b B. C. Strang	6		
H. P. Tillekeratne not out	126		
†R. S. Kaluwitharana c A. Flower b G. J. Whittall	27		
W. P. U. J. C. Vaas st A. Flower b P. A. Strang	8		
K. R. Pushpakumara c B. C. Strang b P. A. Strang	23		
M. Muralitharan not out	1		
L-b 4, w 3, n-b 4	11		

1/19 (1) 2/58 (2) 3/86 (4)   (8 wkts dec.) 350   (no wkt) 30
4/102 (5) 5/216 (3) 6/267 (7)
7/276 (8) 8/340 (9)

K. J. Silva did not bat.

Bowling: *First Innings*—Olonga 26–6–81–0; B. C. Strang 20–6–63–3; A. R. Whittall 31–7–75–0; P. A. Strang 38–11–66–4; G. J. Whittall 16.5–4–48–1; G. W. Flower 2–0–13–0. *Second Innings*—Olonga 3.4–0–17–0; P. A. Strang 3–0–13–0.

Umpires: C. J. Mitchley (South Africa) and K. T. Francis.
Referee: J. R. Reid (New Zealand).

THE AUSTRALIANS IN INDIA, 1996-97

By MIKE COWARD

Australia's tour of India in October 1996 was a disappointment and a setback. They lost the Test match and the five one-day games they contested with India and South Africa in the Titan Cup. Their position as world Test champions – widely proclaimed after their victory in the Caribbean in 1995 – was compromised and, according to the Wisden World Championship table, temporarily lost.

India's solid performance should not be devalued, but the result was probably inevitable. So unsympathetic was the tourists' itinerary that the one-off Test appeared to have more to do with Australian foreign policy than cricket: the Test, played for the new Border-Gavaskar Trophy, was arranged to coincide with a festival designed to strengthen links between the two countries.

Australia arrived seriously under-cooked for their first Test in India for almost ten years. It came after a winter lay-off, a visit to Sri Lanka for another inconsequential limited-overs quadrangular and just one first-class match, rain-affected.

There was no formal mention of the fact, but the visit marked the 60th anniversary of Indo-Australian cricket, which began when Jack Ryder led the Maharaja of Patiala's Australian team to pre-partition India in 1935-36. In view of this, and the fact that the Australian government was intent on improving relations with Delhi, it was ironic that cricketing ties between the two countries were so strained.

The Australian Cricket Board had been in bad odour in India since it directed Mark Taylor's team not to play in Sri Lanka in the World Cup earlier in 1996 and then campaigned against Indian board secretary Jagmohan Dalmiya's bid for the chairmanship of the International Cricket Council. Suffering from sub-continental fatigue syndrome on their third visit to the region in nine months, the Australians were unable to distance themselves from the politicking and it showed in their cricket.

AUSTRALIAN TOURING PARTY

M. A. Taylor (New South Wales) (*captain*), I. A. Healy (Queensland) (*vice-captain*), M. G. Bevan (New South Wales), D. W. Fleming (Victoria), J. N. Gillespie (South Australia), G. B. Hogg (Western Australia), S. G. Law (Queensland), G. D. McGrath (New South Wales), P. E. McIntyre (South Australia), R. T. Ponting (Tasmania), P. R. Reiffel (Victoria), M. J. Slater (New South Wales), M. E. Waugh (New South Wales), S. R. Waugh (New South Wales).

McIntyre replaced S. K. Warne (Victoria), who withdrew before the tour because of finger surgery. A. C. Gilchrist (Western Australia) reinforced the party when Healy was injured during the limited-overs Titan Cup.

Manager: Dr C. Battersby.　*Coach:* G. R. Marsh.

AUSTRALIAN TOUR RESULTS

Test match – Played 1: Lost 1.
First-class matches – Played 2: Lost 1, Drawn 1.
Loss – India.
Draw – Board President's XI.
One-day internationals – Played 6: Lost 5, No result 1. *Losses* – India (2), South Africa (3).
　No result – India.

At Patiala, October 5, 6, 7. Drawn. Toss: Australians. Australians 358 for eight dec. (M. J. Slater 56, R. T. Ponting 58, M. G. Bevan 100 not out, I. A. Healy 49; D. Ganesh five for 103) and 99 for two (M. A. Taylor 41, R. T. Ponting 37 not out); Board President's XI 262 (V. V. S. Laxman 36, P. Dharmani 130 not out; M. E. Waugh six for 68).

Waugh's bowling figures were his best in first-class cricket.

INDIA v AUSTRALIA

Test Match

At Delhi, October 10, 11, 12, 13. India won by seven wickets. Toss: Australia. Test debuts: D. J. Johnson; G. B. Hogg.

Conspiracy theories were inevitable once the bone-dry, fractured and shifting pitch was revealed at this neglected and unprepossessing ground. Would such a substandard pitch have been presented had Shane Warne recovered from delicate finger surgery in time to play? Taylor chose to bat on what could have been mistaken for a third-day strip, but suspicions about the pitch seemed to dominate Australian thinking, and his team's inability to concentrate irritated Taylor beyond measure. He had built his pre-match strategy around the need for occupation of the crease.

In fact Australia were bowled out in 73 overs on the opening day, eight of their wickets falling to spin, and the only man to heed Taylor's advice was their opponents' makeshift opener, Mongia. He constructed a memorable 152 and thus ensured that India's new captain, Tendulkar, would maintain the team's unbeaten record in home Test series since March 1987. An ebullient man, given to incessant appealing when keeping wicket, at the crease Mongia was calm, disciplined and accomplished. This was his maiden Test century, in his 13th match. He held sway for eight hours and 17 minutes to ensure a handsome lead of 179. Given the conditions, that made India unbeatable.

Ganguly and Steve Waugh were the only other batsmen to manage half-centuries, which was testimony to the magnitude of Mongia's performance. Waugh batted for 273 minutes at his second attempt – nine minutes longer than the entire Australian first innings – and remained unconquered on 67 as Kumble and Prasad ran through his team-mates. In the absence of Warne, Kumble carried the standard for the suddenly ubiquitous art of wrist-spin, taking nine wickets for 130 in the match. He had Kapoor and Joshi for company, but Taylor had to turn to leg-spinner McIntyre, playing in only his second Test, and the debutant left-arm wrist-spinner Brad Hogg. McIntyre bowled steadily but without variation or much imagination. Consequently, Taylor had to lean on the tireless pace bowler McGrath, who caused some mutterings by aggressively testing Ganguly's technique and temperament against the shorter-pitched delivery, and also pressed occasional off-spinner Mark Waugh into service.

Though he had no reason to recall the match as a batsman – he scored ten and nought – Tendulkar revealed himself to be a thoughtful and aggressive captain. The Australians were subdued and haunted by the realisation they had failed Allan Border when competing for a trophy partly named in honour of their mate and mentor. But Tendulkar had the satisfaction of becoming the first Indian captain to beat Australia since his own mentor and the other cricketer commemorated by the trophy, Sunil Gavaskar, in 1980-81. There was some hope that India's victory over the generally acknowledged Test champions, completed with a day to spare, would lift the profile of Test cricket in a country obsessed with the shortened form of the game.

Man of the Match: N. R. Mongia.

Close of play: First day, India 57-1 (N. R. Mongia 26*, S. C. Ganguly 19*); Second day, India 319-6 (N. R. Mongia 137*, A. R. Kapoor 8*); Third day, Australia 168-6 (S. R. Waugh 32*, G. B. Hogg 3*).

Australia

M. J. Slater c and b Kumble	44	– (2) c Azharuddin b Johnson 0
*M. A. Taylor lbw b Prasad	27	– (1) c Rathore b Kapoor 37
R. T. Ponting b Kapoor	14	– b Prasad 13
M. E. Waugh c Dravid b Joshi	26	– c Mongia b Kumble 23
S. R. Waugh c Mongia b Kapoor	0	– not out 67
M. G. Bevan lbw b Joshi	26	– c Azharuddin b Kumble 33
†I. A. Healy b Kumble	17	– st Mongia b Kumble.......... 12
G. B. Hogg c Rathore b Kumble	1	– c Rathore b Kumble 4
P. R. Reiffel c Dravid b Kumble	7	– lbw b Kumble 6
P. E. McIntyre not out	6	– lbw b Prasad 16
G. D. McGrath run out	6	– c Mongia b Prasad 0
B 4, l-b 3, n-b 1	8	B 9, l-b 6, w 1, n-b 7..... 23

1/47 (2) 2/81 (3) 3/93 (1) 4/94 (5)   182   1/4 (2) 2/25 (3) 3/72 (4)   234
5/143 (6) 6/144 (4) 7/147 (8)   4/78 (1) 5/145 (6) 6/159 (7)
8/169 (9) 9/170 (7) 10/182 (11)   7/171 (8) 8/191 (9)
                                                             9/232 (10) 10/234 (11)

Bowling: *First Innings*—Prasad 12–4–34–1; Johnson 4–1–12–0; Joshi 23–7–36–2; Kumble 24–7–63–4; Kapoor 10–3–30–2. *Second Innings*—Prasad 13.3–7–18–3; Johnson 12–2–40–1; Kumble 41–12–67–5; Joshi 20–7–52–0; Kapoor 22–5–42–1.

India

V. Rathore c Ponting b Reiffel	5	– b Reiffel 14
†N. R. Mongia b Reiffel	152	– lbw b Reiffel 0
S. C. Ganguly c M. E. Waugh b Hogg	66	– not out 21
*S. R. Tendulkar c M. E. Waugh b McIntyre	10	– b McGrath 0
M. Azharuddin b McGrath	17	– not out 21
R. Dravid c Healy b S. R. Waugh	40	
S. B. Joshi c Ponting b McIntyre	23	
A. R. Kapoor c Ponting b M. E. Waugh	22	
A. Kumble lbw b Reiffel	2	
D. J. Johnson not out	0	
B. K. V. Prasad b McIntyre	3	
B 10, l-b 1, n-b 10	21	W 1, n-b 1.............. 2

1/13 (1) 2/144 (3) 3/169 (4) 4/199 (5)   361   1/1 (2) 2/25 (1) 3/26 (4)   (3 wkts) 58
5/260 (6) 6/303 (7) 7/341 (8)
8/353 (2) 9/354 (9) 10/361 (11)

Bowling: *First Innings*—McGrath 29–10–56–1; Reiffel 17–7–35–3; S. R. Waugh 13–5–25–1; McIntyre 37.4–7–103–3; Hogg 17–3–69–1; M. E. Waugh 18–0–62–1. *Second Innings*—McGrath 7–2–30–1; Reiffel 6–2–24–2; McIntyre 0.2–0–4–0.

Umpires: P. Willey (England) and S. Venkataraghavan.   Referee: J. R. Reid (New Zealand).

Australia's matches v India and South Africa in the Titan Cup (October 19–November 3) may be found in that section.

THE ZIMBABWEANS IN PAKISTAN, 1996-97

By GEOFFREY DEAN

The previous series between Pakistan and Zimbabwe, in Africa in 1994-95, had been an extraordinarily eventful one, shadowed by dissension and allegations of match-rigging and throwing. This month-long tour also exceeded all expectations of newsworthiness, but for different reasons. Several Test batting records fell during an unbeaten double-century from Wasim Akram in the First Test at Sheikhupura, notably the number of sixes hit in one innings. Then, in the Second Test at Faisalabad, Pakistan astonished the cricketing world by selecting a boy, Hasan Raza, who was said to be just 14 years and 227 days old, and thus the youngest ever Test cricketer.

After the match, the Pakistan board's chief executive, Majid Khan, announced that in June Raza's age had been estimated at 15 by a leading radiologist at a Lahore hospital, Dr Zia Faruqi. The Board, sceptical about the validity of birth certificates for members of the squad which played in the Under-15 World Cup in England in August, had insisted that every boy undergo a bone test on his left wrist. Dr Faruqi claimed that an examination of the amount of fusion between the wrist's growth-plates gave an accurate estimate of age. This idea was rejected by other experts (See *Wisden* 1997, page 16), and the matter remained unresolved.

Back on the field, the series was not as one-sided as expected, given Zimbabwe's heavy defeats in Sri Lanka a month earlier. Moreover, they were missing strike bowler Heath Streak, out with a groin strain. But the flattest of pitches in the First Test made a result unlikely, even though Zimbabwe had to bat well on the final day to save the match. An altogether different surface for the Second Test helped to produce a conclusion in two and a half days: home captain Wasim bowled so well that few Test sides could have repelled him. The series was a personal triumph for Wasim, who won both match awards and was named, inevitably, as man of the series.

He then became the first bowler to take 300 wickets in limited-overs internationals when he dismissed Dave Houghton in the first over of the one-day series, won convincingly by Pakistan. For a while, it was unclear whether Pakistan would win that series 2-0 or 3-0: the final game, in Peshawar, was called off because of crowd trouble before being restarted on the advice of police. Match referee Jackie Hendriks considered declaring the match void, but ICC ultimately decided to let the result stand.

ZIMBABWEAN TOURING PARTY

A. D. R. Campbell (Mashonaland) (*captain*), A. Flower (Mashonaland) (*vice-captain*), G. B. Brent (Mashonaland), M. H. Dekker (Matabeleland), G. W. Flower (Mashonaland), D. L. Houghton (Mashonaland), E. Matambanadzo (Mashonaland), M. Mbangwa (Matabeleland), H. K. Olonga (Matabeleland), G. J. Rennie (Mashonaland), B. C. Strang (Mashonaland), P. A. Strang (Mashonaland), A. R. Whittall (Matabeleland), G. J. Whittall (Matabeleland), C. B. Wishart (Mashonaland).

J. A. Rennie (Matabeleland) joined the party to replace the injured Olonga.
Manager: B. Meman.   *Coach:* D. L. Houghton.

ZIMBABWEAN TOUR RESULTS

Test matches – Played 2: Lost 1, Drawn 1.
First-class matches – Played 3: Lost 1, Drawn 2.
Loss – Pakistan.
Draws – Pakistan, PCB Combined XI.
One-day internationals – Played 3: Lost 3.

Note: Matches in this section which were not first-class are signified by a dagger.

At Sahiwal, October 12, 13, 14. Drawn. Toss: Zimbabweans. Zimbabweans 307 for seven dec.
(D. L. Houghton 105, A. Flower 100 not out, Extras 40; Shahid Nazir three for 42) and 203 for
eight dec. (G. W. Flower 75, C. B. Wishart 68 not out; Mohammad Hussain four for 68, Shahid
Afridi three for 78); PCB Combined XI 236 for eight dec. (Shadab Kabir 46, Azam Khan 70,
Hasan Raza 58) and 238 for nine (Sohail Jaffer 36, Mohammad Hussain 58 not out; A. R.
Whittall five for 97, G. W. Flower three for 84).

PAKISTAN v ZIMBABWE

First Test Match

At Sheikhupura, October 17, 18, 19, 20, 21. Drawn. Toss: Zimbabwe. Test debuts: Azam Khan,
Shahid Nazir.

Test cricket's newest venue, the 77th overall and the 16th in Pakistan, had been reconstructed
to international standards so recently that it had never even staged a first-class match before this.
Now it was graced by a remarkable innings from Wasim Akram. His unbeaten 257, in eight
hours ten minutes and 363 balls, was the highest score by a No. 8 in Tests and included 12 sixes,
the most in a Test innings, as well as 22 fours. Wally Hammond's record of ten sixes had stood
since 1932-33, when he scored 336 not out in Auckland. Wasim broke another record of similar
vintage with the help of Saqlain Mushtaq: their stand of 313 in 110 overs was the highest for the
eighth wicket in Tests, beating 246 by Les Ames and Gubby Allen, for England against New
Zealand, in 1931.

Wasim and Saqlain combined at 237 for seven, trailing Zimbabwe by 138, but what looked
likely to be a sizable first-innings deficit was transformed into a lead of 178. Bad light on the
fourth evening and rain next morning may well have cost Pakistan victory, but what really
stymied them was the pitch. Houghton described it as the slowest he had seen: it offered no
bounce and virtually no movement off the seam. Wasim and Waqar Younis got negligible reverse
swing from the locally made Grays balls, which they strongly criticised. Debutant Shahid Nazir
found some swing early on, and, with five wickets in the innings, was largely responsible for
Zimbabwe slipping to 142 for six. Grant Flower and Paul Strang staged a rescue act, adding 131:
Flower reached his second Test hundred, making regular use of his trademark off-drive. Strang
also drove well and had just passed his second Test fifty when his brother Bryan joined him, to
share a stand of 87 and keep him company until he was one short of a maiden hundred. Paul
finished with 106 not out, in five hours, though he was dropped three times.

Some ill-advised shots from the top order left Pakistan an unstable 183 for six. Wasim was
appalled and immediately got his head down. He added 54 with Moin Khan, before Paul Strang
dismissed Moin to become the 18th player to score a hundred and take five wickets in an innings
in the same Test – and the first since Wasim himself in 1989-90. Meanwhile, Wasim was playing
with the sort of application of which few thought him capable. He gave one chance, on 145.
Chiefly, he faced the spin of Strang and Andrew Whittall, playing them almost entirely from the

crease. When the ball was flighted or overpitched, he drove powerfully and cleanly. Most of his 12 sixes went over the straight boundaries, 71 metres away. Saqlain willed himself to survive for seven hours and contributed 79.

Zimbabwe's task of batting out the final day eased when Wasim collided with a boundary board and was unable to bowl more than five overs. With the wicket turning slowly, off-spinner Saqlain bowled 40 overs, but pitched too wide too often; the injured Mushtaq Ahmed was badly missed. Again, Houghton and Grant Flower played key innings, and Andy Flower used up three hours in scoring 18.

Man of the Match: Wasim Akram.

Close of play: First day, Zimbabwe 240-6 (G. W. Flower 98*, P. A. Strang 37*); Second day, Pakistan 189-6 (Moin Khan 3*, Wasim Akram 5*); Third day, Pakistan 395-7 (Wasim Akram 144*, Saqlain Mushtaq 37*); Fourth day, Zimbabwe 38-1 (G. W. Flower 11*, A. D. R. Campbell 14*).

Zimbabwe

G. W. Flower c sub (Shahid Afridi) b Saqlain Mushtaq	.110	– (2) c Shadab Kabir b Saqlain Mushtaq	46
M. H. Dekker lbw b Wasim Akram	14	– (1) c Wasim Akram b Saqlain Mushtaq	13
*A. D. R. Campbell lbw b Shahid Nazir	8	– lbw b Waqar Younis	15
D. L. Houghton run out	43	– b Saqlain Mushtaq	65
†A. Flower lbw b Shahid Nazir	11	– b Shahid Nazir	18
C. B. Wishart lbw b Shahid Nazir	0	– b Shahid Nazir	10
G. J. Whittall c Shadab Kabir b Saqlain Mushtaq	0	– c sub (Shahid Afridi) b Saqlain Mushtaq	32
P. A. Strang not out	.106	– not out	13
A. R. Whittall lbw b Shahid Nazir	0	– not out	0
B. C. Strang b Saqlain Mushtaq	42		
H. K. Olonga b Shahid Nazir	7		
B 9, l-b 16, w 1, n-b 8	34	B 11, l-b 10, n-b 8	29
	375		**(7 wkts) 241**

1/33 (2) 2/41 (3) 3/119 (4) 4/141 (5) 5/141 (6) 6/142 (7) 7/273 (1) 8/274 (9) 9/361 (10) 10/375 (11)

1/13 (1) 2/40 (3) 3/124 (2) 4/159 (4) 5/177 (6) 6/221 (5) 7/232 (7)   (7 wkts) 241

Bowling: *First Innings*—Wasim Akram 28-9-58-1; Waqar Younis 22-3-90-0; Saqlain Mushtaq 37-3-127-3; Shahid Nazir 22.4-3-53-5; Aamir Sohail 6-0-22-0. *Second Innings*—Waqar Younis 20-4-60-1; Shahid Nazir 19-6-45-2; Saqlain Mushtaq 40-15-75-4; Wasim Akram 5-0-16-0; Aamir Sohail 11-6-12-0; Salim Malik 5-1-12-0.

Pakistan

Saeed Anwar st A. Flower b P. A. Strang.		51
Aamir Sohail c A. Flower b P. A. Strang.		46
Shadab Kabir c Houghton b A. R. Whittall		2
Ijaz Ahmed, sen. lbw b Olonga		9
Salim Malik b P. A. Strang		52
Azam Khan lbw b P. A. Strang		14
†Moin Khan c A. R. Whittall b P. A. Strang.		18
*Wasim Akram not out		.257
Saqlain Mushtaq b G. J. Whittall		79
Waqar Younis b G. J. Whittall		0
Shahid Nazir c Dekker b A. R. Whittall..		0
B 10, l-b 8, w 2, n-b 5		25
		553

1/64 (2) 2/77 (3) 3/91 (4) 4/142 (1) 5/176 (6) 6/183 (5) 7/237 (7) 8/550 (9) 9/550 (10) 10/553 (11)

Bowling: Olonga 19-6-60-1; B. C. Strang 10-2-34-0; A. R. Whittall 45.2-7-146-2; P. A. Strang 69-12-212-5; G. J. Whittall 25-5-73-2; G. W. Flower 10-4-10-0.

Umpires: D. L. Orchard (South Africa) and Khizar Hayat.
Referee: J. L. Hendriks (West Indies).

PAKISTAN v ZIMBABWE

Second Test Match

At Faisalabad, October 24, 25, 26. Pakistan won by ten wickets. Toss: Zimbabwe. Test debuts: Hassan Raza, Mohammad Hussain; E. Matambanadzo, M. Mbangwa.

Despite the margin of defeat, Zimbabwe competed bravely until the third morning. The match finished that afternoon, with a full house after the gates were thrown open. But it was effectively settled on the opening morning, when Zimbabwe lost their top five in the first 18 overs as Wasim Akram bowled an inspirational spell.

The attention centred on Pakistan's newest batsman, Hasan Raza, who was hailed as the youngest ever Test player. He was supposedly 14 years and 227 days at the start, and scored a composed 27. Later, the Pakistan board, relying on radiology tests, said that he was up to a year older; it was unclear why they had delayed releasing their information. Still, given that the previously recognised record was Mushtaq Mohammad's 15 years and 124 days, Raza's claim had yet to be disproved.

Unlike at Sheikhupura, conditions were very much to the fast bowlers' liking: the pitch, unusually well-grassed, offered bounce and some pace; there was movement off the seam and the Grays ball swung when new and reverse swung later. Early moisture in the pitch helped the pace bowlers, and the spinners – including another debutant, left-armer Mohammad Hussain – obtained startling first-day turn.

It was a good toss to lose: Wasim admitted that he too would have batted. Swinging and seaming it both ways at pace, he was a fearsome proposition. Five of his six first-innings victims were bowled. Zimbabwe, however, batted poorly, apart from Andy Flower, who resisted for three hours to be last out, before tea.

Fielding a highly inexperienced attack, Zimbabwe did creditably to restrict Pakistan to 267. Their opening bowlers, Everton Matambanadzo and Mpumelelo Mbangwa, both 20, became only the second and third black Zimbabweans to win Test caps (the first, Olonga, had flown home with a groin strain). Both bowled medium-fast out-swingers vigorously, if not always with full control. Saeed Anwar played some exhilarating shots in an attacking 81 with 16 fours. Like several of his colleagues, he got himself out. But, thanks to an aggressive 58 from Moin Khan, Pakistan doubled Zimbabwe's meagre total.

A two-day finish looked possible when both Zimbabwean openers fell within two overs of resuming, though Grant Flower suffered a bad decision. A brilliant counter-attack from Houghton, who added 113 in just 27 overs with Campbell, gave them an outside chance. But Houghton was out first ball next day and, in the next over, Campbell was given out caught behind off his pad, making defeat all but inevitable. Whittall got another bad decision and the last seven wickets fell in 21.4 overs. Wasim took four more to complete his fourth ten-wicket haul in Tests and confirm his role as the dominant figure of the series.

Man of the Match: Wasim Akram.   *Man of the Series:* Wasim Akram.

Close of play: First day, Pakistan 114-3 (Saeed Anwar 69*, Hasan Raza 20*); Second day, Zimbabwe 136-3 (D. L. Houghton 73*, A. D. R. Campbell 52*).

Zimbabwe

G. W. Flower b Wasim Akram	15	– lbw b Wasim Akram	0
M. H. Dekker c Moin Khan b Wasim Akram	19	– lbw b Waqar Younis	0
C. B. Wishart lbw b Waqar Younis	0	– c Salim Malik b Waqar Younis	7
D. L. Houghton b Wasim Akram	1	– lbw b Wasim Akram	73
*A. D. R. Campbell c Moin Khan b Saqlain Mushtaq	9	– c Moin Khan b Shahid Nazir	52
†A. Flower c Mohammad Hussain b Shahid Nazir	61	– c Saeed Anwar b Waqar Younis	23
G. J. Whittall b Wasim Akram	9	– lbw b Shahid Nazir	0
P. A. Strang c Salim Malik b Mohammad Hussain	3	– b Waqar Younis	9
B. C. Strang b Wasim Akram	1	– not out	13
M. Mbangwa b Wasim Akram	0	– (11) lbw b Wasim Akram	2
E. Matambanadzo not out	0	– (10) b Wasim Akram	7
B 4, l-b 10, n-b 1	15	L-b 8, n-b 6	14

1/22 (1) 2/33 (3) 3/34 (4) 4/49 (2)   133   1/0 (1) 2/0 (2) 3/23 (3)   200
5/55 (5) 6/102 (7) 7/111 (8)   4/136 (4) 5/136 (5) 6/140 (7)
8/118 (9) 9/129 (10) 10/133 (6)   7/169 (8) 8/174 (6)
                                                        9/198 (10) 10/200 (11)

Bowling: *First Innings*—Wasim Akram 20–8–48–6; Waqar Younis 11–6–13–1; Saqlain Mushtaq 15–5–28–1; Shahid Nazir 5.5–0–23–1; Mohammad Hussain 6–3–7–1. *Second Innings*—Wasim Akram 18.4–4–58–4; Waqar Younis 15–3–54–4; Saqlain Mushtaq 7–1–34–0; Shahid Nazir 11–5–25–2; Mohammad Hussain 4–1–14–0; Salim Malik 2–0–7–0.

Pakistan

Saeed Anwar c A. Flower b Matambanadzo	81	– not out		50
Aamir Sohail lbw b Matambanadzo	2	– not out		18
Ijaz Ahmed, sen. c A. Flower b Mbangwa	2			
Salim Malik c A. Flower b B. C. Strang	18			
Hasan Raza c Houghton b B. C. Strang	27			
*Wasim Akram b Mbangwa	35			
†Moin Khan c A. Flower b B. C. Strang	58			
Mohammad Hussain run out	0			
Saqlain Mushtaq not out	15			
Waqar Younis b G. W. Flower	23			
Shahid Nazir lbw b P. A. Strang	1			
L-b 4, n-b 1	5	W 1		1
	267			**(no wkt) 69**

1/7 (2) 2/10 (3) 3/67 (4)
4/127 (1) 5/141 (5) 6/194 (6)
7/200 (8) 8/235 (7)
9/264 (10) 10/267 (11)

Bowling: *First Innings*—Matambanadzo 11–0–62–2; Mbangwa 17–1–67–2; B. C. Strang 18–5–53–3; Whittall 7–4–11–0; P. A. Strang 24.1–8–66–1; G. W. Flower 2–0–4–1. *Second Innings*—Matambanadzo 5–0–27–0; Mbangwa 7–3–14–0; B. C. Strang 4.5–1–20–0; P. A. Strang 2–0–8–0.

Umpires: D. B. Cowie (New Zealand) and Mahboob Shah.
Referee: J. L. Hendriks (West Indies).

†PAKISTAN v ZIMBABWE

First One-Day International

At Quetta, October 30. Pakistan won by three wickets. Toss: Zimbabwe. International debuts: G. B. Brent, G. J. Rennie.

Wasim Akram became the first cricketer to take 300 wickets in one-day internationals, in his 208th match, when he trapped Houghton with his fourth ball. That sent Zimbabwe sliding towards 25 for three by the tenth over. They made an excellent recovery, thanks to the Flowers, who added 143: Grant's 91 took just 94 balls. But Pakistan were steered home by Salim Malik, with a fine, unbeaten 72 from 77 balls. Gavin and John Rennie became the third set of brothers to represent Zimbabwe on this tour, following the Flowers and the Strangs, in addition to the Whittall cousins.

Man of the Match: Salim Malik.

Zimbabwe

G. W. Flower c Shahid Afridi b Salim Malik	91	G. J. Rennie run out		0
D. L. Houghton lbw b Wasim Akram	0	P. A. Strang not out		13
J. A. Rennie c Moin Khan b Shahid Nazir	7	G. B. Brent b Saqlain Mushtaq		1
*A. D. R. Campbell b Shahid Nazir	7	A. R. Whittall not out		1
†A. Flower c Shahid Nazir b Saqlain Mushtaq	82	B 5, l-b 7, w 11		23
C. B. Wishart c Wasim Akram b Shahid Afridi	2		**(9 wkts, 50 overs) 237**	
G. J. Whittall run out	10			

1/1 2/14 3/25
4/168 5/175 6/201
7/206 8/228 9/235

Bowling: Wasim Akram 10-1-27-1; Shahid Nazir 7-0-28-2; Azhar Mahmood 4-0-17-0; Saqlain Mushtaq 8-0-40-2; Shahid Afridi 8-0-36-1; Aamir Sohail 6-0-40-0; Salim Malik 7-0-37-1.

Pakistan

Saeed Anwar st A. Flower	†Moin Khan b G. J. Whittall	3
b A. R. Whittall . 26	Hassan Raza run out	11
Shahid Afridi c G. J. Rennie	Azhar Mahmood not out	6
b G. J. Whittall . 28		
Aamir Sohail b J. A. Rennie 55		
Ijaz Ahmed, sen. c Houghton	B 1, l-b 5, w 6	12
b A. R. Whittall . 17		
Salim Malik not out 72	1/45 2/73 3/107 (7 wkts, 49.1 overs) 239	
*Wasim Akram c Houghton	4/160 5/196	
b A. R. Whittall . 9	6/200 7/224	

Saqlain Mushtaq and Shahid Nazir did not bat.

Bowling: J. A. Rennie 10-0-54-1; G. J. Whittall 9.1-0-48-2; Brent 5-0-29-0; A. R. Whittall 10-0-36-3; Strang 10-1-45-0; G. W. Flower 4-0-17-0; Campbell 1-0-4-0.

Umpires: Khizar Hayat and Shakeel Khan.

†PAKISTAN v ZIMBABWE

Second One-Day International

At Lahore, November 1. Pakistan won by nine wickets. Toss: Zimbabwe. International debut: Abdur Razzaq.

Pakistan cruised to victory with more than 21 overs to spare after Saeed Anwar and Shahid Afridi plundered 100 for the first wicket in 10.2 overs. Anwar carried on to an unbeaten 84, from 79 balls, his fourth half-century in five innings against Zimbabwe. But he was upstaged by Afridi, who smashed 66 off just 37 balls, with eight fours and four sixes, after being dropped on nought. A three-pronged pace attack included 18-year-old debutant Abdur Razzaq, who had yet to appear in first-class cricket. The bowlers caused early problems for Zimbabwe, whose only significant contribution was a fifty from Andy Flower.

Man of the Match: Shahid Afridi.

Zimbabwe

G. W. Flower b Shahid Nazir 6	B. C. Strang st Moin Khan	
M. H. Dekker b Wasim Akram 18	b Saqlain Mushtaq .	6
*A. D. R. Campbell lbw b Shahid Nazir . 1	A. R. Whittall not out	4
D. L. Houghton b Abdur Razzaq 25	M. Mbangwa run out	11
†A. Flower c Ijaz Ahmed b Abdur Razzaq 51		
G. J. Whittall st Moin Khan	L-b 12, w 5, n-b 3	20
b Saqlain Mushtaq . 9		
P. A. Strang run out 17	1/18 2/27 3/33 (49.1 overs) 195	
J. A. Rennie c Azam Khan	4/61 5/101 6/127	
b Saqlain Mushtaq . 27	7/161 8/172 9/184	

Bowling: Wasim Akram 9.1-2-26-1; Shahid Nazir 9-0-31-2; Abdur Razzaq 7.3-1-29-2; Saqlain Mushtaq 10-0-46-3; Shahid Afridi 10-0-38-0; Salim Malik 3.3-0-13-0.

Pakistan

Saeed Anwar not out 84	
Shahid Afridi b Rennie 66	
Ijaz Ahmed, sen. not out 32	
B 1, l-b 11, w 1, n-b 1 14	
1/100 (1 wkt, 28.4 overs) 196	

Salim Malik, Hasan Raza, Azam Khan, *Wasim Akram, †Moin Khan, Saqlain Mushtaq, Shahid Nazir and Abdur Razzaq did not bat.

Bowling: Rennie 5–0–28–1; Mbangwa 5.4–0–47–0; P. A. Strang 6–1–44–0; G. J. Whittall 3–0–18–0; B. C. Strang 4–1–21–0; A. R. Whittall 5–0–26–0.

Umpires: Mahboob Khan and Shakoor Rana.

†PAKISTAN v ZIMBABWE

Third One-Day International

At Peshawar, November 3. Pakistan won on scoring-rate, Zimbabwe's target having been revised to 225 from 34 overs. Toss: Pakistan. International debut: Zahoor Elahi.

Several thousand people forced their way into an already packed ground by breaking down a gate, and the resulting trouble cut the match to 40 overs. Seven stoppages followed, with both sides pelted by stones, glass and fruit; Wasim Akram led Pakistan off when Abdur Razzaq was hit. Zimbabwe's target was revised because of the hold-up, but they were already struggling when their best batsman, Grant Flower, became the first victim of a hat-trick by Saqlain Mushtaq, who went on to make it four in five balls. Matambanadzo had claimed three early wickets, but Pakistan's last 20 overs yielded 194, thanks to a top-class 117 in 105 balls from Ijaz Ahmed and Moin Khan's 34 off just 17.

Man of the Match: Ijaz Ahmed, sen.   *Men of the Series:* Wasim Akram and G. W. Flower.

Pakistan

Shahid Afridi c J. A. Rennie		†Moin Khan c Strang b J. A. Rennie	34
b Matambanadzo	0	Salim Malik c A. Flower b G. J. Whittall	0
Zahoor Elahi c Houghton		Saqlain Mushtaq run out	3
b Matambanadzo	1	Shahid Nazir not out	5
Ijaz Ahmed, sen. c G. W. Flower		Abdur Razzaq not out	0
b Matambanadzo	117	L-b 4, w 12, n-b 3	19
Hasan Raza c G. J. Rennie			
b Matambanadzo	12	(9 wkts, 40 overs)	264
Azam Khan c Strang b J. A. Rennie	72		
*Wasim Akram run out	1		

1/0 2/18 3/43 4/194 5/199 6/231 7/251 8/256 9/263

Bowling: Matambanadzo 8–0–32–4; J. A. Rennie 8–0–37–2; G. J. Whittall 8–0–64–1; A. R. Whittall 8–0–62–0; Strang 4–0–33–0; Dekker 4–0–32–0.

Zimbabwe

G. W. Flower c Moin Khan		J. A. Rennie c Moin Khan	
b Saqlain Mushtaq	77	b Saqlain Mushtaq	0
M. H. Dekker lbw b Abdur Razzaq	11	A. R. Whittall c Salim Malik	
P. A. Strang c Wasim Akram		b Saqlain Mushtaq	0
b Shahid Afridi	29	E. Matambanadzo not out	2
D. L. Houghton c Moin Khan		*A. D. R. Campbell absent hurt	
b Shahid Afridi	6	L-b 5, w 6, n-b 4	15
†A. Flower c Wasim Akram			
b Salim Malik	1	(32.1 overs)	147
G. J. Whittall run out	0		
G. J. Rennie b Saqlain Mushtaq	6		

1/34 2/95 3/110 4/118 5/119 6/143 7/143 8/143 9/147

Bowling: Wasim Akram 4–0–20–0; Shahid Nazir 6–0–16–0; Abdur Razzaq 5–0–24–1; Saqlain Mushtaq 6.1–0–28–4; Shahid Afridi 7–0–25–2; Salim Malik 4–0–29–1.

Umpires: Javed Akhtar and Shakoor Rana.   Series referee: J. L. Hendriks (West Indies).

THE SOUTH AFRICANS IN INDIA, 1996-97

By COLIN BRYDEN

While Australia and West Indies embarked on a series grandiosely entitled "The Decider", a Test series of some significance was being played in India.

The Indians had not lost a home series since 1986-87, and had won ten out of 14 Tests at home since 1992-93, the most recent being an emphatic win over Australia in a one-off match at Delhi. South Africa, meanwhile, had not lost any series, or a one-off, since their inaugural Test on rejoining the cricketing world, at Bridgetown in April 1992. They had played enough one-day cricket on the subcontinent not to worry unduly about the conditions. But they soon discovered that Tests were different: they lost the series 2-1, sandwiching a win in Calcutta between defeats in Ahmedabad and Kanpur.

Their cause was not helped by their build-up. Since the first week of 1996, South Africa had played 29 one-day internationals – and won 25. But when they arrived, many of their players had played no first-class cricket in ten months. It was a surprise that the selectors did not freshen up the squad who had played so well in one-day cricket. But three of their young discoveries, Shaun Pollock, Jacques Kallis and (at first) Paul Adams, were all injured. India, in contrast, were starting to gell, having improved during their tour of England. The upshot was an exciting series, uneven in quality, which could have gone either way until the second-last day.

The Indians had the bonus of a late flowering from Mohammad Azharuddin. Relieved of the captaincy, he found sublime batting form: his hundred off 74 balls in Calcutta was extraordinary; his unbeaten 163 in Kanpur clinched the series. Javagal Srinath, the First Test match-winner, and Venkatesh Prasad were an effective new-ball pair, while Anil Kumble had an outstanding series in an unexpected role. Showing a straight bat and good sense, he played vital innings in each Test, and there was no diminution either in his powers as a brisk-paced bowler of leg-spin and top-spin. Although his figures were not sensational, the South Africans never mastered him.

South Africa's batting let them down when conditions were even slightly dubious. The contrast between their performance in Calcutta and the other two Tests was marked. Although Kirsten, Cullinan and Hudson all finished with impressive averages, they made most of their runs in Calcutta – where Kirsten scored twin hundreds. Only the captain, Hansie Cronje, played innings of substance in both Ahmedabad and Kanpur. The loss of fast bowler Allan Donald with a heel injury during the Second Test was a critical blow. He had looked easily the best bowler on either side; although Lance Klusener had the remarkable figures of eight for 64 in the second innings of his debut Test, he lacked Donald's consistency. The left-arm wrist-spinner, Adams, took 14 wickets at 20.28 with a mixture of devastating and dreadful deliveries.

The South Africans were unhappy with conditions in both Ahmedabad and Kanpur, considering Ahmedabad, especially, an unsuitable Test venue – Cronje said the pitch was unsatisfactory and condemned the absence of suitable practice facilities.

SOUTH AFRICAN TOURING PARTY

W. J. Cronje (Free State) (*captain*), G. Kirsten (Western Province) (*vice-captain*), P. R. Adams (Western Province), N. Boje (Free State), D. N. Crookes (Natal), D. J. Cullinan (Transvaal), P. S. de Villiers (Northern Transvaal), A. A. Donald (Free State), H. H. Gibbs (Western Province), A. C. Hudson (Natal), L. Klusener (Natal), B. M. McMillan (Western Province), J. N. Rhodes (Natal), D. J. Richardson (Eastern Province), P. L. Symcox (Natal).

Adams joined the party for the Test series after the one-day Titan Cup. J. B. Commins (Western Province) replaced the injured Rhodes after the First Test and Donald also went home injured after the Second Test.

Manager: R. K. Muzzell.   *Coach:* R. A. Woolmer.

SOUTH AFRICAN TOUR RESULTS

Test matches – Played 3: Won 1, Lost 2.
First-class matches – Played 6: Won 3, Lost 2, Drawn 1.
Wins – India, Karnataka, Board President's XI.
Losses – India (2).
Draw – India A.
One-day internationals – Played 8: Won 6, Lost 2. *Wins* – India (3), Australia (3). *Losses* – India (2).

TEST MATCH AVERAGES

INDIA – BATTING

	T	I	NO	R	HS	100s	Avge	Ct/St
M. Azharuddin	3	6	1	388	163*	2	77.60	4
A. Kumble	3	6	1	199	88	0	39.80	1
R. Dravid	3	6	0	175	56	0	29.16	2
S. R. Tendulkar ...	3	6	0	166	61	0	27.66	1
S. C. Ganguly	2	4	0	86	41	0	21.50	0
N. R. Mongia	3	6	0	116	41	0	19.33	3/1
V. V. S. Laxman ..	2	4	0	77	51	0	19.25	1
J. Srinath	3	5	0	45	19	0	9.00	0
S. B. Joshi	3	6	0	50	16	0	8.33	2
B. K. V. Prasad ..	3	5	2	14	9	0	4.66	0
N. D. Hirwani	2	4	2	9	9	0	4.50	0

Played in one Test: A. R. Kapoor 11, 6*; S. V. Manjrekar 34, 5 (1 ct); W. V. Raman 57, 2 (1 ct).

* *Signifies not out.*

BOWLING

	O	M	R	W	BB	5W/i	Avge
J. Srinath	127.3	33	356	17	6-21	1	20.94
A. Kumble	146.1	26	387	13	4-71	0	29.76
S. B. Joshi	91.3	17	248	8	4-43	0	31.00
B. K. V. Prasad	91	18	259	8	6-104	1	32.37

Also bowled: S. C. Ganguly 3–1–10–0; N. D. Hirwani 40–6–129–2; A. R. Kapoor 21–10–29–2.

SOUTH AFRICA – BATTING

	T	I	NO	R	HS	100s	Avge	Ct
D. J. Cullinan	3	6	1	270	153*	1	54.00	2
G. Kirsten	3	6	0	322	133	2	53.66	2
A. C. Hudson	3	6	1	221	146	1	44.20	3
W. J. Cronje	3	6	1	152	50	0	30.40	0
L. Klusener	2	3	1	53	34*	0	26.50	2
P. S. de Villiers ...	2	4	1	75	67*	0	25.00	2
P. L. Symcox	3	5	1	79	32	0	19.75	0
H. H. Gibbs	2	4	0	62	31	0	15.50	1
D. J. Richardson ...	3	5	1	56	36*	0	14.00	4
B. M. McMillan ...	3	6	1	61	18	0	12.20	8
A. A. Donald	2	3	0	21	17	0	7.00	1
P. R. Adams	3	5	0	14	8	0	2.80	3

Played in one Test: J. N. Rhodes 14, 0 (2 ct).

* Signifies not out.

BOWLING

	O	M	R	W	BB	5W/i	Avge
A. A. Donald	63.2	21	141	10	4-37	0	14.10
P. R. Adams	78.3	14	284	14	6-55	1	20.28
L. Klusener	77.3	16	258	10	8-64	1	25.80
B. M. McMillan ...	89	33	199	6	2-40	0	33.16
P. S. de Villiers	74	26	176	5	2-55	0	35.20
P. L. Symcox	107	22	324	6	2-47	0	54.00

Also bowled: W. J. Cronje 50–22–83–2.

Note: Matches in this section which were not first-class are signified by a dagger.

South Africa's matches v India and Australia in the Titan Cup (October 17–November 6) may be found in that section.

At Cochin, November 10, 11, 12. South Africa won by 244 runs. Toss: South Africans. South Africans 243 (J. N. Rhodes 46, W. J. Cronje 46, D. N. Crookes 45, L. Klusener 32 not out; D. J. Johnson three for 76, R. Ananth four for 72) and 233 (A. C. Hudson 36, D. J. Cullinan 32, W. J. Cronje 49; A. Katti four for 67); Karnataka 115 (F. Khaleel 32; A. A. Donald four for 39, L. Klusener five for 38) and 117 (J. Arun Kumar 33; A. A. Donald three for 29, L. Klusener three for 32).

At Baroda, November 15, 16, 17. South Africa won by ten wickets. Toss: Board President's XI. Board President's XI 179 (S. A. Ankola 63; P. S. de Villiers five for 46, L. Klusener three for 38) and 94 (P. S. de Villiers four for 37, L. Klusener three for 29, B. M. McMillan three for 14); South Africans 206 (A. C. Hudson 39, D. J. Cullinan 31, H. H. Gibbs 74; S. L. V. Raju six for 64) and 70 for no wkt (G. Kirsten 37 not out).

INDIA v SOUTH AFRICA

First Test Match

At Ahmedabad, November 20, 21, 22, 23. India won by 64 runs. Toss: India. Test debut: V. V. S. Laxman.

Devastating pace bowling by Srinath gave India victory on a poor pitch. Though it seemed best suited to the spinners, Srinath's fast, accurate in-swingers and off-cutters brought him career-best figures of six for 21. South Africa crashed for 105 after being set a modest 170 to win.

It was obvious that batting would not be easy on a brown, dusty pitch, and by winning the toss Tendulkar gave India a substantial advantage. But there were frequent changes of fortune and several questionable umpiring decisions. Although Mongia fell early to de Villiers, in the first of umpire Bansal's controversial lbw verdicts, India negotiated the first morning safely enough until Manjrekar misread a top-spinner from the unorthodox left-arm spinner Adams. Thereafter, they struggled against accurate bowling and sharp fielding. Donald was superb, but the two most critical blows were struck by Rhodes. He held a dazzling diving catch at mid-wicket to dismiss Tendulkar and then ran out Azharuddin with a direct hit from cover.

Having restricted India to 223, South Africa needed to bat sensibly. Instead, they slumped to 119 for seven. Bansal gave Cronje out to a ball which pitched well outside leg stump and Cullinan when he was struck on the half-volley at full stretch, but the South Africans were always struggling against the spinners. De Villiers showed the application needed over three hours: with first Symcox, then Donald, he established a 21-run lead.

Donald struck twice before India erased the modest deficit, and they were 38 for three when Tendulkar sliced a slower delivery from McMillan to Rhodes – again – at backward point. It was to be Rhodes's last significant contribution; later, he strained his hamstring badly. Donald had Azharuddin brilliantly caught at second slip by McMillan and, when Dravid was trapped by Symcox, India were just 70 ahead with five down. The 22-year-old debutant Laxman showed a cool head during a 56-run partnership with Kumble.

Needing 170, with nearly two days to get them, South Africa looked to their openers for a solid start before the spinners came on. Instead, Srinath took centre stage. His fifth delivery swung in to Hudson and Bansal's fateful finger rose again (replays suggested it would have missed leg stump). Cullinan edged the next, and South Africa were two down without a run on the board. With Cronje the only batsman to last long, his team seldom looked like reaching the target. Srinath's pace and swing combined perfectly with Kumble's customary accuracy on a crumbling pitch which made driving through the line virtually impossible. From 96 for four, South Africa lost their last six for nine runs. Tendulkar said he could not recall a Test with so many twists and turns.

The match was stopped for ten minutes on the third afternoon when Adams was struck by golf-ball-sized pieces of concrete thrown from the crowd. Azharuddin became the first cricketer to play against all eight other countries, both home and away.

Man of the Match: J. Srinath.

Close of play: First day, India 215-8 (A. Kumble 13*, B. K. V. Prasad 7*); Second day, South Africa 202-8 (P. S. de Villiers 40*, A. A. Donald 4*); Third day, India 172-7 (V. V. S. Laxman 50*, A. Kumble 22*).

India

S. V. Manjrekar b Adams	34	– c Hudson b Donald	5
†N. R. Mongia lbw b de Villiers	9	– c Richardson b Donald	5
R. Dravid lbw b Symcox	24	– lbw b Symcox	34
*S. R. Tendulkar c Rhodes b Symcox	42	– c Rhodes b McMillan	7
M. Azharuddin run out	35	– c McMillan b Donald	24
V. V. S. Laxman lbw b Donald	11	– lbw b Adams	51
S. B. Joshi c Hudson b Donald	16	– c McMillan b Symcox	13
J. Srinath c Cullinan b Donald	14	– lbw b de Villiers	1
A. Kumble c Kirsten b Donald	17	– not out	30
B. K. V. Prasad c Donald b de Villiers	9	– c McMillan b Adams	0
N. D. Hirwani not out	0	– c sub (D. N. Crookes) b Adams	9
L-b 9, n-b 3	12	B 4, l-b 4, n-b 3	11

1/22 (2) 2/63 (1) 3/98 (3) 4/129 (4)   223   1/10 (1) 2/15 (2) 3/38 (4)   190
5/159 (5) 6/165 (6) 7/193 (8)   4/82 (5) 5/91 (3) 6/123 (7)
8/196 (9) 9/221 (10) 10/223 (9)   7/124 (8) 8/180 (6)
                                  9/180 (10) 10/190 (11)

Bowling: *First Innings*—Donald 27–14–37–4; de Villiers 18–5–55–2; McMillan 11–4–20–0; Cronje 5–3–8–0; Adams 17–2–46–1; Symcox 21–5–48–2. *Second Innings*—Donald 15–3–32–3; de Villiers 17–4–45–1; McMillan 9–4–18–1; Symcox 22–8–47–2; Cronje 7–2–10–0; Adams 9.2–4–30–3.

South Africa

A. C. Hudson lbw b Kumble	23	– lbw b Srinath	0
G. Kirsten st Mongia b Kumble	17	– lbw b Joshi	20
D. J. Cullinan lbw b Joshi	43	– c Mongia b Srinath	0
*W. J. Cronje lbw b Hirwani	1	– not out	48
J. N. Rhodes c Manjrekar b Joshi	14	– (7) lbw b Srinath	0
B. M. McMillan b Joshi	8	– (5) c Joshi b Kumble	17
†D. J. Richardson b Hirwani	4	– (6) c Mongia b Srinath	7
P. L. Symcox lbw b Joshi	32	– b Kumble	0
P. S. de Villiers not out	67	– c Azharuddin b Kumble	0
A. A. Donald b Srinath	17	– b Srinath	4
P. R. Adams c Azharuddin b Srinath	1	– b Srinath	0
B 7, l-b 9, n-b 1	17	B 1, l-b 3, w 5	9
	244		**105**

1/29 (2) 2/46 (1) 3/49 (4) 4/95 (5)
5/102 (3) 6/113 (7) 7/119 (6)
8/182 (8) 9/242 (10) 10/244 (11)

1/0 (1) 2/0 (3) 3/40 (2)
4/65 (5) 5/96 (6) 6/96 (7)
7/100 (8) 8/100 (9)
9/105 (10) 10/105 (11)

Bowling: *First Innings*—Srinath 19.1–7–47–2; Prasad 9–2–24–0; Kumble 31–6–76–2; Joshi 24–4–43–4; Hirwani 15–3–38–2. *Second Innings*—Srinath 11.5–4–21–6; Prasad 7–0–18–0; Kumble 12–2–34–3; Joshi 8–1–28–1.

Umpires: G. Sharp (England) and S. K. Bansal. Referee: J. R. Reid (New Zealand).

INDIA v SOUTH AFRICA

Second Test Match

At Calcutta, November 27, 28, 29, 30, December 1. South Africa won by 329 runs. Toss: South Africa. Test debuts: H. H. Gibbs, L. Klusener.

South Africa levelled the series in an invigorating Test watched by an estimated 50,000 people each day. Their batsmen found form on a true pitch and fast outfield and, for the first time, scored four hundreds in one Test. Two came from Kirsten – the third South African to achieve twin centuries, after Alan Melville and Bruce Mitchell – and there was one each for Hudson and Cullinan. The most sensational century, however, came from Azharuddin. He reached it in 74 deliveries, equalling the fourth-quickest Test hundred recorded in terms of balls.

Azharuddin hit debutant Lance Klusener for five successive fours. But Klusener rebounded in remarkable fashion, taking eight for 64 in the second innings, the third-best bowling for South Africa in Tests and the best on debut. He said afterwards he had lacked rhythm in the first innings and, in an unsuccessful team strategy, had peppered Azharuddin with short balls. His triumph came after he shortened his run-up by half a yard and bowled to a fuller length. Klusener had been a surprise selection ahead of de Villiers, and South Africa also introduced 22-year-old Herschelle Gibbs to replace the injured Rhodes. India dropped Manjrekar as Calcutta-born Ganguly returned after a leg injury.

Winning the toss for the first time in eight international fixtures, Cronje chose to bat. There was assistance for the fast bowlers early on, when Hudson was dropped twice off Srinath's bowling. He and Kirsten took full advantage, piling up 236, the second-highest opening stand in South Africa's history. Though Kirsten began more fluently, Hudson gradually found superlative timing. But from 339 for two overnight, South Africa were pegged back to 428, thanks to outstanding pace bowling, especially from Prasad, who was unchanged throughout the second morning and returned a career-best six for 104.

India opened well through Mongia and the promoted Dravid, then slumped, partly due to two good run-outs from Gibbs. Meanwhile, Azharuddin had retired, hit on the elbow by McMillan. But he returned next morning when India slipped to 161 for seven and, with Kumble, managed to double that, setting an Indian record for the eighth wicket. Kumble showed up his team-mates by playing straight for his best Test score, and Azharuddin simply hammered the bowling. He scored his fifty off 35 balls, his century off 74, and pulled Adams for a six to go with his 18 fours before hitting him a return catch.

Kirsten and Cullinan then added 212 to put their team firmly on top again and raise South Africa's second-wicket record. India's eventual target was 467 in just over four sessions. With Donald off the field nursing a severely bruised left heel, Klusener seized the moment. He picked up three wickets by the fourth-day close and the final day was almost all his: he claimed the last five, three of them caught by McMillan at second slip.

Man of the Match: G. Kirsten.

Close of play: First day, South Africa 339-2 (H. H. Gibbs 28*, D. J. Cullinan 29*); Second day, India 152-6 (J. Srinath 9*, A. Kumble 24*); Third day, South Africa 160-1 (G. Kirsten 82*, D. J. Cullinan 60*); Fourth day, India 59-4 (R. Dravid 18*, M. Azharuddin 25*).

South Africa

A. C. Hudson b Prasad	146	– retired hurt	6
G. Kirsten b Srinath	102	– run out	133
H. H. Gibbs lbw b Prasad	31	– c Dravid b Srinath	9
D. J. Cullinan lbw b Prasad	43	– not out	153
*W. J. Cronje b Mongia b Srinath	4	– c and b Kumble	34
B. M. McMillan lbw b Prasad	0	– not out	17
†D. J. Richardson not out	36		
L. Klusener b Prasad	10		
P. L. Symcox b Prasad	13		
A. A. Donald c Laxman b Kumble	0		
P. R. Adams b Kumble	4		
B 6, l-b 24, n-b 9	39	B 1, l-b 11, w 1, n-b 2	15

1/236 (2) 2/296 (1) 3/346 (3) 4/361 (5)   428   1/39 (3) 2/251 (2)   (3 wkts dec.) 367
5/362 (6) 6/363 (4) 7/379 (8)   3/306 (5)
8/421 (9) 9/422 (10) 10/428 (11)

In the second innings A. C. Hudson retired hurt at 18.

Bowling: *First Innings*—Srinath 37-7-107-2; Prasad 35-6-104-6; Joshi 12-1-48-0; Ganguly 3-1-10-0; Kumble 20.1-1-78-2; Hirwani 14-2-51-0. *Second Innings*—Srinath 24.2-2-101-1; Prasad 35-5-0-63-0; Kumble 32-4-101-1; Hirwani 11-1-40-0; Joshi 11-0-50-0.

India

†N. R. Mongia run out	35	– c Cullinan b Klusener	8
R. Dravid c Hudson b McMillan	31	– b McMillan	23
S. C. Ganguly b McMillan	6	– c Richardson b Klusener	0
*S. R. Tendulkar b Donald	18	– c Kirsten b Symcox	2
M. Azharuddin c and b Adams	109	– (6) c McMillan b Klusener	52
V. V. S. Laxman b Donald	14	– (5) b Klusener	1
S. B. Joshi run out	4	– c McMillan b Klusener	1
J. Srinath b Donald	11	– (9) c McMillan b Klusener	19
A. Kumble run out	88	– (8) b Klusener	17
B. K. V. Prasad c Richardson b Adams	1	– not out	3
N. D. Hirwani not out	0	– b Klusener	0
L-b 5, n-b 7	12	L-b 2, n-b 9	11

1/68 (2) 2/71 (1) 3/77 (3) 4/114 (6)   329   1/17 (1) 2/18 (3) 3/27 (4)   137
5/119 (4) 6/119 (7) 7/161 (8)   4/28 (5) 5/88 (2) 6/92 (7)
8/322 (5) 9/324 (10) 10/329 (9)   7/97 (6) 8/132 (9)
                                                                   9/137 (8) 10/137 (11)

In the first innings M. Azharuddin, when 6, retired hurt at 87 and resumed at 161.

Bowling: *First Innings*—Donald 21.2-4-72-3; Klusener 14-1-75-0; Adams 13-1-69-2; McMillan 16-4-52-2; Cronje 6-3-13-0; Symcox 11-1-43-0. *Second Innings*—McMillan 19-8-33-1; Klusener 21.3-4-64-8; Cronje 7-4-10-0; Symcox 6-1-28-1.

Umpires: B. C. Cooray (Sri Lanka) and V. K. Ramaswamy.   Referee: J. R. Reid (New Zealand).

At Nagpur, December 3, 4, 5. Drawn. Toss: South Africans. South Africans 384 for five dec. (W. J. Cronje 53, H. H. Gibbs 200 not out, D. N. Crookes 76; D. Ganesh three for 69) and 492 for three (B. M. McMillan 130, H. H. Gibbs 171, N. Boje 33, L. Klusener 102 not out, W. J. Cronje 30 not out); India A 340 (W. V. Raman 32, V. G. Kambli 98, P. Dharmani 30, S. V. Bahutule 32 not out, A. R. Kapoor 49; L. Klusener three for 38, P. R. Adams five for 108).

Gibbs's 200 not out, his maiden double-hundred, lasted 360 minutes and 287 balls and included 29 fours and four sixes. In the second innings, his 171 lasted 265 minutes and 220 balls and included 21 fours and three sixes. He and McMillan put on 313 for the South Africans' first wicket. Klusener scored his 102 not out from 80 balls.

TWO DOUBLE-HUNDREDS IN A MATCH

244	and	202*	A. E. Fagg	Kent v Essex at Colchester	1938

Nearest Misses

200*	**and**	**171**	**H. H. Gibbs**	**South Africans v India A at Nagpur**	**1996-97**
157*	and	245	W. W. Armstrong	Victoria v South Australia at Melbourne	1920-21
210*	and	157	M. R. Hallam	Leicestershire v Glamorgan at Leicester	1959
216*	and	156*	Zaheer Abbas	Gloucestershire v Surrey at The Oval	1976
215*	and	150*	Zaheer Abbas	Gloucestershire v Somerset at Bath	1981
209	and	146	D. W. Randall	Nottinghamshire v Middlesex at Nottingham	1979
203*	and	143*	M. R. Hallam	Leicestershire v Sussex at Worthing	1961
204	and	142	N. R. Taylor	Kent v Surrey at Canterbury	1990
141	and	222	Saadat Ali	Income Tax Dept v Multan at Multan	1977-78
169	and	185*	G. Gunn	Nottinghamshire v Surrey at Nottingham	1919

INDIA v SOUTH AFRICA

Third Test Match

At Kanpur, December 8, 9, 10, 11, 12. India won by 280 runs. Toss: India.

India maintained their unbeaten record in home series for a tenth season with a crushing victory. They managed only 237 in the first innings, but South Africa struggled even more, allowing India, inspired by a breathtaking century from Azharuddin, to take complete control.

The South Africans were disconcerted by an under-prepared pitch, which had not been rolled for several days and looked badly cracked. It did not deteriorate as much as expected, however, and although batting was never easy on a low, slow surface, it was far from impossible.

India recalled left-handed opener Raman and off-spinner Hirwani in place of Laxman and Hirwani, while de Villiers returned for South Africa's injured spearhead Donald. Raman shared a solid stand of 76 with Mongia before McMillan removed them both. Then, after tea, Ganguly's dismissal by Cronje sparked off a collapse against the unorthodox left-arm spin of Adams, who celebrated each of his six wickets with a cartwheel. Tendulkar made his first Test half-century as captain, battling grimly for more than three hours and striking only two fours, plus a six off Symcox, as he reached 50. He then seemed ready to step up a gear, hitting Adams for two fours in an over, only to sky him to mid-off.

South Africa batted poorly against tight and accurate bowling, especially from Srinath and Kumble. Kumble made the initial breakthrough but Kapoor claimed the vital wickets of Gibbs and Kirsten, each of whom had made twin centuries in this previous match. Again, the middle and lower orders were disappointing, and they were all out 60 behind.

The early loss of Raman gave South Africa hope and, even after India fought their way to 192 for five, a collapse might have given the tourists a chance. Azharuddin ended such thoughts. He was in majestic form and found the ideal partner in the unflappable Dravid, with whom he added 165. Azharuddin's strong wrists and ability to play from the pitch gave the bowlers no margin for error. He reached his 16th Test century in 162 balls with 17 fours, then added another 63 off just 66 balls, with eight more fours and a six.

South Africa, 460 behind, needed to survive ten hours. But their first series defeat since losing to West Indies in April 1992 was effectively sealed at 29 for three on the fourth afternoon. Both Kirsten and Gibbs played down the wrong line, while Cullinan was run out taking a chance against Tendulkar's arm at mid-off. Hudson played a patient three-and-a-half-hour innings. But Joshi, already omitted from the squad for the return Test series in South Africa, had a point to make: he ended an aggressive fifty from Cronje, who drove tamely to cover, and then dismissed McMillan with the fourth ball of the final morning. McMillan tried to sweep against the spin and the substitute, Laxman, ran 15 yards to take a diving catch at square leg. Klusener played some handsome off-side strokes, but only just extended the contest beyond lunch.

Man of the Match: M. Azharuddin.   *Man of the Series*: M. Azharuddin.

Close of play: First day, India 204-6 (S. R. Tendulkar 43*, A. Kumble 5*); Second day, India 7-1 (N. R. Mongia 4*, A. Kumble 0*); Third day, India 270-5 (M. Azharuddin 88*, R. Dravid 33*); Fourth day, South Africa 127-5 (B. M. McMillan 18*, D. J. Richardson 5*).

India

†N. R. Mongia b McMillan	41	– (2) lbw b Klusener	18
W. V. Raman c Klusener b McMillan	57	– (1) lbw b de Villiers	2
S. C. Ganguly lbw b Cronje	39	– (4) c McMillan b Symcox	41
*S. R. Tendulkar c de Villiers b Adams	61	– (5) c Richardson b Klusener	36
R. Dravid lbw b Adams	7	– (7) c McMillan b Adams	56
M. Azharuddin c and b Adams	5	– not out	163
S. B. Joshi c Klusener b Adams	15	– (8) b Adams	16
A. Kumble b Cronje	5	– (3) c Gibbs b de Villiers	42
A. R. Kapoor c de Villiers b Adams	11	– not out	6
J. Srinath c and b Adams	0		
B. K. V. Prasad not out	1		
B 3, l-b 6, n-b 1	10	B 4, l-b 14, n-b 2	20

1/76 (1) 2/111 (2) 3/160 (3) 4/185 (5)   237   1/2 (1) 2/41 (2)   (7 wkts dec.) 400
5/193 (6) 6/193 (7) 7/214 (8)   3/91 (3) 4/121 (4)
8/224 (4) 9/224 (10) 10/237 (9)   5/192 (5) 6/357 (7)
7/385 (8)

Bowling: *First Innings*—de Villiers 15–7–18–0; Klusener 17–4–47–0; Symcox 21–5–57–0; McMillan 18–7–40–2; Adams 19.1–6–55–6; Cronje 10–5–11–2. *Second Innings*—de Villiers 24–10–58–2; Klusener 25–7–72–2; McMillan 16–6–36–0; Cronje 15–5–31–0; Adams 20–1–84–2; Symcox 26–2–101–1.

South Africa

A. C. Hudson lbw b Kumble	15	– c sub (V. V. S. Laxman) b Kumble	31
G. Kirsten c Raman b Kapoor	43	– lbw b Srinath	7
H. H. Gibbs b Kapoor	17	– b Prasad	5
D. J. Cullinan c Azharuddin b Kumble	29	– run out	2
*W. J. Cronje c sub (V. V. S. Laxman) b Kumble	15	– c Tendulkar b Joshi	50
B. M. McMillan b Srinath	1	– c sub (V. V. S. Laxman) b Joshi	18
†D. J. Richardson b Srinath	4	– lbw b Srinath	5
L. Klusener c Dravid b Srinath	9	– not out	34
P. L. Symcox not out	23	– c and b Joshi	11
P. S. de Villiers lbw b Kumble	6	– b Prasad	2
P. R. Adams run out	8	– c Azharuddin b Srinath	1
B 4, l-b 3	7	L-b 14	14

1/34 (1) 2/73 (3) 3/94 (2) 4/121 (4)   177   1/21 (2) 2/26 (3) 3/29 (4)   180
5/126 (6) 6/130 (5) 7/131 (7)   4/97 (5) 5/109 (1) 6/127 (6)
8/144 (8) 9/163 (10) 10/177 (11)   7/138 (7) 8/167 (9)
9/179 (10) 10/180 (11)

Bowling: *First Innings*—Srinath 16–7–42–3; Prasad 14–5–25–0; Kumble 27–2–71–4; Kapoor 8–2–19–2; Joshi 7.3–2–13–0. *Second Innings*—Srinath 19.1–6–38–3; Prasad 11–5–25–2; Kumble 24–11–27–1; Kapoor 13–8–10–0; Joshi 29–9–66–3.

Umpires: D. R. Shepherd (England) and S. Venkataraghavan.
Referee: J. R. Reid (New Zealand).

†INDIA v SOUTH AFRICA

One-Day International

At Mumbai, December 14. India won by 74 runs. Toss: India.

India maintained their advantage in a one-off match, staged as a benefit for former Test batsman Mohinder Amarnath. Batting freely on his home ground, Tendulkar made the most of two lives to score a brisk 114. Jadeja boosted the total with 54 from 44 balls, hitting his fourth six off the last delivery of the innings, bowled by Adams. Few of the South Africans made their mark in reply, and Prasad ended the game by claiming his fourth wicket with four overs to go. Earlier, the match had been interrupted when the crowd responded to Azharuddin's dismissal by throwing plastic water bottles at Adams; Cronje led his team off for 20 minutes.

Man of the Match: S. R. Tendulkar.

India

*S. R. Tendulkar st Kirsten b Boje 114	J. Srinath c Gibbs b Adams 3
W. V. Raman c Cronje b Symcox 29	S. B. Joshi not out 1
M. Azharuddin c Kirsten b Crookes 22	B 1, l-b 4, w 12, n-b 1 18
R. Dravid run out 16	
A. Jadeja not out 54	1/90 2/150 3/188 (6 wkts, 50 overs) 267
R. R. Singh c Symcox b Adams 10	4/202 5/230 6/249

†N. R. Mongia, A. Kumble and B. K. V. Prasad did not bat.

Bowling: de Villiers 5–0–24–0; McMillan 6–0–33–0; Cronje 6–0–36–0; Symcox 10–1–51–1; Boje 10–1–33–1; Crookes 6–0–35–1; Adams 7–0–50–2.

South Africa

A. C. Hudson b Joshi 45	P. L. Symcox not out 3
†G. Kirsten c Azharuddin b Prasad 1	P. S. de Villiers b Srinath 0
*W. J. Cronje c Singh b Prasad 10	P. R. Adams c Mongia b Prasad 0
D. J. Cullinan c Joshi b Singh 44	L-b 13, w 7, n-b 2 22
H. H. Gibbs c Raman b Prasad 31	
D. N. Crookes run out 18	1/2 2/35 3/80 (46 overs) 193
B. M. McMillan c Mongia b Srinath 16	4/122 5/161 6/166
N. Boje c Prasad b Kumble 3	7/174 8/188 9/188

Bowling: Srinath 10–1–40–2; Prasad 8–1–27–4; Joshi 7–0–25–1; Singh 6–0–29–1; Kumble 9–1–34–1; Raman 6–1–25–0.

Umpires: K. Parthasarathy and S. K. Porel.   Referee: J. R. Reid (New Zealand).

OVERSEAS PLAYERS FOR 1998

Derbyshire	Saeed Anwar (Pakistan)	Middlesex	J. L. Langer (Australia)
Durham	D. C. Boon (Australia)*	Northamptonshire	P. R. Reiffel (Australia)
Essex	S. G. Law (Australia)*	Nottinghamshire	P. A. Strang (Zimbabwe)
Glamorgan	Waqar Younis (Pakistan)*	Somerset	Mushtaq Ahmed (Pakistan)*
Gloucestershire	C. A. Walsh (West Indies)	Surrey	Saqlain Mushtaq (Pakistan)*
Hampshire		Sussex	M. G. Bevan (Australia)
Kent	C. L. Hooper (West Indies)	Warwickshire	B. C. Lara (West Indies)
Lancashire	Wasim Akram (Pakistan)*	Worcestershire	T. M. Moody (Australia)*
Leicestershire	P. V. Simmons (West Indies)	Yorkshire	D. S. Lehmann (Australia)*

* Overseas player for same county in 1997. All arrangements subject to alteration.

THE NEW ZEALANDERS IN PAKISTAN, 1996-97

By QAMAR AHMED

New Zealand did themselves unexpectedly proud in Pakistan, sharing the honours in a two-match Test series. Their victory in the First Test at Lahore was their first on a tour of Pakistan in 27 years – the only previous one had been in 1969-70, at the same venue, when Graham Dowling led them to a series win. This time, a jolted Pakistan recovered to take the Second Test, at Rawalpindi, by an innings. But New Zealand ended the short visit – it lasted just over three weeks – with another win, in the third one-day international, having lost the first two. Captain Lee Germon called it "a good tour" and said "the boys have done well and are richer in experience".

They might have done even better but for a growing casualty list. Injury had already forced some changes from the squad that had just played a one-day tournament in Sharjah, and strike bowler Danny Morrison (groin strain) and all-rounder Gavin Larsen (hamstring strain) had to be replaced before the First Test. Even the tour manager, Earle Cooper, flew home, because of a detached retina in his right eye; Tim Murdoch, general manager of New Zealand Cricket, took over.

Pakistan also had their problems. Captain Wasim Akram had to withdraw from the Test series with a shoulder injury which he had carried through the Sharjah tournament and Waqar Younis pulled out of the Second Test with a side strain. But their understudy, the 20-year-old Mohammad Zahid, stepped up to make a sensational debut. He had taken eight New Zealand wickets for a Board XI in a warm-up match at Sahiwal but easily outdid that with 11 for 130 at Rawalpindi. He was the first Pakistani bowler to take ten wickets or more on Test debut. Another talented newcomer, Mohammad Wasim, almost pulled off an unlikely win at Lahore as he scored an unbeaten century, joining Billy Ibadulla, Javed Miandad and Salim Malik as the only Pakistanis to reach three figures on debut. Of the old hands, leg-spinner Mushtaq Ahmed continued his rich vein of form by collecting 18 wickets in the two Tests, and Saeed Anwar and Ijaz Ahmed delighted spectators at Rawalpindi with their strokeplay in a stand of 262.

New Zealand's leading bowler was Simon Doull, who kept his cool when a local paper accused him of ball-tampering at Sahiwal, and bowled with great accuracy on a seaming wicket in the First Test to claim a match-winning eight for 85. On the batting front, Stephen Fleming displayed his consistency in innings of 92 not out and 67, though he was still waiting for his maiden Test hundred, and all-rounder Chris Cairns provided some fireworks in a rapid 93 to turn round New Zealand's second innings at Lahore.

The series was played in a cordial atmosphere, though there were 28 leg-before decisions in seven Test innings and Ijaz and Cairns were fined for dissent during the Second Test. Pakistan were also penalised for their slow over-rate in the same match. But both Tests finished inside four days, despite interruptions caused by bad light, dazzling sunshine and, most unusually, the failure of the authorities to produce a match ball at Rawalpindi.

NEW ZEALAND TOURING PARTY

L. K. Germon (Canterbury) *(captain)*, N. J. Astle (Canterbury), C. L. Cairns (Canterbury), S. B. Doull (Northern Districts), S. P. Fleming (Canterbury), M. J. Greatbatch (Central Districts), C. Z. Harris (Canterbury), M. N. Hart (Northern Districts), G. R. Larsen (Wellington), D. K. Morrison (Auckland), A. C. Parore (Auckland), D. N. Patel (Auckland), C. M. Spearman (Central Districts), J. T. C. Vaughan (Auckland), B. A. Young (Northern Districts).

Manager: L. E. Cooper. *Coach:* S. J. Rixon.

G. R. Jonas (Wellington) and R. J. Kennedy (Otago) replaced the injured Larsen and Morrison. T. J. Murdoch replaced Cooper, who had suffered a detached retina, as manager.

NEW ZEALAND TOUR RESULTS

Test matches – Played 2: Won 1, Lost 1.
First-class matches – Played 3: Won 1, Lost 1, Drawn 1.
Win – Pakistan.
Loss – Pakistan.
Draw – PCB XI.
One-day internationals – Played 3: Won 1, Lost 2.

Note: Matches in this section which were not first-class are signified by a dagger.

At Quaid-e-Azam Stadium, Sahiwal, November 17, 18, 19. Drawn. Toss: New Zealanders. New Zealanders 171 (B. A. Young 47, S. P. Fleming 30; Mohammad Zahid six for 54) and 211 for seven dec. (J. T. C. Vaughan 48, B. A. Young 73, N. J. Astle 30 not out; Aqib Javed three for 38); PCB XI 193 for seven dec. (Zahoor Elahi 34, Sohail Jaffer 30, Mahmood Hamid 39, Ahmer Saeed 33) and 41 for no wkt.

The stadium became Pakistan's 67th first-class ground.

PAKISTAN v NEW ZEALAND

First Test Match

At Lahore, November 21, 22, 23, 24. New Zealand won by 44 runs. Toss: New Zealand. Test debuts: Mohammad Wasim, Zahoor Elahi.

New Zealand won their first Test since November 1994 – since when they had lost eight and drawn seven – and only their second on Pakistan soil. The first, in 1969-70, was also in Lahore. Their key player was Doull, who bowled superbly for match figures of eight for 85. The long-awaited victory arrived half an hour after tea on the fourth day, and it might have been much sooner but for an unbeaten century from 19-year-old debutant Mohammad Wasim.

Scoring was not easy on a pitch of low bounce, and there were 15 lbws given by Shakoor Rana, standing in his first Test for three years, and Zimbabwean Russell Tiffin. Pakistan captain Wasim Akram, who had damaged his shoulder, was missing and Saeed Anwar took over for the first time in a Test. Even without Wasim, New Zealand's first innings was devastated in two sessions by Waqar Younis and Mushtaq Ahmed. Mushtaq picked up three for eight in 16 balls, reducing the score to 83 for six, while Waqar claimed three for 12 in his second spell; it took a last-wicket stand of 38 to prevent a complete rout.

The tourists struck back in the evening: Doull grabbed four wickets as Pakistan slid to 52 for five before bad light spared them the last ten overs. Doull added Salim Malik next morning on his way to career-best figures. But, after the ball was changed, having gone out of shape, a fighting fifty from Moin Khan, including 11 fours, salvaged the innings and provided a lead of 36.

New Zealand's openers wiped out that deficit, before three quick wickets for the spinners, plus another first thing on the third morning, left them 88 for four, which Waqar soon made 101 for five. The turning point came when Cairns, on seven, edged Mushtaq to the gully where Inzamam-ul-Haq dropped him. Reprieved, Cairns hit a superb 93 at more than a run a ball, with 12 fours and three sixes, as he and Fleming added 141 for the sixth wicket. Fleming battled on, with valuable support from Doull in what turned out to be another vital last-wicket stand, and remained unbeaten, eight short of his elusive maiden Test hundred, after 280 minutes. There had been some wayward Pakistani bowling, and Waqar had strained his side, but Mushtaq finished with career-best match figures of ten for 143.

Pakistan were left a target of 276, and humiliation loomed when they lost half their side for 42 by the close. Play was delayed by heavy dew on the fourth day. Then Mohammad Wasim, who had failed to score in the first innings, showed unflinching temperament. Despite being hit on the helmet by a bouncer from Cairns before reaching double figures, he drove and cut with relish. Moin and Mushtaq helped him add 151 for the seventh and eight wickets and he became the fourth Pakistani to score a century on Test debut shortly after tea. He even gave his side an outside chance of victory – they were 45 short when he ran out of partners.

Man of the Match: S. B. Doull.

Close of play: First day, Pakistan 52-5 (Salim Malik 11*, Moin Khan 5*); Second day, New Zealand 88-3 (S. P. Fleming 12*, N. J. Astle 3*); Third day, Pakistan 46-5 (Salim Malik 15*, Mohammad Wasim 0*).

New Zealand

B. A. Young lbw b Waqar Younis	8	– c Mohammad Wasim b Mushtaq Ahmed	36
J. T. C. Vaughan lbw b Shahid Nazir	3	– b Mushtaq Ahmed	11
A. C. Parore c Salim Malik b Saqlain Mushtaq	37	– lbw b Saqlain Mushtaq	15
S. P. Fleming c Salim Malik b Mushtaq Ahmed	19	– not out	92
N. J. Astle lbw b Mushtaq Ahmed	0	– lbw b Mushtaq Ahmed	3
M. J. Greatbatch c Mohammad Wasim b Waqar Younis	18	– b Waqar Younis	1
C. L. Cairns c Inzamam-ul-Haq b Mushtaq Ahmed	4	– lbw b Mushtaq Ahmed	93
C. Z. Harris b Waqar Younis	16	– c Salim Malik b Mushtaq Ahmed	0
*†L. K. Germon lbw b Waqar Younis	0	– lbw b Mushtaq Ahmed	11
D. N. Patel lbw b Mushtaq Ahmed	26	– lbw b Shahid Nazir	0
S. B. Doull not out	15	– st Moin Khan b Saqlain Mushtaq	26
B 4, l-b 5	9	B 6, l-b 16, n-b 1	23

1/6 (2) 2/16 (1) 3/67 (3) 4/70 (5)   155
5/73 (4) 6/83 (7) 7/102 (8)
8/102 (9) 9/117 (6) 10/155 (10)

1/46 (2) 2/59 (1) 3/85 (3)   311
4/88 (5) 5/101 (6) 6/242 (7)
7/242 (8) 8/262 (9)
9/263 (10) 10/311 (11)

Bowling: *First Innings*—Waqar Younis 15–3–48–4; Shahid Nazir 8–3–15–1; Mushtaq Ahmed 22.1–4–59–4; Saqlain Mushtaq 12–3–24–1. *Second Innings*—Waqar Younis 15–6–26–1; Shahid Nazir 16–1–84–1; Mushtaq Ahmed 32–8–84–6; Saqlain Mushtaq 22.2–4–95–2.

Pakistan

*Saeed Anwar b Doull	8	– lbw b Doull	0
Zahoor Elahi c Fleming b Doull	22	– c Young b Patel	6
Ijaz Ahmed, sen. lbw b Cairns	3	– b Doull	8
Inzamam-ul-Haq c Astle b Doull	0	– c Young b Cairns	14
Salim Malik c Young b Doull	21	– (6) c Germon b Doull	21
Mohammad Wasim b Doull	0	– (7) not out	109
†Moin Khan lbw b Vaughan	59	– (6) c Germon b Astle	38
Saqlain Mushtaq lbw b Vaughan	23	– (5) c Fleming b Vaughan	0
Waqar Younis lbw b Vaughan	2	– (10) b Patel	1
Mushtaq Ahmed c Germon b Vaughan	25	– (9) c Fleming b Patel	15
Shahid Nazir not out	13	– c Harris b Patel	1
B 5, l-b 7, n-b 3	15	B 8, l-b 8, n-b 2	18

1/21 (1) 2/29 (3) 3/34 (4) 4/37 (2)   191
5/37 (6) 6/85 (5) 7/141 (7)
8/143 (9) 9/164 (8) 10/191 (10)

1/0 (1) 2/8 (3) 3/25 (4)   231
4/26 (5) 5/42 (2) 6/60 (6)
7/135 (8) 8/211 (9)
9/219 (10) 10/231 (11)

Bowling: *First Innings*—Cairns 19–5–79–1; Doull 16–3–46–5; Harris 1–0–3–0; Vaughan 12.5–2–27–4; Patel 7–2–24–0. *Second Innings*—Doull 16–4–39–3; Cairns 16–5–62–1; Vaughan 14–5–48–1; Patel 15.1–6–36–4; Harris 6–2–20–0; Astle 4–1–10–1.

Umpires: R. B. Tiffin (Zimbabwe) and Shakoor Rana.   Referee: C. W. Smith (West Indies).

PAKISTAN v NEW ZEALAND

Second Test Match

At Rawalpindi, November 28, 29, 30, December 1. Pakistan won by an innings and 13 runs. Toss: Pakistan. Test debut: Mohammad Zahid.

Pakistan struck back to draw the series an hour after lunch on the fourth day. The Test occupied only 258.4 overs, though the opening day saw several hold-ups. One was caused by sunlight dazzling the batsmen after tea, another, more conventionally, by bad light, but the oddest occurred at the start, when play was delayed 20 minutes because the Pakistan Cricket Board had forgotten to supply balls. The match eventually got under way using a ball bought from a local sports shop. The home attack also seemed a touch makeshift: with Waqar Younis joining the injury list, the three pace bowlers started with eight Test caps between them. But 20-year-old Mohammad Zahid rose triumphantly to the occasion, becoming the first Pakistani to take ten wickets in his first Test and finishing with 11 for 130, the seventh-best analysis by any Test debutant. He seized seven wickets as New Zealand's second innings collapsed from 82 without loss to 168 all out. Complementing his efforts, spinner Mushtaq Ahmed claimed eight, taking his haul in his last eight Tests to 63.

MOST WICKETS ON TEST DEBUT

16-136	N. D. Hirwani, India v West Indies at Madras.............................	1987-88
16-137	R. A. L. Massie, Australia v England at Lord's.......................	1972
12-102	F. Martin, England v Australia at The Oval............................	1890
11-82	C. V. Grimmett, Australia v England at Sydney.......................	1924-25
11-96	C. S. Marriott, England v West Indies at The Oval....................	1933
11-112	A. E. Hall, South Africa v England at Cape Town....................	1922-23
11-130	**Mohammad Zahid, Pakistan v New Zealand at Rawalpindi**........	**1996-97**
11-145	A. V. Bedser, England v India at Lord's	1946
11-196	S. F. Burke, South Africa v New Zealand at Cape Town...............	1961-62
11-204	A. L. Valentine, West Indies v England at Manchester................	1950

Zahid struck early on the first day, trapping Vaughan and Parore lbw, while Young gave Mushtaq his 100th wicket in his 26th Test. That was another lbw: there were to be 13 in this match, following 15 at Lahore. New Zealand stumbled to 111 for seven but, by tea, Fleming and Germon had launched a recovery. They put on 81, Fleming hitting 11 fours in 67, and Germon batted into the next day, when he reached a maiden Test fifty.

With Patel's help, New Zealand managed to reach 249. But the home side wiped that out with only one wicket down. Acting-captain Saeed Anwar and Ijaz Ahmed both scored centuries in a stand of 262, easily Pakistan's best for any wicket against New Zealand. Ijaz made 125, including 19 fours and a six, and was fined half his match fee for dissent when Cairns had him lbw; Cairns himself incurred a similar fine when a later appeal was rejected. Anwar, who had been dropped behind the wicket on 115, proceeded to 149 next day. He was eventually caught at long leg, with Inzamam-ul-Haq following one run later. But Salim Malik and night-watchman Mushtaq, who scored a Test-best 42, advanced the score to 375 before the last six fell for 55.

New Zealand trailed by 181, but openers Young and Vaughan survived the last session and took their partnership to 82 in the morning before Vaughan was lbw to Zahid. That opened the floodgates: only Young, who batted for 174 minutes, could defy Zahid's blistering pace. He took five for 47 in 11 overs as the tourists struggled to 137 for six by lunch; he completed his work when he dismissed Patel, also lbw, 53 minutes after the interval.

Man of the Match: Mohammad Zahid.
Men of the Series: Pakistan – Saeed Anwar; New Zealand – S. P. Fleming.

Close of play: First day, New Zealand 215-8 (L. K. Germon 45*, D. N. Patel 6*); Second day, Pakistan 269-2 (Saeed Anwar 130*, Mushtaq Ahmed 1*); Third day, New Zealand 69-0 (B. A. Young 38*, J. T. C. Vaughan 26*).

New Zealand

B. A. Young lbw b Mushtaq Ahmed	39	– c Zahoor Elahi b Mohammad Zahid	61
J. T. C. Vaughan lbw b Mohammad Zahid	12	– lbw b Mohammad Zahid	27
A. C. Parore lbw b Mohammad Zahid	3	– lbw b Mohammad Zahid	6
S. P. Fleming c Moin Khan b Mushtaq Ahmed	67	– (7) c Moin Khan b Shahid Nazir	4
N. J. Astle c Moin Khan b Mushtaq Ahmed	11	– lbw b Mohammad Zahid	1
M. J. Greatbatch c Saeed Anwar b Mush.aq Ahmed	2	– c Saeed Anwar b Mushtaq Ahmed	19
C. L. Cairns c Mohammad Wasim b Mushtaq Ahmed	9	– (8) b Mushtaq Ahmed	11
C. Z. Harris lbw b Mohammad Zahid	1	– (9) lbw b Mohammad Zahid	14
*†L. K. Germon c Moin Khan b Mohammad Zahid	55	– (4) b Mohammad Zahid	0
D. N. Patel c Ijaz Ahmed b Mushtaq Ahmed	21	– lbw b Mohammad Zahid	0
S. B. Doull not out	1	– not out	4
B 4, l-b 14, n-b 10	28	L-b 7, w 1, n-b 13	21

1/33 (2) 2/43 (3) 3/59 (1) 4/77 (5)   249
5/87 (6) 6/110 (7) 7/111 (8)
8/192 (4) 9/241 (9) 10/249 (10)

1/82 (2) 2/105 (3) 3/109 (1)   168
4/112 (4) 5/119 (5) 6/137 (6)
7/137 (7) 8/163 (8)
9/163 (9) 10/168 (10)

Bowling: First Innings—Mohammad Zahid 21–5–64–4; Shahid Nazir 9–4–23–0; Mohammad Akram 12–1–48–0; Mushtaq Ahmed 30–3–87–6; Salim Malik 2–0–9–0. *Second Innings*—Mohammad Zahid 20–3–66–7; Mohammad Akram 7–2–11–0; Mushtaq Ahmed 22–7–52–2; Shahid Nazir 7–1–19–1; Salim Malik 2–0–13–0.

Pakistan

*Saeed Anwar c Doull b Cairns	149	Mohammad Zahid lbw b Astle	0
Zahoor Elahi c Fleming b Cairns	2	Mohammad Akram not out	0
Ijaz Ahmed, sen. lbw b Cairns	125		
Mushtaq Ahmed lbw b Harris	42	L-b 14, n-b 2	16
Inzamam-ul-Haq c Vaughan b Harris	1		
Salim Malik b Cairns	78	1/6 (2) 2/268 (3) 3/290 (1)	430
Mohammad Wasim c Cairns b Doull	5	4/291 (5) 5/375 (4) 6/394 (7)	
†Moin Khan lbw b Doull	2	7/398 (8) 8/419 (9)	
Shahid Nazir c and b Cairns	10	9/420 (10) 10/430 (6)	

Bowling: Doull 31–7–86–2; Cairns 30.4–2–137–5; Vaughan 17–1–72–0; Astle 9–1–31–1; Patel 15–4–33–0; Harris 24–7–57–2.

Umpires: L. H. Barker (West Indies) and Javed Akhtar.   Referee: C. W. Smith (West Indies).

†PAKISTAN v NEW ZEALAND

First One-Day International

At Gujranwala, December 4. Pakistan won by 11 runs. Toss: Pakistan.

Pakistan secured victory when Harris, needing 12 from three balls to win, was caught just inside the boundary. It was off-spinner Saqlain Mushtaq's fifth wicket. The match had been reduced to 46 overs a side because of the sun shining in the batsmen's eyes. Pakistan batted on a green pitch and were in trouble at 71 for five, but Wasim Akram celebrated his return from injury by smashing three sixes and three fours in a quickfire fifty, and Salim Malik ended unbeaten on 73 after hitting the last ball of the innings for six. New Zealand's top order, led by Young, put together some useful partnerships, and never quite lost sight of the target.

Man of the Match: Salim Malik.

Pakistan

Saeed Anwar run out	27	Saqlain Mushtaq c Young b Astle	10
Zahoor Elahi c Young b Kennedy	5	Mushtaq Ahmed not out	3
Ijaz Ahmed, sen. c Harris b Doull	3		
Inzamam-ul-Haq c Germon b Astle	14	B 1, l-b 3, w 17, n-b 1	22
Salim Malik not out	73		—
†Moin Khan c Fleming b Cairns	3	1/11 2/19 3/60 (8 wkts, 46 overs) 228	
*Wasim Akram c Patel b Harris	52	4/61 5/71 6/162	
Shahid Afridi c Patel b Harris	16	7/181 8/197	

Waqar Younis did not bat.

Bowling: Doull 9–0–33–1; Kennedy 9–0–47–1; Cairns 10–0–49–1; Astle 9–1–31–2; Harris 6–0–40–2; Patel 3–0–24–0.

New Zealand

B. A. Young b Waqar Younis	58	S. B. Doull run out	0
C. M. Spearman run out	6	C. Z. Harris c Shahid Afridi	
A. C. Parore lbw b Mushtaq Ahmed	35	b Saqlain Mushtaq	20
S. P. Fleming st Moin Khan		*†L. K. Germon c sub	
b Saqlain Mushtaq	36	(Mohammad Zahid) b Saqlain Mushtaq	2
C. L. Cairns c Moin Khan		R. J. Kennedy not out	0
b Waqar Younis	36	L-b 2, w 8, n-b 3	13
N. J. Astle c Salim Malik			
b Saqlain Mushtaq	11	1/26 2/104 3/117 (45.4 overs) 217	
D. N. Patel st Moin Khan		4/177 5/185 6/185	
b Saqlain Mushtaq	0	7/185 8/200 9/213	

Bowling: Wasim Akram 9–0–45–0; Waqar Younis 9–0–48–2; Saqlain Mushtaq 9.4–0–44–5; Mushtaq Ahmed 9–0–35–1; Shahid Afridi 9–0–43–0.

Umpires: Javed Akhtar and Khizar Hayat.

†PAKISTAN v NEW ZEALAND

Second One-Day International

At Sialkot, December 6. Pakistan won by 46 runs. Toss: Pakistan.

The previous game had been shortened by sunshine; this one was cut to 47 overs by dew. But the Pakistani openers had no problems. Saeed Anwar hit 11 fours and Zahoor Elahi seven fours and five sixes as they ran up an opening stand of 177. Both fell just short of hundreds, and local hero Ijaz Ahmed delighted a capacity crowd of 25,000 with a run-a-ball fifty. No one else passed five, though, as Harris wrecked the middle and lower order. New Zealand lost both openers cheaply, but Parore and Fleming added 118. Once they were gone, however, Pakistan made sure of the series by dismissing the tourists with nearly five overs in hand.

Man of the Match: Saeed Anwar.

Pakistan

Saeed Anwar run out	91	Saqlain Mushtaq b Harris	2
Zahoor Elahi b Cairns	86	Mushtaq Ahmed not out	5
Ijaz Ahmed, sen. c Spearman b Vaughan	59	Salim Malik not out	1
Inzamam-ul-Haq st Germon b Astle	2	L-b 8, w 14, n-b 2	24
*Wasim Akram b Harris	4		—
Shahid Afridi b Harris	2	1/177 2/225 3/242 (9 wkts, 47 overs) 277	
†Moin Khan c Astle b Harris	1	4/247 5/252 6/260	
Waqar Younis st Germon b Harris	0	7/261 8/269 9/276	

Bowling: Doull 8–1–60–0; Kennedy 3–0–24–0; Cairns 8–0–35–1; Vaughan 9–1–55–1; Harris 10–0–42–5; Astle 9–0–53–1.

New Zealand

B. A. Young c Moin Khan		
b Waqar Younis .		5
C. M. Spearman c Moin Khan		
b Wasim Akram .		0
A. C. Parore c Ijaz Ahmed		
b Saqlain Mushtaq .		37
S. P. Fleming c and b Shahid Afridi		88
C. L. Cairns b Saqlain Mushtaq		10
N. J. Astle c Ijaz Ahmed b Salim Malik .		20
C. Z. Harris lbw b Wasim Akram		22
*†L. K. Germon lbw b Shahid Afridi		2

J. T. C. Vaughan c Moin Khan		
b Wasim Akram .		13
S. B. Doull c sub (Mohammad Wasim)		
b Waqar Younis .		1
R. J. Kennedy not out		7
B 9, l-b 3, w 12, n-b 2		26
		—
1/3 2/7 3/125	(42.1 overs)	231
4/146 5/170 6/189		
7/194 8/212 9/219		

Bowling: Wasim Akram 8.1–0–43–3; Waqar Younis 6–0–32–2; Saqlain Mushtaq 8–0–54–2; Mushtaq Ahmed 10–0–42–0; Shahid Afridi 7–0–40–2; Salim Malik 2.5–0–8–1; Ijaz Ahmed 0.1–0–0–0.

Umpires: Khizar Hayat and Mahboob Shah.

†PAKISTAN v NEW ZEALAND

Third One-Day International

At Karachi, December 8. New Zealand won by seven wickets. Toss: Pakistan.

New Zealand ended their tour with their first one-day victory over their hosts on Pakistani soil for 12 years, and did it in style, with seven wickets and 29 balls to spare. A brisk opening stand – 96 in 16 overs – between Young and Astle gave them an excellent start, and Fleming saw them home. Earlier, Saeed Anwar took his aggregate in limited-overs internationals in 1996 to 1,595, though for once he was outshone by his colleagues. Ijaz Ahmed added 108 in 75 balls with Wasim Akram, who hit four fours and five sixes as he took 66 off 39 deliveries. That took Pakistan to 234, but this time it was not enough.

Man of the match: N. J. Astle.
Men of the Series: Pakistan – Saeed Anwar; New Zealand – S. P. Fleming.

Pakistan

Saeed Anwar c Young b Vaughan		16
Zahoor Elahi b Hart		51
Inzamam-ul-Haq st Germon b Hart		7
Ijaz Ahmed, sen. not out		73
Mohammad Wasim c and b Harris		8

*Wasim Akram not out		66
L-b 5, w 5, n-b 3		13
		—
1/38 2/62	(4 wkts, 50 overs)	234
3/103 4/126		

Shahid Afridi, †Moin Khan, Saqlain Mushtaq, Mushtaq Ahmed and Mohammad Zahid did not bat.

Bowling: Doull 4–0–23–0; Vaughan 10–3–59–1; Cairns 9–0–45–0; Astle 8–2–27–0; Hart 10–1–33–2; Harris 9–0–42–1.

New Zealand

B. A. Young c Wasim Akram		
b Shahid Afridi .		32
N. J. Astle run out		60
A. C. Parore c Moin Khan		
b Wasim Akram .		47

S. P. Fleming not out		48
C. L. Cairns not out		25
B 1, l-b 10, w 6, n-b 6		23
		—
1/96 2/99 3/183	(3 wkts, 45.1 overs)	235

M. J. Greatbatch, C. Z. Harris, *†L. K. Germon, J. T. C. Vaughan, M. N. Hart and S. B. Doull did not bat.

Bowling: Wasim Akram 8–0–36–1; Mohammad Zahid 6–0–41–0; Mushtaq Ahmed 10–0–49–0; Saqlain Mushtaq 10–0–43–0; Shahid Afridi 8.1–1–39–1; Ijaz Ahmed 1–0–6–0; Saeed Anwar 2–0–10–0.

Umpires: Mahboob Shah and Shakeel Khan. Series referee: C. W. Smith (West Indies).

THE WEST INDIANS IN AUSTRALIA, 1996-97

By GREG BAUM

Characterised and hyped as a world title "decider", complete with posters of the opposing captains staring like prize-fighters into each other's eyes, this series became a classic of the genre down to its last detail: the victor emerged almost as battered and bloodied as the vanquished.

As Mark Taylor hoisted the Frank Worrell Trophy again after an overwhelming if inconsequential defeat for Australia in the last Test, the best that could be said of the defending champions was also the least expected of them on their own shores: they won. Many heavy blows had been landed and absorbed by both sides. Taylor himself had such a wretched batting series that his place in the team was in the balance, though his captaincy remained as widely admired as ever. His handling of Michael Bevan, so unorthodox of personality and delivery, when the series was still delicately poised in the Fourth Test probably won it for Australia. He became the first Australian captain to win two series against West Indies, though – given the country's cricketing priorities – some of the shine was lost by the team's failure in the one-day competition.

Only one specialist batsman, Matthew Hayden, made a Test century for Australia, and he still could not win over reputable critics who maintained that his front-foot technique was too limited for Test cricket. Shane Warne, recuperating by painstaking degrees from off-season finger surgery and confronted by up to five left-handers at a time in the West Indian order, never took five wickets in an innings. None the less, he did take 22 in total, and was probably denied several others by the serendipitous emergence of Bevan as a bowler.

Injuries, accidents and cumulative stress took a heavy toll, and the expanded and suddenly nervy selection panel exacted another: 16 players appeared for Australia in five different configurations. These did not include Michael Slater, whose shock omission from the First Test was a harbinger of the instability to come.

West Indies, meantime, were wincing from their own wounds, including the knowledge that their decline as the paramount power of world cricket was continuing apace. More than ever, and in stark contrast to Australia, they depended on particular players and pitches. What their Fifth Test victory did above all else was to underline Australia's previous combination of good cricket and good luck in subjugating the two players from whom there was most to fear. West Indies needed Brian Lara and Curtly Ambrose to be at their best, but their big performances were spasmodic and, until the last Test, not contemporaneous.

Lara, having set himself for three or four hundreds, had such a miserable time that he did not reach three figures in aggregate until his last-but-one innings. Further, he restrained his impetuous instincts no better in the pavilion than on the ground. He stormed the Australian dressing-room after what he felt (unjustifiably) was an unfair catch by his old adversary, wicket-keeper Ian Healy, in the Second Test in Sydney. Manager Clive Lloyd, who had made a pact with the Australians to maintain a civil relationship throughout the tour, rebuked him severely. Then, after his century in Perth, Lara accused the Australians of sledging young team-mate Robert Samuels. Next day, he appeared in the middle

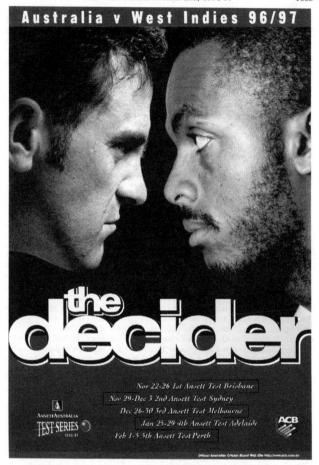

as a runner for Courtney Walsh, provoking such a slanging match that the umpires had to lecture both captains mid-pitch on the game's proprieties. Later, Taylor called him a *provocateur* in the style of Sri Lanka's Arjuna Ranatunga, and Lara left the country estranged from several former friends in the Australian team. Tactically, however, he led the side very skilfully when Walsh was off the field.

Ambrose made his now traditional slow start, with just three wickets in the first two Tests, but responded to suggestions that he was a spent force in the Third and Fifth Tests, thrusting West Indies to resounding victories in both. The academic question that will be debated into the next century is what might have transpired if he had not been invalided out of the Fourth.

This was a bowlers' series: there were, on average, fewer than 30 runs between each fall of wicket all summer, no batsman made more than 370 runs and the last three matches all finished inside or just beyond three days (this, incidentally, has become a characteristic of series between these countries: of 55 scheduled days in their last 11 matches, there have been fewer than 40 played).

The most consistent of the bowlers was Glenn McGrath, with 26 wickets at 17.42. McGrath exercised such a stranglehold over Lara that, during the Third Test, he was emboldened to speak with unusual openness about the anti-Lara strategy Australia were using: the bowlers were either going around the wicket and beating him with away movement or, after several tight overs on off-stump, seducing him with a wider delivery. Bevan emerged to take the wickets Warne could not take, or take them from him, and finished a series in which his place in the side had been uncertain with a batting average of 55 and a bowling average of 17.66.

Australia had other good performers. Mark Waugh played consistently well, making runs when they were needed and not just when they were available, and failed only in that he did not turn any of his four superbly crafted half-centuries into the full measure. Matthew Elliott and Jason Gillespie both emerged as Test-class players, at least until each was cut down by injury, and Greg Blewett re-emerged as one. Hayden, replacing Elliott, made two ducks, but also top-scored twice. Ian Healy's keeping to the spinners was so masterful that an essentially prosaic business became a spectacle in its own right, and his dauntless batting in the first two Tests was crucial to their outcome.

The West Indians ebb and flow in such great tides these days that it is difficult to measure a team's intrinsic worth against them. They went a month in the middle of this tour losing seven consecutive matches, then won eight in succession in the next month, only to crumple again. Their batting was essentially frail: Carl Hooper was consistent and Sherwin Campbell began well, but they made only one fifty between them in the last three Tests and Shivnarine Chanderpaul, that arch-scorer of half-centuries, also declined. Their attack demanded respect, as ever, but at least in the eyes of the Australians lacked a crucial dimension. Hooper, the nearest approximation to a front-line spinner, did not take a wicket until the Fourth Test. Taylor declared then that no team of his would enter a Test on any surface without at least one specialist spinner, which was rather disingenuous since his spinners had just taken 16 wickets.

West Indies were also lamentable in the field, dropping catches, letting ground balls through their fingers and conceding a steady stream of overthrows, byes and no-balls. They compared terribly with Australia's general brilliance, and Healy's in particular, and that was as responsible as any other factor for their eclipse.

Sometimes it is only in the days and weeks after a title fight, when the emotion and adrenalin have subsided, that the toll can truly be reckoned. Duly, it became clear that, for all of Australia's travail, West Indies always had more and deeper troubles. To borrow another imperfect analogy from another sport, Australia won the big points; so, although the margin was seemingly narrow, and the casualties on both sides high, their triumph was morally comprehensive. "The decider", was, after all, decisive.

WEST INDIAN TOURING PARTY

C. A. Walsh (Jamaica) (*captain*), B. C. Lara (Trinidad & Tobago) (*vice-captain*), J. C. Adams (Jamaica), C. E. L. Ambrose (Leeward Islands), K. C. G. Benjamin (Leeward Islands), I. R. Bishop (Trinidad & Tobago), C. O. Browne (Barbados), S. L. Campbell (Barbados), S. Chanderpaul (Guyana), A. F. G. Griffith (Barbados), R. I. C. Holder (Barbados), C. L. Hooper (Guyana), N. A. M. McLean (Windward Islands), J. R. Murray (Windward Islands), R. G. Samuels (Jamaica), P. I. C. Thompson (Barbados).

C. E. Cuffy (Windward Islands) and P. V. Simmons (Trinidad & Tobago) reinforced the party when Benjamin and McLean returned home injured.

Manager: C. H. Lloyd.   *Coach:* M. D. Marshall.

WEST INDIAN TOUR RESULTS

Test matches – Played 5: Won 2, Lost 3.
First-class matches – Played 8: Won 4, Lost 4.
Wins – Australia (2), Western Australia, Victoria.
Losses – Australia (3), Australian XI.
One-day internationals – Played 10: Won 5, Lost 5. *Wins:* Australia (2), Pakistan (3). *Losses:* Australia (2), Pakistan (3).
Other non-first-class matches – Played 7: Won 3, Lost 4. *Wins* – Western Australia, Northern Territory Invitation XI, Australian Country XI. *Losses* – ACB Chairman's XI, Western Australia, Prime Minister's XI, Australia A.

TEST MATCH AVERAGES

AUSTRALIA – BATTING

	T	I	NO	R	HS	100s	Avge	Ct
I. A. Healy........	5	9	3	356	161*	1	59.33	15
M. G. Bevan	4	7	2	275	87*	0	55.00	2
G. S. Blewett......	4	7	1	301	99	0	50.16	4
M. T. G. Elliott	2	4	1	128	78*	0	42.66	1
M. E. Waugh......	5	9	0	370	82	0	41.11	8
M. L. Hayden	3	5	0	177	125	1	35.40	3
S. R. Waugh	4	6	0	188	66	0	31.33	2
R. T. Ponting	2	4	0	110	88	0	27.50	2
S. K. Warne.......	5	7	0	128	30	0	18.28	6
M. A. Taylor	5	9	0	153	43	0	17.00	9
P. R. Reiffel	3	6	0	44	20	0	7.33	2
G. D. McGrath	5	7	2	32	24	0	6.40	2

Played in two Tests: A. J. Bichel 7, 15, 18; J. N. Gillespie 16*, 4*, 2; M. S. Kasprowicz 6, 21; J. L. Langer 12, 0, 19.

* Signifies not out.

BOWLING

	O	M	R	W	BB	5W/i	Avge
G. D. McGrath	200.5	61	453	26	5-50	1	17.42
M. G. Bevan	76.3	10	265	15	6-82	1	17.66
P. R. Reiffel	102.1	22	305	12	5-73	1	25.41
S. K. Warne	217.1	56	594	22	4-95	0	27.00

Also bowled: A. J. Bichel 37.2–6–143–1; G. S. Blewett 23.5–7–64–1; J. N. Gillespie 33–9–94–2; M. S. Kasprowicz 48–9–126–0; R. T. Ponting 1.5–1–0–1; M. E. Waugh 8–1–31–0; S. R. Waugh 25.1–7–63–1.

WEST INDIES – BATTING

	T	I	NO	R	HS	100s	Avge	Ct
C. L. Hooper	5	9	1	362	102	1	45.25	9
S. Chanderpaul	5	9	0	344	82	0	38.22	2
R. G. Samuels	4	8	1	231	76	0	33.00	4
B. C. Lara..........	5	9	0	296	132	1	32.88	8
S. L. Campbell	5	10	1	291	113	1	32.33	3
J. C. Adams	5	9	2	140	74*	0	20.00	3
C. O. Browne	3	5	1	49	25*	0	12.25	15
I. R. Bishop	5	8	0	86	48	0	10.75	1
C. A. Walsh	5	8	4	31	18	0	7.75	2
C. E. L. Ambrose....	4	6	0	39	15	0	6.50	1
K. C. G. Benjamin ...	3	5	0	31	11	0	6.20	1

Played in two Tests: J. R. Murray 53, 34, 25 (4 ct, 1 st). Played in one Test: C. E. Cuffy 2, 3*; A. F. G. Griffith 13, 1; P. V. Simmons 0 (3 ct); P. I. C. Thompson 10*, 6.

* Signifies not out.

BOWLING

	O	M	R	W	BB	5W/i	Avge
C. E. L. Ambrose	160.5	31	444	19	5-43	2	23.36
I. R. Bishop	171.3	30	510	20	3-49	0	25.50
C. A. Walsh	192.3	33	592	19	5-74	2	31.15
K. C. G. Benjamin	117.5	22	362	9	3-34	0	40.22

Also bowled: J. C. Adams 18.5–1–59–1; S. Chanderpaul 3–1–2–1; C. E. Cuffy 33–4–116–2; C. L. Hooper 116–25–317–3; P. V. Simmons 23–5–67–1; P. I. C. Thompson 16–0–80–1.

Note: Matches in this section which were not first-class are signified by a dagger.

†At Lilac Hill, November 4. ACB Chairman's XI won by three wickets. Toss: West Indians. West Indians 256 for nine (50 overs) (R. G. Samuels 31, B. C. Lara 66, R. I. C. Holder 31; B. P. Julian three for 33); ACB Chairman's XI 258 for seven (42 overs) (T. M. Moody 66, B. P. Julian 96 not out; I. R. Bishop four for 44).

†At Perth, November 6 (day/night). Western Australia won by nine wickets. Toss: West Indians. West Indians 127 for eight (31 overs) (J. C. Adams 48 not out); Western Australia 130 for one (19.2 overs) (R. J. Campbell 64 not out, D. R. Martyn 51 not out).

†At Perth, November 7. West Indians won by one wicket. Toss: West Indians. Western Australia 235 for six (50 overs) (M. E. Hussey 56, J. L. Langer 79, D. R. Martyn 37 not out); West Indians 237 for nine (49.4 overs) (S. Chanderpaul 91, C. L. Hooper 51, J. R. Murray 31).

At Perth, November 8, 9, 10. West Indians won by nine wickets. Toss: Western Australia. Western Australia 293 for six dec. (M. P. Lavender 51, D. R. Martyn 44, A. C. Gilchrist 108 not out; C. L. Hooper three for 64) and 170 (M. E. Hussey 37, D. R. Martyn 33, A. C. Gilchrist 36; C. L. Hooper four for 59); West Indians 441 for five dec. (R. G. Samuels 96, S. Chanderpaul 135 not out, C. L. Hooper 84, R. I. C. Holder 68, J. R. Murray 30 not out; M. J. Nicholson three for 94) and 26 for one.

†At Alice Springs, November 12. West Indians won by 48 runs. Toss: West Indians. West Indians 218 for eight (50 overs) (J. C. Adams 67, C. O. Browne 50; M. A. Hatton three for 24); Northern Territory Invitation XI 170 (42.5 overs) (A. C. Gilchrist 64 not out; K. C. G. Benjamin three for 25).

At Hobart, November 15, 16, 17, 18. Australian XI won by ten wickets. Toss: Australian XI. Australian XI 544 for four dec. (M. L. Hayden 224, M. T. G. Elliott 158, G. S. Blewett 89 not out, Extras 44) and 28 for no wkt; West Indians 317 (C. L. Hooper 49, J. C. Adams 47, C. O. Browne 93 not out, N. A. M. McLean 41; A. J. Bichel four for 61, A. M. Stuart four for 104) and 251 (R. G. Samuels 34, S. Chanderpaul 77, B. C. Lara 63; G. S. Blewett five for 29, G. B. Hogg three for 81).

Hayden's 224 lasted 487 minutes and 374 balls and included 23 fours and one six. He put on 323 with Elliott for the Australian XI's first wicket in 352 minutes.

AUSTRALIA v WEST INDIES

First Test Match

At Brisbane, November 22, 23, 24, 25, 26. Australia won by 123 runs. Toss: West Indies. Test debuts: M. T. G. Elliott, M. S. Kasprowicz.

Campbell, whose previous highest score on the tour was 22, made a last-day century and almost saved this match for West Indies. But Bevan, who had never taken a Test wicket as a spinner, took three – including Campbell's – to win it. Meanwhile, Lara and Warne, the celestials in whose hands the match was thought to rest, were by their usual standards little more than bystanders. Thus was established the series' theme: a predictable enough end achieved by not entirely predictable means or agents.

Doubts clouded the prelude. Taylor and Warne were still recovering from off-season surgery and their confrères from a disastrous tour of India. Australia had two new caps, Elliott, the Victorian left-hander, and Kasprowicz, the Queensland pace bowler. Michael Slater's omission caused a sensation. For their part, West Indies had just lost to an Australian XI by ten wickets, and were apprehensive about starting the series with back-to-back Tests.

The Gabba pitch was unusually moist, which made Australia's 11-hour 479 all the more commendable. Mediocrity threatened when Elliott was caught behind off a loose shirt-sleeve for a debut duck, and later when Bevan was caught at slip first ball to re-open speculation about his competence against short bowling, and leave Australia a precarious 196 for five.

Ponting and Taylor made good the first breach with 126 for the second wicket: Taylor by taking to the trenches so completely that he did not hit a boundary before lunch; Ponting, the anointed successor to David Boon at No. 3, with a spirited counter-attack that produced seven fours and a six in that time. Then Steve Waugh and Healy shared 142 for the sixth wicket and

Healy batted indomitably through the rest of the innings for 161 not out. Made in just under six hours and laced with 20 fours, it was his third first-class and Test century and the highest by an Australian wicket-keeper.

West Indies' bowlers had little luck and made none. They pitched too short to both Ponting and Waugh; they should have known better in his case. Thus, for the fifth time in their last six Tests, this celebrated attack conceded more than 400 in the first innings.

Hooper, gifted and remote, made his first century against Australia and, with the combative Chanderpaul, put on 172 to rescue his side from the precipice of 77 for three. Regarded by the Australians as the best right-handed player of Warne in the world, Hooper was typically elegant until the nineties, whereupon his strokeplay became frantic with nerves. His century was literally a close-run thing – an ill-advised call, a direct hit and a judgment so fine that Hooper had to wait several minutes until third umpire Peter Parker gave him the benevolent benefit of a tiny doubt.

Immediately, the match changed. Ponting sprawled to catch Hooper from Steve Waugh, who promptly pulled his hamstring. Taylor, riding a characteristic hunch, gave the ball to Ponting, who claimed Adams, and then Chanderpaul drove at Reiffel and was caught. Warne claimed his first wicket in the 106th over and West Indies, after losing no wickets for more than four hours, lost seven in less than one hour.

Though Australia led by 202, Taylor did not enforce the follow-on: instead Australia spent a little more than two sessions augmenting their total. Mark Waugh made a smooth half-century, Healy set about the flagging bowlers with 45 not out from just 50 balls, and there was a poignant moment when Bevan, still on a pair, edged Bishop gently to slip, where Lara dropped it.

Taylor set a target of 420 from about 120 overs, which history showed to be nearly impossible. But the bookies set a West Indian victory at an absurdly short price: Lara was bristling with shots on the fourth evening, and Warne's forefinger was an unknown quantity. In fact, Lara played an intemperate slash at Reiffel next morning, and second slip Mark Waugh took a white-hot catch in front of his face. The issue then became survival. The pitch was still largely intact, denying Warne his expected spin, but the tireless McGrath threatened constantly from around the wicket and Bevan shocked the batsmen with his bounce. Campbell stood in the breach for nearly seven hours as the others collapsed around him. With the pylons beginning to cast their evening shadows, he played wearily at a straightening ball from Bevan and his brave, vain fight was finished.

Man of the Match: I. A. Healy.   *Attendance:* 51,327.

Close of play: First day, Australia 282-5 (S. R. Waugh 48*, I. A. Healy 47*); Second day, West Indies 61-2 (B. C. Lara 19*, C. L. Hooper 4*); Third day, Australia 8-0 (M. T. G. Elliott 2*, M. A. Taylor 4*); Fourth day, West Indies 89-1 (S. L. Campbell 28*, B. C. Lara 29*).

Australia

*M. A. Taylor b Walsh	43	– (2) c Browne b Benjamin	36
M. T. G. Elliott c Browne b Ambrose	0	– (1) b Bishop	21
R. T. Ponting c Walsh b Benjamin	88	– c Browne b Bishop	9
M. E. Waugh c Browne b Walsh	38	– c Browne b Bishop	57
S. R. Waugh c Lara b Bishop	66		
M. G. Bevan c Samuels b Walsh	0	– (5) c sub (A. F. G. Griffith) b Ambrose	20
†I. A. Healy not out	161	– (6) not out	45
P. R. Reiffel c and b Walsh	20	– (7) run out	11
S. K. Warne c and b Bishop	24		
M. S. Kasprowicz c Benjamin b Bishop	6		
G. D. McGrath b Benjamin	0		
L-b 8, w 3, n-b 22	33	B 1, l-b 3, n-b 14	18
	479	(6 wkts dec.)	**217**

1/4 (2) 2/130 (1) 3/146 (3) 4/196 (4)   1/55 (1) 2/74 (2)   (6 wkts dec.) 217
5/196 (6) 6/338 (5) 7/407 (8)   3/82 (3) 4/137 (5)
8/468 (9) 9/477 (10) 10/479 (11)   5/189 (4) 6/217 (7)

Bowling: *First Innings*—Ambrose 34–4–93–1; Walsh 35–6–112–4; Benjamin 33–6–97–2; Bishop 30–2–105–3; Hooper 19–3–64–0. *Second Innings*—Ambrose 18–2–47–1; Walsh 17–1–58–0; Bishop 13–2–49–3; Benjamin 15–1–52–1; Hooper 2–0–7–0.

West Indies

S. L. Campbell c Warne b Reiffel	18	– lbw b Bevan	113
R. G. Samuels c Healy b McGrath	10	– c Taylor b Warne	29
B. C. Lara c M. E. Waugh b McGrath	26	– c M. E. Waugh b Reiffel	44
C. L. Hooper c Ponting b S. R. Waugh	102	– c Healy b Bevan	23
S. Chanderpaul c M. E. Waugh b Reiffel	82	– b McGrath	14
J. C. Adams lbw b Ponting	0	– lbw b Warne	2
†C. O. Browne c Healy b Reiffel	4	– c Healy b McGrath	20
I. R. Bishop lbw b Warne	0	– c Ponting b Bevan	24
C. E. L. Ambrose c sub (J. N. Gillespie) b Reiffel .	0	– c Warne b McGrath	7
K. C. G. Benjamin lbw b Warne	9	– lbw b McGrath	1
*C. A. Walsh not out	0	– not out	1
L-b 8, w 1, n-b 17	26	B 8, l-b 3, n-b 7	18
	277		**296**

1/30 (2) 2/43 (1) 3/77 (3) 4/249 (4)
5/255 (6) 6/267 (5) 7/268 (8)
8/268 (7) 9/277 (10) 10/277 (9)

1/54 (2) 2/118 (3) 3/154 (4)
4/187 (5) 5/202 (6) 6/241 (7)
7/281 (8) 8/293 (9)
9/293 (1) 10/296 (10)

Bowling: *First Innings*—McGrath 21–7–32–2; Reiffel 24.1–6–58–4; Kasprowicz 22–5–60–0; Warne 27–3–88–2; S. R. Waugh 8.1–1–15–1; M. E. Waugh 4–1–16–0; Ponting 1.5–1–0–1. *Second Innings*—McGrath 29.5–12–60–4; Kasprowicz 13–2–29–0; Warne 41–16–92–2; Reiffel 9–0–58–1; Bevan 14–3–46–3.

Umpires: C. J. Mitchley (South Africa) and S. G. Randell.
Referee: P. L. van der Merwe (South Africa).

AUSTRALIA v WEST INDIES

Second Test Match

At Sydney, November 29, 30, December 1, 2, 3. Australia won by 124 runs. Toss: Australia. Test debut: J. N. Gillespie.

Trailing by merely 27 on first innings, West Indies threw away a position of near-equality with a fielding display of such incompetence that, even when Mark Waugh and Elliott were lying dazed on the ground after a head-on collision, neither was run out. Left again to negotiate survival rather than campaign for victory, the tourists failed, despite an astonishing rearguard innings from Chanderpaul. Lara, sadly, put up a better fight in the dressing-room than on the field as Australia established a 2-0 lead.

Greg Blewett and newcomer Jason Gillespie had replaced the injured Steve Waugh and Reiffel. West Indies were unchanged. Recent innings by pop star Michael Jackson and the Aussie Rules team Sydney Swans had raised apprehensions about the state of the SCG. In the event, pitch and outfield were both like Jackson – a bit of everything in complexion, familiarly eccentric in performance.

The home openers made a merry start, raising 50 before drinks, but, once the new ball's shine dulled, the match was played at an attritional pace: 263 was the most scored on any day. The West Indians reduced Australia to 131 for five – only once in the series did they reach 200 before losing their fifth first-innings wicket – but Blewett and the redoubtable Healy came to the rescue with a stand of 93. Although both fell early next morning, the tail wagged on so that the last five wickets added 200, including 43 for the last between Gillespie and McGrath, who looked aggrieved to be ruled lbw – the only such dismissal for Australia in the first two Tests, compared with nine for West Indies. Walsh took five wickets, but there were none for Ambrose.

Twice in their first innings – at 92 for nought and 229 for four – West Indies were poised to take charge. But both times McGrath reasserted Australia's dominance with a double burst of wickets, including Lara with a superb away-cutter and Adams and Browne with split-finger slower balls he had learned from Craig McDermott. Campbell and Chanderpaul were staunch and Bishop clattered 48, as West Indies reached their first total over 300 in six Tests against Australia.

Two wickets for Bishop that night meant that Elliott and Mark Waugh made necessarily cautious progress on the fourth morning until a moment of mayhem just before lunch. Both changed course as they ran between wickets, neither saw the other, and they collided. Waugh was temporarily stunned, but Elliott – who was batting with great authority – tore a knee cartilage, retired hurt and did not appear again in the series. Somehow West Indies botched the run-out, the nadir of a day of fielding slapstick. It took a heavy toll on morale; Bishop, who had bowled six overs for two runs in the first session, bowled three for 29 in the last. The batsmen exploited this raggedness, stepping up the pace to almost five an over. At Taylor's declaration, West Indies were left 340 to win or a day and a bit to hold out. Waugh opened the bowling with off-spin.

Still this series would not conform to a pattern. West Indies lost three wickets in 20 balls on the last morning, the last of them Lara, who was so sure Healy had not taken the low catch cleanly that – still in his pads – he went to the Australian dressing-room to protest. Manager Clive Lloyd later apologised, though Lara remained unrepentant.

Meanwhile, the elfin Chanderpaul struck back with such abandon that Warne had to be removed from the attack. He reached 50 from just 38 balls and, with Hooper, put on 117 in a bare 95 minutes. That rate of scoring might have delivered victory. But Warne returned and, on the stroke of lunch, conjured a ball that, had it held its line, would have gone to slip; instead, it rounded wickedly on Chanderpaul and cannoned from his pad into his stumps. An hour later, Bevan's wrong 'un fooled not just Hooper, but Taylor at slip. He dropped the snick, kicked it up with his foot as he fell and caught it flat on his back. Taylor got up again; West Indies did not.

Man of the Match: G. D. McGrath.   *Attendance:* 79,581.

Close of play: First day, Australia 224-5 (G. S. Blewett 58*, I. A. Healy 44*); Second day, West Indies 156-3 (C. L. Hooper 27*, S. Chanderpaul 3*); Third day, Australia 77-2 (M. T. G. Elliott 45*, M. E. Waugh 2*); Fourth day, West Indies 27-0 (S. L. Campbell 13*, R. G. Samuels 12*).

Australia

*M. A. Taylor c Chanderpaul b Bishop	27	– (2) c Lara b Bishop	16
M. T. G. Elliott c Lara b Bishop	29	– (1) retired hurt	78
R. T. Ponting c Samuels b Walsh	9	– c Browne b Bishop	4
M. E. Waugh c Lara b Walsh	19	– c Browne b Ambrose	67
M. G. Bevan c Hooper b Benjamin	16	– c Browne b Benjamin	52
G. S. Blewett c Adams b Walsh	69	– not out	47
†I. A. Healy c Lara b Walsh	44	– not out	22
S. K. Warne c Browne b Bishop	28		
M. S. Kasprowicz c Campbell b Walsh	21		
J. N. Gillespie not out	16		
G. D. McGrath lbw b Adams	24		
L-b 10, w 1, n-b 18	29	B 4, l-b 10, w 3, n-b 9	26

1/54 (2) 2/68 (1) 3/73 (3) 4/94 (4)   331   1/51 (2) 2/67 (3)   (4 wkts dec.) 312
5/131 (5) 6/224 (7) 7/245 (6)   3/209 (4) 4/274 (5)
8/283 (9) 9/288 (8) 10/331 (11)

In the second innings M. T. G. Elliott retired hurt at 143.

Bowling: *First Innings*—Ambrose 25–5–73–0; Walsh 30–6–98–5; Benjamin 22–4–69–1; Hooper 14–6–15–0; Bishop 23–5–55–3; Adams 5.5–1–11–1. *Second Innings*—Ambrose 20–2–66–1; Walsh 19–6–36–0; Bishop 20–6–54–2; Benjamin 16–4–46–1; Adams 4–0–21–0; Hooper 27–7–75–0.

West Indies

S. L. Campbell b Blewett	77	– lbw b McGrath 15
R. G. Samuels lbw b McGrath	35	– b Warne 16
B. C. Lara c Healy b McGrath	2	– c Healy b McGrath 1
C. L. Hooper lbw b Warne	27	– c Taylor b Bevan 57
S. Chanderpaul c and b Warne	48	– b Warne 71
J. C. Adams c Bevan b McGrath	30	– c Blewett b McGrath 5
†C. O. Browne c Blewett b McGrath	0	– not out 25
I. R. Bishop c Elliott b Warne	48	– run out 0
C. E. L. Ambrose b Gillespie	9	– b Bevan 0
K. C. G. Benjamin b Gillespie	6	– c Taylor b Warne 4
*C. A. Walsh not out	2	– c McGrath b Warne 18
B 4, l-b 6, n-b 10	20	L-b 2, n-b 1 3

1/92 (2) 2/108 (3) 3/136 (1) 4/166 (4)   **304**   1/33 (1) 2/33 (2) 3/35 (3)   **215**
5/229 (6) 6/229 (7) 7/243 (5)   4/152 (5) 5/157 (6) 6/176 (4)
8/286 (9) 9/298 (10) 10/304 (8)   7/176 (8) 8/176 (9)
                                          9/183 (10) 10/215 (11)

Bowling: *First Innings*—McGrath 31–9–82–4; Kasprowicz 13–2–37–0; Warne 35.2–13–65–3; Gillespie 23–5–62–2; Bevan 11–0–35–0; Blewett 4–0–13–1. *Second Innings*—McGrath 17–7–36–3; Waugh 4–0–15–0; Gillespie 7–2–27–0; Warne 27.4–5–95–4; Bevan 14–2–40–2.

Umpires: D. R. Shepherd (England) and D. B. Hair.
Referee: P. L. van der Merwe (South Africa).

West Indies' matches v Australia and Pakistan in the Carlton & United Series (December 6-17) may be found in that section.

†At Canberra, December 10. Prime Minister's XI won by 58 runs. Toss: Prime Minister's XI. Prime Minister's XI 258 for eight (50 overs) (D. F. Hills 52, M. L. Hayden 45, A. Symonds 33, I. J. Harvey 55 not out, Extras 36); West Indians 200 (43.4 overs) (S. L. Campbell 32, B. C. Lara 32, R. G. Samuels 45; B. E. Young four for 46).

†At Melbourne, December 13 (day/night). Australia A won by six wickets. Toss: West Indians. West Indians 217 for eight (50 overs) (B. C. Lara 33, S. Chanderpaul 72); Australia A 218 for four (44.4 overs) (M. J. Slater 40, D. S. Lehmann 63 not out, I. J. Harvey 67 not out).

At Wangaratta, December 19, 20, 21, 22. West Indians won by six wickets. Toss: Victoria. Victoria 354 (G. R. Vimpani 133, R. P. Larkin 32, D. S. Berry 50, Extras 38; N. A. M. McLean five for 48, J. C. Adams three for 53) and 197 (D. M. Jones 33; K. C. G. Benjamin three for 53, I. R. Bishop three for 40); West Indians 336 (S. L. Campbell 80, B. C. Lara 86, C. L. Hooper 49, J. C. Adams 52; P. R. Reiffel three for 49, I. J. Harvey five for 56) and 219 for four (S. L. Campbell 112 not out, B. C. Lara 46).

AUSTRALIA v WEST INDIES

Third Test Match

At Melbourne, December 26, 27, 28. West Indies won by six wickets. Toss: Australia.
This Test so completely reversed the newly established order that even the aftermath came first. Australia, leading 2-0, made the sort of sweeping changes that losing teams make and then

lost badly. West Indies, hitherto a rabble, made one minor change, as if they were on a winning streak, and so began one that not only accounted for Australia here, but beat them to a place in the one-day finals as well.

Australia lost Elliott because of injury and welcomed back Steve Waugh; they also dropped Ponting, Bevan and Kasprowicz, replacing them with left-handers Langer and Hayden, both playing their first Tests since 1994, and Reiffel. West Indies merely changed wicket-keepers.

Ambrose, enlivened by as difficult a batting pitch as Taylor could remember at Melbourne, promised his team ten wickets and had the first three within an hour, before most of the 72,000 crowd – the biggest at an MCG Test for 21 years – had taken their seats. Langer had retorted with a six off Bishop, but his hesitation and run-out left Australia 27 for four. Steve Waugh, Blewett and Healy fought their way out of the corner, adding 168 for the next two wickets, and were well-bruised for their trouble. But the tail was shot out and they finished at 219.

McGrath matched Ambrose wicket and glare for wicket and glare the next day, despite the bankable resistance of Chanderpaul, who was promoted over Lara to No. 3. He made his 11th fifty in 21 Test innings, but again failed to convert it to a century. Lara, eased down to No. 4, where he stayed for the remaining Tests, waited 22 minutes to break his duck, but found patience no more of a virtue than his urgency in Sydney; he was out four balls later for two and, when Chanderpaul fell, West Indies were teetering at 107 for five.

But Gillespie had broken down with a side strain, and Adams and Murray added 90 for the sixth wicket, Murray swinging freely for as fluent a fifty as any in the series, and Adams patiently batting four hours for an unbeaten 74. West Indies were eight down when they took the lead, but some atypical obduracy from their tail stretched it to 36.

Australia spent three wickets recovering those runs, Ambrose claiming Hayden and Langer for ducks. Walsh chimed in, dismissing Taylor, Mark Waugh and Blewett, West Indies' fielding was for once brilliant and, in less than four hours, Australia were all out for 122. Only Steve Waugh, last out for 37, displayed any fortitude. Ambrose finished with nine of his promised ten wickets, despite a hamstring strain.

West Indies wanted 87 to win, but felt the wrath of McGrath; when Lara fell to him for the fourth time running (for scores of 2, 1, 2 and 2), they were listing badly at 32 for three. Chanderpaul and Hooper bailed them out without needing to take the match into a fourth day. At 2-1, the series had come unexpectedly alive.

Man of the Match: C. E. L. Ambrose.   *Attendance:* 131,671.

Close of play: First day, West Indies 29-1 (R. G. Samuels 10*, S. Chanderpaul 11*); Second day, West Indies 233-9 (J. C. Adams 54*, C. A. Walsh 2*).

Australia

*M. A. Taylor b Ambrose		7 – (2) c Hooper b Walsh	10
M. L. Hayden c Hooper b Ambrose	5	(1) b Ambrose	0
J. L. Langer run out	12	c Hooper b Ambrose	0
M. E. Waugh lbw b Ambrose	0	lbw b Walsh	19
S. R. Waugh c Murray b Bishop	58	b Benjamin	37
G. S. Blewett run out	62	c Murray b Walsh	7
†I. A. Healy c Hooper b Ambrose	36	b Benjamin	0
P. R. Reiffel c Samuels b Benjamin	0	lbw b Benjamin	8
S. K. Warne c Campbell b Bishop	10	c Adams b Ambrose	18
J. N. Gillespie not out	4	lbw b Ambrose	2
G. D. McGrath c Hooper b Ambrose	0	not out	5
L-b 8, n-b 17	25	L-b 4, w 1, n-b 11	16

1/5 (2) 2/26 (1) 3/26 (4) 4/27 (3)	**219**
5/129 (5) 6/195 (7) 7/200 (8)	
8/203 (6) 9/217 (9) 10/219 (11)	

1/0 (1) 2/3 (3) 3/28 (2)	**122**
4/47 (4) 5/64 (6) 6/65 (7)	
7/76 (8) 8/107 (9)	
9/113 (10) 10/122 (5)	

Bowling: First Innings—Ambrose 24.5–7–55–5; Bishop 11–1–31–2; Benjamin 19–2–64–1; Walsh 14–0–43–0; Adams 1–0–4–0; Hooper 5–1–14–0. *Second Innings*—Ambrose 12–4–17–4; Bishop 10–2–26–0; Benjamin 12.5–5–34–3; Walsh 11–4–41–3.

West Indies

S. L. Campbell lbw b McGrath	7	– c Hayden b McGrath	0
R. G. Samuels c Taylor b Warne	17	– lbw b McGrath	13
S. Chanderpaul c and b McGrath	58	– b Reiffel	40
B. C. Lara c Warne b McGrath	2	– c Hayden b McGrath	2
C. L. Hooper run out	7	– not out	27
J. C. Adams not out	74	– not out	1
†J. R. Murray c Reiffel b McGrath	53		
I. R. Bishop lbw b McGrath	0		
C. E. L. Ambrose b Warne	8		
K. C. G. Benjamin b Reiffel	11		
*C. A. Walsh c M. E. Waugh b Warne	4		
B 4, l-b 7, n-b 3	14	N-b 4	4

1/12 (1) 2/62 (2) 3/71 (4) 4/86 (5)   255   1/0 (1) 2/25 (2)   (4 wkts) 87
5/107 (3) 6/197 (7) 7/197 (8)   3/32 (4) 4/82 (3)
8/215 (9) 9/230 (10) 10/255 (11)

Bowling: *First Innings*—McGrath 30–11–50–5; Reiffel 29–8–76–1; Warne 28.1–3–72–3; Gillespie 3–2–5–0; Blewett 9–3–19–0; S. R. Waugh 10–5–22–0. *Second Innings*—McGrath 9–1–41–3; Reiffel 9–2–16–1; Warne 3–0–17–0; Blewett 2.5–0–13–0.

Umpires: S. Venkataraghavan (India) and P. D. Parker.
Referee: P. L. van der Merwe (South Africa).

West Indies' matches v Australia and Pakistan in the Carlton & United Series (January 3-20) may be found in that section.

†At Toowoomba, January 7. West Indians won by 36 runs. Toss: West Indians. West Indians 275 for seven (50 overs) (A. F. G. Griffith 30, S. Chanderpaul 123, R. I. C. Holder 32, S. L. Campbell 65; M. J. Warden three for 39); Australian Country XI 239 (49.5 overs) (A. J. Warren 39, M. S. Curry 49, M. B. Robinson 50 not out).

AUSTRALIA v WEST INDIES

Fourth Test Match

At Adelaide, January 25, 26, 27, 28. Australia won by an innings and 183 runs. Toss: West Indies. Test debuts: A. J. Bichel; A. F. G. Griffith.

In Adelaide four years previously, the sting was in the last ball, when West Indies won by one run. This time, the match and series were as good as decided before the first ball.

The late withdrawal of Ambrose dealt a massive psychological blow to West Indies. But Australia's gamble of playing the enigmatic Bevan as a front-line spinner became a masterstroke. He took ten wickets with his left-arm wrist-spin and scored 85 in an all-round performance of rare efficacy. Early on the fourth morning, West Indies slumped to their second-worst defeat ever at Australia's hands, and Taylor had retained the Frank Worrell Trophy.

Bevan and yet another Queensland fast bowler, Andy Bichel, replaced Reiffel and the injured Gillespie. Though Bevan maintained that he was still a batsman, he was listed at No. 7. The tourists brought in Cuffy, a recent reinforcement, and Thompson for their injured quick bowlers Ambrose and Benjamin, and swapped left-hand openers Samuels and Adrian Griffith.

West Indies betrayed their absent-Ambrose complex by choosing to bat first. It was a token performance: all out in just over three hours. Taylor was bowling Bevan before drinks on the first morning and in tandem with Warne immediately afterwards. Lara played a horrible shot to his first ball from Warne to be caught at mid-on, and what little fight there was in West Indies was snuffed out. McGrath snapped up Hooper, and Bevan took the last four in 28 balls for one run.

Australia then batted the best part of the next 12 hours to make 517. Further failures for Taylor and Langer hardly mattered as their team-mates drove nail after nail into West Indies' coffin. Hayden the imperturbable outlived three chances to arrive after four and a half hours at a stout-hearted maiden century. Mark Waugh, who made a studied 82, shared a three-hour stand of 164.

West Indies were at a low ebb: they missed six catches and a stumping, and had further wickets invalidated by two of their plentiful no-balls. Clive Lloyd said he had not seen worse cricket from a West Indian team. Yet they bowled so beautifully to Hayden on the second morning that it was more than 40 minutes before he added to his overnight score; then, having failed to claim him or Mark Waugh, they yielded to fate. Two of their three wickets on that bleak day were virtually accidental. Wicket-keeper Murray dropped Mark Waugh, only for the ball to bobble up from the flap of his pad back into his gloves. And Steve Waugh, who for two years had kept out the world's best, got such a rank long hop from Chanderpaul that it was on its downward arc when it reached him – and he slashed to cover.

Australia were already 158 ahead when Bevan joined Blewett, and they more than doubled that lead. Blewett breezed to 99 before, having been refused an apparently obvious single by Bevan, was bowled through the gate by Cuffy. But Bevan, anxious to prove his worth as a batsman, laboured five and a half hours for an unbeaten 85. In the circumstances, Taylor was happy enough to indulge that rate of scoring, and Australia finally led by 387.

There was a macabre inevitability about West Indies' second innings. Bevan had Chanderpaul and Campbell caught at slip before Warne even came on to bowl. Lara retorted with a six each off Bevan and Warne as he and Hooper shared 96 in even time for the fourth wicket, but it was no more than a death rattle.

Man of the Match: M. G. Bevan.　　　　*Attendance:* 68,435.

Close of play: First day, Australia 139-2 (M. L. Hayden 66*, M. E. Waugh 31*); Second day, Australia 434-5 (G. S. Blewett 91*, M. G. Bevan 47*); Third day, West Indies 154-6 (B. C. Lara 65*).

West Indies

S. L. Campbell c Healy b McGrath	0	– c Taylor b Bevan	24
A. F. G. Griffith lbw b Bichel	13	– c S. R. Waugh b McGrath	1
S. Chanderpaul c Taylor b Warne	20	– c Taylor b Bevan	8
B. C. Lara c Blewett b Warne	9	– c Healy b Warne	78
C. L. Hooper c M. E. Waugh b McGrath	17	– lbw b Warne	45
J. C. Adams c and b Warne	10	– c M. E. Waugh b Bevan	0
†J. R. Murray c Blewett b Bevan	34	– (8) c Taylor b Bevan	25
I. R. Bishop c Healy b Bevan	1	– (7) c Bevan b Warne	0
*C. A. Walsh c Healy b Bevan	0	– c S. R. Waugh b Bevan	1
C. E. Cuffy c Healy b Bevan	2	– not out	3
P. I. C. Thompson not out	10	– c Hayden b Bevan	6
B 4, l-b 1, n-b 9	14	B 2, l-b 5, n-b 6	13
	130		**204**

1/11 (1) 2/22 (2) 3/45 (4) 4/58 (3)　　　　130
5/72 (5) 6/113 (6) 7/117 (7)
8/117 (9) 9/119 (10) 10/130 (8)

1/6 (2) 2/22 (2) 3/42 (1)　　　　204
4/138 (5) 5/145 (6) 6/154 (7)
7/181 (4) 8/192 (9)
9/196 (8) 10/204 (11)

Bowling: First Innings—McGrath 12–4–21–2; Bichel 10–1–31–1; Bevan 9.5–2–31–4; Warne 16–4–42–3. *Second Innings*—McGrath 17–4–31–1; Bichel 8–4–16–0; Bevan 22.4–3–82–6; Warne 20–4–68–3; Blewett 2–2–0–0.

Australia

*M. A. Taylor lbw b Bishop	11	A. J. Bichel c Lara b Walsh	7
M. L. Hayden st Murray b Hooper	125	G. D. McGrath b Walsh	1
J. L. Langer c Murray b Cuffy	19		
M. E. Waugh c Murray b Hooper	82	B 2, l-b 15, w 4, n-b 20	41
S. R. Waugh c Hooper b Chanderpaul	26		
G. S. Blewett b Cuffy	99		**517**
M. G. Bevan not out	85	1/35 (1) 2/78 (3) 3/242 (4)	
†I. A. Healy c Lara b Thompson	12	4/288 (2) 5/288 (5) 6/453 (6)	
S. K. Warne c Hooper b Bishop	9	7/475 (8) 8/494 (9)	
		9/507 (10) 10/517 (11)	

Bowling: Walsh 37.3–6–101–2; Bishop 34–6–92–2; Cuffy 33–4–116–2; Thompson 16–0–80–1; Hooper 31–7–86–2; Adams 8–0–23–0; Chanderpaul 3–1–2–1.

Umpires: D. R. Shepherd (England) and S. G. Randell. Referee: R. Subba Row (England).

AUSTRALIA v WEST INDIES

Fifth Test Match

At Perth, February 1, 2, 3. West Indies won by ten wickets. Toss: Australia.

Allan Border used to think of Perth Tests as away games for Australia. Four years previously, the curator had provided a pitch lush enough for hay-making; West Indies won in three days and he was sacked. This time, the pitch was so thoroughly cut and compacted that it sported large, longitudinal cracks; West Indies, still fearsome on oddball pitches, again won in three days. The new curator, David Crane, kept his job. WACA officials said he had been undone by the extreme heat before the game.

The last time, defeat cost Australia the series and the trophy they coveted most. Now, it cost only a little pride and its significance was unclear. West Indies maintained their perfect record on this ground – five Tests, five wins – though this was the most hollow. Ambrose and Walsh bade adieu to Australia with bags of five. Lara's *au revoir* was hard-hitting in word and flourishing deed. But the overall balance of the series was unchanged.

For Australia, Reiffel returned and Bevan pushed up to No. 6 and Blewett to No. 3 in place of Langer. For West Indies, Ambrose, Simmons (who had flown in a fortnight previously), Samuels, and Browne replaced Cuffy, Thompson, Griffith and the injured Murray. On an inhumanly hot day – touching 43 degrees Centigrade – Australia batted first, but without conviction. Hayden was out third ball, the ill-starred Taylor was run out by West Indies' slickest fielding of the summer, and they were soon 49 for four. Mark Waugh and Bevan stalled the slide with a stand of 120, Waugh keeping his cool even on this melting day and the mystery of Bevan deepening as he made his highest home Test score on the least likely pitch. The heat forced Walsh to leave the field and acting-captain Lara bowled Ambrose and Bishop in one-over spells. But Ambrose would not be denied and Australia were all out for 243.

Lara came in at 43 for two; when he left, West Indies were in the lead and he had made a century such as only he can make. For him, the cracks closed up and the bounce evened out, or so it seemed. His innings grew like a symphony, two hours for the first fifty, just over an hour for the second, and then a crescendo as he hit Warne for 26 in 14 balls. It was Lara's first century against Australia since his 277 at Sydney four years earlier – and his only first-class hundred on the tour. Samuels kept him dogged company in a stand of 208, batting five and a half hours for 76. His stubbornness, a rash of no-balls and the searing heat revived Australia's propensity towards petulance. Tempers rose and words were exchanged, bringing admonitions from the umpires and, at the press conference, from Lara. Next morning, Lara acted as a runner for Walsh, an unusual gambit for a vice-captain, causing such antagonism that the umpires dressed down both captains on the field.

Even Taylor seemed to lose his captaincy bearings, bowling Warne for only two overs in a session at the height of the Lara–Samuels stand. Eventually, Warne was to dismiss both, half an hour apart, but Hooper's silky fifty helped to stretch the lead to 141. Reiffel took four of the last five – including Simmons, for the third duck of his three-innings tour – and the final wicket came when an ingenious backhand flick from Healy ran out Ambrose, whose bat had jammed in one of the cracks.

Once Ambrose had Taylor caught at the wicket and bowled Blewett with a grubber, it was uncertain which was more cracked, the pitch or Australia's psyche. Only Blewett and Mark Waugh could blame the wicket unconditionally; only Hayden, sixth out for 47, and later Healy and Warne showed any fight. Australia spent eight wickets regaining the lead, and West Indies might not have needed to bat again but for their profligacy with extras. Ambrose bowled 15 no-balls in his last two overs in Australia, an ill-fitting farewell flourish.

The hero of the hour was Walsh, who was carrying a hamstring injury and had not been sure he would bowl at all. He meant to bowl just one over of relief for Ambrose before lunch but ended up bowling 20 unchanged for five wickets. He and Ambrose doffed their caps and bowed to the crowd before the West Indies openers thrashed out the runs needed for victory and the trophy was presented to Taylor. Thus it was that both captains had the last laugh simultaneously, though the bad temper obscured the good humour. It may still be rankling when the teams meet again.

Man of the Match: C. E. L. Ambrose. *Man of the Series:* G. D. McGrath.

Attendance: 27,058.

Close of play: First day, West Indies 25-0 (S. L. Campbell 20*, R. G. Samuels 0*); Second day, West Indies 353-7 (C. L. Hooper 57*, I. R. Bishop 5*).

Australia

M. L. Hayden c Lara b Ambrose	0	– (2) lbw b Hooper	47
*M. A. Taylor run out	2	– (1) c Browne b Ambrose	1
G. S. Blewett c Browne b Simmons	17	– b Ambrose	0
M. E. Waugh c Campbell b Ambrose	79	– c Browne b Walsh	9
S. R. Waugh c Browne b Ambrose	1	– c Hooper b Walsh	0
M. G. Bevan not out	87	– c Simmons b Walsh	15
†I. A. Healy b Ambrose	7	– c Chanderpaul b Walsh	29
P. R. Reiffel c Simmons b Ambrose	0	– c Adams b Walsh	5
S. K. Warne c Browne b Bishop	9	– c Simmons b Bishop	30
A. J. Bichel c Browne b Bishop	15	– c Samuels b Bishop	18
G. D. McGrath c Ambrose b Bishop	0	– not out	2
L-b 10, w 2, n-b 14	26	B 2, l-b 8, w 6, n-b 22	38

1/0 (1) 2/7 (2) 3/45 (5) 4/49 (5)	**243**
5/169 (4) 6/186 (7) 7/186 (8)	
8/216 (9) 9/243 (10) 10/243 (11)	

1/7 (1) 2/17 (3) 3/43 (4)	**194**
4/48 (5) 5/84 (6) 6/105 (2)	
7/110 (8) 8/133 (7)	
9/189 (10) 10/194 (9)	

Bowling: *First Innings*—Ambrose 18–5–43–5; Bishop 18–5–54–3; Walsh 9–0–29–0; Simmons 20–5–58–1; Hooper 15–1–49–0. *Second Innings*—Ambrose 9–2–50–2; Bishop 12.3–1–44–2; Walsh 20–4–74–5; Simmons 3–0–9–0; Hooper 3–0–7–1.

West Indies

S. L. Campbell c Healy b Reiffel	21	– not out	16
R. G. Samuels c M. E. Waugh b Warne	76	– not out	35
S. Chanderpaul c Reiffel b McGrath	3		
B. C. Lara c Healy b Warne	132		
C. L. Hooper c Healy b Reiffel	57		
J. C. Adams c Healy b McGrath	18		
P. V. Simmons c M. E. Waugh b Reiffel	0		
†C. O. Browne c Warne b Reiffel	0		
I. R. Bishop c Taylor b Reiffel	13		
C. E. L. Ambrose run out	15		
*C. A. Walsh not out	5		
B 5, l-b 10, w 1, n-b 28	44	L-b 2, w 1, n-b 3	6

1/30 (1) 2/43 (3) 3/251 (4) 4/275 (2)	**384**
5/331 (6) 6/332 (7) 7/332 (8)	
8/359 (5) 9/367 (9) 10/384 (10)	

(no wkt) 57

Bowling: *First Innings*—McGrath 30–5–86–2; Bichel 18–1–79–0; Reiffel 26–6–73–5; Warne 19–8–55–2; Blewett 6–2–19–0; Bevan 5–0–31–0; S. R. Waugh 7–1–26–0. *Second Innings*—McGrath 4–1–14–0; Reiffel 5–0–24–0; Bichel 1.2–0–17–0.

Umpires: P. Willey (England) and D. B. Hair.   Referee: R. Subba Row (England).

THE PAKISTANIS IN AUSTRALIA, 1996-97

The Pakistanis arrived in December 1996 to take part in the triangular World Series tournament against Australia and West Indies, now known as the Carlton & United Series after its new sponsors. Their warm-up games provided a poor guide to their successful run in that tournament, and they produced several indifferent performances before surging to victory in the series.

PAKISTANI TOURING PARTY

Wasim Akram (PIA) (*captain*), Saeed Anwar (ADBP) (*vice-captain*), Aamir Sohail (Rawalpindi/ Allied Bank), Ijaz Ahmed, sen. (Lahore), Inzamam-ul-Haq (Faisalabad/United Bank), Mohammad Wasim (Rawalpindi), Mohammad Zahid (PIA), Moin Khan (Karachi/PIA), Mushtaq Ahmed (Lahore/United Bank), Saqlain Mushtaq (PIA), Shahid Afridi (Karachi), Shahid Nazir (Faisalabad/National Bank), Waqar Younis (United Bank), Zahoor Elahi (Lahore/ADBP).

Salim Malik withdrew through injury before the tour. Ijaz Ahmed, jun. (Faisalabad/Allied Bank) and Mujahid Jamshed (Lahore/Habib Bank) reinforced the party when Saeed Anwar flew home because of illness.

Tour manager: Yawar Saeed.   *Coach:* Mushtaq Mohammad.

PAKISTANI TOUR RESULTS

First-class match – Played 1: Lost 1.
Loss – Tasmania.
One-day internationals – Played 10: Won 6, Lost 4. *Wins* – Australia (3), West Indies (3). *Losses* – Australia, West Indies (3).
Other non-first-class matches – Played 5: Won 3, Lost 2. *Wins* – Australia A, Hunter Valley Invitation XI, Tasmania. *Losses* – Australian Cricket Academy, Queensland.

Note: Matches in this section which were not first-class are signified by a dagger.

†At Adelaide, December 13. Australian Cricket Academy won by 13 runs. Toss: Pakistanis. Australian Cricket Academy 248 for five (50 overs) (M. G. Dighton 62, B. J. Haddin 45, S. M. Katich 39, D. J. Thornely 36, S. A. J. Craig 34 not out; Saqlain Mushtaq three for 50); Pakistanis 235 (48.4 overs) (Saeed Anwar 56, Zahoor Elahi 61, Mohammad Wasim 37; A. M. Smith three for 40).

Pakistan's matches v Australia and West Indies in the Carlton & United Series (December 15-17) may be found in that section.

At Hobart, December 19, 20, 21. Tasmania won by an innings and 69 runs. Toss: Pakistanis. Pakistanis 299 (Zahoor Elahi 34, Shahid Afridi 80, Mushtaq Ahmed 65; S. Young seven for 64) and 67 (M. W. Ridgway three for 46, J. M. Saint four for ten); Tasmania 435 (J. Cox 200, R. T. Ponting 35, Extras 41; Mushtaq Ahmed four for 97).
Young's seven for 64 was the best analysis for Tasmania since 1983-84. Cox's 200, his maiden double-hundred, lasted 475 minutes and 342 balls and included 19 fours. Tasmania won with a day to spare.

†At Brisbane, December 26 (day/night). Queensland won by 63 runs. Toss: Queensland. Queensland 186 for eight (50 overs) (S. G. Law 31, A. J. Bichel 42 not out; Saqlain Mushtaq three for 49); Pakistanis 123 (38.2 overs) (A. C. Dale five for 28).

†At Sydney, December 28 (day/night). Pakistanis won by three wickets. Toss: Australia A. Australia A 292 for seven (50 overs) (M. J. Di Venuto 63, S. G. Law 76, D. S. Lehmann 69, Extras 31; Shahid Afridi three for 39); Pakistanis 293 for seven (49.5 overs) (Zahoor Elahi 31, Ijaz Ahmed, sen. 123, Inzamam-ul-Haq 59).

†At Newcastle, December 30. Pakistanis won by 25 runs. Toss: Pakistanis. Pakistanis 186 for nine (32 overs) (Zahoor Elahi 69, Inzamam-ul-Haq 55; G. G. Geise five for 20); Hunter Valley Invitation XI 161 (31.2 overs) (S. Lee 35, G. J. Arms 38; Mohammad Zahid three for 25, Saqlain Mushtaq five for 28).

Pakistan's matches v Australia and West Indies in the Carlton & United Series (January 1-20) may be found in that section.

†At Launceston, January 5. Pakistanis won by three wickets. Toss: Tasmania. Tasmania 235 for six (50 overs) (M. J. Di Venuto 39, D. C. Boon 30, S. Young 59 not out, D. J. Marsh 31); Pakistanis 236 for seven (49 overs) (Zahoor Elahi 89, Mohammad Wasim 39).

THE INDIANS IN SOUTH AFRICA
AND ZIMBABWE, 1996-97

By DICKY RUTNAGUR

The Indians arrived in South Africa in mid-December for the second leg of their back-to-back Test series. They had just won the home leg 2-1 on some characteristically Indian wickets. But now it was their turn to play on pitches vastly different from their own. The itinerary, including only two first-class matches outside the three Tests, militated against India, particularly their batsmen, and their difficulties in acclimatising were compounded when their only fixture before the First Test was badly disrupted by rain. Criticism of the itinerary should be aimed at the Indian authorities, however: the length of the tour, or rather its brevity, was their choice. The Tests were followed by a triangular one-day series with Zimbabwe, which South Africa won, before the Indians went to Zimbabwe briefly.

Even allowing for the handicap of inadequate preparation, India were poorly equipped to match South Africa, who won the first two Tests to clinch the rubber and avenge the defeat in the series completed in India only a fortnight earlier. Nevertheless, India came tantalisingly close to winning the Third: they were denied by the weather and Daryll Cullinan.

With 20 wickets at 15.95, fast bowler Allan Donald had an immense influence on the outcome of the series. South Africa's specialist batsmen all took turns at playing major innings but a large part of the gap between the sides was accounted for by the extra depth provided by their all-rounders. Among them, Brian McMillan was outstanding. He was South Africa's highest run-scorer with 296 and headed the averages at 98.66. And a raucous century by Lance Klusener, during a record eighth-wicket partnership with McMillan, was crucial in the Second Test. Batting more sedately, Klusener also helped Cullinan save the final Test.

The heaviest scorer among the specialist batsmen was Cullinan, who made his runs with panache at No. 4. As opener, Andrew Hudson served South Africa well, particularly on a mettlesome Kingsmead pitch in the First Test. His main ally in both innings was the only newcomer to the side, Adam Bacher, the 23-year-old nephew of Ali Bacher, South Africa's chief executive and former captain. Making his debut at the troublesome No. 3 spot, he proved his temperament and technique were equal to the challenge of the pitch, the early fall of the first wicket and the high quality of India's opening bowlers.

The potential strength of India's batting was not fully realised, largely because of a distressing weakness at the top of the order. Vikram Rathore made runs in the two provincial matches, but lacked the technique to play high-class fast bowling on a pitch of any pace, while Woorkeri Raman failed every time. Both were dropped, and Rahul Dravid and Nayan Mongia, the wicket-keeper, were pushed up the order to open. It was only in the final Test, in which the South Africans bowled below their best, that an Indian innings got off to a start worth the name.

Sachin Tendulkar, the captain on whom the Indians were so reliant, recovered from a barren season at home, yet played only one sizeable innings. Azharuddin, too, came good only once, together with Tendulkar at Cape Town when the pair produced a golden partnership, with bold and brilliant batting considered by many observers to be the best they had ever seen. But it could not avert defeat.

And Azharuddin's five remaining innings returned a mere 45 runs – he could not summon the application required. Tendulkar, at least, had the excuse that he got out once to an exceptional ball from Donald and thrice to phenomenal catches. From the Indian viewpoint, one of the gains of a poor series was the advance of Dravid. His 27 not out, calmly made during India's bizarre second-innings collapse for 66 in the First Test, indicated a class confirmed in the final game, when he scored 148 and 81 in times of dire need.

India also depended heavily on their two opening bowlers, Javagal Srinath and Venkatesh Prasad, who were overworked and yet excelled themselves to share almost evenly 35 of the 51 wickets India captured in the series. The lack of a third seamer of quality was an insurmountable obstacle, particularly as the lead spinner, Anil Kumble, was innocuous until the last Test. In the field, the Indians fell far behind their rivals, although Mongia's wicket-keeping was flawless. So was that of his counterpart, Dave Richardson, who, in his 33rd Test, complemented his 119 Test catches with his first stumping.

The series was a refreshing contrast to India's earlier tour of South Africa in 1992-93, when the cricket was attritional, tedious and played in near-empty grounds. It is hard to recall even one dull session in these games. Crowds were not only large, but lively, their enthusiasm creating a magnificent atmosphere. Total attendance figures of 193,739 established a new record for a three-Test series in South Africa.

INDIAN TOURING PARTY

S. R. Tendulkar (Mumbai) (*captain*), A. Kumble (Karnataka) (*vice-captain*), M. Azharuddin (Hyderabad), P. Dharmani (Punjab), R. Dravid (Karnataka), D. Ganesh (Karnataka), S. C. Ganguly (Bengal), D. J. Johnson (Karnataka), S. S. Karim (Bengal), V. V. S. Laxman (Hyderabad), N. R. Mongia (Baroda), B. K. V. Prasad (Karnataka), S. L. V. Raju (Hyderabad), W. V. Raman (Tamil Nadu), V. Rathore (Punjab), J. Srinath (Karnataka).

S. A. Ankola (Mumbai), A. Jadeja (Haryana), S. B. Joshi (Karnataka) and R. R. Singh (Tamil Nadu) replaced Johnson, Raju and Raman for the Standard Bank limited-overs tournament.

Tour manager: Sunil Dev.　　*Coach:* Madan Lal.

INDIAN TOUR RESULTS

Test matches – Played 3: Lost 2, Drawn 1.
First-class matches – Played 5: Lost 2, Drawn 3.
Losses – South Africa (2).
Draws – South Africa, Eastern Province, Free State.
One-day internationals – Played 9: Won 1, Lost 6, Tied 1, No result 1. Abandoned 1. *Win* – Zimbabwe. *Losses* – South Africa (4), Zimbabwe (2). *Tie* – Zimbabwe. *No result* – South Africa. *Abandoned* – Zimbabwe.
Other non-first-class matches – Played 3: Won 1, Lost 1, No result 1. *Win* – Griqualand West. *Loss* – Natal Invitation XI. *No result* – South Africa A.

TEST MATCH AVERAGES

SOUTH AFRICA – BATTING

	T	I	NO	R	HS	100s	Avge	Ct/St
B. M. McMillan	3	6	3	296	103*	1	98.66	5
D. J. Cullinan	3	6	1	291	122*	1	58.20	3
L. Klusener	3	6	2	190	102*	1	47.50	4
A. C. Hudson	3	6	0	224	80	0	37.33	6

	T	I	NO	R	HS	100s	Avge	Ct/St
S. M. Pollock	3	6	2	145	79	0	36.25	1
A. M. Bacher	3	6	0	141	55	0	23.50	3
W. J. Cronje	3	6	0	140	43	0	23.33	1
G. Kirsten	3	6	0	137	103	1	22.83	1
D. J. Richardson	3	5	0	87	39	0	17.40	11/1
A. A. Donald	3	4	1	35	26	0	11.66	0

Played in two Tests: P. R. Adams 2. Played in one Test: H. H. Gibbs 0, 25.

* Signifies not out.

BOWLING

	O	M	R	W	BB	5W/i	Avge
A. A. Donald	119.2	32	319	20	5-40	1	15.95
S. M. Pollock	96	21	231	10	3-25	0	23.10
W. J. Cronje	33.3	13	79	3	2-39	0	26.33
P. R. Adams	79.2	16	262	9	3-45	0	29.11
L. Klusener	77.1	15	241	7	3-75	0	34.42
B. M. McMillan	59.1	10	172	4	2-27	0	43.00

Also bowled: A. M. Bacher 1–0–4–0.

INDIA – BATTING

	T	I	NO	R	HS	100s	Avge	Ct
R. Dravid	3	6	1	277	148	1	55.40	6
S. R. Tendulkar ...	3	6	0	241	169	1	40.16	3
V. V. S. Laxman ...	2	3	2	40	35*	0	40.00	0
S. C. Ganguly	3	6	0	202	73	0	33.66	0
M. Azharuddin	3	6	0	160	115	1	26.66	3
V. Rathore.........	2	4	0	66	44	0	16.50	4
N. R. Mongia	3	6	0	86	50	0	14.33	14
A. Kumble	3	6	1	66	29	0	13.20	0
J. Srinath	3	5	0	63	41	0	12.60	0
B. K. V. Prasad	3	6	2	23	15	0	5.75	0
W. V. Raman	2	4	0	22	16	0	5.50	0
D. Ganesh	2	4	2	4	2*	0	2.00	0

Played in one Test: D. J. Johnson 3, 5.

* Signifies not out.

BOWLING

	O	M	R	W	BB	5W/i	Avge
B. K. V. Prasad	122	15	425	17	5-60	2	25.00
S. C. Ganguly	36	8	85	3	2-36	0	28.33
J. Srinath	148.1	34	517	18	5-104	1	28.72
A. Kumble	155.2	29	384	8	3-40	0	48.00

Also bowled: D. Ganesh 42.5–10–165–1; D. J. Johnson 24–3–91–2; W. V. Raman 15–1–63–0; S. R. Tendulkar 4.4–2–18–0.

Note: Matches in this section which were not first-class are signified by a dagger.

At Port Elizabeth, December 21, 22, 23. Drawn. Toss: Indians. Indians 335 for six dec. (V. Rathore 71, S. C. Ganguly 97, S. R. Tendulkar 62, R. Dravid 31 not out, Extras 31) and 130 for two (V. Rathore 64, R. Dravid 50 not out); Eastern Province 322 for four dec. (P. G. Amm 81, L. J. Koen 44, K. C. Wessels 103 not out, D. J. Callaghan 38, M. W. Rushmere 32 not out).

SOUTH AFRICA v INDIA

First Test Match

At Durban, December 26, 27, 28. South Africa won by 328 runs. Toss: India. Test debut: A. M. Bacher.

Inspired bowling by Donald on a pitch the like of which most of the Indians had never seen before created a three-day finish. India's two innings required a mere 73.2 overs, with Donald claiming nine for 54. Their second innings, 66, fell nine short of the previous lowest against South Africa – by Australia, on the same ground in 1949-50.

The pitch provided excessive bounce as well as movement off the seam. South Africa's own batsmen were discomfited and the match would have been shorter still if India had had a third seamer of quality to support Srinath and Prasad, who bowled magnificently for five in each innings, and held their catches. Adding to the pitch's perils, the sky was overcast at the start, encouraging swing, so it was inevitable that Tendulkar would ask South Africa to bat. India struck early, when Prasad bowled Kirsten through the gate, but then Hudson and Bacher, impressively self-assured, batted until lunch.

Despite the clouds lifting, South Africa lost four wickets in the next session. Bacher was lbw to Srinath's first ball after lunch, Prasad induced edges from Cullinan and Cronje, and Johnson, who had been expensive in the morning, dismissed Gibbs. Hudson, though, had two escapes in the slips, at 39 and 42. His charmed innings finally ended at 80, when Ganguly got him to edge a drive. But by then, McMillan had also been let off: he initiated a recovery which Pollock and Richardson sustained against a tiring attack.

India's reply realised just 100 and lasted barely three hours, with Donald taking five for 40. He produced what he himself pronounced one of the most lethal balls he had ever bowled. It uprooted Tendulkar's off stump, and not only came back at him, but also beat him for pace. Four overs later, Azharuddin mishooked McMillan and, with Donald showing no mercy, the Indians surrendered an hour before tea.

South Africa's second innings featured the only three-figure partnership of the match, between Hudson and Bacher, who scored a distinguished maiden fifty. Once he was out, wickets fell at regular intervals until Mongia took his eighth catch of the match, an Indian Test record, at 185 for nine. But McMillan, who made a robust 51, hooking three sixes off Srinath, and Donald, who survived chances at two and six to bat for almost an hour, added 74.

Facing arrears of 394, India submitted meekly. Donald broke their spirit by dismissing Rathore and Ganguly in his first over. In his third, Raman missed a full toss, and the end was near when Tendulkar and Azharuddin fell to Pollock. Tendulkar was superbly caught in the gully by Kirsten, but Azharuddin gifted his wicket with a heave that would embarrass a No. 11. Dravid, however, showed distinct class in remaining undefeated for two hours.

Man of the Match: A. C. Hudson.   *Attendance:* 41,216.

Close of play: First day, India 2-0 (V. Rathore 2*, W. V. Raman 0*); Second day, South Africa 164-4 (W. J. Cronje 17*, H. H. Gibbs 25*).

South Africa

A. C. Hudson c Mongia b Ganguly	80	– c Tendulkar b Kumble	52
G. Kirsten b Prasad	2	– c Dravid b Prasad	2
A. M. Bacher lbw b Srinath	25	– c Tendulkar b Kumble	55
D. J. Cullinan c Mongia b Prasad	1	– c Mongia b Prasad	3
*W. J. Cronje c Mongia b Prasad	15	– c Mongia b Prasad	17
H. H. Gibbs c Mongia b Johnson	0	– lbw b Srinath	25
B. M. McMillan lbw b Johnson	34	– not out	51
S. M. Pollock not out	23	– c Rathore b Prasad	2
†D. J. Richardson b Prasad	24	– b Srinath	4
L. Klusener c Mongia b Srinath	1	– c Mongia b Srinath	4
A. A. Donald c Rathore b Prasad	5	– c Rathore b Prasad	26
B 4, l-b 10, n-b 11	25	B 7, l-b 6, n-b 5	18

1/8 (2) 2/70 (3) 3/71 (4) 4/99 (5)   235   1/4 (2) 2/115 (3) 3/120 (4)   259
5/113 (6) 6/162 (1) 7/190 (7)   4/120 (1) 5/164 (5) 6/164 (6)
8/229 (9) 9/230 (10) 10/235 (11)   7/171 (8) 8/181 (9)
                                            9/185 (10) 10/259 (11)

Bowling: *First Innings*—Srinath 20–7–36–2; Prasad 19–6–60–5; Johnson 15–2–52–2; Tendulkar 2.4–2–0–0; Kumble 20.2–3–61–0; Ganguly 9–4–12–1. *Second Innings*—Srinath 23–5–80–3; Prasad 25–4–93–5; Johnson 9–1–39–0; Kumble 11–3–26–2; Ganguly 2–0–8–0.

India

V. Rathore c Hudson b Donald	7	– c Richardson b Donald	2
W. V. Raman b Pollock	0	– b Donald	1
S. C. Ganguly c Klusener b Pollock	16	– b Donald	0
*S. R. Tendulkar b Donald	15	– c Kirsten b Pollock	4
M. Azharuddin c Bacher b McMillan	15	– c Klusener b Pollock	8
R. Dravid lbw b McMillan	7	– not out	27
†N. R. Mongia c Richardson b Donald	4	– c Cronje b Klusener	4
A. Kumble not out	13	– c Hudson b Klusener	2
J. Srinath c Cullinan b Donald	0	– run out	7
D. J. Johnson c Bacher b Donald	3	– c Klusener b Pollock	5
B. K. V. Prasad c Richardson b Klusener	4	– c Hudson b Donald	1
B 4, l-b 3, w 2, n-b 7	16	L-b 2, n-b 3	5

1/2 (2) 2/22 (1) 3/36 (3) 4/52 (4)   100   1/2 (1) 2/2 (3) 3/7 (2)   66
5/68 (5) 6/74 (6) 7/74 (7)   4/15 (4) 5/20 (5) 6/25 (7)
8/74 (9) 9/89 (10) 10/100 (11)   7/40 (8) 8/51 (9)
                                            9/59 (10) 10/66 (11)

Bowling: *First Innings*—Donald 16–5–40–5; Pollock 8–2–18–2; Klusener 7.1–2–8–1; McMillan 8–2–27–2. *Second Innings*—Donald 11.1–4–14–4; Pollock 12–4–25–3; Klusener 9–2–16–2; McMillan 2–0–9–0.

Umpires: R. S. Dunne (New Zealand) and D. L. Orchard.
Referee: B. N. Jarman (Australia).

†At Durban, December 30. Natal Invitation XI won by 52 runs. Toss: Natal Invitation XI. Natal Invitation XI 288 for five (55 overs) (N. C. Johnson 80, E. L. R. Stewart 64, J. N. Rhodes 37, D. N. Crookes 63 not out); Indians 236 for seven (55 overs) (W. V. Raman 54, R. Dravid 64, P. Dharmani 38).
The match was arranged after the First Test ended in three days.

SOUTH AFRICA v INDIA

Second Test Match

At Cape Town, January 2, 3, 4, 5, 6. South Africa won by 282 runs. Toss: South Africa. Test debut: D. Ganesh.

A stand of 222 between Tendulkar and Azharuddin not only averted another abbreviated Test but illuminated the game with its sheer brilliance and aggression in the face of adversity. It occupied just 40 overs. Azharuddin, scoring 115 in 110 balls, with 19 fours and a six, provided the major share. But Tendulkar kept going to save India from following on and was last out, after nearly six hours, to an outstanding catch by Bacher at deep mid-wicket.

India were 58 for five when Tendulkar and Azharuddin came together, replying to South Africa's highest total since isolation. It included three centuries. The first, from Kirsten, took nearly five hours; chastened by escapes at nought and ten, he avoided risks, yet batted positively, keeping in step with Cullinan during a partnership of 114. Srinath and Prasad had bowled splendidly when fresh but, once they tired, the attack was innocuous, and a firm, true pitch encouraged aggression. Kirsten was eventually run out off a no-ball and early on the second day South Africa, at 299 for six, were not safe.

But the limited Indian attack stalled as McMillan and Richardson put on 83 before the No. 9, Klusener, launched a spectacular century – 102 in 100 balls, the fastest recorded in terms of balls by a South African Test player – with 13 fours and two pulled sixes. Klusener and McMillan, who also reached a valuable hundred, put on 147, breaking a 94-year-old South African eighth-wicket record. Klusener had not finished. Before the close, he ran out Raman and had experimental opener Dravid playing on. Night-watchman Prasad lasted only one ball against Adams. In the first over next morning, Ganguly steered Donald to second slip. Laxman, after an uneasy half-hour, deflected Pollock down the leg side.

That was the start of the Tendulkar–Azharuddin stand, whose tone belied India's desperate plight. Azharuddin, free of the responsibilities of the captaincy, played the more exotic – and often unorthodox – shots; Tendulkar was more orderly, but attacked in a grand manner. In a six-over spell after lunch, Klusener was hit for 30 and South Africa were forced on to the defensive. Azharuddin constantly took risks and, with the stand at 197, Cronje held a skimming drive at extra cover, but, landing on his elbows, lost his grip. A run later, Tendulkar played a square cut to gully which a juggling Hudson muffed. But an over or two of restraint caused Azharuddin to fret, and he ran himself out with India 50 short of saving the follow-on. Tendulkar averted it with two wickets standing. Strangely, one of the most enjoyable of all Test cricketing afternoons was also a short one. The lunch interval was extended by 15 minutes because the early part of the break had been taken up by a lengthy presentation of the players to President Mandela, who warmly expressed his support for cricket's contribution to the new South Africa. In extreme heat the fielders needed all the rest they could get.

India's recovery continued as they captured three wickets for only 33, but partnerships between Hudson and Cullinan and then McMillan and Pollock played them out of the match. Cronje's declaration, 426 ahead, left South Africa a minimum of 118 overs to bowl India out, but they needed only 67. The openers – this time, Raman and Mongia – were again easy meat and all the middle order played careless shots.

Man of the Match: B. M. McMillan. *Attendance:* 74,009.

Close of play: First day, South Africa 280-4 (W. J. Cronje 35*, B. M. McMillan 13*); Second day, India 29-3 (S. C. Ganguly 19*, S. R. Tendulkar 1*); Third day, South Africa 24-2 (A. C. Hudson 7*, L. Klusener 10*); Fourth day, India 52-3 (S. C. Ganguly 11*, S. R. Tendulkar 6*).

South Africa

A. C. Hudson c Mongia b Prasad	16	– b Srinath	55
G. Kirsten run out	103	– lbw b Ganesh	0
A. M. Bacher c Mongia b Srinath	25	– lbw b Srinath	0
D. J. Cullinan c Mongia b Prasad	77	– (5) b Kumble	55
*W. J. Cronje c Mongia b Srinath	41	– (6) c Dravid b Kumble	18
B. M. McMillan not out	103	– (7) not out	59
S. M. Pollock c Tendulkar b Prasad	1	– (8) not out	40
†D. J. Richardson c Dravid b Srinath	39		
L. Klusener not out	102	– (4) c Dravid b Srinath	12
B 5, l-b 9, n-b 8	22	B 4, l-b 12, w 1	17

1/37 (1) 2/89 (3) 3/203 (2) (7 wkts dec.) 529   1/6 (2) 2/7 (3) (6 wkts dec.) 256
4/251 (4) 5/291 (5) 6/299 (7)   3/33 (4) 4/127 (5)
7/382 (8)   5/133 (1) 6/155 (6)

A. A. Donald and P. R. Adams did not bat.

Bowling: *First Innings*—Srinath 38–8–130–3; Prasad 36–1–114–3; Ganesh 23.5–6–93–0; Kumble 51–7–136–0; Ganguly 9–1–24–0; Raman 5–1–18–0. *Second Innings*—Srinath 18–5–78–3; Ganesh 10–3–38–1; Kumble 25–4–58–2; Prasad 7–1–16–0; Ganguly 2–0–5–0; Raman 10–0–45–0.

India

W. V. Raman run out	5	– c Richardson b Pollock 16
R. Dravid b Klusener	2	– (3) c Richardson b Adams 12
S. C. Ganguly c McMillan b Donald	23	– (4) c McMillan b Pollock 30
B. K. V. Prasad b Adams	0	– (10) st Richardson b Adams 15
*S. R. Tendulkar c Bacher b McMillan	169	– c Klusener b McMillan 9
V. V. S. Laxman c Richardson b Pollock	5	– (7) not out 35
M. Azharuddin run out	115	– (6) c Hudson b Donald.......... 2
†N. R. Mongia lbw b Adams	5	– (2) b Donald 2
A. Kumble c Richardson b Donald	2	– (8) c Richardson b Adams 14
J. Srinath b Pollock	11	– absent hurt
D. Ganesh not out	2	– (9) b Donald 1
L-b 9, n-b 11	20	L-b 1, w 2, n-b 5 8

1/7 (1) 2/24 (2) 3/25 (4) 4/33 (3)	359	1/7 (2) 2/26 (1) 3/44 (3) 144
5/58 (6) 6/280 (7) 7/298 (8)		4/59 (5) 5/61 (6) 6/87 (4)
8/315 (9) 9/340 (10) 10/359 (5)		7/115 (8) 8/121 (9) 9/144 (10)

Bowling: *First Innings*—Donald 24–3–99–2; Pollock 23–2–76–2; Adams 18–5–49–2; Klusener 12–1–88–1; McMillan 6.2–0–22–1; Cronje 9–5–16–0. *Second Innings*—Donald 18–5–40–3; Pollock 12–2–29–2; Klusener 9–3–13–0; McMillan 11–4–16–1; Adams 16.2–4–45–3.

Umpires: D. B. Hair (Australia) and R. E. Koertzen.   Referee: B. N. Jarman (Australia).

†At Kimberley, January 9 (day/night). Indians won by seven wickets. Toss: Griqualand West. Griqualand West 205 for seven (50 overs) (P. H. Barnard 54, W. M. Dry 72; D. J. Johnson three for 26); Indians 206 for three (34.4 overs) (S. C. Ganguly 101, S. R. Tendulkar 51).

At Bloemfontein, January 11, 12, 13. Drawn. Toss: Free State. Free State 320 for seven dec. (H. H. Dippenaar 96, C. F. Craven 76, J. F. Venter 54 not out; D. J. Johnson five for 78) and 259 for two dec. (D. Jordaan 66, G. F. J. Liebenberg 133 not out); Indians 296 for six dec. (V. Rathore 115, V. V. S. Laxman 56 not out, S. S. Karim 53 not out) and 185 for six (V. Rathore 50, R. Dravid 44, V. V. S. Laxman 46 not out; N. Boje three for 59).

SOUTH AFRICA v INDIA

Third Test Match

At Johannesburg, January 16, 17, 18, 19, 20. Drawn. Toss: India.
With only honour and prize money to play for, India almost won. The weather, plus Cullinan's heroic unbeaten century and two-hour eighth-wicket stand with Klusener, saved the day for South Africa.

The pitch was not as lively as expected and the Wanderers did not live up to its reputation for encouraging bowlers on the first morning. However, clouds hung low and it would have been no surprise had India bowled first. The ball did move in the air, but South Africa's pace quartet could not control their line or swing; for the first time in the series, the new ball did India no harm. The openers survived 23 overs, though they scored only 25 – a lot of the bowling did not need playing. It was the very first ball of spin that broke through, an Adams googly finding Rathore's edge. The innings eventually acquired momentum through a fourth-wicket partnership of 145 between Dravid and Ganguly, after Tendulkar, who had promised something substantial, sliced at Cronje's out-swinger. But that was the last wicket South Africa captured on the opening day. Dravid batted in mature fashion, driving in an arc between cover and mid-on, pulling and square-cutting anything short. Ganguly progressed more rapidly, through graceful off-drives.

Overnight rain cost the second morning and, within 20 minutes of resuming, Ganguly edged a ball slanted across him. Azharuddin tried to storm the bowling but left quickly, while Laxman was cut short by a fractured finger. Kumble and Srinath lent Dravid support until he finally holed out, having batted nine hours for 148.

South Africa faced only two balls that night before the light failed. Next morning, Srinath and Prasad bowled superbly; and half an hour after lunch South Africa were 147 for five, Srinath claiming three. The all-rounders turned the tide. McMillan dropped anchor while Pollock flayed the bowling; they put on 112. Then Klusener dug in, and India led by just 89.

They widened this to 355, thanks to their only worthwhile opening stand of the series, 90 from Rathore and Mongia, and a 108-run partnership between Dravid and Ganguly. Dravid missed his second century, but batted with more panache this time.

South Africa were 77 for five, still 278 behind, when a thunderstorm suddenly halted play. The resumption was unduly delayed, though that seemed irrelevant when two more wickets fell in nine overs. But then Klusener settled in to bat most responsibly with Cullinan, who played a magnificent innings of 122 not out in 262 minutes and 194 balls, with 15 fours and a six. It was in the sixth over of the last hour that Klusener was snapped up at short leg. As the light dimmed, so did India's chances; it denied them the use of their quicker bowlers. With four overs remaining, play was called off.

Man of the Match: R. Dravid. *Man of the Series:* A. A. Donald. *Attendance:* 78,514.

Close of play: First day, India 233-3 (R. Dravid 81*, S. C. Ganguly 68*); Second day, South Africa 0-0 (A. C. Hudson 0*, G. Kirsten 0*); Third day, South Africa 321; Fourth day, South Africa 4-1 (G. Kirsten 1*).

India

V. Rathore c Richardson b Adams	13	– lbw b Donald	44
†N. R. Mongia b Donald	21	– c McMillan b Donald	50
R. Dravid c Pollock b Cronje	148	– c Cullinan b Adams	81
*S. R. Tendulkar c McMillan b Cronje	35	– c Richardson b Cronje	9
S. C. Ganguly c McMillan b Klusener	73	– b Adams	60
M. Azharuddin c Hudson b Klusener	18	– lbw b Pollock	2
V. V. S. Laxman retired hurt	0		
A. Kumble c Richardson b Klusener	29	– (7) b Adams	6
J. Srinath c Hudson b Donald	41	– (8) lbw b Donald	4
D. Ganesh c Cullinan b Donald	1	– (9) not out	0
B. K. V. Prasad not out	2	– (10) not out	1
L-b 15, w 5, n-b 9	29	L-b 3, w 4, n-b 2	9

1/25 (1) 2/46 (2) 3/100 (4) 4/245 (5)   410   1/90 (2) 2/109 (1)   (8 wkts dec.) 266
5/266 (6) 6/327 (8) 7/403 (9)   3/124 (4) 4/232 (5)
8/408 (10) 9/410 (3)   5/235 (6) 6/256 (7)
                                        7/265 (8) 8/265 (3)

In the first innings V. V. S. Laxman retired hurt at 266-5.

Bowling: *First Innings*—Donald 32.1–9–88–3; Pollock 30–11–55–0; McMillan 20.5–4–50–0; Klusener 27–6–75–3; Adams 24–6–88–1; Cronje 16.3–5–39–2. *Second Innings*—Donald 18–6–38–3; Klusener 13–1–41–0; Pollock 11–0–28–1; McMillan 11–0–48–0; Adams 21–1–80–3; Bacher 1–0–4–0; Cronje 8–3–24–1.

South Africa

A. C. Hudson c Azharuddin b Kumble	18	– b Kumble	3
G. Kirsten b Prasad	29	– c Rathore b Prasad	1
A. M. Bacher lbw b Srinath	13	– b Prasad	23
D. J. Cullinan c sub (P. Dharmani) b Srinath	33	– not out	122
*W. J. Cronje c Mongia b Srinath	43	– run out	6
B. M. McMillan lbw b Ganguly	47	– c sub (P. Dharmani) b Srinath	2
S. M. Pollock c Mongia b Srinath	79	– b Srinath	0
†D. J. Richardson c Azharuddin b Ganguly	13	– c Azharuddin b Kumble	7
L. Klusener not out	22	– c Dravid b Kumble	49
A. A. Donald b Prasad	4	– not out	0
P. R. Adams c Dravid b Srinath	2		
B 2, l-b 7, w 1, n-b 8	18	B 1, l-b 13, n-b 1	15

1/36 (1) 2/64 (3) 3/73 (2) 4/139 (4)   321   1/4 (1) 2/4 (2) 3/49 (3)   (8 wkts) 228
5/147 (5) 6/259 (6) 7/285 (8)   4/71 (5) 5/76 (6) 6/78 (7)
8/303 (7) 9/318 (10) 10/321 (11)   7/95 (8) 8/222 (9)

Bowling: *First Innings*—Srinath 25.1–3–104–5; Prasad 20–2–83–2; Kumble 25–5–63–1; Ganesh 7–1–26–0; Ganguly 12–1–36–2. *Second Innings*—Srinath 24–6–89–2; Prasad 15–1–59–2; Kumble 23–7–40–3; Ganesh 2–0–8–0; Tendulkar 2–0–18–0; Ganguly 2–2–0–0.

Umpires: P. Willey (England) and C. J. Mitchley.   Series referee: B. N. Jarman (Australia).

India's matches v South Africa and Zimbabwe in the Standard Bank International One-Day Series (January 23–February 13) may be found in that section.

---

†At Pietermaritzburg, January 30 (day/night). No result. Toss: South Africa A. South Africa A 251 for six (50 overs) (L. J. Koen 105, D. N. Crookes 55, M. V. Boucher 42 not out); Indians 94 for five (24.2 overs) (S. R. Tendulkar 37).

†ZIMBABWE v INDIA

First One-Day International

At Queens Sports Club, Bulawayo, February 15. Zimbabwe won by eight wickets, their target having been revised to 136 from 38 overs. Toss: Zimbabwe.

Zimbabwe, who had just pressed India close for a place in the final of the triangular tournament in South Africa, beat them hands down in Bulawayo. Following the 3-0 triumph over England, it gave them a clean sweep of their four home one-day internationals in 1996-97. Rain reduced the match to 44 overs a side and Campbell asked India to bat. They struggled to 95 for six before Robin Singh and Kumble added 64, while Streak returned five for 32, his best one-day international figures. A target of 169 became 136 when showers cut another six overs. Zimbabwe won with 12 overs to spare, Grant Flower leading the way with nine fours in his 61.

Man of the Match: H. H. Streak.

India

V. Rathore c Campbell b Whittall	34	S. B. Joshi lbw b Streak	0
*S. R. Tendulkar c G. W. Flower b Brandes	13	D. Ganesh c and b Streak	4
S. C. Ganguly run out	2	B. K. V. Prasad not out	0
M. Azharuddin c A. Flower b Brandes	24	B 6, l-b 3, w 11, n-b 2	22
A. Jadeja c A. Flower b Streak	0		
R. R. Singh c A. Flower b Streak	45	1/23 2/33 3/68 (43.5 overs) 168
†N. R. Mongia c Waller b Evans	4	4/72 5/84 6/95
A. Kumble c Campbell b Streak	20	7/159 8/159 9/168

Bowling: Brandes 8–1–34–2; Rennie 9–2–38–0; Streak 8.5–0–32–5; Whittall 8–0–29–1; Evans 8–1–19–1; Strang 2–0–7–0.

Zimbabwe

G. W. Flower not out	61	G. J. Whittall not out		19
A. C. Waller b Ganesh	25		B 4, l-b 2, w 3, n-b 1	10
*A. D. R. Campbell c Azharuddin				
b Kumble .	24	1/31 2/96	(2 wkts, 25.5 overs)	139

†A. Flower, D. L. Houghton, C. N. Evans, P. A. Strang, H. H. Streak, E. A. Brandes and J. A. Rennie did not bat.

Bowling: Prasad 6.5–1–35–0; Ganesh 5–0–20–1; Ganguly 2–0–10–0; Singh 4–0–31–0; Kumble 6–2–18–1; Joshi 2–0–19–0.

Umpires: Q. J. Goosen and I. D. Robinson. Referee: B. N. Jarman (Australia).

†ZIMBABWE v INDIA

Second One-Day International

At Harare Sports Club, Harare, February 17. No result (abandoned).
The match was cancelled because of a waterlogged pitch, allowing the Indians to fly home a day early.

THE ZIMBABWEANS IN SOUTH AFRICA, 1996-97

ZIMBABWEAN TOURING PARTY

A. D. R. Campbell (Mashonaland) (*captain*), A. Flower (Mashonaland) (*vice-captain*), E. A. Brandes (Mashonaland), S. V. Carlisle (Mashonaland), C. N. Evans (Mashonaland), G. W. Flower (Mashonaland), D. L. Houghton (Mashonaland), E. Matambanadzo (Mashonaland), J. A. Rennie (Matabeleland), P. A. Strang (Mashonaland), H. H. Streak (Matabeleland), A. C. Waller (Mashonaland), A. R. Whittall (Matabeleland), G. J. Whittall (Matabeleland), C. B. Wishart (Mashonaland).
Manager: A. J. Pycroft. *Coach:* D. L. Houghton.

ZIMBABWEAN TOUR RESULTS

One-day internationals – Played 6: Won 1, Lost 4, Tied 1. *Win* – India. *Losses* – South Africa (3), India. *Tie* – India.
Other non-first-class matches – Played 2: Won 2. *Wins* – North West, Eastern Cape XI.

Note: Matches in this section were not first-class.

At Fochville, January 22 (day/night). Zimbabweans won by 86 runs. Toss: Zimbabweans. Zimbabweans 260 for eight (50 overs) (D. L. Houghton 129 not out; M. J. Lavine four for 27); North West 174 (50 overs) (S. Nicolson 49, B. D. Esterhuysen 40; J. A. Rennie three for 23).
Houghton and John Rennie added 101 unbroken for the Zimbabweans' ninth wicket.

Zimbabwe's matches v South Africa and India in the Standard Bank International One-Day Series (January 25–February 9) may be found in that section.

At Alice, February 5. Zimbabweans won by 83 runs. Zimbabweans 248 for six (50 overs) (A. Flower 95 not out, S. V. Carlisle 52); Eastern Cape XI 165 (40 overs) (S. J. Palframan 55, A. G. Prince 39; C. N. Evans four for 39).

THE AUSTRALIANS IN SOUTH AFRICA, 1996-97

By JACK BANNISTER

Mark Taylor became the first visiting captain to win a Test series in South Africa since they returned to official international cricket in 1991. But although it was Australia's sixth successive series win (excluding a one-off defeat by India), Taylor ended the tour with his position in doubt. His form was such that, after averaging 16 over the three Tests and scoring seven and 17 in the first two one-day internationals, he dropped himself for the remaining five games. He had gone 20 innings without a Test fifty, and the fact that he lasted long enough to reach double figures more often than not led his critics to believe that his decline was not a temporary run of bad luck. Taylor was constantly under fire from the travelling media. But he earned respect and admiration from neutral observers for the unflustered and honest way that he dealt with personal questions.

Australia also won the seven-match one-day international series – South Africa's first defeat in a limited-overs series or tournament on home soil since early 1993. It was a surprise result, as Australia had won only five limited-overs games out of 18 following their defeat in the 1996 World Cup final. South Africa had suffered only two defeats in 24 matches in that time, but paid for their tactical error at Centurion Park, where they opted to risk bowling with a wet ball.

The only disappointing feature of a magnificently successful tour for Australia was the poor attendances at the three Tests. Only 135,209 spectators paid to watch what was billed as the unofficial championship of world cricket – compared with 193,739 who watched India earlier in the summer. The lesson for South African administrators was that two short series are not the best option; future tours by West Indies and England have been scheduled for five Tests each.

Australia won the first two Tests in spite of, not because of, the balance of their side. They opted to play an extra batsman and fielded only three specialist bowlers – Glenn McGrath, Jason Gillespie and Shane Warne – backed up by the emerging wrist-spin of Michael Bevan; had Bevan batted at No. 6, they could have included a third pace bowler. Only the inability of South Africa's batsmen to come to terms with Warne and Bevan enabled this gamble to succeed. It could have failed in the marvellous Second Test at St George's Park, and it did fail at Centurion, when the overworked McGrath finally broke down.

Many records were broken in the First Test at The Wanderers, when Greg Blewett and Steve Waugh added 385 and became the tenth pair of batsmen to bat through an entire day of a Test match. Then Mark Waugh played the key role in the Second Test, scoring 116 to seal a remarkable two-wicket victory. Australia had looked down and out in a low-scoring game on a pitch cynically prepared to tame Warne and Bevan. It was poetic justice that the two wrist-spinners took eight wickets between them.

The effect that the winning margin of the First Test – an innings and 196 runs – had on both sides was reflected in selection policy. Australia fielded the same 11 players in all three Tests, while the home selectors chose 16, with only two changes forced by injury (to Brian McMillan and Shaun Pollock). South Africa's problems stemmed from a top order that was shuffled around in baffling fashion:

there were three inexperienced batsmen in the top six on the poor pitch at Port Elizabeth. It became clear that until they found a class No. 3 South Africa would always struggle against the best opposition.

Gary Kirsten had his first poor series, which meant that it was a mistake to drop the experienced Andrew Hudson and Jonty Rhodes after the First Test. Allan Donald started slowly, but found his top form and rhythm for the Third Test, where eight wickets took him to 155 in his 33 Tests, only 15 behind South Africa's leading wicket-taker, Hugh Tayfield. In the same game, Brett Schultz made an encouraging return to the side after 16 months, and Pat Symcox proved his worth when he replaced Paul Adams. All three helped to propel South Africa to their only win. Adams had never been a threat, and the difference in the spinners' returns – 20 wickets for Australia, seven for South Africa – was a major factor in the visitors' triumph.

And triumph it was, especially for Steve Waugh, who won his third successive Man of the Series award against South Africa. He was the only batsman on either side to exceed 300 runs in the Tests and an average of 78.25 underlined his importance in an inconsistent top order. His brother, Mark, played one of the best fourth-innings Test knocks in living memory, but 93 runs from his other four innings reflected his tendency to sacrifice his wicket to poor strokes. Blewett scored a double-hundred in the First Test, and it said just as much for his temperament as his technique. In the same match, Matthew Elliott enhanced his reputation by making 85 and building a platform for the mammoth partnership between Blewett and Steve Waugh. But Bevan had a poor series with the bat, as did Matthew Hayden, who was dropped for the Ashes tour.

The bowling find of the series was Gillespie. He took 14 wickets, more than any bowler on either side; yet, had Reiffel been fit, he might not have played. Quicker than McGrath, Gillespie used a similar method, bowling from close to the stumps with a high action. He swung the ball away from the right-hander, and played his full part in the Port Elizabeth win with match figures of eight for 103. The home authorities mostly tried to prepare pitches for Donald and Co, but McGrath and Gillespie were the major beneficiaries. Warne's 11 wickets came at an average of 25.63, but he conceded barely two an over; his stock bowling in totally unsuitable conditions in the Second Test showed he is more than a great wrist-spinner, or even a great slow bowler. He is simply a great bowler.

The series was played in good spirit, despite some variable umpiring, particularly in the Third Test when neither Mervyn Kitchen nor Cyril Mitchley distinguished himself. Referee Raman Subba Row disciplined Ian Healy at the end of the game, in which Healy had become only the second wicket-keeper – following Rod Marsh – to claim 300 Test victims. He was suspended for the first two one-day internationals for dissent and throwing his bat after he was given out caught behind. On his return, he took over the captaincy from Taylor.

With their one-day success following their Test series win, Australia swept all before them prior to embarking on their tour of England while, for the first time since their return to Test cricket, South Africa's season ended with players and selectors under fire.

AUSTRALIAN TOURING PARTY

M. A. Taylor (New South Wales) (*captain*), I. A. Healy (Queensland) (*vice-captain*), M. G. Bevan (New South Wales), A. J. Bichel (Queensland), G. S. Blewett (South Australia), M. T. G. Elliott (Victoria), J. N. Gillespie (South Australia), M. L. Hayden (Queensland), J. L. Langer (Western Australia), G. D. McGrath (New South Wales), P. R. Reiffel (Victoria), S. K. Warne (Victoria), M. E. Waugh (New South Wales), S. R. Waugh (New South Wales).

Manager: C. J. Egar. *Coach:* G. R. Marsh.

A. C. Dale (Queensland), M. J. Di Venuto (Tasmania), A. C. Gilchrist (Western Australia), B. P. Julian (Western Australia) and S. G. Law (Queensland) joined the party for the one-day internationals, when Elliott, Hayden, Langer and McGrath went home.

AUSTRALIAN TOUR RESULTS

Test matches – Played 3: Won 2, Lost 1.
First-class matches – Played 6: Won 5, Lost 1.
Wins – South Africa (2), Western Province, Natal, Border.
Loss – South Africa.
One-day internationals – Played 7: Won 4, Lost 3.
Other non-first-class matches – Played 4: Won 4. *Wins* – N. F. Oppenheimer's XI, Boland, Transvaal Invitation XI, Eastern Province Invitation XI.

TEST MATCH AVERAGES

SOUTH AFRICA – BATTING

	T	I	NO	R	HS	100s	Avge	Ct
W. J. Cronje	3	5	1	204	79*	0	51.00	1
D. J. Richardson	3	5	2	124	72*	0	41.33	12
A. M. Bacher	2	4	0	161	96	0	40.25	1
B. M. McMillan	2	4	1	119	55	0	39.66	0
D. J. Cullinan	3	6	1	122	47	0	24.40	3
S. M. Pollock	2	4	1	66	35	0	22.00	0
G. Kirsten	3	6	0	82	43	0	13.66	1
L. Klusener	2	3	0	39	30	0	13.00	0
J. H. Kallis	3	5	0	49	39	0	9.80	0
A. A. Donald	3	5	0	45	21	0	9.00	0
P. R. Adams	2	4	1	21	15	0	7.00	3

Played in one Test: H. H. Gibbs 31, 7; A. C. Hudson 0, 31; J. N. Rhodes 22, 8; B. N. Schultz 2 (1 ct); P. L. Symcox 16.

* Signifies not out.

BOWLING

	O	M	R	W	BB	5W/i	Avge
B. N. Schultz	37	8	91	6	4-52	0	15.16
W. J. Cronje	45.1	16	94	4	2-21	0	23.50
B. M. McMillan	35	7	78	3	2-32	0	26.00
J. H. Kallis	58.4	16	134	5	3-29	0	26.80
S. M. Pollock	38	6	111	4	2-6	0	27.75
A. A. Donald	122	36	325	11	5-36	1	29.54
P. L. Symcox	42	9	111	3	2-49	0	37.00
L. Klusener	66.3	15	185	4	2-23	0	46.25
P. R. Adams	77	11	234	4	2-66	0	58.50

AUSTRALIA – BATTING

	T	I	NO	R	HS	100s	Avge	Ct
S. R. Waugh	3	5	1	313	160	1	78.25	3
G. S. Blewett	3	5	0	271	214	1	54.20	2
M. E. Waugh	3	5	0	209	116	1	41.80	3
M. T. G. Elliott . . .	3	5	0	182	85	0	36.40	2
M. G. Bevan	3	5	1	72	37*	0	18.00	0
M. A. Taylor	3	5	0	80	38	0	16.00	3
I. A. Healy	3	5	1	57	19	0	14.25	11
M. L. Hayden	3	5	0	64	40	0	12.80	4
S. K. Warne	3	5	0	42	18	0	8.40	3
J. N. Gillespie	3	4	3	7	6*	0	7.00	0
G. D. McGrath . . .	3	3	0	11	11	0	3.66	2

* Signifies not out.

BOWLING

	O	M	R	W	BB	5W/i	Avge
M. G. Bevan	62	10	176	9	4-32	0	19.55
J. N. Gillespie	103.4	37	287	14	5-54	1	20.50
G. D. McGrath . . .	111.4	38	289	13	6-86	1	22.23
S. K. Warne	133	47	282	11	4-43	0	25.63

Also bowled: G. S. Blewett 23.3–5–74–1; M. E. Waugh 8–1–38–1; S. R. Waugh 8.3–1–20–1.

Note: Matches in this section which were not first-class are signified by a dagger.

†At NFO Ground, Randjesfontein, February 13. Australians won by 19 runs. Toss: Australians. Australians 284 for seven dec. (M. T. G. Elliott 91, M. L. Hayden 60, S. R. Waugh retired out 72); N. F. Oppenheimer's XI 265 (N. D McKenzie 133).

At Cape Town, February 15, 16, 17. Australians won by 32 runs. Toss: Australians. Australians 439 for four dec. (M. L. Hayden 112, M. A. Taylor 85, M. T. G. Elliott 74, S. R. Waugh 69, G. S. Blewett 48 not out, J. L. Langer 31 not out) and 175 for six dec. (G. S. Blewett 86, M. T. G. Elliott 36; J. H. Kallis four for 46); Western Province 261 for five dec. (G. Kirsten 37, S. G. Koenig 45, J. H. Kallis 31, J. B. Commins 59 not out) and 321 (S. G. Koenig 38, H. H. Gibbs 80, J. B. Commins 51, H. D. Ackerman 37; A. J. Bichel five for 62, M. G. Bevan three for 113).

†At Paarl, February 18 (day/night). Australians won by 50 runs. Toss: Australians. Australians 319 for three (50 overs) (M. A. Taylor 56, M. E. Waugh retired out 101, M. G. Bevan 80 not out, J. L. Langer 57); Boland 269 (47.2 overs) (E. J. Ferreira 38, A. P. Kuiper 48, A. R. Wylie 34, Extras 44; P. R. Reiffel three for 40, G. S. Blewett three for 15).

At Durban, February 20, 21, 22. Australians won by eight wickets. Toss: Natal. Natal 335 (M. L. Bruyns 105, D. M. Benkenstein 103; J. N. Gillespie four for 71, M. G. Bevan three for 56) and 112 (E. L. R. Stewart 49 not out; M. G. Bevan four for 35); Australians 370 (M. T. G. Elliott 38, M. E. Waugh 124, M. G. Bevan 52, S. K. Warne 44; P. L. Symcox four for 117) and 81 for two (I. A. Healy 41 not out, M. T. G. Elliott 35 not out).

†At Soweto, February 25. Australians won by 79 runs. Toss: Australians. Australians 261 for seven (45 overs) (J. L. Langer 63, M. T. G. Elliott 69, M. G. Bevan 49, M. L. Hayden 47; A. J. Hall four for 49); Transvaal Invitation XI 182 (42 overs) (S. Ndima 35, C. E. Eksteen 42, E. W. Kidwell 30 not out; A. J. Bichel three for 21).

SOUTH AFRICA v AUSTRALIA

First Test Match

At Johannesburg, February 28, March 1, 2, 3, 4. Australia won by an innings and 196 runs. Toss: South Africa.

Australia began the series billed as Test cricket's unofficial championship by recording their second biggest victory in 60 Tests against South Africa, who had not lost by an innings since England won at Durban in 1964-65. The match will be remembered for a record-breaking stand between Steve Waugh and Greg Blewett, which spread across three days.

South Africa recalled Rhodes and Kallis, and preferred Hudson as an opener to Bacher; McMillan was unfit. With Reiffel also injured, Australia promoted Gillespie to share the new ball with McGrath, playing Bevan at No. 7 and Healy at No. 8, which theoretically left them a bowler short. But the quality of the bowlers they did have meant Australia were always in charge; 12 of the game's 13 sessions were one-way traffic.

McGrath brilliantly exploited all-too-familiar South African top-order weaknesses in an opening spell of 10–4–10–3 and South Africa slumped to 195 for eight. Only Cronje's 76 represented any worthwhile resistance – until Richardson enhanced his record as the patron saint of apparently lost causes. He hit an unbeaten 72 from 87 balls, including ten fours and a six, to steer his side to a respectable 302 – still at least 100 under par on a good pitch. Only when Richardson was shepherding Donald and Adams through partnerships of 58 and 49 did Australia seem to miss a third pace bowler. Healy backed up McGrath and Gillespie with five catches.

BATSMEN BATTING THROUGHOUT A FULL DAY IN A TEST

J. B. Hobbs and H. Sutcliffe (283-0)	day 3	E v A at Melbourne	1924-25
D. St E. Atkinson and C. C. Depeiza (187-6 to 494-6)	day 4	WI v A at Bridgetown	1954-55
V. Mankad and Pankaj Roy (234-0)	day 1	I v NZ at Madras	1955-56
C. C. Hunte and G. S. Sobers (147-1 to 504-1)	day 3	WI v P at Kingston	1957-58
*G. S. Sobers and F. M. M. Worrell (279-3 to 486-3)	day 5	WI v E at Bridgetown	1959-60
W. M. Lawry and R. B. Simpson (263-0)	day 1	A v WI at Bridgetown	1964-65
G. R. Viswanath and Yashpal Sharma (178-2 to 395-2)	day 2	I v E at Madras	1981-82
A. P. Gurusinha and A. Ranatunga (83-3 to 323-3)	day 5	SL v P at Colombo (PSS)	1985-86
G. R. Marsh and M. A. Taylor (301-0)	day 1	A v E at Nottingham	1989
S. R. Waugh and G. S. Blewett (191-4 to 479-4)	**day 3**	**A v SA at Johannesburg**	**1996-97**

* Sobers and Worrell also batted throughout the fourth day, when the final hour was lost to rain.

Opening Australia's innings next morning, Taylor was unlucky to play on against Pollock. Otherwise, the much vaunted South African pace attack made little impression on an unusually slow pitch, although Donald did bounce out Mark Waugh and the left-hander Elliott – whose elegant off-side play was reminiscent of David Gower – in three balls. That brought in Blewett to join Steve Waugh. Shortly afterwards, rain forced an early close, but next day they rewrote the record books, becoming only the tenth pair of Test batsmen to bat throughout a day. The previous duo watched from the dressing-room – their captain, Taylor, and coach, Geoff Marsh, who scored 301 on the first day of the Trent Bridge Test in 1989.

On that third, wicketless, day, Blewett scored a remorseless 153 and Waugh 123. Waugh's was his 12th hundred in 87 Tests, and Blewett's his third in 14, in which he had also made 99 and four other fifties. Waugh suffered leg cramps after tea but refused to go off, and that final session was worth 101 off 29 overs, following 93 and 94. Blewett's driving and pulling were a revelation, and his 214, in 519 minutes and 421 balls, with 34 fours, beat the previous highest Test score on the ground – Mike Atherton's unbeaten 185, 15 months earlier. Waugh scored 160, in 501 minutes and 366 balls, with 22 fours. When he fell, they had added 385, the second-biggest partnership for the fifth wicket in any Test and the best for any wicket against South Africa, surpassing the 370 by Bill Edrich and Denis Compton at Lord's in 1947.

Taylor's declaration gave his bowlers a minimum of 138 overs to take ten wickets, but they needed only half that. Kallis defended well for almost three hours, but the force was still with Steve Waugh. He ran Hudson out brilliantly and had Cronje caught down the leg side. After that, Warne and Bevan were unstoppable. The last seven wickets fell for 40, with Bevan taking the last four for two runs in 12 balls – two caught at short leg and two bowled. His quickish left-arm wrist-spin was as much a mystery to the batsmen as the wiles of Shane Warne; their combined match figures of 87.4–28–207–12 contrasted vividly with those of Adams, who took one for 163.

Disappointing crowds, amounting to less than 60,000, sat mostly in silence as their side was thrashed. Changes for the Second Test were inevitable.

Men of the Match: G. S. Blewett and S. R. Waugh. *Attendance:* 57,370.

Close of play: First day, South Africa 302; Second day, Australia 191-4 (S. R. Waugh 14*, G. S. Blewett 3*); Third day, Australia 479-4 (S. R. Waugh 137*, G. S. Blewett 156*); Fourth day, South Africa 99-4 (J. H. Kallis 29*, J. N. Rhodes 3*).

South Africa

A. C. Hudson c Healy b McGrath	0	– run out	31
G. Kirsten c Healy b McGrath	9	– b Warne	8
J. H. Kallis c M. E. Waugh b McGrath	6	– b Warne	39
D. J. Cullinan c Healy b McGrath	27	– c Healy b Warne	0
*W. J. Cronje c M. E. Waugh b Warne	76	– c Healy b S. R. Waugh	22
J. N. Rhodes c Healy b Gillespie	22	– lbw b Warne	8
S. M. Pollock c S. R. Waugh b Bevan	35	– not out	14
L. Klusener c Taylor b Bevan	9	– c Hayden b Bevan	0
†D. J. Richardson not out	72	– c Hayden b Bevan	2
A. A. Donald c Healy b Gillespie	21	– b Bevan	0
P. R. Adams lbw b Warne	15	– b Bevan	0
B 1, l-b 3, w 3, n-b 3	10	B 4, l-b 2	6

1/0 (1) 2/15 (3) 3/25 (2) 4/78 (4) 302 1/36 (2) 2/41 (1) 3/46 (4) 130
5/115 (6) 6/165 (7) 7/183 (8) 4/90 (5) 5/108 (6) 6/127 (3)
8/195 (5) 9/253 (10) 10/302 (11) 7/128 (8) 8/130 (9)
9/130 (10) 10/130 (11)

Bowling: First Innings—McGrath 26–8–77–4; Gillespie 17–6–66–2; Warne 27.4–9–68–2; Bevan 17–1–64–2; Blewett 4–0–23–0. *Second Innings*—McGrath 10–5–17–0; Gillespie 11.4–4–24–0; Warne 28–15–43–4; Bevan 15–3–32–4; S. R. Waugh 4–1–4–1; M. E. Waugh 1–0–4–0.

Australia

*M. A. Taylor b Pollock	16	S. K. Warne b Cronje ... 9
M. L. Hayden c Cullinan b Pollock	40	
M. T. G. Elliott c Adams b Donald	85	B 1, l-b 15, w 4, n-b 10 ... 30
M. E. Waugh c Richardson b Donald	26	
S. R. Waugh c Richardson b Kallis	160	1/33 (1) 2/128 (2) (8 wkts dec.) 628
G. S. Blewett c Adams b Klusener	214	3/169 (4) 4/174 (3)
M. G. Bevan not out	37	5/559 (5) 6/577 (6)
†I. A. Healy c Kirsten b Adams	11	7/613 (8) 8/628 (9)

J. N. Gillespie and G. D. McGrath did not bat.

Bowling: Donald 35–7–136–2; Pollock 32–3–105–2; Klusener 37–10–122–1; Kallis 21–4–54–1; Adams 52–7–163–1; Cronje 16.4–5–32–1.

Umpires: S. Venkataraghavan (India) and C. J. Mitchley. *Referee:* R. Subba Row (England).

At East London, March 7, 8. Australians won by an innings and 105 runs. Toss: Australians. Border 117 (J. N. Gillespie seven for 34) and 148 (M. V. Boucher 34, P. C. Strydom 55; A. J. Bichel three for 39, S. K. Warne three for one); Australians 370 for nine dec. (M. T. G. Elliott 41, M. E. Waugh 62, G. S. Blewett 112, I. A. Healy 35, P. R. Reiffel 40 not out).

†At Zwide, March 11. Australians won by 15 runs. Toss: Australians. Australians 243 for four (45 overs) (M. L. Hayden 68, J. L. Langer 56, M. G. Bevan 57 not out); Eastern Province Invitation XI 228 for eight (45 overs) (L. J. Koen 78; M. G. Bevan three for 39).

SOUTH AFRICA v AUSTRALIA

Second Test Match

At Port Elizabeth, March 14, 15, 16, 17. Australia won by two wickets. Toss: Australia.

Mark Waugh's magnificent fourth-innings 116 clinched a wildly fluctuating Test and, with it, the series – South Africa's first home defeat in six series since resuming Test cricket in 1992. Australia began and finished strongly, but for much of the match South Africa seemed bound to square the series. The key was the pitch, which had such a thick mat of grass that it looked like an Essex ground of the 1950s, Westcliff or Clacton maybe. It was automatic that Taylor would bowl.

Australia were unchanged, but South Africa dropped Hudson, Rhodes and Klusener and brought in Bacher, Gibbs and McMillan, now fit again. This meant three inexperienced batsmen in the top six, and they were swept aside by Gillespie's first five-wicket haul for his country. Bowling an impeccable line and length at high speed, he helped to reduce South Africa to 95 for seven. Then the Australians were convinced Richardson was caught behind before scoring, but he remained to add 85 for the eighth wicket with McMillan. A total of 209 was a good one on that pitch. Again, the lack of a third pace bowler hampered Australia, although Warne bowled beautifully in conditions entirely against wrist-spin.

The Australians lost Hayden on the first evening and their reply next day was a peculiar one. They somehow got through the morning with only three wickets down, despite inordinate movement off the greentop. They were helped when Pollock was forced out after tearing a hamstring. The turning point came when Bacher ran out Elliott for 23, the top score of the innings. That started a collapse of seven wickets for 44, and Australia trailed by 101. Donald bowled with fearsome hostility and frequently beat the bat, but Blewett was his only victim in the Test – a statistic almost as extraordinary as the fact that Healy took only one catch. The tourists complained because hessian mats were not used under the tarpaulin covers to reduce overnight sweating, as they were in the First Test. Raman Subba Row exonerated the ground authorities, though he later recommended to ICC that covering should be uniform in each country.

South Africa's openers extended their advantage to 184 as batting conditions improved, which put them almost out of sight. But on the third day, a red mist cost them all ten wickets for 85. Bacher was responsible for another run-out, but this time the victim was his partner, Kallis, and five more dismissals from rash strokes gave Australia a hope of victory. Only Cronje displayed the necessary obduracy, batting for 21 overs until he failed to read a googly from Bevan, who wrapped up the innings with Warne.

Australia needed 270. Though two and a half days remained, another 40 or 50 might have defeated them. But the chance was there and Mark Waugh took it. He later described it as his best innings in any cricket: it lasted nearly five and a half hours and included a six and 17 fours. Stern defence was twinned with innate elegance after he arrived in a crisis – 30 for two. Taylor failed again, and Hayden was comically run out when he and Elliott lunged for the same crease as Cronje burst between them to knock down the other wicket.

Waugh reached his fifty by the close, when Australia were an encouraging 145 for three, with his brother Steve digging in at the other end. But Kallis had Steve caught in the covers and, when Adams bowled Blewett, at 192 for five, South Africa were back in the match. The crowd, though disappointingly small, was close to delirium. Bevan came in to help Waugh to the brink of victory but, with 12 still wanted, Kallis dismissed Waugh and Cronje had Bevan caught at slip. Warne soon followed. Two wickets were left, five needed. But not for Healy the Hirst-Rhodes tactic of getting them in singles – he swung Cronje high over long leg for six.

Man of the Match: M. E. Waugh.   *Attendance:* 44,782.

Close of play: First day, Australia 10-1 (M. A. Taylor 7*, M. T. G. Elliott 1*); Second day, South Africa 83-0 (G. Kirsten 41*, A. M. Bacher 38*); Third day, Australia 145-3 (M. E. Waugh 54*, S. R. Waugh 11*).

South Africa

G. Kirsten c Hayden b Gillespie	0	– b Gillespie	43
A. M. Bacher c Elliott b McGrath	11	– c McGrath b Gillespie	49
J. H. Kallis c Blewett b Gillespie	0	– run out	2
D. J. Cullinan c Warne b Gillespie	34	– lbw b Gillespie	2
*W. J. Cronje b McGrath	0	– c Healy b Bevan	27
H. H. Gibbs b Gillespie	31	– c M. E. Waugh b McGrath	7
B. M. McMillan c S. R. Waugh b Warne	55	– lbw b Bevan	2
S. M. Pollock lbw b Gillespie	0	– lbw b Warne	17
†D. J. Richardson c McGrath b Warne	47	– not out	3
A. A. Donald c and b Warne	9	– c Warne b Bevan	7
P. R. Adams not out	5	– c Taylor b Warne	1
B 8, l-b 8, w 1	17	B 1, l-b 5, n-b 2	8

1/13 (1) 2/17 (3) 3/21 (2) 4/22 (5)   209   1/87 (1) 2/98 (3) 3/99 (2)   168
5/70 (4) 6/95 (6) 7/95 (8)   4/100 (4) 5/122 (6) 6/137 (7)
8/180 (9) 9/204 (7) 10/209 (10)   7/152 (5) 8/156 (8)
                                                                     9/167 (10) 10/168 (11)

Bowling: *First Innings*—McGrath 22–7–66–2; Gillespie 23–10–54–5; Warne 23.4–5–62–3; Blewett 4–2–3–0; Bevan 2–0–8–0. *Second Innings*—McGrath 13–3–43–1; Gillespie 18–4–49–3; S. R. Waugh 4.3–0–16–0; Blewett 7.3–3–16–0; Warne 17.4–7–20–2; Bevan 13–3–18–3.

Australia

M. L. Hayden c Cullinan b Pollock	0	– (2) run out	14
*M. A. Taylor c Richardson b Pollock	8	– (1) lbw b McMillan	13
M. T. G. Elliott run out	23	– c and b Adams	44
M. E. Waugh lbw b Cronje	20	– b Kallis	116
S. R. Waugh c Richardson b McMillan	20	– c Cronje b Kallis	18
G. S. Blewett b Donald	13	– b Adams	7
M. G. Bevan c Richardson b McMillan	0	– c Cullinan b Cronje	24
†I. A. Healy c Bacher b Cronje	5	– not out	10
S. K. Warne lbw b Adams	18	– lbw b Kallis	3
J. N. Gillespie not out	1	– not out	0
G. D. McGrath c Richardson b Kallis	0		
B 1, l-b 7, w 2, n-b 2	12	B 11, l-b 8, w 3	22

1/1 (1) 2/13 (2) 3/48 (4) 4/64 (3)   108   1/23 (1) 2/30 (2)   (8 wkts) 271
5/66 (5) 6/70 (7) 7/85 (8)   3/113 (3) 4/167 (5)
8/86 (6) 9/106 (9) 10/108 (11)   5/192 (6) 6/258 (4)
                                                                     7/258 (7) 8/265 (9)

Bowling: *First Innings*—Donald 23–13–18–1; Pollock 6–3–6–2; Adams 4–0–5–1; McMillan 14–2–32–2; Cronje 14–7–21–2; Kallis 9.4–2–18–1. *Second Innings*—Donald 26–6–75–0; McMillan 21–5–46–1; Cronje 9.3–1–36–1; Kallis 16–7–29–3; Adams 21–4–66–2.

Umpires: S. Venkataraghavan (India) and R. E. Koertzen. Referee: R. Subba Row (England).

SOUTH AFRICA v AUSTRALIA

Third Test Match

At Centurion, March 21, 22, 23, 24. South Africa won by eight wickets. Toss: South Africa.
Though they had won their last six series (excluding the one-off Test in India), the Australians had developed a habit of losing when ahead or already victorious, and it happened again here. They were not helped by their selectors: though the Test series was unchanged, it was decided to send home Elliott, Hayden and Langer before the one-day matches, and the untidy leaking of the news affected morale. Meanwhile, criticism needled the South African players sufficiently to get them on to top form. Schultz, Klusener and Symcox replaced Gibbs, Adams and the injured Pollock, which meant a gamble with an extra bowler. But Donald and Schultz made an outstanding new-ball pair, while Symcox strengthened the spin department.

The pitch looked green enough for Cronje to field first, but the faster bowlers got little help and they relied heavily on batting errors before tea. Hayden and Mark Waugh were bowled by straight deliveries, Elliott was caught hooking, and Taylor's longest innings of the series ended after three and a quarter hours when he chased a wide one and got an inside edge. Steve Waugh and Blewett – together again – put conditions into perspective by adding 80. But, when Blewett was caught behind off Symcox, the last six fell for 37. Schultz, whose last Test had been against England on the same ground 16 months earlier, marked his comeback with three in four overs, including Bevan and Warne, both lbw, in three balls. That followed a controversial decision – one of several by English umpire Merv Kitchen – that Steve Waugh had been caught down the leg side by Richardson. A little later, Richardson also caught Healy to give Donald his 150th wicket in his 33rd Test.

A total of 227 gave South Africa a chance to take control, and they did, but in topsy-turvy fashion. When Kirsten became Healy's 300th Test victim, McMillan, promoted to No. 3, batted solidly to put on 102 with the promising Bacher. By the end of the second day, Bacher had a patient 94 and had helped his side to a small lead with seven wickets standing – ample power to increase it against an attack desperately missing a third fast bowler. He became becalmed next morning, however, scoring only two from 63 balls before he was lbw to McGrath, who took three for 23 in a 14-over spell.

That left South Africa on 262 for seven, and Australia were back in the game. But their unbalanced attack could not prevent Cronje hitting 79, including nine fours and two sixes. He added 68 in 16 overs with Klusener and then 54 for the last two wickets, of which Cronje hit 42. Warne's return was 36–11–89–0, his worst in his last 49 Tests – he took nought for 107 from 22 overs in his third game, against Sri Lanka in 1992-93.

Although Australia trailed by 157 and soon slumped to 28 for three, the Waughs dug in and had taken the score to 94 ten minutes before the close. Then Mark Waugh dragged on an attempted expansive off-drive against Symcox. He had hit seven fours in his 42, but it was a poor dismissal. Donald was irresistible next day, yorking Blewett and Gillespie and getting Warne lbw. Only Steve Waugh held firm, despite a fearful battering in one Donald over. He finished unbeaten with a fighting 60. His match aggregate of 127 in his side's combined total of 412 was a model of concentration; he batted for seven hours and 20 minutes. But Australia went down to their first defeat of the tour on the fourth afternoon.

Healy threw his bat after being given out to a catch claimed by Richardson off Schultz; this earned him a two-match suspension, and highlighted several apparent umpiring errors.

Man of the Match: A. A. Donald.   *Man of the Series:* S. R. Waugh.

Attendance: 33,057.

Close of play: First day, Australia 227; Second day, South Africa 240-3 (A. M. Bacher 94*, P. L. Symcox 5*); Third day, Australia 96-4 (S. R. Waugh 24*, G. S. Blewett 0*).

Australia

*M. A. Taylor c Richardson b Klusener	38	– c Richardson b Donald	5
M. L. Hayden b Schultz	10	– lbw b Schultz	0
M. T. G. Elliott c Schultz b Donald	18	– b Donald	12
M. E. Waugh b Donald	5	– b Symcox	42
S. R. Waugh c Richardson b Schultz	67	– not out	60
G. S. Blewett c Richardson b Symcox	37	– b Donald	0
M. G. Bevan lbw b Schultz	6	– b Symcox	5
†I. A. Healy c Richardson b Donald	19	– c Richardson b Schultz	12
S. K. Warne lbw b Schultz	0	– lbw b Donald	12
J. N. Gillespie not out	6	– b Donald	0
G. D. McGrath b Klusener	0	– b Klusener	11
B 1, l-b 4, w 7, n-b 9	21	B 2, l-b 6, w 4, n-b 14	26

1/23 (2) 2/60 (3) 3/72 (4) 4/110 (1)   227
5/190 (6) 6/197 (5) 7/212 (7)
8/212 (9) 9/226 (8) 10/227 (11)

1/5 (2) 2/10 (1) 3/28 (3)   185
4/94 (4) 5/99 (6) 6/108 (7)
7/131 (8) 8/164 (9)
9/164 (10) 10/185 (11)

Bowling: *First Innings*—Donald 20–5–60–3; Schultz 20–4–52–4; Cronje 5–3–5–0; Klusener 14.5–4–23–2; Symcox 23–4–62–1; Kallis 7–2–20–0. *Second Innings*—Donald 18–5–36–5; Schultz 17–4–39–2; Klusener 14.4–1–40–1; Kallis 5–1–13–0; Symcox 19–5–49–2.

South Africa

G. Kirsten c Healy b McGrath	16	– c Taylor b Blewett	6
A. M. Bacher lbw b McGrath	96	– c Elliott b Gillespie	5
B. M. McMillan b Hayden b M. E. Waugh	55	– not out	7
D. J. Cullinan b McGrath	47	– not out	12
P. L. Symcox c Blewett b Gillespie	16		
J. H. Kallis c S. R. Waugh b McGrath	2		
*W. J. Cronje not out	79		
†D. J. Richardson b McGrath	0		
L. Klusener b Gillespie	30		
A. A. Donald c Healy b Gillespie	8		
B. N. Schultz c Healy b McGrath	2		
B 11, l-b 16, w 1, n-b 5	33	W 1, n-b 1	2

1/26 (1) 2/128 (3) 3/229 (4) 4/252 (5)   384   1/11 (2) 2/15 (1)   (2 wkts) 32
5/255 (6) 6/262 (2) 7/262 (8)
8/330 (9) 9/367 (10) 10/384 (11)

Bowling: *First Innings*—McGrath 40.4–15–86–6; Gillespie 31–13–75–3; Blewett 5–0–19–0; Warne 36–11–89–0; Bevan 15–3–54–0; M. E. Waugh 7–1–34–1. *Second Innings*—Gillespie 3.4–0–19–1; Blewett 3–0–13–1.

Umpires: M. J. Kitchen (England) and C. J. Mitchley. Referee: R. Subba Row (England).

†SOUTH AFRICA v AUSTRALIA

First One-Day International

At East London, March 29. South Africa won by six wickets. Toss: South Africa. International debuts: A. C. Dale, M. J. Di Venuto.

Witless cricket by Australia at a crucial stage wrecked an innings which should have exceeded 250. Law and Waugh scored 50 apiece to take them to 129 for two, but Law's dismissal was quickly followed by the run-outs of Waugh, Blewett and Gilchrist, all within ten overs. Bevan scored 51 not out off 60 balls, but a target of 224 never extended South Africa; they strolled home by six wickets with three overs to spare. Kallis and Cullinan put on 122 in 23 overs, and Cullinan finished unbeaten on 85.

Man of the Match: D. J. Cullinan.   *Attendance:* 14,742.

Australia

*M. A. Taylor c Rhodes b Pollock	7	P. R. Reiffel b Klusener	1
M. J. Di Venuto c Cullinan b Kallis	23	J. N. Gillespie c Cullinan b Klusener	0
S. G. Law c Kallis b Symcox	50	A. C. Dale not out	15
S. R. Waugh run out	50	L-b 1, w 6	7
G. S. Blewett run out	14		
M. G. Bevan not out	51	1/26 2/32 3/129 (9 wkts, 50 overs) 223	
†A. C. Gilchrist run out	1	4/134 5/163 6/169	
S. K. Warne c Cullinan b Donald	4	7/176 8/178 9/178	

Bowling: Pollock 10–1–36–1; Kallis 8–0–42–1; Donald 10–0–37–1; Klusener 6–1–29–2; Symcox 10–0–53–1; Cronje 6–0–25–0.

South Africa

A. M. Bacher c Warne b Reiffel	27	J. N. Rhodes not out	24
H. H. Gibbs c Gilchrist b Dale	10	B 4, l-b 7, w 5, n-b 2	18
J. H. Kallis st Gilchrist b Warne	63		
L. Klusener b Warne	0	1/31 2/48 (4 wkts, 47 overs) 227	
D. J. Cullinan not out	85	3/50 4/172	

*W. J. Cronje, S. M. Pollock, †D. J. Richardson, P. L. Symcox and A. A. Donald did not bat.

Bowling: Reiffel 10–1–44–1; Dale 10–0–55–1; Warne 10–0–36–2; Gillespie 7–0–36–0; Bevan 10–0–45–0.

Umpires: C. J. Mitchley and D. L. Orchard.

†SOUTH AFRICA v AUSTRALIA

Second One-Day International

At Port Elizabeth, March 31. Australia won by seven wickets. Toss: Australia. International debut: L. J. Koen.

A dazzling 115 off 126 balls by Mark Waugh – his tenth hundred in one-day internationals – and a 52-ball fifty from his brother Steve squared the series with five overs to spare. They shared an unbroken partnership of 107. Steady bowling from Reiffel and Dale – who took the first three wickets for five runs – reduced South Africa to 16 for three before a century stand between Kallis and Rhodes. Only two other batsmen managed double figures. In his final appearance of a worrying tour, Taylor scored 17 from 44 balls. But Mark Waugh fluently reached his hundred with successive sixes – he hit three in all, with eight fours. Australia's victory was only their sixth in 19 one-day games since their World Cup final defeat 12 months earlier.

Man of the Match: M. E. Waugh.   *Attendance:* 15,648.

South Africa

A. M. Bacher c Bevan b Dale	3	†D. J. Richardson run out		1
L. J. Koen c M. E. Waugh b Dale	0	P. L. Symcox not out		0
J. H. Kallis b Gillespie	82			
D. J. Cullinan b Dale	0	B 1, l-b 4, w 3, n-b 3		11
J. N. Rhodes c Reiffel b Bevan	57			
*W. J. Cronje b Gillespie	31	1/2 2/4 3/16	(8 wkts, 50 overs)	221
S. M. Pollock c Dale b Warne	9	4/120 5/181 6/183		
L. Klusener not out	27	7/212 8/215		

A. A. Donald did not bat.

Bowling: Reiffel 9–0–33–0; Dale 7–3–18–3; Blewett 10–1–42–0; Gillespie 10–0–51–2; Warne 6–0–39–1; Bevan 8–0–33–1.

Australia

M. E. Waugh not out	115	S. R. Waugh not out	50
*M. A. Taylor c Cullinan b Donald	17	L-b 2, w 2, n-b 3	7
S. G. Law c Rhodes b Symcox	33		
S. K. Warne lbw b Symcox	0	1/47 2/115 3/115 (3 wkts, 45 overs)	222

G. S. Blewett, M. G. Bevan, †A. C. Gilchrist, P. R. Reiffel, J. N. Gillespie and A. C. Dale did not bat.

Bowling: Pollock 8–0–39–0; Kallis 5–0–21–0; Donald 9–1–22–1; Cronje 5–0–25–0; Symcox 10–0–65–2; Klusener 8–1–48–0.

Umpires: R. E. Koertzen and C. J. Mitchley.

†SOUTH AFRICA v AUSTRALIA

Third One-Day International

At Cape Town, April 2 (day/night). South Africa won by 46 runs. Toss: Australia.

South Africa regained their advantage, thanks to a magnificent innings from Rhodes – and a hand injury that prevented Mark Waugh from batting. Australian captain Taylor stepped down, and Healy took over after completing a two-match suspension. Another economical opening spell from Dale, backed up by Gillespie, restricted South Africa to 106 for five after 29 overs, but Rhodes improvised 83 off 78 balls. He received hard-hitting support from Pollock and Bryson as Warne's last two overs went for 29. A target of 246 was too much for Australia's depleted batting order, and Bevan, scoring 82 off 104 balls, offered the only resistance.

Man of the Match: J. N. Rhodes.   *Attendance:* 21,188.

South Africa

L. J. Koen c Di Venuto b Dale	22	†D. J. Richardson run out	4
H. H. Gibbs b Gillespie	28	R. E. Bryson not out	17
J. H. Kallis b Warne	23		
D. J. Cullinan run out	12	L-b 11, w 2, n-b 1	14
J. N. Rhodes not out	83		
*W. J. Cronje b Blewett	3	1/52 2/53 3/80 (8 wkts, 50 overs) 245	
D. N. Crookes c Healy b Gillespie	18	4/101 5/106 6/176	
S. M. Pollock lbw b Warne	21	7/216 8/222	

A. A. Donald did not bat.

Bowling: Reiffel 10–0–47–0; Dale 10–1–26–1; Gillespie 10–1–39–2; Warne 10–0–64–2; Blewett 6–0–30–1; Bevan 4–0–28–0.

Australia

G. S. Blewett b Pollock	6	A. C. Dale not out	12
M. J. Di Venuto run out	13	J. N. Gillespie c Gibbs b Donald	17
S. G. Law c Richardson b Bryson	4	M. E. Waugh absent hurt	
S. R. Waugh b Bryson	0	L-b 4, w 6, n-b 1	11
M. G. Bevan c Kallis b Pollock	82		
*†I. A. Healy c and b Crookes	25	1/14 2/25 3/25 (44.5 overs) 199	
S. K. Warne run out	23	4/25 5/94 6/136	
P. R. Reiffel run out	6	7/157 8/170 9/199	

Bowling: Pollock 8–0–35–2; Bryson 9–0–34–2; Donald 7.5–1–25–1; Kallis 6–0–30–0; Crookes 10–0–42–1; Cronje 4–0–29–0.

Umpires: R. E. Koertzen and D. L. Orchard.

†SOUTH AFRICA v AUSTRALIA

Fourth One-Day International

At Durban, April 5 (day/night). Australia won by 15 runs. Toss: Australia.

Australia squared the series at 2-2 in the penultimate over. They suffered two more run-outs, bringing their total to eight in four matches, and were 83 for five halfway through their innings. Even that owed everything to Blewett, but Gilchrist carried through the recovery, with 77 off 88 balls against some quality pace bowling. Dale's accurate opening spell was his best yet and South Africa subsided from 81 for one to 143 for eight as Bichel struck three times. Pollock kept the target in sight with 41 off 37 balls, but lost the strike and ran out of partners.

Man of the Match: S. M. Pollock.   *Attendance:* 19,524.

Australia

M. J. Di Venuto run out	14	A. J. Bichel lbw b Pollock	17
G. S. Blewett c Crookes b Bryson	53	A. C. Dale not out	10
S. G. Law c Kallis b Pollock	0	J. N. Gillespie not out	5
S. R. Waugh c Crookes b Donald	1	L-b 2, n-b 1	3
M. G. Bevan run out	0		
A. C. Gilchrist c Cronje b Pollock	77	1/30 2/40 3/48 (9 wkts, 50 overs) 211	
*†I. A. Healy c Richardson b Pollock	19	4/50 5/83 6/129	
S. K. Warne b Bryson	12	7/153 8/195 9/198	

Bowling: Pollock 10–1–33–4; Bryson 10–0–47–2; Donald 10–0–37–1; Kallis 7–0–34–0; Crookes 10–0–40–0; Cronje 3–0–18–0.

South Africa

A. M. Bacher lbw b Warne	45
H. H. Gibbs c Waugh b Dale	0
D. J. Cullinan c and b Warne	38
J. H. Kallis run out	1
J. N. Rhodes b Gillespie	1
*W. J. Cronje b Bichel	28
D. N. Crookes b Bichel	17
S. M. Pollock not out	41

†D. J. Richardson lbw b Bichel	0
R. E. Bryson c Warne b Blewett	9
A. A. Donald run out	6
L-b 6, w 4	10
	—
(48.1 overs)	196

1/1 2/81 3/88
4/89 5/89 6/126
7/143 8/143 9/165

Bowling: Dale 10-2-22-1; Bichel 10-0-43-3; Gillespie 9-3-30-1; Law 3-0-16-0; Warne 8.1-1-36-2; Waugh 5-0-25-0; Blewett 3-0-18-1.

Umpires: W. A. Diedricks and D. L. Orchard.

†SOUTH AFRICA v AUSTRALIA

Fifth One-Day International

At Johannesburg, April 8 (day/night). Australia won by eight runs. Toss: Australia.

Di Venuto, one of the players flown in for the one-day internationals, set up Australia with a forceful 89; he hit 11 fours. With Donald conceding 67 in his ten overs, the tourists got to 258. In reply, Cullinan and Kallis scored fifties to redeem a poor start of 31 for three, while Cronje and Pollock, with brisk forties, threatened Australia's hold. Towards the end, Warne had to grip a ball made slippery by dew, but masterly control steered his side home in another tight finish, to take the lead for the first time in the series.

Man of the Match: M. J. Di Venuto.   *Attendance:* 26,766.

Australia

G. S. Blewett c Richardson b Cronje	36
M. J. Di Venuto lbw b Donald	89
S. G. Law c Crookes b Cronje	10
J. N. Gillespie c Gibbs b Donald	26
S. R. Waugh b Bryson	20
M. G. Bevan c Cullinan b Donald	32
A. C. Gilchrist b Pollock	26

*†I. A. Healy not out	3
S. K. Warne not out	6
B 1, l-b 6, w 1, n-b 2	10
	—
(7 wkts, 50 overs)	258

A. J. Bichel and A. C. Dale did not bat.

1/93 2/109 3/160
4/167 5/202
6/244 7/248

Bowling: Pollock 10-1-48-1; Bryson 9-0-47-1; Donald 10-0-67-3; Kallis 1-0-10-0; Crookes 10-0-37-0; Cronje 10-1-42-2.

South Africa

A. M. Bacher c Waugh b Bichel	6
H. H. Gibbs lbw b Dale	22
D. N. Crookes run out	0
D. J. Cullinan b Blewett	53
J. H. Kallis c Waugh b Gillespie	55
J. N. Rhodes c Law b Gillespie	10
*W. J. Cronje not out	40
S. M. Pollock c Law b Warne	40

†D. J. Richardson b Bichel	8
R. E. Bryson not out	4
L-b 6, w 4, n-b 2	12
	—
(8 wkts, 50 overs)	250

A. A. Donald did not bat.

1/27 2/31 3/31
4/132 5/149 6/154
7/227 8/240

Bowling: Dale 10-1-40-1; Bichel 10-0-55-2; Warne 10-0-45-1; Gillespie 10-0-46-2; Bevan 3-0-22-0; Blewett 7-0-36-1.

Umpires: D. F. Becker and S. B. Lambson.

†SOUTH AFRICA v AUSTRALIA

Sixth One-Day International

At Centurion, April 10 (day/night). Australia won by five wickets. Toss: South Africa.

Australia clinched the series 4-2 in an astonishing game that produced 571 runs from 99 overs. The second innings, in which Bevan scored his maiden hundred for Australia while he and Steve Waugh put on 189, an Australian fourth-wicket record, in 28 overs, was played in heavy dew which made conditions farcical. Bowlers could not grip the sopping wet ball properly, and fielders slithered on the outfield. April is too late for floodlit games on the Highveld. Cronje had won the toss but gambled that his bowlers could defend a big score. He himself contributed a run-a-ball 80, and put on 149 with Cullinan. Pollock provided another late boost and a total of 284 seemed fireproof when the tourists lost three wickets reaching 58. Then came the devastating stand between Bevan and Steve Waugh, who did some frantic running to make up for a low boundary count. Their combined 192 runs came off 197 balls, but included only 14 fours and two sixes.

Man of the Match: M. G. Bevan.   *Attendance:* 15,735.

South Africa

A. M. Bacher b Dale	15	D. N. Crookes not out		4
H. H. Gibbs c Healy b Gillespie	33	†D. J. Richardson not out		0
*W. J. Cronje run out	80	L-b 12, w 4, n-b 1		17
D. J. Cullinan c M. E. Waugh b Warne	89			
J. H. Kallis st Healy b Warne	3	1/52 2/77 3/226	(7 wkts, 50 overs)	284
J. N. Rhodes run out	10	4/232 5/232		
S. M. Pollock c Dale b Bichel	33	6/261 7/283		

R. E. Bryson and A. A. Donald did not bat.

Bowling: Dale 10-0-44-1; Bichel 9-0-50-1; Warne 10-1-52-2; Gillespie 9-0-45-1; Blewett 5-0-41-0; Bevan 7-0-40-0.

Australia

M. E. Waugh c Rhodes b Pollock	0	*†I. A. Healy not out		9
G. S. Blewett c Crookes b Pollock	21			
S. G. Law b Cronje	31	L-b 5, w 7, n-b 2		14
S. R. Waugh lbw b Pollock	89			
M. G. Bevan lbw b Bryson	103	1/0 2/36 3/58	(5 wkts, 49 overs)	287
A. C. Gilchrist not out	20	4/247 5/262		

S. K. Warne, A. J. Bichel, A. C. Dale and J. N. Gillespie did not bat.

Bowling: Pollock 10-0-40-3; Bryson 10-0-63-1; Donald 10-1-59-0; Cronje 7-0-46-1; Crookes 6-0-37-0; Kallis 6-0-37-0.

Umpires: D. F. Becker and S. B. Lambson.

†SOUTH AFRICA v AUSTRALIA

Seventh One-Day International

At Bloemfontein, April 13. South Africa won by 109 runs. Toss: Australia.

As in the Tests, Australia relaxed after winning the series, while South Africa, desperate to restore lost reputations, pulled off a conclusive win. They reversed a decision to rest Donald, while Australia gave several regulars a day off, allowing Steve Waugh to captain the team for the first time. South Africa responded with their biggest total against Australia – 310 for six, helped by some loose bowling. Klusener made 92 as an opener and put on 109 with Cronje, who hit six fours and three sixes; then Cullinan scored 57 off 39 balls. Australia lost their top four for 52 and only captain Waugh did himself justice, with a superb 91 off 79 balls. He was last out as South Africa won in just 37 overs.

Man of the Match: L. Klusener.   *Man of the Series:* S. M. Pollock.
Attendance: 14,084.

South Africa

L. Klusener c Blewett b Julian 92	J. N. Rhodes c Blewett b Bichel 0
H. H. Gibbs c Gilchrist b Julian 29	S. M. Pollock not out................. 8
P. L. Symcox run out 26	L-b 4, w 10, n-b 5 19
*W. J. Cronje c Dale b Law 69	
D. J. Cullinan not out................. 57	1/61 2/109 3/218 (6 wkts, 50 overs) 310
J. H. Kallis b Bichel................. 10	4/246 5/290 6/290

D. N. Crookes, †D. J. Richardson and A. A. Donald did not bat.

Bowling: Dale 8–1–70–0; Reiffel 10–0–46–0; Julian 8–0–53–2; Bevan 5–0–35–0; Bichel 10–0–50–2; M. E. Waugh 3.3–0–16–0; Law 5.3–0–36–1.

Australia

M. J. Di Venuto b Klusener 11	P. R. Reiffel c Richardson b Donald 10
M. E. Waugh c Richardson b Klusener .. 3	A. J. Bichel b Klusener 0
B. P. Julian b Pollock................ 0	A. C. Dale not out 1
S. G. Law c Klusener b Cronje 17	L-b 7, w 8, n-b 3 18
*S. R. Waugh b Donald 91	
M. G. Bevan c Klusener b Symcox 29	1/17 2/18 3/18 (37 overs) 201
G. S. Blewett c Crookes b Kallis 18	4/52 5/100 6/139
†A. C. Gilchrist b Symcox............. 3	7/153 8/186 9/193

Bowling: Pollock 8–1–26–1; Klusener 7–1–41–3; Cronje 2–0–9–1; Donald 7–0–37–2; Symcox 9–0–60–2; Kallis 4–0–21–1.

Umpires: W. A. Diedricks and R. E. Koertzen.   Series referee: R. Subba Row (England).

THE SRI LANKANS IN NEW ZEALAND, 1996-97

By PETER BIDWELL

The flak surrounding Lee Germon's sacking as New Zealand captain quickly disappeared in the wake of the team's successes against Sri Lanka in March 1997. Under Germon's Canterbury colleague, Stephen Fleming, New Zealand recovered from a disappointing series against England to beat Sri Lanka in both Tests, and squared the one-day internationals 1-1.

Germon had been dismissed a couple of hours after New Zealand beat England in their final one-day international. He had no idea of his fate when he spoke of the forthcoming Sri Lankan series at the closing ceremony, leading to allegations of plots and poor communication. But Germon had come under mounting pressure through the summer and, when he was injured just before the last Test against England, Fleming demonstrated a refreshing attitude and inventiveness as his stand-in. Though he lost, the selectors and coach Steve Rixon took notice and gave him the job full-time against Sri Lanka.

As one of New Zealand's best batsmen, Fleming commanded instant respect within the team and could hardly have dared ask for a better start, with two wins in his first three Tests at the helm – Germon won only one of his 12 Tests, and lost five. Fleming had been looked on as a future Test captain since he scored 92 on debut against India, just before his 21st birthday. When he was officially elevated, aged 23, he had already played 25 Tests and 60 one-day internationals (Germon had taken over in his debut Test, after one limited-overs game) and he talked confidently about a ten-year reign.

Fleming was lucky to be starting out against Sri Lanka. Though they had won their last two series against New Zealand, who had not beaten them in a Test since 1983-84, they were lacking recent hard matchplay. Rain hampered their preparations, washing out their only first-class warm-up match. They also gave the impression that they had no particular appetite for Test cricket, preferring the shorter game in which they had done so well. This view was backed up by their new coach, Australian Bruce Yardley. Yardley had some way to go to fulfil the Sri Lankan board's dream of making their team the leading Test power by 2000.

Sri Lanka missed the experience and stability of Asanka Gurusinha, who withdrew after being ordered to return from his club in Melbourne for training. Batting hero Aravinda de Silva had damaged his ankle during a brilliant stint for Auckland in New Zealand's limited-overs Shell Cup, and struggled on his return; he never reached double figures in the Tests.

The tourists introduced a promising newcomer in tall left-arm seamer Nuwan Zoysa, aged 18, who could obtain sharp bounce and move the ball into and away from the right-hander. Zoysa had been playing school matches a few months earlier when captain Arjuna Ranatunga spotted him. Yardley likened him to Bruce Reid, his former Western Australian team-mate, but there was also a similarity to Wasim Akram. Sri Lanka's leading Test bowler, off-spinner Muttiah Muralitharan, seemed to have lost confidence, perhaps feeling New Zealand was too close to Australia where his action had been questioned the previous season, and he did not make the impact expected.

New Zealand's Australian coach, Steve Rixon, took time to get to grips with players lacking the ability and bubbling confidence he seemed to expect. By the end of the summer, however, his team looked in better shape. Bryan Young set up New Zealand's first Test win over Sri Lanka with an unbeaten 267. Too often he had been guilty of failing to build on promising starts, but this time he maintained his dominance for five sessions. Blair Pocock and Matt Horne consolidated their places, while Germon's departure enabled Adam Parore to re-establish himself as a wicket-keeper/batsman. Above all, 18-year-old left-arm spinner Daniel Vettori maintained the extraordinary form he showed against England, and took 11 more wickets at 20.09.

SRI LANKAN TOURING PARTY

A. Ranatunga (Sinhalese SC) (*captain*), P. A. de Silva (Nondescripts CC) (*vice-captain*), M. S. Atapattu (Sinhalese SC), K. S. C. de Silva (Nondescripts CC), H. D. P. K. Dharmasena (Bloomfield C and AC), S. T. Jayasuriya (Bloomfield C and AC), R. S. Kaluwitharana (Colts CC), R. S. Mahanama (Bloomfield C and AC), M. Muralitharan (Tamil Union), K. R. Pushpakumara (Nondescripts CC), D. P. Samaraweera (Colts CC), H. P. Tillekeratne (Nondescripts CC), W. P. U. J. C. Vaas (Colts CC), G. P. Wickremasinghe (Sinhalese SC), D. N. T. Zoysa (Sinhalese SC).

A. P. Gurusinha (Sinhalese SC) withdrew before the start of the tour and was replaced by Samaraweera, who was later injured, as was Wickremasinghe. They were replaced by U. D. U. Chandana (Tamil Union) and R. S. Kalpage (Bloomfield C and AC).

Manager: L. R. D. Mendis. *Coach:* B. Yardley.

SRI LANKAN TOUR RESULTS

Test matches – Played 2. Lost 2.
One-day internationals – Played 2. Won 1. Lost 1. Abandoned 1.
Other first-class match – Abandoned v New Zealand A.
Other non-first-class matches – Played 2. Won 1. Drawn 1. *Win* – Central Districts. *Draw* – Northern Districts.

Note: Matches in this section which were not first-class are signified by a dagger.

†At Taupo, February 27, 28. Drawn. Toss: Northern Districts. Northern Districts 116 (M. N. Hart 42; W. P. U. J. C. Vaas six for 22) and 161 for four (M. E. Parlane 65, A. P. O'Dowd 34 not out; M. Muralitharan four for 42); Sri Lankans 256 (R. S. Mahanama 106 retired out, H. P. Tillekeratne 90; G. E. Bradburn six for 22).

Vaas finished off Northern Districts' first innings with a hat-trick. The Sri Lankans lost their last six wickets for four runs, Bradburn claiming five for one.

At Gisborne, March 2, 3, 4. New Zealand A v Sri Lankans. Abandoned.

NEW ZEALAND v SRI LANKA

First Test Match

At Dunedin, March 7, 8, 9, 10. New Zealand won by an innings and 36 runs. Toss: Sri Lanka. Test debut: D. N. T. Zoysa.

New Zealand completed their first home Test win for three years through a remarkable innings from Young backed up by the right-arm swing of Doull. Young scored an unbeaten 267, the seventh double-hundred for New Zealand, and second only to Martin Crowe's 299, also against Sri Lanka, at Wellington in 1990-91. Likewise, New Zealand's total of 586 for seven had been beaten only by their 671 for four in the same match.

Young's one previous Test century, 120 against Pakistan in 1993-94, had set up his team's last home victory. He cut and drove with hardly a blemish, and batted right through the innings for 605 minutes, facing 421 balls and striking 37 fours. He shared century partnerships with Horne and Cairns, while his captain, Fleming, hit 51 in 59 balls out of a stand of 76.

Sri Lanka had put New Zealand in, only to see them bat until tea on the second day. On the first morning, the debutant Zoysa forced several false shots without reward. He deserved better figures than one for 112: his fellow left-armer, Vaas, was far luckier in picking up four. Young was warned of the declaration an hour before it came, and was happy to sacrifice further personal milestones for the team cause. It soon paid off, when Doull and Davis reduced Sri Lanka to 78 for four by stumps. Ranatunga was out first thing next morning and a promising sixth-wicket stand of 56 ended when a ball from Patel stuck between Kaluwitharana's glove and pad, and Fleming raced in to claim a catch before it hit the ground. Umpire Robinson gave it out and referee Burge initially confirmed that the ball was still in play. This was the reverse of the decision made by umpire Hair in similar circumstances in the Christchurch Test three weeks earlier. Burge, who was the referee then as well, later implied that the first ruling had been correct, saying that, in future, he thought such a ball should be considered dead. He called for Law 23 to be reviewed.

Despite an unbeaten 55 from Tillekeratne and some later hitting from Wickremasinghe, Sri Lanka were dismissed for a disappointing 222 and followed on 364 behind. They improved the second time, thanks to a century from Kaluwitharana at No. 7. He scored 103 from as many balls, hitting 13 fours and two sixes. It was still an exceptionally good pitch, and he and Vaas regained some pride in adding 137 for the seventh wicket in 109 minutes.

But, after they had gone, Doull finished off the game with more than a day to spare. Doull's match figures were eight for 140; in the first innings, he had taken his third five-wicket bag of the season, following those against Pakistan and England. He had given New Zealand the bowling edge, but the match award deservedly went to Young, who had been on the pitch throughout.

Man of the Match: B. A. Young.

Close of play: First day, New Zealand 343-4 (B. A. Young 154*, D. L. Vettori 1*); Second day, Sri Lanka 78-4 (A. Ranatunga 13*, H. P. Tillekeratne 7*); Third day, Sri Lanka 37-0 (S. T. Jayasuriya 20*, R. S. Mahanama 15*).

New Zealand

B. A. Young not out	267	D. N. Patel not out 30
B. A. Pocock c Mahanama b Vaas 18		
M. J. Horne c Mahanama b Ranatunga... 66		L-b 14, w 2, n-b 21 37
*S. P. Fleming c Zoysa b Wickremasinghe 51		
N. J. Astle b Vaas 27		1/55 (2) 2/195 (3) (7 wkts dec.) 586
D. L. Vettori c Mahanama b Vaas 1		3/271 (4) 4/337 (5)
C. L. Cairns c Mahanama b Zoysa 70		5/343 (6) 6/466 (7)
†A. C. Parore c Wickremasinghe b Vaas . 19		7/512 (8)

S. B. Doull and H. T. Davis did not bat.

Bowling: Vaas 35-6-144-4; Zoysa 40-6-112-1; Wickremasinghe 25-4-117-1; Muralitharan 33-6-136-0; Ranatunga 5-0-29-1; Jayasuriya 8-0-34-0.

Sri Lanka

S. T. Jayasuriya b Doull	0	– c Parore b Doull	50
R. S. Mahanama lbw b Doull	26	– b Doull	21
M. S. Atapattu lbw b Doull	25	– b Patel	22
P. A. de Silva c Patel b Davis	3	– lbw b Astle	0
*A. Ranatunga c Young b Doull	14	– c Horne b Vettori	13
H. P. Tillekeratne not out	55	– run out	8
†R. S. Kaluwitharana c Fleming b Patel	43	– c and b Vettori	103
W. P. U. J. C. Vaas c Horne b Patel	2	– c and b Davis	57
G. P. Wickremasinghe c Parore b Davis	43	– c Doull b Astle	0
D. N. T. Zoysa c Young b Davis	0	– not out	16
M. Muralitharan c Cairns b Doull	0	– c and b Doull	26
L-b 10, w 1	11	L-b 9, n-b 3	12

1/4 (1) 2/55 (3) 3/58 (2) 4/58 (4)   222   1/49 (2) 2/82 (1) 3/85 (4)   328
5/79 (5) 6/135 (7) 7/141 (8)   4/99 (3) 5/115 (5) 6/133 (6)
8/214 (9) 9/215 (10) 10/222 (11)   7/270 (7) 8/271 (9)
                                                  9/285 (8) 10/328 (11)

Bowling: *First Innings*—Doull 21.2–5–58–5; Davis 19–6–34–3; Horne 6–5–4–0; Astle 3–0–11–0; Patel 22–4–67–2; Vettori 14–5–38–0. *Second Innings*—Doull 20.3–5–82–3; Davis 22–2–79–1; Horne 4–2–18–0; Astle 15–3–51–2; Patel 10–3–36–1; Vettori 15–3–53–2.

Umpires: I. D. Robinson (Zimbabwe) and C. E. King.   Referee: P. J. Burge (Australia).

NEW ZEALAND v SRI LANKA

Second Test Match

At Hamilton, March 14, 15, 16, 17. New Zealand won by 120 runs. Toss: New Zealand. Test debut: K. S. C. de Silva.

Teenage left-arm spinner Daniel Vettori took nine for 130 in his fourth Test to give New Zealand their first series win since their visit to Zimbabwe in 1992-93. It was the first time they had won consecutive Tests since they beat Pakistan twice in 1984-85.

A slow pitch of uneven bounce was below Test standard, and was dug up a few weeks later. Pocock anchored New Zealand's otherwise undistinguished first effort of 222 with 85, an innings whose significance grew clearer as the game developed. It was to be the highest score of the match and further enhanced Pocock's right to the opener's spot. None of his colleagues reached 30 on that first day, and the Sri Lankans struggled even more. Their coach, Bruce Yardley, criticised their lack of patience and shot selection; only Mahanama displayed the necessary commitment, batting 137 minutes for 45. The once-erratic Davis continued his rehabilitation, taking five in an innings for the first time, but Vettori was just behind him with four for 46, his best figures yet, and Sri Lanka conceded a lead of 52.

New Zealand effectively batted them out of the match by extending that to 325, thanks to half-centuries from Young, Fleming and Astle. When off-spinner Muralitharan bowled Fleming, it was his 100th Test wicket – he was the first Sri Lankan to achieve the landmark, in his 27th Test. But, although he picked up six wickets here, he did not seem to bowl with the confidence to put the home batsmen, often suspect against quality spin, under pressure. Vettori, on the other hand, bowled with relish on his own ground. He had come within sight of earning New Zealand victory over England in his second Test; this time he completed the job, improving on the best analysis of his short career yet again by taking another five wickets. He might also have had Dharmasena – he appeared to have bowled him, dislodging one bail, but Parore knocked off the other bail, appealing for a stumping, which was turned down by the third umpire.

Again, Mahanama was Sri Lanka's most determined batsman, holding out more than four hours for his 65, the second-highest score of the match. Their best stand came when he and

Ranatunga added 79 for the fifth wicket; it ended when Ranatunga played a poor shot to be caught by Doull at deep square leg. Aravinda de Silva, the tourists' star on their visit in 1990-91, when he scored 493 in five innings, ended a disastrous series with a total of nine runs. For the second time running, New Zealand had won with a day to spare.

Man of the Match: D. L. Vettori.

Close of play: First day, New Zealand 222; Second day, New Zealand 53-1 (B. A. Young 22*, M. J. Horne 14*); Third day, Sri Lanka 20-2 (R. S. Mahanama 6*, W. P. U. J. C. Vaas 0*).

New Zealand

B. A. Pocock c Tillekeratne b Muralitharan	85	– (2) c Mahanama b Zoysa	7
B. A. Young run out	4	– (1) c Ranatunga b Dharmasena	62
M. J. Horne b Zoysa	21	– st Kaluwitharana b Muralitharan	16
*S. P. Fleming c Mahanama b Zoysa	2	– b Muralitharan	59
N. J. Astle lbw b Zoysa	0	– c Mahanama b Vaas	52
C. L. Cairns c Ranatunga b Dharmasena	10	– c sub (U. D. U. Chandana) b Muralitharan	4
†A. C. Parore run out	25	– run out	2
D. N. Patel c Dharmasena b Muralitharan	13	– c P. A. de Silva b Dharmasena	4
D. L. Vettori b Muralitharan	4	– b Zoysa	6
S. B. Doull c P. A. de Silva b Vaas	20	– c Mahanama b Zoysa	25
H. T. Davis not out	8	– not out	2
B 11, l-b 9, n-b 10	30	B 9, l-b 11, w 7, n-b 7	34

1/19 (2) 2/88 (3) 3/96 (4) 4/100 (5)   **222**   1/14 (2) 2/64 (3) 3/108 (1)   **273**
5/126 (6) 6/172 (7) 7/172 (1)   4/183 (4) 5/198 (5) 6/201 (7)
8/178 (9) 9/203 (8) 10/222 (10)   7/211 (8) 8/239 (5)
                                      9/243 (9) 10/273 (10)

Bowling: First Innings—Vaas 12.4-1-32-1; Zoysa 18-3-47-3; K. S. C. de Silva 15-4-36-0; Dharmasena 22-7-39-1; Muralitharan 22-4-43-3; Jayasuriya 1-0-5-0. *Second Innings*—Vaas 15-3-34-1; Zoysa 22.4-7-53-3; Dharmasena 24-5-75-2; K. S. C. de Silva 10-2-29-0; Muralitharan 26-7-62-3.

Sri Lanka

S. T. Jayasuriya c Astle b Davis	20	– run out	3
R. S. Mahanama lbw b Vettori	45	– lbw b Doull	65
H. P. Tillekeratne c Young b Doull	2	– b Vettori	10
P. A. de Silva c Parore b Vettori	1	– (5) lbw b Doull	5
*A. Ranatunga lbw b Davis	4	– (6) c Doull b Vettori	33
†R. S. Kaluwitharana c Parore b Davis	11	– (7) lbw b Doull	13
H. D. P. K. Dharmasena c Fleming b Davis	27	– (8) not out	38
W. P. U. J. C. Vaas c Pocock b Vettori	28	– (4) c Patel b Vettori	8
D. N. T. Zoysa c Doull b Vettori	14	– c Parore b Vettori	13
K. S. C. de Silva not out	0	– c Young b Davis	0
M. Muralitharan c Parore b Davis	5	– c Cairns b Vettori	7
L-b 9, w 1, n-b 3	13	B 4, l-b 5, w 1	10

1/39 (1) 2/57 (3) 3/58 (4) 4/76 (5)   **170**   1/5 (1) 2/16 (3) 3/40 (4)   **205**
5/87 (2) 6/93 (6) 7/144 (7)   4/50 (5) 5/129 (6) 6/147 (7)
8/154 (8) 9/165 (9) 10/170 (11)   7/152 (2) 8/185 (9)
                                        9/186 (10) 10/205 (11)

Bowling: First Innings—Doull 13-4-19-1; Davis 20.2-3-63-5; Astle 3-1-8-0; Vettori 24-8-46-4; Patel 8-2-25-0. *Second Innings*—Doull 15-4-34-3; Davis 17-4-35-1; Vettori 29.2-8-84-5; Patel 12-5-34-0; Astle 3-1-9-0.

Umpires: Mahboob Shah (Pakistan) and D. B. Cowie. Referee: P. J. Burge (Australia).

†At Napier, March 20. Sri Lankans won by six wickets. Toss: Central Districts. Central Districts 227 (50 overs) (C. M. Spearman 56, M. S. Sinclair 67; U. D. U. Chandana three for 37, S. T. Jayasuriya five for 37); Sri Lankans 228 for four (43.3 overs) (P. A. de Silva 34, A. Ranatunga 96 not out, H. P. Tillekeratne 47 not out).

†NEW ZEALAND v SRI LANKA

First One-Day International

At Auckland, March 22, 23. Abandoned without a ball bowled.

†NEW ZEALAND v SRI LANKA

Second One-Day International

At Christchurch, March 25 (day/night). Sri Lanka won by six wickets. Toss: Sri Lanka.

Sri Lanka reminded their hosts that they were still world one-day champions, winning with more than 14 overs in hand. Jayasuriya hit a dazzling 79 from 63 balls, with eight fours and four sixes. His 29-ball fifty was believed to be the fastest in one-day internationals in New Zealand and he hit 24 off one Doull over – 406644. At the other end, de Silva rediscovered his form, chiming in with six fours and three sixes. Heavy dew under the floodlights made the ball slippery and New Zealand had too small a target to defend; their top eight had reached double figures, but only Harris, with 38, dragged them past 200. Jayasuriya picked up three wickets.

Man of the Match: S. T. Jayasuriya.

New Zealand

B. A. Young b Zoysa	21	S. B. Doull c and b Jayasuriya		1
N. J. Astle c Mahanama b Zoysa	23	D. L. Vettori b de Silva		4
M. J. Horne b Muralitharan	13	H. T. Davis not out		4
*S. P. Fleming run out	31	L-b 1, w 2, n-b 4		7
C. L. Cairns c Dharmasena b Jayasuriya	27			—
†A. C. Parore c and b Jayasuriya	19	1/39 2/49 3/68	(9 wkts, 50 overs)	201
C. Z. Harris not out	38	4/104 5/134 6/142		
G. R. Larsen c de Silva b Muralitharan	13	7/157 8/164 9/170		

Bowling: Vaas 7–0–45–0; Zoysa 7–1–29–2; Dharmasena 10–0–32–0; Muralitharan 10–1–42–2; Jayasuriya 10–0–26–3; Chandana 4–0–22–0; de Silva 2–0–4–1.

Sri Lanka

S. T. Jayasuriya c Larsen b Harris	79	H. P. Tillekeratne not out		13
†R. S. Kaluwitharana c Cairns b Harris	15	B 1, w 3, n-b 2		6
R. S. Mahanama c Cairns b Larsen	4			—
P. A. de Silva b Astle	66	1/68 2/73	(4 wkts, 35.5 overs)	202
*A. Ranatunga not out	19	3/137 4/183		

H. D. P. K. Dharmasena, U. D. U. Chandana, W. P. U. J. C. Vaas, D. N. T. Zoysa and M. Muralitharan did not bat.

Bowling: Doull 5.5–1–38–0; Davis 8–0–58–0; Harris 10–0–38–2; Larsen 5–0–23–1; Vettori 2–0–21–0; Astle 5–0–23–1.

Umpires: C. E. King and D. M. Quested.

†NEW ZEALAND v SRI LANKA

Third One-Day International

At Wellington, March 27. New Zealand won by 69 runs. Toss: Sri Lanka. International debut: A. J. Penn.

Again, New Zealand were put in and made 201, but this time it was enough. Cairns and Parore led the recovery from 91 for five, but Sri Lanka looked good at 87 for three. Then they lost headway against the slow-medium pace of Larsen – who conceded only nine in seven overs – Harris and Astle. The last seven wickets fell for just 45. When de Silva was 15, he appeared to try to prevent Larsen from running him out and refused to leave when umpire Watkin gave him out for obstruction. Watkin reversed his decision and de Silva made 36 before he was ninth out. Afterwards, de Silva was severely reprimanded by referee Peter Burge.

Man of the Match: C. L. Cairns.

New Zealand

B. A. Young lbw b Vaas	2	S. B. Doull c Chandana b Vaas	18
N. J. Astle c Muralitharan b Zoysa	12	A. J. Penn c de Silva b Vaas	1
M. J. Horne c Kaluwitharana		H. T. Davis not out	1
b Muralitharan	14		
*S. P. Fleming c Tillekeratne b Zoysa	9	L-b 8, w 8, n-b 2	18
C. L. Cairns b Vaas	56		—
C. Z. Harris b Muralitharan	5	1/17 2/17 3/28	(49.2 overs) 201
†A. C. Parore run out	39	4/71 5/91 6/125	
G. R. Larsen run out	26	7/156 8/199 9/199	

Bowling: Vaas 9.2–1–26–4; Zoysa 10–1–47–2; Dharmasena 10–0–41–0; Muralitharan 10–1–32–2; Jayasuriya 5–0–30–0; Ranatunga 5–0–17–0.

Sri Lanka

S. T. Jayasuriya b Davis	0	W. P. U. J. C. Vaas c Doull b Astle	0
†R. S. Kaluwitharana lbw b Davis	23	D. N. T. Zoysa not out	3
R. S. Mahanama c Young b Doull	10	M. Muralitharan b Davis	2
P. A. de Silva c Fleming b Davis	36	L-b 13, w 16	29
*A. Ranatunga b Harris	16		—
H. P. Tillekeratne b Astle	8	1/10 2/49 3/57	(37.2 overs) 132
H. D. P. K. Dharmasena st Parore b Harris	2	4/87 5/113 6/116	
U. D. U. Chandana lbw b Astle	3	7/121 8/125 9/126	

Bowling: Penn 2–0–14–0; Davis 8.2–0–35–4; Doull 4–0–21–1; Larsen 7–5–9–0; Harris 10–2–31–2; Astle 6–1–9–3.

Umpires: R. S. Dunne and E. A. Watkin. Series referee: P. J. Burge (Australia).

CRICKET MAX

In October 1997, England sent a 12-man squad to New Zealand for the three-match Cricket Max series against the Max Blacks. Cricket Max, the brainchild of former New Zealand Test batsman Martin Crowe, is a form of one-day cricket in which both teams have two innings of ten overs each, with hits into the "max zone" – an area near the boundary and behind the bowler – counting double. England's side, led by Matthew Maynard, included Test players such as Phillip DeFreitas, Chris Lewis and Robin Smith. Although the Max Blacks were unable to call on New Zealand's stars, who were touring Australia, they had more experience of the format.

England won the first match, at Auckland, by four wickets, thanks to an unbeaten 50 from 17 balls from Dominic Ostler, who finished the series as England's top scorer by far with 152 runs. In all, he hit two twelves, seven eights, a four and three twos. The Max Blacks hit back to win the second match, at Hamilton, by 13 runs and the decider, at Wellington, by ten wickets.

THE INDIANS IN THE WEST INDIES, 1996-97

By TONY COZIER

Both teams had just lost their preceding series – West Indies in Australia, India in South Africa – so both had plenty to play for on India's first tour of the Caribbean for eight years. In the event, they were thoroughly frustrated by the weather.

A potentially gripping finish to the First Test was spoiled by rain on the last day and the last two Tests were so reduced that not even two innings could be completed. The first two of the four one-day internationals were disrupted and had to be decided by the unsatisfactory arrangement of revised targets.

The quality of the cricket was also diminished by slow, featureless pitches in the first two drawn Tests, prompting pleas from both captains for something livelier. They got more than they bargained for at Kensington Oval in Barbados. The hard, well-grassed surface unduly favoured the fast bowlers, who took all but two of the 40 wickets, and produced an astonishing climax. India capitulated for 81 on the fourth day when they needed just 120 for their first victory in the Caribbean for 21 years. West Indies' win was the only outright result of the series.

The exalted batsmen on both sides were seldom seen at their best. Sachin Tendulkar and Brian Lara had their moments, notably Tendulkar's dominant 92 in the first innings in Barbados, Lara's second-innings 78 off 83 balls in Jamaica and his more measured 103 in Antigua. More was expected of the world's two greatest batting stars. The unofficial contest within a contest, to determine the better player, was unresolved. But Lara earned more points for his handling of the team in Barbados, to win his first Test as captain when Courtney Walsh was injured.

Carl Hooper faded badly after a typically elegant 129 in the First Test and Mohammad Azharuddin, who had made three magnificent hundreds in the preceding home and away series against South Africa, was so pathetically out of sorts that his best score in eight innings in Tests and one-day internationals was 40. He was dropped on his return home.

Only Shivnarine Chanderpaul, the 22-year-old West Indies left-hander, and Rahul Dravid, the solid young Indian, prevailed over the conditions to enhance their reputations. Chanderpaul, retained at the No. 3 position to which he was promoted above Lara in Australia, finally gathered the Test and one-day hundreds that had so long eluded him, maintaining his consistency while adding power and range to his strokeplay. He was unchallenged as Man of the Series, an award covering both forms of the game. Dravid, his opposite number at No. 3, was similarly reliable, if comparatively slow, and confirmed the favourable impression he had made since his debut in England the previous summer.

Even though West Indies secured both series, the Tests 1-0 and the internationals 3-1, the teams were well matched. West Indies enjoyed the better of the First Test and India the better of the Second but neither had the re-sources – nor, in India's case, the confidence – to press home their advantage on pitches so sluggish they inhibited both batsmen and bowlers. The exciting scrap in Barbados provided a welcome spark but it was then extinguished by the uncooperative elements in Antigua and Guyana.

Both West Indies and India started with long-standing problems and finished with most unsolved. India were made to suffer for their heavy reliance on the penetrative fast bowling of Javagal Srinath when a recurring shoulder injury ruled him out of the game for at least six months after the first practice session of the tour. Their difficulties at the top of the order led to the revival of Navjot Singh Sidhu's chequered career, the need for his experience over-riding memories of his tetchy withdrawal from the England tour less than a year earlier and his subsequent ban. Sidhu's marathon 201 in the Second Test was a typically determined, single-minded effort. But whether, aged 33, he was the long-term remedy was open to question.

West Indies were no closer to finding a reliable opening pair either, and continued to play musical chairs with their wicket-keepers. The most encouraging development for each team was the emergence of a promising new fast bowler, Franklyn Rose for West Indies and Abey Kuruvilla for India. Rose, an athletic Jamaican well over six feet, had become so disenchanted with the game that he dropped out entirely the previous season. But his form in the Red Stripe Cup and injuries to other contenders gained him a Test debut. He was consistently West Indies' most penetrative bowler. With Walsh and Curtly Ambrose in the twilight of their careers, his arrival was timely. Mervyn Dillon, another tall, sinewy fast bowler in his first first-class season, showed distinct promise in his two Tests, but it was disappointing that, once again, West Indies could find no room for one of their clutch of young leg-spinners.

Kuruvilla, on his first tour, was said to be India's tallest-ever fast bowler at six feet six inches. He used his height, plus his control and variations of pace, learned under the early tutelage of Frank Tyson, to advantage. His consistency helped to compensate for Srinath's absence and the fatigue that took its toll on the worthy Venkatesh Prasad. But the role of stock bowler fell to the overworked leg-spinner Anil Kumble, who sent down more overs and took more wickets than anyone on either side.

At the end, the indelible images were less of dashing batting or incisive bowling than of ground staff trying to dry swampy outfields by the antiquated method of sponges and buckets.

INDIAN TOURING PARTY

S. R. Tendulkar (Mumbai) (*captain*), A. Kumble (Karnataka) (*vice-captain*), M. Azharuddin (Hyderabad), R. Dravid (Karnataka), D. Ganesh (Karnataka), S. C. Ganguly (Bengal), A. Jadeja (Haryana), S. B. Joshi (Karnataka), S. S. Karim (Bengal), A. Kuruvilla (Mumbai), V. V. S. Laxman (Hyderabad), N. R. Mongia (Baroda), B. K. V. Prasad (Karnataka), N. S. Sidhu (Punjab), R. R. Singh (Tamil Nadu), J. Srinath (Karnataka).

N. David (Hyderabad) replaced the injured Srinath.

Manager: D. V. Subba Rao. *Coach:* Madan Lal.

INDIAN TOUR RESULTS

Test matches – Played 5: Lost 1, Drawn 4.
First-class matches – Played 8: Won 1, Lost 1, Drawn 6.
Win – Guyana.
Loss – West Indies.
Draws – West Indies (4), Jamaica, Barbados.
One-day internationals – Played 4: Won 1, Lost 3.
Other non-first-class match – Won v University of West Indies Vice-Chancellor's XI.

TEST MATCH AVERAGES

WEST INDIES – BATTING

	T	I	NO	R	HS	100s	Avge	Ct
S. Chanderpaul	5	8	2	443	137*	1	73.83	1
B. C. Lara	5	8	0	391	103	1	48.87	4
R. I. C. Holder	5	7	1	212	91	0	35.33	6
C. L. Hooper	5	8	1	245	129	1	35.00	3
S. C. Williams	5	8	0	263	128	1	32.87	2
C. O. Browne	3	4	2	64	39*	0	32.00	10
C. E. L. Ambrose . .	5	6	2	126	37	0	31.50	0
F. A. Rose	5	4	1	63	34	0	21.00	0
S. L. Campbell	5	7	0	129	43	0	18.42	1
I. R. Bishop	4	4	0	51	24	0	12.75	2

Played in four Tests: C. A. Walsh 4, 0, 21 (2 ct). Played in two Tests: M. Dillon 0*, 0, 21; J. R. Murray 1, 11, 12* (2 ct).

* Signifies not out.

BOWLING

	O	M	R	W	BB	5W/i	Avge
I. R. Bishop	111.4	26	262	12	4-22	0	21.83
F. A. Rose	141.1	27	402	18	6-100	1	22.33
C. E. L. Ambrose	154.4	49	301	10	5-87	1	30.10
M. Dillon	54	11	148	4	3-92	0	37.00
C. A. Walsh	119.2	32	250	4	1-7	0	62.50

Also bowled: S. Chanderpaul 65–13–156–1; C. L. Hooper 106–36–222–3; B. C. Lara 3–0–16–0; S. C. Williams 3–0–19–0.

INDIA – BATTING

	T	I	NO	R	HS	100s	Avge	Ct
R. Dravid	5	7	2	360	92	0	72.00	5
S. R. Tendulkar	5	6	1	289	92	0	57.80	5
N. S. Sidhu	4	6	0	276	201	1	46.00	1
V. V. S. Laxman . . .	4	6	0	172	64	0	28.66	4
N. R. Mongia	5	5	0	140	78	0	28.00	13
S. B. Joshi	4	4	1	84	43	0	28.00	1
S. C. Ganguly	4	4	0	78	42	0	19.50	2
A. Kumble	5	5	2	58	23*	0	19.33	2
M. Azharuddin	5	5	0	63	31	0	12.60	9
B. K. V. Prasad	5	5	2	10	10*	0	3.33	2
A. Kuruvilla	5	5	0	16	9	0	3.20	0

Played in two Tests: D. Ganesh 8, 6*, 7; A. Jadeja 96, 8.

* Signifies not out.

BOWLING

	O	M	R	W	BB	5W/i	Avge
S. B. Joshi	120.1	28	331	11	3-57	0	30.09
A. Kumble	200.4	44	576	19	5-104	2	30.31
D. Ganesh	34	5	122	4	2-28	0	30.50
A. Kuruvilla.......	172	34	480	13	5-68	1	36.92
B. K. V. Prasad	169.4	43	465	11	5-82	1	42.27

Also bowled: S. C. Ganguly 20–5–59–1; V. V. S. Laxman 15–3–49–0; S. R. Tendulkar 2–0–9–0.

Note: Matches in this section which were not first-class are signified by a dagger.

At Kingston, February 28, March 1, 2, 3. Drawn. Toss: Indians. Jamaica 453 for nine dec. (L. V. Garrick 30, M. D. Ventura 42, T. O. Powell 76, B. S. Murphy 37, L. R. Williams 102 not out, Extras 30) and 190 for four (L. V. Garrick 108, J. C. Adams 53 not out); Indians 323 (V. V. S. Laxman 98, R. Dravid 86, S. C. Ganguly 82 not out; C. A. Walsh four for 44, F. A. Rose three for 67).

WEST INDIES v INDIA

First Test Match

At Kingston, March 6, 7, 8, 9, 10. Drawn. Toss: West Indies. Test debuts: R. I. C. Holder, F. A. Rose; A. Kuruvilla.

Despite a pitch derided for its lack of pace and bounce, which tested the patience and skill of batsmen and bowlers, an intriguing last day was in prospect. Then rain, light but persistent, delayed play until shortly before tea, reduced the maximum number of overs to 58 and enabled India to reach a comfortable draw.

West Indies had created several chances to overwhelm India but each time allowed them to regroup. An exhilarating stand of 147 at a run a minute between Lara and Hooper appeared to have laid the foundation for a mammoth total. But Lara's dismissal for 83, to a low leg-side catch by the wicket-keeper, was a timely strike by the impressive debutant fast bowler Kuruvilla, just before the close. While Hooper advanced to his seventh Test hundred next morning and night-watchman Bishop survived an hour and a half, the last six went for 70. Hooper was Kuruvilla's third wicket, caught at mid-on after striking 17 fours with effortless elegance. Kumble, wicketless through 21 overs on the first day, secured the other five.

India used their seventh opening pair in seven Tests and soon lost Sidhu, playing his first Test since his petulant departure from England the previous May. But Laxman and Dravid had little difficulty adding 95 before Walsh summoned Franklyn Rose for his second spell, an hour into the third day. Observing the "three-quarter length" advocated by coach Malcolm Marshall and a probing off-stump line, he removed Laxman's leg-stump with his sixth ball. To the noisy jubilation of his home crowd, he also dismissed Dravid, Tendulkar and Azharuddin in six overs, and would have had Ganguly for nine had wicket-keeper Murray not muffed a leg-side catch. It was a critical error: Ganguly and the level-headed Mongia steered India away from the follow-on. Rose eventually had Ganguly caught at slip, but Mongia found another able ally in Joshi and the deficit was reduced to 81. Rose became the first West Indian fast bowler to claim six in a Test innings at the first attempt.

By the time they dismissed India on the fourth morning, West Indies needed their foot on the accelerator. With Lara inexplicably kept at No. 4, their advance was stalled by two brief rain-breaks and a period in which they scraped a mere 17 off 11 overs. When Lara did get in, the momentum changed completely. While Kumble's first ten overs cost eight, Lara took 12 off his next, hoisted him for a straight flat six and made 78 off 83 balls, dominating a stand of 122 in an hour and a half with Chanderpaul.

Hooper and Holder batted on in near-darkness that evening to give Walsh the option of an early declaration, but the weather rendered the tactic meaningless.

Man of the Match: F. A. Rose.

Close of play: First day, West Indies 300-4 (C. L. Hooper 87*, I. R. Bishop 3*); Second day, India 108-1 (V. V. S. Laxman 54*, R. Dravid 28*); Third day, India 308-7 (N. R. Mongia 74*, S. B. Joshi 23*); Fourth day, West Indies 241-4 (C. L. Hooper 12*, R. I. C. Holder 21*).

West Indies

S. L. Campbell c Mongia b Joshi	40	– b Kumble	43
S. C. Williams b Kuruvilla	23	– b Kumble	26
S. Chanderpaul c Mongia b Prasad	52	– c Tendulkar b Kuruvilla	48
B. C. Lara c Mongia b Kuruvilla	83	– c Mongia b Kumble	78
C. L. Hooper c Prasad b Kuruvilla	129	– not out	12
I. R. Bishop c Joshi b Kumble	24		
R. I. C. Holder c Azharuddin b Kumble	17	– (6) not out	21
†J. R. Murray lbw b Kumble	1		
C. E. L. Ambrose c Ganguly b Kumble	23		
F. A. Rose not out	14		
*C. A. Walsh b Kumble	4		
L-b 9, n-b 8	17	B 4, l-b 9	13

1/41 (2) 2/96 (1) 3/143 (3) 4/290 (4)   427   1/68 (2) 2/81 (1)   (4 wkts dec.) 241
5/357 (6) 6/368 (5) 7/370 (8)   3/203 (4) 4/203 (3)
8/408 (9) 9/423 (7) 10/427 (11)

Bowling: *First Innings*—Prasad 28-5-104-1; Kuruvilla 30-6-82-3; Kumble 42.4-5-120-5; Joshi 27-6-81-1; Ganguly 7-1-17-0; Laxman 3-0-14-0. *Second Innings*—Prasad 15-2-46-0; Kuruvilla 17-2-56-1; Kumble 23-6-76-3; Joshi 6-1-27-0; Laxman 3-0-14-0; Tendulkar 2-0-9-0.

India

V. V. S. Laxman b Rose	64	– c Holder b Rose	27
N. S. Sidhu lbw b Bishop	10	– c Holder b Walsh	0
R. Dravid c Murray b Rose	43	– not out	51
*S. R. Tendulkar b Rose	7	– not out	15
S. C. Ganguly c Lara b Rose	42		
M. Azharuddin c Lara b Rose	5		
†N. R. Mongia c Holder b Walsh	78		
A. Kumble b Bishop	7		
S. B. Joshi b Bishop	43		
A. Kuruvilla b Rose	0		
B. K. V. Prasad not out	10		
B 5, l-b 9, n-b 23	37	L-b 1, n-b 5	6

1/32 (2) 2/127 (1) 3/140 (3) 4/145 (4)   346   1/6 (2) 2/68 (1)   (2 wkts) 99
5/153 (6) 6/234 (5) 7/248 (8)
8/315 (9) 9/320 (10) 10/346 (9)

Bowling: *First Innings*—Ambrose 25-10-35-0; Bishop 24.5-4-62-3; Rose 33-7-100-6; Walsh 32-6-73-1; Hooper 21-9-40-0; Chanderpaul 11-4-22-0. *Second Innings*—Ambrose 6-3-7-0; Walsh 8-3-7-1; Rose 9-1-23-1; Hooper 16-6-27-0; Chanderpaul 6-0-18-0; Lara 3-0-16-0.

Umpires: M. J. Kitchen (England) and S. A. Bucknor.
Referee: P. L. van der Merwe (South Africa).

WEST INDIES v INDIA

Second Test Match

At Port-of-Spain, March 14, 15, 16, 17, 18. Drawn. Toss: West Indies. Test debut: M. Dillon.

India held the upper hand but lacked the aggression to tighten their grip. Their cause was not helped by another depressingly slow pitch. Runs came at just 2.4 an over and only 26 wickets fell in 429.1 overs. Bowlers' frustrations were accentuated by unsympathetic umpires who granted only two lbw appeals.

West Indies could not get going after Walsh discounted local advice and batted. Their difficulties were typified by Lara, who scratched 14 off 51 balls. When Kumble collected a waist-high return catch off Murray, his fourth wicket, the innings was a shaky 169 for six. It was revived by Holder's positive attitude and his half-century partnerships with Ambrose and the forthright Rose. Holder was nine short of a hundred in his second Test when he was beaten through the air by Joshi, having batted flawlessly for almost five hours.

Ambrose struck with his second ball, pinning Laxman on the back foot in front of middle stump, but West Indies could not claim another wicket until the third ball next morning, when Ambrose breached Dravid's defence with one that kept low. By then, Dravid and Sidhu had added 171 and Sidhu had passed his seventh Test hundred. India consolidated their position as Tendulkar gained confidence. But Sidhu's deceleration cost valuable time. He scored only 94 on the third day, when India advanced by 196 off 90 overs, and he put on 174 with Tendulkar, whose dismissal just before the close, run out by Walsh's snappy pick-up and direct hit from mid-off, was a decisive setback. The following day, no one took a positive lead: India's last seven added only 69 in 30 overs of quality fast bowling, especially from Ambrose and Mervyn Dillon, playing his first Test as replacement for Bishop.

SLOWEST DOUBLE-HUNDREDS IN TEST CRICKET

Minutes	Balls		
777	548	D. S. B. P. Kuruppu, Sri Lanka v New Zealand at Colombo (CCC) .	1986-87
671	**485**	**N. S. Sidhu, India v West Indies at Port-of-Spain**	**1996-97**
656	411	Shoaib Mohammad, Pakistan v New Zealand at Karachi	1990-91
652	426	A. D. Gaekwad, India v Pakistan at Jullundur	1983-84
650	484	S. L. Campbell, West Indies v New Zealand at Bridgetown	1995-96
608	*	R. B. Simpson, Australia v England at Manchester	1964

D. L. Houghton, Zimbabwe v Sri Lanka at Bulawayo, 1994-95, reached 200 in 433 minutes and 524 balls, the second-slowest recorded in terms of balls received.

* Not recorded.

Sidhu needed three-quarters of an hour that morning to score four and reach his first double-century in Tests; two balls later, Ambrose's yorker diverted from his boot into leg stump. Chances in the 170s and his pedestrian rate were the blemishes on Sidhu's marathon, which included a six and 19 fours. Only the Sri Lankan Brendon Kuruppu had scored a slower Test 200 than his 671 minutes.

India's lead of 140 was less formidable than expected and, with the pitch ever slower, their bowlers needed more time than their batsmen had given them to do their work. Williams and Chanderpaul dropped anchor until the final afternoon, ensuring there were no undue alarms: Williams batted with concentration and judgment that had eluded him in 13 previous Tests, arriving at his maiden Test hundred just before lunch. Tired and bored, he finally hoisted a catch in the deep. He had been in just over seven and a half hours, and the match was long since safe.

Man of the Match: N. S. Sidhu.

Close of play: First day, West Indies 239-7 (R. I. C. Holder 71*, F. A. Rose 13*); Second day, India 171-1 (N. S. Sidhu 102*, R. Dravid 57*); Third day, India 367-3 (N. S. Sidhu 196*, S. C. Ganguly 3*); Fourth day, West Indies 118-1 (S. C. Williams 63*, S. Chanderpaul 39*).

West Indies

S. L. Campbell c Prasad b Kumble	8	– lbw b Kuruvilla	4
S. C. Williams c Dravid b Kumble	18	– c Kumble b Joshi	128
S. Chanderpaul c Mongia b Prasad	42	– c Azharuddin b Joshi	79
B. C. Lara c Azharuddin b Joshi	14	– c Azharuddin b Kumble	19
C. L. Hooper c Azharuddin b Kumble	40	– c Laxman b Kumble	14
R. I. C. Holder b Joshi	91	– c Laxman b Joshi	9
†J. R. Murray c and b Kumble	11	– not out	12
C. E. L. Ambrose c Dravid b Kumble	16	– not out	10
F. A. Rose c Dravid b Joshi	34		
*C. A. Walsh c Mongia b Ganguly	0		
M. Dillon not out	0		
L-b 20, n-b 2	22	B 8, l-b 13, n-b 3	24

1/26 (2) 2/29 (1) 3/59 (4) 4/99 (3)   296   1/25 (1) 2/201 (3)   (6 wkts) 299
5/149 (5) 6/169 (7) 7/220 (8)   3/244 (4) 4/252 (2)
8/289 (6) 9/290 (10) 10/296 (9)   5/271 (5) 6/273 (6)

Bowling: *First Innings*—Prasad 26–9–54–1; Kuruvilla 22–9–36–0; Kumble 39–8–104–5; Joshi 22.3–2–79–3; Ganguly 5–3–3–1. *Second Innings*—Prasad 20–7–38–0; Kuruvilla 23–6–47–1; Kumble 40–9–109–2; Joshi 36–11–57–3; Ganguly 3–0–6–0; Laxman 9–3–21–0.

India

V. V. S. Laxman lbw b Ambrose	0	A. Kuruvilla c Murray b Dillon	2
N. S. Sidhu b Ambrose	201	B. K. V. Prasad c Lara b Dillon	0
R. Dravid b Ambrose	57		
*S. R. Tendulkar run out	88	B 9, l-b 11, n-b 8	28
S. C. Ganguly c Chanderpaul b Rose	6		
M. Azharuddin b Ambrose	1	1/0 (1) 2/171 (3) 3/345 (4)	436
†N. R. Mongia b Dillon	17	4/370 (5) 5/371 (6) 6/382 (2)	
A. Kumble not out	12	7/401 (7) 8/420 (10)	
S. B. Joshi c Walsh b Ambrose	24	9/420 (11) 10/436 (9)	

A. Kumble, when 9, retired hurt at 406 and resumed at 420-9.

Bowling: Ambrose 41.4–10–87–5; Walsh 36–11–71–0; Rose 35–6–93–1; Dillon 35–6–92–3; Hooper 28–9–53–0; Chanderpaul 8–1–20–0.

Umpires: S. G. Randell (Australia) and L. H. Barker.
Referee: P. L. van der Merwe (South Africa).

At Bridgetown, March 22, 23, 24. Drawn. Toss: Barbados. Indians 210 (V. V. S. Laxman 36, A. Jadeja 50, N. S. Sidhu 32 not out; D. R. Marshall six for 62) and 166 for five (A. Jadeja 32, V. V. S. Laxman 30, S. C. Ganguly 73 not out; H. R. Bryan three for 37); Barbados 338 for four dec. (P. A. Wallace 69, S. L. Campbell 97, A. F. G. Griffith 43, F. L. Reifer 48 not out, S. N. Proverbs 35).

WEST INDIES v INDIA

Third Test Match

At Bridgetown, March 27, 29, 30, 31. West Indies won by 38 runs. Toss: India.

At the behest of the captains, frustrated by featherbeds, a pitch was prepared with more grass than usual at Kensington Oval. It was also dry and hard and the seven fast bowlers – all six-footers – were encouraged by its progressively uneven bounce and lateral movement. The pitch was widely criticised but produced an intense match and an unforgettable finale: India, requiring just 120 for their first victory in the West Indies since 1975-76, collapsed to their lowest total in the Caribbean amid bacchanalian celebrations. With Walsh forced out by a strained hamstring, Lara became the sixth West Indian to win his first Test as captain.

India read the obvious signs. They brought in fast bowler Ganesh in place of spinner Joshi and chose to bowl. The three pace bowlers duly worked through the batting but could not dislodge Chanderpaul, who entered in the third over and remained unbeaten after nearly seven and a half hours, during which he struck 12 fours and offered no chance. His 137 followed a sequence of 13 scores between 50 and 82 in his previous 18 Tests. His relief was evident as he kissed the pitch. After five wickets fell for 131, he had critical support from Browne, back to keep wicket instead of Murray, and Ambrose.

Tendulkar was near his assertive best as he and Dravid built a commanding position by adding 170. Punishing short and wide bowling and taking advantage of attacking fields, Tendulkar unleashed his full repertoire to score a hooked six off Rose and 14 fours. It took Campbell's leaping catch at gully to dismiss him, for 92, off what television suggested was a no-ball by Bishop. Without Tendulkar, India lost their way on the third day, when 17 wickets fell for 212 runs. As West Indies bowled a fuller length and more direct line, the last seven added only 70. Dravid spent an hour and ten minutes moving from 71 to 78 before playing on to Bishop; Rose rounded off the innings.

India led by a seemingly insignificant 21 but promptly dismissed Williams and Chanderpaul. Lara counter-attacked boldly until falling, for the second time in the match, to a slip catch off Prasad, who took eight wickets in his most threatening performance of the tour. The fast bowlers offered no respite. West Indies were only 86 ahead when last man Dillon joined Ambrose for the innings's highest partnership, 33. It seemed a merry irrelevance.

West Indies had never defended such a meagre target but reminded themselves of their triumph here five years earlier, when South Africa, 122 for two at the start of the last day needing another 79, lost their last eight for 26. India, needing just 120, similarly capitulated next morning against irresistible fast bowling on a capricious pitch.

Rose undermined them with three wickets in an opening burst; Bishop and Ambrose completed the demolition. While Sidhu fended a flier off his throat to slip and Dravid and Azharuddin succumbed to balls that came through at shin height, Tendulkar could not blame the pitch when he edged Bishop's out-swinger low to the left of the solitary slip, Lara. The rest went quietly, amid the Barbadian excitement.

Man of the Match: S. Chanderpaul.

Close of play: First day, West Indies 240-7 (S. Chanderpaul 102*, C. E. L. Ambrose 28*); Second day, India 249-3 (R. Dravid 71*, S. C. Ganguly 21*); Third day, India 2-0 (V. V. S. Laxman 0*, N. S. Sidhu 2*).

West Indies

S. L. Campbell c Azharuddin b Prasad	6	– c Mongia b Ganesh	18
S. C. Williams c Laxman b Ganesh	24	– b Prasad	0
S. Chanderpaul not out	137	– lbw b Kuruvilla	3
*B. C. Lara c Tendulkar b Prasad	19	– c Azharuddin b Prasad	45
C. L. Hooper c Mongia b Ganesh	19	– lbw b Ganesh	4
R. I. C. Holder c Azharuddin b Prasad	5	– c Mongia b Prasad	13
†C. O. Browne c Tendulkar b Kumble	24	– c Mongia b Kuruvilla	1
I. R. Bishop b Prasad	4	– lbw b Kuruvilla	6
C. E. L. Ambrose c Tendulkar b Kuruvilla	37	– not out	18
F. A. Rose run out	11	– c Ganguly b Kuruvilla	4
M. Dillon lbw b Prasad	0	– b Kuruvilla	21
L-b 5, n-b 7	12	L-b 5, n-b 2	7

1/10 (1) 2/40 (2) 3/88 (4) 4/118 (5)　　298　　1/9 (2) 2/18 (3) 3/37 (1)　　140
5/131 (6) 6/187 (7) 7/193 (8)　　　　　　　　　　4/65 (5) 5/86 (4) 6/87 (7)
8/258 (9) 9/290 (10) 10/298 (11)　　　　　　　　7/91 (6) 8/95 (8)
　　　　　　　　　　　　　　　　　　　　　　9/107 (10) 10/140 (11)

Bowling: *First Innings*—Prasad 31.4–9–82–5; Kuruvilla 28–4–88–1; Ganesh 21–2–70–2; Kumble 16–1–44–1; Ganguly 2–1–9–0. *Second Innings*—Prasad 18–6–39–3; Kuruvilla 21–5–68–5; Ganesh 6–1–28–2.

India

V. V. S. Laxman b Ambrose	6	– b Rose	19
N. S. Sidhu c Browne b Rose	26	– c Williams b Rose	3
R. Dravid b Bishop	78	– c Browne b Rose	2
*S. R. Tendulkar c Campbell b Bishop	92	– c Lara b Bishop	4
S. C. Ganguly c Browne b Dillon	22	– b Ambrose	8
M. Azharuddin c Browne b Rose	17	– b Ambrose	9
†N. R. Mongia c Williams b Bishop	1	– b Bishop	5
A. Kumble not out	23	– c Holder b Bishop	1
A. Kuruvilla b Ambrose	0	– (10) c Holder b Ambrose	9
D. Ganesh c Browne b Rose	8	– (9) not out	6
B. K. V. Prasad c Holder b Rose	0	– b Bishop	0
B 2, l-b 12, w 2, n-b 30	46	B 2, l-b 2, n-b 11	15

1/23 (1) 2/42 (2) 3/212 (4) 4/253 (5)   319   1/3 (2) 2/16 (3) 3/32 (1)   81
5/273 (3) 6/275 (7) 7/295 (6)   4/32 (4) 5/45 (5) 6/51 (6)
8/296 (9) 9/319 (10) 10/319 (11)   7/57 (8) 8/66 (7)
                                                 9/80 (10) 10/81 (11)

Bowling: *First Innings*—Ambrose 29–8–74–2; Bishop 28–6–70–3; Dillon 19–5–56–1; Rose 22–4–77–4; Hooper 8–1–28–0. *Second Innings*—Ambrose 15–3–36–3; Bishop 11.5–4–22–4; Rose 9–2–19–3.

Umpires: S. G. Randell (Australia) and L. H. Barker. D. Holder deputised for L. H. Barker on the 2nd day. Referee: P. L. van der Merwe (South Africa).

WEST INDIES v INDIA

Fourth Test Match

At St John's, April 4, 5, 6, 7, 8. Drawn. Toss: West Indies.

Rain, and the Antiguan ground authority's inability to cope with its effects on the overworked outfield, wiped out the first three days and ensured a pointless draw. West Indies pressed for two one-day internationals to be arranged instead, while India wanted the Test extended for a couple more days, dropping their territorial match against Guyana, but they could not agree. Once the weather relented and the ground staff, mainly inmates from the nearby prison, got the outfield into acceptable condition, with help from a hovering helicopter, the Test was played to schedule over two days.

There was time only to score psychological points. India managed more, in spite of Lara's ninth Test hundred, on the same ground as his record 375 against England three years earlier. There was a lackadaisical air to the early West Indies batting until Lara took control. He was kept scoreless for 25 balls but then gathered his runs at a more familiar rate, moving from 90 to 100 with a swept four, his 11th, and a six over long-on off successive balls from Kumble. To the crowd's disappointment, he fell to Prasad, for the third time running, next over. Holder, who had lost little in comparison during a partnership of 142, soon followed, but Browne and the bowlers enjoyed themselves with the bat. When seven, Ambrose joined Sir Garfield Sobers and Malcolm Marshall as the only West Indians to have completed the double of 1,000 runs and 100 wickets in Tests.

Sidhu having succumbed to malarial flu, India tried yet another opening partnership, Jadeja and Laxman. In his first Test of the series, Jadeja used the relaxed atmosphere to compile his highest Test score. He became anxious as he approached his hundred, however, and misjudged a second run to third man; beaten by Williams's accurate return to wicket-keeper Browne, he remained four short.

Man of the Match: B. C. Lara.

Close of play: First day, No play; Second day, No play; Third day, No play; Fourth day, West Indies 252-7 (C. O. Browne 4*).

West Indies

S. L. Campbell run out	10	
S. C. Williams c Tendulkar b Kuruvilla	0	
S. Chanderpaul c Laxman b Kumble	24	
B. C. Lara c Mongia b Prasad	103	
C. L. Hooper c Azharuddin b Joshi	26	
R. I. C. Holder c Mongia b Kumble	56	
†C. O. Browne not out	39	
I. R. Bishop c Dravid b Joshi	17	

C. E. L. Ambrose c Mongia b Kuruvilla	22	
*C. A. Walsh c Dravid b Joshi	21	
F. A. Rose absent ill		
B 1, l-b 5, n-b 9	15	
	333	

1/0 (2) 2/32 (1) 3/40 (3)
4/82 (5) 5/224 (4) 6/230 (6)
7/252 (8) 8/295 (9) 9/333 (10)

Bowling: Prasad 24–5–65–1; Kuruvilla 24–1–69–2; Kumble 36–14–93–2; Joshi 23.4–7–76–3; Ganguly 3–0–24–0.

India

A. Jadeja run out	96	
V. V. S. Laxman c Browne b Walsh	56	
R. Dravid not out	37	
S. B. Joshi not out	10	
L-b 3, n-b 10	13	

1/97 (2) 2/198 (1)   (2 wkts) 212

*S. R. Tendulkar, S. C. Ganguly, M. Azharuddin, †N. R. Mongia, A. Kumble, A. Kuruvilla and B. K. V. Prasad did not bat.

Bowling: Ambrose 9–1–26–0; Bishop 16–3–47–0; Walsh 15–3–37–1; Hooper 15–4–40–0; Chanderpaul 11–0–40–0; Williams 3–0–19–0.

Umpires: B. C. Cooray (Sri Lanka) and S. A. Bucknor.
Referee: P. L. van der Merwe (South Africa).

At Georgetown, April 11, 12, 13, 14. Indians won by 91 runs. Toss: Indians. Indians 341 (A. Jadeja 106, S. C. Ganguly 90, M. Azharuddin 57, R. R. Singh 54; R. D. King seven for 82) and 277 for four dec. (N. S. Sidhu 103, S. C. Ganguly 81, Extras 32); Guyana 300 (S. Chanderpaul 176 not out; D. Ganesh three for 74, S. B. Joshi five for 98) and 227 (Z. A. Haniff 51, N. C. McGarrell 47, M. V. Nagamootoo 56, Extras 35; D. Ganesh three for 25, S. B. Joshi four for 74).

WEST INDIES v INDIA

Fifth Test Match

At Georgetown, April 17, 18, 19, 20, 21. Drawn. Toss: India.

Guyana's notoriously fickle weather once more dogged the Indians. All but one of their six Tests scheduled for Bourda have been seriously disrupted by rain and, in 1975-76, the match was switched to Port-of-Spain as the outfield was a lake. This time, showers left parts of the inadequately covered ground so soft that play was not possible between the end of the uninterrupted first day and the last session of the fourth.

As in Antigua, West Indies proposed abandoning the Test for a one-day game; again, no agreement was reached. Even before the rain, however, the Test had developed into a tiresome tactical impasse. Needing a rare overseas victory to square the series, India took the positive option of omitting a batsman, Ganguly, for a bowler, Ganesh, but were so conscious of their reduced batting power and the need not to waste the toss that they were into the 37th over when Sidhu was second out at 68. Then Tendulkar crashed two of his first four balls to the boundary, threatening to raise the tempo. West Indies, however, resorted to the demeaning tactic of using Chanderpaul to bowl his quick leg-breaks well wide of leg stump from round the wicket, with six fielders on the leg side, for 18 overs after tea. Tendulkar and Dravid made no effort to counter the ploy.

When play resumed, an hour after tea on the fourth day, interest was restricted to personal milestones. Dravid and Tendulkar again fell short of the hundreds they had narrowly missed in previous Tests. But, on the last day, Azharuddin finally gathered the runs he needed to become the fifth Indian – after Sunil Gavaskar, Dilip Vengsarkar, Gundappa Viswanath and Kapil Dev – to pass 5,000, in his 83rd Test. A hundred against West Indies, the only team except Zimbabwe missing from his set, still eluded him: he was caught behind for 31. India batted to the bitter end, scoring 355 at a laborious 2.1 an over.

There was some overdue compensation for a crowd that doubled to around 6,000 on the final afternoon, in the entertainment provided by the batsmen: Williams, Lara, who stroked a delightful 30 – five fours and a six – off 16 balls, and Chanderpaul, opening because Campbell had sinusitis, and reaching 50 for the 15th time in 21 Tests. Even then, the ending was insensitive: the fielders walked off eight overs early, in bright sunshine before an expectant crowd.

Men of the Match: S. Chanderpaul and R. Dravid.

Close of play: First day, India 194-2 (R. Dravid 71*, S. R. Tendulkar 62*); Second day, No play; Third day, No play; Fourth day, India 241-4 (M. Azharuddin 4*, N. R. Mongia 0*).

India

A. Jadeja c Browne b Bishop	8	A. Kuruvilla c Bishop b Hooper 5
N. S. Sidhu c Hooper b Walsh	36	B. K. V. Prasad not out 0
R. Dravid c Hooper b Rose	92	
*S. R. Tendulkar c and b Bishop	83	B 8, l-b 8, w 3, n-b 13........ 32
M. Azharuddin c Browne b Rose	31	
†N. R. Mongia c Hooper b Rose	39	355
A. Kumble c Walsh b Hooper	15	
S. B. Joshi c Browne b Chanderpaul	7	
D. Ganesh c Browne b Hooper	7	

1/32 (1) 2/68 (2) 3/231 (4)
4/241 (3) 5/280 (5) 6/303 (7)
7/320 (8) 8/343 (9)
9/355 (10) 10/355 (6)

Bowling: Ambrose 29–14–36–0; Bishop 31–9–61–2; Rose 33.1–7–90–3; Walsh 28.2–9–62–1; Hooper 18–7–34–3; Chanderpaul 29–8–56–1.

West Indies

S. C. Williams lbw b Kumble	44	†C. O. Browne not out 0
S. Chanderpaul not out	58	B 7, l-b 2, w 1, n-b 2 12
B. C. Lara c Sidhu b Joshi	30	
C. L. Hooper run out	1	1/72 (1) 2/127 (2) 3/145 (4) (3 wkts) 145

S. L. Campbell, R. I. C. Holder, I. R. Bishop, C. E. L. Ambrose, F. A. Rose and *C. A. Walsh did not bat.

Bowling: Prasad 7–0–37–0; Kuruvilla 7–1–34–0; Ganesh 7–2–24–0; Kumble 4–1–30–1; Joshi 5–1–11–1.

Umpires: G. Sharp (England) and E. Nicholls.   Referee: P. L. van der Merwe (South Africa).

†At Port-of-Spain, April 24. Indians won by 32 runs. Toss: Indians. Indians 274 for six (50 overs) (S. C. Ganguly 101, N. S. Sidhu 70, A. Jadeja 38, S. R. Tendulkar 36); University of West Indies Vice-Chancellor's XI 242 (48.1 overs) (S. Chanderpaul 66, J. C. Adams 41, B. C. Lara 57, C. L. Hooper 41; S. B. Joshi four for 36).

†WEST INDIES v INDIA

First One-Day International

At Port-of-Spain, April 26. West Indies won by eight wickets, their target having been revised to 146 from 33 overs. Toss: India.

The rain that wrecked the last two Tests arrived as if on cue to end a prolonged dry spell in Trinidad. Never heavy enough to cause an abandonment, it interrupted India's innings three times and then made a straightforward target even easier for West Indies. India were surprised by a lively pitch after Tendulkar chose to bat, but he did at least gave them a rousing start, belting nine fours in a run-a-ball 44. Once he was out, the first of the showers arrived and no one else could put the innings back on track. Chanderpaul continued his rich vein, with 12 fours in 83 off 87 balls, putting the outcome beyond doubt.

Man of the Match: S. Chanderpaul.

India

*S. R. Tendulkar c Browne b Ambrose	44	S. B. Joshi b Ambrose	8
N. S. Sidhu lbw b Ambrose	5	A. Kuruvilla not out	3
R. Dravid c Hooper b Rose	17	B. K. V. Prasad run out	5
M. Azharuddin b Rose	3	L-b 6, w 20, n-b 5	31
A. Jadeja c Browne b Rose	19		
†N. R. Mongia b Ambrose	29	1/40 2/65 3/71 (48.3 overs)	179
R. R. Singh c Williams b Bishop	2	4/86 5/119 6/123	
A. Kumble c Hooper b Adams	13	7/154 8/171 9/172	

Bowling: Ambrose 9.3–0–36–4; Bishop 7–0–37–1; Walsh 8–0–34–0; Rose 10–2–25–3; Hooper 10–1–33–0; Adams 4–1–8–1.

West Indies

S. C. Williams c Prasad b Kumble 14
S. Chanderpaul c Kuruvilla b Prasad 83
B. C. Lara not out 25
C. L. Hooper not out 9
       B 8, l-b 1, w 8, n-b 1 18

1/43 2/132   (2 wkts, 27.5 overs) 149

J. C. Adams, R. I. C. Holder, †C. O. Browne, I. R. Bishop, C. E. L. Ambrose, F. A. Rose and *C. A. Walsh did not bat.

Bowling: Prasad 7–1–35–1; Kuruvilla 4.5–0–27–0; Kumble 4–0–23–1; Singh 5–0–25–0; Joshi 4–0–19–0; Tendulkar 3–0–11–0.

Umpires: C. E. Cumberbatch and E. Nicholls.

†WEST INDIES v INDIA

Second One-Day International

At Port-of-Spain, April 27. India won by ten wickets, their target having been revised to 113 from 40 overs. Toss: India. International debut: N. David.

India's lesser lights shone brightest in the gloom of another rain-affected match. Kuruvilla and Noel David, in his first international, claimed three wickets each after Prasad had removed Lara first ball; reserve wicket-keeper Karim, replacing the injured Mongia, took two sensational catches plus a slick leg-side stumping. West Indies' total was their lowest in one-day matches against India, whose march to victory was impeded only by the showers that repeatedly swept across the ground. Under heavy cloud cover, Tendulkar and Ganguly passed the revised target with 16.5 of the available 40 overs remaining. It was India's first win in any international in the Caribbean since 1982-83.

Man of the Match: A. Kuruvilla.

West Indies

S. C. Williams lbw b Prasad	3
S. Chanderpaul c Karim b Kuruvilla	12
B. C. Lara c Karim b Prasad	0
C. L. Hooper c Ganguly b Kuruvilla	14
J. C. Adams not out	35
R. I. C. Holder c Karim b Kuruvilla	0
†C. O. Browne c and b Kumble	7
I. R. Bishop c Prasad b David	31

C. E. L. Ambrose c Sidhu b David	4
F. A. Rose b David	5
*C. A. Walsh st Karim b Kumble	3
B 1, l-b 2, w 4	7

1/5 2/5 3/32	(43.5 overs) 121
4/32 5/32 6/44	
7/100 8/107 9/116	

Bowling: Prasad 8–1–22–2; Kuruvilla 10–2–23–3; Kumble 8.5–3–22–2; Ganguly 8–1–26–0; David 8–0–21–3; Tendulkar 1–0–4–0.

India

*S. R. Tendulkar not out	65
S. C. Ganguly not out	39
B 4, l-b 3, w 3, n-b 2	12

(no wkt, 23.1 overs) 116

N. S. Sidhu, R. Dravid, A. Jadeja, M. Azharuddin, †S. S. Karim, A. Kumble, N. David, A. Kuruvilla and B. K. V. Prasad did not bat.

Bowling: Ambrose 6–1–21–0; Rose 7–1–32–0; Walsh 6–1–17–0; Bishop 4–0–35–0; Hooper 0.1–0–4–0.

Umpires: C. E. Cumberbatch and E. Nicholls.

†WEST INDIES v INDIA

Third One-Day International

At St Vincent, April 30. West Indies won by 18 runs. Toss: India.

India were seemingly heading towards another victory while Ganguly and Dravid were comfortably adding 130 in 29 overs for the second wicket, but then collapsed to defeat: their last eight fell for 46 in nine overs thanks to a mixture of hysterical swiping and mindless running. On the best pitch of the tour, Williams made 76 in 110 balls and his stand of 84 with Hooper was the basis of a challenging West Indies total. Tendulkar's dismissal in the fifth over was an early setback for India but Ganguly and Dravid were in charge until panic set in.

Man of the Match: S. C. Williams.

West Indies

S. C. Williams c Singh b Tendulkar	76
S. Chanderpaul lbw b Kuruvilla	5
B. C. Lara b Singh	33
J. C. Adams c Dravid b David	9
C. L. Hooper c and b Kumble	48
R. I. C. Holder c Karim b Prasad	16
O. D. Gibson run out	3
C. E. L. Ambrose b Prasad	13

†C. O. Browne not out	10
F. A. Rose run out	9
*C. A. Walsh not out	0
B 4, l-b 15, w 2, n-b 6	27

1/11 2/71 3/86	(9 wkts, 50 overs) 249
4/170 5/193 6/197	
7/214 8/228 9/248	

Bowling: Prasad 10–0–53–2; Kuruvilla 10–2–34–1; Kumble 10–1–46–1; Singh 7–0–46–1; David 10–1–38–1; Tendulkar 3–0–13–1.

India

*S. R. Tendulkar b Walsh	9	N. David not out	8
S. C. Ganguly c Ambrose b Rose	79	A. Kuruvilla run out	0
R. Dravid b Gibson	74	B. K. V. Prasad run out	0
M. Azharuddin c Hooper b Gibson	24	L-b 11, w 3, n-b 4	18
A. Jadeja b Gibson	9		
R. R. Singh c Adams b Ambrose	4	1/27 2/157 3/185 (48.2 overs) 231	
†S. S. Karim c Lara b Gibson	6	4/201 5/214 6/217	
A. Kumble run out	0	7/219 8/224 9/230	

Bowling: Walsh 9.2–2–26–1; Ambrose 9–1–34–1; Rose 8–0–41–1; Gibson 10–0–61–4; Hooper 8–0–36–0; Adams 4–0–22–0.

Umpires: L. H. Barker and S. A. Bucknor.

†WEST INDIES v INDIA

Fourth One-Day International

At Bridgetown, May 3. West Indies won by ten wickets. Toss: West Indies.

Walsh and Ambrose skilfully exploited the initial life in the pitch to remove Ganguly and Tendulkar in the first five overs. India never fully recovered, despite Jadeja's enterprising 68 and Azharuddin's first convincing innings of the tour. On a pitch that became ideal for strokeplay in the hot sunshine, Chanderpaul and Williams completed victory in an unbroken stand of 200, a West Indies first-wicket record in one-day internationals. Chanderpaul reached his first hundred at this level on the same ground where he had scored his maiden Test hundred five weeks earlier. He made 109 off 134 balls, with a six and 15 fours, to clinch the series 3-1 and take the Man of the Series award including both Tests and one-day internationals.

Man of the Match: S. Chanderpaul. *Man of the Series:* S. Chanderpaul.

India

*S. R. Tendulkar c Lara b Walsh	1	A. Kumble not out	8
S. C. Ganguly b Ambrose	4	N. David not out	1
R. Dravid c Chanderpaul b Rose	30		
M. Azharuddin c Browne b Chanderpaul	40	L-b 1, n-b 3	4
A. Jadeja b Walsh	68		
R. R. Singh c sub (L. V. Garrick) b Gibson	29	1/4 2/6 3/62 (7 wkts, 50 overs) 199	
†S. S. Karim run out	14	4/93 5/168	
		6/187 7/194	

A. Kuruvilla and B. K. V. Prasad did not bat.

Bowling: Walsh 9–3–26–2; Ambrose 10–1–33–1; Gibson 8–0–48–1; Rose 10–1–32–1; Chanderpaul 8–0–36–1; Hooper 5–1–23–0.

West Indies

S. C. Williams not out	78
S. Chanderpaul not out	109
L-b 9, w 1, n-b 3	13

(no wkt, 44.4 overs) 200

B. C. Lara, J. C. Adams, C. L. Hooper, R. I. C. Holder, †C. O. Browne, O. D. Gibson, C. E. L. Ambrose, F. A. Rose and *C. A. Walsh did not bat.

Bowling: Prasad 9–0–45–0; Kuruvilla 6–2–15–0; Kumble 10–2–33–0; David 6–0–38–0; Singh 2–0–7–0; Ganguly 4–0–25–0; Tendulkar 5–0–22–0; Jadeja 2.4–0–6–0.

Umpires: L. H. Barker and S. A. Bucknor. Series referee: P. L. van der Merwe (South Africa).

THE PAKISTANIS IN SRI LANKA, 1996-97

By QAMAR AHMED

Pakistan, having lost at home to the same opponents 19 months earlier, were in danger of losing a series in Sri Lanka for the first time when they toured in April 1997; they were lucky to emerge unscathed, with both Tests drawn, as it seemed that all the odds were against them.

Two of their best batsmen were unavailable, Saeed Anwar because of a viral complaint and Aamir Sohail suspended on disciplinary charges. Their captain, Wasim Akram, and his fellow fast bowler Waqar Younis both withdrew before the First Test, Wasim suffering pain in his bowling shoulder and Waqar with his left leg in plaster because of a hairline fracture in his foot. The heat and humidity of Colombo in April were intense, and the two young pace bowlers, Mohammad Zahid and Shahid Nazir, who had to take on the responsibility of the new-ball attack, both broke down during the Second Test.

Sri Lanka did not escape injury. Their leading bowler, off-spinner Muttiah Muralitharan, injured a finger and damaged a muscle under his bowling arm during the First Test, while left-arm medium-pacer Nuwan Zoysa managed only ten overs before straining a leg muscle. Batsman Roshan Mahanama damaged his toe in practice, though his understudy, Russel Arnold, made a promising start in Test cricket.

On the field, the two-match series was dominated by the stylish batting of Aravinda de Silva, who scored three successive centuries, became the first batsman from any country to score two unbeaten hundreds in the same Test and finished the series with 432 runs at 216.00. Also among the runs were Sanath Jayasuriya and the ever-reliable Hashan Tillekeratne, who both scored centuries. For Pakistan, Ijaz Ahmed hit a hundred in the First Test and Salim Malik a match-saving 155 in the Second, where Moin Khan scored 98. Ijaz's tour deteriorated, however, when referee John Reid fined him 20 per cent of his match fee in the Second Test for using foul language after Ranatunga was out, with a further 30 per cent fine suspended for five months.

The spinners were the most successful bowlers. Muralitharan took a career-best six for 98 before his injury in the First Test, when Saqlain Mushtaq claimed nine for Pakistan and Mushtaq Ahmed six; Saqlain finished the series with 14 wickets for 512 runs from 195.1 overs, a marathon effort. But the slow, dead pitches and the overwhelming heat made bowling an exhausting process and helped to work against either Test reaching a result.

PAKISTANI TOURING PARTY

Wasim Akram (PIA) (*captain*), Ramiz Raja (Allied Bank) (*vice-captain*), Asif Mujtaba (Karachi/PIA), Ijaz Ahmed, sen. (Lahore), Inzamam-ul-Haq (Faisalabad/United Bank), Mohammad Wasim (Rawalpindi), Mohammad Zahid (PIA), Moin Khan (Karachi/PIA), Mushtaq Ahmed (Lahore/United Bank), Salim Elahi (United Bank), Salim Malik (Habib Bank), Saqlain Mushtaq (PIA), Shahid Nazir (Faisalabad/National Bank), Waqar Younis (United Bank).

Abdur Razzaq (Lahore) and Mohammad Hussain (Lahore/United Bank) joined the party when Waqar Younis and Wasim Akram were injured.

Tour manager: Nasim-ul-Ghani.   *Coach:* Mushtaq Mohammad.

PAKISTANI TOUR RESULTS

Tests – Played 2: Drawn 2.
Draws – Sri Lanka (2).
Non-first-class match – Drew v Sri Lankan Board XI.

Note: Matches in this section which were not first-class are signified by a dagger.

†At Bambalapitiya, April 16, 17. Drawn. Toss: Sri Lankan Board XI. Sri Lankan Board XI 301 (R. P. Arnold 140, S. Ranatunga 52; Waqar Younis three for 30, Mohammad Zahid three for 65); Pakistanis 281 for eight (Salim Elahi 106, Salim Malik 100; R. P. Arnold three for seven).

SRI LANKA v PAKISTAN

First Test Match

At R. Premadasa Stadium, Colombo, April 19, 20, 21, 22, 23. Drawn. Toss: Sri Lanka. Test debut: R. P. Arnold.

Sri Lanka led by 158 with seven wickets standing at the start of the final day. But they had little chance of bowling out Pakistan, as their lead spinner, Muralitharan, and medium-pacer Zoysa were both injured. Instead, de Silva batted on, converting his first fifty in 16 Test innings into his ninth Test hundred; by the time he was caught at cover off Mushtaq Ahmed, he had scored 168, striking 14 fours and a six, and there were also half-centuries for Tillekeratne and Jayasuriya. Pakistan had held the advantage when de Silva and Ranatunga combined at 53 for two, just five ahead. They made the match safe, surviving a couple of confident shouts for leg-before as they added 129 on the fourth afternoon.

Ranatunga had decided to bat on winning the toss. Debutant Russel Arnold replaced Mahanama, who had damaged his toe, as Jayasuriya's opening partner and they put on 61 before Mushtaq bowled them both; he also had de Silva stumped, while his fellow-spinner Saqlain Mushtaq accounted for Atapattu. The pitch was at its liveliest that morning but, as it dried out, Sri Lanka eased away from 90 for four. They lost only one more batsman that day, Ranatunga. Tillekeratne was batting serenely and reached his second Test century against Pakistan next day. But the last five wickets fell for 62, mostly to Saqlain, who took five in a Test innings for the first time and was to add four more at the second attempt; he finally had Tillekeratne caught at slip after nearly six hours.

Salim Elahi was lbw offering no stroke to the first ball of Pakistan's reply, but Ijaz Ahmed shared century stands for the next two wickets with acting-captain Ramiz Raja and Salim Malik. Ijaz resumed on the third morning on 90, but almost missed his hundred. He and Malik set off for a single, then both ended up at the non-striker's end as Ranatunga and the keeper effected the run-out. Initially, umpire Shepherd declared Ijaz out. But, after further consultation with TV umpire K. T. Francis, he despatched Malik instead; Ijaz was recalled from the dressing-room and promptly completed his century. Not long after, he was one of three victims claimed by Muralitharan for one run, and Pakistan were 248 for six. The last four wickets, however, added 130, thanks to the stubborn Saqlain, who batted 255 minutes and was last out for 58. Muralitharan had bowled 53 overs of off-spin for a career-best six for 98. But a torn side muscle and a bad finger kept him out of the rest of the series. Sri Lanka had to bat out the remaining two days, but in the end they did so in comfort.

Man of the Match: Saqlain Mushtaq.

Close of play: First day, Sri Lanka 254-5 (H. P. Tillekeratne 65*, R. S. Kaluwitharana 48*); Second day, Pakistan 200-2 (Ijaz Ahmed 90*, Salim Malik 47*); Third day, Pakistan 370-9 (Saqlain Mushtaq 51*, Mohammad Zahid 5*); Fourth day, Sri Lanka 206-3 (P. A. de Silva 79*, H. P. Tillekeratne 20*).

Sri Lanka

S. T. Jayasuriya b Mushtaq Ahmed	31	– (7) c Salim Elahi b Saqlain Mushtaq	62
R. P. Arnold b Mushtaq Ahmed	24	– c Shahid Nazir b Saqlain Mushtaq	15
M. S. Atapattu c Salim Elahi b Saqlain Mushtaq.	0	– (1) c Shahid Nazir b Saqlain Mushtaq	25
P. A. de Silva st Moin Khan b Mushtaq Ahmed.	23	– (3) c Saqlain Mushtaq b Mushtaq Ahmed	168
*A. Ranatunga c Salim Elahi b Asif Mujtaba	49	– (4) c Ramiz Raja b Mushtaq Ahmed	58
H. P. Tillekeratne c Asif Mujtaba b Saqlain Mushtaq	103	– (5) c Ramiz Raja b Saqlain Mushtaq	54
†R. S. Kaluwitharana b Saqlain Mushtaq	57	– (6) c Moin Khan b Shahid Nazir	17
H. D. P. K. Dharmasena b Saqlain Mushtaq	1	– not out	11
W. P. U. J. C. Vaas c Moin Khan b Mohammad Zahid	17	– c sub (Mohammad Hussain) b Mushtaq Ahmed	1
D. N. T. Zoysa lbw b Saqlain Mushtaq	0		
M. Muralitharan not out	8		
B 3, l-b 9, w 1, n-b 4	17	B 3, l-b 4, n-b 5	12

1/61 (1) 2/62 (2) 3/64 (3) 4/90 (4)	330	1/38 (2) 2/53 (1) (8 wkts dec.) 423
5/179 (5) 6/268 (7) 7/280 (8)		3/182 (4) 4/265 (5)
8/322 (6) 9/322 (9) 10/330 (10)		5/315 (6) 6/390 (3)
		7/420 (7) 8/423 (9)

Bowling: *First Innings*—Mohammad Zahid 17-2-44-1; Shahid Nazir 18-6-37-0; Saqlain Mushtaq 44.2-10-89-5; Mushtaq Ahmed 34-2-123-3; Asif Mujtaba 9-2-25-1. *Second Innings*—Mohammad Zahid 11-1-60-0; Shahid Nazir 12-0-61-1; Saqlain Mushtaq 63-13-137-4; Mushtaq Ahmed 39.1-9-94-3; Asif Mujtaba 30-5-64-0.

Pakistan

Salim Elahi lbw b Vaas	0	Mushtaq Ahmed b Muralitharan	26
*Ramiz Raja c Ranatunga b Dharmasena	50	Shahid Nazir c Ranatunga b Muralitharan.	2
Ijaz Ahmed, sen. c Dharmasena b Muralitharan	113	Mohammad Zahid not out	6
Salim Malik run out	58	B 11, l-b 7, n-b 14	32
Inzamam-ul-Haq c sub (R. S. Kalpage) b Muralitharan	12	1/0 (1) 2/102 (2) 3/219 (4)	378
Asif Mujtaba c and b Muralitharan	21	4/247 (5) 5/248 (3) 6/248 (7)	
†Moin Khan b Muralitharan	0	7/298 (6) 8/336 (9)	
Saqlain Mushtaq run out	58	9/349 (10) 10/378 (8)	

Bowling: Vaas 32-6-75-1; Zoysa 10-0-55-0; Dharmasena 52.5-19-93-1; Muralitharan 53-19-98-6; Jayasuriya 3-0-15-0; de Silva 4-0-16-0; Ranatunga 3-1-5-0; Arnold 2-1-3-0.

Umpires: D. R. Shepherd (England) and W. A. U. Wickremasinghe.
Referee: J. R. Reid (New Zealand).

SRI LANKA v PAKISTAN

Second Test Match

At Sinhalese Sports Club, Colombo, April 26, 27, 28, 29, 30. Drawn. Toss: Sri Lanka.
Pakistan flirted with defeat after being set a mammoth target of 426 to win, or most of four sessions to survive. Sri Lanka had declared half an hour after tea on the fourth day as Aravinda

de Silva reached his third successive Test century. He became the first batsman ever to score two unbeaten hundreds in the same Test. But after Pakistan had stumbled to 28 for two, bad light intervened that evening. Next day, Salim Malik scored a polished 155, sharing century partnerships with Ijaz Ahmed and Inzamam-ul-Haq. Pakistan were well out of danger when more bad light ended play seven overs early. A docile pitch and fielding that dropped below Sri Lanka's usual standard helped save the game. Malik was dropped by Kalpage off his own bowling on 42 but went on to his 15th Test century; he had struck 26 fours when he was caught behind attempting a big hit off Silva.

Sri Lanka had made the most of winning the toss, their openers sharing a stand of 95. Then de Silva compiled his tenth century, which he took to 138 not out next day, hitting 19 fours in four and a half hours. But the last three wickets fell within an hour next morning. This time Pakistan opener Salim Elahi lasted three balls of Vaas's first over, and the tourists were in some trouble at 83 for four. Inzamam and Asif Mujtaba started the recovery and Moin Khan scored a fine 98 from 109 balls, with three sixes and nine fours, before he was caught at backward point off Silva. Sajeewa de Silva wrapped up the innings for his first five-wicket haul in Tests, and Sri Lanka led by 39.

They had little difficulty extending that; pace bowlers Mohammad Zahid and Shahid Nazir, themselves understudies for Wasim Akram and Waqar Younis, had broken down, forcing Pakistan to turn to the unlikely new-ball pairing of Malik and Ijaz. They also had a makeshift wicket-keeper in Elahi, Moin having injured his foot. Jayasuriya and Arnold surpassed their previous effort by putting on 157, two short of Sri Lanka's first-wicket record. Jayasuriya advanced to 113 in four and a half hours. But Ranatunga and Aravinda de Silva stepped up a gear, adding 105 in 107 balls; Ranatunga made 66 from 62, with nine fours and three sixes, while de Silva, dropped on 80 by Elahi, reached 103 in 99 balls with 11 fours and a six.

Ranatunga's critics later argued that he should have declared at tea, denying de Silva his landmark in order to gain time to bowl Pakistan out. As it was, after Vaas had removed the openers, the touring batsmen combined sense and defiance for the rest of the match.

Man of the Match: P. A. de Silva. *Man of the Series:* P. A. de Silva.

Close of play: First day, Sri Lanka 281-7 (P. A. de Silva 101*, W. P. U. J. C. Vaas 9*); Second day, Pakistan 146-4 (Inzamam-ul-Haq 43*, Asif Mujtaba 31*); Third day, Sri Lanka 102-0 (S. T. Jayasuriya 61*, R. P. Arnold 29*); Fourth day, Pakistan 28-2 (Ijaz Ahmed 9*, Salim Malik 5*).

Sri Lanka

S. T. Jayasuriya c Mushtaq Ahmed b Saqlain Mushtaq	72	– c sub (Abdur Razzaq) b Saqlain Mushtaq	113
R. P. Arnold run out	37	– b Mushtaq Ahmed	50
M. S. Atapattu c Salim Elahi b Mushtaq Ahmed	14	– run out	4
P. A. de Silva not out	138	– not out	103
*A. Ranatunga c Salim Elahi b Saqlain Mushtaq	4	– st Salim Elahi b Mushtaq Ahmed	66
H. P. Tillekeratne b Mohammad Zahid	10	– not out	24
†R. S. Kaluwitharana b Asif Mujtaba	22		
R. S. Kalpage c Salim Elahi b Saqlain Mushtaq	5		
W. P. U. J. C. Vaas c Salim Elahi b Saqlain Mushtaq	17		
K. S. C. de Silva st Moin Khan b Mushtaq Ahmed	0		
K. J. Silva run out	0		
B 6, l-b 3, n-b 3	12	B 12, l-b 6, w 1, n-b 7	26
	331	(4 wkts dec.)	**386**

1/95 (1) 2/124 (3) 3/124 (2) 4/129 (5) 5/144 (6) 6/204 (7) 7/224 (8) 8/300 (9) 9/321 (10) 10/331 (11)

1/157 (2) 2/171 (3) 3/203 (1) 4/308 (5)

Bowling: First Innings—Mohammad Zahid 12-1-44-1; Shahid Nazir 8-1-50-0; Mushtaq Ahmed 32-6-90-2; Saqlain Mushtaq 45-12-115-4; Asif Mujtaba 15-3-23-1. *Second Innings*—Salim Malik 9-2-33-0; Ijaz Ahmed 5-0-18-0; Saqlain Mushtaq 42.5-4-171-1; Mushtaq Ahmed 33-4-113-2; Asif Mujtaba 6-0-33-0.

Pakistan

Salim Elahi c Tillekeratne b Vaas	0	– (2) c Arnold b Vaas 14
*Ramiz Raja c Arnold b K. S. C. de Silva	36	– (1) c Kaluwitharana b Vaas 0
Ijaz Ahmed, sen. c Arnold b Vaas	4	– c Vaas b Silva................. 47
Salim Malik c Ranatunga b K. S. C. de Silva	24	– c Kaluwitharana b Silva 155
Inzamam-ul-Haq c Kaluwitharana b Vaas	43	– not out 54
Asif Mujtaba c P. A. de Silva b Vaas	49	– c Ranatunga b Atapattu 6
†Moin Khan c Atapattu b Silva	98	
Saqlain Mushtaq b K. S. C. de Silva	23	– (7) not out 5
Mushtaq Ahmed c Atapattu b K. S. C. de Silva	1	
Mohammad Zahid c Kaluwitharana b K. S. C. de Silva	0	
Shahid Nazir not out	0	
L-b 4, w 4, n-b 6	14	L-b 3, n-b 1 4

1/0 (1) 2/13 (3) 3/59 (2) 4/83 (4)   292   1/0 (1) 2/19 (2)   (5 wkts) 285
5/147 (5) 6/238 (6) 7/276 (7)   3/146 (3) 4/267 (4)
8/283 (9) 9/283 (10) 10/292 (8)   5/279 (6)

Bowling: First Innings—Vaas 27–7–60–4; K. S. C. de Silva 24.2–5–85–5; Silva 25–5–91–1; Kalpage 23–8–42–0; Ranatunga 4.1–1–8–0; Arnold 5–3–2–0. *Second Innings*—Vaas 16–7–40–2; K. S. C. de Silva 19–2–73–0; Silva 28–10–71–2; Kalpage 20–6–60–0; Atapattu 4–0–9–1; Arnold 6–0–26–0; Tillekeratne 2–1–3–0.

Umpires: I. D. Robinson (Zimbabwe) and P. Manuel.   Referee: J. R. Reid (New Zealand).

FIFTY YEARS AGO

From WISDEN CRICKETERS' ALMANACK 1948

COMPTON AND EDRICH by R. C. Robertson-Glasgow: "... They seem to be playing not only in front of us and for us, but almost literally with us. Their cricket is communicative. We are almost out of breath at the end of an over by Edrich. We scratch our heads perplexedly at a googly from Compton which refuses to work. We smile with something near to self-satisfaction when, with easy vehemence, he persuades a length-ball from the leg stump to the extra-cover boundary."

NO MAGIC IN FAST BOWLING by C. J. Kortright: "If England can find a real fast bowler who is willing to take a bit of advice from an old-timer, here is a wrinkle he might well remember. He should never forget to try bowling a fast yorker on the leg stump to a newly arrived batsman. It can be a deadly ball to face early in an innings ..."

THE PUBLIC SCHOOLS, 1947 by E. M. Wellings: "Nobody could claim 1947 as a vintage year for Public Schools cricket ... The complaint of cricket masters generally was that few of the younger players had a sound groundwork to their game."

THE SRI LANKANS IN THE WEST INDIES, 1996-97

By CRAIG COZIER

Sri Lanka's first Test tour of the West Indies, 16 years after being granted full status, provided a competitive mini-series in which the home team took the honours but not all the plaudits. The Sri Lankans had paid a brief visit a year earlier, to play a one-day international; this time they arrived in June, unusually late in the year, for two Tests. It was the first season since West Indies began hosting Tests in 1930 that two visiting teams had played Test series in the Caribbean; India had left a month earlier.

World Cup champions Sri Lanka had just chalked up another limited-overs triumph, in the Independence Cup in India, but were seeking to establish their credentials at the longer version of the game, so defeat in the solitary one-day international caused little concern. "We've proved ourselves in the one-day game," said captain Arjuna Ranatunga beforehand. "We now want to do that in the Tests."

By the end of the series, they were closer to that goal. They held first-innings advantage in both Tests but could not find the knockout punch to finish off West Indies when they were down. Each time, the home bowlers clawed their team back into contention, setting up victory in St John's, and rescuing them from the brink at the picturesque Arnos Vale ground in St Vincent, Test cricket's 78th and newest venue, which witnessed a gripping but rain-spoiled draw.

The Sri Lankans were disrupted before they arrived by the loss of front-line fast bowler Chaminda Vaas to a back injury. Fellow left-arm pacer Nuwan Zoysa, the promising teenager, also had back problems and returned home after one match. Their absence provided an opportunity for Ravindra Pushpakumara, who had been on the fringes of the Test side since 1994 but now emerged as the find of the tour. Pushpakumara, whose style was clearly modelled on Waqar Younis, made an early breakthrough in both Tests and claimed five wickets as the unpredictable West Indies batting was routed for 147 in the Second. Only the well-established Curtly Ambrose and Muttiah Muralitharan were more influential.

Muralitharan's prodigious off-breaks baffled the late-order batsmen especially and earned 16 wickets at 15.43. Ambrose thrilled his home crowd on the first day of the series by taking five to reach the coveted landmark of 300 Test wickets. Three West Indians had previously achieved the feat – his captain Courtney Walsh, coach Malcolm Marshall and Lance Gibbs. Walsh was the first to offer congratulations, and the other two were also present to welcome Ambrose into their company.

Once again, West Indies were betrayed by their batsmen. Shivnarine Chanderpaul, their leading scorer against India, was unavailable because of a neck injury and his reliability was clearly missed. Barbadian left-hander Floyd Reifer stepped in but did not look a Test No. 3, while the other specialists put together only one notable innings each. Brian Lara initially appeared uninterested, reporting late for duty before the First Test, for which he was fined half his match fee by team management, and scoring just five in his first three innings. When he put his mind to it, at the last time of asking, he scored a crucial hundred.

Hashan Tillekeratne's involvement in the series lasted only 15 minutes before his forearm was fractured by Walsh. Sri Lanka missed his consistency as much as West Indies missed Chanderpaul's. It was left to the left-handers, Sanath Jayasuriya and captain Arjuna Ranatunga, and the dashing Aravinda de Silva, to carry the batting. Once they were dismissed, a decisive collapse usually followed, leading to eventual defeat in the First Test and the surrender of a winning position in the Second.

With the Tests coming at the end of a protracted West Indian season, public interest was diminished; crowds, especially for St Vincent's maiden Test, were disappointing.

SRI LANKAN TOURING PARTY

A. Ranatunga (Sinhalese SC) (*captain*), P. A. de Silva (Nondescripts CC) (*vice-captain*), R. P. Arnold (Nondescripts CC), M. S. Atapattu (Sinhalese SC), K. S. C. de Silva (Nondescripts CC), H. D. P. K. Dharmasena (Bloomfield C and AC), S. T. Jayasuriya (Bloomfield C and AC), R. S. Kaluwitharana (Colts CC), D. K. Liyanage (Colts CC), R. S. Mahanama (Bloomfield C and AC), M. Muralitharan (Tamil Union), K. R. Pushpakumara (Nondescripts CC), S. Ranatunga (Nondescripts CC), H. P. Tillekeratne (Nondescripts CC), D. N. T. Zoysa (Sinhalese SC).

W. P. U. J. C. Vaas (Colts CC) withdrew because of injury before the start of the tour and was replaced by Pushpakumara. R. S. Kalpage and M. N. Nawaz (both Bloomfield C and AC) replaced the injured Tillekeratne and Zoysa during the tour.

Manager: L. R D. Mendis.   *Coach:* B. Yardley.

SRI LANKAN TOUR RESULTS

Test matches – Played 2: Lost 1, Drawn 1.
First-class matches – Played 3: Lost 1, Drawn 2.
Loss – West Indies.
Draws – West Indies, Leeward Islands.
One-day international – Played 1: Lost 1.
Other non-first-class match – Lost v Trinidad & Tobago.

Note: Matches in this section which were not first-class are signified by a dagger.

†At Pointe-à-Pierre, June 4. Trinidad & Tobago won by three wickets, their target having been revised to 215 from 41 overs. Toss: Sri Lankans. Sri Lankans 226 for eight (50 overs) (M. S. Atapattu 55, H. P. Tillekeratne 49, R. S. Kaluwitharana 42; R. Dhanraj four for 59); Trinidad & Tobago 215 for seven (39.5 overs) (S. Ragoonath 110 not out, I. R. Bishop 53).

†WEST INDIES v SRI LANKA

One-Day International

At Port-of-Spain, June 6. West Indies won by 35 runs. Toss: Sri Lanka. International debuts: D. Ramnarine, F. L. Reifer.

Williams and Lara set the tempo for a formidable total by adding 124 in 22 overs after the pinch-hitters went cheaply. Lara's run-a-ball 67 included six fours and two sixes; Williams hit 12 fours and improved on his career-best for the third straight innings before holing out, ten short of a hundred, to give Jayasuriya one of his five wickets. The closing stages were dominated by an unbeaten 41 in 30 balls from Holder. Sri Lanka made an uncharacteristically slow start, restricted to 28 for two off 11 overs, before Jayasuriya, who had retired hurt, returned to complete a frantic 44 in 28 balls. After he fell, there were defiant fifties by Ranatunga and Dharmasena in a losing cause.

Man of the Match: S. C. Williams.

West Indies

S. C. Williams c Liyanage b Jayasuriya . .	90	R. I. C. Holder not out	41
†J. R. Murray c Muralitharan		L. R. Williams c Dharmasena b Jayasuriya	14
b K. S. C. de Silva .	2	C. E. L. Ambrose not out	9
F. A. Rose c Dharmasena b P. A. de Silva	7	L-b 12, w 4, n-b 3	19
B. C. Lara c Liyanage b Jayasuriya	67		
C. L. Hooper c Kaluwitharana		1/11 2/46 3/170 (7 wkts, 49 overs) 283	
b Jayasuriya .	25	4/184 5/211	
F. L. Reifer c Atapattu b Jayasuriya	9	6/220 7/254	

D. Ramnarine and *C. A. Walsh did not bat.

Bowling: Liyanage 9–1–36–0; K. S. C. de Silva 7–0–58–1; P. A. de Silva 3–0–20–1; Muralitharan 10–1–58–0; Dharmasena 10–0–41–0; Jayasuriya 10–0–58–5.

Sri Lanka

S. T. Jayasuriya c S. C. Williams		H. D. P. K. Dharmasena not out	51
b L. R. Williams .	44	D. K. Liyanage c and b L. R. Williams . .	43
M. S. Atapattu c Hooper b Walsh	1	M. Muralitharan not out	5
P. A. de Silva c Hooper b Ambrose	7		
*A. Ranatunga c Ambrose b Ramnarine . .	53	L-b 9, w 8, n-b 2	19
H. P. Tillekeratne c Reifer			
b L. R. Williams .	2	1/6 2/19 3/39 (8 wkts, 49 overs) 248	
R. S. Mahanama c Rose b Ramnarine . . .	14	4/89 5/121 6/139	
†R. S. Kaluwitharana b Hooper	9	7/150 8/241	

K. S. C. de Silva did not bat.

S. T. Jayasuriya, when 7, retired hurt at 8 and resumed at 39.

Bowling: Ambrose 7–1–19–1; Walsh 8–1–27–1; L. R. Williams 8–0–56–3; Rose 6–0–45–0; Hooper 10–1–40–1; Ramnarine 10–0–52–2.

Umpires: L. H. Barker and E. Nicholls.   Referee: Talat Ali (Pakistan).

At St John's, June 8, 9, 10. Drawn. Toss: Leeward Islands. Sri Lankans 192 for six dec. (R. S. Mahanama 65, A. Ranatunga 35) and 398 for four dec. (R. P. Arnold 158, M. S. Atapattu 118, P. A. de Silva 80); Leeward Islands 148 (R. Morton 31, R. D. Jacobs 35; M. Muralitharan four for 34) and 128 for no wkt (J. Mitchum 50 not out, A. Adams 68 not out).

WEST INDIES v SRI LANKA

First Test Match

At St John's, June 13, 14, 15. West Indies won by six wickets. Toss: West Indies. Test debut: F. L. Reifer.

Victory with more than two days to spare flattered West Indies, who needed their bowlers to pull them out of a hole dug by their batsmen. Ambrose was soon closing in on his 300th Test wicket, dismissing three men in the first half-hour on a damp, grassy pitch. But he was the only bowler to hit the right length consistently and, when he was relieved, Jayasuriya and Ranatunga turned things round with a brave stand of 110. Both collected body bruises as the ball darted around and bounced disconcertingly off a good length.

Sri Lankan coach Bruce Yardley complained about a "crap pitch" and argued that play should not have started before tea. But for all the devil in it, his batsmen survived the most testing period. After Ranatunga was run out, Tillekeratne, rashly batting without an arm guard, dropped his wrists and had his right forearm fractured by Walsh. Jayasuriya was eventually bowled driving over Hooper's faster ball; typically harsh on anything short, he had hit nine fours and two sixes in 223 minutes. Bishop collected his 150th wicket in 36 Tests as Kaluwitharana trod on his stumps, then Ambrose returned to achieve his own landmark when Sajeewa de Silva skied to cover. He was the fourth West Indian to take 300 wickets, in his 71st Test, and the 12th bowler in all.

What looked like a solid reply by West Indies on the first afternoon became a collapse next day, thanks to some indisciplined batting. Lara appeared unlucky to be given out to a keeper's catch, but it was an inspired spell by Pushpakumara that jolted the top order. Muralitharan swept aside the lower half in 35 balls, clean bowling the last three without conceding a run. After Campbell had gone for 50, the last six wickets tumbled for 21.

Ambrose quickly put his stamp on proceedings again, removing the dangerous Jayasuriya third ball and adding two more wickets as Sri Lanka extended their lead to 75. This time, his colleagues offered proper support to regain the initiative. The best stand, between Aravinda de Silva and Ranatunga, added only 44 before Bishop claimed both in his second over, and Dharmasena found no one to stay with him.

Sri Lanka were all out in 35 overs, leaving West Indies a target of 187, which appeared far from straightforward in a low-scoring match. But Williams and Campbell reeled off some breathtaking shots and raced to 160, West Indies' highest opening stand since Gordon Greenidge and Desmond Haynes put on a record 298, also at St John's, against England in 1989-90. Williams was the more fluent, hitting 12 fours and two sixes in 155 minutes before he was caught at long-on. Campbell also squandered his wicket, as did Lara, second ball, while debutant Floyd Reifer followed one run later. But victory was secured half an hour before tea.

Man of the Match: C. E. L. Ambrose.

Close of play: First day, West Indies 56-1 (S. L. Campbell 24*, F. L. Reifer 10*); Second day, Sri Lanka 151-8 (K. S. C. de Silva 2*, M. Muralitharan 0*).

Sri Lanka

S. T. Jayasuriya b Hooper	85	– c Hooper b Ambrose	0
R. S. Mahanama c Browne b Ambrose	1	– c Browne b Ambrose	14
R. P. Arnold c Williams b Ambrose	0	– c Browne b Ambrose	12
P. A. de Silva b Walsh b Ambrose	0	– c Browne b Bishop	47
*A. Ranatunga run out	42	– c Rose b Bishop	13
H. P. Tillekeratne retired hurt	1	– absent hurt	
†R. S. Kaluwitharana hit wkt b Bishop	23	– (6) c Browne b Walsh	16
H. D. P. K. Dharmasena c Browne b Ambrose	29	– (7) c Walsh b Rose	31
K. R. Pushpakumara c Reifer b Bishop	1	– (8) c Williams b Rose	8
K. S. C. de Silva c Reifer b Ambrose	6	– (9) not out	2
M. Muralitharan not out	6	– (10) c Williams b Rose	0
B 4, l-b 11, n-b 14	29	L-b 2, n-b 7	9

1/19 (2) 2/19 (3) 3/23 (4) 4/133 (5)   223   1/0 (1) 2/17 (3) 3/41 (2)   152
5/171 (1) 6/206 (7) 7/210 (9)   4/85 (5) 5/91 (4) 6/113 (6)
8/216 (8) 9/223 (10)   7/140 (8) 8/151 (7) 9/152 (10)

In the first innings H. P. Tillekeratne retired hurt at 139.

Bowling: *First Innings*—Ambrose 13.1–3–37–5; Bishop 15–3–44–2; Walsh 11–0–46–0; Rose 10–2–32–0; Hooper 19–2–49–1. *Second Innings*—Ambrose 9–0–41–3; Walsh 10–0–37–1; Rose 9–1–43–3; Bishop 7–0–29–2.

West Indies

S. L. Campbell c Muralitharan b K. S. C. de Silva	50	– c Mahanama b Muralitharan	79
S. C. Williams c Arnold b Pushpakumara	21	– c sub (D. K. Liyanage)	
		b Muralitharan	83
F. L. Reifer c Kaluwitharana b Pushpakumara	29	– b Dharmasena	1
B. C. Lara c Kaluwitharana b Pushpakumara	0	– c sub (D. K. Liyanage)	
		b Muralitharan	4
C. L. Hooper lbw b Muralitharan	27	– not out	6
R. I. C. Holder c and b Dharmasena	28	– not out	0
†C. O. Browne c Jayasuriya b Muralitharan	0		
I. R. Bishop b Muralitharan	5		
C. E. L. Ambrose not out	11		
F. A. Rose b Muralitharan	0		
*C. A. Walsh b Muralitharan	0		
B 4, l-b 6, n-b 8	18	B 4, l-b 2, w 1, n-b 9	16

1/40 (2) 2/94 (3) 3/97 (4) 4/122 (1)   189   1/160 (2) 2/178 (1)   (4 wkts) 189
5/168 (5) 6/168 (6) 7/172 (7)   3/182 (4) 4/183 (3)
8/189 (8) 9/189 (10) 10/189 (11)

Bowling: *First Innings*—K. S. C. de Silva 13–1–56–1; Pushpakumara 15–2–62–3; Dharmasena 8–4–19–1; Muralitharan 23.4–13–34–5; Jayasuriya 1–0–8–0. *Second Innings*—K. S. C. de Silva 9–2–35–0; Pushpakumara 8–0–38–0; Muralitharan 21.2–5–72–3; Dharmasena 7–1–21–1; Jayasuriya 4–0–17–0.

Umpires: R. S. Dunne (New Zealand) and L. H. Barker.   Referee: Talat Ali (Pakistan).

WEST INDIES v SRI LANKA

Second Test Match

At St Vincent, June 20, 21, 22, 23, 24. Drawn. Toss: Sri Lanka.

A tense finish to a memorable inaugural Test at picturesque Arnos Vale was spoiled by bad light and showers. Sri Lanka had dominated most of the exchanges, but when the umpires offered Arjuna Ranatunga the light late on the final day, he was relieved to come off at 233 for eight, still 36 from victory.

West Indies' carefree batting again let them down. Sent in on a pitch holding no terrors, they lasted 44.4 overs: only Hooper applied himself. Williams top-edged a hook in Pushpakumara's first over and Reifer was plumb lbw next ball. Lara made it five for three, lobbing back to Sajeewa de Silva, and they never really recovered. The last five wickets fell for 21 as Muralitharan combined with Pushpakumara, who induced one of Hooper's few mistakes, a firm drive that found mid-on. That ended two and three-quarter hours' exquisite batting in which Hooper hit a six and ten fours.

Sri Lanka replied with a flourish and closed ten ahead with only three men out. But they could not recapture their momentum next day, when West Indies fought back gallantly, with defensive fields supported by cleverly orchestrated lines of attack. From 178 for three, the last seven Sri Lankans subsided for 44. Jayasuriya, who had batted aggressively against the new ball to run up 80 in 107 deliveries, with 11 fours, needed 41 more balls to score another ten. He was lbw padding out a drifter from Hooper, who completed his best first-class figures, five for 26.

The deficit was only 75 and West Indies' batsmen soon made up for their first-innings indiscretions, with Lara stealing the show. After three failures and a fine for arriving late for the First Test, he accumulated a determined century, his tenth in Tests. He raised his bat again at 111, aware he had amassed 4,000 Test runs, before he miscued Dharmasena to mid-wicket. He had struck 11 fours and a six and batted 266 minutes and 207 balls. When Lara was out, West Indies led by 197. Holder and Ambrose stretched that with an eighth-wicket stand of 53 before Muralitharan wrapped up the innings, taking his haul for the series to 16. He finished by dismissing Walsh for his 25th Test duck, which passed Danny Morrison's record.

By the end of the rain-interrupted fourth day, the match hung in the balance, with Sri Lanka 97 for two pursuing 269. West Indies had held a marginal edge when Aravinda de Silva unleashed a calculated assault, lashing 34 in 28 balls, including 18 from Bishop's third over. He lost Mahanama on the final, sunny morning, but he and Arjuna Ranatunga took lunch at 179 for three, just 90 from their goal.

Heavy rain swept across the ground to wipe out the next session. Then, after tea, Walsh bowled de Silva with a perfect off-stump yorker. As the tension mounted, no one else could establish a stand with Ranatunga; he remained unbeaten on 72 after more than three hours when the weather had the final say.

Man of the Match: C. L. Hooper.

Close of play: First day, Sri Lanka 157-3 (S. T. Jayasuriya 80*, A. Ranatunga 0*); Second day, West Indies 19-0 (S. L. Campbell 13*, S. C. Williams 6*); Third day, West Indies 128-2 (B. C. Lara 30*, F. L. Reifer 15*); Fourth day, Sri Lanka 97-2 (R. S. Mahanama 26*, P. A. de Silva 34*).

West Indies

S. L. Campbell c Mahanama b Dharmasena	20	– b Pushpakumara	33
S. C. Williams c Kaluwitharana b Pushpakumara	0	– c Jayasuriya b Muralitharan	46
F. L. Reifer lbw b Pushpakumara	0	– (4) c Kaluwitharana b Pushpakumara	18
B. C. Lara c and b K. S. C. de Silva	1	– (3) c Jayasuriya b Dharmasena	115
C. L. Hooper c Atapattu b Pushpakumara	81	– c Kaluwitharana b Dharmasena	34
R. I. C. Holder c Atapattu b Muralitharan	16	– hit wkt b Muralitharan	34
I. R. Bishop b Muralitharan	11	– lbw b Muralitharan	0
†C. O. Browne lbw b Pushpakumara	0	– lbw b Muralitharan	0
C. E. L. Ambrose b Pushpakumara	7	– c Kaluwitharana b K. S. C. de Silva	31
F. A. Rose b Muralitharan	1	– not out	0
*C. A. Walsh not out	1	– b Muralitharan	0
B 3, l-b 2, n-b 3	9	B 4, l-b 21, n-b 7	32
	147		**343**

1/2 (2) 2/2 (3) 3/5 (4) 4/34 (1)   1/62 (1) 2/92 (2) 3/143 (4)
5/92 (6) 6/126 (7) 7/133 (8)   4/240 (5) 5/272 (3) 6/276 (7)
8/140 (5) 9/145 (10) 10/147 (9)   7/286 (8) 8/339 (9)
      9/343 (6) 10/343 (11)

Bowling: *First Innings*—K. S. C. de Silva 13–2–46–1; Pushpakumara 12.4–1–41–5; Dharmasena 7–0–26–1; Muralitharan 12–1–28–3. *Second Innings*—K. S. C. de Silva 17–1–62–1; Pushpakumara 19–2–81–2; Muralitharan 41–13–113–5; Dharmasena 25–4–62–2.

Sri Lanka

S. T. Jayasuriya lbw b Hooper	90	– b Walsh	17
R. S. Mahanama c Browne b Rose	28	– c Browne b Bishop	29
M. S. Atapattu c Hooper b Rose	7	– b Walsh	10
P. A. de Silva c Lara b Hooper	35	– b Walsh	78
*A. Ranatunga c Lara b Walsh	13	– not out	72
S. Ranatunga c Hooper b Walsh	9	– (7) run out	0
†R. S. Kaluwitharana c Browne b Ambrose	7	– (6) hit wkt b Walsh	2
H. D. P. K. Dharmasena b Hooper	10	– c Browne b Ambrose	7
K. R. Pushpakumara c Browne b Hooper	0		
K. S. C. de Silva not out	4	– not out	1
M. Muralitharan c Reifer b Hooper	4	– (9) c Holder b Ambrose	0
B 2, l-b 3, n-b 10	15	L-b 3, n-b 14	17
	222	(8 wkts)	**233**

1/62 (2) 2/75 (3) 3/151 (4) 4/178 (5)   1/26 (1) 2/55 (3)
5/185 (1) 6/196 (7) 7/211 (8)   3/118 (2) 4/189 (4)
8/211 (9) 9/215 (6) 10/222 (11)   5/193 (6) 6/208 (7)
      7/231 (8) 8/231 (9)

Bowling: *First Innings*—Ambrose 9–1–34–1; Walsh 22–3–62–2; Rose 12–1–44–2; Bishop 7–0–51–0; Hooper 13.4–5–26–5. *Second Innings*—Ambrose 15–1–51–2; Walsh 24–2–73–4; Rose 6–1–24–0; Bishop 14–1–61–1; Hooper 9–3–21–0.

Umpires: D. B. Cowie (New Zealand) and S. A. Bucknor.   Referee: Talat Ali (Pakistan).

SINGER WORLD SERIES, 1996-97

By TRENT BOUTS

As in the World Cup six months earlier, Kalashnikovs and body searches were as characteristic of this tournament as the cricket itself. The result was just the same too. After Zimbabwe and India had been seen off, Sri Lanka – who won all their games – beat Australia in the final.

The Australians mended important fences simply by coming to Sri Lanka, which they had refused to do in the World Cup. But, largely at their behest, a fortune was spent on security. Weeks after a terrorist train bombing had once again brought tragedy to Colombo, the players were rarely allowed outside their hotel at night, though they did once take a bus to a restaurant 50 metres away.

The security worked, though – except when the sons of a local official tossed water on to the Australian players in their viewing area. And the tournament's success was a fillip for Sri Lankan morale, especially as the team were once again magnificent. Sanath Jayasuriya and Romesh Kaluwitharana provided the high-octane starts that have revolutionised one-day cricket, and Aravinda de Silva was sublime. In four innings, he scored 334 without losing his wicket.

All three visiting teams had new captains. Ian Healy led Australia because Mark Taylor had a back strain; Sachin Tendulkar had recently been appointed to succeed Mohammad Azharuddin, and Alistair Campbell took over Zimbabwe because Andy Flower had decided the triple strain of captaincy, wicket-keeping and batting was too much.

In contrast, Arjuna Ranatunga had nearly eight years' experience of leading his team, and chalked up his 50th win in limited-overs internationals during the competition. Tendulkar asked wicket-keeper Nayan Mongia to open with him in one game and once threw the new ball to leg-spinner Anil Kumble. Neither move was a roaring success, but each signalled a bolder brand of Indian cricket.

Note: Matches in this section were not first-class.

AUSTRALIA v ZIMBABWE

At R. Premadasa Stadium, Colombo, August 26 (day/night). Australia won by 125 runs. Toss: Australia. International debut: G. B. Hogg.

Healy kept to Australia's usual habit of batting after winning the toss. On a sound if sluggish pitch, they were never troubled. Slater scored his first one-day fifty since March 1995 and Steve Waugh made 82 off 70 balls. Campbell had talked of a bolder Zimbabwean approach, but it came to nothing. Indeed, Shah, returning to international cricket after nearly two years, was the only batsman to reach 20; he advanced to 41, taking up 30 overs, before becoming the first victim of left-arm wrist-spinner Brad Hogg, promoted because Warne had stayed at home after finger surgery.

Man of the Match: S. R. Waugh.

Australia

M. J. Slater c Strang b Whittall	50	G. B. Hogg not out	11
M. E. Waugh b Strang	18		
R. T. Ponting c and b Whittall	53	B 1, l-b 8, w 3, n-b 3	15
S. R. Waugh c Campbell b Whittall	82		
S. G. Law b Streak	20	1/48 2/92 3/167 (7 wkts, 50 overs)	263
M. G. Bevan c Campbell b Brandes	9	4/230 5/240	
*†I. A. Healy b Brandes	5	6/242 7/263	

P. R. Reiffel, D. W. Fleming and G. D. McGrath did not bat.

Bowling: Streak 10–1–50–1; Brandes 10–1–47–2; Strang 9–0–41–1; G. W. Flower 6–0–28–0; Whittall 10–0–53–3; Dekker 3–0–17–0; Shah 2–0–18–0.

Zimbabwe

G. W. Flower c Ponting b Fleming	7	P. A. Strang b M. E. Waugh	9
A. H. Shah c M. E. Waugh b Hogg	41	H. H. Streak b M. E. Waugh	0
†A. Flower lbw b Fleming	0	E. A. Brandes c Hogg b M. E. Waugh	17
*A. D. R. Campbell lbw b McGrath	9	L-b 4, w 10, n-b 7	21
C. B. Wishart b Healy b Reiffel	0		
G. J. Whittall b Reiffel	11	1/16 2/16 3/33 (41 overs)	138
C. N. Evans c Healy b S. R. Waugh	15	4/35 5/56 6/98	
M. H. Dekker not out	8	7/100 8/120 9/120	

Bowling: McGrath 7–2–13–1; Fleming 7–0–24–2; Reiffel 6–1–23–2; S. R. Waugh 7–2–24–1; Hogg 9–2–26–1; M. E. Waugh 5–1–24–3.

Umpires: K. T. Francis and W. A. U. Wickremasinghe.

SRI LANKA v INDIA

At R. Premadasa Stadium, Colombo, August 28 (day/night). Sri Lanka won by nine wickets. Toss: India.

Tendulkar launched himself into captaincy with a century. But his 110, off 138 balls, was made to look pedestrian by Jayasuriya, who scored an unbeaten 120 off just 128. He saw Sri Lanka home with nine wickets and 5.4 overs to spare, but had to be carried from the field because of cramp. Already tired after bowling ten overs, he had skipped tea, believing his innings would be brief. After Jayasuriya and Kaluwitharana had raised Sri Lanka's first-wicket record to 129, de Silva scored a composed 49 not out – an *hors d'oeuvre* to what was to become a feast.

Man of the Match: S. T. Jayasuriya.

India

A. Jadeja run out	0	R. Dravid not out	7
*S. R. Tendulkar run out	110	J. Srinath not out	1
S. C. Ganguly c de Silva b Dharmasena	16	B 1, l-b 3, w 9, n-b 3	16
M. Azharuddin st Kaluwitharana b Jayasuriya	58	1/4 2/57 3/186 (5 wkts, 50 overs)	226
V. G. Kambli run out	18	4/217 5/218	

†N. R. Mongia, A. Kumble, A. R. Kapoor and B. K. V. Prasad did not bat.

Bowling: Vaas 9–2–35–0; Pushpakumara 6–0–23–0; Dharmasena 10–0–59–1; Muralitharan 10–0–42–0; Jayasuriya 10–1–39–1; de Silva 5–0–24–0.

Sri Lanka

S. T. Jayasuriya not out	120
†R. S. Kaluwitharana b Tendulkar	53
P. A. de Silva not out	49
L-b 3, w 2, n-b 3	8

1/129   (1 wkt, 44.2 overs) 230

A. P. Gurusinha, *A. Ranatunga, H. P. Tillekeratne, R. S. Mahanama, H. D. P. K. Dharmasena, W. P. U. J. C. Vaas, K. R. Pushpakumara and M. Muralitharan did not bat.

Bowling: Srinath 8–0–33–0; Prasad 6–0–47–0; Kapoor 10–2–51–0; Kumble 10–1–40–0; Tendulkar 6–0–29–1; Jadeja 2.2–0–13–0; Ganguly 2–0–14–0.

Umpires: S. A. Bucknor and C. J. Mitchley.

SRI LANKA v AUSTRALIA

At R. Premadasa Stadium, Colombo, August 30 (day/night). Sri Lanka won by four wickets. Toss: Australia. International debuts: J. N. Gillespie, D. S. Lehmann.

Sri Lanka delighted a packed house with a reprise of their World Cup victory. There was a special roar when Australian captain Healy was out – caught Ranatunga, bowled Muralitharan. Healy had cast aspersions on Ranatunga in a recent book and Muralitharan was considered a martyr because of allegations of throwing during Sri Lanka's torrid tour of Australia seven months before. Loud boos followed Healy all the way to the middle, but they were nothing to the cheers that saw him off. As in the World Cup final, Sri Lanka had some early scares; they were gravely ill at 81 for five, after Fleming took three wickets in eight balls. But, strangely, Fleming and McGrath were left in the outfield while de Silva and Mahanama provided a 115-run transfusion.

Man of the Match: P. A. de Silva.

Australia

M. E. Waugh c and b Jayasuriya	50	J. N. Gillespie st Kaluwitharana	
M. J. Slater run out	9	b Chandana	6
S. G. Law c Tillekeratne b Dharmasena	13	D. W. Fleming c Chandana b Jayasuriya	3
M. G. Bevan c Vaas b Dharmasena	56	G. D. McGrath not out	8
S. R. Waugh b Muralitharan	22	L-b 3, n-b 2	5
R. T. Ponting not out	46		
D. S. Lehmann st Kaluwitharana		1/21 2/52 3/97 (9 wkts, 50 overs) 228	
b Chandana	2	4/149 5/157 6/163	
*†I. A. Healy c Ranatunga b Muralitharan	8	7/178 8/198 9/203	

Bowling: Vaas 7–0–29–0; de Silva 4–0–25–0; Dharmasena 9–0–49–1; Muralitharan 10–0–41–2; Jayasuriya 10–0–43–2; Chandana 10–0–38–3.

Sri Lanka

S. T. Jayasuriya c Healy b Fleming	44	R. S. Mahanama b McGrath	50
†R. S. Kaluwitharana b S. R. Waugh	8	U. D. U. Chandana not out	14
A. P. Gurusinha run out	16	L-b 3, w 7, n-b 6	16
P. A. de Silva not out	83		
*A. Ranatunga lbw b Fleming	0	1/22 2/78 3/78 (6 wkts, 45.5 overs) 232	
H. P. Tillekeratne lbw b Fleming	1	4/78 5/81 6/196	

H. D. P. K. Dharmasena, W. P. U. J. C. Vaas and M. Muralitharan did not bat.

Bowling: S. R. Waugh 5–1–36–1; Law 2–0–23–0; McGrath 9.5–0–44–1; Fleming 8–1–26–3; Gillespie 6–0–27–0; M. E. Waugh 5–0–29–0; Lehmann 6–0–26–0; Bevan 4–0–18–0.

Umpires: S. A. Bucknor and C. J. Mitchley.

INDIA v ZIMBABWE

At Sinhalese Sports Club, Colombo, September 1. India won by seven wickets. Toss: India.

The Zimbabweans put on a better show than in their first match, chiefly thanks to Andy Flower and Wishart, who added 84. Kumble was unusually late into the Indian attack but, when he did come on, claimed four for 33 in ten overs. This offered Zimbabwe some hope that their leg-spinner, Paul Strang, might give them a chance; instead, he was thrashed for 73. Tendulkar and Jadeja opened in the Sri Lankan manner, scoring 91 in the first 15 overs. There was an attempt, supported by referee John Reid, to reduce Zimbabwe's total to 225, because the television camera had missed umpire Samarasinghe signalling a wide against Prasad; the scorers remained adamant that they had seen and acknowledged the signal.

Man of the Match: A. Jadeja.

Zimbabwe

*A. D. R. Campbell c Tendulkar b Prasad	10	H. H. Streak b Kumble	2
P. A. Strang st Mongia b Joshi	19	A. H. Shah c Azharuddin b Prasad	6
†A. Flower c Prasad b Kumble	78	B. C. Strang not out	1
C. N. Evans c Mongia b Joshi	4	L-b 12, w 9, n-b 2	23
G. W. Flower b Kumble	26		
C. B. Wishart c Joshi b Kumble	53	1/22 2/50 3/61	(49.4 overs) 226
G. J. Whittall run out	1	4/117 5/201 6/204	
M. H. Dekker c Kumble b Srinath	3	7/217 8/218 9/220	

Bowling: Srinath 10–2–42–1; Prasad 7.4–0–42–2; Joshi 10–1–37–2; Jadeja 5–0–20–0; Tendulkar 4–0–20–0; Kumble 10–2–33–4; Ganguly 3–0–20–0.

India

A. Jadeja c A. Flower b Evans	68	V. G. Kambli not out	29
*S. R. Tendulkar c B. C. Strang b Streak	40		
S. C. Ganguly c B. C. Strang b P. A. Strang	36	L-b 1, w 9, n-b 6	16
M. Azharuddin not out	40	1/91 2/148 3/161 (3 wkts, 43.5 overs) 229

R. Dravid, †N. R. Mongia, S. B. Joshi, J. Srinath, A. Kumble and B. K. V. Prasad did not bat.

Bowling: Streak 10–1–46–1; B. C. Strang 7.5–0–52–0; P. A. Strang 10–0–73–1; Whittall 9–0–28–0; G. W. Flower 2–0–10–0; Evans 5–0–19–1.

Umpires: B. C. Cooray and T. M. Samarasinghe.

SRI LANKA v ZIMBABWE

At Sinhalese Sports Club, Colombo, September 3. Sri Lanka won by six wickets. Toss: Sri Lanka. International debut: A. R. Whittall.

Play was delayed eight minutes while the umpires hunted for the bails, which turned up in a groundsman's pocket. Even then, momentum was sluggish: Wickremasinghe bowled five wides in his first over. Evans hit a career-best 96, with six fours and three sixes almost exclusively to the mid-wicket boundary, and lifted Zimbabwe to a respectable 227. That suddenly looked threatening when Olonga, making a rare limited-overs appearance, blasted out both openers. But his second spell was delayed until de Silva's century, with 13 fours and a six at better than a run a ball, was in the book and Sri Lanka's clean sweep in the qualifiers was certain.

Man of the Match: P. A. de Silva.

Zimbabwe

G. W. Flower c Kaluwitharana		C. B. Wishart c Chandana b Ranatunga ..	7
b Pushpakumara .	0	C. N. Evans not out	96
P. A. Strang c Kaluwitharana		G. J. Whittall not out	15
b Pushpakumara .	24		
A. Flower c Kaluwitharana		L-b 7, w 13................	20
b Wickremasinghe .	11		
*A. D. R. Campbell st Kaluwitharana		1/13 2/48 3/48 (5 wkts, 50 overs)	227
b Muralitharan .	54	4/66 5/180	

†W. R. James, H. H. Streak, H. K. Olonga and A. R. Whittall did not bat.

Bowling: Wickremasinghe 9–1–32–1; Pushpakumara 6–0–28–2; Muralitharan 10–1–36–1; Ranatunga 5–0–22–1; Chandana 10–0–48–0; Jayasuriya 10–1–54–0.

Sri Lanka

S. T. Jayasuriya b Olonga	5	H. P. Tillekeratne not out.............	34
†R. S. Kaluwitharana c Wishart b Olonga	12	B 1, l-b 2, w 8, n-b 4.........	15
A. P. Gurusinha run out	15		
P. A. de Silva not out 127		1/18 2/25 (4 wkts, 47 overs)	228
*A. Ranatunga c Olonga b A. R. Whittall	20	3/100 4/129	

M. S. Atapattu, U. D. U. Chandana, G. P. Wickremasinghe, K. R. Pushpakumara and M. Muralitharan did not bat.

Bowling: Streak 8–0–24–0; Olonga 6–0–47–2; G. J. Whittall 5–0–26–0; A. R. Whittall 10–1–30–1; Strang 10–0–50–0; Campbell 4–0–24–0; G. W. Flower 1–0–10–0; Evans 3–0–14–0.

Umpires: S. A. Bucknor and C. J. Mitchley.

AUSTRALIA v INDIA

At Sinhalese Sports Club, Colombo, September 6. Australia won by three wickets. Toss: Australia.

Postponed a day and shortened to 45 overs by rain, the contest to claim the remaining berth in the final was a flat affair until a spate of wickets late in Australia's chase. A brave stand of 100 in 20 overs by left-handers Ganguly and Joshi rescued India from a humiliating 89 for six. Then Kambli missed a sitter at mid-wicket offered by Steve Waugh, who put on 113 with Law. India were luckier after umpire Francis turned down an appeal for run out against Healy. Boos from those watching the replay prompted him to call for the TV verdict and Healy was given out. But Bevan drove the winning boundary with three balls to spare.

Man of the Match: S. R. Waugh.

India

†N. R. Mongia c Bevan b McGrath	38	J. Srinath run out	2
*S. R. Tendulkar c S. R. Waugh		A. Kumble c S. R. Waugh b M. E. Waugh	0
b McGrath .	7	B. K. V. Prasad not out	6
R. Dravid b Reiffel	13		
M. Azharuddin c M. E. Waugh b Reiffel .	3	L-b 3, w 11, n-b 4	18
V. G. Kambli c Healy b McGrath.......	1		
A. Jadeja c and b S. R. Waugh........	6	1/32 2/64 3/67 (41 overs)	201
S. C. Ganguly lbw b Bevan	59	4/68 5/72 6/89	
S. B. Joshi b Bevan	48	7/189 8/191 9/194	

Bowling: McGrath 9–1–33–3; Fleming 6–0–25–0; Reiffel 5–0–37–2; S. R. Waugh 6–0–20–1; Hogg 5–0–33–0; M. E. Waugh 7–0–36–1; Bevan 3–0–14–2.

Australia

M. J. Slater c Azharuddin b Prasad	29	G. B. Hogg b Kumble		2
M. E. Waugh c Tendulkar b Joshi	23	P. R. Reiffel not out		1
R. T. Ponting lbw b Joshi	0	L-b 2, w 4, n-b 3		9
S. R. Waugh st Mongia b Kumble	55			
S. G. Law c Dravid b Prasad	67	1/50 2/50 3/69	(7 wkts, 44.3 overs)	202
M. G. Bevan not out	12	4/182 5/185		
*†I. A. Healy run out	4	6/194 7/197		

D. W. Fleming and G. D. McGrath did not bat.

Bowling: Srinath 6–0–32–0; Prasad 9–0–53–2; Joshi 9–1–23–2; Kumble 8.3–1–36–2; Tendulkar 8–0–38–0; Jadeja 4–0–18–0.

Umpires: B. C. Cooray and K. T. Francis.

QUALIFYING TABLE

	Played	Won	Lost	Points	Net run-rate
Sri Lanka	3	3	0	6	0.49
Australia	3	2	1	4	0.74
India	3	1	2	2	−0.01
Zimbabwe	3	0	3	0	−1.17

Net run-rate was calculated by subtracting runs conceded per over from runs scored per over.

FINAL

SRI LANKA v AUSTRALIA

At R. Premadasa Stadium, Colombo, September 7. Sri Lanka won by 50 runs. Toss: Australia.

Australia had always won when chasing a Sri Lankan target, so Healy fielded first. But the new Sri Lankan game laughs at precedent. The visitors paid dearly for missing both Jayasuriya and Kaluwitharana, and the 100 came up in the 13th over with only one of them out. Later de Silva lifted Reiffel for successive sixes to reach 75 not out from 64 balls. The Australians might have been hard-pressed to beat 234 in 50 overs, but this was a 35-over game because overnight rain had delayed the start. Although Steve Waugh scored a run-a-ball fifty in his 200th one-day international, Sri Lanka were always on top. They fielded only one pace bowler, Vaas, but leg-spinner Chandana took four wickets, suggesting they had the depth to hold sway in one-day cricket for some time.

Man of the Match: P. A. de Silva.   *Man of the Series:* P. A. de Silva.

Sri Lanka

S. T. Jayasuriya c Law b McGrath	27	*A. Ranatunga not out		39
†R. S. Kaluwitharana c and b Lehmann	58	B 1, l-b 1, w 2, n-b 2		6
A. P. Gurusinha c Bevan b McGrath	29			
P. A. de Silva not out	75	1/42 2/104 3/131	(3 wkts, 35 overs)	234

H. P. Tillekeratne, R. S. Mahanama, U. D. U. Chandana, H. D. P. K. Dharmasena, W. P. U. J. C. Vaas and M. Muralitharan did not bat.

Bowling: McGrath 7–0–35–2; Fleming 7–0–53–0; Reiffel 4–0–43–0; Lehmann 5–0–29–1; S. R. Waugh 7–0–31–0; M. E. Waugh 5–0–41–0.

Australia

M. E. Waugh run out	9	P. R. Reiffel c Mahanama b Chandana	12
M. J. Slater c Chandana b Vaas	8	D. W. Fleming not out	1
R. T. Ponting c Jayasuriya b Vaas	17	G. D. McGrath c Mahanama b Chandana	0
S. R. Waugh c and b Chandana	55		
S. G. Law c Muralitharan b Dharmasena	31	L-b 3, w 4, n-b 2	9
M. G. Bevan b Dharmasena	7		
D. S. Lehmann st Kaluwitharana		1/17 2/26 3/48	(33 overs) 184
b Muralitharan	15	4/104 5/129 6/145	
*†I. A. Healy c Muralitharan b Chandana	20	7/151 8/183 9/183	

Bowling: Vaas 5–0–23–2; Gurusinha 2–0–17–0; de Silva 3–0–18–0; Muralitharan 7–0–28–1; Jayasuriya 5–0–27–0; Dharmasena 5–0–33–2; Chandana 6–0–35–4.

Umpires: S. A. Bucknor and C. J. Mitchley. Series referee: J. R. Reid (New Zealand).

SAHARA CUP, 1996-97

By R. MOHAN

Canadians hearing the scoreline "Pakistan 3, India 2" in September 1996 may have assumed they were hearing an ice hockey or baseball result. In fact, the Toronto Cricket, Skating & Curling Club had just become the cricket world's latest off-shore venue for official one-day internationals, hosting five games between India and Pakistan. It was not ideal – the playing field was no better than that of a college campus and the local pitch technology was primitive. Moreover, the torrential rains brought by Hurricane Fran washed out the first two scheduled days and gave the pitches no time to recover between matches.

The other unfortunate consequence of the wet weather was that three of the four planned weekend games had to be staged on weekdays, in front of very small crowds. The one match played on a Saturday attracted 5,000, mainly expatriate Indians, Pakistanis and West Indians; a similar number arrived the following day for the series decider but left disappointed. The real target audience, however, was the aspiring middle class of the Indian subcontinent, who could follow the matches on an American television channel beamed out of Singapore. The promoters agreed to a multi-million dollar five-year deal revolving round the television rights; if the series proved one thing, it was that the clicking turnstile is no longer the index of marketing success.

But Toronto also provided a peaceful setting for matches which have so often proved incendiary in India or Pakistan. There were no riots, despite rival fans rubbing shoulders in the temporary stands, nor were there any reports of suicides or smashing of televisions after Pakistan, who came from behind twice, won the fifth and final match. The atmosphere was also friendly on the field. "After all, it's a game," commented victorious captain Wasim Akram.

Note: Matches in this section were not first-class.

INDIA v PAKISTAN

First One-Day International

At Toronto, September 16. India won by eight wickets. Toss: India. International debut: Azhar Mahmood.

The series made a belated start, after rain prevented any play over the weekend. Atmosphere was distinctly lacking, with only 750 watching on the Monday. The match was reduced to 33 overs a side and the pitch was still damp. India's bowling was spot on after Saeed Anwar, with 46 from 34 balls, and Ijaz Ahmed had taken Pakistan to 80 for one; only tailender Saqlain Mushtaq lifted them past 150. Timing the ball was not easy, but Tendulkar gave impetus to India's chase with a run-a-ball 89, including nine fours and three sixes, and settled the issue by adding 65 in nine overs with Azharuddin.

Man of the Match: S. R. Tendulkar.

Pakistan

Aamir Sohail c Dravid b Srinath	12	
Saeed Anwar c and b Kumble	46	
Ijaz Ahmed, sen. lbw b Srinath	35	
Inzamam-ul-Haq c Kumble b Prasad	5	
Salim Malik c Joshi b Kumble	3	
Shadab Kabir c Azharuddin b Kumble	0	
*Wasim Akram run out	9	
†Moin Khan c Tendulkar b Srinath	2	
Azhar Mahmood c Joshi b Prasad	6	
Saqlain Mushtaq not out	22	
Waqar Younis not out	6	
L-b 13, w 2, n-b 9	24	

1/44 2/80 3/90 4/98 5/108 6/123 7/131 8/135 9/148   (9 wkts, 33 overs) 170

Bowling: Srinath 7–0–23–3; Prasad 7–0–38–2; Jadeja 4–0–30–0; Joshi 6–0–22–0; Kumble 7–0–32–3; Tendulkar 2–0–12–0.

India

†N. R. Mongia b Waqar Younis	9
*S. R. Tendulkar not out	89
R. Dravid c Aamir Sohail b Salim Malik	39
M. Azharuddin not out	30
L-b 2, w 3, n-b 1	6

1/18 2/108   (2 wkts, 29.5 overs) 173

V. G. Kambli, A. Jadeja, S. C. Ganguly, S. B. Joshi, J. Srinath, A. Kumble and B. K. V. Prasad did not bat.

Bowling: Waqar Younis 6–0–30–1; Wasim Akram 6.5–0–37–0; Azhar Mahmood 4–0–19–0; Aamir Sohail 3–0–25–0; Saqlain Mushtaq 6–0–39–0; Salim Malik 4–0–21–1.

Umpires: L. H. Barker and D. R. Shepherd.

INDIA v PAKISTAN

Second One-Day International

At Toronto, September 17. Pakistan won by two wickets. Toss: Pakistan.

With the pitch playing far better, a stand of 161 between Azharuddin, who passed 6,000 runs in his 222nd one-day international, and Dravid set up a stiff target. Saeed Anwar's early brilliance kept Pakistan on the ball: he hit 80 from 78 balls, with three sixes and six fours. But the match turned back India's way when he holed out off Tendulkar. Salim Malik revived the chase, but Pakistan were 221 for eight, needing 44 at a run a ball, when Saqlain Mushtaq joined him. He provided durable company and, ignoring a twisted ankle, Malik cut the penultimate ball of the match from Joshi through the gap at point for a boundary.

Man of the Match: Salim Malik.

India

†N. R. Mongia c Wasim Akram	A. Jadeja not out 21
b Azhar Mahmood . 18	J. Srinath c Wasim Akram
*S. R. Tendulkar c Wasim Akram	b Saqlain Mushtaq . 0
b Azhar Mahmood . 20	S. C. Ganguly not out 11
R. Dravid b Saqlain Mushtaq 90	
M. Azharuddin c Azhar Mahmood	
b Mushtaq Ahmed . 88	B 4, l-b 5, w 3, n-b 1 13
V. G. Kambli c Aamir Sohail	
b Mushtaq Ahmed . 3	1/32 2/44 3/205 (6 wkts, 50 overs) 264
	4/214 5/245 6/245

S. B. Joshi, A. Kumble and B. K. V. Prasad did not bat.

Bowling: Wasim Akram 10–1–52–0; Waqar Younis 6–0–37–0; Azhar Mahmood 9–2–38–2; Mushtaq Ahmed 9–0–47–2; Saqlain Mushtaq 10–0–39–2; Aamir Sohail 5–0–33–0; Salim Malik 1–0–9–0.

Pakistan

Saeed Anwar c Joshi b Tendulkar 80	Mushtaq Ahmed c and b Srinath 4
Aamir Sohail c Mongia b Prasad 0	Saqlain Mushtaq not out 11
Ijaz Ahmed, sen. c Mongia b Prasad 13	
Inzamam-ul-Haq c Dravid b Kumble 29	B 4, l-b 11, w 9 24
Salim Malik not out 70	
†Moin Khan c Azharuddin b Joshi 14	1/10 2/44 3/115 (8 wkts, 49.5 overs) 266
*Wasim Akram c Ganguly b Srinath 20	4/144 5/169 6/214
Azhar Mahmood run out 1	7/215 8/221

Waqar Younis did not bat.

Bowling: Srinath 10–0–53–2; Prasad 10–0–54–2; Joshi 9.5–1–57–1; Jadeja 3–0–20–0; Kumble 10–0–32–1; Tendulkar 7–0–35–1.

Umpires: L. H. Barker and D. L. Orchard.

INDIA v PAKISTAN

Third One-Day International

At Toronto, September 18. India won by 55 runs. Toss: India.

Three matches in three days were fast wearing out the pitch. For the first time, the run-ups were dry enough for Wasim Akram and Waqar Younis to exploit their pace; India lost their last five for 12 runs. But their fast bowlers found similar encouragement, taking Pakistan's first three wickets for 16. Then leg-spinner Kumble came into his own, claiming four for 12 in seven overs despite some late striking from Moin Khan. Mongia equalled the world record of five dismissals in a limited-overs international and became the only wicket-keeper to have done it twice.

Man of the Match: R. Dravid.

India

†N. R. Mongia lbw b Wasim Akram 2	J. Srinath c Saqlain Mushtaq
*S. R. Tendulkar c Aamir Sohail	b Wasim Akram . 3
b Wasim Akram . 2	A. R. Kapoor c Mushtaq Ahmed
R. Dravid c Salim Elahi	b Saqlain Mushtaq . 0
b Saqlain Mushtaq . 46	A. Kumble run out 2
M. Azharuddin st Moin Khan	B. K. V. Prasad not out 0
b Aamir Sohail . 38	L-b 8, w 7 15
V. G. Kambli st Moin Khan	
b Mushtaq Ahmed . 29	1/5 2/14 3/88 (50 overs) 191
A. Jadeja b Wasim Akram 23	4/103 5/133 6/179
S. B. Joshi run out 31	7/183 8/189 9/189

Bowling: Wasim Akram 9–0–35–4; Waqar Younis 7–1–15–0; Azhar Mahmood 5–1–28–0; Mushtaq Ahmed 10–2–29–1; Aamir Sohail 9–1–31–1; Saqlain Mushtaq 10–0–45–2.

Pakistan

Saeed Anwar c Tendulkar b Kumble	 28	Saqlain Mushtaq c Tendulkar b Prasad	... 9
Salim Elahi c Kambli b Srinath	 4	Mushtaq Ahmed st Mongia b Joshi	 1
Aamir Sohail c Mongia b Prasad	 1	Waqar Younis not out	 0
Ijaz Ahmed, sen. c Mongia b Prasad	 0	B 1, l-b 10, w 3	 14
Salim Malik lbw b Kumble	 27		—
Azhar Mahmood b Kumble	 10	1/9 2/12 3/16	(42.4 overs) 136
*Wasim Akram st Mongia b Kumble	 0	4/63 5/66 6/66	
†Moin Khan c Mongia b Srinath	 42	7/91 8/124 9/131	

Bowling: Srinath 7.4–0–20–2; Prasad 9–3–22–3; Kapoor 6–0–27–0; Joshi 9–1–27–1; Kumble 7–2–12–4; Tendulkar 4–0–17–0.

Umpires: D. L. Orchard and D. R. Shepherd.

INDIA v PAKISTAN

Fourth One-Day International

At Toronto, September 21. Pakistan won by 97 runs. Toss: India.

Before a 5,000-strong crowd, the only full house of the series, Pakistan drew level for the second time. On a fresh pitch, Ijaz Ahmed scored a fine 90 – in 110 balls, with seven fours and a six – and Inzamam made a sparkling 40 before, as so often, he was run out. They had almost doubled the score from an uncertain 91 for four and Pakistan finished on a high of 258; Srinath and Prasad conceded a combined 102 in their 19 overs. Wasim Akram fired out the Indian openers, Saqlain Mushtaq tied down the middle order with three for nine in seven overs, and Waqar Younis ensured there were no late heroics.

Man of the Match: Ijaz Ahmed.

Pakistan

Saeed Anwar b Prasad	 35	Saqlain Mushtaq not out	 10
Aamir Sohail c Srinath b Joshi	 23	Waqar Younis not out	 0
Salim Elahi lbw b Srinath	 1		
Ijaz Ahmed, sen. b Kumble	 90	B 3, l-b 8, w 4	 15
Salim Malik run out	 1		—
Inzamam-ul-Haq run out	 40	1/42 2/43 3/84	(8 wkts, 50 overs) 258
†Moin Khan st Mongia b Tendulkar	 33	4/91 5/177 6/214	
*Wasim Akram c Prasad b Kumble	 10	7/235 8/248	

Mushtaq Ahmed did not bat.

Bowling: Srinath 9–0–52–1; Prasad 10–0–50–1; Jadeja 1–0–8–0; Kapoor 8–0–34–0; Joshi 9–1–45–1; Kumble 10–0–36–2; Tendulkar 3–0–22–1.

India

†N. R. Mongia c Ijaz Ahmed b Wasim Akram .	0	A. R. Kapoor c Moin Khan b Waqar Younis . 19
*S. R. Tendulkar c Salim Malik b Wasim Akram .	3	A. Kumble c Aamir Sohail b Salim Malik 16
R. Dravid c Moin Khan b Saqlain Mushtaq .	25	J. Srinath c Saqlain Mushtaq b Waqar Younis . 10
M. Azharuddin c Salim Elahi b Saqlain Mushtaq .	16	B. K. V. Prasad not out 0
V. G. Kambli run out	6	B 8, l-b 7, w 3 18
A. Jadeja st Moin Khan b Salim Malik ..	47	—
S. B. Joshi c Moin Khan b Saqlain Mushtaq .	1	1/4 2/9 3/41 (39.2 overs) 161
		4/58 5/63 6/64
		7/118 8/148 9/160

Bowling: Wasim Akram 6–2–11–2; Waqar Younis 8–0–51–2; Saqlain Mushtaq 7–1–9–3; Aamir Sohail 10–0–36–0; Mushtaq Ahmed 7–0–33–0; Salim Malik 1.2–0–6–2.

Umpires: L. H. Barker and D. R. Shepherd.

INDIA v PAKISTAN

Fifth One-Day International

At Toronto, September 23. Pakistan won by 52 runs. Toss: Pakistan.

More rain washed out Sunday, disappointing around 5,000 spectators, some from as far as New York. Very few attended on Monday when Pakistan took the series. They grabbed first use of a pitch which did not allow the ball to come on to the bat. The out-of-touch Aamir Sohail anchored the innings, and Salim Malik, Pakistan's most capped one-day player with 235 games, passed 6,000 runs. They promised to set a target well out of India's reach until a comedy of run-out errors dissipated the tail. Wasim Akram and Waqar Younis, who was swinging the ball splendidly, then made the most of the worn pitch. As the asking-rate climbed, the anxious batsmen tried to charge Mushtaq Ahmed; they paid the penalty as he collected five wickets in a limited-overs international for the first time. Though Mushtaq's team triumphed, it was his fellow leg-spinner, Kumble, who was named man of the series. He was easily the leading bowler, with 13 wickets at 12.23.

Man of the Match: Mushtaq Ahmed.   *Man of the Series:* A. Kumble.

Pakistan

Aamir Sohail c Jadeja b Kumble	44	Saqlain Mushtaq run out	0
Saeed Anwar c Dravid b Kapoor	14	Waqar Younis not out	12
Ijaz Ahmed, sen. c and b Kumble	27	Mushtaq Ahmed not out	5
Shadab Kabir c Dravid b Kumble	0	B 1, l-b 21, w 4, n-b 1	27
Salim Malik b Prasad	43		
Inzamam-ul-Haq c Prasad b Kapoor	9	1/44 2/95 3/99	(9 wkts, 50 overs) 213
†Moin Khan run out	15	4/108 5/135 6/174	
*Wasim Akram run out	17	7/195 8/195 9/197	

Bowling: Srinath 10-0-40-0; Prasad 10-0-32-1; Kapoor 10-0-36-2; Joshi 10-1-36-0; Kumble 10-0-47-3.

India

A. Jadeja b Mushtaq Ahmed	20	A. R. Kapoor c Ijaz Ahmed	
*S. R. Tendulkar run out	23	b Mushtaq Ahmed	18
R. Dravid c sub (Shahid Nazir)		A. Kumble not out	8
b Mushtaq Ahmed	20	B. K. V. Prasad c Saeed Anwar	
S. B. Joshi c Salim Malik		b Saqlain Mushtaq	19
b Mushtaq Ahmed	2		
M. Azharuddin c Inzamam-ul-Haq			
b Mushtaq Ahmed	2	B 7, l-b 3, w 15	25
S. C. Ganguly lbw b Aamir Sohail	12	1/46 2/62 3/66	(45.5 overs) 161
J. Srinath run out	2	4/70 5/92 6/96	
†N. R. Mongia c Wasim Akram		7/99 8/127 9/128	
b Saqlain Mushtaq	10		

Bowling: Wasim Akram 8-2-16-0; Waqar Younis 8-0-27-0; Saqlain Mushtaq 7.5-0-34-2; Aamir Sohail 10-1-27-1; Mushtaq Ahmed 10-0-36-5; Salim Malik 2-0-11-0.

Umpires: L. H. Barker and D. L. Orchard.   Series referee: C. W. Smith.

SAMEER FOUR NATIONS CUP, 1996-97

By LUKE ALFRED

Kenya followed up their official debut in the 1996 World Cup by staging their first senior international tournament, commemorating the centenary of the earliest recorded match played in the country. The Kenyans could not emulate their triumph over West Indies in February, losing to all three of their rivals, though they gave Pakistan a scare. Pakistan eventually squeezed through to join South Africa in the final by the smallest possible fraction of net run-rate; had Sri Lanka scored one more run in their last game, they would have qualified. South Africa won the final easily, having produced their familiar all-conquering one-day form except for one aberration, against Sri Lanka. Allan Donald was named player of the tournament for his 14 wickets.

But it was a teenager batting for the first time in a senior international, in the qualifying game between Pakistan and Sri Lanka, who grabbed the world headlines. Shahid Afridi scored a century from 37 balls, shattering the 48-ball record Sanath Jayasuriya of Sri Lanka had set when the teams met in Singapore the previous April. Afridi was a late selection, summoned from the Under-19 tour of the West Indies for his leg-spin because Mushtaq Ahmed was unfit. Saeed Anwar (acting-captain after Wasim Akram was called home to his sick father) sent him in as a pinch-hitter at No. 3 and changed the course of the tournament. Crowds at the Nairobi Gymkhana were good, rising to around 10,000 for the final, with up to 4,000 at the lesser venues.

Note: Matches in this section were not first-class.

KENYA v SRI LANKA

At Nairobi Gymkhana, Nairobi, September 28. Sri Lanka won by seven wickets. Toss: Sri Lanka. International debuts: S. Gupta; K. S. C. de Silva.

Kenya's best moments in their first home one-day international came when Edward Odumbe reduced Sri Lanka to seven for two at the beginning of his four expensive overs. He also caught Aravinda de Silva off his brother Maurice's bowling, but by then Sri Lanka were well on their way. They completed victory with nearly 20 overs to spare as Kaluwitharana reached a maiden hundred in limited-overs internationals from 89 balls. Earlier, Muralitharan bowled his off-spin with verve and economy, taking four for 18; Kenya were a feeble 93 for eight, but Hitesh Modi, an accomplished left-hander, and Asif Karim enabled them to double that.

Man of the Match: M. Muralitharan.

Kenya

D. Chudasama b Vaas	0	E. Odumbe b Muralitharan	5
†K. Otieno lbw b K. S. C. de Silva	2	Asif Karim run out	24
S. Gupta b Muralitharan	41	Rajab Ali not out	1
S. Tikolo lbw b K. S. C. de Silva	5		
*M. Odumbe c Kaluwitharana		L-b 8, w 11, n-b 1	20
b Ranatunga	3		
Hitesh Modi not out	78	1/0 2/7 3/14	(9 wkts, 50 overs) 188
T. Odoyo b Muralitharan	9	4/31 5/65 6/83	
M. Suji c Gurusinha b Muralitharan	0	7/85 8/93 9/182	

Bowling: Vaas 10–2–40–1; K. S. C. de Silva 8–0–27–2; Ranatunga 3–0–10–1; Dharmasena 10–1–39–0; Muralitharan 10–4–18–4; Chandana 5–0–22–0; Jayasuriya 4–0–24–0.

Sri Lanka

S. T. Jayasuriya lbw b E. Odumbe	5	*A. Ranatunga not out	25
†R. S. Kaluwitharana not out	100	L-b 1, w 4	5
A. P. Gurusinha lbw b E. Odumbe	0		
P. A. de Silva c E. Odumbe b M. Odumbe	55	1/5 2/7 3/128	(3 wkts, 30.4 overs) 190

H. P. Tillekeratne, U. D. U. Chandana, H. D. P. K. Dharmasena, W. P. U. J. C. Vaas, K. S. C. de Silva and M. Muralitharan did not bat.

Bowling: Rajab Ali 4–0–23–0; E. Odumbe 4–1–29–2; Suji 5.4–0–48–0; Asif Karim 7–0–42–0; Odoyo 6–0–34–0; M. Odumbe 4–0–13–1.

Umpires: I. D. Robinson and R. B. Tiffin.

PAKISTAN v SOUTH AFRICA

At Nairobi Gymkhana, Nairobi, September 29. South Africa won by 62 runs. Toss: Pakistan.

Rhodes joined Cullinan at 38 for three to add 232 in 34 overs, a fourth-wicket record for all limited-overs internationals. Both batted crisply, with Rhodes slightly more aggressive: he scored 121 from 114 balls and Cullinan 124 from 117. Pakistan needed 6.44 an over and had more chance than the final margin suggested. Salim Elahi scored a dangerous 54 and Ijaz Ahmed, who had tormented South Africa before, looked capable of setting up a fine win. He made 88 from 63 deliveries before misjudging Donald's slower ball. Rhodes and McMillan contributed to three run-outs in an immaculate fielding display.

Man of the Match: J. N. Rhodes.

South Africa

A. C. Hudson lbw b Waqar Younis	2	†D. J. Richardson not out	11
G. Kirsten lbw b Wasim Akram	15	P. S. de Villiers b Saqlain Mushtaq	3
D. J. Cullinan c Salim Malik b Waqar Younis	.124	C. R. Matthews not out	0
P. L. Symcox lbw b Wasim Akram	0	B 1, l-b 18, w 8, n-b 3	30
J. N. Rhodes run out	.121		
*W. J. Cronje c Ijaz Ahmed b Saqlain Mushtaq	11	1/12 2/37 3/38 (8 wkts, 50 overs)	321
B. M. McMillan lbw b Saqlain Mushtaq	4	4/270 5/299 6/305	
		7/312 8/316	

A. A. Donald did not bat.

Bowling: Wasim Akram 10–0–42–2; Waqar Younis 9–0–48–2; Shahid Nazir 7–0–54–0; Azhar Mahmood 9–0–73–0; Saqlain Mushtaq 10–0–42–3; Salim Malik 3–0–26–0; Ijaz Ahmed 2–0–17–0.

Pakistan

Saeed Anwar run out	1	Saqlain Mushtaq b Donald	0
Salim Elahi c Richardson b McMillan	54	Waqar Younis b de Villiers	28
Saeed Azad lbw b de Villiers	14	Shahid Nazir not out	5
Ijaz Ahmed, sen. c Cronje b Donald	88	B 5, l-b 4, w 6	15
Salim Malik run out	0		
†Moin Khan run out	31	1/1 2/48 3/115 (42.3 overs)	259
*Wasim Akram b Donald	8	4/117 5/189 6/200	
Azhar Mahmood b Symcox	15	7/210 8/210 9/229	

Bowling: de Villiers 8.3–0–39–2; Matthews 6–0–44–0; Donald 8–0–29–3; McMillan 8–0–49–1; Cronje 2–0–21–0; Symcox 9–0–60–1; Cullinan 1–0–8–0.

Umpires: S. K. Bansal and R. B. Tiffin.

SOUTH AFRICA v SRI LANKA

At Nairobi Club, Nairobi, October 1. Sri Lanka won by two wickets. Toss: South Africa.

South Africa were uncharacteristically jittery on a less than satisfactory pitch – originally laid by the late Don Pringle, Derek's father – which helped the spinners. Ranatunga permed his bowlers magnificently and the Sri Lankans fielded like demons, Mahanama catching a screamer in the covers to dismiss Hudson. Cullinan rode his luck to play his shots and McMillan reverse-swept a six, but they were all out with eight overs to go. Sri Lankan openers Jayasuriya and Kaluwitharana raced to 69 in nine overs. At 130 for six, however, South Africa seemed to have regained control until Dharmasena batted thoughtfully to steer his side home.

Man of the Match: S. T. Jayasuriya.

South Africa

A. C. Hudson c Mahanama b Vaas		7
G. Kirsten c Muralitharan b Dharmasena		28
P. L. Symcox c Ranatunga		
b K. S. C. de Silva		9
D. J. Cullinan b P. A. de Silva		51
J. N. Rhodes c Gurusinha b Muralitharan		7
*W. J. Cronje b Muralitharan		15
D. N. Crookes c Vaas b Jayasuriya		10
B. M. McMillan not out		25

†D. J. Richardson run out		1
P. S. de Villiers c sub		
(U. D. U. Chandana) b Muralitharan		5
A. A. Donald b Muralitharan		0
L-b 5, w 6		11
		—
1/16 2/33 3/45	(42 overs)	169
4/69 5/105 6/132		
7/136 8/137 9/167		

Bowling: Vaas 5–1–13–1; K. S. C. de Silva 7–0–28–1; Dharmasena 8–0–36–1; Muralitharan 10–1–35–4; Jayasuriya 8–0–29–1; P. A. de Silva 4–1–23–1.

Sri Lanka

S. T. Jayasuriya c Cullinan b Symcox		45
†R. S. Kaluwitharana c Symcox		27
A. P. Gurusinha run out		22
P. A. de Silva c Cullinan b Donald		3
*A. Ranatunga lbw b Crookes		11
R. S. Mahanama lbw b de Villiers		10
H. P. Tillekeratne c McMillan		
b de Villiers		13

H. D. P. K. Dharmasena not out		18
W. P. U. J. C. Vaas b Donald		13
K. S. C. de Silva not out		4
L-b 1, w 1, n-b 2		4
		—
1/69 2/82 3/85	(8 wkts, 40.4 overs)	170
4/110 5/113 6/130		
7/144 8/166		

M. Muralitharan did not bat.

Bowling: de Villiers 8–1–37–2; McMillan 6–0–38–0; Donald 9.4–2–35–2; Symcox 10–1–20–2; Crookes 7–0–39–1.

Umpires: I. D. Robinson and R. B. Tiffin.

KENYA v PAKISTAN

At Aga Khan Sports Club, Nairobi, October 2. Pakistan won by four wickets. Toss: Kenya. International debuts: A. Suji; Shahid Afridi.

Kenya hoped for a repeat of their shock World Cup victory over West Indies when they reduced Pakistan to 61 for five, but Salim Malik and Moin Khan averted ignominy. The home team had stumbled themselves, subsiding to 62 for seven, mainly to Saqlain Mushtaq. But Chudasama scored a patient fifty while Odoyo chipped in with some fluent shots through mid-wicket. Odoyo then struck with the ball, taking three early wickets as Pakistan tottered. Kenya were left to regret the lack of an extra wicket-taking bowler.

Man of the Match: T. Odoyo.

Kenya

D. Chudasama c Saeed Azad		
b Salim Malik		51
†K. Otieno c Ramiz Raja b Waqar Younis		25
S. Gupta c Moin Khan b Waqar Younis		0
S. Tikolo run out		6
*M. Odumbe b Saqlain Mushtaq		1
Hitesh Modi c Salim Malik		
b Saqlain Mushtaq		3
Asif Karim run out		0

A. Suji c Shahid Afridi b Saqlain Mushtaq		4
T. Odoyo c and b Salim Malik		32
M. Suji not out		6
E. Odumbe b Shahid Nazir		2
L-b 3, w 15		18
		—
1/38 2/40 3/51	(47 overs)	148
4/54 5/58 6/58		
7/62 8/129 9/142		

Bowling: Waqar Younis 10–2–31–2; Shahid Nazir 9–2–31–1; Saqlain Mushtaq 10–1–27–3; Shahid Afridi 10–0–32–0; Salim Malik 8–0–24–2.

Pakistan

*Saeed Anwar c Otieno b M. Suji	27	†Moin Khan not out	50
Salim Elahi b Odoyo	14	Saqlain Mushtaq not out	8
Ijaz Ahmed, sen. lbw b M. Suji	3	B 4, l-b 5, w 6, n-b 4	19
Ramiz Raja b Odoyo	0		
Salim Malik b A. Suji	27	1/39 2/45 3/48 (6 wkts, 40.2 overs)	149
Saeed Azad b Odoyo	1	4/52 5/61 6/115	

Shahid Afridi, Waqar Younis and Shahid Nazir did not bat.

Bowling: M. Suji 10–0–42–2; E. Odumbe 2–0–13–0; Odoyo 10-2-25–3; Asif Karim 10–1–32–0; M. Odumbe 4–1–12–0; A. Suji 4.2–2–16–1.

Umpires: S. K. Bansal and I. D. Robinson.

KENYA v SOUTH AFRICA

At Nairobi Gymkhana, Nairobi, October 3. South Africa won by 202 runs. Toss: South Africa. International debut: H. H. Gibbs.

Kenya were completely outclassed, surviving only half their 50 overs. They collapsed before the hostility and the well-disguised slower ball of Donald, who finished with a career-best six for 23 and became the first South African to take 100 wickets in limited-overs internationals. None of the Kenyans reached 30; in contrast, most of South Africa's top order weighed in, with Cronje, coming good after a poor run, and Rhodes adding 101 – almost as many as Kenya managed in total – for the fifth wicket. They marched imperiously to 305, with slow left-armer Asif Karim the only Kenyan bowler to go for less than five an over.

Man of the Match: A. A. Donald.

South Africa

A. C. Hudson lbw b Onyango	27	†D. J. Richardson run out	3
G. Kirsten c Chudasama b Asif Karim	66	P. S. de Villiers not out	20
P. L. Symcox c Odoyo b Asif Karim	35		
H. H. Gibbs st Otieno b Odumbe	17	· L-b 5, w 12, n-b 1	18
J. N. Rhodes run out	54		—
*W. J. Cronje not out	63	1/77 2/116 3/158 (8 wkts, 50 overs)	305
D. N. Crookes lbw b Odoyo	1	4/161 5/262 6/264	
B. M. McMillan run out	1	7/266 8/276	

A. A. Donald did not bat.

Bowling: M. Suji 9–0–47–0; Odoyo 9–0–54–1; Onyango 3–0–45–1; A. Suji 6–0–38–0; Asif Karim 10–0–44–2; Odumbe 10–0–53–1; Tikolo 3–0–19–0.

Kenya

D. Chudasama b Donald	29	A. Suji b Donald	10
†K. Otieno lbw b McMillan	0	L. Onyango b Donald	4
S. Gupta c Crookes b McMillan	2	M. Suji not out	0
S. Tikolo c Crookes b McMillan	9	L-b 6, w 8, n-b 1	15
*M. Odumbe lbw b Donald	19		
Hitesh Modi c sub (N. Boje) b Crookes	14	1/2 2/20 3/42 (25.1 overs)	103
T. Odoyo lbw b Donald	0	4/68 5/75 6/77	
Asif Karim lbw b Donald	1	7/79 8/93 9/103	

Bowling: McMillan 4–0–17–3; de Villiers 3–0–25–0; Symcox 4–0–18–0; Donald 9–0–23–6; Crookes 5.1–0–14–1.

Umpires: S. K. Bansal and R. B. Tiffin.

PAKISTAN v SRI LANKA

At Nairobi Gymkhana, Nairobi, October 4. Pakistan won by 82 runs. Toss: Sri Lanka.

Sensational batting by teenage leg-spinner Shahid Afridi swept Pakistan into the final. He was promoted to No. 3 – he had not batted in his only previous international – and dashed to a hundred in 37 balls, 11 fewer than the limited-overs international record set by Jayasuriya against Pakistan in Singapore six months earlier. He was said to be 16 years 217 days old, but he looked older, and the ages of several established Pakistani players had recently been challenged. His brilliance was not in dispute. In all, he scored 102 from 40 balls, with 11 sixes (equalling Jayasuriya's record) and six fours, out of 126 for the second wicket. The full innings was 06104006006611662644006614110410600224100. He took 41 off the 11 balls he faced from Jayasuriya, whose ten overs went for 94, though he also managed three wickets. The ground was not especially small, and most of the sixes went into the car park, anyway. They would have been sixes almost anywhere. Nor were they slogs; it was an exhibition of wonderful clean hitting. After Afridi was out, Saeed Anwar scored a more sedate 115 from 120 balls and Pakistan galloped to 371, the second-highest total ever scored in a one-day international. Sri Lanka had little hope of winning, but could still reach the final ahead of Pakistan on net run-rate if they scored 290. When Waqar Younis reduced them to 27 for four, that looked unlikely. But Aravinda de Silva scored an intelligent, unflustered 122 from 116 balls, sharing century stands with Ranatunga and Dharmasena. Sri Lanka entered the final over, from Waqar, needing 11 to qualify; Vaas hit a six and a four, then was bowled with one ball remaining.

Man of the Match: Shahid Afridi.

Pakistan

*Saeed Anwar c Mahanama		Waqar Younis c Dharmasena b Jayasuriya	12
b Muralitharan	.115	Azhar Mahmood run out	0
Salim Elahi c Muralitharan b Dharmasena	23	Saqlain Mushtaq not out	13
Shahid Afridi c Muralitharan		Shahid Nazir not out	6
b K. S. C. de Silva	.102		
Ramiz Raja c Gurusinha b Muralitharan	7	L-b 7, w 17, n-b 2	26
Salim Malik c Ranatunga b P. A. de Silva	43		
Ijaz Ahmed, sen. st Kaluwitharana		1/60 2/186 3/207 (9 wkts, 50 overs)	371
b Jayasuriya	6	4/299 5/314 6/322	
†Moin Khan c Dharmasena b Jayasuriya	18	7/335 8/336 9/364	

Bowling: K. S. C. de Silva 6–0–47–1; Vaas 7–0–44–0; Dharmasena 7–0–48–1; Jayasuriya 10–0–94–3; Muralitharan 10–0–73–2; P. A. de Silva 10–0–58–1.

Sri Lanka

S. T. Jayasuriya c Shahid Nazir		H. D. P. K. Dharmasena c Saeed Anwar	
b Waqar Younis	2	b Saqlain Mushtaq	51
†R. S. Kaluwitharana c Moin Khan		W. P. U. J. C. Vaas b Waqar Younis	16
b Waqar Younis	19	M. Muralitharan st Moin Khan	
A. P. Gurusinha b Waqar Younis	1	b Saqlain Mushtaq	0
P. A. de Silva st Moin Khan		K. S. C. de Silva not out	0
b Saqlain Mushtaq	.122	L-b 10, w 12, n-b 1	23
R. S. Mahanama lbw b Waqar Younis	0		
*A. Ranatunga c Moin Khan		1/4 2/26 3/27 (49.5 overs)	289
b Shahid Afridi	52	4/27 5/151 6/160	
H. P. Tillekeratne b Saqlain Mushtaq	3	7/270 8/279 9/279	

Bowling: Waqar Younis 8.5–0–52–5; Shahid Nazir 2–0–32–0; Azhar Mahmood 5–2–39–0; Saqlain Mushtaq 10–2–33–4; Salim Malik 10–0–58–0; Shahid Afridi 10–0–43–1; Saeed Anwar 1–0–8–0; Ijaz Ahmed 3–0–14–0.

Umpires: I. D. Robinson and R. B. Tiffin.

QUALIFYING TABLE

	Played	*Won*	*Lost*	*Points*	*Net run-rate*
South Africa	3	2	1	4	1.518
Pakistan.	3	2	1	4	0.497
Sri Lanka	3	2	1	4	0.495
Kenya	3	0	3	0	−2.395

The top three teams tied on points and could not be separated on the basis of head-to-head results. South Africa and Pakistan went through on net run-rate, calculated by subtracting runs conceded per over from runs scored per over.

FINAL

PAKISTAN v SOUTH AFRICA

At Nairobi Gymkhana, Nairobi, October 6. South Africa won by seven wickets. Toss: Pakistan.

A large crowd watched a disappointingly one-sided final. South Africa knocked off their target with more than ten overs in hand after Pakistan failed to extend their innings past the 47th over. Most of their top order scored solidly, but no one bettered Ijaz Ahmed's 47. Donald took his haul of wickets to 14 in four games and Crookes's off-spin helped to finish off the tail. Hudson and Kirsten raised 77 for South Africa's first wicket in reply and Kirsten was still there at the end, unbeaten on 118, an innings he had been threatening throughout the tournament, though he was dropped twice on 32. Shahid Afridi proved he was an accomplished leg-spinner as well as a batsman, taking all three wickets. Afterwards, Kirsten was fined ten per cent of his match fee for wearing the South African flag as a bandana; ICC regulations insisted that such items should be white when white clothing is worn. Mike Doherty, the team manager, was fined the same amount for not passing on the referee's instruction to Kirsten to remove the bandana. Subsequently, ICC softened the rules and agreed to allow national colours.

Man of the Match: G. Kirsten.   *Man of the Series:* A. A. Donald.

Pakistan

*Saeed Anwar c Richardson b Donald . . .	32	Azhar Mahmood lbw b Crookes	3
Salim Elahi c Kirsten b de Villiers	30	Waqar Younis c Donald b Crookes	3
Shahid Afridi c Richardson b Donald	14	Saqlain Mushtaq not out	2
Ijaz Ahmed, sen. c Richardson			
b McMillan .	47	L-b 3, w 9	12
Salim Malik c and b Symcox	24		
Ramiz Raja c and b Crookes	3	1/58 2/78 3/90 (46.2 overs)	203
Saeed Azad c Cronje b Donald	31	4/138 5/143 6/170	
†Moin Khan b McMillan	2	7/174 8/185 9/195	

Bowling: McMillan 10–0–55–2; de Villiers 8–0–40–1; Donald 8.2–0–32–3; Cronje 1–0–8–0; Symcox 9–0–35–1; Crookes 10–0–30–3.

South Africa

A. C. Hudson c Saqlain Mushtaq		J. N. Rhodes not out	16
b Shahid Afridi .	42		
G. Kirsten not out	118		
P. L. Symcox b Shahid Afridi	0	B 1, l-b 3, w 6, n-b 2	12
D. J. Cullinan c Saqlain Mushtaq			
b Shahid Afridi .	16	1/77 2/77 3/125 (3 wkts, 39.2 overs)	204

*W. J. Cronje, D. N. Crookes, B. M. McMillan, †D. J. Richardson, P. S. de Villiers and A. A. Donald did not bat.

Bowling: Waqar Younis 9–0–49–0; Azhar Mahmood 6–0–31–0; Saqlain Mushtaq 10–1–41–0; Shahid Afridi 10–0–48–3; Salim Malik 3.2–0–25–0; Saeed Anwar 1–0–6–0.

Umpires: S. K. Bansal and I. D. Robinson.   Series referee: M. H. Denness.

TITAN CUP, 1996-97

By GREG BAUM

The quirky nature of these trilateral one-day competitions came through bizarrely when India, who did not secure a place in the final until the last over of the last qualifying game, won the Titan Cup by soundly beating South Africa, who had won all six of their qualifying matches by solid margins.

For South Africa, it was an unfortunate repeat of their experience in the World Cup, when they won all five qualifying matches only to be eliminated in the quarter-finals. It meant that they had won 11 of their 13 one-day matches in India and Pakistan in 1996, but no trophy. For India, it meant the usual: lionisation and a showering of wealth for the players, a new halo for their captain, Sachin Tendulkar, and instant forgiveness for their mediocre form in the qualifying games, where they were comfortably beaten three times by South Africa and, though they beat Australia twice, did so unconvincingly.

Australia did not win a single match. They lost to South Africa three times and twice threw away winning positions against India (their other fixture was washed out). Following their defeat by Sri Lanka in the Singer World Series final in September, it amounted to Australia's worst losing streak in one-day cricket. Yet, if they had beaten India as they should have done in their last match, they would have made the final – and, given the importance of the toss in the final, would have stood a good chance of winning the Cup.

As it was, India went through, won the toss and batted first, then, as the pitch died in the clammy night, kept luckless South Africa to 185. The last act was symbolic: the Man of the Series, Donald, batting for only the second time in a one-day international in 1996 (such was South Africa's dominance, he hardly needed to) was bowled first ball by Kumble, the Man of the Final.

Note: Matches in this section were not first-class.

INDIA v SOUTH AFRICA

At Hyderabad, October 17 (day/night). South Africa won by 47 runs. Toss: South Africa. International debut: S. Somasunder.

India, on a high from their Test win over Australia in Delhi, came quickly back to earth as South Africa rattled up 261. Kirsten, who hit 84 from 81 balls, and Hudson led the way with a speedy opening stand of 74 and, though Kumble checked them with three wickets, Cronje and McMillan rounded off the innings. India were in trouble from the early loss of Tendulkar. Dravid played well for 62, but only Azharuddin and Ganguly gave support, and India were all out for 214. It was Azharuddin's 226th one-day international, which put him past Kapil Dev's Indian record.

Man of the Match: G. Kirsten.

South Africa

A. C. Hudson c Azharuddin b Prasad	34	B. M. McMillan run out	32
G. Kirsten c Azharuddin b Kumble	84	†D. J. Richardson not out	9
P. L. Symcox b Kumble	3	L-b 4, w 2, n-b 2	8
D. J. Cullinan c Prasad b Joshi	16		
J. N. Rhodes c and b Jadeja	10	1/74 2/85 3/128 (7 wkts, 50 overs)	261
*W. J. Cronje not out	63	4/145 5/158	
D. N. Crookes b Kumble	2	6/166 7/242	

A. A. Donald and P. S. de Villiers did not bat.

Bowling: Srinath 9–1–45–0; Prasad 10–0–45–1; Joshi 10–0–64–1; Kumble 10–0–42–3; Tendulkar 5–0–28–0; Jadeja 6–0–33–1.

India

S. Somasunder run out	9	S. B. Joshi run out	2
*S. R. Tendulkar c Cullinan b de Villiers	11	A. Kumble c Hudson b Donald	9
R. Dravid c Rhodes b Crookes	62	B. K. V. Prasad c Crookes b de Villiers	0
M. Azharuddin c Cullinan b Crookes	32	B 5, l-b 14, w 4	23
S. C. Ganguly c Symcox b Donald	31		
A. Jadeja c Cronje b Donald	15	1/19 2/30 3/97 (46.3 overs)	214
†N. R. Mongia run out	3	4/144 5/171 6/178	
J. Srinath not out	17	7/180 8/188 9/206	

Bowling: de Villiers 8.3–1–27–2; McMillan 8–1–30–0; Donald 9–0–43–3; Cronje 2–0–11–0; Symcox 10–0–43–0; Crookes 9–1–41–2.

Umpires: H. S. Sekhon and R. C. Sharma.

AUSTRALIA v SOUTH AFRICA

At Indore, October 19. South Africa won by seven wickets. Toss: Australia.

Australia made a solid start until both openers were run out by the brilliant South Africans; the loss of Mark Waugh just as he was moving into his shots was especially devastating. The middle order floundered against the spinners, and it needed a Bevan half-century to take them past 200. Kirsten and Hudson soon put the target in perspective with a rollicking opening stand of 118 in 104 minutes, and Kirsten proceeded to his seventh one-day hundred, with aplomb that was only slightly shaken when the scoreboard turned out to have signalled the century four runs early. It took him another 20 minutes to get there properly. With no genuine fifth bowler, the Australians were helpless to slow South Africa, who won without fuss.

Man of the Match: G. Kirsten.

Australia

*M. A. Taylor run out	39	G. B. Hogg not out	11
M. E. Waugh run out	50	P. R. Reiffel not out	6
R. T. Ponting c Richardson b Donald	35	L-b 4, w 1, n-b 4	9
S. R. Waugh st Richardson b Symcox	1		
S. G. Law c and b Crookes	1	1/85 2/99 3/103 (7 wkts, 50 overs)	219
M. G. Bevan b Donald	56	4/106 5/167	
†I. A. Healy c Rhodes b Donald	11	6/197 7/204	

J. N. Gillespie and G. D. McGrath did not bat.

Bowling: de Villiers 10–0–38–0; McMillan 9–0–48–0; Donald 10–0–57–3; Crookes 10–0–39–1; Symcox 10–0–28–1; Cronje 1–0–5–0.

South Africa

A. C. Hudson c Taylor b McGrath	53	J. N. Rhodes not out	19
G. Kirsten not out	105	B 5, l-b 14, w 3, n-b 7	29
D. J. Cullinan b McGrath	0		—
*W. J. Cronje c Healy b Gillespie	14	1/118 2/129 3/175 (3 wkts, 46.1 overs)	220

B. M. McMillan, D. N. Crookes, †D. J. Richardson, P. L. Symcox, P. S. de Villiers and A. A. Donald did not bat.

Bowling: McGrath 10–1–42–2; Reiffel 10–1–34–0; Gillespie 10–0–51–1; Hogg 7.1–0–37–0; Law 6–0–23–0; M. E. Waugh 3–0–14–0.

Umpires: S. Banerjee and S. Deo.

INDIA v AUSTRALIA

At Bangalore, October 21 (day/night). India won by two wickets. Toss: Australia.

Taylor at last made his maiden one-day century in his 98th match and, with Steve Waugh, established a sound position. But a late collapse left Australia to defend a modest 215. India were quickly in trouble as night fell and, when Tendulkar was eighth out at 164, defeat seemed inevitable. Then bowlers Srinath and Kumble gave the tale a final twist with an unbroken match-winning stand of 52 in seven overs. That averted any repetition of the crowd disturbance which followed Azharuddin's disgruntled response to his lbw dismissal; there had been 17 minutes of plastic bottle throwing and peace was restored only after Azharuddin appealed to the crowd.

Man of the Match: S. R. Tendulkar.

Australia

M. E. Waugh c Tendulkar b Prasad	4	G. B. Hogg not out	3
*M. A. Taylor c Azharuddin b Tendulkar	105		
M. J. Slater c Mongia b Prasad	3	B 1, l-b 4, w 3, n-b 2	10
S. R. Waugh c Ganguly b Joshi	41		—
M. G. Bevan c Kumble b Prasad	36	1/9 2/23 3/115 (7 wkts, 50 overs)	215
S. G. Law lbw b Kumble	5	4/197 5/204	
†I. A. Healy c Tendulkar b Kumble	8	6/212 7/215	

J. N. Gillespie, D. W. Fleming and G. D. McGrath did not bat.

Bowling: Srinath 10–2–35–0; Prasad 10–0–37–3; Kumble 10–0–40–2; Joshi 10–1–42–1; Ganguly 2–0–11–0; Tendulkar 8–0–45–1.

India

S. Somasunder b McGrath	7	J. Srinath not out	30
*S. R. Tendulkar lbw b S. R. Waugh	88	A. Kumble not out	16
R. Dravid lbw b Fleming	6		
M. Azharuddin lbw b Gillespie	1	B 1, l-b 8, w 12, n-b 1	22
S. C. Ganguly run out	4		—
A. Jadeja run out	27	1/30 2/41 3/42 (8 wkts, 48.5 overs)	216
†N. R. Mongia c McGrath b S. R. Waugh	14	4/47 5/126 6/157	
S. B. Joshi b Fleming	1	7/164 8/164	

B. K. V. Prasad did not bat.

Bowling: McGrath 9.5–2–27–1; Fleming 10–1–39–2; Gillespie 10–1–44–1; Hogg 10–0–45–0; S. R. Waugh 9–0–52–2.

Umpires: S. K. Bansal and S. K. Porel.

INDIA v SOUTH AFRICA

At Jaipur, October 23. South Africa won by 27 runs. Toss: India. International debut: P. Dharmani.

South Africa's openers departed early for once, though not before Kirsten had broken Lara's record of 1,349 one-day runs in a calendar year (later in the series, Tendulkar overtook Kirsten). None the less, Cullinan and Cronje shared 113 to set South Africa up for another challenging score, Cullinan stroking his effortless way to his third one-day hundred. Ganguly opened with Tendulkar and they put on 126, but their scoring-rate was moderate and, although Azharuddin later blazed a half-century, India fell 28 short.

Man of the Match: D. J. Cullinan.

South Africa

A. C. Hudson lbw b Prasad	5	B. M. McMillan not out	19
G. Kirsten c Joshi b Kumble	29	†D. J. Richardson not out	8
D. J. Cullinan st Mongia b Kumble	106	L-b 3, w 4, n-b 3	10
*W. J. Cronje c and b Joshi	58		—
J. N. Rhodes lbw b Jadeja	4	1/5 2/55 3/168	(6 wkts, 50 overs) 249
D. N. Crookes lbw b Jadeja	10	4/180 5/204 6/232	

P. L. Symcox, P. S. de Villiers and A. A. Donald did not bat.

Bowling: Srinath 10–0–45–0; Prasad 9–0–42–1; Kumble 10–0–49–2; Joshi 10–0–41–1; Tendulkar 3–0–22–0; Jadeja 8–0–47–2.

India

S. C. Ganguly b Donald	54	A. Kumble b Donald	1
*S. R. Tendulkar c Kirsten b McMillan	64	†N. R. Mongia not out	8
R. Dravid c Richardson b McMillan	0	L-b 8, w 9	17
M. Azharuddin not out	56		—
J. Srinath b Symcox	4	1/126 2/126 3/148	(7 wkts, 50 overs) 222
A. Jadeja b McMillan	10	4/153 5/191	
P. Dharmani b de Villiers	8	6/207 7/208	

S. B. Joshi and B. K. V. Prasad did not bat.

Bowling: de Villiers 10–2–28–1; McMillan 9–1–32–3; Donald 10–0–49–2; Symcox 10–0–38–1; Crookes 4–0–32–0; Cronje 7–0–35–0.

Umpires: S. Chowdhury and J. Kurushinkal.

AUSTRALIA v SOUTH AFRICA

At Faridabad, October 25. South Africa won by two wickets. Toss: Australia. International debut: A. C. Gilchrist.

Australia again looked set for a big score, and again faltered, losing their last five for three runs to squander the industry of their early batsmen. Donald took four for nought with his last seven balls, the first victim being wicket-keeper Adam Gilchrist, who had flown in to replace the injured Healy. Pinch-hitter Symcox set South Africa on the path to victory after the early loss of Kirsten, and Cullinan guided them home with an unbeaten 71. But they suffered their own late collapse and the margin was merely two wickets. Reiffel, with four for 35, almost stole it for Australia.

Man of the Match: A. A. Donald.

Australia

*M. A. Taylor c McMillan b Symcox	... 42	P. R. Reiffel b Donald	0
M. E. Waugh c Richardson b McMillan	.. 16	D. W. Fleming not out	1
R. T. Ponting st Richardson b Symcox	... 17	G. D. McGrath c Cronje b Donald	1
S. R. Waugh c McMillan b Boje	 40	B 1, l-b 8, w 3, n-b 4	16
M. G. Bevan c Hudson b Boje	 12		—
S. G. Law run out	 52	1/34 2/72 3/107	(47.3 overs) 215
†A. C. Gilchrist b Donald	 18	4/128 5/162 6/212	
G. B. Hogg lbw b Donald	 0	7/212 8/212 9/214	

Bowling: de Villiers 9–0–35–0; McMillan 9–0–41–1; Cronje 2–0–12–0; Donald 8.3–0–31–4; Symcox 10–0–43–2; Boje 9–0–44–2.

South Africa

A. C. Hudson run out	 32	N. Boje c S. R. Waugh b Hogg	 6
G. Kirsten b Fleming	 1	P. S. de Villiers not out	 0
P. L. Symcox c Bevan b Reiffel	 26		
D. J. Cullinan not out	 71	L-b 9, w 3, n-b 2	 14
J. N. Rhodes b Reiffel	 42		—
*W. J. Cronje c Gilchrist b Reiffel	 0	1/3 2/40 3/77	(8 wkts, 47.2 overs) 218
B. M. McMillan run out	 21	4/142 5/142 6/184	
†D. J. Richardson c Gilchrist b Reiffel	... 5	7/205 8/214	

A. A. Donald did not bat.

Bowling: Fleming 8.2–1–53–1; Reiffel 10–0–35–4; McGrath 10–1–50–0; Hogg 8–1–23–1; Law 3–0–14–0; M. E. Waugh 8–1–34–0.

Umpires: B. A. Jamula and M. R. Singh.

INDIA v AUSTRALIA

At Cuttack, October 27. No result (abandoned).

Steady rain led the umpires to call off the match at noon, thus giving Australia what was to remain their only point of the tournament.

INDIA v SOUTH AFRICA

At Rajkot, October 29. South Africa won by five wickets. Toss: India.

With Ganguly injured, Sidhu returned as opener after completing his suspension for walking out on the England tour. But it was fast bowler Srinath, sent in at No. 3, who starred with a thumping half-century. The rest of India's batting was again lame. De Villiers bowled nine overs for just 19 and Donald took another three wickets, giving him 15 at 14.06 in the series to date, a remarkable effort for a fast bowler in India. South Africa were weakened when illness ruled out Hudson and McMillan, but Rhodes seized the moment with a lovely half-century.

Man of the Match: J. N. Rhodes.

India

*S. R. Tendulkar lbw b Donald	 28	A. R. Kapoor lbw b Klusener	 0
N. S. Sidhu run out	 2	A. Kumble b Donald	 12
J. Srinath b Symcox	 53	B. K. V. Prasad not out	 1
R. Dravid run out	 21	L-b 4, w 3, n-b 3	 10
M. Azharuddin c Richardson b Boje	 9		—
A. Jadeja b Donald	 26	1/7 2/48 3/105	(48.1 overs) 185
†N. R. Mongia c and b Boje	 3	4/111 5/122 6/128	
S. B. Joshi c Cullinan b Klusener	 20	7/169 8/170 9/172	

Bowling: de Villiers 9–1–19–0; Klusener 9–0–54–2; Donald 9.1–1–31–3; Symcox 10–0–37–1; Boje 10–0–38–2; Cronje 1–0–2–0.

South Africa

G. Kirsten c Jadeja b Joshi	38
H. H. Gibbs c Tendulkar b Prasad	35
D. J. Cullinan c Kumble b Joshi	6
*W. J. Cronje run out	27
J. N. Rhodes c Jadeja b Prasad	54
N. Boje not out	13
†D. J. Richardson not out	4
L-b 7, w 3, n-b 1	11
1/62 2/72 3/88 (5 wkts, 48.4 overs)	188
4/151 5/184	

P. L. Symcox, L. Klusener, P. S. de Villiers and A. A. Donald did not bat.

Bowling: Srinath 8–0–26–0; Prasad 9–0–38–2; Kumble 9.4–1–40–0; Joshi 10–0–32–2; Kapoor 10–0–32–0; Tendulkar 2–0–13–0.

Umpires: V. Chopra and B. S. Rao.

AUSTRALIA v SOUTH AFRICA

At Gauhati, November 1. South Africa won by eight wickets. Toss: Australia.

Australia at last mounted what seemed a competitive total after a dashing partnership of 124 between Bevan, who made a career-best 79, and Slater, the out-of-favour opener who reappeared in the middle order because Mark Waugh was injured. They took severe toll of Klusener, but he had his revenge, coming in at No. 3 to stroke 88 and, backed by Hudson and Cullinan, delivering victory with a full five overs to spare. South Africa completed a clean sweep of the qualifying series.

Man of the Match: P. L. Symcox.

Australia

*M. A. Taylor c Rhodes b Symcox	38
S. G. Law c Cullinan b Klusener	22
S. R. Waugh c McMillan b Boje	37
M. G. Bevan c Symcox b Donald	79
R. T. Ponting b Boje	0
M. J. Slater not out	53
†A. C. Gilchrist run out	0
G. B. Hogg not out	0
L-b 7, w 2	9
1/38 2/94 3/113 (6 wkts, 50 overs)	238
4/113 5/237 6/237	

P. R. Reiffel, D. W. Fleming and G. D. McGrath did not bat.

Bowling: McMillan 10–2–35–0; Symcox 10–0–32–1; Klusener 7–0–55–1; Donald 9–0–47–1; Boje 10–0–43–2; Cronje 4–0–19–0.

South Africa

A. C. Hudson c Hogg b Law	68
G. Kirsten b Hogg	27
L. Klusener not out	88
D. J. Cullinan not out	43
L-b 1, w 4, n-b 8	13
1/60 2/133 (2 wkts, 45 overs)	239

*W. J. Cronje, J. N. Rhodes, P. L. Symcox, B. M. McMillan, †D. J. Richardson, N. Boje and A. A. Donald did not bat.

Bowling: Fleming 7–0–37–0; Reiffel 10–1–51–0; Hogg 8–0–42–1; McGrath 6–0–41–0; Waugh 4–0–24–0; Law 10–0–43–1.

Umpires: K. Murali and K. Parthasarathy.

INDIA v AUSTRALIA

At Mohali, November 3 (day/night). India won by five runs. Toss: Australia.

India scraped through in the match to decide South Africa's opponents in the final. Sent in by Taylor, who wanted to avoid bowling with a ball affected by the evening dew, they had mocked him by rattling up 289, equalling their highest score against Australia. Tendulkar, Azharuddin and Dravid were murderous on a perfect pitch. But Taylor and the rejuvenated Slater replied in kind. When Australia began the last ten overs needing 62 with six wickets in hand, it seemed they must win. Then a series of accidents left them to get six from the last over with one wicket standing. Tendulkar brought himself on and appealed for lbw first ball; he did not get it, but wicket-keeper Mongia ran out Hogg as he tried to steal a leg-bye.

Man of the Match: M. Azharuddin.

India

*S. R. Tendulkar c Law b M. E. Waugh . 62	A. Jadeja not out	25
N. S. Sidhu run out	11	†N. R. Mongia not out	19
J. Srinath st Healy b M. E. Waugh	3	L-b 7, w 2, n-b 4	13
M. Azharuddin c M. E. Waugh b McGrath 94		
R. Dravid c Taylor b Law	56	1/54 2/75 3/95 (6 wkts, 50 overs) 289
R. R. Singh c Slater b Law	6	4/205 5/217 6/253

S. B. Joshi, A. Kumble and B. K. V. Prasad did not bat.

Bowling: McGrath 10–0–52–1; Reiffel 10–1–52–0; Gillespie 9–0–63–0; M. E. Waugh 9–0–38–2; Law 10–0–65–2; Hogg 2–0–12–0.

Australia

M. E. Waugh b Singh	37	P. R. Reiffel b Kumble	9
*M. A. Taylor lbw b Kumble	78	J. N. Gillespie b Kumble	2
S. G. Law c Azharuddin b Singh	0	G. D. McGrath not out	8
S. R. Waugh st Mongia b Joshi	33	L-b 6, w 4, n-b 2	12
M. G. Bevan b Prasad	40		
M. J. Slater lbw b Srinath	52	1/84 2/84 3/151 (49.1 overs) 284
†I. A. Healy run out	2	4/155 5/241 6/248
G. B. Hogg run out	11	7/250 8/265 9/273

Bowling: Srinath 10–0–62–1; Prasad 10–0–68–1; Kumble 10–0–42–3; Singh 7–0–45–2; Joshi 10–0–50–1; Jadeja 2–0–11–0; Tendulkar 0.1–0–0–0.

Umpires: A. V. Jayaprakash and S. K. Sharma.

QUALIFYING TABLE

	Played	Won	Lost	No result	Points	Net run-rate
South Africa	6	6	0	0	12	0.48
India	6	2	3	1	5	−0.29
Australia	6	0	5	1	1	−0.30

Net run-rate was calculated by subtracting runs conceded per over from runs scored per over.

FINAL

INDIA v SOUTH AFRICA

At Mumbai, November 6 (day/night). India won by 35 runs. Toss: India.

The toss was crucial. Tendulkar won it, and took advantage of the pitch while it was still good, leading the way for India with 67. But the scoring-rate slowed until one-time opener Jadeja arrived at No. 7 to thrash 43 not out from 42 balls, including successive sixes from off-spinner Symcox. India's 220 was worthier than it looked, and Tendulkar increased the pressure by keeping the field up, forcing South Africa to try to hit over the top on a pitch that got ever slower. At 96 for seven, the game was lost, though Richardson and Symcox momentarily threatened to recover it with a breezy stand of 88. It was too much to ask.

Man of the Match: A. Kumble.   *Man of the Series: A. A. Donald.*

India

S. V. Manjrekar c Richardson b de Villiers	7
*S. R. Tendulkar c Cronje b Boje	67
J. Srinath c de Villiers b Donald	5
M. Azharuddin c Richardson b Boje	26
R. Dravid b de Villiers	31
R. R. Singh run out	5
A. Jadeja not out	43
†N. R. Mongia c Boje b de Villiers	15
S. B. Joshi not out	8
L-b 6, w 5, n-b 2	13

1/34 2/43 3/91 (7 wkts, 50 overs) 220
4/137 5/147
6/153 7/204

A. Kumble and B. K. V. Prasad did not bat.

Bowling: de Villiers 10–3–32–3; Klusener 4–0–26–0; Donald 10–1–36–1; Cronje 6–0–27–0; Symcox 10–0–42–0; Boje 10–0–51–2.

South Africa

A. C. Hudson c Azharuddin b Prasad	7
G. Kirsten c Dravid b Kumble	23
L. Klusener c Dravid b Prasad	7
D. J. Cullinan c Azharuddin b Singh	31
J. N. Rhodes c Joshi b Kumble	6
*W. J. Cronje c Joshi b Singh	6
N. Boje c Azharuddin b Joshi	3
†D. J. Richardson c Singh b Prasad	43
P. L. Symcox st Mongia b Kumble	46
P. S. de Villiers not out	0
A. A. Donald b Kumble	0
L-b 1, w 11, n-b 1	13

1/19 2/29 3/49 (47.2 overs) 185
4/60 5/84 6/92
7/96 8/184 9/185

Bowling: Srinath 10–0–45–0; Prasad 9–0–28–3; Kumble 8.2–0–25–4; Singh 10–1–40–2; Joshi 10–0–46–1.

Umpires: V. K. Ramaswamy and S. Venkataraghavan.
Series referee: J. R. Reid (New Zealand).

SINGER CHAMPIONS TROPHY, 1996-97

Pakistan won their ninth trophy in 20 limited-overs tournaments at Sharjah, a return to form after three barren visits. It looked as if New Zealand would keep them out when they dismissed Pakistan for 160 in the final, but captain Wasim Akram led the fightback and New Zealand collapsed for 119.

Pakistan had also made a bad start to their qualifying matches, when Sri Lanka bowled them out in 36 overs, but won their remaining three games, with Saeed Anwar scoring two unbeaten centuries and a fifty. He averaged 92.66 during the tournament – six of his 11 one-day centuries have come at Sharjah. Waqar Younis was named Man of the Series, however, for his 13 wickets at 11.76.

There was considerable confusion about who should join Pakistan in the final when New Zealand and Sri Lanka finished level on three points. Referee Mike Smith, of England, initially announced that Sri Lanka should go through on their superior net run-rate, a decision which ICC chief executive David Richards appeared to confirm. But New Zealand officials pointed out ICC One-Day International Regulation 11.1, introduced before the 1996 World Cup. This said that, when teams finished on equal points with equal wins, the team which won the preliminary matches between them should be higher placed, with net run-rate coming into play only if they could not be separated by this method. New Zealand had won their first match with Sri Lanka and tied the second, and it was eventually agreed that they should qualify. It was an encouraging beginning for their new coach, Steve Rixon, but a disappointing end for his opposite number and fellow-Australian Dav Whatmore, who was about to leave the Sri Lankan team to coach Lancashire.

Pakistan won $US30,000 dollars with the trophy and New Zealand took $US15,000. The Cricketers' Benefit Fund paid out $US35,000 each to Pakistan Test players Talat Ali, Sadiq Mohammad and Ijaz Ahmed. Crowds were mostly disappointing, except for the final.

Note: Matches in this section were not first-class.

NEW ZEALAND v SRI LANKA

At Sharjah, November 7. New Zealand won by 29 runs. Toss: Sri Lanka.

New Zealand set off with what turned out to be a crucial victory. They were rescued by Cairns, who came in at 25 for three after Sri Lanka put them in to bat; he hit 71, including four sixes, and added 73 in 14 overs with Harris. That was easily the biggest stand of the match. Doull dismissed dashing openers Jayasuriya and Kaluwitharana cheaply and Sri Lanka's middle order could not score quickly enough. Cairns took their final wicket in the last over but, with 30 runs still required, the result had already become inevitable.

Man of the Match: C. L. Cairns.

New Zealand

C. M. Spearman c Chandana b K. S. C. de Silva . 39	*†L. K. Germon c K. S. C. de Silva b Vaas . 20
N. J. Astle c and b K. S. C. de Silva 0	D. N. Patel b Vaas 0
A. C. Parore lbw b Vaas 0	S. B. Doull not out 1
S. P. Fleming c Tillekeratne b Vaas 1	B 1, l-b 6, w 6, n-b 4......... 17
C. L. Cairns c Kaluwitharana b Chandana . 71	
M. J. Greatbatch c and b Muralitharan ... 23	1/7 2/7 3/25 (8 wkts, 50 overs) 206
C. Z. Harris not out 34	4/48 5/92 6/165
	7/205 8/205

D. K. Morrison did not bat.

Bowling: Vaas 9–1–22–4; K. S. C. de Silva 8–1–37–2; Dharmasena 7–0–31–0; Muralitharan 10–0–37–1; Jayasuriya 7–0–39–0; Chandana 9–0–33–1.

Sri Lanka

S. T. Jayasuriya c Astle b Doull 15	W. P. U. J. C. Vaas c Harris b Cairns ... 1
†R. S. Kaluwitharana lbw b Doull 16	M. Muralitharan b Cairns.............. 3
A. P. Gurusinha c Doull b Patel 27	K. S. C. de Silva not out 0
P. A. de Silva c Harris b Morrison 47	L-b 7, w 6.................. 13
*A. Ranatunga b Harris 3	
H. P. Tillekeratne c Doull b Morrison ... 41	1/23 2/40 3/83 (49.1 overs) 177
U. D. U. Chandana c Cairns b Harris 4	4/88 5/131 6/142
H. D. P. K. Dharmasena b Astle 7	7/158 8/162 9/175

Bowling: Morrison 9–0–28–2; Doull 7–1–29–2; Cairns 9.1–0–39–2; Astle 6–1–20–1; Patel 10–2–26–1; Harris 8–0–28–2.

Umpires: I. D. Robinson and G. Sharp.

PAKISTAN v SRI LANKA

At Sharjah, November 8. Sri Lanka won by 75 runs. Toss: Pakistan.

Pakistan were humiliated, bowled out with 14 overs to spare: Ijaz Ahmed was their only batsman to pass 15. A target of barely four an over was still possible when they were 126 for six, needing 81 from 19 overs. Then Ijaz was run out for 49 and the last three wickets fell for just five more runs. Jayasuriya claimed three for 15 to complete a fine all-round performance. Earlier, he had hit 33 from 34 balls to give Sri Lanka a promising start, though his team-mates could not keep up his scoring-rate after he became one of Wasim Akram's four victims.

Man of the Match: S. T. Jayasuriya.

Sri Lanka

S. T. Jayasuriya c Ijaz Ahmed b Wasim Akram .	33	H. P. Tillekeratne c Ijaz Ahmed b Saqlain Mushtaq .	20
†R. S. Kaluwitharana c Waqar Younis b Wasim Akram .	12	H. D. P. K. Dharmasena b Wasim Akram .	1
A. P. Gurusinha lbw b Shahid Afridi	32	M. Muralitharan b Wasim Akram	4
P. A. de Silva c Salim Malik b Waqar Younis .	4	K. S. C. de Silva not out	1
*A. Ranatunga c Saqlain Mushtaq b Salim Malik .	23		
R. S. Mahanama c Aamir Sohail b Saqlain Mushtaq .	37	L-b 6, w 16, n-b 3	25
W. P. U. J. C. Vaas c Shahid Afridi b Salim Malik .	14	1/25 2/64 3/79 (49.3 overs)	206
		4/119 5/133 6/158	
		7/191 8/194 9/204	

Bowling: Wasim Akram 10–0–42–4; Shahid Nazir 7–0–38–0; Waqar Younis 8–0–21–1; Saqlain Mushtaq 9.3–0–32–2; Shahid Afridi 9–0–37–1; Salim Malik 6–0–30–2.

Pakistan

Saeed Anwar c Kaluwitharana b K. S. C. de Silva .	7	*Wasim Akram b Jayasuriya	12
Shahid Afridi c Mahanama b K. S. C. de Silva .	7	†Moin Khan c and b Jayasuriya	10
		Saqlain Mushtaq c and b P. A. de Silva ..	1
Aamir Sohail c Kaluwitharana b Muralitharan .	14	Waqar Younis b Jayasuriya	2
		Shahid Nazir not out	1
Ijaz Ahmed, sen. run out	49	W 6, n-b 1.................	7
Azam Khan c Jayasuriya b Muralitharan .	15	1/11 2/29 3/38 (36 overs)	131
Salim Malik c Kaluwitharana b K. S. C. de Silva .	6	4/84 5/93 6/109	
		7/126 8/127 9/129	

Bowling: Vaas 6–1–12–0; K. S. C. de Silva 10–0–48–3; Muralitharan 7–1–33–2; Ranatunga 3–0–15–0; Jayasuriya 5–1–15–3; P. A. de Silva 5–2–8–1.

Umpires: S. K. Bansal and G. Sharp.

NEW ZEALAND v PAKISTAN

At Sharjah, November 10. Pakistan won by four wickets. Toss: New Zealand.

Saeed Anwar pulled Pakistan back on course, scoring an unbeaten 104 to win the match with 21 balls to spare. He hit three fours and two sixes in 132 balls. But Pakistan slumped to 86 for five before first Moin Khan and then Wasim Akram provided him with some support. Parore had played a similar role for New Zealand. He helped them to recover from five for three, and was finally run out at 189 for nine in the penultimate over, seven short of his hundred, as Saqlain Mushtaq mopped up the tail.

Man of the Match: Saeed Anwar.

New Zealand

C. M. Spearman c Moin Khan b Wasim Akram .	0	*†L. K. Germon b Saqlain Mushtaq	7
N. J. Astle b Waqar Younis............	0	D. N. Patel b Saqlain Mushtaq	7
A. C. Parore run out.................	93	S. B. Doull st Moin Khan b Saqlain Mushtaq .	14
S. P. Fleming lbw b Waqar Younis	1	D. K. Morrison not out	1
C. L. Cairns c Saqlain Mushtaq b Mushtaq Ahmed .	26	L-b 3, w 9, n-b 3	15
M. J. Greatbatch c Waqar Younis b Mushtaq Ahmed .	10	1/0 2/0 3/5 (50 overs)	197
		4/56 5/73 6/135	
C. Z. Harris run out	23	7/162 8/176 9/189	

Bowling: Wasim Akram 10–1–57–1; Waqar Younis 10–0–38–2; Saqlain Mushtaq 10–1–31–3; Mushtaq Ahmed 10–0–30–2; Shahid Afridi 10–0–38–0.

Pakistan

Saeed Anwar not out	...104	†Moin Khan st Germon b Astle	....	15
Aamir Sohail c Germon b Morrison	 6	*Wasim Akram not out	....	28
Shahid Afridi b Cairns	 20	L-b 3, w 7	....	10
Ijaz Ahmed, sen. c Germon b Cairns	 4			—
Salim Malik c Fleming b Astle	 7	1/15 2/45 3/53	(6 wkts, 46.3 overs)	198
Azam Khan run out	 4	4/67 5/86 6/135		

Saqlain Mushtaq, Waqar Younis and Mushtaq Ahmed did not bat.

Bowling: Morrison 7–0–44–1; Doull 8–1–30–0; Cairns 8.3–0–33–2; Astle 9–1–25–2; Patel 10–0–41–0; Harris 4–0–22–0.

Umpires: S. K. Bansal and I. D. Robinson.

NEW ZEALAND v SRI LANKA

At Sharjah, November 11. Tied. Toss: New Zealand.

Morrison brought about the first tie in a Sharjah international when he dismissed Sajeewa de Silva and Muralitharan in his last four balls. He had had Kaluwitharana caught behind in his first over, and his career-best analysis of five for 34 also included the key wicket of Ranatunga, who seemed to have victory in reach when Sri Lanka needed only 11 from five overs. Jayasuriya had made it look easy while he was running up 53 in 66 balls. But most batsmen found it hard going: the highest score of the match was Astle's 66, and his chief supporter, Greatbatch, made 35 without any boundaries.

Man of the Match: D. K. Morrison.

New Zealand

C. M. Spearman c Mahanama		*†L. K. Germon not out	......	11
b K. S. C. de Silva .	2	D. N. Patel run out	....	3
N. J. Astle c Mahanama b Muralitharan . .	66	S. B. Doull not out	....	0
A. C. Parore c Kaluwitharana				
b K. S. C. de Silva .	0			
S. P. Fleming b K. S. C. de Silva	 13	B 3, l-b 4, w 8	....	15
C. L. Cairns run out	 11			—
M. J. Greatbatch c Vaas b P. A. de Silva .	35	1/8 2/8 3/29	(8 wkts, 50 overs)	169
C. Z. Harris st Kaluwitharana		4/61 5/136 6/144		
b P. A. de Silva .	13	7/160 8/167		

D. K. Morrison did not bat.

Bowling: Vaas 10–1–25–0; K. S. C. de Silva 8–2–18–3; Muralitharan 10–2–22–1; Ranatunga 2–0–20–0; Chandana 4–0–17–0; Jayasuriya 9–0–32–0; P. A. de Silva 7–0–28–2.

Sri Lanka

S. T. Jayasuriya run out	 53	W. P. U. J. C. Vaas not out	....	17
†R. S. Kaluwitharana c Germon		K. S. C. de Silva b Morrison	....	0
b Morrison .	0	M. Muralitharan c Fleming b Morrison	..	0
M. S. Atapattu c and b Morrison	 16			
P. A. de Silva b Doull	 1	B 1, l-b 5, w 4, n-b 2	....	12
H. P. Tillekeratne c Germon b Cairns	 22			—
*A. Ranatunga c Germon b Morrison	 34	1/1 2/31 3/39	(48 overs)	169
R. S. Mahanama lbw b Cairns	 0	4/82 5/98 6/98		
U. D. U. Chandana c Germon b Astle	... 14	7/140 8/159 9/169		

Bowling: Morrison 10–0–34–5; Doull 9–2–37–1; Cairns 10–1–44–2; Harris 10–1–24–0; Patel 6–0–16–0; Astle 3–0–8–1.

Umpires: I. D. Robinson and G. Sharp.

PAKISTAN v SRI LANKA

At Sharjah, November 12. Pakistan won by eight wickets. Toss: Sri Lanka.

Saeed Anwar scored another unbeaten century to steer Pakistan into the final. He made 112 in 125 balls, with seven fours and a six, and it looked as if he and his opening partner Aamir Sohail could reach their target unaided as they put on 173 in 39 overs. Though two wickets fell in quick succession, Pakistan still completed an overwhelming victory. Ranatunga had taken first use of the pitch but his batting stars got little from it.

Man of the Match: Saeed Anwar.

Sri Lanka

S. T. Jayasuriya c Moin Khan		U. D. U. Chandana c Moin Khan	
b Waqar Younis .	1	b Saqlain Mushtaq .	0
†R. S. Kaluwitharana run out	12	K. S. C. de Silva c Aamir Sohail	
M. S. Atapattu run out	58	b Waqar Younis .	3
P. A. de Silva lbw b Wasim Akram	0	M. Muralitharan c Wasim Akram	
H. P. Tillekeratne c Moin Khan		b Saqlain Mushtaq .	1
b Mushtaq Ahmed .	34		
*A. Ranatunga c Wasim Akram		L-b 10, w 11, n-b 1	22
b Waqar Younis .	27		——
W. P. U. J. C. Vaas c Shahid Afridi		1/9 2/29 3/30	(50 overs) 189
b Salim Malik .	0	4/105 5/132 6/132	
R. S. Mahanama not out	31	7/166 8/166 9/182	

Bowling: Wasim Akram 7–1–31–1; Waqar Younis 10–0–28–3; Saqlain Mushtaq 10–1–36–2; Mushtaq Ahmed 10–0–39–1; Shahid Afridi 9–0–34–0; Salim Malik 4–0–11–1.

Pakistan

Saeed Anwar not out	112	†Moin Khan not out	4
Aamir Sohail c K. S. C. de Silva		W 4, n-b 3	7
b Jayasuriya .	65		——
Hasan Raza c Chandana b Muralitharan . .	5	1/173 2/188	(2 wkts, 46.4 overs) 193

Shahid Afridi, Ijaz Ahmed, sen., Salim Malik, *Wasim Akram, Saqlain Mushtaq, Waqar Younis and Mushtaq Ahmed did not bat.

Bowling: Vaas 8–1–23–0; K. S. C. de Silva 10–0–36–0; Muralitharan 8.4–0–57–1; P. A. de Silva 6–0–18–0; Jayasuriya 9–1–35–1; Chandana 5–0–24–0.

Umpires: S. K. Bansal and G. Sharp.

NEW ZEALAND v PAKISTAN

At Sharjah, November 13. Pakistan won by four wickets. Toss: Pakistan.

As in their previous encounter, Parore and Saeed Anwar dominated the batting, though they were upstaged by Waqar Younis, who took six for 44. Only Parore stood firm as Waqar reduced his side to 60 for six, until Germon joined him in a stand of 115, equalling the seventh-wicket record in one-day internationals. New Zealand's hopes of defending a target of 193 suffered when Doull strained a hamstring in his first over. Anwar set off as if hoping to repeat his feat of three consecutive hundreds at Sharjah in 1993-94, only to fall for 54, from 37 balls with six fours and two sixes. Moin Khan completed the victory, which left New Zealand and Sri Lanka tied on points; New Zealand were declared finalists after protracted consultation among officials.

Man of the Match: Waqar Younis.

New Zealand

B. A. Young lbw b Shahid Nazir	2	D. N. Patel b Waqar Younis	2
C. M. Spearman c Moin Khan		S. B. Doull not out	3
b Shahid Nazir	2	D. K. Morrison c Salim Malik	
A. C. Parore c Shahid Afridi		b Saqlain Mushtaq	0
b Waqar Younis	78		
N. J. Astle c Moin Khan b Waqar Younis	6	L-b 5, w 20, n-b 3	28
C. L. Cairns b Waqar Younis	18		
M. J. Greatbatch lbw b Waqar Younis	0	1/2 2/7 3/28 (50 overs) 192	
C. Z. Harris lbw b Waqar Younis	1	4/57 5/57 6/60	
*†L. K. Germon run out	52	7/175 8/187 9/191	

Bowling: Waqar Younis 10-1-44-6; Shahid Nazir 7-1-35-2; Mushtaq Ahmed 10-0-30-0; Saqlain Mushtaq 10-1-30-1; Shahid Afridi 7-1-26-0; Salim Malik 6-0-22-0.

Pakistan

*Saeed Anwar c Greatbatch b Harris	54	Shahid Afridi b Cairns	3
Aamir Sohail c Parore b Cairns	25	Saqlain Mushtaq not out	5
Ijaz Ahmed, sen. c Germon b Astle	16	L-b 3, w 9, n-b 2	14
Salim Malik c Germon b Morrison	41		
Hasan Raza lbw b Cairns	1	1/66 2/101 3/109 (6 wkts, 48.3 overs) 196	
†Moin Khan not out	37	4/113 5/181 6/187	

Waqar Younis, Mushtaq Ahmed and Shahid Nazir did not bat.

Bowling: Morrison 8-0-46-1; Doull 0.2-0-7-0; Astle 9.4-0-29-1; Patel 10-2-60-0; Harris 10-1-27-1; Cairns 10-2-18-3; Spearman 0.3-0-6-0.

Umpires: S. K. Bansal and I. D. Robinson.

QUALIFYING TABLE

	Played	Won	Lost	Tied	Points	Net run-rate
Pakistan	4	3	1	0	6	−0.17
New Zealand	4	1	2	1	3	0.02
Sri Lanka	4	1	2	1	3	0.15

New Zealand qualified for the final because they had taken more points than Sri Lanka in their head-to-head games. Net run-rate was calculated by subtracting runs conceded per over from runs scored per over.

FINAL

NEW ZEALAND v PAKISTAN

At Sharjah, November 15. Pakistan won by 41 runs. Toss: New Zealand.

The Champions Trophy was within New Zealand's grasp when their attack, despite lacking its spearhead of Morrison and Doull, bowled out Pakistan for 160. Saeed Anwar failed for once and Pakistan's best effort came from Salim Malik, with 40, though Moin Khan hit three sixes near the end. In reply, only two New Zealanders reached double figures. Their chase seemed to be progressing smoothly at 66 for one, stumbled when Parore was out in the 20th over and collapsed when Greatbatch went at 98, just after completing his fifty. The last seven wickets fell for 21 in 51 balls; Wasim Akram finished with three and the spinners picked up two each.

Man of the Match: Wasim Akram.   *Man of the Series:* Waqar Younis.

Pakistan

Saeed Anwar c Fleming b Vaughan	1	Saqlain Mushtaq lbw b Harris		0
Aamir Sohail st Germon b Patel	16	Waqar Younis run out		0
Shahid Afridi c Greatbatch b Larsen	21	Mushtaq Ahmed not out		4
Ijaz Ahmed, sen. c Fleming b Astle	10	L-b 12, w 2		14
Salim Malik lbw b Cairns	40			
Azam Khan c Greatbatch b Harris	22	1/4 2/32 3/51	(48.5 overs)	160
†Moin Khan lbw b Cairns	32	4/63 5/116 6/120		
*Wasim Akram c Vaughan b Patel	0	7/120 8/138 9/145		

Bowling: Vaughan 8–0–33–1; Larsen 9–1–22–1; Cairns 9.5–0–24–2; Astle 3–0–7–1; Harris 9–2–32–2; Patel 10–2–30–2.

New Zealand

B. A. Young b Wasim Akram	5	*†L. K. Germon lbw b Wasim Akram		5
M. J. Greatbatch c Ijaz Ahmed b Mushtaq Ahmed	52	D. N. Patel lbw b Shahid Afridi		1
A. C. Parore lbw b Saqlain Mushtaq	22	J. T. C. Vaughan not out		1
N. J. Astle c Mushtaq Ahmed b Saqlain Mushtaq	8	G. R. Larsen b Shahid Afridi		0
S. P. Fleming lbw b Waqar Younis	4	W 5, n-b 6		11
C. L. Cairns lbw b Wasim Akram	8	1/7 2/66 3/81	(36.5 overs)	119
C. Z. Harris c Shahid Afridi b Mushtaq Ahmed	2	4/98 5/102 6/111 7/114 8/117 9/119		

Bowling: Wasim Akram 8–1–20–3; Waqar Younis 8–0–22–1; Saqlain Mushtaq 8–0–32–2; Shahid Afridi 2.5–0–14–2; Mushtaq Ahmed 10–0–31–2.

Umpires: S. K. Bansal and G. Sharp. Series referee: M. J. K. Smith.

CARLTON & UNITED SERIES, 1996-97

By ROBERT CRADDOCK

In the year that Australia introduced a brewer, Carlton & United, as the new sponsor for their one-day international series, the home side produced a performance that went totally flat. Australia failed to qualify for the finals for the first time since the World Series' inaugural year in 1979-80, when West Indies and England squeezed them out. This time they lagged behind West Indies and Pakistan, and it was Pakistan who won the trophy, for the first time in six attempts.

It seemed a formality that Australia would make the finals when they won their first two games. But they then lost five in a row to make their last match, a victory over Pakistan, a non-event. Before that win Australia had lost 11 of their last 13 one-day games and pundits were asking whether the side that once led the world in this form of cricket had been overtaken by teams playing with more spark and invention. Senior players were privately concerned that team-mates were playing conservatively, to protect their places, rather than displaying the type of bravado and risk-taking exemplified by World Cup holders Sri Lanka. Unusually, their fielding at times slipped below the standard of the opposition.

In contrast, Pakistan's dazzling fleet of young go-getters were a joy to watch. Leg-spinner Shahid Afridi introduced a rocket-like faster ball which snared a bagful of wickets, off-spinner Saqlain Mushtaq troubled batsmen with a mystery ball that turned away from the right-handers, and batsman Mohammad Wasim displayed the cool calculation his top order tended to lack. As usual, Pakistan could be brilliant or terrible, with not much in between, but Saqlain was a dominant force throughout the competition, challenging the notion that off-spinners were becoming the dinosaurs of the modern game.

West Indies' form reversed Australia's – they lost two matches, won their next five to head the table, then lost their last qualifier and went on to lose the finals. Brian Lara was judged man of the series for a mid-tournament form surge which included two centuries and lit up his summer . . . but only briefly: he struggled for most of the Test series.

Note: Matches in this section were not first-class.

AUSTRALIA v WEST INDIES

At Melbourne, December 6 (day/night). Australia won by five wickets. Toss: West Indies. International debut: N. A. M. McLean.

This match reinforced the feeling that West Indies lacked the killer touch. They had Australia waist-deep in trouble at 90 for four in the 32nd over, but the home side slipped the noose; Blewett, a cool head in a crisis, advanced his rehabilitation with a well-paced 57 to see them home with eight balls to spare. The pitch was fresh and bouncy and, when the lights came on at 3.45 after early rain, no batsman looked at home. But it was not quite challenging enough to excuse West Indies' top order. Chanderpaul was their anchor again when Lara's looseness put his side under pressure.

Man of the Match: G. S. Blewett.   *Attendance:* 42,442.

West Indies

S. L. Campbell c Healy b Gillespie	31	K. C. G. Benjamin b Warne	8
R. G. Samuels c Waugh b Gillespie	7	C. E. L. Ambrose run out	2
B. C. Lara c Warne b Moody	5	*C. A. Walsh not out	8
S. Chanderpaul c Healy b Blewett	54	L-b 10, w 1, n-b 3	14
C. L. Hooper run out	7		
J. C. Adams lbw b Moody	5	1/11 2/38 3/64	(49.2 overs) 172
†J. R. Murray c Blewett b Warne	24	4/73 5/81 6/120	
N. A. M. McLean c and b Waugh	7	7/135 8/150 9/153	

Bowling: Reiffel 10–2–26–0; Gillespie 10–0–39–2; Moody 10–1–25–2; Blewett 6.2–0–27–1; Warne 10–0–34–2; Waugh 3–0–11–1.

Australia

*M. A. Taylor b McLean	29	T. M. Moody not out	3
M. E. Waugh c Murray b Benjamin	27		
R. T. Ponting lbw b McLean	5	L-b 17, w 3, n-b 8	28
G. S. Blewett not out	57		
M. G. Bevan st Murray b Hooper	3	1/59 2/70 3/78	(5 wkts, 48.4 overs) 173
S. G. Law b Hooper	21	4/90 5/161	

†I. A. Healy, P. R. Reiffel, S. K. Warne and J. N. Gillespie did not bat.

Bowling: Ambrose 10–3–19–0; Walsh 9–0–34–0; Benjamin 9.4–0–43–1; McLean 10–1–33–2; Hooper 10–0–27–2.

Umpires: P. D. Parker and S. G. Randell.

AUSTRALIA v WEST INDIES

At Sydney, December 8 (day/night). Australia won by eight wickets. Toss: West Indies. International debut: A. F. G. Griffith.

For most of the summer, West Indies' tail disappeared quicker than that of a field mouse scurrying behind a barn door. Here, they lost their last six for 19 off the final 37 balls of another limp innings. Five of them went to Warne, who mesmerised the bottom order in 15 balls to transform nought for 29 into a career-best five for 33. Twice he bowled for hat-tricks. A West Indies total of 161 was quite inadequate. Waugh, relishing the absence of pressure to score quickly, lobbed along to be 83 not out when Australia won with eight overs to spare.

Man of the Match: S. K. Warne. *Attendance:* 35,860.

West Indies

S. L. Campbell lbw b Blewett	38	K. C. G. Benjamin lbw b Warne	3
A. F. G. Griffith c Taylor b Reiffel	1	C. E. L. Ambrose not out	5
B. C. Lara c Healy b Moody	26	*C. A. Walsh b Warne	0
C. L. Hooper c Healy b Reiffel	41	L-b 4, w 1, n-b 5	10
J. C. Adams c Healy b Blewett	22		
R. I. C. Holder b Warne	7	1/8 2/62 3/91	(48.3 overs) 161
†J. R. Murray c Bevan b Warne	8	4/124 5/142 6/147	
N. A. M. McLean c Reiffel b Warne	0	7/147 8/155 9/155	

Bowling: McGrath 9-1-26-0; Reiffel 10-1-26-2; Moody 10-0-38-1; Warne 9.3-1-33-5; Blewett 10-0-34-2.

Australia

M. E. Waugh not out	83
*M. A. Taylor c Holder b Ambrose	17
R. T. Ponting b Walsh	44
G. S. Blewett not out	12
W 1, n-b 5	6

1/39 2/137 (2 wkts, 42 overs) 162

M. G. Bevan, S. G. Law, T. M. Moody, †I. A. Healy, P. R. Reiffel, S. K. Warne and G. D. McGrath did not bat.

Bowling: Walsh 8-0-30-1; Benjamin 10-1-38-0; Ambrose 8-1-27-1; McLean 7-0-27-0; Hooper 5-0-24-0; Adams 4-1-16-0.

Umpires: D. B. Hair and T. A. Prue.

AUSTRALIA v PAKISTAN

At Adelaide, December 15. Pakistan won by 12 runs. Toss: Pakistan.

Australia's unexpected slide began with a narrow defeat induced by clever bowling from leg-spinner Shahid Afridi and off-spinner Saqlain Mushtaq. Afridi rocketed a fast ball through Blewett's defences and Saqlain turned several away from the right-handers without any discernible change in his action. Saqlain took a career-best five for 29 and the mystery of his leg-break intensified when captain Wasim Akram said, "He won't even tell me how he bowls it." Australia lost their composure and folded from 192 for five to 211 all out, chasing 224. After a month of under-achievement by West Indies, this day lit up the summer: it introduced a Pakistan side full of excitement, passion and fresh, unorthodox players.

Man of the Match: Saqlain Mushtaq. *Attendance:* 21,103.

Pakistan

Aamir Sohail c Healy b Bevan	67	Saqlain Mushtaq c M. E. Waugh b Warne	3
Zahoor Elahi run out	21	Waqar Younis b Warne	2
Mohammad Wasim c Taylor b Bevan	44	Mushtaq Ahmed not out	0
Ijaz Ahmed, sen. c Taylor b Blewett	18	L-b 3, w 6, n-b 5	14
Inzamam-ul-Haq c Blewett b McGrath	34		
*Wasim Akram st Healy b Warne	7	1/39 2/141 3/142	(49.5 overs) 223
†Moin Khan st Healy b Warne	7	4/170 5/191 6/205	
Shahid Afridi c Warne b McGrath	6	7/213 8/220 9/223	

Bowling: McGrath 10-2-45-2; Reiffel 7-1-34-0; Moody 10-1-38-0; Warne 9.5-1-52-4; Bevan 8-0-32-2; Blewett 5-0-19-1.

Australia

*M. A. Taylor c Moin Khan b Saqlain Mushtaq . 28	P. R. Reiffel run out 1
M. E. Waugh b Waqar Younis 24	S. K. Warne c Ijaz Ahmed b Saqlain Mushtaq . 11
R. T. Ponting run out 19	G. D. McGrath not out 0
S. R. Waugh c Mohammad Wasim b Saqlain Mushtaq . 57	
G. S. Blewett b Shahid Afridi 12	L-b 5, w 11, n-b 1 17
M. G. Bevan b Wasim Akram 30	
T. M. Moody st Moin Khan b Saqlain Mushtaq . 8	1/39 2/76 3/81 (47.5 overs) 211
†I. A. Healy c Mohammad Wasim b Saqlain Mushtaq . 4	4/106 5/174 6/192 7/194 8/195 9/211

Bowling: Wasim Akram 10-1-44-1; Waqar Younis 8-1-33-1; Saqlain Mushtaq 8.5-0-29-5; Mushtaq Ahmed 9-0-43-0; Shahid Afridi 10-0-49-1; Aamir Sohail 2-0-8-0.

Umpires: R. A. Emerson and D. J. Harper.

PAKISTAN v WEST INDIES

At Adelaide, December 17. West Indies won by seven wickets. Toss: West Indies.

West Indies' revival was ignited by two unexpected sparks: Adams's finger-spin and keeper Murray's big hitting. The team had been warned by manager Clive Lloyd that a new, more willing generation would be shuffled in if they did not bridge the gap between reputation and results. Winning the toss helped, as the pitch was fresh before mellowing. Then Adams's unpretentious left-arm tweakers yielded five for 37, as batsmen tried shots they could not contemplate against the near-perfect line of Ambrose, who conceded only 16 in 9.4 overs. Later, Murray gave West Indies a flying start, with 86 off 79 balls; they won with a resounding 14 overs in hand.

Man of the Match: J. R. Murray.   *Attendance:* 8,696.

Pakistan

Aamir Sohail c Adams b Benjamin 11	Saqlain Mushtaq b Adams 6
Zahoor Elahi run out 51	Mushtaq Ahmed run out 1
Ijaz Ahmed, sen. b Ambrose 16	Waqar Younis not out 2
Inzamam-ul-Haq c Chanderpaul b Adams . . 12	L-b 8, w 3 11
Mohammad Wasim lbw b Ambrose 37	
Shahid Afridi c Campbell b Adams 3	1/21 2/66 3/93 (48.4 overs) 176
*Wasim Akram c Hooper b Adams 3	4/97 5/102 6/105 7/143 8/163 9/171
†Moin Khan b Adams 23	

Bowling: Walsh 8-2-24-0; Benjamin 8-0-42-1; McLean 2-0-13-0; Ambrose 9.4-3-16-2; Hooper 7-1-23-0; Adams 10-0-37-5; Chanderpaul 4-0-13-0.

West Indies

S. L. Campbell c Aamir Sohail b Mushtaq Ahmed . 24	B. C. Lara not out 31
†J. R. Murray lbw b Shahid Afridi 86	C. L. Hooper not out 10
S. Chanderpaul c Aamir Sohail b Shahid Afridi . 21	L-b 3, w 1, n-b 1 5
	1/69 2/128 3/137 (3 wkts, 36.1 overs) 177

J. C. Adams, R. G. Samuels, N. A. M. McLean, K. C. G. Benjamin, C. E. L. Ambrose and *C. A. Walsh did not bat.

Bowling: Wasim Akram 5-1-27-0; Waqar Younis 5-1-28-0; Saqlain Mushtaq 5-0-43-0; Mushtaq Ahmed 10-0-32-1; Shahid Afridi 8.1-1-31-2; Aamir Sohail 3-0-13-0.

Umpires: D. J. Harper and T. A. Prue.

AUSTRALIA v PAKISTAN

At Sydney, January 1 (day/night). Pakistan won by four wickets. Toss: Australia.

Following their Melbourne Test defeat, Australia's mid-summer crisis continued before a barbaric crowd. The game halted six times as intruders swept the ground: one moron, after a seven-hour drinking binge, crash-tackled the stumps, sparking a week-long media debate about crowd control. All Australia's top six reached double figures but none got to 50. A total of 199 was vulnerable on a flat pitch and it was a serious blow when seamer Reiffel limped off with a hamstring strain. Warne, who took four for 37, did his best to launch a salvage operation but was like a lone frogman trying to raise the *Titanic*. Surprisingly, he received the match award ahead of Aamir Sohail, who scored 52, took two spectacular catches, one off his own bowling, and bowled Blewett. Two policewomen, who danced the macarena when the band played the tune during the interval, delighted spectators but were given a warning by their superiors.

Man of the Match: S. K. Warne.   *Attendance:* 37,476.

Australia

*M. A. Taylor run out 11	P. R. Reiffel c and b Aamir Sohail 3
M. E. Waugh c Moin Khan	S. K. Warne c Ijaz Ahmed
b Wasim Akram . 12	b Saqlain Mushtaq . 11
S. G. Law c Zahoor Elahi	G. D. McGrath c Aamir Sohail
b Mushtaq Ahmed . 23	b Saqlain Mushtaq . 1
S. R. Waugh b Saqlain Mushtaq 42	L-b 7, w 2, n-b 1 10
M. G. Bevan c and b Shahid Afridi 27	
G. S. Blewett b Aamir Sohail 33	1/24 2/24 3/75 (47.1 overs) 199
T. M. Moody run out 4	4/96 5/154 6/156
†I. A. Healy not out 22	7/165 8/173 9/191

Bowling: Wasim Akram 8–1–35–1; Shahid Nazir 7–0–31–0; Aamir Sohail 9–0–33–2; Saqlain Mushtaq 7.1–2–23–3; Mushtaq Ahmed 7–0–38–1; Shahid Afridi 9–0–32–1.

Pakistan

Aamir Sohail lbw b Warne 52	*Wasim Akram st Healy b Law 11
Shahid Afridi c Blewett b Warne 34	†Moin Khan not out 17
Zahoor Elahi c and b Warne 0	L-b 5, w 2 7
Ijaz Ahmed, sen. c Bevan b Law 58	
Inzamam-ul-Haq b Warne 8	1/54 2/54 3/129 (6 wkts, 45.3 overs) 203
Mohammad Wasim not out 16	4/153 5/160 6/180

Saqlain Mushtaq, Mushtaq Ahmed and Shahid Nazir did not bat.

Bowling: McGrath 10–1–41–0; Reiffel 3.3–2–18–0; Blewett 0.3–0–12–0; Warne 10–1–37–4; Moody 2–0–6–0; Bevan 10–0–35–0; M. E. Waugh 5.3–1–27–0; Law 4–0–22–2.

Umpires: R. A. Emerson and S. G. Randell.

PAKISTAN v WEST INDIES

At Brisbane, January 3 (day/night). West Indies won by six wickets. Toss: West Indies.

"We are on a roll," trumpeted Walsh after his side won their fourth successive tour game and their second in the tournament. Pakistan never recovered from 12 for two against the relentless accuracy of the West Indian fast bowling troupe. The talking point of the night, however, was the storming Australian international debut of stringbean Pakistan pace bowler Mohammad Zahid. In a Test-style confrontation, he captured the Gabba crowd's attention by livening up Lara with speed and lift and eventually snared him with a snick behind. Hooper branded the 21-year-old Zahid the fastest bowler he had faced on tour.

Man of the Match: C. L. Hooper.   *Attendance:* 15,873.

Pakistan

Aamir Sohail c Murray b Walsh	9	Saqlain Mushtaq c Murray b Bishop	4
Shahid Afridi c Griffith b Walsh	2	Shahid Nazir c Ambrose b Bishop	8
Zahoor Elahi c McLean b Bishop	14	Mohammad Zahid not out	0
Ijaz Ahmed, sen. c Murray b Walsh	59	L-b 9, w 6, n-b 7	22
Inzamam-ul-Haq c McLean b Ambrose	1		—
Mohammad Wasim run out	34	1/12 2/12 3/45	(49.5 overs) 197
*Wasim Akram run out	1	4/47 5/120 6/124	
†Moin Khan c Samuels b Bishop	43	7/157 8/184 9/192	

Bowling: Walsh 10–1–40–3; Bishop 9.5–1–38–4; Ambrose 10–0–26–1; McLean 4–0–21–0; Hooper 10–0–38–0; Adams 6–0–25–0.

West Indies

S. L. Campbell b Saqlain Mushtaq	35	J. C. Adams not out	33
†J. R. Murray b Wasim Akram	15		
A. F. G. Griffith run out	2	L-b 7, w 2, n-b 2	11
B. C. Lara c Moin Khan			—
b Mohammad Zahid	48	1/26 2/37	(4 wkts, 48.1 overs) 198
C. L. Hooper not out	54	3/78 4/124	

R. G. Samuels, N. A. M. McLean, I. R. Bishop, C. E. L. Ambrose and *C. A. Walsh did not bat.

Bowling: Wasim Akram 9–0–30–1; Mohammad Zahid 10–2–29–1; Shahid Nazir 8–0–37–0; Saqlain Mushtaq 10–2–38–1; Shahid Afridi 6.1–0–39–0; Aamir Sohail 5–0–18–0.

Umpires: R. A. Emerson and D. J. Harper.

AUSTRALIA v WEST INDIES

At Brisbane, January 5 (day/night). West Indies won by seven wickets. Toss: Australia. International debuts: A. J. Bichel, A. M. Stuart.

West Indies methodically and nervelessly reeled in Australia's 281 for four, a total which made the home side 4-1 on favourites with the bookmakers at the break. It was the best chase in the history of Australian one-day internationals, apart from New Zealand's 297 to beat England at Adelaide in 1982-83. There were three sublime centuries: Lara and Mark Waugh cancelled each other out with identical scores – 102 from 114 balls. But West Indies were given the edge by Hooper, who scored a run-a-ball 110 and secured victory with seven balls to spare after a beautifully timed chase. This was West Indies' 15th win in their 17 one-day internationals at the Gabba.

Man of the Match: C. L. Hooper.   *Attendance:* 21,801.

Australia

M. E. Waugh run out	102	G. S. Blewett not out	18
*M. A. Taylor c Murray b McLean	26	L-b 7, w 3, n-b 8	18
S. G. Law c Lara b Bishop	93		—
S. R. Waugh run out	6	1/57 2/202	(4 wkts, 50 overs) 281
M. G. Bevan not out	18	3/227 4/253	

T. M. Moody, †I. A. Healy, S. K. Warne, A. J. Bichel and A. M. Stuart did not bat.

Bowling: Walsh 8–0–50–0; Bishop 10–2–33–1; Ambrose 9–0–53–0; McLean 6–0–23–1; Hooper 7–0–52–0; Chanderpaul 2–0–16–0; Adams 8–0–47–0.

West Indies

S. L. Campbell c Healy b Bichel	6	J. C. Adams not out	34
†J. R. Murray c Moody b Stuart	21	B 4, l-b 4, w 3	11
B. C. Lara c Bevan b Stuart	102		—
C. L. Hooper not out	110	1/21 2/45 3/199	(3 wkts, 48.5 overs) 284

S. Chanderpaul, R. G. Samuels, N. A. M. McLean, I. R. Bishop, C. E. L. Ambrose and *C. A. Walsh did not bat.

Bowling: Bichel 10–1–57–1; Stuart 10–0–48–2; Moody 6.5–0–50–0; Warne 9–0–51–0; Bevan 10–0–46–0; S. R. Waugh 3–0–24–0.

Umpires: P. D. Parker and S. G. Randell.

AUSTRALIA v PAKISTAN

At Hobart, January 7. Pakistan won by 29 runs. Toss: Pakistan. International debut: Mujahid Jamshed.

Australia's lamentable one-day form stretched to ten losses in 12 matches, and the headlines were devoted to Taylor's confession that he considered pulling out to find his form in the Sheffield Shield before the Tests resumed. Pakistan did a lot wrong and still won. They batted first on a seaming wicket and lost their top three for ducks, they included two spinners in conditions perfect for pace, and conceded 28 sundries when runs were like gold bars. A substandard, spiteful Bellerive Oval pitch demanded scrapping, unattractive cricket. Cool-headed youngster Mohammad Wasim played straight to conquer its variable bounce but few followed his lead. Set just 150, Australia batted timidly. Having rested three strike bowlers, Pakistan had to hunt for options: debutant Mujahid Jamshed put up his hand, despite not having bowled in a couple of seasons, and took one for six in four overs – enhancing Pakistan's reputation for hauling in talent from unexpected quarters.

Man of the Match: Mohammad Wasim. *Attendance:* 11,542.

Pakistan

Aamir Sohail c Healy b McGrath	0	Shahid Afridi c Blewett b Stuart	3
Zahoor Elahi lbw b Bichel	0	Saqlain Mushtaq run out	2
Ijaz Ahmed, sen. c S. R. Waugh b Bichel.	0	Mohammad Zahid run out	1
Inzamam-ul-Haq c McGrath b Blewett	10	L-b 10, w 12	22
Mohammad Wasim c Taylor b Warne	54		
Mujahid Jamshed c S. R. Waugh b Bichel	23	1/4 2/4 3/7 (45.2 overs)	149
†Moin Khan not out	33	4/28 5/78 6/116	
*Wasim Akram st Healy b Warne	1	7/121 8/132 9/136	

Bowling: McGrath 8–1–21–1; Bichel 10–3–17–3; Stuart 10–1–35–1; Blewett 10–2–31–1; Warne 7.2–0–35–2.

Australia

*M. A. Taylor c Moin Khan		S. K. Warne c Zahoor Elahi	
b Wasim Akram.	6	b Mohammad Zahid.	4
M. E. Waugh c Moin Khan b Ijaz Ahmed	18	A. J. Bichel lbw b Shahid Afridi	2
S. G. Law c Ijaz Ahmed		A. M. Stuart b Shahid Afridi	1
b Mujahid Jamshed.	21	G. D. McGrath not out	0
S. R. Waugh b Wasim Akram	5		
M. G. Bevan lbw b Wasim Akram	24	L-b 6, w 9, n-b 13	28
G. S. Blewett c Mohammad Wasim			
b Mohammad Zahid.	9	1/29 2/38 3/52 (41.3 overs)	120
†I. A. Healy c Wasim Akram		4/68 5/93 6/102	
b Saqlain Mushtaq.	2	7/115 8/118 9/120	

Bowling: Wasim Akram 8–2–13–3; Mohammad Zahid 10–1–53–2; Ijaz Ahmed 10–0–28–1; Mujahid Jamshed 4–1–6–1; Saqlain Mushtaq 8–1–13–1; Shahid Afridi 1.3–0–1–2.

Umpires: T. A. Prue and S. G. Randell.

PAKISTAN v WEST INDIES

At Perth, January 10 (day/night). West Indies won by five wickets. Toss: West Indies.

This was West Indies' seventh successive victory, following seven successive defeats, and included Lara's 11th one-day international century – his second in consecutive innings. His 103 not out enabled his team to scale the lofty peak of Pakistan's 257 for seven. Pakistan had started slowly, mustering just 75 off their first 25 overs. But Ijaz Ahmed senior, often a high achiever under pressure, thumped 94 off 81 balls to provide a fuel-injected finish. West Indian keeper Murray thrashed 62 off 66 in their opening overs to set the stage; Lara then dominated it.

Man of the Match: B. C. Lara. *Attendance:* 13,852.

Pakistan

Aamir Sohail c Hooper b Walsh	9	Mujahid Jamshed not out	3
Zahoor Elahi c Griffith b Adams	32	Ijaz Ahmed, jun. not out	3
Mohammad Wasim c Lara b Chanderpaul	53	L-b 7, w 8, n-b 4	19
Ijaz Ahmed, sen. run out	94		
Shahid Afridi st Murray b Hooper	29	1/14 2/71 3/151 (7 wkts, 50 overs)	257
*Wasim Akram c Adams b Thompson	10	4/200 5/245	
†Moin Khan c Adams b Walsh	5	6/247 7/252	

Saqlain Mushtaq and Mohammad Zahid did not bat.

Bowling: Walsh 10–2–38–2; Bishop 9–1–60–0; Hooper 10–1–38–1; Thompson 9–1–46–1; Adams 9–1–52–1; Chanderpaul 3–0–16–1.

West Indies

S. L. Campbell b Wasim Akram	21	J. C. Adams run out	8
†J. R. Murray st Moin Khan b Aamir Sohail	62	R. G. Samuels not out	7
B. C. Lara not out	103	B 2, l-b 13, w 2, n-b 2	19
C. L. Hooper b Saqlain Mushtaq	3		
S. Chanderpaul st Moin Khan b Ijaz Ahmed, jun.	35	1/60 2/93 3/102 (5 wkts, 48.4 overs)	258
		4/219 5/242	

A. F. G. Griffith, I. R. Bishop, *C. A. Walsh and P. I. C. Thompson did not bat.

Bowling: Wasim Akram 10–1–39–1; Mohammad Zahid 10–0–41–0; Saqlain Mushtaq 10–0–45–1; Aamir Sohail 10–0–53–1; Shahid Afridi 6–0–52–0; Ijaz Ahmed, jun. 2–0–9–1; Ijaz Ahmed, sen. 0.4–0–4–0.

Umpires: R. A. Emerson and D. J. Harper.

AUSTRALIA v WEST INDIES

At Perth, January 12. West Indies won by four wickets. Toss: Australia.

West Indies produced their third classic victory in a week to eliminate Australia from the finals, but it represented the peak of their form. Lara simply took the breath away, scoring 90 off 110, including 40 off 24 balls at the death. Rarely had Warne received such a battering: his last three overs went for 31 after he bowled the first seven into a difficult breeze for just 15. With an improbable 66 needed off 42 balls, Lara, who started poorly, switched on the afterburners to smack Warne over the mid-on and mid-off fences. Samuels joined the party with 36 off 24 balls. They found so many gaps in the field that the match resembled an eight-a-side contest.

Man of the Match: B. C. Lara. *Attendance:* 27,985.

Australia

M. E. Waugh c Adams b Chanderpaul	92	†I. A. Healy not out	16
*M. A. Taylor b Ambrose	18	S. K. Warne not out	10
S. G. Law c and b Adams	14	L-b 8, w 7, n-b 9	24
S. R. Waugh c Griffith b Chanderpaul	29		
T. M. Moody c Adams b Hooper	0	1/63 2/92 3/147 (7 wkts, 50 overs)	267
M. G. Bevan c Griffith b Ambrose	35	4/148 5/181	
G. S. Blewett run out	29	6/217 7/251	

A. J. Bichel and G. D. McGrath did not bat.

Bowling: Walsh 10–0–53–0; Bishop 9–0–49–0; Ambrose 10–0–53–2; Adams 9–0–53–1; Hooper 8–0–35–1; Chanderpaul 4–0–16–2.

West Indies

S. L. Campbell c Taylor b Warne	15	R. G. Samuels not out 36
†J. R. Murray c Law b Bevan	56	A. F. G. Griffith not out.............. 0
B. C. Lara c Law b Warne	90	B 1, l-b 11, w 3 15
S. Chanderpaul run out...............	49	
J. C. Adams c S. R. Waugh b Moody	0	1/60 2/80 3/165 (6 wkts, 49.2 overs) 269
C. L. Hooper c McGrath b Moody	8	4/168 5/179 6/265

I. R. Bishop, C. E. L. Ambrose and *C. A. Walsh did not bat.

Bowling: McGrath 10–0–37–0; Bichel 7.2–0–52–0; Warne 10–1–46–2; Law 6–0–31–0; Bevan 10–0–45–1; Moody 6–0–46–2.

Umpires: D. B. Hair and T. A. Prue.

PAKISTAN v WEST INDIES

At Sydney, January 14 (day/night). Pakistan won by eight wickets. Toss: Pakistan.

Defeat snapped West Indies' eight-match winning streak and proved that you should never sacrifice winning momentum to give players a game. They rested Ambrose, Lara and Walsh and began a spiral into two weeks of poor form which culminated in losing the decisive Adelaide Test. Fringe pace bowlers Thompson and McLean struggled in the front line as Pakistan cruised home with ten overs in hand. Earlier, a collapse of eight wickets for 25 wasted the solidity of Chanderpaul, as Saqlain Mushtaq, displaying the cunning of an old sweat, took four for 17 with near-flawless control. This gave him 15 at 13.86 in the tournament; by its end, he was widely lauded as the best off-spinner in the world.

Man of the Match: Saqlain Mushtaq.   *Attendance:* 19,011.

West Indies

S. L. Campbell c Inzamam-ul-Haq		*C. L. Hooper c Aamir Sohail
b Waqar Younis	3	b Waqar Younis . 1
†J. R. Murray c Ijaz Ahmed, jun.		I. R. Bishop not out 2
b Saqlain Mushtaq	22	N. A. M. McLean run out 1
S. Chanderpaul c Wasim Akram		P. I. C. Thompson b Wasim Akram 2
b Mushtaq Ahmed	72	
A. F. G. Griffith c Aamir Sohail		B 6, l-b 4, w 5 15
b Saqlain Mushtaq	47	
R. I. C. Holder lbw b Saqlain Mushtaq	2	1/10 2/50 3/156 (47.3 overs) 181
J. C. Adams b Saqlain Mushtaq	11	4/159 5/160 6/165
R. G. Samuels lbw b Waqar Younis	3	7/169 8/176 9/179

Bowling: Wasim Akram 8.3–1–17–1; Waqar Younis 10–1–35–3; Saqlain Mushtaq 9–0–17–4; Mushtaq Ahmed 9–0–51–1; Aamir Sohail 8–0–35–0; Ijaz Ahmed, jun. 3–0–16–0.

Pakistan

Aamir Sohail b Adams	55
Inzamam-ul-Haq c Murray b Thompson	42
Zahoor Elahi not out.................	31
Ijaz Ahmed, sen. not out	43
B 1, w 7, n-b 4	12

1/90 2/125   (2 wkts, 39.2 overs) 183

*Wasim Akram, †Moin Khan, Mujahid Jamshed, Ijaz Ahmed, jun., Saqlain Mushtaq, Mushtaq Ahmed and Waqar Younis did not bat.

Bowling: Bishop 7–0–20–0; Thompson 10–1–64–1; McLean 5–0–28–0; Hooper 6–0–21–0; Adams 8–2–30–1; Chanderpaul 3.2–0–19–0.

Umpires: P. D. Parker and S. G. Randell.

AUSTRALIA v PAKISTAN

At Melbourne, January 16 (day/night). Australia won by three wickets. Toss: Pakistan.

With Australia already out of the finals, this was a meaningless match. But it came to life when lively pace bowler Anthony Stuart became only the second Australian to take a hat-trick at this level, following Bruce Reid, against New Zealand in 1985-86. Stuart was playing his third international, aged 27. As a teenager, he was a wicket-keeper, but found his niche in bowling history when Moin Khan edged a perfectly pitched leg-cutter to slip, and he finished with five for 26. Even then, his team struggled. Opener Inzamam-ul-Haq rallied Pakistan from 29 for five to reach 181, and Australia looked no certainties at 110 for four. But Bevan's cool 79 saw them home.

Man of the Match: A. M. Stuart.   *Attendance:* 48,218.

Pakistan

Aamir Sohail c Lehmann b Stuart	6	Saqlain Mushtaq not out	30
Inzamam-ul-Haq c Stuart b Bevan	64	Mushtaq Ahmed st Healy b Bevan	9
Zahoor Elahi c Bichel b Stuart	1	Waqar Younis not out	1
Ijaz Ahmed, sen. c Healy b Stuart	2	L-b 1, w 3, n-b 2	6
Mohammad Wasim c Healy b Stuart	0		—
†Moin Khan c Taylor b Stuart	0	1/19 2/20 3/29 (9 wkts, 50 overs) 181	
*Wasim Akram run out	33	4/29 5/29 6/92	
Shahid Afridi c Stuart b Bevan	29	7/130 8/146 9/177	

Bowling: Bichel 8–2–31–0; Stuart 10–1–26–5; McGrath 10–0–40–0; Warne 10–2–37–0; Bevan 10–1–36–3; Lehmann 2–0–10–0.

Australia

*M. A. Taylor lbw b Wasim Akram	8	†I. A. Healy b Wasim Akram	0
G. S. Blewett c Moin Khan b Wasim Akram	2	S. K. Warne lbw b Shahid Afridi	2
S. R. Waugh c Wasim Akram b Saqlain Mushtaq	20	A. J. Bichel not out	16
M. G. Bevan not out	79	L-b 7, w 9, n-b 1	17
S. G. Law c Mohammad Wasim b Waqar Younis	28	1/9 2/14 3/54 (7 wkts, 49.3 overs) 182	
D. S. Lehmann lbw b Wasim Akram	10	4/110 5/139	
		6/139 7/148	

A. M. Stuart and G. D. McGrath did not bat.

Bowling: Wasim Akram 10–1–25–4; Waqar Younis 10–0–36–1; Saqlain Mushtaq 10–0–37–1; Mushtaq Ahmed 10–0–28–0; Shahid Afridi 9–0–48–1; Aamir Sohail 0.3–0–1–0.

Umpires: D. B. Hair and P. D. Parker.

QUALIFYING TABLE

	Played	Won	Lost	Points	Net run-rate
West Indies	8	5	3	10	−0.01
Pakistan	8	4	4	8	0.09
Australia	8	3	5	6	−0.08

Net run-rate was calculated by subtracting runs conceded per over from runs scored per over.

Player of the Preliminaries: B. C. Lara.

PAKISTAN v WEST INDIES

First Final Match

At Sydney, January 18 (day/night). Pakistan won by four wickets. Toss: Pakistan.

Pakistan all-rounder Shahid Afridi won the nickname Kid Dynamite for his explosive batting and devastating fast ball; both were in the groove on this tour, and particularly in this match. He slogged 53 off 54 balls after his leg-spin netted three for 33 to give his side command of a one-sided final. West Indies had started well, with an opening stand of 99. But then they lost seven for 24. Waqar Younis, who had been hampered by a hip injury, found his best form of the summer: with his wicked toe-seeking in-swinger hooping late, he whipped out the middle order and became one of the few bowlers to rock Chanderpaul's stumps. Pakistan jogged home with almost 12 overs to spare.

Attendance: 32,331.

West Indies

S. L. Campbell b Shahid Afridi	52	I. R. Bishop not out	18	
†J. R. Murray c and b Mushtaq Ahmed	48	C. E. L. Ambrose lbw b Waqar Younis	0	
B. C. Lara c and b Shahid Afridi	0	*C. A. Walsh not out	2	
S. Chanderpaul b Waqar Younis	11	B 1, l-b 7, w 2, n-b 3	13	
P. V. Simmons lbw b Waqar Younis	0		—	
J. C. Adams lbw b Shahid Afridi	2	1/99 2/100 3/117	(9 wkts, 50 overs) 179	
R. G. Samuels lbw b Waqar Younis	1	4/120 5/121 6/123		
R. I. C. Holder run out	32	7/123 8/176 9/176		

Bowling: Wasim Akram 10-0-23-0; Waqar Younis 10-1-43-4; Saqlain Mushtaq 10-1-32-0; Mushtaq Ahmed 10-0-40-1; Shahid Afridi 10-0-33-3.

Pakistan

Inzamam-ul-Haq c Chanderpaul b Walsh	5	Mujahid Jamshed b Chanderpaul	1	
Shahid Afridi c Walsh b Bishop	53	*Wasim Akram not out	1	
Zahoor Elahi c Murray b Ambrose	4	B 4, l-b 7, w 3, n-b 6	20	
Ijaz Ahmed, sen. c Adams b Walsh	60		—	
Mohammad Wasim run out	3	1/13 2/40 3/93	(6 wkts, 38.2 overs) 185	
†Moin Khan not out	38	4/99 5/170 6/171		

Saqlain Mushtaq, Mushtaq Ahmed and Waqar Younis did not bat.

Bowling: Ambrose 9-1-35-1; Walsh 10-1-29-2; Bishop 8-0-36-1; Simmons 5-0-34-0; Adams 3-0-19-0; Chanderpaul 3.2-0-21-1.

Umpires: D. B. Hair and S. G. Randell.

PAKISTAN v WEST INDIES

Second Final Match

At Melbourne, January 20 (day/night). Pakistan won by 62 runs. Toss: Pakistan.

Pakistan were deserving World Series victors at their sixth attempt. Fast bowlers ruled on a difficult, seaming pitch which allowed no batsman to reach 50. Pakistan batted and made just 165. But Wasim Akram was at his unpredictable best. He started off with three wides, then made Campbell tread on his stumps next ball. From that point, he was all over the West Indians like a wasp, while Waqar trapped Murray with his first delivery. West Indies were already doomed at 85 for seven – Campbell, Murray, Hooper, Adams and Simmons having managed just one run between them – when the MCG's floodlight system cut out for 24 minutes. A quick-thinking ground announcer played the Rolling Stones number *Start Me Up*. West Indian spirits were further lowered when, five days before the Fourth Test, their spearhead, Ambrose, suffered a thigh injury while batting.

Player of the Finals: Shahid Afridi.   *Attendance:* 23,045.

Pakistan

Aamir Sohail c Lara b Cuffy	16	Saqlain Mushtaq c Murray b Cuffy	4
Shahid Afridi c Lara b Walsh	0	Waqar Younis b Ambrose	4
Zahoor Elahi c Lara b Walsh	0	Shahid Nazir not out	0
Ijaz Ahmed, sen. c Murray b Simmons	45	L-b 12, w 4, n-b 5	21
Inzamam-ul-Haq run out	5		
Mohammad Wasim c Adams b Ambrose	41		(48.3 overs) 165
*Wasim Akram run out	3	1/2 2/6 3/38	
†Moin Khan c Simmons b Adams	26	4/53 5/96 6/102	
		7/137 8/154 9/159	

Bowling: Ambrose 9.3–2–17–2; Walsh 9–1–24–2; Cuffy 9–1–33–2; Hooper 10–0–35–0; Simmons 9–2–30–1; Adams 2–0–14–1.

West Indies

S. L. Campbell hit wkt b Wasim Akram	0	R. I. C. Holder b Shahid Afridi	20
†J. R. Murray lbw b Waqar Younis	0	C. E. L. Ambrose not out	31
B. C. Lara c Moin Khan b Shahid Nazir	19	*C. A. Walsh b Saqlain Mushtaq	0
S. Chanderpaul c Moin Khan		C. E. Cuffy b Waqar Younis	4
b Wasim Akram	10	B 1, l-b 7, w 10	18
C. L. Hooper c Shahid Afridi			
b Wasim Akram	0	1/3 2/3 3/31	(40.3 overs) 103
J. C. Adams c Moin Khan b Shahid Nazir	1	4/31 5/32 6/41	
P. V. Simmons b Shahid Nazir	0	7/42 8/89 9/90	

Bowling: Wasim Akram 7–2–17–3; Waqar Younis 6.3–1–17–2; Shahid Nazir 10–3–14–3; Saqlain Mushtaq 10–0–26–1; Shahid Afridi 7–0–21–1.

Umpires: P. D. Parker and S. G. Randell.
Series referees: P. L. van der Merwe (South Africa) and R. Subba Row (England).

STANDARD BANK INTERNATIONAL ONE-DAY SERIES, 1996-97

By R. MOHAN

South Africa ran out winners of another limited-overs tournament, but not without a last-minute alarm. As so often, they were clearly the strongest team in the league stages, winning six games out of six. The first attempt to stage the final against India was ended by rain. The replay featured a remarkable late-night run-chase, which seemingly carried India within reach of a reduced target and offered them the chance to overturn South Africa's form, as they had done in the equivalent tournament on Indian soil three months before. But they came a cropper in the final stages, leaving their hosts triumphant.

The tournament saw South African captain Hansie Cronje re-emerge as an effective batsman and an inspirational leader. His poor form in the preceding Test series against India had placed him under some pressure, but here he scored 274 runs in seven innings, and was dismissed only twice.

Although they finished third, Zimbabwe demonstrated that they were a vastly improved side, as their whitewash of England in a recent one-day series had suggested. They surprised South Africa more than once, tied their first match with the Indians, won the second – their maiden victory over India – and entered the last game ahead of them on points, with a good chance of reaching the final. India had to win in less than 41 overs to squeeze through on net run-rate; Sachin Tendulkar finally rediscovered his own form to beat the target with nine balls to spare.

Note: Matches in this section were not first-class.

SOUTH AFRICA v INDIA

At Bloemfontein, January 23 (day/night). South Africa won by 39 runs. Toss: South Africa. International debut: S. S. Karim.

Despite an anchoring innings from Kirsten and some touches of class from Cullinan, South Africa's batting seemed below par until Rhodes provided a late spurt. Striking out in the middle order, he hit 57 in 39 balls; he and Cronje scored at nine an over in the final ten. India, whose top order still looked shaky after losing the Test series, were never in the hunt chasing 271. But Saba Karim, stepping up as wicket-keeper because Mongia was injured, scored a well-made fifty, as had Azharuddin. Klusener ran through the tail to pick up five.

Man of the Match: J. N. Rhodes. *Attendance:* 13,732.

South Africa

A. C. Hudson c Tendulkar b Prasad	15	*W. J. Cronje not out	44
G. Kirsten c Singh b Prasad	73	L-b 6, w 7, n-b 2	15
L. Klusener run out	15		
D. J. Cullinan c Jadeja b Kumble	51	1/36 2/54 (4 wkts, 50 overs)	270
J. N. Rhodes not out	57	3/165 4/168	

S. M. Pollock, †D. J. Richardson, P. L. Symcox, C. R. Matthews and A. A. Donald did not bat.

Bowling: Srinath 10-0-50-0; Prasad 10-1-63-2; Ankola 10-0-45-0; Kumble 9-0-44-1; Singh 8-0-40-0; Jadeja 3-0-22-0.

India

S. C. Ganguly c Rhodes b Donald	40	S. A. Ankola b Klusener	3
*S. R. Tendulkar b Pollock	0	A. Kumble c Richardson b Klusener	7
J. Srinath c Cullinan b Klusener	37	B. K. V. Prasad not out	10
M. Azharuddin b Klusener	52	B 1, l-b 3, w 10, n-b 4	18
R. Dravid b Symcox	8		
A. Jadeja c Richardson b Cronje	1	1/14 2/87 3/107 (47.4 overs)	231
R. R. Singh b Symcox	0	4/128 5/129 6/136	
†S. S. Karim b Klusener	55	7/179 8/183 9/211	

Bowling: Pollock 8-0-46-1; Matthews 5-0-31-0; Donald 9-0-43-1; Klusener 8.4-0-42-5; Symcox 10-0-38-2; Cronje 7-1-27-1.

Umpires: S. B. Lambson and C. J. Mitchley.

SOUTH AFRICA v ZIMBABWE

At Centurion, January 25 (day/night). South Africa won by five wickets. Toss: Zimbabwe.

Zimbabwe had recently won their one-day series with England 3-0, and had hopes of giving their South African neighbours a similar shock when Brandes and Rennie reduced them to seven for three. But Cullinan continued his recent form, while Cronje rediscovered his. They put on 123 for the fifth wicket and Cronje completed an easy enough victory, in the process passing 3,000 runs in his 102nd one-day international. Zimbabwe's 211 had always looked inadequate, with no one offering much support to Grant Flower, who survived Donald's opening burst to score a patient 90.

Man of the Match: D. J. Cullinan. *Attendance:* 15,705.

Zimbabwe

G. W. Flower c Hudson b Donald	90	H. H. Streak b Donald	9
A. C. Waller c Cullinan b Pollock	0	E. A. Brandes run out	2
*A. D. R. Campbell c sub (J. H. Kallis)		J. A. Rennie not out	0
b Cullinan	15		
†A. Flower c Richardson b Cronje	16	L-b 4, w 6, n-b 1	11
C. B. Wishart c Donald b Cronje	8		—
D. L. Houghton c Cullinan b Klusener	8	1/2 2/53 3/85	(48.5 overs) 211
G. J. Whittall c Richardson b Donald	13	4/99 5/110 6/157	
P. A. Strang b Donald	39	7/171 8/203 9/211	

Bowling: Pollock 10-0-33-1; Matthews 0.1-0-4-0; Cronje 8.5-0-34-2; Klusener 9-0-38-1; Donald 9.5-0-37-4; Symcox 10-0-54-0; Cullinan 1-0-7-1.

South Africa

A. C. Hudson lbw b Brandes	0	S. M. Pollock not out	20
G. Kirsten c Campbell b Rennie	4		
L. Klusener b Rennie	1	L-b 1, w 5, n-b 5	11
D. J. Cullinan c A. Flower b Streak	73		—
J. N. Rhodes c G. W. Flower b Streak	16	1/0 2/5 3/7	(5 wkts, 46.1 overs) 212
*W. J. Cronje not out	87	4/43 5/166	

†D. J. Richardson, P. L. Symcox, C. R. Matthews and A. A. Donald did not bat.

Bowling: Brandes 8-2-31-1; Rennie 7-1-28-2; Streak 10-0-51-2; Whittall 8-0-42-0; Strang 10-0-43-0; G. W. Flower 3.1-0-16-0.

Umpires: D. F. Becker and C. J. Mitchley.

INDIA v ZIMBABWE

At Paarl, January 27 (day/night). Tied. Toss: Zimbabwe.

India needed two to win off the last ball; Brandes, who had strangled their chase with five wickets, bowled it wide of leg stump. As the batsmen ran a bye, the keeper aimed the ball at the near wicket and missed; Brandes pounced on it and threw down the wicket at the other end to run out Robin Singh. Umpire Koertzen gave him out, but also signalled "wide"; the Zimbabweans did not realise at first that they had only tied. Houghton and Evans had boosted Zimbabwe's total to 236 in the slog overs, and India were in trouble at 110 for five. But Singh, scoring 48 off 32 balls, helped them to catch up with an asking-rate which had risen to 11 an over and they came within a whisker of victory.

Man of the Match: E. A. Brandes and R. R. Singh.　　*Attendance:* 8,442.

Zimbabwe

G. W. Flower b Ankola	28	C. N. Evans b Kumble	40
A. C. Waller b Prasad	6	H. H. Streak not out	4
†A. Flower run out	7	L-b 8, w 9, n-b 4	21
P. A. Strang c Kumble b Prasad	47		—
*A. D. R. Campbell c Jadeja b Srinath	61	1/17 2/32 3/51	(8 wkts, 50 overs) 236
D. L. Houghton c Prasad b Kumble	13	4/145 5/172 6/179	
G. J. Whittall c and b Prasad	9	7/211 8/236	

E. A. Brandes and J. A. Rennie did not bat.

Bowling: Srinath 10-0-34-1; Prasad 10-1-49-3; Singh 7-2-33-0; Ankola 8-1-32-1; Kumble 10-0-58-2; Tendulkar 5-0-22-0.

India

S. C. Ganguly c G. W. Flower b Evans	38	A. Kumble b Brandes		4
*S. R. Tendulkar c Campbell b Brandes	6	S. A. Ankola run out		9
J. Srinath b Brandes	8	B. K. V. Prasad not out		1
M. Azharuddin b Brandes	6	B 3, l-b 9, w 11		23
R. Dravid run out	23			
A. Jadeja b Brandes	32	1/10 2/22 3/40	(49.5 overs)	236
†S. S. Karim c and b Strang	38	4/85 5/110 6/166		
R. R. Singh run out	48	7/176 8/204 9/229		

Bowling: Brandes 9.5–1–41–5; Rennie 3–0–17–0; Whittall 7–0–28–0; Streak 10–0–52–0; Evans 10–0–48–1; Strang 10–0–38–1.

Umpires: W. A. Diedricks and R. E. Koertzen.

SOUTH AFRICA v ZIMBABWE

At Cape Town, January 29 (day/night). South Africa won by five wickets. Toss: Zimbabwe. International debut: R. E. Bryson.

South Africa's third straight win made them near-certainties to reach the final, but it was a drab game on a grey day. The highlight came from Zimbabwe's player-coach Houghton, who reminded some of Ian Botham as he smashed 57 in 44 balls, with eight fours. It was a sporting pitch and South Africa did not achieve a target of 227 without a struggle, but Kirsten gave them a steady start and Rhodes calmly pulled them through.

Man of the Match: D. L. Houghton.　　　*Attendance:* 19,469.

Zimbabwe

G. W. Flower b Pollock	0	D. L. Houghton not out		57
A. C. Waller b Bryson	52	G. J. Whittall not out		26
†A. Flower run out	13	B 1, l-b 4, w 5, n-b 8		18
P. A. Strang c Rhodes b Symcox	11			—
C. N. Evans c and b Pollock	19	1/1 2/49 3/77	(6 wkts, 50 overs)	226
*A. D. R. Campbell c Rhodes b Cronje	30	4/100 5/125 6/176		

H. H. Streak, E. A. Brandes and J. A. Rennie did not bat.

Bowling: Pollock 10–0–50–2; Bryson 10–0–41–1; Donald 10–0–44–0; Klusener 10–0–38–0; Symcox 4–0–16–1; Cronje 6–0–32–1.

South Africa

A. C. Hudson c Strang b Brandes	26	S. M. Pollock not out		26
G. Kirsten run out	55			
L. Klusener c G. W. Flower b Rennie	19	L-b 4, w 5, n-b 3		12
D. J. Cullinan c Campbell b Whittall	33			—
J. N. Rhodes not out	36	1/50 2/84 3/131	(5 wkts, 47 overs)	229
*W. J. Cronje b Rennie	22	4/154 5/187		

†D. J. Richardson, P. L. Symcox, R. E. Bryson and A. A. Donald did not bat.

Bowling: Brandes 10–1–51–1; Rennie 10–1–51–2; Streak 8–0–34–0; Whittall 8–0–42–1; Strang 7–0–26–0; Evans 4–0–21–0.

Umpires: R. E. Koertzen and D. L. Orchard.

SOUTH AFRICA v ZIMBABWE

At Johannesburg, January 31 (day/night). South Africa won by four wickets. Toss: Zimbabwe.

Yet again, the resilient Zimbabweans seemed capable of pulling off a surprise win. Forced into a corner at 61 for four, they recovered to reach 256, with handsome contributions from the late order to supplement a half-century from opener Grant Flower. Then Brandes rocked South Africa by firing out their top three as the total limped to 16. But it was the South Africans' turn to stage a recovery. Cronje and Pollock, who scored a career-best 75 from 85 balls, made sure of victory by putting on 137, and Cronje finished the job.

Man of the Match: W. J. Cronje.　　　*Attendance:* 26,224.

Zimbabwe

G. W. Flower b Cronje 62	H. H. Streak b Donald 12
A. C. Waller c and b Donald 1	E. A. Brandes not out 1
†A. Flower c Richardson b Donald 0	
C. B. Wishart c Richardson b Pollock .. 24	L-b 5, w 7, n-b 1 13
*A. D. R. Campbell run out 5	
D. L. Houghton c Rhodes b Symcox ... 57	1/6 2/6 3/51 (8 wkts, 50 overs) 256
G. J. Whittall c Cronje b Donald 41	4/61 5/154 6/168
P. A. Strang not out 40	7/231 8/247

E. Matambanadzo did not bat.

Bowling: Donald 10-1-46-4; Bryson 8-1-44-0; Pollock 10-1-43-1; Klusener 7-0-39-0; Symcox 10-0-55-1; Cronje 5-1-24-1.

South Africa

A. C. Hudson lbw b Brandes 1	S. M. Pollock b Streak 75
G. Kirsten lbw b Brandes 7	†D. J. Richardson not out 11
L. Klusener c Whittall b Brandes 5	B 3, l-b 7, w 16 26
D. J. Cullinan b Whittall 30	
J. N. Rhodes c Campbell b Matambanadzo 34	1/4 2/15 3/16 (6 wkts, 48.3 overs) 259
*W. J. Cronje not out 70	4/72 5/102 6/239

P. L. Symcox, R. E. Bryson and A. A. Donald did not bat.

Bowling: Brandes 10-1-45-3; Streak 9-0-44-1; Whittall 9-0-47-1; Matambanadzo 8.3-0-53-1; Strang 10-0-48-0; G. W. Flower 2-0-12-0.

Umpires: D. F. Becker and S. B. Lambson.

SOUTH AFRICA v INDIA

At Port Elizabeth, February 2. South Africa won by six wickets. Toss: India.

Kallis, recalled to the South African side, won the match for them with an unhurried, elegant 79. The Indian batting had left something to be desired on an unusually slow pitch. With Tendulkar in poor form, Dravid was promoted to open; he responded with a fifty, and Azharuddin matched him. But when Donald removed them in quick succession, India folded. A target of 180 meant they had to bowl out rather than contain their opponents; their attempt started well enough, but Kallis stepped up the pace when required.

Man of the Match: J. H. Kallis.   *Attendance:* 16,633.

India

S. C. Ganguly run out 0	A. Kumble not out 11
R. Dravid c Cronje b Donald 50	S. A. Ankola run out 8
J. Srinath c Richardson b Kallis 3	
*S. R. Tendulkar b Donald 1	L-b 3, w 4, n-b 1 8
M. Azharuddin c Rhodes b Donald 57	
A. Jadeja lbw b Kallis 15	1/0 2/7 3/11 (9 wkts, 50 overs) 179
†S. S. Karim c Bacher b Adams 8	4/116 5/118 6/130
R. R. Singh c Donald b Pollock 18	7/147 8/168 9/179

B. K. V. Prasad did not bat.

Bowling: Pollock 10-1-37-1; Kallis 8-2-23-2; Donald 10-2-40-3; Klusener 8-0-28-0; Adams 10-1-31-1; Cronje 4-0-17-0.

South Africa

A. M. Bacher b Kumble 13	*W. J. Cronje not out 20
G. Kirsten c Azharuddin b Prasad 6	L-b 9, w 1, n-b 2 12
J. H. Kallis c Ankola b Singh 79	
D. J. Cullinan c Jadeja b Singh 21	1/8 2/47 (4 wkts, 45.1 overs) 180
J. N. Rhodes not out 29	3/89 4/152

S. M. Pollock, L. Klusener, †D. J. Richardson, A. A. Donald and P. R. Adams did not bat.

Bowling: Srinath 7.1–2–24–0; Prasad 9–0–41–1; Kumble 9–0–30–1; Ankola 10–0–42–0; Singh 10–0–34–2.

Umpires: R. E. Koertzen and D. L. Orchard.

SOUTH AFRICA v INDIA

At East London, February 4 (day/night). South Africa won by six wickets. Toss: India.

India's latest opening pair, Ganguly and Dravid, gave India an excellent platform by putting on 117. But the middle order lost their way, with Tendulkar hitting to mid-wicket and Azharuddin bowled by Donald. Only Robin Singh, with 32 off 22 balls, got them to 232. Kirsten scored an assured 82, which settled the innings nicely, and, though the win did not come until the final over, South Africa were always in control of the asking-rate. Having completed the group stage with six straight wins, they had a week to rest before the final.

Men of the Match: S. C. Ganguly and G. Kirsten.   *Attendance:* 15,242.

India

S. C. Ganguly run out	83	†S. S. Karim not out	7
R. Dravid run out	53		
*S. R. Tendulkar c Cullinan b Klusener	14	L-b 7, w 3, n-b 1	11
M. Azharuddin b Donald	13		
A. Jadeja c Cronje b Klusener	19	1/117 2/150 3/171 (5 wkts, 50 overs) 232	
R. R. Singh not out	32	4/176 5/216	

J. Srinath, A. Kumble, S. B. Joshi and B. K. V. Prasad did not bat.

Bowling: Pollock 10–2–26–0; Kallis 6–0–34–0; Klusener 10–0–58–2; Donald 10–1–38–1; Cronje 9–1–37–0; Adams 5–0–32–0.

South Africa

A. M. Bacher c Dravid b Kumble	14	*W. J. Cronje not out	21
G. Kirsten c Kumble b Prasad	82	B 1, l-b 7, w 2, n-b 3	13
D. J. Cullinan st Karim b Joshi	32		
J. H. Kallis not out	52	1/44 2/134 (4 wkts, 49.2 overs) 236	
J. N. Rhodes lbw b Srinath	22	3/142 4/200	

S. M. Pollock, L. Klusener, †D. J. Richardson, A. A. Donald and P. R. Adams did not bat.

Bowling: Srinath 10–0–50–1; Prasad 9.2–1–43–1; Kumble 10–1–36–1; Singh 6–0–31–0; Joshi 10–0–48–1; Tendulkar 3–0–17–0; Jadeja 1–0–3–0.

Umpires: W. A. Diedricks and D. L. Orchard.

INDIA v ZIMBABWE

At Centurion, February 7 (day/night). Zimbabwe won by three wickets, their target having been revised to 171 from 34 overs. Toss: India.

Having tied at Paarl 11 days earlier, and once before at Indore in 1993-94, Zimbabwe finally completed their first win over India at the 14th attempt (they had first met in the 1983 World Cup). Play was frequently interrupted by rain, and India never recovered sufficiently from a poor start to manage an imposing total. Still, Zimbabwe's revised target looked unassailable when they were 78 for six. But Evans relaunched their innings with three sixes and a four, out of 43 in 47 balls. Strang also hit out and Streak made short work of scoring the nine needed from the final over.

Men of the Match: C. N. Evans and P. A. Strang.   *Attendance:* 8,722.

India

S. C. Ganguly c Strang b Whittall	31
R. Dravid c A. Flower b Rennie	12
J. Srinath c Evans b Streak	9
*S. R. Tendulkar c Waller b Campbell	41
M. Azharuddin st A. Flower b Strang	44
A. Jadeja run out	36
R. R. Singh run out	11
†S. S. Karim run out	10

A. Kumble c A. Flower b Brandes	7
S. A. Ankola c Whittall b Brandes	0
B. K. V. Prasad not out	0
L-b 6, w 9	15

1/25 2/46 3/67   (48.4 overs) 216
4/137 5/161 6/195
7/198 8/216 9/216

Bowling: Brandes 9.4–0–44–2; Rennie 8–1–26–1; Streak 10.2–2–42–1; Whittall 5–0–20–1; Strang 9–0–43–1; Evans 2–0–13–0; Campbell 2–0–8–1; G. W. Flower 3–0–14–0.

Zimbabwe

A. C. Waller c Ganguly b Prasad	2
G. W. Flower b Ankola	28
†A. Flower c Karim b Singh	9
G. J. Whittall run out	4
*A. D. R. Campbell run out	10
D. L. Houghton c Kumble b Singh	13
C. N. Evans c Azharuddin b Kumble	43

P. A. Strang not out	31
H. H. Streak not out	11
L-b 8, w 7, n-b 5	20

1/16 2/46 3/53   (7 wkts, 33.4 overs) 171
4/55 5/77
6/78 7/149

E. A. Brandes and J. A. Rennie did not bat.

Bowling: Srinath 7–0–32–0; Prasad 6.4–0–39–1; Kumble 7–0–31–1; Ankola 5–0–32–1; Singh 7–1–18–2; Tendulkar 1–0–11–0.

Umpires: D. F. Becker and C. J. Mitchley.

INDIA v ZIMBABWE

At Benoni, February 9. India won by six wickets. Toss: India.

With Zimbabwe two points ahead going into the last group game, India had to overtake their 240 in 40.5 overs or less to slip past them onto the final on net run-rate. That meant getting cracking early. But Tendulkar returned to the top of the order and to his fluent best, scoring a chanceless 104, his 11th one-day international hundred, off 97 balls, with a six and eight fours. Even when he was out, India needed 83 from 80 balls. But Jadeja and Robin Singh completed the task in a spirited stand. Zimbabwe's captain, Campbell, had also regained his touch, scoring 86, but it was not to be enough.

Man of the Match: S. R. Tendulkar.   *Attendance:* 12,148.

Zimbabwe

G. W. Flower c Jadeja b Joshi	40
S. V. Carlisle c Mongia b Srinath	3
*A. D. R. Campbell b Srinath	86
G. J. Whittall c Dravid b Kumble	20
†A. Flower b Joshi	35
D. L. Houghton c Kumble b Joshi	1
C. N. Evans not out	17
P. A. Strang c Azharuddin b Kumble	6

H. H. Streak b Srinath	3
E. A. Brandes not out	8
B 3, l-b 6, w 10, n-b 2	21

1/18 2/79 3/128   (8 wkts, 50 overs) 240
4/191 5/195 6/212
7/219 8/225

J. A. Rennie did not bat.

Bowling: Srinath 10–0–35–3; Prasad 10–1–45–0; Singh 5–0–31–0; Kumble 10–0–53–2; Joshi 10–1–40–3; Tendulkar 3–0–16–0; Ganguly 2–0–11–0.

India

S. C. Ganguly c Carlisle b Rennie	12
*S. R. Tendulkar c Campbell b Evans	104
M. Azharuddin b Rennie	2
R. Dravid b Whittall	17
A. Jadeja not out	56

R. R. Singh not out	38
L-b 2, w 6, n-b 4	12

1/19 2/34   (4 wkts, 39.2 overs) 241
3/119 4/158

†N. R. Mongia, J. Srinath, S. B. Joshi, A. Kumble and B. K. V. Prasad did not bat.

Bowling: Brandes 5.2–0–50–0; Rennie 9–0–36–2; Streak 9–0–62–0; Whittall 6–0–36–1; Strang 5–0–30–0; Evans 5–0–25–1.

Umpires: D. F. Becker and W. A. Diedricks.

QUALIFYING TABLE

	Played	Won	Lost	Tied	Points	Net run-rate
South Africa	6	6	0	0	12	0.39
India	6	1	4	1	3	−0.18
Zimbabwe	6	1	4	1	3	−0.23

India and Zimbabwe tied on points and could not be separated on the basis of head-to-head results. India went through on net run-rate, calculated by subtracting runs conceded per over from runs scored per over.

FINAL

SOUTH AFRICA v INDIA

At Durban, February 12 (day/night). No result. Toss: India.

The first attempt to stage the final was ended by rain; South Africa were in firm control, but a result could not be declared as they had not faced 25 overs of their reply to India's 191. The match was still counted as an international under ICC rules. Tendulkar reached 5,000 runs in his 141st game before he was controversially given out, caught by Rhodes at point; television replays suggested that the ball might have been grounded before the catch was completed.

India

S. C. Ganguly run out	18	A. Kumble c Klusener b Donald	3
*S. R. Tendulkar c Rhodes b Klusener	32	S. B. Joshi not out	3
R. Dravid c Kirsten b Cronje	33	B. K. V. Prasad not out	2
M. Azharuddin run out	60	B 1, l-b 2, w 4	7
A. Jadeja b Donald	10		
R. R. Singh run out	16	1/43 2/54 3/116 (9 wkts, 50 overs)	191
†N. R. Mongia c Hudson b Klusener	7	4/138 5/163 6/177	
J. Srinath c Richardson b Pollock	0	7/177 8/184 9/187	

Bowling: Donald 10–2–23–2; Pollock 10–1–31–1; Kallis 4–0–27–0; Klusener 10–1–35–2; Symcox 10–0–49–0; Cronje 6–1–23–1.

South Africa

A. C. Hudson c Joshi b Srinath	7
G. Kirsten not out	20
J. H. Kallis not out	8
L-b 2, w 4, n-b 1	7

1/18 (1 wkt, 14.3 overs) 42

D. J. Cullinan, J. N. Rhodes, *W. J. Cronje, S. M. Pollock, L. Klusener, †D. J. Richardson, P. L. Symcox and A. A. Donald did not bat.

Bowling: Srinath 7–2–12–1; Prasad 7–1–26–0; Singh 0.3–0–2–0.

Umpires: R. E. Koertzen and C. J. Mitchley.

SOUTH AFRICA v INDIA

At Durban, February 13 (day/night). South Africa won by 16 runs, India's target having been revised to 251 from 40 overs. Toss: South Africa.

The pitch played better than on the previous day, and most of South Africa's top order contributed to getting sufficient runs on the board. Rain interrupted the match again, but there was time to set India a reduced target, which they pursued with gusto. Tendulkar smashed 45 off 33 balls, with a six and seven fours, and added 66 with Dravid at eight an over. Cronje had him caught off a well-disguised slower ball, but Dravid kept cranking up the rate, supported by Azharuddin. The chase only petered out when Azharuddin fell to a fine diving catch by Rhodes and Dravid drove to Kirsten on the mid-wicket boundary.

Man of the Match: R. Dravid.   *Man of the Series:* W. J. Cronje.   *Attendance:* 20,259.

South Africa

A. C. Hudson c Karim b Srinath	19	†D. J. Richardson not out	15
G. Kirsten c Dravid b Singh	51	R. E. Bryson not out	2
J. H. Kallis lbw b Singh	49		
D. J. Cullinan b Kumble	60	L-b 8, w 3, n-b 4	15
J. N. Rhodes b Tendulkar	41		—
*W. J. Cronje b Prasad	10	1/44 2/130 3/130 (8 wkts, 50 overs) 278
S. M. Pollock lbw b Prasad	0	4/221 5/242 6/242	
L. Klusener b Kumble	16	7/244 8/266	

A. A. Donald did not bat.

Bowling: Srinath 10–0–50–1; Prasad 10–1–43–2; Kumble 10–0–45–2; Ankola 7–0–50–0; Singh 10–0–63–2; Tendulkar 3–0–19–1.

India

S. C. Ganguly c Donald b Pollock	5	S. A. Ankola b Donald	0
*S. R. Tendulkar c Bryson b Cronje	45	A. Kumble run out	6
R. Dravid c Kirsten b Klusener	84	B. K. V. Prasad not out	2
M. Azharuddin c Rhodes b Pollock	45	B 1, l-b 4, w 2, n-b 3	10
A. Jadeja c Hudson b Klusener	18		—
R. R. Singh run out	15	1/18 2/84 3/165 (39.2 overs) 234
†S. S. Karim b Donald	3	4/198 5/210 6/224	
J. Srinath c Cullinan b Donald	1	7/224 8/224 9/230	

Bowling: Pollock 6–0–39–2; Bryson 7–0–47–0; Donald 7.2–0–48–3; Cronje 8–0–35–1; Klusener 8–0–42–2; Kallis 3–0–18–0.

Umpires: R. E. Koertzen and C. J. Mitchley.   Series referee: B. N. Jarman (Australia).

SINGER AKAI CUP, 1996-97

Sri Lanka returned to their World Cup winning form as they claimed their second trophy in 14 visits to Sharjah. One man dominated the competition from start to finish: Aravinda de Silva, who scored 410 runs at 102.50 when no other batsman totalled 200. It was a satisfying return after the disappointment of their last visit, for the Singer Champions Trophy the previous November, when they could not reach the final and de Silva, after scoring 47 in his first game, managed only five in his last three innings.

Pakistan won that November tournament, but this time they were weakened by the absence of Saeed Anwar, suffering from a virus, and Aamir Sohail, banned for making allegations about match-fixing. They lost all their games with Sri Lanka, though they beat Zimbabwe twice.

The Zimbabweans' confidence in this form of the game was growing and they pulled off a surprise win over Sri Lanka, whom they caught off their guard. That meant that, for the second time in 1997, Zimbabwe entered the last qualifying match of a triangular tournament with a chance of reaching the final. In South Africa, two months earlier, India had squeezed them out on net run-rate; this time, Pakistan beat them comprehensively.

Beneficiaries of the tournament were Waqar Younis and Saeed Ahmed, who were awarded $US35,000 each by the Cricketers' Benefit Fund, and Aslam Khokhar, Israr Bhatti and Zulfiqar Ahmed, with $US10,000 each.

Note: Matches in this section were not first-class.

SRI LANKA v ZIMBABWE

At Sharjah, April 3. Sri Lanka won by seven wickets. Toss: Sri Lanka. International debut: D. P. Viljoen.

De Silva set the pattern for the tournament, ensuring Sri Lanka's victory with the biggest innings of the game. He was out looking for the winning hit, having added 107 with Atapattu to level the scores. De Silva hit nine fours and a six in his 60, during which he became the first Sri Lankan to pass 6,000 runs in limited-overs internationals, in his 200th match. Earlier, Zimbabwe's most forceful innings came from Wishart, who made 32 in 36 balls. But with Vaas taking three wickets for a tidy 25, they could not set a sufficiently challenging target.

Man of the Match: P. A. de Silva.

Zimbabwe

G. W. Flower b Zoysa	12	H. H. Streak run out	11
C. B. Wishart run out	32	E. A. Brandes not out	10
*A. D. R. Campbell lbw b Vaas	2	A. R. Whittall c Kaluwitharana b Vaas	4
D. P. Viljoen st Kaluwitharana		E. Matambanadzo not out	0
b Dharmasena	17	B 3, l-b 7, w 4, n-b 3	17
†A. Flower b Muralitharan	38		
S. V. Carlisle c Tillekeratne		1/31 2/34 3/65 (9 wkts, 50 overs) 187
b Muralitharan	6	4/77 5/100 6/139
P. A. Strang b Vaas	38	7/169 8/180 9/186

Bowling: Vaas 10–2–25–3; Zoysa 10–0–46–1; Muralitharan 10–1–39–2; de Silva 10–0–34–0; Dharmasena 10–0–33–1.

Sri Lanka

S. T. Jayasuriya c Wishart b Strang	56	*A. Ranatunga not out	0
†R. S. Kaluwitharana c Wishart b Brandes	0	B 6, l-b 3, w 11	20
M. S. Atapattu not out	52		
P. A. de Silva c Strang b G. W. Flower	60	1/1 2/80 3/187 (3 wkts, 45.4 overs) 188

R. S. Mahanama, H. P. Tillekeratne, H. D. P. K. Dharmasena, W. P. U. J. C. Vaas, D. N. T. Zoysa and M. Muralitharan did not bat.

Bowling: Brandes 7–0–33–1; Matambanadzo 7–0–38–0; Whittall 10–0–30–0; Streak 7–1–22–0; Strang 10–0–41–1; G. W. Flower 4.4–0–15–1.

Umpires: D. B. Cowie and R. S. Dunne.

PAKISTAN v SRI LANKA

At Sharjah, April 4. Sri Lanka won by 19 runs. Toss: Pakistan.

Sri Lanka and Aravinda de Silva cruised onwards. This time, de Silva and Atapattu equalled Sri Lanka's all-wicket record, 184, in 39 overs after joining forces at a perilous four for two. Both fell just short of centuries. In reply, Shahid Afridi, scorer of cricket's fastest international hundred when the two teams met in Nairobi in October, raced to 67 in 55 balls, with four fours and five sixes. Salim Malik added a brisk fifty but the loss of three wickets in four balls at 190 sabotaged their chase, and only Moin Khan kept them going throughout 50 overs.

Man of the Match: P. A. de Silva.

Sri Lanka

S. T. Jayasuriya lbw b Waqar Younis	3	W. P. U. J. C. Vaas b Saqlain Mushtaq		0
†R. S. Kaluwitharana lbw b Wasim Akram	0	H. P. Tillekeratne run out		1
M. S. Atapattu c Mushtaq Ahmed		H. D. P. K. Dharmasena not out		3
b Salim Malik	94	M. Muralitharan not out		4
P. A. de Silva st Moin Khan				
b Saqlain Mushtaq	97	L-b 6, w 12		18
*A. Ranatunga c Ramiz Raja				
b Saqlain Mushtaq	20	1/3 2/4 3/188 (8 wkts, 50 overs)		243
R. S. Mahanama c Waqar Younis		4/222 5/232 6/232		
b Wasim Akram	3	7/233 8/238		

K. S. C. de Silva did not bat.

Bowling: Wasim Akram 10–1–52–2; Waqar Younis 7–1–34–1; Saqlain Mushtaq 10–0–47–3; Mushtaq Ahmed 10–0–44–0; Shahid Afridi 9–1–39–0; Salim Malik 4–0–21–1.

Pakistan

Ramiz Raja b K. S. C. de Silva	6	*Wasim Akram st Kaluwitharana		
Shahid Afridi c K. S. C. de Silva		b Muralitharan		0
b Jayasuriya	67	Mushtaq Ahmed run out		0
Ijaz Ahmed, sen. c K. S. C. de Silva		Saqlain Mushtaq run out		1
b Dharmasena	18	Waqar Younis not out		9
Salim Malik lbw b Muralitharan	51			
Inzamam-ul-Haq c Kaluwitharana		L-b 7, w 4, n-b 5		16
b Jayasuriya	9			
Mohammad Wasim c Tillekeratne		1/21 2/84 3/111 (9 wkts, 50 overs)		224
b Muralitharan	17	4/140 5/173 6/190		
†Moin Khan not out	30	7/190 8/190 9/197		

Bowling: Vaas 8–0–45–0; K. S. C. de Silva 7–0–24–1; Muralitharan 10–0–38–3; Dharmasena 7–0–39–1; Jayasuriya 10–0–42–2; P. A. de Silva 8–1–29–0.

Umpires: R. S. Dunne and C. J. Mitchley.

PAKISTAN v ZIMBABWE

At Sharjah, April 6. Pakistan won by 93 runs. Toss: Pakistan.

Zimbabwe got only halfway to their target, capitulating with 18 overs to spare. They were all out for 94, their lowest total in one-day internationals, after their openers had made a promising start with 39. Four were run out as the Pakistani bowlers tied the batsmen down. In contrast, Pakistan had started badly, with Matambanadzo removing two of the top three for a single apiece. But first Salim Malik, then Inzamam-ul-Haq, whose 46 was easily the highest score of the match, led the recovery. Though the innings fell away again, it was to prove far too much for Zimbabwe.

Man of the Match: Inzamam-ul-Haq.

Pakistan

Ramiz Raja c A. Flower b Streak	20	*Wasim Akram b Streak		5
Shahid Afridi c Carlisle b Matambanadzo	1	Saqlain Mushtaq run out		3
Ijaz Ahmed, sen. c Streak		Mushtaq Ahmed not out		16
b Matambanadzo	1	Waqar Younis run out		10
Salim Malik b Strang	33	L-b 6, w 7, n-b 1		14
Inzamam-ul-Haq c and b G. J. Whittall	46			
Mohammad Wasim c Streak		1/6 2/9 3/58 (50 overs)		187
b G. J. Whittall	27	4/67 5/138 6/143		
†Moin Khan c Brandes b Streak	11	7/157 8/157 9/164		

Bowling: Brandes 8–0–24–0; Matambanadzo 8–0–25–2; Streak 10–1–37–3; Strang 10–2–29–1;
A. R. Whittall 4–0–29–0; G. J. Whittall 10–0–37–2.

Zimbabwe

C. B. Wishart run out	29	P. A. Strang c Ramiz Raja
G. W. Flower run out	14	b Shahid Afridi . 8
E. A. Brandes b Wasim Akram	2	H. H. Streak run out 1
*A. D. R. Campbell		A. R. Whittall lbw b Mushtaq Ahmed ... 0
c and b Saqlain Mushtaq .	8	E. Matambanadzo run out 0
G. J. Whittall c Ijaz Ahmed		
b Waqar Younis .	1	L-b 1, w 5 6
†A. Flower not out	21	
S. V. Carlisle c Wasim Akram		1/39 2/47 3/57 4/58 5/61 (31.4 overs) 94
b Mushtaq Ahmed .	4	6/78 7/87 8/90 9/93

Bowling: Wasim Akram 7–0–25–1; Waqar Younis 6–1–14–1; Mushtaq Ahmed 7–0–20–2;
Saqlain Mushtaq 5–0–23–1; Shahid Afridi 6.4–1–11–1.

Umpires: D. B. Cowie and C. J. Mitchley.

PAKISTAN v SRI LANKA

At Sharjah, April 7. Sri Lanka won by 51 runs. Toss: Sri Lanka.

Sri Lanka entered the final with their third successive win, while Aravinda de Silva earned his
third successive match award. He came in at 11 for two and added 124 with Jayasuriya on his
way to his eighth one-day international century. He was dismissed by the final ball of the innings
for 134 in 131 balls, with 11 fours and four sixes. Pakistan needed five an over, but only Ramiz
Raja and Inzamam-ul-Haq, with 62 in 66 balls, made much headway. Both fell to Muralitharan,
whose fellow off-spinner, Dharmasena, finished the job with time to spare.

Man of the Match: P. A. de Silva.

Sri Lanka

S. T. Jayasuriya c Waqar Younis		R. S. Mahanama c Moin Khan
b Salim Malik .	67	b Shahid Afridi . 12
†R. S. Kaluwitharana		H. P. Tillekeratne
lbw b Waqar Younis .	3	c and b Saqlain Mushtaq . 13
M. S. Atapattu lbw b Waqar Younis	0	H. D. P. K. Dharmasena not out 10
P. A. de Silva c Waqar Younis		B 1, l-b 5, w 3, n-b 2 11
b Saqlain Mushtaq .	134	
*A. Ranatunga c Wasim Akram		1/9 2/11 3/135 4/137 (7 wkts, 50 overs) 251
b Salim Malik .	1	5/171 6/193 7/251

W. P. U. J. C. Vaas, M. Muralitharan and K. S. C. de Silva did not bat.

Bowling: Wasim Akram 7–0–34–0; Waqar Younis 8–0–60–2; Saqlain Mushtaq 10–0–42–2;
Mushtaq Ahmed 6–0–37–0; Shahid Afridi 10–0–30–1; Salim Malik 9–0–42–2.

Pakistan

Sajid Ali c Kaluwitharana		Mohammad Wasim c Kaluwitharana
b K. S. C. de Silva .	15	b Jayasuriya . 1
Shahid Afridi c sub (R. S. Kalpage)		Mushtaq Ahmed run out 2
b Vaas .	7	Saqlain Mushtaq not out 4
Ramiz Raja c Jayasuriya b Muralitharan .	47	Waqar Younis c Mahanama b Dharmasena 3
Salim Malik c and b Muralitharan	8	
Inzamam-ul-Haq c Tillekeratne		L-b 1, w 3, n-b 1 5
b Muralitharan .	62	
†Moin Khan c Mahanama b Dharmasena .	19	1/9 2/29 3/49 (45.4 overs) 200
*Wasim Akram c Kaluwitharana		4/126 5/156 6/186
b Dharmasena .	27	7/187 8/192 9/196

Bowling: Vaas 6–0–21–1; K. S. C. de Silva 7–0–28–1; Muralitharan 9–1–47–3; Dharmasena
9.4–0–27–3; P. A. de Silva 5–0–30–0; Jayasuriya 9–0–46–1.

Umpires: D. B. Cowie and C. J. Mitchley.

SRI LANKA v ZIMBABWE

At Sharjah, April 8. Zimbabwe won by 50 runs. Toss: Zimbabwe.

Sri Lanka's only slip in the tournament was Zimbabwe's only triumph – their second win in ten meetings between the sides. Zimbabwe elected to bat and the Flowers put them on course, with Campbell and Guy Whittall taking charge of the mid-innings. The target was just over four an over but, with Jayasuriya resting, the Sri Lankans were uncharacteristically slow. None of them bettered Mahanama's 42, and even Aravinda de Silva took 61 balls to score 32. As the pressure mounted, the last five wickets crashed for five runs in three overs. Streak and Strang bowled especially tightly, taking four for 28 in 15.1 overs between them.

Man of the Match: G. J. Whittall.

Zimbabwe

G. W. Flower lbw b Kalpage	28	
C. B. Wishart c Mahanama b Pushpakumara	0	
†A. Flower c Chandana b Kalpage	42	
P. A. Strang c Tillekeratne b Kalpage	11	
*A. D. R. Campbell c Atapattu b Muralitharan	30	
G. J. Whittall c and b Muralitharan	44	
D. P. Viljoen st Kaluwitharana b Chandana	22	
H. H. Streak c Mahanama b Chandana	14	
E. A. Brandes c Mahanama	2	
A. R. Whittall lbw b K. S. C. de Silva	3	
E. Matambanadzo c Mahanama b K. S. C. de Silva	1	
L-b 2, w 3, n-b 1	6	

1/3 2/68 3/73 4/91 5/157 6/164 7/197 8/198 9/201 (49.5 overs) 203

Bowling: Pushpakumara 7–0–34–1; K. S. C. de Silva 6.5–0–12–2; Kalpage 9–1–38–3; Muralitharan 10–0–39–2; Chandana 9–0–41–2; Atapattu 8–0–37–0.

Sri Lanka

R. S. Mahanama c and b Strang	42	
†R. S. Kaluwitharana c Streak b Matambanadzo	4	
M. S. Atapattu run out	14	
P. A. de Silva c G. W. Flower b Brandes	32	
*A. Ranatunga c A. Flower b Strang	0	
H. P. Tillekeratne c Viljoen b G. J. Whittall	36	
R. S. Kalpage c Matambanadzo b A. R. Whittall	7	
U. D. U. Chandana b A. R. Whittall	0	
M. Muralitharan b Streak	1	
K. R. Pushpakumara not out	2	
K. S. C. de Silva lbw b Streak	0	
B 1, l-b 2, w 11, n-b 1	15	

1/14 2/59 3/69 4/69 5/131 6/148 7/149 8/149 9/149 (46.1 overs) 153

Bowling: Brandes 6–0–24–1; Matambanadzo 5–1–18–1; Streak 8.1–2–12–2; Strang 7–3–16–2; G. J. Whittall 10–0–42–1; A. R. Whittall 10–0–38–2.

Umpires: R. S. Dunne and C. J. Mitchley.

PAKISTAN v ZIMBABWE

At Sharjah, April 9. Pakistan won by 32 runs. Toss: Pakistan.

As each team had one win to its name before this match, they were playing for a place in the final. Zimbabwe had high hopes when their seamers had Pakistan reeling at 51 for seven after 19 overs. But Moin Khan organised the tail, especially Saqlain Mushtaq, to add another 100 runs. When Zimbabwe set out in pursuit of just over three an over, Waqar Younis removed both openers cheaply and two further bursts of wickets saw their involvement in the tournament ended with nearly ten overs to spare.

Man of the Match: Moin Khan.

Pakistan

Inzamam-ul-Haq run out	14	Saqlain Mushtaq c G. W. Flower	
Sajid Ali b Matambanadzo	4	b Streak	20
Ijaz Ahmed, sen. c A. R. Whittall		Mushtaq Ahmed not out	5
b Brandes	19	Waqar Younis not out	8
Salim Malik c A. Flower b Brandes	0		
Mohammad Wasim lbw b Streak	3	B 1, l-b 6, w 4	11
*Wasim Akram c Strang			
b Matambanadzo	1	1/8 2/34 3/34 (9 wkts, 50 overs)	151
†Moin Khan c A. R. Whittall b Streak	61	4/40 5/41 6/43	
Shahid Afridi b Streak	5	7/51 8/128 9/140	

Bowling: Brandes 10-4-39-2; Matambanadzo 8-0-27-2; Streak 10-2-18-4; Strang 10-0-32-0; G. J. Whittall 8-1-18-0; A. R. Whittall 4-1-10-0.

Zimbabwe

C. B. Wishart b Waqar Younis	5	E. A. Brandes st Moin Khan	
G. W. Flower c Ijaz Ahmed		b Mushtaq Ahmed	0
b Waqar Younis	1	A. R. Whittall c Wasim Akram	
†A. Flower b Mushtaq Ahmed	28	b Mushtaq Ahmed	0
P. A. Strang b Saqlain Mushtaq	26	E. Matambanadzo not out	5
*A. D. R. Campbell b Saqlain Mushtaq	0	L-b 5, w 4	9
G. J. Whittall c Moin Khan			
b Mushtaq Ahmed	0	1/5 2/14 3/57 (40.1 overs)	119
D. P. Viljoen run out	25	4/57 5/58 6/76	
H. H. Streak lbw b Waqar Younis	20	7/94 8/94 9/94	

Bowling: Wasim Akram 7-1-11-0; Waqar Younis 5.1-2-14-3; Saqlain Mushtaq 9-1-37-2; Shahid Afridi 9-1-25-0; Mushtaq Ahmed 10-0-27-4.

Umpires: D. B. Cowie and C. J. Mitchley.

QUALIFYING TABLE

	Played	Won	Lost	Points	Net run-rate
Sri Lanka	4	3	1	6	0.20
Pakistan	4	2	2	4	0.28
Zimbabwe	4	1	3	2	-0.46

Net run-rate was calculated by subtracting runs conceded per over from runs scored per over.

FINAL

PAKISTAN v SRI LANKA

At Sharjah, April 11. Sri Lanka won by four wickets. Toss: Pakistan.

Sri Lanka were back on target as Aravinda de Silva steered them home with four balls in hand to secure their second trophy at Sharjah and a couple more awards for himself. It was not his most dazzling display of the tournament – he struck only three fours – but he was still there at the end, unbeaten on 87. Pakistan chose to bat first, a decision which they seemed to have justified when Salim Malik and Inzamam-ul-Haq took them to 185 for three. But once they were separated, the last seven fell for 29 runs in six overs. Though Kaluwitharana was dismissed by the third ball of Sri Lanka's innings, it was only a temporary setback for his colleagues.

Man of the Match: P. A. de Silva.   *Man of the Tournament:* P. A. de Silva.

Pakistan

Ramiz Raja c Ranatunga			
b K. S. C. de Silva .	12	Waqar Younis c P. A. de Silva b Vaas ..	1
Sajid Ali c Tillekeratne b Muralitharan ..	28	Saqlain Mushtaq c Mahanama	
Ijaz Ahmed, sen. b Jayasuriya	33	b K. S. C. de Silva .	1
Salim Malik b Muralitharan............	58	Mushtaq Ahmed not out..............	0
Inzamam-ul-Haq run out	61	B 1, l-b 1, w 5, n-b 1........	8
†Moin Khan c Mahanama b Muralitharan.	1		
*Wasim Akram b Dharmasena	3	1/19 2/68 3/87 (49.2 overs) 214	
Shahid Afridi b Vaas	8	4/183 5/185 6/194	
		7/208 8/210 9/212	

Bowling: Vaas 9.2–1–32–2; K. S. C. de Silva 9–0–35–2; Muralitharan 10–0–42–3; Dharmasena 9–1–30–1; Jayasuriya 5–0–31–1; P. A. de Silva 7–0–42–0.

Sri Lanka

S. T. Jayasuriya lbw b Waqar Younis....	13	H. P. Tillekeratne c Ijaz Ahmed	
†R. S. Kaluwitharana c Ijaz Ahmed		b Saqlain Mushtaq .	7
b Wasim Akram .	0	H. D. P. K. Dharmasena not out	3
M. S. Atapattu lbw b Mushtaq Ahmed ...	29		
P. A. de Silva not out	87	L-b 11, w 2, n-b 4	17
*A. Ranatunga c and b Salim Malik	28		
R. S. Mahanama c Mushtaq Ahmed		1/1 2/35 3/67 (6 wkts, 49.2 overs) 215	
b Saqlain Mushtaq .	31	4/133 5/193 6/204	

W. P. U. J. C. Vaas, M. Muralitharan and K. S. C. de Silva did not bat.

Bowling: Wasim Akram 10–1–30–1; Waqar Younis 8–0–43–1; Saqlain Mushtaq 9.2–0–41–2; Mushtaq Ahmed 10–0–41–1; Shahid Afridi 5–0–24–0; Salim Malik 7–0–25–1.

Umpires: R. S. Dunne and C. J. Mitchley.   Series referee: Hanumant Singh.

PEPSI INDEPENDENCE CUP, 1996-97

By R. MOHAN

India staged a quadrangular one-day tournament in the unusually late month of May to celebrate the fiftieth anniversary of the country's independence. They evaded the worst of the intense summer heat by starting the games in the afternoon and playing on under floodlights, now erected at most of the major grounds thanks to the profits of the World Cup.

But India were not able to celebrate on the field. They won only one match, against New Zealand, before being swept away by their neighbours, Sri Lanka and Pakistan. Sri Lanka added another trophy to their growing list, hitting peak form in the finals, where they passed 300 in both games, thanks to the offensive set up by Sanath Jayasuriya and elegantly sustained by Aravinda de Silva and Arjuna Ranatunga.

But Pakistan – whose bowling was severely weakened by the absence of Wasim Akram, Waqar Younis and Mushtaq Ahmed, all in England with their counties – would long remember their victory over India in the final group match. Left-hander Saeed Anwar scored the highest innings ever made in a one-day international, plundering 194 off the Indian bowling to beat Viv Richards's 13-year-old record. It was his 12th century in this form of the game; Tendulkar had also reached 12 during the tournament, and only Desmond Haynes, with 17, remained ahead of them. One well-known name was not around: Mohammad Azharuddin, the former Indian captain, was left out of the squad after his poor tour of the Caribbean.

Note: Matches in this section were not first-class.

NEW ZEALAND v PAKISTAN

At Mohali, May 9 (day/night). New Zealand won by 22 runs. Toss: Pakistan.

Invited to bat, Astle and Young shared an opening stand of 155, punishing Pakistan's depleted attack on a splendid pitch. New Zealand were 234 for one in the 41st over. But after Astle was stumped, for his fourth century in one-day internationals, they lost momentum against the tight bowling of Saqlain Mushtaq. Pakistan needed 286 and Shahid Afridi gave them a chance, racing to 59 from 46 balls. New Zealand's slow bowlers put the brakes on, however, backed up by some fine catches inside the fielding circle. Astle completed an excellent game by taking four wickets, including key batsmen Ijaz Ahmed and Salim Malik.

Man of the Match: N. J. Astle.

New Zealand

B. A. Young b Abdur Razzaq	59	†A. C. Parore not out	16
N. J. Astle st Moin Khan b Shahid Afridi	117	G. R. Larsen not out	1
M. J. Horne b Saqlain Mushtaq	45	L-b 2, w 9, n-b 2	13
C. L. Cairns b Aqib Javed	17		
*S. P. Fleming c and b Saqlain Mushtaq	9	1/155 2/234 3/236 (7 wkts, 50 overs)	285
C. Z. Harris b Saqlain Mushtaq	4	4/256 5/264	
D. N. Patel run out	4	6/264 7/282	

A. J. Penn and H. T. Davis did not bat.

Bowling: Abdur Razzaq 7–0–45–1; Aqib Javed 8–0–70–1; Shahid Afridi 10–0–49–1; Saqlain Mushtaq 10–0–38–3; Mohammad Hussain 5–0–36–0; Salim Malik 10–0–45–0.

Pakistan

Saeed Anwar c Harris b Penn	17	Abdur Razzaq st Parore b Astle	8
Shahid Afridi b Larsen	59	Saqlain Mushtaq not out	6
*Ramiz Raja run out	11	Aqib Javed not out	6
Ijaz Ahmed, sen. lbw b Astle	50	L-b 2, w 7, n-b 3	12
Salim Malik c Harris b Astle	47		
Inzamam-ul-Haq c Harris b Patel	30	1/45 2/92 3/106 (9 wkts, 50 overs)	263
†Moin Khan c Fleming b Astle	16	4/189 5/220 6/232	
Mohammad Hussain c Davis b Larsen	1	7/242 8/243 9/256	

Bowling: Penn 6–0–50–1; Davis 6–0–39–0; Harris 10–2–34–0; Larsen 10–0–46–2; Patel 10–0–49–1; Astle 8–0–43–4.

Umpires: K. T. Francis and S. Venkataraghavan.

PAKISTAN v SRI LANKA

At Gwalior, May 12 (day/night). Pakistan won by 30 runs. Toss: Pakistan.

Aqib Javed dismissed Sri Lanka's top three in his opening spell and later added Aravinda de Silva to leave them 59 for four in the 11th over. That stopped the Sri Lankan pursuit of 290 in its tracks. Salim Malik inflicted further fatal blows with two wickets in an over, and the batsmen were also impeded by a 16-minute break when the floodlights broke down. Aqib passed 150 one-day international wickets during this innings, and Saqlain Mushtaq 100. Earlier, Shahid Afridi celebrated the chance to bat first by whipping 52 off 29 balls; Pakistan had the 50 up in their eighth over, and Ramiz Raja and Malik ensured a large total.

Man of the Match: Aqib Javed.

Pakistan

Saeed Anwar st Kaluwitharana	Salim Malik b Vaas 49
b Muralitharan . 36	Inzamam-ul-Haq b K. S. C. de Silva 22
Shahid Afridi c Kaluwitharana	†Moin Khan not out 23
b K. S. C. de Silva . 52	Mohammad Hussain not out 17
*Ramiz Raja c P. A. de Silva	B 4, l-b 3, w 5 12
b K. S. C. de Silva . 49	
Ijaz Ahmed, sen. c Mahanama	1/74 2/112 3/158　(6 wkts, 50 overs) 289
b Jayasuriya . 29	4/190 5/219 6/260

Azhar Mahmood, Saqlain Mushtaq and Aqib Javed did not bat.

Bowling: Vaas 10–1–71–1; K. S. C. de Silva 10–0–59–3; Dharmasena 10–0–54–0; Muralitharan 10–1–39–1; Jayasuriya 10–0–59–1.

Sri Lanka

S. T. Jayasuriya lbw b Aqib Javed 0	H. D. P. K. Dharmasena
†R. S. Kaluwitharana b Aqib Javed 7	lbw b Saqlain Mushtaq . 28
M. S. Atapattu c Ijaz Ahmed b Aqib Javed 0	W. P. U. J. C. Vaas b Aqib Javed 15
P. A. de Silva c Ijaz Ahmed	M. Muralitharan c Azhar Mahmood
b Aqib Javed . 33	b Saqlain Mushtaq . 7
*A. Ranatunga c Azhar Mahmood	K. S. C. de Silva not out 13
b Salim Malik . 58	L-b 10, w 1, n-b 4 15
H. P. Tillekeratne c Inzamam-ul-Haq	
b Salim Malik . 29	1/0 2/0 3/25　　　(49.5 overs) 259
R. S. Mahanama c Ijaz Ahmed	4/59 5/134 6/134
b Saqlain Mushtaq . 54	7/205 8/229 9/243

Bowling: Aqib Javed 10–1–35–5; Azhar Mahmood 5–0–36–0; Saqlain Mushtaq 9.5–0–43–3; Shahid Afridi 8–0–58–0; Salim Malik 10–0–46–2; Mohammad Hussain 7–0–31–0.

Umpires: R. S. Dunne and S. Venkataraghavan.

INDIA v NEW ZEALAND

At Bangalore, May 14 (day/night). India won by eight wickets. Toss: New Zealand.

Astle almost reached his second century in as many games, scoring 92 in 111 balls, with ten fours, but New Zealand slid from a promising 109 for one to an inadequate final total of 220, with four run-outs. That was due to poor running as much as brilliant fielding. India's batsmen found the New Zealand bowling no trouble at all. Tendulkar and Ganguly put on 169 in 32 overs and Tendulkar continued to complete his 12th century in one-day internationals. He had made 117 from 136 balls, with 13 fours and two sixes, when he was bowled with his team needing only five to win.

Man of the Match: S. R. Tendulkar.

New Zealand

B. A. Young c Kumble b Joshi 17	G. R. Larsen b Joshi 12
N. J. Astle b Singh 92	A. J. Penn not out 7
M. J. Horne run out 23	H. T. Davis not out 0
*S. P. Fleming run out 13	L-b 4, w 1, n-b 3 8
C. L. Cairns lbw b Singh 3	
C. Z. Harris c and b Kumble 3	1/59 2/109 3/136　(9 wkts, 50 overs) 220
†A. C. Parore run out 32	4/147 5/154 6/166
D. N. Patel run out 10	7/185 8/209 9/219

Bowling: Prasad 10–0–40–0; Kuruvilla 6–1–37–0; Kumble 10–1–30–1; Joshi 10–0–47–2; Singh 7–0–27–2; Tendulkar 7–0–35–0.

India

S. C. Ganguly c Parore b Larsen		62
*S. R. Tendulkar b Astle		117
R. Dravid not out		21
V. G. Kambli not out		4
L-b 1, w 13, n-b 3		17

1/169 2/216   (2 wkts, 42.3 overs) 221

A. Jadeja, R. R. Singh, †N. R. Mongia, A. Kumble, S. B. Joshi, A. Kuruvilla and B. K. V. Prasad did not bat.

Bowling: Penn 8.3–0–59–0; Davis 5–0–54–0; Larsen 8–2–26–1; Harris 7–1–26–0; Patel 7–0–30–0; Astle 7–0–25–1.

Umpires: Javed Akhtar and D. L. Orchard.

INDIA v SRI LANKA

At Mumbai, May 17 (day/night). Sri Lanka won by five wickets. Toss: India.

India lost Ganguly to the first ball of the match and were in dire straits when Tendulkar slashed to deep third man in the fourth over. Jadeja joined Dravid at 29 for three and revived the innings with a stand of 95, while Robin Singh added a run-a-ball maiden fifty. But Vaas bowled with such economy that he conceded only 13 runs, including just one in the 50th over. A moderate target of 226 soon shrank as Jayasuriya blazed his way to the highest score by a Sri Lankan in one-day internationals – 151 off 121 balls, with 17 fours and four sixes, beating Aravinda de Silva's 145 against Kenya in the 1996 World Cup. Sri Lanka won with nine overs to spare.

Man of the Match: S. T. Jayasuriya.

India

S. C. Ganguly b Vaas	0		†N. R. Mongia not out	21
*S. R. Tendulkar c Dharmasena			A. Kumble c Muralitharan b Vaas	0
b K. S. C. de Silva	2			
R. Dravid b Muralitharan	61		L-b 6, w 7, n-b 1	14
V. G. Kambli c Tillekeratne				
b K. S. C. de Silva	4		1/0 2/4 3/29 (7 wkts, 50 overs) 225	
A. Jadeja b Jayasuriya	72		4/124 5/182	
R. R. Singh b K. S. C. de Silva	51		6/224 7/225	

S. B. Joshi, A. Kuruvilla and B. K. V. Prasad did not bat.

Bowling: Vaas 10–3–13–2; K. S. C. de Silva 10–0–59–3; Muralitharan 10–0–37–1; Dharmasena 10–2–38–0; Jayasuriya 8–0–55–1; P. A. de Silva 2–0–17–0.

Sri Lanka

S. T. Jayasuriya not out	151		H. P. Tillekeratne c Mongia b Kuruvilla	6
†R. S. Kaluwitharana c Tendulkar			R. S. Mahanama not out	4
b Kuruvilla	0			
M. S. Atapattu run out	38		B 4, l-b 2, w 7	13
P. A. de Silva lbw b Kumble	0			
*A. Ranatunga c sub (G. K. Khoda)			1/8 2/146 3/151 (5 wkts, 40.5 overs) 229	
b Kumble	17		4/194 5/220	

H. D. P. K. Dharmasena, W. P. U. J. C. Vaas, M. Muralitharan and K. S. C. de Silva did not bat.

Bowling: Prasad 10–1–57–0; Kuruvilla 7–1–22–2; Kumble 10–0–55–2; Joshi 9.5–0–56–0; Singh 2–0–20–0; Tendulkar 2–0–13–0.

Umpires: R. S. Dunne and D. L. Orchard.

NEW ZEALAND v SRI LANKA

At Hyderabad, May 20 (day/night). Sri Lanka won by 52 runs. Toss: Sri Lanka. International debuts: C. D. McMillan, S. B. O'Connor.

Debutant seamer Shayne O'Connor quickly removed Jayasuriya and Aravinda de Silva. Those blows, plus the persistence of off-spinner Patel, who shared the new ball, and the slow medium-pacers, Larsen and Astle, choked Sri Lanka's usual free-scoring style. While Mahanama tried to anchor the innings, it was left to Kaluwitharana, demoted to No. 7 after a run of poor scores, to ensure that it went past 200. Once again, New Zealand started well – they were 96 for two at the halfway mark – but then, after Fleming swept and missed at de Silva, they subsided against Sri Lanka's slow bowlers, who each picked up two wickets.

Man of the Match: R. S. Kaluwitharana.

Sri Lanka

S. T. Jayasuriya c Cairns b O'Connor	4	W. P. U. J. C. Vaas b Larsen		0
M. S. Atapattu run out	41	M. Muralitharan not out		9
P. A. de Silva b O'Connor	9	K. S. C. de Silva lbw b Larsen		0
*A. Ranatunga c Parore b Larsen	15	B 5, l-b 6, w 3, n-b 2		16
H. P. Tillekeratne b Astle	29			
R. S. Mahanama c McMillan b O'Connor	41	1/6 2/23 3/68	(48.3 overs)	214
†R. S. Kaluwitharana c Cairns b Astle	44	4/85 5/126 6/173		
H. D. P. K. Dharmasena run out	6	7/188 8/194 9/210		

Bowling: O'Connor 9–0–44–3; Patel 10–0–37–0; Larsen 9.3–1–43–3; Harris 10–0–30–0; Astle 8–1–37–2; Cairns 2–0–12–0.

New Zealand

B. A. Young c Kaluwitharana b K. S. C. de Silva	22	†A. C. Parore c Tillekeratne b Dharmasena		9
N. J. Astle c Kaluwitharana b Vaas	9	D. N. Patel c Muralitharan b Dharmasena		5
M. J. Horne st Kaluwitharana b Jayasuriya	41	G. R. Larsen b Muralitharan		1
*S. P. Fleming lbw b P. A. de Silva	24	S. B. O'Connor c Tillekeratne b Muralitharan		0
C. L. Cairns c P. A. de Silva b Jayasuriya	6	B 1, l-b 5, w 2, n-b 1		9
C. D. McMillan st Kaluwitharana b P. A. de Silva	10	1/29 2/31 3/97	(44.5 overs)	162
C. Z. Harris not out	26	4/103 5/120 6/120		
		7/140 8/147 9/152		

Bowling: Vaas 6–2–23–1; K. S. C. de Silva 6–2–13–1; Muralitharan 9.5–1–49–2; Dharmasena 6–0–28–2; P. A. de Silva 10–1–22–2; Jayasuriya 7–1–21–2.

Umpires: S. K. Bansal and Javed Akhtar.

INDIA v PAKISTAN

At Chennai (formerly Madras), May 21 (day/night). Pakistan won by 35 runs. Toss: Pakistan.

Saeed Anwar broke the record for the highest individual innings in a one-day international by scoring 194, from 146 balls, with 22 fours and five sixes, three in succession off Kumble, which went for 226664. He beat the previous record, Viv Richards's unbeaten 189 for West Indies against England at Old Trafford in 1984, by five, and might have reached a double-hundred had he not top-edged a sweep to be caught at fine leg in the 47th over. It was a remarkable exhibition of controlled aggression, even if he was helped by a runner, Shahid Afridi, for most of the innings (he was suffering from heat exhaustion and loss of fluid). India were left a target of 328. They began on a poor note when Inzamam-ul-Haq took an athletic catch to dismiss Tendulkar, but Dravid sustained them with his maiden hundred in limited-overs internationals – also briefly assisted by a runner, Tendulkar, until the fielding side objected. They soon fell behind, however, after he pushed a catch to mid-wicket, one of five wickets for Aqib Javed. Afterwards, Tendulkar said Anwar's innings was the best he had seen, and the former Test bowler Bishen Bedi said batting like that comes "once in a lifetime". Some observers – including TV commentator Glenn Turner – diluted their praise by noting that his runner made the innings much easier, given the extreme heat. Anwar himself said: "To beat India in India is something special. Only we know the pressure we were subjected to back at home after our loss at Bangalore in the World Cup." In contrast to past bitterness in India–Pakistan matches, the 45,000 crowd gave him a standing ovation.

Man of the Match: Saeed Anwar.

Pakistan

Saeed Anwar c Ganguly b Tendulkar	194	Mohammad Hussain not out	 7
Shahid Afridi c Ganguly b Kuruvilla	 5		
*Ramiz Raja b Singh	 22	B 1, l-b 8, w 3	 12
Ijaz Ahmed, sen. lbw b Kumble	 39		
Inzamam-ul-Haq not out	 39	1/8 2/97 3/213	(5 wkts, 50 overs) 327
†Moin Khan b Tendulkar	 9	4/297 5/315	

Salim Malik, Azhar Mahmood, Saqlain Mushtaq and Aqib Javed did not bat.

Bowling: Prasad 9–0–63–0; Kuruvilla 10–2–50–1; Kumble 9–1–58–1; Joshi 4–0–36–0; Singh 9–0–50–1; Tendulkar 9–0–61–2.

India

*S. R. Tendulkar c Inzamam-ul-Haq		S. B. Joshi c Moin Khan b Aqib Javed	.. 2
b Aqib Javed .	4	A. Kumble c and b Saqlain Mushtaq	 0
S. C. Ganguly c Saqlain Mushtaq		A. Kuruvilla c Mohammad Hussain	
b Aqib Javed .	33	b Aqib Javed .	1
R. Dravid c Shahid Afridi b Aqib Javed.	.107	B. K. V. Prasad c Moin Khan	
V. G. Kambli c Ijaz Ahmed		b Saqlain Mushtaq .	2
b Mohammad Hussain .	65	L-b 7, w 8, n-b 1	 16
A. Jadeja c sub (Mohammad Wasim)			
b Salim Malik .	4	1/9 2/61 3/195	(49.2 overs) 292
R. R. Singh run out	 35	4/209 5/247 6/275	
†N. R. Mongia not out	 23	7/279 8/281 9/284	

Bowling: Aqib Javed 10–0–61–5; Azhar Mahmood 4–0–24–0; Saqlain Mushtaq 9.2–0–46–2; Shahid Afridi 10–0–56–0; Salim Malik 6–0–46–1; Mohammad Hussain 10–0–52–1.

Umpires: K. T. Francis and D. L. Orchard.

QUALIFYING TABLE

	Played	Won	Lost	Points	Net run-rate
Pakistan	3	2	1	4	0.29
Sri Lanka	3	2	1	4	0.48
India	3	1	2	2	−0.33
New Zealand	3	1	2	2	−0.45

Pakistan led the table because they had won their head-to-head game with Sri Lanka, although Sri Lanka had a better net run-rate (calculated by subtracting runs conceded per over from runs scored per over). India won their head-to-head game with New Zealand so were placed higher.

PAKISTAN v SRI LANKA

First Final Match

At Mohali, May 24 (day/night). Sri Lanka won by 115 runs. Toss: Sri Lanka.

Pakistan's weak and inexperienced bowling was put to the sword as Sri Lanka ran riot, to reach the seventh-highest total in one-day internationals. Jayasuriya scored an entertaining 96, off 67 balls, missing his century when he just failed to clear long-off. He had put on 148 with Atapattu, a Sri Lankan first-wicket record. There was to be no respite as Aravinda de Silva and Ranatunga added 153 for the third wicket. All the top four passed 50 and three of them reached 80, showing just the right mix of aggression and safe batting, with singles seemingly there for the asking. Pakistan had no realistic hopes of making 340 once Sajeewa de Silva sent their top three back to the pavilion before 50 was on the board. Moin Khan slashed his way to 57 off 60 balls at No. 7, but it was too little, too late, and with two men injured and unable to bat, they folded by the 44th over.

Man of the Match: S. T. Jayasuriya.

Sri Lanka

S. T. Jayasuriya c sub (Mohammad Wasim) b Mohammad Hussain . 96		†R. S. Kaluwitharana not out	1
M. S. Atapattu lbw b Mohammad Hussain 53		D. K. Liyanage not out	1
P. A. de Silva st Moin Khan b Saqlain Mushtaq . 90		L-b 8, w 8, n-b 2	18
*A. Ranatunga st Moin Khan b Saqlain Mushtaq . 80		1/148 2/184 (4 wkts, 50 overs) 339 3/337 4/338	

H. P. Tillekeratne, R. S. Mahanama, H. D. P. K. Dharmasena, M. Muralitharan and K. S. C. de Silva did not bat.

Bowling: Aqib Javed 9–0–64–0; Abdur Razzaq 5–0–41–0; Saqlain Mushtaq 10–0–72–2; Shahid Afridi 10–0–63–0; Mohammad Hussain 10–0–56–2; Salim Malik 6–0–35–0.

Pakistan

Saeed Anwar c Liyanage b K. S. C. de Silva . 14		Saqlain Mushtaq c Atapattu b P. A. de Silva .	18
Shahid Afridi c Atapattu b K. S. C. de Silva . 18		Aqib Javed lbw b Dharmasena	5
Mohammad Hussain b K. S. C. de Silva . 8		Inzamam-ul-Haq absent hurt	
*Ramiz Raja run out 42		Abdur Razzaq absent hurt	
Ijaz Ahmed, sen. c sub (U. D. U. Chandana) b Dharmasena . 23		L-b 1, w 8, n-b 1	10
Salim Malik b P. A. de Silva . 29		1/30 2/41 3/49 (8 wkts, 43.5 overs) 224	
†Moin Khan not out 57		4/85 5/141 6/143 7/212 8/224	

Bowling: Liyanage 6–0–40–0; K. S. C. de Silva 7–0–40–3; Dharmasena 6.5–0–33–2; Muralitharan 7–0–48–0; P. A. de Silva 10–1–39–2; Jayasuriya 7–0–23–0.

Umpires: R. S. Dunne and S. Venkataraghavan.

PAKISTAN v SRI LANKA

Second Final Match

At Calcutta, May 27 (day/night). Sri Lanka won by 85 runs. Toss: Sri Lanka.

Another piece of luck with the toss and another dynamic display from Jayasuriya helped Sri Lanka to settle the best-of-three finals in two games. They were also helped by the support of a crowd estimated at 85,000, the most to attend Eden Gardens when India were not playing. Jayasuriya – who made 55 from 40 balls – and Atapattu opened with 69 in ten overs, then Aravinda de Silva kept up the impetus with a classy 57 from 49 balls. Ranatunga added another fifty and Sri Lanka passed 300 for the second match running. Pakistan made a poor start, with both openers holing out off unconventional shots as they tried to clear the infield. Ijaz Ahmed and Ramiz Raja added 98 but, once Ijaz fell to a smart stumping, they could not sustain the chase.

Man of the Match: P. A. de Silva.   *Man of the Series:* S. T. Jayasuriya.

Sri Lanka

S. T. Jayasuriya c sub (Azhar Mahmood) b Arshad Khan .	55	R. S. Mahanama b Salim Malik	27
M. S. Atapattu c sub (Hasan Raza) b Arshad Khan .	29	H. D. P. K. Dharmasena b Saqlain Mushtaq .	16
†R. S. Kaluwitharana lbw b Shahid Afridi	5	M. Muralitharan not out	0
P. A. de Silva b Saqlain Mushtaq	57	K. S. C. de Silva lbw b Saqlain Mushtaq .	0
*A. Ranatunga run out	59		
H. P. Tillekeratne c sub (Hasan Raza) b Salim Malik .	38	L-b 6, w 13, n-b 1	20
W. P. U. J. C. Vaas c Ijaz Ahmed b Saqlain Mushtaq .	3	1/69 2/90 3/110 (49.4 overs) 309 4/177 5/250 6/254 7/276 8/304 9/308	

Bowling: Aqib Javed 6–0–49–0; Arshad Khan 10–0–54–2; Shahid Afridi 5–0–40–1; Saqlain Mushtaq 9.4–0–53–4; Mohammad Hussain 9–0–46–0; Salim Malik 10–0–61–2.

Pakistan

Saeed Anwar c Muralitharan b Vaas	6	Mohammad Hussain not out	18
Shahid Afridi c P. A. de Silva b K. S. C. de Silva .	17	Saqlain Mushtaq b P. A. de Silva	0
*Ramiz Raja b Dharmasena	76	Arshad Khan run out	0
Ijaz Ahmed, sen. st Kaluwitharana b Jayasuriya	55	Aqib Javed run out	4
Salim Malik lbw b Muralitharan	2	B 4, l-b 8, w 10, n-b 2	24
Mohammad Wasim st Kaluwitharana b Muralitharan .	20	1/14 2/34 3/132 (43.1 overs) 224	
†Moin Khan c Atapattu b Muralitharan . .	2	4/135 5/193 6/195 7/204 8/207 9/207	

Bowling: Vaas 7–0–40–1; K. S. C. de Silva 6–0–41–1; Dharmasena 8.1–0–23–1; Muralitharan 10–0–40–3; Jayasuriya 7–0–42–1; P. A. de Silva 5–0–26–1.

Umpires: R. S. Dunne and D. L. Orchard.
Series referees: Hanumant Singh (India) and A. M. Ibrahim (Zimbabwe).

INTERNATIONAL UMPIRES' PANEL

On December 21, 1993, the International Cricket Council announced the formation of an international umpires' panel, backed by sponsorship from National Grid. Each Full Member of ICC was to nominate two officials – apart from England, who named four, because of their large number of professional umpires and the fact that most Tests take place during the English winter. A third-country member of the panel was to stand with a "home" umpire, not necessarily from the panel, in every Test staged from February 1994. Teams would have no right of objection to appointments. In 1997, National Grid renewed their sponsorship until 2000.

The following umpires were on the panel from September 1997:

L. H. Barker (West Indies), S. A. Bucknor (West Indies), B. C. Cooray (Sri Lanka), D. B. Cowie (New Zealand), R. S. Dunne (New Zealand), K. T. Francis (Sri Lanka), D. B. Hair (Australia), Javed Akhtar (Pakistan), M. J. Kitchen (England), R. E. Koertzen (South Africa), C. J. Mitchley (South Africa), V. K. Ramaswamy (India), S. G. Randell (Australia), I. D. Robinson (Zimbabwe), Salim Badar (Pakistan), G. Sharp (England), D. R. Shepherd (England), R. B. Tiffin (Zimbabwe), S. Venkataraghavan (India), P. Willey (England).

Note: Compared with the 1996-97 list, Javed Akhtar and Salim Badar have replaced Khizar Hayat and Mahboob Shah, R. E. Koertzen has replaced D. L. Orchard and V. K. Ramaswamy has replaced S. K. Bansal. West Indies were due to name a replacement for L. H. Barker after England's tour in early 1998.

THE ICC CARLSBERG TROPHY, 1996-97

By DAVID TOWNSEND

Amid scenes of wild excitement, some of it spilling over into hysteria, Bangladesh scrambled a leg-bye off the last ball of the ICC Trophy final to defeat Kenya. They thus claimed top ranking for the first time among ICC's Associate Member countries. Both teams qualified for the 1999 World Cup, along with Scotland, who beat Ireland in the third-place play-off. But the other dominant force in the sixth ICC Trophy, held in Kuala Lumpur in Malaysia, was rain.

The final, at the Tenaga Sports Ground in Kuala Lumpur, stretched over two days. The first was dominated by a magnificent century from Steve Tikolo, the second by the largely untried theories of Messrs Duckworth and Lewis, the gurus of rain-reduced matches. Though no one played a major innings like Tikolo's, Bangladesh doggedly pursued a revised target of 166 from 25 overs and hit the 11 they needed off the final over – helped in part by Kenya's confusion over whether they needed 166 or 167.

Victory was celebrated with fervour by 4,000 Bangladeshi fans – mostly immigrant building workers. As captain Akram Khan accepted the trophy, four collapsed and needed medical attention. Happily, all recovered. At home in Dhaka, another man had been shot dead during the revelling that followed Bangladesh's semi-final win against Scotland, which put them through to the World Cup for the first time. Thus a country where support runs deep enough to provide 30,000 crowds for club matches began to move towards the cricketing status its people deserve.

Kenya, who had also been runners-up when they hosted the previous ICC Trophy, in 1993-94, could console themselves that Maurice Odumbe, named Player of the Tournament, Steve Tikolo and Martin Suji could challenge for a place in many Test teams, that their fielding was outstanding, and that, with a wicket-keeper and three bowlers among their top five batsmen, there was plenty of scope for strengthening their line-up.

Bangladesh, by contrast, were short of star players – though their supporters would argue that there were 11 of them. Their batting was admirably flexible, they bowled tightly, using several options, and, most importantly, they had the nerve to cope with the expectations of a fanatical following.

The prospect that failure could result in their houses being burned down was not one that worried the players of Scotland or Ireland, although the Irish might have benefited from a sharper focus: they offered eight easy catches as they lost the battle for third place. Scotland coach Jim Love, the former Yorkshire batsman, was proud that his charges had achieved so much on their first appearance in the Trophy. But he knew he would have to work hard, and perhaps recruit a couple of seasoned English county players, for Scotland to put up a showing in the World Cup. Ireland, who had lost their semi-final to Kenya by only seven runs, looked better organised up to that point and took out their frustration at not qualifying by recording their first competitive win over an English county – Middlesex – within the month.

Two days were needed to complete all the matches in the later stages, and it seemed a strange decision to hold such an important tournament in March and April, Kuala Lumpur's wettest months. Malaysia's bid to the International Cricket Council had stated that on the ''odd day'' it would rain for 30 minutes and be playable ten minutes later. This may have been true of the "odd day", but the routine experience of the second and third weeks was of torrential downpours and flooded outfields.

Holland, World Cup qualifiers four years earlier, were particularly unlucky with the rain. Having reached the last eight, they lost a finely balanced match to Ireland through a Duckworth/Lewis calculation after rain halted Ireland's reply. Their next game, against Hong Kong, was started but then washed out. Then they were obliged to attend a dinner on the eve of their remaining game – one they had to win to reach the semis – and could not leave before the King of Malaysia, who, by local custom, spent the evening with his back turned to the other guests. For a while next day, it looked as though Holland's luck had changed. But Bangladesh, who had also attended the dinner, recovered from losing early wickets to reach an unfavourable revised target with some comfort.

Ironically, the best weather of the tournament favoured the often one-sided and irrelevant first-round games. Kenya, the favourites, won all their five games in Group A, though they started slowly, scraping past Singapore's meagre 89 by only two wickets. But they hit top form to trounce Ireland by 119 runs and dismiss the United States for 32 in their final game. The Americans, boasting former Test batsman Faoud Bacchus and Derek Kallicharran, Alvin's brother, in a predominantly West Indian line-up, had had Ireland on the ropes in what proved to have been the group's second-place decider, but Mark Patterson inspired a late rally and a two-wicket victory.

Bangladesh also maintained a 100 per cent record, in Group B, where a one-wicket last-ball win by Denmark was to bring an early end to the United Arab Emirates' defence of the Trophy. That Danish victory, heroically completed by an injured Thomas Hansen, was all the more commendable as the UAE again fielded more "overseas players" than any other team. After they had won the Trophy in Nairobi in 1993-94 with a team that controversially included ten foreign-born players, ICC changed its residential qualification rules to demand a minimum of seven citizens in every team. But, in a typical fudge, any country which thought this would be too much of a handicap was allowed to claim special dispensation. The UAE did and, alone among the 22 Associate Members, were allowed to field sides containing only six citizens. ICC also caved in under the threat of legal action by Italy and granted Benito Giordano temporary registration, although he was born in Warrington, lived just outside Manchester, and did not qualify to play for his parents' country under any interpretation of the existing rule. But the Italians argued that under their national law, he had the right to be considered Italian, and ICC later changed their regulations.

Holland pipped Canada on net run-rate in Group C after their final, head-to-head match was abandoned. Five hundred Moslem fundamentalists had invaded the ground, refusing to believe that Israel, the subject of their protest, had been moved to another venue. The early exit of Bermuda, semi-finalists in 1994, was a surprise. As in Nairobi, Hong Kong were the surprise success of the first round. They beat the Bermudans with two balls to spare. Despite employing former Australian coach Bob Simpson, Bermuda then lost their final match to group winners Scotland.

Other celebrity coaches included Sandeep Patil of India, who worked with the Kenyans, and West Indian legend Gordon Greenidge, who proved his devotion to the Bangladeshi cause when he was seen on hands and knees mopping up the outfield. Greenidge's former Test colleagues, Roger Harper and Larry Gomes, assisted the USA and Canada.

The difference in playing standards among the 22 Associates – the 23rd and most recent, Nepal, did not take part – was highlighted by some of the records set during the tournament. East and Central Africa sank to a new low when they were dismissed for 26 in 15.2 overs by Holland, Asim Khan taking a Trophy-best seven for nine. Those two records are unlikely to be beaten if ICC follows through a move to end such mis-matches by separating the Associates into two divisions. This has already been agreed in principle. Under the likeliest plan, the next tournament will be contested by the top 12 from this one. It would be a sensible change: that royal dinner, scheduled to fit in with the King's diary rather than the business of qualifying for the World Cup, had highlighted a growing schism between the "serious" teams and those, like Gibraltar and Argentina, for whom the tournament is primarily a social event.

For the most part, the tournament was more efficiently organised, both on and off the field, than in Kenya, mainly because ICC officials were more involved, but the bustle, noise and climate of Kuala Lumpur were an irritation to those who had enjoyed the quiet charm and ambience of Nairobi. After three weeks of rain, inconsistent matting pitches, high humidity, congested traffic and more rain, it was not only the Israelis who were quietly relieved to clear Malaysian air space. No team were more relieved than the Scots, who had been pessimistic enough to book their return flight before the closing stages. They were unable to get later bookings and made three unsuccessful journeys to the airport before the president of the Malaysian Cricket Association used his influence to get them away.

Notes: Matches in this section were not first-class.

The Duckworth/Lewis method for deciding the result of rain-affected matches was used in this tournament.

GROUP A

At Victoria Institute, March 24. Ireland won by 192 runs. Toss: Gibraltar. Ireland 278 for two (50 overs) (J. D. Curry 52, D. A. Lewis 127 not out, J. D. R. Benson 73); Gibraltar 86 (32.2 overs) (Extras 31; M. W. Patterson four for 22).

At Kelab Aman, March 24. Kenya won by seven wickets. Toss: Israel. Israel 154 for eight (50 overs) (D. Silver 36; T. Odoyo three for 22); Kenya 157 for three (31.2 overs) (S. Tikolo 71 not out).

At PKNS, March 24. USA won by 106 runs. Toss: Singapore. USA 229 for eight (50 overs) (S. F. A. F. Bacchus 36, D. I. Kallicharran 60 not out, K. Dennis 40); Singapore 123 for nine (50 overs) (Extras 40; D. I. Kallicharran three for 22).

At Rubber Research Institute, March 25. USA won by 189 runs. Toss: USA. USA 312 for six (50 overs) (P. Singh 69, R. Denny 34, A. D. Texeira 44, S. F. A. F. Bacchus 100 not out; N. Churaman three for 64); Gibraltar 123 for nine (50 overs) (C. Rocca 35, Extras 31; D. I. Kallicharran three for 24).

At Royal Selangor Club, March 25. Kenya won by two wickets. Toss: Singapore. Singapore 89 (44.4 overs) (M. Suji three for nine); Kenya 90 for eight (30 overs) (G. S. Wilson four for 25, R. S. R. Martens three for 30).

At Royal Military College, March 26. Ireland won by ten wickets. Toss: Ireland. Israel 88 (31.5 overs) (G. D. Harrison three for 19, N. G. Doak four for nine); Ireland 89 for no wkt (17.2 overs) (J. D. Curry 51 not out).

The Israel total included 24 wides.

At Tenaga Sports Ground (Kilat Kelab), March 27. Ireland won by two wickets. Toss: Ireland. USA 212 (50 overs) (R. Denny 44, A. D. Texeira 40, A. Ali 32; N. G. Doak three for 27, J. D. Curry three for 28); Ireland 215 for eight (49.1 overs) (D. A. Lewis 37, J. D. R. Benson 31).

At Victoria Institute, March 27. Singapore won by 65 runs. Toss: Singapore. Singapore 204 (49.5 overs) (A. J. Ranggi 38, R. T. Y. Mohammed 33, G. S. Wilson 50; R. Ashton four for 54); Israel 139 (43.4 overs) (D. Silver 40; G. S. Wilson three for 17, S. Muruthi three for 22).

At Tenaga Sports Ground (Kilat Kelab), March 28. Singapore won on a revised calculation in a rain-affected match. Toss: Gibraltar. Singapore 198 (49.3 overs) (K. M. Deshpande 60, R. T. Y. Mohammed 65; N. Churaman three for 38); Gibraltar 162 for six (44.4 overs) (C. Rocca 58).

At Rubber Research Institute, March 29. Kenya won by 119 runs. Toss: Ireland. Kenya 247 for seven (50 overs) (S. Tikolo 31, M. Odumbe 99 not out, Hitesh Modi 49); Ireland 128 for nine (50 overs) (N. G. Doak 35; S. Tikolo three for 28).

At Royal Military College, March 29. USA won by seven wickets. Toss: Israel. Israel 105 (47 overs) (N. Islam three for 15); USA 108 for three (24 overs) (R. Denny 44 not out, S. F. A. F. Bacchus 33 not out).

At Rubber Research Institute, March 30. Gibraltar won by two wickets. Toss: Gibraltar. Israel 87 (41 overs) (N. Churaman five for 14, G. De'ath three for 12); Gibraltar 88 for eight (34.2 overs).

At Kelab Aman, March 30. Ireland won by ten wickets. Toss: Singapore. Singapore 110 (46.5 overs) (G. S. Wilson 31; M. W. Patterson three for 27); Ireland 113 for no wkt (10.2 overs) (J. D. Curry 65 not out, A. D. Patterson 44 not out).

At University of Malaysia, March 30. Kenya won by 211 runs. Toss: Kenya. Kenya 243 for seven (50 overs) (Asif Karim 34, K. Otieno 50, M. Odumbe 83); USA 32 (19 overs) (M. Suji five for seven, S. Tikolo four for 17).

	Played	Won	Lost	Points
Kenya	5	5	0	10
Ireland	5	4	1	8
USA	5	3	2	6
Singapore	5	2	3	4
Gibraltar	5	1	4	2
Israel	5	0	5	0

GROUP B

At University of Malaysia, March 24. Bangladesh won by five wickets. Toss: Argentina. Argentina 138 (48.3 overs) (B. I. Irigoyen 30 not out; Enam-ul-Haque three for 18, Naim-ur-Rahman three for 21); Bangladesh 142 for five (24 overs) (Ather Ali Khan 39 not out, Naim-ur-Rahman 53; C. J. Tunon three for 42).

At Rubber Research Institute, March 24. Denmark won by 31 runs. Toss: Denmark. Denmark 143 (47.2 overs) (M. Lund 43; S. N. Jeevandrum four for 22); Malaysia 112 (41.5 overs) (Extras 33; M. H. Andersen five for 19).

At Royal Selangor Club, March 24. United Arab Emirates won by seven wickets. Toss: West Africa. West Africa 72 (40.2 overs) (Arshad Laiq four for 14); United Arab Emirates 73 for three (14.1 overs).

At PKNS, March 25. Bangladesh won by nine wickets. Toss: Bangladesh. West Africa 82 (39.1 overs) (Minhaz-ul-Abedin three for eight); Bangladesh 83 for one (19.4 overs) (Naim-ur-Rahman 42 not out).

At Royal Military College, March 25. Malaysia won by 81 runs. Toss: Argentina. Malaysia 189 (50 overs) (M. A. Williams 56 not out; B. I. Irigoyen four for 27, A. R. P. Rivero four for 47); Argentina 108 (40.5 overs).

At University of Malaysia, March 26. Denmark won by one wicket. Toss: United Arab Emirates. United Arab Emirates 147 (46.2 overs) (Arshad Laiq 46; S. Vestergaard three for 16, S. R. M. Sorensen three for 19); Denmark 148 for nine (50 overs) (M. H. Andersen 30, Extras 31).

At Rubber Research Institute, March 27. West Africa won by five wickets. Toss: Argentina. Argentina 77 (38.1 overs) (D. Idowu four for 14); West Africa 79 for five (20.1 overs) (B. I. Irigoyen three for 35).

At Royal Selangor Club, March 27. Bangladesh won by five wickets. Toss: Denmark. Denmark 98 (47.4 overs); Bangladesh 99 for five (33.5 overs) (Ather Ali Khan 32, Amin-ul-Islam 33).

At PKNS, March 27. United Arab Emirates won by two wickets. Toss: Malaysia. Malaysia 140 (49.3 overs) (R. M. Selvaratnam 30); United Arab Emirates 141 for eight (47.5 overs) (Azhar Saeed 33; S. Navaratnam three for 41).

At Kelab Aman, March 28. Malaysia won on a revised calculation in a rain-affected match. Toss: Malaysia. Malaysia 170 (48.1 overs) (R. Menon 49 not out, Extras 33; U. Ntinu three for 19); West Africa 123 for eight (44 overs).

At PKNS, March 29. Denmark won by 150 runs. Toss: Argentina. Denmark 226 for eight (50 overs) (J. S. Jensen 43, B. Singh 57, M. H. Andersen 52 not out, Extras 33; G. F. Arizaga three for 46); Argentina 76 (35.1 overs) (Extras 30; S. K. Kristensen three for 16).

At Kelab Aman, March 29. Bangladesh won by 110 runs. Toss: United Arab Emirates. Bangladesh 205 (49.3 overs) (Minhaz-ul-Abedin 37, Enam-ul-Haque 37; Saleem Raza four for 23); United Arab Emirates 95 (34.3 overs).

At Victoria Institute, March 30. United Arab Emirates won by eight wickets. Toss: Argentina. Argentina 189 for seven (50 overs) (M. J. Paterlini 77 not out, Extras 32); United Arab Emirates 190 for two (31.3 overs) (Azhar Saeed 66 not out, Arshad Laiq 66, M. V. Perera 32 not out).

At Royal Military College, March 30. Denmark won by eight wickets. Toss: West Africa. West Africa 105 (45.5 overs) (A. Kpundeh 30; S. Vestergaard three for 15, S. K. Kristensen three for 24); Denmark 106 for two (22.5 overs) (J. S. Jensen 46 not out, C. R. Pedersen 34 not out).

At Tenaga Sports Ground (Kilat Kelab), March 30. Bangladesh won by 59 runs. Toss: Bangladesh. Bangladesh 211 for nine (50 overs) (Minhaz-ul-Abedin 42, Akram Khan 39, Khaled Mammud 33; R. Menon three for 43); Malaysia 152 for eight (50 overs) (M. A. Williams 58).

	Played	Won	Lost	Points
Bangladesh...............	5	5	0	10
Denmark	5	4	1	8
United Arab Emirates	5	3	2	6
Malaysia.................	5	2	3	4
West Africa	5	1	4	2
Argentina	5	0	5	0

GROUP C

At Royal Military College, March 24. Holland won by eight wickets. Toss: Holland. East and Central Africa 26 (15.2 overs) (A. Khan seven for nine); Holland 27 for two (5.3 overs).

East and Central Africa's total was the lowest in ICC Trophy games, and Khan's bowling figures of 7.2–1–9–7 were the best.

At University of Malaysia, March 25. Canada won by four wickets. Toss: Fiji. Fiji 128 (41.1 overs) (T. Batina 30; S. Rana five for 29; Canada 130 for six (38.2 overs) (L. Bhansingh 40 not out, M. Johnson 34; N. D. Maxwell three for 16).

S. Rana took a hat-trick.

At Tenaga Sports Ground (Kilat Kelab), March 25. Holland won by ten wickets. Toss: Namibia. Namibia 90 (48.5 overs) (B. W. Ackerman 36 not out; R. P. Lefebvre three for 14, A. Khan four for 24); Holland 91 for no wkt (23.5 overs) (T. B. M. de Leede 46 not out, R. P. Lefebvre 35 not out).

At Kelab Aman, March 26. Canada won by 60 runs. Toss: Namibia. Canada 264 for eight (50 overs) (I. Liburd 53, M. Diwan 125, B. F.ajadurai 62; R. van Schoor three for 44); Namibia 204 (43.2 overs) (D. Keulder 41, B. G. Murgatroyd 37; S. Seeram four for 50).

At Royal Selangor Club, March 26. Fiji won by 35 runs. Toss: East and Central Africa. Fiji 111 (40.3 overs) (N. D. Maxwell 33); East and Central Africa 76 (44 overs) (A. Tawatatau three for eight, T. Batina three for seven).

At PKNS, March 28. Namibia won by one wicket. Toss: Namibia. East and Central Africa 143 (48.1 overs) (B. Musoke 30); Namibia 144 for nine (46.5 overs) (D. Kotze 37, M. van Schoor 32; Y. S. Patel three for 28).

At Royal Military College, March 28. Holland won by six wickets. Toss: Fiji. Fiji 96 (41.2 overs) (J. Rouse 30; R. P. Lefebvre four for 16, P. E. Cantrell four for ten); Holland 100 for four (20.5 overs) (T. B. M. de Leede 48).

At Victoria Institute, March 29. Canada won by four wickets. Toss: East and Central Africa. East and Central Africa 179 (50 overs) (Y. S. Patel 64; I. Liburd four for 38, B. Seebaran three for 21); Canada 180 for six (46.3 overs) (N. Isaacs 51, I. Liburd 47 not out; C. M. Gomm three for 22).

At Royal Selangor Club, March 29. Fiji won by 105 runs. Toss: Namibia. Fiji 178 for six (50 overs) (L. Sorovakatini 37, Extras 32; R. van Vuuren four for 39); Namibia 73 (33.5 overs) (A. Tawatatau four for nine).

At PKNS, March 30. Canada v Holland. Abandoned.

Islamic fundamentalists prevented the match taking place, mistakenly believing that Israel were playing. The teams agreed to share the points rather than stage a replay.

	Played	Won	Lost	No result	Points
Holland	4	3	0	1	7
Canada	4	3	0	1	7
Fiji.	4	2	2	0	4
Namibia	4	1	3	0	2
East and Central Africa	4	0	4	0	0

Holland took first place on net run-rate.

GROUP D

At Tenaga Sports Ground (Kilat Kelab), March 24. Bermuda won by seven wickets. Toss: Bermuda. Italy 128 for eight (50 overs) (W. A. E. Manders three for 18); Bermuda 129 for three (31.1 overs) (C. J. Smith 43 not out, C. M. Marshall 47).

At Victoria Institute, March 25. Hong Kong won by three wickets. Toss: Hong Kong. Bermuda 227 for nine (50 overs) (A. Steede 65, W. A. E. Manders 65; M. Hussain three for 37, M. Zubair three for 31); Hong Kong 228 for seven (49.4 overs) (M. R. Farcy 65, R. Sharma 69; R. Blades three for 42).

At Kelab Aman, March 25. Scotland won by six wickets. Toss: Papua New Guinea. Papua New Guinea 120 (36.1 overs) (Extras 37; K. Thomson three for 37, K. L. P. Sheridan three for 12); Scotland 121 for four (38.1 overs) (G. Salmond 37 not out).

At Rubber Research Institute, March 26. Scotland won by 87 runs. Toss: Hong Kong. Scotland 221 for six (50 overs) (M. J. Smith 67, G. Salmond 34, M. J. D. Allingham 35 not out); Hong Kong 134 (40.4 overs) (J. P. Fordham 32; J. A. R. Blain three for 23, J. G. Williamson three for 26, S. R. Kennedy three for 15).

At PKNS, March 26. Papua New Guinea won by 101 runs. Toss: Italy. Papua New Guinea 219 for four (50 overs) (J. Ovia 94, C. Amini 45 not out, Extras 34); Italy 118 (48.4 overs) (Extras 31; K. Ilaraki three for 33).

At University of Malaysia, March 28. Bermuda won by 121 runs. Toss: Papua New Guinea. Bermuda 204 for nine (50 overs) (J. Tucker 104; T. Raka four for 27); Papua New Guinea 83 (28.2 overs) (I. Morea 38; B. D. Perinchief four for 33).

At Royal Selangor Club, March 28. Hong Kong won by 145 runs. Toss: Italy. Hong Kong 282 (49.4 overs) (S. J. Brew 39, J. P. Fordham 36, M. Hussain 39; A. Qureshi three for 67, B. Giordano three for 35, S. V. de Mel three for 40); Italy 137 (41 overs) (B. Giordano 32, Extras 31; D. A. Jones three for 14).

At Tenaga Sports Ground (Kilat Kelab), March 29. Hong Kong won by 81 runs. Toss: Hong Kong. Hong Kong 232 for eight (50 overs) (R. Sharma 57, M. I. N. Eames 33, J. P. Fordham 71, Extras 32); Papua New Guinea 151 (42.1 overs) (J. Ovia 62; S. J. Brew three for 22).

At University of Malaysia, March 29. Scotland won by 131 runs. Toss: Scotland. Scotland 273 (48.1 overs) (I. L. Philip 71, B. G. Lockie 58, G. Salmond 43, Extras 33; S. V. de Mel three for 43); Italy 142 (37.2 overs) (I. R. Beven four for 20).

At Royal Selangor Club, March 30. Scotland won by 57 runs. Toss: Scotland. Scotland 231 for eight (50 overs) (I. L. Philip 49, B. G. Lockie 33, G. Salmond 44, J. G. Williamson 42, Extras 30; J. Tucker three for 25); Bermuda 174 (50 overs) (Extras 36; M. J. D. Allingham three for 34).

	Played	Won	Lost	Points
Scotland	4	4	0	8
Hong Kong	4	3	1	6
Bermuda	4	2	2	4
Papua New Guinea	4	1	3	2
Italy	4	0	4	0

QUARTER-FINAL GROUP MATCHES

GROUP E

At Tenaga Sports Ground (Kilat Kelab), April 1. Kenya won on a revised calculation in a rain-affected match. Toss: Kenya. Kenya 303 for six (50 overs) (S. Tikolo 93, M. Odumbe 148 not out; S. Seeram three for 46); Canada 126 for seven (48 overs) (A. Suji three for 38).

At Rubber Research Institute, April 1. Scotland won by 45 runs. Toss: Scotland. Scotland 167 (48 overs) (G. Salmond 59; S. R. M. Sorensen three for 29, P. Jensen four for 25); Denmark 122 (45.4 overs) (I. R. Beven four for 23).

At Royal Military College, April 2. No result. Toss: Canada. Canada 99 for four (29.4 overs) (I. Liburd 39) v Scotland.

At Kelab Aman, April 2. No result. Toss: Kenya. Kenya 33 for four (9.4 overs) v Denmark.

At Royal Selangor Club, April 4. Denmark won by seven runs. Toss: Denmark. Denmark 126 (48.1 overs) (Extras 37; I. Liburd three for 14, D. Maxwell three for 21); Canada 119 (27.2 overs) (N. Isaacs 43; T. M. Hansen five for 51).

At PKNS, April 4. Kenya won on a revised calculation in a rain-affected match. Toss: Kenya. Kenya 153 (48.2 overs) (S. Tikolo 32; S. Gourlay three for 26, I. R. Beven three for 34); Scotland 37 for three (23 overs) (M. Suji three for 18).

	Played	Won	Lost	No result	Points
Kenya	3	2	0	1	5
Scotland	3	1	1	1	3
Denmark	3	1	1	1	3
Canada	3	0	2	1	1

Scotland qualified for the semi-finals because they had won their head-to-head game with Denmark.

GROUP F

At PKNS, April 1. Bangladesh won by seven wickets. Toss: Bangladesh. Hong Kong 145 (45.2 overs) (M. R. Farcy 38; Mohammad Rafiq three for 20); Bangladesh 148 for three (38.2 overs) (Amin-ul-Islam 53 not out).

At Kelab Aman, April 1. Ireland won on a revised calculation in a rain-affected match. Toss: Ireland. Holland 211 for eight (50 overs) (B. Zuiderent 38, P. E. Cantrell 53 not out); Ireland 91 for three (23 overs) (J. D. Curry 30).

At Royal Selangor Club, April 2. No result. Toss: Ireland. Ireland 129 (49.1 overs) (N. G. Doak 32; Hasib-ul-Hassan three for 21); Bangladesh 24 for no wkt (6.4 overs).

At Tenaga Sports Ground (Kilat Kelab), April 2. No result. Toss: Hong Kong. Hong Kong 170 (47.5 overs) (J. P. Fordham 34; A. Khan four for 28); Holland 16 for no wkt (5.2 overs).

At Rubber Research Institute, April 4. Bangladesh won by a higher comparative score in a reduced-overs match. Toss: Bangladesh. Holland 171 (49.5 overs) (P. E. Cantrell 37, R. F. van Oosterom 40); Bangladesh 141 for seven (31.4 overs) (Akram Khan 68 not out; R. P. Lefebvre three for eight).

At Kelab Aman, April 4. Ireland won by 51 runs. Toss: Hong Kong. Ireland 223 for seven (50 overs) (J. D. R. Benson 33, A. R. Dunlop 54, Extras 35; R. Sharma three for 29); Hong Kong 172 (45.3 overs) (S. J. Brew 50, Extras 33; P. G. Gillespie three for 42, P. McCrum three for 30).

	Played	Won	Lost	No result	Points
Bangladesh	3	2	0	1	5
Ireland	3	2	0	1	5
Holland	3	0	2	1	1
Hong Kong	3	0	2	1	1

Bangladesh took first place on net run-rate.

SEMI-FINALS

At Tenaga Sports Ground (Kilat Kelab), April 6, 7. Kenya won by seven runs. Toss: Ireland. Kenya 215 for eight (50 overs) (K. Otieno 51, M. Odumbe 67; P. McCrum four for 51); Ireland 208 for nine (50 overs) (J. D. R. Benson 35, D. Heasley 51; Asif Karim four for 28).

At Tenaga Sports Ground (Kilat Kelab), April 8, 9. Bangladesh won by 72 runs. Toss: Scotland. Bangladesh 243 for seven (50 overs) (Khaled Masud 70, Amin-ul-Islam 57, Minhaz-ul-Abedin 39 not out); Scotland 171 (44.5 overs) (I. L. Philip 37, J. G. Williamson 39 not out; Enam-ul-Haque three for 31, Mohammad Rafiq four for 25).

THIRD-PLACE PLAY-OFF

IRELAND v SCOTLAND

At Tenaga Sports Ground (Kilat Kelab), April 10, 11. Scotland won by a higher comparative score in a reduced-overs match. Toss: Ireland.

A storm submerged the outfield after 19 overs and, on resumption 25 hours later, five overs were docked from each innings. The Irish bowling and fielding had lost their edge and Smith led Scotland to a steady 187 for eight. The Duckworth/Lewis method raised Ireland's target to 192 – because they were approaching the reduced number of overs with all their wickets intact – but that became academic. Their batsmen panicked, offering up five boundary catches, and were dismissed for 141. Left-arm spinner Sheridan picked up four, but slow medium-pacer Kennedy bowled the key spell, conceding just 14 in nine overs.

Man of the Match: M. J. Smith.

Close of play: Scotland 56-1 (19 overs) (D. R. Lockhart 19*, M. J. Smith 13*).

Scotland

I. L. Philip c Doak b McCrum 11	I. R. Beven c A. D. Patterson
D. R. Lockhart c Benson b Doak 21	b M. W. Patterson . 3
M. J. Smith run out 49	S. R. Kennedy not out 4
*G. Salmond st A. D. Patterson b Curry . 7	L-b 4, w 22 26
J. G. Williamson c and b M. W. Patterson 27	
M. J. D. Allingham run out 22	1/19 2/75 3/94 4/132 (8 wkts, 45 overs) 187
†A. G. Davies b Heasley 17	5/136 6/172 7/177 8/187

K. L. P. Sheridan and K. Thomson did not bat.

Bowling: Gillespie 5–1–10–0; McCrum 7–1–14–1; Heasley 8–0–44–1; M. W. Patterson 8–0–42–2; Harrison 8–0–34–0; Doak 6–0–28–1; Curry 3–0–11–1.

Ireland

J. D. Curry c Salmond b Thomson 7	G. D. Harrison c Lockhart b Williamson . 16
†A. D. Patterson c Davies b Thomson ... 6	M. W. Patterson c Kennedy b Williamson 6
D. A. Lewis c Thomson b Allingham 11	P. McCrum not out 2
*J. D. R. Benson c Smith b Sheridan 26	B 1, l-b 1, w 15, n-b 6 23
N. G. Doak c Thomson b Sheridan 7	
A. R. Dunlop c Salmond b Sheridan 10	1/9 2/20 3/46 (39 overs) 141
D. Heasley c Lockhart b Sheridan 18	4/72 5/80 6/88
P. G. Gillespie st Davies b Beven 9	7/111 8/115 9/137

Bowling: Beven 9–0–35–1; Thomson 6–1–27–2; Kennedy 9–3–14–0; Allingham 3–0–13–1; Sheridan 9–1–34–4; Williamson 3–0–16–2.

Umpires: D. B. Hair (Australia) and S. Venkataraghavan (India).

FINAL

BANGLADESH v KENYA

At Tenaga Sports Ground (Kilat Kelab), April 12, 13. Bangladesh won by a higher comparative score in a reduced-overs match. Toss: Bangladesh.

After a delayed start, Steve Tikolo struck 147 from 152 balls, with 12 fours and three sixes. Odumbe supported him in a solid stand of 138, and Kenya reached an imposing 241 for seven.

and Martin Suji removed Naim-ur-Rahman's middle stump first ball. But, though wickets fell, Bangladesh kept the asking-rate in sight. Khaled Masud hit the first ball of the final over for six and they needed one from the last delivery. But Odumbe mistakenly believed 166 was Kenya's revised total, not the target, and set a field to defend against two runs. Hasib-ul-Hassan ran through for a winning leg-bye.

Man of the Man: S. Tikolo. *Man of the Tournament:* M. Odumbe.
Close of play: Kenya 241-7 (50 overs).

Kenya

Asif Karim b Saif-ul-Islam	0	Hitesh Modi not out	12
S. K. Gupta c and b Khaled Mammud	16	A. Suji st Khaled Masud	
†K. Otieno lbw b Saif-ul-Islam	2	b Mohammad Rafiq	1
S. Tikolo c Saif-ul-Islam		B 1, l-b 9, w 9	19
b Khaled Mammud	147		
*M. Odumbe st Khaled Masud		1/0 2/15 3/58 (7 wkts, 50 overs)	241
b Mohammad Rafiq	43	4/196 5/212	
T. Odoyo b Mohammad Rafiq	1	6/230 7/241	

D. Tikolo, M. Suji and B. Patel did not bat.

Bowling: Saif-ul-Islam 9–0–39–2; Hasib-ul-Hassan 6–0–15–0; Ather Ali Khan 5–0–22–0; Khaled Mammud 7–1–31–2; Enam-ul-Haque 10–0–41–0; Naim-ur-Rahman 4–0–21–0; Mohammad Rafiq 6–1–40–3; Akram Khan 3–0–22–0.

Bangladesh

Naim-ur-Rahman b M. Suji	0	Khaled Mammud st Otieno b Odumbe	5
Mohammad Rafiq c Odumbe b A. Suji	26	Hasib-ul-Hassan not out	4
Minhaz-ul-Abedin c Patel b Odoyo	26		
Amin-ul-Islam b Asif Karim	37	B 3, l-b 4, w 5	12
*Akram Khan c Odoyo b Odumbe	22		
Enam-ul-Haque c Gupta b Asif Karim	5	1/0 2/50 3/63 (8 wkts, 25 overs)	166
Saif-ul-Islam c Odumbe b Asif Karim	14	4/116 5/118 6/123	
†Khaled Masud not out	15	7/139 8/151	

Ather Ali Khan did not bat.

Bowling: M. Suji 4–0–28–1; S. Tikolo 4–0–29–0; Odoyo 5–0–27–1; A. Suji 5–0–26–1; Asif Karim 4–0–31–3; Odumbe 3–0–18–2.

Umpires: D. B. Hair (Australia) and S. Venkataraghavan (India).
Director of Referees: J. R. Reid (New Zealand).

ICC TROPHY FINALS

1979	SRI LANKA beat Canada by 60 runs at Worcester.
1982	ZIMBABWE beat Bermuda by five wickets at Leicester.
1986	ZIMBABWE beat Holland by 25 runs at Lord's.
1990	ZIMBABWE beat Holland by six wickets at The Hague.
1993-94	UNITED ARAB EMIRATES beat Kenya by two wickets at Nairobi.
1996-97	BANGLADESH beat Kenya by a higher comparative score at Kuala Lumpur.

ICC RANKINGS

Countries which failed to qualify for the quarter-finals played in a plate competition for the Philip Snow Trophy. This was won by Bermuda, who beat United Arab Emirates by 57 runs in the final. After the tournament, ICC were able to produce a ranking system for all Associate Members. This is likely to be used at the next ICC Trophy to split the teams into two divisions and prevent mismatches. The standings were: 1 Bangladesh: 2 Kenya; 3 Scotland; 4 Ireland; 5 Denmark; 6 Holland; 7 Canada; 8 Hong Kong; 9 Bermuda; 10 United Arab Emirates; 11 Fiji; 12 United States; 13 Papua New Guinea; 14 Singapore; 15 Namibia; 16 Malaysia; 17 East and Central Africa; 18 West Africa; 19 Gibraltar; 20 Argentina; 21= Israel and Italy; 23 Nepal*.

* *Nepal became Associates only in 1996, and did not participate in the 1997 Trophy.*

ENGLAND UNDER-19 IN PAKISTAN, 1996-97

By GARETH A. DAVIES

England's Under-19 tour of Pakistan was a resounding success. Under the mature captaincy of Andrew Flintoff, a squad of emerging cricketers played confident, aggressive cricket, made friends and showed mental toughness in some hard-fought four-day unofficial Tests. They won the three-match series 1-0, thanks to a two-wicket victory at Faisalabad, and went 2-0 up in the one-day internationals before losing the third – only their second defeat in 12 matches, eight of which they won.

"We saw some of the inconsistencies of youth but, when we were in a difficult position, we came out fighting," said tour manager Phil Neale. Former Test cricketer Haroon Rashid, coaching Pakistan Under-19, believed they had adapted to the conditions as well as any England side he had seen. Never mind that lunch failed to materialise one day, or that bed was once a store-room floor in a biscuit factory, the players remained undaunted.

The main difference between the sides was their new-ball attack. England had the cut and thrust of Surrey's Alex Tudor and Ben Hollioake; Pakistan had Abdur Razzaq, a wiry fast bowler operating alone. Tudor and Hollioake took 29 wickets between them in the four-day series: Hollioake, who also batted usefully, made his senior international debut a few months later, while Tudor was invited to train with the Test squad. The leading run-scorers were Middlesex wicket-keeper/batsman David Nash, with 227, and captain Flintoff, who made 200.

There was considerable local interest in the tour; highlights of the four-day games were broadcast nightly on television, while the one-day series was shown in full.

ENGLAND UNDER-19 TOURING PARTY

A. Flintoff (Lancashire) (*captain*), G. J. Batty (Yorkshire), D. A. Cosker (Glamorgan), I. N. Flanagan (Essex), J. A. Graham (Durham), S. J. Harmison (Durham), B. C. Hollioake (Surrey), N. D. Martin (Middlesex), Z. C. Morris (Yorkshire), D. C. Nash (Middlesex), S. D. Peters (Essex), J. C. Powell (Essex), C. M. W. Read (Gloucestershire), D. J. Sales (Northamptonshire), A. J. Tudor (Surrey).

S. R. G. Francis (Hampshire) and P. J. Franks (Nottinghamshire) replaced the injured Harmison and Martin.

Manager: P. A. Neale. *Coach:* J. Abrahams. *Physiotherapist:* S. M. B. Robertson.

ENGLAND UNDER-19 TOUR RESULTS

Matches – Played 12: Won 8, Lost 2, Drawn 2.

Note: Matches in this section were not first-class.

At KRL Cricket Ground, Rawalpindi, November 26. England Under-19 won by 58 runs. Toss: Rawalpindi Under-19. England Under-19 273 for three (45 overs) (I. N. Flanagan 41, A. Flintoff 38, B. C. Hollioake 133 not out, Extras 33); Rawalpindi Under-19 215 for six (45 overs) (Nauman Ashraf 52, Faisal Mushtaq 34, Mohammad Shaban 45, Extras 35; J. C. Powell three for 38).

At Chaudhry Rehmat Ali Cricket Ground, Islamabad, November 27. England Under-19 won by 29 runs. Toss: Islamabad Under-19. England Under-19 194 (38.2 overs) (D. J. Sales 63; Abrar Aziz three for 30, Asif Mehmood three for 28); Islamabad Under-19 165 for nine (40 overs) (Bilal Asad 58; D. A. Cosker three for 33).

At National Stadium, Karachi, November 29, 30, December 1. Karachi Under-19 won by nine wickets. Toss: England Under-19. England Under-19 238 (D. J. Sales 46, B. C. Hollioake 35, C. M. W. Read 30; Shahid Afridi five for 51) and 181 (J. A. Graham 41, B. C. Hollioake 38; Kashif Ibrahim four for 57, Shahid Afridi four for 46, Mohammad Farrukh three for seven); Karachi Under-19 294 for six dec. (Mohammad Farrukh 69, Hasan Raza 124, Majid Mujtaba 39) and 126 for one (Mohammad Farrukh 69 not out, Farhan Adil 49).

At Montgomery Cricket Club Ground, Sahiwal, December 3, 4, 5. England Under-19 won by 224 runs. Toss: England Under-19. England Under-19 195 (I. N. Flanagan 64 not out; Wasim Majid four for 56) and 212 for six dec. (I. N. Flanagan 30, C. M. W. Read 73, B. C. Hollioake 57; Ahmed Ali four for 44); Multan Under-19 82 (B. C. Hollioake three for 30, D. A. Cosker five for 14) and 101 (J. C. Powell three for 48, G. J. Batty four for 22).

Flanagan carried his bat for 84 overs in England's first innings.

PAKISTAN UNDER-19 v ENGLAND UNDER-19

First Unofficial Test

At Iqbal Stadium, Faisalabad, December 8, 9, 10, 11. England Under-19 won by two wickets. Toss: Pakistan Under-19.

England scraped home on the final morning, despite a collapse of five wickets for 22 which gave Pakistan the scent of an unexpected win. But the home side had left it too late. They had scored a workmanlike 256 in their first innings, with Hasan Raza, already a Test player though allegedly under 15, scoring 64. In reply, a promising stand of 92 between Flintoff and Sales suggested England would take the lead. After their departure, however, only Hollioake sparkled, with 47 from 50 balls, as six went down for 38. On the third day, Tudor bowled with menacing swing to tear the heart out of Pakistan's top order for the second time. They then capitulated to the well-controlled left-arm spin of Cosker and were all out for 123, leaving a target of 150. At the close of the second day, England looked comfortable on 99 for three, after another significant contribution from Sales. But their nerves were severely tested in the morning.

Man of the Match: A. J. Tudor.

Close of play: First day, Pakistan Under-19 248-9 (Shoaib Malik 28*, Fazal-e-Akbar 7*); Second day, England Under-19 230; Third day, England Under-19 99-3 (A. Flintoff 2*, C. M. W. Read 12*).

Pakistan Under-19

Farhan Adil c Batty b Cosker	26	– c Flintoff b Cosker	30
Shahid Qambrani c Batty b Cosker	68	– b Tudor	2
Adil Nisar lbw b Tudor	10	– c Nash b Hollioake	1
*Shadab Kabir c Read b Hollioake	0	– c sub (S. D. Peters) b Tudor	1
Hasan Raza b Tudor	64	– b Tudor	3
Kashif Ibrahim b Tudor	4	– c and b Cosker	2
†Mohammad Shakil lbw b Cosker	3	– c and b Cosker	16
Shoaib Malik not out	28	– c Nash b Cosker	10
Abdur Razzaq c and b Batty	22	– not out	27
Imran Tahir c Hollioake b Batty	0	– c Hollioake b Cosker	0
Fazal-e-Akbar b Tudor	7	– b Batty	9
B 2, l-b 3, w 2, n-b 17	24	B 6, l-b 9, n-b 7	22

1/91 2/112 3/113 4/124 5/129   256   1/8 2/15 3/25 4/46 5/52   123
6/142 7/212 8/246 9/246   6/57 7/78 8/100 9/100

Bowling: *First Innings*—Tudor 22.1–3–79–4; Hollioake 12–3–43–1; Flintoff 8–1–19–0; Cosker 28–8–79–3; Batty 13–6–22–2; Powell 5–3–9–0. *Second Innings*—Tudor 14–2–43–3; Hollioake 8–1–12–1; Cosker 17–12–36–5; Flintoff 1–1–0–0; Batty 10.3–5–17–1.

England Under-19

I. N. Flanagan c Mohammad Shakil b Abdur Razzaq	11	– lbw b Abdur Razzaq	0
J. A. Graham c Mohammad Shakil b Abdur Razzaq	13	– (7) not out	11
D. J. Sales c Shadab Kabir b Imran Tahir	45	– c sub (Taufeeq Umar) b Imran Tahir	46
*A. Flintoff c Shadab Kabir b Shoaib Malik	52	– lbw b Imran Tahir	26
†D. C. Nash c Mohammad Shakil b Shoaib Malik	19	– (10) not out	1
B. C. Hollioake c Hasan Raza b Shoaib Malik	47	– c Shadab Kabir b Imran Tahir	8
C. M. W. Read c Mohammad Shakil b Shoaib Malik	8	– (5) c Farhan Adil b Shoaib Malik	19
G. J. Batty c Adil Nisar b Imran Tahir	5	– (2) lbw b Imran Tahir	27
A. J. Tudor c Farhan Adil b Imran Tahir	3	– (8) c Mohammad Shakil b Imran Tahir	0
J. C. Powell b Abdur Razzaq	12	– (9) lbw b Shoaib Malik	0
D. A. Cosker not out	0		
B 8, l-b 4, n-b 3	15	B 5, l-b 6, n-b 1	12

1/24 2/29 3/121 4/125 5/192	230	1/0 2/76 3/79	(8 wkts) 150
6/204 7/213 8/215 9/220		4/123 5/135 6/138	
		7/138 8/145	

Bowling: *First Innings*—Abdur Razzaq 15.4–0–71–3; Fazal-e-Akbar 7–1–30–0; Imran Tahir 34–12–71–3; Shoaib Malik 23–10–38–4; Kashif Ibrahim 1–0–8–0. *Second Innings*—Abdur Razzaq 9–1–38–1; Fazal-e-Akbar 7–2–18–0; Imran Tahir 18–7–47–5; Shoaib Malik 17–7–36–2.

Umpires: Afzal Ahmed and Saqib Qurashi.

At LCCA Ground, Lahore, December 14, 15, 16. England Under-19 won by 338 runs. Toss: England Under-19. England Under-19 389 for five dec. (S. D. Peters 30, D. C. Nash 100 not out, D. J. Sales 189, Extras 34; Sajid Ali three for 33) and 181 for nine dec. (I. N. Flanagan 49, G. J. Batty 57; Taufeeq Umar four for 46); Lahore City Under-19 133 (J. C. Powell four for 22, Z. C. Morris three for 36) and 99 (Z. C. Morris six for 30, J. C. Powell three for eight).

In the first innings, England were 78 for four; Nash and Sales added 274 for the fifth wicket. Sales's 189 lasted 192 minutes and 158 balls and included 29 fours and three sixes.

PAKISTAN UNDER-19 v ENGLAND UNDER-19

Second Unofficial Test

At Sheikhupura Stadium, Sheikhupura, December 19, 20, 21, 22. Drawn. Toss: England Under-19.
The tourists fielded three spinners – Cosker, Batty and Powell – who took one wicket between them. First, England ran up an impressive 361, thanks to a solid 74 from opener Peters and an unbeaten century from Nash. They strengthened their grip when Tudor and Hollioake had Pakistan reeling at 99 for seven, but Abdur Razzaq almost single-handedly held England at bay. He had already carried the attack to them when he claimed seven wickets with his pace. Now, he batted nearly four hours for 85 to restrict the deficit to 139. England extended their advantage by 50 that night. On the last morning, however, they lost their way, with five wickets going for 30 as Razzaq took his match haul to ten. Nash persevered, scoring 87, but the visitors toiled too long, wary of losing their 1-0 lead. They eventually left a target of 345 – and too little time to bowl Pakistan out. Only one wicket fell in 26 overs before the captains agreed to a draw.

Man of the Match: Abdur Razzaq.

Close of play: First day, England Under-19 224-5 (D. C. Nash 47*); Second day, Pakistan Under-19 95-6 (Shadab Kabir 16*, Humayun Farhat 31*); Third day, England Under-19 50-2 (D. J. Sales 18*, A. Flintoff 17*).

England Under-19

S. D. Peters c Farhan Adil b Jan Nisar Khan	74	– b Abdur Razzaq	11
J. A. Graham b Abdur Razzaq	2	– b Jan Nisar Khan	0
D. J. Sales lbw b Abdur Razzaq	6	– c Imran Tahir b Hasan Raza	46
*A. Flintoff c Humayun Farhat b Abdur Razzaq	33	– lbw b Fahad Khan	43
†D. C. Nash not out	108	– run out	87
B. C. Hollioake b Abdur Razzaq	37	– c Shadab Kabir b Hasan Raza	0
C. M. W. Read lbw b Hasan Raza	45	– lbw b Abdur Razzaq	1
G. J. Batty c Humayun Farhat b Abdur Razzaq	1	– c Humayun Farhat b Abdur Razzaq	0
A. J. Tudor b Abdur Razzaq	10	– run out	5
J. C. Powell c Humayun Farhat b Abdur Razzaq	0	– not out	3
D. A. Cosker lbw b Imran Tahir	5		
B 14, l-b 9, w 5, n-b 12	40	B 2, l-b 2, w 2, n-b 3	9

1/18 2/30 3/108 4/153 5/224   361   1/4 2/22 3/84   (9 wkts dec.) 205
6/317 7/326 8/347 9/347   4/123 5/126 6/134
                                           7/134 8/153 9/205

Bowling: *First Innings*—Abdur Razzaq 38–9–118–7; Jan Nisar Khan 17–2–32–1; Imran Tahir 33.3–8–82–1; Fahad Khan 33–6–85–0; Shadab Kabir 5–0–12–0; Hasan Raza 4–1–9–1. *Second Innings*—Abdur Razzaq 17–2–55–3; Jan Nisar Khan 6–0–15–1; Imran Tahir 28–6–80–0; Fahad Khan 12–2–20–1; Hasan Raza 10–2–30–2; Saeed Anwar 0.3–0–1–0.

Pakistan Under-19

Saeed Anwar, jun. c Read b Tudor	5	– not out	68
Shahid Qambrani c Read b Hollioake	20	– c sub (Z. C. Morris) b Hollioake	8
Farhan Adil c Flintoff b Tudor	12	– not out	21
Mohammad Salim run out	1		
Hasan Raza c Cosker b Tudor	0		
*Shadab Kabir c Hollioake b Powell	30		
Jan Nisar Khan c Flintoff b Hollioake	0		
†Humayun Farhat c Read b Hollioake	32		
Abdur Razzaq c Read b Tudor	85		
Fahad Khan not out	18		
Imran Tahir b Tudor	0		
B 9, l-b 6, w 4	19	B 1, l-b 1, n-b 1	3

1/16 2/42 3/46 4/47 5/49   222   1/25   (1 wkt) 100
6/51 7/99 8/137 9/218

Bowling: *First Innings*—Tudor 23.5–6–52–5; Hollioake 27–9–63–3; Cosker 20–5–50–0; Batty 4–1–10–0; Powell 18–7–32–1. *Second Innings*—Hollioake 4–0–21–1; Cosker 7–2–31–0; Batty 7–2–15–0; Powell 5–1–17–0; Peters 2–0–10–0; Graham 1–0–4–0.

Umpires: Azhar Hassan and Rab Nawaz.

PAKISTAN UNDER-19 v ENGLAND UNDER-19

Third Unofficial Test

At Gaddafi Stadium, Lahore, December 26, 27, 28, 29. Drawn. Toss: Pakistan Under-19.

England's ambition to finish the Test series with another win was evident when Hollioake and Tudor reduced Pakistan to 29 for four on an overcast morning. But Ahmar Saeed played a determined captain's innings, backed up by Abdur Razzaq, whose watchful fifty was punctuated by powerful strokes. They eventually scored 237, with the aggressive Hollioake returning six for 40. England then ran into trouble themselves in the face of some prodigious swing from Razzaq.

A battling half-century from Hollioake helped them reach 244 on the third morning, a lead of just seven. It was Pakistan's last chance to level the series. Hasan Raza made a fluent 69 as they attempted to set England a target. Needing 201 from 37 overs, however, on a pitch of ever more variable bounce, the tourists wanted nothing more than a draw.

Man of the Match: B. C. Hollioake.

Men of the Series: Pakistan – Abdur Razzaq; England – B. C. Hollioake.

Close of play: First day, Pakistan Under-19 189-6 (Ahmar Saeed 65*, Mohammad Shakil 2*); Second day, England Under-19 167-7 (B. C. Hollioake 44*); Third day, Pakistan Under-19 132-5 (Hasan Raza 38*, Abdur Razzaq 24*).

Pakistan Under-19

Mohammad Farrukh c Read b Tudor	4	– (2) c Read b Hollioake 22
Saeed Anwar, jun. c Read b Hollioake	1	– (1) b Hollioake 5
Mohammad Salim c Cosker b Hollioake	10	– c Hollioake b Batty............ 21
Hasan Raza c Cosker b Hollioake	2	– b Franks 69
*Ahmar Saeed lbw b Hollioake	77	– lbw b Tudor.................... 0
Bazid Khan run out	26	– c Read b Batty 15
Abdur Razzaq c Franks b Batty	57	– b Hollioake 33
†Mohammad Shakil lbw b Franks	21	– lbw b Batty 10
Shoaib Malik not out	11	– not out 8
Waqas Ahmed lbw b Hollioake	5	– b Franks 2
Imran Tahir c Morris b Hollioake	0	– not out 5
B 4, l-b 13, w 1, n-b 5..............	23	B 5, l-b 10, n-b 2 17

1/12 2/12 3/14 4/29 5/84   237   1/12 2/31 3/33   (9 wkts dec.) 207
6/181 7/221 8/229 9/237   4/62 5/75 6/164
                                     7/192 8/192 9/194

In the second innings Hasan Raza, when 0, retired hurt at 33-2 and resumed at 62.

Bowling: *First Innings*—Tudor 20–6–43–1; Hollioake 22.4–8–40–6; Franks 17–7–35–1; Cosker 22–9–56–0; Batty 17–7–24–1; Morris 8–2–20–0; Flintoff 2–0–2–0. *Second Innings*—Tudor 25–7–64–1; Hollioake 25–12–35–3; Franks 12–2–24–2; Batty 22–7–51–3; Cosker 11–4–18–0.

England Under-19

S. D. Peters lbw b Abdur Razzaq	9	– c Shoaib Malik b Abdur Razzaq .. 7
G. J. Batty lbw b Imran Tahir	32	– b Waqas Ahmed 1
D. J. Sales c Imran Tahir b Abdur Razzaq	16	– c Mohammad Shakil
		b Abdur Razzaq . 12
*A. Flintoff c Ahmar Saeed b Imran Tahir	30	– c Mohammad Shakil
		b Abdur Razzaq . 16
†D. C. Nash b Imran Tahir	0	– not out 12
B. C. Hollioake c Saeed Anwar b Shoaib Malik	67	– not out 9
C. M. W. Read c Saeed Anwar b Shoaib Malik	14	
Z. C. Morris b Abdur Razzaq	0	
A. J. Tudor b Abdur Razzaq	34	
D. A. Cosker c Mohammad Farrukh b Shoaib Malik	5	
P. J. Franks not out	1	
B 5, l-b 5, w 4, n-b 22.............	36	L-b 2, w 5 7

1/38 2/62 3/105 4/105 5/124   244   1/15 2/19 3/39 4/48   (4 wkts) 64
6/158 7/167 8/210 9/232

Bowling: *First Innings*—Abdur Razzaq 20.4–3–55–4; Waqas Ahmed 8–1–40–0; Imran Tahir 29–9–76–3; Shoaib Malik 32–10–63–3. *Second Innings*—Abdur Razzaq 13–4–33–3; Waqas Ahmed 8–3–14–1; Hasan Raza 2–1–2–0; Imran Tahir 4–3–4–0; Shoaib Malik 3–0–9–0.

Umpires: Khalid Aziz and Mian Aslam.

At Aitchison College Ground, Lahore, January 2. England Under-19 won by 39 runs. Toss: Combined Under-19 XI. England Under-19 169 for eight (40 overs) (D. C. Nash 49, C. M. W. Read 35, Extras 35); Combined Under-19 XI 130 (38.2 overs) (Kamran Akmal 35; G. J. Batty five for 19).

At Jinnah Stadium, Gujranwala, January 4. First unofficial one-day international: England Under-19 won by 26 runs. Toss: Pakistan Under-19. England Under-19 160 for seven (38 overs) (S. D. Peters 34, D. J. Sales 62; Abdur Razzaq three for 20); Pakistan Under-19 134 (35.2 overs) (Hasan Raza 48; A. J. Tudor three for 13, G. J. Batty four for 28).

At Jinnah Stadium, Sialkot, January 6. Second unofficial one-day international: England Under-19 won by three runs. Toss: Pakistan Under-19. England Under-19 232 for five (40 overs) (S. D. Peters 46, D. J. Sales 43, B. C. Hollioake 40 not out, D. C. Nash 49); Pakistan Under-19 210 (39.5 overs) (Mohammad Farrukh 39, Hasan Raza 90; A. J. Tudor three for 36).

At National Stadium, Karachi, January 8. Third unofficial one-day international: Pakistan Under-19 won by two wickets. Toss: England Under-19. England Under-19 232 for seven (50 overs) (J. A. Graham 51, D. C. Nash 76; Fazal-e-Akbar three for 29); Pakistan Under-19 235 for eight (49.5 overs) (Ahmar Saeed 63, Farhan Adil 66; A. J. Tudor three for 43).

Pakistan were 80 for five; Ahmar Saeed and Farhan Adil added 128 for the sixth wicket.

THE DUCKWORTH/LEWIS METHOD

In 1997, the ECB's limited-overs competitions adopted a new method to revise targets in interrupted games, devised by Frank Duckworth of the Royal Statistical Society and Tony Lewis of the University of the West of England. The system aims to preserve any advantage that one team has established before the interruption. It uses the idea that teams have two resources from which they make runs – an allocated number of overs and ten wickets. Traditional run-rate calculations relied only on the overs available, and ignored wickets lost. It also takes into account when the interruption occurs, because of the different scoring-rates typical of different stages of an innings.

The system has been modified for 1998. It now uses one unified table, instead of several, with 60 rows, covering matches of any length up to 60 overs, and ten columns, from nought to nine wickets down. Each figure in the table gives the percentage of the total runs in an innings that would, on average, be scored with a certain number of overs left and wickets lost.

If overs are lost, the table is used to calculate the percentage of runs the team would be expected to score in those missing overs. This is obtained by reading off the figure for the number of overs left and wickets down when play stops and subtracting from it the corresponding figure for the number of overs remaining when it resumes.

If the first innings is complete and the second innings is interrupted, the target to be beaten is reduced by the percentage of the innings lost. If the suspension occurs between innings, as in the ICC Trophy final between Bangladesh and Kenya at Kuala Lumpur in April 1997, only one figure is required: the percentage of the innings remaining for the reduced number of overs with no wicket lost.

Kenya scored 241 from 50 overs, but rain restricted Bangladesh to 25 overs. On the traditional average run-rate, losing half their overs would have halved the target to 121. But they had all ten wickets, so had more than half their run-scoring resources. The table showed that, on average, 25 overs should yield 68.7 per cent of a 50-over total. Bangladesh's target was set at 166 (68.7 per cent of 241 = 165.56), which they reached off the final ball.

The system also covers interruptions to the first innings, multiple interruptions and innings terminated by rain.

ENGLISH COUNTIES OVERSEAS, 1996-97

Scorecards of first-class matches played by English counties on pre-season tours to other countries.

NATAL v LEICESTERSHIRE

At Durban, March 25, 26, 27. Natal won by an innings and one run. Toss: Leicestershire.

Watson's 200 not out, his maiden double-hundred, lasted 501 minutes and 375 balls and included 16 fours and one six.

Close of play: First day, Natal 40-1 (D. J. Watson 21*, E. L. R. Stewart 4*); Second day, Natal 430-4 (D. J. Watson 161*, N. C. Johnson 9*).

Leicestershire

D. L. Maddy c Forde b Botha	50	– c Watson b Gilder	2
I. J. Sutcliffe c Stewart b Johnson	1	– c Sugden b Gilder	0
B. F. Smith c Forde b Benkenstein	27	– c Forde b Gilder	5
*J. J. Whitaker c Forde b Botha	10	– lbw b Storey	105
V. J. Wells c Johnson b Storey	61	– c Watson b Botha	8
†P. A. Nixon c Forde b Storey	15	– c Forde b Crookes	51
J. M. Dakin c Sugden b Johnson	12	– c Bruyns b Storey	23
D. J. Millns c Bruyns b Johnson	1	– c Bruyns b Crookes	17
G. J. Parsons b Benkenstein	16	– not out	14
A. R. K. Pierson c Sugden b Storey	27	– c and b Crookes	1
M. T. Brimson not out	12	– c Forde b Botha	10
B 6, l-b 2, n-b 12	20	B 5, l-b 2, w 4, n-b 3	14

1/2 2/62 3/97 4/119 5/166   252   1/2 2/3 3/7 4/45 5/160   250
6/185 7/195 8/196 9/231   6/199 7/210 8/229 9/234

Bowling: *First Innings*—Gilder 12–1–33–0; Johnson 17–6–52–3; Benkenstein 13–2–33–2; Storey 15–1–49–3; Botha 14–4–35–2; Crookes 14–5–42–0. *Second Innings*—Gilder 12–1–30–3; Johnson 10–3–41–0; Botha 16–2–61–3; Storey 16–2–43–2; Crookes 25–6–51–2; Benkenstein 3–0–17–0.

Natal

D. J. Watson not out	200	C. B. Sugden not out	23
M. L. Bruyns lbw b Wells	14		
E. L. R. Stewart c Nixon b Dakin	36	L-b 7, n-b 6	13
*D. M. Benkenstein c Dakin b Brimson	89		
D. N. Crookes c Whitaker b Brimson	110	1/30 2/90 3/260	(5 wkts dec.) 503
N. C. Johnson c Parsons b Pierson	18	4/419 5/448	

†K. A. Forde, A. G. Botha, G. M. Gilder and K. G. Storey did not bat.

Bowling: Millns 18–3–90–0; Parsons 22–5–57–0; Wells 15–2–54–1; Pierson 26–2–121–1; Brimson 34–5–104–2; Dakin 10–0–39–1; Maddy 7–2–31–0.

Umpires: R. B. Shah and B. A. Williams.

MATABELELAND INVITATION XI v WORCESTERSHIRE

At Bulawayo Athletic Club, March 28, 29, 30. Worcestershire won by 18 runs. Toss: Worcestershire. County debut: R. J. Chapman.

Streak took a wicket in each of his first three overs without conceding a run.

Close of play: First day, Matabeleland Invitation XI 44-0 (T. R. Gripper 17*, D. P. Viljoen 21*); Second day, Worcestershire 156-4 (D. A. Leatherdale 28*, G. R. Haynes 4*).

Worcestershire

T. S. Curtis c Peck b Streak	0	– c Abrams b Rennie	7
W. P. C. Weston c A. R. Whittall b Streak	1	– c Abrams b Streak	10
G. A. Hick c Campbell b Olonga	22	– c A. R. Whittall b Mbangwa	32
V. S. Solanki c Gripper b Streak	0	– run out	61
D. A. Leatherdale b Olonga	18	– c and b Rennie	44
G. R. Haynes c Olonga b Mbangwa	11	– b Olonga	29
*†S. J. Rhodes c A. R. Whittall b Streak	46	– c G. J. Whittall b A. R. Whittall	22
S. R. Lampitt c Campbell b A. R. Whittall	13	– not out	22
P. J. Newport c Campbell b Mbangwa	5	– lbw b A. R. Whittall	5
R. K. Illingworth c A. R. Whittall b Olorga	14	– not out	14
R. J. Chapman not out	7		
L-b 2, w 1, n-b 5	8	B 6, l-b 4, w 1, n-b 6	17

1/0 2/1 3/1 4/26 5/40	145	1/18 2/24 3/70	(8 wkts dec.) 263
6/62 7/93 8/102 9/126		4/138 5/178 6/220	
		7/222 8/232	

Bowling: *First Innings*—Streak 15.4–6–20–4; Rennie 13–5–25–0; Olonga 14–3–38–3; Mbangwa 12–3–16–2; G. J. Whittall 5–0–12–0; A. R. Whittall 13–2–32–1. *Second Innings*—Rennie 14.5–3–44–2; Streak 13.1–4–27–1; Olonga 13–2–53–1; Mbangwa 7–1–30–1; G. J. Whittall 8–1–23–0; A. R. Whittall 23–4–66–2; Viljoen 3–0–10–0.

Matabeleland Invitation XI

T. R. Gripper c Hick b Haynes	45	– c Rhodes b Newport	0
D. P. Viljoen b Newport	25	– c Rhodes b Chapman	9
†D. J. R. Campbell c Rhodes b Illingworth	29	– lbw b Lampitt	46
G. J. Whittall c and b Illingworth	2	– c Solanki b Illingworth	40
M. D. Abrams lbw b Lampitt	0	– c Curtis b Hick	45
*H. H. Streak not out	19	– c Lampitt b Hick	1
J. A. Rennie c Solanki b Newport	20	– c Rhodes b Hick	8
G. Peck run out	3	– c Haynes b Hick	17
A. R. Whittall c Illingworth b Hick	0	– c Curtis b Chapman	23
H. K. Olonga c Curtis b Hick	17	– not out	29
M. Mbangwa (did not bat)		– st Rhodes b Illingworth	2
L-b 6, w 1, n-b 1	8	L-b 1, w 1	2

1/56 2/97 3/105 4/107 5/109	(9 wkts dec.) 168	1/0 2/22 3/77 4/103 5/104	222
6/141 7/147 8/148 9/168		6/116 7/162 8/167 9/211	

Bowling: *First Innings*—Newport 16–6–21–2; Chapman 13–4–27–0; Lampitt 17–7–44–1; Haynes 17–6–21–1; Illingworth 18–4–32–2; Hick 4.4–0–17–2. *Second Innings*—Newport 9–0–34–1; Chapman 10–0–40–2; Lampitt 6–1–20–1; Haynes 4–0–19–0; Illingworth 17.2–4–30–2; Hick 14–2–59–4; Solanki 2–0–19–0.

Umpires: C. Coventry and E. G. R. Gilmour.

TRANSVAAL v NOTTINGHAMSHIRE

At Johannesburg, April 11, 12, 13. Drawn. Toss: Nottinghamshire.
Close of play: First day, Transvaal 60-2 (H. A. Manack 22*, N. D. McKenzie 5*); Second day, Nottinghamshire 98-4 (P. Johnson 21*, C. M. Tolley 8*).

Nottinghamshire

P. R. Pollard c McKenzie b Eksteen	79		
R. T. Robinson c Pothas b Terbrugge	10 – (1) c Pothas b Kidwell	4
U. Afzaal c Pothas b Hall	4 – b Eksteen	37
G. F. Archer c Manack b Bodi	25 – b Terbrugge	22
A. A. Metcalfe c Kidwell b Bodi	12 – (2) b Terbrugge	1
*P. Johnson c Pothas b Terbrugge	13 – (5) not out	88
C. M. Tolley b Kidwell	22 – (6) not out	51
†W. M. Noon b Eksteen	0		
R. A. Pick c Pothas b Terbrugge	17		
M. N. Bowen not out	28		
J. A. Afford b Terbrugge	13		
L-b 5, w 7, n-b 5	17	B 5, l-b 7, w 1, n-b 2	15

1/21 2/30 3/93 4/107 5/122   240   1/3 2/7 3/58 4/72   (4 wkts dec.) 218
6/181 7/181 8/181 9/216

Bowling: *First Innings*—Kidwell 11–1–50–1; Terbrugge 19.3–3–54–4; Hall 11–1–52–1; Laing 5–3–9–0; Bodi 8–1–39–2; Eksteen 15–5–31–2. *Second Innings*—Kidwell 14–3–50–1; Terbrugge 17–9–32–2; Eksteen 22–5–56–1; Hall 12–5–28–0; Bodi 3–0–16–0; Laing 3–1–10–0; McKenzie 3–0–14–0.

Transvaal

H. A. Manack c Noon b Bowen	30 – (2) lbw b Bowen	23
M. R. Benfield c Pollard b Bowen	26 – (1) c Archer b Bowen	4
D. R. Gain c sub (M. P. Dowman) b Bowen	5 – b Bowen	88
N. D. McKenzie lbw b Tolley	14 – c Noon b Bowen	0
D. R. Laing c Noon b Pick	41 – lbw b Afzaal	24
†N. Pothas c Noon b Afford	6 – b Afzaal	50
A. J. Hall lbw b Afford	13 – b Afzaal	5
*C. E. Eksteen c Noon b Afford	19 – not out	3
G. H. Bodi run out	18 – not out	0
D. J. Terbrugge c sub (R. T. Bates) b Archer	2		
E. W. Kidwell not out	0		
B 3, l-b 6, w 1, n-b 1	11	B 1, l-b 8, w 2, n-b 2	13

1/43 2/53 3/73 4/79 5/118   185   1/17 2/49 3/49 4/100   (7 wkts) 210
6/134 7/149 8/176 9/185   5/176 6/197 7/206

Bowling: *First Innings*—Pick 13–6–34–1; Tolley 22–4–49–1; Bowen 17–4–43–3; Afford 11.1–4–39–3; Afzaal 7–3–5–0; Archer 4–1–6–1. *Second Innings*—Pick 13–5–24–0; Bowen 13–0–56–4; Tolley 13–1–36–0; Afzaal 21–4–62–3; Archer 6–0–23–0.

Umpires: D. F. Becker and T. Dry.

SHEFFIELD SHIELD PLAYER OF THE YEAR

The Sheffield Shield Player of the Year Award for 1996-97 was won by Andy Bichel of Queensland. The award, instituted in 1975-76, is adjudicated by the umpires over the course of the season. Each of the two umpires standing in each of the 30 Sheffield Shield matches (excluding the final) allocated marks of 3, 2 and 1 to the three players who most impressed them during the game. Bichel earned 17 votes in only three Shield matches, one ahead of Michael Hussey of Western Australia who played in 11. Jamie Cox of Tasmania won the Player of the Year award sponsored by Lord's Taverners and decided by his fellow players.

CRICKET IN AUSTRALIA, 1996-97

By JOHN MACKINNON

Andy Bichel

In the year Australia established themselves beyond dispute as the best team in the world, domestic cricket ended once again in a triumph for Queensland. After 68 years in which, infamously, they never won the Sheffield Shield, they won it for the second time in three seasons.

They went to Perth for the final not only as runners-up to Western Australia but also as clear underdogs. They were one of three teams tied on 28 points to Western Australia's runaway 42. In the event, theirs was only the second away win in 15 finals; the first was also in Perth, where New South Wales won the inaugural final in 1982-83.

Queensland started their season emphatically enough with three straight wins, but there followed a barren period of three months before victory in their last game, against South Australia, just earned them second position. Several stalwarts were missing from the previous year, notably Allan Border, who had retired at last, and Carl Rackemann, Greg Rowell and Dirk Tazelaar, no longer required by the state selectors. In mid-season, Craig McDermott, who had not managed to play a single game, gave up his own battle for fitness. Although he was only 31, he had been struggling against injury for years. His final record was an imposing 677 first-class wickets at 28.10, 291 of them in Tests, at 28.63. Only Dennis Lillee had taken more wickets for Australia.

For all these losses, Queensland were brilliantly served by their pace bowlers, especially Michael Kasprowicz, Andy Bichel and Adam Dale – no side visiting the Gabba reached 200 in their first innings. Although the youngest – he was 25 by the end of the season – Kasprowicz was the most experienced and his form for Queensland was unrelenting. But he was dropped from the Test side after failing to take a wicket in two matches against West Indies; before long, his place was taken by his 26-year-old team-mate Bichel, who played only three games for Queensland but collected 25 wickets, as well as earning enough umpires' votes to win the Shield Player of the Year award. Dale, a club cricketer from Victoria who had looked the part as a limited-overs bowler for Queensland the previous season, finally made his first-class debut at 27 and took a wicket in his first over. He bowled with miserly control and virtually won the final, cleverly exploiting the breeze to pick up nine wickets. It was no surprise when he was called up for the one-day internationals in South Africa.

Trevor Barsby retired and will be missed both by his team and by spectators, who appreciated his daring strokeplay. But his fellow-opener Matthew Hayden looked likely to be back with Queensland for the time being, after an unconvincing stint in the Test side. Stuart Law, the only Queenslander to have captained a Shield-winning team – twice – had a solid season but seemed to have been earmarked as a one-day specialist by the national selectors. English-born Andrew Symonds, who had finally decided to throw in his lot with Australia, found his second full state season better than his first, though his impetuosity was still a problem. Matthew Mott was the best of the other batsmen.

Western Australia dominated one-day cricket and the regular first-class season. After an opening Shield defeat by Tasmania, they did not lose again until the final. Not only did they top the Shield table by 14 points, they also won all their matches in the Mercantile Mutual Cup, finishing with a comfortable eight-wicket win over Queensland for the one-day title. They lost the Shield final to the same opponents three weeks later; the batting, so positive and productive all season, fell apart when it mattered most. Michael Hussey, in his second full season, and Ryan Campbell, in his first, had established a dynamic opening partnership, an ideal platform for Justin Langer, Damien Martyn, Tom Moody and Adam Gilchrist.

But in the final, with Langer on tour in South Africa, Western Australia foundered as Hussey, Campbell and Martyn scored a grand match aggregate of 17. Their captain, Moody, saved them from disgrace with a second-innings 152. He enjoyed a terrific year with bat and ball and in the field and, at 31, earned another run in Australia's one-day team. Brendon Julian and Jo Angel shared 66 wickets, despite injuries, and off-spinner Brett Mulder reappeared after ten years in the wilderness, destroyed New South Wales in Perth with figures of five for two, and finished as the leading spinner in the national averages. Wicket-keeper Gilchrist made 62 dismissals for the second year running and equalled the Shield record of 54 he had set jointly with Wade Seccombe of Queensland in 1995-96. He also had a taste of captaincy in Moody's absence.

New South Wales were kept out of the final by Queensland only on "quotient" and could point to some close games which, if won, would have carried them through. In reality, third place flattered them; their last win owed as much to a desperate declaration by Tasmania, who were also in with a chance of the final, as to their own merit. The combination of Greg Matthews as captain and Geoff Lawson as coach was no recipe for compatibility. Lawson's one-year contract was terminated; his successor, the popular Steve Small, also had to settle for a one-year term from the paranoid New South Wales Cricket Association. Matthews turned 37 in December and his best days seemed well behind him. His fielding looked brittle, especially to his own bowling, but he retained his quirky enthusiasm, appeared rather fitter than some of his younger charges, and became the first bowler to pass 400 wickets for New South Wales. An intemperate stroke in the Delhi Test in October consigned Michael Slater to a full term of domestic cricket, with orders to reassess his shot selection. But his former Test partner, Mark Taylor, was having a worse time, with 252 first-class runs at 16.80 and a mere 99 at 16.50 for New South Wales. The brightest star was the 32-year-old all-rounder Brad McNamara, whose brisk medium-pace and determined batting rarely let his side down. Of the others, Anthony Stuart showed promise for Australia in one-day cricket, taking a hat-trick against Pakistan, but Phil Alley's lack of control undermined his potential and the once-vaunted spin attack was of little consequence. Phil Emery marked his 100th state appearance by scoring his first century.

An outright win in their last match would have put Tasmania and not Queensland into the Shield final. However, they found Matthews and a flat Sydney pitch equally uncompromising. Despite making two declarations, they lacked the bowling to get them home. An early win in Perth was encouraging but it was double success against South Australia in February that put them into contention. Ricky Ponting, another international player put out to grass with the same brief as Slater, found his feet and his very best form with three consecutive hundreds. Even more prolific was 27-year-old Jamie Cox, with 1,349, including five centuries. Voted the Lord's Taverners Cricketer of the Year by his peers, he capped a wonderful season with twin hundreds in that crucial game in Sydney. He also shared five century partnerships with fellow-opener Dene Hills, four of them over 150. With the exciting Michael Di Venuto, captain David Boon and the dependable Shaun Young to follow, runs were plentiful. Wickets were harder to come by: Young was the best of the bowlers, with 35. Daniel Marsh moved over from Adelaide to provide some variety with his left-arm spin.

Two of Victoria's three wins came from unlikely fourth-innings chases at the MCG, both featuring outstanding centuries by Graeme Vimpani. His success was all the more noteworthy given the fragile nature of the rest of Victoria's batting. Matthew Elliott looked set for a sensational season before his crippling collision with Mark Waugh while batting in the Second Test, and Dean Jones ultimately succumbed to an ankle operation. David Saker and Ian Harvey bowled tirelessly while keeper Darren Berry returned to the side, after his controversial displacement in 1995-96, as a much improved batsman and made 45 dismissals, second only to Gilchrist. Tony Dodemaide had a difficult year, but was rewarded when he became the first Victorian to complete the double of 3,000 runs and 300 wickets for his state.

South Australia made only a token defence of their title. Tim May and Paul Nobes had retired, and James Brayshaw turned to sports journalism in mid-season. Jamie Siddons combined coaching with captaincy and, judging by some erratic batting, needed urgent relief from either or both. Left-hand batsman Darren Lehmann stood supreme among his embattled colleagues, without attracting much attention from the national selectors. The Australian Cricket Board did call him up for a promotional mission to Alice Springs when he should have been helping his team score 170 to beat England A, an arrogant decision that insulted the visitors; justice prevailed when South Australia lost by 12. At 21, Jason Gillespie was the youngest and arguably the most talented of Australia's emerging fast bowlers. Greg Blewett made only one Shield appearance; his absence highlighted South Australia's lack of resources.

The day-night experiment in first-class cricket had a rough time. The yellow ball was superseded by an orange one, which was easier to see but condemned by spinners past and present for being hard to grip. Meanwhile, the crowds stayed away, except in Perth, where Victoria's visit attracted 13,085. In 1997-98, the international programme was to allow state teams to field full-strength sides for at least four matches, a small boost for the competition, and restored the tradition of a Sydney Test over the New Year. Over seven weeks in December to January 1996-97, the prime holiday period, only three days of Test cricket were played (the time taken by West Indies to beat Australia in Melbourne) compared to 14 days of the limited-overs Carlton & United series.

Halfway through the season, the Australian Cricket Board sacked its chief executive, Graham Halbish, and refused to announce its reasons; the acrimony attending his departure was not a secret and it seemed that the Board, and its new chairman Denis Rogers, were alarmed by the extent that Halbish appeared to be pursuing his own agenda. Halbish had also been embarrassingly critical of ICC. Four months elapsed before his successor was named as Malcolm Speed, who had an administrative background in basketball but possessed valuable experience of negotiating with Asian countries. Halbish dramatically reappeared as a consultant to the Australian Cricketers' Association, the players' union, which is run by Tim May. Halbish was expected to negotiate future player contracts, but the Board refused to meet him on the grounds that he possessed confidential information about their finances, although they were later persuaded to back down, following legal advice. The argument simmered quietly during the Ashes tour of England and flared up again later in 1997, with a threat of strike action. Australian cricket, its international standing at a peak, suddenly found itself facing a domestic crisis.

FIRST-CLASS AVERAGES, 1996-97

BATTING

(Qualification: 500 runs)

	M	I	NO	R	HS	100s	Avge
J. L. Langer (*WA*)	8	14	4	771	274*	3	77.10
M. T. G. Elliott (*Vic*)	5	10	2	577	187	2	72.12
J. Cox (*Tas*).............	11	21	1	1,349	200	5	67.45
M. G. Bevan (*NSW*)	7	12	3	561	150*	1	62.33
R. T. Ponting (*Tas*)	10	18	2	960	159	3	60.00
M. P. Mott (*Qld*)........	6	10	0	590	150	1	59.00
S. R. Waugh (*NSW*)	7	12	1	609	186*	2	55.36
M. L. Hayden (*Qld*)	8	14	2	648	224	2	54.00
D. S. Lehmann (*SA*)	11	19	1	960	255	2	53.33
G. R. Vimpani (*Vic*)	8	15	0	752	161	3	50.13
T. M. Moody (*WA*)	9	14	1	621	152	3	47.76
S. G. Law (*Qld*)	10	16	3	617	144	1	47.46
M. E. Hussey (*WA*)	12	22	2	928	147	2	46.40
M. E. Waugh (*NSW*).....	7	13	0	564	159	1	43.38
T. J. Barsby (*Qld*)	11	19	1	765	111	2	42.50
D. M. Jones (*Vic*)	7	13	0	521	152	2	40.07
M. J. Di Venuto (*Tas*) ...	11	20	0	799	130	2	39.95
A. C. Gilchrist (*WA*)	12	17	2	591	108*	1	39.40
S. Young (*Tas*)	11	18	4	548	113	2	39.14
R. J. Campbell (*WA*)	11	19	1	672	113	1	37.33
M. J. Slater (*NSW*)	10	19	0	703	102	1	37.00
D. C. Boon (*Tas*)	11	17	0	628	118	1	36.94
D. R. Martyn (*WA*)	12	20	1	701	108	2	36.89
D. F. Hills (*Tas*)	11	21	2	701	124*	2	36.89
D. J. Marsh (*Tas*)	11	19	5	500	97	0	35.71
A. Symonds (*Qld*).......	11	18	1	604	111	1	35.52
S. Lee (*NSW*)	9	17	2	506	101*	1	33.73
L. D. Harper (*Vic*).......	10	19	2	543	100*	1	31.94
J. P. Maher (*Qld*)	11	19	2	532	95	0	31.29
D. S. Berry (*Vic*)........	11	20	1	590	148	1	31.05
J. D. Siddons (*SA*).......	11	21	0	631	101	1	30.04
G. R. Parker (*SA*)	10	19	2	500	112	1	29.41
T. J. Nielsen (*SA*)	11	20	2	521	110*	1	28.94

* Signifies not out.

BOWLING

(Qualification: 20 wickets)

	O	M	R	W	BB	5W/i	Avge
J. C. Scuderi (SA)	130.4	32	399	23	5-43	1	17.34
G. D. McGrath (NSW)	229.5	67	567	29	5-50	1	19.55
A. J. Bichel (Qld).........	239.2	64	650	30	6-56	4	21.66
A. C. Dale (Qld)..........	454.5	170	927	42	6-38	2	22.07
J. Angel (WA)	274.5	81	685	31	4-20	0	22.09
B. E. McNamara (NSW)....	235.2	53	741	33	5-19	3	22.45
T. M. Moody (WA).........	357.4	94	926	38	7-41	1	24.36
B. Mulder (WA)	242.2	60	578	23	6-65	2	25.13
M. S. Kasprowicz (Qld)....	466.4	131	1,226	48	5-64	3	25.54
B. P. Julian (WA)	318	78	908	35	7-48	2	25.94
B. N. Creevey (Qld).......	198.1	45	588	22	6-70	2	26.72
I. J. Harvey (Vic)	315.4	81	965	35	7-44	3	27.57
P. J. S. Alley (NSW)	194.5	40	641	23	5-89	1	27.86
S. K. Warne (Vic).........	314.1	87	795	27	4-95	0	29.44
P. R. Reiffel (Vic)	225.1	59	596	20	5-73	1	29.80
A. M. Stuart (NSW)	186.1	41	643	21	5-63	1	30.61
S. A. Muller (Qld)	216.3	43	645	21	5-76	1	30.71
S. Young (Tas)	366.5	102	1,096	35	7-64	2	31.31
P. W. Jackson (Qld)	351.2	111	789	23	5-85	1	34.30
M. W. Ridgway (Tas)......	298.3	64	978	28	6-88	1	34.92
C. R. Miller (Tas)	433.3	113	1,143	32	4-48	0	35.71
D. J. Saker (Vic)	426	119	1,210	32	4-22	0	37.81
B. E. Young (SA)	303.1	67	903	23	4-111	0	39.26
P. E. McIntyre (SA)	492.5	114	1,413	35	6-64	2	40.37
J. P. Marquet (Tas)	289.2	59	1,028	25	4-107	0	41.12
M. S. Garnaut (WA)	309	81	953	23	4-51	0	41.43
D. W. Fleming (Vic).......	318.4	72	979	23	4-66	0	42.56
D. J. Marsh (Tas)	352	89	955	22	3-55	0	43.40

SHEFFIELD SHIELD, 1996-97

	Played	Won	Lost	Drawn	1st-inns Points	Points	Quotient
Western Australia	10	6	1	3	6	42	1.399
Queensland	10	4	1	5	4	28	1.193
New South Wales	10	4	4	2	4	28	1.050
Tasmania	10	3	4	3	10	28	1.066
Victoria	10	3	5	2	2	19.7*	0.730
South Australia	10	2	7	1	2	14	0.738

Final: Queensland beat Western Australia by 160 runs.

Queensland finished ahead of New South Wales by virtue of their superior quotient, New South Wales ahead of Tasmania by virtue of more outright wins.

* 0.3 points deducted for slow over-rate.
  Outright win = 6 pts; lead on first innings in a drawn or lost game = 2 pts.
  Quotient = runs per wicket scored divided by runs per wicket conceded.

Under Australian Cricket Board playing conditions, two extras are scored for every no-ball bowled whether scored off or not. Any runs scored off the bat are credited to the batsman, while byes and leg-byes are counted as no-balls, in accordance with Law 24.9, in addition to the initial penalty.

*In the following scores, * by the name of a team indicates that they won the toss.*

At Brisbane, November 6, 7, 8, 9. Queensland won by nine wickets. Tasmania 168 (D. F. Hills 60, M. J. Di Venuto 66; A. J. Bichel six for 63, A. C. Dale three for 29) and 176 (A. J. Daly 42, C. R. Miller 41; A. C. Dale four for 44, S. A. Muller four for 35); Queensland* 244 (M. L. Love 46, A. Symonds 35, G. I. Foley 82 not out; C. R. Miller three for 67, J. M. Saint three for 44) and 101 for one (T. J. Barsby 48 not out). *Queensland 6 pts.*

Dale dismissed Cox in the first over of his first-class debut. Lights were used on the second evening.

At Sydney, November 8, 9, 10, 11. New South Wales won by 58 runs. New South Wales* 264 (S. R. Waugh 38, M. G. Bevan 79, S. Lee 40, G. R. J. Matthews 45; D. W. Fleming three for 48) and 353 for eight dec. (M. J. Slater 69, M. G. Bevan 150 not out, S. Lee 40, P. A. Emery 34; B. A. Williams four for 63); Victoria 161 (W. G. Ayres 55, D. W. Fleming 34; A. M. Stuart five for 63) and 398 (M. T. G. Elliott 187, D. S. Berry 148; S. C. G. MacGill four for 72, D. A. Freedman three for 92). *New South Wales 6 pts, Victoria −0.3 pts.*

Victoria were 89 for five in their second innings before Elliott and Berry, who scored his maiden hundred, added 290 in 277 minutes, a Victorian sixth-wicket record. Their last five wickets then fell for 19.

At Bankstown, November 15, 16, 17, 18. Queensland won by seven wickets. New South Wales* 296 (M. A. Taylor 53, S. R. Waugh 106, G. R. J. Matthews 47; M. S. Kasprowicz five for 110) and 141 (S. R. Waugh 35); Queensland 330 (T. J. Barsby 79, M. L. Love 37, A. Symonds 111; S. Nikitaras three for 76) and 108 for three (T. J. Barsby 68). *Queensland 6 pts.*

Symonds scored a century in the last session of the second day. Matthews became New South Wales's leading wicket-taker when he passed the 394 of state coach Geoff Lawson.

At Melbourne, November 15, 16, 17, 18. Victoria won by nine wickets. Victoria* 345 for nine dec. (D. M. Jones 152, I. J. Harvey 70, D. S. Berry 47; J. C. Scuderi three for 49) and 38 for one; South Australia 84 (J. C. Scuderi 34; D. J. Saker four for 22, S. K. Warne three for 25) and 298 (B. A. Johnson 52, G. R. Parker 112, Extras 30; I. J. Harvey seven for 44). *Victoria 6 pts.*

Berry made eight dismissals (seven catches and one stumping) in South Australia's first innings, equalling the Australian record, and 11 in the match, equalling his own state record. Jones became the first batsman to score 9,000 runs for Victoria.

At Perth, November 15, 16, 17, 18. Tasmania won by 141 runs. Tasmania 473 for six dec. (D. F. Hills 111, J. Cox 62, M. J. Di Venuto 130, R. T. Ponting 67, D. C. Boon 42, S. Young 31 not out) and 252 for four dec. (D. F. Hills 68, J. Cox 116, R. T. Ponting 36); Western Australia* 326 for four dec. (M. E. Hussey 33, J. L. Langer 143 not out, T. M. Moody 114) and 258 (M. E. Hussey 90, D. R. Martyn 70, R. J. Campbell 44, J. M. Allen 30; J. P. Marquet three for 91, C. R. Miller four for 48, S. Young three for 41). *Tasmania 6 pts.*

Hills and Cox shared opening stands of 112 and 152. In Western Australia's first innings, Langer and Moody added 231 for the fourth wicket.

At Brisbane, November 29, 30, December 1, 2. Queensland won by eight wickets. Victoria* 162 (B. J. Hodge 45, B. A. Williams 31; A. J. Bichel five for 46) and 277 (W. G. Ayres 56, B. J. Hodge 51, L. D. Harper 36, D. S. Berry 48; A. J. Bichel five for 69); Queensland 305 (T. J. Barsby 59, M. L. Love 34, A. Symonds 77, G. I. Foley 37, W. A. Seccombe 42; D. J. Saker three for 99) and 137 for two (M. L. Hayden 73 not out, M. L. Love 39). *Queensland 6 pts.*

Berry made five catches and a stumping in Queensland's first innings.

At Adelaide, November 29, 30, December 1, 2. Western Australia won by five wickets. South Australia* 277 (D. S. Lehmann 47, J. C. Scuderi 55, Extras 45; B. P. Julian four for 77, T. M. Moody three for 30) and 325 (D. S. Lehmann 46, J. A. Brayshaw 96, G. R. Parker 80; B. P. Julian five for 98, M. S. Garnaut four for 81); Western Australia 318 (J. L. Langer 116, D. R. Martyn 96; J. C. Scuderi four for 42) and 288 for five (M. E. Hussey 37, J. L. Langer 45, D. R. Martyn 43, T. M. Moody 89 not out, A. C. Gilchrist 36). *Western Australia 6 pts.*

At Hobart, November 29, 30, December 1, 2. Drawn. New South Wales* 403 for nine dec. (M. J. Slater 76, G. R. J. Matthews 34, B. E. McNamara 137 not out, P. J. S. Alley 54 not out; M. W. Ridgway three for 101) and 225 for three dec. (S. Lee 101 not out, K. J. Roberts 54); Tasmania 327 for nine dec. (J. Cox 49, M. J. Di Venuto 50, D. C. Boon 41, S. Young 108 not out; A. M. Stuart three for 77, B. E. McNamara four for 72) and 268 for nine (J. Cox 67, D. C. Boon 77; P. J. S. Alley four for 69). *New South Wales 2 pts.*

McNamara and Alley shared an unbroken stand of 138 for New South Wales's last wicket; both scored career-bests. In their second innings, Lee scored 100 before lunch on the final day. Tasmania were set 302 in 81 overs: their last pair, Mark Atkinson and Ridgway, survived 14 balls to draw.

At Hobart, December 6, 7, 8, 9. Drawn. Tasmania* 481 for eight dec. (M. J. Di Venuto 119, D. C. Boon 118, S. Young 113, A. J. Daly 33, D. J. Marsh 42 not out; I. J. Harvey three for 81) and 311 for two dec. (D. F. Hills 124 not out, J. Cox 132, D. J. Saker 66 not out; B. J. Stacey 32, B. A. Williams 37; M. W. Ridgway three for 78) and 204 for three (W. G. Ayres 56, D. M. Jones 36, I. J. Harvey 62 not out, L. D. Harper 37 not out). *Tasmania 2 pts.*

At Brisbane, December 19, 20, 21, 22. Drawn. New South Wales 190 (S. R. Waugh 55, M. E. Waugh 31; M. S. Kasprowicz three for 74, A. J. Bichel six for 56) and 445 for nine (S. R. Waugh 186 not out, M. E. Waugh 159, Extras 30; M. S. Kasprowicz three for 99, A. J. Bichel three for 127); Queensland* 549 (J. P. Maher 91, S. G. Law 144, A. Symonds 50, I. A. Healy 88, A. J. Bichel 58, Extras 36; G. D. McGrath three for 114, S. C. G. MacGill three for 64). *Queensland 2 pts.*

Adam Dale had figures of 19–14–17–1 in New South Wales's first innings. Maher and Law put on 244 for Queensland's third wicket. In New South Wales's second innings, the Waughs added 273 for the third wicket.

At Perth, December 20, 21, 22, 23. Drawn. South Australia* 258 (M. P. Faull 35, D. S. Lehmann 52, J. A. Brayshaw 73; B. P. Julian three for 54, T. M. Moody three for 67) and 381 for seven (G. S. Blewett 66, J. D. Siddons 81, J. N. Gillespie 58, D. S. Lehmann 46, G. R. Parker 52 not out, Extras 41; B. P. Julian three for 85); Western Australia 560 for eight dec. (J. L. Langer 274 not out, D. R. Martyn 104, A. C. Gilchrist 40, G. B. Hogg 46, B. P. Julian 32 not out; J. N. Gillespie five for 64). *Western Australia 2 pts.*

This was Brayshaw's last match before retirement. Langer's career-best 274 not out lasted 485 minutes and 379 balls and included 30 fours and a six. He and Martyn added 238 for Western Australia's third wicket.

At Adelaide, January 3, 4, 5, 6. New South Wales won by 143 runs. New South Wales* 415 (C. J. Richards 76, S. Lee 43, K. J. Roberts 44, G. R. J. Matthews 58, P. A. Emery 49, B. E. McNamara 50; S. P. George three for 70, P. E. McIntyre three for 140) and 173 for three dec. (R. J. Davison 67 not out, S. Lee 67); South Australia 137 (S. M. Thompson four for 56) and 308 (M. P. Faull 68, D. S. Lehmann 97, B. E. Young 91 not out; P. J. S. Alley five for 89, S. M. Thompson three for 81). *New South Wales 6 pts.*

At Perth, January 3, 4, 5, 6 (day/night). Western Australia won by seven wickets. Victoria* 332 (G. R. Vimpani 37, D. M. Jones 32, R. P. Larkin 104, I. J. Harvey 55, Extras 31; J. Angel three for 59) and 283 (G. R. Vimpani 88, D. M. Jones 75, Extras 34; B. P. Julian four for 44, J. Angel three for 74); Western Australia 495 (M. E. Hussey 147, R. J. Campbell 74, J. L. Langer 42, D. R. Martyn 108, A. C. Gilchrist 67; A. I. C. Dodemaide four for 67, B. J. Stacey four for 122) and 121 for three (M. E. Hussey 50, J. L. Langer 30 not out; B. J. Stacey three for 44). *Western Australia 6 pts.*

13,085 watched the game over four days.

At Sydney, January 9, 10, 11, 12. Western Australia won by nine wickets. New South Wales* 126 (J. Angel four for 20, M. S. Garnaut four for 51) and 337 (R. J. Davison 99, M. J. Slater 34, K. J. Roberts 30, P. A. Emery 33, P. J. S. Alley 45 not out; G. B. Hogg three for 73); Western Australia 244 (M. E. Hussey 33, A. C. Gilchrist 32, G. B. Hogg 59, Extras 30; B. E. McNamara five for 75) and 220 for one (R. J. Campbell 50, M. E. Hussey 81 not out, J. L. Langer 70 not out). *Western Australia 6 pts.*

18 wickets fell on the first day.

At Melbourne, January 9, 10, 11, 12. Victoria won by one wicket. Tasmania* 359 for seven dec. (M. J. Di Venuto 35, D. C. Boon 75, S. Young 50, D. J. Marsh 97, M. N. Atkinson 50 not out; A. I. C. Dodemaide three for 75) and 264 for four dec. (D. F. Hills 38, J. Cox 38, R. T. Ponting 94 not out, D. C. Boon 52); Victoria 284 for nine dec. (G. R. Vimpani 62, L. D. Harper 37, R. P. Larkin 39, D. S. Berry 38, A. I. C. Dodemaide 41 not out; D. J. Marsh three for 64) and 340 for nine (G. R. Vimpani 113, R. P. Larkin 70, L. D. Harper 40, D. S. Berry 50 not out; D. J. Marsh three for 55, C. R. Miller three for 48). *Victoria 6 pts, Tasmania 2 pts.*

Victoria, set 340 in 80 overs, won with three balls to spare.

At Adelaide, January 10, 11, 12, 13. South Australia won by nine wickets. South Australia* 527 for six dec. (M. P. Faull 50, D. S. Lehmann 255, J. D. Siddons 61, T. J. Nielsen 110 not out; M. S. Kasprowicz four for 93) and 51 for one; Queensland 227 (M. L. Hayden 38, T. J. Dixon 43, W. A. Seccombe 59; P. E. McIntyre six for 64) and 350 (M. L. Hayden 69, T. J. Dixon 33, J. P. Maher 33, G. I. Foley 72, A. C. Dale 31, P. W. Jackson 49; P. E. McIntyre four for 133, B. E. Young four for 111). *South Australia 6 pts.*

Lehmann's career-best 255 lasted 496 minutes and 377 balls and included 26 fours and one six. He added 260 for South Australia's sixth wicket with Nielsen.

At Sydney, January 23, 24, 25, 26 (day/night). New South Wales won by an innings and 169 runs. South Australia* 154 (G. R. Parker 44; B. E. McNamara three for 42, S. Lee three for 15) and 117 (B. E. McNamara five for 19, S. Lee three for 32); New South Wales 440 for six dec. (M. J. Slater 102, K. J. Roberts 119, G. R. J. Matthews 109 not out, B. E. McNamara 47 not out, Extras 33). *New South Wales 6 pts.*

Originally scheduled as a day match starting on January 24; the attendance on the first day was approximately 150.

At Hobart, January 24, 25, 26, 27. Western Australia won by seven wickets. Tasmania* 314 (J. Cox 96, M. J. Di Venuto 65, M. N. Atkinson 44; J. Angel four for 71, B. Mulder three for 85) and 175 (M. J. Di Venuto 43, D. J. Marsh 32; T. M. Moody seven for 41); Western Australia 312 (M. E. Hussey 83, R. J. Campbell 78, R. M. Baker 48, A. C. Gilchrist 36; M. W. Ridgway six for 88) and 180 for three (M. E. Hussey 87, R. J. Campbell 45). *Western Australia 6 pts, Tasmania 2 pts.*

Off-spinner Brett Mulder played his first Shield game for ten years. Hussey and Campbell shared opening stands of 139 and 106; Western Australia collapsed from 210 for one to 312 all out.

At Brisbane, January 30, 31, February 1, 2 (day/night). Drawn. Queensland 179 (T. J. Dixon 37, W. A. Seccombe 35; M. S. Garnaut three for 45, K. M. Harvey three for 30) and 412 (T. J. Barsby 107, J. P. Maher 76, S. G. Law 56, A. Symonds 39, W. A. Seccombe 36, B. N. Creevey 32 not out; J. Angel three for 70, K. M. Harvey three for 94); Western Australia* 183 (D. R. Martyn 38, T. M. Moody 30; M. S. Kasprowicz three for 49, A. C. Dale five for 43) and 273 for five (D. R. Martyn 35, T. M. Moody 136, S. M. Katich 65 not out). *Western Australia 2 pts.*

In Western Australia's first innings, Michael Hussey was out hit wicket when the bat slipped from his hands when he was driving; it flew over his head and cart-wheeled into the stumps.

At Melbourne, January 30, 31, February 1, 2 (day/night). Victoria won by two wickets. New South Wales 290 (M. J. Slater 71, C. J. Richards 58, P. A. Emery 32, B. E. McNamara 69; D. J. Saker four for 71, D. W. Fleming four for 66) and 264 (R. J. Davison 88, C. J. Richards 39, P. J. S. Alley 56; D. J. Saker three for 54, D. W. Fleming three for 60); Victoria* 164 (D. J. Saker 40 not out, D. W. Fleming 36; B. E. McNamara five for 30) and 391 for eight (G. R. Vimpani 161, M. T. G. Elliott 65, I. J. Harvey 88; B. E. McNamara three for 98). *Victoria 6 pts, New South Wales 2 pts.*

Victoria's fourth-innings total was their best to win for 65 years.

At Adelaide, February 1, 2, 3, 4. Tasmania won by ten wickets. South Australia* 293 (D. S. Lehmann 76, J. D. Siddons 55, D. S. Webber 41, B. E. Young 56 not out; J. P. Marquet three for 57) and 142 (D. S. Lehmann 31, G. R. Parker 37; S. Young five for 26); Tasmania 425 (D. F. Hills 59, J. Cox 94, M. J. Di Venuto 42, R. T. Ponting 39, D. J. Marsh 58, M. N. Atkinson 58, Extras 39; S. P. George three for 112, P. Wilson three for 55) and 11 for no wkt. *Tasmania 6 pts.*

At Melbourne, February 5, 6, 7, 8. Drawn. Queensland* 229 for nine dec. (W. A. Seccombe 103, P. W. Jackson 31 retired hurt; I. J. Harvey five for 45) and 355 for four dec. (M. P. Mott 150, T. J. Dixon 34, J. P. Maher 95, S. G. Law 45 not out); Victoria 191 (R. P. Larkin 52, I. J. Harvey 31, A. M. Smith 36; B. N. Creevey five for 32) and 213 for eight (G. R. Vimpani 32, B. P. Ricci 43, I. J. Harvey 31). *Queensland 2 pts.*

Victoria's ninth-wicket pair, Tony Dodemaide and David Saker, played out the last 90 minutes to draw.

At Hobart, February 11, 12, 13, 14. Tasmania won by five wickets. South Australia* 387 (M. P. Faull 62, B. A. Johnson 91, J. C. Scuderi 70, T. J. Nielsen 64; J. P. Marquet four for 107, D. J. Marsh three for 67) and 209 for five dec. (M. P. Faull 65, G. R. Parker 68 not out, B. E. Young 30; C. R. Miller three for 28); Tasmania 248 (R. T. Ponting 126; M. A. Harrity three for 73, J. C. Scuderi five for 43) and 351 for five (J. Cox 57, R. T. Ponting 145 not out, D. C. Boon 30, S. Young 32, D. J. Marsh 49 not out; B. E. Young three for 87). *Tasmania 6 pts, South Australia 2 pts.*

Tasmania, set 349 off 84 overs, won with 20 balls to spare after Cox reached 1,000 runs for the season and Ponting scored his second hundred of the match.

At Perth, February 14, 15, 16, 17. Drawn. Western Australia 414 (R. J. Campbell 53, M. W. Goodwin 127, D. R. Martyn 62, T. M. Moody 37, M. P. Atkinson 43 not out; S. A. Muller five for 76) and 320 for eight (R. J. Campbell 55, M. W. Goodwin 77, A. C. Gilchrist 43, M. P. Atkinson 45 not out, Extras 42); Queensland* 400 (M. P. Mott 90, J. P. Maher 56, S. G. Law 41, A. Symonds 45, G. I. Foley 53, W. A. Seccombe 45; M. S. Garnaut three for 87, T. M. Moody four for 73). *Western Australia 2 pts.*

When 13 in the first innings, Moody became Western Australia's leading run-scorer, passing Mike Veletta's 8,038.

At Adelaide, March 7, 8, 9, 10. South Australia won by 161 runs. South Australia* 216 (B. A. Johnson 46, J. D. Siddons 37, J. C. Scuderi 37; D. J. Saker three for 74, D. W. Fleming three for 46, I. J. Harvey three for 19) and 449 for nine dec. (M. P. Faull 54, D. S. Lehmann 167, J. D. Siddons 51, T. J. Nielsen 46, B. E. Young 70 not out); Victoria 241 (B. J. Hodge 50, I. J. Harvey 73; P. Wilson three for 49, P. E. McIntyre four for 90) and 263 (R. P. Larkin 56, D. S. Berry 41, L. D. Harper 52, A. M. Smith 33; P. E. McIntyre five for 88). *South Australia 6 pts, Victoria 2 pts.*

At Hobart, March 7, 8, 9, 10. Drawn. Tasmania* 408 (R. T. Ponting 159, S. Young 92, D. J. Marsh 52, M. N. Atkinson 48 not out; B. N. Creevey three for 76) and 263 for nine dec. (J. Cox 74, M. J. Di Venuto 56, D. C. Boon 37; M. S. Kasprowicz four for 70, P. W. Jackson five for 85); Queensland 283 (T. J. Barsby 39, M. P. Mott 74, A. Symonds 43, G. I. Foley 77; M. W. Ridgway four for 76) and 198 for four (T. J. Barsby 59, S. G. Law 74 not out). *Tasmania 2 pts.*

Ponting scored his third hundred in successive first-class innings.

At Perth, March 7, 8. Western Australia won by nine wickets. New South Wales* 89 (B. Mulder five for two) and 217 (M. J. Slater 47, G. R. J. Matthews 31, B. E. McNamara 33; B. Mulder six for 65); Western Australia 228 (R. J. Campbell 64, A. C. Gilchrist 66, B. P. Julian 51; G. R. J. Matthews six for 66) and 80 for one (M. W. Goodwin 46 not out). *Western Australia 6 pts.*

Mulder's first-innings analysis was 6-4-2-5.

At Sydney, March 13, 14, 15, 16. New South Wales won by six wickets. Tasmania* 463 for seven dec. (J. Cox 143, M. J. Di Venuto 65, R. T. Ponting 64, D. C. Boon 52, M. N. Atkinson 45 not out, Extras 46) and 290 for five dec. (D. F. Hills 75, J. Cox 125, C. R. Miller 37 not out; S. C. G. MacGill four for 78); New South Wales 449 (M. J. Slater 87, R. J. Davison 36, J. L. Arnberger 71, K. J. Roberts 56, P. A. Emery 100 not out; S. Young three for 100) and 305 for four (R. J. Davison 63, M. J. Slater 79, J. L. Arnberger 57, S. Lee 75 not out). *New South Wales 6 pts, Tasmania 2 pts.*

Cox scored a hundred in each innings and became only the second batsman to pass 6,000 for Tasmania, following Boon. Slater and Davison shared a century opening stand in each innings. Emery scored his maiden century in his 100th match for New South Wales, who were set 305 in 67 overs and won with two to spare; the match featured 1,507 runs for the loss of 26 wickets.

At Brisbane, March 13, 14, 15, 16. Queensland won by 137 runs. Queensland 277 (T. J. Barsby 34, M. P. Mott 33, A. Symonds 43, G. I. Foley 34, B. N. Creevey 48 not out, Extras 36; P. Wilson three for 53, B. N. Wigney three for 76) and 218 (M. P. Mott 60, S. G. Law 50, A. Symonds 35; P. Wilson three for 44, J. C. Scuderi three for 19); South Australia* 160 (J. D. Siddons 82, T. J. Nielsen 34; M. S. Kasprowicz five for 64, A. C. Dale four for 40) and 198 (M. P. Faull 64, D. S. Lehmann 31, T. J. Nielsen 41; M. S. Kasprowicz four for 55). *Queensland 6 pts.*

At Melbourne, March 13, 14, 15, 16. Western Australia won by an innings and 29 runs. Victoria* 205 (M. R. Foster 32, S. J. Craig 90; J. Angel four for 32, B. P. Julian three for 38) and 224 (L. D. Harper 100 not out; B. P. Julian seven for 48); Western Australia 458 for nine dec. (M. E. Hussey 138, R. J. Campbell 113, M. W. Goodwin 90, B. P. Julian 37; D. W. Fleming four for 85). *Western Australia 6 pts.*

Campbell scored 113, his maiden hundred, in 106 balls and 125 minutes; Harper's maiden hundred took 252 balls and 313 minutes.

FINAL

WESTERN AUSTRALIA v QUEENSLAND

At Perth, March 21, 22, 23, 24, 25. Queensland won by 160 runs. Toss: Queensland.

Second-placed Queensland needed an outright win to claim their second Sheffield Shield and took the initiative from the start. They had scored 100 without loss when Barsby holed out for 67 just before lunch. After that, they lost some momentum, but Mott shared another century partnership with Law and 320 looked a more than decent total when Dale dismissed Western Australia's in-form openers, Hussey and Campbell, for five. The home side never recovered. There was nothing in the pitch to account for their failures, but Dale swung the ball well in the breeze to claim six victims and Kasprowicz bowled with rare pace. Only the Zimbabwean-born Goodwin showed much resistance – his 63 was more than twice the next highest score. Queensland led by 155 and Barsby was prominent again when they resumed. Defying gastric problems, he batted for five hours, added 131 with Law and scored his 15th first-class century. The performance had special significance as this was Barsby's 100th Shield game, and his last before retirement. To win the Shield, Western Australia had to score 465 or bat nearly two days for a draw, but after 40 minutes they were 18 for four and down if not quite out. Their captain, Moody, had already bowled more than 50 overs and taken eight wickets; now he embarked on seven hours of defiance, which yielded 152 before he played a tired shot at Kasprowicz and was last out. Queensland won with three hours to spare, only the second visiting team to prevail in 15 Shield finals.

Close of play: First day, Queensland 266-4 (A. Symonds 16*, G. I. Foley 3*); Second day, Western Australia 164-9 (M. S. Garnaut 2*, B. Mulder 5*); Third day, Queensland 259-6 (W. A. Seccombe 6*, P. W. Jackson 10*); Fourth day, Western Australia 166-5 (T. M. Moody 66*, A. C. Gilchrist 36*).

Queensland

T. J. Barsby c Garnaut b Mulder	67	– (2) c Gilchrist b Garnaut 111
M. P. Mott c Campbell b Angel	86	– (1) c Goodwin b Garnaut 1
J. P. Maher c Gilchrist b Julian	8	– c Moody b Mulder 10
*S. G. Law c Garnaut b Hogg	70	– c Gilchrist b Moody 72
A. Symonds c Julian b Moody	27	– run out 30
G. I. Foley c Gilchrist b Moody	17	– c Gilchrist b Julian 2
†W. A. Seccombe c Gilchrist b Julian	3	– c Gilchrist b Moody 10
B. N. Creevey lbw b Moody	0	– (9) c Gilchrist b Moody 0
P. W. Jackson not out	6	– (8) not out 22
A. C. Dale c Julian b Moody	15	– c Martyn b Angel 0
M. S. Kasprowicz c Goodwin b Angel	1	– c Angel b Moody 26
L-b 7, w 1, n-b 12	20	L-b 16, w 1, n-b 8 25

1/100 2/112 3/227 4/258 5/281   320   1/20 2/56 3/187 4/236 5/238   309
6/296 7/296 8/296 9/317   6/241 7/275 8/275 9/276

Bowling: *First Innings*—Angel 18–7–56–2; Garnaut 9–1–36–0; Julian 31–6–74–2; Mulder 27–8–75–4; Martyn 2–0–4–0; Hogg 6–0–27–1. *Second Innings*—Angel 19–8–40–1; Julian 18–7–36–1; Garnaut 13–2–46–2; Moody 23.4–4–76–4; Mulder 18–2–62–1; Hogg 7–0–24–0; Martyn 5–1–9–0.

Western Australia

M. E. Hussey lbw b Dale	5	– b Dale	5
R. J. Campbell c Seccombe b Dale	0	– c Barsby b Dale	0
M. W. Goodwin lbw b Dale	63	– lbw b Jackson	5
D. R. Martyn c Maher b Kasprowicz	7	– c Foley b Kasprowicz	0
*T. M. Moody c Law b Jackson	23	– c Symonds b Kasprowicz	152
G. B. Hogg lbw b Kasprowicz	1	– c Seccombe b Kasprowicz	30
†A. C. Gilchrist c Barsby b Dale	23	– c Barsby b Kasprowicz	48
B. P. Julian c Law b Dale	0	– c Seccombe b Dale	8
J. Angel c Law b Dale	28	– c Maher b Jackson	13
M. S. Garnaut not out	2	– c Law b Kasprowicz	7
B. Mulder c Maher b Kasprowicz	6	– not out	4
B 5, l-b 2	7	B 5, l-b 11, w 2, n-b 14	32

1/2 2/5 3/16 4/51 5/74   165   1/2 2/9 3/10 4/18 5/99   304
6/101 7/101 8/152 9/157   6/185 7/206 8/246 9/300

Bowling: *First Innings*—Kasprowicz 20.1–9–42–3; Dale 22–9–38–6; Creevey 10–1–37–0; Jackson 16–3–41–1. *Second Innings*—Kasprowicz 41.3–14–83–5; Dale 27–9–46–3; Jackson 29–6–74–2; Creevey 17–3–58–0; Law 2–0–3–0; Foley 6–2–24–0.

Umpires: D. B. Hair and P. D. Parker.

SHEFFIELD SHIELD WINNERS

1892-93	Victoria	1923-24	Victoria
1893-94	South Australia	1924-25	Victoria
1894-95	Victoria	1925-26	New South Wales
1895-96	New South Wales	1926-27	South Australia
1896-97	New South Wales	1927-28	Victoria
1897-98	Victoria	1928-29	New South Wales
1898-99	Victoria	1929-30	Victoria
1899-1900	New South Wales	1930-31	Victoria
1900-01	Victoria	1931-32	New South Wales
1901-02	New South Wales	1932-33	New South Wales
1902-03	New South Wales	1933-34	Victoria
1903-04	New South Wales	1934-35	Victoria
1904-05	New South Wales	1935-36	South Australia
1905-06	New South Wales	1936-37	Victoria
1906-07	New South Wales	1937-38	New South Wales
1907-08	Victoria	1938-39	South Australia
1908-09	New South Wales	1939-40	New South Wales
1909-10	South Australia	1940-46	No competition
1910-11	New South Wales	1946-47	Victoria
1911-12	New South Wales	1947-48	Western Australia
1912-13	South Australia	1948-49	New South Wales
1913-14	New South Wales	1949-50	New South Wales
1914-15	Victoria	1950-51	Victoria
1915-19	No competition	1951-52	New South Wales
1919-20	New South Wales	1952-53	South Australia
1920-21	New South Wales	1953-54	New South Wales
1921-22	Victoria	1954-55	New South Wales
1922-23	New South Wales	1955-56	New South Wales

1956-57	New South Wales		1977-78	Western Australia
1957-58	New South Wales		1978-79	Victoria
1958-59	New South Wales		1979-80	Victoria
1959-60	New South Wales		1980-81	Western Australia
1960-61	New South Wales		1981-82	South Australia
1961-62	New South Wales		1982-83	New South Wales
1962-63	Victoria		1983-84	Western Australia
1963-64	South Australia		1984-85	New South Wales
1964-65	New South Wales		1985-86	New South Wales
1965-66	New South Wales		1986-87	Western Australia
1966-67	Victoria		1987-88	Western Australia
1967-68	Western Australia		1988-89	Western Australia
1968-69	South Australia		1989-90	New South Wales
1969-70	Victoria		1990-91	Victoria
1970-71	South Australia		1991-92	Western Australia
1971-72	Western Australia		1992-93	New South Wales
1972-73	Western Australia		1993-94	New South Wales
1973-74	Victoria		1994-95	Queensland
1974-75	Western Australia		1995-96	South Australia
1975-76	South Australia		1996-97	Queensland
1976-77	Western Australia			

New South Wales have won the Shield 42 times, Victoria 25, South Australia and Western Australia 13, Queensland 2, Tasmania 0.

MERCANTILE MUTUAL INSURANCE CUP

Note: Matches in this section were not first-class.

At Adelaide, October 12. Victoria won by 30 runs. Victoria 238 for four (50 overs) (D. M. Jones 93 not out, B. J. Hodge 50, I. J. Harvey 41); South Australia* 208 for nine (50 overs) (G. S. Blewett 61, G. R. Parker 42 not out; I. J. Harvey three for 29).

At North Sydney, October 13. Western Australia won by four wickets. New South Wales 242 for seven (50 overs) (R. Chee Quee 36, C. J. Richards 109, M. T. Haywood 37; J. Angel three for 54, K. M. Harvey three for 42); Western Australia* 246 for six (46.4 overs) (J. L. Langer 54, R. J. Campbell 34, D. R. Martyn 37, A. C. Gilchrist 61 not out).

At Brisbane, October 18 (day/night). Queensland won by five wickets. New South Wales* 169 (49.2 overs) (R. Chee Quee 47, T. H. Bayliss 36, B. E. McNamara 33 not out); Queensland 173 for five (45.2 overs) (M. L. Hayden 75 not out, J. P. Maher 40; A. M. Stuart four for 22).

At Brisbane, October 27. Western Australia won by four wickets. Queensland 214 (50 overs) (M. L. Hayden 64, W. A. Seccombe 32; K. M. Harvey four for 37); Western Australia* 218 for six (49.2 overs) (M. P. Lavender 75, D. R. Martyn 53).

At Carlton, October 27. Victoria won by 58 runs. Victoria* 250 for four (50 overs) (M. T. G. Elliott 59, W. G. Ayres 39, D. M. Jones 100 not out, M. R. Foster 31 not out); Tasmania 192 (45.4 overs) (D. F. Hills 39, M. J. Di Venuto 31, D. C. Boon 52, D. J. Marsh 30; S. K. Warne five for 35).

At Sydney, November 1. New South Wales won by seven wickets. Tasmania* 173 (46.4 overs) (D. F. Hills 30; B. E. McNamara six for 25); New South Wales 174 for three (39.2 overs) (S. Lee 63, K. J. Roberts 55 not out, T. H. Bayliss 35 not out).

At Adelaide, November 3. Queensland won by seven wickets. South Australia 134 (47.5 overs) (T. J. Nielsen 35); Queensland* 138 for three (37.3 overs) (M. L. Love 58 not out, G. I. Foley 38 not out; P. Wilson three for 19).

At Brisbane, November 10. Queensland won by 40 runs. Queensland* 275 for five (50 overs) (J. P. Maher 91, M. L. Love 38, G. I. Foley 46 not out); Tasmania 235 (47.5 overs) (M. J. Di Venuto 78, R. T. Ponting 46; S. A. Prestwidge four for 43).

At Perth, December 18 (day/night). Western Australia won by 39 runs. Western Australia* 210 for nine (50 overs) (A. C. Gilchrist 37, T. M. Moody 102 not out); South Australia 171 (46.1 overs) (M. P. Faull 38, J. A. Brayshaw 37; T. M. Moody four for 30).

At Perth, January 17 (day/night). Western Australia won by five wickets. Victoria* 143 (43.5 overs) (R. P. Larkin 61; B. P. Julian three for 24, K. M. Harvey three for 17); Western Australia 146 for five (43.1 overs) (R. J. Campbell 34, A. C. Gilchrist 32).

At Adelaide, February 8. South Australia won by four wickets. New South Wales 178 (49.5 overs) (B. E. McNamara 63; P. Wilson three for 18, M. A. Harrity three for 26, B. A. Johnson three for 46); South Australia* 179 for six (43.5 overs) (B. A. Johnson 37, D. S. Lehmann 33).

At Hobart, February 8. Western Australia won by 26 runs. Western Australia 222 (49.1 overs) (M. E. Hussey 82, T. M. Moody 44, M. P. Atkinson 31; M. W. Ridgway four for 37, R. T. Ponting three for 34); Tasmania* 196 (48.5 overs) (R. T. Ponting 64; T. M. Moody three for 32, J. Stewart three for 29).

At Melbourne, February 9. Queensland won by 78 runs. Queensland 240 for six (50 overs) (J. P. Maher 111 not out, G. I. Foley 52; D. W. Lowery three for 51); Victoria* 162 for seven (50 overs) (D. J. Saker 32, A. M. Smith 41 not out).

At Sydney, February 15. New South Wales won by 23 runs. New South Wales 152 for nine (46 overs) (T. H. Bayliss 30); Victoria* 129 for eight (46 overs) (G. R. Vimpani 35; G. R. Robertson three for 24).

At Hobart, February 16. Tasmania won by 115 runs. Tasmania 260 for five (50 overs) (M. J. Di Venuto 129 not out, S. Young 64; S. P. George three for 64); South Australia* 145 (28.4 overs) (D. S. Lehmann 65; S. Young three for 63, P. J. Hutchison five for 27).

Western Australia 10 pts, Queensland 8 pts, New South Wales 4 pts, Victoria 4 pts, South Australia 2 pts, Tasmania 2 pts.

Semi-finals

At Brisbane, February 22. Queensland won by 17 runs. Queensland* 265 for five (50 overs) (J. P. Maher 37, S. G. Law 93, G. I. Foley 66); New South Wales 248 for nine (50 overs) (R. Chee Quee 52, K. J. Roberts 47, P. A. Emery 49, G. R. Robertson 33 not out; A. C. Dale four for 48).

At Perth, February 23. Western Australia won by three wickets. Victoria* 191 for eight (50 overs) (D. J. Saker 47 not out; K. M. Harvey three for 45); Western Australia 193 for seven (42.5 overs) (R. J. Campbell 50, D. R. Martyn 50).

Final

At Perth, March 2. Western Australia won by eight wickets. Queensland 148 (40.1 overs) (G. I. Foley 34 not out; M. P. Atkinson three for 33); Western Australia* 149 for two (35 overs) (R. J. Campbell 50, D. R. Martyn 48 not out, T. M. Moody 37 not out).

CRICKET IN SOUTH AFRICA, 1996-97

By COLIN BRYDEN and ANDREW SAMSON

Jonty Rhodes

Any complacency in South African cricket at the end of the previous season was swept away in 1996-97. Having been unbeaten in a series since they returned to Test cricket in 1991-92 with a one-off defeat by West Indies, the national team lost two rubbers, both by 2-1, away in India and at home to Australia. In between, South Africa won a return series against India by 2-0. Even the country's proud reputation in one-day cricket took a knock: Australia followed up their Test triumphs by winning a limited-overs series 4-3. The balance sheet nevertheless showed a record of 19 wins in 27 one-day matches during the season against seven defeats, with one no-result.

South Africa's frailties at international level, in particular a crushing innings defeat in the First Test against Australia, prompted vigorous debate in a nation which does not take kindly to defeat. Eddie Barlow, a Test star before South Africa's isolation, called for the sacking of the selectors, chaired by his old team-mate Peter Pollock, and took a sideswipe at the coach, former England player Bob Woolmer. Kepler Wessels, their first Test captain of the new era, questioned the mental fortitude of the team led by his one-time protégé Hansie Cronje.

At the end of the season, the United Cricket Board announced that, for the first time, more than a million paying spectators had attended matches. A record was not unexpected, however, with an unprecedented six Tests and 18 limited-overs internationals. But the board was dismayed to find that attendances fell away during the Australian tour, which had been planned as the highlight of the season. The three Tests against India, some of which were played during the holiday season, drew excellent crowds, with 193,739 paying spectators. The three against Australia drew 135,209. Playing two Tests in six weeks at the Wanderers in Johannesburg did not bring the expected dividend: the Australians forged their innings victory in a 28,000-seater stadium that was only once more than half full.

Attendances at the four-day Supersport Series, formerly the Castle Cup, were predictably pathetic: only 68,235 watched nine provinces playing a total of 36 matches. Less than two decades ago, almost as many would watch one match, the traditional New Year encounter between Western Province and Transvaal at Newlands. Then, of course, there were neither the counter-attractions of internationals nor the seductions of night cricket. The domestic limited-overs competition, now sponsored by Standard Bank, continued to be popular, attracting 267,594 spectators to 66 matches, although the experiment of playing a best-of-three final, in late April, with autumn's chill starting to bite, was unsuccessful.

A common criticism of domestic cricket, uniting both Barlow and Woolmer, was that there were too many teams and not enough quality. The promotion of Griqualand West meant that nine provinces contested the Supersport Series and, with the national players seldom in action, concerns about standards were well founded. No fewer than 11 teams took part in the Standard Bank League, with Easterns (formerly Eastern Transvaal) and North West (formerly Western Transvaal) joining the nine senior sides.

The gulf which has grown between provincial and international cricket was illustrated by the fact that six batsmen averaged 80 or better over five innings in the Supersport Series, with another eight managing 50 or more. It was not simply a case of good pitches leading to tall scores; seven bowlers claimed five or more wickets at less than 20 apiece. Rather, it seemed, too few outstanding players were swimming in too large a pool.

Adam Bacher, nephew of the board's managing director, Ali, took full advantage. In Transvaal's opening Supersport match, he made 210 and 112 not out against Griqualand West in Kimberley, to become the first player in South African first-class cricket to score a double-century and a century in the same match. (Herschelle Gibbs achieved the same feat three weeks later on tour in Nagpur.) Bacher headed the competition averages with 710 runs at 101.42. His early form earned him a call-up to the national team where, not surprisingly, he found the going somewhat tougher, although he finished the season with a dogged innings of 96 in the final Test against Australia. Another who prospered in provincial cricket was Jonty Rhodes, who made three successive centuries for Natal, though the national selectors mostly needed him just for one-day games.

While the batsmen flourished, the best bowlers were seldom in action for their provinces. Allan Donald, South Africa's outstanding player with an astounding 99 wickets in the international season (41 in Tests at 19.14, 58 in limited-overs internationals at 17.51), played only two limited-overs games and no first-class matches for Free State. Lance Klusener, having made a dramatic Test debut when he took eight for 64 in India's second innings at Calcutta, played only one match in Natal's successful campaign. His team-mate and fellow fast bowler, Shaun Pollock, did appear four times, but that was mainly due to the fact that he had to regain fitness after an ankle operation before reclaiming his place in the national side.

At the insistence of the national selectors, neither Klusener nor Pollock played for Natal in their final Supersport match against Western Province. Pollock had been withdrawn from the same fixture a year earlier, when a draw helped Western Province pip Natal for the title; this time, Natal led them by 17 points and needed only bonus points to become champions, so their sense of grievance was more muted.

Despite the healthy performances at the top of the first-class averages, there was concern about the quality and depth of both batting and bowling. Although there was satisfying progress by youngsters such as Bacher, Gibbs, Jacques Kallis, Hylton "H.D." Ackerman and Dale Benkenstein, the quest for reliable Test batsmen remained a priority. South Africa's depth in fast bowling was severely tested as injuries and the ravages of increasing years took a toll, although the successful return to Test cricket of the injury-plagued left-arm fast bowler Brett Schultz at the end of the season was heartening. The youngster Paul

Adams was matched as the best of the slow bowlers by the 36-year-old off-spinner Pat Symcox.

Natal were worthy winners of the Supersport Series, which despite its racy name is now South Africa's main first-class competition. Benkenstein was appointed captain at the age of 22 and proved an inspired choice. As well as leading with flair and imagination, he improved enormously as a batsman, hitting three centuries and averaging 55.09. He made a fourth century in Natal's match against the Australians and batted particularly well against Shane Warne. Natal's strength was in their depth of all-rounders and their ability to overcome the absence of up to six players on national team duty. Under coach Graham Ford, they have developed a host of fine young players. Among those who made good progress were opening batsman Doug Watson and left-arm fast bowler Gary Gilder. All-rounder Derek Crookes made a substantial contribution after returning from the national team's tour of India.

Natal also broke a long drought in limited-overs cricket when they won the Standard Bank Cup. This was a knockout competition staged in March and April between the top six teams in the Standard Bank League, held in October to December, plus Kenya and Mashonaland, who reached the semi-finals with something close to the Zimbabwean Test team, then lost to Natal after several leading players left to fulfil overseas contracts. The league had been won by Northern Transvaal, also under a new captain, Mark Davis.

Western Province, like Natal, had to play for most of the season without a host of international stars, and had the frustration of finishing runners-up in all three competitions. Their captain, John Commins, led a reliable batting line-up, but the team was handicapped when Adams was away by the lack of a wicket-taking spinner. Border, one of the smallest provinces, had an excellent season, finishing third in the Supersport Series under their new captain, Pieter Strydom. All-rounder Piet Botha was outstanding, as was Peter Kirsten in his last season, while Mark Boucher emerged as a highly talented young wicket-keeper/batsman. Another old-stager, Wessels, scored a lot of runs for Eastern Province, as did Louis Koen, but the bowling was disappointing, with the exception of former West Indian international Eldine Baptiste, who was the leading Supersport wicket-taker with 38 at 19.81. Mornantau Hayward, an exciting young fast bowler, took 24 wickets at 16.04 in one-day cricket but was unable to extend that form into the four-day games.

Transvaal had a disappointing season, although there were several good individual performers, notably batsmen Bacher and Neil McKenzie, left-arm spinner Clive Eksteen and the pace bowlers Ross Veenstra and Wayne Kidwell. Free State did not have the attack to back up their reliable batsmen, Louis Wilkinson, Hendrik Dippenaar and Deon Jordaan. Boland were hit hard when promising fast bowler Roger Telemachus missed five matches through injury; their leading batsmen were Adrian Kuiper, who hinted it might be his last season, and Kenny Jackson.

Griqualand West struggled on their return to the senior competition after a long absence. Martyn Gidley, Pieter Barnard and the captain, Mickey Arthur, batted well but the bowling was weak. Their only victory was over Northern Transvaal, who had a season of wild contrasts, heading the Standard Bank League but then recording a succession of dismal performances in the Supersport Series, where they managed one draw to seven defeats. Their B team did top the second, non-first-class, division of the UCB Bowl, which included Namibia. The first-class division was headed by Eastern Province B.

One feature of the season was the provision for floodlights to be switched on in first-class matches to augment fading light. This was resorted to frequently, not always to the delight of provincial treasurers. The new ruling was of particular relevance to Natal, where the sun sets earlier than further west. Chief executive Cassim Docrat said: "For us it was a huge success. The lights came on in virtually every game and definitely helped us to get results."

Six years after the unification of South Africa's cricket authorities, concern continued to be expressed about the fact that senior provincial sides still did not reflect the nation's multi-ethnic reality. Affirmative action is compulsory up to provincial B team level, where 40 black cricketers played in 1996-97. A total of 11 home-grown black players were selected for senior provincial teams, where merit remains the only qualification. Black players are emerging strongly at age-group level and the process is expected to accelerate, although the slow pace of integration in clubs remains a problem. – C.B.

Note: Western Transvaal changed their name to North West before the 1996-97 season. In 1997-98 Transvaal became known as Gauteng, and Northern Transvaal as Northerns.

FIRST-CLASS AVERAGES, 1996-97

BATTING

(Qualification: 8 innings, average 40.00)

	M	I	NO	R	HS	100s	Avge
J. B. Commins (*W. Province*)	7	10	4	598	200*	2	99.66
I. L. Howell (*Border*).............	8	9	5	300	102*	1	75.00
J. N. Rhodes (*Natal*)	7	11	2	589	156*	3	65.44
K. C. Wessels (*E. Province*)	9	14	2	736	179	2	61.33
B. M. McMillan (*W. Province*)	7	13	5	490	103*	1	61.25
A. M. Bacher (*Transvaal*)	10	19	2	1,012	210	4	59.52
D. M. Benkenstein (*Natal*)	10	15	1	806	129	4	57.57
L. J. Koen (*E. Province*)	9	16	1	859	186	2	57.26
H. H. Gibbs (*W. Province*)	6	11	1	553	163*	2	55.30
H. D. Ackerman (*W. Province*)	9	14	3	573	122	2	52.09
M. Strydom (*North West*)	5	10	1	464	129	1	51.55
M. J. Mitchley (*Easterns*)	5	10	1	462	201*	2	51.33
D. N. Crookes (*Natal*).............	7	10	1	453	128*	2	50.33
D. L. Haynes (*W. Province*)	8	13	1	600	202*	1	50.00
P. G. Amm (*E. Province*)	5	8	1	340	105	1	48.57
H. H. Dippenaar (*Free State*)	9	16	1	716	151*	1	47.73
M. W. Rushmere (*E. Province*).....	9	15	4	521	89*	0	47.36
M. V. Boucher (*Border*)	9	17	5	566	71	0	47.16
J. H. Kallis (*W. Province*)	10	16	2	656	143	2	46.85
U. H. Goedeke (*Natal B*)..........	5	8	2	275	102*	1	45.83
D. Jordaan (*Free State*)	9	16	0	703	117	1	43.93
D. J. Watson (*Natal*)	10	16	3	571	200*	1	43.92
P. H. Barnard (*Griqualand W.*).....	8	15	0	652	212	1	43.46
M. G. Beamish (*E. Province*)	8	15	0	633	164	3	42.20
S. C. Pope (*Border*).............	8	13	3	417	103	1	41.70
P. N. Kirsten (*Border*)	9	17	1	666	173*	2	41.62
G. F. J. Liebenberg (*Free State*)	9	16	1	618	133*	1	41.20
D. R. Gain (*Transvaal*)	6	11	1	408	88	0	40.80

* *Signifies not out.*

BOWLING

(Qualification: 20 wickets)

	O	M	R	W	BB	5W/i	Avge
D. G. Payne (*W. Province B*)	182.5	49	434	24	5-20	2	18.08
S. M. Pollock (*Natal*)	269	62	660	36	5-48	1	18.33
K. G. Storey (*Natal*)	280.4	60	741	38	7-58	2	19.50
E. A. E. Baptiste (*E. Province*)	327.3	87	753	38	5-37	3	19.81
H. S. Williams (*Boland*)	220.3	61	511	25	6-57	2	20.44
R. E. Veenstra (*Transvaal*)	239.3	60	680	33	5-36	1	20.60
A. A. Donald (*South Africa*)	241.2	68	644	31	5-36	2	20.77
P. J. Botha (*Border*)	283.3	70	698	33	5-35	2	21.15
A. J. Hall (*Transvaal*)	166.5	55	455	21	4-29	0	21.66
A. G. Botha (*Natal*)	172.1	37	464	21	4-52	0	22.09
C. E. Eksteen (*Transvaal*)	393.2	107	904	40	5-83	1	22.60
G. M. Gilder (*Natal*)	314.5	72	868	38	5-57	2	22.84
T. Bosch (*Natal*)	218.1	67	470	20	5-15	1	23.50
B. T. Player (*Free State*)	204.3	46	588	24	4-41	0	24.50
S. A. Cilliers (*Free State*)	217.2	48	672	27	5-69	1	24.88
D. N. Crookes (*Natal*)	229	58	625	25	7-114	2	25.00
V. C. Drakes (*Border*)	201.3	34	552	22	8-59	1	25.09
A. V. Birrell (*E. Province*)	252.4	43	812	32	8-134	2	25.37
B. N. Schultz (*W. Province*)	352	62	1,113	42	5-49	3	26.50
R. E. Bryson (*N. Transvaal*)	222.2	46	642	23	5-84	1	27.91
J. F. Venter (*Free State*)	256.3	71	718	25	6-96	1	28.72
N. C. Johnson (*Natal*)	205.3	50	575	20	3-52	0	28.75
P. L. Symcox (*Natal*)	246.2	48	678	22	4-26	0	30.81
C. W. Henderson (*Boland*)	322.2	85	779	25	5-107	1	31.16
E. W. Kidwell (*Transvaal*)	320.4	66	1,044	32	4-54	0	32.62
S. Elworthy (*N. Transvaal*)	258.2	67	804	24	4-71	0	33.50
M. Ntini (*Border*)	222.1	26	847	25	6-49	1	33.88
M. W. Pringle (*W. Province*)......	345.1	68	1,057	30	4-26	0	35.23
G. A. Roe (*Griqualand W.*).......	299.3	55	901	21	4-74	0	42.90

SUPERSPORT SERIES, 1996-97

	Played	Won	Lost	Drawn	Bonus Points Batting	Bonus Points Bowling	Points
Natal	8	5	1	2	32	28	110
Western Province	8	4	1	3	28	27	95
Border	8	4	1	3	25	25	90
Eastern Province	8	4	3	1	25	23	88
Transvaal	8	3	3	2	24	28	82
Free State	8	3	1	4	22	25	77
Boland	8	3	4	1	14	26	70
Griqualand West	8	1	6	1	18	16	44
Northern Transvaal	8	0	7	1	15	22	37

Outright win = 10 pts.

Bonus points are awarded for the first 100 overs of each team's first innings. One batting point is awarded for the first 150 runs and for every subsequent 50. One bowling point is awarded for the third wicket taken and for every subsequent two.

In the following scores, * by the name of a team indicates that they won the toss.

At Boland Bank Park, Paarl, November 1, 2, 3, 4. Boland won by 195 runs. Boland 268 (L. D. Ferreira 127, D. J. Millns 37; G. A. Roe three for 56, C. V. English five for 65) and 260 (K. C. Jackson 70, A. P. Kuiper 63; V. A. Walsh three for 58, G. A. Roe three for 69, B. N. Benkenstein three for 35); Griqualand West* 250 (J. M. Arthur 31, M. I. Gidley 39, P. H. Barnard 64, F. C. Brooker 34; C. W. Henderson three for 69) and 83 (R. Telemachus six for 21). *Boland 16 pts, Griqualand West 6 pts.*

At Kingsmead, Durban, November 1, 2, 3, 4. Border won by four wickets. Natal* 332 (D. M. Benkenstein 129, M. L. Bruyns 73, S. M. Pollock 66; V. C. Drakes eight for 59) and 257 (D. J. Watson 75, D. M. Benkenstein 41, S. M. Pollock 77, K. A. Forde 38; V. C. Drakes three for 42, P. J. Botha three for 55); Border 205 (F. J. C. Cronje 42, M. V. Boucher 30, V. C. Drakes 41; S. M. Pollock three for 35) and 385 for six (P. J. Botha 49, F. J. C. Cronje 67, P. N. Kirsten 90, P. C. Strydom 61, M. V. Boucher 36 not out, S. J. Palframan 30). *Border 14 pts, Natal 8 pts.*

At Newlands, Cape Town, November 1, 2, 3, 4. Western Province won by 38 runs. Western Province* 220 (H. D. Ackerman 51, J. B. Commins 81 not out; S. Elworthy three for 77, R. E. Bryson four for 64) and 399 (R. Maron 35, S. G. Koenig 97, D. L. Haynes 71, J. B. Commins 38, E. O. Simons 61, P. Kirsten 43; R. E. Bryson three for 83); Northern Transvaal 355 (R. F. Pienaar 95, R. B. Richardson 56, D. J. van Zyl 35, S. Elworthy 40; A. Martyn three for 73) and 226 (R. F. Pienaar 43, S. Elworthy 34, I. Pistorius 32 not out; M. W. Pringle three for 82). *Western Province 14 pts, Northern Transvaal 8 pts.*

At Newlands, Cape Town, November 14, 15, 16, 17. Western Province won by an innings and 65 runs. Boland* 239 (L. D. Ferreira 39, D. J. Millns 44; P. R. Adams four for 68) and 205 (A. P. Kuiper 33; A. Martyn three for 32, A. C. Dawson five for 30); Western Province 509 for seven dec. (D. L. Haynes 33, S. G. Koenig 119, H. D. Ackerman 65, J. B. Commins 148 not out, E. O. Simons 38, A. C. Dawson 64; C. W. Henderson three for 163). *Western Province 18 pts, Boland 4 pts.*

At Buffalo Park, East London, November 15, 16, 17, 18. Drawn. Border 261* (P. N. Kirsten 32, P. C. Strydom 35, M. V. Boucher 51; Q. Ferreira three for 64); Eastern Province 338 for five (P. G. Amm 81 not out, L. J. Koen 64, K. C. Wessels 70, D. J. Callaghan 74). *Border 5 pts, Eastern Province 8 pts.*
There was no play on the final two days.

At Kimberley Country Club, Kimberley, November 15, 16, 17, 18. Transvaal won by 93 runs. Transvaal* 440 for six dec. (A. M. Bacher 210, N. D. McKenzie 84, D. R. Laing 80) and 194 for four dec. (A. M. Bacher 112 not out, N. Pothas 37); Griqualand West 327 (J. M. Arthur 47, M. I. Gidley 52, P. H. Barnard 93, R. A. Koster 32, W. Bossenger 45; R. E. Veenstra three for 40, C. E. Eksteen four for 105) and 214 (M. I. Gidley 39, C. Light 38, R. A. Koster 74; C. E. Eksteen four for 72, R. E. Veenstra three for 35). *Transvaal 17 pts, Griqualand West 3 pts.*
Bacher's 210, his maiden double-hundred, lasted 423 minutes and 341 balls and included 24 fours and three sixes. In the second innings, he became the first player to score a double-hundred and a hundred in the same first-class match in South Africa.

At Centurion Park, Centurion, November 15, 16, 17. Free State won by an innings and five runs. Free State 349 (G. F. J. Liebenberg 49, L. J. Wilkinson 87, J. F. Venter 76, F. D. Stephenson 36, B. T. Player 48; R. E. Bryson five for 84, P. Joubert three for 52); Northern Transvaal* 190 (A. J. Seymore 34, R. F. Pienaar 60, D. J. van Zyl 37; F. D. Stephenson three for 61, B. T. Player three for 45, H. Botha three for 31) and 154 (S. Elworthy 30; F. D. Stephenson four for 21, S. A. Cilliers three for 65, B. T. Player three for 13). *Free State 18 pts, Northern Transvaal 4 pts.*

At St George's Park, Port Elizabeth, November 29, 30, December 1, 2. Eastern Province won by 89 runs. Eastern Province* 476 for six dec. (M. W. Rushmere 63, L. J. Koen 186, K. C. Wessels 40, D. J. Callaghan 102, G. Morgan 48) and 185 for three dec. (P. G. Amm 42, L. J. Koen 46, K. C. Wessels 64 not out); Griqualand West 266 (J. M. Arthur 86, W. E. Schonegevel 32, W. M. Dry 33, C. V. English 33; E. A. E. Baptiste five for 60) and 306 (P. H. Barnard 42, B. N. Benkenstein 68, W. M. Dry 56; T. G. Shaw four for 67, G. T. Love four for 38). *Eastern Province 19 pts, Griqualand West 4 pts.*

At Springbok Park, Bloemfontein, November 29, 30, December 1, 2. Drawn. Western Province 446 (S. G. Koenig 52, J. H. Kallis 143, D. B. Rundle 81 not out, A. C. Dawson 59; J. F. Venter three for 94); Free State* 280 (G. F. J. Liebenberg 90, J. F. Venter 41, P. J. L. Radley 44; M. W. Pringle four for 61, A. Martyn four for 76) and 483 for two (D. Jordaan 80, G. F. J. Liebenberg 91, H. H. Dippenaar 151 not out, L. J. Wilkinson 139 not out). *Free State 4 pts, Western Province 7 pts.*

In Free State's second innings, Dippenaar and Wilkinson shared an unbroken stand of 300 for the third wicket.

At Centurion Park, Centurion, November 29, 30, December 1, 2. Natal won by 286 runs. Natal 360 (P. J. R. Steyn 45, E. L. R. Stewart 78, N. C. Johnson 69, S. M. Pollock 32, K. A. Forde 30, T. Bosch 31; S. Elworthy four for 71, R. E. Bryson three for 79) and 261 for nine dec. (E. L. R. Stewart 48, D. M. Benkenstein 87, S. M. Pollock 33; M. J. G. Davis three for 70); Northern Transvaal* 121 (G. M. Gilder five for 57, T. Bosch four for 19) and 214 (R. B. Richardson 68, M. J. R. Rindel 60; S. M. Pollock five for 48, A. G. Botha three for 39). *Natal 19 pts, Northern Transvaal 4 pts.*

At Wanderers Stadium, Johannesburg, November 29, 30, December 1. Transvaal won by an innings and three runs. Transvaal 308 (A. M. Bacher 58, N. D. McKenzie 80, D. R. Laing 76; R. Telemachus four for 71, C. W. Henderson four for 107); Boland* 146 (L. D. Ferreira 30, W. S. Truter 32; C. E. Eksteen four for 38) and 159 (D. J. Millns 32; R. E. Veenstra four for 48, A. J. Hall three for 14). *Transvaal 17 pts, Boland 3 pts.*

At Kingsmead, Durban, December 12, 13, 14. Natal won by eight wickets. Boland* 133 (D. J. Millns 42; S. M. Pollock four for 22, G. M. Gilder four for 36) and 201 (K. C. Jackson 43, R. C. Oosthuizen 32; G. M. Gilder five for 60); Natal 198 (D. M. Benkenstein 50, S. M. Pollock 33, K. A. Forde 32; D. J. Millns four for 64, H. S. Williams six for 57) and 137 for two (D. J. Watson 51 not out, J. N. Rhodes 40 not out). *Natal 15 pts, Boland 4 pts.*

At Kimberley Country Club, Kimberley, December 13, 14, 15, 16. Drawn. Free State* 493 (H. H. Dippenaar 50, L. J. Wilkinson 75, C. F. Craven 109, B. T. Player 133 not out; G. A. Roe three for 116); Griqualand West 340 (J. M. Arthur 57, M. I. Gidley 52, P. H. Barnard 52, W. M. Dry 42, R. A. Koster 37, B. N. Benkenstein 30; B. T. Player four for 41, J. F. Venter three for 112) and 222 for six (J. M. Arthur 39, M. I. Gidley 76 not out, R. A. Koster 41). *Griqualand West 6 pts, Free State 6 pts.*

At Wanderers Stadium, Johannesburg, December 13, 14, 15, 16. Transvaal won by 160 runs. Transvaal* 334 (D. R. Laing 128, A. J. Hall 60; L. D. Botha three for 52, E. A. E. Baptiste four for 65) and 272 for three dec. (A. M. Bacher 114, M. R. Benfield 43, N. D. McKenzie 53 not out); Eastern Province 261 (M. W. Rushmere 43, K. C. Wessels 51, G. Morgan 65 not out, T. G. Shaw 37; R. E. Veenstra five for 36) and 185 (L. J. Koen 75, D. J. Callaghan 34; C. E. Eksteen four for 74). *Transvaal 18 pts, Eastern Province 6 pts.*

At Newlands, Cape Town, December 13, 14, 15. Western Province won by eight wickets. Border 210 (P. J. Botha 34, M. V. Boucher 71; B. N. Schultz three for 61, A. C. Dawson three for 31) and 185 (M. V. Boucher 68 not out; M. W. Pringle four for 26, B. N. Schultz five for 69); Western Province* 290 (D. L. Haynes 99, C. R. Matthews 96; M. Ntini six for 49) and 106 for two (S. G. Koenig 42). *Western Province 17 pts, Border 6 pts.*

At Boland Bank Park, Paarl, December 26, 27, 28. Boland won by 55 runs. Boland* 170 (A. P. Kuiper 74; S. Elworthy three for 52) and 179 (L. D. Ferreira 38, K. C. Jackson 62; M. J. G. Davis six for 80); Northern Transvaal 117 (H. S. Williams four for 31, C. M. Willoughby three for 28) and 177 (M. van Jaarsveld 37, I. Pistorius 33, M. J. G. Davis 32; C. W. Henderson three for 52). *Boland 15 pts, Northern Transvaal 4 pts.*

At Buffalo Park, East London, December 29, 30, 31, January 1. Border won by five wickets. Transvaal* 291 (R. E. Veenstra 135 not out, A. J. Hall 78; P. J. Botha five for 38) and 162 (K. R. Rutherford 30, M. R. Benfield 53; V. C. Drakes three for 56, P. J. Botha four for 47); Border 319 for eight dec. (P. J. Botha 30, P. N. Kirsten 106, I. L. Howell 102 not out; E. W. Kidwell four for 97, S. Jacobs three for 42) and 135 for five (M. V. Boucher 44 not out, P. C. Strydom 45 not out; R. E. Veenstra three for 48). *Border 18 pts, Transvaal 6 pts.*

At St George's Park, Port Elizabeth, January 3, 4, 5, 6. Eastern Province won by five wickets. Western Province* 401 for two dec. (D. L. Haynes 202 not out, J. H. Kallis 94, H. D. Ackerman 45 not out, Extras 33) and 228 for six dec. (J. H. Kallis 79, H. D. Ackerman 102 not out; E. A. E. Baptiste three for 48); Eastern Province 300 for nine dec. (L. J. Koen 128, M. W. Rushmere 74, T. G. Shaw 37 not out; M. W. Pringle four for 79) and 331 for five (K. C. Wessels 179, D. J. Callaghan 88; M. W. Pringle three for 75). *Eastern Province 14 pts, Western Province 9 pts.*

Haynes's 202 not out, his sixth double-hundred, lasted 439 minutes and 333 balls and included 21 fours and four sixes.

At Kingsmead, Durban, January 3, 4, 5, 6. Drawn. Natal* 282 (J. N. Rhodes 33, D. M. Benkenstein 100, N. C. Johnson 50, P. L. Symcox 30) and 349 for seven dec. (M. L. Bruyns 48, D. N. Crookes 52, J. N. Rhodes 156 not out, D. J. Watson 33 not out); Free State 160 (H. H. Dippenaar 81; T. Bosch three for 40, P. L. Symcox three for 34) and 312 for nine (D. Jordaan 81, G. F. J. Liebenberg 34, H. H. Dippenaar 93, P. J. L. Radley 58 not out; D. N. Crookes seven for 114). *Natal 7 pts, Free State 5 pts.*

At Centurion Park, Centurion, January 10, 11, 12, 13. Border won by six wickets. Northern Transvaal 334 for seven dec. (B. J. Sommerville 62, A. J. Seymore 47, M. J. R. Rindel 33, D. J. van Zyl 57, S. Elworthy 51, M. J. G. Davis 38 not out) and 155 (A. J. Seymore 58, D. J. van Zyl 35; P. J. Botha five for 35); Border* 271 for five dec. (P. J. Botha 62, P. B. du Plessis 33, P. N. Kirsten 49, M. V. Boucher 45, P. C. Strydom 52 not out) and 220 for four (B. M. White 63, P. J. Botha 77, P. N. Kirsten 36). *Border 16 pts, Northern Transvaal 6 pts.*

At Buffalo Park, East London, January 17, 18, 19, 20. Drawn. Border* 331 (P. C. Strydom 100, S. C. Pope 103, I. L. Howell 46; H. S. Williams four for 74, C. J. Vorster three for 76) and 201 for four dec. (P. J. Botha 34, B. M. White 54, M. V. Boucher 68 not out); Boland 277 (W. S. Truter 95, K. C. Jackson 44, A. R. Wylie 74; P. A. N. Emslie three for 36) and 219 for seven (L. D. Ferreira 53, A. Wessels 44, K. C. Jackson 90 not out; I. L. Howell three for 46). *Border 6 pts, Boland 6 pts.*

At St George's Park, Port Elizabeth, January 17, 18, 19. Natal won by an innings and 46 runs. Eastern Province* 265 (L. J. Koen 43, K. C. Wessels 61, M. W. Rushmere 37; D. N. Crookes four for 62) and 118 (E. A. E. Baptiste 39; D. N. Crookes three for 27, P. L. Symcox four for 26); Natal 429 (D. J. Watson 47, E. L. R. Stewart 138, J. N. Rhodes 108, P. L. Symcox 45 not out; E. A. E. Baptiste three for 77). *Natal 18 pts, Eastern Province 4 pts.*

At Springbok Park, Bloemfontein, January 17, 18, 19. Free State won by 192 runs. Free State 251 (D. Jordaan 57, C. F. Craven 64, J. F. Venter 40; E. W. Kidwell four for 54, R. E. Veenstra three for 61) and 246 (D. Jordaan 66, J. F. Venter 57, N. Boje 33; A. J. Hall three for 51, S. Jacobs three for 52); Transvaal* 197 (N. Pothas 100 not out; N. W. Pretorius three for 29, B. T. Player three for 42) and 108 (N. W. Pretorius four for 26, S. A. Cilliers three for 24). *Free State 17 pts, Transvaal 5 pts.*

At Kimberley Country Club, Kimberley, January 17, 18, 19. Western Province won by an innings and five runs. Griqualand West 298 (M. I. Gidley 117, W. M. Dry 31, C. V. English 51; C. R. Matthews four for 44) and 167 (J. M. Arthur 46; B. N. Schultz five for 49, C. R. Matthews three for 34); Western Province* 470 for five dec. (D. L. Haynes 91, J. H. Kallis 40 not out, H. H. Gibbs 49, J. B. Commins 200 not out, H. D. Ackerman 47). *Western Province 19 pts, Griqualand West 4 pts.*

Pieter Koortzen of Griqualand West took a wicket with his first ball in first-class cricket. Commins's 200 not out, his maiden double-hundred, lasted 287 minutes and 233 balls and included 14 fours and eight sixes.

At Springbok Park, Bloemfontein, February 1, 2, 3, 4. Drawn. Free State 401 (D. Jordaan 68, J. F. Venter 101, N. Boje 34, H. C. Bakkes 35, P. J. L. Radley 38) and 273 for nine dec. (D. Jordaan 117, G. F. J. Liebenberg 46, H. H. Dippenaar 54; P. C. Strydom four for 52); Border* 367 for nine dec. (B. M. White 37, P. J. Botha 136, P. N. Kirsten 56, M. V. Boucher 53; H. C. Bakkes six for 43) and 222 for five (B. M. White 38, P. C. Strydom 31, S. C. Pope 68 not out, I. L. Howell 36 not out). *Free State 7 pts, Border 7 pts.*

At Kingsmead, Durban, February 1, 2, 3. Natal won by an innings and 156 runs. Griqualand West 91 (J. M. Arthur 37; T. Bosch five for 15) and 166 (C. V. English 41, P. H. Barnard 33, R. A. Koster 30; D. N. Crookes five for 43); Natal* 413 for three dec. (D. J. Watson 52, E. L. R. Stewart 82, D. N. Crookes 128 not out, D. M. Benkenstein 101 not out). *Natal 20 pts, Griqualand West 1 pt.*

At Boland Bank Park, Paarl, February 2, 3, 4, 5. Eastern Province won by six wickets. Boland* 204 (K. C. Jackson 120; E. A. E. Baptiste three for 38, A. Badenhorst three for 52) and 237 (A. P. Kuiper 82, A. R. Wylie 61; T. G. Shaw three for 52); Eastern Province 262 (M. G. Beamish 38, M. W. Rushmere 89 not out, G. Morgan 64; J. D. Albanie four for 37, C. W. Henderson three for 79, A. P. Kuiper three for 56) and 181 for four (M. G. Beamish 76, L. J. Koen 40 not out; C. J. Vorster three for 44). *Eastern Province 16 pts, Boland 5 pts.*

At Kimberley Country Club, Kimberley, February 7, 8, 9, 10. Griqualand West won by ten wickets. Northern Transvaal 363 (A. J. Seymore 132, M. van Jaarsveld 109, S. Elworthy 34; V. A. Walsh three for 87, G. A. Roe four for 74) and 185 (M. van Jaarsveld 30, M. J. R. Rindel 35; A. J. Swanepoel three for 31); Griqualand West* 541 for six dec. (M. I. Gidley 61, P. H. Barnard 212, W. M. Dry 74, F. C. Brooker 45, B. N. Benkenstein 62 not out; M. J. G. Davis three for 116) and ten for no wkt. *Griqualand West 16 pts, Northern Transvaal 4 pts.*

Barnard's 212, his maiden double-hundred, lasted 408 minutes and 329 balls and included 26 fours and two sixes.

At Wanderers Stadium, Johannesburg, February 8, 9, 10, 11. Drawn. Transvaal* 371 (N. D. McKenzie 139, S. Jacobs 85; B. N. Schultz five for 64) and 263 for eight dec. (M. R. Benfield 33, C. E. Eksteen 32, K. R. Rutherford 126 not out); Western Province 227 (H. H. Gibbs 47, E. O. Simons 80, P. Kirsten 50; E. W. Kidwell three for 34, C. E. Eksteen four for 65) and 352 for seven (H. H. Gibbs 103, H. D. Ackerman 122, E. O. Simons 58 not out; R. A. Lyle three for 40). *Transvaal 5 pts, Western Province 5 pts.*

At Boland Bank Park, Paarl, February 14, 15, 16, 17. Boland won by five wickets. Free State* 254 (H. H. Dippenaar 46, L. J. Wilkinson 46, J. F. Venter 59, W. J. Cronje 45; H. S. Williams five for 48) and 264 (D. Jordaan 44, G. F. J. Liebenberg 35, H. H. Dippenaar 40, W. J. Cronje 52, H. C. Bakkes 43; C. J. Vorster three for 51); Boland 264 (B. C. Baguley 77, A. P. Kuiper 49, M. M. Brink 34, C. J. Vorster 49; J. F. Venter six for 96) and 256 for five (W. S. Truter 33, A. P. Kuiper 117 not out, A. Wessels 56 not out; J. F. Venter four for 109). *Boland 17 pts, Free State 7 pts.*

At Buffalo Park, East London, February 14, 15, 16, 17. Border won by 40 runs. Border* 400 (P. J. Botha 34, P. N. Kirsten 173 not out, S. C. Pope 38, I. L. Howell 46, D. Taljard 32; G. A. Roe three for 84, M. I. Gidley three for 59) and 192 for five dec. (P. J. Botha 90 not out, S. C. Pope 30); Griqualand West 253 (J. M. Arthur 37, P. H. Barnard 79, F. C. Brooker 38; D. Taljard three for 33) and 299 (J. M. Arthur 67, W. Bossenger 82, C. V. English 31, P. H. Barnard 30; M. Ntini four for 73, D. Taljard three for 34). *Border 18 pts, Griqualand West 4 pts.*

At St George's Park, Port Elizabeth, February 14, 15, 16, 17. Eastern Province won by 206 runs. Eastern Province* 432 for nine dec. (M. G. Beamish 37, C. C. Bradfield 38, L. J. Koen 87, K. C. Wessels 58, M. W. Rushmere 66, D. J. Richardson 41, E. A. E. Baptiste 50; R. E. Bryson three for 77, S. Elworthy four for 95) and 161 for two dec. (C. C. Bradfield 50 not out, L. J. Koen 75); Northern Transvaal 272 (R. F. Pienaar 30, G. Dros 54, R. B. Richardson 69, D. J. J. de Vos 31 not out; E. A. E. Baptiste five for 56) and 115 (E. A. E. Baptiste five for 37). *Eastern Province 16 pts, Northern Transvaal 4 pts.*

At Wanderers Stadium, Johannesburg, February 14, 15, 16, 17. Natal won by 145 runs. Natal* 407 (D. J. Watson 42, J. N. Rhodes 137, N. C. Johnson 34, L. Klusener 38; C. E. Eksteen five for 83) and 241 for eight dec. (A. C. Hudson 49, J. N. Rhodes 43, L. Klusener 33; C. E. Eksteen four for 75); Transvaal 241 (A. M. Bacher 35, K. R. Rutherford 88; L. Klusener four for 61, S. M. Pollock four for 58) and 262 (A. M. Bacher 43, D. J. Cullinan 78, Z. de Bruyn 39, N. Pothas 38; S. M. Pollock four for 61, P. L. Symcox four for 76). *Natal 19 pts, Transvaal 5 pts.*

Rhodes's 137 was his third hundred in successive first-class innings.

At Springbok Park, Bloemfontein, March 7, 8, 9, 10. Free State won by 74 runs. Free State 178 (D. Jordaan 42, M. N. van Wyk 49, N. Boje 31; A. Badenhorst four for 39) and 275 (G. F. J. Liebenberg 85, W. J. Cronje 40, M. N. van Wyk 31; T. G. Shaw four for 81, E. A. E. Baptiste three for 61); Eastern Province* 198 (L. J. Koen 57, K. C. Wessels 57; N. W. Pretorius three for 59, S. A. Cilliers five for 69) and 181 (M. W. Rushmere 40, E. A. E. Baptiste 48, T. G. Shaw 40). *Free State 15 pts, Eastern Province 5 pts.*

At Centurion Park, Centurion, March 7, 8, 9, 10. Drawn. Transvaal 201 for six dec. (A. M. Bacher 102, A. J. Hall 44 not out; S. Elworthy three for 42) and 71 for one (N. D. McKenzie 43 not out); Northern Transvaal* 164 (R. F. Pienaar 55, M. van Jaarsveld 38; E. W. Kidwell four for 58, R. E. Veenstra three for 45). *Northern Transvaal 3 pts, Transvaal 6 pts.*

At Newlands, Cape Town, March 7, 8, 9, 10. Drawn. Western Province 433 for three dec. (D. L. Haynes 83, J. H. Kallis 138, H. H. Gibbs 163 not out) and 222 (B. M. McMillan 63, C. R. Matthews 64; D. N. Crookes three for 72); Natal* 359 (A. C. Hudson 32, N. C. Johnson 52, D. M. Benkenstein 46, D. N. Crookes 96, E. L. R. Stewart 44; B. N. Schultz three for 95) and 55 for one (A. C. Hudson 35 not out). *Western Province 6 pts, Natal 4 pts.*

Gibbs added 116 to his overnight score on the second morning. He and Kallis added 257 for Western Province's third wicket.

CHAMPIONS

Currie Cup			
1889-90	Transvaal	1955-56	Western Province
1890-91	Kimberley	1958-59	Transvaal
1892-93	Western Province	1959-60	Natal
1893-94	Western Province	1960-61	Natal
1894-95	Transvaal	1962-63	Natal
1896-97	Western Province	1963-64	Natal
1897-98	Western Province	1965-66	Natal/Transvaal (Tied)
1902-03	Transvaal	1966-67	Natal
1903-04	Transvaal	1967-68	Natal
1904-05	Transvaal	1968-69	Transvaal
1906-07	Transvaal	1969-70	Transvaal/W. Province (Tied)
1908-09	Western Province	1970-71	Transvaal
1910-11	Natal	1971-72	Transvaal
1912-13	Natal	1972-73	Transvaal
1920-21	Western Province	1973-74	Natal
1921-22	Transvaal/Natal/W. Prov. (Tied)	1974-75	Western Province
1923-24	Transvaal	1975-76	Natal
1925-26	Transvaal	1976-77	Natal
1926-27	Transvaal	1977-78	Western Province
1929-30	Transvaal	1978-79	Transvaal
1931-32	Western Province	1979-80	Transvaal
1933-34	Natal	1980-81	Natal
1934-35	Transvaal	1981-82	Western Province
1936-37	Natal	1982-83	Transvaal
1937-38	Natal/Transvaal (Tied)	1983-84	Transvaal
1946-47	Natal	1984-85	Transvaal
1947-48	Natal	1985-86	Western Province
1950-51	Transvaal	1986-87	Transvaal
1951-52	Natal	1987-88	Transvaal
1952-53	Western Province	1988-89	Eastern Province
1954-55	Natal	1989-90	E. Province/W. Province (Shared)

Castle Cup

1990-91	Western Province	1994-95	Natal
1991-92	Eastern Province	1995-96	Western Province
1992-93	Orange Free State	*Supersport Series*	
1993-94	Orange Free State	1996-97	Natal

Transvaal have won the title outright 24 times, Natal 20, Western Province 15, Eastern Province and Orange Free State 2, Kimberley 1. The title has been shared five times as follows: Transvaal 4, Natal and Western Province 3, Eastern Province 1.

UCB BOWL, 1996-97

Division 1

	Played	Won	Lost	Drawn	Bonus Points Batting	Bonus Points Bowling	Points
Eastern Province B	5	2	1	2	21	17	57†
Easterns	5	2	1	2	17	15	52
Natal B	5	1	1	3	15	20	43†
North West	5	1	1	3	15	18	42†
Western Province B	5	1	2	2	16	16	42
Transvaal B	5	0	1	4	19	16	35

Division 2 (not first-class)

	Played	Won	Lost	Drawn	Bonus Points Batting	Bonus Points Bowling	Points
Northern Transvaal B	5	2	1	2	14	15	48†
Zimbabwe Board XI	5*	2	1	1	15	10	44†
Free State B	5*	1	1	2	14	15	37†
Border B	5	1	0	4	12	16	35†
Namibia	5	0	2	3	15	18	33
Boland B	5	0	1	4	15	15	30

* The match between Zimbabwe Board XI and Free State B was abandoned.
Northern Transvaal B were promoted in place of Transvaal B.

Outright win = 10 pts.
Bonus points are awarded for the first 85 overs of each team's first innings. One batting point is awarded for the first 100 runs and for every subsequent 50. One bowling point is awarded for the second wicket taken and for every subsequent two up to eight.
† Points deducted for slow over-rate.

Note: First innings closed at 100 overs.

*In the following scores, * by the name of a team indicates that they won the toss.*

Division 1

At Wanderers Stadium, Johannesburg, October 31, November 1, 2. Eastern Province B won by six wickets. Transvaal B 277 (M. R. Benfield 41, G. A. Pollock 115; P. P. Bruce three for 55) and 247 (M. R. Benfield 122, D. R. Gain 62; G. T. Love three for 65, A. V. Birrell five for 62); Eastern Province B* 401 for four dec. (P. G. Amm 105, M. G. Beamish 164, G. C. Victor 95) and 125 for four (G. C. Victor 69 not out). *Eastern Province B 21 pts, Transvaal B 6 pts.*

At Willowmoore Park, Benoni, November 1, 2, 3. Easterns won by 180 runs. Easterns* 290 for seven (C. R. Norris 75, T. A. Marsh 39, T. Blake 64 not out, G. P. Cooke 36; M. J. Lavine four for 58) and 302 for six dec. (M. J. Mitchley 55, C. R. Norris 55, A. G. Pollock 36, T. A. Marsh 52 not out, G. Myburgh 45; L. C. R. Jordaan three for 78); North West 290 (L. P. Vorster 30, M. J. Lavine 107, M. Strydom 87; J. R. Meyer three for 56, C. R. Norris four for 72) and 122 (C. R. Norris four for 14, P. V. Simmons three for 43). *Easterns 17 pts, North West 7 pts.*

At Kingsmead, Durban, November 14, 15, 16. Drawn. Natal B 251 for six (J. Buxton-Forman 70, N. J. Parsons 84, A. G. Botha 41 not out) and 178 for five (C. B. Sugden 85 not out, U. H. Goedeke 40; B. N. Schultz three for 43); Western Province B* 277 (R. Maron 41, S. Hofmeyr 30, F. Davids 65, G. de Kock 36; G. M. Gilder four for 66, K. G. Storey three for 82). *Natal B 5 pts, Western Province B 6 pts.*

At Wanderers Stadium, Johannesburg, November 15, 16, 17. Drawn. North West 160 (E. G. Poole 33; A. J. Hall four for 29) and 254 (S. Nicolson 70, M. Strydom 30, L. P. Vorster 69; A. J. Hall three for 74, A. V. Griffiths three for 61); Transvaal B* 247 for eight dec. (D. R. Gain 82, R. P. Snell 35, A. J. Hall 48 not out; D. Rossouw five for 61) and 53 for three. *Transvaal B 7 pts, North West 5 pts.*

At Kingsmead, Durban, November 28, 29, 30. Eastern Province B won by seven wickets. Natal B* 225 (J. Buxton-Forman 60, G. S. Katz 42, U. H. Goedeke 52; A. Badenhorst four for 51, A. V. Birrell four for 46) and 203 (M. Badat 45, G. S. Katz 54, R. B. MacQueen 42; L. D. Botha six for 59); Eastern Province B 174 (A. G. Prince 34, G. C. Victor 30; K. G. Storey five for 51, R. B. MacQueen four for 44) and 255 for three (C. C. Bradfield 39, A. G. Prince 125 not out, G. C. Victor 51). *Eastern Province B 16 pts, Natal B 7 pts.*

At Newlands, Cape Town, November 29, 30, December 1. Easterns won by 28 runs. Easterns* 304 for nine dec. (M. J. Mitchley 201 not out, C. R. Norris 50; D. G. Payne three for 68, D. Q. MacHelm three for 90) and 96 (C. R. Norris 31; D. G. Payne five for 26); Western Province B 191 (H. Pangarker 34, G. de Kock 50; J. R. Meyer six for 43) and 181 (H. Pangarker 44; C. R. Norris four for 47). *Easterns 19 pts, Western Province B 6 pts.*

Mitchley's 201 not out, his maiden double-hundred, lasted 335 minutes and 244 balls and included 31 fours and two sixes.

At Old Grey, Port Elizabeth, December 12, 13, 14. Western Province B won by ten wickets. Eastern Province B* 241 (M. G. Beamish 108, C. N. du Plessis 30, A. V. Birrell 34; D. B. Rundle three for 57) and 178 (A. G. Prince 78, P. Botha 40; D. B. Rundle three for 42, G. de Kock three for eight); Western Province B 298 (F. Davids 52 retired not out, H. Pangarker 92, S. Hofmeyr 51; A. Badenhorst three for 81, P. Botha three for 43, S. Abrahams three for 81) and 123 for no wkt (R. Maron 65 not out, F. B. Touzel 52 not out). *Western Province B 18 pts, Eastern Province B 6 pts.*

Davids retired overnight in order to join the senior Western Province team in their match against Border.

At Witrand Cricket Field, Potchefstroom, December 12, 13, 14. Drawn. Natal B 299 for eight (B. A. Nash 64, U. H. Goedeke 102 not out, K. G. Storey 34 not out) and 142 (G. S. Katz 58; M. Strydom six for 55); North West* 210 (G. M. Hewitt 52, M. Strydom 34, E. G. Poole 43; K. G. Storey seven for 58, R. B. MacQueen three for 95) and 73 for two (M. Strydom 37 not out). *North West 7 pts, Natal B 7 pts.*

At Willowmoore Park, Benoni, December 13, 14, 15. Drawn. Easterns 340 (M. J. Mitchley 119, G. Myburgh 32, T. A. Marsh 61, A. G. Pollock 30; S. Jacobs five for 63) and 274 for seven dec. (J. S. Lerm 30, P. V. Simmons 102, G. Myburgh 44; N. A. Fusedale three for 92); Transvaal B* 301 for five dec. (H. A. Manack 137 not out, G. Brophy 68, D. R. Gain 46; A. G. Pollock three for 40) and 129 for three (J. M. Henderson 30, Z. de Bruyn 70 not out). *Easterns 7 pts, Transvaal B 8 pts.*

At St George's Park, Port Elizabeth, January 10, 11, 12. Drawn. Easterns* 231 (C. R. Norris 61, P. V. Simmons 35, J. J. van der Watt 31; G. T. Love four for 51, A. V. Birrell three for 76) and 282 for nine (M. J. Mitchley 34, J. S. Lerm 38, T. A. Marsh 30, A. G. Pollock 56 not out; A. V. Birrell eight for 134); Eastern Province B 350 for three dec. (M. G. Beamish 105, C. C. Bradfield 163, J. Bryant 48 not out). *Eastern Province B 8 pts, Easterns 4 pts.*

At Kingsmead, Durban, January 16, 17, 18. Drawn. Transvaal B 249 (R. P. Snell 31, G. Elliott 67, N. A. Fusedale 44; K. G. Storey four for 65); Natal B* 253 for eight (J. Buxton-Forman 41, C. B. Sugden 71, B. A. Nash 44; Z. de Bruyn three for 58, N. A. Fusedale three for 59). *Natal B 7 pts, Transvaal B 7 pts.*

At Newlands, Cape Town, January 17, 18. North West won by 27 runs. North West* 116 (L. P. Vorster 33; D. G. Payne five for 20) and 221 (M. Strydom 91, D. Rossouw 49, M. van Schalkwyk 31; D. G. Payne three for 57); Western Province B 193 (H. Pangarker 31, F. Davids 33, M. T. Solomons 32, D. G. Payne 41 not out; M. J. Lavine three for 57, M. van Schalkwyk four for 17) and 117 (R. Maron 34; F. Baird four for 33, D. Rossouw four for 30). *North West 15 pts, Western Province B 6 pts.*

At Newlands, Cape Town, February 5, 6, 7. Drawn. Transvaal B* 385 for seven (H. A. Manack 173, D. R. Gain 42, R. P. Snell 46, N. A. Fusedale 44 not out; D. Q. MacHelm three for 76) and 256 (D. R. Gain 47, Z. de Bruyn 34, R. P. Snell 52, G. H. Bodi 33; G. de Kock three for 29); Western Province B 350 for eight (H. Pangarker 144, F. Davids 38, G. de Kock 67, D. G. Payne 33 not out; Z. de Bruyn six for 120). *Western Province B 6 pts, Transvaal B 7 pts.*

At Fanie du Toit Stadium, Potchefstroom, February 13, 14, 15. Drawn. Eastern Province B* 300 for nine dec. (D. Sontundu 47, A. G. Prince 51, G. C. Victor 63, C. N. du Plessis 42; M. Strydom three for 77) and 273 (G. C. Victor 79, G. Morgan 39, C. N. du Plessis 46, J. Kemp 35; J. N. Dreyer three for 64); North West 373 for eight dec. (M. Strydom 129, B. D. Esterhuysen 58, M. C. Venter 46, M. J. Lavine 49; A. V. Birrell three for 94) and 162 for eight (S. Nicolson 57, M. C. Venter 30; G. T. Love three for 36, A. V. Birrell four for 75). *North West 8 pts, Eastern Province B 6 pts.*

At Willowmoore Park, Benoni, February 14, 15, 16. Natal B won by 176 runs. Natal B 227 (M. L. Bruyns 48, B. A. Nash 51; A. G. Pollock four for 52) and 244 for one dec. (M. L. Bruyns 103, P. J. R. Steyn 100 not out); Easterns* 149 (K. G. Storey four for 39, A. G. Botha three for 15) and 146 (G. Myburgh 35, J. S. Lerm 32; K. G. Storey three for 31, A. G. Botha four for 52). *Natal B 17 pts, Easterns 5 pts.*

OTHER FIRST-CLASS MATCHES

Natal v Leicestershire (March 25, 26, 27) and Transvaal v Nottinghamshire (April 11, 12, 13) may be found in English Counties Overseas, 1996-97.

Note: Matches in the following two competitions were not first-class.

STANDARD BANK LEAGUE, 1996-97

	Played	Won	Lost	No Result	Points
Northern Transvaal	10	8	2	0	16
Western Province	10	8	2	0	16
Natal	10	6	2	2	14
Eastern Province	10	5	1	4	14
Griqualand West	10	5	4	1	11
Transvaal	10	4	5	1	9
Free State	10	3	6	1	7
Boland	10	3	6	1	7
Border	10	3	6	1	7
North West	10	2	7	1	5
Easterns	10	1	7	2	4

Northern Transvaal finished ahead of Western Province by virtue of winning their head-to-head match. Natal finished ahead of Eastern Province by virtue of more wins.

STANDARD BANK CUP, 1996-97

Quarter-finals

At Newlands, Cape Town, February 19 (day/night). Western Province won by eight runs. Western Province* 188 (44.5 overs) (J. H. Kallis 50, J. B. Commins 30; S. Jacobs three for 28); Transvaal 180 for eight (45 overs) (N. Pothas 44, A. J. Hall 57 not out).

At St George's Park, Port Elizabeth, February 26 (day/night). Eastern Province's target having been revised to 243 from 41 overs. Mashonaland won by three runs. Mashonaland 268 for eight (45 overs) (G. W. Flower 100, E. A. Brandes 32 not out; M. Hayward three for 47); Eastern Province* 239 for nine (41 overs) (G. C. Victor 62, M. W. Rushmere 64).

At Kimberley Country Club, Kimberley, March 5 (day/night). No result. Northern Transvaal* 237 for seven (45 overs) (M. J. R. Rindel 62, M. van Jaarsveld 38, D. J. Smith 30 not out; A. J. Swanepoel three for 52); Griqualand West four for no wkt (0.1 over).
Replayed on March 21.

At Kingsmead, Durban, March 12 (day/night). Natal won by 104 runs. Natal 240 for six (45 overs) (D. J. Watson 85, D. N. Crookes 72; B. Patel three for 19); Kenya* 136 (42.5 overs) (N. C. Johnson four for 19, P. L. Symcox three for 22).

At Kimberley Country Club, Kimberley, March 21 (day/night). Northern Transvaal won by 123 runs. Northern Transvaal* 233 for five (45 overs) (M. J. R. Rindel 109, R. F. Pienaar 47, D. J. J. de Vos 30 not out; A. J. Swanepoel three for 43); Griqualand West 110 (35 overs) (R. A. Koster 59; S. Elworthy three for 22, R. E. Bryson four for 17).

Semi-finals

At Kingsmead, Durban, April 18 (day/night). Natal won by 75 runs, Mashonaland's target having been revised to 211 from 26 overs. Natal* 309 for eight (45 overs) (L. Klusener 36, N. C. Johnson 86, D. N. Crookes 30; J. N. Rhodes 85; E. A. Brandes three for 51); Mashonaland 135 for seven (26 overs) (A. D. R. Campbell 55 not out; P. L. Symcox three for 19).

At Centurion Park, Centurion, April 20. No result. Western Province* 230 for seven (45 overs) (H. H. Gibbs 39, J. H. Kallis 86, H. D. Ackerman 32, E. O. Simons 30; P. S. de Villiers three for 41); Northern Transvaal 30 for no wkt (4.3 overs).
Replayed on April 21.

At Centurion Park, Centurion, April 21. Western Province won by 73 runs. Western Province* 215 for seven (45 overs) (H. D. Ackerman 57, B. M. McMillan 33, E. O. Simons 59 not out; S. Elworthy three for 28); Northern Transvaal 142 (34.2 overs) (M. van Jaarsveld 41, A. J. Seymore 34; A. C. Dawson three for 30).

Finals

At Newlands, Cape Town, April 25 (day/night). Western Province won by six wickets. Natal* 174 (42.1 overs) (L. Klusener 34, N. C. Johnson 49, D. M. Benkenstein 30; E. O. Simons three for 24); Western Province 175 for four (42.3 overs) (G. Kirsten 62, H. H. Gibbs 30, J. H. Kallis 43).

At Kingsmead, Durban, April 27. Natal won by three wickets. Western Province* 238 for seven (45 overs) (G. Kirsten 63, H. H. Gibbs 40, H. D. Ackerman 42, B. M. McMillan 31); Natal 239 for seven (44.2 overs) (A. C. Hudson 37, D. J. Watson 60, J. N. Rhodes 46 not out).

At Kingsmead, Durban, April 28. Natal won by two wickets. Western Province 228 for eight (45 overs) (G. Kirsten 33, J. H. Kallis 56, H. D. Ackerman 40, E. O. Simons 35); Natal* 232 for eight (44.2 overs) (D. J. Watson 53, P. L. Symcox 40, J. N. Rhodes 31, D. M. Benkenstein 37 not out).

COCA-COLA CRICKET WEEK, 1996-97

South Africa's 54th annual Cricket Week, formerly known as Nuffield Week, reverted to concentrating on Under-18 cricket, after two years during which Under-19 players had taken part. For the first time, matches were organised in two competitive leagues, with ten teams in each. The hosts, Easterns, took the Gold Cup and Western Province, who won all their five matches, the Platinum Cup. At the end of the week, a South African Schools XI was selected to play a 50-over game against Easterns, who won by one wicket.

The team was: P. K. Hearle (Transvaal, *captain*), J. de Nobrega (Western Province), C. Jantjes (Easterns), P. Joubert (Northern Transvaal), M. Morkel (Transvaal), R. Munnik (Western Province), T. Ngxoweni (Border), R. Sierra (Transvaal), M. Street (Transvaal), A. van der Berg (Transvaal), J. J. van der Wath (Easterns). Twelfth man R. Petersen (Eastern Province).

CRICKET IN THE WEST INDIES, 1996-97

By TONY COZIER

Floyd Reifer

With home series against India and Sri Lanka, comprising seven Tests and five one-day internationals, and the Red Stripe Cup expanded from 16 matches to 30, the 1996-97 season was the longest and most congested West Indies cricket has known. For a host of reasons, many unexpected and unavoidable, it proved too much.

The West Indies Cricket Board had long recognised that the five first-class matches provided by the previous format of the Red Stripe Cup, in which the six teams played each other only once, were inadequate either for a decent competition or for the proper development of players. But the lack of funds had precluded an enlargement until increased sponsorship, mainly from Cable & Wireless, and the revenue from television rights helped turn around the Board's financial position.

As it happened, rain, which also affected both Test series, completely eliminated Guyana's first three home games, effectively destroying their chances of the championship and reducing those of their visitors. Meanwhile, Barbados reeled off three successive victories to build a virtually insurmountable lead, with the unfortunate consequence of appreciably diminishing interest among players and public. The situation was compounded by disruptive breaks – of up to 26 days – to accommodate the Tests and one-day internationals against India.

Attendances declined so much that they could be reckoned in dozens, rather than hundreds or thousands, even though admission prices were significantly reduced and, in some last-round matches, erased altogether. At its annual meeting in May, the Board promised a new format for 1997-98 that "should provide for a more exciting and interesting competition for the public and the sponsors as well as the cricketers themselves". The WICB's vice-president, Alloy Lequay, observed that the players had not enjoyed the expanded season any more than the spectators. In fact, the 1997-98 programme reverted to the old format of the teams playing each other only once.

The players' attitudes were reflected in the inconsistency of team and individual performances, the worrying decline in batting standards and the absence from the later games, through injury or just plain tiredness, of some of the leading players. In the 27 Cup matches played, there were only four totals above 400, against 34 instances of teams bowled out for under 200, of which 15 were below 150. This batting deficiency was mirrored in the seven Tests against India and Sri Lanka, in which West Indies managed just one total over 400 and three under 200. Only ten batsmen averaged 40 or more, of whom eight had already earned international caps. Floyd Reifer, the tall, upright Barbadian who had toured Sri Lanka with the A team late in 1996, was the tournament's leading scorer with 756 at 44.47, and earned selection for the two Tests against Sri Lanka; Suruj Ragoonath, the attacking Trinidad & Tobago opener in his ninth season, was the only other non-international batsman to reach the 40 barrier, though Philo Wallace of Barbados, with 709 at 39.38, was close.

Rohan Kanhai, the former Test captain now coaching Jamaica, noted that generally substandard pitches affected the younger players. "We need our young batsmen to play on good pitches to improve their technique and confidence," he said. "When you have slow pitches, you can't ask them to go out and play shots."

One of Kanhai's charges was the only new batsman to create an impression – Leon Garrick, aged 20, who hit hundreds opening for Jamaica against Trinidad & Tobago and the touring Indians in the space of a couple of weeks. But the long season took its toll: he finished with a pair against Barbados, and a Cup average below 30. Two promising young left-handers, Barbadian Adrian Griffith, just back from the Australian trip, and Tony Powell of Jamaica, who had been on the A tour of Sri Lanka, were eventually dropped from their island teams; the Leewards' captain Dave Joseph, another seemingly on the edge of Test selection, declined so markedly that he averaged only 17.92.

In the circumstances, it was a season for bowlers. As Curtly Ambrose and Courtney Walsh reached the twilight of their careers and injuries sidelined three fast bowlers who had toured Australia – Kenny Benjamin, Cameron Cuffy and Nixon McLean – three more emerged to scotch fears that the long-standing legacy of pace was at an end. Franklyn Rose, the tall, athletic Jamaican, returned after a self-imposed absence in 1995-96 to become the Cup's leading wicket-taker with 45 at 15.42 and make an impressive entry into the Test side. He was joined in two Tests by another well-built fast bowler, 22-year-old Mervyn Dillon of Trinidad & Tobago, whose 32 wickets in his debut season confirmed Malcolm Marshall's assessment of his potential after seeing him bowl for Hampshire's Second Eleven. Reon King, 21, who had shown promise in the Under-19 series against England in 1994-95, made an emphatic return for Guyana in their last four Cup matches, with 18 wickets, and took seven for 82 against the Indians.

Ottis Gibson, the experienced all-rounder who spearheaded Barbados's varied attack, took 44 wickets, only one behind Rose, but, as usual, spinners were also prominent. Four orthodox left-armers, Winston Reid of Barbados, Warrington Phillip of the Leewards, Roy Marshall of the Windwards and Neil McGarrell of Guyana, and the young leg-spinners Dinanath Ramnarine of Trinidad & Tobago, Mahendra Nagamootoo of Guyana and Rawl Lewis of the Windwards were all extensively used and all had more than 25 wickets. Yet spin was again all but ignored by the Test selectors. Lewis, who enjoyed a successful A tour of Sri Lanka, was included in the squad for all five Tests against India without making the side.

Barbados, led by opening batsman Wallace, achieved their 15th championship since the inauguration of the Shell Shield in 1965-66 by winning six of their ten matches outright. Their flying start came before the return of the West Indies squad from Australia. Such a sequence prompted public debate as to whether their five tourists – former captain Courtney Browne, Sherwin Campbell, Roland

Holder, Griffith and Patterson Thompson – should be reinstated automatically on their return. Predictably, they were: Barbados were promptly beaten, at home in three days, by the Leeward Islands, fuelling more critical comment.

It was to be a temporary setback. They formalised their success in the penultimate round by inflicting on the woeful Windwards the first two-day defeat in a regional match since 1938-39. Their celebrations when they received the Cup were a little muted, though; they had just lost their final match, at home to Jamaica, who thus ensured second place.

The Leeward Islands were weakened by injuries to their two Test fast bowlers, which limited Ambrose to three matches and Benjamin to one. This hampered their efforts to regain the Cup they had won the previous year, when they benefited from what turned out to have been a short-lived experiment, a Cup final, to beat table-leaders Trinidad & Tobago. Yet the Leewards clinched third place with a comprehensive three-day victory over the Trinidadians on a substandard pitch at the Queen's Park Oval, when they were missing both star bowlers plus Test opener Stuart Williams.

There was continuing concern over the Windward Islands, the only team never to have won the regional first-class title. They lost eight of their nine matches outright (their fixture in Guyana was rained off), and were all out under 200 twelve times. Oddly, their captain, Test wicket-keeper Junior Murray, registered the highest score of the season, 218, in their last match against Guyana, who were also without a win, and their fast bowler Casper Davis had the best individual figures, seven for 58 against Jamaica.

The limited-overs tournament for the Shell/Sandals Trophy was also enlarged – by the admission of ICC Associates Canada and Bermuda – but this was completed without a hitch. Staged in October, it was divided into two groups of four teams, the leaders meeting in the final. As in 1995-96, when rain obliged them to share the title, Guyana and Trinidad & Tobago qualified, but this time it was an epic match. Phil Simmons scored an unbeaten 80 off 67 balls, but Guyana appeared on course for victory until they lost their last six wickets for six runs; they were beaten by only nine runs when leg-spinner Rajindra Dhanraj took a hat-trick in the final over.

Neither Bermuda, coached by the former Australian captain and coach Bob Simpson, nor Canada won a match, but neither was disgraced. Bermuda came within three runs of victory in their opening game against the Windwards while Canada dismissed Trinidad & Tobago, led by Brian Lara and including Simmons and Ragoonath, for 194 but could not reach their target.

Consolidating its development programme, the WICB repeated the Under-15 tournament, introduced the previous year; Barbados foreshadowed their seniors' success by taking the title in March. The Board also announced that it would arrange more regular tours for its A and Under-19 teams and appointed former Jamaica and West Indies off-spinner Reg Scarlett administrator of coaching. Scarlett, now 62 and well-known for his work in the development of grassroots cricket at the Haringey Cricket College in London, was to co-ordinate a more structured programme through a cadre of regional coaches.

The A team visited Sri Lanka at the end of 1996, winning two unofficial Tests but losing the one-day series, while the Under-19s hosted the Pakistanis in August to October, drawing three youth Tests and winning the limited-overs games 2-1. The tour was marred by the arrest in Jamaica of Pakistan player Zeeshan Pervez on a rape charge. He was allowed to return to Pakistan on bail, and acquitted when he returned for the trial in January.

FIRST-CLASS AVERAGES, 1996-97

BATTING

(Qualification: 300 runs)

	M	I	NO	R	HS	100s	Avge
C. B. Lambert (*Guyana*)	4	8	1	454	159	2	64.85
S. Chanderpaul (*Guyana*)	11	18	4	815	176*	2	58.21
S. Ragoonath (*T & T*)	8	14	3	625	128	2	56.81
J. C. Adams (*Jamaica*)	8	15	2	572	73	0	44.00
C. L. Hooper (*Guyana*)	12	20	2	791	129	3	43.94
B. C. Lara (*T & T*)	13	22	0	965	135	3	43.86
F. L. Reifer (*Barbados*)	14	25	2	940	200	2	40.86
J. R. Murray (*Windward I.*)	8	15	1	547	218	2	39.07
R. D. Jacobs (*Leeward I.*)	10	15	3	464	107	1	38.66
S. C. Williams (*Leeward I.*)	16	26	1	964	141	4	38.56
R. I. C. Holder (*Barbados*)	15	26	2	908	111	2	37.83
P. A. Wallace (*Barbados*)	12	21	0	787	121	1	37.47
K. L. T. Arthurton (*Leeward I.*)	9	15	1	488	95	0	34.85
L. V. Garrick (*Jamaica*)...........	10	20	1	640	138	2	33.68
S. L. Campbell (*Barbados*)	15	25	1	790	109	1	32.91
D. Williams (*T & T*)	9	13	1	360	55	0	30.00
R. G. Samuels (*Jamaica*)	8	16	2	417	90*	0	29.78
R. N. Lewis (*Windward I.*)	9	18	5	366	55*	0	28.15
L. A. Roberts (*T & T*).............	8	13	1	319	65	0	26.58
A. F. G. Griffith (*Barbados*)	8	13	0	339	123	1	26.07
L. R. Williams (*Jamaica*)..........	10	17	4	331	102*	1	25.46
D. S. Morgan (*Jamaica*)	9	15	1	343	63	0	24.50
J. A. R. Sylvester (*Windward I.*)	7	14	0	332	70	0	23.71
B. M. Watt (*Windward I.*)	9	18	0	422	64	0	23.44
N. A. De Groot (*Guyana*)	8	15	1	328	63	0	23.42
T. O. Powell (*Jamaica*)	8	15	0	317	76	0	21.13
I. R. Bishop (*T & T*)	13	17	0	315	111	1	18.52

* Signifies not out.

BOWLING

(Qualification: 20 wickets)

	O	M	R	W	BB	5W/i	Avge
F. A. Rose (*Jamaica*).............	420.5	84	1,306	71	6-63	4	18.39
L. R. Williams (*Jamaica*)	252.3	60	648	33	6-26	1	19.63
C. E. L. Ambrose (*Leeward I.*)	268.3	75	575	29	5-37	2	19.82
W. E. Reid (*Barbados*)	348	109	812	40	4-72	0	20.30
R. D. King (*Guyana*)	185.4	35	542	26	7-82	3	20.84
C. A. Davis (*Windward I.*)	202.1	42	613	29	7-58	3	21.13
O. D. Gibson (*Barbados*).........	322.4	64	990	46	5-57	1	21.52
R. A. Marshall (*Windward I.*)	273.4	59	654	30	3-15	0	21.80
H. R. Bryan (*Barbados*)..........	266.1	61	820	37	5-39	1	22.16
D. Ramnarine (*T & T*)	365.1	89	848	38	5-69	1	22.31
C. A. Walsh (*Jamaica*)	365.2	78	883	39	6-39	2	22.64
I. R. Bishop (*T & T*)	360.3	71	1,006	43	5-82	1	23.39
B. S. Murphy (*Jamaica*)	203.2	49	496	21	5-85	1	23.61
M. J. Morgan (*Windward I.*)	180.2	34	628	24	4-32	0	26.16
R. M. Powell (*Leeward I.*)	283	70	655	23	3-31	0	28.47
W. D. Phillip (*Leeward I.*)	452.2	123	1,024	35	7-104	3	29.25

	O	M	R	W	BB	5W/i	Avge
M. Dillon (*T & T*)	324.1	58	1,068	36	4-94	0	29.66
M. V. Nagamootoo (*Guyana*)	321.5	80	872	29	4-59	0	30.06
R. N. Lewis (*Windward I.*)	286.2	37	899	27	5-160	1	33.29
N. C. McGarrell (*Guyana*)	387.2	111	924	27	7-84	1	34.22

RED STRIPE CUP, 1996-97

	Played	Won	Lost	Drawn	Abandoned	1st-inns Points	Points
Barbados	10	6	2	2	0	8	112
Jamaica	10	4	2	3	1	13	93
Leeward Islands	10	4	2	3	1	0	80
Trinidad & Tobago	10	3	2	5	0	8	76
Guyana	10	0	1	6	3	8	44
Windward Islands	10	0	8	1	1	19	27

Guyana's home matches against Leeward Islands, Jamaica and Windward Islands were abandoned because of rain.

Win = 16 pts; draw = 4 pts; abandoned match = 4 pts; 1st-innings lead in a drawn match = 4 pts; 1st-innings lead in a lost match = 5 pts.

In the following scores, * by the name of a team signifies that they won the toss.

At Kensington Oval, Bridgetown, January 24, 25, 26, 27. Barbados won by ten wickets. Guyana 156 (A. R. Percival 30; O. D. Gibson four for 58, W. E. Reid three for 36) and 294 (C. B. Lambert 145, A. R. Percival 91; O. D. Gibson three for 60, W. E. Reid three for 76); Barbados* 448 for eight dec. (P. A. Wallace 74, F. L. Reifer 151 not out, T. E. Rollock 53, O. D. Gibson 41, H. R. Bryan 40 not out, Extras 45; K. G. Darlington three for 105) and four for no wkt. *Barbados 16 pts.*

At Webster Park, The Valley (Anguilla), January 24, 25, 26, 27. Drawn. Jamaica 332 (D. S. Morgan 63, N. O. Perry 41, F. A. Rose 96, Extras 38; J. E. S. Joseph three for 122) and 199 for five (L. V. Garrick 34, W. E. Cuff 36, T. O. Powell 32, D. S. Morgan 31 not out, B. S. Murphy 43 not out; L. C. Weekes three for 46); Leeward Islands* 234 (M. D. Liburd 40, R. D. Jacobs 30, L. C. Weekes 31 not out; B. S. Murphy five for 85). *Leeward Islands 4 pts, Jamaica 8 pts.*

At Queen's Park Oval, Port-of-Spain, January 24, 25, 26, 27. Trinidad & Tobago won by four wickets. Trinidad & Tobago* 302 (L. A. Roberts 39, M. Bodoe 46, D. Williams 53, D. Ramnarine 43; R. A. Marshall three for 55) and 80 for six (D. Thomas three for 21); Windward Islands 140 (B. M. Watt 30; D. Ramnarine three for 21, R. Dhanraj four for 18) and 238 (J. A. R. Sylvester 66, B. M. Watt 57, R. A. Marshall 34, R. N. Lewis 35 not out; M. Persad four for 55). *Trinidad & Tobago 16 pts.*

At Kensington Oval, Bridgetown, January 31, February 1, 2, 3. Barbados won by seven wickets. Trinidad & Tobago 165 (L. A. Roberts 52, R. A. M. Smith 47; T. E. Rollock six for 15) and 253 (M. Bodoe 49, R. A. M. Smith 48, K. Mason 49; P. T. Collins three for 38); Barbados* 238 (F. L. Reifer 50, R. L. Hoyte 31, O. D. Gibson 49; R. Dhanraj three for 59, D. Ramnarine three for 39) and 186 for three (S. N. Proverbs 112 not out, R. L. Hoyte 39 not out; M. Dillon three for 43). *Barbados 16 pts.*

At Albion, Berbice, January 31, February 1, 2, 3. Guyana v Leeward Islands. Abandoned without a ball bowled. *Guyana 4 pts, Leeward Islands 4 pts.*

At Mindoo Phillip Park, Castries (St Lucia), January 31, February 1, 2, 3. Jamaica won by 31 runs. Jamaica 77 (C. A. Davis three for seven, R. A. Marshall three for 15) and 184 (L. V. Garrick 44; M. J. Morgan four for 33, R. N. Lewis four for 37); Windward Islands* 104 (F. A. Rose three for 26) and 126 (D. Thomas 33 not out; F. A. Rose four for 25). *Jamaica 16 pts, Windward Islands 5 pts.*

At Everest CC, Georgetown, February 7, 8, 9, 10. Guyana v Jamaica. Abandoned without a ball bowled. *Guyana 4 pts, Jamaica 4 pts.*

The match was switched from Bourda, which was under water, to the Everest club ground. But persistent rain prevented its debut as a first-class venue.

At Recreation Ground, St John's, February 7, 8, 9, 10. Drawn. Leeward Islands 352 (S. C. Joseph 30, D. R. E. Joseph 66, K. L. T. Arthurton 49, R. D. Jacobs 107; D. Ramnarine four for 90); Trinidad & Tobago* 26 for two. *Leeward Islands 4 pts, Trinidad & Tobago 4 pts.*

At Queen's Park, St George's (Grenada), February 8, 9, 10. Barbados won by 51 runs. Barbados 161 (P. A. Wallace 37, O. D. Gibson 33; M. J. Morgan four for 32, R. N. Lewis three for 56) and 167 (O. D. Gibson 30, H. R. Bryan 42 not out; D. Thomas three for 22, R. A. Marshall three for 36); Windward Islands* 166 (D. Thomas 30, R. N. Lewis 55 not out; O. D. Gibson four for 56, W. E. Reid three for 28) and 111 (J. A. R. Sylvester 37; O. D. Gibson three for 37). *Barbados 16 pts, Windward Islands 5 pts.*

The referee restaged the toss after both captains, Dawnley Joseph of the Windwards and Philo Wallace claimed they had won it. Substituting as wicket-keeper – and wearing his pads under his trousers – Wallace took five catches in the Windwards' second innings.

At Kensington Oval, Bridgetown, February 14, 15, 16. Leeward Islands won by eight wickets. Leeward Islands* 339 (S. C. Williams 141, S. C. Joseph 49, L. C. Weekes 38 not out; O. D. Gibson three for 84, W. E. Reid four for 79) and 117 for two (S. C. Williams 50 not out, S. C. Joseph 44); Barbados 141 (R. I. C. Holder 53; H. A. G. Anthony three for 35) and 311 (P. A. Wallace 42, A. F. G. Griffith 42, R. I. C. Holder 111; W. D. Phillip six for 78). *Leeward Islands 16 pts.*

At Bourda, Georgetown, February 14, 15, 16, 17. Guyana v Windward Islands. Abandoned without a ball bowled. *Guyana 4 pts, Windward Islands 4 pts.*

At Guaracara Park, Pointe-à-Pierre, February 14, 15, 16, 17. Drawn. Jamaica* 349 (L. V. Garrick 138, J. C. Adams 66, T. O. Powell 30, D. S. Morgan 33; I. R. Bishop three for 76, M. Dillon three for 100) and 201 for five dec. (R. G. Samuels 34, L. V. Garrick 64, J. C. Adams 67); Trinidad & Tobago 256 (B. C. Lara 135, D. Williams 36; L. R. Williams three for 55) and 118 for five (S. Ragoonath 54 not out, B. C. Lara 30). *Trinidad & Tobago 4 pts, Jamaica 8 pts.*

Returning from the Australian tour, Phil Simmons scored a pair – his fourth and fifth successive ducks after he failed to score in the one-day international finals and the Fifth Test.

At Kaiser SC, Discovery Bay, February 21, 22, 23. Barbados won by 121 runs. Barbados* 184 (P. A. Wallace 34, F. L. Reifer 50, R. I. C. Holder 58; D. S. McKenzie four for 35) and 223 (S. L. Campbell 34, R. I. C. Holder 54, O. D. Gibson 36; F. A. Rose five for 62); Jamaica 180 (Extras 36; P. I. C. Thompson three for 27, H. R. Bryan four for 42) and 106 (B. S. Murphy 34; P. I. C. Thompson three for 33, H. R. Bryan three for 16). *Barbados 16 pts.*

The Kaiser Sports Club in Jamaica staged its first first-class match. Murphy hit four sixes off one over from Winston Reid in Jamaica's first innings.

At Webster Park, The Valley (Anguilla), February 21, 22, 23, 24. Leeward Islands won by two runs. Leeward Islands* 168 (S. C. Williams 30, M. D. Liburd 33, R. D. Jacobs 50 not out; C. A. Davis four for 30, R. N. Lewis three for 50) and 236 (K. L. T. Arthurton 95, R. M. Powell 34; C. A. Davis five for 43, R. A. Marshall three for 56); Windward Islands 199 (J. A. R. Sylvester 35, R. N. Lewis 46; H. A. G. Anthony three for 32, R. M. Powell three for 31) and 203 (J. R. Murray 52, R. N. Lewis 35 not out; J. C. Maynard three for 41, R. M. Powell three for 35). *Leeward Islands 16 pts, Windward Islands 5 pts.*

At Queen's Park Oval, Port-of-Spain, February 21, 22, 23, 24. Drawn. Trinidad & Tobago 305 (L. A. Roberts 65, P. V. Simmons 78, D. Williams 40; N. C. McGarrell seven for 84) and 204 for nine dec. (S. Ragoonath 39, B. C. Lara 72; N. C. McGarrell four for 63, M. V. Nagamootoo four for 59); Guyana* 241 (N. A. De Groot 53, S. Chanderpaul 60, C. L. Hooper 38, Extras 31; D. Ramnarine five for 69) and three for no wkt. *Trinidad & Tobago 8 pts, Guyana 4 pts.*

At Bourda, Georgetown, February 28, March 1, 2, 3. Drawn. Barbados 240 (P. A. Wallace 62, A. F. G. Griffith 36, C. O. Browne 78; C. L. Hooper five for 52) and 211 for five dec. (S. L. Campbell 58 not out, P. A. Wallace 69, Extras 31; N. C. McGarrell four for 69); Guyana* 164 (C. B. Lambert 34, S. Chanderpaul 30, Extras 32; O. D. Gibson five for 57) and 263 for seven (C. B. Lambert 45, N. A. De Groot 47, C. L. Hooper 101, Extras 35; O. D. Gibson three for 80). *Guyana 4 pts, Barbados 8 pts.*

At Windsor Park, Roseau (Dominica), February 28, March 1, 2, 3. Trinidad & Tobago won by ten wickets. Windward Islands* 199 (J. R. Murray 100; I. R. Bishop three for 20, D. Ramnarine three for 47) and 214 (J. A. R. Sylvester 70, B. M. Watt 36, R. N. Lewis 40, Extras 35; M. Dillon three for 65); Trinidad & Tobago 370 (S. Ragoonath 120, L. A. Roberts 41, B. C. Lara 53, R. A. M. Smith 62; M. J. Morgan three for 64, R. A. Marshall three for 116) and 44 for no wkt (S. Ragoonath 33 not out). *Trinidad & Tobago 16 pts.*

At Albion, Berbice, March 20, 21, 22, 23. Drawn. Guyana* 281 (C. B. Lambert 55, C. L. Hooper 119; I. R. Bishop five for 82, D. Ramnarine four for 80) and 263 for two (C. B. Lambert 159, N. A. De Groot 63); Trinidad & Tobago 413 (D. Ganga 54, P. V. Simmons 116, S. Ragoonath 44, D. Williams 31, I. R. Bishop 50, Extras 36; N. C. McGarrell three for 125). *Guyana 4 pts, Trinidad & Tobago 8 pts.*

At Chedwin Park, St Catherine (Jamaica), March 20, 21, 22, 23. Jamaica won by 251 runs. Jamaica 156 (J. C. Adams 35, T. O. Powell 40, B. S. Murphy 35; C. E. L. Ambrose four for 16, R. M. Powell three for 44) and 337 for nine dec. (L. V. Garrick 50, M. D. Ventura 96, J. C. Adams 73, T. O. Powell 31; W. D. Phillip seven for 104); Leeward Islands* 145 (R. D. Jacobs 33; C. A. Walsh three for 32, F. A. Rose six for 63) and 97 (F. A. Rose five for 36, L. R. Williams three for 37). *Jamaica 16 pts.*

At Kaiser SC, Discovery Bay, April 10, 11, 12. Jamaica won by ten wickets. Windward Islands* 117 (L. R. Williams six for 26) and 161 (C. A. Walsh five for 49, F. A. Rose three for 42); Jamaica 276 (R. G. Samuels 69, T. O. Powell 44, L. R. Williams 35, S. G. B. Ford 44; C. A. Davis seven for 58) and four for no wkt. *Jamaica 16 pts.*

At Warner Park, Basseterre (St Kitts), April 10, 11, 12, 13. Barbados won by 81 runs. Barbados* 275 (F. L. Reifer 61, R. I. C. Holder 107; C. M. Tuckett three for 57) and 212 for seven dec. (S. L. Campbell 46, R. I. C. Holder 57, P. A. Wallace 37, W. E. Reid 37 not out; W. D. Phillip three for 76); Leeward Islands 152 (S. C. Williams 31; H. R. Bryan five for 39, D. K. Marshall three for 29) and 254 (S. C. Williams 118, D. R. E. Joseph 34; W. E. Reid three for 61, D. K. Marshall four for 70). *Barbados 16 pts.*

Leg-spinner Marshall took three wickets in four balls in the penultimate over to secure victory for Barbados.

At Sabina Park, Kingston, May 9, 10, 11, 12. Drawn. Jamaica 206 (J. C. Adams 52, D. S. Morgan 30; R. D. King four for 47, M. V. Nagamootoo three for 61) and 251 (S. G. B. Ford 32, D. S. Morgan 51, L. R. Williams 35, B. S. Murphy 31; R. D. King five for 56, M. V. Nagamootoo three for 75); Guyana* 271 (N. A. De Groot 61, C. L. Hooper 73, N. C. McGarrell 30, Extras 30; B. S. Murphy four for 43) and 116 for one (S. Chanderpaul 56 not out, C. L. Hooper 46). *Jamaica 4 pts, Guyana 8 pts.*

On the third day, 125 runs were scored in 88.2 overs (Guyana 193-5 to 271, Jamaica 47-3) – the fewest in a full day's first-class cricket in the West Indies.

At Queen's Park Oval, Port-of-Spain, May 9, 10, 11, 12. Drawn. Barbados 394 (S. L. Campbell 109, A. F. G. Griffith 60, F. L. Reifer 48, W. E. Reid 31, Extras 66; M. Dillon four for 94) and 288 (S. L. Campbell 41, P. A. Wallace 31, R. I. C. Holder 35, W. E. Reid 54 not out, D. K. Marshall 42; I. R. Bishop four for 51); Trinidad & Tobago* 361 (S. Ragoonath 128, I. R. Bishop 111, Extras 52; H. R. Bryan three for 75, W. E. Reid four for 72) and 99 for one (S. Ragoonath 73). *Trinidad & Tobago 4 pts, Barbados 8 pts.*

There were 66 extras in Barbados's first innings (26 byes, 12 leg-byes, 28 no-balls), a tournament record. Barbados went on to concede 52 (two byes, 20 leg-byes and 30 no-balls) in Trinidad & Tobago's reply.

At Arnos Vale, St Vincent, May 9, 10, 11, 12. Leeward Islands won by six wickets. Leeward Islands 390 (S. C. Williams 111, J. Mitchum 89, K. L. T. Arthurton 78, R. M. Powell 37, Extras 37; C. A. Davis five for 70, M. J. Morgan three for 77) and 107 for four (S. C. Williams 30, R. D. Jacobs 56 not out); Windward Islands* 158 (U. Pope 34; W. K. L. Quinn three for 28) and 337 (K. K. Sylvester 56, J. R. Murray 38, B. M. Watt 64, K. Martin 65, R. A. Marshall 46; W. K. L. Quinn three for 40). *Leeward Islands 16 pts.*

In the Windwards' first innings, Arthurton returned figures of 7.2–5–3–2.

At Kensington Oval, Bridgetown, May 16, 17. Barbados won by an innings and 191 runs. Windward Islands 82 (O. D. Gibson three for 16, P. T. Collins four for 36) and 161 (J. R. Murray 48; W. E. Reid three for 52); Barbados* 434 for eight dec. (P. A. Wallace 121, F. L. Reifer 200, R. L. Hoyte 50 not out, Extras 30; R. N. Lewis five for 160). *Barbados 16 pts.*

Barbados became the first team to win a first-class match in the West Indies in two days since Trinidad beat British Guiana by ten wickets, also at Bridgetown, in 1938-39. Reifer's 200, his maiden double-hundred, lasted 307 minutes and 226 balls and included 27 fours and three sixes. He put on 275 for the third wicket with Wallace.

At Sabina Park, Kingston, May 16, 17, 18, 19. Trinidad & Tobago won by 45 runs. Trinidad & Tobago* 160 (B. C. Lara 30, K. Mason 36; F. A. Rose three for 39, B. S. Murphy three for 22) and 245 (B. C. Lara 39, D. Williams 55, Extras 39; F. A. Rose four for 89); Jamaica 226 (L. V. Garrick 44, R. G. Samuels 46, J. C. Adams 35, L. R. Williams 32 not out; M. Dillon three for 53, R. Dhanraj four for 65) and 134 (R. G. Samuels 55; M. Dillon three for 41, I. R. Bishop three for nine, R. Dhanraj three for 49). *Trinidad & Tobago 16 pts, Jamaica 5 pts.*

Bishop's full second-innings figures were 13–8–9–3.

At Grove Park, Charlestown (Nevis), May 16, 17, 18, 19. Drawn. Guyana* 257 (A. Haniff 31, R. R. Sarwan 77, V. Nagamootoo 36, R. D. King 30; W. D. Phillip three for 72) and 264 (A. Haniff 62, Z. A. Haniff 71; W. D. Phillip five for 108, R. M. Powell three for 85); Leeward Islands 221 (K. L. T. Arthurton 61, R. D. Jacobs 37, R. M. Powell 51; N. C. McGarrell three for 46, M. V. Nagamootoo four for 88) and 129 for one (F. A. Adams 69 not out, K. L. T. Arthurton 45 not out). *Leeward Islands 4 pts, Guyana 8 pts.*

At Kensington Oval, Bridgetown, May 23, 24, 25, 26. Jamaica won by eight wickets. Barbados 258 (P. A. Wallace 47, F. L. Reifer 59, Extras 35; F. A. Rose three for 63) and 180 (P. A. Wallace 53, Extras 32; C. A. Walsh six for 39); Jamaica* 282 (W. W. Hinds 84, D. S. Morgan 54, S. G. B. Ford 36 not out; O. D. Gibson four for 57, P. T. Collins four for 40) and 157 for two (R. G. Samuels 90 not out, J. C. Adams 50 not out). *Jamaica 16 pts.*

At Queen's Park Oval, Port-of-Spain, May 23, 24, 25. Leeward Islands won by 55 runs. Leeward Islands 208 (E. Waldron 43, K. L. T. Arthurton 70; D. Ramnarine three for 44, D. Rampersaud three for 13) and 95 (R. D. Jacobs 39 not out; D. Ramnarine four for 28); Trinidad & Tobago* 110 (S. Ragoonath 31; W. K. L. Quinn four for 39) and 138 (B. C. Lara 52; M. Mills five for 33). *Leeward Islands 16 pts.*

Lara took five catches in the Leewards' second innings, equalling the West Indian fielding record.

At Tanteen, St George's (Grenada), May 23, 24, 25, 26. Drawn. Windward Islands* 446 (J. R. Murray 218, B. M. Watt 50, K. Martin 35, M. J. Morgan 35, A. Sandford 30 not out, Extras 31; M. V. Nagamootoo four for 104) and 177 for nine dec. (J. A. R. Sylvester 54; R. D. King five for 43, M. V. Nagamootoo four for 67); Guyana 315 (Z. A. Haniff 66, R. R. Sarwan 54, V. Nagamootoo 33, N. C. McGarrell 73; R. N. Lewis four for 104) and 125 for eight (T. M. Dowlin 30; M. J. Morgan three for 42). *Windward Islands 8 pts, Guyana 4 pts.*

Tanteen staged its first first-class match, because Grenada's main ground, Queen's Park, was undergoing improvements. Nicholas De Groot became Guyana's fourth captain in eight matches in 1996-97, following Clayton Lambert, Carl Hooper and Shivnarine Chanderpaul. Murray's 218, his maiden double-hundred, lasted 440 minutes and 317 balls and included 26 fours and a six.

SHELL SHIELD AND RED STRIPE CUP WINNERS

The Shell Shield was replaced by the Red Stripe Cup after the 1986-87 season.

1965-66	Barbados	1981-82	Barbados
1966-67	Barbados	1982-83	Guyana
1967-68	No competition	1983-84	Barbados
1968-69	Jamaica	1984-85	Trinidad & Tobago
1969-70	Trinidad	1985-86	Barbados
1970-71	Trinidad	1986-87	Guyana
1971-72	Barbados	1987-88	Jamaica
1972-73	Guyana	1988-89	Jamaica
1973-74	Barbados	1989-90	Leeward Islands
1974-75	Guyana	1990-91	Barbados
1975-76 { Trinidad		1991-92	Jamaica
{ Barbados		1992-93	Guyana
1976-77	Barbados	1993-94	Leeward Islands
1977-78	Barbados	1994-95	Barbados
1978-79	Barbados	1995-96	Leeward Islands
1979-80	Barbados	1996-97	Barbados
1980-81	Combined Islands		

Barbados have won the title outright 14 times, Guyana 5, Jamaica 4, Leeward Islands and Trinidad/Trinidad & Tobago 3, Combined Islands 1. Barbados and Trinidad also shared the title once.

OTHER FIRST-CLASS MATCH

At Kensington Oval, Bridgetown, September 23, 24, 25, 26. Drawn. Barbados 163 (F. L. Reifer 32, R. I. C. Holder 76; S. G. Cronje five for 43) and 356 for five (A. F. G. Griffith 123, F. L. Reifer 56, R. O. Hurley 122); Free State* 322 (G. F. J. Liebenberg 131, H. H. Dippenaar 111; J. H. Williams three for 57, R. O. Hurley five for 66).

SHELL/SANDALS TROPHY, 1996-97

Zone A (in Guyana)

At Enmore, Demerara, October 4. Windward Islands won by two runs. Windward Islands* 209 (49.5 overs) (U. Pope 30, J. R. Murray 40, R. A. Marshall 44; R. W. Blades four for 30); Bermuda 207 for nine (50 overs) (C. J. Smith 52, G. S. Smith 54; C. E. Cuffy three for 33, C. A. Davis three for 34).

At Bourda, Georgetown, October 4. Guyana won by seven wickets. Barbados 147 (47.5 overs) (P. A. Wallace 41; M. V. Nagamootoo three for 30, S. Chanderpaul three for 19); Guyana* 148 for three (39 overs) (C. B. Lambert 68, S. Chanderpaul 42 not out).

At Enmore, Demerara, October 5. Barbados won by five wickets. Bermuda* 216 for nine (50 overs) (C. J. Smith 69, D. A. Minors 36; O. D. Gibson four for 36); Barbados 220 for five (45.2 overs) (P. A. Wallace 87, R. I. C. Holder 55).

At Bourda, Georgetown, October 5. Guyana won by six wickets. Windward Islands 131 (41.4 overs) (J. R. Murray 35 not out; S. Chanderpaul three for 18); Guyana* 135 for four (42.2 overs) (S. Chanderpaul 58 not out).

At Hampton Court, Essequibo, October 8. Windward Islands won by three wickets. Barbados* 165 (46 overs) (A. F. G. Griffith 37; D. Thomas three for 18); Windward Islands 166 for seven (46 overs) (A. J. Pierre 39, N. A. M. McLean 41 not out; W. E. Reid four for 20).

At Bourda, Georgetown, October 8. Guyana won by ten wickets. Bermuda 108 (42.2 overs) (M. V. Nagamootoo three for 29); Guyana* 113 for no wkt (17.5 overs) (C. B. Lambert 41 not out, Sudesh Dhaniram 63 not out).

At Bourda, Georgetown, October 10. Barbados won by eight wickets. Bermuda 215 for eight (50 overs) (A. B. Steede 47; J. H. Williams three for 33, W. E. Reid three for 17); Barbados* 216 for two (47.1 overs) (S. L. Campbell 46 retired hurt, A. F. G. Griffith 57, R. I. C. Holder 60 not out).

At Hampton Court, Essequibo, October 10. Guyana won by eight wickets. Windward Islands* 152 for six (50 overs) (D. A. Joseph 39); Guyana 155 for two (36.4 overs) (C. B. Lambert 81 not out).

At Albion, Berbice, October 12. Windward Islands won by 37 runs. Windward Islands* 228 for six (50 overs) (D. A. Joseph 67, A. J. Pierre 61, L. Stephen 31, N. A. M. McLean 31; C. M. Marshall three for 46); Bermuda 191 (50 overs) (C. M. Marshall 86, Extras 32).

At Blairmont, Berbice, October 12. Guyana won by 78 runs. Guyana* 270 for seven (50 overs) (C. B. Lambert 91, S. Chanderpaul 35, C. L. Hooper 72 not out; W. E. Reid four for 43); Barbados 192 for nine (50 overs) (A. F. G. Griffith 32, F. L. Reifer 47; M. V. Nagamootoo three for 47, S. Chanderpaul three for 44).

At Blairmont, Berbice, October 13. Windward Islands won by one wicket. Barbados* 232 for nine (42 overs) (R. L. Hoyte 50, A. E. Proverbs 47, R. I. C. Holder 65; C. A. Davis three for 66); Windward Islands 233 for nine (41.5 overs) (D. A. Joseph 42, A. J. Pierre 69).

At Albion, Berbice, October 13. Guyana won by 108 runs. Guyana* 234 for five (43 overs) (R. A. Harper 44, A. R. Percival 42, S. Chanderpaul 69 not out); Bermuda 126 for six (42 overs) (J. J. Tucker 43).

Guyana 12 pts, Windward Islands 8 pts, Barbados 4 pts, Bermuda 0 pts.

Zone B (in Jamaica)

At Jarrett Park, Montego Bay, October 4. No result. Jamaica* 268 for five (50 overs) (D. S. Morgan 133 not out, J. C. Adams 71); Canada 17 for one (12 overs).

At Chedwin Park, St Catherine, October 4. Leeward Islands won by eight wickets. Trinidad & Tobago 116 (48.5 overs) (A. Lawrence 32; K. L. T. Arthurton four for 25); Leeward Islands* 117 for two (31.4 overs) (S. C. Williams 50, K. L. T. Arthurton 44 not out).

At Jarrett Park, Montego Bay, October 6. No result. Trinidad & Tobago* 251 for three (42 overs) (S. Ragoonath 75, B. C. Lara 127) v Canada.

At Sabina Park, Kingston, October 6. Leeward Islands won by eight runs. Leeward Islands 229 (50 overs) (K. L. T. Arthurton 62, D. R. E. Joseph 39, R. M. Powell 42; K. H. Powell four for 33, J. C. Adams three for 44); Jamaica* 221 for nine (50 overs) (J. C. Adams 84, T. O. Powell 41; K. C. G. Benjamin four for 33).

At Sabina Park, Kingston, October 8. Leeward Islands won by eight wickets. Canada 74 (39 overs) (C. E. L. Ambrose three for six, L. C. Weekes three for 18); Leeward Islands* 75 for two (17.2 overs) (S. C. Williams 34 not out).

At Kaiser SC, Discovery Bay, October 8. Trinidad & Tobago won by 47 runs. Trinidad & Tobago* 221 for eight (50 overs) (S. Ragoonath 63, B. C. Lara 64; R. C. Haynes four for 38); Jamaica 174 (46.2 overs) (R. G. Samuels 33, J. C. Adams 42).

At Sabina Park, Kingston, October 10. Trinidad & Tobago won by 32 runs, Canada's target having been revised to 176 from 40 overs. Trinidad & Tobago* 194 (46.1 overs) (L. A. Roberts 37, B. C. Lara 53; M. Rajadurai four for 20); Canada 143 (37.5 overs) (A. Glegg 37, L. Bhansingh 45; R. Dhanraj five for 35).

At Kaiser SC, Discovery Bay, October 10. Jamaica won by one wicket. Leeward Islands 243 for eight (50 overs) (M. D. Liburd 48, K. L. T. Arthurton 118; C. A. Walsh three for 40, L. R. Williams three for 55); Jamaica* 246 for nine (49 overs) (R. G. Samuels 60, S. G. B. Ford 46 not out).

At Chedwin Park, St Catherine, October 12. Jamaica won by seven wickets. Canada 174 for six (50 overs) (I. Liburd 78); Jamaica* 175 for three (32 overs) (J. C. Adams 53 not out, T. O. Powell 45, L. R. Williams 35 not out).

At Sabina Park, Kingston, October 12. Trinidad & Tobago won by eight wickets. Leeward Islands 110 (29 overs) (D. R. E. Joseph 33; R. Dhanraj three for 29, D. Ramnarine four for 23); Trinidad & Tobago* 113 for two (26 overs) (B. C. Lara 67 not out).

At Chedwin Park, St Catherine, October 13. Leeward Islands won by 104 runs. Leeward Islands* 304 for five (50 overs) (S. C. Williams 47, M. D. Liburd 77, J. Mitchum 39, D. R. E. Joseph 51, S. C. Joseph 41, Extras 40); Canada 200 for seven (50 overs) (P. Prashad 48, I. Liburd 71, D. Maxwell 30).

At Sabina Park, Kingston, October 13. Trinidad & Tobago won by five wickets. Jamaica 193 (50 overs) (J. C. Adams 64, N. O. Perry 34; R. Dhanraj four for 40); Trinidad & Tobago* 196 for five (48.1 overs) (A. Lawrence 81, L. A. Roberts 52; J. C. Adams three for 34).

Trinidad & Tobago 9 pts, Leeward Islands 8 pts, Jamaica 5 pts, Canada 2 pts.

Final

At Bourda, Georgetown, Guyana, October 19. Trinidad & Tobago won by nine runs. Trinidad & Tobago* 236 for four (50 overs) (L. A. Roberts 33, B. C. Lara 51, P. V. Simmons 80 not out); Guyana 227 (49.3 overs) (K. F. Semple 71, S. Chanderpaul 88; R. Dhanraj four for 16).
Dhanraj completed Trinidad & Tobago's victory with a hat-trick in the final over.

WEST INDIES A IN SRI LANKA

At Maitland Crescent, Colombo (CCC), November 2, 3, 4. Drawn. Board President's XI* 340 (G. R. P. Peiris 30, S. I. Fernando 56, S. Jayantha 97, D. P. M. Jayawardene 50, Extras 34; R. A. Harper three for 46, R. N. Lewis three for 86); West Indies A 343 for six (P. A. Wallace 125, D. R. E. Joseph 93, T. O. Powell 50).

At Welagedera Stadium, Kurunegala, November 7, 8, 9, 10. First Unofficial Test: West Indies A won by ten wickets. Sri Lanka A 269 (M. S. Atapattu 104, S. K. L. de Silva 33, R. S. Kalpage 44; C. E. Cuffy three for 48, R. A. Harper three for 42) and 204 (M. S. Atapattu 30 retired not out, S. Jayantha 39, R. S. Kalpage 35, Extras 30; C. E. Cuffy seven for 84); West Indies A* 470 for nine dec. (S. C. Williams 39, P. A. Wallace 124, F. L. Reifer 96, T. O. Powell 87, R. A. Harper 51) and five for no wkt.
Atapattu was withdrawn to join the senior Sri Lankan squad in the Singer Champions Trophy in Sharjah.

At Maitland Place, Colombo (SSC), November 13, 14, 15, 16. Second Unofficial Test: West Indies A won by nine wickets. West Indies A 220 (S. C. Williams 52, P. A. Wallace 56, T. O. Powell 42, R. A. Harper 40 not out; G. P. Wickremasinghe three for 65, R. S. Kalpage six for 51) and 231 (P. A. Wallace 71, O. D. Gibson 39; K. J. Silva three for 46, R. S. Kalpage six for 62); Sri Lanka A* 287 (D. P. Samaraweera 73, M. N. Nawaz 36, S. Ranatunga 39, R. S. Kalpage 34 not out; R. A. Harper five for 61, R. N. Lewis three for 87) and 95 (R. A. Harper four for 26, R. N. Lewis four for 23).

At Uyanwatte Stadium, Matara, November 20, 21, 22, 23. Third Unofficial Test: Drawn. West Indies A* 523 for nine dec. (S. C. Williams 170, P. A. Wallace 31, F. L. Reifer 60, D. R. E. Joseph 43, T. O. Powell 47, R. D. Jacobs 100 not out; R. S. Kalpage three for 130); Sri Lanka A 108 (M. N. Nawaz 44; N. B. Francis four for 32) and 118 for two (D. P. Samaraweera 41 not out, M. N. Nawaz 38).
West Indies A won the Test series 2-0, but lost the subsequent one-day internationals 2-1.

CRICKET IN NEW ZEALAND, 1996-97

By TERRY POWER

Chris Harris

In New Zealand, the ups exceeded the downs in 1996-97. On the Test front, the national team began promisingly by drawing 1-1 in Pakistan. They then lost at home to England, but the administration had realised the danger of surrendering March to winter sports and arranged a visit from Sri Lanka to fill the gap. This turned out to be doubly worthwhile, as it provided New Zealand with their first home series win since 1989-90. In all, they won three Tests, lost three and drew one, all against higher-rated nations, the first time since 1989-90 that wins were not exceeded by defeats.

Two longstanding problems, the opening partnership and the spin bowling, both showed strong improvement. Personnel problems seemed to ease as the team coach, Australian Steve Rixon, gained acceptance. There had been a disastrously inconsistent series of selections – absurdly, 18 players bowled for New Zealand during 1996-97 and three recent Test bowlers could not make their provincial teams by the time the season ended. But two inspired decisions were immediately rewarded: the installation of Stephen Fleming as captain and the introduction of left-arm spinner Daniel Vettori.

On the down side, one-day international results were less encouraging and the Test batting was still filled with dashers at the expense of grafters. "It's like a druggie looking for a fix," said Rixon. "They just have to hit a four an over." Administratively, routine communications and other simple matters, such as dealing with the aftermath of rain, were repeatedly mishandled. Though the number of days allocated to domestic first-class cricket rose from 64 to a hundred, New Zealand cricket indulged its inclination to jump on every bandwagon available when it adopted Cricket Max, a highly commercial vehicle developed by Martin Crowe and Sky TV. This ten-overs slog, which started with four stumps, took pride of place on midsummer Sundays, mish-mashed with the four-day games, and some players went straight from Cricket Max into the Tests. "I don't think an enormous amount of thought went into the programme," said Rixon. Money is needed to keep cricket going, but the prime object of playing in or organising matches should be to maximise the amount of enjoyable high-calibre cricket, not to make profits.

The season's most important decision was the change of captain between the England and Sri Lanka series. The sacking of Lee Germon was messy, but the change itself was justifiable. Germon had an admirable, jaw-jutting determination and sense of duty, most evident in the World Cup quarter-final against Australia at Madras in 1996, when he put himself in at No. 3, after several others had failed there, and made 89. But he was never the country's best wicket-keeper – a department in which New Zealand does have strength in depth – and rarely looked a batsman of international calibre. The claims of his Canterbury team-mate Fleming, the most talented if not yet most productive batsman, and a naturally gracious leader who might hold his place for a decade (he was only 23 when appointed), became irresistible.

The international player of the year was Simon Doull. The previous season, he had been refused a place in both the home Tests against Zimbabwe and the West Indies tour party. But at 27, he had his first full international season and proved a world-class attacking swing bowler, with 31 Test wickets at 21.38. He was also an effective tail-end hitter and a better fielder than most pace bowlers. The discovery of the season, however, was the 18-year-old Vettori, a slow left-armer from Northern Districts, who made his debut against England after his school exams and was named Man of the Match in the Second Test against Sri Lanka. No young unknown spinner had done so well since Bill Merritt went on New Zealand's inaugural tour of England in 1927, when he was 18, and took 107 wickets. Vettori's public comments showed he was sensible as well as scholarly; he was sure that picking a second spinner would have won the Christchurch Test against England, where he bowled 57 overs in the second innings. His Hamilton coach, Dave Richardson, believed he could become an outstanding captain, "the New Zealand Richie Benaud".

Domestic first-class cricket began two months earlier than in 1995-96 to accommodate the expansion of the Shell Trophy. There were eight rounds of four-day games instead of five: after every province had played every other once, each of the top three played each of the bottom three to settle who would go through to the final. Post-season, a plan was launched for a regional contest, above Shell Trophy level, for 1997-98.

The regular international players were available for the middle and later rounds of the one-day Shell Cup, but only for the final of the first-class Trophy. Canterbury were rewarded for what was, by provincial standards, unusual strength in depth, which enabled them to fill the numerous gaps left by international calls. They took the Trophy without losing a match, and scored 777, a national record, in the final against Otago, to complete the double: they had already retained the Cup. Chris Harris, dropped for the home Tests after numerous failures, showed he could concentrate for long periods with two double-centuries, plus 198 in the final, and an average of 139.16. Craig McMillan, captain of the 1996 Under-19 tour of England, also scored three hundreds, and his 809 first-class runs were a Canterbury record. All-rounder Mark Priest took 41 wickets at 24.95 with his left-arm spin and made 357 runs at 44.62 – but continued to be ignored by the selectors. Left-arm pace bowler Geoff Allott made an important contribution before Test calls and subsequent injury curtailed his season.

Otago earned the other berth in the Trophy final after losing their two opening first-class matches. Under their new captain, 22-year-old Robbie Lawson, they won through with a string of five outright victories. Double international Jeff Wilson, free to play as the All Blacks had no tour, had two excellent games – then dropped out with a recurring rugby injury. Glamorgan captain Matthew Maynard, who had prospered with Northern Districts in the early 1990s, could not reach 50 in either competition. But Matt Horne, transferring from Auckland, where he never had a secure place, was a much more successful import: three centuries and brilliant fielding took him into the Test team. The consistent Lawson and Chris Gaffaney – more strokes, but less sound – formed a promising opening pair. The rotund expatriate South African surgeon, Michael Austen, who must be the biggest doctor in first-class cricket since W. G. Grace, made the slowest century in New Zealand domestic cricket to earn a draw in the final, though that was not enough to deny Canterbury. Two young left-arm quick bowlers, Shayne O'Connor and David Sewell, both did well, and O'Connor made his international debut in India in May. Paul Wiseman, who, like Horne, had found a more secure tenure in Otago than in Auckland, took 40 wickets, and looked the likeliest successor to Test off-spinner Dipak Patel, who announced his retirement after the season.

Along with Canterbury, Northern Districts provided most of the national team but, lacking their resources to plug the gaps, they finished third. By mid-summer, their batting had become unreliable, a situation exacerbated by the Hamilton pitch. Captain Blair Pocock was not wanted for the one-day internationals, so was available more than most; he began with a century and was their best batsman, steady rather than prolific. Matthew Bell still looked solid without making big scores. There were two startling developments on the bowling front. Alex Tait, a wiry medium-pacer who calls himself a "donkey bowler", blossomed to take 53 wickets at 16.32, including the first 16-in-a-match in New Zealand first-class cricket. No one except Jim Laker, with his 19 in the Manchester Test of 1956, had taken more than 16 since before the Second World War. And they had Vettori.

Central Districts won both Cricket Max titles. The highlight of their season was Andrew Penn's rise to the Test squad, and to the top of the bowling averages with 36 wickets at 15.33, through his penetrative, brisk right-arm accuracy. Their best batsmen, both second-season youngsters, were Mathew Sinclair and Matthew Walker.

Wellington were Shell Cup finalists but, as captain Roger Twose's batting fortunes slumped, so did their performances. Gavin Larsen, though mostly a bowler nowadays, was their most successful batsman. Steven Hotter, left-arm fast-medium, was periodically hostile and took 30 wickets, including a hat-trick against Otago. Defending Trophy champions Auckland finished last this time; a selection panel shake-up followed. Danny Morrison and captain Justin Vaughan, both dumped after the First Test against England, bowled better and better as the season went on, but no one managed a century.

FIRST-CLASS AVERAGES, 1996-97

BATTING

(Qualification: 5 innings, average 35.00)

	M	I	NO	R	HS	100s	Avge
C. Z. Harris (*Canterbury*)	5	7	1	835	251*	3	139.16
C. D. McMillan (*Canterbury*)	8	12	1	809	159	3	73.54
B. A. Young (*N. Districts*)	6	11	1	510	267*	1	51.00
M. J. Horne (*Otago*)	10	17	0	843	124	3	49.58
M. S. Sinclair (*C. Districts*)	8	16	1	722	189	1	48.13
N. J. Astle (*Canterbury*)	6	10	1	411	160	2	45.66
M. W. Priest (*Canterbury*)	8	11	3	357	63*	0	44.62

	M	I	NO	R	HS	100s	Avge
M. D. J. Walker (*C. Districts*)	5	9	1	340	84	0	42.50
G. R. Stead (*Canterbury*)	8	12	2	405	124	1	40.50
C. B. Gaffaney (*Otago*)	9	18	2	642	194	2	40.12
S. P. Fleming (*Canterbury*)	6	10	0	390	129	1	39.00
B. A. Pocock (*N. Districts*)	11	18	0	682	137	1	37.88
C. D. Cumming (*Canterbury*)	6	9	1	287	90*	0	35.87
S. M. Lynch (*Auckland*)	8	16	1	536	94	0	35.73
L. G. Howell (*C. Districts*)	10	19	2	604	91	0	35.52
G. R. Larsen (*Wellington*)	3	6	0	211	76	0	35.16

* *Signifies not out.*

BOWLING

(Qualification: 20 wickets)

	O	M	R	W	BB	5W/i	Avge
A. J. Penn (*C. Districts*)	237.1	79	552	36	6-36	4	15.33
A. R. Tait (*N. Districts*)	377.2	120	865	53	9-48	4	16.32
C. J. Drum (*Auckland*)	198.4	56	523	30	6-47	1	17.43
D. L. Vettori (*N. Districts*)	350.5	111	762	36	5-61	3	21.16
J. T. C. Vaughan (*Auckland*) ..	178.2	55	425	20	8-27	1	21.25
D. K. Morrison (*Auckland*)	203.2	46	574	27	5-66	1	21.25
S. J. Hotter (*Wellington*)	229.5	52	641	30	6-69	3	21.36
S. B. O'Connor (*Otago*)......	190.5	43	602	28	6-55	2	21.50
R. J. Kennedy (*Otago*)	208.1	50	563	25	4-44	0	22.52
G. I. Allott (*Canterbury*)	224	44	689	30	6-60	1	22.96
S. B. Doull (*New Zealand*) ...	175.3	49	492	21	5-58	2	23.42
P. J. Wiseman (*Otago*)	365.1	80	968	40	8-66	3	24.20
D. G. Sewell (*Otago*)	234.3	47	851	35	8-31	2	24.31
M. W. Priest (*Canterbury*)	451.5	133	1,023	41	6-146	3	24.95
S. E. Bond (*Canterbury*)	175	43	530	21	5-59	1	25.23
H. T. Davis (*Wellington*)	276.2	69	769	29	5-63	1	26.51
W. A. Wisneski (*Canterbury*) .	257.5	79	745	27	4-37	0	27.59
A. J. Gale (*Otago*)	228.4	65	595	20	4-43	0	29.75

SHELL TROPHY, 1996-97

	Played	Won	Lost	Drawn	1st-inns Points	Points
Canterbury..............	7	6	0	1	24	74*
Otago...................	8	5	3	0	24	61†
Northern Districts	8	3	4	1	20	44
Central Districts	8	3	4	1	8	32
Wellington..............	7	2	5	0	8	26*
Auckland	8	2	5	1	8	18†

The second match between Wellington and Canterbury was abandoned.

Final: Canterbury drew with Otago and took the Trophy by virtue of leading the table.

Win = 8 pts; lead on first innings = 4 pts.
* *Two points each in abandoned match.*
† *Points deducted for slow over-rate.*

Under New Zealand Cricket playing conditions, two extras are scored for every no-ball bowled whether scored off or not. Any runs scored off the bat are credited to the batsman, while byes and leg-byes are counted as no-balls, in accordance with Law 24.9, in addition to the initial penalty.

In the following scores, * by the name of a team indicates that they won the toss.

At Lancaster Park, Christchurch, November 25, 26, 27, 28. Drawn. Northern Districts 518 for four dec. (B. A. Pocock 137, M. D. Bell 55, G. E. Bradburn 148 not out, M. E. Parlane 142); Canterbury* 549 (B. R. Hartland 30, D. J. Murray 153, B. J. K. Doody 38, C. D. McMillan 159, G. R. Stead 42, M. W. Priest 67 not out). *Canterbury 4 pts.*

This was the first match in New Zealand in which both teams passed 500, though on November 1 the pitch had staged the Third Rugby League Test against Great Britain. Bradburn and Parlane added 259 for Northern Districts' fourth wicket.

At Victoria Park, Wanganui, November 25, 26, 27, 28. Central Districts won by three wickets. Otago 227 (M. J. Horne 124; A. J. Penn four for 84) and 271 (R. A. Lawson 44, M. J. Horne 90, C. B. Gaffaney 49; A. J. Penn six for 54); Central Districts* 263 (L. G. Howell 41, M. S. Sinclair 85, G. R. Loveridge 49 not out; P. J. Wiseman five for 80) and 236 for seven (M. D. J. Walker 34, M. S. Sinclair 83, D. M. Cooper 48; K. R. O'Dowda three for 27). *Central Districts 12 pts.*

Horne took his aggregate to 521 in his last five first-class innings; he had scored 113 and 190 in his only two matches for Auckland in 1995-96.

At Basin Reserve, Wellington, November 25, 26, 27, 28. Wellington won by ten wickets. Auckland 119 (R. A. Jones 39; S. J. Hotter four for 33, R. G. Petrie four for 32) and 246 (R. A. Jones 41, S. J. Peterson 40, S. M. Lynch 79 not out, Extras 47; S. J. Hotter three for 69, R. G. Petrie three for 34, H. T. Davis three for 74); Wellington* 365 (P. J. B. Chandler 177, R. G. Twose 63, R. G. Petrie 45; C. J. Drum four for 51, H. D. Barton three for 60) and one for no wkt. *Wellington 12 pts.*

At Eden Park, Auckland, November 30, December 1, 2, 3. Drawn. Auckland 109 (A. C. Barnes 41; A. J. Penn six for 36, G. R. Loveridge four for 23) and 198 for four dec. (M. J. Clark 42, A. C. Barnes 45, S. J. Peterson 49 not out); Central Districts* 61 (C. M. Brown five for 21) and 77 for seven (K. P. Walmsley three for 17, C. M. Brown three for 17). *Auckland 4 pts.*

At Harry Barker Reserve, Gisborne, November 30, December 1, 2, 3. Northern Districts won by an innings and 23 runs. Northern Districts* 474 (B. A. Pocock 53, M. D. Bell 43, G. E. Bradburn 45, M. E. Parlane 104, R. G. Hart 78, A. R. Tait 70, Extras 42; S. J. Hotter five for 99, M. R. Jefferson three for 100); Wellington 238 (P. J. B. Chandler 32, J. D. Wells 52, R. G. Petrie 44; C. W. Ross three for 69, S. A. Thomson three for 47) and 213 (P. J. B. Chandler 69, S. W. Weenink 40, S. J. Blackmore 34; A. R. Tait three for 25, S. B. Styris six for 42). *Northern Districts 12 pts.*

At Centennial Park, Oamaru, November 30, December 1, 2. Canterbury won by 122 runs. Canterbury 162 (B. J. K. Doody 79; J. W. Wilson five for 34, P. J. Wiseman three for 19) and 303 (C. D. McMillan 129, M. W. Priest 48; P. J. Wiseman five for 88); Otago* 191 (R. A. Lawson 98; G. I. Allott six for 60) and 152 (J. W. Wilson 69 not out; G. I. Allott four for 49, W. A. Wisneski four for 37). *Canterbury 8 pts, Otago 4 pts.*

Wilson took five wickets for 11 in the first hour of the match; on the final afternoon, he came in at 74 for six and scored 69 of the last 78 runs.

At Basin Reserve, Wellington, January 17, 18. Otago won by ten wickets. Wellington* 147 (R. G. Twose 49, S. J. Hotter 33; S. B. O'Connor five for 43) and 135 (G. R. Larsen 37; P. J. Wiseman eight for 66); Otago 250 (M. J. Horne 103, M. H. Richardson 59, S. B. O'Connor 40 not out; S. J. Hotter six for 69, H. T. Davis three for 62) and 36 for no wkt. *Otago 12 pts.*

Hotter took a hat-trick in Otago's first innings.

At Dudley Park, Rangiora, January 20, 21, 22, 23. Canterbury won by an innings and 11 runs. Central Districts* 347 (L. G. Howell 49, M. J. Greatbatch 141, C. J. M. Furlong 33, Extras 44; M. W. Priest four for 92) and 185 (C. M. Spearman 96; M. W. Priest five for 57); Canterbury 543 for eight dec. (D. J. Murray 41, C. Z. Harris 251 not out, M. W. Priest 56, M. E. L. Lane 61, W. A. Wisneski 40). *Canterbury 12 pts.*

Harris's 251 not out, his maiden double-hundred, lasted 647 minutes and 531 balls, included 29 fours and was a Canterbury record.

At Lancaster Park, Christchurch, January 27, 28, 29, 30. Canterbury won by an innings and 32 runs. Wellington* 212 (J. M. Aiken 50, J. D. Wells 69; C. Z. Harris four for 22) and 245 (D. S. McHardy 46, R. G. Petrie 80, C. J. Nevin 36, M. R. Jefferson 35; M. W. Priest four for 59); Canterbury 489 (C. D. Cumming 44, C. Z. Harris 93, C. D. McMillan 157, G. R. Stead 43, M. A. Hastings 52, Extras 35; R. G. Petrie four for 78, G. R. Jonas four for 49). *Canterbury 12 pts.*

Three Canterbury players and two from Wellington were required to leave after two days to join New Zealand A against England. Under NZC rules, replacements were allowed, but the start was delayed for an hour on the first day when Wellington objected to Canterbury naming Stephen Fleming and Nathan Astle, who were still playing in the First Test. The objection was upheld and the toss retaken. McMillan scored his third hundred of the season, equalling Walter Hadlee's Canterbury record set in 1947-48.

At Trafalgar Park, Nelson, January 27, 28, 29, 30. Northern Districts won by 155 runs. Northern Districts* 386 (M. D. Bell 66, M. N. Hart 47, M. D. Bailey 101, S. B. Styris 38 not out, Extras 40; A. J. Penn five for 89) and 194 (D. J. Nash 41; C. J. M. Furlong seven for 72); Central Districts 245 (L. G. Howell 49, M. D. J. Walker 84, C. J. M. Furlong 59; A. R. Tait four for 50, D. L. Vettori five for 61) and 180 (M. D. J. Walker 37, M. S. Sinclair 70; A. R. Tait three for 45, D. L. Vettori three for 81, G. E. Bradburn four for 12). *Northern Districts 12 pts.*

Vettori, who was 18 on the first day, took eight wickets on his Trophy debut, his second first-class match. A week later, he played in the Second Test against England.

At Carisbrook, Dunedin, January 27, 28, 29, 30. Otago won by ten wickets. Auckland* 272 (R. T. King 44, S. M. Lynch 85, S. J. Peterson 71, J. M. Mills 40 not out; S. B. O'Connor four for 83, R. J. Kennedy four for 44) and 307 (J. C. Forrest 34, R. A. Jones 99, A. C. Barnes 52, R. T. King 62, Extras 31; S. B. O'Connor six for 55); Otago 548 for eight dec. (R. A. Lawson 39, C. B. Gaffaney 194, M. J. Horne 112, M. P. Maynard 35, M. H. Richardson 36, S. B. O'Connor 47, A. J. Gale 36 not out; C. J. Drum four for 102) and 34 for no wkt. *Otago 12 pts.*

Gaffaney reached his maiden 100 in 99 minutes and 103 balls and went on to 194, out of 303, in 272 minutes and 230 balls.

At Trust Bank Park, Hamilton, February 3, 4, 5, 6. Auckland won by 212 runs. Auckland* 126 (S. M. Lynch 37; A. R. Tait nine for 48) and 245 (J. C. Forrest 34, R. A. Jones 54, A. C. Barnes 89 not out; A. R. Tait seven for 82); Northern Districts 127 (S. B. Styris 35; D. K. Morrison three for 38, C. J. Drum four for 33) and 32 (D. K. Morrison three for five, C. J. Drum four for 13, J. T. C. Vaughan three for six). *Auckland 8 pts, Northern Districts 4 pts.*

Tait became the first New Zealander to take 16 wickets in a match, and the first to take nine in an innings since Mark Priest in 1989-90. But Northern Districts lost, their second-innings 32 being the lowest total in their 40-year history.

At Eden Park, Auckland, February 10, 11, 12, 13. Canterbury won by six wickets. Auckland 293 (S. M. Lynch 68, J. T. C. Vaughan 38, H. D. Barton 76 not out; W. A. Wisneski four for 83, M. W. Priest four for 104) and 100 (J. T. C. Vaughan 30; W. A. Wisneski four for 37, M. W. Priest five for 31); Canterbury* 301 (C. D. Cumming 60, C. D. McMillan 44, M. W. Priest 50, G. A. Muir 44, M. A. Hastings 47 not out) and 93 for four (G. R. Stead 40 not out; D. K. Morrison four for 19). *Canterbury 12 pts.*

At Queen Elizabeth Park, Masterton, February 10, 11, 12, 13. Central Districts won by eight wickets. Wellington 263 (G. R. Larsen 76, R. G. Petrie 42, C. J. Nevin 36 not out, Extras 42; A. J. Penn four for 43) and 166 (P. J. B. Chandler 33, R. G. Twose 39, R. G. Petrie 32 not out; A. J. Penn five for 55); Central Districts* 411 (M. S. Sinclair 189, L. G. Howell 66, M. J. Greatbatch 31, Extras 34; G. R. Jonas four for 113, H. T. Davis four for 88) and 19 for two. *Central Districts 12 pts.*

At Molyneux Park, Alexandra, February 10, 11, 12, 13. Otago won by five wickets. Northern Districts 141 (M. D. Bailey 47; D. G. Sewell six for 58) and 236 (D. J. Nash 38, R. G. Hart 49; D. G. Sewell four for 72); Otago* 304 (A. J. Gale 44, M. P. Maynard 33, M. H. Richardson 40, S. A. Robinson 50, S. B. O'Connor 43; A. R. Tait six for 104) and 74 for five (M. P. Maynard 47 not out; A. R. Tait three for 33). *Otago 12 pts.*

Tait took his aggregate of wickets to 32 in three successive matches.

At Lancaster Park, Christchurch, February 23, 24, 25, 26. Canterbury won by seven wickets. Auckland* 172 (S. M. Lynch 55; S. E. Bond five for 59, M. W. Priest three for 25) and 233 (A. C. Barnes 31, S. M. Lynch 94, H. D. Barton 39; M. A. Hastings four for 37); Canterbury 223 (C. D. Cumming 46, B. J. K. Doody 93, C. D. McMillan 41; C. J. Drum six for 47) and 184 for three (C. D. Cumming 90 not out, B. J. K. Doody 33). *Canterbury 12 pts.*

At Trust Bank Park, Hamilton, February 23, 24, 25, 26. Wellington won by 14 runs. Wellington 247 (P. J. B. Chandler 34, S. J. Blackmore 78, Extras 37; A. R. Tait four for 59, D. L. Vettori five for 82) and 212 (P. J. B. Chandler 49, R. G. Petrie 56, C. J. Nevin 42; D. L. Vettori four for 79, G. E. Bradburn three for 46); Northern Districts* 244 (D. J. Nash 76, S. B. Styris 56; S. J. Hotter six for 77) and 201 (J. A. Yovich 78; G. R. Jonas four for 51, S. J. Hotter five for 48). *Wellington 12 pts.*
In Northern District's first innings, Nash and Styris added 95 for the ninth wicket; in their second innings, Yovich and Tait added 83 for the tenth wicket.

At Queen's Park, Invercargill, February 23, 24, 25. Otago won by five wickets. Central Districts 74 (D. G. Sewell eight for 31) and 348 (C. M. Spearman 87, M. S. Sinclair 66, L. G. Howell 63, C. J. M. Furlong 34; S. B. O'Connor three for 51, A. J. Gale three for 66); Otago* 347 (R. A. Lawson 49, C. B. Gaffaney 100, M. H. Richardson 98 not out, M. G. Croy 33; L. J. Hamilton three for 65) and 77 for five (L. J. Hamilton four for 26). *Otago 12 pts.*

At Eden Park Outer Oval, Auckland, March 15, 16, 17. Northern Districts won by ten wickets. Auckland* 229 (A. C. Barnes 81; J. A. Yovich five for 66) and 180 (R. A. Jones 79; A. R. Tait three for 29, G. E. Bradburn four for 40, M. N. Hart three for 54); Northern Districts 351 (M. D. Bell 36, M. E. Parlane 34, G. E. Bradburn 88, M. N. Hart 61, A. R. Tait 36; D. K. Morrison three for 66) and 59 for no wkt (A. P. O'Dowd 31 not out). *Northern Districts 12 pts.*

At Horton Park, Blenheim, March 15, 16, 17, 18. Canterbury won by four wickets. Central Districts* 285 (G. P. Sulzberger 35, L. G. Howell 91, M. D. J. Walker 33, C. O. Findlay 30, Extras 35; W. A. Wisneski three for 68) and 392 (G. P. Sulzberger 56, M. S. Sinclair 78, L. G. Howell 45, M. D. J. Walker 63; M. W. Priest six for 146); Canterbury 537 (C. Z. Harris 206, G. R. Stead 124, C. D. McMillan 67, Extras 52; C. E. Bulfin five for 111) and 142 for six (C. D. McMillan 47, G. R. Stead 31 not out; C. E. Bulfin four for 53). *Canterbury 12 pts.*
Harris's 206 lasted 468 minutes and 387 balls and included 28 fours. He became the second New Zealander to score two double-hundreds in a domestic season, following J. S. Hiddleston in 1925-26, and added 290 for Canterbury's fifth wicket with Stead. In the second innings, he made nought.

At Basin Reserve, Wellington, March 15, 16, 17, 18. Otago won by three wickets. Wellington 285 (G. R. Larsen 56, G. J. Wilkinson 57, M. R. Jefferson 35 not out, Extras 31; S. B. O'Connor three for 48, R. J. Kennedy three for 55) and 317 (S. J. Blackmore 102, G. J. Wilkinson 96, C. J. Nevin 32 not out, Extras 43; R. J. Kennedy four for 55, D. G. Sewell three for 58); Otago* 292 (R. A. Lawson 79, C. B. Gaffaney 58, M. H. Richardson 49, Extras 34; G. R. Larsen five for 33) and 311 for seven (R. A. Lawson 63, C. B. Gaffaney 74, M. H. Austen 42, M. G. Croy 35, Extras 33; M. R. Jefferson three for 41). *Otago 12 pts.*
Lawson and Gaffaney shared century opening stands in both Otago innings.

At Trust Bank Park, Hamilton, March 22, 23, 24, 25. Central Districts won by six wickets. Northern Districts 353 for nine dec. (B. A. Pocock 69, M. D. Bell 73, M. E. Parlane 37, M. N. Hart 60, R. G. Hart 33 not out; C. E. Bulfin three for 64) and forfeited second innings; Central Districts* 34 for two dec. and 320 for four (C. M. Spearman 57, M. S. Sinclair 99 not out, M. J. Greatbatch 72, M. D. J. Walker 33 not out, Extras 45). *Central Districts 8 pts, Northern Districts 4 pts.*
With Sinclair facing on 99 and Central Districts needing four to win, Grant Bradburn bowled four wides down the leg side; he claimed he was trying for a leg-side stumping but was fined $100 for "unacceptable conduct".

At Molyneux Park, Alexandra, March 22, 23, 24, 25. Auckland won by three wickets. Otago 126 (C. B. Gaffaney 36; J. T. C. Vaughan eight for 27) and 179 (R. A. Lawson 42, M. H. Austen 50; D. K. Morrison five for 66, A. C. Barnes three for 37); Auckland* 137 (R. A. Jones 54, Extras 34; D. G. Sewell three for 48, A. J. Gale four for 43) and 169 for seven (S. M. Lynch 60; A. J. Gale three for 40). *Auckland 12 pts.*
Vaughan returned career-best bowling figures in his last match as Auckland captain before leaving for England.

At Basin Reserve, Wellington, March 22, 23, 24, 25. Abandoned without a ball bowled. *Wellington 2 pts, Canterbury 2 pts.*

FINAL

CANTERBURY v OTAGO

At Lancaster Park, Christchurch, March 29, 30, 31, April 1. Drawn. Toss: Canterbury.

Second-placed Otago needed an outright win to take the Shell Trophy, but Canterbury scored 777 over the first two days and bowled them out for just 189. Then Austen scored the slowest century in New Zealand domestic cricket, enabling Otago to achieve an unlikely draw. Canterbury's total was the highest ever made in New Zealand, beating 752 for eight by New South Wales on tour in 1923-24 – also against Otago. It was the more remarkable because the square had been used for rugby the previous week. Harris was at the heart of the innings: when he hit a full toss to short mid-wicket, he was two short of becoming the first batsman to score three double-hundreds in a New Zealand season, and he did match the Canterbury record of three centuries, set by Walter Hadlee in 1947-48 and equalled by his team-mate McMillan earlier in 1996-97. Harris batted for 576 minutes and 469 balls and hit 21 fours and two sixes. He shared in three century partnerships and was well out-scored by his partners: McMillan made 94 during a stand of 124 – almost managing a fourth century the season – and Astle scored 160 out of 236. Astle then took six wickets – including four of the last five, which fell for three runs. Following on, Otago limped to 116 for seven, still 472 behind. But Austen, who reached 100 in 464 minutes and 390 balls, and batted on for another 16 minutes, added 146 with Wiseman to save face.

Man of the Match: N. J. Astle.

Close of play: First day, Canterbury 415-4 (C. Z. Harris 69*, N. J. Astle 64*); Second day, Canterbury 777; Third day, Otago 101-2 (M. H. Austen 15*, M. J. Horne 14*).

Canterbury

G. R. Stead b O'Connor	44	†M. E. L. Lane c Gaffaney b Wiseman	6
*D. J. Murray lbw b O'Connor	59	W. A. Wisneski c and b Wiseman	5
S. P. Fleming c Austen b Morland	66	S. E. Bond not out	3
C. Z. Harris c Lawson b Wiseman	198		
C. D. McMillan c Croy b Sewell	94	B 1, l-b 11, w 1, n-b 16	29
N. J. Astle b Morland	160		
C. L. Cairns lbw b Gale	57	1/71 2/170 3/183 4/307 5/543	777
M. W. Priest c Croy b Wiseman	56	6/676 7/739 8/763 9/770	

Bowling: O'Connor 37–5–140–2; Sewell 19–3–107–1; Gale 34–8–106–1; Wiseman 47.1–5–172–4; Morland 63–11–163–2; Richardson 15–5–46–0; Horne 5–1–16–0; Austen 3–0–15–0.

Otago

*R. A. Lawson lbw b Astle	24	– lbw b Wisneski	15
C. B. Gaffaney c McMillan b Bond	16	– lbw b Harris	48
M. H. Austen c Fleming b Priest	15	– not out	100
M. J. Horne c Murray b Astle	98	– c Lane b Bond	17
M. H. Richardson lbw b Bond	14	– c Wisneski b Bond	0
†M. G. Croy b Harris b Astle	14	– b Wisneski	0
S. B. O'Connor c Priest b Astle	0	– b Wisneski	0
A. J. Gale c Stead b Astle	0	– lbw b Harris	5
P. J. Wiseman b Bond	0	– c Stead b McMillan	73
N. D. Morland b Astle	0	– not out	15
D. G. Sewell not out	0		
B 1, l-b 7	8	B 11, l-b 9, w 1, n-b 12	33

1/32 2/51 3/68 4/97 5/166   189   1/20 2/76 3/104 4/106   (8 wkts) 306
6/186 7/186 8/187 9/188   5/107 6/107 7/116 8/262

Bowling: *First Innings*—Wisneski 14–4–39–0; Bond 15–4–43–3; Astle 8.4–2–22–6; Harris 13–7–24–0; Priest 20–6–53–1. *Second Innings*—Wisneski 21–10–39–3; Bond 24–10–57–2; Astle 22–9–45–0; Priest 43–16–57–0; Harris 31–7–59–2; McMillan 7–2–13–1; Stead 3–0–16–0; Fleming 2–2–0–0.

Umpires: B. F. Bowden and E. A. Watkin.

PLUNKET SHIELD AND SHELL TROPHY WINNERS

The Plunket Shield was replaced by the Shell Trophy after the 1974-75 season.

1921-22	Auckland	1949-50	Wellington	1973-74	Wellington
1922-23	Canterbury	1950-51	Otago	1974-75	Otago
1923-24	Wellington	1951-52	Canterbury	1975-76	Canterbury
1924-25	Otago	1952-53	Otago	1976-77	Otago
1925-26	Wellington	1953-54	Central Districts	1977-78	Auckland
1926-27	Auckland	1954-55	Wellington	1978-79	Otago
1927-28	Wellington	1955-56	Canterbury	1979-80	Northern Districts
1928-29	Auckland	1956-57	Wellington	1980-81	Auckland
1929-30	Wellington	1957-58	Otago	1981-82	Wellington
1930-31	Canterbury	1958-59	Auckland	1982-83	Wellington
1931-32	Wellington	1959-60	Canterbury	1983-84	Canterbury
1932-33	Otago	1960-61	Wellington	1984-85	Wellington
1933-34	Auckland	1961-62	Wellington	1985-86	Otago
1934-35	Canterbury	1962-63	Northern Districts	1986-87	Central Districts
1935-36	Wellington	1963-64	Auckland	1987-88	Otago
1936-37	Auckland	1964-65	Canterbury	1988-89	Auckland
1937-38	Auckland	1965-66	Wellington	1989-90	Wellington
1938-39	Auckland	1966-67	Central Districts	1990-91	Auckland
1939-40	Auckland	1967-68	Central Districts	1991-92	Central Districts / Northern Districts
1940-45	No competition	1968-69	Auckland	1992-93	Northern Districts
1945-46	Canterbury	1969-70	Otago	1993-94	Canterbury
1946-47	Auckland	1970-71	Central Districts	1994-95	Auckland
1947-48	Otago	1971-72	Otago	1995-96	Auckland
1948-49	Canterbury	1972-73	Wellington	1996-97	Canterbury

Auckland and Wellington have won the title outright 18 times, Canterbury and Otago 13, Central Districts 5, Northern Districts 3. Central Districts and Northern Districts also shared the title once.

SHELL CUP, 1996-97

Note: Matches in this section were not first-class.

Play-offs

At Eden Park, Auckland, January 8. Northern Districts won by seven runs. Northern Districts 223 for nine (50 overs) (B. A. Young 60, M. E. Parlane 43; J. T. C. Vaughan three for 31); Auckland* 216 for nine (50 overs) (A. C. Parore 61, P. A. de Silva 32, S. M. Lynch 49).

At Lancaster Park, Christchurch, January 8. Wellington won by 37 runs. Wellington* 247 for nine (50 overs) (P. J. B. Chandler 106, R. G. Twose 100; C. L. Cairns six for 37); Canterbury 210 (47 overs) (S. P. Fleming 32, L. K. Germon 60; G. R. Larsen three for 35).

At Lancaster Park, Christchurch, January 12. Canterbury won by seven wickets. Northern Districts 133 (37.5 overs) (W. A. Wisneski three for 27, G. A. Muir three for 24); Canterbury* 137 for three (27.3 overs) (D. J. Murray 38, C. D. McMillan 44).

Final

At Basin Reserve, Wellington, January 15. Canterbury won by 123 runs. Canterbury* 204 for seven (50 overs) (C. D. McMillan 38, C. L. Cairns 42, M. W. Priest 35 not out); Wellington 81 (33.5 overs) (M. W. Priest three for 15).
   Twelve spectators were arrested after alcohol-related disturbances.

CRICKET IN INDIA, 1996-97

By R. MOHAN and SUDHIR VAIDYA

Wasim Jaffer

Bombay, now known as Mumbai, won the Ranji Trophy for the 33rd time in its 63 years, but in an untraditional manner; the Indian Board decided to stage the final under lights at a neutral venue. The players of Mumbai and fellow-finalists Delhi were not best pleased by the change; after six months playing in daylight with red balls, they were required to switch to white balls, which had to be replaced every 50 overs, for the floodlit games.

Indian-made white balls were judged incapable of taking the soaking from the dew as night fell or of retaining their colour in the dusty environment, so a set of 18 Australian balls had to be rushed from the Board Secretary's office in Calcutta to Gwalior, where the match was taking place. Even then, and despite the frequent replacements, the lack of a prominent seam on the balls made life hard for the bowlers. The pitch was flat enough already in the summer conditions of early April.

Mumbai prevailed, partly because they won the toss and partly because their powerful batting line-up had the temperament for running up huge totals. They scored 630 in 202.2 overs, with centuries from Jatin Paranjpe, who added 173 for the second wicket with his captain, Sanjay Manjrekar, and Amol Muzumdar, who batted patiently with the tailenders to consolidate the upper order's work. In reply, Ajay Sharma and Ashu Dani shared a third-wicket stand of 313 to take Delhi to 385 for two. Slow left-armer Nilesh Patel bowled 74.1 overs to tip the scales Mumbai's way and a first-innings lead of 71 was enough to give them the trophy when the match petered out after five days.

The fact that the spinners had to bowl a negative line to defend their total reflected India's weakness in spotting or grooming bowlers. The best ones they do have are rarely available to play in the domestic tournaments as the national team followed a hectic schedule – from arriving in England in May 1996 to leaving the Caribbean in May 1997, they played 15 Tests and 31 one-day internationals in venues from Colombo to Canada. Karnataka, the defending Ranji champions, suffered heavily from national calls, finished fifth in South Zone and did not advance to the next stage.

That next stage underwent a reform in 1996-97. The old ''pre-quarter-final'' knockouts that used to whittle down the 15 teams qualifying from the regional zones were replaced by a Super League, which provided more meaningful league cricket than the zones, with their conspicuous mismatches, could offer. The teams were divided into three round-robin groups of five and the top two from each group advanced to the final stages. Mumbai and Delhi earned a bye to the semi-finals with the other four contesting two "quarter-finals".

The extra matches, as well as the growing imbalance between batsmen and bowlers – Indian pitches are getting ever flatter, through age and over-use – created a spate of batting records. Two Delhi batsmen, Raman Lamba and Ajay Sharma, passed the record aggregate for a Ranji season, set by Woorkeri Raman with 1,018 in 1988-89; Lamba scored 1,034 at 73.85 and Sharma 1,033 at 114.78. Sharma scored five centuries, culminating in 176 in the final, to pass Brijesh Patel's record of 26 Ranji hundreds, and in all first-class matches he reached 1,198 at 99.83. Hrishikesh Kanitkar, of semi-finalists Maharashtra, and Rahul Sapru of Uttar Pradesh also scored five hundreds, and Kanitkar reached four figures in all first-class cricket. But the averages were headed by the teenager Wasim Jaffer of Mumbai, who scored 314 against Saurashtra to lift himself to 115.33. It was his second first-class match, and he was three months short of his 19th birthday.

Slow bowlers earned the most rewards: Bhaskaran Ramprakash took 14 in Kerala's match against Karnataka, including eight for 25 in the second innings, on his way to 53 wickets in the season. His fellow off-spinner Rajesh Chauhan of Madhya Pradesh was the leading wicket-taker with 60, and the Punjabi slow left-armer Bharati Vij was close behind with 58.

There were some seamers who managed to rise above the conditions, however; medium-pacer Obaid Kamal took seven for 74 for Central Zone in their Duleep Trophy semi-final against West Zone. Central Zone reached 500 twice in that match, with four out of five batsmen making centuries in the second innings, before the declaration set West Zone an unlikely target of 760. Even then, they clung on to draw.

In the other semi-final (as the Ranji Trophy had expanded, the Duleep had dropped its own league and reverted to a knockout format), South Zone pulled off a surprise win over North Zone by successfully chasing 391 in the fourth innings. Sandagoppan Ramesh and Sridharan Sharath added 255 for the fifth wicket. But the team was badly depleted, losing ten players to the Test side and India A, and succumbed to Central Zone in the final. Central won the title for the first time since 1971-72, thanks to Zakir Hussain, a trainee from Dennis Lillee's academy, who took nine in the match on his first appearance in the competition, and Sapru, who scored 161 in their second innings.

Bowlers did achieve a better balance with batsmen in the one-day tournaments, in which the totals were far lower. This was predictable as the Deodhar Trophy was played in January, when the northern centres are noticeably wintry and there is always some assistance for seamers, especially in the first session. East Zone won the Deodhar championship, winning three of their four games. As in 1994-95, Mumbai achieved a first-class and limited-overs double, adding the Wills Trophy to the Ranji. – R.M.

FIRST-CLASS AVERAGES, 1996-97

BATTING

(Qualification: 600 runs)

	M	I	NO	R	HS	100s	Avge
Wasim Jaffer (*Mumbai*)	7	10	4	692	314*	2	115.33
Ajay Sharma (*Delhi*)	10	13	1	1,198	220*	5	99.83
R. Lamba (*Delhi*)	10	14	0	1,034	250	3	73.85
R. V. Sapru (*Uttar Pradesh*)	10	16	3	949	185*	5	73.00
R. Nayyar (*Himachal Pradesh*)	8	13	3	717	170	4	71.70
H. H. Kanitkar (*Maharashtra*)	11	16	2	1,003	205	5	71.64
S. S. Sugwekar (*Maharashtra*)	10	14	1	928	193	3	71.38
S. Sharath (*Tamil Nadu*)	8	12	1	774	151	3	70.36
S. V. Manjrekar (*Mumbai*)	11	11	1	675	150	2	67.50
A. A. Muzumdar (*Mumbai*)	12	16	2	942	214*	4	67.28
A. S. Kaypee (*Haryana*)	8	14	4	619	135*	2	61.90
C. S. Pandit (*Madhya Pradesh*)	12	16	1	873	189	3	58.20
V. Rathore (*Punjab*)	10	17	0	982	254	4	57.76
K. S. More (*Baroda*)	8	13	0	714	180	1	54.92
S. Abbas Ali (*Madhya Pradesh*)	10	15	1	761	198	3	54.35
J. Dani (*Delhi*)	10	14	1	696	215	2	53.53
V. Dahiya (*Delhi*)	12	17	3	738	134	1	52.71
Ajay Mehra (*Punjab*)	9	14	2	630	200*	1	52.50
S. S. Bhave (*Maharashtra*)	11	16	0	832	168	2	52.00
Jitender Singh (*Haryana*)	10	18	2	807	230	2	50.43
V. Pratap (*Hyderabad*)	10	16	1	754	136	1	50.26
Rizwan Shamshad (*Uttar Pradesh*) . . .	10	19	5	694	120*	2	49.57
K. N. A. Padmanabhan (*Kerala*)	11	18	5	615	200	2	47.30
G. K. Khoda (*Rajasthan*)	8	13	0	609	124	1	46.84
S. Raul (*Orissa*)	9	17	2	698	173	1	46.53
A. R. Khurasia (*Madhya Pradesh*)	10	17	0	790	209	2	46.47
V. G. Kambli (*Mumbai*)	11	13	0	604	111	1	46.46
R. S. Gavaskar (*Bengal*)	10	16	2	648	109	1	46.28
M. V. Sridhar (*Hyderabad*)	10	16	1	621	94	0	41.40
Jai P. Yadav (*Madhya Pradesh*)	12	20	0	825	108	2	41.25
S. Ramesh (*Tamil Nadu*)	10	18	1	655	146	2	38.52

* Signifies not out.

BOWLING

(Qualification: 30 wickets)

	O	M	R	W	BB	5W/i	Avge
Sukhbinder Singh (*Assam*)	183	51	435	31	7-99	4	14.03
P. Jain (*Haryana*)	333.2	79	879	44	7-72	4	19.97
B. Ramprakash (*Kerala*)	508.1	136	1,136	53	8-25	6	21.43
N. M. Kulkarni (*Mumbai*)	443.3	145	904	41	6-51	5	22.04
S. Raul (*Orissa*)	345.1	92	845	38	6-44	4	22.23
P. Thakur (*Haryana*)	400.1	80	1,133	47	6-32	1	24.10
Obaid Kamal (*Uttar Pradesh*)	367.2	86	948	39	7-74	4	24.30
B. Vij (*Punjab*)	527.1	108	1,449	58	7-55	6	24.98
N. D. Hirwani (*Bengal*)	409.1	106	1,045	41	6-51	3	25.48
A. S. Wassan (*Delhi*)	335.4	70	1,049	41	5-48	3	25.58
U. Chatterjee (*Bengal*)	459.3	138	1,030	40	6-115	2	25.75
A. Kuruvilla (*Mumbai*)	298	64	852	33	5-36	1	25.81

	O	M	R	W	BB	5Wfi	Avge
D. Ganesh (*Karnataka*)	279	38	961	37	6-84	4	25.97
R. K. Chauhan (*Madhya Pradesh*) ...	753.3	223	1,588	60	7-52	7	26.46
Zakir Hussain (*Railways*)	305.5	39	902	32	5-31	2	28.18
K. V. P. Rao (*Bihar*)	438.1	110	1,095	38	6-47	2	28.81
Iqbal Siddiqui (*Maharashtra*)	337.3	64	960	33	5-99	2	29.09
Sandeep Sharma (*Punjab*)	360	95	908	31	4-65	0	29.29
R. R. Singh (*Delhi*)	302	58	931	30	6-80	2	31.03
K. N. A. Padmanabhan (*Kerala*)	415.1	96	1,044	32	6-99	1	32.62
Avinash Kumar (*Bihar*)	502.2	123	1,307	40	6-42	1	32.67
S. V. Bahutule (*Mumbai*)	503.2	112	1,316	39	4-25	0	33.74
R. Sanghvi (*Delhi*)	381	89	1,114	32	6-75	2	34.81

Note: The names of some Indian cities have been changed by their state governments. Bombay is now officially Mumbai and Madras is Chennai.

*In the following scores, * by the name of a team indicates that they won the toss.*

IRANI CUP, 1996-97

Ranji Trophy Champions (Karnataka) v Rest of India

At M. Chinnaswamy Stadium, Bangalore, September 22, 23, 24, 25, 26. Karnataka won by five wickets. Rest of India* 203 (P. Dharmani 84, S. S. Karim 72; D. Ganesh six for 84, K. Katti three for 23) and 288 (G. K. Khoda 67, V. V. S. Laxman 78, P. Dharmani 72, R. Sanghvi 40 not out; D. Ganesh five for 89); Karnataka 356 (J. Arun Kumar 93, R. Vijay 93, P. V. Shashikanth 69; N. D. Hirwani six for 129) and 139 for five (S. Siriguppi 62 not out).

DULEEP TROPHY, 1996-97

At Feroz Shah Kotla Ground, Delhi, November 20, 21, 22, 23, 24. Drawn. East Zone* 276 (D. Gandhi 71, P. K. Amre 67, S. Raul 50; R. Sanghvi five for 45) and 472 for nine dec. (P. K. Amre 95, S. S. Karim 190, U. Chatterjee 69, A. Sarkar 35; Sandeep Sharma three for 63); North Zone 506 (A. Jadeja 74, Ajay Sharma 67, R. Nayyar 108, V. Dahiya 134, Sandeep Sharma 35, B. Vij 32; U. Chatterjee six for 115) and 91 for two (Sandeep Sharma 44 not out).

At Feroz Shah Kotla Ground, Delhi, November 27, 28, 29, 30, December 1. Drawn. Central Zone* 503 (A. R. Khurasia 45, R. V. Sapru 85, C. S. Pandit 189, Obaid Kamal 55, R. K. Chauhan 54; A. Ankola three for 101, A. Kuruvilla three for 97, S. V. Bahutule three for 108) and 500 for three dec. (G. K. Khoda 124, A. R. Khurasia 126, Rizwan Shamshad 120 not out, R. V. Sapru 100 not out); West Zone 244 (S. S. Bhave 75, V. G. Kambli 34, S. S. Dighe 44, H. J. Parsana 52; Obaid Kamal seven for 74) and 280 for eight (S. S. Bhave 86, A. V. Kale 37, V. G. Kambli 38; R. K. Chauhan three for 70).

At Nahar Singh Stadium, Faridabad, November 27, 28, 29, 30, December 1. South Zone won by five wickets. North Zone* 344 (V. Rathore 150, Ajay Sharma 80, Extras 39; D. J. Johnson four for 82, D. Ganesh three for 64) and 332 (A. Jadeja 89, V. Rathore 84, N. S. Sidhu 30, R. Nayyar 40; B. Ramprakash five for 100, K. N. A. Padmanabhan three for 65); South Zone 286 (W. V. Raman 51, S. Sharath 40, R. R. Singh 84, M. S. K. Prasad 60; Sandeep Sharma three for 62, F. Ghayas four for 54) and 393 for five (W. V. Raman 31, S. Sharath 140, R. Vijay 34, S. Ramesh 143 not out, R. R. Singh 37).

In South Zone's second innings, Sharath and Ramesh put on 255 for the fifth wicket.

At PCA Stadium, Mohali, Chandigarh, December 4, 5, 6, 7, 8. Central Zone won by 161 runs. Central Zone 264 (G. K. Khoda 72, A. R. Khurasia 37, C. S. Pandit 46; B. Ramprakash five for 85) and 359 (G. K. Khoda 68, R. V. Sapru 161, S. B. Bangar 36; J. Gokulkrishnan four for 81); South Zone* 225 (M. V. Sridhar 90; Obaid Kamal three for 53, Zakir Hussain four for 68) and 237 (A. Pathak 58, S. Ramesh 77, R. R. Singh 50; Obaid Kamal four for 79, Zakir Hussain five for 88).

DULEEP TROPHY WINNERS

1961-62	West Zone	1974-75	South Zone	1987-88	North Zone
1962-63	West Zone	1975-76	South Zone	1988-89	{ North Zone
1963-64	West Zone	1976-77	West Zone		{ West Zone
1964-65	West Zone	1977-78	West Zone	1989-90	South Zone
1965-66	South Zone	1978-79	North Zone	1990-91	North Zone
1966-67	South Zone	1979-80	North Zone	1991-92	North Zone
1967-68	South Zone	1980-81	West Zone	1992-93	North Zone
1968-69	West Zone	1981-82	West Zone	1993-94	North Zone
1969-70	West Zone	1982-83	North Zone	1994-95	North Zone
1970-71	South Zone	1983-84	North Zone	1995-96	South Zone
1971-72	Central Zone	1984-85	South Zone	1996-97	Central Zone
1972-73	West Zone	1985-86	West Zone		
1973-74	North Zone	1986-87	South Zone		

RANJI TROPHY, 1996-97

Central Zone

At Karnail Singh Stadium, Delhi, October 22, 23, 24, 25. Drawn. Madhya Pradesh* 329 (A. R. Khurasia 39, Raja Ali 70, P. K. Dwevedi 61, Extras 35; Javed Zaman three for 53) and 89 for eight (A. R. Khurasia 34; Zakir Hussain five for 31); Railways 122 (H. S. Sodhi four for 46, M. Majithia four for 18) and 313 (Z. Zuffri 55, K. Bharathan 34, D. Sudhakar 51, M. Suresh Kumar 33, M. Kartik 47; S. Pandey four for 63, R. K. Chauhan five for 112). *Railways 3 pts, Madhya Pradesh 5 pts.*

Zakir Hussain took five for 31 on first-class debut.

At VCA Ground, Nagpur, October 22, 23, 24, 25. Drawn. Uttar Pradesh* 263 for three dec. (M. S. Mudgal 81, R. Sharma 60, Jyoti P. Yadav 54, Rizwan Shamshad 55 not out); Vidarbha 158 for five (Mohammad Shabir 68). *Vidarbha 2 pts, Uttar Pradesh 2 pts.*

At Nehru Stadium, Indore, October 30, 31, November 1, 2. Drawn. Madhya Pradesh* 199 (P. K. Dwevedi 34, S. Abbas Ali 82; M. S. Doshi four for 64, P. K. Hedaoo three for 50, A. Kale three for 29) and 281 for eight dec. (Jai P. Yadav 45, A. R. Khurasia 72, C. S. Pandit 37, P. K. Dwevedi 35, S. Abbas Ali 45; P. K. Hedaoo five for 115); Vidarbha 173 (U. S. Phate 34, K. S. M. Iyer 40 not out; M. Majithia six for 59) and 106 for three (Mohammad Shabir 30, L. S. Rajput 40 not out). *Madhya Pradesh 5 pts, Vidarbha 3 pts.*

At Mansarovar Stadium, Jaipur, October 30, 31, November 1, 2. Drawn. Uttar Pradesh* 490 (R. Sharma 32, Rizwan Shamshad 49, R. V. Sapru 185 not out, S. A. Shukla 35, G. K. Pandey 101, Extras 38; Mohammad Aslam three for 132) and 285 for three (M. S. Mudgal 101, Jyoti P. Yadav 113, Rizwan Shamshad 51 not out); Rajasthan 364 (G. K. Khoda 93, R. J. Kanwat 47, N. Negi 87; Obaid Kamal five for 92). *Rajasthan 3 pts, Uttar Pradesh 5 pts.*

At Jayanti Stadium, Bhilai, November 7, 8, 9, 10. Madhya Pradesh won by an innings and 17 runs. Rajasthan* 227 (G. K. Khoda 39, V. Joshi 54, R. J. Kanwat 68, Mohammad Aslam 30; S. S. Lahore three for 77, R. K. Chauhan seven for 62) and 333 (G. K. Khoda 52, V. Joshi 137, A. S. Parmar 37, Abhay Sharma 30; R. K. Chauhan five for 93); Madhya Pradesh 577 (K. K. Patel 74, S. Abbas Ali 198, C. S. Pandit 116, P. K. Dwevedi 80, R. K. Chauhan 38; Mohammad Aslam three for 173). *Madhya Pradesh 8 pts.*

At Karnail Singh Stadium, Delhi, November 7, 8, 9, 10. Railways won by 110 runs. Railways* 163 (S. B. Bangar 47, P. S. Rawat 35, D. Sudhakar 48; P. K. Hedaoo four for 59) and 172 (S. B. Bangar 35; U. V. Gandhe four for 32); Vidarbha 130 (Y. T. Ghare 31, U. V. Gandhe 32; M. Kartik six for 28) and 95 (M. Suresh Kumar four for 21, M. Kartik three for 27). *Railways 8 pts.*
  Kartik took a hat-trick in Vidarbha's first innings.

At Mansarovar Stadium, Jaipur, December 16, 17, 18, 19. Drawn. Railways* 338 (S. B. Bangar 87, V. Z. Yadav 37, D. Sudhakar 69, K. Bharathan 63, Extras 32; P. Krishnakumar three for 92, D. Pal Singh three for 51) and 160 for four (S. B. Bangar 72 not out, D. Sudhakar 48); Rajasthan 374 (A. Jain 45, P. Krishnakumar 110, N. Negi 119, Extras 39; Iqbal Thakur three for 88). *Rajasthan 5 pts, Railways 3 pts.*
  Krishnakumar and Negi put on 218 for Rajasthan's seventh wicket.

At Green Park, Kanpur, December 16, 17, 18, 19. Drawn. Uttar Pradesh* 460 (M. S. Mudgal 51, R. Sharma 98, R. V. Sapru 86, G. K. Pandey 64, Obaid Kamal 44; R. K. Chauhan five for 132) and 92 for one (Rizwan Shamshad 51 not out); Madhya Pradesh 330 (Jai P. Yadav 94, A. R. Khurasia 36, S. Abbas Ali 62, C. S. Pandit 60; S. A. Shukla three for 37). *Uttar Pradesh 5 pts, Madhya Pradesh 3 pts.*

At Green Park, Kanpur, December 24, 25, 26, 27. Drawn. Uttar Pradesh* 267 (Jyoti P. Yadav 79, S. A. Shukla 41, S. Bajpai 31 not out; Iqbal Thakur five for 84, S. B. Bangar three for 46) and 209 (M. S. Mudgal 36, Rizwan Shamshad 36; Iqbal Thakur four for 42, M. Suresh Kumar three for 42); Railways 343 (V. Z. Yadav 30, Z. Zuffri 86, Y. Gowda 37, A. Kapoor 45, K. Bharathan 39 not out, Zakir Hussain 30; Obaid Kamal five for 98) and 33 for no wkt. *Uttar Pradesh 3 pts, Railways 5 pts.*

At VCA Ground, Nagpur, December 24, 25, 26, 27. Drawn. Vidarbha* 308 (Mohammad Shabir 31, U. I. Ghani 38, L. S. Rajput 56, P. K. Hedaoo 74; P. Krishnakumar three for 43, Mohammad Aslam five for 95) and 345 for eight (R. Shahane 41, L. S. Rajput 123, M. S. Doshi 43, Y. Chandurkar 30 not out; Mohammad Aslam four for 104); Rajasthan 396 (A. D. Sinha 35, G. K. Khoda 60, A. S. Parmar 74, R. J. Kanwat 52, V. Joshi 75 not out, N. Negi 49; P. K. Hedaoo three for 121, U. V. Gandhe three for 76). *Vidarbha 3 pts, Rajasthan 5 pts.*

Madhya Pradesh 21 pts, Railways 19 pts, Uttar Pradesh 15 pts, Rajasthan 13 pts, Vidarbha 8 pts. Madhya Pradesh, Railways and Uttar Pradesh qualified for the Super League.

East Zone

At Eden Gardens, Calcutta, November 3, 4, 5, 6. Drawn. Bengal* 188 (N. Haldipur 64, R. S. Gavaskar 43, Chetan Sharma 38; D. S. Mohanty five for 52, R. B. Biswal three for 47) and 293 for nine dec. (D. Gandhi 31, R. S. Gavaskar 55, S. S. Karim 66, U. Chatterjee 30, Chetan Sharma 37; D. S. Mohanty four for 91, R. B. Biswal four for 109); Orissa 181 (P. Jayachandra 37, S. Raul 35, R. R. Parida 46; U. Chatterjee three for 27, N. D. Hirwani six for 86) and 185 for five (P. R. Mohapatra 35, S. S. Das 68, S. Raul 42 not out). *Bengal 5 pts, Orissa 3 pts.*
  Rohan Gavaskar, son of former Indian captain Sunil, made his first-class debut; Mohanty took nine wickets, also on debut.

At Keenan Stadium, Jamshedpur, November 3, 4, 5, 6. Bihar won by an innings and 29 runs. Bihar* 474 (D. Chakraborty 111, M. Yadav 44, Rajiv Kumar 129 not out, Sunil Kumar 105, Avinash Kumar 38 not out); Tripura 150 (K. Burman 48; K. V. P. Rao six for 47, Avinash Kumar three for 42) and 295 (P. Debnath 37, K. Burman 36; D. K. Singh five for 24). *Bihar 8 pts.*
  Chakraborty scored 111 on first-class debut.

At North-East Frontier Railway Stadium, Maligaon, Gauhati, November 12, 13, 14, 15. Bengal won by eight wickets. Assam* 162 (S. Sawant 32, V. Samant 36; U. Chatterjee five for 34, A. Varma three for 35) and 233 (S. Sawant 53, Sukhbinder Singh 80 not out, I. Hussain 36; U. Chatterjee three for 82, A. Varma three for 59, S. Singh three for 71); Bengal 279 (N. Haldipur 91, P. K. Amre 85; Sukhbinder Singh four for 84, S. Sawant three for 44) and 117 for two (N. Haldipur 35, R. S. Gavaskar 52 not out). *Bengal 8 pts.*

In Assam's second innings, Sukhbinder Singh and Hussain put on 100 for the last wicket.

At Tata Digwadi Stadium, Dhanbad, November 12, 13, 14, 15. Bihar won by nine wickets. Orissa* 247 (S. Raul 37, G. Gopal 42, S. C. Mohanty 56; K. V. P. Rao three for 57) and 193 (P. Jayachandra 62, S. S. Das 52, S. Raul 30; Avinash Kumar three for 74, J. Patel three for 30); Bihar 369 (M. Yadav 33, Tarun Kumar 31, Avinash Kumar 139, D. K. Singh 34 not out; S. Raul six for 106) and 72 for one (M. Yadav 40). *Bihar 8 pts.*

At North-East Frontier Railway Stadium, Maligaon, Gauhati, December 11, 12, 13, 14. Orissa won by eight wickets. Assam 212 (S. Saikia 59, S. Sawant 35, G. Dutta 54 not out; S. Raul three for 32, Syed Khan three for 54) and 262 (A. Das 39, S. Saikia 50, Rajinder Singh 39, S. Sawant 35, G. Dutta 38; D. S. Mohanty three for 70); Orissa* 216 (P. Jayachandra 84, R. Seth 37; G. Dutta four for 64, Sukhbinder Singh four for 54) and 260 for two (P. R. Mohapatra 102 not out, S. S. Das 85, S. Raul 65 not out). *Orissa 8 pts.*

At Eden Gardens, Calcutta, December 11, 12, 13, 14. Bengal won by an innings and 35 runs. Tripura 96 (S. T. Banerjee three for 23, A. Sarkar four for 39, U. Chatterjee three for 19) and 151 (K. Burman 36, T. Chanda 34, R. Deb-Burman 33 not out; U. Chatterjee four for 48, A. Varma four for 24); Bengal* 282 (A. Varma 34, R. S. Gavaskar 46, S. J. Kalyani 31, S. S. Karim 30, A. Sarkar 57 not out; Pawan Kumar five for 85). *Bengal 8 pts.*

At North-East Frontier Railway Stadium, Maligaon, Gauhati, December 20, 21, 22, 23. Assam won by four wickets. Bihar* 150 (V. Khullar 75; Sukhbinder Singh five for 35, Indrajit Singh three for 45) and 263 (V. Khullar 53, J. Patel 57; Sukhbinder Singh seven for 99); Assam 293 (S. Saikia 56, G. Dutta 32, Sukhbinder Singh 89, V. Samant 89; Avinash Kumar three for 112, K. V. P. Rao five for 63) and 123 for six (K. V. P. Rao four for 43). *Assam 8 pts.*

At Polytechnic Ground, Agartala, December 20, 21, 22, 23. Orissa won by 188 runs. Orissa* 183 (S. S. Das 72; S. Roy seven for 50) and 267 (S. S. Das 53, A. Khatua 79, R. R. Parida 50; H. Yadav seven for 80); Tripura 123 (S. Lahiri 54; S. Raul six for 44) and 139 (S. Raul four for 44, S. C. Mohanty four for 35). *Orissa 8 pts.*

At Eden Gardens, Calcutta, December 28, 29, 30, 31. Drawn. Bihar 243 (Tariq-ur-Rehman 53, Tarun Kumar 36, Rajiv Kumar 56; N. D. Hirwani four for 57) and 41 for one; Bengal* 750 for seven dec. (A. Varma 98, N. Haldipur 113, R. S. Gavaskar 70, P. K. Amre 78, S. J. Kalyani 35, U. Chatterjee 120, H. Feroze 152 not out, S. T. Banerjee 50, Extras 34; Avinash Kumar three for 216). *Bengal 5 pts, Bihar 3 pts.*

At Polytechnic Ground, Agartala, December 28, 29, 30, 31. Assam won by an innings and 327 runs. Assam* 524 for eight dec. (D. Bora 50, S. Sawant 63, N. Bordoloi 151 not out, Sukhbinder Singh 167, V. Samant 37; C. Sanyal three for 127, H. Yadav three for 120); Tripura 65 (Sukhbinder Singh five for 20) and 132 (R. Chowdhary 67; Sukhbinder Singh five for 41). *Assam 8 pts.*

Bordoloi and Sukhbinder Singh put on 263 for Assam's seventh wicket. Sukhbinder completed the double of 100 or more runs and ten or more wickets for the second match running.

Bengal 26 pts, Bihar 19 pts, Orissa 19 pts, Assam 16 pts, Tripura 0 pt. Bengal, Bihar and Orissa qualified for the Super League.

North Zone

At Feroz Shah Kotla Ground, Delhi, October 24, 25, 26, 27. Delhi won by two wickets. Services* 249 (Narinder Singh 37, S. Verma 32, P. Maitreya 51, K. K. Dixit 78; M. Prabhakar four for 31, A. S. Wassan three for 50) and 318 (Chinmoy Sharma 117, J. P. Pandey 52, M. V.

Rao 56 not out; R. Sanghvi six for 75); Delhi 350 (M. Prabhakar 44, Ajay Sharma 56, V. Dahiya 72, A. S. Wassan 48; K. K. Dixit three for 73) and 221 for eight (A. Dani 58, Ajay Sharma 68, S. Dogra 31; M. V. Rao seven for 59). *Delhi 8 pts.*

At Police Stadium, Chamba, October 24, 25, 26, 27. Haryana won by an innings and 260 runs. Haryana* 456 for nine dec. (Jitender Singh 230, N. R. Goel 63; Jaswant Rai three for 126); Himachal Pradesh 99 (N. Gaur 36; P. Thakur six for 32) and 97 (P. Thakur four for 41, P. Jain six for 25). *Haryana 8 pts.*

Jitender Singh's 230, his maiden double-hundred, lasted 518 minutes and 368 balls and included 28 fours and two sixes.

At Gandhi Ground, Amritsar, October 24, 25, 26, 27. Punjab won by an innings and 91 runs. Punjab* 485 (Ajay Mehra 30, V. Rathore 254, D. Mongia 32, M. Mehra 105; Abdul Qayyum four for 97, A. Gupta four for 199); Jammu and Kashmir 225 (Kanwaljit Singh 97, Sanjay Sharma 55; B. Vij seven for 55) and 169 (Kanwaljit Singh 63, V. Bhaskar 35; Sandeep Sharma three for 25, B. Vij four for 23). *Points cancelled.*

Rathore's 254 lasted 474 minutes and 326 balls and included 26 fours and five sixes. All points in Jammu and Kashmir matches were cancelled after they failed to attend their last two fixtures.

At Nahar Singh Stadium, Faridabad, October 31, November 1, 2, 3. Haryana won by eight wickets. Jammu and Kashmir* 283 (A. Gupta 99, V. Bhaskar 96; R. P. Singh four for 64, P. Thakur four for 89) and 268 (R. Gill 79, A. Gupta 102; P. Jain three for 74); Haryana 464 (Jitender Singh 33, Shafiq Khan 95, N. R. Goel 42, A. S. Kaypee 135 not out, V. S. Yadav 70, P. Jain 37; Sanjay Sharma three for 102, P. Bali three for 74) and 89 for two (N. R. Goel 30 not out). *Points cancelled.*

At Paddal Stadium, Mandi, October 31, November 1, 2, 3. Punjab won by six wickets. Himachal Pradesh* 305 (N. Gaur 36, Chetan Kumar 89, Virender Sharma 37, Jaswant Rai 31; B. Vij five for 92) and 268 (R. Nayyar 110 not out, Virender Sharma 45; B. Vij six for 90); Punjab 482 (Ajay Mehra 84, V. Rathore 167, D. Mongia 115, Extras 36; Jaswant Rai five for 121) and 92 for four (Jaswant Rai four for 42). *Punjab 8 pts.*

At Gandhi Ground, Amritsar, November 6, 7, 8, 9. Drawn. Haryana* 249 (A. S. Kaypee 56, V. S. Yadav 47, P. Thakur 46; Sandeep Sharma three for 42, B. Vij three for 79) and 307 (Jitender Singh 62, N. R. Goel 55, R. Puri 64, Shafiq Khan 44; B. Bhushan four for 69, Chaman Lal three for 93); Punjab 222 (V. Rathore 104; P. Thakur three for 95, P. Jain three for 19) and 134 for five (Sandeep Sharma 80 not out). *Punjab 3 pts, Haryana 5 pts.*

At Air Force Complex, Palam, Delhi, November 7, 8, 9, 10. Services won by nine wickets. Services* 430 (P. Maitreya 60, Chinmoy Sharma 207, Extras 36; Jaswant Rai four for 123) and 81 for one (Narinder Singh 32 not out); Himachal Pradesh 125 (N. Gaur 35; Arun Sharma three for 15, K. K. Dixit three for 51) and 380 (N. Gaur 128, R. Nayyar 148; S. Ghag three for 44). *Services 8 pts.*

Chinmoy Sharma's 207, his maiden double-hundred, lasted 329 minutes and 325 balls and included 24 fours.

At Feroz Shah Kotla Ground, Delhi, November 13, 14, 15, 16. Delhi won by an innings and 155 runs. Delhi 486 for five dec. (A. Dani 215, Ajay Sharma 78, S. Dogra 101 not out, V. Dahiya 42 not out; Jaswant Rai four for 158); Himachal Pradesh* 188 (R. Nayyar 99; A. S. Wassan three for 73, F. Ghayas three for 29) and 143 (Raj Kumar 41; A. S. Wassan three for 29, F. Ghayas three for 23). *Delhi 8 pts.*

Dani's 215, his maiden double-hundred, lasted 503 minutes and 412 balls and included 24 fours.

At Air Force Complex, Palam, Delhi, November 13, 14, 15, 16. Haryana won by eight wickets. Haryana* 375 (Syed Khan 67, A. S. Kaypee 113, R. Puri 48; M. V. Rao three for 63, Arun Sharma three for 91) and 69 for two (N. R. Goel 33 not out); Services 115 (P. Maitreya 32; Dhanraj Singh four for 37, P. Thakur four for 23) and 325 (Sarabjit Singh 64, Chinmoy Sharma 70, M. V. Rao 57; Dhanraj Singh three for 63, P. Jain three for 92). *Haryana 8 pts.*

At Feroz Shah Kotla Ground, Delhi, December 11, 12, 13, 14. Drawn. Punjab* 351 (V. Rathore 30, N. S. Sidhu 132, D. Mongia 38, M. Mehra 77; R. R. Singh six for 80) and 190 for five (V. Rathore 30, R. Sodhi 43, Bhupinder Singh, jun. 68); Delhi 604 for nine dec. (A. Dani 33, R. Lamba 250, Akash Malhotra 120, M. Prabhakar 40, V. Dahiya 61 not out, A. S. Wassan 33, Extras 34; B. Bhushan three for 100, B. Vij five for 178). *Delhi 5 pts, Punjab 3 pts.*

Lamba's 250 lasted 617 minutes and 429 balls and included 29 fours and three sixes. He put on 291 for Delhi's third wicket with Akash Malhotra.

At Indira Stadium, Una, December 11, 12, 13, 14. Himachal Pradesh won by an innings and 42 runs. Himachal Pradesh* 385 (Jasminder Singh 61, R. Nayyar 170, Chetan Kumar 80; Abdul Qayyum five for 110, Idris three for 54); Jammu and Kashmir 187 (Idris 63, Vijay Sharma 31; Surinder Singh five for 41, Jaswant Rai four for 67) and 156 (Sandeep Chandel five for 25). *Points cancelled.*

At Feroz Shah Kotla Ground, Delhi, December 18, 19, 20, 21. Delhi v Jammu and Kashmir. Abandoned.

The Jammu and Kashmir players did not attend this or their game v Services below.

At Air Force Complex, Palam, Delhi, December 18, 19, 20, 21. Punjab won by an innings and 148 runs. Services* 238 (P. Maitreya 78, Chinmoy Sharma 42; B. Vij six for 88) and 182 (S. Verma 57; B. Vij five for 43); Punjab 568 for four dec. (Ajay Mehra 84, R. Sodhi 55, N. S. Sidhu 81, D. Mongia 207 not out, Bhupinder Singh, jun. 56, M. Mehra 50 not out, Extras 35). *Punjab 8 pts.*

Mongia's 207 not out, his maiden double-hundred, lasted 568 minutes and 331 balls and included 23 fours.

At Nehru Stadium, Gurgaon, December 24, 25, 26, 27. Drawn. Haryana* 268 (Jatinder Singh 98, V. S. Yadav 68; M. Prabhakar three for 38, R. R. Singh five for 52) and 449 for six (A. Jadeja 154, N. R. Goel 135, A. S. Kaypee 80, Extras 41; O. Wilson three for 85); Delhi 326 (A. Dani 40, R. Lamba 60, V. Dahiya 51, Ajay Sharma 35, N. Chopra 42, R. Sanghvi 41; P. Thakur four for 93). *Haryana 3 pts, Delhi 5 pts.*

In Haryana's second innings, Jadeja and Goel put on 294 for the second wicket.

At Air Force Complex, Palam, Delhi, December 24, 25, 26, 27. Services v Jammu and Kashmir. Abandoned.

Delhi 26 pts, Haryana 24 pts, Punjab 22 pts, Services 8 pts, Himachal Pradesh 0 pt, Jammu and Kashmir 0 pt. Delhi, Haryana and Punjab qualified for the Super League.

South Zone

At Vizzy Stadium, Vizianagram, October 25, 26, 27, 28. Drawn. Andhra* 302 (A. Pathak 123, B. S. Naik 55, V. Vinay Kumar 48) and 119 for six (R. V. C. Prasad 64 not out; S. L. V. Raju three for 37); Hyderabad 290 (A. Nandakishore 46, V. V. S. Laxman 61, Yuvraj Singh 50, N. P. Singh 48 not out; H. Ramkishen four for 131, K. Chakradhar Rao four for 95). *Andhra 5 pts, Hyderabad 3 pts.*

At Gymkhana Ground, Kampal, Panaji, October 25, 26, 27, 28. Goa won by an innings and 81 runs. Goa 346 (V. B. Chandrasekhar 88, R. Naik 55, J. Gokulkrishnan 36, S. Y. Dhuri 51, S. Signapurkar 33 not out, Extras 31; D. Ganesh five for 92); Karnataka* 114 (S. Somasunder 70; J. Gokulkrishnan seven for 54) and 151 (J. Arun Kumar 38, P. V. Shashikanth 32; J. Gokulkrishnan four for 60, Sayyad Khalid three for 36). *Goa 8 pts.*

At Municipal Stadium, Thalassery, October 25, 26, 27, 28. Drawn. Tamil Nadu* 397 (S. Ramesh 33, S. Sharath 151, R. Paul 84; B. Ramprakash three for 85, C. T. K. Masood three for 104) and 73 for three (R. Paul 32); Kerala 330 (S. Oasis 72, A. S. Kudva 82, B. Ramprakash 60, K. N. A. Padmanabhan 31 not out; S. Subramaniam three for 70, R. Chandramouli three for 112). *Kerala 3 pts, Tamil Nadu 5 pts.*

At Arlem Breweries Ground, Margao, November 3, 4, 5, 6. Drawn. Tamil Nadu* 326 (K. Srinath 34, S. Sharath 86, H. Badani 94, R. Paul 42; Y. C. Barde three for 60, N. Kalekar three for 68) and 264 for four dec. (K. Srinath 33, S. Ramesh 38, S. Sharath 94, H. Badani 80 not out; A. Shetty three for 79); Goa 253 (A. Shetty 63, S. Y. Dhuri 65, S. V. Kamat 30; D. K. Devanand three for 65) and 80 for three. *Goa 3 pts, Tamil Nadu 5 pts.*

At M. Chinnaswamy Stadium, Bangalore, November 3, 4, 5, 6. Drawn. Hyderabad* 358 (G. A. Shetty 75, V. V. S. Laxman 67, V. Pratap 34, M. V. Sridhar 33, N. David 65, R. Sridhar 36; D. Ganesh four for 96, R. Ananth three for 68) and 231 (M. V. Sridhar 31, S. L. V. Raju 36 not out; D. J. Johnson three for 72, D. Ganesh three for 96); Karnataka 335 (F. Khaleel 76, R. Vijay 116, P. V. Shashikanth 46; N. P. Singh three for 70). *Karnataka 3 pts, Hyderabad 5 pts.*

At Gymkhana Ground, Secunderabad, November 10, 11, 12, 13. Hyderabad won by six wickets. Kerala* 245 (S. Shankar 62, S. Oasis 66; S. L. V. Raju three for 49, Kanwaljit Singh four for 72) and 112 (S. Manoj 34; N. David four for 35); Hyderabad 203 (A. Nandakishore 47, M. V. Sridhar 55; K. N. A. Padmanabhan four for 47) and 158 for four (V. V. S. Laxman 56, M. V. Sridhar 61). *Hyderabad 8 pts.*

Kerala wicket-keeper V. Kamaruddin made four catches and two stumpings in Hyderabad's first innings.

At M. A. Chidambaram Stadium, Chennai, November 12, 13, 14, 15. Tamil Nadu v Karnataka. Abandoned due to rain. *Tamil Nadu 2 pts, Karnataka 2 pts.*

At Trishna Stadium, Ukkunagaram, Vishakhapatnam, November 17, 18, 19, 20. Kerala won by an innings and 49 runs. Andhra* 76 (B. Ramprakash four for 26, K. N. A. Padmanabhan three for 17) and 159 (A. Pathak 80; C. T. K. Masood five for 53); Kerala 284 (K. N. Balasubramaniam 37, S. Shankar 43, S. Oasis 43, K. Chandrasekhar 72 not out; K. Chakradhar Rao four for 70). *Kerala 8 pts.*

At Gymkhana Ground, Kampal Panaji, December 12, 13, 14, 15. Goa won by ten wickets. Goa 371 (V. B. Chandrasekhar 194, S. Upadhyaya 45, S. Y. Dhuri 35, B. K. P. Misquin 32; H. Ramkishen seven for 126) and 37 for no wkt; Andhra* 141 (Madhusudhan Raju 35; S. V. Kamat four for 38, J. Gokulkrishnan three for 50) and 265 (A. Pathak 58, R. V. C. Prasad 141 not out; Sayyad Khalid five for 53). *Goa 8 pts.*

Prasad carried his bat through Andhra's second innings.

At Gymkhana Ground, Secunderabad, December 20, 21, 22, 23. Drawn. Tamil Nadu* 424 (S. Sharath 35, R. R. Singh 59, H. Badani 164, R. Paul 100; Kanwaljit Singh four for 74) and 146 for five (S. Ramesh 65, S. Sriram 51); Hyderabad 395 (G. A. Shetty 93, M. V. Sridhar 94, R. Sridhar 58, Extras 46; S. Subramaniam five for 84). *Hyderabad 3 pts, Tamil Nadu 5 pts.*

At M. Chinnaswamy Stadium, Bangalore, December 20, 21, 22, 23. Karnataka won by 208 runs. Karnataka* 237 (R. Vijay 63, P. V. Shashikanth 30, S. Siriguppi 34; H. Ramkishen three for 67, K. Chakradhar Rao three for 59, Y. S. Ranganath three for 67) and 290 for eight dec. (S. Somasunder 43, R. Vijay 68, S. Sriram 39, S. B. Joshi 72 not out; H. Ramkishen three for 91, K. Chakradhar Rao three for 111); Andhra 120 (S. B. Joshi five for 57, K. Katti three for nine) and 199 (B. S. Naik 45; S. B. Joshi six for 97). *Karnataka 8 pts.*

At Victoria College Ground, Palghat, December 20, 21, 22, 23. Kerala won by seven wickets. Goa* 276 (S. Signapurkar 30, J. Gokulkrishnan 104 not out, B. K. P. Misquin 52; B. Ramprakash five for 109, C. T. K. Masood three for 47) and 153 (V. B. Chandrasekhar 31, B. K. P. Misquin 49; B. Ramprakash six for 34); Kerala 281 (K. N. Balasubramaniam 36, S. Shankar 32, S. Oasis 57, B. Ramprakash 30, S. Manoj 47, Extras 34; P. J. Rodrigues four for 57, Sayyad Khalid four for 85) and 153 for three (K. N. Balasubramaniam 32, S. Shankar 55 not out, S. Oasis 46). *Kerala 8 pts.*

At M. A. Chidambaram Stadium, Chennai, December 27, 28, 29, 30. Tamil Nadu won by an innings and 16 runs. Tamil Nadu* 457 (S. Ramesh 146, R. C. Vasant Kumar 35, S. Sriram 30, R. R. Singh 150; H. Ramkishen three for 108, K. Chakradhar Rao four for 179); Andhra 262 (A. Pathak 114, K. S. T. Sai 33, Madhusudhan Raju 39; S. Subramaniam three for 50, S. Sriram three for 37) and 179 (K. S. T. Sai 48, B. S. Naik 92; R. Chandramouli three for 46, W. D. Balaji Rao five for 47). *Tamil Nadu 8 pts.*

At Gymkhana Ground, Secunderabad, December 28, 29, 30, 31. Drawn. Hyderabad 393 (S. Kiran Kumar 59, V. Pratap 94, N. David 70, R. Sridhar 49, N. P. Singh 74; J. Gokulkrishnan four for 94, N. Kalekar five for 104) and 305 for eight dec. (V. Pratap 136, N. David 105; Y. C. Barde three for 101); Goa* 192 (S. Upadhyaya 39, R. Naik 61, S. Y. Dhuri 35; V. Vardhan four for 51) and 46 for no wkt. *Hyderabad 5 pts, Goa 3 pts.*

At Victoria College Ground, Palghat, December 28, 29, 30, 31. Kerala won by six wickets. Karnataka* 153 (S. Oasis three for 28, B. Ramprakash six for 52) and 74 (B. Ramprakash eight for 25); Kerala 161 (A. S. Kudva 60; S. B. Joshi five for 68) and 69 for four (R. Ananth three for 17). *Kerala 8 pts.*

Kerala 27 pts, Tamil Nadu 25 pts, Hyderabad 24 pts, Goa 22 pts, Karnataka 13 pts, Andhra 5 pts. Kerala, Tamil Nadu and Hyderabad qualified for the Super League.

West Zone

At IPCL Sports Complex Ground, Baroda, October 27, 28, 29, 30. Drawn. Baroda 205 (K. S. More 59, J. J. Martin 31; H. J. Parsana four for 57) and 229 for nine dec. (A. C. Bedade 76, M. S. Narula 44 not out; H. J. Parsana four for 64); Saurashtra* 151 (B. M. Jadeja 30, H. J. Parsana 37, C. C. Mankad 32 not out; Sukhbir Singh three for 34, T. B. Arothe five for 38) and 108 for five. *Baroda 5 pts, Saurashtra 3 pts.*

At Wankhede Stadium, Mumbai, October 27, 28, 29, 30. Mumbai won by an innings and 190 runs. Mumbai* 451 (S. V. Manjrekar 50, A. A. Muzumdar 214 not out, S. K. Kulkarni 30, P. L. Mhambrey 97; D. T. Patel four for 118); Gujarat 113 (N. D. Modi 37; A. Kuruvilla five for 36, S. V. Bahutule four for 25) and 148 (Maqbul Malam 35; S. V. Bahutule three for 39). *Mumbai 5 pts.*
   Muzumdar's 214 not out lasted 611 minutes and 453 balls and included 16 fours. He put on 230 for Mumbai's eighth wicket with Mhambrey.

At Poona Club, Pune, November 4, 5, 6, 7. Maharashtra won by an innings and 70 runs. Maharashtra 547 for nine dec. (H. H. Kanitkar 205, S. S. Sugwekar 57, S. V. Jedhe 158; D. Barot four for 118); Gujarat* 280 (N. D. Modi 33, P. H. Patel 31, M. H. Parmar 134, N. A. Patel 31; M. S. Kulkarni four for 59, Iqbal Siddiqui three for 63) and 197 (Maqbul Malam 47, N. D. Modi 51, U. S. Belsare 48; S. V. Ranjane four for 49, Iqbal Siddiqui four for 49). *Maharashtra 8 pts.*
   Kanitkar's 205, his maiden double-hundred, lasted 533 minutes and 409 balls and included 22 fours. He put on 279 for Maharashtra's third wicket with Jedhe.

At Municipal Ground, Rajkot, November 4, 5, 6, 7. Drawn. Saurashtra* 595 for four dec. (S. S. Tanna 141, S. H. Kotak 89, B. M. Jadeja 132 not out, P. J. Bhatt 123, H. J. Parsana 100 not out; A. Yalvigi three for 125); Mumbai 647 for four (Wasim Jaffer 314 not out, S. K. Kulkarni 239, S. V. Bahutule 72). *Saurashtra 3 pts, Mumbai 5 pts.*
   Wasim Jaffer's 314 not out lasted 680 minutes and 501 balls and included 47 fours. He added 459 for Mumbai's first wicket, five short of the national record, with Kulkarni, whose 239 lasted 518 minutes and 421 balls and included 31 fours and a six. Jaffer was 18 years and 264 days old and became the second-youngest player to score a triple-hundred, following Javed Miandad, aged 17 years and 312 days, for Karachi Whites in 1974-75. It was his second first-class match.

At Sardar Patel Stadium, Ahmedabad, December 12, 13, 14, 15. Baroda won by an innings and 105 runs. Gujarat* 139 (M. H. Parmar 50, T. Varasani 36; S. S. Hazare five for 29) and 218 (N. D. Modi 42, A. Desai 41, P. H. Patel 51; Sukhbir Singh four for 32, R. A. Swarup five for 69); Baroda 462 (R. A. Swarup 134, K. S. More 55, C. C. Williams 62, J. J. Martin 106 not out, Extras 45; D. T. Patel four for 66, B. N. Mehta four for 146). *Baroda 8 pts.*

At Nehru Stadium, Pune, December 12, 13, 14, 15. Drawn. Maharashtra* 335 (S. S. Bhave 101, S. V. Jedhe 35, R. R. Kanade 81, Extras 35; A. Kuruvilla four for 102, S. V. Bahutule four for 100) and 304 (S. S. Sugwekar 121, R. R. Kanade 40, S. V. Ranjane 47; N. M. Kulkarni five for 65); Mumbai 381 (J. V. Paranjpe 165, S. K. Kulkarni 36, S. A. Ankola 40) and 21 for one. *Maharashtra 3 pts, Mumbai 5 pts.*

At Wankhede Stadium, Mumbai, December 20, 21, 22, 23. Mumbai won by nine wickets. Baroda 117 (R. A. Swarup 42; P. L. Mhambrey five for 34) and 189 (R. A. Swarup 37, K. S. More 79; S. V. Bahutule three for 39); Mumbai* 283 (S. V. Manjrekar 77, A. A. Muzumdar 42, V. G. Kambli 69; Sukhbir Singh four for 39, R. A. Swarup six for 121) and 24 for one. *Mumbai 8 pts.*

At Western Railway Ground, Rajkot, December 20, 21, 22, 23. Maharashtra won by an innings and 27 runs. Saurashtra* 208 (S. H. Kotak 93, B. M. Jadeja 33; S. V. Jedhe five for 47) and 247 (J. Motiwaras 52, B. J. Dutta 37, H. J. Parsana 41, N. P. Rana 47; S. V. Jedhe four for 80); Maharashtra 482 for nine dec. (S. S. Bhave 74, S. S. Sugwekar 44, H. H. Kanitkar 121, R. R. Kanade 37, I. Kamtekar 63, P. Y. Chitale 48; S. A. Shukla four for 128, H. J. Parsana three for 153). *Maharashtra 8 pts.*

At IPCL Sports Complex Ground, Baroda, December 28, 29, 30, 31. Drawn. Baroda 438 (R. A. Swarup 44, J. J. Martin 56, K. S. More 180, T. B. Arothe 99; Iqbal Siddiqui five for 99) and 48 for one (R. A. Swarup 31 not out); Maharashtra* 495 (S. S. Bhave 87, H. H. Kanitkar 42, A. V. Kale 150, R. R. Kanade 42, I. Kamtekar 62 not out; S. S. Hazare five for 158). *Baroda 3 pts, Maharashtra 5 pts.*

At Municipal Ground, Rajkot, December 28, 29, 30, 31. Drawn. Gujarat* 324 (N. D. Modi 106, M. H. Parmar 58, B. N. Mehta 73; H. J. Parsana five for 74) and 252 for nine dec. (T. Varasani 109 not out, P. H. Patel 42, B. N. Mehta 43; S. A. Shukla four for 61); Saurashtra 359 (J. Motiwaras 31, P. J. Bhatt 101, H. J. Parsana 85, S. A. Shukla 41; B. N. Mehta five for 126) and 103 for two (H. J. Parsana 68 not out). *Saurashtra 5 pts, Gujarat 3 pts.*

Mumbai 26 pts, Maharashtra 24 pts, Baroda 16 pts, Saurashtra 11 pts, Gujarat 3 pts. Mumbai, Maharashtra and Baroda qualified for the Super League.

Super League Group A

At Nehru Stadium, Pune, January 20, 21, 22, 23. Drawn. Madhya Pradesh* 334 (Jai P. Yadav 107, C. S. Pandit 96, Raja Ali 45; Iqbal Siddiqui four for 104) and 274 for two (Jai P. Yadav 96, K. K. Patel 36 not out, H. S. Sodhi 120 not out); Maharashtra 519 for five dec. (S. S. Bhave 52, S. S. Sugwekar 193, H. H. Kanitkar 60, S. V. Jedhe 144 not out, N. Dixit 50). *Maharashtra 5 pts, Madhya Pradesh 3 pts.*

At PCA Stadium, Mohali, Chandigarh, January 20, 21, 22, 23. Punjab won by seven wickets. Kerala 206 (A. S. Kudva 33, S. Oasis 32, S. Manoj 45 not out; B. Bhushan three for 51, Harvinder Singh five for 71) and 90 (B. Bhushan four for 33, Harvinder Singh six for 36); Punjab* 176 (Bhupinder Singh, jun. 62, Harvinder Singh 36; S. Oasis four for 59, K. A. Sunil three for 41) and 122 for three (N. S. Sidhu 77 not out). *Punjab 8 pts.*

At Nehru Stadium, Pune, January 29, 30, 31, February 1. Maharashtra won by nine wickets. Kerala 133 (Iqbal Siddiqui three for 49, B. D. Kakad three for 35) and 356 (K. N. Balasubramaniam 48, S. Shankar 45, K. N. A. Padmanabhan 161 not out; S. V. Jedhe four for 53); Maharashtra* 447 for three dec. (S. S. Bhave 168, S. S. Sugwekar 94, H. H. Kanitkar 100, A. V. Kale 72 not out) and 43 for one (S. S. Sugwekar 32 not out). *Maharashtra 8 pts.*

At Barabati Stadium, Cuttack, January 29, 30, 31, February 1. Madhya Pradesh won by 118 runs. Madhya Pradesh* 275 (Jai P. Yadav 95, A. R. Khurasia 45, Raja Ali 58; D. S. Mohanty three for 64, S. Raul three for 45, S. C. Mohanty three for 60) and 154 (K. K. Patel 64; S. Raul five for 31, S. C. Mohanty three for 67); Orissa 156 (S. S. Das 40, S. Raul 36; R. K. Chauhan five for 42) and 155 (S. Raul 36, R. Seth 32; R. K. Chauhan seven for 52). *Madhya Pradesh 8 pts.*
Chauhan took 12 wickets in a match for the second time in the season. S. Abbas Ali of Madhya Pradesh took seven catches in the match.

At Maharani Usharaje Trust Ground, Indore, February 7, 8, 9, 10. Drawn. Madhya Pradesh* 439 (A. R. Khurasia 57, K. K. Patel 79, S. Abbas Ali 147, C. S. Pandit 48, Raja Ali 56; C. T. K. Masood four for 55); Kerala 273 (K. N. Balasubramaniam 35, S. Oasis 54, Feroz Rashid 45; H. S. Sodhi four for 70, S. S. Lahore three for 48) and 226 for six (K. N. Balasubramaniam 52, K. N. A. Padmanabhan 43, S. Oasis 52 not out; R. K. Chauhan three for 66, S. S. Lahore three for 64). *Madhya Pradesh 5 pts, Kerala 3 pts.*

At PCA Stadium, Mohali, Chandigarh, February 7, 8, 9, 10. Drawn. Orissa 312 (P. R. Mohapatra 50, S. Raul 64, R. R. Parida 35, B. Mullik 44, Extras 40; B. Bhushan five for 72) and 146 for three (P. R. Mohapatra 80 not out); Punjab* 434 for eight dec. (Ajay Mehra 200 not out, Bhupinder Singh, jun. 48, R. Saini 39, M. Mehra 32, A. R. Kapoor 38, Extras 44; Ajay Barik three for 119). *Punjab 5 pts, Orissa 3 pts.*

Ajay Mehra's 200 not out, his maiden double-hundred, lasted 718 minutes and 500 balls and included 24 fours.

At Nehru Stadium, Pune, February 16, 17, 18, 19. Drawn. Maharashtra 417 (S. S. Sugwekar 169, H. H. Kanitkar 159, R. R. Kanade 40; B. Bhushan three for 113, A. R. Kapoor three for 96) and 307 (S. S. Sugwekar 85, H. H. Kanitkar 32, S. V. Jedhe 45, R. R. Kanade 40; Sandeep Sharma four for 65, A. R. Kapoor three for 72, B. Vij three for 105); Punjab* 380 (N. S. Sidhu 87, Amit Sharma 63, R. Saini 74, Sandeep Sharma 83; M. S. Kulkarni three for 85, S. V. Jedhe three for 78) and 85 for no wkt (Ajay Mehra 37 not out, D. Mongia 48 not out). *Maharashtra 5 pts, Punjab 3 pts.*

In Maharashtra's first innings, Sugwekar and Kanitkar put on 309 for the second wicket.

At Barabati Stadium, Cuttack, February 16, 17, 18, 19. Drawn. Kerala* 535 (S. Shankar 34, K. N. A. Padmanabhan 200, S. Oasis 135, A. S. Kudva 51, Feroz Rashid 63 not out; S. Raul six for 143); Orissa 253 (P. Jayachandra 40, P. Das 53, G. Gopal 48; K. N. A. Padmanabhan six for 99) and 291 (Alekh Barik 45, P. R. Mohapatra 36, R. R. Parida 94, B. Mullik 41; K. Chandrasekhar three for 47). *Orissa 3 pts, Kerala 5 pts.*

Padmanabhan's 200, his maiden double-hundred, lasted 670 minutes and 483 balls and included 22 fours. He put on 290 for Kerala's third wicket with Oasis.

At Captain Roop Singh Stadium, Gwalior, February 25, 26, 27, 28. Drawn. Punjab* 330 (Ajay Mehra 79, Bhupinder Singh, jun. 55, P. Dharmani 44, M. Mehra 51, A. R. Kapoor 42; H. S. Sodhi three for 59, R. K. Chauhan four for 92) and 326 for six (V. Rathore 98, Bhupinder Singh, jun. 30, R. Saini 63, A. R. Kapoor 53 not out; S. S. Lahore four for 84); Madhya Pradesh 396 (Jai P. Yadav 82, H. S. Sodhi 40, P. K. Dwevedi 34, C. S. Pandit 111, R. K. Chauhan 34; B. Vij four for 143, A. R. Kapoor five for 94). *Madhya Pradesh 5 pts, Punjab 3 pts.*

At Barabati Stadium, Cuttack, February 25, 26, 27, 28. Drawn. Orissa* 432 (Alekh Barik 36, S. Raul 173, B. Mullik 64, P. Das 67; P. Y. Chitale five for 102) and 231 for five (S. Raul 55, R. R. Parida 111 not out; S. V. Jedhe three for 43); Maharashtra 339 (S. S. Bhave 32, H. H. Kanitkar 39, S. V. Jedhe 34, R. R. Kanade 52, I. Kamtekar 78 not out; Baljit Singh three for 98, S. Satpathy three for 66). *Orissa 5 pts, Maharashtra 3 pts.*

Madhya Pradesh 21 pts, Maharashtra 21 pts, Punjab 19 pts, Orissa 11 pts, Kerala 8 pts. Madhya Pradesh and Maharashtra qualified for the quarter-finals.

Super League Group B

At IPCL Sports Complex Ground, Baroda, January 20, 21, 22, 23. Drawn. Baroda 439 (C. C. Williams 64, J. J. Martin 114, K. S. More 82, T. B. Arothe 72; Iqbal Thakur four for 89, S. B. Bangar three for 70); Railways* 223 (S. Yadav 33, Y. Gowda 77 not out; R. A. Swarup five for 68, V. N. Buch three for 62) and 246 for five (S. Yadav 82, Y. Gowda 100 not out). *Baroda 5 pts, Railways 3 pts.*

At Feroz Shah Kotla Ground, Delhi, January 20, 21, 22, 23. Drawn. Tamil Nadu* 255 (R. C. Vasant Kumar 31, S. Sharath 60, S. Mahesh 82; M. Prabhakar three for 60, R. R. Singh three for 60) and 171 for six (S. Sriram 57, H. Badani 30, P. Rajesh 34 not out; N. Chopra three for 52); Delhi 413 for five dec. (A. Dani 40, R. Lamba 64, V. Dahiya 95, Ajay Sharma 128, Akash Malhotra 56 not out). *Delhi 5 pts, Tamil Nadu 3 pts.*

At IPCL Sports Complex Ground, Baroda, January 29, 30, 31, February 1. Drawn. Baroda* 238 (J. J. Martin 37, K. S. More 60, T. B. Arothe 75; A. Sarkar five for 50) and 316 for six dec. (R. A. Swarup 97, C. C. Williams 42, K. S. More 85, T. B. Arothe 42 not out; N. D. Hirwani three for 117); Bengal 181 (N. Haldipur 33, P. K. Amre 55; Sukhbir Singh four for 53, T. B. Arothe four for 30) and 199 for five (N. Haldipur 50, D. Gandhi 57, R. S. Gavaskar 49). *Baroda 5 pts, Bengal 3 pts.*

At Karnail Singh Stadium, Delhi, January 29, 30, 31, February 1. Delhi won by an innings and 135 runs. Delhi* 457 (R. Lamba 87, Ajay Sharma 220 not out, N. Chopra 84; K. Parida six for 121); Railways 205 (S. Yadav 83; A. S. Wassan four for 47, N. Chopra six for 78) and 117 (Zakir Hussain 31, K. Bharathan 44; A. S. Wassan five for 48). *Delhi 8 pts.*
   Ajay Sharma's 220 not out lasted 473 minutes and 362 balls and included 18 fours and three sixes.

At Feroz Shah Kotla Ground, Delhi, February 7, 8, 9, 10. Delhi won by two wickets. Baroda* 287 (C. C. Williams 62, J. J. Martin 51, K. S. More 32, H. R. Jadhav 32; F. Ghayas four for 82, R. R. Singh three for 73) and 242 (J. J. Martin 37, T. B. Arothe 78, V. N. Buch 38; A. S. Wassan five for 49); Delhi 384 (R. Lamba 69, Ajay Sharma 118, S. Dogra 41, N. Chopra 53, A. S. Wassan 42; Sukhbir Singh four for 100) and 146 for eight (R. Lamba 37, Akash Malhotra 38; Sukhbir Singh four for 73). *Delhi 8 pts.*
   Ajay Sharma's 118 was his third hundred in successive innings.

At M. A. Chidambaram Stadium, Chennai, February 7, 8, 9, 10. Drawn. Bengal* 247 (R. S. Gavaskar 69, P. K. Amre 33, S. J. Kalyani 30, A. Varma 51; D. K. Devanand three for 68, S. Mahesh three for 55) and 295 for five (D. Gandhi 182, R. S. Gavaskar 34); Tamil Nadu 425 for eight dec. (S. Sriram 99, H. Badani 62, S. Sharath 131, R. Paul 37; A. Varma three for 90, N. D. Hirwani three for 105). *Tamil Nadu 5 pts, Bengal 3 pts.*

At Eden Gardens, Calcutta, February 16, 17, 18. Bengal won by 168 runs. Bengal* 383 (R. S. Gavaskar 36, A. Varma 162, A. K. Das 81; A. S. Wassan four for 111, R. R. Singh four for 107) and 245 for six dec. (D. Gandhi 61, P. K. Amre 55, A. K. Das 66; A. S. Wassan five for 73); Delhi 251 (R. Lamba 45, Akash Malhotra 71, P. Joshi 32, V. Dahiya 35; U. Chatterjee three for 82, N. D. Hirwani three for 40) and 209 (P. Joshi 67, V. Dahiya 40; U. Chatterjee three for 102, N. D. Hirwani six for 51). *Bengal 8 pts.*

At Karnail Singh Stadium, Delhi, February 16, 17, 18, 19. Railways won by an innings and 65 runs. Tamil Nadu* 157 (R. Paul 36, S. Subramaniam 40, S. Chandramouli 33; Zakir Hussain four for 66, Javed Zaman five for 45) and 135 (S. Ramesh 61; Javed Zaman four for 20, R. R. Parida four for 20); Railways 357 (S. B. Bangar 122, Z. Zuffri 108, Y. Gowda 42; S. Mahesh three for 83, D. K. Devanand seven for 74). *Railways 8 pts.*

At Eden Gardens, Calcutta, February 25, 26, 27, 28. Drawn. Railways* 455 for nine dec. (S. Yadav 50, Y. Gowda 96, P. S. Rawat 56, Zakir Hussain 97, M. Kartik 74; S. Majumdar four for 105, Abdul Masud three for 110); Bengal 244 (D. Gandhi 34, A. K. Das 43, U. Chatterjee 52, Extras 38; Javed Zaman three for 29, R. R. Parida three for 44) and 126 for five (D. Gandhi 36, R. S. Gavaskar 30 not out). *Bengal 3 pts, Railways 5 pts.*

At M. A. Chidambaram Stadium, Chennai, February 25, 26, 27, 28. Tamil Nadu won by five wickets. Tamil Nadu* 415 (T. Karunamurthy 31, S. Sriram 172, J. Ashique Ali 55, S. Mahesh 49, S. Subramaniam 33; M. Kadri four for 99, R. A. Swarup three for 97) and 180 for five (T. Karunamurthy 39, S. Sriram 31, T. Jabbar 59 not out); Baroda 193 (R. A. Swarup 93, C. C. Williams 35; M. Venkataramana five for 63, S. Subramaniam three for 49) and 399 for seven dec. (A. C. Bedade 102 not out, J. J. Martin 115, K. S. More 61, M. Kadri 81; S. Subramaniam three for 105). *Tamil Nadu 8 pts.*

Delhi 21 pts, Bengal 17 pts, Railways 16 pts, Tamil Nadu 16 pts, Baroda 10 pts. Delhi qualified for the semi-finals and Bengal for the quarter-finals.

Super League Group C

At Keenan Stadium, Jamshedpur, January 20, 21, 22, 23. Mumbai won by an innings and 14 runs. Bihar* 161 (Tariq-ur-Rehman 43, Rajiv Kumar 49; N. M. Kulkarni six for 51) and 143 (Tariq-ur-Rehman 58 not out; A. Kuruvilla three for 28, S. V. Bahutule four for 35); Mumbai 318 for nine dec. (Wasim Jaffer 65, J. V. Paranjpe 84, S. V. Manjrekar 70, S. V. Bahutule 53; Anil Kumar four for 102). *Mumbai 8 pts.*

At Gymkhana Ground, Secunderabad, January 20, 21, 22, 23. Hyderabad won by an innings and 42 runs. Hyderabad 343 (G. A. Shetty 71, V. Pratap 93, V. Vardhan 39, Extras 38; S. Pandey five for 106); Haryana* 114 (N. David four for 26) and 187 (A. S. Kaypee 62, V. S. Yadav 43; N. David three for 42). *Hyderabad 8 pts.*

At Nahar Singh Stadium, Faridabad, January 29, 30, 31, February 1. Drawn. Uttar Pradesh* 345 (Jyoti P. Yadav 93, M. S. Mudgal 38, R. V. Sapru 118, G. K. Pandey 37; S. Pandey three for 93, Iqbal Thakur three for 81) and 267 for five (R. Sharma 40, Jyoti P. Yadav 85, M. S. Mudgal 35 not out, Rizwan Shamshad 53 not out); Haryana 471 for nine dec. (Jitender Singh 229 not out, N. R. Goel 37, R. Puri 62, V. S. Yadav 37, P. Jain 48; A. L. Gera five for 133, G. K. Pandey three for 124). *Haryana 5 pts, Uttar Pradesh 3 pts.*

Jitender Singh's 229 not out, his second double-hundred of the season, lasted 601 minutes and 484 balls and included 23 fours.

At Gymkhana Ground, Secunderabad, January 29, 30, 31, February 1. Drawn. Hyderabad 265 (G. A. Shetty 116, V. Pratap 30, D. Vinay Kumar 30 not out; K. V. P. Rao three for 63, Avinash Kumar three for 82) and 279 for nine dec. (V. Pratap 60, M. V. Sridhar 81, N. David 65; K. V. P. Rao three for 88, Avinash Kumar four for 84); Bihar* 260 (Sunil Kumar 63, Tarun Kumar 36, Somnath Jha 42, Avinash Kumar 44; N. P. Singh three for 66, S. L. V. Raju four for 65) and 172 for four (Sunil Kumar 40, C. M. Jha 60, Tarun Kumar 33 not out). *Hyderabad 5 pts, Bihar 3 pts.*

At Moin-ul-Haq Stadium, Patna, February 7, 8, 9, 10. Haryana won by 24 runs. Haryana* 362 (N. R. Goel 86, R. Puri 130, Syed Khan 43, Dhanraj Singh 41; Avinash Kumar three for 100) and 169 for nine dec. (Syed Khan 47; Avinash Kumar six for 42); Bihar 281 (C. M. Jha 57, Tariq-ur-Rehman 82; P. Jain seven for 72) and 226 (C. M. Jha 63, Tariq-ur-Rehman 52, Rajiv Kumar 38; P. Jain five for 79). *Haryana 8 pts.*

At K. D. Singh "Babu" Stadium, Lucknow, February 7, 8, 9, 10. Mumbai won by eight wickets. Mumbai* 342 (Wasim Jaffer 106, S. V. Manjrekar 50, A. A. Muzumdar 88, Extras 36; Obaid Kamal four for 71) and 27 for two; Uttar Pradesh 151 (Rizwan Shamshad 41, G. K. Pandey 32; A. Kuruvilla three for 59, N. M. Kulkarni four for 40) and 214 (R. V. Sapru 52; N. M. Kulkarni five for 73). *Mumbai 8 pts.*

At Keenan Stadium, Jamshedpur, February 16, 17, 18, 19. Drawn. Bihar* 329 (Sunil Kumar 44, C. M. Jha 44, Tariq-ur-Rehman 118 not out, V. Khullar 35; S. Bajpai three for 49, G. K. Pandey three for 27) and 213 for five dec. (Sunil Kumar 34, Anant Prakash 30, C. M. Jha 37, Tariq-ur-Rehman 62, Tarun Kumar 35 not out); Uttar Pradesh 289 (R. Sharma 41, S. A. Shukla 51, Rizwan Shamshad 107, G. K. Pandey 44; K. V. P. Rao four for 117, Avinash Kumar four for 103) and 194 for six (M. S. Mudgal 45, S. A. Shukla 37, G. K. Pandey 50 not out; K. V. P. Rao three for 61). *Bihar 5 pts, Uttar Pradesh 3 pts.*

At Gymkhana Ground, Secunderabad, February 16, 17, 18, 19. Mumbai won by an innings and 82 runs. Hyderabad 240 (G. A. Shetty 48, R. Sridhar 36; A. Kuruvilla three for 35, R. Pawar three for 71) and 218 (A. Nandakishore 43, V. Pratap 61, S. Yadav 37; N. M. Kulkarni five for 87); Mumbai* 540 (A. A. Muzumdar 138, V. G. Kambli 111, S. V. Manjrekar 150, J. V. Paranjpe 51; Kanwaljit Singh three for 150, R. Sridhar three for 155). *Mumbai 8 pts.*

At Gymkhana Ground, Secunderabad, February 25, 26, 27, 28. Drawn. Uttar Pradesh* 314 (S. A. Shukla 145, Manoj Singh 30, G. K. Pandey 45) and 272 for five dec. (M. S. Mudgal 94, R. V. Sapru 101 not out); Hyderabad 292 (V. Pratap 78, S. Yadav 70; Obaid Kamal six for 120) and 107 for one (A. Nandakishore 43 not out, M. V. Sridhar 56 not out). *Hyderabad 3 pts, Uttar Pradesh 5 pts.*

Uttar Pradesh wicket-keeper Mudgal took six catches in Hyderabad's first innings.

At Wankhede Stadium, Mumbai, February 25, 26, 27, 28. Mumbai won by four wickets. Haryana 303 (R. Puri 38, V. S. Yadav 80, Shafiq Khan 84; M. P. Patel five for 65) and 234 (A. S. Kaypee 82, Shafiq Khan 64; R. Pawar five for 93); Mumbai* 330 (M. V. Joglekar 80, S. K. Kulkarni

126; P. Jain five for 67, P. Thakur three for 125) and 208 for six (A. A. Muzumdar 82, V. G. Kambli 71; P. Thakur four for 79). *Mumbai 8 pts.*

Mumbai wicket-keeper Kulkarni took six catches in Haryana's first innings.

Mumbai 32 pts, Hyderabad 16 pts, Haryana 13 pts, Uttar Pradesh 11 pts, Bihar 8 pts. Mumbai qualified for the semi-finals and Hyderabad for the quarter-finals.

Quarter-finals

At Maharani Usharaje Trust Ground, Indore, March 17, 18, 19, 20. Drawn. Madhya Pradesh were declared winners by virtue of their first-innings lead. Madhya Pradesh* 464 (K. K. Patel 37, A. R. Khurasia 209, C. S. Pandit 34, D. Bundela 72; U. Chatterjee three for 110) and 425 for five dec. (Jai P. Yadav 108, S. Abbas Ali 75, P. K. Dwevedi 57, D. Bundela 102 not out, R. K. Chauhan 54 not out); Bengal 420 (N. Haldipur 63, R. S. Gavaskar 109, A. Varma 30, A. K. Das 49, G. Shome, jun. 88, Extras 31; R. K. Chauhan three for 121) and 54 for two.

Khurasia's 209 lasted 406 minutes and 247 balls and included 20 fours and five sixes.

At Nehru Stadium, Pune, March 17, 18, 19, 20. Maharashtra won by seven wickets. Hyderabad* 226 (A. Nandakishore 47, V. Pratap 76; M. S. Kulkarni four for 71, S. Inamdar three for 50) and 230 (V. Pratap 50, D. Vinay Kumar 32, S. Yadav 52, N. P. Singh 62; Iqbal Siddiqui four for 46, H. H. Kanitkar three for 41); Maharashtra 287 (H. H. Kanitkar 37, S. V. Jedhe 40, A. V. Kale 30, I. Kamtekar 53, S. M. Kondhalkar 37; S. L. V. Raju three for 54) and 172 for three (S. S. Bhave 86, S. S. Sugwekar 56).

Semi-finals

At Maharani Usharaje Trust Ground, Indore, March 27, 28, 29, 30, 31. Drawn. Mumbai were declared winners by virtue of their first-innings lead. Madhya Pradesh* 369 (Jai P. Yadav 34, K. K. Patel 38, A. R. Khurasia 32, P. K. Dwevedi 45, C. S. Pandit 40, M. Majithia 75, R. K. Chauhan 43; N. M. Kulkarni five for 81, S. V. Bahutule three for 98) and 291 for seven dec. (Jai P. Yadav 37, P. K. Dwevedi 39, S. Abbas Ali 102 not out, H. S. Sodhi 58; S. V. Bahutule four for 75); Mumbai 532 (Wasim Jaffer 65, J. V. Paranjpe 47, S. V. Manjrekar 114, A. A. Muzumdar 125, V. G. Kambli 41, A. Agarkar 32, A. Ranade 41; R. K. Chauhan six for 191) and 25 for no wkt.

Chauhan bowled 93.5 of the 230.5 overs in Mumbai's first innings.

At Nehru Stadium, Pune, March 27, 28, 29, 30, 31. Drawn. Delhi were declared winners by virtue of their first-innings lead. Delhi* 656 (V. Dahiya 85, R. Lamba 192, Ajay Sharma 144, Akash Malhotra 61, N. Chopra 74 not out, F. Ghayas 32; S. Inamdar four for 163, H. H. Kanitkar three for 113) and 264 for two (V. Dahiya 74, R. Lamba 101, A. Dani 50 not out); Maharashtra 524 (H. H. Kanitkar 174, A. V. Kale 54, S. V. Jedhe 38, I. Kamtekar 36, R. R. Kanade 54, Iqbal Siddiqui 48 not out, M. S. Kulkarni 43, Extras 43; R. R. Singh three for 168).

Dahiya and Lamba put on 214 and 192 for Delhi's first wicket, and Lamba scored a century in each innings.

Final

At Captain Roop Singh Stadium, Gwalior, April 5, 6, 7, 8, 9 (day/night). Drawn. Mumbai were declared winners by virtue of their first-innings lead. Mumbai* 630 (Wasim Jaffer 58, J. V. Paranjpe 111, S. V. Manjrekar 78, A. A. Muzumdar 144, V. G. Kambli 89, A. Agarkar 39, S. V. Bahutule 44); Delhi 559 (R. Lamba 42, A. Dani 178, Ajay Sharma 176, N. Chopra 43, Extras 33; N. M. Kulkarni four for 143).

Dani and Ajay Sharma put on 313 for Delhi's third wicket.

RANJI TROPHY WINNERS

1934-35	Bombay	1955-56	Bombay	1976-77	Bombay
1935-36	Bombay	1956-57	Bombay	1977-78	Karnataka
1936-37	Nawanagar	1957-58	Baroda	1978-79	Delhi
1937-38	Hyderabad	1958-59	Bombay	1979-80	Delhi
1938-39	Bengal	1959-60	Bombay	1980-81	Bombay
1939-40	Maharashtra	1960-61	Bombay	1981-82	Delhi
1940-41	Maharashtra	1961-62	Bombay	1982-83	Karnataka
1941-42	Bombay	1962-63	Bombay	1983-84	Bombay
1942-43	Baroda	1963-64	Bombay	1984-85	Bombay
1943-44	Western India	1964-65	Bombay	1985-86	Delhi
1944-45	Bombay	1965-66	Bombay	1986-87	Hyderabad
1945-46	Holkar	1966-67	Bombay	1987-88	Tamil Nadu
1946-47	Baroda	1967-68	Bombay	1988-89	Delhi
1947-48	Holkar	1968-69	Bombay	1989-90	Bengal
1948-49	Bombay	1969-70	Bombay	1990-91	Haryana
1949-50	Baroda	1970-71	Bombay	1991-92	Delhi
1950-51	Holkar	1971-72	Bombay	1992-93	Punjab
1951-52	Bombay	1972-73	Bombay	1993-94	Bombay
1952-53	Holkar	1973-74	Karnataka	1994-95	Bombay
1953-54	Bombay	1974-75	Bombay	1995-96	Karnataka
1954-55	Madras	1975-76	Bombay	1996-97	Mumbai

Bombay/Mumbai have won the Ranji Trophy 33 times, Delhi 6, Baroda, Holkar and Karnataka 4, Bengal, Hyderabad, Madras/Tamil Nadu and Maharashtra 2, Haryana, Nawanagar, Punjab and Western India 1.

CEAT CRICKETER OF THE YEAR

The second CEAT International Cricketer of the Year was Venkatesh Prasad of India. Judges Sunil Gavaskar, Clive Lloyd and Ian Chappell have devised a system awarding points for performances in Tests and limited-overs internationals. A player earns one point for a score of 50 and another for every 25 runs thereafter in that innings, with a three-point bonus for a hundred and a six-point bonus for a double-hundred. Two wickets in an innings earn one point, with another for every subsequent wicket in that innings, and a three-point bonus for five in the innings and a six-point bonus for ten in the match. Every catch and every stumping is worth one point. The judges make monthly assessments and add the CEAT Efficiency Quotient. In 1996-97, Prasad scored 92 points, beating Wasim Akram of Pakistan (87) and his own team-mate Anil Kumble (85). The previous winner was Brian Lara of West Indies.

CRICKET IN PAKISTAN, 1996-97

By ABID ALI KAZI

Asif Mujtaba

The 1996-97 season was less eventful than the previous one, in which Pakistan co-hosted the World Cup, but it saw some success coming Pakistan's way. After a satisfying tour of England, in which they took the Tests 2-0, Pakistan staged home series against Zimbabwe, winning 1-0, and New Zealand, drawing 1-1. In April, they drew two Tests in Sri Lanka.

But some of their best performances came in the limited-overs game. As well as winning the one-day series with Zimbabwe and New Zealand, they won the Sahara Cup, against India in Canada, the Singer Champions Trophy in Sharjah and, for the first time, the Australian one-day tournament, now known as the Carlton & United Series. They were finalists in three other tournaments, in Kenya, Sharjah and India. Shahid Afridi achieved fame in Kenya with a 37-ball century, the fastest ever in one-day internationals, while the visit to India saw Saeed Anwar score 194, the highest ever. But the controversy which had dogged Pakistan in recent years still haunted them, with Aamir Sohail excluded from the team for a while after making further allegations concerning match-fixing. After the Independence Cup, they lost their coach, Mushtaq Mohammad, in a dispute over pay; another former Test player, Haroon Rashid, replaced him.

As usual, the domestic programme received little attention in comparison with the glittering progress of the national team. Not only were the two first-class competitions, the Quaid-e-Azam Trophy and the PCB Patron's Trophy, staged concurrently with the home Tests: the semi-finals and finals of the Quaid-e-Azam Trophy clashed with the opening two rounds of the Patron's Trophy. The four city teams involved lost several players because the commercial teams have first claim on the cricketers they employ. Faisalabad were led in their semi-final by their manager, Tanvir Shaukat, who had not appeared in the first team for seven years.

Lahore City won the Quaid-e-Azam for only the third time in its 39 years. They beat Karachi Whites by one wicket in a low-scoring final which lasted only three days out of five. Abdur Razzaq, making his first-class debut although he had already played two one-day internationals, took nine wickets and, batting at No. 10, scored the winning runs. It was a dramatic change of fortune for Lahore, who were scratched from the competition the previous season after a dispute in their game with Karachi Blues. United Bank won the Patron's Trophy for the first time. Hasnain Kazim swung the ball on a seaming pitch to take 11 for 128, securing a convincing 306-run victory over Habib Bank in the final. But United Bank unexpectedly withdrew their team at the start of the 1997-98 season; the bank was laying off employees, including its cricketers. The Trophy was still contested by eight teams, however. WAPDA, winners of the non-first-class Grade II, were promoted to replace bottom-placed PNSC, but the losing finalists, Khan Research Laboratories, were also elevated because of their overall record and the company's investment in cricket's infrastructure, by developing the KRL Cricket Ground in Rawalpindi to international standard.

The board had cut back the number of first-class Quaid-e-Azam teams from ten to the original eight, but this lasted for only one season. It was announced that the bottom team, Bahawalpur, would not be relegated in 1997-98, while both the finalists from Grade II, winners Gujranwala and runners-up Multan, would be promoted.

Allied Bank won the one-day Wills Kings Cup, beating National Bank under floodlights in the final in March. The semi-finals were also played as day/night games, and were the first domestic matches in Pakistan to be played under lights. Bangladesh were invited to join the final rounds of the competition, as part of their preparation for the ICC Trophy in Malaysia a few weeks later. They lost all their four matches, but the experience must have been helpful, as they won the ICC Trophy to qualify for the 1999 World Cup.

The National Under-19 Junior Cup final was won by Karachi Whites, who beat Lahore City at the start of October - the opposite of the later Quaid-e-Azam result. Pakistan also welcomed Under-19 teams from England and Australia.

No one scored 1,000 first-class runs in 1996-97; there were fewer opportunities, with only 68 first-class matches played, down from 100 in the previous season, when there was a Pentangular Trophy. Asif Mujtaba, of Karachi Blues and PIA, was the leading run-scorer. He made 913 in 19 innings at 57.06, which also enabled him to head the averages for the second season running. Ijaz Ahmed, jun. was only two runs behind with 911 in 23 innings for Faisalabad and Allied Bank. A dramatic Test debut by Mohammad Zahid of PIA, in which he took 11 wickets to seal victory over New Zealand, helped him to the top of the bowling averages, with 31 wickets at just 12.29. But Kabir Khan of Peshawar and Habib Bank collected most wickets, 71 at 19.77. Aqib Javed took nine for 51 in an innings, including a hat-trick, for Allied Bank against Habib Bank. Wasim Yousufi was the leading wicket-keeper with 38 catches and four stumpings in his 14 matches for Peshawar and United Bank.

FIRST-CLASS AVERAGES, 1996-97

BATTING

(Qualification: 500 runs)

	M	I	NO	R	HS	100s	Avge
Asif Mujtaba (*Karachi Blues/PIA*)	11	19	3	913	116	2	57.06
Mohammad Wasim (*Rawalpindi*)	8	14	2	630	109*	3	52.50
Mujahid Jamshed (*Lahore City/Habib Bank*)	10	16	1	771	129	3	51.40
Manzoor Elahi (*Lahore City/ADBP*)	13	19	3	730	113	1	45.62
Ghulam Ali (*Karachi Blues/PIA*)	10	19	5	636	142	2	45.42
Iqbal Saleem (*Karachi Whites/Allied Bank*)	9	14	1	573	207	2	44.07
Zahoor Elahi (*Lahore City*)	8	14	1	571	153	2	43.92

	M	I	NO	R	HS	100s	Avge
Jahangir Khan, sen. (*Peshawar*)	7	12	0	522	147	1	43.50
Ijaz Ahmed, jun. (*Faisalabad/Allied Bank*)	13	23	1	911	151	2	41.40
Salim Elahi (*United Bank*)	9	16	2	546	78	0	39.00
Basit Ali (*Karachi Blues/United Bank*)	12	21	0	784	100	1	37.33
Wasim Yousufi (*Peshawar/United Bank*)	14	23	3	724	100*	1	36.20
Shahid Nawaz (*Lahore City*)	9	16	0	576	94	0	36.00
Moin-ul-Atiq (*Karachi Whites/Habib Bank*)	11	20	3	611	129	2	35.94
Akhtar Sarfraz (*Peshawar/National Bank*)	12	22	2	700	135	2	35.00
Mansoor Rana (*Lahore City/ADBP*)	13	21	3	620	117	1	34.44
Azam Khan (*Karachi Blues/Pakistan Customs*)	9	17	1	529	70	0	33.06
Aamer Hanif (*Karachi Whites/Allied Bank*)	13	24	1	735	134	1	31.95
Mohammad Ramzan (*Faisalabad/United Bank*)	14	25	2	731	112	1	31.78
Shahid Javed (*Rawalpindi/Habib Bank*)	13	21	4	538	73	0	31.64
Sohail Jaffer (*Karachi Whites/PIA*)	11	17	0	537	72	0	31.58
Sher Ali (*Bahawalpur/PNSC*)	10	18	1	528	123*	1	31.05
Shakeel Ahmed (*Peshawar/Habib Bank*)	14	25	1	716	123	1	29.83
Shahid Anwar (*Lahore City/National Bank*)	12	23	1	630	105	1	28.63
Aaley Haider (*Karachi Whites/Allied Bank*)	11	20	0	572	124	1	28.60
Mohammad Nawaz (*Islamabad/Allied Bank*)	12	22	0	587	83	0	26.68
Azhar Shafiq (*Bahawalpur/Pakistan Customs*)	14	27	1	689	123	1	26.50
Iqbal Imam (*Karachi Whites/United Bank*)	15	25	2	520	88*	0	22.60

* *Signifies not out.*

BOWLING

(Qualification: 25 wickets)

	O	M	R	W	BB	5W/i	Avge
Mohammad Zahid (*PIA*)	133.3	24	381	31	7-66	3	12.29
Asif Mujtaba (*Karachi Blues/PIA*)	198.3	76	342	26	5-60	2	13.15
Hasnain Kazim (*United Bank*)	107	17	369	25	6-41	2	14.76
Mushtaq Ahmed (*Lahore City*)	157.1	36	436	28	6-66	3	15.57
Aamer Hanif (*Karachi Whites/Allied Bank*)	195.5	48	488	30	5-57	1	16.26
Aqib Javed (*Islamabad/Allied Bank*)	282	48	852	50	9-51	4	17.04
Naeem Akhtar (*Rawalpindi*)	172.2	35	428	25	5-37	2	17.12
Azhar Mahmood (*Islamabad/United Bank*)	393.5	106	1,011	59	7-65	3	17.13
Ata-ur-Rehman (*Lahore City/Allied Bank*)	138.2	23	431	25	5-56	2	17.24
Azhar Shafiq (*Bahawalpur/Pakistan Customs*)	218.1	30	756	43	6-56	4	17.58
Mohammad Asif (*Lahore City/ADBP*)	422.2	86	959	53	5-20	3	18.09
Akram Raza (*Faisalabad/Habib Bank*)	373.3	96	967	51	5-49	2	18.96
Kabir Khan (*Peshawar/Habib Bank*)	456	101	1,404	71	8-70	6	19.77
Ali Hussain Rizvi (*Karachi Whites/Pak. Customs*)	360.1	64	1,090	54	6-123	4	20.18
Salman Fazal (*Karachi Whites/National Bank*)	352.5	83	808	39	6-42	4	20.71
Mohammad Hussain (*Lahore City/United Bank*)	448.1	158	1,015	48	6-81	3	21.14
Naseer Shaukat (*Faisalabad*)	189.1	29	664	30	6-51	4	22.13
Murtaza Hussain (*Bahawalpur/PNSC*)	528.3	129	1,442	64	5-43	4	22.53
Shoaib Akhtar (*Rawalpindi/ADBP*)	426.4	88	1,633	69	5-58	6	23.66
Mohammad Zahid (*Bahawalpur/Allied Bank*)	300.3	76	782	33	4-44	0	23.69
Ali Gauhar (*Karachi Blues/United Bank*)	405.3	96	1,244	52	6-55	3	23.92
Nadeem Khan (*Karachi Blues/PIA*)	552.3	149	1,308	54	6-35	3	24.22
Arshad Khan (*Peshawar/Allied Bank*)	347.4	69	878	36	6-74	2	24.38
Nadeem Ghauri (*Habib Bank*)	246.3	62	639	26	7-101	1	24.57
Haaris Khan (*Karachi Blues/Pakistan Customs*)	333.3	77	836	34	6-131	2	24.58
Athar Laeeq (*Karachi Blues/National Bank*)	306.5	68	935	38	6-57	3	24.60
Manzoor Elahi (*Lahore City/ADBP*)	262.5	64	699	28	8-43	2	24.96
Nadeem Afzal (*Faisalabad/PIA*)	239	44	776	30	7-70	2	25.86
Naeem Tayyab (*Karachi Whites/National Bank*)	321.4	67	808	31	6-88	3	26.06
Bilal Rana (*Islamabad/Allied Bank*)	392	102	984	36	6-26	4	27.33
Aamir Nazir (*Lahore City/Allied Bank*)	205.3	30	767	28	4-27	0	27.39

QUAID-E-AZAM TROPHY, 1996-97

	Played	Won	Lost	Drawn	1st-inns Points	Points
Karachi Whites	7	4	2	1	10	50
Lahore City	7	3	3	1	8	38
Faisalabad	7	3	2	2	6	36
Islamabad	7	3	3	1	6	36
Karachi Blues	7	3	4	0	6	36
Rawalpindi	7	3	1	3	4	34
Peshawar	7	2	3	2	8	28
Bahawalpur	7	2	5	0	0	20

Outright win = 10 pts; lead on first innings in a won or drawn game = 2 pts.

Semi-finals: Lahore City beat Islamabad by virtue of their first-innings lead; Karachi Whites beat Faisalabad by an innings and 119 runs. **Final:** Lahore City beat Karachi Whites by one wicket.

*In the following scores, * by the name of a team indicates that they won the toss.*

At Bahawal Stadium, Bahawalpur, October 4, 5, 6, 7. Bahawalpur won by 148 runs. Bahawalpur 112 (Aamir Sohail 51; Salman Fazal five for 13) and 244 (Sher Ali 52, Nasir Jam 32, Faisal Elahi 42 not out; Naeem Tayyab four for 55, Ali Hussain Rizvi three for 59); Karachi Whites* 160 (Iqbal Imam 44, Javed Qadir 32; Murtaza Hussain four for 67, Mohammad Zahid three for 51) and 48 (Murtaza Hussain four for 27). *Bahawalpur 10 pts.*

At National Stadium, Karachi, October 4, 5, 6, 7. Karachi Blues won by four wickets. Lahore City 253 (Zahoor Elahi 124; Athar Laeeq three for 107, Ali Gauhar six for 55) and 331 (Zahoor Elahi 41, Shahid Anwar 57, Shahid Nawaz 62, Mansoor Rana 33, Manzoor Elahi 45, Extras 49; Athar Laeeq four for 89, Ali Gauhar four for 81); Karachi Blues* 370 (Shoaib Mohammad 54, Asif Mujtaba 66, Mahmood Hamid 94, Nadeem Khan 59; Maqsood Rana three for 72, Mohammad Hussain four for 86) and 218 for six (Azam Khan 56, Manzoor Akhtar 62, Tahir Rashid 40 not out; Maqsood Rana three for 74). *Karachi Blues 12 pts.*

Lahore City wicket-keeper Ahsan Raza took five catches in Karachi Blues' first innings.

At Arbab Niaz Stadium, Peshawar, October 4, 5, 6, 7. Drawn. Peshawar 322 (Jahangir Khan, sen. 77, Wajahatullah Wasti 67, Wasim Yousufi 65; Nadeem Afzal five for 69) and 262 for seven (Jahangir Khan, sen. 45, Wasim Yousufi 100 not out, Sajid Shah 43; Saadat Gul four for 53); Faisalabad* 258 (Mohammad Ramzan 51, Akram Raza 77 not out, Naseer Shaukat 35, Extras 45; Kabir Khan six for 64, Sajid Shah three for 61). *Peshawar 2 pts.*

At KRL Cricket Ground, Rawalpindi, October 4, 5, 6, 7. Drawn. Rawalpindi 299 for nine dec. (Arif Butt 37, Asif Mahmood 62, Naseer Ahmed 42, Nadeem Abbasi 33, Raja Afaq 52; Bilal Rana four for 135, Aqib Javed five for 51); Islamabad* 187 for six (Mufeez Murtaza 36, Asif Ali 58, Zaheer Abbasi 50 not out; Naeem Akhtar three for 51).

The match did not start until 2.45 p.m. on the second day because of rain and a wet pitch.

At Chaudhry Rehmat Ali Cricket Ground, Islamabad, October 10, 11, 12, 13. Peshawar won by an innings and 43 runs. Peshawar* 523 (Jahangir Khan, sen. 147, Akhtar Sarfraz 87, Wajahatullah Wasti 86, Wasim Yousufi 84, Extras 42; Azhar Mahmood four for 118); Islamabad 203 (Raj Hans 106; Kabir Khan eight for 70) and 277 (Mohammad Nawaz 65, Bilal Rana 56, Azhar Mahmood 68; Arshad Khan six for 74). *Peshawar 12 pts.*

Islamabad wicket-keeper Aamir Nazir took four catches and one stumping in Peshawar's innings.

At National Stadium, Karachi, October 10, 11, 12, 13. Karachi Blues won by ten wickets. Bahawalpur 128 (Nasir Jam 31; Athar Laeeq five for 35) and 361 (Bilal Moin 83, Saifullah 57, Aamir Sohail 93, Murtaza Hussain 42 not out; Athar Laeeq five for 86, Ali Gauhar three for 85); Karachi Blues* 458 (Ghulam Ali 42, Saeed Azad 32, Asif Mujtaba 63, Basit Ali 31, Mahmood Hamid 157, Moin Khan 46, Ali Gauhar 40 not out; Azhar Shafiq three for 97, Murtaza Hussain five for 151) and 32 for no wkt. *Karachi Blues 12 pts.*

Mahmood Hamid and Ali Gauhar added 118 runs for Karachi Blues' tenth wicket.

At Gaddafi Stadium, Lahore, October 10, 11, 12, 13. Karachi Whites won by 179 runs. Karachi Whites 224 (Aamer Hanif 36, Javed Qadir 36; Manzoor Elahi eight for 43) and 283 (Javed Sami 42, Kashif Ahmed 35, Aamer Hanif 82, Iqbal Imam 48; Manzoor Elahi four for 79); Lahore City* 102 (Shahid Iqbal three for 33, Baqar Rizvi five for 33) and 226 (Shahid Anwar 52, Javed Hayat 32, Manzoor Elahi 57; Baqar Rizvi three for 38, Aamer Hanif four for 53). *Karachi Whites 12 pts.*

Lahore City wicket-keeper Ahsan Raza took five catches in Karachi Whites' first innings.

At KRL Cricket Ground, Rawalpindi, October 10, 11, 12. Faisalabad won by eight wickets. Rawalpindi* 148 (Shahid Javed 56 not out; Akram Raza four for 48, Mohammad Nawaz three for 16) and 159 (Shahid Javed 39; Akram Raza five for 49, Naved Nazir three for 43); Faisalabad 272 (Javed Iqbal 60, Ijaz Ahmed, jun. 41, Bilal Ahmed 58, Saadat Gul 44; Shoaib Akhtar five for 58, Mohammad Riaz four for 77) and 36 for two. *Faisalabad 12 pts.*

At Bahawal Stadium, Bahawalpur, October 16, 17, 18. Lahore City won by 260 runs. Lahore City* 219 (Zahoor Elahi 58, Shahid Nawaz 37, Manzoor Elahi 37; Murtaza Hussain five for 84, Mohammad Zahid four for 61) and 271 (Shahid Nawaz 94, Manzoor Elahi 40 not out; Mohammad Zahid three for 86, Murtaza Hussain four for 104); Bahawalpur 108 (Mohammad Asif five for 20, Mohammad Hussain five for 30) and 122 (Bilal Moin 52 not out; Mohammad Asif five for 33, Mohammad Hussain five for 86). *Lahore City 12 pts.*

Mohammad Asif and Mohammad Hussain took ten wickets each for Lahore City. Murtaza Hussain took nine wickets and Mohammad Zahid seven for Bahawalpur.

At Chaudhry Rehmat Ali Cricket Ground, Islamabad, October 16, 17, 18, 19. Islamabad won by 153 runs. Islamabad* 342 (Mohammad Nawaz 33, Naved Ahmed 44, Raj Hans 63, Bilal Rana 69, Qaiser Mahmood 57; Naved Nazir four for 106, Akram Raza four for 71) and 226 for nine dec. (Mohammad Nawaz 62, Ehsan Butt 60; Saadat Gul three for 53, Ijaz Ahmed, jun. three for 36); Faisalabad 205 (Ijaz Ahmed, jun. 34, Mohammad Nawaz 49; Azhar Mahmood seven for 65) and 210 (Mohammad Saleem 71; Azhar Mahmood three for 51, Fahad Khan four for 63). *Islamabad 12 pts.*

Both teams included players called Mohammad Nawaz.

At KCCA Stadium, Karachi, October 16, 17. Karachi Whites won by ten wickets. Karachi Blues* 123 (Irfanullah 39; Salman Fazal six for 42) and 187 (Sajid Ali 32, Hasan Raza 96; Iqbal Imam seven for 71); Karachi Whites 233 (Maisam Hasnain 44, Mohammad Masroor 93 not out; Nadeem Khan six for 79) and 81 for no wkt (Maisam Hasnain 32 not out, Kamran Hussain 47 not out). *Karachi Whites 12 pts.*

At Arbab Niaz Stadium, Peshawar, October 16, 17, 18, 19. Drawn. Peshawar 309 (Akhtar Sarfraz 104 not out, Shakeel Ahmed 56, Idrees Baig 56; Shoaib Akhtar four for 114, Naeem Akhtar three for 61) and 164 (Jahangir Khan, sen. 75; Shoaib Akhtar five for 74); Rawalpindi* 260 (Mohammad Wasim 63, Shahid Javed 65, Naseer Ahmed 49; Kabir Khan six for 100). *Peshawar 2 pts.*

At UBL Sports Complex, Karachi, October 22, 23, 24. Islamabad won by three wickets. Karachi Blues* 138 (Aqib Javed five for 25, Azhar Mahmood four for 40) and 233 (Saeed Azad 66, Basit Ali 83; Aqib Javed four for 61, Azhar Mahmood six for 94); Islamabad 254 (Mohammad Nawaz 62, Zaheer Abbasi 69; Ali Gauhar three for 72, Athar Laeeq four for 90) and 121 for seven (Zaheer Abbasi 33 not out; Ali Gauhar six for 70). *Islamabad 12 pts.*

At National Stadium, Karachi, October 22, 23, 24, 25. Drawn. Karachi Whites 479 (Iqbal Saleem 207, Aaley Haider 124, Shahid Iqbal 31; Naseer Shaukat five for 157, Nadeem Butt five for 108) and 231 for five dec. (Javed Sami 37, Aamer Hanif 80 not out, Aaley Haider 41, Mohammad

Javed 31 not out); Faisalabad* 358 (Amjad Ali 77, Ijaz Ahmed, jun. 63, Mohammad Nawaz 58, Bilal Ahmed 54, Naseer Shaukat 47, Extras 32; Baqar Rizvi three for 84, Aamer Hanif four for 49) and 238 for five (Mohammad Ramzan 66, Amjad Ali 31, Mohammad Saleem 44, Ijaz Ahmed, jun. 43). *Karachi Whites 2 pts.*
Iqbal Saleem's 207 lasted 441 minutes and 290 balls and included 22 fours. He added 240 runs for Karachi Whites' fifth wicket with Aaley Haider.

At Gaddafi Stadium, Lahore, October 22, 23, 24, 25. Drawn. Lahore City 285 (Zahoor Elahi 81, Extras 30; Shoaib Akhtar three for 80, Naeem Akhtar three for 65) and 284 (Shahid Anwar 31, Mansoor Rana 59, Manzoor Elahi 75 not out, Extras 30; Shoaib Akhtar five for 129, Naeem Akhtar three for 73); Rawalpindi* 252 (Zubair Nadeem 42, Naseer Ahmed 80, Extras 34; Ata-ur-Rehman five for 87, Naeem Ashraf four for 82) and 252 for seven (Mohammad Wasim 100, Naseer Ahmed 58; Ata-ur-Rehman four for 72). *Lahore City 2 pts.*
Rawalpindi wicket-keeper Mohammad Nadeem took five catches in Lahore City's second innings.

At Arbab Niaz Stadium, Peshawar, October 22, 23, 24. Bahawalpur won by eight wickets. Peshawar 216 (Akhtar Sarfraz 53, Wasim Yousufi 37, Extras 34; Azhar Shafiq five for 83, Murtaza Hussain five for 43) and 165 (Wasim Yousufi 38; Azhar Shafiq five for 61, Murtaza Hussain three for 22); Bahawalpur* 189 (Sher Ali 53, Yousuf Youhana 46; Kabir Khan five for 52) and 197 for two (Sher Ali 123 not out). *Bahawalpur 10 pts.*

At Iqbal Stadium, Faisalabad, October 28, 29, 30. Faisalabad won by 88 runs. Faisalabad 244 (Mohammad Ramzan 68, Naseer Shaukat 70 not out, Ijaz Mahmood 39; Azhar Shafiq four for 57, Mohammad Zahid four for 48) and 191 (Ijaz Mahmood 56; Azhar Shafiq for 58, Mohammad Zahid three for 34); Bahawalpur* 108 (Tariq Aziz 35; Kashif Elahi three for 38, Naseer Shaukat six for 51) and 239 (Azhar Shafiq 60, Nasir Jam 37, Murtaza Hussain 31, Yousuf Youhana 48; Naseer Shaukat three for 59). *Faisalabad 12 pts.*

At National Stadium, Karachi, October 28, 29, 30. Karachi Whites won by nine wickets. Peshawar* 236 (Jahangir Khan, sen. 41, Akhtar Sarfraz 37, Abdus Salam 90; Aamer Hanif five for 57, Ali Hussain Rizvi three for 42) and 166 (Shakeel Ahmed 43; Ali Hussain Rizvi four for 60); Karachi Whites 289 (Aamer Hanif 134, Aaley Haider 59, Iqbal Imam 32; Kabir Khan four for 62, Jan Nisar Khan three for 44) and 114 for one (Moin-ul-Atiq 68 not out, Kashif Ahmed 30 not out). *Karachi Whites 12 pts.*
Aamer Hanif scored a hundred in Karachi Whites' first innings and took five wickets in Peshawar's first innings. Karachi Whites wicket-keeper Iqbal Saleem took five catches in Peshawar's second innings.

At LCCA Ground, Lahore, October 28, 29, 30. Lahore City won by an innings and 139 runs. Lahore City* 493 (Zahoor Elahi 153, Mujahid Jamshed 129, Zahid Umar 30, Shahid Anwar 70; Bilal Rana six for 179); Islamabad 171 (Naved Ahmed 72; Mushtaq Ahmed six for 66) and 183 (Mohammad Nawaz 52, Ehsan Butt 32, Qaiser Mahmood 31; Mushtaq Ahmed four for 88, Mohammad Asif three for 32). *Lahore City 12 pts.*
Zahoor Elahi and Mujahid Jamshed added 281 in 265 minutes for Lahore City's first wicket.

At Pindi Cricket Stadium, Rawalpindi, October 28, 29, 30, 31. Rawalpindi won by five wickets. Karachi Blues 303 (Shadab Kabir 40, Basit Ali 88, Ahmer Saeed 37; Naeem Akhtar five for 45) and 166 (Mohammad Akram five for 57, Shoaib Akhtar four for 75); Rawalpindi* 253 (Mohammad Wasim 105, Shahid Javed 49; Zafar Iqbal three for 65, Haaris Khan five for 56) and 218 for five (Tasawwur Hussain 75, Mohammad Wasim 66; Shahid Mahboob three for 56). *Rawalpindi 10 pts.*

At Iqbal Stadium, Faisalabad, November 3, 4, 5. Lahore City won by five wickets. Faisalabad* 226 (Mohammad Ramzan 40, Mohammad Nawaz 39, Naseer Shaukat 32, Ata-ur-Rehman four for 63, Imran Tahir four for 83; Mohammad Asif three for 36); Lahore City 296 (Intikhab Alam 82, Shahid Nawaz 42, Mansoor Rana 43, Tahir Mahmood 52; Saeed Ajmal four for 72) and 106 for five (Tahir Mahmood 46 not out). *Lahore City 12 pts.*

At Chaudhry Rehmat Ali Cricket Ground, Islamabad, November 3, 4, 5. Islamabad won by five wickets. Bahawalpur* 114 (Sajjad Akhtar 37; Ghulam Abbas three for 27, Bilal Rana six for 26) and 222 (Saifullah 54, Extras 30; Bilal Rana five for 55); Islamabad 166 (Zaheer Abbasi 35; Murtaza Hussain four for 78, Khalid Butt four for 27) and 172 for five (Zaheer Abbasi 52, Naved Ahmed 43, Ehsan Butt 41 not out; Mohammad Zahid four for 68). *Islamabad 12 pts.*
Khalid Butt took a wicket with his first ball in first-class cricket.

At National Stadium, Karachi, November 3, 4, 5, 6. Karachi Blues won by five wickets. Peshawar 269 (Jahangir Khan, sen. 33, Akhtar Sarfraz 77, Asmatullah Khan 33, Wajahatullah Wasti 51, Abdus Salam 36; Humayun Hussain three for 71, Imranullah six for 75) and 259 (Akhtar Sarfraz 69, Abdus Salam 37, Jan Nisar Khan 50 not out, Arshad Khan 32; Nadeem Khan four for 77, Humayun Hussain three for 45); Karachi Blues* 312 (Ahmer Saeed 74, Asif Mujtaba 116; Kabir Khan five for 75, Fazal-e-Akbar three for 97) and 217 for five (Ahmer Saeed 55, Asif Mujtaba 39, Basit Ali 84). *Karachi Blues 12 pts.*

At Asghar Ali Shah Stadium, Karachi, November 3, 4, 5, 6. Rawalpindi won by 120 runs. Rawalpindi 251 (Shahid Naqi 41, Mohammad Wasim 33, Naeem Akhtar 43, Shakeel Ahmed 66; Ali Hussain Rizvi five for 83) and 162 (Naeem Akhtar 72; Aamer Hanif four for 55); Karachi Whites* 190 (Iqbal Saleem 34, Sohail Jaffer 33, Aaley Haider 34; Shoaib Akhtar four for 46, Shakeel Ahmed four for 53) and 103 (Shoaib Akhtar three for 30, Naeem Akhtar five for 37). *Rawalpindi 12 pts.*

At Bahawal Stadium, Bahawalpur, November 9, 10, 11. Rawalpindi won by 143 runs. Rawalpindi 188 (Naseer Ahmed 89 not out; Murtaza Hussain five for 77) and 281 (Mohammad Wasim 77, Naseer Ahmed 89, Naeem Akhtar 33; Murtaza Hussain four for 108); Bahawalpur* 175 (Azhar Shafiq 50; Tauqeer Hussain four for 63, Iftikhar Asghar four for 32) and 151 (Saifullah 40, Murtaza Hussain 33; Shoaib Akhtar three for 34, Tauqeer Hussain three for 43). *Rawalpindi 12 pts.*

At Iqbal Stadium, Faisalabad, November 9, 10, 11. Faisalabad won by 58 runs. Faisalabad 184 (Naseer Shaukat 72, Kamal Merchant 33; Ali Gauhar five for 61) and 174 (Fida Hussain 55, Inzamam-ul-Haq 32; Ali Gauhar four for 72, Imranullah four for 51); Karachi Blues* 82 (Naseer Shaukat five for 23, Saadat Gul five for 35) and 218 (Shadab Kabir 43, Asif Mujtaba 58, Mahmood Hamid 45; Naseer Shaukat five for 45, Kamal Merchant three for 27). *Faisalabad 12 pts.*

At Chaudhry Rehmat Ali Cricket Ground, Islamabad, November 9, 10, 11. Karachi Whites won by 13 runs. Karachi Whites 181 (Iqbal Imam 34; Ghulam Abbas four for 53, Bilal Rana three for 66) and 215 (Aamer Hanif 48, Sohail Jaffer 72, Iqbal Saleem 32 not out; Raj Hans five for 74, Bilal Rana three for 84); Islamabad* 127 (Bilal Rana 44 not out; Rashid Hanif seven for 36) and 256 (Zaheer Abbasi 56, Ehsan Butt 88, Bilal Rana 38; Naeem Tayyab six for 88). *Karachi Whites 12 pts.*

Rashid Hanif took a wicket with his first ball in first-class cricket, and seven for 36 in the innings.

At Arbab Niaz Stadium, Peshawar, November 9, 10. Peshawar won by an innings and 163 runs. Lahore City 103 (Sohail Idrees 55; Ijaz Elahi five for 27, Arshad Khan four for 28) and 53 (Kabir Khan five for 29, Ijaz Elahi four for 23); Peshawar* 319 (Jahangir Khan, sen. 42, Wajahatullah Wasti 77, Kabir Khan 57, Zulfiqar Ali 42 not out; Inamullah Khan eight for 109). *Peshawar 12 pts.*

Lahore City's second innings lasted 17.2 overs.

Semi-finals

At Asghar Ali Shah Stadium, Karachi, November 16, 17, 18, 19. Karachi Whites won by an innings and 119 runs. Karachi Whites* 554 (Nasir Khan 45, Mansoor Khan 43, Nasir Ali 167, Iqbal Saleem 182, Rashid Hanif 50, Abdullah Khan 43 not out; Saeed Ajmal seven for 220); Faisalabad 237 (Mohammad Saleem 107, Kamal Merchant 30, Zaheer Ahmed 38; Kashif Ibrahim five for 29, Rashid Hanif three for 67) and 198 (Amjad Ali 42, Mohammad Younis 58; Naeem Tayyab five for 47, Rashid Hanif four for 84).

Nasir Ali and Iqbal Saleem added 301 runs for Karachi Whites' fourth wicket. Faisalabad manager Tanvir Shaukat played his first first-team match for seven years.

At Pindi Cricket Stadium, Rawalpindi, November 16, 17, 18, 19. Drawn. Lahore City were declared winners by virtue of their first-innings lead. Lahore City 301 (Sohail Idrees 55, Aamer Manzoor 41, Shahid Nawaz 39, Ghaffar Kazmi 39, Waqas Ahmed 37; Ghulam Abbas three for 91, Bilal Rana five for 59) and 38 for one; Islamabad* 299 (Naved Ahmed 31, Ehsan Butt 77, Asif Ali 34, Bilal Rana 63, Extras 33; Ijaz Khan four for 64, Shahid Khan three for 70).

Final

At Makli Cricket Ground, Thatta, November 23, 24, 25. Lahore City won by one wicket. Karachi Whites 242 (Nasir Khan 35, Shahid Afridi 30, Extras 30; Masood Anwar five for 81) and 120 (Abdur Razzaq seven for 51, Shahid Khan three for 53); Lahore City* 214 (Shahid Nawaz 75) and 149 for nine (Shahid Nawaz 81; Kashif Ibrahim five for 37, Shahid Afridi three for 32).

   Lahore City won the five-day final with two days to spare. Abdur Razzaq, making his first-class debut three weeks after he played two limited-overs internationals against Zimbabwe, took nine wickets in the match.

QUAID-E-AZAM TROPHY WINNERS

1953-54	Bahawalpur	1970-71	Karachi Blues	1984-85	United Bank
1954-55	Karachi	1972-73	Railways	1985-86	Karachi
1956-57	Punjab	1973-74	Railways	1986-87	National Bank
1957-58	Bahawalpur	1974-75	Punjab A	1987-88	PIA
1958-59	Karachi	1975-76	National Bank	1988-89	ADBP
1959-60	Karachi	1976-77	United Bank	1989-90	PIA
1961-62	Karachi Blues	1977-78	Habib Bank	1990-91	Karachi Whites
1962-63	Karachi A	1978-79	National Bank	1991-92	Karachi Whites
1963-64	Karachi Blues	1979-80	PIA	1992-93	Karachi Whites
1964-65	Karachi Blues	1980-81	United Bank	1993-94	Lahore City
1966-67	Karachi	1981-82	National Bank	1994-95	Karachi Blues
1968-69	Lahore	1982-83	United Bank	1995-96	Karachi Blues
1969-70	PIA	1983-84	National Bank	1996-97	Lahore City

PCB PATRON'S TROPHY, 1996-97

	Played	Won	Lost	Drawn	1st-inns Points	Points
PIA	7	4	1	2	8	48
ADBP	7	3	0	4	10	40
United Bank	7	3	0	4	8	38
Habib Bank	7	2	1	4	10	30
Allied Bank	7	2	3	2	8	28
National Bank........	7	1	4	2	4	14
Pakistan Customs	7	1	4	2	2	12
PNSC	7	0	3	4	0	0

   Outright win = 10 pts; lead on first innings in a won or drawn game = 2 pts.

Semi-finals: Habib Bank beat ADBP by virtue of their first-innings lead; United Bank beat PIA by 52 runs. **Final:** United Bank beat Habib Bank by 306 runs.

At KRL Cricket Ground, Rawalpindi, November 16, 17, 18, 19. Drawn. ADBP 146 (Sabih Azhar 32; Shehzad Butt five for 42) and 221 for six (Mujahid Hameed 38, Mansoor Rana 76, Javed Hayat 38 not out; Ali Gauhar three for 40); United Bank* 331 (Salim Elahi 75, Basit Ali 32, Wasim Yousufi 51, Inzamam-ul-Haq 34, Tauseef Ahmed 33, Extras 38; Mohammad Asif four for 75). *United Bank 2 pts.*

At Defence Cricket Stadium, Karachi, November 16, 17, 18, 19. Drawn. Allied Bank* 349 (Ramiz Raja 53, Ijaz Ahmed, jun. 67, Manzoor Akhtar 124, Rashid Latif 38; Sajjad Akbar four for 94) and 204 for nine dec. (Mohammad Nawaz 83; Mohsin Kamal four for 43); PNSC 260 (Majid Saeed 38, Zeeshan Siddiqi 36, Sajjad Akbar 35, Tahir Mahmood 31; Aamir Nazir three for 51, Mohammad Zahid four for 44) and 157 for nine (Bilal Moin 35, Sajjad Akbar 38, Sajid Shah 50). *Allied Bank 2 pts.*

At UBL Sports Complex, Karachi, November 16, 17, 18, 19. Drawn. PIA* 325 (Rizwan-uz-Zaman 91, Shoaib Mohammad 54, Ghulam Ali 35, Asif Mujtaba 83; Kabir Khan four for 83, Nadeem Ghauri three for 52) and 187 for two (Rizwan-uz-Zaman 50, Ghulam Ali 101 not out); Habib Bank 356 (Shakeel Ahmed 69, Mujahid Jamshed 102, Tahir Rashid 73, Akram Raza 34, Extras 40; Nadeem Khan four for 115, Asif Mujtaba five for 60). *Habib Bank 2 pts.*
Habib Bank wicket-keeper Tahir Rashid took five catches in PIA's first innings.

At National Stadium, Karachi, November 16, 17, 18, 19. National Bank won by seven wickets. Pakistan Customs 341 (Naved Latif 44, Azhar Shafiq 123, Mohammad Masroor 33, Aamer Iqbal 32, Extras 37; Mohammad Javed four for 70) and 148 (Naved Latif 35, Azhar Shafiq 52; Shahid Anwar six for two); National Bank* 422 (Shahid Anwar 105, Sajid Ali 69, Tahir Shah 43, Mohammad Javed 52, Shahid Tanvir 64; Nadeem Iqbal four for 134, Azhar Shafiq three for 75, Ali Hussain Rizvi three for 71) and 69 for three (Azhar Shafiq three for 26). *National Bank 12 pts.*
Shahid Anwar's analysis was 4.5–4–2–6, as Pakistan Customs collapsed from 145 for three to 148 all out in their second innings. He also scored 105.

At National Stadium, Karachi, November 22, 23, 24, 25. Drawn. ADBP 461 for seven dec. (Mujahid Hameed 187, Mansoor Rana 117, Manzoor Elahi 66, Extras 48; Sajjad Akbar three for 93); PNSC* 306 (Sher Ali 73, Majid Saeed 85, Nasir Wasti 39, Extras 39; Shoaib Akhtar five for 90, Mohammad Asif three for 60) and 260 for three (Majid Saeed 115 not out, Nasir Wasti 84, Sajjad Akbar 31 not out; Shoaib Akhtar three for 73). *ADBP 2 pts.*

At Defence Cricket Stadium, Karachi, November 22, 23, 24, 25. Drawn. Pakistan Customs* 184 (Aamer Iqbal 57; Shahid Mahmood three for 62, Nadeem Ghauri four for 39) and 375 (Azhar Shafiq 33, Naved Latif 62, Azam Khan 70, Kamran Haider 47, Ziauddin 44; Nadeem Ghauri four for 71, Shahid Mahmood three for 98); Habib Bank 316 (Shakeel Ahmed 67, Mujahid Jamshed 120, Shahid Javed 38, Tahir Rashid 54; Ali Hussain Rizvi six for 123) and 100 for two (Shakeel Ahmed 33, Moin-ul-Atiq 38 not out). *Habib Bank 2 pts.*
Nadeem Ghauri took a hat-trick and wicket-keeper Tahir Rashid took four catches and one stumping in Pakistan Customs' second innings.

At Asghar Ali Shah Stadium, Karachi, November 22, 23, 24, 25. PIA won by nine wickets. National Bank* 203 (Zafar Iqbal 79, Naeem Tayyab 47 not out; Mohammad Zahid six for 49) and 151 (Tahir Shah 30, Zafar Iqbal 54; Mohammad Zahid four for 59, Nadeem Afzal three for 61, Nadeem Khan three for 14); PIA 289 (Ghulam Ali 47, Asif Mujtaba 59, Sohail Jaffer 62, Extras 30; Athar Laeeq three for 79, Naeem Tayyab five for 55) and 66 for one. *PIA 12 pts.*
PIA wicket-keeper Javed Qadir took four catches and one stumping in National Bank's second innings.

At UBL Sports Complex, Karachi, November 22, 23, 24, 25. Drawn. Allied Bank 358 (Aamir Sohail 46, Ijaz Ahmed, jun. 150, Aamer Hanif 52; Shehzad Butt five for 114, Azhar Mahmood three for 71) and 170 for three dec. (Aamir Sohail 59, Aamer Hanif 57, Bilal Rana 32 not out; Ali Gauhar three for 63); United Bank* 235 (Mohammad Ramzan 73; Mohammad Akram six for 56) and 219 for seven (Javed Sami 46, Mohammad Hussain 34, Wasim Yousufi 49 not out; Ata-ur-Rehman four for 53). *Allied Bank 2 pts.*

At Bahawal Stadium, Bahawalpur, November 28, 29, 30. ADBP won by seven wickets. Allied Bank 113 (Mohammad Asif four for 15) and 150 (Ehsan Butt 44; Raja Afaq three for 35); ADBP* 133 (Manzoor Elahi 32, Javed Hayat 36 not out; Aamir Nazir four for 27, Arshad Khan five for 52) and 131 for three (Atif Rauf 32 not out, Javed Hayat 47 not out). *ADBP 12 pts.*

At Multan Cricket Club Stadium, Multan, November 28, 29, 30, December 1. Habib Bank won by nine wickets. Habib Bank 299 (Shakeel Ahmed 37, Moin-ul-Atiq 49, Mujahid Jamshed 31, Anwar Miandad 43, Shahid Javed 40, Akram Raza 33 not out, Extras 34; Salman Fazal six for 62) and 122 for one (Shakeel Ahmed 31, Mujahid Jamshed 52 not out); National Bank* 76 (Kabir Khan four for 16, Nadeem Ghauri three for 18, Akram Raza three for 29) and 341 (Akhtar Sarfraz 135, Naeem Ashraf 44, Zafar Iqbal 43, Extras 31; Nadeem Ghauri seven for 101, Akram Raza three for 109). *Habib Bank 12 pts.*

At Montgomery Cricket Club Ground, Sahiwal, November 28, 29, 30. PIA won by six wickets. Pakistan Customs 202 (Azam Khan 46, Haaris Khan 50 not out; Nadeem Khan three for 57) and 97 (Nadeem Afzal three for 38, Asif Mujtaba four for 30, Nadeem Khan three for 18); PIA* 170 (Sohail Jaffer 38; Shahid Ali five for 36) and 130 for four (Zahid Fazal 33, Asif Mujtaba 35 not out, Nadeem Khan 37 not out; Haaris Khan three for 40). *PIA 10 pts.*

This ground was previously called Montgomery Biscuit Factory Ground.

At Quaid-e-Azam Stadium, Sahiwal, November 28, 29, 30, December 1. United Bank won by seven wickets. PNSC* 206 (Majid Saeed 41, Sajjad Ali 40; Tauseef Ahmed three for 53, Mohammad Hussain four for 51) and 182 (Majid Saeed 46, Sajjad Ali 33, Tahir Mahmood 41; Mohammad Hussain six for 81); United Bank 348 (Salim Elahi 59, Basit Ali 100, Mohammad Hussain 55 not out, Wasim Yousufi 49) and 41 for three (Sajid Shah three for 17). *United Bank 12 pts.*

At Railways Stadium, Lahore, December 4, 5, 6. ADBP won by 301 runs. ADBP* 177 (Sabih Azhar 36, Manzoor Elahi 46, Javed Hayat 37; Haaris Khan four for 56, Ali Hussain Rizvi four for 49) and 339 for nine dec. (Ghaffar Kazmi 43, Sabih Azhar 65, Atif Rauf 105, Manzoor Elahi 45; Haaris Khan six for 131); Pakistan Customs 113 (Azam Khan 56; Mohammad Asif five for 31) and 102 (Mohammad Asif four for 28). *ADBP 12 pts.*

At Bohranwala Ground, Faisalabad, December 4, 5, 6, 7. PIA won by eight wickets. Allied Bank 111 (Aamir Sohail 37; Nadeem Khan six for 35, Asif Mujtaba four for 27) and 327 (Aamir Sohail 132, Ijaz Ahmed, jun. 81; Wasim Haider four for 27, Asif Mujtaba five for 74); PIA* 324 (Asif Mujtaba 100, Sohail Jaffer 43, Javed Qadir 44 not out, Extras 43; Aamir Nazir three for 79, Aamir Sohail four for 76, Arshad Khan three for 56) and 117 for two (Ghulam Ali 68 not out). *PIA 12 pts.*

Asif Mujtaba scored a hundred in PIA's first innings and took five wickets in Allied Bank's second innings (eight in the match).

At Sheikhupura Stadium, Sheikhupura, December 4, 5, 6, 7. Drawn. Habib Bank 391 (Shakeel Ahmed 30, Moin-ul-Atiq 129, Tahir Rashid 70, Akram Raza 41, Naved Anjum 42, Extras 37; Murtaza Hussain four for 89) and 286 for eight (Shakeel Ahmed 123, Anwar Miandad 49; Shahid Hussain five for 83); PNSC* 284 (Majid Saeed 58, Sajjad Akbar 110, Shahid Hussain 43; Kabir Khan four for 87, Akram Raza three for 33). *Habib Bank 2 pts.*

At LCCA Ground, Lahore, December 4, 5, 6, 7. United Bank won by 150 runs. United Bank 168 (Iqbal Imam 71 not out; Athar Laeeq six for 57, Salman Fazal three for 31) and 296 (Mohammad Ramzan 112, Salim Elahi 46, Wasim Yousufi 52; Salman Fazal five for 102); National Bank* 195 (Shahid Anwar 64, Naeem Ashraf 40; Mohammad Hussain three for 42, Tauseef Ahmed three for 32) and 119 (Shehzad Butt three for 25, Tauseef Ahmed five for 36). *United Bank 10 pts.*

At Municipal Stadium, Gujranwala, December 10, 11, 12, 13. Drawn. National Bank 277 (Shahid Anwar 58, Saeed Azad 43, Aamer Gul 60, Wasim Arif 36; Mohammad Ali four for 110, Mohammad Asif three for 42) and 189 for six dec. (Sajid Ali 41, Penalty runs 40; Mubashir Nazir three for 55, Mohammad Ali three for 83); ADBP* 290 (Ghaffar Kazmi 48, Mansoor Rana 35, Javed Hayat 39, Bilal Ahmed 53; Maqsood Rana five for 76, Zafar Iqbal three for 35) and 57 for three (Athar Laeeq three for 28). *ADBP 2 pts.*

At Gaddafi Stadium, Lahore, December 10, 11, 12, 13. Habib Bank won by 11 runs. Habib Bank 354 (Mujahid Jamshed 83, Naved Anjum 83, Asadullah Butt 64 not out; Aqib Javed three for 83, Mohammad Akram four for 114) and 131 (Aqib Javed nine for 51); Allied Bank* 188 (Ramiz Raja 65; Kabir Khan four for 40, Shakeel Khan three for 38) and 286 (Ijaz Ahmed, jun. 88, Ramiz Raja 93; Asadullah Butt three for 96, Shakeel Khan four for 80). *Habib Bank 12 pts.*

Aqib Javed took a hat-trick in Habib Bank's second innings, earning career-best figures of nine for 51 and 12 for 134 in the match. But Allied Bank incurred a 20-run penalty for their slow over-rate in that innings, which proved enough to give Habib Bank victory.

At Jinnah Stadium, Sialkot, December 10, 11, 12, 13. Drawn. Pakistan Customs 198 (Kashif Ahmed 33, Azam Khan 38; Umar Rasheed three for 40, Mohammad Hussain three for 54) and 291 (Azhar Shafiq 91, Kashif Ahmed 59, Azam Khan 39; Azhar Mahmood five for 81); United Bank* 226 (Salim Elahi 63, Mohammad Hussain 78; Nadeem Ashraf five for 81) and 64 for no wkt (Salim Elahi 35 not out). *United Bank 2 pts.*

At Montgomery Cricket Club Ground, Sahiwal, December 10, 11, 12, 13. PIA won by ten wickets. PNSC* 152 (Tahir Mahmood 42; Zahid Ahmed five for 35) and 204 (Tahir Mahmood 33, Mazhar Qayyum 41, Sajjad Akbar 44 not out; Zahid Ahmed six for 71); PIA 331 (Ghulam Ali 68, Zahid Fazal 62, Zahid Ahmed 68, Javed Qadir 52, Extras 36; Murtaza Hussain three for 92) and 26 for no wkt. *PIA 12 pts.*
   Zahid Ahmed took a hat-trick in PNSC's first innings.

At KRL Cricket Ground, Rawalpindi, December 16, 17, 18, 19. Allied Bank won by an innings and 93 runs. National Bank* 171 (Zafar Iqbal 46 not out; Aamir Nazir four for 51) and 212 (Sajid Ali 54, Naeem Tayyab 41 not out; Aqib Javed four for 53, Aamir Nazir four for 70); Allied Bank 476 (Mohammad Nawaz 83, Ijaz Ahmed, jun. 151, Aaley Haider 50, Aamer Hanif 46, Arshad Khan 31, Aqib Javed 65; Mohammad Javed five for 75). *Allied Bank 12 pts.*

At Railways Stadium, Lahore, December 16, 17, 18, 19. Pakistan Customs won by three wickets. PNSC 125 (Nadeem Ashraf three for 31; Ali Hussain Rizvi five for 38) and 147 (Tahir Mahmood 44, Sajjad Akbar 35; Ali Hussain Rizvi five for 59, Haaris Khan four for 42); Pakistan Customs* 136 (Azhar Shafiq 34, Kashif Ahmed 43; Shahid Hussain four for 40, Sajjad Akbar four for 13) and 137 for seven (Azam Khan 39 not out; Murtaza Hussain four for 49). *Pakistan Customs 12 pts.*

At Gaddafi Stadium, Lahore, December 16, 17, 18, 19. United Bank won by 113 runs. United Bank 163 (Azhar Mahmood 69; Nadeem Afzal seven for 70) and 252 (Mohammad Ramzan 37, Salim Elahi 38, Iqbal Imam 88 not out, Wasim Yousufi 40; Nadeem Afzal three for 51, Adnan Naeem three for 75); PIA* 79 (Hasnain Kazim four for 36) and 223 (Asif Mujtaba 96, Wasim Haider 57, Extras 30; Hasnain Kazim four for 52, Umar Rasheed three for 20, Azhar Mahmood three for 63). *United Bank 12 pts.*
   United Bank wicket-keeper Wasim Yousufi took five catches in PIA's first innings and eight in the match.

At LCCA Ground, Lahore, December 17, 18, 19, 20. ADBP won by six wickets. Habib Bank 259 (Shahid Javed 39, Asadullah Butt 83, Naved Anjum 77, Extras 30; Shoaib Akhtar five for 89) and 221 (Idrees Baig 32, Asadullah Butt 44; Javed Hayat six for 49); ADBP* 298 (Atif Rauf 46, Javed Hayat 57, Manzoor Elahi 88 not out; Nadeem Ghauri four for 129, Akram Raza five for 113) and 183 for four (Mohammad Nadeem 41, Sabih Azhar 37, Mansoor Rana 46 not out, Javed Hayat 42 not out; Akram Raza four for 65). *ADBP 12 pts.*

At KRL Cricket Ground, Rawalpindi, December 22, 23, 24, 25. Drawn. ADBP 264 (Mansoor Rana 37, Manzoor Elahi 113, Mohammad Asif 31; Wasim Haider three for 66, Nadeem Khan three for 73) and 84 for two (Ghaffar Kazmi 33); PIA* 356 for eight dec. (Ghulam Ali 142, Sohail Jaffer 70, Extras 70; Mohammad Ali five for 89). *PIA 2 pts.*

At Arbab Niaz Stadium, Peshawar, December 22, 23, 24, 25. Allied Bank won by 118 runs. Allied Bank 330 (Masroor Hussain 48, Ramiz Raja 100, Aamer Hanif 66, Arshad Khan 30; Ali Hussain Rizvi four for 107) and 185 (Aaley Haider 45; Azhar Shafiq six for 56); Pakistan Customs* 187 (Muzaffar Abbasi 68; Aqib Javed three for 42, Mohammad Akram three for 64) and 210 (Muzaffar Abbasi 44; Aqib Javed seven for 64). *Allied Bank 12 pts.*

At Municipal Stadium, Gujranwala, December 22, 23, 24, 25. Drawn. Habib Bank 247 (Mujahid Jamshed 38, Shahid Javed 73, Naved Anjum 43, Akram Raza 39; Mohammad Hussain three for 60); United Bank* 224 for five (Mohammad Ramzan 44 retired hurt, Mansoor Akhtar 101 retired hurt, Extras 42; Akram Raza three for 28).

At Pindi Cricket Stadium, Rawalpindi, December 22, 23, 24, 25. Drawn. National Bank 269 (Aamer Gul 37, Akhtar Sarfraz 63; Sajid Shah five for 89) and 205 for five (Wasim Arif 35, Sajid Ali 52, Shahid Anwar 41 not out; Mohsin Kamal three for 59); PNSC* 259 (Sher Ali 77, Tahir Mahmood 38, Mazhar Qayyum 52, Extras 30; Naeem Ashraf three for 90, Maqsood Rana five for 42). *National Bank 2 pts.*

Semi-finals

At National Stadium, Karachi, December 28, 29, 30, 31. Drawn. Habib Bank were declared winners by virtue of their first-innings lead. Habib Bank 343 (Moin-ul-Atiq 112, Mujahid Jamshed 60, Asadullah Butt 43, Extras 38; Shoaib Akhtar five for 110) and 346 for four (Shakeel Ahmed 53, Moin-ul-Atiq 81, Mujahid Jamshed 61, Idrees Baig 50, Shahid Javed 58 not out); ADBP* 244 (Ghaffar Kazmi 76, Mansoor Rana 51 not out; Kabir Khan three for 106, Akram Raza four for 30).

At Pindi Cricket Stadium, Rawalpindi, December 28, 29, 30, 31. United Bank won by 52 runs. United Bank 272 (Basit Ali 84, Mohammad Hussain 48; Nadeem Khan six for 63) and 249 (Salim Elahi 31, Basit Ali 72; Nadeem Khan four for 97, Asif Mujtaba four for 47); PIA* 213 (Asif Mujtaba 71, Sohail Jaffer 49; Azhar Mahmood four for 76, Tauseef Ahmed four for 32) and 256 (Shoaib Mohammad 33, Zahid Fazal 43, Sohail Jaffer 39; Azhar Mahmood three for 42).

Final

At Gaddafi Stadium, Lahore, January 4, 5, 6, 7, 8. United Bank won by 306 runs. United Bank 338 (Mohammad Ramzan 43, Salim Elahi 78, Shehzad Butt 88, Aamer Bashir 30, Extras 50; Asadullah Butt three for 59, Akram Raza three for 33) and 294 (Mohammad Ramzan 70, Salim Elahi 46, Basit Ali 74, Azhar Mahmood 39; Asadullah Butt five for 77, Shakeel Khan three for 73); Habib Bank* 145 (Tahir Rashid 43, Akram Raza 41 not out; Hasnain Kazim six for 41, Azhar Mahmood three for 36) and 181 (Naved Anjum 92; Hasnain Kazim five for 87, Azhar Mahmood four for 56).

AYUB TROPHY AND PCB (BCCP) PATRON'S TROPHY WINNERS

The Ayub Trophy was replaced by the BCCP Trophy after the 1969-70 season, by the BCCP Patron's Trophy after the 1971-72 season and by the PCB Patron's Trophy after the 1994-95 season.

1960-61	Railways-Quetta	1975-76	National Bank	1987-88	Habib Bank
1961-62	Karachi	1976-77	Habib Bank	1988-89	Karachi
1962-63	Karachi	1977-78	Habib Bank	1989-90	Karachi Whites
1964-65	Karachi	1978-79	National Bank	1990-91	ADBP
1965-66	Karachi Blues	†1979-80	IDBP	1991-92	Habib Bank
1967-68	Karachi Blues	†1980-81	Rawalpindi	1992-93	Habib Bank
1969-70	PIA	†1981-82	Allied Bank	1993-94	ADBP
1970-71	PIA	†1982-83	PACO	1994-95	Allied Bank
1971-72	PIA	1983-84	Karachi Blues	1995-96	ADBP
1972-73	Karachi Blues	1984-85	Karachi Whites	1996-97	United Bank
1973-74	Railways	1985-86	Karachi Whites		
1974-75	National Bank	1986-87	National Bank		

† The competition was not first-class between 1979-80 and 1982-83, when it served as a qualifying competition for the Quaid-e-Azam Trophy.

WILLS KINGS CUP, 1996-97

Note: This match was not first-class.

Final

At Gaddafi Stadium, Lahore, March 13 (day/night). Allied Bank won by six wickets. National Bank 251 for nine (50 overs) (Sajid Ali 115, Mohammad Javed 34, Naeem Ashraf 35; Aqib Javed four for 46, Manzoor Akhtar three for 53); Allied Bank* 252 for four (42.1 overs) (Ramiz Raja 102 not out, Manzoor Akhtar 33, Aamer Hanif 38 not out; Naeem Ashraf three for 42).

The semi-finals of this tournament were the first matches to be played under floodlights in Pakistani domestic cricket.

CRICKET IN SRI LANKA, 1996-97

By GERRY VAIDYASEKERA and SA'ADI THAWFEEQ

Romesh Kaluwitharana

Sri Lanka's national team continued to shine in limited-overs cricket, collecting three more one-day trophies to follow up their triumph in the 1996 World Cup. But their plans to become a major Test power seemed to stall; after defeating novices Zimbabwe 2-0 at home, they lost away to New Zealand (whom they had beaten in their last two series) and West Indies and drew at home to Pakistan. They continued to look to Australia, so successful in Test cricket, for help. After Dav Whatmore, who had coached them to the World Cup, left to join Lancashire, the Sri Lankan board appointed Western Australian Bruce Yardley.

Out of the limelight, the domestic season continued, overshadowed by controversy. The holders of the P. Saravanamuttu Trophy, Colombo, found themselves fighting to defend not their title but their very right to take part in the tournament. They had not prepared a pitch for their opening match against Sinhalese Sports Club at the end of November, and the umpires declared the game abandoned. Colombo had asked for it to be rescheduled to another date, because of incessant rain earlier in the week. But they gave the tournament committee only a day's notice of their problem, whereas the rules stated that ten days' notice should normally be given before rescheduling. The executive committee of the Board of Control suspended Colombo from the trophy, and the two matches which they did play in December were excluded from the tournament table. (Old Dharmapalians were also suspended for providing an unsuitable pitch in the non-first-class Segment B of the competition.) Colombo's last resort, an appeal to the sports minister, failed. By then, their players had been given permission to join other clubs for the remainder of the season; they had argued successfully that they were being deprived of their livelihood for a matter which was entirely the responsibility of the club officials.

Colombo pursued their feud by querying the eligibility of board officials to stand for re-election at the AGM in March. The constitution stated that, apart from the treasurers, no one should be nominated for office who had not played in a major tournament. There were moves to make the rules more explicit, by specifying the number of major tournament matches required from candidates, to prevent them from qualifying by spending an afternoon on the field.

The executive committee had already decided that the national team should be drawn only from those cricketers who had played for at least 60 per cent of the season in the major domestic tournaments (not necessarily first-class). Exceptions could be made for national players contracted to overseas first-class teams – in the English County Championship or Australian Sheffield Shield, for example – but those appearing in minor competitions should return at least two weeks before a tour. This contributed to the decision of Test batsman Asanka Gurusinha, already smarting at being fined for remarks about the national team, to remain with his club in Melbourne rather than returning for Sri Lanka's tour of New Zealand.

It was also decided that, in 1997-98, the 15 teams of the Sara Trophy's first-class Segment A would again be divided into two groups, with the two leading clubs from each group advancing to semi-finals. But in 1996-97, the Trophy was contested by a round-robin league, as in the previous season, with no knockout stages. The champions were Bloomfield, who won all their last nine matches and were unbeaten. Runners-up Sinhalese also won nine and lost none, but Bloomfield were comfortably ahead on points. It was a double triumph for Bloomfield, who had beaten Tamil Union in the final of the Division I limited-overs tournament in December.

The leading run-scorer of the season was Test wicket-keeper Romesh Kaluwitharana, of Colombo Colts, who made 1,270 runs at 70.55. He scored six hundreds – four of them in succession from late January to mid-February. Lanka de Silva of Kurunegala was the only other player to reach four figures, with 1,032, but took 25 innings to Kaluwitharana's 18. Bandula Ranjith of Singha took 70 wickets at 16.40, including nine in an innings against Antonians and eight in an innings against Galle. But the best figures came from Mario Villavarayan, who had used the board's dispensation to move from Colombo to Bloomfield. He took nine for 15 in 11.1 overs to seal Bloomfield's innings victory over Police.

Test captain Arjuna Ranatunga and Hemantha Wickremaratne shared an unbeaten stand of 317 for Sinhalese's fifth wicket against Sebastianites, breaking the Sri Lankan all-wicket record of 315 set by Sampath Perera and Ruwan Kalpage of Bloomfield the previous year. Ranatunga made 200 not out, the only first-class double-hundred of the season, though both Mahela Jayawardene, also of Sinhalese, and Kaluwitharana managed two hundreds in a match. Kalpage was the season's leading all-rounder, making an important contribution to Bloomfield's success, with 731 runs at 45.68 and 61 wickets at 20.13.

Matara were the non-first-class Segment B champions, after winning five of their first six preliminary matches; Moors, relegated from Segment A the previous season, won all six but finished runners-up. Sebastianites led the Division II tournament. Burgher, promoted to the first-class competition after winning the B title in 1995-96, took the Six-a-Side MasterCard Trophy, which they organised in their centenary year. The Lanka Lions won the ninth Sharjah Floodlight Cricket Tournament, the Al Kabeer Cup, and a Colombo District Cricket Association team, led by Test opener Chandika Hathurusinghe, reached the semi-finals of the Mom-ul-Dowlah Gold Cup in Hyderabad.

In schools cricket, St Sebastian's College of Moratuwa claimed the Coca-Cola Bottlers' Trophy, winning seven of their 17 matches outright. The outstanding individual performance came from 17-year-old Dhammika Vaas Gunawardene of Maris Stella College, who scored 310 against St Peter's College at Negombo,

believed to be the first triple-hundred by a Sri Lankan schoolboy. His first
hundred took 121 balls, the second 50 and the third only 35, and he hit 14 sixes
and 36 fours. In the same fixture, his team-mate Ranga Dias took ten for 34 in
an innings. Sudanga Fernando of Trinity also took all ten, against St Anthony's,
and included a hat-trick. Chintaka Jayasinghe of Dharmapala College scored
1,000 runs for the third successive season, including four consecutive hundreds,
two of them against Royal at Pannipitiya. His second century of the match, an
unbeaten 106, took only fifty balls.

FIRST-CLASS AVERAGES, 1996-97

BATTING

(Qualification: 600 runs, average 30.00)

	M	I	NO	R	HS	100s	Avge
H. P. Tillekeratne (*Nondescripts CC*)	13	14	4	840	143	5	84.00
R. S. Kaluwitharana (*Colts CC*)	13	18	0	1,270	179	6	70.55
A. Ranatunga (*Sinhalese SC*)	11	13	2	680	200*	1	61.81
R. P. A. H. Wickremaratne (*Sinhalese SC*)	12	15	3	688	130	2	57.33
S. I. Fernando (*Colts CC*)	14	21	3	887	178*	2	49.27
G. R. P. Peiris (*Nondescripts CC*)	11	14	1	640	125	2	49.23
M. S. Atapattu (*Sinhalese SC*)	13	19	4	721	135*	3	48.06
S. T. Jayasuriya (*Bloomfield C and AC*)	13	21	1	954	129	2	47.70
D. P. M. Jayawardene (*Sinhalese SC*)	12	17	3	644	106*	2	46.00
R. S. Kalpage (*Bloomfield C and AC*)	15	22	6	731	160*	1	45.68
S. K. L. de Silva (*Kurunegala Youth CC*)	14	25	1	1,032	109	4	43.00
A. S. Jayasinghe (*Tamil Union C and AC*)	13	19	1	773	183	2	42.94
E. M. I. Galagoda (*Burgher RC*)	13	23	1	913	117	1	41.50
M. N. Nawaz (*Bloomfield C and AC*)	12	20	1	758	124	2	39.89
J. Kulatunga (*Colts CC*)	12	18	2	634	118	1	39.62
S. T. Perera (*Bloomfield C and AC*)	13	21	3	700	102*	1	38.88
S. Ranatunga (*Nondescripts CC*)	17	25	4	805	97	0	38.33
R. C. Liyanage (*Police SC*)	12	22	2	741	86	0	37.05
E. F. M. U. Fernando (*Colombo CC/Antonians SC*)	11	18	1	610	105	1	35.88
C. Mendis (*Colts CC*)	13	20	0	714	131	2	35.70
D. Rajapakse (*Burgher RC*)	13	22	1	743	101*	1	35.38
R. P. Arnold (*Nondescripts CC*)	17	24	1	813	131	3	35.34
D. P. Samaraweera (*Colts CC*)	13	21	1	664	100	1	33.20
S. Jayantha (*Singha SC*)	12	23	1	726	97	0	33.00
A. S. Wewalwala (*Singha SC*)	12	24	3	667	74	0	31.76

* *Signifies not out.*

BOWLING

(Qualification: 30 wickets, average 25.00)

	O	M	R	W	BB	5W/i	Avge
S. D. Anurasiri (*Panadura SC*)	325.5	148	474	39	7-84	5	12.15
M. Muralitharan (*Tamil Union C and AC*)	389	101	972	66	7-55	6	14.72
A. D. B. Ranjith (*Singha SC*)	369	81	1,148	70	9-29	7	16.40
C. N. Bandaratilleke (*Tamil Union C and AC*)	393.3	77	1,001	58	8-78	4	17.25
K. G. Perera (*Antonians SC*)	469	156	993	57	7-49	3	17.42
W. P. U. J. C. Vaas (*Colts CC*)	361.5	94	945	51	6-12	2	18.52
P. K. Serasinghe (*Police SC*)	401.4	87	996	53	7-55	3	18.79

	O	M	R	W	BB	5W/i	Avge
D. N. T. Zoysa (*Sinhalese SC*)	273	58	811	42	7-58	2	19.30
U. C. Hathurusinghe (*Tamil Union C and AC*)	250.5	68	700	36	8-29	4	19.44
T. T. Samaraweera (*Colts CC*)	260.2	67	743	38	5-8	2	19.55
K. S. C. de Silva (*Nondescripts CC*)	259.4	52	755	38	6-48	2	19.86
K. R. Pushpakumara (*Nondescripts CC*)	243.3	39	858	43	6-43	6	19.95
R. S. Kalpage (*Bloomfield C and AC*)	496.4	124	1,228	61	7-37	3	20.13
C. D. U. S. Weerasinghe (*Nondescripts CC*)	176.1	24	683	33	8-77	4	20.69
D. K. Liyanage (*Colts CC*)	228	37	800	37	5-26	2	21.62
A. Rideegammana (*Galle CC*)	392.1	98	1,017	46	5-54	2	22.10
A. W. R. Madurasinghe (*Kurunegala Youth CC*)	325.1	91	753	34	5-49	1	22.14
V. H. K. Ranaweera (*Police SC*)	294.2	51	936	41	5-39	2	22.82
A. W. Ekanayake (*Kurunegala Youth CC*)	361.5	66	1,075	47	5-41	3	22.87
R. P. Arnold (*Nondescripts CC*)	322.2	71	941	41	7-84	1	22.95
K. J. Silva (*Sinhalese SC*)	490.2	134	1,287	56	6-42	3	22.98
G. P. Wickremasinghe (*Sinhalese SC*)	263.4	45	913	39	6-82	1	23.41
P. Perera (*Kalutara Town CC*)	292.1	71	824	35	6-41	3	23.54
P. W. Gunaratne (*Bloomfield C and AC*)	248.4	46	765	32	6-71	1	23.90
K. E. A. Upashantha (*Colts CC*)	220.1	44	769	32	4-48	0	24.03
I. S. Gallage (*Panadura SC*)	259.2	49	899	36	5-72	2	24.97

P. SARAVANAMUTTU TROPHY, 1996-97

	Played	Won	Lost	Drawn	1st-inns Points	Bonus Points	Points
Bloomfield C and AC	13	9	0	4	18	129.5	255.5
Sinhalese SC	13	9	0	4	6	109	223
Colts CC	13	6	0	7	30	119.5	221.5
Tamil Union C and AC	13	7	2	4	12	101.5	197.5
Nondescripts CC	13	5	3	5	18	91	169
Kurunegala Youth CC	13	3	5	5	18	68.5	122.5
Police SC	13	3	4	6	12	67	115
Burgher RC	13	1	4	8	24	76	112
Sebastianites C and AC	13	1	3	9	24	64.5	100.5
Antonians SC	13	2	5	6	12	63.5	99.5
Panadura SC	13	1	3	9	28	59	99
Singha SC	13	3	9	1	0	61	97
Galle CC	13	1	3	9	16	55	83
Kalutara Town CC	13	0	10	3	10	34.5	44.5

Colombo CC were suspended from the tournament; the two matches they played, against Nondescripts and Bloomfield, are not shown in the above table.

Outright win = 12 pts; 1st-innings lead in drawn game = 6 pts; 1st-innings lead in lost game = 4 pts.

In the following scores, * by the name of a team indicates that they won the toss.

At Havelock Park, Colombo (BRC), November 29, 30, December 1. Drawn. Kurunegala Youth CC 153 (A. W. Ekanayake 82; D. Ekanayake five for 33, C. S. Perera three for 30) and 290 (R. R. Jaymon 51, A. W. Ekanayake 45, M. W. Kumara 35, A. W. R. Madurasinghe 33, R. K. B. Amunugama 39; A. P. Ranaweera three for 66, S. Madanayake three for 48); Burgher RC* 142 (C. U. Jayasinghe 38; M. W. Kumara three for 40, A. W. Ekanayake three for 37, A. W. R. Madurasinghe three for 18) and 103 for no wkt (A. P. Ranaweera 61 not out, E. M. I. Galagoda 32 not out).

At Maitland Crescent, Colombo (CCC), November 29, 30, December 1. Colombo SC v Sinhalese CC. Abandoned.

The umpires abandoned the game on the opening day, after defending champions Colombo failed to provide a suitable pitch, citing rain. They played two more matches, against Nondescripts and Bloomfield, but were then suspended from the tournament. None of Colombo's matches counted towards the final table.

At Havelock Park, Colombo (Colts), November 29, 30, December 1. Drawn. Bloomfield C and AC 262 (N. Bopage 81, I. P. P. Batuwitarachchi 70; W. P. U. J. C. Vaas four for 65, T. T. Samaraweera three for 40) and 178 for four dec. (S. T. Perera 83, I. P. P. Batuwitarachchi 51 not out); Colts CC* 185 (T. T. Samaraweera 41 not out, W. P. U. J. C. Vaas 31; P. W. Gunaratne three for 51, H. Boteju three for 29) and one for no wkt.

At Galle Esplanade, Galle, November 29, 30, December 1. Drawn. Galle CC 109 (I. D. Gunawardene three for eight, A. Priyantha six for 30) and 187 (C. K. Hewamanna 54, M. M. de Silva 53; V. H. K. Ranaweera three for 44, A. Priyantha three for 47); Police SC* 176 (R. C. Liyanage 38, W. N. M. Soysa 64; A. Rideegammana four for 37) and 111 for six (I. D. Gunawardene 30; S. M. Faumi three for 29).

At Panadura Esplanade, Panadura, November 29, 30, December 1. Drawn. Nondescripts CC 253 for six dec. (R. P. Arnold 70, S. D. Rajapakse 46, A. Gunawardene 35, C. I. Dunusinghe 34 not out); Panadura SC* 138 (S. E. D. Ruwan 32; R. P. Arnold three for 40) and 107 for three (S. E. D. Ruwan 46 not out, S. Kumara 37).

At Moratuwa Stadium, Moratuwa, November 29, 30, December 1. Drawn. Sebastianites C and AC 302 (S. K. Silva 111, D. Bodiyabaduge 31, M. Peiris 43, Anusha Perera 36; C. M. Hathurusinghe four for 61) and 312 for seven (M. S. Mendis 100, S. K. Silva 83, A. Fernando 36; C. N. Bandaratilleke six for 95); Tamil Union C and AC* 180 (C. P. Jayasinghe 38, D. N. Nadarajah 40 not out; G. R. M. A. Perera five for 49).

At Maitland Crescent, Colombo (CCC), December 6, 7, 8. Nondescripts CC won by six wickets. Nondescripts CC 362 for nine dec. (R. P. Arnold 62, G. R. P. Peiris 40, H. P. Tillekeratne 108, S. Ranatunga 78, Extras 42; M. Villavarayan four for 93, N. Dabare three for 58) and 108 for four (A. Gunawardene 48); Colombo CC* 148 (Sanjeewa Silva 31, V. S. K. Waragoda 75; K. R. Pushpakumara six for 59) and 321 (Sanjeewa Silva 38, A. P. Dalugoda 116, M. Villavarayan 48; K. R. Pushpakumara four for 73, K. S. C. de Silva four for 60).

At Havelock Park, Colombo (Colts), December 6, 7, 8. Drawn. Colts CC* 194 (J. Kulatunga 48 not out, N. Ranatunga 34, Extras 31; Anura Perera four for 67) and 300 for eight dec. (C. Mendis 80, R. S. Kaluwitharana 45, M. T. Sampath 36, D. K. Liyanage 60 not out, N. Ranatunga 35; Anura Perera three for 88); Sebastianites C and AC 242 (M. S. Mendis 70, Anusha Perera 51; D. K. Liyanage three for 71, T. T. Samaraweera four for 55) and 171 for nine (Extras 34; N. Ranatunga three for 42).

At Galle Esplanade, Galle, December 6, 7, 8. Singha SC won by 18 runs. Singha SC* 173 (S. Jayantha 37, A. D. B. Ranjith 41; S. Jayasekera three for 67, A. Rideegammana four for 42) and 117 (H. Premasiri 47; A. Rideegammana four for 31); Galle CC 137 (N. Shiroman 48; A. D. B. Ranjith eight for 50) and 135 (A. D. B. Ranjith seven for 48).

At Tyronne Fernando Stadium, Moratuwa, December 6, 7, 8. Kurunegala Youth CC won by eight wickets. Kalutara Town CC* 142 (H. S. S. Fonseka 70; A. W. Ekanayake three for 52, R. Herath three for 15) and 249 (T. M. Dilshan 91, P. C. Seeman 37; A. W. R. Madurasinghe three for 53, R. Herath five for 96); Kurunegala Youth CC 334 (S. K. L. de Silva 108, R. R. Jaymon 102; P. Perera three for 62) and 58 for two.

At Panadura Esplanade, Panadura, December 6, 7, 8. Drawn. Bloomfield C and AC 403 (I. P. P. Batuwitarachchi 109, P. B. Dassanayake 119, B. de Silva 66, Extras 32; I. S. Gallage five for 100) and 250 for eight dec. (S. T. Jayasuriya 42, S. T. Perera 53, R. S. Kalpage 31, I. P. P. Batuwitarachchi 44; S. Kumara three for 40); Panadura SC* 295 (S. E. D. Ruwan 58, B. P. Perera 46, S. Kumara 58, S. D. Anurasiri 37; R. S. Kalpage three for 61, P. P. Wickremasinghe four for 82).

At Police Park, Colombo, December 6, 7, 8. Drawn. Police SC* 158 (H. M. L. Sagara three for 56, J. A. Mahindaratne four for 29) and 300 for eight dec. (A. Priyantha 49, R. C. Liyanage 37, I. D. Gunawardene 93; J. A. Mahindaratne four for 78); Burgher RC 123 (E. M. I. Galagoda 47; W. N. M. Soysa five for 44, P. K. Serasinghe three for 35) and 175 for nine (D. Rajapakse 48; W. N. M. Soysa four for 61, P. K. Serasinghe four for 65).

At P. Saravanamuttu Stadium, Colombo, December 6, 7, 8. Sinhalese SC won by ten wickets. Tamil Union C and AC* 312 (C. P. Jayasinghe 46, U. D. U. Chandana 83, Extras 34; G. P. Wickremasinghe three for 32) and 97 (G. P. Wickremasinghe three for 28, K. J. Silva six for 42); Sinhalese SC 334 (M. S. Atapattu 106, R. P. A. H. Wickremaratne 77, Extras 49; M. Muralitharan five for 120) and 76 for no wkt (D. P. M. Jayawardene 54 not out).

At Braybrooke Place, Colombo, December 13, 14, 15. Drawn. Galle CC 205 (D. D. Wickremasinghe 31, S. M. Faumi 43; K. G. Perera four for 37); Antonians SC* 105 for six (V. S. Sittamige 38).

At Havelock Park, Colombo (BRC), December 13, 14, 15. Drawn. Kalutara Town CC 160 (C. N. Hettiarachchi 45; D. Madurapperuma six for 45) and 257 (T. M. Dilshan 51, H. S. S. Fonseka 60, C. N. Hettiarachchi 52, P. C. Seeman 45; S. Madanayake five for 36); Burgher RC* 266 for nine dec. (E. M. I. Galagoda 117, U. Hettiarachchi 41; C. N. Hettiarachchi five for 51) and 19 for four.

At Maitland Crescent, Colombo (CCC), December 13, 14, 15. Drawn. Colombo CC* 292 (Sanjeewa Silva 39, Y. N. Tillekeratne 37, E. F. M. U. Fernando 55, M. Villavarayan 61; P. P. Wickremasinghe four for 63, B. de Silva three for 21); Bloomfield C and AC 183 for seven (S. T. Jayasuriya 73, I. P. P. Batuwitarachchi 34, P. B. Dassanayake 36 not out; N. Dabare three for 40).

At Havelock Park, Colombo (Colts), December 13, 14, 15. Drawn. Tamil Union C and AC 232 (S. I. de Saram 54, U. D. U. Chandana 67; N. Ranatunga three for 53, T. T. Samaraweera five for 50); Colts CC* 413 for nine (C. Mendis 32, R. S. Kaluwitharana 162, T. T. Samaraweera 56, J. Kulatunga 45; M. Muralitharan three for 117).

At Maitland Place, Colombo (NCC), December 13, 14, 15. Drawn. Sinhalese SC 57 for four (K. S. C. de Silva three for 23) v Nondescripts CC*.

At Moratuwa Stadium, Moratuwa, December 13, 14, 15. Drawn. Sebastianites C and AC* 196 (D. Bodiyabaduge 55; I. S. Gallage three for 61, S. Kumara three for 37); Panadura SC 159 for three (B. P. Perera 43, S. N. Liyanage 51 not out).

At Galle Esplanade, Galle, December 27, 28, 29. Galle CC won by 123 runs. Galle CC* 235 (N. Shiroman 36, D. D. Wickremasinghe 81; P. Perera three for 73, C. R. P. Silva four for 82) and 218 for six dec. (N. Shiroman 53, A. Rideegammana 32, S. M. Faumi 39 not out, M. M. de Silva 30 not out); Kalutara Town CC 112 (M. M. de Silva six for 27) and 218 (P. Perera 64, R. D. Kottachchi 49; J. C. Gamage three for 19).

At Welagedera Stadium, Kurunegala, December 27, 28, 29. Kurunegala Youth CC won by two wickets. Singha SC 128 (R. K. B. Amunugama three for 46, A. W. R. Madurasinghe three for 15) and 187 (W. M. J. Kumudu 35, S. Jayantha 56, A. S. Wewalwala 53, P. Chandana 32; A. W. R. Madurasinghe four for 67, R. Herath three for 41); Kurunegala Youth CC* 147 (D. Hunukumbura 32, A. W. R. Madurasinghe 34; A. D. B. Ranjith three for 45, A. S. Wewalwala five for 40) and 170 for eight (S. K. L. de Silva 59, R. R. Jaymon 38; W. K. Jayalath three for 43).

At Police Park, Colombo, December 27, 28, 29. Drawn. Police SC* 138 (R. C. Liyanage 66; K. G. Perera four for 20) and 300 for seven dec. (R. C. Liyanage 47, W. N. M. Soysa 73, R. R. Wimalasiri 66 not out, M. N. C. Silva 30; K. Dharmasena three for 41); Antonians SC 145 (T. P. Kodikara 44; P. K. Serasinghe six for 38) and 156 for six (P. N. Wanasinghe 56, V. S. Sittamige 34, W. A. M. P. Perera 30 not out).

At Tyronne Fernando Stadium, Moratuwa, December 27, 28, 29. Nondescripts CC won by an innings and 26 runs. Sebastianites C and AC* 172 (S. K. Silva 58, M. Peiris 31; K. R. Pushpakumara six for 64) and 102 (S. K. Silva 35; K. R. Pushpakumara five for 26, R. P. Arnold three for 29); Nondescripts CC 300 for nine dec. (R. P. Arnold 116, C. I. Dunusinghe 34 not out; M. H. A. Jabbar three for 97).

At Maitland Place, Colombo (SSC), December 27, 28, 29. Drawn. Bloomfield C and AC 161 (R. S. Mahanama 39; D. N. T. Zoysa three for 44, G. P. Wickremasinghe three for 37) and 300 for five (S. T. Jayasuriya 89, S. T. Perera 102 not out, R. S. Mahanama 42; G. P. Wickremasinghe three for 42); Sinhalese SC* 352 for nine dec. (A. A. W. Gunawardene 34, D. P. M. Jayawardene 60, M. S. Atapattu 44, A. Ranatunga 31, R. P. A. H. Wickremaratne 84, G. P. Wickremasinghe 48; R. S. Kalpage four for 72).

At P. Saravanamuttu Stadium, Colombo, December 27, 28, 29. Tamil Union C and AC won by ten wickets. Tamil Union C and AC* 310 (U. D. U. Chandana 53, G. R. K. Wijekoon 92 not out, A. S. Jayasinghe 95; I. S. Gallage four for 64) and 15 for no wkt; Panadura SC 144 (S. E. D. Ruwan 32, I. Amithakeerthi 36 not out; M. Muralitharan five for 28) and 177 (D. Prasanna 38; C. M. Hathurusinghe six for 72).

At P. Saravanamuttu Stadium, Colombo, January 3, 4, 5. Singha SC won by seven wickets. Antonians SC 81 (A. D. B. Ranjith nine for 29) and 295 (S. Jayawardene 45, V. S. Sittamige 34, W. A. M. P. Perera 57, N. Devarajan 53 not out; A. D. B. Ranjith four for 101, S. Sanjeewa three for 67); Singha SC* 268 (H. Premasiri 34, S. Jayantha 61, A. S. Wewalwala 62; P. N. Wanasinghe three for 43, K. G. Perera three for 27) and 112 for three (H. Premasiri 32, A. S. Wewalwala 40 not out).

At Havelock Park, Colombo (Colts), January 3, 4, 5. Colts CC won by an innings and 190 runs. Colts CC* 446 for five dec. (D. P. Samaraweera 100, C. Mendis 102, R. S. Kaluwitharana 150, T. T. Samaraweera 50 not out); Panadura SC 105 (R. R. K. Wimalasena 30 not out; K. E. A. Upashantha four for 48, D. K. Liyanage five for 26) and 151.

At Galle Esplanade, Galle, January 3, 4, 5. Drawn. Galle CC* 267 (N. Shiroman 35, A. Rideegammana 71, D. Sudarshana 30, S. M. Faumi 31, H. Rajapakse 36 not out; D. Arnolda three for 55, D. Madurapperuma three for 55) and 232 (N. Shiroman 55, D. Sudarshana 91; J. A. Mahindaratne three for 48, D. Rajapakse three for 43); Burgher RC 354 (D. Arnolda 129 not out, S. Madanayake 110; S. M. Faumi three for 105, A. Rideegammana five for 87).

Arnolda and Madanayake added 222, a Sri Lankan eighth-wicket record.

At Maitland Place, Colombo (NCC), January 3, 4, 5. Drawn. Bloomfield C and AC* 364 (S. T. Jayasuriya 75, R. S. Mahanama 111, R. S. Kalpage 71; R. P. Arnold three for 89) and 212 for six dec. (S. T. Jayasuriya 72, M. N. Nawaz 84); Nondescripts CC 316 (G. R. P. Peiris 85, A. Gunawardene 108, H. P. Tillekeratne 71; R. S. Kalpage four for 110, S. T. Jayasuriya four for 54) and 73 for three (S. Ranatunga 31 not out).

At Police Park, Colombo, January 3, 4, 5. Police SC won by six wickets. Kurunegala Youth CC 76 (V. H. K. Ranaweera five for 39, A. Priyantha three for 21) and 208 (A. W. Ekanayake 67, R. K. B. Amunugama 33 not out; A. Priyantha four for 29); Police SC* 133 (R. C. Liyanage 46; R. K. B. Amunugama five for 61, A. W. Ekanayake three for 19) and 152 for four (R. C. Liyanage 53 not out, R. R. Wimalasiri 32 not out).

At Maitland Place, Colombo (SSC), January 3, 4, 5. Sinhalese SC won by an innings and 24 runs. Sebastianites C and AC 222 (W. D. J. Abeywardene 75, M. Peiris 43, D. Bodiyabaduge 35 not out; S. B. Dodanwela four for 42, D. P. M. Jayawardene three for 30) and 207 (Anusha Perera 90, M. Peiris 35; G. P. Wickremasinghe six for 82, S. B. Dodanwela three for 44); Sinhalese SC* 453 for four dec. (A. A. W. Gunawardene 36, M. S. Atapattu 60, A. Ranatunga 200 not out, R. P. A. H. Wickremaratne 102 not out).

Ranatunga's 200 not out lasted 203 balls and included 22 fours and four sixes. He added 317 for Sinhalese's fifth wicket with Wickremaratne, in 250 minutes and 59 overs; it was an all-wicket record in Sri Lankan first-class cricket.

At Havelock Park, Colombo (Colts), January 10, 11, 12. Colts CC won by 384 runs. Colts CC* 295 (D. P. Samaraweera 90, R. S. Kaluwitharana 52, M. T. Sampath 35, T. T. Samaraweera 32; P. K. Serasinghe four for 60) and 302 for seven dec. (D. P. Samaraweera 47, S. I. Fernando 44, T. T. Samaraweera 68, J. Kulatunga 89); Police SC 57 (K. E. A. Upashantha three for 18, T. T. Samaraweera five for eight) and 156 (S. I. Fernando four for 35, B. Perera four for 43).

At Welagedera Stadium, Kurunegala, January 10, 11, 12. Bloomfield C and AC won by 134 runs. Bloomfield C and AC 411 for seven dec. (S. T. Jayasuriya 31, M. N. Nawaz 57, H. D. P. K. Dharmasena 155 not out, R. S. Kalpage 74, P. B. Dassanayake 33; M. W. Kumara three for 104) and 113 for six dec. (A. W. Ekanayake three for 22); Kurunegala Youth CC* 264 (R. Kariyawasam 42, D. Hunukumbura 54, R. R. Jaymon 60, S. Malmeewala 32; P. W. Gunaratne six for 71) and 126 (P. W. Gunaratne four for 40, S. T. Jayasuriya three for 35).

At Maitland Place, Colombo (NCC), January 10, 11, 12. Drawn. Nondescripts CC 412 for eight dec. (G. R. P. Peiris 39, P. K. Rajapakse 88, H. P. Tillekeratne 143, C. I. Dunusinghe 50 not out) and 188 for one dec. (R. P. Arnold 49, G. R. P. Peiris 100 not out, S. Ranatunga 33 not out); Burgher RC* 326 (D. Rajapakse 67, C. R. Perera 46, D. Arnolda 61, S. K. B. Tennekoon 53) and 127 for three (M. Rajapakse 37, E. M. I. Galagoda 35; E. A. R. de Silva three for 39).

At Panadura Esplanade, Panadura, January 10, 11, 12. Drawn. Panadura SC* 294 (S. E. D. Ruwan 36, S. Kumara 74, S. N. Liyanage 77, I. Amithakeerthi 31 not out; J. C. Gamage four for 34, S. M. Faumi three for 54, H. Rajapakse three for 77) and 150 for four dec. (S. E. D. Ruwan 61 not out); Galle CC 188 (H. Rajapakse 45, J. C. Gamage 32; S. D. Anurasiri six for 36, S. Kumara three for 65) and 45 for one.

At Moratuwa Stadium, Moratuwa, January 10, 11, 12. Drawn. Antonians SC 275 (P. N. Wanasinghe 70, W. A. M. P. Perera 30, N. Devarajan 50, Extras 43; Anusha Perera four for 40) and 127 for five (T. P. Kodikara 37); Sebastianites C and AC* 260 (C. M. Wickremasinghe 40, M. S. Mendis 34, A. P. Dalugoda 52, Extras 31; K. G. Perera six for 64).

At Maitland Place, Colombo (SSC), January 10, 11, 12. Sinhalese SC won by an innings and 167 runs. Kalutara Town CC 109 (C. N. Hettiarachchi 31, R. D. Kottachchi 30 not out; D. N. T. Zoysa five for 33, S. B. Dodanwela three for 24) and 74 (D. N. T. Zoysa four for 16, S. B. Dodanwela four for 49); Sinhalese SC* 350 (D. P. M. Jayawardene 51, M. Perera 50, R. P. A. H. Wickremaratne 52, R. S. Jayawardene 89, G. P. Wickremasinghe 32, Extras 30; P. Perera five for 70, R. Chandana three for 141).

At P. Saravanamuttu Stadium, Colombo, January 10, 11, 12. Tamil Union C and AC won by an innings and 196 runs. Tamil Union 448 for nine dec. (S. Herathge 36, U. D. U. Chandana 104, G. R. K. Wijekoon 117, C. N. Bandaratilleke 77); Singha SC* 133 (A. S. Wewalwala 38 not out; G. R. K. Wijekoon three for 22, M. Muralitharan four for 26, U. D. U. Chandana three for 30) and 119 (S. Jayantha 35, Extras 30; U. D. U. Chandana six for 25).

At Reid Avenue, Colombo, January 17, 18, 19. Bloomfield C and AC won by ten wickets. Burgher RC 283 (M. Rajapakse 46, S. Jayasundera 31, D. Madurapperuma 40, C. S. Perera 39 not out; A. P. R. Shaman three for 59) and 141 (E. M. I. Gallage 32; R. S. Kalpage three for 34, H. D. P. K. Dharmasena five for 27); Bloomfield C and AC* 410 for nine dec. (S. T. Jayasuriya 43, R. S. Mahanama 94, M. N. Nawaz 49, H. D. P. K. Dharmasena 194, Extras 35; H. M. L. Sagara four for 131, D. Madurapperuma three for 86) and 17 for no wkt.

At Havelock Park, Colombo (Colts), January 17, 18, 19. Drawn. Singha SC 328 (H. Premasiri 71, S. Jayantha 77, A. S. Wewalwala 32, S. Sanjeewa 72 not out, Extras 39; S. I. Fernando five for 45) and 281 (S. Jayantha 73, S. Sanjeewa 54; K. E. A. Upashantha four for 66); Colts CC* 380 (C. Mendis 131, T. T. Samaraweera 117, R. K. Liyanage 47; A. D. B. Ranjith six for 132) and 136 for six (R. S. Kaluwitharana 34, S. I. Fernando 30, J. Kulatunga 32; A. D. B. Ranjith three for 64).

At Maitland Place, Colombo (NCC), January 17, 18, 19. Nondescripts CC won by an innings and 22 runs. Kalutara Town CC 114 (V. S. Sittamige 34; K. R. Pushpakumara five for 65, K. S. C. de Silva three for 26) and 165 (N. M. Tillekeratne 46, R. D. Kottachchi 52; K. R. Pushpakumara six for 43, K. S. C. de Silva three for 47); Nondescripts CC* 301 (G. R. P. Peiris 125, A. Gunawardene 68, C. I. Dunusinghe 32; R. Chandana three for 41, M. Bandara three for 57).

At Panadura Esplanade, Panadura, January 17, 18, 19. Drawn. Panadura SC 156 (I. Amithakeerthi 37; V. H. K. Ranaweera three for 53, M. N. C. Silva three for four, P. K. Serasinghe three for 36) and 230 for six dec. (S. Kumara 58, B. P. Perera 35; P. K. Serasinghe four for 69); Police SC* 84 (S. D. Anurasiri five for 21) and 121 for nine (I. S. Gallage four for 36, S. D. Anurasiri five for 36).

Police wicket-keeper M. Kudagodage made four catches and two stumpings in Panadura's first innings.

At Moratuwa Stadium, Moratuwa, January 17, 18, 19. Drawn. Sebastianites C and AC* 307 (Sanjeewa Silva 129, C. M. Wickremasinghe 36, A. P. Dalugoda 50, Extras 31; M. M. de Silva five for 72) and 315 for seven (M. S. Mendis 53, S. K. Silva 59, Primal Salgado 47, Anusha Perera 32, A. Fernando 51 not out; M. M. de Silva five for 109); Galle CC 349 (N. Shiroman 103, D. D. Wickremasinghe 91, D. Sudarshana 64, S. M. Faumi 31; G. R. M. A. Perera four for 62).

At P. Saravanamuttu Stadium, Colombo, January 17, 18, 19. Tamil Union C and AC won by an innings and 55 runs. Tamil Union C and AC* 370 (C. P. Jayasinghe 40, U. D. U. Chandana 56, V. S. K. Waragoda 138, N. de Silva 39; S. Jayawardene three for 72, K. G. Perera three for 50, Y. N. Tillekeratne four for 65); Antonians SC 179 (T. P. Kodikara 54, Y. N. Tillekeratne 32; M. Muralitharan seven for 55) and 136 (T. P. Kodikara 36; M. Muralitharan three for 23, C. N. Bandaratilleke four for 41).

At Reid Avenue, Colombo, January 24, 25, 26. Bloomfield C and AC won by 416 runs. Bloomfield C and AC 432 for three dec. (P. B. Dassanayake 55, R. S. Mahanama 176, M. N. Nawaz 101, R. S. Kalpage 52 not out) and 250 for eight dec. (N. Bopage 57, R. S. Kalpage 50, A. P. R. Shaman 73; C. R. P. Silva three for 94); Kalutara Town CC* 125 (R. S. Kalpage three for 38, H. D. P. K. Dharmasena four for 27) and 141 (N. M. Tillekeratne 64; R. S. Kalpage seven for 37).

At Havelock Park, Colombo (BRC), January 24, 25, 26. Drawn. Sebastianites C and AC* 340 (A. P. Dalugoda 51, M. Peiris 36, Anusha Perera 45, A. Fernando 92 not out, Extras 30; W. C. Labrooy four for 102, H. M. L. Sagara three for 74) and 161 for five (A. P. Dalugoda 45 not out; W. C. Labrooy four for 71); Burgher RC 433 for nine dec. (M. Rajapakse 66, E. M. I. Galagoda 81, D. Rajapakse 101 not out, S. K. B. Tennekoon 62, W. C. Labrooy 31; Anura Perera six for 87).

At Havelock Park, Colombo (Colts), January 24, 25, 26. Drawn. Antonians SC* 303 (T. P. Kodikara 68, M. Prasanga 31, E. F. M. U. Fernando 30, P. N. Wanasinghe 110, Extras 31; D. Hettiarachchi three for 51, T. T. Samaraweera three for 43) and 241 (M. Prasanga 73, E. F. M. U. Fernando 67; W. P. U. J. C. Vaas four for 57, T. T. Samaraweera three for 51); Colts CC 458 for four dec. (D. P. Samaraweera 35, S. Janaka 62, S. I. Fernando 144 not out, R. S. Kaluwitharana 149, D. K. Liyanage 30, Extras 31).

Fernando and Kaluwitharana added 267 for Colts' third wicket.

At Galle Esplanade, Galle, January 24, 25, 26. Sinhalese SC won by 134 runs. Sinhalese SC* 196 (U. N. K. Fernando 71, R. P. A. H. Wickremaratne 34; A. Rideegammana three for 64, M. M. de Silva six for 47) and 335 for eight dec. (M. S. Atapattu 135 not out, U. N. K. Fernando 77, S. H. S. M. K. Silva 35; H. Rajapakse three for 69); Galle CC 225 (S. Kodituwakku 52, C. K. Hewamana 42, D. Sudarshana 57, S. M. Faumi 33; D. N. T. Zoysa three for 23, R. S. Jayawardene three for 29) and 172 (A. Rideegammana 64; D. N. T. Zoysa four for 46).

At Welagedera Stadium, Kurunegala, January 24, 25, 26. Drawn. Tamil Union C and AC* 350 (D. N. Nadarajah 38, U. D. U. Chandana 37, V. S. K. Waragoda 75, G. R. K. Wijekoon 81, C. N. Bandaratilleke 32; M. W. Kumara three for 73, A. W. Ekanayake four for 88) and 287 for four dec. (A. S. Jayasinghe 100, D. N. Nadarajah 102 not out, V. S. K. Waragoda 43); Kurunegala Youth CC 261 (S. K. L. de Silva 109, Extras 34; C. M. Hathurusinghe four for 42, C. N. Bandaratilleke three for 38).

At Panadura Esplanade, Panadura, January 24, 25, 26. Panadura SC won by 126 runs. Panadura SC* 169 (S. D. Anurasiri 32; K. P. J. Warnaweera three for 43, W. K. Jayalath three for 53) and 176 (S. N. Liyanage 32, D. Prasanna 33 not out; A. D. B. Ranjith four for 63); Singha SC 90 (K. C. Silva five for 41) and 129 (S. Jayantha 31; S. D. Anurasiri six for 42).

At Havelock Park, Colombo (BRC), January 31, February 1, 2. Sinhalese SC won by seven wickets. Sinhalese SC* 394 (M. Perera 106, M. S. Atapattu 61, R. S. Jayawardene 60, A. Ranatunga 88, Extras 33; W. C. Labrooy five for 90) and 67 for three (W. C. Labrooy three for 47); Burgher RC 204 (E. M. I. Galagoda 41, S. K. B. Tennekoon 44, W. C. Labrooy 32; D. N. T. Zoysa four for 61, K. J. Silva three for 49) and 255 (D. Rajapakse 50, W. C. Labrooy 65 not out, H. M. L. Sagara 48; G. P. Wickremasinghe three for 58).

In Burgher's second innings, Labrooy and Sagara added 118 for the ninth wicket.

At Havelock Park, Colombo (Colts), January 31, February 1, 2. Colts CC won by an innings and 106 runs. Colts CC* 413 for six dec. (S. I. Fernando 49, R. S. Kaluwitharana 179, J. Kulatunga 118; A. W. Ekanayake three for 120); Kurunegala Youth CC 197 (C. P. Handunettige 82, H. Liyanage 50 not out; D. K. Liyanage five for 42) and 110 (W. P. U. J. C. Vaas six for 12).

At Maitland Place, Colombo (NCC), January 31, February 1, 2. Drawn. Galle CC 326 (A. Rideegamamma 100, D. D. Wickremasinghe 103 not out, S. M. Faumi 30, Extras 33; D. Samarasinghe four for 47) and 44 for one; Nondescripts CC* 401 for five dec. (G. R. P. Peiris 61, S. Ranatunga 80, A. Gunawardene 120 not out, H. P. Tillekeratne 110 not out; S. M. Faumi four for 111).

Gunawardene and Tillekeratne added 239 for Nondescripts' sixth wicket.

At Panadura Esplanade, Panadura, January 31, February 1, 2. Drawn. Panadura SC* 384 (R. C. Galappathi 31, S. Kumara 142, B. P. Perera 67, I. Amithakeerthi 41, Extras 33; S. Jayawardene three for 66) and 183 for six (R. C. Galappathi 69, S. Kumara 57 not out; D. Surendra five for 95); Antonians SC 214 (Y. N. Tillekeratne 69, E. F. M. U. Fernando 61 not out; S. D. Anurasiri seven for 84).

At Moratuwa Stadium, Moratuwa, January 31, February 1, 2. Drawn. Kalutara Town CC* 229 (H. S. S. Fonseka 91, Extras 30; A. P. Dalugoda four for 65) and 322 for eight dec. (H. S. S. Fonseka 40, P. Perera 133, T. M. Dilshan 111; Primal Salgado five for 42); Sebastianites C and AC 412 for nine dec. (S. K. Silva 71, S. Silva 36, Anusha Perera 36, A. Fernando 113, R. Yasalal 54, Extras 30; V. S. Sittamige three for 48) and 46 for three (S. Silva 33).

At P. Saravanamuttu Stadium, Colombo, January 31, February 1, 2. Tamil Union C and AC won by seven wickets. Police SC* 197 (W. N. M. Soysa 53; M. Muralitharan four for 44, C. N. Bandaratilleke three for 27) and 206 (A. Priyantha 56, R. C. Liyanage 51; M. Muralitharan six for 75); Tamil Union C and AC 236 (A. S. Jayasinghe 38, V. S. K. Waragoda 84, N. de Silva 38, G. R. K. Wijekoon 34; V. H. K. Ranaweera four for 67) and 168 for three (U. D. U. Chandana 104 not out; V. H. K. Ranaweera three for 52).

At Reid Avenue, Colombo, February 7, 8, 9. Bloomfield C and AC won by an innings and 125 runs. Galle CC* 172 (A. Rideegamamma 77; P. W. Gunaratne three for 20, A. P. R. Shaman three for 31) and 104 (N. Shiroman 48; M. Villavarayan three for 18, P. P. Wickremasinghe five for 26); Bloomfield C and AC 401 for six dec. (S. T. Jayasuriya 129, R. S. Kalpage 92 not out, P. B. Dassanayake 92, A. P. R. Shaman 34 not out).

At Havelock Park, Colombo (Colts), February 7, 8, 9. Colts CC won by 101 runs. Colts CC 403 (D. P. Samaraweera 82, S. I. Fernando 68, S. Janaka 85, J. Kulatunga 65; W. C. Labrooy three for 124, H. M. L. Sagara three for 99, D. Madurapperuma three for 48) and 179 for eight dec. (D. P. Samaraweera 30, S. Janaka 58, J. Kulatunga 36; H. M. L. Sagara three for 41); Burgher RC* 302 (E. M. I. Galagoda 93, D. Rajapakse 37, D. Madurapperuma 49 not out; W. P. U. J. C. Vaas three for 78) and 179 (E. M. I. Galagoda 49, C. R. Perera 31, W. C. Labrooy 40 not out; W. P. U. J. C. Vaas six for 48).

At Tyronne Fernando Stadium, Moratuwa, February 7, 8, 9. Drawn. Kurunegala Youth CC* 258 (R. J. Jaymon 57, R. R. Jaymon 48, S. K. L. de Silva 30; I. S. Gallage five for 72, K. P. Ratnaweera four for 95) and 172 for eight (S. K. L. de Silva 60, H. Liyanage 34; I. Amithakeerthi four for 50); Panadura SC 193 (S. Kumara 36; M. W. Kumara six for 64).

At Maitland Place, Colombo (NCC), February 7, 8, 9. Nondescripts CC won by an innings and 28 runs. Police SC* 102 (R. R. Wimalasiri 32; C. D. U. S. Weerasinghe six for 32) and 142 (A. Priyantha 39; K. S. C. de Silva six for 48, R. P. Arnold four for 38); Nondescripts CC 272 (R. P. Arnold 131, P. K. Rajapakse 47; V. H. K. Ranaweera five for 83).

At Maitland Place, Colombo (SSC), February 7, 8, 9. Sinhalese Sports Club won by an innings and 126 runs. Singha SC 136 (H. Premasiri 51; S. B. Dodanwela five for 39, C. Boteju three for 41) and 143 (S. G. S. Silva 39, H. Premasiri 30; D. N. T. Zoysa seven for 58); Sinhalese SC* 405 for seven dec. (M. Perera 42, D. P. M. Jayawardene 54, M. S. Atapattu 91, R. S. Jayawardene 67, A. Ranatunga 43, R. P. A. H. Wickremaratne 34, D. N. T. Zoysa 32 not out; S. Jayantha three for 79).

At P. Saravanamuttu Stadium, Colombo, February 7, 8, 9. Tamil Union C and AC won by an innings and 78 runs. Kalutara Town CC* 119 (H. S. S. Fonseka 39; C. N. Bandaratilleke six for 50, M. Muralitharan three for 25) and 160 (R. C. Perera 55; C. N. Bandaratilleke three for 27, U. D. U. Chandana three for 51); Tamil Union C and AC 357 (S. P. Herathge 46, U. C. Hathurusinghe 121, V. S. K. Waragoda 55, Extras 32; P. Perera five for 66, R. D. Kottachchi three for 68).

At Reid Avenue, Colombo, February 14, 15, 16. Bloomfield C and AC won by an innings and 150 runs. Bloomfield C and AC* 417 for seven dec. (S. T. Perera 40, H. D. P. K. Dharmasena 93, R. S. Kalpage 160 not out; V. H. K. Ranaweera three for 108); Police SC 204 (W. N. M. Soysa 35, A. Senasinghe 36, Extras 35; R. S. Kalpage three for 36) and 63 (M. Villavarayan nine for 15).

Villavarayan's second-innings analysis was 11.1–6–15–9.

At Havelock Park, Colombo (Colts), February 14, 15, 16. Drawn. Colts CC 453 for five dec. (D. P. Samaraweera 39, C. Mendis 30, S. I. Fernando 178 not out, R. S. Kaluwitharana 157; M. M. de Silva three for 152) and 258 for six dec. (R. S. Kaluwitharana 107, S. I. Fernando 43; A. Rideegammana three for 68); Galle CC* 176 (S. Kodituwakku 32, C. K. Hewamanna 44; W. P. U. J. C. Vaas four for 50, K. E. A. Upashantha three for 38, B. Perera three for 63) and 233 for eight (S. Kodituwakku 43, D. Sudarshana 57, S. M. Faumi 30 not out, C. K. Hewamanna 33; W. P. U. J. C. Vaas three for 50, B. Perera four for 113).

Kaluwitharana's twin centuries were his third and fourth in successive innings. In Colts' first innings, he added 277 for the third wicket with Fernando.

At Welagedera Stadium, Kurunegala, February 14, 15, 16. Kurunegala Youth CC won by 109 runs. Kurunegala Youth CC* 189 (R. J. Jaymon 30, S. K. L. de Silva 80, A. H. Bandaranayake 34; K. R. Pushpakumara five for 50) and 250 (S. K. L. de Silva 104; R. P. Arnold seven for 84); Nondescripts CC 153 (S. D. Rajapakse 36, A. Gunawardene 38; M. W. Kumara three for 82, A. W. Ekanayake five for 41) and 177 (A. Gunawardene 30; A. W. R. Madurasinghe five for 49).

At Panadura Esplanade, Panadura, February 14, 15, 16. Drawn. Burgher RC* 213 (D. Madurapperuma 41, D. Rajapakse 55, C. R. Perera 39; I. S. Gallage three for 56, K. C. Silva three for 33) and 235 for six (M. Rajapakse 61, D. Rajapakse 46, S. K. B. Tennekoon 53 not out, Extras 31); Panadura SC 420 (R. C. Galappathi 43, S. Kumara 43, S. N. Liyanage 48, I. Amithakeerthi 137 not out, I. S. Gallage 38, Extras 42; D. Madurapperuma three for 70, D. Rajapakse three for 33).

At Moratuwa Stadium, Moratuwa, February 14, 15, 16. Sebastianites C and AC won by an innings and 24 runs. Singha SC 101 (W. M. J. Kumudu 44; Anura Perera five for 34, Primal Salgado three for 13) and 182 (S. Jayantha 69 not out; Anura Perera four for 49, A. P. Dalugoda four for 31); Sebastianites C and AC* 307 (M. S. Mendis 51, C. M. Wickremasinghe 59, A. P. Dalugoda 80, A. Fernando 38; A. D. B. Ranjith three for 73).

At Maitland Place, Colombo (SSC), February 14, 15, 16. Sinhalese SC won by an innings and 14 runs. Antonians SC 206 (V. S. Sittamige 38, K. Dharmasena 37 not out; G. P. Wickremasinghe four for 61) and 197 (M. Prasanga 31, V. S. Sittamige 53; D. N. T. Zoysa four for 68); Sinhalese SC* 417 for six dec. (A. A. W. Gunawardene 158 not out, R. P. A. H. Wickremaratne 130, D. P. M. Jayawardene 46; P. N. Wanasinghe five for 131).

At Air Force Ground, Katunayake, February 21, 22, 23. Nondescripts CC won by eight wickets. Antonians SC 107 (E. F. M. U. Fernando 35; D. Samarasinghe three for 21, S. Jayaratne three for 45, N. Saranasekera four for 22) and 197 (S. Jayawardene 120; D. Maiarachchi three for 32); Nondescripts CC* 118 (R. P. Arnold 36 not out; P. N. Wanasinghe six for 42, K. G. Perera three for 11) and 190 for two (D. Maiarachchi 79, S. Ranatunga 84 not out).

At Reid Avenue, Colombo, February 21, 22, 23. Bloomfield C and AC won by an innings and 60 runs. Bloomfield C and AC 419 for eight dec. (N. Bopage 46, P. B. Ediriweera 82, S. K. Perera 33, S. T. Perera 69, S. Abeynayake 62, P. P. Wickremasinghe 39, B. de Silva 62; W. C. Chrishantha three for 48); Singha SC* 216 (W. M. J. Kumudu 48, S. G. S. Silva 43, T. Achintha 47; A. P. R. Shaman four for 45, B. de Silva four for 47) and 143 (T. Achintha 38; R. L. Perera four for 38, W. G. S. Wijenayake five for 38).

At Panadura Esplanade, Panadura, February 21, 22, 23. Drawn. Kalutara Town CC 203 (N. M. Tillekeratne 78, P. Perera 41, R. D. Kottachchi 33; I. Amithakeerthi five for six) and 231 for eight (T. M. Dilshan 93, P. Perera 56; K. P. Ratnaweera four for 63); Panadura SC* 115 (B. P. Perera 41; P. Perera six for 41).

At Moratuwa Stadium, Moratuwa, February 21, 22, 23. Drawn. Police SC 284 (A. Priyantha 57, R. C. Liyanage 70, M. N. C. Silva 58 not out; A. P. Dalugoda four for 50); Sebastianites C and AC* 302 for eight (Sanjeewa Silva 135, Anusha Perera 50 not out).

At P. Saravanamuttu Stadium, Colombo, February 21, 22, 23. Drawn. Tamil Union C and AC 285 (S. P. Herathge 60, U. C. Hathurusinghe 85, A. S. Jayasinghe 47, S. I. de Saram 31, Extras 30; A. Rideegammana five for 54) and 197 (N. de Silva 35; A. Rideegammana three for 41, M. M. de Silva four for 60); Galle CC* 282 (D. D. Wickremasinghe 63, H. U. G. Samarawickreme 66; C. N. Bandaratilleke eight for 78).

At Maitland Place, Colombo (SSC), February 22, 23, 24. Sinhalese SC won by ten wickets. Kurunegala Youth CC 263 (S. K. L. de Silva 50, H. Liyanage 56, S. S. Guruge 66, R. K. B. Amunugama 37; S. B. Dodanwela four for 46, D. P. M. Jayawardene three for 56) and 191 (R. J. Jaymon 38, R. R. Jaymon 32, S. S. Guruge 30; S. H. S. M. K. Silva three for 47, K. J. Silva six for 78); Sinhalese SC* 392 (U. N. K. Fernando 92, C. N. Fernando 107, S. H. S. M. K. Silva 44, C. Boteju 53 not out; M. W. Kumara three for 102, R. K. B. Amunugama three for 88) and 63 for no wkt (M. Perera 37 not out).

At Reid Avenue, Colombo, February 28, March 1, 2. Bloomfield C and AC won by 250 runs. Bloomfield C and AC* 389 (P. B. Ediriweera 64, S. K. Perera 46, S. T. Perera 34, A. P. R. Shaman 117, Extras 34; P. N. Wanasinghe three for 65) and 180 for six dec. (P. B. Ediriweera 33, S. K. Perera 34, S. T. Perera 54 not out, A. P. R. Shaman 31; P. N. Wanasinghe four for 74); Antonians SC 265 (T. P. Kodikara 88, Y. N. Tillekeratne 46, E. F. M. U. Fernando 39; W. G. S. Wijenayake four for 66) and 54 (R. L. Perera five for 26, A. P. R. Shaman three for eight).
In Antonians' first innings, Sampath Perera made two catches and four stumpings. In their second innings, Laksiri Perera took a hat-trick.

At Havelock Park, Colombo (BRC), February 28, March 1, 2. Tamil Union C and AC won by an innings and 17 runs. Tamil Union C and AC 444 for six dec. (S. P. Herathge 35, G. R. K. Wijekoon 73, S. I. de Saram 35, A. S. Jayasinghe 183, D. N. Nadarajah 52 not out, N. de Silva 52; W. C. Labrooy three for 106); Burgher RC* 291 (E. M. I. Galagoda 72, D. Rajapakse 79, D. Maduraperuma 59 not out; U. C. Hathurusinghe seven for 158, C. N. Bandaratilleke three for 61) and 136 (U. Hettiarachchi 38; U. C. Hathurusinghe eight for 29).
Jayasinghe reached his hundred in 79 balls and 103 minutes.

At Panadura Esplanade, Panadura, February 28, March 1, 2. Colts CC won by an innings and 75 runs. Kalutara Town CC 130 (B. Perera four for 21) and 200 (N. M. Tillekeratne 55, T. M. Dilshan 67; B. Perera three for 71); Colts CC* 405 for seven dec. (S. Janaka 148, S. Attanayake 46, M. T. Sampath 50, J. Kulatunga 61, K. E. A. Upashantha 35, Extras 41).
Kalutara Town fielded only ten players.

At Welagedera Stadium, Kurunegala, February 28, March 1, 2. Drawn. Kurunegala Youth CC* 329 for seven dec. (L. Karunaratne 32, S. K. L. de Silva 109, H. Liyanage 82, R. Kariyawasam 32, S. S. Guruge 37); Sebastianites C and AC 275 (M. S. Mendis 57, Sanjeewa Silva 69, A. P. Dalugoda 45; R. Kariyawasam four for 102, A. W. R. Madurasinghe three for 66).

At Maitland Place, Colombo (NCC), February 28, March 1, 2. Nondescripts Cricket Club won by an innings and two runs. Nondescripts CC* 382 (S. Ranatunga 97, R. P. Arnold 104, E. A. R. de Silva 36; W. C. Chrishantha four for 106); Singha SC 193 (W. M. J. Kumudu 38, S. G. S. Silva

55, A. S. Wewalwala 43; C. D. U. S. Weerasinghe five for 66) and 187 (A. S. Wewalwala 36, H. Premasiri 32; R. P. Arnold three for 59, C. D. U. S. Weerasinghe five for 69).

At Police Ground, Colombo, February 28, March 1, 2. Drawn. Sinhalese SC 345 (A. A. W. Gunawardene 135, A. Kapilaratne 58, C. N. Fernando 54; V. H. K. Ranaweera three for 48); Police SC* 293 for seven (A. Priyantha 79, R. C. Liyanage 83, M. N. C. Silva 41; K. J. Silva five for 80).

At Havelock Park, Colombo (BRC), March 7, 8, 9. Burgher RC won by an innings and 73 runs. Burgher RC* 265 (E. M. I. Galagoda 77, D. Rajapakse 44, M. Rajapakse 38; A. D. B. Ranjith four for 53, K. P. J. Warnaweera three for 89, W. K. Jayalath three for 54); Singha SC 64 (S. Madanayake four for 15) and 128 (A. S. Wewalwala 74; S. Madanayake three for 39).

At Maitland Place, Colombo (NCC), March 7, 8, 9. Tamil Union C and AC won by eight wickets. Nondescripts CC* 257 (G. R. P. Peiris 38, D. Maiarachchi 74, S. Ranatunga 35, A. T. Weerappuli 50 not out; C. N. Bandaratilleke six for 78, U. C. Hathurusinghe four for 55) and 194 (S. Ranatunga 82; U. C. Hathurusinghe seven for 63); Tamil Union C and AC 410 (U. C. Hathurusinghe 46, S. P. Herathge 52, S. I. de Saram 105, A. S. Jayasinghe 65, D. N. Nadarajah 63; S. Jayaratne five for 106, S. Ranatunga three for 38) and 42 for two.

At Police Park, Colombo, March 7, 8, 9. Police SC won by ten wickets. Kalutara Town CC 166 (C. N. Hettiarachchi 68; A. Priyantha three for 38, R. R. Wimalasiri three for 22) and 160 (N. M. Tillekeratne 63, Piyal Salgado 32; P. K. Serasinghe seven for 55); Police SC* 311 (R. C. Liyanage 86, W. N. M. Soysa 46, A. Priyantha 47, I. D. Gunawardene 52; R. Chandana three for 60, R. D. Kottachchi five for 60) and 19 for no wkt.

At Tyronne Fernando Stadium, Moratuwa, March 8, 9, 10. Bloomfield C and AC won by an innings and 65 runs. Bloomfield C and AC* 424 for five dec. (P. B. Dassanayake 96, P. B. Ediriweera 68, M. N. Nawaz 124, S. T. Perera 87); Sebastianites C and AC 121 (R. Handunettige 43; R. S. Kalpage four for 46, S. Dissanayake four for 26) and 238 (D. Bodiyabaduge 30, R. Yasalal 139; R. S. Kalpage three for 72, S. Dissanayake four for 73).

At Reid Avenue, Colombo, March 14, 15, 16. Bloomfield C and AC won by 238 runs. Bloomfield C and AC* 303 (M. N. Nawaz 95, N. Bopage 41, A. P. R. Shaman 76; U. C. Hathurusinghe five for 129, C. N. Bandaratilleke three for 89) and 224 (M. N. Nawaz 37, S. T. Perera 36, A. P. R. Shaman 30, S. Dissanayake 39; U. C. Hathurusinghe four for 91); Tamil Union C and AC 190 (G. R. K. Wijekoon 56, A. S. Jayasinghe 42; P. W. Gunaratne three for 32, B. de Silva five for 88) and 99 (V. S. K. Waragoda 31; B. de Silva six for 22).

Bloomfield recorded their ninth successive win, which was to bring them the Sara Trophy.

At Havelock Park, Colombo (BRC), March 14, 15, 16. Drawn. Burgher RC* 278 (A. P. Ranaweera 35, E. M. I. Galagoda 33, S. K. B. Tennekoon 40, C. R. Perera 74; K. G. Perera three for 36) and 322 (A. P. Ranaweera 56, E. M. I. Galagoda 64, M. Rajapakse 42, S. K. B. Tennekoon 43, D. Rajapakse 56; K. G. Perera four for 58); Antonians SC 254 (E. F. M. U. Fernando 105, V. S. Sittamige 62; S. Madanayake five for 47) and 11 for one.

At Havelock Park, Colombo (Colts), March 14, 15, 16. Colts CC won by four wickets. Nondescripts CC* 256 (S. Ranatunga 61, S. Jayaratne 33, Extras 31; D. K. Liyanage three for 66) and 331 (G. R. P. Peiris 62, A. T. Weerappuli 65, C. I. Dunusinghe 41, J. Pradeep 37; B. Perera three for 56); Colts CC 349 (S. Janaka 72, S. I. Fernando 80, N. Ranatunga 57; C. D. U. S. Weerasinghe eight for 77) and 239 for six (S. I. Fernando 33, J. Kulatunga 52, D. K. Liyanage 49 not out, S. Attanayake 34 not out; C. D. U. S. Weerasinghe three for 80).

At Panadura Esplanade, Panadura, March 14, 15, 16. Singha SC won by five wickets. Kalutara Town CC* 191 (N. M. Tillekeratne 40, N. Hettiarachchi 42; A. D. B. Ranjith five for 68, W. K. Jayalath four for 26) and 145 (A. D. B. Ranjith five for 30, A. S. Wewalwala three for 20); Singha SC 193 (S. G. S. Silva 58, A. S. Wewalwala 51; P. Perera four for 57, C. R. P. Silva three for 56) and 146 for five (T. Achintha 36, A. S. Wewalwala 47 not out).

At Air Force Ground, Katunayake, March 14, 15, 16. Drawn. Galle CC* 248 (C. M. Withanage 60, D. Sudarshana 61, H. Rajapakse 38, M. M. de Silva 34) and 266 for nine dec. (S. Kodituwakku 74, H. U. G. Samarawickreme 34, S. M. Faumi 46; R. Kariyawasam four for 95, A. W. Ekanayake five for 66); Kurunegala Youth CC 204 (R. Kariyawasam 87, A. W. R. Madurasinghe 35; S. M. Faumi three for 32, A. Rideegammana three for 44) and 198 for four (R. J. Jaymon 74, S. K. L. de Silva 61).

At Police Park, Colombo, March 28, 29, 30. Police SC won by nine wickets. Singha SC 126 (W. M. J. Kumudu 34; A. Priyantha four for 38, P. K. Serasinghe five for 38) and 103 (A. S. Wewalwala 46; P. K. Serasinghe three for 49); Police SC* 226 (W. N. M. Soysa 42, R. R. Wimalasiri 59, M. N. C. Silva 45; W. K. Jayalath four for 53, A. D. B. Ranjith five for 76) and four for one.

At Antonians School Ground, Wattala, March 29, 30, 31. Antonians SC won by 135 runs. Antonians SC* 167 (S. Jayawardene 33, N. Devarajan 35; C. R. P. Silva four for 68, R. D. Kottachchi three for five) and 228 (T. P. Kodikara 30, E. F. M. U. Fernando 83; H. S. S. Fonseka three for 30); Kalutara Town CC 189 (T. M. Sampath 38, H. S. S. Fonseka 47; K. G. Perera seven for 49) and 71 (P. N. Wanasinghe three for 15, K. G. Perera five for 31).

At Reid Avenue, Colombo, March 29, 30, 31. Sinhalese SC won by four wickets. Panadura SC 374 (S. E. D. Ruwan 36, I. Amithakeerthi 105, B. P. Perera 110, Extras 39; C. Boteju three for 56, H. Perera three for 61) and 190 (S. E. D. Ruwan 38, Extras 32; C. Boteju three for 44, C. N. Fernando five for 25); Sinhalese SC* 270 (A. A. W. Gunawardene 83, V. Wijegunawardene 74, R. P. A. H. Wickremaratne 64 not out; I. S. Gallage three for 85, K. P. Ratnaweera four for 59) and 295 for six (A. A. W. Gunawardene 45, R. P. A. H. Wickremaratne 48, P. Viswanath 61 not out, C. N. Fernando 99).

At Antonians School Ground, Wattala, April 4, 5, 6. Antonians SC won by an innings and 58 runs. Kurunegala Youth CC* 148 (H. Liyanage 37, S. S. Guruge 36) and 70 (S. K. L. de Silva 35; S. Jayawardene five for 40, K. G. Perera three for four); Antonians SC 276 (Y. N. Tillekeratne 135 not out, K. Dharmasena 31; A. W. Ekanayake five for 86).

At Havelock Park, Colombo (Colts), April 4, 5, 6. Drawn. Colts CC* 336 (C. Mendis 86, T. T. Samaraweera 34, S. Attanayake 46 not out, B. Perera 59, Extras 35; D. P. M. Jayawardene five for 72) and 233 for eight dec. (D. P. Samaraweera 30, S. I. Fernando 54, S. Janaka 50; S. H. S. M. K. Silva four for 35); Sinhalese SC 190 (D. P. M. Jayawardene 100 not out; D. K. Liyanage three for 41, K. E. A. Upashantha three for 47) and 222 for four (V. Wijegunawardene 42, D. P. M. Jayawardene 106 not out).

In Colts' first innings, Attanayake and Perera added 102 for the tenth wicket. Jayawardene scored unbeaten centuries in both Sinhalese innings.

P. SARAVANAMUTTU TROPHY WINNERS

The competition was known as the Lakspray Trophy in 1988-89 and 1989-90.

1988-89 {	Nondescripts CC	1993-94	Nondescripts CC
	Sinhalese SC	1994-95 {	Bloomfield C and AC
1989-90	Sinhalese SC		Sinhalese SC
1990-91	Sinhalese SC	1995-96	Colombo CC
1991-92	Colts CC	1996-97	Bloomfield C and AC
1992-93	Sinhalese SC		

CRICKET IN ZIMBABWE, 1996-97

By JOHN WARD

Grant Flower

Zimbabwe's most encouraging season as a Test-playing nation began in some disarray. The Test team had lost its coach, John Hampshire, whose contract was not renewed, and its captain, Andy Flower, who resigned after three years of intense pressure combining the role with those of wicket-keeper and leading batsman.

Alistair Campbell was appointed to lead the tour of Sri Lanka in August, just before his 24th birthday. Here Zimbabwe suffered their two most humiliating defeats in Test cricket but, with three key players missing, the odds were stacked against them. Still, Campbell did a positive job in difficult circumstances and was confirmed as captain.

The team improved in Pakistan, when David Houghton returned as player-coach. But then a visit from England started a run of unprecedented success, particularly in the limited-overs game. Widespread criticism of Mike Atherton's team diverted attention from how well Zimbabwe played. Perhaps they were fortunate to escape with two Test draws, but they matched England for most of the First Test and adjusted better in the Second to what used to be regarded as typical English conditions. The one-day series was a triumph: they won two narrow victories through superior handling of pressure, while the third was their most convincing yet.

Further improvement was evident during a triangular series in South Africa, in which they beat India once and were prevented from reaching their first one-day final only by a brilliant century from Sachin Tendulkar. It was in South Africa that manager Andy Pycroft noted the team had developed its own brand of cricket. Dynamic in the field, they communicated their enjoyment more effectively than the clinical South Africans, and always attempted to fight their way out of difficulty, a fresh approach which won them many supporters.

The season closed with a visit to Sharjah, where they beat World Cup-holders Sri Lanka and again had a chance of reaching the final. They bowled and fielded magnificently, though conditions did not suit their batting. When Zimbabwe strike their best form in all three departments simultaneously, they will be a handful for anyone. More exposure to Test cricket would surely bring progress here too.

The new leadership deserved much credit. Campbell's calm captaincy was backed by Houghton's innovative coaching and role as mentor to the many younger players, who could not speak highly enough of him. The enterprising selectors, headed by John Traicos, brought several new players out of nowhere. Notable successes included two 20-year-old black pace bowlers, Mpumelelo Mbangwa and Everton Matambanadzo, taken to Pakistan with very little first-class cricket behind them. They dropped out when Heath Streak, Eddo Brandes and Henry Olonga returned, but remained contenders. Some promising young batsmen added to Zimbabwe's depth.

Several established players enjoyed the most fruitful seasons of their short careers. Campbell himself, previously criticised for throwing his wicket away, thrived on the responsibilities of captaincy and showed a new maturity with the bat, especially under pressure. Grant Flower, hitherto a dour opener, widened his range of strokes and gained confidence. Brandes, often distracted by his chicken farm, was able to devote more time to the game and forced his way back into the team. His hat-trick at the expense of three of England's top batsmen in the final one-day international was his most notable achievement; had Streak been fully fit, they would have made a formidable opening attack. Campbell also acknowledged the value of Brandes's constant quiet encouragement of the youngsters. Paul Strang made tremendous strides. He bowled with a skill not far short of the world's top three leg-spinners, Shane Warne, Mushtaq Ahmed and Anil Kumble, fielded brilliantly (mainly at backward point), scored a Test century against Wasim Akram and Waqar Younis, and improvised with success in the one-day game.

Before the domestic season began, the Zimbabwe Cricket Union had decided on the radical step of reducing the Logan Cup competition from four teams to just two, Mashonaland and Matabeleland, in an effort to raise the quality of first-class cricket. They were to play each other in a best-of-three competition before the England tour. While this solved one problem, it gave rise to another. The bulk of Zimbabwe's talent is still based in Harare, and the Matabeles proved no match for the Mashonas. Mashonaland recorded two comfortable victories, although Matabeleland, captained by John Rennie, did force a high-scoring draw in between. In that match, Grant Flower made 243 not out, the highest innings since the tournament became first-class. A one-day competition between the two was even more one-sided: Mashonaland won all three games with ease and there was no competitive atmosphere. Furthermore, several international players could not get into Mashonaland's first team, were relegated to the B side and played no first-class cricket. The need for a better solution provided the ZCU with much food for thought.

Although the ZCU recognises the importance of Logan Cup cricket, it does not always receive enough backing from the local associations. Matches are poorly advertised, administrative involvement is low and, at times, not even a full scoreboard is in operation. Given such neglect, the public virtually ignores the competition and even the players do not always take it very seriously. Local boards should consider employing a full-time administrator to handle these games more professionally.

One of the Logan Cup's most successful players was the young Sussex professional engaged by Mashonaland, James Kirtley. Not only did he take a hat-trick in the final Logan Cup match – only Brandes had previously achieved the feat in Zimbabwean first-class cricket – but he also played a significant part in Mashonaland's victory over England. Gary Fellows, from the Yorkshire Cricket Academy, played in two Logan Cup matches for Matabeleland.

Another area needing attention was the Zimbabwe Board XI's role in South Africa's UCBSA Bowl. This competition had also been revamped, with Zimbabwe assigned to a non-first-class division. The team is not far off a national second eleven and generally contains more than one Test cricketer, but suffered from frequent changes of personnel, as well as wet weather. The outstanding performance for the Board XI was a magnificent 266 by captain Andy Waller against Namibia in Windhoek. Waller enjoyed his best season, culminating in his well-deserved, if belated, Test debut, against England. Like Brandes, he first represented his country in the 1987-88 World Cup, but his business had hindered his availability. Finding a capable manager for his tobacco farm meant he could commit himself more fully. In February, however, he announced his retirement from international cricket, aged 37. He was probably one of the last of Zimbabwe's true amateur cricketers and will be sadly missed.

The international players had a little more opportunity for match practice in the Dunlop National League, which was won by Alexandra Club of Harare. The Vigne Cup, for clubs in Harare, was won by Harare Sports Club. It was played on Sundays, between National League fixtures, but the top players were rarely available.

At the ZCU prize-giving and awards ceremony, Grant Flower won the Player of the Season award, while Matambanadzo won the Bob Nixon Trophy for the best Under-21 player. The Australian High Commission and Qantas jointly sponsor a promising young player to spend three weeks at the Australian Cricket Academy in Adelaide; this season the prize was won by Dirk Viljoen, another youngster who had been plunged into international cricket, at Sharjah, with some success.

The ZCU considered the possibility of moving away from Harare Sports Club and acquiring its own home, probably at the Showgrounds, just to the west of the city centre. The development programme continued to make progress, although lack of finance still hampered expansion in rural areas. Concrete pitches, net facilities and coaches are regularly provided in schools, but little is available in public areas and parks. At Chitungwiza, a black township just south of Harare, the ZCU hoped to acquire a five-acre site for a cricket ground from the town council. But the shortage of kit, which is also very expensive, remained a major problem.

There is still a feeling that black cricketers should be coming through more quickly. But when Conrad Hunte, the former West Indian Test player now working as the national development coach in South Africa, was asked for his advice, he pointed to the lack of a cricket culture among the blacks of Zimbabwe. That was in sharp contrast to the culture of the West Indies, and he thought that it would be some years before black cricketers could form a majority in the national side.

FIRST-CLASS AVERAGES, 1996-97

BATTING

(Qualification: 200 runs)

	M	I	NO	R	HS	100s	Avge
A. Flower (*Mashonaland*)	5	6	2	270	112	1	67.50
A. D. R. Campbell (*Mashonaland*) . . .	5	8	2	370	84	0	61.66
G. W. Flower (*Mashonaland*)	7	11	2	477	243*	1	53.00
M. H. Dekker (*Matabeleland*)	4	6	0	309	104	1	51.50
C. B. Wishart (*Mashonaland*)	5	8	3	250	110	1	50.00
P. A. Strang (*Mashonaland*)	7	7	2	236	103*	1	47.20
D. L. Houghton (*Mashonaland*)	6	7	0	311	110	1	44.42
W. R. James (*Matabeleland*)	4	7	1	255	74	0	42.50
S. V. Carlisle (*Mashonaland*)	4	6	0	243	131	1	40.50
G. J. Whittall (*Matabeleland*)	6	10	0	316	159	1	31.60
H. H. Streak (*Matabeleland*)	6	9	2	204	67	0	29.14

* *Signifies not out.*

BOWLING

(Qualification: 10 wickets)

	O	M	R	W	BB	5W/i	Avge
R. J. Kirtley (*Mashonaland*)	71.1	19	172	14	5-53	2	12.28
P. A. Strang (*Mashonaland*)	365.3	92	906	36	5-45	3	25.16
H. H. Streak (*Matabeleland*)	180	41	475	17	4-20	0	27.94
H. K. Olonga (*Matabeleland*) . . .	125	22	458	15	3-70	0	30.53
B. C. Strang (*Mashonaland*)	173.4	50	436	12	5-50	1	36.33

LONRHO LOGAN CUP, 1996-97

This was played between Mashonaland and Matabeleland, in a best-of-three series. No match points were awarded. Mashonaland won 2-0.

*In the following scores, * by the name of a team indicates that they won the toss.*

At Bulawayo Athletic Club, Bulawayo, October 4, 5, 6. Mashonaland won by eight wickets. Matabeleland 118 (M. H. Dekker 32; B. C. Strang five for 50, P. A. Strang five for 45) and 279 (M. H. Dekker 90, M. D. Abrams 34, M. Ranchod 56 not out, H. K. Olonga 33; E. Matambanadzo three for 76, P. A. Strang five for 103); Mashonaland* 314 (D. P. Viljoen 47, A. D. R. Campbell 76, D. L. Houghton 67, A. Flower 61; H. K. Olonga three for 70, D. Vaghmaria three for 44) and 85 for two (G. W. Flower 44 not out).

Andrew Whittall made his first-class debut in Zimbabwe, having previously represented the country in limited-overs internationals in Sri Lanka and captained Cambridge University.

At Alexandra Sports Club, Harare, November 15, 16, 17. Drawn. Mashonaland* 503 for four dec. (G. W. Flower 243 not out, S. V. Carlisle 96, A. C. Waller 104); Matabeleland 448 (G. J. Whittall 159, M. H. Dekker 55, H. H. Streak 47, W. R. James 52, M. Ranchod 33, J. A. Rennie 57 not out; E. A. Brandes four for 107).

Flower's 243 not out, his highest score and a Logan Cup first-class record, lasted 542 minutes and 367 balls and included 25 fours and a six. Waller hit his maiden first-class century, 12 seasons after his debut in 1984-85.

At Bulawayo Athletic Club, Bulawayo, November 22, 23, 24. Mashonaland won by 213 runs. Mashonaland 477 for six dec. (S. V. Carlisle 131, C. B. Wishart 110, A. Flower 73 not out, P. A. Strang 103 not out; A. R. Whittall three for 119) and forfeited second innings; Matabeleland* 69 for four dec. and 195 (G. M. Fellows 50, W. R. James 74; R. J. Kirtley five for 56).

With much time lost to rain, Matabeleland declared at their overnight total on the second evening and Mashonaland forfeited their second innings to reach a result. Kirtley took a hat-trick, only the second in Zimbabwean first-class cricket, following Eddo Brandes in 1988-89.

LONRHO LOGAN CUP WINNERS

1993-94	Mashonaland Under-24
1994-95	Mashonaland
1995-96	Matabeleland
1996-97	Mashonaland

OTHER FIRST-CLASS MATCHES

Western Province in Zimbabwe

At Alexandra Sports Club, Harare, September 26, 27, 28. Drawn. Western Province* 303 (M. C. de Villiers 84, S. G. Koenig 67, A. C. Dawson 30 not out; P. A. Strang four for 111) and 237 for nine dec. (S. G. Koenig 49, J. B. Commins 104, D. B. Rundle 41; P. A. Strang four for 110, G. J. Rennie three for 15); Mashonaland XI 276 for eight dec. (B. C. Strang 68, C. B. Wishart 53, A. D. R. Campbell 32; A. Martyn four for 46) and 74 for four (C. B. Wishart 30 not out).

Matabeleland Invitation XI v Worcestershire (March 28, 29, 30) may be found in English Counties Overseas, 1996-97.

ONE HUNDRED YEARS AGO

From JOHN WISDEN'S CRICKETERS' ALMANACK FOR 1898

FIVE CRICKETERS OF THE YEAR – MR. GILBERT L. JESSOP: "We have never before produced a batsman of quite the same stamp. We have harder hitters, but perhaps never one who could, in twenty minutes or half-an-hour, so entirely change the fortunes of a game."

MEETING OF COUNTY SECRETARIES – The Programme for 1898: "Mr. H. Perkins [secretary of MCC] . . . thought their gatherings had been a great success. The county programme had grown to such gigantic proportions that it could not well be arranged by correspondence. Difficulties must necessarily arise, but they were more readily disposed of when the secretaries met in conference. Whatever the difficulties might be, they usually disappeared after a little lunch (laughter)."

DERBYSHIRE: "The Derbyshire season was of unvaried disappointment and disaster from start to finish . . . There appeared to be a spell overhanging the Derbyshire Eleven, which they were never able to break and nothing they did seemed for the best."

CRICKET IN BANGLADESH, 1996-97

By UTPAL SHUVRO

Cricket in Bangladesh entered a new era when the national team won the 1997 ICC Trophy in Kuala Lumpur, thus achieving their goal of a place in the 1999 World Cup and doing so as champions of the non-Test-playing nations.

Not since independence from Pakistan in 1971 had the country celebrated with such togetherness. When the team won their semi-final against Scotland and thus made sure of their World Cup place, processions started all over the country and young people began sprinkling coloured water. Ecstasy was not without its share of undesirable excess: three fatalities were reported. However, good sense prevailed soon. This was evident when Bangladesh beat Kenya in the final: the country seemed to be bathed in a serene spirit of joy. Hundreds of thousands of people thronged the airport to receive the heroes. Each player was given a new car. And Gordon Greenidge, the West Indian batsman whose inspired coaching helped Bangladesh turn a dream into reality, was made a Bangladeshi citizen as a special honour.

The dream had been there for some time. Bangladesh have been competing in the ICC Trophy since it started in 1979. Twice, in 1982 and 1990, they reached the semi-finals. Unfortunately for them, on both occasions they ran into Zimbabwe, then the dominant team among the ICC Associate Members. When it was first announced that three Associates would take part in the 1996 World Cup alongside the nine Test-playing countries, Bangladeshi cricket-lovers began visualising – not illogically – their national team among the élite. It was not to be. In Nairobi in 1994 they lost to the United Arab Emirates, Holland and Kenya, and these three, not Bangladesh, reached the World Cup. This time Bangladesh exacted revenge over each of them.

It was Zimbabwe's entry into the Test family that helped expand Bangladesh's horizons. The success of the country's subcontinental neighbours was also inspiring. Cricket has a long tradition in Bangladesh. Pakistan played their first home Test match in Dhaka in 1955, and it was a regular Test venue until independence 16 years later. After that, cricket took some time to win its place back – the country was ravaged by war, cricket was labelled élitist in certain quarters, and there was propaganda against it. But the love of the players overcame this.

After a short tour by an MCC team, led by E. A. Clark, in 1976-77, Bangladesh were granted Associate Membership of ICC. Now the country, like Kenya, has one-day international status. Saber Hossain Chowdhury, president of the Bangladesh Cricket Board, was optimistic that Test status could come by 2000, though performances later in 1997 were not encouraging. In some respects, the authorities have already begun thinking anew. Bangladesh now have the right to play first-class matches against Kenya or existing first-class teams. This means adjusting domestic competitions, which up to now have been limited-overs in nature. There is a zone-based national championship in the longer form but, compared to the glamour of the Dhaka league championship, this has been rather ineffectual and pointless.

Club-level competition is the basis of the game's popularity and charm in Bangladesh. Star international cricketers like Wasim Akram, Arjuna Ranatunga, Sanath Jayasuriya, Neil Fairbrother and Richard Illingworth have played in the league championship. While other ICC Associate Members are still wrestling with the problem of popularising the game, in Bangladesh it has already become a craze. A match between popular clubs like Abahani and Mohammedan usually draws a crowd above 35,000.

In 1993 the ICC chief executive, David Richards, was surprised to see a turn-out of about 15,000 for a league match at the Dhaka Stadium between two rather unfancied clubs. He was even more astonished when he was told everyone had had to pay.

Since Test status is the ultimate target, the longer version of the game is now the priority. Already, the decision has been taken to turn the popular domestic competitions into two-day, 80-overs-a-side affairs, and the national champion-ships will include three-day games. School level competition is quite organised in Bangladesh, with about 500 schools taking part in the main competition. Greenidge, who has been in charge of the national team since September 1996, has also been asked to take charge of shaping young talent across the whole country.

The Kuala Lumpur success has brought other benefits. Although the Dhaka Stadium was built for cricket, it eventually became a multi-purpose venue. Before the ICC triumph, football and cricket authorities were engaged in a long drawn-out struggle over the control of the stadium. In the reception ceremony for the homecoming heroes, the Prime Minister officially announced that a separate stadium would be built for cricket at Maghbazar, near the city centre. Until this new facility is available, the Dhaka Stadium has been allocated to cricket.

Improvement has also been hampered by the lack of good, true playing surfaces. The fact that the ICC Trophy was played on artificial surfaces meant matches had to be played on synthetic turf to acclimatise the players. Now work is going on to prepare a quality natural turf.

Understandably, everything else that happened in the 1996-97 season paled before the ICC success. Nevertheless, it was a lively domestic season. Abahani Krira Chakra pocketed both the big titles: the league championship and the Damal Summer Tournament. Their rivals, Mohammedan Sporting Club, failed miserably, despite having the services of two star Sri Lankans, Ranatunga and Jayasuriya. As they suffered their worst season for some years, it was Kalabagan who finished runners-up to Abahani in the championship.

CRICKET IN KENYA, 1997

By JASMER SINGH

Kenyan cricket perhaps recorded its best year, and in July 1997 took another step up the game's ladder. Along with Bangladesh, Kenya were granted a special one-day international status by ICC, enabling them to arrange both internationals and first-class matches. They marked their promotion by organising a three-nation tournament in October with both Bangladesh and Zimbabwe, the newest of the Test-playing countries. It was not as financially successful as the four-nation tournament a year earlier (reported on page 1145) and it showed that Zimbabwe were a class above their two rivals, their experience and professionalism shining through. However, it also enabled the Kenyans to consider themselves once again the best of the non-Test countries.

Kenya's promotion came after a successful run in the ICC Trophy in Kuala Lumpur. They won all the matches leading up to the final, barring one no-result, but then lost a rain-affected match to Bangladesh on the last ball. They had the consolation of providing the Man of the Match in the final, Steve Tikolo, and the Man of the Tournament, Maurice Odumbe, who made 493 runs in all.

In Nairobi six months later, in more familiar conditions, they looked clearly superior and easily beat the Bangladeshis twice. In the opening game, at the Gymkhana ground, the Kenyan openers Kennedy Otieno and Deepak Chudasama got the tournament off to a remarkable start and broke the heart of the Bangladeshi bowlers with a first-wicket stand of 225, beating the 11-year-old one-day international record of 212 set by David Boon and Geoff Marsh of Australia.

Six days after that, Thomas Odoyo and Tony Suji beat the seventh-wicket record, with a stand of 119 against Zimbabwe. This did not save the Kenyans from defeat, however. Just before the tournament, New Zealand stopped in Nairobi, on their way to Zimbabwe, and played a three-day match and two one-day matches, which did not have international status. The three-day match was drawn and New Zealand won the one-dayers.

These games have made Kenya aware that they still have some way to go before they can compete with the very best. But there have been enough successes and individual achievements to enable the game to maintain its momentum, as the efforts continue to develop it at grassroots level and spread it across the country.

After the tournament in October, Suji, his brother Martin, Odoyo, Odumbe and Tikolo all left to play club cricket in South Africa – the first three in Cape Town, the other two in Soweto. At home, Nairobi Gymkhana won the national league for the second successive year, with Aga Khan second.

CRICKET IN DENMARK, 1997

By PETER S. HARGREAVES

It was a good year for Danish cricket, even though Denmark failed to qualify for the 1999 World Cup. They finished level on points with Scotland in their quarter-final group in the ICC Trophy in Malaysia, and lost out only because the Scots had won their head-to-head match. This represented a major improvement on their showing in 1994, when they failed to qualify for the quarter-finals. They were ranked fifth in the tournament and can thus be regarded as No. 14 in the world.

A powerful attack spearheaded by Søren Sørenson led Denmark to comfortable wins over West Africa, Argentina, Malaysia and Canada, and there was also a morale-boosting one-wicket victory against United Arab Emirates, the champions from 1994. Kenya, the eventual runners-up, were reduced to 33 for four in a game that was never finished because of bad weather. The side was all-amateur and Danish-born.

However, when the squad returned home, four senior players announced their retirement – among them Søren Henriksen, the captain, and Sørenson. The summer became a process of rebuilding, which began with three matches against a PIA side from Pakistan that included several Test players. Denmark won those easily, but learned more from tough matches on English turf against Sussex and Hampshire. A well-prepared side then travelled north of the border, where they recorded their first-ever victory against the Scots in Scotland, thanks to a fine innings from Aftab Ahmed.

At home, it had been decided in 1996 to reduce the top division from ten teams to eight. Matches were also brought into line with the ICC standard of 50 overs, with fielding circles and a maximum of ten overs per bowler. The holders Svanholm adjusted well enough to win their 17th title, but they had to beat Glostrup, always their sternest opponents, in their final match. Glostrup had already defeated Svanholm early in the season, and in the semi-final of the knockout cup. Denmark's No. 3 club, Herning, triumphed in the final, when their spin attack baffled the Glostrup batsmen.

At the foot of the table, the Aalborg-Chang club suffered relegation for the first time in living memory, and Nykøbing Mors, the winners of the second division, replaced them. There was also a successful challenge from Ishøj, runners-up in the second division, against Husum. Ishøj's promotion means that there are two Pakistani clubs in the first division for the first time.

The best batting average belonged to Niels Bindslev, who hit 498 runs for KB at just under 50. Aftab Ahmed of Nørrebro, who had topped the averages himself for the previous two seasons, had to be content with the highest aggregate – 613 runs. Both men did much to keep their sides in the truncated first division. Among the bowlers, Søren Vestergaard maintained his extraordinary strike-rate, collecting 19 wickets at 6.73 apiece from only 57 overs. His season was restricted by injury and appearances for Warwickshire's Second Eleven. For Glostrup, 41-year-old Steen Thomsen bowed out after 25 years by taking 24 wickets at just under 16.

In June, Jørgen Holmen, the chairman of Danish cricket for the last 12 years, was appointed chairman of the Associate Member Nations of ICC. And in September a new turf pitch was laid at Brøndby.

CRICKET IN THE NETHERLANDS, 1997

By DAVID HARDY

After ten years of rapid progress, Dutch cricket took a step back in 1997. Holland's record over the previous three ICC Trophies consisted of two second places and one third place – the last of which won them entry to the 1996 World Cup – but they could only manage sixth in the 1997 tournament.

There had been little time for new players and management to gel after the exodus that had followed the World Cup. Five senior players – including the captain Steven Lubbers and Barbadian-born opener Nolan Clarke – retired in 1996, as did coach David Trist and manager John Wories. Tim de Leede became captain, and John Bell, from Australia, coach. They could still call on the services of Roland Lefebvre, naturalised Australian Peter Cantrell and the stars of 1996, Klaas Jan van Noortwijk and Bas Zuiderent. But it was too tall an order, and Holland will miss the 1999 World Cup in England.

Bell paid the price for failure – both in the ICC Trophy and on the preceding tour of South Africa, where Holland won only one of their seven matches. He was deposed, and during the Dutch summer a replacement was found in the shape of the Barbadian Emmerson Trotman, who has been playing and coaching at various clubs around the country for 20 years. Under Trotman's aegis, Holland took on three English counties: a NatWest game against Worcestershire at New Road, where Holland lost by 111 runs despite 99 from Zuiderent, the annual friendly against Leicestershire at HCC The Hague, which surprisingly resulted in a home win; and a Scarborough Festival game in which Yorkshire avenged their defeat of the previous year, winning by 82 runs.

In a damp domestic season, Schiedam's Excelsior CC won their third successive Premier League (*Hoofdklasse*). They were weakened by the departure of Trotman, who continued his playing career with Gandhi CC, but were well served by Australian/Zimbabwean professional Murray Goodwin, who made 945 runs at 59.06. Two teams (Amsterdam CC and Kampong from Utrecht) were relegated in order to reduce the League from 12 to ten teams, while another – Gandhi – survived a play-off against Koninklijke UD from the first division. That kept one of Holland's two grass wickets, Koninklijke's home strip at Deventer, out of the top flight for another year.

For the first time in many years, no one topped 1,000 runs or 50 wickets, though Kampong's professional Jeremy Bray finished only seven runs short. The top Dutch batsman was once again de Leede, with 980 runs at 57.64. De Leede combined a number of roles with great aplomb; as well as being the national captain, he was also Voorburg's player-coach, and enjoyed his best season yet with the ball – 39 wickets at 14.10. The most remarkable achievement of the season, however, was the milestone of 1,000 Premier League victims, reached by VOC's wicket-keeper, Rene Schoonheim. It was forty years since Schoonheim, a dentist in his fifties, had made his debut in the national league.

There were two contrasting events in May, both in the Amsterdam suburb of Amstelveen. The 11-year-old clubhouse of Amsterdam CC – the only purpose-built cricket pavilion in the country – was burned down. The good news was that the grass wicket at neighbouring club VRA was officially opened, coinciding almost exactly with an announcement from Lord's that Amstelveen would host a group match in the 1999 World Cup – South Africa v Kenya. Such are the highs and lows of an emerging cricket nation.

CRICKET ROUND THE WORLD, 1997

ARGENTINA

In the ICC Trophy in Malaysia, Argentina lost all five of their qualifying matches. This sums up the sadly diminished playing standards. Only four clubs are left playing the game, and the oldest of them, Hurlingham (founded 1888) won the Championship, thanks largely to the talents of captain Brian Roberts and the coaching skills of Roland Lefebvre. But the game is far from dead and, in December 1997, Argentina provided some hope for their cricketing future when a young local team – average age 22 – easily retained The Economist Cup, with easy wins over their three South American opponents, Brazil, Chile and Peru. The 19-year-old opening batsman Matias Paterlini scored 206 runs in the three matches without being dismissed, including 114 not out against Brazil. – David Parsons.

BELGIUM

Belgian cricket had a good 1997 domestically, but almost disappeared from the international scene. The national team hardly played at all, though club cricket was contested with great passion. The Championship was won by Pakistan (Greens) and the Cup by the Pakistan CC of Belgium. Ayub Khan scored 96 not out for them in the final. Farooq Malik of Royal Brussels was the leading batsman overall, averaging 56.80. The most welcome development, however, was the growth of women's cricket. Royal Brussels and Antwerp, as well as the Luxembourg Maidens, all put out sides. Clubs have become noticeably more family-minded, running youth teams, informal matches and midweek evening games for company teams. – Colin Wolfe.

BRUNEI DARUSSALAM

The highlight of the season was the performance of the national side. Sarawak and Sabah were soundly defeated in the Borneo Cup. Then the team took part for the first time in the Malaysian Cricket Association Division Two competition and almost came out as winners. Only a bad batting performance against Trengganu let them down. Brunei beat the eventual winners, Malaysian Armed Forces, by 79 runs. Our fast bowler Sidek was magnificent with 14 wickets for 85 runs overall. As recently as 1995, there was just one annual game – against Sabah. The domestic tournament, the Select Offshore Services League, was more closely fought than for many years, and Cavaliers and Panaga tied for the title, with Yachties a single point adrift in third place. There is still no cricket ground in the capital, Bandar Seri Begawan, and two-thirds of the teams face a 150-mile round trip for their day of enjoyment under the tropical sun. The hope that this situation will improve also burns on. – Derek Thursby.

CANADA

Canada made strides towards their goal of limited-over international status by 2000 and prepared their bid to hold the ICC Trophy in 2001. The India and Pakistan teams returned to Toronto to play another series of Sahara Cup games, and they gave both physical and spiritual support. The money from these visits should enable five turf pitches to be constructed in 1997-98. The Indians were outstandingly patient and graceful when they played a practice match against the national team when the rain could easily have led them to call it off; and the Canadian-born spinner Barry Seebaran was delighted with his two for 23. West Indies invited Canada to join the Red Stripe Bowl again in 1997-98. Though they failed to qualify for the finals, Muneeb Diwan's 130 from 154 balls against a Leeward Islands attack led by Curtly Ambrose and Kenny Benjamin helped the team confidence. With Larry Gomes as coach, Canada came seventh in the ICC Trophy, enough to salvage a qualifying place for the Commonwealth Games. – Geoff Edwards.

CAYMAN ISLANDS

A record 16 teams – 12 senior and four at Under-15 level – took part in competition in 1997. The Byrite Sports Club completed the double, winning both the First Division and the knockout final. The leading performers were the Wight twins, Christopher and David. Christopher scored 373 runs at an average of 74.60, while David took 22 wickets at ten each. In September, the Cayman public were treated to a Cable and Wireless-sponsored Weekend with the Stars, featuring Courtney Walsh, Jimmy Adams and Ian Bishop, who took part in an exhibition match and coached local youngsters. The year also saw the founding of the first women's cricket organisation in the Caymans. – Jimmy Powell.

CHINA

The 1997 Peking Cricket Club season got off to a shaky start when two of the six sides in the PCC League, Sri Lanka and Bangladesh, failed to form teams. Then Pakistan, who had cleaned up most of the honours in 1996, suddenly withdrew without explanation. The remaining three teams, England, Australia and India, soldiered on before the League ground to a halt when India lost too many players due to a rash of Embassy postings. The season ended on a high note, however, with the most successful Beijing International Cricket Sixes yet. Sponsored by Allied Pickfords, the Beijing Sixes is now truly on the map. Spread over two days, it featured 12 teams including the Barcelona Cricket Club, a South African team led by Clive Rice and a Racal UK team from England, plus teams from Hong Kong, Japan and South Korea. Racal won the Cup, but the multi-national and multi-ethnic tournament was thoroughly enjoyed by everyone involved. – Tony Fisher.

CUBA

There is a trophy cabinet in the Havana Golf Club that hasn't been opened for 39 years. When the deposed ruler Batista left the island in the hands of Fidel Castro and Che Guevara on New Year's Eve 1958, someone took the keys to Miami. But if you look long enough through the dust and the rust you can see that there, among the baseball and golf trophies, is unmistakably a silver cup with a man wielding a cricket bat on top.

Cricket was brought to Cuba by black sugar workers and slaves from the English-speaking Caribbean. And, until the 1960s when private sports clubs were abolished, the game was widely played in the sugar regions of the east. "We had a proper team and ground in my town, Manati," said Donald Pancho Muir. "It's a car workshop now. The local Cubans never really took to the game, but the club kept going because of the immigrant interest. We had a great time. There were teams in five other places that we used to play. There was always a party after the match."

In 1955 and 1960, Club Manati were invited to play in Montego Bay, Jamaica. "We lost more than we won," said Pancho, "but we had genuinely good players like Hilary 'Drinki' Pendas, and Rafael Bood. I think there is still a team in Baragua, and I heard of something going on in Cayo Mambi. But it is sad the game isn't played here much any more. We could have been good."

In the past 12 months, however, the game has shown signs of a come-back. A British journalist, Ian Katz, working on a story at the Guantanamo airbase, was approached by the Anglo-West Indian Cultural Association to explain the rules of cricket to their youth section, with a view to starting a team. When he got back to England he sent them a bat and a ball. Months later, another British journalist brought them pads and gloves and another bat. And the British Embassy sent one of their men in Havana, Ed Hobart, who plays for the expats and diplomats' team in the capital, to give them a training session.

"It was a chastening experience," said Hobart. "They were so eager to learn they copied everything you showed them exactly. There was one lad who after ten minutes' practice on a stone courtyard was playing classic cover drives and square cuts as if he had been coached from five years old." The Guantanamo team had their first game against another eastern team, Ciego de Avila, late in 1997. "We can't predict when games will be," said Robertson Claxton, the club president. "It depends when the opposition can get the petrol."

There are 11 million people living in Cuba, an island that dwarfs every other in the Caribbean. They play baseball to a high enough standard to suggest that the art of throwing a ball and using a bat to hit it comes very naturally. And the idea of a game that can take five days would not frighten a population accustomed to queuing four hours to travel on the back of a lorry to the next town. If the Cubans can find a Spanish translation of the Laws, the West Indies and the world had better watch out. – John Duncan (*The Guardian*).

CZECH REPUBLIC

About 25 players are now attached to the Prague Cricket Club, which organised a six-a-side tournament in 1997 and played a two-day game in Vienna. The tournament was reported in the Prague papers, but there were more jokes about tea and cakes than serious mention of the cricket. "Basically, people here think it's croquet," said one member. However, at least one Czech who came along to try the game learned it was not croquet: he had his finger broken by a ball from British diplomat Steve O'Connor that lifted sharply. This was not surprising as he was bowling on a mat laid on a rugby field. An urgent search is now under way for a proper pitch. Most players are British expats, though the club did unearth a talented Pakistani batsman; unfortunately, he was in a refugee camp and is believed to have been deported. Passing players keen for a game should contact Tony Brennan at the British Embassy.

EUROPEAN NATIONS CUP

France retained the Nations Cup at Zuoz, Switzerland, in astonishing circumstances. They beat Germany by one run in a pulsating 50-over final. The unwitting hero was France's last man, David Bordes, who was hit on the forehead, and staggered through for a single at the end of the French innings before collapsing with a fractured skull. With two balls left, Germany, chasing 267, were 260 for nine: a top-edge fumbled by third man plopped over the rope for six. The Germans completed the two runs they needed for victory while the last ball was still skying to mid-on, where Valentin Brumant eventually caught it. So the Bordes head-bye proved a match-winner. He had to spend the next two weeks in hospital, and was ill for some time but, happily, was able to resume playing indoor cricket before Christmas. Bordes normally bats with a helmet but did not bother this time because he had only the one ball to face. In a group game against Switzerland, Germany scored 467 for one in their 50 overs including an unbroken stand of 349 between Shamaz Khan, a Pakistani-born naturalised German, and Abdul Bhatti. Shamaz scored 200 not out and Bhatti 179 not out. – Simon Hewitt/Brian Fell.

FIJI

Fiji did better than ever before in the ICC Trophy, and the placing of 11th was very satisfying, ensuring that the team should be among the elite when ICC splits Associate Members into two divisions. Interestingly, the Fijian players who shone were those who have had the chance to play in overseas club competitions. We intend to continue with our policy of placing promising players abroad, mainly in Australia, whenever possible. Our preparation was greatly helped by two events: firstly, the invitation to play in the Asia Cricket Council Trophy in Malaysia in 1996, and the kind assistance with our costs that made participation possible; and, secondly, the visit by MCC in February 1997. We have laid our first pitch of turf on a concrete base in Suva, and have plans for 12 more in the near future. The annual Crompton Cup clashed with the ICC Trophy, and so was held on a reduced basis: Suva beat Koma in the final. – Peter Knight.

FRANCE

Richie Benaud, who has French ancestry and a home near Nice, delighted Gallic cricket in October by agreeing to become honorary patron of France Cricket – the new ruling body of the game in France – and offering to advise on coaching and development. The Benaud oui-oui came soon after a two-day, 700-mile, inspection by ICC chief executive David Richards and Jørgen Holmen, chairman of the Associate Members, in connection with French hopes for promotion from Affiliate to Associate status in 1998. France retained their position as European

Nations Cup holders, with an extraordinary win over Germany (see separate report). At home, Paris Université landed a League and Cup double and Château de Thoiry retained the national indoor title. The Picardy town of Chauny, who lost to Thoiry in the indoor final, now have more than 90 school cricketers, including 35 girls. Five new grounds were built in 1997. Three of these were at St-Aulaye (Dordogne), and Wimereux and Arras in the north. The most notable was at the Domaine des Ormes in Brittany, on a site that includes a golf course, a hotel and the national cricket office. The unluckiest was Robin Marlar's ground (complete with turf wicket) at Mollans-sur-Ouveze, Provence, which was wrecked by wild boar, who dug their snouts into the turf and almost ploughed it up. "Hampshire Hogs on tour, I expect," said Marlar. The ground has had to be temporarily abandoned. – Simon Hewitt.

GERMANY

This was the busiest season yet for German cricket, including an expanded domestic programme and a ten-day tour by MCC, 87 years after an invitation was first sent. MCC were unable to oblige in 1910, but in 1997 played five games and were in danger of an upset against a combined West Region and North Rhine Westphalia XI at Osnabrück, when they won by just 15 runs. They won their other games, including a match against the German national team, comfortably. North Rhine Westphalia was the main area of growth in 1997 and a new league started there, which was won by Rheydter SV. However, DSSC Berlin again became German champions in the competition between the regional league champions – Hamburg Youth (North), who were runners-up, Rheydter, Hassloch Cosmopolitans (West) and Pak Orient Munich (South). There was further good news for Berlin when the authorities confirmed that the main pitch in the Olympic Stadium grounds would be kept for the use of cricketers, despite the departure of British troops. Two ICC officials inspected the country's cricket after Germany applied to upgrade from Affiliate to Associate Membership; a decision is expected in 1998. – Brian Fell.

GIBRALTAR

The 1997 season was one of the longest in memory, starting with the ICC Trophy in March and extending into mid-October. Gibraltar improved on their performance in Kenya three years earlier, beating Israel in the competition proper and Argentina in the Plate. The dominance of the local season established by the Gibraltar Cricket Club continued: their team won three of the four domestic competitions, including the Murto Cup, which had eluded them since the war. A new club, Calpe, joined the senior ranks with a team made up almost exclusively of youngsters. This augurs well for the future, as does the appointment of a Youth Development Officer, David Gelling. – T. J. Finlayson.

GREECE

Cricket in Corfu, where the locals have played cricket since early in the 19th century, is about to enter the modern age with the construction of a new purpose-built stadium. Another ground is being built in the resort area of Acharavi, and two more are planned. There are eight teams on the island. Corfiot cricket has had its own lexicon since 1900 and, with Greece now belatedly attached to ICC, there is the prospect of a new and exciting era. – Steve Bunce.

ISRAEL

Israel did not do well on the field in the ICC Trophy, except for some gutsy performances in the opening game against Kenya. But the team withstood the political barrage with great honour. Israel does not have diplomatic relations with Malaysia, and much careful work went into getting our squad there. Full marks to the Malaysian Cricket Association and their government for their help in making our stay a success. In July, the quadrennial Maccabi Games, for Jewish sportsmen and women throughout the world, were held in Israel. Six teams took part in the cricket, and the gold medal surprisingly went to Australia, who beat South Africa by two wickets, even though the South African top four all had first-class experience, and included the triple-centurion Terence Lazard. Israel beat Britain for the bronze. The improvement can be credited to Roland Lefebvre, whose coaching left an indelible mark, and to the excellent playing facilities at our new HQ. The shock of the season was the relegation to Division Two of Ashdod, the 1996 champions. Lions Lod did the double, easily beating Tel Aviv in a play-off for the League and, more controversially, beating Netanya on run-rate in the Cup final. The match was held up because the sun was shining in the batsmen's eyes. Shortly after it resumed, play was abandoned because of bad light. – Stanley Perlman.

ITALY

Their performance in the ICC Trophy came as a great disappointment to Italy, but the result of the year was the national team's victory over Durham at Whitburn in August. Against a side containing nine players who had played first-class cricket in 1997, Italy fielded brilliantly to restrict the county to 134 for nine, and won the game thanks to a painstaking 45 not out by Benito Giordano, the Cheshire-born Neapolitan. Giordano and opener Andrea Amati were the heroes of another surprising result, a six-wicket win over Denmark Under-23 in Rome to square a two-game series. Pianoro won the pennant, their third in four years, beating Capanelle in the final. – Simone Gambino.

JAPAN

Tokyo Bay had a triumphant season. They easily won the Gunma Cup, which is restricted to Japanese nationals, but also achieved unexpected success in the Kanto Cup, which was originally organised for the foreign community. With ten Japanese and one Australian in their side, they reached the final against Fuji and had every hope of completing the double. Unfortunately, the match was rained off and the trophy shared. Enthusiasm for the game is growing, and 1998 should be a big year for Japanese cricket, with the staging of UK98, a festival of British culture. The Japanese players remain hazy about the world game. A trivia quiz organised around the British Ambassador's Challenge Cup (for beginners) included the question: "Name four past or present England Test players." Three of the five teams named Atherton, two of them Hick; the only other names to appear were Lewis, Bradman, Donald and either Trevor Bailey or Bayley – they are the same in Japanese script. However, Japan's best fielder, Jin Shibata, is now known to his team-mates as "Jonty". As the game takes hold, an independent Japanese lexicon is appearing. Howzat is still used for an appeal, but backing up has become "leading", a helmet is "metto" and that most valuable piece of protective equipment is known as "a cup". – Trevor Bayley.

MAURITIUS

There are now five teams on Mauritius with a small but dedicated group keeping the game alive. Competitive, good-standard, matches are played by expatriates – mainly Indians and Sri Lankans – on Sundays at the Police Grounds in Vacoas, where there is a matting wicket. The Maurindia club has now begun a regular series with the Seychelles Cricket Association, playing two matches there in July and in Mauritius in October. However, cricket remains strange and unfathomable to most Mauritians, and efforts to promote cricket among schoolchildren have been largely unsuccessful, owing to lack of finance. – Vinod Vetath.

NEPAL

Nepal became an Associate Member of ICC in 1996, which did not allow enough time for a team to prepare for the 1997 ICC Trophy. But towards the end of 1997 an Under-19 team played in the Asian Cricket Council tournament in Hong Kong and beat both Malaysia and Thailand. Nepal is hoping to stage the next ACC Trophy tournament, and four turf pitches are due to be completed in Kathmandu in the first half of 1998. Talks have been going on with Tribhuvan University to upgrade their stadium for cricket. The national competition, the Jai Trophy, was organised at the ex-British Gurkha camp at Dharan and was won by the team from the eastern district of Sausari. – Jai Kumar Shah.

NORWAY

Cricket survives and thrives in Norway, despite the problems caused by the very harsh winters. Football as well as cricket is a summer sport, and so there is a shortage of available playing space. It took a long while to persuade the authorities that a patch of grass was not quite enough. The big breakthrough came in 1996 when, after a lot of hard work and persuasion, the Oslo Sports Council agreed to provide an artificial pitch and two practice wickets. The climate has caused some teething problems, but these will be overcome. Already, the better facilities have helped standards, and in 1998 nine teams will compete for the league title. Most of the players are migrants from Asia, and one of the teams is Sri Lankan. When they play, the whole family attends, and local residents have been intrigued to see a crowd of 200 watching cricket at 10 a.m. on a Sunday. – Bob Gibb.

SEYCHELLES

Cricket in Seychelles is in a somewhat parlous state. The Seychelles Cricket Association is laughingly referred to as the Sri Lankan Cricket Association, for without their expatriates there would be no cricket here. For eight years I have been taking young players to practise, but the locals kick a football around and across the wicket, disrupting the cricket so much that many are scared to attend. Still, five teams are playing. We are obliged to play with a mat on a football field, which is positively lethal; everybody now wears a helmet when batting. Our reciprocal matches with Mauritius have been rather one-sided in their favour. We have support from our National Sports Council, but they are obliged to give priority to sports which are enjoyed by the Seychellois, which is unlikely ever to include cricket. – Antony Coster.

SINGAPORE

Singapore's focus is on development of youth cricket and facilities, and 1997 was a year of progress. About 2,000 boys are now playing, compared to 100 five years ago; 51 schools and colleges are involved, and there is fierce competition. There are eight full-time professional coaches, and national squads at four different age levels. Our adult team in the ICC Trophy at Kuala Lumpur was not as strong as originally hoped, but performed exceedingly well to come 14th in the final rankings. There are now 23 clubs in the national league, split into three divisions; Division One was very hard fought, with Singapore Cricket Club narrowly beating Indian Association. The Kallang ground has been completely renovated, with a new square constructed and a new pavilion to come. We hope to host one-day internationals there in 1998. – Chris Pianca.

SOUTH KOREA

The game is alive and well in Korea, and the standard has improved in recent years, despite fairly basic facilities and the peculiar problems of playing in an environment where cricket is unknown. After the cricketers lost a battle with Korean Customs over excessive import duties on equipment, two of the six new stumps broke during the first game. In the autumn, the final of the Gillette Kimchi Cup had to be postponed because the playing surface – a rubber mat and felt carpet – had disappeared, together with the shed where they had been stored after the semi-finals. Little did we know that the US military authorities, who are responsible for the UN compound where we play, had marked the shed for demolition – nor that the contractor would not realise the vital importance of the equipment. Cricketers are resourceful in emergency, though: a new mat and felt were acquired locally, enabling the Pakistan team to beat the Rest of the World and win the Cup. The final of the spring competition was ruined by a thunderstorm: no new date could be arranged, and All Stars were awarded the Cup for having led the league table, a decision sportingly endorsed by India, the other finalists. – Olivier de Braekeleer.

SPAIN

The year 1997 proved to be one of stagnation for Spanish cricket. The promised funding from central government failed to become a reality, and the inability to find a major sponsor hindered progress. However, there was both a National League and National Cup, supported by seven of the possible ten clubs. The League was won by Marbella, but they lost the Cup final to Javea. For the first time, competitive cricket was played in the Canary Islands. The Club de Cricket Canarias joined the League. Their first match in Gran Canaria against Sporting Alfas proved to be an interesting experience, in that the mat – placed in the centre of a grass football field – was too short, and bowling could take place from one end only. The introduction of the Canaries was welcomed, but the cost of travel for each match, more than £2,000 per team, is likely to hamper progress. – Clive Woodbridge.

SWITZERLAND

A new rule in the League was that each team should include two Swiss-born players. Three of the nine clubs found this impracticable, and so only six participated. The competition was split into two mini-leagues to reduce travelling, and Berne beat Basle by 124 runs in the final. The annual Zuoz Festival was severely hit by flooding. – Bryan Pattison.

UGANDA

Uganda is unique in African cricket: it is the only country where the game is played mainly by the African community. When the country was enduring its national nightmare of tyranny and civil war in the 1970s and early 1980s, and nearly all Asians and Europeans left the country, a small group of enthusiasts kept the game alive in near-impossible circumstances. Under the Amin regime, cricket was regarded as elitist and the team was often denied permission to play abroad. Once, the square used by the national team was churned up by being used for the start and finish of a motor rally – at the insistence of the sports minister. Now, with the country reviving, Ugandan cricket is reviving too. In 1997 Uganda won the annual quadrangular tournament against the other countries affiliated to ICC as East and Central Africa (Malawi, Tanzania and Zambia) for only the second time in three decades. In 1998 Uganda hope to break away from this group and achieve Associate Membership of ICC in their own right. Playing standards are not a match for neighbouring Kenya, but the Ugandans' tour of England in 1995, when they won ten games out of 12 against strong club sides, suggests that the team could be a force in future ICC Trophies.

UNITED STATES

American cricket politics remained confused and combustible in 1997. The effect was that ICC was forced to abandon its dream of staging its 1998 mini-World Cup at Disney World in Florida. The USA Cricket Association had done a deal with a marketing group which would have made such a tournament a legal minefield. ICC decided to back off, but insisted it would definitely stage fixtures in Florida by 1999. The Association, regarded by its opponents as moribund, has been at loggerheads with both ICC and an internal dissident group which formed itself into the USA Cricket Federation. At the end of 1997 there were some hopes that new elections might produce a ruling body that would satisfy everyone. However, international administrators have refused to rule out the possibility of stepping in and setting up a fresh organisation. In a confused fashion, the game has been booming across America, in areas with heavy populations of immigrants from the Caribbean and the subcontinent. Cricketing internet sites, in particular, report huge interest from America.

VANUATU

One of the highlights each year now in this South Pacific nation is the visit of the Ginger Meggs XI, for a one-day friendly. In 1997 they made their fourth annual visit with a team including a number of well-known Australian players, past and present: Simon Cook, who made his Test debut for Australia in November 1997, acquired his first international experience at Independence Park in Port Vila. In 1998 we hope to hold the inaugural Vanuatu Sixes tournament, aimed at club and social teams throughout the region, to coincide with the Ginger Meggs visit. It should be noted that the boundary at Independence Park drops around 30 feet from the top to the bottom; there is a magnificent view of the harbour. In 1997 we were able to send a young player, Abraham Nasak, on a one-month scholarship to the Australian Institute of Sport. Also in 1997 the South Efate Traditional Cricket Association was established to run a women's competition, mainly in the villages near Port Vila. Wearing island dresses, they play the modified version of the game that has long been played in the South Pacific, using rough-hewn bats that weigh up to four kilos. – Mark Stafford.

HONG KONG SIXES

Pakistan, captained by Wasim Akram, won the Hong Kong Sixes in September 1997 with a dramatic win over England in the final. They needed 22 to win when the last over began, bowled by the England captain Adam Hollioake. Zahoor Elahi scored three fours and a six and, with the help of two wides, won the game for Pakistan. Bangladesh produced the surprise results by beating both India and Australia. The tournament was held less than three months after Britain handed its former colony over to China, and was thus the first major cricket competition on Communist soil.

PART SIX:
ADMINISTRATION AND LAWS

INTERNATIONAL CRICKET COUNCIL

On June 15, 1909, representatives of cricket in England, Australia and South Africa met at Lord's and founded the Imperial Cricket Conference. Membership was confined to the governing bodies of cricket in countries within the British Commonwealth where Test cricket was played. India, New Zealand and West Indies were elected as members on May 31, 1926, Pakistan on July 28, 1952, Sri Lanka on July 21, 1981, and Zimbabwe on July 8, 1992. South Africa ceased to be a member of ICC on leaving the British Commonwealth in May, 1961, but was elected as a Full Member on July 10, 1991.

On July 15, 1965, the Conference was renamed the International Cricket Conference and new rules were adopted to permit the election of countries from outside the British Commonwealth. This led to the growth of the Conference, with the admission of Associate Members, who were each entitled to one vote, while the Foundation and Full Members were each entitled to two votes, on ICC resolutions. On July 12, 13, 1989, the Conference was renamed the International Cricket Council and revised rules were adopted.

On July 7, 1993, ICC ceased to be administered by MCC and became an independent organisation with its own chief executive, the headquarters remaining at Lord's. The category of Foundation Member, with its special rights, was abolished. On October 1, 1993, Sir Clyde Walcott became the first non-British chairman of ICC.

On June 16, 1997, ICC became an incorporated body, with an executive board and a president instead of a chairman. Jagmohan Dalmiya became ICC's first president.

Officers

President: J. Dalmiya. *Chief Executive:* D. L. Richards.
Chairman of Committees: Cricket: Sir Clyde Walcott; *Development:* Dr A. Bacher; *Finance and Marketing:* E. Mani; *Associate Members:* J. Holmen.
Executive Board: The six officers listed above sit on the board *ex officio.* They are joined by Sir John Anderson (New Zealand), S. Z. A. S. Bukhari (Pakistan), P. Chingoka (Zimbabwe), S. H. Chowdhury (Bangladesh), Raj Singh Dungarpur (India), HRH Tunku Imran (Malaysia), K. Mackerdhuj (South Africa), Lord MacLaurin (England), D. Ranatunga (Sri Lanka), J. Rayani (Kenya), D. W. Rogers (Australia), P. H. O. Rousseau (West Indies).

Constitution

President: Each Full Member has the right, by rotation, to appoint ICC's president. In 1997, India named J. Dalmiya to serve until 2000. Australia has nominated M. A. Gray to serve from 2000 to 2003. Subsequent presidents will serve for two years.

Chief Executive: Appointed by the Council. D. L. Richards was appointed in 1993; his contract has been extended until 2003.

Membership

Full Members: Australia, England, India, New Zealand, Pakistan, South Africa, Sri Lanka, West Indies and Zimbabwe.

Associate Members*: Argentina (1974), Bangladesh (1977), Bermuda (1966), Canada (1968), Denmark (1966), East and Central Africa (1966), Fiji (1965), Gibraltar (1969), Hong Kong (1969), Ireland (1993), Israel (1974), Italy (1995), Kenya (1981), Malaysia (1967), Namibia (1992), Nepal (1996), Netherlands (1966), Papua New Guinea (1973), Scotland (1994), Singapore (1974), United Arab Emirates (1990), USA (1965) and West Africa (1976).

Affiliate Members*: Austria (1992), Bahamas (1987), Belgium (1991), Belize (1997), Brunei (1992), Cayman Islands (1997), France (1987), Germany (1991), Greece (1995), Japan (1989), Portugal (1996), Spain (1992), Sweden (1997), Switzerland (1985), Thailand (1995) and Vanuatu (1995).

* *Year of election shown in parentheses.*

The following governing bodies for cricket shall be eligible for election.

Full Members: The governing body for cricket recognised by ICC of a country, or countries associated for cricket purposes, or a geographical area, from which representative teams are qualified to play official Test matches.

Associate Members: The governing body for cricket recognised by ICC of a country, or countries associated for cricket purposes, or a geographical area, which does not qualify as a Full Member but where cricket is firmly established and organised.

Affiliate Members: The governing body for cricket recognised by ICC of a country, or countries associated for cricket purposes, or a geographical area (which is not part of one of those already constituted as a Full or Associate Member) where ICC recognises that cricket is played in accordance with the Laws of Cricket. Affiliate Members have no right to vote or to propose or second resolutions at ICC meetings.

ENGLAND AND WALES CRICKET BOARD

The England and Wales Cricket Board (ECB) became responsible for the administration of all cricket – professional and recreational – in England and Wales on January 1, 1997. It took over the functions of the Cricket Council, the Test and County Cricket Board and the National Cricket Association which had run the game in England and Wales since 1968. The Management Committee is answerable to the First-Class Forum on matters concerning the first-class game and to the Recreational Forum on matters concerning the non-professional game. Each of the forums elects four members to the Management Committee.

Officers

Chairman: Lord MacLaurin of Knebworth. *Chief Executive:* T. M. Lamb.

Management Committee: Lord MacLaurin (*chairman*), D. L. Acfield, R. Bennett, A. J. Cross, B. G. K. Downing, P. J. Edwards, F. H. Elliott, B. G. Ford, P. W. Gooden, R. Jackson, R. D. V. Knight, F. D. Morgan, J. B. Pickup, A. Wheelhouse.

Chairmen of Committees: First-Class Forum: F. D. Morgan; *Recreational Forum:* J. B. Pickup; *Cricket Advisory Committee:* D. L. Acfield; *England Management Advisory Committee:* R. Bennett; *Finance Advisory Committee:* B. G. Ford; *Marketing Advisory Committee:* B. G. K. Downing; *Discipline Standing Committee:* G. Elias QC; *Registration Standing Committee:* A. Wheelhouse.

Deputy Chief Executive and Finance Director: C. A. Barker; *Director of Cricket Operations:* J. D. Carr; *Marketing Director:* T. D. M. Blake; *Corporate Affairs Director:* R. Peel; *Technical Director:* H. Morris; *National Development Manager:* K. R. Pont; *International Teams Director:* S. J. Pack; *Cricket Operations Manager (First-Class):* A. Fordham; *Cricket Operations Manager (Recreational):* F. Kemp.

THE MARYLEBONE CRICKET CLUB

The Marylebone Cricket Club evolved out of the White Conduit Club in 1787, when Thomas Lord laid out his first ground in Dorset Square. Its members revised the Laws in 1788 and gradually took responsibility for cricket throughout the world. However, it relinquished control of the game in the UK in 1968 and the International Cricket Council finally established its own secretariat in 1993. MCC still owns Lord's and remains the guardian of the Laws. It calls itself "a private club with a public function" and aims to support cricket everywhere, especially at grassroots level and in countries where the game is least developed.

Patron: HER MAJESTY THE QUEEN

Officers

President: 1996-98 – A. C. D. Ingleby-Mackenzie.

Treasurer: M. E. L. Melluish.   *Chairman of Finance:* D. L. Hudd.

Trustees: Lord Griffiths, D. R. W. Silk, J. C. Woodcock.

Hon. Life Vice-Presidents: Sir Donald Bradman, D. G. Clark, Lord Cowdrey, G. H. G. Doggart, D. J. Insole, F. G. Mann, C. H. Palmer, C. G. A. Paris, E. W. Swanton, J. J. Warr.

Secretary: R. D. V. Knight.

Assistant Secretaries: J. W. Booth (Head of Finance), J. A. Jameson (Cricket), C. W. W. Rea (Marketing), J. R. Smith (Administration).   *Personal Assistant to Secretary:* Miss S. A. Lawrence. *Curator:* S. E. A. Green.

MCC Committee, elected members 1997-98: Lord Alexander, E. R. Dexter, D. J. C. Faber, C. A. Fry, Sir Michael Jenkins, A. R. Lewis, D. R. Male, M. C. J. Nicholas, Sir Tim Rice, D. Rich, J. A. F. Vallance, A. W. Wreford.

Chairmen of main sub-committees: Lord Cowdrey (Cricket); B. M. Thornton (Estates); R. V. C. Robins (General Purposes).   *Chairmen of specialist sub-committees:* R. P. Hodson (Players and Fixtures); B. A. Sharp (Tennis and Squash); T. M. B. Sissons (Marketing); H. M. Wyndham (Arts and Libraries).

PROFESSIONAL CRICKETERS' ASSOCIATION

The Professional Cricketers' Association was formed in 1967 (as the Cricketers' Association) to represent the first-class county playing staffs, and to promote and protect professional players' interests. During the 1970s, it succeeded in establishing pension schemes and a minimum wage. In 1995, David Graveney became the Association's general secretary and first full-time employee. In 1997, the organisation set up its own marketing company to raise regular revenue and fund improved benefits for members of the PCA during and after their playing careers.

President: M. W. Gatting.   *Chairman:* M. V. Fleming.   *General Secretary:* D. A. Graveney.   *Managing Director, PCA Management:* R. H. Bevan.

EUROPEAN CRICKET COUNCIL

On June 16, 1997, the eight-year-old European Cricket Federation was superseded by the European Cricket Council, bringing together all European ICC members, plus Israel. These were England (Full Member); Denmark, Gibraltar, Ireland, Israel, Italy, Netherlands and Scotland (Associate Members); Austria, Belgium, France, Germany, Greece, Portugal, Spain, Sweden and Switzerland (Affiliate Members); and Luxembourg and Malta (applicants for Affiliate status).

Chairman: D. J. Insole.   *European Development Officer:* N. E. F. Laughton.

ADDRESSES

INTERNATIONAL CRICKET COUNCIL

D. L. Richards, The Clock Tower, Lord's Cricket Ground, London NW8 8QN (0171-266 1818; fax 0171-266 1777).

Full Members

AUSTRALIA: Australian Cricket Board, M. Speed, 90 Jolimont Street, Jolimont, Victoria 3002 (00 61 3 9653 9999; fax 00 61 3 9653 9922).

ENGLAND: England and Wales Cricket Board, T. M. Lamb, Lord's Ground, London NW8 8QZ (0171-432 1200; fax 0171-289 5619).

INDIA: Board of Control for Cricket in India, J. Y. Lele, Sanmitra, Anandpura, Baroda 390 001 (00 91 265 428833; fax 00 91 265 431122).

NEW ZEALAND: New Zealand Cricket Inc., C. Doig, PO Box 958, 109 Cambridge Terrace, Christchurch (00 64 3 366 2964; fax 00 64 3 365 7491).

PAKISTAN: Pakistan Cricket Board, Majid Khan, Gaddafi Stadium, Ferozepur Road, Lahore 54600 (00 92 42 575 4737/9936; fax 00 92 42 571 1860).

SOUTH AFRICA: United Cricket Board of South Africa, Dr A. Bacher, PO Box 55009, Northlands 2116, Transvaal (00 27 11 880 2810; fax 00 27 11 880 6578).

SRI LANKA: Board of Control for Cricket in Sri Lanka, D. Ranatunga, 58 Campbell Place, Colombo 10 (00 94 1 691601/691602; fax 00 94 1 691439).

WEST INDIES: West Indies Cricket Board, G. S. Camacho, Factory Road, PO Box 616 W, Woods Centre, St John's, Antigua (00 1 268 460 5462/5465; fax 00 1 268 460 5452/5453).

ZIMBABWE: Zimbabwe Cricket Union, D. Arnott, PO Box 2739, Harare (00 263 4 704616/704617/704618; fax 00 263 4 729370).

Associate and Affiliate Members

ARGENTINA: Argentine Cricket Association, B. C. Roberts, ACA Sede Central, J. M. Gutierrez 3829, 1425 Buenos Aires (00 54 1 802 6166; fax 00 54 1 802 6692).

AUSTRIA: Austrian Cricket Association, A. Simpson-Parker, Benidikt-Schellingergasse 22/16, A-1150 Vienna (00 43 1 985 7070; fax 00 43 1 985 9477).

BAHAMAS: Bahamas Cricket Association, S. Deveaux, Government House, PO Box 1001, Nassau (00 1 242 322 1875; fax 00 1 242 322 4659).

BANGLADESH: Bangladesh Cricket Control Board, S. H. Chowdhury, National Stadium No. 1, Dhaka 1000 (00 880 2 955 6343; fax 00 880 2 956 3414).

BELGIUM: Belgian Cricket Federation, P. Larivière, Konigin Astridlaan 98, B-2800 Mechelen (00 32 3 233 2605; fax 00 32 3 226 1654).

BELIZE: Belize National Cricket Association, Mrs V. Parks, Burnham Manse, 88 Albert Street, Belize City (00 501 2 77380/72330; fax 00 501 2 30936).

BERMUDA: Bermuda Cricket Board of Control, R. Outerbridge, PO Box HM992, Hamilton HM DX (00 1 441 292 8958; fax 00 1 441 292 8959).

BRUNEI: Brunei Darussalam National Cricket Association, S. Langton, PO Box 667, MPC, Badar Seri Begawan 3706, Brunei Darussalam (00 673 2 452889; fax 00 673 2 452890).

CANADA: Canadian Cricket Association, G. Edwards, 46 Port Street East, Mississauga, Ontario L5G 1C1 (00 1 905 278 5000; fax 00 1 905 278 5005).

CAYMAN ISLANDS: Cayman Islands Cricket Association, J. Powell, PO Box 1201 GT, George Town, Grand Cayman (00 1 345 945 5589; fax 00 1 345 945 5558).

DENMARK: Danish Cricket Association, J. Holmen, Idraettens Hus, 2605 Brøndby (00 45 4326 2160; fax 00 45 4326 2163).

EAST AND CENTRAL AFRICA: East and Central African Cricket Conference, T. B. McCarthy, PO Box 34321, Lusaka 1010, Zambia (00 260 1 226 011; fax 00 260 1 224 454/235 450).

FIJI: Fiji Cricket Association, P. I. Knight, PO Box 300, Suva (00 679 301 499/300 321; fax 00 679 301 618).

FRANCE: France Cricket, O. Dubaut, 41 Rue de Fécamp, 75012 Paris (00 33 1 44 68 89 30; fax 00 33 1 44 68 96 00).

GERMANY: Deutscher Cricket Bund, B. Fell, Luragogasse 5, D-94032 Passau (00 49 851 34307; fax 00 49 851 32815).

GIBRALTAR: Gibraltar Cricket Association, T. J. Finlayson, 21 Sandpits House, Withams Road (00 350 79461; also fax).

GREECE: Greek Cricket Federation, C. Evangelos, 1 Artis Street, PO Box 361, Corfu 49100 (00 30 661 30560; fax 00 30 661 25702).

HONG KONG: Hong Kong Cricket Association, J. A. Cribbin, Room 1019, Sports House, 1 Stadium Path, So Kon Po, Causeway Bay (00 852 250 48102; fax 00 852 257 78486).

IRELAND: Irish Cricket Union, D. Scott, 45 Foxrock Park, Foxrock, Dublin 18 (00 353 1 289 3943; also fax).

ISRAEL: Israel Cricket Association, S. Perlman, PO Box 65085, Tel-Aviv 61650 (00 972 3 642 5529; fax 00 972 3 641 7071).

ITALY: Associazione Italiana Cricket, S. Gambino, Via S. Ignazio 9, 00186 Roma (00 39 6 689 6989; fax 00 39 6 687 8684).

JAPAN: Japan Cricket Association, R. G. Martineau, c/o Office of Cricket Development and Promotion, Amagawa Oshima Machi 2-8-17, Maebashi City 379-21 (00 81 272 23 3976; also fax).

KENYA: Kenya Cricket Association, M. Jaffer, PO Box 45870, Nairobi (00 254 2 214288; fax 00 254 2 213240).

MALAYSIA: Malaysian Cricket Association, K. Selveratnam, 1st Floor, Wisma OCM, Jalan Hang Jebat, 50150 Kuala Lumpur (00 60 3 201 6761; fax 00 60 3 201 3878).

NAMIBIA: Namibia Cricket Board, L. Pieters, PO Box 457, Windhoek 9000 (00 264 61 263128/263129; fax 00 264 61 215149).

NEPAL: Cricket Association of Nepal, B. R. Pandey, Dasharath Stadium, PO Box 925 and 1432, Kathmandu (00 977 1 224782; fax 00 977 1 231166/226692).

NETHERLANDS: Royal Netherlands Cricket Board, A. de la Mar, Neiuwe Kalfjeslaan 21-B, 1182 AA Amstelveen (00 31 20 645 1705; fax 00 31 20 645 1715).

PAPUA NEW GUINEA: Papua New Guinea Cricket Board of Control, W. Satchell, PO Box 83, Konedobu NCD (00 675 321 1070; fax 00 675 321 7974).

PORTUGAL: Cricket Association of Portugal, J. Simpson, Vila D'Acia, Rua do Pinhal s/n, Bicesse, P-2765 Estoril (00 351 1 469 0178; also fax).

SCOTLAND: Scottish Cricket Union, R. W. Barclay, Caledonia House, South Gyle, Edinburgh EH12 9DQ (0131 317 7247; fax 0131 317 7103).

SINGAPORE: Singapore Cricket Association, A. Kalaver, 15 Stadium Road, National Stadium, Singapore 397718 (00 65 348 6566; fax 00 65 348 6506).

SPAIN: Asociacion Española de Cricket, C. E. Woodbridge, Apartado de Correos 137, 03581 Alfaz-Playa, Alicante (00 34 6 686 6965; also fax).

SWEDEN: Sweden Cricket Board, C. Bertilson, Enskedevagen 81 12238, Enskede (00 46 8 6496167; fax 00 46 40 911467).

SWITZERLAND: Swiss Cricket Association, B. Pattison, 9 Chemin du Bois-Contens, CH-1291 Commugny (00 41 22 767 2923; fax 00 41 22 767 9191).

THAILAND: Thailand Cricket League, T. Karnasuta, 17th Floor, Silom Complex Building, 191 Silom Road, Bangkok 10500 (00 66 2 231 3888 ext 167/168; fax 00 66 2 231 3870).

UNITED ARAB EMIRATES: Emirates Cricket Board, M. Khan, Sharjah Cricket Stadium, PO Box 88, Sharjah (00 971 6 322 991; fax 00 971 6 334 741).

USA: United States of America Cricket Association, R. Craig, c/o Consulate General of Barbados, 800 Second Avenue, New York NY 10017 (00 1 212 867 8435; fax 00 1 212 986 1030).

VANUATU: Vanuatu Cricket Association, M. Stafford, c/o Stafford and Associates, PO Box 734, Port Vila, Vanuatu (00 678 26104; fax 00 678 26105).

WEST AFRICA: West Africa Cricket Conference, Mrs Tayo Oreweme, Tafawa Balewa Square, Cricket Pavilion, Race Course, Lagos, Nigeria (00 234 1 261 4152; fax 00 234 1 261 4960).

UK ADDRESSES

ENGLAND AND WALES CRICKET BOARD: T. M. Lamb, Lord's Ground, London NW8 8QZ (0171-432 1200; fax 0171-289 5619).

MARYLEBONE CRICKET CLUB: R. D. V. Knight, Lord's Ground, London NW8 8QN (0171-289 1611; fax 0171-289 9100. Tickets 0171-432 1066; fax 0171-432 1061. Administration 0171-432 1046. Membership 0171-432 1026).

First-Class Counties

DERBYSHIRE: County Ground, Nottingham Road, Derby DE21 6DA (01332-383211; fax 01332-290251).

DURHAM: County Ground, Riverside, Chester-le-Street, County Durham DH3 3QR (0191-387 1717; fax 0191-387 1616).

ESSEX: County Ground, New Writtle Street, Chelmsford CM2 0PG (01245-252420; fax 01245-491607).

GLAMORGAN: Sophia Gardens, Cardiff CF1 9XR (01222-343478; fax 01222-377044).

GLOUCESTERSHIRE: Phoenix County Ground, Nevil Road, Bristol BS7 9EJ (0117-924 5216; fax 0117-924 1193).

HAMPSHIRE: Northlands Road, Southampton SO9 2TY (01703-333788; fax 01703-330121).

KENT: St Lawrence Ground, Old Dover Road, Canterbury CT1 3NZ (01227-456886; fax 01227-762168).

LANCASHIRE: County Cricket Ground, Old Trafford, Manchester M16 0PX (0161-282 4000; fax 0161-282 4100).

LEICESTERSHIRE: County Ground, Grace Road, Leicester LE2 8AD (0116-283 1880/2128; fax 0116-244 0363).

MIDDLESEX: Lord's Cricket Ground, London NW8 8QN (0171-289 1300/286 1310; fax 0171-289 5831).

NORTHAMPTONSHIRE: County Ground, Wantage Road, Northampton NN1 4TJ (01604-632917; fax 01604-232855).

NOTTINGHAMSHIRE: County Cricket Ground, Trent Bridge, Nottingham NG2 6AG (0115-982 1525; fax 0115-945 5730).

SOMERSET: County Ground, St James's Street, Taunton TA1 1JT (01823-272946; fax 01823-332395).

SURREY: The Oval, London SE11 5SS (0171-582 6660; fax 0171-735 7769).

SUSSEX: County Ground, Eaton Road, Hove BN3 3AN (01273-732161; fax 01273-771549).

WARWICKSHIRE: County Ground, Edgbaston, Birmingham B5 7QU (0121-446 4422; fax 0121-446 4544).

WORCESTERSHIRE: County Ground, New Road, Worcester WR2 4QQ (01905-748474; fax 01905-748005).

YORKSHIRE: Headingley Cricket Ground, Leeds LS6 3BU (0113-278 7394; fax 0113-278 4099).

Minor Counties

MINOR COUNTIES CRICKET ASSOCIATION: D. J. M. Armstrong, Thorpe Cottage, Mill Common, Ridlington, North Walsham NR28 9TY (01692-650563).

BEDFORDSHIRE: D. J. F. Hoare, 5 Brecon Way, Bedford MK41 8DF (01234-266648).

BERKSHIRE: C. M. S. Crombie, Orchard Cottage, Waltham St Lawrence, Reading, Berkshire RG10 0JH (01734-343387 home/fax).

BUCKINGHAMSHIRE: K. A. Beaumont, 49 Amersham Road, Little Chalfont, Amersham, Buckinghamshire HP6 6SW (01494-763516).

CAMBRIDGESHIRE: P. W. Gooden, The Redlands, Oakington Road, Cottenham, Cambridge CB4 4TW (01954-250429).

CHESHIRE: J. B. Pickup, 2 Castle Street, Northwich, Cheshire CW8 1AB (01606-74970 home, 01606-74301 business; fax 01606-871034).

CORNWALL: The Rev. Canon Kenneth Rogers, The Rectory, Priory Road, Bodmin, Cornwall PL31 2AB (01208-73867).

CUMBERLAND: K. Ion, 47 Beech Grove, Stanwix, Carlisle, Cumbria CA3 9BG (01228-28858).

DEVON: G. R. Evans, Blueberry Haven, 20 Boucher Road, Budleigh Salterton, Devon EX9 6JF (01395-445216 home, 01392-258406 business; fax 01392-411697).

DORSET: K. H. House, The Barn, Higher Farm, Bagber Common, Sturminster Newton, Dorset DT10 2HB (01258-473394).

HEREFORDSHIRE: P. Sykes, 5 Dale Drive, Holmer Grange, Hereford HR4 9RF (01432-264703 home, 01432-382684 business).

HERTFORDSHIRE: D. S. Dredge, "Trevellis", 38 Santers Lane, Potters Bar, Hertfordshire EN6 2BX (01707-658377 home, 0171-359 3579 business).

LINCOLNSHIRE: C. A. North, "Koorah", Whisby Road, Whisby Moor, Lincoln LN6 9BY (01522-681636).

NORFOLK: S. J. Skinner, 27 Colkett Drive, Old Catton, Norwich NR6 7ND (01603-485940 home – weekend, 01354-659026 – midweek, 01733-412152 business).

NORTHUMBERLAND: A. B. Stephenson, Northumberland County Cricket Club, Osborne Avenue, Jesmond, Newcastle-upon-Tyne NE2 1JS (0191-281 2738).

OXFORDSHIRE: A. W. Moss, 14 Croft Avenue, Kidlington, Oxford OX5 2HU (01865-372399, also fax).

SHROPSHIRE: N. H. Birch, 8 Port Hill Close, Shrewsbury, Shropshire SY3 8RR (01743-233650).

STAFFORDSHIRE: W. S. Bourne, 10 The Pavement, Brewood, Staffordshire ST19 9BZ (01902-850325 home, 01902-23038 business).

SUFFOLK: T. J. Pound, 94 Henley Road, Ipswich IP1 4NJ (01473-213288 home, 01473-232121 business).

WALES MINOR COUNTIES: W. Edwards, 59a King Edward Road, Swansea SA1 4LN (01792-462233; fax 01792-643931).

WILTSHIRE: C. R. Sheppard, 45 Ipswich Street, Swindon SN2 1DB (01793-511811 home, 01793-530784 business, 0831-565866 mobile).

Other Bodies

ASSOCIATION OF CRICKET UMPIRES AND SCORERS: G. J. Bullock, PO Box 399, Camberley, Surrey GU16 5ZJ (01276-27962).

BRITISH UNIVERSITIES SPORTS ASSOCIATION: J. Ellis, 8 Union Street, London SE1 1SZ (0171-357 8555).

CLUB CRICKET CONFERENCE: D. Franklin, 361 West Barnes Lane, New Malden, Surrey KT3 6JF (0181-949 4001).

COMBINED SERVICES: Major R. W. K. Ross-Hurst, c/o Army Sports Control Board, Clayton Barracks, Aldershot, Hampshire GU11 2BG.

ENGLISH SCHOOLS' CRICKET ASSOCIATION: K. S. Lake, 38 Mill House, Woods Lane, Cottingham, Hull HU16 4HQ.

EUROPEAN CRICKET COUNCIL: N. E. F. Laughton, Europe Office, Lord's Ground, London NW8 8QN (0171-432 1019; fax 0171-432 1018).

LEAGUE CRICKET CONFERENCE: N. Edwards, 1 Longfield, Freshfield, Formby, Merseyside.

MIDLAND CLUB CRICKET CONFERENCE: D. R. Thomas, 4 Silverdale Gardens, Wordsley, Stourbridge, W. Midlands DY8 5NU.

PROFESSIONAL CRICKETERS' ASSOCIATION: D. A. Graveney, 1 St Paul's Road, Clifton, Bristol BS8 1LZ. PCA MANAGEMENT: R. H. Bevan, Hawkstone Park, Weston-under-Redcastle, Shrewsbury, Shropshire SY4 5UY (01939-200202; fax 01939-200699).

SCARBOROUGH CRICKET FESTIVAL: Colin T. Adamson, Cricket Ground, North Marine Road, Scarborough, North Yorkshire YO12 7TJ.

WOMEN'S CRICKET ASSOCIATION: Warwickshire County Cricket Ground, Edgbaston Road, Birmingham B5 7QX (0121-440 0567; fax/answerphone 0121-440 0520).

Cricket Associations and Societies

COUNCIL OF CRICKET SOCIETIES, THE: B. Rickson, 31 Grange Avenue, Cheadle Hulme, Cheshire SK8 5EN.

COUNTY CRICKET SUPPORTERS ASSOCIATION: Miss F. J. Walker, 12 Grasmere Drive, Linton Croft, Wetherby, West Yorkshire LS22 6GP.

CRICKET MEMORABILIA SOCIETY: A. Sheldon, 29 Highclere Road, Crumpsall, Manchester M8 4WH.

CRICKET SOCIETY, THE: E. R. Budd, 16 Storey Court, 39 St John's Wood Road, London NW8 8QX.

CRICKET STATISTICIANS AND HISTORIANS, ASSOCIATION OF: P. Wynne-Thomas, 3 Radcliffe Road, West Bridgford, Nottingham NG2 5FF.

NATIONAL CRICKET MEMBERSHIP SCHEME: c/o Cricket Lore, 22 Grazebrook Road, London N16 0HS.

SCOTLAND, CRICKET SOCIETY OF: A. J. Robertson, 5 Riverside Road, Eaglesham, Glasgow G76 0DQ.

WOMBWELL CRICKET LOVERS' SOCIETY: M. Pope, 59 Wood Lane, Treeton, Rotherham, South Yorkshire S60 5QR.

CRIME AND PUNISHMENT

ICC CODE OF CONDUCT – BREACHES AND PENALTIES IN 1996-97

S. R. Waugh   Australia v India, one-day international at Colombo.
Dissent over calling of wides.   Fine of 30 per cent of match fee, suspended for three months, by J. R. Reid.

G. Kirsten   South Africa v Pakistan, one-day international at Nairobi.
Wearing a coloured bandana with white clothing.   Fined 10 per cent of match fee by M. H. Denness.

M. Doherty
(South African manager)   South Africa v Pakistan, one-day international at Nairobi.
Not responding to referee's request to remove Kirsten's bandana.   Fined 10 per cent of match fee by M. H. Denness.

H. H. Gibbs   South Africa v India, 2nd Test at Calcutta.
Commercial logo on arm guard.   Fined 15 per cent of match fee by J. R. Reid.

V. V. S. Laxman   India v South Africa, 2nd Test at Calcutta.
Commercial logo on pads.   Fined 15 per cent of match fee by J. R. Reid.

C. L. Cairns   New Zealand v Pakistan, 2nd Test at Rawalpindi.
Dissent when lbw appeal rejected.   Fined 50 per cent of match fee by C. W. Smith.

Ijaz Ahmed, sen.   Pakistan v New Zealand, 2nd Test at Rawalpindi.
Dissent when given lbw.   Fined 50 per cent of match fee by C. W. Smith.

H. H. Streak   Zimbabwe v England, 1st Test at Bulawayo.
Told press he was surprised umpire had not called him for wides.   Fined 15 per cent of match fee by Hanumant Singh.

D. J. Johnson   India v South Africa, 1st Test at Durban.
Implied dissent when given out caught.   Severely reprimanded by B. N. Jarman.

Aamir Sohail   Pakistan v Australia, one-day international at Melbourne.
Dissent when given out: twice asked umpire to consult TV replay, swore and threw bat.   Suspended for one one-day international by R. Subba Row.

P. Dharmani   India v South Africa, 3rd Test at Johannesburg.
Continued aggressive appeal after bat-pad verdict not given.   Fined 25 per cent of match fee by B. N. Jarman.

S. C. Ganguly   India v South Africa, 3rd Test at Johannesburg.
Continued aggressive appeal after bat-pad verdict not given.   Fined 25 per cent of match fee by B. N. Jarman.

M. Azharuddin   India v South Africa, 3rd Test at Johannesburg.
Dissent when given out.   Severely reprimanded by B. N. Jarman.

I. A. Healy   Australia v South Africa, 3rd Test at Centurion.
Dissent when given out.   Suspended for two one-day internationals by R. Subba Row.

P. A. de Silva   Sri Lanka v New Zealand, one-day international at Wellington.
Dissent when given out.   Severely reprimanded by P. J. Burge.

Ijaz Ahmed, sen.   Pakistan v Sri Lanka, 2nd Test at Colombo (SSC).
Verbal abuse of dismissed batsman.   Fined 20 per cent of match fee, with further 30 per cent fine suspended for five months from July 1997, by J. R. Reid.

N. R. Mongia   India v Sri Lanka, one-day international at Mumbai.
Excessive appeals (twice).   Severely reprimanded by A. M. Ibrahim.

No action was taken by the referees in the 1997 series in England.

THE LAWS OF CRICKET

(1980 CODE)

As updated in 1992. World copyright of MCC and reprinted by permission of MCC. Copies of the "Laws of Cricket" may be obtained from Lord's Cricket Ground.

INDEX TO THE LAWS

LAW 1. THE PLAYERS

1. Number of Players and Captain

A match is played between two sides each of 11 players, one of whom shall be captain. In the event of the captain not being available at any time, a deputy shall act for him.

2. Nomination of Players

Before the toss for innings, the captain shall nominate his players, who may not thereafter be changed without the consent of the opposing captain.

Note

> **(a) More or Less than 11 Players a Side**
> A match may be played by agreement between sides of more or less than 11 players, but not more than 11 players may field.

LAW 2. SUBSTITUTES AND RUNNERS: BATSMAN OR FIELDSMAN LEAVING THE FIELD: BATSMAN RETIRING: BATSMAN COMMENCING INNINGS

1. Substitutes

In normal circumstances, a substitute shall be allowed to field only for a player who satisfies the umpires that he has become injured or become ill during the match. However, in very exceptional circumstances, the umpires may use their discretion to allow a substitute for a player who has to leave the field for other wholly acceptable reasons, subject to consent being given by the opposing captain. If a player wishes to change his shirt, boots, etc., he may leave the field to do so (no changing on the field), but no substitute will be allowed.

2. Objection to Substitutes

The opposing captain shall have no right of objection to any player acting as substitute in the field, nor as to where he shall field; however, no substitute shall act as wicket-keeper.

3. Substitute not to Bat or Bowl

A substitute shall not be allowed to bat or bowl.

4. A Player for whom a Substitute has Acted

A player may bat, bowl or field even though a substitute has acted for him.

5. Runner

A runner shall be allowed for a batsman who, during the match, is incapacitated by illness or injury. The person acting as runner shall be a member of the batting side and shall, if possible, have already batted in that innings.

6. Runner's Equipment

The player acting as runner for an injured batsman shall wear the same external protective equipment as the injured batsman.

7. Transgression of the Laws by an Injured Batsman or Runner

An injured batsman may be out should his runner break any one of Laws 33 (Handled the Ball), 37 (Obstructing the Field) or 38 (Run Out). As striker he remains himself subject to the Laws. Furthermore, should he be out of his ground for any purpose and the wicket at the wicket-keeper's end be put down he shall be out under Law 38 (Run Out) or Law 39 (Stumped), irrespective of the position of the other batsman or the runner, and no runs shall be scored.

When not the striker, the injured batsman is out of the game and shall stand where he does not interfere with the play. Should he bring himself into the game in any way, then he shall suffer the penalties that any transgression of the Laws demands.

8. Fieldsman Leaving the Field

No fieldsman shall leave the field or return during a session of play without the consent of the umpire at the bowler's end. The umpire's consent is also necessary if a substitute is required for a fieldsman, when his side returns to the field after an interval. If a member of the fielding side leaves the field or fails to return after an interval and is absent from the field for longer than 15 minutes, he shall not be permitted to bowl after his return until he has been on the field for at least that length of playing time for which he was absent. This restriction shall not apply at the start of a new day's play.

9. Batsman Leaving the Field or Retiring

A batsman may leave the field or retire at any time owing to illness, injury or other unavoidable cause, having previously notified the umpire at the bowler's end. He may resume his innings at the fall of a wicket, which for the purposes of this Law shall include the retirement of another batsman.

If he leaves the field or retires for any other reason he may resume his innings only with the consent of the opposing captain.

When a batsman has left the field or retired and is unable to return owing to illness, injury or other unavoidable cause, his innings is to be recorded as "retired, not out". Otherwise it is to be recorded as "retired, out".

10. Commencement of a Batsman's Innings

A batsman shall be considered to have commenced his innings once he has stepped on to the field of play.

Note

(a) Substitutes and Runners

For the purpose of these Laws, allowable illnesses or injuries are those which occur at any time after the nomination by the captains of their teams.

LAW 3.   THE UMPIRES

1. Appointment

Before the toss for innings, two umpires shall be appointed, one for each end, to control the game with absolute impartiality as required by the Laws.

2. Change of Umpires

No umpire shall be changed during a match without the consent of both captains.

3. Special Conditions

Before the toss for innings, the umpires shall agree with both captains on any special conditions affecting the conduct of the match.

4. The Wickets

The umpires shall satisfy themselves before the start of the match that the wickets are properly pitched.

5. Clock or Watch

The umpires shall agree between themselves and inform both captains before the start of the match on the watch or clock to be followed during the match.

6. Conduct and Implements

Before and during a match the umpires shall ensure that the conduct of the game and the implements used are strictly in accordance with the Laws.

7. Fair and Unfair Play

The umpires shall be the sole judges of fair and unfair play.

8. Fitness of Ground, Weather and Light

(a) The umpires shall be the sole judges of the fitness of the ground, weather and light for play.

    (i) However, before deciding to suspend play, or not to start play, or not to resume play after an interval or stoppage, the umpires shall establish whether both captains (the batsmen at the wicket may deputise for their captain) wish to commence or to continue in the prevailing conditions; if so, their wishes shall be met.

    (ii) In addition, if during play the umpires decide that the light is unfit, only the batting side shall have the option of continuing play. After agreeing to continue to play in unfit light conditions, the captain of the batting side (or a batsman at the wicket) may appeal against the light to the umpires, who shall uphold the appeal only if, in their opinion, the light has deteriorated since the agreement to continue was made.

(b) After any suspension of play, the umpires, unaccompanied by any of the players or officials, shall, on their own initiative, carry out an inspection immediately the conditions improve and shall continue to inspect at intervals. Immediately the umpires decide that play is possible they shall call upon the players to resume the game.

9. Exceptional Circumstances

In exceptional circumstances, other than those of weather, ground or light, the umpires may decide to suspend or abandon play. Before making such a decision the umpires shall establish, if the circumstances allow, whether both captains (the batsmen at the wicket may deputise for their captain) wish to continue in the prevailing conditions; if so, their wishes shall be met.

10. Position of Umpires

The umpires shall stand where they can best see any act upon which their decision may be required.

Subject to this over-riding consideration, the umpire at the bowler's end shall stand where he does not interfere with either the bowler's run-up or the striker's view.

The umpire at the striker's end may elect to stand on the off instead of the leg side of the pitch, provided he informs the captain of the fielding side and the striker of his intention to do so.

11. Umpires Changing Ends

The umpires shall change ends after each side has had one innings.

12. Disputes

All disputes shall be determined by the umpires, and if they disagree the actual state of things shall continue.

13. Signals

The following code of signals shall be used by umpires who will wait until a signal has been answered by a scorer before allowing the game to proceed.

Boundary	– by waving the arm from side to side.
Boundary 6	– by raising both arms above the head.
Bye	– by raising an open hand above the head.
Dead Ball	– by crossing and re-crossing the wrists below the waist.
Leg-bye	– by touching a raised knee with the hand.
No-ball	– by extending one arm horizontally.
Out	– by raising the index finger above the head. If not out, the umpire shall call "not out".
Short Run	– by bending the arm upwards and by touching the nearer shoulder with the tips of the fingers.
Wide	– by extending both arms horizontally.

14. Correctness of Scores

The umpires shall be responsible for satisfying themselves on the correctness of the scores throughout and at the conclusion of the match. See Law 21.6 (Correctness of Result).

Notes

(a) Attendance of Umpires
The umpires should be present on the ground and report to the ground executive or the equivalent at least 30 minutes before the start of a day's play.

(b) Consultation between Umpires and Scorers
Consultation between umpires and scorers over doubtful points is essential.

(c) Fitness of Ground
The umpires shall consider the ground as unfit for play when it is so wet or slippery as to deprive the bowlers of a reasonable foothold, the fieldsmen, other than the deep-fielders, of the power of free movement, or the batsmen of the ability to play their strokes or to run between the wickets. Play should not be suspended merely because the grass and the ball are wet and slippery.

(d) Fitness of Weather and Light
The umpires should suspend play when they consider that the conditions are so bad that it is unreasonable or dangerous to continue.

LAW 4. THE SCORERS

1. Recording Runs

All runs scored shall be recorded by scorers appointed for the purpose. Where there are two scorers they shall frequently check to ensure that the score-sheets agree.

2. Acknowledging Signals

The scorers shall accept and immediately acknowledge all instructions and signals given to them by the umpires.

LAW 5.   THE BALL

1. Weight and Size

The ball, when new, shall weigh not less than $5\frac{1}{2}$ ounces/155.9g, nor more than $5\frac{3}{4}$ ounces/163g; and shall measure not less than $8\frac{13}{16}$ inches/22.4cm, nor more than 9 inches/22.9cm in circumference.

2. Approval of Balls

All balls used in matches shall be approved by the umpires and captains before the start of the match.

3. New Ball

Subject to agreement to the contrary, having been made before the toss, either captain may demand a new ball at the start of each innings.

4. New Ball in Match of Three or More Days' Duration

In a match of three or more days' duration, the captain of the fielding side may demand a new ball after the prescribed number of overs has been bowled with the old one. The governing body for cricket in the country concerned shall decide the number of overs applicable in that country, which shall be not less than 75 six-ball overs (55 eight-ball overs).

5. Ball Lost or Becoming Unfit for Play

In the event of a ball during play being lost or, in the opinion of the umpires, becoming unfit for play, the umpires shall allow it to be replaced by one that in their opinion has had a similar amount of wear. If a ball is to be replaced, the umpires shall inform the batsman.

Note

> **(a) Specifications**
> The specifications, as described in 1 above, shall apply to top-grade balls only. The following degrees of tolerance will be acceptable for other grades of ball.
>
> (i) *Men's Grades 2–4*
> Weight: $5\frac{5}{16}$ ounces/150g to $5\frac{13}{16}$ ounces/165g.
> Size: $8\frac{11}{16}$ inches/22.0cm to $9\frac{1}{16}$ inches/23.0cm.
>
> (ii) *Women's*
> Weight: $4\frac{15}{16}$ ounces/140g to $5\frac{5}{16}$ ounces/150g.
> Size: $8\frac{1}{4}$ inches/21.0cm to $8\frac{7}{8}$ inches/22.5cm.
>
> (iii) *Junior*
> Weight: $4\frac{11}{16}$ ounces/133g to $5\frac{1}{16}$ ounces/143g.
> Size: $8\frac{1}{16}$ inches/20.5cm to $8\frac{11}{16}$ inches/22.0cm.

LAW 6.   THE BAT

1. Width and Length

The bat overall shall not be more than 38 inches/96.5cm in length; the blade of the bat shall be made of wood and shall not exceed $4\frac{1}{4}$ inches/10.8cm at the widest part.

Note

> (a) The blade of the bat may be covered with material for protection, strengthening or repair. Such material shall not exceed $\frac{1}{16}$ inch/1.56mm in thickness.

LAW 7.   THE PITCH

1. Area of Pitch

The pitch is the area between the bowling creases – see Law 9 (The Bowling and Popping Creases). It shall measure 5 feet/1.52m in width on either side of a line joining the centre of the middle stumps of the wickets – see Law 8 (The Wickets).

2. Selection and Preparation

Before the toss for innings, the executive of the ground shall be responsible for the selection and preparation of the pitch; thereafter the umpires shall control its use and maintenance.

3. Changing Pitch

The pitch shall not be changed during a match unless it becomes unfit for play, and then only with the consent of both captains.

4. Non-Turf Pitches

In the event of a non-turf pitch being used, the following shall apply:

(a) Length: That of the playing surface to a minimum of 58 feet/17.68m.

(b) Width: That of the playing surface to a minimum of 6 feet/1.83m.

See Law 10 (Rolling, Sweeping, Mowing, Watering the Pitch and Re-marking of Creases) Note (a).

LAW 8. THE WICKETS

1. Width and Pitching

Two sets of wickets, each 9 inches/22.86cm wide, and consisting of three wooden stumps with two wooden bails upon the top, shall be pitched opposite and parallel to each other at a distance of 22 yards/20.12m between the centres of the two middle stumps.

2. Size of Stumps

The stumps shall be of equal and sufficient size to prevent the ball from passing between them. Their tops shall be 28 inches/71.1cm above the ground, and shall be dome-shaped except for the bail grooves.

3. Size of Bails

The bails shall be each $4\frac{3}{8}$ inches/11.1cm in length and when in position on the top of the stumps shall not project more than $\frac{1}{2}$ inch/1.3cm above them.

Notes

(a) **Dispensing with Bails**
In a high wind the umpires may decide to dispense with the use of bails.

(b) **Junior Cricket**
For junior cricket, as defined by the local governing body, the following measurements for the wickets shall apply:

Width – 8 inches/20.32cm.
Pitched – 21 yards/19.20m.
Height – 27 inches/68.58cm.
Bails – each $3\frac{7}{8}$ inches/9.84cm in length and should not project more than $\frac{1}{2}$ inch/1.3cm above the stumps.

LAW 9. THE BOWLING, POPPING AND RETURN CREASES

1. The Bowling Crease

The bowling crease shall be marked in line with the stumps at each end and shall be 8 feet 8 inches/2.64m in length, with the stumps in the centre.

2. The Popping Crease

The popping crease, which is the back edge of the crease marking, shall be in front of and parallel with the bowling crease. It shall have the back edge of the crease marking 4 feet/1.22m from the centre of the stumps and shall extend to a minimum of 6 feet/1.83m on either side of the line of the wicket.

The popping crease shall be considered to be unlimited in length.

3. The Return Crease

The return crease marking, of which the inside edge is the crease, shall be at each end of the bowling crease and at right angles to it. The return crease shall be marked to a minimum of 4 feet/1.22m behind the wicket and shall be considered to be unlimited in length. A forward extension shall be marked to the popping crease.

LAW 10.   ROLLING, SWEEPING, MOWING, WATERING THE PITCH AND RE-MARKING OF CREASES

1. Rolling

During the match the pitch may be rolled at the request of the captain of the batting side, for a period of not more than seven minutes before the start of each innings, other than the first innings of the match, and before the start of each day's play. In addition, if, after the toss and before the first innings of the match, the start is delayed, the captain of the batting side may request to have the pitch rolled for not more than seven minutes. However, if in the opinion of the umpires the delay has had no significant effect upon the state of the pitch, they shall refuse any request for the rolling of the pitch.

The pitch shall not otherwise be rolled during the match.

The seven minutes' rolling permitted before the start of a day's play shall take place not earlier than half an hour before the start of play and the captain of the batting side may delay such rolling until ten minutes before the start of play should he so desire.

If a captain declares an innings closed less than 15 minutes before the resumption of play, and the other captain is thereby prevented from exercising his option of seven minutes' rolling or if he is so prevented for any other reason, the time for rolling shall be taken out of the normal playing time.

2. Sweeping

Such sweeping of the pitch as is necessary during the match shall be done so that the seven minutes allowed for rolling the pitch, provided for in 1 above, is not affected.

3. Mowing

(a) **Responsibilities of Ground Authority and of Umpires**
All mowings which are carried out before the toss for innings shall be the responsibility of the ground authority; thereafter they shall be carried out under the supervision of the umpires. See Law 7.2 (Selection and Preparation).

(b) **Initial Mowing**
The pitch shall be mown before play begins on the day the match is scheduled to start, or in the case of a delayed start on the day the match is expected to start. See 3(a) above (Responsibilities of Ground Authority and of Umpires).

(c) **Subsequent Mowings in a Match of Two or More Days' Duration**
In a match of two or more days' duration, the pitch shall be mown daily before play begins. Should this mowing not take place because of weather conditions, rest days or other reasons, the pitch shall be mown on the first day on which the match is resumed.

(d) **Mowing of the Outfield in a Match of Two or More Days' Duration**
In order to ensure that conditions are as similar as possible for both sides, the outfield shall normally be mown before the commencement of play on each day of the match, if ground and weather conditions allow. See Note (b) to this Law.

4. Watering

The pitch shall not be watered during a match.

5. Re-marking Creases

Whenever possible the creases shall be re-marked.

6. Maintenance of Foot-holes

In wet weather, the umpires shall ensure that the holes made by the bowlers and batsmen are cleaned out and dried whenever necessary to facilitate play. In matches of two or more days' duration, the umpires shall allow, if necessary, the re-turfing of foot-holes made by the bowler in his delivery stride, or the use of quick-setting fillings for the same purpose, before the start of each day's play.

7. Securing of Footholds and Maintenance of Pitch

During play, the umpires shall allow either batsman to beat the pitch with his bat and players to secure their footholds by the use of sawdust, provided that no damage to the pitch is so caused, and Law 42 (Unfair Play) is not contravened.

Notes

(a) Non-turf Pitches
The above Law 10 applies to turf pitches.
   The game is played on non-turf pitches in many countries at various levels. Whilst the conduct of the game on these surfaces should always be in accordance with the Laws of Cricket, it is recognised that it may sometimes be necessary for governing bodies to lay down special playing conditions to suit the type of non-turf pitch used in their country.
   In matches played against touring teams, any special playing conditions should be agreed in advance by both parties.

(b) Mowing of the Outfield in a Match of Two or More Days' Duration
If, for reasons other than ground and weather conditions, daily and complete mowing is not possible, the ground authority shall notify the captains and umpires, before the toss for innings, of the procedure to be adopted for such mowing during the match.

(c) Choice of Roller
If there is more than one roller available, the captain of the batting side shall have a choice.

LAW 11.   COVERING THE PITCH

1. Before the Start of a Match

Before the start of a match, complete covering of the pitch shall be allowed.

2. During a Match

The pitch shall not be completely covered during a match unless prior arrangement or regulations so provide.

3. Covering Bowlers' Run-up

Whenever possible, the bowlers' run-up shall be covered, but the covers so used shall not extend further than 4 feet/1.22m in front of the popping crease.

Note

(a) Removal of Covers
The covers should be removed as promptly as possible whenever the weather permits.

LAW 12.   INNINGS

1. Number of Innings

A match shall be of one or two innings of each side according to agreement reached before the start of play.

2. Alternate Innings

In a two-innings match each side shall take their innings alternately except in the case provided for in Law 13 (The Follow-on).

3. The Toss

The captains shall toss for the choice of innings on the field of play not later than 15 minutes before the time scheduled for the match to start, or before the time agreed upon for play to start.

4. Choice of Innings

The winner of the toss shall notify his decision to bat or to field to the opposing captain not later than ten minutes before the time scheduled for the match to start, or before the time agreed upon for play to start. The decision shall not thereafter be altered.

5. Continuation after One Innings of Each Side

Despite the terms of 1 above, in a one-innings match, when a result has been reached on the first innings, the captains may agree to the continuation of play if, in their opinion, there is a prospect of carrying the game to a further issue in the time left. See Law 21 (Result).

Notes

    (a) Limited Innings – One-innings Match
    In a one-innings match, each innings may, by agreement, be limited by a number of overs or by a period of time.

    (b) Limited Innings – Two-innings Match
    In a two-innings match, the first innings of each side may, by agreement, be limited to a number of overs or by a period of time.

LAW 13.   THE FOLLOW-ON

1. Lead on First Innings

In a two-innings match the side which bats first and leads by 200 runs in a match of five days or more, by 150 runs in a three-day or four-day match, by 100 runs in a two-day match, or by 75 runs in a one-day match, shall have the option of requiring the other side to follow their innings.

2. Day's Play Lost

If no play takes place on the first day of a match of two or more days' duration, 1 above shall apply in accordance with the number of days' play remaining from the actual start of the match.

LAW 14.   DECLARATIONS

1. Time of Declaration

The captain of the batting side may declare an innings closed at any time during a match, irrespective of its duration.

2. Forfeiture of Second Innings

A captain may forfeit his second innings, provided his decision to do so is notified to the opposing captain and umpires in sufficient time to allow seven minutes' rolling of the pitch. See Law 10 (Rolling, Sweeping, Mowing, Watering the Pitch and Re-marking of Creases). The normal ten-minute interval between innings shall be applied.

LAW 15.   START OF PLAY

1. Call of Play

At the start of each innings and of each day's play, and on the resumption of play after any interval or interruption, the umpire at the bowler's end shall call "play".

2. Practice on the Field

At no time on any day of the match shall there be any bowling or batting practice on the pitch.

No practice may take place on the field if, in the opinion of the umpires, it could result in a waste of time.

3. Trial Run-up

No bowler shall have a trial run-up after ''play'' has been called in any session of play, except at the fall of a wicket when an umpire may allow such a trial run-up if he is satisfied that it will not cause any waste of time.

LAW 16.   INTERVALS

1. Length

The umpire shall allow such intervals as have been agreed upon for meals, and ten minutes between each innings.

2. Luncheon Interval – Innings Ending or Stoppage within Ten Minutes of Interval

If an innings ends or there is a stoppage caused by weather or bad light within ten minutes of the agreed time for the luncheon interval, the interval shall be taken immediately.

The time remaining in the session of play shall be added to the agreed length of the interval but no extra allowance shall be made for the ten-minute interval between innings.

3. Tea Interval – Innings Ending or Stoppage within 30 Minutes of Interval

If an innings ends or there is a stoppage caused by weather or bad light within 30 minutes of the agreed time for the tea interval, the interval shall be taken immediately.

The interval shall be of the agreed length and, if applicable, shall include the ten-minute interval between innings.

4. Tea Interval – Continuation of Play

If, at the agreed time for the tea interval, nine wickets are down, play shall continue for a period not exceeding 30 minutes or until the innings is concluded.

5. Tea Interval – Agreement to Forgo

At any time during the match, the captains may agree to forgo a tea interval.

6. Intervals for Drinks

If both captains agree before the start of a match that intervals for drinks may be taken, the option to take such intervals shall be available to either side. These intervals shall be restricted to one per session, shall be kept as short as possible, shall not be taken in the last hour of the match, and in any case shall not exceed five minutes.

The agreed times for these intervals shall be strictly adhered to, except that if a wicket falls within five minutes of the agreed time then drinks shall be taken out immediately.

If an innings ends or there is a stoppage caused by weather or bad light within 30 minutes of the agreed time for a drinks interval, there will be no interval for drinks in that session.

At any time during the match the captains may agree to forgo any such drinks interval.

Notes

(a) Tea Interval – One-day Match

In a one-day match, a specific time for the tea interval need not necessarily be arranged, and it may be agreed to take this interval between the innings of a one-innings match.

(b) Changing the Agreed Time of Intervals

In the event of the ground, weather or light conditions causing a suspension of play, the umpires, after consultation with the captains, may decide in the interests of time-saving to bring forward the time of the luncheon or tea interval.

LAW 17. CESSATION OF PLAY

1. Call of Time

The umpire at the bowler's end shall call "time" on the cessation of play before any interval or interruption of play, at the end of each day's play, and at the conclusion of the match. See Law 27 (Appeals).

2. Removal of Bails

After the call of "time", the umpires shall remove the bails from both wickets.

3. Starting a Last Over

The last over before an interval or the close of play shall be started provided the umpire, after walking at his normal pace, has arrived at his position behind the stumps at the bowler's end before time has been reached.

4. Completion of the Last Over of a Session

The last over before an interval or the close of play shall be completed unless a batsman is out or retires during that over within two minutes of the interval or the close of play or unless the players have occasion to leave the field.

5. Completion of the Last Over of a Match

An over in progress at the close of play on the final day of a match shall be completed at the request of either captain, even if a wicket falls after time has been reached.

If, during the last over, the players have occasion to leave the field, the umpires shall call "time" and there shall be no resumption of play and the match shall be at an end.

6. Last Hour of Match – Number of Overs

The umpires shall indicate when one hour of playing time of the match remains according to the agreed hours of play. The next over after that moment shall be the first of a minimum of 20 six-ball overs (15 eight-ball overs), provided a result is not reached earlier or there is no interval or interruption of play.

7. Last Hour of Match – Intervals between Innings and Interruptions of Play

If, at the commencement of the last hour of the match, an interval or interruption of play is in progress or if, during the last hour, there is an interval between innings or an interruption of play, the minimum number of overs to be bowled on the resumption of play shall be reduced in proportion to the duration, within the last hour of the match, of any such interval or interruption.

The minimum number of overs to be bowled after the resumption of play shall be calculated as follows:

(a) In the case of an interval or interruption of play being in progress at the commencement of the last hour of the match, or in the case of a first interval or interruption, a deduction shall be made from the minimum of 20 six-ball overs (or 15 eight-ball overs).

(b) If there is a later interval or interruption, a further deduction shall be made from the minimum number of overs which should have been bowled following the last resumption of play.

(c) These deductions shall be based on the following factors:

(i) The number of overs already bowled in the last hour of the match or, in the case of a later interval or interruption, in the last session of play.

(ii) The number of overs lost as a result of the interval or interruption allowing one six-ball over for every full three minutes (or one eight-ball over for every full four minutes) of interval or interruption.

(iii) Any over left uncompleted at the end of an innings to be excluded from these calculations.

(iv) Any over of the minimum number to be played which is left uncompleted at the start of an interruption of play to be completed when play is resumed and to count as one over bowled.

(v) An interval to start with the end of an innings and to end ten minutes later; an interruption to start on the call of "time" and to end on the call of "play".

(d) In the event of an innings being completed and a new innings commencing during the last hour of the match, the number of overs to be bowled in the new innings shall be calculated on the basis of one six-ball over for every three minutes or part thereof remaining for play (or one eight-ball over for every four minutes or part thereof remaining for play); or alternatively on the basis that sufficient overs be bowled to enable the full minimum quota of overs to be completed under circumstances governed by (a), (b) and (c) above. In all such cases the alternative which allows the greater number of overs shall be employed.

8. Bowler Unable to Complete an Over during Last Hour of the Match

If, for any reason, a bowler is unable to complete an over during the period of play referred to in 6 above, Law 22.7 (Bowler Incapacitated or Suspended during an Over) shall apply.

LAW 18.   SCORING

1. A Run

The score shall be reckoned by runs. A run is scored:

(a) So often as the batsmen, after a hit or at any time while the ball is in play, shall have crossed and made good their ground from end to end.

(b) When a boundary is scored. See Law 19 (Boundaries).

(c) When penalty runs are awarded. See 6 below.

2. Short Runs

(a) If either batsman runs a short run, the umpire shall call and signal "one short" as soon as the ball becomes dead and that run shall not be scored. A run is short if a batsman fails to make good his ground on turning for a further run.

(b) Although a short run shortens the succeeding one, the latter, if completed, shall count.

(c) If either or both batsmen deliberately run short the umpire shall, as soon as he sees that the fielding side have no chance of dismissing either batsman, call and signal "dead ball" and disallow any runs attempted or previously scored. The batsmen shall return to their original ends.

(d) If both batsmen run short in one and the same run, only one run shall be deducted.

(e) Only if three or more runs are attempted can more than one be short and then, subject to (c) and (d) above, all runs so called shall be disallowed. If there has been more than one short run the umpires shall instruct the scorers as to the number of runs disallowed.

3. Striker Caught

If the striker is caught, no run shall be scored.

4. Batsman Run Out

If a batsman is run out, only that run which was being attempted shall not be scored. If, however, an injured striker himself is run out, no runs shall be scored. See Law 2.7 (Transgression of the Laws by an Injured Batsman or Runner).

5. Batsman Obstructing the Field

If a batsman is out Obstructing the Field, any runs completed before the obstruction occurs shall be scored unless such obstruction prevents a catch being made, in which case no runs shall be scored.

6. Runs Scored for Penalties

Runs shall be scored for penalties under Laws 20 (Lost Ball), 24 (No-ball), 25 (Wide-ball), 41.1 (Fielding the Ball) and for boundary allowances under Law 19 (Boundaries).

7. Batsman Returning to Wicket he has Left

If, while the ball is in play, the batsmen have crossed in running, neither shall return to the wicket he has left, even though a short run has been called or no run has been scored as in the case of a catch. Batsmen, however, shall return to the wickets they originally left in the cases of a boundary and of any disallowance of runs and of an injured batsman being, himself, run out. See Law 2.7 (Transgression by an Injured Batsman or Runner).

Note

(a) **Short Run**

A striker taking stance in front of his popping crease may run from that point without penalty.

LAW 19.   BOUNDARIES

1. The Boundary of the Playing Area

Before the toss for innings, the umpires shall agree with both captains on the boundary of the playing area. The boundary shall, if possible, be marked by a white line, a rope laid on the ground, or a fence. If flags or posts only are used to mark a boundary, the imaginary line joining such points shall be regarded as the boundary. An obstacle, or person, within the playing area shall not be regarded as a boundary unless so decided by the umpires before the toss for innings. Sightscreens within, or partially within, the playing area shall be regarded as the boundary and when the ball strikes or passes within or under or directly over any part of the screen, a boundary shall be scored.

2. Runs Scored for Boundaries

Before the toss for innings, the umpires shall agree with both captains the runs to be allowed for boundaries, and in deciding the allowance for them, the umpires and captains shall be guided by the prevailing custom of the ground. The allowance for a boundary shall normally be four runs, and six runs for all hits pitching over and clear of the boundary line or fence, even though the ball has been previously touched by a fieldsman. Six runs shall also be scored if a fieldsman, after catching a ball, carries it over the boundary. See Law 32 (Caught) Note (a). Six runs shall not be scored when a ball struck by the striker hits a sightscreen full pitch if the screen is within, or partially within, the playing area, but if the ball is struck directly over a sightscreen so situated, six runs shall be scored.

3. A Boundary

A boundary shall be scored and signalled by the umpire at the bowler's end whenever, in his opinion:

(a) A ball in play touches or crosses the boundary, however marked.

(b) A fieldsman with ball in hand touches or grounds any part of his person on or over a boundary line.

(c) A fieldsman with ball in hand grounds any part of his person over a boundary fence or board. This allows the fieldsman to touch or lean on or over a boundary fence or board in preventing a boundary.

4. Runs Exceeding Boundary Allowance

The runs completed at the instant the ball reaches the boundary shall count if they exceed the boundary allowance.

5. Overthrows or Wilful Act of a Fieldsman

If the boundary results from an overthrow or from the wilful act of a fieldsman, any runs already completed and the allowance shall be added to the score. The run in progress shall count provided that the batsmen have crossed at the instant of the throw or act.

Note

(a) Position of Sightscreens

Sightscreens should, if possible, be positioned wholly outside the playing area, as near as possible to the boundary line.

LAW 20.   LOST BALL

1. Runs Scored

If a ball in play cannot be found or recovered, any fieldsman may call "lost ball" when six runs shall be added to the score; but if more than six have been run before "lost ball" is called, as many runs as have been completed shall be scored. The run in progress shall count provided that the batsmen have crossed at the instant of the call of "lost ball".

2. How Scored

The runs shall be added to the score of the striker if the ball has been struck, but otherwise to the score of byes, leg-byes, no-balls or wides as the case may be.

LAW 21.   THE RESULT

1. A Win – Two-innings Matches

The side which has scored a total of runs in excess of that scored by the opposing side in its two completed innings shall be the winner.

2. A Win – One-innings Matches

(a) One-innings matches, unless played out as in 1 above, shall be decided on the first innings, but see Law 12.5 (Continuation after One Innings of Each Side).

(b) If the captains agree to continue play after the completion of one innings of each side in accordance with Law 12.5 (Continuation after One Innings of Each Side) and a result is not achieved on the second innings, the first innings result shall stand.

3. Umpires Awarding a Match

(a) A match shall be lost by a side which, during the match, (i) refuses to play, or (ii) concedes defeat, and the umpires shall award the match to the other side.

(b) Should both batsmen at the wickets or the fielding side leave the field at any time without the agreement of the umpires, this shall constitute a refusal to play and, on appeal, the umpires shall award the match to the other side in accordance with (a) above.

4. A Tie

The result of a match shall be a tie when the scores are equal at the conclusion of play, but only if the side batting last has completed its innings.

   If the scores of the completed first innings of a one-day match are equal, it shall be a tie but only if the match has not been played out to a further conclusion.

5. A Draw

A match not determined in any of the ways as in 1, 2, 3 and 4 above shall count as a draw.

6. Correctness of Result

Any decision as to the correctness of the scores shall be the responsibility of the umpires. See Law 3.14 (Correctness of Scores).

If, after the umpires and players have left the field in the belief that the match has been concluded, the umpires decide that a mistake in scoring has occurred, which affects the result, and provided time has not been reached, they shall order play to resume and to continue until the agreed finishing time unless a result is reached earlier.

If the umpires decide that a mistake has occurred and time has been reached, the umpires shall immediately inform both captains of the necessary corrections to the scores and, if applicable, to the result.

7. Acceptance of Result

In accepting the scores as notified by the scorers and agreed by the umpires, the captains of both sides thereby accept the result.

Notes

(a) Statement of Results
The result of a finished match is stated as a win by runs, except in the case of a win by the side batting last when it is by the number of wickets still then to fall.

(b) Winning Hit or Extras
As soon as the side has won, see 1 and 2 above, the umpire shall call "time", the match is finished, and nothing that happens thereafter other than as a result of a mistake in scoring (see 6 above) shall be regarded as part of the match.

However, if a boundary constitutes the winning hit – or extras – and the boundary allowance exceeds the number of runs required to win the match, such runs scored shall be credited to the side's total and, in the case of a hit, to the striker's score.

LAW 22.   THE OVER

1. Number of Balls

The ball shall be bowled from each wicket alternately in overs of either six or eight balls according to agreement before the match.

2. Call of "Over"

When the agreed number of balls has been bowled, and as the ball becomes dead or when it becomes clear to the umpire at the bowler's end that both the fielding side and the batsmen at the wicket have ceased to regard the ball as in play, the umpire shall call "over" before leaving the wicket.

3. No-ball or Wide-ball

Neither a no-ball nor a wide-ball shall be reckoned as one of the over.

4. Umpire Miscounting

If an umpire miscounts the number of balls, the over as counted by the umpire shall stand.

5. Bowler Changing Ends

A bowler shall be allowed to change ends as often as desired, provided only that he does not bowl two overs consecutively in an innings.

6. The Bowler Finishing an Over

A bowler shall finish an over in progress unless he be incapacitated or be suspended under Law 42.8 (The Bowling of Fast Short-pitched Balls), 9 (The Bowling of Fast High Full Pitches), 10 (Time Wasting) and 11 (Players Damaging the Pitch). If an over is left incomplete for any reason at the start of an interval or interruption of play, it shall be finished on the resumption of play.

7. Bowler Incapacitated or Suspended during an Over

If, for any reason, a bowler is incapacitated while running up to bowl the first ball of an over, or is incapacitated or suspended during an over, the umpire shall call and signal "dead ball" and another bowler shall be allowed to bowl or complete the over from the same end, provided only that he shall not bowl two overs, or part thereof, consecutively in one innings.

8. Position of Non-striker

The batsman at the bowler's end shall normally stand on the opposite side of the wicket to that from which the ball is being delivered, unless a request to do otherwise is granted by the umpire.

LAW 23.   DEAD BALL

1. The Ball Becomes Dead

When:

    (a) It is finally settled in the hands of the wicket-keeper or the bowler.

    (b) It reaches or pitches over the boundary.

    (c) A batsman is out.

    (d) Whether played or not, it lodges in the clothing or equipment of a batsman or the clothing of an umpire.

    (e) A ball lodges in a protective helmet worn by a member of the fielding side.

    (f) A penalty is awarded under Law 20 (Lost Ball) or Law 41.1 (Fielding the Ball).

    (g) The umpire calls "over" or "time".

2. Either Umpire Shall Call and Signal "Dead Ball"

When:

    (a) He intervenes in a case of unfair play.

    (b) A serious injury to a player or umpire occurs.

    (c) He is satisfied that, for an adequate reason, the striker is not ready to receive the ball and makes no attempt to play it.

    (d) The bowler drops the ball accidentally before delivery, or the ball does not leave his hand for any reason other than in an attempt to run out the non-striker (See Law 24.5 – Bowler Attempting to Run Out Non-striker before Delivery).

    (e) One or both bails fall from the striker's wicket before he receives delivery.

    (f) He leaves his normal position for consultation.

    (g) He is required to do so under Law 26.3 (Disallowance of Leg-byes), etc.

3. The Ball Ceases to be Dead

When:

    (a) The bowler starts his run-up or bowling action.

4. The Ball is Not Dead

When:

    (a) It strikes an umpire (unless it lodges in his dress).

    (b) The wicket is broken or struck down (unless a batsman is out thereby).

    (c) An unsuccessful appeal is made.

    (d) The wicket is broken accidentally either by the bowler during his delivery or by a batsman in running.

    (e) The umpire has called "no-ball" or "wide".

Notes

(a) **Ball Finally Settled**
Whether the ball is finally settled or not – see 1(a) above – must be a question for the umpires alone to decide.

(b) **Action on Call of ''Dead Ball''**
   (i) If ''dead ball'' is called prior to the striker receiving a delivery, the bowler shall be allowed an additional ball.
   (ii) If ''dead ball'' is called after the striker receives a delivery, the bowler shall not be allowed an additional ball, unless a ''no-ball'' or ''wide'' has been called.

LAW 24. NO-BALL

1. Mode of Delivery

The umpire shall indicate to the striker whether the bowler intends to bowl over or round the wicket, overarm or underarm, right or left-handed. Failure on the part of the bowler to indicate in advance a change in his mode of delivery is unfair and the umpire shall call and signal ''no-ball''.

2. Fair Delivery – The Arm

For a delivery to be fair the ball must be bowled, not thrown – see Note (a) below. If either umpire is not entirely satisfied with the absolute fairness of a delivery in this respect he shall call and signal ''no-ball'' instantly upon delivery.

3. Fair Delivery – The Feet

The umpire at the bowler's wicket shall call and signal ''no-ball'' if he is not satisfied that in the delivery stride:
   (a) The bowler's back foot has landed within and not touching the return crease or its forward extension; or
   (b) Some part of the front foot whether grounded or raised was behind the popping crease.

4. Bowler Throwing at Striker's Wicket before Delivery

If the bowler, before delivering the ball, throws it at the striker's wicket in an attempt to run him out, the umpire shall call and signal ''no-ball''. See Law 42.12 (Batsman Unfairly Stealing a Run) and Law 38 (Run Out).

5. Bowler Attempting to Run Out Non-striker before Delivery

If the bowler, before delivering the ball, attempts to run out the non-striker, any runs which result shall be allowed and shall be scored as no-balls. Such an attempt shall not count as a ball in the over. The umpire shall not call ''no-ball''. See Law 42.12 (Batsman Unfairly Stealing a Run).

6. Infringement of Laws by a Wicket-keeper or a Fieldsman

The umpire shall call and signal ''no-ball'' in the event of the wicket-keeper infringing Law 40.1 (Position of Wicket-keeper) or a fieldsman infringing Law 41.2 (Limitation of On-side Fieldsmen) or Law 41.3 (Position of Fieldsmen).

7. Revoking a Call

An umpire shall revoke the call ''no-ball'' if the ball does not leave the bowler's hand for any reason. See Law 23.2 (Either Umpire Shall Call and Signal ''Dead Ball'').

8. Penalty

A penalty of one run for a no-ball shall be scored if no runs are made otherwise.

9. Runs from a No-ball

The striker may hit a no-ball and whatever runs result shall be added to his score. Runs made otherwise from a no-ball shall be scored no-balls.

10. Out from a No-ball

The striker shall be out from a no-ball if he breaks Law 34 (Hit the Ball Twice) and either batsman may be run out or shall be given out if either breaks Law 33 (Handled the Ball) or Law 37 (Obstructing the Field).

11. Batsman Given Out off a No-ball

Should a batsman be given out off a no-ball the penalty for bowling it shall stand unless runs are otherwise scored.

Notes

(a) Definition of a Throw

A ball shall be deemed to have been thrown if, in the opinion of either umpire, the process of straightening the bowling arm, whether it be partial or complete, takes place during that part of the delivery swing which directly precedes the ball leaving the hand. This definition shall not debar a bowler from the use of the wrist in the delivery swing.

(b) No-ball Not Counting in Over

A no-ball shall not be reckoned as one of the over. See Law 22.3 (No-ball or Wide-ball).

LAW 25.   WIDE-BALL

1. Judging a Wide

If the bowler bowls the ball so high over or so wide of the wicket that, in the opinion of the umpire, it passes out of reach of the striker, standing in a normal guard position, the umpire shall call and signal "wide-ball" as soon as it has passed the line of the striker's wicket.

The umpire shall not adjudge a ball as being wide if:

(a) The striker, by moving from his guard position, causes the ball to pass out of his reach.

(b) The striker moves and thus brings the ball within his reach.

2. Penalty

A penalty of one run for a wide shall be scored if no runs are made otherwise.

3. Ball Coming to Rest in Front of the Striker

If a ball which the umpire considers to have been delivered comes to rest in front of the line of the striker's wicket, "wide" shall not be called. The striker has a right, without interference from the fielding side, to make one attempt to hit the ball. If the fielding side interfere, the umpire shall replace the ball where it came to rest and shall order the fieldsmen to resume the places they occupied in the field before the ball was delivered.

The umpire shall call and signal "dead ball" as soon as it is clear that the striker does not intend to hit the ball, or after the striker has made an unsuccessful attempt to hit the ball.

4. Revoking a Call

The umpire shall revoke the call if the striker hits a ball which has been called "wide".

5. Ball Not Dead

The ball does not become dead on the call of "wide-ball" – see Law 23.4 (The Ball is Not Dead).

6. Runs Resulting from a Wide

All runs which are run or result from a wide-ball which is not a no-ball shall be scored wide-balls, or if no runs are made one shall be scored.

7. Out from a Wide

The striker shall be out from a wide-ball if he breaks Law 35 (Hit Wicket), or Law 39 (Stumped). Either batsman may be run out and shall be out if he breaks Law 33 (Handled the Ball), or Law 37 (Obstructing the Field).

8. Batsman Given Out off a Wide

Should a batsman be given out off a wide, the penalty for bowling it shall stand unless runs are otherwise made.

Note

(a) Wide-ball Not Counting in Over
A wide-ball shall not be reckoned as one of the over – see Law 22.3 (No-ball or Wide-ball).

LAW 26.   BYE AND LEG-BYE

1. Byes

If the ball, not having been called "wide" or "no-ball", passes the striker without touching his bat or person, and any runs are obtained, the umpire shall signal "bye" and the run or runs shall be credited as such to the batting side.

2. Leg-byes

If the ball, not having been called "wide" or "no-ball", is unintentionally deflected by the striker's dress or person, except a hand holding the bat, and any runs are obtained the umpire shall signal "leg-bye" and the run or runs so scored shall be credited as such to the batting side.

Such leg-byes shall be scored only if, in the opinion of the umpire, the striker has:

    (a) Attempted to play the ball with his bat; or

    (b) Tried to avoid being hit by the ball.

3. Disallowance of Leg-byes

In the case of a deflection by the striker's person, other than in 2(a) and (b) above, the umpire shall call and signal "dead ball" as soon as one run has been completed or when it is clear that a run is not being attempted, or the ball has reached the boundary.

On the call and signal of "dead ball" the batsmen shall return to their original ends and no runs shall be allowed.

LAW 27.   APPEALS

1. Time of Appeals

The umpires shall not give a batsman out unless appealed to by the other side which shall be done prior to the bowler beginning his run-up or bowling action to deliver the next ball. Under Law 23.1 (g) (The Ball Becomes Dead), the ball is dead on "over" being called; this does not, however, invalidate an appeal made prior to the first ball of the following over provided "time" has not been called – see Law 17.1 (Call of Time).

2. An Appeal "How's That?"

An appeal "How's That?" shall cover all ways of being out.

3. Answering Appeals

The umpire at the bowler's wicket shall answer appeals before the other umpire in all cases except those arising out of Law 35 (Hit Wicket) or Law 39 (Stumped) or Law 38 (Run Out) when this occurs at the striker's wicket.

When either umpire has given a batsman not out, the other umpire shall, within his jurisdiction, answer the appeal or a further appeal, provided it is made in time in accordance with 1 above (Time of Appeals).

4. Consultation by Umpires

An umpire may consult with the other umpire on a point of fact which the latter may have been in a better position to see and shall then give his decision. If, after consultation, there is still doubt remaining the decision shall be in favour of the batsman.

5. Batsman Leaving his Wicket under a Misapprehension

The umpires shall intervene if satisfied that a batsman, not having been given out, has left his wicket under a misapprehension that he has been dismissed.

6. Umpire's Decision

The umpire's decision is final. He may alter his decision, provided that such alteration is made promptly.

7. Withdrawal of an Appeal

In exceptional circumstances the captain of the fielding side may seek permission of the umpire to withdraw an appeal provided the outgoing batsman has not left the playing area. If this is allowed, the umpire shall cancel his decision.

LAW 28.   THE WICKET IS DOWN

1. Wicket Down

The wicket is down if:

(a) Either the ball or the striker's bat or person completely removes either bail from the top of the stumps. A disturbance of a bail, whether temporary or not, shall not constitute a complete removal, but the wicket is down if a bail in falling lodges between two of the stumps.

(b) Any player completely removes with his hand or arm a bail from the top of the stumps, provided that the ball is held in that hand or in the hand of the arm so used.

(c) When both bails are off, a stump is struck out of the ground by the ball, or a player strikes or pulls a stump out of the ground, providing that the ball is held in the hand(s) or in the hand of the arm so used.

2. One Bail Off

If one bail is off, it shall be sufficient for the purpose of putting the wicket down to remove the remaining bail, or to strike or pull any of the three stumps out of the ground in any of the ways stated in 1 above.

3. All the Stumps Out of the Ground

If all the stumps are out of the ground, the fielding side shall be allowed to put back one or more stumps in order to have an opportunity of putting the wicket down.

4. Dispensing with Bails

If, owing to the strength of the wind, it has been agreed to dispense with the bails in accordance with Law 8, Note (a) (Dispensing with Bails), the decision as to when the wicket is down is one for the umpires to decide on the facts before them. In such circumstances and if the umpires so decide, the wicket shall be held to be down even though a stump has not been struck out of the ground.

Note

(a) Remaking the Wicket

If the wicket is broken while the ball is in play, it is not the umpire's duty to remake the wicket until the ball has become dead – see Law 23 (Dead Ball). A member of the fielding side, however, may remake the wicket in such circumstances.

LAW 29.   BATSMAN OUT OF HIS GROUND

1. When out of his Ground

A batsman shall be considered to be out of his ground unless some part of his bat in his hand or of his person is grounded behind the line of the popping crease.

LAW 30.   BOWLED

1. Out Bowled

The striker shall be out *Bowled* if:

  (a) His wicket is bowled down, even if the ball first touches his bat or person.

  (b) He breaks his wicket by hitting or kicking the ball on to it before the completion of a stroke, or as a result of attempting to guard his wicket. See Law 34.1 (Out Hit the Ball Twice).

Note

(a) Out Bowled – Not lbw

The striker is out bowled if the ball is deflected on to his wicket even though a decision against him would be justified under Law 36 (lbw).

LAW 31.   TIMED OUT

1. Out Timed Out

An incoming batsman shall be out *Timed Out* if he wilfully takes more than two minutes to come in – the two minutes being timed from the moment a wicket falls until the new batsman steps on to the field of play.

If this is not complied with and if the umpire is satisfied that the delay was wilful and if an appeal is made, the new batsman shall be given out by the umpire at the bowler's end.

2. Time to be Added

The time taken by the umpires to investigate the cause of the delay shall be added at the normal close of play.

Notes

(a) Entry in Scorebook

The correct entry in the scorebook when a batsman is given out under this Law is "timed out", and the bowler does not get credit for the wicket.

(b) Batsmen Crossing on the Field of Play

It is an essential duty of the captains to ensure that the in-going batsman passes the out-going one before the latter leaves the field of play.

LAW 32. CAUGHT

1. Out Caught

The striker shall be out *Caught* if the ball touches his bat or if it touches below the wrist his hand or glove, holding the bat, and is subsequently held by a fieldsman before it touches the ground.

2. A Fair Catch

A catch shall be considered to have been fairly made if:

    (a) The fieldsman is within the field of play throughout the act of making the catch.

        (i) The act of making the catch shall start from the time when the fieldsman first handles the ball and shall end when he both retains complete control over the further disposal of the ball and remains within the field of play.

        (ii) In order to be within the field of play, the fieldsman may not touch or ground any part of his person on or over a boundary line. When the boundary is marked by a fence or board the fieldsman may not ground any part of his person over the boundary fence or board, but may touch or lean over the boundary fence or board in completing the catch.

    (b) The ball is hugged to the body of the catcher or accidentally lodges in his dress or, in the case of the wicket-keeper, in his pads. However, a striker may not be caught if a ball lodges in a protective helmet worn by a fieldsman, in which case the umpire shall call and signal "dead ball". See Law 23 (Dead Ball).

    (c) The ball does not touch the ground even though a hand holding it does so in effecting the catch.

    (d) A fieldsman catches the ball, after it has been lawfully played a second time by the striker, but only if the ball has not touched the ground since being first struck.

    (e) A fieldsman catches the ball after it has touched an umpire, another fieldsman or the other batsman. However, a striker may not be caught if a ball has touched a protective helmet worn by a fieldsman.

    (f) The ball is caught off an obstruction within the boundary provided it has not previously been agreed to regard the obstruction as a boundary.

3. Scoring of Runs

If a striker is caught, no run shall be scored.

Notes

    (a) Scoring from an Attempted Catch
    When a fieldsman carrying the ball touches or grounds any part of his person on or over a boundary marked by a line, six runs shall be scored.

    (b) Ball Still in Play
    If a fieldsman releases the ball before he crosses the boundary, the ball will be considered to be still in play and it may be caught by another fieldsman. However, if the original fieldsman returns to the field of play and handles the ball, a catch may not be made.

LAW 33. HANDLED THE BALL

1. Out Handled the Ball

Either batsman on appeal shall be out *Handled the Ball* if he wilfully touches the ball while in play with the hand not holding the bat unless he does so with the consent of the opposite side.

Note

    (a) Entry in Scorebook
    The correct entry in the scorebook when a batsman is given out under this Law is "handled the ball", and the bowler does not get credit for the wicket.

LAW 34.   HIT THE BALL TWICE

1. Out Hit the Ball Twice

The striker, on appeal, shall be out *Hit the Ball Twice* if, after the ball is struck or is stopped by any part of his person, he wilfully strikes it again with his bat or person except for the sole purpose of guarding his wicket: this he may do with his bat or any part of his person other than his hands, but see Law 37.2 (Obstructing a Ball From Being Caught).

For the purpose of this Law, a hand holding the bat shall be regarded as part of the bat.

2. Returning the Ball to a Fieldsman

The striker, on appeal, shall be out under this Law if, without the consent of the opposite side, he uses his bat or person to return the ball to any of the fielding side.

3. Runs from Ball Lawfully Struck Twice

No runs except those which result from an overthrow or penalty – see Law 41 (The Fieldsman) – shall be scored from a ball lawfully struck twice.

Notes

(a) Entry in Scorebook
The correct entry in the scorebook when the striker is given out under this Law is ''hit the ball twice'', and the bowler does not get credit for the wicket.

(b) Runs Credited to the Batsman
Any runs awarded under 3 above as a result of an overthrow or penalty shall be credited to the striker, provided the ball in the first instance has touched the bat, or, if otherwise, as extras.

LAW 35.   HIT WICKET

1. Out Hit Wicket

The striker shall be out *Hit Wicket* if, while the ball is in play:

(a) His wicket is broken with any part of his person, dress, or equipment as a result of any action taken by him in preparing to receive or in receiving a delivery, or in setting off for his first run, immediately after playing, or playing at, the ball.

(b) He hits down his wicket whilst lawfully making a second stroke for the purpose of guarding his wicket within the provisions of Law 34.1 (Out Hit the Ball Twice).

Notes

(a) Not Out Hit Wicket
A batsman is not out under this Law should his wicket be broken in any of the ways referred to in 1(a) above if:

(i) It occurs while he is in the act of running, other than in setting off for his first run immediately after playing at the ball, or while he is avoiding being run out or stumped.

(ii) The bowler after starting his run-up or bowling action does not deliver the ball; in which case the umpire shall immediately call and signal ''dead ball''.

(iii) It occurs whilst he is avoiding a throw-in at any time.

LAW 36.   LEG BEFORE WICKET

1. Out lbw

The striker shall be out *lbw* in the circumstances set out below:

(a) Striker Attempting to Play the Ball
The striker shall be out lbw if he first intercepts with any part of his person, dress or equipment a fair ball which would have hit the wicket and which has not previously touched his bat or a hand holding the bat, provided that:

(i) The ball pitched in a straight line between wicket and wicket or on the off side of the striker's wicket, or was intercepted full pitch; and

(ii) The point of impact is in a straight line between wicket and wicket, even if above the level of the bails.

(b) Striker Making No Attempt to Play the Ball

The striker shall be out lbw even if the ball is intercepted outside the line of the off stump if, in the opinion of the umpire, he has made no genuine attempt to play the ball with his bat, but has intercepted the ball with some part of his person and if the other circumstances set out in (a) above apply.

LAW 37. OBSTRUCTING THE FIELD

1. Wilful Obstruction

Either batsman, on appeal, shall be out *Obstructing the Field* if he wilfully obstructs the opposite side by word or action.

2. Obstructing a Ball From Being Caught

The striker, on appeal, shall be out should wilful obstruction by either batsman prevent a catch being made.

This shall apply even though the striker causes the obstruction in lawfully guarding his wicket under the provisions of Law 34. See Law 34.1 (Out Hit the Ball Twice).

Notes

(a) Accidental Obstruction

The umpires must decide whether the obstruction was wilful or not. The accidental interception of a throw-in by a batsman while running does not break this Law.

(b) Entry in Scorebook

The correct entry in the scorebook when a batsman is given out under this Law is "obstructing the field", and the bowler does not get credit for the wicket.

LAW 38. RUN OUT

1. Out Run Out

Either batsman shall be out *Run Out* if in running or at any time while the ball is in play – except in the circumstances described in Law 39 (Stumped) – he is out of his ground and his wicket is put down by the opposite side. If, however, a batsman in running makes good his ground he shall not be out run out if he subsequently leaves his ground, in order to avoid injury, and the wicket is put down.

2. "No-ball" Called

If a no-ball has been called, the striker shall not be given run out unless he attempts to run.

3. Which Batsman Is Out

If the batsmen have crossed in running, he who runs for the wicket which is put down shall be out; if they have not crossed, he who has left the wicket which is put down shall be out. If a batsman remains in his ground or returns to his ground and the other batsman joins him there, the latter shall be out if his wicket is put down.

4. Scoring of Runs

If a batsman is run out, only that run which is being attempted shall not be scored. If, however, an injured striker himself is run out, no runs shall be scored. See Law 2.7 (Transgression of the Laws by an Injured Batsman or Runner).

Notes

(a) Ball Played on to Opposite Wicket

If the ball is played on to the opposite wicket, neither batsman is liable to be run out unless the ball has been touched by a fieldsman before the wicket is broken.

(b) Entry in Scorebook
The correct entry in the scorebook when a batsman is given out under this Law is "run out", and the bowler does not get credit for the wicket.

(c) Run Out off a Fieldsman's Helmet
If, having been played by a batsman, or having come off his person, the ball rebounds directly from a fieldsman's helmet on to the stumps, with either batsman out of his ground, the batsman shall be "not out".

LAW 39.   STUMPED

1. Out Stumped

The striker shall be out *Stumped* if, in receiving the ball, not being a no-ball, he is out of his ground otherwise than in attempting a run and the wicket is put down by the wicket-keeper without the intervention of another fieldsman.

2. Action by the Wicket-keeper

The wicket-keeper may take the ball in front of the wicket in an attempt to stump the striker only if the ball has touched the bat or person of the striker.

Note

(a) Ball Rebounding from Wicket-keeper's Person
The striker may be out stumped if, in the circumstances stated in 1 above, the wicket is broken by a ball rebounding from the wicket-keeper's person or equipment other than a protective helmet or is kicked or thrown by the wicket-keeper on to the wicket.

LAW 40.   THE WICKET-KEEPER

1. Position of Wicket-keeper

The wicket-keeper shall remain wholly behind the wicket until a ball delivered by the bowler touches the bat or person of the striker, or passes the wicket, or until the striker attempts a run.

In the event of the wicket-keeper contravening this Law, the umpire at the striker's end shall call and signal "no-ball" at the instant of delivery or as soon as possible thereafter.

2. Restriction on Actions of the Wicket-keeper

If the wicket-keeper interferes with the striker's right to play the ball and to guard his wicket, the striker shall not be out except under Laws 33 (Handled the Ball), 34 (Hit the Ball Twice), 37 (Obstructing the Field) and 38 (Run Out).

3. Interference with the Wicket-keeper by the Striker

If, in the legitimate defence of his wicket, the striker interferes with the wicket-keeper, he shall not be out, except as provided for in Law 37.2 (Obstructing a Ball From Being Caught).

LAW 41.   THE FIELDSMAN

1. Fielding the Ball

The fieldsman may stop the ball with any part of his person, but if he wilfully stops it otherwise, five runs shall be added to the run or runs already scored; if no run has been scored five penalty runs shall be awarded. The run in progress shall count provided that the batsmen have crossed at the instant of the act. If the ball has been struck, the penalty shall be added to the score of the striker, but otherwise to the score of byes, leg-byes, no-balls or wides as the case may be.

2. Limitation of On-side Fieldsmen

The number of on-side fieldsmen behind the popping crease at the instant of the bowler's delivery shall not exceed two. In the event of infringement by the fielding side the umpire at the striker's end shall call and signal "no-ball" at the instant of delivery or as soon as possible thereafter.

3. Position of Fieldsmen

Whilst the ball is in play and until the ball has made contact with the bat or the striker's person or has passed his bat, no fieldsman, other than the bowler, may stand on or have any part of his person extended over the pitch (measuring 22 yards/20.12m×10 feet/3.05m). In the event of a fieldsman contravening this Law, the umpire at the bowler's end shall call and signal "no-ball" at the instant of delivery or as soon as possible thereafter. See Law 40.1 (Position of Wicket-keeper).

4. Fieldsmen's Protective Helmets

Protective helmets, when not in use by members of the fielding side, shall be placed, if above the surface, only on the ground behind the wicket-keeper. In the event of the ball, when in play, striking a helmet whilst in this position, five penalty runs shall be awarded as laid down in Law 41.1 and Note (a).

Note

(a) Batsmen Changing Ends
The five runs referred to in 1 and 4 above are a penalty and the batsmen do not change ends solely by reason of this penalty.

LAW 42.   UNFAIR PLAY

1. Responsibility of Captains

The captains are responsible at all times for ensuring that play is conducted within the spirit of the game as well as within the Laws.

2. Responsibility of Umpires

The umpires are the sole judges of fair and unfair play.

3. Intervention by the Umpire

The umpires shall intervene without appeal by calling and signalling "dead ball" in the case of unfair play, but should not otherwise interfere with the progress of the game except as required to do so by the Laws.

4. Lifting the Seam

A player shall not lift the seam of the ball for any reason. Should this be done, the umpires shall change the ball for one of similar condition to that in use prior to the contravention. See Note (a).

5. Changing the Condition of the Ball

Any member of the fielding side may polish the ball provided that such polishing wastes no time and that no artificial substance is used. No one shall rub the ball on the ground or use any artificial substance or take any other action to alter the condition of the ball.

In the event of a contravention of this Law, the umpires, after consultation, shall change the ball for one of similar condition to that in use prior to the contravention.

This Law does not prevent a member of the fielding side from drying a wet ball, or removing mud from the ball. See Note (b).

6. Incommoding the Striker

An umpire is justified in intervening under this Law and shall call and signal "dead ball" if, in his opinion, any player of the fielding side incommodes the striker by any noise or action while he is receiving a ball.

7. Obstruction of a Batsman in Running

It shall be considered unfair if any fieldsman wilfully obstructs a batsman in running. In these circumstances the umpire shall call and signal "dead ball" and allow any completed runs and the run in progress, or alternatively any boundary scored.

8. The Bowling of Fast Short-pitched Balls

The bowling of fast short-pitched balls is unfair if, in the opinion of the umpire at the bowler's end, it constitutes an attempt to intimidate the striker. See Note (d).

Umpires shall consider intimidation to be the deliberate bowling of fast short-pitched balls which by their length, height and direction are intended or likely to inflict physical injury on the striker. The relative skill of the striker shall also be taken into consideration.

In the event of such unfair bowling, the umpire at the bowler's end shall adopt the following procedure:

(a) In the first instance the umpire shall call and signal "no-ball", caution the bowler and inform the other umpire, the captain of the fielding side and the batsmen of what has occurred.

(b) If this caution is ineffective, he shall repeat the above procedure and indicate to the bowler that this is a final warning.

(c) Both the above caution and final warning shall continue to apply even though the bowler may later change ends.

(d) Should the above warnings prove ineffective the umpire at the bowler's end shall:

(i) At the first repetition call and signal "no-ball" and when the ball is dead direct the captain to take the bowler off forthwith and to complete the over with another bowler, provided that the bowler does not bowl two overs or part thereof consecutively. See Law 22.7 (Bowler Incapacitated or Suspended during an Over).

(ii) Not allow the bowler, thus taken off, to bowl again in the same innings.

(iii) Report the occurrence to the captain of the batting side as soon as the players leave the field for an interval.

(iv) Report the occurrence to the executive of the fielding side and to any governing body responsible for the match, who shall take any further action which is considered to be appropriate against the bowler concerned.

9. The Bowling of Fast High Full Pitches

The bowling of fast high full pitches is unfair.

A fast high full-pitched ball is defined as a ball that passes, or would have passed, on the full above waist height of a batsman standing upright at the crease. Should a bowler bowl a fast high full-pitched ball, either umpire shall call and signal "no-ball" and adopt the procedure of caution, final warning, action against the bowler and reporting as set out in Law 42.8.

10. Time Wasting

Any form of time wasting is unfair.

(a) In the event of the captain of the fielding side wasting time or allowing any member of his side to waste time, the umpire at the bowler's end shall adopt the following procedure:

(i) In the first instance he shall caution the captain of the fielding side and inform the other umpire of what has occurred.

(ii) If this caution is ineffective he shall repeat the above procedure and indicate to the captain that this is a final warning.

(iii) The umpire shall report the occurrence to the captain of the batting side as soon as the players leave the field for an interval.

(iv) Should the above procedure prove ineffective the umpire shall report the occurrence to the executive of the fielding side and to any governing body responsible for that match, who shall take appropriate action against the captain and the players concerned.

(b) In the event of a bowler taking unnecessarily long to bowl an over the umpire at the bowler's end shall adopt the procedures, other than the calling of "no-ball", of caution, final warning, action against the bowler and reporting as set out in 8 above.

(c) In the event of a batsman wasting time (See Note (e)) other than in the manner described in Law 31 (Timed Out), the umpire at the bowler's end shall adopt the following procedure:

(i) In the first instance he shall caution the batsman and inform the other umpire at once, and the captain of the batting side, as soon as the players leave the field for an interval, of what has occurred.

(ii) If this proves ineffective, he shall repeat the caution, indicate to the batsman that this is a final warning and inform the other umpire.

(iii) The umpire shall report the occurrence to both captains as soon as the players leave the field for an interval.

(iv) Should the above procedure prove ineffective, the umpire shall report the occurrence to the executive of the batting side and to any governing body responsible for that match, who shall take appropriate action against the player concerned.

11. Players Damaging the Pitch

The umpires shall intervene and prevent players from causing damage to the pitch which may assist the bowlers of either side. See Note (c).

(a) In the event of any member of the fielding side damaging the pitch, the umpire shall follow the procedure of caution, final warning and reporting as set out in 10(a) above.

(b) In the event of a bowler contravening this Law by running down the pitch after delivering the ball, the umpire at the bowler's end shall first caution the bowler. If this caution is ineffective the umpire shall adopt the procedures, other than the calling of ''no-ball'', as set out in 8 above.

(c) In the event of a batsman damaging the pitch the umpire at the bowler's end shall follow the procedures of caution, final warning and reporting as set out in 10(c) above.

12. Batsman Unfairly Stealing a Run

Any attempt by the batsman to steal a run during the bowler's run-up is unfair. Unless the bowler attempts to run out either batsman – see Law 24.4 (Bowler Throwing at Striker's Wicket before Delivery) and Law 24.5 (Bowler Attempting to Run Out Non-striker before Delivery) – the umpire shall call and signal ''dead ball'' as soon as the batsmen cross in any such attempt to run. The batsmen shall then return to their original wickets.

13. Player's Conduct

In the event of a player failing to comply with the instructions of an umpire, criticising his decisions by word or action, or showing dissent, or generally behaving in a manner which might bring the game into disrepute, the umpire concerned shall, in the first place, report the matter to the other umpire and to the player's captain, requesting the latter to take action. If this proves ineffective, the umpire shall report the incident as soon as possible to the executive of the player's team and to any governing body responsible for the match, who shall take any further action which is considered appropriate against the player or players concerned.

Notes

(a) **The Condition of the Ball**
Umpires shall make frequent and irregular inspections of the condition of the ball.

(b) **Drying of a Wet Ball**
A wet ball may be dried on a towel or with sawdust.

(c) **Danger Area**
The danger area on the pitch, which must be protected from damage by a bowler, shall be regarded by the umpires as the area contained by an imaginary line 4 feet/1.22m from the popping crease, and parallel to it, and within two imaginary and parallel lines drawn down the pitch from points on that line 1 foot/30.48cm on either side of the middle stump.

(d) Fast Short-pitched Balls

As a guide, a fast short-pitched ball is one which pitches short and passes, or would have passed, above the shoulder height of the striker standing in a normal batting stance at the crease.

(e) Time Wasting by Batsmen

Other than in exceptional circumstances, the batsman should always be ready to take strike when the bowler is ready to start his run-up.

CHANGE IN THE LAWS

The following change in the Laws of Cricket has been made since the publication of *Wisden* in 1997.

Law 3 (Umpires) Note (d) has been amended from ''The umpires should suspend play only when they consider that the conditions are so bad that it is unreasonable or dangerous to continue'' to ''The umpires should suspend play when they consider [etc]''.

REGULATIONS OF THE INTERNATIONAL CRICKET COUNCIL

Extracts

1. Standard Playing Conditions

In July 1995, ICC Full Members adopted standard playing conditions to apply to all Tests and one-day internationals for an initial three-year period. These include the following:

Duration of Test Matches

Test matches shall be of five days' scheduled duration. The two participating countries may:

(a) Provide for a rest day during the match, and/or a reserve day after the scheduled days of play.

(b) Play on any scheduled rest day, conditions and circumstances permitting, should a full day's play be lost on any day prior to the rest day.

(c) Play on any scheduled reserve day, conditions and circumstances permitting, should a full day's play be lost on any day. Play shall not take place on more than five days.

(d) Make up time lost in excess of five minutes in each day's play owing to circumstances outside the game, other than acts of God.

Hours of Play and Minimum Overs in the Day in Test Matches

1. Start and cessation times shall be determined by the home board, subject to there being six hours scheduled for play per day (Pakistan a minimum of five and a half hours).

(a) Play shall continue on each day until the completion of a minimum number of overs or until the scheduled or rescheduled cessation time, whichever is the later. The minimum number of overs to be completed, unless an innings ends or an interruption occurs, shall be:

(i) on days other than the last day – a minimum of 90 overs.

(ii) on the last day – a minimum of 75 overs (or 15 overs per hour) for playing time other than the last hour when a minimum of 15 six-ball overs shall be bowled. All calculations with regard to suspensions of play or the start of a new innings shall be based on one over for each full four minutes. If, however, at any time after 30 minutes of the last hour have elapsed both captains (the batsmen at the wicket may act for their captain) accept that there is no prospect of a result to the match, they may agree to cease play at that time.

Subject to weather and light, except in the last hour of the match, in the event of play being suspended for any reason other than normal intervals, the playing time on that day shall be extended by the amount of time lost up to a maximum of one hour. The minimum number of overs to be bowled shall be in accordance with the provisions of this clause and the cessation time shall be rescheduled accordingly.

(b) When an innings ends, a minimum number of overs shall be bowled from the start of the new innings. The number of overs to be bowled shall be calculated at the rate of one over for each full four minutes to enable a minimum of 90 overs to be bowled in a day. The last hour of the match shall be excluded from this calculation (see (a) (ii)).

Where a change of innings occurs during a day's play in the event of the team bowling second being unable to complete its overs by the scheduled cessation time, play shall continue until the required number of overs have been completed.

2. Either captain may decide to play 30 minutes (a minimum eight overs) extra time at the end of any day other than the last day if, in their opinion, it would bring about a definite result on that day. If it is decided to play such extra time, the whole period shall be played out even though the possibility of finishing the match may have disappeared before the full period has expired. The time by which play is extended on any day shall be deducted from the total number of hours of play remaining and the match shall end earlier on the final day by that amount of time.

Use of Lights: Experimental Condition for one year from September 1, 1997, subject to both Boards' agreement before the tour

If, in the opinion of the umpires, natural light is deteriorating to an unfit level, they shall authorise the ground authorities to use the available artificial lighting so that the match can continue in acceptable conditions.

The lights are only to be used to enable a full day's play to be completed as provided for in Clause 1 above. In the event of power failure or lights malfunction, the existing provisions of Clause 1 shall apply.

Once the lights have been turned on, they must remain on for the remainder of the day's play.

The Bowling of Fast, Short-Pitched Balls: Law 42.8

1. A bowler shall be limited to two fast, short-pitched deliveries per over.

2. A fast, short-pitched ball is defined as a ball which passes or would have passed above the shoulder height of the batsman standing upright at the crease.

3. In the event of a bowler bowling more than two fast, short-pitched deliveries in an over, either umpire shall call and signal ''no-ball'' on each occasion.

4. The penalty for a fast, short-pitched no-ball shall be two runs, plus any runs scored from the delivery.

5. The umpire shall call and signal ''no-ball'' and then raise the other arm across the chest.

Where a bowler delivers a third fast, short-pitched ball in one over which is also a no-ball under Law 24, e.g. a front-foot no-ball, the penalty will be two runs plus any runs scored from that delivery, i.e. the greater penalty will apply. The umpire shall also adopt the procedures of caution, final warning, action against the bowler and reporting as set out in Law 42.8.

The above Regulation is not a substitute for Law 42.8 (as amended below), which umpires are able to apply at any time:

The bowling of fast, short-pitched balls is unfair if the umpire at the bowler's end considers that, by their repetition and taking into account their length, height and direction, they are likely to inflict physical injury on the striker, irrespective of the protective clothing and equipment he may be wearing. The relative skill of the striker shall also be taken into consideration.

The umpire at the bowler's end shall adopt the procedures of caution, final warning, action against the bowler and reporting as set out in Law 42.8.

New Ball: Law 5.4

The captain of the fielding side shall have the choice of taking a new ball any time after 80 overs have been bowled with the previous ball.

Ball Lost or Becoming Unfit for Play: Law 5.5

In the event of a ball during play being lost or, in the opinion of the umpires, being unfit for play through normal use, the umpires shall allow it to be replaced by one that in their opinion has had a similar amount of wear. If the ball is to be replaced, the umpires shall inform the batsmen.

Practice on the Field: Law 15.2

At no time on any day of the match shall there be any bowling or batting practice on the pitch or the square, except in official netted practice pitch areas. In addition there shall be no bowling or batting practice on any part of the square or the area immediately parallel to the match pitch after the commencement of play on any day. Any fielder contravening this Law may not bowl his next over.

No practice may take place on the field if, in the opinion of the umpires, it could result in a waste of time.

Fieldsman Leaving the Field: Law 2.8

No fieldsman shall leave the field or return during a session of play without the consent of the umpire at the bowler's end. The umpire's consent is also necessary if a substitute is required for a fieldsman at the start of play or when his side returns to the field after an interval.

If a member of the fielding side does not take the field at the start of play, leaves the field, or fails to return after an interval and is absent from the field longer than 15 minutes, he shall not be permitted to bowl in that innings after his return until he has been on the field for at least that length of playing time for which he was absent. In the event of a follow-on, this restriction will, if necessary, continue into the second innings. Nor shall he be permitted to bat unless or until, in the aggregate, he has returned to the field and/or his side's innings has been in progress for at least that length of playing time for which he has been absent or, if earlier, when his side has lost five wickets. The restrictions shall not apply if he has suffered an external blow (as opposed to an internal injury such as a pulled muscle) while participating earlier in the match and consequently been forced to leave the field, nor if he has been absent for exceptional and acceptable reasons (other than injury or illness) and consent for a substitute has been granted by the opposing captain.

2. Classification of First-Class Matches

1. Definitions

A match of three or more days' duration between two sides of 11 players played on natural turf pitches on international standard grounds and substantially conforming with standard playing conditions shall be regarded as a first-class fixture.

2. Rules

(a) Full Members of ICC shall decide the status of matches of three or more days' duration played in their countries.

(b) In matches of three or more days' duration played in countries which are not Full Members of ICC, except Bangladesh and Kenya (see 2.3 (k) below):

(i) If the visiting team comes from a country which is a Full Member of ICC, that country shall decide the status of matches.

(ii) If the visiting team does not come from a country which is a Full Member of ICC, or is a Commonwealth team composed of players from different countries, ICC shall decide the status of matches.

Notes

(a) Governing bodies agree that the interest of first-class cricket will be served by ensuring that first-class status is *not* accorded to any match in which one or other of the teams taking part cannot on a strict interpretation of the definition be adjudged first-class.

(b) In case of any disputes arising from these Rules, the Chief Executive of ICC shall refer the matter for decision to the Council, failing unanimous agreement by postal communication being reached.

3. First-Class Status

The following matches shall be regarded as first-class, subject to the provisions of 2.1 (Definitions) being complied with:

(a) **In Great Britain and Ireland:** (i) County Championship matches. (ii) Official representative tourist matches from Full Member countries unless specifically excluded. (iii) MCC v any first-class county. (iv) Oxford v Cambridge and either University against first-class counties. (v) Scotland v Ireland.

(b) **In Australia:** (i) Sheffield Shield matches. (ii) Matches played by teams representing states of the Commonwealth of Australia between each other or against opponents adjudged first-class.

(c) **In India:** (i) Ranji Trophy matches. (ii) Duleep Trophy matches. (iii) Irani Trophy matches. (iv) Matches played by teams representing state or regional associations affiliated to the Board of Control between each other or against opponents adjudged first-class. (v) All three-day matches played against representative visiting sides.

(d) **In New Zealand:** (i) Shell Trophy matches. (ii) Matches played by teams representing major associations of the North and South Islands, between each other or against opponents adjudged first-class.

(e) **In Pakistan:** (i) Matches played by teams representing divisional associations affiliated to the Pakistan Cricket Board, between each other or against teams adjudged first-class. (ii) Quaid-e-Azam Trophy matches. (iii) PCB Patron's Trophy matches. (iv) PCB Pentangular Trophy matches.

(f) **In South Africa:** (i) Supersport Series four-day matches between Boland, Border, Eastern Province, Free State, Gauteng, Griqualand West, Natal, Northerns, Western Province. (ii) The United Cricket Board Bowl competition three-day matches between Easterns, North West and the B teams of Eastern Province, Natal, Northerns and Western Province.

(g) **In Sri Lanka:** (i) Matches of three days or more against touring sides adjudged first-class. (ii) Inter-Club Division I tournament matches played over three days for the P. Saravanamuttu Trophy.

(h) **In West Indies:** Matches played by teams representing Barbados, Guyana, Jamaica, the Leeward Islands, Trinidad & Tobago and the Windward Islands, either for the President's Cup or against other opponents adjudged first-class.

(i) **In Zimbabwe:** (i) Matches of three days or more against touring sides adjudged first-class. (ii) Logan Cup competition three-day matches between Mashonaland, Mashonaland A and Matabeleland.

(j) **In all Full Member countries represented on the Council:** (i) Test matches and matches against teams adjudged first-class played by official touring teams. (ii) Official Test Trial matches. (iii) Special matches between teams adjudged first-class by the governing body or bodies concerned.

(k) **In Bangladesh and Kenya:** (i) Matches between a Full Member and either country. (ii) Matches between teams adjudged first-class and either country. (iii) Matches between both countries.

3. Classification of One-Day International Matches

The following shall be classified as one-day internationals:

(a) All matches played between the Full Member countries of ICC as part of an official tour itinerary.

(b) All matches played as part of an official tournament by Full Member countries. These need not necessarily be held in a Full Member country.

(c) All matches played in the official World Cup competition, including matches involving Associate Member countries.

(d) All matches between the Full Members and Bangladesh or Kenya.

(e) Matches between Bangladesh and Kenya on natural turf pitches conforming with standard playing conditions.

4. Qualification Rules for Test Matches and One-Day International Matches

Qualification by Birth

A cricketer is qualified to play in Tests, one-day internationals or any other representative cricket match for the country of his birth provided he has not played in Tests, one-day internationals or, after October 1, 1994, in any other representative cricket match for any other Member country during the two immediately preceding years.

Qualification by Residence

A cricketer is qualified to play in Tests, one-day internationals or in any other representative cricket match for any Full or Associate Member country in which he has resided for at least 183 days in each of the four immediately preceding years provided that he has not played in Tests, one-day internationals or, after October 1, 1994, in any other representative cricket match for any other Member country during that period of four years.

Notes: "Representative cricket match" means any cricket match in which a team representing a Member country at Under-19 level or above takes part, including Tests and one-day internationals.

The governing body for cricket of any Member country may impose more stringent qualification rules for that country.

ICC CODE OF CONDUCT

1. The captains are responsible at all times for ensuring that play is conducted within the spirit of the game as well as within the Laws.

2. Players and team officials shall not at any time engage in conduct unbecoming to an international player or team official which could bring them or the game into disrepute.

3. Players and team officials must at all times accept the umpire's decision. Players must not show dissent at the umpire's decision.

4. Players and team officials shall not intimidate, assault or attempt to intimidate or assault an umpire, another player or a spectator.

5. Players and team officials shall not use crude or abusive language (known as "sledging") nor make offensive gestures.

6. Players, umpires and team officials shall not use or in any way be concerned in the use or distribution of illegal drugs.

7. Players, umpires and team officials shall not disclose or comment upon any alleged breach of the Code or upon any hearing, report or decision arising from such breach.

8. Players, umpires and team officials shall not make any public pronouncement or media comment which is detrimental either to the game in general; or to a particular tour in which they are involved; or about any tour between other countries which is taking place; or to relations between the Boards of the competing teams.

9. Players, umpires and team officials shall not engage, directly or indirectly, in betting, gambling or any form of financial speculation on the outcome of any cricket match to which this Code applies and in which the player is a participant or with which a team official is associated or on any event which, in the opinion of the referee, shall be connected with any such cricket match the purpose (or pretended purpose) of which is to benefit such player or team official either directly or indirectly whether financially or otherwise. Players, umpires and team officials shall not accept any form of inducement which is considered by the referee to be likely to affect the performance of any player involved in any such cricket match adversely.

REGULATIONS FOR FIRST-CLASS MATCHES IN BRITAIN, 1997

Hours of Play

Four-day matches:

1st, 2nd, 3rd days .... 11.00 a.m. to 6.30 p.m.
4th day .... 11.00 a.m. to 6.00 p.m.

Three-day matches:

1st, 2nd days .... 11.30 a.m. to 6.30 p.m. (11.00 a.m. to 6.30 p.m. in tourist matches and Oxford v Cambridge)
3rd day .... 11.00 a.m. to 6.00 p.m.

Note: The hours of play, including intervals, are brought forward by half an hour for matches scheduled to start in September.

(i) (In Championship and tourist matches) Play shall continue on each day until the completion of a minimum number of overs or until the scheduled cessation time, whichever is the later. The minimum number of overs, unless an innings ends or an interruption occurs, shall be 104 on days other than the last day, and 80 on the last day before the last hour (98 and 75 respectively in tourist matches).

(ii) Where there is a change of innings during the day (except during an interval or suspension of play), two overs will be deducted from the minimum number.

(iii) If interruptions for weather or light occur, other than in the last hour of the match, the minimum number of overs shall be reduced by one over for each full $3\frac{3}{4}$ minutes (4 in tourist matches) of the aggregate playing time lost.

(iv) On the last day, if any of the minimum of 80 overs (75 in tourist matches), or as recalculated, have not been bowled when one hour of scheduled playing time remains, the last hour of the match shall be the hour immediately following the completion of those overs.

(v) Law 17.6 and 17.7 will apply except that a minimum of 16 six-ball overs (15 in tourist matches) shall be bowled in the last hour, and *all* calculations with regard to suspensions of play or the start of a new innings shall be based on one over for each full $3\frac{3}{4}$ (4) minutes. (In all matches) If, however, at 5.30 p.m. both captains accept that there is no prospect of a result or of either side gaining any further first-innings bonus points, they may agree to cease play at that time or at any time after 5.30 p.m.

(vi) (In all matches) The captains may agree or, in the event of disagreement, the umpires may decide to play 30 minutes (a minimum eight overs in Championship and tourist matches, or ten in other domestic matches) extra time at the end of any day other than the last day if, in their opinion, it would bring about a definite result on that day. In the event of the possibility of a finish disappearing before the full period has expired, the whole period must be played out. The time by which play is extended on any day shall be deducted from the total number of hours remaining in the match, and the match shall end earlier on the last day by the actual amount of time by which play was extended.

(vii) (In Championship and tourist matches) Notwithstanding any other provision, there shall be no further play on any day, other than the last day, if a wicket falls or a batsman retires, or if the players leave the field during the last minimum over within two minutes of the scheduled cessation time or thereafter.

(viii) An over completed on resumption of a new day's play shall be disregarded in calculating minimum overs for that day.

(ix) Fractions are to be ignored in all calculations re the number of overs.

(x) The scoreboard shall show the total number of overs bowled with the ball in use and the minimum number remaining to be bowled in a day.

Intervals

Lunch: 1.15 p.m. to 1.55 p.m. (1st, 2nd [3rd] days) in Championship and tourist matches and Oxford v Cambridge, 1.30 p.m. to 2.10 p.m. in others

1.00 p.m. to 1.40 p.m. (final day)

In the event of lunch being taken early because an innings ends or because of a stoppage caused by weather or bad light within ten minutes of the scheduled time (Law 16.2), the interval shall be limited to 40 minutes.

Tea: (Championship matches) A tea interval of 20 minutes shall normally be taken at 4.10 p.m. (3.40 p.m. on final day), or when 32 overs or less remain to be bowled (except on final day). The over in progress shall be completed unless a batsman is out or retires during that over within two minutes of the interval or the players have occasion to leave the field.

If an innings ends or there is a stoppage caused by weather within 30 minutes of the scheduled time, the tea interval shall be taken immediately. There will be no tea interval if the scheduled timing for the cessation of play is earlier than 5.30 p.m.

(Other matches) 4.10 p.m. to 4.30 p.m. (1st, 2nd [3rd] days), 3.40 p.m. to 4.00 p.m. (final day).

Substitutes

(Domestic matches only) Law 2.1 will apply, but in addition:

No substitute may take the field until the player for whom he is to substitute has been absent from the field for five consecutive complete overs, with the exception that if a fieldsman sustains an obvious, serious injury or is taken ill, a substitute shall be allowed immediately. In the event of any disagreement between the two sides as to the seriousness of an injury or illness, the umpires shall adjudicate. If a player leaves the field during an over, the remainder of that over shall not count in the calculation of the five complete overs.

A substitute shall be allowed by right immediately in the event of a cricketer currently playing in a Championship match being required to join the England team for a Test match (or one-day international). Such a substitute may be permitted to bat or bowl in that match, subject to the approval of the ECB. The cricketer who is substituted shall take no further part in the match, even though he may not be required by England. If batting at the time, he shall retire "not out" and his substitute may be permitted to bat later in that innings subject to the approval of the ECB.

Fieldsman Leaving the Field

ICC regulations apply (see pages 1366) but without mention of the follow-on, except in tourist matches, and with the explanation that "external blow" should include, but not be restricted to, collisions with boundary boards, clashes of heads, heavy falls etc.

New Ball

The captain of the fielding side shall have the choice of taking the new ball after 100 overs (80 in tourist matches) have been bowled with the old one.

Covering of Pitches and Bowler's Run-up

(Domestic matches) The whole pitch shall be covered:

(a) The night before the match and, if necessary, until the first ball is bowled; and whenever necessary and possible at any time prior to that during the preparation of the pitch.

(b) On each night of the match and, if necessary, throughout any rest days.

(c) In the event of play being suspended on account of bad light or rain, during the specified hours of play.

The bowler's run-up shall be covered to a distance of at least ten yards, with a width of four yards, as will the areas ten feet either side of the length of the pitch.

Declarations

Law 14 will apply, but, in addition, a captain may also forfeit his first innings, subject to the provisions set out in Law 14.2. If, due to weather conditions, a County Championship match has not started when less than eight hours' playing time remains, the first innings of each side shall automatically be forfeited and a one-innings match played.

RAISING THE STANDARD

THE PROPOSALS

ECB chairman Lord MacLaurin and chief executive Tim Lamb unveiled the board's proposals for the future of cricket in England and Wales, a document entitled "Raising the Standard", on August 5. Its stated aim was to enable cricketers from schoolchildren to Test players to perform to their maximum potential; a successful and vibrant England team was at the top of the agenda, but cricket in general should be more competitive, more appealing and more exciting.

School and youth cricket

The Board proposed rationalising the organisation of the game at school, junior and youth level. In schools, a new "development game" – one step up from Kwik Cricket – should be introduced to expose more secondary schoolchildren to cricket. Links between schools and local clubs should be encouraged. County boards should help to organise inter-school and inter-district cricket and co-ordinate junior county representative cricket, ensuring that the best young cricketers did not suffer from competing demands. The youth game should be encouraged to adopt "time" cricket rather than limited overs. At Under-17 and Under-19 levels, players should be introduced to the two-day "grade" format, so that batsmen could learn to play longer innings and bowlers to take wickets rather than contain the batting.

Adult cricket below first-class level

The report recognised the enormous divide between the recreational and first-class games, and argued that England were weakened by having to draw on a relatively small closed shop of contracted professionals. It aimed to enable players to progress seamlessly from club and non-first-class representative cricket upwards. Three potential feeders for the first-class game were identified: the top tier of club cricket, the Minor Counties and County-Board sides, and the present competition for the first-class counties' Second Elevens. The report proposed the introduction of a national network of Premier Leagues for top clubs, building on existing leagues, by 1999. These would ideally play two-day "grade" cricket and take part in a new national knockout cup. Meanwhile, the Second Eleven competition would be wound down from 1998, and there would be a move towards integrating the Second Elevens with the 20 Minor Counties in a 38-county competition playing two-day "grade" cricket. First-class counties would employ fewer contracted cricketers – enough to provide a first-class squad rather than both a first and second team – and the players thus released would strengthen the Premier Leagues and compete for another chance to enter the first-class game. Further universities, in addition to Oxford and Cambridge, should be established as centres of cricketing excellence. Elsewhere in recreational cricket, the ECB would integrate with the Women's Cricket Association, and also promote cricket for disabled people.

First-class cricket

The report argued that there should be fewer first-class matches, to create a better balance between matchplay, rest and practice. Top county players currently played approximately 100 days a year, and internationals even more. More time off, more and better coaching and better practice facilities were recommended. The county programme should be more competitive, appealing to spectators (and staged when they were free to attend), and should give counties greater financial independence, while preserving all 18 first-class counties as centres of excellence. The current four-day Championship format, as opposed to three-day games on uncovered pitches, would be maintained. The report rejected the argument for two divisions with promotion and relegation, on the grounds that it would penalise counties providing Test players, discourage gambling on youth, threaten the survival of the poorer counties, and provide either eight matches per team (too few) or 16 (too many). It also rejected a competition of regional teams sitting above the County Championship, though matches between regional teams and touring Test sides were proposed.

The report's preferred option was a three-conference system in which each team would play 14 first-class matches. The 18 counties would be divided into three groups, A, B and C. Each team in Conference A would play each team in Conferences B and C – a total of 12 matches. The A teams would thus compete against each other on equal terms, by facing exactly the same opponents, but would not actually play each other. The season would end with three rounds of play-offs, in which the top teams in each of the three conferences would play each other (A v B, B v C, C v A) for the title of Champion County; the second-placed teams would play each other to determine fourth to sixth placings; and so on down to the bottom three teams, whose play-offs would determine 16th to 18th placings. Prize money would be guaranteed for the top six teams, and for the winners of the other four groups of play-offs, so that there would be something at stake even for the three teams at the bottom of the conferences. Batting and bowling points would be used at the conference stage, but other systems, such as first-innings points, might be used in the play-offs.

One-day cricket

It was proposed that, from 1999, the NatWest Trophy should be remodelled on the lines of the FA Cup. The number of teams competing would rise from 32 to 60 – 18 first-class counties, the 38 County Board teams, Ireland, Scotland, Holland and Denmark. The 42 non-first-class teams would contest the opening two rounds, competing for 14 places in the third round, when the 18 first-class counties would join in; all non-first-class qualifiers would be guaranteed home fixtures. The Benson and Hedges Cup would be abandoned after 1998, and the Sunday League superseded by a 50-overs National League. This would split the 18 first-class counties into two divisions (to be determined by 1998 Sunday League placings), with promotion and relegation (three up, three down) in future seasons. Counties would play the other eight teams in their own division twice, and the nine teams in the other division once, making 25 games. Flexible schedules would enable counties to stage midweek fixtures, floodlight or daylight, if they so wished.

FIRST-CLASS FORUM

The First-Class Forum met at Lord's on September 2 to discuss the proposals contained in "Raising the Standard". They expressed little enthusiasm for the proposed three-conference format for the County Championship and several asked for the option of a two-division Championship with promotion and relegation instead. On September 8, the ECB wrote to Forum members offering three alternatives to the conferences: two divisions; the existing round-robin Championship; or an enhanced version of the existing Championship with the top eight teams competing in a Super Cup knockout in May and June the following season. The bottom four teams would be drawn against one another when the first-class counties entered the third round of the NatWest Trophy.

ECB MEETINGS

The First-Class Forum and Recreational Forum both met at Lord's on September 15 to vote on the proposals in "Raising the Standard". The proposed changes to the recreational game were accepted. However, the First-Class Forum rejected major structural change to the County Championship. The two-division format was rejected along with the conferences. Seven of the 18 counties supported two divisions: the six who play on Test grounds plus Worcestershire. It was agreed to retain the single-division Championship, with a Super Cup for the top eight and penalties for the bottom four in the NatWest Trophy draw, as proposed on September 8.

The planned increase in one-day county cricket was also rejected. The two-division National League was agreed but with teams playing only those in their own division i.e. 16 fixtures not 25. The expanded NatWest Trophy was accepted, with the abolition of the Benson and Hedges Cup and Sunday League. The First-Class Forum agreed in principle to reduce county staffs and to improve cricket management and practice facilities. For the time being, England players would remain contracted to counties, not to the ECB, and overseas players would remain on the same basis as in 1997. The home international programme would include five or six Tests and six or seven one-day internationals. The tourists would also play regional teams, though these should not replace traditional county matches.

In 1998, the Second Eleven Championship would be reduced, and a new one-day competition for the 38 County Board teams would be introduced, while the County Boards of the first-class counties would also play a two-day knockout competition with a view to combining with the Minor Counties equivalent at a later date. Oxford and Cambridge would retain their first-class status for the present, with the possibility kept open of such status being extended to other universities.

OTHER MEETINGS AND DECISIONS IN 1997

ENGLAND SELECTORS' APPOINTMENT

On March 13, the ECB's England Management Advisory Committee appointed David Graveney chairman of selectors. It was the first time the appointment had been made in this manner; under the old TCCB, England selectors were elected by the counties. Graveney had put himself forward a year earlier but withdrew when his employers, the Cricketers' Association, told him the role would conflict with his job as their general secretary. But now that the chairman's former disciplinary duties had been transferred to the Management Committee, the Association cleared him to stand. Mike Gatting and Graham Gooch were also appointed selectors. Gooch and Graveney, who had served as selectors the previous year, were to hold office until February 28, 1999, Gatting until February 28, 1998.

ICC SPECIAL MEETING

At a special general meeting held in Kuala Lumpur on March 23, the International Cricket Council agreed on a new governmental structure to end the bitterness created at the 1996 annual meeting, when the organisation failed to agree on a new chairman. The plan was based on proposals drawn up by Sir John Anderson, chairman of New Zealand Cricket. Instead of a chairman, ICC will have a president, an appointment which will be assigned to a member country, who can then nominate an individual to serve in the role for three years. India was unanimously chosen as the first President country, starting in June 1997, to be followed by Australia in 2000. However, policy and direction of ICC will now be vested in an executive board to include representatives of all nine Test-playing countries and three Associates. Three committees will report to the executive covering cricket, development, and finance and marketing. ICC also agreed to become incorporated.

ENGLAND SPONSORSHIP DEAL

On March 26, the ECB announced that mobile phone company Vodafone would be England's sponsors from the winter of 1997-98 until 2001, replacing Tetley Bitter. They would also sponsor England A, the England women's team – from the summer of 1997 – and the children's game of Kwik Cricket.

MCC ANNUAL GENERAL MEETING

The 210th annual general meeting of the Marylebone Cricket Club was held on May 7. Colin Ingleby-Mackenzie, in the first of his two years as president, took the chair. It was announced that the committee, after canvassing members' views by post, had decided to ban smoking in the Long Room on match days. Membership of the club on December 31, 1996, was 19,743, made up of 17,108 full members, 1,948 associate members, 575 honorary members and 112 senior members. There were 9,071 candidates awaiting election. In 1996, 400 vacancies arose.

Following the AGM, a special meeting was held to approve a change to Law 3 Note (d) of the Laws of Cricket.

ICC ANNUAL CONFERENCE

ICC met at Lord's on June 16 and 17 and confirmed the new corporate structure agreed at Kuala Lumpur. The executive board appointed chairmen for the three main committees: Sir Clyde Walcott of West Indies, the retiring ICC chairman, for the cricket committee; Dr Ali Bacher of South Africa for development; and Ehsan Mani of Pakistan for finance and marketing. These three and the chairman of the Associate Members, Jørgen Holmen of Denmark, were to sit on the executive board alongside the 12 national representatives, the president, Jagmohan Dalmiya, and chief executive David Richards, who was given a second five-year contract, until 2003. A sub-committee was established to investigate options for a Test World Championship and report back in December. An application from Bangladesh for Test status was rejected, but they and Kenya were granted full one-day international status in games with Full Members of ICC and with each other, and first-class status in three or four-day games with Full Members, other recognised first-class teams and each other. To further development of cricket in non-Test countries, a new five-region structure was approved in principle, and ICC was to employ a development manager. ICC agreed to stage regular triangular one-day international tournaments at Disney World in Florida and approved participation of Commonwealth countries in the 1998 Commonwealth Games in Malaysia. Belize, the Cayman Islands and Sweden were granted Affiliate status.

ICC CRICKET COMMITTEE MEETING

After a meeting of the nine Test captains on July 11, which reported to ICC's cricket committee on July 12, ICC agreed that Test grounds equipped with floodlights could switch them on if bad light threatened play. All international venues were to provide at least one absorbent roller to help in removing water from the pitch. Umpires in doubt about clean catches were authorised to ask the third umpire to consult TV replays. The number of bouncers allowed in an over would remain at two. Teams would no longer be fined for slow over-rates if they dismissed their opponents inside 50 overs (in a Test innings) or 33 (in one-day internationals).

THE CRICKET FOUNDATION

In August, the Cricket Foundation announced awards totalling £2.5 million to the boards of the 38 first-class and minor counties. These ranged from £107,535 for Middlesex to £32,000 for Suffolk. There were also grants to Durham University, the Channel Islands, the Isle of Wight and the children's game of Kwik Cricket. The money, a proportion of the ECB's profits from international cricket and TV revenue, was to be used to pay regional development officers, provide expenses for junior county teams, improve coaching in schools and train groundsmen, umpires, scorers and administrators. It was the second year that the money had been distributed through the Foundation.

FIRST-CLASS FORUM

At a meeting at Lord's on December 4, the First-Class Forum voted by ten to eight against the proposal that selectors should have the right to withdraw England players from county matches for rest or coaching. The ECB had offered the counties affected £500 compensation per day per player rested. Counties promised that they would remain sympathetic to the selectors' requests, as they had been throughout the 1997 season. The Forum asked the ECB Management Board to review the contractual arrangements of England players. It also agreed that the maximum number of players registered on each county playing staff should be reduced from 35 to 30, a move supported by the Professional Cricketers' Association.

ICC MEETING

ICC met in Calcutta on December 8 and 9. It was announced that the limited-overs tournament for all nine Full Members planned to take place in Disney World in September/October 1998 would now take place in Sharjah. (In January it was moved yet again, to Dhaka.) The sub-committee investigating the options for a Test World Championship was to continue its work and report again at Lord's in June 1998.

ENGLAND SELECTORS' APPOINTMENT

On December 22, the England Management Advisory Committee agreed to extend the terms of England selectors David Graveney and Graham Gooch to August 31, 1999, and that of Mike Gatting until the end of February 2000. The renewed appointments were to provide continuity, especially during the build-up to the World Cup.

ERRATA

WISDEN, 1950

Page 297   H. L. Jackson's second-innings bowling figures should read 12–0–45–0, not 2–0–45–0.

WISDEN, 1984

Page 1029   The South African bowling averages should include N. V. Radford of Transvaal, with 943 runs, 34 wkts, avge 27.73, two five-wicket innings and best bowling 5-39.

Page 1095   In Canterbury's second innings against Otago, K. B. K. Ibadulla's analysis should read 17.2–7–22–5.

WISDEN, 1988

Page 1019   The one-day international between England and West Indies at Melbourne on January 30 was a day/night game.

WISDEN, 1994

Page 1039   In the First Test between Sri Lanka and New Zealand at Moratuwa, Sri Lanka's first wicket fell at 26, not 27, and Mahanama and Gurusinha added 138, a record for Sri Lanka's second wicket against New Zealand.

WISDEN, 1997

Page 33   Umpire Dickie Bird stood in 68 one-day internationals, not 71.

Page 941   In the National Club Championship, Scarborough lost to Sheffield Collegiate, not Sheffield Colliery.

Page 1406   Graham Kersey died in Queensland, not Western Australia.

Page 1418   T. B. Werapitiya played for Trinity College, Kandy, not against them.

PART SEVEN: MISCELLANEOUS

CHRONICLE OF 1997

JANUARY

3 Eddo Brandes takes hat-trick in Harare to give Zimbabwe 3-0 win over England in one-day international series. **12** Graham Halbish sacked as chief executive of the Australian Cricket Board. Australia fail to reach final of World Series for first time since 1979-80. **28** Australia retain the Frank Worrell Trophy with victory over West Indies in Adelaide and become clear leaders of Wisden World Championship. Danny Morrison, the world record holder for Test ducks, shares last-wicket stand of 106 with Nathan Astle to deny England victory in the Auckland Test. **30** Craig McDermott retires.

FEBRUARY

5 Alex Tait takes 16 wickets for Northern Districts against Auckland, the most in a first-class match in New Zealand. **18** England win Christchurch Test to complete their first overseas series win for five years.

MARCH

3 Steve Waugh and Greg Blewett put on 385 for Australia's fifth wicket at Johannesburg, then the 12th-highest partnership in Test history. **4** Lee Germon sacked as New Zealand captain. South Africa lose to Australia in Johannesburg by an innings and 196 runs, their biggest defeat in 47 years. **8** Yorkshire members vote to leave Headingley and build a new ground at Wakefield. Bryan Young scores 267 not out against Sri Lanka in Dunedin, the second-highest Test score by a New Zealander. **10** Desmond Haynes retires. **13** David Graveney named as chairman of England selectors. **17** In Port Elizabeth, Australia complete victory in Test series over South Africa. **19** Sussex committee ousted. **23** ICC agree new structure for governing cricket, with a rotating presidency and an 18-man executive. **25** Queensland win the Sheffield Shield for the second time, becoming the first team in 14 years to win a final away. **31** India, needing only 120 to beat West Indies in the Bridgetown Test, are bowled out for 81.

APRIL

13 Bangladesh win the ICC Trophy; they qualify for the 1999 World Cup, along with Kenya and Scotland. **23** Denis Compton dies, aged 78. **29** In Colombo, Aravinda de Silva becomes the first batsman ever to score two unbeaten centuries in a Test match.

MAY

19 British Government announces that tobacco advertising will be banned, signalling end of Benson and Hedges Cup. **21** Saeed Anwar scores 194 for Pakistan against India, beating Viv Richards's 13-year-old record score in one-day internationals. **27** Mike Gatting resigns as Middlesex captain after 14 years.

JUNE

5 Australia bowled out for 118 by England at Edgbaston on first day of Ashes series. **6** Nasser Hussain scores 207, the highest score for England v Australia since 1985. **7** Mark Taylor scores century for Australia, to avert possible resignation. **8** England win Edgbaston Test by nine wickets to take 1-0 lead in Ashes. **11** John Emburey retires from first-class cricket. **12** Derbyshire captain Dean Jones walks out. **13** Curtly Ambrose takes his 300th Test wicket. **14** Sir Colin Cowdrey made a life peer in Queen's Birthday Honours. Glamorgan bowled out by Middlesex for 31, the lowest Championship score in 14 years. **20** Mike Atherton breaks Peter May's record when he captains England in a Test for the 42nd time. **21** England bowled out for 77 in Lord's Test, the lowest Ashes score since 1948; Glenn McGrath takes eight for 38. **25** Keith Piper of Warwickshire banned for one match for use of cannabis.

JULY

3 Dean Headley becomes first third-generation Test cricketer. **6** Steve Waugh becomes first player since 1946-47 to score two centuries in an Ashes Test. **7** Australia win Old Trafford Test to level Ashes series 1-1. **20** Alistair Brown of Surrey becomes first player to score a double-century in the Sunday League. **23** Warwickshire stage Sunday League match v Somerset on a Wednesday night, concluding at 11.38 p.m. – the first ever floodlit match in a major UK competition. **26** Graham Gooch retires. **28** Australia win Headingley Test to go 2-1 up in Ashes.

AUGUST

5 ECB unveil plan to divide County Championship into three ''conferences''. **6** Sri Lanka score 952 for six against India in Colombo, the highest total in Tests; Sanath Jayasuriya scores 340, the fourth-highest Test innings; with Roshan Mahanama, he puts on 576, a record for Tests and one short of the record stand in all first-class cricket. **10** Australia win Trent Bridge Test and make sure of winning Ashes for the fifth successive series. **23** Australia, needing 124 to win The Oval Test, are bowled out for 104, making final score in Ashes series 3-2.

SEPTEMBER

14 Inzamam-ul-Haq of Pakistan banned for two matches after fighting with a spectator in Toronto. **15** Counties reject radical reform of County Championship. **20** Glamorgan win Championship for first time in 28 years.

OCTOBER

8 In Rawalpindi, Azhar Mahmood and Mushtaq Ahmed of Pakistan equal the Test last-wicket record stand of 151, v South Africa. Azhar makes a hundred on Test debut, as did Ali Naqvi two days earlier. **10** Kennedy Otieno and Deepak Chudasama of Kenya break the world-record opening stand in a one-day international with 225 v Bangladesh. **24** Phil Tufnell fined £1,000 plus costs with suspended 18-month ban for failing to take ECB drugs test. **27** Pakistan lose Faisalabad Test, and series. Needing 146 to beat South Africa, they are bowled out for 92.

NOVEMBER

20 Pakistan score their biggest Test win over West Indies: an innings and 19 runs in Peshawar. England coach David Lloyd given contract until August 1999. **21** Floodlights switched on for the first time during a Test, because of bad light during Australia v New Zealand at Perth. **23** Australian players drop plans for strike over pay and conditions and agree to more talks. **27** Jamie Siddons passes David Hookes's career record of 9,364 Sheffield Shield runs.

DECEMBER

9 West Indies lose Karachi Test and are beaten 3-0 in three-Test series in Pakistan. **17** MCC committee asks members to support the admission of women. **19** England win Champions' Trophy in Sharjah. **29** Australia win Women's World Cup before 50,000 crowd in Calcutta.

The following were also among items reported in the media during 1997:

Twenty-eight prisoners broke down two doors and walked out of a minimum-security jail in Guyana in protest after guards turned off a radio broadcast of the First Test between Australia and West Indies. (*Red Stripe Caribbean Cricket Quarterly*, January)

Australia's Anti-Discrimination Board reported that Britons complained of racial abuse more than any other ethnic group in the country, and said the level of complaints rose during England cricket tours. Chris Puplick, the board chairman, said expatriates were often upset by TV commentators saying that Poms would play better cricket if they washed more. He added that most complaints were unjustified, and indicated hypersensitivity rather than racial hatred. (*Daily Telegraph*, January 3)

Alec Kock from Durban, known as "the Fat Fan", claimed to be cricket's first sponsored supporter. A café chain offered him and his friends free food and drinks round the country if he entertained the customers as well as he entertained spectators sitting near him at the Newlands Test. (*Cape Times*, January 7)

Sanath Jayasuriya was voted Sri Lanka's Man of the Year in a competition organised by the *Midweek Mirror*. Sixty per cent of readers who voted chose him, and a panel of judges set up to evaluate the results picked him unanimously in 15 minutes. They said he made "all the people of this country – irrespective of their race, religion or social status – proud and happy to be Sri Lankans". (*Midweek Mirror*, Colombo, January 8)

West Indian cricketer Franklyn Stephenson, who plays for South African team Free State, was cut and bruised after being set upon in a racial attack outside a bar in Bloemfontein. (*The Pioneer*, January 28)

The Movement for Justice, led by the former Pakistan captain Imran Khan, failed to win any of the 217 National Assembly seats contested in the Pakistani general elections. (*Daily Telegraph*, February 5)

Members of Oatlands Park Cricket Club, near Weybridge, Surrey, were thwarted when the local council vetoed a plan to build on their ground. The members voted the club out of existence in response to a £4 million offer from developers to buy the ground. The 109 members stood to gain about £50,000 each. Local residents claimed the club had been run down after members narrowly rejected an offer in 1988. (*The Times*, March 3/July 28)

Mike Atherton opened a new sports hall at his old school, Manchester Grammar, which – in breach of tradition – was named after Atherton rather than the high master. The current high master, Dr Martin Stephen, said Atherton was an ideal role model. (*Manchester Evening News*, March 11)

Former Labour leader Neil Kinnock, now a European Commissioner, resigned as honorary president of the Royal Brussels Cricket Club after members complained that he had failed to attend a match or social function in his two years in office. (*Daily Telegraph*, March 14)

Laura Joyce, 14, said by the Middlesex junior coach to be one of the best female players of her age in Britain, was barred from an Easter training school at Lord's because of her sex. (*Daily Telegraph*, March 20)

Satish Samant of the MIG Cricket Club in Bandra, India, scored 310 in 135 balls against the Jayco Sports Club. Samant hit 33 fours and 18 sixes. (*Times of India*, March 28)

In Lincolnshire, a friendly between Bardney and Horncastle was halted by a hang-glider which crashed into Horncastle fielder John Hague as he was running in to field a ball on the boundary. Hague received a glancing blow on the head. "I nearly didn't play because I'd woken up with a migraine," said Hague. "Being biffed on the head by a hang-glider was all I needed." The pilot said he had been trying to avoid a field of crops. The players helped him remove his broken glider before all of them, including Hague, carried on. (*Horncastle News*, April 16) The newspaper headlined the item "Bad Flight Stopped Play".

Phil Hutchings, 65, of Abbotsbury, Dorset, claimed a hat-trick after taking two wickets with his last delivery of 1996 and another with his first of 1997 – against the same opponents, Burley. (*The Times*, April 18)

Batsmen at the Melbourne Town club, Derbyshire, have been asked not to hit sixes on one side of the pitch to avoid irritating residents in a new housing development. Cricket has been played on the ground for 77 years; the houses were erected in 1996. (*The Times*, April 19)

Players from the Whitchurch club in Bristol abandoned their game to chase two burglars they saw stealing a video from a nearby house. They eventually cornered the men in a nearby field. (*Evening Post*, Bristol, April 21)

Basdeo Debideen, who is under sentence of death in the Port-of-Spain state prison, has written to *The Cricketer* magazine asking for a pen-pal. (*Daily Telegraph*, April 23)

Groundsman Brian Lucas had his false teeth crushed by his roller at the Perkins Cricket Club in Shropshire. They shot out of his mouth when he sneezed. (*Daily Mail*, April 30)

Yasin Ghodiwallah, a 12-year-old boy at Little Ilford School, London, died after being hit in the chest by a full toss while batting in an under-14 match against Rokeby School. (*Daily Telegraph*, May 8)

Thirty staff from Leeds Metropolitan University signed a letter protesting against the award of an honorary degree to the former England captain and manager Ray Illingworth, saying it "risks sending out the worst kind of message to the region's Asian and black population". This followed Devon Malcolm's suggestion – later retracted – that Illingworth's treatment of him on the 1995-96 South African tour might have been racially motivated. (*The Guardian*, May 13)

A 30-year-old milkmaid, Karen Grabham, has been poached by the men's third team at Brompton Ralph, Somerset, after averaging 67 for the local women's team. (*Daily Telegraph*, May 13)

Regulars at The Brewery Tap in Idle, Yorkshire, are to contest an annual game against the Bradford Campaign for Real Ale for the ashes of the pub team's former umpire, Keith Narey. Mr Narey, 50, died after a drinking binge to celebrate the Labour Party's election victory. (*Daily Telegraph*, May 14)

Lord MacLaurin, chairman of the England and Wales Cricket Board, resigned as chairman of the UK Sports Council after the election of the Labour Government. Lord MacLaurin had publicly supported the Conservatives in the election, and the new Sports Minister Tony Banks had warned: "Let's say we'll have an interesting relationship. But I think it will be a short one." (*The Guardian*, May 15)

Bowls players at Frensham, Surrey, complained that the local cricketers next door were hitting the wrong bowlers for six by continually hitting the ball over the fence on to their green. "It does tend to spoil the enjoyment," said bowls club president John Chuter. "We are always having to look over our shoulders." (*Daily Mail*, May 27)

A Cornwall League Division One match between Helston and Falmouth was held up for 90 minutes after thousands of bees swarmed on to the ground. Two players were stung and bee specialists had to be called to collect the swarm before play could resume. (*The West Briton*, Truro, May 29)

A 15ft swarm of bees stopped play for seven minutes in an England women's training match at Wellingborough. The bees headed straight for the scorebox, but scorers Pat Siderfin and Sue Robinson slammed the shutters, and the swarm eventually settled on a nearby hawthorn bush. (*The Times*, May 31)

The club at Congleton, Cheshire, have agreed to play all their fixtures away until they can afford a seven-metre high net round the ground to protect nearby homes. (*Daily Express*, May 31)

The thatched pavilion at Wellingborough School, where Northamptonshire used to play, has been completely destroyed by fire. The school's honours boards were lost, along with a signed picture of W. G. Grace. Arson was suspected. (*Kettering Evening Telegraph*, June 2)

Chris Davis was timed out under Law 31 while playing for Frenchay against Twyford House in the Bristol and District League. Davis was lazing on the boundary with his girlfriend when three wickets fell quickly. He dashed to the pavilion, but was given out as soon as he got on to the pitch. Frenchay still won. (*Evening Post*, Bristol, June 3)

Neighbours objected to the new sign at the Cricketers pub in Chelmsford, which showed an anonymous, helmeted, batsman wearing blue. It replaced a sign showing Ian Botham, Mike Gatting and Graham Gooch in whites. (*Daily Telegraph*, June 7)

The landlord of cricket's most historic pub, the Bat and Ball Inn at Hambledon, complained that letters sent there from all over the cricketing world were being delayed for several days because the Post Office officially considered the pub to be in the neighbouring parish of Clanfield. (*Sunday Telegraph*, June 8)

The Sri Lankan Health Department has acquired a new blood-testing machine for use by the country's hospitals. The Health Minister, A. H. M. Fowze, said that under the old system various errors occurred, including a case when the technician was watching a cricket match on TV while testing a male patient and told him he was pregnant. (*Daily News*, Colombo, June 10)

Viv Richards has flown to Brunei to coach one of the sons of the Sultan of Brunei, believed to be the world's richest man. Ian Botham had previously done the job. (*The Times*, June 10)

William Bruce, aged nine, took ten wickets in an innings with his leg-breaks for King's Junior School, Canterbury, for the second year running. This time he had figures of ten for 36 – including five stumpings – in an under-11s match against Wellesley House school. (*The Times*, June 11)

West Wight Middle School on the Isle of Wight were bowled out for nought, chasing Ryde School's 162 for no wicket. The Ryde cricket master, Chris Ody, said: "The West Wight boys performed in a dignified and sporting manner." (*Daily Express*, June 21)

Donna Underdown of Gillingham, Dorset, was told it would cost her £50 to visit the lavatory while watching her son play cricket for Gillingham's Second Eleven. The club play at the council-owned leisure centre but had not paid their annual fee. Mrs Underdown was eventually allowed in, and the players were told to go behind the trees. (*Daily Telegraph*, June 21)

Rye Cricket Club in Sussex, founded in 1754, has been told by the town council it must end the ancient practice of using Rye's official seal on its caps and sweaters. "The seal is being debased and degraded," said Councillor Frank Palmer. "People could use it to forge town council paper." The club chairman, Commander Colin Marsh, called the decision "pomposity and bureaucracy gone mad". (*Sunday Telegraph*, June 22)

Players complained when an electricity company erected a 30ft pole a few yards from the square at Thornton Watlass, Yorkshire. A spokesman for Northern Electric said that his workers could be forgiven for not realising it was a cricket field: the ground has a road running through it, and the pub wall forms part of the boundary. (*Sunday Telegraph*, June 22)

An Essex woman won £62,623 by betting £159,000 that the Lord's Test would end in a draw. Bookmakers William Hill refused to name her, but a spokesman said: "She'd be the one in the middle of the road pointing towards Lord's and doing a rain dance." (*Daily Telegraph*, June 25)

Dave Elliott, 43, took ten for 33 for Downend A against Patchway, and celebrated by drinking a yard of ale. (*Evening Post*, Bristol, June 27)

The first and second elevens from Hampsthwaite, who play in the Nidderdale League in Yorkshire, were both involved in a tie on the same day. The first team, their opponents Studley Royal, and the second team and their opponents Bagby and Balk all scored 148. In both cases the end came when the Hampsthwaite batsman at the non-striker's end was run out off the last ball of the 44th over. (*The Times*, June 28)

A Hampshire League match was declared void because Southampton Travellers fielded 12 men against Hamble Aerostructures. The mistake was only discovered at the drinks interval when one of the fielders complained that he had not got a drink. (*Daily Telegraph*, July 12)

The Glamorgan player Alun Evans scored the first 51 runs of the innings for a Select XI at Gowerton against Kenthurst of New South Wales. His opening partner, Chris Morgan, was out for nought with the score on 47. Evans went on to make 89. (*South Wales Evening Post*, July 17)

The Manchester United footballer David Beckham has been chosen as the "Brylcreem Boy", the advertising role originally made famous by the late Denis Compton, who was paid £1,000 by the company. Beckham is believed to be earning £1 million. (*Daily Telegraph*, July 18)

New Zealand has banned a Nike advert showing a ball bowled by Shane Warne turning into a chainsaw. The country's advertising watchdog said the advert showed violence "in a gratuitous and wantonly destructive manner and was likely to encourage violent behaviour". (*Daily Telegraph*, July 26)

A 20-year-old man poisoned himself in southern Sri Lanka after being scolded by his mother for playing too much cricket. Visantha Kumara left a note saying he was "sacrificing his life for the game of cricket" and asked that he be buried with a bat and ball in his coffin so he should be a better cricketer when he is reborn. (*Divaina*, Colombo, July 29)

The Westmorland League match between Milnthorpe and Burneside was declared a draw after being referred to Lord's. Milnthorpe claimed they had won because Burneside's ninth wicket fell to the last ball of the match, and the No. 11 had gone home to attend a social engagement. MCC advised that, since the game was over, it did not matter where the No. 11 was. (*League Cricket Review*, August)

Matthew Crease, 26, of the Frinton-on-Sea club, has been banned for life from the Two Counties Championship, covering Essex and Suffolk, after being involved in two incidents of dissent. He swore at an umpire who no-balled him for throwing, and had to be escorted from the field after refusing to believe he had been stumped. "It's Walt Disney stuff," said his club captain David Leyton. "You can't ban someone for life. He's a lovely gentle guy off the field." (*The Sun/Daily Telegraph*, August 8)

A 33-year-old Sri Lankan cricket fan, Ranasinghe Sarath, committed suicide by hanging himself in a well when Sanath Jayasuriya failed to beat Brian Lara's record Test score. (*Sunday Island*, Colombo, August 10)

Sir Garry Sobers won a prize believed to be around £200,000 in the Lotto, the Barbados lottery. (*The Times*, August 20)

Anil Kumar scored 343 in a schools match in Chennai (formerly Madras). Playing for St Bede's against Don Bosco in the Tamil Nadu Under-19 Championship, Kumar faced just 161 balls and hit 25 sixes and 30 fours out of a total of 606 for seven. (*The Hindu*, August 21)

A coaching class for under-16s in Nottinghamshire offered free by Sir Garry Sobers was cancelled when only nine youngsters signed up. Tom Meldrum, 12, one of the nine due to attend, said that when he mentioned the class to his cricket-loving friends they asked "Garry Who?" (*Daily Mail*, August 22)

Darren Bloomfield of the Essex club Tiptree United claimed a hat-trick spread over three separate matches. Bloomfield, an occasional off-spinner, was brought on with nine wickets down against Chappel and Wakes Colne, and ended the innings first ball. The same thing happened two weeks later against Cavaliers. The following week he was brought on earlier against Dedham, and took a wicket first ball again. He said he hoped the club might start bowling him more regularly. (*Essex Chronicle*, August 22)

A Vauxhall Astra driven by 80-year-old Grace Cummins collided with three other cars and slightly injured a player's wife during the game between Curdridge and Denmead in Hampshire. The driver's foot got jammed between the brake and the accelerator, and she careered round the outfield before she could free it. (*News of the World*, August 24)

Bodie, a Jack Russell terrier, found his 500th lost ball for the club at Shanklin, Isle of Wight. (*Daily Telegraph*, August 30)

The former England player Jim Parks, 65, played what he said would be his final match, for an Old England XI at Haywards Heath. He was out fourth ball for nought. (*Daily Telegraph*, August 30)

Arthur Cuthbertson, a 70-year-old slow left-arm bowler from Caversham, Berkshire, took nine for 38, including a hat-trick, against Whitchurch, immediately after undergoing two eye operations. "At least I can see the stumps again," he said. (*Sunday Times*, August 31)

The Second Eleven match between Melksham and Bathford in Wiltshire was interrupted so that players could light bonfires to disperse an invasion of flying ants. In Cornwall, the match between Lanner and St Day was abandoned after a similar attack; an attempt to solve the problem by pouring boiling water on the ground proved unsuccessful. (*Daily Telegraph*, September 6)

Two clubs in the North Yorkshire and South Durham League, Norton and Preston-on-Tees B, were deemed to have lost matches they called off on the day of the funeral of Diana, Princess of Wales. The decision cost Norton a chance of winning the league; their opponents, Darlington, said they were happy to rearrange the game. No major sporting fixtures took place that day. Frank Cook, the local Labour MP, called the decision "diabolical". (*The Times*, September 11)

Hundreds of cricket lovers threw stones at the cable TV office in Jammu, Northern India, after the company failed to relay an India-Pakistan one-day international from Toronto. Police charged the crowd to restore order. (*Times of India*, September 15)

Brian Lara shot 84 and 87, missing the cut, in the qualifying tournament for the Trinidad & Tobago golf team at the Caribbean Championships. (*Red Stripe Caribbean Cricket Quarterly*, October)

Mike Atherton led a team of six past and present England players to victory at boules over a French team, which included the national captain. The game, in Reims, was part of Atherton's benefit year. (*The Independent*, October 3)

Sanath Jayasuriya broke yet another record when his interview on Sri Lanka TV was shown on October 6: so many sets were switched on that the nation's electricity demand rose above 1,000 megawatts for the first time ever. (*Daily News*, Colombo, October 11)

Stuart Hensman of the Redback Cricket Club in Sydney went in to bat, having told team-mates he would have to retire after half an hour because of an urgent appointment. He was late for the appointment, but only just, after scoring 140 from 56 balls. (*North Shore Times*, Sydney, October 17)

Fast bowler Rachi Kariyawasam, 15, took ten for 12 in five overs, including a hat-trick, for Springvale against Endeavour Hills in an Under-16 match in Melbourne. Endeavour Hills were 49 for nought before Kariyawasam came into the attack, and were bowled out for 70. (*Sunday Herald Sun*, Melbourne, October 19)

Sir Raymond Ferrall, 91, who played for Tasmania in the 1930s, was stabbed in the hand after confronting a burglar at his home. The intruder fled. (*Hobart Mercury*, October 21)

Winston Davis, the 39-year-old former West Indian fast bowler, has been left paralysed after falling from a tree on his home island of St Vincent. (*The Guardian*, November 5)

Geoffrey Boycott has put his Yorkshire farmhouse up for sale at £600,000 so that he could move to a seafront home at Sandbanks, Dorset. His friend Dickie Bird said he was shocked. "He's a born and bred Yorkshireman and I thought he would never leave." (*Daily Telegraph*, November 5)

Steven "Spud" Davidson, who plays for Glenaladale in Victorian country cricket, scored an unbeaten 132 out of 232 – a week after taking ten for 64 in a different match. (*Herald Sun*, Melbourne, November 12)

A bad smell stopped play today at Newlands, on the first day of the first-class match between Western Province and Free State. Players and umpires raced off with shirts and jerseys pulled over their heads, and handkerchiefs stuffed into their mouths. Western Province chief executive Arthur Turner said: "It was a terrible, bad eggs, ammonia, kind of smell. It was almost overpowering." A small explosion in the nearby brewery turned out to be responsible. (*Reuters*, November 15)

Dean Gunawardana scored 102 not out, all in boundaries, for Silverton Under-11s in a Dandenong District Association match. He hit seven sixes and 15 fours. (*Herald Sun*, Melbourne, November 19)

Geoffrey Boycott's TV commentaries have made him a cult figure in India. One group of schoolboys were given six of the best by their headmaster for constantly imitating Boycott and describing everything as "roobbish". (*The Times*, December 24)

The following item was received too late for inclusion in the Chronicle of 1996:

A local cricketer shot dead an opponent during a match in Kashmir, after an umpire's decision went against his team. The player pulled out a revolver and fired at the opposition, killing Ghulam Hassan and wounding two others, before fleeing. (*Asian Age*, November 21, 1996)

Contributions from readers for this feature are very welcome, particularly if the items are from local or non-UK newspapers. Please send cuttings to the editor at The Oaks, Newton St Margarets, Herefordshire HR2 0QN, England. The title and date of publication should be clearly marked.

CRICKET BOOKS, 1997

By LESLIE THOMAS

It is not easy to write about cricket of the past, especially of the remote past. To distil the excitement, drama, skill and sunshine of a June afternoon into a few pages is beyond most writers. After a lapse of seasons, or even one season, 4 for 31 becomes what it actually is, three numbers and three letters.

Sometimes the old hands found it just as difficult, even when the events they described were very recent history. If you burrow into the *Manchester Guardian* files for 1948, you will find that coverage of Bradman's famous last Test innings at The Oval consisted of simply this: "Hollies drew Barnes forward with his leg-break and had him beautifully caught at the wicket, and drew Bradman even further forward and bowled him with his googly." Perhaps the fault lay in the communications of those days: perhaps the carrier pigeon was due to fly off.

Reading through the great pyramid of cricket books which have yet again appeared this year, it is too apparent that the achievement of clothing mere numbers with anything like the pleasure and romance of the great game is beyond most attempts, certainly beyond the ingenuity of ghost writers. John Gaustad, owner of Sportspages bookshop, has suggested that cricket books are hidebound, and that the market is in danger. Anyone who has undertaken the serious task of writing these reviews for *Wisden* will nod. There are too many cricket books.

At least one of the 1997 crop, however, has been a major best-seller. Charlie Chaplin called his life story **My Autobiography**, and so has Dickie Bird. Both are the sagas of little men, born in poor circumstances, feeling their ways somewhat tentatively through life, falling into holes, but eventually triumphing by the talent of being able to put on a performance when necessary. Dickie Bird, although nowhere near as rich as Chaplin, has had the happier life and, of course, he is thankfully still around to enjoy it. His timidity and unsophisticated readiness to laugh at himself, even when the situations are not particularly laughable, go to make a good story, almost bowling-analysis and batting-average free.

There is a lot of "it could only happen to me" in his tale, and certainly one of the wisest things he did when setting out to tell it was to enlist the assistance, not of one of the cricket circuit scribes, but of Keith Lodge, the sports editor of his local *Barnsley Chronicle*. This gives the book an authentic Yorkshire accent, and Dickie's story rings true throughout. You can almost hear him telling some fairly lame yarn and then huffing a bit before adding: "We had a good laugh about it after."

Michael Parkinson writes the introduction with affection and sincerity. When Parky confesses that someone loves cricket, and knows cricket, more than he does, it's strong praise. They knew each other (and Geoffrey Boycott) in Barnsley. Their fathers grafted in the coal mines. They kicked footballs and played wall-cricket, pretending to be famous, and of course one day they all were. It is not difficult to picture them scuffling in their short trousers and scraggy school ties.

Harold Bird's father warned him about cigarettes and whisky and wild women, and he heeds his dad (dead five years after retiring from the 18-inch coal seam) to this day. He never wanted to smoke; he only once thought of getting married (to a South African blonde who, by the sound of her, might have been worth a try); and when he is presented with an exclusive bottle of gin, he puts it on his dresser at home as an ornament.

Dickie Bird might easily have spent a stiff-collared sort of life: a harmless bachelor, a Yorkshire bank clerk, well liked but with a suspicion of eccentricity. But he could play cricket, although even this was only to an extent. He was the almost perpetual twelfth man for Yorkshire, so good with the drinks and towels that he suspected he owed his place to his conscientiousness. Yorkshire appear to have appreciated his cricketing ability rather less. Returning in perspiring triumph from scoring 181 against Glamorgan on a difficult track, he was told that he was being dropped for the next match.

When he went to Leicestershire he was frankly unhappy. Too nice to go into reasons, he thought it was a bad time. His patience and good nature found their true home only when he failed at playing and became an umpire. The ordered and meticulous way in which he has gone about his business in the middle before big crowds is much in contrast to the often lone and slightly pathetic man who experiences such sadly funny adventures just getting to a match.

The most touching tale of the lot would make an elegant short story: stranded in Nigeria by a series of African misunderstandings, he is rescued by relays of expats who know their way around and finally get him sorted out. He is endearingly grateful. Before they arrived he was almost in tears; sometimes he really does cry – like the August day in 1980 when MCC members turned nasty and tried to bully him into restarting the Centenary Test against Australia when the ground was soaked.

In a tough, often spiteful, world (the cricket world, that is), we should be glad for a pilgrim like Dickie Bird. One winter's day, Bob Wilson, the coach at Lord's, saw Dickie standing in the middle, in front of the empty stands, practising his umpiring signals. You can almost imagine he was wearing his school shorts.

Brian Johnston was another legend – forever "Johnners". He used to call me Tommers, which is not very different in sound to my actual name. I often wondered what he would have made of the stalwart Gloucestershire batsman Jack Crapp. Now Jonathan Agnew, formerly of Leicestershire and currently of *Test Match Special*, has written **Over to You, Aggers**. (There must be an end to this joke somewhere. But I suppose these names are marginally preferable to Hickie and Suchie and suchlike.)

Agnew, burnished and furnished with earphones and a pad, appears on the front cover of his story, and, as if they could not think of anything better, the same photograph is reproduced on the back. Why are the jackets of cricket books so dire? Of the current batch only Robert Low's *W.G.* is of any quality. At least Agnew is a cheerful soul. There's something to laugh at in his tale, which is more than can be said for the chronicles of some of those still in the game. He has, as you would expect, done the writing himself. It's not Cardus, nor Frank Keating, but it is all his own work.

Agnew does get serious about the recurring dirt-on-the-ball drama. He was required by the BBC to make a judgment, and while drawing back from the word "cheat", he made it known that he thought Atherton was up to dirty work and ought to resign as captain. Atherton's book denies that he broke any rules. Agnew asserts that since it is against the rules to rub the ball on the earth, it is logically wrong to rub the earth on the ball. But I think he is on crumbly ground there. It is not the same thing at all.

A few crises before that one came the fiasco of the barmaid and the unfortunate Gatting. There is a tale that a gloomy MCC member approached E. W. Swanton at Lord's and murmured: "Don't you think, Jim, that English cricket has reached a new low?" "Not at all," Swanton is said to have replied. "It's English barmaids who have reached a new low."

Mike Gatting, a good and brave batsman, appears to have unwittingly become the fall-guy of the English game. First there was the fatal reverse sweep, then the unplayable leg-break; he fell out with the umpire and in with the barmaid. No fewer than three of the current crop of cricket books mention that he cannot spell "Faisalabad". In **The Botham Report**, Ian Botham makes the fair point that Gatting and every England captain since have been on a hiding to nothing. Most of the blame for this Botham puts irrevocably on the shoulders of the men who have run, and he says ruined, the English game over the past years. Ted Dexter, Raman Subba Row and, naturally, Ray Illingworth are put in the stocks and we are invited to throw things. On occasions it is difficult not to accept the invitation.

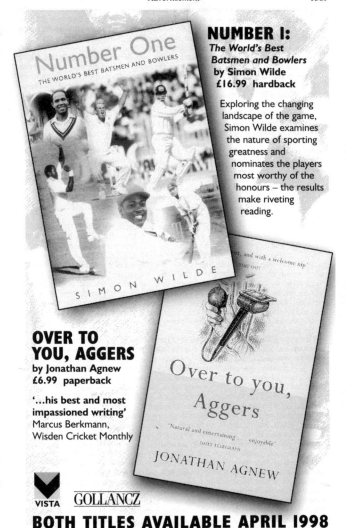

Botham's book, punchily written with Peter Hayter, has a quoted theme: "What is wrong with English cricket – and how I intend to put it right". Just how Botham intends to be *in a position* to put it right is not made clear, although there may be a clue in his belief that a one-man controller, a supremo, is the answer to all the ills. It was just that Ray Illingworth was the wrong man.

Botham rails at the loonier moments of the past decade, like Ted Dexter asking who could forget Malcolm Devon, and the unidentified committeeman who said that county cricket was all right in its present form because it gave pensioners somewhere to go in the daytime. This gentleman could not have answered Botham's questionnaire, sent to all county chairmen, executives, captains and coaches, since 100 per cent of the replies said that changes were needed in the game. Not many knew how to make them, and how many actually replied to the canvass is not stated. Few of Botham's answers are entirely revolutionary, and the reader is left, with the author, to wonder how many will be implemented in the next decade. Or will cricket be a dead duck?

Robert Low's splendid biography **W.G.**, the shortest title of the year and also its nearest thing to a literary cricket book, is handsome in every aspect. From the cover, Grace in his prime – with the West Country eyes, the smoky whiskers, and the too-tight, slightly ridiculous cap – stares out as though you were about to bowl to him and he knew he was going to hit you out of the ground.

This year is the one hundred and fiftieth anniversary of Grace's birth. He played family cricket in the garden of their house at Downend outside Bristol, under the supervision of Martha, his mother, of whom Richard Daft – no mean judge – said: "She knew ten times more about cricket than any lady I ever met." Gloucestershire batsmen were expected to doff their caps to her when they came back from the wicket and she would often point out the error which caused their dismissal.

Grace, eminent Victorian though he was, would still, I think, have recognised the modern stories and crises contained in the other books of 1997. He was an amateur who earned more from the game than any professional of his day. He courted controversy in this country and in Australia, was belligerent and frequently self-seeking, but he was the life and soul of cricket. Wherever he played, there the crowds gathered. Imagine what today's tabloids would make of his action in literally kidnapping Billy Midwinter from the Australian touring team at Lord's so that he could play for Gloucestershire against Surrey at The Oval. And yet he was a man of immense heart and kindness.

The feats and the figures apart, Robert Low's triumph in this book is to clothe the man with real and recognisable personality: his appetite for life and profit, his almost childlike joys and sorrows. I found the later pages extremely moving. The Golden Age, as the author memorably notes, had ended in the trenches. Grace, in 1915, had become an old man sitting in his south-east London house shuddering with fear as Zeppelins showered bombs (Woolwich Arsenal was only up the road). When he died a few days later, Berlin trumpeted an almost symbolic victory, although what the Germans would have made of it, I cannot imagine.

No modern cricketer is as distinctive as Grace. But no other international athlete looks like Jack Russell. He peers from the front cover of his autobiography with that grandad moustache, that ragged hair and that battered hat, his eyes sharp and narrow, his smile only a half-smile, like some guileful old gardener giving tips for the potting shed. With a moustache like his, it is a mystery how he ever keeps wicket like he does. Much of Jack Russell remains a mystery in any case, even after reading what amounts to his true confessions in **Unleashed**, written with Patrick Murphy.

Russell once said to me, while I was nervously contemplating captaining a charity team: "Enjoy it – you'll play better." I did too. His deep enjoyment of cricket, in the most trying and even dangerous circumstances, shines through the story. Unlike Mike Atherton, who seems to have been born on the cricket field, Russell had a full West Country childhood: "a grubby-haired little kid" (in the Laurie Lee country around Stroud) playing soldiers, dreaming of being a hero.

You get the feeling that if he had *been* a soldier, he would have been in the trenches before most. The huge patriotism – jingoism really – sounds sometimes strange in these days. On the far side of the world he listens to the Queen's Speech while his wife in Gloucestershire holds the telephone close to the television set. He has already (at 34) made arrangements for his own funeral, with the coffin carried on an army tank and "Land of Hope and Glory" sung full blast.

This complex, sentimental, skilful and courageous man is also honest to the point where most people would have kept quiet. He was a teenage drunk, sometimes too smashed to see straight behind the stumps the next morning: he was on the dole and played pool to increase his earnings. (Not that this is particularly reprehensible. Few young men on the giro have any secondary skills.) He has a curious dislike of his own real name, having once threatened to "deck" the 6ft 4in Peter Martin for referring to him as "Robert", yet he has none of the everyday aggression of the eponymous dog. In fact, the title *Unleashed* strikes me as being scarcely appropriate, and to add the word "Barking" across the corner of the jacket totally misleading. Russell is not mad, he's unusual.

True grit

While I was engaged with **Athers**, David Norrie's authorised biography of the England captain, I had a clear dream of Atherton batting at Lord's and reaching 94 not out before I woke. Determined that he should score his century there, I forced myself back to sleep and Atherton duly obliged. When I awoke he was 102 and had just been caught off his glove.

Most biographies (and certainly autobiographies) have their real interest in the early days of the subject. Struggles, childhood, learning to be famous, in other words *getting there*. After the major step, or leap, has been achieved, the charm somehow diminishes. With this book, the reverse is the case. Michael Atherton's progression, from the six-year-old with the dauntingly straight bat and the gritty expression to his days at Manchester Grammar School and Cambridge, pass with hardly a trouble in sight. I would have liked to have heard more of his time at university: the place deserted in the holidays while he worked alone at his desk so he could play cricket in term-time. But these years apparently swanned by, nothing untoward happening to our hero. Even his early cricket days seemed unruffled and easily fulfilled. It was when he became England's captain, his heart's desire, that Atherton's troubles began.

Norrie makes all the running with the criticism of Ray Illingworth and the general staff at Lord's, but Atherton still bats cannily. At the end of each section he adds a few slightly languid lines ("Illy and I got on well generally") as though, now the storm is past, he has no further interest in it. I defy anyone reading the "grit on the ball" episode again not to wonder if everyone in cricket had gone bonkers.

Atherton, Norrie spells out, did nothing illegal by rubbing the ball with earth. Neither umpire believed he had altered the condition of the ball (and certainly not the game, which the South Africans cruised). But with all the escalation of a stage farce, scene followed ludicrous scene, the main players being the bumptious referee, Peter Burge, Illingworth, and Atherton himself ("I panicked") with a comic chorus which included, needless to say, Members of Parliament, the Headmasters' Conference, and Church notables. And it was all started by some numbskull in Johannesburg telephoning the local television station. No wonder the Germans and the French think it's a game for madmen.

Atherton's photograph on the jacket of the book, grinning and cap awry, has a touch of Just William. So has his general off-pitch demeanour, apparently. His dressing-room corner is like a tip, according to his team-mates. Nor does he seem a particularly interesting man, as some private men are. We hear that he likes to go to the Lake District, but there is no information as to what he does there. Does he walk?

Does he swim in Windermere? Does he recite Wordsworth or Coleridge? His nearest friend, his only close friend perhaps, Neil Fairbrother, says that Atherton's love life could be written on the back of a postage stamp. Atherton's two girlfriends (consecutive) are only mentioned in passing, and we are told that he has taken to fly-fishing.

But when it comes to cricket, he is a considerable player. His sometimes lonely battles, when all around him are losing heads and wickets, tell most about the man. Atherton appears almost a shadow outside the gates of a cricket ground. All he cares about is the bat, the ball and the battle. England should be grateful for that.

After all these years of lore and legend it appears, according to Peter Wynne-Thomas, that much of the misty history of cricket is bunk. In **The History of Cricket: From The Weald to The World**, he questions long-held beliefs, including the accepted theory that shepherds, needing only to keep half an eye on the sheep, invented the game using wicket gates and crooks as implements. He also thinks that MCC is at least 43 years older than it thinks it is. In 1744, he says, it met in Pall Mall at the Star and Garter, where the Jockey Club also used to meet. Did one club beget the other? Well, it's a nice idea.

More than a little to the author's surprise, I suspect, Simon Hughes's book **A Lot of Hard Yakka** won the William Hill Sports Book of the Year award, the first time a cricket book has achieved this. This in itself is astonishing, considering the number that appear every season, and the supposed niche, as far as quality is concerned, that they claim. I mentioned to Hughes that I had enjoyed his tale of a cricketer's beginnings, his life in and out of the game, and his eventual departure from it, but that I thought it was a terrible title. Amiable chap that he is, he agreed. Yakka is an Australianism, meaning work, endeavour, experience (I think). Subtitled "Triumph and torment: a county cricketer's life", it makes a breezy and irreverent read.

I recall how horrified I was to read in an American definitions book that "Shiver my timbers" is a well-known cricket expression. The solecism does not appear in **The Language of Cricket** by John Eddowes, but there are others. *Wisden Cricketers' Almanack*, for example, appears bereft of its final 'k'.

Sir Arthur Conan Doyle's main claim to cricket fame was that he bowled W. G. Grace (his only first-class wicket). He also captained P. G. Wodehouse at Lord's. Murray Hedgcock has edited **Wodehouse at the Wicket** with extracts from various cricketing adventures concerning Psmith and Jeeves. It raised a distant smile. A more contemporary grin is raised by Mark Bussell's **Linseed and Fishpaste**, surely the first book ever to have a cover featuring a curly-edged sandwich. I think its subtitle, "Confessions of a Cricket nut", should have been at the top of the page, because that is what it enjoyably is.

Les Jackson: A Derbyshire Legend by Mike Carey is a little book about a great-hearted man. Like Fred Trueman, who writes an admiring foreword, he came up from the mines and into the sunshine of cricket. Jackson also occupies several pages in Stephen Chalke's **Runs In The Memory**, a marvellously evocative recollection of county cricket in the 1950s. Since the author was born only in 1948, he patently took to the game straight from the cradle. He was only just born when Glamorgan won their first County Championship, but he retells here the enjoyable story of the relationship between the formidable captain, Wilf Wooller, and the self-doubting Willie Jones. Chalke says that Willie so lacked confidence that he used to get his wife to ring up to see if he had been selected for the team. He scored two hundreds in a fortnight in 1948, but still wondered if Glamorgan would renew his contract.

The Glory Days of Cricket by Ashley Mote is the story of the birth of the game at Broadhalfpenny Down. It is a wonderfully researched book, redolent with the famous old names of Hambledon – the Nyrens, Noah Mann, Lumpy Stevens. With a name like his, the author himself would not look out of place in the old scoresheets.

From Arlott to Aggers (that name again) is a mostly pictorial celebration of 40 years of the cheery club of *Test Match Special*, edited by Peter Baxter and Phil

McNeill. The tale of The Ball That Bowled Gatting is told yet again as it is, very naturally, in Shane Warne's **My Own Story**, written with Mark Ray. Warne says it is as great a moment as he has experienced. His book is one of the customary batch out of Australia, including **Under the Southern Cross**, David Boon's autobiography, this is a most finely produced book. Despite being priced lower than many of its contemporaries, this is a most finely produced book. What a pleasure to handle, let alone own, a volume as carefully put together as this! The binding, the paper, the design are all excellent, and the redoubtable Boon comes through with credit.

On Top Down Under: Australia's Cricket Captains is a revised paperback edition of Ray Robinson's book, first published in 1975. In an edition updated by Gideon Haigh, he tells the stories of the men who have led Australia since 1877. There are some intriguing pictures, including one of Syd Gregory looking not unlike a turn-of-the-century David Boon.

On the wall of my study I have a *Vanity Fair* drawing of Sammy Woods, ball half-hidden by his shirt cuff, sizing up the batsman. The same cartoon occupies the front of **Sammy: The Sporting Life of S. M. J. Woods** by Clifford Jiggens, the story of a cricketer who, at the end of the last century, plied his trade in both Australia and England. He played for *both* countries at Test level and W. G. Grace described him as "a giant in size, in strength and pluck". Sammy had enough pluck to describe Grace as "an artful old toad". Ah, but what a toad, who still casts a spell 150 years after his birth.

Leslie Thomas is a best-selling popular novelist and travel writer. He is a member of the Lord's Taverners and a cricket fanatic, still playing aged 66. He is usually sent in when the other batsman is scoring too slowly and the captain wants someone to run him out.

ADDITIONAL REVIEWS

Matthew Engel writes: A small avalanche of books arrived too late to be included in Leslie Thomas's review. Several of them came out of the 1997 Ashes series. Traditionally, these books sell best when England win. But there is no recent evidence to tell us whether that still applies and, anyway, the traditional sort of tour or Test series book seems to have vanished, to be replaced by something a bit less obvious. Rob Steen's book **Poms and Cobbers** sees the drama of the summer mainly through four pairs of eyes; they belong to two players, Robert Croft and Matthew Elliott, plus Mark Ray, who is an extremely original and clever photographer, and Steen himself.

The book works, because Steen was lucky/shrewd enough to pick two players who had fascinating series: Elliott ascending to glory, Croft plummeting to earth. Steen himself is a gifted, worldly writer (who sometimes does not know when to give over), and he brings plenty out of his subjects. My favourite moment comes when Croft muses on his argy-bargy with Mark Ilott in the NatWest semi-final. "I do think it has been blown out of proportion. It was announced after the third bong on *News at Ten*; if I'm not mistaken, it took precedence over a famine."

David Hopps's "Alternative Story of an Ashes Year" is entitled **We're Right Behind You, Captain!** There are two captains involved here: Mike Atherton, as captain of England, and Hopps himself, as captain of Thorner Mexborough CC of the Wetherby and District League. If Hopps abuses Atherton's leadership, you can be sure that he does so with some feeling and the experience of leading a truly inadequate cricket team. It is an engaging way of looking at the game, and Hopps gamely quotes some of his own players, satirising the dilemmas that afflict a *Guardian* writer when he is made captain of anything: "Do *I* prefer you in front of square or behind? Well, I don't *really* have an opinion. Which would *you* prefer? Which position could you most *relate* to? Where do *you* feel more comfortable? Where do you think you could most *grow* as a human being?''

Ashes Summer is harder to read than the other two, but will probably prove easier to sell. It is a joint diary from the two vice-captains, Nasser Hussain and Steve Waugh. (Hussain was ''helped'' by Paul Newman; Waugh seems able to do his own pen-wielding). Both have plenty to talk about. ''It was the first time I can remember being content after getting out,'' says Hussain of his 207 at Edgbaston. Waugh is disarmingly matter-of-fact about his two hundreds at Old Trafford: ''My second hundred was finally secured with a push through mid-wicket off Robert Croft. The elation was not as intense as in the first innings, but the satisfaction was the same ...''

The nearest thing to an old-fashioned Ashes book is **Ashes 97: Two Views from the Boundary** by two political scientists from Manchester University, Norman Geras and Ian Holliday. Dignified in their own field, they attend cricket as unashamed fans. They pinch the corporate guests' seats when they are absent (i.e. most of the time); they play Scrabble when it rains. They do not know the players' nicknames, but they experienced every day of the summer as spectators, and I have a curious feeling that this book will weather well as a social document of cricket-watching.

Yet another biography of Ian Botham has appeared: **No Surrender** by Dave Bowler. It is perhaps encouraging that publishers think there is still mileage in Beefy. But there is not a lot more anyone can say. And, though Bowler is thoughtful and sympathetic, he has no special access or insights to offer. Trueman books also go on for ever. **Fred Trueman Talking Cricket** has the old stories, gilded handsomely by Don Mosey, and, heaven knows, people still laugh at them after dinner, so who can complain? Martin Johnson, lately of *The Independent*, now of the *Daily Telegraph*, is one of the few people now adding to the game's vein of humour. His writings have been collected by a fan, Andrew Green, under the title of Johnson's famous phrase about England: **Can't Bat, Can't Bowl, Can't Field**. Johnson has less ego per ton of talent than any writer I have ever met and he is mordantly, often mercilessly, funny. His drawback is that he works best being sardonic, and finds it hard to move into another gear. But then he spent ten years covering England, so that is hardly surprising.

Reference book of the year must be **Limited-Overs International Cricket: The Complete Record** by Bill Frindall. It is, as you would expect, meticulously done and as user-friendly as a book with 1,119 one-day scorecards can possibly be. There is a disagreement between ICC and *Wisden* on the one hand, and Frindall on the other, over the status of matches that are started, rained off at an early stage and then replayed. It is not Grant Flower's fault that it rained when he was 25 not out at Patna at 1995-96, and it seems reasonable to me that these runs should count. Frindall disagrees, vehemently, and has included these scores only as what he nicely calls ''a grumbling appendix''.

Finally: two very different books from Australia. **The Summer Game**, Gideon Haigh's history of the Australian game between the era of Bradman and the Chappells, is evocative, charming and finely woven, a serious addition to social history. **Wildmen of Cricket** by Ken Piesse and Brian Hansen is unashamedly breathless and sensationalist. I was still recovering from the surprise that ''wildmen'' had suddenly become one word when I reached No. 2 on the list of wildmen: Sir Donald Bradman. That could make some readers really wild.

BOOKS RECEIVED IN 1997

ASHES 1997

Geras, Norman and Holliday, Ian **Ashes 97: Two Views from the Boundary** (Baseline Books, PO Box 8, Tisbury, Wilts SP3 6TG, £9.99)

Hopps, David **We're Right Behind You, Captain! The Alternative Story of an Ashes Year** Foreword by Matthew Engel (Robson Books, £17.95)

Hussain, Nasser and Waugh, Steve **Ashes Summer: A Personal Diary of the 1997 England v Australia Test Series** (Collins Willow, £14.99)

Steen, Rob with Robert Croft and Matthew Elliott **Poms and Cobbers: The Ashes 1997 – An Inside View** (Andre Deutsch, £17.99)

GENERAL

Bassano, Brian **MCC in South Africa 1938-39** Forewords by Len Wilkinson and Norman Gordon (J. W. McKenzie, 12 Stoneleigh Park Road, Ewell, Surrey KT19 0QT, £18. Limited edition of 250 copies, signed by Len Wilkinson and the author, £38)

Baxter, Peter, Agnew, Jonathan and Lloyd, David **Out of the Rough: England in Zimbabwe and New Zealand** (Andre Deutsch, £15.99)

Baxter, Peter and McNeill, Phil, eds. **From Arlott to Aggers: 40 Years of Test Match Special** Foreword by Sir Colin Cowdrey (Andre Deutsch, £14.99)

Botham, Ian with Peter Hayter **The Botham Report** (Collins Willow, £16.99)

Bussell, Mark **Linseed and Fishpaste: Confessions of a Cricket nut** (Headline, £14.99)

Chalke, Stephen **Runs In The Memory: County Cricket in the 1950s** Illustrated by Ken Taylor (Fairfield Books, 17 St George's Road, Fairfield Park, Bath BA1 6EY, £15.95 inc. p&p)

Haigh, Gideon **The Summer Game: Australian Test Cricket 1949-71** (Text Publishing, Melbourne, $A39.95)

Licudi, Adam with Wasim Raja **Cornered Tigers: A History of Pakistan's Test Cricket** Foreword by Hanif Mohammad (Hansib Caribbean, PO Box 2773, St John's, Antigua; from the author, 53 Oxford Road South, London W4 3DD, £16.95 + p&p)

Mote, Ashley **The Glory Days of Cricket: The Extraordinary Story of Broadhalfpenny Down** (Robson Books, £22.95)

Piesse, Ken and Hansen, Brian **Wildmen of Cricket Volume 1.** Foreword by Greg Chappell (Brian Hansen Publications, PO Box 698, Mount Waverley, Victoria 3149, $A24.95 + $A5 p&p in Australia)

Qureshi, Ehsan A. ed. **Wills World Cup 1996** Foreword by Imran Khan (Sports Publications, GPO Box 1021, Karachi, Pakistan, Rs 300 or $US10)

Robinson, Ray and Haigh, Gideon **On Top Down Under: Australia's Cricket Captains – revised edition** (Wakefield Press, $A27.95; Andre Deutsch, £8.99)

Sharpham, Peter **The 1899 Australians in England** Foreword by Lindsay Hassett (J. W. McKenzie, address as above, £18)

Simons, R. G. **Cricket in Hertfordshire** Foreword by Henry Blofeld (from Tony Gibbs, 19 Huggins Lane, Welham Green, Herts AL9 7LJ, £25)

Simpson, Bob **The Reasons Why: A decade of coaching, a lifetime of cricket** (Harper Sports, $A24.95; £14.99)

Thorburn, Gordon and Baxter, John **Village Cricket: The genuine article** Foreword by David Byas (Fido Publishing, Appleby-in-Westmorland, Cumbria CA16 6BD, £8.99)

Trueman, Fred and Mosey, Don **Fred Trueman Talking Cricket** (Hodder & Stoughton, £16.99)

Waugh, Steve **Steve Waugh's World Cup Diary** (Harper Sports, Sydney, $A30; in UK from Sportspages, 94-96 Charing Cross Road, London WC2H 0JG and Barton Square, St Ann's Square, Manchester M2 7HA, £10.99)

West, Alan comp. **Fifty Years of the Lancashire Cricket Federation 1947-1997/The Memoirs of Jim Gledhill** (from Duncan Sutcliffe, 3 East View Cottage, Church Road, Todmorden OL14 8HP, £10 + £1.50 p&p)

Willis, Ron **The Ashes People, Shaken and Stirred** (Suite 2, 116 Acomb Road, York YO2 4EY, £7 + £1.55 p&p in UK, £2.75 EU, £5 US, £5.50 Australia)

Wynne-Thomas, Peter **The History of Cricket: From The Weald to The World.** Foreword by Richie Benaud (The Stationery Office, £25)

ANTHOLOGY

Gideon Haigh's **Australian Cricket Anecdotes** (Oxford University Press, Melbourne, $A29.95; in UK, £16.99)

Hedgcock, Murray ed. **Wodehouse at the Wicket** (Hutchinson, £12.99)

Johnson, Martin **Can't Bat, Can't Bowl, Can't Field: The Best Cricket Writing of Martin Johnson** Foreword by David Gower (Collins Willow, £16.99)

AUTOBIOGRAPHY

Agnew, Jonathan **Over to You, Aggers** (Victor Gollancz, £16.99)

Bird, Dickie **My Autobiography** Foreword by Michael Parkinson (Hodder & Stoughton, £17.99)

Boon, David **Under the Southern Cross** (Harper Sports, $A29.95; £14.99)

Frith, David **Caught England, Bowled Australia: A cricket slave's complex story** (Eva Press, 17 Lyon Road, London SW19 2SE, £18 + £1.99 p&p)

Healy, Ian with Robert Craddock **The Ian Healy Story: Playing for Keeps** (Swan Publishing, Perth, $A24.95; in UK from Sportspages, 94-96 Charing Cross Road, London WC2H 0JG and Barton Square, St Ann's Square, Manchester M2 7HA, £17.95)

Hughes, Simon **A Lot of Hard Yakka: Triumph and torment: a county cricketer's life** (Headline, £16.99)

Russell, Jack with Patrick Murphy **Unleashed: Barking?** (Collins Willow, £15.99)

Snow, Philip **The Years of Hope: Cambridge, Colonial Administration in the South Seas and Cricket** (The Radcliffe Press, £24.50)

Snow, Philip **A Time of Renewal: Clusters of Characters, C. P. Snow and Coups** (The Radcliffe Press, £24.50)

Warne, Shane with Mark Ray **My Own Story** (Bookman Projects, £9.99)

BIOGRAPHY

Bowler, Dave **No Surrender: The life and times of Ian Botham** (Orion, £18.99)

Carey, Mike **Les Jackson: A Derbyshire Legend** (Tranters, Markeaton Printing Works, Derby DE22 3AX, £9.50 inc. p&p, £15 hardback, signed by Les Jackson)

Jiggens, Clifford **Sammy: The Sporting Life of S. M. J. Woods** (Sansom & Co, 22 Canynge Square, Bristol BS8 3LA, £14.99)

Low, Robert **W. G.: A Life of W. G. Grace** (Richard Cohen Books, £18.99)

Norrie, David **Athers: the Authorised Biography of Michael Atherton** (Headline, £17.99)

Searle, Andrew **S. F. Barnes: His Life and Times** (Empire Publications, 62 Charles St, Manchester M1 7DF, £14.95 + £2 p&p)

Simons, Grenville **William Yardley: Master of Bat and Burlesque** (Wisteria Books, Wisteria Cottage, Birt St, Birtsmorton, Worcs WR13 6AW, £15 + £1.50 p&p)

PICTORIAL

Hignell, Andrew comp. **Glamorgan County Cricket Club** Part of The Archive Photograph series (Chalford Publishing, St Mary's Mill, Chalford, Glos, GL6 8NX, £9.99)

Pope, Mick comp. **Yorkshire County Cricket Club** Part of The Archive Photograph series (Chalford Publishing, address as above, £9.99)

CARTOONS

Hall, Robert **Chirping Cricket Club v A. Village** Illustrations by Richard Walker. Last Word by Allan Lamb (Last Word Publications, Woodcote, Seaview, Isle of Wight PO34 5BJ, no price given)

REFERENCE

Arnold, Peter and Wynne-Thomas, Peter **The Ultimate Encyclopedia of Cricket** (Carlton/Hodder & Stoughton, £19·99)

Eddowes, John **The Language of Cricket** (Carcanet, £9.95)

Winch, Jonty **Cricket in Southern Africa: Two hundred years of achievements and records** (Windsor Publishers, PO Box 621, Rosettenville, South Africa, no price given)

STATISTICAL

Ambrose, Don comp. **1873: A Statistical Survey** and **1874** (ACS, 3 Radcliffe Road, West Bridgford, Nottingham NG2 5FF, £4.50 and £5.50 respectively)

Bailey, Philip J. comp. **First-Class County Matches 1902** (ACS, address as above, £13.00)

Bailey, Philip J. comp. **Sri Lanka First-Class Matches 1992-93** and **1993-94** (ACS, address as above, £4.50 and £5.95 respectively)

Frindall, Bill **Limited-Overs International Cricket: The Complete Record** (Headline, £35)

Griffiths, Peter **Complete First-Class Match List: Volume 2 1914/15-1944/45** and **Volume 3 1945-1962/63** (ACS, address as above, £7 each)

Griffiths, Peter and Senior, Darren **I.C.C. Trophy 1997: Kuala Lumpur, Malaysia** (ACS, address as above, £8.50)

Harte, Wesley **C. S. Dempster: His Record Innings-by-Innings** (ACS, address as above, £6)

Hatton, Les **Worcestershire County Cricket Club First-Class Records 1899-1996** (Limlow Books, Blue Bell House, 2-4 Main Street, Scredington, Sleaford, Lincs NG34 0AE, £8.75 + 50p p&p)

Isaacs, Vic and Richard comp. **Gillette Cup and NatWest Trophy Record Book 1963-1996** (ACS, address as above, £9.95)

Isherwood, Robin and Bailey, Philip comp. **Natal Cricketers** (ACS, address as above, £3)

Kazi, Abid Ali comp. **First-Class Cricket in Pakistan: Volume I 1947-48 to 1952-53** (Pakistan Association of Cricket Statisticians and Scorers, 31, 30th Street, F-6/1, Islamabad, Rs 250; in UK from Limlow Books, address as above, £15)

Lambert, Dennis **Leicestershire County Cricket Club First-Class Records 1894-1996** (Limlow Books, address as above, £8.75 + 50p p&p)

Ledbetter, Jim ed. **First-Class Cricket: A Complete Record 1933** (Limlow Books, address as above, £16.95 + £1.50 p&p)

Ledbetter, Jim comp. **Trent Bridge Test Records 1899-1996** (ACS, address as above, £6.95)

Overson, Chris **Tony Lock: His Record Innings-by-Innings** (ACS, address as above, £8.95)

Percival, Tony, comp. **Cheshire Cricketers 1822-1996** (ACS, address as above, £3)

Phipps, Ian **Doug Wright: His Record Innings-by-Innings** (ACS, address as above, £7.95)

Sandiford, Keith A. P. **Frank Worrell: His Record Innings-by-Innings** (ACS, address as above, £5.95)

Sheen, Steven and Bartlett, Kit **Tom Hayward: His Record Innings-by-Innings** (ACS, address as above, £6.95)

Stanford, Arthur and Collin, Marion R. **99 Not Out: Scorecards and Statistics of Women's Test Matches 1934-1996** (ACS, address as above, £8.50)

Ward, John comp. **Zimbabwe First-Class Matches 1996-97** (ACS, address as above, £1.99)

Webster, Ray comp. **First-Class Cricket in Australia: Volume 2: 1945-46 to 1976-77** (from Ray Webster, PO Box 1074, Glen Waverley, Victoria 3150, $A80 + $10 p&p; in UK from Limlow Books, address as above, £45 inc. p&p)

Wilkinson, Roy D. **Yorkshire County Cricket Club First-Class Records 1863-1996** (Limlow Books, address as above, £9.50 + 50p p&p)

FIRST-CLASS COUNTY YEARBOOKS, 1997

Derbyshire (£5), Durham (£6), Essex (£7), Glamorgan (£5), Gloucestershire (£3), Hampshire (£6.50), Kent (£4.99), Lancashire (£6), Leicestershire (£6.95), Middlesex (£8), Northamptonshire (£7.50), Nottinghamshire (£4.50), Somerset (£6.50), Surrey (£5), Sussex (£6), Warwickshire (£5), Worcestershire (£5), Yorkshire (£11.50). 1998 prices may change. Some counties may add charges for p&p.

OTHER HANDBOOKS AND ANNUALS

Bader, Nauman ed. **PCB Wills Cricket Annual 1996-97** (from Limlow Books, Blue Bell House, 2-4 Main Street, Scredington, Sleaford, Lincs NG34 0AE, £21 inc. p&p in UK)

Bailey, Philip comp. **ACS International Cricket Year Book 1997** (ACS, 3 Radcliffe Road, West Bridgford, Nottingham NG2 5FF, £9.95)

Berry, Mike ed. **Minor Counties Cricket 1997 Annual** (from Mike Berry, Idsworth, 3 Fair Close, Frankton, Rugby, Warwicks CV23 9PL, £3)

Bryden, Colin ed. **Mutual & Federal South African Cricket Annual 1996** (UCBSA/Mutual & Federal, PO Box 1120 Johannesburg 2000; in UK from Appleby's Books, 15 Southey Street, Keswick, Cumbria CA12 4EG, £16.50 inc. p&p)

Frindall, Bill ed. **NatWest Playfair Cricket Annual 1997** (Headline, £4.99)

Frith, David ed. **Test Match Year 1996-1997** (Penguin, £9.99)

Hatton, Les comp. **ACS First Class Counties Second Eleven Annual** (ACS, address as above, £4.95)

Hawkes, Chris ed. **The Cricketers' Who's Who, 1997** Foreword by Hugh Morris (Lennard/Queen Anne Press, £12.99)

Lemmon, David ed. **Benson and Hedges Cricket Year: Sixteenth Edition** (Bloomsbury, £20)

Maxwell, Jim ed. **ABC Cricket 1997 Ashes Tour** (Australian Broadcasting Commission, $A4.95)

Maxwell, Jim ed. **ABC Cricket 1997-98** (Australian Broadcasting Commission, $A4.95)

Menon, Mohandras ed. **Cricontrol Statistical Annual 1996-97** (Board of Control for Cricket in India)

Miller, Allan ed. **Allan's Australian Cricket Annual 1997** (from Allan Miller, PO Box 974, Busselton, WA 6280, $A35; in UK from Sport in Print, 3 Radcliffe Road, West Bridgford, Nottingham NG2 5FF, £18.50 inc. p&p)

The W. M. Mann Guide to Scottish Cricket 1997 (Scottish Cricket Union, £4)

FICTION

Spartak, Steve **The Sinister Case of the Lost Over Before Tea** (from the author, 55 Roden St, London N7 6QJ or from Sportspages, 94-96 Charing Cross Road, London WC2H 0JG and Barton Square, St Ann's Square, Manchester M2 7HA, £5.50)

CHILDREN'S FICTION

Cattell, Bob **League of Champions** and **Blaze of Glory** (Red Fox, £3.50 each)

REPRINTS AND UPDATES

Bentley, Henry **Book of Cricket Matches: 1786 to 1822** (with two supplements, 1823 to 1825) Facsimile edition with new preface by David Rayvern Allen (Roger Heavens, 2 Lowfields, Little Eversden, Cambs CB3 7HJ, £50 + £3.50 p&p)

Dawson, Graham and Wat, Charlie **Test Cricket Lists: Third edition** (Five Mile Press, Melbourne $A19.95; in UK from Chris Lloyd, 463 Ashley Road, Parkstone, Dorset BH14 0AX, £9.95)

Hopps, David **Free as a Bird: The Life and Times of Harold "Dickie" Bird** Foreword by Geoffrey Boycott. Paperback edition (Pan, £5.99)

Lamb, Allan with Jack Bannister **My Autobiography** Paperback edition with additional chapter (Collins Willow, £5.99)

Lillywhite, Frederick **Frederick Lillywhite's Scores and Biographies: Volume II 1827-1840** and **Volume III 1841-1848** (Facsimile edition, from Roger Heavens, address as above, £50 each + £3.50 p&p each in Europe, £4.50 or £10 airmail elsewhere)

Philpott, Peter **The Art of Wrist-Spin Bowling** Paperback edition (Crowood Press, £12.99)

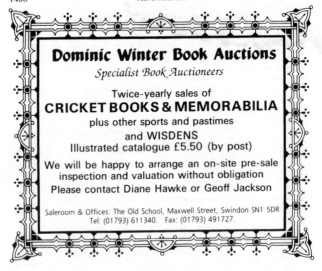

Rayvern Allen, David ed. **In the Covers: The Best Cricket Writing of the Year (1996)** Paperback edition (Headline, £6.99)

Reeve, Dermot with Patrick Murphy **Winning Ways** Paperback edition (Boxtree, £6.99)

John Wisden's Cricketers' Almanacks for 1902, 1903, 1916, 1917, 1918 and **1919** Facsimile edition (Willows Publishing, 17 The Willows, Stone, Staffs ST15 0DE, £46 (1902), £48 (1903), £40 (1917-19) inc. p&p UK, £2 (1902-03) or £3 (1917-19) extra overseas; £5 extra for version with facsimile of original hard cloth cover; 1916 available only in original hard cloth version at £45 or £48 overseas)

PERIODICALS

Australian Cricket (monthly October to March) ed. Ken Piesse (EMAP Australia, PO Box 746, Darlinghurst, NSW 2010, $A4.95, $A25.48 per year, $A72.40 for 12 issues overseas)

The Cricketer International (monthly) editorial director Richard Hutton (Beech Hanger, Ashurst, Tunbridge Wells, Kent TN3 9ST, £2.60)

The Cricketer Quarterly: Facts and Figures ed. Richard Lockwood (The Cricketer International, address as above, £2.90)

Cricket Lore (ten per volume, frequency variable) ed. Richard Hill (Cricket Lore, 22 Grazebrook Road, London N16 0HS, £35 per volume)

The Cricket Statistician (quarterly) ed. Philip J. Bailey (ACS, 3 Radcliffe Road, West Bridgford, Nottingham NG2 5FF, £2.50, free to ACS members)

Cricket World (most months) editorial director Michael Blumberg (157 Praed Street, London W2 1RL, £2.35)

Inside Edge (Australia, monthly) managing editor Norman Tasker (ACP Publishing, 54 Park Street, Sydney, NSW 2000, $A5.20)

The Journal of the Cricket Society (twice yearly) ed. Clive W. Porter (from Mr P. Ellis, 63 Groveland Road, Beckenham, Kent BR3 3PX, £5 to non-members)

League Cricket Review (monthly in summer) ed. Andy Searle (Empire Publications, 62 Charles Street, Manchester M1 7DF, £1.50)

Minor Counties News (details from Mike Berry, Idsworth, 3 Fair Close, Frankton, Rugby, Warwicks CV23 9PL)

Red Stripe Caribbean Quarterly ed. Tony Cozier (Cozier Publishing, PO Box 40W, Worthing, Christ Church, Barbados, annual subscription £12 Europe, $BDS22 Barbados, $BDS28/$US14 rest of West Indies, $US18 US, $Can24 Canada, $US24 elsewhere)

SA Cricket Action (nine issues a year) ed. Chris Whales (PO Box 1144, Cape Town 8000, R9.95. Subscriptions: (00 27) 21 461 9752)

The Scottish Cricketer (three issues a year) editorial director Terry Brennan (4 Belhaven Terrace, Dowanhill, Glasgow G12 0TF, £1.50)

Wicket Maiden Quarterly ed. Alex Picker (223 Perry Road, Nottingham NG5 1GN, £1.25)

Wisden Cricket Monthly ed. Tim de Lisle (The New Boathouse, 136-142 Bramley Road, London W10 6SR, £2.60. Subscriptions: 01483 733895)

INDEX

Heavens, Roger **An Index to Frederick Lillywhite's/Haygarth's Cricket Scores and Biographies of Celebrated Cricketers: Volumes I to XV, 1746-1878** (Roger Heavens, 2 Lowfields, Little Eversden, Cambs CB3 7HJ; I to XI £4.95 each inc. p&p, XII to XIV £9.95, XV free with the set)

THE CRICKET SOCIETY LITERARY AWARD

The Cricket Society Literary Award, sponsored by Coopers & Lybrand, has been presented since 1970 to the author of the cricket book judged as best of the year. The 1998 award went to Ashley Mote for **The Glory Days of Cricket: The Extraordinary Story of Broadhalfpenny Down**.

CRICKET VIDEOS, 1997

By SIMON BRIGGS

Australia responded smartly to England's commanding start to the Ashes summer, but not as smartly as Sky Sports. Sky rushed out **Battle for the Ashes, Part One** – a neat compilation of highlights from the one-day internationals and the First Test – within a fortnight of England's triumph at Edgbaston. But they confirmed that there were no plans to release Part Two, "for obvious reasons". Their market was England rather than Australia.

So the **Cover Point** series of monthly video magazines provided the only visual record of the next five Tests. Short interviews with key players from each game added a new dimension to its familiar clips and tips formula, and turned up some unexpectedly interesting titbits. Glenn McGrath, speaking after his eight for 38 at Lord's, ascribed his poor early form to the fact that he had been charging in too fast and spoiling the rhythm of his body action.

There was vintage footage from Australia's Channel Nine in a series called **The Tests of Time**. The video featuring the first Test of England's 1979-80 tour included a cameo of Dennis Lillee's infamous aluminium bat. He opted for the willow in the second innings, but his dismissal caused further excitement in the commentary box: "Lillee, caught Willey, bowled Dilley!" cried Tony Cozier. "That's the scoreline we had all hoped for this season!"

The black-and-white era was brought to life by **All Time Greats Masterclass**, filmed in 1930 and boasting Jack Hobbs, Wally Hammond, Maurice Tate and Percy Chapman among its models. And a 1990 interview with another all-time great was re-released by Cover Point under the title **Don Bradman – Genius**. The excellence of its action footage made up for some creaky production values, which is more than could be said for two contrived compilations: **The A to Z of Cricket** and **Great Moments in Cricket**.

Harry Brind's **Groundsmanship – a Year in the Life of a Cricket Ground** was available to ECB-affiliated clubs, but not to the general public. As far as the layman was concerned, it was absorbing but rather slow-moving – a little like the job itself, one suspects. And a few more glimpses of groundsman Micky Hunt at work could be found on **Lord's Uncovered**, a guided tour of the "cathedral of cricket". Even those who know the ground intimately might be intrigued by its pictures of the Australian team processing through the members in the Long Room, or of Father Time being restored last summer. Keith Miller described his own experience of MCC members: "If you make a hundred, the men stand aside – 'Well done, Miller.' Then make a duck, and walk through the same crowd, and you feel as if you're in a mortuary."

VIDEOS RECEIVED IN 1997

The A to Z of Cricket (IMC Video, £10.99)

Battle for the Ashes, Part One (Sky Sports, £9.99)

Cover Point Video magazine (Cover Point Cricket Ltd, 113 Upper Tulse Hill, London SW2 2RD, £11.99 each or ten issues a year for £89.99 in UK)

Cricket: All Time Greats Masterclass (Historic Sports Video, £9.99)

Don Bradman – Genius (Sharp Focus/Cover Point, £16.49 inc. p&p in UK)

Great Moments in Cricket (Classic Pictures Video, £10.99)

Groundsmanship (ECB Video, available free of charge to affiliated clubs)

Lord's Uncovered (ITN/MCC, £12.99)

The Tests of Time (Visual Entertainment, 362 Swan St, Richmond, Vic 3121, $A29.95)

UK prices are Recommended Retail Prices.

CRICKET AND THE MEDIA IN 1997

1. DAVID McKIE in London

The Times thought it worth a place on page one. "Sporting euphoria vanishes" it announced on July 5 over a story which, though it also mentioned the collapse of the British challenge at Wimbledon, was mainly about England's slump to Shane Warne, who had just put Australia in command in the Third Test at Old Trafford. For readers with even the mildest sense of history, the curious thing about this report was that euphoria should ever have been there in the first place.

Only four months earlier, there had been universal agreement that English cricket had hit rock bottom. The precise moment of that collision was a matter of choice. The seven-wicket defeat by largely part-time Mashonaland? An England collapse in the third one-day match with Zimbabwe, engineered by the out-swing bowling of a *chicken farmer*? Or the failure of English bowlers in the Auckland Test to dismiss Danny Morrison, who, said Simon Barnes in *The Times*, could "claim without false modesty to be the worst batsman in the history of Test cricket"? "The man," *The Guardian's* Mike Selvey snorted, "is a ferret who goes in after the rabbits. In short, he cannot bat his eyelids." The word nadir was used several times, and might have been used more often but for the sense that nadirs of English cricket had been proclaimed before, only for worse to follow. The coming summer would see the arrival of the all-powerful Australians. Even deeper humiliations threatened.

Then suddenly everything changed – in media perception, if not in real life. The Australians were seen to be struggling. The captain, Mark Taylor, just couldn't bat: calls by Ian Chappell and other Australian commentators for the captain to be sacked were joyously reproduced in the British press. *The Mirror* mockingly presented him with a bat three feet wide, labelled "Duckbats Inc." and plastered with ducks, an event to which he reacted with better grace than *The Mirror* deserved. And Warne couldn't bowl. "Shane can't grip his balls," enthused a back-page headline in *The Sun*. That was "Taylor's excuse for flop Warne".

England's one day successes whipped up a conviction that any nadirs this summer would be Australia's rather than England's. "It is time to be cocky," wrote Alan Fraser of the *Daily Mail* after the one-day series. "It is time to shout from the highest hill: we beat the Aussies. Correction: we murdered the Aussies." "Here in real life," wrote Lord Deedes in the *Daily Telegraph*, "was the sort of ascent from the abyss against the odds which A. E. W. Mason had in mind when he wrote *The Four Feathers*."

Even Fred Trueman was caught up in the general spirit of celebration. "Take it from me," he wrote in *The People* before the Edgbaston Test, "Devon Malcolm will be brought back to shatter what little remains of Australia's Ashes hopes. And in my book, that's good news for England, because we'll never have a better chance to win back the little urn and Big Dev – our quickest bowler – is the man to provide the firepower." "England's performance in the First Test," Trueman wrote a week later, "has revitalised the whole country and I reckon we have not had such a boost in sporting morale since Alf Ramsey's boys won the World Cup in 1966. They have shown what I have been saying ever since the Australians arrived. World champions! They're not all they're cracked up to be." He was not wholly enthusiastic about England's bowling: "Devon Malcolm," he said, "would not have been in the team if I had my way." "Our men," *The Times* purred in a leader page comment, "wore clean, pressed whites, and proper caps, and smiles of good rapport. They played with spontaneity, a far cry from their ochre humour on the recent Zimbabwe tour."

But despite all the shaving and ironing, it couldn't last, and it didn't. "It's time to take sweet revenge on wily Warne," said the *Mail* headline over a piece by Nasser Hussain (as told to Brian Scovell) on the eve of Old Trafford. Hussain was more cautious than his headline suggested, but here was hubris, and just round the corner as usual was nemesis: Hussain c Healy b Warne 13. "England froze in bewilderment yesterday when the perverse Manchester sunshine brought the warmth and magic flooding back into Shane Warne's fingers," Peter Johnson wrote in the *Mail* on July 5 as glory made its customary departure. "The problem, I fear," Ian Wooldridge reflected in the same paper, "is largely created by my trade, which tends to deal in emotive headlines from either extremity of the critical spectrum. Thus yesterday's idol is tomorrow's idiot... The splendid Birmingham victory was greeted with such an embarrassing blast of jingoistic triumphalism that it was always on the cards that they'd be skittled out for next to nothing at Lord's and on the rack again at Old Trafford."

Worse was to follow. "England's cricket here," Alan Lee of *The Times* reported from Headingley, "had become limp, clueless, fatalistic... Their batting crumbled pitifully on the second morning and their bowling, initially menacing, was reduced by yesterday to anaemic compliance. Their fielding, recently so sharp, was shambolic." *The Express* sports page issued an apology: "In common with other newspapers, we might have given the impression that England were capable of winning the Ashes..." Inside, Ray Illingworth recommended that Atherton be dismissed. "What a bunch of pansies!" ran a headline in *The Mirror* after Trent Bridge. "That's England, NOT the flowers," the paper explained.

The Oval made things seem brighter again. It also changed calculations on the future of Mike Atherton. After the Trent Bridge fiasco, the *Mail* ran a disdainful piece under the headline: "Dead duck: Michael Atherton – you are charged with impersonating an England cricket captain." After England's bad opening day at The Oval, *The Sun* published under the headline "Ather n'Out" a picture of the shot which had cost the captain his wicket. "This was the moment," it claimed, "when Mike Atherton knew he was finished as England skipper." Not exactly. England won the game, Atherton went away to consider his future quietly. That was not good enough for Geoff Boycott. "The way the selectors and management are carrying on," he said in *The Sun* (as told to John Etheridge), "you would think Michael Atherton is the King of England. He is being given the fawning, reverential treatment normally afforded to the reigning monarch." (This was five days before the death of Diana, Princess of Wales, revealed that the public no longer fawned over monarchs.) Michael, Boycott conceded, was not a bad man. He was not a criminal. He was not even our worst ever captain. But he still ought to go. He stayed.

Amidst it all, one group which rarely troubles the scorers also caught the eye of the media – the scorers themselves – initially when difficulties with the Duckworth/Lewis system for setting target scores in rain-affected limited-overs matches ("makes $E = mc^2$ look like a bit of fun with an abacus" – Paul Weaver, *The Guardian*) made its inventors the most talked-about double act since the discoverers of the Hale-Bopp comet. Then the scorers threatened to strike over various grievances, the chief of which was the choice of a BBC man to be the official scorer on the winter tour again. It never seemed likely. "I do not think scorers are sufficiently militant to go on strike," their man at The Oval, Keith Booth, was quoted as saying. He was right. Eventually they withdrew their earlier threat to boycott all Sunday League games on August 31 – though not before they had made history as perhaps the only group threatening industrial action ever to earn a sympathetic editorial comment from the *Daily Telegraph*.

2. GIDEON HAIGH in Melbourne

Winter 1997 in Australia offered two enticing competitions: one traditional, in the form of the Ashes; the other newer but growing more familiar, of Cricket versus the Rest of the World of Sport. Arriving at Heathrow in May, Mark Taylor's men were confident they had England's measure. But could they prevail in the battle for column inches and screen time against Australian Rules football, two loggerheaded rugby league competitions, the Bledisloe Cup in rugby union, soccer, Wimbledon, sundry Grands Prix and four golf majors?

As it happened, they more than punched their weight . . . if in a fashion quite impossible to forecast. For not only did the Ashes campaign prove quite the most entertaining of the last decade, but dressing-room dramas and commercial argy-bargy exerted a critical influence on the way events were seen. And not seen.

Preliminaries were inauspicious. After cut-throat series against West Indies and South Africa, few journalists were enthused by the prospect of watching Australia mete out six of the best to an English side incapable of matching Zimbabwe six months before. Writers at *The Australian*, in particular, left little doubt of their voting intentions at a future plebiscite on an Australian republic. "It is difficult to understand why England is still so widely regarded as a champagne series," griped its correspondent, Malcolm Conn. "Playing the beleaguered Poms is cheap and unfulfilling." Columnist Mike Coward was even more damning: "Apart from sentiment and tradition, England has nothing to do with cricket's real world at the end of the 20th century." Sentiment and tradition, of course, being things cricket should have no truck with. But perhaps they were merely echoing some of their own players. In the pre-tour *ABC Cricket Magazine*, Mark Waugh also implied a walkover in the offing: "They [England] just haven't got the toughness you need to win Test cricket consistently. Man-for-man they are not that far behind us, but they lack hunger."

One dissonant note as the tourists arrived was the captain's protracted spell in the batting dumps, which caused Ron Reed of the *Herald Sun* to liken the team to a Formula One racing car with a loose steering wheel. Among those urging Taylor to fall on his Stuart Surridge were an unlikely coalition of former coach Bob Simpson and the brothers Chappell. Greg of that ilk even turned amateur psychologist in the *Sunday Herald Sun*, contending that Taylor was a "classic case of denial" and "in no fit state to carry on".

Taylor's redemptive 129 at Edgbaston a week later, consequently, became the greatest cricketing come-back since Graham Gooch's hair. "Edge of abyss to the highest peak" shrieked the front page of the *Herald Sun*, while beneath ran reams from a breathless Reed: "Of all the many thousands of runs that have been scored in 120 years and 287 games of Test cricket between Australia and England, no more emotional shot has been played than the gentle push for a single that took Mark Taylor to his century at Edgbaston."

The story of virtue triumphant came complete with several juicy subplots: it emerged that another Australian sporting icon, Olympic swimmer Kieren Parkins, had spurred on Taylor with an inspirational fax; and that Taylor's wife Judy had cleaned up by standing by her man at the betting tent. Most fulsome praise, however, flowed on the broadsheet editorial pages of *The Australian*, where its omnicompetent conservative columnist Frank Devine explored parallels between Taylor's innings and Gary Cooper in *High Noon*, with its "eerily topical theme tune: 'If I'm a man I must be brave/And I must face the deadly killer/Or lie a coward, a craven coward/Or lie a coward in my grave'."

But Taylor's new lease of life – and England's – were by now competing for space with a local controversy over the maltreatment of Test match telecasts by the owners of free-to-air rights: Kerry Packer's mighty Nine Network, which had gone to such lengths to get the cricket 20 years earlier. With play starting at 8 p.m. Eastern Australian time, Nine chose not to disrupt its prime-time schedules and began showing the cricket only after lunch. Full service was available only to pay-TV viewers. Anyone in Melbourne turning on their sets to verify that Australia were really losing eight wickets before lunch on the first day of the series would instead have seen the celebrity panellists of *The Footy Show* cross-examining a touring troupe of Sumo wrestlers.

Nine defended itself on ratings grounds, chief executive David Leckie telling the *Herald Sun*: "You cannot disregard the viewers who choose to watch your regular programming week-in, week-out, and who would be appalled." Many people were appalled anyway. "No wonder Michael Jordan is No. 1 hero to our schoolchildren," blustered Victorian sports minister Tom Reynolds in *The Age*.

Nine could claim victory at the box office, where its evening ratings remained consistently strong. But, as a piece of public relations, it was a disaster. McGrath's opening salvos at Lord's and Jason Gillespie's lethal seven for 37 at Leeds, for instance, were supplanted by such telefodder as *Butterbox Babies*, *All-American Murder* and *Television: The Way We Were*. And of Steve Waugh's Manchester majesty, Nine viewers saw nothing at all: the Test had been dumped on the ABC to make way for the broadcast of rain from Wimbledon. But the *pièce de résistance* was Nine's approach to the last day of the Fourth Test. It featured live coverage of one delivery, an apparent sign-off from anchorman Greg Ritchie, a ten-minute ad break and, unannounced, a replay of the first session. As "You've Lost Us" of Barooga wrote to the *Herald Sun*: "Great work with the cricket, Channel Nine. Now can we look forward to seeing the last ten minutes of a movie before you show the beginning?"

Australia's eventual retention of the Ashes restored the cheery mood, Devine of *The Australian* again leading the cheers for Taylor after seeing him *en famille* amid his Trent Bridge triumph: "It is hard to think of a more resplendent demonstration of masculinity."

In all the on- and off-field theatre, however, probably the tour's most significant story was overlooked. As the First Test unfolded, the respected *Sunday Age* scribe Mark Ray reported that Australian Test cricketers had, under the auspices of their new Australian Cricketers' Association, recently discussed strike action "as part of a fight for better pay and conditions with the Australian Cricket Board". Rather remarkably, no member of the travelling troupe in England elected to pursue the story. But, as the 1997-98 season dawned, the alert was sounded again. No cricketers, no cricket. That would allow Channel Nine to show *Butterbox Babies* in peace.

CRICKET ON THE INTERNET, 1997

By DAVID HOPPS

One of the most peculiar experiences of the last English summer was to switch on the radio during the Oval Test and hear the *Test Match Special* team apprehensively advancing their knowledge of the Internet. What they sought to inform their listeners, in between deliveries, was that thanks to the Net, the *TMS* broadcast could now be heard worldwide, all for the cost of a local phone call. There were times when it all sounded like a counselling session for a group of technophobes.

The Internet's rise in popularity continued throughout 1997. Armed with a personal computer complete with the appropriate software, you could link up to the expanding worldwide web of computer information and entertainment. In the case of *TMS*, this caused some clashing of two diverse worlds. Merely announcing the web site's address on air proved challenging enough for some of the commentary team (Jonathan Agnew honourably excepted), who contentedly flaunted their inability to know a dot from a backslash.

Nevertheless, for *TMS* to broadcast via the Internet was a marvellous way to celebrate its 40th anniversary. Messages of congratulation were sent by e-mail (the equally flourishing electronic mail service) from places as far removed as Argentina and the Solomon Islands. For the first time *TMS* offered a truly worldwide service. It had yet to catch on, however, in the Internet epicentre of southern California.

In 1997, cricket and the Internet truly joined forces. It would have been inconceivable, even 12 months earlier, that a national newspaper would specifically consign a cricket writer to Internet duties for the whole of an Ashes series, but that was my own fate on behalf of the web site run jointly by *The Guardian* and *Wisden*. While I laboured over daily running copy, some newspaper-reading friends innocently enquired whether I had left the paper. There were times when I wondered that, too. But when the Ashes series was at its peak, a web site response as high as 100 hits (or callers) per second suggested that interest was higher than many perceived.

The *Guardian/Wisden* site had its rivals, though both the *Daily Telegraph* and *The Times*, for instance, satisfied themselves by carrying their correspondent's Ashes reports on their electronic sports pages. In all cases, the Internet was being explored uncertainly. Among newspaper executives, the debate continues as to whether it can prove a money-making venture, and whether it enhances press coverage or threatens to be the canker that will one day destroy it.

The launching of the official site of the ECB and MCC was also to be welcomed, coming as it did after sites from most of the other Test nations; indeed, after some first-class counties. Even then the welcome was not entirely unreserved. I wondered, and still do, whether it is healthy for the ECB, the modern administrators of the English game, to be linked so formally to a body which these days is little more than a private members' club. A touch more independence might have been advisable. Some MCC members, not without justification, also felt it inappropriate that the site was developed through the pointed sponsorship of Microsoft, the all-consuming computer software company; Lord's, argued some MCC loyalists, should not be used for advertising purposes, whatever might take place at The Oval. The official site of ECB and

MCC, in partnership with the Microsoft Network, carries the usual mix of news, reports and statistics. Throughout the winter, it offered more unusual service. The really homesick cricket lover could call up a small, "live" picture of Lord's, updated every minute, taken by a camera positioned at the top of the pavilion.

Such a proliferation of sites offered a new challenge to CricInfo, the most established cricket site. CricInfo claims to be "a non-profit organisation dependent on volunteer help". This ensures that it is not entirely reliable – two Yorkshire bowlers called Hutchinson were supposedly near the top of the first-class bowling averages last summer – but for statistical breadth, and especially for news on Asian cricket, CricInfo is unsurpassed.

And, if all these sites are not satisfying enough, call up a search engine such as "excite.com" or "yahoo.com", type in the word "cricket", ignore all references to jumping chirping insects and see what you can find. Up-to-date information is not always as obtainable as it might be, as this apology on an amateur site on Zimbabwe indicates: "Well, it's all been happening in Zimbabwe cricket. And here I am back from my holidays and too busy to do anything. This page will be updated asap." Time-consuming work, these web pages.

Selection of sites:

Wisden: www.wisden.com
Guardian/Wisden: www.thecricketsite.co.uk
CricInfo: www.cricket.org
ECB/MCC: www.lords.org
Australian Cricket Board: www.acb.com.au
Press Association cricket index: www.pa.press.net/sport/cricket

Although this is only a brief selection, many of these pages carry links to other sites. Internet addresses are always liable to change.

CRICKETANA IN 1997

By DAVID FRITH

The stock markets may have swayed and rattled towards the end of 1997, but the cricketana business continued to flourish without so much as a serious blip. The year was probably the most active and lucrative to date for memorabilia. If cricket did not quite have a counterpart to the quarter-million pounds paid for a mere replica of the Jules Rimet World Cup, or Jimi Hendrix's guitar, which fetched three times that, there was a top bid of £21,172 (including premium) for a 1930 Bradman bat at Phillips, and just on $A30,000 each (about £13,000) for Victor Trumper's 1899 cap and 1902 tour diary.

These last two items were in the sale of the year: the Ramamurthy Collection, sold in 413 lots by Christie's in Melbourne. Srikantan Ramamurthy, an Indian-born Australian, banked almost $A400,000 for his treasures, gathered over 35 years, and enjoyed not only freedom from the VAT and capital gains tax which would have haunted a resident of the UK, but also better prices overall than he might have done in London. Some delectable articles inspired a frenzy of bidding: $A6,325 for a signed photograph of the 1888 Australians, $A9,775 for a Clem Hill bat, thousands of dollars for signed Bradman photos and for team groups (Australia 1910-11 raised $A4,830), and big cheques for Trumper's cuff links, silverware and signed portraits (one made $A2,760). An exceptional item was Hugh Trumble's 1893 hat-band, the earliest relic of the Australian green-and-gold colours, sold for $A1,610.

In June, Christie's in London handled the sale of pictures from Peter MacKinnon's large collection. Collectors and dealers competed for an exquisite array of watercolours, oils and lithographs. The highest bid, £18,820, was for the original of *Cricket at Parker's Piece* (1846). Later in this sale, Jack Hobbs's richly filled autograph album made £2,823. But a set of six engraved pewter beakers, over 150 years old, sold for only £3,293, £1,000 less than in the 1987 MCC sale.

The other major auction-house for cricket, Phillips, also ventured to Melbourne. They offered Don Tallon's blazer ($A4,400), an 1880 tankard presented to Harry Boyle ($A2,750), and an imaginative painting of a fast bowler by Colvin Smith ($A6,600); Ray Lindwall's admirers would hope he was not the model, as suggested. A Trumper photo with a substandard signature made $A1,650, further causing onlookers to reflect that they really ought to cease being astonished by events in the sale-room.

In London, Phillips hammered bats associated with George Bonnor (£1,411), Patsy Hendren (£647), Hobbs (£6,116), and another of Bradman's (1938: £13,527), as well as Harold Larwood's book on the Bodyline tour, inscribed to his bowling partner Bill Voce (£506). An elderly man secured an old cast-iron turnstile from Trent Bridge for £176. He remarked: "I'm not sure what my wife's going to say." There were few more dramatic prices than the £5,646 paid for a copy of Thomas Boxall's 1804 instructional book, with John Small's name

on the endpaper. In 1966, this gem was bought for £58 at the J. W. Goldman sale.

Some big fish were caught away from the major venues. At Hampton's Godalming saleroom, a copy of W. G. Grace's *Cricket*, decorated with nearly 500 old signatures, fetched £5,881. At a Cricket Memorabilia Society auction, where buyers are spared any premium, James Lillywhite's contracts for Australian teams at Southport made over £2,000 each. Knight's of Norwich and Vennett-Smith of Nottingham shift great quantities of ephemera, and people are on the lookout for possible items at antiques fairs and jumble sales all over the cricket world. This is the bottom end, where bargains might just occasionally still be snapped up. There is another (sometimes slightly lunatic) end: the bat Mike Atherton used to withstand his siege in Johannesburg in 1995-96 was bought at a benefit dinner for £11,000.

CRICKET EQUIPMENT IN 1997

By NORMAN HARRIS

Even the humble cricket manufacturer in his supposed cottage industry understands the scientific point that protection from a high-speed hard ball is a matter not of resistance but of rapid energy-absorption. The analogy is with the runaway vehicle slowed better by deep sand than by the brick wall.

Some makers have even used a material, Confor, that was developed to line the cockpits of jet fighters and racing cars. And one of the makers at the cutting edge, Hunts County, is now exploring an air-cell material used in the mid-soles of running shoes.

One of the considerations here is that the protective material not only has to cushion the blow, but it has to recover, just as the human body does. Batting against Yorkshire in 1997, Durham's Mike Roseberry had the bad luck to be hit on the same spot – on the bottom hand – by two consecutive balls from Peter Hartley. His finger was badly bruised, and the assumption was that slow recovery made the damage worse the second time. That is not a factor in the one-off car crash, but it is, of course, in the rapidly repeated heel-strike of the runner.

Cricket's quest for new, high-tech materials is impressive, but it contains a hint of futility. The fact that such advances have to come second-hand from motor sports and road-running underlines the fact that the cricket equipment market is a small one, with little scope for research and development. Further, do players want to pay for the best protective equipment that money can buy?

Players seem to prefer the comfortable glove to the most protective one. Remember the St Peters glove, which looked like a huge mitten, pioneered by Tony Greig in the 1970s? The bigger area is still said to provide more effective distribution of the force of the ball, but batsmen have not been interested. Nick Knight, who had enthusiastically endorsed the Confor glove when it first appeared in 1996, was not wearing it when he was struck in Auckland, suffering a break that delayed his appearance in the 1997 county season.

But the game will continue to prompt the occasional imaginative and eye-catching innovation. Such is the Amoeba, a bat grip which is mouldable when heated, enabling the batsman to press his hands into it and create indentations that become permanent. Thus the grip is literally grooved in – which brings to mind the former New Zealand opener John Wright, who says he once glued one of his gloves to the handle to ensure that an errant hand remained correctly positioned.

The Amoeba was marketed as an aid which would help youngsters to adopt and maintain the right grip. Its attraction for established cricketers was less clear, though Warwickshire's Neil Smith is said to have "played with it a bit". The grooves that are made are quite deep, which suggests that the fingers would be fixed in position even more securely than Wright's. Whether or not it is desirable to have no movement of the hands (in relation to the handle) during stroke-making seems a key question.

Balls produced less controversy in 1997 than they had been doing. No news was good news for Dukes, whose balls were seldom the focus of the sort of mid-pitch debates which dogged the Reader balls that were used in the 1996 Tests. Inevitably, though, ball-movement sometimes appeared irrational. The Headingley Test was such a case, even allowing for the reputation of this ground. Each new ball seemed almost unplayable, whilst runs flowed against the old: a customary pattern, it is true, but here it was greatly exaggerated.

One possible question prompted by this was whether different grounds hasten the wear and softening of a ball. Could, for example, concrete or brickwork just beyond the boundary line be a significant factor? Might it not be valuable to keep used balls and relate their condition to the venue, the weather, and the scores? Certainly this should not entail any logistical problems in a professional sport. Or perhaps we prefer to keep cricket research-free, thus preserving the mystique?

One traditional element of the cricket scene which no one can wish to preserve is the playing square that remains damp from poor or missing covering. This happened at both Old Trafford and Leicester on one Saturday in 1997 which might have had a critical bearing on the County Championship. Lord's also suffered the loss of a session on one fine Saturday – ruining the end of the Middlesex-Leicestershire match – as the soggy Tavern side of the square was just left to itself to dry out.

Cricket groundsmen have their "water hogs" and "whales" to draw off surface water, but their ground-maintenance industry is unable to help with the drying of turf that is simply damp. At Canterbury, a small industrial hot-air drier was hired on one occasion, but was ineffectual. Contrast that with the job done by a hovering helicopter at some other sporting venues. What cricket needs is the helicopter effect produced by purpose-designed machinery. And in England the need is immense.

CRICKET GROUNDS IN 1997

The chances of a new major English Test ground to greet the next millennium – or even the millennium after that – receded dramatically as Yorkshire's plans to move from Headingley to their own home on a site outside Wakefield became bogged down in legal arguments and recrimination.

In January 1998, Yorkshire and their landlord Paul Caddick announced new talks with a view to the club staying at Headingley and the ground being redeveloped. Only if this proved impossible would the club blow the dust off its plans to build a new stadium at Durkar, near Wakefield.

Yorkshire turned out to have severely underestimated the difficulties of getting out of the 99-year lease, signed in 1982, with their landlords, the Leeds Cricket, Football and Athletic Co, in effect the Leeds Rhinos Rugby League club. Caddick, the property developer who now controls the Rhinos, has adamantly opposed Yorkshire's departure.

Yorkshire members voted 3-1 in March 1997 to back the move to Wakefield. But Caddick fought back with a glossy brochure showing how a rebuilt Headingley might look – and writs claiming £17 million damages, which could theoretically have cost the county's members £2,000 each.

Relations between Caddick and the Yorkshire administration were frosty throughout 1997, and both Caddick and Sir Lawrence Byford, the Yorkshire president, agreed to stay out of future negotiations. Meanwhile, the ground itself grew shabbier, and Yorkshire's chances of getting the funding it wanted for the move grew slimmer as funds from the National Lottery began to flow less freely.

Another well-known ground was definitely reprieved. Obsequies were already being said for St Helen's at Swansea, which actually staged a one-day international seven weeks before Headingley did – England v New Zealand in 1973. Many of Glamorgan's great occasions took place there, and 25,000 watched a famous win over the South Africans in 1951.

But after the demolition of the huge terrace, ground capacity had dwindled to 3,000. The place was becoming increasingly decrepit, and neither the Swansea rugby club nor the City Council seemed especially anxious for county cricket to go on. But a supporters' group, the St Helen's Balconiers, raised £10,000 to keep cricket on the ground, and Glamorgan decided to take the four-day and one-day fixtures against Surrey there in 1998.

There is one unexpected venue on this year's fixture list. Middlesex are playing the Championship match against Essex and their NatWest second-round match (if they get through) at the Walker Cricket Ground, Southgate. It will be the sixth ground used by Middlesex for a Championship fixture this century, after Lord's, The Oval and Chelmsford (in emergency), Hornsey (used once in 1959) and Uxbridge, which will retain its cricket week.

However, Middlesex have to play more fixtures away from Lord's while the pitches are relaid. Southgate was chosen because of its good facilities, and because of its convenience for large numbers of both Middlesex and Essex members. It staged a Sunday League game in 1991 but has not had a first-class fixture since 1859.

Lord's, where the new Grand Stand and the gherkin-shaped media centre have both been under construction, was one of many English grounds alive with the sound of hammering in advance of the 1999 World Cup. Glamorgan were beginning a complete rebuilding programme at their Sophia Gardens headquarters; Northamptonshire started work on an indoor school on the old football ground. Nottinghamshire were revitalising the Radcliffe Road end of Trent Bridge. Yorkshire, however, could only gnash their teeth in frustration.

CRICKET AND STAMPS IN 1997

By MARCUS WILLIAMS

Nearly 48 years after his final first-class appearance, Sir Donald Bradman was still setting records in 1997, when he became the first living person apart from a member of the Royal Family to appear on Australian postage stamps. On January 23, a pair of 45-cent stamps was issued to mark the inaugural "Legends Award", established to honour a prominent person who has made an outstanding contribution to the Australian identity and heritage. The stamps, which were printed as adjoining pairs, show a photograph-style portrait of the Don from his heyday in the late 1930s and square leg's view of one of his famous straight drives.

Several more cricketing legends featured in a set of stamps issued by Alderney on August 21 to commemorate 150 years of the game on the island, among them the founder of this Almanack, John Wisden himself. He was accompanied by W. G. Grace, Sir Pelham Warner, Harold Larwood and the best-known voice in cricket, John Arlott, who retired to the island after his broadcasting and journalistic career, and was depicted with a glass of one of his favourite tipples in his hand. Another Alderney resident, Ian Botham, appeared in this issue – batting, not drinking – but Alderney, like many postal authorities, still observes the rule that royalty should be the only living people on stamps. So Botham was shown only on an unvalued stamp (lacking the Queen's head), printed alongside the other five values in a souvenir sheet.

Test cricketers of more recent vintage appeared on stamps issued on May 1 by the Caribbean island of Nevis, which is more relaxed about this philatelic tradition. These celebrated three players born within its shores who have been selected for West Indies: Elquemedo Willett, Keith Arthurton and Stuart Williams. The only other Nevisian to have played Test cricket, Derick Parry, did not wish to appear, for undisclosed reasons. Willett, a slow left-armer was the first man from any of the Leeward Islands to play in Tests, in 1972-73 – preceding such luminaries as Viv Richards, Andy Roberts, and Curtly Ambrose.

One of the Windward Islands, St Vincent, joined the cricket stamp producers of 1997 on June 20 with a pair to mark the inaugural Test match – against Sri Lanka – at Arnos Vale, the 78th Test ground. One showed the ground; the other depicted Alfie Roberts, who died in 1996, the first from any of the small islands to play a Test. The rest of the year's issues involved the ICC Trophy: Malaysia marked the sixth staging of the tournament in March with three stamps, and on September 4 Bangladesh celebrated their victory over Kenya in the final, and qualification for the 1999 World Cup, with a single stamp.

CHARITIES IN 1997

THE LORD'S TAVERNERS, accredited by the ECB as cricket's national charity for the recreational game, distributed more than £1.7 million during 1997. This was raised to give young people, particularly those with special needs, a sporting chance. Half the money raised in 1997 was distributed direct to grassroots cricket. The other half was used largely to provide 26 New Horizons minibuses – bringing the number presented since 1980 to 438.

The Secretary, The Lord's Taverners, 22 Queen Anne's Gate, London SW1H 9AA. Telephone: 0171-222 0707.

THE JOHN ARLOTT MEMORIAL TRUST Living Villages Appeal closed in 1997, having raised more than £85,000 for housing and recreational projects in English villages. Projects which benefited included a John Arlott Memorial Playground in Timberscombe, Somerset; a recreation ground in New Alresford, Hampshire; a low-cost housing project in East Tytherley, Hampshire; and cricket nets and surfaces in Kendal, Cumbria, and Northchurch, Hertfordshire. The annual John Arlott Rioja Dinner took place in October, raising additional funds for affordable housing in Preston, Kent. It is hoped that the dinner will continue, under the auspices of the Rural Housing Trust.

Janet Hart, Prince Consort House, 27-29 Albert Embankment, London SE1 7TJ. Telephone: 0171-793 8114.

THE BRIAN JOHNSTON MEMORIAL TRUST was launched in 1995. Its aims are to foster cricket (a) for young people, (b) in the community, and (c) for players with disabilities. Brian Johnston Scholarships are available for young cricketers of potential who are in need of financial help, and Brian Johnston Awards are given to inner city schools which present projects to establish cricket in their area. The Johnners Cricket Week is to be held from June 20 to 28, 1998, and clubs everywhere are invited to participate and raise funds for themselves and the Trust. Christopher Martin-Jenkins became chairman of the Trust in 1997.

Chief Executive: Christopher Atkinson, PO Box 3897, Lord's Cricket Ground, London NW8 8QG. Telephone: 0171-224 1005. Fax: 0171-224 0431.

THE PRIMARY CLUB, which was one of Brian Johnston's favourite charities, raises money for sporting and recreational facilities for the blind and partially sighted. Membership is nominally restricted to players who have been dismissed first ball in any form of cricket. Started in 1955, the club raises money by donations and a wide variety of members' activities – both in the UK and overseas. In 1997 it sponsored the British Blind Sport cricket knockout final on the Nursery Ground at Lord's. A complete gymnasium was built for the children at Dorton House School in Sevenoaks.

Hon. Secretary: Robert Fleming, 5 South Villas, Camden Square, London NW1 9BS. Telephone: 0171-267 3316. Fax: 0171-485 6808.

THE HORNSBY PROFESSIONAL CRICKETERS FUND was established in 1928, from the estate of J. H. J. Hornsby, who played for Middlesex, MCC and the Gentlemen. It provides money to assist "former professional cricketers [not necessarily first-class] or their wives, widows until remarriage, children and other dependents, provided the persons concerned shall be in necessitous circumstances''. Assistance is given by monthly allowances, special grants or, in certain cases, loans. Donations, requests for help or information about potential recipients are all welcome.

Clerk to the Trustees: A. K. James, ''Dunroamin'', 65 Keyhaven Road, Milford-on-Sea, Lymington, Hampshire SO41 0QX. Telephone: 01590-644720.

THE PROFESSIONAL CRICKETERS' ASSOCIATION CHARITY was founded in 1983 to relieve financial hardship amongst present or former members of the Association, anyone who has played cricket for a first-class county or their ''wives, widows, children, parents and dependents''. It is becoming the custom for cricketers in their benefit year to donate half of one per cent of their proceeds to the fund. Donations are welcome; also requests for help and information about cricketers who may be in need.

Chairman of the Trustees: Harold Goldblatt, 60 Doughty Street, London WC1N 2LS. Telephone: 0171-405 9855.

THE CRICKET SOCIETY TRUST was first started in 1958, and became a registered charity in 1992. It helps disadvantaged people by providing remedial and recreational facilities through the enjoyment of cricket, and in 1997 made donations of both kit and cash. The aim is to target specific small projects and problems not always reached by bigger donors.

Hon. Secretary: K. F. C. Merchant, 16 Louise Road, Rayleigh, Essex SS6 8LW.

THE CRICKET FOUNDATION was reconstituted in 1996 with the help of £10 million of funding promised by the first-class game over a four-year period. The Foundation exists to support youth and grassroots cricket, mainly by helping training and education in all aspects of the game. It is run from the ECB offices but operates independently of the Board, with Ossie Wheatley as chairman of the trustees.

Secretary: Terry Bates, ECB, Lord's Ground, London NW8 8QZ.

GRANT AID FOR CRICKET, 1997

During the last three years, Britain's National Lottery has made a substantial impact on the development of the game. In all, there have been 400 awards to cricket organisations, adding up to a total value of £47,678,506; applicants are required to provide at least 35 per cent of the overall budget for themselves. Cricket has received more capital awards than any other sport and benefited from many multi-sport grants which include provision for cricket. However, proposed Government changes may mean less money in future.

The biggest grant during 1997 was the £4.2 million given to Nottinghamshire CCC for reconstruction at the Radcliffe Road End of Trent Bridge.

Northamptonshire received over £1 million for an indoor cricket school. County clubs also received support from the Foundation for Sports and the Arts. Durham, Glamorgan, Gloucestershire and Nottinghamshire each received the maximum of £250,000.

For further information on these and other potential donors – several of which will consider grants for much smaller projects – consult the booklet *Sources of Grant Aid for Cricket*, which is available from the ECB at Lord's. Mike Turner, author of the booklet, is available to give advice to clubs on 0116-283 1615.

LABOUR RELATIONS IN 1997

1. THE AUSTRALIAN PLAYERS IN 1997

By MARK RAY

Play was almost halted in the one-day internationals in Australia at the end of 1997 for a reason far removed from rain or bad light. The newly formed Australian Cricketers' Association (ACA) took the grievances of professional cricketers to the top of the game's agenda for the first time since the Packer split 20 years earlier, and came close to strike action. Led by the star players – Mark Taylor, Shane Warne, Steve Waugh and Ian Healy – the ACA's campaign for a better deal gathered quiet momentum during the 1997 Ashes tour and almost reached a showdown during the Perth Test against New Zealand in November. The ACA drew back from the brink, at least temporarily, conscious that it was losing the battle for public sympathy. But anyone within the game who thought the Association would be another meek and mild organisation, content to ask politely for a few more crumbs, realised they had been proved wrong; and there was no doubt that its leadership had strong support from the members.

The main demand was for pay increases for all Australian first-class players, based on a set percentage of the game's revenue, plus the implementation of a career structure for state players. The ACA also wanted a say in tour programming, which the Australian Cricket Board (ACB) saw as an attempt to take over the running of cricket.

In 1997-98 most Sheffield Shield players were earning between \$A35,000 (less than £15,000) and \$A50,000 (about £20,000), though they were expected to do several months of pre-season training, the intensity of which has increased markedly in the past decade. However, as the battle raged, the Board released the 1996-97 incomes of the regular international players: these varied from \$A275,000 (about £120,000) to \$A485,000 (more than £200,000). This focused attention on the game's elite, encouraging the public to believe the nation's best cricketers were being greedy.

The players did have one major victory when the Board agreed, for the first time, to release details of its finances. And the players certainly got under the skin of their employers. In January 1997, the ACB had sacked its chief executive officer, Graham Halbish, a major factor apparently being a clash betwen Halbish and Board chairman Denis Rogers. A few months later, the ACA's President, former Test off-spinner Tim May, announced that Halbish had joined the Association as chief adviser and negotiator.

At first, the Board said they would not deal with Halbish, but they were forced to back down on legal advice. Halbish eventually also took a step back, but another key figure on the players' side was James Erskine, former head of the Australian arm of Mark McCormack's organisation, the International Management Group. The ACB saw Erskine as a man who had wider ambitions within cricket; Erskine denied any ulterior motives. After the Perth Test, things went quiet and private negotiations resumed. But early in 1998 there had been no advance and the players' patience was wearing thin. Strike Stops Play was still not out of the question.

2. THE ENGLISH SCORERS

By PAUL WEAVER

When county cricket scorers threatened strike action last season, the response was one of amused incredulity. It was like being told that Aunt Sally had gone to an industrial tribunal. If David Steele was the bank manager who went to war, in Clive Taylor's memorable image, this was the Ledger Clerks' Uprising. The scorers are the surviving gofers of the game. Even umpires have publishers and sponsors these days, and it is difficult to say that the likes of Chester, Buller, Alley and Pepper were exactly put upon. The scorers, however, underpaid and overworked, are traditionally exploited by their counties. Sometimes they are used as general factotums who, at the drop of a sharpened stubby pencil, will pay the team's hotel bill, organise the bags and give young players wise counsel.

They are no fools. Anybody who can embrace new technology and engage in hand-to-hand combat with the Duckworth/Lewis method (a scoring system the umpires took one look at and ran away from) and emerge scarred but triumphant must be respected. Thomas Henwood's famous 1842 portrait "The Scorer", depicting a rather myopic William Davies of Lewes Priory, surrounded by bottles, is a little dated.

For some years, the scorers had felt miffed that they received nothing from the ECB for computer scoring, despite the fact that the Board had done a deal with the Press Association to send their work down the wire. At least two county scorers do the job for nothing. Mostly, they receive pittance pay and a few expenses. They are often retired men of private means whose love of the game is rewarded with a close association with the team. There are some perks. They can take their wives to a certain number of games. At the NatWest Final they get one of the commemorative medallions, though both Benson and Hedges and Cornhill have refused to do even this. Then there is the possibility of being chosen to spend the winter abroad scoring for the England team – and this is what all the trouble is about.

Malcolm Ashton, who had worked for the BBC but was not a county scorer, and therefore not a full member of the Association of County Cricket Scorers, was told he would tour with England in the West Indies, his third winter in the job. When Ashton was first appointed for the tour of South Africa in 1995-96, the then Test and County Cricket Board said it would probably be for two years but that the position would be reviewed annually and applications sought each summer. Last year the ECB did not ask for applications and, in a Sunday League programme, announced that Ashton was once again their choice.

There was already some resentment among the scorers that the job had become "in-house". Alex Davis of Warwickshire went on the two tours when his county chairman Mike Smith was manager, and the Essex scorer Clem Driver was appointed when Graham Gooch and Keith Fletcher were in charge of the England side. "But Alex and Clem were full and respected members of the Association," said Keith Gerrish, secretary of the ACCS. "When Ashton got the job I felt it was because Ray Illingworth wanted a bridge partner. We had no argument with Ashton personally. He obviously does a good job. But it seemed to us that the board was not playing fair, and several scorers were annoyed." The Surrey scorer, Keith Booth, called an extraordinary general meeting in July to discuss strike action on Sunday, August 31. The ECB were sufficiently worried to line up scabs for manual scoring.

Ultimately, the scorers did not get close to striking. There was not even a vote on the issue at their July meeting, and at least one said he would leave the Association rather than his post. The ACCS is hardly a militant organisation. When the Certification Office for Trade Unions and Employers' Associations told them they could join last year, the horrified officers of the ACCS hurriedly rewrote their constitution so that they were no longer eligible.

"I prefer dialogue to confrontation," said Mr Gerrish. "The trouble is, when you confront someone he often digs his heels in."

CRICKET PEOPLE IN 1997

By SIMON BRIGGS

Until December, Australian Test cricketer ZOË GOSS was best known as the only woman to have taken Brian Lara's wicket. Now she can also claim the dubious honour of being the first woman cricketer to have posed nude in a magazine (Chris Lewis is thought to have been the first man). The photographs, which appeared in Australia's *Total Sport* magazine, depicted Goss lying on an uncomfortable-looking bed of cricket balls; some modesty was preserved. Newspapers following up the story were told that the shoot had been just "a bit of fun", though its timing – shortly before Australia departed for the women's World Cup in India – seemed intended to raise the profile of the women's game. But Goss, who was not selected for the World Cup squad, was unhappy that the pictures had been reproduced in Sydney's Sunday papers. "I'm dirty about that," she said.

JASON BARRY, one of cricket's most enthusiastic evangelists, made more progress towards his goal of playing the game in 100 different countries by the end of the millennium (see *Wisden* 1997, page 1392). What began as a bet and then became a fundraising enterprise has now developed into a one-man mission to promote cricket as an Olympic sport. The International Olympic Committee refuse to consider a sport for inclusion unless it can be proved that it is played in more than 100 countries – and Barry reckons he now has 45 to go. In 1997 he added 12, mostly in the West Indies, to the 43 that he visited in 1996. He then paused for a brief sabbatical, taking up a teaching post at Brookhouse College in Leicestershire, but in 1998 he plans to continue his quest in Mongolia and Malaysia, among other places. Barry generally travels alone and funds himself, though increased press coverage has meant more sponsors have come forward, notably the Sandals hotel chain in the West Indies, and he has raised over £52,000 for Save the Children and other charities. In playing terms, he managed to acquit himself reasonably well until his 50th game, in Jamaica, where he was dismissed for a third-ball duck, his only one to date. Wes Hall promised him he could play his 100th game at Sabina Park to make up for it. However, the aborted Test there in January 1998 may have made that idea less enticing.

Only a truly dedicated fan would support England at Tests in South Africa, Zimbabwe and New Zealand, at the one-day international tournament in Sharjah, and even at the Hong Kong Sixes. Especially one who can't see. FRED RAFFLE has been blind since he was four but, since retiring from his post as head of rehabilitation studies at the University of Central England a couple of years ago, he has indulged his passion for cricket by following England all over the world. His regular travelling companion is Barry Dudleston, the first-class umpire and head of travel company Sun Sports. Raffle has contacts in the media as well: he met Don Shepherd and Eddie Bevan, *Wisden*'s Glamorgan correspondent and a broadcaster with BBC Wales, while watching Glamorgan play Sussex at Hove in 1990. Now Raffle attends almost all the county's matches with his dog Iva, named after I. V. A. Richards, and sits with Bevan in the commentary box. Bevan describes him as ''an encyclopaedia of knowledge about the game, and very popular with the players.'' Raffle was unavailable for comment at the time of writing, as he and his wife had taken a holiday to Sri Lanka – a holiday which just happened to coincide with the arrival of the England A team.

Another candidate for the title of cricket fan of the year was PEGGY FAIRBOURNE, a schoolteacher from Stowmarket, Suffolk, who was pictured in newspapers with a poster reading ''Stay Captain Athers''. The photographs appeared after England's Test win at The Oval, and a week later, against most expectations, Atherton decided that he would remain in the job. Fairbourne, the mother of two grown-up children, was already well-known to the England team as a source of home-baked cakes. She did not think she was the main influence on Mike Atherton's decision: ''He's not going to be swayed by me – he already knows I'm his No. 1 fan. That's what I put at the bottom of my letters to him: 'Your No. 1 Suffolk Fan and Crazy Cake Lady.' ''

England's flying start to the Ashes prompted the Barmy Army to release a single entitled *We Are England*. The lyrics went ''We are England, we are mighty / In our hearts we know that this will be our year / We are rising from the Ashes / And there's no other team on earth we need to fear.'' But according to PAUL BURNHAM, one of the three men who copyrighted the Barmy Army name in 1994, ''the single didn't come out until Trent Bridge, by which time the whole summer had gone a bit dead. In the end we sold somewhere between 600 and 700 copies, which wasn't bad, all things considered.'' Burnham, who is known to other members of the army as Leafy, left his job as a broker with a spread betting firm in December. He hoped that the sale and promotion of Barmy Army merchandise might constitute a full-time job, but early indications were not promising. ''The ECB seem unwilling to let us sell shirts within cricket grounds, and I can't see it being commercially viable if we have to stay outside.''

Former Sussex fast bowler ED GIDDINS, who was banned from county cricket for 18 months after testing positive for cocaine, kept himself busy during the first of his blank winters selling Christmas trees. ''Geezer'', as he is known on the circuit, joined forces with Surrey batsman Nadeem Shahid, and the pair operated from a rented property in South London. But Giddins was keen to stress that he was also working hard on his fitness. He told the *Daily Mail*'s Mike Dickson that ''after shutting up the shop every night we go off to the gym, do a hard workout and then it's home for an early night. Party time is over.'' It's not the most eccentric career move that Giddins has made; his CV already lists stints as a ski instructor, topless barman, landscape gardener and dustman. In 1998, he will be bowling for Warwickshire.

A former professional cricketer played a key role in a complicated political imbroglio in Scotland. BADAR ISLAM, an all-rounder who turned out for West of Scotland, Poloc, Kelburne and Clydeside in the 1970s, stood in the General

Election as an independent candidate for the seat of Glasgow Govan. He polled 319 votes; the Labour candidate, Mohammed Sarwar, became Britain's first Moslem MP when he won with 14,216. But in the *News of the World* just a fortnight later Islam claimed that Sarwar gave him £5,000 to run a low-profile campaign that would fall short of splitting the Asian vote. Sarwar responded with a lawsuit against the *News of the World*, but he was suspended from the Labour Party and soon facing charges of electoral fraud. The case was due to be tried in 1998.

For Bridgend Town Cricket Club in South Wales, the 1998 New Year's Honours' List was a particular cause for celebration. CHARLIE GRIFFITHS, who has served the club in just about every capacity, was awarded an MBE for his considerable services to the game. Griffiths was born into a cricketing family – both his father and uncle represented the town in the early years of the century – and he can hardly remember a time when the club wasn't the most important thing in his life. A talented wicket-keeper and middle-order bat, he would perhaps have played first-class cricket had not the war intervened. Instead he devoted himself first to preparing the Bridgend pitch, then to the administration of the club and, since 1975, to enthusing 70 or more boys – many of whom had never picked up a bat before – in the art of cricket. When vandals burnt down the pavilion in 1991, Griffiths immediately set about raising funds. Seven years and £175,000 later, work is about to begin on the replacement. And at the age of 74, he still keeps wicket when the Fourth Eleven is short of a player.

Another MBE went to a member of a famous cricketing family. MERVYN MANSELL was honoured for services to Ealing Cricket Club, and youth cricket in Middlesex – specifically, 43 years spent coaching and organising colts' cricket. The unusual, and perhaps unique, feature of this award is that Mansell's late brother Percy received the same honour 36 years earlier for his services to cricket. Percy Mansell's MBE was given for his work in Rhodesia, where he spent most of his life; he played 13 times for South Africa and scored 90 in the Headingley Test of 1951. There are three other Mansells, including Mervyn's wife and daughter, involved in coaching in West London, and two of the latest generation are heavily involved in under-11 and under-nine cricket. Quite a dynasty.

One cricket-loving prime minister, John Major, bit the electoral dust in 1997. But another maintained his grip on power. Most outside media interest in the Pakistan election focused on Imran Khan's wholly unsuccessful campaign. In fact, the winner was another cricketer: NAWAZ SHARIF, the most powerful first-class player in world politics since the 1960s, when Sir Alec Douglas-Home was British prime minister. Nawaz was not quite in the Imran class on the field, however. He played one first-class match, when he opened the batting for Pakistan Railways v PIA B in the quarter-finals of the Patron's Trophy in 1973-74. His team won by an innings and 68 – and went on to win the tournament. But Nawaz was out for a duck, didn't bowl and didn't take a catch. He romped home in the election, though.

Additional research: Hugh Chevallier

OBITUARY

ASHMORE, FAVELL MAY, died on April 30, 1997, aged 79. Fay Ashmore worked for MCC for 40 years up to 1986, first as personal assistant to the secretary, Colonel R. S. Rait Kerr, then in the museum. Her late husband, Bill, played twice for Middlesex. She is believed to have been the first woman to act as scorer at Lord's, in 1944.

AVERY, ALFRED VICTOR, died on May 10, 1997, aged 82. "Sonny" Avery played 268 matches for Essex between 1935 and 1954 and, after the war, joined forces with Dickie Dodds to give the county one of the circuit's most durable opening partnerships. Avery was the neater, more solid player of the two, though inclined to make mistakes. Doug Insole recalled that, if asked what the ball did when he got out, Avery would shrug and say: "Nothing much, skip. Lazy old shot." Sometimes he was right, and many judges thought that Avery only needed more steel to have been a really good player. He made 79 for The Rest against an England attack headed by Voce and Bedser in a Test trial at Canterbury in 1946. He was a good player of in-swing and a powerful cutter who held the bat low down and often suffered injured hands as a result. Avery coached briefly at Gloucestershire and then at Monmouth School; Dodds visited him in hospital days before he died.

BAIRSTOW, DAVID LESLIE, was found hanged at his home on January 5, 1998. He was 46. Reports said he had been suffering from depression: his wife was ill, he had financial troubles, he faced a drink-driving charge and was in pain from his own injuries. The news stunned cricket, especially as Bairstow had always seemed the most indomitable and least introspective of men, and led to much comment on the problems faced by retired sportsmen.

David "Bluey" Bairstow was not merely the Yorkshire wicket-keeper but almost the embodiment of the county's cricket throughout the 1970s and 1980s. He arrived in county cricket amid a blaze of publicity when he was drafted from grammar school in Bradford into the Yorkshire side as an 18-year-old on the day he sat an English Literature A-level. He was allowed to sit the exam at 7 a.m., then went out and caught five Gloucestershire batsmen over the next three days. From then on, he was a regular, and while Yorkshire's affairs swirled turbulently around him, Bairstow was always there: loud, combative, combustible. "He wasn't a great wicket-keeper and he wasn't a great batsman," said his team-mate Phil Carrick, "but he was a great cricketer." His fighting qualities overrode any technical deficiencies, and he did equal a world record by taking 11 catches against Derbyshire at Scarborough in 1981. But he was at his best when batting in one-day games when victory was improbable but just short of impossible: in the Benson and Hedges Cup at Derby in 1981, he was joined by Mark Johnson, the No. 11 and a debutant, with Yorkshire 80 short of victory. Bairstow hit nine sixes in an innings that left everyone on the ground aghast; Yorkshire won with Bairstow on 103, and Johnson four. He was picked for the Oval Test against India in 1979, made a brisk 59 in the second innings, and went to Australia for the post-Packer tour that winter. Though Bob Taylor played in the Tests, Bairstow was a regular in the one-day games, and played a succession of small but vital innings. Most famously, Graham Stevenson walked out to join him at the SCG with 35 wanted from six overs. "Evening, lad," said Bairstow. "We can piss this." Which they duly did.

He played two more Tests the following summer, and one on the 1980-81 tour of the West Indies, but he could not force his way into the team again. In 1984, he became captain of Yorkshire, after Geoff Boycott's supporters had seized control of the club. With the rest of Yorkshire torn asunder, depending on whether they worshipped Boycott

[*Patrick Eagar*

David Bairstow: Yorkshire through and through.

or loathed him, Bairstow seemed the last man to believe he was still leading a normal cricket team. His three years of captaincy were, in Derek Hodgson's words, "a series of uphill cavalry charges". The attack was appallingly weak – his main tactic was to shout "C'mon Arn" at his weary spearhead Sidebottom – but Bairstow's sheer willpower saved Yorkshire from utter collapse; indeed, having been bottom of the Championship the year before he took over, they improved slightly in each of his seasons in charge. He was perhaps the only unequivocally popular man in Yorkshire. Bairstow believed he could intimidate the bowling simply by announcing that he was going to whack the ball back over the bowler's head, and often enough he kept his promise. His wicket-keeping, never beautiful but usually efficient, seemed to deteriorate at the same time, possibly because his insecurity kept him playing through injuries that should have been rested. When he was appointed, the committee had wanted him to play only as a batsman. But he refused, causing Steve Rhodes to move to Worcestershire.

Both the captaincy and, in 1990, his place in the Yorkshire team had to be prised from him, but Bairstow had a last hurrah in the Caribbean in March 1990 when he was on a pre-season tour with Yorkshire, and an injury-hit England team stretched the Laws by calling him in to keep wicket as a substitute against Barbados. His 961 career catches have been bettered by only six wicket-keepers in history, though he had only 138 stumpings, putting him 14th in the list of all-time dismissals. His son Andrew played briefly for Derbyshire. His thoughts never seemed private, and he was a firm believer that there was no dispute that could not be settled by a shouting-match over a pint or six. Even after he died, people wrote of David Bairstow's "unquenchable spirit". But in the end, the stress of life outside cricket meant his spirit was quenched, and crushed.

BALL, PETER, who died of leukaemia on November 11, 1997, aged 54, was an innovative journalist who pioneered coverage of participation sports while sports editor of *Time Out*. He later moved to Lancashire and covered northern football and cricket for *The Times*. His books included two editions of *The Book of Cricket Quotations* (with David Hopps); he also ghosted Graeme Fowler's autobiography, *Fox on the Run*.

BARKATULLAH KHAN, who died of cancer in October 1996, aged 29, was a fast-medium bowler who took 263 first-class wickets for Karachi and National Bank. As a youngster, he took 66 wickets for National Bank when they won the Quaid-e-Azam Trophy in 1986-87. He toured Zimbabwe that year with the Pakistan B team. Barkatullah played on until 1993-94 despite a serious leg injury – reportedly caused when he hit it on the corner of his bed. Doctors eventually recommended amputation, an option he rejected.

BAYLEY, HENRY PETER, died on December 29, 1996, aged 80. Peter Bayley was a batsman from British Guiana who scored 268 against Barbados in 1937-38, which stood as a team record for almost 60 years until eclipsed by Shivnarine Chanderpaul. He put on 381 for the fourth wicket with C. S. Persaud. Bayley toured England in 1939 without getting in the Test team or making much impression. He later became a radio commentator.

BEWICKE, Major CALVERLEY, died in February 1997, aged 82. Verly Bewicke kept wicket for Eton in 1932 and 1933 and played for Free Foresters and I Zingari. He was also a well-known racehorse trainer who trained the first mare to win the Cheltenham Gold Cup, Kerstin in 1958.

BLAND, ROBERT DENNIS FRASER, who died on April 10, 1997, aged 85, was a left-arm medium-pace bowler who had a good record at Shrewsbury School, and made 33 appearances for Nottinghamshire as an amateur between 1929 and 1934. He later became a stockbroker.

BOND, ANDREW, who died on July 28, 1997, aged 60, was instrumental in bringing cricket to the Costa Blanca. He was a founder of two clubs, Javea and Sporting Alfas. Bond retired to Spain, having previously played league cricket for Milnrow.

BOWLING, KENNETH, died on December 7, 1997, aged 66, having just gone for his regular five-mile jog. Ken Bowling was a prolific batsman for Leyland who played one game for Lancashire in 1954 but failed to cement his place against competition from contemporaries like Bob Barber and Geoff Pullar. He was the nephew of the Lancashire and England player Jack Iddon.

BRADMAN, Lady, died on September 14, 1997, aged 88. Jessie Bradman was the beloved wife of Sir Donald for 65 years. He called it ''the greatest partnership of my life''. Jessie Menzies grew up on a farm in Glenquarry, New South Wales, and at 11 was sent to school in Bowral, eight miles away. To cut down the travelling, the Bradman family agreed to let her stay at their house during the week. It took Don and Jessie just over ten years to graduate from playmates to man and wife. By the time they were married, Don was already cricket's biggest name; their honeymoon was spent on a tour of North America where she met a succession of Hollywood stars. Throughout Bradman's glorious but often troubled career, she remained staunch. He was desperate to guard her privacy but in the early years she was a very public figure and sometimes had to fulfil quasi-monarchical duties; she did so with a natural ease and grace. The Bradmans' elder son died soon after his birth, and their other children both survived serious illnesses. She was never heard to complain, certainly not when she herself became gravely ill. Lady Bradman was a good horsewoman, tennis player and golfer herself; later she became a silversmith and worked hard for charity.

BRAGGER, JUNE, who died on June 27, 1997, aged 68, played five women's Tests for England between 1963 and 1966. She later became an umpire.

BRATCHFORD, JAMES DAVID, died on a plane returning from the US on October 5, 1997, aged 68. Jim Bratchford was a Queensland stalwart of the 1950s who was close to a place on the 1956 England tour, but was hit all round the SCG in a Test trial, and overlooked. He remained a successful Shield player, as a forceful bat and lively swing bowler who achieved the Australian double of 1,000 runs and 100 wickets in his career. He scored two centuries, and took six for 57 against Victoria in 1958-59. Bratchford was from the Toombul club and came up with Ken Mackay and Wally Grout. He captained Queensland in his last season, when he came third in the Shield bowling averages.

BULLOCK, KENNETH REGINALD, died on June 29, 1997, aged 70. Ken Bullock, who was born in Portsmouth, went to Canada as a child and was for many years one of the country's leading cricket figures. He was a useful wicket-keeper and played club cricket for half a century. He served as the country's ICC delegate for 14 years.

BURKE, CECIL, died on August 4, 1997, aged 83. Cec Burke, known as "The Burglar" – for his wicket-taking methods rather than a non-cricketing sideline – bowled well-flighted leg-breaks for Auckland and played for New Zealand in the Test against Australia at Wellington in 1945-46. He dismissed Bill Brown and Keith Miller. Burke toured England in 1949, taking 54 wickets on the tour including six for 23 against Derbyshire, but Tom Burtt was chosen ahead of him in the Test team.

CAMERON, EWEN HENRY JOHN, who died on January 12, 1997, aged 75, was a country schoolteacher and left-arm medium-fast bowler from upcountry Otago. Cameron was belatedly given his chance to play for the province in 1953-54 when he was 32. On his debut he bowled 32 overs and took two for 30, but was chosen for only four more matches. He was famous locally for writing musicals.

CASSELS, Field Marshal Sir ARCHIBALD JAMES HALKETT, DSO KBE GCB, who died on December 13, 1996, aged 89, was a successful schoolboy batsman at Rugby, and played five first-class matches for the Europeans in India and the Army, with a highest score of 72 against the RAF in 1932. He led the liberation of Le Havre and St Valéry, became GOC of the 51st Highland Division and eventually Chief of the General Staff.

CASTLE, FREDERICK, died on May 17, 1997, aged 88. Fred Castle was the headmaster of Oldfield Boys' School in Bath who began playing for Somerset aged 37, and turned out mostly during the holidays in the four seasons after the war, captaining the side twice. At county level, his batting was only moderately successful – he averaged barely 20 – but his good nature and his range of accomplishments made him a popular figure. He was a skilful raconteur and baritone, and rivalled Jack Mercer as the best performer of card tricks the county circuit ever saw.

CATCHLOVE, WALTER EVERED, who died on April 12, 1997, aged 90, scored an unbeaten 103 for South Australia against Queensland in 1931-32. He played eight other matches for the state in the early 1930s.

CHEETHAM, ALBERT GEORGE, died on May 23, 1997, aged 81. Bert Cheetham bowled the first ball for Australia in the first Victory Test at Lord's in 1945, and took seven wickets in three of these celebratory games. He played 20 times for New South Wales before the war, taking 35 wickets and making a top score of 85.

CHIVERS, ALFRED PERCIVAL, died on July 11, 1997, aged 88. "Perce" Chivers was a fast-medium bowler who took ten wickets for 145 in his three first-class matches for Victoria in 1929-30. However, he was never given a Sheffield Shield game. His wife of 64 years died the day after he did.

CLARKE, CHARLES CYRIL, who died in 1997, aged 86, played 25 games for Derbyshire between 1929 and 1933, and three for Sussex in 1947, but failed to pass 35 and did not bowl. He undoubtedly had ability at club level: he moved to Kendal to play and coach and was known as the Conjuror, because he was magic on the field. He later managed a white-elephant shop.

COMBES, GEOFFREY ARTHUR, who died on February 4, 1997, aged 83, was a slow left-armer who played eight matches for Tasmania in the 1930s and one in 1946-47. Playing for a Tasmania Combined XI against MCC in 1936-37, he outbowled Clarrie Grimmett, taking one for 50 in 22 overs during an innings when Barnett and Hardstaff cut loose.

COMPTON, DENIS CHARLES SCOTT, CBE, who died on April 23, 1997, aged 78, was not just a great cricketer but a character who transcended the game and became what would now be called a national icon. In the years after the war, when the British were still finding the joys of victory elusive, the exuberance of Compton's batting and personality became a symbol of national renewal. Almost single-handed (though his pal Bill Edrich helped), he ensured that cricket returned to its pre-war place in the nation's affections. Only Ian Botham has ever come remotely close to matching this achievement.

Compton was a remarkable batsman: loose-limbed with broad shoulders and powerful forearms. He could play all the strokes, though he rarely straight-drove. What made him special was his audacity: he would take risks, standing outside the crease even to quickish bowlers, challenging them to bowl anything other than the length he wanted. He took 622 wickets, mostly with his chinamen, and any other player might have turned this skill into a career; Compton regarded them as a bit of a party trick. His running between the wickets was never good, but it seemed to get worse after he retired and became the source of a thousand after-dinner jokes. In reality, it was never a disastrous weakness.

Denis Compton was born in Hendon, on May 23, 1918, and described his childhood as both "poorish" and "happy". His father was a self-employed decorator who became a lorry driver when his business foundered. He was also a keen cricketer, as was Leslie, Denis's elder brother. They played against the lamp-posts in Alexandra Road and at Bell Lane Elementary School, and Compton's talent was obvious at once. At 12, he was playing for his father's team, and North London Schools against South London Schools at Lord's. He made 88. Two years later, watched by Sir Pelham Warner, he made 114 at Lord's for the Elementary Schools against C. F. Tufnell's XI and led his team to a crushing victory. He joined the Lord's staff in 1933, and three years later got a game for the county, as an 18-year-old against Sussex in the Whitsun match. Compton batted at No. 11: he scored 14 in an important last-wicket stand with Gubby Allen that gave Middlesex first-innings points; the umpire Bill Bestwick supposedly said later that he only gave Compton lbw because he was desperate for a pee.

Next match he was No. 8 and facing Larwood with confidence. Then he was No. 7, scoring 87 against Northamptonshire. In one game, the captain Walter Robins came down the pitch after he had driven a fast bowler for two consecutive fours. "You know what to look out for now, don't you?" "No, skipper." "Well, he'll bounce one at you." "If he does, I shall hook him." And he did – into the Mound Stand. Before June was out he scored a hundred, in an hour and three-quarters, at Northampton. By the time the season was over and he had passed a thousand runs, Warner, then chairman of the Test selectors, called him "the best young batsman who has come out since Walter Hammond was a boy".

THAT'S THE STYLE

Give your hair the double benefit of Brylcreem . .

[*Patrick Eagar*

The Brylcreem Boy: an advert from *Wisden* 1950.

But Compton had no time to relax. In September he made his Football League debut for Arsenal on the left wing against Derby County, scored the opening goal in a 2-2 draw, and was called "the success of the afternoon" by the *Daily Express*. Soon he was being marked out as a future England footballer as well as cricketer, despite criticism, which Compton always accepted, that he was inclined to prefer pretty ball-play to anything else. In cricket, the golden youth's progress turned out to be stoppable only by the Germans. In 1937 he scored 1,980 runs and was picked by England against New Zealand at The Oval. He scored 65 and was run out, flukily, while backing up. That year, as Patsy Hendren retired, Bill Edrich qualified for Middlesex. Len Hutton also made his Test debut. Thus started both the great partnership and the great rivalry that were to dominate post-war cricket. The contrast between the serious-minded Hutton and the insouciant Compton would be the great divide in English cricket for years, and small boys of all ages invariably inclined to one or the other.

Next time Compton batted for England, against Australia at Trent Bridge in 1938, he made 102; then came a match-saving yet exuberant 76 not out at Lord's. But he contributed just a single when Hutton scored his 364 at The Oval. Compton preferred to play football rather than tour South Africa – the 10-day Test at Durban would not have suited him – but in 1939 was back to top cricketing form, scoring 2,468 runs, including 120 against West Indies at Lord's, when he put on 248 with Hutton in two hours 20 minutes. There is no telling what this generation of batsmen might have achieved had they not been so rudely interrupted. Possibly, in the absence of equally compelling bowlers, they might have got bored. They never had the chance to find out. Soon Compton was a special constable and then a member of the Royal Artillery, posted first to East Grinstead which still allowed the chance of weekend football. (He won 12 wartime and Victory match football caps for England, which did not officially count, but many contemporaries agreed that he was now the best outside-left in the country.) In 1944 he was sent to India as a sergeant-major supposedly in charge of getting men fit to defeat Japan; his lenient approach to this task enhanced his popularity with the men, and the Allies still won the war. He was able to fit in 17 first-class matches in India as well. His performances included a century for East Zone against the Australian Services, which was interrupted by rioters for several minutes when he was in the nineties. The line "Mr Compton, you very good player but the game must stop" became one of the catch-phrases of his friendship with Keith Miller, which ended only with Compton's death. Compton also appeared, in the casual manner of that era, in the extraordinary Ranji Trophy final of 1944-45, then the highest-scoring match ever, between Holkar and Bombay.

Compton struggled at first in 1946, and his first 12 months of post-war cricket are sometimes thought of as a failure. He was still the leading scorer with 2,403 runs in 1946, and made a hundred in each innings at the Adelaide Test the following February.

ON COMPTON . . .

I doubt if any game at any period has thrown up anyone to match his popular appeal in the England of 1947 to 1949. – E. W. Swanton.

Wicked rumours enhanced the legend: that Denis had probably just arrived from a night on the town, ripped off his dinner jacket, picked up the nearest bat and walked straight to the wicket. Sometimes he had. The point was that as often as not what followed was an innings of breathtaking *élan*. – Ian Wooldridge, *Daily Mail*.

His feet never needed to be informed what to do and, if they got him into a tangle, his instincts usually got him out of it. He could feather a late cut from three yards down the pitch or drive past cover point's left hand from a foot outside the leg stump or sweep when he seemed to be standing on gully's toes. If he were to come out and play against Shane Warne, the cricket would bring the country to a standstill. – John Woodcock, *The Times*.

Had he been playing in this day and age there would not have been an unsponsored inch of him. – Michael Parkinson, *Daily Telegraph*.

Mike Atherton once asked me at an England selection meeting: "Just how good was Denis Compton?" "I can't tell you, Mike," I replied, "because you just wouldn't believe me." – Fred Titmus.

Because Compton had been touring, he missed that icy, fuel-rationed winter which for many people in Britain was tougher than anything produced by the war. Thus the stage was set for the greatest cricket season any individual has ever had. Compton did not really hit form until the season was a month old, and did not emerge into his full glory until the sun came out, and the series against South Africa began. He scored 753 of his 3,816 runs that summer in the Tests. But somehow, in the mind's eye of a generation, he was always batting at Lord's in a county match: hair tousled, the ball racing past cover point or backward of square. An exile in Australia complained: "I hardly expected him to score 18 hundreds in a season. I thought him too good a player for that sort of thing." He was assured that Compton had just played his natural game and the centuries – like his aggregate, a record for any season – had been almost incidental. Even more incidentally, Compton and Edrich took Middlesex to the Championship. The only cloud in that perfect summer came in the very last county match at Lord's: Compton had to retire to the pavilion because of knee trouble. He came out to make a second-innings

DENIS COMPTON'S RECORD FOR EACH TEAM

Batting and Fielding

	M	I	NO	R	HS	100s	50s	Avge	Ct
L. E. G. Ames's XI	1	2	0	30	24	0	0	15.00	0
Cavaliers XI	2	4	0	146	103	1	0	36.50	0
Commonwealth XI	3	4	1	160	74*	0	2	534.33	1
East Zone	1	2	0	101	101	1	0	50.50	0
England	78	131	15	5,807	278	17	28	50.06	49
England XI	10	12	0	398	132	1	2	33.16	5
Europeans	2	4	1	301	124*	1	2	100.33	2
A. E. R. Gilligan's XI	1	1	0	24	24	0	0	24.00	0
Holkar	3	4	1	372	249*	1	1	124.00	2
MCC	86	133	15	7,166	300	25	32	60.72	68
Middlesex	296	485	49	21,781	252*	67	106	49.95	263
C. K. Nayudu's XI	1	2	0	138	100	1	0	69.00	0
T. N. Pearce's XI	2	4	0	109	45	0	0	27.25	1
Players	14	25	3	889	150	1	4	40.40	15
The Rest	2	4	0	169	103	1	0	42.25	1
Services	3	5	0	394	123	3	0	78.80	2
South	4	7	1	271	101	1	1	45.16	2
South African XI	1	2	1	260	135	2	0	260.00	1
South of England	4	7	1	376	87*	0	4	62.66	2
Sir P. F. Warner's XI	1	1	0	50	50	0	1	50.00	2
Total	515	839	88	38,942	300	123	183	51.85	416

Bowling

	Balls	R	W	BB	5W/i	10W/m	Avge
L. E. G. Ames's XI	54	51	1	1-40	–	–	51.00
Cavaliers XI	138	122	3	3-88	–	–	40.66
Commonwealth XI	168	100	2	1-34	–	–	50.00
England	2,716	1,410	25	5-70	1	0	56.40
England XI	434	279	3	1-14	–	–	93.00
Europeans	196	95	2	2-51	–	–	47.50
A. E. R. Gilligan's XI	60	37	1	1-37	–	–	37.00
Holkar	120	67	1	1-19	–	–	67.00
MCC	5,002	2,792	84	7-36	2	1	33.23
Middlesex	26,564	14,124	477	6-63	16	2	29.61
C. K. Nayudu's XI	60	47	0	–	–	–	–
Players	325	207	9	3-28	–	–	23.00
The Rest	54	40	1	1-14	–	–	40.00
Services	228	166	2	2-63	–	–	83.00
South	374	243	2	1-84	–	–	121.50
South African XI	141	93	5	3-28	–	–	18.60
South of England	170	157	3	1-22	–	–	52.33
Sir P. F. Warner's XI	24	44	1	1-44	–	–	44.00
Total	36,828	20,074	622	7-36	19	3	32.27

Statistics: Brian Croudy

century, another against the South Africans, and a further 246 – the knee strapped – for Middlesex against The Rest at The Oval.

But from then on the words Compton and knee were to go together almost as easily as Compton and Edrich. Apparently, it was first damaged in a collision with the Charlton goalkeeper Sid Hobbins in 1938, but it now became increasingly troublesome to him, and a constant source of worry for the public too. There were still many great innings – two big Test hundreds in 1948 against Bradman's invincible Australians, an astounding 300 in three hours against an admittedly weak North-Eastern Transvaal team a few months later – but they came less certainly. As a cricketer his zenith had been so high that the only possible way was down. He was, however, now much more than a cricketer. On the 1948-49 tour of South Africa, he approached the journalist Reg Hayter with a suitcase full of unopened letters. Hayter started to go through them and found one from the *News of the World* offering £2,000 a year for a weekly column. Then he found another, written a few months later, withdrawing the offer because there had been no reply. Hayter introduced Compton to Bagenal Harvey, who became the first sportsman's agent, and did the famous deal in which Compton slicked down his hair and became forever identified with Brylcreem.

In the spring of 1950 he was still able to come out of footballing semi-retirement, get into the Arsenal team during their FA Cup run and get a winner's medal at Wembley, where they beat Liverpool 2-0. But in the Whitsun game against Sussex, his knee gave way and he missed much of that summer. He failed horribly in the Tests in Australia in the winter. In May 1951, after being appointed joint captain of Middlesex with Edrich, he scored 909 runs, more than in May 1947, but Compton's knee was by now entering national folklore. His appearances were becoming curtailed, and his ambition less intense. The runs still kept coming: he made the hit that won the Ashes in 1953, and in 1954, against Pakistan, there came both his highest Test score, 278 at Trent Bridge, and the innings he was inclined to regard as his best, 53 on a wet pitch at The Oval. He scored 492 in the 1955 Tests against South Africa. That November he had his right kneecap removed; his surgeon kept it as a souvenir, before giving it to MCC as part of the Lord's archive. Compton's biographer, Tim Heald, examined it and reported that it was like "a medium-sized mushroom, honey-coloured and honey-combed".

The operation enabled him to carry on playing for another two seasons, and to tour South Africa in 1956-57. He left county cricket as triumphantly as he entered it, hitting 143 in three hours in his final match as a professional for Middlesex in 1957. Thereafter he made occasional appearances as an amateur, scored his 123rd first-class hundred for the Cavaliers on a sociable trip to Jamaica in January 1964, and finally bowed out with a fifty for MCC against Lancashire later that year.

By then, he had become a thoroughly successful ex-cricketer, commentating for the BBC, writing pieces for the *Sunday Express* that were usually absurdly optimistic about the talents of iffy young cricketers, and using his natural readiness to have a drink and a chat with anyone to win accounts (successfully) for advertising agencies, first Royds then McCanns. He remained a bit of a roisterer into old age and maintained the friendships of his playing days until death. Edrich and Miller were at the top of this list; but it extended to all the South Africans he had found such chivalrous opponents and generous hosts. This led him to take the pro-white South Africa side in the disputes that followed his retirement and to be used on occasion – such as the 1983 debate over sending an MCC team to South Africa – by those with dubious motives. He never lost the slightly chaotic ingenuousness that was responsible for the suitcase of letters: he was always unpunctual and would arrive, as Michael Parkinson put it, in a cloud of dust even when he was walking with a stick. His home life was successful only serially, but his third and last wife provided two daughters to add to his earlier families, which helped keep him young. He was always young at heart, even towards the end when the pain from his hip merged with the pain from his knee. He died in hospital at Windsor on St George's Day, following complications from his third hip operation. His memorial service at Westminster Abbey created more applications for tickets than any in 30 years.

Cricket was hugely fortunate that such a gifted sportsman graced the game with his presence. It was doubly blessed that he was a man of modesty, charm and good nature.

CONSTABLE, BERNARD, who died on May 15, 1997, aged 76, was one of the unsung heroes of the great Surrey side of the 1950s. He played 434 matches for the county, starting in 1939 and finishing in 1964, and indeed got better as he aged. His best season came in 1961, when he was 40 and had had a kneecap removed: he scored 1,799 runs that year. As a batsman, he was technically correct and outstanding against spin, a vital skill given the pitches Surrey prepared in that era. He was a brilliant cover point, and a first-rate student of cricket's intricacies. "He knew the game inside out and every first-class player inside out," said Micky Stewart. "I learned more about cricket from Bernie Constable than from anyone else." He will be remembered best as an Oval character. Though his family were boat builders, by the Thames at East Molesey, he was regarded as the epitome of the cock-sparrer Cockney, an image he played up to with his confident strut round the field and his willingness to argue with anyone, including his captain, Stuart Surridge. "On your toes, Bernie," Surridge once shouted when Constable slipped on a sodden outfield at Leicester. "On me toes?" he roared back. "I'm on me knees." He would complain just as loudly if he disagreed with Surridge's field placings. "What do you need three of them over there for? Give 'em a fourth and they can play cards." The highlight of his career might have been the unbeaten 205 – in under five hours – he made against Somerset at The Oval in 1952. But it was probably the moment he ran two against Glamorgan, while Wilf Wooller was debating with the umpire about whether a disputed catch was fair or not.

CUMBERBATCH, CHESTER ST CLAIR, died in September 1996, aged 82. Chessie Cumberbatch appeared for Barbados as a batsman in the 1930s. He played only five matches, but these included the two games against the MCC team in 1934-35. His best score came in his last match: 59 against British Guiana in 1938-39.

DICKINSON, DAVID CHRISTOPHER, who died on August 25, 1997, aged 67, opened the bowling for the Cambridge team that won the 1953 University Match.

DIVE, MARY CLOUSTON, OAM, died on September 10, 1997 aged 84. "Mollie" Dive was captain of the Australian women's team in all her seven Tests, winning three and losing only one. She made two fifties, and led the team to victory over England in the 1948-49 series.

DIXON, PATRICK LESLIE, died on November 5, 1996, aged 80. Les Dixon played 30 matches for Queensland, and had some success as a fast-medium bowler before the war. He took 26 wickets in his first season, 1936-37, including five for 66 against South Australia and, though he never did as well again, missed only two matches over four seasons. He was a wartime pilot before being shot down and captured by the Germans. He returned to the Queensland team later but found wicket-taking more difficult, and retired to concentrate on banking. In his mid-seventies he could shoot his age at golf.

DYAL, REDVERS DUNDONALD, died on May 7, 1997, aged 96. "King" Dyal was a lovable exhibitionist and one of the sights of Barbados. He attended every major match at Kensington Oval for four decades: a tall, slim, pipe-smoking figure wearing a brightly-coloured suit, which he would change at each interval before making a re-entrance that would often attract more attention than the cricket. He claimed never to have worked in his life. He died in poverty and was buried at sea; former West Indies Cricket Board president Peter Short delivered a eulogy.

ELGOOD, BERNARD CYRIL, died on July 10, 1997, aged 75. "Bruno" Elgood was in the 1948 Cambridge side and made hundreds against Sussex and Middlesex.

FARMAN, ROY NEWSON, who died on July 1, 1996, aged 69, was a left-handed batsman who captained Auckland to the Plunket Shield in 1958-59. He was 31, had played only two first-class matches before that season, and was a completely unexpected choice to lead the side. However, in his first match he scored a battling unbeaten 96 against Wellington and, though he never repeated that success, he proved a shrewd leader and kept the team happy. His form declined the following year, and he dropped out of first-class cricket after just 11 matches.

FENNER, DEREK ALFRED, who died on September 6, 1997, aged 63, played just one first-class match, for Cambridge University in 1954, but bowled left-arm spin in Surrey club cricket for nearly half a century. He became headmaster of Alleyn's School.

FREWIN, LESLIE, who died on August 27, 1997, aged 80, was the head of publicity of Elstree Studios, whose stunts included having a mink bikini designed for Diana Dors to wear at the Cannes Film Festival. Frewin was chairman of the Lord's Taverners for three years, and his 32 books included *The Boundary Book*, a successful celebrity anthology which raised a huge sum for charity when it was first published in 1962.

GALLOWAY, PAUL WARREN, who died on August 20, 1996, aged 52, after a long illness, was a gritty if unstylish opening batsman for South Australia when they won the Sheffield Shield in 1968-69. He made four fifties, including 78 against New South Wales, and regularly paved the way for big innings by Les Favell or the Chappells. But he played only two games after that season.

GIBSON, NORMAN ALAN STANLEY, died on April 10, 1997, aged 73. Alan Gibson was one of the most remarkable men ever to broadcast or write about cricket. He was president of the Oxford Union and gained a first in history. Perhaps no one has brought more literacy or classical knowledge to the reporting of any game. Men with his background expect to become cabinet ministers at least, and Gibson often seemed conscious of this; a sense of failure may explain the demons that regularly afflicted him. He came from an unmoneyed background – his father was a Baptist preacher – and joined BBC West Region in 1948 in search of security. It became clear that he was a natural broadcaster, with a honeyed voice, a wonderful sense of cadence, a turn of phrase and an eye for the telling detail. In 1962 he was finally promoted to *Test Match Special*. When Gibson commentated on the same match as John Arlott, listeners were given a stream of description, wit, and both general and cricketing erudition that remains unsurpassed. Unfortunately, Gibson had the same weakness as Arlott without the same capacity to conceal it. Finally, the incidents of drunkenness on air became too reckless, and he was dropped – without ever being told why. He did, however, have a second flowering as his county match reports in *The Times* attained cult status. He described his experience at or going to the cricket with occasional, tangential references to the actual game. There was generally some disastrous experience to report from Didcot Station, where he usually had to change trains. There was the mysterious GRIP (The Glorious Red-headed Imperturbable Pamela), the barmaid in the Hammond Bar at Bristol. And he baffled Peter Lees, who ran the press bar at Lord's, by rechristening him Bardolph. The overall result was usually uproarious. He was, however, capable of ignoring some peripheral event like a century or a hat-trick; and as the years went by, humourless sub-editors lost patience.

Despite his taste for drink – perhaps a reaction against his Nonconformist background – Gibson was not a clubbable man. He rarely went into press boxes, and would sit alone, fending off bores, writing his copy in fountain pen while nursing a gigantic whisky, cleverly diluted so that it looked like a half of lager. Eventually, after his second marriage had broken down, he drifted into a nursing home, and in the last years the shadows took over. Much of his life – Didcot might have been a metaphor – was a source of torment as well as humour. He had a spell in a psychiatric hospital, which he wrote about in his autobiography *A Mingled Yarn*. His history, *The Cricket Captains of England*, was a wonderful read. He was a Liberal candidate in the 1959 election and remained a Baptist lay preacher. Gibson spoke at Sir Neville Cardus's memorial service in 1975 and read from William Blake:

> Joy and woe are woven fine
> A clothing for the soul divine.
> Under every grief and pine
> Runs a thread of silken twine.

It perhaps summed up Alan Gibson's own life better than Sir Neville's.

GREENE, EDMUND ARNOLD, died on May 20, 1997, aged 76. "Soldier" Greene was a Barbadian bowler who was surprisingly quick off ten paces and dismissed four batsmen, all of whom played Tests, on his debut for Barbados against Trinidad in 1943-44. He played eight first-class matches in all.

GUY, JOHN BERNARD, who died on February 7, 1997, aged 80, was a batsman who played six matches for Oxford University in the two seasons before the war, without getting a Blue, and one match for Kent in 1938. He also appeared twice for Warwickshire in 1950.

HAMPSHIRE, JOHN, who died on May 23, 1997, aged 83, was a fast bowler who played for Yorkshire Second Eleven for many years in the 1930s but got only three chances in the first team, all in 1937. He took five wickets in all – the last of them Denis Compton's – for only 109. Hampshire became a police sergeant in Rotherham and captained Rotherham Town in the Yorkshire League. His son John played for England.

HANLEY, ROBIN, was found dead in a hotel car park at Eastbourne on September 12, 1996, aged 28. He played five matches for Sussex between 1990 and 1992 as a middle-order batsman. His highest score in county cricket was 28, but he was a prolific scorer in both second-team and club cricket, making three hundreds for Sussex Second Eleven in 1990, and a double-century for Eastbourne in the Sussex League in 1992. Hanley was working at the hotel as a waiter when he died and apparently fell from the fourth-floor window of his room. At the inquest, the coroner, David Wadman, recorded a verdict of accidental death, having found no evidence of heavy drinking or drugs, nor any reason why Hanley should take his own life: he had been looking forward to going to Spain to be with his fiancée. "I suspect Robin went to the window to open it further . . . Whether this is what happened, or he leaned out to take the air, we will never know, but he lost his balance."

HARBOTTLE, Brigadier MICHAEL NEALE, OBE, who died on May 1, 1997, aged 80, played one innings in his only first-class match, and scored 156, for the Army against Oxford University at Camberley in 1938. Harbottle emerged as a talented left-handed batsman at Marlborough. He was rejected by the Navy because of bunions, but these did not bother the Army and he became captain of the Sandhurst XI. In the 1960s he became chief of staff for the UN peace-keeping force in Cyprus and was later an organiser of Generals for Peace and Disarmament.

HARRIS, WILFRED ERNEST, who died on December 4, 1996, aged 77, appeared for Glamorgan in 1938 while still a schoolboy. He played only five games in all, the last in 1947, but was an all-rounder for the powerful St Fagans club for half a century.

HARVEY-WALKER, ASHLEY JOHN, was shot dead in a bar in Johannesburg on April 28, 1997, aged 52. A gunman apparently walked in, shouted his name and fired when he responded. It was a bizarre end for an engaging cricketer associated with the good humour of the Derbyshire dressing-room in the 1970s. Harvey-Walker made an immediate impact when he became the first Derbyshire player to score a century on debut. This came on the less than fierce occasion of a match against Oxford University at Burton-on-Trent in 1971 when he was already 26. Though he played 81 matches over eight seasons, he was rarely sure of his place, and his successes were spasmodic. He was a fine striker of the ball and once hit Pat Pocock on to the top deck of the Oval pavilion; the fast bowlers, however, usually found him out. John Arlott once christened him "Ashley Hearty-Whacker", though the Derby press box usually preferred "Ashley Harvey-Wider", a reference to his occasional off-breaks. These, however, came good spectacularly at Ilkeston in 1978. Derbyshire went into the match without a recognised spinner and found themselves on a disintegrating pitch; Eddie Barlow gave Harvey-Walker the new ball, and he took seven for 35 as Surrey collapsed for 77 – though Derbyshire still lost. Harvey-Walker will be best remembered for the incident in the famous match at Buxton in 1975, when Derbyshire were caught on a snow-affected pitch with the ball bouncing dangerously. He handed something wrapped in a hanky to umpire Dickie Bird: his false teeth. As the ball looped to short leg when he was seven, Harvey-Walker is supposed to have let out a gummy cry of "Catch it!" After retirement, he played in the Bradford League then emigrated to South Africa. He worked as assistant groundsman at The Wanderers and only a month before his death helped prepare the pitch for the Test against Australia. He also had an interest in an inner-city bar, a business prone to produce murderous disputes.

HAYNES, MICHAEL WILLIAM, who died on September 18, 1997, aged 61, played nine matches for Nottinghamshire as a batsman between 1959 and 1961.

HOLT, JOHN KENNETH CONSTANTINE, OD, died on July 2, 1997, aged 73. "J.K." Holt – also known as J.K. junior, as his father was one of Jamaica's earliest star players – showed formidable batting form for West Indies in the Test series against England in 1953-54. He was given out lbw for 94 on his Test debut at Sabina Park, his home ground. There was a near riot, and umpire Perry Burke had to be escorted home. Holt made up for this in the next Test at Bridgetown, scoring 166 with a stunning exhibition of strokeplay that made his partner, Frank Worrell, look comparatively ordinary. He made runs in the next two Tests as well: 48 not out, 64 and 40. From then on his Test form declined, though he was appointed vice-captain for the tour of India and Pakistan in 1958-59, and scored 123 in the high-scoring draw at Delhi. He was always a strong cutter and puller, and batted on for Jamaica until 1961-62. Holt was awarded Jamaica's highest honour, the Order of Distinction, in 1976. But against Australia in 1954-55 he had dropped several catches, and the crowds at Bridgetown, who had cheered his century a year earlier, turned against him. Leslie Hylton, the former Jamaican fast bowler, was about to be executed for murdering his wife, and one group of spectators held up a placard: "Save Hylton," it said, "Hang Holt."

HURST, GORDON THOMAS, who died on July 5, 1996, aged 75, was a leg-spinner who played nine games for Sussex between 1947 and 1949, but was then much troubled by a shoulder injury. He took six for 80 against Warwickshire at Hove in his first season.

JAGDISH LAL, who died on March 3, 1997, aged 75, played for six different teams in the Ranji Trophy: Northern India, Hyderabad, United Provinces, Services, Patiala and Railways; he was a railway official, frequently transferred. He shared an opening stand of 273 with Nazar Mohammad against North-West Frontier Province in 1941-42, which remained a Ranji record for 28 years. Jagdish's son, Arun Lal, played 16 Tests for India in the 1980s.

JAYARATNE, MAHINDA PARAKRAMA, died on March 15, 1997, aged 29, two days after being shot by a gunman who arrived by motorcycle at his home in Sri Lanka. Jayaratne was a medium-pace bowler for North-Western Province and Kurunegala between 1989 and 1993, and when he was killed was running the campaign for a candidate in municipal elections.

JENNINGS, JACK, who died on April 11, 1997, aged 94, was Northamptonshire's travelling physiotherapist for many years. He was also the masseur on England's tour of Australia in 1965-66 and to the UK team at three Olympics. Jennings had particular faith in the restorative properties of sherry and raw egg. Before concentrating on cricket, he had been trainer of Northampton Town FC and was caretaker manager for the club's first three games ever in the Second Division after they were promoted in 1963: they won them all.

JEPSON, ARTHUR, who died on July 17, 1997, aged 82, was a miner's son who left his pit village to play for Nottinghamshire just before the war and rapidly established a reputation as a medium-paced bowler and lower-order slogger. He mostly bowled at the other end from Harold Butler and, though he could not match Butler's pace, swung the ball sharply enough to take 1,051 wickets before he retired in 1959. He switched to umpiring the following year, and that was enough to turn "Jeppo" into a minor institution. He umpired four Tests, and controlled games with a booming voice and a lugubrious air – half-weary, half-humorous – that was all his own. The most famous Jeppo anecdote concerns the 1971 Gillette semi-final at Old Trafford which went on past nightfall. Jack Bond, the Lancashire captain, complained about the light. "What's that up there?" asked Jepson. "The moon," said Bond. "Well, how far do you want to see then?" came the triumphant answer. David Lloyd was once bowling for Lancashire when Jepson said to him: "I hope you don't mind me mentioning this but you're the worst bowler I've ever seen. Fred Price was a bad 'un, but you're worse."

KEITH, HEADLEY JAMES, who died on November 17, 1997, aged 70, was a left-hand batsman, strong off the back foot, who was an important component of the powerful Natal batting line-up of the 1950s. Keith failed to make a successful transition into Test cricket, though he toured both Australia and England, and in 1952-53 became the first South African to score two centuries in a match in Australia: against Victoria at the MCG. He made his debut in the Melbourne Test, scoring 40 not out to seal victory and square the series; he also made 57 in the Lord's Test of 1955 and 73 at Leeds two Tests later. Both times he was watchful rather than dominant. Keith played eight Tests in all, but did little in the others. He was a useful slow left-armer at Currie Cup level.

KISCHENCHAND, GOGUMAL HARISINGHANI, who died on April 16, 1997, aged 72, was a small right-handed batsman, with an ungainly stance, who was a prolific scorer in Ranji Trophy cricket but had a disastrous record in Test cricket. He played five times for India, and on every occasion was out for a duck. In Australia in 1947-48 he was out for nought in each of his four second innings; recalled at Lucknow against Pakistan five years later, he got nought in the first innings. He did score some runs, including 44 in the low-scoring and rain-ruined Test at Sydney, but his Test average of 8.90 compares oddly with his overall average of just under 50. He represented Sind, Saurashtra, Baroda, Gujarat and Delhi in the Ranji, and also played for Hindus in the Bombay Pentangular.

LAMB, DAVID, who died on October 15, 1997, aged 58, after being mugged in Paris, had been secretary of Cumberland since 1992.

LEABEATER, LEONARD RAYMOND, died on June 1, 1996, aged 89. Len Leabeater scored 128 in 146 minutes, including 100 between lunch and tea, on his first-class debut for New South Wales against Tasmania in 1929-30. He played three Shield games in 1931-32 when the Test players were away, and scored two fifties, but work demands prevented him playing any more, and he finished his first-class career with 315 runs at an average of 45.00.

LEDWARD, JOHN ALLAN, MBE, died on July 22, 1997, aged 88. Jack Ledward was secretary of the Victorian Cricket Association for 20 years, and of the Australian Cricket Board of Control for six, from 1954 to 1960. He captained the Richmond club and played for Victoria for five seasons before the war, scoring 76 on his debut against Tasmania in 1934-35.

LEESON, PATRICK GEORGE, who died on May 12, 1997, aged 81, played one match for Worcestershire in 1936.

LITHGOW, Lt-Col WILLIAM SAMUEL PLENDERLEATH, who died on August 8, 1997, aged 77, played for Oxford in 1939 but did not gain a Blue. Later, asked what he had read, he said "cricket and rugger". He became a highly successful *chef d'équipe* and chairman of selectors of the British Olympic equestrian team.

LORD, REGINALD ARTHUR, died on June 10, 1997, aged 92. "Rex" Lord had a 50-year association with St Bede's Prep School, Eastbourne – he was still teaching four mornings a week when he was 88 – and developed the cricket interests of generations of boys. He played a single first-class match in each of the three years he was at Oxford, though the last was against the university, for H. D. G. Leveson Gower's XI.

MACPHERSON, ARCHIBALD IAN STEWART, who died on April 20, aged 83, played four times for Scotland in 1934 and 1935. He was a well-known surgeon.

McWATT, CLIFFORD AUBREY, died on July 12, 1997, aged 75, after a car crash in Canada. Cliff McWatt played for British Guiana from 1943-44 to 1956-57, and was one of the wicket-keepers tried by West Indies after Clyde Walcott injured his back and was forced to give up the job. McWatt was a useful left-hand batsman and a nimble keeper, who was Walcott's deputy on the 1948-49 tour of India but did not get his Test chance until five years later. Then he played in all five Tests against England in 1953-54, making some useful runs at No. 8, though his chancy style led one headline writer to call him McCatt – for his many lives. In Georgetown, his eighth-wicket stand with J.K. Holt (who was to die a few days before him) might have saved the follow-on. But with the stand on 99, McWatt was run out. Though McWatt himself later said he was out by about two yards, the crowd began hurling missiles at the umpire, "Badge" Menzies, and play was halted for ten minutes. McWatt was chosen once more against Australia a year later. He emigrated to Canada in 1986 but remained a close follower of the game.

MAKHIJA, SEWARAM MULCHAND, who died on October 27, 1997, aged 78, was a well-known umpire in Indian domestic cricket in the 1950s and 1960s.

MANLEY, MICHAEL NORMAN, who died on March 7, 1997, aged 72, was prime minister of Jamaica from 1972 to 1980 and again from 1989 to 1992. Cricket was one of his many enthusiasms; he was present at Sabina Park as a ten-year-old when Manny Martindale broke Bob Wyatt's jaw. While out of power in the 1980s, Manley wrote *A History of West Indies Cricket*, which was factually flawed but notable for its understanding of the game's cultural context.

MANT, GILBERT PALMER, who died on February 16, 1997, aged 94, was the last surviving journalist who covered the Bodyline tour in 1932-33. He was Sydney-born but working in London for Reuters, who chose him ahead of the future *Wisden* editor, Sydney Southerton, to cover the tour for both them and the Press Association. With few newspaper correspondents there, he was thus the major source of information for people in Britain. Unfortunately, Douglas Jardine ignored him; when Mant introduced himself on the *Orontes*, Jardine simply said "I see" and returned to his book. Mant's Australian accent did not help and, as the tour developed, he did not have enough of a reputation to break out of the factual straitjacket of the agency reporter and denounce England's tactics. He wrote a book, *A Cuckoo in the Bodyline Nest*, which Reuters refused to let him publish when he told them it would be anti-Jardine. It finally appeared 60 years later, when he was in his nineties, by which time it added little new information. When Mant returned to Australia, he had a successful career as a war correspondent and columnist: "The Way I See It" appeared in the *Sydney Sun* for many years.

MARKS, LYNN ALEXANDER, who died suddenly on December 7, 1997, aged 55, was a hard-hitting left-handed opener. His finest hour came when he made 185 for New South Wales at the Adelaide Oval in 1964-65 and shared a second-wicket stand of 378 with Doug Walters. He played the next year for South Australia, then returned to New South Wales, and was close to selection for the 1968 tour of England. The following season Marks was hit in the face by a bouncer from Laurie Mayne of Western Australia, suffered a fractured cheekbone, and retired from the game. His father Alec and his brother Neil also hit centuries for New South Wales. Neil said: "Lynn believed the opener's job was to wear the shine off the new ball. He tried to do it by bouncing the ball off the roads outside the oval."

MILLER, Dr HAMISH DAVID SNEDDON, died on April 24, 1997, aged 54; he had had a history of heart trouble. Miller was an English-born, South African-bred, quickish out-swing bowler who played for Glamorgan from 1963 to 1966 in between spells with Western Province and Orange Free State. Peter Walker recommended him to Glamorgan after watching him in South Africa. Miller was a sort of prototype one-day cricketer, a good lower-order hitter and field. He became an expert in mining engineering, and eventually head of the mining department of the University of Missouri.

MUZZELL, JACK KENDALL, who died on August 11, 1996, aged 90, was a fast bowler for Border from 1928-29 to 1934-35. He took 11 for 109 against Natal at Queenstown in 1929-30. His sons Peter and Robbie were also first-class cricketers.

NAYLOR, JOHN EDWARD, who died on June 26, 1996, aged 65, was a slow left-arm bowler who played once for Yorkshire in 1953.

NAYUDU, PRAKASH, who died on March 12, 1997, aged 60, played 14 matches for Madhya Pradesh, making his debut in 1957-58, with a score of 64 against Vidharba. He was India's junior table tennis champion and the son of C. K. Nayudu, the country's first Test captain. He later became a senior police officer.

NYALCHAND, SHAH, who died on January 3, 1997, aged 77, was a left-arm medium-pace bowler who had remarkable bowling figures in his only Test for India. He was chosen to play at Lucknow against Pakistan in their second official Test and, on a jute-matting pitch, bowled 64 overs and took three for 97. However, Nazar Mohammad carried his bat and Pakistan won by an innings. Nyalchand never played for India again. He remained a stalwart in the Ranji Trophy for more than two decades, making his debut for Western India in 1939-40, going on to play for Gujarat and then captaining

Saurashtra. In the last match of the 1961-62 season against Baroda he took 11 for 64, including a hat-trick spanning both innings. Frank Worrell once called him "the king of matting wickets".

OAKES, JOHN YPRES, died on July 4, 1997, aged 81. Jack Oakes was born at Horsham, where his father was groundsman, on March 29, 1916, as the British struggled to hold on to the town that gave him his middle name. He grew into a burly cricketer, who bowled off-breaks and hit the ball hard, though more often for quick forties than for major scores. He joined Sussex in 1937, and returned after the war, but often lost his place when there was a surfeit of amateurs, and he left acrimoniously in 1951 after he was accused of not trying in a Second Eleven match. He went on to play for Northumberland and became groundsman at Tynedale. He and his brother Charlie constitute one of the many pairs of brothers to have played for Sussex.

O'BRIEN, LEO PATRICK JOSEPH, who died on March 13, 1997, aged 89, was the oldest Australian Test cricketer, and his death left Sir Donald Bradman as the sole survivor from either side of the Bodyline series. He played for Australia only five times, but these included the Second and Fifth Tests of 1932-33, and he was at the other end when MCC were playing an Australian XI at Melbourne earlier in the tour and he saw five fielders going on to the leg side for Woodfull. "It's the right-hander down that end," he reputedly told the fielders, trying to be helpful. "I'm the left-hander." He made a determined 46 that day, and was picked for the Melbourne Test. He made 10 and 11 in Australia's only victory, but came back in the last Test at Sydney to make 61. O'Brien was not picked to tour England in 1934, but went to South Africa in 1935-36 and scored 59 and 48 in his two Tests, which were both won by an innings. His final appearance was against England at Sydney the following season, when he scored 0 and 17; he had gone by the next game when Australia began to turn the series round. He was a left-handed bat of the most determined sort, who played for the Melbourne club Richmond before making his debut for Victoria in 1929-30. O'Brien was also a first-rate baseball player, and an amateur boxer who won every fight except his last. Later, he worked for the tax department, coached in Asia and bred racehorses as a hobby. He was a friendly man and sociable cricketer, who kept playing into his seventies, and for more than fifty years of his life played at least one match a year on the MCG.

OSBORNE, HAROLD, died on November 9, 1997, aged 87. "Ossie" Osborne was Sussex's honorary librarian and archivist for 21 years.

PARKER, ANTHONY JOHN, died on October 30, 1997, aged 71. John Parker was a gregarious broadcaster and journalist whose varied career included being locked up by the Rhodesian government, a spell as sports editor of Independent Television News, and reporting county cricket for the *Sunday Times*. He wrote the Tillingfold series of novels, updating Hugh de Selincourt's classic, *The Cricket Match*. The fourth of his six children was Paul Parker, who played one Test for England.

PARRIS, JAMES LAMBERT, died on May 29, 1997, aged 91. "Puss" Parris was a Barbadian leg-spinner who was highly successful in club cricket and played 15 matches for the island over a 21-year span from 1925-26.

PARTRIDGE, REGINALD JOSEPH, died on February 1, 1997, aged 84. Reg Partridge was a stalwart of the Northamptonshire attack throughout the worst years of the club's history. Partridge, from Wollaston, took a day off from his boot factory to attend a trial in 1929, only to discover that no one from the club had turned up to watch him. He came back a second time, more successfully, and began a career more wearying than work in any factory. He finally retired from first-class cricket in 1948, just before the club's revival, having played 277 first-class games for a team that had won only a handful of them. Partridge bowled medium-pacers, sometimes varying them with off-breaks, which provided his best figures: nine for 66 against Warwickshire in 1934. He took 638 wickets, one of them the most prized of all – when Bradman came to the County Ground in 1938. The Western Brothers, a variety duo who wrote topical songs at the time, marked the occasion:

> Partridge must feel such a cocky young bird
> Bradman is out for two!

He batted as dependably as anyone in the team's continual crises. Partridge remained a local celebrity: he became groundsman at the well-appointed British Timken company ground outside Northampton and led the firm's team to six County League titles in eight years in the 1950s.

PRATT, DEREK EDWARD, who died on January 10, 1997, aged 71, was a batsman and leg-spinner from South London who played club cricket for Banstead and got nine games for Surrey between 1954 and 1957, some of them alongside his brother Ronnie. He later played for Bedfordshire.

PRICE, CHARLES FREDERICK THOMAS, who died on January 19, 1997, aged 79, was a member of the Australian Services team of 1945. He was with the team throughout its exhausting schedule, including the tour of the Australian states. Price was an unorthodox left-arm bowler, who bowled quickish chinamen and kept a very steady length. He played in the first two of the Victory Tests in England, took seven useful wickets for 99, scored 35 in the first innings at Lord's from No. 10 and was batting with Cec Pepper when the Australians completed their thrilling win. Price played 14 first-class matches for the Services, but moved upcountry on his return home and never appeared in a major fixture for his home state, New South Wales.

PROVIS, THOMAS ANTHONY JAMES, died on June 8, 1997, aged 77. Tom Provis was born in Birmingham and flew into Denmark with the liberation forces to settle and become one of the country's most prominent cricketers. He was the only non-Dane to play in the so-called continental Tests against Holland before 1983, and he took 1,371 wickets in Danish cricket at barely nine runs each. He served in many roles as an administrator and co-wrote *The Story of Continental Cricket* in 1969.

PUTNER, FRANK WILLIAM, who died on March 25, 1997, aged 84, played 11 games for Middlesex in 1933 and 1934. In 1934 he scored 126 not out for the MCC Young Professionals in the annual fixture against the Young Amateurs. He later ran various pubs in London and the Home Counties.

RAPER, JAMES RHODES STANLEY, died on March 9, 1997, aged 87. Stanley Raper ran a West Riding wool business and was captain of the Yorkshire Second Eleven from 1939 to 1948, in an era when that was a position of some prestige and authority in itself. He also captained the first team in one of his three first-class appearances: he led a weakened side to Yorkshire's first defeat against Nottinghamshire in 24 years, at Bramall Lane in 1947. Five of his grandsons played for the Harrow XI, and four of them captained the side against Eton at Lord's, as did his son Brian.

ROBINSON, GLENN, who died on January 19, 1997, aged 16, from meningitis, was one of the most promising young players in County Durham. He was a first-team player for the Durham Senior League club Philadelphia and was expected to represent the county Under-17s in 1997.

ROY, AMBAR, who died on September 19, 1997, aged 52, from malaria, was a left-hand batsman who played four Tests for India, against New Zealand and Australia, in 1969-70. He scored a fighting 48 in his first Test innings, but did little thereafter. However, he was an effective Ranji Trophy player for almost two decades: perhaps the most talented left-hander to come from Bengal. He was a Bengal selector for 15 years and was credited for spotting the talent of Sourav Ganguly. He was also a national selector from 1984 to 1986. Roy was a nephew of the Indian opening batsman Pankaj Roy.

SCHOFIELD, BRYAN, who died on October 27, 1997, aged 62, had been sponsorship manager of Cornhill Insurance since 1983 and an important figure in Cornhill's continuing support for Test cricket in England.

SCOTT, Lt-Col HAROLD ELDON, who died on January 29, 1997, aged 89, was an all-rounder who played four matches in 1937, two for the Army and two for Sussex. His father and brother were also first-class cricketers.

SCOTT-BROWNE, IAN FREDERICK BACHE, who died on January 4, 1997, aged 69, after many years of illness, was a businessman and Surrey committee member who moved over to become secretary of the county from 1978 to 1988. He was among the pioneers of modern cricket administration, placing emphasis on the need for commercialism – though he was still paid an old-fashioned, uncommercial, salary. He had been captain of Streatham CC and a four-handicap golfer.

SEEDAT, DAWOOD MOHOMED, who died on May 1, 1997, aged 71, captained Natal in the segregated non-white tournaments of the 1950s. He was a fast-medium left-armer who once took six for ten, including a hat-trick, against Eastern Province.

SEWTER, JAMES WALTER, died on October 26, 1997, aged 81. Jim Sewter was a genial pipe-smoker who brought an air of relaxed calm to county scoreboxes for most of his 19 seasons as Worcestershire scorer, though the calm dissipated after the introduction of computers. He continued scoring until the month before he died, and recorded the unbroken partnership of 438 between Graeme Hick and Tom Moody in his final match. He had previously been transport manager for the British Sugar Corporation in Kidderminster. This job was busiest in the winter, when the harvested sugar beet came in, enabling him to have time off for cricket in the summer, when he bowled fast for Kidderminster in the Birmingham League.

SHEFFIELD, JAMES ROY, died in New Zealand on November 16, 1997, aged 90. Roy Sheffield was probably the only Essex wicket-keeper ever to be arrested on suspicion of being a Bolivian spy. He was a small, agile man who kept wicket in 177 games for Essex between 1929 and 1936. Though he was an efficient keeper, Sheffield's batting shone only intermittently – he scored 85 not out on his debut against Warwickshire, and made a century at Hove in his last season, but did little in between. Sheffield was more notable for his off-season adventures. In 1932-33, while England's most famous cricketers were involved in the Bodyline series, he was working as a cowboy in South America and trying to canoe down the River Paraguay. There was a war going on between Paraguay and Bolivia, and the Paraguayans arrested Sheffield and locked him up until a British businessman intervened. He later wrote a novel based on the incident, entitled *Bolivian Spy*? A year later he spent two months walking through the Drakensberg Mountains and Basutoland. Essex did not retain him after 1936 and he left for New Zealand, meeting his future wife on the boat, and never returned to England. He played three games for Wellington in 1938-39, but later concentrated on his canoeing. He competed in the 50-mile Waikato River Marathon when he was well into his eighties; the Essex secretary Peter Edwards visited him in 1992 and described him as astonishingly fit. He died a few days after his daughter, a BBC producer who had been visiting him, was knocked off her bike and killed.

SHERRARD, PATRICK, who died on January 11, 1997, aged 78, was a first-class cricketer for one week in May 1938. He turned out for Cambridge against Northamptonshire and, on finishing there, set off for The Parks, where he scored 53 for Leicestershire against Oxford. He also won a rugby Blue.

SKINNER, ALFRED GRAHAM, who died in 1997, aged 86, played for Buckinghamshire between 1928 and 1952. He also served in India and scored 125 for Bengal against Nawanagar in the 1936-37 Ranji Trophy final.

SMITH, CYRIL GERALD DOUGLAS, who died on December 7, 1997, was a member of the Worcestershire committee from 1926 to 1976 and a club trustee until he died. He helped guide the club's finances through some very difficult years.

SMITH, FRANK BRUNTON, died on July 6, 1997, aged 75. Brun Smith, otherwise known as "Runty", was a small, aggressive batsman who was a crowd favourite in Christchurch and played four Tests for New Zealand, two of them on the England tour of 1949. He made a vital 96, full of wristy square cuts, in just two hours at Headingley, and an unbeaten 54 in the second innings. During his 96 he is supposed to have warned the slips: "I'll hole out to one of you jokers before long." He often did, but not that time. After scoring 23 at Lord's, he lost his place to John Reid. Smith had reached his peak the previous season at home when his three Plunket Shield matches for Canterbury included 153 in 163 minutes against Otago and 146, only slightly slower, in Auckland. He was principal of various primary schools in Christchurch. His father Frank and son Geoff also played for Canterbury, making them the province's only three-generation family. Dick Brittenden wrote of him: "He was often lucky, if the failure of a startled slips fieldsman to catch a crimson blur soaring overhead can be regarded as luck for the batsman ... Brilliance in stroke production, eagerness to get on with the game, beautiful fielding and a cheerful and engaging personality made Smith one of the most popular players of his day. He would have been remarkable in any generation."

SPENCE, ROBERT, who died on February 17, 1997, aged 76, was treasurer of the Queensland Cricket Association from 1963 to 1988. He was also scorer in 150 first-class matches, including 16 Tests.

SPERRY, JAMES, died on April 21, 1997, aged 87. Jim Sperry was a miner at Bagworth Colliery who came up to bowl quickish left-arm in-swing for Leicestershire from 1937 to 1952. He took seven for 19 against Hampshire in 1939, but even as a 41-year-old in 1951 managed 62 wickets at 22 each. "He appeared frail, but would bowl loyally until the point of fatigue," wrote Philip Snow. "A rather lugubrious, pallid countenance hid unfailing amiability. He was a man of excellent team spirit." Sperry was the oldest Leicestershire cricketer when he died.

SPOONER, RICHARD THOMPSON, died on December 20, 1997, aged 77. Dick Spooner did not play first-class cricket until he was 28, but then established himself as Warwickshire's wicket-keeper/batsman for more than a decade. He was a wicket-keeper in the modern style, agile rather than elegant, but he also had the enormous plus of his no-nonsense left-hand batting. Usually, he opened the innings, and in Warwickshire's title-winning season of 1951 he topped their averages as well, scoring 1,767 Championship runs, with four centuries. He was picked for the 1951-52 tour of India, when England sent a substandard team, and played in all five Tests, scoring 71 and 92 at Calcutta. He had no chance of being picked ahead of Godfrey Evans, and played only two further Tests, both times when Evans was injured: at Port-of-Spain in 1953-54, and The Oval in 1955, when England wanted left-handers to counter Trevor Goddard's defensive bowling. In that game he got a pair but did not concede a bye. Contemporaries, however, considered him the perfect deputy, and in *Cricket Cauldron*

Alex Bannister called him "a grand team man", who was more concerned than anyone for Evans's welfare on the West Indies tour. Spooner was one of several north-easterners to join Warwickshire after the war. He was loud on the field, with definite views on most cricketing subjects, and a distinctive broken nose. In retirement, he became a groundsman in Devon.

SPRING, LEICESTER RUSSELL, who died on May 31, 1997, aged 88, was a fast-medium bowler who played three matches for Auckland in 1936-37 and twice dismissed Walter Hadlee. He founded the *Whakatane Beacon* newspaper and by 1953 was able to buy his first racehorse, Rising Fast, which won nine races out of 11, including the Melbourne Cup.

STOCKER, Sir JOHN DEXTER, MC TD PC, who died on December 27, 1996, aged 78, was an all-round cricketer who represented Westminster School and Wimbledon CC. He became a Lord Justice of Appeal and, in 1993, President of Surrey.

STOW, Sir JOHN MONTAGUE, GCMG KCVO, who died in January 1997, aged 85, was the last Governor of Barbados and the first Governor-General. As a colonial official in the Caribbean, his skill at cricket – as well as his deep distaste for racial barriers – made him a popular figure. He captained St Lucia in the Windward Islands tournament of 1951-52 when he was the island's administrator. He had played for Harrow against Eton in 1930.

SUNNUCKS, PETER REGAN, who died in February 1997, aged 80, played 66 times for Kent in the 1930s and two more in 1946. He opened the batting at Colchester with Arthur Fagg in 1938, when Fagg scored two double-hundreds; Sunnucks put on 283 with him in the second innings before being run out for 82. Sunnucks himself scored just one first-class century, 162 against Nottinghamshire the previous season.

TATE, CECIL FREDERICK, who died on August 7, 1997, aged 89, was a slow left-armer who played four matches for Derbyshire in 1928 and seven for Warwickshire in the early 1930s. He was the younger brother (there was a 13-year gap) of Maurice Tate and son of Fred, both of whom played for England.

TAYLOR, NORMAN CYRIL, who died on April 20, 1997, aged 90, was a member of the Worcestershire committee for about 40 years, and was one of the instigators of the tradition of tea in the Worcester ladies' pavilion. He claimed to have seen all or part of every Worcestershire home match since 1926.

THOMAS, JOHN BRINLEY GEORGE, OBE, died on April 11, 1997, aged 79. Bryn Thomas was probably the best-known journalist in Wales. He was chief rugby writer of the *Western Mail* for 36 years; his prose was knowledgable, if verbose, but he was known everywhere as simply "JBG". In the summer he wrote widely about cricket, partly as "Arthurian" of the *Daily Telegraph*, and as the Glamorgan correspondent for *Wisden* from 1979 to 1984.

TOWNSEND, DAVID CHARLES HUMPHERY, who died on January 27, 1997, aged 84, was the last man to play cricket for England without ever playing for a first-class county. Townsend was picked for the 1934-35 tour of West Indies on the strength of his form for Oxford University. He played, opening each time with Bob Wyatt, in the last three Tests of the series, and top-scored with 36 in the second innings of his debut when England were all out for 107. But his highest score otherwise was 16. The Townsends were a cricketing dynasty: six members of the family have played first-class cricket, including David's grandfather Frank, his father Charles, and his son Jonathan; Charles Townsend also played two Tests, in 1899. No other family is known to have produced four generations of first-class cricketers. David Townsend was steady rather than outstanding amongst a gifted generation at Winchester, and was ill during his first summer at Oxford. But, in 1933, he blossomed with 734 runs, including 195 against the Free Foresters, and *Wisden* approvingly noted his fine physique, his patience, his power and his attractive range of strokes. The following year he hit peak form when it then mattered, at Lord's: his 193 remains the sixth-highest score in the 152 official University matches. In style and impact, it was overshadowed by a blistering hundred from F. G. H. Chalk, but it was enough to gain him an invitation from MCC for the winter. Thereafter, he went back to Norton-on-Tees, County Durham, where he was born and died, and took over the family law firm in Stockton. He practised as a solicitor for more than 50 years and played for the Norton club and Durham, whom he captained from 1937 to 1947.

VAVASOUR Bt, Commander Sir GEOFFREY WILLIAM, DSC, who died in July, aged 82, played one first-class match for the Combined Services, at Northampton in 1947.

WANSBOROUGH, SYLVIA NANCY, who died on August 13, 1997, aged 82, toured Australasia with the England women's team in 1948-49 when she was Nancy Joy, but played no Tests. She later campaigned on behalf of former mental patients, and for the provision of sheltered employment as part of their rehabilitation.

WARBURTON, ROBERT, died on June 17, 1997, aged 70. Bob Warburton was a member of the Lancashire administrative staff for 44 years up to 1991. He was assistant secretary for 35 years and developed the Supporters' Association.

WEBSTER, JACK, who died on October 25, 1997, aged 79, was a Harrow School master briefly elevated to be captain of Northamptonshire in the middle of the 1946 season when Peter Murray-Willis resigned. He led the team on his Championship debut. As a fast-medium bowler, he continued playing for the county in holiday time for the next ten years, occasionally deputising as captain. Webster had won Blues at Cambridge for both cricket and soccer.

WESTON, ALAN GIBBONS, who died on June 10, 1997, aged 89, played five games as an amateur batsman for Leicestershire in 1933 and 1934.

WHITTAKER, GEOFFREY JAMES, died on April 20, 1997, aged 80. Geoff Whittaker joined Surrey before the war and was still on the fringe of the team when they began to dominate cricket in the 1950s. He was a big hitter who struck nine sixes when he made 148 at Northampton in 1949; his highest score, 185 not out against Kent in 1951, took only four hours. That was his best year, and he scored 1,439 runs – with 32 sixes – but, as Surrey began their seven Championship seasons, his form fell away. He left in 1953 to become coach at Victoria College, Jersey, where he lived for the rest of his life.

WILLIAMS, ERNEST ALBERT VIVIAN, died on April 13, 1997, aged 83. "Foffie" Williams was a Barbadian all-rounder who played four Tests for West Indies, all against England: one in 1939, the others in 1947-48. He was primarily a bowler who could vary his pace quite markedly from very sharp to slow-medium, but his two most famous performances came with the bat. In 1935-36 Williams scored 131 not out and shared an eighth-wicket stand of 255 for Barbados against Trinidad with Manny Martindale. In 1947-48 he came into the Test team as a late replacement for Frank Worrell, and hit the first six balls he faced in the second innings for boundaries: 6644 off Jim Laker, and then two more fours off Jack Ikin. He reached 50 in half an hour, and finished with 72 in 63 minutes. Williams played football for Barbados and became the country's chief sports officer. He was a man of firm views on many subjects, and strongly opposed the life ban on West Indian players who went on the rebel tour to South Africa; he stopped going to Kensington Oval in protest.

WINWOOD, THOMAS LAWSON, who died in November 1997, aged 87, was an amateur who played 18 matches for Worcestershire in the early 1930s. Batting at No. 7, he made 104 in just two hours against Hampshire at Worcester in the county's last home match of 1930.

WOOLLER, WILFRED, who died on March 10, 1997, aged 84, was one of the greatest all-round sportsmen Wales ever produced. More than that, he was one of the nation's richest – and certainly most combative – characters. He was captain of Glamorgan for 14 years, secretary for 30 and club president for the six years before he died. He had 18 rugby caps for Wales, played soccer for Cardiff and was later fearsome at bowls. Even when he was in his seventies, it was always likely that Wilf's latest exploit would be the talk of the principality. He was brave and bull-headed, on and off the field. There will be never be another.

Wooller was a North Walian – which some South Walians say accounted for his extraordinary character – born at Rhos-on-Sea, the son of a successful but mild-mannered businessman who moved from Manchester. He became famous when he was still at Rydal School, though he was 20 years old, having failed his first attempt to get into Cambridge. He was chosen to play for the Welsh rugby team at Twickenham and starred in their first-ever win there. He played in another historic victory, against the All-Blacks, two years later. His cricket developed more slowly and, when he did eventually reach Cambridge, he did not play in his freshman year, but won Blues in 1935 and 1936.

By then, Wooller was already making headlines of the sort that would follow him all his life: a drunken adventure involving the theft of a receiver from a phone box resulted in a £5 fine from the magistrates and a headline in the national press: NIGHT TIME EXPLOITS OF CAMBRIDGE BLUE. He got a job with a Cardiff coal firm, who made him spend the next two summers supervising the company's operations at docksides in places like Algiers, so it was 1938 before he could play for Glamorgan. He finally came into the side against Yorkshire, opened the bowling with Jack Mercer, swung the new ball sharply and took five for 90. The following year he made a hundred against the West Indians. But his cricket career had barely started when the war came, and he was shipped overseas. In 1942 Wooller found himself against a force even he could not take on single-handed and was obliged to surrender to the Japanese with the rest of his regiment. When he returned from Changi Jail – emotionally and physically fragile – he began to throw himself into Championship cricket for the first time, aged 34. He had a fair season in 1946, and the captain Johnnie Clay recommended him as his successor; Wooller became secretary as well, and for the next three decades would be synonymous with Glamorgan cricket. At once, he gave the team a sense of purpose – deriving from a mixture of rugby fervour, military strategy and his own remarkable personality – and in 1948 it paid off: "I left nothing to chance, and when playing at Swansea even consulted the tide tables." Glamorgan travelled around the country with a small lorry carrying a large mangle and some blankets; if it rained, the players would spread the blankets on the field and keep putting them through the wringer. They fielded like demons and the then-newest of the counties became champions for the first time.

Glamorgan remained a force in the Championship for most of the Wooller years. Wooller himself became a formidable all-rounder and did the double in 1954. He never played Test cricket, and lost the opportunity because of business commitments: he made himself unavailable when he had a chance of the vice-captaincy on the 1948-49 tour of South Africa, and captaincy to India in 1951-52. He was a Test selector from 1955 to 1961. Even when he was secretary and off the field, he still effectively *was* Glamorgan, and he found it desperately hard to moderate the constant involvement that had characterised his captaincy. Not only that, he was supplementing his rotten pay by writing and broadcasting, so he was often chief prosecutor as well. He never minced words on any subject – most particularly politics, where he became a ferocious supporter of sporting contact with South Africa. "These antis make me puke," he said and called them "lefties, weirdos or odd bods – some of them may be all three."

Even now, almost everyone in Wales has a Wilf anecdote. He took on fast bowlers with bat and mouth: "Bugger off, Tyson. You're not fast enough to hurt me." "You're slow, Loader. How did I ever pick you for England?" He was 46 at that time, and facing a fusillade of bouncers. His own players were never exempt. There is some dispute about exactly which opponent he said had just scored the worst double-century he had ever seen, but he probably said it every time anyone reached 200 against his teams. There is no question about the authenticity of the dispute at Swansea when Wooller, as secretary, became incensed about Brian Close's tactics as captain of Somerset and announced over the loudspeaker: "In view of Somerset's negative approach to this game, we are willing to refund the admission money of any spectator who wishes to call at the county office."

Having retired from the club completely, he chafed even more against non-involvement and he became a trenchant critic of the club's policies as Glamorgan drifted into years of failure – on the air, in his *Sunday Telegraph* column, the letters pages or the bar. He was usually right. However furious the dispute, he would always have a drink with opponents. His exemplary family life emphasised the softness that lay underneath. Those who hated him always did so with a tinge of affection; those who loved him did so with a touch of exasperation. He was always "that bloody Wilf Wooller".

WREFORD-BROWN, ANTHONY JOHN, who died in 1997, aged 84, played a handful of first-class games for various teams in the 1930s, including Oxford University and Sussex. He was a well-known sociable cricketer and taught generations at Charterhouse, where he was a housemaster for 15 years. His father was one of the last of the great Corinthian footballers.

CAREER FIGURES

This list covers all Test cricketers whose deaths are reported above.

	Tests				First-class			
	Runs	Avge	Wkts	Avge	Runs	Avge	Wkts	Avge
Bairstow, D. L.	125	20.83	–	–	13,961	26.44	9	34.22
Burke, C.	4	2.00	2	15.00	959	17.43	200	25.99
Compton, D. C. S.	5,807	50.06	25	56.40	38,942	51.85	622	32.27
Holt, J. K., jun.	1,066	36.75	1	20.00	4,258	41.33	5	35.40
Keith, H. J.	318	21.20	0	–	3,203	30.50	79	27.51
Kischenchand, G.	89	8.90	–	–	7,218	49.43	37	32.24
McWatt, C. A.	202	28.85	1	16.00	1,673	28.84	2	52.50
Nyalchand, S.	7	7.00	3	32.33	420	7.63	235	22.57
O'Brien, L. P. J.	211	26.37	–	–	3,303	36.70	3	42.33
Roy, A.	91	13.00	–	–	7,163	43.15	29	34.86
Smith, F. B.	237	47.40	–	–	2,643	33.03	1	76.00
Spooner, R. T.	354	27.23	–	–	13,851	27.26	0	–
Townsend, D. C. H.	77	12.83	0	–	1,801	29.04	6	83.50
Williams, E. A. V.	113	18.83	9	26.77	1,479	26.89	116	29.19

DIRECTORY OF BOOK DEALERS

AARDVARK BOOKS "Copperfield", High Street, Harmston, Lincoln LN5 9SN. Tel: 01522-722671. Peter Taylor specialises in Wisdens. Send SAE for list. Wisden cleaning and repair service available. Wisdens purchased, *any* condition.

TIM BEDDOW, 62a Stanmore Road, Edgbaston, Birmingham B16 9TB. Tel: 0956-456112 (mobile); fax: 0121-770 9645. Visit my stall at Edgbaston. New books from £1.00. Large selection of Wisdens available. Open every first-team game. Send SAE for catalogue.

BODYLINE BOOKS: Specialist dealer in antique, second-hand and new cricket books. For my latest maga-logue of books for sale, editorial and poetry, send 38p stamp to: **150A Harbord Street, London SW6 6PH. Tel: 0171-385 2176; e-mail: cricket@dircon.co.uk.**

BOUNDARY BOOKS, Southlands, Sandy Lane, Goostrey, Cheshire CW4 8NT. Tel: 01477-533106; fax 01477-544529. Second-hand and antiquarian cricket books and autographs. Catalogues issued. Viewing by appointment at Stockport offices.

PETER BRIGHT, 11 Ravens Court, Ely, Cambridgeshire CB6 3ED. Tel: 01353-661727. Antiquarian and second-hand cricket books bought and sold. Occasional catalogues. Representative stock held at **The Bookshop, 24 Magdalene Street, Cambridge.**

CRICKET BOOKS, 'Headingley', 3 Pruiti Crescent, Lesmurdie, Western Australia 6076. Tel: (08) 9291-8704; fax: (08) 9291-8735. Second-hand and antiquarian cricket books and memorabilia bought and sold. Catalogues issued. Want-lists welcome.

IAN DYER Cricket Books, 29 High Street, Gilling West, Richmond, North Yorkshire DL10 5JG. Wisdens, antiquarian, second-hand books, printed ephemera bought/sold. **Tel/fax: 01748-822786; e-mail: iandyercricketbooks@btinternet.com. Catalogue also at www.bibliofind.com/iandyercricketbooks.html.**

K. FAULKNER, 65 Brookside, Wokingham, Berkshire RG41 2ST. Tel: 0118-978 5255. Cricket books, Wisdens, memorabilia bought and sold. Telephone enquiries welcome. Permanent display in Gloucestershire CCC Shop, Nevil Road, Bristol BS7 9EJ. Open all year.

E. O. KIRWAN, 3 Pine Tree Garden, Oadby, Leicestershire LE2 5UT. Tel: 0116-271 4267 (evenings and weekends only). Second-hand and antiquarian cricket books, Wisdens, autograph material and cricket ephemera of all kinds.

J. W. McKENZIE, 12 Stoneleigh Park Road, Ewell, Epsom, Surrey KT19 0QT. Tel: 0181-393 7700; fax: 0181-393 1694. Specialists in antiquarian second-hand cricket books, particularly Wisdens, since 1969. Catalogues sent on request. Publishers of rare cricket books. Shop premises open regular business hours.

ROGER PAGE, 10 Ekari Court, Yallambie, Victoria 3085, Australia. Tel: (03) 9435-6332; fax: (03) 9432-2050. Dealer in new and second-hand cricket books. Distributor of overseas cricket annuals and magazines. Agent for Cricket Statisticians and Cricket Memorabilia Society.

RED ROSE BOOKS, 196 Belmont Road, Astley Bridge, Bolton BL1 7AR. Tel/fax: 01204-598080. Specialist in antiquarian and second-hand cricket books. Catalogue available on request. Collections purchased.

WILLIAM H. ROBERTS, The Crease, 113 Hill Grove, Salendine Nook, Huddersfield, West Yorkshire HD3 3TL. Tel/fax: 01484-654463. Second-hand/antiquarian cricket books, Wisdens, autograph material and memorabilia bought and sold. Catalogues sent on request.

CHRISTOPHER SAUNDERS, Orchard Books, Kingston House, High Street, Newnham on Severn, Gloucestershire GL14 1BB. Tel: 01594-516030; fax: 01594-517273. Office/bookroom by appointment. Second-hand/antiquarian cricket books and memorabilia bought and sold. Full-time bookseller for 17 years.

SPORTSPAGES, Caxton Walk, 94-96 Charing Cross Road, London WC2H 0JG. Tel: 0171-240 9604; fax: 0171-836 0104. Barton Square, St Ann's Square, Manchester M2 7HA. Tel: 0161-832 8530; fax: 0161-832 9391. New cricket books, audio and videotapes, including imports, especially from Australasia; retail and mail order service.

STUART TOPPS, 40 Boundary Avenue, Wheatley Mills, Doncaster, South Yorkshire DN2 5QU. Tel: 01302-366044. Our 88-page catalogue of cricket books, Wisdens, booklets, brochures and county yearbooks is always available.

WISTERIA BOOKS, Wisteria Cottage, Birt Street, Birtsmorton, Malvern WR13 6AW. Tel: 01684-833578. Visit our family-run stall at county grounds for new, second-hand, antiquarian cricket books and ephemera, or contact Grenville Simons at the address above. Send SAE for catalogue.

MARTIN WOOD, Dept WIS, 2 St John's Road, Sevenoaks, Kent TN13 3LW. Tel: 01732-457205. Since 1970 Martin Wood has posted 26,000 parcels of cricket books worldwide. For latest catalogue, please send 26p stamp to the above address.

AUCTIONEERS

CHRISTIE'S inaugural cricket sale was the MCC Bicentenary Sale of 1987. Since then sales have been held on a regular basis at London, South Kensington, with 19 June and 11 September as the planned dates for this year's sales.

DOMINIC WINTER, Specialist Book Auctioneers & Valuers, The Old School, Maxwell Street, Swindon SN1 5DR. Tel: 01793-611340; fax: 01793-491727. Twice-yearly auction sales of sports books and memorabilia, including Wisdens.

PHILLIPS have held specialised cricket auctions since 1978, highlighted by the celebrated Hal Cohen Collection in 1995. Free valuations and collection undertaken by Mike Ashton on **01222-396453.**

T. VENNETT-SMITH, 11 Nottingham Road, Gotham, Nottinghamshire NG11 0HE. Tel: 0115-983 0541. Auctioneers and valuers. Twice-yearly auctions of cricket and sports memorabilia. The cricket auction run by cricketers for cricket lovers worldwide.

DIRECTORY OF CRICKET SUPPLIERS

CRICKET EQUIPMENT

DUNCAN FEARNLEY, 17 Vigo Place, Brickyard Road, Aldridge, Walsall WS9 8UG. Tel: 01922-457733; fax: 01922-452659. Makers of the finest hand-made English willow bats, and suppliers of a complete range of cricket equipment, including pads, gloves, clothing, footwear and accessories.

GUNN & MOORE LTD, 119/121 Stanstead Road, Forest Hill, London SE23 1HJ. Tel: 0181-291 3344; fax: 0181-699 4008. Gunn & Moore, established in 1885, are the world's most comprehensive provider of cricket bats, equipment, footwear and clothing.

READERS – The largest UK manufacturers of leather and plastic cricket balls. Distributors of Albion C & D cricket helmets. Contact Graham Brown for more information. **Invicta Works, Teston, Maidstone, Kent ME18 5AW. Tel: 01622-812230.**

BOWLING MACHINES

STUART & WILLIAMS (BOLA), 6 Brookfield Road, Cotham, Bristol BS6 5PQ; e-mail: info@bola.co.uk; web site: http://www.bola.co.uk. Manufacturers of bowling machines and ball throwing machines for all sports. Machines for recreational and commercial application. UK and overseas.

CLOTHING

LUKE EYRES, Freepost, Denny Industrial Estate, Pembroke Avenue, Waterbeach, Cambridge CB5 8BR. Tel: 01353-863125. 100% wool, cotton or acrylic sweaters as supplied to major county clubs, international cricket teams and schools.

McLELLAN SPORTS, 94–96 Moorside Road, Swinton, Manchester M27 0HJ. Tel: 0161-794 1169. Cricket caps, shirts, sweaters and tracksuits made to your design. Full range of embroidered leisurewear. Catalogue available.

COACHING AIDS

WIZARD CRICKET CO LTD, Units 1 & 2, Aston Works, Aston, Near Brampton, Oxford OX18 2DQ. Designers, manufacturers and retailers of cricket coaching equipment, with special emphasis on the developing cricketer. **Tel: (44) 01993-852037; fax: 01993-852038; e-mail: WizCricket@aol.com.**

GAMES

CORPORATE GAMES 96 LTD, Holcombe House, Gravel Hill, Ludlow, Shropshire SY8 1QU. The second edition of the Wisden Hicpac contains another 600 questions. Concentrating on the previous season, it naturally complements the Almanack. This collectable is therefore an esssential for all Almanack enthusiasts.

WILLOW & WICKET COMPUTER CRICKET LTD, Freepost, PO Box 2515, Eastbourne, Sussex BN21 4BR. Fax: 01323-430554. Designers and sole suppliers of the ever-popular Willow & Wicket[R] range of computer cricket games.

LIMITED EDITION PRINTS

DD DESIGNS, 40 Willowbank, Tamworth, Staffordshire B78 3LS. Tel: 01827-69950. Specialists in signed limited edition prints. Official producer of Wisden's ''Cricketers of the Year'' sets and other art portfolios.

MAIL ORDER/RETAIL CRICKET SPECIALISTS

FORDHAM SPORTS CRICKET EQUIPMENT SPECIALIST, 81 Robin Hood Way, Kingston Vale, London SW15 3PU. Largest range of branded stock in UK at discount prices. 1,000 bats in stock. **Free catalogue 0181-974 5654**.

PAVILION AND GROUND EQUIPMENT

E. A. COMBS LIMITED, Pulteney Works, London E18 1PS. Tel: 0181-530 4216. Pavilion clocks for permanent and temporary siting. Wide choice of sizes and styles to suit any ground.

COURTYARD DESIGNS, Suckley, Worcestershire WR6 5EH. Tel: 01886-884640; fax: 01886-884444. Classic wooden pavilions made to the highest standards from weatherboard and clay tile roofs. Full colour brochure and testimonials.

POWER PRECISION & FABRICATION LTD, Greenhill Works, Gunnislake, Cornwall PL18 9AS. Tel/fax: 01822-832608. Manufacture new and re-conditioned grounds rollers. New machine uses water ballast, adjustable from 1-2¼ tonnes, swivel seat enables forward-facing driving.

J. M. SMITH, Saw Mill Yard, Bobbins Mill Close, Steeton, West Yorkshire BD20 6PZ. Manufacturer of mobile wicket covers, portable and static net frames. Installer and supplier of artificial surfaces. **Tel: 01535-654520**.

STADIA SPORTS INTERNATIONAL LTD, Ely, Cambridgeshire CB6 3NP, England. Tel: 01353-668686. Manufacturers of quality sightscreens, scoreboxes and faces, net cages, synthetic wickets and wicket covers. Full colour catalogue available.

PITCHES (NON-TURF)

CARPETITION LTD, 14 Kaffir Road, Huddersfield HD2 2AN. Tel: 01484-428777; fax: 01484-423251. Manufacturers of "Tufturf" cricket wickets for match and practice in lengths as required. Sample and quotation on request.

CLUB SURFACES LIMITED, The Barn, Bisham Grange, Marlow, Buckinghamshire SL7 1RS. Tel: 01628-485969; fax: 01628-471944. ClubTurf, world-leading pitch since 1978, with 4,500 installations, including Lord's, Old Trafford. Contact Derek Underwood for information pack.

J. M. SMITH, Saw Mill Yard, Bobbins Mill Close, Steeton, West Yorkshire BD20 6PZ. Installer and supplier of artificial surfaces. Manufacturer of mobile wicket covers, portable and static net frames. **Tel: 01535-654520**.

PITCHES (TURF)

C. H. BINDER LTD, Moreton, Ongar, Essex CM5 0HY. Tel: 01277-890246; fax: 01277-890105. Sole suppliers nationwide of ONGAR LOAM for cricket squares, grass seed, fertilisers etc. Collections available.

SOCIETIES

CRICKET MEMORABILIA SOCIETY. Hon. Secretary, Tony Sheldon, 29 Highclere Road, Crumpsall, Manchester M8 4WH. Tel/fax: 0161-740 3714. For collectors worldwide – meetings, speakers, auctions, magazines, directory, merchandise, but most of all friendship.

CRICKET TOURS (OVERSEAS)

ALL-WAYS SPORTS TRAVEL, 4 The Green, Chalfont St Giles, Buckinghamshire HP8 4QF. Tel: 01494-875757; fax: 01494-874747. Specialist tour operators to the South Pacific. Worldwide cricket supporters' tours include Australia, New Zealand and South Africa.

MIKE BURTON SPORTS TRAVEL, Bastion House, Brunswick Road, Gloucester GL1 1JJ. Tel: 01452-412444; fax: 01452-892098; e-mail: sportstours@mikeburtongroup.co.uk. The number one in cricket, specialist sports tour operator. Worldwide destinations for supporter groups, clubs, schools and colleges. UK cricket tours always available.

GULLIVERS SPORTS TRAVEL, Tewkesbury, Gloucestershire GL20 7BJ. **Tel: 01684-293175; fax: 01684-297926; e-mail: gulliver@gullivers-sports.co.uk.** The best quality tours for supporters, clubs and schools – official tour operator Cricket World Cup 1999.

SPORT ABROAD, the official travel agent for the ECB, are the acknowledged experts in arranging cricket supporters' tours (Australia v England 1998-99), corporate hospitality and club and school tours, at home and overseas. **Tel/fax: 01306-744345/744380.**

SUN LIVING, 10 Milton Court, Ravenshead, Nottingham NG15 9BD. Tel: 01623-795365; fax: 01623-797421. Worldwide specialists in cricket tours for all levels and ages, plus our ever popular supporters' tours. ABTA and ATOL bonded.

SUNSPORT TOURS & TRAVEL, Hamilton House, 66 Palmerston Road, Northampton NN1 5EX. Tel: 01604-631626; fax: 01604-631628. Fully bonded tour operator. England supporter tours – Australia: November–February 1998–99. Club, school playing tours and sports business travel, worldwide.

CRICKET TOURS (UK)

CLIFF VIEW HOTEL, Ventnor, Isle of Wight PO38 1SQ. **Tel: 01983-852226.** Hotel with coastal views and beach close by. Long experience with touring sides, open-ended bar – evening bar snacks.

INDEX OF UNUSUAL OCCURRENCES

INDEX TO TEST MATCHES

THE DAY OF THE BIG NUMBERS

By TONY COZIER

For close on 20 years, the lives of the gentle, amiable people of the enchanting island nation of Sri Lanka have been dominated and depressed by a gruesome civil war. Cricket has been the one endeavour that has provided a positive focal point. In March 1996, a mere two months after a terrorist bomb blast in the heart of Colombo killed nearly 100 people, Sri Lanka's cricketers were holding the World Cup aloft on a rainy night in Lahore, and their countrymen blew their horns, set off fireworks and riotously celebrated the achievement in every town and village.

The victory in the final against Australia asserted Sri Lanka's status as world leader in the one area to which all its people could relate. The West Indies, similarly small and impoverished, had long since appreciated the importance of such success to the psyche of the populace. In Sri Lanka's case, acceptance of their credentials was constrained, as their less myopic followers might agree. They might have been champions of the world in the shortened form of the game, but they knew they had yet to prove themselves in the traditional Tests, the real standard by which all cricket is still judged.

It was this realisation, along with as placid a pitch as it is possible for any ground staff to produce, that was responsible more than anything else for Sri Lanka's accumulation of phenomenal run-scoring records at Colombo's Premadasa Stadium in the First Test against India in August 1997.

The left-handed opener Sanath Jayasuriya made 340, the fourth-highest individual score in Tests. This was not the swashbuckling Jayasuriya of one-day cricket, not the better-than-a-run-a-ball belter who had made a mockery of the shortened game's conventions. Now, over 799 minutes, he allowed himself only two sixes off the 578 balls he received. There were 36 fours as he made a point of stroking the ball across the grass.

His second-wicket partnership of 576 with Roshan Mahanama, which lasted 753 minutes and carried through two unbroken days, was the biggest for any Test wicket by over 100 runs (surpassing the 467 Sri Lanka themselves conceded to New Zealanders Martin Crowe and Andrew Jones in Wellington more than six years earlier). Mahanama, a sound but limited batsman with a modest Test record, amassed 225 and, when he was out, the brilliant Aravinda de Silva duly helped himself to yet another hundred as Sri Lanka's eventual total of 952 for six surpassed England's 903 for seven, against Australia at The Oval in the late summer of 1938, as Test cricket's Everest. Had they been so minded, they could have aimed for and achieved 1,000, for 13 overs were still available. But, by then, everyone agreed that enough was enough.

A recitation of such statistics is relevant, for they superseded all else once the flat, bare, hard pitch was turned over to the umpires. The weather remained blissfully sunny and warm throughout – not as uncomfortably hot as it can be in Colombo – and the outfield, carefully manicured, offered little hindrance even to well-timed pushes. In like conditions at the Antigua Recreation Ground in April 1994, I had watched another left-hander, Brian Lara, accumulate Test cricket's previous triple-hundred and then carry on until it was the highest.

Fifteen wickets fell over the five days then; 14 did now. As Navjot Singh Sidhu, Sachin Tendulkar and Mohammad Azharuddin all exploited the benefits, compiling effortless hundreds while India occupied most of the first two days before declaring on 537 for eight, the cricketing public of Colombo showed little interest. As elsewhere, but even more understandably, they have become more attracted to the limited-overs game. Just a few days earlier, they had packed the ground as Sri Lanka secured yet another one-day championship, the Asia Cup, at the same venue over the same neighbouring opponents.

But even when Jayasuriya and Mahanama were responding in kind, there were never more than a couple of thousand spectators scattered around the vast, concrete stadium. Jayasuriya, a man with forearms like Popeye's, is always pleasing to watch, but there must be some point to a sporting contest, beyond personal records. It was soon unmistakably evident that there was none in this, except in the cause of Sri Lankan pride.

By the time the last day arrived, Jayasuriya was 326 and Lara's 375 was tantalisingly close. He had not offered a sniff of a chance and was in such control that it seemed inevitable to the whole of Sri Lanka, and most of the cricketing world as well, that a new king of batting would be crowned next day. In anticipation of the momentous event, the gates were thrown open and radio stations urged fans to fill the stadium, to acclaim a cricketer who was already a hero, following his performances in the World Cup.

They duly obliged. They arrived, 30,000 of them, with their flags and their drums and their expectations, well before Jayasuriya received his first ball of the final day. They cheered when he stroked three off-side boundaries and closed the gap between himself and Lara to 35. Suddenly, an eerie hush enveloped the ground. First, Mahanama was lbw, playing back to Anil Kumble. Then, two balls later, Jayasuriya stabbed uncertainly at an off-break that Rajesh Chauhan somehow made bounce and turn, and Sourav Ganguly collected the simple catch two yards away at silly point. Jayasuriya had tears in his eyes as he shuffled away to sympathetic pats on the back from relieved, but understanding, Indians. There were thousands of others with tears in their eyes too.

With his twinkling footwork and flashing blade, de Silva was soon dispelling the collective disappointment and, into the afternoon, it became clear that the crowd's day would still be rewarded by a piece of history. De Silva had the honour of creating it, his boundary carrying Sri Lanka to heights no team had ever previously achieved in Tests.

Now Sri Lanka had not only the World Cup but also several records to prove that they were not merely one-day wonders. It was cause for more celebration. The government committed a plot of land valued at four million rupees ($US69,000) to each member of the team and the Sri Lankan Board of Control awarded Jayasuriya and Mahanama $US25,000 for their partnership. Heaven knows how much more they had stuffed into their pockets and mail boxes by grateful fans.

Theirs had been a remarkable feat of endurance and concentration, for neither wavered through all the hours at the wicket. Yet was it really cricket? Greg Chappell, Barry Richards and Ravi Shastri were all commentating on TV, and each berated the lack of purpose to the match. It was driving another nail into the coffin of Test cricket, they agreed. Sa'adi Thawfeeq, the respected writer for Sri Lanka's *Daily News*, took up the theme: "Unless the Premadasa Stadium pitch is relaid and made competitive to both batsmen and bowlers, Test matches should not be played there."

Chauhan and Nilesh Kulkarni, the two Indian spinners, would readily agree. This was Chauhan's come-back Test after doubts over his action had threatened

[*Anuruddha Lokuhapuarachchi*

his career. His 78 overs yielded him a solitary wicket. It was the tall left-armer Kulkarni's debut. Late on the second afternoon, he became the 12th bowler to take a wicket with his first ball on Test debut, Marvan Atapattu edging a catch to the keeper; but he sent down another 419 after that without anything to show. In contrast, Sri Lanka's cricket had plenty to show the world, which still does not accept its all-round credentials. Sri Lanka tour England this summer for the first time in seven years: they have been granted one solitary Test match.

Tony Cozier, the Barbados-based commentator and journalist, was in Colombo to commentate for WorldTel. The formal report of this and all other Tests of the 1997-98 season will be in Wisden *1999.*

TEST MATCHES, 1997-98

Full details of these Tests, and others too late for inclusion, will appear in the 1999 edition of *Wisden*.

SRI LANKA v INDIA

First Test Match

At R. Premadasa Stadium, Colombo, August 2, 3, 4, 5, 6. Drawn. Toss: India.

India

†N. R. Mongia c Jayawardene b Pushpakumara	7	A. Kumble not out	27
N. S. Sidhu c Kaluwitharana b Vaas	111	R. K. Chauhan c Vaas b Jayasuriya	23
R. Dravid c and b Jayasuriya	69	A. Kuruvilla c Atapattu b Pushpakumara	9
*S. R. Tendulkar c Jayawardene b Muralitharan	143	B 10, n-b 12	22
M. Azharuddin c and b Muralitharan	126		
S. C. Ganguly c Mahanama b Jayasuriya	0	1/36 2/183 3/230 (8 wkts dec.) 537	

1/36 2/183 3/230 (8 wkts dec.) 537
4/451 5/451 6/479
7/516 8/537

N. M. Kulkarni and B. K. V. Prasad did not bat.

Bowling: Vaas 23–5–80–1; Pushpakumara 19.3–2–97–2; Jayawardene 2–0–6–0; Muralitharan 65–9–174–2; Silva 39–3–122–0; Jayasuriya 18–3–45–3; Atapattu 1–0–3–0.

Sri Lanka

S. T. Jayasuriya c Ganguly b Chauhan	340	†R. S. Kaluwitharana not out	14
M. S. Atapattu c Mongia b Kulkarni	26	W. P. U. J. C. Vaas not out	11
R. S. Mahanama lbw b Kumble	225		
P. A. de Silva c Prasad b Ganguly	126	B 28, l-b 9, w 7, n-b 14	58
*A. Ranatunga run out	86		
D. P. M. Jayawardene c Kulkarni b Ganguly	66	1/39 2/615 3/615 (6 wkts dec.) 952	

1/39 2/615 3/615 (6 wkts dec.) 952
4/790 5/921 6/924

K. J. Silva, K. R. Pushpakumara and M. Muralitharan did not bat.

Bowling: Prasad 24–1–88–0; Kuruvilla 14–2–74–0; Chauhan 78–8–276–1; Kumble 72–7–223–1; Kulkarni 70–12–195–1; Ganguly 9–0–53–2; Tendulkar 2–1–2–0; Dravid 2–0–4–0.

Umpires: S. G. Randell (Australia) and K. T. Francis. Referee: J. R. Reid (New Zealand).

Sri Lanka scored the biggest total in Test history and the third biggest in first-class cricket. After Kulkarni dismissed Atapattu with his first ball in Test cricket, Jayasuriya and Mahanama added 576 for the second wicket in 753 minutes, the highest partnership in Test cricket and only one short of the all-wicket first-class record. They batted together throughout the third and fourth days, the first time a pair of Test batsmen had survived two complete and uninterrupted days. Jayasuriya made the fourth-highest individual Test score, batting for 799 minutes and 578 balls and hitting 36 fours and two sixes. Ranatunga became the first Sri Lankan to pass 4,000 Test runs.

Second Test: At Sinhalese Sports Club, Colombo, August 9, 10, 11, 12, 13. Drawn. Toss: India. Sri Lanka 332 (S. T. Jayasuriya 32, R. S. Mahanama 37, P. A. de Silva 146, M. Muralitharan 39; D. S. Mohanty four for 78) and 415 for seven dec. (S. T. Jayasuriya 199, R. S. Mahanama 35, P. A. de Silva 120; A. Kumble three for 106); India 375 (S. R. Tendulkar 139, S. C. Ganguly 147; K. S. C. de Silva three for 101, M. Muralitharan four for 99) and 281 for five (A. Jadeja 73, M. Azharuddin 108 not out, S. C. Ganguly 45; M. Muralitharan three for 96).

Jayasuriya took his aggregate to 571, a record for a two-Test series; when 95 in the second innings, he reached 1,000 Test runs in 1997. De Silva scored two centuries in a Test for the second time in four months and became the second Sri Lankan to pass 4,000 Test runs. The series was drawn 0-0.

ZIMBABWE v NEW ZEALAND

First Test: At Harare, September 18, 19, 20, 21, 22. Drawn. Toss: New Zealand. Zimbabwe 298 (G. W. Flower 104, G. J. Whittall 33, P. A. Strang 42; H. T. Davis three for 57, C. L. Cairns five for 50) and 311 for nine dec. (G. J. Rennie 57, G. W. Flower 151; S. B. O'Connor three for 73); New Zealand 207 (S. P. Fleming 52, A. C. Parore 42 not out; B. C. Strang three for 29) and 304 for eight (B. A. Pocock 52, C. M. Spearman 33, C. L. Cairns 71 not out, A. C. Parore 51, C. Z. Harris 41; A. G. Huckle three for 84).

Zimbabwe fielded three sets of brothers, the Flowers, the Rennies and the Strangs, a record for any Test country. Grant Flower became the first batsman to score two hundreds in a Test for Zimbabwe. Fleming took five catches in Zimbabwe's first innings and seven in all, equalling the innings and match records for Test fielders.

Second Test: At Bulawayo, September 25, 26, 27, 28, 29. Drawn. Toss: Zimbabwe. Zimbabwe 461 (G. J. Rennie 57, G. W. Flower 83, A. Flower 39, G. J. Whittall 203 not out, D. L. Houghton 32; S. B. O'Connor three for 80, C. L. Cairns three for 97, D. L. Vettori four for 165) and 227 for eight dec. (G. W. Flower 49, G. J. Whittall 45, A. D. R. Campbell 59 not out); New Zealand 403 (C. M. Spearman 47, N. J. Astle 96, C. Z. Harris 71, D. L. Vettori 90; P. A. Strang three for 110, A. G. Huckle six for 109) and 275 for eight (B. A. Pocock 62, S. P. Fleming 75; A. G. Huckle five for 146).

Whittall scored Zimbabwe's third Test double-hundred. Huckle took 11 for 255 in his second Test and became the first bowler to take ten or more wickets for Zimbabwe. Fifteen of New Zealand's 18 wickets fell to leg-spin, and the other three to run-outs. The series was drawn 0-0.

PAKISTAN v SOUTH AFRICA

First Test: At Rawalpindi, October 6, 7, 8, 9, 10. Drawn. Toss: Pakistan. Pakistan 456 (Ali Naqvi 115, Azhar Mahmood 128 not out, Waqar Younis 45, Mushtaq Ahmed 59; A. A. Donald three for 108, S. M. Pollock three for 74) and 182 for six (Inzamam-ul-Haq 56, Azhar Mahmood 50 not out); South Africa 403 (G. Kirsten 98, A. M. Bacher 50, J. H. Kallis 61, S. M. Pollock 48, D. J. Richardson 45 not out, Extras 48; Mushtaq Ahmed three for 126, Saqlain Mushtaq five for 129).

Naqvi and Mahmood both scored hundreds on Test debut, the first time two newcomers had achieved this in the same Test innings. Mahmood's century was his first in first-class cricket, and he put on 151 with Mushtaq Ahmed, equalling the Test last-wicket record.

Second Test: At Sheikhupura, October 17, 18, 19, 20, 21. Drawn. Toss: South Africa. South Africa 402 (G. Kirsten 56, A. M. Bacher 96, W. J. Cronje 50, S. M. Pollock 82, L. Klusener 58; Mushtaq Ahmed four for 122); Pakistan 53 for one (Ali Naqvi 30 not out).

Dave Richardson missed his first Test since South Africa returned to international cricket in 1991-92; he had played 38 in succession. Mark Boucher was flown in to keep wicket in his place. Rain restricted the match to 132.3 overs.

Third Test: At Faisalabad, October 24, 25, 26, 27. South Africa won by 53 runs. Toss: South Africa. South Africa 239 (G. Kirsten 100 not out, P. L. Symcox 81; Wasim Akram four for 42,

Mushtaq Ahmed three for 81) and 214 (P. L. Symcox 55, L. Klusener 38; Mushtaq Ahmed four for 58, Saqlain Mushtaq three for 36); Pakistan 308 (Inzamam-ul-Haq 96, Moin Khan 80, Aamir Sohail 38, Waqar Younis 34) and 92 (Moin Khan 32; P. L. Symcox three for eight, S. M. Pollock five for 37).

Kirsten carried his bat. In the fourth innings, Pakistan needed only 146 to win but were bowled out inside 38 overs; Pollock took four wickets in seven balls and Symcox three in 14. South Africa took the series 1-0.

AUSTRALIA v NEW ZEALAND

First Test: At Brisbane, November 7, 8, 9, 10, 11. Australia won by 186 runs. Toss: New Zealand. Australia 373 (M. A. Taylor 112, I. A. Healy 68, P. R. Reiffel 77; S. B. Doull four for 70, C. L. Cairns four for 90) and 294 for six dec. (G. S. Blewett 91, R. T. Ponting 73 not out; C. L. Cairns three for 54); New Zealand 349 (B. A. Pocock 57, S. P. Fleming 91, C. D. McMillan 54, C. L. Cairns 64; S. K. Warne four for 106) and 132 (B. A. Young 45, A. C. Parore 39 not out; G. D. McGrath five for 32, S. K. Warne three for 54).

Taylor took his 40th catch off Warne's bowling, beating the previous Test record for a fielder/ bowler pairing, 39 by Garry Sobers off Lance Gibbs.

Second Test: At Perth, November 20, 21, 22, 23. Australia won by an innings and 70 runs. Toss: New Zealand. New Zealand 217 (A. C. Parore 30, C. D. McMillan 54, C. L. Cairns 52; S. K. Warne four for 83) and 174 (A. C. Parore 63; S. H. Cook five for 39); Australia 461 (M. T. G. Elliott 42, M. E. Waugh 86, S. R. Waugh 96, I. A. Healy 85, P. R. Reiffel 54, S. K. Warne 36; S. B. O'Connor three for 109, C. L. Cairns four for 95).

Floodlights were switched on after tea on the opening day because of bad light, the first time they had been used in a Test. Mark Waugh hit a ball from Daniel Vettori 130 yards on to the roof of a five-storey stand. Cook took five in an innings on Test debut.

Third Test: At Hobart, November 27, 28, 29, 30, December 1. Drawn. Toss: Australia. Australia 400 (M. T. G. Elliott 114, G. S. Blewett 99, I. A. Healy 68; S. B. Doull three for 87, S. B. O'Connor three for 101) and 138 for two dec. (M. A. Taylor 66 not out, G. S. Blewett 56); New Zealand 251 for six dec. (B. A. Young 31, M. J. Horne 133, A. C. Parore 44; S. R. Waugh three for 20) and 223 for nine (M. J. Horne 31, N. J. Astle 40, C. D. McMillan 41, A. C. Parore 41; S. K. Warne five for 88).

Blewett was out for 99 for the second time in Tests, only minutes after Sourav Ganguly of India fell for 99 in the Nagpur Test against Sri Lanka. New Zealand's last-wicket pair survived 64 balls to draw, but Australia took the series 2-0.

PAKISTAN v WEST INDIES

First Test: At Peshawar, November 17, 18, 19, 20. Pakistan won by an innings and 19 runs. Toss: West Indies. West Indies 151 (D. Williams 31, C. E. L. Ambrose 30; Mushtaq Ahmed five for 35) and 211 (S. L. Campbell 66, B. C. Lara 37; Wasim Akram four for 65, Mushtaq Ahmed five for 71); Pakistan 381 (Saeed Anwar 65, Ijaz Ahmed, sen. 65, Inzamam-ul-Haq 92 not out, Moin Khan 58; C. A. Walsh five for 78, I. R. Bishop three for 76).

Wasim regained the Pakistan captaincy and led them to their biggest victory over West Indies – until the next game – in three and a half days.

Second Test: At Rawalpindi, November 29, 30, December 1, 2, 3. Pakistan won by an innings and 29 runs. Toss: Pakistan. West Indies 303 (S. L. Campbell 78, S. Chanderpaul 95, D. Williams 48; Waqar Younis three for 99, Azhar Mahmood four for 53) and 139 (S. L. Campbell 34, C. L. Hooper 73 not out; Wasim Akram four for 42); Pakistan 471 (Aamir Sohail 160, Inzamam-ul-Haq 177, Extras 53; C. A. Walsh five for 143, F. A. Rose three for 92).

Sohail and Inzamam added 323, a third-wicket record for any country against West Indies. Pakistan wrapped up the second innings in only 41 overs, increasing the margin of their biggest Test win over West Indies for the second match running.

Third Test: At Karachi, December 6, 7, 8, 9. Pakistan won by ten wickets. Toss: West Indies. West Indies 216 (S. L. Campbell 50, S. C. Williams 33, B. C. Lara 36; Wasim Akram four for 76, Saqlain Mushtaq four for 54) and 212 (B. C. Lara 37, C. L. Hooper 106; Wasim Akram four for 42, Saqlain Mushtaq four for 26); Pakistan 417 (Aamir Sohail 160, Ijaz Ahmed, sen. 151, Extras 31; C. A. Walsh four for 74, M. Dillon five for 111) and 15 for no wkt.

Sohail, who scored 160 for the second time in successive innings, and Ijaz opened with 298, a Pakistani first-wicket record in Tests, before all ten fell for 119. Pakistan took the series 3-0. It was only their second series win over West Indies, and their first since 1958-59; they were the first team to whitewash West Indies since 1928, when England, under Percy Chapman, beat them 3-0 in their inaugural Test series.

INDIA v SRI LANKA

First Test: At Mohali, November 19, 20, 21, 22, 23. Drawn. Toss: India. Sri Lanka 369 (S. T. Jayasuriya 53, M. S. Atapattu 108, R. S. Mahanama 42, P. A. de Silva 33, A. Ranatunga 30, H. D. P. K. Dharmasena 37 not out; J. Srinath four for 92, A. Kuruvilla four for 88) and 251 for six (M. S. Atapattu 31, P. A. de Silva 110 not out, Extras 34; J. Srinath three for 75); India 515 for nine dec. (N. R. Mongia 57, N. S. Sidhu 131, R. Dravid 34, M. Azharuddin 53, S. C. Ganguly 109, A. Kuruvilla 35 not out, Extras 43; M. Muralitharan three for 174).

After scoring four ducks in his previous two Tests in India, Atapattu scored his maiden Test hundred. De Silva scored his seventh hundred in seven Tests.

Second Test: At Nagpur, November 26, 27, 28, 29, 30. Drawn. Toss: India. India 485 (N. S. Sidhu 79, R. Dravid 92, M. Azharuddin 62, S. C. Ganguly 99, A. Kumble 78, Extras 36; K. R. Pushpakumara five for 122) v Sri Lanka.

Rain prevented any play after lunch on the third day.

Third Test: At Mumbai, December 3, 4, 5, 6, 7. Drawn. Toss: Sri Lanka. India 512 (N. S. Sidhu 35, R. Dravid 93, S. C. Ganguly 173, S. R. Tendulkar 148; K. R. Pushpakumara three for 108, H. D. P. K. Dharmasena three for 144) and 181 for nine dec. (N. S. Sidhu 43, R. Dravid 85; H. D. P. K. Dharmasena five for 57); Sri Lanka 361 (S. T. Jayasuriya 50, M. S. Atapattu 98, H. D. P. K. Dharmasena 40, P. A. de Silva 66, Extras 35; R. K. Chauhan four for 48) and 166 for seven (S. T. Jayasuriya 37, M. S. Atapattu 31, R. S. Mahanama 35; A. Kumble three for 56, R. K. Chauhan four for 59).

Ganguly and Tendulkar added 256 in the first innings, an Indian record for the fourth wicket in Tests. The series was drawn 0-0. India had drawn ten and lost two of their 12 Tests in 1997; Sri Lanka had drawn eight and lost three of their 11.

AUSTRALIA v SOUTH AFRICA

First Test: At Melbourne, December 26, 27, 28, 29, 30. Drawn. Toss: Australia. Australia 309 (S. R. Waugh 96, R. T. Ponting 105; A. A. Donald three for 74, P. L. Symcox four for 69) and

257 (M. A. Taylor 59, R. T. Ponting 32, P. R. Reiffel 79 not out; A. A. Donald six for 59, S. M. Pollock three for 56); South Africa 186 (G. Kirsten 83, B. M. McMillan 48; M. S. Kasprowicz three for 28, S. K. Warne three for 64) and 273 for seven (A. M. Bacher 39, J. H. Kallis 101, W. J. Cronje 70; S. K. Warne three for 97).

Donald and Dave Richardson became South Africa's leading wicket-taker and wicket-keeper respectively, passing Hugh Tayfield's total of 170 Test wickets and John Waite's 141 Test dismissals.

Second Test: At Sydney, January 2, 3, 4, 5. Australia won by an innings and 21 runs. Toss: South Africa. South Africa 287 (A. M. Bacher 39, W. J. Cronje 88, H. H. Gibbs 54; S. K. Warne five for 75) and 113 (J. H. Kallis 45, P. L. Symcox 38; S. K. Warne six for 34); Australia 421 (M. T. G. Elliott 32, M. E. Waugh 100, S. R. Waugh 85, R. T. Ponting 62, I. A. Healy 46 not out; A. A. Donald three for 81, S. M. Pollock three for 71).

Warne took his 300th wicket in his 63rd Test; he was the second Australian to reach the landmark, after Dennis Lillee, and the second spinner, after West Indian Lance Gibbs.

Third Test: At Adelaide, January 30, 31, February 1, 2, 3. Drawn. Toss: South Africa. South Africa 517 (A. M. Bacher 64, G. Kirsten 77, W. J. Cronje 73, H. H. Gibbs 37, B. M. McMillan 87 not out, S. M. Pollock 40, L. Klusener 38, P. L. Symcox 54; M. S. Kasprowicz three for 125) and 193 for six dec. (G. Kirsten 108 not out, A. M. Bacher 41; S. C. G. MacGill three for 22); Australia 350 (M. A. Taylor 169 not out, G. S. Blewett 31, M. E. Waugh 63; S. M. Pollock seven for 87) and 227 for seven (M. E. Waugh 115 not out, S. R. Waugh 34; L. Klusener four for 67).

Ian Healy became the first wicket-keeper to play in 100 Tests. South Africa were 305 for seven; the tail added 212. Taylor carried his bat and was on the field for nearly 24 hours before falling for six in the second innings. Australia took the series 1-0. This was Australia's ninth successive series win, going back to 1994, excluding their defeat in a single Test against India in October 1996. Dave Richardson subsequently announced his retirement from international cricket, having made 152 dismissals in 42 Tests.

SRI LANKA v ZIMBABWE

First Test: At Kandy, January 7, 8, 9, 10, 11. Sri Lanka won by eight wickets. Toss: Sri Lanka. Sri Lanka 469 for nine dec. (M. S. Atapattu 223, P. A. de Silva 75, H. P. Tillekeratne 44; P. A. Strang three for 123, A. R. Whittall three for 73) and ten for two; Zimbabwe 140 (G. J. Rennie 53, P. A. Strang 35; M. Muralitharan five for 23, K. J. Silva three for 27) and 338 (G. W. Flower 38, M. W. Goodwin 70, A. Flower 67, A. D. R. Campbell 40, P. A. Strang 33; M. Muralitharan seven for 94).

Atapattu scored the first double-hundred in Tests at Kandy to set up the follow-on. Muralitharan's 12 for 117 were the best Test figures for Sri Lanka.

Second Test: At Sinhalese Sports Club, Colombo, January 14, 15, 16, 17, 18. Sri Lanka won by five wickets. Toss: Zimbabwe. Zimbabwe 251 (G. J. Rennie 50, G. W. Flower 41, M. W. Goodwin 73, A. D. R. Campbell 44; S. D. Anurasiri three for 65) and 299 (G. W. Flower 52, M. W. Goodwin 39, A. Flower 105 not out, A. D. R. Campbell 37; M. Muralitharan three for 73); Sri Lanka 225 (M. S. Atapattu 48, A. Ranatunga 52, R. S. Kaluwitharana 51; P. A. Strang four for 77) and 326 for five (S. T. Jayasuriya 68, P. A. de Silva 143 not out, A. Ranatunga 87 not out; H. H. Streak four for 84).

Muralitharan became the first Sri Lankan to take 150 Test wickets, in his 36th Test. De Silva scored his fifth hundred in his last six Test innings at Sinhalese Sports Club. He and Ranatunga shared an unbroken stand of 189, a Sri Lankan sixth-wicket Test record, to complete a 2-0 series win. Zimbabwean coach David Houghton made an official complaint about the umpiring; he was banned from the ground for the following two limited-overs internationals for his public remarks on the subject.

THE WISDEN WORLD CHAMPIONSHIP

Australia dominated the Wisden World Championship in 1997. And, in February 1998, after their victory in the home series against South Africa, they took an unprecedented lead over all their rivals.

When the Championship began in 1996, South Africa were the leaders. But their failure to win this year's Adelaide Test meant that Australia went five points clear, making it improbable that they could be caught before 1999, if then. After losing to India in Delhi in October 1996, they won five successive series: against West Indies, New Zealand and South Africa at home, and away in South Africa and England.

The Wisden Championship – unofficial but gaining widespread acceptance – is intended as a prototype of an official Test match Championship, which *Wisden* has been advocating since 1995. The principle was accepted by the International Cricket Council last year. However, the form it would take remained a matter of dispute, perhaps irreconcilable. Some people within ICC were fighting hard for a World Cup-style Championship over a short period of time; others regarded that as absurd.

In the meantime, the Wisden Championship goes on. It is an effective measure of Test nations' standings and, unlike any of the dozens of other schemes submitted to the Almanack since this debate began, very simple.

It takes account of the most recent series, both home and away, between each pair of countries. Teams receive two points for winning a series, and one for drawing. A one-off Test counts as a series. Not every country has played every other one, and fixtures not renewed since 1990 are excluded. The number of points minus the series played determines the standings.

THE WISDEN CHAMPIONSHIP TABLE

(as at February 25, 1998)

		Series played	Points	Difference
1.	Australia	14	23	+9
2.	South Africa	13	17	+4
	West Indies	13	17	+4
4.	India	14	15	+1
	Pakistan	13	14	+1
6.	Sri Lanka	15	13	−2
7.	England	14	11	−3
8.	Zimbabwe	10	5	−5
9.	New Zealand	16	7	−9

Previous leaders: October 13–December 12, 1996 South Africa; December 12–January 28, 1997 Australia, South Africa and West Indies (joint); Australia have led since January 28, 1997.

The standings are updated regularly in *Wisden Cricket Monthly* and on Wisden's web site, www.wisden.com. A fuller account of the Championship can be found in *Wisden* 1997, pages 18-19.

FIXTURES, 1998

* Indicates Sunday play.   † Not first-class.

All County Championship matches are of four days' duration. Other first-class matches are of three days' duration unless stated.

Tuesday, April 14

Cambridge	Cambridge U. v Northants
Oxford	Oxford U. v Sussex

Friday, April 17

Derby*	Derbys v Notts
Bristol	Glos v Glam
Canterbury	Kent v Middx
The Oval	Surrey v Northants
Hove*	Sussex v Lancs
Birmingham	Warwicks v Durham
Worcester	Worcs v Essex
Leeds	Yorks v Somerset
Cambridge*	Cambridge U. v Leics
Oxford	Oxford U. v Hants

Thursday, April 23

Chester-le-Street	Durham v Glos
Chelmsford	Essex v Sussex
Cardiff	Glam v Kent
Southampton	Hants v Northants
Manchester	Lancs v Middx
Leicester	Leics v Worcs
Taunton	Somerset v Notts
The Oval	Surrey v Warwicks
Leeds	Yorks v Derbys

Tuesday, April 28

†Benson and Hedges Cup (1 day)

Derby	Derbys v Durham
Southampton	Hants v Surrey
Taunton	Somerset v Kent
Leeds	Yorks v Worcs
Oxford	†British Univs v Northants (1 day)

Wednesday, April 29

†Benson and Hedges Cup (1 day)

Cardiff	Glam v Essex
Manchester	Lancs v Warwicks
Lord's	Middx v Sussex
Luton	Minor Counties v Northants

Thursday, April 30

†Benson and Hedges Cup (1 day)

Taunton	Somerset v British Univs
The Oval	Surrey v Glos

Friday, May 1

†Benson and Hedges Cup (1 day)

Oxford	British Univs v Hants
Dublin (Castle Avenue)	Ireland v Glam
Leicester	Leics v Lancs
Nottingham	Notts v Minor Counties
Birmingham	Warwicks v Northants
Worcester	Worcs v Derbys

Saturday, May 2

†Benson and Hedges Cup (1 day)

Canterbury	Kent v Glos
Nottingham	Notts v Leics
Linlithgow	Scotland v Yorks
Hove	Sussex v Essex

Monday, May 4

†Benson and Hedges Cup (1 day)

Derby	Derbys v Yorks
Chelmsford	Essex v Ireland
Bristol	Glos v Somerset
Leicester	Leics v Warwicks
Northampton	Northants v Notts
The Oval	Surrey v British Univs
Worcester	Worcs v Scotland

Tuesday, May 5

†Benson and Hedges Cup (1 day)

Lord's	Middx v Ireland
Lakenham	Minor Counties v Lancs
Taunton	Somerset v Hants
Hove	Sussex v Glam

Wednesday, May 6

†Benson and Hedges Cup (1 day)

Chester-le-Street	Durham v Scotland
Bristol	Glos v British Univs

Canterbury   Kent v Surrey
Lakenham   Minor Counties v
                      Warwicks
Northampton   Northants v Leics
Lord's   †MCC v MCC Young
                      Cricketers (1 day)

Thursday, May 7

†Benson and Hedges Cup (1 day)

Chester-le-Street   Durham v Worcs
Chelmsford   Essex v Middx
Southampton   Hants v Kent
Nottingham   Notts v Lancs

Friday, May 8

†Benson and Hedges Cup (1 day)

Leicester   Leics v Minor Counties
Forfar   Scotland v Derbys
The Oval   Surrey v Somerset

Saturday, May 9

†Benson and Hedges Cup (1 day)

Oxford   British Univs v Kent
Cardiff   Glam v Middx
Bristol   Glos v Hants
Eglinton   Ireland v Sussex
Manchester   Lancs v Northants
Birmingham   Warwicks v Notts
Leeds   Yorks v Durham

Monday, May 11

Oxford   Oxford U. v Worcs

Wednesday, May 13

Derby   Derbys v Warwicks
Chester-le-Street   Durham v Essex
Bristol   Glos v Leics
Southampton   Hants v Surrey
Canterbury   Kent v Lancs
Lord's   Middx v Somerset
Northampton   Northants v Yorks
Nottingham   Notts v Sussex
Cambridge   Cambridge U. v Glam

Thursday, May 14

Worcester   Worcs v South Africans

Saturday, May 16

Oxford   †Oxford U. v
                      Cambridge U. (1 day)

Sunday, May 17

Arundel   †Duke of Norfolk's XI v
                      South Africans (1 day)

Monday, May 18

Cambridge   Cambridge U. v Durham
Oxford   Oxford U. v Warwicks

Tuesday, May 19

Canterbury   †Kent v South Africans
                      (1 day)
Lord's   †MCC v Scotland
                      (2 days)

Thursday, May 21

The Oval   †ENGLAND v SOUTH
                      AFRICA (1st 1-day
                      Texaco Trophy)
Chelmsford*   Essex v Lancs
Gloucester*   Glos v Yorks
Canterbury*   Kent v Durham
Leicester*   Leics v Hants
Uxbridge*   Middx v Worcs
Northampton*   Northants v Glam
Taunton*   Somerset v Surrey
Horsham*   Sussex v Derbys
Birmingham*   Warwicks v Notts

Saturday, May 23

Manchester   †ENGLAND v SOUTH
                      AFRICA (2nd 1-day
                      Texaco Trophy)

Sunday, May 24

Leeds   †ENGLAND v SOUTH
                      AFRICA (3rd 1-day
                      Texaco Trophy)

Wednesday, May 27

†Benson and Hedges Cup – Quarter-finals
(1 day)

Stone   †Minor Counties v
                      South Africans (1 day)

Friday, May 29

Chesterfield*   Derbys v Leics
Lord's*   Middx v Glam
Nottingham*   Notts v Durham
The Oval*   Surrey v Kent
Worcester*   Worcs v Sussex
Bristol*   Glos v South Africans
                      (4 days)
Oxford   Oxford U. v Yorks

Wednesday, June 3

Chesterfield	Derbys v Glos
Ilford	Essex v Notts
Southampton	Hants v Glam
Tunbridge Wells	Kent v Sussex
Lord's	Middx v Durham
Northampton	Northants v Lancs
Taunton	Somerset v Warwicks
The Oval	Surrey v Worcs
Leeds	Yorks v Leics

Thursday, June 4

Birmingham*	ENGLAND v SOUTH AFRICA (1st Cornhill Test, 5 days)

Tuesday, June 9

†Benson and Hedges Cup – Semi-finals
(1 day)

Wednesday, June 10

Leicester or Nottingham	†Leics or Notts v South Africans (1 day)

Or Warwicks if both Leics and Notts in B&H Cup semi-finals.

Cambridge	Cambridge U. v Derbys
Oxford	Oxford U. v Notts

Subject to involvement in B&H Cup semi-finals.

Thursday, June 11

Chester-le-Street	Durham v Northants
Chelmsford	Essex v Surrey
Cardiff	Glam v Worcs
Bristol	Glos v Warwicks
Manchester	Lancs v Somerset
Leicester	Leics v Kent
Leeds	Yorks v Hants

Friday, June 12

Arundel*	Sussex v South Africans

Saturday, June 13

Oxford	Oxford U. v Middx

Wednesday, June 17

Chester-le-Street	Durham v Yorks
Cardiff	Glam v Leics
Basingstoke	Hants v Derbys
Canterbury	Kent v Notts
Northampton	Northants v Middx
Bath	Somerset v Essex
Hove	Sussex v Warwicks
Worcester	Worcs v Glos

Thursday, June 18

Lord's*	ENGLAND v SOUTH AFRICA (2nd Cornhill Test, 5 days)
Manchester*	Lancs v Surrey

Wednesday, June 24

†NatWest Trophy – First Round
(1 day)

Chester (Boughton Hall CC)	Cheshire v Essex
Derby	Derbys v Cumberland
Exmouth	Devon v Yorks
Bournemouth	Dorset v Hants
Cardiff	Glam v Beds
Bristol	Glos v Northants
Canterbury	Kent v Cambs
Manchester	Lancs v Sussex
Leicester	Leics v Staffs
Lord's	Middx v Herefordshire
Lakenham	Norfolk v Durham
Edinburgh	Scotland v Worcs
Taunton	Somerset v Holland
The Oval	Surrey v Bucks
Colwyn Bay	Wales v Notts
Birmingham	Warwicks v Ireland
Cambridge	British Univs v South Africans

Friday, June 26

Leicester*	Leics v Sussex
Southgate*	Middx v Essex
Nottingham*	Notts v Glam
Taunton*	Somerset v Hants
Birmingham*	Warwicks v Lancs
Lord's	†Eton v Harrow (1 day)

Saturday, June 27

Canterbury*	Kent v Oxford U.
Leeds*	Yorks v Cambridge U.

Sunday, June 28

Northampton	†Northants v South Africans (1 day)

Tuesday, June 30

Glasgow	†Triple Crown Tournament (3 days)

Wednesday, July 1

Derby	Derbys v Essex
Darlington	Durham v Leics
Swansea	Glam v Surrey
Southampton	Hants v Glos

Maidstone	Kent v Yorks
Nottingham	Notts v Middx
Hove	Sussex v Somerset
Worcester	Worcs v Northants
Lord's	Oxford U. v Cambridge U.

Thursday, July 2

Manchester*	ENGLAND v SOUTH AFRICA (3rd Cornhill Test, 5 days)

Wednesday, July 8

†NatWest Trophy – Second Round (1 day)

Bournemouth or Southampton	Dorset or Hants v Cheshire or Essex
Cardiff or Luton	Glam or Beds v Leics or Staffs
Bristol or Northampton	Glos or Northants v Surrey or Bucks
Manchester or Hove	Lancs or Sussex v Devon or Yorks
Southgate or Brockhampton	Middx or Herefordshire v Norfolk or Durham
Edinburgh or Worcester	Scotland or Worcs v Derbys or Cumberland
Swansea or Nottingham	Wales or Notts v Somerset or Holland
Birmingham or Belfast	Warwicks or Ireland v Kent or Cambs
Amsterdam	†Holland v South Africans (1 day)

Unless Holland in NWT 2nd round.

Friday, July 10

Downpatrick	†Ireland v South Africans (1 day)
Scarborough	†Tim Rice's International XI v The Yorkshiremen (1 day)

Saturday, July 11

Lord's	†BENSON AND HEDGES CUP FINAL (1 day)
Scarborough	†Yorks v Durham (1 day)

Sunday, July 12

Dublin (Castle Avenue)	†Ireland v South Africans (1 day)

Southampton or Taunton	†Hants or Somerset v Sri Lankans (1 day)

Glos to play Sri Lankans if both Hants and Somerset in B&H Cup final.

Monday, July 13

Scarborough	†Tim Rice's XI v Yorks (1 day)

Tuesday, July 14

Cheltenham	Glos v Sussex
Lytham	Lancs v Worcs
Leicester	Leics v Northants
Chester-le-Street	Durham v South Africans
Taunton	Somerset v Sri Lankans

Wednesday, July 15

Southend	Essex v Kent
Guildford	Surrey v Middx
Birmingham	Warwicks v Hants
Scarborough	Yorks v Notts

Saturday, July 18

Derby*	Derbys v South Africans
Cardiff*	Glam v South Africans
Lord's	†MCC v Rest of the World (Diana, Princess of Wales Memorial Match, 1 day)

Wednesday, July 22

Colwyn Bay	Glam v Lancs
Cheltenham	Glos v Surrey
Portsmouth	Hants v Notts
Lord's	Middx v Yorks
Northampton	Northants v Derbys
Taunton	Somerset v Durham

Thursday, July 23

Nottingham*	ENGLAND v SOUTH AFRICA (4th Cornhill Test, 5 days)
Birmingham*	Warwicks v Essex

Friday, July 24

Leicester*	Leics v Sri Lankans (4 days)

Tuesday, July 28

†NatWest Trophy – Quarter-finals (1 day)

Wednesday, July 29

Chelmsford or Worcester	†Essex or Worcs v South Africans (1 day)

Or Derbys if both Essex and Worcs in NWT quarter-finals.

Thursday, July 30

Derby	Derbys v Kent
Southampton	Hants v Durham
Manchester	Lancs v Leics
Nottingham	Notts v Northants
The Oval*	Surrey v Sussex
Birmingham*	Warwicks v Glam
Worcester	Worcs v Yorks
Harrogate	†England Under-19 v Pakistan Under-19 (1st 1-day)

Friday, July 31

Chelmsford*	Essex v South Africans
Lord's*	Middx v Sri Lankans (4 days)

Saturday, August 1

Chester-le-Street	†England Under-19 v Pakistan Under-19 (2nd 1-day)

Monday, August 3

Chester-le-Street	†England Under-19 v Pakistan Under-19 (3rd 1-day)

Wednesday, August 5

Chelmsford	Essex v Glam
Canterbury	Kent v Hants
Manchester	Lancs v Glos
Leicester	Leics v Somerset
Lord's	Middx v Warwicks
Eastbourne	Sussex v Durham
Kidderminster	Worcs v Notts
Lakenham	†ECB XI v Sri Lankans (1 day)

Thursday, August 6

Leeds*	ENGLAND v SOUTH AFRICA (5th Cornhill Test, 5 days)

The Oval*	Surrey v Derbys

Friday, August 7

Northampton	†Northants v Sri Lankans (1 day)

Sunday, August 9

Milton Keynes (Campbell Park)	†Northants v Sri Lankans (1 day)

Tuesday, August 11

†NatWest Trophy – 1st Semi-final (1 day)

Canterbury or Manchester	†Kent or Lancs v Sri Lankans (1 day)

Or Warwicks if both Kent and Lancs in NWT semi-finals.

Wednesday, August 12

†NatWest Trophy – 2nd Semi-final (1 day)

Manchester or Leeds	†First-Class Counties Select XI v South Africans (1 day)

Friday, August 14

Nottingham	†SOUTH AFRICA v SRI LANKA (1-day Triangular Tournament)
Derby*	Derbys v Worcs
Chester-le-Street*	Durham v Glam
Bristol*	Glos v Kent
Portsmouth*	Hants v Essex
Taunton*	Somerset v Northants
Hove*	Sussex v Middx
Leeds*	Yorks v Lancs
Worcester	†England Under-19 v Pakistan Under-19 (1st Unofficial Test, 4 days)

Sunday, August 16

Lord's	†ENGLAND v SRI LANKA (1-day Triangular Tournament)

Monday, August 17

†AON Trophy Semi-finals (1 day)

Tuesday, August 18

| Birmingham | †ENGLAND v SOUTH AFRICA (1-day Triangular Tournament) |

†AON Trophy Semi-finals (1 day)
(if not played on August 17)

Wednesday, August 19

Chester-le-Street	Durham v Lancs
Colchester	Essex v Glos
Canterbury	Kent v Worcs
Leicester	Leics v Middx
Northampton	Northants v Warwicks
Nottingham	Notts v Surrey
Taunton	Somerset v Derbys
Hove	Sussex v Sri Lankans

If Sri Lanka not in Triangular final.

Thursday, August 20

| Lord's | †TRIANGULAR TOURNAMENT FINAL (1 day) |
| Cardiff* | Glam v Yorks |

Saturday, August 22

| Southampton* | Hants v Sri Lankans |

Tuesday, August 25

| Taunton | England Under-19 v Pakistan Under-19 (2nd Unofficial Test, 4 days) |

Wednesday, August 26

Derby	Derbys v Durham
Northampton	Northants v Kent
Worksop	Notts v Leics
Hove	Sussex v Hants
Worcester	Worcs v Warwicks
Scarborough	Yorks v Essex
Lord's	†ECB 38-County Final (1 day)

Thursday, August 27

| The Oval* | ENGLAND v SRI LANKA (Cornhill Test, 5 days) |
| Bristol* | Glos v Somerset |

Friday, August 28

| Lord's | †National Club Championship Final (1 day) |

Sunday, August 30

| Hove* | Sussex v Glam |
| Lord's | †National Village Championship Final (1 day) |

Monday, August 31

| Southampton | Hants v Middx |
| Chelmsford | England Under-19 v Pakistan Under-19 (3rd Unofficial Test, 4 days) |

Tuesday, September 1

Bristol	Glos v Northants
Manchester	Lancs v Derbys
Taunton	Somerset v Worcs
Birmingham	Warwicks v Leics
Leeds	Yorks v Surrey

Saturday, September 5

| Lord's | †NATWEST TROPHY FINAL (1 day) |

Monday, September 7

†AON Trophy Final (1 day)

Wednesday, September 9

Chester-le-Street	Durham v Surrey
Cardiff	Glam v Derbys
Canterbury	Kent v Somerset
Leicester	Leics v Essex
Lord's	Middx v Glos
Northampton	Northants v Sussex
Worcester	Worcs v Hants
Leeds	Yorks v Warwicks

Friday, September 11		Cardiff*	Glam v Somerset
		Manchester*	Lancs v Hants
Nottingham*	Notts v Lancs	Nottingham*	Notts v Glos
		The Oval*	Surrey v Leics
Thursday, September 17		Hove*	Sussex v Yorks
		Birmingham*	Warwicks v Kent
Derby*	Derbys v Middx	Worcester*	Worcs v Durham
Chelmsford*	Essex v Northants		

Australia A are also scheduled to tour in 1998, but their fixtures remained unconfirmed when Wisden *went to press.*

†AXA LEAGUE, 1998

All matches are of one day's duration.

APRIL

19 – Glos v Glam (Bristol); Kent v Middx (Canterbury); Surrey v Northants (The Oval); Warwicks v Durham (Birmingham); Worcs v Essex (Worcester); Yorks v Somerset (Leeds).

21 – **(Tuesday)** Derbys v Notts (Derby); Sussex v Lancs (Hove) (day/night).

26 – Durham v Glos (Chester-le-Street); Essex v Sussex (Chelmsford); Glam v Kent (Cardiff); Hants v Northants (Southampton); Lancs v Middx (Manchester); Leics v Worcs (Leicester); Somerset v Notts (Taunton); Surrey v Warwicks (The Oval); Yorks v Derbys (Leeds).

MAY

3 – Middx v Glam (Lord's); Sussex v Hants (Arundel); Worcs v Durham (Worcester).

10 – Glam v Somerset (Cardiff); Glos v Kent (Bristol); Hants v Essex (Southampton); Lancs v Derbys (Manchester); Notts v Durham (Nottingham); Warwicks v Leics (Birmingham); Yorks v Surrey (Leeds).

17 – Derbys v Warwicks (Derby); Durham v Essex (Chester-le-Street); Glos v Leics (Bristol); Hants v Surrey (Southampton); Kent v Lancs (Canterbury); Middx v Somerset (Lord's); Northants v Yorks (Northampton); Notts v Sussex (Nottingham).

19 – **(Tuesday)** Derbys v Leics (Derby); Glam v Yorks (Cardiff); Middx v Essex (Uxbridge); Notts v Glos (Nottingham); Somerset v Northants (Taunton); Worcs v Sussex (Worcester).

25 – **(Monday)** Essex v Lancs (Chelmsford); Glos v Yorks (Gloucester); Kent v Durham (Canterbury); Leics v Hants (Leicester); Middx v Worcs (Uxbridge); Northants v Glam (Northampton); Somerset v Surrey (Taunton); Sussex v Derbys (Horsham); Warwicks v Notts (Birmingham).

31 – Essex v Northants (Ilford); Somerset v Warwicks (Taunton).

JUNE

7 – Derbys v Glos (Chesterfield); Hants v Glam (Southampton); Kent v Sussex (Tunbridge Wells); Middx v Durham (Lord's); Northants v Lancs (Northampton); Yorks v Leics (Leeds).

14 – Derbys v Middx (Derby); Durham v Northants (Chester-le-Street); Essex v Surrey (Chelmsford); Glam v Worcs (Cardiff); Glos v Warwicks (Bristol); Lancs v Somerset (Manchester); Leics v Kent (Leicester); Yorks v Hants (Leeds).

17 – **(Wednesday)** Lancs v Surrey (Manchester) (day/night).

21 – Durham v Yorks (Chester-le-Street); Glam v Leics (Pontypridd); Hants v Derbys (Basingstoke); Kent v Notts (Canterbury); Northants v Middx (Northampton); Somerset v Essex (Bath); Sussex v Warwicks (Hove); Worcs v Glos (Worcester).

28 – Surrey v Worcs (The Oval).

JULY

1 – **(Wednesday)** Warwicks v Lancs (Birmingham) (day/night).

5 – Derbys v Essex (Derby); Durham v Leics (Darlington); Glam v Surrey (Swansea); Hants v Glos (Southampton); Kent v Yorks (Maidstone); Notts v Middx (Nottingham); Sussex v Somerset (Hove); Worcs v Northants (Worcester).

12 – Derbys v Worcs (Derby); Notts v Glam (Nottingham); Surrey v Leics (The Oval); Warwicks v Kent (Birmingham).

Note: Matches involving B&H Cup finalists to be played on July 13 or 14.

14 – **(Tuesday)** Warwicks v Hants (Birmingham) (day/night).

18 – **(Saturday)** Glos v Sussex (Cheltenham); Leics v Northants (Leicester).

19 – Essex v Kent (Southend); Glos v Northants (Cheltenham); Somerset v Hants (Taunton); Surrey v Middx (Guildford); Yorks v Notts (Scarborough).

20 – **(Monday)** Lancs v Worcs (Manchester) (day/night); Sussex v Middx (Hove) (day/night).

21 – **(Tuesday)** Warwicks v Essex (Birmingham) (day/night).

26 – Glam v Lancs (Colwyn Bay); Glos v Surrey (Cheltenham); Hants v Notts (Portsmouth); Middx v Yorks (Lord's); Northants v Derbys (Northampton); Somerset v Durham (Taunton).

AUGUST

2 – Derbys v Kent (Derby); Hants v Durham (Southampton); Lancs v Leics (Manchester); Notts v Northants (Nottingham); Worcs v Yorks (Worcester).

3 – **(Monday)** Surrey v Sussex (The Oval) (day/night); Warwicks v Glam (Birmingham) (day/night).

5 – **(Wednesday)** Surrey v Derbys (The Oval) (day/night).

9 – Essex v Glam (Chelmsford); Kent v Hants (Canterbury); Lancs v Glos (Manchester); Leics v Somerset (Leicester); Middx v Warwicks (Lord's); Sussex v Durham (Eastbourne); Worcs v Notts (Worcester).

23 – Durham v Lancs (Chester-le-Street); Essex v Glos (Colchester); Kent v Worcs (Canterbury); Leics v Sussex (Leicester); Northants v Warwicks (Northampton); Notts v Surrey (Nottingham); Somerset v Derbys (Taunton).

24 – **(Monday)** Yorks v Lancs (Leeds) (day/night).

25 – **(Tuesday)** Glos v Somerset (Bristol) (day/night).

30 – Derbys v Durham (Derby); Hants v Middx (Southampton); Northants v Kent (Northampton); Notts v Leics (Nottingham); Warwicks v Worcs (Birmingham); Yorks v Essex (Scarborough).

SEPTEMBER

3 – **(Thursday)** Sussex v Glam (Hove) (day/night).

6 – Durham v Glam (Chester-le-Street); Essex v Notts (Chelmsford); Lancs v Hants (Manchester); Leics v Middx (Leicester); Somerset v Worcs (Taunton); Surrey v Kent (The Oval); Sussex v Yorks (Hove).

Note: Matches involving NWT finalists to be played on September 8.

9 – **(Wednesday)** Notts v Lancs (Nottingham) (day/night).

13 – Durham v Surrey (Chester-le-Street); Glam v Derbys (Cardiff); Kent v Somerset (Canterbury); Leics v Essex (Leicester); Middx v Glos (Lord's); Northants v Sussex (Northampton); Worcs v Hants (Worcester); Yorks v Warwicks (Leeds).

†MINOR COUNTIES CHAMPIONSHIP, 1998

Unless otherwise indicated, all matches are of two days' duration.

MAY

24 – Berks v Herefordshire (Hurst CC); Devon v Dorset (Bovey Tracey); Lincs v Beds (Sleaford); Wilts v Wales (Swindon CC).

26 – Bucks v Suffolk (Marlow).

31 – *Berks v Wales (Reading CC); *Cumberland v Herts (Askam); *Herefordshire v Dorset (Kington); *Lincs v Staffs (Bourne); *Northumberland v Bucks (Jesmond); *Salop v Oxon (St Georges, Telford).

JUNE

2 – *Cheshire v Oxon (Toft); Cumberland v Bucks (Netherfield); Northumberland v Herts (Benwell Hill).

8 – Cumberland v Norfolk (Barrow).

10 – Cambs v Suffolk (Saffron Walden); *Staffs v Norfolk (Stone).

14 – *Beds v Cumberland (Bedford CC); *Dorset v Salop (Bournemouth); *Lincs v Northumberland (Grantham); Oxon v Wales (Banbury); *Wilts v Berks (Corsham).

15 – Cornwall v Cheshire (Werrington).

16 – *Cambs v Northumberland (Wisbech); Staffs v Bucks (Longton).

17 – Devon v Cheshire (Mount Wise, Plymouth).

28 – *Herefordshire v Devon (Colwall).

JULY

1 – Cambs v Staffs (March).

5 – Beds v Northumberland (Henlow); Berks v Cornwall (Reading CC); *Bucks v Norfolk (Slough); Devon v Wilts (Torquay); *Herts v Suffolk (Shenley Park); Lincs v Cumberland (Lincoln Lindum); Wales v Salop (Pontypridd).

7 – Cambs v Cumberland (Fenner's, Cambridge); Oxon v Cornwall (Christ Church, Oxford).

12 – Cheshire v Berks (New Brighton); *Cornwall v Dorset (St Austell); Herts v Bucks (Long Marston); Lincs v Cambs (Cleethorpes); *Suffolk v Beds (Ipswich School); Wilts v Oxon (South Wilts CC).

13 – Northumberland v Staffs (Jesmond).

14 – Salop v Berks (Bridgnorth).

15 – Cumberland v Staffs (Millom).

22 – *Cambs v Bucks (Fenner's, Cambridge); Norfolk v Herts (Lakenham).

26 – Bucks v Beds (Aylesbury); *Norfolk v Lincs (Lakenham); Oxon v Devon (Thame); Salop v Herefordshire (Oswestry); Suffolk v Northumberland (Copdock CC); *Wales v Cornwall (Swansea); *Wilts v Cheshire (Marlborough).

27 – *Staffs v Herts (Cannock).

28 – *Berks v Devon (Finchampstead); Dorset v Cheshire (Weymouth); Herefordshire v Cornwall (Brockhampton); Norfolk v Northumberland (Lakenham).

AUGUST

2 – Beds v Herts (Southill Park); *Cheshire v Wales (Boughton Hall, Chester); *Devon v Salop (Exmouth); Dorset v Oxon (Bournemouth); Herefordshire v Wilts (Brockhampton).

3 – Norfolk v Cambs (Lakenham).

4 – Cornwall v Salop (Falmouth).

5 – Suffolk v Lincs (Ransomes, Ipswich).

9 – Beds v Norfolk (Dunstable CC); *Cornwall v Wilts (Camborne); Herts v Lincs (Hitchin); *Oxon v Herefordshire (Aston Rowant); Wales v Dorset (Pontarddulais).

11 – *Cumberland v Suffolk (Carlisle).

13 – Staffs v Suffolk (Brewood).

16 – *Beds v Cambs (Luton); Cheshire v Herefordshire (Bowdon); Dorset v Berks (Bournemouth); Salop v Wilts (Wellington); Wales v Devon (Colwyn Bay).

23 – Berks v Oxon (Falkland CC); Bucks v Lincs (Beaconsfield); Cheshire v Salop (Alderley Edge); Cornwall v Devon (Truro); Herefordshire v Wales (Dales CC, Leominster); Herts v Cambs (Hertford); Northumberland v Cumberland (Jesmond); Staffs v Beds (Leek); Suffolk v Norfolk (Mildenhall); Wilts v Dorset (Westbury).

SEPTEMBER

6 – Final.

* Played under "grade" rules, in which a single-innings match is contested over two days, with provision for second innings if time and conditions permit.

†SECOND ELEVEN CHAMPIONSHIP, 1998

Unless otherwise stated, all matches are of three days' duration.

APRIL

22 – Kent v Yorks (Canterbury); Notts v Derbys (Nottingham).

28 – Leics v Glos (Hinckley Town CC); Warwicks v Hants (Knowle & Dorridge; 4 days).

29 – Essex v Kent (Saffron Walden); Surrey v Notts (Oxted CC); Sussex v Derbys (Eastbourne).

MAY

5 – Derbys v Yorks (Chesterfield; 4 days); Worcs v Northants (Worcester; 4 days).

6 – Glos v Durham (Bristol University); Lancs v Surrey (Manchester); Warwicks v Kent (Stratford-upon-Avon CC).

13 – Essex v Glos (Chelmsford); Somerset v Northants (Taunton); Surrey v Leics (The Oval); Yorks v Notts (Park Avenue, Bradford).

19 – Glos v Lancs (Bristol).

20 – Derbys v Essex (Abbotsholme School); Hants v Glam (Southampton); Notts v Warwicks (Nottingham); Sussex v Worcs (Hove); Yorks v Leics (Bingley).

26 – Worcs v Glos (Kidderminster; 4 days); Yorks v Glam (Marske).

27 – Derbys v Warwicks (Abbotsholme School); Kent v Surrey (Maidstone); Northants v Hants (Campbell Park, Milton Keynes).

JUNE

2 – Sussex v Kent (Hove; 4 days).

3 – Glam v Durham (Pontypridd); Glos v Middx (Bristol); Notts v Hants (Nottingham); Worcs v Somerset (Worcester).

9 – Derbys v Glos (Chesterfield; 4 days); Middx v Essex (Southgate CC; 4 days).

10 – Lancs v Somerset (Northern CC); Northants v Durham (Campbell Park, Milton Keynes); Sussex v Yorks (Horsham); Worcs v Glam (Halesowen).

16 – Notts v Leics (Nottingham; 4 days); Yorks v Durham (Middlesbrough; 4 days).

17 – Glam v Essex (Panteg); Hants v Derbys (Finchampstead); Middx v Worcs (Lensbury); Somerset v Kent (Taunton); Surrey v Northants (The Oval); Warwicks v Sussex (Coventry and North Warwicks).

23 – Durham v Lancs (Hartlepool; 4 days); Hants v Glos (Southampton); Northants v Middx (Dunstable Town).

24 – Essex v Somerset (Chelmsford); Glam v Derbys (Pontarddulais); Kent v Leics (Ashford); Notts v Surrey (Worksop).

29 – Glos v Somerset (Bristol; 4 days).

30 – Northants v Warwicks (Northampton; 4 days); Yorks v Worcs (Harrogate; 4 days).

JULY

1 – Essex v Hants (Wickford); Glam v Leics (Abergavenny); Middx v Kent (Harrow); Notts v Durham (Collingham CC); Surrey v Sussex (The Oval).

7 – Warwicks v Worcs (Studley CC; 4 days).

8 – Durham v Sussex (Ropery Lane, Chester-le-Street); Essex v Northants (Chelmsford); Kent v Lancs (Canterbury); Middx v Derbys (Harrow); Somerset v Notts (Taunton); Surrey v Glam (The Oval); Yorks v Hants (Todmorden).

14 – Surrey v Middx (The Oval; 4 days).

15 – Kent v Glam (Folkestone); Lancs v Warwicks (Fleetwood); Northants v Leics (Northampton); Notts v Glos (Nottingham High School); Sussex v Somerset (Middleton-on-Sea).

21 – Essex v Surrey (Coggeshall; 4 days); Lancs v Yorks (Blackpool; 4 days).

22 – Durham v Derbys (Chester-le-Street); Glam v Warwicks (Usk); Kent v Northants (Eltham); Leics v Worcs (Hinckley Town CC); Sussex v Middx (Hastings).

29 – Derbys v Lancs (Cheadle CC); Durham v Worcs (Stockton CC); Hants v Surrey (Bournemouth Sports Club); Leics v Essex (Oakham School); Middx v Notts (Vine Lane, Uxbridge); Northants v Glam (Wellingborough School); Somerset v Yorks (Clevedon).

AUGUST

4 – Hants v Sussex (Southampton; 4 days).

5 – Glam v Middx (Cardiff); Lancs v Worcs (Middleton); Notts v Northants (Worksop College); Somerset v Surrey (Taunton); Warwicks v Essex (Moseley CC).

10 – Kent v Hants (Eltham; 4 days); Leics v Sussex (Oakham School).

11 – Somerset v Glam (North Perrott; 4 days).

12 – Durham v Essex (Sunderland); Glos v Warwicks (Hatherley & Reddings CC, Cheltenham); Middx v Yorks (Lensbury); Worcs v Notts (Barnt Green CC).

19 – Derbys v Somerset (Derby); Durham v Kent (South Shields); Glos v Sussex (Bristol); Notts v Lancs (Cleethorpes); Warwicks v Surrey (Walmley CC); Worcs v Essex (Ombersley); Yorks v Northants (York).

25 – Glam v Glos (Pontypridd; 4 days); Leics v Derbys (Leicester; 4 days).

26 – Essex v Yorks (Chelmsford); Kent v Notts (Tunbridge Wells); Lancs v Middx (Manchester); Somerset v Hants (Weston-super-Mare).

SEPTEMBER

1 – Derbys v Notts (Chesterfield; 4 days); Northants v Glos (Northampton).

2 – Essex v Lancs (Colchester); Surrey v Durham (Oxted CC); Warwicks v Middx (Kenilworth Wardens CC); Worcs v Hants (Worcester).

9 – Derbys v Northants (Derby); Hants v Lancs (Southampton); Sussex v Notts (Hove; 4 days); Warwicks v Yorks (Birmingham).

14 – Leics v Lancs (Leicester).

Second Eleven fixtures were subject to confirmation when Wisden *went to press.*

†AON TROPHY, 1998

All matches are of one day's duration.

APRIL

28 – Essex v Kent (Saffron Walden).

30 – Lancs v Yorks (Manchester).

MAY

1 – Glos v Somerset (Bristol).

5 – Glam v Somerset (Cardiff); MCC Young Cricketers v Essex (Shenley Park).

6 – Leics v Middx (Hinckley Town).

7 – Somerset v Hants (Taunton).

11 – Lancs v Notts (Manchester); Leics v Minor Counties (Leicester); MCC Young Cricketers v Sussex (Shenley Park); Somerset v Glam (Taunton); Surrey v Essex (The Oval); Warwicks v Middx (West Bromwich Dartmouth CC).

12 – Minor Counties v Middx (Dunstable); Yorks v Notts (Castleford).

14 – Lancs v Derbys (Manchester).

18 – Derbys v Notts (Belper Meadows); Essex v MCC Young Cricketers (Saffron Walden).

19 – Hants v Glam (Southampton).

20 – Middx v Minor Counties (Uxbridge CC).

25 – Derbys v Lancs (Duffield CC); Worcs v Somerset (Worcester).

26 – Derbys v Durham (Glossop); Kent v Surrey (Maidstone); Middx v Leics (Uxbridge).

28 – Lancs v Durham (Urmston).

JUNE

1 – MCC Young Cricketers v Surrey (Shenley Park); Somerset v Worcs (Taunton).

2 – Leics v Warwicks (Hinckley Town CC); Yorks v Lancs (Elland).

4 – Warwicks v Minor Counties (Griff & Coton).

8 – Derbys v Yorks (Dunstall); Kent v Sussex (Maidstone); Notts v Lancs (Worksop College).

9 – Minor Counties v Leics (Banbury).

10 – Kent v MCC Young Cricketers (Maidstone).

11 – Warwicks v Leics (Leamington CC).

12 – Minor Counties v Warwicks (Wolverhampton); Surrey v MCC Young Cricketers (The Oval).

15 – Glam v Glos (Ebbw Vale); Hants v Somerset (Southampton); Sussex v MCC Young Cricketers (East Grinstead); Yorks v Durham (Marske).

16 – Middx v Northants (Lensbury).

22 – Durham v Lancs (Seaton Carew); Glam v Worcs (Newport); Hants v Glos (Southampton); Sussex v Surrey (Hove); Warwicks v Northants (Solihull); Yorks v Derbys (Park Avenue, Bradford).

23 – Notts v Yorks (Welbeck CC); Sussex v Kent (Hove).

29 – Hants v Worcs (Southampton); Northants v Minor Counties (Northampton).

30 – Essex v Sussex (Chelmsford); Notts v Durham (Farnsfield CC); Surrey v Kent (The Oval).

JULY

3 – Somerset v Glos (Taunton).

6 – Durham v Notts (Boldon); Kent v Essex (Canterbury); Northants v Middx (Campbell Park, Milton Keynes); Surrey v Sussex (The Oval); Worcs v Hants (Worcester).

7 – Glos v Glam (Lydney); Leics v Northants (Lutterworth).

13 – Durham v Yorks (Stockton CC); Northants v Warwicks (Northampton); Notts v Derbys (Notts Unity Casuals CC); Sussex v Essex (Haywards Heath); Worcs v Glos (Worcester).

20 – Essex v Surrey (Coggeshall); Minor Counties v Northants (North Runcton); Worcs v Glam (Worcester).

21 – Durham v Derbys (Chester-le-Street); Glos v Worcs (Cheltenham).

22 – Glos v Hants (Bristol).

27 – Glam v Hants (Ammanford); Middx v Warwicks (Ealing); MCC Young Cricketers v Kent (Shenley Park); Northants v Leics (Tring).

Semi-finals to be played on August 17 or 18.

Final to be played on September 7 (reserve day September 8).

†WOMEN'S CRICKET, 1998

MAY

23 Wellingborough   England trial matches (4 days)

JULY

5 Finchley	England Under-21 v Australians (1 day)
7 Shenley Park	South of England v Australians (1 day)
9 Oxton	North of England v Australians (1 day)
12 Scarborough	ENGLAND v AUSTRALIA (1st one-day international)
15 Derby	ENGLAND v AUSTRALIA (2nd one-day international)
18 Hove	ENGLAND v AUSTRALIA (3rd one-day international)
19 Southampton	ENGLAND v AUSTRALIA (4th one-day international)
21 Lord's	ENGLAND v AUSTRALIA (5th one-day international)
25 Cambridge	Area Championship (5 days)

31 Sittingbourne (Gore Court)	England A v Australians (3 days)

AUGUST

5 Guildford	ENGLAND v AUSTRALIA (1st Test, 4 days)
11 Harrogate	ENGLAND v AUSTRALIA (2nd Test, 4 days)
16 Colwall & Malvern	Cricket Week (6 days)
17 Rochdale	President's XI v Australians (3 days)
21 Worcester	ENGLAND v AUSTRALIA (3rd Test, 4 days)

SEPTEMBER

6 Milton Keynes (Campbell Park)	Premier League final
12 Milton Keynes (Campbell Park)	England Under-21 v Chairman's XI
13 Wolverhampton	National Club Knockout/Plate finals

COMMONWEALTH GAMES

The 1998 Commonwealth Games, to be held in Kuala Lumpur in September 1998, will include cricket for the first time. Sixteen teams are due to take part: Australia, Bangladesh, Barbados, Canada, Guyana, India, Jamaica, Kenya, Malaysia, New Zealand, Pakistan, Scotland, South Africa, Sri Lanka, Zimbabwe and (provisionally) Northern Ireland. England declined to participate.

According to the provisional schedule, limited-overs fixtures will be played every day between September 9, the opening day of Games competition, and September 19, except September 11.